VICTORIAN LITERATURE
1830–1900

VICTORIAN
LITERATURE
1830–1900

DOROTHY MERMIN

Cornell University

HERBERT F. TUCKER

University of Virginia

THOMSON

HEINLE

Australia Canada Mexico Singapore Spain United Kingdom United States

Victorian Literature
1830 - 1900
Dorothy Mermin and Herbert F. Tucker

Publisher: *Earl McPeek*
Acquisitions Editor: *Bill Hoffman*
Market Strategist: *John Meyers*
Developmental Editor: *Michell Phifer*
Project Editor: *Joyce Fink*
Art Director: *Sue Hart*
Production Manager: *Linda McMillan*

Printed in the United States of America
2 3 4 5 6 7 8 9 10   06 05 04 03

For more information contact Heinle, 25 Thomson Place, Boston, MA 02210 USA,
or you can visit our Internet site at http://www.heinle.com

ISBN: 0-1550-7177-7

Library of Congress Catalog Card Number: 2001086294

THE SELECTIONS

This anthology of poetry and nonfiction prose addresses the enlarged prospect that opens for literary study at the beginning of the twenty-first century. We have as a matter of course made ample provision for the principal poets and prose writers who traditionally represent (along with novelists) "Victorian literature." Among these we include, as anthologists before us have done, natural and social scientists who were essential contributors to Victorian literary culture. The familiar loose and baggy canon has lately opened up as well, however, to voices that spoke in their own time from the periphery of high culture, and has readmitted others that were devalued—even more drastically than the canonical Victorians were—by the anti-Victorian reaction that accompanied literary modernism. We have sought to give these voices, muted for much of the twentieth century, a fresh hearing.

Many of the newly audible voices belong to women. In the Victorian period, for the first time in English literature, women not only published in abundance but were taken seriously by their contemporaries, even if they were rarely acknowledged to be in the first rank. Writers excluded from the canon by class rather than gender are harder to find, partly because class has proven a sturdier barrier than gender to entering the general literary conversation, and partly because writing for Victorian publication meant, as a rule, enrolling in the middle class. As for bringing forward authors from the overseas British Empire, we have not even tried: colonial voices are heard in this anthology only as they are mediated through the Victorians themselves. Despite a dramatic widening of the circle of readers and authors that was effected by improvements in popular education on the one hand, and by the ease and cheapness of publication and distribution networks on the other, Victorian literature remained almost entirely the preserve of the white, Christian, British middle class—a fact inevitably reflected in this anthology.

Victorian studies have always been contextually oriented, and recent trends towards convergence between literary and historical disciplines have reinforced this orientation. We begin, therefore, with five sections of *Contexts*: sequences of short selections providing a quick survey of major topics. Our five categories are arbitrary and overlapping. Bishop Colenso, for instance, who wrote a notorious book explaining how his faith in the literal accuracy of the Old Testament was destroyed by the Zulus he was trying to convert, appears under the rubric "Faith, Doubt, and Knowledge"; but his demonstration that colonial encounters could reverberate unexpectedly at home evidently bears on issues of "Travel and Empire" too. The women's petition against the Contagious Diseases Acts tells as much about social class as about "Gender and Sexuality," the category in which we have placed it here. Social class, poverty, and national self-definition are officially covered in our first *Contexts* section; but like gender, race, empire, science, and religion, these topics crop up all over the book. Their ubiquity demonstrates their importance; their interpenetration is as thorough an illustration as our book can provide of the loose but systematic integrity of the culture on which Victorian literature rests, and broods. Our final *Contexts* section, on poetics, collects some important documents on a more strictly literary subject that is addressed and exemplified in many parts of the anthology.

The *Contexts* selections have been ruthlessly trimmed in order to highlight essential issues, provide pungent examples of contemporary styles, and afford breadth of coverage. In the *Authors* selections that form the bulk of the book we have aimed instead to err on the side of generosity. For writers whose importance is now largely historical, whose output was small, or who published mostly after 1900 the selections are relatively brief. We have tried to avoid excerpting poetry. Long poems composed of separate lyrics are, along with the dramatic monologue, the most characteristic of Victorian poetic forms, and to read them piecemeal is to miss much of their meaning and value. We therefore almost always give poems and poetic sequences entire or not at all (the main exception being the indispensable *Aurora Leigh*). For prose, however, we often admit extracts. This should suit readers unused to the leisurely expansiveness of Victorian disquisition; in any case, since much of the finest Victorian prose consists of whole books or long essays, excerpting is unavoidable. We incorporate a variety of prose styles and genres, including letters, newspaper and commission reports, notebooks, petitions, statutes, and practical manuals. Both the *Authors* and the *Contexts* sections contain numerous examples of an important genre that crested during the Victorian era: autobiographical writing. Autobiography can bring home like no other genre the tone and texture of personal experience, and it feeds our abiding interest in the ways people both live and imagine their lives. The autobiographical selections cover a wide range: poverty and prosperity, childhood and parenthood, public success and private crisis, women's experience and men's. Biographies, which the Victorians also were the first to produce and consume in large quantities, are represented here by the most fascinating of them all, Elizabeth Gaskell's *Life of Charlotte Brontë*.

Since it is impossible to represent Victorian fiction adequately we have not attempted to represent it at all. Several major novelists appear here in other roles, though, and the creed of fictional realism is brilliantly set forth in the passage from George Eliot's *Adam Bede* that appears in our final *Contexts* section. We urge our readers to remember that the Victorian period was the great age of the English novel, which catered to an ever-increasing public, undermined traditional hierarchies of genre, and became the prevalent literary form of an emerging mass-culture democracy. The novel's determinants and traces can be seen everywhere in this book: the concern with current social issues, the emphasis on character-drawing and anecdote in both poetry and prose, the displacement of high-born romantic heroes and heroines by contemporary men and women struggling along in ordinary life, and the valorization of simple affections and humane sympathy. Although men educated in the classics still dominated the higher ranks of literature, one no more needed Greek and Latin to write a novel than to read one. As the proliferation of relatively inexpensive books and periodicals sustained a vast public unversed (and uninterested) in the high-cultural traditions of the past, every genre and mode responded to mounting pressures to meet that public on its own terms. Even the great counter-movements of Aestheticism and Decadence, with their late-century rebellion against the ugliness of modern life and the values of the marketplace, can be defined in large part by their resistance to the formal unwieldiness, unfastidious popularity, and mainstream moralism of the novel. Reasons of space have defeated our wish to represent the rich stratifications of stage drama; but the one play we could never omit, Wilde's *The Importance of Being Earnest*, offers a wonderfully thorough send-up of the melodramatic sensationalism that links Victorian stagecraft to Victorian fiction.

While we have chosen some works with an eye to their contemporary popularity or impact, and others because they concern matters of great interest today, our final criterion has been, inevitably, literary value. If we didn't think something was well written and likely to please or intrigue readers today, we didn't put it in. What "well written" means we know better than to try to define, but we can point to the immense stylistic range of our selections: from the plainness of William Barnes' country poems and the hard-hitting essays of Harriet Martineau and John Stuart Mill, to the superfine weft of Pater's spidery prose, the verbal fireworks of a Hopkins sonnet, or the elegant implication of a lyric by the female couple who called themselves Michael Field.

Our eldest authors were born with the first industrial steam engines, before the American Revolution; our youngest survived into the Cold War and the atomic age. Given so long a chronological sweep, we have had to police our boundaries by excluding most writers whose work falls primarily before 1830 or after 1900. Thus Mary Shelley, William Wordsworth, Letitia Landon, and others who were active during our period (but are included, more appropriately, in the companion volume *British Literature 1780–1830*, edited by Anne Mellor and Richard Matlak) are absent here. And while we give selections from the Victorian writings of authors whose work appeared mostly in the next century, we rigorously limit these to titles composed or published by the century's end.

THE APPARATUS

Dates of publication are indicated on the right after each work. If a text was significantly changed for republication, or if a significant interval elapsed between periodical and book issue, we give two dates. Dates of composition, when known and of interest, appear on the left.

We have fought against the temptation to write footnotes that preempt interpretation. Nor do we define words that can be found in a good dictionary, unless they are unusually difficult or might mislead readers unfamiliar with subsidiary or nineteenth-century meanings. Instead, we briefly identify people, places, events, oddities, quotations, and allusions whenever we can.[1] Besides simply providing information, our annotation of allusions serves to define the range of reference within which Victorian literature operated. In particular, it graphically demonstrates the degree to which the culture was saturated not just with the stories and ideas of the Bible but with its language, familiar to Victorians from church, family reading and instruction, and the ingrained habit of consulting Scripture to feed a settled or enthusiastic faith, combat doubt or confess it. The frequency of allusion to Greek and Latin myths and texts suggests that the classical languages were still considered prerequisites for entrance into literary culture. Their possession and display marked writers and readers as having undergone the expensive, impractical education that was given to the sons of privilege—and that was coveted by the numerous women and several men in this anthology who, against considerable odds, acquired something like it on their own. Also noteworthy is a tendency among early Victorian writers to draw on medieval history and literature (usually as a reservoir of idealized community feeling), supplemented among later writers by reference to the artistic productions of the Renaissance (with its

---

[1]When we can't provide identification of an item, we pass it by in silence, refraining from confessional footnotes like this one.

ideology of individual genius). The density of cultural allusion to all these traditions in Aesthetic and Decadent writings, visible from afar as a cloud of fine print across the bottom of our later pages, is a telling sign of how those movements went about their business. Of the authors' own notes, we have transcribed those that seem most interesting, silently excising others.

Readers puzzled by an unannotated name or title should check the table of contents or index, since we have not identified writers or works that appear elsewhere in the book. The frequency with which our authors mention or allude to each other is an indication of how small the Victorian literary world was, based in a few London publishing houses and in a burgeoning but still limited set of periodicals that "everybody" read. Most of the men attended the same two universities and moved in overlapping social circles; the relatively small number of women who achieved literary notice sought out each other's acquaintance, sympathy, and support; and many authors of either sex were linked by ties of friendship and intellectual influence. Our writers thus as a rule inhabited, and exploited, known networks of professional relationship. It is an interesting question to what extent this cultural inbreeding reflected a living community of letters within industrial society and to what extent it portended (what in any case it eventually produced and bequeathed to later media) the rise of a celebrity culture.

In addition to written material we provide, after page 684, a small gallery of visual images—illustrations, advertisements, covers, and representative pages—from Victorian books and journals. We hope these will give some idea of how Victorian texts looked when they were in their original settings rather than in a large double-columned anthology. In particular, they demonstrate the intimate connection between word and picture that characterized publishing on almost every level throughout the century. We start with the brash, cheerful, exuberantly miscellaneous inventiveness of *Punch*, followed by the conservative medievalism, both social and architectural, of Pugin. From the more literary end of the cultural scale there is, first, Holman Hunt's *Lady of Shalott*, which complements the pictorial qualities of the poetry with the narrative qualities of illustration; this is from Moxon's lavish gift edition of Tennyson's *Poems*, which contained illustrations commissioned from a range of artists that included several PreRaphaelites. Next, Dante Rossetti gives graphic equivalents for the mingled seductiveness and playfulness of his sister's "Goblin Market" in a book design well suited to the clean lines of her verse. The much ridiculed early- and mid-century gift annuals also specialize in female beauty: we reproduce an image of a lovely woman reading a Valentine's-day letter, along with an advertisement that promises to enhance the beauty of readers with Oriental herbs and oils. A book cover designed by Beardsley and a title page by Ricketts evoke the paradoxes of the decadent fin de siècle: its appetite and refinement, its mystique, melancholia, and self-conscious make-believe. At almost the same time, but in a very different key from the cool intensity of aestheticism, a crudely drawn frontispiece to a book by William Booth charts a vision of Britain sunk in poverty and sin but saved by the Salvation Army at home and emigration abroad. Our final picture shows the aging Queen's profile—apparently disapproving yet infallibly familiar—enlisted in a jubilee year to sell a product of Empire for the English home.

At the end of the book readers will find a four-fold chronology offering a coordinated overview of cultural, social, and political events. Last of all we offer a set of highly selective bibliographies. Since electronic sources of information can be consulted nowadays with ever-increasing ease, the bibliographies point toward only the most reliable information and the most noteworthy guides to interpretation available in book and article form.

Acknowledgments

This book could not have come into being without many kinds of assistance, for which we are deeply grateful. We thank first of all the Victorianists who reviewed our selections and gave us encouragement and good advice: James Eli Adams, Cornell University; Steven Dillon, Bates College; Antony Harrison, North Carolina State University; Elizabeth Helsinger, The Universisty of Chicago; James Kincaid, University of Southern California; Christine Krueger, Marquette University; Robert Newsom, University of California, Irvine; Lawrence Poston, University of Illinois at Chicago; Matthew Rowlinson, Dartmouth College.

Katherine Reagan, Curator of Rare Books and Manuscripts at Cornell University Library, helped us discover Victorian images; Jennifer Conklin and Felicia Johnson of the Cornell and University of Virginia libraries captured them for us.

We have had substantial research support from Zubair Amir, Gina Franco, Andrea Gazzaniga, Sarah Heidt, Jen Hill, and Sonam Singh at Cornell, and from student assistants Hessa Albader, Sandy Alexandre, Emily Etherington, Sarah Evans, Jessie Kokrda, David Mongillo, Zora Tucker, and Annie Wagner at Virginia.

We also thank the many colleagues who generously offered their scholarly expertise when we found ourselves stumped in the course of annotation, and VICTORIA listmembers for internet-free, archive-deep wisdom.

Finally, we gratefully acknowledge the firm and patient support of staff at Harcourt College Publishers: Tia Black for guidance in early stages and Michell Phifer, senior development editor, for stamina till the end; Bill Hoffman, senior acquisitions editor; Joyce Fink, project editor; Sue Hart, senior art director; and Linda McMillan, production manager.

~ CONTENTS ~

WILLIAM BARNES
(1801–1886)   257

HARRIET MARTINEAU
(1802–1876)   263

JOHN STUART MILL
(1806–1873)   297

ELIZABETH BARRETT BROWNING
(1806–1861)   338

ALFRED TENNYSON
(1809–1892)   380

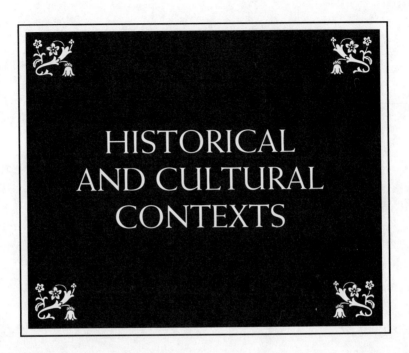

HISTORICAL
AND CULTURAL
CONTEXTS

The Condition of England

BRITANNIA SAILED HOME in 1815 from her victory over France at Waterloo and the redistribution of European power at the Congress of Vienna to take her place at the top of the diplomatic and commercial world. She retained that place without serious challenge through the end of the century. But peace and prosperity soon gave rise to questions that two decades of mobilization for war had muted. What was Britain? Who had a stake in the nation? Who had a say in its government? Between 1815 and 1837 the United Kingdom had changed crowned heads more often than in all the hundred years before, and the monarch who came to the throne in 1837, Victoria, was a teenager. To some observers this instability at the top symbolized something that ran much deeper, a sudden nationwide disposition toward change. If war had consolidated British identity at the beginning of the century, the focal issue around 1830 was reform itself. As Romantic nationalism gave way to Victorian reformism, the prospect of changing things, be they legislatures, schools, or sewage systems, aroused the concern of an entire public.

That a nation's character should be formed on reformism is an unlikely paradox. But it became a reality once British society, based on age-old relationships among government, landowners, the church, and the laboring poor, came to seem outmoded and inadequate to nearly everybody concerned. Things started to change all at once, it appeared, and at breakneck speed. A spate of 1820s legislation removed barriers to citizenship for religious minorities. The hotly contested Reform Bill of 1832 gave votes to something like one-fifth of the men in the country, those who paid a certain level of tax. Traditions of locally based charity were scrapped in favor of a harshly rationalized national system that after 1834 forced all but the wretchedest paupers into the labor market and the rest into punitively unpleasant "workhouses." In 1845 Parliament abolished the Corn Laws, tariffs on grain that had long favored entrenched landholders over emergent manufacturers and the hungry poor. These experiments in national policy signaled the arrival of the middle classes as modern Britain's effective rulers: a people commercially and technologically confident, urban and indeed suburban in stance, relatively unafraid of innovation, but by the same token far from sure who they were or ought to be. Reformism—questioning, repairing, reimagining all that came to hand—was not only a public program, it was a national state of mind.

The ongoing crisis of collective self-awareness generated an obsessive concern with taking stock, measuring progress or decline, and projecting profit and loss in reports and tabulations that seized eagerly on the new science of statistics. A new class of writer stepped forth: the secular sage—a category that includes authors as diverse as Thomas Carlyle, Harriet

Martineau, and John Ruskin. From such authors, Victorian readers sought a balm for the anxiety that accompanied their reformist zeal, but as often as not what they found was a fresh formulation of their doubts. Placing the natural and cultural world in question, the Victorians inevitably summoned themselves for interrogation as well. For perhaps the first time in history, they were a people who saw their age in terms much like those in which we seek to understand it now: they apprehended their own position, that is, not as natural and inevitable but as a problem for historical and cultural analysis. Thus the title for this Contexts section, "The Condition of England," was put into wide circulation when the arch-sage Carlyle posed it around 1830 as, emphatically, a "question."

Resoundingly affirmative answers were quickly supplied in such London spectacles as the 1851 "Great Exhibition of the Industry of All Nations" (Britain foremost, of course) and the Duke of Wellington's ostentatious funeral in 1852. These extravaganzas converted both national know-how and national grief to the purposes of state aggrandizement, and they were enthusiastically replayed in Victoria's Jubilees of 1887 and 1897. But in a subtler sense the question of British identity conditioned public discussion of a much wider range of topics. In the 1830s and 1840s the conservative Oxford Movement, asserting the primacy of the Church of England over secular political concerns and reaffirming the ritual traditions it inherited from Roman Catholicism, spurred a contest for the nation's soul that was decided in favor of toleration, and thus of functionally secular citizenship; Parliament and the ancient national universities were opened, as the century advanced, to Catholics, Jews, and Protestants who did not subscribe to the established Church. New and highly popular narratives of British history bristled with implications for the contemporary scene (including, from our Authors section, Carlyle's *Past and Present* and T. B. Macaulay's *History of England*). Philology came out of the study into the street with middlebrow books on the English language that were also celebrations of "Englishness" or "Britishness," the two terms serenely meshing in a mainstream harmony that blended English, Welsh, Scottish, and Anglo-Irish voices. By the end of the century the Queen's English, having assimilated its constituent regional dialects, was lavishly saluted by a monumental *New English Dictionary* (1884–1928, now the *OED*). The great *Encyclopaedia Britannica* (9th edition, 1875–1889) and the Revised Version of the English Bible (1881–1885) were similar monuments reinforcing national self-awareness and self-confidence. These late-century developments—plus one that holds particular interest for users of this anthology, the inauguration of English literature as a university subject—kept in public view the vital question of the English: where they had come from, what they might amount to, who in the world they were.

Knowing who they were meant deciding who they were not; yet the Victorians' attempts at self-definition by exclusion kept coming to grief. For one thing, military actions in the Crimea (1853), India (1857), Jamaica (1864), and with increasing frequency elsewhere as the Empire became fully extended in the last quarter of the century, stretched the traditional British sense of sea-girt borders to an unprecedented global extreme. The tally of lives lost and families broken in missionary or merchant or colonial service kept before everyone's mind the high cost of policing foreign frontiers. At the same time, the incessant importation into Britain of foreign persons and things brought crises of definition firmly home. The railroads that spanned the island between 1830 and 1850 drew Britons closer together than ever, enriching the thousands who held shares in rail, iron, and coal companies, and synchronizing household clocks to a single standard time. But those English railroads were increasingly built by Irish laborers, who poured across the Irish Sea as famine decimated their island in the 1840s to form a permanent class of resident aliens in the appalling British slums. The Irish became, if not English, then a part of what England was, and in time they were joined by a reflux of immigrants and returning career emigrants from outposts in South Africa or Saskatchewan or New Zealand or Kashmir. These strangers were rarely welcome, but as they settled in and grew familiar, they ensured that the question of English identity would not go away.

What made the new immigrants hardest for Britain to disown was the presence of their homegrown counterparts who lived a few streets away, the urban working class. The containment of this element posed the greatest unsolved problem in Victorian national self-definition, and it furnishes the leading theme of the excerpts that follow. For the commercial and industrial advance on which the middle class rose had bred a crowd of native strangers whose Englishness middle-class Victorians could neither deny nor fully accept. By requiring a constant supply of factory and domestic labor, the bourgeois way of life continually re-created its shadow underclass. Not only that, but every time the ruling order drew an official line demarcating its own position, it quickened the self-consciousness of the underclass it was excluding, which found increasingly articulate and effective expression in 1840s Chartism, 1860s reform agitation, and 1880s labor organizing. The 1860s gave the ballot to a majority of factory workmen, the 1870s gave public education to their children, and the 1880s, which produced a vigorous trade unionism, extended the vote to their country cousins laboring in agricultural production. By the turn of the twentieth century the new national goals of universal literacy and male suffrage were all but realized.

In his 1845 novel *Sybil, or the Two Nations*, the future prime minister Benjamin Disraeli described England's rich and poor as "two nations between whom there is no contact and no sympathy; we are as ignorant of each other's feelings as if we were dwellers in different zones or different planets." This was half the truth; the other half was that awareness of the two-nations crisis was itself central to Victorian national feeling. To be sure, the polite literature of the age seldom represented working-class reality. But that reality was constantly presupposed, whether as an implied otherness defining bourgeois gentility, as the fate to which the trapdoor of unsteady class relations could at any moment deliver a lady or gentleman who misstepped, or as a menace whose gathered force required incessant surveillance and whose strengthening will wrested concessions from reluctant policy-makers. The unignorable, intractable presence of the poor also made itself felt in middle-class writing through the swell of humanitarian sensibility that established Florence Nightingale as the most adulated person in the land. In poetry the problems of poverty were most often represented by the figure of the prostitute, who haunts Victorian literature—and this anthology. For many women writers, the lower classes figured as objects for philanthropy, for sisterhood across class lines, and for expanding the limits of bourgeois female activity and experience.

The excerpts that follow present stages in the shifting correlation between Britain's national identity (an ideal of unity) and Britain's class identities (a reality of differentiation and struggle). Victorian literature was an overwhelmingly middle-class enterprise; fringe figures like William Cobbett and William Booth wrote for a middle-class audience, while writers like James Kay-Shuttleworth and Sidney Webb earned baronial titles in recognition of their essentially bourgeois service in government. Consequently, nearly all that our selections have to say about the lower orders is constrained by the limits of a middle-class outlook. Those limits, along with some fervent efforts to transcend them, are our topic here: it is not just in their account of themselves, but in their attempt to account for others, that the Victorians show us who they were.

A Note on British Money: Currency was reckoned throughout the nineteenth century in pounds (£), shillings (s), pence (d), and farthings. Four farthings made a penny, 12 pence a shilling, 20 shillings a pound. Other coins in circulation included the guinea (worth 21 shillings, £1.1s), the sovereign (one pound), the crown (5s.), and the half-crown (2s.6d, two shillings sixpence). Shifts in wages, prices, and the relative value of goods and services during the nineteenth century alone—not to mention developments since then—make any simple rule for conversion to today's currency impossible.

WILLIAM COBBETT

(1763–1835)

In 1819 William Cobbett, who as a soldier and militant journalist had been in and out of trouble on both sides of the Atlantic for more than three decades, exhumed the bones of the great revolutionary Tom Paine from a New York farmyard for repatriation to Britain as relics of a national hero. Everything about this flamboyant scheme—including its failure when the bones got lost en route—was characteristic of its projector. For in the lens of Cobbett's fierce populism we see how the first decades of the nineteenth century had refracted Paine's international Enlightenment into a spotlight focused, with impassioned practicality, on issues resolutely national. *Cobbett's Weekly Political Register* from 1802 until the reporter's death launched hard-hitting volleys against whatever abuse lay closest to hand. The swing in opinion from Cobbett's youthful Toryism to his installation, in the Reform year 1832, as a sort of people's-tribune MP (member of Parliament) marks him ideologically as a loose cannon. But he remained staunch in opposition to the market forces that he saw transforming England in the image of the Great Wen (his name for London) and delivering his countrymen into the grip of what he was among the first to call the System: the interlocking commercial, financial, and state interests that, in the name of progress, were oppressing ordinary people and eviscerating their folkways. Cobbett spent his last decade travelling, lecturing, and writing to such people. The result was the serially published *Rural Rides*, which represent Cobbett's regionally specific concern for the land (as productive resource, as national idea) and for the common life of the English, as well as his forthright style, ranging curiosity, and sharp eye for an anecdote.

from **Rural Rides**

Cambridge, 28 March 1830

. . . I had not time sufficient for a lecture, but I explained to them briefly the real cause of the distress which prevailed; I warned the farmers particularly against the consequences of hoping that this distress would remove itself. I portrayed to them the effects of the taxes;[1] and showed them that we owe this enormous burden to the want of being fairly represented in parliament. Above all things, I did that which I never fail to do, showed them the absurdity of grumbling at the six millions a year given in relief to the poor, while they were silent and seemed to think nothing of the sixty millions of taxes collected by the government at London, and I asked them how any man of property could have the impudence to call upon the labouring man to serve in the militia, and to deny that that labouring man had, in case of need, a clear right to a share of the produce of the land. I explained to them how the poor were originally relieved; told them that the revenues of the livings, which had their foundation in *charity*, were divided amongst the poor. The demands for repair of the churches and the clergy themselves; I explained to them how church-rates and poor-rates came to be introduced; how the burden of maintaining the poor came to be thrown upon the people at large; how the nation had sunk by degrees ever since the event called the Reformation; and pointing towards the cathedral I said, "Can you believe, gentlemen, that when that magnificent pile was reared, and when all the fine monasteries, hospitals, schools, and other resorts of piety and charity existed in this town and neighbourhood; can you believe that Ely[2] was the miserable little place that it now is; and that that England which had never heard of the name of *pauper* contained the crowds of miserable creatures that it now contains, some starving at stone-cracking by the way-side, and others drawing loaded waggons on that way?" . . .

A young man in the room (I having come to a pause) said, "But, sir, were there no poor in Catholic times?" "Yes," said I, "to be sure there were. The Scripture says that the poor shall never cease out of the land;[3] and there are five hundred texts of Scripture enjoining on all men to be good and kind to the poor. It is necessary to the existence of civil society that there should be poor. Men have two motives to industry and care in all the walks of life: one to acquire wealth; but the other and stronger to avoid poverty. If there were no poverty, there would be no industry, no enterprise. But this poverty is not to be made a punishment unjustly severe. Idleness, extravagance, are offences against morality; but they are not offences of that heinous nature to justify the infliction of starvation by way of punishment. It is, therefore, the duty of every man that is able; it is particularly the duty of every government, and it was a duty faithfully executed by the Catholic church, to take care that no human being should perish for want in a land of plenty; and to take care, too, that no one should be deficient of a sufficiency of food and raiment, not only to sustain life, but also to sustain health." The young man said: "I thank you, sir; I am answered."

Spittal, near Lincoln, 19 April 1830

. . . It is time for me now, withdrawing myself from these objects visible to the eye, to speak of the state of *the people*, and of the manner in which their affairs are affected by the workings of the system. With regard to the labourers, they are, everywhere, miserable. The wages for those who are employed on the land are, through all the counties that I have come, twelve shillings a week for married men, and less for single ones; but a large part of them are not even at this season employed on the land. The farmers, for want of means of profitable employment, suffer the men to fall upon the parish;[4] and they are employed in digging and breaking stone for the roads; so that the roads are nice and smooth for the sheep and cattle to walk on in their way to the all-devouring jaws of the Jews and other tax-eaters in London and its vicinity. None of the best meat, except by mere accident, is consumed here. To-day (the 20th of April), we have seen hundreds upon hundreds of sheep, as fat as hogs, go by this inn door, their toes, like those of the foot marks at the entrance of the lion's den, all pointing towards the Wen; and the landlord gave us for dinner a little skinny, hard leg of old ewe mutton! Where the man got it, I cannot imagine. Thus it is: every good thing is literally driven or carried away out of the country. In walking out yesterday, I saw

[1] **taxes:** Cobbett's protest is twofold: that funds long ago intended for poverty relief have been appropriated by the Church establishment, which reserves as clergymen's **livings** (stipends and perks of office) revenue that ought to be distributed in charity; and that unmet needs have consequently devolved in the form of legislated taxation (**church-** and **poor-rates**) on working people who in 1830 are eligible for the **militia** but not the vote.

[2] **Ely:** Cambridgeshire cathedral town.

[3] **the poor . . . the land:** Deuteronomy 15:11.

[4] **fall upon the parish:** depend on locally administered charity.

three poor fellows digging stone for the roads, who told me that they never had anything but bread to eat, and water to wash it down. One of them was a widower with three children; and his pay was eighteenpence a day; that is to say, about three pounds of bread a day each, for six days in the week; nothing for Sunday, and nothing for lodging, washing, clothing, candle light, or fuel! Just such was the state of things in France at the eve of the Revolution! Precisely such; and precisely the same were the *causes*. Whether the effect will be the same, I do not take upon myself positively to determine. Just on the other side of the hedge, while I was talking to these men, I saw about two hundred fat sheep in a rich pasture. I did not tell them what I might have told them; but I explained to them why the farmers were unable to give them a sufficiency of wages. They listened with great attention; and said that they did believe that the farmers were in great distress themselves. . . .

Lord Stanhope[5] cautioned his brother peers, a little while ago, against the angry feeling which was *rising up in the poor against the rich*. His lordship is a wise and humane man, and this is evident from all his conduct. Nor is this angry feeling confined to the counties in the south, where the rage of the people, from the very nature of the local circumstances, is more formidable; woods and coppices and dingles and by-lanes and sticks and stones ever at hand, being resources[6] unknown in counties like this. When I was at St. Ives, in Huntingdonshire, an open country, I sat with the farmers, and smoked a pipe by way of preparation for evening service, which I performed on a carpenter's bench in a wheelwright's shop; my friends, the players, never having gained any regular settlement in that grand mart for four-legged fat meat, coming from the Fens, and bound to the Wen.[7] While we were sitting, a hand-bill was handed round the table, advertising *farming stock for sale*; and amongst the implements of husbandry "an *excellent fire-engine, several steel traps, and spring guns!*"[8] And

that is the life, is it, of an English *farmer?* I walked on about six miles of the road from Holbeach to Boston. I have before observed upon the inexhaustible riches of this land. At the end of about five miles and three quarters I came to a public-house, and thought I would get some breakfast; but the poor woman, with a tribe of children about her, had not a morsel of either meat or bread! At a house called an inn, a little further on, the landlord had no meat except a little bit of chine of bacon; and though there were a good many houses near the spot, the landlord told me that the people were become so poor that the butchers had left off killing meat in the neighbourhood. Just the state of things that existed in France on the eve of the Revolution. On that very spot I looked round me and counted more than two thousand fat sheep in the pastures! How long, how long, good God! is this state of things to last? How long will these people starve in the midst of plenty? How long will fire-engines, steel traps, and spring guns be, in such a state of things, a protection to property? When I was at Beverley, a gentleman told me, it was Mr. Dawson of that place, that some time before a farmer had been sold up by his landlord; and that, in a few weeks afterwards, the farmhouse was on fire, and that when the servants of the landlord arrived to put it out, they found the handle of the pump taken away and that the homestead was totally destroyed. This was told me in the presence of several gentlemen, who all spoke of it as a fact of perfect notoriety.

Leicester, 26 April 1830

The march of circumstances is precisely what it was in France just previous to the French Revolution. If the aristocracy were wise they would put a stop to that march. The middle class are fast sinking down to the state of the lower class. *A community of feeling* between these classes, and that feeling an angry one, is what the aristocracy has to dread. As far as the higher clergy are concerned, this community of feeling is already complete. A short time will extend the feeling to every other branch; and then the hideous consequences make their appearance. Reform; a radical reform of the parliament; this reform *in time*; this reform, which would reconcile the middle class to the aristocracy, and give renovation to that which has now become a mass of decay and disgust; this reform, given with a good grace, and not taken by force, is the only refuge for the aristocracy of this kingdom. Just as it was in France. All the tricks of financiers have been tried in vain; and by and by some trick more pompous

---

[5]**Lord Stanhope:** Philip Henry Stanhope (1805–1875), who entered Parliament in 1830 as a conservative, but backed several liberal causes.

[6]**resources:** i.e., in support of popular rebellion, the fen country lacking **coppices** (thickets) and **dingles** (wooded valleys) for ambush and hideout.

[7]**Fens:** flatlands northeast of London, which city Cobbett nicknamed **the Wen** (tumor).

[8]*fire-engine, traps, guns:* farmers' defenses against arson and trespass. Disaffected farm workers were setting fire to crops across the country.

and foolish than the rest, Sir Henry Parnell's[9] trick, perhaps, or something equally foolish, would blow the whole concern into the air.

Worcester, 18 May 1830

In tracing myself from Leicester to this place, I begin at Lutterworth, in Leicestershire, one of the prettiest country towns that I ever saw; that is to say, prettiest *situated*. At this place they have, in the church (they say), the identical *pulpit* from which Wickliffe[10] preached! This was not his birthplace; but he was, it seems, priest of this parish. . . .

. . . I set off from Lutterworth early on the 29th of April, stopped to breakfast at Birmingham, got to Wolverhampton by two o'clock (a distance altogether of about 50 miles), and lectured at six in the evening. I repeated, or rather continued, the lecturing on the 30th and on the 3rd of May. On the 6th of May went to Dudley, and lectured there: on the 10th of May, at Birmingham; on the 12th and 13th, at Shrewsbury; and on the 14th came here.

Thus have I come through countries of corn and meat and iron and coal; and from the banks of the Humber to those of the Severn I find all the people who do not share in the taxes[11] in a state of distress, greater or less; *mortgagers* all frightened out of their wits; *fathers* trembling for the fate of their children; and *working people* in the most miserable state, and, as they ought to be, in the *worst of temper*. These will, I am afraid, be the *state-doctors* at last! The farmers are cowed down: the poorer they get the more cowardly they are.

---

[9]**Sir Henry Parnell** (1776–1842): designer of a banking scheme that had nearly broken the Bank of England.

[10]John **Wickliffe** (1330?–1384): theological reformer and translator of the Bible into English.

[11]**Humber, Severn**: rivers in NE and SW England; Cobbett has traversed the midlands from coast to coast. **share in the taxes**: benefit from state expenditures.

Every one of them sees the cause of his suffering, and sees general ruin at hand; but every one hopes that by some trick, some act of meanness, some contrivance, *he shall escape*. So that there is no hope of any change for the better but from the *working people*. The farmers will sink to a very low state; and thus the Thing (barring *accidents*) may go on, until neither farmer nor tradesman will see a joint of meat on his table once in a quarter of a year. It appears likely to be precisely as it was in France: it is now just what France was at the close of the reign of Louis XV. It has been the fashion to ascribe the *French Revolution* to the writings of Voltaire, Rousseau, Diderot,[12] and others. These writings had *nothing at all* to do with the matter: no, *nothing at all*. The *Revolution* was produced by *taxes*, which at last became unbearable; by debts of the state; but, in fact, by the despair of the people, produced by the weight of the taxes.

It is curious to observe how ready the supporters of tyranny and taxation are to ascribe rebellions and revolutions to disaffected leaders; and particularly to writers; and as these supporters of tyranny and taxation have had the press at their command; have had generally the absolute command of it, they have caused this belief to go down from generation to generation. It will not do for them to ascribe revolutions and rebellions to the true cause; because then the rebellions and revolutions would be justified; and it is their object to cause them to be condemned. Infinite delusion has prevailed in this country in consequence of the efforts of which I am now speaking. Voltaire was just as much a cause of the French Revolution as I have been the cause of imposing these sixty millions of taxes. The French Revolution was produced by the grindings of taxation; and this I will take an opportunity very soon of proving, to the conviction of every man in the kingdom who chooses to read.

1830

---

[12]**Voltaire** (Francois-Marie Arouet, 1694–1778), Jean-Jacques **Rousseau** (1712–1778), Denis **Diderot** (1713–1784): freethinking writers of the French Enlightenment.

PETER GASKELL

(1806?–1841)

Having entered the Royal College of Surgeons in 1828, five years later "P. Gaskell, Esq., Surgeon" published *The Manufacturing Population of England*, which was revised and enlarged in 1836 into the book excerpted here. He died at 35 in a London suburb, but clearly he had spent time in the northern English cities that were the laboratory of the industrial revolution, chiefly Manchester, where his in-law Elizabeth Gaskell the novelist also lived. When Friedrich Engels published the communist classic *The Condition of the Working Class in England* (in German, 1845), he decried Gaskell's laissez-faire bias but trusted him as "an objective observer" of the factory scene. Objective or not, Gaskell was indubitably earnest. Written all over his 1836 title page is the methodical character of an era that, awaking with a start to the fallout from its new industrial order, made industrious diagnosis the first step toward a cure: *Artisans and Machinery: The Moral and Physical Condition of the Manufacturing Population Considered with Reference to Mechanical Substitutes for Human Labour*. At the beginning and end of our selection Gaskell respectfully alludes to official committees that were appointed, with what seems in retrospect a touching bureaucratic naiveté, to look into and mend problems rooted in a wholesale revolution in economic and human relations. Still, Gaskell's account matters for its early registration of the impact mechanical technology had on families as well as muscles, for its scientific appraisal of morals as a social problem and of religion as a cultural fixative, and above all for its apprehension that industrialization was not just a regional aberration but a transformative shock to the entire national system.

from Artisans and Machinery

The great importance of the subjects discussed in the following pages will be understood, by saying that they involve questions of the highest interest to our commercial relations, and the welfare of the entire kingdom. The declension of the most numerous class of artisans in Great Britain, from comfort, morality, independence, and loyalty, to misery, demoralization, dependence, and discontent, is the painful picture now presented by the domestic manufacturers. The handloom weavers, whether of cotton, linen, worsted, or silk, and the multitudes engaged in bobbin-net,[1] lace, and other manufacturing processes, still carried on as household labour, together with all other industrious classes, on whose path steam-machinery is advancing, present a most interesting and anxious subject for examination.

The domestic labourers were at one period a most loyal and devoted body of men. "Lancashire," says an intelligent witness before the Select Committee[2] of Hand-Loom Weavers in 1834, "was a particularly loyal county. There was a call made upon their patriotism at one time to repel the gigantic power of Buonaparte, and it was not made in vain: there were 30,000 volunteers stepped forward in the county, and upwards of 20,000 were hand-loom weavers. Durst any Government call upon the services of such a people, living upon three shillings a week?"

Unparalleled distress, and long-continued privations, have, it is to be feared, operated prejudicially upon the minds of this large class of artisans. "I have not merited these things!" says another witness: "I am a loyal man, strongly attached to the institutions of my country. I am a

---

[1]**bobbin-net**: loose mesh netting.

[2]**Select Committee**: one of many set up by Parliament to investigate labor crises caused by industrialization.

friend to social order, and I never shall act upon any other principle myself; but I cannot think I ought tamely to submit to perish without a struggle; and I am confident, that, unless something be done to prevent it, any accidental cause, such as an advance of the price of provisions, or a deficiency of crops, must bring thousands of us to a premature grave. This is the exact condition of things."

Nor can any wonder be felt that men should grow discontented and dissatisfied who labour fourteen or sixteen hours daily, and earn from four to six shillings per week, and who see not the most remote probability that their condition will be improved. Upwards of a million of human beings are literally starving, and the number is constantly on the increase, hand-weaving being the only refuge for the adult labourer, since the spread of the factory system.

Irreligion and general immorality must ever attend hopeless poverty. Men thus circumstanced become reckless and dispirited, and it is painful to witness the growth of unfavourable dispositions in classes who have been driven to destitution by causes far beyond their control. The evidence given before the Committee above mentioned, both by the masters and men, is not less startling than true.

It would have been well if steam and mechanism, in breaking up a healthy, contented, and moral body of labourers, had provided another body, possessing the same excellent qualities, as men and citizens: but it has not been so. . . .

The trains of facts and reasonings on the substitution of steam-machinery for human labour bring the Author into direct collision with many eminent writers on political economy. In entering into the contest, he is aware that he shall have to encounter much opposition; but his facts are undeniable, and his deductions are illustrated by every-day experience.

It is a new era in the history of commerce that an active and increasing trade should be the index, not to the improvement of the condition of the working classes, but to their poverty and degradation: it is an era at which Great Britain has arrived; and it behoves every man, anxious for the well-being of his country, to turn his attention to this extraordinary fact. (Preface)

. . . The greatest misfortune—the most unfavourable change which has resulted from factory labour—is the breaking up of these family ties, the consequent abolition of the domestic circle, and the perversion of all the social obligations which should exist between parent and child on the one hand, and between children themselves on the other.

The age at which a child became useful to its parents so long as the great mass of manufactures was manual and confined to private dwelling-houses, was from fourteen to sixteen. At an earlier age it was useful in a minor degree, but that was the period at which it became an auxiliary to the incomings of the family by regular working.

Before this it was a mere child, entirely dependent upon the exertions of its parents or older brothers and sisters for support. During this time it was taught, by daily experience, habits of subordination to its seniors. The period at which it ranked itself by the side of the efficient portions of the household was a happy medium between too early an application and too late a procrastination of its physical energies, for the child was sufficiently matured, in its material organization, to bear without injury moderate and continued exertion; and no time had, as yet, been allowed for the acquirement of slothful habits. It came, too, at a time when the first impulses of puberty were beginning to stir new associations in his mind. These it checked by keeping him occupied, while he was removed from the influence of bad example, and laboured in an open workshop, free from the stimulus of warmth, and in the presence of his sisters, brothers, and parents, the very best anodyne for allaying and keeping in due restraint his nascent passions, whilst his moral and social instincts were under a process of incessant cultivation.

The same observations apply with still greater force to the females of the family. With them labour commenced at a somewhat earlier period, or they supplied the place of their mother in the household offices, leaving her at liberty to work for their sustenance, if such a course of proceeding was deemed necessary, or forced upon them by the pressure of circumstances. Whichever it was, she was kept from promiscuous intercourse[3] with the other sex, at an age when it was of the utmost importance, her young sensibilities rendering her peculiarly liable to powerful and irresistible impressions. It is true that the sports of her own sex were to some extent libidinous, but to these she was not admitted till a much later period; and these, though coarse and highly objectionable, rarely ended in mischief, being considered as a sort of prelude to marriage, a custom certainly "more honoured in the breach than in the observance."[4]

Her occupations and feelings were therefore exclusively home-bred, and no idea existed that distinct or detached interests could intervene betwixt her parents and herself.

---

[3]**promiscuous intercourse**: unsupervised companionship.

[4]**"more honoured . . . observance"**: *Hamlet* 1.4.18.

It is in these respects that the family of the factory labourer offers such strong contrasts and unhappy differences to their precursors in manufacturing industry.

In the first place, there is no home labour. Home becomes therefore a mere shelter, in which their meals are hastily swallowed, and which offers them repose for the night. It has no endearing recollections which bind it on their memories—no hold upon their imaginations.

In the next place, the various members not only do not labour under their own roof, but they do not labour in common, nor in one mill; or if in one mill, so separated, that they have no opportunity of exchanging a single glance or a word throughout the long hours they are engaged there. Children are thus entirely removed from parental guardianship; and not only so, but they are brought into immediate contact with parties, generally of their own age, equally removed with themselves from inspection, and equally unchecked by a consciousness that the eye of a brother, sister, or parent may be fixed upon them. They are placed, too, under the control of an overlooker or spinner, who, from a sense of duty to his employer or himself, if moved by no baser feeling, treats them frequently with harshness,[5] making no allowance for childish simplicity, bashfulness, delicacy, or female failings; and this is most fatal to self-esteem, which nothing so soon injures or destroys as unworthy treatment, suffered in themselves or witnessed in others, without the power of redress, or even of appeal.

Again, they are subjected on all sides to the influence of vicious examples—are placed in a heated atmosphere, and have no occupation, save watching the passage of a thread or the revolution of a spindle. The mind is but little engaged,—there is no variety for it to feed upon, and it has none of the pure excitements which home affords. It becomes crowded with images of the very opposite quality, and no opportunity is given for the growth of modesty, on the one hand, or of the social obligations of brother, sister, or child, on the other.

The next evil which removes factory labour another step still more widely apart from the condition of domestic manufacture is, that the wages of children have become, either by universal consent, or by the growth of disobedience, payable to the person earning them. This has led to another crying and grievous misfortune, namely, that each

child ceases to view itself as a subordinate agent in the household; so far indeed loses the character and bearing of a child, that it pays over to its natural protector a stated sum for food and lodging; thus detaching itself from parental subjection and control. The members, therefore, of a spinner's or weaver's family become a body of distinct individuals, occupying occasionally, but by no means universally, the same home, each paying its quota to the joint expenses, and considering themselves as lodgers merely, and appropriating any surplus which may remain of their wages to their own private purposes, accountable to no one for the mode in which it happens to be used or wasted.

It is to be feared, that the mischiefs resulting from such an unnatural arrangement must, in the first instance, be saddled upon the errors of parents—such a dereliction from filial duty being hardly likely to happen spontaneously on the side of the children; and that a plan originally adopted in a few cases by the family of idle and depraved parents,—and many such are to be found, who would willingly live upon the toil of their children,—has become general, in consequence of the lowering in the reciprocal confidence and affection which ought to exist between parent and child.

In numerous examples, then, at the present day, parents are become the keepers of lodging-houses for their offspring, between whom little intercourse exists beyond that relating to pecuniary profit and loss. In a vast number of others, children have been entirely driven away from their homes, either by unnatural treatment, or they have voluntarily deserted them, and taken up their abode in other asylums, for the sake of saving a small sum, in the amount of payment required for food and house-room.

This disruption of all the ties of home is one of the most fatal consequences of the factory system. The social relations which should distinguish the members of the same family are destroyed. The domestic virtues, man's natural instincts, and the affections of the heart, are deadened and lost. The feelings and actions which should be the charm of the fire-side—which should prepare young men and young women for fulfilling the duties of parents—are displaced by a selfishness utterly repugnant to all such sacred obligations. Tenderness of manner—solicitude during sickness—the foregoing of personal gratification for the sake of others—submission to home restraint—these are partially lost, and their place occupied by individual independence—private avarice—the withholding assistance, however slight, from those around them, who have a natural claim upon their generosity—calculations and arrangements, based solely upon sordid motives,—with a gradual extinction of those sympathies and feelings, which are alone fitted to afford

---

[5]The extraordinary charges made against the factories in this respect are gross exaggerations. Cruelty has existed, and does exist amongst the spinners, but by no means in the shape generally supposed. [Gaskell's note]

happiness—a wearing away of the more delicate shades of character, leaving nothing but attention to the simple wants of nature, in addition to the depraved appetites which are the result of other circumstances connected with their condition,—and in the end reducing them, as a mass, to a heartless assemblage of separate and conflicting individuals, each striving for their "own hand," uninfluenced by the more gentle, the more noble, and the more humanized cares, aspirations, and feelings, which could alone render them estimable as fathers, mothers, brothers and sisters. . . . (Chapter 5)

. . . Inquiries made amongst these classes have shewn, that often there is no belief in the superintending care of a beneficent Creator—none, of a state of future rewards or punishments; and that materialism has placed them, in these respects, upon a level with the beasts that perish.[6] In numerous other examples, where even some knowledge was found on religious subjects, it failed in producing its salutary influence upon morals, in consequence of apathy and indifference.

Thus, deprived of the most ennobling characteristic of the human mind, what wonder can be felt that it is a wild waste, overgrown with noxious weeds, which choke and destroy the seeds of a better harvest, scattered as they are so thinly and so rarely over its surface. The savage, roaming through his native wilderness, bows down with reverence before the objects he has been taught to worship; and however degraded these are, they are such as his condition leads him to fear or to love; and he looks forward to the "spirit land" as his place of rest. Thus, he is religious in the only way in which his untutored mind and limited observation will permit, and thus far he is superior to that portion of the operative manufacturers which acknowledges no God—which worships no image—which regards no hereafter. The savage, indeed, from his familiarity with the operations of nature, in all their wild wonders, is impressed with her power, and yields obedience to the dictates of a whispering consciousness that there is—that there must be—a *cause* for all he sees around him. But how differently placed is the factory labourer! He knows nothing of nature—her very face is hidden and obscured from him, and he is surrounded and hemmed in by a vast circle of human inventions. He is at perpetual warfare with the world and with himself, and his bad passions are consequently in constant play. Thus combating—the pure and holy impulses of religion can find no home with him, but, like the dove hanging with trembling wing over the agitated waters of the deluge, they seek a refuge in the ark of some more peaceful bosom, and leave him occupied solely by his own impure sensations.

The immoralities which stain the character of the most vindictive and ignorant of savage nations have never exhibited any cruelty or depravity more glaring than this, and the simple fact tells more forcibly the immoral and degraded state of the factory population than the most graphic description or the most minute detail.

It has been said that the vast body of hand-loom weavers and domestic manufacturers have been hitherto in a great measure free from combination.[7] It is with pain, but without surprise, that we find that of late their unparalleled distress has given rise to many discussions, and that the most strenuous efforts are making to unite them, scattered as they are over a wide extent of territory, into one general and efficient community. Committees have been already formed at Preston, Manchester, Wigan, Bradford, Warrington,[8] and are likely to extend to Scotland, and into the ribbon, stocking-weaving, and bobbin-net district. (Chapter 11)

1836

---

[6]**beasts that perish**: Psalm 49:20.

[7]**combination**: trade union organizing.

[8]**Preston . . . Warrington**: manufacturing towns in N England.

THE PEOPLE'S CHARTER

We print here in its earliest version the document that gave its name to Chartism, the principal British working-class movement of the first half of the nineteenth century. The Charter came into being in 1837 when an economic depression brought to the boil resentments that had simmered ever since the 1832 Reform Bill expressly excluded all but the well-to-do from voting and the 1834 Poor Law, adding insult to injury, dismantled traditional community supports for the indigent. By 1839 the national movement was strong enough to hold conventions in London and Birmingham; after Parliament refused to consider the six-point Chartist petition, an armed uprising in Newport (Wales) led to the imprisonment and deportation of many movement leaders. A second petition in 1842 bearing three million signatures was also rejected out of hand by Parliament, and Chartism languished while better-funded reformers carried the day in 1845 against the Corn Law price supports for grain—a victory of industrial over landed interests that by making food cheaper diminished lower-class unrest. Chartism flared up once more when poor harvests in 1848 coincided with revolutionary activity across Europe, but again the petition failed to get parliamentary approval. With the prosperity of the 1850s, Chartist energies were diverted from electoral politics into efforts for cultural and educational reform, nourishing eventually the more comprehensive Reform Bills of 1868 and 1884 and the Education Act of 1870. The diversity among signatories even of the 1837 Charter—working-class organizers, radical MPs, and leaders from Ireland— indicates both the strength of the movement and its fatal diffuseness. Chartism spoke for large numbers of people aroused by a range of discontents, but this same variety divided the movement on aims and tactics, especially in regard to civil disobedience and violence.

The Six Points
of the People's Charter

1. A VOTE for every man twenty-one years of age, of sound mind, and not undergoing punishment for crime.

2. THE BALLOT—To protect the elector in the exercise of his vote.

3. NO PROPERTY QUALIFICATION for Members of Parliament—thus enabling the constituencies to return the man of their choice, be he rich or poor.

4. PAYMENT OF MEMBERS, thus enabling an honest tradesman, working man, or other person, to serve a constituency, when taken from his business to attend to the interests of the Country.

5. EQUAL CONSTITUENCIES, securing the same amount of representation for the same number of electors, instead of allowing small constituencies to swamp the votes of large ones.

6. ANNUAL PARLIAMENTS, thus presenting the most effectual check to bribery and intimidation, since though a constituency might be bought once in seven years (even with the ballot), no purse could buy a constituency (under a system of universal suffrage) in each ensuing twelve-month; and since members, when elected for a year, would not be able to defy and betray their constituents as

now. Subjoined are the names of the gentlemen who embodied these principles into the document called the "People's Charter" at an influential meeting held at the British Coffee House, London, on the 7th of June 1837:

Daniel O'Connell, Esq., M.P.[1]
John Arthur Roebuck, Esq., M.P.[2]
John Temple Leader, Esq., M.P.[3]
Charles Hindley, Esq., M.P.[4]
Thomas Perronet Thompson, Esq., M.P.[5]

William Sharman Crawford, Esq., M.P.[6]
Mr Henry Hetherington.[7]
Mr John Cleave.[8]

Mr James Watson.[9]
Mr Richard Moore.[10]
Mr William Lovett.[11]
Mr Henry Vincent.[12]

---

[1]**Daniel O'Connell** (1775–1847): Irish MP for Cork and Clare, orator and activist called "the Liberator"; advocated Catholic Emancipation and Irish independence.

[2]**John Arthur Roebuck** (1801–1879): Utilitarian lawyer, speaker, and author; MP for Bath and Sheffield.

[3]**John Temple Leader** (1810–1903): radical MP for Westminster and Bridgewater.

[4]**Charles Hindley** (1800–1857): cotton industrialist and pacifist; MP from greater Manchester.

[5]**Thomas Peronnet Thompson** (1783–1869): army general, publicist, and philosophical radical; MP for Bradford.

[6]**William Sharman Crawford** (1781–1861): MP for Dundalk and Rochdale, Ireland.

[7]**Henry Hetherington** (1792–1849): radical printer, trade-union advocate, and publisher of *The Poor Man's Guardian* (circulation 20,000).

[8]**John Cleave** (1790?–1847): printer and editor of *Cleave's Weekly Police Gazette* (circulation 40,000).

[9]**James Watson** (1799–1874): radical freethinker and publisher of works by Paine, Byron, and Shelley.

[10]**Richard Moore** (1810–1878): artisan and radical political reformer.

[11]**William Lovett** (1800–1877): self-educated artisan intellectual and activist, chief draftsman of the Charter.

[12]**Henry Vincent** (1813–1878): journalist, lecturer, and agitator; sentenced to a year in prison for advocating armed insurrection, 1838.

JAMES KAY-SHUTTLEWORTH

(1804–1877)

After taking his medical degree in Edinburgh, James Kay (he assumed his wife's name later) moved to Manchester, seat of all that was most exciting about British industrialization in the 1830s—and, to a medical man like Kay, all that was most appalling. Kay served on the board of health there, then on the commission administering the new national Poor Law. In 1839 he became secretary of a national Committee of Council studying popular education, which had received intermittent attention since 1800 and was now a threadbare crazy quilt of religious and private initiatives. It was in the increasingly important area of educational reform that Kay-Shuttleworth found the life's work for which he was made Sir James a decade later; and in the career that led him from treating disease to confronting its social causes in poverty and ignorance, and then to administering institutional remedies through education, may be seen a widening circle of national concern that was typical of his generation. As early as 1832, in an essay on the Manchester working classes that was heavy with laissez-faire ideology, we find him tentatively affirming that "the ignorant are . . . properly, the care of the state" and proposing "a system of national education so extensive and liberal as to supply the wants of the whole labouring population." Fifteen years later, fortified with his authority as an education commissioner, he could invoke "the national will" and argue for state education by analogy with the army, the law, and such new public exertions as city lighting, sewerage, and water supply. In the pamphlet excerpted here, Kay-Shuttleworth is still finding his way, across moral persuasions (Do right by the poor!) and prudential warnings (Or else!), toward a national consensus that would, in the Education Act of 1870, lay the first cornerstone of the twentieth-century British welfare state.

from Recent Measures for the Promotion of Education in England

All plans which have been proposed for promoting National Education in England by calling into operation the powers of the Executive Government, have necessarily been subjected to the most searching scrutiny. The advocates of education must not, however, accept the earnestness with which public attention is directed to this subject as a measure of the degree in which the necessity of an extension and improvement of the elementary education of the poorer classes is recognised. It is indeed generally known that even the art of reading has been acquired by a portion only of the rising population, and by a smaller part of the adult working class; and that, as respects the rudimentary knowledge which might develop the understanding, and afford the labourer a clear view of his social position,—its duties, its difficulties, and rewards,— and thus enable him better to employ the powers with which Providence has gifted him, to promote his own comfort and the well-being of society, he is generally destitute, and, what is worse, abandoned to the ill-regulated and often pernicious agencies by which he is surrounded. It is commonly confessed that no sufficient means exist to train the habits of the children of our poorer classes,—to inspire them with healthful, social, and household sympathies,—with a love of domestic peace and social order,—with an enlightened reverence for revealed truth,— and with the sentiment of piety and devotion. . . .

. . . Our political atmosphere has been comparatively serene; our social institutions have not suffered the shock of any disastrous revolution; our country has not been ravaged, as has been the fate of every Continental state, by any

armies. The great territorial possessions of our aristocracy, are but so many stores of wealth and power, by which the civilisation of the people might be promoted. In every English proprietor's domain there ought to be, as in many there are, school-houses with well trained masters, competent and zealous to rear the population in obedience to the laws, in submission to their superiors, and to fit them to strengthen the institutions of their country by their domestic virtues, their sobriety, their industry, and forethought,— by the steadiness of purpose with which they pursue their daily labour,—by the enterprise with which they recover from calamity,—and by the strength of heart with which they are prepared to grapple with the enemies of their country. How striking is the contrast which the estates of the landed proprietors of almost all other European countries bear in all that relates to material wealth—to the domains of our English aristocracy! On the Continent you are met on every side by the proofs of meagre or exhausted resources. In England we have no excuse; we have proofs of how much can be affected, and at how little cost, by the well directed energy of individuals; and we have in our eye examples among our peerage which cannot but be imitated as soon as they are generally known and appreciated.

Our great commercial cities and manufacturing towns contain middle classes whose wealth, enterprise, and intelligence have no successful rivals in Europe; they have made this country the mart of the whole earth; they have covered the seas with their ships, exploring every inlet, estuary, or river which affords them a chance of successful trade. They have colonised almost every accessible region; and from all these sources, as well as from the nightly and daily toil of our working classes in mines, in manufactories, and workshops, in every form of hardy and continued exertion on the sea and on the shore, wealth has been derived, which has supported England in unexampled struggles; yet between the merchants and manufacturers of this country and the poorer class there is little or no alliance, excepting that of mutual interest. But the critical events of this very hour are full of warning, that the ignorance—nay the barbarism—of large portions of our fellow-countrymen, can no longer be neglected, if we are not prepared to substitute a military tyranny or anarchy for the moral subjection which has hitherto been the only safeguard of England. At this hour military force alone retains in subjection great masses of the operative population, beneath whose outrages, if not thus restrained, the wealth and institutions of society would fall. The manufacturers and merchants of England must know what interest they have in the civilisation of the working population; and ere this we trust they are conscious, not merely how deep is their stake in the moral, intellectual, and religious advancement of the labouring class, but how deep is their responsibility to employ for this end the vast resources at their command.

In one other respect England stands in the strongest contrast with the Continental States as to the extent of her means for educational improvement. It is scarcely credible that, with primary education in utter ruin, we should possess educational endowments to the extent of half a million annually, which are either, to a large extent, misapplied, or are used for the support of such feeble and inefficient methods of instruction as to render little service to the community. Whenever the Government shall bend its efforts to combine, for the national advantage, all these great resources, we have no fears for our country. We perceive in it energies possessed by no other nation—partly attributable to the genius of our race; to a large extent derived from the spirit of our policy, which has admitted constant progression in our social institutions; in no small degree to our insular situation, which makes the sea at once the guardian of our liberties and the source of our wealth. But any further delay in the adoption of energetic measures for the elementary education of her working classes is fraught both with intestine and foreign danger—no one can stay the physical influences of wealth—some knowledge the people will acquire by the mere intercourse of society—many appetites are stimulated by a mere physical advancement. With increasing wants comes an increase of discontent, among a people who have only knowledge enough to make them eager for additional enjoyments, and have never yet been sufficiently educated to frame rational wishes and to pursue them by rational means. The mere physical influences of civilisation will not, we fear, make them more moral or religious, better subjects of the State, or better Christians, unless to these be superadded the benefits of an education calculated to develope the entire moral and intellectual capacity of the whole population.

A great change has taken place in the moral and intellectual state of the working classes during the last half century. Formerly, they considered their poverty and sufferings as inevitable, as far as they thought about their origin at all; now, rightly or wrongly, they attribute their sufferings to political causes; they think that by a change in political institutions their condition can be enormously ameliorated. The great Chartist petition, recently presented by Mr. Attwood,[1] affords ample evidence of the prevalence of the restless desire for organic changes, and for violent political measures, which pervades the manufacturing districts, and which is every day increasing. This agitation is no recent matter; it has assumed various other forms in the last thirty years, in all of which the manufacturing population have shown how readily masses of ignorance, discontent, and suffering may be misled. At no period within our memory have the manufacturing districts been free from some form of agitation for unattainable objects referable to these causes. At one period, Luddism[2] prevailed; at another machine-breaking; at successive periods the Trades' Unions have endeavoured in strikes, by hired bands of ruffians, and by assassination, to sustain the rate of wages above that determined by the natural laws of trade; panics have been excited among the working classes, and severe runs upon the Savings' Banks effected from time to time. At one time they have been taught to believe that they could obtain the same wages if an eight hours' bill were passed as if the law permitted them to labour twelve hours in the day; and mills were actually worked on this principle for some weeks, to rivet the conviction in the minds of the working class. The agitation becomes constantly more systematic and better organised, because there is a greater demand for it among the masses, and it is more profitable to the leaders. It is vain to hope that this spirit will subside spontaneously, or that it can be suppressed by coercion. Chartism, an armed political monster, has at length sprung from the soil on which the struggle for the forcible repression of these evils has occurred. It is as certain as any thing future is certain, that the anarchical spirit of the Chartist association will, if left to the operation of the causes now in activity, become every year more formidable. The Chartists think that it is in the power

---

[1]Thomas **Attwood** (1783–1856): Reform Bill advocate, MP from 1832 to 1839, when he presented the People's Charter before the House of Commons.

[2]**Luddism**: sabotage intended to stop industrialization; Luddites, taking their name from one Ned Lud, smashed machinery in middle and N England (1811–1816).

of Government to raise the rate of wages by interfering between the employer and the workman; they imagine that this can be accomplished by a maximum of prices and minimum of wages, or some similar contrivance; and a considerable portion of them believe that the burden of taxation and of all 'fixed charges' (to use Mr. Attwood's expression) ought to be reduced by issuing inconvertible paper, and thus depreciating the currency. They are confident that a Parliament chosen by universal suffrage would be so completely under the dominion of the working classes as to carry these measures into effect; and therefore they petition for universal suffrage, treating all truly remedial measures as unworthy of their notice, or as obstacles to the attainment of the only objects really important. Now the sole effectual means of preventing the tremendous evils with which the anarchical spirit of the manufacturing population threatens the country is, by giving the working people a good secular education, to enable them to understand the true causes which determine their physical condition and regulate the distribution of wealth among the several classes of society. Sufficient intelligence and information to appreciate these causes might be diffused by an education which could easily be brought within the reach of the entire population, though it would necessarily comprehend more than the mere mechanical rudiments of knowledge.

We are far from being alarmists; we write neither under the influence of undue fear, nor with a wish to inspire undue fear into others. The opinions which we have expressed are founded on a careful observation of the proceedings and speeches of the Chartists, and of their predecessors in agitation in the manufacturing districts for many years, as reported in their newspapers; and have been as deliberately formed as they are deliberately expressed. We confess that we cannot contemplate with unconcern the vast physical force which is now moved by men so ignorant and so unprincipled as the Chartist leaders; and without expecting such internal convulsions as may deserve the name of *civil war*, we think it highly probable that persons and property will, in certain parts of the country, be so exposed to violence as materially to affect the prosperity of our manufactures and commerce, to shake the mutual confidence of mercantile men, and to diminish the stability of our political and social institutions. That the country will ultimately recover from these internal convulsions we think, judging from its past history, highly probable; but the recovery will be effected by the painful process of teaching the working classes, by actual experience, that the violent measures which they desire do not tend to improve their condition. (Chapter 1)

1839

CHARLES DICKENS

(1812–1870)

The leading Victorian novelist perhaps needs no introduction here, but the investigative reporter may. Dickens was the son of a government clerk, and his first professional writing was reportage of debates on the floor of the House of Commons. The work he did for periodicals like the *Morning Chronicle* and *Monthly Magazine* accustomed him to writing for deadlines and for strong, immediate effect. Dickens never forgot the correlation between the routinized rhythms of journalism and of the machine age; and, having established himself as a serial novelist during the 1840s, he returned to his journalist roots at decade's end and founded two magazines. For one of these, *Household Words*, he traveled north in the winter of 1854 to cover the prolonged factory-workers' strike in Preston. Emergent trade unions and industrial strikes were new and terrifying phenomena regarded by the ruling classes as lawless, insurrectionary threats to property, profits, and the entire civil order. Ambivalent loyalties suffuse Dickens' account: a "foreigner" yet familiarly received among the conferring strike leaders, he lets them speak for themselves in a sympathetic transcript yet cannot dispense with dialectal markers of their difference from the middle classes. The reader's sense of entering a combat zone in virtual civil war is heightened by an introductory dialogue on the train (here omitted), in which a John Bullish passenger hectors Dickens on the necessity of crushing all insurgency flat.

from On Strike

HOUSEHOLD WORDS
A Weekly Journal.
Conducted by Charles Dickens.
Saturday, February 11, 1854.
Vol. 8, No. 203]   *[Price 2d.*

. . . When I got to Preston,[1] it was four o'clock in the afternoon. The day being Saturday and market-day, a foreigner might have expected, from among so many idle and not over-fed people as the town contained, to find a turbulent, ill-conditioned crowd in the streets. But, except for the cold smokeless factory chimneys, the placards at the street corners, and the groups of working people attentively reading them, nor foreigner nor Englishman could have had the least suspicion that there existed any interruption to the usual labours of the place. The placards thus perused were not remarkable for their logic certainly, and did not make the case particularly clear; but, considering that they emanated from, and were addressed to, people who had been out of employment for three-and-twenty consecutive weeks, at least they had little passion in them, though they had not much reason. . . .

That evening, the Delegates from the surrounding districts were coming in, according to custom, with their subscription lists for the week just closed. These delegates meet on Sunday as their only day of leisure; when they have made their reports, they go back to their homes and their Monday's work. On Sunday morning, I repaired to the Delegates' meeting.

These assemblages take place in a cockpit,[2] which, in the better times of our fallen land, belonged to the late Lord Derby for the purposes of the intellectual recreation implied in its name. I was directed to the cockpit up a narrow lane, tolerably crowded by the lower sort of working people. Personally, I was quite unknown in the town, but every one made way for me to pass, with great civility, and perfect good humour. Arrived at the cockpit door, and expressing my desire to see and hear, I was handed through the crowd, down into the pit, and up again, until I found myself seated on the topmost circular bench, within one of the secretary's table, and within three of the chairman. Behind the chairman was a great crown on top of a pole, made of particoloured calico, and strongly suggestive of May-day. There was no other symbol or ornament in the place.

It was hotter than any mill or factory I have ever been in; but there was a stove down in the sanded pit, and delegates were seated close to it, and one particular delegate often warmed his hands at it, as if he were chilly. The air was so intensely close and hot, that at first I had but a confused perception of the delegates down in the pit, and the dense crowd of eagerly listening men and women (but not very many of the latter) filling all the benches and choking such narrow standing-room as there was. When the atmosphere cleared a little on better acquaintance, I found the question under discussion to be, Whether the Manchester Delegates in attendance from the Labor Parliament,[3] should be heard?

If the Assembly, in respect of quietness and order, were put in comparison with the House of Commons, the Right Honorable the Speaker himself would decide for Preston. The chairman was a Preston weaver, two or three and fifty years of age, perhaps; a man with a capacious head, rather long dark hair growing at the sides and back, a placid attentive face, keen eyes, a particularly composed manner, a quiet voice, and a persuasive action of his right arm. Now look'ee heer my friends. See what t' question is. T' question

---

[1]**Preston:** industrial city in Lancashire (NW England), site of the first cotton-spinning mill in 1777 and of a long and bitter strike at the time of Dickens' visit.

[2]**cockpit:** place constructed for cockfighting and gambling.

[3]**Labor Parliament:** national body of delegates from local workers' organizations, modeled on Chartist "People's Parliament."

is, sholl these heer men be heerd. Then 't cooms to this, what ha' these men got t' tell us? Do they bring mooney? If they bring mooney t'ords t' expences o' this strike, they're welcome. For, Brass, my friends, is what we want, and what we must ha' (hear hear hear!). Do they coom to us wi' any suggestion for the conduct of this strike? If they do, they're welcome. Let 'em give us their advice and we will hearken to 't. But, if these men coom heer, to tell us what t' Labor parliament is, or what Ernest Jones's[4] opinions is, or t' bring in politics and difference amoong us when what we want is 'armony, brotherly love, and con-cord; then I say t' you, decide for yoursel' carefully, whether these men ote to be heerd in this place. (Hear hear hear! and No no no!) Chairman sits down, earnestly regarding delegates, and holding both arms of his chair. Looks extremely sensible; his plain coarse working man's shirt collar easily turned down over his loose Belcher neckerchief.[5] Delegate who has moved that Manchester delegates be heard, presses motion—Mr. Chairman, will that delegate tell us, as a man, that these men have anything to say concerning this present strike and lock-out, for we have a deal of business to do, and what concerns this present strike and lock-out is our business and nothing else is. (Hear hear hear!)—Delegate in question will not compromise the fact; these men want to defend the Labor Parliament from certain charges made against them.—Very well, Mr. Chairman, Then I move as an amendment that you do not hear these men now, and that you proceed wi' business—and if you don't I'll look after you, I tell you that. (Cheers and laughter)—Coom lads, prove 't then!—Two or three hands for the delegates; all the rest for the business. Motion lost, amendment carried, Manchester deputation not to be heard. . . .

Perhaps the world could not afford a more remarkable contrast than between the deliberate collected manner of these men proceeding with their business, and the clash and hurry of the engines among which their lives are passed. Their astonishing fortitude and perseverance; their high sense of honor among themselves; the extent to which they are impressed with the responsibility that is upon them of setting a careful example, and keeping their order out of any harm and loss of reputation; the noble readiness in them to help one another, of which most medical practitioners and working clergymen can give so many affecting examples; could scarcely ever be plainer to an ordinary observer of human nature than in this cockpit. To hold, for a minute, that the great mass of them were not sincerely actuated by the belief that all these qualities were bound up in what they were doing, and that they were doing right, seemed to me little short of an impossibility. As the different delegates (some in the very dress in which they had left the mill last night) reported the amounts sent from the various places they represented, this strong faith on their parts seemed expressed in every tone and every look that was capable of expressing it. One man was raised to enthusiasm by his pride in bringing so much; another man was ashamed and depressed because he brought so little; this man triumphantly made it known that he could give you, from the store in hand, a hundred pounds in addition next week, if you should want it; and that man pleaded that he hoped his district would do better before long; but I could as soon have doubted the existence of the walls that enclosed us, as the earnestness with which they spoke (many of them referring to the children who were to be born to labor after them) of "this great, this noble, gallant, godlike struggle." Some designing and turbulent spirits among them, no doubt there are; but I left the place with a profound conviction that their mistake is generally an honest one, and that it is sustained by the good that is in them, and not by the evil.

Neither by night nor by day was there any interruption to the peace of the streets. Nor was this an accidental state of things, for the police records of the town are eloquent to the same effect. I traversed the streets very much, and was, as a stranger, the subject of a little curiosity among the idlers; but I met with no rudeness or ill-temper. More than once, when I was looking at the printed balance-sheets to which I have referred, and could not quite comprehend the setting forth of the figures, a bystander of the working class interposed with his explanatory forefinger and helped me out. Although the pressure in the cockpit on Sunday was excessive, and the heat of the room obliged me to make my way out as I best could before the close of the proceedings, none of the people whom I put to inconvenience showed the least impatience; all helped me, and all cheerfully acknowledged my word of apology as I passed. It is very probable, notwithstanding, that they may have supposed from my being there at all—I and my companion were the only persons present, not of their own order—that I was there to carry what I heard and saw to the opposite side; indeed one speaker seemed to intimate as much. . . .

In any aspect in which it can be viewed, this strike and lock-out is a deplorable calamity. In its waste of time, in its waste of a great people's energy, in its waste of wages, in its waste of wealth that seeks to be employed, in its encroach-

---

[4]**Ernest Jones** (1819–1869): Chartist barrister, orator, and poet.

[5]**Belcher neckerchief:** polka-dot kerchief worn around the neck, named after early 19th-century boxer Jim Belcher.

ment on the means of many thousands who are laboring from day to day, in the gulf of separation it hourly deepens between those whose interests must be understood to be identical or must be destroyed, it is a great national affliction. But, at this pass, anger is of no use, starving it of no use—for what will that do, five years hence, but overshadow all the mills in England with the growth of a bitter remembrance?—political economy is a mere skeleton unless it has a little human covering and filling out, a little human bloom upon it, and a little human warmth in it. Gentlemen are found, in great manufacturing towns, ready enough to extol imbecile mediation with dangerous madmen abroad;[6] can none of them be brought to think of authorised media-

tion and explanation at home? I do not suppose that such a knotted difficulty as this, is to be at all untangled by a morning-party in the Adelphi;[7] but I would entreat both sides now so miserably opposed, to consider whether there are no men in England, above suspicion, to whom they might refer the matters in dispute, with a perfect confidence above all things in the desire of those men to act justly, and in their sincere attachment to their countrymen of every rank and to their country. Masters right, or men right; masters wrong, or men wrong; both right, or both wrong; there is certain ruin to both in the continuance or frequent revival of this breach. And from the ever-widening circle of their decay, what drop in the social ocean shall be free!

1854

---

[6]**madmen abroad:** Britain had entered the Crimean War in October 1853.

[7]**Adelphi** Terrace: fashionable London club.

HENRY MAYHEW
(1812–1887)

At 15 Henry Mayhew ran away from Westminster, one of the best boarding schools in England. He tried his luck as a midshipman and a lawyer but threw both chances over. At 20 and again at 30, while writing plays and journalism in London, he helped found two magazines, one of which folded and one of which, the phenomenally successful *Punch,* he quit after a year's editorship. At 35 he declared bankruptcy, walking away from his debts and, thanks to a timely change in the law, from prison too. And then at 40, having collaborated with his brother on several novels, Mayhew started publishing in serial format his masterpiece, *London Labour and the London Poor.* The original edition of this compendium of urban sociology and ethnography (1851–1852) was a vast opus, and the enlarged edition of a decade later, which included substantial contributions by other hands, filled four hefty volumes. Much of the work's impact was due to the sheer wealth of fact—narrative, tabular, statistical, graphic data—that Mayhew's diligence amassed. This quantitative aspect of *London Labour* baffles representation in an anthology like this. But there is also a qualitative side to Mayhew, which emerges in his anecdotal literary descriptions of how poor people lived at mid-century in the biggest city in the Western world. Mayhew's methods as an interviewer are not scientifically objective; but they took him where not even Charles Dickens knew to go in the 1850s, and his successes are largely due to the subjective involvement he risked with his informants. This bankrupt and vagabond literary hustler was better placed than most of his class to divine where the London poor were coming from.

from London Labour and the London Poor

THE LONDON STREET MARKETS ON A SATURDAY NIGHT

The street-sellers are to be seen in the greatest numbers at the London street markets on a Saturday night. Here, and in the shops immediately adjoining, the working-classes generally purchase their Sunday's dinner; and after pay-time on Saturday night, or early on Sunday morning, the crowd in the New-cut, and the Brill in particular, is almost impassable. Indeed, the scene in these parts has more of the character of a fair than a market. There are hundreds of stalls, and every stall has its one or two lights; either it is illuminated by the intense white light of the new self-generating gas-lamp, or else it is brightened up by the red smoky flame of the old-fashioned grease lamp.[1] One man shows off his yellow haddock with a candle stuck in a bundle of firewood; his neighbour makes a candlestick of a huge turnip, and the tallow gutters over its sides; whilst the boy shouting "Eight a penny, stunning pears!" has rolled his dip[2] in a thick coat of brown paper, that flares away with the candle. Some stalls are crimson with the fire shining through the holes beneath the baked chestnut stove; others have handsome octohedral lamps, while a few have a candle shining through a sieve: these, with the sparkling ground-glass globes of the tea-dealers' shops, and the butchers' gaslights streaming and fluttering in the wind, like flags of flame, pour forth such a flood of light, that at a distance the atmosphere immediately above the spot is as lurid as if the street were on fire.

The pavement and the road are crowded with purchasers and street-sellers. The housewife in her thick shawl, with the market-basket on her arm, walks slowly on, stopping now to look at the stall of caps, and now to cheapen[3] a bunch of greens. Little boys, holding three or four onions in their hand, creep between the people, wriggling their way through every interstice, and asking for custom in whining tones, as if seeking charity. Then the tumult of the thousand different cries of the eager dealers, all shouting at the top of their voices, at one and the same time, is almost bewildering. "So-old again," roars one. "Chestnuts all 'ot, a penny a score," bawls another. "An 'aypenny a skin, blacking," squeaks a boy. "Buy, buy, buy, buy, buy—bu-u-uy!" cries the butcher. "Half-quire of paper for a penny," bellows the street stationer. "An 'aypenny a lot ing-uns." "Two-pence a pound grapes." "Three a penny Yarmouth bloaters."[4] "Who'll buy a bonnet for fourpence?" "Pick 'em out cheap here! three pair for a halfpenny, bootlaces." "Now's your time! beautiful whelks, a penny a lot." "Here's ha'p'orths," shouts the perambulating confectioner. "Come and look at 'em! here's toasters!" bellows one with a Yarmouth bloater stuck on a toasting-fork. "Penny a lot, fine russets," calls the apple woman: and so the Babel goes on.

One man stands with his red-edged mats hanging over his back and chest, like a herald's coat; and the girl with her basket of walnuts lifts her brown-stained fingers to her mouth, as she screams, "Fine warnuts! sixteen a penny, fine war-r-nuts." A bootmaker, to "ensure custom", has illuminated his shop-front with a line of gas, and in its full glare stands a blind beggar, his eyes turned up so as to show only "the whites," and mumbling some begging rhymes, that are drowned in the shrill notes of the bamboo-flute-player next to him. The boy's sharp cry, the woman's cracked voice, the gruff, hoarse shout of the man, are all mingled together. Sometimes an Irishman is heard with his "fine ating apples"; or else the jingling music of an unseen organ breaks out, as the trio of street singers rest between the verses.

Then the sights, as you elbow your way through the crowd, are equally multifarious. Here is a stall glittering with new tin saucepans; there another, bright with its blue and yellow crockery, and sparkling with white glass. Now you come to a row of old shoes arranged along the pavement; now to a stand of gaudy tea-trays; then to a shop with red handkerchiefs and blue checked shirts, fluttering backwards and forwards, and a counter built up outside on the kerb, behind which are boys beseeching custom. At the door of a tea-shop, with its hundred white globes of light, stands a man delivering bills, thanking the public for past favours, and "defying competition." Here, alongside the road, are some half-dozen headless tailors' dummies, dressed in Chesterfields and fustian jackets, each labelled, "Look at the prices," or "Observe the quality." After this is a butcher's shop, crimson and white with meat piled up to the first-floor, in front of which the butcher himself, in his blue coat, walks up and down, sharpening his knife on the steel that hangs to his waist. A little further on stands the clean

---

[1]**gas-lamp:** burning vapor from coal or lime, began during early 1800s to supplant oil or **grease lamp** in theatrical and city lighting.

[2]**dip:** candle made by dipping a wick into melted tallow.

[3]**cheapen:** bargain for.

[4]**blacking:** substance used to blacken leather. **ing-uns:** onions. **Yarmouth bloaters:** smoked herring.

family, begging; the father with his head down as if in shame, and a box of lucifers held forth in his hand—the boys in newly-washed pinafores, and the tidily got-up mother with a child at her breast. This stall is green and white with bunches of turnips—that red with apples, the next yellow with onions, and another purple with pickling cabbages. One minute you pass a man with an umbrella turned inside up and full of prints; the next, you hear one with a peepshow of Mazeppa, and Paul Jones the pirate,[5] describing the pictures to the boys looking in at the little round windows. Then is heard the sharp snap of the percussion-cap from the crowd of lads firing at the target for nuts; and the moment afterwards, you see a black man half-clad in white, and shivering in the cold with tracts in his hand, or else you hear the sounds of music from "Frazier's Circus", on the other side of the road, and the man outside the door of the penny concert, beseeching you to "Be in time—be in time!" as Mr. Somebody is just about to sing his favourite song of the "Knife Grinder." Such, indeed, is the riot, the struggle, and the scramble for a living, that the confusion and uproar of the New-cut on Saturday night have a bewildering and saddening effect upon the thoughtful mind.

Each salesman tries his utmost to sell his wares, tempting the passerby with his bargains. The boy with his stock of herbs offers "a double 'andful of fine parsley for a penny"; the man with the donkey-cart filled with turnips has three lads to shout for him to their utmost, with their "Ho! ho! hi-i-i! What do you think of this here? a penny a bunch—hurrah for free trade! *Here's* your turnips!" Until it is seen and heard, we have no sense of the scramble that is going on throughout London for a living. The same scene takes place at the Brill—the same in Leather-lane—the same in Tottenham-court-road—the same in Whitecross-street; go to whatever corner of the metropolis you please, either on a Saturday night or a Sunday morning, and there is the same shouting and the same struggling to get the penny profit out of the poor man's Sunday dinner.

Since the above description was written, the New Cut has lost much of its noisy and brilliant glory. In consequence of a New Police regulation, "stands" or "pitches" have been forbidden, and each coster, on a market night, is now obliged, under pain of the lock-up house, to carry his tray, or keep moving with his barrow. The gay stalls have been replaced by deal boards, some sodden with wet fish, others stained purple with blackberries, or brown with wal-nut-peel; and the bright lamps are almost totally superseded by the dim, guttering candle. Even if the pole under the tray or "shallow" is seen resting on the ground, the policeman on duty is obliged to interfere. . . .

The Life of a Coster-Lad[6]

One lad that I spoke to gave me as much of his history as he could remember. He was a tall stout boy, about sixteen years old, with a face utterly vacant. His two heavy lead-coloured eyes stared unmeaningly at me, and, beyond a constant anxiety to keep his front lock curled on his cheek, he did not exhibit the slightest trace of feeling. He sank into his seat heavily and of a heap, and when once settled down he remained motionless, with his mouth open and his hands on his knees—almost as if paralyzed. He was dressed in all the slang beauty of his class, with a bright red handkerchief and unexceptionable boots.

"My father" he told me in a thick unimpassioned voice, "was a waggoner, and worked the country roads. There was two on us at home with mother, and we used to play along with the boys of our court, in Golding-lane, at buttons and marbles. I recollects nothing more than this—only the big boys used to cheat like bricks and thump us if we grumbled—that's all I recollects of my infancy, as you calls it. Father I've heard tell died when I was three and brother only a year old. It was worse luck for us!—Mother was so easy with us. I once went to school for a couple of weeks, but the cove[7] used to fetch me a wipe over the knuckles with his stick, and as I wasn't going to stand that there, why you see I ain't no great schollard. We did as we liked with mother, she was so precious easy, and I never learned anything but playing buttons and making leaden 'bonces,'[8] that's all," (here the youth laughed slightly). "Mother used to be up and out very early washing in families—anything for a living. She was a good mother to us. We was left at home with the key of the room and some bread and butter for dinner. Afore she got into work—and it was a goodish long time— we was shocking hard up, and she pawned nigh everything. Sometimes, when we hadn't no grub at all, the other lads, perhaps, would give us some of their bread and butter, but often our stomachs used to ache with the hunger, and we would cry when we was werry far gone. She used to be at work from six in the morning till ten o'clock at night, which

---

[5]**Mazeppa:** Polish hero of an adventure poem by Byron (1819). John **Paul Jones** (1747–1792), American privateer and naval hero.

[6]**Coster:** street seller of perishable goods.

[7]**cove:** guy (Cockney slang).

[8]**bonces:** large marbles.

was a long time for a child's belly to hold out again, and when it was dark we would go and lie down on the bed and try and sleep until she came home with the food. I was eight year old then.

"A man as know'd mother, said to her, 'Your boy's got nothing to do, let him come along with me and yarn a few ha'pence,' and so I became a coster. He gave me 4*d.* a morning and my breakfast. I worked with him about three year, until I learnt the markets, and then I and brother got baskets of our own, and used to keep mother. One day with another, the two of us together could make 2*s.* 6*d* by selling greens of a morning, and going round to the publics with nuts of an evening, till about ten o'clock at night. Mother used to have a bit of fried meat or a stew ready for us when we got home, and by using up the stock as we couldn't sell, we used to manage pretty tidy. When I was fourteen I took up with a girl. She lived in the same house as we did, and I used to walk out of a night with her and give her half-pints of beer at the publics. She were about thirteen, and used to dress werry nice, though she weren't above middling pretty. Now I'm working for another man as gives me a shilling a week, victuals, washing, and lodging, just as if I was one of the family.

"On a Sunday I goes out selling, and all I yarns I keeps. As for going to church why, I can't afford it,—besides, to tell the truth, I don't like it well enough. Plays, too, ain't in my line much; I'd sooner go to a dance—it's more livelier. The 'penny gaffs'[9] is rather more in my style; the songs are out and out, and makes our gals laugh. The smuttier the better, I thinks; bless you! the gals likes it as much as we do. If we lads ever has a quarrel, why, we fights for it. If I was to let a cove off once, he'd do it again; but I never give a lad a chance, so long as I can get anigh him. I never heard about Christianity, but if a cove was to fetch me a lick of the head, I'd give it him again, whether he was a big 'un or a little 'un. I'd precious soon see a henemy of mine shot afore I'd forgive him,—where's the use? Do I understand what behaving to your neighbour is?—In coorse I do. If a feller as lives next me wanted a basket of mine as I wasn't using, why, he might have it; if I was working it though, I'd see him further![10] I can understand that all as lives in a court is neighbours; but as for policemen, they're nothing to me, and I should like to pay 'em all off well. No; I never heerd about this here creation you speaks about. In coorse God Almighty made the world, and the poor bricklayers' labourers built the houses afterwards—that's *my* opinion; but I can't say, for I've never been in no schools, only always hard at work, and knows nothing about it. I have heerd a little about our Saviour,—they seem to say he were a goodish kind of a man; but if he says as how a cove's to forgive a feller as hits you, I should say he know'd nothing about it. In coorse the gals the lads goes and lives with thinks our walloping 'em wery cruel of us, but we don't. Why don't we?—why, because we don't. Before father died, I used sometimes to say my prayers, but after that mother was too busy getting a living to mind about my praying. Yes, I knows!—in the Lord's prayer they says, 'Forgive us our trespasses, as we forgives them as trespasses agin us.' It's a very good thing, in coorse, but no costers can't do it." . . .

OF THE COSTER-GIRLS

The costermongers, taken as a body, entertain the most imperfect idea of the sanctity of marriage. To their undeveloped minds it merely consists in the fact of a man and woman living together, and sharing the gains they may each earn by selling in the street. The father and mother of the girl look upon it as a convenient means of shifting the support of their child over to another's exertions; and so thoroughly do they believe this to be the end and aim of matrimony, that the expense of a church ceremony is considered as a useless waste of money, and the new pair are received by their companions as cordially as if every form of law and religion had been complied with.

The notions of morality among these people agree strangely, as I have said, with those of many savage tribes—indeed, it would be curious if it were otherwise. They are a part of the Nomades of England, neither knowing nor caring for the enjoyments of home. The hearth, which is so sacred a symbol to all civilized races as being the spot where the virtues of each succeeding generation are taught and encouraged, has no charms to them. The tap-room is the father's chief abiding place; whilst to the mother the house is only a better kind of *tent*. She is away at the stall, or hawking her goods from morning till night, while the children are left to play away the day in the court or alley, and pick their morals out of the gutter. So long as the limbs gain strength the parent cares for nothing else. As the younger ones grow up, their only notions of wrong are formed by what the policeman will permit them to do. If we, who have known from babyhood the kindly influences of a home, require, before we are thrust out into the world to get a living for ourselves, that our perceptions of good and evil should

---

[9] 'penny gaffs': cheap popular theaters or music halls.

[10] I'd see him further!: I'd tell him to get lost!

be quickened and brightened (the same as our perceptions of truth and falsity) by the experience and counsel of those who are wiser and better than ourselves,—if, indeed, it needed a special creation and example to teach the best and strongest of us the law of right, how bitterly must the children of the street-folk require tuition, training, and advice, when from their very cradles (if, indeed, they ever know such luxuries) they are doomed to witness in their parents, whom they naturally believe to be their superiors, habits of life in which passion is the sole rule of action, and where every appetite of our animal nature is indulged in without the least restraint.

I say thus much because I am anxious to make others feel, as I do myself, that *we* are the culpable parties in these matters. That they poor things should do as they do is but human nature—but that *we* should allow them to remain thus destitute of every blessing vouchsafed to ourselves—that we should willingly share what we enjoy with our brethren at the Antipodes, and yet leave those who are nearer and who, therefore, should be dearer to us, to want even the commonest moral necessaries is a paradox that gives to the zeal of our Christianity a strong savour of the chicanery of Cant.

The costermongers strongly resemble the North American Indians in their conduct to their wives. They can understand that it is the duty of the woman to contribute to the happiness of the man, but cannot feel that there is a reciprocal duty from the man to the woman. The wife is considered as an inexpensive servant, and the disobedience of a wish is punished with blows. She must work early and late, and to the husband must be given the proceeds of her labour. Often when the man is in one of his drunken fits—which sometimes last two or three days continuously—she must by her sole exertions find food for herself and him too. To live in peace with him, there must be no murmuring, no tiring under work, no fancied cause for jealousy—for if there be, she is either beaten into submission or cast adrift to begin life again—as another's leavings.

The story of one coster-girl's life may be taken as a type of the many. When quite young she is placed out to nurse with some neighbour, the mother—if a fond one—visiting the child at certain periods of the day, for the purpose of feeding it, or sometimes, knowing the round she has to make, having the infant brought to her at certain places, to be "suckled." As soon as it is old enough to go alone, the court is its play-ground, the gutter its school-room, and under the care of an elder sister the little one passes the day, among children whose mothers like her own are too busy out in the streets helping to get the food, to be able to mind

the family at home. When the girl is strong enough, she in her turn is made to assist the mother by keeping guard over the younger children, or, if there be none, she is lent out to carry about a baby, and so made to add to the family income by gaining her sixpence weekly. Her time is from the earliest years fully occupied; indeed, her parents cannot afford to keep her without doing and getting *something*. Very few of the children receive the least education. "The parents," I am told, "never give their minds to learning, for they say, 'What's the use of it? *that* won't yarn a gal a living.'" Everything is sacrificed—as, indeed, under the circumstances it must be—in the struggle to live—aye! and to live *merely*. Mind, heart, soul, are all absorbed in the belly. The rudest form of animal life, physiologists tell us, is simply a locomotive stomach. Verily, it would appear as if our social state had a tendency to make the highest animal sink into the lowest. . . .

After a girl has once grown accustomed to a street-life, it is almost impossible to wean her from it. The muscular irritability begotten by continued wandering makes her unable to rest for any time in one place, and she soon, if put to any *settled* occupation, gets to crave for the severe exercise she formerly enjoyed. The least restraint will make her sigh after the perfect liberty of the coster's "roving life." As an instance of this I may relate a fact that has occurred within the last six months. A gentleman of high literary repute, struck with the heroic strugglings of a coster Irish girl to maintain her mother, took her to his house, with a view of teaching her the duties of a servant. At first the transition was a painful one to the poor thing. Having travelled barefoot through the streets since a mere child, the pressure of shoes was intolerable to her, and in the evening or whenever a few minutes' rest could be obtained, the boots were taken off, for with them on she could enjoy no ease. The perfect change of life, and the novelty of being in a new place, reconciled her for some time to the loss of her liberty. But no sooner did she hear from her friends, that sprats were again in the market, than, as if there were some magical influence in the fish, she at once requested to be freed from the confinement, and permitted to return to her old calling.

Such is the history of the lower class of girls, though this lower class, I regret to say, constitutes by far the greater portion of the whole. Still I would not for a moment have it inferred that *all* are bad. There are many young girls getting their living, or rather helping to get the living of others in the streets, whose goodness, considering the temptations and hardships besetting such an occupation, approximates to the marvellous. As a type of the more prudent class of coster-girls, I would cite the following narrative received from the lips of a young woman in answer to a series of questions.

THE LIFE OF A COSTER-GIRL

I wished to have obtained a statement from the girl whose portrait is here given, but she was afraid to give the slightest information about the habits of her companions, lest they should recognize her by the engraving and persecute her for the revelations she might make. After disappointing me some dozen times, I was forced to seek out some other coster girl.

The one I fixed upon was a fine-grown young woman of eighteen. She had a habit of curtseying to every question that was put to her. Her plaid shawl was tied over the breast, and her cotton-velvet bonnet was crushed in with carrying her basket. She seemed dreadfully puzzled where to put her hands, at one time tucking them under her shawl, warming them at the fire, or measuring the length of her apron, and when she answered a question she invariably addressed the fireplace. Her voice was husky from shouting apples. . . .

"Only last night father was talking about religion. We often talks about religion. Father has told me that God made the world, and I've heerd him talk about the first man and woman as was made and lived—it must be more than a hundred years ago—but I don't like to speak on what I don't know. Father, too, has told me about our Saviour what was nailed on a cross to suffer for such poor people as we is. Father has told us, too, about his giving a great many poor people a penny loaf and a bit of fish each, which proves him to have been a very kind gentleman. The Ten Commandments was made by him, I've heerd say, and he performed them too among other miracles. Yes! this is part of what our Saviour tells us. We are to forgive everybody, and do nobody no injury. I don't think I could forgive an enemy if she injured me very much; I'm sure I don't know why I couldn't, unless it is that I'm poor, and never learnt to do it. If a gal stole my shawl and didn't return it back or give me the value on it, I couldn't forgive her; but if she told me she lost it off her back, I shouldn't be so hard on her. We poor gals ain't very religious, but we are better than the men. We all of us thanks God for everything—even for a fine day; as for sprats, we always says they're God's blessing for the poor, and thinks it hard of the Lord Mayor not to let 'em come in afore the ninth of November, just because he wants to dine off them—which he always do. Yes, we knows for certain that they eats plenty of sprats at the Lord Mayor's 'blanket'.

They say in the Bible that the world was made in six days: the beasts, the birds, the fish, and all—and sprats was among them in coorse. There was only one house at that time as was made, and that was the Ark for Adam and Eve and their family. It seems very wonderful indeed how all this world was done so quick. I should have thought that England alone would have took double the time; shouldn't you, sir? But then it says in the Bible, God Almighty's a just and true God, and in coorse time would be nothing to him. When a good person is dying, we says, 'The Lord has called upon him, and he must go,' but I can't think what it means, unless it is that an angel comes—like when we're a-dreaming—and tells the party he's wanted in heaven. I know where heaven is; it's above the clouds, and they're placed there to prevent us seeing into it. That's where all the good people go, but I'm afeerd,"—she continued solemnly—"there's very few costers among the angels—'specially those as deceives poor gals.

"No, I don't think this world could well go on for ever. There's a great deal of ground in it, certainly, and it seems very strong at present; but they say there's to be a flood on the earth, and earthquakes, and that will destroy it. The earthquake ought to have took place some time ago, as people tells me, but I never heerd any more about it. If we cheats in the streets. I know we shan't go to Heaven; but it's very hard upon us, for if we didn't cheat we couldn't live, profits is so bad. It's the same with the shops, and I suppose the young men there won't go to Heaven neither; but if people won't give the money, both costers and tradesmen must cheat, and that's very hard. Why, look at apples! customers want them for less than they cost us, and so we are forced to shove in bad ones as well as good ones; and if we're to suffer for that, it does seem to be dreadful cruel."

Curious and extravagant as this statement may perhaps appear to the uninitiated, nevertheless it is here given as it was spoken; and it was spoken with an earnestness that proved the poor girl looked upon it as a subject, the solemnity of which forced her to be truthful. (Volume 1)

OF THE MUD-LARKS

There is another class who may be termed river-finders, although their occupation is connected only with the shore; they are commonly known by the name of "mud-larks", from being compelled, in order to obtain the articles they seek, to wade sometimes up to their middle through the mud left on the shore by the retiring tide. These poor creatures are certainly about the most deplorable in their appearance of any I have met with in the course of my inquiries. They may be seen of all ages, from mere childhood to positive decrepitude, crawling among the barges at the various wharfs along the river; it cannot be said that they are clad in rags, for they are scarcely half covered by the tattered indescribable things that serve them for clothing; their bodies are grimed with the foul soil of the river, and their torn garments stiffened up like boards with dirt of every possible description.

Among the mud-larks may be seen many old women, and it is indeed pitiable to behold them, especially during the winter, bent nearly double with age and infirmity, paddling and groping among the wet mud for small pieces of coal, chips of wood, or any sort of refuse washed up by the tide. These women always have with them an old basket or an old tin kettle, in which they put whatever they chance to find. It usually takes them a whole tide to fill this receptacle, but when filled, it is as much as the feeble old creatures are able to carry home.

The mud-larks generally live in some court or alley in the neighbourhood of the river, and, as the tide recedes, crowds of boys and little girls, some old men, and many old women, may be observed loitering about the various stairs, watching eagerly for the opportunity to commence their labours. When the tide is sufficiently low they scatter themselves along the shore, separating from each other, and soon disappear among the craft lying about in every direction. This is the case on both sides of the river, as high up as there is anything to be found, extending as far as Vauxhall-bridge, and as low down as Woolwich.[11] The mud-larks themselves, however, know only those who reside near them, and whom they are accustomed to meet in their daily pursuits; indeed, with but few exceptions, these people are dull, and apparently stupid; this is observable particularly among the boys and girls, who, when engaged in searching the mud, hold but little converse one with another. The men and women may be passed and repassed, but they notice no one; they never speak, but with a stolid look of wretchedness they plash their way through the mire, their bodies bent down while they peer anxiously about, and occasionally stoop to pick up some paltry treasure that falls in their way.

The mud-larks collect whatever they happen to find, such as coals, bits of old-iron, rope, bones, and copper nails that drop from ships while lying or repairing along shore. Copper nails are the most valuable of all the articles they

find, but these they seldom obtain, as they are always driven from the neighbourhood of a ship while being new-sheathed. Sometimes the younger and bolder mud-larks venture on sweeping some empty coal-barge, and one little fellow with whom I spoke, having been lately caught in the act of so doing, had to undergo for the offence seven days' imprisonment in the House of Correction: this, he says, he liked much better than mud-larking, for while he staid there he wore a coat and shoes and stockings, and though he had not over much to eat, he certainly was never afraid of going to bed without anything at all—as he often had to do when at liberty. He thought he would try it on again in the winter, he told me, saying, it would be so comfortable to have clothes and shoes and stockings then, and not be obliged to go into the cold wet mud of a morning.

The coals that the mud-larks find, they sell to the poor people of the neighbourhood at 1*d.* per pot, holding about 14 lbs. The iron and bones and rope and copper nails which they collect, they sell at the rag-shops. They dispose of the iron at 5 lbs. for 1*d.*, the bones at 3 lbs. a 1*d.*, rope at ½*d.* per lb. wet, and ¾*d.* per lb. dry, and copper nails at the rate of 4*d.* per lb. They occasionally pick up tools, such as saws and hammers; these they dispose of to the seamen for biscuit and meat, and sometimes sell them at the rag-shops for a few halfpence. In this manner they earn from 2½*d.* to 8*d.* per day, but rarely the latter sum; their average gains may be estimated at about 3*d.* per day. The boys, after leaving the river, sometimes scrape their trousers, and frequent the cab-stands, and try to earn a trifle by opening the cab-doors for those who enter them, or by holding gentlemen's horses. Some of them go, in the evening, to a ragged school,[12] in the neighbourhood of which they live; more, as they say, because other boys go there, than from any desire to learn.

At one of the stairs in the neighbourhood of the pool, I collected about a dozen of these unfortunate children; there was not one of them over twelve years of age, and many of them were but six. It would be almost impossible to describe the wretched group, so motley was their appearance, so extraordinary their dress, and so stolid and inexpressive their countenances. Some carried baskets, filled with the produce of their morning's work, and others old tin kettles with iron handles. Some, for want of these articles, had old hats filled with the bones and coals they had picked up; and others, more needy still, had actually taken the caps from their own heads, and filled them with what they had happened to find.

---

[11]**Vauxhall Bridge:** spans Thames River, W of central London. **Woolwich:** in borough of Greenwich, E of central London.

[12]**ragged school:** charity school for poor children.

The muddy slush was dripping from their clothes and uten-sils, and forming a puddle in which they stood. There did not appear to be among the whole group as many filthy cot-ton rags to their backs as, when stitched together, would have been sufficient to form the material of one shirt. . . . (Volume 2)

STREET CLOWN

He was a melancholy-looking man, with the sunken eyes and other characteristics of semi-starvation, whilst his face was scored with lines and wrinkles, telling of paint and pre-mature age.

I saw him performing in the streets with a school of ac-robats soon after I had been questioning him, and the readi-ness and business-like way with which he resumed his professional buffoonery was not a little remarkable. His story was more pathetic than comic, and proved that the life of a street clown is, perhaps, the most wretched of all existence. Jest as he may in the street, his life is literally no joke at home. . . .

"Frequently when I am playing the fool in the streets, I feel very sad at heart. I can't help thinking of the bare cup-boards at home; but what's that to the world? I've often and often been at home all day when it has been wet, with no food at all, either to give my children or take myself, and have gone out at night to the public-houses to sing a comic song or play the funnyman for a meal—you may imagine with what feelings for the part—and when I've come home I've call'd my children up from their beds to share the loaf I had brought back with me. I know three or more clowns as miserable and bad off as myself. The way in which our pro-fession is ruined is by the stragglers or outsiders, who are often men who are good tradesmen. They take to the clown's business only at holiday or fair time, when there is a little money to be picked up at it, and after that they go back to their own trades; so that, you see, we, who are obliged to continue at it the year through, are deprived of even the little bit of luck we should otherwise have. I know only of another regular street clown in London besides my-self. Some schools of acrobats, to be sure, will have a comic character of some kind or other, to keep the pitch up; that is, to amuse the people while the money is being collected: but these, in general, are not regular clowns. They are mostly dressed and got up for the occasion. They certainly don't do anything else but the street comic business, but they are not pantomimists by profession. The street clowns generally go out with dancers and tumblers. There are some street clowns to be seen with the Jacks-in-the-greens; but they are mostly sweeps, who have hired their dress for the two or three days, as the case may be. I think there are three regular clowns in the metropolis, and one of these is not a professional: he never smelt the sawdust, I know, sir. The most that I have known have been shoemakers before tak-ing to the business. When I go out as a street clown, the first thing I do is a comic medley dance; and then after that I crack a few jokes, and that is the whole of my entertain-ment. The first part of the medley dance is called 'the good St Anthony' (I was the first that ever danced the polka[13] in the streets); then I do a waltz, and wind up with a hornpipe. After that I go through a little burlesque business. I fan my-self, and one of the school asks me whether I am out of breath? I answer, 'No, the breath is out of me.' The leading questions for the jokes are all regularly prepared before-hand. The old jokes always go best with our audiences. The older they are, the better for the streets. I know, indeed, of nothing new in the joking way; but even if there was, and it was in anyway deep, it would not do for the public thor-oughfares. I have read a great deal of 'Punch,'[14] but the jokes are nearly all too high there; indeed, I can't say I think very much of them myself. The principal way in which I've got up my jokes is through associating with other clowns. We don't make our jokes ourselves; in fact, I never knew one clown who did. I must own that the street clowns like a lit-tle drop of spirits, and occasionally a good deal. They are in a measure obligated to it. I can't fancy a clown being funny on small beer; and I never in all my life knew one who was a teetotaller. I think such a person would be a curious charac-ter, indeed. Most of the street clowns die in the work-houses. In their old age they are generally very wretched and poverty-stricken. I can't say what I think will be the end of me. I daren't think of it, sir."

A few minutes afterwards I saw this man dressed as Jim Crow,[15] with his face blackened, dancing and singing in the streets as if he was the lightest-hearted fellow in all London. (Volume 3)

1861

---

[13]**polka**: Bohemian folk dance that swept Europe and America in the 1840s.

[14]**"Punch"**: illustrated periodical published since 1841; Mayhew was among the first editors. See plate facing page 684.

[15]**Jim Crow**: blackface minstrel routine popular in 1840s London.

WALTER BAGEHOT

(1826–1877)

Born into a Unitarian family of merchants and bankers, Bagehot (rhymes with *gadget*) had a brilliant career at the still new, nonsectarian University of London and then, after a few unhappy years as a law student, settled into a career in shipping and finance. He practiced political, economic, and literary journalism on the side for a decade, until in 1860 he succeeded his father-in-law as editor of *The Economist,* an influential journal whose statistical and analytic reach he extended even as he broadened its outlook on larger questions of social policy. Bagehot's writings demonstrate a versatility remarkable even among the Victorians: sane and witty essays in literary criticism, an experimental study applying new evolutionary theory to cultural development (*Physics and Politics,* 1872), and the work we excerpt here. Appearing just at the epoch of the second Reform Bill, *The English Constitution* anatomizes with cheerful if Machiavellian candor how the British government has evolved to meet the needs of mass society on an imperial scale. Gray MPs and unglamorous bureaucrats hold the (real) power and get the work done, while a celebrity class of royals and nobles meet the (also real) popular need for frequent enactment of the nation's greatness at a symbolic level. Like all political and social analysis of its day, Bagehot's takes for granted an immense disparity between classes in the constitutional monarchy of which the British were so proud. He proposes that the apparently useless hereditary trappings of government performed important cultural work by helping to hold an outdated, unwieldy, and apparently illogical political system together in rapidly changing social and economic times.

from The English Constitution

. . . No one can approach to an understanding of the English institutions, or of others which, being the growth of many centuries, exercise a wide sway over mixed populations, unless he divide them into two classes. In such constitutions there are two parts (not indeed separable with microscopic accuracy, for the genius of great affairs abhors nicety of division): first, those which excite and preserve the reverence of the population—the *dignified* parts, if I may so call them; and next, the *efficient* parts—those by which it, in fact, works and rules. There are two great objects which every constitution must attain to be successful, which every old and celebrated one must have wonderfully achieved: every constitution must first *gain* authority, and then *use* authority; it must first win the loyalty and confidence of mankind, and then employ that homage in the work of government.

There are indeed practical men who reject the dignified parts of government. They say, we want only to attain results, to do business: a constitution is a collection of political means for political ends, and if you admit that any part of a constitution does no business, or that a simpler machine would do equally well what it does, you admit that this part of the constitution, however dignified or awful it may be, is nevertheless in truth useless. And other reasoners, who distrust this bare philosophy, have propounded subtle arguments to prove that these dignified parts of old governments are cardinal components of the essential apparatus, great pivots of substantial utility; and so they manufactured fallacies which the plainer school have well exposed. But both schools are in error. The dignified parts of government are those which bring it force—which attract its motive power. The efficient parts only employ that power. The comely parts of a government *have* need, for they are those upon which its vital strength depends. They may not do anything definite that a simpler polity would not do better; but they are the preliminaries, the needful pre-requisites of *all* work. They raise the army, though they do not win the battle.

Doubtless, if all subjects of the same government only thought of what was useful to them, and if they all thought the same thing useful, and all thought that same thing could be attained in the same way, the efficient members of a constitution would suffice, and no impressive adjuncts would be needed. But the world in which we live is organized far otherwise.

The most strange fact, though the most certain in nature, is the unequal development of the human race. If we look back to the early ages of mankind, such as we seem in the faint distance to see them—if we call up the image of those dismal tribes in lake villages, or on wretched beaches—scarcely equal to the commonest material needs, cutting down trees slowly and painfully with stone tools, hardly resisting the attacks of huge, fierce animals—without culture, without leisure, without poetry, almost without thought—destitute of morality, with only a sort of magic for religion; and if we compare that imagined life with the actual life of Europe now, we are overwhelmed at the wide contrast—we can scarcely conceive ourselves to be of the same race as those in the far distance. There used to be a notion—not so much widely asserted as deeply implanted, rather pervadingly latent than commonly apparent in political philosophy—that in a little while, perhaps ten years or so, all human beings might, without extraordinary appliances, be brought to the same level. But now, when we see by the painful history of mankind at what point we began, by what slow toil, what favourable circumstances, what accumulated achievements, civilized man has become at all worthy in any degree so to call himself—when we realize the tedium of history and the painfulness of results—our perceptions are sharpened as to the relative steps of our long and gradual progress. We have in a great community like England crowds of people scarcely more civilized than the majority of two thousand years ago; we have others, even more numerous, such as the best people were a thousand years since. The lower orders, the middle orders, are still, when tried by what is the standard of the educated "ten thousand," narrow-minded, unintelligent, incurious. It is useless to pile up abstract words. Those who doubt should go out into their kitchens. Let an accomplished man try what seems to him most obvious, most certain, most palpable in intellectual matters, upon the housemaid and the footman, and he will find that what he says seems unintelligible, confused, and erroneous—that his audience think him mad and wild when he is speaking what is in his own sphere of thought the dullest platitude of cautious soberness. Great communities are like great mountains—they have in them the primary, secondary, and tertiary strata of human

progress; the characteristics of the lower regions resemble the life of old times rather than the present life of the higher regions. And a philosophy which does not ceaselessly remember, which does not continually obtrude, the palpable differences of the various parts, will be a theory radically false, because it has omitted a capital reality—will be a theory essentially misleading, because it will lead men to expect what does not exist, and not to anticipate that which they will find. . . .

The brief description of the characteristic merit of the English Constitution is, that its dignified parts are very complicated and somewhat imposing, very old and rather venerable; while its efficient part, at least when in great and critical action, is decidedly simple and rather modern. We have made, or rather stumbled on, a constitution which—though full of every species of incidental defect, though of the worst *workmanship* in all out-of-the-way matters of any constitution in the world—yet has two capital merits: it contains a simple efficient part which, on occasion, and when wanted, *can* work more simply and easily, and better, than any instrument of government that has yet been tried; and it contains likewise historical, complex, august, theatrical parts, which it has inherited from a long past—which *take* the multitude—which guide by an insensible but an omnipotent influence the associations of its subjects. Its essence is strong with the strength of modern simplicity; its exterior is august with the Gothic grandeur of a more imposing age. . . . (Chapter 1)

. . . The characteristic of the English Monarchy is that it retains the feelings by which the heroic kings governed their rude age, and has added the feelings by which the constitutions of later Greece ruled in more refined ages. We are a more mixed people than the Athenians, or probably than any political Greeks. We have progressed more unequally. The slaves in ancient times were a separate order; not ruled by the same laws, or thoughts, as other men. It was not necessary to think of them in making a constitution: it was not necessary to improve them in order to make a constitution possible. The Greek legislator had not to combine in his polity men like the labourers of Somersetshire, and men like Mr. Grote.[1] He had not to deal with a community in which primitive barbarism lay as a recognized basis to acquired civilization. *We have.* We have no slaves to keep down by spe-

---

[1]George **Grote** (1794–1871): author of the 12-volume *History of Greece* (1846–1856), vice chancellor of University of London.

cial terrors and independent legislation. But we have whole classes unable to comprehend the idea of a constitution—unable to feel the least attachment to impersonal laws. Most do indeed vaguely know that there are some other institutions besides the Queen, and some rules by which she governs. But a vast number like their minds to dwell more upon her than upon anything else, and therefore she is inestimable. A Republic has only difficult ideas in government; a Constitutional Monarchy has an easy idea too; it has a comprehensible element for the vacant many, as well as complex laws and notions for the inquiring few.

A *family* on the throne is an interesting idea also. It brings down the pride of sovereignty to the level of petty life. No feeling could seem more childish than the enthusiasm of the English at the marriage of the Prince of Wales.[2] They treated as a great political event, what, looked at as a matter of pure business, was very small indeed. But no feeling could be more like common human nature as it is, and as it is likely to be. The women—one half the human race at least—care fifty times more for a marriage than a ministry. All but a few cynics like to see a pretty novel touching for a moment the dry scenes of the grave world. A princely marriage is the brilliant edition of a universal fact, and as such, it rivets mankind. We smile at the *Court Circular*; but remember how many people read the *Court Circular*![3] Its use is not in what it says, but in those to whom it speaks. They say that the Americans were more pleased at the Queen's letter to Mrs. Lincoln,[4] than at any act of the English Government. It was a spontaneous act of intelligible feeling in the midst of confused and tiresome business. Just so a royal family sweetens politics by the seasonable addition of nice and pretty events. It introduces irrelevant facts into the business of government, but they are facts which speak to "men's bosoms" and employ their thoughts.

To state the matter shortly, Royalty is a government in which the attention of the nation is concentrated on one person doing interesting actions. A Republic is a government in which that attention is divided between many, who are all doing uninteresting actions. Accordingly, so long as the human heart is strong and the human reason weak, Roy-

alty will be strong because it appeals to diffused feeling, and Republics weak because they appeal to the understanding. . . . (Chapter 2)

. . . The order of nobility is of great use, too, not only in what it creates, but in what it prevents. It prevents the rule of wealth—the religion of gold. This is the obvious and natural idol of the Anglo-Saxon. He is always trying to make money; he reckons everything in coin; he bows down before a great heap, and sneers as he passes a little heap. He has a "natural instinctive admiration of wealth for its own sake." And within good limits the feeling is quite right. So long as we play the game of industry vigorously and eagerly (and I hope we shall long play it, for we must be very different from what we are if we do anything better), we shall of necessity respect and admire those who play successfully, and a little despise those who play unsuccessfully. Whether this feeling be right or wrong, it is useless to discuss; to a certain degree, it is involuntary: it is not for mortals to settle whether we will have it or not; nature settles for us that, within moderate limits, we must have it. But the admiration of wealth in many countries goes far beyond this; it ceases to regard in any degree the skill of acquisition; it respects wealth in the hands of the inheritor just as much as in the hands of the maker; it is a simple envy and love of a heap of gold as a heap of gold. From this our aristocracy preserves us. There is no country where a "poor devil of a millionaire is so ill off as in England." The experiment is tried every day, and every day it is proved that money alone—money *pur et simple*—will not buy "London Society." Money is kept down, and, so to say, cowed by the predominant authority of a different power.

But it may be said that this is no gain; that worship for worship, the worship of money is as good as the worship of rank. Even granting that it were so, it is a great gain to society to have two idols; in the competition of idolatries, the true worship gets a chance. But it is not true that the reverence for rank—at least, for hereditary rank—is as base as the reverence for money. As the world has gone, manner has been half-hereditary in certain castes, and manner is one of the fine arts. It is the *style* of society; it is in the daily-spoken intercourse of human beings what the art of literary expression is in their occasional written intercourse. In reverencing wealth we reverence not a man, but an appendix to a man; in reverencing inherited nobility, we reverence the probable possession of a great faculty—the faculty of bringing out what is in one. The unconscious grace of life *may* be in the middle classes: finely-mannered persons are born everywhere; but it *ought* to be in the aristocracy; and a man

---

[2]**Prince of Wales**: Victoria's son and successor, the future Edward VII, married Princess Alexandra of Denmark in 1863.

[3]*Court Circular*: record of affairs at the royal court, published in daily newspapers.

[4]**letter to Mrs. Lincoln**: after assassination of Abraham Lincoln in 1865.

must be born with a hitch in his nerves if he has not some of it. It is a physiological possession of the race, though it is sometimes wanting in the individual.

There is a third idolatry from which that of rank preserves us, and perhaps it is the worst of any—that of office. The basest deity is a subordinate *employé*, and yet just now in civilized governments it is the commonest. In France and all the best of the Continent it rules like a superstition. It is to no purpose that you prove that the pay of petty officials is smaller than mercantile pay; that their work is more monotonous than mercantile work; that their mind is less useful and their life more tame. They are still thought to be greater and better. They are *decorés*; they have a little red on the left breast of their coat, and no argument will answer that. In England, by the odd course of our society, what a theorist would desire has in fact turned up. The great offices, whether permanent or parliamentary, which require mind now give social prestige, and almost only those. An Under-Secretary of State with £2,000 a-year is a much greater man than the director of a finance company with £5,000, and the country saves the difference. But except in a few offices like the Treasury, which were once filled with aristocratic people, and have an odour of nobility at second-hand, minor place is of no social use. A big grocer despises the exciseman; and what in many countries would be thought impossible, the exciseman envies the grocer. Solid wealth tells where there is no artificial dignity given to petty public functions. A clerk in the public service is "nobody"; and you could not make a common Englishman see why he should be anybody. . . . (Chapter 4)

. . . We are ruled by the House of Commons; we are, indeed, so used to be so ruled, that it does not seem to be at all strange. But of all odd forms of government, the oddest really is government by a *public meeting*. Here are 658 persons, collected from all parts of England, different in nature, different in interests, different in look and language. If we think what an empire the English is, how various are its components, how incessant its concerns, how immersed in history its policy: if we think what a vast information, what a nice discretion, what a consistent will ought to mark the rulers of that empire,—we shall be surprised when we see them. We see a changing body of miscellaneous persons, sometimes few, sometimes many, never the same for an hour; sometimes excited but mostly dull and half weary,—impatient of eloquence, catching at any joke as an alleviation. These are the persons who rule the British empire,—who rule England,—who rule Scotland,—who rule Ireland,—who rule a great

deal of Asia,—who rule a great deal of Polynesia,—who rule a great deal of America, and scattered fragments everywhere.

Paley[5] said many shrewd things, but he never said a better thing than that it was much harder to make men see a difficulty than comprehend the explanation of it. The key to the difficulties of most discussed and unsettled questions is commonly in their undiscussed parts; they are like the background of a picture which looks obvious, easy, just what any one might have painted, but which, in fact, sets the figures in their right position, chastens them, and makes them what they are. Nobody will understand parliament government who fancies it an easy thing, a natural thing, a thing not needing explanation. You have not a perception of the first elements in this matter till you know that government by a *club* is a standing wonder. . . . (Chapter 5)

. . . The middle classes—the ordinary majority of educated men—are in the present day the despotic power in England. "Public opinion," nowadays, "is the opinion of the bald-headed man at the back of the omnibus." It is *not* the opinion of the aristocratical classes as such; or of the most educated or refined classes as such; it is simply the opinion of the ordinary mass of educated, but still commonplace, mankind. If you look at the mass of the constituencies, you will see that they are not very interesting people; and perhaps if you look behind the scenes and see the people who manipulate and work the constituencies, you will find that these are yet more uninteresting. The English constitution in its palpable form is this—the mass of the people yield obedience to a select few; and when you see this select few, you perceive that though not of the lowest class, nor of an unrespectable class, they are yet of a heavy sensible class— the last people in the world to whom, if they were drawn up in a row, an immense nation would ever give an exclusive preference.

In fact, the mass of the English people yield a deference rather to something else than to their rulers. They defer to what we may call the *theatrical show* of society. A certain state passes before them; a certain pomp of great men; a certain spectacle of beautiful women; a wonderful scene of wealth and enjoyment is displayed, and they are coerced by it. Their imagination is bowed down; they feel they are not equal to the life which is revealed to them. Courts and aristocracies have the great quality which rules

---

[5]William **Paley** (1743–1805): Anglican theologian and philosopher.

the multitude, though philosophers can see nothing in it—visibility. Courtiers can do what others cannot. A common man may as well try to rival the actors on the stage in their acting, as the aristocracy in *their* acting. The higher world, as it looks from without, is a stage on which the actors walk their parts much better than the spectators can. This play is played in every district. Every rustic feels that his house is not like my lord's house; his life like my lord's life; his wife like my lady. The climax of the play is the Queen: nobody supposes that their house is like the court; their life like her life; her orders like their orders. There is in England a certain charmed spectacle which imposes on the many, and guides their fancies as it will. As a rustic on coming to London finds himself in the presence of a great show and vast exhibition of inconceivable mechanical things, so by the structure of our society he finds himself face to face with a great exhibition of political things which he could not have imagined, which he could not make—to which he feels in himself scarcely anything analogous.

Philosophers may deride this superstition, but its results are inestimable. By the spectacle of this august society, countless ignorant men and women are induced to obey the few nominal electors—the £10 borough renters, and the £50 county renters[6]—who have nothing imposing about them, nothing which would attract the eye or fascinate the fancy. What impresses men is not mind, but the result of mind. And the greatest of these results is this wonderful spectacle of society, which is ever new, and yet ever the same; in which accidents pass and essence remains; in which one generation dies and another succeeds, as if they were birds in a cage, or animals in a menagerie; of which it seems almost more than a metaphor to treat the parts as limbs of a perpetual living thing, so silently do they seem to change, so wonderfully and so perfectly does the conspicuous life of the new year take the place of the conspicuous life of last year. The apparent rulers of the English nation are like the most imposing personages of a splendid procession: it is by them the mob are influenced; it is they whom the spectators cheer. The real rulers are secreted in second-rate carriages; no one cares for them or asks about them, but they are obeyed implicitly and unconsciously by reason of the splendour of those who eclipsed and preceded them. (Chapter 8)

1867

---

[6]**renters**: taxpayers, here those whose tax rates confer voting rights.

SIDNEY WEBB

(1859–1947)

One of the major British intellectuals of his day, Sidney Webb had a lower-middle-class upbringing and went to work in the civil service, earning his higher education in night school and admission to the bar in 1884. In that year the Fabian Society was founded as a sort of moderate socialist think-tank aiming to influence national policy by educational and persuasive means. At the urging of fellow member George Bernard Shaw, Webb made his practical mark in 1887 with *Facts for Socialists,* and the next year he delivered the lecture excerpted here, which Shaw included in the widely read volume *Fabian Essays in Socialism.* In 1892 Webb won a seat on the London County Council, where he remained until 1910, and also won the hand of the heiress and intellectual Beatrice Potter, with whom he jointly authored *The History of Trade Unionism* (1894) and *Industrial Democracy* (1897). The latter was soon translated into Russian by another recently married couple, V. Lenin and N. Krupskaya. A founder of the London School of Economics in 1895, Sidney Webb became a Labour MP in the 1920s and a baron in 1929. His ashes and Beatrice Webb's were buried in Westminster Abbey.

These twentieth-century honors attest the eventual triumph of a welfare policy and a collectivist orientation for which, in the following excerpt, we see the young Fabian lecturer framing an initial case as he recapitulates nineteenth-century intellectual history from a socialist-Darwinian point of view.

from The Basis of Socialism: Historic

THE NEW SYNTHESIS

It need hardly be said that the social philosophy of the time did not remain unaffected by the political evolution and the industrial development. Slowly sinking into men's minds all this while was the conception of a new social nexus, and a new end of social life. It was discovered (or rediscovered) that a society is something more than an aggregate of so many individual units—that it possesses existence distinguishable from those of any of its components. A perfect city became recognized as something more than any number of good citizens—something to be tried by other tests, and weighed in other balances than the individual man. The community must necessarily aim, consciously or not, at its continuance as a community; its life transcends that of any of its members; and the interests of the individual unit must often clash with those of the whole. Though the social organism has itself evolved from the union of individual men, the individual is now created by the social organism of which he forms a part: his life is born of the larger life; his attributes are moulded by the social pressure; his activities, inextricably interwoven with others, belong to the activity of the whole. Without the continuance and sound health of the social organism, no man can now live or thrive; and its persistence is accordingly his paramount end. His conscious motive for action may be, nay, always must be, individual to himself; but where such action proves inimical to the social welfare, it must sooner or later be checked by the whole, lest the whole perish through the error of its member. The conditions of social health are accordingly a matter for scientific investigation. There is, at any moment, one particular arrangement of social relations which involves the minimum of human misery then and there possible amid the "niggardliness of nature."[1] Fifty years ago it would have been assumed that absolute freedom in the sense of individual or "manly" independence, plus a criminal code, would spontaneously result in such an arrangement for each particular nation; and the effect was the philosophic apotheosis of *Laisser Faire*. To-day every student is aware that no such optimistic assumption is warranted by the facts of life. We know now that in natural selection at the stage of development where the existence of civilized mankind is at stake, the units selected from are not individuals, but societies. Its action at earlier stages, though analogous, is quite dissimilar. Among the lower animals physical strength or agility is the favored quality; if some heaven-sent genius among the cuttlefish developed a delicate poetic faculty, this high excellence would not delay his succumbing to his hulking neighbor. When, higher up in the scale, mental cunning became the favored attribute, an extra brain convolution, leading primitive man to the invention of fire or tools, enabled a comparatively puny savage to become the conqueror and survivor of his fellows.

Brain culture accordingly developed apace; but we do not yet thoroughly realize that this has itself been superseded as the "selected" attribute, by social organization. The cultivated Athenians, Saracens, and Provençals[2] went down in the struggle for existence before their respective competitors, who, individually inferior, were in possession of a, at that time, more valuable social organization. The French nation was beaten in the last war,[3] not because the average German was an inch and a half taller than the average Frenchman, or because he had read five more books, but because the German social organism, was, for the purposes of the time, superior in efficiency to the French. If we desire to hand on to the after-world our direct influence, and not merely the memory of our excellence, we must take even more care to improve the social organism of which we form part, than to perfect our own individual developments. Or

---

[1] **"niggardliness of nature"**: quoting J. S. Mill, *Principles of Political Economy* (1848).

[2] **Athenians, Saracens, and Provençals**: defeated by, respectively, the 4th-century BCE Macedonians, the medieval Crusaders, and the 5th-century Goths.

[3] **last war**: the Franco-Prussian War (1870–1871).

rather, the perfect and fitting development of each individual is not necessarily the utmost and highest cultivation of his own personality, but the filling, in the best possible way, of his humble function in the great social machine. We must abandon the self-conceit of imagining that we are independent units, and bend our jealous minds, absorbed in their own cultivation, to this subjection to the higher end, the Common Weal. Accordingly, conscious "direct adaptation" steadily supplants the unconscious and wasteful "indirect adaptation" of the earlier form of the struggle for existence; and with every advance in sociological knowledge, Man is seen to assume more and more, not only the mastery of "things," but also a conscious control over social destiny itself. . . .

The result of this development of Sociology is to compel a revision of the relative importance of liberty and equality as principles to be kept in view in social administration. In Bentham's[4] celebrated "ends" to be aimed at in a civil code, liberty stands predominant over equality, on the ground that full equality can be maintained only by the loss of security for the fruits of labor. That exposition remains as true as ever; but the question for decision remains, how much liberty? . . .

. . . For he cannot escape the lesson of the century, taught alike by the economists, the statesmen, and the "practical men," that complete individual liberty, with unrestrained private ownership of the instruments of wealth production, is irreconcilable with the common weal. The free struggle for existence among ourselves menaces our survival as a healthy and permanent social organism. Evolution, Professor Huxley declares, is the substitution of consciously regulated co-ordination among the units of each organism, for blind anarchic competition. Thirty years ago Herbert Spencer demonstrated the incompatibility of full private property in land with the modern democratic State; and almost every economist now preaches the same doctrine. The Radical is rapidly arriving, from practical experience, at similar conclusions; and the steady increase of the government regulation of private enterprise, the growth of municipal administration, and the rapid shifting of the burden of taxation directly to rent and interest, mark in treble lines the statesman's unconscious abandonment of the old Individualism, and our irresistible glide into collectivist Socialism.

It was inevitable that the Democracy should learn this lesson. With the masses painfully conscious of the failure of Individualism to create a decent social life for four-fifths of the people, it might have been foreseen that Individualism could not survive their advent to political power. If private property in land and capital necessarily keeps the many workers permanently poor (through no fault of their own), in order to make the few idlers rich (from no merit of their own), private property in land and capital will inevitably go the way of the feudalism which is superseded. The economic analysis confirms the rough generalization of the suffering people. The history of industrial evolution points to the same result; and for two generations the world's chief ethical teachers have been urging the same lesson. No wonder the heavens of Individualism are rolling up before our eyes like a scroll; and even the Bishops believe and tremble.

It is, of course, possible, as Sir Henry Maine[5] and others have suggested, that the whole experience of the century is a mistake, and that political power will once more swing back into the hands of a monarch or an aristocratic oligarchy. It is, indeed, want of faith in Democracy which holds back most educated sympathisers with Socialism from frankly accepting its principles. What the economic side of such political atavism would be it is not easy to forecast. The machine industry and steam power could hardly be dismissed with the caucus and the ballot-box. So long, however, as Democracy in political administration continues to be the dominant principle, Socialism may be quite safely predicted as its economic obverse, in spite of those freaks or aberrations of Democracy which have already here and there thrown up a short-lived monarchy or a romantic dictatorship. Every increase in the political power of the proletariat will most surely be used by them for their economic and social protection. In England, at any rate, the history of the century serves at once as their guide and their justification.

1889

---

[4]Jeremy **Bentham** (1748–1832): leading Utilitarian philosopher.

[5]**Sir Henry Maine** (1822–1888): jurist and legal historian.

WILLIAM BOOTH

(1829–1912)

At the age of 15 William Booth, an apprentice pawnbroker, was born again as a Christian evangelist convinced that eternal damnation awaited the unconverted. He left his native Nottingham to rescue souls in London, first as a Methodist sectarian preacher and then, starting in 1865, at a mission he founded in the East End slums. When he reorganized this Christian Mission on a British military model in 1878 and named himself General Booth, the Salvation Army was launched on what became a campaign against sin and the degradation of poverty throughout the English-speaking world. Braving years of ridicule and persecution, the Salvation Army became such a household word that in 1902 an appreciative Edward VII required Booth's presence at his coronation. The best-seller Booth wrote in 1890 with the help of popular journalist W. T. Stead, *In Darkest England,* summoned the attention of late Victorian readers home from the reaches of empire and toward the misery within their own neglected inner cities. The book's strident call to battle sounded a deep connection of "civilization" with "savagery," which would also resonate in such 1890s works as Bram Stoker's *Dracula* and Joseph Conrad's *Heart of Darkness.* Even as Booth pointed the modern missionary to England's own doorstep and hearth, his work with immigrant and emigrant populations—not to mention the booming export of the Salvation Army itself around the world—showed to what extent domestic distress and homelessness now had to be treated as local symptoms of global ills. (This worldwide continuum receives vivid graphic representation in the plate facing page 685.)

from In Darkest England and the Way Out

This summer the attention of the civilised world has been arrested by the story which Mr. Stanley has told of "Darkest Africa" and his journeyings across the heart of the Lost Continent. In all that spirited narrative of heroic endeavour, nothing has so much impressed the imagination, as his description of the immense forest, which offered an almost impenetrable barrier to his advance. . . .

It is a terrible picture, and one that has engraved itself deep on the heart of civilisation. But while brooding over the awful presentation of life as it exists in the vast African forest, it seemed to me only too vivid a picture of many parts of our own land. As there is a darkest Africa is there not also a darkest England? Civilisation, which can breed its own barbarians, does it not also breed its own pygmies? May we not find a parallel at our own doors, and discover within a stone's throw of our cathedrals and palaces similar horrors to those which Stanley has found existing in the great Equatorial forest?

The more the mind dwells upon the subject, the closer the analogy appears. The ivory raiders who brutally traffic in the unfortunate denizens of the forest glades, what are they but the publicans who flourish on the weakness of our poor? The two tribes of savages, the human baboon and the handsome dwarf, who will not speak lest it impede him in his task, may be accepted as the two varieties who are continually present with us—the vicious, lazy lout, and the toiling slave. They, too, have lost all faith of life being other than it is and has been. As in Africa, it is all trees, trees, trees with no other world conceivable; so is it here—it is all vice and poverty and crime. To many the world is all slum, with the Workhouse as an intermediate purgatory before the grave. And just as Mr. Stanley's Zanzibaris lost faith, and could only be induced to plod on in brooding sullenness of dull despair, so the most of our social reformers, no matter how cheerily they may have started off, with forty pioneers swinging blithely their axes as they force their way into the wood, soon become depressed and despairing. Who can battle against the ten thousand million trees? Who can hope to make headway against the innumerable adverse conditions which doom the dweller in Darkest England to eternal and immutable misery? What wonder is it that many of the warmest hearts and enthusiastic workers feel disposed to repeat the lament of the old English chronicler,[1] who, speaking of the evil days which fell upon our forefathers in the reign of Stephen, said "It seemed to them as if God and his Saints were dead."

An analogy is as good as a suggestion; it becomes wearisome when it is pressed too far. But before leaving it, think for a moment how close the parallel is, and how strange it is that so much interest should be excited by a narrative of human squalor and human heroism in a distant continent, while greater squalor and heroism not less magnificent may be observed at our very doors.

The Equatorial Forest traversed by Stanley resembles that Darkest England of which I have to speak, alike in its vast extent—both stretch, in Stanley's phrase, "as far as from Plymouth to Peterhead;"[2] its monotonous darkness, its malaria and its gloom, its dwarfish de-humanized inhabitants, the slavery to which they are subjected, their privations and their misery. That which sickens the stoutest heart, and causes many of our bravest and best to fold their hands in despair, is the apparent impossibility of doing more than merely to peck at the outside of the endless tangle of monotonous undergrowth; to let light into it, to make a road clear through it, that shall not be immediately choked up by the ooze of the morass and the luxuriant parasitical growth of the forest—who dare hope for that? At present, alas, it would seem as though no one dares even to hope! It is the great Slough of Despond[3] of our time.

And what a slough it is no man can gauge who has not waded therein, as some of us have done, up to the very neck for long years. Talk about Dante's Hell, and all the horrors and cruelties of the torture-chamber of the lost! The man who walks with open eyes and with bleeding heart through the shambles of our civilisation needs no such fantastic images of the poet to teach him horror. Often and often, when I have seen the young and the poor and the helpless go down before my eyes into the morass, trampled underfoot by beasts of prey in human shape that haunt these regions, it seemed as if God were no longer in His world, but that in His stead reigned a fiend, merciless as Hell, ruthless as the grave. Hard it is, no doubt, to read in Stanley's pages of the slave-traders coldly arranging for the surprise of a village, the capture of the inhabitants, the massacre of those who resist, and the violation of all the women; but the stony streets of London, if they could but speak, would tell of tragedies as awful, of ruin as complete, of ravishments as horrible, as if we were in Central Africa; only the ghastly devastation is covered, corpse-like, with the artificialities and hypocrisies of modern civilisation.

The lot of a negress in the Equatorial Forest is not, perhaps, a very happy one, but is it so very much worse than that of many a pretty orphan girl in our Christian capital? We talk about the brutalities of the dark ages, and we profess to shudder as we read in books of the shameful exaction of the rights of feudal superior. And yet here, beneath our very eyes, in our theatres, in our restaurants, and in many other places, unspeakable though it be but to name it, the same hideous abuse flourishes unchecked. A young penniless girl, if she be pretty, is often hunted from pillar to post by her employers, confronted always by the alternative—Starve or Sin. And when once the poor girl has consented to buy the right to earn her living by the sacrifice of her virtue, then she is treated as a slave and an outcast by the very men who have ruined her. Her word becomes unbelievable, her life an ignominy, and she is swept downward ever downward, into the bottomless perdition of prostitution. But there, even in the lowest depths, excommunicated by Humanity and outcast from God, she is far nearer the pitying heart of the One true Saviour than all the men who forced her down, aye, and than all the Pharisees and Scribes who stand silently by while these fiendish wrongs are perpetrated before their very eyes.

The blood boils with impotent rage at the sight of these enormities, callously inflicted, and silently borne by these miserable victims. Nor is it only women who are the victims, although their fate is the most tragic. Those firms which reduce sweating[4] to a fine art, who systematically and deliberately defraud the workman of his pay, who grind the faces of the poor, and who rob the widow and the orphan, and who for a pretence make great professions

---

[1]**chronicler**: the Peterborough Chronicle for 1137, trans. Benjamin Thorpe (1861): "they said openly that Christ and his saints slept."

[2]"**from Plymouth to Peterhead**": Stanley's estimate of the Congo jungle, equivalent in extent to a line drawn between Britain's SW and NE points.

[3]**Slough of Despond**: from John Bunyan's *Pilgrim's Progress* (1678).

[4]**sweating**: labor under sweatshop conditions.

of public-spirit and philanthropy, these men nowadays are sent to Parliament to make laws for the people. The old prophets sent them to Hell—but we have changed all that. They send their victims to Hell, and are rewarded by all that wealth can do to make their lives comfortable. Read the House of Lords' Report on the Sweating System, and ask if any African slave system, making due allowance for the superior civilisation, and therefore sensitiveness, of the victims, reveals more misery.

Darkest England, like Darkest Africa, reeks with malaria. The foul and fetid breath of our slums is almost as poisonous as that of the African swamp. Fever is almost as chronic there as on the Equator. Every year thousands of children are killed off by what is called defects of our sanitary system. They are in reality starved and poisoned, and all that can be said is that, in many cases, it is better for them that they were taken away from the trouble to come.

Just as in Darkest Africa it is only a part of the evil and misery that comes from the superior race who invade the forest to enslave and massacre its miserable inhabitants, so with us, much of the misery of those whose lot we are considering arises from their own habits. Drunkenness and all manner of uncleanness, moral and physical, abound. Have you ever watched by the bedside of a man in delirium tremens? Multiply the sufferings of that one drunkard by the hundred thousand, and you have some idea of what scenes are being witnessed in all our great cities at this moment. As in Africa streams intersect the forest in every direction, so the gin-shop stands at every corner with its River of the Water of Death flowing seventeen hours out of the twenty-four for the destruction of the people. A population sodden with drink, steeped in vice, eaten up by every social and physical malady, these are the denizens of Darkest England amidst whom my life has been spent, and to whose rescue I would now summon all that is best in the manhood and womanhood of our land.

But this book is no mere lamentation of despair. For Darkest England, as for Darkest Africa, there is a light beyond. I think I see my way out, a way by which these wretched ones may escape from the gloom of their miserable existence into a higher and happier life. Long wandering in the Forest of the Shadow of Death at our doors, has familiarised me with its horrors; but while the realisation is a vigorous spur to action it has never been so oppressive as to extinguish hope. Mr. Stanley never succumbed to the terrors which oppressed his followers. He had lived in a larger life, and knew that the forest, though long, was not interminable. Every step forward brought him nearer his destined goal, nearer to the light of the sun, the clear sky, and the rolling uplands of the grazing land. Therefore he did not despair. The Equatorial Forest was, after all, a mere corner of one quarter of the world. In the knowledge of the light outside, in the confidence begotten by past experience of successful endeavour, he pressed forward; and when the 160 days' struggle was over, he and his men came out into a pleasant place where the land smiled with peace and plenty, and their hardships and hunger were forgotten in the joy of a great deliverance.

So I venture to believe it will be with us. But the end is not yet. We are still in the depths of the depressing gloom. It is in no spirit of light-heartedness that this book is sent forth into the world as if it was written some ten years ago.

If this were the first time that this wail of hopeless misery had sounded on our ears the matter would have been less serious. It is because we have heard it so often that the case is so desperate. The exceeding bitter cry of the disinherited has become to be as familiar in the ears of men as the dull roar of the streets or as the moaning of the wind through the trees. And so it rises unceasing, year in and year out, and we are too busy or too idle, too indifferent or too selfish, to spare it a thought. Only now and then, on rare occasions, when some clear voice is heard giving more articulate utterance to the miseries of the miserable men, do we pause in the regular routine of our daily duties, and shudder as we realise for one brief moment what life means to the inmates of the Slums. But one of the grimmest social problems of our time should be sternly faced, not with a view to the generation of profitless emotion, but with a view to its solution.

Is it not time? There is, it is true, an audacity in the mere suggestion that the problem is not insoluble that is enough to take away the breath. But can nothing be done? If, after full and exhaustive consideration, we come to the deliberate conclusion that nothing can be done, and that it is the inevitable and inexorable destiny of thousands of Englishmen to be brutalised into worse than beasts by the condition of their environment, so be it. But if, on the contrary, we are unable to believe that this "awful slough," which engulfs the manhood and womanhood of generation after generation, is incapable of removal; and if the heart and intellect of mankind alike revolt against the fatalism of despair, then, indeed, it is time, and high time, that the question were faced in no mere dilettante spirit, but with a resolute determination to make an end of the crying scandal of our age.

What a satire it is upon our Christianity and our civilisation, that the existence of these colonies of heathens and savages in the heart of our capital should attract so little attention! It is no better than a ghastly mockery—theologians might use a stronger word—to call by the name of One who came to seek and to save that which was lost those Churches which in the midst of lost multitudes either sleep in apathy or display a fitful interest in a chasuble.[5] Why all this apparatus of temples and meeting-houses to save men from perdition in a world which is to come, while never a helping hand is stretched out to save them from the inferno of their present life? Is it not time that, forgetting for a moment their wranglings about the infinitely little or infinitely obscure, they should concentrate all their energies on a united effort to break this terrible perpetuity of perdition, and to rescue some at least of those for whom they profess to believe their Founder came to die?

Before venturing to define the remedy, I begin by describing the malady. But even when presenting the dreary picture of our social ills, and describing the difficulties which confront us, I speak not in despondency but in hope. "I know in whom I have believed."[6] I know, therefore do I speak. Darker England is but a fractional part of "Greater England." There is wealth enough abundantly to minister to its social regeneration so far as wealth can, if there be but heart enough to set about the work in earnest. And I hope and believe that the heart will not be lacking when once the problem is manfully faced, and the method of its solution plainly pointed out. (Chapter 1)

1890

---

[5]**chasuble**: priestly vestment revived for use by High-Church Victorians.

[6]**"I know . . . believed"**: 2 Timothy 1:12.

FAITH, DOUBT, AND KNOWLEDGE

WHAT COUNTED AS the truth about elementary and ultimate reality underwent profound change during the nineteenth century, both in the substance of people's beliefs and in the grounds on which those beliefs were based. During the century's early decades a climate of militant reaction against freethinking—tainted by association with revolutionary developments in the national enemy, France—welded the state as rigidly as ever to the episcopal Church of England (or Anglican Church), which had been established three centuries before. But the first Victorian generation saw in reform a middle way between revolution and reaction, and undertook to institute an empire of peaceful commerce in a new spirit of religious toleration. Roman Catholics, Jews, and Dissenters (Protestants who worshiped outside the Church) were all gradually accorded rights of citizenship in a state that, while still nominally Anglican, was becoming unmistakably secular in all practical respects. At the same time, the Church itself began to weather severe internal schism. Sweeping through parishes across the 1820s, evangelical revivalism vested the essence of religion not in doctrinal correctness but in personal and inward redemption. The emphasis thus placed on untutored individual experience prompted in alarmed clergy and parishioners a counter-emphasis on dogma, liturgy, and priestly prerogative (conspicuously represented by John Keble and John Henry Newman among our major authors). As ecclesiastical conflict broke out into the open with a spate of polemical publications, the authority of Anglicanism—taken comparatively for granted during the long eighteenth century—now seemed a matter open to testing, negotiation, and reconstruction. Small wonder that by midcentury, when government office and university matriculation ceased to depend on Church membership, many sober Victorians publicly advocated disestablishing the Church itself.

That experimentation, reconstruction, and reform were the order of the Victorian day was largely due to the increasing power of nineteenth-century science. By 1830 scientists had been pursuing for two centuries a program of experimental demonstration and verification that derived knowledge from methodically skeptical inquiry rather than the affirmation of learned authorities. This empirical spirit had existed in more or less peaceful subordination to the spirit of religion from Francis Bacon's time at the start of the seventeenth century through Adam Smith's at the close of the eighteenth. By the second quarter of the new century, however, recent achievements had so boosted science's prestige that the customary equilibrium between scientific and religious truths was in danger. It was up to the Victorians to work out a fresh solution.

From the 1830s forward, scientific discovery, theory, and technical accomplishment were at the center of British public debate. As science dramatically extended its explanatory reach into the natural world, its technological offshoots contributed to the industrial reorganization of more and more people's lives. Truths that the Bible had long sponsored about the size and shape of the universe, or the length of recorded history—one cherished extrapolation set the Creation, with scrupulous precision, in 4004 BCE—met with shock after shock. Concurrently, new processes for farming, mining, and manufacture were adopted in every corner of the kingdom, while improvements in transportation drew the corners closer together. Where man had wrought so much, fortified by scientific progress, Victorians wondered what was left for God to do; or at least they wondered what need remained for a God beyond the laws of change that science was busily codifying.

The distinctive note that sounded across the Victorian struggle of knowledge with faith was one of cautiously optimistic compromise. Not even an astronomer of John Herschel's eminence, or a biologist of Charles Darwin's, could presuppose anything like the public reception science has commanded during the twentieth century. Indeed, the prestige of science in our day owes a debt to the tact with which such writers tempered their often revolutionary assertions to suit Victorian ears. Part of the rhetorical interest of the following selections lies in the accommodation their authors make between new scientific results and the preexisting articles of faith they had to impute to their readers—if only because the authors had encountered some version of the faith/knowledge conflict in themselves. Religion retained ascendancy in 1830 and for some time thereafter. Its cultural grasp weakened with the decades, however, as defense of the faith cracked under the pressures of modernity, and the militancy of the Church spent itself in civil broils. A conservative camp with "High Church" traditionalists on one wing and "Low Church" fundamentalists on the other issued fulminations so stubbornly purist that in the end their party forfeited a serious place in the national debate. In the meantime, a liberal camp of "Broad Church" intellectuals set out to rescue Christianity by redefining it on historicist, psychological, even anthropological premises that were themselves drawn from contemporary science.

The note of conciliation that we hear on either side of the debate—audible in the selections that follow and also in the fully orchestrated polemics of major authors like the staunch ecclesiastic Newman and the scientific bulldog Thomas Henry Huxley—is a genuine note, often a moving one. Yet it also bespeaks a struggle for possession of a common ground that was shifting fast under Victorian writers' feet. Amid a climate of change, special power was vested in narratives of change itself; and the contest of belief with knowledge pitted the scriptural account of human development against the vastly longer and less flattering account advanced by science. Somewhat like a Victorian serial narrative, this account reached the public in three chief phases. For the generations of 1830, then 1860, and then 1890 geology, then biology, and then anthropology provided compelling histories that resituated humankind, formerly the focal point of a morally charged cosmos, within material and social systems whose dynamic evolution was explained with reference to the impersonal operations of uniform law. This law might by the faithful be imaginatively identified with God—as in the end of Tennyson's *In Memoriam* or Meredith's "Lucifer in Starlight"—but conversely it might be brought round to bear on cultural productions including the Bible itself. The leading accomplishments of nineteenth-century science were its master narratives, which attempted natural history writing on the most ambitious scale, embracing the evolution of organism and species, planet and cosmos (see Herbert Spencer's "Progress," page 694). The greatest stroke of the Victorian culture wars may have been the recruitment of biblical scholarship in the service of just such a master narrative. Modern textual scholars practicing what was known as the Higher Criticism subjected to a scientific, evolutionary understanding both the history *in* the Bible and the history *of* the Bible, its composition and interpretation. The coup de grace, during an era that saw the rise of modern social science and history writing, was Victorian intellectuals' reconception of religious doctrine as a truth in transit: a necessary yet waning phase within a cultural evolution destined to supersede it.

JOHN HERSCHEL

(1792–1871)

In 1838 the knighting of Herschel as Sir John confirmed his repetition, in a Victorian key, of scientific eminence that his immigrant father Sir William had attained before him by discovering the planet Uranus (an event commemorated by Keats in a sonnet) and propounding the theories of nebulae and double stars. The son's contributions to physics and astronomy, while significant, were eclipsed by his labors as a scientific administrator and publicist. John Herschel refined his father's theories, gave currency across Europe to the wave hypothesis of light, and pioneered the use of chemically sensitized paper for photography. He also took a leading part in Victorian social engineering by working on projects for national and imperial education at school and university levels, supporting the Great Exhibition of 1851, and composing diplomatic defenses of science like the excerpt given here. Herschel writes the judicious, balanced prose of the eighteenth century in which he was born, and his style communicates a rational confidence in the capacity of open discussion to produce the truth. Given a fair field, he affirms, scientific understanding of the natural order may look forward to an exponential advance: the "wealth and civilization" that science augments will in turn, as more and more amateurs involve themselves in the observation of facts and dissemination of ideas, promote further increase in the knowledge that sustains progress. Herschel's is a temperate optimism typical of his generation, which came into its own just as the first wave of reformist legislation was making its way through Parliament.

from A Preliminary Discourse on the Study of Natural Philosophy

. . . Nothing can be more unfounded than the objection which has been taken, *in limine*,[1] by persons, well meaning perhaps, certainly narrow-minded, against the study of natural philosophy, and indeed against all science,—that it fosters in its cultivators an undue and overweening self-conceit, leads them to doubt the immortality of the soul, and to scoff at revealed religion. Its natural effect, we may confidently assert, on every well constituted mind is and must be the direct contrary. No doubt, the testimony of natural reason, on whatever exercised, must of necessity stop short of those truths which it is the object of revelation to make known; but, while it places the existence and principal attributes of a Deity on such grounds as to render

---

[1]*in limine:* at the outset.

doubt absurd and atheism ridiculous, it unquestionably opposes no natural or necessary obstacle to further progress: on the contrary, by cherishing as a vital principle an unbounded spirit of enquiry, and ardency of expectation, it unfetters the mind from prejudices of every kind, and leaves it open and free to every impression of a higher nature which it is susceptible of receiving, guarding only against enthusiasm and self-deception by a habit of strict investigation, but encouraging, rather than suppressing, every thing that can offer a prospect or a hope beyond the present obscure and unsatisfactory state. The character of the true philosopher is to hope all things not impossible, and to believe all things not unreasonable. He who has seen obscurities which appeared impenetrable in physical and mathematical science suddenly dispelled, and the most barren and unpromising fields of enquiry converted, as if by inspiration, into rich and inexhaustible springs of knowledge and power on a simple change of our point of view, or by merely bringing to bear on them some principle which it never occurred before to try, will surely be the very last to acquiesce in any dispiriting prospects of either the present or future destinies of mankind; while, on the other hand, the boundless views of intellectual and moral as well as material relations which open on him on all hands in the course of these pursuits, the knowledge of the trivial place he occupies in the scale of creation, and the sense continually pressed upon him of his own weakness and incapacity to suspend or modify the slightest movement of the vast machinery he sees in action around him, must effectually convince him that humility of pretension, no less than confidence of hope, is what best becomes his character.

But while we thus vindicate the study of natural philosophy from a charge at one time formidable from the pertinacity and acrimony with which it was urged, and still occasionally brought forward to the distress and disgust of every well constituted mind, we must take care that the testimony afforded by science to religion, be its extent or value what it may, shall be at least independent, unbiassed, and spontaneous. We do not here allude to such reasoners as would make all nature bend to their narrow interpretations of obscure and difficult passages in the sacred writings: such a course might well become the persecutors of Galileo and the other bigots of the fifteenth and sixteenth centuries, but can only be adopted by dreamers in the present age. But, without going these lengths, it is no uncommon thing to find persons, earnestly attached to science and anxious for its promotion, who yet manifest a morbid sensibility on points of this kind,—who exult and applaud when any fact starts up explanatory (as they suppose) of some scriptural allusion, and who feel pained and disappointed when the general course of discovery in any department of science runs wide of the notions with which particular passages in the Bible may have impressed themselves. To persons of such a frame of mind it ought to suffice to remark, on the one hand, that truth can never be opposed to truth, and, on the other, that error is only to be effectually confounded by searching deep and tracing it to its source. Nevertheless, it were much to be wished that such persons, estimable and excellent as they for the most part are, before they throw the weight of their applause or discredit into the scale of scientific opinion on such grounds, would reflect, first, that the credit and respectability of *any* evidence may be destroyed by tampering with its *honesty*; and, secondly, that this very disposition of mind implies a lurking mistrust in its own principles, since the grand and indeed only character of truth is its capability of enduring the test of universal experience, and coming unchanged out of every possible form of *fair* discussion. . . . (Part 1, Chapter 1)

. . . It cannot be supposed, that all the indications of nature continually passed unremarked, or that much good observation and shrewd reasoning on it failed to perish unrecorded, before the invention of printing enabled every one to make his ideas known to all the world. The moment this took place, however, the sparks of information from time to time struck out, instead of glimmering for a moment, and dying away in oblivion, began to accumulate into a genial glow, and the flame was at length kindled which was speedily to acquire the strength and rapid spread of a conflagration. The universal excitement in the minds of men throughout Europe, which the first out-break of modern science produced, has been already spoken of. But even the most sanguine anticipators could scarcely have looked forward to that steady, unintermitted progress which it has since maintained, nor to that rapid succession of great discoveries which has kept up the interest of the first impulse still vigorous and undiminished. It may truly, indeed, be said, that there is scarcely a single branch of physical enquiry which is either stationary, or which has not been, for many years past, in a constant state of advance, and in which the progress is not, at this moment, going on with accelerated rapidity.

Among the causes of this happy and desirable state of things, no doubt we are to look, in the first instance, to that great increase in wealth and civilization which has at once afforded the necessary leisure and diffused the taste for intellectual pursuits among numbers of mankind, which have long been and still continue steadily progressive in every principal European state, and which the increase and fresh establishment of civilized communities in every distant region are rapidly spreading over the whole globe. It is not, however, merely the increased number of cultivators of science, but their enlarged opportunities, that we have here to consider, which, in all those numerous departments of natural research that require local information, is in fact the most important consideration of all. To this cause we must trace the great extension which has of late years been conferred on every branch of natural history, and the immense contributions which have been made, and are daily making, to the departments of zoology and botany, in all their ramifications. It is obvious, too, that all the information that can possibly be procured, and reported, by the most enlightened and active travellers, must fall infinitely short of what is to be obtained by individuals actually resident upon the spot. Travellers, indeed, may make collections, may snatch a few hasty observations, may note, for instance, the distribution of geological formations in a few detached points, and now and then witness remarkable local phenomena; but the resident alone can make continued series of regular observations, such as the scientific determination of climates, tides, magnetic variations, and innumerable other objects of that kind, requires; can alone mark all the details of geological structure, and refer each stratum, by a careful and long continued observation of its fossil contents, to its true epoch; can alone note the habits of the animals of his country, and the limits of its vegetation, or obtain a satisfactory knowledge of its mineral contents, with a thousand other particulars essential to that complete acquaintance with our globe as a whole, which is beginning to be understood by the extensive designation of physical geography. Besides which, ought not to be omitted multiplied opportunities of observing and recording those extraordinary phenomena of nature which offer an intense interest, from the rarity of their occurrence as well as the instruction they are calculated to afford. To what, then, may we not look forward, when a spirit of scientific enquiry shall have spread through those vast regions in which the process of civilization, its sure precursor, is actually commenced and in active progress? And what may we not expect from the exertions of powerful minds called into action under circumstances totally different from any which have yet existed in the world, and over an extent of territory far surpassing that which has hitherto produced the whole harvest of human intellect? . . .

Finally, when we look back on what has been accomplished in science, and compare it with what remains to be done, it is hardly possible to avoid being strongly impressed with the idea that we have been and are still executing the labour by which succeeding generations are to profit. In a few instances only have we arrived at those general axiomatic laws which admit of direct deductive inference, and place the solutions of physical phenomena before us as so many problems, whose principles of solution we fully possess, and which require nothing but acuteness of reasoning to pursue even into their farthest recesses. In fewer still have we reached that command of abstract reasoning itself which is necessary for the accomplishment of so arduous a task. Science, therefore, in relation to our faculties, still remains boundless and unexplored, and, after the lapse of a century and a half from the æra of Newton's discoveries, during which every department of it has been cultivated with a zeal and energy which have assuredly met their full return, we remain in the situation in which he figured himself,—standing on the shore of a wide ocean, from whose beach we may have culled some of those innumerable beautiful productions it casts up with lavish prodigality, but whose acquisition can be regarded as no diminution of the treasures that remain.

But this consideration, so far from repressing our efforts, or rendering us hopeless of attaining any thing intrinsically great, ought rather to excite us to fresh enterprise, by the prospect of assured and ample recompense from that inexhaustible store which only awaits our continued endeavours. "It is no detraction from human capacity to suppose it incapable of infinite exertion, or of exhausting an infinite subject."[2] In whatever state of knowledge we may conceive man to be placed, his progress towards a yet higher state need never fear a check, but must continue till the last existence of society.

It is in this respect an advantageous view of science, which refers all its advances to the discovery of general laws, and to the inclusion of what is already known in generalizations of still higher orders; inasmuch as this view of the subject represents it, as it really is, essentially incomplete, and incapable of being fully embodied in any system, or embraced by any single mind. Yet it must be recollected that, so far as our experience has hitherto gone, every advance towards generality has at the same time been a step towards simplification. It is only when we are wandering and lost in the mazes of particulars, or entangled in fruitless attempts to work our way downwards in the thorny paths of applications, to which our reasoning powers are incompetent, that nature appears complicated:—the moment we contemplate it as it is, and attain a position from which we can take a commanding view, though but of a small part of its plan, we never fail to recognize that sublime simplicity on which the mind rests satisfied that it has attained the truth. (Part 3, Chapter 6)

1830

---

[2]"**It is . . . infinite subject**": William Jackson (1730–1803), *The Four Ages* (1798).

MARY SOMERVILLE

(1780–1872)

Born a decade before Herschel (whom she knew and outlived), still actively reading new science books in her nineties, Somerville left behind not just the charmingly temperate memoir anthologized here but also notable achievements of scientific synthesis: *The Mechanism of the Heavens* and *The Connection of the Physical Sciences*, both published to acclaim during the 1830s. She received the education in female accomplishments that was thought suitable to an admiral's daughter. But she possessed in addition an unslaked curiosity, a stubborn persistence, and what her own daughter in editing the memoir wonderingly called "a singular power of abstraction" that "rendered her entirely independent of outward circumstances." These gifts had led Somerville, by the time of her second marriage, to study Newton's abstruse *Principia* in the original Latin, and to grasp higher mathematical applications with which few contemporary men of science were conversant but to which her books were instrumental in giving broader currency.

Science and mathematics were regarded across the nineteenth century as subjects unsuited to the female mind. But in the earlier decades science was not regularly taught to British boys either; science was not a profession, and few scientists held university posts or conducted research in academic institutions. The amateur status of science, while it would eventually yield to heavily gendered late-Victorian professionalism, made it possible in Somerville's day for a woman of wealth and genius to make her way as a scientist. Her serene retrospect across nearly a century of ideological turmoil bears witness to the lifelong accommodation she contrived between the restrictions her gender imposed and the scientific aspiration that overcame them, and between the troublesome findings of science and an unshaken piety.

from Personal Recollections
From Early Life to Old Age

... I was often invited with my mother to the tea-parties given either by widows or maiden ladies who resided at Burntisland.[1] A pool of commerce used to be keenly contested till a late hour at these parties, which bored me exceedingly, but I there became acquainted with a Miss Ogilvie, much younger than the rest, who asked me to go and see fancy works she was doing, and at which she was very clever. I went next day, and after admiring her work, and being told how it was done, she showed me a monthly magazine with coloured plates of ladies' dresses, charades, and puzzles. At the end of a page I read what appeared to me to be simply an arithmetical question; but on turning the page I was surprised to see strange looking lines mixed with letters, chiefly X'es and Y's, and asked; "What is that?" "Oh," said Miss Ogilvie, "it is a kind of arithmetic: they call it Algebra; but I can tell you nothing about it." And we talked about other things; but on going home I thought I would look if any of our books could tell me what was meant by Algebra.

In Robertson's "Navigation"[2] I flattered myself that I had got precisely what I wanted; but I soon found that I was

---

[1]**Burntisland**: seacoast town in E Scotland where Somerville grew up. **commerce**: a card game.

[2]**"Navigation"**: *The Elements of Navigation* (1754) by John **Robertson** (1712–1776).

mistaken. I perceived, however, that astronomy did not consist in star-gazing,[3] and as I persevered in studying the book for a time, I certainly got a dim view of several subjects which were useful to me afterwards. Unfortunately not one of our acquaintances or relations knew anything of science or natural history; nor, had they done so, should I have had courage to ask any of them a question, for I should have been laughed at. I was often very sad and forlorn; not a hand held out to help me. . . .

Nasmyth,[4] an exceedingly good landscape painter had opened an academy for ladies in Edinburgh, a proof of the gradual improvement which was taking place in the education of the higher classes; my mother, very willingly allowed me to attend it. The class was very full. I was not taught to draw, but looked on while Nasmyth painted; then a picture was given me to copy, the master correcting the faults. Though I spoilt canvas, I had made some progress by the end of the season. Mr. Nasmyth, besides being a good artist, was clever, well-informed, and had a great deal of conversation. One day I happened to be near him while he was talking to the Ladies Douglas about perspective. He said, "You should study Euclid's Elements of Geometry; the foundation not only of perspective, but of astronomy and all mechanical science." Here, in the most unexpected manner, I got the information I wanted, for I at once saw that it would help me to understand some parts of Robertson's "Navigation;" but as to going to a bookseller and asking for Euclid the thing was impossible! Besides I did not yet know anything definite about Algebra, so no more could be done at that time; but I never lost sight of an object which had interested me from the first. . . .

On returning to Burntisland, I played on the piano as diligently as ever, and painted several hours every day. At this time, however, a Mr. Craw came to live with us as tutor to my youngest brother, Henry. He had been educated for the kirk, was a fair Greek and Latin scholar, but, unfortunately for me, was no mathematician. He was a simple, good-natured kind of man, and I ventured to ask him about algebra and geometry, and begged him, the first time he went to Edinburgh, to buy me something elementary on these subjects, so he soon brought me "Euclid" and Bonnycastle's "Algebra," which were the books used in the schools

at that time. Now I had got what I so long and earnestly desired. I asked Mr. Craw to hear me demonstrate a few problems in the first book of "Euclid," and then I continued the study alone with courage and assiduity, knowing I was on the right road. Before I began to read algebra I found it necessary to study arithmetic again, having forgotten much of it. I never was expert at addition, for, in summing up a long column of pounds, shillings, and pence, in the family account book, it seldom came out twice the same way. In after life I, of course, used logarithms for the higher branches of science.

I had to take part in the household affairs, and to make and mend my own clothes. I rose early, played on the piano, and painted during the time I could spare in the daylight hours, but I sat up very late reading Euclid. The servants, however, told my mother "It was no wonder the stock of candles was soon exhausted, for Miss Mary sat up reading till a very late hour;" whereupon an order was given to take away my candle as soon as I was in bed. I had, however, already gone through the first six books of Euclid, and now I was thrown on my memory, which I exercised by beginning at the first book, and demonstrating in my mind a certain number of problems every night, till I could nearly go through the whole. My father came home for a short time, and, somehow or other, finding out what I was about, said to my mother, "Peg, we must put a stop to this, or we shall have Mary in a strait jacket one of these days. There was X., who went raving mad about the longitude!" . . . (Chapter 3)

We went frequently to see Mr. Babbage[5] while he was making his Calculating-machines. He had a transcendant intellect, unconquerable perseverance, and extensive knowledge on many subjects, besides being a first-rate mathematician. I always found him most amiable and patient in explaining the structure and use of the engines. The first he made could only perform arithmetical operations. Not satisfied with that, Mr. Babbage constructed an analytical engine, which could be so arranged as to perform all kinds of mathematical calculations, and print each result.

Nothing has afforded me so convincing a proof of the unity of the Deity as these purely mental conceptions of numerical and mathematical science which have been by slow degrees vouchsafed to man, and are still granted in these latter times by the Differential Calculus, now superseded by the Higher Algebra, all of which must have existed in that sublimely omniscient Mind from eternity.

---

[3]**star-gazing:** Many people evidently think the science of astronomy consists entirely in observing the stars, for I have been frequently asked if I passed my nights looking through a telescope, and I have astonished the enquirers by saying I did not even possess one. [Somerville's note]

[4]Alexander **Nasmyth** (1768–1840): painter and amateur scientist.

[5]Charles **Babbage** (1792–1871): see page 55.

Many of our friends had very decided and various religious opinions, but my husband[6] and I never entered into controversy; we had too high a regard for liberty of conscience to interfere with any one's opinions, so we have lived on terms of sincere friendship and love with people who differed essentially from us in religious views, and in all the books which I have written I have confined myself strictly and entirely to scientific subjects, although my religious opinions are very decided.

Timidity of character, probably owing to early education, had a great influence on my daily life; for I did not assume my place in society in my younger days; and in argument I was instantly silenced, although I often knew, and could have proved, that I was in the right. The only thing in which I was determined and inflexible was in the prosecution of my studies. They were perpetually interrupted, but always resumed at the first opportunity. No analysis is so difficult as that of one's own mind, but I do not think I err much in saying that perseverance is a characteristic of mine. . . . (Chapter 9)

— LETTER FROM LORD BROUGHAM[7] TO DR. SOMERVILLE —

MY DEAR SIR,

I fear you will think me very daring for the design I have formed against Mrs. Somerville, and still more for making you my advocate with her; through whom I have every hope of prevailing. There will be sent to you a prospectus, rules, and a preliminary treatise of our Society for Diffusing Useful Knowledge, and I assure you I speak without any flattery when I say that of the two subjects which I find it most difficult to see the chance of executing, there is one, which—unless Mrs. Somerville will undertake—none else can, and it must be left undone, though about the most interesting of the whole, I mean an account of the Mécanique Céleste; the other is an account of the Principia,[8] which I

have some hopes of at Cambridge. The kind of thing wanted is such a description of that divine work as will both explain to the unlearned the sort of thing it is—the plan, the vast merit, the wonderful truths unfolded or methodized—and the calculus by which all this is accomplished, and will also give a somewhat deeper insight to the uninitiated. Two treatises would do this. No one without trying it can conceive how far we may carry ignorant readers into an understanding of the depths of science, and our treatises have about 100 to 800 pages of space each, so that one might give the more popular view, and another the analytical abstracts and illustrations. In England there are now not twenty people who know this great work, except by name; and not a hundred who know it even by name. My firm belief is that Mrs. Somerville could add two cyphers to each of those figures. Will you be my counsel in this suit? Of course our names are concealed, and no one of our council but myself needs to know it.

Yours ever most truly,
H. BROUGHAM. . . .

THIS letter surprised me beyond expression. I thought Lord Brougham must have been mistaken with regard to my acquirements, and naturally concluded that my self-acquired knowledge was so far inferior to that of the men who had been educated in our universities that it would be the height of presumption to attempt to write on such a subject, or indeed on any other. A few days after this Lord Brougham came to Chelsea himself, and Somerville joined with him in urging me at least to make the attempt. I said, "Lord Brougham, you must be aware that the work in question never can be popularized, since the student must at least know something of the differential and integral calculi, and as a preliminary step I should have to prove various problems in physical mechanics and astronomy. Besides, La Place never gives diagrams or figures, because they are not necessary to persons versed in the calculus, but they would be indispensable in a work such as you wish me to write. I am afraid I am incapable of such a task: but as you both wish it so much, I shall do my very best upon condition of secrecy, and that if I fail the manuscript shall be put into the fire." Thus suddenly and unexpectedly the whole character and course of my future life was changed.

I rose early and made such arrangements with regard to my children and family affairs that I had time to write afterwards; not, however, without many interruptions. A man can always command his time under the plea of business, a woman is not allowed any such excuse. At Chelsea I was

---

[6]**husband:** William Somerville, her second husband (married 1812). In 1807 her first husband had left her a widow with two young sons.

[7]Lord Henry **Brougham:** statesman, legal and educational reformer, founder of the Society for the Diffusion of Useful Knowledge (1825) and of the secular University of London (1828). Letter of March 27, 1827.

[8]*Mécanique Céleste:* published 1798 by Marquis Pierre Simon de Laplace (1749–1827). *Principia Mathematica:* published 1687 by Sir Isaac Newton.

always supposed to be at home, and as my friends and acquaintances came so far out of their way on purpose to see me, it would have been unkind and ungenerous not to receive them. Nevertheless, I was sometimes annoyed when in the midst of a difficult problem some one would enter and say, "I have come to spend a few hours with you." However, I learnt by habit to leave a subject and resume it again at once, like putting a mark into a book I might be reading; this was the more necessary as there was no fire-place in my little room, and I had to write in the drawing-room in winter. Frequently I hid my papers as soon as the bell announced a visitor, lest anyone should discover my secret. . . .

I was a considerable time employed in writing this book, but I by no means gave up society, which would neither have suited Somerville nor me. We dined out, went to evening parties, and occasionally to the theatre. As soon as my work was finished I sent the manuscript to Lord Brougham, requesting that it might be thoroughly examined, criticised and destroyed according to promise if a failure. I was very nervous while it was under examination, and was equally surprised and gratified that Sir John Herschel, our greatest astronomer, and perfectly versed in the calculus, should have found so few errors. . . . (Chapter 11)

. . . I am now in my 92nd year (1872), still able to drive out for several hours; I am extremely deaf, and my memory of ordinary events, and especially of the names of people, is failing, but not for mathematical and scientific subjects. I am still able to read books on the higher algebra for four or five hours in the morning, and even to solve the problems. Sometimes I find them difficult, but my old obstinacy remains, for if I do not succeed to-day, I attack them again on the morrow. I also enjoy reading about all the new discoveries and theories in the scientific world, and on all branches of science. . . .

Though far advanced in years, I take as lively an interest as ever in passing events. I regret that I shall not live to know the result of the expedition to determine the currents of the ocean, the distance of the earth from the sun determined by the transits of Venus, and the source of the most renowned of rivers, the discovery of which will immortalise the name of Dr. Livingstone.[9] But I regret most of all that I shall not see the suppression of the most atrocious system of slavery that ever disgraced humanity—that made known to the world by Dr. Livingstone and by Mr. Stanley, and which Sir Bartle Frere[10] has gone to suppress by order of the British Government.

The Blue Peter[11] has been long flying at my foremast, and now that I am in my ninety-second year I must soon expect the signal for sailing. It is a solemn voyage, but it does not disturb my tranquillity. Deeply sensible of my utter unworthiness, and profoundly grateful for the innumerable blessings I have received, I trust in the infinite mercy of my Almighty Creator. I have every reason to be thankful that my intellect is still unimpaired, and, although my strength is weakness, my daughters support my tottering steps, and, by incessant care and help, make the infirmities of age so light to me that I am perfectly happy. (Chapter 18)

1874

---

[9]David **Livingstone** (1813–1873): explorer who undertook in 1865 to reach the source of the Nile and was rescued in 1871 by journalist H. M. **Stanley**.

[10]Sir **Bartle Frere** (1815–1884): colonial administrator sent to Zanzibar in 1872 to negotiate suppression of the African slave trade.

[11]**Blue Peter**: flag hoisted to indicate a ship's immediate departure.

CHARLES LYELL

(1797–1875)

Knighted in 1848 like Herschel a decade before him, Lyell led a life that illustrated not only the growing prestige of science but its transformation from a hobby into a professional career. Born to riches, he trained half-heartedly as a lawyer; but his manifest gifts as a geological observer and theorizer led this talented amateur to an appointment as professor of geology at the new, nondenominational University of London. The man who had read for the law made his mark as a scientific author by the success with which he reduced the history of the planet to law or, as the quietly bold title of his three-volume masterwork put it, to *Principles*.

Against the interventionist (and ultimately creationist) view that the earth had at intervals been subject to unpredictable cataclysm, Lyell proposed a narrative of smooth change, which read in the rocks testimony to the operation of uniform causes working as steadily in the present as they had worked eons ago. The implications of such uniformitarianism were earthshaking indeed: they rendered God, from the standpoint of scientific explanation, practically superfluous. On one hand Lyell's theory shrank the role that geological catastrophism had assigned to God's ever-present superintendence of the world, and on the other hand it extended the reach of earthly time immensely beyond the received biblical account. Every notable man and woman of Victorian letters seems to have read Lyell: we trace him in FitzGerald and Eliot, and confront him in Tennyson and Hardy; his influence on Spencer, Huxley, and above all Darwin can hardly be overestimated.

from Principles of Geology

. . . When we compare the result of observations in the last thirty years with those of the three preceding centuries, we cannot but look forward with the most sanguine expectations to the degree of excellence to which geology may be carried, even by the labours of the present generation. Never, perhaps, did any science, with the exception of astronomy, unfold, in an equally brief period, so many novel and unexpected truths, and overturn so many preconceived opinions. The senses had for ages declared the earth to be at rest, until the astronomer taught that it was carried through space with inconceivable rapidity. In like manner was the surface of this planet regarded as having remained unaltered since its creation, until the geologist proved that it had been the theatre of reiterated change, and was still the subject of slow but never ending fluctuations. The discovery of other systems in the boundless regions of space

was the triumph of astronomy—to trace the same system through various transformations— to behold it at successive eras adorned with different hills and valleys, lakes and seas, and peopled with new inhabitants, was the delightful meed of geological research. By the geometer were measured the regions of space, and the relative distances of the heavenly bodies—by the geologist myriads of ages were reckoned, not by arithmetical computation, but by a train of physical events—a succession of phenomena in the animate and inanimate worlds—signs which convey to our minds more definite ideas than figures can do, of the immensity of time.

Whether our investigation of the earth's history and structure will eventually be productive of as great practical benefits to mankind, as a knowledge of the distant heavens, must remain for the decision of posterity. It was not till astronomy had been enriched by the observations of many centuries, and had made its way against popular prejudices to the establishment of a sound theory, that its application to the useful arts was most conspicuous. The cultivation of geology began at a later period; and in every step which it has hitherto made towards sound theoretical principles, it has had to contend against more violent prepossessions. The practical advantages already derived from it have not been inconsiderable: but our generalizations are yet imperfect, and they who follow may be expected to reap the most valuable fruits of our labour. Meanwhile the charm of first discovery is our own, and as we explore this magnificent field of inquiry, the sentiment of a great historian of our times may continually be present to our minds, that "he who calls what has vanished back again into being, enjoys a bliss like that of creating."[1] (Volume 1, Chapter 4)

We have seen that, during the progress of geology, there have been great fluctuations of opinion respecting the nature of the causes to which all former changes of the earth's surface are referrible. The first observers conceived that the monuments which the geologist endeavours to decipher, relate to a period when the physical constitution of the earth differed entirely from the present, and that, even after the creation of living beings, there have been causes in action distinct in kind or degree from those now forming part of the economy of nature. These views have been gradually modified, and some of them entirely abandoned in proportion as observations have been multiplied, and the signs of former mutations more skilfully interpreted. Many appearances, which for a long time were regarded as indicating mysterious and extraordinary agency, are finally recognized as the necessary result of the laws now governing the material world; and the discovery of this unlooked for conformity has induced some geologists to infer that there has never been any interruption to the same uniform order of physical events. The same assemblage of general causes, they conceive, may have been sufficient to produce, by their various combinations, the endless diversity of effects, of which the shell of the earth has preserved the memorials, and, consistently with these principles, the recurrence of analogous changes is expected by them in time to come.

Whether we coincide or not in this doctrine, we must admit that the gradual progress of opinion concerning the succession of phenomena in remote eras, resembles in a singular manner that which accompanies the growing intelligence of every people, in regard to the economy of nature in modern times. In an early stage of advancement, when a great number of natural appearances are unintelligible, an eclipse, an earthquake, a flood, or the approach of a comet, with many other occurrences afterwards found to belong to the regular course of events, are regarded as prodigies. The same delusion prevails as to moral phenomena, and many of these are ascribed to the intervention of demons, ghosts, witches, and other immaterial and supernatural agents. By degrees, many of the enigmas of the moral and physical world are explained, and, instead of being due to extrinsic and irregular causes, they are found to depend on fixed and invariable laws. The philosopher at last becomes convinced of the undeviating uniformity of secondary causes, and, guided by his faith in this principle, he determines the probability of accounts transmitted to him of former occurrences, and often rejects the fabulous tales of former ages, on the ground of their being irreconcilable with the experience of more enlightened ages. . . . (Volume 1, Chapter 5).

. . . Our estimate, indeed, of the value of all geological evidence, and the interest derived from the investigation of the earth's history, must depend entirely on the degree of confidence which we feel in regard to the permanency of the laws of nature. Their immutable constancy alone can enable us to reason from analogy, by the strict rules of induction, respecting the events of former ages, or, by a comparison of the state of things at two distinct geological epochs, to arrive at the knowledge of general principles in the economy of our terrestrial system.

The uniformity of the plan being once assumed, events which have occurred at the most distant periods in the animate and inanimate world will be acknowledged to throw light on each other, and the deficiency of our information respecting some of the most obscure parts of the present creation will be removed. For as by studying the external configuration of the existing land and its inhabitants, we may restore in imagination the appearance of the ancient continents which have passed away, so may we obtain from the deposits of ancient seas and lakes an insight into the nature of the subaqueous processes now in operation, and of many forms of organic life, which, though now existing, are veiled from our sight. Rocks, also produced by subterranean fire in former ages at great depths in the bowels of the earth, present us, when upraised by gradual movements, and exposed to the light of

---

[1] **"he who calls . . . of creating":** Barthold Niebuhr (1776–1831), *History of Rome* (a milestone of the new German historiography, English translation 1828).

heaven, with an image of those changes which the deep-seated volcano may now occasion in the nether regions. Thus, although we are mere sojourners on the surface of the planet, chained to a mere point in space, enduring but for a moment of time, the human mind is not only enabled to number worlds beyond the unassisted ken of mortal eye, but to trace the events of indefinite ages before the creation of our race, and is not even withheld from penetrating into the dark secrets of the ocean, or the interior of the solid globe; free, like the spirit which the poet described as animating the universe,

> Thro' Heav'n, and Earth, and Oceans depth he throws
> His Influence round, and kindles as he goes.[2]

(Volume 1, Chapter 9)   *1830*

---

[2]**Thro' Heav'n . . . he goes:** Dryden's translation of Virgil, *Eclogues* 4.221–22.

WILLIAM WHEWELL

(1794–1866)

In 1829 the will of the Earl of Bridgewater funded a series of treatises "On the Power, Wisdom, and Goodness of God, as manifested in the Creation "—that is, on what the religious mind in response to Enlightenment science had come to call natural theology. The high-ranking bishops who administered the bequest sought out authors of undoubted orthodoxy to survey such fields as anatomy, physiology, zoology, chemistry, and geology, culling from each the evidence of a divine designer's benevolent hand. Of these authors the most conspicuously qualified was Whewell (pronounced like *hue* and *jewel*), at once an ordained Anglican priest and a distinguished mathematician who had written on mechanics and dynamics and who currently held a professorship in mineralogy at Cambridge. Whewell went on to become vice chancellor there and published on a variety of topics that no academic today would dare to compass, including moral philosophy, mathematical pedagogy, and the science of tides.

Whewell's Bridgewater treatise confidently embraces as its twofold theme nothing less than the earth and the heavens. Our selection from a chapter on "The Nebular Hypothesis" shows how Whewell's philosophically deductive intellect takes the recent findings of science in stride. He submits them to the test of a logic that declares the emerging facts to be, if not positive inducements to faith, then at any rate harmonious with the teachings of the Church; and he underscores the Church's capacity to furnish what science cannot: a "resting place or satisfaction for the mind."

from Astronomy and General Physics, Considered With Reference to Natural Theology

We have referred to Laplace,[1] as a profound mathematician, who has strongly expressed the opinion, that the arrangement by which the stability of the solar system is secured is not the result of chance; that *"a primitive cause* has directed the planetary motions." This author, however, having arrived, as we have done, at this conviction, does not draw from it the conclusion which has appeared to us so irresistible, that "the admirable arrangement of the solar system cannot but be the work of an intelligent and most powerful being." He quotes these expressions, which are those of Newton, and points at them as instances where that great philosopher had deviated from the method of true philosophy. He himself proposes an hypothesis concerning the nature of the *primitive cause* of which he conceives the existence to be thus probable: and this hypothesis, on account of the facts which it attempts to combine, the view of the universe which it presents, and the eminence of the person by whom it is propounded, deserves our notice.

1. Laplace conjectures that in the original condition of the solar system, the sun revolved upon his axis, surrounded by an atmosphere which, in virtue of an excessive heat, extended far beyond the orbits of all the planets, the planets as yet having no existence. The heat gradually diminished, and as the solar atmosphere contracted by cooling, the rapidity of its rotation increased by the laws of rotatory motion, and an exterior zone of vapour was detached from the rest, the central attraction being no longer able to overcome the increased centrifugal force. This zone of vapour might in some cases retain its form, as we see it in Saturn's ring; but more usually the ring of vapour would break into several masses, and these would generally coalesce into one mass, which would revolve about the sun. Such portions of the solar atmosphere, abandoned successively at different distances, would form "planets in the state of vapour." These masses of vapour, it appears from mechanical considerations, would have each its rotatory motion, and as the cooling of the vapour still went on, would each produce a planet, which might have satellites and rings, formed from the planet in the same manner as the planets were formed from the atmosphere of the sun.

It may easily be conceived that all the primary motions of a system so produced would be nearly circular, nearly in the plane of the original equator of the solar rotation, and in the direction of that rotation. Reasons are offered also to show that the motions of the satellites thus produced and the motions of rotation of the planets must be in the same direction. And thus it is held that the hypothesis accounts for the most remarkable circumstances in the structure of the solar system: namely, the motions of the planets in the same direction, and almost in the same plane; the motions of the satellites in the same direction as those of the planets; the motions of rotation of these different bodies still in the same direction as the other motions, and in planes not much different; the small excentricity of the orbits of the planets, upon which condition, along with some of the preceding ones, the stability of the system depends; and the position of the source of light and heat in the centre of the system.

It is not necessary for the purpose, nor suitable to the plan of the present treatise, to examine, on physical grounds, the probability of the above hypothesis. It is proposed by its author, with great diffidence, as a conjecture only. We might, therefore, very reasonably put off all discussion of the bearings of this opinion upon our views of the government of the world, till the opinion itself should have assumed a less indistinct and precarious form. It can be no charge against our doctrines, that there is a difficulty in reconciling with them arbitrary guesses and half-formed theories. We shall, however, make a few observations upon this *nebular hypothesis*, as it may be termed.

2. If we grant, for a moment, the hypothesis, it by no means proves that the solar system was formed without the intervention of intelligence and design. It only transfers our view of the skill exercised, and the means employed, to another part of the work. For, how came the sun and its atmosphere to have such materials, such motions, such a constitution, that these consequences followed from their primordial condition? How came the parent vapour thus to be capable of coherence, separation, contraction, solidification? How came the laws of its motion, attraction, repulsion, condensation, to be so fixed, as to lead to a beautiful and harmonious system in the end? How came it to be neither too fluid nor too tenacious, to contract neither too quickly nor too slowly, for the successive formation of the several planetary bodies? How came that substance, which at one time was a luminous vapour, to be at a subsequent period, solids and fluids of many various kinds? What but design and intelligence prepared and tempered this previously existing element, so that it should by its natural changes produce such an orderly system?

---

[1]Marquis Pierre Simon de **Laplace** (1749–1827): eminent French scientist, whose revolutionary *System of the World* (1795) and *Celestial Mechanics* (1798) appeared in English translation within his lifetime.

And if in this way we suppose a planet to be produced, what sort of a body would it be?—something, it may be presumed, resembling a large meteoric stone. How comes this mass to be covered with motion and organization, with life and happiness? What primitive cause stocked it with plants and animals, and produced all the wonderful and subtle contrivances which we find in their structure, all the wide and profound mutual dependencies which we trace in their economy? Was man, with his thought and feeling, his powers and hopes, his will and conscience, also produced as an ultimate result of the condensation of the solar atmosphere? Except we allow a prior purpose and intelligence presiding over this material "primitive cause," how irreconcilable is it with the evidence which crowds in upon us on every side!

3. In the next place, we may observe concerning this hypothesis, that it carries us back to the beginning of the present system of things; but that it is impossible for our reason to stop at the point thus presented to it. The sun, the earth, the planets, the moons were brought into their present order out of a previous state, and, as is supposed in the theory, by the natural operation of laws. But how came that previous state to exist? We are compelled to suppose that it, in like manner, was educed from a still prior state of things; and this, again, must have been the result of a condition prior still. Nor is it possible for us to find, in the tenets of the nebular hypothesis, any resting place or satisfaction for the mind. The same reasoning faculty, which seeks for the origin of the present system of things, and is capable of assenting to, or dissenting from the hypothesis propounded by Laplace as an answer to this inquiry, is necessarily led to seek, in the same manner, for the origin of any previous system of things, out of which the present may appear to have grown: and must pursue this train of enquiries unremittingly, so long as the answer which it receives describes a mere assemblage of matter and motion; since it would be to contradict the laws of matter and the nature of motion, to suppose such an assemblage to be the *first* condition.

The reflection just stated, may be illustrated by the further consideration of the Nebular Hypothesis. This opinion refers us, for the origin of the solar system, to a sun surrounded with an atmosphere of enormously elevated temperature, revolving and cooling. But as we ascend to a still earlier period, what state of things are we to suppose?—a still higher temperature, a still more diffused atmosphere. Laplace conceives that, in its primitive state, the sun consisted in a diffused luminosity so as to resemble those nebulæ among the fixed stars, which are seen by the aid of the telescope, and which exhibit a nucleus, more or less bril-

liant, surrounded by a cloudy brightness. "This anterior state was itself preceded by other states, in which the nebulous matter was more and more diffuse, the nucleus being less and less luminous. We arrive," Laplace says, "in this manner, at a nebulosity so diffuse, that its existence could scarcely be suspected.". . .

It appears then that the highest point to which this series of conjectures can conduct us, is "an extremely diffused nebulosity," attended, we may suppose, by a far higher degree of heat, than that which, at a later period of the hypothetical process, keeps all the materials of our earth and planets in a state of vapour. Now is it not impossible to avoid asking, whence was this light, this heat, this diffusion? How came the laws which such a state implies, to be already in existence? Whether light and heat produce their effects by means of fluid vehicles or otherwise, they have complex and varied laws which indicate the existence of some subtle machinery for their action. When and how was this machinery constructed? Whence too that enormous expansive power which the nebulous matter is supposed to possess? And if, as would seem to be supposed in this doctrine, all the material ingredients of the earth existed in this diffuse nebulosity, either in the state of vapour, or in some state of still greater expansion, whence were they and their properties? how came there to be of each simple substance which now enters into the composition of the universe, just so much and no more? Do we not, far more than ever, require an origin of this origin? an explanation of this explanation? Whatever may be the merits of the opinion as a physical hypothesis, with which we do not here meddle, can it for a moment prevent our looking beyond the hypothesis, to a First Cause, an Intelligent Author, an origin proceeding from free volition, not from material necessity?

But again: let us ascend to the highest point of the hypothetical progression: let us suppose the nebulosity diffused throughout all space, so that its course of running into patches is not yet begun. How are we to suppose it distributed? Is it equably diffused in every part? clearly not; for if it were, what should cause it to gather into masses, so various in size, form and arrangement? The separation of the nebulous matter into distinct nebulæ implies necessarily some original inequality of distribution; some determining circumstances in its primitive condition. Whence were these circumstances? this inequality? we are still compelled to seek some ulterior agency and power.

Why must the primeval condition be one of change at all? Why should not the nebulous matter be equably diffused throughout space, and continue for ever in its state of equable diffusion, as it must do, from the absence of all cause to determine the time and manner of its separation? why should this nebulous matter grow cooler and cooler? why should it not retain for ever the same degree of heat, whatever heat be? If heat be a fluid, if to cool be to part with this fluid, as many philosophers suppose, what becomes of the fluid heat of the nebulous matter, as the matter cools down? Into what unoccupied region does it find its way?

Innumerable questions of the same kind might be asked, and the conclusion to be drawn is, that every new physical theory which we include in our view of the universe, involves us in new difficulties and perplexities, if we try to erect it into an ultimate and final account of the existence and arrangement of the world in which we live. With the evidence of such theories, considered as scientific generalizations of ascertained facts, with their claims to a place in our natural philosophy, we have here nothing to do. But if they are put forwards as a disclosure of the ultimate cause of that which occurs, and as superseding the necessity of looking further or higher; if they claim a place in our Natural Theology, as well as our Natural Philosophy; we conceive that their pretensions will not bear a moment's examination.

Leaving then to other persons and to future ages to decide upon the scientific merits of the nebular hypothesis, we conceive that the final fate of this opinion can not, in sound reason, affect at all the view which we have been endeavouring to illustrate;—the view of the universe as the work of a wise and good Creator. Let it be supposed that the point to which this hypothesis leads us, is the ultimate point of physical science: that the farthest glimpse we can obtain of the material universe by our natural faculties, shows it to us occupied by a boundless abyss of luminous matter: still we ask, how space came to be thus occupied, how matter came to be thus luminous? If we establish by physical proofs, that the first fact which can be traced in the history of the world, is that "there was light;" we shall still be led, even by our natural reason, to suppose that before this could occur, "God said, let there be light." (Book 2, Chapter 7)

1833

CHARLES BABBAGE

(1792–1871)

As impressive as the advance of science was that of technology, which probably made a more direct impact on the conduct and quality of Victorian people's lives. Before turning thirty Babbage had impeccable scientific credentials, but his distinction arises from the practical uses to which he put his mathematical gifts. A pioneering statistician, he was also an industrial designer both pragmatic and visionary, fearless alike on the factory floor and in the boardroom. Babbage's chief claim on us today is his farsighted conception of the "analytical engine": a steam-driven calculating machine, which he never perfected but which was a forerunner of the modern computer.

The following selection from Babbage's book on industrial technology displays several aspects of that drive for efficiency which impelled the Victorian reformist. His minute description of manual processes for straightening and pointing wire is a triumphant vindication of the division of labor that reveals, almost casually, the technocrat's habitual conversion of human skill into a mathematized coefficient for equations relating money, materiel, and time. "A man, his wife, and a child" are present in Babbage's text, but it is easy to miss them: the difficulty of spotting the human beings in the picture suggests how nearly invisible family values had become within a system of manufacture that was speedily transforming thousands of family lives. From the thrifty style of such descriptions Babbage ascends to the poetry of technology, a hymn to the magically smooth operation of a printing-house, in whose swift dissemination of contemporary intelligence *The Economy of Machinery* proudly participates. Our selection concludes with Babbage's technological version of the benevolent futurism already instanced in Herschel and Lyell: "design" and "power," so important in early nineteenth-century writing about natural theology and the sublime, are now co-opted by a committed engineer's veneration for human invention and its virtually limitless mechanical multiplication.

from On the Economy of Machinery and Manufactures

. . . As the clear apprehension of this principle, upon which a great part of the economy arising from the division of labour depends, is of considerable importance, it may be desirable to point out its precise and numerical application in some specific manufacture. The art of making needles is, perhaps, that which I should have selected for this illustration, as comprehending a very large number of processes remarkably different in their nature; but the less difficult art of pin-making, has some claim to attention, from its having been used by Adam Smith[1]. . . .

Straightening the Wire.—The coil of wire now passes into the hands of a woman, assisted by a boy or girl. A few nails, or iron pins, not quite in line, are fixed into one end of a wooden table about twenty feet in length; the end of the wire is passed alternately between these nails, and is then pulled to the other end of the table. The object of this process is to straighten the wire, which had acquired considerable curvature in the small coils in which it had been wound. The length thus straightened is cut off, and the remainder of the coil is drawn into similar lengths. About seven nails or pins are employed in straightening the wire, and their adjustment is a matter of some nicety. It seems, that by passing the wire between the first three nails or pins, a bend is produced in an opposite direction to that which the wire had in the coil; this bend, by passing the next two nails, is reduced to another less curved in the first direction, and so on till the curve of the wire may at last be confounded with a straight line.

Pointing.—(a.) A man next takes about three hundred of these straightened pieces in a parcel, and putting them into a gauge, cuts off from one end, by means of a pair of shears,

moved by his foot, a portion equal in length to rather more than six pins. He continues this operation until the entire parcel is reduced into similar pieces. (b.) The next step is to sharpen the ends: for this purpose the operator sits before a *steel mill*, which is kept rapidly revolving: it consists of a cylinder about six inches in diameter, and two and a half inches broad, faced with steel, which is cut in the manner of a file. Another cylinder is fixed on the same axis at a few inches distant; the file on the edge of which is of a finer kind, and is for finishing off the points. The workman now takes up a parcel of the wires between the finger and thumb of each hand, and presses the ends obliquely on the mill, taking care with his fingers and thumbs to make each wire slowly revolve upon its axis. Having thus pointed all the pieces at one end, he reverses them, and performs the same operation on the others. This process requires considerable skill, but it is not unhealthy; whilst the similar process in needle-making is remarkably destructive of health. (c.) The pieces now pointed at both ends, are next placed in gauges, and the pointed ends are cut off, by means of shears, to the proper length of which the pins are to be made. The remaining portions of the wire are now equal to about four pins in length, and are again pointed at each end, and their lengths again cut off. This process is repeated a third time, and the small portion of wire left in the middle is thrown amongst the waste, to be melted along with the dust arising from the sharpening. It is usual for a man, his wife, and a child, to join in performing these processes; and they are paid at the rate of five farthings[2] per pound. They can point from thirty-four to thirty-six and a half pounds per day, and gain from 6s. 6d to 7s., which may be apportioned thus; 5s. 6d. the man, 1s. the woman, 6d. to the boy or girl. . . .

It appears from the analysis we have given of the art of pin-making, that it occupies rather more than seven hours and a half of time, for ten different individuals working in

---

[1]**Adam Smith** (1723–1790): author of *The Wealth of Nations* (1776), classic work of political economy.

[2]**farthing:** one-fourth of a penny. See note on Victorian money, page 6.

succession on the same material, to convert it into a pound of pins; and that the total expense of their labour, each being paid in the joint ratio of his skill and of the time he is employed, amounts very nearly to 1s. 1d. But . . . it appears that the wages earned by persons employed vary from 4½d. per day up to 6s., and consequently the skill which is required for their respective employments may be measured by those sums. Now it is evident, that if one person were required to make the whole pound of pins, he must have skill enough to earn about 5s. 3d. per day, whilst he is pointing the wires or cutting off the heads from the spiral coils,— and 6s. when he is whitening the pins; which three operations together would occupy little more than the seventeenth part of his time. It is also apparent, that during more than one half of his time he must be earning only 1s. 3d. per day, in putting on the heads; although his skill, if properly employed, would, in the same time, produce nearly five times as much. If, therefore, we were to employ, for all the processes, the man who whitens the pins, and who earns 6s. per day, even supposing that he could make the pound of pins in an equally short time, yet we must pay him for his time 46.14 pence, or about 3s. 10d. *The pins would therefore cost, in making, three times and three quarters as much as they now do by the application of the division of labour.* . . . (Chapter 19)

    . . . The experience of the past, has stamped with the indelible character of truth, the maxim, that *"Knowledge is power."* It not merely gives to its votaries control over the mental faculties of their species, but is itself the generator of physical force. The discovery of the expansive power of steam, its condensation, and the doctrine of latent heat, has already added to the population of this small island, millions of hands. But the source of this power is not without limit, and the coal-mines of the world may ultimately be exhausted. Without adverting to the theory, that new deposites [sic] of that mineral are now accumulating under the sea, at the estuaries of some of our larger rivers; without anticipating the application of other fluids requiring a less supply of caloric than water:—we may remark that the sea itself offers a perennial source of power hitherto almost unapplied. The tides, twice in each day, raise a vast mass of water, which might be made available for driving machinery. But supposing heat still to remain necessary, when the exhausted state of our coal-fields renders it expensive: long before that period arrives, other methods will probably have been invented for producing it. In some districts, there are springs of hot water, which have flowed for centuries unchanged in temperature. In many parts of the island of Ischia, by deepening the sources of the hot springs only a few feet, the water boils; and there can be little doubt that, by boring a short distance, steam of high pressure would issue from the orifice.[3]

In Iceland, the sources of heat are still more plentiful; and their proximity to large masses of ice, seems almost to point out the future destiny of that island. The ice of its glaciers may enable its inhabitants to liquefy the gases with the least expenditure of mechanical force; and the heat of its volcanoes may supply the power necessary for their condensation. Thus, in a future age, *power* may become the staple commodity of the Icelanders, and of the inhabitants of other volcanic districts; and possibly the very process by which they will procure this article of exchange for the luxuries of happier climates may, in some measure, tame the tremendous element which occasionally devastates their provinces.

Perhaps to the sober eye of inductive philosophy, these anticipations of the future may appear too faintly connected with the history of the past. When time shall have revealed the future progress of our race, those laws which are now obscurely indicated, will then become distinctly apparent; and it may possibly be found that the dominion of mind over the material world advances with an ever-accelerating force.

Even now, the imprisoned winds which the earliest poet made the Grecian warrior bear for the protection of his fragile bark; or those which, in more modern times, the Lapland wizards sold to the deluded sailors;—these, the unreal creations of fancy or of fraud, called, at the command of science, from their shadowy existence, obey a holier spell: and the unruly masters of the poet and the seer become the obedient slaves of civilized man.

Nor have the wild imaginings of the satirist been quite unrivalled by the realities of after years: as if in mockery of the College of Laputa, light almost solar has been extracted from the refuse of fish; fire has been sifted by the lamp of Davy;[4] and machinery has been taught arithmetic instead of poetry.

---

[3] In 1828, the author of these pages visited Ischia, with a committee of the Royal Academy of Naples, deputed to examine the temperature and chemical constitution of the springs in that island. During the few first days, several springs which had been represented in the instructions as under the boiling temperature, were found, on deepening the excavations, to rise to the boiling point. [Babbage's note] **Ischia**: volcanic island in the Bay of Naples.

[4] **Laputa**: island governed by mathematicians and scientists in Swift's *Gulliver's Travels* (1726); Babbage evidently conflates this episode with Gulliver's visit to the Academy of Lagado. Sir Humphry **Davy** (1778–1829): leading chemist of his day. **machinery**: Babbage's own invention, the proto-computer.

In whatever light we examine the triumphs and achievements of our species over the creation submitted to its power, we explore new sources of wonder. But if science has called into real existence the visions of the poet—if the accumulating knowledge of ages has blunted the sharpest and distanced the loftiest of the shafts of the satirist, the philosopher has conferred on the moralist an obligation of surpassing weight. In unveiling to him the living miracles which teem in rich exuberance around the minutest atom, as well as throughout the largest masses of ever-active matter, he has placed before him resistless evidence of immeasurable design. Surrounded by every form of animate and inanimate existence, the sun of science has yet penetrated but through the outer fold of Nature's majestic robe; but if the philosopher were required to separate, from amongst those countless evidences of creative power, one being, the masterpiece of its skill; and from that being to select one gift, the choicest of all the attributes of life;—turning within his own breast, and conscious of those powers which have subjugated to his race the external world, and of those higher powers by which he has subjugated to himself that creative faculty which aids his faltering conceptions of a deity,—the humble worshipper at the altar of truth would pronounce that being,—man; that endowment,—human reason.

But however large the interval that separates the lowest from the highest of those sentient beings which inhabit our planet, all the results of observation, enlightened by all the reasonings of the philosopher, combine to render it probable that, in the vast extent of creation, the proudest attribute of our race is but, perchance, the lowest step in the gradation of intellectual existence. For, since every portion of our own material globe, and every animated being it supports, afford, on more scrutinizing inquiry, more perfect evidence of design, it would indeed be most unphilosophical to believe that those sister spheres, obedient to the same law, and glowing with light and heat radiant from the same central source—and that the members of those kindred systems, almost lost in the remoteness of space, and perceptible only from the countless multitude of their congregated globes—should each be no more than a floating chaos of unformed matter;——or, being all the work of the same Almighty architect, that no living eye should be gladdened by their forms of beauty, that no intellectual being should expand its faculties in decyphering their laws. (Conclusion)

1832

ROBERT CHAMBERS

(1802–1871)

The anonymous publication of *Vestiges of the Natural History of Creation* was in one sense self-protective, since so provocative a book would inevitably expose its author to detraction. In another sense, though, Chambers' anonymity constituted a polemical demand that the book be evaluated, not on its party affiliation or authorial prestige, but on the strength of its argument. That argument amounted to a unified field theory of law-governed change across an entire span of natural phenomena from galaxies to babies: all the Bridgewater treatises, so to speak, reconceived according to Lyell's uniformitarianism and purposely made available to the nonspecialist reader in an accessible style. An enterprising publisher and the talented author already of some thirty books, Chambers had studied both his scientific sources and his bourgeois audience. As Benjamin Disraeli's conservative novel *Tancred* (1847), mocking the book under the title "The Revelations of Chaos," had an ingenue enthuse, "It explains everything, and is written in a very agreeable style."

The very title was telling, and one Bridgewater author reprehended it as a contradiction in terms. How, asked Whewell, could divine *creation* be said to have any *natural history* at all?

Did not the divine order constitute a supernatural history prior to nature and logically distinct from it? To maintain the sufficiency of a merely natural understanding of the creation was to commit at once a heresy and a major category mistake. Just this, however, was what Chambers had indeed maintained, interpreting the fossil record as evidence for a regular and comprehensible history of unmiraculous millennia, and in the process stirring up a controversy that kept his book in the hands of readers through ten revised editions. By the time Darwin's *Origin of Species* appeared, sales of *Vestiges* had reached the then extraordinary figure of 20,000 copies. Its readers included Mill, Barrett Browning, Tennyson, Darwin, Eliot, and Nightingale. When Huxley snorted at *Vestiges* as a "work of fiction," that was because the chief scientific publicist of the rising generation knew a formidable precursor when he saw one.

from Vestiges of the Natural History of Creation

. . . If we could suppose a number of persons of various ages presented to the inspection of an intelligent being newly introduced into the world, we cannot doubt that he would soon become convinced that men had once been boys, that boys had once been infants, and, finally, that all had been brought into the world in exactly the same circumstances. Precisely thus, seeing in our astral system many thousands of worlds in all stages of formation, from the most rudimental to that immediately preceding the present condition of those we deem perfect, it is unavoidable to conclude that all the perfect have gone through the various stages which we see in the rudimental. This leads us at once to the conclusion that the whole of our firmament was at one time a diffused mass of nebulous matter, extending through the space which it still occupies. So also, of course, must have been the other astral systems. Indeed, we must presume the whole to have been originally in one connected mass, the astral systems being only the first division into parts, and solar systems the second.

The first idea which all this impresses upon us is, that the formation of bodies in space is *still and at present in progress*. . . .

Another and more important consideration arises from the hypothesis; namely, as to the means by which the grand process is conducted. The nebulous matter collects around nuclei by virtue of the law of attraction. The agglomeration brings into operation another physical law, by force of which the separate masses of matter are either made to rotate singly, or, in addition to that single motion, are set into a coupled revolution in ellipses. Next centrifu-

gal force comes into play, flinging off portions of the rotating masses, which become spheres by virtue of the same law of attraction, and are held in orbits of revolution round the central body by means of a composition between the centrifugal and gravitating forces. All, we see, is done by certain laws of matter, so that it becomes a question of extreme interest, what are such laws? All that can yet be said, in answer, is, that we see certain natural events proceeding in an invariable order under certain conditions, and thence infer the existence of some fundamental arrangement which, for the bringing about of these events, has a force and certainty of action similar to, but more precise and unerring than those arrangements which human society makes for its own benefit, and calls laws. It is remarkable of physical laws, that we see them operating on every kind of scale as to magnitude, with the same regularity and perseverance. The tear that falls from childhood's cheek is globular, through the efficacy of that same law of mutual attraction of particles which made the sun and planets round. The rapidity of Mercury is quicker than that of Saturn, for the same reason that, when we wheel a ball round by a string and make the string wind up round our fingers, the ball always flies quicker and quicker as the string is shortened. Two eddies in a stream, as has been stated, fall into a mutual revolution at the distance of a couple of inches, through the same cause which makes a pair of suns link in mutual revolution at the distance of millions of miles. There is, we might say, a sublime simplicity in this indifference of the grand regulations to the vastness or minuteness of the field of their operation. Their being uniform, too, throughout space, as far as we can scan it, and their being so unfailing in their tendency to operate, so that only the proper conditions are presented, afford to our minds matter for the

gravest consideration. Nor should it escape our careful notice that the regulations on which all the laws of matter operate, are established on a rigidly accurate mathematical
basis. Proportions of numbers and geometrical figures rest
at the bottom of the whole. All these considerations, when
the mind is thoroughly prepared for them, tend to raise our
ideas with respect to the character of physical laws, even
though we do not go a single step further in the investigation. But it is impossible for an intelligent mind to stop
there. We advance from law to the cause of law, and ask,
What is that? Whence have come all these beautiful regulations? Here science leaves us, but only to conclude, from
other grounds, that there is a First Cause to which all others
are secondary and ministrative, a primitive almighty will, of
which these laws are merely the mandates. That great
Being, who shall say where is his dwelling-place, or what
his history! Man pauses breathless at the contemplation of a
subject so much above his finite faculties, and only can
wonder and adore! (Chapter 1)

    . . . A candid consideration of all these circumstances
can scarcely fail to introduce into our minds a somewhat
different idea of organic creation from what has hitherto
been generally entertained. That God created animated beings, as well as the terraqueous theatre of their being, is a
fact so powerfully evidenced, and so universally received,
that I at once take it for granted. But in the particulars of
this so highly supported idea, we surely here see cause for
some re-consideration. It may now be inquired,—In what
way was the creation of animated beings effected? The ordinary notion may, I think, be not unjustly described as
this,—that the Almighty author produced the progenitors
of all existing species by some sort of personal or immediate
exertion. But how does this notion comport with what we
have seen of the gradual advance of species, from the humblest to the highest? How can we suppose an immediate exertion of this creative power at one time to produce
zoophytes, another time to add a few marine mollusks, another to bring in one or two conchifers, again to produce
crustaceous fishes, again perfect fishes, and so on to the
end? This would surely be to take a very mean view of the
Creative Power—to, in short, anthropomorphize it, or reduce it to some such character as that borne by the ordinary
proceedings of mankind. And yet this would be unavoidable; for that the organic creation was thus progressive
through a long space of time, rests on evidence which nothing can overturn or gainsay. Some other idea must then be
come to with regard to *the mode* in which the Divine Author

proceeded in the organic creation. Let us seek in the history
of the earth's formation for a new suggestion on this point.
We have seen powerful evidence, that the construction of
this globe and its associates, and inferentially that of all the
other globes of space, was the result, not of any immediate
or personal exertion on the part of the Deity, but of natural
laws which are expressions of his will. What is to hinder our
supposing that the organic creation is also a result of natural
laws, which are in like manner an expression of his will?
More than this, the fact of the cosmical arrangements being
an effect of natural law, is a powerful argument for the organic arrangements being so likewise, for how can we suppose that the august Being who brought all these countless
worlds into form by the simple establishment of a natural
principle flowing from his mind, was to interfere personally
and specially on every occasion when a new shell-fish or
reptile was to be ushered into existence on *one* of these
worlds? Surely this idea is too ridiculous to be for a moment
entertained.

    It will be objected that the ordinary conceptions of
Christian nations on this subject are directly derived from
Scripture, or, at least, are in conformity with it. If they were
clearly and unequivocally supported by Scripture, it may
readily be allowed that there would be a strong objection to
the reception of any opposite hypothesis. But the fact is,
however startling the present announcement of it may be,
that the first chapter of the Mosaic record is not only not in
harmony with the ordinary ideas of mankind respecting
cosmical and organic creation, but is opposed to them, and
only in accordance with the views here taken. When we
carefully peruse it with awakened minds, we find that all the
procedure is represented primarily and pre-eminently as
flowing *from commands and expressions of will, not from direct acts.*
Let there be light—let there be a firmament—let the dry
land appear—let the earth bring forth grass, the herb, the
tree—let the waters bring forth the moving creature that
hath life—let the earth bring forth the living creature after
his kind—these are the terms in which the principal acts are
described. The additional expressions,—God made the firmament—God made the beast of the earth, &c., occur sub-
ordinately, and only in a few instances; they do not
necessarily convey a different idea of the mode of creation,
and indeed only appear as alternative phrases, in the usual
duplicative manner of Eastern narrative. Keeping this in
view, the words used in a subsequent place, "God *formed* man
in his own image," cannot well be understood as implying
any more than what was implied before,—namely, that man
was produced in consequence of an expression of the Divine will to that effect. Thus, the scriptural objection

quickly vanishes, and the prevalent ideas about the organic creation appear only as a mistaken inference from the text, formed at a time when man's ignorance prevented him from drawing therefrom a just conclusion. At the same time, I freely own that I do not think it right to adduce the Mosaic record, either in objection to, or support of any natural hypothesis, and this for many reasons, but particularly for this, that there is not the least appearance of an intention in that book to give philosophically exact views of nature.

To a reasonable mind the Divine attributes must appear, not diminished or reduced in any way, by supposing a creation by law, but infinitely exalted. It is the narrowest of all views of the Deity, and characteristic of a humble class of intellects, to suppose him acting constantly in particular ways for particular occasions. It, for one thing, greatly detracts from his foresight, the most undeniable of all the attributes of Omnipotence. It lowers him towards the level of our own humble intellects. Much more worthy of him it surely is, to suppose that all things have been commissioned by him from the first, though neither is he absent from a particle of the current of natural affairs in one sense, seeing that the whole system is continually supported by his providence. Even in human affairs, if I may be allowed to adopt a familiar illustration, there is a constant progress from specific action for particular occasions, to arrangements which, once established, shall continue to answer for a great multitude of occasions. Such plans the enlightened readily form for themselves, and conceive as being adopted by all who have to attend to a multitude of affairs, while the ignorant suppose every act of the greatest public functionary to be the result of some special consideration and care on his part alone. Are we to suppose the Deity adopting plans which harmonize only with the modes of procedure of the less enlightened of our race? Those who would object to the hypothesis of a creation by the intervention of law, do not perhaps consider how powerful an argument in favour of the existence of God is lost by rejecting this doctrine. When all is seen to be the result of law, the idea of an Almighty Author becomes irresistible, for the creation of a law for an endless series of phenomena—an act of intelligence above all else that we can conceive—could have no other imaginable source, and tells, moreover, as powerfully for a sustaining as for an originating power. . . . (Chapter 12)

. . . But the idea that any of the lower animals have been concerned in any way with the origin of man—is not this degrading? Degrading is a term, expressive of a notion of the human mind, and the human mind is liable to prejudices which prevent its notions from being invariably correct. Were we acquainted for the first time with the circumstances attending the production of an individual of our race, we might equally think them degrading, and be eager to deny them, and exclude them from the admitted truths of nature. Knowing this fact familiarly and beyond contradiction, a healthy and natural mind finds no difficulty in regarding it complacently. Creative Providence has been pleased to order that it should be so, and it must therefore be submitted to. Now the idea as to the progress of organic creation, if we become satisfied of its truth, ought to be received precisely in this spirit. It has pleased Providence to arrange that one species should give birth to another, until the second highest gave birth to man, who is the very highest: be it so, it is our part to admire and to submit. The very faintest notion of there being anything ridiculous or degrading in the theory—how absurd does it appear, when we remember that every individual amongst us actually passes through the characters of the insect, the fish, and reptile, (to speak nothing of others,) before he is permitted to breathe the breath of life! But such notions are mere emanations of false pride and ignorant prejudice. He who conceives them little reflects that they, in reality, involve the principle of a contempt for the works and ways of God. For it may be asked, if He, as appears, has chosen to employ inferior organisms as a generative medium for the production of higher ones, even including ourselves, what right have we, his humble creatures, to find fault? There is, also, in this prejudice, an element of unkindliness towards the lower animals, which is utterly out of place. These creatures are all of them part products of the Almighty Conception, as well as ourselves. All of them display wondrous evidences of his wisdom and benevolence. All of them have had assigned to them by their Great Father a part in the drama of the organic world, as well as ourselves. Why should they be held in such contempt? Let us regard them in a proper spirit, as parts of the grand plan, instead of contemplating them in the light of frivolous prejudices, and we shall be altogether at a loss to see how there should be any degradation in the idea of our race having been genealogically connected with them. (Chapter 14)

. . . It may be asked,—Is the existing human race the only species designed to occupy the grade to which it is here referred? Such a question evidently ought not to be answered rashly; and I shall therefore confine myself to the admission that, judging by analogy, we might expect to see several varieties of the being, homo. There is no other family approaching to this in importance, which presents but one species. The corvidæ, our parallel in aves, consist of several distinct genera and sub-genera. It is startling to find such an appearance of imperfection in the circle to which man belongs, and the ideas which rise in consequence are not less startling. Is our race but the initial of the grand crowning type? Are there yet to be species superior to us in organization, purer in feeling, more powerful in device and act, and who shall take a rule over us! There is in this nothing improbable on other grounds. The present race, rude and impulsive as it is, is perhaps the best adapted to the present state of things in the world; but the external world goes through slow and gradual changes, which may leave it in time a much serener field of existence. There may then be occasion for a nobler type of humanity, which shall complete the zoological circle on this planet, and realize some of the dreams of the purest spirits of the present race. (Chapter 15)

1844

CHARLES CHRISTIAN HENNELL

(1809–1850)

The advancing knowledge that rewrote the nineteenth-century book of nature was also brought to bear, in the form of textual scholarship and interpretation, on the nineteenth-century book of books, the Bible. The remaining excerpts in this section of contexts record the impact of new learning on the status and meaning of Scripture. The Higher Criticism, as Victorians called it, led many Christians to reconceive the basis of their faith in more or less radical ways that included the tolerationist Broad Church, the progressive Christian Socialist movement, and, in militant reaction to these outgrowths of liberalism, the ritualist Anglo-Catholicism that was centered in the Oxford Movement. Other seekers departed from the Church altogether into forms of atheism, humanism, spiritualism, and above all—there is no Victorian coinage that speaks more eloquently than this one—agnosticism.

By way of introduction to this religious ferment, and the outwardly dull respectabilities that often went with it, consider the wedding in 1843 of the London merchant Charles Hennell to Rufa Brabant, a physician's daughter. That the ceremony was a Unitarian one already says something, since Unitarianism dissented from the established Church so far as to question the divinity of Christ. Officiating was the Reverend W. J. Fox, a prominent preacher and at the same time a literary mentor to liberal intellectuals who included the young Browning and Mill. Among the bridesmaids was Mary Ann Evans, who was soon to become a distinguished translator, essayist, and editor, and would eventually become, under the pseudonym George Eliot, the most revered of Victorian novelists. The Hennells' wedding can remind us that the comparatively small world of early-Victorian literary culture was a system of distinct if intersecting orbits, where the provincialism of the commercial middle classes might coexist with surprisingly cosmopolitan free thought. The bride at the time was translating from the German original D. F. Strauss' boldly secular biography *The Life of Jesus*, a milestone of the Higher Criticism that would be set in Victorian place a few years later when her bridesmaid took over and finished the job.

Hennell's *Inquiry* owes its place in literary history to the decisive shake it gave to the evangelical piety of the future George Eliot. It deserves a place here for its application of scientific uniformitarianism to religious history. Winnowing from its husk of primitive myth and miracle, as he sees it, the ethical essence of Christianity, Hennell attaches an unswerving moralism to a progressivism that resonates with the claims of science. The difficulty of determining whether the "time" in his final sentence anticipates life after death, or life after the consummation of science, is an effect worthy of Victorian writers much better known.

from An Inquiry Concerning the Origin of Christianity

. . . The following pages are the result of an investigation . . . pursued for some time with the expectation that, at least, the principal miraculous facts supposed to lie at the foundation of Christianity would be found to be impregnable; but it was continued with a gradually increasing conviction that the true account of the life of Jesus Christ, and of the spread of his religion, would be found to contain no deviation from the known laws of nature, nor to require, for their explanation, more than the operation of human motives and feelings, acted upon by the peculiar circumstances of the age and country whence the religion originated. . . .

Although the belief in the miraculous origin of Christianity forms at present a prominent feature in the creeds of all sects of professing Christians, it would be an unnecessary and perhaps injudicious limitation to hold that the relinquishment of this belief is equivalent to an entire renunciation of the Christian religion. Whatever be men's conclusions concerning the much-debated question of the nature and powers of Jesus Christ, no conclusions of this kind need obstruct their perception of the general excellence of the moral system which is connected with his name, nor impede their acknowledgment of the beneficial influence which the Scriptures exercise over mankind, nor lead to hostility towards the ancient and useful institutions which the sanction of Christ and his followers has caused almost universally to accompany the admission of his religion. Most of the doctrines of Christianity are admitted to be so much in accordance with the purest dictates of natural reason, that, on recognizing the latter as the supreme guide, no violent disruption of the habits and associations of the religious world is necessary. The philosophizing tone adopted by many of the most distinguished modern advocates of religion renders the transition easy from Christianity as a divine revelation to Christianity as the purest form yet existing of natural religion. The contemplation of the Creator may still be indulged, and lessons of morality and wisdom still sought, according to the forms which Christianity has consecrated. The transference of the sanction from a supposed revelation to natural reason will be so little prejudicial to these high exercises of the mind, that, on the contrary, it will extend their interest by allowing them wider scope, and by rendering them more susceptible of all the improvements which experience, circumstances, and growing intelligence, suggest. Christianity will no longer be fettered by the necessity of a continual adaptation to written precept, but will assume a position allowing it to expand freely according to the wants of each successive age, and to advance with the advancement of mankind.

The author of this volume would therefore willingly have it considered as employed in the real service of Christianity, rather than as an attack upon it. Many doctrines, which were once thought to be essential parts of the system, have been successively dismissed into the class of its corruptions; yet, after the wound occasioned by the separation has been healed, Christianity has been found to remain still vigorous, and has even appeared more sightly as relieved from an excrescence. And, now, if the progress of inquiry should lead men to carry the pruning-knife nearer to the root than they had at first contemplated, and to consign even the whole of the miraculous relations in the New Testament to the same list as the prodigies of Hindoo or Romish superstition, we may still find enough left in Christianity to maintain its name and power amidst growing knowledge and civilization. And this will be in that purer moral spirit, and those higher views of the nature of man, the progress of which, although naturally coincident with the advancement of the human mind, received so vigorous an impulse from the life of Jesus, that this spirit and these views have come to be indissolubly associated with the idea, and expressed under the name, of Christianity.

Christianity, thus regarded as a system of elevated thought and feeling, will not be injured by being freed from those fables, and those views of local or temporary interest, which hung about its origin. It will, on the contrary, be placed on a surer basis; for it need no longer appeal for its support to the uncertain evidence of events which happened nearly two thousand years ago, a species of evidence necessarily attainable only by long and laborious research, impracticable to most men, and unsatisfactory and harassing even to those who have most means of pursuing it; but it will rest its claims on an evidence clearer, simpler, and always at hand,—the thoughts and feelings of the human mind itself. Thus, whatever in it is really true and excellent,[1] will meet with a ready attestation in every breast, and, in the improvement of the human mind, find an ever-increasing evidence. (Preface)

. . . That the resurrection of Jesus was intended as a pledge to mankind of a general resurrection, is a delightful idea. But the only safe basis for such a belief is historical evidence. If this fail to establish the fact, the agreeable nature of the belief is so far from proving it, that it rather furnishes an explanation of the general prevalence of the belief in the face of insufficient evidence.

It is not pretended that the foregoing pages prove the absolute impossibility of Christ's miracles and resurrection. If we be so determined, we may still indulge in the belief of them, by overlooking difficulties, inventing hypotheses, and concluding that the whole is a trial of our faith. But if the reasoner will still hold the reality of these miracles, to what scheme must he have recourse? That God has caused a deviation from the course of nature for the instruction of mankind, and has left the account of it to be conveyed to them by means which, on the closest examination, occasion it to bear a strong resemblance to human fictions; a supposition so monstrous and perplexing, that, notwithstanding the value of the supposed lesson, our minds turn at last from this mode of teaching in weariness, and resolve to be contented to learn where we are sure, at least, that the lessons proceed from God himself—and that is in nature.

The miraculous birth, works, resurrection, and ascension of Christ, being thus successively surrendered, to be classed amongst the fables of an obscure age, what remains of Christianity? and what is there in the life and doctrine of Jesus that they should still claim the attention and respect of mankind in remote ages? This: Christianity forms a striking passage in the history of human nature, and appears as one of the most prominent of the means employed in its improvement. It no longer boasts of a special divine origin, but shares in that which the Theist attributes to the world and the whole order of its events. It has presented to the world a system of moral excellence; it has led forth the principles of humanity and benevolence from the recesses of the schools and groves, and compelled them to take an active part in the affairs of life. It has consolidated the moral and religious sentiments into a more definite and influential form than had before existed, and thereby constituted an engine which has worked powerfully towards humanizing and civilizing the world. . . .

. . . Science and philosophy are, however, yet in their infancy, and especially as regards their application to subjects supposed to be connected with morality and religion. The belief that Revelation had assumed these subjects as her own peculiar ground, has hitherto impeded the growth of free inquiry upon them amongst nations most competent to the task.[2] Released from this restraint, and having unbounded scope to traverse the creation in search of evidence, mankind may reach points in moral discovery which at present would be at once pronounced visionary. The

---

[1]**whatever in it is really true and excellent**: compare Philippians 4:8.

[2]Whenever any great revolutions in opinion have been in progress, it has appeared to many that the ties of morality were being unloosed, and that the mental world was falling into the darkest confusion. Such was the idea of the heathens whilst Christianity was throwing down their venerable ancient deities. Eunapius, a heathen sophist, who wrote in the time of the emperor Theodosius I, giving an account of an Egyptian Philosopher named Antoninus, says, "He foretold to all his disciples that, after his death, there would be no temples, but that the magnificent and sacred temple of Serapis would be laid in ruinous heaps, and that fabulous confusion and unformed darkness would tyrannize over the best parts of the earth. All which things time has brought to pass."

We see at present the incipient upheavings of another of these revolutions—the subversion of the belief in miraculous revelations, and the gradual advance of a system of natural religion, of which we cannot yet predict the whole creed, but of which we may already perceive two essential features, the recognition of a God, and that of an inherent moral nature in man. As the clearing away of the antiquated piles of the old law made way for the simpler structure of faith in Christ, so will the release from the exclusive authority of written precept enable men to hear more distinctly the voice of the moral nature within them. Reformed Judaism will be succeeded by reformed Christianity, and each change appear the transition to a more perfect law of liberty. [Hennell's note]

achievements of mechanical and chemical science may be equalled or outdone by those of moral and intellectual research; and a clearer confession be forced out of nature concerning the character of the Creator, and the ultimate destination of man. In the mean time may it not be, that the feelings of the human heart have anticipated the laborious operations of the intellect, and that Christianity has taken the advance of philosophy in ministering to the deepest wants of man?

Let not, then, the mind which is compelled to renounce its belief in miraculous revelations deem itself bound to throw aside, at the same time, all its most cherished associations. Its generous emotions and high contemplations may still find an occasion for exercise in the review of the interesting incidents which have for ever consecrated the plains of Palestine; but it may also find pleasure in the thought that, for this exercise no single spot of earth, and no one page of its history, furnishes the exclusive theme. Whatever dimness may gather from the lapse of time and the obscurity of records about the events of a distant age, these capabilities of the mind itself remain, and always will remain, in full freshness and beauty. Other Jerusalems will excite the glow of patriotism, other Bethanies exhibit the affections of home,[3] and other minds of benevolence and energy seek to hasten the approach of the kingdom of man's perfection. Nor can scriptures ever be wanting—the scriptures of the physical and of the moral world—the book of the universe. Here the page is open, and the language intelligible to all men; no transcribers have been able to interpolate or erase its texts; it stands before us in the same genuineness as when first written; the simplest understanding can enter with delight into criticism upon it; the volume does not close, leaving us to thirst for more, but another and another epistle still meets the inquisitive eye, each signed with the author's own hand, and bearing undoubted characters of divine inspiration. Unable at present to comprehend the whole, we can still feel the privilege of looking into it at pleasure, of knowing a part, and of attempting the opening of further leaves. And if, after its highest efforts, the mind be compelled to sink down, acknowledging its inability, in some parts, to satisfy itself with any clear conclusion, it may remain serene at least, persuaded that God will not cause any soul to fare the worse for not knowing what he has given it no means to know. Enough is understood to enable us to see, in the Universe itself, a Son which tells us of a Father, and in all the natural beauty and moral excellence which meet us in the world an ever-present Logos, which reveals the grace and truth of its invisible source. Enough is understood to convince us that, to have a place on this beautiful planet, on almost any terms, is an unspeakable privilege; that virtue produces the highest happiness, whether for this or another world; and that there does exist an encircling mysterious Intelligence, which, as it appears to manifest its energy in arrangements for the general welfare of the creation, must ensure a provision for all the real interests of man. From all our occasional excursions into the abysses of the unseen world, and from all our efforts to reach upwards to the hidden things of God, both reason and piety bid us return tranquilly to our accustomed corner of the earth, to use and enjoy fully our present lot, and to repose implicitly upon the higher wisdom in whose disposal we stand, whilst indulging the thought that a time is appointed when the cravings of the heart and of the intellect will be satisfied, and the enigma of our own and the world's existence be solved. (Conclusion)

1838

---

[3]**other Bethanies:** see John 11:1–45, where Mary and Martha mourn Lazarus at their **home** in Bethany.

BENJAMIN JOWETT

(1817–1893)

As the Bridgewater treatises stood to questions of faith and knowledge in the first great era of reform (1828–1832), so stood *Essays and Reviews* in the second (1867–1870). Both comprised essays by established clergymen-scholars affiliated with the great national universities and schools, and both addressed a schism between religion and science by seeking to contain it. One generation's fissure, however, had become another's crevasse. Where earlier Christian apologists had wielded the Bible as a weapon with which to intimidate the still tentative scientific vanguard, now their successors were clearly on the defensive. What they had to defend, first of all, was their former weapon: the truth and consistency of Scripture kept disintegrating under critical analysis and requiring sophisticated efforts of repair. The tactics of interpretive recovery that were proposed in *Essays and Reviews* scandalized Church authorities, who condemned the book's liberalism not only in word but also in deed. Several contributors were brought to trial; and the author excerpted here, Benjamin Jowett, lost ten years' income from his post at Oxford on suspicion of heresy.

For this and other reasons Jowett was a famous figure at Oxford, where for half a century as student, tutor, and eventually Master of Balliol College he witnessed the transformation of the university from a nearly medieval pasture for the sons of gentlemen to a nearly modern institution of higher learning. Jowett's own learning lay in Greek studies, where he produced not only translations of Plato and Thucydides but also a scholarly edition of St. Paul's epistles. The copresence of classical and biblical texts in his own scholarship gives special point to his most famous recommendation: "read Scripture like any other book," he advised, with a view to discerning, in a phrase that the Oxford-trained Arnold and Pater laid to heart, "things as they truly are." The aim of *Essays and Reviews* was not simply to question authority, but to free the Bible and its readers to "create a new interest" and "a new kind of authority." Church authorities, of course, had a vested interest of their own; and they were not amused.

from On the Interpretation of Scripture

. . . Modes of interpreting vary as time goes on; they partake of the general state of literature or knowledge. It has not been easily or at once that mankind have learned to realize the character of sacred writings—they seem almost necessarily to veil themselves from human eyes as circumstances change; it is the old age of the world only that has at length understood its childhood. (Or rather perhaps is beginning to understand it, and learning to make allowance for its own deficiency of knowledge; for the infancy of the human race, as of the individual, affords but few indications of the workings of the mind within.) More often than we suppose, the great sayings and doings upon the earth, "thoughts that breathe and words that burn,"[1] are lost in a sort of chaos to the apprehension of those that come after. Much of past history is dimly seen and receives only a conventional interpretation, even when the memorials of it remain. There is a time at which the freshness of early literature is lost; mankind have turned rhetoricians, and no longer write or feel in the spirit which created it. . . .

The book itself remains as at the first unchanged amid the changing interpretations of it. The office of the

---

[1]**"thoughts . . . that burn"**: Thomas Gray (1716–1771), "The Progress of Poesy" (1757), 110.

interpreter is not to add another, but to recover the original one: the meaning, that is, of the words as they struck on the ear or flashed before the eyes of those who first heard and read them. He has to transfer himself to another age; to imagine that he is a disciple of Christ or Paul; to disengage himself from all that follows. The history of Christendom is nothing to him; but only the scene at Galilee or Jerusalem, the handful of believers who gathered themselves together at Ephesus, or Corinth, or Rome. His eye is fixed on the form of one like the Son of man, or of the Prophet who was girded with a garment of camel's hair, or of the Apostle who had a thorn in the flesh.[2] The greatness of the Roman Empire is nothing to him; it is an inner not an outer world that he is striving to restore. All the after-thoughts of theology are nothing to him; they are not the true lights which light him in difficult places. His concern is with a book in which, as in other ancient writings, are some things of which we are ignorant; which defect of our knowledge cannot however be supplied by the conjectures of fathers or divines. The simple words of that book he tries to preserve absolutely pure from the refinements or distinctions of later times. He acknowledges that they are fragmentary, and would suspect himself, if out of fragments he were able to create a well-rounded system, or a continuous history. The greater part of his learning is a knowledge of the text itself; he has no delight in the voluminous literature which has overgrown it. He has no theory of interpretation; a few rules guarding against common errors are enough for him. His object is to read Scripture like any other book, with a real interest and not merely a conventional one. He wants to be able to open his eyes and see or imagine things as they truly are. . . .

. . . In natural science it is felt to be useless to build on assumptions; in history we look with suspicion on *à priori*[3] ideas of what ought to have been; in mathematics, when a step is wrong, we pull the house down until we reach the point at which the error is discovered. But in theology it is otherwise; there the tendency has been to conceal the unsoundness of the foundation under the fairness and loftiness of the superstructure. It has been thought safer to allow arguments to stand which, although fallacious, have been on

the right side, than to point out their defect. And thus many principles have imperceptibly grown up which have overridden facts. . . .

. . . Any true doctrine of inspiration must conform to all well-ascertained facts of history or of science. The same fact cannot be true and untrue, any more than the same words can have two opposite meanings. The same fact cannot be true in religion when seen by the light of faith, and untrue in science when looked at through the medium of evidence or experiment. It is ridiculous to suppose that the sun goes round the earth in the same sense in which the earth goes round the sun; or that the world appears to have existed, but has not existed during the vast epochs of which geology speaks to us.[4] But if so, there is no need of elaborate reconcilements of revelation and science; they reconcile themselves the moment any scientific truth is distinctly ascertained. As the idea of nature enlarges, the idea of revelation also enlarges; it was a temporary misunderstanding which severed them. And as the knowledge of nature which is possessed by the few is communicated in its leading features at least to the many, they will receive with it a higher conception of the ways of God to man. It may hereafter appear as natural to the majority of mankind to see the providence of God in the order of the world as it once was to appeal to interruptions of it. . . .

. . . The sciences of geology and comparative philology are steadily gaining ground; many of the guesses of twenty years ago have become certainties, and the guesses of today may hereafter become so. Shall we peril religion on the possibility of their untruth? On such a cast to stake the life of a man implies not only a recklessness of facts, but a misunderstanding of the nature of the Gospel. If it is fortunate for science, it is perhaps more fortunate for Christian truth, that the admission of Galileo's discovery has for ever settled the principle of the relations between them. . . .

. . . As the time has come when it is no longer possible to ignore the results of criticism, it is of importance that Christianity should be seen to be in harmony with them. That objections to some received views should be valid, and yet that they should be always held up as the objections of infidels, is a mischief to the Christian cause. It is a mischief that critical observations which any intelligent man can

---

[2]**Son of man**: one of Jesus' preferred titles. **Prophet**: John the Baptist (Matthew 3:4). **Apostle**: St Paul, who described himself as struggling with a **thorn in the flesh** (2 Corinthians 12:7) and who wrote biblical epistles to the early churches at **Ephesus, Corinth,** and **Rome**.

[3]*à priori*: derived from first principles, not experience.

[4]**the world appears to have existed**: doctrine espoused by Philip Gosse in *Omphalos: An Attempt to Untie the Geological Knot* (1857), which argued that the fossil record had been embedded in the rocks by God at the creation, just as Adam had been created with a navel (Greek *omphalos*).

make for himself, should be ascribed to atheism or unbelief. It would be a strange and almost incredible thing that the Gospel, which at first made war only on the vices of mankind, should now be opposed to one of the highest and rarest of human virtues—the love of truth. And that in the present day the great object of Christianity should be, not to change the lives of men, but to prevent them from changing their opinions; that would be a singular inversion of the purposes for which Christ came into the world. The Christian religion is in a false position when all the tendencies of knowledge are opposed to it. Such a position cannot be long maintained, or can only end in the withdrawal of the educated classes from the influences of religion. It is a grave consideration whether we ourselves may not be in an earlier stage of the same religious dissolution, which seems to have gone further in Italy and France.[5] The reason for thinking so is not to be sought in the external circumstances of our own or any other religious communion, but in the progress of ideas with which Christian teachers seem to be ill at ease. Time was when the Gospel was before the age; when it breathed a new life into a decaying world—when the difficulties of Christianity were difficulties of the heart only, and the highest minds found in its truths not only the rule of their lives, but a well-spring of intellectual delight. Is

it to be held a thing impossible that the Christian religion, instead of shrinking into itself, may again embrace the thoughts of men upon the earth? Or is it true that since the Reformation "all intellect has gone the other way"? and that in Protestant countries reconciliation is as hopeless as Protestants commonly believe to be the case in Catholic?

Those who hold the possibility of such a reconcilement or restoration of belief, are anxious to disengage Christianity from all suspicion of disguise or unfairness. They wish to preserve the historical use of Scripture as the continuous witness in all ages of the higher things in the heart of man, as the inspired source of truth and the way to the better life. They are willing to take away some of the external supports, because they are not needed and do harm; also, because they interfere with the meaning. They have a faith, not that after a period of transition all things will remain just as they were before, but that they will all come round again to the use of man and to the glory of God. When interpreted like any other book, by the same rules of evidence and the same canons of criticism, the Bible will still remain unlike any other book; its beauty will be freshly seen, as of a picture which is restored after many ages to its original state; it will create a new interest and make for itself a new kind of authority by the life which is in it. It will be a spirit and not a letter; as it was in the beginning, having an influence like that of the spoken word, or the book newly found. . . .

1860

---

[5]**Italy and France:** Roman Catholic countries where, Jowett warns, intolerant dogmatism has provoked infidelity and revolution.

JOHN WILLIAM COLENSO

(1814–1883)

Colenso rose from provincial obscurity to respectable appointments as a mathematics teacher, and thence to a colonial bishopric—maintained with honor amid much adversity— in the Natal province of South Africa. An earnest, practical plainness distinguished his advocacy on behalf of the Zulus and their culture, which he tried to defend against colonial maladministration. This same plainness, together with Colenso's rational cast of mind, forbade his settling anywhere along the range of equivocations that sufficed so many of his clerical brethren, once the Zulus for whom he was translating the Bible pointed out impossibilities in its story. "I have arrived at the conviction," this Anglican bishop declared, "that the

Pentateuch, as a whole, cannot possibly have been written by Moses, or by any one acquainted personally with the facts which it professes to describe, and, further, that the (so-called) Mosaic narrative, by whomsoever written, and though imparting to us, as I fully believe it does, revelations of the Divine Will and Character, cannot be regarded as *historically true."*

At home in England, the idea of a missionary bishop's conversion by the "savages" he had been sent to convert struck some witnesses as hilarious, others as wicked. Colenso was excommunicated by ecclesiastical superiors, only to be reinstated as bishop by the secular courts of law. The trials of Bishop Colenso, like the concurrent furor over *Essays and Reviews,* show how the personal conflict between faith and knowledge entailed larger Victorian conflicts between institutions and consciences, and also between Anglican traditions and rapidly broadening intellectual and geographical horizons.

from The Pentateuch and Book of Joshua Critically Examined

Since I have had the charge of this Diocese, I have been closely occupied in the study of the Zulu tongue, and in translating the Scriptures into it. Through the blessing of God, I have now translated the New Testament completely, and several parts of the Old, among the rest the books of Genesis and Exodus. In this work I have been aided by intelligent natives; and, having also published a Zulu Grammar and Dictionary, I have acquired sufficient knowledge of the language, to be able to have intimate communion with the native mind, while thus engaged with them, so as not only to avail myself freely of their criticisms, but to appreciate fully their objections and difficulties. Thus, however, it has happened that I have been brought again face to face with questions, which caused me some uneasiness in former days, but with respect to which I was then enabled to satisfy my mind sufficiently for practical purposes, and I had fondly hoped to have laid the ghosts of them at last for ever. Engrossed with parochial and other work in England, I did what, probably, many other clergymen have done under similar circumstances,—I contented myself with silencing, by means of the specious explanations, which are given in most commentaries, the ordinary objections against the historical character of the early portions of the Old Testament, and settled down into a willing acquiescence in the general truth of the narrative, whatever difficulties might still hang

about particular parts of it. In short, the doctrinal and devotional portions of the Bible were what were needed most in parochial duty. And, if a passage of the Old Testament formed at any time the subject of a sermon, it was easy to draw from it practical lessons of daily life, without examining closely into the historical truth of the narrative. It is true, there were one or two stories, which presented great difficulties, too prominent not to be noticed, and which were brought every now and then before us in the Lessons of the Church, such, for instance, as the account of the Creation and the Deluge. But, on the whole, I found so much of Divine Light and Life in these and other parts of the Sacred Book, so much wherewith to feed my own soul and the souls of others, that I was content to take all this for granted, as being true in the main, however wonderful, and as being at least capable, in an extreme case, of *some* sufficient explanation.

Here, however, as I have said, amidst my work in this land, I have been brought face to face with the very questions which I then put by. While translating the story of the Flood, I have had a simple-minded, but intelligent, native,—one with the docility of a child, but the reasoning powers of mature age,—look up, and ask, "Is all that true? Do you really believe that all this happened thus,—that all the beasts, and birds, and creeping things, upon the earth, large and small, from hot countries and cold, came thus by pairs, and entered into the ark with Noah? And did Noah gather food for them *all,* for the beasts and birds of prey, as well as the rest?" My heart answered in the words of the Prophet, "Shall a man speak lies in the name of the LORD?" Zech.xiii.3. I dared not do so. My own knowledge of some branches of science, of Geology in particular, had been much increased since I left England; and I now knew for certain, on geological grounds, a fact, of which I had only had misgivings before, viz. that a *Universal* Deluge, such as the Bible manifestly speaks of, could not possibly have taken place in the way described in the Book of Genesis, not to mention other difficulties which the story contains. . . .

. . . Certainly, there are not a few points, on which I differ strongly from those writers.[1] But I cannot think it to be a fair way of proceeding to point out, as the *apparent consequence* of the course they are pursuing, that it will necessarily lead to infidelity or atheism. It may be so with some; must it, therefore, be so with all? The same, of course, might have been said, and probably was said, freely, and just as truly, by the Jews of St. Paul and others, and, in later times, by members of the Romish Church of our own Reformers. Our duty, surely, is to follow the Truth, wherever it leads us, and to leave the consequences in the hands of God. . . .

. . . There are very many, who appreciate to some extent the difficulties of the traditionary view, but yet are unable to satisfy themselves that it is wholly untenable, and live in a state of painful uncertainty, which they would gladly have terminated, though even by the sharp pang of one decisive stroke, which shall sever their connection with it once and for ever.

I believe that there are not a few among the more highly educated classes of society in England, and multitudes among the more intelligent operatives, who are in danger of drifting into irreligion and practical atheism, under this dim sense of the unsoundness of the popular view, combined with a feeling of distrust of their spiritual teachers, as if *these* must be either ignorant of facts, which to themselves are patent, or, at least, insensible to the difficulties which those facts involve, or else, being aware of their existence, and feeling their importance, are consciously ignoring them. It has been said by some, "Why make this disturbance? Why publish to the world matters like these, about which theologians may have doubts?" I answer, that they are not theologians only, who are troubled with such doubts, and that we have a duty to discharge towards that large body of our brethren,—*how* large it is impossible to say, but, probably, much larger than is commonly imagined,—who not only doubt, but disbelieve, many important parts of the Mosaic narrative, as well as to those, whose faith may be more simple and unenquiring, though not, therefore, necessarily, more deep and sincere, than theirs. We cannot expect such as these to look to us for comfort and help in their religious perplexities, if they cannot place entire confidence in our honesty of purpose and good faith,—if they have any reason to suppose that we are willing to keep back any part of the truth, and are afraid to state the plain facts of the case, as we know them. . . . (Preface to Part 1)

1862

---

[1] **those writers:** contributors to *Essays and Reviews* (1860).

JOHN TYNDALL

(1820–1893)

Tyndall, like his more celebrated friend and ally Huxley, made his way up from poverty to become at once a respected researcher and a major promoter of science within the public arena. It was Tyndall who explained how the molecular scattering of sunlight makes the sky blue; this readiness to gratify a common curiosity nicely exemplifies the responsibility Victorian scientists felt to court the public as well as inform it. Thus in the lecture represented here we find him equally attentive to his announced topic (the scientific status of the soul) and to the ideological climate within which such a topic must be delicately framed if it is to be well received. Awareness of this climate was no doubt sharpened as Tyndall—Irish-bred, German-trained, and London-employed—returned home to address scientists within a Protestant enclave of Roman Catholic, politically unstable Ireland.

Like other writers in this section, Tyndall prefers a scientific to a religious understanding. What distinguishes his approach from theirs is the confidence with which he advances the standard of science into the stronghold of mystery where, by the last third of the century, the religious mind has made its retreat. No longer merely contending like Herschel for an unprejudiced hearing, Tyndall can afford to confide, without any concession to immaterial metaphysics, that science too has mysterious charms. Our selection picks up the second half of an imaginary debate between a disciple of Lucretius (94-55 BCE) and Bishop Joseph Butler (1692–1752). The former is an exponent of atomistic materialism, the latter an antimaterialist whose philosophical vindication of mind over matter Tyndall appropriates on modern science's terms of reverence for the unknown dimensions within matter itself. The way he magnifies "the vision of the mind" on "beyond the range of the senses" recalls Whewell's earlier refusal to rest cosmological explanation anywhere short of a First Cause—a similarity underscoring the difference forty years have made in the respective Victorian positions of religion and science. We begin with the Lucretian materialist's concluding arguments for identifying the mind with the brain and proceed at once to the Bishop's rejoinder.

from Address before the British Association Assembled at Belfast

"... The brain may change from health to disease, and through such a change the most exemplary man may be converted into a debauchee or a murderer. My very noble and approved good master had, as you know, threatenings of lewdness introduced into his brain by his jealous wife's philter; and, sooner than permit himself to run even the risk of yielding to these base promptings, he slew himself. How could the hand of Lucretius have been thus turned against himself if the real Lucretius remained as before? Can the brain or can it not act in this distempered way without the intervention of the immortal reason? If it can, then it is a prime mover which requires only healthy regulation to render it reasonably self-acting, and there is no apparent need of your immortal reason at all. If it cannot, then the immortal reason, by its mischievous activity in operating upon a broken instrument, must have the credit of committing every imaginable extravagance and crime. I think, if you will allow me to say so, that the gravest consequences are likely to flow from your estimate of the body. To regard the brain as you would a staff or an eyeglass—to shut your eyes to all its mystery, to the perfect correlation of its condition and our consciousness, to the fact that a slight excess or de-

fect of blood in it produces the very swoon to which you refer, and that in relation to it our meat and drink and air and exercise have a perfectly transcendental value and significance—to forget all this, does, I think, open a way to innumerable errors in our habits of life, and may possibly in some cases initiate and foster that very disease, and consequent mental ruin, which a wiser appreciation of this mysterious organ would have avoided."

I can imagine the bishop thoughtful after hearing this argument. He was not the man to allow anger to mingle with the consideration of a point of this kind. After due reflection, and having strengthened himself by that honest contemplation of the facts which was habitual with him, and which includes the desire to give even adverse facts their due weight, I can suppose the bishop to proceed thus: "... You are a Lucretian, and from the combination and separation of insensate atoms deduce all terrestrial things, including organic forms and their phenomena. Let me tell you, in the first instance, how far I am prepared to go with you. I admit that you can build crystalline forms out of this play of molecular force; that the diamond, amethyst, and snow-star, are truly wonderful structures which are thus produced. I will go further and acknowledge that even a tree or flower might in this way be organized. Nay, if you can show me an animal without sensation, I will concede to you that it also might be put together by the suitable play of molecular force.

"Thus far our way is clear; but now comes my difficulty. Your atoms are individually without sensation, much more are they without intelligence. May I ask you, then, to try your hand upon this problem? Take your dead hydrogen-atoms, your dead oxygen-atoms, your dead carbon-atoms, your dead nitrogen-atoms, your dead phosphorus-atoms, and all the other atoms, dead as grains of shot, of which the brain is formed. Imagine them separate and sensationless, observe them running together and forming all imaginable combinations. This, as a purely mechanical process, is *seeable* by the mind. But can you see, or dream, or in any way imagine, how out of that mechanical act, and from these individually dead atoms, sensation, thought, and emotion, are to arise? Are you likely to extract Homer out of the rattling of dice, or the Differential Calculus out of the clash of billiard-balls? I am not all bereft of this *Vorstellungskraft*[1] of which you speak, nor am I, like so many of my brethren, a mere vacuum as regards scientific knowledge. I can follow a particle of musk until it reaches the olfactory nerve; I can follow the waves of sound until their tremors reach the water of the labyrinth and set the otoliths and Corti's fibres[2] in motion; I can also visualize the waves of ether as they cross the eye and hit the retina. Nay, more, I am able to pursue to the central organ the motion thus imparted at the periphery, and to see in idea the very molecules of the brain thrown into tremors. My insight is not baffled by these physical processes. What baffles and bewilders me, is the notion that from those physical tremors things so utterly incongruous with them as sensation, thought, and emotion, can be derived. You may say, or think, that this issue of consciousness from the clash of atoms is not more incongruous than the flash of light from the union of oxygen and hydrogen. But I beg to say that it is. For such incongruity as the flash possesses is that which I now force upon your attention. The flash is an affair of consciousness, the objective counterpart of which is a vibration. It is a flash only by your interpretation. *You* are the cause of the apparent incongruity, and *you* are the thing that puzzles me. I need not remind you that the great Leibnitz[3] felt the difficulty which I feel, and that to get rid of this monstrous deduction of life from death he displaced your atoms by his monads, which were more or less

perfect mirrors of the universe, and out of the summation and integration of which he supposed all the phenomena of life—sentient, intellectual, and emotional—to arise.

"Your difficulty, then, as I see you are ready to admit, is quite as great as mine. You cannot satisfy the human understanding in its demand for logical continuity between molecular processes and the phenomena of consciousness. This is a rock on which materialism must inevitably split whenever it pretends to be a complete philosophy of life. What is the moral, my Lucretian? You and I are not likely to indulge in ill-temper in the discussion of these great topics, where we see so much room for honest differences of opinion. But there are people of less wit or more bigotry (I say it with humility) on both sides, who are ever ready to mingle anger and vituperation with such discussions. There are, for example, writers of note and influence at the present day who are not ashamed to assume the 'deep personal sin' of a great logician to be the cause of his unbelief in a theologic dogma. And there are others who hold that we, who cherish our noble Bible, wrought as it has been into the constitution of our forefathers, and by inheritance into us, must necessarily be hypocritical and insincere. Let us disavow and discountenance such people, cherishing the unswerving faith that what is good and true in both our arguments will be preserved for the benefit of humanity, while all that is bad or false will disappear."

I hold the bishop's reasoning to be unanswerable, and his liberality to be worthy of imitation. . . .

At the outset of this Address it was stated that physical theories which lie beyond experience are derived by a process of abstraction from experience. It is instructive to note from this point of view the successive introduction of new conceptions. The idea of the attraction of gravitation was preceded by the observation of the attraction of iron by a magnet, and of light bodies by rubbed amber. The polarity of magnetism and electricity appealed to the senses, and thus became the substratum of the conception that atoms and molecules are endowed with definite, attractive, and repellent poles, by the play of which definite forms of crystalline architecture are produced. Thus molecular force becomes *structural*. It required no great boldness of thought to extend its play into organic Nature, and to recognize in molecular force the agency by which both plants and animals are built up. In this way out of experience arise conceptions which are wholly ultra-experiential. None of the atomists of antiquity had any notion of this play of molecular polar force, but they had experience of gravity as manifested by falling bodies. Abstracting from this, they permitted their atoms to fall eternally through empty space.

---

[1] *Vorstellungskraft*: a term from German philosophy, defined earlier in the lecture as the power of "mental presentation."

[2] **otoliths, Corti's fibres**: organelles of the ear.

[3] Gottfried Wilhelm **Leibnitz** (1646–1716) posited the existence of **monads**, in his 1714 *Monadologia*, as dimensionless building blocks of the universe.

Democritus[4] assumed that the larger atoms moved more rapidly than the smaller ones, which they therefore could overtake, and with which they could combine. Epicurus, holding that empty space could offer no resistance to motion, ascribed to all the atoms the same velocity; but he seems to have overlooked the consequence that under such circumstances the atoms could never combine. Lucretius cut the knot by quitting the domain of physics altogether, and causing the atoms to move together by a kind of volition.

Was the instinct utterly at fault which caused Lucretius thus to swerve from his own principles? Diminishing gradually the number of progenitors, Mr. Darwin comes at length to one "primordial form;" but he does not say, as far as I remember, how he supposes this form to have been introduced. He quotes with satisfaction the words of a celebrated author and divine who had "gradually learned to see that it is just as noble a conception of the Deity to believe He created a few original forms, capable of self-development into other and needful forms, as to believe that He required a fresh act of creation to supply the voids caused by the action of his laws."[5] What Mr. Darwin thinks of this view of the introduction of life I do not know. But the anthropomorphism, which it seemed his object to set aside, is as firmly associated with the creation of a few forms as with the creation of a multitude. We need clearness and thoroughness here. Two courses, and two only, are possible. Either let us open our doors freely to the conception of creative acts, or, abandoning them, let us radically change our notions of matter. If we look at matter as pictured by Democritus, and as defined for generations in our scientific text-books, the notion of any form of life whatever coming out of it is utterly unimaginable. The argument placed in the mouth of Bishop Butler suffices, in my opinion, to crush all such materialism as this. But those who framed these definitions of matter were not biologists, but mathematicians, whose labors referred only to such accidents and properties of matter as could be expressed in their formulæ. The very intentness with which they pursued mechanical science turned their thoughts aside from the science of life. May not their imperfect definitions be the real cause of our present dread? Let us reverently, but honestly, look the question in the face. Divorced from matter, where is life to be found? Whatever our *faith* may say, our *knowledge* shows them to be indissolubly joined. Every meal we eat, and every cup we drink, illustrates the mysterious control of mind by matter.

Trace the line of life backward, and see it approaching more and more to what we call the purely physical condition. . . . Believing as I do in the continuity of Nature, I cannot stop abruptly where our microscopes cease to be of use. Here the vision of the mind authoritatively supplements the vision of the eye. By an intellectual necessity I cross the boundary of the experimental evidence, and discern in that matter which we, in our ignorance of its latent powers, and notwithstanding our professed reverence for its creator, have hitherto covered with opprobrium, the promise and potency of all terrestrial life.

If you ask me whether there exists the least evidence to prove that any form of life can be developed out of matter, without demonstrable antecedent life, my reply is that evidence considered perfectly conclusive by many has been adduced; and that were some of us who have pondered this question to follow a very common example, and accept testimony because it falls in with our belief, we also should eagerly close with the evidence referred to. But there is in the true man of science a wish stronger than the wish to have his beliefs upheld; namely, the wish to have them true. And this stronger wish causes him to reject the most plausible support if he has reason to suspect that it is vitiated by error. Those to whom I refer as having studied this question, believing the evidence offered in favor of "spontaneous generation" to be thus vitiated, cannot accept it. They know full well that the chemist now prepares from inorganic matter a vast array of substances which were some time ago regarded as the sole products of vitality. They are intimately acquainted with the structural power of matter as evidenced in the phenomena of crystallization. They can justify scientifically their *belief* in its potency, under the proper conditions, to produce organisms. But in reply to your question they will frankly admit their inability to point to any satisfactory experimental proof that life can be developed save from demonstrable antecedent life. As already indicated, they draw the line from the highest organisms through lower ones down to the lowest, and it is the prolongation of this line by the intellect beyond the range of the senses that leads them to the conclusion which Bruno so boldly enunciated.[6]

---

[4]**Democritus**: 5th-century Greek philosopher, proponent of atomic theory later adopted by the Athenian **Epicurus** (341-270 BCE), on whose ideas the Roman poet **Lucretius** (94-55 BCE) based his didactic epic *De Rerum Natura* (On the Nature of Things).

[5]*Origin of Species*, chapter 15. The **celebrated author** quoted is Charles Kingsley (1819–1875).

---

[6]Bruno was a "pantheist," not an "atheist" or a "materialist." [Tyndall's note] Giordano **Bruno** (1548–1600): speculative polymath who went to the stake in Rome rather than recant heterodox theories.

The "materialism" here professed may be vastly differ-ent from what you suppose. . . . For when I say I see you, and that I have not the least doubt about it, the reply is that what I am really conscious of is an affection of my own retina. And if I urge that I can check my sight of you by touching you, the retort would be that I am equally trans-gressing the limits of fact; for what I am really conscious of is, not that you are there, but that the nerves of my hand have undergone a change. All we hear, and see, and touch, and taste, and smell, are, it would be urged, mere variations of our own condition, beyond which, even to the extent of a hair's breadth, we cannot go. That any thing answering to our impressions exists outside of ourselves is not a *fact*, but an *inference*, to which all validity would be denied by an ide-alist like Berkeley, or by a skeptic like Hume.[7] Mr. Spencer takes another line. With him, as with the uneducated man, there is no doubt or question as to the existence of an exter-nal world. But he differs from the uneducated, who think that the world really *is* what consciousness represents it to be. Our states of consciousness are mere *symbols* of an out-side entity which produces them and determines the order of their succession, but the real nature of which we can never know. In fact, the whole process of evolution is the manifestation of a power absolutely inscrutable to the intel-lect of man. As little in our day as in the days of Job can man by searching find this power out. Considered funda-mentally, then, it is by the operation of an insoluble mys-tery that life on earth is evolved, species differentiated, and mind unfolded from their prepotent elements in the immea-surable past. There is, you will observe, no very rank mate-rialism here. . . .

. . . Man the *object* is separated by an impassable gulf from man the *subject*. There is no motor energy in intellect to carry it without logical rupture from the one to the other.

Further, the doctrine of evolution derives man in his totality from the interaction of organism and environment through countless ages past. The human understanding, for example—that faculty which Mr. Spencer has turned so skillfully round upon its own antecedents—is itself a re-sult of the play between organism and environment through cosmic ranges of time. Never surely did prescrip-tion plead so irresistible a claim. But then it comes to pass that, over and above his understanding, there are many

other things appertaining to man whose prescriptive rights are quite as strong as those of the understanding itself. It is a result, for example, of the play of organism and environ-ment that sugar is sweet, and that aloes are bitter, that the smell of henbane differs from the perfume of a rose. Such facts of consciousness (for which, by-the-way, no adequate reason has yet been rendered) are quite as old as the un-derstanding; and many other things can boast an equally ancient origin. Mr. Spencer at one place refers to that most powerful of passions—the amatory passion—as one which, when it first occurs, is antecedent to all relative experience whatever; and we may pass its claim as being at least as an-cient and valid as that of the understanding. Then there are such things woven into the texture of man, as the feel-ing of awe, reverence, wonder—and not alone the sexual love just referred to, but the love of the beautiful, physical, and moral, in Nature, poetry, and art. There is also that deep-set feeling which, since the earliest dawn of history, and probably for ages prior to all history, incorporated it-self in the religions of the world. You who have escaped from these religions into the high-and-dry light of the in-tellect may deride them; but in so doing you deride acci-dents of form merely, and fail to touch the immovable basis of the religious sentiment in the nature of man. To yield this sentiment reasonable satisfaction is the problem of problems at the present hour. And grotesque in relation to scientific culture as many of the religions of the world have been and are—dangerous, nay, destructive, to the dearest privileges of freemen as some of them undoubtedly have been, and would, if they could, be again—it will be wise to recognize them as the forms of a force, mischie-vous, if permitted to intrude on the region of *knowledge*, over which it holds no command, but capable of adding, in the region of *poetry* and *emotion*, inward completeness and dignity to man.

Feeling, I say again, dates from as old an origin and as high a source as intelligence; and it equally demands its range of play. The wise teacher of humanity will recognize the necessity of meeting this demand, rather than of resist-ing it on account of errors and absurdities of form. What we should resist, at all hazards, is the attempt made in the past, and now repeated, to found upon this elemental bias of man's nature a system which should exercise despotic sway over his intellect. I have no fears as to such a consumma-tion. Science has already to some extent leavened the world: it will leaven it more and more; and I should look upon the light of science breaking in upon the minds of the youth of Ireland, and strengthening gradually to the perfect day, as a surer check to any intellectual or spiritual tyranny

---

[7]Bishop George **Berkeley** (1685–1753): idealist philosopher in the Lockean line of British thought leading through David **Hume** (1711–1776) toward Kantian and utilitarianism developments dur-ing the 19th century.

which now threatens this island, than the laws of princes or the swords of emperors. We fought and won our battle even in the Middle Ages: should we doubt the issue of another conflict with our broken foe?

The impregnable position of science may be described in a few words. We claim, and we shall wrest, from theology the entire domain of cosmological theory. All schemes and systems which thus infringe upon the domain of science must, *in so far as they do this*, submit to its control, and relinquish all thought of controlling it. Acting otherwise proved disastrous in the past, and it is simply fatuous to-day. Every

system which would escape the fate of an organism too rigid to adjust itself to its environment must be plastic to the extent that the growth of knowledge demands. When this truth has been thoroughly taken in, rigidity will be relaxed, exclusiveness diminished, things now deemed essential will be dropped, and elements now rejected will be assimilated. The lifting of the life is the essential point; and as long as dogmatism, fanaticism, and intolerance, are kept out, various modes of leverage may be employed to raise life to a higher level. . . .

1873

ANNIE BESANT
(1847–1933)

The case of Mary Somerville shows that not all Victorians who felt the force of scientific advance lost their faith; that of Annie Besant shows that not all lapses of faith were due to the new science. The adventure in homemade Higher Criticism with which our selection begins gave the teenaged Besant a genuine scare in 1866 but left her faith intact. It was her later trauma as a young mother and clergyman's wife, helplessly nursing a child in pain, that detached her from Christian orthodoxy. Besant's late Victorian quest led at midlife through British secularism, socialism, trade-unionism, and feminism (she wrote this book at around the time of her prosecution for a pamphlet on birth control). She then went on to India, where she encountered Hindu traditions and took a leading part in early movements for national independence. For a quarter century she served as president of the Theosophical Society, which drew from the world's religious writings and rituals an esoteric alternative to the materialism of science.

Besant's long spiritual quest arose in private conscience and branched into many varieties of public witness. Few of these impinged directly on scientific or technological advance; and the last, theosophy, in certain respects sidestepped modern knowledge for the sake of timeless wisdom. Still, the vivid standoff that concludes our selection—where the irresistible force of a twentysomething inquirer collides with the immovable object of a septuagenarian archconservative churchman robed as Grand Inquisitor—would hardly take the rhetorical, virtually allegorical form it does had not "the face of Truth," as Besant calls it, been sculpted and worn by the contending prospects for human betterment that this section of our anthology represents.

from **Autobiographical Sketches**

. . . That Easter was memorable to me for another cause. It saw waked and smothered my first doubt. That some people did doubt the historical accuracy of the Bible I knew, for one or two of the Harrow[1] masters were friends of Colenso, the heretic Bishop of Natal, but fresh from my Patristic studies, I looked on heretics with blind horror, possibly the stronger from its very vagueness, and its ignorance of what it feared. My mother objected to my reading controversial books which dealt with the points at issue between Christianity and Freethought, and I did not care for her favorite Stanley, who might have widened my views, regarding him (on the word of Pusey)[2] as "unsound in the faith once delivered to the saints." I had read Pusey's book on "Daniel the prophet," and, knowing nothing of the criticisms he attacked, I felt triumphant at his convincing demonstrations of their error, and felt sure that none but the wilfully blind could fail to see how weak were the arguments of the heretic writers. That stately preface of his was one of my favorite pieces of reading, and his dignified defence against all novelties of "that which must be old because it is eternal, and must be unchangeable because it is true," at once charmed and satisfied me. The delightful vagueness of Stanley, which just suited my mother's broad views, because it *was* vague and beautiful, was denounced by Pusey—not unwarrantably—as that "variegated use of words which destroys all definiteness of meaning." When she would bid me not be uncharitable to those with whom I differed in matters of religion, I would answer in his words, that "charity to error is treason to truth," and that to speak out the truth unwaveringly as it was revealed, was alone "loyalty to God and charity to the souls of men."

Judge, then, of my terror at my own results when I found myself betrayed into writing down some contradictions from the Bible. With that poetic dreaming which is one of the charms of Catholicism, whether English or Roman, I threw myself back into the time of the first century as the "Holy Week" of 1866 approached. In order to facilitate the realisation of those last sacred days of God incarnate on earth, working out man's salvation, I resolved to write a brief history of that week, compiled from the four gospels, meaning then to try and realise each day the occurrences that had happened on the corresponding date in A.D. 33, and so to follow those "blessed feet" step by step, till they were

" . . . nailed for our advantage to the bitter cross."[3]

With the fearlessness which springs from ignorance I sat down to my task. . . . I had been getting more and more uneasy and distressed as I went on, but when I found that the Jews would not go into the judgment hall lest they should be defiled, because they desired to eat the passover, having previously seen that Jesus had actually eaten the passover with his disciples the evening before; when after writing down that he was crucified at 9 a.m., and that there was darkness over all the land from 12 to 3 p.m., I found that three hours after he was crucified he was standing in the judgment hall, and that at the very hour at which the miraculous darkness covered the earth; when I saw that I was writing a discord instead of a harmony, I threw down my pen and shut up my Bible. The shock of doubt was, however, only momentary. I quickly recognised it as a temptation of the devil, and I shrank back horror-striken and penitent for the momentary lapse of faith. I saw that these apparent contradictions were really a test of faith, and that there would be no credit in believing a thing in which there were no difficulties. *Credo quia impossibile*,[4] I repeated Tertullian's words at first doggedly, at last triumphantly. I fasted as penance for my involuntary sin of unbelief. I remembered that the Bible must not be carelessly read, and that St. Peter had warned us that there were in it "some things hard to be understood, which they that are unlearned and unstable wrest unto their own destruction."[5] I shuddered at the "destruction" to the edge of which my unlucky "harmony" had drawn me, and resolved that I would never again venture on a task for which I was so evidently unfitted. Thus the first doubt was caused, and though swiftly trampled down, it had none the less raised its head. It was stifled, not answered, for all my religious training had led me to regard a doubt as a sin to be repented of, not examined. And it left in my mind the dangerous feeling that there were some things into which it was safer not to enquire too closely; things which must be accepted on faith, and not too narrowly

---

[1]**Harrow:** prestigious boys' school in greater London.

[2]A. P. **Stanley** (1815–1881): liberal Oxford professor who defended Bishop **Colenso** (see page 69) against High Church assailants like E. B. **Pusey** (1800–1882), whose interview with Besant appears here.

[3]**"nailed . . . bitter cross":** *1 Henry IV* 1.1.27 (slightly misquoted).

[4]*Credo quia impossibile:* "I believe it because it is impossible." **Tertullian** (155?–220): early Church apologist.

[5]**"some things . . . destruction":** 2 Peter 3:16.

scrutinised. The awful threat: "He that believeth not shall be damned," sounded in my ears, and, like the angel with the flaming sword, barred the path of all too curious enquiry. (Chapter 4)

In the spring of 1871 both my children were taken ill with hooping-cough. The boy, Digby, vigorous and merry, fought his way through it with no danger, and with comparatively little suffering; Mabel, the baby, had been delicate since her birth; there had been some little difficulty in getting her to breathe after she was born, and a slight tendency afterwards to lung-delicacy. She was very young for so trying a disease as hooping-cough, and after a while bronchitis set in, and was followed by congestion of the lungs. For weeks she lay in hourly peril of death; we arranged a screen round the fire like a tent, and kept it full of steam to ease the panting breath, and there I sat all through those weary weeks with her on my lap, day and night. The doctor said that recovery was impossible, and that in one of the fits of coughing she must die; the most distressing thing was that at last the giving of a drop or two of milk brought on the terrible convulsive choking, and it seemed cruel to torture the apparently dying child. . . .

Not unnaturally, when the child was out of danger, I collapsed from sheer exhaustion, and I lay in bed for a week. But an important change of mind dated from those silent weeks with a dying child on my knees. There had grown up in my mind a feeling of angry resentment against the God who had been for weeks, as I thought, torturing my helpless baby. For some months a stubborn antagonism to the Providence who ordained the sufferings of life had been steadily increasing in me, and this sullen challenge, "Is God good?" found voice in my heart during those silent nights and days. My mother's sufferings, and much personal unhappiness, had been intensifying the feeling, and as I watched my baby in its agony, and felt so helpless to relieve, more than once the indignant cry broke from my lips: "How canst thou torture a baby so? What has she done that she should suffer so? Why dost thou not kill her at once, and let her be at peace?" More than once I cried aloud: "O God, take the child, but do not torment her." All my personal belief in God, all my intense faith in his constant direction of affairs, all my habit of continual prayer and of realisation of his presence, were against me now. To me he was not an abstract idea, but a living reality, and all my mother-heart rose up in rebellion against this person in whom I believed, and whose individual finger I saw in my baby's agony. . . .

Everyone who has doubted after believing knows how, after the first admitted and recognised doubt, others rush in like a flood, and how doctrine after doctrine starts up in new and lurid light, looking so different in aspect from the fair faint outlines in which it had shone forth in the soft mists of faith. The presence of evil and pain in the world made by a "good God," and the pain falling on the innocent, as on my seven months' old babe; the pain here reaching on into eternity unhealed; these, while I yet believed, drove me desperate, and I believed and hated, instead of like the devils, "believed and trembled." Next, I challenged the righteousness of the doctrine of the Atonement, and while I worshipped and clung to the suffering Christ, I hated the God who required the death-sacrifice at his hands. And so for months the turmoil went on, the struggle being all the more terrible for the very desperation with which I strove to cling to some planks of the wrecked ship of faith on the tossing sea of doubt. . . .

No one who has not felt it knows the fearful agony caused by doubt to the earnestly religious mind. There is in this life no other pain so horrible. The doubt seems to shipwreck everything, to destroy the one steady gleam of happiness "on the other side" that no earthly storm could obscure; to make all life gloomy with a horror of despair, a darkness that may verily be felt. Fools talk of Atheism as the outcome of foul life and vicious thought. They, in their shallow heartlessness, their brainless stupidity, cannot even dimly imagine the anguish of the mere penumbra of the eclipse of faith, much less the horror of that great darkness in which the orphaned soul cries out into the infinite emptiness: "Is it a Devil who has made this world? Are we the sentient toys of an Almighty Power, who sports with our agony, and whose peals of awful mocking laughter echo the wailings of our despair?" (Chapter 6)

On recovering from that prostrating physical pain, I came to a very definite decision. I resolved that, whatever might be the result, I would take each dogma of the Christian religion, and carefully and thoroughly examine it, so that I should never again say "I believe" where I had not proved. So, patiently and steadily, I set to work. . . .

. . . . Worst of all the puzzles, perhaps, was that of the existence of evil and of misery, and the racking doubt whether God *could* be good, and yet look on the evil and the misery of the world unmoved and untouched. It seemed so impossible to believe that a Creator could be either cruel enough to be indifferent to the misery, or weak enough to be unable to stop it: the old dilemma faced me unceasingly. "If he can prevent it, and does not, he is not good; if he wishes to prevent it, and cannot, he is not almighty;" and out of this I could find no way of escape. Not yet had any doubt of the existence of God crossed my mind. . . .

Despite reading and argument, my scepticism grew only deeper and deeper. The study of W. R. Greg's "Creed of Christendom," of Matthew Arnold's "Literature and Dogma,"[6] helped to widen the mental horizon, while making a return to the old faith more and more impossible. The church services were a weekly torture, but feeling as I did that I was only a doubter, I spoke to none of my doubts. It was possible, I felt, that all my difficulties might be cleared up, and I had no right to shake the faith of others while in uncertainty myself. Others had doubted and had afterwards believed; for the doubter silence was a duty; the blinded had better keep their misery to themselves. I found some practical relief in parish work of a non-doctrinal kind, in nursing the sick, in trying to brighten a little the lot of the poor of the village. But here, again, I was out of sympathy with most of those around me. . . .

In the summer and autumn of 1872 I was a good deal in London with my mother. My health had much broken down, and after a severe attack of congestion of the lungs, my recovery was very slow. One Sunday in London, I wandered into St. George's Hall, in which Mr. Charles Voysey was preaching, and there I bought some of his sermons. To my delight I found that someone else had passed through the same difficulties as I about hell and the Bible and the atonement and the character of God, and had given up all these old dogmas, while still clinging to belief in God. I went to St. George's Hall again on the following Sunday, and in the little ante-room, after the service, I found myself in a stream of people, who were passing by Mr. and Mrs. Voysey, some evidently known to him, some strangers, many of the latter thanking him for his morning's work. As I passed in my turn I said: "I must thank you for very great help in what you have said this morning," for indeed the possibility opened of a God who was really "loving unto every man," and in whose care each was safe for ever, had come like a gleam of light across the stormy sea of doubt and distress on which I had been tossing for nearly twelve months. On the following Sunday, I saw them again, and was cordially invited down to their Dulwich home, where they gave welcome to all in doubt. I soon found that the Theism they professed was free from the defects which revolted me in Christianity. It left me God as a Supreme

Goodness, while rejecting all the barbarous dogmas of the Christian faith. I now read Theodore Parker's "Discourse on Religion," Francis Newman's "Hebrew Monarchy,"[7] and other works, many of the essays of Miss Frances Power Cobbe and of other Theistic writers, and I no longer believed in the old dogmas and hated while I believed; I no longer doubted whether they were true or not; I shook them off, once for all, with all their pain, and horror, and darkness, and felt, with relief and joy inexpressible, that they were all but the dreams of ignorant and semi-savage minds, not the revelation of a God. The last remnant of Christianity followed swiftly these cast-off creeds, though, in parting with this, one last pang was felt. It was the doctrine of the Deity of Christ. The whole teaching of the Broad Church School tends, of course, to emphasise the humanity at the expense of the Deity of Christ, and when the eternal punishment and the substitutionary atonement had vanished, there seemed to be no sufficient reason left for so stupendous a miracle as the incarnation of the Deity. I saw that the idea of incarnation was common to all Eastern creeds, not peculiar to Christianity; the doctrine of the unity of God repelled the doctrine of the incarnation of a portion of the Godhead. But the doctrine was dear from association; there was something at once soothing and ennobling in the idea of a union between Man and God, between a perfect man and divine supremacy, between a human heart and an almighty strength. Jesus as God was interwoven with all art, with all beauty in religion; to break with the Deity of Jesus was to break with music, with painting, with literature; the Divine Child in his mother's arms, the Divine Man in his Passion and in his triumph, the human friend encircled with the majesty of the Godhead— did inexorable Truth demand that this ideal figure, with all its pathos, its beauty, its human love, should pass into the Pantheon of the dead Gods of the Past? (Chapter 7)

Yet one other effort I made to save myself from the difficulties I foresaw in connexion with this final breach with Christianity. There was one man who had in former days wielded over me a great influence, one whose writings had guided and taught me for many years—Dr. Pusey,[8] the

---

[6]**W. R. Greg** (1809–1881): manufacturer, administrator, and author, whose 1851 book, like **Arnold's** (1873), represented the Higher Criticism of Scripture.

[7]**Theodore Parker** (1810–1860): American Unitarian who published his *Discourse* in 1842. **Francis Newman** (1805–1897): British Unitarian whose liberal views in *History of the Hebrew Monarchy* (1847) differ sharply from those of his famous brother John Henry Newman.

[8]**Pusey:** see note 2 page 76.

venerable leader of the Catholic party in the Church, the learned Patristic scholar, full of the wisdom of antiquity. He believed in Christ as God; what if I put my difficulties to him? If he resolved them for me I should escape the struggle I foresaw; if he could not resolve them, then no answer to them was to be hoped for. My decision was quickly made; being with my mother, I could write to him unnoticed, and I sat down and put my questions clearly and fully, stating my difficulties and asking him whether, out of his wider knowledge and deeper reading, he could resolve them for me. I wish I could here print his answer, together with two or three other letters I received from him, but the packet was unfortunately stolen from my desk and I have never recovered it. Dr. Pusey advised me to read Liddon's "Bampton Lectures,"[9] referred me to various passages, chiefly from the Fourth Gospel, if I remember rightly, and invited me to go down to Oxford and talk over my difficulties. Liddon's "Bampton Lectures" I had thoroughly studied, and the Fourth Gospel had no weight with me, the arguments in favor of its Alexandrian origin being familiar to me, but I determined to accept his invitation to a personal interview, regarding it as the last chance of remaining in the Church.

To Oxford, accordingly, I took the train, and made my way to the famous Doctor's rooms. I was shown in, and saw a short, stout gentleman, dressed in a cassock, and looking like a comfortable monk; but the keen eyes, steadfastly gazing straight into mine, told me of the power and subtlety hidden by the unprepossessing form. The head was fine and impressive, the voice low, penetrating, drilled into a somewhat monotonous and artificially subdued tone. I quickly found that no sort of enlightenment could possibly result from our interview. He treated me as a penitent going to confession, seeking the advice of a director, not as an enquirer struggling after truth, and resolute to obtain some firm standing-ground in the sea of doubt, whether on the shores of orthodoxy or of heresy. He would not deal with the question of the Deity of Jesus as a question for argument; he reminded me: "You are speaking of your judge," when I pressed some question. The mere suggestion of an imperfection in Jesus' character made him shudder in positive pain, and he checked me with raised hand, and the rebuke: "You are blaspheming; the very thought is a terrible sin." I asked him if he could recommend to me any books which would throw light on the subject: "No, no, you have read too much already. You must pray; you

must pray." Then, as I said that I could not believe without proof, I was told: "Blessed are they that have not seen, and yet have believed,"[10] and my further questioning was checked by the murmur: "O my child, how undisciplined! how impatient!". Truly, he must have found in me—hot, eager, passionate in my determination to know, resolute not to profess belief while belief was absent—but very little of that meek, chastened, submissive spirit to which he was accustomed in the penitents wont to seek his counsel as their spiritual guide. In vain did he bid me pray as though I believed; in vain did he urge the duty of blind submission to the authority of the Church, of yielding, unreasoning faith, which received but questioned not. He had no conception of the feelings of the sceptical spirit; his own faith was solid as a rock—firm, satisfied, unshakeable; he would as soon have committed suicide as have doubted of the infallibility of the "Universal Church."

"It is not your duty to ascertain the truth," he told me sternly. "It is your duty to accept and to believe the truth as laid down by the Church; at your peril you reject it; the responsibility is not yours so long as you dutifully accept that which the Church has laid down for your acceptance. Did not the Lord promise that the presence of the Spirit should be ever with his Church, to guide her into all truth?"

"But the fact of the promise and its value are the very points on which I am doubtful," I answered.

He shuddered. "Pray, pray," he said. "Father, forgive her, for she knows not what she says."

It was in vain I urged that I had everything to gain and nothing to lose by following his directions, but that it seemed to me that fidelity to truth forbade a pretended acceptance of that which was not believed.

"Everything to lose? Yes, indeed. You will be lost for time and lost for eternity."

"Lost or not," I rejoined, "I must and will try to find out what is true, and I will not believe till I am sure."

"You have no right to make terms with God," he answered, "as to what you will believe and what you will not believe. You are full of intellectual pride."

I sighed hopelessly. Little feeling of pride was there in me just then, and I felt that in this rigid unyielding dogmatism there was no comprehension of my difficulties, no help for me in my strugglings. I rose and, thanking him for his courtesy, said that I would not waste his time further, that I must go home and just face the difficulties out, openly leaving the Church and taking the consequences. Then for the first time his serenity was ruffled.

---

[9]H. P. **Liddon** (1829–1890): conservative divine who delivered the 1866 **Bampton Lectures** at Oxford on *The Divinity of Our Lord and Saviour Jesus Christ* and wrote a 3-volume life of Pusey.

---

[10]"**Blessed . . . have believed**": John 20:29.

"I forbid you to speak of your disbelief," he cried. "I forbid you to lead into your own lost state the souls for whom Christ died."

Slowly and sadly I took my way back to the station, knowing that my last chance of escape had failed me. I recognised in this famous divine the spirit of the priest, which could be tender and pitiful to the sinner, repentant, humble, submissive, craving only for pardon and for guidance, but which was iron to the doubter, to the heretic, and would crush out all questionings of "revealed truth," silencing by force, not by argument, all challenge of the traditions of the Church. Out of such men were made the Inquisitors of the Middle Ages, perfectly conscientious, perfectly rigid, perfectly merciless to the heretic. To them heretics were and are centres of infectious disease, and charity to them "the worst cruelty to the souls of men." Certain that they hold "by no merit of our own, but by the mercy of our God the one truth which he hath revealed," they can permit no questionings, they can accept nought but the most complete submission. But while man aspires after truth, while his brain yearns after knowledge, while his intellect soars upward into the heaven of speculation and "beats the air with tireless wing," so long shall those who demand faith be met by challenge for proof, and those who would blind him shall be defeated by his determination to gaze unblenching on the face of Truth, even though her eyes should turn him into stone. . . . (Chapter 8)

1885

3

GENDER AND SEXUALITY

GENDER ROLES WERE often conveniently defined during the Victorian period by a division of the world into "separate spheres." According to this scheme, men spent their days in the competitive, alienating public sphere, building Britain's greatness. Women remained safe at home in the private sphere of tenderness, sympathy, piety, self-sacrifice, and love, providing nurture and uplift for men and children. But of course so simple a system did not fully correspond to reality. It ignored most people below the middle class: the divinely feminine "angel in the house" (a phrase taken, not altogether fairly, from Coventry Patmore's poem and later popularized by Virginia Woolf) could afford to stay at home and employ at least one or two servants to assist in the hard, dirty labor of keeping a Victorian household warm, clean, and fed. There were thousands of unmarried middle-class women, furthermore, for whom there was no room in the family home, who had little choice except to live in someone else's house as a governess or emigrate to the colonies. Even in prosperous circumstances many women grew restive in the narrow space allotted them, as did many men in the corresponding masculine role. Queen Victoria herself was a figure of paradox: at the head of a nation in which women had no political rights, she was a confidently autocratic woman who believed that women should be subordinate to their husbands and were unsuited for public life. And when her initially exemplary widow's mourning did not abate with the passage of years, she was censured for neglecting public duties to indulge a private grief.

The "woman question"—that is, what women's status in society should be—perplexed the nineteenth century, issuing most famously in Sigmund Freud's plaintive query: What do women want? Not surprisingly, Victorian women wanted many different things. Most, probably, accepted their assigned position. But many of them wanted more opportunities for education and employment, the right to control their own property even if they were married, and the right to vote and hold public office.

In the course of the century, women's legal rights were significantly augmented. They began to participate in government on the local level, but they did not gain the right to vote in parliamentary elections until well into the next century. Women were expected to guard the welfare of the nation by means of "influence": to raise the tone of public affairs by making their sons and husbands better men and therefore better civic agents. An appeal against women's suffrage signed in 1889 by a few eminent women and many wives of eminent men argued that the right to vote, by decreasing women's sympathy and disinterestedness, would erode their moral influence. Motherhood, or the potential for it, was taken to be woman's defining characteristic, making her loving and self-sacrificing—and also physically, psychologically, and practically unfit for any kind of public life. As Eliza Lynn Linton succinctly put it in 1891, "The cradle lies across the door of the polling-booth and bars the way to the senate."

Theoretical distinctions of gender were protected and reinforced by sexually segregated education. Boys at the higher social levels—including most of those who became prominent writers and intellectuals—usually went at an early age to schools where they learned to survive in a self-contained and often brutal all-male social system. During most of the century the education of such boys consisted largely in the study of Latin and Greek, the mark of both social and gender superiority. Girls went to school away from home less often and for shorter periods. Usually they had a more varied curriculum than boys, including modern languages, painting and drawing, or playing music—studies often denigrated as "accomplishments" acquired only to attract men. Intellectually ambitious girls bitterly resented their exclusion from the classical studies that seemed the indispensable foundation of high culture: many, from Elizabeth Barrett Browning to Augusta Webster, became proficient in Latin and Greek by sitting in on their brothers' lessons and studying on their own. Higher education was concentrated in a small number of universities, and much feminist effort went toward the admission of women to at least partial membership, a goal that was achieved in the 1870s.

Increasing educational opportunities helped women qualify for employment outside the home, which (like involvement in politics) was generally considered deleterious to true womanhood; working for money brought middle-class women's social status and personal purity into question. One of the few ways of earning money open to women was writing, which could be done at home with little expense and no special training. The rising popularity of prose fiction, with its large female audiences and (for most of the century) relatively low prestige, made an opening into literary life that women gladly seized; the first women before the twentieth century to earn a secure place in the English canon of high culture were nineteenth-century novelists: Jane Austen, the Brontës, George Eliot. At the same time, Elizabeth Barrett Browning and Christina Rossetti were the first women poets widely accepted as at least potentially the equal of men. Harriet Martineau was regarded by many as ranking close to, if not actually among, the most authoritative writers of nonfictional prose. In periodicals, which formed a large part of literary production at all levels of culture, the custom of anonymity enabled women reviewers and essayists to speak with a man's authority. Several church-related periodicals were in effect written by and for women, and by the 1860s journals of expressly feminist allegiance appeared. Women often wrote about what were classified as feminine subjects—love, domestic virtue, and the wrongs of the oppressed (slaves, the poor and outcast, animals)—as well as about women's lives and their place in the social system.

The Victorian period remained one of male dominance. Still, that dominance was steadily contested, and not just by women. Many men did not fit, or did not wish to fit, established gender roles. The lives and work of clergymen, poets, and male novelists, for instance, belonged in many ways to the private sphere. Men as well as women thought the highest humanity should combine what were too simply taken to be exclusively male or female traits. Thomas Hughes, the author of the most influential school story of all time, *Tom Brown's Schooldays* (1857), insisted that true manliness should include such stereotypically feminine virtues as tenderness and thoughtfulness for others.

Conceptions of sexual orientation, like gender, were vexed and contested. Intense affection between boys or men flourished in the sexually segregated schools and universities; a friendship for which no adequate language existed inspired the central poem of the Victorian period, Tennyson's *In Memoriam* (1850). After midcentury such affectionate relationships tended more and more to be seen in specifically sexual terms. In the last decades of the century homosexuality became the object of increasing attention and definition, the word itself first appearing in English in 1892. Efforts to repress and punish it also increased, but "the love that dare not speak its name" (a phrase made famous during the trial of Oscar Wilde) spoke audibly if not quite openly in the literature of the fin de siècle. The excerpts from the *Memoirs* of John Addington Symonds that are printed here show the tensions and contradictions that were associated with the idea of homosexuality, even among its most sympathetic and intelligent analysts.

As the century progressed sexuality and gender came more and more under the purview of science. Darwin studied the role of sexual selection in the evolution of animals and men. Anthropologists examined gender as an aspect of human history. Doctors argued that physiology did (or did not) set the limits of what women could learn and do, and by the end of the century homosexuality, even as it became criminalized, could be seen as a matter of pathology rather than morality. When one considers the great variety of ways in which the Victorians wrote, spoke, and thought about sexuality, it is clear that the period which was regarded in the twentieth century as the heyday of sexual repression harbored a troubled awareness of the complexities of sexuality and gender, to which nearly all of Victorian literature testifies.

SARAH STICKNEY ELLIS

(1812–1872)

The Women of England was the first in a series of immensely popular conduct books for women by Sarah Stickney Ellis. Ellis was the wife of an eminent missionary, the adoptive mother of her dead sisters' children, active in various educational projects for girls, and the author of many didactic works of fiction and poetry. Her books are addressed to middle-class women, whom she charges with the task of maintaining "the home comforts, and fireside virtues for which [England] is so justly celebrated." She worries, like many moralists before and after, that women have come to prefer mental cultivation and the arts of luxury and leisure to old-fashioned domestic usefulness and "the place appointed . . . by providence." That place, she argues, is defined by self-sacrifice and service.

The subordinate position of women in Victorian England became vividly clear to girls when they saw their brothers in possession of education, freedom, money, and prestige that were denied to themselves. In the passage that follows Ellis unsparingly defines the obligations of sisters to brothers in an ideal middle-class family.

from The Women of England

. . . Brothers and sisters are so associated in English homes, as materially to promote each other's happiness, by the habits of kindness and consideration which they cultivate; and when a strong friendship can be formed between such parties, it is perhaps one of the most faithful and disinterested of any which the aspect of human life presents. A young man of kind and social feelings is often glad to find in his sister, a substitute for what he afterwards ensures more permanently in a wife; and young women are not backward in returning this affection by a love as confiding, and almost as tender as they are capable of feeling. Their intercourse has also the endearing charm of early association, which no later-formed acquaintance can supply. They have shared the sunny hours of childhood together; and when the young man goes forth into the world, the love of his sister is like a talisman about his heart. Women, however, must be watchful and studious to establish this intimate connexion, and to keep entire the golden cord by which they are thus bound. Affection does not come by relationship alone; and never yet was the affection of man fully and lastingly engaged by woman, without some means being adopted on her part to increase or preserve his happiness. The childish and most unsatisfactory fondness that means nothing but "I love you," goes but a little way to reach the heart of man; but let his home be made more comfortable, let his peculiarities of habit and temper be studiously consulted, and social and familiar gratifications provided for his daily use; and, unless he is ungrateful beyond the common average of mankind, he will be sure to regard the source from whence his comforts flow with extreme complacency, and not unfrequently with affection.

On the other hand, let the sister possess all that ardour of attachment which young ladies are apt to believe they feel, let her hang about his neck at parting, and bathe his face with her tears; if she has not taken the trouble to rise and prepare his early meal, but has allowed him to depend upon the servant, or to prepare it for himself; it is very questionable whether that brother can be made to believe in her affection; and certainly he will be far from feeling its value. If, again, they read some interesting volume together, if she lends her willing sympathy, and blends her feelings with his, entering into all the trains of thought and recollection which two congenial minds are capable of awakening in each other; and if, after the book is closed, he goes up into his chamber late on the Saturday night, and finds his linen[1]

unaired, buttonless, and unattended to, with the gloves he had ten times asked to have mended, remaining untouched, where he had left them; he soon loses the impression of the social hour he had been spending, and wishes, that, instead of an idle sister, he had a faithful and industrious wife. He reasons, and reasons rightly, that while his sister is willing to share with him all that is most agreeable to herself, she is by no means willing to do for his sake what is not agreeable, and he concludes his argument with the conviction, that notwithstanding her professions, hers is not true affection.

I do not mean that sisters ought to be the servants of their brothers, or that they should not, where domestics abound, leave the practical part of these duties to them. All that is wanted is stronger evidence of their watchfulness and their solicitude for their brother's real comfort. The manner in which this evidence shall be given, must still be left to their judgment, and their circumstances. There are, however a few simple rules, by which I should suppose all kindly affectioned women would be willing to be guided. No woman in the enjoyment of health should allow her brother to prepare his own meals at any time of the day, if it were possible for her to do it for him. No woman should allow her brother to put on linen in a state of dilapidation, to wear gloves or stockings in want of mending, or to return home without finding a neat parlour, a place to sit down without asking for it, and a cheerful invitation to partake of necessary refreshment.

All this I believe is often faithfully done, where the brother is a gentlemanly, attractive, and prepossessing person—in short, a person to be proud of in company, and pleased with in private; but a brother is a brother still, even where these attractions do not exist: where the duty is most irksome, the moral responsibility is precisely the same, as where it is most pleasing. Besides, who knows what female influence may not effect? It is scarcely probable that a younger brother, treated by his sisters with perpetual contempt, almost bordering upon disgust, regarded as an intolerable bore, and got rid of by every practicable means, will grow up into a companionable, interesting, and social man; or if he should, he would certainly reserve these qualities for exercise beyond the circle of his own fireside, and for the benefit of those who could appreciate him better than his sisters.

The virtue of consideration, in the intercourse of sisters with brothers, is never more felt than in the sacred duty of warning them of moral evil, and encouraging them in moral good. Here we see in an especial manner the advantages arising from habits of personal attention and kindness. A woman who stands aloof from the common offices of domestic usefulness, may very properly extend her advice to a husband, a brother, or a son; but when she has faithfully

---

[1]linen: shirts.

pointed out the fault she would correct, she must leave the object of her solicitude, with his wounded self-love unhealed, and his irritated feelings unrelieved. She has done her duty, and the impression most frequently remaining upon the mind of the other party is, either that she has done it in anger, or that it is impossible she can love a being of whom she entertains such hard thoughts.

The sister who is accustomed to employ her hands in the services of domestic life, is, on these occasions, rich in resources. She feels the pain she has been compelled to give, and calculates how much she has to make up. It is a time for tenfold effort; but it must be effort without display. In a gentle and unobtrusive manner, she does some extra service for her brother, choosing what would otherwise be degrading in its own nature, in order to prove in the most delicate manner, that though she can see a fault in him, she still esteems herself his inferior, and though she is cruel enough to point it out, her love is yet so deep and pure as to sweeten every service she can render him.

It is impossible for the human heart to resist this kind of evidence, and hence arises the strong influence that women possess over the moral feelings of those with whom they are intimately associated.

If such, then, be the effect of kindness and consideration upon the heart of man, what must we expect when it operates in all its force and all its sweetness upon that of woman. In her intercourse with man, it is impossible but that woman should feel her own inferiority; and it is right that it should be so. Yet, feeling this, it is also impossible but that the weight of social and moral duties she is called upon to perform, must, to an unsanctified spirit, at times appear oppressive. She has innumerable sources of disquietude, too, in which no man can partake; and from the very weakness and susceptibility of her own nature, she has need of sympathies which it would be impossible for him to render. She does not meet him upon equal terms. Her part is to make sacrifices, in order that his enjoyment may be enhanced. She does this with a willing spirit; but, from error of judgment, or from want of consideration, she does it so often without producing any adequate result, and so often without grateful acknowledgment, that her spirit sometimes sinks within her, and she shrinks back from the cares and anxieties of every day, with a feeling that the burden of life is too heavy to be borne.

Nor is man to be blamed for this. He knows not half the foolish fears that agitate her breast. He could not be made to know, still less to understand, the intensity of her capability of suffering from slight, and what to him would appear inadequate causes. But women *do* know what their sex is formed to suffer; and for this very reason, there is sometimes a bond existing between sisters, the most endearing, the most pure and disinterested, of any description of affection which this world affords. . . . (Chapter 8)

1838

SARAH LEWIS

Woman's Mission is perhaps the clearest exposition and most serious defense of the doctrine that a woman finds her best work and true happiness at home. Guardian of a sacred domestic space, sequestered from the pollution of the public world, she is responsible for instilling the highest moral and spiritual values into her children and preserving them in her husband. Lewis makes it clear that the idealization of domesticity and the family came at the cost of considerable self-sacrifice for women—all the more acceptable in turn, however, because according to Victorian orthodoxy self-sacrifice was woman's highest virtue. In accordance with its insistence that women should remain in the private, domestic sphere, this very influential book was published anonymously, and almost nothing—not even when she was born or died—is known of Sarah Lewis beyond her name.

from Woman's Mission

... Spirits are not finely touched,
But to fine issues.

Shakespeare[1]

The age in which we live is pre-eminently one of novelty,—new plans, new discoveries, new truths, new opinions, at least, whether true or chimerical. Some of these relate to the position, political and social, of woman, whose importance in the scale of humanity no rational being, above all no Christian, can doubt. The "last at the cross, and the first at the sepulchre,"[2] are dignified in the eyes of all Christian believers by the noble qualities of unworldliness and self-devotion; and it is one among many of the internal and collateral evidences of Christianity, that its historians have so beautifully and faithfully portrayed the distinction between man's and woman's devotedness.

That the sex, characterized by such noble moral development, is destined to exercise no unimportant influence on the political and social condition of mankind, we must all believe; indeed, the united testimony of ages leaves this an undoubted fact. There is a popular cry raised of injustice and oppression on the part of the other sex. Yet men, in all ages, have shown a sufficient willingness to allow woman a share of influence, sometimes a very undue share. There is no hyperbole in the phrase,—"Vainqueurs des vainqueurs de la terre;"[3] and this influence is so powerful, and so generally felt, that it becomes a question whether it is used as it ought to be,—for good.

But, it is said, it is degrading to work by influence instead of by power,—indirectly instead of directly,—as subordinates, not as principals. Here is the question at issue. Would mankind be benefited by the exchange of influence for power in the case of woman? would the greatest possible good be procured by bringing her out of her present sphere into the arena of public life, by introducing to our homes and to our hearths the violent dissensions, the hard and rancorous feelings, engendered by political strife? It is really difficult to approach the subject in the form to which it has by some writers been reduced, with any degree of gravity; and it is somewhat to the credit of the other sex, that it has

not more frequently been treated with the keen and indelicate satire which it deserves, and might provoke. Yet we are not one iota behind these fiery champions of womanhood, in exalted notions of its dignity and mission. We are as anxious as they can be that women should be roused to a sense of their own importance; but we affirm, that it is not so much social institutions that are wanting to women, but women who are wanting to themselves. We claim for them no less an office than that of instruments (under God) for the regeneration of the world,—restorers of God's image in the human soul. Can any of the warmest advocates of the political rights of woman claim or assert for her a more exalted mission,—a nobler destiny! That she will best accomplish this mission by moving in the sphere which God and nature have appointed, and not by quitting that sphere for another, it is the object of these pages to prove. (Introduction)

... It is by no means my intention to assert, that women should be passive and indifferent spectators of the great political questions, which affect the well-being of the community, neither can I repeat the old adage, that "women have nothing to do with politics;" they have, and ought to have, much to do with politics. But in what way? It has been maintained, that their public participation in them would be fatal to the best interests of society. How then are women to interfere in politics? As moral agents; as representatives of the moral principle; as champions of the right in preference to the expedient; by their endeavours to instil into their relatives of the other sex the uncompromising sense of duty and self-devotion, which ought to be *their* ruling principles! The immense influence which women possess will be most beneficial, if allowed to flow in its natural channels, viz.—domestic ones,—because it is of the utmost importance to the existence of influence, that purity of motive be unquestioned. It is by no means affirmed, that women's political feelings are always guided by the abstract principles of right and wrong; but they are surely more likely to be so, if they themselves are restrained from the public expression of them. Participation in scenes of popular emotion has a natural tendency to warp conscience and overcome charity. Now conscience and charity (or love) are the very essence of woman's beneficial influence, therefore everything tending to blunt the one and sour the other is sedulously to be avoided by her. It is of the utmost importance to men to feel, in consulting a wife, a mother, or a sister, that they are appealing *from* their passions and prejudices, and not *to* them as embodied in a second self: nothing tends to give

---

[1]*Measure for Measure* 1.1.35–36.

[2]"last . . . sepulchre": see Matthew 27:61.

[3]"Vainqueurs . . . terre": conquerors of the conquerors of the earth.

opinions such weight as the certainty, that the utterer of them is free from all petty or personal motives. The beneficial influence of woman is nullified if once her motives, or her personal character, come to be the subject of attack; and this fact alone ought to induce her patiently to acquiesce in the plan of seclusion from public affairs.

It supposes, indeed, some magnanimity in the possessors of great powers and widely-extended influence, to be willing to exercise them with silent unostentatious vigilance. There must be a deeper principle than usually lies at the root of female education, to induce women to acquiesce in the plan which, assigning to them the responsibility, has denied them the *éclat*[4] of being reformers of society. Yet it is, probably, exactly in proportion to their reception of this truth, and their adoption of it into their hearts, that they will fulfil their own high and lofty mission; precisely because the manifestation of such a spirit is the one thing needful for the re-

generation of society. It is from her being the depository and disseminator of such a spirit, that woman's influence is principally derived. It appears to be for this end that Providence has so lavishly endowed her with moral qualities, and, above all, with that of love,—the antagonist spirit of selfish-worldliness,—that spirit which, as it is vanquished or victorious, bears with it the moral destinies of the world! Now it is proverbially as well as scripturally true, that love "seeketh not its own"[5] interest, but the good of others, and finds its highest honour, its highest happiness, in so doing. This is precisely the spirit which can never be too much cultivated by women, because it is the spirit by which their highest triumphs are to be achieved: it is they who are called upon to show forth its beauty, and to prove its power; everything in their education should tend to develope self-devotion and self-renunciation. . . . (Chapter 5)

1839

---

[4]*éclat*: renown.

[5]"**seeketh not its own**": see 1 Corinthians 13:5.

BARBARA LEIGH SMITH BODICHON
(1827–1891)

Perhaps the most important feminist activist in Victorian Britain, Barbara Leigh Smith Bodichon was a professional painter as well as a leading proponent of women's education, employment, and legal and political rights. She was one of the organizers of the Married Women's Property Committee in 1855, formed the first major women's suffrage committee in 1865, and worked effectively to found Girton College, Cambridge (1869), the first women's college connected with one of the two major universities. In *Women and Work* (1857) she made the case for widening employment opportunities.

The *Brief Summary* printed here was her most politically efficacious publication, setting forth with devastating precision women's status under the law. Published as a very cheap pamphlet in 1854, with new editions in 1856 and 1869, it inspired feminist activism and won the support of almost all women writers, even those who were cool or hostile to feminism, for reforming the laws that denied married women the right to their own earnings. The legal conditions that Bodichon outlines here with tight-lipped restraint and occasional flashes of indignation reveal the skeleton beneath the surface of Ellis' and Lewis' mollifying rhetoric.

from A Brief Summary, in Plain Language, of the Most Important Laws of England Concerning Women

The Queen Regnant[1] in all respects fills the office of King; she has the same rights, prerogative and duties; and all that is said in the words of the law of the regal office, is as applicable to the Queen Regnant as to a King.

A Queen Consort is considered by the law as unlike other married women. She can herself purchase land and make leases, receive gifts from her husband, and sue, and be sued alone. She is the only wife in England who has these rights.

— LEGAL CONDITION OF UNMARRIED WOMEN OR SPINSTERS —

A single woman has the same rights to property, to protection from the laws, and must pay the same taxes to the state, as a man. . . .

A woman duly qualified can vote upon parish[2] questions, and for parish officers, overseers, surveyors, vestry clerks, &c.

If a woman's father or mother die intestate (*i.e.* without a will) she takes an equal share with her brothers and sisters of the personal property (*i.e.* goods, chattels, moveables,[3] leases for years of houses or land, stock shares, &c.,) but her eldest brother, if she have one, and his children, even daughters, will take the *real* property (*i.e.*, not personal property, but all other, as freehold houses, and lands, &c.) as the heir-at-law, males and their issue being preferred to females; if, however, she have sisters only, then all the sisters take the real property equally. If she be an only child, and has no parent surviving, she is entitled to all the intestate real and personal property.

The Church and nearly all offices under government are closed to women. The Post office affords some little employment to them; but there is no important office which they can practically hold, with the single exception of that of sovereign. The professions of law and medicine, whether or not closed by law, are in England closed in fact. Women may engage in trade, and may occupy inferior situations, such as matron of a charity, sextoness of a church; and some

parochial offices are open to them. Women are occasionally governors of prisons for women, overseers of the poor, and parish clerks. A woman may be a ranger of a park. . . .

Any person guilty of certain fraudulent practices to procure the defilement of any woman or girl, under the age of twenty-one, commits a misdemeanor, and may be imprisoned with or without hard labour for a term not exceeding two years. Unless a promise of marriage has been made in writing, or overheard, a seduced woman has no remedy against her seducer.

Her father may maintain an action against the seducer, it being supposed that he stands in the place of a master, and sustains a loss of service in consequence of the pregnancy of his daughter. . . .

— LAWS CONCERNING THE CHILDREN OF SINGLE WOMEN —

Illegitimate children belong to the mother, and the father, even if avowed, cannot take possession of them. If a woman who is able to maintain her bastard child, fails to do so and it becomes chargeable to the parish,[4] she may be punished as a rogue and a vagabond. . . .

— LAWS CONCERNING WOMEN IN OTHER RELATIONSHIPS —

A single woman can act as agent for another person, and as an agent, legally execute delegated authority. A *wife* can so act if her husband do not dissent.

An unmarried woman can be invested with a trust, but if she marry, the complexities and difficulties are great, from her inability to enter alone into deeds and assurances.

A single woman can act as executrix under a will, but a wife cannot accept an executorship without her husband's consent.

A woman can hold the office of administratrix to an intestate personalty, that is to the personal property of a deceased person dying without a will; and administration will be granted to her if she be next of kin to the intestate. But a wife cannot so act without the consent of her husband.

If a man place a woman in his house, and treat her as his wife, he is responsible for her debts to the same extent as if she were married to him. . . .

— LAWS CONCERNING MARRIED WOMEN —

Matrimony is a civil and indissoluble contract between a consenting man and woman of competent capacity. . . .

---

[1]**Regnant**: reigning. **Queen Consort**: wife of the king.

[2]**parish**: area of local government. **vestry**: governing body of a church.

[3]**moveables**: furniture.

[4]**chargeable to the parish**: supported by local authorities.

A man and wife are one person in law; the wife loses all her rights as a single woman, and her existence is, as it were absorbed in that of her husband. He is civilly responsible for her wrongful acts, and in some cases for her contracts; she lives under his protection or cover, and her condition is called coverture.

In theory, a married woman's body belongs to her husband; she is in his custody, and he can enforce his right by a writ of habeas corpus; but in practice this is greatly modified.

The belief that a man can rid himself of his wife by going through the farce of a sale, and exhibiting his wife with a halter round her neck is a vulgar error. This disgusting exhibition, which has often been seen in our country, is a misdemeanor, and can be punished with fine and imprisonment.

The author of a recent publication asserts that a man may lend his wife; a man may not lend, let out, or sell his wife; such transactions are considered as being against public decency, and are misdemeanors.

A wife's personal property before marriage (such as stock, shares, money in hand, money at the bank, jewels, household goods, clothes, etc.) becomes absolutely her husband's, unless when settled in trust for her, and he may assign or dispose of it at his pleasure, whether he and his wife live together or not. . . .

A husband is liable for the price of such goods as he allows his wife, as his agent, to order; she may have more power than any other agent, but her power is of the same kind; for if a wife orders goods without the knowledge of the husband, it is not at all certain that a legal decision will oblige him to pay for them; it mainly depends on what the jury thinks are domestic necessaries, or requisite for the position of the family.

Neither the Courts of Common Law nor of Equity, have any direct power to oblige a man to support his wife. But the Divorce[5] or Matrimonial Court, on granting a judicial separation may decree that the husband shall pay *alimony* to the wife for her support, and when a wife becomes chargeable to the parish, the magistrate may, upon application of the parish officers direct the husband to pay for her maintenance. A wife, whose husband without valid reason refuses to support her, may rent lodgings, take up goods etc., suitable to her station, for which the creditors can compel the husband to pay.

A husband has the possession and usafruct[6] of his wife's freehold property during the joint existence of himself and her; that is to say he has absolute possession of them as long as they both live. If the wife dies without children, the property goes to her heir, but if she has borne a child capable of inheriting, her husband holds possession until his death, when it passes to her heir; but on surviving her husband, her freeholds revert to her.

Money earned by a married woman belongs absolutely to her husband; that and all sources of income, excepting those mentioned above, and included in the term personal property. And her receipt for the earnings is not legal. The husband can claim the money notwithstanding such payment.

By the express permission of her husband, a wife can make a will of her personal property; for by such a permission he gives up his right. But he may revoke his leave at any time before *probate* (i.e., the exhibiting and proving a Will in Court).

The legal custody of children belongs to the father. During the life–time of a sane father, the mother has no rights over her children, except limited power over young infants, and the father may take them from her and dispose of them as he thinks fit. If there be a legal separation of the parents, and there be neither agreement nor order in Court, giving the custody of the children to either parent, then the *right to the custody of the child* (except for the nutriment of infants) belongs legally to the father.

A married woman cannot sue or be sued for contracts, nor can she enter into them except as the agent of her husband; that is to say, neither her word nor her deed is binding in law, and persons giving a wife credit have no remedy against her. There are some exceptions, as where she contracts debts upon estates settled to her separate use, or where a wife carries on trade separately, according to the custom of London, etc.

A husband is liable for his wife's debts contracted before marriage, and also for her breaches of trust committed before marriage.

Neither a husband nor a wife can be witness against or for the other in criminal cases, not even after the death or divorce of either.

A wife cannot bring actions unless the husband's name is joined.

As the wife is presumed to act under the command and control of her husband, she is excused from punishment for

---

[5]**Common Law:** unwritten law of England, derived from judicial precedent. Civil cases not remediable under common law were heard by **Courts of Equity,** of which Chancery became the most notorious—satirized in Dickens' *Bleak House* (1853) and abolished in 1873. The **Divorce** Court was established in 1857, but divorce remained rare and expensive.

[6]**usafruct** (usufruct): right of temporary possession.

certain offences, such as theft, burglary, house-breaking, etc. if committed in his presence, unless it is proved that she did not act under his influence. A wife cannot be found guilty of concealing her felon husband, or of concealing a felon guilty with her husband. She cannot be convicted of stealing from her husband or of setting his house on fire, as they are one person in law. A husband and wife cannot be found guilty of a conspiracy to which they themselves only are parties, as that offence cannot be committed by one person. . . .

— USUAL PRECAUTION AGAINST THE LAWS CONCERNING THE PROPERTY OF MARRIED WOMEN —

Where a woman has consented to a proposal of marriage she cannot dispose or give away her property without the knowledge of her betrothed; if she make any such disposition without his knowledge, even if he be ignorant of the existence of the property, the disposition will not be legal.

It is usual before marriage, in order to secure a wife and her children against the power of the husband, to make with his consent a settlement of some property on the wife, or to make an agreement before marriage that a settlement shall be made subsequently. It is in the power of the Court of Chancery to enforce the performance of such agreements.

Although the Common Law does not allow a married woman to possess any property, yet in respect of property settled for her separate use, equity endeavours to treat her as a single woman. She can acquire such property by contract before marriage with her husband, or by gift from him or other persons, and can, unless forbidden by the settlements, deal with it as she pleases.

There are great difficulties and complexities in making settlements, and they should always be drawn by a competent lawyer.

When a wife's property is stolen, the property (as it legally belongs to the husband) must be laid as his in the indictment.

— SEPARATION AND DIVORCE —

. . . The Divorce and Matrimonial Court decrees either a judicial separation or a divorce.

Judicial separation may be decreed at the suit of the husband for adultery, or upon any of the grounds for which he might, if he be pleased, sue for a divorce. At the suit of the wife, it may be decreed for cruelty, adultery, etc., also for the grounds on which she might, if she pleased, sue for a divorce.

Divorce is an absolute dissolution of the marriage, after which the parties are free to re-marry.

At the suit of the husband it may be decreed for adultery; and at the suit of the wife for adultery coupled with cruelty or desertion, and for certain aggravated cases of adultery.

A woman who has been deserted by her husband can obtain an order from the Divorce and Matrimonial Court, or from a magistrate, freeing her subsequent earnings and subsequently acquired property from the husband and his creditors. This protection to a wife is most valuable to working women. . . .

Upon a judicial separation all the property subsequently acquired by the wife, becomes her own, and devolves after her death as if she were single. She is considered to be a single woman for purposes of contract, bringing actions; and her husband is not liable for what she does. . . .

— LAWS CONCERNING A WIDOW —

A widow recovers her real property, but if there be a settlement she is restricted by its provisions. She recovers her chattels real,[7] if her husband has not disposed of them by will or otherwise.

A wife's paraphernalia (*i.e.* her clothes and ornaments) which her husband owns during her life-time, and which his creditors can seize for his debts, becomes her property on his death.

A widow is liable for any debts which she contracted before marriage, and which have been left unpaid during her marriage.

The widow is not bound to bury her dead husband, that being the duty of his legal representative.

If a man die intestate, his widow, if there are children, is entitled to one-third of the personalty;[8] if there are no children, to one half; the other is distributed among the next of kin of the husband, among whom the widow is not counted. If there is no next of kin, the moiety[9] goes to the Crown.

A husband can, by will, deprive a wife of all right in his personalty. . . .

1854, 1869

---

[7]**chattels real**: estates held for a term of years, as opposed to a freehold, held for life.

[8]**personalty**: personal goods or belongings.

[9]**moiety**: half.

ELIZA LYNN LINTON

(1822–1898)

The most notorious antifeminist Victorian woman writer (she excoriated feminist activists as the "Shrieking Sisterhood"), Eliza Lynn Linton was also one of the first professional woman journalists. She was independent, industrious, shrewd, and successful. At the age of thirty-six she married a widower with several children and supported the family until the couple separated. Her views varied over time, but a broad streak of radicalism underlay the conservative positions that brought most of her success. The daughter of a clergyman, in religion she was agnostic, and her novel *The True History of Joshua Davidson* (1872) is a vigorous attack on the British political, economic, and religious system. For a while she supported some of the goals of the women's movement, but in "The Girl of the Period"—her best-known work, with a title that became a popular catchphrase—she condemned modern women in the name of traditional values. As in her own life, however, we may see signs of contradiction even in this essay: by allowing no intermediate possibilities between angelic domesticity and sexual corruption, Linton indirectly shows the desperate situation of women whose only hope lay in marriage—a situation for which the feminists she castigated prescribed just such independence and employment as Linton herself enjoyed. The essay speaks, furthermore, in the assumed voice of a man.

The Girl of the Period

Time was when the stereotyped phrase, "a fair young English girl," meant the ideal of womanhood; to us, at least, of home birth and breeding. It meant a creature generous, capable, and modest; something franker than a Frenchwoman, more to be trusted than an Italian, as brave as an American but more refined, as domestic as a German and more graceful. It meant a girl who could be trusted alone if need be, because of the innate purity and dignity of her nature, but who was neither bold in bearing nor masculine in mind; a girl who, when she married, would be her husband's friend and companion, but never his rival; one who would consider their interest identical, and not hold him as just so much fair game for spoil; who would make his house his true home and place of rest, not a mere passage-place for vanity and ostentation to go through; a tender mother, an industrious housekeeper, a judicious mistress. We thought we had the pick of creation in this fair young English girl of ours, and envied no other men their own. We admired the languid grace and subtle fire of the South; the docility and

childlike affectionateness of the East seemed to us sweet and simple and restful; the vivacious sparkle of the trim and sprightly Parisienne was a pleasant little excitement when we met with it in its own domain; but our allegiance never wandered from our brown-haired girls at home, and our hearts were less vagrant than our fancies. This was in the old time, and when English girls were content to be what God and nature had made them. Of late years we have changed the pattern, and have given to the world a race of women as utterly unlike the old insular ideal as if we had created another nation altogether. The girl of the period, and the fair young English girl of the past, have nothing in common save ancestry and their mother-tongue; and even of this last the modern version makes almost a new language, through the copious additions it has received from the current slang of the day.

The girl of the period is a creature who dyes her hair and paints her face, as the first articles of her personal religion; whose sole idea of life is plenty of fun and luxury; and whose dress is the object of such thought and intellect as she possesses. Her main endeavour in this is to outvie her neighbours in the extravagance of fashion. No matter whether, as in the time of crinolines,[1] she sacrificed decency, or, as now, in the time of trains, she sacrifices cleanliness; no matter either, whether she makes herself a nuisance and an inconvenience to every one she meets. The girl of the period has done away with such moral muffishness as consideration for others, or regard for counsel and rebuke. It was all very well in old-fashioned times, when fathers and mothers had some authority and were treated with respect, to be tutored and made to obey, but she is far too fast and flourishing to be stopped in mid-career by these slow old morals; and as she dresses to please herself, she does not care if she displeases every one else. Nothing is too extraordinary and nothing too exaggerated for her vitiated taste; and things which in themselves would be useful reforms if let alone become monstrosities worse than those which they have displaced so soon as she begins to manipulate and improve. If a sensible fashion lifts the gown out of the mud, she raises hers midway to her knee. If the absurd structure of wire and buckram, once called a bonnet, is modified to something that shall protect the wearer's face without putting out the eyes of her companion, she cuts hers down to four straws and a rosebud, or a tag of lace and a bunch of glass beads. If there is a reaction against an excess of Rowland's Macassar,[2] and hair shiny and sticky with grease is thought less nice than if left clean and healthily crisp, she dries and frizzes and sticks hers out on end like certain savages in Africa, or lets it wander down her back like Madge Wildfire's,[3] and thinks herself all the more beautiful the nearer she approaches in look to a maniac or a negress. With purity of taste she has lost also that far more precious purity and delicacy of perception which sometimes mean more than appears on the surface. What the *demi-monde*[4] does in its frantic efforts to excite attention, she also does in imitation. If some fashionable *dévergondée en évidence* is reported to have come out with her dress below her shoulder-blades, and a gold strap for all the sleeve thought necessary, the girl of the period follows suit next day; and then wonders that men sometimes mistake her

for her prototype, or that mothers of girls not quite so far gone as herself refuse her as a companion for their daughters. She has blunted the fine edges of feeling so much that she cannot understand why she should be condemned for an imitation of form which does not include imitation of fact; she cannot be made to see that modesty of appearance and virtue ought to be inseparable, and that no good girl can afford to appear bad, under penalty of receiving the contempt awarded to the bad.

This imitation of the *demi-monde* in dress leads to something in manner and feeling, not quite so pronounced perhaps, but far too like to be honourable to herself or satisfactory to her friends. It leads to slang, bold talk, and fastness; to the love of pleasure and indifference to duty; to the desire of money before either love or happiness; to uselessness at home, dissatisfaction with the monotony of ordinary life, and horror of all useful work; in a word, to the worst forms of luxury and selfishness, to the most fatal effects arising from want of high principle and absence of tender feeling. The girl of the period envies the queens of the *demi-monde* far more than she abhors them. She sees them gorgeously attired and sumptuously appointed, and she knows them to be flattered, fêted, and courted with a certain disdainful admiration of which she catches only the admiration while she ignores the disdain. They have all for which her soul is hungering, and she never stops to reflect at what a price they have bought their gains, and what fearful moral penalties they pay for their sensuous pleasures. She sees only the coarse gilding on the base token, and shuts her eyes to the hideous figure in the midst, and the foul legend written round the edge. It is this envy of the pleasures, and indifference to the sins, of these women of the *demi-monde* which is doing such infinite mischief to the modern girl. They brush too closely by each other, if not in actual deeds, yet in aims and feelings; for the luxury which is bought by vice with the one is the thing of all in life most passionately desired by the other, though she is not yet prepared to pay quite the same price. Unfortunately, she has already paid too much—all that once gave her distinctive national character. No one can say of the modern English girl that she is tender, loving, retiring, or domestic. The old fault so often found by keen-sighted Frenchwomen, that she was so fatally *romanesque*,[5] so prone to sacrifice appearances and social advantages for love, will never be set down to the girl of the period. Love indeed is the last thing she thinks of, and the least of the dangers besetting her. Love in a

---

[1]**crinolines**: wide stiff petticoats popular at midcentury that exposed women's underwear when they bent over. **trains**: long extensions of a skirt that trailed in the dirt.

[2]**Rowland's Macassar**: hair oil made by Rowland and Son. (see pp. 684–685)

[3]**Madge Wildfire**: poor madwoman in Scott's *The Heart of Midlothian* (1818).

[4]*demi-monde*: women of doubtful reputation. *dévergondée en évidence*: shameless and conspicuous woman.

---

[5]*romanesque*: romantic.

cottage, that seductive dream which used to vex the heart and disturb the calculations of prudent mothers, is now a myth of past ages. The legal barter of herself for so much money, representing so much dash, so much luxury and pleasure—that is her idea of marriage; the only idea worth entertaining. For all seriousness of thought respecting the duties or the consequences of marriage, she has not a trace. If children come, they find but a stepmother's cold welcome from her; and if her husband thinks that he has married anything that is to belong to him—*a tacens et placens uxor*[6] pledged to make him happy—the sooner he wakes from his hallucination and understands that he has simply married some one who will condescend to spend his money on herself, and who will shelter her indiscretions behind the shield of his name, the less severe will be his disappointment. She has married his house, his carriage, his balance at the banker's, his title; and he himself is just the inevitable condition clogging the wheel of her fortune; at best an adjunct, to be tolerated with more or less patience as may chance. For it is only the old-fashioned sort, not girls of the period *pur sang*,[7] that marry for love, or put the husband before the banker. But she does not marry easily. Men are afraid of her; and with reason. They may amuse themselves with her for an evening, but they do not take her readily for life. Besides, after all her efforts, she is only a poor copy of the real thing; and the real thing is far more amusing than the copy, because it is real. Men can get that whenever they like; and when they go into their mothers' drawing-rooms, to see their sisters and their sisters' friends, they want something of quite different flavour. *Toujours perdrix*[8] is bad providing all the world over; but a continual weak imitation of *toujours perdrix* is worse. If we must have only one kind of thing, let us have it genuine; and the queens of St. John's Wood in their unblushing honesty, rather than their imitators and make-believes in Bayswater and Belgravia.[9] For, at whatever cost of shocked self-love or pained modesty it may be, it cannot be too plainly told to the modern English girl that the net result of her present manner of life is to assimilate her as

nearly as possible to a class of women whom we must not call by their proper—or improper—name. And we are willing to believe that she has still some modesty of soul left hidden under all this effrontery of fashion, and that, if she could be made to see herself as she appears to the eyes of men, she would mend her ways before too late.

It is terribly significant of the present state of things when men are free to write as they do of the women of their own nation. Every word of censure flung against them is two-edged, and wounds those who condemn as much as those who are condemned; for surely it need hardly be said that men hold nothing so dear as the honour of their women, and that no one living would willingly lower the repute of his mother or his sisters. It is only when these have placed themselves beyond the pale of masculine respect that such things could be written as are written now; when they become again what they were once they will gather round them the love and homage and chivalrous devotion which were then an English-woman's natural inheritance. The marvel, in the present fashion of life among women, is how it holds its ground in spite of the disapprobation of men. It used to be an old-time notion that the sexes were made for each other, and that it was only natural for them to please each other, and to set themselves out for that end. But the girl of the period does not please men. She pleases them as little as she elevates them; and how little she does that, the class of women she has taken as her models of itself testifies. All men whose opinion is worth having prefer the simple and genuine girl of the past, with her tender little ways and pretty bashful modesties, to this loud and rampant modernization, with her false red hair and painted skin, talking slang as glibly as a man, and by preference leading the conversation to doubtful subjects. She thinks she is piquante and exciting when she thus makes herself the bad copy of a worse original; and she will not see that though men laugh with her they do not respect her, though they flirt with her they do not marry her; she will not believe that she is not the kind of thing they want, and that she is acting against nature and her own interests when she disregards their advice and offends their taste. We do not see how she makes out her account, viewing her life from any side; but all we can do is to wait patiently until the national madness has passed, and our women have come back again to the old English ideal, once the most beautiful, the most modest, the most essentially womanly in the world.

1868

---

[6]*tacens et placens uxor:* silent and agreeable wife.

[7]*pur sang:* genuine.

[8]*toujours perdrix:* partridge (for dinner) every day (i.e., luxury).

[9]**St. John's Wood:** district of London where one would expect to find kept mistresses; respectable and rich women lived in **Bayswater** and **Belgravia.**

THE LADIES' NATIONAL ASSOCIATION FOR THE REPEAL OF THE CONTAGIOUS DISEASES ACT

The dark side of the Victorian obsession with female virtue was a fascination with the figure of the prostitute, which appeared in many, often contradictory guises: the seductive or dangerous embodiment of uncontrolled female sexuality, the victim of male vice and the sexual double standard, the helpless object of oppressive social forces, the agent of physical infection, the symbol of social disease. Much philanthropic effort was devoted to the material rescue and moral salvation of prostitutes. Such activity offered middle-class women an opportunity to cross class boundaries and express solidarity with their less fortunate sisters as well as to improve the moral and physical health of society. The prostitute or "fallen woman" haunts much of Victorian literature, addressed in this anthology from very different points of view in Dante Gabriel Rossetti's "Jenny," Augusta Webster's "A Castaway," and Amy Levy's "Magdalen."

To protect the armed services from venereal disease, Parliament passed the Contagious Diseases Act in 1864 authorizing police in garrison towns to arrest any woman suspected of being a prostitute. Women adjudged to be prostitutes were subject to medical inspection. In 1866 and 1869 the legislation was extended to other parts of the country, and despite vigorous opposition from women it remained in force until 1886. The petition reprinted here formally objects to the law's unfair and degrading treatment of women and its implicit sanctioning of male vice. Published in the London *Daily News*, it was signed by 128 women, including Florence Nightingale; the author was presumably Harriet Martineau, the first signatory.

[Petition]

There are two Acts of Parliament—one passed in 1866, the other in 1869—called the Contagious Diseases Acts. These Acts are in force in some of our garrison towns, and in large districts around them. Unlike all other laws for the repression of contagious diseases, to which both men and women are liable, these two apply to women only, men being wholly exempt from their penalties. The law is ostensibly framed for a certain class of women, but in order to reach these, all the women residing within the districts where it is in force are brought under the provisions of the Acts. Any woman can be dragged into court, and required to prove that she is not a common prostitute. The magistrate can condemn her, if a policeman swears only that he "has good cause to believe" her to be one. The accused has to rebut,

not positive evidence, but the state of mind of her accuser. When condemned, the sentence is as follows:—To have her person outraged by the periodical inspection of a surgeon, through a period of twelve months; or, resisting that, to be imprisoned, with or without hard labour—first for a month, next for three months—such imprisonment to be continuously renewed through her whole life unless she submit periodically to the brutal requirements of this law. Women arrested under false accusations have been so terrified at the idea of encountering the public trial necessary to prove their innocence, that they have, under the intimidation of the police, signed away their good name and their liberty by making what is called a "voluntary submission" to appear periodically for twelve months for surgical examination. Women who, through dread of imprisonment, have been induced to register themselves as common prostitutes, now pursue their traffic under the sanction of Parliament; and the houses where they congregate, so long as the government surgeons are satisfied with the health of their inmates, enjoy, practically, as complete a protection as a church or a school.

We, the undersigned, enter our solemn protest against these Acts—

1. Because, involving as they do such a momentous change in the legal safeguards hitherto enjoyed by women in common with men, they have been passed, not only without the knowledge of the country, but unknown to Parliament[1] itself; and we hold that neither the representatives of the people nor the press fulfil the duties which are expected of them, when they allow such legislation to take place without the fullest discussion.

2. Because, so far as women are concerned, they remove every guarantee of personal security which the law has established and held sacred, and put their reputation, their freedom, and their persons absolutely in the power of the police.

3. Because the law is bound, in any country professing to give civil liberty to its subjects, to define clearly an offence which it punishes.

4. Because it is unjust to punish the sex who are the victims of a vice, and leave unpunished the sex who are the main cause, both of the vice and its dreaded consequences; and we consider that the liability to arrest, forced surgical examination, and where this is resisted, imprisonment with hard labour, to which these Acts subject women, are punishments of the most degrading kind.

---

[1] **unknown to Parliament**: the legislation was said to have been passed by Parliament without proper consideration.

5. Because, by such a system, the path of evil is made more easy to our sons, and to the whole of the youth of England; inasmuch as a moral restraint is withdrawn the moment the State recognises and provides convenience for the practice of a vice which it thereby declares to be necessary and venial.

6. Because these measures are cruel to the women who come under their action—violating the feelings of those whose sense of shame is not wholly lost, and further brutalising even the most abandoned.

7. Because the disease which these Acts seek to remove has never been removed by any such legislation. The advocates of the system have utterly failed to show, by statistics or otherwise, that these regulations have in any case, after several years' trial, and when applied to one sex only, diminished disease, reclaimed the fallen, or improved the general morality of the country. We have, on the contrary, the strongest evidence to show that in Paris and other continental cities, where women have long been outraged by this forced inspection, the public health and morals are worse than at home.

8. Because the conditions of this disease, in the first instance, are moral, not physical. The moral evil through which the disease makes its way separates the case entirely from that of the plague or other scourges, which have been placed under police control or sanitary care. We hold that we are bound, before rushing into the experiment of legalising a revolting vice, to try to deal with the causes of the evil, and we dare to believe that with wiser teaching and more capable legislation those causes would not be beyond control.

1869

THOMAS HUGHES

(1822–1896)

Thomas Hughes's *Tom Brown's Schooldays* (1857) set the tone for generations of school stories (and indeed for the organization of many later schools) through its idealized picture of Rugby, one of the foremost of Britain's elite "public" schools. The book balances Tom Brown's sturdy boyishness with the delicate spiritual and intellectual nature of Tom's best friend, showing how each can learn from and become more like the other. Although both Tom and his friend become star cricketers, Hughes later deplored the increasing emphasis on athletic prowess in the culture of the schools.

Hughes became a lawyer and a judge, worked for "Christian Socialism," and was an active founder and administrator of a Working Men's College in London. *The Manliness of Christ* was written for Sunday afternoon readings at this College; it is designed to combat the idea that members of such groups as the Young Men's Christian Association are unmanly, or that Christianity appeals "mainly to men's fears—to that in them which is timid and shrinking, rather than to that which is courageous and outspoken." In Hughes's view, true manliness includes the best qualities of both women and men; his emphasis on self-sacrifice suggests that women can and do show it as well.

from The Manliness of Christ

One . . . precaution we must take at the outset of our inquiry, and that is, to settle for ourselves, without diverging into useless metaphysics, what we mean by "manliness, manfulness, courage." My friends of the Christian Guild[1] seemed to assume that these words all have the same meaning, and denote the same qualities. Now, is this so? I think not, if we take the common use of the words. "Manliness and manfulness" are synonymous, but they embrace more than we ordinarily mean by the word "courage;" for instance, tenderness, and thoughtfulness for others. They include that courage which lies at the root of all manliness, but is, in fact, only its lowest or rudest form. Indeed, we must admit that it is not exclusively a human quality at all, but one which we share with other animals, and which some of them—for instance, the bulldog and weasel—exhibit with a certainty and a thoroughness which is very rare amongst mankind. . . .

. . . True manliness is as likely to be found in a weak as in a strong body. Other things being equal, we may perhaps admit (though I should hesitate to do so) that a man with a highly-trained and developed body will be more courageous than a weak man. But we must take this caution with us, that a great athlete may be a brute or a coward, while a truly manly man can be neither.

Having got thus far, and satisfied ourselves what is not of the essence of manliness, though often assumed to be so (as by the promoters of the Christian Guild), let us see if we cannot get on another step, and ascertain what is of that essence. And here it may be useful to take a few well-known instances of courageous deeds and examine them; because if we can find out any common quality in them we shall have lighted on something which is of the essence of, or inseparable from, that manliness which includes courage—that manliness of which we are in search.

I will take two or three at hazard from a book in which they abound, and which was a great favorite here some years ago, as I hope it is still, I mean Napier's "Peninsular War."[2] . . .

---

[1] **Christian Guild**: a proposed organization making physical courage or prowess a condition of membership.

[2] Sir William **Napier** (1785–1860): *History of the War in the Peninsula* (1828–1840). Britain fought in the **Peninsular War** against Napoleon in Spain and Portugal.

Captain Wright[3] gave the word for the men to fall in on deck by companies, knowing that the sea below them was full of sharks, and that the ship could not possibly float till the boats came back; and the men fell in, knowing this also, and stood at attention without uttering a word, till she heeled over and went down under them. And Napier, with all his delight in physical force and prowess, and his intense appreciation of the qualities which shine most brightly in the fiery action of battle, gives the palm to these when he writes, "The records of the world furnish no parallel to this self-devotion." He was no mean judge in such a case; and, if he is right, as I think he is, do we not get another side-light on our inquiry, and find that the highest temper of physical courage is not to be found, or perfected, in action but in repose? All physical effort relieves the strain, and makes it easier to persist unto death, under the stimulus and excitement of the shock of battle, or of violent exertion of any kind, than when the effort has to be made with grounded arms. In other words, may we not say that in the face of danger self-restraint is after all the highest form of self-assertion, and a characteristic of manliness as distinguished from courage?

But we have only been looking hitherto at one small side of a great subject, at the courage which is tested in times of terror, on the battle-field, in the sinking ship, the poisoned mine, the blazing house. Such testing times come to few, and to these not often in their lives. But, on the other hand, the daily life of every one of us teems with occasions which will try the temper of our courage as searchingly, though not as terribly, as battle-field or fire or wreck. For we are born into a state of war; with falsehood and disease and wrong and misery, in a thousand forms, lying all around us, and the voice within calling on us to take our stand as men in the eternal battle against these.

And in this life-long fight, to be waged by every one of us single-handed against a host of foes, the last requisite for a good fight, the last proof and test of our courage and manfulness, must be loyalty to truth—the most rare and difficult

of all human qualities. For such loyalty, as it grows in perfection, asks ever more and more of us, and sets before us a standard of manliness always rising higher and higher.

And this is the great lesson which we shall learn from Christ's life, the more earnestly and faithfully we study it. "For this end was I born, and for this cause came I into the world, to bear witness to the truth."[4] To bear this witness against avowed and open enemies is comparatively easy. But to bear it against those we love, against those whose judgment and opinions we respect, in defense or furtherance of that which approves itself as true to our own inmost conscience, this is the last and abiding test of courage and of manliness. How natural, nay, how inevitable it is, that we should fall into the habit of appreciating and judging things mainly by the standards in common use amongst those we respect and love. But these very standards are apt to break down with us when we are brought face to face with some question which takes us ever so little out of ourselves and our usual moods. At such times we are driven to admit in our hearts that we, and those we respect and love, have been looking at and judging things, not truthfully, and therefore not courageously and manfully, but conventionally. And then comes one of the most searching of all trials of courage and manliness, when a man or woman is called to stand by what approves itself to their consciences as true, and to protest for it through evil report and good report, against all discouragement and opposition from those they love or respect. The sense of antagonism instead of rest, of distrust and alienation instead of approval and sympathy, which such times bring, is a test which tries the very heart and reins, and it is one which meets us at all ages, and in all conditions of life. Emerson's hero[5] is the man who, "taking both reputation and life in his hand, will with perfect urbanity dare the gibbet and the mob, by the absolute truth of his speech and rectitude of his behavior." And, even in our peaceful and prosperous England, absolute truth of speech and rectitude of behavior will not fail to bring their fiery trials, if also in the end their exceeding great rewards. . . .

1879

---

[3]**Captain Wright:** commanded the *Birkenhead*, where (in words Hughes quotes earlier) "four hundred men . . . calmly and without a murmur accepted death in a horrible form rather than endanger the women and children saved in the boats."

[4]"**For this end . . . truth**": apocryphal gospel of Nicodemus (3:2).

[5]**Emerson's hero:** see Ralph Waldo Emerson (1803–1882), "Heroism" (1841).

LABOUCHÈRE AMENDMENT

The Criminal Law bill passed by Parliament in 1885 was concerned mostly with the protection of girls and the suppression of brothels. As amended by Henry du Pré Labouchère (1831–1912), a Radical Member of Parliament, it also extended existing criminal sanctions against specific sexual acts to include an indeterminately wide range of public or private behavior carried out between men. By threatening them with disgrace, ruin, and imprisonment, the amendment also made homosexual men peculiarly vulnerable to blackmail. The most notorious victim of the Labouchère amendment was Oscar Wilde, sentenced in 1895 to two years' imprisonment with hard labor. The sensational trials that led to Wilde's conviction made him the representative example of the newly defined category of "the homosexual" and reinforced the connection in the public mind between homosexuality and contemporary art.

Female homosexuality was not subject to legal sanction.

from Criminal Law Amendment Act

Any male person who, in public or private, commits, or is a party to the commission of, or procures or attempts to procure the commission by any male person of, any act of gross indecency with another male person, shall be guilty of a misdemeanor, and, being convicted thereof, shall be liable, at the discretion of the court, to be imprisoned for any term not exceeding two years, with or without hard labour.

1885

JOHN ADDINGTON SYMONDS

(1840–1893)

The author of learned, brilliant, beautifully written studies in literature and art culminating in his seven-volume *Renaissance in Italy* (1875–1886), John Addington Symonds attempted to come to terms with his homosexuality in his *Memoirs*, which he wanted withheld from publication until after he and his wife were dead. The work remained unpublished until 1984.

The *Memoirs* demonstrate the ignorance and repugnance associated with homosexuality in the second half of the nineteenth century. They also demonstrate its prevalence. Symonds gives an unusually candid account of what he and others summed up as "vice" at Harrow, one of England's most prestigious schools for boys. Toward the end of his life he found in the burgeoning medico-scientific studies of sexuality a way of addressing a topic that had been taboo even to himself. He began the *Memoirs*, he said, "to supply material for the ethical psychologist and the student of mental pathology," and he contributed historical information and case studies (including his own) to Havelock Ellis' *Sexual Inversion* (1897), the first volume in Ellis' influential *Studies in the Psychology of Sex*. In his writing as in his life, Symonds vacillates between the guilty fear that homosexuality is abnormal and corrupt, and the conviction, based on his own experience and his reading of classical history and literature, that it can be natural, beautiful, and good. The *Memoirs* also demonstrate the "Decadent" mingling of erotic, aesthetic, and religious experience that characterizes much late Victorian literature and art.

from Memoirs

One thing at Harrow very soon arrested my attention. It was the moral state of the school. Every boy of good looks had a female name, and was recognized either as a public prostitute or as some bigger fellow's "bitch." Bitch was the word in common usage to indicate a boy who yielded his person to a lover. The talk in the dormitories and the studies was incredibly obscene. Here and there one could not avoid seeing acts of onanism, mutual masturbation, the sports of naked boys in bed together. There was no refinement, no sentiment, no passion; nothing but animal lust in these occurrences. They filled me with disgust and loathing. My school-fellows realized what I had read in Swift about the Yahoos.[1] . . .

Nothing could have been worse for a boy of my temperament than this unhealthy state of things. It poisoned and paralysed my moral nature, confused my judgement, perplexed my thoughts about religion. Had it not been for a strong physical repulsion, I should certainly have taken to bad courses. As it was, I began to coquette with vice. I fell in love with a handsome powerful boy called Huysche, and I remember stealing his hymnbook from his seat in chapel; but I never spoke to him. I also fell in love with Eliot Yorke, who used to come to my room; but I kept at a respectful distance from him. There must have happened some change in my manner or appearance; for a very depraved lad, whom I had known for three years, on one occasion finding me alone in my room, suddenly dared to throw his arms round me, kissed me, and thrust his hand into my trousers. At that moment I nearly gave way to sensuality. I was narcotized by the fellow's contact and the forecast of coming pleasure. But in this, as in all other cases, the inclination for vulgar lust was wanting. That saved me from self-abasement and traffic with the unclean thing.

A fatigued cynicism took possession of me. My health, which had never been good, suffered. I neglected my work. At the same time, my self-consciousness became enormously developed. I felt a terrible new sense of power. For the first time I seemed able to survey myself and the world, to grasp the facts of human nature from a point of view outside my inner and outer egotism. It is certain that, though I grew unhealthily and perversely during this period, I grew fast and to some purpose. I acquired then a certain disengagement from things which are not essential, a certain habit of doubting appearances and disdaining trifles. This attitude of mind has, I believe, been useful to me. But the price paid in disillusion and moral befoulment outweighed the gain of mental grit.

The progress of a lad of seventeen has to be reckoned not by years but by months.

We were reading Plato's *Apology* in the sixth form. I bought Cary's crib, and took it with me to London on an *exeat*[2] in March. My hostess, a Mrs Bain, who lived in Regent's Park, treated me to a comedy one evening at the Haymarket. I forget what the play was—except that there was a funny character in it, who set the house in a roar by his enunciation of this sentence: "Smythers please, not Smithers; Smithers is a different party, and moves in quite a different sphere." When we returned from the play, I went to bed and began to read my Cary's Plato. It so happened that I stumbled on the *Phaedrus*. I read on and on, till I reached the end. Then I began the *Symposium*;[3] and the sun was shining on the shrubs outside the ground-floor room in which I slept, before I shut the book up.

I have related these insignificant details because that night was one of the most important nights of my life; and

---

[1]**Yahoos:** in Jonathan **Swift**'s *Gulliver's Travels* (1726), book 4.

[2]**Cary's crib:** literal translation used illegitimately by students to cheat on their schoolwork, by Henry **Cary** (1804–1870). *exeat:* permission to leave school.

[3]*Phaedrus, Symposium:* Platonic dialogues in which love of a beautiful male is said to be a stage in the ascent to love of true beauty and wisdom.

when anything of great gravity has happened to me, I have always retained a firm recollection of trifling facts which formed its context.

Here in the *Phaedrus* and the *Symposium*—in the myth of the Soul and the speeches of Pausanias, Agathon, and Diotima—I discovered the true *liber amoris*[4] at last, the revelation I had been waiting for, the consecration of a long-cherished idealism. It was just as though the voice of my own soul spoke to me through Plato, as though in some antenatal experience I had lived the life of a philosophical Greek lover.

Harrow vanished into unreality. I had touched solid ground. I had obtained the sanction of the love which had been ruling me from childhood. Here was the poetry, the philosophy of my own enthusiasm for male beauty, expressed with all the magic of unrivalled style. And, what was more, I now became aware that the Greek race—the actual historical Greeks of antiquity—treated this love seriously, invested it with moral charm, endowed it with sublimity.

For the first time I saw the possibility of resolving in a practical harmony the discords of my instincts. I perceived that masculine love had its virtue as well as its vice, and stood in this respect upon the same ground as normal sexual appetite. I understood, or thought I understood, the relation which those dreams of childhood and the brutalities of vulgar lust at Harrow bore to my higher aspiration after noble passion. . . .

On the first Sunday morning after my arrival,[5] I attended service in Bristol Cathedral. It was a radiant forenoon and the light streamed in from those large southern windows. My ritualistic pranks with Vickers at Harrow had this much of reality in them, that they indicated a natural susceptibility to the aesthetic side of religion—I felt a real affection and a natural reverence for grey Gothic churches. The painted glass and heraldries in this cathedral, crusaders crosslegged on their tombs, carved woodwork and high-built organ lofts, the monuments to folk long dead, and, over all, the quiring voices and reverberations of sweet sacred music, touched me to the quick at a thousand sensitive points. There was no real piety, however, in my mood. My soul was lodged in Hellas;[6] and the Christian in me stirred only, like a torpid snake, sunned by the genial warmth of art.

On this, the morning of all mornings in my life, my eyes fell on a chorister who sat nearly opposite the stall which I had taken. His voice charmed me by its sharp ethereal melancholy. In timbre and quality it had something of a wood instrument; and because of my love for it, I have ever since been sensitive to the notes of hautbois and clarinet. As I gazed and listened through the psalms and service and litany, I felt that a new factor had been introduced into my life. The voice dominated. But the boy who owned that voice seemed the only beautiful, the only flawless being I had ever seen.

From the church I walked home, enveloped in a dream. All that afternoon and evening I dreamed of Willie Dyer. I have forgotten how I discovered his name. At earliest daybreak I leaned from my bedroom window, sending my soul out to him, greeting the cathedral tower beneath me. This went on for two or three days. Ah, those April mornings—that hush of thin-leaved trees and dewy lawns, those notes of blackbirds, the stillness of the sleeping town, the poetry of flooding light, the steady thrill of flooding love!

There had been nothing like to this emotion in my past experience. It precipitated the turbid mixture of my blood and brains. I saw ahead of me the goal to which I had been tending. The close blind alley into which I had blundered at Harrow, and from which there was no escape, seemed now to expand into infinities of free and liberal experience.

I was so intoxicated with the moment that I demanded nothing from the future. I did not inquire how—my present mood of feeling squared with the philosophy of love I had imbibed from Plato. . . .

We met then on the morning of 10 April 1858. Swallows were wheeling in sunlight round the tower. The clock struck. I took Willie's slender hand into my own and gazed into his large brown eyes fringed with heavy lashes. A quite indescribable effluence of peace and satisfaction, blent with yearning, flowed from his physical presence and inundated my whole being with some healing and refreshing influence.

From that morning I date the birth of my real self. Thirty-two years have elapsed since then; and still I can hardly hold the pen when I attempt to write about it.

Much sentimental nonsense has been talked about first love. Yet I am speaking the bare truth when I say my affection for this boy exhausted my instinctive faculty of loving. I have never felt the same unreasoned and unreasoning emotion for any other human being.

I could not marry him; modern society provided no bond of comradeship whereby we might have been united. So my first love flowed to waste. I was unable to deal justly with him; the mortification of the anomalous position he and I were placed in did much to degrade my character.

---

[4]*liber amoris*: book of love.

[5]**arrival**: at home.

[6]**Hellas**: ancient Greece. **snake**: see P. B. Shelley's *Hellas* (1822), 1060–65.

These things, however, were not felt at once. From 10 April in that year 1858, for many months to come, I used either to see Willie or wrote to him daily. He returned my affection with a simple loyal love. Our intimacy, though clandestine—though we two boys, the elder by three years and the younger, met together and exchanged our hearts without the sanction of family or friends—was wholly respectful and absolutely free from evil. More than a year elapsed before I dared to do more than touch his hand. Twice only in my life did I kiss him on the lips. The first time I did so I almost fainted from the intense rapture of the contact. We were together alone, I well remember, in a clearing of Leigh Woods—where the red quarries break down from tufted yews and dwarf beeches and wych elms plumed upon the cliff to the riverside. The afternoon sunlight fell upon glossy ivy, bluebells and late flowering anemones. We were lying side by side. The plash of paddle wheels and the chant of sailors working a seagoing vessel down the Avon, rose up to us between the two long kisses which I took.

Leigh Woods used to be our favourite resort. In those days there was no suspension bridge. We crossed the ferry, and clambered up the sides of Nightingale Valley until we found some coign of vantage where we rested. Not a soul disturbed our solitude. The wild rabbits were not more innocent of guile than we were.

I still possess a white anemone gathered on the spot of that first kiss. It marks the place in my Theocritus, where this phrase occurs:

$$\mathring{\eta} \,\,\rho\alpha\,\, \tau\acute{o}\tau'\,\, \mathring{\eta}\sigma\alpha\nu$$
$$\chi\rho\acute{\upsilon}\sigma\epsilon\iota o\iota\,\, \pi\acute{\alpha}\lambda\alpha\iota\,\, \mathring{\alpha}\nu\delta\rho\epsilon\varsigma,\,\, \mathring{o}\tau'\,\, \mathring{\alpha}\nu\tau\epsilon\phi\acute{\iota}\lambda\eta\sigma'\,\, \mathring{o}\,\, \phi\iota\lambda\eta\theta\epsilon\acute{\iota}\varsigma.^{[7]}$$

Gratitude mingled with my love for Willie. He had delivered my soul from the Egyptian house of Harrow bondage.[8] He enabled me to realize an ideal of a passionate and yet pure love between friend and friend. All the 'rich foreshadowings of the world'[9] which filled my boyhood with the vision of a comrade, seemed at the time to be made actual in him. He restored me to a healthy state of nerves by the sweet magnetism of his presence. In him too I found the final satisfaction of that dim aesthetic ecstasy which I called religion.

Music and the grandeur of Gothic aisles, the mystery of winter evenings in cathedral choirs, when the tumultuous vibrations of the organ shook the giant windows and made the candles in their sconces tremble, took from him a poetry that pierced into my heart and marrow. . . . (Chapter 5)

. . . After our wedding[10] my wife and I were driven to Brighton by a Norfolk coachman, who had been in Mr North's service many years.

It requires all the romance and passion of Romeo and Juliet to make a double bedroom in an English town hotel appear poetical. Marriage begins ill which begins with a prosaic tour through inns. The first joys of nuptial intercourse ought not to be remembered in connection with places so common, so sordid and so trivial.

I shall not forget the repulsion stirred in me by that Brighton bedroom or the disillusion caused by my first night of marriage. Disagreeable as it is, I cannot omit to tell the truth about these things, since they are all-important for the object I have in writing my memoirs.

I had never had anything at all to do with any woman in the way of sex. I had only a vague notion about the structure of the female body. I had never performed any sexual act with any one, and I did not know how to go about it. I firmly expected that some extraordinary and ecstatic enthusiasm would awake in me at the mere contact of a woman's body in bed, although I was aware that the presence of women did not disturb my senses in the ballroom or a carriage. I also anticipated that nature would take care of herself when it came to the consummation of marriage.

To my surprise and annoyance, I felt myself rather uncomfortable than otherwise by the side of my wife, oppressed with shyness, and not at all carried away by passionate enthusiasm. Dearly as I loved her, and ardently as I desired through marriage to enter into the state of normal manhood, I perceived that this thing which we had to do together was not what either of us imperatively required. I felt no repugnance at first, but no magnetic thrill of attraction. A deep sense of disappointment came over me when I found that the

> Corps feminin, qui tant est tendre,
> Polly, souef, si précieux[11]

---

[7]$\mathring{\eta}\,\,\rho\alpha$ . . . $\phi\iota\lambda\eta\theta\epsilon\acute{\iota}\varsigma$: Men were in the golden age long ago, when the beloved youth loved in return. Theocritus, *Idylls* 12.15–16. **Theocritus:** Greek pastoral poet, 3d century BCE.

[8]**Egyptian . . . bondage:** see Exodus 1–14.

[9]**"rich foreshadowings . . . world":** Tennyson, *The Princess* (1847), 7.293.

[10]**wedding:** in 1864.

[11]**Corps feminin . . . précieux:** the female body, which is so tender, polished, sweet, so precious; from François Villon, *Le Testament* (1461), 325–26.

did not exercise its hoped-for magic. What was worse, nature refused to show me how the act should be accomplished. This was due to no defect in me. The organ of sex was vigorous enough and ready to perform its work. My own ineptitude prevented me for several nights from completing the marital function; and at last I found the way by accident—after having teased and hurt both my wife and myself, besides suffering dismally from the humiliating absurdity of the situation. She afterwards told me that such manifest proofs of my virginity were agreeable to her. But all the romance and rapture of sexual intercourse, on which I had so fondly counted, were destroyed by this sordid experience. I also discovered that the physical contact of a woman, though it did not actually disgust me, left me very cold. There was something in it nauseous, and cohabitation in my case meant only the mechanical relief of nature.

Truly we civilized people of the nineteenth century are more backward than the African savages in all that concerns this most important fact of human life. We allow young men and women to contract permanent relations involving sex, designed for procreation, without instructing them in the elementary science of sexual physiology. We do all that lies in us to keep them chaste, to develop and refine their sense of shame, while we leave them to imagine what they like about the nuptial connection. Then we fling them naked into bed together, modest, alike ignorant, mutually embarrassed by the awkward situation, trusting that they will blunder upon the truth by instinct. We forget that this is a dangerous test of their affection and their self-respect; all the more dangerous in proportion as they are highly cultivated, refined and sensitive. Instead of the supreme embrace occurring, as it ought to do, and does in properly instructed people, as an episode, inevitable and consummative of the long chord of passion, it has to be stupidly sought out amid circumstances of abasement which generate repugnance.

I have known cases of marriage spoiled from the commencement by this idiotic system of let-alone education. . . . (Chapter 9)

. . . It is a singular life history;[12] and yet, for aught I know, it may be commoner than I imagine. A town-bred boy, burdened with physical ailments, shy and sensitive, above the average in mental faculty, but ill-adapted to the ordinary course of English education. Emotion wakes in him; and just when the first faint stirrings of sex before the age of puberty are felt, he discerns the masterful attraction of the male. He feels it dimly and grotesquely at the commencement, then distinctly, overpoweringly, in dreams and waking fancies. It connects itself with the impressions he derives from art, from poetry, from nature. Remaining a timid, reserved, refined child, he goes to a great public school, is ailing there, incapable of joining his comrades in their games, inferior to the best of them in scholarship. His life passes like a turbid vision of the night. The vicious habits of the boys around him repel him with a keen repugnance, He is poisoned by discovering the secret of his headmaster.[13] Plato's paiderastic[14] dialogues bring a sudden revelation, and he devotes himself to the study of Greek love. All this while he forms himself surely, blindly, into a literary being with an absorbing passion for persons of his own sex. He falls in love shyly, purely, imaginatively, with a boy of little less than his own age. This leads to nothing but the torture of caressed emotion, the thrilling of some coarser chords which he resolutely masters. He goes to Oxford, begins to discover his mental force, dreams continually, carries off the usual academical prizes, but cares little for such success. At root he is love-laden, love-smitten, wounded. Suffering comes to him, through his own fault in part, but more through the malice of a treacherous friend. Determined to trample down his abnormal inclinations, he marries a woman for whom he feels the strongest admiration and the firmest friendship, but not the right quality of sexual passion. Soon afterwards he falls ill, and is pronounced consumptive. Incapable of following a profession, he spends years in seeking health, with his wife, with children growing up. At length, when he has reached the age of twenty-nine, he yields to the attraction of the male. And this is the strange point about the man, that now for the first time he attains to self-mastery and self-control. Contemporaneously with his first indulged passion, he begins to write books, and rapidly becomes an author of distinction. The indecision of the previous years is replaced by a firm volition and a consciousness of power. He can deal more effectively with men and women, is better company, learns to write with greater force. He seems to draw strength from the congenital malady which has now come to the surface. Upon the verge of fifty, this man is younger and wholesomer than when he went to Harrow at thirteen. He is

---

[12]These last paragraphs of the book summarize its narrative.

[13]Charles John Vaughan (1816–1897) was blackmailed into resigning as **headmaster** of Harrow by Symonds' father when Symonds told him that Vaughan had sent love letters to a schoolboy.

[14]**paiderastic**: concerning love for boys.

easier to live with than when he married at twenty-four. He has to some extent surmounted his consumptive tendencies. He has made himself a name in literature. Altogether he is more of a man than when he repressed and pent within his soul those fatal and abnormal inclinations. Yet he belongs to a class abhorred by society and is, by English law, a criminal. What is the meaning, the lesson, the conclusion to be drawn from this biography? . . .

Few situations in life are more painful than this: that a man, gifted with strong intellectual capacity, and exercised in all the sleights of criticism, should sit down soberly to contemplate his own besetting vice. In pleasant moments, when instinct prevails over reason, when the broadway of sensual indulgence invites his footing, the man plucks primroses of frank untutored inclination. They have for him, then, only the fragrance of wayside flowers, blossoms upon the path of exquisite experience. But, when he comes to frigid reason's self again, when he tallies last night's deeds with today's knowledge of fact and moral ordinance, he awakes to the reality of a perpetual discord between spontaneous appetite and acquired respect for social law. By the light of his clear brain he condemns the natural action of his appetite; and what in moments of self-abandonment to impulse appeared a beauteous angel, stands revealed before him as a devil abhorred by the society he clings to. The agony of this struggle between self-yielding to desire and love, and self-scourging by a trained discipline of analytic reflection, breaks his nerve. The only exit for a soul thus plagued is suicide. Two factors, equally unconquerable, flesh and the reason, animal joy in living and mental perception that life is a duty, war in the wretched victim of their equipoise. While he obeys the flesh, he is conscious of no wrong-doing. When he awakes from the hypnotism of the flesh, he sees his own misdoing not in the glass of truth to his nature, but in the mirror of convention. He would fain have less of sense or less of intellect. Why was he not born a savage or a normal citizen? The quarrel drives him into blowing his brains out, or into idiocy. (Chapter 17)

1984

EMPIRE AND TRAVEL

WHAT IT MEANT to be British during the nineteenth century was inflected by increasingly complex interactions with the wider world. After finally defeating Napoleon in 1815 Britain was involved in no major European wars for almost a century, except in the distant Crimea during the 1850s. Instead, British power and influence spread outward around the globe until it could routinely be remarked that "the sun never sets on the British Empire." With the aid of improvements in steamships, railroads, the telegraph, bookkeeping, and finance—and also guns—British people and practices and industrial products flowed outward, as raw materials, profits, and data flowed back.

The colonies offered a safety valve for a crowded, industrialized country. Young men of the ruling classes found employment and scope for ambition in military or government service or commercial enterprises abroad. Well-to-do families sent their black sheep to the colonies and paid them to stay there. Charitable organizations helped poor people to emigrate, while the government disposed of criminals and rebels (especially in Ireland) by transporting them to penal colonies (especially in Australia). Unmarried women often found husbands in the colonies, where women were scarce. Restless spirits traveled in search of excitement and adventure; missionaries sought to spread Christianity and "civilization"; scientists and artists pursued materials for their work.

Many of these travelers returned, often with money acquired abroad—sometimes large fortunes, more often government or military pensions or the modest fruits of labor and trade—as well as new and less insular ideas. Information was accumulated and organized, feeding an insatiable desire to learn what the world was like and to describe it scientifically. Explorers "discovered" and mapped regions hitherto unseen by Europeans, often writing bestselling books and becoming popular heroes. Charles Darwin and Thomas Huxley founded their scientific careers on observations made during long sea voyages. Travelers and residents abroad painstakingly acquired botanical and zoological specimens and sent them back for specialists to classify, or collected data for the burgeoning discipline of anthropology. Cultural artifacts ancient and modern, specimens living and dead, made their way to Britain for display in exhibitions and in the zoos, gardens, and museums that proliferated during the Victorian period. Fashion imitated Middle-Eastern, Japanese, and Chinese styles of home furnishing, decoration, and art, bringing the exotic into private homes.

In the underlying metaphor of colonialism, both populous areas of the Orient and apparently "empty" lands were gendered female, passive objects of masculine European enterprise and proving grounds of male identity. Most colonists and all government and military officials were men. But gender counted for less than class in nineteenth-century hierarchy, and class less than race, so European women often found in the wider world an exhilarating freedom and authority that were denied them at home. Sometimes, following the careers of their fathers or husbands to distant lands, they drooped under the difficulties of keeping house in inhospitable climates among alien people, but many women enjoyed surmounting difficulties and delighted in what was new and strange. Many traveled alone, as missionaries, artists, or scientific explorers, or simply as tourists.

British colonialism changed in the course of the century and was at all times diverse and contested. In India, where the British had ruled since the eighteenth century, they were a small band of alien intruders who mostly put in their time and (if they survived) went home. In Canada, Australia, and New Zealand, on the other hand, the relatively small indigenous populations were pushed aside by settlers who meant to stay. In the Caribbean, Europeans had accumulated wealth from slave plantations, but abolitionist fervor in Britain had led to the abolition of the slave trade in 1807 and of slavery in British possessions during the 1830s. Parts of Africa were acquired relatively late and, except for South Africa (where great riches could be acquired in mining), were considered relatively unimportant. In the first part of the century, many people thought colonial expansion a waste of energy, population, and money. Even as late as 1876, when the Queen was pronounced Empress of India, there was by no means unanimous approval. The belligerent imperialist spirit expressed by Rudyard Kipling belongs mostly to later decades, when the full ideology of imperialism arose to meet the challenge of European rivals and indigenous opponents.

The latter part of the century also saw a hardening of racist attitudes. Abolitionist fervor, which persisted in Britain until the end of the American Civil War, relied on at least minimal notions of human equality. For missionaries, similarly, religious conversion mattered more than race or nation. But after midcentury rigid pseudo-scientific and hierarchical notions of race increasingly gained ground, with the British taking for granted not only the inherent "racial" superiority of light-skinned northern Europeans over darker peoples, but also the right—indeed, the duty—of Europeans to impose their culture and political power on everyone else.

Increasingly, too, uprisings of subjected peoples against imperial power aroused angrily repressive measures. The Indian Revolt (more often called the "Mutiny") of 1857, in which atrocities were committed on both sides, frightened and enraged the British public. A rebellion in Jamaica in 1866 was put down with appalling cruelty by Governor Edward Eyre, whose subsequent trial in England split the cultural elite into two violently opposing parties, one (including John Stuart Mill, Charles Darwin, and Thomas Huxley) urging that Eyre be punished for unlawful abuse of authority, the other (including Thomas Carlyle, John Ruskin, Charles Dickens, Alfred Tennyson, and John Tyndall) defending Eyre as the bulwark of "civilization" against "barbarism." Local wars in Africa, especially South Africa, also focused racist attitudes. Evolutionary thought, meanwhile, reinforced the idea that "primitive" cultures and peoples must necessarily give way to "civilized" ones.

In literature, especially prose fiction, the colonies figure in various ways, being equally convenient as the source of a character's (often ill-gotten) fortune and as a misfit's destination. Visitors from the colonies enliven stories set in the British Isles with irruptions of mystery, danger, or romance. Adventure stories set in exotic locations, especially for boys, were immensely popular, as were the innumerable books of travels that appeared throughout the century. Serious observers of the wider world (including most of those included here) generally felt some admiration for the people they wrote about, and tried to imagine, although through a racialized lens, a non-European point of view. And as English in creolized and standardized forms became the foremost language for business, administration, diplomacy, and education, English literature itself came to exert an unprecedented influence throughout much of the world.

AUSTEN HENRY LAYARD

(1817–1894)

As a child Henry Layard loved the *Arabian Nights* and daydreamed of the Orient. At the age of twenty-two, bored and restless after six years of study and work as a lawyer, he made his way to the Middle East. He delighted in the beauty of the country, the fascination of ancient ruins, and the excitements of travel and political unrest, working unofficially and often in secret for the British ambassador in Constantinople while pursuing archaeological research. In 1845 he began excavating the Assyrian ruins at Nimrud (which he mistook for the ancient city of Nineveh, named in the Bible and in ancient Greek and Roman texts), in what is now Iraq and was then under Turkish control. As many as possible of the giant sculptures, bas-reliefs, and inscribed stones that he unearthed were shipped to London. *Nineveh and Its Remains* (1849) tells the story of the excavation and gives a scholarly account of Assyrian civilization. Along with the abridged version excerpted here, it made its author famous and started him on a distinguished political and diplomatic career.

Layard saw remnants of a legendary, long-vanished civilization rise like an apparition from the bowels of the earth. With dreamlike strangeness, it was geographically and culturally remote and yet, through the Bible and the *Arabian Nights*, deeply familiar. The beautiful works Layard recovered challenged British classically based canons of taste; at the same time, it was taken for granted that they belonged not where they were made or found but in the British Museum, where they thrilled and appalled Dante Gabriel Rossetti (see "The Burden of Nineveh," pages 804–806) and still make a stunning display. Layard's intense excitement, his assumption of authority, and his casually scornful depiction of awestruck native observers are characteristic of Victorian travel writing.

from A Popular Account of Discoveries at Nineveh

. . . On reaching the ruins I descended into the new trench, and found the workmen, who had already seen me, as I approached, standing near a heap of baskets and cloaks.

Whilst Awad[1] advanced and asked for a present to celebrate the occasion, the Arabs withdrew the screen they had hastily constructed, and disclosed an enormous human head

---

[1]Sheik **Awad**: hired by Layard as superintendent of the excavations.

sculptured in full out of the alabaster of the country. They had uncovered the upper part of a figure, the remainder of which was still buried in the earth. I saw at once that the head must belong to a winged lion or bull, similar to those of Khorsabad and Persepolis. It was in admirable preservation. The expression was calm, yet majestic, and the outline of the features showed a freedom and knowledge of art, scarcely to be looked for in works of so remote a period. The cap had three horns, and, unlike that of the human-headed bulls hitherto found in Assyria, was rounded and without ornament at the top.

I was not surprised that the Arabs had been amazed and terrified at this apparition. It required no stretch of imagination to conjure up the most strange fancies. This gigantic head, blanched with age, thus rising from the bowels of the earth, might well have belonged to one of those fearful beings which are pictured in the traditions of the country, as appearing to mortals, slowly ascending from the regions below. One of the workmen, on catching the first glimpse of the monster, had thrown down his basket and had run off towards Mosul as fast as his legs could carry him. I learnt this with regret, as I anticipated the consequences.

Whilst I was superintending the removal of the earth, which still clung to the sculpture, and giving directions for the continuation of the work, a noise of horsemen was heard, and presently Abd-ur-rahman,[2] followed by half his tribe, appeared on the edge of the trench. As soon as the two Arabs had reached the tents, and published the wonders they had seen, every one mounted his mare and rode to the mound to satisfy himself of the truth of these inconceivable reports. When they beheld the head they all cried together, "There is no God but God, and Mahommed is his Prophet!" It was some time before the Sheikh could be prevailed upon to descend into the pit, and convince himself that the image he saw was of stone. "This is not the work of men's hands," exclaimed he, "but of those infidel giants of whom the Prophet, peace be with him! has said, that they were higher than the tallest date tree; this is one of the idols which Noah, peace be with him! cursed before the flood." In this opinion, the result of a careful examination, all the bystanders concurred.

I now ordered a trench to be dug due south from the head in the expectation of finding a corresponding figure, and before night-fall reached the object of my search about twelve feet distant. Engaging two or three men to sleep near the sculptures, I returned to the village, and celebrated the day's discovery by a slaughter of sheep, of which all the Arabs near partook. As some wandering musicians chanced to be at Selamiyah, I sent for them, and dances were kept up during the greater part of the night. On the following morning Arabs from the other side of the Tigris, and the inhabitants of the surrounding villages, congregated on the mound. Even the women could not repress their curiosity, and came in crowds, with their children, from afar. My Cawass[3] was stationed during the day in the trench, into which I would not allow the multitude to descend. . . .

I ascertained by the end of March the existence of a second pair of winged human-headed lions, differing from those previously discovered in form, the human shape being continued to the waist, and being furnished with human arms, as well as with the legs of the lion. In one hand each figure carried a goat or stag, and in the other, which hung down by the side, a branch with three flowers. They formed a northern entrance into the chamber of which the lions previously described were the western portal. I completely uncovered the latter, and found them to be entire. They were about twelve feet in height, and the same number in length. The body and limbs were admirably portrayed; the muscles and bones, although strongly developed to display the strength of the animal, showed at the same time a correct knowledge of its anatomy and form. Expanded wings sprung from the shoulder and spread over the back; a knotted girdle, ending in tassels, encircled the loins. These sculptures, forming an entrance, were partly in full and partly in relief. The head and fore-part, facing the chamber, were in full; but only one side of the rest of the slab was sculptured, the back being placed against the wall of sun-dried bricks. That the spectator might have both a perfect front and side view of the figures, they were furnished with five legs; two were carved on the end of the slab to face the chamber, and three on the side. The relief of the body and limbs was high and bold, and the slab was covered, in all parts not occupied by the image, with inscriptions in the cuneiform character. The remains of color could still be traced in the eyes—the pupils being painted black, and the rest filled up with an opaque white pigment; but on no other parts of the sculpture. These magnificent specimens of Assyrian art were in perfect preservation; the most minute lines in the details of the wings and in the ornaments had been retained with their original freshness.

I used to contemplate for hours these mysterious emblems, and muse over their intent and history. What more

---

[2]**Abd-ur-rahman:** sheik of a nearby **tribe.**

[3]**Cawass:** consular guard.

noble forms could have ushered the people into the temple of their gods? What more sublime images could have been borrowed from nature, by men who sought, unaided by the light of revealed religion, to embody their conception of the wisdom, power, and ubiquity of a Supreme Being? They could find no better type of intellect and knowledge than the head of the man; of strength, than the body of the lion; of ubiquity, than the wings of the bird. These winged human-headed lions were not idle creations, the offspring of mere fancy; their meaning was written upon them. They had awed and instructed races which flourished 3000 years ago. Through the portals which they guarded, kings, priests, and warriors had borne sacrifices to their altars, long before the wisdom of the East had penetrated to Greece, and had furnished its mythology with symbols recognised of old by the Assyrian votaries. They may have been buried, and their existence may have been unknown, before the foundation of the eternal city.[4] For twenty-five centuries they had been hidden from the eye of man, and they now stood forth once more in their ancient majesty. But how changed was the scene around them! The luxury and civilisation of a mighty nation had given place to the wretchedness and ignorance of a few half-barbarous tribes. The wealth of temples, and the riches of great cities, had been succeeded by ruins and shapeless heaps of earth. Above the spacious hall in which they stood, the plough had passed and the corn now waved. Egypt has monuments no less ancient and no less wonderful; but they have stood forth for ages to testify her early power and renown; whilst those before me had but now appeared to bear witness, in the words of the prophet, that once "the Assyrian was a cedar in Lebanon with fair branches and with a shadowing shroud of an high stature; and his top was among the thick boughs . . . his height was exalted above all the trees of the field, and his boughs were multiplied, and his branches became long, because of the multitude of waters when he shot forth. All the fowls of heaven made their nests in his boughs, and under his branches did all the beasts of the fields bring forth their young, and under his shadow dwelt all great nations;" for now is "Nineveh a desolation and dry like a wilderness, and flocks lie down in the midst of her: all the beasts of the nations, both the cormorant and bittern, lodge in the upper lintels of it; their voice sings in the windows; and desolation is in the thresholds."[5] . . . . (Chapter 3)

1851

---

[4]**eternal city**: Rome, legendarily founded 753 BCE.

[5]**"the Assyrian . . . thresholds"**: Ezekiel, xxxi. 3., &c.; Zephaniah, ii. 13. and 14. [Layard's note]

RICHARD BURTON

(1821–1890)

Tall, dark, swashbuckling Richard Burton was perhaps the most glamorous and gifted of the Victorian romantic adventurers. Having provoked the authorities at Oxford into expelling him, he joined the army in India, where he threw himself into the study of languages and customs and often lived in disguise among the native population. As an explorer, he went on major expeditions to parts of Arabia and East Africa where few or no Europeans had ventured before; as British consul in West Africa, South America, Syria, and Trieste he used his official posts as jumping-off points for further explorations. He mastered more than two dozen languages and gathered ethnographic information wherever he went. He also produced more than forty books, of which the most notable were travel narratives and a series of literary translations including the *Arabian Nights* and the *Kama Sutra*, the ancient Sanskrit manual of the art of love. But a reckless contempt for authority hampered his career, even though he was married to a respectable aristocrat, Isabel, and was awarded a knighthood in 1886.

In 1853 Burton traveled through Arabia disguised as an Afghan doctor from India on pilgrimage to Mecca. The project for which he obtained official support was primarily geographic and ethnographic, but his real object was to visit the holiest cities of Islam, which nonbelievers were forbidden on pain of death to enter. His account in the *Pilgrimage* is crammed with footnotes (omitted here) about history, geography, climate, religion, medical matters, buildings, domestic life, food and drink, conditions of travel, and other aspects of Arab culture. Like many English people he was fascinated by the desert, where "man meets man." The *Pilgrimage* depicts a dangerous adventure and a quintessentially Romantic outsider-hero whose scorn for stay-at-home enervation extends equally to the passive Arab and the lazy Londoner.

Our second excerpt is from Burton's account of his disastrous quest for the Holy Grail of Victorian explorers, the source of the Nile; it describes his first sight of Lake Tanganyika. In Burton's African books the assumption of racial and cultural superiority that undergirds his fascination with distant people and places shows itself in its most virulent form. Here he expresses in primarily aesthetic terms the imperialist impulse to subsume everything in the world into European discourse, even as his imagination responds with awe and delight to exotic abundance.

from **Personal Narrative of a Pilgrimage to El-Medinah and Meccah**

. . . In thirteen days we had passed from the clammy grey fog, that atmosphere of industry which kept us at anchor off the Isle of Wight, through the liveliest air of the inland sea,[1] whose sparkling blue and purple haze spread charms even on Africa's beldame features, and now we are sitting silent and still, listening to the monotonous melody of the East— the soft night-breeze wandering through starlit skies and tufted trees, with a voice of melancholy meaning.

And this is the Arab's Kayf.[2] The savouring of animal existence; the passive enjoyment of mere sense; the pleasant languor, the dreamy tranquillity, the airy castle-building, which in Asia stand in lieu of the vigorous, intensive, passionate life of Europe. It is the result of a lively, impressible, excitable nature, and exquisite sensibility of nerve,—a facility for voluptuousness unknown to northern regions; where

happiness is placed in the exertion of mental and physical powers; where "Ernst ist das Leben;"[3] where niggard earth commands ceaseless sweat of brow, and damp chill air demands perpetual excitement, exercise, or change, or adventure, or dissipation, for want of something better. In the East, man requires but rest and shade: upon the bank of a bubbling stream, or under the cool shelter of a perfumed tree, he is perfectly happy, smoking a pipe, or sipping a cup of coffee, or drinking a glass of sherbet, but above all things deranging body and mind as little as possible; the trouble of conversations, the displeasures of memory, and the vanity of thought being the most unpleasant interruptions to his Kayf. No wonder that Kayf is a word untranslatable in our mother-tongue! . . . (Chapter 1)

. . . To conclude this subject, the Tawarah still retain many characteristics of the Bedouin race.[4] The most good-humoured and sociable of men, they delight in a jest, and may readily be managed by kindness and courtesy. Yet they are passionate, nice upon points of honor, revengeful and easily offended where their peculiar prejudices are misunderstood. I have always found them pleasant companions, and deserving of respect, for their hearts are good, and their

---

[1]**Isle of Wight:** off the British coast. **inland sea:** Mediterranean. Burton is now in Alexandria, Egypt.

[2]**Kayf:** In a coarser sense "kayf" is applied to all manner of intoxication. Sonnini is not wrong when he says, "the Arabs give the name of Kayf to the voluptuous relaxation, the delicious stupor, produced by the smoking of hemp." [Burton's note]

---

[3]**"Ernst . . . Leben":** life is earnest.

[4]**Tawarah:** Arab tribes. **Bedouin:** nomadic Arabs of the desert.

courage is beyond a doubt. Those travellers who complain of their insolence and extortion may have been either ignorant of their language or offensive to them by assumption of superiority,—in the Desert man meets man,—or physically unfitted to acquire their esteem.

We journeyed on till near sunset through the wilderness without ennui. It is strange how the mind can be amused amid scenery that presents so few objects to occupy it. But in such a country every slight modification of form or color rivets observation: the senses are sharpened, and the perceptive faculties, prone to sleep over a confused shifting of scenery, act vigorously when excited by the capability of embracing each detail. Moreover desert views are eminently suggestive; they appeal to the Future, not to the Past; they arouse because they are by no means memorial. To the solitary wayfarer there is an interest in the wilderness unknown to Cape seas and Alpine glaciers, and even to the rolling Prairie,—the effect of continued excitement on the mind, stimulating its powers to their pitch. Above, through a sky terrible in its stainless beauty, and the splendors of a pitiless blinding glare, the Simoom[5] caresses you like a lion with flaming breath. Around lie drifted sand heaps, upon which each puff of wind leaves its trace in solid waves, flayed rocks, the very skeletons of mountains, and hard unbroken plains, over which he who rides is spurred by the idea that the bursting of a water-skin, or the pricking of a camel's hoof would be a certain death of torture,—a haggard land infested with wild beasts, and wilder men,—a region whose very fountains murmur the warning words "Drink and away!" What can be more exciting? what more sublime? Man's heart bounds in his breast at the thought of measuring his puny force with Nature's might, and of emerging triumphant from the trial. This explains the Arab's proverb, "Voyaging is a Victory." In the Desert even more than upon the ocean, there is present death: hardship is there, and piracies, and shipwreck—solitary, not in crowds, where, as the Persians say, "Death is a Festival,"—and this sense of danger, never absent, invests the scene of travel with an interest not its own.

Let the traveller who suspects exaggeration leave the Suez road for an hour or two, and gallop northwards over the sands: in the drear silence, the solitude, and the fantastic desolation of the place, he will feel what the Desert may be. And then the Oases, and little lines of fertility—how soft and how beautiful!—even though the Wady El Ward (the Vale of Flowers) be the name of some stern flat upon which a handful of wild shrubs blossom while struggling through a cold season's ephemeral existence.

---

[5]**Simoom**: sandstorm, wind.

In such circumstances the mind is influenced through the body. Though your mouth glows, and your skin is parched, yet you feel no languor, the effect of humid heat; your lungs are lightened, your sight brightens, your memory recovers its tone, and your spirits become exuberant; your fancy and imagination are powerfully aroused, and the wildness and sublimity of the scenes around you stir up all the energies of your soul—whether for exertion, danger, or strife. Your morale improves: you become frank and cordial, hospitable and single-minded: the hypocritical politeness and the slavery of civilisation are left behind you in the city. Your senses are quickened: they require no stimulants but air and exercise,—in the Desert spirituous liquors excite only disgust. There is a keen enjoyment in mere animal existence. The sharp appetite disposes of the most indigestible food, the sand is softer than a bed of down, and the purity of the air suddenly puts to flight a dire cohort of diseases. Hence it is that both sexes, and every age, the most material as well as the most imaginative of minds, the tamest citizen, the most peaceful student, the spoiled child of civilisation, all feel their hearts dilate, and their pulses beat strong, as they look down from their dromedaries upon the glorious Desert. Where do we hear of a traveller being disappointed by it? It is another illustration of the ancient truth that Nature returns to man, however unworthily he has treated her. And believe me, gentle reader, that when once your tastes have conformed to the tranquillity of such travel, you will suffer real pain in returning to the turmoil of civilisation. You will anticipate the bustle and the confusion of artificial life, its luxury and its false pleasures, with repugnance. Depressed in spirits, you will for a time after your return feel incapable of mental or bodily exertion. The air of cities will suffocate you, and the care-worn and cadaverous countenances of citizens will haunt you like a vision of judgment. . . . (Chapter 8)

1855

from The Lake Regions of Central Africa

. . . Nothing, in sooth, could be more picturesque than this first view of the Tanganyika Lake, as it lay in the lap of the mountains, basking in the gorgeous tropical sunshine. Below and beyond a short foreground of rugged and precipitous hill-fold, down which the foot-path zigzags painfully, a narrow strip of emerald green, never sere and marvellously fertile, shelves towards a ribbon of glistening yellow sand, here bordered by sedgy rushes, there cleanly and clearly cut by the breaking wavelets. Further in front stretch the waters, an expanse of the lightest and softest blue, in breadth varying from thirty to thirty-five miles, and sprinkled by the crisp east-wind with tiny crescents of snowy foam. The background in front is a high and broken wall of steel-coloured mountain, here flecked and capped with pearly mist, there standing sharply pencilled against the azure air; its yawning chasms, marked by a deeper plum-colour, fall towards dwarf hills of mound-like proportions, which apparently dip their feet in the wave. To the south, and opposite the long low point, behind which the Malagarazi River discharges the red loam suspended in its violent stream, lie the bluff headlands and capes of Uguhha, and, as the eye dilates, it falls upon a cluster of outlying islets, speckling a sea-horizon. Villages, cultivated lands, the frequent canoes of the fishermen on the waters, and on a nearer approach the murmurs of the waves breaking upon the shore, give a something of variety, of movement, of life to the landscape, which, like all the fairest prospects in these regions, wants but a little of the neatness and finish of Art,—mosques and kiosks, palaces and villas, gardens and orchards—contrasting with the profuse lavishness and magnificence of nature, and diversifying the unbroken *coup d'œil*[1] of excessive vegetation, to rival, if not to excel, the most admired scenery of the classic regions. The riant shores of this vast crevasse appeared doubly beautiful to me after the silent and spectral mangrove-creeks on the East-African seaboard, and the melancholy, monotonous experience of desert and jungle scenery, tawny rock and sun-parched plain or rank herbage and flats of black mire. Truly it was a revel for soul and sight! Forgetting toils, dangers, and the doubtfulness of return, I felt willing to endure double what I had endured; and all the party seemed to join with me in joy. . . . (Chapter 18)

1860

---

[1]*coup d'œil*: look.

ISABEL BURTON

(1831–1896)

Isabel Arundell was walking along a seaside promenade in France, bored and restless after a glittering London debut, when she saw Richard Burton and fell instantly in love. The Arundells were an aristocratic Catholic family; Burton, belonging neither to their class nor to their religion, just returned from India with no money and a brilliant but dubious reputation, was hardly a fit suitor for their daughter. Five years later, however, Richard and Isabel formed a secret engagement, and in 1861, ten years after their first meeting, they married. They lived together in Brazil, Syria, and Trieste, and she sometimes accompanied him to wilder areas. "A traveler's wife," she explained in *The Inner Life of Syria, Palestine, and the Holy Land* (1875),

> must cultivate certain capabilities—ride well, walk, swim, shoot, and learn to defend herself if attacked, so as not to be entirely dependent upon the husband; also to make the bed, arrange the tent, cook the dinner if necessary, wash the clothes by the river side, mend and spread them to dry—for his comfort; nurse the sick, bind and dress wounds, pick up a language, make a camp of natives love, respect, and obey her; groom her own horse, saddle him, learn to wade him through rivers; sleep on the ground with the saddle for a pillow, and generally learn to rough it, and do without comforts.

Besides publishing two books about her travels and a biography of her husband, Burton left materials for an autobiography that was completed by W. H. Wilkins (1860–1905) after she died. She also contributed to her husband's literary endeavors, dealing with publishers, helping to edit and proofread his works, writing a preface in which she criticized his tolerance of polygamy, and working with him to expurgate the *Arabian Nights* for a "Household Edition." Her happiest time was in Damascus, where Burton was consul from 1869 to 1871, as shown in the following excerpt.

from The Romance of Isabel Lady Burton: The Story of Her Life

. . . I must add that when we were in the East Richard and I made a point of leading two lives. We were always thoroughly English in our Consulate, and endeavoured to set an example of the way in which England should be represented abroad, and in our official life we strictly conformed to English customs and conventions; but when we were off duty, so to speak, we used to live a great deal as natives, and so obtained experience of the inner Eastern life. Richard's friendship with the Mohammedans, and his perfect mastery of the Arabic and Persian languages and literature, naturally put him into intimate relations with the oriental authorities and the Arab tribes, and he was always very popular among them, with one exception, and that was the Turkish Wali, or Governor, aforesaid. Richard was my guide in all things; and since he adapted himself to the native life, I endeavoured to adapt myself to it also, not only because it was my duty, but because I loved it. For instance, though we always wore European dress in Damascus and Beyrout, we wore native dress in the desert. I always wore the men's dress on our expeditions in the desert and up the country. By that I mean the dress of the Arab men. This is not so dreadful as Mrs. Grundy[1] may suppose, as it was all drapery, and does not show the figure. There was nothing but the face to show the curious whether you were a man or a woman, and I used to tuck my *kuffiyyah* up to only show my eyes. When we wore Eastern clothes, we always ate as the Easterns ate. If I went to a bazar, I frequently used to dress like a Moslem woman with my face covered, and sit in the shops and let my Arab maid do the talking. They never suspected me, and so I heard all their gossip and entered into something of their

lives. The women frequently took me into the mosque in this garb, but to the harím[2] I always went in my European clothes. Richard and I lived the Eastern life thoroughly, and we loved it.

We went to every kind of ceremony, whether it was a circumcision, or a wedding, or a funeral, or a dervish dance, or anything that was going on; and we mixed with all classes, and religions, and races, and tongues. I remember my first invitation was to a grand *fête* to celebrate the circumcision of a youth about ten years of age. He was very pretty, and was dressed in gorgeous garments covered with jewellery. Singing, dancing, and feasting went on for about three days. The ceremony took place quite publicly. There was a loud clang of music and firing of guns to drown the boy's cries, and with one stroke of a circular knife the operation was finished in a second. The part cut off was then handed round on a silver salver, as if to force all present to attest that the rite had been performed. I felt quite sick, and English modesty overpowered curiosity, and I could not look. Later on, when I grew more used to Eastern ways, I was forced to accept the compliment paid to the highest rank, and a great compliment to me as a Christian, to hold the boy in my arms whilst the ceremony was being performed. It was rather curious at first to be asked to a circumcision, as one might be asked to a christening in England or a "small and early."[3]

For the first three months of my life at Damascus I only indulged in short excursions, but Richard went away on longer expeditions, often for days, sometimes on business and sometimes to visit the Druze chiefs. I have said that our house was about a quarter of an hour from Damascus, and whilst Richard was away on one of these expeditions I broke through a stupid rule. It was agreed that I could never

---

[1] **Mrs. Grundy:** personification of censorious propriety. *kuffiyyah:* head covering.

[2] **harím:** harem, women's part of the house.

[3] **"small and early":** small evening party that ends early.

dine out or go to a *soirée* in Damascus, because after sunset the roads between Damascus and our house on the hillside were infested with Kurds. I was tired of being "gated"[4] in this way, so I sent to the Chief of the Police, and told him I intended to dine out when I chose and where I chose, and to return at all hours—any hours I pleased. He looked astonished, so I gave him a present. He looked cheerful, and I then told him to make it his business that I was never to be attacked or molested. I showed him my revolver, and said, "I will shoot the first man who comes within five yards of me or my horse." I went down twice to Damascus while Richard was away the first time, and I found all the gates of the city open and men posted with lanterns everywhere. I took an escort of four of my servants, and I told them plainly that the first man who ran away I would shoot from behind. I came back one night at eleven o'clock, and another at two o'clock in the morning, and nothing happened.

When I knew that Richard was coming back from the desert, I rode out to meet him about eight miles. I did not meet him until sunset. He said he knew a short cut to Damascus across the mountains, but we lost our way. Night came on, and we were wandering about amongst the rocks and precipices on the mountains. We could not see our hands before our faces. Our horses would not move, and we had to dismount, and grope our way, and lead them. Richard's horse was dead-beat, and mine was too fiery; and we had to wait till the moon rose, reaching home at last half dead with fatigue and hunger.

Our daily life at Damascus, when we were not engaged in any expedition or excursion, was much as follows: We rose at daybreak. Richard went down every day to his Consulate in the city at twelve o'clock, and remained there till four or five. We had two meals a day—breakfast at 11 a.m., and supper at dusk. At the breakfast any of our friends and acquaintances who liked used to drop in and join us; and immediately after our evening meal we received friends, if any came. If not, Richard used to read himself to sleep, and I did the same. Of Richard's great and many activities at Damascus, of his difficult and dangerous work, of his knowledge of Eastern character and Eastern languages, of his political and diplomatic talents, all of which made him just the man for the place, I have written elsewhere. Here I have to perform the infinitely harder task of speaking of myself. But in writing of my daily life at Damascus I must not forget that my first and best work was to interest myself in all my husband's pursuits, and to be, as far as he would allow me to be, his companion, his private secretary, and his *aide-de-camp*. Thus I saw and learnt much, not only of native life, but also of high political matters. I would only say that my days were all too short: I wish they had been six hours longer. When not helping Richard, my work consisted of looking after my house, servants, stables and horses, of doing a little gardening, of reading, writing, and studying, of trying to pick up Arabic, of receiving visits and returning them, of seeing and learning Damascus thoroughly, and looking after the poor and sick who came in my way. I often also had a gallop over the mountains and plains; or I went shooting, either on foot or on horseback. The game was very wild round Damascus, but I got a shot at red-legged partridges, wild duck, quail, snipe, and woodcock, and I seldom came home with an empty bag. The only time I ever felt lonely was during the long winter nights when Richard was away. In the summer I did not feel lonely, because I could always go and smoke a narghîleh[5] with the women at the water-side in a neighbour's garden. But in the winter it was not possible to do this. So I used to occupy myself with music or literature, or with writing these rough notes, which I or some one else will put together some day. But more often than not I sat and listened to the stillness, broken ever and anon by weird sounds outside.

So passed our life at Damascus. (Chapter 12)

1897

GEORGE OTTO TREVELYAN

(1838–1928)

The Revolt or "Mutiny" of 1857 decisively changed British attitudes toward India. Indian troops killed their British officers, the British retaliated, and violence spread across the country. The immediate cause was believed to be a rumor spread among the troops that they had been issued rifle cartridges greased with cows' and pigs' fat: since the cartridges had to be bitten before being loaded, this would have meant violating both Hindu and Moslem religious taboos. The most notorious events occurred at Cawnpore, in northern India, where British women and children were hacked to death and their bodies thrown into a well. When the British regained control they killed large numbers of people, including civilians, with great cruelty. The British government then took over the administration of India from the East India Company, sent more troops, and thereafter attended more seriously to the business of administration and control. Racist attitudes hardened among the British: Indians were popularly depicted as cruel, treacherous, lascivious, and superstitious, and their political grievances aroused little support.

The events at Cawnpore produced a flood of writing, of which the young George Trevelyan's account was probably, after the reports in periodicals, the most influential. In 1862 Trevelyan had gone to India, where he served for a year as private secretary to his father, the minister of finance. He quickly produced a series of letters from a fictional Englishman, which appeared first in periodicals and then, much revised, as a book. Our first selection describes the pleasant life of an English administrator in peaceful times; other letters record Trevelyan's deepening conviction that too many Englishmen were crudely unsympathetic and ferociously unjust to the native population of India. *Cawnpore*, in which he endeavors to see how the uprising appeared from the Indian point of view even as he voices his belief in European superiority, was written after his return to England.

Trevelyan entered Parliament as a Liberal in 1865. He later held high political office, became an eminent historian, and wrote a biography of his uncle, Thomas Babington Macaulay.

from The Indian Civil Service

I have lately witnessed some phases of life in India which have little in common with Calcutta grandeur and civilisation. To begin with the travelling, I spent sixteen hours on the four hundred miles between the capital and Patna, and eighteen hours on the forty miles between Patna and Mofussilpore. I started late in the evening in the time-honoured palanquin.[1] My suite comprised sixteen bearers, two men with torches, and four porters carrying my baggage. At five o'clock next afternoon we had still an hour's journey before us; so that I sent on the bearers and the baggage, and walked into the station alone.

It was nearly dark when I arrived at the Collectorate,[2] where my cousin Tom welcomed me warmly, if the idea of warmth can be connected with anything pleasant in such a climate as this. There was a large dinner-party in the evening, and every guest on his arrival was duly acquainted

---

[1]palanquin: a covered conveyance carried by four or six **bearers**.

[2]**Collectorate**: The Collector of revenue was magistrate and chief administrator in an Indian district.

with my having performed the last four miles of my journey on foot. It was very amusing to observe the incredulity with which this statement was received by some, and the hilarity which it excited in others. One or two old Indians were seriously put out at such a piece of enthusiastic folly; and a young Assistant-magistrate, who had won the mile race at Eton, and who, in the long vacation before he came out, had discovered three passes in Switzerland, talked of my "superabundant energy" with the languid pity of an Oriental voluptuary. From the moment when he is cheated in the purchase of his first buggy by a third-hand dealer in Calcutta, to the time when, amidst an escort of irregular cavalry, he dashes through wondering villages in all the state of a Lieutenant-Governor, your true civil servant never goes a-foot on the high-road for a hundred yards together. And this does not proceed from indolence or effeminacy: for a Mofussil[3] official, on the most dim rumour of bear or tiger, will carry his gun for days over ground that would heartily disgust an English sportsman. But horses and grooms and fodder are so cheap out here, and the standard of incomes so high, that no one need walk except for pleasure; and the pleasure of walking in Bengal is, to say the very least, equivocal. . . .

The Indian Civil Service is undoubtedly a very fine career. Here is Tom Goddard, in his thirty-first year, in charge of a population as numerous as that of England in the reign of Elizabeth. His Burghley is a Joint Magistrate of eight-and-twenty, and his Walsingham an Assistant-Magistrate who took his degree at Christ Church[4] within the last fifteen months. These, with two or three Superintendents of Police,—and last, but by no means least, a Judge, who in rank and amount of salary, stands to Tom in the position which the Lord Chancellor holds to the Prime Minister,— are the only English officials in a province a hundred and twenty miles by seventy. . . .

Work in India is so diversified as to be always interesting. During the cold season, the Collector travels about his district, pitching his camp for a night at one place, and for three days at another; while at the larger towns he may find sufficient business to occupy him for a week. Tent-life in the winter months is very enjoyable, especially to a man who has his heart in his duties. It is pleasant, after having spent the forenoon in examining schools and inspecting infirmaries, and quarrelling about the sites of bridges with the Superintending Engineer in the Public Works Department, to take a light tiffin, and start off with your gun and your Assistant-Magistrate on a roundabout ride to the next camping-ground. It is pleasant to dismount at a likely piece of grass, and, flushing a bouncing black partridge, to wipe the eye[5] of your subordinate; and then to miss a hare, which your bearer knocks over with a stick, pretending to find the marks of your shot in its fore-quarter. It is pleasant, as you reach the rendezvous in the gloaming, rather tired and very dusty, to find your tents pitched, and your soup and curry within a few minutes of perfection, and your kitmudgar[6] with a bottle of lemonade, just drawn from its cool bed of saltpetre, and the head man of the village ready with his report of a deadly affray that would have taken place if you had come in a day later. Is not this better than the heartsickness of briefs deferred; the dreary chambers, and the hateful lobby;[7] the hopeless struggle against the sons of attorneys and the nephews of railway-directors; the petition to be put into one of the law offices, that you may eat a piece of bread? Is it not better than grinding year after year at the school-mill, teaching the young idea how to turn good English verses into bad Latin; stopping the allowances, and paring down the journey-money, and crowding as many particles into an iambic line as the metre will bear? Is it not better than hanging wearily on at college; feeling your early triumphs turn to bitterness; doubting whether to class yourself with the old or the young; seeing around you an ever-changing succession of lads, who, as fast as they grow to be friends and companions to you, pass away into the world, and are no more seen?

During ten months in the year the Collector resides at the station. The Government does not provide its servants with house-room; but they seldom experience any inconvenience in finding suitable accommodation, for the native landlords make a point of reserving for every official the residence which had been occupied by his predecessor. No advance in terms will tempt them to let the Judge's bungalow to any but the Judge, or to turn the Joint Sahib[8] out of the dwelling which has been appropriated to Joint Sahibs ever since that class of functionaries came into being. They charge a very moderate rent, which includes the cost of

---

[3]**Mofussil**: rural districts.

[4]William Cecil, 1st Baron **Burghley** (1520–1598), Sir Francis **Walsingham** (1532–1590): principal advisers to Elizabeth I. **Christ Church**: a college of Oxford University.

[5]**wipe the eye**: kill the game another shooter missed.

[6]**kitmudgar**: servant who waits at table.

[7]Hope **deferred** maketh the heart sick (Proverbs 13:12). **briefs**: case summaries for a lawyer's use; to receive a brief is to be hired to conduct a case in court. **chambers**: lawyers' offices. **lobby**: of Parliament

[8]**Sahib**: title used to address Englishmen.

gardeners and sweepers for the use of the tenant. This is an effect of the passion for conferring obligations upon men in authority which exists in the mind of every Hindoo. The life of a Collector in the Mofussil is varied and bustling even in the hot weather. He rises at daybreak, and goes straight from his bed to the saddle. Then off he gallops across fields bright with dew to visit the scene of the late Dacoit[9] robbery; or to see with his own eyes whether the crops of the Zemindar who is so unpunctual with his assessment have really failed; or to watch with fond parental care the progress of his pet embankment. Perhaps he has a run with the bobbery pack of the station, consisting of a superannuated foxhound, four beagles, a greyhound, the doctor's retriever, and a Skye terrier belonging to the Assistant-Magistrate, who unites in his own person the offices of M. F. H., huntsman, and whipper-in. They probably start a jackal, who gives them a smart run of ten minutes, and takes refuge in a patch of sugar-cane: whence he steals away in safety while the pack are occupied in mobbing a fresh fox and a brace of wolf-cubs, to the delight of a remarkably full field of five sportsmen, with one pair of top-boots amongst them. On their return, the whole party adjourn to the subscription swimming-bath, where they find their servants ready with clothes, razors, and brushes. After a few headers, and "chota hasaree," or "little breakfast," of tea and toast, flavoured with the daily papers and scandal about the Commissioner, the Collector returns to his bungalow, and settles down to the hard business of the day. Seated under a punkah in his veranda, he works through the contents of one despatch-box after another; signing orders, and passing them on to the neighbouring Collectors; dashing through drafts, to be filled up by his subordinates; writing Reports, Minutes, Digests, letters of explanation, of remonstrance, of warning, of commendation. Noon finds him quite ready for a *déjeûner à la fourchette*,[10] the favourite meal in the Mofussil, where the tea-tray is lost amidst a crowd of dishes,—fried fish, curried fowl, roast kid and mint-sauce, and mango-fool. Then he sets off in his buggy to Cutcherry, where he spends the afternoon in hearing and deciding questions connected with land and revenue. If the cases are few, and easy to be disposed of, he may get away in time for three or four games at rackets in the new court of glaring white plaster, which a rich native has built, partly as a speculation, and partly to please the Sahibs. Otherwise, he drives with his wife on the race-course; or plays at billiards with the Inspector of Police; or, if horticulturally inclined, superintends the labours of his Mollies.[11] Then follows dinner, and an hour of reading or music. By ten o'clock he is in bed, with his little ones asleep in cribs, enclosed within the same mosquito curtains as their parents. . . .

The drawbacks of Indian life begin to be severely felt when it becomes necessary to send the first-born home.[12] From that period, until his final retirement, there is little domestic comfort for the father of the family. After two or three years have gone by, and two or three children have gone home, your wife's spirits are no longer what they were. She is uneasy for days after a letter has come in with the Brighton[13] post-mark. At last there arrives a sheet of paper scrawled over in a large round hand, and smeared with tears and dirty fingers, which puts her beside herself. You wake two or three times in the night always to find her crying at your side; and the next morning you write to the agent of the P. and O. to engage places for a lady and ayah.[14] At the end of the six months she writes to say that the doctor has insisted on the child's going to Nice[15] for the winter, and that she must stay to take him; and shortly afterwards you receive a communication from your mother-in-law, to the effect that you must give her daughter another summer in England, under pain of the lifelong displeasure of that estimable relative. And so it goes on till, after the lapse of some three or four years, your wife joins you at the Presidency[16] in a state of wild delight at meeting you, and intense misery at finding herself again in India. Within the next two hot seasons she has had three fevers. She tries the hills, but it will not do; and at last you make up your mind to the inevitable, and run down to Calcutta to take your seat at the Board of Revenue and despatch her to England, with a tacit understanding that she is never to return. Then you settle down into confirmed bachelor habits, until one day in August, when all Chowringhee is a vast vapour-bath, you feel, in the region of your liver, an unusually smart touch of the pain which has been constantly recurring during the last eighteen months, and it strikes you that your

---

[9]**Dacoit:** robber band. **Zemindar:** Indian landowner who paid revenues to the British. **bobbery:** poor quality. **M.F.H.:** Master of Foxhounds; head of the hunt.

[10]*déjeûner à la fourchette:* fork luncheon.

[11]**Mollies:** gardeners.

[12]**send . . . home:** Children were sent back to England for schooling and to escape the dangers of the climate.

[13]**Brighton:** in England.

[14]**P. and O.:** Peninsular and Orient shipping company. **ayah:** Indian nurse for children.

[15]**Nice:** city in S France.

[16]**Presidency:** seat of government of one of three divisions of the East India Company's territory.

clever idle son will be more likely to pass his competitive examination if you are on the spot to superintend his studies. So you resign your seat in Council, accept a farewell dinner from your friends, who by this time comprise nearly the whole of Calcutta society, and go on board at Garden Reach, under a salute from the guns of Fort William and an abusive article in the *Hurkaru*[17] on your infatuated predilection for the natives. . . .

1863, 1905

from Cawnpore

. . . We had, indeed, been negligent. We had been improvident even to madness. Some twenty thousand European troops were scattered over the continent of India, for the security of which seventy thousand are now held to be barely sufficient. In the May of 1857, from Meerut in the Northwest, to Dinapore in the South-east, two weak British regiments only were to be found. In these days, a battalion of English infantry may be placed at any important city in our dominions within the twenty-four hours. Then, all the field-batteries throughout the entire region of Oude, with a single exception, were manned by native gunners and drivers. Now, in every station on the plains, the artillerymen, the trained workmen of warfare, without whom in modern times an armed force is helpless, are one and all our own countrymen. Then, our only communication was along roads which the first rains turned into strips of bog, and up rivers treacherous with crossing current and changing sandbanks. Now, through the heart of every province, there runs, or soon will run, those lines of rail and lines of wire, which defy alike season and distance. . . . (Chapter 1)

. . . As soon as the Rubicon[1] of insurrection had been passed,—as soon as the gauntlet of sedition had been thrown,—the first care of the mutineers was to get rid of all who had been the witnesses of their guilt, and who might hereafter be the judges. No sepoy felt secure of his neck and plunder as long as one solitary Englishman remained on Indian soil. The revolted soldier desired with a nervous and morbid anxiety to get quit of the Sahibs by fair means or foul. He did not care to expose us to unnecessary misery and humiliation; to torture our men, or to outrage our women. His sole object was to see the last of us: to get done with us for good and for ever. Ignorant beyond conception of European geography and statistics, he had convinced himself that, if once the Anglo-Indians of every sex and age were killed off, from the Governor-General to the Sergeant-major's baby, there did not exist the wherewithal to replace them. He conceived that Great Britain had been drained dry of men to recruit the garrison of our Asiatic empire; that our home population consisted of nurses and children, of invalids who had left the East for a while in quest of health, and veterans who had retired to live at ease on their share of the treasures of Hindostan. He fancied that the tidings of a general massacre of our people would render our island a home of helpless mourners: he found that those tidings changed it into a nest of pitiless avengers. He believed our power to be a chimera, and he discovered it to be a hydra. He learned too late that he had digged a pit[2] for himself, and had fallen into the ditch which he had made: that his mischief and his violent dealings had come down upon his own head: that Englishmen were many, and that, when the occasion served, their feet too were not slow to shed blood: that our soldiers could kill within the year more heathen than our missionaries had converted in the course of a century: that our social science talk about the sacredness of human life, and our May Meeting[3] talk concerning our duty towards those benighted souls for whom Christ died, meant that we were to forgive most of those who had never injured us, and seldom hang an innocent Hindoo if we could catch a guilty one: that the great principles of mercy and justice and charity must cease to be eternally true until the injured pride of a mighty nation had been satisfied, its wrath glutted, and its sway restored.

But though apprehension and dislike had inspired the rebels with a determination to destroy every Englishman off the face of the land, had they no feeling of ruth for the sufferings and the fate of our women? Never in European warfare has the sword been deliberately pointed at a female breast; save during those rare seasons, indelible from memory and inexpiable by national remorse, when, after the mad carnage of a successful escalade, drunkenness and

---

[17]*Hurkaru:* English-language periodical published in Bengal.

[1]**Rubicon:** river crossed by Julius Caesar, marking the start of a war; a decisive, irrevocable step. **sepoy:** Indian soldier under British command.

[2]**chimera:** fantastic mythical beast. **hydra:** mythical many-headed snakelike beast whose heads grow back when cut off. **digged a pit:** see Psalms 7:15–16.

[3]**May Meeting:** annual meeting of religious and philanthropic societies.

licence have ruled the hour. If the Nana[4] knew the valour and strength of our officers too well to allow him to be merciful, how came it that he did not respect the weakness of our ladies? No one can rightly read the history of the mutineers unless he constantly takes into account the wide and radical difference between the views held by Europeans and Asiatics with reference to the treatment and position of the weaker sex. We who live among the records and associations of chivalry still make it our pride to regard women as goddesses. The Hindoos, who allow their sisters and daughters few or no personal rights; the Mohammedans, who do not even allow them souls; cannot bring themselves to look upon them as better than playthings. The pride of a Mussulman servant is painfully wounded by a scolding from the mistress of the house, and he takes every opportunity of showing his contempt for her by various childish impertinences. Among the numberless symptoms of our national eccentricity, that which seems most extraordinary to a native is our submitting to be governed by a woman. And as a Hindoo fails to appreciate the social standing of an English lady, so it is to be feared that he gives her little credit for her domestic virtues. Her free and unrestrained life excites in his mind the most singular and unjust ideas. To see women walking in public, driving about in open carriages, dining, and talking, and dancing with men connected with them neither by blood nor marriage, never fails to produce upon him a false and unfortunate impression. And therefore it happened that a sepoy corporal, whose estimate of a European lady was curiously compounded of contempt, disapprobation, and misconception, was little adapted to entertain for her sentiments of knightly tenderness and devotion. In the eyes of such a man every Englishwoman was but the mother of an English child, and every English child was a sucking tyrant. The wolves, with their mates and whelps, had been hounded into their den, and now or never was the time to smoke them out, and knock on the head the whole of that formidable brood. And so, on the first Saturday of that June,—these, bent on a wholesale butchery: those, prepared to play the man for their dear life, and for lives dearer still,—with widely different hope, but with equal resolution, on either side of the meagre rampart, besiegers and besieged mustered for the battle. (Chapter 2)

1865

---

[4]**Nana** Sahib (1821?–1859?): a leader of the sepoys at Cawnpore.

JAMES ANTHONY FROUDE

(1818–1894)

At a time when the colonies were regarded by many in Britain as an unnecessary burden, James Anthony Froude—an eminent journalist and historian, and Carlyle's biographer—wielded his considerable rhetorical powers to argue that they drained off excess population, provided a wholesome alternative to the industrialization and urbanization of England, and established loyal offshoots of the mother country around the globe. He set forth his case most fully in *Oceana, or England and Her Colonies* (1886), describing his travels to places in South Africa, Australia, New Zealand, and North America where Europeans, driving out or destroying relatively small indigenous populations, came to settle rather than rule. Froude's conception of a greater Britain, globally united by language, religion, and (not least) literary tradition, resumes and extends the Condition of England question treated in our first Contexts section. At the same time, his concern with national degeneracy in the essay printed here—published in 1870, the year Parliament finally instituted compulsory elementary education—forms part of the combustible mix of eugenics with economics that would impel fin-de-siècle imperialism.

from England and Her Colonies

During the last quarter of a century, nearly four million British subjects—English, Irish, and Scots—have become citizens, more or less prosperous, of the United States of America. We have no present quarrel with the Americans; we trust most heartily that we may never be involved in any quarrel with them; but undoubtedly from the day that they became independent of us, they became our rivals. They constitute the one great power whose interests and whose pretensions compete with our own, and in so far as the strength of nations depends on the number of thriving men and women composing them, the United States have been made stronger, the English empire weaker, to the extent of those millions and the children growing of them. The process is still continuing. Emigration remains the only practical remedy for the evils of Ireland. England and Scotland contain as many people as in the present condition of industry they can hold. The annual increase of the population has to be drafted off and disposed of elsewhere, and while the vast proportion of it continues to be directed on the shores of the Republic, those who leave us, leave us for the most part resenting the indifference with which their loss is regarded. They part from us as from a hard stepmother. They are exiles from a country which was the home of their birth; which they had no desire to leave, but which drives them from her at the alternative of starvation.

England at the same time possesses dependencies of her own, not less extensive than the United States, not less rich in natural resources, not less able to provide for these expatriated swarms, where they would remain attached to her Crown, where their well-being would be our well-being, their brains and arms our brains and arms, every acre which they could reclaim from the wilderness, so much added to English soil, and themselves and their families fresh additions to our national stability. . . .

Now it is against all experience that any nation can long remain great which does not possess, or having once possessed has lost, a hardy and abundant peasantry. Athens lost her dependencies, and in two generations the sun of Athens had set. The armies which made the strength of the Roman republic were composed of the small freeholders of Latium and afterwards of Italy. When Rome became an empire, the freeholder disappeared; the great families bought up the soil and cultivated it with slaves, and the decline and fall followed by inevitable consequence. . . . The life of cities brings with it certain physical consequences, for which no antidote and no preventive has yet been discovered. When vast numbers of people are crowded together, the air they breathe becomes impure, the water polluted. The hours of work are unhealthy, occupation passed largely within doors thins the blood and wastes the muscles and creates a craving for drink, which reacts again as poison. The town child rarely sees the sunshine; and light, it is well known, is one of the chief feeders of life. What is worse, he rarely or never tastes fresh milk or butter; or even bread which is unbewitched. The rate of mortality may not be perceptibly affected. The Bolton operative may live as long as his brother on the moors, but though bred originally perhaps in the same country home he has not the same bone and stature, and the contrast between the children and grandchildren will be increasingly marked. Any one who cares to observe a gathering of operatives in Leeds or Bradford and will walk afterwards through Beverley[1] on a market day, will see two groups which, comparing man to man, are like pigmies beside giants. A hundred labourers from the wolds would be a match for a thousand weavers. The tailor confined to his shop-board has been called the ninth part of a man. There is nothing special in the tailor's work so to fractionize him beyond other indoor trades. We shall be breeding up a nation of tailors. In the great engine factories and iron works we see large sinewy men, but they are invariably country born. Their children dwindle as if a blight was on them. Artisans and operatives of all sorts who work in confinement are so exhausted at the end of their day's labour that the temptations of the drink-shop are irresistible. As towns grow drunkenness grows, and with drunkenness comes diminished stamina and physical decrepitude. . . .

If we are to take hostages of the future we require an agricultural population independent of and beside the towns. We have no longer land enough in England commensurate with our present dimensions, and the land that we have lies under conditions which only a revolution can again divide among small cultivators. A convulsion which would break up the great estates would destroy the entire constitution. It is not the law of the land, it is not custom, it is not the pride of family, which causes the agglomeration. It is an economic law which legislation can no more alter than it can alter the law of gravity.

The problem is a perfectly simple one. Other nations, once less powerful or not more powerful than ourselves, are growing in strength and numbers, and we too must grow if we intend to remain on a level with them. Here at home we

---

[1]**Bolton, Leeds, Bradford:** great industrial cities. **Beverley:** a beautiful market town.

have no room to grow except by the expansion of towns which are already overgrown, which we know not certainly that we can expand. If we succeed it can be only under conditions unfavourable and probably destructive to the physical constitution of our people, and our greatness will be held by a tenure which in the nature of things must become more and more precarious.

Is there then no alternative? Once absolutely our own, and still easily within our reach, are our eastern and western colonies, containing all and more than all that we require. We want land on which to plant English families where they may thrive and multiply without ceasing to be Englishmen. The land lies ready to our hand. The colonies contain virgin soil sufficient to employ and feed five times as many people as are now crowded into Great Britain and Ireland. Nothing is needed but arms to cultivate it; while here, among ourselves, are millions of able-bodied men unwillingly idle, clamouring for work, with their families starving on their hands. What more simple than to bring the men and the land together? Everything which we could most desire exactly meeting what is most required is thrust into our hands, and this particular moment is chosen to tell the colonies that we do not want them and they may go. The land, we are told impatiently, is no longer ours. A few years ago it was ours, but to save the Colonial Office trouble we made it over to the local governments, and now we have no more rights over it than we have over the prairies of Texas. If it were so, the more shame to the politicians who let drop so precious an inheritance. But the colonies, it seems, set more value than we do on the prosperity of the empire. They care little for the profit or pleasure of individual capitalists. They see their way more clearly perhaps because their judgment is not embarrassed by considerations of the Chancellor of the Exchequer's budget. Conscious that their relations with us cannot continue on their present footing, their ambition is to draw closer to us, to be absorbed in a united empire. From them we have no difficulty to fear, for in consenting they have everything to gain. They are proud of being English subjects. Every able-bodied workman who lands on their shores is so much added to their wealth as well as ours. If we do not attempt to thrust paupers and criminals on them, but send labourers and their families adequately provided, they will absorb our people by millions,

while in desiring to remain attached to England they are consulting England's real interests as entirely as their own. Each husband and wife as they establish themselves will be a fresh root for the old tree, struck into a new soil. . . .

For emigration, the first step is the only hard one; to do for England what Ireland did for itself, and at once spread over the colonies the surplus population for whom we can find no employment at home. Once established on a great scale, emigration supports itself. Every Irishman who now goes to the United States, has his expenses paid by those who went before him, and who find it their own interest, where there is such large elbow-room, to attract the labour of their friends. It would cost us money—but so do wars; and for a great object we do not shrink from fighting. Let it be once established that an Englishman emigrating to Canada, or the Cape, or Australia, or New Zealand, did not forfeit his nationality, that he was still on English soil as much as if he was in Devonshire or Yorkshire, and would remain an Englishman while the English empire lasted; and if we spent a quarter of the sums which were sunk in the morasses at Balaclava in sending out and establishing two millions of our people in those colonies, it would contribute more to the essential strength of the country than all the wars in which we have been entangled from Agincourt to Waterloo.[2] No further subsidies would be needed to feed the stream. Once settled they would multiply and draw their relations after them, and at great stations round the globe there would grow up, under conditions the most favourable which the human constitution can desire, fresh nations of Englishmen. So strongly placed, and with numbers growing in geometrical proportion, they would be at once feeding-places of our population, and self-supporting imperial garrisons themselves unconquerable. With our roots thus struck so deeply into the earth, it is hard to see what dangers, internal or external, we should have cause to fear, or what impediments could then check the indefinite and magnificent expansion of the English Empire. . . .

1870, 1871

---

[2]**Balaclava**: site of a battle (1854) in the Crimean War. England defeated France at **Agincourt** in 1415 and at **Waterloo** in 1815.

EDWARD BURNETT TYLOR

(1832–1917)

At sixteen Edward Tylor joined his Quaker family's brass business. In his mid-twenties, having gone to America to look for business opportunities, he traveled for four months in Mexico and became fascinated by the people he saw there. When he returned to England he educated himself in the subject matter of current ethnology, particularly comparative linguistics and mythology, and in 1896 he became Oxford University's first professor of anthropology. Arguing from a Victorian liberal position that all humankind was essentially one, his major work, *Primitive Culture*, developed an evolutionary model of cultural development with European peasants as the link between primitive "savages" and "civilized" modern Europeans. In the spirit of Darwin, Tylor tried to show that people everywhere had similar mental processes, even if the higher intellectual faculties developed only in more advanced societies. Although he was long regarded as having founded modern cultural anthropology as the "scientific" study of human societies, his hierarchical presuppositions (loosely but clearly correlated with skin color, hemisphere, and latitude) are very different from the cultural relativism and pluralism that later informed the discipline. It should be noted that Tylor, like other pioneering nineteenth-century anthropologists, worked largely from materials compiled by explorers, missionaries, colonial and military officials, and other travelers rather than doing fieldwork himself.

from Primitive Culture

Culture or Civilization, taken in its wide ethnographic sense, is that complex whole which includes knowledge, belief, art, morals, law, custom, and any other capabilities and habits acquired by man as a member of society. The condition of culture among the various societies of mankind, in so far as it is capable of being investigated on general principles, is a subject apt for the study of laws of human thought and action. On the one hand, the uniformity which so largely pervades civilization may be ascribed, in great measure, to the uniform action of uniform causes; while on the other hand its various grades may be regarded as stages of development or evolution, each the outcome of previous history, and about to do its proper part in shaping the history of the future. To the investigation of these two great principles in several departments of ethnography, with especial consideration of the civilization of the lower tribes as related to the civilization of the higher nations, the present volumes are devoted. . . .

Surveyed in a broad view, the character and habit of mankind at once display that similarity and consistency of phenomena which led the Italian proverb-maker to declare that "all the world is one country," "tutto il mondo è paese." To general likeness in human nature on the one hand, and to general likeness in the circumstances of life on the other, this similarity and consistency may no doubt be traced, and they may be studied with especial fitness in comparing races near the same grade of civilization. Little respect need be had in such comparisons for date in history or for place on the map; the ancient Swiss lake-dweller may be set beside the mediæval Aztec, and the Ojibwa of North America beside the Zulu of South Africa. As Dr. Johnson contemptuously said when he had read about Patagonians and South Sea Islanders in Hawkesworth's Voyages,[1] "one set of savages is like another." How true a generalization this really

---

[1] Samuel **Johnson's** (1709–1784) friend John **Hawkesworth** (1715?–1773) published an official account of various voyages to the South Seas in 1773.

is, any Ethnological Museum may show. Examine for instance the edged and pointed instruments in such a collection; the inventory includes hatchet, adze, chisel, knife, saw, scraper, awl, needle, spear and arrow-head, and of these most or all belong with only differences of detail to races the most various. So it is with savage occupations; the wood-chopping, fishing with net and line, shooting and spearing game, fire-making, cooking, twisting cord and plaiting baskets, repeat themselves with wonderful uniformity in the museum shelves which illustrate the life of the lower races from Kamchatka to Tierra del Fuego, and from Dahome to Hawaii. Even when it comes to comparing barbarous hordes with civilized nations, the consideration thrusts itself upon our minds, how far item after item of the life of the lower races passes into analogous proceedings of the higher, in forms not too far changed to be recognized, and sometimes hardly changed at all. Look at the modern European peasant using his hatchet and his hoe, see his food boiling or roasting over the log-fire, observe the exact place which beer holds in his calculation of happiness, hear his tale of the ghost in the nearest haunted house, and of the farmer's niece who was bewitched with knots in her inside till she fell into fits and died. If we choose out in this way things which have altered little in a long course of centuries, we may draw a picture where there shall be scarce a hand's breadth difference between an English ploughman and a negro of Central Africa. . . .

. . . By comparing the various stages of civilization among races known to history, with the aid of archæological inference from the remains of pre-historic tribes, it seems possible to judge in a rough way of an early general condition of man, which from our point of view is to be regarded as a primitive condition, whatever yet earlier state may in reality have lain behind it. This hypothetical primitive condition corresponds in a considerable degree to that of modern savage tribes, who, in spite of their difference and distance, have in common certain elements of civilization, which seem remains of an early state of the human race at large. If this hypothesis be true, then, notwithstanding the continual interference of degeneration, the main tendency of culture from primæval up to modern times has been from savagery towards civilization. On the problem of this relation of savage to civilized life, almost every one of the thousands of facts discussed in the succeeding chapters has its direct bearing. Survival in Culture, placing all along the course of advancing civilization way-marks full of meaning to those who can decipher their signs, even now sets up in our midst primæval monuments of barbaric thought and life. Its investigation tells strongly in favour of the view that

the European may find among the Greenlanders or Maoris many a trait for reconstructing the picture of his own primitive ancestors. . . . (Chapter 1)

. . . Arrest and decline in civilization are to be recognized as among the more frequent and powerful operations of national life. That knowledge, arts, and institutions should decay in certain districts, that peoples once progressive should lag behind and be passed by advancing neighbours, that sometimes even societies of men should recede into rudeness and misery—all these are phenomena with which modern history is familiar. In judging of the relation of the lower to the higher stages of civilization, it is essential to gain some idea how far it may have been affected by such degeneration. What kind of evidence can direct observation and history give as to the degradation of men from a civilized condition towards that of savagery? In our great cities, the so-called "dangerous classes" are sunk in hideous misery and depravity. If we have to strike a balance between the Papuans of New Caledonia and the communities of European beggars and thieves, we may sadly acknowledge that we have in our midst something worse than savagery. But it is not savagery; it is broken down civilization. Negatively, the inmates of a Whitechapel casual ward[2] and of a Hottentot kraal agree in their want of the knowledge and virtue of the higher culture. But positively, their mental and moral characteristics are utterly different. Thus, the savage life is essentially devoted to gaining subsistence from nature, which is just what the proletarian life is not. Their relations to civilized life—the one of independence, the other of dependence—are absolutely opposite. To my mind the popular phrases about "city savages" and "street Arabs" seem like comparing a ruined house to a builder's yard. . . .

It is apparent, from such general inspection of this ethnological problem, that it would repay a far closer study than it has as yet received. As the evidence stands at present, it appears that when in any race some branches much excel the rest in culture, this more often happens by elevation than by subsidence. But this elevation is much more apt to be produced by foreign than by native action. Civilization is a plant much oftener propagated than developed. As regards the lower races, this accords with the results of European intercourse with savage tribes during the last three

---

[2]**Whitechapel casual ward:** hospital ward for the poor in East End of London. **Hottentot:** now pejorative name for the Khoikhoin people of South Africa. **kraal:** village, community.

or four centuries; so far as these tribes have survived the process, they have assimilated more or less of European culture and risen towards the European level, as in Polynesia, South Africa, South America. Another important point becomes manifest from this ethnological survey. The fact that, during so many thousand years of known existence, neither the Aryan nor the Semitic stock appears to have thrown off any direct savage offshoot recognizable by the age-enduring test of language, tells, with some force, against the probability of degradation to the savage level ever happening from high-level civilization. . . .

In the various branches of the problem which will henceforward occupy our attention, that of determining the relation of the mental condition of savages to that of civilized men, it is an excellent guide and safeguard to keep before our minds the theory of development in the material arts. Throughout all the manifestations of the human intellect, facts will be found to fall into their places on the same general lines of evolution. The notion of the intellectual state of savages as resulting from decay of previous high knowledge, seems to have as little evidence in its favour as that stone celts are the degenerate successors of Sheffield[3] axes, or earthen grave-mounds degraded copies of Egyptian pyramids. The study of savage and civilized life alike avail us to trace in the early history of the human intellect, not gifts of transcendental wisdom, but rude shrewd sense taking up the facts of common life and shaping from them schemes of primitive philosophy. It will be seen again and again, by examining such topics as language, mythology, custom, religion, that savage opinion is in a more or less rudimentary state, while the civilized mind still bears vestiges, neither few nor slight, of a past condition from which savages represent the least, and civilized men the greatest advance. Throughout the whole vast range of the history of human thought and habit, while civilization has to contend not only with survival from lower levels, but also with degeneration within its own borders, it yet proves capable of overcoming both and taking its own course. History within its proper field, and ethnography over a wider range, combine to show that the institutions which can best hold their own in the world gradually supersede the less fit ones, and that this incessant conflict determines the general resultant course of culture. I will venture to set forth in mythic fashion how progress, aberration, and retrogression in the general course of culture contrast themselves in my own mind. We may fancy ourselves looking on Civilization, as in personal figure she traverses the world; we see her lingering or resting by the way, and often deviating into paths that bring her toiling back to where she had passed by long ago; but, direct or devious, her path lies forward, and if now and then she tries a few backward steps, her walk soon falls into a helpless stumbling. It is not according to her nature, her feet were not made to plant uncertain steps behind her, for both in her forward view and in her onward gait she is of truly human type. (Chapter 2)

1871

---

[3]**celts**: prehistoric chisels. **Sheffield**: major center of Victorian steelmaking.

HENRY MORTON STANLEY

(1841–1904)

In Henry Morton Stanley's accounts of his travels, late British imperialism displays with unabashed complacency its self-righteous rapacity, its violence, its contempt for indigenous populations, and its assumption that the earth belongs to Europeans and especially to Englishmen. Stanley himself had struggled hard to forge his English identity. Brought up from the age of six in a brutally inhumane workhouse (an institution for the poor), he had made his way in 1859 from England to America, where he took the name of a friendly cotton broker in New Orleans, became an American citizen, and served on both sides in the Civil War before becoming a correspondent for American newspapers and an African explorer based in Britain. During 1874–1877 and 1879–1884 he was in Central Africa almost continuously. He helped to establish the Belgian regime in the Congo that became infamous for its cruelty and inspired Joseph Conrad's *Heart of Darkness* (1899).

In Darkest Africa records a large armed expedition (1887–1890) during which Stanley lost many of his forces but made wide-ranging explorations in areas of East Africa that then came under British rule. Back in England he was received as a hero; becoming once more a British subject, he was awarded official honors and served in Parliament from 1895 to 1900. He also became famous for comically exemplifying Victorian travel writers' insistence on maintaining a well-bred British nonchalance even in the most unlikely circumstances. When, on an arduous expedition in Central Africa to find the missionary-explorer David Livingstone, Stanley came upon him at last, he took off his hat and inquired, "Dr. Livingstone, I presume?"

from In Darkest Africa

. . . This was on the 28th day of June, and until the 5th of December, for 160 days, we marched through the forest, bush and jungle, without ever having seen a bit of greensward of the size of a cottage chamber floor. Nothing but miles and miles, endless miles of forest, in various stages of growth and various degrees of altitude, according to the ages of the trees, with varying thickness of undergrowth according to the character of the trees which afforded thicker or slighter shade. It is to the description of the march through this forest and to its strange incidents I propose to confine myself for the next few chapters, as it is an absolutely unknown region opened to the gaze and knowledge of civilized man for the first time since the waters disappeared and were gathered into the seas, and the earth became dry land. Beseeching the reader's patience, I promise to be as little tedious as possible, though there is no

other manuscript or missal, printed book or pamphlet, this spring of the year of our Lord 1890, that contains any account of this region of horrors other than this book of mine.

With the temperature of 86° in the shade we travelled along a path very infrequently employed, which wound under dark depths of bush. It was a slow process, interrupted every few minutes by the tangle. The bill-hooks and axes, plied by fifty men, were constantly in requisition; the creepers were slashed remorselessly, lengths of track one hundred yards or so were as fair as similar extents were difficult.

At noon we looked round the elbow of the Aruwimi, which is in view of Yambuya,[1] and saw above, about four miles, another rapid with its glancing waters as it waved in rollers in the sunshine; the rapids of Yambuya were a little below us. Beneath the upper rapids quite a fleet of canoes

---

[1]Yambuya: a series of villages.

hovered about it. There was much movement and stir, owing, of course, to the alarm that the Yambuyas had communicated to their neighbours. At 4 p.m. we observed that the point we had gazed at abreast of the rapids consisted of islands. These were now being crowded with the women and children of Yankondé, whom as yet we had not seen. About a hundred canoes formed in the stream crowded with native warriors, and followed the movements of the column as it appeared and disappeared in the light and into the shadows, jeering, mocking, and teasing.

The head of the column arrived at the foot of a broad cleared road, twenty feet wide and three hundred yards long, and at the further end probably three hundred natives of the town of Yankondé stood gesticulating, shouting, with drawn bows in their hands. In all my experience of Africa I had seen nothing of this kind. The pioneers halted, reflecting, and remarking somewhat after this manner: "What does this mean? The pagans have carved a broad highway out of the bush to their town for us, and yet there they are at the other end, ready for a fight! It is a trap, lads, of some kind, so look sharp."

With the bush they had cut they had banked and blocked all passage to the forest on either side of the road for some distance. But, with fifty pairs of sharp eyes searching around above and below, we were not long in finding that this apparent highway through the bush bristled with skewers six inches long sharpened at both ends, which were driven into the ground half their length, and slightly covered with green leaves so carelessly thrown over them that we had thought at first these strewn leaves were simply the effect of clearing bush.

Forming two lines of twelve men across the road, the first line was ordered to pick out the skewers, the second line was ordered to cover the workers with their weapons, and at the first arrow shower to fire. A dozen scouts were sent on either flank of the road to make their way into the village through the woods. We had scarcely advanced twenty yards along the cleared way before volumes of smoke broke out of the town, and a little cloud of arrows came towards us, but falling short. A volley was returned, the skewers were fast being picked out, and an advance was steadily made until we reached the village at the same time that the scouts rushed out of the underwood, and as all the pioneers were pushed forward the firing was pretty lively, under cover of which the caravan pressed through the burning town to a village at its eastern extremity, as yet unfired.

Along the river the firing was more deadly. The very noise was sufficient to frighten a foe so prone as savages to rely on the terrors of sound, but unfortunately the noise was as hurtful as it was alarming. Very many, I fear, paid the penalty of the foolish challenge. The blame is undoubtedly due to the Yambuyas, who must have invented fables of the most astounding character to cause their neighbours to attempt stopping a force of nearly four hundred rifles.

It was nearly 9 p.m. before the rear-guard entered camp. Throughout the night the usual tactics were resorted to by the savages to create alarm and disturbance, such as vertically dropping assegais[2] and arrows heavily tipped with poison, with sudden cries, whoops, howls, menaces, simultaneous blasts of horn-blowing from different quarters, as though a general attack was about to be made. Strangers unacquainted with the craftiness of these forest satyrs might be pardoned for imagining that daylight only was required for our complete extermination. Some of these tactics I knew before in younger days, but there was still something to be gleaned from the craft of these pure pagans. The camp was surrounded by sentries, and the only orders given were to keep strict silence and sharpen their eyesight.

In the morning a narrow escape was reported. A man had wakened to find a spear buried in the earth, penetrating his sleeping cloth and mat on each side of him, slightly pinning him to his bedding. Two were slightly wounded with arrows. . . . (Chapter 7)

1890

---

[2]**assegais**: spears.

MARY KINGSLEY

(1862–1900)

The daughter of a globe-trotting physician and his cook, who married four days before she was born, Mary Kingsley grew up in almost total isolation, with no schooling except what she could forage in her father's library or her younger brother's schoolbooks. Her self-education centered on science; her imagination was fired by travel books. In 1884 the family moved to Cambridge, but her mother's chronic invalidism forced Kingsley to spend much of her time at home. After both parents died in 1892, she fulfilled her long-standing dream of traveling to Africa. On foot and in dugout canoes she made her way through West African swamps and forests, wearing long black skirts, white blouses, stays, and hairpins, collecting specimens of fish and other creatures, and studying indigenous legal and religious systems.

After her second trip, Kingsley became a successful lecturer and wrote two very popular books. She responded with delight to the beauty of the natural world and defended African customs, including polygamy. She hoped the British would learn to see the colonies as opportunities for mutually satisfactory trade, without attempting to impose European values or interfere with local culture. "The fascination of the African point of view," she wrote, "is as sure to linger in your mind as the malaria in your body. Never then will you be able to attain to the gay, happy cocksureness regarding the Deity and the Universe of those people who stay at home." The relentlessly facetious tone of her lively narrative barely disguises her attachment to the people and places she describes, while downplaying her own courage and fortitude. Restless to go "home" to West Africa, she went as a nurse with British troops to South Africa, where she died of fever caught nursing Boer prisoners of war.

from Travels in West Africa

... It was the beginning of August '93 when I first left England for "the Coast." Preparations of quinine[1] with postage partially paid arrived up to the last moment, and a friend hastily sent two newspaper clippings, one entitled "A Week in a Palm-oil Tub," which was supposed to describe the sort of accommodation, companions, and fauna likely to be met with on a steamer going to West Africa, and on which I was to spend seven to The Graphic contributor's one; the other

from *The Daily Telegraph*, reviewing a French book of "Phrases in common use" in Dahomey. The opening sentence in the latter was, "Help, I am drowning." Then came the inquiry, "If a man is not a thief?" and then another cry, "The boat is upset." "Get up, you lazy scamps," is the next exclamation, followed almost immediately by the question, "Why has not this man been buried?" "It is fetish[2] that has killed him, and he must lie here exposed with nothing on him until only the bones remain," is the cheerful answer. This sounded discouraging to a person whose occupation would necessitate going about considerably in boats, and whose fixed desire was to study fetish. So with a feeling of foreboding gloom I left London for Liverpool—none the

---

[1]**"Coast"**: of W Africa. Kingsley landed first in Sierra Leone; these excerpts describe part of an inland journey in Gabon (then the French Congo). **quinine**: used medicinally, primarily to bring down fever.

[2]**fetish**: animistic religious beliefs.

more cheerful for the matter-of-fact manner in which the steamboat agents had informed me that they did not issue return tickets by the West African lines of steamers. . . . (Introduction)

. . . About four o'clock we struck some more plantations, and passing through these, came to a path running north-east, down which we went. I must say the forest scenery here was superbly lovely. Along this mountain side cliff to the mangrove-swamp the sun could reach the soil, owing to the steepness and abruptness and the changes of curves of the ground; while the soft steamy air which came up off the swamp swathed everything, and although unpleasantly strong in smell to us, was yet evidently highly agreeable to the vegetation. Lovely wine palms and rafia palms, looking as if they had been grown under glass, so deliciously green and profuse was their feather-like foliage, intermingled with giant red woods, and lovely dark glossy green lianes, blooming in wreaths and festoons of white and mauve flowers, which gave a glorious wealth of beauty and colour to the scene. Even the monotony of the mangrove-belt alongside gave an additional charm to it, like the frame round a picture.

As we passed on, the ridge turned N. and the mangrove line narrowed between the hills. Our path now ran east and more in the middle of the forest, and the cool shade was charming after the heat we had had earlier in the day. We crossed a lovely little stream coming down the hillside in a cascade; and then our path plunged into a beautiful valley. We had glimpses through the trees of an amphitheatre of blue mist-veiled mountains coming down in a crescent before us, and on all sides, save due west where the mangrove-swamp came in. Never shall I forget the exceeding beauty of that valley, the foliage of the trees round us, the delicate wreaths and festoons of climbing plants, the graceful delicate plumes of the palm trees, interlacing among each other, and showing through all a background of soft, pale, purple-blue mountains and forest, not really far away, as the practised eye knew, but only made to look so by the mist, which has this trick of giving suggestion of immense space without destroying the beauty of detail. Those African misty forests have the same marvellous distinctive quality that Turner[3] gives one in his greatest pictures. I am no artist, so I do not know exactly what it is, but I see it is there. I luxuriated in the exquisite beauty of that

valley, little thinking or knowing what there was in it besides beauty, as Allah "in mercy hid the book of fate."[4] On we went among the ferns and flowers until we met a swamp, a different kind of swamp to those we had heretofore met, save the little one last mentioned. This one was much larger, and a gem of beauty; but we had to cross it. It was completely furnished with characteristic flora. Fortunately when we got to its edge we saw a woman crossing before us, but unfortunately she did not take a fancy to our appearance, and instead of staying and having a chat about the state of the roads, and the shortest way to N'dorko, she bolted away across the swamp. I noticed she carefully took a course, not the shortest, although that course immersed her to her arm-pits. In we went after her, and when things were getting unpleasantly deep, and feeling highly uncertain under foot, we found there was a great log of a tree under the water which, as we had seen the lady's care at this point, we deemed it advisable to walk on. All of us save one, need I say that one was myself, effected this with safety. As for me, when I was at the beginning of the submerged bridge, and busily laying about in my mind for a definite opinion as to whether it was better to walk on a slippy tree trunk bridge you could see, or on one you could not, I was hurled off by that inexorable fate that demands of me a personal acquaintance with fluvial and paludial ground deposits; whereupon I took a header, and am thereby able to inform the world, that there is between fifteen and twenty feet of water each side of that log. I conscientiously went in on one side, and came up on the other. The log, I conjecture, is dum or ebony, and it is some fifty feet long; anyhow it is some sort of wood that won't float. I really cannot be expected, by the most exigent of scientific friends, to go botanising under water without a proper outfit. Gray Shirt says it is a bridge across an under-swamp river. Having survived this and reached the opposite bank, we shortly fell in with a party of men and women, who were taking, they said, a parcel of rubber to Holty's.[5] They told us N'dorko was quite close, and that the plantations we saw before us were its outermost ones, but spoke of a swamp, a bad swamp. We knew it, we said, in the foolishness of our hearts thinking they meant the one we had just forded, and leaving them resting, passed on our way; half-a-mile further on we were wiser and sadder, for then we stood on the rim of one of the biggest swamps I have ever seen south of the

---

[3] J. M. W. **Turner** (1775–1851): English landscape painter.

[4] "**in . . . fate**": see Alexander Pope, "An Essay on Man" (1733) 1.77.

[5] **Gray Shirt**: like **Singlet** (below), a name bestowed by Kingsley. **Holty's**: agent for the trading firm of John Holt.

Rivers. It stretched away in all directions, a great sheet of filthy water, out of which sprang gorgeous marsh plants, in islands, great banks of screw pine, and coppices of wine palm, with their lovely fronds reflected back by the still, mirror-like water, so that the reflection was as vivid as the reality, and above all remarkable was a plant,[6] new and strange to me, whose pale-green stem came up out of the water and then spread out in a flattened surface, thin, and in a peculiarly graceful curve. This flattened surface had growing out from it leaves, the size, shape and colour of lily of the valley leaves; until I saw this thing I had held the wine palm to be the queen of grace in the vegetable kingdom, but this new beauty quite surpassed her.

Our path went straight into this swamp over the black rocks forming its rim, in an imperative, no alternative, "Come-along-this-way" style. Singlet, who was leading, carrying a good load of bottled fish and a gorilla specimen, went at it like a man, and disappeared before the eyes of us close following him, then and there down through the water. He came up, thanks be, but his load is down there now, worse luck. Then I said we must get the rubber carriers who were coming this way to show us the ford; and so we sat down on the bank a tired, disconsolate, dilapidated-looking row, until they arrived. When they came up they did not plunge in forthwith; but leisurely set about making a most nerve-shaking set of preparations, taking off their clothes, and forming them into bundles, which, to my horror, they put on the tops of their heads. The women carried the rubber on their backs still, but rubber is none the worse for being under water. The men went in first, each holding his gun high above his head. They skirted the bank before they struck out into the swamp, and were followed by the women and by our party, and soon we were all up to our chins.

We were two hours and a quarter passing that swamp. I was one hour and three-quarters; but I made good weather of it, closely following the rubber-carriers, and only going in right over head and all twice. Other members of my band were less fortunate. One finding himself getting out of his depth, got hold of a palm frond and pulled himself into deeper water still, and had to roost among the palms until a special expedition of the tallest men went and gathered him like a flower. Another got himself much mixed up and scratched because he thought to make a short cut through screw pines. He did not know the screw pine's little ways, and he had to have a special relief expedition. One and all, we got horribly infested with leeches, having a frill of them round our necks like astrachan collars, and our hands covered with them, when we came out. The depth of the swamp is very uniform, at its ford we went in up to our necks, and climbed up on to the rocks on the hither side out of water equally deep.

Knowing you do not like my going into details on such matters, I will confine my statement regarding our leeches, to the fact that it was for the best that we had some trade salt with us. It was most comic to see us salting each other; but in spite of the salt's efficacious action I was quite faint from loss of blood, and we all presented a ghastly sight as we made our way on into N'dorko. Of course the bleeding did not stop at once, and it attracted flies and—but I am going into details, so I forbear. . . . (Chapter 13)

1897

---

[6]**a plant**: Specimen placed in Herbarium at Kew. [Kingsley's note] **Kew** is a botanical garden in London.

THE FUNCTION OF POETRY

A READER WHO approaches Victorian writing about poetry with expectations formed on Romantic defenses or Modernist manifestos will probably be disappointed. Perhaps only Matthew Arnold and Oscar Wilde are in the highest rank of poet-critics; the vein of meditation on language and verse in Gerard Manley Hopkins' journals and letters, while glorious, is a glorious exception. It is not that Victorian poets had less to say about their art than those who came before or after. They wrote about the theory and practice of poetry often, and incisively; but they did this best in their poems. In Elizabeth Barrett Browning's *Aurora Leigh* the narrator-protagonist both examines and enacts the role of a poet in Victorian society. The young Robert Browning's elliptical opus *Sordello* (1840) is about a poet trying to tell the story of a poet trying to understand what being a poet means. Alfred Tennyson's friend Arthur Hallam speaks eloquently about Tennyson's early poetics in the essay excerpted here, but the poet himself gives a more complex and troubled account of the matter in "The Lady of Shalott." So it is with poets who were also serious essayists: while A. C. Swinburne's rhapsodism inspired his book on Blake, its full expression required the surge of his verses; and Augusta Webster's dramatic monologues put to proof the issues of language and identity she discussed as a columnist in prose. These poets were enacting their ideas; they were not hiding them. Still, the student of Victorian poetics will seek in vain for direct authorial statements of purpose like those of S. T. Coleridge or T. S. Eliot.

The major Victorian prose writers also wrote about poetry from time to time, usually with genuine engagement but rarely with their usual clarity and penetration. There is something endearing in the candid philistinism with which Charles Darwin in his autobiography confesses his immunity to sublime verse and his preference for novels with happy endings, and even in Thomas Carlyle's crotchety assertions that Browning and others should abandon poetry for prose. But the frequent obtuseness of critical response among essayists powerfully susceptible to imaginative influence is harder to understand: Cardinal Newman's fondness for the puerile oriental fantasias of Robert Southey; John Ruskin's contempt for Romantic projections of imaginative feeling onto inanimate nature, which he calls the "pathetic fallacy"; Arnold's dismissal of Dryden and Pope as "classics of our prose" and of Chaucer and Burns as lacking in "high seriousness."

Such parochial reactions in high places reveal a structural opposition within the Victorian literary system: an opposition between the experience of literature and critical analysis, between feeling a poem and thinking about it. Newman's surrender to romantic fantasy and Ruskin's reproof of Romantic fancy are two sides of the same coin; and Arnold's verdict against the great satirists and humorists shows that, when it came to poetry, the side of feeling was uppermost. Victorian literary theory wanted to keep poetry as a haven for emotion, safe from violation by the chilly analytics of science and business. The reviews of poetry that swelled Victorian periodicals might be effusive or opprobrious about the poet's soul and quote the poetry at great length, but they rarely came to grips with specific passages—as if close reading were bad manners. Nothing illustrates this better than John Stuart Mill's rigorously logical conclusion that poetry is spontaneous feeling, transfused immediately from poet to reader, and so unaware of its audience as to seem accidentally "overheard." Mill framed this argument shortly after regular doses of lyric poetry had helped rescue him from depression brought on by inveterate intellectual analysis; poetry had worked for the young Utilitarian, and in order to maximize its utility he wanted it pure—which is to say, as free as possible from contamination by the brain. No wonder the analytic faculty of Victorian criticism slumbered, or else burrowed back into creative writing to produce, as the era's salient new genres, the hybrid verse novel and the ironic, self-critical dramatic monologue.

Victorian poetry was not in itself escapist, as has sometimes been charged; but there is a sense in which the operative Victorian poetic was. Where poets aimed to *make* poetry, readers and reviewers and critics aimed to *use* it—an aim largely governed by the general rise in Victorian consumerism, with its diversification of market desires and satisfactions. The term *literature*, which had once denoted all the kinds of writing belonging to the province of letters (history, philosophy, and so on), was gradually restricted to the sense it retains today, for which the former name was *poetry*. *Poetry* in turn came to mean verse and to be associated especially with lyric modes of intimacy and introspection. Mill's early question "What is poetry?" thus became an inquiry into what poetry did or might do for the reader or for the culture. What use was poetry? Detractors trivialized it as a leisure-time hobby, acknowledging its prestige in former ages but affirming its supersession, in all things that mattered, by the efficiency of prose and the modern division of intellectual labor. Defenders, remarkably, conceded this major premise—poetry's disconnection from the currency of the modern—only to conjure from it a new prestige. They claimed an aura for poetry that was entirely separate from the force that drove business and ran society. Poetry had essential cultural work to do in the training of sensibility and the preservation of feeling, the multiplication of refined enjoyments and the refurbishing of the restless human spirit. But it could do this work only by staying out of the world's way, in its separate aesthetic sphere. The use of poetry lay precisely in being, as Wilde said all art was, "quite useless."

Much of the smartest Victorian work in poetics appears in essays and poems elsewhere in this anthology. The excerpts here should serve to outline the main lines of Victorian concern with the quality of literary feeling and with the uses to which such feeling may be put. George Eliot's topic is prose fiction, not poetry; yet her stress on "the secret of deep human sympathy" implicitly unites novelists and poets in their moral responsibility to connect sympathetic feeling and social duty. Alfred Austin and Robert Buchanan around 1870 take this responsibility for granted, while worrying both that contemporary poetry is feebly inauthentic and that it stimulates sympathies of entirely the wrong kind. At either end of the period Arthur Hallam and Arthur Symons assert poetry's duty to render sensation with originality and truth—virtues that were forced into near identity by avant-garde reactions against the pressures of industrial society.

The pervasive presence of vividly gendered images and categories in all these writings is neither a coincidence nor a deliberate editorial contrivance. Gendered discourse was intrinsic to Victorian poetics. Hallam focused on Tennyson's "female characters," Eliot produced "an old woman bending over her flower-pot," Austin and Buchanan showed signs of free-floating sexual panic, Symons evinced the ambiguously effete manner of the fin-de-siècle aesthete, because poetry itself had assumed a conventionally feminine position within culture. Revered in theory but disregarded in practice, atop a fine pedestal off on the sidelines, poetry had a paradoxical status that those who wrote about it might deplore or exploit, but could not ignore.

ARTHUR HENRY HALLAM

(1811–1833)

The cerebral hemorrhage that killed Arthur Hallam at twenty-two extinguished a promise so impressive that figures of great renown—Alfred Tennyson the Poet Laureate and W. E. Gladstone the Prime Minister—later remembered it as the most brilliant of their generation. Hallam was born to signal advantages: education at Eton and Cambridge, travel abroad, wealth, and the cachet of his father's fame as an historian. To these gifts of privilege he added an open and affectionate sensibility, as well as a personal charisma that made him a debating star at Eton, put him at the head of the Cambridge "Apostles" (an ambitious and distinguished undergraduate society), and sufficed years later to inspire Gladstone's poignant reminiscences and Tennyson's masterpiece *In Memoriam A. H. H.* Hallam's *Remains in Verse and Prose*, privately published in 1834, displayed a modest poetic talent, an impressive command of reading in ancient and modern languages, a fund of rhetorical self-confidence, and some accomplished literary criticism and speculative philosophy. The most important piece he himself saw into print, excerpted here, was a review in the out-of-the-way *Englishman's Magazine* of Tennyson's 1830 *Poems, Chiefly Lyrical*. The conversancy Hallam shows with Romantic poetry, which he treats as nearly contemporary but not quite—Keats and Shelley had been alive within the decade, Wordsworth and Coleridge were living yet—shows that early nineteenth-century poetics were very much under construction, and that Hallam stood ready to challenge Wordsworth's critical authority publicly by appealing at the distance of a half-generation to the still controversial poetic practice of Shelley and Keats. The emphasis Hallam places on sensation rather than reflection, and the intuitive subtlety of sense which he identifies as modern poetry's cutting edge, chart a course that major developments in Victorian and then modernist poetics will follow. The certainty that Hallam composed his review with the approval of Tennyson, whose intimate friend he was and to whose sister he had just become engaged, gives extra weight to its ideas about the predominance of mood and the fusion of perception with emotion.

from On Some of the Characteristics of Modern Poetry, and on the Lyrical Poems of Alfred Tennyson

... It is not true, as his[1] exclusive admirers would have it, that the highest species of poetry is the reflective; it is a gross fallacy, that because certain opinions are acute or profound, the expression of them by the imagination must be eminently beautiful. Whenever the mind of the artist suffers itself to be occupied, during its periods of creation, by any other predominant motive than the desire of beauty, the result is false in art.

Now there is undoubtedly no reason why he may not find beauty in those moods of emotion, which arise from the combinations of reflective thought; and it is possible that he may delineate these with fidelity, and not be led astray by any suggestions of an unpoetical mood. But though possible, it is hardly probable; for a man whose reveries take a reasoning turn, and who is accustomed to measure his ideas by their logical relations rather than the congruity of the sentiments to which they refer, will be apt to mistake the pleasure he has in knowing a thing to be true, for the pleasure he would have in knowing it to be beautiful, and so will pile his thoughts in a rhetorical battery, that they may convince, instead of letting them flow in a natural course of contemplation, that they may enrapture.

It would not be difficult to shew, by reference to the most admired poems of Wordsworth, that he is frequently chargeable with this error; and that much has been said by him which is good as philosophy, powerful as rhetoric, but false as poetry. Perhaps this very distortion of the truth did more in the peculiar juncture of our literary affairs to enlarge and liberalize the genius of our age, than could have been effected by a less sectarian temper.

However this may be, a new school of reformers soon began to attract attention, who, professing the same independence of immediate favor, took their stand on a different region of Parnassus from that occupied by the Lakers,[2] and one, in our opinion, much less liable to perturbing currents of air from ungenial climates. We shall not hesitate to express our conviction, that the cockney school (as it was termed in derision from a cursory view of its accidental circumstances) contained more genuine inspiration, and adhered more steadily to that portion of truth which it embraced, than any *form* of art that has existed in this country since the days of Milton. Their *caposetta* was Mr. Leigh Hunt,[3] who did little more than point the way, and was diverted from his aim by a thousand personal predilections and political habits of thought.

But he was followed by two men of very superior make; men who were born poets, lived poets, and went poets to their untimely graves. Shelley and Keats were indeed of opposite genius; that of the one was vast, impetuous, and sublime, the other seemed to be "fed with honeydew," and to have "drunk the milk of Paradise."[4] Even the softness of Shelley comes out in bold, rapid, comprehensive strokes; he has no patience for minute beauties, unless they can be massed into a general effect of grandeur. On the other hand, the tenderness of Keats cannot sustain a lofty flight; he does not generalize or allegorize Nature; his imagination works with few symbols, and reposes willingly on what is given freely.

Yet in this formal opposition of character there is, it seems to us, a groundwork of similarity sufficient for the purposes of classification, and constituting a remarkable point in the progress of literature. They are both poets of sensation rather than reflection. Susceptible of the slightest impulse from external nature, their fine organs trembled into emotion at colors, and sounds, and movements, unperceived or unregarded by duller temperaments. Rich and clear were their perceptions of visible forms; full and deep their feelings of music. So vivid was the delight attending the simple exertions of eye and ear, that it became mingled more and more with their trains of active thought, and tended to absorb their whole being into the energy of sense. Other poets *seek* for images to illustrate their conceptions; these men had no need to seek; they lived in a world of images; for the most important and extensive portion of their life consisted in those emotions which are immediately conversant with the sensation. Like the hero of Goethe's novel, they would hardly have been affected by what is called the pathetic parts of a book; but the *merely beautiful*

---

[1]**his**: Wordsworth's. Hallam has in mind the Preface to *Lyrical Ballads* (1800).

[2]**Parnassus**: Greek mountain haunt of the Muses. **Lakers**: Wordsworth, Coleridge, and Robert Southey lived for a time together in the Lake District (NW England).

[3]**Leigh Hunt** (1784–1859): London-based poet and journalist whose essays made him head (*caposetta*) of the so-called **cockney school** including Shelley and Keats.

[4]**"fed ... Paradise"**: from Coleridge's "Kubla Khan" (1816) 53–54.

passages, "those from which the spirit of the author looks clearly and mildly forth,"[5] would have melted them to tears. Hence they are not descriptive, they are picturesque. They are not smooth and *negatively* harmonious; they are full of deep and varied melodies.

This powerful tendency of imagination to a life of immediate sympathy with the external universe, is not nearly so liable to false views of art as the opposite disposition of purely intellectual contemplation. For where beauty is constantly passing before "that inward eye, which is the bliss of solitude;"[6] where the soul seeks it as a perpetual and necessary refreshment to the sources of activity and intuition; where all the other sacred ideas of our nature, the idea of good, the idea of perfection, the idea of truth, are habitually contemplated through the medium of this predominant mood, so that they assume its colour, and are subject to its peculiar laws, there is little danger that the ruling passion of the whole mind will cease to direct its creative operations, or the energetic principle of love for the beautiful sink, even for a brief period, to the level of a mere notion in the understanding.

We do not deny that it is, on other accounts, dangerous for frail humanity to linger with fond attachment in the vicinity of sense. Minds of this description are especially liable to moral temptations; and upon them, more than any, it is incumbent to remember, that their mission as men, which they share with their fellow-beings, is of infinitely higher interest than their mission as artists, which they possess by rare and exclusive privilege. But it is obvious that, critically speaking, such temptations are of slight moment. Not the gross and evident passions of our nature, but the elevated and less separable desires, are the dangerous enemies which misguide the poetic spirit in its attempts at self-cultivation. That delicate sense of fitness which grows with the growth of artist feelings, and strengthens with their strength, until it acquires a celerity and weight of decision hardly inferior to the correspondent judgments of conscience, is weakened by every indulgence of heterogeneous aspirations, however pure they may be, however lofty, however suitable to human nature.

We are therefore decidedly of opinion that the heights and depths of art are most within the reach of those who have received from nature the "fearful and wonderful"[7] con-

stitution we have described, whose poetry is a sort of magic, producing a number of impressions, too multiplied, too minute, and too diversified to allow of our tracing them to their causes, because just such was the effect, even so boundless and so bewildering, produced on their imaginations by the real appearance of Nature.

These things being so, our friends of the new school had evidently much reason to recur to the maxim laid down by Mr. Wordsworth, and to appeal from the immediate judgment of lettered or unlettered contemporaries to the decision of a more equitable posterity. How should they be popular, whose senses told them a richer and ampler tale than most men could understand, and who constantly expressed, because they constantly felt, sentiments of exquisite pleasure or pain, which most men were not permitted to experience? The public very naturally derided them as visionaries, and gibbeted *in terrorem*[8] those inaccuracies of diction occasioned sometimes by the speed of their conceptions, sometimes by the inadequacy of language to their peculiar conditions of thought.

But it may be asked, does not this line of argument prove too much? Does it not prove that there is a barrier between these poets and all other persons so strong and immovable, that, as has been said of the Supreme Essence, we must be themselves before we can understand them in the least? Not only are they not liable to sudden and vulgar estimation, but the lapse of ages, it seems, will not consolidate their fame, nor the suffrages of the wise few produce any impression, however remote or slow matured, on the judgment of the incapacitated many.

We answer, this is not the import of our argument. Undoubtedly the true poet addresses himself, in all his conceptions, to the common nature of us all. Art is a lofty tree, and may shoot up far beyond our grasp, but its roots are in daily life and experience. Every bosom contains the elements of those complex emotions which the artist feels, and every head can, to a certain extent, go over in itself the process of their combination, so as to understand his expressions and sympathize with his state. But this requires exertion; more or less, indeed, according to the difference of occasion, but always some degree of exertion. For since the emotions of the poet, during composition, follow a regular law of association, it follows that to accompany their progress up to the harmonious prospect of the whole, and to perceive the proper dependence of every step on that which preceded, it is absolutely necessary *to start from the same*

---

[5]"those . . . forth": from *Wilhelm Meisters Lehrjahre* (1795–1796) by Johann Wolfgang von **Goethe** (1749–1832), book 5, chapter 6.

[6]"that . . . bliss of solitude": Wordsworth, "I Wandered Lonely as a Cloud" (1807) 21–22.

[7]"fearful and wonderful:" see Psalm 139:14.

[8]*in terrorem*: as a warning.

point, i.e. clearly to apprehend that leading sentiment of the poet's mind, by their conformity to which the host of suggestions are arranged.

Now this requisite exertion is not willingly made by the large majority of readers. It is so easy to judge capriciously, and according to indolent impulse! For very many, therefore, it has become *morally* impossible to attain the author's point of vision, on account of their habits, or their prejudices, or their circumstances; but it is never *physically* impossible, because nature has placed in every man the simple elements, of which art is the sublimation. Since then this demand on the reader for activity, when he wants to peruse his author in a luxurious passiveness, is the very thing that moves his bile, it is obvious that those writers will be always most popular who require the least degree of exertion. Hence, whatever is mixed up with art, and appears under its semblance, is always more favorably regarded than art free and unalloyed. Hence, half the fashionable poems in the world are mere rhetoric, and half the remainder are, perhaps, not liked by the generality for their substantial merits. Hence, likewise, of the really pure compositions, those are most universally agreeable which take for their primary subject the *usual* passions of the heart, and deal with them in a simple state, without applying the transforming powers of high imagination. Love, friendship, ambition, religion, &c., are matters of daily experience even amongst unimaginative tempers. The forces of association, therefore, are ready to work in these directions, and little effort of will is necessary to follow the artist.

For the same reason, such subjects often excite a partial power of composition, which is no sign of a truly poetic organization. We are very far from wishing to depreciate this class of poems, whose influence is so extensive, and communicates so refined a pleasure. We contend only that the facility with which its impressions are communicated is no proof of its elevation as a form of art, but rather the contrary.

What, then, some may be ready to exclaim, is the pleasure derived by most men, from Shakespeare, or Dante, or Homer, entirely false and factitious? If these are really masters of their art, must not the energy required of the ordinary intelligences that come in contact with their mighty genius, be the greatest possible? How comes it then, that they are popular? Shall we not say, after all, that the difference is in the power of the author, not in the tenor of his meditations? Those eminent spirits find no difficulty in conveying to common apprehensions their lofty sense and profound observation of Nature. They keep no aristocratic state, apart from the sentiments of society at large; they speak to the hearts of all, and by the magnetic force of their conceptions, elevate inferior intellects into a higher and purer atmosphere.

The truth contained in this observation is undoubtedly important; geniuses of the most universal order, and assigned by destiny to the most propitious era of a nation's literary development, have a clearer and a larger access to the minds of their compatriots than can ever open to those who are circumscribed by less fortunate circumstances. In the youthful periods of any literature there is an expansive and communicative tendency in mind which produces unreservedness of communion, and reciprocity of vigor between different orders of intelligence.

Without abandoning the ground which has always been defended by the partizans of Mr. Wordsworth, who declare with perfect truth, that the number of real admirers of what is really admirable in Shakespeare and Milton is much fewer than the number of apparent admirers might lead one to imagine, we may safely assert that the intense thoughts set in circulation by those "orbs of song" and their noble satellites "in great Eliza's golden time,"[9] did not fail to awaken a proportionable intensity of the nature of numberless auditors. Some might feel feebly, some strongly; the effect would vary according to the character of the recipient; but upon none was the stirring influence entirely unimpressive. The knowledge and power thus imbibed became a part of national existence; it was ours as Englishmen; and amid the flux of generations and customs we retain unimpaired this privilege of intercourse with greatness.

But the age in which we live comes late in our national progress. That first raciness and juvenile vigor of literature, when nature "wantoned as in her prime, and played at will her virgin fancies" is gone, never to return. Since that day we have undergone a period of degradation. "Every handicraftsman has worn the mask of Poesy." It would be tedious to repeat the tale so often related of the French contagion[10] and the heresies of the Popian school.

With the close of the last century came an era of reaction, an era of painful struggle to bring our over-civilised condition of thought into union with the fresh productive spirit that brightened the morning of our literature. But

---

[9]"**orbs of song**": Wordsworth, *The Excursion* (1814) 1.249. "**in great Eliza's golden time**": Wordsworth, *The White Doe of Rylstone* (1807) 1.42.

[10]"**wantoned . . . virgin fancies**": see Wordsworth, *Descriptive Sketches* (1793), 40, 784. "**Every handicraftsman . . .**": adapted from Keats, "Sleep and Poetry" (1817) 200–01. **French contagion**: 17th- and 18th-century influence of neoclassicism.

repentance is unlike innocence; the laborious endeavor to restore has more complicated methods of action than the freedom of untainted nature. Those different powers of poetic disposition, the energies of Sensitive,[11] of Reflective, of Passionate Emotion, which in former times were intermingled, and derived from mutual support an extensive empire over the feelings of men, were now restrained within separate spheres of agency. The whole system no longer worked harmoniously, and by intrinsic harmony acquired external freedom; but there arose a violent and unusual action in the several component functions, each for itself, all striving to reproduce the regular power which the whole had once enjoyed.

Hence the melancholy which so evidently characterises the spirit of modern poetry; hence that return of the mind upon itself and the habit of seeking relief in idiosyncrasies rather than community of interest. In the old times the poetic impulse went along with the general impulse of the nation; in these it is a reaction against it, a check acting for conservation against a propulsion towards change.

We have indeed seen it urged in some of our fashionable publications, that the diffusion of poetry must be in the direct ratio of the diffusion of machinery, because a highly civilized people must have new objects of interest, and thus a new field will be open to description. But this notable argument forgets that against this *objective* amelioration may be set the decrease of *subjective* power, arising from a prevalence of social activity, and a continual absorption of the higher feelings into the palpable interests of ordinary life. The French Revolution may be a finer theme than the war of Troy; but it does not so evidently follow that Homer is to find his superior.

Our inference, therefore, from this change in the relative position of artists to the rest of the community is, that modern poetry in proportion to its depth and truth is likely to have little immediate authority over public opinion. Admirers it will have; sects consequently it will form; and these strong under-currents will in time sensibly affect the principal stream. Those writers whose genius, though great, is not strictly and essentially poetic, become mediators between

the votaries of art and the careless cravers for excitement. Art herself, less manifestly glorious than in her periods of undisputed supremacy, retains her essential prerogatives, and forgets not to raise up chosen spirits who may minister to her state and vindicate her title.

One of the faithful Islâm, a poet in the truest and highest sense, we are anxious to present to our readers. He has yet written little and published less; but in these "preludes of a loftier strain"[12] we recognize the inspiring god. Mr. Tennyson belongs decidedly to the class we have already described as Poets of Sensation. He sees all the forms of nature with the "eruditus oculus,"[13] and his ear has a fairy fineness. There is a strange earnestness in his worship of beauty which throws a charm over his impassioned song, more easily felt than described, and not to be escaped by those who have once felt it. We think he has more definiteness and roundness of general conception than the late Mr. Keats, and is much more free from blemishes of diction and hasty capriccios of fancy. He has also this advantage over that poet and his friend Shelley, that he comes before the public unconnected with any political party or peculiar system of opinions. Nevertheless, true to the theory we have stated, we believe his participation in their characteristic excellences is sufficient to secure him a share of their unpopularity.

The volume of "Poems, chiefly Lyrical," does not contain above 154 pages; but it shews us much more of the character of its parent mind, than many books we have known of much larger compass and more boastful pretensions. The features of original genius are clearly and strongly marked. The author imitates nobody; we recognise the spirit of his age, but not the individual form of this or that writer. His thoughts bear no more resemblance to Byron or Scott, Shelley or Coleridge, than to Homer or Calderón, Firdúsí or Calidasa.[14]

We have remarked five distinctive excellencies of his own manner. First, his luxuriance of imagination, and at the same time his control over it. Secondly his power of embodying himself in ideal characters, or rather moods of character, with such extreme accuracy of adjustment, that the circumstances of the narration seem to have a natural correspondence with the predominant feeling, and, as it

---

[11]We are aware that this is not the right word, being appropriated by common use to a different signification. Those who think the caution given by Caesar should not stand in the way of urgent occasion, may substitute "sensuous"; a word in use amongst our elder divines, and revived by a few bold writers in our own time. [Hallam's note] **Caesar** famously cautioned his wife against the mere appearance of impropriety.

[12]**"preludes of a loftier strain"**: from Shelley's "Dedication" to *The Revolt of Islam* (1818) 83.

[13]**"eruditus oculus"**: trained eye.

[14]Pedro **Calderón** de la Barca (1600–1681): Spanish dramatist. **Firdúsí**: 10th-century Persian poet. **Calidasa**: 5th-century Sanskrit poet and dramatist.

were, to be evolved from it by assimilative force. Thirdly his vivid, picturesque delineation of objects, and the peculiar skill with which he holds all of them *fused*, to borrow a metaphor from science, in a medium of strong emotion. Fourthly, the variety of his lyrical measures, and exquisite modulation of harmonious words and cadences to the swell and fall of the feelings expressed. Fifthly, the elevated habits of thought, implied in these compositions, and imparting a mellow soberness of tone, more impressive, to our minds, than if the author had drawn up a set of opinions in verse, and sought to instruct the understanding rather than to communicate the love of beauty to the heart. . . .

A considerable portion of this book is taken up with a very singular and very beautiful class of poems on which the author has evidently bestowed much thought and elaboration. We allude to the female characters, every trait of which presumes an uncommon degree of observation and reflection. Mr. Tennyson's way of proceeding seems to be this. He collects the most striking phenomena of individual minds until he arrives at some leading fact, which allows him to lay down an axiom or law; and then, working on the law thus attained, he clearly discerns the tendency of what new particulars his invention suggests, and is enabled to impress an individual freshness and unity on ideal combinations. These expressions of character are brief and coherent; nothing extraneous to the dominant fact is admitted, nothing illustrative of it, and, as it were, growing out of it, is rejected. They are like summaries of mighty dramas. We do not say this method admits of such large luxuriance of power as that of our real dramatists; but we contend that it is a new species of poetry, a graft of the lyric on the dramatic, and Mr. Tennyson deserves the laurel of an inventor, an enlarger of our modes of knowledge and power. . . .

1831

GEORGE ELIOT (MARY ANN EVANS)

(1819–1880)

In her twenties the fervid Evangelical who would become the most esteemed of Victorian novelists moved with her father from the countryside to the Midlands manufacturing town of Coventry. There she found intellectual nurture among Unitarians and freethinkers, lost her former Christian faith, and replaced it with a powerfully moralized agnosticism that drew on the latest Continental ideas in social and cultural theory. By the early 1850s in London she had become the anonymous English translator of skeptical blockbusters from Germany (Strauss's biography of Jesus, Feuerbach's anthropological interpretation of Christianity); a contributing editor, also anonymous, of the liberal *Westminster Review*; and the scrupulously proper but technically scandalous partner of G. H. Lewes, a versatile man of letters who was married without hope of divorce. Later in the decade she embarked as "George Eliot" on a career in prose fiction, first with a set of three tales about small-town life and then, in 1859, with the full-scale historical novel *Adam Bede*, from which the following discussion is taken.

Eliot's apology for the bland worldliness of her Rev. Mr. Irwine, a mere supporting character, turns into an eloquent critical defense of the novel as a literary form and, further, of the representational realism that by 1860 had become the dominant Victorian criterion in art. Poems, plays, histories, statues, paintings—all concurred in a version of the ordinary whose touchstone was bourgeois experience, apprehended from a worldly modern viewpoint and corroborated by a wealth of chiefly domestic things. For Eliot this enumerative realism of description entailed an ethical realism of prescription enjoining sympathy, toleration, and affirmation of the common life. The homely aesthetic that Eliot here enunciates spoke not just for the novel but for other literary genres practiced by a diversity of writers: T. B. Macaulay's history, A. H. Clough's poetry, Margaret Oliphant's memoirs. The mode became so fully naturalized that a succession of avant-garde manifestoes and experiments have labored now for a century and a half to remind the public that realism is not natural, just normal, and that it traffics not in essences but in conventions of representation. The realist conventions that Eliot warmed to in Dutch paintings, and followed in *Adam Bede*, have consistently defined the center from which all such creative departures keep having to depart, even in media undreamed of in her lifetime.

from Adam Bede
In Which the Story Pauses a Little

"This Rector of Broxton is little better than a pagan!" I hear one of my readers exclaim. "How much more edifying it would have been if you had made him give Arthur some truly spiritual advice! You might have put into his mouth the most beautiful things—quite as good as reading a sermon."

Certainly I could, if I held it the highest vocation of the novelist to represent things as they never have been and never will be. Then, of course, I might refashion life and character entirely after my own liking; I might select the most unexceptionable type of clergyman, and put my own admirable opinions into his mouth on all occasions. But it happens, on the contrary, that my strongest effort is to avoid any such arbitrary picture, and to give a faithful account of men and things as they have mirrored themselves in my mind. The mirror is doubtless defective; the outlines will sometimes be disturbed, the reflection faint or confused; but I feel as much bound to tell you as precisely as I can what that reflection is, as if I were in the witness-box narrating my experience on oath.

Sixty years ago—it is a long time, so no wonder things have changed—all clergymen were not zealous; indeed there is reason to believe that the number of zealous clergymen was small, and it is probable that if one among the small minority had owned the livings of Broxton and Hayslope in the year 1799, you would have liked him no better than you like Mr. Irwine. Ten to one, you would have thought him a tasteless, indiscreet, methodistical[1] man. It is

so very rarely that facts hit that nice medium required by our own enlightened opinions and refined taste! Perhaps you will say, "Do improve the facts a little, then; make them more accordant with those correct views which it is our privilege to possess. The world is not just what we like; do touch it up with a tasteful pencil, and make believe it is not quite such a mixed entangled affair. Let all people who hold unexceptionable opinions act unexceptionably. Let your most faulty characters always be on the wrong side, and your virtuous ones on the right. Then we shall see at a glance whom we are to condemn, and whom we are to approve. Then we shall be able to admire, without the slightest disturbance of our prepossessions: we shall hate and despise with that true ruminant relish which belongs to undoubting confidence."

But, my good friend, what will you do then with your fellow-parishioner who opposes your husband in the vestry?—with your newly-appointed vicar, whose style of preaching you find painfully below that of his regretted predecessor?—with the honest servant who worries your soul with her one failing?—with your neighbor, Mrs. Green, who was really kind to you in your last illness, but has said several ill-natured things about you since your convalescence?—nay, with your excellent husband himself, who has other irritating habits besides that of not wiping his shoes? These fellow-mortals, every one, must be accepted as they are: you can neither straighten their noses, nor brighten their wit, nor rectify their dispositions; and it is these people—amongst whom your life is passed—that it is needful you should tolerate, pity, and love: it is these more or less ugly, stupid, inconsistent people, whose movements of goodness you should be able to admire—for whom you should cherish all possible hopes, all possible patience. And I would not, even if I had the choice, be the clever novelist who could create a world so much better than this, in which we get up in the morning to do our daily work, that you

---

[1]**methodistical:** fanatically evangelical. Eliot's novel is set at a date when revivalism was sweeping the English countryside, and her heroine is an open-air methodist preacher.

would be likely to turn a harder, colder eye on the dusty streets and the common green fields—on the real breathing men and women, who can be chilled by your indifference or injured by your prejudice; who can be cheered and helped onward by your fellow-feeling, your forbearance, your out-spoken, brave justice.

So I am content to tell my simple story, without trying to make things seem better than they were; dreading nothing, indeed, but falsity, which, in spite of one's best efforts, there is reason to dread. Falsehood is so easy, truth so difficult. The pencil is conscious of a delightful facility in drawing a griffin[2]—the longer the claws, and the larger the wings, the better; but that marvellous facility which we mistook for genius is apt to forsake us when we want to draw a real unexaggerated lion. Examine your words well, and you will find that even when you have no motive to be false, it is a very hard thing to say the exact truth, even about your own immediate feelings—much harder than to say something fine about them which is *not* the exact truth.

It is for this rare, precious quality of truthfulness that I delight in many Dutch paintings, which lofty-minded people despise. I find a source of delicious sympathy in these faithful pictures of a monotonous homely existence, which has been the fate of so many more among my fellow-mortals than a life of pomp or of absolute indigence, of tragic suffering or of world-stirring actions. I turn, without shrinking, from cloud-borne angels, from prophets, sibyls, and heroic warriors, to an old woman bending over her flower-pot, or eating her solitary dinner, while the noonday light, softened perhaps by a screen of leaves, falls on her mob-cap,[3] and just touches the rim of her spinning-wheel, and her stone jug, and all those cheap common things which are the precious necessaries of life to her;—or I turn to that village wedding, kept between four brown walls, where an awkward bridegroom opens the dance with a high-shouldered, broad-faced bride, while elderly and middle-aged friends look on, with very irregular noses and lips, and probably with quart-pots in their hands, but with an expression of unmistakable contentment and good-will. "Foh!" says my idealistic friend, "what vulgar details! What good is there in taking all these pains to give an exact likeness of old women and clowns? What a low phase of life!—what clumsy, ugly people!"

But bless us, things may be lovable that are not altogether handsome, I hope? I am not at all sure that the majority of the human race have not been ugly, and even among those "lords of their kind," the British, squat figures, ill-shapen nostrils, and dingy complexions are not startling exceptions. Yet there is a great deal of family love amongst us. I have a friend or two whose class of features is such that the Apollo[4] curl on the summit of their brows would be decidedly trying; yet to my certain knowledge tender hearts have beaten for them, and their miniatures—flattering, but still not lovely—are kissed in secret by motherly lips. I have seen many an excellent matron, who could never in her best days have been handsome, and yet she had a packet of yellow love-letters in a private drawer, and sweet children showered kisses on her sallow cheeks. And I believe there have been plenty of young heroes, of middle stature and feeble beards, who have felt quite sure they could never love anything more insignificant than a Diana, and yet have found themselves in middle life happily settled with a wife who waddles. Yes! thank God; human feeling is like the mighty rivers that bless the earth: it does not wait for beauty—it flows with resistless force and brings beauty with it.

All honor and reverence to the divine beauty of form! Let us cultivate it to the utmost in men, women, and children—in our gardens and in our houses. But let us love that other beauty too, which lies in no secret of proportion, but in the secret of deep human sympathy. Paint us an angel, if you can, with a floating violet robe, and a face paled by the celestial light; paint us yet oftener a Madonna, turning her mild face upward and opening her arms to welcome the divine glory; but do not impose on us any æsthetic rules which shall banish from the region of Art those old women scraping carrots with their work-worn hands, those heavy clowns taking holiday in a dingy pot-house, those rounded backs and stupid weather-beaten faces that have bent over the spade and done the rough work of the world—those homes with their tin pans, their brown pitchers, their rough curs, and their clusters of onions. In this world there are so many of these common coarse people, who have no picturesque sentimental wretchedness! It is so needful we should remember their existence, else we may happen to leave them quite out of our religion and philosophy, and frame lofty theories which only fit a world of extremes. Therefore let Art always remind us of them; therefore let us always have men ready to give the loving pains of a life to the faithful representing of commonplace things—men who see beauty in these commonplace things, and delight in showing how kindly the light of heaven falls on them. There are few prophets in the world; few sublimely beautiful women; few heroes. I can't afford to give all my love and reverence to such rarities: I want

---

[2] **griffin:** fabulous creature with a lion's body and bird's head.

[3] **mob-cap:** small indoors bonnet worn by women.

[4] **Apollo:** classical sun god, standard of masculine beauty.

a great deal of those feelings for my every-day fellow-men, especially for the few in the foreground of the great multitude, whose faces I know, whose hands I touch, for whom I have to make way with kindly courtesy. Neither are picturesque lazzaroni[5] or romantic criminals half so frequent as your common laborer, who gets his own bread, and eats it vulgarly but creditably with his own pocket-knife. It is more needful that I should have a fibre of sympathy connecting me with that vulgar citizen who weighs out my sugar in a vilely assorted cravat and waistcoat, than with the handsomest rascal in red scarf and green feathers;—more needful that my heart should swell with loving admiration at some trait of gentle goodness in the faulty people who sit at the same hearth with me, or in the clergyman of my own parish, who is perhaps rather too corpulent, and in other respects is

not an Oberlin or a Tillotson,[6] than at the deeds of heroes whom I shall never know except by hearsay, or at the sublimest abstract of all clerical graces that was ever conceived by an able novelist.

And so I come back to Mr. Irwine, with whom I desire you to be in perfect charity, far as he may be from satisfying your demands on the clerical character. Perhaps you think he was not—as he ought to have been—a living demonstration of the benefits attached to a national church? But I am not sure of that; at least I know that the people in Broxton and Hayslope would have been very sorry to part with their clergyman, and that most faces brightened at his approach. . . . (Book 2, Chapter 17)

1859

---

[5]lazzaroni: Neapolitan term for the poor.

---

[6]Johann Friedrich **Oberlin** (1740–1826): humanitarian French pastor. John **Tillotson** (1630–1694): Anglican archbishop and renowned preacher.

ALFRED AUSTIN

(1835–1913)

Austin's two decades as poet laureate constitute his claim to fame, but his acceptance of the position in 1896 after it had gone begging for three years made him a laughingstock. Nobody thought him a match for his predecessor Tennyson, but then by the time Tennyson died nobody thought much of the laureateship either. The offer came to Austin through political channels, in recognition more of his strictly conservative journalism than of his creative output. That output had been substantial, however, and had included novels, patriotic lyrics, poetical dramas, dramatical poems, and a steady stream of pretty aggressive literary criticism. It is Austin's critical impulse, particularly from the 1860s, that shows his temper to best advantage. Much of his early verse is satirical, displaying an eye for manners that is sometimes trenchant if also sometimes just mean-spirited. He was one of the few competent Victorians to take up improvisatory satire where Byron had left off, and the serially expanded verse narrative he began publishing in 1862 as *The Human Tragedy* reads a little like a Tory *Don Juan*. Austin's loose and jaunty irony is also on display in the following excerpt from *The Poetry of the Period*, which works some telling variations on a perception that was widely shared by better artists than Austin, among them the leading PreRaphaelites and late-century aestheticists: the perception that commercial culture and traditional poetics were incompatible. Austin's rather automatic sexism (manly concentration versus nude dancing girls) may betray a nervous indebtedness to Eliza Lynn Linton's conservative philippic "The Girl of the Period," published two years before (see page 91).

from The Poetry of the Period

. . . Art is not like dry-goods, whatever some people may think or indolently assume to the contrary. The law of demand and supply breaks down when once you pass the limits of craft, and invade the region of art. Though the material and labour requisite for the production of art must be paid for somehow, all the money in the world cannot produce one stroke of art, any more than it can produce the notes of a nightingale. The proper conditions alone can produce that, and demand is not one of them, much less all of them. Financial patronage—whether it be the patronage of wealthy, cultured dilettanti, of a luxurious, getting-on, and aspiring public, or of a centralized and tasteful State—is equally powerless to evoke manifestations of art if the social conditions are wanting to its development. Financial patronage may found academies, distribute prizes, confer laureateships, instigate unbounded competition. But what then? Great art, whether it be poetry or any other of its branches, bears as much resemblance to birthday odes, or poems that run through innumerable editions, as a monarch of the forest does to a faultless park-paling, or a wind-stirred group of water-reeds to an exquisitely-finished cane-bottomed chair. Naturally this age, having plenty of money, and having procured with it an immense amount of desirable things—underground railways, ocean steamers, splendid carriages and horses, rare and long-kept vintages, enormous mirrors, miles of lace, new colours, exciting novels by eminent hands, newspapers without end, gorgeous spectacles, naked dancing-girls, deft cooks, many courses, and a mild religion—is desirous of having great art likewise, which it has always heard is a good thing, and which, moreover, it fancies that it has got. For why should it not have it? It is quite ready to pay for it. To pay what for it? That is the question. Ready money. Alas! ready money is not the price of great art. Great art is to be reached only through spontaneity, simplicity, faith, unconscious earnestness, and manly concentration. It is idle to inquire if the age would make a sacrifice of its artificiality, its self-consciousness, its feminine infirmities, its scepticism, its distracted aims, in order to obtain it, since it would argue a complete metamorphosis of the age into something different from what it is; and ages are just as powerless to change their character as leopards to change their skins. It can offer money, favourable criticisms, and the *entrée* to its most conspicuous drawing-rooms—for it has got these things to give. But the contemporary social atmosphere and climate are no more within its gift or control than is the direction of the winds, the stir of volcanoes, the tumult of the sea, or the electricity of the air. These are not the commodities of market overt,[1] and the heavens have not yet been assailed by the law of demand and supply.

Here, then, we touch firm ground. We bring the poet *en rapport* with his age, and at best he can but say what he has got to say. The more his own disposition is in harmony with that of his time, the more complete, lucid, and satisfactory will be his poetry. If he clashes with it, the conflict will be evident in his verse—with discord, incompleteness, and obscurity as the result. It stands to reason that it must be so; for the resultant of two forces pushing in much the same direction is of necessity both simpler and stronger than that of the two forces pulling in different directions. Of this truth Mr. Tennyson is a most remarkable example. He has never once, as I have previously remarked, betrayed the slightest symptom of possessing the highest of poetical gifts. There is not one sublime passage in the whole of his works; and, what is more, there is no attempt at one. Yet I repeat my opinion that he must be conceded the first place among living English poets, though some of them have occasionally aimed at higher flights than any he has dreamed of. For whilst they are partly of the age, and partly at issue with it, he is of his age almost wholly and solely. . . .

Now, what is the temper of the age in which we live? Is intellectual concord one of its characteristics? On the contrary, is not intellectual discord its very mark and note? It is an age blown about "with every wind of doctrine."[2] It cannot make up its mind on any one single subject, except that to have plenty of money is a good thing; and even on that point it has occasional miserable qualms of conscience, being ever and anon half-disposed to suspect that, after all, hair shirts and serge[3] are better than purple and fine linen. It entertains the most serious doubts as to Christianity save as an historical phenomenon; and though it cannot bring itself really to believe in the old pagan deities, it would like vastly to revivify them. It is by no means sure even as to the existence of God; and if there be one, what He is like completely baffles its power of deciding. Between the doctrine that men have no souls, and that tables and pianos have, it swings in painful and ludicrous oscillation. What is the best

---

[1] **market overt:** the open market.

[2] **"with every wind of doctrine":** Ephesians 4:14.

[3] **hair shirts:** rough undergarments of horse or camel hair worn by ascetics as penance and here associated, like woolen **serge,** with bygone simplicity.

form of government; what the desirable state of society; what man's mission—what woman's; who ought to rule and who obey, or whether anybody ought to obey at all; whether marriage be an obsolete institution, or one deserving of rehabilitation; whether troops of nude dancing-girls be an indecent spectacle, or only an agreeably exciting entertainment: on all these, and indeed on every fundamental matter, it is in a hopeless plight of doubt and bewilderment. It consoles itself by asserting that, if it is wanting in decision, it is remarkable for toleration. It is a tolerant age. No doubt it is; though I may observe it would be rather extraordinary, not to say scandalous, if, under the circumstances, it were anything else. Still, toleration is a good thing, however brought about, and has its merits. But it has its drawbacks also, and I will name two of them. A tolerant age never produced great deeds or great poets, and it never will. Strong and practically unanimous convictions and passionate earnestness are wanted for those two products. The convictions of the community are in a state of pitiable flux, and its passions are quiescent, save in the pursuit of puny personal objects. On every conceivable subject the country is torn by what we might call factions, if any of them had vigour enough to deserve that name. What wonder, then, if it can find no adequate voice, no really one great poet, to give its feelings utterance? Its feelings are so complex and unmarshalled that it requires a number of small ambiguous voices to represent each particular shade of its many moods and yearnings. It is not satisfied with anything, and least of all is it satisfied with itself. . . . (Chapter 8)

1870

ROBERT BUCHANAN

(1841–1901)

The enabling premise of the *ad hominem* attack to which Buchanan owes his narrow niche in literary history is that avant-garde art outrages sexual decency. The rhetorically interesting position in which this premise places him—along with modern columnists who publicize in descriptive detail the museum exhibitions they find obscene—is that of retailing at second hand the soiled goods he decries. It is not clear that this position embarrassed Buchanan, whose full essay quoted a lot more naughty PreRaphaelite verse than our excerpt represents, and thus repeatedly shared with his *Contemporary Review* reader the satisfactions (virtually advertised in the essay's title) of having his cheesecake and banning it too. At one telling point he complains both that Rossetti's poem "Jenny" is indecent and that it owes a large debt to a poem by Buchanan himself. The ideological whiplash here—softened a little by Buchanan's having published his attack pseudonymously, a strategy that Rossetti's rejoinder "The Stealthy School" hit back at (see pages 816–819)—suggests that Buchanan's real indignation arose from something other than prudery. Under cover of sex surveillance we find him targeting a system of literary hucksterism, puffery, and coterie-protection in which the Pre-Raphaelites were patently complicit.

But then he was complicit in it too. A tailor's son from Glasgow who wrote his way to prominence, Buchanan had inside experience of the London literary hustle: he worked hard at keeping his name before the public with a series of turgidly ambitious poetic narratives and dramas, several novels, and the sort of high-profile journalism that not only elicited Rossetti's public reply but embroiled Buchanan in a (successful) lawsuit against Swinburne for libel. That Buchanan eventually became reconciled with both men is part of the larger story our excerpt conveys. He saw, with Alfred Austin a year before, that a rampant commercialism was hostile to the poet's higher calling; but he also saw that if poetry was to circulate at all, under the new order, it must commodify itself. Buchanan's actual quarrel with Rossetti was over who offered the better commodity, which is to say who knew better how to negotiate a place for modern poetry without selling out to either titillation or rectitude. The market has long since declared for Rossetti, but Buchanan's finger in the trade wind can remind us how difficult good forecasting was at the time.

from The Fleshly School of Poetry: Mr. D. G. Rossetti

If, on the occasion of any public performance of Shakespeare's great tragedy, the actors who perform the parts of Rosencranz and Guildenstern[1] were, by a preconcerted arrangement and by means of what is technically known as "gagging," to make themselves fully as prominent as the leading character, and to indulge in soliloquies and business strictly belonging to Hamlet himself, the result would be, to say the least of it, astonishing; yet a very similar effect is produced on the unprejudiced mind when the "walking gentlemen"[2] of the fleshly school of poetry, who bear precisely the same relation to Mr. Tennyson as Rosencranz and Guildenstern do to the Prince of Denmark in the play, obtrude their lesser identities and parade their smaller idiosyncrasies in the front rank of leading performers. In their own place, the gentlemen are interesting and useful. Pursuing still the theatrical analogy, the present drama of poetry might be cast as follows: Mr. Tennyson supporting the part of Hamlet, Mr. Matthew Arnold that of Horatio, Mr. Bailey that of Voltimand, Mr. Buchanan that of Cornelius, Messrs. Swinburne and Morris the parts of Rosencranz and Guildenstern, Mr. Rossetti that of Osric, and Mr. Robert Lytton,[3] that of "A Gentleman." It will be seen that we have left no place for Mr. Browning, who may be said, however, to play the leading character in his own peculiar fashion on alternate nights.

This may seem a frivolous and inadequate way of opening our remarks on a school of verse-writers which some people regard as possessing great merits; but in good truth, it is scarcely possible to discuss with any seriousness the pretensions with which foolish friends and small critics have surrounded the fleshly school, which, in spite of its spasmodic[4] ramifications in the erotic direction, is merely one of the many sub-Tennysonian schools expanded to supernatural dimensions, and endeavouring by affectations all its own to overshadow its connection with the great original. In the sweep of one single poem, the weird and doubtful "Vivien,"[5] Mr. Tennyson has concentrated all the epicene force which, wearisomely expanded, constitutes the characteristic of the writers at present under consideration; and if in "Vivien" he has indicated for them the bounds of sensualism in art, he has in *Maud*, in the dramatic person of the hero, afforded distinct precedent for the hysteric tone and overloaded style which is now so familiar to readers of Mr. Swinburne. The fleshliness of "Vivien" may indeed be described as the distinct quality held in common by all the members of the last sub-Tennysonian school, and it is a quality which becomes unwholesome when there is no moral or intellectual quality to temper and control it. Fully conscious of this themselves, the fleshly gentlemen have bound themselves by solemn league and covenant to extol fleshliness as the distinct and supreme end of poetic and pictorial art; to aver that poetic expression is greater than poetic thought, and by inference that the body is greater

---

[1]**Rosencranz** and **Guildenstern**: Hamlet's former schoolmates, who carried out Buchanan's premise in Tom Stoppard's 1967 comedy *Rosencrantz and Guildenstern Are Dead.*

[2]**"walking gentlemen"**: walk-ons, bit players.

[3]Philip James **Bailey** (1816–1902), Edward **Robert** Bulwer **Lytton,** pseud. Owen Meredith (1831–1891): poets whose major works—respectively, *Festus* (first edition, 1839) and *Lucile* (1863)— enjoyed brisk sales.

[4]**spasmodic**: allusion to the "Spasmodist" school of poets who flared and sputtered in the 1850s, and whose impulsive, grandiose poetics were thought influential on Tennyson's *Maud* and Barrett Browning's *Aurora Leigh.*

[5]**"Vivien"**: one of the original 1859 *Idylls of the King* (later titled "Merlin and Vivien").

than the soul, and sound superior to sense; and that the poet, properly to develop his poetic faculty, must be an intellectual hermaphrodite, to whom the very facts of day and night are lost in a whirl of aesthetic terminology. After Mr. Tennyson has probed the depths of modern speculation in a series of commanding moods, all right and interesting in him as the reigning personage, the walking gentlemen, knowing that something of the sort is expected from all leading performers, bare their roseate bosoms and aver that *they* are creedless; the only possible question here being, if any disinterested person cares twopence whether Rosencranz, Guildenstern, and Osric are creedless or not—their self-revelation on that score being so perfectly gratuitous? But having gone so far, it was and is too late to retreat. Rosencranz, Guildenstern, and Osric, finding it impossible to risk an individual bid for the leading business,[6] have arranged all to play leading business together, and mutually to praise, extol, and imitate each other; and although by these measures they have fairly earned for themselves the title of the Mutual Admiration School, they have in a great measure succeeded in their object—to the general stupefaction of a British audience. It is time, therefore, to ascertain whether any of these gentlemen has actually in himself the making of a leading performer. When the *Athenæum*,[7]—once more cautious in such matters—advertised nearly every week some interesting particular about Mr. Swinburne's health, Mr. Morris's holiday-making, or Mr. Rossetti's genealogy, varied with such startling statements as "We are informed that Mr. Swinburne dashed off his noble ode *at a sitting*," or "Mr. Swinburne's songs have already reached a second edition," or "Good poetry seems to be in demand; the first edition of Mr. O'Shaughnessy's[8] poems is exhausted;" when the *Academy* informed us that "During the past year or two Mr. Swinburne has written several novels" (!), and that some review or other is to be praised for giving Mr. Rossetti's poems "the attentive study which they demand"—when we read these things we might or might not know pretty well how and where they originated; but to a provincial eye, perhaps, the whole thing really looked like leading business. It would be scarcely worth while, however, to inquire into the pretensions of the writers on

merely literary grounds, because sooner or later all literature finds its own level, whatever criticism may say or do in the matter; but it unfortunately happens in the present case that the fleshly school of verse-writers are, so to speak, public offenders, because they are diligently spreading the seeds of disease broadcast wherever they are read and understood. Their complaint too is catching, and carries off many young persons. What the complaint is, and how it works, may be seen on a very slight examination of the works of Mr. Dante Gabriel Rossetti, to whom we shall confine our attention in the present article.

Mr. Rossetti has been known for many years as a painter of exceptional powers, who, for reasons best known to himself, has shrunk from publicly exhibiting his pictures, and from allowing anything like a popular estimate to be formed of their qualities. He belongs, or is said to belong, to the so-called Pre-Raphaelite school, a school which is generally considered to exhibit much genius for colour, and great indifference to perspective. It would be unfair to judge the painter by the glimpses we have had of his works, or by the photographs which are sold of the principal paintings. Judged by the photographs, he is an artist who conceives unpleasantly, and draws ill. Like Mr. Simeon Solomon,[9] however, with whom he seems to have many points in common, he is distinctively a colourist, and of his capabilities in colour we cannot speak, though we should guess that they are great; for if there is any good quality by which his poems are specially marked, it is a great sensitiveness to hues and tints as conveyed in poetic epithet. These qualities, which impress the casual spectator of the photographs from his pictures, are to be found abundantly among his verses. There is the same thinness and transparence of design, the same combination of the simple and the grotesque, the same morbid deviation from healthy forms of life, the same sense of weary, wasting, yet exquisite sensuality; nothing virile, nothing tender, nothing completely sane; a superfluity of extreme sensibility, of delight in beautiful forms, hues, and tints, and a deep-seated indifference to all agitating forces and agencies, all tumultuous griefs and sorrows, all the thunderous stress of life, and all the straining storm of speculation. Mr. Morris is often pure, fresh, and wholesome as his own great model; Mr. Swinburne startles us more than once by some fine flash of insight; but the mind of Mr. Rossetti is like a glassy mere, broken only by the dive of some water-bird or the hum of winged insects, and brooded over by an atmosphere of insufferable closeness,

---

[6]**leading business**: parts for leading actors.

[7]*Athenaeum, Academy*: 19th-century literary journals whose readership overlapped that of the *Contemporary Review*, which published Buchanan's salvo and Rossetti's reply.

[8]Arthur **O'Shaughnessy** (1844–1881): poet with PreRaphaelite connections.

---

[9]**Simeon Solomon** (1840–1905): PreRaphaelite painter.

with a light blue sky above it, sultry depths mirrored within it, and a surface so thickly sown with waterlilies that it retains its glassy smoothness even in the strongest wind. Judged relatively to his poetic associates, Mr. Rossetti must be pronounced inferior to either. He cannot tell a pleasant story like Mr. Morris, nor forge alliterative thunderbolts like Mr. Swinburne. It must be conceded, nevertheless, that he is neither so glibly imitative as the one, nor so transcendently superficial as the other.

Although he has been known for many years as a poet as well as a painter—as a painter and poet idolized by his own family and personal associates—and although he has once or twice appeared in print as a contributor to magazines, Mr. Rossetti did not formally appeal to the public until rather more than a year ago, when he published a copious volume of poems, with the announcement that the book, although it contained pieces composed at intervals during a period of many years, "included nothing which the author believes to be immature." This work was inscribed to his brother, Mr. William Rossetti,[10] who, having written much both in poetry and criticism, will perhaps be known to bibliographers as the editor of the worst edition of Shelley which has yet seen the light. No sooner had the work appeared than the chorus of eulogy began. "The book is satisfactory from end to end," wrote Mr. Morris in the *Academy*; "I think these lyrics, with all their other merits, the most complete of their time; nor do I know what lyrics of any time are to be called *great*, if we are to deny the title to these." On the same subject Mr. Swinburne went into a hysteria of admiration: "golden affluence," "jewel-coloured words," "chastity of form," "harmonious nakedness," "consummate fleshly sculpture," and so on in Mr. Swinburne's well-known manner when reviewing his friends. Other critics, with a singular similarity of phrase, followed suit. Strange to say, moreover, no one accused Mr. Rossetti of naughtiness. What had been heinous in Mr. Swinburne was majestic exquisiteness in Mr. Rossetti. Yet we question if there is anything in the unfortunate *Poems and Ballads*[11] quite so questionable on the score of thorough nastiness as many pieces in Mr. Rossetti's collection. Mr. Swinburne was wilder, more outrageous, more blasphemous, and his subjects were more atrocious in themselves; yet the hysterical tone slew the animalism, the furiousness of epithet lowered the sensation; and the first feeling of disgust at such themes

as "Laus Veneris" and "Anactoria," faded away into comic amazement. It was only a little mad boy letting off squibs; not a great strong man, who might be really dangerous to society. "I *will* be naughty!" screamed the little boy; but, after all, what did it matter? It is quite different, however, when a grown man, with the self-control and easy audacity of actual experience, comes forward to chronicle his amorous sensations, and, first proclaiming in a loud voice his literary maturity, and consequent responsibility, shamelessly prints and publishes such a piece of writing as this sonnet on "Nuptial Sleep;"—

> At length their long kiss severed, with sweet smart:
> And as the last slow sudden drops are shed
> From sparkling eaves when all the storm has fled,
> So singly flagged the pulses of each heart.
> Their bosoms sundered, with the opening start
> Of married flowers to either side outspread
> From the knit stem; yet still their mouths, burnt red,
> Fawned on each other where they lay apart.
>
> Sleep sank them lower than the tide of dreams,
> And their dreams watched them sink, and slid away.
> Slowly their souls swam up again, through gleams
> Of watered light and dull drowned waifs of day;
> Till from some wonder of new woods and streams
> He woke, and wondered more: for there she lay.

This, then, is "the golden affluence of words, the firm outline, the justice and chastity of form." Here is a full-grown man, presumably intelligent and cultivated, putting on record for other full-grown men to read, the most secret mysteries of sexual connection, and that with so sickening a desire to reproduce the sensual mood, so careful a choice of epithet to convey mere animal sensations, that we merely shudder at the shameless nakedness. We are no purists in such matters. We hold the sensual part of our nature to be as holy as the spiritual or intellectual part, and we believe that such things must find their equivalent in all; but it is neither poetic, nor manly, nor even human, to obtrude such things as the themes of whole poems. It is simply nasty. Nasty as it is, we are very mistaken if many readers do not think it nice. English society of one kind purchases the *Day's Doings*.[12] English society of another kind goes into ecstasy over Mr. Solomon's pictures—pretty pieces of morality,

---

[10]**William** Michael **Rossetti** (1829–1919): literary editor and art critic.

[11]*Poems and Ballads*: Swinburne's notorious volume of 1866.

[12]*Day's Doings: An Illustrated Journal of Romantic Events, Reports, Sporting and Theatrical News*: published weekly 1870–1872.

such as "Love dying by the breath of Lust." There is not much to choose between the two objects of admiration, except that painters like Mr. Solomon lend actual genius to worthless subjects, and thereby produce veritable monsters—like the lovely devils that danced round Saint Anthony.[13] Mr. Rossetti owes his so-called success to the same causes. In poems like "Nuptial Sleep," the man who is too sensitive to exhibit his pictures, and so modest that it takes him years to make up his mind to publish his poems, parades his private sensations before a coarse public, and is gratified by their applause.

It must not be supposed that all Mr. Rossetti's poems are made up of trash like this. Some of them are as noteworthy for delicacy of touch as others are for shamelessness of exposition. They contain some exquisite pictures of nature, occasional passages of real meaning, much beautiful phraseology, lines of peculiar sweetness, and epithets chosen with true literary cunning. But the fleshly feeling is everywhere. . . .

. . . There is very little writing in the volume spontaneous in the sense that some of Swinburne's verses are spontaneous; the poems all look as if they had taken a great deal of trouble. The grotesque mediævalism of "Stratton Water" and "Sister Helen," the mediæval classicism of "Troy Town," the false and shallow mysticism of "Eden Bower," are one and all essentially imitative, and must have cost the writer much pains. It is time, indeed, to point out that Mr. Rossetti is a poet possessing great powers of assimilation and some faculty for concealing the nutriment on which he feeds. Setting aside the *Vita Nuova*[14] and the early Italian poems, which are familiar to many readers by his own excellent translations, Mr. Rossetti may be described as a writer who has yielded to an unusual extent to the complex influences of the literature surrounding him at the present moment. He has the painter's imitative power developed in proportion to his lack of the poet's conceiving imagination. He reproduces to a nicety the manner of an old ballad, a trick in which Mr. Swinburne is also an adept. Cultivated readers, moreover, will recognise in every one of these poems the tone of Mr. Tennyson broken up by the style of Mr. and Mrs. Browning, and disguised here and there by the eccentricities of the Pre-Raphaelites. The "Burden of Nineveh" is a philosophical edition of "Recollections of the Arabian Nights;" "A Last Confession" and

"Dante at Verona" are, in the minutest trick and form of thought, suggestive of Mr. Browning; and that the sonnets have been largely moulded and inspired by Mrs. Browning can be ascertained by any critic who will compare them with the *Sonnets from the Portuguese.* . . .

. . . Whether he is writing of the holy Damozel, or of the Virgin herself, or of Lilith, or Helen, or of Dante, or of Jenny the street-walker, he is fleshly all over, from the roots of his hair to the tip of his toes; never a true lover merging his identity into that of the beloved one; never spiritual, never tender; always self-conscious and aesthetic. "Nothing," says a modern writer, "in human life is so utterly remorseless—not love, not hate, not ambition, not vanity—as the artistic or aesthetic instinct morbidly developed to the suppression of conscience and feeling;" and at no time do we feel more fully impressed with this truth than after the perusal of "Jenny," in some respects the finest poem in the volume, and in all respects the poem best indicative of the true quality of the writer's humanity. It is a production which bears signs of having been suggested by Mr. Buchanan's quasi-lyrical poems, which it copies in the style of title, and particularly by "Artist and Model,"[15] but certainly Mr. Rossetti cannot be accused, as the Scottish writer has been accused, of maudlin sentiment and affected tenderness. The two first lines are perfect:—

> Lazy laughing languid Jenny,
> Fond of a kiss and fond of a guinea;

And the poem is a soliloquy of the poet—who has been spending the evening in dancing at a casino—over his partner, whom he has accompanied home to the usual style of lodgings occupied by such ladies, and who has fallen asleep with her head upon his knee, while he wonders, in a wretched pun—

> Whose person or whose purse may be
> The lodestar of your reverie?

The soliloquy is long, and in some parts beautiful, despite a very constant suspicion that we are listening to an emasculated Mr. Browning, whose whole tone and gesture, so to speak, is occasionally introduced with startling fidelity; and there are here and there glimpses of actual thought and insight, over and above the picturesque

---

[13]**Saint Anthony** of Egypt (3rd–4th century): ascetic hermit whose demonic temptations formed a favorite theme for painters.

[14]*Vita Nuova* (*New Life*): Dante's narrative of erotic conversion, translated by Rossetti in *The Early Italian Poets* (1861).

[15]**"Artist and Model:** A Love Poem": dramatic monologue published by Buchanan shortly before this review.

touches which belong to the writer's true profession, such as that where, at daybreak—

> lights creep in
> Past the gauze curtains half drawn to,
> And *the Lamp's doubled shade grows blue.*

What we object to in this poem is not the subject, which any writer may be fairly left to choose for himself; nor anything particularly vicious in the poetic treatment of it; nor any bad blood bursting through in special passages. But the whole tone, without being more than usually coarse, seems heartless. There is not a drop of piteousness in Mr. Rossetti. He is just to the outcast, even generous; severe to the seducer; sad even at the spectacle of lust in dimity and fine ribbons. Notwithstanding all this, and a certain delicacy and refinement of treatment unusual with this poet, the poem repels and revolts us, and we like Mr. Rossetti least after its perusal. We are angry with the fleshly person at last. The "Blessed Damozel" puzzled us, the "Song of the Bower" amused us, the love-sonnet depressed and sickened us, but "Jenny," though distinguished by less special viciousness of thought and style than any of these, fairly makes us lose patience. We detect its fleshliness at a glance; we perceive that the scene was fascinating less through its human tenderness than because it, like all the others, possessed an inherent quality of animalism. . . .

1871

ARTHUR SYMONS

(1865–1945)

The 1890s had their apotheosis in Oscar Wilde, their epitome in Arthur Symons. Symons made a coterie name with the enameled lyrics of *Silhouettes* (1892) and *London Nights* (1895), contributed to the aesthete organ *The Yellow Book,* and in 1896 became literary editor of a fashionable journal, *The Savoy,* alongside art editor Aubrey Beardsley. The two essays excerpted here frame the 1890s between the old century and the new. "The Decadent Movement in Literature," first published in an American magazine in 1893, diagnoses the degeneracy of a culture burdened by its own abundance—a condition that Symons' own grave and highly allusive style constantly illustrates. Risking health and balance for the sake of exotically refined excitements, high-strung nineties artists and audiences seemed to be fulfilling Robert Buchanan's spluttering prophecy from two decades before, but now at a pitch of nervous sophistication where the "fleshly school" thinned out into something like a spiritual discipline. Symons wrote about the Parisian avant-garde, for a self-selected elite of cultural adepts whose connoisseurship amounted, as they saw it, to psychological research. His rhetoric of "exactitude" and "precision" claims for aesthetic experimentation the prestige that had accrued during the century to scientific experimentation; the expert discrimination of impression and nuance, he implies, is hard and even dangerous work.

Symons came to know the danger of hyperaestheticism at first hand in 1908 when a severe nervous breakdown put an effective end to his literary career. Earlier, however, he had glimpsed in *The Symbolist Movement* a quasi-religious light at the end of the Decadent tunnel. Here Symons proposes the self-conscious pursuit of the poetic image as a cure rather than a symptom of the contemporary condition, clearing the way to twentieth-century modernism.

At the same time, in both the essays excerpted here Symons recapitulates major Victorian categories from which the modernists (though they hated to admit it) learned to think about poetics in the first place. Symons throws in his lot with Arthur Hallam on sensation, and against George Eliot on "the accidents of daily life"; he divides his topic along the lines drawn between subjective and objective poets in Browning's *Essay on Shelley*, between classic and modern modes in Arnold's 1853 *Preface*; and his invocation of early Carlyle rings with an 1899 intention to transmit one century's most vital literary ideas to the next.

from **The Decadent Movement in Literature**

The latest movement in European literature has been called by many names, none of them quite exact or comprehensive—Decadence, Symbolism, Impressionism, for instance. It is easy to dispute over words, and we shall find that Verlaine objects to being called a Decadent, Maeterlinck to being called a Symbolist, Huysmans[1] to being called an Impressionist. These terms, as it happens, have been adopted as the badge of little separate cliques, noisy, brainsick young people who haunt the brasseries of the Boulevard Saint-Michel,[2] and exhaust their ingenuities in theorizing over the works they cannot write. But, taken frankly as epithets which express their own meaning, both Impressionism and Symbolism convey some notion of that new kind of literature which is perhaps more broadly characterized by the word Decadence. The most representative literature of the day—the writing which appeals to, which has done so much to form, the younger generation—is certainly not classic, nor has it any relation with that old antithesis of the Classic, the Romantic. After a fashion it is no doubt a decadence; it has all the qualities that mark the end of great periods, the qualities that we find in the Greek, the Latin, decadence: an intense self-consciousness, a restless curiosity in research, an over-subtilizing refinement upon refinement, a spiritual and moral perversity. If what we call the classic is indeed the supreme art—those qualities of perfect simplicity, perfect sanity, perfect proportion, the supreme qualities—then this representative literature of to-day, in-teresting, beautiful, novel as it is, is really a new and beautiful and interesting disease.

Healthy we cannot call it, and healthy it does not wish to be considered. The Goncourts, in their prefaces, in their *Journal*, are always insisting on their own malady, *la névrose*.[3] It is in their work, too, that Huysmans notes with delight *"le style tacheté et faisandé"*—high-flavoured and spotted with corruption—which he himself possesses in the highest degree. "Having desire without light, curiosity without wisdom, seeking God by strange ways, by ways traced by the hands of men; offering rash incense upon the high places to an unknown God, who is the God of darkness"—that is how Ernest Hello,[4] in one of his apocalyptic moments, characterizes the nineteenth century. And this unreason of the soul—of which Hello himself is so curious a victim—this unstable equilibrium, which has overbalanced so many brilliant intelligences into one form or another of spiritual confusion, is but another form of the *maladie fin de siècle*.[5] For its very disease of form, this literature is certainly typical of a civilization grown over-luxurious, over-inquiring, too languid for the relief of action, too uncertain for any emphasis in opinion or in conduct. It reflects all the moods, all the manners, of a sophisticated society; its very artificiality is a way of being true to nature; simplicity, sanity, proportion—the classic qualities—how much do we possess them in our life, our surroundings, that we should look to find them in our literature—so evidently the literature of a decadence?

Taking the word Decadence, then, as most precisely expressing the general sense of the newest movement in literature, we find that the terms Impressionism and Symbolism define correctly enough the two main branches of that

---

[1]Paul-Marie **Verlaine** (1844–1896): French lyric poet. Maurice **Maeterlinck** (1862–1949): Belgian playwright. Joris-Karl **Huysmans** (1848–1907): French novelist.

[2]**brasseries**: bistros. **Boulevard Saint-Michel**: main street of the Latin Quarter in Paris.

[3]Edmund-Louis-Antoine **Goncourt** (1822–1896), Jules-Alfred **Goncourt** (1830–1870): brothers who collaboratively published art criticism, fiction, and journals of private life. *la névrose*: neurosis.

[4]**Ernest Hello** (1828–1885): French Catholic apologist.

[5]*maladie fin de siècle*: turn-of-the-century disease.

movement. Now Impressionist and Symbolist have more in common than either supposes; both are really working on the same hypothesis, applied in different directions. What both seek is not general truth merely, but *la vérité vraie*,[6] the very essence of truth—the truth of appearances to the senses, of the visible world to the eyes that see it; and the truth of spiritual things to the spiritual vision. The Impressionist, in literature as in painting, would flash upon you in a new, sudden way so exact an image of what you have just seen, just as you have seen it, that you may say, as a young American sculptor, a pupil of Rodin, said to me on seeing for the first time a picture of Whistler's, "Whistler seems to think his picture upon canvas—and there it is!" Or you may find, with Sainte-Beuve,[7] writing of Goncourt, the "soul of the landscape"—the soul of whatever corner of the visible world has to be realized. The Symbolist, in this new, sudden way, would flash upon you the "soul" of that which can be apprehended only by the soul—the finer sense of things unseen, the deeper meaning of things evident. And naturally, necessarily, this endeavour after a perfect truth to one's impression, to one's intuition—perhaps an impossible endeavour—has brought with it, in its revolt from ready-made impressions and conclusions, a revolt from the ready-made of language, from the bondage of traditional form, of a form become rigid. In France, where this movement began and has mainly flourished, it is Goncourt who was the first to invent a style in prose really new, impressionistic, a style which was itself almost sensation. It is Verlaine who has invented such another new style in verse. . . .

. . . To fix the last fine shade, the quintessence of things; to fix it fleetingly; to be a disembodied voice, and yet the voice of a human soul: that is the ideal of Decadence, and it is what Paul Verlaine has achieved.

And certainly, so far as achievement goes, no other poet of the actual group in France can be named beside him or near him. But in Stéphane Mallarmé,[8] with his supreme pose as the supreme poet, and his two or three pieces of exquisite verse and delicately artificial prose to show by way of result, we have the prophet and pontiff of the movement, the mystical and theoretical leader of the great emancipa-

tion. No one has ever dreamed such beautiful, impossible dreams as Mallarmé: no one has ever so possessed his soul in the contemplation of masterpieces to come. All his life he has been haunted by the desire to create, not so much something new in literature, as a literature which should itself be a new art. He has dreamed of a work into which all the arts should enter, and achieve themselves by a mutual interdependence—a harmonizing of all the arts into one supreme art—and he has theorized with infinite subtlety over the possibilities of doing the impossible. Every Tuesday for the last twenty years he has talked more fascinatingly, more suggestively, than anyone else has ever done, in that little room in the Rue de Rome, to that little group of eager young poets. "A seeker after something in the world, that is there in no satisfying measure or not at all,"[9] he has carried his contempt for the usual, the conventional, beyond the point of literary expression, into the domain of practical affairs. Until the publication, quite recently, of a selection of *Vers et Prose*,[10] it was only possible to get his poems in a limited and expensive edition, lithographed in facsimile of his own clear and elegant handwriting. An aristocrat of letters, Mallarmé has always looked with intense disdain on the indiscriminate accident of universal suffrage. He has wished neither to be read nor to be understood by the bourgeois intelligence, and it is with some deliberateness of intention that he has made both issues impossible. Catulle Mendès defines him admirably as "a difficult author," and in his latest period he has succeeded in becoming absolutely unintelligible. His early poems, *L'Après-midi d'un Faune, Hérodiade*,[11] for example, and some exquisite sonnets, and one or two fragments of perfectly polished verse, are written in a language which has nothing in common with every-day language—symbol within symbol, image within image; but symbol and image achieve themselves in expression without seeming to call for the necessity of a key. The latest poems (in which punctuation is sometimes entirely suppressed, for our further bewilderment) consist merely of a sequence of symbols, in which every word must be taken in a sense with which its ordinary significance has nothing to do. Mallarmé's contortion of the French language, so far

---

[6]*la vérité vraie:* the true truth.

[7]Auguste **Rodin** (1840–1917): French sculptor. James Abbott McNeill **Whistler** (1834–1903): American painter. Charles-Augustin **Saint-Beuve** (1804–1869): French literary critic.

[8]Stéphane **Mallarmé** (1842–1898): French leader of the Symbolist movement.

[9]"**A seeker . . . or not at all**": Pater's phrase for the painter Antoine Watteau (1684–1721) in *Imaginary Portraits* (1887).

[10]*Vers et Prose* (Verse and Prose, 1887, 1891).

[11]**Catulle Mendès** (1841–1909): French poet, novelist, and critic. *L'Après-midi d'un Faune* (Afternoon of a Faun, 1876). *Hérodiade* (1869).

as mere style is concerned, is curiously similar to the kind of depravation which was undergone by the Latin language in its decadence. It is, indeed, in part a reversion to Latin phraseology, to the Latin construction, and it has made, of the clear and flowing French language, something irregular, unquiet, expressive, with sudden surprising felicities, with nervous starts and lapses, with new capacities for the exact noting of sensation. Alike to the ordinary and to the scholarly reader it is painful, intolerable; a jargon, a massacre. Supremely self-confident, and backed, certainly, by an ardent following of the younger generation, Mallarmé goes on his way, experimenting more and more audaciously, having achieved by this time, at all events, a style wholly his own. Yet the *chef d'oeuvre inconnu*[12] seems no nearer completion, the impossible seems no more likely to be done. . . .

. . . Joris Karl Huysmans demands a prominent place in any record of the Decadent movement. His work, like that of the Goncourts, is largely determined by the *maladie fin de siècle*—the diseased nerves that, in his case, have given a curious personal quality of pessimism to his outlook on the world, his view of life. Part of his work—*Marthe, Les Sœurs Vatard, En Menage, A Vau-l'eau*[13]—is a minute and searching study of the minor discomforts, the commonplace miseries of life, as seen by a peevishly disordered vision, delighting, for its own self-torture, in the insistent contemplation of human stupidity, of the sordid in existence. Yet these books do but lead up to the unique masterpiece, the astonishing caprice of *A Rebours*, in which he has concentrated all that is delicately depraved, all that is beautifully, curiously poisonous, in modern art. *A Rebours* is the history of a typical Decadent—a study, indeed, after a real man, but a study which seizes the type rather than the personality. In the sensations and ideas of Des Esseintes[14] we see the sensations and ideas of the effeminate, over-civilized, deliberately abnormal creature who is the last product of our society: partly the father, partly the offspring, of the perverse art that he adores. Des Esseintes creates for his solace, in the wilderness of a barren and profoundly uncomfortable world, an artificial paradise. His Thébaïde raffinée[15] is furnished elaborately for candle-light, equipped with the pictures, the books, that satisfy his sense of the exquisitely abnormal. He delights in the Latin of Apuleius and Petronius, in the French of Baudelaire, Goncourt, Verlaine, Mallarmé, Villiers; in the pictures of Gustave Moreau, of Odilon Redon.[16] He delights in the beauty of strange, unnatural flowers, in the melodic combination of scents, in the imagined harmonies of the sense of taste. And at last, exhausted by these spiritual and sensory debauches in the delights of the artificial, he is left (as we close the book) with a brief, doubtful choice before him—madness or death, or else a return to nature, to the normal life.

Since *A Rebours*, Huysmans has written one other remarkable book, *La-Bas*, a study in the hysteria and mystical corruption of contemporary Black Magic. But it is on that one exceptional achievement, *A Rebours*, that his fame will rest; it is there he has expressed not merely himself, but an epoch. And he has done so in a style which carries the modern experiments upon language to their furthest development. Formed upon Goncourt and Flaubert, it has sought for novelty, *l'image peinte*,[17] the exactitude of colour, the forcible precision of epithet, wherever words, images, or epithets are to be found. Barbaric in its profusion, violent in its emphasis, wearying in its splendour, it is—especially in regard to things seen—extraordinarily expressive, with all the shades of a painter's palette. Elaborately and deliberately perverse, it is in its very perversity that Huysmans' work—so fascinating, so repellent, so instinctively artificial—comes to represent, as the work of no other writer can be said to do, the main tendencies, the chief results, of the Decadent movement in literature.

1893

---

[12]**chef d'oeuvre inconnu**: unknown masterpiece.

[13]*Marthe* (*Martha, The Story of a Girl*, 1876), *Les Soeurs Vatard* (*The Vatard Sisters*, 1879), *En Menage* (*Housekeeping*, 1881), *A Vau-l'eau* (*Down Stream*, 1882): novels mingling impressionism and naturalist detail. Symons goes on to discuss Huysmans's Decadent classic *A Rebours* (*Against the Grain*, 1884)—the mysterious "yellow book" in chapters 10 and 11 of Wilde's *The Picture of Dorian Gray*—and *Là-Bas* (*Down There*, 1891), a novel based on satanist cult practices.

[14]**Des Esseintes**: protagonist of *A Rebours*.

---

[15]**Thébaïde raffinée**: deep, refined solitude.

[16]Lucius **Apuleius** (2nd century): author of the protonovel *The Golden Ass*. Gaius **Petronius** Arbiter (1st century): author of the *Satyricon*. Charles **Baudelaire** (1821–1867): poet and critic. Auguste **Villiers** de l'Isle Adam (1838–1889): author of the Symbolist drama *Axël* (1886) and of the Gothic *Contes cruels* (*Cruel Tales*, 1883). **Gustave Moreau** (1826–1898): French Symbolist painter of erotic mythological canvasses. **Odilon Redon** (1840–1916): French Symbolist painter of the macabre.

[17]*l'image peinte*: the painted image.

~

from The Symbolist Movement in Literature

"It is in and through Symbols that man, consciously or un-consciously, lives, works, and has his being: those ages, moreover, are accounted the noblest which can the best recognise symbolical worth, and prize it highest."

Carlyle[1]

Without symbolism there can be no literature; indeed, not even language. What are words themselves but symbols, al-most as arbitrary as the letters which compose them, mere sounds of the voice to which we have agreed to give cer-tain significations, as we have agreed to translate these sounds by those combinations of letters? Symbolism began with the first words uttered by the first man, as he named every living thing; or before them, in heaven, when God named the world into being. And we see, in these begin-nings, precisely what Symbolism in literature really is: a form of expression, at the best but approximate, essentially but arbitrary, until it has obtained the force of a conven-tion, for an unseen reality apprehended by the conscious-ness. It is sometimes permitted to us to hope that our convention is indeed the reflection rather than merely the sign of that unseen reality. We have done much if we have found a recognisable sign.

"A symbol," says Comte Goblet d'Alviella, in his book on *The Migration of Symbols*,[2] "might be defined as a represen-tation which does not aim at being a reproduction." Origi-nally, as he points out, used by the Greeks to denote "the two halves of the tablet they divided between themselves as a pledge of hospitality," it came to be used of every sign, formula, or rite by which those initiated in any mystery made themselves secretly known to one another. Gradually the word extended its meaning, until it came to denote every conventional representation of idea by form, of the

unseen by the visible. "In a Symbol," says Carlyle, "there is concealment and yet revelation: hence therefore, by Si-lence and by Speech acting together, comes a double sig-nificance." And, in that fine chapter of *Sartor Resartus*, he goes further, vindicating for the word its full value: "In the Symbol proper, what we can call a Symbol, there is ever, more or less distinctly and directly, some embodiment and revelation of the Infinite; the Infinite is made to blend itself with the Finite, to stand visible, and as it were, attainable there."

It is in such a sense as this that the word Symbolism has been used to describe a movement which, during the last generation, has profoundly influenced the course of French literature. All such words, used of anything so living, variable, and irresponsible as literature, are, as symbols themselves must so often be, mere compromises, mere indi-cations. Symbolism, as seen in the writers of our day, would have no value if it were not seen also, under one disguise or another, in every great imaginative writer. What distin-guishes the Symbolism of our day from the Symbolism of the past is that it has now become conscious of itself, in a sense in which it was unconscious even in Gérard de Ner-val,[3] to whom I trace the particular origin of the literature which I call Symbolist. The forces which mould the thought of men change, or men's resistance to them slack-ens; with the change of men's thought comes a change of literature, alike in its inmost essence and in its outward form: after the world has starved its soul long enough in the contemplation and the re-arrangement of material things, comes the turn of the soul; and with it comes the literature of which I write in this volume, a literature in which the vis-ible world is no longer a reality, and the unseen world no longer a dream. . . .

. . . It is all an attempt to spiritualise literature, to evade the old bondage of rhetoric, the old bondage of exteriority. Description is banished that beautiful things may be evoked, magically; the regular beat of verse is broken in order that words may fly, upon subtler wings. Mystery is no longer feared, as the great mystery in whose midst we are islanded was feared by those to whom that unknown sea was only a great void. We are coming closer to nature, as we seem to shrink from it with something of horror, disdaining to cata-logue the trees of the forest. And as we brush aside the acci-dents of daily life, in which men and women imagine

---

[1]**"It is in and through Symbols . . .":** Carlyle, *Sartor Resartus* (1834), book 3, chapter 3, from which Symons' subsequent quota-tions also come.

[2]**Comte Goblet d'Alviella** (1846–1925): author of *The Migration of Symbols* (1894).

[3]**Gérard de Nerval** (1808–1855): French Romantic poet and the subject of Symons' first chapter.

that they are alone touching reality, we come closer to humanity, to everything in humanity that may have begun before the world and may outlast it.

Here, then, in this revolt against exteriority, against rhetoric, against a materialistic tradition; in this endeavour to disengage the ultimate essence, the soul, of whatever exists and can be realised by the consciousness; in this dutiful waiting upon every symbol by which the soul of things can be made visible; literature, bowed down by so many burdens, may at last attain liberty, and its authentic speech. In attaining this liberty, it accepts a heavier burden; for in speaking to us so intimately, so solemnly, as only religion had hitherto spoken to us, it becomes itself a kind of religion, with all the duties and responsibilities of the sacred ritual. (Introduction)

1899

AUTHORS

JOHN KEBLE

(1792–1866)

Home-schooled in a village, Keble distinguished himself as a scholarship student at Oxford, where he was ordained in 1815 and spent his twenties as a fellow and tutor. He returned home as a curate to assist his ailing father with parish duties and stayed nearly a decade, composing the devotional lyrics that were published anonymously in 1827 as *The Christian Year*. Modeled on the Anglican liturgical calendar, soothing in tone and lucidly orthodox in content, Keble's cycle of poems went into nearly a hundred editions in his lifetime. Its success won him appointment as Professor of Poetry at Oxford from 1831 to 1841, when he published his lectures (in Latin, the language he used in delivering them, like every incumbent before Matthew Arnold). These lectures articulated what Keble's poems exemplified: a Wordsworthian poetic of spontaneous and sympathetic feeling, tempered by the conservative, domestic modesty that governed English poetry during the 1820s and 1830s. Having married in 1836, Keble accepted the country vicarage in Hampshire that he would hold for the rest of his life, mingling village responsibilities with a prominent national role in the issues that embroiled the Victorian Church.

These issues arose from the rivalry of ecclesiastical with secular interests in determining the character of the modern British state. Keble, a traditionalist to the backbone, inveighed against liberalism in an 1833 sermon called "National Apostasy," which launched the High Church Oxford Movement in defense of sacramental ritual, approved doctrine, and the prerogative and authority of the priesthood. In this cause Keble joined John Henry Newman and other writers of the influential *Tracts for the Times* (1833–1841); he also prepared scholarly editions of orthodox Catholic and Anglican divines. These labors were sometimes reactionary to the point of unworldliness, yet the author of *The Christian Year* pursued them with a lively sense of his contemporary audience, ministering shrewdly to public anxieties about changing community and family patterns by upholding the Church as a safeguard for both. In the shelter of God's house, Keble affirmed in a later collection of verses for children and parents, *Lyra Innocentium* (*The Innocents' Harp*, 1846), lay the proper ground for an English home. By midcentury he and his fellow Tractarians had been defeated by Broad Church liberalism; but the most significant poetic testament on the winning side, Tennyson's *In Memoriam*, would probably not have assumed the firmly stanzaic shape, calendrical sequence, or lay-pastoral therapeutic posture it did if Keble had not shown the way. This arch-conservative provides a benchmark from which to measure Victorian change, even as the staying power of his *Christian Year*, like the unslaked thirst for such instructive reading as his posthumous twelve-volume *Sermons*, cautions us against overestimating the pace of that change.

from The Christian Year

Septuagesima Sunday[1]

The invisible things of Him from the creation of the world
are clearly seen, being understood by the things which are
made. *Romans* i:20.

There is a book, who runs may read,
    Which heavenly truth imparts,
And all the lore its scholars need,
    Pure eyes and Christian hearts.

The works of God above, below,
    Within us and around,
Are pages in that book, to shew
    How God himself is found.

The glorious sky embracing all
    Is like the Maker's love,   10
Wherewith encompass'd, great and small
    In peace and order move.

The Moon above, the Church below,
    A wondrous race they run,
But all their radiance, all their glow,
    Each borrows of its Sun.

The Saviour lends the light and heat
    That crowns his holy hill;
The saints, like stars, around his seat,
    Perform their courses still[2]   20

The saints above are stars in Heaven—
    What are the saints on earth?
Like trees they stand whom God has given[3]
    Our Eden's happy birth.

Faith is their fix'd unswerving root,
    Hope their unfading flower,
Fair deeds of charity their fruit,
    The glory of their bower.

The dew of heaven is like thy grace,[4]
    It steals in silence down;   30

But where it lights, the favour'd place
    By richest fruits is known.

One Name above all glorious names
    With its ten thousand tongues
The everlasting sea proclaims,
    Echoing angelic songs.

The raging Fire[5], the roaring Wind,
    Thy boundless power display:
But in the gentler breeze we find
    Thy Spirit's viewless way[6]   40

Two worlds are ours: 'tis only Sin
    Forbids us to descry
The mystic heaven and earth within,
    Plain as the sea and sky.

Thou, who hast given me eyes to see
    And love this sight so fair,
Give me a heart to find out Thee,
    And read Thee every where.

                  1827

Eleventh Sunday after Trinity[1]

Is it a time to receive money, and to receive garments, and
olive yards, and vineyards, and sheep, and oxen, and men
servants, and maid servants? 2 *Kings* v. 26.

Is this a time to plant and build,
Add house to house, and field to field,
When round our walls the battle lowers,
When mines are sprung beneath our towers,
And watchful foes are stealing round
To search and spoil the holy ground?

Is this a time for moonlight dreams
Of love and home by mazy streams,
For Fancy with her shadowy toys,
Aerial hopes and pensive joys,   10
While souls are wandering far and wide,
And curses swarm on every side?

---

[1]**Septuagesima Sunday**: third Sunday before Lent.
[2]**still**: Dan. xii.3. [Keble's note]
[3]**given**: Isaiah lx.21. [Keble's note]
[4]**grace**: Psalm lxviii. 9. [Keble's note]

[5]**Fire**: Hebrews xii.29. [Keble's note]
[6]**way**: St. John iii.8. [Keble's note]
[1]**Trinity**: eighth Sunday after Easter.

No—rather steel thy melting heart
To act the martyr's sternest part,
To watch, with firm unshrinking eye,
Thy darling visions as they die,
Till all bright hopes, and hues of day
Have faded into twilight gray.

Yes—let them pass without a sigh,
And if the world seem dull and dry,   20
If long and sad thy lonely hours,
And winds have rent thy sheltering bowers,
Bethink thee what thou art and where,
A sinner in a life of care.

The fire of Heaven is soon to fall,
(Thou know'st it) on this earthly ball;
Then many a soul, the price of blood,
Mark'd by th' Almighty's hand for good,
Shall feel the o'erflowing whirlwinds sweep—
And will the blessed Angels weep?   30

Then in his wrath shall GOD uproot
The trees He set, for lack of fruit,
And drown in rude tempestuous blaze
The towers His hand had deign'd to raise;
In silence, ere that storm begin,
Count o'er His mercies and thy sin.

Pray only that thine aching heart,
From visions vain content to part,
Strong for Love's sake its woe to hide,
May cheerful wait the cross beside,   40
Too happy if, that dreadful day,
Thy life be given thee for a prey.[2]

Snatch'd sudden from th' avenging rod,
Safe in the bosom of thy GOD,
How wilt thou then look back, and smile
On thoughts that bitterest seem'd erewhile,
And bless the pangs that made thee see,
This was no world of rest for thee.

     1827

---

[2]**prey**: Jeremiah xlv.4, 5. The Lord saith thus: Behold, that which I have built will I break down, and that which I have planted I will pluck up, even this whole land. And seekest thou great things for thyself? seek them not, for, behold, I will bring evil upon all flesh, saith the Lord; but thy life will I give unto **thee for a prey** in all places whither thou goest. [Keble's note]

All Saints' Day[1]

> Hurt not the earth, neither the sea, nor the trees, till we have sealed the servants of our God in their foreheads. *Revelations* vii. 3.

Why blow'st thou not, thou wintry wind,
    Now every leaf is brown and sere,
And idly droops, to thee resign'd,
    The fading chaplet of the year?
Yet wears the pure aerial sky
Her summer veil, half drawn on high,
Of silvery haze, and dark and still
The shadows sleep on every slanting hill.

How quiet shews the woodland scene!
    Each flower and tree, its duty done,   10
Reposing in decay serene,
    Like weary men when age is won,
Such calm old age as conscience pure
And self-commanding hearts ensure,
Waiting their summons to the sky,
Content to live, but not afraid to die.

Sure if our eyes were purg'd to trace
    God's unseen armies hovering round,
We should behold by angels' grace
    The four strong winds of Heaven fast bound, 20
Their downward sweep a moment staid
On ocean cove and forest glade,
Till the last flower of autumn shed
Her funeral odours on her dying bed.

So in thine awful armoury, Lord,
    The lightnings of the judgment day
Pause yet awhile, in mercy stor'd,
    Till willing hearts wear quite away
Their earthly stains; and spotless shine
On every brow in light divine   30
The cross by angel hands impress'd,
The seal of glory won and pledge of promis'd rest.

Little they dream, those haughty souls
    Whom empires own with bended knee,
What lowly fate their own controuls,
    Together link'd by Heaven's decree;—

---

[1]**All Saints' Day**: November 1.

As bloodhounds hush their baying wild
To wanton with some fearless child,
So Famine waits, and War with greedy eyes,
Till some repenting heart be ready for the skies.   40

Think ye the spires that glow so bright
    In front of yonder setting sun,
Stand by their own unshaken might?
    No—where th' upholding grace is won,
We dare not ask, nor Heaven would tell,
But sure from many a hidden dell,
From many a rural nook unthought of there,
Rises for that proud world the saints' prevailing prayer.

On, champions blest, in Jesus' name,
    Short be your strife, your triumph full,   50
Till every heart have caught your flame,
    And lighten'd of the world's misrule
Ye soar those elder saints to meet,
Gather'd long since at Jesus' feet,
No world of passions to destroy,
Your prayers and struggles o'er, your task all praise and joy.

                                                    1827

~

from Sermon on National Apostasy[1]

Advertisement to the First Edition

Since the following pages were prepared for the press, the calamity,[2] in anticipation of which they were written, has actually overtaken this portion of the Church of God. The Legislature of England and Ireland, (*the members of which are not even bound to profess belief in the Atonement,*) this body has virtually usurped the commission of those whom our Saviour entrusted with *at least one voice* in making ecclesiastical laws, on matters wholly or partly spiritual. The same Legislature has also ratified, to its full extent, this principle; —that the Apostolical Church in this realm is henceforth only to stand, in the eye of the State, as *one sect among many*, depending, for any preeminence she may still appear to retain,

merely upon the accident of her having a strong party in the country.

It is a moment, surely, full of deep solicitude to all those members of the Church who still believe her authority divine, and the oaths and obligations, by which they are bound to her, undissolved and indissoluble by calculations of human expediency. Their anxiety turns not so much on the consequences, to the State, of what has been done, (*they are but too evident,*) as on the line of conduct which they are bound themselves to pursue. How may they continue their communion with the Church *established*, (hitherto the pride and comfort of their lives,) without any taint of those Erastian Principles[3] on which she now is avowedly to be governed? What answer can we make henceforth to the partisans of the Bishop of Rome,[4] when they taunt us with being a mere Parliamentarian Church? And how, consistently with our present relations to the State, can even the doctrinal purity and integrity of the MOST SACRED ORDER be preserved?

The attention of all who love the Church is most earnestly solicited to these questions. They are such, it will be observed, as cannot be answered by appealing to precedents in English History, because, at most, such could only shew, that the difficulty might have been raised before. It is believed, that there are hundreds, nay thousands of Christians, and that soon there will be tens of thousands, unaffectedly anxious to be rightly guided with regard to these and similar points. And they are mooted thus publicly, for the chance of eliciting, from competent judges, a correct and early opinion.

If, under such trying and delicate circumstances, one could venture to be positive about any thing, it would seem safe to say, that in such measure as it may be thought incumbent on the Church, or on Churchmen, to submit to any profane intrusion, it must at least be their sacred duty, to declare, promulgate, and record, their full conviction, that it *is* intrusion; that they yield to it as they might to any other tyranny, but do from their hearts deprecate and abjure it. This seems the least that can be done: unless we would have our children's children say, "There was once here a glorious Church, but it was betrayed into the hands of Libertines for the real or affected love of a little temporary peace and good order."

---

[1]**Apostasy**: renunciation of faith.

[2]**calamity**: Parliament's 1833 reorganization of Anglican bishoprics in Ireland, which Keble saw as a sacrilege, and as the most recent in a series of steps towards the secularization of Britain, one of which released MPs from subscribing to the doctrine of Christ's **Atonement**.

[3]**Erastian principles**: assertions of the state's supremacy in church affairs.

[4]**Bishop of Rome**: the pope.

Sermon on National Apostasy

*As for me, God forbid that I should sin against the Lord in
ceasing to pray for you: but I will teach you the good and
the right way. 1 Samuel xii. 23*

That portion,[5] in particular, of the history of the chosen
people, which drew from Samuel, the truest of patriots, the
wise and noble sentiment in the text, must ever be an unpleasing and perplexing page of Scripture, to those, who
would fain persuade themselves, that a nation, even a Christian nation, may do well enough, as such, without God, and
without His Church. For what if the Jews were bound to the
Almighty by ties common to no other people? What if He
had condescended to know them in a way in which He was
as yet unrevealed to all families of the earth besides? What
if, as their relation to Him was nearer, and their ingratitude
more surpassing, so they might expect more exemplary
punishment? Still, after all has been said, to exaggerate their
guilt, in degree, beyond what is supposed possible in any
nation whatever now, what can it come to, in kind and in
substance, but only this,—that they rejected God? that they
wished themselves rid of the moral restraint implied in His
peculiar presence and covenant? They said, what the
prophet Ezekiel, long after, represents their worthy posterity as saying, "We will be as the heathen, the families of the
countries.[6] Once for all, we will get rid of these disagreeable, unfashionable scruples, which throw us behind, as we
think, in the race of worldly honour and profit." Is this indeed a tone of thought, which Christian nations cannot fall
into? Or, if they should, has it ceased to be displeasing to
God? In other words, has He forgotten to be angry with
impiety and practical atheism? Either this must be affirmed,
or men must own, (what is clear at once to plain unsophisti-
cated readers,) that this first overt act, which began the
downfall of the Jewish nation, stands on record, with its
fatal consequences, for a perpetual warning to all nations, as
well as to all individual Christians, who, having accepted
God for their King, allow themselves to be weary of subjec-

tion to Him, and think they should be happier if they were
freer, and more like the rest of the world. . . .

What are the symptoms, by which one may judge
most fairly, whether or no a nation, as such, is becoming
alienated from God and Christ?

And what are the particular duties of sincere Christians, whose lot is cast by Divine Providence in a time of
such dire calamity?

The conduct of the Jews, in asking for a king, may furnish an ample illustration of the first point: the behaviour of
Samuel, then and afterwards, supplies as perfect a pattern of
the second, as can well be expected from human nature.

The case is at least possible, of a nation, having for
centuries acknowledged, as an essential part of its theory of
government, that, as a Christian nation, she is also a part of
Christ's Church, and bound, in all her legislation and policy, by the fundamental rules of that Church—the case is, I
say, conceivable, of a government and people, so constituted, deliberately throwing off the restraint, which in
many respects such a principle would impose on them, nay,
disavowing the principle itself; and that, on the plea, that
other states, as flourishing or more so in regard of wealth
and dominion, do well enough without it. Is not this desiring, like the Jews, to have an earthly king over them, when
the Lord their God is their King? Is it not saying in other
words, "We will be as the heathen, the families of the countries," the aliens to the Church of our Redeemer?

To such a change, whenever it takes place, the immediate impulse will probably be given by some pretence of
danger from without—such as, at the time now spoken of,
was furnished to the Israelites by an incursion of the children of Ammon,[7] or by some wrong or grievance in the executive government, such as the malversation[8] of Samuel's
sons, to whom he had deputed his judicial functions. Pretences will never be hard to find; but, in reality, the movement will always be traceable to the same decay or want of
faith, the same deficiency in Christian resignation and
thankfulness, which leads so many, as individuals, to disdain
and forfeit the blessings of the Gospel. Men not impressed
with religious principle attribute their ill success in life,—
the hard times they have to struggle with,—to any thing
rather than their own ill-desert: and the institutions of the
country, ecclesiastical and civil, are always at hand to bear
the blame of whatever seems to be going amiss. . . .

---

[5]**that portion**: The context for Keble's sermon **text** is 1 Samuel
11–12, where against God's will the Israelites make Saul their king.

[6]**"We will be . . . countries"**: Ezekiel 20:32.

[7]**Ammon**: see 2 Samuel 10.

[8]**malversation**: corruption in office.

[handwritten margin notes: Strong felt deeply voice / cove clever ol England / moves away from / Forward? needs to be more inclusive]

The charge might perhaps surprise many of them, just as, in other times and countries, the impatient patrons of innovation are surprised, at finding themselves rebuked on religious grounds. Perhaps the Jews pleaded the express countenance, which the words of their Law, in one place, seemed, by anticipation, to lend to the measure they were urging. And so, in modern times, when liberties are to be taken, and the intrusive passions of men to be indulged, precedent and permission, or what sounds like them, may be easily found and quoted for every thing. But Samuel, in God's name, silenced all this, giving them to understand, that in His sight the whole was a question of motive and purpose, not of ostensible and colourable argument;—in His sight, I say, to Whom we, as well as they, are nationally responsible for much more than the soundness of our deductions as matter of disputation, or of law; we are responsible for the meaning and temper in which we deal with His Holy Church, established among us for the salvation of our souls.

These, which have been hitherto mentioned as omens and tokens of an Apostate[9] Mind in a nation, have been suggested by the portion itself of sacred history, to which I have ventured to direct your attention. There are one or two more, which the nature of the subject, and the palpable tendency of things around us, will not allow to be passed over.

One of the most alarming, as a symptom, is the growing indifference, in which men indulge themselves, to other men's religious sentiments. Under the guise of charity and toleration we are come almost to this pass; that no difference, in matters of faith, is to disqualify for our approbation and confidence, whether in public or domestic life. Can we conceal it from ourselves, that every year the practice is becoming more common, of trusting men unreservedly in the most delicate and important matters, without one serious inquiry, whether they do not hold principles which make it impossible for them to be loyal to their Creator, Redeemer, and Sanctifier? Are not offices conferred, partnerships formed, intimacies courted,—nay, (what is almost too painful to think of,) do not parents commit their children to be educated, do they not encourage them to intermarry, in houses, on which Apostolical Authority[10] would rather teach them to set a mark, as unfit to be entered by a faithful servant of Christ?

---

[9]**Apostate**: religious renegade.

[10]**Apostolical Authority**: claimed by the Church of England (which denied it to Rome), in direct descent from Jesus' charge to the apostle Peter (Matthew 16:18).

I do not now speak of public measures only or chiefly; many things of that kind may be thought, whether wisely or no, to become from time to time necessary, which are in reality as little desired by those who lend them a seeming concurrence, as they are, in themselves, undesirable. But I speak of the spirit which leads men to exult in every step of that kind; to congratulate one another on the supposed decay of what they call an exclusive system.

Very different are the feelings with which it seems natural for a true Churchman to regard such a state of things, from those which would arise in his mind on witnessing the mere triumph of any given set of adverse opinions, exaggerated or even heretical as he might deem them. He might feel as melancholy,—he could hardly feel so indignant.

But this is not a becoming place, nor are these safe topics, for the indulgence of mere feeling. The point really to be considered is, whether, according to the coolest estimate, the fashionable liberality of this generation be not ascribable, in a great measure, to the same temper which led the Jews voluntarily to set about degrading themselves to a level with the idolatrous Gentiles? And, if it be true any where, that such enactments are forced on the Legislature by public opinion, is APOSTASY too hard a word to describe the temper of that nation?

The same tendency is still more apparent, because the fair gloss of candour and forbearance is wanting, in the surly or scornful impatience often exhibited, by persons who would regret passing for unbelievers, when Christian motives are suggested, and checks from Christian principles attempted to be enforced on their public conduct. I say, "their public conduct," more especially; because in that, I know not how, persons are apt to be more shameless, and readier to avow the irreligion that is in them;—amongst other reasons, probably, from each feeling that he is one of a multitude, and fancying, therefore, that his responsibility is divided.

For example:—whatever be the cause, in this country of late years, (though we are lavish in professions of piety,) there has been observable a growing disinclination, on the part of those bound by VOLUNTARY OATHS, to whatever reminds them of their obligation; a growing disposition to explain it all away. We know what, some years ago, would have been thought of such uneasiness, if betrayed by persons officially sworn, in private, legal, or commercial life. If there be any subjects or occasions, now, on which men are inclined to judge of it more lightly, it concerns them deeply to be quite sure, that they are not indulging or encouraging a profane dislike of God's awful Presence; a general tendency, as a people, to leave Him out of all their thoughts.

They will have the more reason to suspect themselves, in proportion as they see and feel more of that impatience under pastoral authority, which our Saviour Himself has taught us to consider as a never-failing symptom of an unchristian temper. "He that heareth you, heareth Me; and he that despiseth you, despiseth Me."[11] Those words of divine truth put beyond all sophistical exception, what common sense would lead us to infer, and what daily experience teaches,—that disrespect to the Successors of the Apostles, as such, is an unquestionable symptom of enmity to Him, who gave them their commission at first, and has pledged Himself to be with them for ever. Suppose such disrespect general and national, suppose it also avowedly grounded not on any fancied tenet of religion, but on mere human reasons of popularity and expediency, either there is no meaning at all in these emphatic declarations of our Lord, or that nation, how highly soever she may think of her own religion and morality, stands convicted in His sight of a direct disavowal of His Sovereignty.

To this purpose it may be worth noticing, that the ill-fated chief, whom God gave to the Jews, as the prophet tells us, in His anger, and whose disobedience and misery were referred by himself to his "fearing the people, and obeying their voice,"[12] whose conduct, therefore, may be fairly taken as a sample of what public opinion was at that time supposed to require—his first step in apostasy was, perhaps, an intrusion on the sacrificial office, certainly an impatient breach of his engagement with Samuel, as the last and greatest of his crimes was persecuting David, whom he well knew to bear God's special commission. God forbid, that any Christian land should ever, by her prevailing temper and policy, revive the memory and likeness of Saul, or incur a sentence of reprobation like his. But if such a thing should be, the crimes of that nation will probably begin in infringement on Apostolical Rights; she will end in persecuting the true Church; and in the several stages of her melancholy career, she will continually be led on from bad to worse by vain endeavours at accommodation and compromise with evil. Sometimes toleration may be the word, as with Saul when he spared the Amalekites; sometimes state security, as when he sought the life of David; sometimes sympathy with popular feeling, as appears to have been the case, when violating solemn treaties, he attempted to exterminate the remnant of the Gibeonites, in his zeal for the children of Israel and Judah. Such are the sad but obvious results of separating religious resignation altogether from men's notions of civil duty. . . .

1833

---

[11]"He . . . despiseth Me": Luke 10:16.

[12]"fearing . . . voice": see 1 Samuel 15:24; the **chief** is Saul, whose royal misdeeds the paragraph goes on to enumerate.

THOMAS CARLYLE

(1795–1881)

To the strict Scots Calvinists of rural Ecclefechan, the angular, shy, and very bright son of stonemason James Carlyle seemed made for the ministry. And so he was, but in an unforeseen way that bypassed the kirk and led through German ideas and London journalism to his installation as the first of the Victorian prose sages, minister-provocateur to a doubt-swept generation. What to make of Thomas Carlyle is a problem that has always worried his students (among them Emerson and Nietzsche, William Morris and George Bernard Shaw), but the person it worried most was Carlyle himself, especially during the 1820s as he successively tested on theology, mathematics, geology, the law, and philosophy a keen mind impatient with formal teaching and hungry for a spiritual fulfillment that would be compatible with intellectual freedom. By 1830 he had settled on literature as the least unsatisfactory compromise between his needs for elbow room and for an earnest engagement with life. He was focused and steadied by marriage in 1826 to his former pupil Jane Welsh of Edinburgh, a woman whose own ready wit and spirited, frustrated ambition made her one of the sharpest letter-writers of the day. Beset by chronic indigestion and bouts of depression, Thomas entered his thirties on a poor, isolated sheep farm Jane had inherited in Craigenputtoch, the middle of Scottish nowhere. From this improbable quarter he launched a literary career, producing autobiographical fiction that nobody liked and a stream of translations and articles, mostly about German books and ideas, that earned him a firm if small circle of admirers in London, where the couple eventually settled in 1834.

Carlyle's early readers admired in equal measure what he had to say and how he said it. In essays like "Signs of the Times" he fabricated a prose style that compounded allusive learning and Biblical sonority with a managed outlandishness, stamping the page with a voice whose Teutonical transcendentalism and Scotch spleen could soar or swoop with attention-grabbing unpredictability. These idiosyncrasies emerge in force with Carlyle's masterpieces of the next decade, *Sartor Resartus* (1833) and *The French Revolution* (1837), experimental works resistant to anthologization. In the former, an extravaganza serially published in a humor magazine, a bewildered English editor strives to blend an account of the "Philosophy of Clothes" expounded by Professor Diogenes Teufelsdröckh (God-born Devil-dung) with a biography assembled out of laundry bags; the latter, a thousand-page history of the crisis that precipitated nineteenth-century Europe, imposes on a solid structure of documentation bold techniques of montage and panorama, with a soundtrack running the gamut from sermon to wisecrack. Carlyle's birth date marks him as a contemporary of Byron, Shelley, and Keats, whose early deaths removed them from the literary scene before he entered it; and his work of the 1830s keeps faith with the Romantic program of recasting the genres that shape literary meaning. That work endeavors at once to make sense of the world and to make readers aware of the means—rhetorical, imaginative, often unconscious—by which sense gets made.

As fame came to Carlyle at the end of the decade, he turned a culture critic's eye on current events in *Chartism* and *Past and Present*, works that increasingly echoed the Old Testament prophets' clamor for justice and appeal to root causes. Beneath the moral vehemence, however, one looks in vain for any anchorage more substantial than awed reverence before the drift of power or spirit of the age. This central mystery, or dynamic vacuity, may be seen both as the secret of Carlyle's influence and as his Achilles' heel. For some contemporaries it made him a confidence man or ethical desperado, for others an inspired modern improviser denouncing guilt and upholding duty as honestly as possible. Many readers find something rather like it in the writings of Carlyle's prophetic heirs, from John Ruskin and Matthew Arnold to Walter Pater and Oscar Wilde. And most will hesitate whether to consider Carlyle's fulminations against free-market abuses and the cash nexus reactionary or revolutionary, protofascist or protosocialist (a conundrum sharpened by his place here between the conservative Keble and the liberal Macaulay). His meditation *On Heroes* declares both that a healthy people follows leaders of genius and that the genius of leadership involves an instinctual responsiveness to the people's will. The analogy to literary genius and cultural authority under mass-market conditions was not lost on Carlyle himself.

After *Past and Present* he wrote biographies of two ruler-heroes, Oliver Cromwell (1845) and Frederick the Great of Prussia (1858–1865). These voluminous productions maintained Carlyle's position without advancing it; and his ongoing commentary on events of the 1850s and 1860s likewise exhibits a brittleness of style and attitude that was often the price exacted of Victorian public intellectuals by their success. Younger writers overtook him during the second half of the century in both narrative and essay forms, but his example had touched them all, not least Dickens, George Eliot, and other masters of the Victorian social novel. In later years Carlyle became a fixture in the literary heavens for ready reference, allusion, and parody: a perennial outsider, but also the unofficial prophet, minister, and moral authority to thousands. When J. A. M. Whistler titled his *second* most famous oil portrait simply *Arrangement in Grey and Black, No. 2* (1873), it was because the grizzled sitter's profile was one he could count on every gallery-goer to recognize.

— Sense of movement

from Signs of the Times

... The repeal of the Test Acts, and then of the Catholic disabilities,[1] has struck many of their admirers with an indescribable astonishment. Those things seemed fixed and immovable; deep as the foundations of the world; and lo, in a moment they have vanished, and their place knows them no more! Our worthy friends mistook the slumbering Leviathan[2] for an island; often as they had been assured, that Intolerance was, and could be nothing but a Monster; and so, mooring under the lee, they had anchored comfortably in his scaly rind, thinking to take good cheer; as for some space they did. But now their Leviathan has suddenly dived under; and they can no longer be fastened in the stream of time; but must drift forward on it, even like the rest of the world: no very appalling fate, we think, could they but understand it; which, however, they will not yet, for a season. Their little island is gone; sunk deep amid confused eddies; and what is left worth caring for in the universe? What is it to them that the great continents of the earth are still standing; and the polestar and all our loadstars, in the heavens, still shining and eternal? Their cherished little haven is gone, and they will not be comforted! And therefore, day after day, in all manner of periodical or perennial publications, the most lugubrious predictions are sent forth. The King has virtually abdicated; the Church is a widow, without jointure; public principle is gone; private honesty is going; society, in short, is fast falling in pieces; and a time of unmixed evil is come on us.

Society Falling Apart

At such a period, it was to be expected that the rage of prophecy should be more than usually excited. Accordingly, the Millennarians have come forth on the right hand, and the Millites on the left. The Fifth-monarchy men prophesy from the Bible, and the Utilitarians from Bentham. The one

---

[1]**repeal ... disabilities:** In 1828 and 1829 Parliament struck down 150-year-old laws discriminating against nonmembers in the Church of England.

[2]**Leviathan:** see *Paradise Lost* 1.201–08.

not the Good & the life ... busy life

announces that the last of the seals[3] is to be opened, positively, in the year 1860; and the other assures us that "the greatest-happiness principle" is to make a heaven of earth, in a still shorter time. We know these symptoms too well, to think it necessary or safe to interfere with them. Time and the hours will bring relief to all parties. The grand encourager of Delphic or other noises is—the Echo. Left to themselves, they will the sooner dissipate, and die away in space.

Meanwhile, we too admit that the present is an important time; as all present time necessarily is. The poorest Day that passes over us is the conflux of two Eternities; it is made up of currents that issue from the remotest Past, and flow onwards into the remotest Future. We were wise indeed, could we discern truly the signs of our own time; and by knowledge of its wants and advantages, wisely adjust our own position in it. Let us, instead of gazing idly into the obscure distance, look calmly around us, for a little, on the perplexed scene where we stand. Perhaps, on a more serious inspection, something of its perplexity will disappear, some of its distinctive characters and deeper tendencies more clearly reveal themselves; whereby our own relations to it, our own true aims and endeavours in it, may also become clearer.

Were we required to characterise this age of ours by any single epithet, we should be tempted to call it, not an Heroical, Devotional, Philosophical, or Moral Age, but, above all others, the Mechanical Age. It is the Age of Machinery, in every outward and inward sense[4] of that word; the age which, with its whole undivided might, forwards, teaches and practises the great art of adapting means to ends. Nothing is now done directly, or by hand; all is by rule and calculated contrivance. For the simplest operation, some helps and accompaniments, some cunning abbreviating process is in readiness. Our old modes of exertion are all discredited, and thrown aside. On every hand, the living artisan is driven from his workshop, to make room for a speedier, inanimate one. The shuttle drops from the fingers of the weaver, and falls into iron fingers that ply it faster. The sailor furls his sail, and lays down his oar; and bids a strong, unwearied servant, on vaporous wings, bear him through the waters. Men have crossed oceans by steam; the Birmingham Fire-king has visited the fabulous East; and the

genius of the Cape, were there any Camoens now to sing it, has again been alarmed, and with far stranger thunders than Gama's.[5] There is no end to machinery. Even the horse is stripped of his harness, and finds a fleet fire-horse yoked in his stead. Nay, we have an artist that hatches chickens by steam; the very brood-hen is to be superseded! For all earthly, and for some unearthly purposes, we have machines and mechanic furtherances; for mincing our cabbages, for casting us into magnetic sleep. We remove mountains, and make seas our smooth highway; nothing can resist us. We war with rude Nature; and, by our resistless engines, come off always victorious, and loaded with spoils.

What wonderful accessions have thus been made, and are still making, to the physical power of mankind; how much better fed, clothed, lodged and, in all outward respects, accommodated men now are, or might be, by a given quantity of labour, is a grateful reflection which forces itself on every one. What changes, too, this addition of power is introducing into the Social System; how wealth has more and more increased, and at the same time gathered itself more and more into masses, strangely altering the old relations, and increasing the distance between the rich and the poor, will be a question for Political Economists, and a much more complex and important one than any they have yet engaged with.

But leaving these matters for the present, let us observe how the mechanical genius of our time has diffused itself into quite other provinces. Not the external and physical alone is now managed by machinery, but the internal and spiritual also. Here too nothing follows its spontaneous course, nothing is left to be accomplished by old natural methods. Everything has its cunningly devised implements, its preëstablished apparatus; it is not done by hand, but by machinery. Thus we have machines for Education: Lancastrian machines; Hamiltonian machines;[6] monitors, maps and emblems. Instruction, that mysterious communing of Wisdom with Ignorance, is no longer an indefinable tentative process, requiring a study of individual aptitudes, and a perpetual variation of means and methods, to attain the same end; but a secure, universal, straightforward business, to be conducted in the gross, by proper mechanism, with such intellect as comes to hand. Then, we have Religious

---

[3]**Millennarians, Fifth-monarchy men**: Puritan extremists from the mid-17th-century English civil war. **Millites**: adherents of James and John Stuart Mill, **Utilitarian** followers of Jeremy **Bentham** (1748–1832). **the last of the seals**: opened in Revelation 8:1.

[4]**inward sense**: alludes to Greek root of *machine*: a means to an end.

[5]**Birmingham**: early industrial center pioneering steam power. Luis de **Camoens** (1524–1580): author of the Portuguese epic *The Lusiads*, where Vasco da **Gama**'s rounding the African **Cape** forms a key episode.

[6]Joseph **Lancaster** (1778–1838) streamlined primary education by making older pupils **monitors** to teach beginners. James **Hamilton** (1769–1829) developed a system for linguistic instruction.

machines, of all imaginable varieties; the Bible-Society,[7] professing a far higher and heavenly structure, is found, on inquiry, to be altogether an earthly contrivance; supported by collection of moneys, by fomenting of vanities, by puffing, intrigue and chicane; a machine for converting the Heathen. It is the same in all other departments. Has any man, or any society of men, a truth to speak, a piece of spiritual work to do; they can nowise proceed at once and with the mere natural organs, but must first call a public meeting, appoint committees, issue prospectuses, eat a public dinner; in a word, construct or borrow machinery, wherewith to speak it and do it. Without machinery they were hopeless, helpless; a colony of Hindoo weavers squatting in the heart of Lancashire. Mark, too, how every machine must have its moving power, in some of the great currents of society; every little sect among us, Unitarians, Utilitarians, Anabaptists, Phrenologists, must have its Periodical, its monthly or quarterly Magazine;—hanging out, like its windmill, into the *popularis aura*,[8] to grind meal for the society.

With individuals, in like manner, natural strength avails little. No individual now hopes to accomplish the poorest enterprise single-handed and without mechanical aids; he must make interest with some existing corporation, and till his field with their oxen. In these days, more emphatically than ever, "to live, signifies to unite with a party, or to make one." Philosophy, Science, Art, Literature, all depend on machinery. No Newton, by silent meditation, now discovers the system of the world from the falling of an apple; but some quite other than Newton stands in his Museum, his Scientific Institution, and behind whole batteries of retorts, digesters and galvanic piles[9] imperatively "interrogates Nature,"—who, however, shows no haste to answer. In defect of Raphaels, and Angelos, and Mozarts, we have Royal Academies[10] of Painting, Sculpture, Music; whereby the languishing spirit of Art may be strengthened, as by the more generous diet of a Public Kitchen. Literature, too, has its Paternoster-row[11] mechanism, its Trade-dinners, its Editorial conclaves, and huge subterranean, puffing bellows; so that books are not only printed, but, in a great measure, written and sold, by machinery.

National culture, spiritual benefit of all sorts, is under the same management. No Queen Christina, in these times, needs to send for her Descartes; no King Frederick for his Voltaire,[12] and painfully nourish him with pensions and flattery: any sovereign of taste, who wishes to enlighten his people, has only to impose a new tax, and with the proceeds establish Philosophic Institutes. Hence the Royal and Imperial Societies, the Bibliothèques, Glyptothèques, Technothèques,[13] which front us in all capital cities; like so many well-finished hives, to which it is expected the stray agencies of Wisdom will swarm of their own accord, and hive and make honey. In like manner, among ourselves, when it is thought that religion is declining, we have only to vote half-a-million's worth of bricks and mortar, and build new churches. In Ireland it seems they have gone still farther, having actually established a "Penny-a-week Purgatory-Society"! Thus does the Genius of Mechanism stand by to help us in all difficulties and emergencies, and with his iron back bears all our burdens.

These things, which we state lightly enough here, are yet of deep import, and indicate a mighty change in our whole manner of existence. For the same habit regulates not our modes of action alone, but our modes of thought and feeling. Men are grown mechanical in head and in heart, as well as in hand. They have lost faith in individual endeavour, and in natural force, of any kind. Not for internal perfection, but for external combinations and arrangements, for institutions, constitutions,—for Mechanism of one sort or other, do they hope and struggle. Their whole efforts, attachments, opinions, turn on mechanism, and are of a mechanical character. . . .

Nay, our whole Metaphysics itself, from Locke's[14] time downwards, has been physical; not a spiritual philosophy, but a material one. The singular estimation in which his Essay was so long held as a scientific work (an estimation grounded, indeed, on the estimable character of the man) will one day be thought a curious indication of the spirit of these times. His whole doctrine is mechanical, in its aim and origin, in its method and its results. It is not a philosophy of the mind: it is a mere discussion concerning the origin of our consciousness, or ideas, or whatever else they are

---

[7]British and Foreign **Bible-Society**: founded 1804 to supply cheap Bibles worldwide in vernacular translation.

[8]*popularis aura*: public opinion (from Horace, *Odes* 3.2.20).

[9]**retorts, digesters, galvanic piles**: chemical and electrical apparatus.

[10]**Royal Academy** of Arts: founded 1768.

[11]**Paternoster Row**: London publishing district.

[12]**Queen Christina** (1626–1689) summoned the French philosopher René **Descartes** (1596–1650) to the Swedish court, where he died. **King Frederick** (1712–1786) a century later patronized the French man of letters **Voltaire** (1694–1778) at the Prussian court.

[13]**Bibliothèques, Glyptothèques, Technothèques**: collections of books, sculptures, crafts.

[14]**John Locke** (1632–1704): author of *An Essay Concerning Human Understanding* (1690).

Good life   Spiritual fulfillm...
Spiritual ...
intellectional bliss

called; a genetic history of what we see *in* the mind. The grand secrets of Necessity and Freewill, of the Mind's vital or non-vital dependence on Matter, of our mysterious relations to Time and Space, to God, to the Universe, are not, in the faintest degree, touched on in these inquiries; and seem not to have the smallest connexion with them. . . .

This condition of the two great departments of knowledge,—the outward, cultivated exclusively on mechanical principles; the inward, finally abandoned, because, cultivated on such principles, it is found to yield no result,—sufficiently indicates the intellectual bias of our time, its all-pervading disposition towards that line of inquiry. In fact, an inward persuasion has long been diffusing itself, and now and then even comes to utterance, That, except the external, there are no true sciences; that to the inward world (if there be any) our only conceivable road is through the outward; that, in short, what cannot be investigated and understood mechanically, cannot be investigated and understood at all. We advert the more particularly to these intellectual propensities, as to prominent symptoms of our age, because Opinion is at all times doubly related to Action, first as cause, then as effect; and the speculative tendency of any age will therefore give us, on the whole, the best indications of its practical tendency.

Nowhere, for example, is the deep, almost exclusive faith we have in Mechanism more visible than in the Politics of this time. Civil government does by its nature include much that is mechanical, and must be treated accordingly. We term it indeed, in ordinary language, the Machine of Society, and talk of it as the grand working wheel from which all private machines must derive, or to which they must adapt, their movements. Considered merely as a metaphor, all this is well enough; but here, as in so many other cases, the "foam hardens itself into a shell," and the shadow we have wantonly evoked stands terrible before us and will not depart at our bidding. Government includes much also that is not mechanical, and cannot be treated mechanically; of which latter truth, as appears to us, the political speculations and exertions of our time are taking less and less cognisance.

Nay, in the very outset, we might note the mighty interest taken in *mere political arrangements,* as itself the sign of a mechanical age. The whole discontent of Europe takes this direction. The deep, strong cry of all civilised nations,—a cry which, every one now sees, must and will be answered, is: Give us a reform of Government! A good structure of legislation, a proper check upon the executive, a wise arrangement of the judiciary, is *all* that is wanting for human happiness. The Philosopher of this age is not a Socrates, a

Plato, a Hooker, or Taylor,[15] who inculcates on men the necessity and infinite worth of moral goodness, the great truth that our happiness depends on the mind which is within us, and not on the circumstances which are without us; but a Smith, a De Lolme,[16] a Bentham, who chiefly inculcates the reverse of this,—that our happiness depends entirely on external circumstances; nay, that the strength and dignity of the mind within us is itself the creature and consequence of these. Were the laws, the government, in good order, all were well with us; the rest would care for itself! Dissentients from this opinion, expressed or implied, are now rarely to be met with; widely and angrily as men differ in its application, the principle is admitted by all.

Equally mechanical, and of equal simplicity, are the methods proposed by both parties for completing or securing this all-sufficient perfection of arrangement. It is no longer the moral, religious, spiritual condition of the people that is our concern, but their physical, practical, economical condition, as regulated by public laws. Thus is the Body-politic more than ever worshipped and tendered; but the Soul-politic less than ever. Love of country, in any high or generous sense, in any other than an almost animal sense, or mere habit, has little importance attached to it in such reforms, or in the opposition shown them. Men are to be guided only by their self-interests. Good government is a good balancing of these; and, except a keen eye and appetite for self-interest, requires no virtue in any quarter. To both parties it is emphatically a machine: to the discontented, a "taxing-machine;" to the contented, a "machine for securing property." Its duties and its faults are not those of a father, but of an active parish-constable.[17]

Thus it is by the mere condition of the machine, by preserving it untouched, or else by reconstructing it, and oiling it anew, that man's salvation as a social being is to be insured and indefinitely promoted. Contrive the fabric of law aright, and without farther effort on your part, that divine spirit of Freedom, which all hearts venerate and long for, will of herself come to inhabit it; and under her healing wings every noxious influence will wither, every good and salutary one more and more expand. Nay, so devoted are we to this principle, and at the same time so curiously mechanical, that a new trade, specially grounded on it, has

---

[15]Richard **Hooker** (1554–1600), Jeremy **Taylor** (1613–1667): Anglican divines.

[16]Adam **Smith** (1723–1790): economist. Jean-Louis **De Lolme** (1740–1806): Swiss author of *The English Constitution* (1771).

[17]**parish-constable:** township official.

Spiritual vacuum — emptiness

arisen among us, under the name of "Codification," or code-making in the abstract; whereby any people, for a reasonable consideration, may be accommodated with a patent code;—more easily than curious individuals with patent breeches, for the people does *not* need to be measured first.

To us who live in the midst of all this, and see continually the faith, hope and practice of every one founded on Mechanism of one kind or other, it is apt to seem quite natural, and as if it could never have been otherwise. Nevertheless, if we recollect or reflect a little, we shall find both that it has been, and might again be otherwise. The domain of Mechanism,—meaning thereby political, ecclesiastical or other outward establishments,—was once considered as embracing, and we are persuaded can at any time embrace, but a limited portion of man's interests, and by no means the highest portion.   Fulfillment?

To speak a little pedantically, there is a science of *Dynamics* in man's fortunes and nature, as well as of *Mechanics*. There is a science which treats of, and practically addresses, the primary, unmodified forces and energies of man, the mysterious springs of Love, and Fear, and Wonder, of Enthusiasm, Poetry, Religion, all which have a truly vital and *infinite* character; as well as a science which practically addresses the finite, modified developments of these, when they take the shape of immediate "motives," as hope of reward, or as fear of punishment.

Now it is certain, that in former times the wise men, the enlightened lovers of their kind, who appeared generally as Moralists, Poets or Priests, did, without neglecting the Mechanical province, deal chiefly with the Dynamical; applying themselves chiefly to regulate, increase and purify the inward primary powers of man; and fancying that herein lay the main difficulty, and the best service they could undertake. But a wide difference is manifest in our age. For the wise men, who now appear as Political Philosophers, deal exclusively with the Mechanical province; and occupying themselves in counting-up and estimating men's motives, strive by curious checking and balancing, and other adjustments of Profit and Loss, to guide them to their true advantage: while, unfortunately, those same "motives" are so innumerable, and so variable in every individual, that no really useful conclusion can ever be drawn from their enumeration. But though Mechanism, wisely contrived, has done much for man in a social and moral point of view, we cannot be persuaded that it has ever been the chief source of his worth or happiness. Consider the great elements of human enjoyment, the attainments and possessions that exalt man's life to its present height, and see what part of

these he owes to institutions, to Mechanism of any kind; and what to the instinctive, unbounded force, which Nature herself lent him, and still continues to him. Shall we say, for example, that Science and Art are indebted principally to the founders of Schools and Universities? Did not Science originate rather, and gain advancement, in the obscure closets of the Roger Bacons, Keplers, Newtons; in the workshops of the Fausts and the Watts;[18] wherever, and in what guise soever Nature, from the first times downwards, had sent a gifted spirit upon the earth? Again, were Homer and Shakspeare members of any beneficed guild, or made Poets by means of it? Were Painting and Sculpture created by forethought, brought into the world by institutions for that end? No; Science and Art have, from first to last, been the free gift of Nature; an unsolicited, unexpected gift; often even a fatal one. These things rose up, as it were, by spontaneous growth, in the free soil and sunshine of Nature. They were not planted or grafted, nor even greatly multiplied or improved by the culture or manuring of institutions. Generally speaking, they have derived only partial help from these; often enough have suffered damage. They made constitutions for themselves. They originated in the Dynamical nature of man, not in his Mechanical nature.

Or, to take an infinitely higher instance, that of the Christian Religion, which, under every theory of it, in the believing or unbelieving mind, must ever be regarded as the crowning glory, or rather the life and soul, of our whole modern culture: How did Christianity arise and spread abroad among men? Was it by institutions, and establishments and well-arranged systems of mechanism? Not so; on the contrary, in all past and existing institutions for those ends, its divine spirit has invariably been found to languish and decay. It arose in the mystic deeps of man's soul; and was spread abroad by the "preaching of the word,"[19] by simple, altogether natural and individual efforts; and flew, like hallowed fire, from heart to heart, till all were purified and illuminated by it; and its heavenly light shone, as it still shines, and (as sun or star) will ever shine, through the whole dark destinies of man. Here again was no Mechanism; man's highest attainment was accomplished Dynamically, not Mechanically.

Nay, we will venture to say, that no high attainment, not even any far-extending movement among men, was ever

---

[18]**Roger Bacon** (1220?–1292): early scientific experimenter. Johannes **Kepler** (1571–1630): German astronomer. **Faust**: early 16th-century astrologer and magician, subsequently a literary legend. James **Watt** (1736–1819): inventor.

[19]**"preaching of the word"**: see Acts 8:4.

delivns ↳ not solve problem

accomplished otherwise. Strange as it may seem, if we read History with any degree of thoughtfulness, we shall find that the checks and balances of Profit and Loss have never been the grand agents with men; that they have never been roused into deep, thorough, all-pervading efforts by any computable prospect of Profit and Loss, for any visible, finite object; but always for some invisible and infinite one. The Crusades took their rise in Religion; their visible object was, commercially speaking, worth nothing. It was the boundless Invisible world that was laid bare in the imaginations of those men; and in its burning light, the visible shrunk as a scroll. Not mechanical, nor produced by mechanical means, was this vast movement. No dining at Freemasons' Tavern,[20] with the other long train of modern machinery; no cunning reconciliation of "vested interests," was required here: only the passionate voice of one man, the rapt soul looking through the eyes of one man; and rugged, steel-clad Europe trembled beneath his words, and followed him whither he listed. In later ages it was still the same. The Reformation had an invisible, mystic and ideal aim; the result was indeed to be embodied in external things; but its spirit, its worth, was internal, invisible, infinite. Our English Revolution too originated in Religion. Men did battle, in those old days, not for Purse-sake, but for Conscience-sake. Nay, in our own days it is no way different. The French Revolution itself had something higher in it than cheap bread and a Habeas-corpus act. Here too was an Idea; a Dynamic, not a Mechanic force. It was a struggle, though a blind and at last an insane one, for the infinite, divine nature of Right, of Freedom, of Country.

Thus does man, in every age, vindicate, consciously or unconsciously, his celestial birthright. Thus does Nature hold on her wondrous, unquestionable course; and all our systems and theories are but so many froth-eddies or sand-banks, which from time to time she casts up, and washes away. When we can drain the Ocean into mill-ponds, and bottle-up the Force of Gravity, to be sold by retail, in gas-jars; then may we hope to comprehend the infinitudes of man's soul under formulas of Profit and Loss; and rule over this too, as over a patent engine, by checks, and valves, and balances. . . .

To define the limits of these two departments[21] of man's activity, which work into one another, and by means of one another, so intricately and inseparably, were by its nature an impossible attempt. Their relative importance, even to the wisest mind, will vary in different times, according to the special wants and dispositions of those times. Meanwhile, it seems clear enough that only in the right coördination of the two, and the vigorous forwarding of *both*, does our true line of action lie. Undue cultivation of the inward or Dynamical province leads to idle, visionary, impracticable courses, and, especially in rude eras, to Superstition and Fanaticism, with their long train of baleful and well-known evils. Undue cultivation of the outward, again, though less immediately prejudicial, and even for the time productive of many palpable benefits, must, in the long-run, by destroying Moral Force, which is the parent of all other Force, prove not less certainly, and perhaps still more hopelessly, pernicious. This, we take it, is the grand characteristic of our age. By our skill in Mechanism, it has come to pass, that in the management of external things we excel all other ages; while in whatever respects the pure moral nature, in true dignity of soul and character, we are perhaps inferior to most civilised ages.

In fact, if we look deeper, we shall find that this faith in Mechanism has now struck its roots down into man's most intimate, primary sources of conviction; and is thence sending up, over his whole life and activity, innumerable stems,—fruit-bearing and poison-bearing. The truth is, men have lost their belief in the Invisible, and believe, and hope, and work only in the Visible; or, to speak it in other words: This is not a Religious age. Only the material, the immediately practical, not the divine and spiritual, is important to us. The infinite, absolute character of Virtue has passed into a finite, conditional one; it is no longer a worship of the Beautiful and Good; but a calculation of the Profitable. Worship, indeed, in any sense, is not recognised among us, or is mechanically explained into Fear of pain, or Hope of pleasure. Our true Deity is Mechanism. It has subdued external Nature for us, and we think it will do all other things. We are Giants in physical power: in a deeper than metaphorical sense, we are Titans, that strive, by heaping mountain on mountain, to conquer Heaven also. . . .

To what extent theological Unbelief, we mean intellectual dissent from the Church, in its view of Holy Writ, prevails at this day, would be a highly important, were it not, under any circumstances, an almost impossible inquiry. But the Unbelief, which is of a still more fundamental character, every man may see prevailing, with scarcely any but the faintest contradiction, all around him; even in the Pulpit itself. Religion in most countries, more or less in every country, is no longer what it was, and should be,—a thousand-voiced

---

[20]**Freemasons' Tavern**: popular London meeting place, built 1776.

[21]**two departments**: outward mechanical technique, inward moral force.

beauty in Art ↳ helps us be more refined.

psalm from the heart of Man to his invisible Father, the fountain of all Goodness, Beauty, Truth, and revealed in every revelation of these; but for the most part, a wise prudential feeling grounded on mere calculation; a matter, as all others now are, of Expediency and Utility; whereby some smaller quantum of earthly enjoyment may be exchanged for a far larger quantum of celestial enjoyment. Thus Religion too is Profit, a working for wages; not Reverence, but vulgar Hope or Fear. Many, we know, very many we hope, are still religious in a far different sense; were it not so, our case were too desperate: but to witness that such is the temper of the times, we take any calm observant man, who agrees or disagrees in our feeling on the matter, and ask him whether our *view* of it is not in general well-founded.

Literature too, if we consider it, gives similar testimony. At no former era has Literature, the printed communication of Thought, been of such importance as it is now. We often hear that the Church is in danger; and truly so it is,—in a danger it seems not to know of: for, with its tithes in the most perfect safety, its functions are becoming more and more superseded. The true Church of England, at this moment, lies in the Editors of its Newspapers. These preach to the people daily, weekly; admonishing kings themselves; advising peace or war, with an authority which only the first Reformers, and a long-past class of Popes, were possessed of; inflicting moral censure; imparting moral encouragement, consolation, edification; in all ways diligently "administering the Discipline of the Church." It may be said too, that in private disposition the new Preachers somewhat resemble the Mendicant Friars of old times: outwardly full of holy zeal; inwardly not without stratagem, and hunger for terrestrial things. But omitting this class, and the boundless host of watery personages who pipe, as they are able, on so many scrannel straws,[22] let us look at the higher regions of Literature, where, if anywhere, the pure melodies of Poesy and Wisdom should be heard. Of natural talent there is no deficiency: one or two richly-endowed individuals even give us a superiority in this respect. But what is the song they sing? Is it a tone of the Memnon Statue,[23] breathing music as the *light* first touches it? A "liquid wisdom," disclosing to our sense the deep, infinite harmonies of Nature and man's soul? Alas, no! It is not a matin or vesper hymn to the Spirit of Beauty, but a fierce clashing of cymbals, and shouting of multitudes, as children pass through the fire to

Moloch![24] Poetry itself has no eye for the Invisible. Beauty is no longer the god it worships, but some brute image of Strength; which we may well call an idol, for true Strength is one and the same with Beauty, and its worship also is a hymn. The meek, silent Light can mould, create and purify all Nature; but the loud Whirlwind, the sign and product of Disunion, of Weakness, passes on, and is forgotten. How widely this veneration for the physically Strongest has spread itself through Literature, any one may judge who reads either criticism or poem. We praise a work, not as "true," but as "strong;" our highest praise is that it has "affected" us, has "terrified" us. All this, it has been well observed, is the "maximum of the Barbarous," the symptom, not of vigorous refinement, but of luxurious corruption. It speaks much, too, for men's indestructible love of truth, that nothing of this kind will abide with them; that even the talent of a Byron cannot permanently seduce us into idol-worship; that he too, with all his wild siren charming, already begins to be disregarded and forgotten.

Again, with respect to our Moral condition: here also, he who runs may read[25] that the same physical, mechanical influences are everywhere busy. For the "superior morality," of which we hear so much, we too would desire to be thankful: at the same time, it were but blindness to deny that this "superior morality" is properly rather an "inferior criminality," produced not by greater love of Virtue, but by greater perfection of Police; and of that far subtler and stronger Police, called Public Opinion. This last watches over us with its Argus eyes more keenly than ever; but the "inward eye" seems heavy with sleep. Of any belief in invisible, divine things, we find as few traces in our Morality as elsewhere. It is by tangible, material considerations that we are guided, not by inward and spiritual. Self-denial, the parent of all virtue, in any true sense of that word, has perhaps seldom been rarer: so rare is it, that the most, even in their abstract speculations, regard its existence as a chimera. Virtue is Pleasure, is Profit; no celestial, but an earthly thing. Virtuous men, Philanthropists, Martyrs are happy accidents; their "taste" lies the right way! In all senses, we worship and follow after Power; which may be called a physical pursuit. No man now loves Truth, as Truth must be loved, with an infinite love; but only with a finite love, and as it were *par amours*.[26] Nay, properly speaking, he does not *believe* and know it, but only "*thinks*" it, and that "there is every

---

[22]**scrannel straws:** see Milton's "Lycidas" 124.

[23]**Memnon Statue:** colossal Egyptian head near Thebes that emitted sound when warmed by the morning sun.

[24]**Moloch:** ancient Mideast deity to whom **children** were sacrificed.

[25]**he who runs may read:** see Habakkuk 2:2.

[26]*par amours:* in casual flirtation.

[handwritten: Treadmill not getting anywhere]

probability"! He preaches it aloud, and rushes courageously forth with it,—if there is a multitude huzzaing at his back; yet ever keeps looking over his shoulder, and the instant the huzzaing languishes, he too stops short.

In fact, what morality we have takes the shape of Ambition, of "Honour": beyond money and money's worth, our only rational blessedness is Popularity. It were but a fool's trick to die for conscience. Only for "character," by duel, or, in case of extremity, by suicide, is the wise man bound to die. By arguing on the "force of circumstances," we have argued away all force from ourselves; and stand leashed together, uniform in dress and movement, like the rowers of some boundless galley. This and that may be right and true; *but* we must not do it. Wonderful "Force of Public Opinion"! We must act and walk in all points as it prescribes; follow the traffic it bids us, realise the sum of money, the degree of "influence" it expects of us, *or* we shall be lightly esteemed; certain mouthfuls of articulate wind will be blown at us, and this what mortal courage can front? Thus, while civil liberty is more and more secured to us, our moral liberty is all but lost. Practically considered, our creed is Fatalism; and, free in hand and foot, we are shackled in heart and soul with far straiter than feudal chains. Truly may we say, with the Philosopher, "the deep meaning of the Laws of Mechanism lies heavy on us;" and in the closet, in the marketplace, in the temple, by the social hearth, encumbers the whole movements of our mind, and over our noblest faculties is spreading a nightmare sleep. . . .

Meanwhile, that great outward changes are in progress can be doubtful to no one. The time is sick and out of joint. Many things have reached their height; and it is a wise adage that tells us, "the darkest hour is nearest the dawn." Wherever we can gather indication of the public thought, whether from printed books, as in France or Germany, or from Carbonari[27] rebellions and other political tumults, as in Spain, Portugal, Italy and Greece, the voice it utters is the same. The thinking minds of all nations call for change. There is a deep-lying struggle in the whole fabric of society; a boundless grinding collision of the New with the Old. The French Revolution, as is now visible enough, was not the parent of this mighty movement, but its offspring. Those two hostile influences, which always exist in human things, and on the constant intercommunion of which depends their health and safety, had lain in separate masses, accumulating through generations, and France was the

scene of their fiercest explosion; but the final issue was not unfolded in that country: nay it is not yet anywhere unfolded. Political freedom is hitherto the object of these efforts; but they will not and cannot stop there. It is towards a higher freedom than mere freedom from oppression by his fellow-mortal, that man dimly aims. Of this higher, heavenly freedom, which is "man's reasonable service," all his noble institutions, his faithful endeavours and loftiest attainments, are but the body, and more and more approximated emblem.

On the whole, as this wondrous planet, Earth, is journeying with its fellows through infinite Space, so are the wondrous destinies embarked on it journeying through infinite Time, under a higher guidance than ours. For the present, as our astronomy informs us, its path lies towards *Hercules*, the constellation of *Physical Power*: but that is not our most pressing concern. Go where it will, the deep HEAVEN will be around it. Therein let us have hope and sure faith. To reform a world, to reform a nation, no wise man will undertake; and all but foolish men know, that the only solid, though a far slower reformation, is what each begins and perfects on *himself*.

[handwritten: 1829]

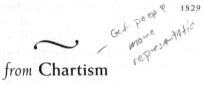

[handwritten: Get people more representatio]

from Chartism

Finest Peasantry in the World

The New Poor-Law[1] is an announcement, sufficiently distinct, that whosoever will not work ought not to live. Can the poor man that is willing to work, always find work, and live by his work? Statistic Inquiry, as we saw, has no answer to give. Legislation presupposes the answer—to be in the affirmative. A large postulate; which should have been made a proposition of; which should have been demonstrated, made indubitable to all persons! A man willing to work, and unable to find work, is perhaps the saddest sight that Fortune's inequality exhibits under this sun. Burns[2] expresses feelingly what thoughts it gave him: a poor man seeking *work*; seeking leave to toil that he might be fed and

---

[27]**Carbonari**: Italian secret society that led a **rebellion** in Naples in 1820.

[1]**New Poor-Law**: 1834 statute that forced able-bodied workers into the labor market by eliminating relief for those earning less than subsistence wages.

[2]Robert **Burns** (1759–1796): poet whose Scottish and English songs gave voice to the common people.

[handwritten: Work should be spiritually fulfilling.]

sheltered! That he might but be put on a level with the four-footed workers of the Planet which is his! There is not a horse willing to work but can get food and shelter in requital; a thing this two-footed worker has to seek for, to solicit occasionally in vain. He is nobody's two-footed worker; he is not even anybody's slave. And yet he is a *two*-footed worker; it is currently reported there is an immortal soul in him, sent down out of Heaven into the Earth; and one beholds him *seeking* for this!—Nay what will a wise Legislature say, if it turn out that he cannot find it; that the answer to their postulate proposition is not affirmative but negative?

There is one fact which Statistic Science has communicated, and a most astonishing one; the inference from which is pregnant as to this matter. Ireland has near seven millions of working people, the third unit of whom, it appears by Statistic Science, has not for thirty weeks each year as many third-rate potatoes as will suffice him. It is a fact perhaps the most eloquent that was ever written down in any language, at any date of the world's history. Was change and reformation needed in Ireland? Has Ireland been governed and guided in a "wise and loving" manner? A government and guidance of white European men which has issued in perennial hunger of potatoes to the third man extant,—ought to drop a veil over its face, and walk out of court under conduct of proper officers; saying no word; expecting now of a surety sentence either to change or die. All men, we must repeat, were made by God, and have immortal souls in them. The Sanspotato[3] is of the selfsame stuff as the superfinest Lord Lieutenant. Not an individual Sanspotato human scarecrow but had a Life given him out of Heaven, with Eternities depending on it; for once and no second time. With Immensities in him, over him and round him; with feelings which a Shakspeare's speech would not utter; with desires illimitable as the Autocrat's of all the Russias! Him various thrice-honoured persons, things and institutions have long been teaching, long been guiding, governing: and it is to perpetual scarcity of third-rate potatoes, and to what depends thereon, that he has been taught and guided. Figure thyself, O high-minded, clear-headed, clean-burnished reader, clapt by enchantment into the torn coat and waste hunger-lair of that same root-devouring brother man!—

[3]**Sanspotato**: Carlyle's wry coinage (*French Revolution* 3.7.6), based on the nickname given destitute Parisian insurgents: "Sansculottes" (the trouserless). The conditions described here antedated the Irish Famine by nearly a decade.

Social anomalies are things to be defended, things to be amended; and in all places and things, short of the Pit itself, there is some admixture of worth and good. Room for extenuation, for pity, for patience! And yet when the general result has come to the length of perennial starvation, argument, extenuating logic, pity and patience on that subject may be considered as drawing to a close. It may be considered that such arrangement of things will have to terminate. That it has all just men for its natural enemies. That all just men, of what outward colour soever in Politics or otherwise, will say: This cannot last, Heaven disowns it, Earth is against it; Ireland will be burnt into a black unpeopled field of ashes rather than this should last.—The woes of Ireland, or "justice to Ireland," is not the chapter we have to write at present. It is a deep matter, an abysmal one, which no plummet of ours will sound. For the oppression has gone far farther than into the economics of Ireland; inwards to her very heart and soul. The Irish National character is degraded, disordered; till this recover itself, nothing is yet recovered. Immethodic, headlong, violent, mendacious: what can you make of the wretched Irishman? "A finer people never lived," as the Irish lady said to us; "only they have two faults, they do generally lie and steal: barring these"—! A people that knows not to speak the truth, and to act the truth, such people has departed from even the possibility of well-being. Such people works no longer on Nature and Reality; works now on Phantasm, Simulation, Nonentity; the result it arrives at is naturally not a thing but no-thing,—defect even of potatoes. Scarcity, futility, confusion, distraction must be perennial there. Such a people circulates not order but disorder, through every vein of it;—and the cure, if it is to be a cure, must begin at the heart: not in his condition only but in himself must the Patient be all changed. Poor Ireland! And yet let no true Irishman, who believes and sees all this, despair by reason of it. Cannot he too do something to withstand the unproductive falsehood, there as it lies accursed around him, and change it into truth, which is fruitful and blessed? Every mortal can and shall himself be a true man: it is a great thing, and the parent of great things;—as from a single acorn the whole earth might in the end be peopled with oaks! Every mortal can do something: this let him faithfully do, and leave with assured heart the issue to a Higher Power!

We English pay, even now, the bitter smart of long centuries of injustice to our neighbour Island. Injustice, doubt it not, abounds; or Ireland would not be miserable. The Earth is good, bountifully sends food and increase; if man's unwisdom did not intervene and forbid. It was an evil day when Strigul[4] first meddled with that people. He could not extirpate them: could they but have agreed together, and extirpated him! Violent men there have been, and merciful; unjust rulers, and just; conflicting in a great element of violence, these five wild centuries now; and the violent and unjust have carried it, and we are come to *this*. England is guilty towards Ireland; and reaps at last, in full measure, the fruit of fifteen generations of wrongdoing.

But the thing we had to state here was our inference from that mournful fact of the third Sanspotato,—coupled with this other well-known fact that the Irish speak a partially intelligible dialect of English, and their fare across by steam is four-pence sterling! Crowds of miserable Irish darken all our towns. . . .

But now, on the whole, it seems to us, English Statistic Science, with floods of the finest peasantry in the world streaming in on us daily, may fold up her Danaides reticulations[5] on this matter of the Working Classes; and conclude, what every man who will take the statistic spectacles off his nose, and look, may discern in town or country: That the condition of the lower multitude of English labourers approximates more and more to that of the Irish competing with them in all markets; that whatsoever labour, to which mere strength with little skill will suffice, is to be done, will be done not at the English price, but at an approximation to the Irish price: at a price superior as yet to the Irish, that is, superior to scarcity of third-rate potatoes for thirty weeks yearly; superior, yet hourly, with the arrival of every new steamboat, sinking nearer to an equality with that. Half-a-million handloom weavers, working fifteen hours a-day, in perpetual inability to procure thereby enough of the coarsest food; English farm-labourers at nine shillings and at seven shillings a-week; Scotch farm-labourers who, "in districts the half of whose husbandry is that of cows, taste no milk, can procure no milk:" all these things are credible to us; several of them are known to us by the best evidence, by eyesight. With all this it is consistent that the wages of "skilled labour," as it is called, should in many cases be higher than they ever were: the giant Steamengine in a giant English Nation will here create violent demand for labour, and will there annihilate

demand. But, alas, the great portion of labour is not skilled: the millions are and must be skilless, where strength alone is wanted; ploughers, delvers, borers, hewers of wood and drawers of water; menials of the Steamengine, only the *chief* menials and immediate *body*-servants of which require skill. English Commerce stretches its fibres over the whole earth; sensitive literally, nay quivering in convulsion, to the farthest influences of the earth. The huge demon of Mechanism smokes and thunders, panting at his great task, in all sections of English land; changing his *shape* like a very Proteus;[6] and infallibly, at every change of shape, *oversetting* whole multitudes of workmen, and as if with the waving of his shadow from afar, hurling them asunder, this way and that, in their crowded march and course of work or traffic; so that the wisest no longer knows his whereabout. With an Ireland pouring daily in on us, in these circumstances; deluging us down to its own waste confusion, outward and inward, it seems a cruel mockery to tell poor drudges that *their* condition is improving.

New Poor-Law! *Laissez faire, laissez passer!*[7] The master of horses, when the summer labour is done, has to feed his horses through the winter. If he said to his horses: "Quadrupeds, I have no longer work for you; but work exists abundantly over the world: are you ignorant (or must I read you Political-Economy Lectures) that the Steamengine always in the long-run creates additional work? Railways are forming in one quarter of this earth, canals in another, much cartage is wanted; somewhere in Europe, Asia, Africa or America, doubt it not, ye will find cartage: go and seek cartage, and good go with you!" They, with protrusive upper lip, snort dubious; signifying that Europe, Asia, Africa and America lie somewhat out of their beat; that what cartage may be wanted there is not too well known to them. *They* can find no cartage. They gallop distracted along highways, all fenced in to the right and to the left: finally, under pains of hunger, they take to leaping fences; eating foreign property, and—we know the rest. Ah, it is not a joyful mirth, it is sadder than tears, the laugh Humanity is forced to, at *Laissez-faire* applied to poor peasants in a world like our Europe of the year 1839! . . .

1839

---

[4]Richard FitzGilbert, Earl of Pembroke and **Strigul:** Anglo-Norman lord whose 1170 invasion initiated the conquest of Ireland.

[5]**Danaides:** the daughters of Danaüs were condemned in the classical underworld to fetch water in leaky woven (**reticulated**) sieves.

[6]**Proteus:** shape-shifting Greek sea god.

[7]*Laissez faire* (Leave it alone): free-market slogan imported around 1825 from 18th-century French political economists. *Laissez passer!*: Make way!

from On Heroes, Hero-Worship, and the Heroic in History

The Hero as Divinity

[Tuesday, 5th May 1840.][1]

We have undertaken to discourse here for a little on Great Men, their manner of appearance in our world's business, how they have shaped themselves in the world's history, what ideas men formed of them, what work they did;—on Heroes, namely, and on their reception and performance; what I call Hero-worship and the Heroic in human affairs. Too evidently this is a large topic; deserving quite other treatment than we can expect to give it at present. A large topic; indeed, an illimitable one; wide as Universal History itself. For, as I take it, Universal History, the history of what man has accomplished in this world, is at bottom the History of the Great Men who have worked here. They were the leaders of men, these great ones; the modellers, patterns, and in a wide sense creators, of whatsoever the general mass of men contrived to do or to attain; all things that we see standing accomplished in the world are properly the outer material result, the practical realisation and embodiment, of Thoughts that dwelt in the Great Men sent into the world: the soul of the whole world's history, it may justly be considered, were the history of these. Too clearly it is a topic we shall do no justice to in this place!

One comfort is, that Great Men, taken up in any way, are profitable company. We cannot look, however imperfectly, upon a great man, without gaining something by him. He is the living light-fountain, which it is good and pleasant to be near. The light which enlightens, which has enlightened the darkness of the world; and this not as a kindled lamp only, but rather as a natural luminary shining by the gift of Heaven; a flowing light-fountain, as I say, of native original insight, of manhood and heroic nobleness;—in whose radiance all souls feel that it is well with them. On any terms whatsoever, you will not grudge to wander in

such neighbourhood for a while. These Six classes of Heroes, chosen out of widely-distant countries and epochs, and in mere external figure differing altogether, ought, if we look faithfully at them, to illustrate several things for us. Could we see *them* well, we should get some glimpses into the very marrow of the world's history. How happy, could I but, in any measure, in such times as these, make manifest to you the meanings of Heroism; the divine relation (for I may well call it such) which in all times unites a Great Man to other men; and thus, as it were, not exhaust my subject, but so much as break ground on it! At all events, I must make the attempt.

It is well said, in every sense, that a man's religion is the chief fact with regard to him. A man's, or a nation of men's. By religion I do not mean here the church-creed which he professes, the articles of faith which he will sign and, in words or otherwise, assert; not this wholly, in many cases not this at all. We see men of all kinds of professed creeds attain to almost all degrees of worth or worthlessness under each or any of them. This is not what I call religion, this profession and assertion; which is often only a profession and assertion from the outworks of the man, from the mere argumentative region of him, if even so deep as that. But the thing a man does practically believe (and this is often enough *without* asserting it even to himself, much less to others); the thing a man does practically lay to heart, and know for certain, concerning his vital relations to this mysterious Universe, and his duty and destiny there, that is in all cases the primary thing for him, and creatively determines all the rest. That is his *religion*; or, it may be, his mere scepticism and *no-religion*: the manner it is in which he feels himself to be spiritually related to the Unseen World or No-World; and I say, if you tell me what that is, you tell me to a very great extent what the man is, what the kind of things he will do. Of a man or of a nation we inquire, therefore, first of all, What religion they had? Was it Heathenism,—plurality of gods, mere sensuous representation of this Mystery of Life, and for chief recognised element therein Physical Force? Was it Christianism; faith in an Invisible, not as real only, but as the only reality; Time, through every meanest moment of it, resting on Eternity; Pagan empire of Force displaced by a nobler supremacy, that of Holiness? Was it Scepticism, uncertainty and inquiry whether there was an Unseen World, any Mystery of Life except a mad one;—doubt as to all this, or perhaps unbelief and flat denial? Answering of this question is giving us the soul of the history of the man or nation. The thoughts they had were the parents of the actions they did; their feelings

---

[1] Our selection comes from the first of six lectures delivered to a paying London audience in May 1840 and published the next year. The subsequent types of hero were the prophet, poet, priest, man of letters, and king.

were parents of their thoughts: it was the unseen, and spiritual in them that determined the outward and actual;—their religion, as I say, was the great fact about them. In these Discourses, limited as we are, it will be good to direct our survey chiefly to that religious phasis of the matter. That once known well, all is known. We have chosen as the first Hero in our series, Odin the central figure of Scandinavian Paganism; an emblem to us of a most extensive province of things. Let us look for a little at the Hero as Divinity, the oldest primary form of Heroism.

Surely it seems a very strange-looking thing this Paganism; almost inconceivable to us in these days. A bewildering, inextricable jungle of delusions, confusions, falsehoods, and absurdities, covering the whole field of Life! A thing that fills us with astonishment, almost, if it were possible, with incredulity,—for truly it is not easy to understand that sane men could ever calmly, with their eyes open, believe and live by such a set of doctrines. That men should have worshipped their poor fellow-man as a God, and not him only, but stocks and stones, and all manner of animate and inanimate objects; and fashioned for themselves such a distracted chaos of hallucinations by way of Theory of the Universe: all this looks like an incredible fable. Nevertheless it is a clear fact that they did it. Such hideous inextricable jungle of misworships, misbeliefs, men, made as we are, did actually hold by, and live at home in. This is strange. Yes, we may pause in sorrow and silence over the depths of darkness that are in man; if we rejoice in the heights of purer vision he has attained to. Such things were and are in man; in all men; in us too.

Some speculators have a short way of accounting for the Pagan religion: mere quackery, priestcraft, and dupery, say they; no sane man ever did believe it,—merely contrived to persuade other men, not worthy of the name of sane, to believe it! It will be often our duty to protest against this sort of hypothesis about men's doings and history; and I here, on the very threshold, protest against it in reference to Paganism, and to all other *isms* by which man has ever for a length of time striven to walk in this world. They have all had a truth in them, or men would not have taken them up. Quackery and dupery do abound; in religions, above all in the more advanced decaying stages of religions, they have fearfully abounded: but quackery was never the originating influence in such things; it was not the health and life of such things, but their disease, the sure precursor of their being about to die! Let us never forget this. It seems to me a most mournful hypothesis, that of quackery giving birth to any faith even in savage men. Quackery gives birth to nothing; gives death to all things.

We shall not see into the true heart of anything, if we look merely at the quackeries of it; if we do not reject the quackeries altogether; as mere diseases, corruptions, with which our and all men's sole duty is to have done with them, to sweep them out of our thoughts as out of our practice. Man everywhere is the born enemy of lies. I find Grand Lamaism itself to have a kind of truth in it. Read the candid, clear-sighted, rather sceptical Mr. Turner's *Account of his Embassy*[2] to that country, and see. They have their belief, these poor Thibet people, that Providence sends down always an Incarnation of Himself into every generation. At bottom some belief in a kind of Pope! At bottom still better, belief that there is a *Greatest* Man; that *he* is discoverable; that, once discovered, we ought to treat him with an obedience which knows no bounds! This is the truth of Grand Lamaism; the "discoverability" is the only error here. The Thibet priests have methods of their own of discovering what Man is Greatest, fit to be supreme over them. Bad methods: but are they so much worse than our methods,—of understanding him to be always the eldest-born of a certain genealogy? Alas, it is a difficult thing to find good methods for!—We shall begin to have a chance of understanding Paganism, when we first admit that to its followers it was, at one time, earnestly true. Let us consider it very certain that men did believe in Paganism; men with open eyes, sound senses, men made altogether like ourselves; that we, had we been there, should have believed in it. Ask now, What Paganism could have been?

Another theory, somewhat more respectable, attributes such things to Allegory. It was a play of poetic minds, say these theorists; a shadowing-forth, in allegorical fable, in personification and visual form, of what such poetic minds had known and felt of this Universe. Which agrees, add they, with a primary law of human nature, still everywhere observably at work, though in less important things, That what a man feels intensely, he struggles to speak-out of him, to see represented before him in visual shape, and as if with a kind of life and historical reality in it. Now doubtless there is such a law, and it is one of the deepest in human nature; neither need we doubt that it did operate fundamentally in this business. The hypothesis which ascribes Paganism wholly or mostly to this agency, I call a little more respectable; but I cannot yet call it the true hypothesis. Think, would *we* believe, and take with us as our life-guidance, an allegory, a poetic sport? Not sport but earnest is what we should require. It is a most earnest thing to be

---

[2]Samuel **Turner** (1749–1802) published his *Account* in 1800.

alive in this world; to die is not sport for a man. Man's life never was a sport to him; it was a stern reality, altogether a serious matter to be alive!

I find, therefore, that though these Allegory theorists are on the way towards truth in this matter, they have not reached it either. Pagan Religion is indeed an Allegory, a Symbol of what men felt and knew about the Universe; and all Religions are symbols of that, altering always as that alters: but it seems to me a radical perversion, and even *inversion*, of the business, to put that forward as the origin and moving cause, when it was rather the result and termination. To get beautiful allegories, a perfect poetic symbol, was not the want of men; but to know what they were to believe about this Universe, what course they were to steer in it; what, in this mysterious Life of theirs, they had to hope and to fear, to do and to forbear doing. The *Pilgrim's Progress*[3] is an Allegory, and a beautiful, just and serious one: but consider whether Bunyan's Allegory could have *preceded* the Faith it symbolises! The Faith had to be already there, standing believed by everybody;—of which the Allegory could *then* become a shadow; and, with all its seriousness, we may say a *sportful* shadow, a mere play of the Fancy, in comparison with that awful Fact and scientific certainty which it poetically strives to emblem. The Allegory is the product of the certainty, not the producer of it; not in Bunyan's nor in any other case. For Paganism, therefore, we have still to inquire, Whence came that scientific certainty, the parent of such a bewildered heap of allegories, errors, and confusions? How was it, what was it?

Surely it were a foolish attempt to pretend "explaining," in this place, or in any place, such a phenomenon as that far-distant distracted cloudy imbroglio of Paganism,—more like a cloudfield than a distant continent of firm land and facts! It is no longer a reality, yet it was one. We ought to understand that this seeming cloudfield was once a reality; that not poetic allegory, least of all that dupery and deception was the origin of it. Men, I say, never did believe idle songs, never risked their soul's life on allegories: men in all times, especially in early earnest times, have had an instinct for detecting quacks, for detesting quacks. Let us try if, leaving out both the quack theory and the allegory one, and listening with affectionate attention to that far-off confused rumour of the Pagan ages, we cannot ascertain so much as this at least, That there was a kind of fact at the heart of them; that they too were not mendacious and distracted, but in their own poor way true and sane!

You remember that fancy of Plato's,[4] of a man who had grown to maturity in some dark distance, and was brought on a sudden into the upper air to see the sun rise. What would his wonder be, his rapt astonishment at the sight we daily witness with indifference! With the free open sense of a child, yet with the ripe faculty of a man, his whole heart would be kindled by that sight, he would discern it well to be Godlike, his soul would fall down in worship before it. Now, just such a childlike greatness was in the primitive nations. The first Pagan Thinker among rude men, the first man that began to think, was precisely this child-man of Plato's. Simple, open as a child, yet with the depth and strength of a man. Nature had as yet no name to him; he had not yet united under a name the infinite variety of sights, sounds, shapes and motions, which we now collectively name Universe, Nature, or the like,—and so with a name dismiss it from us. To the wild deep-hearted man all was yet new, not veiled under names or formulas; it stood naked, flashing-in on him there, beautiful, awful, unspeakable. Nature was to this man, what to the Thinker and Prophet it for ever is, *preternatural*. This green flowery rock-built earth, the trees, the mountains, rivers, many-sounding seas;—that great deep sea of azure that swims overhead; the winds sweeping through it; the black cloud fashioning itself together, now pouring out fire, now hail and rain; what *is* it? Ay, what? At bottom we do not yet know; we can never know at all. It is not by our superior insight that we escape the difficulty; it is by our superior levity, our inattention, our *want* of insight. It is by *not* thinking that we cease to wonder at it. Hardened round us, encasing wholly every notion we form, is a wrappage of traditions, hearsays, mere *words*. We call that fire of the black thunder-cloud "electricity," and lecture learnedly about it, and grind the like of it out of glass and silk: but *what* is it? What made it? Whence comes it? Whither goes it? Science has done much for us; but it is a poor science that would hide from us the great deep sacred infinitude of Nescience,[5] whither we can never penetrate, on which all science swims as a mere superficial film. This world, after all our science and sciences, is still a miracle; wonderful, inscrutable, *magical* and more, to whosoever will *think* of it.

That great mystery of TIME, were there no other; the illimitable, silent, never-resting thing called Time, rolling, rushing on, swift, silent, like an all-embracing ocean-tide, on which we and all the Universe swim like exhalations,

---

[3]*Pilgrim's Progress* (1678): by John **Bunyan** (1628–1688).

[4]**Plato**: see *Republic*, book 7.
[5]**Nescience**: ignorance.

like apparitions which *are*, and then *are not*: this is for ever very literally a miracle; a thing to strike us dumb,—for we have no word to speak about it. This Universe, ah me— what could the wild man know of it; what can we yet know? That it is a Force, and thousandfold Complexity of Forces; a Force which is *not we*. That is all; it is not we, it is altogether different from *us*. Force, Force, everywhere Force; we ourselves a mysterious Force in the centre of that. "There is not a leaf rotting on the highway but has Force in it: how else could it rot?" Nay surely, to the Atheistic Thinker, if such a one were possible, it must be a miracle too, this huge illimitable whirlwind of Force, which envelops us here; neverresting whirlwind, high as Immensity, old as Eternity. What is it? God's creation, the religious people answer; it is the Almighty God's! Atheistic science babbles poorly of it, with scientific nomenclatures, experiments and what-not, as if it were a poor dead thing, to be bottled-up in Leyden jars[6] and sold over counters: but the natural sense of man, in all times, if he will honestly apply his sense, proclaims it to be a living thing,—ah, an unspeakable, godlike thing; towards which the best attitude for us, after never so much science, is awe, devout prostration and humility of soul; worship if not in words, then in silence.

But now I remark further: What in such a time as ours it requires a Prophet or Poet to teach us, namely, the strippingoff of those poor undevout wrappages, nomenclatures and scientific hearsays,—this, the ancient earnest soul, as yet unencumbered with these things, did for itself. The world, which is now divine only to the gifted, was then divine to whosoever would turn his eye upon it. He stood bare before it face to face. "All was Godlike or God:"—Jean Paul[7] still finds it so; the giant Jean Paul, who has power to escape out of hearsays: but there then were no hearsays. Canopus shining-down over the desert, with its blue diamond brightness (that wild blue spirit-like brightness, far brighter than we ever witness here), would pierce into the heart of the wild Ishmaelitish[8] man, whom it was guiding through the solitary waste there. To his wild heart, with all feelings in it, with no *speech* for any feeling, it might seem a little eye, that

Canopus, glancing-out on him from the great deep Eternity; revealing the inner Splendour to him. Cannot we understand how these men *worshipped* Canopus; became what we call Sabeans, worshipping the stars? Such is to me the secret of all forms of Paganism. Worship is transcendent wonder; wonder for which there is now no limit or measure; that is worship. To these primeval men, all things and everything they saw exist beside them were an emblem of the Godlike, of some God.

And look what perennial fibre of truth was in that. To us also, through every star, through every blade of grass, is not a God made visible, if we will open our minds and eyes? We do not worship in that way now: but is it not reckoned still a merit, proof of what we call a "poetic nature," that we recognise how every object has a divine beauty in it; how every object still verily is 'a window through which we may look into Infinitude itself'? He that can discern the loveliness of things, we call him Poet, Painter, Man of Genius, gifted, lovable. . . .

And now if worship even of a star had some meaning in it, how much more might that of a Hero! Worship of a Hero is transcendent admiration of a Great Man. I say great men are still admirable; I say there is, at bottom, nothing else admirable! No nobler feeling than this of admiration for one higher than himself dwells in the breast of man. It is to this hour, and at all hours, the vivifying influence in man's life. Religion I find stand upon it; not Paganism only, but far higher and truer religions,—all religion hitherto known. Hero-worship, heartfelt prostrate admiration, submission, burning, boundless, for a noblest godlike Form of Man,—is not that the germ of Christianity itself? The greatest of all Heroes is One—whom we do not name here! Let sacred silence meditate that sacred matter; you will find it the ultimate perfection of a principle extant throughout man's whole history on earth.

Or coming into lower, less *unspeakable* provinces, is not all Loyalty akin to religious Faith also? Faith is loyalty to some inspired Teacher, some spiritual Hero. And what therefore is loyalty proper, the life-breath of all society, but an effluence of Hero-worship, submissive admiration for the truly great? Society is founded on Hero-worship. All dignities of rank, on which human association rests, are what we may call a *Heroarchy* (Government of Heroes),—or a Hierarchy, for it is "sacred" enough withal! The Duke means *Dux*, Leader; King is *Kön-ning, Kan-ning*, Man that *knows or cans*.[9]

---

[6]**Leyden jar:** early battery, invented during the 1740s in Holland.

[7]**Jean Paul:** pen name of J. P. F. Richter (1763–1825), German novelist and humorist.

[8]**Canopus:** 2nd-brightest star. **Ishmaelitish:** see Genesis 16, where the fugitive Hagar bears a "wild" son, Ishmael. His descendants were claimed as ancestors of the nomadic Arabs and the S Arabian people of Sheba, or **Sabeans**.

---

[9]**King:** Carlyle's etymology is intriguing but wrong: the word stems from *kin*.

Society everywhere is some representation, not *in*supportably inaccurate, of a graduated Worship of Heroes;—reverence and obedience done to men really great and wise. Not *in*supportably inaccurate, I say! They are all as bank-notes, these social dignitaries, all representing gold;—and several of them, alas, always are *forged* notes. We can do with some forged false notes; with a good many even; but not with all, or the most of them forged! No: there have to come revolutions then; cries of Democracy, Liberty and Equality, and I know not what:—the notes being all false, and no gold to be had for *them*, people take to crying in their despair that there is no gold, that there never was any!—"Gold," Heroworship, *is* nevertheless, as it was always and everywhere, and cannot cease till man himself ceases.

I am well aware that in these days Hero-worship, the thing I call Hero-worship, professes to have gone out, and finally ceased. This, for reasons which it will be worth while some time to inquire into, is an age that as it were denies the existence of great men; denies the desirableness of great men. Show our critics a great man, a Luther[10] for example, they begin to what they call "account" for him; not to worship him, but take the dimensions of him,—and bring him out to be a little kind of man! He was the "creature of the Time," they say; the Time called him forth, the Time did everything, he nothing—but what we the little critic could have done too! This seems to me but melancholy work. The Time call forth? Alas, we have known Times *call* loudly enough for their great man; but not find him when they called! He was not there; Providence had not sent him; the Time, *calling* its loudest, had to go down to confusion and wreck because he would not come when called.

For if we will think of it, no Time need have gone to ruin, could it have *found* a man great enough, a man wise and good enough: wisdom to discern truly what the Time wanted, valour to lead it on the right road thither; these are the salvation of any Time. But I liken common languid Times, with their unbelief, distress, perplexity, with their languid doubting characters and embarrassed circumstances, impotently crumbling-down into ever worse distress towards final ruin;—all this I liken to dry dead fuel, waiting for the lightning out of Heaven that shall kindle it. The great man, with his free force direct out of God's own hand, is the lightning. His word is the wise healing word which all can believe in. All blazes round him now,

when he has once struck on it, into fire like his own. The dry mouldering sticks are thought to have called him forth. They did want him greatly; but as to calling him forth—!—Those are critics of small vision, I think, who cry: "See, is it not the sticks that made the fire?" No sadder proof can be given by a man of his own littleness than disbelief in great men. There is no sadder symptom of a generation than such general blindness to the spiritual lightning, with faith only in the heap of barren dead fuel. It is the last consummation of unbelief. In all epochs of the world's history, we shall find the Great Man to have been the indispensable saviour of his epoch;—the lightning, without which the fuel never would have burnt. The History of the World, I said already, was the Biography of Great Men.

Such small critics do what they can to promote unbelief and universal spiritual paralysis: but happily they cannot always completely succeed. In all times it is possible for a man to arise great enough to feel that they and their doctrines are chimeras and cobwebs. And what is notable, in no time whatever can they entirely eradicate out of living men's hearts a certain altogether peculiar reverence for Great Men; genuine admiration, loyalty, adoration, however dim and perverted it may be. Hero-worship endures for ever while man endures. . . .

. . . We all love great men; love, venerate and bow down submissive before great men: nay can we honestly bow down to anything else? Ah, does not every true man feel that he is himself made higher by doing reverence to what is really above him? No nobler or more blessed feeling dwells in man's heart. And to me it is very cheering to consider that no sceptical logic, or general triviality, insincerity and aridity of any Time and its influences can destroy this noble inborn loyalty and worship that is in man. In times of unbelief, which soon have to become times of revolution, much down-rushing, sorrowful decay and ruin is visible to everybody. For myself, in these days, I seem to see in this indestructibility of Hero-worship the everlasting adamant lower than which the confused wreck of revolutionary things cannot fall. The confused wreck of things crumbling and even crashing and tumbling all round us in these revolutionary ages, will get down so far; *no* farther. It is an eternal corner-stone, from which they can begin to build themselves up again. That man, in some sense or other, worships Heroes; that we all of us reverence and must ever reverence Great Men: this is, to me, the living rock amid all rushings-down whatsoever;—the one fixed point in modern revolutionary history, otherwise as if bottomless and shoreless.

---

[10]Martin **Luther** (1483–1546) returns in Carlyle's 4th lecture, "The Hero as Priest."

So much of truth, only under an ancient obsolete ves-ture, but the spirit of it still true, do I find in the Paganism of old nations. Nature is still divine, the revelation of the workings of God; the Hero is still worshipable: this, under poor cramped incipient forms, is what all Pagan religions have struggled, as they could, to set forth. I think Scandina-vian Paganism, to us here, is more interesting than any other. It is, for one thing, the latest; it continued in these re-gions of Europe till the eleventh century: eight-hundred years ago the Norwegians were still worshippers of Odin. It is interesting also as the creed of our fathers; the men whose blood still runs in our veins, whom doubtless we still resem-ble in so many ways. Strange: they did believe that, while we believe so differently. Let us look a little at this poor Norse creed, for many reasons. We have tolerable means to do it; for there is another point of interest in these Scandi-navian mythologies: that they have been preserved so well.

In that strange island Iceland,—burst-up, the geol-ogists say, by fire from the bottom of the sea; a wild land of barrenness and lava; swallowed many months of every year in black tempests, yet with a wild gleaming beauty in sum-mertime; towering up there, stern and grim, in the North Ocean; with its snow jokuls,[11] roaring geysers, sulphur-pools and horrid volcanic chasms, like the waste chaotic battle-field of Frost and Fire;—where of all places we least looked for Literature or written memorials, the record of these things was written down. On the seaboard of this wild land is a rim of grassy country, where cattle can subsist, and men by means of them and of what the sea yields; and it seems they were poetic men these, men who had deep thoughts in them, and uttered musically their thoughts. Much would be lost, had Iceland not been burst-up from the sea, not been discovered by the Northmen! The old Norse Poets were many of them natives of Iceland.

Sæmund,[12] one of the early Christian Priests there, who perhaps had a lingering fondness for Paganism, col-lected certain of their old Pagan songs, just about becom-ing obsolete then,—Poems or Chants of a mythic, prophetic, mostly all of a religious character: that is what Norse critics call the *Elder* or Poetic *Edda*. *Edda*, a word of uncertain etymology, is thought to signify *Ancestress*. Snorro Sturleson, an Iceland gentleman, an extremely notable per-sonage, educated by this Sæmund's grandson, took in hand next, near a century afterwards, to put together, among

several other books he wrote, a kind of Prose Synopsis of the whole Mythology; elucidated by new fragments of tra-ditionary verse. A work constructed really with great inge-nuity, native talent, what one might call unconscious art; altogether a perspicuous clear work, pleasant reading still: this is the *Younger* or Prose *Edda*. By these and the numerous other *Sagas*, mostly Icelandic, with the commentaries, Ice-landic or not, which go on zealously in the North to this day, it is possible to gain some direct insight even yet; and see that old Norse system of Belief, as it were, face to face. Let us forget that it is erroneous Religion; let us look at it as old Thought, and try if we cannot sympathise with it somewhat.

The primary characteristic of this old Northland Mythology I find to be Impersonation of the visible work-ings of Nature. Earnest simple recognition of the workings of Physical Nature, as a thing wholly miraculous, stupen-dous, and divine. What we now lecture of as Science, they wondered at, and fell down in awe before, as Religion. The dark hostile Powers of Nature they figure to themselves as "*Jötuns*," Giants, huge shaggy beings of a demonic character. Frost, Fire, Sea-tempest; these are Jötuns. The friendly Pow-ers again, as Summer-heat, the Sun, are Gods. The empire of this Universe is divided between these two; they dwell apart, in perennial internecine feud. The Gods dwell above in Asgard, the Garden of the Asen, or Divinities; Jötunheim, a distant dark chaotic land, is the home of the Jötuns.

Curious all this; and not idle or inane, if we will look at the foundation of it! The power of *Fire*, or *Flame*, for in-stance, which we designate by some trivial chemical name, thereby hiding from ourselves the essential character of wonder that dwells in it as in all things, is with these old Northmen, Loke, a most swift subtle *Demon*, of the brood of the Jötuns. The savages of the Ladrones Islands[13] too (say some Spanish voyagers) thought Fire, which they never had seen before, was a devil or god, that bit you sharply when you touched it, and that lived upon dry wood. From us too no Chemistry, if it had not Stupidity to help it, would hide that Flame is a wonder. What *is* Flame?—*Frost* the old Norse Seer discerns to be a monstrous hoary Jötun, the Giant *Thrym*, *Hrym*; or *Rime*, the old word now nearly obsolete here, but still used in Scotland to signify hoar-frost. *Rime* was not then as now a dead chemical thing, but a living Jötun or Devil; the monstrous Jötun *Rime* drove home his Horses at night, sat "combing their manes,"—which Horses

---

[11]**jokuls:** mountains permanently covered in snow.

[12]**Sæmund** Frode Sigfússon (1056–1133): chronicler credited (erroneously) with compiling the *Poetic Edda*.

---

[13]**Ladrones:** Magellan's name for the W Pacific islands since named the Marianas.

were *Hail-Clouds*, or fleet *Frost-Winds*. His Cows—No, not his, but a kinsman's, the Giant Hymir's Cows are *Icebergs*: this Hymir "looks at the rocks" with his devil-eye, and they *split* in the glance of it.

Thunder was not then mere Electricity, vitreous or resinous;[14] it was the God Donner (Thunder) or Thor,— God also of beneficent Summer-heat. The thunder was his wrath; the gathering of the black clouds is the drawing-down of Thor's angry brows; the fire-bolt bursting out of Heaven is the all-rending Hammer flung from the hand of Thor: he urges his loud chariot over the mountain-tops,— that is the peal; wrathful he "blows in his red beard,"—that is the rustling stormblast before the thunder begin. Balder again, the White God, the beautiful, the just and benignant (whom the early Christian Missionaries found to resemble Christ), is the Sun,—beautifulest of visible things; wondrous too, and divine still, after all our Astronomies and Almanacs! But perhaps the notablest god we hear-tell-of is one of whom Grimm[15] the German Etymologist finds trace: the God *Wünsch*, or Wish. The God *Wish*; who could give us all that we *wished*! Is not this the sincerest and yet rudest voice of the spirit of man? The *rudest* ideal that man ever formed; which still shows itself in the latest forms of our spiritual culture. Higher considerations have to teach us that the God *Wish* is not the true God.

Of the other Gods or Jötuns I will mention only for etymology's sake, that Sea-tempest is the Jötun *Aegir*, a very dangerous Jötun;—and now to this day, on our river Trent, as I learn, the Nottingham bargemen, when the River is in a certain flooded state (a kind of backwater, or eddying swirl it has, very dangerous to them), call it *Eager*; they cry out, "Have a care, there is the *Eager* coming!" Curious; that word surviving, like the peak of a submerged world! The *oldest* Nottingham bargemen had believed in the God Aegir. Indeed our English blood too in good part is Danish, Norse; or rather, at bottom, Danish and Norse and Saxon have no distinction, except a superficial one,—as of Heathen and Christian, or the like. But all over our Island we are mingled largely with Danes proper,—from the incessant invasions there were: and this, of course, in a greater proportion along the east coast; and greatest of all, as I find, in the North Country. From the Humber upwards, all over Scotland, the

Speech of the common people is still in a singular degree Icelandic; its Germanism has still a peculiar Norse tinge. They too are "Normans," Northmen,—if that be any great beauty!—

Of the chief god, Odin, we shall speak by and by. Mark at present so much; what the essence of Scandinavian and indeed of all Paganism is: a recognition of the forces of Nature as godlike, stupendous, personal Agencies,—as Gods and Demons. Not inconceivable to us. It is the infant Thought of man opening itself, with awe and wonder, on this ever-stupendous Universe. To me there is in the Norse System something very genuine, very great and manlike. A broad simplicity, rusticity, so very different from the light gracefulness of the old Greek Paganism, distinguishes this Scandinavian System. It is Thought; the genuine Thought of deep, rude, earnest minds, fairly opened to the things about them; a face-to-face and heart-to-heart inspection of the things,—the first characteristic of all good Thought in all times. Not graceful lightness, half-sport, as in the Greek Paganism; a certain homely truthfulness and rustic strength, a great rude sincerity, discloses itself here. It is strange, after our beautiful Apollo statues and clear smiling mythuses,[16] to come down upon the Norse Gods "brewing ale" to hold their feast with Aegir, the Sea-Jötun; sending out Thor to get the caldron for them in the Jötun country; Thor, after many adventures, clapping the Pot on his head, like a huge hat, and walking off with it,—quite lost in it, the ears of the Pot reaching down to his heels! A kind of vacant hugeness, large awkward gianthood, characterises that Norse System; enormous force, as yet altogether untutored, stalking helpless with large uncertain strides. Consider only their primary mythus of the Creation. The Gods, having got the Giant Ymer slain, a Giant made by "warm wind," and much confused work, out of the conflict of Frost and Fire,—determined on constructing a world with him. His blood made the Sea; his flesh was the Land, the Rocks his bones; of his eyebrows they formed Asgard their Gods'-dwelling; his skull was the great blue vault of Immensity, and the brains of it became the Clouds. What a Hyper-Brobdingnagian[17] business! Untamed Thought, great, giantlike, enormous;— to be tamed in due time into the compact greatness, not giantlike, but godlike and stronger than gianthood, of the Shakspeares, the Goethes!—Spiritually as well as bodily these men are our progenitors.

[14]**vitreous, resinous**: reference to electric properties of glass and amber.

[15]Jacob **Grimm** (1785–1863): German folklorist and linguist who published a compendium of German myths in the 1830s and, with his brother Wilhelm (1786–1859), undertook a huge etymological dictionary of German in 1838.

[16]**mythuses**: plural of *mythus*, Carlyle's preferred term for *myth*.

[17]**Brobdingnagian**: from the land of Swift's giants in *Gulliver's Travels* (1726).

Power in the Word   *Value of Art magical core*

I like, too, that representation they have of the Tree Igdrasil. All Life is figured by them as a Tree. Igdrasil, the Ash-tree of Existence, has its roots deep-down in the kingdoms of Hela or Death; its trunk reaches up heaven-high, spreads its boughs over the whole Universe: it is the Tree of Existence. At the foot of it, in the Death-kingdom, sit Three *Nornas*, Fates,— the Past, Present, Future; watering its roots from the Sacred Well. Its "boughs," with their buddings and disleafings,— events, things suffered, things done, catastrophes,—stretch through all lands and times. Is not every leaf of it a biography, every fibre there an act or word? Its boughs are Histories of Nations. The rustle of it is the noise of Human Existence, on-wards from of old. It grows there, the breath of Human Passion rustling through it;—or stormtost, the stormwind howling through it like the voice of all the gods. It is Igdrasil, the Tree of Existence. It is the past, the present, and the future; what was done, what is doing, what will be done; "the infinite conjugation of the verb *To do*." Considering how human things circulate, each inextricably in communion with all,—how the word I speak to you today is borrowed, not from Ulfila the Mœsogoth[18] only, but from all men since the first man began to speak,—I find no similitude so true as this of a Tree. Beautiful; altogether beautiful and great. The "*Machine* of the Universe,"—alas, do but think of that in contrast!

Well, it is strange enough this old Norse view of Nature; different enough from what we believe of Nature. Whence it specially came, one would not like to be compelled to say very minutely! One thing we may say: It came from the thoughts of Norse men;—from the thought, above all, of the *first* Norse man who had an original power of thinking. The First Norse "man of genius," as we should call him! Innumerable men had passed by, across this Universe, with a dumb vague wonder, such as the very animals may feel; or with a painful, fruitlessly inquiring wonder, such as men only feel;—till the great Thinker came, the *original* man, the Seer; whose shaped spoken Thought awakes the slumbering capability of all into Thought. It is ever the way with the Thinker, the spiritual Hero. What he says, all men were not far from saying, were longing to say. The Thoughts of all start up, as from painful enchanted sleep, round his Thought; answering to it, Yes, even so! Joyful to men as the dawning of day from night;—*is* it not, indeed, the awakening for them from no-being into being, from

death into life? We still honour such a man; call him Poet, Genius, and so forth: but to these wild men he was a very magician, a worker of miraculous unexpected blessing for them; a Prophet, a God!—Thought once awakened does not again slumber; unfolds itself into a System of Thought; grows, in man after man, generation after generation,—till its full stature is reached, and *such* System of Thought can grow no further, but must give place to another.

For the Norse people, the Man now named Odin, and Chief Norse God, we fancy, was such a man. A Teacher, and Captain of soul and of body; a Hero, of worth *immeasurable*; admiration for whom, transcending the known bounds, became adoration. Has he not the power of articulate Thinking; and many other powers, as yet miraculous? So, with boundless gratitude, would the rude Norse heart feel. Has he not solved for them the sphinx-enigma of this Universe; given assurance to them of their own destiny there? By him they know now what they have to do here, what to look for hereafter. Existence has become articulate, melodious by him; he first has made Life alive!—We may call this Odin, the origin of Norse Mythology: Odin, or whatever name the First Norse Thinker bore while he was a man among men. His view of the Universe once promulgated, a like view starts into being in all minds; grows, keeps ever growing, while it continues credible there. In all minds it lay written, but invisibly, as in sympathetic ink;[19] at his word it starts into visibility in all. Nay, in every epoch of the world, the great event, parent of all others, is it not the arrival of a Thinker in the world? . . .

How the man Odin came to be considered a *god*, the chief god?—that surely is a question which nobody would wish to dogmatise upon. I have said, his people knew no *limits* to their admiration of him; they had as yet no scale to measure admiration by. Fancy your own generous heart's-love of some greatest man expanding till it *transcended* all bounds, till it filled and overflowed the whole field of your thought! Or what if this man Odin,—since a great deep soul, with the afflatus and mysterious tide of vision and impulse rushing on him he knows not whence, is ever an enigma, a kind of terror and wonder to himself,—should have felt that perhaps *he* was divine; that *he* was some effluence of the "*Wuotan*," "*Movement*," Supreme Power and Divinity, of whom to his rapt vision all Nature was the awful Flame-image; that some effluence of *Wuotan*[20] dwelt here in

---

[18]**Ulfila**: 4th-century missionary to the **Goths** of **Moesia** (Bulgaria), reputed creator of the Gothic alphabet he used in translating the Bible.

[19]**sympathetic ink**: invisible ink.

[20]*Wuotan*: Carlyle has earlier derived Wotan/Odin's name from "*Wading*, force of *Movement*."

[handwritten: Self — Is it how world sees us or how we see ourself]

him! He was not necessarily false; he was but mistaken, speaking the truest he knew. A great soul, any sincere soul, knows not *what* he is,—alternates between the highest height and the lowest depth; can, of all things, the least measure—Himself! What others take him for, and what he guesses that he may be; these two items strangely act on one another, help to determine one another. With all men reverently admiring him; with his own wild soul full of noble ardours and affections, of whirlwind chaotic darkness and glorious new light; a divine Universe bursting all into godlike beauty round him, and no man to whom the like ever had befallen, what could he think himself to be? "Wuotan?" All men answered, "Wuotan!"—

And then consider what mere Time will do in such cases; how if a man was great while living, he becomes tenfold greater when dead. What an enormous *camera-obscura* magnifier is Tradition! How a thing grows in the human Memory, in the human Imagination, when love, worship, and all that lies in the human Heart, is there to encourage it. And in the darkness, in the entire ignorance; without date or document, no book, no Arundel-marble;[21] only here and there some dumb monumental cairn. Why, in thirty or forty years, were there no books, any great man would grow *mythic*, the contemporaries who had seen him, being once all dead. And in three-hundred years, and in three-thousand years—!—To attempt *theorising* on such matters would profit little: they are matters which refuse to be *theoremed* and diagramed; which Logic ought to know that she *cannot* speak of. Enough for us to discern, far in the uttermost distance, some gleam as of a small real light shining in the centre of that enormous camera-obscura image; to discern that the centre of it all was not a madness and nothing, but a sanity and something.

This light, kindled in the great dark vortex of the Norse mind, dark but living, waiting only for light; this is to me the centre of the whole. How such light will then shine out, and with wondrous thousandfold expansion spread itself, in forms and colours, depends not on *it*, so much as on the National Mind recipient of it. The colours and forms of your light will be those of the *cut-glass* it has to shine through. . . .

Thus if the man Odin himself have vanished utterly, there is this huge Shadow of him which still projects itself over the whole History of his People. For this Odin once admitted to be God, we can understand well that the whole Scandinavian Scheme of Nature, or dim No-scheme, whatever it might before have been, would now begin to develop itself altogether differently, and grow thenceforth in a new manner. What this Odin saw into, and taught with his runes and his rhymes,[22] the whole Teutonic People laid to heart and carried forward. His way of thought became their way of thought:—such, under new conditions, is the history of every great thinker still. In gigantic confused lineaments, like some enormous camera-obscura shadow thrown upwards from the dead deeps of the Past, and covering the whole Northern Heaven, is not that Scandinavian Mythology in some sort the Portraiture of this man Odin? The gigantic image of *his* natural face, legible or not legible there, expanded and confused in that manner! Ah, Thought, I say, is always Thought. No great man lives in vain. The History of the world is but the Biography of great men.

To me there is something very touching in this primeval figure of Heroism; in such artless, helpless, but hearty entire reception of a Hero by his fellow-men. Never so helpless in shape, it is the noblest of feelings, and a feeling in some shape or other perennial as man himself. If I could show in any measure, what I feel deeply for a long time now, That it is the vital element of manhood, the soul of man's history here in our world,—it would be the chief use of this discoursing at present. We do not now call our great men Gods, nor admire *without* limit; ah no, *with* limit enough! But if we have no great men, or do not admire at all,—that were a still worse case.

This poor Scandinavian Hero-worship, that whole Norse way of looking at the Universe, and adjusting oneself there, has an indestructible merit for us. A rude childlike way of recognising the divineness of Nature, the divineness of Man; most rude, yet heartfelt, robust, giantlike; betokening what a giant of a man this child would yet grow to!—It was a truth, and is none. Is it not as the half-dumb stifled voice of the long-buried generations of our own Fathers, calling out of the depths of ages to us, in whose veins their blood still runs: "This then, this is what *we* made of the world: this is all the image and notion we could form to ourselves of this great mystery of a Life and Universe. Despise it not. You are raised high above it, to large free scope of vision; but you too are not yet at the top. No, your notion too, so much enlarged, is but a partial, imperfect one; that matter is a thing no man will ever, in time or out of time, comprehend; after thousands of years of ever-new expansion, man will find

---

[21]**marble**: ornate family tomb, like those at **Arundel** Castle in S England.

[22]**runes, rhymes**: Odin was credited with inventing letters and poetry.

himself but struggling to comprehend again a part of it: the thing is larger than man, not to be comprehended by him; an Infinite thing!"

The essence of the Scandinavian, as indeed of all Pagan Mythologies, we found to be recognition of the divineness of Nature; sincere communion of man with the mysterious invisible Powers visibly seen at work in the world round him. This, I should say, is more sincerely done in the Scandinavian than in any Mythology I know. Sincerity is the great characteristic of it. Superior sincerity (far superior) consoles us for the total want of old Grecian grace. Sincerity, I think, is better than grace. I feel that these old Northmen were looking into Nature with open eye and soul: most earnest, honest; childlike, and yet manlike; with a great-hearted simplicity and depth and freshness, in a true, loving, admiring, unfearing way. A right valiant, true old race of men. Such recognition of Nature one finds to be the chief element of Paganism: recognition of Man, and his Moral Duty, though this too is not wanting, comes to be the chief element only in purer forms of religion. Here, indeed, is a great distinction and epoch in Human Beliefs; a great landmark in the religious development of Mankind. Man first puts himself in relation with Nature and her Powers, wonders and worships over those; not till a later epoch does he discern that all Power is Moral, that the grand point is the distinction for him of Good and Evil, of *Thou shalt* and *Thou shalt not.* . . .

That the man Odin, speaking with a Hero's voice and heart, as with an impressiveness out of Heaven, told his People the infinite importance of Valour, how man thereby became a god; and that his People, feeling a response to it in their own hearts, believed this message of his, and thought it a message out of Heaven, and him a Divinity for telling it them: this seems to me the primary seed-grain of the Norse Religion, from which all manner of mythologies, symbolic practices, speculations, allegories, songs and sagas would naturally grow. Grow,—how strangely! I called it a small light shining and shaping in the huge vortex of Norse darkness. Yet the darkness itself was *alive;* consider that. It was the eager inarticulate uninstructed Mind of the whole Norse People, longing only to become articulate, to go on articulating ever further! The living doctrine grows, grows;—like a Banyan-tree; the first *seed* is the essential thing: any branch strikes itself down into the earth, becomes a new root; and so, in endless complexity, we have a whole wood, a whole jungle, one seed the parent of it all. Was not the whole Norse Religion, accordingly, in some sense, what we called "the

enormous shadow of this man's likeness"? Critics trace some affinity in some Norse mythuses, of the Creation and suchlike, with those of the Hindoos. The Cow Adumbla, "licking the rime from the rocks," has a kind of Hindoo look. A Hindoo Cow, transported into frosty countries. Probably enough; indeed we may say undoubtedly, these things will have a kindred with the remotest lands, with the earliest times. Thought does not die, but only is changed. The first man that began to think in this Planet of ours, he was the beginner of all. And then the second man, and the third man;—nay, every true Thinker to this hour is a kind of Odin, teaches men *his* way of thought, spreads a shadow of his own likeness over sections of the History of the World. . . . (Lecture 1)

1841

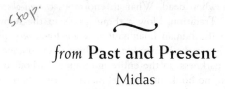

from **Past and Present**
Midas

The condition of England, on which many pamphlets are now in the course of publication, and many thoughts unpublished are going on in every reflective head, is justly regarded as one of the most ominous, and withal one of the strangest, ever seen in this world. England is full of wealth, or multifarious produce, supply for human want in every kind; yet England is dying of inanition. With unabated bounty the land of England blooms and grows; waving with yellow harvests; thick-studded with workshops, industrial implements, with fifteen millions of workers, understood to be the strongest, the cunningest and the willingest our Earth ever had; these men are here; the work they have done, the fruit they have realized is here, abundant, exuberant on every hand of us: and behold, some baleful fiat as of Enchantment has gone forth, saying, "Touch it not, ye workers, ye master-workers, ye master-idlers; none of you can touch it, no man of you shall be the better for it; this is enchanted fruit!" On the poor workers such fiat falls first, in its rudest shape; but on the rich master-workers too it falls; neither can the rich master-idlers, nor any richest or highest man escape, but all are like to be brought low with it, and made "poor" enough, in the money sense or a far fataller one.

Of these successful skilful workers some two millions, it is now counted, sit in Workhouses, Poor-law Prisons; or have "out-door relief" flung over the wall to them,—the workhouse Bastille being filled to bursting, and the strong

Poor-law[1] broken asunder by a stronger. They sit there, these many months now; their hope of deliverance as yet small. In workhouses, pleasantly so-named, because work cannot be done in them. Twelve hundred thousand workers in England alone; their cunning right-hand lamed, lying idle in their sorrowful bosom; their hopes, outlooks, share of this fair world, shut in by narrow walls. They sit there, pent up, as in a kind of horrid enchantment; glad to be imprisoned and enchanted, that they may not perish starved. The picturesque Tourist, in a sunny autumn day, through this bounteous realm of England, descries the Union Workhouse on his path. "Passing by the Workhouse of St. Ives in Huntingdonshire, on a bright day last autumn," says the picturesque Tourist, "I saw sitting on wooden benches, in front of their Bastille and within their ring-wall and its railings, some half-hundred or more of these men. Tall robust figures, young mostly or of middle age; of honest countenance, many of them thoughtful and even intelligent-looking men. They sat there, near by one another; but in a kind of torpor, especially in a silence, which was very striking. In silence: for, alas, what word was to be said? An Earth all lying round, crying, Come and till me, come and reap me;—yet we here sit enchanted! In the eyes and brows of the men hung the gloomiest expression, not of anger, but of grief and shame and manifold inarticulate distress and weariness; they returned my glance with a glance that seemed to say, 'Do not look at us. We sit enchanted here, we know not why. The Sun shines and the Earth calls; and, by the governing Powers and Impotences of this England, we are forbidden to obey. It is impossible, they tell us!' There was something that reminded me of Dante's Hell in the look of all this; and I rode swiftly away."

So many hundred thousands sit in workhouses: and other hundred thousands have not yet got even workhouses; and in thrifty Scotland itself, in Glasgow or Edinburgh City, in their dark lanes, hidden from all but the eye of God, and of rare Benevolence the minister of God, there are scenes of woe and destitution and desolation, such as, one may hope, the Sun never saw before in the most barbarous regions where men dwelt. Competent witnesses, the

brave and humane Dr. Alison,[2] who speaks what he knows, whose noble Healing Art in his charitable hands becomes once more a truly sacred one, report these things for us: these things are not of this year, or of last year, have no reference to our present state of commercial stagnation, but only to the common state. Not in sharp fever-fits, but in chronic gangrene of this kind is Scotland suffering. A Poor-law, any and every Poor-law, it may be observed, is but a temporary measure; an anodyne, not a remedy: Rich and Poor, when once the naked facts of their condition have come into collision, cannot long subsist together on a mere Poor-law. True enough:—and yet, human beings cannot be left to die! Scotland too, till something better come, must have a Poor-law, if Scotland is not to be a byword among the nations. O, what a waste is there; of noble and thrice-noble national virtues; peasant Stoicisms, Heroisms; valiant manful habits, soul of a Nation's worth,—which all the metal of Potosí[3] cannot purchase back; to which the metal of Potosí, and all you can buy with *it*, is dross and dust!

Why dwell on this aspect of the matter? It is too indisputable, not doubtful now to any one. Descend where you will into the lower class, in Town or Country, by what avenue you will, by Factory Inquiries, Agricultural Inquiries, by Revenue Returns, by Mining-Labourer Committees, by opening your own eyes and looking, the same sorrowful result discloses itself: you have to admit that the working body of this rich English Nation has sunk or is fast sinking into a state, to which, all sides of it considered, there was literally never any parallel. At Stockport Assizes[4]—and this too has no reference to the present state of trade, being of date prior to that—a Mother and a Father are arraigned and found guilty of poisoning three of their children, to defraud a "burial-society" of some £3 8s. due on the death of each child: they are arraigned, found guilty; and the official authorities, it is whispered, hint that perhaps the case is not solitary, that perhaps you had better not probe farther into that department of things. This is in the autumn of 1841; the crime itself is of the previous year or season. "Brutal savages, degraded Irish," mutters the idle reader of Newspapers; hardly lingering on this incident. Yet it is an incident worth lingering on; the depravity, savagery and degraded Irishism being never so well admitted. In the British land, a

---

[1]**Poor-law:** Under the Poor Law Amendment Act of 1834, able-bodied paupers had to labor in exchange for room and board in sordid **workhouses**, which were in any case not adequate to accommodate the numbers impoverished during the slump of the late 1830s and early 1840s—a circumstance illustrating the **stronger** law of economics, if not of physics.

[2]**Dr. Alison:** see note 33 page 192.

[3]**Potosí:** silver mining center in S Bolivia.

[4]**Stockport Assizes:** court sessions in Manchester, center of the industrial north.

human Mother and Father, of white skin and professing the Christian religion, had done this thing; they, with their Irishism and necessity and savagery, had been driven to do it. Such instances are like the highest mountain apex emerged into view; under which lies a whole mountain region and land, not yet emerged. A human Mother and Father had said to themselves, What shall we do to escape starvation? We are deep sunk here, in our dark cellar; and help is far.—Yes, in the Ugolino Hunger-tower[5] stern things happen; best-loved little Gaddo fallen dead on his Father's knees!—The Stockport Mother and Father think and hint: Our poor little starveling Tom, who cries all day for victuals, who will see only evil and not good in this world: if he were out of misery at once; he well dead, and the rest of us perhaps kept alive? It is thought, and hinted; at last it is done. And now Tom being killed, and all spent and eaten, Is it poor little starveling Jack that must go, or poor little starveling Will?—What a committee of ways and means!

In starved sieged cities, in the uttermost doomed ruin of old Jerusalem fallen under the wrath of God, it was prophesied and said, "The hands of the pitiful women have sodden their own children."[6] The stern Hebrew imagination could conceive no blacker gulf of wretchedness; that was the ultimatum of degraded god-punished man. And we here, in modern England, exuberant with supply of all kinds, besieged by nothing if it be not by invisible Enchantments, are we reaching that?—How come these things? Wherefore are they, wherefore should they be?

Nor are they of the St. Ives[7] workhouses, of the Glasgow lanes, and Stockport cellars, the only unblessed among us. This successful industry of England, with its plethoric wealth, has as yet made nobody rich; it is an enchanted wealth, and belongs yet to nobody. We might ask, Which of us has it enriched? We can spend thousands where we once spent hundreds; but can purchase nothing good with them. In Poor and Rich, instead of noble thrift and plenty, there is idle luxury alternating with mean scarcity and inability. We have sumptuous garnitures for our Life, but have forgotten to *live* in the middle of them. It is an enchanted wealth; no man of us can yet touch it. The class of men who feel that they are truly better off by means of it, let them give us their name!

Many men eat finer cookery, drink dearer liquors,—with what advantage they can report, and their Doctors can: but in the heart of them, if we go out of the dyspeptic stomach, what increase of blessedness is there? Are they better, beautifuller, stronger, braver? Are they even what they call "happier?" Do they look with satisfaction on more things and human faces in this God's-Earth; do more things and human faces look with satisfaction on them? Not so. Human faces gloom discordantly, disloyally on one another. Things, if it be not mere cotton and iron things, are growing disobedient to man. The Master Worker is enchanted, for the present, like his Workhouse Workman; clamours, in vain hitherto, for a very simple sort of "Liberty": the liberty "to buy where he finds it cheapest, to sell where he finds it dearest". With guineas jingling in every pocket, he was no whit richer; but now, the very guineas threatening to vanish, he feels that he is poor indeed. Poor Master Worker! And the Master Unworker,[8] is not he in a still fataller situation? Pausing amid his game-preserves, with awful eye,—as he well may! Coercing fifty-pound tenants; coercing, bribing, cajoling; doing what he likes with his own. His mouth full of loud futilities, and arguments to prove the excellence of his Corn-law; and in his heart the blackest misgiving, a desperate half-consciousness that his excellent Corn-law is *in*defensible, that his loud arguments for it are of a kind to strike men too literally *dumb*.

To whom, then, is this wealth of England wealth? Who is it that it blesses; makes happier, wiser, beautifuller, in any way better? Who has got hold of it, to make it fetch and carry for him, like a true servant, not like a false mock-servant; to do him any real service whatsoever? As yet no one. We have more riches than any Nation ever had before; we have less good of them than any Nation ever had before. Our successful industry is hitherto unsuccessful; a strange success, if we stop here! In the midst of plethoric plenty, the people perish;[9] with gold walls, and full barns, no man feels himself safe or satisfied. Workers, Master Workers, Unworkers, all men, come to a pause; stand fixed, and cannot farther. Fatal paralysis spreading inwards, from the extremities, in St. Ives workhouses, in Stockport cellars, through all limbs, as if towards the heart itself. Have we actually got enchanted, then; accursed by some god?—

---

[5]**Ugolino**: imprisoned and starved with his children in a **tower** (Dante, *Inferno* 33).

[6]**"The hands . . . children"**: Lamentations 4:10.

[7]**St. Ives**: town in Cambridgeshire.

[8]**Master Unworker**: the idle-rich aristocrat, in distinction from the middle-class **Master Worker** and indigent **Workhouse Workman**. The **Corn-law** tariffs, abolished in 1845, favored aristocratic landowners by propping up agricultural prices.

[9]**the people perish**: see Proverbs 29:18.

Midas longed for gold, and insulted the Olympians. He got gold, so that whatsoever he touched became gold— and he, with his long ears, was little the better for it. Midas had misjudged the celestial music-tones; Midas had insulted Apollo and the gods: the gods gave him his wish, and a pair of long ears, which also were a good appendage to it. What a truth in these old Fables! (Book 1, Chapter 1)

The Sphinx

How true, for example, is that other old Fable of the Sphinx, who sat by the wayside, propounding her riddle to the passengers, which if they could not answer she destroyed them! Such a Sphinx is this Life of ours, to all men and societies of men. Nature, like the Sphinx, is of womanly celestial loveliness and tenderness; the face and bosom of a goddess, but ending in claws and the body of a lioness. There is in her a celestial beauty—which means celestial order, pliancy to wisdom; but there is also a darkness, a ferocity, fatality, which are infernal. She is a goddess, but one not yet disimprisoned; one still half-imprisoned,—the articulate, lovely still encased in the inarticulate, chaotic. How true! And does she not propound her riddles to us? Of each man she asks daily, in mild voice, yet with a terrible significance, 'Knowest thou the meaning of this Day? What thou canst do To-day; wisely attempt to do?' Nature, Universe, Destiny, Existence, howsoever we name this grand unnameable Fact in the midst of which we live and struggle, is as a heavenly bride and conquest to the wise and brave, to them who can discern her behests and do them; a destroying fiend to them who cannot. Answer her riddle, it is well with thee. Answer it not, pass on regarding it not, it will answer itself; the solution for thee is a thing of teeth and claws; Nature is a dumb lioness, deaf to thy pleadings, fiercely devouring. Thou art not now her victorious bridegroom; thou art her mangled victim, scattered on the precipices, as a slave found treacherous, recreant, ought to be and must.

With Nations it is as with individuals: Can they rede the riddle of Destiny? This English Nation, will it get to know the meaning of *its* strange new To-day? Is there sense enough extant, discoverable anywhere or anyhow, in our united twenty-seven million heads to discern the same; valour enough in our twenty-seven million hearts to dare and do the bidding thereof? It will be seen!—

The secret of gold Midas, which he with his long ears never could discover, was, That he had offended the Supreme Powers;—that he had parted company with the eternal inner Facts of this Universe, and followed the tran-

sient outer Appearances thereof; and so was arrived *here*. Properly it is the secret of all unhappy men and unhappy nations. Had they known Nature's right truth, Nature's right truth would have made them free.[10] They have become enchanted; stagger spell-bound, reeling on the brink of huge peril, because they were not wise enough. They have forgotten the right Inner True, and taken up with the Outer Shamtrue. They answer the Sphinx's question *wrong*. Foolish men cannot answer it aright! Foolish men mistake transitory semblance for eternal fact, and go astray more and more.

Foolish men imagine that because judgement for an evil thing is delayed, there is no justice, but an accidental one, here below. Judgement for an evil thing is many times delayed some day or two, some century or two, but it is sure as life, it is sure as death! In the centre of the world-whirlwind, verily now as in the oldest days, dwells and speaks a God. The great soul of the world is *just*. O brother, can it be needful now, at this late epoch of experience, after eighteen centuries of Christian preaching for one thing, to remind thee of such a fact; which all manner of Mahometans, old Pagan Romans, Jews, Scythians[11] and heathen Greeks, and indeed more or less all men that God made, have managed at one time to see into; nay which thou thyself, till "redtape" strangled the inner life of thee, hadst once some inkling of: That there *is* justice here below; and even, at bottom, that there is nothing else but justice! Forget that, thou hast forgotten all. Success will never more attend thee: how can it now? Thou hast the whole Universe against thee. No more success: mere sham-success, for a day and days; rising ever higher—towards its Tarpeian Rock. Alas, how, in thy soft-hung Longacre[12] vehicle, of polished leather to the bodily eye, of redtape philosophy, of expediencies, clubroom moralities, Parliamentary majorities to the mind's eye, thou beautifully rollest: but knowest thou whitherward? It is towards the *road's end*. Old use-and-wont; established methods, habitudes, *once* true and wise; man's noblest tendency, his perseverance, and man's ignoblest, his inertia; whatsoever of noble and ignoble Conservatism there is in men and Nations, strongest always in the strongest men and Nations: all this is as a road to thee, paved smooth through the abyss—till all this *end*. Till men's bitter necessities can endure thee no more. Till Nature's patience with thee is done; and there is no road or footing any farther, and the abyss yawns sheer!—

---

[10]**truth . . . free:** see John 8:32.

[11]**Scythians:** ancient nomadic inhabitants of Russia.

[12]**Tarpeian Rock:** Roman cliff from which criminals were thrown to death. **Longacre:** London carriage-shop district.

Parliament and the Courts of Westminster are venerable to me; how venerable; grey with a thousand years of honourable age! For a thousand years and more, Wisdom and faithful Valour, struggling amid much Folly and greedy Baseness, not without most sad distortions in the struggle, have built them up; and they are as we see. For a thousand years, this English Nation has found them useful or supportable; they have served this English Nation's want; *been* a road to it through the abyss of Time. They are venerable, they are great and strong. And yet it is good to remember always that they are not the venerablest, nor the greatest, nor the strongest! Acts of Parliament are venerable; but if they correspond not with the writing on the "Adamant Tablet",[13] what are they? Properly their one element of venerableness, of strength or greatness, is, that they at all times correspond therewith as near as by human possibility they can. They are cherishing destruction in their bosom every hour that they continue otherwise.

Alas, how many causes that can plead well for themselves in the Courts of Westminster; and yet in the general Court of the Universe, and free Soul of Man, have no word to utter! Honourable Gentlemen may find this worth considering, in times like ours. And truly, the din of triumphant Law-logic, and all shaking of horse-hair wigs and learned-sergeant gowns[14] having comfortably ended, we shall do well to ask ourselves withal, What says that high and highest Court to the verdict? For it is the Court of Courts, that same; where the universal soul of Fact and very Truth sits President;—and thitherward, more and more swiftly, with a really terrible increase of swiftness, all causes do in these days crowd for revisal—for confirmation, for modification, for reversal with costs. Dost thou know that Court; hast thou had any Law-practice there? What, didst thou never enter; never file any petition of redress, reclaimer, disclaimer, or demurrer, written as in thy heart's blood, for thy own behoof or another's; and silently await the issue? Thou knowest not such a Court? Hast merely heard of it by faint tradition as a thing that was or had been? Of thee, I think, we shall get little benefit.

For the gowns of learned-sergeants are good; parchment records, fixed forms, and poor terrestrial Justice, with or without horse-hair, what sane man will not reverence these? And yet, behold, the man is not sane but insane, who considers these alone as venerable. Oceans of horse-hair, continents of parchment, and learned-sergeant eloquence, were it continued till the learned tongue wore itself small in the indefatigable learned mouth, cannot make unjust just. The grand question still remains, Was the judgement just? If unjust, it will not and cannot get harbour for itself, or continue to have footing in this Universe, which was made by other than One Unjust. Enforce it by never such statuting, three readings, royal assents; blow it to the four winds with all manner of quilted trumpeters and pursuivants,[15] in the rear of them never so many gibbets and hangmen, it will not stand, it cannot stand. From all souls of men, from all ends of Nature, from the Throne of God above, there are voices bidding it: Away, away! Does it take no warning; does it stand, strong in its three readings, in its gibbets and artillery-parks? The more woe is to it, the frightfuller woe. It will continue standing for its day, for its year, for its century, doing evil all the while; but it has One enemy who is Almighty: dissolution, explosion, and the everlasting Laws of Nature incessantly advance towards it; and the deeper its rooting, more obstinate its continuing, the deeper also and huger will its ruin and overturn be.

In this God's-World, with its wild-whirling eddies and mad foam-oceans, where men and nations perish as if without law, and judgement for an unjust thing is sternly delayed, dost thou think that there is therefore no justice? It is what the fool hath said in his heart.[16] It is what the wise, in all times, were wise because they denied, and knew forever not to be. I tell thee again, there is nothing else but justice. One strong thing I find here below: the just thing, the true thing. My friend, if thou hadst all the artillery of Woolwich[17] trundling at thy back in support of an unjust thing; and infinite bonfires visibly waiting ahead of thee, to blaze centuries long for thy victory on behalf of it—I would advise thee to call halt, to fling down thy baton, and say, "In God's name, No!" Thy "success"? Poor devil, what will thy success amount to? If the thing is unjust, thou hast not succeeded; no, not though bonfires blazed from North to South, and bells rang, and editors wrote leading-articles, and the just thing lay trampled out of sight, to all mortal eyes an abolished and annihilated thing. Success? In few years thou wilt be dead and dark,—all cold, eyeless, deaf;

---

[13]**"Adamant Tablet"**: see Jeremiah 17:1. **cherishing . . . bosom**: see 1 Kings 1:2

[14]**wigs**: worn in court by gowned British lawyers, of whom one high rank were called **sergeants**.

[15]Bills under parliamentary consideration may have several **readings** before passage and **royal assent. pursuivants**: attenders to a herald, whose royal message came with **trumpeters**' fanfare.

[16]**the fool . . . in his heart**: see Psalm 14:1.

[17]**Woolwich**: site of the state arsenal, E of London.

no blaze of bonfires, ding-dong of bells or leading-articles visible or audible to thee again at all forever: What kind of success is that!—

It is true, all goes by approximation in this world; with any not insupportable approximation we must be patient. There is a noble Conservatism as well as an ignoble. Would to Heaven, for the sake of Conservatism itself, the noble alone were left, and the ignoble, by some kind severe hand, were ruthlessly lopped away, forbidden evermore to show itself! For it is the right and noble alone that will have victory in this struggle; the rest is wholly an obstruction, a postponement and fearful imperilment of the victory. Towards an eternal centre of right and nobleness, and of that only, is all this confusion tending. We already know whither it is all tending; what will have victory, what will have none! The Heaviest will reach the centre. The Heaviest, sinking through complex fluctuating media and vortices, has its deflexions, its obstructions, nay at times its resiliences, its reboundings; whereupon some blockhead shall be heard jubilating, "See, your Heaviest ascends!"—but at all moments it is moving centreward, fast as is convenient for it; sinking, sinking; and, by laws older than the World, old as the Maker's first Plan of the World, it has to arrive there.

Await the issue. In all battles, if you await the issue, each fighter has prospered according to his right. His right and his might, at the close of the account, were one and the same. He has fought with all his might, and in exact proportion to all his right he has prevailed. His very death is no victory over him. He dies indeed; but his work lives, very truly lives. A heroic Wallace,[18] quartered on the scaffold, cannot hinder that his Scotland become, one day, a part of England: but he does hinder that it become, on tyrannous unfair terms, a part of it; commands still, as with a god's voice, from his old Valhalla and Temple of the Brave, that there be a just real union as of brother and brother, not a false and merely semblant one as of slave and master. If the union with England be in fact one of Scotland's chief blessings, we thank Wallace withal that it was not the chief curse. Scotland is not Ireland: no, because brave men rose there, and said, "Behold ye must not tread us down like slaves; and ye shall not,—and cannot!" Fight on, thou brave true heart, and falter not, through dark fortune and through bright. The cause thou fightest for, so far as it is true, no far-

ther, yet precisely so far, is very sure of victory. The falsehood alone of it will be conquered, will be abolished, as it ought to be: but the truth of it is part of Nature's own Laws, co-operates with the World's eternal Tendencies, and cannot be conquered.

The *dust* of controversy, what is it but the *falsehood* flying off from all manner of conflicting true forces, and making such a loud dust-whirlwind,—that so the truths alone may remain, and embrace brother-like in some true resulting force! It is ever so. Savage fighting Heptarchies:[19] their fighting is an ascertainment, who has the right to rule over whom; that out of such waste-bickering Saxondom a peacefully co-operating England may arise. Seek through this Universe; if with other than owl's eyes, thou wilt find nothing nourished there, nothing kept in life, but what has right to nourishment and life. The rest, look at it with other than owl's eyes, is not living; is all dying, all as good as dead! Justice was ordained from the foundations of the world; and will last with the world and longer.

From which I infer that the inner sphere of Fact, in this present England as elsewhere, differs infinitely from the outer sphere and spheres of Semblance. That the Temporary , here as elsewhere, is too apt to carry it over the Eternal. That he who dwells in the temporary Semblances, and does not penetrate into the eternal Substance, will *not* answer the Sphinx-riddle of To-day, or of any Day. For the substance alone is substantial; that *is* the law of Fact; if you discover not that, Fact, who already knows it, will let you also know it by and by!

What is Justice? that, on the whole, is the question of the Sphinx to us. The law of Fact is, that Justice must and will be done. The sooner the better; for the Time grows stringent, frightfully pressing! "What is Justice?" ask many, to whom cruel Fact alone will be able to prove responsive. It is like jesting Pilate asking, What is Truth?[20] Jesting Pilate had not the smallest chance to ascertain what was Truth. He could not have known it, had a god shown it to him. Thick serene opacity, thicker than amaurosis, veiled those smiling eyes of his to Truth; the inner *retina* of them was gone paralytic, dead. He looked at Truth; and discerned her not, there where she stood. "What is Justice?" The clothed embodied Justice that sits in Westminster Hall, with penal-

---

[18]Sir William **Wallace** (d. 1305): Scottish national hero. **Valhalla**: hall of slain heroes in Norse mythology.

[19]**Heptarchies**: the seven feuding Anglo-Saxon kingdoms of 7th- and 8th-century England.

[20]**What is Truth?**: John 18:38. **amaurosis**: disease of the optic nerve.

ties, parchments, tipstaves, is very visible. But the *unembod-ied* Justice, whereof that other is either an emblem, or else is a fearful indescribability, is not so visible! For the unembod-ied Justice is of Heaven; a Spirit, and Divinity of Heaven,— *in*visible to all but the noble and pure of soul. The impure ignoble gaze with eyes, and she is not there. They will prove it to you by logic, by endless Hansard Debatings,[21] by bursts of Parliamentary eloquence. It is not consolatory to behold! For properly, as many men as there are in a Na-tion who *can* withal see Heaven's invisible Justice, and know it to be on Earth also omnipotent, so many men are there who stand between a Nation and perdition. So many, and no more. Heavy-laden England, how many hast thou in this hour? The Supreme Power sends new and ever new, all *born* at least with hearts of flesh and not of stone;—and heavy Misery itself, once heavy enough, will prove didactic!— (Book 1, Chapter 2)

Gospel of Mammonism[22]

Reader, even Christian Reader as thy title goes, hast thou any notion of Heaven and Hell? I rather apprehend, not. Often as the words are on our tongue, they have got a fabu-lous or semi-fabulous character for most of us, and pass on like a kind of transient similitude, like a sound signifying little.

Yet it is well worth while for us to know, once and al-ways, that they are not a similitude, nor a fable nor semi-fable; that they are an everlasting highest fact! "No Lake of Sicilian or other sulphur[23] burns now anywhere in these ages," sayest thou? Well, and if there did not! Believe that there does not; believe it if thou wilt, nay hold by it as a real increase, a rise to higher stages, to wider horizons and em-pires. All this has vanished, or has not vanished; believe as thou wilt as to all this. But that an Infinite of Practical Im-portance, speaking with strict arithmetical exactness, an *Infi-nite*, has vanished or can vanish from the Life of any Man: this thou shalt not believe! O brother, the Infinite of Terror, of Hope, of Pity, did it not at any moment disclose itself to thee, indubitable, unnameable? Came it never, like the gleam of *preter*natural Oceans, like the voice of old Eterni-ties, far-sounding through thy heart of hearts? Never? Alas,

it was not thy Liberalism then; it was thy Animalism! The Infinite is more sure than any other fact. But only men can discern it; mere building beavers, spinning arachnes, much more the predatory vulturous and vulpine species, do not discern it well!—

"The word Hell," says Sauerteig,[24] "is still frequently in use among the English People: but I could not without diffi-culty ascertain what they meant by it. Hell generally signi-fies the Infinite Terror, the thing a man *is* infinitely afraid of, and shudders and shrinks from, struggling with his whole soul to escape from it. There is a Hell therefore, if you will consider, which accompanies man, in all stages of his his-tory, and religious or other development: but the Hells of men and Peoples differ notably. With Christians it is the in-finite terror of being found guilty before the Just Judge. With old Romans, I conjecture, it was the terror not of Pluto, for whom probably they cared little, but of doing un-worthily, doing unvirtuously,[25] which was their word for un*man*fully. And now what is it, if you pierce through his Cants, his oft-repeated Hearsays, what he calls his Wor-ships and so forth,—what is it that the modern English soul does, in very truth, dread infinitely, and contemplate with entire despair? What *is* his Hell, after all these reputable, oft-repeated Hearsays, what is it? With hesitation, with as-tonishment, I pronounce it to be: The terror of 'Not suc-ceeding;' of not making money, fame, or some other figure in the world,—chiefly of not making money! Is not that a somewhat singular Hell?"

Yes, O Sauerteig, it is very singular. If we do not "suc-ceed", where is the use of us? We had better never have been born. "Tremble intensely," as our friend the Emperor of China[26] says: *there* is the black Bottomless of Terror; what Sauerteig calls the "Hell of the English!"—But indeed this Hell belongs naturally to the Gospel of Mammonism, which also has its corresponding Heaven. For there *is* one Reality among so many Phantasms; about one thing we are entirely in earnest: The making of money. Working Mammonism does divide the world with idle game-preserving Dilettan-tism:—thank Heaven that there is even a Mammonism, *any-*thing we are in earnest about! Idleness is worst, Idleness alone is without hope: work earnestly at anything, you will

---

[21]Thomas **Hansard** (1776–1833): publisher of House of Com-mons debates in a record still informally known by his name.

[22]**Mammonism**: worship of Mammon, demon of avarice; see Matthew 6:24.

[23]**sulphur**: mined in **Sicily**, traditionally the fuel of hell.

[24]**Sauerteig**: Carlyle's impersonation of a German tourist.

[25]**Pluto**: Roman god, ruler of the dead, whose confusion with the god of wealth, Plutus, Carlyle here exploits. **unvirtuously**: from Latin *vir*, man.

[26]**Emperor of China**: forced by British arms to an 1842 commer-cial treaty; thus, ironically, Britain's **friend**.

by degrees learn to work at almost all things. There is endless hope in work, were it even work at making money.

True, it must be owned, we for the present, with our Mammon-Gospel, have come to strange conclusions. We call it a Society; and go about professing openly the totallest separation, isolation. Our life is not a mutual helpfulness; but rather, cloaked under due laws-of-war, named "fair competition" and so forth, it is a mutual hostility. We have profoundly forgotten everywhere that *Cash-payment* is not the sole relation of human beings; we think, nothing doubting, that *it* absolves and liquidates all engagements of man. "My starving workers?" answers the rich Millowner: "Did not I hire them fairly in the market? Did I not pay them, to the last sixpence, the sum covenanted for? What have I to do with them more?"—Verily Mammon-worship is a melancholy creed. When Cain, for his own behoof, had killed Abel, and was questioned, "Where is thy brother?" he too made answer, "Am I my brother's keeper?" Did I not pay my brother *his* wages, the thing he had merited from me?

O sumptuous Merchant-Prince, illustrious game-preserving Duke, is there no way of "killing" thy brother but Cain's rude way! "A good man by the very look of him, by his very presence with us as a fellow wayfarer in this Life-pilgrimage, *promises* so much": woe to him if he forget all such promises, if he never know that they are given! To a deadened soul, seared with the brute Idolatry of Sense, to whom going to Hell is equivalent to not making money, all "promises", and moral duties, that cannot be pleaded for in Courts of Requests,[27] address themselves in vain. Money he can be ordered to pay, but nothing more. I have not heard in all Past History, and expect not to hear in all Future History, of any Society anywhere under God's Heaven supporting itself on such Philosophy. The Universe is not made so; it is made otherwise than so. The man or nation of men that thinks it is made so, marches forward nothing doubting, step after step; but marches—whither we know! In these last two centuries of Atheistic Government (near two centuries now, since the blessed restoration of his Sacred Majesty, and Defender of the Faith, Charles Second),[28] I reckon that we have pretty well exhausted what of 'firm earth' there was for us to march on;—and are now, very ominously, shuddering, reeling, and let us hope trying to recoil, on the cliff's edge!—

For out of this that we call Atheism come so many other *isms* and falsities, each falsity with its misery at its heels!—A SOUL is not like wind (*spiritus*, or breath) contained within a capsule; the ALMIGHTY MAKER is not like a Clockmaker that once, in old immemorial ages, having *made* his Horologe of a Universe, sits ever since and sees it go! Not at all. Hence comes Atheism; come, as we say, many other *isms*; and as the sum of all, comes Valetism,[29] the *reverse* of Heroism; sad root of all woes whatsoever. For indeed, as no man ever saw the above-said wind-element enclosed within its capsule, and finds it at bottom more deniable than conceivable; so too he finds, in spite of Bridgewater Bequests, your Clockmaker[30] Almighty an entirely questionable affair, a deniable affair;—and accordingly denies it, and along with it so much else. Alas, one knows not what and how much else! For the faith in an Invisible, Unnameable, Godlike, present everywhere in all that we see and work and suffer, is the essence of all faith whatsoever; and that once denied, or still worse, asserted with lips only, and out of bound prayerbooks only, what other thing remains believable? That Cant well-ordered is marketable Cant; that Heroism means gas-lighted Histrionism;[31] that seen with "clear eyes" (as they call Valet-eyes), no man is a Hero, or ever was a Hero, but all men are Valets and Varlets. The accursed practical quintessence of all sorts of Unbelief! For if there be now no Hero, and the Histrio himself begin to be seen into, what hope is there for the seed of Adam here below? We are the doomed everlasting prey of the Quack; who, now in this guise, now in that, is to filch us, to pluck and eat us, by such modes as are convenient for him. For the modes and guises I care little. The Quack once inevitable, let him come swiftly, let him pluck and eat me;—swiftly, that I may at least have done with him; for in his Quack-world I can have no wish to linger. Though he slay me, yet will I *not* trust in him. Though he conquer nations, and have all the Flunkeys of the Universe shouting at his heels, yet will I know well that *he* is an Inanity; that for him and his there is no continuance appointed, save only in Gehenna and the Pool.[32] Alas, the Atheist world, from its utmost

---

[27]**Courts of Requests:** small-claims courts.

[28]**Charles II** (restored in 1660) was notorious for dissipation.

[29]**Valetism:** reference to the epigram "No man is a hero to his valet" (Marshal Catinat, 1637–1712).

[30]A **bequest** from the Earl of **Bridgewater** commissioned a series of treatises illustrating Natural Theology, the view that a clocklike world revealed a **Clockmaker** deity. See page 52.

[31]**Histrionism:** theatricality (from Latin *histrio*, actor).

[32]**Gehenna and the Pool:** hell; from Hinnom, fiery scene of child sacrifice in Jeremiah 32:35. **seven-feet Hats:** London advertising gimmick discussed in Carlyle's previous chapter. **Unveracities:** fakes (Carlyle's coinage).

summits of Heaven and Westminster Hall, downwards through poor seven-feet Hats and "Unveracities fallen hungry," down to the lowest cellars and neglected hunger-dens of it, is very wretched.

One of Dr. Alison's Scotch facts struck us much.[33] A poor Irish Widow, her husband having died in one of the Lanes of Edinburgh, went forth with her three children, bare of all resource, to solicit help from the Charitable Establishments of that City. At this Charitable Establishment and then at that she was refused; referred from one to the other, helped by none;—till she had exhausted them all; till her strength and heart failed her: she sank down in typhus-fever; died, and infected her Lane with fever, so that "seventeen other persons" died of fever there in consequence. The humane Physician asks thereupon, as with a heart too full for speaking, Would it not have been *economy* to help this poor Widow? She took typhus-fever, and killed seventeen of you!—Very curious. The forlorn Irish Widow applies to her fellow-creatures, as if saying, "Behold I am sinking, bare of help: ye must help me! I am your sister, bone of your bone; one God made us: ye must help me!" They answer, "No; impossible; thou art no sister of ours." But she proves her sisterhood; her typhus-fever kills *them*: they actually were her brothers, though denying it! Had human creature ever to go lower for a proof?

For, as indeed was very natural in such case, all government of the Poor by the Rich has long ago been given over to Supply-and-demand, Laissez-faire and such like, and universally declared to be "impossible." "You are no sister of ours; what shadow of proof is there? Here are our parchments, our padlocks, proving indisputably our money-safes to be *ours*, and you to have no business with them. Depart! It is impossible!"—Nay, what wouldst thou thyself have us do? cry indignant readers. Nothing, my friends,—till you have got a soul for yourselves again. Till then all things are "impossible." Till then I cannot even bid you buy, as the old Spartans would have done, two-pence worth of powder and lead, and compendiously shoot to death this poor Irish Widow: even that is "impossible" for you. Nothing is left but that she prove her sisterhood by dying, and infecting you with typhus. Seventeen of you lying dead will not deny such proof that she *was* flesh of your flesh;[34] and perhaps some of the living may lay it to heart.

---

[33]**much** . . . *Observations on the Management of the Poor in Scotland:* By William Pulteney Alison, M.D. (Edinburgh, 1840). [Carlyle's note]

[34]**flesh of your flesh**: see Genesis 2:23.

"Impossible": of a certain two-legged animal with feathers it is said, if you draw a distinct chalk-circle round him, he sits imprisoned, as if girt with the iron ring of Fate; and will die there, though within sight of victuals,—or sit in sick misery there, and be fatted to death. The name of this poor two-legged animal is—Goose; and they make of him, when well fattened, *Pâté de foie gras*, much prized by some! (Book 3, Chapter 2)

Happy

All work, even cotton-spinning, is noble; work is alone noble: be that here said and asserted once more. And in like manner, too, all dignity is painful; a life of ease is not for any man, nor for any god. The life of all gods figures itself to us as a Sublime Sadness,—earnestness of Infinite Battle against Infinite Labour. Our highest religion is named the "Worship of Sorrow." For the son of man there is no noble crown, well worn, or even ill worn, but is a crown of thorns!—These things, in spoken words, or still better, in felt instincts alive in every heart, were once well known.

Does not the whole wretchedness, the whole *Atheism* as I call it, of man's ways, in these generations, shadow itself for us in that unspeakable Life-philosophy of his: The pretension to be what he calls "happy?" Every pitifullest whipster that walks within a skin has his head filled with the notion that he is, shall be, or by all human and divine laws ought to be, "happy." His wishes, the pitifullest whipster's, are to be fulfilled for him; his days, the pitifullest whipster's, are to flow on in ever-gentle current of enjoyment, impossible even for the gods. The prophets preach to us, Thou shalt be happy; thou shalt love pleasant things, and find them. The people clamour, Why have we not found pleasant things?

We construct our theory of Human Duties, not on any Greatest-Nobleness Principle, never so mistaken; no, but on a Greatest-Happiness Principle. "The word *Soul* with us, as in some Slavonic dialects, seems to be synonymous with *Stomach*." We plead and speak, in our Parliaments and elsewhere, not as from the Soul, but from the Stomach;—wherefore, indeed, our pleadings are so slow to profit. We plead not for God's Justice; we are not ashamed to stand clamouring and pleading for our own "interests," our own rents and trade-profits; we say, They are the "interests" of so many; there is such an intense desire in us for them! We demand Free-Trade, with much just vociferation and benevolence, That the poorer classes, who are terribly ill-off at present, may have cheaper New-Orleans bacon. Men ask on Free-trade platforms, How can the indomitable spirit of Englishmen be kept up without plenty of bacon? We shall become a ruined Nation!—Surely, my friends, plenty of bacon is good and indispensable: but, I doubt, you will never get even bacon by aiming only at that. You are men, not animals of prey, well-used or ill-used! Your Greatest-Happiness Principle seems to me fast becoming a rather unhappy one,—What if we should cease babbling about "happiness", and leave *it* resting on its own basis, as it used to do!

A gifted Byron rises in his wrath; and feeling too surely that he for his part is not "happy", declares the same in very violent language, as a piece of news that may be interesting. It evidently has surprised him much. One dislikes to see a man and poet reduced to proclaim on the streets such tidings: but on the whole, as matters go, that is not the most dislikable. Byron speaks the *truth* in this matter. Byron's large audience indicates how true it is felt to be.

"Happy", my brother? First of all, what difference is it whether thou art happy or not! To-day becomes Yesterday so fast, all To-morrows become Yesterdays; and then there is no question whatever of the "happiness", but quite another question. Nay, thou hast such a sacred pity left at least for thyself, thy very pains, once gone over into Yesterday, become joys to thee. Besides, thou knowest not what heavenly blessedness and indispensable sanative virtue was in them; thou shalt only know it after many days, when thou art wiser!—A benevolent old Surgeon sat once in our company, with a Patient fallen sick by gormandizing, whom he had just, too briefly in the Patient's judgement, been examining. The foolish Patient still at intervals continued to break in on our discourse, which rather promised to take a philosophic turn: "But I have lost my appetite," said he, objurgatively, with a tone of irritated pathos; "I have no appetite; I can't eat!"—"My dear fellow," answered the Doctor in mildest tone, "it isn't of the slightest consequence";—and continued his philosophical discoursings with us!

Or does the reader not know the history of that Scottish iron Misanthrope? The inmates of some town-mansion, in those Northern parts, were thrown into the fearfullest alarm by indubitable symptoms of a ghost inhabiting the next house, or perhaps even the partition-wall! Ever at a certain hour, with preternatural gnarring, growling and screeching, which attended as running bass, there began, in a horrid, semi-articulate, unearthly voice, this song: "Once I was hap-hap-happy, but now I'm *mees*-erable! Clack-clack-clack, gnarr-r-r, whuz-z: Once I was hap-hap-happy, but

now I'm *mees*-erable!"—Rest, rest, perturbed spirit;[35]—or indeed, as the good old Doctor said: My dear fellow, it isn't of the slightest consequence! But no; the perturbed spirit could not rest; and to the neighbours, fretted, affrighted, or at least insufferably bored by him, it *was* of such consequence that they had to go and examine in his haunted chamber. In his haunted chamber, they find that the perturbed spirit is an unfortunate—Imitator of Byron? No, is an unfortunate rusty Meat-jack,[36] gnarring and creaking with rust and work; and this, in Scottish dialect, is *its* Byronian musical Life-philosophy, sung according to ability!

Truly, I think the man who goes about pothering and uproaring for his "happiness",—pothering, and were it ballot-boxing, poem-making, or in what way soever fussing and exerting himself,—he is not the man that will help us to "get our knaves and dastards arrested"! No; he rather is on the way to increase the number,—by at least one unit and his tail! Observe, too, that this is all a modern affair; belongs not to the old heroic times, but to these dastard new times. "Happiness our being's end and aim,"[37] all that very paltry speculation, is at bottom, if we will count well, not yet two centuries old in the world.

The only happiness a brave man ever troubled himself with asking much about was, happiness enough to get his work done. Not "I can't eat!" but "I can't work!" that was the burden of all wise complaining among men. It is, after all, the one unhappiness of a man. That he cannot work; that he cannot get his destiny as a man fulfilled. Behold, the day is passing swiftly over, our life is passing swiftly over; and the night cometh, wherein no man can work.[38] The night once come, our happiness, our unhappiness,—it is all abolished; vanished, clean gone; a thing that has been: "not of the slightest consequence" whether we were happy as eupeptic Curtis, as the fattest pig of Epicurus, or unhappy as Job with potsherds, as musical Byron with Giaours[39] and sensibilities of the heart; as the unmusical Meat-jack with hard labour and rust! But our work,—behold that is not abolished, that has not vanished: our work, behold, it remains, or the want of it remains;—for endless Times and Eternities, remains;

---

[35]**Rest, rest, perturbed spirit**: *Hamlet* 1.5.182.

[36]**Meat-jack**: machine to turn the spit over a roasting fire.

[37]**"Happiness . . . aim"**: Pope, *Essay on Man* (1734) 4.1.

[38]**the night . . . work**: John 9:4.

[39]William **Curtis** (1752–1829): MP, Lord Mayor of London, gourmet. **Epicurus** (341–270 BCE): Greek philosopher of pleasure. *The Giaour*: oriental verse tale by **Byron** (1813).

and that is now the sole question with us for evermore! Brief brawling Day, with its noisy phantoms, its poor paper-crowns tinsel-guilt, is gone; and divine everlasting Night, with her star-diadems, with her silences and her veracities, is come! What hast thou done, and how? Happiness, unhappiness: all that was but the *wages* thou hadst; thou has spent all that, in sustaining thyself hitherward; not a coin of it remains with thee, it is all spent, eaten: and now thy work, where is thy work? Swift, out with it, let us see thy work!

Of a truth, if man were not a poor hungry dastard, and even much of a blockhead withal, he would cease criticizing his victuals to such extent; and criticize himself rather, what he does with his victuals! (Book 3, Chapter 4)

1843

THOMAS BABINGTON MACAULAY

(1800–1859)

His prose aglow with conviction, Thomas Babington Macaulay blazoned around the English-speaking world opinions few of which can have surprised the evangelical editor and abolitionist crusader who was his father. After finishing at Cambridge, Macaulay rocketed into public view in 1825 with literary and political essays, published in the liberal *Edinburgh Review*, that attacked (along with other targets) slavery and the religious intolerance prevalent among cultural conservatives like John Keble. At thirty he was in Parliament acquiring a name for eloquence in the cause of Reform. Soon after passage of the 1832 Bill he moved to India for four years on the Supreme Council, where he was instrumental in overhauling the educational system and penal code—in the spirit of beefy chauvinism that our selection from his official Minute exhales—at a salary that set him up for life as an independent man of letters keeping house with his sisters in London.

Macaulay's writing henceforth was predominantly historical. He steadily published articles that, collected in 1843 as *Critical and Historical Essays*, were popular throughout the century. He produced a poetry hit in the *Lays of Ancient Rome* (1842), pre-imperial Roman legends rendered into briskly stirring versions of the vernacular British ballad. The crowning work of his last twenty years was *The History of England from the Accession of James II* (1848–1855), four stout volumes that sold like a serial novel because they read like one. Packed with vividly drawn characters and teeming with documentary social detail of a sort that was new to ambitious history writing, the work was driven by a plot of national importance: the emergence of Britain from the twilights of fanaticism and feudal privilege to play a leading role, on the enlightened eighteenth-century stage, as the world's paragon of political toleration, commercial enterprise, and strong common sense.

All Macaulay's writings were crafted to vindicate those developments in contemporary life whose pulse meant progress. This is not quite the same as endorsement of the status quo—Macaulay brought great energy to projects of reform—but it resembles such an endorsement closely enough to explain his fall from favor in the twentieth century. An intellectual climate that prizes nuance and self-critique finds Macaulay's Whiggish confidence abrasively smug, and it is tempting to reduce his force to bullying caricature, his clarity to mere orderliness. Some of the outcomes he struggled for have become established ills that the world now struggles against; so the publicist whose glib assumption of British superiority supported an imperialist mission will be read today with a measure of annoyance, if he is read at all.

Yet his is a Victorian voice that we would have to invent should we be so careless as to lose him. His unshakable faith in the convergence between Britain's destiny and the direction of world progress, as well as in the bond between individual liberties and the sanctity of property, equipped him to inscribe the ideological high watermark to which, by midcentury, the middle class had risen. Thousands shared this faith, though none could express it in so victorious a march of sentences. Macaulay mastered the balanced Augustan prose of the previous century, beating its resources of parallelism and contrast on the anvil of a relentlessly argumentative purpose. Like his eighteenth-century stylistic models Addison and Johnson, he wrote to entertain and instruct, but he also and always wrote to win. Exultation may not be the richest of literary tempers; still, it is no more alien to literature than to life, and the selections that follow register, in solid brass, a manic side without which the mood swings of Victorian writing cannot be rightly appreciated. Macaulay's sweeping contrast in the *History* between Britain's past and present offers, as a bonus, a practical orientation to where the country stood at midcentury—or, rather, to the phase it took itself to be passing through with accelerating speed.

from Minute on Indian Education

... We now come to the gist of the matter.[1] We have a fund to be employed as Government shall direct for the intellectual improvement of the people of this country. The simple question is, what is the most useful way of employing it?

All parties seem to be agreed on one point, that the dialects commonly spoken among the natives of this part of India, contain neither literary nor scientific information, and are, moreover, so poor and rude that, until they are enriched from some other quarter, it will not be easy to translate any valuable work into them. It seems to be admitted on all sides, that the intellectual improvement of those classes of the people who have the means of pursuing higher studies can at present be effected only by means of some language not vernacular amongst them.

What then shall that language be? One-half of the Committee maintain that it should be the English. The other half strongly recommend the Arabic and Sanscrit. The whole question seems to me to be, which language is the best worth knowing?

I have no knowledge of either Sanscrit or Arabic.—But I have done what I could to form a correct estimate of their value. I have read translations of the most celebrated Arabic and Sanscrit works. I have conversed both here and at home with men distinguished by their proficiency in the Eastern tongues. I am quite ready to take the Oriental learning at the valuation of the Orientalists themselves. I have never found one among them who could deny that a single shelf of a good European library was worth the whole native literature of India and Arabia. The intrinsic superiority of the Western literature is, indeed, fully admitted by those members of the Committee who support the Oriental plan of education.

It will hardly be disputed, I suppose, that the department of literature in which the Eastern writers stand highest is poetry. And I certainly never met with any Orientalist who ventured to maintain that the Arabic and Sanscrit poetry could be compared to that of the great European nations. But when we pass from works of imagination to works in which facts are recorded, and general principles investigated, the superiority of the Europeans becomes absolutely immeasurable. It is, I believe, no exaggeration to say, that all the historical information which has been collected from all the books written in the Sanscrit language is less valuable than what may be found in the most paltry abridgments used at preparatory schools in England. In every branch of physical or moral philosophy, the relative position of the two nations is nearly the same.

How, then, stands the case? We have to educate a people who cannot at present be educated by means of their mother-tongue. We must teach them some foreign language. The claims of our own language it is hardly necessary to recapitulate. It stands preeminent even among the languages of the west. It abounds with works of imagination not inferior to the noblest which Greece has bequeathed to us; with models of every species of eloquence; with historical compositions, which, considered merely as narratives, have seldom been surpassed, and which, considered as vehicles of ethical and political instruction, have never been equalled; with just and lively representations of human life and human nature; with the most profound speculations on metaphysics, morals, government, jurisprudence, and trade; with full and correct information respecting every experimental science

---

[1]**gist of the matter:** whether the curriculum in colonial India is to transmit native culture in Sanskrit and Arabic or western culture in English. Macaulay wrote this minute as a charter member of the Supreme Council set up in 1834 to bring India under the coordinated rule of the British state and the longstanding East India Company.

which tends to preserve the health, to increase the comfort, or to expand the intellect of man. Whoever knows that language has ready access to all the vast intellectual wealth, which all the wisest nations of the earth have created and hoarded in the course of ninety generations. It may safely be said, that the literature now extant in that language is of far greater value than all the literature which three hundred years ago was extant in all the languages of the world together. Nor is this all. In India, English is the language spoken by the ruling class. It is spoken by the higher class of natives at the seats of Government. It is likely to become the language of commerce throughout the seas of the East. It is the language of two great European communities which are rising, the one in the south of Africa, the other in Australasia; communities which are every year becoming more important, and more closely connected with our Indian empire. Whether we look at the intrinsic value of our literature, or at the particular situation of this country, we shall see the strongest reason to think that, of all foreign tongues, the English tongue is that which would be the most useful to our native subjects.

The question now before us is simply whether, when it is in our power to teach this language, we shall teach languages in which, by universal confession, there are no books on any subject which deserve to be compared to our own; whether, when we can teach European science, we shall teach systems which, by universal confession, whenever they differ from those of Europe, differ for the worse; and whether, when we can patronise sound Philosophy and true History, we shall countenance, at the public expense, medical doctrines, which would disgrace an English farrier,—Astronomy, which would move laughter in girls at an English boarding school,—History, abounding with kings thirty feet high, and reigns thirty thousand years long,—and Geography, made up of seas of treacle and seas of butter.

We are not without experience to guide us. History furnishes several analogous cases, and they all teach the same lesson. There are in modern times, to go no further, two memorable instances of a great impulse given to the mind of a whole society,—of prejudices overthrown,—of knowledge diffused,—of taste purified,—of arts and sciences planted in countries which had recently been ignorant and barbarous.

The first instance to which I refer, is the great revival of letters among the Western nations at the close of the fifteenth and the beginning of the sixteenth century. At that time almost every thing that was worth reading was contained in the writings of the ancient Greeks and Romans. Had our ancestors acted as the Committee of Public Instruc-

tion has hitherto acted; had they neglected the language of Cicero and Tacitus,[2] had they confined their attention to the old dialects of our own island; had they printed nothing and taught nothing at the universities but Chronicles in Anglo-Saxon, and Romances in Norman-French, would England have been what she now is? What the Greek and Latin were to the contemporaries of More and Ascham,[3] our tongue is to the people of India. The literature of England is now more valuable than that of classical antiquity. I doubt whether the Sanscrit literature be as valuable as that of our Saxon and Norman progenitors. In some departments,—in History, for example, I am certain that it is much less so.

Another instance may be said to be still before our eyes. Within the last hundred and twenty years, a nation which has previously been in a state as barbarous as that in which our ancestors were before the crusades, has gradually emerged from the ignorance in which it was sunk, and has taken its place among civilized communities.—I speak of Russia. There is now in that country a large educated class, abounding with persons fit to serve the state in the highest functions, and in no wise inferior to the most accomplished men who adorn the best circles of Paris and London. There is reason to hope that this vast empire, which in the time of our grandfathers was probably behind the Punjab,[4] may, in the time of our grandchildren, be pressing close on France and Britain in the career of improvement. And how was this change effected? Not by flattering national prejudices: not by feeding the mind of the young Muscovite with the old women's stories which his rude fathers had believed: not by filling his head with lying legends about St. Nicholas: not by encouraging him to study the great question, whether the world was or was not created on the 13th of September: not by calling him "a learned native," when he has mastered all these points of knowledge: but by teaching him those foreign languages in which the greatest mass of information had been laid up, and thus putting all that information within his reach. The languages of Western Europe civilized Russia. I cannot doubt that they will do for the Hindoo what they have done for the Tartar.

And what are the arguments against that course which seems to be alike recommended by theory and by experience? It is said that we ought to secure the co-operation of

---

[2]Marcus Tullius **Cicero** (106–43 BCE): Roman jurist and author. **Tacitus** (56–120): Roman historian.

[3]Sir Thomas **More** (1477–1535): statesman and author. Roger **Ascham** (1515–1568): Tudor humanist and educator.

[4]**Punjab:** N region of Indian subcontinent.

the native public, and that we can do this only by teaching Sanscrit and Arabic.

I can by no means admit that when a nation of high intellectual attainments undertakes to superintend the education of a nation comparatively ignorant, the learners are absolutely to prescribe the course which is to be taken by the teachers. It is not necessary, however, to say any thing on this subject. For it is proved by unanswerable evidence that we are not at present securing the co-operation of the natives. It would be bad enough to consult their intellectual taste at the expense of their intellectual health. But we are consulting neither;—we are withholding from them the learning for which they are craving, we are forcing on them the mock-learning which they nauseate. . . .

1835

~

from History of England

I purpose to write the history of England from the accession of King James the Second down to a time which is within the memory of men still living.[1] I shall recount the errors which, in a few months, alienated a loyal gentry and priesthood from the House of Stuart. I shall trace the course of that revolution which terminated the long struggle between our sovereigns and their parliaments, and bound up together the rights of the people and the title of the reigning dynasty. I shall relate how the new settlement was, during many troubled years, successfully defended against foreign and domestic enemies; how, under that settlement, the authority of law and the security of property were found to be compatible with a liberty of discussion and of individual action never before known; how, from the auspicious union of order and freedom, sprang a prosperity of which the annals of human affairs had furnished no example; how our country, from a state of ignominious vassalage, rapidly rose to the place of umpire among European powers; how her opulence and her martial glory grew together; how, by wise and resolute good faith, was gradually established a public credit fruitful of marvels which to the statesmen of any former age would have seemed incredible; how a gigantic commerce gave birth to a maritime power, compared with which every other maritime power, ancient or modern, sinks into insignificance; how Scotland, after ages of enmity, was at length united to England, not merely by legal bonds, but by indissoluble ties of interest and affection; how, in America, the British colonies rapidly became far mightier and wealthier than the realms which Cortes and Pizarro had added to the dominions of Charles the Fifth;[2] how in Asia, British adventurers founded an empire not less splendid and more durable than that of Alexander.

Nor will it be less my duty faithfully to record disasters mingled with triumphs, and great national crimes and follies far more humiliating than any disaster. It will be seen that even what we justly account our chief blessings were not without alloy. It will be seen that the system which effectually secured our liberties against the encroachments of kingly power gave birth to a new class of abuses from which absolute monarchies are exempt. It will be seen that, in consequence partly of unwise interference, and partly of unwise neglect, the increase of wealth and the extension of trade produced, together with immense good, some evils from which poor and rude societies are free. It will be seen how, in two important dependencies of the crown, wrong was followed by just retribution; how imprudence and obstinacy broke the ties which bound the North American colonies to the parent state; how Ireland, cursed by the domination of race over race, and of religion over religion, remained indeed a member of the empire, but a withered and distorted member, adding no strength to the body politic, and reproachfully pointed at by all who feared or envied the greatness of England.

Yet, unless I greatly deceive myself, the general effect of this chequered narrative will be to excite thankfulness in all religious minds, and hope in the breasts of all patriots. For the history of our country during the last hundred and sixty years is eminently the history of physical, of moral, and of intellectual improvement. Those who compare the age on which their lot has fallen with a golden age which exists only in their imagination may talk of degeneracy and decay: but no man who is correctly informed as to the past will be disposed to take a morose or desponding view of the present.

I should very imperfectly execute the task which I have undertaken if I were merely to treat of battles and sieges, of

[1]**history of England:** Macaulay's thousand-page epic focuses on the "Glorious Revolution," which deposed **James II** (reigned 1685–1688), last of the **House of Stuart**, and installed William of Orange (reigned 1688–1702). The narrative begins around 1660 with the Restoration period (avoiding the midcentury upheaval of the English Civil War) and comes to rest with the prospect of a stable 18th-century United Kingdom under the Hanoverian succession (1714). Macaulay died without bringing his narrative up to what **men still living** could recall in 1840, when he began to write.

[2]**Charles V** (1500–1558): King of Spain and Holy Roman Emperor during the New World conquests of **Cortes** in Mexico and **Pizarro** in Peru.

the rise and fall of administrations, of intrigues in the palace, and of debates in the parliament. It will be my endeavour to relate the history of the people as well as the history of the government, to trace the progress of useful and ornamental arts, to describe the rise of religious sects and the changes of literary taste, to portray the manners of successive generations, and not to pass by with neglect even the revolutions which have taken place in dress, furniture, repasts, and public amusements. I shall cheerfully bear the reproach of having descended below the dignity of history, if I can succeed in placing before the English of the nineteenth century a true picture of the life of their ancestors. . . . (Chapter 1)

State of England in 1685

I intend, in this chapter, to give a description of the state in which England was at the time when the crown passed from Charles the Second to his brother.[3] Such a description, composed from scanty and dispersed materials, must necessarily be very imperfect. Yet it may perhaps correct some false notions which would make the subsequent narrative unintelligible or uninstructive.

If we would study with profit the history of our ancestors, we must be constantly on our guard against that delusion which the well known names of families, places, and offices naturally produce, and must never forget that the country of which we read was a very different country from that in which we live. In every experimental science there is a tendency towards perfection. In every human being there is a wish to ameliorate his own condition. These two principles have often sufficed, even when counteracted by great public calamities and by bad institutions, to carry civilisation rapidly forward. No ordinary misfortune, no ordinary misgovernment, will do so much to make a nation wretched, as the constant progress of physical knowledge and the constant effort of every man to better himself will do to make a nation prosperous. It has often been found that profuse expenditure, heavy taxation, absurd commercial restrictions, corrupt tribunals, disastrous wars, seditions, persecutions, conflagrations, inundations, have not been able to destroy capital so fast as the exertions of private citizens have been able to create it. It can easily be proved that, in our own land, the national wealth has, during at least six centuries, been almost uninterruptedly increasing; that it was greater under the Tudors than under the Plantagenets; that it was greater under the Stuarts than under the Tudors;

that, in spite of battles, sieges, and confiscations, it was greater on the day of the Restoration than on the day when the Long Parliament met;[4] that, in spite of maladministration, of extravagance, of public bankruptcy, of two costly and unsuccessful wars, of the pestilence and of the fire, it was greater on the day of the death of Charles the Second than on the day of his Restoration. This progress, having continued during many ages, became at length, about the middle of the eighteenth century, portentously rapid, and has proceeded, during the nineteenth, with accelerated velocity. In consequence partly of our geographical and partly of our moral position, we have, during several generations, been exempt from evils which have elsewhere impeded the efforts and destroyed the fruits of industry. While every part of the Continent, from Moscow to Lisbon, has been the theatre of bloody and devastating wars, no hostile standard has been seen here but as a trophy. While revolutions have taken place all around us, our government has never once been subverted by violence. During more than a hundred years there has been in our island no tumult of sufficient importance to be called an insurrection; nor has the law been once borne down either by popular fury or by regal tyranny: public credit has been held sacred: the administration of justice has been pure: even in times which might by Englishmen be justly called evil times, we have enjoyed what almost every other nation in the world would have considered as an ample measure of civil and religious freedom. Every man has felt entire confidence that the state would protect him in the possession of what had been earned by his diligence and hoarded by his selfdenial. Under the benignant influence of peace and liberty, science has flourished, and has been applied to practical purposes on a scale never before known. The consequence is that a change to which the history of the old world furnishes no parallel has taken place in our country. Could the England of 1685 be, by some magical process, set before our eyes, we should not know one landscape in a hundred or one building in ten thousand. The country gentleman would not recognise his own fields. The inhabitant of the town would not recognise his own street. Everything has been changed, but the great features of nature, and a few massive and durable works of human art. We might find out Snowdon and Windermere, the Cheddar Cliffs and Beachy Head. We might find out here and there a Norman minster, or a castle

---

[3]**Charles II** (reigned 1660–1685): elder brother to James II.

[4]The **Plantagenet** line yielded in 1485 to the **Tudors,** succeeded in 1603 by the **Stuarts,** whose fall dated from the sitting of the **Long Parliament** in 1642.

which witnessed the wars of the Roses.[5] But, with such rare exceptions, everything would be strange to us. Many thousands of square miles which are now rich corn land and meadow, intersected by green hedgerows, and dotted with villages and pleasant country seats, would appear as moors overgrown with furze, or fens abandoned to wild ducks. We should see straggling huts built of wood and covered with thatch, where we now see manufacturing towns and seaports renowned to the farthest ends of the world. The capital itself would shrink to dimensions not much exceeding those of its present suburb on the south of the Thames. Not less strange to us would be the garb and manners of the people, the furniture and the equipages, the interior of the shops and dwellings. Such a change in the state of a nation seems to be at least as well entitled to the notice of a historian as any change of the dynasty or of the ministry.[6] . . .

The increase of the people has been great in every part of the kingdom, but generally much greater in the northern than in the southern shires. In truth a large part of the country beyond Trent[7] was, down to the eighteenth century, in a state of barbarism. Physical and moral causes had concurred to prevent civilisation from spreading to that region. The air was inclement; the soil was generally such as required skilful and industrious cultivation; and there could be little skill or industry in a tract which was often the theatre of war, and which, even when there was nominal peace, was constantly desolated by bands of Scottish marauders. Before the union of the two British crowns, and long after that union, there was as great a difference between Middlesex and Northumberland[8] as there now is between Massachusetts and the settlements of those squatters who, far to the west of the Mississippi, administer a rude justice with the rifle and the dagger. In the reign of Charles the Second, the traces left by ages of slaughter and pillage were distinctly perceptible, many miles south of the Tweed,[9] in the face of the country and in the lawless manners of the people. There was still a large class of mosstroopers, whose calling was to plunder dwellings and to drive away whole herds of cattle. It was found necessary, soon after the Restoration, to enact laws of great severity for the prevention of these outrages. The magistrates of Northumberland and Cumberland were authorised to raise bands of armed men for the defence of property and order; and provision was made for meeting the expense of these levies by local taxation. The parishes were required to keep bloodhounds for the purpose of hunting the freebooters. Many old men who were living in the middle of the eighteenth century could well remember the time when those ferocious dogs were common. Yet, even with such auxiliaries, it was often found impossible to track the robbers to their retreats among the hills and morasses. For the geography of that wild country was very imperfectly known. Even after the accession of George the Third, the path over the fells from Borrowdale[10] to Ravenglas was still a secret carefully kept by the dalesmen, some of whom had probably in their youth escaped from the pursuit of justice by that road. The seats of the gentry and the larger farmhouses were fortified. Oxen were penned at night beneath the overhanging battlements of the residence, which was known by the name of the Peel. The inmates slept with arms at their sides. Huge stones and boiling water were in readiness to crush and scald the plunderer who might venture to assail the little garrison. No traveller ventured into that country without making his will. The Judges on circuit, with the whole body of barristers, attorneys, clerks, and serving men, rode on horseback from Newcastle to Carlisle,[11] armed and escorted by a strong guard under the command of the Sheriffs. It was necessary to carry provisions; for the country was a wilderness which afforded no supplies. The spot where the cavalcade halted to dine, under an immense oak, is not yet forgotten. The irregular vigour with which criminal justice was administered shocked observers whose lives had been passed in more tranquil districts. Juries, animated by hatred and by a sense of common danger, convicted housebreakers and cattle

---

[5]**Snowdon**: tallest Welsh mountain. **Windermere**: largest English lake. **Cheddar Cliffs**: limestone gorge in SW England. **Beachy Head**: chalk cliff on the SE English Channel coast. **wars of the Roses**: 15th-century civil wars.

[6]**ministry**: During the interval which has elapsed since this chapter was written, England has continued to advance rapidly in material prosperity. I have left my text nearly as it originally stood; but I have added a few notes which may enable the reader to form some notion of the progress which has been made during the last nine years; and, in general, I would desire him to remember that there is scarcely a district which is not more populous, or a source of wealth which is not more productive, at present than in 1848. (1857) [Macaulay's note]

[7]**Trent**: river flowing through N Midlands S of Yorkshire to the North Sea.

[8]**union**: Scotland joined England and Wales to form the United Kingdom in 1704. **Middlesex**: county surrounding London. **Northumberland**: far NE England.

---

[9]**Tweed**: river forming English-Scottish border. **mosstroopers**: border bandits. **Cumberland**: far NW England.

[10]**George III**: assumed the throne in 1760. **Borrowdale**: in NW England's Lake District, where the mountains are called **fells**.

[11]**from Newcastle to Carlisle**: from NE to NW England.

stealers with the promptitude of a court martial in a mutiny; and the convicts were hurried by scores to the gallows. Within the memory of some whom this generation has seen, the sportsman who wandered in pursuit of game to the sources of the Tyne found the heaths round Keeldar Castle[12] peopled by a race scarcely less savage than the Indians of California, and heard with surprise the half naked women chaunting a wild measure, while the men with brandished dirks danced a war dance. . . .

We should be much mistaken if we pictured to ourselves the squires of the seventeenth century as men bearing a close resemblance to their descendants, the county members and chairmen of quarter sessions with whom we are familiar. The modern country gentleman generally receives a liberal education, passes from a distinguished school to a distinguished college, and has ample opportunity to become an excellent scholar. He has generally seen something of foreign countries. A considerable part of his life has generally been passed in the capital; and the refinements of the capital follow him into the country. There is perhaps no class of dwellings so pleasing as the rural seats of the English gentry. In the parks and pleasure grounds, nature, dressed yet not disguised by art, wears her most alluring form. In the buildings, good sense and good taste combine to produce a happy union of the comfortable and the graceful. The pictures, the musical instruments, the library, would in any other country be considered as proving the owner to be an eminently polished and accomplished man. A country gentleman who witnessed the Revolution[13] was probably in receipt of about a fourth part of the rent which his acres now yield to his posterity. He was, therefore, as compared with his posterity, a poor man, and was generally under the necessity of residing, with little interruption, on his estate. To travel on the Continent, to maintain an establishment in London, or even to visit London frequently, were pleasures in which only the great proprietors could indulge. It may be confidently affirmed that of the squires whose names were then in the Commissions of Peace and Lieutenancy not one in twenty went to town once in five years, or had ever in his life wandered so far as Paris. Many lords of manors had received an education differing little from that of their menial servants. The heir of an estate often passed his boyhood and youth at the seat of his family with no better tutors than grooms and gamekeepers, and scarce attained learning enough to sign his name to a Mit-

timus.[14] If he went to school and to college, he generally returned before he was twenty to the seclusion of the old hall, and there, unless his mind were very happily constituted by nature, soon forgot his academical pursuits in rural business and pleasures. His chief serious employment was the care of his property. He examined samples of grain, handled pigs, and, on market days, made bargains over a tankard with drovers and hop merchants. His chief pleasures were commonly derived from field sports and from an unrefined sensuality. His language and pronunciation were such as we should now expect to hear only from the most ignorant clowns. His oaths, coarse jests, and scurrilous terms of abuse, were uttered with the broadest accent of his province. It was easy to discern, from the first words which he spoke, whether he came from Somersetshire or Yorkshire.[15] He troubled himself little about decorating his abode, and, if he attempted decoration, seldom produced anything but deformity. The litter of a farmyard gathered under the windows of his bedchamber, and the cabbages and gooseberry bushes grew close to his hall door. His table was loaded with coarse plenty; and guests were cordially welcomed to it. But, as the habit of drinking to excess was general in the class to which he belonged, and as his fortune did not enable him to intoxicate large assemblies daily with claret or canary, strong beer was the ordinary beverage. The quantity of beer consumed in those days was indeed enormous. For beer then was to the middle and lower classes, not only all that beer now is, but all that wine, tea, and ardent spirits now are. It was only at great houses, or on great occasions, that foreign drink was placed on the board. The ladies of the house, whose business it had commonly been to cook the repast, retired as soon as the dishes had been devoured, and left the gentlemen to their ale and tobacco. The coarse jollity of the afternoon was often prolonged till the revellers were laid under the table.

It was very seldom that the country gentleman caught glimpses of the great world; and what he saw of it tended rather to confuse than to enlighten his understanding. His opinions respecting religion, government, foreign countries and former times, having been derived, not from study, from observation, or from conversation with enlightened companions, but from such traditions as were current in his own small circle, were the opinions of a child. He adhered to them, however, with the obstinacy which is generally found in ignorant men accustomed to be

---

[12]**Tyne, Keeldar Castle:** in NE England.

[13]**the Revolution:** the bloodless coup of 1688.

[14]**Mittimus:** justice's warrant placing a suspect in custody.

[15]**Somersetshire, Yorkshire:** southern and northern counties.

fed with flattery. His animosities were numerous and bitter.
He hated Frenchmen and Italians, Scotchmen and Irish-
men, Papists and Presbyterians, Independents and Baptists,
Quakers and Jews. Towards London and Londoners he felt
an aversion which more than once produced important political effects. His wife and daughter were in tastes and acquirements below a housekeeper or a stillroom maid[16] of
the present day. They stitched and spun, brewed gooseberry wine, cured marigolds, and made the crust for the
venison pasty.

From this description it might be supposed that the
English esquire of the seventeenth century did not materially differ from a rustic miller or alehouse keeper of our
time. There are, however, some important parts of his character still to be noted, which will greatly modify this estimate. Unlettered as he was and unpolished, he was still in
some most important points a gentleman. . . . His ignorance
and uncouthness, his low tastes and gross phrases, would, in
our time, be considered as indicating a nature and a breeding thoroughly plebeian. Yet he was essentially a patrician,
and had, in large measure, both the virtues and the vices
which flourish among men set from their birth in high
place, and used to respect themselves and to be respected
by others. It is not easy for a generation accustomed to find
chivalrous sentiments only in company with liberal studies
and polished manners to imagine to itself a man with the
deportment, the vocabulary, and the accent of a carter, yet
punctilious on matters of genealogy and precedence, and
ready to risk his life rather than see a stain cast on the honour of his house. It is however only by thus joining together
things seldom or never found together in our own experience, that we can form a just idea of that rustic aristocracy
which constituted the main strength of the armies of
Charles the First, and which long supported, with strange fidelity, the interest of his descendants. . . .

. . . There is reason to believe that, in 1685, London
had been, during about half a century, the most populous
capital in Europe. The inhabitants, who are now at least
nineteen hundred thousand, were then probably little more
than half a million. London had in the world only one commercial rival, now long ago outstripped, the mighty and opulent Amsterdam. English writers boasted of the forest of
masts and yardarms which covered the river from the Bridge
to the Tower, and of the stupendous sums which were collected at the Custom House in Thames Street. There is, indeed, no doubt that the trade of the metropolis then bore a

far greater proportion than at present to the whole trade of
the country; yet to our generation the honest vaunting of
our ancestors must appear almost ludicrous. The shipping
which they thought incredibly great appears not to have exceeded seventy thousand tons. This was, indeed, then more
than a third of the whole tonnage of the kingdom, but is
now less than a fourth of the tonnage of Newcastle, and is
nearly equalled by the tonnage of the steam vessels of the
Thames. The customs of London amounted, in 1685, to
about three hundred and thirty thousand pounds a year. In
our time the net duty paid annually, at the same place, exceeds ten millions.

Whoever examines the maps of London which were
published towards the close of the reign of Charles the Second will see that only the nucleus of the present capital
then existed. The town did not, as now, fade by imperceptible degrees into the country. No long avenues of villas,
embowered in lilacs and laburnums, extended from the
great centre of wealth and civilisation almost to the boundaries of Middlesex and far into the heart of Kent and Surrey. In the east, no part of the immense line of warehouses
and artificial lakes which now stretches from the Tower to
Blackwall had even been projected. On the west, scarcely
one of those stately piles of building which are inhabited
by the noble and wealthy was in existence; and Chelsea,
which is now peopled by more than forty thousand human
beings, was a quiet country village with about a thousand
inhabitants. On the north, cattle fed, and sportsmen wandered with dogs and guns, over the site of the borough of
Marylebone, and over far the greater part of the space now
covered by the boroughs of Finsbury and of the Tower
Hamlets. Islington was almost a solitude; and poets loved
to contrast its silence and repose with the din and turmoil
of the monster London. On the south the capital is now
connected with its suburb by several bridges, not inferior
in magnificence and solidity to the noblest works of the
Cæsars. In 1685, a single line of irregular arches, overhung
by piles of mean and crazy houses, and garnished, after a
fashion worthy of the naked barbarians of Dahomy,[17] with
scores of mouldering heads, impeded the navigation of the
river. . . .

The whole character of the City has, since that time,
undergone a complete change. At present the bankers, the
merchants, and the chief shopkeepers repair thither on six
mornings of every week for the transaction of business: but

---

[16]**stillroom maid:** domestic servant responsible for the pantry.

[17]**Dahomy:** W African kingdom (18th–19th centuries) in present-
day Benin.

they reside in other quarters of the metropolis, or at suburban country seats surrounded by shrubberies and flower gardens. This revolution in private habits has produced a political revolution of no small importance. The City is no longer regarded by the wealthiest traders with that attachment which every man naturally feels for his home. It is no longer associated in their minds with domestic affections and endearments. The fireside, the nursery, the social table, the quiet bed are not there. Lombard Street and Threadneedle Street are merely places where men toil and accumulate. They go elsewhere to enjoy and to expend. On a Sunday, or in an evening after the hours of business, some courts and alleys, which a few hours before had been alive with hurrying feet and anxious faces, are as silent as the glades of a forest. The chiefs of the mercantile interest are no longer citizens.[18] They avoid, they almost contemn, municipal honours and duties. Those honours and duties are abandoned to men who, though useful and highly respectable, seldom belong to the princely commercial houses of which the names are renowned throughout the world. . . .

The chief cause which made the fusion of the different elements of society so imperfect was the extreme difficulty which our ancestors found in passing from place to place. Of all inventions, the alphabet and the printing press alone excepted, those inventions which abridge distance have done most for the civilisation of our species. Every improvement of the means of locomotion benefits mankind morally and intellectually as well as materially, and not only facilitates the interchange of the various productions of nature and art, but tends to remove national and provincial antipathies, and to bind together all the branches of the great human family. In the seventeenth century the inhabitants of London were, for almost every practical purpose, farther from Reading[19] than they now are from Edinburgh, and farther from Edinburgh than they now are from Vienna.

The subjects of Charles the Second were not, it is true, quite unacquainted with that principle which has, in our own time, produced an unprecedented revolution in human affairs, which has enabled navies to advance in face of wind and tide, and brigades of troops, attended by all their baggage and artillery, to traverse kingdoms at a pace equal to that of the fleetest race horse. The Marquess of Worcester[20] had recently observed the expansive power of moisture rar-

efied by heat. After many experiments he had succeeded in constructing a rude steam engine, which he called a fire water work, and which he pronounced to be an admirable and most forcible instrument of propulsion. But the Marquess was suspected to be a madman, and known to be a Papist. His inventions, therefore, found no favourable reception. His fire water work might, perhaps, furnish matter for conversation at a meeting of the Royal Society, but was not applied to any practical purpose. There were no railways, except a few made of timber, on which coals were carried from the mouths of the Northumbrian pits to the banks of the Tyne. There was very little internal communication by water. A few attempts had been made to deepen and embank the natural streams, but with slender success. Hardly a single navigable canal had been even projected. The English of that day were in the habit of talking with mingled admiration and despair of the immense trench by which Lewis the Fourteenth had made a junction between the Atlantic and the Mediterranean. They little thought that their country would, in the course of a few generations, be intersected, at the cost of private adventurers, by artificial rivers making up more than four times the length of the Thames, the Severn, and the Trent together. . . .

In one respect it must be admitted that the progress of civilisation has diminished the physical comforts of a portion of the poorest class. It has already been mentioned that, before the Revolution, many thousands of square miles, now enclosed and cultivated, were marsh, forest, and heath. Of this wild land much was, by law, common, and much of what was not common by law was worth so little that the proprietors suffered it to be common in fact. In such a tract, squatters and trespassers were tolerated to an extent now unknown. The peasant who dwelt there could, at little or no charge, procure occasionally some palatable addition to his hard fare, and provide himself with fuel for the winter. He kept a flock of geese on what is now an orchard rich with apple blossoms. He snared wild fowl on the fen which has long since been drained and divided into corn fields and turnip fields. He cut turf among the furze bushes on the moor which is now a meadow bright with clover and renowned for butter and cheese. The progress of agriculture and the increase of population necessarily deprived him of these privileges. But against this disadvantage a long list of advantages is to be set off. Of the blessings which civilisation and philosophy bring with them a large proportion is common to all ranks, and would, if withdrawn, be missed as painfully by the labourer as by the peer. The market-place which the rustic can now reach with his cart in an hour was, a hundred and sixty years ago, a day's

---

[18]**citizens:** city dwellers.

[19]**Reading:** city 40 miles W of London.

[20]Edward Somerset, **Marquess of Worcester** (1601–1667): royalist and inventor.

journey from him. The street which now affords to the artisan, during the whole night, a secure, a convenient, and a brilliantly lighted walk was, a hundred and sixty years ago, so dark after sunset that he would not have been able to see his hand, so ill paved that he would have run constant risk of breaking his neck, and so ill watched that he would have been in imminent danger of being knocked down and plundered of his small earnings. Every bricklayer who falls from a scaffold, every sweeper of a crossing who is run over by a carriage, may now have his wounds dressed and his limbs set with a skill such as, a hundred and sixty years ago, all the wealth of a great lord like Ormond, or of a merchant prince like Clayton,[21] could not have purchased. Some frightful diseases have been extirpated by science; and some have been banished by police. The term of human life has been lengthened over the whole kingdom, and especially in the towns. The year 1685 was not accounted sickly; yet in the year 1685 more than one in twenty-three of the inhabitants of the capital died. At present only one inhabitant of the capital in forty dies annually. The difference in salubrity between the London of the nineteenth century and the London of the seventeenth century is very far greater than the difference between London in an ordinary year and London in a year of cholera.

Still more important is the benefit which all orders of society, and especially the lower orders, have derived from the mollifying influence of civilisation on the national character. The groundwork of that character has indeed been the same through many generations, in the sense in which the groundwork of the character of an individual may be said to be the same when he is a rude and thoughtless schoolboy and when he is a refined and accomplished man. It is pleasing to reflect that the public mind of England has softened while it has ripened, and that we have, in the course of ages, become, not only a wiser, but also a kinder people. There is scarcely a page of the history or lighter literature of the seventeenth century which does not contain some proof that our ancestors were less humane than their posterity. The discipline of workshops, of schools, of private families, though not more efficient than at present, was infinitely harsher. Masters, well born and bred, were in the habit of beating their servants. Pedagogues knew no way of imparting knowledge but by beating their pupils. Husbands, of decent station, were not ashamed to beat their wives.

The implacability of hostile factions was such as we can scarcely conceive. Whigs were disposed to murmur because Stafford was suffered to die without seeing his bowels burned before his face. Tories reviled and insulted Russell[22] as his coach passed from the Tower to the scaffold in Lincoln's Inn Fields. As little mercy was shown by the populace to sufferers of a humbler rank. If an offender was put into the pillory, it was well if he escaped with life from the shower of brickbats and paving stones. If he was tied to the cart's tail, the crowd pressed round him, imploring the hangman to give it the fellow well, and make him howl. Gentlemen arranged parties of pleasure to Bridewell on court days for the purpose of seeing the wretched women who beat hemp there whipped. A man pressed to death for refusing to plead, a woman burned for coining, excited less sympathy than is now felt for a galled horse or an overdriven ox. Fights compared with which a boxing match is a refined and humane spectacle were among the favourite diversions of a large part of the town. Multitudes assembled to see gladiators hack each other to pieces with deadly weapons, and shouted with delight when one of the combatants lost a finger or an eye. The prisons were hells on earth, seminaries of every crime and of every disease. At the assizes the lean and yellow culprits brought with them from their cells to the dock an atmosphere of stench and pestilence which sometimes avenged them signally on bench, bar, and jury. But on all this misery society looked with profound indifference. Nowhere could be found that sensitive and restless compassion which has, in our time, extended a powerful protection to the factory child, to the Hindoo widow, to the negro slave, which pries into the stores and watercasks of every emigrant ship, which winces at every lash laid on the back of a drunken soldier, which will not suffer the thief in the hulks[23] to be ill fed or overworked, and which has repeatedly endeavoured to save the life even of the murderer. It is true that compassion ought, like all other feelings, to be under the government of reason, and has, for want of such government, produced some ridiculous and some deplorable effects. But the more we study the annals of the past, the more shall we rejoice that we live in a merciful age, in an age in which cruelty is abhorred, and in which pain, even when deserved, is inflicted reluctantly and from a sense of duty. Every class doubtless has gained largely by this great moral change: but the class which has

---

[21]James Butler, Duke of **Ormonde** (1610–1688): royalist magnate. Sir Robert **Clayton** (1629–1707): London businessman and politician.

[22]William Lord **Russell** (1639–1683): executed for a royal assassination plot.

[23]**hulks**: dismantled ships used as prisons.

gained most is the poorest, the most dependent, and the most defenceless.

The general effect of the evidence which has been submitted to the reader seems hardly to admit of doubt. Yet, in spite of evidence, many will still image to themselves the England of the Stuarts as a more pleasant country than the England in which we live. It may at first sight seem strange that society, while constantly moving forward with eager speed, should be constantly looking backward with tender regret. But these two propensities, inconsistent as they may appear, can easily be resolved into the same principle. Both spring from our impatience of the state in which we actually are. That impatience, while it stimulates us to surpass preceding generations, disposes us to overrate their happiness. It is, in some sense, unreasonable and ungrateful in us to be constantly discontented with a condition which is constantly improving. But, in truth, there is constant improvement precisely because there is constant discontent. If we were perfectly satisfied with the present, we should cease to contrive, to labour, and to save with a view to the future. And it is natural that, being dissatisfied with the present, we should form a too favourable estimate of the past.

In truth we are under a deception similar to that which misleads the traveller in the Arabian desert. Beneath the caravan all is dry and bare: but far in advance, and far in the rear, is the semblance of refreshing waters. The pilgrims hasten forward and find nothing but sand where an hour before they had seen a lake. They turn their eyes and see a lake where, an hour before, they were toiling through sand. A similar illusion seems to haunt nations through every stage of the long progress from poverty and barbarism to the highest degrees of opulence and civilisation. But, if we resolutely chase the mirage backward, we shall find it recede before us into the regions of fabulous antiquity. It is now the fashion to place the golden age of England in times when noblemen were destitute of comforts the want of which would be intolerable to a modern footman, when farmers and shopkeepers breakfasted on loaves the very sight of which would raise a riot in a modern workhouse, when to have a clean shirt once a week was a privilege reserved for the higher class of gentry, when men died faster in the purest country air than they now die in the most pestilential lanes of our towns, and when men died faster in the lanes of our towns than they now die on the coast of Guiana. We too shall, in our turn, be outstripped, and in our turn be envied. It may well be, in the twentieth century, that the peasant of Dorsetshire may think himself miserably paid with twenty shillings a week; that the carpenter at

Greenwich[24] may receive ten shillings a day; that labouring men may be as little used to dine without meat as they now are to eat rye bread; that sanitary police and medical discoveries may have added several more years to the average length of human life; that numerous comforts and luxuries which are now unknown, or confined to a few, may be within the reach of every diligent and thrifty working man. And yet it may then be the mode to assert that the increase of wealth and the progress of science have benefited the few at the expense of the many, and to talk of the reign of Queen Victoria as the time when England was truly merry England, when all classes were bound together by brotherly sympathy, when the rich did not grind the faces of the poor, and when the poor did not envy the splendour of the rich. (Chapter 3)

The Interregnum

. . . The highest eulogy which can be pronounced on the revolution of 1688 is this, that it was our last revolution. Several generations have now passed away since any wise and patriotic Englishman has meditated resistance to the established government. In all honest and reflecting minds there is a conviction, daily strengthened by experience, that the means of effecting every improvement which the constitution requires may be found within the constitution itself.

Now, if ever, we ought to be able to appreciate the whole importance of the stand which was made by our forefathers against the House of Stuart.[25] All around us the world is convulsed by the agonies of great nations. Governments which lately seemed likely to stand during ages have been on a sudden shaken and overthrown. The proudest capitals of Western Europe have streamed with civil blood. All evil passions, the thirst of gain and the thirst of vengeance, the antipathy of class to class, the antipathy of race to race, have broken loose from the control of divine and human laws. Fear and anxiety have clouded the faces and depressed the hearts of millions. Trade has been suspended, and industry paralysed. The rich have become poor; and the poor have become poorer. Doctrines hostile to all sciences, to all arts, to all industry, to all domestic charities, doctrines which, if carried into effect, would, in

---

[24]**Dorsetshire:** rural county in SW England. **Greenwich:** borough E of central London.

[25]**Stuart:** This passage was written in November 1848. [Macaulay's note] The year 1848 witnessed revolution, and violent repression, across the Continent.

thirty years, undo all that thirty centuries have done for mankind, and would make the fairest provinces of France and Germany as savage as Congo or Patagonia, have been avowed from the tribune and defended by the sword. Europe has been threatened with subjugation by barbarians, compared with whom the barbarians who marched under Attila and Alboin[26] were enlightened and humane. The truest friends of the people have with deep sorrow owned that interests more precious than any political privileges were in jeopardy, and that it might be necessary to sacrifice even liberty in order to save civilisation. Meanwhile in our island the regular course of government has never been for a day interrupted. The few bad men who longed for license and plunder have not had the courage to confront for one moment the strength of a loyal nation, rallied in firm array round a parental throne. And, if it be asked what has made us to differ from others, the answer is that we never lost what others are wildly and blindly seeking to regain. It is because we had a preserving revolution in the seventeenth century that we have not had a destroying revolution in the nineteenth. It is because we have freedom in the midst of servitude that we have order in the midst of anarchy. For the authority of law, for the security of property, for the peace of our streets, for the happiness of our homes, our gratitude is due, under Him who raises and pulls down nations at his pleasure, to the Long Parliament, to the Convention, and to William of Orange. (Chapter 10)

1848–1861

---

[26]**Alboin**: Germanic king who conquered N Italy in the 6th century.

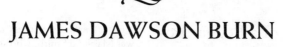

JAMES DAWSON BURN

(1801?–1889?)

That we have to guess his dates of birth and death suggests how very little we know about Burn. His anonymously published autobiography records, as the subtitle puts it, the "vicissitudes of a strangely chequered life" that sent him all over the British Isles and led from vagrancy and odd jobs to the comparative security of the hatter's trade. When changes in industry and fashion doomed the makers of felt hats to financial ruin, Burn awakened to working-class radicalism, which he then exchanged in the 1840s for organizing activity on behalf of the fraternal and apolitical Odd Fellows, all the while supporting a large family on barkeeping, debt-collection, and whatever else turned up. One thing that turned up was a string of lecturing and writing opportunities, on the strength of which this self-taught survivor produced the *Autobiography of a Beggar Boy* in 1855. The book went into several printings and even a new edition in 1882, after Burn had published several other books of observations on working-class experience in Britain and America.

This career recalls the rising slope of self-help that was so dear to the Victorian imagination, and at times Burn squints hard enough through rosy spectacles to make himself over on that progressive model. A good-faith effort to identify with middle-class values appears throughout the *Autobiography*: in Burn's hearty superiority to the superstitious folkways and helpless incompetence of his parents, in the stylistic and allusive badges of his hard-won literary skill and learning, in the satisfaction with which he implies that the progress of the nation means that he has progressed along with it—to the point of revisiting in Letter 11 new and improved versions of traumatic primal scenery from Letter 1. But Burn sees that his circumstances do not fit this fundamentally bourgeois slant. He respects, even envies, the middle-class mythology of personal pluck and commercial redemption; but when it comes to the direction of his own life, linear progress keeps getting blindsided by a counterstory of radical contingency, in which things just happen and nothing adds up. As picaresque anecdotes crowd out the long view, and casual impulse or sheer accident cancels good intentions, Burn keeps an autobiographical faith that runs deeper than ideology by shaping his experience on the model of vagrant dependency itself. His recurrent self-image as a football, or a piece of shipwrecked flotsam saved by random kindness, bespeaks thousands of obscure lives for which the standard Victorian narrative made scant room. Like a handful of other workingmen's memoirs, Burn's book showed the comfortable reader a way of life that was chronically uncomfortable and virtually invisible, and whose hiddenness the book's anonymity aptly represented. Burn's book surpasses others of its kind by playing out the class tensions contained in its title and remaining the autobiography, precisely, of a beggar boy.

from Autobiography of a Beggar Boy

Aberdeen, September 20th, 1854.

My dear Thomas[1],—I have often thought of giving you some account of my early history. I have now made up my mind to do so, in the hope that my numerous trials and difficulties, and the experience of my chequered life, may be of service to you in guiding your steps in the path of duty. . . .

. . . Like a large number of my own class, I was born in poverty, nursed in sorrow, and reared in difficulties, hardships, and privations. It is only such as have passed through the various substrata of civilized society who can justly appreciate the feelings and sufferings of the thousands who continually live as it were by chance. When we know the numerous petty shifts and dishonest subterfuges which characterize the conduct of a large portion of those members of society whose position places them out of the reach of want, we cannot feel surprised at the dishonest practices of that miserable class of beings who hang upon the outskirts of civilization. The man who can dine is very differently situated to the poor wretch who, after he has had one meal of victuals, has no idea where or when he may be blessed with another! Those members of society who are blessed with a regular supply of food and raiment may be said to be antipodes to the accidental feeders, and their modes of thinking are, in every sense of the word, as opposite as are their ways of living!

You have only known me since I was what may be termed a free man; or, in other words, since I became independent by the application of my energies to honest industry. To attain this position was with me a work of years of toil and ardent hope. The great majority of young men who are put to trades are generally prepared in some measure, ere they are sent to masters, to pass their probation for the duties of life. You will learn, as you proceed, that my case, upon entering into the busy arena of the world, was very different.

Where or how I came into the world I have no very definite idea. The first place I found myself in was a garret in the main street of Dumfries. The date of this extraordinary occurrence I have lately learned was somewhere about the year 1806.[2] Among the first great events of my life, I remember the circumstance of having been held up in my

mother's arms to witness an execution; the person's name was Maitland Smith, who suffered death for the murder of a cattle dealer, in Dumfries, in 1806. From this effort of memory, I conclude that I must have been from three to four years of age at that time. My mother then was earning her living by carding hatters' wool, which I believe to have been a very laborious occupation. Poor woman! she had been unfortunate in placing her affections upon my father, who had deceived her, and left her with myself in her arms as a recompense for her lost honour and slighted affections. Shortly after this event she must have left the North of Ireland, and migrated to Dumfries; how long she remained there I have no recollection. The next event which clings to my memory was my mother's marriage with a discharged soldier, whose health and constitution had been sacrificed before the altar of patriotism and glory in the Peninsular war.[3] This gentleman's name was William McNamee. What sort of a figure he made in the war I know not, but I am aware he was no ordinary person in the estimation of all who had the honour of seeing him. In height he was upwards of six feet, and as perpendicular as the gable-end of a house; his bones were so poorly protected with anything in the shape of muscle, that he looked like the frame of a man being set up. The first time I saw him, and ever after, he wore buckskin smalls (a part of the uniform of the foot guards); his limbs were so slender that he put one in mind of Death's shanks in Burns's inimitable *Death and Doctor Hornbook*.[4] Whether it was the fashion to wear the hair long at that period I cannot say, but Mac wore his hanging down upon his shoulders; the colour was that of a dark chestnut, and it hung in graceful natural curls. When a young man he must have been very good-looking; his face was still prepossessing, and his bearing characterized by a commanding military air. The marriage was celebrated in a common lodging-house in Gretna Green. I believe the ceremony was performed by a knight of the hammer.[5] How long the marriage festivities were kept up I cannot say; but this I know, that after this event the world became to me a scene of continual vicissitudes and hardships. It is true, I had a reversionary interest in it; and how I turned this patrimony to

---

[1]**Thomas:** Burn's eldest son, to whom the autobiography is addressed in a sequence of 13 letters, mostly undated.

[2]**Dumfries:** market town in SW Scotland. **1806:** the revised edition gives 1804; Burn had no firm knowledge of when he was born.

[3]**Peninsular war:** pitted British armies with Spanish and Portuguese insurgents against Napoleon's army of occupation, 1808–1814.

[4]**smalls:** breeches. *Death and Doctor Hornbook:* poetic satire from 1780s by Robert **Burns** (1759–1796).

[5]**Gretna Green:** Scottish village near English border, famous venue for hasty marriages. **knight of the hammer:** blacksmith.

account will be seen in the sequel. My new-found father and good mentor was a man who possessed a goodly share of common sense; he had seen a good deal of service while in the army, having been in several general engagements, and was with the Duke of York in his memorable Dutch campaign.[6] His scholastic attainments, I believe, were limited to reading and writing imperfectly. He was a member of the Church of Rome, and a rigid observer of all its forms. Poor man! he had one failing, but this one was followed by a thousand others; if he once tasted intoxicating liquors he had no power to close the safety-valve until he either became prostrated, or his finances were exhausted. When he was in his sober moments, Mac was as honest a man as the sun could shine upon, and strange to say, when under the influence of drink he was quite the reverse. The most dangerous of his drunken foibles was an everlasting propensity for polemical discussion, accompanied by an obstinacy of character like that of Goldsmith's village schoolmaster—

"For e'en though vanquished, he could argue still."[7]

This superabundance of religious zeal often caused him to receive treatment, anything but in keeping with the charity of the Gospel. Like the majority of his countrymen, (the name will indicate that he was an Irishman,) the mind of my step-father was largely surcharged with strong feelings of religious prejudice. It will be remembered that people professing Catholicism in those days were marked with the hateful *brand* of the national stigma. They were therefore continually labouring under a painful sense of their unmerited wrongs. The members of the Church of Rome, though British subjects, and contributing to the national wealth, and submitting to all the conditions of society, were debarred nearly all the rights and privileges of common citizens. They were not only continually subject to the gross and brutal attacks of the ignorant, but their wrongs were frequently used as stepping-stones to state preferment by the rich and powerful. It was thus that the deadly embers of religious animosity were kept alive, and one class of society was continually made the foot-ball of the other. I have no doubt but my step-father's mind must have been soured by the overbearing conduct of his comrades while in the army, who took occasion to prove their sense of religion by a system of heartless persecution,

which was at that time sure to find favour with their superiors. Of course this was no justification of his foolish conduct: I merely mention it as matter of palliation. Men who are goaded by the unjust treatment of their fellows, seldom regulate their conduct by the principles of reason: unmerited wrongs are sure to produce a spirit of revenge; and in my opinion he would be more than man, or less than man, who could passively submit to such degradation. From the above traits in my step-father's character, it will be seen what manner of man he was; it may, therefore, be readily imagined that a mind so formed would necessarily exercise no small influence over the building up of my own.

McNamee had never learned any trade, having gone to serve his country when he was little more than a boy. After his constitution had been fairly shattered, he very imprudently took his discharge upon request, by which means his long service of twenty-eight years was unrequited. When my mother put herself under the protection of this gallant defender of his country, he was making an honourable living by appealing to the charitably disposed members of society. I believe she had been earning her own living, as a travelling merchant, by retailing to her patrons such small wares as she could carry in a basket.

Shortly after the marriage, it was arranged that my mother should continue her business, and that my father should take me along with him, in order to increase the commiseration of the benevolent public in his behalf. As I was said to be the oldest of three, and rather a prepossessing looking little fellow, I was considered a pretty good subject to stimulate the kindly feelings of all good Christians. My existence up to this eventful period may be said to have been in the dream-land which lies beyond the confines of memory. It is true I recollect some little land-marks, which left their impress upon my plastic memory; but their importance is of so infantile a character, that I deem them worthy of undisturbed repose. My capacity for thinking was at this time beginning to expand, and my mind began to chronicle passing events. In the course of a few years after this, I had passed through a life full of hardships and romantic adventures. Within the space of two years I had been the inmate of every jail in the south of Scotland. My poor father's love of drink, and his religious dogmatism, continually embroiled him in scrapes, and, being his squire, of course I always came in for a share of his rewards. I have still a vague remembrance of nearly being made food for a colony of rats in the tolbooth of Moffat.[8] . . .

---

[6]**Dutch campaign:** British forces under the **Duke of York** (1763–1827) fought the French twice in the Netherlands during the 1790s, sustaining heavy losses.

[7]**"For e'en though . . . still":** Oliver Goldsmith, "The Deserted Village" (1770) l. 212.

---

[8]**tolbooth:** jail. **Moffat:** hill town in SW Scotland.

People who look down from the comfortable eminence of social life, will necessarily imagine that all class
distinctions will cease to exist among the wandering *nomads*,
who live upon the charity of the well-disposed. In this they
are very much mistaken. In whatever walk of life men are
placed, talent will always take the lead. Among beggars,
there is an aristocracy as exclusive as any that prevails
among the higher orders of society. The difference between a common beggar, who earns his daily bread by
cadging for *scran*,[9] and the genteel high-flyer, is as marked
as the distinction between a peasant and a peer. The man
who can successfully pass himself off as the innocent victim
of an awful calamity, can afford to live in a very superior
style to the common every-day beggar, who receives alms
as a matter of course. The one can generally afford to live
like a lord, while the life of the other is a dull round of
drudgery. Vagrants are not wanting in ambition; and the
genius of one successful member is sure to stimulate the energy of some of his compeers. I have known men made up
for the charity market in a hundred different ways; I have
even seen some adepts in the profession who were able to
personate half a dozen characters, and successively impose
upon the feelings of the benevolent in each. While we were
in the neighbourhood of Hytee, there were three men, and
the same number of females, who were all first-class professionals: these fellows could make themselves up in an astonishing variety of ways, and they continued to go over the
same ground with undiminished success in fresh guises.
One day, one of these fellows was ruined by fire, and the
next he lost his all by shipwreck; then again he was the victim of a foul conspiracy, by which he was robbed out of his
patrimony. No man can be a successful actor unless he can
identify himself in the mind of the audience as the real
Simon Pure;[10] it must, therefore, be admitted that the *artistes*
I have alluded to above were no mean ornaments to their
honourable profession.

Amongst the wanderers in these days, there were a
great number in Scotland who carried the meal *poke*. Many
of the farmers' wives kept what was then called an *aumous*[11]
dish; this was a small turned wooden dish, and was filled according to the deserts of the claimants or the feeling of the
donor. Those who did not keep one of these vessels, were
in the habit of measuring the amount of their alms by a single handful of meal, or by a double handful, which was

styled a *goupen fou'*. Some people gave alms in oatmeal, and
others in barley-meal. The oatmeal was always preferred by
the applicants, inasmuch as they could always find a ready
market for it, and at better price than could be obtained for
the barley. I know not whether it arises from the march of
intellect and the progress of scientific knowledge, but I find
there is one class of beggars who used to excite the sympathies of the good people on the north side of the Border,
who appear to have gone down into the greedy gulf of
oblivion. I allude to the handbarrow beggars. These human
counter-irritants for acting upon the best feelings of our nature, were at one time a source of infinite trouble to the
people in the wild sequestered parts of the country. The
manner in which these dilapidated and crumpled-up fragments of the *genus homo*[12] were transported from one locality
to another, imposed no small tax upon the time and kindly
feelings of all who were honoured with a visit. These creatures were either seated upon their barrows, or reclined
upon soft couches, and when one of them was set down at a
farmer's door, it required two able-bodied people to remove
the living lumber to the next house. This was frequently no
easy task, as the meal pokes were often as heavy as their
owners. Now it often happened when one of these animals
was planted at the door of a farm-house, especially in the
summer season, when there would only be a single female at
home, the he, or she, and the barrow would have to remain
until the servants came to their victuals. In many instances,
these living loads had to be carried several miles before they
could be deposited at the door of another farm-house. I
knew one case where a lady of this class was made to find
the use of her limbs, by those who had charge of removing
her taking it into their heads to souse her into a comfortable
cold bath in the river Esk, which they had occasion to ford.
Her ladyship, instead of "taking up her bed and walking,"
arose from her bed and ran!!! After her bath she was no
more seen in the beautiful valley of the Esk.[13]

Up to the period I am writing of, which would be
somewhere about the year 1809, I had twice narrowly escaped drowning. While my step-father continued sober, he
treated me with all possible kindness, and not unfrequently
evinced as much real affection for me as if I had been his
own child; but unfortunately when he was in drink, and, of
course, got into trouble, I was continually made his *scape
goat*, and all his sins were sure to be visited upon my devoted
head. About six months after the Dumfries expedition, my

---

[9]*scran*: table scraps.

[10]**real Simon Pure**: real McCoy.

[11]*poke*: bag. *aumous*: for alms, charity.

---

[12]*genus homo*: human kind.

[13]**Esk**: in SE Scotland. **"taking up . . . walking"**: see John 5:8.

father had been drinking for some days in New Galloway, a small place in the wilds of Kirkcudbrightshire.[14] After he could remain no longer in this town, he sallied forth late in the evening of a cold October day, and he knew not whither. In the course of a short time we had arrived upon a wild and desolate moor, the face of the sky was covered as with a pall, and the rain fell in torrents. I can never forget how he dragged me along the dreary waste he knew not whither. His tall, gaunt figure, was frequently brought into fearful relief by the flashes of lightning which followed the fitful claps of thunder, and he looked like the genius of the storm, with a young victim in his hand ready for a peace offering. During that awful night we floundered through its dreary hours, and had so frequently measured our lengths amid the bogs and swamps of the moor, that we actually became a part of it. By daylight we found ourselves in the neighbourhood of a lonely shepherd's cottage. The inmates of this house kindly received us; we were both completely exhausted, and I believe if we had not met this relief at the time we did we should have both perished. As it was I could not be removed for eight days in consequence of having been seized with a fever.

During the whole of this time my mother had been very industrious; but the great misfortune with her was, she had no sooner accumulated a little property than her thoughtless husband squandered it in dissipation. Poor fellow! there never was a man in the world with a better set of good intentions; but as a set-off to these unfinished virtues, he possessed a stock of evil ones which were like Pharaoh's lean kine[15]—they continually devoured the good ones. Being a creature of impulse, his whole life was a continual round of sinning and repenting; and I firmly believe that he was as honest in his resolves of amendment as he was industrious in crushing his good intentions. In consequence of his frequent rounds of dissipation he was subject to fits of *delirium tremens*. At that time I had no idea of the cause of this fearful malady, and as a consequence was often nearly frightened out of my life. The first circumstance of this kind occurred at a place called Wark; this is a small village upon North Tyne, twelve miles from Hexham, in Northumberland.[16] My father had been drinking in this place for some days; whether he was obliged to leave the place surreptitiously, or did so upon his own account, I cannot say; but this I do know, that I shall never forget the occasion as long

as I live. We left Wark between ten and eleven o'clock at night, in the middle of winter; he had made up his mind to go to Hexham, but instead of taking the direct road by Chollorford, he forded the Tyne, and took the road by Barrisford, which was at least three miles further round. How he got safely through the river I cannot imagine, but it must have been attended with no small danger; all I now remember is that we were both as wet as water could make us.

We had not proceeded on our journey more than half-a-mile after having forded the river, when my father brought up in the middle of the road. Up to this time, he had been talking to himself a great deal of incoherent and disjointed stuff. This was an ordinary occurrence with poor Mac, when under the influence of the *jolly god*. The moment we came to a dead stand, he pointed his hand to the devil, who was standing on the middle of the highway, at the comfortable distance of about five yards in advance of us. We stood still for a few minutes, during which time my father seemed resolving the matter over in his mind, as to whether he should retrace his steps or go on. At last, he crossed himself, and we moved forward. The devil, in the most friendly and accommodating manner, did the same. In order to satisfy himself of Satan's identity, my father made an attempt to pass him; but, however fast we walked, we were not able to lessen the distance a single inch, or, however slow we paced the ground, our relative positions remained unchanged. My poor little heart fluttered like a new-caught bird in a cage, and I was in a state of the most indescribable fear. I did not see the devil, but imagined we were in the company of thousands. My father was a person who, under ordinary circumstances, possessed a large amount of moral courage; but he must have been more than mortal who could encounter the devil single-handed, and that devil a *blue* one.[17] For some time, the perspiration exuded from every pore of his skin, and every now and again he crossed himself, cursed, or mumbled a prayer! All this time he grasped my trembling hand with convulsive energy, and I clung to him for my very life, and did not dare to turn my eyes either to the right or the left. Although the night was extremely cold and my clothes were saturated with water, the powerful emotion of fear must have sent my blood galloping through my system: otherwise I must have perished. Our journey home was one of continual mental suffering. Every bush and tree, and every gust of wind, were to me as many devils, and, during the whole time, my father

---

[14]**Kirkcudbrightshire**: in SW Scotland.

[15]**Pharaoh's lean kine**: see Genesis 41:1–4.

[16]**Northumberland**: in NE England.

---

[17]**blue devil**: traditional hallucination from alcoholic delirium tremens.

continued talking to himself and blackguarding his satanic majesty, who still acted as our pilot. When we arrived at Hexham Bridge, our unsocial companion silently took his leave of us, after having travelled over fifteen miles of a bleak and solitary road. It would be impossible for me to describe my own sufferings during that dreadful night. My father continued to see and to hold converse with the devil for some days after, and it was more than a month before he recovered from the effects of his debauch and nocturnal journey with the Master of the Blues!

. . . I can well remember the marked difference in the etiquette of the English and Scottish beggars; at that time, the manners and habits of these strollers were as different as it is well possible to conceive. The English beggars were then characterized by an independent, free, and easy style; of course the distinctions of class were rigidly maintained on both sides of the Border, but in all cases the Scotch were far behind the *genteel civilisation* of their southern neighbours. The manners of these people, I imagine, are formed and regulated much in the same way as those of gentlemen's servants.

I have found that nearly every class of people in the kingdom have a moral code of their own, and every body of men has its own standard of perfection. Your professional pickpocket looks down with contempt upon a knight of the *scranbag*, and the *highflyer* turns up his genteel proboscis at the common cadger. A lady who may have shared the bed, board, and affections of an aristocratic letter-writer, would feel herself as much humbled in allying herself with a plebeian *charity irritator*, as my Lord Noodle's[18] some time affection receiver would have in espousing one of his lordship's ploughmen. From what I have witnessed in my early life, of the manners, habits and feelings of the wandering tribes of humanity in Great Britain, I am the better able to reflect upon their modes, and compare them with those whose position is higher up in the social scale. Honesty may be said to be the basis of human virtue. This consciousness of what is right is liable in the minds of certain people to an amazing amount of latitude. In some people, the perception of this principle becomes "small by degrees, and beautifully less." In comparing men's actions and motives, I have found that the difference is very frequently only in the degree, for instance, I have seen a beggar barter his wife for a pot of ale, and I have known a nobleman who got clear of his better half for 40s. damages. I remember when in York, along with my father and mother, we were lodging in a house where there were about fifty travellers, male and female, congregated; among this heterogeneous group of all ages, conditions, and nationalities, there was one jovial young fellow who found himself inconvenienced by the possession of a very good looking young woman—I should think her age was not more than nineteen. This pair of turtle-doves had been moistening their clays pretty freely for three or four days. At the expiration of this time, the gay Lothario,[19] either sated with love or full of generosity, kindly transferred his lovely nymph to the keeping of another gentleman, and gave him half-a-gallon of beer into the bargain. I have no doubt such a transaction as this would be highly offensive to the feelings of people trained in the genteel walks of life; yet it is no uncommon thing for the young fast sailors among our aristocracy to act in the same manner—with this difference in their favour, namely, that they have had the despoiling of their victims and covering their families with shame and ignominy before they cast them off.

After a good many vicissitudes and two incarcerations, we arrived in London, and took up our abode in that sylvan retreat where the motley inhabitants spoke all tongues, from Kerry to Constantinople—Church-lane in St. Giles. "Sad thy tale, thou idle page!"[20] The ruthless hand of progress has swept this place of a *million* memories, and many a thousand dark deeds from the map of the world! If I remember correctly, we paid nine-pence a-night for one bed in a large barrack of a building, the proprietor of which kept a provision-shop. This fellow was both as ugly and as dirty as if he had been bespoke so. The very atmosphere of London, or else its *gin*, very soon produced an exhilarating effect upon the nervous system of my father. In the course of a few days, his libations had reduced us to the most miserable state of destitution, and, to add to our hapless condition, we were left among strangers, many of whom were brutalized into heartless grinning savages by drunkenness. . . .

. . . During these small events, which went to make up the history of my father's life, my own years were increasing, and impressions were being made upon my undeveloped sensibility, which stamped themselves upon my memory, or passed like shadows.

---

[18]**Lord Noodle**: caricature from *Bleak House* (1853) by Dickens, to whom Burn dedicated the first edition.

[19]**gay Lothario**: rakish lady-killer.

[20]**St. Giles**: notorious slum in N London. "**Sad thy . . . page**": opening line of Robert Burns' "On Reading in a Newspaper the Death of John M'leod" (1787).

I was a thing without a mind, and might be said to have neither body nor soul of my own—that plastic part of my nature, which was to become my only patrimony, was being moulded under the most degrading influences and corrupt examples. It is true, and strangely so, whether McNamee was drunk or sober, he never forgot to pray, morning and evening: and it was an amiable trait in his character that, whether in prosperity or adversity, he never let any of us forget the duty we owed to God, and our dependence upon his Divine will. I owe him an eternal debt of gratitude for having left an indelible impression of the noblest aspiration of his mind upon my own. This redeeming living reality of his existence haunts me in my happiest waking dreams, and causes me to revere his memory with a holy affection. I often think that there is a soft and holy influence steals over our souls when our memories call up the living forms of those who taught us to lift our eyes to Heaven, and say, "Our Father who art in Heaven!" I know that other influences have wound themselves round my existence, and that I had received impressions of men and things which were well calculated to cramp the energies, and strengthen the bonds of my mental slavery. These peculiar circumstances were inseparable from my condition, and it required no small effort, in after life, to cast off the silent working influences of such an education. . . . (Letter 1)

. . . . The time I am now writing of was towards the end of the year 1819, during that year the whole country was in a state of feverish excitement. The Prince Regent had used every exertion to blast the character of his wife,[21] and hand down her name to posterity with infamy. This event called forth one universal feeling of indignation in the public mind against the Prince and his sycophantic abettors. I am not aware of any circumstance in my time wherein the English people gave such unequivocal and unanimous proof of their love of justice. The fact was, that the more thoughtful members of the community saw that the national character was being compromised, and I believe their unmistakable protest was the means of saving the honour of the nation. From this date up to the year 1832, the country was in a dangerous state of transition. Commerce was crippled in almost every possible way, and the taxes hung like a dead weight upon the industrial energies of the people. The legislative functions were solely in the hands of men who were wedded to aristocratic notions, and government patronage flowed in one muddy and corrupt channel, while the members of Parliament, instead of representing the feelings of the nation, continued to serve their own sinister ends at the expense of the people.

The introduction of machinery was then creating a panic among the working classes, especially in the manufacturing districts. Men who had spent their time, and wasted their energies in the various occupations, were doomed to see their labour superseded by an entire new power. The working men had not then learnt the science of political economy; and even if they had, it would have afforded them little or no relief. Men with hungry bellies have small thought to spare upon abstract principles of speculative philosophy. Under all circumstances, and in all countries, the necessities of the time among the great industrial masses must produce the ruling feeling of the hour. To live has ever been, and ever will be, the great battle of the people.

In reviewing the critical position of the country at that time, and reflecting upon the severe ordeal through which the people have passed, we have much reason to be thankful that the national barque has weathered the storm. It is true that the people were occasionally guilty of trifling excesses but it must be borne in mind, that in many instances they were goaded into acts of insubordination by the greatness of their sufferings. The manner in which the unoffending and defenceless people were treated at *Peterloo*,[22] in Manchester, in 1819, afforded a melancholy proof of the utter disregard of the men in power to the feelings and wants of the industrious classes. The circumstances connected with this cold-blooded event will remain like so many foul stains upon the page of England's history.

I may observe, that in the early part of the nineteenth century, the middle class element was only in its infancy, and it was not until the wonderful discoveries of Watt, Cartwright and Stephenson[23] were brought into operation that this useful body in the state began to assume its proper position. During the last thirty years, the extraordinary

---

[21]**wife**: The marital difficulties of Princess Charlotte and the future George IV, then **Prince Regent**, furnished the burgeoning media with scandals that polarized the nation. Burn's sympathies typify his consistent opposition to aristocratic privilege and identification of working-class with middle-class interests.

[22]*Peterloo*: name popularly given (after Waterloo) to the lethal 1819 cavalry assault on peaceful protesters in St. Peter's Field, Manchester.

[23]James **Watt** (1736–1819): developer of steam-engine. Edmund **Cartwright** (1743–1823): inventor of textile machinery. George **Stephenson** (1781–1848): pioneer in railroad engineering.

energy and directing power of this body have attained for it a moral force unprecedented in the history of the country; and I think it may be justly said, that whatever social advantages we now enjoy over those of the preceding age, are in a great measure due to the well-timed exertions of this now powerful class. If the signs of the times are to be interpreted by their own manifestations, I certainly think we are upon the eve of one of those social changes which will entirely alter the political aspect of affairs in this country. After repeated trials, the aristocracy have been found wanting in the management of the state; as business men, they are proved to be not up to the mark; and it would appear, from the broad expression of public opinion, that John Bull, while he is both able and willing to pay his servants, is determined to put his affairs into the hands of men who can manage them in a business-like manner. In all cases where men are invested with power, it necessarily follows that a good deal of it must be discretionary and irresponsible; in state affairs this is particularly so, and I think the more such a condition of things can be narrowed within the limits of a responsible system, the better for the nation. A system may be made to approximate perfection, though it be not in the nature of man to arrive at such a state. (Letter 5)

. . . Since I had become a loyal and independent journeyman hatter,[24] my career up to the time of my arrival at home had only been so-so. Before I went to the trade my life had been like a feather on the stream, and I was being continually whirled along from one eddy to another. My own impulses had little or nothing to do in producing the varied colours in the ever-changing views of my living kaleidoscope. Notwithstanding my altered condition,—when you might suppose that judgment, matured by experience, should have taken the helm, and quietly steered me along the ocean of life, avoiding the quicksands of dissipation, and the misty headlands of speculation,—I am sorry to say you will find that my life still continued to be the mere sport of fate, and instead of regulating my feelings by the rule of reason, my passions dragged me headlong through the by-ways of folly. I do not wish you to understand that I was guilty of such conduct as would affect my character or position in society by indolence, roguery, or dissipation; on the contrary, I was both temperate and industrious, and I can say with the confidence of truth that I never lost half a

day from my employment through drink as long as I continued the servant of another man. My follies were of quite a different character, which you will observe as you proceed with my narrative.

I obtained employment as soon as I arrived at home, and for some time diligently applied myself to my work. In this year (1831) the agitation for a reform in the House of Commons was gathering strength over the whole of Great Britain, and the whole of the manufacturing towns were beginning to show unmistakable symptoms of a determination that would not submit to a denial. Meetings were being held in Birmingham, Manchester, Sheffield, Leeds, Glasgow, and Edinburgh. These meetings, though generally composed of the working classes, were supported by several members of the aristocracy, many of the liberal gentlemen, and more especially by large numbers of the influential merchants and manufacturers. Before the passing of the Reform Bill, the country may be said to have been divided into two sections, namely, the Tories and the Whigs. The good old self-willed Tories had long possessed the power and patronage, and the consequence was, that the stream of government favour flowed in one channel, while the power was frequently used to crush the rights and liberties of the people. The liberal party were, therefore, galled by an unjust exclusion from the honours and emoluments of office. The real strength of the Tory party was in the machinery they had been able to keep in motion over the whole of the country. This machinery was composed of all the working elements under Government, from the lord-lieutenants of counties to petty constables. On the other hand, the Whigs were numerically strong, and carried with them a considerable moral power; but their greatest strength lay in the sympathy and hearty support of the working population. The antagonism of party feeling was mixed up with the whole of men's actions, and the nation seemed plunged in the boiling vortex of party strife.

A short time after I returned home, meetings were being held by the working-men in all the districts of Glasgow. The hatters, as a body, had never made themselves conspicuous by identifying themselves with any political movement; however, upon this occasion they became infected with the common feeling, and a general meeting of the trade was held in order to co-operate with the other public bodies. By this time the Radicals of the west of Scotland had appointed a central committee. This body of men had the power of calling general meetings of the combined trades, and also of organising large meetings of the whole working population; they also suggested the rate of the levies, which were made from time to time, in order to carry

---

[24]**hatter:** Burn was apprenticed to a hatter in 1822 and advanced to **journeyman** in five years.

on the war. At the meeting of my own trade, I was appointed to represent the hatters at the general meetings of
the delegates from the various bodies in the west of Scotland. My maiden speech at the first general meeting I
attended got me elected a member of the Central Committee.[25] Here, then, I got into the gulf-stream of political agitation, and was carried onward with amazing velocity. I was
seized with a wild enthusiasm, and for the time became politically mad; my pride, too, was flattered, by being made a
leader in the camp of the people. From this date I took an
active part in all the proceedings of both the Whig and the
Radical parties in Glasgow for several years. . . .

From the time I became a member of this body, until
long after the passing of the Reform Bill, my mind was continually directed to some business connected with it. Indeed, there was rarely a single night in the week that my
time was not occupied, either in sub-committees, or on the
general committee. The most dangerous feature connected
with these meetings was the everlasting adjournments to
the taverns after business hours. In this little political squad
every man was as full of self-consequence and legislative importance as if each were a political Atlas, and the battles of
the committee were frequently fought a second time o'er
the *gill stoup*.[26] After I had been a member of the Trades'
Committee about six months, I was also elected a member
of the standing committee of the Reform Association. This
body was composed of the resident gentry, merchants and
manufacturers of the Whig party. You may well imagine,
that if I was not a person of importance, I thought myself
so. I know that nothing great can be attained by man without the salutary spur of ambition, and that he who would
honestly serve his fellow-men must be self-sacrificing. I dare
say I was a good deal actuated by a true spirit of patriotism;
but if I had done the same duty, with anything like the
amount of zeal, to my family, I could now have looked back
upon the past with a feeling of satisfaction very different to
what I possess. In looking at my political career from my
present position, I have reason to be thankful that I passed
through the dangerous ordeal without sustaining greater
loss. It was so far fortunate for me that I never indulged in
drinking habits, and I never lost time from my employment.

During the year 1832, several open-air meetings were
held on the Green of Glasgow. Some of these gatherings I
believe to have been the largest political meetings ever held

in Great Britain. The manifestation of public feeling displayed at some of these meetings produced no small effect
upon the Legislature. The meeting which took place during
the time the Duke of Wellington held the seals of office,
and had the whole of the administrative power vested in
his own person, gave such a demonstration of outraged
feeling and disappointment, that the country became
greatly alarmed, and the Sovereign was obliged to recall
Earl Grey.[27] During the whole of my life I never witnessed
such a display of self-possessed determination. Many of the
flags and emblems indicated the feelings of the people in
the most unmistakable language. The portraits of the King
and Queen were turned upside down, and burned amid the
execrations of above 200,000 people. There was no boisterous mirth among that vast assemblage of human beings; all
feeling of levity was checked by the serious symbols which
were so numerously displayed. In various parts of the meeting brawny arms were seen to cling to weapons of death,
and death's-heads and cross-bones gave the meeting a
solemn import. I had the marshalling of the whole of these
out-door displays, and in all cases they passed off with the
utmost order; but upon the occasion of the one above alluded to, I was somewhat afraid that the leaders had raised a
power they could not subdue. . . . (Letter 8)

. . . I continued to struggle on in the Hatter's Arms[28] until
1839, when I found that my business had become so hopelessly irredeemable that I was obliged to give it up. At that
time I had some political acquaintances in Greenock, who
got me persuaded to hang out my sign in that amphibious
town. This was another of my false steps, which was purely
caused by want of calculation. I removed my family to that
place, after having taken a spirit-cellar in one of the low
streets in the town. I very soon found that I had made a serious blunder in coming to this town. I know of no business
in the whole catalogue of commerce, so utterly contemptible and truly degrading as that of keeping a spirit cellar in a poor locality; and before I had been in this place a
month I was heartily sick of it, and felt myself humbled in
the lowest degree. The tavern business is sufficiently bad in
all conscience; but when compared with the other, in a

---

[25]**Central Committee**: composed of representatives from various
trades.

[26]*gill stoup*: glass of liquor.

---

[27]**Earl Grey** (1764–1845): reforming Whig leader who assumed
power when the **Wellington** government collapsed in 1830.

[28]**Hatter's Arms**: Burn had become a tavern-keeper when
changes in fashion and industry permanently depressed the market
for felt hats. **Greenock**: waterfront town in SW Scotland.

moral point of view, it is immeasurably superior. There is something truly revolting to every right feeling of humanity, to live, as it were, upon the degradation of the unfortunate members of society. It is true that this infamous traffic is legalized by the law of the country; but it is equally true, that the law is one of blood, murder, and crime, which stains the black catalogue of our social condition. I could not for the soul within me apply myself to this loathsome business; and in my endeavour to make it somewhat select, I tried to weed the wheat from the chaff of my customers, but in doing so ruined the business entirely.

While I was in Greenock I had in some measure identified myself with the Charter movement,[29] but up to that time the agitation had been conducted upon something like rational principles, if I except the mad conduct of a few of the leaders. About this time, the People's Parliament was holding its sittings, and its sage members, in the abundance of their wisdom, had propounded the sacred month. If the devil had been legislating for the people, his satanic majesty could not have devised a better plan for their destruction. A meeting was held in Greenock, in order to carry this hellish suggestion into execution; and I was not only invited to attend, but was pressed to take the chair. At this meeting I told the working men of Greenock that if they wished to cover themselves with infamy, by assisting in bringing the industry of the nation to a stand, they would do well to proceed. I told them also that one of the immediate consequences of their conduct would be, to let loose the whole vagabondage of the country, who would rob, plunder, and murder the innocent and defenceless members of society, and that the honest and well-conducted would have the credit of it. Such, however, was the infatuation of the more unthinking, that I had the pleasure of being branded with the character of a renegade and a traitor to the cause. I did not blame the working classes, who were then paying men to think for them, and in whose wisdom and prudence they had trusted the management of their affairs; but I certainly felt disgusted with the mercenary horde, who were not only deceiving them, but were also guilty of the treachery of misleading them. Perhaps there never was a greater farce played off upon the credulity of the working classes of Great Britain than that of the People's Parliament. I grant that there were a few honest men among the members of that august body, but I certainly think their judgment was

of a very questionable character. On the other hand, the great majority of the members were a set of hungry knaves, who embraced the opportunity of turning their spouting qualifications to their own mercenary account. . . .

Before I had left the "Hatter's Arms," a lodge of Odd Fellows[30] of the Independent Order of the Manchester Unity was opened in my house. This was the first introduction of the society into the west of Scotland, and in a short time it spread its branches over the whole of that part of the country, which was in a great measure owing to my labours, as you will learn by and by. I had paid a good deal of attention to the character of this institution, and was satisfied that if it was conducted properly it would be of signal service to the working classes, as it offered them the advantages of mutual assistance in case of sickness or death. I knew that many futile attempts had been made during the whole of the beginning of the nineteenth century, by the working men of Great Britain, to institute Friendly Societies,[31] whereby they could make suitable provision against the hour of trouble. In nine cases out of every ten, these praiseworthy efforts ended in failure, in consequence of the societies being founded upon a wrong basis. The fact was, that in all these attempts the men were working in the dark, inasmuch as they had no data to direct them. Indeed, it is only within the last thirty years that public attention has been directed to this branch of political economy. During that time the labours of Neison,[32] and other actuaries, have furnished statistical tables, which are now used as infallible charts both for Friendly Societies and Insurance Companies. I took it into my head to give a lecture upon the character and objects of Odd Fellowship. After having arranged the heads of my subject, I delivered a lecture both in Glasgow and Greenock; after which I published it in the form of a pamphlet. I realized a few pounds from this labour, but during the whole time I suffered the most excruciating pain, so much so, that in a very short time the hair of my head had changed from black to gray.

In the latter end of the year 1839, I was sent for by the Odd Fellows of Edinburgh, to deliver a lecture in the Freemason's Hall there. I went as requested, but owing to my trouble it was with the greatest possible difficulty I was

---

[29]**Charter:** on Chartism see page 14. **People's Parliament:** Chartist Convention of 1839, which called for a **sacred month** of general strike.

[30]**Odd Fellows:** fraternal organization dating from mid-18th century.

[31]**Friendly Societies:** co-ops pooling funds for mutual aid.

[32]F.G.P. **Neison:** statistician who in the 1840s improved principles of group averaging used to compute mortality rate and life expectancy.

enabled to perform the duties of my mission. When I returned home, I was seized with typhus fever of the most virulent character; and to fill the cup of my bitter sorrow, my whole family, with the exception of my wife, were prostrated at the same time.

I never was the man to repine under affliction. The difference between life and death with me has always been a thing of small moment, inasmuch as I have always had an unlimited confidence in the goodness of God, and a just appreciation of my own infinite littleness. Upon this occasion, I owed my life to the medical skill, and unwearied attention, of my friend Dr. Archibald Johnston; and while I am writing this, I feel an inward satisfaction in thus giving expression to the lasting and grateful sense I feel of his never-to-be-forgotten kindness.

I have often had opportunities of witnessing the untiring zeal, anxious solicitude, love, and devotion of women, when ministering at the couch of sickness. But in all my experience I never knew a case of so much heroic devotion, self-abnegation, unwearied attention, and self-sustaining love, as that exhibited by my own wife upon this occasion. During nine days and nights she never had her clothes off, and she was the only nurse we had to wait upon six patients. The younger members of the family soon recovered, but I lingered for two months. When I was just sufficiently recovered to move about the house, the over-strained system of my wife gave way, and she, too, became prostrated. It certainly was a very fortunate circumstance, that she was blessed with strength and courage to see us all through our illness, before she was seized with the disease herself. I feel called upon in this place, both as an act of duty and gratitude, to state, that as soon as my calamity became known to the Odd Fellows' Lodges, several of them sent me various sums of money. "The Banks of Clyde," in Greenock, of which I was a member, cleared me on their books, and sent me three pounds ten shillings. I may here remark, that I had long been out of benefit in consequence of not being able to pay my contribution. One of the lodges in Edinburgh sent two pounds. One of the country lodges also sent the same sum; and two of the town lodges sent five pounds between them. My sufferings, and those of my family, are very common-place things in the abodes of poverty. My condition was therefore by no means singular; but the manifestation of generous feeling, and the substantial proof of friendly regard I received from a large body of my fellow-men was certainly something to feel proud of. You will therefore perceive, that though I have had my small troubles in passing along the rugged highway of the world, I have frequently had my path smoothed by the generous conduct of my fellow-men. Believe me, Dear Thomas, the choicest blessing of heaven to man is the truly godlike feeling of kindness. However unbounded our knowledge, the magnitude of our thoughts, or the profundity of our genius, if we have not the electricity of love in our hearts, sufficient to make us feel for the sufferings of others, the chief end of our creation is unfulfilled. The man who dries the tears of sorrow, and relieves the wants of suffering humanity with acts of charity, is the greatest among the sons of men. . . . (Letter 9)

. . . I am now about introducing you to the last scene in the shifting drama of my truly chequered life, up to the present time. In the month of May, 1853, I was offered employment from a gentleman to whom I had been recommended by a mutual friend. The conditions of the engagement offered were more liberal than I had been accustomed to for some time; I was therefore not slow in accepting the offer. The character of the business was perfectly new to me; but I had every confidence in being equal to it, and have since both justified my own anticipations, and the expectations of my employer. Since I have been in my present business,[33] I have travelled over the most of England and Scotland, and have therefore passed over many of those scenes that were once familiar to me; and have had many opportunities of comparing the past with the present state of things.

In September of 1854 I travelled from Newton-stewart to Dumfries. This was within a few months of forty years after my runaway exploit. The old widow's house that sheltered me at the ferry-town of Cree had disappeared; but the farm-house on the way-side where I slept on the Sunday evening was still unchanged. In several places, as I passed along, I found that the highway had been completely altered. Modern improvement was everywhere visible. I found villages where formerly there was not the vestige of a house; and in other places ruins, where I had formerly seen cheerful dwellings. I could see no greater change in that part of the country than what was observable in the condition of the soil; everywhere the hand of industry was abundantly visible in the improved state of the land. In one place, hundreds of acres of moorland was reclaimed; and in another, what had been a deep bog was drained, and bearing a rich harvest of grain. The character of the modern dwellings in all the country districts is highly indicative of the improved taste and condition of the people. . . .

---

[33]**my present business:** debt collection.

. . . From my own experience and observation, I would say that the progress of transition has been more rapid in Scotland than in any other part of the United Kingdom. The social condition of the people is as different from what it was fifty years ago, as it is possible to imagine. The annual visits of Her Majesty within the last fourteen years has made that part of her kingdom the regular resort of a large portion of the higher and middle class English. At one time, I could flatter myself that I was one in five hundred thousand, if not a million, of old George the Third's subjects who had made the grand tour of England and Scotland!! Fifty years ago, a journey from Scotland to London, was a very important undertaking, and the preparation for such an event was greater than would be now necessary for a journey to Hong Kong. I dispute that your modern traveller would manifest so much curiosity on witnessing the frowning batteries of Malta, the heterogeneous mixture of Eastern races in the dark dingy streets of Grand Cairo, the little old fashioned dirty town of Aden, with its noise and bustle of landing and embarking passengers, or the tropical luxurance of Ceylon with its herds of hill coolies,—as your traveller of fifty years ago, would have done upon his first visit to Berwick-upon-Tweed,[34] with its crumbling walls and narrow Gothic bridge;—Newcastle-upon-Tyne, with its side resting on a comfortable travelling declivity, at an angle of forty-five degrees;—the quiet town of Durham, with its zigzag streets and sombre cathedral;—and the good city of York with its narrow street, double-ribbed houses, and splendid minster. But we must remember this is the age of the rail, electric telegraph, and a general desire for everybody to be everywhere. I sometimes feel a melancholy regret at the loss of our old-fashioned method of transit by the stage-coach; there was really something cheerful and exhilarating in seeing a good whip managing his four-in-hand in all the pride of his profession, and listening to a jolly bluff guard, sounding his warning horn. It was pleasant to hear the slang of the clerks of the stable, with their sly observations and rude jests, as they changed the 'osses for the next stage. It was also a pleasant consolation for the hungry traveller, while in the act of masticating a half-crown dinner, to be warned by the guard's horn, that it was time for him to discontinue his knife and fork operations, if he desired to proceed on his journey! A knowing set of fellows were the stage-coach guards, they had a sly look, and a familiar leer, for all the pretty girls on the road,

and Dan O'Connell[35] could never beg with more independence than they. A capital race of sportsmen were the guards, and they could bag more game in a season than any lord duke, although they seldom used fowling pieces.

It would be a tedious task to enumerate the many changes which have come over the face of society in my time. The application of steam to machinery has been the means of introducing a great number of new trades. Then came the railways, with their surprising interest and revolutionizing influence, creating a thousand new wants and calling into existence a great variety of new branches of industry. Electricity, too, has been made subservient to many modern improvements in several of the arts. India-rubber and gutta percha have been turned to a hundred valuable purposes, of both utility and ornament. While new trades and professions have sprung into existence in rapid succession; numbers of old ones have tumbled out of both use and memory; and should the social system progress upon anything like the same ratio during the next fifty years, we will be like Paddy when in love—"Faith, not ourselves at all at all." Fifty years ago, we were the most inartistic people imaginable. The decorations of the cottage, and even the farm-house, were confined to a few stupid prints and rude wood-cuts; a tiger, or a funny looking shepherdess stuck in the centre of a rough and tasteless made tea-tray, and perhaps a few stucco dolls, with a parrot beautifully daubed with green paint on each wing. The old prints and wood-cuts are now displaced by elegant designs, either engraved or lithographed—the ill-informed and badly executed tray has given place to beautiful specimens of art on iron and *papier maché*—the stucco dolls and natural history ornaments of fifty years ago have been superseded by splendid works of art in bronze and imitation Parian marble.[36] The farmers' wives, in many instances, make their butter by steam and send it to market by the rail. Fish are now caught in the Frith of Forth[37] in the morning, and stewed over fires in London for the next day's dinner. The cheap postage regulation has made men write who never wrote before; and the steam-press has caused those who read but little to read the more. The very day-light has found a rival in gas; and our thoughts are scarcely able to keep up with the ideas we are in the habit of sending along our magic

---

[34]**Berwick-upon-Tweed:** English border town; Burn goes on to mention cities in northern England.

[35]**Dan O'Connell:** like **Paddy** in the next paragraph, a generic Irishman, named here after the parliamentary orator and Chartist (1775–1847).

[36]**Parian:** from Paros, Aegean island famous for **marble**.

[37]**Frith of Forth:** frith (estuary) of the Forth River in E Scotland.

wires. The dispatch of fifty years ago is the miserable delay of the present age, and men seem now to be in such haste, that they are ready to kick both time and space out of the market. . . . (Letter 11)

My dear Thomas.—Like a man that has accomplished a long and arduous journey, and who, while seated on a rising ground, feels a melancholy pleasure in surveying the dangers and difficulties through which he has passed, I cannot help, like Lot's wife, casting one long lingering look behind.[38] The past is fraught with dear-bought lessons of experience; the present only exists in the mind, while the thought rushes through it with the speed of lightning. For aught I know, the future may be to me a dark passage of misery, without the buoyant energy of youth or manhood to spur me in the last battle of life. I think a cursory *résumé* may enable you to seize hold of the salient points in my character, whereby you may take advantage of the lessons it is calculated to impress upon the mind of the thoughtful. During the first twelve years of my life, I was dragged through all the various scenes, and conditions consequent to the *Nomadic* existence of a vagrant. Although this unenviable state was surrounded with innumerable hardships, and even occasional privations, yet it was not without its sunny spots. The storms which passed with even the greatest violence over my head, only lasted for the time being, and after their fury was over, the calm of forgetfulness reigned supreme. The morning of life is the legitimate time for hunting the butterfly on the wing. It is then we pull the beautiful flowers in the very wantonness of thoughtless pleasure, and it is then we follow our untamed *wills* in the madness of delight. Many and many times, the dewy eve has found me wandering by the clear running brook, through some shady dell, or twisting the green rushes into conical hats in some quiet nook, in complete forgetfulness of all the world; while the lash awaited me when night or hunger drove me to my temporary home.

The time I spent under my father's roof was one of continual suffering. Physical hardships were nothing new to me, but I had never before been treated with the freezing coldness of neglect. Had I remained in Ireland, I think my natural energy of mind would have been crushed, and I might have remained a ragged outcast during life. My conduct in leaving under the circumstances gave early proof of my determination of character. Settling down to the business of a country life was indicative of my desire to follow the pursuits of honest industry. During the last two years I was with my mother, I had large sums of money continuously passing through my hands without abusing the trust reposed in me; at such a time, and under such guidance, this was no bad proof of my honesty. During the next three years, I was like a feather on the ocean of life, dashed here and there by the conflicting circumstances of my condition. Although I was an atom in the world of life, I was never without an individuality; in all my miserable littleness, I possessed a mind far above my position; and though I often wandered in the gloomy valley, bordering on despair, the lamp of hope never ceased to burn and light me on my way. My great struggle in the battle of life was to find my proper position in society. You have seen how I suffered, and braved every difficulty in the attainment of my level.

I think I am fairly entitled to credit for one act of wise determination, and that was in serving my apprenticeship to a trade. I look upon this as the grand turning point in my existence; to me it was the half-way house between the desert of my youth, and the sunny lands of my manhood. I have reason to reflect with pleasure upon my conduct as a journeyman; I entirely escaped the leading vice of the profession at the time, which was intemperance. And although I was a young man, when compared to many of my co-mates, who were intelligent, and well conducted, my judgment was uniformly looked up to in almost every case of emergency. My political career was one of pride, folly and stupidity. As a commercial man, I wanted ballast; and my credulity too frequently made me forget my own interest in consideration for the feelings of others. As a publican, I was above the business, and as a necessary consequence it got above me! The next three years of my life, after leaving Glasgow, may be found in the chapter of accidents. When I went to my trade I had all the wild associations of my vagrant existence clinging to my memory; and when I left Glasgow, a ruined man, the flesh-pots of Egypt[39] held their fascinating sway over my feelings, like dreams of past enjoyments. In my moments of sadness, I have had the folly to think that my fall was unmerited; but a little sound reflection would banish the thought, and again and again I have resolved to improve the future by the dear-bought experience of the past.

During my wedded life I have had sixteen births, and twelve deaths to provide for. In the course of events these were things of absorbing interest for the time being, and

---

[38]**Lot's wife:** see Genesis 19. **one long lingering look:** adapting Thomas Gray, "Elegy Written in a Country Churchyard" (1747), 88.

[39]**flesh-pots of Egypt:** see Exodus 16:1–3.

they have all been surrounded with many feelings of much joy and no little sorrow. I have always been blessed with the enjoyment of domestic love and sincerity; my family and fireside have therefore ever been my first and last consideration. The soothing pleasures and quiet enjoyments of home have always exercised a pleasing influence over my mind, and when the toils, trials, and vexations of the world have pressed upon me with their cankering cares and corroding anxieties, the approving smile of my hoping and confiding wife would chase the melancholy gloom from my heart. The innocent prattle and joyous gambols of my children have always been a source of real pleasure to me; and now I frequently delight to unbend myself, and occasionally become a part of themselves. In my sad moments, I have sometimes felt my ire kindling at their boisterous mirth, but I have checked the rising spleen, when I reflected that youth is the season when their little laughing batteries should be charged with the electricity of pure hilarity. The wise man hath said, that "there is a time for all things;"[40] and it is surely soon enough to encounter the cares of the world when reason has been assisted to her throne by the experience of years!

You have now before you an honest history of my life up to the present time. I am aware you will find much to blame, but in this respect your censure will not be more severe than my own. You will also find some little to commend; and, on the whole, you will not fail to find much useful matter for reflection. I think you will agree with me, that I have passed through many severe and dangerous trials, and on some occasions suffered no small hardships. The battle of my life is well calculated to prove to young men what energy and determination of character are able to accomplish when rightly directed. It is true that I had frequent opportunities of doing more, and turning my position to a more fortunate account; but in looking at the other side of the picture, if I had gone with the strong tide of my circumstances in early life, I should have remained a vagrant still, if not something worse!

Many of my historical notices will be new to you; and I have necessarily had to speak much about the manners and habits of those who immediately preceded you in the journey of life.

In my little time I have witnessed many strange reverses in the fortunes of others. Upon more occasions than one, I have been enabled to assist in supplying the necessities of those who were once in such a position that I would have been glad of the crumbs that fell from their tables. On the other hand, I have seen scores of men run up the scale of society, some by sheer plodding, some by the force of their genius, and others by less honourable methods. Between forty and fifty years ago, I was a bare-footed and ragged urchin, unworthy of notice, unless I was in somebody's way; like others in the same condition, I was sometimes relieved through a feeling of kindness, and at others to save further importunity!! Like St. Paul, I may therefore be said to have been all things to all men.[41] The ground that I walked over as a beggar, I have also traversed in the character of a gentleman, and upon more occasions than one, at the houses where I once sought alms, I have been saluted with the respect due to rank far above my own. For the last two years, I have held a situation of considerable responsibility, during that time I have come in contact with many of the first-class commercial men in the United Kingdom. And what is of no small importance to myself, I have the entire confidence of my employer. My home is the abode of happiness, and my own, and the lives of my family gently glide down the stream of existence in peace and contentment. Whether the remainder of my journey be rough or smooth, providence alone can decide; and in the language of Jacob on leaving the home of his father, I would say,—"If God shall be with me, and shall keep me in the way by which I shall walk, and shall give me bread to eat and raiment to put on, and I shall return prosperously to my father's house, the Lord shall be my God."[42] (Letter 13)

1855

---

[40]"there is . . . things": see Ecclesiastes 3:1.

[41]**St. Paul:** see Corinthians 9:22.

[42]"**If God shall . . . be my god**": see Genesis 28:20–21.

JOHN HENRY NEWMAN

(1801–1890)

In Newman we encounter the shock of a formidable modern intellect devoted to principles and aims with which modern intellectuals rarely grapple, and for which *conservative* seems too meek a label. *Apologia pro Vita Sua (Defense of His Life)*, an autobiography written to rebut the charges of deceit and hypocrisy that opponents launched at Newman's defection from the Anglican to the Roman Catholic Church, has persuaded readers from all denominations—or from none—that a firm assurance of God's "luminously self-evident" reality formed the axis on which his excruciatingly protracted conversion turned. Another lifelong principle of consistency was his fidelity to the concept of authority, which he ultimately found enshrined in Catholic tradition, hierarchy, and dogma, yet which he also identified with the force and uniqueness of personality itself. The submission Newman made to appointed authority was radical, indeed ferocious; and its ferocity measures the power of the inquiring, supple, tenacious mind—the "living intelligence, by which I write, and argue, and act"—that was most itself when most conscious of obedience.

A chaste and monastic sensibility like Newman's might have been more at home in an earlier epoch or a different culture. He was born, however, into the heyday of commercial individualism, a London banker's eldest son. As a pious and susceptible teenager he conformed to the spirit of the age so far as to undergo an evangelical conversion, which bathed his conventional Anglicanism in the new light of an individualized relationship with his savior. A brilliant undergraduate career at Oxford led to appointment there as a college tutor and parish vicar, and in the 1820s Newman confirmed the convictions from which most of his writing would proceed: that the intimacy of his personal faith required a counterbalancing submission to the institutional authority embodied in a church; that without this authority the human intellect, whether in himself or in the world at large, was an unstoppable and dangerous force; and that the secular culture around him was bent with reckless ingenuity on casting all such authority to the winds.

These convictions made Newman a foe to everything in modern life that fostered liberalism—a word his controversialist writings use often, and with a sinister slither that portends, behind each local skirmish, the one great battle with evil. Opposition was a role he relished during the 1830s, when from the center of the influential Oxford Movement he warned Church and nation about the perils of rampant individualism and liberal Reform. In sermons, works of historical scholarship, letters to the editor, and especially the dozens of propaganda pamphlets he and his "Tractarian" associates issued as *Tracts for the Times*, Newman championed the principle of authority in a prose that the pressure of events tempered into a tool, and weapon, of surpassing versatility. Thus, a politician's slick endorsement of the benefits people might enjoy at the library drew from Newman an astonishing exhibition of polemical brilliance, *The Tamworth Reading Room*. In this series of letters to the *Times*, Newman cut right to the bone of contention: whether "useful knowledge" offered adequately useful answers to the most urgent human questions, and whether its proponents were not in effect secular missionaries seeking to replace revealed wisdom with science, the church with the library and the lab.

As the Oxford Movement flagged, Newman moved further to the ecclesiastical right and into the arms of Rome, where he was ordained a Catholic priest in 1846. Anglicans, who had been anticipating this apparently inevitable betrayal for years, worried how many of their children the charismatic teacher would take with him. Catholics rejoiced, supporting Newman's 1847 foundation of an "Oratory" or community of priests in Birmingham and naming him Rector of the new Catholic University in Dublin during the 1850s. There he delivered the lectures on education that became *The Idea of a University*. Newman's stated task was the definition of a modern curriculum and the place of theology within it; his theme, as usual, went deeper into bedrock, assaying the relative educational merits of experimentation and commitment, free inquiry and ultimate principles. The fifth of his nine Discourses, included here, offers a classic statement of the case for liberal education—a case that for Newman requires completion by truths of an altogether different order. An accommodatingly suave prose conveys the aplomb of the churchman who later wrote a guidebook for believers (*Grammar of Assent*, 1870) and became a Cardinal in 1879.

Meanwhile, however, remote provincial Dublin and industrial Birmingham were a far cry from Oxford. Newman mourned for lost friendships and chafed at the marginal position in English public life to which his conversion relegated him. So when in 1864 the welterweight Anglican polemicist Rev. Charles Kingsley smeared him in a national magazine with broad hints of jesuitical duplicity, the old Tractarian warrior saw his chance and leapt. Here was an opportunity to justify himself at last before the readership he had once commanded. In a conversion narrative that drew on the archive of a lifetime's diaries and letters, he defended his own honest Englishness, while at the same time vindicating the Catholic Church that many of his countrymen feared and reviled as an alien compound of superstition and intrigue. The result, composed in a matter of weeks, was the *Apologia pro Vita Sua*: his most characteristic work, and his greatest. Kingsley's provocation called on all Newman had—the combatant's verve, the logician's exactitude, the nostalgia of the man of feeling—with a tonal range to match: the boyish candor of the opening reminiscences, the staccato crisis of vocation at the end of chapter 1, the organic power of the declaration of faith that concludes our selection from chapter 5. In its narrative as in its sentences, the book maximizes the tension between Newman's distinctive selfhood and his will to self-surrender. Like nearly everything he wrote, the *Apologia* arises from a discrete occasion only to transcend it; part of the greatness of its writing inheres in his conviction that writing, however great, is not enough to live by.

from **The Tamworth Reading Room**

(*Addressed to the Editor of* The Times. *By Catholicus.*)

Secular Knowledge in Contrast with Religion

Sir,—Sir Robert Peel's[1] position in the country, and his high character, render it impossible that his words and

deeds should be other than public property. This alone would furnish an apology for my calling the attention of your readers to the startling language, which many of them doubtless have already observed, in the Address which this most excellent and distinguished man has lately delivered upon the establishment of a Library and Reading Room at Tamworth; but he has superseded the need of apology altogether, by proceeding to present it to the public in the form of a pamphlet. His speech, then becomes important, both from the name and the express act of its author. At the same time, I must allow that he has not published it in the fulness in which it was spoken. Still it seems to me right and fair, or rather imperative, to animadvert upon it

---

[1]**Sir Robert Peel** (1788–1850), MP for Tamworth in the Midlands, had delivered an address in favor of secular education at the opening of a library he had endowed there.

as it has appeared in your columns, since in that shape it will have the widest circulation. A public man must not claim to harangue the whole world in newspapers, and then to offer his second thoughts to such as choose to buy them at a bookseller's.

I shall surprise no one who has carefully read Sir Robert's Address, and perhaps all who have not, by stating my conviction, that, did a person take it up without looking at the heading, he would to a certainty set it down as a production of the years 1827 and 1828,—the scene Gower Street, the speaker Mr. Brougham or Dr. Lushington,[2] and the occasion, the laying the first stone, or the inauguration, of the then-called London University. I profess myself quite unable to draw any satisfactory line of difference between the Gower Street and the Tamworth Exhibition, except, of course, that Sir Robert's personal religious feeling breaks out in his Address across his assumed philosophy. I say assumed, I might say affected;—for I think too well of him to believe it genuine.

On the occasion in question, Sir Robert gave expression to a theory of morals and religion, which of course, in a popular speech, was not put out in a very dogmatic form, but which, when analyzed and fitted together, reads somewhat as follows:—

Human nature, he seems to say, if left to itself, becomes sensual and degraded. Uneducated men live in the indulgence of their passions; or, if they are merely taught to read, they dissipate and debase their minds by trifling or vicious publications. Education is the cultivation of the intellect and heart, and Useful Knowledge is the great instrument of education. It is the parent of virtue, the nurse of religion; it exalts man to his highest perfection, and is the sufficient scope of his most earnest exertions.

Physical and moral science rouses, transports, exalts, enlarges, tranquillizes, and satisfies the mind. Its attractiveness obtains a hold over us; the excitement attending it supersedes grosser excitements; it makes us know our duty, and thereby enables us to do it; by taking the mind off itself, it destroys anxiety; and by providing objects of admiration, it soothes and subdues us.

And, in addition, it is a kind of neutral ground, on which men of every shade of politics and religion may meet together, disabuse each other of their prejudices, form intimacies, and secure co-operation.

This, it is almost needless to say, is the very theory, expressed temperately, on which Mr. Brougham once expatiated in the Glasgow[3] and London Universities. Sir R. Peel, indeed, has spoken with somewhat of his characteristic moderation; but for his closeness in sentiment to the Brougham of other days, a few parallels from their respective Discourses will be a sufficient voucher.

For instance, Mr. Brougham, in his Discourses upon Science, and in his Pursuit of Knowledge under Difficulties,[4] wrote about the "pure delight" of physical knowledge, of its "pure gratification," of its "tendency to purify and elevate man's nature," of its "elevating and refining it," of its "giving a dignity and *importance* to the enjoyment of life." Sir Robert, pursuing the idea, shows us its importance even in death, observing, that physical knowledge supplied the thoughts from which "a great experimentalist professed *in his last illness* to derive some pleasure and some consolation, when most other sources of consolation and pleasure were closed to him."

Mr. Brougham talked much and eloquently of "the *sweetness* of knowledge," and "the *charms* of philosophy," of students "smitten with the love of knowledge," of "*wooing* truth with the unwearied ardour of a *lover*," of "keen and overpowering *emotion*, of *ecstasy*," of "the absorbing *passion* of knowledge," of "the *strength* of the passion, and the exquisite pleasure of its *gratification*." And Sir Robert, in less glowing language, but even in a more tender strain than Mr. Brougham, exclaims, "If I can only persuade you to enter upon that delightful path, I am sanguine enough to believe that there *will be opened to you gradual charms and temptations* which will induce you to persevere."

Mr. Brougham naturally went on to enlarge upon "bold and successful adventures in the pursuit;—such, perhaps, as in the story of Paris and Helen, or Hero and Leander;" of "daring ambition in its course to greatness," of "enterprising spirits," and their "brilliant feats," of "adventurers of the world of intellect," and of "the illustrious vanquishers of fortune." And Sir Robert, not to be outdone, echoes back "aspirations for knowledge and distinction," "simple determination of overcoming difficulties," "premiums on skill and intelligence," "mental activity," "steamboats and railroads," "producer and consumer," "spirit of inquiry afloat;" and at length he breaks

----

[2]Lord Henry Peter **Brougham** (1778–1868), Dr. Stephen **Lushington** (1782–1873): founders of the nonsectarian University of London.

[3]**Glasgow**: where Brougham spoke on his inauguration as university rector, 1825.

[4]**Pursuit of Knowledge under Difficulties** (1830): written not by Brougham but by his associate George Craik in the Society for the Diffusion of Useful Knowledge.

out into almost conventical[5] eloquence, crying, "Every newspaper *teems with notices* of publications written upon *popular principles*, detailing all the recent discoveries of science, and their connexion with improvements in arts and manufactures. *Let me earnestly entreat you* not to neglect the *opportunity* which we are now willing to afford you! *It will not be our fault* if the ample page of knowledge, rich with the spoils of time, is not unrolled to you! *We tell you*," etc., etc.

Mr. Brougham pronounces that a man by "learning truths wholly new to him," and by "satisfying himself of the grounds on which known truths rest," "will enjoy a *proud consciousness* of having, by his own exertions become a *wiser*, and *therefore* a more *exalted* creature." Sir Robert runs abreast of this great sentiment. He tells us, in words which he adopts as his own, that a man "in becoming *wiser* will become *better*:" he will "rise *at once* in the scale of intellectual and moral existence, and by being accustomed to such contemplations, he will feel the *moral dignity* of his nature *exalted*."

Mr. Brougham, on his inauguration at Glasgow, spoke to the ingenuous youth assembled on the occasion, of "the benefactors of mankind, when they rest from their pious labours, looking down upon the blessings with which their toils and sufferings have clothed the scene of their former existence;" and in his Discourse upon Science declared it to be "no mean reward of our labour to become acquainted with the prodigious genius of those who have almost exalted the nature of man above his destined sphere;" and who "hold a station apart, rising over *all* the great teachers of mankind, and spoken of reverently, as if Newton and La Place[6] were not the names of mortal men." Sir Robert cannot, of course, equal this sublime flight; but he succeeds in calling Newton and others "those mighty spirits which have made the *greatest* (though imperfect) advances towards the understanding of 'the Divine Nature and Power.'"

Mr. Brougham talked at Glasgow about putting to flight the "evil spirits of *tyranny and persecution* which haunted the long night now gone down the sky," and about men "no longer suffering themselves to be led *blindfold in ignorance*;" and in his Pursuit of Knowledge he speaks of Pascal[7] having, "under the influence of certain religious views, during a period of *depression*, conceived scientific pursuits to be little better than abuse of his time and faculties." Sir Robert, fainter in tone, but true to the key, warns his hearers,—"Do not be deceived by the sneers that you hear against knowledge, which are uttered by men who *want to depress you*, and keep you depressed to the level of their *own contented ignorance*."

Mr. Brougham laid down at Glasgow the infidel principle, or, as he styles it, "the great truth," which "has gone forth to all the ends of the earth, that man shall no more render account to man for his belief, over which he has himself no control." And Dr. Lushington applied it in Gower Street to the College then and there rising, by asking, "Will any one argue for establishing a *monopoly* to be enjoyed by the few who are of one *denomination* of the Christian Church only?" And he went on to speak of the association and union of all *without exclusion or restriction*, of "friendships cementing the bond of charity, and softening the asperities which *ignorance and separation* have fostered." Long may it be before Sir Robert Peel professes the great principle itself! even though, as the following passages show, he is inconsistent enough to think highly of its application in the culture of the mind. He speaks, for instance, of "this preliminary and fundamental rule, that no works of *controversial divinity* shall enter into the library (applause),"— of "the institution being open to all persons of all descriptions, without reference to political opinions, or *religious creed*,"—and of "an edifice in which men of all political opinions and *all religious feelings* may unite in the furtherance of knowledge, without the *asperities* of party feeling." Now, that British society should consist of persons of different religions, is this a positive standing evil, to be endured at best as unavoidable, or a topic of exultation? Of exultation, answers Sir Robert; the greater differences the better, the more the merrier. So we must interpret his tone.

It is reserved for few to witness the triumph of their own opinions; much less to witness it in the instance of their own direct and personal opponents. Whether the Lord Brougham of this day feels all that satisfaction and inward peace which he attributes to success of whatever kind in intellectual efforts, it is not for me to decide; but that he has achieved, to speak in his own style, a mighty victory, and is leading in chains behind his chariot-wheels, a great captive, is a fact beyond question.

Such is the reward in 1841 for unpopularity in 1827.

What, however, is a boast to Lord Brougham, is in the same proportion a slur upon the fair fame of Sir Robert Peel, at least in the judgment of those who have hitherto thought well of him. Were there no other reason against the doctrine propounded in the Address which has been the subject

---

[5]**conventical**: suited to a conventicle or Dissenting house of worship.

[6]Pierre-Simon, Marquis de **Laplace** (1749–1827): astronomer and physicist.

[7]Blaise **Pascal** (1623–1662): French mathematician and philosopher.

of these remarks, (but I hope to be allowed an opportunity of assigning others,) its parentage would be a grave *primâ facie* difficulty in receiving it. It is, indeed, most melancholy to see so sober and experienced a man practising the antics of one of the wildest performers of this wild age; and taking off the tone, manner, and gestures of the versatile ex-Chancellor, with a versatility almost equal to his own.

Yet let him be assured that the task of rivalling such a man is hopeless, as well as unprofitable. No one can equal the great sophist. Lord Brougham is inimitable in his own line. (Letter 1)

Secular Knowledge Not the Principle of Moral Improvement

A distinguished Conservative statesman tells us from the town-hall of Tamworth that "in becoming wiser a man will become better," meaning by wiser more conversant with the facts and theories of physical science; and that such a man will "rise *at once* in the scale of intellectual and *moral* existence." "That," he adds, "is my belief." He avows, also, that the fortunate individual whom he is describing, by being "accustomed to such contemplations, will feel the *moral dignity of his nature exalted.*" He speaks also of physical knowledge as "being the means of useful occupation and rational recreation;" of "the pleasures of knowledge" superseding "the indulgence of sensual appetite," and of its "contributing to the intellectual and *moral improvement* of the community." Accordingly, he very consistently wishes it to be set before "the female as well as the male portion of the population;" otherwise, as he truly observes, "great injustice would be done to the well-educated and virtuous women" of the place. They are to "have equal power and equal influence with others." It will be difficult to exhaust the reflections which rise in the mind on reading avowals of this nature.

The first question which obviously suggests itself is *how* these wonderful moral effects are to be wrought under the instrumentality of the physical sciences. Can the process be analyzed and drawn out, or does it act like a dose or a charm which comes into general use empirically? Does Sir Robert Peel mean to say, that whatever be the occult reasons for the result, so it is; you have but to drench the popular mind with physics, and moral and religious advancement follows on the whole, in spite of individual failures? Yet where has the experiment been tried on so large a scale as to justify such anticipations? Or rather, does he mean, that, from the nature of the case, he who is imbued with science and literature, unless adverse influences interfere, cannot but be a better man? It is

natural and becoming to seek for some clear idea of the meaning of so dark an oracle. To know is one thing, to do is another; the two things are altogether distinct. A man knows he should get up in the morning,—he lies a-bed; he knows he should not lose his temper, yet he cannot keep it. A labouring man knows he should not go to the ale-house, and his wife knows she should not filch when she goes out charing;[8] but, nevertheless, in these cases, the consciousness of a duty is not all one with the performance of it. There are, then, large families of instances, to say the least, in which men may become wiser, without becoming better; what, then, is the meaning of this great maxim in the mouth of its promulgators?

Mr. Bentham[9] would answer, that the knowledge which carries virtue along with it, is the knowledge how to take care of number one—a clear appreciation of what is pleasurable, what painful, and what promotes the one and prevents the other. An uneducated man is ever mistaking his own interest, and standing in the way of his own true enjoyments. Useful Knowledge is that which tends to make us more useful to ourselves;—a most definite and intelligible account of the matter, and needing no explanation. But it would be a great injustice, both to Lord Brougham and to Sir Robert, to suppose, when they talk of Knowledge being Virtue, that they are Benthamizing. Bentham had not a spark of poetry in him; on the contrary, there is much of high aspiration, generous sentiment, and impassioned feeling in the tone of Lord Brougham and Sir Robert. They speak of knowledge as something "pulchrum," fair and glorious, exalted above the range of ordinary humanity, and so little connected with the personal interest of its votaries, that, though Sir Robert does *obiter*[10] talk of improved modes of draining, and the chemical properties of manure, yet he must not be supposed to come short of the lofty enthusiasm of Lord Brougham, who expressly panegyrizes certain ancient philosophers who gave up riches, retired into solitude, or embraced a life of travel, smit with a sacred curiosity about physical or mathematical truth.

Here Mr. Bentham, did it fall to him to offer a criticism, doubtless would take leave to inquire whether such language was anything better than a fine set of words "signifying nothing,"[11]—flowers of rhetoric, which bloom, smell sweet, and die. But it is impossible to suspect so grave and practical a man as Sir Robert Peel of using words literally

---

[8]**charing**: paid housecleaning.

[9]Jeremy **Bentham** (1748–1832): principal exponent of Utilitarian philosophy.

[10]"**pulchrum**": beautiful. *obiter*: incidentally.

[11]"**signifying nothing**": *Macbeth* 5.5.27.

without any meaning at all; and though I think at best they have not a very profound meaning, yet, such as it is, we ought to attempt to draw it out.

Now, without using exact theological language, we may surely take it for granted, from the experience of facts, that the human mind is at best in a very unformed or disordered state; passions and conscience, likings and reason, conflicting,—might rising against right, with the prospect of things getting worse. Under these circumstances, what is it that the School of philosophy in which Sir Robert has enrolled himself proposes to accomplish? Not a victory of the mind over itself—not the supremacy of the law—not the reduction of the rebels—not the unity of our complex nature—not an harmonizing of the chaos—but the mere lulling of the passions to rest by turning the course of thought; not a change of character, but a mere removal of temptation. This should be carefully observed. When a husband is gloomy, or an old woman peevish and fretful, those who are about them do all they can to keep dangerous topics and causes of offence out of the way, and think themselves lucky, if, by such skilful management, they get through the day without an outbreak. When a child cries, the nurserymaid dances it about, or points to the pretty black horses out of window, or shows how ashamed poll-parrot or poor puss must be of its tantrums. Such is the sort of prescription which Sir Robert Peel offers to the good people of Tamworth. He makes no pretence of subduing the giant nature, in which we were born, of smiting the loins of the domestic enemies of our peace, of overthrowing passion and fortifying reason; he does but offer to bribe the foe for the nonce with gifts which will avail for that purpose just so long as they *will* avail, and no longer.

This was mainly the philosophy of the great Tully, except when it pleased him to speak as a disciple of the Porch. Cicero handed the recipe to Brougham, and Brougham has passed it on to Peel. If we examine the old Roman's meaning in "*O philosophia, vitae dux*,"[12] it was neither more nor less than this,—that, *while* we were thinking of philosophy, we were not thinking of anything else; we did not feel grief, or anxiety, or passion, or ambition, or hatred all that time, and the only point was to keep thinking of it. How to keep thinking of it was *extra artem*.[13] If a man was in grief, he was

to be amused; if disappointed, to be excited; if in a rage, to be soothed; if in love, to be roused to the pursuit of glory. No inward change was contemplated, but a change of external objects; as if we were all White Ladies or Undines,[14] our moral life being one of impulse and emotion, not subjected to laws, not consisting in habits, not capable of growth. When Cicero was outwitted by Caesar, he solaced himself with Plato; when he lost his daughter, he wrote a treatise on Consolation. Such, too, was the philosophy of that Lydian city, mentioned by the historian, who in a famine played at dice to stay their stomachs.

And such is the rule of life advocated by Lord Brougham; and though, of course, he protests that knowledge "must invigorate the mind as well as entertain it, and refine and elevate the character, while it gives listlessness and weariness their most agreeable excitement and relaxation," yet his notions of vigour and elevation, when analyzed, will be found to resolve themselves into a mere preternatural excitement under the influence of some stimulating object, or the peace which is attained by there being nothing to quarrel with. He speaks of philosophers leaving the care of their estates, or declining public honours, from the greater desirableness of Knowledge; envies the shelter enjoyed in the University of Glasgow from the noise and bustle of the world; and, *apropos* of Pascal and Cowper,[15] "so mighty," says he, "is the power of intellectual occupation, to make the heart forget, *for the time*, its most prevailing griefs, and to change its deepest gloom to sunshine."

Whether Sir Robert Peel meant all this, which others before him have meant, it is impossible to say; but I will be bound, if he did not mean this, he meant nothing else, and his words will certainly insinuate this meaning, wherever a reader is not content to go without any meaning at all. They will countenance, with his high authority, what in one form or other is a chief error of the day, in very distinct schools of opinion,—that our true excellence comes not from within, but from without; not wrought out through personal struggles and sufferings, but following upon a passive exposure to influences over which we have no control. They will countenance the theory that diversion is the instrument of improvement, and excitement the condition of right action; and whereas diversions cease to be diversions if they are constant, and excitements by their very nature have a crisis and run through a course, they will tend to make novelty ever in request, and will set the great teachers

---

[12] **Tully:** Marcus Tullius **Cicero** (106–43 BCE), Roman jurist and orator. **Porch:** the Athenian *stoa* (colonnade or porch), from which stoicism takes its name. "*O philosophia, vitae dux*": O philosophy, guide of life (from the "Hymn to Philosophy" in Cicero's *Nature of the Gods*).

[13] *extra artem*: beyond his skill.

---

[14] **White Ladies, Undines**: fantastical female beings.

[15] William **Cowper** (1731–1800): English poet.

of morals upon the incessant search after stimulants and sedatives, by which unruly nature may, *pro re natâ*,[16] be kept in order.

Hence, be it observed, Lord Brougham, in the last quoted sentence, tells us, with much accuracy of statement, that "intellectual occupation made the heart" of Pascal or Cowper "*for the time* forget its griefs." He frankly offers us a philosophy of expedients: he shows us how to live by medicine. Digestive pills half an hour before dinner, and a posset at bedtime at the best; and at the worst, dram-drinking and opium,—the very remedy against broken hearts, or remorse of conscience, which is in request among the many, in gin-palaces *not* intellectual.

And if these remedies be but of temporary effect at the utmost, more commonly they will have no effect at all. Strong liquors, indeed, do for a time succeed in their object; but who was ever consoled in real trouble by the small beer of literature or science? "Sir," said Rasselas,[17] to the philosopher who had lost his daughter, "mortality is an event by which a wise man can never be surprised." "Young man," answered the mourner, "you speak like one that hath never felt the pangs of separation. What comfort can truth or reason afford me? of what effect are they now but to tell me that my daughter will not be restored?" Or who was ever made more humble or more benevolent by being told, as the same practical moralist words it, "to concur with the great and unchangeable scheme of universal felicity, and co-operate with the general dispensation and tendency of the present system of things"? Or who was made to do any secret act of self-denial, or was steeled against pain, or peril, by all the lore of the infidel La Place, or those other "mighty spirits" which Lord Brougham and Sir Robert eulogize? Or when was a choleric temperament ever brought under by a scientific King Canute[18] planting his professor's chair before the rising waves? And as to the "keen" and "ecstatic" pleasures which Lord Brougham, not to say Sir Robert, ascribes to intellectual pursuit and conquest, I cannot help thinking that in that line they will find themselves outbid in the market by gratifications much closer at hand, and on a level with the meanest capacity. Sir Robert makes it a boast that women are to be members of his institution; it is hardly necessary to remind so

accomplished a classic, that Aspasia[19] and other learned ladies in Greece are no very encouraging precedents in favour of the purifying effects of science. But the strangest and most painful topic which he urges, is one which Lord Brougham has had the good taste altogether to avoid,—the power, not of religion, but of scientific knowledge, on a death-bed; a subject which Sir Robert treats in language which it is far better to believe is mere oratory than is said in earnest.

Such is this new art of living, offered to the labouring classes,—we will say, for instance, in a severe winter, snow on the ground, glass falling, bread rising, coal at 20d. the cwt.,[20] and no work.

It does not require many words, then, to determine that, taking human nature as it is actually found, and assuming that there is an Art of life, to say that it consists, or in any essential manner is placed, in the cultivation of Knowledge, that the mind is changed by a discovery, or saved by a diversion, and can thus be amused into immortality,—that grief, anger, cowardice, self-conceit, pride, or passion, can be subdued by an examination of shells or grasses, or inhaling of gases, or chipping of rocks, or calculating the longitude, is the veriest of pretences which sophist or mountebank ever professed to a gaping auditory. If virtue be a mastery over the mind, if its end be action, if its perfection be inward order, harmony, and peace, we must seek it in graver and holier places than in Libraries and Reading Rooms. (Letter 2)

Secular Knowledge Not the Antecedent of Moral Improvement

. . . I suppose we may readily grant that the science of the day is attended by more lively interest, and issues in more entertaining knowledge, than the study of the New Testament. Accordingly, Lord Brougham fixes upon such science as the great desideratum of human nature, and puts aside faith under the nickname of opinion. I wish Sir Robert Peel had not fallen into the snare, insulting doctrine by giving it the name of "controversial divinity."

However, it will be said that Sir Robert, in spite of such forms of speech, differs essentially from Lord Brougham: for he goes on, in the latter part of the Address which has occasioned these remarks, to speak of Science as leading to Christianity. "I can never think it possible," he

---

[16]*pro re natâ*: in an improvised way.

[17]**Rasselas**: protagonist of *Rasselas* (1759), philosophical novel by Samuel Johnson (1709–1784). Newman returns to this passage in *Idea of a University* page 237.

[18]**King Canute** (995–1035): Danish ruler who sought to command the tide.

[19]**Aspasia**: mistress of Athenian statesman Pericles (5th century BCE).

[20]**20d. the cwt**: twenty pence per hundred pounds' weight.

says, "that a mind can be so constituted, that after being familiarized with the great truth of observing in every object of contemplation that nature presents the manifest proofs of a Divine Intelligence, if you range even from the organization of the meanest weed you trample upon, or of the insect that lives but for an hour, up to the magnificent structure of the heavens, and the still more wonderful phenomena of the soul, reason, and conscience of man; I cannot believe that any man, accustomed to such contemplations, can return from them with any other feelings than those of enlarged conceptions of the Divine Power, and greater reverence for the name of the Almighty Creator of the universe." A long and complicated sentence, and no unfitting emblem of the demonstration it promises. It sets before us a process and deduction. Depend on it, it is not so safe a road and so expeditious a journey from premiss and conclusion as Sir Robert anticipates. The way is long, and there are not a few halfway houses and traveller's rests along it; and who is to warrant that the members of the Reading Room and Library will go steadily on to the goal he would set before them? And when at length they come to "Christianity," pray how do the roads lay between it and "controversial divinity"? Or, grant the Tamworth readers to *begin* with "Christianity" as well as science, the same question suggests itself, What *is* Christianity? Universal benevolence? Exalted morality? Supremacy of law? Conservatism? An age of light? An age of reason?—Which of them all?

Most cheerfully do I render to so religious a man as Sir Robert Peel the justice of disclaiming any insinuation on my part, that he has any intention at all to put aside Religion; yet his words either mean nothing, or they do, both on their surface, and when carried into effect, mean something very irreligious.

And now for one plain proof of this.

It is certain, then, that the multitude of men have neither time nor capacity for attending to many subjects. If they attend to one, they will not attend to the other; if they give their leisure and curiosity to this world, they will have none left for the next. We cannot be everything; as the poet says, *"non omnia possumus omnes."*[21] We must make up our minds to be ignorant of much, if we would know anything. And we must make our choice between risking Science, and risking Religion. Sir Robert indeed says, "Do not believe that you have not time for rational recreation. It is the idle man who wants time for everything." However, this seems to me rhetoric; and what I have said to be the matter of fact, for the truth of which I appeal, not to argument, but to the

proper judges of facts,—common sense and practical experience; and if they pronounce it to be a fact, then Sir Robert Peel, little as he means it, does unite with Lord Brougham in taking from Christianity what he gives to Science.

I will make this fair offer to both of them. Every member of the Church Established shall be eligible to the Tamworth Library on one condition—that he brings from the "public minister of religion," to use Sir Robert's phrase, a ticket in witness of his proficiency in Christian knowledge. We will have no "controversial divinity" in the Library, but a little out of it. If the gentlemen of the Knowledge School will but agree to teach town and country Religion first, they shall have a *carte blanche* from me to teach anything or everything else second. Not a word has been uttered or intended in these Letters against Science; I would treat it, as they do *not* treat "controversial divinity," with respect and gratitude. They caricature doctrine under the name of controversy. I do not nickname science infidelity. I call it by their own name, "useful and entertaining knowledge;" and I call doctrine "Christian knowledge:" and, as thinking Christianity something more than useful and entertaining, I want faith to come first, and utility and amusement to follow.

That persons indeed are found in all classes, high and low, busy and idle, capable of proceeding from sacred to profane knowledge, is undeniable; and it is desirable they should do so. It is desirable that talent for particular departments in literature and science should be fostered and turned to account, wherever it is found. But what has this to do with this general canvass of *"all* persons of all descriptions without reference to religious creed, who shall have attained *the age of fourteen?"* Why solicit "the working classes, without distinction of party, political opinion, or religious profession;" that is, whether they have heard of a God or no? Whence these cries rising on our ears, of "Let me entreat you!" "Neglect not the opportunity!" "It will not be our fault!" "Here is an access for you!" very like the tones of a street preacher, or the cad[22] of an omnibus,—little worthy of a great statesman and a religious philosopher?

However, the Tamworth Reading Room admits of one restriction, which is not a little curious, and has no very liberal sound. It seems that all *"virtuous* women" may be members of the Library; that "great injustice would be done to the *well-educated and virtuous* women of the town and neighborhood" had they been excluded. A very emphatic silence is maintained about women not virtuous. What does this mean? Does it mean to exclude them, while bad *men* are admitted? Is this accident or design, sinister and insidious,

---

[21] we can't do everything (Virgil, *Eclogues* 8.63)

[22] **cad:** driver of a horse-drawn bus.

against a portion of the community? What has virtue to do with a Reading Room? It is to *make* its members virtuous; it is to "exalt the *moral dignity* of their nature;" it is to provide "charms and temptations" to allure them from sensuality and riot. To whom but to the vicious ought Sir Robert to discourse about "opportunities," and "access," and "moral improvement;" and who else would prove a fitter experiment, and a more glorious triumph, of scientific influences? And yet he shuts out all but the well-educated and virtuous.

Alas, that bigotry should have left the mark of its hoof on the great "fundamental principle of the Tamworth Institution"! Sir Robert Peel is bound in consistency to attempt its obliteration. But if that is impossible, as many will anticipate, why, O why, while he is about it, why will he not give us just a little more of it? *Cannot* we prevail on him to modify his principle, and to admit into his library none but "well-educated and virtuous" *men?* (Letter 4)

Secular Knowledge Not a Principle of Action

People say to me, that it is but a dream to suppose that Christianity should regain the organic power in human society which once it possessed. I cannot help that; I never said it could. I am not a politician; I am proposing no measures, but exposing a fallacy, and resisting a pretence. Let Benthamism reign, if men have no aspirations; but do not tell them to be romantic, and then solace them with glory; do not attempt by philosophy what once was done by religion. The ascendency of Faith may be impracticable, but the reign of Knowledge is incomprehensible. The problem for statesmen of this age is how to educate the masses, and literature and science cannot give the solution.

Not so deems Sir Robert Peel; his firm belief and hope is, "that an increased sagacity will administer to an exalted faith; that it will make men not merely believe in the cold doctrines of Natural Religion, but that it will so prepare and temper the spirit and understanding, that they will be better qualified to comprehend the great scheme of human redemption." He certainly thinks that scientific pursuits have some considerable power of impressing religion upon the mind of the multitude. I think not, and will now say why.

Science gives us the grounds or premises from which religious truths are to be inferred; but it does not set about inferring them, much less does it reach the inference;—that is not its province. It brings before us phenomena, and it leaves us, if we will, to call them works of design, wisdom, or benevolence; and further still, if we will, to proceed to confess an Intelligent Creator. We have to take its facts, and

to give them a meaning, and to draw our own conclusions from them. First comes Knowledge, then a view, then reasoning, and then belief. This is why Science has so little of a religious tendency; deductions have no power of persuasion. The heart is commonly reached, not through the reason, but through the imagination, by means of direct impressions, by the testimony of facts and events, by history, by description. Persons influence us, voices melt us, looks subdue us, deeds inflame us. Many a man will live and die upon a dogma: no man will be a martyr for a conclusion. A conclusion is but an opinion; it is not a thing which *is*, but which *we are* "certain about;" and it has often been observed, that we never say we are certain without implying that we doubt. To say that a thing *must* be, is to admit that it *may not* be. No one, I say, will die for his own calculations; he dies for realities. This is why a literary religion is so little to be depended upon; it looks well in fair weather, but its doctrines are opinions, and, when called to suffer for them, it slips them between its folios, or burns them at its hearth. And this again is the secret of the distrust and raillery with which moralists have been so commonly visited. They say and do not. Why? Because they are contemplating the fitness of things, and they live by the square, when they should be realizing their high maxims in the concrete. . . .

Life is not long enough for a religion of inferences; we shall never have done beginning, if we determine to begin with proof. We shall ever be laying our foundations; we shall turn theology into evidences, and divines into textuaries. We shall never get at our first principles. Resolve to believe nothing, and you must prove your proofs and analyze your elements, sinking further and further, and finding "in the lowest depth a lower deep,"[23] till you come to the broad bosom of scepticism. I would rather be bound to defend the reasonableness of assuming that Christianity is true, than to demonstrate a moral governance from the physical world. Life is for action. If we insist on proofs for everything, we shall never come to action: to act you must assume, and that assumption is faith. . . . (Letter 6)

Secular Knowledge without Personal Religion Tends to Unbelief

. . . There are two ways, then, of reading Nature—as a machine and as a work. If we come to it with the assumption that it is a creation, we shall study it with awe; if assuming it to be a system, with mere curiosity. Sir Robert does not

---

[23]"in . . . a lower deep": *Paradise Lost* 4.76 (the speaker is Satan).

make this distinction. He subscribes to the belief that the man "accustomed to such contemplations, *struck with awe* by the manifold proofs of infinite power and infinite wisdom, will yield more ready and hearty assent—yes, the assent of the heart, and not only of the understanding, to the pious exclamation, 'O Lord, how glorious are Thy works!'" He considers that greater insight into Nature will lead a man to say, "How great and wise is the Creator, who has done this!" True: but it is possible that his thoughts may take the form of "How clever is the creature who has discovered it!" and self-conceit may stand proxy for adoration. This is no idle apprehension. Sir Robert himself, religious as he is, gives cause for it; for the first reflection that rises in his mind, as expressed in the above passage, *before* his notice of Divine Power and Wisdom, is, that "the man accustomed to such contemplations will feel the *moral dignity of his nature exalted.*" But Lord Brougham speaks out. "The delight," he says, "is inexpressible of *being able to follow*, as it were, with our eyes, the marvellous works of the Great Architect of Nature." And more clearly still: "One of the most *gratifying treats* which science affords us is *the knowledge of the extraordinary powers* with which the human mind is endowed. No man, until he has studied philosophy, can have a just idea of the great things for which Providence has fitted his understanding, the extraordinary disproportion which there is between his natural strength and the powers of his mind, and the force which he derives from these powers. When we survey the marvellous truths of astronomy, we are first of all lost in the feeling of immense space, and of the comparative insignificance of this globe and its inhabitants. But there soon arises a *sense of gratification and of new wonder* at perceiving how so insignificant a creature has been *able to reach such a knowledge* of the unbounded system of the universe." So, this is the religion we are to gain from the study of Nature; how miserable! The god we attain is our own mind; our veneration is even professedly the worship of self.

The truth is that the system of Nature is just as much connected with Religion, where minds are not religious, as a watch or a steam-carriage. The material world, indeed, is infinitely more wonderful than any human contrivance; but wonder is not religion, or we should be worshipping our railroads. What the physical creation presents to us in itself is a piece of machinery, and when men speak of a Divine Intelligence as its Author, this god of theirs is not the Living and True, unless the spring is the god of a watch, or steam the creator of the engine. Their idol, taken at advantage (though it is *not* an idol, for they do not worship it), is the animating principle of a vast and complicated system; it is subjected to laws, and it is connatural and co-extensive with

matter. Well does Lord Brougham call it "the great architect of nature;" it is an instinct, or a soul of the world, or a vital power; it is not the Almighty God.

It is observable that Lord Brougham does not allude to any *relation* as existing between his *god* and ourselves. He is filled with awe, it seems, at the powers of the human mind, as displayed in their analysis of the vast creation. Is not this a fitting time to say a word about gratitude towards Him who gave them? Not a syllable. What we gain from his contemplation of Nature is "a gratifying treat," the knowledge of the "great things for which Providence has fitted man's understanding;" our admiration terminates in man; it passes on to no prototype. I am not quarrelling with his result as illogical or unfair; it is but consistent with the principles with which he started. Take the system of Nature by itself, detached from the axioms of Religion, and I am willing to confess—nay, I have been expressly urging—that it does not force us to take it for *more* than a system; but why, then, persist in calling the study of it religious, when it can be treated, and is treated, thus atheistically? Say that Religion hallows the study, not that the study is a true ground of Religion. The essence of Religion is the idea of a Moral Governor, and a particular Providence; now let me ask, is the doctrine of moral governance and a particular providence conveyed to us through the physical sciences at all? Would they be physical sciences if they treated of morals? Can physics teach moral matters without ceasing to be physics? But are not virtue and vice, and responsibility, and reward and punishment, anything else than moral matters, and are *they* not of the essence of Religion? In what department, then, of physics are they to be found? Can the problems and principles they involve be expressed in the differential calculus? Is the galvanic battery a whit more akin to conscience and will, than the mechanical powers? What we seek is what concerns us, the traces of a Moral Governor; even religious minds cannot discern these in the physical sciences; astronomy witnesses divine power, and physics divine skill; and all of them divine beneficence; but which teaches of divine holiness, truth, justice, or mercy? Is that much of a Religion which is silent about duty, sin, and its remedies? Was there ever a Religion which was without the idea of an expiation?

Sir Robert Peel tells us, that physical science imparts "pleasure and *consolation*" on a death-bed. Lord Brougham confines himself to the "gratifying treat;" but Sir Robert ventures to speak of "consolation." Now, if we are on trial in this life, and if death be the time when our account is gathered in, is it at all serious or real to be talking of "consoling" ourselves at such a time with scientific subjects? Are these topics to suggest to us the thought of the Creator or not? If not, are they better than story books, to beguile the mind from what lies before it? But, if they are to speak of Him, can a dying man find rest in the mere notion of his Creator, when he knows Him also so awfully as his Moral Governor and his Judge? Meditate indeed on the wonders of Nature on a death-bed! Rather stay your hunger with corn grown in Jupiter, and warm yourself by the Moon. . . . (Letter 7)

1841, 1872

~

from **The Idea of a University**

Knowledge Its Own End

A university may be considered with reference either to its Students or to its Studies; and the principle, that all Knowledge is a whole and the separate Sciences parts of one, which I have hitherto been using in behalf of its studies, is equally important when we direct our attention to its students. Now then I turn to the students, and shall consider the education which, by virtue of this principle, a University will give them; and thus I shall be introduced, Gentlemen, to the second question, which I proposed to discuss, viz., whether and in what sense its teaching, viewed relatively to the taught, carries the attribute of Utility along with it.

— 1. —

I have said that all branches of knowledge are connected together, because the subject-matter of knowledge is intimately united in itself, as being the acts and the work of the Creator. Hence it is that the Sciences, into which our knowledge may be said to be cast, have multiplied bearings one on another, and an internal sympathy, and admit, or rather demand, comparison and adjustment. They complete, correct, balance each other. This consideration, if well-founded, must be taken into account, not only as regards the attainment of truth, which is their common end, but as regards the influence which they exercise upon those whose education consists in the study of them. I have said already, that to give undue prominence to one is to be unjust to another; to neglect or supersede these is to divert those from their proper object. It is to unsettle the boundary lines between science and science, to disturb their action, to destroy the harmony which binds them together. Such a proceeding will have a corresponding effect when introduced into a place of education. There is no science but tells a different tale, when viewed as a portion of a whole, from what it is likely to suggest when taken by itself, without the safeguard, as I may call it, of others.

Let me make use of an illustration. In the combination of colours, very different effects are produced by a difference in their selection and juxta-position; red, green, and white, change their shades, according to the contrast to which they are submitted. And, in like manner, the drift and meaning of a branch of knowledge varies with the company in which it is introduced to the student. If his reading is confined simply to one subject, however such division of labour may favour the advancement of a particular pursuit, a point into which I do not here enter, certainly it has a tendency to contract his mind. If it is incorporated with others, it depends on those others as to the kind of influence which it exerts upon him. Thus the Classics, which in England are the means of refining the taste, have in France subserved the spread of revolutionary and deistical doctrines. In Metaphysics, again, Butler's Analogy of Religion,[1] which has had so much to do with the conversion to the Catholic faith of members of the University of Oxford, appeared to Pitt and others, who had received a different training, to operate only in the direction of infidelity. And so again, Watson, Bishop of Llandaff,[2] as I think he tells us in the narrative of his life, felt the science of Mathematics to indispose the mind to religious belief, while others see in its investigations the best parallel, and thereby defence, of the Christian Mysteries. In like manner, I suppose, Arcesilas[3] would not have handled logic as Aristotle, nor Aristotle have criticized poets as Plato; yet reasoning and poetry are subject to scientific rules.

It is a great point then to enlarge the range of studies which a University professes, even for the sake of the students; and, though they cannot pursue every subject which is open to them, they will be the gainers by living among those and under those who represent the whole circle. This I conceive to be the advantage of a seat of universal learning, considered as a place of education. An assemblage of learned men, zealous for their own sciences, and rivals of each other, are brought, by familiar intercourse and for the sake of intellectual peace, to adjust together the claims and relations of their respective subjects of investigation. They learn to respect, to consult, to aid each other. Thus is

---

[1] Joseph **Butler** (1692–1752): Anglican bishop, author of *The Analogy of Religion, Natural and Revealed* (1736). William **Pitt** (1708–1778): **Whig** statesman.

[2] Richard **Watson** (1737–1810): author of autobiographical *Anecdotes* (1817).

[3] **Arcesilas** (315?–240 BCE) denied the possibility of absolute knowledge.

created a pure and clear atmosphere of thought, which the student also breathes, though in his own case he only pursues a few sciences out of the multitude. He profits by an intellectual tradition, which is independent of particular teachers, which guides him in his choice of subjects, and duly interprets for him those which he chooses. He apprehends the great outlines of knowledge, the principles on which it rests, the scale of its parts, its lights and its shades, its great points and its little, as he otherwise cannot apprehend them. Hence it is that his education is called "Liberal." A habit of mind is formed which lasts through life, of which the attributes are, freedom, equitableness, calmness, moderation, and wisdom; or what in a former Discourse[4] I have ventured to call a philosophical habit. This then I would assign as the special fruit of the education furnished at a University, as contrasted with other places of teaching or modes of teaching. This is the main purpose of a University in its treatment of its students.

And now the question is asked me, What is the *use* of it? and my answer will constitute the main subject of the Discourses which are to follow.

— 2. —

Cautious and practical thinkers, I say, will ask of me, what, after all, is the gain of this Philosophy, of which I make such account, and from which I promise so much. Even supposing it to enable us to exercise the degree of trust exactly due to every science respectively, and to estimate precisely the value of every truth which is anywhere to be found, how are we better for this master view of things, which I have been extolling? Does it not reverse the principle of the division of labour? will practical objects be obtained better or worse by its cultivation? to what then does it lead? where does it end? what does it do? how does it profit? what does it promise? Particular sciences are respectively the basis of definite arts, which carry on to results tangible and beneficial the truths which are the subjects of the knowledge attained; what is the Art of this science of sciences? what is the fruit of such a Philosophy? what are we proposing to effect, what inducements do we hold out to the Catholic community, when we set about the enterprise of founding a University?

I am asked what is the end of University Education, and of the Liberal or Philosophical Knowledge which I conceive it to impart: I answer, that what I have already said,

has been sufficient to show that it has a very tangible, real, and sufficient end, though the end cannot be divided from that knowledge itself. Knowledge is capable of being its own end. Such is the constitution of the human mind, that any kind of knowledge, if it be really such, is its own reward. And if this is true of all knowledge, it is true also of that special Philosophy, which I have made to consist in a comprehensive view of truth in all its branches, of the relations of science to science, of their mutual bearings, and their respective values. What the worth of such an acquirement is, compared with other objects which we seek,— wealth or power or honour or the conveniences and comforts of life, I do not profess here to discuss; but I would maintain, and mean to show, that it is an object, in its own nature so really and undeniably good, as to be the compensation of a great deal of thought in the compassing, and a great deal of trouble in the attaining.

Now, when I say that Knowledge is, not merely a means to something beyond it, or the preliminary of certain arts into which it naturally resolves, but an end sufficient to rest in and to pursue for its own sake, surely I am uttering no paradox, for I am stating what is both intelligible in itself, and has ever been the common judgment of philosophers and the ordinary feeling of mankind. I am saying what at least the public opinion of this day ought to be slow to deny, considering how much we have heard of late years, in opposition to Religion, of entertaining, curious, and various knowledge. I am but saying what whole volumes have been written to illustrate, viz., by a "selection from the records of Philosophy, Literature, and Art, in all ages and countries, of a body of examples, to show how the most unpropitious circumstances have been unable to conquer an ardent desire for the acquisition of knowledge."[5] That further advantages accrue to us and redound to others by its possession, over and above what it is in itself, I am very far indeed from denying; but, independent of these, we are satisfying a direct need of our nature in its very acquisition; and, whereas our nature, unlike that of the inferior creation, does not at once reach its perfection, but depends, in order to it, on a number of external aids and appliances, Knowledge, as one of the principal of these, is valuable for what its very presence in us does for us after the manner of a habit, even though it be turned to no further account, nor subserve any direct end.

---

[4]**Discourse:** Newman's preceding lecture, on the "Bearing of Other Branches of Knowledge on Theology."

[5]**"selection . . . knowledge":** citing George Craik, *The Pursuit of Knowledge under Difficulties* (1830).

— 3. —

Hence it is that Cicero, in enumerating the various heads of mental excellence, lays down the pursuit of Knowledge for its own sake, as the first of them. "This pertains most of all to human nature," he says, "for we are all of us drawn to the pursuit of Knowledge; in which to excel we consider excellent, whereas to mistake, to err, to be ignorant, to be deceived, is both an evil and a disgrace."[6] And he considers Knowledge the very first object to which we are attracted, after the supply of our physical wants. After the calls and duties of our animal existence, as they may be termed, as regards ourselves, our family, and our neighbours, follows, he tells us, "the search after truth. Accordingly, as soon as we escape from the pressure of necessary cares, forthwith we desire to see, to hear, and to learn; and consider the knowledge of what is hidden or is wonderful a condition of our happiness."

This passage, though it is but one of many similar passages in a multitude of authors, I take for the very reason that it is so familiarly known to us; and I wish you to observe, Gentlemen, how distinctly it separates the pursuit of Knowledge from those ulterior objects to which certainly it can be made to conduce, and which are, I suppose, solely contemplated by the persons who would ask of me the use of a University or Liberal Education. So far from dreaming of the cultivation of Knowledge directly and mainly in order to our physical comfort and enjoyment, for the sake of life and person, of health, of the conjugal and family union, of the social tie and civil security, the great Orator implies, that it is only after our physical and political needs are supplied, and when we are "free from necessary duties and cares," that we are in a condition for "desiring to see, to hear, and to learn." Nor does he contemplate in the least degree the reflex or subsequent action of Knowledge, when acquired, upon those material goods which we set out by securing before we seek it; on the contrary, he expressly denies its bearing upon social life altogether, strange as such a procedure is to those who live after the rise of the Baconian[7] philosophy, and he cautions us against such a cultivation of it as will interfere with our duties to our fellow-creatures. "All these methods," he says, "are engaged in the investigation of truth; by the pursuit of which to be carried off from public occupations is a transgression of duty. For the praise of virtue lies altogether in action; yet intermissions often

occur, and then we recur to such pursuits; not to say that the incessant activity of the mind is vigorous enough to carry us on in the pursuit of knowledge, even without any exertion of our own." The idea of benefiting society by means of "the pursuit of science and knowledge" did not enter at all into the motives which he would assign for their cultivation.

This was the ground of the opposition which the elder Cato[8] made to the introduction of Greek Philosophy among his countrymen, when Carneades and his companions, on occasion of their embassy, were charming the Roman youth with their eloquent expositions of it. The fit representative of a practical people, Cato estimated every thing by what it produced; whereas the Pursuit of Knowledge promised nothing beyond Knowledge itself. He despised that refinement or enlargement of mind of which he had no experience.

— 4. —

Things, which can bear to be cut off from every thing else and yet persist in living, must have life in themselves; pursuits, which issue in nothing, and still maintain their ground for ages, which are regarded as admirable, though they have not as yet proved themselves to be useful, must have their sufficient end in themselves, whatever it turn out to be. And we are brought to the same conclusion by considering the force of the epithet, by which the knowledge under consideration is popularly designated. It is common to speak of "*liberal* knowledge," of the "*liberal* arts and studies," and of a "*liberal* education," as the especial characteristic or property of a University and of a gentleman; what is really meant by the word? Now, first, in its grammatical sense it is opposed to *servile*; and by "servile work" is understood, as our catechisms inform us, bodily labour, mechanical employment, and the like, in which the mind has little or no part. Parallel to such servile works are those arts, if they deserve the name, of which the poet speaks;[9] which owe their origin and their method to hazard, not to skill; as, for instance, the practice and operations of an empiric. As far as this contrast may be considered as a guide into the meaning of the word, liberal education and liberal pursuits are exercises of mind, of reason, of reflection.

---

[6]"**This . . . disgrace**": from *De Officiis* (On Duties) by **Cicero** (106–43 BCE).

[7]**Baconian**: in the scientific tradition inaugurated by Sir Francis Bacon (1561–1626).

[8]Marcus Porcius **Cato** (234–149 BCE): Roman patriot. **Carneades** (213–129 BCE): Greek skeptic and rhetorician.

[9]**the poet**: Agathon (5th century BCE), Athenian tragic playwright whom Newman quotes in a note from the *Ethics* of Aristotle (384–322 BCE).

But we want something more for its explanation, for there are bodily exercises which are liberal, and mental exercises which are not so. For instance, in ancient times the practitioners in medicine were commonly slaves; yet it was an art as intellectual in its nature, in spite of the pretence, fraud, and quackery with which it might then, as now, be debased, as it was heavenly in its aim. And so in like manner, we contrast a liberal education with a commercial education or a professional; yet no one can deny that commerce and the professions afford scope for the highest and most diversified powers of mind. There is then a great variety of intellectual exercises, which are not technically called "liberal;" on the other hand, I say, there are exercises of the body which do receive that appellation. Such, for instance, was the palæstra,[10] in ancient times; such the Olympic games, in which strength and dexterity of body as well as of mind gained the prize. In Xenophon we read of the young Persian nobility being taught to ride on horseback and to speak the truth; both being among the accomplishments of a gentleman. War, too, however rough a profession, has ever been accounted liberal, unless in cases when it becomes heroic, which would introduce us to another subject.

Now comparing these instances together, we shall have no difficulty in determining the principle of this apparent variation in the application of the term which I am examining. Manly games, or games of skill, or military prowess, though bodily, are, it seems, accounted liberal; on the other hand, what is merely professional, though highly intellectual, nay, though liberal in comparison of trade and manual labour, is not simply called liberal, and mercantile occupations are not liberal at all. Why this distinction? because that alone is liberal knowledge, which stands on its own pretensions, which is independent of sequel, expects no complement, refuses to be *informed* (as it is called) by any end, or absorbed into any art, in order duly to present itself to our contemplation. The most ordinary pursuits have this specific character, if they are self-sufficient and complete; the highest lose it, when they minister to something beyond them. It is absurd to balance, in point of worth and importance, a treatise on reducing fractures with a game of cricket or a fox-chase; yet of the two the bodily exercise has that quality which we call "liberal," and the intellectual has it not. And so of the learned professions altogether, considered merely as professions; although one of them be

the most popularly beneficial, and another the most politically important, and the third the most intimately divine of all human pursuits, yet the very greatness of their end, the health of the body, or of the commonwealth, or of the soul, diminishes, not increases, their claim to the appellation "liberal," and that still more, if they are cut down to the strict exigencies of that end. If, for instance, Theology, instead of being cultivated as a contemplation, be limited to the purposes of the pulpit or be represented by the catechism, it loses,—not its usefulness, not its divine character, not its meritoriousness (rather it gains a claim upon these titles by such charitable condescension),—but it does lose the particular attribute which I am illustrating; just as a face worn by tears and fasting loses its beauty, or a labourer's hand loses its delicateness;—for Theology thus exercised is not simple knowledge, but rather is an art or a business making use of Theology. And thus it appears that even what is supernatural need not be liberal, nor need a hero be a gentleman, for the plain reason that one idea is not another idea. And in like manner the Baconian Philosophy, by using its physical sciences in the service of man, does thereby transfer them from the order of Liberal Pursuits to, I do not say the inferior, but the distinct class of the Useful. And, to take a different instance, hence again, as is evident, whenever personal gain is the motive, still more distinctive an effect has it upon the character of a given pursuit; thus racing, which was a liberal exercise in Greece, forfeits its rank in times like these, so far as it is made the occasion of gambling.

All that I have been now saying is summed up in a few characteristic words of the great Philosopher.[11] "Of possessions," he says, "those rather are useful, which bear fruit; those *liberal, which tend to enjoyment*. By fruitful, I mean, which yield revenue; by enjoyable, where *nothing accrues of consequence beyond the using*."

— 5. —

Do not suppose, that in thus appealing to the ancients, I am throwing back the world two thousand years, and fettering Philosophy with the reasonings of paganism. While the world lasts, will Aristotle's doctrine on these matters last, for he is the oracle of nature and of truth. While we are men, we cannot help, to a great extent, being Aristotelians, for the great Master does but analyze the thoughts, feelings, views, and opinions of human kind. He has told us the meaning of our own words and ideas, before we were born.

---

[10]**palaestra**: outdoor gymnasium. **Xenophon** (434–355 BCE): Greek historian.

[11]**Philosopher**: Aristotle, whose *Rhetoric* Newman here cites.

In many subject-matters, to think correctly, is to think like Aristotle, and we are his disciples whether we will or no, though we may not know it. Now, as to the particular instance before us, the word "liberal" as applied to Knowledge and Education, expresses a specific idea, which ever has been, and ever will be, while the nature of man is the same, just as the idea of the Beautiful is specific, or of the Sublime, or of the Ridiculous, or of the Sordid. It is in the world now, it was in the world then; and, as in the case of the dogmas of faith, it is illustrated by a continuous historical tradition, and never was out of the world, from the time it came into it. There have indeed been differences of opinion from time to time, as to what pursuits and what arts came under that idea, but such differences are but an additional evidence of its reality. That idea must have a substance in it, which has maintained its ground amid these conflicts and changes, which has ever served as a standard to measure things withal, which has passed from mind to mind unchanged, when there was so much to colour, so much to influence any notion or thought whatever, which was not founded in our very nature. Were it a mere generalization, it would have varied with the subjects from which it was generalized; but though its subjects vary with the age, it varies not itself. The palæstra may seem a liberal exercise to Lycurgus, and illiberal to Seneca; coach-driving and prize-fighting may be recognized in Elis,[12] and be condemned in England; music may be despicable in the eyes of certain moderns, and be in the highest place with Aristotle and Plato,—(and the case is the same in the particular application of the idea of Beauty, or of Goodness, or of Moral Virtue, there is a difference of tastes, a difference of judgments)—still these variations imply, instead of discrediting, the archetypal idea, which is but a previous hypothesis or condition, by means of which issue is joined between contending opinions, and without which there would be nothing to dispute about.

I consider, then, that I am chargeable with no paradox, when I speak of a Knowledge which is its own end, when I call it liberal knowledge, or a gentleman's knowledge, when I educate for it, and make it the scope of a University. And still less am I incurring such a charge, when I make this acquisition consist, not in Knowledge in a vague and ordinary sense, but in that Knowledge which I have especially called Philosophy or, in an extended sense of the word, Science; for whatever claims Knowledge has to be considered as a good, these it has in a higher degree when it is viewed not vaguely, not popularly, but precisely and transcendently as

Philosophy. Knowledge, I say, is then especially liberal, or sufficient for itself, apart from every external and ulterior object, when and so far as it is philosophical, and this I proceed to show.

— 6. —

Now bear with me, Gentlemen, if what I am about to say, has at first sight a fanciful appearance. Philosophy, then, or Science, is related to Knowledge in this way:—Knowledge is called by the name of Science or Philosophy, when it is acted upon, informed, or if I may use a strong figure, impregnated by Reason. Reason is the principle of that intrinsic fecundity of Knowledge, which, to those who possess it, is its especial value, and which dispenses with the necessity of their looking abroad for any end to rest upon external to itself. Knowledge, indeed, when thus exalted into a scientific form, is also power; not only is it excellent in itself, but whatever such excellence may be, it is something more, it has a result beyond itself. Doubtless; but that is a further consideration, with which I am not concerned. I only say that, prior to its being a power, it is a good; that it is, not only an instrument, but an end. I know well it may resolve itself into an art, and terminate in a mechanical process, and in tangible fruit; but it also may fall back upon that Reason which informs it, and resolve itself into Philosophy. In one case it is called Useful Knowledge, in the other Liberal. The same person may cultivate it in both ways at once; but this again is a matter foreign to my subject; here I do but say that there are two ways of using Knowledge, and in matter of fact those who use it in one way are not likely to use it in the other, or at least in a very limited measure. You see, then, here are two methods of Education; the end of the one is to be philosophical, of the other to be mechanical; the one rises towards general ideas, the other is exhausted upon what is particular and external. Let me not be thought to deny the necessity, or to decry the benefit, of such attention to what is particular and practical, as belongs to the useful or mechanical arts; life could not go on without them; we owe our daily welfare to them; their exercise is the duty of the many, and we owe to the many a debt of gratitude for fulfilling that duty. I only say that Knowledge, in proportion as it tends more and more to be particular, ceases to be Knowledge. It is a question whether Knowledge can in any proper sense be predicated of the brute creation; without pretending to metaphysical exactness of phraseology, which would be unsuitable to an occasion like this, I say, it seems to me improper to call that passive sensation, or perception of things, which brutes seem to possess, by the name of Knowledge. When I speak of

---

[12]**Lycurgus**: ancient Spartan lawgiver. **Seneca** (4 BCE–65): Roman stoic. **Elis**: Greek city-state.

Knowledge, I mean something intellectual, something which grasps what it perceives through the senses; something which takes a view of things; which sees more than the senses convey; which reasons upon what it sees, and while it sees; which invests it with an idea. It expresses itself, not in a mere enunciation, but by an enthymeme: it is of the nature of science from the first, and in this consists its dignity. The principle of real dignity in Knowledge, its worth, its desirableness, considered irrespectively of its results, is this germ within it of a scientific or a philosophical process. This is how it comes to be an end in itself; this is why it admits of being called Liberal. Not to know the relative disposition of things is the state of slaves or children; to have mapped out the Universe is the boast, or at least the ambition, of Philosophy.

Moreover, such knowledge is not a mere extrinsic or accidental advantage, which is ours to-day and another's to-morrow, which may be got up from a book, and easily forgotten again, which we can command or communicate at our pleasure, which we can borrow for the occasion, carry about in our hand, and take into the market; it is an acquired illumination, it is a habit, a personal possession, and an inward endowment. And this is the reason, why it is more correct, as well as more usual, to speak of a University as a place of education, than of instruction, though, when knowledge is concerned, instruction would at first sight have seemed the more appropriate word. We are instructed, for instance, in manual exercises, in the fine and useful arts, in trades, and in ways of business; for these are methods, which have little or no effect upon the mind itself, are contained in rules committed to memory, to tradition, or to use, and bear upon an end external to themselves. But education is a higher word; it implies an action upon our mental nature, and the formation of a character; it is something individual and permanent, and is commonly spoken of in connexion with religion and virtue. When, then, we speak of the communication of Knowledge as being Education, we thereby really imply that that Knowledge is a state or condition of mind; and since cultivation of mind is surely worth seeking for its own sake, we are thus brought once more to the conclusion, which the word "Liberal" and the word "Philosophy" have already suggested, that there is a Knowledge, which is desirable, though nothing come of it, as being of itself a treasure, and a sufficient remuneration of years of labour.

— 7. —

This, then, is the answer which I am prepared to give to the question with which I opened this Discourse. Before going on to speak of the object of the Church in taking up Philosophy, and the uses to which she puts it, I am prepared to maintain that Philosophy is its own end, and, as I conceive, I have now begun the proof of it. I am prepared to maintain that there is a knowledge worth possessing for what it is, and not merely for what it does; and what minutes remain to me to-day I shall devote to the removal of some portion of the indistinctness and confusion with which the subject may in some minds be surrounded.

It may be objected then, that, when we profess to seek Knowledge for some end or other beyond itself, whatever it be, we speak intelligibly; but that, whatever men may have said, however obstinately the idea may have kept its ground from age to age, still it is simply unmeaning to say that we seek Knowledge for its own sake, and for nothing else; for that it ever leads to something beyond itself, which therefore is its end, and the cause why it is desirable;—moreover, that this end is twofold, either of this world or of the next; that all knowledge is cultivated either for secular objects or for eternal; that if it is directed to secular objects, it is called Useful Knowledge, if to eternal, Religious or Christian Knowledge;—in consequence, that if, as I have allowed, this Liberal Knowledge does not benefit the body or estate, it ought to benefit the soul; but if the fact be really so, that it is neither a physical or a secular good on the one hand, nor a moral good on the other, it cannot be a good at all, and is not worth the trouble which is necessary for its acquisition.

And then I may be reminded that the professors of this Liberal or Philosophical Knowledge have themselves, in every age, recognized this exposition of the matter, and have submitted to the issue in which it terminates; for they have ever been attempting to make men virtuous; or, if not, at least have assumed that refinement of mind was virtue, and that they themselves were the virtuous portion of mankind. This they have professed on the one hand; and on the other, they have utterly failed in their professions, so as ever to make themselves a proverb among men, and a laughing-stock both to the grave and the dissipated portion of mankind, in consequence of them. Thus they have furnished against themselves both the ground and the means of their own exposure, without any trouble at all to any one else. In a word, from the time that Athens was the University of the world, what has Philosophy taught men, but to promise without practising, and to aspire without attaining? What has the deep and lofty thought of its disciples ended in but eloquent words? Nay, what has its teaching ever meditated, when it was boldest in its remedies for human ill, beyond charming us to sleep by its lessons, that we might feel nothing at all? like some melodious air, or rather like those strong and transporting perfumes, which at first spread their sweetness over every thing they touch, but in a little while do but offend in proportion as they once pleased us. Did Philosophy support Cicero under the disfavour of the fickle populace, or nerve Seneca to oppose an imperial tyrant? It abandoned Brutus, as he sorrowfully confessed, in his greatest need, and it forced Cato, as his panegyrist strangely boasts, into the false position of defying heaven. How few can be counted among its professors, who, like Polemo, were thereby converted from a profligate course, or like Anaxagoras, thought the world well lost in exchange for its possession? The philosopher in Rasselas taught a superhuman doctrine, and then succumbed without an effort to a trial of human affection.[13]

"He discoursed," we are told, "with great energy on the government of the passions. His look was venerable, his action graceful, his pronunciation clear, and his diction elegant. He showed, with great strength of sentiment and variety of illustration, that human nature is degraded and debased, when the lower faculties predominate over the higher. He communicated the various precepts given, from time to time, for the conquest of passion, and displayed the happiness of those who had obtained the important victory, after which man is no longer the slave of fear, nor the fool of hope. . . . He enumerated many examples of heroes immoveable by pain or pleasure, who looked with indifference on those modes or accidents to which the vulgar give the names of good and evil."

Rasselas in a few days found the philosopher in a room half darkened, with his eyes misty, and his face pale. "Sir," said he, "you have come at a time when all human friendship is useless; what I suffer cannot be remedied, what I have lost cannot be supplied. My daughter, my only daughter, from whose tenderness I expected all the comforts of my age, died last night of a fever." "Sir," said the prince, "mortality is an event by which a wise man can never be surprised; we know that death is always near, and it should therefore always be expected." "Young man," answered the philosopher, "you speak like one who has never felt the pangs of separation." "Have you, then, forgot the precept," said Rasselas, "which you so powerfully enforced? . . . con-

sider that external things are naturally variable, but truth and reason are always the same." "What comfort," said the mourner, "can truth and reason afford me? Of what effect are they now, but to tell me that my daughter will not be restored?"

— 8. —

Better, far better, to make no professions, you will say, than to cheat others with what we are not, and to scandalize them with what we are. The sensualist, or the man of the world, at any rate is not the victim of fine words, but pursues a reality and gains it. The Philosophy of Utility, you will say, Gentlemen, has at least done its work; and I grant it,—it aimed low, but it has fulfilled its aim. If that man of great intellect who has been its Prophet[14] in the conduct of life played false to his own professions, he was not bound by his philosophy to be true to his friend or faithful in his trust. Moral virtue was not the line in which he undertook to instruct men; and though, as the poet calls him, he were the "meanest" of mankind, he was so in what may be called his private capacity and without any prejudice to the theory of induction. He had a right to be so, if he chose, for any thing that the Idols of the den or the theatre had to say to the contrary. His mission was the increase of physical enjoyment and social comfort;[15] and most wonderfully, most awfully has he fulfilled his conception and his design. Almost day by day have we fresh and fresh shoots, and buds, and blossoms, which are to ripen into fruit, on that magical tree of Knowledge which he planted, and to which none of us perhaps, except the very poor, but owes, if not his present life, at least his daily food, his health, and general wellbeing. He was the divinely provided minister of temporal benefits to all of us so great, that, whatever I am forced to think of him as a man, I have not the heart, from mere gratitude, to speak of him severely. And, in spite of the tendencies of his philosophy, which are, as we see at this day, to depreciate, or to trample on Theology, he has himself, in his writings, gone out of his way, as if with a prophetic misgiving of those tendencies, to insist on it as the instrument of that beneficent Father, who, when He came on earth in

---

[13]Marcus Junius **Brutus** (85–42 BCE): assassin of Julius Caesar. **Polemo:** taught at the 4th-century BCE Academy in Athens. **Anaxagoras:** 5th-century BCE philosopher and scientist banished for his opinions. *Rasselas* (1759): philosophical novel by Samuel Johnson (1709–1784).

[14]**Prophet:** Bacon, called "meanest" by Pope in *Essay on Man* (1734) 4.282.

[15]**comfort:** It will be seen that on the whole I agree with Lord Macaulay in his Essay on Bacon's Philosophy. I do not know whether he would agree with me. [Newman's note, referring to **Macaulay's** 1837 essay "Lord Bacon"] **Idols:** Bacon's name in *Novum Organum* (1620) for prevalent errors.

visible form, took on Him first and most prominently the office of assuaging the bodily wounds of human nature. And truly, like the old mediciner in the tale, "he sat diligently at his work, and hummed, with cheerful countenance, a pious song;" and then in turn "went out singing into the meadows so gaily, that those who had seen him from afar might well have thought it was a youth gathering flowers for his beloved, instead of an old physician gathering healing herbs in the morning dew."[16]

Alas, that men, in the action of life or in their heart of hearts, are not what they seem to be in their moments of excitement, or in their trances or intoxications of genius,—so good, so noble, so serene! Alas, that Bacon too in his own way should after all be but the fellow of those heathen philosophers who in their disadvantages had some excuse for their inconsistency, and who surprise us rather in what they did say than in what they did not do! Alas, that he too, like Socrates or Seneca, must be stripped of his holy-day coat, which looks so fair, and should be but a mockery amid his most majestic gravity of phrase; and, for all his vast abilities, should, in the littleness of his own moral being, but typify the intellectual narrowness of his school! However, granting all this, heroism after all was not his philosophy:— I cannot deny he has abundantly achieved what he proposed. His is simply a Method whereby bodily discomforts and temporal wants are to be most effectually removed from the greatest number; and already, before it has shown any signs of exhaustion, the gifts of nature, in their most artificial shapes and luxurious profusion and diversity, from all quarters of the earth, are, it is undeniable, by its means brought even to our doors, and we rejoice in them.

— 9. —

Useful Knowledge then, I grant, has done its work; and Liberal Knowledge as certainly has not done its work,—that is, supposing, as the objectors assume, its direct end, like Religious Knowledge, is to make men better; but this I will not for an instant allow, and, unless I allow it, those objectors have said nothing to the purpose. I admit, rather I maintain, what they have been urging, for I consider Knowledge to have its end in itself. For all its friends, or its enemies, may say, I insist upon it, that it is as real a mistake to burden it with virtue or religion as with the mechanical arts. Its direct business is not to steel the soul against temptation or to

console it in affliction, any more than to set the loom in motion, or to direct the steam carriage; be it ever so much the means or the condition of both material and moral advancement, still, taken by and in itself, it as little mends our hearts as it improves our temporal circumstances. And if its eulogists claim for it such a power, they commit the very same kind of encroachment on a province not their own as the political economist who should maintain that his science educated him for casuistry or diplomacy. Knowledge is one thing, virtue is another; good sense is not conscience, refinement is not humility, nor is largeness and justness of view faith. Philosophy, however enlightened, however profound, gives no command over the passions, no influential motives, no vivifying principles. Liberal Education makes not the Christian, not the Catholic, but the gentleman. It is well to be a gentleman, it is well to have a cultivated intellect, a delicate taste, a candid, equitable, dispassionate mind, a noble and courteous bearing in the conduct of life;—these are the connatural qualities of a large knowledge; they are the objects of a University; I am advocating, I shall illustrate and insist upon them; but still, I repeat, they are no guarantee for sanctity or even for conscientiousness, they may attach to the man of the world, to the profligate, to the heartless,—pleasant, alas, and attractive as he shows when decked out in them. Taken by themselves, they do but seem to be what they are not; they look like virtue at a distance, but they are detected by close observers, and on the long run; and hence it is that they are popularly accused of pretence and hypocrisy, not, I repeat, from their own fault, but because their professors and their admirers persist in taking them for what they are not, and are officious in arrogating for them a praise to which they have no claim. Quarry the granite rock with razors, or moor the vessel with a thread of silk; then may you hope with such keen and delicate instruments as human knowledge and human reason to contend against those giants, the passion and the pride of man.

Surely we are not driven to theories of this kind, in order to vindicate the value and dignity of Liberal Knowledge. Surely the real grounds on which its pretensions rest are not so very subtle or abstruse, so very strange or improbable. Surely it is very intelligible to say, and that is what I say here, that Liberal Education, viewed in itself, is simply the cultivation of the intellect, as such, and its object is nothing more or less than intellectual excellence. Every thing has its own perfection, be it higher or lower in the scale of things; and the perfection of one is not the perfection of another. Things animate, inanimate, visible, invisible, all are good in their kind, and have a *best* of themselves,

---

[16]Fouqué's Unknown Patient. [Newman's note] F. H. K. de la Motte, Baron **Fouqué** (1777–1843): German storyteller and playwright.

which is an object of pursuit. Why do you take such pains with your garden or your park? You see to your walks and turf and shrubberies; to your trees and drives; not as if you meant to make an orchard of the one, or corn or pasture land of the other, but because there is a special beauty in all that is goodly in wood, water, plain, and slope, brought all together by art into one shape, and grouped into one whole. Your cities are beautiful, your palaces, your public buildings, your territorial mansions, your churches; and their beauty leads to nothing beyond itself. There is a physical beauty and a moral: there is a beauty of person, there is a beauty of our moral being, which is natural virtue; and in like manner there is a beauty, there is a perfection, of the intellect. There is an ideal perfection in these various subject-matters, towards which individual instances are seen to rise, and which are the standards for all instances whatever. The Greek divinities and demigods, as the statuary has moulded them, with their symmetry of figure, and their high forehead and their regular features, are the perfection of physical beauty. The heroes, of whom history tells, Alexander, or Cæsar, or Scipio, or Saladin,[17] are the representatives of that magnanimity or self-mastery which is the greatness of human nature. Christianity too has its heroes, and in the supernatural order, and we call them Saints. The artist puts before him beauty of feature and form; the poet, beauty of mind; the preacher, the beauty of grace: then intellect too, I repeat, has its beauty, and it has those who aim at it. To open the mind, to correct it, to refine it, to enable it to know, and to digest, master, rule, and use its knowledge, to give it power over its own faculties, application, flexibility, method, critical exactness, sagacity, resource, address, eloquent expression, is an object as intelligible (for here we are inquiring, not what the object of a Liberal Education is worth, nor what use the Church makes of it, but what it is in itself), I say, an object as intelligible as the cultivation of virtue, while, at the same time, it is absolutely distinct from it.

— 10. —

This indeed is but a temporal object, and a transitory possession; but so are other things in themselves which we make much of and pursue. The moralist will tell us that man, in all his functions, is but a flower which blossoms and fades, except so far as a higher principle breathes upon him, and makes him and what he is immortal. Body and mind are carried on into an eternal state of being by the gifts of Di-

vine Munificence; but at first they do but fail in a failing world; and if the powers of intellect decay, the powers of the body have decayed before them, and, as an Hospital or an Alms-house, though its end be ephemeral, may be sanctified to the service of religion, so surely may a University, even were it nothing more than I have as yet described it. We attain to heaven by using this world well, though it is to pass away; we perfect our nature, not by undoing it, but by adding to it what is more than nature, and directing it towards aims higher than its own. (Discourse 5)

1852, 1873

from Apologia pro Vita Sua

History of My Religious Opinions to the Year 1833

It may easily be conceived how great a trial it is to me to write the following history of myself; but I must not shrink from the task. The words, "Secretum meum mihi,"[1] keep ringing in my ears; but as men draw towards their end, they care less for disclosures. Nor is it the least part of my trial, to anticipate that, upon first reading what I have written, my friends may consider much in it irrelevant to my purpose; yet I cannot help thinking that, viewed as a whole, it will effect what I propose to myself in giving it to the public.

I was brought up from a child to take great delight in reading the Bible; but I had no formed religious convictions till I was fifteen. Of course I had a perfect knowledge of my Catechism.

After I was grown up, I put on paper my recollections of the thoughts and feelings on religious subjects, which I had at the time that I was a child and a boy,—such as had remained on my mind with sufficient prominence to make me then consider them worth recording. Out of these, written in the Long Vacation of 1820, and transcribed with additions in 1823, I select two, which are at once the most definite among them, and also have a bearing on my later convictions.

1. "I used to wish the Arabian Tales were true: my imagination ran on unknown influences, on magical powers, and talismans. . . . I thought life might be a dream, or I an Angel, and all this world a deception, my fellow-angels by a

---

[17]**Scipio:** 2nd-century BCE Roman general. **Saladin** (1137–1193): sultan who stymied the Third Crusade.

[1]**"Secretum meum mihi":** my secret is my own (Isaiah 24:16, Latin Bible).

playful device concealing themselves from me, and deceiving me with the semblance of a material world."

Again: "Reading in the Spring of 1816 a sentence from [Dr. Watts's] *Remnants of Time*,[2] entitled 'the Saints unknown to the world,' to the effect, that 'there is nothing in their figure or countenance to distinguish them,' &c., &c., I supposed he spoke of Angels who lived in the world, as it were disguised."

2. The other remark is this: "I was very superstitious, and for some time previous to my conversion" [when I was fifteen] "used constantly to cross myself on going into the dark."

Of course I must have got this practice from some external source or other; but I can make no sort of conjecture whence; and certainly no one had ever spoken to me on the subject of the Catholic religion, which I only knew by name. The French master was an *émigré* Priest, but he was simply made a butt, as French masters too commonly were in that day, and spoke English very imperfectly. There was a Catholic family in the village,[3] old maiden ladies we used to think; but I knew nothing about them. I have of late years heard that there were one or two Catholic boys in the school; but either we were carefully kept from knowing this, or the knowledge of it made simply no impression on our minds. My brother[4] will bear witness how free the school was from Catholic ideas.

I had once been into Warwick Street Chapel, with my father, who, I believe, wanted to hear some piece of music; all that I bore away from it was the recollection of a pulpit and a preacher, and a boy swinging a censer.

When I was at Littlemore,[5] I was looking over old copy-books of my school days, and I found among them my first Latin verse-book; and in the first page of it there was a device which almost took my breath away with surprise. I have the book before me now, and have just been showing it to others. I have written in the first page, in my schoolboy hand, "John H. Newman, February 11th, 1811, Verse Book;" then follow my first Verses. Between "Verse" and "Book" I have drawn the figure of a solid cross upright, and next to it is, what may indeed be meant for a necklace, but what I cannot make out to be anything else than a set of beads suspended, with a little cross attached. At this time I was not quite ten years old. I suppose I got these ideas from some romance, Mrs. Radcliffe's or Miss Porter's;[6] or from some religious picture; but the strange thing is, how, among the thousand objects which meet a boy's eyes, these in particular should so have fixed themselves in my mind, that I made them thus practically my own. I am certain there was nothing in the churches I attended, or the prayer books I read, to suggest them. It must be recollected that Anglican churches and prayer books were not decorated in those days as I believe they are now.

When I was fourteen, I read Paine's *Tracts against the Old Testament*, and found pleasure in thinking of the objections which were contained in them. Also, I read some of Hume's *Essays*; and perhaps that on *Miracles*. So at least I gave my Father to understand; but perhaps it was a brag. Also, I recollect copying out some French verses, perhaps Voltaire's,[7] in denial of the immortality of the soul, and saying to myself something like "How dreadful, but how plausible!"

When I was fifteen, (in the autumn of 1816,) a great change of thought took place in me. I fell under the influences of a definite Creed, and received into my intellect impressions of dogma, which, through God's mercy, have never been effaced or obscured. Above and beyond the conversations and sermons of the excellent man, long dead, the Rev. Walter Mayers, of Pembroke College, Oxford, who was the human means of this beginning of divine faith in me, was the effect of the books which he put into my hands, all of the school of Calvin. One of the first books I read was a work of Romaine's;[8] I neither recollect the title nor the contents, except one doctrine, which of course I do not include among those which I believe to have come from a divine source, viz. the doctrine of final perseverance. I received it at once, and believed that the inward conversion of which I was conscious, (and of which I still am more certain than that I have hands and feet,) would last into the next life, and that I was elected to eternal glory. I have no

---

[2]*Remnants of Time: The Improvement of the Mind* (1741), by Nonconformist divine and hymn writer Isaac **Watts** (1674–1748).

[3]**village:** Ealing, near London.

[4]**brother:** Francis William Newman (1805–1897), a scholar whose unorthodox religious views were very different from his brother's and well publicized.

[5]**Littlemore:** village in the parish near Oxford where Newman was vicar from 1828 and where he lived in cottage retirement from 1842 until his conversion in 1845.

---

[6]Ann **Radcliffe** (1764–1823): leading Gothic novelist of the 1790s. Jane **Porter** (1776–1850) and her sister Anna Maria **Porter** (1780–1832): pioneers of the historical novel.

[7]Thomas **Paine** (1737–1809): notorious radical and deist. David **Hume** (1711–1776): skeptical philosopher. **Voltaire** (1694–1778): philosopher and provocateur.

[8]William **Romaine** (1714–1795): Calvinist author.

consciousness that this belief had any tendency whatever to lead me to be careless about pleasing God. I retained it till the age of twenty-one, when it gradually faded away; but I believe that it had some influence on my opinions, in the direction of those childish imaginations which I have already mentioned, viz. in isolating me from the objects which surrounded me, in confirming me in my mistrust of the reality of material phenomena, and making me rest in the thought of two and two only absolute and luminously self-evident beings, myself and my Creator;—for while I considered myself predestined to salvation, my mind did not dwell upon others, as fancying them simply passed over, not predestined to eternal death. I only thought of the mercy to myself.

The detestable doctrine last mentioned is simply denied and abjured, unless my memory strangely deceives me, by the writer who made a deeper impression on my mind than any other, and to whom (humanly speaking) I almost owe my soul,—Thomas Scott[9] of Aston Sandford. I so admired and delighted in his writings, that, when I was an Under-graduate, I thought of making a visit to his Parsonage, in order to see a man whom I so deeply revered. I hardly think I could have given up the idea of this expedition, even after I had taken my degree; for the news of his death in 1821 came upon me as a disappointment as well as a sorrow. I hung upon the lips of Daniel Wilson,[10] afterwards Bishop of Calcutta, as in two sermons at St. John's Chapel he gave the history of Scott's life and death. I had been possessed of his *Force of Truth* and *Essays* from a boy; his *Commentary* I bought when I was an Under-graduate.

What, I suppose, will strike any reader of Scott's history and writings, is his bold unworldliness and vigorous independence of mind. He followed truth wherever it led him, beginning with Unitarianism;[11] and ending in a zealous faith in the Holy Trinity. It was he who first planted deep in my mind that fundamental truth of religion. With the assistance of Scott's *Essays*, and the admirable work of Jones of Nayland, I made a collection of Scripture texts in proof of the doctrine, with remarks (I think) of my own upon them,

before I was sixteen; and a few months later I drew up a series of texts in support of each verse of the Athanasian Creed. These papers I have still.

Besides his unworldliness, what I also admired in Scott was his resolute opposition to Antinomianism,[12] and the minutely practical character of his writings. They show him to be a true Englishman, and I deeply felt his influence; and for years I used almost as proverbs what I considered to be the scope and issue of his doctrine, *Holiness rather than peace,* and *Growth the only evidence of life.*

Calvinists make a sharp separation between the elect and the world; there is much in this that is cognate or parallel to the Catholic doctrine; but they go on to say, as I understand them, very differently from Catholicism,—that the converted and the unconverted can be discriminated by man, that the justified are conscious of their state of justification, and that the regenerate cannot fall away. Catholics on the other hand shade and soften the awful antagonism between good and evil, which is one of their dogmas, by holding that there are different degrees of justification, that there is a great difference in point of gravity between sin and sin, that there is the possibility and the danger of falling away, and that there is no certain knowledge given to any one that he is simply in a state of grace, and much less that he is to persevere to the end:—of the Calvinistic tenets the only one which took root in my mind was the fact of heaven and hell, divine favour and divine wrath, of the justified and unjustified. The notion that the regenerate and the justified were one and the same, and that the regenerate, as such, had the gift of perseverance, remained with me not many years, as I have said already.

This main Catholic doctrine of the warfare between the city of God and the powers of darkness was also deeply impressed upon my mind by a work of a character very opposite to Calvinism, Law's *Serious Call.*[13]

From this time I have held with a full inward assent and belief the doctrine of eternal punishment, as delivered by our Lord Himself, in as true a sense as I hold that of eternal happiness; though I have tried in various ways to make that truth less terrible to the imagination.

Now I come to two other works, which produced a deep impression on me in the same Autumn of 1816, when I was fifteen years old, each contrary to each, and planting in

---

[9]**Thomas Scott** (1747–1821): Biblical commentator and theologian.

[10]**Daniel Wilson** (1778–1858): evangelical preacher at St. John's Chapel, London.

[11]**Unitarianism**: liberal Protestant position repudiating the doctrine of the Trinity. William **Jones** (1726–1800): author of *The Catholic Doctrine of the Trinity* (1756). **Athanasian Creed**: formal profession of Trinitarian faith dating from 5th century.

[12]**Antinomianism**: doctrine that faith alone is sufficient for salvation.

[13]William **Law** (1686–1761): author of *A Serious Call to a Devout and Holy Life* (1729).

me the seeds of an intellectual inconsistency which disabled me for a long course of years. I read Joseph Milner's *Church History;*[14] and was nothing short of enamoured of the long extracts from St. Augustine, St. Ambrose, and the other Fathers which I found there. I read them as being the religion of the primitive Christians: but simultaneously with Milner I read Newton *On the Prophecies,* and in consequence became most firmly convinced that the Pope was the Antichrist predicted by Daniel, St. Paul, and St. John. My imagination was stained by the effects of this doctrine up to the year 1843; it had been obliterated from my reason and judgment at an earlier date; but the thought remained upon me as a sort of false conscience. Hence came that conflict of mind, which so many have felt besides myself,—leading some men to make a compromise between two ideas, so inconsistent with each other,—driving others to beat out the one idea or the other from their minds,—and ending in my own case, after many years of intellectual unrest, in the gradual decay and extinction of one of them,—I do not say in its violent death, for why should I not have murdered it sooner, if I murdered it at all?

I am obliged to mention, though I do it with great reluctance, another deep imagination, which at this time, the autumn of 1816, took possession of me,—there can be no mistake about the fact; viz. that it would be the will of God that I should lead a single life. This anticipation, which has held its ground almost continuously ever since,—with the break of a month now and a month then, up to 1829, and, after that date, without any break at all,—was more or less connected in my mind with the notion, that my calling in life would require such a sacrifice as celibacy involved; as, for instance, missionary work among the heathen, to which I had a great drawing for some years. It also strengthened my feeling of separation from the visible world of which I have spoken above. . . .

The *Christian Year*[15] made its appearance in 1827. It is not necessary, and scarcely becoming, to praise a book which has already become one of the classics of the language. When the general tone of religious literature was so nerveless and impotent, as it was at that time, Keble struck an original note and woke up in the hearts of thousands a new music, the music of a school, long unknown in England. Nor can I pretend to analyze, in my own instance,

the effect of religious teachings so deep, so pure, so beautiful. I have never till now tried to do so; yet I think I am not wrong in saying, that the two main intellectual truths which it brought home to me, were the same two, which I had learned from Butler,[16] though recast in the creative mind of my new master. The first of these was what may be called, in a large sense of the word, the Sacramental system; that is, the doctrine that material phenomena are both the types and the instruments of real things unseen,—a doctrine, which embraces in its fulness, not only what Anglicans, as well as Catholics, believe about Sacraments properly so called; but also the article of "the Communion of Saints;" and likewise the Mysteries of the faith. The connexion of this philosophy of religion with what is sometimes called "Berkeleyism"[17] has been mentioned above; I knew little of Berkeley at this time except by name; nor have I ever studied him.

On the second intellectual principle which I gained from Mr. Keble, I could say a great deal; if this were the place for it. It runs through very much that I have written, and has gained for me many hard names. Butler teaches us that probability is the guide of life. The danger of this doctrine, in the case of many minds, is, its tendency to destroy in them absolute certainty, leading them to consider every conclusion as doubtful, and resolving truth into an opinion, which it is safe indeed to obey or to profess, but not possible to embrace with full internal assent. If this were to be allowed, then the celebrated saying, "O God, if there be a God, save my soul, if I have a soul!" would be the highest measure of devotion:—but who can really pray to a Being, about whose existence he is seriously in doubt?

I considered that Mr. Keble met this difficulty by ascribing the firmness of assent which we give to religious doctrine, not to the probabilities which introduced it, but to the living power of faith and love which accepted it. In matters of religion, he seemed to say, it is not merely probability which makes us intellectually certain, but probability as it is put to account by faith and love. It is faith and love which give to probability a force which it has not in itself. Faith and love are directed towards an Object; in the vision of that Object they live; it is that Object, received in faith

---

[14]Joseph **Milner** (1744–1797): coauthor of *A History of the Church of Christ* (1794–1809). Thomas **Newton** (1642–1727): author of *Dissertations on the Prophecies* (1754–1758).

[15]*Christian Year*: Keble's cycle of devotional poems; see page 157.

[16]Bishop Joseph **Butler** (1692–1752): author of the *Analogy of Religion* (1736).

[17]"**Berkeleyism**": idealist philosophy of Bishop George Berkeley (1685–1753) in which existence depends on perception, the universe on God's omniscience.

and love, which renders it reasonable to take probability as sufficient for internal conviction. Thus the argument from Probability, in the matter of religion, became an argument from Personality, which in fact is one form of the argument from Authority.

In illustration, Mr. Keble used to quote the words of the Psalm: "I will guide thee with mine *eye*. Be ye not like to horse and mule, which have no understanding; whose mouths must be held with bit and bridle, lest they fall upon thee."[18] This is the very difference, he used to say, between slaves, and friends or children. Friends do not ask for literal commands; but, from their knowledge of the speaker, they understand his half-words, and from love of him they anticipate his wishes. Hence it is, that in his Poem for St. Bartholomew's Day, he speaks of the "Eye of God's word;" and in the note quotes Mr. Miller, of Worcester College, who remarks in his Bampton Lectures,[19] on the special power of Scripture, as having "this Eye, like that of a portrait, uniformly fixed upon us, turn where we will." The view thus suggested by Mr. Keble, is brought forward in one of the earliest of the *Tracts for the Times*.[20] In No. 8 I say, "The Gospel is a Law of Liberty. We are treated as sons, not as servants; not subjected to a code of formal commandments, but addressed as those who love God, and wish to please Him."

I did not at all dispute this view of the matter, for I made use of it myself; but I was dissatisfied, because it did not go to the root of the difficulty. It was beautiful and religious, but it did not even profess to be logical; and accordingly I tried to complete it by considerations of my own, which are to be found in my *University Sermons, Essay on Ecclesiastical Miracles*, and *Essay on Development of Doctrine*.[21] My argument is in outline as follows: that that absolute certitude which we were able to possess, whether as to the truths of natural theology, or as to the fact of a revelation, was the result of an *assemblage* of concurring and converging probabilities, and that, both according to the constitution of the human mind and the will of its Maker; that certitude was a

habit of mind, that certainty was a quality of propositions; that probabilities which did not reach to logical certainty, might suffice for a mental certitude; that the certitude thus brought about might equal in measure and strength the certitude which was created by the strictest scientific demonstration; and that to possess such certitude might in given cases and to given individuals be a plain duty, though not to others in other circumstances:—

Moreover, that as there were probabilities which sufficed for certitude, so there were other probabilities which were legitimately adapted to create opinion; that it might be quite as much a matter of duty in given cases and to given persons to have about a fact an opinion of a definite strength and consistency, as in the case of greater or of more numerous probabilities it was a duty to have a certitude; that accordingly we were bound to be more or less sure, on a sort of (as it were) graduated scale of assent, viz. according as the probabilities attaching to a professed fact were brought home to us, and as the case might be, to entertain about it a pious belief, or a pious opinion, or a religious conjecture, or at least, a tolerance of such belief, or opinion or conjecture in others; that on the other hand, as it was a duty to have a belief, of more or less strong texture, in given cases, so in other cases it was a duty not to believe, not to opine, not to conjecture, not even to tolerate the notion that a professed fact was true, inasmuch as it would be credulity or superstition, or some other moral fault, to do so. This was the region of Private Judgment in religion; that is, of a Private Judgment, not formed arbitrarily and according to one's fancy or liking, but conscientiously, and under a sense of duty. . . .

Hurrell Froude[22] was a pupil of Keble's, formed by him, and in turn reacting upon him. I knew him first in 1826, and was in the closest and most affectionate friendship with him from about 1829 till his death in 1836. He was a man of the highest gifts,—so truly many-sided, that it would be presumptuous in me to attempt to describe him, except under those aspects in which he came before me. Nor have I here to speak of the gentleness and tenderness of nature, the playfulness, the free elastic force and graceful versatility of mind, and the patient winning considerateness in discussion, which endeared him to those to whom he opened his heart; for I am all along engaged upon matters of belief and opinion, and am introducing others into my narrative, not for their own sake, or because I love and have

---

[18]"**I will guide . . . upon thee**": Psalm 32:8–9.

[19]**Bampton Lectures**: delivered annually on topics in divinity at Oxford since 1780; John **Miller's** 1817 lectures concerned "The Adaptation of Holy Scripture to the Real State of Human Nature."

[20]*Tracts for the Times*: chief organ of the Oxford Movement for conservative reform within the Church. Newman wrote over one-fourth of the 90 tracts published between 1833 and 1841.

[21]*University . . . Doctrine*: works Newman published 1842–1845. He discusses certitude in his *Grammar of Assent* (1870).

---

[22]Richard **Hurrell Froude** (1803–1836): Tractarian controversialist and poet.

loved them, so much as because, and so far as, they have influenced my theological views. In this respect then, I speak of Hurrell Froude,—in his intellectual aspect,—as a man of high genius, brimful and overflowing with ideas and views, in him original, which were too many and strong even for his bodily strength, and which crowded and jostled against each other in their effort after distinct shape and expression. And he had an intellect as critical and logical as it was speculative and bold. Dying prematurely, as he did, and in the conflict and transition-state of opinion, his religious views never reached their ultimate conclusion, by the very reason of their multitude and their depth. His opinions arrested and influenced me, even when they did not gain my assent. He professed openly his admiration of the Church of Rome, and his hatred of the Reformers. He delighted in the notion of an hierarchical system, of sacerdotal power, and of full ecclesiastical liberty. He felt scorn of the maxim, "The Bible and the Bible only is the religion of Protestants;" and he gloried in accepting Tradition as a main instrument of religious teaching. He had a high severe idea of the intrinsic excellence of Virginity; and he considered the Blessed Virgin its great Pattern. He delighted in thinking of the Saints; he had a vivid appreciation of the idea of sanctity, its possibility and its heights; and he was more than inclined to believe a large amount of miraculous interference as occurring in the early and middle ages. He embraced the principle of penance and mortification. He had a deep devotion to the Real Presence,[23] in which he had a firm faith. He was powerfully drawn to the Medieval Church, but not to the Primitive.

He had a keen insight into abstract truth; but he was an Englishman to the backbone in his severe adherence to the real and the concrete. He had a most classical taste, and a genius for philosophy and art; and he was fond of historical inquiry, and the politics of religion. He had no turn for theology as such. He set no sufficient value on the writings of the Fathers, on the detail or development of doctrine, on the definite traditions of the Church viewed in their matter, on the teaching of the Ecumenical Councils, or on the controversies out of which they arose. He took an eager courageous view of things on the whole. I should say that his power of entering into the minds of others did not equal his other gifts; he could not believe, for instance, that I really held the Roman Church to be Antichristian. On many points he would not believe but that I agreed with him,

when I did not. He seemed not to understand my difficulties. His were of a different kind, the contrariety between theory and fact. He was a high Tory of the Cavalier stamp, and was disgusted with the Toryism of the opponents of the Reform Bill.[24] He was smitten with the love of the Theocratic Church; he went abroad and was shocked by the degeneracy which he thought he saw in the Catholics of Italy.

It is difficult to enumerate the precise additions to my theological creed which I derived from a friend to whom I owe so much. He taught me to look with admiration towards the Church of Rome, and in the same degree to dislike the Reformation. He fixed deep in me the idea of devotion to the Blessed Virgin, and he led me gradually to believe in the Real Presence.

There is one remaining source of my opinions to be mentioned, and that far from the least important. In proportion as I moved out of the shadow of that Liberalism which had hung over my course, my early devotion towards the Fathers returned; and in the Long Vacation of 1828 I set about to read them chronologically, beginning with St. Ignatius and St. Justin. About 1830 a proposal was made to me by Mr. Hugh Rose, who with Mr. Lyall[25] (afterwards Dean of Canterbury) was providing writers for a Theological Library, to furnish them with a History of the Principal Councils. I accepted it, and at once set to work on the Council of Nicæa. It was to launch myself on an ocean with currents innumerable; and I was drifted back first to the ante-Nicene history, and then to the Church of Alexandria.[26] The work at last appeared under the title of *The Arians of the Fourth Century*; and of its 422 pages, the first 117 consisted of introductory matter, and the Council of Nicæa did not appear till the 254th, and then occupied at most twenty pages.

---

[24]**Reform Bill**: 1832 act of Parliament liberalizing voting franchise, opposed by Tories out of mere prudence, not on the high **Cavalier** grounds from which conservatives like Froude and Newman decried not just Reform but the 16th-century **Reformation**.

[25]**St. Ignatius** of Antioch (1st century), **St. Justin** Martyr (2nd century). **Hugh Rose** (1795–1838): theologian and editor. William Rowe **Lyall** (1788–1857): churchman, periodical and encyclopedia editor.

[26]**Council of Nicaea** (325): first ecumenical conclave, where the anti-Trinitarian heresy of **Arianism** was condemned. Newman's studies, including the Anglican apologetics of **Bishop** George **Bull** (1634–1710), led him back before the **Nicene** epoch to theological controversialists from the **Church of Alexandria**, among them St. **Clement** (2nd century), **Origen** (2nd–3rd century) and St. **Dionysius** (3rd century).

---

[23]**Real Presence**: doctrine that Christ's body and blood are actually present in eucharistic bread and wine.

I do not know when I first learnt to consider that Antiquity was the true exponent of the doctrines of Christianity and the basis of the Church of England; but I take it for granted that the works of Bishop Bull, which at this time I read, were my chief introduction to this principle. The course of reading, which I pursued in the composition of my volume, was directly adapted to develope it in my mind. What principally attracted me in the ante-Nicene period was the great Church of Alexandria, the historical centre of teaching in those times. Of Rome for some centuries comparatively little is known. The battle of Arianism was first fought in Alexandria; Athanasius, the champion of the truth, was Bishop of Alexandria; and in his writings he refers to the great religious names of an earlier date, to Origen, Dionysius, and others, who were the glory of its see, or of its school. The broad philosophy of Clement and Origen carried me away; the philosophy, not the theological doctrine; and I have drawn out some features of it in my volume, with the zeal and freshness, but with the partiality, of a neophyte. Some portions of their teaching, magnificent in themselves, came like music to my inward ear, as if the response to ideas, which, with little external to encourage them, I had cherished so long. These were based on the mystical or sacramental principle, and spoke of the various Economies or Dispensations of the Eternal. I understood these passages to mean that the exterior world, physical and historical, was but the manifestation to our senses of realities greater than itself. Nature was a parable: Scripture was an allegory: pagan literature, philosophy, and mythology, properly understood, were but a preparation for the Gospel. The Greek poets and sages were in a certain sense prophets; for "thoughts beyond their thought to those high bards were given."[27] There had been a directly divine dispensation granted to the Jews; but there had been in some sense a dispensation carried on in favour of the Gentiles. He who had taken the seed of Jacob for His elect people had not therefore cast the rest of mankind out of His sight. In the fulness of time both Judaism and Paganism had come to nought; the outward framework, which concealed yet suggested the Living Truth, had never been intended to last, and it was dissolving under the beams of the Sun of Justice which shone behind it and through it. The process of change had been slow; it had been done not rashly, but by rule and measure, "at sundry times and in divers manners,"[28] first one

disclosure and then another, till the whole evangelical doctrine was brought into full manifestation. And thus room was made for the anticipation of further and deeper disclosures, of truths still under the veil of the letter, and in their reason to be revealed. The visible world still remains without its divine interpretation; Holy Church in her sacraments and her hierarchical appointments, will remain, even to the end of the world, after all but a symbol of those heavenly facts which fill eternity. Her mysteries are but the expressions in human language of truths to which the human mind is unequal. It is evident how much there was in all this in correspondence with the thoughts which had attracted me when I was young, and with the doctrine which I have already associated with the *Analogy* and the *Christian Year*.

It was, I suppose, to the Alexandrian school and to the early Church, that I owe in particular what I definitely held about the Angels. I viewed them, not only as the ministers employed by the Creator in the Jewish and Christian dispensations, as we find on the face of Scripture, but as carrying on, as Scripture also implies, the Economy of the Visible World. I considered them as the real causes of motion, light, and life, and of those elementary principles of the physical universe, which, when offered in their developments to our senses, suggest to us the notion of cause and effect, and of what are called the laws of nature. This doctrine I have drawn out in my Sermon for Michaelmas day, written in 1831. I say of the Angels, "Every breath of air and ray of light and heat, every beautiful prospect, is, as it were, the skirts of their garments, the waving of the robes of those whose faces see God." Again, I ask what would be the thoughts of a man who, "when examining a flower, or a herb, or a pebble, or a ray of light, which he treats as something so beneath him in the scale of existence, suddenly discovered that he was in the presence of some powerful being who was hidden behind the visible things he was inspecting,—who, though concealing his wise hand, was giving them their beauty, grace, and perfection, as being God's instrument for the purpose,—nay, whose robe and ornaments those objects were, which he was so eager to analyze?" . . .

While I was engaged in writing my work upon the Arians, great events were happening at home and abroad, which brought out into form and passionate expression the various beliefs which had so gradually been winning their way into my mind. Shortly before, there had been a Revolution in France;[29] the Bourbons had been dismissed: and I held that it was unchristian for nations to cast off their

---

[27]**"thoughts . . . were given"**: quoting Keble's poem for "Third Sunday after Lent" from *The Christian Year*.

[28]**"at sundry times . . . manners"**: Hebrews 1:1.

[29]**Revolution in France**: the July Revolution of 1830.

governors, and, much more, sovereigns who had the divine right of inheritance. Again, the great Reform Agitation was going on around me as I wrote. The Whigs had come into power; Lord Grey had told the Bishops to set their house in order, and some of the Prelates had been insulted and threatened in the streets of London. The vital question was, how were we to keep the Church from being liberalized? there was such apathy on the subject in some quarters, such imbecile alarm in others; the true principles of Churchmanship seemed so radically decayed, and there was such distraction in the councils of the Clergy. Blomfield, the Bishop of London of the day, an active and open-hearted man, had been for years engaged in diluting the high orthodoxy of the Church by the introduction of members of the Evangelical body into places of influence and trust. He had deeply offended men who agreed in opinion with myself, by an off-hand saying (as it was reported) to the effect that belief in the Apostolical succession had gone out with the Non-jurors.[30] "We can count you," he said to some of the gravest and most venerated persons of the old school. And the Evangelical party itself, with their late successes, seemed to have lost that simplicity and unworldliness which I admired so much in Milner and Scott. It was not that I did not venerate such men as Ryder, the then Bishop of Lichfield, and others of similar sentiments, who were not yet promoted out of the ranks of the Clergy,[31] but I thought little of the Evangelicals as a class. I thought they played into the hands of the Liberals. With the Establishment thus divided and threatened, thus ignorant of its true strength, I compared that fresh vigorous Power of which I was reading in the first centuries. In her triumphant zeal on behalf of that Primeval Mystery, to which I had had so great a devotion from my youth, I recognized the movement of my Spiritual Mother. "Incessu patuit Dea."[32] The self-conquest of her Ascetics, the patience of her Martyrs, the irresistible determination of her Bishops, the joyous swing of her advance, both exalted and abashed me. I said to myself, "Look on this picture and

on that;"[33] I felt affection for my own Church, but not tenderness; I felt dismay at her prospects, anger and scorn at her do-nothing perplexity. I thought that if Liberalism once got a footing within her, it was sure of the victory in the event. I saw that Reformation principles were powerless to rescue her. As to leaving her, the thought never crossed my imagination; still I ever kept before me that there was something greater than the Established Church, and that that was the Church Catholic and Apostolic, set up from the beginning, of which she was but the local presence and the organ. She was nothing, unless she was this. She must be dealt with strongly, or she would be lost. There was need of a second reformation.

At this time I was disengaged from College duties, and my health had suffered from the labour involved in the composition of my Volume. It was ready for the Press in July, 1832, though not published till the end of 1833. I was easily persuaded to join Hurrell Froude and his Father, who were going to the south of Europe for the health of the former.

We set out in December, 1832. It was during this expedition that my Verses which are in the *Lyra Apostolica*[34] were written;—a few indeed before it, but not more than one or two of them after it. Exchanging, as I was, definite Tutorial work, and the literary quiet and pleasant friendships of the last six years, for foreign countries and an unknown future, I naturally was led to think that some inward changes, as well as some larger course of action, were coming upon me. At Whitchurch, while waiting for the down mail to Falmouth, I wrote the verses about my Guardian Angel, which begin with these words: "Are these the tracks of some unearthly Friend?" and which go on to speak of "the vision" which haunted me:—that vision is more or less brought out in the whole series of these compositions.

I went to various coasts of the Mediterranean; parted with my friends at Rome; went down for the second time to Sicily without companion, at the end of April; and got back to England by Palermo in the early part of July. The strangeness of foreign life threw me back into myself; I found pleasure in historical sites and beautiful scenes, not in men and manners. We kept clear of Catholics throughout our tour. I had a conversation with the Dean of Malta, a most pleasant man, lately dead; but it was about the Fathers,

---

[30]Charles James **Blomfield** (1786–1857): bishop, classicist, and lukewarm Tractarian. **Apostolical succession:** unbroken transfer of Church authority from St. Peter (Matthew 16:18) to the present Pope or (for Anglicans) Archbishop of Canterbury. **Non-jurors:** Anglican clergymen who refused in 1688 to swear allegiance to William and Mary because of their previous oath to the Stuart kings.

[31]Henry **Ryder** (1777–1836): promoted in 1815 to **Bishop** from the rank-and-file **Clergy**.

[32]**Primeval Mystery:** the Trinity. "**Incessu . . . Dea**": Her step showed her to be a goddess (*Aeneid* 1.405, where Venus appears).

[33]"**Look on . . . that**": *Hamlet* 3.4.54.

[34]*Lyra Apostolica:* hymns by Newman and other Tractarians published periodically in the High Church *British Magazine* and then as a book in 1836.

and the Library of the great church. I knew the Abbate Santini, at Rome, who did no more than copy for me the Gregorian tomes. Froude and I made two calls upon Monsignore (now Cardinal) Wiseman[35] at the Collegio Inglese, shortly before we left Rome. Once we heard him preach at a church in the Corso. I do not recollect being in a room with any other ecclesiastics except a Priest at Castro-Giovanni in Sicily, who called on me when I was ill, and with whom I wished to hold a controversy. As to Church Services, we attended the Tenebræ, at the Sestine, for the sake of the Miserere;[36] and that was all. My general feeling was, "All, save the spirit of man, is divine." I saw nothing but what was external; of the hidden life of Catholics I knew nothing. I was still more driven back into myself, and felt my isolation. England was in my thoughts solely, and the news from England came rarely and imperfectly. The Bill for the Suppression of the Irish Sees[37] was in progress, and filled my mind. I had fierce thoughts against the Liberals.

It was the success of the Liberal cause which fretted me inwardly. I became fierce against its instruments and its manifestations. A French vessel was at Algiers; I would not even look at the tricolour. On my return, though forced to stop twenty-four hours at Paris, I kept indoors the whole time, and all that I saw of that beautiful city was what I saw from the Diligence. The Bishop of London had already sounded me as to my filling one of the Whitehall preacherships, which he had just then put on a new footing; but I was indignant at the line which he was taking, and from my Steamer I had sent home a letter declining the appointment by anticipation, should it be offered to me. At this time I was specially annoyed with Dr. Arnold,[38] though it did not last into later years. Some one, I think, asked, in conversation at Rome, whether a certain interpretation of Scripture was Christian? it was answered that Dr. Arnold took it; I interposed, "But is *he* a Christian?" The subject went out of my head at once; when afterwards I was taxed with it, I could

say no more in explanation, than (what I believe was the fact) that I must have had in mind some free views of Dr. Arnold about the Old Testament:——I thought I must have meant, "Arnold answers for the interpretation, but who is to answer for Arnold?" It was at Rome, too, that we began the *Lyra Apostolica* which appeared monthly in the *British Magazine*. The motto shows the feeling of both Froude and myself at the time: we borrowed from M. Bunsen a Homer, and Froude chose the words in which Achilles, on returning to the battle, says, "You shall know the difference, now that I am back again."[39]

Especially when I was left by myself, the thought came upon me that deliverance is wrought, not by the many but by the few, not by bodies but by persons. Now it was, I think, that I repeated to myself the words, which had ever been dear to me from my school days, "Exoriare aliquis!"— now too, that Southey's beautiful poem of *Thalaba*,[40] for which I had an immense liking, came forcibly to my mind. I began to think that I had a mission. There are sentences of my letters to my friends to this effect, if they are not destroyed. When we took leave of Monsignore Wiseman, he had courteously expressed a wish that we might make a second visit to Rome; I said with great gravity, "We have a work to do in England." I went down at once to Sicily, and the presentiment grew stronger. I struck into the middle of the island, and fell ill of a fever at Leonforte. My servant thought that I was dying, and begged for my last directions. I gave them, as he wished; but I said, "I shall not die." I repeated, "I shall not die, for I have not sinned against light, I have not sinned against light." I never have been able quite to make out what I meant.

I got to Castro-Giovanni, and was laid up there for nearly three weeks. Towards the end of May I left for Palermo, taking three days for the journey. Before starting from my inn in the morning of May 26th or 27th, I sat down on my bed, and began to sob violently. My servant, who had acted as my nurse, asked what ailed me. I could only answer him, "I have a work to do in England."

I was aching to get home; yet for want of a vessel I was kept at Palermo for three weeks. I began to visit the

[35]Nicholas **Wiseman** (1802–1865): Rector of the English College in Rome, supporter of the Oxford Movement, leader of Catholics in England after 1850, when he became Archbishop of Westminster.

[36]**Tenebrae**: evening mass, at which was sung a setting of Psalm 51, the Miserere.

[37]**Bill . . . Sees**: to reduce the Anglican Church in predominantly Catholic Ireland, in Newman's view an illegitimate act of state intervention.

[38]**Thomas Arnold** (1795–1842): Oxford liberal theologian and scholar, reforming headmaster of Rugby, father of Matthew Arnold.

[39]**Christian K. J. Bunsen** (1791–1860): Prussian scholar, liberal theologian, and diplomatic representative at the Vatican and later in England. "**You shall know . . . again**": *Iliad* 18.125.

[40]"**Exoriare aliquis!**": Rise up, somebody! (Dido's call for vengeance, *Aeneid* 4.625). *Thalaba the Destroyer* (1801): oriental fantasy by Robert **Southey** (1774–1843), whose romantic epics were endeared to Newman by extravagant moral intensity.

Churches, and they calmed my impatience, though I did not attend any services. I knew nothing of the Presence of the Blessed Sacrament there. At last I got off in an orange boat, bound for Marseilles. Then it was that I wrote the lines, "Lead, kindly light," which have since become well known. We were becalmed a whole week in the Straights of Bonifacio.[41] I was writing verses the whole time of my passage. At length I got to Marseilles and set off for England. The fatigue of travelling was too much for me, and I was laid up for several days at Lyons. At last I got off again, and did not stop night or day, (except a compulsory delay at Paris,) till I reached England, and my mother's house. My brother had arrived from Persia only a few hours before. This was on the Tuesday. The following Sunday, July 14th, Mr. Keble preached the Assize Sermon in the University Pulpit. It was published under the title of "National Apostasy."[42] I have ever considered and kept the day, as the start of the religious movement of 1833. (Chapter 1)

History of My Religious Opinions from 1839 to 1841

And now that I am about to trace, as far as I can, the course of that great revolution of mind, which led me to leave my own home, to which I was bound by so many strong and tender ties, I feel overcome with the difficulty of satisfying myself in my account of it, and have recoiled from the attempt, till the near approach of the day, on which these lines must be given to the world, forces me to set about the task. For who can know himself, and the multitude of subtle influences which act upon him? And who can recollect, at the distance of twenty-five years, all that he once knew about his thoughts and his deeds, and that, during a portion of his life, when, even at the time, his observation, whether of himself or of the external world, was less than before or after, by very reason of the perplexity and dismay which weighed upon him,—when, in spite of the light given to him according to his need amid his darkness, yet a darkness it emphatically was? And who can suddenly gird himself to a new and anxious undertaking, which he might be able indeed to perform well, were full and calm leisure allowed him to look through every thing that he had written, whether in published works or private letters? yet again, granting that calm contemplation of the past, in itself so desirable, who could afford to be leisurely and deliberate,

while he practises on himself a cruel operation, the ripping up of old griefs, and the venturing again upon the *infandum dolorem*[43] of years, in which the stars of this lower heaven were one by one going out? I could not in cool blood, nor except upon the imperious call of duty, attempt what I have set myself to do. It is both to head and heart an extreme trial, thus to analyze what has so long gone by, and to bring out the results of that examination. I have done various bold things in my life: this is the boldest: and, were I not sure I should after all succeed in my object, it would be madness to set about it.

In the spring of 1839 my position in the Anglican Church was at its height. I had supreme confidence in my controversial *status*, and I had a great and still growing success, in recommending it to others. I had in the foregoing autumn been somewhat sore at the Bishop's Charge,[44] but I have a letter which shows that all annoyance had passed from my mind. In January, if I recollect aright, in order to meet the popular clamour against myself and others, and to satisfy the Bishop, I had collected into one all the strong things which they, and especially I, had said against the Church of Rome, in order to their insertion among the advertisements appended to our publications. Conscious as I was that my opinions in religion were not gained, as the world said, from Roman sources, but were, on the contrary, the birth of my own mind and of the circumstances in which I had been placed, I had a scorn of the imputations which were heaped upon me. It was true that I held a large bold system of religion, very unlike the Protestantism of the day, but it was the concentration and adjustment of the statements of great Anglican authorities, and I had as much right to hold it, as the Evangelical, and more right than the Liberal party could show, for asserting their own respective doctrines. As I declared on occasion of Tract 90, I claimed, in behalf of who would in the Anglican Church, the right of holding with Bramhall a comprecation[45] with the Saints, and the Mass all but Transubstantiation with Andrewes, or

---

[41]**Bonifacio:** strait between Sardinia and Corsica.

[42]**"National Apostasy":** see pages161–163 for Keble's sermon.

[43]*infandum dolorem:* unspeakable sorrow (*Aeneid* 2.3).

[44]**Bishop's Charge:** insistence from above that Newman refrain from defending Tract 90, in which he had deliberately interpreted the articles of Anglican belief in a Catholic sense, and that the *Tracts for the Times* be stopped.

[45]**comprecation:** praying *with*, not *to* or *about*. **Transubstantiation:** doctrine that bread and wine at the Mass actually become Christ's body and blood. **Bramhall, Hooker,** and others are 16th- and 17th-century Anglican authorities.

with Hooker that Transubstantiation itself is not a point for Churches to part communion upon, or with Hammond that a General Council, truly such, never did, never shall err in a matter of faith, or with Bull that man had in paradise and lost on the fall, a supernatural habit of grace, or with Thorndike that penance is a propitiation for post-baptismal sin, or with Pearson that the all-powerful name of Jesus is not otherwise given than in the Catholic Church. "Two can play at that," was often in my mouth, when men of Protestant sentiments appealed to the Articles, Homilies, or Reformers; in the sense that, if they had a right to speak loud, I had the liberty to speak out as well as they, and had the means, by the same or parallel appeals, of giving them tit for tat. I thought that the Anglican Church was tyrannized over by a mere party, and I aimed at bringing into effect the promise contained in the motto to the *Lyra*, "They shall know the difference now." I only asked to be allowed to show them the difference. . . .

The Long Vacation of 1839 began early. There had been a great many visitors to Oxford from Easter to Commemoration; and Dr. Pusey's[46] party had attracted attention, more, I think, than in any former year. I had put away from me the controversy with Rome for more than two years. In my *Parochial Sermons* the subject had at no time been introduced: there had been nothing for two years, either in my Tracts or in the *British Critic*, of a polemical character. I was returning, for the Vacation, to the course of reading which I had many years before chosen as especially my own. I have no reason to suppose that the thoughts of Rome came across my mind at all. About the middle of June I began to study and master the history of the Monophysites.[47] I was absorbed in the doctrinal question. This was from about June 13th to August 30th. It was during this course of reading that for the first time a doubt came upon me of the tenableness of Anglicanism. I recollect on the 30th of July mentioning to a friend, whom I had accidentally met, how remarkable the history was; but by the end of August I was seriously alarmed.

I have described in a former work, how the history affected me. My stronghold was Antiquity; now here, in the middle of the fifth century, I found, as it seemed to me, Christendom of the sixteenth and the nineteenth centuries reflected. I saw my face in that mirror, and I was a Monophysite. The Church of the *Via Media* was in the position of the Oriental communion, Rome was, where she now is; and the Protestants were the Eutychians. Of all passages of history, since history has been, who would have thought of going to the sayings and doings of old Eutyches, that *delirus senex*, as (I think) Petavius calls him, and to the enormities of the unprincipled Dioscorus,[48] in order to be converted to Rome!

Now let it be simply understood that I am not writing controversially, but with the one object of relating things as they happened to me in the course of my conversion. With this view I will quote a passage from the account, which I gave in 1850, of my reasonings and feelings in 1839:

> It was difficult to make out how the Eutychians or Monophysites were heretics, unless Protestants and Anglicans were heretics also; difficult to find arguments against the Tridentine[49] Fathers, which did not tell against the Fathers of Chalcedon; difficult to condemn the Popes of the sixteenth century, without condemning the Popes of the fifth. The drama of religion, and the combat of truth and error, were ever one and the same. The principles and proceedings of the Church now, were those of the Church then; the principles and proceedings of heretics then, were those of Protestants now. I found it so,—almost fearfully; there was an awful similitude, more awful, because so silent and unimpassioned, between the dead records of the past and the feverish chronicle of the present. The shadow of the fifth century was on the sixteenth. It was like a spirit rising from the troubled waters of the old world, with the shape and lineaments of the new. The Church then, as now, might be called peremptory and stern, resolute, overbearing, and relentless; and

---

[46]**Long Vacation:** summer break between academic terms. Edward **Pusey** (1800–1882): highly dogmatic and visible Oxford Tractarian.

[47]**Monophysites:** 5th-century heretics who sought compromise between **Eutyches'** extreme view that Christ's divinity and humanity formed "one nature" (Greek *mono-* + *physis*) and Pope **Leo's** denunciation of that view at the Council of **Chalcedon** (see below). For Newman this ancient attempt to steer a middle course or *Via Media* prefigures the current, untenable position of the Anglican Church between Protestantism and Roman Catholicism.

[48]*delirus senex:* crazy old man. **Petavius:** 17th-century French writer on doctrinal history. **Dioscorus:** eastern Patriarch excommunicated for Monophysite heresy.

[49]**Tridentine:** from the Council of Trent (1545–1563), at which the Church of Rome defined its position against the challenge of Protestantism.

heretics were shifting, changeable, reserved, and deceitful, ever courting civil power, and never agreeing together, except by its aid; and the civil power was ever aiming at comprehensions, trying to put the invisible out of view, and substituting expediency for faith. What was the use of continuing the controversy, or defending my position, if, after all, I was forging arguments for Arius or Eutyches, and turning devil's advocate against the much-enduring Athanasius and the majestic Leo? Be my soul with the Saints! and shall I lift up my hand against them? Sooner may my right hand forget her cunning, and wither outright, as his who once stretched it out against a prophet of God! anathema to a whole tribe of Cranmers, Ridleys, Latimers, and Jewels! perish the names of Bramhall, Ussher, Taylor, Stillingfleet, and Barrow[50] from the face of the earth, ere I should do ought but fall at their feet in love and in worship, whose image was continually before my eyes, and whose musical words were ever in my ears and on my tongue!

Hardly had I brought my course of reading to a close, when the *Dublin Review* of that same August was put into my hands, by friends who were more favourable to the cause of Rome than I was myself. There was an article in it on the "Anglican Claim" by Dr. Wiseman. This was about the middle of September. It was on the Donatists,[51] with an application to Anglicanism. I read it, and did not see much in it. The Donatist controversy was known to me for some years, as has appeared already. The case was not parallel to that of the Anglican Church. St. Augustine in Africa wrote against the Donatists in Africa. They were a furious party who made a schism within the African Church, and not beyond its limits. It was a case of Altar against Altar, of two occupants of the same See, as that between the Non-jurors in England and the Established Church; not the case of one Church against another, as of Rome against the Oriental Monophysites. But my friend, an anxiously religious man, now, as then, very dear to me, a Protestant still, pointed out the palmary words of St. Augustine, which were contained

in one of the extracts made in the Review, and which had escaped my observation. "Securus judicat orbis terrarum."[52] He repeated these words again and again, and, when he was gone, they kept ringing in my ears. "Securus judicat orbis terrarum;" they were words which went beyond the occasion of the Donatists: they applied to that of the Monophysites. They gave a cogency to the Article, which had escaped me at first. They decided ecclesiastical questions on a simpler rule than that of Antiquity; nay, St. Augustine was one of the prime oracles of Antiquity; here then Antiquity was deciding against itself. What a light was hereby thrown upon every controversy in the Church! not that, for the moment, the multitude may not falter in their judgment,—not that, in the Arian hurricane, Sees more than can be numbered did not bend before its fury, and fall off from St. Athanasius,—not that the crowd of Oriental Bishops did not need to be sustained during the contest by the voice and the eye of St. Leo; but that the deliberate judgment, in which the whole Church at length rests and acquiesces, is an infallible prescription and a final sentence against such portions of it as protest and secede. Who can account for the impressions which are made on him? For a mere sentence, the words of St. Augustine, struck me with a power which I never had felt from any words before. To take a familiar instance, they were like the "Turn again Whittington" of the chime; or, to take a more serious one, they were like the "Tolle, lege,—Tolle, lege," of the child, which converted St. Augustine himself.[53] "Securus judicat orbis terrarum!" By those great words of the ancient Father, interpreting and summing up the long and varied course of ecclesiastical history, the theory of the *Via Media* was absolutely pulverized.

I became excited at the view thus opened upon me. I was just starting on a round of visits; and I mentioned my state of mind to two most intimate friends: I think to no others. After a while, I got calm, and at length the vivid impression upon my imagination faded away. What I thought about it on reflection, I will attempt to describe presently. I had to determine its logical value, and its bearing upon my

---

[50]**forget her cunning**: Psalm 137:5. **Cranmers . . . Barrow**: 16th- and 17th-century Anglican divines.

[51]**Donatists**: 4th-century African schismatics opposed by St. Augustine (354–430).

[52]**"Securus . . . terrarum"**: The whole world judges securely (that they who separate from the rest of the world are wrong).

[53]Dick **Whittington**: 15th-century Lord Mayor of London who, according to legend, as a runaway boy turned back to his master on hearing the church bells say, "**Turn again**, Whittington." "**Tolle, lege**" (Take up and read): the voice **Augustine** hears in book 8 of his *Confessions*, where on opening the Bible he is converted to Christianity.

duty. Meanwhile, so far as this was certain,—I had seen the shadow of a hand upon the wall. It was clear that I had a good deal to learn on the question of the Churches, and that perhaps some new light was coming upon me. He who has seen a ghost, cannot be as if he had never seen it. The heavens had opened and closed again. The thought for the moment had been, "The Church of Rome will be found right after all." . . . (Chapter 3)

Position of My Mind Since 1845

From the time that I became a Catholic, of course I have no further history of my religious opinions to narrate. In saying this, I do not mean to say that my mind has been idle, or that I have given up thinking on theological subjects; but that I have had no variations to record, and have had no anxiety of heart whatever. I have been in perfect peace and contentment; I never have had one doubt. I was not conscious to myself, on my conversion, of any change, intellectual or moral, wrought in my mind. I was not conscious of firmer faith in the fundamental truths of Revelation, or of more self-command; I had not more fervour; but it was like coming into port after a rough sea; and my happiness on that score remains to this day without interruption.

Nor had I any trouble about receiving those additional articles, which are not found in the Anglican Creed. Some of them I believed already, but not any one of them was a trial to me. I made a profession of them upon my reception with the greatest ease, and I have the same ease in believing them now. I am far of course from denying that every article of the Christian Creed, whether as held by Catholics or by Protestants, is beset with intellectual difficulties; and it is simple fact, that, for myself, I cannot answer those difficulties. Many persons are very sensitive of the difficulties of Religion; I am as sensitive of them as any one; but I have never been able to see a connexion between apprehending those difficulties, however keenly, and multiplying them to any extent, and on the other hand doubting the doctrines to which they are attached. Ten thousand difficulties do not make one doubt, as I understand the subject; difficulty and doubt are incommensurate. There of course may be difficulties in the evidence; but I am speaking of difficulties intrinsic to the doctrines themselves, or to their relations with each other. A man may be annoyed that he cannot work out a mathematical problem, of which the answer is or is not given to him, without doubting that it admits of an answer, or that a certain particular answer is the true one. Of all points of faith, the being of a God is, to my own apprehen-

sion, encompassed with most difficulty, and yet borne in upon our mind with most power.

People say that the doctrine of Transubstantiation is difficult to believe; I did not believe the doctrine till I was a Catholic. I had no difficulty in believing it, as soon as I believed that the Catholic Roman Church was the oracle of God, and that she had declared this doctrine to be part of the original revelation. It is difficult, impossible, to imagine, I grant;—but how is it difficult to believe? Yet Macaulay thought it so difficult to believe, that he had need of a believer in it of talents as eminent as Sir Thomas More,[54] before he could bring himself to conceive that the Catholics of an enlightened age could resist "the overwhelming force of the argument against it." "Sir Thomas More," he says, "is one of the choice specimens of wisdom and virtue; and the doctrine of transubstantiation is a kind of proof charge. A faith which stands that test, will stand any test." But for myself, I cannot indeed prove it, I cannot tell *how* it is; but I say, "Why should it not be? What's to hinder it? What do I know of substance or matter? just as much as the greatest philosophers, and that is nothing at all;"—so much is this the case, that there is a rising school of philosophy now, which considers phenomena to constitute the whole of our knowledge in physics. The Catholic doctrine leaves phenomena alone. It does not say that the phenomena go; on the contrary, it says that they remain; nor does it say that the same phenomena are in several places at once. It deals with what no one on earth knows any thing about, the material substances themselves. And, in like manner, of that majestic Article of the Anglican as well as of the Catholic Creed,—the doctrine of the Trinity in Unity. What do I know of the Essence of the Divine Being? I know that my abstract idea of three is simply incompatible with my idea of one; but when I come to the question of concrete fact, I have no means of proving that there is not a sense in which one and three can equally be predicated of the Incommunicable God.

But I am going to take upon myself the responsibility of more than the mere Creed of the Church; as the parties accusing me are determined I shall do. They say, that now, in that I am a Catholic, though I may not have offences of my own against honesty to answer for, yet, at least, I am answerable for the offences of others, of my co-religionists, of my brother priests, of the Church herself. I am quite

---

[54]**Sir Thomas More** (1477–1535): Catholic martyr to the Anglican Reformation. Newman quotes **Macaulay**'s 1840 review of Ranke's *History of the Popes*.

willing to accept the responsibility; and, as I have been able, as I trust, by means of a few words, to dissipate, in the minds of all those who do not begin with disbelieving me, the suspicion with which so many Protestants start, in forming their judgment of Catholics, viz. that our Creed is actually set up in inevitable superstition and hypocrisy, as the original sin of Catholicism; so now I will proceed, as before, identifying myself with the Church and vindicating it,—not of course denying the enormous mass of sin and error which exists of necessity in that world-wide multi-form Communion,—but going to the proof of this one point, that its system is in no sense dishonest, and that therefore the upholders and teachers of that system, as such, have a claim to be acquitted in their own persons of that odious imputation.

Starting then with the being of a God, (which, as I have said, is as certain to me as the certainty of my own existence, though when I try to put the grounds of that certainty into logical shape I find a difficulty in doing so in mood and figure to my satisfaction,) I look out of myself into the world of men, and there I see a sight which fills me with unspeakable distress. The world seems simply to give the lie to that great truth, of which my whole being is so full; and the effect upon me is, in consequence, as a matter of necessity, as confusing as if it denied that I am in existence myself. If I looked into a mirror, and did not see my face, I should have the sort of feeling which actually comes upon me, when I look into this living busy world, and see no reflexion of its Creator. This is, to me, one of those great difficulties of this absolute primary truth, to which I referred just now. Were it not for this voice, speaking so clearly in my conscience and my heart, I should be an atheist, or a pantheist, or a polytheist when I looked into the world. I am speaking for myself only; and I am far from denying the real force of the argument in proof of a God, drawn from the general facts of human society and the course of history, but these do not warm me or enlighten me; they do not take away the winter of my desolation, or make the buds unfold and the leaves grow within me, and my moral being rejoice. The sight of the world is nothing else than the prophet's scroll, full of "lamentations, and mourning, and woe."[55]

To consider the world in its length and breadth, its various history, the many races of man, their starts, their fortunes, their mutual alienation, their conflicts; and then their ways, habits, governments, forms of worship; their enterprises, their aimless courses, their random achievements and acquirements, the impotent conclusion of long-standing facts, the tokens so faint and broken of a superintending design, the blind evolution of what turn out to be great powers or truths, the progress of things, as if from unreasoning elements, not towards final causes, the greatness and littleness of man, his far-reaching aims, his short duration, the curtain hung over his futurity, the disappointments of life, the defeat of good, the success of evil, physical pain, mental anguish, the prevalence and intensity of sin, the pervading idolatries, the corruptions, the dreary hopeless irreligion, that condition of the whole race, so fearfully yet exactly described in the Apostle's words, "having no hope and without God in the world,"[56]—all this is a vision to dizzy and appal; and inflicts upon the mind the sense of a profound mystery, which is absolutely beyond human solution.

What shall be said to this heart-piercing, reason-bewildering fact? I can only answer, that either there is no Creator, or this living society of men is in a true sense discarded from His presence. Did I see a boy of good make and mind, with the tokens on him of a refined nature, cast upon the world without provision, unable to say whence he came, his birthplace or his family connexions, I should conclude that there was some mystery connected with his history, and that he was one, of whom, from one cause or other, his parents were ashamed. Thus only should I be able to account for the contrast between the promise and the condition of his being. And so I argue about the world;—if there be a God, *since* there is a God, the human race is implicated in some terrible aboriginal calamity. It is out of joint with the purposes of its Creator. This is a fact, a fact as true as the fact of its existence; and thus the doctrine of what is theologically called original sin becomes to me almost as certain as that the world exists, and as the existence of God.

And now, supposing it were the blessed and loving will of the Creator to interfere in this anarchical condition of things, what are we to suppose would be the methods which might be necessarily or naturally involved in His purpose of mercy? Since the world is in so abnormal a state, surely it would be no surprise to me, if the interposition were of necessity equally extraordinary—or what is called miraculous. But that subject does not directly come into the scope of my present remarks. Miracles as evidence, involve a process of reason, or an argument; and of course I am

---

[55]"lamentations . . . woe": Ezekiel 2:10.

[56]"having . . . in the world": Ephesians 2:12.

thinking of some mode of interference which does not immediately run into argument. I am rather asking what must be the face-to-face antagonist, by which to withstand and baffle the fierce energy of passion and the all-corroding, all-dissolving scepticism of the intellect in religious inquiries? I have no intention at all of denying, that truth is the real object of our reason, and that, if it does not attain to truth, either the premiss or the process is in fault; but I am not speaking here of right reason, but of reason as it acts in fact and concretely in fallen man. I know that even the unaided reason, when correctly exercised, leads to a belief in God, in the immortality of the soul, and in a future retribution; but I am considering the faculty of reason actually and historically; and in this point of view, I do not think I am wrong in saying that its tendency is towards a simple unbelief in matters of religion. No truth, however sacred, can stand against it, in the long run; and hence it is that in the pagan world, when our Lord came, the last traces of the religious knowledge of former times were all but disappearing from those portions of the world in which the intellect had been active and had had a career.

And in these latter days, in like manner, outside the Catholic Church things are tending,—with far greater rapidity than in that old time from the circumstance of the age,—to atheism in one shape or other. What a scene, what a prospect, does the whole of Europe present at this day! and not only Europe, but every government and every civilization through the world, which is under the influence of the European mind! Especially, for it most concerns us, how sorrowful, in the view of religion, even taken in its most elementary, most attenuated form, is the spectacle presented to us by the educated intellect of England, France, and Germany! Lovers of their country and of their race, religious men, external to the Catholic Church, have attempted various expedients to arrest fierce wilful human nature in its onward course, and to bring it into subjection. The necessity of some form of religion for the interests of humanity, has been generally acknowledged: but where was the concrete representative of things invisible, which would have the force and the toughness necessary to be a breakwater against the deluge? Three centuries ago the establishment of religion, material, legal, and social, was generally adopted as the best expedient for the purpose, in those countries which separated from the Catholic Church; and for a long time it was successful; but now the crevices of those establishments are admitting the enemy. Thirty years ago, education was relied upon: ten years ago there was a hope that wars would cease for ever, under the influence of commercial enterprise and the reign of the useful and fine arts; but will any one venture to say that there is any thing any where on this earth, which will afford a fulcrum for us, whereby to keep the earth from moving onwards?

The judgment, which experience passes whether on establishments or on education, as a means of maintaining religious truth in this anarchical world, must be extended even to Scripture, though Scripture be divine. Experience proves surely that the Bible does not answer a purpose for which it was never intended. It may be accidentally the means of the conversion of individuals; but a book, after all, cannot make a stand against the wild living intellect of man, and in this day it begins to testify, as regards its own structure and contents, to the power of that universal solvent, which is so successfully acting upon religious establishments.

Supposing then it to be the Will of the Creator to interfere in human affairs, and to make provisions for retaining in the world a knowledge of Himself, so definite and distinct as to be proof against the energy of human scepticism, in such a case,—I am far from saying that there was no other way,—but there is nothing to surprise the mind, if He should think fit to introduce a power into the world, invested with the prerogative of infallibility in religious matters. Such a provision would be a direct, immediate, active, and prompt means of withstanding the difficulty; it would be an instrument suited to the need; and, when I find that this is the very claim of the Catholic Church, not only do I feel no difficulty in admitting the idea, but there is a fitness in it, which recommends it to my mind. And thus I am brought to speak of the Church's infallibility, as a provision, adapted by the mercy of the Creator, to preserve religion in the world, and to restrain that freedom of thought, which of course in itself is one of the greatest of our natural gifts, and to rescue it from its own suicidal excesses. And let it be observed that, neither here nor in what follows, shall I have occasion to speak directly of Revelation in its subject-matter, but in reference to the sanction which it gives to truths which may be known independently of it,—as it bears upon the defence of natural religion. I say, that a power, possessed of infallibility in religious teaching, is happily adapted to be a working instrument, in the course of human affairs, for smiting hard and throwing back the immense energy of the aggressive, capricious, untrustworthy intellect:—and in saying this, as in the other things that I have to say, it must still be recollected that I am all along bearing in mind my main purpose, which is a defence of myself.

I am defending myself here from a plausible charge brought against Catholics, as will be seen better as I proceed. The charge is this:—that I, as a Catholic, not only make profession to hold doctrines which I cannot possibly believe in my heart, but that I also believe in the existence of a power on earth, which at its own will imposes upon men any new set of *credenda*, when it pleases, by a claim to infallibility;[57] in consequence, that my own thoughts are not my own property; that I cannot tell that to-morrow I may not have to give up what I hold to-day, and that the necessary effect of such a condition of mind must be a degrading bondage, or a bitter inward rebellion relieving itself in secret infidelity, or the necessity of ignoring the whole subject of religion in a sort of disgust, and of mechanically saying every thing that the Church says, and leaving to others the defence of it. As then I have above spoken of the relation of my mind towards the Catholic Creed, so now I shall speak of the attitude which it takes up in the view of the Church's infallibility.

And first, the initial doctrine of the infallible teacher must be an emphatic protest against the existing state of mankind. Man had rebelled against his Maker. It was this that caused the divine interposition: and to proclaim it must be the first act of the divinely-accredited messenger. The Church must denounce rebellion as of all possible evils the greatest. She must have no terms with it; if she would be true to her Master, she must ban and anathematize it. This is the meaning of a statement of mine, which has furnished matter for one of those special accusations to which I am at present replying: I have, however, no fault at all to confess in regard to it; I have nothing to withdraw, and in consequence I here deliberately repeat it. I said, "The Catholic Church holds it better for the sun and moon to drop from heaven, for the earth to fail, and for all the many millions on it to die of starvation in extremest agony, as far as temporal affliction goes, than that one soul, I will not say, should be lost, but should commit one single venial sin, should tell one wilful untruth, or should steal one poor farthing without excuse." I think the principle here enunciated to be the mere preamble in the formal credentials of the Catholic Church, as an Act of Parliament might begin with a *"Whereas."* It is because of the intensity of the evil which has possession of mankind, that a suitable antagonist has been provided against it; and the initial act of that divinely-commissioned power is of course to deliver her challenge and to defy the enemy. Such a preamble then gives a mean-

ing to her position in the world, and an interpretation to her whole course of teaching and action.

In like manner she has ever put forth, with most energetic distinctness, those other great elementary truths, which either are an explanation of her mission or give a character to her work. She does not teach that human nature is irreclaimable, else wherefore should she be sent? not, that it is to be shattered and reversed, but to be extricated, purified, and restored; not, that it is a mere mass of hopeless evil, but that it has the promise upon it of great things, and even now, in its present state of disorder and excess, has a virtue and a praise proper to itself. But in the next place she knows and she preaches that such a restoration, as she aims at effecting in it, must be brought about, not simply through certain outward provisions of preaching and teaching, even though they be her own, but from an inward spiritual power or grace imparted directly from above, and of which she is the channel. She has it in charge to rescue human nature from its misery, but not simply by restoring it on its own level, but by lifting it up to a higher level than its own. She recognizes in it real moral excellence though degraded, but she cannot set it free from earth except by exalting it towards heaven. It was for this end that a renovating grace was put into her hands; and therefore from the nature of the gift, as well as from the reasonableness of the case, she goes on, as a further point, to insist, that all true conversion must begin with the first springs of thought, and to teach that each individual man must be in his own person one whole and perfect temple of God, while he is also one of the living stones[58] which build up a visible religious community. And thus the distinctions between nature and grace, and between outward and inward religion, become two further articles in what I have called the preamble of her divine commission.

Such truths as these she vigorously reiterates, and pertinaciously inflicts upon mankind; as to such she observes no half-measures, no economical reserve, no delicacy or prudence. "Ye must be born again,"[59] is the simple, direct form of words which she uses after her Divine Master: "your whole nature must be re-born; your passions, and your affections, and your aims, and your conscience, and your will, must all be bathed in a new element, and reconsecrated to your Maker,— and, the last not the least, your intellect." It was for repeating these points of her teaching in my own way, that certain passages of one of my Volumes have been

---

[57]*credenda:* things to be believed. **infallibility:** authority not expressly vested in the Pope until the first Vatican Council met in 1869—a proceeding hotly debated beforehand and opposed by Newman as inflammatory and untimely.

---

[58]**living stones:** see 1 Peter 2:4–5.

[59]**"Ye . . . born again":** John 3:7.

brought into the general accusation which has been made against my religious opinions. The writer has said that I was demented if I believed, and unprincipled if I did not believe, in my own statement, that a lazy, ragged, filthy, story-telling beggar-woman, if chaste, sober, cheerful, and religious, had a prospect of heaven, such as was absolutely closed to an accomplished statesman, or lawyer, or noble, be he ever so just, upright, generous, honourable, and conscientious, unless he had also some portion of the divine Christian graces;—yet I should have thought myself defended from criticism by the words which our Lord used to the chief priests, "The publicans and harlots go into the kingdom of God before you."[60] And I was subjected again to the same alternative of imputations, for having ventured to say that consent to an unchaste wish was indefinitely more heinous than any lie viewed apart from its causes, its motives, and its consequences: though a lie, viewed under the limitation of these conditions, is a random utterance, an almost outward act, not directly from the heart, however disgraceful and despicable it may be, however prejudicial to the social contract, however deserving of public reprobation; whereas we have the express words of our Lord to the doctrine that "whoso looketh on a woman to lust after her, hath committed adultery with her already in his heart."[61] On the strength of these texts, I have surely as much right to believe in these doctrines which have caused so much surprise, as to believe in original sin, or that there is a supernatural revelation, or that a Divine Person suffered, or that punishment is eternal.

Passing now from what I have called the preamble of that grant of power, which is made to the Church, to that power itself, Infallibility, I premise two brief remarks:— 1. on the one hand, I am not here determining any thing about the essential seat of that power, because that is a question doctrinal, not historical and practical; 2. nor, on the other hand, am I extending the direct subject-matter, over which that power of Infallibility has jurisdiction, beyond religious opinion:—and now as to the power itself.

This power, viewed in its fulness, is as tremendous as the giant evil which has called for it. It claims, when brought into exercise but in the legitimate manner, for otherwise of course it is but quiescent, to know for certain the very meaning of every portion of that Divine Message in detail, which was committed by our Lord to His Apostles. It claims to know its own limits, and to decide what it can de-

termine absolutely and what it cannot. It claims, moreover, to have a hold upon statements not directly religious, so far as this,—to determine whether they indirectly relate to religion, and, according to its own definitive judgment, to pronounce whether or not, in a particular case, they are simply consistent with revealed truth. It claims to decide magisterially, whether as within its own province or not, that such and such statements are or are not prejudicial to the *Depositum*[62] of faith, in their spirit or in their consequences, and to allow them, or condemn and forbid them, accordingly. It claims to impose silence at will on any matters, on controversies, of doctrine, which on its own *ipse dixit*,[63] it pronounces to be dangerous, or inexpedient, or inopportune. It claims that, whatever may be the judgment of Catholics upon such acts, these acts should be received by them with those outward marks of reverence, submission, and loyalty, which Englishmen, for instance, pay to the presence of their sovereign, without expressing any criticism on them on the ground that in their matter they are inexpedient, or in their manner violent or harsh. And lastly, it claims to have the right of inflicting spiritual punishment, of cutting off from the ordinary channels of the divine life, and of simply excommunicating, those who refuse to submit themselves to its formal declarations. Such is the infallibility lodged in the Catholic Church, viewed in the concrete, as clothed and surrounded by the appendages of its high sovereignty: it is, to repeat what I said above, a supereminent prodigious power sent upon earth to encounter and master a giant evil.

And now, having thus described it, I profess my own absolute submission to its claim. I believe the whole revealed dogma as taught by the Apostles, as committed by the Apostles to the Church, and as declared by the Church to me. I receive it, as it is infallibly interpreted by the authority to whom it is thus committed, and (implicitly) as it shall be, in like manner, further interpreted by that same authority till the end of time. I submit, moreover, to the universally received traditions of the Church, in which lies the matter of those new dogmatic definitions which are from time to time made, and which in all times are the clothing and the illustration of the Catholic dogma as already defined. And I submit myself to those other decisions of the Holy See, theological or not, through the organs which it has itself appointed, which, waiving the question of their infallibility, on the lowest ground come to me with a claim to be accepted and obeyed. Also, I consider that, gradually

---

[60]"The publicans . . . before you": Matthew 21:31.

[61]"whoso looketh . . . in his heart": Matthew 5:28.

[62]*Depositum:* doctrine committed to the Church for safekeeping.

[63]*ipse dixit:* say-so.

and in the course of ages, Catholic inquiry has taken certain definite shapes, and has thrown itself into the form of a science, with a method and a phraseology of its own, under the intellectual handling of great minds, such as St. Athanasius, St. Augustine, and St. Thomas;[64] and I feel no temptation at all to break in pieces the great legacy of thought thus committed to us for these latter days.

All this being considered as the profession which I make *ex animo*,[65] as for myself, so also on the part of the Catholic body, as far as I know it, it will at first sight be said that the restless intellect of our common humanity is utterly weighed down, to the repression of all independent effort and action whatever, so that, if this is to be the mode of bringing it into order, it is brought into order only to be destroyed. But this is far from the result, far from what I conceive to be the intention of that high Providence who has provided a great remedy for a great evil,—far from borne out by the history of the conflict between Infallibility and Reason in the past, and the prospect of it in the future. The energy of the human intellect "does from opposition grow;" it thrives and is joyous, with a tough elastic strength, under the terrible blows of the divinely-fashioned weapon, and is never so much itself as when it has lately been overthrown. It is the custom with Protestant writers to consider that, whereas there are two great principles in action in the his-

---

[64]**St. Athanasius** (293–373): theologian of the Alexandrian Church. **St. Thomas** Aquinas (1224–1274): leading medieval theologian.

[65]*ex animo*: from the soul, sincerely.

tory of religion, Authority and Private Judgment, they have all the Private Judgment to themselves, and we have the full inheritance and the superincumbent oppression of Authority. But this is not so; it is the vast Catholic body itself, and it only, which affords an arena for both combatants in that awful, never-dying duel. It is necessary for the very life of religion, viewed in its large operations and its history, that the warfare should be incessantly carried on. Every exercise of Infallibility is brought out into act by an intense and varied operation of the Reason, both as its ally and as its opponent, and provokes again, when it has done its work, a re-action of Reason against it; and, as in a civil polity the State exists and endures by means of the rivalry and collision, the encroachments and defeats of its constituent parts, so in like manner Catholic Christendom is no simple exhibition of religious absolutism, but presents a continuous picture of Authority and Private Judgment alternately advancing and retreating as the ebb and flow of the tide;—it is a vast assemblage of human beings with wilful intellects and wild passions, brought together into one by the beauty and the Majesty of a Superhuman Power,—into what may be called a large reformatory or training-school, not as if into a hospital or into a prison, not in order to be sent to bed, not to be buried alive, but (if I may change my metaphor) brought together as if into some moral factory, for the melting, refining, and moulding, by an incessant, noisy process, of the raw material of human nature, so excellent, so dangerous, so capable of divine purposes. . . . (Chapter 5)

1864

WILLIAM BARNES

(1801–1886)

William Barnes was born, lived, and died in the Dorsetshire Vale of Blackmore, the most placid corner of Britain's most picturesque rural county. A farm boy, he ran a country school until 1835, moving thereafter to the county seat, Dorchester, where he continued teaching into his sixties. He married and raised a family, was ordained a curate, and earned a divinity degree from Cambridge. He also published a good deal of journalistic, creative, and scholarly work, the most important being *Poems of Rural Life in the Dorset Dialect* (1844, 1859, 1862), which won the esteem of major contemporaries from Alfred Tennyson to Thomas Hardy and Gerard Manley Hopkins by their sweetness of feeling and strength of craft. Like Robert Burns and other modern poets with pronounced regional roots, Barnes was fluent in what he called National English—the very term a pointed reminder that the genteel London intonation which prevailed during the nineteenth century was nothing but a dialect with clout—yet he wrote most freely and precisely in the accents of his Dorset home. His best work fuses familiar emotion both with an unusually direct presentation of imagery and with a special feeling for language itself: when the words that enumerate a landscape or record a loss belong to a dwindling dialect, those words share the precious fragility of the way of life they bespeak. Thus in "The Turnstile" the moving reticence of a bereaved father is heightened by the reader's awareness of other losses in store: loss of footpaths and country ways, loss of the folk animism that can glimpse in a homely turnstile the sympathetic ache of empty "spreaden eärmes," loss of the speech in which such a vision finds unaffected voice.

The poet's cherishing of the empowered, endangered word led Barnes afield into translations from Italian and Biblical Greek and gave him considerable self-taught expertise in Welsh and Anglo-Saxon. His armchair philology is represented here by brief excerpts from *An Outline of English Speech-Craft* (1878), a work whose crackpot charm stands out at once, but whose perennially poetic concern with right naming it would be a mistake to dismiss. The prefatory offer of a guided tour through "our village," on the lookout for "many things of which we want to speak every day" but for which "our Queen's English" wants the words, is finally the same offer that Barnes's poems make: to behold, along the byways of language and culture, the overlooked places where meaning dwells. In his fascination with a disappearing local dialect, Barnes resembles those of his contemporaries who collected folk songs at home or curious customs and artifacts from "primitive" cultures abroad, and he anticipates the arts and crafts movement theorized by John Ruskin and spearheaded by William Morris later in the century. All these Victorian activities were part of a widespread Romantic resistance to the centralized, rationalized, homogeneous culture that industrial society was in the process of producing.

Travelers to Barnes's Dorset who anticipate dialect trouble can practice on the two versions of "Shellbrook." Most of the trouble disappears if one just reads s for the Dorset z, ʃ for v, -ing for -en, and lets the umlaut vowels ä, ӳ, and so on reveal how many diphthongs (long vowels squeezed double) our own dialects contain.

The Hwomestead

If I had all the land my zight
    Can overlook vrom Chalwell hill,
Vrom Sherborn left to Blanvord right,
    Why I could be but happy still.
An' I be happy wi' my spot
O' freehold ground an' mossy cot,
An' shoulden get a better lot
    If I had all my will.

My orcha'd's wide, my trees be young;
    An' they do bear such heavy crops,   10
Their boughs, lik' onion-rwopes a-hung,
    Be all a-trigg'd to year,[1] wi' props.
I got some geärden groun' to dig,
A parrock,[2] an' a cow an' pig;
I got zome cider vor to swig,
    An' eäle o' malt an' hops.

I'm landlord o' my little farm,
    I'm king 'ithin my little pleäce;
I don't break laws, an' don't do harm,
    An' ben't a-feär'd o' noo man's feäce.   20
When I'm a-cover'd wi' my thatch,
Noo man do deäre to lift my latch;
Where honest han's do shut the hatch,[3]
    There fear do leäve the pleäce.

My lofty elem trees do screen
    My brown-ruf'd house, an' here below,
My geese do strut athirt[4] the green,
    An' hiss an' flap their wings o' snow;
As I do walk along a rank
Ov apple trees, or by a bank,   30
Or zit upon a bar or plank,
    To zee how things do grow.

1844

---

[1]**a-trigg'd to year**: supported this year.

[2]**parrock**: paddock, pen.

[3]**hatch**: waist-high gate.

[4]**athirt**: athwart, across.

The Väices That Be Gone

When evenèn sheädes o' trees do hide
A body by the hedge's zide,
An' twitt'rèn birds, wi' playsome flight,
Do vlee to roost at comèn night,
Then I do saunter out o' zight
    In orcha'd, where the pleäce woonce rung
    Wi' laughs a-laugh'd an' zongs a-zung
        By väices that be gone.

There's still the tree that bore our swing,
An' others where the birds did zing;   10
But long-leav'd docks do overgrow
The groun' we trampled beäre below,
Wi' merry skippèns to an' fro
    Bezide the banks, where Jim did zit
    A-playen o' the clarinit
        To väices that be gone.

How mother, when we us'd to stun
Her head wi' all our naïsy fun,
Did wish us all a-gone vrom hwome:
An' now that zome be dead, an' zome   20
A-gone, an' all the pleäce is dum',
    How she do wish, wi' useless tears,
    To have ageän about her ears
        The väices that be gone.

Vor all the maïdens an' the bwoys
But I, be marri'd off all woys,
Or dead an' gone; but I do bide
At hwome, alwone, at mother's zide,
An' often, at the evenèn-tide,
    I still do saunter out, wi' tears,   30
    Down drough the orcha'd, where my ears
        Do miss the väices gone.

1844

The Child an' the Mowers

O, aye! they had woone child bezide,
    An' a finer your eyes never met,
'Twer a dear little fellow that died
    In the zummer that come wi' such het;[1]

---

[1]**het**: heat. Based on an actual occurrence in Barnes' neighborhood.

By the mowers, too thoughtless in fun,
    He wer then a-zent off vrom our eyes,
Vrom the light ov the dew-dryèn zun,—
    Aye! vrom days under blue-hollow'd skies.

He went out to the mowers in meäd,
    When the zun wer a-rose to his height,   10
An' the men wer a-swingèn the sneäd,[2]
    Wi' their eärms in white sleeves, left an' right;
An' out there, as they rested at noon,
    O! they drench'd en vrom eäle-horns[3] too deep,
Till his thoughts wer a-drown'd in a swoon;
    Aye! his life wer a-smother'd in sleep.

Then they laid en there-right on the ground,
    On a grass-heap, a-zweltren wi' het,
Wi' his heäir all a-wetted around
    His young feäce, wi' the big drops o' zweat;   20
In his little left palm he'd a-zet,
    Wi' his right hand, his vore-vinger's tip,
As vor zome'hat he woulden vorget,—
    Aye! zome thought that he woulden let slip.

Then they took en in hwome to his bed,
    An' he rose vrom his pillow noo mwore,
Vor the curls on his sleek little head
    To be blown by the wind out o' door.
Vor he died while the haÿ russled grey
    On the staddle[4] so leätely begun;   30
Lik' the mown-grass a-dried by the day,—
    Aye! the zwath-flow'r's a-killed by the zun.

                       1862

~

The Turnstile

Ah! sad wer we as we did peäce
The wold church road, wi' downcast feäce,
The while the bells, that mwoan'd so deep
Above our child a-left asleep,
Wer now a-zingèn all alive
Wi' tother bells to meäke the vive.[1]

But up at woone pleäce we come by,
'Twer hard to keep woone's two eyes dry;
On Steän-cliff road, 'ithin the drong,[2]
Up where, as vo'k do pass along,   10
The turnèn stile, a-païnted white,
Do sheen by day an' show by night.
Vor always there, as we did goo
To church, thik stile did let us drough,[3]
Wi' spreaden eärms that wheel'd to guide
Us each in turn to tother zide.
An' vu'st ov all the traïn he took
My wife, wi' winsome gaït an' look;
An' then zent on my little maïd,
A-skippèn onward, overjaÿ'd   20
To reach ageän the pleäce o' pride,
Her comely mother's left han' zide.
An' then, a-wheelèn roun', he took
On me, 'ithin his third white nook.
An' in the fourth, a-sheäkèn wild,
He zent us on our giddy child.
But eesterday he guided slow
My downcast Jenny, vull o'woe,
An' then my little maïd in black,
A-walkèn softly on her track;   30
An' after he'd a-turn'd ageän,
To let me goo along the leäne,
He had noo little bwoy to vill
His last white eärms, an' they stood still.

                       1862

~

Shellbrook

When out by Shellbrook, round by stile and tree,
With longer days and sunny hours come on,
With spring and all its sunny showers come on,
With May and all its shining flowers come on,
How merry, young with young would meet in glee.

And there, how we in merry talk went by
The foam below the river bay, all white,

---

[2]**sneäd**: scythe blade.

[3]**en**: him. **eäle-horns**: ale-horns.

[4]**staddle**: lower part of a haystack.

[1]**vive**: happy sound.

---

[2]**drong**: narrow lane.

[3]**thik**: that same. **drough**: through.

And blossom on the green-leav'd may, all white,
And chalk beside the dusty way, all white,
Where glitt'ring water match'd with blue the sky.   10

Or else in winding paths and lanes, along
The timb'ry hillocks, sloping steep, we roam'd;
Or down the dells and dingles deep we roam'd;
Or by the bending brook's wide sweep we roam'd
On holidays, with merry laugh or song.

But now, the frozen churchyard wallings keep
The patch of tower-shaded ground, all white,
Where friends can find the frosted mound, all white
With turfy sides upswelling round, all white
With young offsunder'd from the young in sleep.   20
1862

Shellbrook [Dorset]¹

Then out at Shellbrook, roun' by stile an' tree,
Wi' longer days an' zunny hours a-come,
Wi' spring an' all the zunny show'rs a-come,
Wi' Maÿ an' all its sheenèn flow'rs a-come,
How sweet vor young wi' young to meet in glee.

An' there how we in merry talk did goo
By foam below the river baÿ, all white,
By blossom on the green-leaved Maÿ, all white,
By chalk bezide the dousty waÿ, all white,
Where glitt'rèn waters match'd the sky wi' blue.   10

Or else in windèn paths by vield or drong,²
We over knaps³ a-slopèn steep did wind,
Or down the dells a-zinkèn deep did wind,
Or where the bendèn brook did zweep did wind,
All young wi' young in merry laugh or zong.

But now the winter-vrozen churchyard wall do keep
The plot o' tower-sheäded ground all white,
Where friends can vind the vrosted mound, all white,
Wi' turf a-zwellèn up so round, all white,
Wi' young a-sunder'd vrom the young in sleep.   20
1868 ?   *1962*

---

¹Barnes published "Shellbrook" only in its National English
form, leaving this dialect version in manuscript.

²**drong**: narrow lane.

³**knaps**: hillocks.

---

from An Outline of English Speech-Craft

— FORE-SAY¹ —

This little book was not written to win prize or praise; but it
is put forth as one small trial, weak though it may be, towards the upholding of our own strong old Anglo-Saxon
speech, and the ready teaching of it to purely English minds
by their own tongue.

Speech was shapen of the breath-sounds of speakers,
for the ears of hearers, and not from speech-tokens (letters)
in books, for men's eyes, though it is a great happiness that
the words of man can be long holden and given over to the
sight; and therefore I have shapen my teaching as that of a
speech of breath-sounded words, and not of lettered ones;
and though I have, of course, given my thoughts in a book,
for those whom my voice cannot reach, I believe that the
teaching matter of it may all be put forth to a learner's mind,
and readily understood by him, without book or letters. So,
for consonants and vowels, as letters, I put breath-pennings
and free-breathings,² and these names would be good for
any speech, of the lettering of which a learner might know
nothing. On the grounds here given, I have not begun with
orthography, the writing or spelling of our speech, or of any
other, while as yet the teaching or learning of the speech itself is unbegun.

I have tried to teach English by English, and so have
given English words for most of the lore-words (scientific
terms), as I believe they would be more readily and more
clearly understood, and, since we can better keep in mind
what we do than what we do not understand, they would
be better remembered. There is, in the learning of that
charmingly simple and yet clear speech, pure Persian, now
much mingled with Arabic, a saddening check; for no
sooner does a learner come to the time-words³ than he is

---

¹**Fore-say**: prologue. In this book Barnes practices what he
preaches, reclaiming or coining Saxon versions of the school terms
derived from Latin and Greek. To the coinages glossed in the text
or notes may be added a few others: mark-word (adjective), time-
taking (clause), mate-penning (alliteration), twy-meaning (ambiguity), overcarrying (metaphor), heads of matter (table of contents),
clue to matters handled (index).

²**breath-pennings**: consonants, which "pen" (confine) the spoken flow of **free-breathings** (vowels).

³**time-words**: verbs.

told that he should learn, what is then put before him, an outline of Arabic Grammar. And there are tokens that, ere long, the English youth will want an outline of the Greek and Latin tongues ere he can well understand his own speech. . . .

To any friend who has ever asked me whether I do not know some other tongues beside English, my answer has been "No; I do not know English itself." How many men do? And how should I know all of the older English, and the mighty wealth of English words which the English Dialect Society[4] have begun to bring forth; words that are not all of them other shapes of our words of book-English, or words of their very meanings, but words of meanings which dictionaries of book-English should, but cannot give, and words which should be taken in hundreds (by careful choice) into our Queen's English? If a man would walk with me through our village, I could show him many things of which we want to speak every day, and for which we have words of which Johnson[5] knew nothing.

Some have spoken of cultivated languages as differing from uncultivated ones, and of the reducing of a speech to a grammatical form.

What is the meaning of "cultivate" as a time word about a speech? The Latin dictionary does not help us to its meaning, and it might be that of the French *cultiver*, from which we should have, by the wonted changes, to *cultive*. The Romans said *colere deum* and *colere agrum*,[6] but not *agrum cultivare*; and we may believe that *colo*, with *deus* or *ager*, bore the same meaning, "to keep or hold (with good care)," and a speech is cultivated by the speaking as well as by the writing of it, and a speech which is sounding over a whole folkland every moment of the day cannot be uncultivated. "Not with good care," it may be said. Yes; most people speak as well as they can, as they write as well as they can, from the utterer of a fine rede-speech (oration), and the clergyman who gives unwritten sermons, down to the lowly maiden who dresses as finely as she can; and to

try to dress herself well is a token that she will try to express herself well.

King Finow, of the Tonga Islands, gave a fine speech, as Mr. Mariner[7] tells us, at his coming to the throne; and it may be well said that he made it, as he had made it in thought, ere he came to the meeting.

What is meant by the reducing of a speech to a grammatical form, or to grammar, is not very clear. If a man would write a grammar of a speech, of which there is yet none, what could he do but show it forth as it is in the shape which its best speakers over the land hold to be its best? To hold that a tongue had no shape, or a bad one, ere a grammar of it was written, seems much like saying that a man had no face, or a bad one, till his likeness was taken.

— SPEECH-TRIMMING —

The putting of speech into trim; *trim* being a truly good form or state. To *trim* a shrub, a bonnet, or a boat, is to put it into trim.

The first care in speech-trimming is that we should use words which give most clearly the meaning and thoughts of our mind, though it is not likely that unclear thought will find a clear outwording; and either of the two, as clear or unclear, helps to clearen or bemuddle the other.

With most English minds, and with all who have not learned the building of Latin and Greek words, English ones may be used with fewer mistakes of meaning than would words from those tongues; though Englishmen should get a clearer insight into English word-building ere they could hope to keep English words to their true sundriness of meaning.

The so-seeming miswordings (solœcisms)[8] of writers in the Latinised and Greekish speech-trimming are not uncommon or unmarkworthy. . . .

Some say "Mrs. A. has had *twins*," or "Alfred was one of *twins*." A twin is a *twain*, a *two*, or a couple of things of the same name or kind; and twins of children must be at least four. I should say "Alfred was one of *a* twin." In the latter case it would be correct to say "There is *one* or a *twain* of fat men," &c., in which *is* would match both. . . .

[4]**English Dialect Society**: organization whose occasional publications culminated in a 6-volume dictionary issued between 1898 and 1905.

[5]Samuel **Johnson** (1709–1784): author and critic whose *Dictionary of the English Language* (1755) was important in standardizing and stabilizing modern English.

[6]*colere deum*: to revere a god. *colere agrum*: to till a field.

[7]William **Mariner** (1791–1853): author of *An Account of the Natives of the Tonga Islands in the South Pacific Ocean, with an Original Grammar and Vocabulary of Their Language* (1827).

[8]**soloecisms**: linguistic improprieties.

— THE GOODNESS OF A SPEECH —

The goodness of a speech should be sought in its clearness to the hearing and mind, clearness of its breath-sounds, and clearness of meaning in its words; in its fulness of words for all the things and time-takings which come, with all their sundrinesses, under the minds of men of the speech, in their common life; in sound-sweetness to the ear, and glibness to the tongue. As to fulness, the speech of men who know thoroughly the making of its words may be fullened from its own roots and stems, quite as far as has been fullened Greek or German, so that they would seldom feel a stronger want of a foreign word than was felt by those men who, having the words *rail* and *way*, made the word *railway* instead of calling it *chemin de fer*, or, going to the Latin, *via ferrea*,[9] or than Englishmen felt with *steam* and *boat*, to go to the Greeks for the name of the *steamboat*, for which Greek had no name at all. The fulness of English has not risen at the rate of the inbringing of words from other tongues, since many new words have only put out as many old ones, as:—

immediately,   anon,

(no saving of time here),

ignite,   kindle,
annual,   yearly,
machine,   jinny. . . .

There came out in print some time ago a statement wonderful to me, that it had been found that the poor landfolk of one of our shires had only about two hundred words in their vocabulary, with a hint that Dorset rustics were not likely to be more fully worded. There can be shown to any writer two hundred thing-names, known to every man and woman of our own village, for things of the body and dress of a labourer, without any mark-words, or time-words, or others, and without leaving the man for his house, or garden, or the field, or his work.

1878

---

[9] *chemin de fer, via ferrea:* French and Latin for "iron road."

HARRIET MARTINEAU

(1802–1876)

Harriet Martineau, author of many books and hundreds of essays, was the most prominent female public intellectual in early Victorian England. She believed fervently in equality and made it her business to speak out for the oppressed: slaves, the poor, the disabled, servants, children, and women. Her moral courage, social sympathies, and intellectual range and rigor won the admiration of many who disliked her radical views.

Martineau was born the sixth of eight children in Norwich, where her father was a manufacturer. Her parents tried to educate their daughters as well as their sons so that they could, if necessary, support themselves. For a few years Martineau attended an unusually good day school that was primarily for boys. She also read voraciously and studied systematically in philosophy, Latin, Biblical commentaries, and other subjects. By the age of sixteen severe deafness had isolated her even within her family and made social intercourse difficult, and throughout life she suffered from severe bouts of illness. But the collapse of the family business after her father's death when she was in her twenties forced her to exert herself effectually to earn a living, and she became a professional writer.

Her success began with *Illustrations of Political Economy* (1832–1833), a series of short sketches designed to teach working-class readers how to live in accordance with the harsh laissez-faire economic principles of Adam Smith. By 1834 ten thousand copies a month were being sold—an enormous number for that time—and Martineau was accepted as an authority on the subject. In later years she modified her extreme laissez-faire principles, accepting the need for state intervention in matters of public health, education, and the welfare of children, but she never lost her belief in the paramount value of freedom. She also retained her belief in the "greatest happiness principle" of utilitarianism: the idea that a society should be measured by the amount of human happiness it produces.

The success of her *Political Economy* pamphlets enabled her to set out in 1834 on a two-year tour of America. She was determined to avoid the haphazard generalizations of ordinary tourists, and on her way to America began drafting *How to Observe Morals and Manners*, in which she outlined the beginnings of a science of sociology. She took detailed notes as she travelled, and she tried to see as wide as possible a range of people and institutions, to examine the moral system underlying the facts she observed, and to avoid cultural bias. In America, she liked the egalitarian behavior that offended other English travelers, but her commitments to democracy, equality, and freedom were often affronted. She had already published fiery praise of the abolition movement, and she detested not only slavery in the South but racial prejudice in the North. She was shocked, too, by the treatment of American Indians. She arrived to find herself famous—she was invited to the White House and had dinner with former President James Madison—but her continued support of the abolitionists sometimes brought social ostracism and physical danger. Her travels produced two books, a systematic analytical account called *Society in America* (1837) and the more touristic *Retrospect of Western Travel* (1838).

The diversity of her writing was as prodigious as its quantity. She wrote two novels: *Deerbrook* (1839), set in an English village and modeled on Jane Austen, and *The Hour and the Man* (1841), a celebration of François Toussaint-L'Ouverture (1744–1803), the black hero of the Haitian slave rebellion of 1791. She wrote a history of England from 1816 to 1846 (published 1849–1850) that sees the immediate past as part of an ongoing movement of ever-increasing liberty, democracy, and human happiness. In two books about India she warned against expanding British rule or imposing British customs and beliefs abroad. Whatever happened to her, she wrote about. Her frequently reprinted "Letter to the Deaf" draws on her own experience to give advice to the disabled, and five years as a house-bound invalid produced among other works a volume of practical and moral advice, *Life in the Sickroom* (1843). The essay on domestic service reprinted here treats this humble, everyday subject with her habitual attentive seriousness and sets forth for the mistress's edification the point of view of the maid. As in this essay, she wrote frequently about women's lives, but although she was a strong believer in women's rights she kept somewhat aloof from the feminist movement. She gave a higher priority to the general extension of the franchise than to extending it to women. If women were adequately educated, she thought, they would find themselves able to "obtain whatever they show themselves fit for."

Perhaps her boldest publication was *Eastern Life Present and Past* (1848), written after a journey to the Middle East during which she observed social and natural phenomena and reflected on the origins of Christianity. Christianity, she concluded, was based on Egyptian legends, not historical facts. Raised as a Unitarian (that is, a believer in Christianity but not in the divinity of Christ), she had been fervent in her devotion if increasingly rationalistic in her belief, but she now ceased to believe either in a divinity as conventionally understood or in personal immortality. When she reported the results of her inquiry in her usual forthright fashion, reviewers were appalled and some of her neighbors stopped speaking to her.

In 1855 when she thought she was dying she wrote her *Autobiography*, which was published after her death two decades later. Her sympathetic attention to childhood here and elsewhere is part of a trend that accelerated throughout the nineteenth century; her childish experiences of loneliness and moral oppression recall scenes from Victorian novels. Although she lacks analytical tools such as have become second nature to post-Freudian readers, she records dreams and apparently nonsensical memories in the confidence that these are significant psychological data. The vividness of her early recollections may be due to the fact that she drew on versions written as early as 1831, and the book as a whole shows her training in the presentation of observed facts, her practice of taking herself as one among many objects for observation and analysis, and her habitual struggle to represent herself truthfully, at whatever sacrifice of vanity.

Unlike her close contemporary the parliamentary insider Thomas Babington Macaulay, for whom British history was also a triumphant tale of progress, Martineau wrote from the periphery of social, political, and cultural power. Her sympathies turned instinctively to the underdog. Determined to tell the truth at any cost, she was often mocked and reviled. If she was praised for the masculine power of her intellect, she was also scorned as unfeminine. But she declared herself "probably the happiest single woman in England." "My business in life," she said in her *Autobiography*, "has been to think and learn, and to speak out with absolute freedom what I have thought and learned," and she rejoiced in the intellectual emancipation by which she became "a free rover on the broad, bright, breezy common of the universe."

from Letter to the Deaf

MY DEAR COMPANIONS,

The deafness under which I have now for some years past suffered, has become, from being an almost intolerable grievance, so much less of one to myself and my friends, than such a deprivation usually is, that I have often of late longed to communicate with my fellow-sufferers, in the hope of benefiting, by my experience, some to whom the discipline is newer than to myself.

I have for some time done what I could in private conversation; but it never occurred to me to print what I had to say, till it was lately not only suggested to me, but urged upon me as a duty. I adopt this method as the only means of reaching you all; and I am writing with the freedom which I should use in a private letter to each of you. It does not matter what may be thought of anything I now say, or of my saying it in this manner, by those who do not belong to our fraternity. I write merely for those who are deeply concerned in the subject of my letter. The time may come when I shall tell the public some of our secrets, for other purposes than those which are now before me. At present I address only you; and as there is no need for us to tell our secrets to one another, there may be little here to interest any but ourselves. I am afraid I have nothing to offer to those of you who have been deaf from early childhood. Your case is very different from mine, as I have reason to know through my intimacy with a friend who became deaf at five years old. Before I was so myself, I had so prodigious a respect for this lady, (which she well deserves,) that if she could have heard the lightest whisper in which a timid girl ever spoke, I should not have dared to address her. Circumstances directed her attention towards me, and she began a correspondence, by letter, which flattered me, and gave me courage to converse with her when we met, and our acquaintance grew into an intimacy which enabled me at last to take a very bold step;— to send her a sonnet, in allusion to our common infirmity; my deafness being then new, and the uppermost thing in my mind day and night. I was surprised and mortified at her not seeming to enter into what I had no doubt in the world must touch her very nearly; but I soon understood the reason. When we came to compare our experiences, we were amused to find how differently we felt, and had always felt, about our privation. Neither of us, I believe, much envies the other, though neither of us pretends to strike the balance of evil. She had suffered the most privations, and I the most pain.

Nothing can be more different than the two cases necessarily are. Nine-tenths of my miseries arose from false shame; and, instead of that false shame, the early deaf entertain themselves with a sort of pride of singularity, and usually contrive to make their account of this, as of other infirmities, by obtaining privileges and indulgences, for which they care much more than for advantages which they have never known and cannot appreciate. My friend and I have principles, major and minor, on which our methods of managing our infirmity are founded; but some of the minor principles, and all the methods, are as different as might be expected from the diversity of the experience which has given rise to them. Nothing can be better for her than her own management, and, of course, I think the same of my own for myself, or I should change it. Before I dismiss this lady, I must mention that I am acquainted with several deaf ladies; so that no one but herself and our two families can know whom I have been referring to.

I am afraid some of you may be rather surprised at the mention of plans, and methods, and management,—for, alas! we are but too apt to shrink from regularly taking in hand our own case. We are left to our own weakness in this respect. We can have but little help,—and we usually have none, but much hinderance. I do not mean by this, to find any fault with our neighbours. I have met with too much sympathy, (as far as sympathy is possible,) with too much care, and generosity, and tenderness, to have the least inclination to complain of any body connected with me. I only mean that this very tenderness is hurtful to us in as far as it encourages us to evade our enemy, instead of grappling with it; to forget our infirmity, from hour to hour, if we can, and to get over the present occasion somehow, without thinking of the next. This would be considered a strange way of meeting any other kind of evil and its consequences in our case are most deplorable. If we see that the partially deaf are often unscrupulous about truth, inquisitive, irritable or morose, suspicious, low-spirited, or ill-mannered, it is owing to this. It is impossible for *us* to deny that if principles are ever needed, if methods are ever of use as supports and guides, it must be in a case where each of us must stand alone in the midst of temptations and irritations which beset us every hour, and against which no defence of habit has been set up, and no bond of companionship can strengthen us. What these temptations and irritations are, we all know:—the almost impossibility of not seeming to hear when we do not,—the persuasion that people are taking advantage of us in what they say,—that they are discussing us, or laughing at us,—that they do not care for us as long as they are merry,—that the friend who takes the pains to talk to us might make us less conspicuous if he would,—the vehement desire that we might be let alone, and the sense of neglect if too long let alone; all these, absurd and wicked fancies as they are seen to be when fairly set down, have beset us all in our time; have they not? For my own part, though I am never troubled with them now, I have so vivid a remembrance of them all, that I believe a thousand years would not weaken the impression. Surely that degree of suffering which lashes us into a temporary misanthropy when our neighbours are happiest, which makes us fly to our chambers, and lock ourselves in, to hide the burning tears which spring at the mirth of those we love best, which seduces us into falsehood or thanklessness to God and man, is enough to justify and require the most careful fixing of principles, and framing of methods. We might as well let our hearts and minds—our happiness—take their chance without discipline in this.

The first thing to be done is to fix upon our principle. This is easy enough. To give the least possible pain to others is the right principle: how to apply it requires more consideration. Let me just observe, that we are more inexcusable in forsaking our principle here than in any other case, and than the generality of people are in the generality of cases. Principles are usually forsaken from being forgotten,—from the occasion for them not being perceived. We have no such excuse while beginning to act upon our principle. We cannot forget,—we cannot fail to perceive the occasion, for five minutes together, that we spend in society. By the time that we become sufficiently at ease to be careless, habit may, if we choose, have grown up to support our principle, and we may be safe.

Our principle requires that we should boldly review our case, and calmly determine for ourselves what we will give up, and what struggle to retain. It is a miserable thing to get on without a plan from day to day, nervously watching whether our infirmity lessens or increases, or choosing to take for granted that we shall be rid of it; or hopelessly and indolently giving up every thing but a few selfish gratifications, or weakly refusing to resign what we can no longer enjoy. We must ascertain the probability for the future, if we can find physicians humane enough to tell us the truth: and where it cannot be ascertained, we must not delay making provision for the present. The greatest difficulty here arises from the mistaken kindness of friends. The physician had rather not say, as mine said to me, "I consider yours a bad case." The parent entreats to be questioned about any thing that passes; brothers and sisters wish that music should be kept up; and, what is remarkable, every body has a vast deal of advice to give, if the subject be fairly mentioned; though every body helps, by false tenderness, to make the subject too sacred an one to be touched upon. We sufferers are the persons to put an end to all this delusion and mismanagement. Advice must go for nothing with us in a case where nobody is qualified to advise. We must cross-question our physician, and hold him to it till he has told us all. We must destroy the sacredness of the subject, by speaking of it ourselves; not perpetually and sentimentally, but, when occasion arises, boldly, cheerfully, and as a plain matter of fact. When every body about us gets to treat it as a matter of fact, our daily difficulties are almost gone; and when we have to do with strangers, the simple, cheerful declaration, "I am very deaf," removes almost all trouble. . . .

How much less pain there is in calmly estimating the enjoyments from which we must separate ourselves, or bravely saying, for once and for ever, "Let them go," than in feeling them waste and dwindle, till their very shadows escape from our grasp! With the best management, there is quite enough, for some of us, of this wasting and dwindling, when we find, at the close of each season, that we are finally parting with something, and at the beginning of each that we have lost something since the last. We miss first the song of the skylark, and then the distant nightingale, and then one bird after another, till the loud thrush itself seems to have vanished; and we go in the way of every twittering under the eaves, because we know that that will soon be silenced too. But I need not enlarge upon this to you. I only mean to point out the prudence of lessening this kind of pain to the utmost, by making a considerable effort at first; and the most calculating prudence becomes a virtue, when it is certain that as much must at best be gone through as will afflict our friends, and may possibly overpower ourselves, our temper and deportment, if not our principles and our affections. I do not know how sufficiently to enforce these sacrifices being made with frankness and simplicity; and nothing so much needs enforcing. If our friends were but aware how cruel an injury is the false delicacy which is so common, they would not encourage our false shame as they do. If they have known anything of the bondage of ordinary false shame, they may imagine something of our suffering in circumstances of irremediable singularity. Instead of putting the singularity out of sight, they should lead us to acknowledge it in words, prepare for it in habits, and act upon it in social intercourse. If they will not assist us here, we must do it for ourselves. Our principle, again, requires this. Thus only can we save others from being uneasy in our presence, and sad when they think of us. That we can thus alone make ourselves sought and beloved is an inferior consideration, though an important one to us, to whom warmth and kindliness are as peculiarly animating as sunshine to the caged bird. This frankness, simplicity, and cheerfulness, can only grow out of a perfect acquiescence in our circumstances. Submission is not enough. Pride fails at the most critical moment. Nothing short of acquiescence will preserve the united consistency and cheerfulness of our acknowledgment of infirmity. Submission will bemoan it while making it. Pride will put on indifference while making it. But hearty acquiescence cannot fail to bring forth cheerfulness. The thrill of delight which arises during the ready agreement to profit by pain—(emphatically the joy with which no stranger intermeddleth)—must subside like all other emotions; but it does not depart without leaving the spirit lightened and cheered; and every visitation leaves it in a more genial state than the last.

And now, what may we struggle for? I dare say the words of the moralist lie as deep down in your hearts as in my own: "We must not repine, but we may lawfully struggle!" I go further, and say that we are bound to struggle. Our principle requires it. We must struggle for whatever may be had, without encroaching on the comfort of others. With this limitation, we must hear all we can, for as long as we can. Yet how few of us will use the helps we might have! How seldom is a deaf person to be seen with a trumpet![1] I should have been diverted, if I had not been too much vexed, at the variety of excuses that I have heard on this head since I have been much in society. The trumpet makes the sound disagreeable; or is of no use; or is not wanted in a noise, because we hear better in a noise; nor in quiet, because we hear very fairly in quiet; or we think our friends do not like it; or we ourselves do not care for it, if it does not enable us to hear general conversation; or—a hundred other reasons just as good. Now, dear friends, believe me, these are but excuses. I have tried them all in turn, and I know them to be so. The sound soon becomes anything but disagreeable; and the relief to the nerves, arising from the use of such a help, is indescribable. None but the totally deaf can fail to find some kind of trumpet that will be of use of them, if they choose to look for it properly, and give it a fair trial. That it is not wanted in a noise is usually true; but we are seldom in a noise; and quiet is our greatest enemy, (next to darkness, when the play of the countenance is lost to us.) To reject a tête-à-tête in comfort because the same means will not afford us the pleasure of general conversation, is not very wise. Is it? As for the fancy, that our friends do not like it, it is a mistake, and a serious mistake. I can speak confidently of this. By means of galvanism,[2] (which I do not, from my own experience, recommend,) I once nearly recovered my hearing for a few weeks. It was well worth while being in a sort of nervous fever during those weeks, and more deaf than ever afterwards, for the enlightenment which I gained during the interval on various subjects, of which the one that concerns us now, is,—the toil that our friends undergo on our account. This is the last topic on which I should speak to you, but for the prevalent unwillingness in our fraternity to use such helps as much as their own nerves. Of course, my friends could not suddenly accommodate their speech to my improved hearing; and I was absolutely shocked when I found what efforts they had been making for my sake. I vowed that I would never again bestow an unkind thought on their natural mistakes, or be restive under their inapplicable instructions; and, as for carrying a trumpet, I liked it no better than my brethren till then; but now, if it would in any degree ease my friends that I should wear a fool's cap and bells, I would do it. Any of you who may have had this kind of experience, are, I should think, using trumpets. I entreat those of you who have not been so made aware of your state, to take my word for what you are obliging your friends to undergo. You know that we can be no judges of the degree of effort necessary to make us hear. We might as well try to echo the skylark. I speak plainly, it may seem harshly; but I am sure you would thank me ere long if I could persuade you to encounter this one struggle to make the most of your remnant of one of God's prime blessings.

Another struggle must be to seize or make opportunities for preserving or rectifying our associations, as far as they are connected with the sense which is imperfect. Hunger and thirst after all sounds that you can obtain, without trouble to others, and without disturbing your own temper; and do it the more strenuously and cheerfully, the more reason you have to apprehend the increase of your infirmity. The natural desire to obtain as much pleasure as we can, while we can, would prompt us to this; but my appetite was much sharpened during the interval I spoke of; as yours would be, if you had such an interval. I was dismayed to find, not only what absurd notions I had formed on some small points, but how materially some very important processes of association had been modified by the failure of the sense of hearing. In consequence of the return and increase of the infirmity, I have now no distinct notion of what these intellectual faults are: but the certainty then

---

[1] **trumpet:** trumpet-shaped tube used to assist hearing.

[2] **galvanism:** electric stimulus applied therapeutically to nerves.

impressed that they exist, has taught me more than one lesson. I carry about with me the consciousness of an intellectual perversion which I can never remedy in this world, and of which neither I nor any one else can ascertain the extent, nor even the nature. This does not afflict me, because it would be as unreasonable to wish it otherwise, as to pray for wings which should carry us up to the milky-way; but it has stimulated me to devise every possible means of checking and delaying the perversion. We ought all to do so; losing no opportunity of associating sounds with other objects of sense, and of catching every breath of sound that passes us. We should note street cries; we should entice children to talk to us; we should linger in the neighbourhood of barrel organs, and go out of our way to walk by a dashing stream. We cannot tell how much wisdom we may at last find ourselves to have gained, by running out among the trees, when the quick coming and going of the sunshine tells us that the winds are abroad. Some day will show us from how much folly the chirp of an infant's voice may have saved us. I go so far as to recommend, certainly not any place of worship for purposes of experiment, but the theatre and the House of Commons; even when "the sough[3] of words without the sense" is all that can be had. The human voice is music, and carries sense, even then; and every tone is worth treasuring, when tones are likely to become scarce, or to cease. You will understand that it is only to those who can rule their own spirits that I recommend such an exercise as this last. If you cannot bear to enjoy less than the people about you, and in a different manner; or if you neglect what you came for, in mourning what you have lost, you are better at home. Nothing is worth the sacrifice of your repose of mind.

What else may we struggle for? For far more in the way of knowledge than I can now even intimate. I am not going to make out, as some would have me, that we lose nothing after all; that what we lose in one way we gain in another, and so on; pursuing a line of argument equally insulting to our own understandings, and to the wisdom and benignity of Him who framed that curious instrument, the ear, and strung the chords of its nerves, and keeps up the perpetual harmonies of the atmosphere for its gratification. The ear was not made that men should be happier without it. To attempt to persuade *you* so, would above all be folly. But, in some sense, there is a compensation to us, if we choose to accept it; and it is to improve this to the utmost that I would urge you and stimulate myself. We *have* some accomplish-

ments which we may gratefully acknowledge, while the means by which we gain them must prevent our being proud of them. We are good physiognomists—good perceivers in every way, and have (if we are not idle) rather the advantage over others in the power of abstract reasoning. This union of two kinds of power, which in common cases are often cultivated at the expense of each other, puts a considerable amount of accurate knowledge within easier reach of us than of most other people. We must never forget what a vast quantity we must forego, but neither must we lose sight of whatever is peculiarly within our power. We have more time, too, than anybody else: more than the laziest lordling, who does nothing but let his ears be filled with nonsense from morning till night. The very busiest of our fraternity has, I should think, time every day for as much thought as is good for him, between the hours of rising and of rest.

These advantages make it incumbent upon us to struggle for such compensation as is placed before us. We must set ourselves to gather knowledge from whatever we see and touch, and to digest it into wisdom during the extra time which is our privilege. What the sage goes out into the field at eventide to seek, we can have at table, or in the thronged streets at noonday,—opportunity for meditation, one of the chief means of wisdom. If to us the objects of sight are more vivid in their beauty, and more distinct in their suggestions than to others,—if to us there is granted more leisure, and stronger inducement to study the movements of the mind within, from us may be expected a degree of certain kinds of attainment, in which it is as much of a sin as a misfortune for us to be deficient.

Finally, we, like all who are placed in uncommon circumstances, are so situated that our mental and moral constitution can scarcely fail of being either very weak or very strong. If we are dull and slow of observation, and indolent in thought, there is little chance of our being much wiser than infants; whereas, if we are acute and quick of observation, (and for us there is no medium,) and disposed for thought, nothing is likely to prevent our going on to be wiser continually. In like manner, there is an awful alternative as to our morals. If we cannot stand our trial, we must become selfish in principle, sour in temper, and disagreeable in manners. If we are strong enough for our discipline, we cannot fail to come out of it with principles strengthened, affections expanded, temper under control, and manners graced by the permanent cheerfulness of a settled mind and a heart at ease. If you can make this last your lot, you have little more to fear. If you have brought vigour out of this conflict, you are not likely to be unnerved. If, in your enforced

---

[3]**sough**: murmur as of wind or water.

solitude, you have cultivated instead of losing your sympathies, you can scarcely afterwards grow selfish. If, as your enjoyments were failing you, you have improved your serenity,
your cheerfulness will probably be beyond the reach of circumstances. The principal check which must be put upon
these happy anticipations, is the fear that while the privations cannot be lessened, the pain of it may disappear too
soon and too entirely. I now suffer little or no pain from my
privation, (except at moments when comparisons are forced
upon me before I am ready for them;) and I cannot help
dreading a self-deception, to avoid which I would gladly endure over again all I have suffered. I had infinitely rather hear
the perpetual sense of privation than become unaware of any
thing that is true,—of my intellectual deficiencies, of my dis-
qualifications for society, of my errors in matters of fact, and
of the burdens which I necessarily impose on those who surround me. My dependence for being reminded of these
things is,—not on those who incur trouble and sacrifice for
my sake, but on the few occasional mortifications which I
still meet with, and which are always welcomed for the sake
of their office. We can never get beyond the necessity of
keeping in full view the worst and the best that can be made
of our lot. The worst is, either to sink under the trial, or to be
made callous by it. The best is, to be as wise as is possible
under a great disability, and as happy as is possible under
great privation. Believe me, with deep respect,

Your affectionate sister,
HARRIET MARTINEAU.
1834

~

from Society in America
Political Non-Existence of Women

One of the fundamental principles announced in the Declaration of Independence is, that governments derive their
just powers from the consent of the governed. How can the
political condition of women be reconciled with this?

Governments in the United States have power to tax
women who hold property; to divorce them from their husbands; to fine, imprison, and execute them for certain offences. Whence do these governments derive their powers?
They are not "just," as they are not derived from the consent
of the women thus governed.

Governments in the United States have power to enslave certain women; and also to punish other women for
inhuman treatment of such slaves. Neither of these powers
are "just;" not being derived from the consent of the
governed.

Governments decree to women in some States half
their husbands' property; in others one-third. In some, a
woman, on her marriage, is made to yield all her property to
her husband; in others, to retain a portion, or the whole, in
her own hands. Whence do governments derive the unjust
power of thus disposing of property without the consent of
the governed?

The democratic principle condemns all this as wrong;
and requires the equal political representation of all rational
beings. Children, idiots, and criminals, during the season of
sequestration, are the only fair exceptions.

The case is so plain that I might close it here; but it is
interesting to inquire how so obvious a decision has been so
evaded as to leave to women no political rights whatever.
The question has been asked, from time to time, in more
countries than one, how obedience to the laws can be required of women, when no woman has, either actually or
virtually, given any assent to any law. No plausible answer
has, as far as I can discover, been offered; for the good reason, that no plausible answer can be devised. The most
principled democratic writers on government have on this
subject sunk into fallacies, as disgraceful as any advocate of
despotism has adduced. In fact, they have thus sunk from
being, for the moment, advocates of despotism. Jefferson in
America, and James Mill at home, subside, for the occasion,
to the level of the author of the Emperor of Russia's Catechism for the young Poles.[1]

Jefferson says,[2] "Were our State a pure democracy, in
which all the inhabitants should meet together to transact
all their business, there would yet be excluded from their
deliberations,

"1. Infants, until arrived at years of discretion;
"2. Women, who, to prevent depravation of morals, and
     ambiguity of issue, could not mix promiscuously in the
     public meetings of men;
"3. Slaves, from whom the unfortunate state of things with
     us takes away the rights of will and of property."

If the slave disqualification, here assigned, were shifted
up under the head of Women, their case would be nearer

---

[1]James Mill (1773–1836): Utilitarian philosopher, economist,
historian; father of John Stuart Mill, and author of an 1820 essay on
government. In 1831 **Russia** crushed a Polish rebellion against its
rule.

[2]**Jefferson**: Correspondence vol. iv, p. 295. [Martineau's note]

the truth than as it now stands. Woman's lack of will and of property, is more like the true cause of her exclusion from the representation, than that which is actually set down against her. As if there could be no means of conducting public affairs but by promiscuous meetings! As if there would be more danger in promiscuous meetings for political business than in such meetings for worship, for oratory, for music, for dramatic entertainments,—for any of the thousand transactions of civilized life! The plea is not worth another word.

Mill says, with regard to representation, in his Essay on Government, "One thing is pretty clear; that all those individuals, whose interests are involved in those of other individuals, may be struck off without inconvenience. . . . In this light, women may be regarded, the interest of almost all of whom is involved, either in that of their fathers or in that of their husbands."

The true democratic principle is, that no person's interests can be, or can be ascertained to be, identical with those of any other person. This allows the exclusion of none but incapables.

The word "almost," in Mr. Mill's second sentence, rescues women from the exclusion he proposes. As long as there are women who have neither husbands nor fathers, his proposition remains an absurdity.

The interests of women who have fathers and husbands can never be identical with theirs, while there is a necessity for laws to protect women against their husbands and fathers. This statement is not worth another word.

Some who desire that there should be an equality of property between men and women, oppose representation, on the ground that political duties would be incompatible with the other duties which women have to discharge. The reply to this is, that women are the best judges here. God has given time and power for the discharge of all duties; and, if he had not, it would be for women to decide which they would take, and which they would leave. But their guardians follow the ancient fashion of deciding what is best for their wards. The Emperor of Russia discovers when a coat of arms and title do not agree with a subject prince. The King of France early perceives that the air of Paris does not agree with a free-thinking foreigner. The English Tories feel the hardship that it would be to impose the franchise on every artizan, busy as he is in getting his bread. The Georgian planter perceives the hardship that freedom would be to his slaves. And the best friends of half the human race peremptorily decide for them as to their rights, their duties, their feelings, their powers. In all these cases, the persons thus cared for feel that the abstract decision

rests with themselves; that, though they may be compelled to submit, they need not acquiesce.

It is pleaded that half of the human race does acquiesce in the decision of the other half, as to their rights and duties. And some instances, not only of submission, but of acquiescence, there are. Forty years ago, the women of New Jersey went to the poll, and voted, at state elections. The general term, "inhabitants," stood unqualified;—as it will again, when the true democratic principle comes to be fully understood. A motion was made to correct the inadvertence; and it was done, as a matter of course; without any appeal, as far as I could learn, from the persons about to be injured. Such acquiescence proves nothing but the degradation of the injured party. It inspires the same emotions of pity as the supplication of the freed slave who kneels to his master to restore him to slavery, that he may have his animal wants supplied, without being troubled with human rights and duties. Acquiescence like this is an argument which cuts the wrong way for those who use it.

But this acquiescence is only partial; and, to give any semblance of strength to the plea, the acquiescence must be complete. I, for one, do not acquiesce. I declare that whatever obedience I yield to the laws of the society in which I live is a matter between, not the community and myself, but my judgment and my will. Any punishment inflicted on me for the breach of the laws, I should regard as so much gratuitous injury; for to those laws I have never, actually or virtually, assented. I know that there are women in England who agree with me in this—I know that there are women in America who agree with me in this. The plea of acquiescence is invalidated by us.

It is pleaded that, by enjoying the protection of some laws, women give their assent to all. This needs but a brief answer. Any protection thus conferred is, under woman's circumstances, a boon bestowed at the pleasure of those in whose power she is. A boon of any sort is no compensation for the privation of something else; nor can the enjoyment of it bind to the performance of anything to which it bears no relation.

Because I, by favour, may procure the imprisonment of the thief who robs my house, am I, unrepresented, therefore bound not to smuggle French ribbons? The obligation not to smuggle has a widely different derivation.

I cannot enter upon the commonest order of pleas of all,—those which relate to the virtual influence of woman; her swaying the judgment and will of man through the heart; and so forth. One might as well try to dissect the morning mist. I knew a gentleman in America who told me how much rather he had be a woman than the man he is;—

a professional man, a father, a citizen. He would give up all this for a woman's influence. I thought he was mated too soon. He should have married a lady, also of my acquaintance, who would not at all object to being a slave, if ever the blacks should have the upper hand; "it is so right that the one race should be subservient to the other!" Or rather,—I thought it a pity that the one could not be a woman, and the other a slave; so that an injured individual of each class might be exalted into their places, to fulfil and enjoy the duties and privileges which they despise, and, in despising, disgrace.

The truth is, that while there is much said about "the sphere of woman," two widely different notions are entertained of what is meant by the phrase. The narrow, and, to the ruling party, the more convenient notion is that sphere appointed by men, and bounded by their ideas of propriety;—a notion from which any and every woman may fairly dissent. The broad and true conception is of the sphere appointed by God, and bounded by the powers which he has bestowed. This commands the assent of man and woman; and only the question of powers remains to be proved.

That woman has power to represent her own interests, no one can deny till she has been tried. The modes need not be discussed here: they must vary with circumstances. The fearful and absurd images which are perpetually called up to perplex the question,—images of women on woolsacks[3] in England, and under canopies in America, have nothing to do with the matter. The principle being once established, the methods will follow, easily, naturally, and under a remarkable transmutation of the ludicrous into the sublime. The kings of Europe would have laughed mightily, two centuries ago, at the idea of a commoner, without robes, crown, or sceptre, stepping into the throne of a strong nation. Yet who dared to laugh when Washington's super-royal voice greeted the New World from the presidential chair, and the old world stood still to catch the echo?

The principle of the equal rights of both halves of the human race is all we have to do with here. It is the true democratic principle which can never be seriously controverted, and only for a short time evaded. Governments can derive their just powers only from the consent of the governed.

1837

---

[3]**woolsacks**: seats for judges, especially the Lord Chancellor, in the House of Lords.

from **Retrospect of Western Travel**

First Sight of Slavery

"Ed io, ch'avea di riguardar desio
La condicion, che tal fortezza serra,
Com' i fù dentro, l'occhio intorno invio,
E veggio ad ogni man grande campagna
Piena ad duolo, e di tormento rio."

Dante.1

From the day of my entering the States till that of my leaving Philadelphia, I had seen society basking in one bright sunshine of good will. The sweet temper and kindly manners of the Americans are so striking to foreigners, that it is some time before the dazzled stranger perceives that, genuine as is all this good, evils as black as night exist along with it. I had been received with such hearty hospitality everywhere, and had lived among friends so conscientious in their regard for human rights, that though I had heard of abolition riots, and had observed somewhat of the degradation of the blacks, my mind had not yet been really troubled about the enmity of the races. The time of awakening must come. It began just before I left Philadelphia.

I was calling on a lady whom I had heard speak with strong horror of the abolitionists (with whom I had then no acquaintance); and she turned round upon me with the question whether I would not prevent, if I could, the marriage of a white person with a person of colour. I saw at once the beginning of endless troubles in this inquiry, and was very sorry it had been made: but my determination had been adopted long before, never to evade the great question of colour; never to provoke it; but always to meet it plainly in whatever form it should be presented. I replied that I would never, under any circumstances, try to separate persons who really loved, believing such to be truly those whom God hath joined: but I observed that the case she put was one not likely to happen, as I believed the blacks were no more disposed to marry the whites than the whites to marry the blacks. "You are an amalgamationist!" cried she. I told her that the party term was new to me; but that she must give what name she pleased to the principle I had

---

[1]**Dante**: "And I, who wanted to see the condition of those such a fortress enclosed, as soon as I was inside looked around and saw on every side a great plain full of grief and guilty torment." *Inferno* 9.107–111.

declared in answer to her question. This lady is an eminent religionist, and denunciations spread rapidly from her. The day before I left Philadelphia, my old shipmate, the Prussian physician, arrived there, and lost no time in calling to tell me, with much agitation, that I must not go a step further south; that he had heard on all hands, within two hours of his arrival, that I was an amalgamationist, and that my having published a story against slavery would be fatal to me in the slave States. I did not give much credit to the latter part of this news; and saw plainly that all I had to do was to go straight on. I really desired to see the working of the slave system, and was glad that my having published against its principles divested me altogether of the character of a spy, and gave me an unquestioned liberty to publish the results of what I might observe. In order to see things as they were, it was necessary that people's minds should not be prepossessed by my friends as to my opinions and conduct; and I therefore forbade my Philadelphia friends to publish in the newspapers, as they wished, an antidote to the charges already current against me.

The next day I first set foot in a slave State, arriving in the evening at Baltimore. I dreaded inexpressibly the first sight of a slave, and could not help speculating on the lot of every person of colour I saw from the windows, the first few days. The servants in the house where I was were free blacks.

Before a week was over, I perceived that all that is said in England of the hatred of the whites to the blacks in America is short of the truth. The slanders that I heard of the free blacks were too gross to injure my estimation of any but those who spoke them. In Baltimore the bodies of coloured people exclusively are taken for dissection, "because the whites do not like it, and the coloured people cannot resist." It is wonderful that the bodily structure can be (with the exception of the colouring of the skin) thus assumed to be the pattern of that of the whites; that the exquisite nervous system, the instrument of moral as well as physical pleasures and pains, can be nicely investigated, on the ground of its being analogous with that of the whites; that not only the mechanism, but the sensibilities of the degraded race should be argued from to those of the exalted order, and that men come from such a study with contempt for these brethren in their countenances, hatred in their hearts, and insult on their tongues. These students are the men who cannot say that the coloured people have not nerves that quiver under moral injury, nor a brain that is on fire with insult, nor pulses that throb under oppression. These are the men who should stay the hand of the rash and ignorant possessors of power who crush the being of

creatures, like themselves, "fearfully and wonderfully made." But to speak the right word, to hold out the helping hand, these searchers into man have not light nor strength.

It was in Baltimore that I heard Miss Edgeworth[2] denounced as a woman of no intelligence or delicacy, whose works could never be cared for again, because, in Belinda, poor Juba was married, at length, to an English farmer's daughter! The incident is so subordinate that I had entirely forgotten it: but a clergyman's lady threw the volume to the opposite corner of the floor when she came to the page. As I have said elsewhere, Miss Edgeworth is worshipped throughout the United States; but it is in spite of this terrible passage,—this clause of a sentence in Belinda,—which nobody in America can tolerate, while no one elsewhere ever, I should think, dreamed of finding fault with it.

A lady from New England, staying in Baltimore, was one day talking over slavery with me, her detestation of it being great, when I told her I dreaded seeing a slave. "You have seen one," said she. "You were waited on by a slave yesterday evening." She told me of a gentleman who let out and lent out his slaves to wait at gentlemen's houses, and that the tall handsome mulatto who handed the tea at a party the evening before was one of these. I was glad it was over for once; but I never lost the painful feeling caused to a stranger by intercourse with slaves. No familiarity with them, no mirth and contentment on their part ever soothed the miserable restlessness caused by the presence of a deeply-injured fellow-being. No wonder or ridicule on the spot avails anything to the stranger. He suffers, and must suffer from this, deeply and long, as surely as he is human and hates oppression.

The next slave that I saw, knowing that it was a slave, was at Washington, where a little negro child took hold of my gown in the passage of our boarding-house, and entered our drawing-room with me. She shut the door softly, as asking leave to stay. I took up a newspaper. She sat at my feet, and began amusing herself with my shoe-strings. Finding herself not discouraged, she presently begged play by peeping at me above and on each side the newspaper. She was a bright-eyed, merry-hearted child,—confiding, like other children, and dreading no evil, but doomed, hopelessly doomed to ignorance, privation, and moral degradation. When I looked at her, and thought of the fearful disobedience to the first of moral laws, the cowardly treachery, the

---

[2]Maria **Edgeworth** (1767–1849): British novelist and nonfiction author; **Juba** is a black servant in her novel *Belinda* (1801).

cruel abuse of power involved in thus dooming to blight a being so helpless, so confiding, and so full of promise, a horror came over me which sickened my very soul. To see slaves is not to be reconciled to slavery.

At Baltimore and Washington again I was warned, in various stealthy ways, of perils awaiting me in the South. I had no means of ascertaining the justness of these warnings but by going on; and turning back for such vague reasons was not to be thought of. So I determined to say no word to my companions (who were in no danger), but to see the truth for myself. The threats proved idle, as I suspected they would. Throughout the South I met with very candid and kind treatment.—I mention these warnings partly because they are a fact connected with the state of the country; and partly because it will afterwards appear that the stranger's real danger lies in the north and west, over which the south had, in my case, greatly the advantage in liberality.

1837

~

from How to Observe Morals and Manners

Requisites for Observation

"Inest sua gratia parvis."

"Les petites choses n'ont de valeur que de la part de ceux qui peuvent s'élever aux grandes."—De Jouy.[1]

There is no department of inquiry in which it is not full as easy to miss truth as to find it, even when the materials from which truth is to be drawn are actually present to our senses. A child does not catch a gold fish in water at the first trial, however good his eyes may be, and however clear the water; knowledge and method are necessary to enable him to take what is actually before his eyes and under his hand. So it is with all who fish in a strange element for the truth which is living and moving there: the powers of observation must be trained, and habits of method in arranging the materials presented to the eye must be acquired before the student possesses the requisites for understanding what he contemplates.

The observer of Men and Manners stands as much in need of intellectual preparation as any other student. This is not, indeed, generally supposed, and a multitude of travellers act as if it were not true. Of the large number of tourists who annually sail from our ports, there is probably not one who would dream of pretending to make observations on any subject of physical inquiry, of which he did not understand even the principles. If, on his return from the Mediterranean, the unprepared traveller was questioned about the geology of Corsica, or the public buildings of Palermo, he would reply, "Oh, I can tell you nothing about that—I never studied geology; I know nothing about architecture." But few, or none, make the same avowal about the morals and manners of a nation. Every man seems to imagine that he can understand men at a glance; he supposes that it is enough to be among them to know what they are doing; he thinks that eyes, ears, and memory are enough for morals, though they would not qualify him for botanical or statistical observation; he pronounces confidently upon the merits and social condition of the nations among whom he has travelled; no misgiving ever prompts him to say, "I can give you little general information about the people I have been seeing; I have not studied the principles of morals; I am no judge of national manners."

There would be nothing to be ashamed of in such an avowal. No wise man blushes at being ignorant of any science which it has not suited his purposes to study, or which it has not been in his power to attain. No linguist wrings his hands when astronomical discoveries are talked of in his presence; no political economist covers his face when shown a shell or a plant which he cannot class; still less should the artist, the natural philosopher, the commercial traveller,[2] or the classical scholar, be ashamed to own himself unacquainted with the science which, of all the sciences which have yet opened upon men, is, perhaps, the least cultivated, the least definite, the least ascertained in itself, and the most difficult in its application.

In this last characteristic of the science of Morals lies the excuse of as many travellers as may decline pronouncing on the social condition of any people. Even if the generality of travellers were as enlightened as they are at present ignorant about the principles of Morals, the difficulty of putting those principles to interpretative uses would deter the wise from making the hasty decisions, and uttering the large judgments, in which travellers have hitherto been wont to

---

[1] *"Inest . . . parvis"*: "Small things have their own kind of grace." *"Les petites choses . . . grandes"*: "Little things are valuable only for people who can rise to big ones" (Etienne **De Jouy**, 1764–1846).

[2] **natural philosopher**: scientist. **Commercial traveller**: traveling salesman.

indulge. In proportion as men become sensible how infinite are the diversities in man, how incalculable the varieties and influences of circumstances, rashness of pretension and decision will abate, and the great work of classifying the moral manifestations of society will be confided to the philosophers, who bear the same relation to the science of society as Herschel does to astronomy, and Beaufort to hydrography.[3]

Of all the tourists who utter their decisions upon foreigners, how many have begun their researches at home? Which of them would venture upon giving an account of the morals and manners of London, though he may have lived in it all his life? Would any one of them escape errors as gross as those of the Frenchman who published it as a general fact that people in London always have, at dinner parties, soup on each side, and fish at four corners? Which of us would undertake to classify the morals and manners of any hamlet in England, after spending the summer in it? What sensible man seriously generalizes upon the manners of a street, even though it be Houndsditch or Cranbourn-Alley? Who pretends to explain all the proceedings of his next-door neighbour? Who is able to account for all that is said and done by the dweller in the same house,—by parent, child, brother, or domestic? If such judgments were attempted, would they not be as various as those who make them? And would they not, after all, if closely looked into, reveal more of the mind of the observer than of the observed?

If it be thus with us at home, amidst all the general resemblances, the prevalent influences which furnish an interpretation to a large number of facts, what hope of a trustworthy judgment remains for the foreign tourist, however good may be his method of travelling, and however long his absence from home? He looks at all the people along his line of road, and converses with a few individuals from among them. If he diverges from time to time, from the high road,—if he winds about among villages, and crosses mountains, to dip into the hamlets of the valleys,—he still pursues only a line, and does not command the expanse; he is furnished, at best, with no more than a sample of the people; and whether they be indeed a sample, must remain a conjecture which he has no means of verifying. He converses, more or less, with, perhaps, one man in ten thousand of those he sees; and of the few with whom he converses, no two are alike in powers and in training, or

perfectly agree in their views on any one of the great subjects which the traveller professes to observe; the information afforded by one is contradicted by another; the fact of one day is proved error by the next; the wearied mind soon finds itself overwhelmed by the multitude of unconnected or contradictory particulars, and lies passive to be run over by the crowd. The tourist is no more likely to learn, in this way, the social state of a nation, than his valet would be qualified to speak of the meteorology of the country from the number of times the umbrellas are wanted in the course of two months. His children might as well undertake to exhibit the geological formation of the country from the pebbles they picked up in a day's ride.

I remember some striking words addressed to me, before I set out on my travels, by a wise man, since dead. "You are going to spend two years in the United States," said he. "Now just tell me,—do you expect to understand the Americans by the time you come back? You do not: that is well. I lived five-and-twenty years in Scotland, and I fancied I understood the Scotch; then I came to England, and supposed I should soon understand the English. I have now lived five-and-twenty years here, and I begin to think I understand neither the Scotch nor the English."

What is to be done? Let us first settle what is not to be done.

The traveller must deny himself all indulgence of peremptory decision, not only in public on his return, but in his journal, and in his most superficial thoughts. The experienced and conscientious traveller would word the condition differently. Finding peremptory decision more trying to his conscience than agreeable to his laziness, he would call it not indulgence, but anxiety; he enjoys the employment of collecting materials, but would shrink from the responsibility of judging a community.

The traveller must not generalise on the spot, however true may be his apprehension—however firm his grasp, of one or more facts. A raw English traveller in China was entertained by a host who was intoxicated, and a hostess who was red-haired; he immediately made a note of the fact that all the men in China were drunkards, and all the women red-haired. A raw Chinese traveller in England was landed by a Thames waterman who had a wooden leg. The stranger saw that the wooden leg was used to stand in the water with, while the other was high and dry. The apparent economy of the fact struck the Chinese; he saw in it strong evidence of design, and wrote home that in England one-legged men are kept for watermen, to the saving of all injury to health, shoe, and stocking, from standing in the river. These anecdotes exhibit but a slight exaggeration of

---

[3]Sir William **Herschel** (1738–1822): astronomer. Sir Francis **Beaufort** (1774–1857): rear-admiral and student of the earth's waters.

the generalising tendencies of many modern travellers. They are not so much worse than some recent tourists' tales, as they are better than the old narratives of "men whose heads do grow beneath their shoulders."[4]

Natural philosophers do not dream of generalising with any such speed as that used by the observers of men; yet they might do it with more safety, at the risk of an incalculably smaller mischief. The geologist and the chemist make a large collection of particular appearances, before they commit themselves to propound a principle drawn from them, though their subject matter is far less diversified than the human subject, and nothing of so much importance as human emotions,—love and dislike, reverence and contempt, depends upon their judgment. If a student in natural philosophy is in too great haste to classify and interpret, he misleads, for a while, his fellow-students (not a very large class;) he vitiates the observations of a few successors; his error is discovered and exposed; he is mortified, and his too docile followers are ridiculed, and there is an end; but if a traveller gives any quality which he may have observed in a few individuals as a characteristic of a nation, the evil is not speedily or easily remediable. Abject thinkers, passive readers, adopt his words; parents repeat them to their children; and townspeople spread the judgment into the villages and hamlets—the strongholds of prejudice; future travellers see according to the prepossessions given them, and add their testimony to the error, till it becomes the work of a century to reverse a hasty generalisation. It was a great mistake of a geologist to assign a wrong level to the Caspian Sea; and it is vexatious that much time and energy should have been devoted to account for an appearance which, after all, does not exist. It is provoking to geologists that they should have wasted a great deal of ingenuity in finding reasons for these waters being at a different level from what is now found that they have; but the evil is over; the "pish!" and the "pshaw!" are said; the explanatory and apologetical notes are duly inserted in new editions of geological works, and nothing more can come of the mistake. But it is difficult to foresee when the British public will believe that the Americans are a mirthful nation, or even that the French are not almost all cooks or dancing-masters. A century hence, probably, the Americans will continue to believe that all the English make a regular study of the art of conversation; and the lower orders of French will be still telling their children that half the people in England hang or drown themselves every November. As long as travellers

generalise on morals and manners as hastily as they do, it will probably be impossible to establish a general conviction that no civilised nation is ascertainably better or worse than any other on this side barbarism, the whole field of morals being taken into the view. As long as travellers continue to neglect the safe means of generalisation which are within the reach of all, and build theories upon the manifestations of individual minds, there is little hope of inspiring men with that spirit of impartiality, mutual deference, and love, which are the best enlighteners of the eyes and rectifiers of the understanding.

Above all things, the traveller must not despair of good results from his observations. Because he cannot establish true conclusions by imperfect means, he is not to desist from doing any thing at all. Because he cannot safely generalise in one way, it does not follow that there is no other way. There are methods of safe generalisation of which I shall speak by-and-by. But, if there were not such within his reach, if his only materials were the discourse, the opinions, the feelings, the way of life, the looks, dress, and manners of individuals, he might still afford important contributions to science by his observations on as wide a variety of these as he can bring within his mental grasp. The experience of a large number of observers would in time yield materials from which a cautious philosopher might draw conclusions. It is a safe rule, in morals as in physics, that no fact is without its use. Every observer and recorder is fulfilling a function; and no one observer or recorder ought to feel discouragement, as long as he desires to be useful rather than shining; to be the servant rather than the lord of science, and a friend to the home-stayers rather than their dictator.

One of the wisest men living writes to me, "No books are so little to be trusted as travels. All travellers do and must generalise too rapidly. Most, if not all, take a fact for a principle, or the exception for the rule, more or less; and the quickest minds, which love to reason and explain more than to observe with patience, go most astray. My faith in travels received a mortal wound when I travelled. I read, as I went along, the books of those who had preceded me, and found that we did not see with the same eyes. Even descriptions of nature proved false. The traveller had viewed the prospect at a different season, or in a different light, and substituted the transient for the fixed. Still I think travels useful. Different accounts give means of approximation to truth; and by-and-by what is fixed and essential in a people will be brought out."

It ought to be an animating thought to a traveller that, even if it be not in his power to settle any one point

---

[4] "men whose heads . . . shoulders": *Othello* 1.3.143–144.

respecting the morals and manners of an empire, he can in-fallibly aid in supplying means of approximation to truth, and of bringing out "what is fixed and essential in a people." This should be sufficient to stimulate his exertions and sat-isfy his ambition. (Part 1, Introduction)

Philosophical Requisites

"Only I believe that this is not a bow for every man to shoot in that counts himself a teacher, but will require sinews al-most equal to those which Homer gave Ulysses: yet I am withal persuaded that it may prove much more easy in the essay than it now seems at a distance."   Milton.[5]

There are two parties to the work of observation on Morals and Manners—the observer and the observed. This is an important fact which the traveller seldom dwells upon as he ought; yet a moment's consideration shows that the mind of the observer—the instrument by which the work is done, is as essential as the material to be wrought. If the instrument be in bad order it will furnish a bad product, be the material what it may. In this chapter I shall point out what requisites the traveller ought to make sure that he is possessed of be-fore he undertakes to offer observations on the Morals and Manners of a people.

He must have made up his mind as to what it is that he wants to know. In physical science, great results may be ob-tained by hap-hazard experiments; but this is not the case in Morals. A chemist can hardly fail of learning something by putting any substances together, under new circumstances, and seeing what will arise out of the combination; and some striking discoveries happened in this way, in the infancy of the science: though no one doubts that more knowledge may be gained by the chemist who has an aim in his mind, and who conducts his experiment on some principle. In Morals, the latter method is the only one which promises any useful results. In the workings of the social system, all the agents are known in the gross—all are determined. It is not their nature, but the proportions in which they are com-bined, which have to be ascertained.

What does the traveller want to know? He is aware that, wherever he goes, he will find men, women, and chil-dren; strong men, and weak men; just men and selfish men.

He knows that he will every where find a necessity for food, clothing, and shelter; and every where some mode of gen-eral agreement how to live together. He knows that he will every where find birth, marriage and death; and therefore domestic affections. What results from all these elements of social life does he mean to look for?

For want of settling this question, one traveller sees nothing truly, because the state of things is not consistent with his speculations as to how human beings ought to live together; another views the whole with prejudice, because it is not like what he has been accustomed to see at home; yet each of these would shrink from the recognition of his folly, if it were fully placed before him. The first would be ashamed of having tried any existing community by an arbi-trary standard of his own—an act much like going forth into the wilderness to see kings' houses full of men in soft raiment; and the other would perceive that different nations may go on judging one another by themselves till dooms-day, without in any way improving the chance of self-advancement and mutual understanding. Going out with the disadvantage of a habit of mind uncounteracted by an in-tellectual aim, will never do. The traveller may as well stay at home, for any thing he will gain in the way of social knowledge.

The two considerations just mentioned must be sub-ordinated to the grand one,—the only general one,—of the relative amount of human happiness. Every element of social life derives its importance from this great considera-tion. The external conveniences of men, their internal emotions and affections, their social arrangements, gradu-ate in importance precisely in proportion as they affect the general happiness of the section of the race among whom they exist. Here then is the wise traveller's aim,—to be kept in view to the exclusion of prejudice, both philosoph-ical and national. He must not allow himself to be per-plexed or disgusted by seeing the great ends of human association pursued by means which he could never have devised, and to the practice of which he could not recon-cile himself. He is not to conclude unfavorably about the diet of the multitude because he sees them swallowing blubber, or scooping out water-melons, instead of regaling themselves with beef and beer. He is not to suppose their social meetings a failure because they eat with their fin-gers, instead of with silver forks, or touch foreheads in-stead of making a bow. He is not to conclude against domestic morals, on account of a diversity of methods of entering upon marriage. He might as well judge of the minute transactions of manners all over the world by what he sees in his native village. There, to leave the door open

---

[5]**Milton:** from *Of Education* (1644).

or to shut it bears no relation to morals, and but little to manners; whereas, to shut the door is as cruel an act in a Hindoo hut as to leave it open in a Greenland cabin. In short, he is to prepare himself to bring whatever he may observe to the test of some high and broad principle, and not to that of a low comparative practice. To test one people by another, is to argue within a very small segment of a circle; and the observer can only pass backwards and forwards at an equal distance from the point of truth. To test the morals and manners of a nation by a reference to the essentials of human happiness, is to strike at once to the centre, and to see things as they are. (Part 1, Chapter 1)

1838

from Domestic Service[1]

. . . The misunderstanding between the richer and poorer classes of Great Britain is the growth of many centuries. Both parties are ignorant and unjust in blaming any existing individuals of their foes for the ill-temper of the present hour. This temper is, in all, original sin, imputable to a remote generation of their fathers. It was once true that laws were made to gratify the rich and coerce the poor; and this ancient fact makes the poor hate the rich of the present day as oppressors. It would probably require a century of unalloyed good works on the part of the aristocracy of England to dissolve this traditionary enmity. It has been true from the day that Cain rose against Abel, that men have hated those whom they have injured; and the lofty few of every land have therefore always misregarded the lowly many, believing them turbulent, malicious, inaccessible to kindness, to be reached only by flattery, while deserving little but contempt. When not to be used as creatures, they have been treated as foes.—While the two classes have been thus regarding each other, nothing that an individual here and there could say or do could avail to improve the relation. A just and benevolent employer finds his efforts spent in vain upon the callous temper and immovable prejudices of his work-people: and an enlightened operative[2] may act the mediator for a life-time without enabling the capitalist to

enter into the feelings of his labourers, or the labourers to put faith in their employer. The opposing currents of feeling are so strong that it is not only impossible to make them mingle, but individuals are carried along with them, let the strongest-hearted struggle as they may. Much impotent passion might be saved if it were clearly understood that this mutual misunderstanding is of ancient origin, and has been growing for centuries, nourished by many influences, and tending towards a radical change (gradually or suddenly produced) in the organization of society. Not only would much vituperation and secret hatred be obviated, but those who would fain see a promise of a better state of things would perceive in what direction they may work with some rational hope of ameliorating our social condition.

Any one relation of employers and employed serves as an exponent of the rest. The principles and feelings which govern the relation are much alike in all. But if there is one which more certainly than any other includes all the feelings which have descended through a hundred generations of rich and poor, it is that of Domestic Service. We have headed our article with its name, and we propose to look a little into its actual state. It is important, both in itself and because it is symptomatic of some things out of itself.

One proof of the bad state of this very relation is the fact that the subject of Domestic Service is considered a low, trifling, and almost ludicrous one. Men know very little about it, and would fain appear to know less than they do. The very words call up in their minds images of mops and brooms, or of squabbles about giving away cold meat, summonses of pilfering cooks to police offices, and such disagreeable things. Men never think of the subject if they can help it: they put away all knowledge of it as a nuisance. They consider it an evil which it is their wives' business to manage and to bear. A gentleman swore at a police office lately, that he had never seen his housemaid; and he was actually unable to identify her. This state of feeling with regard to the relation is itself a proof that it is in a wrong state: for, when viewed without prejudice, it is plain that the relation is an extremely important, and ought to be a very interesting one to all the parties involved in it. Seriously and impartially viewed, the case is this. One party (men as well as women) depends on the other for the cleanliness and security of home, with the comfort of every hour spent in it,—for the care of the children, and the preservation of the property, and the maintenance of the respectability of the house. These are serious matters enough. On the other hand, the employed party depends on the employers for the necessaries of life; in a great degree for health; for ease of mind, self-respect, and for the justice,

---

[1]From an essay reviewing books such as those mentioned below; *Westminster Review* 31 (August 1838), 405–432.

[2]**operative**: industrial worker.

kindliness and sympathy which are absolutely necessary to make the lot of the labourer endurable. These are more serious matters still. When householders look on their servants as mere sweepers of parlours and bakers of bread, it is no wonder that they are careless and ignorant about them. But it is a fault so to look upon them: and if he remembers that they are human beings exerting their human powers for the service of all whom he most loves,—that they are inmates of his house, dependent on him for protection, comfort, and, above all, self-respect, any good man will be shocked that he could treat such a relation with levity.

The numbers concerned show that the relation is important in itself. The number of domestic servants in the United Kingdom is considerably above a million. The census of 1831 presents us for the first time with the estimate.[3] Seventy-five in a thousand of the female population, and eighteen in a thousand of the male population are domestic servants. It is strange that this large class has been the subject of so little philosophical observation and reflection, that it is difficult to find in any history of any country accounts of the state of Domestic Service (except where the portents and catastrophes of slavery force themselves upon the attention of the historian). Travellers omit the subject in their survey of society; and social moralists at home seem to know little of domestic servants as a class,—of their common feelings, prejudices, and characteristics of mind and manners,—and much less of the causes of these. Yet domestics are as much a class, marked by characteristics, as agriculturalists, mechanics,[4] and tradespeople. These characteristics vary with situation and circumstance. The domestics of England are as unlike those of Scotland, as those of Scotland are unlike those of Ireland. The French servants, again, differ from the English as widely as the Americans from the French. In all countries the causes of these different characteristics lie deep; and, like all deep-lying causes, will sooner or later peremptorily demand research, contemplation, and the forethought which it would be wise to exercise early. . . .

. . . In the view which we are about to take of domestic service we regard chiefly the domestics of the middle classes. Because the opulent keep many servants, it is too commonly supposed that the greater number of servants belong to the opulent. But, since the opulent are few, and householders are many, this is a great mistake; and one bad consequence of it is, that the evils of the relation are much underrated. The vices of fashionable families, above and below stairs, are bad enough; and the housekeeper of a nobleman's family may be of kindred temper with the tyrannical mistress of a single maid: but the worst woes of the system are found among families of a lower rank, where the bulk of the domestics of the country serve. This is the proper scene of the relation; and to this will our observation be chiefly directed. It is the lot of the thousands rather than the tens which it is important to contemplate.

The peculiarity in the life of domestic service is subjection to the will of another. There may be more or less of this, avowedly or virtually, in other modes of life; but of no other is it the distinguishing peculiarity. An artisan contracts to supply a want for a money recompense, retaining the power of doing the work in his own way, and the choice of doing as much or as little as he pleases, subject to his own necessities, and not to the will of his employer. A servant enters a family for the very purpose of fulfilling the will of the employer; and obedience to orders is the first requisite demanded. The wages are given in return for the obedience of service quite as much as for the industry itself. If there be here and there a master or mistress in England who allows to servants their own uncontrolled way of doing the business of the family, demanding only results, such is an exception to the general rule; and the freedom thus permitted is commonly found, in the present state of the parties, to be as injurious to the habits of the domestics as to the comfort of the employer. Such cases are very rare, and more commonly result from indolence than from any principle. The general agreement is, that the domestic is to do the work appointed by the employer, and as the employer appoints.

How troublesome and fundamentally vicious an arrangement this is, becomes apparent when we consider the difficulty of settling where this obedience to another's will is to stop, and that the system is a *tertium quid*[5] from the mixture of two other systems quite opposite in their principles—slavery and contract for the fruits of labour. The element of obedience to the employer's will is introduced into the contract for labour,—the first supposes the parties to be unequal; the last supposes them to be equal. The relation

---

[3]**estimate:** In England female servants are 77 in a thousand: in Wales 102: in Scotland 88: in Ireland 63. The total number is 923,646. Men servants are in England 16 in a thousand of the entire male population: in Wales 8½: in Scotland 17 ½: in Ireland 26. The total number is 211,966. [Martineau's note]

[4]**mechanics:** manual workers, artisans.

[5]*tertium quid:* a third thing.

resulting from elements so discordant is naturally what we see it—irksome and injurious to both parties.

The limits of obedience to the employer's will cannot be settled by law, nor by mutual agreement, when the contract of service is formed; and it cannot be left, with any hope of peace and comfort, to the judgment and feelings of the parties, as the occasions arise. The judgment and feelings of the parties differ as their position to each other. Very few individuals are to be trusted with irresponsible power over other human beings; and those few are not to be looked for among such as are themselves suffering under arbitrary power, as every woman is. The condition of women is the worst preparation for their use of power; and the power which they hold is abused as any wise observer would anticipate that it must be. The negro slave uses his dog and his ass as his master uses him; and women treat their servants as they have been treated by those who have the control of their lot. On the other hand, the party controlled is ignorant and prejudiced; as far from rationality of obedience as the superior one from rationality of control. How is it possible that disputes should not arise? And where there are not disputes, there is apt to be slavish submission—grudging, but timid; or a yielding of points by the mistress, ending in quarrel when the consequent encroachment has grown too provoking to be borne. Hence we see mistresses interfering with the dress of their maid-servants, forbidding them to wear white gowns, or silk gowns, or any other gowns than it seems in "ladies'" eyes proper that "maid-servants" should wear. The natural consequence of this species of meddling is fraud and lying. The maids keep their white or their silk gowns at a friend's house, or smuggle them out in a bundle, the children of the families perhaps acting as spies, and reporting of hidden finery, or accepting bribes not to speak of it.—This is no trifle, though it may appear one. There is no more fruitful cause of quarrel in this relation than the mistress's interference with the personal habits of her domestics. They are tenacious, as they have a right to be, of their independence in the management of their own affairs; and mistresses are sadly apt to forget that, however much wiser their views about the expenditure of ten or twelve guineas a year may be than those of the owners, they have no right to make others act upon their views.—The very common regulation about "followers"[6] is another ground of contention—another occasion for imperiousness on the one hand, and discontent on the other. It is doubtless most convenient to the mistress that

her servants should never have any visitors; but how stands the case with the servants? They have the same need to see the faces of their family and friends that their mistress has: if it be possible to obtain the indulgence secretly they will do it: if not, they will leave their place, as they would leave a prison or an exile.—Then there is the whole class of cases, of servants being desired to do what they think wrong; cases which often arise merely from the mistress being unaware of the ideas and feelings which are in her servants' minds. There are multitudes of cases where domestics are disturbed at the way of passing the Sunday—at being obliged to attend at the same church with the family when their own opinions would lead them to another,—and at the long-standing grievance of being desired to declare the family not at home when they are in the house.—Again, there is the stubbornness of servants, induced by their position, through which they refuse to discharge offices, much wanted at the moment, but which they declare not to be in their bond. These refusals, being a struggle for right against supposed despotism, are usually made about matters of small importance in themselves, and at times selected for their peculiar inconvenience, and in an irritating spirit of defiance.— Here we may as well stop; for there is no end to the heart-burnings which arise from the false practice of promising and exacting obedience where the limits of the obedience cannot be defined—where it is not sanctioned by natural relation, nor sanctified by natural affection. Co-operation is natural and practicable enough, under a bond of mutual interest: but obedience is spurious if it springs from anything but respect or love.

The system of Domestic Service in England is a compound, as we have said, from two other systems quite opposite in their principles,—slavery, and contract for the fruits of labour. It combines some of the worst features of each;—the requisition of obedience and subjection to caprice of the first, and the uncertainty of maintenance of the last. The slave-owner, whatever else he may do, cannot avoid maintaining his slaves till their last breath is drawn. The subjects of his despotism are certain of having their animal wants supplied so long as they live. The domestic servant, gaining the invaluable power of quitting a service at pleasure, and being always free to form a new contract, loses the certainty of a maintenance, and has rarely, in the best circumstances, a prospect of providing for old age. This uncertainty, and the positive evils of frequent change of place, together with ignorance of their actual rights, induce in multitudes a subjection to authority, a slavishness of soul, under which the best results of the system of contract are lost. It is hard to tell which is worst,—perpetual struggle for the upper hand

---

[6]**"followers"**: men who court servant women.

in small matters between mistress and servants, or this slavish subjection from helplessness and fear. Free, friendly intercourse is scarcely possible in this relation in England, where the employer is always looking upon the ancient aspect of the relation, and the employed upon the modern. The fault does not lie in individuals. The most just and kind-hearted employer cannot make friends of her domestics, except in a few rare cases; for there is jealousy in their minds,—minds so unenlightened that if jealousy is got rid of, it gives place only to presumption or servility. The best-natured servant cannot make a friend of her mistress, because she has been brought up with the notion that the interests of the two parties are in direct opposition; and the requisition of obedience is sure to come in, from time to time, to check the best feelings of the very best minds of the class.

The case thus stated appears to be very bad: and in England it is very bad. In some European countries it is an easier and pleasanter, and in America it is a far more righteous one. Whence arises the eminent badness of it in England? One most important fact appears to be, that the fierce evils of the Norman Conquest are smouldering in this relation.[7] The old Saxon enmity burns in the bosoms of the working classes of England; and in none so naturally as in those who have to render service to superior rank. The evil of arbitrary rank, imposed originally by foreign force, is the ingredient which poisons all our social relations; and domestic service among the rest. The sufferers under it are unconscious of the cause. Thousands upon thousands struggle and inflict, who never heard the name of Saxon or Norman. A multitude yet unborn are destined to carry out the consequences of the battle of Hastings. Many a student is perfectly unconscious, while poring over the old historians in his library, that the catastrophe is working out in his own kitchen. Many a child looks at pictures of arrows going astray in the New Forest, who little thinks that the difficulties he is witness to between mamma and the maids date further back than poor Sir Walter Tyrrel's[8] running away. The feelings have been transmitted, without the traditions of those times, among the common people of England. They may not have heard of the sour grapes their fathers ate, but they feel their own teeth set on edge. By custom of ages, domestic service may have come to be considered a

natural and proper destination; there may be no longer any recoil from entering into the relation itself; but there is a set of feelings roused by any casual opposition of will, of which the sufferer can give no account, but in which the attentive observer discerns an historical record of the oppressions practised seven centuries ago. No one doubts the relation of the poachers[9] of the present day to the humbled Saxons, who were reduced to the midnight use of the clap-net, while their Norman masters made the woods and heaths of the vanquished ring at noon with the clamour of their dogs and the whistle of their falconers. It is no less clear, that the exasperated feelings of the insulted and oppressed Saxons perpetually re-appear, more or less diluted, in the touchiness, the coldness, the reserve, and the occasional treachery of the domestic servants of the present day. That exasperation was quite strong enough to spread itself over many more than seven centuries. The lands of the Saxons were seized, their property plundered, their homes defiled, their pride mocked, their prejudices outraged, and, in connexion with all this, service was exacted. The very name of service was thereby poisoned in the minds of millions of people, and through hundreds of their generations. The poison is working yet, whether the time and manner of its infusion are recognized or not. There appears little rational hope that it will work itself out imperceptibly and vanish. . . .

We have instanced Conquest as one great cause, and the earliest in date, of the enmity between the classes of employers and employed; but it is far from being the only one. By introducing feudal principles and practices, by imposing a foreign aristocracy on a people reluctant to serve them, it fatally divided the nation against itself; but the division has been aggravated by other influences. Of these, the most disastrous are such as tend to sour the temper of the lower classes, even more than those which go to inflate the pride of the higher; and among such the spirit of asceticism is pre-eminent.

The most fatal consequences of asceticism are always found among the poor and ignorant. The rich and educated are scarcely touched by it, in comparison. Even if their asceticism goes such lengths as to compel them to strip themselves of their external advantages, they have the pleasure of giving away what they had: and there remains to them the inexhaustible wealth of a cultivated understanding and an enlarged imagination. A learned man or an able thinker in La Trappe, may probably be in possession of more means

---

[7]**Norman Conquest**: conquest of England and its **Saxon** inhabitants by the Normans in 1066 at the **Battle of Hastings**.

[8]**Sir Walter Tyrrel** (fl. 1100): thought to have shot William II (reigned 1087–1100) with an **arrow**.

---

[9]**poachers**: illegal catchers of game. A **clap-net,** for catching birds, is shut by pulling a string.

of temporal happiness than a peasant of La Vendée,[10] in the highest peasant state of La Vendée. But place peasants and artizans under the influences of asceticism, and you take from them all that lightens their lives, and relieves their cares, and nourishes the spirit of joy within them. Social intercourse is the life of the poor man's mind. It is to him instead of books and thought. It is his intellectual exercise; it is his spiritual delight. Take this from him, or throw restraint over it, or debase it for him, and you do what in you lies towards making him a machine, or a brute, or a fiend, according as he tends to stupidity, or sensuality, or activity. A wholesale trial of the effects of this treatment has been now going on among us for many generations; and they are what we see. Our labouring classes are precluded by law or religious custom from social assemblies of almost every kind. Here and there may be seen a fair. When the squire's son comes of age, the tenantry are feasted in the park, and there is some jumping in sacks and running after pigs with soaped tails: but there are no spontaneous meetings of the workmen and workwomen of the land, like those of their employers, for the pleasure of meeting, for mirth and dancing, without patronage, without permission, without regard to anything beyond the delights of the hour. Instead of this, there is in large cities a corrupt attendance upon bad penny theatres, and stealthy dances at low public houses, where there is a full knowledge of the amusement being illegal; the house not being licensed to have music in it. In the country, the labourers resort to the beer-shops, for want of any amusement in which their wives and daughters can join. In both town and country there are multitudes who rarely meet their neighbours at all. None of these methods are likely to be sweeteners of the temper. If instead of them our working classes could forget, when work is over, what their employers will think and say; if they could innocently frolic, like the working classes of some other countries, much of the spirit of enmity would evaporate in sympathy and social mirth, and their condition would appear less burdensome to themselves, and less desperate in the apprehensions of others. . . .

The alienation between different classes has also been much increased by the growth of the commercial spirit in this country. This spirit is eminently selfish. However magnificent may be its collateral effects and ultimate results, its immediate influences are clearly unfavourable to free mutual trust; and this in regard to classes quite as much as to individuals. With poverty pressing behind, and ambition hanging out her lures before, men and orders of men are treading on the heels of men and orders of men, and social struggle is the characteristic of the time. No one's position is fixed, at least of our town population. There are not, as of old, families and generations born to service, and having no other idea than of dying in it: nor are there numbers, as it is to be hoped there will be hereafter, who are satisfied with service, from an enlightened view of its real dignity, and the value of the security it offers. The lottery of commerce is preferred to the sure gains of service, wherever the choice is possible; and every one feels depressed who has not a prospect of rising. The actual wealth of the country has enormously increased, and the multitude are dissatisfied with any position which prevents their trying to get in a hand to snatch a share. Though the class of domestic servants may not be conscious that this is the present state of affairs, the jealousy and restlessness consequent upon it extend to them, and impair the chances of tranquillity and content.

The reserve and unsociableness of the national character can scarcely be assigned as a separate cause, it being a necessary product from all the rest: but it now operates as a hindrance to reconciliation. Offences are brooded over which might be explained away; anger becomes treachery through concealment; and, what is far worse than even all this, there is no promise of an intermission of offence. Where two opposing parties live side by side in complete ignorance of one another's feelings, the one in spirit of carelessness and contempt, and the other in a state of irritability and resentment, they cannot but be wounding each other incessantly. If tempers were open, not only would there be no score, but every disagreement would be a warning against future disagreements. As it is, with the reserved tempers of the English, the score mounts up, and it is left to future generations to pay the awful reckoning. . . .

A favourite device for the amelioration of servants is the circulation of tracts written for them. But in these publications the supposition is made throughout, of the obligation lying all on one side. The reader might imagine that it is by act of pure favour that the services of a domestic are accepted at all. Gratitude is preached throughout—gratitude for lodging, food, and clothing; gratitude for health being regarded; gratitude for notice; gratitude for promotion; gratitude, in short, for whatever may be claimed and whatever is earned, as well as for whatever may be bestowed. All this while, not a syllable is breathed about any reciprocity

---

[10]**La Trappe:** Cistercian Abbey in France known for its strict rule of silence, prayer, manual labor, and seclusion from the world. **La Vendée:** poor and extremely religious area of France, site of counterrevolutionary activity during the French Revolution.

of duty; and the one moral lesson taught is servility. Servants are to be blind to their employers' faults, patient under wrongs and sufferings: nowhere is there to be found a hint of the duty of resistance to oppression, of steady rejection of insult. For the reward of labour, the exhorted are referred to another world; for support they are offered, not human sympathy, but religious exercises. They are to be content under the selfish rule of man, as if it were the paternal government of God. Where such exhortations are received, the fruits are seen in hypocrisy and servility, and the authors have to answer for transforming the free-minded of God's creation into a serpent-like groveller that carries a sting. But such exhortations rarely take effect. If kings and princesses were to write preachments on conduct, for the benefit of bankers, merchants and manufacturers, and their families, the royal directions for conduct to superiors would not greatly alter the demeanour of the middle classes, unless the minds of the writers were above mere royalty—were sympathetic. Minds are wrought upon by the like-minded, not by those who, through wealth or station, can overrule the outward fortune. The books which will work at length upon the minds of the labouring classes will be books proceeding from those classes, or from minds which are in sympathy with theirs, and not with the adverse party. It is absolutely necessary for the writers of the "Industrial Series" to bear this constantly in mind, if they propose from their publications any lasting results. In the one whose title stands at the head of this article, "The Maid of All Work," that class of domestics is viewed throughout as a large, important, honourable body, possessed of rights, and independent of patronage. The instruction offered is given in virtue of the youth and inexperience, and not the station of the reader: instead of passive obedience and non-resistance, we find recommendations of honour, generosity, and forbearance; affection instead of gratitude; aspiration instead of content. It must be a matter of experiment how far writings of the kind can be made congenial to the minds of young people of the labouring class by those who are not of them. It will soon be proved which of these two strains of sentiment is most acceptable to the persons addressed.

A little work came under our notice lately, "Mrs Audley," which is rather a favourable specimen of the books of advice written for servants. Some kind-hearted ladies of our acquaintance have bought several copies to give away; and we can only hope that the effect upon other people's tempers may be less irritating than on our own. The heroine's first service was as Maid of All Work at a village blacksmith's. She was required to be extremely thankful for her lot; and there was no end to the self-felicitations put into her mouth for being placed in the following circumstances.—She was a growing girl when she took the situation: she rose at five; got up without waking the children, two of whom slept with her. She went out to milk the cows; when she came back, she washed and dressed the children, and got breakfast ready. While the family breakfasted, she made the beds, then snatched her own meal, and took the children out to walk. On her return, she prepared dinner; then there was cleaning and putting away the dishes; then another walk with the children; then supper; then clearing away again; then washing the children and putting them to bed. She might then sew with her mistress, or go to rest.— Now, the work at a village blacksmith's must be done,— (except the taking out the children for a walk twice a day, by the person who does all the hard work of the house:)— the business must be done, and at a great expense of fatigue to somebody: but it is too much to require a girl to be unboundedly grateful for two pound ten a year in return for work which would kill off most growing girls in two years. Writers of this class of books seem to think that servant-girls have not the same sort of nerves and muscles that other people have; that they can stand all day long, and be up early and late, and yet be blameable if they go to sleep over their book or their meditations on Sundays, when they are required to sit still almost all day. These writers seem to suppose that God and man cannot be sufficiently thanked by a girl who has food, one-third of a bed, and two pound ten a year, without proper time to economize her money. This will not go down with any but the most servile of servant-girls. They may take the work and wages for want of something better; but they will not accept them as a boon, but put up with them as an evil. And what is an evil if not excessive toil with miserable pay? If the writers of such tracts will inquire, they will find that, next to governesses, the largest class of female patients in lunatic asylums is Maids of All Work. . . .

It is commonly said that Education is the remedy for this, as for other social evils. This is true; but the education must begin with the master. What is commonly called education is a great good; but if it has failed to teach employers the truth which lies at the bottom of social reform, it will probably fail to impart it to the employed. This great truth is, that *mutual service is honourable, and not disgraceful.* Reading and writing, the study of history, science, and art, have not yet enlightened the aristocracies of the earth upon this matter; and they may be sure that no charity schools will of themselves make the labouring classes wise upon the point. Domestic servants in England are not untrustworthy and unamiable because they suppose that the world is as flat as

Salisbury Plain, or because they cannot spell, or because they believe that gipsies can tell their fortunes; but because they feel themselves an oppressed and degraded class. A Louisiana slave is scandalised at her mistress taking up the tongs; and an English maid-servant is discomposed at the lady of the house choosing to make a pudding, or iron her husband's cravats. In their eyes, the ladies are degrading themselves by doing useful things, which are "servants' work." Slave and servant are completely in the wrong here; ignorant and immoral in their views and feelings: but they are so because their employers are wrong, ignorant, and immoral first. Long before the Norman conquest, long before the prevalence of feudal pride in Europe, long before the day of the princes, nobles, and priests, who committed all that was most worthy to be done by human hands to thralls, serfs, and churls, there was One who declared that those who would be chief must be servants, and that he himself came not to be ministered unto but to minister. Long ago as this was, and followed as this Teacher has been, these sayings of his are barely beginning to be understood, even now. The classes which, as the most enlightened, lead society, have yet to be initiated into the great doctrine of the glory of Service; and the less educated classes must follow up their better convictions before social safety and comfort can be attained. Here is where the proposed remedy of education must begin. The better convictions must be shown in practice, and not only in preaching. There is no use in masters telling their servants that every one respects the industrious, while they themselves are seen to pay the most honour to the lazy and luxurious. There is no use in mistresses assuring their maids that there is great credit in humble usefulness, when they themselves, pining in idleness, will not touch their household burdens with one of their fingers. Men and maid-servants will go on to believe from what they see, rather than from what they are told: and while gentlemen continue to be distinguished by their retinue, and ladies are waited upon as much from ostentation and laziness as for convenience, country girls will have visions of swinging upon a gate all day, and town maids will languish on sofas when their mistresses are abroad, and footmen will lord it over footboys, and gentlemen's gentlemen[11] will stipulate that their bed-curtains shall close at the foot. The probability is, as we have already intimated, that the struggle for a supposed state of privilege (authority and idleness) will continue till a crisis comes, which shall reveal that all this is no privilege at all, but a curse; but happy are

they meantime who may learn this by an easier and safer discipline, and who, being themselves convinced of the glory and beauty of mutual service, may so diffuse their own convictions as to cheer and strengthen the hearts of those of their fellow-beings whose lot is to serve.

Women are especially called on to do this. Men of all ranks have usually more or less real business to do,—more or less actual service to render to society by head or hand work. Women are unhappily precluded from much of this. Women are more distinctly divided into the two classes of those who must work, and those who need not or cannot. As might be expected, the worst kinds of aristocratic tyranny are found among women who do not work; and they have it in their power to inflict more misery by their tyranny than their husbands can generally impose. They meet their retribution, speedily and certainly; but the retribution serves only to increase the evil, while the rectifying principle is hidden in darkness. From the commercial troubles of this country, as from the political troubles of France, multitudes of women, delicately reared, have been thrown upon their own resources; and if for some, for many, the struggle has seemed too hard, for many more it has been proved to be fraught with blessings. The blessedness of work, the heavenly fruits of toil, have been experienced by hundreds or thousands who, but for adversity, might now have been perishing, body and spirit, from *ennui*. To such is the charge committed of ameliorating the relation of Domestic Service in England. As many of these as have seen with their own eyes the dignity of ministering, in preference to being ministered to; as many as have felt in their own hearts the glow arising from intellectual and moral exercise; as many as have enjoyed the amusement of manual occupations, when pride has been cast behind and prejudice overcome, are the sisters, and are bound to be the saviors, of the domestic servants of society. Their own experience, if they let it work, will have made them reasonable—will have made them sympathising—will have fitted them to be, in this relation, apostolic. They will not only be just and gentle and affectionate mistresses themselves, but they will take the lead in the improvement of the system. They will break up, be it in the minds of many or few, the fatal persuasion of an opposition of interests between the employers and the employed; and this black cloud-canopy once rent asunder, no one knows how much sunshine may be let down into the region where this million of our people, and their children after them, are to spend their lives. The self-education of the employing class—the study of the philosophy of Work, and the cultivation of sympathy with human feelings, will help to rectify the position of the one party;

---

[11]**gentlemen's gentlemen**: valets.

and the influence of their improvement upon those beneath them will tend to dissolve the prejudices and temper the feelings of the other. These seem the only means of breaking up the evils of our social oppositions of every kind, without breaking up society itself. This is a grave consideration, and one which all householders should lay to heart. It is not only themselves and their kitchen inmates who are concerned in their mutual intercourse; nor even the present million of domestics who are dispersed through the homes of the land; but the interests of the future society which, according to the preparation made by us, will be a natural and noble offspring of our present social organisation, or will arise from its ashes.

1838

~

from Eastern Life, Present and Past

The Hareem

I saw two hareems in the East; and it would be wrong to pass them over in an account of my travels; though the subject is as little agreeable as any I can have to treat. I cannot now think of the two mornings thus employed without a heaviness of heart greater than I have ever brought away from Deaf and Dumb Schools, Lunatic Asylums, or even Prisons. As such are my impressions of hareems, of course I shall not say whose they were that I visited. Suffice it that one was at Cairo and the other at Damascus.

The royal hareems were not accessible while I was in Egypt. The Pasha's[1] eldest daughter, the widow of Defterdar Bey, was under her father's displeasure, and was, in fact, a prisoner in her own house. While her father did not visit her, no one else could: and while she was secluded, her younger sister could not receive visitors: and thus their hareems were closed.—The one which I saw was that of a gentleman of high rank; and as good a specimen as could be seen. The misfortune was that there was a mistake about the presence of an interpreter. A lady was to have met us who spoke Italian or French: but she did not arrive; and the morning therefore passed in dumb show: and we could not repeat our visit on a subsequent day, as we were invited to do. We lamented this much at the time: but our subsequent experience of what is to be learned in a hareem with the aid of an intelligent and kind interpretress convinced us that we had not lost much.

Before I went abroad, more than one sensible friend had warned me to leave behind as many prejudices as possible; and especially on this subject, on which the prejudices of Europeans are the strongest. I was reminded of the wide extent, both of time and space, in which polygamy had existed; and that openness of mind was as necessary to the accurate observation of this institution as of every other. I had really taken this advice to heart: I had been struck by the view taken by Mr. Milnes in his beautiful poem of "The Hareem,"[2] and I am sure I did meet this subject with every desire to investigate the ideas and general feelings involved in it. I learned a very great deal about the working of the institution; and I believe I apprehend the thoughts and feelings of the persons concerned in it: and I declare that if we are to look for a hell upon earth, it is where polygamy exists: and that, as polygamy runs riot in Egypt, Egypt is the lowest depth of this hell. I always before believed that every arrangement and prevalent practice had some one fair side, some one redeeming quality: and diligently did I look for this fair side in regard to polygamy: but there is none. The longer one studies the subject, and the deeper one penetrates into it,—the more is one's mind confounded with the intricacy of its iniquity, and the more does one's heart feel as if it would break.

I shall say but little of what I know. If there were the slightest chance of doing any good, I would speak out at all hazards; I would meet all the danger, and endure all the disgust. But there is no reaching the minds of any who live under the accursed system. It is a system which belongs to a totally different region of ideas from ours: and there is nothing to appeal to in the minds of those who, knowing the facts of the institution, can endure it: and at home, no one needs appealing to and convincing. Any plea for liberality that we meet at home proceeds from some poetical fancy, or some laudable desire for impartiality in the absence of knowledge of the facts. Such pleas are not operative enough to render it worth while to shock and sadden many hearts by statements which no one should be required needlessly to endure. I will tell only something of what I saw; and but little of what I thought and know.

At ten o'clock one morning, Mrs. Y.[3] and I were home from our early ride, and dressed for a visit to a hareem of a high order. The lady to whose kindness we mainly owed

---

[1] Ibrahim **Pasha** (1789–1848): viceroy of Egypt.

[2] Richard Monckton **Milnes** (1809–1885) praised the protective seclusion of Eastern women in "**The Hareem**" (1844).

[3] **Mrs. Y.**: Martineau travelled with Richard Vaughan Yates (1785–1856), a Unitarian philanthropist, and his wife.

this opportunity accompanied us, with her daughter. We had a disagreeable drive in the carriage belonging to the hotel, knocking against asses, horses and people all the way. We alighted at the entrance of a paved passage leading to a court, which we crossed: and then, in a second court, we were before the entrance of the hareem.

A party of eunuchs stood before a faded curtain, which they held aside when the gentlemen of our party and the dragomen[4] had gone forward. Retired some way behind the curtain stood, in a half circle, eight or ten slave girls, in an attitude of deep obeisance. Two of them then took charge of each of us, holding us by the arms above the elbows, to help us upstairs.—After crossing a lobby at the top of the stairs, we entered a handsome apartment, where lay the chief wife,—at that time an invalid.—The ceiling was gaily painted; and so were the walls, the latter with curiously bad attempts at domestic perspective. There were four handsome mirrors; and the curtains in the doorway were of a beautiful shawl fabric, fringed and tasselled. A Turkey carpet not only covered the whole floor, but was turned up at the corners. Deewáns[5] extended round nearly the whole room,—a lower one for ordinary use, and a high one for the seat of honour. The windows, which had a sufficient fence of blinds, looked upon a pretty garden, where I saw orange trees and many others, and the fences were hung with rich creepers.

On cushions on the floor lay the chief lady, ill and miserable-looking. She rose as we entered; but we made her lie down again: and she was then covered with a silk counterpane. Her dress was, as we saw when she rose, loose trowsers of blue striped cotton under her black silk jacket: and the same blue cotton appeared at the wrists, under her black sleeves. Her head-dress was of black net, bunched out curiously behind. Her hair was braided down the sides of this head-dress behind, and the ends were pinned over her forehead. Some of the black net was brought round her face, and under the chin, showing the outline of a face which had no beauty in it, nor traces of former beauty, but which was interesting to-day from her manifest illness and unhappiness. There was a strong expression of waywardness and peevishness about the mouth, however. She wore two handsome diamond rings; and she and one other lady had watches and gold chains. She complained of her head; and her left hand was bound up: she made signs, by pressing her bosom, and imitating the dan-

dling of a baby, which, with her occasional tears, persuaded my companions that she had met with some accident and had lost her infant. On leaving the hareem, we found that it was not a child of her own that she was mourning, but that of a white girl in the hareem: and that the wife's illness was wholly from grief for the loss of this baby;—a curious illustration of the feelings and manners of the place! The children born in large hareems are extremely few: and they are usually idolised, and sometimes murdered. It is known that in the houses[6] at home which morally most resemble these hareems (though little enough externally), when the rare event of the birth of a child happens, a passionate joy extends over the wretched household:—jars are quieted, drunkenness is moderated, and there is no self-denial which the poor creatures will not undergo during this gratification of their feminine instincts. They will nurse the child all night in illness, and pamper it all day with sweetmeats and toys; they will fight for the possession of it, and be almost heartbroken at its loss: and lose it they must; for the child always dies,—killed with kindness, even if born healthy. This natural outbreak of feminine instinct takes place in the too populous hareem, when a child is given to any one of the many who are longing for the gift: and if it dies naturally, it is mourned as we saw, through a wonderful conquest of personal jealousy by this general instinct. But when the jealousy is uppermost,— what happens then?—why, the strangling the innocent in its sleep,—or the letting it slip from the window into the river below,—or the mixing poison with its food;—the mother and the murderess, always rivals and now fiends, being shut up together for life. If the child lives, what then? If a girl, she sees before her from the beginning the nothingness of external life, and the chaos of interior existence, in which she is to dwell for life. If a boy, he remains among the women till ten years old, seeing things when the eunuchs come in to romp, and hearing things among the chatter of the ignorant women, which brutalise him for life before the age of rationality comes. But I will not dwell on these hopeless miseries.

A sensible-looking old lady, who had lost an eye, sat at the head of the invalid: and a nun-like elderly woman, whose head and throat were wrapped in unstarched muslin, sat behind for a time, and then went away, after an affectionate salutation to the invalid.—Towards the end of the visit, the husband's mother came in,—looking like a little old man in her coat trimmed with fur. Her countenance was cheerful

---

[4]**dragomen:** interpreters, guides.

[5]**Deewáns:** benches, couches.

[6]**houses:** houses of prostitution.

and pleasant. We saw, I think, about twenty more women,—some slaves,—most or all young—some good-looking, but none handsome. Some few were black; and the rest very light:—Nubians or Abyssinians and Circassians,[7] no doubt. One of the best figures, as a picture, in the hareem, was a Nubian girl, in an amber-coloured watered silk, embroidered with black, looped up in festoons, and finished with a black bodice. The richness of the gay printed cotton skirts and sleeves surprised us: the finest shawls could hardly have looked better. One graceful girl had her pretty figure well shown by a tight-fitting black dress. Their heads were dressed much like the chief lady's. Two, who must have been sisters, if not twins, had patches between the eyes. One handmaid was barefoot, and several were without shoes. Though there were none of the whole large number who could be called particularly pretty individually, the scene was, on the whole, exceedingly striking, as the realisation of what one knew before, but as in a dream. The girls went and came in, but, for the most part, stood in a half circle. Two sat on their heels for a time: and some went to play in the neighbouring apartments.

Coffee was handed to us twice, with all the well-known apparatus of jewelled cups, embroidered tray cover, and gold-flowered napkins. There were chibouques,[8] of course: and sherbets in cut glass cups. The time was passed in attempts to have conversation by signs; attempts which are fruitless among people of the different ideas which belong to different races. How much they made out about us, we do not know: but they inquired into the mutual relationships of the party, and put the extraordinary questions which are always put to ladies who visit the hareems.—A young lady of my acquaintance, of the age of eighteen, but looking younger, went with her mother to a hareem in Cairo (not the one I have been describing), and excited great amazement when obliged to confess that she had not either children or a husband. One of the wives threw her arms about her, entreated her to stay for ever, said she should have any husband she liked, but particularly recommended her own, saying that she was sure he would soon wish for another wife, and she had so much rather it should be my young friend, who would amuse her continually, than anybody else that she could not be so fond of. Everywhere they pitied us European women heartily, that we had to go about travelling, and appearing in the streets without

being properly taken care of—that is, watched. They think us strangely neglected in being left so free, and boast of their spy system and imprisonment as tokens of the value in which they are held.

The mourning worn by the lady who went with us was the subject of much speculation: and many questions were asked about her home and family. To appease the curiosity about her home, she gave her card. As I anticipated, this did not answer. It was the great puzzle of the whole interview. At first the poor lady thought it was to do her head good: then, she fidgetted about it, in the evident fear of omitting some observance: but at last, she understood that she was to keep it. When we had taken our departure, however, a eunuch was sent after us to inquire of the dragoman what "the letter" was which our companion had given to the lady.

The difficulty is to get away, when one is visiting a hareem. The poor ladies cannot conceive of one's having anything to do; and the only reason they can understand for the interview coming to an end is the arrival of sunset, after which it would, they think, be improper for any woman to be abroad. And the amusement to them of such a visit is so great that they protract it to the utmost, even in such a case as ours to-day, when all intercourse was conducted by dumb show. It is certainly very tiresome; and the only wonder is that the hostesses can like it. To sit hour after hour on the deewán, without any exchange of ideas, having our clothes examined, and being plied with successive cups of coffee and sherbet, and pipes, and being gazed at by a half-circle of girls in brocade and shawls, and made to sit down again as soon as one attempts to rise, is as wearisome an experience as one meets with in foreign lands.—The weariness of heart is, however, the worst part of it. I noted all the faces well during our constrained stay; and I saw no trace of mind in any one, except in the homely one-eyed old lady. All the younger ones were dull, soulless, brutish, or peevish. How should it be otherwise, when the only idea of their whole lives is that which, with all our interests and engagements, we consider too prominent with us? There cannot be a woman of them all who is not dwarfed and withered in mind and soul by being kept wholly engrossed with that one interest,—detained at that stage in existence which, though most important in its place, is so as a means to ulterior ends. The ignorance is fearful enough: but the grossness is revolting.

At the third move, and when it was by some means understood that we were waited for, we were permitted to go,—after a visit of above two hours. The sick lady rose from her cushions, notwithstanding our opposition, and we

---

[7]**Nubians, Abyssinians:** from NE Africa. **Circassians:** from the Caucasus.

[8]**chibouques:** tobacco pipes.

were conducted forth with much observance. On each side of the curtain which overhung the outer entrance stood a girl with a bottle of rose-water, some of which was splashed in our faces as we passed out.

We had reached the carriage when we were called back;—his Excellency was waiting for us. So we visited him in a pretty apartment, paved with variegated marbles, and with a fountain in the centre. His Excellency was a sensible-looking man, with gay, easy, and graceful manners. He lamented the mistake about the interpreter, and said we must go again, when we might have conversation. He insisted upon attending us to the carriage, actually passing between the files of beggars which lined the outer passage. The dragoman was so excessively shocked by this degree of condescension that we felt obliged to be so too, and remonstrated, but in vain. He stood till the door was shut and the whip was cracked. He is a liberal-minded man, and his hareem is nearly as favourable a specimen as could be selected for a visit; but what is this best specimen? I find these words written down on the same day in my journal: written, as I well remember, in heaviness of heart:—"I am glad of the opportunity of seeing a hareem: but it leaves an impression of discontent and uneasiness which I shall be glad to sleep off. And I am not conscious that there is prejudice in this. I feel that a visit to the worst room in the rookery in St. Giles's[9] would have affected me less painfully. There are there at least the elements of a rational life, however perverted; while here humanity is wholly and hopelessly baulked. It will never do to look on this as a case for cosmopolitan philosophy to regard complacently, and require a good construction for. It is not a phase of natural early manners. It is as pure a conventionalism as our representative monarchy, or German heraldry, or Hindoo caste; and the most atrocious in the world."

And of this atrocious system Egypt is the most atrocious example. It has unequalled facilities for the importation of black and white slaves, and these facilities are used to the utmost; yet the population is incessantly on the decline. But for the importation of slaves, the upper classes, where polygamy runs riot, must soon die out, so few are the children born, and so fatal to health are the arrangements of society. The finest children are those born of Circassian or Georgian[10] mothers; and but for these we should soon hear little more of an upper class in Egypt.—Large numbers are brought from the south,—the girls to be made attendants or concubines in the hareem, and the boys to be made, in a vast proportion, those guards to the female part of the establishment whose mere presence is a perpetual insult and shame to humanity. The business of keeping up the supply of these miserable wretches—of whom the Pasha's eldest daughter has fifty for her exclusive service—is in the hands of the Christians of Asyoot.[11] It is these Christians who provide a sufficient supply, and cause a sufficient mortality to keep the number of the sexes pretty equal, in consideration of which we cannot much wonder that Christianity does not appear very venerable in the eyes of Mohammedans.

These eunuchs are indulged in regard to dress, personal liberty, and often the possession of office, domestic, military, or political. When retained as guards of the hareem, they are in their master's confidence,—acting as his spies, and indispensable to the ladies as a medium of communication with the world, and as furnishing their amusements,—being at once playmates and servants. It is no unusual thing for the eunuchs to whip the ladies away from a window, whence they had hoped for amusement; or to call them opprobrious names; or to inform against them to their owner: and it is also no unusual thing for them to romp with the ladies, to obtain their confidence, and to try their dispositions. Cases have been known of one of them becoming the friend of some poor girl of higher nature and tendencies than her companions; and even of a closer attachment, which is not objected to by the proprietor of both. It is a case too high for his jealousy, so long as he knows that the cage is secure. It has become rather the fashion to extenuate the lot of the captive of either sex: to point out how the Nubian girl, who would have ground corn, and woven garments, and nursed her infants in comparative poverty all her days, is now surrounded by luxury, and provided for for life: and how the Circassian girl may become a wife of the son of her proprietor, and hold a high rank in the hareem: and how the wretched brothers of these slaves may rise to posts of military command or political confidence; but it is enough to see them to be disabused of all impressions of their good fortune. It is enough to see the dull and gross face of the handmaid of the hareem, and to remember at the moment the cheerful, modest countenance of the Nubian girl, busy about her household tasks, or of the Nubian mother, with her infants hanging about her as she looks, with face open to the sky, for her husband's return from the field, or meets him on the river bank. It is enough to observe the wretched health, and abject, or

---

[9] **rookery in St. Giles's:** very poor tenements in a London slum.

[10] **Georgian:** from Georgia (Russia).

[11] **Asyoot:** in upper Egypt.

worn, or insolent look of the guard of the hareem, and to remember that he ought to have been the head of a household of his own, however humble: and in this contrast of what is with what ought to have been, slavery is seen to be fully as detestable here as anywhere else. These two hellish practices, slavery and polygamy, which, as practices, can clearly never be separated, are here avowedly connected; and, in that connection, are exalted into a double institution, whose working is such as to make one almost wish that the Nile would rise to cover the tops of the hills, and sweep away the whole abomination. Till this happens there is, in the condition of Egypt, a fearful warning before the eyes of all men. The Egyptians laugh at the marriage arrangements of Europe, declaring that virtual polygamy exists everywhere, and is not improved by hypocritical concealment. The European may see, when startled by the state of Egypt, that virtual slavery is indispensably required by the practice of polygamy; virtual proprietorship of the women involved, without the obligations imposed by actual proprietorship; and cruel oppression of the men who should have been the husbands of these women. And again, the Carolina planter, who knows as well as any Egyptian that polygamy is a natural concomitant of slavery, may see in the state of Egypt and the Egyptians what his country and his children must come to, if either of those vile arrangements is permitted which necessitates the other.

It is scarcely needful to say that those benevolent persons are mistaken who believe that slavery in Egypt has been abolished by the Pasha, and the importation of slaves effectually prohibited. Neither the Pasha nor any other human power can abolish slavery while polygamy is an institution of the country, the proportion of the sexes remaining in Egypt what it is, there and everywhere else.

The reason assigned by Montesquieu[12] for polygamy throughout the East has no doubt something in it:—that women become so early marriageable that the wife cannot satisfy the needs of the husband's mind and heart: and that therefore he must have both a bride and a companion of whom he may make a friend. How little there is in this to excuse the polygamy of Egypt may be seen by an observation of the state of things there and in Turkey, where the same religion and natural laws prevail as in Egypt. In Egypt, the difficulty would be great of finding a wife of any age who could be the friend of a man of any sense: and in Turkey, where the wives are of a far higher order, polygamy is rare, and women are not married so young. It is not usual there to find such disparity of years as one finds in Egypt between the husband and his youngest wife. The cause assigned by Montesquieu is true in connection with a vicious state of society: but it is not insuperable, and it will operate only as long as it is wished for. If any influence could exalt the ideas of marriage, and improve the training of women in Egypt, it would soon be seen that men would prefer marrying women of nearly their own age, and would naturally remain comparatively constant: but before this experiment can be tried, parents must have ceased to become restless when their daughter reaches eleven years old, and afraid of disgrace if she remains unmarried long after that.

I was told, while at Cairo, of one extraordinary family where there is not only rational intercourse and confidence at home, and some relaxation of imprisonment, but the young ladies read!—and read French and Italian! I asked what would be the end of this: and my informant replied that whether the young ladies married or not, they would sooner or later sink down, he thought, into a state even less contented than the ordinary. There could be no sufficient inducement for secluded girls, who never saw anybody wiser than themselves, to go on reading French and Italian books within a certain range. For want of stimulus and sympathy, they would stop; and then, finding themselves dissatisfied among the nothings which fill the life of other women, they would be very unhappy. The exceptional persons under a bad state of things, and the beginners under an improving system, must ever be sufferers,—martyrs of their particular reformation. To this they may object less than others would for them, if they are conscious of the personal honour and general blessing of their martyrdom.

The youngest wife I ever saw (except the swathed and veiled brides we encountered in the streets of Egyptian cities) was in a Turkish hareem which Mrs. Y. and I visited at Damascus. I will tell that story now, that I may dismiss the subject of this chapter. I heartily dreaded this second visit to a hareem, and braced myself up to it as one does to an hour at the dentist's, or to an expedition into the City[13] to prove a debt. We had the comfort of a good and pleasant interpreter; and there was more mirth and nonsense than in the Cairo hareem; and therefore somewhat less disgust and constraint: but still it was painful enough. We saw the seven wives of three gentlemen, and a crowd of attendants and visitors. Of the seven, two had been the wives of the head

---

[12]Charles-Louis de Secondat **Montesquieu** (1689–1755) discussed polygamy in **The Persian Letters** (1721) and **The Spirit of Laws** (1748).

---

[13]**City:** financial district of London.

of the household, who was dead: three were the wives of his eldest son, aged twenty-two; and the remaining two were the wives of his second son, aged fifteen. The youngest son, aged thirteen, was not yet married; but he would be thinking about it soon.—The pair of widows were elderly women, as merry as girls, and quite at their ease. Of the other five, three were sisters:—that is, we conclude, half-sisters,—children of different mothers in the same hareem. It is evident at a glance what a tragedy lies under this; what the horrors of jealousy must be among sisters thus connected for life,—three of them between two husbands in the same house! And we were told that the jealousy had begun, young as they were, and the third having been married only a week.—This young creature, aged twelve, was the bride of the husband of fifteen. She was the most conspicuous person in the place, not only for the splendour of her dress, but because she sat on the deewán, while the others sat or lounged on cushions on the raised floor. The moment we took our seats I was struck with compassion for this child,—she looked so grave, and sad, and timid. While the others romped and giggled, pushing and pulling one another about, and laughing at jokes among themselves, she never smiled, but looked on listlessly. I was determined to make her laugh before we went away; and at last she relaxed somewhat,—smiling, and growing grave again in a moment: but at length she really and truly laughed; and when we were shown the whole hareem, she also slipped her bare and dyed feet into her pattens[14] inlaid with mother-of-pearl, and went into the courts with us, nestling to us, and seeming to lose the sense of her new position for the time: but there was far less of the gaiety of a child about her than in the elderly widows. Her dress was superb;—a full skirt and bodice of geranium-coloured brocade, embossed with gold flowers and leaves; and her frill and ruffles were of geranium-coloured gauze. Her eyebrows were frightful,—joined and prolonged by black paint. Her head was covered with a silk net, in almost every mesh of which were stuck jewels or natural flowers: so that her head was like a bouquet sprinkled with diamonds. Her nails were dyed black; and her feet were dyed black in chequers. Her complexion, called white, was of an unhealthy yellow: and indeed we did not see a healthy complexion among the whole company; nor anywhere among women who were secluded from exercise, while pampered with all the luxuries of Eastern living.

Besides the seven wives, a number of attendants came in to look at us, and serve the pipes and sherbet; and a few ladies from a neighbouring hareem; and a party of Jewesses, with whom we had some previous acquaintance. Mrs. Y. was compelled to withdraw her lace veil, and then to take off her bonnet: and she was instructed that the street was the place for her to wear her veil down, and that they expected to see her face. Then her bonnet went round, and was tried on many heads,—one merry girl wearing it long enough to surprise many new-comers with the joke.—My gloves were stretched and pulled all manner of ways, in their attempts to thrust their large, broad brown hands into them, one after another. But the great amusement was my trumpet.[15] The eldest widow, who sat next me, asked for it, and put it to her ear; when I said "Bo!" When she had done laughing, she put it to her next neighbour's ear, and said "Bo!" and in this way it came round to me again. But in two minutes, it was asked for again, and went round a second time,—everybody laughing as loud as ever at each "Bo!"—and then a third time! Could one have conceived it!—The next joke was on behalf of the Jewesses, four or five of whom sat in a row on the deewán. Almost everybody else was puffing away at a chibouque or a nargeeleh, and the place was one cloud of smoke. The poor Jewesses were obliged to decline joining us; for it happened to be Saturday: they must not smoke on the Sabbath. They were naturally much pitied: and some of the young wives did what was possible for them. Drawing in a long breath of smoke, they puffed it forth in the faces of the Jewesses, who opened mouth and nostrils eagerly to receive it. Thus was the Sabbath observed, to shouts of laughter.

A pretty little blue-eyed girl of seven was the only child we saw. She nestled against her mother; and the mother clasped her closely, lest we should carry her off to London. She begged we would not wish to take her child to London, and said she "would not sell her for much money."—One of the wives was pointed out to us as particularly happy in the prospect of becoming a mother; and we were taken to see the room in which she was to lie in, which was all in readiness, though the event was not looked for for more than half a year. She was in the gayest spirits, and sang and danced. While she was lounging on her cushions, I thought her the handsomest and most graceful, as well as the happiest, of the party: but when she rose to dance, the charm was destroyed for ever. The dancing is utterly disgusting. A pretty Jewess of twelve years old danced, much in the same way; but with downcast eyes and an air of modesty. While the dancing went on, and the smoking, and

---

[14]**pattens**: thick-soled shoes.

[15]**trumpet**: trumpet-shaped tube used to assist hearing.

drinking coffee and sherbet, and the singing, to the accompaniment of a tambourine, some hideous old hags came in successively, looked and laughed, and went away again. Some negresses made a good background to this thoroughly Eastern picture. All the while, romping, kissing, and screaming went on among the ladies, old and young. At first, I thought them a perfect rabble; but when I recovered myself a little, I saw that there was some sense in the faces of the elderly women.—In the midst of all this fun, the interpretess assured us "there is much jealousy every day"; jealousy of the favoured wife; that is, in this case, of the one who was pointed out to us by her companions as so eminently happy, and with whom they were romping and kissing, as with the rest. Poor thing! even the happiness of these her best days is hollow: for she cannot have, at the same time, peace in the hareem and her husband's love.

They were so free in their questions about us, and so evidently pleased when we used a similar impertinence about them, that we took the opportunity of learning a good deal of their way of life. Mrs. Y. and I were consulting about noticing the bride's dress, when we found we had put off too long: we were asked how we liked her dress, and encouraged to handle the silk. So I went on to examine the bundles of false hair that some of them wore; the pearl bracelets on their tattooed arms, and their jewelled and inlaid pattens.—In answer to our question what they did in the way of occupation, they said "Nothing": but when we inquired whether they never made clothes or sweetmeats, they replied "Yes."—They earnestly wished us to stay always; and they could not understand why we should not. My case puzzled them particularly. I believe they took me for a servant; and they certainly pitied me extremely for having to go about without being taken care of. They asked what I did: and Mrs. Y., being anxious to do me all honour, told them I had written many books: but the information was thrown away, because they did not know what a book was. Then we informed them that I lived in a field among mountains, where I had built a house; and that I had plenty to do; and we told them in what way: but still they could make nothing of it but that I had brought the stones with my own hands, and built the house myself. There is nothing about which the inmates of hareems seem to be so utterly stupid as about women having anything to do. That time should be valuable to a woman, and that she should have any business on her hands, and any engagements to observe, are things quite beyond their comprehension.

The pattens I have mentioned are worn to keep the feet and flowing dress from the marble pavement, which is often wetted for coolness. I think all the ladies here had bare feet. When they left the raised floor on which they sat, they slipped their feet into their high pattens, and went stumping about, rather awkwardly. I asked Dr. Thompson, who has admission as a physician into more houses than any other man could familiarly visit, whether he could not introduce skipping-ropes upon these spacious marble floors. I see no other chance of the women being induced to take exercise. They suffer cruelly from indigestion,—gorging themselves with sweet things, smoking intemperately, and passing through life with more than half the brain almost unawakened, and with scarcely any exercise of the limbs. Poor things! our going was a great amusement to them, they said; and they showed this by their entreaties to the last moment that we would not leave them yet, and that we would stay always.—"And these," as my journal says, "were human beings, such as those of whom Christ made friends!—The chief lady gave me roses as a farewell token.—The Jewish ladies, who took their leave with us, wanted us to visit at another house: but we happily had not time.—I am thankful to have seen a hareem under favourable circumstances; and I earnestly hope I may never see another."

I kept those roses, however. I shall need no reminding of the most injured human beings I have ever seen,—the most studiously depressed and corrupted women whose condition I have witnessed: but I could not throw away the flowers which so found their way into my hand as to bespeak for the wrongs of the giver the mournful remembrance of my heart. (Chapter 22)

1848

~

from Autobiography
First Period: To Eight Years Old

My first recollections are of some infantine impressions which were in abeyance for a long course of years, and then revived in an inexplicable way,— as by a flash of lightning over a far horizon in the night. There is no doubt of the genuineness of the remembrance, as the facts could not have been told me by any one else. I remember standing on the threshold of a cottage, holding fast by the doorpost, and putting my foot down, in repeated attempts to reach the ground. Having accomplished the step, I toddled (I remember the uncertain feeling) to a tree before the door, and tried to clasp and get round it; but the rough bark hurt my hands. At night of the same day, in bed, I was disconcerted by the coarse feel of the sheets,—so much less smooth and cold than those at home; and I was alarmed by the creaking of the bedstead when I moved. It was a turn-up bedstead in a cottage, or small farm-house at Carleton, where I was sent for my health, being a delicate child. My mother's account of things was that I was all but starved to death in the first weeks of my life,—the wetnurse being very poor, and holding on to her good place after her milk was going or gone. The discovery was made when I was three months old, and when I was fast sinking under diarrhœa. My bad health during my whole childhood and youth, and even my deafness, was always ascribed by my mother to this. However it might be about that, my health certainly was very bad till I was nearer thirty than twenty years of age; and never was poor mortal cursed with a more beggarly nervous system. The long years of indigestion by day and night-mare terrors are mournful to think of now.—Milk has radically disagreed with me, all my life: but when I was a child, it was a thing unheard of for children not to be fed on milk: so, till I was old enough to have tea at breakfast, I went on having a horrid lump at my throat for hours of every morning, and the most terrific oppressions in the night. Sometimes the dim light of the windows in the night seemed to advance till it pressed upon my eyeballs, and then the windows would seem to recede to an infinite distance. If I laid my hand under my head on the pillow, the hand seemed to vanish almost to a point, while the head grew as big as a mountain. Sometimes I was panic struck at the head of the stairs, and was sure I could never get down; and I could never cross the yard to the garden without flying and panting, and fearing to look behind, because a wild beast was after me. The starlight sky was the worst; it was always coming down, to stifle and crush me, and rest upon my head. I do not remember any dread of thieves or ghosts in particular; but things as I actually saw them were dreadful to me; and it now appears to me that I had scarcely any respite from the terror. My fear of persons was as great as any other. To the best of my belief, the first person I was ever not afraid of was Aunt Kentish, who won my heart and my confidence when I was sixteen. My heart was ready enough to flow out; and it often did: but I always repented of such expansion, the next time I dreaded to meet a human face.—It now occurs to me, and it may be worth while to note it,—what the extremest terror of all was about. We were often sent to walk on the Castle Hill at Norwich. In the wide area below, the residents were wont to expose their feather-beds, and to beat them with a stick. That sound,—a dull shock,—used to make my heart stand still: and it was no use my standing at the rails above, and seeing the process. The striking of the

blow and the arrival of the sound did not correspond; and this made matters worse. I hated that walk; and I believe for that reason. My parents knew nothing of all this. It never occurred to me to speak of any thing I felt most: and I doubt whether they ever had the slightest idea of my miseries. It seems to me now that a little closer observation would have shown them the causes of the bad health and fitful temper which gave them so much anxiety on my account; and I am sure that a little more of the cheerful tenderness which was in those days thought bad for children, would have saved me from my worst faults, and from a world of suffering.

My hostess and nurse at the above-mentioned cottage was a Mrs. Merton, who was, as was her husband, a Methodist or melancholy Calvinist of some sort. The family story about me was that I came home the absurdest little preacher of my years (between two and three) that ever was. I used to nod my head emphatically, and say "Never ky for tyfles:" "Dooty fust, and pleasure afterwards," and so forth: and I sometimes got courage to edge up to strangers, and ask them to give me—"a maxim." Almost before I could join letters, I got some sheets of paper, and folded them into a little square book, and wrote, in double lines, two or three in a page, my beloved maxims. I believe this was my first effort at book-making. It was probably what I picked up at Carleton that made me so intensely religious as I certainly was from a very early age. The religion was of a bad sort enough, as might be expected from the urgency of my needs; but I doubt whether I could have got through without it. I pampered my vain-glorious propensities by dreams of divine favour, to make up for my utter deficiency of self-respect: and I got rid of otherwise incessant remorse by a most convenient confession and repentance, which relieved my nerves without at all, I suspect, improving my conduct.

To revert to my earliest recollections:—I certainly could hardly walk alone when our nursemaid took us,—including my sister Elizabeth, who was eight years older than myself,—an unusual walk; through a lane, (afterwards called by us the "Spinner's Lane") where some Miss Taskers, acquaintances of Elizabeth's and her seniors, were lodging, in a cottage which had a fir grove behind it. Somebody set me down at the foot of a fir, where I was distressed by the slight rising of the ground at the root, and by the long grass, which seemed a terrible entanglement. I looked up the tree, and was scared at its height, and at that of so many others. I was comforted with a fir-cone; and then one of the Miss Taskers caught me up in her arms and kissed me; and I was too frightened to cry till we got away.—I was not more than two years old when an impression of touch occurred to me which remains vivid to this day. It seems indeed as if impressions of touch were at that age more striking than those from the other senses. I say this from observation of others besides myself; for my own case is peculiar in that matter. Sight, hearing and touch were perfectly good in early childhood; but I never had the sense of smell; and that of taste was therefore exceedingly imperfect.—On the occasion I refer to, I was carried down a flight of steep back stairs, and Rachel (a year and a half older than I) clung to the nursemaid's gown, and Elizabeth was going before, (still quite a little girl) when I put down my finger ends to feel a flat velvet button on the top of Rachel's bonnet. The rapture of the sensation was really monstrous, as I remember it now. Those were our mourning bonnets for a near relation; and this marks the date, proving me to have been only two years old.

I was under three when my brother James[1] was born. That day was another of the distinct impressions which flashed upon me in after years. I found myself within the door of the best bedroom,—an impressive place from being seldom used, from its having a dark, polished floor, and from the awful large gay figures of the chintz bed hangings. That day the curtains were drawn, the window blinds were down, and an unknown old woman, in a mob cap, was at the fire, with a bundle of flannel in her arms. She beckoned to me, and I tried to go, though it seemed impossible to cross the slippery floor. I seem to hear now the pattering of my feet. When I arrived at her knee, the nurse pushed out with her foot a tiny chair, used as a foot-stool, made me sit down on it, laid the bundle of flannel across my knees, and opened it so that I saw the little red face of the baby. I then found out that there was somebody in the bed,—seeing a nightcap on the pillow. This was on the 21st of April, 1805. I have a distinct recollection of some incidents of that summer. My mother did not recover well from her confinement, and was sent to the sea, at Yarmouth. On our arrival there, my father took me along the old jetty,—little knowing what terror I suffered. I remember the strong grasp of his large hand being some comfort; but there were holes in the planking of the jetty quite big enough to let my foot through; and they disclosed the horrible sight of waves flowing and receding below, and great tufts of green weeds swaying to and fro. I remember the sitting-room at our lodgings, and my mother's dress as she sat picking shrimps, and letting me try to help her.—Of all my many fancies, perhaps none was so terrible as a dream that I had at four

years old. The impression is as fresh as possible now; but I cannot at all understand what the fright was about. I know nothing more strange than this power of re-entering, as it were, into the narrow mind of an infant, so as to compare it with that of maturity; and therefore it may be worth while to record that piece of precious nonsense,—my dream at four years old. I imagine I was learning my letters then from cards, where each letter had its picture,—as a stag for S. I dreamed that we children were taking our walk with our nursemaid out of St. Austin's Gate (the nearest bit of country to our house). Out of the public-house there came a stag, with prodigious antlers. Passing the pump, it crossed the road to us, and made a polite bow, with its head on one side, and with a scrape of one foot, after which it pointed with its foot to the public-house, and spoke to me, inviting me in. The maid declined, and turned to go home. Then came the terrible part. By the time we were at our own door, it was dusk, and we went up the steps in the dark; but in the kitchen it was bright sunshine. My mother was standing at the dresser, breaking sugar; and she lifted me up, and set me in the sun, and gave me a bit of sugar. Such was the dream which froze me with horror! Who shall say why?— But my panics were really unaccountable. They were a matter of pure sensation, without any intellectual justification whatever, even of the wildest kind. A magic-lantern[2] was exhibited to us on Christmas-day, and once or twice in the year besides. I used to see it cleaned by daylight, and to handle all its parts,—understanding its whole structure; yet, such was my terror of the white circle on the wall, and of the moving slides, that, to speak the plain truth, the first apparition always brought on bowel-complaint; and, at the age of thirteen, when I was pretending to take care of little children during the exhibition, I could never look at it without having the back of a chair to grasp, or hurting myself, to carry off the intolerable sensation. My bitter shame may be conceived; but then, I was always in a state of shame about something or other. I was afraid to walk in the town, for some years, if I remember right, for fear of meeting two people. One was an unknown old lady who very properly rebuked me one day for turning her off the very narrow pavement of London Lane, telling me, in an awful way, that little people should make way for their elders. The other was an unknown farmer, in whose field we had been gleaning (among other trespassers) before the shocks were carried. This man left the field after us, and followed us into

---

[1]James Martineau (1805–1900) became a Unitarian divine and moral philosopher.

[2]**magic-lantern:** instrument that projects a magnified image of a picture on glass.

the city,—no doubt, as I thought, to tell the Mayor, and send the constable after us. I wonder how long it was before I left off expecting that constable. There were certain little imps, however, more alarming still. Our house was in a narrow street; and all its windows, except two or three at the back, looked eastwards. It had no sun in the front rooms, except before breakfast in summer. One summer morning, I went into the drawing-room, which was not much used in those days, and saw a sight which made me hide my face in a chair, and scream with terror. The drops of the lustres on the mantle-piece, on which the sun was shining, were somehow set in motion, and the prismatic colours danced vehemently on the walls. I thought they were alive,—imps of some sort; and I never dared go into that room alone in the morning, from that time forward. I am afraid I must own that my heart has beat, all my life long, at the dancing of prismatic colours on the wall.

I was getting some comfort, however, from religion by this time. The Sundays began to be marked days, and pleasantly marked, on the whole. I do not know why crocuses were particularly associated with Sunday at that time; but probably my mother might have walked in the garden with us, some early spring Sunday. My idea of Heaven was of a place gay with yellow and lilac crocuses. My love of gay colours was very strong. When I was sent with the keys to a certain bureau in my mother's room, to fetch miniatures of my father and grandfather, to be shown to visitors, I used to stay an unconscionable time, though dreading punishment for it, but utterly unable to resist the fascination of a certain watch-ribbon kept in a drawer there. This ribbon had a pattern in floss silk, gay and beautifully shaded; and I used to look at it till I was sent for, to be questioned as to what I had been about. The young wild parsley and other weeds in the hedges used to make me sick with their luscious green in spring. One crimson and purple sunrise I well remember, when James could hardly walk alone, and I could not therefore have been more than five. I awoke very early, that summer morning, and saw the maid sound asleep in her bed, and "the baby" in his crib. The room was at the top of the house; and some rising ground beyond the city could be seen over the opposite roofs. I crept out of bed, saw James's pink toes showing themselves invitingly through the rails of his crib, and gently pinched them, to wake him. With a world of trouble I got him over the side, and helped him to the window, and upon a chair there. I wickedly opened the window, and the cool air blew in; and yet the maid did not wake. Our arms were smutted with the blacks on the window-sill, and our bare feet were corded with the impression of the rush-bottomed chair; but we were not found out. The sky was

gorgeous, and I talked very religiously to the child. I remember the mood, and the pleasure of expressing it, but nothing of what I said.

I must have been a remarkably religious child, for the only support and pleasure I remember having from a very early age was from that source. I was just seven when the grand event of my childhood took place,—a journey to Newcastle to spend the summer (my mother and four of her children) at my grandfather's; and I am certain that I cared more for religion before and during that summer than for anything else. It was after our return, when Ann Turner, daughter of the Unitarian Minister there, was with us, that my piety first took a practical character; but it was familiar to me as an indulgence long before. While I was afraid of everybody I saw, I was not in the least afraid of God. Being usually very unhappy, I was constantly longing for heaven, and seriously, and very frequently planning suicide in order to get there. I was sure that suicide would not stand in the way of my getting there. I knew it was considered a crime; but I did not feel it so. I had a devouring passion for justice;—justice, first to my own precious self, and then to other oppressed people. Justice was precisely what was least understood in our house, in regard to servants and children. Now and then I desperately poured out my complaints; but in general I brooded over my injuries, and those of others who dared not speak; and then the temptation to suicide was very strong. No doubt, there was much vindictiveness in it. I gloated over the thought that I would make somebody care about me in some sort of way at last: and, as to my reception in the other world, I felt sure that God could not be very angry with me for making haste to him when nobody else cared for me, and so many people plagued me. One day I went to the kitchen to get the great carving knife, to cut my throat; but the servants were at dinner; and this put it off for that time. By degrees, the design dwindled down into running away. I used to lean out of the window, and look up and down the street, and wonder how far I could go without being caught. I had no doubt at all that if I once got into a farm-house, and wore a woollen petticoat, and milked the cows, I should be safe, and that nobody would inquire about me any more.—It is evident enough that my temper must have been very bad. It seems to me now that it was downright devilish, except for a placability which used to annoy me sadly. My temper might have been early made a thoroughly good one, by the slightest indulgence shown to my natural affections, and any rational dealing with my faults: but I was almost the youngest of a large family, and subject, not only to the rule of severity to which all were liable, but also to the rough and contemptuous treatment of the elder children, who meant no harm, but injured me irreparably. I had no self-respect, and an unbounded need of approbation and affection. My capacity for jealousy was something frightful. When we were little more than infants, Mr. Thomas Watson, son of my father's partner, one day came into the yard, took Rachel up in his arms, gave her some grapes off the vine, and carried her home, across the street, to give her Gay's Fables,[3] bound in red and gold. I stood with a bursting heart, beating my hoop, and hating every body in the world. I always hated Gay's Fables, and for long could not abide a red book. Nobody dreamed of all this; and the 'taking down' system was pursued with me as with the rest, issuing in the assumed doggedness and wilfulness which made me desperately disagreeable during my youth, to every body at home. The least word or tone of kindness melted me instantly, in spite of the strongest predeterminations to be hard and offensive. Two occasions stand out especially in my memory, as indeed almost the only instances of the enjoyment of tenderness manifested to myself individually.

When I was four or five years old, we were taken to a lecture of Mr. Drummond's, for the sake, no doubt, of the pretty shows we were to see,—the chief of which was the Phantasmagoria of which we had heard, as a fine sort of magic-lantern. I did not like the darkness, to begin with; and when Minerva[4] appeared, in a red dress, at first extremely small, and then approaching, till her owl seemed coming directly upon me, it was so like my nightmare dreams that I shrieked aloud. I remember my own shriek. A pretty lady who sat next us, took me on her lap, and let me hide my face in her bosom, and held me fast. How intensely I loved her, without at all knowing who she was! From that time we knew her, and she filled a large space in my life; and above forty years after, I had the honour of having her for my guest in my own house. She was Mrs. Lewis Cooper, then the very young mother of two girls of the ages of Rachel and myself, of whom I shall have to say more presently.—The other occasion was when I had a terrible ear-ache one Sunday. The rest went to chapel in the afternoon; and my pain grew worse. Instead of going into the kitchen to the cook, I wandered into a lumber room at the top of the house. I laid my aching ear against the cold iron screw of a bedstead, and howled with pain; but nobody came to me. At last, I heard the family come home from chapel. I heard them go into the parlour, one after another,

and I knew they were sitting round the fire in the dusk. I stole down to the door, and stood on the mat, and heard them talking and laughing merrily. I stole in, thinking they would not observe me, and got into a dark corner. Presently my mother called to me, and asked what I was doing there. Then I burst out,—that my ear ached so I did not know *what* to do! Then she and my father both called me tenderly, and she took me on her lap, and laid the ear on her warm bosom. I was afraid of spoiling her starched muslin handkerchief with the tears which *would* come; but I was very happy, and wished that I need never move again. Then of course came remorse for all my naughtiness; but I was always suffering that, though never, I believe, in my whole childhood, being known to own myself wrong. I must have been an intolerable child: but I need not have been so.

I was certainly fond of going to chapel before that Newcastle era which divided my childhood into two equal portions: but my besetting troubles followed me even there. My passion for justice was baulked there, as much as any where. The duties preached were those of inferiors to superiors, while the *per contra*[5] was not insisted on with any equality of treatment at all. Parents were to bring up their children "in the nurture and admonition of the Lord,"[6] and to pay servants due wages; but not a word was ever preached about the justice due from the stronger to the weaker. I used to thirst to hear some notice of the oppression which servants and children had (as I supposed universally) to endure, in regard to their feelings, while duly clothed, fed and taught: but nothing of the sort ever came; but instead, a doctrine of passive obedience which only made me remorseful and miserable. I was abundantly obedient in act; for I never dreamed of being otherwise; but the interior rebellion kept my conscience in a state of perpetual torture. As far as I remember, my conscience was never of the least use to me; for I always concluded myself wrong about every thing, while pretending entire complacency and assurance. My moral discernment was almost wholly obscured by fear and mortification.—Another misery at chapel was that I could not attend to the service, nor refrain from indulging in the most absurd vain-glorious dreams, which I was ashamed of, all the while. The Octagon Chapel at Norwich has some curious windows in the roof;—not skylights, but letting in light indirectly. I used to sit staring up at those windows, and looking for angels to come for me, and take me to heaven, in sight of all the congrega-

---

[3]*Fables* (1727): by John **Gay** (1685–1732).

[4]**Minerva**: Roman goddess of wisdom whose symbol is an owl.

[5]*per contra*: in return.

[6]"in the nurture . . . of the Lord": Ephesians 6:4.

tion,—the end of the world being sure to happen while we were at chapel. I was thinking of this, and of the hymns, the whole of the time, it now seems to me. It was very shocking to me that I could not pray at chapel. I believe that I never did in my life. I prayed abundantly when I was alone; but it was impossible to me to do it in any other way; and the hypocrisy of appearing to do so was a long and sore trouble to me.—All this is very painful; but I really remember little that was not painful at that time of my life.—To be sure, there was Nurse Ayton, who used to come, one or two days in the week, to sew. She was kind to me, and I was fond of her. She told us long stories about her family; and she taught me to sew. She certainly held the family impression of my abilities,—that I was a dull, unobservant, slow, awkward child. In teaching me to sew, she used to say (and I quite acquiesced) that "slow and sure" was the maxim for me, and "quick and well" was the maxim for Rachel. I was not jealous about this,—it seemed to me so undeniable. On one occasion only I thought Nurse Ayton unkind. The back of a rickety old nursing-chair came off when I was a playing on it; and I was sure she could save me from being scolded by sewing it on again. I insisted that she could sew *anything*. This made my mother laugh when she came up; and so I forgave nurse: and I believe that was our only quarrel.

My first political interest was the death of Nelson.[7] I was then four years old. My father came in from the counting-house at an unusual hour, and told my mother, who cried heartily. I certainly had some conception of a battle, and of a great man being a public loss. It always rent my heart-strings (to the last day of her life,) to see and hear my mother cry; and in this case it was clearly connected with the death of a great man. I had my own notions of Bonaparte too. One day, at dessert, when my father was talking anxiously to my mother about the expected invasion, for which preparations were made all along the Norfolk coast, I saw them exchange a glance, because I was standing staring, twitching my pinafore with terror. My father called me to him, and took me on his knee, and I said "But, papa, what will you do if Boney comes?" "What will I do?" said he, cheerfully, "Why, I will ask him to take a glass of Port with me,"—helping himself to a glass as he spoke. That wise reply was of immense service to me. From the moment I knew that "Boney" was a creature who could take a glass of wine, I dreaded him no more. Such was my induction into the department of foreign affairs. As to social matters,—my

passion for justice was cruelly crossed, from the earliest time I can remember, by the imposition of passive obedience and silence on servants and tradespeople, who met with a rather old-fashioned treatment in our house. We children were enough in the kitchen to know how the maids avenged themselves for scoldings in the parlour, before the family and visitors, to which they must not reply; and for being forbidden to wear white gowns, silk gowns, or any thing but what strict housewives approved. One of my chief miseries was being sent with insulting messages to the maids,—e.g., to "bid them not be so like cart-horses overhead," and the like. On the one hand, it was a fearful sin to alter a message; and, on the other, it was impossible to give such an one as that: so I used to linger and delay to the last moment, and then deliver something civil, with all imaginable sheepishness, so that the maids used to look at one another and laugh. Yet, one of my most heartfelt sins was towards a servant who was really a friend of my mother's, and infinitely respected, and a good deal loved, by us children,—Susan Ormsby, who came to live with us just before James was born, and staid till that memorable Newcastle journey, above four years afterwards. When she was waiting at dinner one day, I stuck my knife upright, in listening to something, so that the point cut her arm. I saw her afterwards washing it at the pump; and she shook her head at me in tender reproach. My heart was bursting; but I dared not tell her how sorry I was. I never got over it, or was happy with her again; and when we were to part, the night before our journey, and she was kissing us with tears, it was in dumb grief and indignation that I heard her tell my mother that children do not feel things as grown people do, and that they could not think of any thing else when they were going a journey.

One more fact takes its place before that journey,—the awakening of a love of money in me. I suspect I have had a very narrow escape of being an eminent miser. A little more, or a little less difficulty, or another mode of getting money would easily have made me a miser. The first step, as far as I remember, was when we played cards, one winter evening, at our uncle Martineau's, when I was told that I had won twopence. The pavement hardly seemed solid when we walked home,—so elated was I. I remember equal delight when Mrs. Meadows Taylor gave us children twopence when we expected only a halfpenny, to buy string for a top: but in this last case it was not the true *amor nummi*,[8] as in the other. The same avarice was excited in the same way, a few

---

[7]Horatio **Nelson** (1758–1805): naval commander, killed at the battle of Trafalgar in the war against France.

[8]*amor nummi*: love of money.

years later, when I won eighteen-pence at cards, on a visit. The very sight of silver and copper was transporting to me, without any thought of its use. I stood and looked long at money, as it lay in my hand. Yet, I do not remember that this passion ever interfered with my giving away money, though it certainly did with my spending it otherwise. I certainly was very close, all my childhood and youth. I may as well mention here that I made rules and kept them, in regard to my expenditure, from the time I had an allowance. I believe we gave away something out of our first allowance of a penny a week. When we had twopence, I gave away half. The next advance was to half-a-guinea a quarter, to buy gloves and sashes: then to ten pounds a year (with help) for clothes; then fifteen, and finally twenty, without avowed help. I sewed indefatigably all those years,—being in truth excessively fond of sewing, with the amusement of either gossipping, or learning poetry by heart, from a book, lying open under my work. I never had the slightest difficulty in learning any amount of verse; and I knew enough to have furnished me for a wandering reciter,—if there had been such a calling in our time,—as I used to wish there was. While thus busy, I made literally all my clothes, as I grew up, except stays and shoes. I platted bonnets at one time, knitted stockings as I read aloud, covered silk shoes for dances, and made all my garments. Thus I squeezed something out of the smaller allowance, and out of the fifteen pounds, I never spent more than twelve in dress; and never more than fifteen pounds out of the twenty. The rest I gave away, except a little which I spent in books. The amount of time spent in sewing now appears frightful; but it was the way in those days, among people like ourselves. There was some saving in our practice of reading aloud, and in mine of learning poetry in such mass: but the censorious gossip which was the bane of our youth drove prose and verse out of the field, and wasted more of our precious youthful powers and dispositions than any repentance and amendment in after life could repair. This sort of occupation, the sewing however, was less unfitting than might now appear, considering that the fortunes of manufacturers, like my father, were placed in jeopardy by the war, and that there was barely a chance for my father ever being able to provide fortunes for his daughters. He and my mother exercised every kind of self-denial to bring us up qualified to take care of ourselves. They pinched themselves in luxuries to provide their girls, as well as their boys, with masters and schooling; and they brought us up to an industry like their own,—the boys in study and business, and the girls in study and household cares. Thus was I saved from being a literary lady who could not sew; and when, in after years, I have been insulted by admiration at not being helpless in regard to household employments, I have been wont to explain, for my mother's sake, that I could make shirts and puddings, and iron and mend, and get my bread by my needle, if necessary,—(as it once was necessary, for a few months,) before I won a better place and occupation with my pen.

1855, 1877

JOHN STUART MILL

(1806–1873)

"Autobiography of a steam-engine," snorted Carlyle at the posthumous memoir of his friend with the industrial name; today the irresistible analogy is to a computer. Mill's first chapter accesses childhood memories like a batch of uploaded text files; the depression that hit him in early manhood is fixed by plugging human feeling into working memory like a new microchip. The low-key hum of clear and neutral prose underscores his account of what can seem little more than a highly efficient, incredibly well stocked brain or, as Mill conceded, looking back on what he had been at twenty, "a mere reasoning machine." That he himself put matters this way, however, should make us think twice. In fact, the *Autobiography* is a brave, ambitious, and often moving work, put together across two decades (Mill began it in 1853 when afraid he was dying from tuberculosis) with considerable narrative and rhetorical skill. It is an educational case study by a man who was at once the victim and the beneficiary of a mind-boggling experiment in home schooling that gave him, he quietly observes, a quarter-century's head start on conventionally educated peers. Mill's serious learning not only started amazingly early but never stopped, during a lifetime of exercise in the habits of open-mindedness he advocated in *On Liberty* and *The Subjection of Women*. As a result the *Autobiography* may be read as an allegory of the intellectual history of the first half of the nineteenth century. Force-fed in the rationalist tradition of the eighteenth-century Enlightenment by his Utilitarian father, Mill found that mental survival required a course of self-guided reading in the rival tradition of Romantic idealism, to which his "Coleridge" essay pays homage.

The *Autobiography* plays out this dialectical movement of the European mind in a psychodrama of poignant intensity. The "manufactured man," as people called him, wins his way towards an affective life which has been systematically denied by the rigorous training given his juvenile intellect, and which leads him, through a precocious midlife crisis, to cultivate responsiveness to nature and art, relationships with other people, and the late-blooming exercise of a will of his own. Spinning an atheistic, postreligious myth of self-actualization, Mill finds himself between two towering personalities. One is his father James Mill, a major intellectual whom the book represents as his son's sole teacher (and indeed sole parent, since Mill, having nothing nice to say about his mother, says nothing at all). The *Autobiography* ambivalently narrates his partial liberation from this overwhelming paternal influence, through the counterforce of Harriet Taylor, a married woman with whom he fell in love in 1830 and whom he married on her widowhood after two decades' emotional and intellectual intimacy. Within this mythic psychodrama James Mill represents the head, Harriet Taylor the heart; and it is to her impassioned originality and practical comprehension that he credits all that is best in his work. Both his father's son and his wife's husband, Mill remains bound by emotional as well as ideological ties to respect the competing claims of each.

This attentiveness to both sides—sides of himself, of a question, of the partisan debate informing public discourse in his lifetime—constituted Mill's working definition of intellectual virtue. It structured nearly everything he published: significant statements in psychology, aesthetics, and poetics (including "What Is Poetry?" excerpted here); books on logic and political economy; essays in government, philosophy, and the history of ideas; and editorial labors for journals of Utilitarian and liberal opinion. Nearly as impressive as the breadth of topics Mill addressed was the basis of continental, classical, and British learning from which he addressed them. Nor was his knowledge altogether bookish. From the age of seventeen and for most of his writing life Mill held a regular job in London preparing reports on business matters for the East India Company, from which he retired in 1858. He won election to the House of Commons between 1865 and 1868 as an independent radical who, when the Second Reform Bill was substantially enlarging the electorate, proposed giving votes to women too.

These experiences all contributed to the judicious balance that is a hallmark of Mill's work. He never takes up the pen except to argue a case, but his persuasiveness owes much to a patient habit of lending his mind to the position of actual or imputed adversaries. In this sense *On Liberty* practices what it preaches about a healthy society's need for uncensored controversy. Likewise *The Subjection of Women* strikes the most telling blow for its difficult, unpopular case by the penetration with which Mill imagines and draws forth, as symptoms of the sexism he seeks to remove, the ingrained prejudices that stand in the way of a fair hearing. The flair and brilliance of these later essays suggest that the typically matte finish of Mill's style represents the deliberate choice of a writer who means to convince rather than compel, to take us with him and not push us along. Having called Wordsworth "the poet of unpoetical natures" (natures, that is, like Mill's own), Mill in turn might be called the rhetorician of unrhetorical natures, attentive to the quiet grace of reasonableness itself.

from What Is Poetry?[1]

It has often been asked, What is Poetry? And many and various are the answers which have been returned. The vulgarest of all—one with which no person possessed of the faculties to which Poetry addresses itself can ever have been satisfied—is that which confounds poetry with metrical composition: yet to this wretched mockery of a definition, many have been led back, by the failure of all their attempts to find any other that would distinguish what they have been accustomed to call poetry, from much which they have known only under other names.

That, however, the word "poetry" *does* import something quite peculiar in its nature, something which may exist in what is called prose as well as in verse, something which does not even require the instrument of words, but can speak through those other audible symbols called musical sounds, and even through the visible ones, which are the language of sculpture, painting, and architecture; all this, as

we believe, is and must be felt, though perhaps indistinctly, by all upon whom poetry in any of its shapes produces any impression beyond that of tickling the ear. To the mind, poetry is either nothing, or it is the better part of all art whatever, and of real life too; and the distinction between poetry and what is not poetry, whether explained or not, is felt to be fundamental.

Where everyone feels a difference, a difference there must be. All other appearances may be fallacious, but the appearance of a difference is itself a real difference. Appearances too, like other things, must have a cause, and that which can *cause* anything, even an illusion, must be a reality. And hence, while a half-philosophy disdains the classifications and distinctions indicated by popular language, philosophy carried to its highest point may frame new ones, but never sets aside the old, content with correcting and regularizing them. It cuts fresh channels for thought, but it does not fill up such as it finds ready made, but traces, on the contrary, more deeply, broadly, and distinctly, those into which the current has spontaneously flowed.

Let us then attempt, in the way of modest inquiry, not to coerce and confine nature within the bounds of an arbitrary definition, but rather to find the boundaries which she herself has set, and erect a barrier round them; not calling mankind to account for having misapplied the word "poetry,"

---

[1]First published in the *Monthly Repository* for January 1833, this essay was revised and combined with another in 1859 as "Thoughts on Poetry and Its Varieties."

but attempting to clear up to them the conception which they already attach to it, and to bring before their minds as a distinct *principle* that which, as a vague *feeling*, has really guided them in their actual employment of the term.

The object of poetry is confessedly to act upon the emotions; and therein is poetry sufficiently distinguished from what Wordsworth[2] affirms to be its logical opposite, namely, not prose, but matter of fact or science. The one addresses itself to the belief, the other to the feelings. The one does its work by convincing or persuading, the other by moving. The one acts by presenting a proposition to the understanding, the other by offering interesting objects of contemplation to the sensibilities.

This, however, leaves us very far from a definition of poetry. We have distinguished it from one thing, but we are bound to distinguish it from everything. To present thoughts or images to the mind for the purpose of acting upon the emotions, does not belong to poetry alone. It is equally the province (for example) of the novelist: and yet the faculty of the poet and the faculty of the novelist are as distinct as any other two faculties; as the faculty of the novelist and of the orator, or of the poet and the metaphysician. The two characters may be united, as characters the most disparate may; but they have no natural connection.

Many of the finest poems are in the form of novels, and in almost all good novels there is true poetry. But there is a radical distinction between the interest felt in a novel as such, and the interest excited by poetry; for the one is derived from *incident*, the other from the representation of *feeling*. In one, the source of the emotion excited is the exhibition of a state or states of human sensibility; in the other, of a series of states of mere outward circumstances. Now, all minds are capable of being affected more or less by representations of the latter kind, and all, or almost all, by those of the former; yet the two sources of interest correspond to two distinct and (as respects their greatest development) mutually exclusive characters of mind. So much is the nature of poetry dissimilar to the nature of fictitious narrative, that to have a really strong passion for either of the two, seems to presuppose or to superinduce a comparative indifference to the other.

At what age is the passion for a story, for almost any kind of story, merely as a story, the most intense?—in childhood. But that also is the age at which poetry, even of the simplest description, is least relished and least understood; because the feelings with which it is especially conversant are yet undeveloped, and not having been even in the slightest degree experienced, cannot be sympathized with. In what stage of the progress of society, again, is storytelling most valued, and the storyteller in greatest request and honor?—in a rude state; like that of the Tartars and Arabs at this day, and of almost all nations in the earliest ages. But in this state of society there is little poetry except ballads, which are mostly narrative, that is, essentially *stories*, and derive their principal interest from the *incidents*. Considered as poetry, they are of the lowest and most elementary kind: the feelings depicted, or rather indicated, are the simplest our nature has; such joys and griefs as the immediate pressure of some outward event excites in rude minds, which live wholly immersed in outward things, and have never, either from choice or a force they could not resist, turned themselves to the contemplation of the world within. Passing now from childhood, and from the childhood of society, to the grown-up men and women of this most grown-up and unchildlike age—the minds and hearts of greatest depth and elevation are commonly those which take greatest delight in poetry; the shallowest and emptiest, on the contrary, are, by universal remark, the most addicted to novel reading. This accords, too, with all analogous experience of human nature. The sort of persons whom not merely in books but in their lives, we find perpetually engaged in hunting for excitement from without, are invariably those who do not possess, either in the vigor of their intellectual powers or in the depth of their sensibilities, that which would enable them to find ample excitement nearer at home. The same persons whose time is divided between sight-seeing, gossip, and fashionable dissipation, take a natural delight in fictitious narrative; the excitement it affords is of the kind which comes from without. Such persons are rarely lovers of poetry, though they may fancy themselves so, because they relish novels in verse. But poetry, which is the delineation of the deeper and more secret workings of the human heart, is interesting only to those to whom it recalls what they have felt, or whose imagination it stirs up to conceive what they could feel, or what they might have been able to feel, had their outward circumstances been different.

Poetry, when it is really such, is truth; and fiction also, if it is good for anything, is truth: but they are different truths. The truth of poetry is to paint the human soul truly: the truth of fiction is to give a true picture of *life*. The two kinds of knowledge are different, and come by different ways, come mostly to different persons. Great poets are often proverbially ignorant of life. What they know has come by observation of themselves; they have found *there* one highly delicate, and sensitive, and refined specimen of human nature, on which the laws of human emotion are written in large characters, such as can be read off without

---

[2]**Wordsworth**: in the Preface to *Lyrical Ballads* (1800).

much study: and other knowledge of mankind, such as comes to men of the world by outward experience, is not indispensable to them as poets: but to the novelist such knowledge is all in all; he has to describe outward things, not the inward man; actions and events, not feelings; and it will not do for him to be numbered among those who, as Madame Roland said of Brissot,[3] know man but not *men*.

All this is no bar to the possibility of combining both elements, poetry and narrative or incident, in the same work, and calling it either a novel or a poem; but so may red and white combine on the same human features, or on the same canvas; and so may oil and vinegar, though opposite natures, blend together in the same composite taste. There is one order of composition which requires the union of poetry and incident, each in its highest kind—the dramatic. Even there the two elements are perfectly distinguishable, and may exist of unequal quality, and in the most various proportion. The incidents of a dramatic poem may be scanty and ineffective, though the delineation of passion and character may be of the highest order; as in Goethe's glorious "Torquato Tasso"[4]; or again, the story as a mere story may be well got up for effect, as is the case with some of the most trashy productions of the Minerva press:[5] it may even be, what those are not, a coherent and probable series of events, though there be scarcely a feeling exhibited which is not exhibited falsely, or in a manner absolutely commonplace. The combination of the two excellencies is what renders Shakespeare so generally acceptable, each sort of readers finding in him what is suitable to their faculties. To the many he is great as a storyteller, to the few as a poet.

In limiting poetry to the delineation of states of feeling, and denying the name where nothing is delineated but outward objects, we may be thought to have done what we promised to avoid—to have not *found*, but *made* a definition, in opposition to the usage of the English language, since it is established by common consent that there is a poetry called *descriptive*. We deny the charge. Description is not poetry because there is descriptive poetry, no more than science is poetry because there is such a thing as a didactic poem; no more, we might almost say, than Greek or Latin is poetry because there are Greek and Latin poems. But an object which admits of being described, or a truth which may fill a

place in a scientific treatise, may *also* furnish an occasion for the generation of poetry, which we thereupon choose to call descriptive or didactic. The poetry is not in the object itself, nor in the scientific truth itself, but in the state of mind in which the one and the other may be contemplated. The mere delineation of the dimensions and colors of external objects is not poetry, no more than a geometrical ground plan of St. Peter's or Westminster Abbey is painting. Descriptive poetry consists, no doubt, in description, but in description of things as they appear, not as they *are*; and it paints them not in their bare and natural lineaments, but arranged in the colors and seen through the medium of the imagination set in action by the feelings. If a poet is to describe a lion, he will not set about describing him as a naturalist would, nor even as a traveler would, who was intent upon stating the truth, the whole truth, and nothing but the truth. He will describe him by *imagery*, that is, by suggesting the most striking likenesses and contrasts which might occur to a mind contemplating the lion, in the state of awe, wonder, or terror, which the spectacle naturally excites, or is, on the occasion, supposed to excite. Now this is describing the lion professedly, but the state of excitement of the spectator really. The lion may be described falsely or in exaggerated colors, and the poetry be all the better; but if the human emotion be not painted with the most scrupulous truth, the poetry is bad poetry, i.e., is not poetry at all, but a failure.

Thus far our progress towards a clear view of the essentials of poetry has brought us very close to the last two attempts at a definition of poetry which we happen to have seen in print, both of them by poets and men of genius. The one is by Ebenezer Elliott, the author of "Corn-Law Rhymes,"[6] and other poems of still greater merit. "Poetry," says he, "is impassioned truth." The other is by a writer in *Blackwood's Magazine*, and comes, we think, still nearer the mark. We forget his exact words, but in substance he defined poetry, "man's thoughts tinged by his feelings." There is in either definition a near approximation to what we are in search of. Every truth which man can announce, every thought, even every outward impression, which can enter into his consciousness, may become poetry when shown through any impassioned medium, when invested with the coloring of joy, or grief, or pity, or affection, or admiration, or reverence, or awe, or even hatred or terror: and, unless so colored, nothing, be it as interesting as it may, is poetry. But both these definitions fail to discriminate between poetry and eloquence. Eloquence, as well as poetry, is impassioned truth; eloquence, as well as

---

[3] Jeanne-Marie **Roland** (1734–1793): French revolutionary and memoirist. Jacques–Pierre **Brissot** (1754–1793): journalist and fellow revolutionary.

[4] *Torquato Tasso* (1789): verse play by Johann Wolfgang von **Goethe** (1749–1832) about the life of the 16th-century Italian poet.

[5] *Minerva press*: late 18th-century publisher of sentimental novels.

[6] Ebenezer **Elliott** (1781–1849): author of philippics against the English Corn Laws, *Corn-Law Rhymes* (1831–1846).

poetry, is thoughts colored by the feelings. Yet common apprehension and philosophic criticism alike recognize a distinction between the two: there is much that everyone would call eloquence, which no one would think of classing as poetry. A question will sometimes arise, whether some particular author is a poet; and those who maintain the negative commonly allow, that though not a poet, he is a highly *eloquent* writer.

The distinction between poetry and eloquence appears to us to be equally fundamental with the distinction between poetry and narrative, or between poetry and description. It is still farther from having been satisfactorily cleared up than either of the others, unless, which is highly probable, the German artists and critics have thrown some light upon it which has not yet reached us. Without a perfect knowledge of what they have written, it is something like presumption to write upon such subjects at all, and we shall be the foremost to urge that, whatever we may be about to submit, may be received, subject to correction from *them.*

Poetry and eloquence are both alike the expression or uttering forth of feeling. But if we may be excused the seeming affectation of the antithesis, we should say that eloquence is *heard*, poetry is *overheard*. Eloquence supposes an audience; the peculiarity of poetry appears to us to lie in the poet's utter unconsciousness of a listener. Poetry is feeling confessing itself to itself, in moments of solitude, and bodying itself forth in symbols which are the nearest possible representations of the feeling in the exact shape in which it exists in the poet's mind. Eloquence is feeling pouring itself forth to other minds, courting their sympathy, or endeavoring to influence their belief, or move them to passion or to action. . . .

1833

from Coleridge

The name of Coleridge[1] is one of the few English names of our time which are likely to be oftener pronounced, and to become symbolical of more important things, in proportion as the inward workings of the age manifest themselves more and more in outward facts. Bentham[2] excepted, no Englishman of recent date has left his impress so deeply in the opinions and mental tendencies of those among us who attempt to enlighten their practice by philosophical meditation. If it be true, as Lord Bacon[3] affirms, that a knowledge of the speculative opinions of the men between twenty and thirty years of age is the great source of political prophecy, the existence of Coleridge will show itself by no slight or ambiguous traces in the coming history of our country; for no one has contributed more to shape the opinions of those among its younger men, who can be said to have opinions at all.

The influence of Coleridge, like that of Bentham, extends far beyond those who share in the peculiarities of his religious or philosophical creed. He has been the great awakener in this country of the spirit of philosophy, within the bounds of traditional opinions. He has been, almost as truly as Bentham, "the great questioner of things established;"[4] for a questioner needs not necessarily be an enemy. By Bentham, beyond all others, men have been led to ask themselves, in regard to any ancient or received opinion, Is it true? and by Coleridge, What is the meaning of it? The one took his stand *outside* the received opinion, and surveyed it as an entire stranger to it: the other looked at it from within, and endeavored to see it with the eyes of a believer in it; to discover by what apparent facts it was at first suggested, and by what appearances it has ever since been rendered continually credible,—has seemed, to a succession of persons, to be a faithful interpretation of their experience. Bentham judged a proposition true or false as it accorded or not with the result of his own inquiries; and did not search very curiously into what might be meant by the proposition, when it obviously did not mean what he thought true. With Coleridge, on the contrary, the very fact that any doctrine had been believed by thoughtful men, and received by whole nations or generations of mankind, was part of the problem to be solved; was one of the phenomena to be accounted for. And, as Bentham's short and easy method of referring all to the selfish interests of aristocracies or priests or lawyers, or some other species of impostors, could not satisfy a man who saw so much farther into the complexities of the human intellect and feelings, he considered the long or extensive prevalence of any opinion as a presumption that it was not altogether a fallacy; that, to its first authors at least, it was the result of a struggle to express in words something which had a reality to them, though perhaps not to many of those who have since received the doctrine by mere tradition. The long duration of

---

[1]Samuel Taylor **Coleridge** (1772–1834): poet, critic, and philosopher.

[2]Jeremy **Bentham** (1748–1832): proponent of the Utilitarian doctrine based on the greatest happiness of the greatest number.

[3]Francis **Bacon, Lord** Verulam (1561–1626): English philosopher and statesman.

[4]"**the great questioner . . . established**": Mill quotes his own 1838 essay "Bentham," to which "Coleridge" forms a complement.

a belief, he thought, is at least proof of an adaptation in it to some portion or other of the human mind: and if, on digging down to the root, we do not find, as is generally the case, some truth, we shall find some natural want or requirement of human nature which the doctrine in question is fitted to satisfy; among which wants the instincts of selfishness and of credulity have a place, but by no means an exclusive one. From this difference in the points of view of the two philosophers, and from the too rigid adherence of each to his own, it was to be expected that Bentham should continually miss the truth which is in the traditional opinions, and Coleridge that which is out of them and at variance with them. But it was also likely that each would find, or show the way to finding, much of what the other missed.

It is hardly possible to speak of Coleridge, and his position among his cotemporaries, without reverting to Bentham: they are connected by two of the closest bonds of association,—resemblance and contrast. It would be difficult to find two persons of philosophic eminence more exactly the contrary of one another. Compare their modes of treatment of any subject, and you might fancy them inhabitants of different worlds. They seem to have scarcely a principle or a premise in common. Each of them sees scarcely any thing but what the other does not see. Bentham would have regarded Coleridge with a peculiar measure of the good-humored contempt with which he was accustomed to regard all modes of philosophizing different from his own. Coleridge would probably have made Bentham one of the exceptions to the enlarged and liberal appreciation which (to the credit of *his* mode of philosophizing) he extended to most thinkers of any eminence from whom he differed. But contraries, as logicians say, are but *quæ in eodem genere maxime distant,*—the things which are farthest from one another in the same kind. These two agreed in being the men, who, in their age and country, did most to enforce, by precept and example, the necessity of a philosophy. They agreed in making it their occupation to recall opinions to first principles; taking no proposition for granted without examining into the grounds of it, and ascertaining that it possessed the kind and degree of evidence suitable to its nature. They agreed in recognizing that sound theory is the only foundation for sound practice; and that whoever despises theory, let him give himself what airs of wisdom he may, is self-convicted of being a quack. If a book were to be compiled containing all the best things ever said on the rule-of-thumb school of political craftsmanship, and on the insufficiency for practical purposes of what the mere practical man calls experience, it is difficult to say whether the collection would be more indebted to the writings of Bentham or of

Coleridge. They agreed, too, in perceiving that the groundwork of all other philosophy must be laid in the philosophy of the mind. To lay this foundation deeply and strongly, and to raise a superstructure in accordance with it, were the objects to which their lives were devoted. They employed, indeed, for the most part, different materials; but as the materials of both were real observations, the genuine product of experience, the results will, in the end, be found, not hostile, but supplementary, to one another. Of their methods of philosophizing, the same thing may be said: they were different, yet both were legitimate logical processes. In every respect, the two men are each other's "completing counterpart:" the strong points of each correspond to the weak points of the other. Whoever could master the premises and combine the methods of both would possess the entire English philosophy of his age. Coleridge used to say that every one is born either a Platonist or an Aristotelian:[5] it may be similarly affirmed, that every Englishman of the present day is by implication either a Benthamite or a Coleridgian; holds views of human affairs which can only be proved true on the principles either of Bentham or of Coleridge. In one respect, indeed, the parallel fails. Bentham so improved and added to the system of philosophy he adopted, that, for his successors, he may almost be accounted its founder; while Coleridge, though he has left, on the system he inculcated, such traces of himself as cannot fail to be left by any mind of original powers, was anticipated in all the essentials of his doctrine by the great Germans of the latter half of the last century, and was accompanied in it by the remarkable series of their French expositors and followers. Hence, although Coleridge is to Englishmen the type and the main source of that doctrine, he is the creator rather of the shape in which it has appeared among us than of the doctrine itself.

The time is yet far distant, when, in the estimation of Coleridge, and of his influence upon the intellect of our time, any thing like unanimity can be looked for. As a poet, Coleridge has taken his place. The healthier taste, and more intelligent canons of poetic criticism, which he was himself mainly instrumental in diffusing, have at length assigned to him his proper rank, as one among the great (and, if we look to the powers shown rather than to the amount of actual achievement, among the greatest) names in our literature. But, as a philosopher, the class of thinkers has scarcely yet arisen by whom he is to be judged. The limited philosophical

---

[5]**Platonist:** follower of the idealist and formalist thought of Plato (427–348 BCE). **Aristotelian:** follower of Plato's materialist and developmentalist pupil Aristotle (384–322 BCE).

public of this country is as yet too exclusively divided between those to whom Coleridge and the views which he promulgated or defended are every thing, and those to whom they are nothing. A true thinker can only be justly estimated when his thoughts have worked their way into minds formed in a different school; have been wrought and moulded into consistency with all other true and relevant thoughts; when the noisy conflict of half-truths, angrily denying one another, has subsided, and ideas which seemed mutually incompatible have been found only to require mutual limitations. This time has not yet come for Coleridge. The spirit of philosophy in England, like that of religion, is still rootedly sectarian. Conservative thinkers and Liberals, transcendentalists and admirers of Hobbes and Locke,[6] regard each other as out of the pale of philosophical intercourse; look upon each other's speculations as vitiated by an original taint, which makes all study of them, except for purposes of attack, useless, if not mischievous. An error much the same as if Kepler had refused to profit by Ptolemy's or Tycho's[7] observations, because those astronomers believed that the sun moved round the earth; or as if Priestley and Lavoisier, because they differed on the doctrine of phlogiston,[8] had rejected each other's chemical experiments. It is even a still greater error than either of these. For among the truths long recognized by Continental philosophers, but which very few Englishmen have yet arrived at, one is, the importance, in the present imperfect state of mental and social science, of antagonist modes of thought; which, it will one day be felt, are as necessary to one another in speculation, as mutually checking powers are in a political constitution. A clear insight, indeed, into this necessity, is the only rational or enduring basis of philosophical tolerance; the only condition under which liberality in matters of opinion can be any thing better than a polite synonyme for indifference between one opinion and another.

All students of man and society who possess that first requisite for so difficult a study, a due sense of its difficulties, are aware that the besetting danger is not so much of embracing falsehood for truth, as of mistaking part of the truth for the whole. It might be plausibly maintained, that in almost every one of the leading controversies, past or present, in social philosophy, both sides were in the right in what they affirmed, though wrong in what they denied; and that, if either could have been made to take the other's views in addition to its own, little more would have been needed to make its doctrine correct. Take, for instance, the question, how far mankind have gained by civilization. One observer is forcibly struck by the multiplication of physical comforts; the advancement and diffusion of knowledge; the decay of superstition; the facilities of mutual intercourse; the softening of manners; the decline of war and personal conflict; the progressive limitation of the tyranny of the strong over the weak; the great works accomplished throughout the globe by the co-operation of multitudes: and he becomes that very common character, the worshipper of "our enlightened age." Another fixes his attention, not upon the value of these advantages, but upon the high price which is paid for them; the relaxation of individual energy and courage; the loss of proud and self-relying independence; the slavery of so large a portion of mankind to artificial wants; their effeminate shrinking from even the shadow of pain; the dull, unexciting monotony of their lives, and the passionless insipidity, and absence of any marked individuality, in their characters; the contrast between the narrow mechanical understanding, produced by a life spent in executing by fixed rules a fixed task, and the varied powers of the man of the woods, whose subsistence and safety depend at each instant upon his capacity of extemporarily adapting means to ends; the demoralizing effect of great inequalities in wealth and social rank; and the sufferings of the great mass of the people of civilized countries, whose wants are scarcely better provided for than those of the savage, while they are bound by a thousand fetters in lieu of the freedom and excitement which are his compensations. One who attends to these things, and to these exclusively, will be apt to infer that savage life is preferable to civilized; that the work of civilization should as far as possible be undone; and, from the premises of Rousseau, he will not improbably be led to the practical conclusions of Rousseau's disciple, Robespierre.[9]

---

[6]**transcendentalists**: adherents of modern philosophical idealism. Thomas **Hobbes** (1588–1679): skeptical monarchist philosopher. John **Locke** (1632–1704): empiricist philosopher, founder of the British Enlightenment.

[7]Johannes **Kepler** (1571–1630): German discoverer of planetary laws elucidating the Copernican system. **Ptolemy**: 2nd-century Alexandrian astronomer. **Tycho** Brahe (1546–1601): Danish astronomer.

[8]Joseph **Priestley** (1733–1804): English scientist and radical. Antoine-Laurent **Lavoisier** (1743–1794): French scientist, founder of modern chemistry. **phlogiston**: hypothetical principle of heat, disproved by Lavoisier.

---

[9]Jean-Jacques **Rousseau** (1712–1778): Swiss philosopher and writer. **Robespierre** (1758–1794): head of Revolutionary France during the Reign of Terror.

No two thinkers can be more entirely at variance than the two we have supposed,—the worshippers of civilization and of independence, of the present and of the remote past. Yet all that is positive in the opinions of either of them is true: and we see how easy it would be to choose one's path, if either half of the truth were the whole of it; and how great may be the difficulty of framing, as it is necessary to do, a set of practical maxims which combine both. . . .

. . . But most of all ought an enlightened Radical or Liberal to rejoice over such a Conservative as Coleridge. For such a Radical must know, that the Constitution and Church of England, and the religious opinions and political maxims professed by their supporters, are not mere frauds, nor sheer nonsense; have not been got up originally, and all along maintained, for the sole purpose of picking people's pockets; without aiming at, or being found conducive to, any honest end during the whole process. Nothing, of which this is a sufficient account, would have lasted a tithe of five, eight, or ten centuries, in the most improving period and (during much of that period) the most improving nation in the world. These things, we may depend upon it, were not always without much good in them, however little of it may now be left: and reformers ought to hail the man as a brother-reformer who points out what this good is; what it is which we have a right to expect from things established; which they are bound to do for us, as the justification of their being established; so that they may be recalled to it, and compelled to do it, or the impossibility of their any longer doing it may be conclusively manifested. What is any case for reform good for, until it has passed this test? What mode is there of determining whether a thing is fit to exist, without first considering what purposes it exists for, and whether it be still capable of fulfilling them? . . .

. . . We do not pretend to have given any sufficient account of Coleridge; but we hope we may have proved to some, not previously aware of it, that there is something, both in him and in the school to which he belongs, not unworthy of their better knowledge. We may have done something to show, that a Tory philosopher cannot be wholly a Tory, but must often be a better Liberal than Liberals themselves; while he is the natural means of rescuing from oblivion truths which Tories have forgotten, and which the prevailing schools of Liberalism never knew.

And, even if a Conservative philosophy were an absurdity, it is well calculated to drive out a hundred absurdities worse than itself. Let no one think that it is nothing to accustom people to give a reason for their opinion, be the opinion ever so untenable, the reason ever so insufficient. A person accustomed to submit his fundamental tenets to the test of reason will be more open to the dictates of reason on every other point. Not from him shall we have to apprehend the owl-like dread of light, the drudge-like aversion to change, which were the characteristics of the old unreasoning race of bigots. A man accustomed to contemplate the fair side of Toryism (the side that every attempt at a philosophy of it must bring to view), and to defend the existing system by the display of its capabilities as an engine of public good,—such a man, when he comes to administer the system, will be more anxious than another person to realize those capabilities, to bring the fact a little nearer to the specious theory. "Lord, enlighten thou our enemies," should be the prayer of every true reformer; sharpen their wits, give acuteness to their perceptions, and consecutiveness and clearness to their reasoning powers. We are in danger from their folly, not from their wisdom: their weakness is what fills us with apprehension, not their strength.

For ourselves, we are not so blinded by our particular opinions as to be ignorant that in this, and in every other country of Europe, the great mass of the owners of large property, and of all the classes intimately connected with the owners of large property, are, and must be expected to be, in the main, Conservative. To suppose that so mighty a body can be without immense influence in the commonwealth, or to lay plans for effecting great changes, either spiritual or temporal, in which they are left out of the question, would be the height of absurdity. Let those who desire such changes ask themselves if they are content that these classes should be, and remain, to a man, banded against them; and what progress they expect to make, or by what means, unless a process of preparation shall be going on in the minds of these very classes, not by the impracticable method of converting them from Conservatives into Liberals, but by their being led to adopt one liberal opinion after another as a part of Conservatism itself. The first step to this is to inspire them with the desire to systematize and rationalize their own actual creed: and the feeblest attempt to do this has an intrinsic value; far more, then, one which has so much in it, both of moral goodness and true insight, as the philosophy of Coleridge.

1840

from **On Liberty**

Of the Liberty of Thought and Discussion

The time, it is to be hoped, is gone by when any defence would be necessary of the "liberty of the press" as one of the securities against corrupt or tyrannical government. No argument, we may suppose, can now be needed, against permitting a legislature or an executive, not identified in interest with the people, to prescribe opinions to them, and determine what doctrines or what arguments they shall be allowed to hear. This aspect of the question, besides, has been so often and so triumphantly enforced by preceding writers, that it needs not be specially insisted on in this place. Though the law of England, on the subject of the press, is as servile to this day as it was in the time of the Tudors, there is little danger of its being actually put in force against political discussion, except during some temporary panic, when fear of insurrection drives ministers and judges from their propriety;[1] and, speaking generally, it is not, in constitutional countries, to be apprehended that the government, whether completely responsible to the people or not, will often attempt to control the expression of opinion, except when in doing so it makes itself the organ of the general intolerance of the public. Let us suppose, therefore, that the government is entirely at one with the peo-

---

[1] **propriety:** These words had scarcely been written, when, as if to give them an emphatic contradiction, occurred the Government Press Prosecutions of 1858. That ill-judged interference with the liberty of public discussion has not, however, induced me to alter a single word in the text, nor has it at all weakened my conviction that, moments of panic excepted, the era of pains and penalties for political discussion has, in our own country, passed away. For, in the first place, the prosecutions were not persisted in; and, in the second, they were never, properly speaking, political prosecutions. The offence charged was not that of criticizing institutions, or the acts or persons of rulers, but of circulating what was deemed an immoral doctrine, the lawfulness of Tyrannicide.

If the arguments of the present chapter are of any validity, there ought to exist the fullest liberty of professing and discussing, as a matter of ethical conviction, any doctrine, however immoral it may be considered. It would, therefore, be irrelevant and out of place to examine here, whether the doctrine of Tyrannicide deserves that title. I shall content myself with saying, that the subject has been at all times one of the open questions of morals; that the act of a private citizen in striking down a criminal, who, by raising himself above the law, has placed himself beyond the reach of legal punishment or control, has been accounted by whole nations, and by some of the best and wisest of men, not a crime, but an act of exalted virtue; and that, right or wrong, it is not of the nature of assassination, but of civil war. As such, I hold that the instigation to it, in a specific case, may be a proper subject of punishment, but only if an overt act has been followed, and at least a probable connection can be established between the act and the instigation. Even then, it is not a foreign government, but the very government assailed, which alone, in the exercise of self-defence, can legitimately punish attacks directed against its own existence. [Mill's note]

ple, and never thinks of exerting any power of coercion unless in agreement with what it conceives to be their voice. But I deny the right of the people to exercise such coercion, either by themselves or by their government. The power itself is illegitimate. The best government has no more title to it than the worst. It is as noxious, or more noxious, when exerted in accordance with public opinion, than when in opposition to it. If all mankind minus one, were of one opinion, and only one person were of the contrary opinion, mankind would be no more justified in silencing that one person, than he, if he had the power, would be justified in silencing mankind. Were an opinion a personal possession of no value except to the owner; if to be obstructed in the enjoyment of it were simply a private injury, it would make some difference whether the injury was inflicted only on a few persons or on many. But the peculiar evil of silencing the expression of an opinion is, that it is robbing the human race; posterity as well as the existing generation; those who dissent from the opinion, still more than those who hold it. If the opinion is right, they are deprived of the opportunity of exchanging error for truth: if wrong, they lose, what is almost as great a benefit, the clearer perception and livelier impression of truth, produced by its collision with error.

It is necessary to consider separately these two hypotheses, each of which has a distinct branch of the argument corresponding to it. We can never be sure that the opinion we are endeavouring to stifle is a false opinion; and if we were sure, stifling it would be an evil still.

First: the opinion which it is attempted to suppress by authority may possibly be true. Those who desire to suppress it, of course deny its truth; but they are not infallible. They have no authority to decide the question for all mankind, and exclude every other person from the means of judging. To refuse a hearing to an opinion, because they are sure that it is false, is to assume that *their* certainty is the same thing as *absolute* certainty. All silencing of discussion is an assumption of infallibility. Its condemnation may be allowed to rest on this common argument, not the worse for being common.

Unfortunately for the good sense of mankind, the fact of their fallibility is far from carrying the weight in their practical judgment, which is always allowed to it in theory; for while every one well knows himself to be fallible, few think it necessary to take any precautions against their own fallibility, or admit the supposition that any opinion of which they feel very certain, may be one of the examples of the error to which they acknowledge themselves to be liable. Absolute princes, or others who are accustomed to

judgement

unlimited deference, usually feel this complete confidence in their own opinions on nearly all subjects. People more happily situated, who sometimes hear their opinions disputed, and are not wholly unused to be set right when they are wrong, place the same unbounded reliance only on such of their opinions as are shared by all who surround them, or to whom they habitually defer: for in proportion to a man's want of confidence in his own solitary judgment, does he usually repose, with implicit trust, on the infallibility of "the world" in general. And the world, to each individual, means the part of it with which he comes in contact; his party, his sect, his church, his class of society: the man may be called, by comparison, almost liberal and large-minded to whom it means anything so comprehensive as his own country or his own age. Nor is his faith in this collective authority at all shaken by his being aware that other ages, countries, sects, churches, classes, and parties have thought, and even now think, the exact reverse. He devolves upon his own world the responsibility of being in the right against the dissentient worlds of other people; and it never troubles him that mere accident has decided which of these numerous worlds is the object of his reliance, and that the same causes which make him a Churchman in London, would have made him a Buddhist or a Confucian in Pekin. Yet it is as evident in itself as any amount of argument can make it, that ages are no more infallible than individuals; every age having held many opinions which subsequent ages have deemed not only false but absurd; and it is as certain that many opinions, now general, will be rejected by future ages, as it is that many, once general, are rejected by the present.

The objection likely to be made to this argument, would probably take some such form as the following. There is no greater assumption of infallibility in forbidding the propagation of error, than in any other thing which is done by public authority on its own judgment and responsibility. Judgment is given to men that they may use it. Because it may be used erroneously, are men to be told that they ought not to use it at all? To prohibit what they think pernicious, is not claiming exemption from error, but fulfilling the duty incumbent on them, although fallible, of acting on their conscientious conviction. If we were never to act on our opinions, because those opinions may be wrong, we should leave all our interests uncared for, and all our duties unperformed. An objection which applies to all conduct can be no valid objection to any conduct in particular.

It is the duty of governments, and of individuals, to form the truest opinions they can; to form them carefully, and never impose them upon others unless they are quite sure of being right. But when they are sure (such reasoners may say), it is not conscientiousness but cowardice to shrink from acting on their opinions, and allow doctrines which they honestly think dangerous to the welfare of mankind, either in this life or in another, to be scattered abroad without restraint, because other people, in less enlightened times, have persecuted opinions now believed to be true. Let us take care, it may be said, not to make the same mistake: but governments and nations have made mistakes in other things, which are not denied to be fit subjects for the exercise of authority: they have laid on bad taxes, made unjust wars. Ought we therefore to lay on no taxes, and, under whatever provocation, make no wars? Men, and governments, must act to the best of their ability. There is no such thing as absolute certainty, but there is assurance sufficient for the purposes of human life. We may, and must, assume our opinion to be true for the guidance of our own conduct: and it is assuming no more when we forbid bad men to pervert society by the propagation of opinions which we regard as false and pernicious.

I answer, that it is assuming very much more. There is the greatest difference between presuming an opinion to be true, because, with every opportunity for contesting it, it has not been refuted, and assuming its truth for the purpose of not permitting its refutation. Complete liberty of contradicting and disproving our opinion, is the very condition which justifies us in assuming its truth for purposes of action; and on no other terms can a being with human faculties have any rational assurance of being right.

When we consider either the history of opinion, or the ordinary conduct of human life, to what is it to be ascribed that the one and the other are no worse than they are? Not certainly to the inherent force of the human understanding; for, on any matter not self-evident, there are ninety-nine persons totally incapable of judging of it, for one who is capable; and the capacity of the hundredth person is only comparative; for the majority of the eminent men of every past generation held many opinions now known to be erroneous, and did or approved numerous things which no one will now justify. Why is it, then, that there is on the whole a preponderance among mankind of rational opinions and rational conduct? If there really is this preponderance—which there must be, unless human affairs are, and have always been, in an almost desperate state—it is owing to a quality of the human mind, the source of everything respectable in man, either as an intellectual or as a moral being, namely, that his errors are corrigible. He is capable of rectifying his mistakes by discussion and experience. Not by experience alone. There must be discussion, to show how experience is to be interpreted. Wrong opinions and practices gradually yield to fact and argument: but facts and arguments, to produce any effect on the mind, must be brought before it. Very few facts are able to tell their own story, without comments to bring out their meaning. The whole strength and value, then, of human judgment, depending on the one property, that it can be set right when it is wrong, reliance can be placed on it only when the means of setting it right are kept constantly at hand. In the case of any person whose judgment is really deserving of confidence, how has it become so? Because he has kept his mind open to criticism of his opinions and conduct. Because it has been his practice to listen to all that could be said against him; to profit by as much of it as was just, and expound to himself, and upon occasion to others, the fallacy of what was fallacious. Because he has felt, that the only way in which a human being can make some approach to knowing the whole of a subject, is by hearing what can be said about it by persons of every variety of opinion, and studying all modes in which it can be looked at by every character of mind. No wise man ever acquired his wisdom in any mode but this; nor is it in the nature of human intellect to become wise in any other manner. The steady habit of correcting and completing his own opinion by collating it with those of others, so far from causing doubt and hesitation in carrying it into practice, is the only stable foundation for a just reliance on it: for, being cognizant of all that can, at least obviously, be said against him, and having taken up his position against all gainsayers knowing that he has sought for objections and difficulties, instead of avoiding them, and has shut out no light which can be thrown upon the subject from any quarter—he has a right to think his judgment better than that of any person, or any multitude, who have not gone through a similar process.

It is not too much to require that what the wisest of mankind, those who are best entitled to trust their own judgment, find necessary to warrant their relying on it, should be submitted to by that miscellaneous collection of a few wise and many foolish individuals, called the public. The most intolerant of churches, the Roman Catholic Church, even at the canonization of a saint, admits, and listens patiently to, a "devil's advocate." The holiest of men, it appears, cannot be admitted to posthumous honors, until all that the devil could say against him is known and weighed. If even the Newtonian philosophy were not permitted to be questioned, mankind could not feel as complete assurance of its truth as they now do. The beliefs which we have most warrant for, have no safeguard to rest on, but a standing invitation to the whole world to prove them unfounded. If the challenge is not accepted, or is accepted and the attempt

fails, we are far enough from certainty still; but we have done the best that the existing state of human reason admits of; we have neglected nothing that could give the truth a chance of reaching us: if the lists are kept open, we may hope that if there be a better truth, it will be found when the human mind is capable of receiving it; and in the meantime we may rely on having attained such approach to truth, as is possible in our own day. This is the amount of certainty attainable by a fallible being, and this the sole way of attaining it.

Strange it is, that men should admit the validity of the arguments for free discussion, but object to their being "pushed to an extreme;" not seeing that unless the reasons are good for an extreme case, they are not good for any case. Strange that they should imagine that they are not assuming infallibility when they acknowledge that there should be free discussion on all subjects which can possibly be *doubtful*, but think that some particular principle or doctrine should be forbidden to be questioned because it is *so certain*, that is, because *they are certain* that it is certain. To call any proposition certain, while there is any one who would deny its certainty if permitted, but who is not permitted, is to assume that we ourselves, and those who agree with us, are the judges of certainty, and judges without hearing the other side.

In the present age—which has been described as "destitute of faith, but terrified at scepticism,"[2]—in which people feel sure, not so much that their opinions are true, as that they should not know what to do without them—the claims of an opinion to be protected from public attack are rested not so much on its truth, as on its importance to society. There are, it is alleged, certain beliefs, so useful, not to say indispensable to well-being, that it is as much the duty of governments to uphold those beliefs, as to protect any other of the interests of society. In a case of such necessity, and so directly in the line of their duty, something less than infallibility may, it is maintained, warrant, and even bind, governments, to act on their own opinion, confirmed by the general opinion of mankind. It is also often argued, and still oftener thought, that none but bad men would desire to weaken these salutary beliefs; and there can be nothing wrong, it is thought, in restraining bad men, and prohibiting what only such men would wish to practise. This mode of thinking makes the justification of restraints on discussion not a question of the truth of doctrines, but of their

---

[2]**destitute of faith . . . scepticism**": from Thomas Carlyle's "On Sir Walter Scott" (1838).

usefulness; and flatters itself by that means to escape the responsibility of claiming to be an infallible judge of opinions. But those who thus satisfy themselves, do not perceive that the assumption of infallibility is merely shifted from one point to another. The usefulness of an opinion is itself matter of opinion: as disputable, as open to discussion and requiring discussion as much, as the opinion itself. There is the same need of an infallible judge of opinions to decide an opinion to be noxious, as to decide it to be false, unless the opinion condemned has full opportunity of defending itself. And it will not do to say that the heretic may be allowed to maintain the utility or harmlessness of his opinion, though forbidden to maintain its truth. The truth of an opinion is part of its utility. If we would know whether or not it is desirable that a proposition should be believed, is it possible to exclude the consideration of whether or not it is true? In the opinion, not of bad men, but of the best men, no belief which is contrary to truth can be really useful: and can you prevent such men from urging that plea, when they are charged with culpability for denying some doctrine which they are told is useful, but which they believe to be false? Those who are on the side of received opinions, never fail to take all possible advantage of this plea; you do not find *them* handling the question of utility as if it could be completely abstracted from that of truth: on the contrary, it is, above all, because their doctrine is "the truth," that the knowledge or the belief of it is held to be so indispensable. There can be no fair discussion of the question of usefulness, when an argument so vital may be employed on one side, but not on the other. And in point of fact, when law or public feeling do not permit the truth of an opinion to be disputed, they are just as little tolerant of a denial of its usefulness. The utmost they allow is an extenuation of its absolute necessity or of the positive guilt of rejecting it.

In order more fully to illustrate the mischief of denying a hearing to opinions because we, in our own judgment, have condemned them, it will be desirable to fix down the discussion to a concrete case; and I choose, by preference, the cases which are least favourable to me—in which the argument against freedom of opinion, both on the score of truth and on that of utility, is considered the strongest. Let the opinions impugned be the belief in a God and in a future state, or any of the commonly received doctrines of morality. To fight the battle on such ground, gives a great advantage to an unfair antagonist; since he will be sure to say (and many who have no desire to be unfair will say it internally), Are these the doctrines which you do not deem sufficiently certain to be taken under the protection of law? Is the belief in a God one of the opinions, to feel sure of

which, you hold to be assuming infallibility? But I must be permitted to observe, that it is not the feeling sure of a doctrine (be it what it may) which I call an assumption of infallibility. It is the undertaking to decide that question *for others*, without allowing them to hear what can be said on the contrary side. And I denounce and reprobate this pretension not the less, if put forth on the side of my most solemn convictions. However positive any one's persuasion may be, not only of the falsity, but of the pernicious consequences—not only of the pernicious consequences, but (to adopt expressions which I altogether condemn) the immorality and impiety of an opinion; yet if, in pursuance of that private judgment, though backed by the public judgment of his country or his cotemporaries, he prevents the opinion from being heard in its defence, he assumes infallibility. And so far from the assumption being less objectionable or less dangerous because the opinion is called immoral or impious, this is the case of all others in which it is most fatal. These are exactly the occasions on which the men of one generation commit those dreadful mistakes which excite the astonishment and horror of posterity. It is among such that we find the instances memorable in history, when the arm of the law has been employed to root out the best men and the noblest doctrines; with deplorable success as to the men, though some of the doctrines have survived to be (as if in mockery) invoked, in defence of similar conduct towards those who dissent from *them*, or from their received interpretation.

Mankind can hardly be too often reminded, that there was once a man named Socrates, between whom and the legal authorities and public opinion of his time, there took place a memorable collision. Born in an age and country abounding in individual greatness, this man has been handed down to us by those who best knew both him and the age, as the most virtuous man in it; while *we* know him as the head and prototype of all subsequent teachers of virtue, the source equally of the lofty inspiration of Plato and the judicious utilitarianism of Aristotle, *"i maëstri di color che sanno,"*[3] the two headsprings of ethical as of all other philosophy. This acknowledged master of all the eminent thinkers who have since lived—whose fame, still growing after more than two thousand years, all but outweighs the whole remainder of the names which make his native city illustrious—was put to death by his countrymen, after a judicial conviction, for impiety and immorality. Impiety, in

---

[3] *"i maëstri . . . sanno"*: the masters among those who know (adapting Dante, *Inferno* 4. 131).

denying the gods recognized by the State; indeed his accuser asserted (see the "Apologia") that he believed in no gods at all. Immorality, in being, by his doctrines and instructions, a "corrupter of youth." Of these charges the tribunal, there is every ground for believing, honestly found him guilty, and condemned the man who probably of all then born had deserved best of mankind, to be put to death as a criminal.

To pass from this to the only other instance of judicial iniquity, the mention of which, after the condemnation of Socrates, would not be an anti-climax: the event which took place on Calvary[4] rather more than eighteen hundred years ago. The man who left on the memory of those who witnessed his life and conversation, such an impression of his moral grandeur, that eighteen subsequent centuries have done homage to him as the Almighty in person, was ignominiously put to death, as what? As a blasphemer. Men did not merely mistake their benefactor; they mistook him for the exact contrary of what he was, and treated him as that prodigy of impiety, which they themselves are now held to be, for their treatment of him. The feelings with which mankind now regard these lamentable transactions, especially the latter of the two, render them extremely unjust in their judgment of the unhappy actors. These were, to all appearance, not bad men—not worse than men most commonly are, but rather the contrary; men who possessed in a full, or somewhat more than a full measure, the religious, moral, and patriotic feelings of their time and people: the very kind of men who, in all times, our own included, have every chance of passing through life blameless and respected. The high-priest who rent his garments when the words were pronounced, which, according to all the ideas of his country, constituted the blackest guilt, was in all probability quite as sincere in his horror and indignation, as the generality of respectable and pious men now are in the religious and moral sentiments they profess; and most of those who now shudder at his conduct, if they had lived in his time and been born Jews, would have acted precisely as he did. Orthodox Christians who are tempted to think that those who stoned to death the first martyrs must have been worse men than they themselves are, ought to remember that one of those persecutors was Saint Paul.

Let us add one more example, the most striking of all, if the impressiveness of an error is measured by the wisdom and virtue of him who falls into it. If ever any one, possessed of power, had grounds for thinking himself the best and most enlightened among his cotemporaries, it was the Emperor Marcus Aurelius.[5] Absolute monarch of the whole civilized world, he preserved through life not only the most unblemished justice, but what was less to be expected from his Stoical breeding, the tenderest heart. The few failings which are attributed to him, were all on the side of indulgence: while his writings, the highest ethical product of the ancient mind, differ scarcely perceptibly, if they differ at all, from the most characteristic teachings of Christ. This man, a better Christian in all but the dogmatic sense of the word, than almost any of the ostensibly Christian sovereigns who have since reigned, persecuted Christianity. Placed at the summit of all the previous attainments of humanity, with an open, unfettered intellect, and a character which led him of himself to embody in his moral writings the Christian ideal, he yet failed to see that Christianity was to be a good and not an evil to the world, with his duties to which he was so deeply penetrated. Existing society he knew to be in a deplorable state. But such as it was, he saw or thought he saw, that it was held together and prevented from being worse, by belief and reverence of the received divinities. As a ruler of mankind, he deemed it his duty not to suffer society to fall in pieces; and saw not how, if its existing ties were removed, any others could be formed which could again knit it together. The new religion openly aimed at dissolving these ties: unless, therefore, it was his duty to adopt that religion, it seemed to be his duty to put it down. Inasmuch then as the theology of Christianity did not appear to him true or of divine origin; inasmuch as this strange history of a crucified God was not credible to him, and a system which purported to rest entirely upon a foundation to him so wholly unbelievable, could not be foreseen by him to be that renovating agency which, after all abatements, it has in fact proved to be; the gentlest and most amiable of philosophers and rulers, under a solemn sense of duty, authorized the persecution of Christianity. To my mind this is one of the most tragical facts in all history. It is a bitter thought, how different a thing the Christianity of the world might have been, if the Christian faith had been adopted as the religion of the empire under the auspices of Marcus Aurelius instead of those of Constantine. But it would be equally unjust to him and false to truth, to deny, that no one plea which can be urged for punishing anti-Christian

---

[4]**Calvary**: site of the crucifixion of Jesus.

[5]**Marcus Aurelius** Antoninus (121–180): Roman emperor (161–180) and stoic philosopher.

teaching, was wanting to Marcus Aurelius for punishing, as he did, the propagation of Christianity. No Christian more firmly believes that Atheism is false, and tends to the dissolution of society, than Marcus Aurelius believed the same things of Christianity; he who, of all men then living, might have been thought the most capable of appreciating it. Unless any one who approves of punishment for the promulgation of opinions, flatters himself that he is a wiser and better man than Marcus Aurelius—more deeply versed in the wisdom of his time, more elevated in his intellect above it—more earnest in his search for truth, or more single-minded in his devotion to it when found;—let him abstain from that assumption of the joint infallibility of himself and the multitude, which the great Antoninus made with so unfortunate a result.

Aware of the impossibility of defending the use of punishment for restraining irreligious opinions, by any argument which will not justify Marcus Antoninus, the enemies of religious freedom, when hard pressed, occasionally accept this consequence, and say, with Dr. Johnson, that the persecutors of Christianity were in the right;[6] that persecution is an ordeal through which truth ought to pass, and always passes successfully, legal penalties being, in the end, powerless against truth, though sometimes beneficially effective against mischievous errors. This is a form of the argument for religious intolerance, sufficiently remarkable not to be passed without notice.

A theory which maintains that truth may justifiably be persecuted because persecution cannot possibly do it any harm, cannot be charged with being intentionally hostile to the reception of new truths; but we cannot commend the generosity of its dealing with the persons to whom mankind are indebted for them. To discover to the world something which deeply concerns it, and of which it was previously ignorant; to prove to it that it had been mistaken on some vital point of temporal or spiritual interest, is as important a service as a human being can render to his fellow-creatures, and in certain cases, as in those of the early Christians and of the Reformers, those who think with Dr. Johnson believe it to have been the most precious gift which could be bestowed on mankind. That the authors of such splendid benefits should be requited by martyrdom; that their reward should be to be dealt with as the vilest of criminals, is not, upon this theory, a deplorable

error and misfortune, for which humanity should mourn in sackcloth and ashes, but the normal and justifiable state of things. The propounder of a new truth, according to this doctrine, should stand, as stood, in the legislation of the Locrians,[7] the proposer of a new law, with a halter round his neck, to be instantly tightened if the public assembly did not, on hearing his reasons, then and there adopt his proposition. People who defend this mode of treating benefactors, can not be supposed to set much value on the benefit; and I believe this view of the subject is mostly confined to the sort of persons who think that new truths may have been desirable once, but that we have had enough of them now.

But, indeed, the dictum that truth always triumphs over persecution, is one of those pleasant falsehoods which men repeat after one another till they pass into commonplaces, but which all experience refutes. History teems with instances of truth put down by persecution. If not suppressed forever, it may be thrown back for centuries. To speak only of religious opinions: the Reformation broke out at least twenty times before Luther, and was put down. Arnold of Brescia was put down. Fra Dolcino was put down. Savonarola was put down. The Albigeois were put down. The Vaudois were put down. The Lollards were put down. The Hussites were put down.[8] Even after the era of Luther, wherever persecution was persisted in, it was successful. In Spain, Italy, Flanders, the Austrian empire, Protestantism was rooted out; and, most likely, would have been so in England, had Queen Mary lived, or Queen Elizabeth died. Persecution has always succeeded, save where the heretics were too strong a party to be effectually persecuted. No reasonable person can doubt that Christianity might have been extirpated in the Roman empire. It spread, and became predominant, because the persecutions were only occasional, lasting but a short time, and separated by long intervals of almost undisturbed propagandism. It is a piece of idle sentimentality that truth, merely as truth, has any inherent power denied to error, of prevailing against the dungeon and the stake. Men are not more zealous for truth than they often are for error, and a sufficient application of legal

---

[6]Samuel **Johnson** (1709–1784): conservative whose remarks on **persecution** and martyrdom (May 1773) appear in James Boswell's 1791 *Life of Johnson*.

[7]**Locrians**: ancient Greek tribe.

[8]The Protestant **Reformation** led by Martin **Luther** (1483–1546) was anticipated by individuals such as **Arnold of Brescia** (1100–1155), **Fra Dolcino** (early 14th century), Girolamo **Savonarola** (1452–1498), and by communities such as the **Vaudois** or Waldenses (12th century), **Albigeois** (early 13th century), **Lollards** (1382–1414), and **Hussites** (15th century).

or even of social penalties will generally succeed in stopping the propagation of either. The real advantage which truth has, consists in this, that when an opinion is true, it may be extinguished once, twice, or many times, but in the course of ages there will generally be found persons to rediscover it, until some one of its reappearances falls on a time when from favourable circumstances it escapes persecution until it has made such head as to withstand all subsequent attempts to suppress it.

It will be said, that we do not now put to death the introducers of new opinions: we are not like our fathers who slew the prophets, we even build sepulchres to them. It is true we no longer put heretics to death; and the amount of penal infliction which modern feeling would probably tolerate, even against the most obnoxious opinions, is not sufficient to extirpate them. But let us not flatter ourselves that we are yet free from the stain even of legal persecution. Penalties for opinion, or at least for its expression, still exist by law; and their enforcement is not, even in these times, so unexampled as to make it at all incredible that they may some day be revived in full force. In the year 1857, at the summer assizes of the county of Cornwall, an unfortunate man,[9] said to be of unexceptionable conduct in all relations of life, was sentenced to twenty-one months imprisonment, for uttering, and writing on a gate, some offensive words concerning Christianity. Within a month of the same time, at the Old Bailey, two persons, on two separate occasions,[10] were rejected as jurymen, and one of them grossly insulted by the judge and one of the counsel, because they honestly declared that they had no theological belief; and a third, a foreigner,[11] for the same reason, was denied justice against a thief. This refusal of redress took place in virtue of the legal doctrine, that no person can be allowed to give evidence in a court of justice, who does not profess belief in a God (any god is sufficient) and in a future state; which is equivalent to declaring such persons to be outlaws, excluded from the protection of the tribunals; who may not only be robbed or assaulted with impunity, if no one but themselves, or persons of similar opinions, be present, but

any one else may be robbed or assaulted with impunity, if the proof of the fact depends on their evidence. The assumption on which this is grounded, is that the oath is worthless, of a person who does not believe in a future state; a proposition which betokens much ignorance of history in those who assent to it (since it is historically true that a large proportion of infidels in all ages have been persons of distinguished integrity and honor); and would be maintained by no one who had the smallest conception how many of the persons in greatest repute with the world, both for virtues and for attainments, are well known, at least to their intimates, to be unbelievers. The rule, besides, is suicidal, and cuts away its own foundation. Under pretence that atheists must be liars, it admits the testimony of all atheists who are willing to lie, and rejects only those who brave the obloquy of publicly confessing a detested creed rather than affirm a falsehood. A rule thus self-convicted of absurdity so far as regards its professed purpose, can be kept in force only as a badge of hatred, a relic of persecution; a persecution, too, having the peculiarity that the qualification for undergoing it is the being clearly proved not to deserve it. The rule, and the theory it implies, are hardly less insulting to believers than to infidels. For if he who does not believe in a future state necessarily lies, it follows that they who do believe are only prevented from lying, if prevented they are, by the fear of hell. We will not do the authors and abettors of the rule the injury of supposing, that the conception which they have formed of Christian virtue is drawn from their own consciousness.

These, indeed, are but rags and remnants of persecution, and may be thought to be not so much an indication of the wish to persecute, as an example of that very frequent infirmity of English minds, which makes them take preposterous pleasure in the assertion of a bad principle, when they are no longer bad enough to desire to carry it really into practice. But unhappily there is no security in the state of the public mind, that the suspension of worse forms of legal persecution, which has lasted for about the space of a generation, will continue. In this age the quiet surface of routine is as often ruffled by attempts to resuscitate past evils, as to introduce new benefits. What is boasted of at the present time as the revival of religion, is always, in narrow and uncultivated minds, at least as much the revival of bigotry; and where there is the strongest permanent leaven of intolerance in the feelings of a people, which at all times abides in the middle classes of this country, it needs but little to provoke them into actively persecuting those whom they have never ceased to think proper

---

[9]**man:** Thomas Pooley, Bodmin Assizes, July 31, 1857. In December following, he received a free pardon from the Crown. [Mill's note]

[10]**occasions:** George Jacob Holyoake, August 17, 1857; Edward Truelove, July 1857. [Mill's note]

[11]**foreigner:** Baron de Gleichen, Marlborough Street Police Court, August 4, 1857. [Mill's note]

objects of persecution.[12] For it is this—it is the opinions men entertain, and the feelings they cherish, respecting those who disown the beliefs they deem important, which makes this country not a place of mental freedom. For a long time past, the chief mischief of the legal penalties is that they strengthen the social stigma. It is that stigma which is really effective, and so effective is it, that the profession of opinions which are under the ban of society is much less common in England, than is, in many other countries, the avowal of those which incur risk of judicial punishment. In respect to all persons but those whose pecuniary circumstances make them independent of the good will of other people, opinion, on this subject, is as efficacious as law; men might as well be imprisoned, as excluded from the means of earning their bread. Those whose bread is already secured, and who desire no favors from men in power, or from bodies of men, or from the public, have nothing to fear from the open avowal of any opinions, but to be ill-thought of and ill-spoken of, and this it ought not to require a very heroic mould to enable them to bear. There is no room for any appeal *ad misericordiam*[13] in behalf of such per-

sons. But though we do not now inflict so much evil on those who think differently from us, as it was formerly our custom to do, it may be that we do ourselves as much evil as ever by our treatment of them. Socrates was put to death, but the Socratic philosophy rose like the sun in heaven, and spread its illumination over the whole intellectual firmament. Christians were cast to the lions, but the Christian Church grew up a stately and spreading tree, overtopping the older and less vigorous growths, and stifling them by its shade. Our merely social intolerance, kills no one, roots out no opinions, but induces men to disguise them, or to abstain from any active effort for their diffusion. With us, heretical opinions do not perceptibly gain or even lose, ground in each decade or generation; they never blaze out far and wide, but continue to smoulder in the narrow circles of thinking and studious persons among whom they originate, without ever lighting up the general affairs of mankind with either a true or a deceptive light. And thus is kept up a state of things very satisfactory to some minds, because, without the unpleasant process of fining or imprisoning anybody, it maintains all prevailing opinions outwardly undisturbed, while it does not absolutely interdict the exercise of reason by dissentients afflicted with the malady of thought. A convenient plan for having peace in the intellectual world, and keeping all things going on therein very much as they do already. But the price paid for this sort of intellectual pacification, is the sacrifice of the entire moral courage of the human mind. A state of things in which a large portion of the most active and inquiring intellects find it advisable to keep the genuine principles and grounds of their convictions within their own breasts, and attempt, in what they address to the public, to fit as much as they can of their own conclusions to premises which they have internally renounced, cannot send forth the open, fearless characters, and logical, consistent intellects who once adorned the thinking world. The sort of men who can be looked for under it, are either mere conformers to commonplace, or time-servers for truth whose arguments on all great subjects are meant for their hearers, and are not those which have convinced themselves. Those who avoid this alternative, do so by narrowing their thoughts and interests to things which can be spoken of without venturing within the region of principles, that is, to small practical matters, which would come right of themselves, if but the minds of mankind were strengthened and enlarged, and which will never be made effectually right until then; while that which would strengthen and enlarge men's minds, free and daring speculation on the highest subjects, is abandoned.

Those in whose eyes this reticence on the part of heretics is no evil, should consider in the first place, that in

---

[12]**persecution**: Ample warning may be drawn from the large infusion of the passions of a persecutor, which mingled with the general display of the worst parts of our national character on the occasion of the Sepoy insurrection. The ravings of fanatics or charlatans from the pulpit may be unworthy of notice; but the heads of the Evangelical party have announced as their principle, for the government of Hindoos and Mahomedans, that no schools be supported by public money in which the Bible is not taught, and by necessary consequence that no public employment be given to any but real or pretended Christians. An Under-Secretary of State, in a speech delivered to his constituents on the 12th of November, 1857, is reported to have said: "Toleration of their faith" (the faith of a hundred millions of British subjects), "the superstition which they called religion, by the British Government, had had the effect of retarding the ascendency of the British name, and preventing the salutary growth of Christianity . . . Toleration was the great cornerstone of the religious liberties of this country; but do not let them abuse that precious word toleration. As he understood it, it meant the complete liberty to all, freedom of worship, *among Christians, who worshipped upon the same foundation*. It meant toleration of all sects and denominations of *Christians who believed in the one mediation*." I desire to call attention to the fact, that a man who has been deemed fit to fill a high office in the government of this country, under a liberal Ministry, maintains the doctrine that all who do not believe in the divinity of Christ are beyond the pale of toleration. Who, after this imbecile display, can indulge the illusion that religious persecution has passed away, never to return? [Mill's note] **Sepoy insurrection**: 1857 uprising in India; see page 115.

[13]*ad misericordiam*: to pity.

consequence of it there is never any fair and thorough discussion of heretical opinions; and that such of them as could not stand such a discussion, though they may be prevented from spreading, do not disappear. But it is not the minds of heretics that are deteriorated most, by the ban placed on all inquiry which does not end in the orthodox conclusions. The greatest harm done is to those who are not heretics, and whose whole mental development is cramped, and their reason cowed, by the fear of heresy. Who can compute what the world loses in the multitude of promising intellects combined with timid characters, who dare not follow out any bold, vigorous, independent train of thought, lest it should land them in something which would admit of being considered irreligious or immoral? Among them we may occasionally see some man of deep conscientiousness, and subtile and refined understanding, who spends a life in sophisticating with an intellect which he cannot silence, and exhausts the resources of ingenuity in attempting to reconcile the promptings of his conscience and reason with orthodoxy, which yet he does not, perhaps, to the end succeed in doing. No one can be a great thinker who does not recognize, that as a thinker it is his first duty to follow his intellect to whatever conclusions it may lead. Truth gains more even by the errors of one who, with due study and preparation, thinks for himself, than by the true opinions of those who only hold them because they do not suffer themselves to think. Not that it is solely, or chiefly, to form great thinkers, that freedom of thinking is required. On the contrary, it is as much, and even more indispensable, to enable average human beings to attain the mental stature which they are capable of. There have been, and may again be, great individual thinkers, in a general atmosphere of mental slavery. But there never has been, nor ever will be, in that atmosphere, an intellectually active people. Where any people has made a temporary approach to such a character, it has been because the dread of heterodox speculation was for a time suspended. Where there is a tacit convention that principles are not to be disputed; where the discussion of the greatest questions which can occupy humanity is considered to be closed, we cannot hope to find that generally high scale of mental activity which has made some periods of history so remarkable. Never when controversy avoided the subjects which are large and important enough to kindle enthusiasm, was the mind of a people stirred up from its foundations, and the impulse given which raised even persons of the most ordinary intellect to something of the dignity of thinking beings. Of such we have had an example in the condition of Europe during the times immediately following the Reformation; another, though limited to the Continent and to a more cultivated class, in

the speculative movement of the latter half of the eighteenth century; and a third, of still briefer duration, in the intellectual fermentation of Germany during the Goethian and Fichtean period.[14] These periods differed widely in the particular opinions which they developed; but were alike in this, that during all three the yoke of authority was broken. In each, an old mental despotism had been thrown off, and no new one had yet taken its place. The impulse given at these three periods has made Europe what it now is. Every single improvement which has taken place either in the human mind or in institutions, may be traced distinctly to one or other of them. Appearances have for some time indicated that all three impulses are well-nigh spent; and we can expect no fresh start, until we again assert our mental freedom. . . . (Chapter 2)

1859

from The Subjection of Women

The object of this Essay is to explain as clearly as I am able, the grounds of an opinion which I have held from the very earliest period when I had formed any opinions at all on social or political matters, and which, instead of being weakened or modified, has been constantly growing stronger by the progress of reflection and the experience of life: That the principle which regulates the existing social relations between the two sexes—the legal subordination of one sex to the other—is wrong in itself, and now one of the chief hindrances to human improvement; and that it ought to be replaced by a principle of perfect equality, admitting no power or privilege on the one side, nor disability on the other.

The very words necessary to express the task I have undertaken, show how arduous it is. But it would be a mistake to suppose that the difficulty of the case must lie in the insufficiency or obscurity of the grounds of reason on which my conviction rests. The difficulty is that which exists in all cases in which there is a mass of feeling to be contended against. So long as an opinion is strongly rooted in the feelings, it gains rather than loses in stability by having a preponderating weight of argument against it. For if it were accepted as a result of argument, the refutation of the argument might shake the solidity of the conviction; but when it rests solely on feeling, the worse it fares in argumentative

---

[14]Johann Wolfgang von **Goethe** (1749–1832), Johann Gottlieb **Fichte** (1762–1814).

contest, the more persuaded its adherents are that their feeling must have some deeper ground, which the arguments do not reach; and while the feeling remains, it is always throwing up fresh intrenchments of argument to repair any breach made in the old. And there are so many causes tending to make the feelings connected with this subject the most intense and most deeply-rooted of all those which gather round and protect old institutions and customs, that we need not wonder to find them as yet less undermined and loosened than any of the rest by the progress of the great modern spiritual and social transition; nor suppose that the barbarisms to which men cling longest must be less barbarisms than those which they earlier shake off.

In every respect the burthen is hard on those who attack an almost universal opinion. They must be very fortunate as well as unusually capable if they obtain a hearing at all. They have more difficulty in obtaining a trial, than any other litigants have in getting a verdict. If they do extort a hearing, they are subjected to a set of logical requirements totally different from those exacted from other people. In all other cases, the burthen of proof is supposed to lie with the affirmative. If a person is charged with a murder, it rests with those who accuse him to give proof of his guilt, not with himself to prove his innocence. If there is a difference of opinion about the reality of any alleged historical event, in which the feelings of men in general are not much interested, as the Siege of Troy for example, those who maintain that the event took place are expected to produce their proofs, before those who take the other side can be required to say anything; and at no time are these required to do more than show that the evidence produced by the others is of no value. Again, in practical matters, the burthen of proof is supposed to be with those who are against liberty; who contend for any restriction or prohibition; either any limitation of the general freedom of human action, or any disqualification or disparity of privilege affecting one person or kind of persons, as compared with others. The *à priori*[1] presumption is in favour of freedom and impartiality. It is held that there should be no restraint not required by the general good, and that the law should be no respecter of persons, but should treat all alike, save where dissimilarity of treatment is required by positive reasons, either of justice or of policy. But of none of these rules of evidence will the benefit be allowed to those who maintain the opinion I profess. It is useless for me to say that those who maintain the doctrine that men have a right to command and women are

under an obligation to obey, or that men are fit for government and women unfit, are on the affirmative side of the question, and that they are bound to show positive evidence for the assertions, or submit to their rejection. It is equally unavailing for me to say that those who deny to women any freedom or privilege rightly allowed to men, having the double presumption against them that they are opposing freedom and recommending partiality, must be held to the strictest proof of their case, and unless their success be such as to exclude all doubt, the judgment ought to go against them. These would be thought good pleas in any common case; but they will not be thought so in this instance. Before I could hope to make any impression, I should be expected not only to answer all that has ever been said by those who take the other side of the question, but to imagine all that could be said by them—to find them in reasons, as well as answer all I find: and besides refuting all arguments for the affirmative, I shall be called upon for invincible positive arguments to prove a negative. And even if I could do all this, and leave the opposite party with a host of unanswered arguments against them, and not a single unrefuted one on their side, I should be thought to have done little; for a cause supported on the one hand by universal usage, and on the other by so great a preponderance of popular sentiment, is supposed to have a presumption in its favour, superior to any conviction which an appeal to reason has power to produce in any intellects but those of a high class.

I do not mention these difficulties to complain of them; first, because it would be useless; they are inseparable from having to contend through people's understandings against the hostility of their feelings and practical tendencies: and truly the understandings of the majority of mankind would need to be much better cultivated than has ever yet been the case, before they can be asked to place such reliance in their own power of estimating arguments, as to give up practical principles in which they have been born and bred and which are the basis of much of the existing order of the world, at the first argumentative attack which they are not capable of logically resisting. I do not therefore quarrel with them for having too little faith in argument, but for having too much faith in custom and the general feeling. It is one of the characteristic prejudices of the reaction of the nineteenth century against the eighteenth, to accord to the unreasoning elements in human nature the infallibility which the eighteenth century is supposed to have ascribed to the reasoning elements. For the apotheosis of Reason we have substituted that of Instinct; and we call everything instinct which we find in ourselves and for which we cannot trace any rational

---

[1] *à priori*: proceeding from axioms, not experience.

foundation. This idolatry, infinitely more degrading than the other, and the most pernicious of the false worships of the present day, of all of which it is now the main support, will probably hold its ground until it gives way before a sound psychology, laying bare the real root of much that is bowed down to as the intention of Nature and the ordinance of God. As regards the present question, I am willing to accept the unfavourable conditions which the prejudice assigns to me. I consent that established custom, and the general feeling, should be deemed conclusive against me, unless that custom and feeling from age to age can be shown to have owed their existence to other causes than their soundness, and to have derived their power from the worse rather than the better parts of human nature. I am willing that judgment should go against me, unless I can show that my judge has been tampered with. The concession is not so great as it might appear; for to prove this, is by far the easiest portion of my task.

The generality of a practice is in some cases a strong presumption that it is, or at all events once was, conducive to laudable ends. This is the case, when the practice was first adopted, or afterwards kept up, as a means to such ends, and was grounded on experience of the mode in which they could be most effectually attained. If the authority of men over women, when first established, had been the result of a conscientious comparison between different modes of constituting the government of society; if, after trying various other modes of social organization—the government of women over men, equality between the two, and such mixed and divided modes of government as might be invented—it had been decided, on the testimony of experience, that the mode in which women are wholly under the rule of men, having no share at all in public concerns, and each in private being under the legal obligation of obedience to the man with whom she has associated her destiny, was the arrangement most conducive to the happiness and well being of both; its general adoption might then be fairly thought to be some evidence that, at the time when it was adopted, it was the best: though even then the considerations which recommended it may, like so many other primeval social facts of the greatest importance, have subsequently, in the course of ages, ceased to exist. But the state of the case is in every respect the reverse of this. In the first place, the opinion in favour of the present system, which entirely subordinates the weaker sex to the stronger, rests upon theory only; for there never has been trial made of any other: so that experience, in the sense in which it is vulgarly opposed to theory, cannot be pretended to have pronounced any verdict. And in the second place, the adoption of this system of inequality never was the result of deliberation, or forethought, or any social ideas, or any notion whatever of what conduced to the benefit of humanity or the good order of society. It arose simply from the fact that from the very earliest twilight of human society, every woman (owing to the value attached to her by men, combined with her inferiority in muscular strength) was found in a state of bondage to some man. Laws and systems of polity always begin by recognising the relations they find already existing between individuals. They convert what was a mere physical fact into a legal right, give it the sanction of society, and principally aim at the substitution of public and organized means of asserting and protecting these rights, instead of the irregular and lawless conflict of physical strength. Those who had already been compelled to obedience became in this manner legally bound to it. Slavery, from being a mere affair of force between the master and the slave, became regularized and a matter of compact among the masters, who, binding themselves to one another for common protection, guaranteed by their collective strength the private possessions of each, including his slaves. In early times, the great majority of the male sex were slaves, as well as the whole of the female. And many ages elapsed, some of them ages of high cultivation, before any thinker was bold enough to question the rightfulness, and the absolute social necessity, either of the one slavery or of the other. By degrees such thinkers did arise: and (the general progress of society assisting) the slavery of the male sex has, in all the countries of Christian Europe at least (though, in one of them, only within the last few years)[2] been at length abolished, and that of the female sex has been gradually changed into a milder form of dependence. But this dependence, as it exists at present, is not an original institution, taking a fresh start from considerations of justice and social expediency—it is the primitive state of slavery lasting on, through successive mitigations and modifications occasioned by the same causes which have softened the general manners, and brought all human relations more under the control of justice and the influence of humanity. It has not lost the taint of its brutal origin. No presumption in its favour, therefore, can be drawn from the fact of its existence. The only such presumption which it could be supposed to have, must be grounded on its having lasted till now, when so many other things which came down from the same odious source have been done away with. And this, indeed, is what makes it strange to ordinary ears, to

---

[2] **last few years:** Russia abolished serfdom in 1861.

hear it asserted that the inequality of rights between men and women has no other source than the law of the strongest. . . .

. . . Whatever gratification of pride there is in the possession of power, and whatever personal interest in its exercise, is in this case not confined to a limited class, but common to the whole male sex. Instead of being, to most of its supporters, a thing desirable chiefly in the abstract, or, like the political ends usually contended for by factions, of little private importance to any but the leaders; it comes home to the person and hearth of every male head of a family, and of every one who looks forward to being so. The clodhopper exercises, or is to exercise, his share of the power equally with the highest nobleman. And the case is that in which the desire of power is the strongest: for every one who desires power, desires it most over those who are nearest to him, with whom his life is passed, with whom he has most concerns in common, and in whom any independence of his authority is oftenest likely to interfere with his individual preferences. If, in the other cases specified, powers manifestly grounded only on force, and having so much less to support them, are so slowly and with so much difficulty got rid of, much more must it be so with this, even if it rests on no better foundation than those. We must consider, too, that the possessors of the power have facilities in this case, greater than in any other, to prevent any uprising against it. Every one of the subjects lives under the very eye, and almost, it may be said, in the hands, of one of the masters—in closer intimacy with him than with any of her fellow-subjects; with no means of combining against him, no power of even locally overmastering him, and, on the other hand, with the strongest motives for seeking his favour and avoiding to give him offence. In struggles for political emancipation, everybody knows how often its champions are bought off by bribes, or daunted by terrors. In the case of women, each individual of the subject-class is in a chronic state of bribery and intimidation combined. In setting up the standard of resistance, a large number of the leaders, and still more of the followers, must make an almost complete sacrifice of the pleasures or the alleviations of their own individual lot. If ever any system of privilege and enforced subjection had its yoke tightly riveted on the necks of those who are kept down by it, this has. I have not yet shown that it is a wrong system: but every one who is capable of thinking on the subject must see that even if it is, it was certain to outlast all other forms of unjust authority. And when some of the grossest of the other forms still exist in many civilized countries, and have only recently been got rid of in others,

it would be strange if that which is so much the deepest rooted had yet been perceptibly shaken anywhere. There is more reason to wonder that the protests and testimonies against it should have been so numerous and so weighty as they are.

Some will object, that a comparison cannot fairly be made between the government of the male sex and the forms of unjust power which I have adduced in illustration of it, since these are arbitrary, and the effect of mere usurpation, while it on the contrary is natural. But was there ever any domination which did not appear natural to those who possessed it? There was a time when the division of mankind into two classes, a small one of the masters and a numerous one of slaves, appeared, even to the most cultivated minds, to be a natural, and the only natural, condition of the human race. No less an intellect, and one which contributed no less to the progress of human thought, than Aristotle, held this opinion without doubt or misgiving; and rested it on the same premises on which the same assertion in regard to the dominion of men over women is usually based, namely that there are different natures among mankind, free natures, and slave natures; that the Greeks were of a free nature, the barbarian races of Thracians[3] and Asiatics of a slave nature. But why need I go back to Aristotle? Did not the slaveowners of the Southern United States maintain the same doctrine, with all the fanaticism with which men cling to the theories that justify their passions and legitimate their personal interests? Did they not call heaven and earth to witness that the dominion of the white man over the black is natural, that the black race is by nature incapable of freedom, and marked out for slavery? some even going so far as to say that the freedom of manual labourers is an unnatural order of things anywhere. Again, the theorists of absolute monarchy have always affirmed it to be the only natural form of government; issuing from the patriarchal, which was the primitive and spontaneous form of society, framed on the model of the paternal, which is anterior to society itself, and, as they contend, the most natural authority of all. Nay, for that matter, the law of force itself, to those who could not plead any other, has always seemed the most natural of all grounds for the exercise of authority. Conquering races hold it to be Nature's own dictate that the conquered should obey the conquerors, or, as they euphoniously paraphrase it, that the feebler and more unwarlike races should submit to the braver and manlier. The

---

[3]**Thracians:** ancient inhabitants of SE Balkan region.

smallest acquaintance with human life in the middle ages, shows how supremely natural the dominion of the feudal nobility over men of low condition appeared to the nobility themselves, and how unnatural the conception seemed, of a person of the inferior class claiming equality with them, or exercising authority over them. It hardly seemed less so to the class held in subjection. The emancipated serfs and burgesses, even in their most vigorous struggles, never made any pretension to a share of authority; they only demanded more or less of limitation to the power of tyrannizing over them. So true is it that unnatural generally means only uncustomary, and that everything which is usual appears natural. The subjection of women to men being a universal custom, any departure from it quite naturally appears unnatural. But how entirely, even in this case, the feeling is dependent on custom, appears by ample experience. Nothing so much astonishes the people of distant parts of the world, when they first learn anything about England, as to be told that it is under a queen: the thing seems to them so unnatural as to be almost incredible. To Englishmen this does not seem in the least degree unnatural, because they are used to it; but they do feel it unnatural that women should be soldiers or members of parliament. In the feudal ages, on the contrary, war and politics were not thought unnatural to women, because not unusual; it seemed natural that women of the privileged classes should be of manly character, inferior in nothing but bodily strength to their husbands and fathers. The independence of women seemed rather less unnatural to the Greeks than to other ancients, on account of the fabulous Amazons[4] (whom they believed to be historical), and the partial example afforded by the Spartan women; who, though no less subordinate by law than in other Greek states, were more free in fact, and being trained to bodily exercises in the same manner with men, gave ample proof that they were not naturally disqualified for them. There can be little doubt that Spartan experience suggested to Plato, among many other of his doctrines, that of the social and political equality of the two sexes.[5]

But, it will be said, the rule of men over women differs from all these others in not being a rule of force: it is accepted voluntarily; women make no complaint, and are consenting parties to it. In the first place, a great number of women do not accept it. Ever since there have been women able to make their sentiments known by their writings (the

only mode of publicity which society permits to them), an increasing number of them have recorded protests against their present social condition: and recently many thousands of them, headed by the most eminent women known to the public, have petitioned Parliament[6] for their admission to the Parliamentary Suffrage. The claim of women to be educated as solidly, and in the same branches of knowledge, as men, is urged with growing intensity, and with a great prospect of success; while the demand for their admission into professions and occupations hitherto closed against them, becomes every year more urgent. Though there are not in this country, as there are in the United States, periodical Conventions and an organized party to agitate for the Rights of Women, there is a numerous and active Society[7] organized and managed by women, for the more limited object of obtaining the political franchise. Nor is it only in our own country and in America that women are beginning to protest, more or less collectively, against the disabilities under which they labour. France, and Italy, and Switzerland, and Russia now afford examples of the same thing. How many more women there are who silently cherish similar aspirations, no one can possibly know; but there are abundant tokens how many *would* cherish them, were they not so strenuously taught to repress them as contrary to the proprieties of their sex. It must be remembered, also, that no enslaved class ever asked for complete liberty at once. When Simon de Montfort[8] called the deputies of the commons to sit for the first time in Parliament, did any of them dream of demanding that an assembly, elected by their constituents, should make and destroy ministries, and dictate to the king in affairs of state? No such thought entered into the imagination of the most ambitious of them. The nobility had already these pretensions; the commons pretended to nothing but to be exempt from arbitrary taxation, and from the gross individual oppression of the king's officers. It is a political law of nature that those who are under any power of ancient origin, never begin by complaining of the power itself, but only of its oppressive exercise. There is never any want of women who complain of ill usage by their husbands. There would be infinitely more, if

---

[6]**petitioned Parliament:** Mill introduced this petition in the House of Commons in 1866.

[7]**Conventions:** held in the United States regularly after the Seneca Falls Convention, 1848. **Society:** Kensington Society, founded 1865, later the London Society for Women's Suffrage.

[8]**Simon de Montfort:** leader of 13th-century baronial revolt against Henry III.

---

[4]**Amazons:** mythological race of warrior women.

[5]**Plato:** see *Republic*, book 5.

complaint were not the greatest of all provocatives to a repetition and increase of the ill usage. It is this which frus-
trates all attempts to maintain the power but protect the
woman against its abuses. In no other case (except that of a
child) is the person who has been proved judicially to have
suffered an injury, replaced under the physical power of the
culprit who inflicted it. Accordingly wives, even in the most
extreme and protracted cases of bodily ill usage, hardly ever
dare avail themselves of the laws made for their protection:
and if, in a moment of irrepressible indignation, or by the
interference of neighbours, they are induced to do so, their
whole effort afterwards is to disclose as little as they can,
and to beg off their tyrant from his merited chastisement.

All causes, social and natural, combine to make it unlikely that women should be collectively rebellious to the
power of men. They are so far in a position different from
all other subject classes, that their masters require something more from them than actual service. Men do not want
solely the obedience of women, they want their sentiments.
All men, except the most brutish, desire to have, in the
woman most nearly connected with them, not a forced
slave but a willing one, not a slave merely, but a favourite.
They have therefore put everything in practice to enslave
their minds. The masters of all other slaves rely, for maintaining obedience, on fear; either fear of themselves, or religious fears. The masters of women wanted more than
simple obedience, and they turned the whole force of education to effect their purpose. All women are brought up
from the very earliest years in the belief that their ideal of
character is the very opposite to that of men; not self-will,
and government by self-control, but submission, and yielding to the control of others. All the moralities tell them that
it is the duty of women, and all the current sentimentalities
that it is their nature, to live for others; to make complete
abnegation of themselves, and to have no life but in their affections. And by their affections are meant the only ones
they are allowed to have—those to the men with whom
they are connected, or to the children who constitute an
additional and indefeasible tie between them and a man.
When we put together three things—first, the natural attraction between opposite sexes; secondly, the wife's entire
dependence on the husband, every privilege or pleasure she
has being either his gift, or depending entirely on his will;
and lastly, that the principal object of human pursuit, consideration, and all objects of social ambition, can in general
be sought or obtained by her only through him, it would be
a miracle if the object of being attractive to men had not
become the polar star of feminine education and formation
of character. And, this great means of influence over the

minds of women having been acquired, an instinct of selfishness made men avail themselves of it to the utmost as a
means of holding women in subjection, by representing to
them meekness, submissiveness, and resignation of all individual will into the hands of a man, as an essential part of
sexual attractiveness. Can it be doubted that any of the
other yokes which mankind have succeeded in breaking,
would have subsisted till now if the same means had existed,
and had been as sedulously used, to bow down their minds
to it? If it had been made the object of the life of every
young plebeian to find personal favour in the eyes of some
patrician, of every young serf with some seigneur; if domestication with him, and a share of his personal affections, had
been held out as the prize which they all should look out
for, the most gifted and aspiring being able to reckon on
the most desirable prizes; and if, when this prize had been
obtained, they had been shut out by a wall of brass from all
interests not centering in him, all feelings and desires but
those which he shared or inculcated; would not serfs and
seigneurs, plebeians and patricians, have been as broadly
distinguished at this day as men and women are? and would
not all but a thinker here and there, have believed the distinction to be a fundamental and unalterable fact in human
nature?

The preceding considerations are amply sufficient to
show that custom, however universal it may be, affords in
this case no presumption, and ought not to create any prejudice, in favour of the arrangements which place women in
social and political subjection to men. But I may go farther,
and maintain that the course of history, and the tendencies
of progressive human society, afford not only no presumption in favour of this system of inequality of rights, but a
strong one against it; and that, so far as the whole course of
human improvement up to this time, the whole stream of
modern tendencies, warrants any inference on the subject,
it is, that this relic of the past is discordant with the future,
and must necessarily disappear.

For, what is the peculiar character of the modern
world—the difference which chiefly distinguishes modern
institutions, modern social ideas, modern life itself, from
those of times long past? It is, that human beings are no
longer born to their place in life, and chained down by an
inexorable bond to the place they are born to, but are free
to employ their faculties, and such favourable chances as
offer, to achieve the lot which may appear to them most desirable. Human society of old was constituted on a very different principle. All were born to a fixed social position, and
were mostly kept in it by law, or interdicted from any means
by which they could emerge from it. As some men are born

white and others black, so some were born slaves and others freemen and citizens; some were born patricians, others plebeians; some were born feudal nobles, others commoners and *roturiers*.[9] A slave or serf could never make himself free, nor, except by the will of his master, become so. In most European countries it was not till towards the close of the middle ages, and as a consequence of the growth of regal power, that commoners could be ennobled. Even among nobles, the eldest son was born the exclusive heir to the paternal possessions, and a long time elapsed before it was fully established that the father could disinherit him. Among the industrious classes, only those who were born members of a guild, or were admitted into it by its members, could lawfully practise their calling within its local limits; and nobody could practise any calling deemed important, in any but the legal manner—by processes authoritatively prescribed. Manufacturers have stood in the pillory for presuming to carry on their business by new and improved methods. In modern Europe, and most in those parts of it which have participated most largely in all other modern improvements, diametrically opposite doctrines now prevail. Law and government do not undertake to prescribe by whom any social or industrial operation shall or shall not be conducted, or what modes of conducting them shall be lawful. These things are left to the unfettered choice of individuals. Even the laws which required that workmen should serve an apprenticeship, have in this country been repealed: there being ample assurance that in all cases in which an apprenticeship is necessary, its necessity will suffice to enforce it. The old theory was, that the least possible should be left to the choice of the individual agent; that all he had to do should, as far as practicable, be laid down for him by superior wisdom. Left to himself he was sure to go wrong. The modern conviction, the fruit of a thousand years of experience, is, that things in which the individual is the person directly interested, never go right but as they are left to his own discretion; and that any regulation of them by authority, except to protect the rights of others, is sure to be mischievous. This conclusion, slowly arrived at, and not adopted until almost every possible application of the contrary theory had been made with disastrous result, now (in the industrial department) prevails universally in the most advanced countries, almost universally in all that have pretensions to any sort of advancement. . . .

The social subordination of women thus stands out an isolated fact in modern social institutions; a solitary breach of what has become their fundamental law; a single relic of an old world of thought and practice exploded in everything else, but retained in the one thing of most universal interest; as if a gigantic dolmen, or a vast temple of Jupiter Olympius, occupied the site of St. Paul's[10] and received daily worship, while the surrounding Christian churches were only resorted to on fasts and festivals. This entire discrepancy between one social fact and all those which accompany it, and the radical opposition between its nature and the progressive movement which is the boast of the modern world, and which has successively swept away everything else of an analogous character, surely affords, to a conscientious observer of human tendencies, serious matter for reflection. . . .

Even the preliminary knowledge, what the differences between the sexes now are, apart from all question as to how they are made what they are, is still in the crudest and most incomplete state. Medical practitioners and physiologists have ascertained, to some extent, the differences in bodily constitution; and this is an important element to the psychologist: but hardly any medical practitioner is a psychologist. Respecting the mental characteristics of women; their observations are of no more worth than those of common men. It is a subject on which nothing final can be known, so long as those who alone can really know it, women themselves, have given but little testimony, and that little, mostly suborned. It is easy to know stupid women. Stupidity is much the same all the world over. A stupid person's notions and feelings may confidently be inferred from those which prevail in the circle by which the person is surrounded. Not so with those whose opinions and feelings are an emanation from their own nature and faculties. It is only a man here and there who has any tolerable knowledge of the character even of the women of his own family. I do not mean, of their capabilities; these nobody knows, not even themselves, because most of them have never been called out. I mean their actually existing thoughts and feelings. Many a man thinks he perfectly understands women, because he has had amatory relations with several, perhaps with many of them. If he is a good observer, and his experience extends to quality as well as quantity, he may have learnt something of one narrow department of their nature—an important department, no doubt. But of all the rest of it, few persons are generally more ignorant, because there

---

[9]*roturiers:* persons of low rank.

[10]**dolmen:** prehistoric standing stone formation. **Jupiter Olympius:** supreme deity of ancient Rome. **St. Paul's:** chief London cathedral.

are few from whom it is so carefully hidden. The most favourable case which a man can generally have for studying the character of a woman, is that of his own wife: for the opportunities are greater, and the cases of complete sympathy not so unspeakably rare. And in fact, this is the source from which any knowledge worth having on the subject has, I believe, generally come. But most men have not had the opportunity of studying in this way more than a single case: accordingly one can, to an almost laughable degree, infer what a man's wife is like, from his opinions about women in general. To make even this one case yield any result, the woman must be worth knowing, and the man not only a competent judge, but of a character so sympathetic in itself, and so well adapted to hers, that he can either read her mind by sympathetic intuition, or has nothing in himself which makes her shy of disclosing it. Hardly anything, I believe, can be more rare than this conjunction. It often happens that there is the most complete unity of feeling and community of interests as to all external things, yet the one has as little admission into the internal life of the other as if they were common acquaintance. Even with true affection, authority on the one side and subordination on the other prevent perfect confidence. Though nothing may be intentionally withheld, much is not shown. In the analogous relation of parent and child, the corresponding phenomenon must have been in the observation of every one. As between father and son, how many are the cases in which the father, in spite of real affection on both sides, obviously to all the world does not know, nor suspect, parts of the son's character familiar to his companions and equals. The truth is, that the position of looking up to another is extremely unpropitious to complete sincerity and openness with him. The fear of losing ground in his opinion or in his feelings is so strong, that even in an upright character, there is an unconscious tendency to show only the best side, or the side which, though not the best, is that which he most likes to see: and it may be confidently said that thorough knowledge of one another hardly ever exists, but between persons who, besides being intimates, are equals. How much more true, then, must all this be, when the one is not only under the authority of the other, but has it inculcated on her as a duty to reckon everything else subordinate to his comfort and pleasure, and to let him neither see nor feel anything coming from her, except what is agreeable to him. All these difficulties stand in the way of a man's obtaining any thorough knowledge even of the one woman whom alone, in general, he has sufficient opportunity of studying. When we further consider that to understand one woman is not necessarily to understand any other woman; that even if he

could study many women of one rank, or of one country, he would not thereby understand women of other ranks or countries; and even if he did, they are still only the women of a single period of history; we may safely assert that the knowledge which men can acquire of women, even as they have been and are, without reference to what they might be, is wretchedly imperfect and superficial, and always will be so, until women themselves have told all that they have to tell. . . .

One thing we may be certain of—that what is contrary to women's nature to do, they never will be made to do by simply giving their nature free play. The anxiety of mankind to interfere in behalf of nature, for fear lest nature should not succeed in effecting its purpose, is an altogether unnecessary solicitude. What women by nature cannot do, it is quite superfluous to forbid them from doing. What they can do, but not so well as the men who are their competitors, competition suffices to exclude them from; since nobody asks for protective duties and bounties in favour of women; it is only asked that the present bounties and protective duties in favour of men should be recalled. If women have a greater natural inclination for some things than for others, there is no need of laws or social inculcation to make the majority of them do the former in preference to the latter. Whatever women's services are most wanted for, the free play of competition will hold out the strongest inducements to them to undertake. And, as the words imply, they are most wanted for the things for which they are most fit; by the apportionment of which to them, the collective faculties of the two sexes can be applied on the whole with the greatest sum of valuable result.

The general opinion of men is supposed to be, that the natural vocation of a woman is that of a wife and mother. I say, is supposed to be, because, judging from acts—from the whole of the present constitution of society—one might infer that their opinion was the direct contrary. They might be supposed to think that the alleged natural vocation of women was of all things the most repugnant to their nature; insomuch that if they are free to do anything else—if any other means of living, or occupation of their time and faculties, is open, which has any chance of appearing desirable to them—there will not be enough of them who will be willing to accept the condition said to be natural to them. If this is the real opinion of men in general, it would be well that it should be spoken out. I should like to hear somebody openly enunciating the doctrine (it is already implied in much that is written on the subject)—"It is necessary to society that women should marry and produce children. They will not do so unless they are compelled. Therefore it is necessary to compel them." The merits of the case would then be clearly defined. It would be exactly that of the slaveholders of South Carolina and Louisiana. "It is necessary that cotton and sugar should be grown. White men cannot produce them. Negroes will not, for any wages which we choose to give. *Ergo* they must be compelled." An illustration still closer to the point is that of impressment.[11] Sailors must absolutely be had to defend the country. It often happens that they will not voluntarily enlist. Therefore there must be the power of forcing them. How often has this logic been used! and, but for one flaw in it, without doubt it would have been successful up to this day. But it is open to the retort—First pay the sailors the honest value of their labour. When you have made it as well worth their while to serve you, as to work for other employers, you will have no more difficulty than others have in obtaining their services. To this there is no logical answer except "I will not:" and as people are now not only ashamed, but are not desirous, to rob the labourer of his hire, impressment is no longer advocated. Those who attempt to force women into marriage by closing all other doors against them, lay themselves open to a similar retort. If they mean what they say, their opinion must evidently be, that men do not render the married condition so desirable to women, as to induce them to accept it for its own recommendations. It is not a sign of one's thinking the boon one offers very attractive, when one allows only Hobson's choice, "that or none."[12] And here, I believe, is the clue to the feelings of those men, who have a real antipathy to the equal freedom of women. I believe they are afraid, not lest women should be unwilling to marry, for I do not think that any one in reality has that apprehension; but lest they should insist that marriage should be on equal conditions; lest all women of spirit and capacity should prefer doing almost anything else, not in their own eyes degrading, rather than marry, when marrying is giving themselves a master, and a master too of all their earthly possessions. And truly, if this consequence were necessarily incident to marriage, I think that the apprehension would be very well founded. I agree in thinking it probable that few women, capable of anything else, would, unless under an irresistible *entrainement*,[13] rendering them for the time insensible to anything but itself, choose such a lot, when any other means were open to them of filling a conventionally hon-

ourable place in life: and if men are determined that the law of marriage shall be a law of despotism, they are quite right, in point of mere policy, in leaving to women only Hobson's choice. But, in that case, all that has been done in the modern world to relax the chain on the minds of women, has been a mistake. They never should have been allowed to receive a literary education. Women who read, much more women who write, are, in the existing constitution of things, a contradiction and a disturbing element: and it was wrong to bring women up with any acquirements but those of an odalisque,[14] or of a domestic servant. (Chapter 1)

1869

from **Autobiography**
Childhood and Early Education

It seems proper that I should prefix to the following biographical sketch, some mention of the reasons which have made me think it desirable that I should leave behind me such a memorial of so uneventful a life as mine. I do not for a moment imagine that any part of what I have to relate, can be interesting to the public as a narrative, or as being connected with myself. But I have thought that in an age in which education, and its improvement, are the subject of more, if not of profounder study than at any former period of English history, it may be useful that there should be some record of an education which was unusual and remarkable, and which, whatever else it may have done, has proved how much more than is commonly supposed may be taught, and well taught, in those early years which, in the common modes of what is called instruction, are little better than wasted. It has also seemed to me that in an age of transition in opinions, there may be somewhat both of interest and of benefit in noting the successive phases of any mind which was always pressing forward, equally ready to learn and to unlearn either from its own thoughts or from those of others. But a motive which weighs more with me than either of these, is a desire to make acknowledgment of the debts which my intellectual and moral development owes to other persons; some of them of recognised eminence, others less known than they deserve to be, and the one to whom most of all is due, one whom the world had no opportunity of knowing. The reader whom these things do not interest,

---

[11]**impressment:** forcible conscription into service.

[12]**Hobson's choice:** false option between the thing offered and nothing at all.

[13]*entrainement:* infatuation.

---

[14]**odalisque:** female slave or concubine in a harem.

has only himself to blame if he reads farther, and I do not desire any other indulgence from him than that of bearing in mind, that for him these pages were not written.

I was born in London, on the 20th of May, 1806, and was the eldest son of James Mill, the author of the History of British India.[1] My father, the son of a petty tradesman and (I believe) small farmer, at Northwater Bridge, in the county of Angus, was, when a boy, recommended by his abilities to the notice of Sir John Stuart, of Fettercairn, one of the Barons of the Exchequer in Scotland, and was, in consequence, sent to the University of Edinburgh, at the expense of a fund established by Lady Jane Stuart (the wife of Sir John Stuart) and some other ladies for educating young men for the Scottish Church. He there went through the usual course of study, and was licensed as a Preacher, but never followed the profession; having satisfied himself that he could not believe the doctrines of that or any other Church. For a few years he was a private tutor in various families in Scotland, among others that of the Marquis of Tweeddale, but ended by taking up his residence in London, and devoting himself to authorship. Nor had he any other means of support until 1819, when he obtained an appointment in the India House.[2]

In this period of my father's life there are two things which it is impossible not to be struck with: one of them unfortunately a very common circumstance, the other a most uncommon one. The first is, that in his position, with no resource but the precarious one of writing in periodicals, he married and had a large family; conduct than which nothing could be more opposed, both as a matter of good sense and of duty, to the opinions which, at least at a later period of life, he strenuously upheld. The other circumstance, is the extraordinary energy which was required to lead the life he led, with the disadvantages under which he laboured from the first, and with those which he brought upon himself by his marriage. It would have been no small thing, had he done no more than to support himself and his family during so many years by writing, without ever being in debt, or in any pecuniary difficulty; holding, as he did, opinions, both in politics and in religion, which were more odious to all persons of influence, and to the common run of prosperous Englishmen in that generation than either before or since; and being not only a man whom nothing would have induced to write against his convictions, but one who invari-

ably threw into everything he wrote, as much of his convictions as he thought the circumstances would in any way permit: being, it must also be said, one who never did anything negligently; never undertook any task, literary or other, on which he did not conscientiously bestow all the labour necessary for performing it adequately. But he, with these burdens on him, planned, commenced, and completed, the History of India; and this in the course of about ten years, a shorter time than has been occupied (even by writers who had no other employment) in the production of almost any other historical work of equal bulk, and of anything approaching to the same amount of reading and research. And to this is to be added, that during the whole period, a considerable part of almost every day was employed in the instruction of his children: in the case of one of whom, myself, he exerted an amount of labour, care, and perseverance rarely, if ever, employed for a similar purpose, in endeavouring to give, according to his own conception, the highest order of intellectual education.

A man who, in his own practice, so vigorously acted up to the principle of losing no time, was likely to adhere to the same rule in the instruction of his pupil. I have no remembrance of the time when I began to learn Greek, I have been told that it was when I was three years old. My earliest recollection on the subject, is that of committing to memory what my father termed vocables, being lists of common Greek words, with their signification in English, which he wrote out for me on cards. Of grammar, until some years later, I learnt no more than the inflexions of the nouns and verbs, but, after a course of vocables, proceeded at once to translation; and I faintly remember going through Æsop's Fables, the first Greek book which I read. The Anabasis,[3] which I remember better, was the second. I learnt no Latin until my eighth year. At that time I had read, under my father's tuition, a number of Greek prose authors, among whom I remember the whole of Herodotus, and of Xenophon's Cyropædia and Memorials of Socrates; some of the lives of the philosophers by Diogenes Laertius; part of Lucian, and Isocrates ad Demonicum and Ad Nicoclem.[4] I also read, in 1813, the first six dialogues (in the common arrangement) of Plato, from the Euthyphron to the Theoctetus inclusive: which last dialogue, I venture to

---

[1]James Mill (1773–1836): Utilitarian philosopher and economist who wrote *History of British India* (1817).

[2]India House: London office of the East India Company.

---

[3]*Anabasis* (Upcountry March): military narrative by Greek historian Xenophon (431–350? BCE).

[4]Herodotus (5th century BCE), Diogenes Laertius (3rd century BCE): Greek historians. Lucian (2nd century BCE): author of dialogues and satires. Isocrates (436–338 BCE): Athenian orator.

think, would have been better omitted, as it was totally impossible I should understand it. But my father, in all his teaching, demanded of me not only the utmost that I could do, but much that I could by no possibility have done. What he was himself willing to undergo for the sake of my instruction, may be judged from the fact, that I went through the whole process of preparing my Greek lessons in the same room and at the same table at which he was writing: and as in those days Greek and English lexicons were not, and I could make no more use of a Greek and Latin lexicon than could be made without having yet begun to learn Latin, I was forced to have recourse to him for the meaning of every word which I did not know. This incessant interruption, he, one of the most impatient of men, submitted to, and wrote under that interruption several volumes of his History and all else that he had to write during those years.

The only thing besides Greek, that I learnt as a lesson in this part of my childhood, was arithmetic: this also my father taught me: it was the task of the evenings, and I well remember its disagreeableness. But the lessons were only a part of the daily instruction I received. Much of it consisted in the books I read by myself, and my father's discourses to me, chiefly during our walks. From 1810 to the end of 1813 we were living in Newington Green,[5] then an almost rustic neighbourhood. My father's health required considerable and constant exercise, and he walked habitually before breakfast, generally in the green lanes towards Hornsey. In these walks I always accompanied him, and with my earliest recollections of green fields and wild flowers, is mingled that of the account I gave him daily of what I had read the day before. To the best of my remembrance, this was a voluntary rather than a prescribed exercise. I made notes on slips of paper while reading, and from these in the morning walks, I told the story to him; for the books were chiefly histories of which I read in this manner a great number. . . .[6]

In my eighth year I commenced learning Latin, in conjunction with a younger sister, to whom I taught it as I went on, and who afterwards repeated the lessons to my father: and from this time, other sisters and brothers being successively added as pupils, a considerable part of my day's work consisted of this preparatory teaching. It was a part which I greatly disliked; the more so, as I was held responsible for the lessons of my pupils, in almost as full a sense as for my

own: I, however, derived from this discipline the great advantage, of learning more thoroughly and retaining more lastingly the things which I was set to teach: perhaps, too, the practice it afforded in explaining difficulties to others, may even at that age have been useful. In other respects, the experience of my boyhood is not favourable to the plan of teaching children by means of one another. The teaching, I am sure, is very inefficient as teaching, and I well know that the relation between teacher and taught is not a good moral discipline to either. I went in this manner through the Latin grammar, and a considerable part of Cornelius Nepos and Cæsar's Commentaries,[7] but afterwards added to the superintendence of these lessons, much longer ones of my own.

In the same year in which I began Latin, I made my first commencement in the Greek poets with the Iliad. After I had made some progress in this, my father put Pope's translation[8] into my hands. It was the first English verse I had cared to read, and it became one of the books in which for many years I most delighted: I think I must have read it from twenty to thirty times through. I should not have thought it worth while to mention a taste apparently so natural to boyhood, if I had not, as I think, observed that the keen enjoyment of this brilliant specimen of narrative and versification is not so universal with boys, as I should have expected both *à priori*[9] and from my individual experience. . . .

. . . During the same years I learnt elementary geometry and algebra thoroughly, the differential calculus, and other portions of the higher mathematics far from thoroughly: for my father, not having kept up this part of his early acquired knowledge, could not spare time to qualify himself for removing my difficulties, and left me to deal with them, with little other aid than that of books: while I was continually incurring his displeasure by my inability to solve difficult problems for which he did not see that I had not the necessary previous knowledge.

As to my private reading, I can only speak of what I remember. History continued to be my strongest predilection, and most of all ancient history. Mitford's Greece[10] I read

---

[5]**Newington Green, Hornsey:** suburbs in N London.

[6]We omit a long paragraph itemizing some two dozen titles of history, travel, and adventure writing in English.

[7]**Cornelius Nepos** (100–25 BCE): Roman imperial biographer. Julius **Caesar's** *Commentaries* (58–47 BCE): military memoir.

[8]Alexander **Pope** (1688–1744): translated *Iliad* in 1720.

[9]*à priori:* as a matter of principle. We again omit the bulk of a detailed syllabus, some 30 Latin and Greek authors.

[10]William **Mitford** (1744–1827): author of *History of Greece* (1784–1818).

continually; my father had put me on my guard against the Tory prejudices of this writer, and his perversions of facts for the whitewashing of despots, and blackening of popular institutions. These points he discoursed on, exemplifying them from the Greek orators and historians, with such effect that in reading Mitford my sympathies were always on the contrary side to those of the author, and I could, to some extent, have argued the point against him: yet this did not diminish the ever new pleasure with which I read the book. Roman history, both in my old favourite, Hooke, and in Ferguson,[11] continued to delight me. A book which, in spite of what is called the dryness of its style, I took great pleasure in, was the Ancient Universal History, through the incessant reading of which, I had my head full of historical details concerning the obscurest ancient people, while about modern history, except detached passages, such as the Dutch War of Independence,[12] I knew and cared comparatively little. A voluntary exercise, to which throughout my boyhood I was much addicted, was what I called writing histories. I successively composed a Roman History, picked out of Hooke; an Abridgement of the Ancient Universal History; a History of Holland, from my favourite Watson[13] and from an anonymous compilation; and in my eleventh and twelfth year I occupied myself with writing what I flattered myself was something serious. This was no less than a History of the Roman Government, compiled (with the assistance of Hooke) from Livy and Dionysius: of which I wrote as much as would have made an octavo volume, extending to the epoch of the Licinian Laws.[14] It was, in fact, an account of the struggles between the patricians and plebeians, which now engrossed all the interest in my mind which I had previously felt in the mere wars and conquests of the Romans. I discussed all the constitutional points as they arose: though quite ignorant of Niebuhr's researches, I, by such lights as my father had given me, vindicated the Agrarian Laws on the evidence of Livy,[15] and upheld, to the

best of my ability, the Roman Democratic party. A few years later, in my contempt of my childish efforts, I destroyed all these papers, not then anticipating that I could ever feel any curiosity about my first attempts at writing and reasoning. My father encouraged me in this useful amusement, though, as I think judiciously, he never asked to see what I wrote; so that I did not feel that in writing it I was accountable to any one, nor had the chilling sensation of being under a critical eye.

But though these exercises in history were never a compulsory lesson, there was another kind of composition which was so, namely, writing verses, and it was one of the most disagreeable of my tasks. Greek and Latin verses I did not write, nor learnt the prosody of those languages. My father, thinking this not worth the time it required, contented himself with making me read aloud to him, and correcting false quantities. I never composed at all in Greek, even in prose, and but little in Latin. Not that my father could be indifferent to the value of this practice, in giving a thorough knowledge of these languages, but because there really was not time for it. The verses I was required to write were English. When I first read Pope's Homer, I ambitiously attempted to compose something of the same kind, and achieved as much as one book of a continuation of the Iliad. There, probably, the spontaneous promptings of my poetical ambition would have stopped; but the exercise, begun from choice, was continued by command. Conformably to my father's usual practice of explaining to me, as far as possible, the reasons for what he required me to do, he gave me, for this, as I well remember, two reasons highly characteristic of him: one was, that some things could be expressed better and more forcibly in verse than in prose: this, he said, was a real advantage. The other was, that people in general attached more value to verse than it deserved, and the power of writing it, was, on this account, worth acquiring. He generally left me to choose my own subjects, which, as far as I remember, were mostly addresses to some mythological personage or allegorical abstraction; but he made me translate into English verse many of Horace's shorter poems: I also remember his giving me Thomson's "Winter"[16] to read, and afterwards making me attempt (without book) to write something myself on the same subject. The verses I wrote were, of course, the merest rubbish, nor did I ever attain any facility of versification, but the practice may have been useful in making it easier for me, at a later period, to acquire readiness of expression. I had read,

---

[11]Nathaniel **Hooke** (d. 1763), Adam **Ferguson** (1723–1816): historians of ancient Rome.

[12]*An Universal History from the Earliest Account of Time to the Present* (1736–1744). **Dutch War of Independence** (1568–1648): revolt of the Netherlands against Spain.

[13]Robert **Watson** (1730?–1781): author of *The History of the Reign of Philip II, King of Spain* (1777).

[14]**Licinian Laws**: 4th-century BCE Roman reform establishing plebeians' rights.

[15]Barthold Georg **Niebuhr** (1776–1831): path-breaking German historian noted for his critical approach to sources. **Livy** (60? BCE–17): Roman historian.

[16]**Horace** (65–8 BCE): Latin lyric poet. "**Winter**" forms part of *The Seasons* (1744) by James **Thomson** (1700–1748).

up to this time, very little English poetry. Shakspeare my father had put into my hands, chiefly for the sake of the historical plays, from which, however, I went on to the others.
My father never was a great admirer of Shakspeare, the
English idolatry of whom he used to attack with some
severity. He cared little for any English poetry except Milton (for whom he had the highest admiration), Goldsmith,
Burns, and Gray's Bard, which he preferred to his Elegy:
perhaps I may add Cowper and Beattie.[17] He had some
value for Spenser, and I remember his reading to me (unlike
his usual practice of making me read to him), the first book
of the Fairie Queene; but I took little pleasure in it. The poetry of the present century he saw scarcely any merit in, and
I hardly became acquainted with any of it till I was grown
up to manhood, except the metrical romances of Walter
Scott, which I read at his recommendation and was intensely delighted with; as I always was with animated narrative. Dryden's Poems were among my father's books, and
many of these he made me read, but I never cared for any of
them except Alexander's Feast, which, as well as many of
the songs in Walter Scott, I used to sing internally, to a
music of my own: to some of the latter, indeed, I went so far
as to compose airs, which I still remember. Cowper's short
poems I read with some pleasure, but never got far into the
longer ones; and nothing in the two volumes interested me
like the prose account of his three hares. In my thirteenth
year I met with Campbell's poems,[18] among which Lochiel,
Hohenlinden, The Exile of Erin, and some others, gave me
sensations I had never before experienced from poetry.
Here, too, I made nothing of the longer poems, except the
striking opening of Gertrude of Wyoming, which long kept
its place in my feelings as the perfection of pathos.

During this part of my childhood, one of my greatest
amusements was experimental science; in the theoretical,
however, not the practical sense of the word; not trying experiments—a kind of discipline which I have often regretted not having had—nor even seeing, but merely reading
about them. I never remember being so wrapt up in any
book, as I was in Joyce's Scientific Dialogues;[19] and I was
rather recalcitrant to my father's criticisms of the bad rea-

soning respecting the first principles of physics, which
abounds in the early part of that work. I devoured treatises
on Chemistry, especially that of my father's early friend and
schoolfellow, Dr. Thomson,[20] for years before I attended a
lecture or saw an experiment.

From about the age of twelve, I entered into another
and more advanced stage in my course of instruction; in
which the main object was no longer the aids and appliances of thought, but the thoughts themselves. This commenced with Logic, in which I began at once with the
Organon, and read it to the Analytics[21] inclusive, but profited little by the Posterior Analytics, which belong to a
branch of speculation I was not yet ripe for. Contemporaneously with the Organon, my father made me read the whole
or parts of several of the Latin treatises on the scholastic
logic; giving each day to him, in our walks, a minute account of what I had read, and answering his numerous and
searching questions. After this, I went in a similar manner,
through the "Computatio sive Logica" of Hobbes,[22] a work
of a much higher order of thought than the books of the
school logicians, and which he estimated very highly; in my
own opinion beyond its merits, great as these are. It was his
invariable practice, whatever studies he exacted from me, to
make me as far as possible understand and feel the utility of
them: and this he deemed peculiarly fitting in the case of
the syllogistic logic, the usefulness of which had been impugned by so many writers of authority. I well remember
how, and in what particular walk, in the neighbourhood of
Bagshot Heath (where we were on a visit to his old friend
Mr. Wallace, then one of the Mathematical Professors at
Sandhurst)[23] he first attempted by questions to make me
think on the subject, and frame some conception of what
constituted the utility of the syllogistic logic, and when I
had failed in this, to make me understand it by explanations.
The explanations did not make the matter at all clear to me
at the time; but they were not therefore useless; they remained as a nucleus for my observations and reflections to
crystallize upon; the import of his general remarks being interpreted to me, by the particular instances which came

---

[17]Oliver **Goldsmith** (1730–1774). Robert **Burns** (1759–1796).
Thomas **Gray** (1716–1771): author of *The Bard* (1757) and "**Elegy
Written in a Country Churchyard**" (1751). William **Cowper**
(1731–1800). James **Beattie** (1735–1803).

[18]Thomas **Campbell** (1777–1844): Scottish poet whose cited
works date from first decade of 19th century.

[19]Jeremiah **Joyce** (1763–1816): author of *Scientific Dialogues, Intended for the Instruction and Entertainment of Young People* (1800).

[20]Thomas **Thomson** (1773–1852): author of *A System of Chemistry*
(1802).

[21]*Organon*: a compilation of Aristotle's logical treatises. *Analytics*:
Aristotle's writings in logical theory.

[22]Thomas **Hobbes** (1588–1679): philosopher and political
theorist.

[23]**Bagshot Heath**: open land SW of London in Surrey, near
Sandhurst, military academy founded 1799. William **Wallace**
(1768–1843): mathematician.

under my notice afterwards. My own consciousness and experience ultimately led me to appreciate quite as highly as he did, the value of an early practical familiarity with the school logic. I know of nothing, in my education, to which I think myself more indebted for whatever capacity of thinking I have attained. The first intellectual operation in which I arrived at any proficiency, was dissecting a bad argument, and finding in what part the fallacy lay: and though whatever capacity of this sort I attained, was due to the fact that it was an intellectual exercise in which I was most perseveringly drilled by my father, yet it is also true that the school logic, and the mental habits acquired in studying it, were among the principal instruments of this drilling. I am persuaded that nothing, in modern education, tends so much, when properly used, to form exact thinkers, who attach a precise meaning to words and propositions, and are not imposed on by vague, loose, or ambiguous terms. The boasted influence of mathematical studies is nothing to it; for in mathematical processes, none of the real difficulties of correct ratiocination occur. It is also a study peculiarly adapted to an early stage in the education of philosophical students, since it does not presuppose the slow process of acquiring, by experience and reflection, valuable thoughts of their own. They may become capable of disentangling the intricacies of confused and self-contradictory thought, before their own thinking faculties are much advanced; a power which, for want of some such discipline, many otherwise able men altogether lack; and when they have to answer opponents, only endeavour, by such arguments as they can command, to support the opposite conclusion, scarcely even attempting to confute the reasonings of their antagonists; and, therefore, at the utmost, leaving the question, as far as it depends on argument, a balanced one.

During this time, the Latin and Greek books which I continued to read with my father were chiefly such as were worth studying, not for the language merely, but also for the thoughts. This included much of the orators, and especially Demosthenes,[24] some of whose principal orations I read several times over, and wrote out, by way of exercise, a full analysis of them. My father's comments on these orations when I read them to him were very instructive to me. He not only drew my attention to the insight they afforded into Athenian institutions, and the principles of legislation and government which they often illustrated, but pointed out the skill and art of the orator—how everything important to his purpose was said at the exact mo-

ment when he had brought the minds of his audience into the state most fitted to receive it; how he made steal into their minds, gradually and by insinuation, thoughts which, if expressed in a more direct manner would have roused their opposition. Most of these reflections were beyond my capacity of full comprehension at the time; but they left seed behind, which germinated in due season. At this time I also read the whole of Tacitus, Juvenal, and Quintilian.[25] The latter, owing to his obscure style and to the scholastic details of which many parts of his treatise are made up, is little read, and seldom sufficiently appreciated. His book is a kind of encyclopædia of the thoughts of the ancients on the whole field of education and culture; and I have retained through life many valuable ideas which I can distinctly trace to my reading of him, even at that early age. It was at this period that I read, for the first time, some of the most important dialogues of Plato, in particular the Gorgias, the Protagoras, and the Republic. There is no author to whom my father thought himself more indebted for his own mental culture, than Plato, or whom he more frequently recommended to young students. I can bear similar testimony in regard to myself. The Socratic method, of which the Platonic dialogues are the chief example, is unsurpassed as a discipline for correcting the errors, and clearing up the confusions incident to the *intellectus sibi permissus*,[26] the understanding which has made up all its bundles of associations under the guidance of popular phraseology. The close, searching *elenchus* by which the man of vague generalities is constrained either to express his meaning to himself in definite terms, or to confess that he does not know what he is talking about; the perpetual testing of all general statements by particular instances; the siege in form which is laid to the meaning of large abstract terms, by fixing upon some still larger class-name which includes that and more, and dividing down to the thing sought—marking out its limits and definition by a series of accurately drawn distinctions between it and each of the cognate objects which are successively parted off from it—all this, as an education for precise thinking, is inestimable, and all this, even at that age, took such hold of me that it became part of my own mind. I have felt ever

---

[24]**Demosthenes** (384–322 BCE): Athenian statesman.

[25]**Tacitus** (1st and 2nd century): Roman orator and historian. **Juvenal** (1st and 2nd century): Roman satiric poet. **Quintilian** (1st century): Roman rhetorician.

[26]*intellectus sibi permissus*: the mind left to itself (from Francis Bacon's 1620 *Novum Organum*, book 1). *elenchus*: cross-examination, Socrates' method of eliciting truth by short question and answer.

since that the title of Platonist belongs by far better right to those who have been nourished in, and have endeavoured to practise Plato's mode of investigation, than to those who are distinguished only by the adoption of certain dogmatical conclusions, drawn mostly from the least intelligible of his works, and which the character of his mind and writings makes it uncertain whether he himself regarded as anything more than poetic fancies, or philosophic conjectures.

In going through Plato and Demosthenes, since I could now read these authors, as far as the language was concerned, with perfect ease, I was not required to construe them sentence by sentence, but to read them aloud to my father, answering questions when asked: but the particular attention which he paid to elocution (in which his own excellence was remarkable) made this reading aloud to him a most painful task. Of all things which he required me to do, there was none which I did so constantly ill, or in which he so perpetually lost his temper with me. He had thought much on the principles of the art of reading, especially the most neglected part of it, the inflections of the voice, or *modulation* as writers on elocution call it (in contrast with *articulation* on the one side, and *expression* on the other), and had reduced it to rules, grounded on the logical analysis of a sentence. These rules he strongly impressed upon me, and took me severely to task for every violation of them: but I even then remarked (though I did not venture to make the remark to him) that though he reproached me when I read a sentence ill, and *told* me how I ought to have read it, he never, by reading it himself, *showed* me how it ought to be read. A defect running through his otherwise admirable modes of instruction, as it did through all his modes of thought, was that of trusting too much to the intelligibleness of the abstract, when not embodied in the concrete. . . .

Though Ricardo's great work[27] was already in print, no didactic treatise embodying its doctrines, in a manner fit for learners, had yet appeared. My father, therefore, commenced instructing me in the science by a sort of lectures, which he delivered to me in our walks. He expounded each day a portion of the subject, and I gave him next day a written account of it, which he made me rewrite over and over again until it was clear, precise, and tolerably complete. In this manner I went through the whole extent of the science; and the written outline of it which resulted from my daily *compte rendu*, served him afterwards as notes from which to

write his Elements of Political Economy.[28] After this I read Ricardo, giving an account daily of what I read, and discussing, in the best manner I could, the collateral points which offered themselves in our progress.

On Money, as the most intricate part of the subject, he made me read in the same manner Ricardo's admirable pamphlets, written during what was called the Bullion controversy; to these succeeded Adam Smith;[29] and in this reading it was one of my father's main objects to make me apply to Smith's more superficial view of political economy, the superior lights of Ricardo, and detect what was fallacious in Smith's arguments, or erroneous in any of his conclusions. Such a mode of instruction was excellently calculated to form a thinker; but it required to be worked by a thinker, as close and vigorous as my father. The path was a thorny one, even to him, and I am sure it was so to me, notwithstanding the strong interest I took in the subject. He was often, and much beyond reason, provoked by my failures in cases where success could not have been expected; but in the main his method was right, and it succeeded. I do not believe that any scientific teaching ever was more thorough, or better fitted for training the faculties, than the mode in which logic and political economy were taught to me by my father. Striving, even in an exaggerated degree, to call forth the activity of my faculties, by making me find out everything for myself, he gave his explanations not before, but after, I had felt the full force of the difficulties; and not only gave me an accurate knowledge of these two great subjects, as far as they were then understood, but made me a thinker on both. I thought for myself almost from the first, and occasionally thought differently from him, though for a long time only on minor points, and making his opinion the ultimate standard. At a later period I even occasionally convinced him, and altered his opinion on some points of detail: which I state to his honour, not my own. It at once exemplifies his perfect candour, and the real worth of his method of teaching.

At this point concluded what can properly be called my lessons: when I was about fourteen I left England for more than a year; and after my return, though my studies went on under my father's general direction, he was no longer my schoolmaster. I shall therefore pause here, and

---

[27]David **Ricardo** (1772–1823): English economist, whose **great work** was *Principles of Political Economy and Taxation* (1817).

[28]*compte rendu:* account rendered. James Mill published *Elements of Political Economy* in 1821.

[29]**Bullion controversy:** early 19th-century debate over the gold standard and currency control by the Bank of England. **Adam Smith** (1723–1790): political economist.

turn back to matters of a more general nature connected with the part of my life and education included in the preceding reminiscences.

In the course of instruction which I have partially retraced, the point most superficially apparent is the great effort to give, during the years of childhood an amount of knowledge in what are considered the higher branches of education, which is seldom acquired (if acquired at all) until the age of manhood. The result of the experiment shows the ease with which this may be done, and places in a strong light the wretched waste of so many precious years as are spent in acquiring the modicum of Latin and Greek commonly taught to schoolboys; a waste which has led so many educational reformers to entertain the ill-judged proposal of discarding these languages altogether from general education. If I had been by nature extremely quick of apprehension, or had possessed a very accurate and retentive memory, or were of a remarkably active and energetic character, the trial would not be conclusive; but in all these natural gifts I am rather below than above par; what I could do, could assuredly be done by any boy or girl of average capacity and healthy physical constitution: and if I have accomplished anything, I owe it, among other fortunate circumstances, to the fact that through the early training bestowed on me by my father, I started, I may fairly say, with an advantage of a quarter of a century over my contemporaries.

There was one cardinal point in this training, of which I have already given some indication, and which, more than anything else, was the cause of whatever good it effected. Most boys or youths who have had much knowledge drilled into them, have their mental capacities not strengthened, but overlaid by it. They are crammed with mere facts, and with the opinions or phrases of other people, and these are accepted as a substitute for the power to form opinions of their own: and thus the sons of eminent fathers, who have spared no pains in their education, so often grow up mere parroters of what they have learnt, incapable of using their minds except in the furrows traced for them. Mine, however, was not an education of cram. My father never permitted anything which I learnt to degenerate into a mere exercise of memory. He strove to make the understanding not only go along with every step of the teaching, but, if possible, precede it. Anything which could be found out by thinking I never was told, until I had exhausted my efforts to find it out for myself. As far as I can trust my remembrance, I acquitted myself very lamely in this department; my recollection of such matters is almost wholly of failures, hardly ever of success. It is true the failures were often in things in which success in so early a stage of my progress, was almost impossible. I remember at some time in my thirteenth year, on my happening to use the word idea, he asked me what an idea was; and expressed some displeasure at my ineffectual efforts to define the word: I recollect also his indignation at my using the common expression that something was true in theory but required correction in practice; and how, after making me vainly strive to define the word theory, he explained its meaning, and showed the fallacy of the vulgar form of speech which I had used; leaving me fully persuaded that in being unable to give a correct definition of Theory, and in speaking of it as something which might be at variance with practice, I had shown unparalleled ignorance. In this he seems, and perhaps was, very unreasonable; but I think, only in being angry at my failure. A pupil from whom nothing is ever demanded which he cannot do, never does all he can.

One of the evils most liable to attend on any sort of early proficiency, and which often fatally blights its promise, my father most anxiously guarded against. This was self-conceit. He kept me, with extreme vigilance, out of the way of hearing myself praised, or of being led to make self-flattering comparisons between myself and others. From his own intercourse with me I could derive none but a very humble opinion of myself; and the standard of comparison he always held up to me, was not what other people did, but what a man could and ought to do. He completely succeeded in preserving me from the sort of influences he so much dreaded. I was not at all aware that my attainments were anything unusual at my age. If I accidentally had my attention drawn to the fact that some other boy knew less than myself—which happened less often than might be imagined—I concluded, not that I knew much, but that he, for some reason or other, knew little, or that his knowledge was of a different kind from mine. My state of mind was not humility, but neither was it arrogance. I never thought of saying to myself, I am, or I can do, so and so. I neither estimated myself highly nor lowly: I did not estimate myself at all. If I thought anything about myself, it was that I was rather backward in my studies, since I always found myself so, in comparison with what my father expected from me. I assert this with confidence, though it was not the impression of various persons who saw me in my childhood. They, as I have since found, thought me greatly and disagreeably self-conceited; probably because I was disputatious, and did not scruple to give direct contradictions to things which I heard said. I suppose I acquired this bad habit from having been encouraged in an unusual degree to talk on matters beyond my age, and with grown persons, while I never had inculcated on me the usual respect for them. My father did not correct this ill-breeding and impertinence, probably from not being aware of it, for I was always too much in awe of him to be otherwise than extremely subdued and quiet in his presence. Yet with all this I had no notion of any superiority in myself; and well was it for me that I had not. I remember the very place in Hyde Park where, in my fourteenth year, on the eve of leaving my father's house for a long absence, he told me that I should find, as I got acquainted with new people, that I had been taught many things which youths of my age did not commonly know; and that many persons would be disposed to talk to me of this, and to compliment me upon it. What other things he said on this topic I remember very imperfectly; but he wound up by saying, that whatever I knew more than others, could not be ascribed to any merit in me, but to the very unusual advantage which had fallen to my lot, of having a father who was able to teach me, and willing to give the necessary trouble and time; that it was no matter of praise to me, if I knew more than those who had not had a similar advantage, but the deepest disgrace to me if I did not. I have a distinct remembrance, that the suggestion thus for the first time made to me, that I knew more than other youths who were considered well educated, was to me a piece of information, to which, as to all other things which my father told me, I gave implicit credence, but which did not at all impress me as a personal matter. I felt no disposition to glorify myself upon the circumstance that there were other persons who did not know what I knew; nor had I ever flattered myself that my acquirements, whatever they might be, were any merit of mine: but, now when my attention was called to the subject, I felt that what my father had said respecting my peculiar advantages was exactly the truth and common sense of the matter, and it fixed my opinion and feeling from that time forward.

It is evident that this, among many other of the purposes of my father's scheme of education, could not have been accomplished if he had not carefully kept me from having any great amount of intercourse with other boys. He was earnestly bent upon my escaping not only the corrupting influence which boys exercise over boys, but the contagion of vulgar modes of thought and feeling; and for this he was willing that I should pay the price of inferiority in the accomplishments which schoolboys in all countries chiefly cultivate. The deficiencies in my education were principally in the things which boys learn from being turned out to shift for themselves, and from being brought together in large numbers. From temperance and much walking, I grew up healthy and hardy, though not muscular; but I could do no feats of skill or physical strength, and knew none of the ordinary bodily exercises. It was not that play, or time for it, was refused me. Though no holidays were allowed, lest the

habit of work should be broken, and a taste for idleness acquired, I had ample leisure in every day to amuse myself; but as I had no boy companions, and the animal need of physical activity was satisfied by walking, my amusements, which were mostly solitary, were in general, of a quiet, if not a bookish turn, and gave little stimulus to any other kind even of mental activity than that which was already called forth by my studies: I consequently remained long, and in a less degree have always remained, inexpert in anything requiring manual dexterity; my mind, as well as my hands, did its work very lamely when it was applied, or ought to have been applied, to the practical details which, as they are the chief interest of life to the majority of men, are also the things in which whatever mental capacity they have, chiefly shows itself: I was constantly meriting reproof by inattention, inobservance, and general slackness of mind in matters of daily life. My father was the extreme opposite in these particulars: his senses and mental faculties were always on the alert; he carried decision and energy of character in his whole manner and into every action of life: and this, as much as his talents, contributed to the strong impression which he always made upon those with whom he came into personal contact. But the children of energetic parents, frequently grow up unenergetic, because they lean on their parents, and the parents are energetic for them. The education which my father gave me, was in itself much more fitted for training me to *know* than to *do*. Not that he was unaware of my deficiencies; both as a boy and as a youth I was incessantly smarting under his severe admonitions on the subject. There was anything but insensibility or tolerance on his part towards such shortcomings: but, while he saved me from the demoralizing effects of school life, he made no effort to provide me with any sufficient substitute for its practicalizing influences. Whatever qualities he himself, probably, had acquired without difficulty or special training, he seems to have supposed that I ought to acquire as easily. He had not, I think, bestowed the same amount of thought and attention on this, as on most other branches of education; and here, as well in some other points of my tuition, he seems to have expected effects without causes. (Chapter 1)

Moral Influences in Early Youth
My Father's Character and Opinions

In my education, as in that of everyone, the moral influences, which are so much more important than all others, are also the most complicated, and the most difficult to specify with any approach to completeness. Without attempting the hopeless task of detailing the circumstances by which, in this respect, my early character may have been shaped, I shall confine myself to a few leading points, which form an indispensable part of any true account of my education.

I was brought up from the first without any religious belief, in the ordinary acceptation of the term. My father, educated in the creed of Scotch Presbyterianism, had by his own studies and reflections been early led to reject not only the belief in Revelation, but the foundations of what is commonly called Natural Religion. I have heard him say, that the turning point of his mind on the subject was reading Butler's Analogy.[30] That work, of which he always continued to speak with respect, kept him, as he said, for some considerable time, a believer in the divine authority of Christianity; by proving to him, that whatever are the difficulties in believing that the Old and New Testaments proceed from, or record the acts of, a perfectly wise and good being, the same and still greater difficulties stand in the way of the belief, that a being of such a character can have been the Maker of the universe. He considered Butler's argument as conclusive against the only opponents for whom it was intended. Those who admit an omnipotent as well as perfectly just and benevolent maker and ruler of such a world as this, can say little against Christianity but what can, with at least equal force, be retorted against themselves. Finding, therefore, no halting place in Deism, he remained in a state of perplexity, until, doubtless after many struggles, he yielded to the conviction, that, concerning the origin of things nothing whatever can be known. This is the only correct statement of his opinion; for dogmatic atheism he looked upon as absurd; as most of those, whom the world has considered Atheists, have always done. These particulars are important, because they show that my father's rejection of all that is called religious belief, was not, as many might suppose, primarily a matter of logic and evidence: the grounds of it were moral, still more than intellectual. He found it impossible to believe that a world so full of evil was the work of an Author combining infinite power with perfect goodness and righteousness. His intellect spurned the subtleties by which men attempt to blind themselves to this open contradiction. The Sabæan, or Manichæan theory of a Good and an Evil Principle,[31] struggling against each other for the government of the universe, he would not have equally condemned; and I have heard him express surprise,

that no one revived it in our time. He would have regarded it as a mere hypothesis; but he would have ascribed to it no depraving influence. As it was, his aversion to religion, in the sense usually attached to the term, was of the same kind with that of Lucretius:[32] he regarded it with the feelings due not to a mere mental delusion, but to a great moral evil. He looked upon it as the greatest enemy of morality: first, by setting up fictitious excellences,—belief in creeds, devotional feelings, and ceremonies, not connected with the good of human-kind,—and causing these to be accepted as substitutes for genuine virtues: but above all, by radically vitiating the standard of morals; making it consist in doing the will of a being, on whom it lavishes indeed all the phrases of adulation, but whom in sober truth it depicts as eminently hateful. I have a hundred times heard him say, that all ages and nations have represented their gods as wicked, in a constantly increasing progression, that mankind have gone on adding trait after trait till they reached the most perfect conception of wickedness which the human mind can devise, and have called this God, and prostrated themselves before it. This ne plus ultra[33] of wickedness he considered to be embodied in what is commonly presented to mankind as the creed of Christianity. Think (he used to say) of a being who would make a Hell—who would create the human race with the infallible foreknowledge, and therefore with the intention, that the great majority of them were to be consigned to horrible and everlasting torment. The time, I believe, is drawing near when this dreadful conception of an object of worship will be no longer identified with Christianity; and when all persons, with any sense of moral good and evil, will look upon it with the same indignation with which my father regarded it. My father was as well aware as any one that Christians do not, in general, undergo the demoralizing consequences which seem inherent in such a creed, in the manner or to the extent which might have been expected from it. The same slovenliness of thought, and subjection of the reason to fears, wishes, and affections, which enable them to accept a theory involving a contradiction in terms, prevents them from perceiving the logical consequences of the theory. Such is the facility with which mankind believe at one and the same time things inconsistent with one another, and so few are those who draw from what they receive as truths, any consequences but those recommended to them by their feelings, that multitudes have held the undoubting

---

[30]Joseph **Butler** (1692–1752): Anglican bishop, author of *The Analogy of Religion* (1736).

[31]**Sabaean, Manichaean:** forms of theological dualism.

[32]**Lucretius** (1st century BCE): Latin poet and philosopher.

[33]*ne plus ultra:* extreme point.

belief in an Omnipotent Author of Hell, and have nevertheless identified that being with the best conception they were able to form of perfect goodness. Their worship was not paid to the demon which such a Being as they imagined would really be, but to their own ideal of excellence. The evil is, that such a belief keeps the ideal wretchedly low; and opposes the most obstinate resistance to all thought which has a tendency to raise it higher. Believers shrink from every train of ideas which would lead the mind to a clear conception and an elevated standard of excellence, because they feel (even when they do not distinctly see) that such a standard would conflict with many of the dispensations of nature, and with much of what they are accustomed to consider as the Christian creed. And thus morality continues a matter of blind tradition, with no consistent principle, nor even any consistent feeling, to guide it.

It would have been wholly inconsistent with my father's ideas of duty, to allow me to acquire impressions contrary to his convictions and feelings respecting religion: and he impressed upon me from the first, that the manner in which the world came into existence was a subject on which nothing was known: that the question, "Who made me?" cannot be answered, because we have no experience or authentic information from which to answer it; and that any answer only throws the difficulty a step further back, since the question immediately presents itself, "Who made God?" He, at the same time, took care that I should be acquainted with what had been thought by mankind on these impenetrable problems. I have mentioned at how early an age he made me a reader of ecclesiastical history; and he taught me to take the strongest interest in the Reformation, as the great and decisive contest against priestly tyranny for liberty of thought. . . .

. . . For passionate emotions of all sorts, and for everything which has been said or written in exaltation of them, he professed the greatest contempt. He regarded them as a form of madness. "The intense" was with him a bye-word of scornful disapprobation. He regarded as an aberration of the moral standard of modern times, compared with that of the ancients, the great stress laid upon feeling. Feelings, as such, he considered to be no proper subjects of praise or blame. Right and wrong, good and bad, he regarded as qualities solely of conduct—of acts and omissions; there being no feeling which may not lead, and does not frequently lead, either to good or to bad actions: conscience itself, the very desire to act right, often leading people to act wrong. Consistently carrying out the doctrine, that the object of praise and blame should be the discouragement of wrong conduct and the encouragement of right, he refused to let his praise or blame be influenced by the motive of the agent. . . .

It will be admitted, that a man of the opinions, and the character, above described, was likely to leave a strong moral impression on any mind principally formed by him, and that his moral teaching was not likely to err on the side of laxity or indulgence. The element which was chiefly deficient in his moral relation to his children was that of tenderness. I do not believe that this deficiency lay in his own nature. I believe him to have had much more feeling than he habitually showed, and much greater capacities of feeling than were ever developed. He resembled most Englishmen in being ashamed of the signs of feeling, and by the absence of demonstration, starving the feelings themselves. If we consider further that he was in the trying position of sole teacher, and add to this that his temper was constitutionally irritable, it is impossible not to feel true pity for a father who did, and strove to do, so much for his children, who would have so valued their affection, yet who must have been constantly feeling that fear of him was drying it up at its source. This was no longer the case later in life, and with his younger children. They loved him tenderly: and if I cannot say so much of myself, I was always loyally devoted to him. As regards my own education, I hesitate to pronounce whether I was more a loser or gainer by his severity. It was not such as to prevent me from having a happy childhood. And I do not believe that boys can be induced to apply themselves with vigour, and what is so much more difficult, perseverance, to dry and irksome studies, by the sole force of persuasion and soft words. Much must be done, and much must be learnt, by children, for which rigid discipline, and known liability to punishment, are indispensable as means. It is, no doubt, a very laudable effort, in modern teaching, to render as much as possible of what the young are required to learn, easy and interesting to them. But when this principle is pushed to the length of not requiring them to learn anything *but* what has been made easy and interesting, one of the chief objects of education is sacrificed. I rejoice in the decline of the old brutal and tyrannical system of teaching, which, however, did succeed in enforcing habits of application; but the new, as it seems to me, is training up a race of men who will be incapable of doing anything which is disagreeable to them. I do not, then, believe that fear, as an element in education, can be dispensed with; but I am sure that it ought not to be the main element; and when it predominates so much as to preclude love and confidence on the part of the child to those who should be the unreservedly trusted advisers of after years, and perhaps to seal up the fountains of frank and spontaneous communicativeness in the child's nature, it is an evil for which a large abatement must be made from the benefits, moral and intellectual, which may flow from any other part of the education. (Chapter 2)

A Crisis in My Mental History. One Stage Onward

For some years after this time I wrote very little, and nothing regularly, for publication: and great were the advantages which I derived from the intermission. It was of no common importance to me, at this period, to be able to digest and mature my thoughts for my own mind only, without any immediate call for giving them out in print. Had I gone on writing, it would have much disturbed the important transformation in my opinions and character, which took place during those years. The origin of this transformation, or at least the process by which I was prepared for it, can only be explained by turning some distance back.

From the winter of 1821, when I first read Bentham,[34] and especially from the commencement of the Westminster Review, I had what might truly be called an object in life: to be a reformer of the world. My conception of my own happiness was entirely identified with this object. The personal sympathies I wished for were those of fellow labourers in this enterprise. I endeavoured to pick up as many flowers as I could by the way; but as a serious and permanent personal satisfaction to rest upon, my whole reliance was placed on this; and I was accustomed to felicitate myself on the certainty of a happy life which I enjoyed, through placing my happiness in something durable and distant, in which some progress might be always making, while it could never be exhausted by complete attainment. This did very well for several years, during which the general improvement going on in the world and the idea of myself as engaged with others in struggling to promote it, seemed enough to fill up an interesting and animated existence. But the time came when I awakened from this as from a dream. It was in the autumn of 1826. I was in a dull state of nerves, such as everybody is occasionally liable to; unsusceptible to enjoyment or pleasurable excitement; one of those moods when what is pleasure at other times, becomes insipid or indifferent; the state, I should think, in which converts to Methodism usually are,

when smitten by their first "conviction of sin."[35] In this frame of mind it occurred to me to put the question directly to myself: "Suppose that all your objects in life were realized; that all the changes in institutions and opinions which you are looking forward to, could be completely effected at this very instant: would this be a great joy and happiness to you?" And an irrepressible self-consciousness distinctly answered, "No!" At this my heart sank within me: the whole foundation on which my life was constructed fell down. All my happiness was to have been found in the continual pursuit of this end. The end had ceased to charm, and how could there ever again be any interest in the means? I seemed to have nothing left to live for.

At first I hoped that the cloud would pass away of itself; but it did not. A night's sleep, the sovereign remedy for the smaller vexations of life, had no effect on it. I awoke to a renewed consciousness of the woful fact. I carried it with me into all companies, into all occupations. Hardly anything had power to cause me even a few minutes' oblivion of it. For some months the cloud seemed to grow thicker and thicker. The lines in Coleridge's "Dejection"—I was not then acquainted with them—exactly describe my case:

"A grief without a pang, void, dark and drear,
    A drowsy, stifled, unimpassioned grief,
    Which finds no natural outlet or relief
    In word, or sigh, or tear."[36]

In vain I sought relief from my favourite books; those memorials of past nobleness and greatness from which I had always hitherto drawn strength and animation. I read them now without feeling, or with the accustomed feeling *minus* all its charm; and I became persuaded, that my love of mankind, and of excellence for its own sake, had worn itself out. I sought no comfort by speaking to others of what I felt. If I had loved any one sufficiently to make confiding my griefs a necessity, I should not have been in the condition I was. I felt, too, that mine was not an interesting, or in any way respectable distress. There was nothing in it to attract sympathy. Advice, if I had known where to seek it, would have been most precious. The words of Macbeth to the physician[37] often occurred to my thoughts. But there

---

[34]Jeremy **Bentham** (1748–1832): English jurist and philosopher; earliest proponent of the Utilitarian doctrine promoting the greatest happiness of the greatest number. *Westminster Review*: liberal periodical founded in 1824 by Bentham and James Mill.

[35]**Methodism**: evangelical revivalism within the 18th-century Church of England. "**conviction of sin**": spiritual crisis preceding evangelical conversion.

[36]"**A grief . . . or tear**": "**Dejection: An Ode**" (1802) 21–24.

[37]**Macbeth**: "Canst thou not minister to a mind diseased?" (*Macbeth* 5.3.40).

was no one on whom I could build the faintest hope of such assistance. My father, to whom it would have been natural to me to have recourse in any practical difficulties, was the last person to whom, in such a case as this, I looked for help. Everything convinced me that he had no knowledge of any such mental state as I was suffering from, and that even if he could be made to understand it, he was not the physician who could heal it. My education, which was wholly his work, had been conducted without any regard to the possibility of its ending in this result; and I saw no use in giving him the pain of thinking that his plans had failed, when the failure was probably irremediable, and, at all events, beyond the power of *his* remedies. Of other friends, I had at that time none to whom I had any hope of making my condition intelligible. It was however abundantly intelligible to myself; and the more I dwelt upon it, the more hopeless it appeared.

My course of study had led me to believe, that all mental and moral feelings and qualities, whether of a good or of a bad kind, were the results of association;[38] that we love one thing, and hate another, take pleasure in one sort of action or contemplation, and pain in another sort, through the clinging of pleasurable or painful ideas to those things, from the effect of education or of experience. As a corollary from this, I had always heard it maintained by my father, and was myself convinced, that the object of education should be to form the strongest possible associations of the salutary class; associations of pleasure with all things beneficial to the great whole, and of pain with all things hurtful to it. This doctrine appeared inexpugnable; but it now seemed to me, on retrospect, that my teachers had occupied themselves but superficially with the means of forming and keeping up these salutary associations. They seemed to have trusted altogether to the old familiar instruments, praise and blame, reward and punishment. Now, I did not doubt that by these means, begun early, and applied unremittingly, intense associations of pain and pleasure, especially of pain, might be created, and might produce desires and aversions capable of lasting undiminished to the end of life. But there must always be something artificial and casual in associations thus produced. The pains and pleasures thus forcibly associated with things, are not connected with them by any natural tie; and it is therefore, I thought, essential to the

durability of these associations, that they should have become so intense and inveterate as to be practically indissoluble, before the habitual exercise of the power of analysis had commenced. For I now saw, or thought I saw, what I had always before received with incredulity—that the habit of analysis has a tendency to wear away the feelings: as indeed it has, when no other mental habit is cultivated, and the analysing spirit remains without its natural complements and correctives. The very excellence of analysis (I argued) is that it tends to weaken and undermine whatever is the result of prejudice; that it enables us mentally to separate ideas which have only casually clung together: and no associations whatever could ultimately resist this dissolving force, were it not that we owe to analysis our clearest knowledge of the permanent sequences in nature; the real connexions between Things, not dependent on our will and feelings; natural laws, by virtue of which, in many cases, one thing is inseparable from another in fact; which laws, in proportion as they are clearly perceived and imaginatively realized, cause our ideas of things which are always joined together in Nature, to cohere more and more closely in our thoughts. Analytic habits may thus even strengthen the associations between causes and effects, means and ends, but tend altogether to weaken those which are, to speak familiarly, a *mere* matter of feeling. They are therefore (I thought) favourable to prudence and clear-sightedness, but a perpetual worm at the root both of the passions and of the virtues; and, above all, fearfully undermine all desires, and all pleasures, which are the effects of association, that is, according to the theory I held, all except the purely physical and organic; of the entire insufficiency of which to make life desirable, no one had a stronger conviction than I had. These were the laws of human nature, by which, as it seemed to me, I had been brought to my present state. All those to whom I looked up, were of opinion that the pleasure of sympathy with human beings, and the feelings which made the good of others, and especially of mankind on a large scale, the object of existence, were the greatest and surest sources of happiness. Of the truth of this I was convinced, but to know that a feeling would make me happy if I had it, did not give me the feeling. My education, I thought, had failed to create these feelings in sufficient strength to resist the dissolving influence of analysis, while the whole course of my intellectual cultivation had made precocious and premature analysis the inveterate habit of my mind. I was thus, as I said to myself, left stranded at the commencement of my voyage, with a well-equipped ship and a rudder, but no sail; without any real desire for the ends which I had been so carefully fitted out to work for: no delight in virtue, or the general good,

---

[38]**association**: according to associationism, which dominated English psychology in the later 18th and early 19th centuries, repeated sensations became correlated in the mind as kindred images or ideas.

but also just as little in anything else. The fountains of vanity and ambition seemed to have dried up within me, as completely as those of benevolence. I had had (as I reflected) some gratification of vanity at too early an age: I had obtained some distinction, and felt myself of some importance, before the desire of distinction and of importance had grown into a passion: and little as it was which I had attained, yet having been attained too early, like all pleasures enjoyed too soon, it had made me *blasé* and indifferent to the pursuit. Thus neither selfish nor unselfish pleasures were pleasures to me. And there seemed no power in nature sufficient to begin the formation of my character anew, and create in a mind now irretrievably analytic, fresh associations of pleasure with any of the objects of human desire.

These were the thoughts which mingled with the dry heavy dejection of the melancholy winter of 1826-7. During this time I was not incapable of my usual occupations. I went on with them mechanically, by the mere force of habit. I had been so drilled in a certain sort of mental exercise, that I could still carry it on when all the spirit had gone out of it. I even composed and spoke several speeches at the debating society,[39] how, or with what degree of success, I know not. Of four years continual speaking at that society, this is the only year of which I remember next to nothing. Two lines of Coleridge, in whom alone of all writers I have found a true description of what I felt, were often in my thoughts, not at this time (for I had never read them), but in a later period of the same mental malady:

> "Work without hope draws nectar in a sieve,
>   And hope without an object cannot live."[40]

In all probability my case was by no means so peculiar as I fancied it, and I doubt not that many others have passed through a similar state; but the idiosyncrasies of my education had given to the general phenomenon a special character, which made it seem the natural effect of causes that it was hardly possible for time to remove. I frequently asked myself, if I could, or if I was bound to go on living, when life must be passed in this manner. I generally answered to myself, that I did not think I could possibly bear it beyond a year. When, however, not more than half that duration of time had elapsed, a small ray of light broke in upon my gloom. I was reading, accidentally, Marmontel's

"Memoires,"[41] and came to the passage which relates his father's death, the distressed position of the family, and the sudden inspiration by which he, then a mere boy, felt and made them feel that he would be everything to them—would supply the place of all that they had lost. A vivid conception of the scene and its feelings came over me, and I was moved to tears. From this moment my burden grew lighter. The oppression of the thought that all feeling was dead within me, was gone. I was no longer hopeless: I was not a stock or a stone. I had still, it seemed, some of the material out of which all worth of character, and all capacity for happiness, are made. Relieved from my ever present sense of irremediable wretchedness, I gradually found that the ordinary incidents of life could again give me some pleasure; that I could again find enjoyment, not intense, but sufficient for cheerfulness, in sunshine and sky, in books, in conversation, in public affairs; and that there was, once more, excitement, though of a moderate kind, in exerting myself for my opinions, and for the public good. Thus the cloud gradually drew off, and I again enjoyed life: and though I had several relapses, some of which lasted many months, I never again was as miserable as I had been.

The experiences of this period had two very marked effects on my opinions and character. In the first place, they led me to adopt a theory of life very unlike that on which I had before acted, and having much in common with what at that time I certainly had never heard of, the anti-self-consciousness theory of Carlyle. I never, indeed, wavered in the conviction that happiness is the test of all rules of conduct, and the end of life. But I now thought that this end was only to be attained by not making it the direct end. Those only are happy (I thought) who have their minds fixed on some object other than their own happiness; on the happiness of others, on the improvement of mankind, even on some art or pursuit, followed not as a means, but as itself an ideal end. Aiming thus at something else, they find happiness by the way. The enjoyments of life (such was now my theory) are sufficient to make it a pleasant thing, when they are taken *en passant*,[42] without being made a principal object. Once make them so, and they are immediately felt to be insufficient. They will not bear a scrutinizing examination. Ask yourself whether you are happy, and you cease to be so. The only chance is to treat, not happiness, but some end external to it, as the purpose of

---

[39]**debating society:** Speculative Society, founded by Mill and friends in 1825.

[40]**"Work . . . cannot live":** Coleridge, "Work Without Hope" (1825) 13–14.

[41]Jean-François **Marmontel** (1723–1799): French author of *Mémoires d'un père* (*A Father's Memoirs*, 1804).

[42]*en passant:* in passing.

life. Let your self-consciousness, your scrutiny, your self-interrogation, exhaust themselves on that; and if otherwise fortunately circumstanced you will inhale happiness with the air you breathe, without dwelling on it or thinking about it, without either forestalling it in imagination, or putting it to flight by fatal questioning. This theory now became the basis of my philosophy of life. And I still hold to it as the best theory for all those who have but a moderate degree of sensibility and of capacity for enjoyment, that is, for the great majority of mankind.

The other important change which my opinions at this time underwent, was that I, for the first time, gave its proper place, among the prime necessities of human well-being, to the internal culture of the individual. I ceased to attach almost exclusive importance to the ordering of outward circumstances, and the training of the human being for speculation and for action.

I had now learnt by experience that the passive susceptibilities needed to be cultivated as well as the active capacities, and required to be nourished and enriched as well as guided. I did not, for an instant, lose sight of, or undervalue, that part of the truth which I had seen before; I never turned recreant to intellectual culture, or ceased to consider the power and practice of analysis as an essential condition both of individual and of social improvement. But I thought that it had consequences which required to be corrected, by joining other kinds of cultivation with it. The maintenance of a due balance among the faculties, now seemed to me of primary importance. The cultivation of the feelings became one of the cardinal points in my ethical and philosophical creed. And my thoughts and inclinations turned in an increasing degree towards whatever seemed capable of being instrumental to that object.

I now began to find meaning in the things which I had read or heard about the importance of poetry and art as instruments of human culture. . . .

This state of my thoughts and feelings made the fact of my reading Wordsworth for the first time (in the autumn of 1828), an important event in my life. I took up the collection of his poems from curiosity, with no expectation of mental relief from it, though I had before resorted to poetry with that hope. In the worst period of my depression, I had read through the whole of Byron (then new to me), to try whether a poet, whose peculiar department was supposed to be that of the intenser feelings, could rouse any feeling in me. As might be expected, I got no good from this reading, but the reverse. The poet's state of mind was too like my own. His was the lament of a man who had worn out all pleasures, and who seemed to think that life, to all who possess the good things of it, must necessarily be the vapid, uninteresting thing which I found it. His Harold and Manfred had the same burden on them which I had; and I was not in a frame of mind to desire any comfort from the vehement sensual passion of his Giaours, or the sullenness of his Laras.[43] But while Byron was exactly what did not suit my condition, Wordsworth was exactly what did. I had looked into the Excursion[44] two or three years before, and found little in it; and I should probably have found as little, had I read it at this time. But the miscellaneous poems, in the two-volume edition of 1815 (to which little of value was added in the latter part of the author's life), proved to be the precise thing for my mental wants at that particular juncture.

In the first place, these poems addressed themselves powerfully to one of the strongest of my pleasurable susceptibilities, the love of rural objects and natural scenery; to which I had been indebted not only for much of the pleasure of my life, but quite recently for relief from one of my longest relapses into depression. In this power of rural beauty over me, there was a foundation laid for taking pleasure in Wordsworth's poetry; the more so, as his scenery lies mostly among mountains, which, owing to my early Pyrenean excursion,[45] were my ideal of natural beauty. But Wordsworth would never have had any great effect on me, if he had merely placed before me beautiful pictures of natural scenery. Scott does this still better than Wordsworth, and a very second-rate landscape does it more effectually than any poet. What made Wordsworth's poems a medicine for my state of mind, was that they expressed, not mere outward beauty, but states of feeling, and of thought coloured by feeling, under the excitement of beauty. They seemed to be the very culture of the feelings, which I was in quest of. In them I seemed to draw from a source of inward joy, of sympathetic and imaginative pleasure, which could be shared in by all human beings; which had no connexion with struggle or imperfection, but would be made richer by every improvement in the physical or social condition of mankind. From them I seemed to learn what would be the perennial sources of happiness, when all the greater evils of life shall have been removed. And I felt myself at once better and happier as I came under their influence. There have certainly been, even in our own age, greater poets than Wordsworth; but poetry of deeper and loftier feeling could

---

[43]**Harold . . . Laras:** see *Childe Harold's Pilgrimage* (1812–1818), *Manfred* (1817), *The Giaour* (1813), and *Lara* (1814).

[44]*The Excursion:* Wordsworth's long philosophical poem of 1814.

[45]**Pyrenean excursion:** in 1820–1821.

not have done for me at that time what his did. I needed to be made to feel that there was real, permanent happiness in tranquil contemplation. Wordsworth taught me this, not only without turning away from, but with a greatly increased interest in the common feelings and common destiny of human beings. And the delight which these poems gave me, proved that with culture of this sort, there was nothing to dread from the most confirmed habit of analysis. . . .

In giving an account of this period of my life, I have only specified such of my new impressions as appeared to me, both at the time and since, to be a kind of turning points, marking a definite progress in my mode of thought. But these few selected points give a very insufficient idea of the quantity of thinking which I carried on respecting a host of subjects during these years of transition. Much of this, it is true, consisted in rediscovering things known to all the world, which I had previously disbelieved, or disregarded. But the rediscovery was to me a discovery, giving me plenary possession of the truths, not as traditional platitudes, but fresh from their source: and it seldom failed to place them in some new light, by which they were reconciled with, and seemed to confirm while they modified, the truths less generally known which lay in my early opinions, and in no essential part of which I at any time wavered. All my new thinking only laid the foundation of these more deeply and strongly, while it often removed misapprehension and confusion of ideas which had perverted their effect. For example, during the later returns of my dejection, the doctrine of what is called Philosophical Necessity[46] weighed on my existence like an incubus. I felt as if I was scientifically proved to be the helpless slave of antecedent circumstances; as if my character and that of all others had been formed for us by agencies beyond our control, and was wholly out of our own power. I often said to myself, what a relief it would be if I could disbelieve the doctrine of the formation of character by circumstances; and remembering the wish of Fox[47] respecting the doctrine of resistance to governments, that it might never be forgotten by kings, nor remembered by subjects, I said that it would be a blessing if the doctrine of necessity could be believed by all quoad[48] the characters of others and disbelieved in regard to their own. I pondered painfully on the subject, till gradually I saw light through it. I perceived, that the word Necessity, as a name for the doctrine of Cause and Effect applied to human action, carried

with it a misleading association; and that this association was the operative force in the depressing and paralysing influence which I had experienced: I saw that though our character is formed by circumstances, our own desires can do much to shape those circumstances; and that what is really inspiriting and ennobling in the doctrine of freewill, is the conviction that we have real power over the formation of our own character; that our will, by influencing some of our circumstances, can modify our future habits or capabilities of willing. All this was entirely consistent with the doctrine of circumstances, or rather, was that doctrine itself, properly understood. From that time I drew in my own mind, a clear distinction between the doctrine of circumstances, and Fatalism; discarding altogether the misleading word Necessity. The theory, which I now for the first time rightly apprehended, ceased altogether to be discouraging, and besides the relief to my spirits, I no longer suffered under the burden, so heavy to one who aims at being a reformer in opinions, of thinking one doctrine true, and the contrary doctrine morally beneficial. The train of thought which had extricated me from this dilemma, seemed to me, in after years, fitted to render a similar service to others; and it now forms the chapter on Liberty and Necessity in the concluding Book of my System of Logic. . . .

I have already mentioned Carlyle's earlier writings as one of the channels through which I received the influences which enlarged my early narrow creed; but I do not think that those writings, by themselves, would ever have had any effect on my opinions. What truths they contained, though of the very kind which I was already receiving from other quarters, were presented in a form and vesture less suited than any other to give them access to a mind trained as mine had been. They seemed a haze of poetry and German metaphysics, in which almost the only clear thing was a strong animosity to most of the opinions which were the basis of my mode of thought; religious scepticism, utilitarianism, the doctrine of circumstances, and the attaching any importance to democracy, logic, or political economy. Instead of my having been taught anything, in the first instance, by Carlyle, it was only in proportion as I came to see the same truths through media more suited to my mental constitution, that I recognised them in his writings. Then, indeed, the wonderful power with which he put them forth made a deep impression upon me, and I was during a long period one of his most fervent admirers; but the good his writings did me, was not as philosophy to instruct, but as poetry to animate. Even at the time when our acquaintance commenced, I was not sufficiently advanced in my new modes of thought, to appreci-

---

[46]**Philosophical Necessity**: strict causal fatalism.

[47]Charles James **Fox** (1749–1806): statesman.

[48]*quoad*: with respect to.

ate him fully; a proof of which is, that on his showing me the manuscript of Sartor Resartus, his best and greatest work, which he had just then finished, I made little of it; though when it came out about two years afterwards in Fraser's Magazine I read it with enthusiastic admiration and the keenest delight. I did not seek and cultivate Carlyle less on account of the fundamental differences in our philosophy. He soon found out that I was not "another mystic," and when for the sake of my own integrity I wrote to him a distinct profession of all those of my opinions which I knew he most disliked, he replied that the chief difference between us was that I "was as yet consciously nothing of a mystic." I do not know at what period he gave up the expectation that I was destined to become one; but though both his and my opinions underwent in subsequent years considerable changes, we never approached much nearer to each other's modes of thought than we were in the first years of our acquaintance. I did not, however, deem myself a competent judge of Carlyle. I felt that he was a poet, and that I was not; that he was a man of intuition, which I was not; and that as such, he not only saw many things long before me, which I could only when they were pointed out to me, hobble after and prove, but that it was highly probable he could see many things which were not visible to me even after they were pointed out. I knew that I could not see round him, and could never be certain that I saw over him; and I never presumed to judge him with any definiteness, until he was interpreted to me by one[49] greatly the superior of us both—who was more a poet than he, and more a thinker than I—whose own mind and nature included his, and infinitely more. . . . (Chapter 5)

1873

---

[49]**one:** Harriet Taylor (1807–1858), radical author whom Mill met in 1830 and married in 1851.

ELIZABETH BARRETT BROWNING

(1806–1861)

Elizabeth Barrett Browning was in her lifetime the most widely respected woman poet who had ever written in English. Her intellectual power, high moral seriousness, and varied and daring subject matter, along with the pathos and artistry of her verse, made her the supreme example from which to argue that women could—or could not—be great poets. The drama of her life, meanwhile, cast her as a fairy-tale heroine: immured for long years in solitude, rescued by a gallant lover, living blissfully ever after.

The eldest of twelve children, Elizabeth Barrett spent a happy, lively childhood in a fantastical turreted country mansion built by her father from the profits of a slave plantation in Jamaica. She read voraciously, wrote poems, and daydreamed of marrying a great poet and being one herself. She yearned to study Greek, which she imagined (with some justification) held the key to the male stronghold of high literary culture, and when a tutor came to prepare her younger brother for one of the great public schools, she shared the lessons; when her brother went off to boarding school, she studied by herself until a classical scholar living nearby allowed her to read with him. The range and depth of her mastery of Greek literature, rare even for a man and almost unheard-of in a woman, gave her the confidence and authority to enter the cultural arena.

In adolescence a mysterious illness (attributed by the family to a spinal injury from riding her pony) brought her near death, and for most of her life thereafter she was an invalid. In 1835 her father, having lost much of his fortune, sold his country estate and moved the family to London. In 1840 her brother drowned while visiting her at the seaside, where she had been sent to alleviate a serious bout of tuberculosis; the accident left her overwhelmed by grief and guilt. She spent the next several years in London, confined day and night to one room where, feeding largely on morphine (prescribed by her doctors) and coffee and admitting almost no visitors, she conducted epistolary friendships with men and women of letters and developed a flourishing literary career.

She had dreamed as a girl of being "the feminine of Homer," the first and greatest of women poets. This ambition was both exorbitant and realizable. Surveying the literary tradition in 1845, she wrote: "I look everywhere for grandmothers, and see none." Despising the weakness that was considered "feminine," she aspired beyond the narrow ground of love and tears to which women poets were mostly consigned. She began instead with a small Homeric epic, *The Battle of Marathon*, which her father paid to have privately printed when she was fourteen. Her first properly published volumes were *An Essay on Mind* (1826), centered on a philosophical poem in the style of Pope, and a translation of Aeschylus' knotty and difficult *Prometheus Bound* (1833). These works sedulously followed the male poetic tradition. She began to challenge that tradition, however, in her next long poems: a vision of the crucifixion, and a sequel to Milton that took up the story of Adam and Eve after the fall. Profoundly religious in the evangelical mode of her parents and scornful of established churches, she found in Christianity a validation of female experience—defined as suffering, humility, and love—that gave her access to sources of knowledge and power that were closed, she asserted, to all pre-Christian poets and indeed to most Christian men.

Her long poems won respect, but her most popular ones were ballad romances, often with a feminist or ironical edge. And then her own life became a romance. In January 1845 Robert Browning, enchanted by the "strange new music" of her poetry, sent her what was very like a love letter. They corresponded, she eventually allowed him to visit, and they became secretly engaged. She was hesitant to let him bind himself to her, since she was almost six years older and assumed to be incurably ill. Her father, moreover, was convinced that his children owed him absolute obedience and refused to let any of them marry. But in September 1846 the two poets eloped to Italy and for the rest of her life lived mostly in Florence; her health improved, and she gave birth to a son. She was much the more famous of the two, although both were renowned for the difficulty of their verse.

The Brownings' love affair produced two major literary works: the letters in which the two poets conducted much of their courtship, and *Sonnets from the Portuguese*. Reviving the Renaissance tradition of the amatory sonnet sequence, *Sonnets* inaugurates a distinctive Victorian literary form: the long, quasi-autobiographical lyric sequence that juxtaposes poetic convention and day-to-day contemporary life. *Sonnets from the Portuguese* takes the point of view of a woman who is both the (conventionally male) poet-speaker-lover whose desire fuels the poem and also the (conventionally female) object of poetic desire. Among her other mature works were poems in support of American abolitionism, a cause resonant for her with the guilty awareness that her family's wealth had come from slavery. She also passionately supported the *Risorgimento*, the Italian struggle for reunification and liberation from foreign rule. In *Aurora Leigh*, a verse novel in nine books, she tells the story of a girl who becomes a very successful poet and then marries the man she loves—a story that, except for the author's own example, would have seemed highly unlikely.

Barrett Browning's reputation went through many vicissitudes even in her lifetime. Contemporary critics who admired her work often objected to its obscurity, difficulty, daring and unusual imagery, and experiments in diction and rhyme. For some readers her attacks on tyranny—slavery, the industrial exploitation of children, the oppression of subject nations, the sexual double standard, male domination of women—made her a heroine. For others, such boldness was offensively unfeminine. Her conjugal and maternal devotion, along with her diminutive person, soft voice, gentle manner, and social reclusiveness, seemed angelic to many contemporaries, and her comparatively early death and her widower's devotion made this impression easy to sustain. In the backlash against all things "Victorian," however, these qualities lost their luster. To modernist eyes her political commitments seemed aesthetically crude, her verse sentimental, diffuse, and undisciplined. The continuing popularity of *Sonnets from the Portuguese* among ordinary readers further discredited her; the uncharacteristically simple "How do I love thee?" became a joke. Because most of her best poems are very long, she has not fared well in anthologies. But for many Victorian women, and then again after feminist criticism rediscovered her in the twentieth century, she became the "grandmother"—the female precursor she herself had sought in vain.

A Seaside Walk

— 1 —

We walked beside the sea
After a day which perished silently
Of its own glory—like the princess weird
Who, combating the Genius, scorched and seared,
Uttered with burning breath, "Ho! victory!"
And sank adown, a heap of ashes pale:
    So runs the Arab tale.[1]

— 2 —

The sky above us showed
A universal and unmoving cloud
On which the cliffs permitted us to see   10
Only the outline of their majesty,
As master-minds when gazed at by the crowd:
And shining with a gloom, the water grey
    Swang in its moon-taught way.

— 3 —

Nor moon, nor stars were out:
They did not dare to tread so soon about,
Though trembling, in the footsteps of the sun:
The light was neither night's nor day's, but one
Which, life-like, had a beauty in its doubt,
And silence's impassioned breathings round   20
    Seemed wandering into sound.

— 4 —

O solemn-beating heart
Of nature! I have knowledge that thou art
Bound unto man's by cords he cannot sever;
And, what time they are slackened by him ever,
So to attest his own supernal part,
Still runneth thy vibration fast and strong
    The slackened cord along:

— 5 —

For though we never spoke
Of the grey water and the shaded rock,   30
Dark wave and stone unconsciously were fused
Into the plaintive speaking that we used

---

[1]**Arab tale:** *The Arabian Nights* 1, Second Royal Mendicant's Tale
(continuation).

Of absent friends and memories unforsook;
And, had we seen each other's face, we had
    Seen haply, each was sad.

                                1838

Felicia Hemans

To L. E. L., Referring to her Monody on the Poetess.[1]

— 1 —

Thou bay-crowned living. One that o'er the bay-crowned[2]
    Dead art bowing,
And o'er the shadeless moveless brow the vital shadow
    throwing,
And o'er the sighless songless lips the wail and music
    wedding,
And dropping o'er the tranquil eyes the tears not of their
    shedding!—

— 2 —

Take music from the silent Dead whose meaning is
    completer,
Reserve thy tears for living brows where all such tears are
    meeter,
And leave the violets in the grass to brighten where thou
    treadest,
No flowers for her! no need of flowers, albeit "bring
    flowers!" thou saidest.

— 3 —

Yes, flowers, to crown the "cup and lute," since both may
    come to breaking,
Or flowers, to greet the "bride"—the heart's own beating
    works its aching;   10
Or flowers, to soothe the "captive's" sight, from earth's
    free bosom gathered,
Reminding of his earthly hope, then withering as it
    withered:

---

[1]**Felicia Hemans** (1793–1835), Letitia Landon (**L. E. L.**,
1802–1838): most notable women poets of the early 19th century.
monody (poem lamenting a death): Landon's "Stanzas on the Death
of Mrs. Hemans" (1838).

[2]Poets traditionally were **crowned** with laurel or **bay** leaves.

— 4 —

But bring not near the solemn corse a type of human
    seeming,
Lay only dust's stern verity upon the dust undreaming:
And while the calm perpetual stars shall look upon it solely,
Her spherèd soul shall look on *them* with eyes more bright
    and holy.

— 5 —

Nor mourn, O living One, because her part in life was
    mourning:
Would she have lost the poet's fire for anguish of the
    burning?
The minstrel harp, for the strained string? the tripod, for
    the afflated[3]
Woe? or the vision, for those tears in which it shone
    dilated?   20

— 6 —

Perhaps she shuddered while the world's cold hand her
    brow was wreathing,
But never wronged that mystic breath which breathed
    in all her breathing,
Which drew, from rocky earth and man, abstractions high
    and moving,
Beauty, if not the beautiful, and love, if not the loving.

— 7 —

Such visionings have paled in sight; the Saviour she
    descrieth,
And little recks *who* wreathed the brow which on His
    bosom lieth:
The whiteness of His innocence o'er all her garments,
    flowing,
There learneth she the sweet "new song" she will not
    mourn in knowing.

— 8 —

Be happy, crowned and living One! and as thy dust
    decayeth
May thine own England say for thee what now for Her it
    sayeth—   30
"Albeit softly in our ears her silver song was ringing,

The foot-fall of her parting soul is softer than
    her singing."

1835, 1838

The Cry of the Children

"Φεῦ, φεῦ, τί προσδέρκεσθέ μ' ὄμμασιν, τέκνα;"
—*Medea.*[1]

— 1 —

Do ye hear the children weeping, O my brothers,
    Ere the sorrow comes with years?
They are leaning their young heads against their mothers,
    And *that* cannot stop their tears.
The young lambs are bleating in the meadows,
    The young birds are chirping in the nest,
The young fawns are playing with the shadows,
    The young flowers are blowing toward the west—
But the young, young children, O my brothers,
    They are weeping bitterly!   10
They are weeping in the playtime of the others,
    In the country of the free.

— 2 —

Do you question the young children in the sorrow
    Why their tears are falling so?
The old man may weep for his to-morrow
    Which is lost in Long Ago;
The old tree is leafless in the forest,
    The old year is ending in the frost,
The old wound, if stricken, is the sorest,
    The old hope is hardest to be lost: 20
But the young, young children, O my brothers,
    Do you ask them why they stand
Weeping sore before the bosoms of their mothers,
    In our happy Fatherland?

— 3 —

They look up with their pale and sunken faces,
    And their looks are sad to see,

---

[3]**tripod:** seat from which the priestess of Apollo at Delphi delivered oracles. **afflated:** inspired.

[1]"Φεῦ, φεῦ, τί προσδέρκεσθέ μ' ὄμμασιν, τέκνα;": " Alas, alas, why do you look at me with your eyes, children?" Euripides, *Medea* 1040.

For the man's hoary anguish draws and presses
    Down the cheeks of infancy;
"Your old earth," they say, "is very dreary,
    Our young feet," they say, "are very weak;   30
Few paces have we taken, yet are weary—
    Our grave-rest is very far to seek:
Ask the aged why they weep, and not the children,
    For the outside earth is cold,
And we young ones stand without, in our bewildering,
    And the graves are for the old.

— 4 —

"True," say the children, "it may happen
    That we die before our time:
Little Alice died last year, her grave is shapen
    Like a snowball, in the rime.   40
We looked into the pit prepared to take her:
    Was no room for any work in the close clay!
From the sleep wherein she lieth none will wake her,
    Crying, 'Get up, little Alice! it is day.'
If you listen by that grave, in sun and shower,
    With your ear down, little Alice never cries;
Could we see her face, be sure we should not know her,
    For the smile has time for growing in her eyes:
And merry go her moments, lulled and stilled in
    The shroud by the kirk-chime.   50
It is good when it happens," say the children,
    "That we die before our time."

— 5 —

Alas, alas, the children! they are seeking
    Death in life, as best to have:
They are binding up their hearts away from breaking,
    With a cerement from the grave.
Go out, children, from the mine and from the city,
    Sing out, children, as the little thrushes do;
Pluck your handfuls of the meadow-cowslips pretty,
    Laugh aloud, to feel your fingers let them
        through!   60
But they answer, "Are your cowslips of the meadows
    Like our weeds anear the mine?
Leave us quiet in the dark of the coal-shadows,
    From your pleasures fair and fine!

— 6 —

"For oh," say the children, "we are weary,
    And we cannot run or leap;
If we cared for any meadows, it were merely
    To drop down in them and sleep.

Our knees tremble sorely in the stooping,
    We fall upon our faces, trying to go;   70
And, underneath our heavy eyelids drooping
    The reddest flower would look as pale as snow.
For, all day, we drag our burden tiring
    Through the coal-dark, underground;
Or, all day, we drive the wheels of iron
    In the factories, round and round.

— 7 —

"For all day the wheels are droning, turning;
    Their wind comes in our faces,
Till our hearts turn, our heads with pulses burning,
    And the walls turn in their places: 80
Turns the sky in the high window, blank and reeling,
    Turns the long light that drops adown the wall,
Turn the black flies that crawl along the ceiling:
    All are turning, all the day, and we with all.
And all day the iron wheels are droning,
    And sometimes we could pray,
'O ye wheels' (breaking out in a mad moaning),
    'Stop! be silent for to-day!' "

— 8 —

Ay, be silent!   Let them hear each other breathing
    For a moment, mouth to mouth!   90
Let them touch each other's hands, in a fresh wreathing
    Of their tender human youth!
Let them feel that this cold metallic motion
    Is not all the life God fashions or reveals:
Let them prove their living souls against the notion
    That they live in you, or under you, O wheels!
Still, all day, the iron wheels go onward,
    Grinding life down from its mark;
And the children's souls which God is calling sunward,
    Spin on blindly in the dark.   100

— 9 —

Now tell the poor young children, O my brothers,
    To look up to Him and pray;
So the blessed One who blesseth all the others,
    Will bless them another day.
They answer, "Who is God that He should hear us,
    While the rushing of the iron wheels is stirred?
When we sob aloud, the human creatures near us
    Pass by, hearing not, or answer not a word.
And *we* hear not (for the wheels in their resounding)
    Strangers speaking at the door: 110

Is it likely God, with angels singing round Him,
    Hears our weeping any more?

— 10 —

"Two words, indeed, of praying we remember,
    And at midnight's hour of harm,
'Our Father,' looking upward in the chamber,
    We say softly for a charm.[2]
We know no other words except 'Our Father,'
    And we think that, in some pause of angels' song,
God may pluck them with the silence sweet to gather,
    And hold both within His right hand which is
       strong.   120
'Our Father!'   If He heard us, He would surely
    (For they call Him good and mild)
Answer, smiling down the steep world very purely,
    'Come and rest with me, my child.'

— 11 —

"But, no!" say the children, weeping faster,
    "He is speechless as a stone:
And they tell us, of His image is the master
    Who commands us to work on.
Go to!" say the children,—"up in Heaven,
    Dark, wheel-like, turning clouds are all we find. 130
Do not mock us; grief has made us unbelieving:
    We look up for God, but tears have made us blind."
Do you hear the children weeping and disproving,
    O my brothers, what ye preach?
For God's possible is taught by His world's loving,
    And the children doubt of each.

— 12 —

And well may the children weep before you!
    They are weary ere they run;
They have never seen the sunshine, nor the glory
    Which is brighter than the sun.   140

They know the grief of man, without its wisdom;
    They sink in man's despair, without its calm;
Are slaves, without the liberty in Christdom,
    Are martyrs, by the pang without the palm:[3]
Are worn as if with age, yet unretrievingly
    The harvest of its memories cannot reap,—
Are orphans of the earthly love and heavenly.
    Let them weep! let them weep!

— 13 —

They look up with their pale and sunken faces,
    And their look is dread to see,   150
For they mind you of their angels in high places,
    With eyes turned on Deity.
"How long," they say, "how long, O cruel nation,
    Will you stand, to move the world, on a child's heart,—
Stifle down with a mailed heel its palpitation,
    And tread onward to your throne amid the mart?
Our blood splashes upward, O gold-heaper,
    And your purple shows your path!
But the child's sob in the silence curses deeper
    Than the strong man in his wrath."   160

1843, 1844

Bertha in the Lane ✓

— 1 —

Put the broidery-frame away,
    For my sewing is all done:
The last thread is used to-day,
    And I need not join it on.
Though the clock stands at the noon
I am weary.   I have sewn,
Sweet, for thee, a wedding-gown.

— 2 —

Sister, help me to the bed,
    And stand near me, Dearest-sweet.
Do not shrink nor be afraid,   10
    Blushing with a sudden heat!
No one standeth in the street?—
By God's love I go to meet,
Love I thee with love complete.

---

[2]**"Our Father"** . . . **charm:** A fact rendered pathetically historical by Mr. Horne's report of his Commission. The name of the poet of "Orion" and "Cosmo de' Medici" has, however, a change of associations, and comes in time to remind me that we have some noble poetic heat of literature still,—however open to the reproach of being somewhat gelid in our humanity. [Barrett Browning's note] Richard Hengist **Horne** (1803–1884), poet, critic, and Barrett Browning's collaborator, wrote the report of a Parliamentary **Commission** investigating child labor in mines and manufacturing; this poem aroused support for corrective legislation.

[3]**palm:** palm-leaf, symbol of victory or martyrdom.

— 3 —

Lean thy face down; drop it in
    These two hands, that I may hold
'Twixt their palms thy cheek and chin,
    Stroking back the curls of gold:
'Tis a fair, fair face, in sooth—
Larger eyes and redder mouth   20
Than mine were in my first youth.

— 4 —

Thou art younger by seven years—
    Ah!—so bashful at my gaze,
That the lashes, hung with tears,
    Grow too heavy to upraise?
I would wound thee by no touch
Which thy shyness feels as such.
Dost thou mind me, Dear, so much?

— 5 —

Have I not been nigh a mother
    To thy sweetness—tell me, Dear?   30
Have we not loved one another
    Tenderly, from year to year,
Since our dying mother mild
Said with accents undefiled,
"Child, be mother to this child!"

— 6 —

Mother, mother, up in heaven,
    Stand up on the jasper sea,
And be witness I have given
    All the gifts required of me,—
Hope that blessed me, bliss that crowned,   40
Love that left me with a wound,
Life itself that turneth round!

— 7 —

Mother, mother, thou art kind,
    Thou art standing in the room,
In a molten glory shrined
    That rays off into the gloom!
But thy smile is bright and bleak
Like cold waves—I cannot speak,
I sob in it, and grow weak.

— 8 —

Ghostly mother, keep aloof
    One hour longer from my soul,   50

For I still am thinking of
    Earth's warm-beating joy and dole!
On my finger is a ring
Which I still see glittering
When the night hides everything.

— 9 —

Little sister, thou art pale!
    Ah, I have a wandering brain—
But I lose that fever-bale,
    And my thoughts grow calm again.   60
Lean down closer—closer still!
I have words thine ear to fill,
And would kiss thee at my will.

— 10 —

Dear, I heard thee in the spring,
    Thee and Robert—through the trees,—
When we all went gathering
    Boughs of May-bloom for the bees.
Do not start so! think instead
How the sunshine overhead
Seemed to trickle through the shade.   70

— 11 —

What a day it was, that day!
    Hills and vales did openly
Seem to heave and throb away
    At the sight of the great sky:
And the silence, as it stood
In the glory's golden flood,
Audibly did bud, and bud.

— 12 —

Through the winding hedgerows green,
    How we wandered, I and you,
With the bowery tops shut in,   80
    And the gates that showed the view!
How we talked there; thrushes soft
Sang our praises out, or oft
Bleatings took them from the croft:

— 13 —

Till the pleasure grown too strong
    Left me muter evermore,
And, the winding road being long,
    I walked out of sight, before,
And so, wrapt in musings fond,

Issued (past the wayside pond)   90
On the meadow-lands beyond.

— 14 —

I sate down beneath the beech
    Which leans over to the lane,
And the far sound of your speech
    Did not promise any pain;
And I blessed you full and free,
With a smile stooped tenderly
O'er the May-flowers on my knee.

— 15 —

But the sound grew into word
    As the speakers drew more near—   100
Sweet, forgive me that I heard
    What you wished me not to hear.
Do not weep so, do not shake,
Oh,—I heard thee, Bertha, make
Good true answers for my sake.

— 16 —

Yes, and HE too! let him stand
    In thy thoughts, untouched by blame.
Could he help it, if my hand
    He had claimed with hasty claim?
That was wrong perhaps—but then   110
Such things be—and will, again.
Women cannot judge for men.

— 17 —

Had he seen thee when he swore
    He would love but me alone?
Thou wast absent, sent before
    To our kin in Sidmouth town.
When he saw thee who art best
Past compare, and loveliest,
He but judged thee as the rest.

— 18 —

Could we blame him with grave words,   120
    Thou and I, Dear, if we might?
Thy brown eyes have looks like birds
    Flying straightway to the light:
Mine are older.—Hush!—look out—
Up the street! Is none without?
How the poplar swings about!

— 19 —

And that hour—beneath the beech,
    When I listened in a dream,
And he said in his deep speech
    That he owed me all *esteem*,—   130
Each word swam in on my brain
With a dim, dilating pain,
Till it burst with that last strain.

— 20 —

I fell flooded with a dark,
    In the silence of a swoon.
When I rose, still cold and stark,
    There was night; I saw the moon
And the stars, each in its place,
And the May-blooms on the grass,
Seemed to wonder what I was.   140

— 21 —

And I walked as if apart
    From myself, when I could stand,
And I pitied my own heart,
    As if I held it in my hand—
Somewhat coldly, with a sense
Of fulfilled benevolence,
And a "Poor thing" negligence.

— 22 —

And I answered coldly too,
    When you met me at the door;
And I only *heard* the dew   150
    Dripping from me to the floor:
And the flowers, I bade you see,
Were too withered for the bee,—
As my life, henceforth, for me.

— 23 —

Do not weep so—Dear,—heart-warm!
    All was best as it befell.
If I say he did me harm,
    I speak wild,—I am not well.
All his words were kind and good—
He esteemed me. Only, blood —   160
Runs so faint in womanhood!

— 24 —

Then I always was too grave,—
    Like the saddest ballad sung,—

With that look, besides, we have
  In our faces, who die young.
I had died, Dear, all the same;
Life's long, joyous, jostling game
Is too loud for my meek shame.

— 25 —

We are so unlike each other,
  Thou and I, that none could guess   170
We were children of one mother,
  But for mutual tenderness.
Thou art rose-lined from the cold,
And meant verily to hold
Life's pure pleasures manifold.

— 26 —

I am pale as crocus grows
  Close beside a rose-tree's root;
Whosoe'er would reach the rose,
  Treads the crocus underfoot.
I, like May-bloom on thorn-tree,   180
Thou, like merry summer-bee,—
Fit that I be plucked for thee!

— 27 —

Yet who plucks me?—no one mourns,
  I have lived my season out,
And now die of my own thorns
  Which I could not live without.
Sweet, be merry! How the light
Comes and goes! If it be night,
Keep the candles in my sight.

— 28 —

Are there footsteps at the door?   190
  Look out quickly. Yea, or nay?
Some one might be waiting for
  Some last word that I might say.
Nay? So best!—so angels would
Stand off clear from deathly road,
Not to cross the sight of God.

— 29 —

Colder grow my hands and feet.
  When I wear the shroud I made,
Let the folds lie straight and neat,
  And the rosemary be spread,   200
That if any friend should come,

(To see *thee*, Sweet!) all the room
May be lifted out of gloom.

— 30 —

And, dear Bertha, let me keep
  On my hand this little ring,
Which at nights, when others sleep,
  I can still see glittering!
Let me wear it out of sight,
In the grave,—where it will light
All the dark up, day and night.   210

— 31 —

On that grave drop not a tear!
  Else, though fathom-deep the place,
Through the woollen shroud I wear
  I shall feel it on my face.
Rather smile there, blessèd one,
Thinking of me in the sun,
Or forget me—smiling on!

— 32 —

Art thou near me? nearer! so—
  Kiss me close upon the eyes,
That the earthly light may go   220
  Sweetly, as it used to rise
When I watched the morning-grey
Strike, betwixt the hills, the way
He was sure to come that day.

— 33 —

So,—no more vain words be said!
  The hosannas nearer roll.
Mother, smile now on thy Dead,
  I am death-strong in my soul.
Mystic Dove alit on cross,
Guide the poor bird of the snows   230
Through the snow-wind above loss!

— 34 —

Jesus, Victim, comprehending
  Love's divine self-abnegation,
Cleanse my love in its self-spending,
  And absorb the poor libation!
Wind my thread of life up higher,
Up, through angels' hands of fire!
I aspire while I expire.

1844

Grief

I tell you, hopeless grief is passionless;
That only men incredulous of despair,
Half-taught in anguish, through the midnight air
Beat upward to God's throne in loud access
Of shrieking and reproach. Full desertness,
In souls as countries, lieth silent-bare
Under the blanching, vertical eye-glare
Of the absolute Heavens. Deep-hearted man, express
Grief for thy Dead in silence like to death—
Most like a monumental statue set   10
In everlasting watch and moveless woe
Till itself crumble to the dust beneath.
Touch it; the marble eyelids are not wet:
If it could weep, it could arise and go.

                                          1844

To George Sand[1]

A Desire

Thou large-brained woman and large-hearted man,
Self-called George Sand! whose soul, amid the lions
Of thy tumultuous senses, moans defiance
And answers roar for roar, as spirits can:
I would some mild miraculous thunder ran
Above the applauded circus, in appliance
Of thine own nobler nature's strength and science,
Drawing two pinions, white as wings of swan,
From thy strong shoulders, to amaze the place
With holier light! that thou to woman's claim   10
And man's, mightst join beside the angel's grace
Of a pure genius sanctified from blame,
Till child and maiden pressed to thine embrace
To kiss upon thy lips a stainless fame.

                                          1844

---

[1]**George Sand** (Amandine Aurore Lucie Dupin, Baronne Dudevant, 1804–1876): French author of poetic, passionate, idealistic novels; her habit of wearing men's clothing, her divorce, her notorious love affairs, and her novels shocked many contemporaries.

To George Sand

A Recognition

True genius, but true woman! dost deny
The woman's nature with a manly scorn,
And break away the gauds and armlets worn
By weaker women in captivity?
Ah, vain denial! that revolted cry
Is sobbed in by a woman's voice forlorn,—
Thy woman's hair, my sister, all unshorn
Floats back dishevelled strength in agony,
Disproving thy man's name: and while before
The world thou burnest in a poet-fire,   10
We see thy woman-heart beat evermore
Through the large flame. Beat purer, heart, and
    higher,
Till God unsex thee on the heavenly shore
Where unincarnate spirits purely aspire!

                                          1844

The Runaway Slave
at Pilgrim's Point[1]

— 1 —

I stand on the mark beside the shore
    Of the first white pilgrim's bended knee,
Where exile turned to ancestor,
    And God was thanked for liberty.
I have run through the night, my skin is as dark,
I bend my knee down on this mark . .
    I look on the sky and the sea.

— 2 —

O pilgrim-souls, I speak to you!
    I see you come out proud and slow
From the land of the spirits pale as dew,   10
    And round me and round me ye go!
O pilgrims, I have gasped and run
All night long from the whips of one
    Who in your names works sin and woe.

---

[1]**The Runaway Slave**: written for an American antislavery journal, the 1848 *Liberty Bell*.

— 3 —

And thus I thought that I would come
    And kneel here where ye knelt before,
And feel your souls around me hum
    In undertone to the ocean's roar;
And lift my black face, my black hand,
Here, in your names, to curse this land   20
    Ye blessed in freedom's evermore.

— 4 —

I am black, I am black!
    And yet God made me, they say,
But if He did so, smiling back
    He must have cast his work away
Under the feet of his white creatures,
With a look of scorn,—that the dusky features
    Might be trodden again to clay.

— 5 —

And yet he has made dark things
    To be glad and merry as light.   30
There's a little dark bird, sits and sings;
    There's a dark stream ripples out of sight;
And the dark frogs chant in the safe morass,
And the sweetest stars are made to pass
    O'er the face of the darkest night.

— 6 —

But *we* who are dark, we are dark!
    Ah God, we have no stars!
About our souls in care and cark
    Our blackness shuts like prison-bars.
The poor souls crouch so far behind,   40
That never a comfort can they find
    By reaching through the prison-bars.

— 7 —

Indeed we live beneath the sky,
    That great smooth Hand of God stretched out
On all His children fatherly,
    To save them from the dread and doubt
Which would be, if, from this low place,
All opened straight up to His face
    Into the grand eternity.

— 8 —

And still God's sunshine and His frost,   50
    They make us hot, they make us cold,

As if we were not black and lost;
    And the beasts and birds, in wood and fold,
Do fear and take us for very men!
Could the weep-poor-will or the cat of the glen
    Look into my eyes and be bold?

— 9 —

I am black, I am black!—
    But, once, I laughed in girlish glee,
For one of my colour stood in the track
    Where the drivers drove, and looked at me,   60
And tender and full was the look he gave—
Could a slave look *so* at another slave?—
    I look at the sky and the sea.

— 10 —

And from that hour our spirits grew
    As free as if unsold, unbought.
Oh, strong enough, since we were two,
    To conquer the world, we thought!
The drivers drove us day by day;
We did not mind, we went one way,
    And no better a freedom sought.   70

— 11 —

In the sunny ground between the canes,
    He said "I love you" as he passed:
When the shingle-roof rang sharp with the rains,
    I heard how he vowed it fast.
While others shook he smiled in the hut,
As he carved me a bowl of the cocoa-nut
    Through the roar of the hurricanes.

— 12 —

I sang his name instead of a song,
    Over and over I sang his name—
Upward and downward I drew it along   80
    My various notes,—the same, the same!
I sang it low, that the slave-girls near
Might never guess from aught they could hear,
    It was only a name—a name.

— 13 —

I look on the sky and the sea.
    We were two to love, and two to pray,—
Yes, two, O God, who cried to Thee,
    Though nothing didst Thou say.
Coldly Thou sat'st behind the sun!

And now I cry who am but one,   90
    Thou wilt not speak to-day.—

— 14 —

We were black, we were black.
    We had no claim to love and bliss,
What marvel, if each went to wrack?
    They wrung my cold hands out of his,—
They dragged him . . . where? . . I crawled to touch
His blood's mark in the dust! . . not much,
    Ye pilgrim-souls, . . though plain as *this!*

— 15 —

Wrong, followed by a deeper wrong!
    Mere grief's too good for such as I.   100
So the white men brought the shame ere long
    To strangle the sob of my agony.
They would not leave me for my dull
Wet eyes!—it was too merciful
    To let me weep pure tears and die.

— 16 —

I am black, I am black!
    I wore a child upon my breast . . .
An amulet that hung too slack,
    And, in my unrest, could not rest.
Thus we went moaning, child and mother,   110
One to another, one to another,
    Until all ended for the best.

— 17 —

For hark! I will tell you low . . low . .
    I am black, you see,—
And the babe who lay on my bosom so,
    Was far too white . . too white for me;
As white as the ladies who scorned to pray
Beside me at church but yesterday,
    Though my tears had washed a place for my knee.

— 18 —

My own, own child! I could not bear   120
    To look in his face, it was so white.
I covered him up with a kerchief there;
    I covered his face in close and tight:
And he moaned and struggled, as well might be.
For the white child wanted his liberty—
    Ha, ha! he wanted the master-right.

— 19 —

He moaned and beat with his head and feet,
    His little feet that never grew—
He struck them out, as it was meet,
    Against my heart to break it through.   130
I might have sung and made him mild—
But I dared not sing to the white-faced child
    The only song I knew.

— 20 —

I pulled the kerchief very close:
    He could not see the sun, I swear,
More then, alive, than now he does
    From between the roots of the mango . . . where?
. . I know where.   Close! a child and mother
Do wrong to look at one another,
    When one is black and one is fair.   140

— 21 —

Why, in that single glance I had
    Of my child's face, . . I tell you all,
I saw a look that made me mad!
    The *master's* look, that used to fall
On my soul like his lash . . or worse!—
And so, to save it from my curse,
    I twisted it round in my shawl.

— 22 —

And he moaned and trembled from foot to head,
    He shivered from head to foot;
Till, after a time, he lay instead   150
    Too suddenly still and mute.
I felt, beside, a stiffening cold . .
I dared to lift up just a fold, . .
    As in lifting a leaf of the mango-fruit.

— 23 —

But *my* fruit . . . ha, ha!—there, had been
    (I laugh to think on't at this hour!)
Your fine white angels (who have seen
    Nearest the secret of God's power)
And plucked my fruit to make them wine,
And sucked the soul of that child of mine,   160
    As the humming-bird sucks the soul of the flower.

— 24 —

Ha, ha, the trick of the angels white!
    They freed the white child's spirit so.

I said not a word, but, day and night,
  I carried the body to and fro,
And it lay on my heart like a stone . . as chill.
—The sun may shine out as much as he will:
  I am cold, though it happened a month ago.

— 25 —

From the white man's house and the black man's hut
  I carried the little body on.   170
The forest's arms did round us shut,
  And silence through the trees did run.
They asked no question as I went,—
They stood too high for astonishment,—
  They could see God sit on his throne.

— 26 —

My little body, kerchiefed fast,
  I bore it on through the forest . . on;
And when I felt it was tired at last,
  I scooped a hole beneath the moon.
Through the forest-tops the angels far,   180
With a white sharp finger from every star,
  Did point and mock at what was done.

— 27 —

Yet when it was all done aright, . .
  Earth, 'twixt me and my baby, strewed, . .
All, changed to black earth, . . nothing white, . .
  A dark child in the dark!—ensued
Some comfort, and my heart grew young.
I sate down smiling there and sung
  The song I learnt in my maidenhood.

— 28—

And thus we two were reconciled,   190
  The white child and black mother, thus;
For, as I sang it soft and wild,
  The same song, more melodious,
Rose from the grave whereon I sate,
It was the dead child singing that,
  To join the souls of both of us.

— 29 —

I look on the sea and the sky!
  Where the pilgrims' ship first anchored lay
The free sun rideth gloriously,
  But the pilgrim-ghosts have slid away   200
Through the earliest streaks of the morn.

My face is black, but it glares with a scorn
  Which they dare not meet by day.

— 30 —

Ah!—in their 'stead, their hunter sons!
  Ah, ha! they are on me—they hunt in a ring—
Keep off! I brave you all at once—
  I throw off your eyes like snakes that sting!
You have killed the black eagle at nest, I think.
Did you never stand still in your triumph, and shrink
  From the stroke of her wounded wing?   210

— 31 —

(Man, drop that stone you dared to lift!—)
  I wish you who stand there five a-breast,
Each, for his own wife's joy and gift,
  A little corpse as safely at rest
As mine in the mangos!—Yes, but *she*
May keep live babies on her knee,
  And sing the song she likes the best.

— 32 —

I am not mad: I am black.
  I see you staring in my face—
I know you staring, shrinking back,   220
  Ye are born of the Washington-race.
And this land is the free America.
And this mark on my wrist . . (I prove what I say)
  Ropes tied me up here to the flogging-place.

— 33 —

You think I shrieked then? Not a sound!
  I hung, as a gourd hangs in the sun.
I only cursed them all around
  As softly as I might have done
My very own child.—From these sands
Up to the mountains, lift your hands,   230
  O slaves, and end what I begun!

— 34 —

Whips, curses; these must answer those!
  For in this UNION, you have set
Two kinds of men in adverse rows,
  Each loathing each; and all forget
The seven wounds in Christ's body fair,
While HE sees gaping everywhere
  Our countless wounds that pay no debt.

— 35 —

Our wounds are different. Your white men
    Are, after all, not gods indeed,   240
Nor able to make Christs again
    Do good with bleeding.   *We* who bleed
(Stand off!) we help not in our loss!
We are too heavy for our cross,
    And fall and crush you and your seed.

— 36 —

I fall, I swoon! I look at the sky.
    The clouds are breaking on my brain.
I am floated along, as if I should die
    Of liberty's exquisite pain.
In the name of the white child waiting for me   250
In the death-dark where we may kiss and agree,
White men, I leave you all curse-free
    In my broken heart's disdain!

        1848, 1850

Hiram Powers' "Greek Slave"[1]

They say Ideal beauty cannot enter
The house of anguish. On the threshold stands
An alien Image with enshackled hands,
Called the Greek Slave! as if the artist meant her
(That passionless perfection which he lent her,
Shadowed not darkened where the sill expands)
To so confront man's crimes in different lands
With man's ideal sense. Pierce to the centre,
Art's fiery finger, and break up ere long
The serfdom of this world. Appeal, fair stone,   10
From God's pure heights of beauty against man's
    wrong!
Catch up in thy divine face, not alone
East griefs but west, and strike and shame the strong,
By thunders of white silence, overthrown.

        1850

---

[1]**Hiram Powers** (1805–1873): American sculptor whose "Greek Slave" represents a Greek Christian girl enslaved by the Turks. Here she also represents slavery in America.

Sonnets from the Portuguese[1]

— 1 —

I thought once how Theocritus[2] had sung
Of the sweet years, the dear and wished-for years,
Who each one in a gracious hand appears
To bear a gift for mortals, old or young:
And, as I mused it in his antique tongue,
I saw, in gradual vision through my tears,
The sweet, sad years, the melancholy years,
Those of my own life, who by turns had flung
A shadow across me. Straightway I was 'ware,
So weeping, how a mystic Shape did move   10
Behind me, and drew me backward by the hair;[3]
And a voice said in mastery, while I strove,—
"Guess now who holds thee?"—"Death," I said. But, there,
The silver answer rang,—"Not Death, but Love."

— 2 —

But only three in all God's universe
Have heard this word thou hast said,—Himself, beside
Thee speaking, and me listening! and replied
One of us . . . *that* was God, . . . and laid the curse
So darkly on my eyelids, as to amerce[4]
My sight from seeing thee,—that if I had died,
The deathweights, placed there, would have signified
Less absolute exclusion.   "Nay" is worse
From God than from all others, O my friend!
Men could not part us with their worldly jars,   10
Nor the seas change us, nor the tempests bend;
Our hands would touch for all the mountain bars:
And, heaven being rolled between us at the end,
We should but vow the faster for the stars.

— 3 —

Unlike are we, unlike, O princely Heart!
Unlike our uses and our destinies.
Our ministering two angels look surprise

---

[1]**Portuguese:** allusion to Barrett Browning's "Catarina to Camoens," in which a Portuguese woman expresses her love for the epic poet Luís Vaz de Camões (1524?–1580).

[2]**Theocritus:** Greek poet, (308?–240? BCE), Idyl 15.

[3]The goddess Athena draws Achilles **backward by the hair** in *Iliad* 1.197.

[4]**amerce:** deprive.

On one another, as they strike athwart
Their wings in passing.   Thou, bethink thee, art
A guest for queens to social pageantries,
With gages[5] from a hundred brighter eyes
Than tears even can make mine, to play thy part
Of chief musician.   What hast *thou* to do
With looking from the lattice-lights at me,   10
A poor, tired, wandering singer, singing through
The dark, and leaning up a cypress tree?
The chrism[6] is on thine head,—on mine, the dew,—
And Death must dig the level where these agree.

— 4 —

Thou hast thy calling to some palace-floor,
Most gracious singer of high poems! where
The dancers will break footing, from the care
Of watching up thy pregnant lips for more.
And dost thou lift this house's latch too poor
For hand of thine? and canst thou think and bear
To let thy music drop here unaware
In folds of golden fulness at my door?
Look up and see the casement broken in,
The bats and owlets builders in the roof!   10
My cricket chirps against thy mandolin.
Hush, call no echo up in further proof
Of desolation! there's a voice within
That weeps . . . as thou must sing . . . alone, aloof.

— 5 —

I lift my heavy heart up solemnly,
As once Electra her sepulchral urn,[7]
And, looking in thine eyes, I overturn
The ashes at thy feet.   Behold and see
What a great heap of grief lay hid in me,
And how the red wild sparkles dimly burn
Through the ashen greyness.   If thy foot in scorn
Could tread them out to darkness utterly,
It might be well perhaps.   But if instead
Thou wait beside me for the wind to blow   10
The grey dust up, . . . those laurels[8] on thine head,

_____

[5]**gages**: challenges, pledges to do battle.

[8]**chrism**: consecrated oil.

[7]In Sophocles' *Electra*, Orestes gives his sister **Electra**, who does not recognize him, an **urn** that he says contains Orestes' funeral **ashes**.

[8]A wreath of **laurels** or bay leaves symbolizes poetic fame.

O my Belovèd, will not shield thee so,
That none of all the fires shall scorch and shred
The hair beneath.   Stand farther off then!   go.

— 6 —

Go from me.   Yet I feel that I shall stand
Henceforward in thy shadow.   Nevermore
Alone upon the threshold of my door
Of individual life, I shall command
The uses of my soul, nor lift my hand
Serenely in the sunshine as before,
Without the sense of that which I forbore—
Thy touch upon the palm.   The widest land
Doom takes to part us, leaves thy heart in mine
With pulses that beat double.   What I do   10
And what I dream include thee, as the wine
Must taste of its own grapes.   And when I sue
God for myself, He hears that name of thine,
And sees within my eyes the tears of two.

— 7 —

The face of all the world is changed, I think,
Since first I heard the footsteps of thy soul
Move still, oh, still, beside me, as they stole
Betwixt me and the dreadful outer brink
Of obvious death, where I, who thought to sink,
Was caught up into love, and taught the whole
Of life in a new rhythm.   The cup of dole
God gave for baptism, I am fain to drink,
And praise its sweetness, Sweet, with thee anear.
The names of country, heaven, are changed
          away   10
For where thou art or shalt be, there or here;
And this . . . this lute and song . . . loved yesterday,
(The singing angels know) are only dear
Because thy name moves right in what they say.

— 8 —

What can I give thee back, O liberal
And princely giver, who hast brought the gold
And purple of thine heart, unstained, untold,
And laid them on the outside of the wall
For such as I to take or leave withal,
In unexpected largesse? am I cold,
Ungrateful, that for these most manifold
High gifts, I render nothing back at all?
Not so; not cold,—but very poor instead.
Ask God who knows.   For frequent tears have
          run   10

The colours from my life, and left so dead
And pale a stuff, it were not fitly done
To give the same as pillow to thy head.
Go farther! let it serve to trample on.

— 9 —

Can it be right to give what I can give?
To let thee sit beneath the fall of tears
As salt as mine, and hear the sighing years
Re-sighing on my lips renunciative
Through those infrequent smiles which fail to live
For all thy adjurations? O my fears,
That this can scarce be right! We are not peers,
So to be lovers; and I own, and grieve,
That givers of such gifts as mine are, must
Be counted with the ungenerous. Out, alas!   10
I will not soil thy purple with my dust,
Nor breathe my poison on thy Venice-glass,[9]
Nor give thee any love—which were unjust.
Beloved, I only love thee! let it pass.

— 10 —

Yet, love, mere love, is beautiful indeed
And worthy of acceptation. Fire is bright,
Let temple burn, or flax; an equal light
Leaps in the flame from cedar-plank or weed:
And love is fire. And when I say at need
I love thee . . . mark! . . . I love thee—in thy sight
I stand transfigured, glorified aright,
With conscience of the new rays that proceed
Out of my face toward thine. There's nothing low
In love, when love the lowest: meanest creatures   10
Who love God, God accepts while loving so.
And what I *feel*, across the inferior features
Of what I *am*, doth flash itself, and show
How that great work of Love enhances Nature's.

— 11 —

And therefore if to love can be desert,
I am not all unworthy. Cheeks as pale
As these you see, and trembling knees that fail
To bear the burden of a heavy heart,—
This weary minstrel-life that once was girt
To climb Aornus,[10] and can scarce avail
To pipe now 'gainst the valley nightingale
A melancholy music,—why advert

To these things? O Belovèd, it is plain
I am not of thy worth nor for thy place!   10
And yet, because I love thee, I obtain
From that same love this vindicating grace,
To live on still in love, and yet in vain,—
To bless thee, yet renounce thee to thy face.

— 12 —

Indeed this very love which is my boast,
And which, when rising up from breast to brow,
Doth crown me with a ruby large enow
To draw men's eyes and prove the inner cost,—
This love even, all my worth, to the uttermost,
I should not love withal, unless that thou
Hadst set me an example, shown me how,
When first thine earnest eyes with mine were crossed,
And love called love. And thus, I cannot speak
Of love even, as a good thing of my own: 10
Thy soul hath snatched up mine all faint and weak,
And placed it by thee on a golden throne,—
And that I love (O soul, we must be meek!)
Is by thee only, whom I love alone.

— 13 —

And wilt thou have me fashion into speech
The love I bear thee, finding words enough,
And hold the torch out, while the winds are rough,
Between our faces, to cast light on each?—
I drop it at thy feet. I cannot teach
My hand to hold my spirit so far off
From myself—me—that I should bring thee proof
In words, of love hid in me out of reach.
Nay, let the silence of my womanhood
Commend my woman-love to thy belief,—   10
Seeing that I stand unwon, however wooed,
And rend the garment of my life, in brief,
By a most dauntless, voiceless fortitude,
Lest one touch of this heart convey its grief.

— 14 —

If thou must love me, let it be for nought
Except for love's sake only. Do not say
"I love her for her smile—her look—her way
Of speaking gently,—for a trick of thought
That falls in well with mine, and certes brought
A sense of pleasant ease on such a day"—
For these things in themselves, Belovèd, may
Be changed, or change for thee,—and love, so wrought,
May be unwrought so. Neither love me for

---

[9]**poison** was believed to shatter delicate **Venetian glass**.

[10]**Aornus** (Aornos): mountain in India.

Thine own dear pity's wiping my cheeks dry,—   10
A creature might forget to weep, who bore
Thy comfort long, and lose thy love thereby!
But love me for love's sake, that evermore
Thou mayst love on, through love's eternity.

— 15 —

Accuse me not, beseech thee, that I wear
Too calm and sad a face in front of thine;
For we two look two ways, and cannot shine
With the same sunlight on our brow and hair.
On me thou lookest with no doubting care,
As on a bee shut in a crystalline;
Since sorrow hath shut me safe in love's divine,
And to spread wing and fly in the outer air
Were most impossible failure, if I strove
To fail so.   But I look on thee—on thee—   10
Beholding, besides love, the end of love,
Hearing oblivion beyond memory;
As one who sits and gazes from above,
Over the rivers to the bitter sea.

— 16 —

And yet, because thou overcomest so,
Because thou art more noble and like a king,
Thou canst prevail against my fears and fling
Thy purple round me, till my heart shall grow
Too close against thine heart henceforth to know
How it shook when alone.   Why, conquering
May prove as lordly and complete a thing
In lifting upward, as in crushing low!
And as a vanquished soldier yields his sword
To one who lifts him from the bloody earth,   10
Even so, Belovèd, I at last record,
Here ends my strife.   If thou invite me forth,
I rise above abasement at the word.
Make thy love larger to enlarge my worth.

— 17 —

My poet, thou canst touch on all the notes
God set between His After and Before,
And strike up and strike off the general roar
Of the rushing worlds a melody that floats
In a serene air purely.   Antidotes
Of medicated music, answering for
Mankind's forlornest uses, thou canst pour
From thence into their ears.   God's will devotes
Thine to such ends, and mine to wait on thine.
How, Dearest, wilt thou have me for most use?   10

A hope, to sing by gladly? or a fine
Sad memory, with thy songs to interfuse?
A shade, in which to sing—of palm or pine?
A grave, on which to rest from singing?   Choose.

— 18 —

I never gave a lock of hair away
To a man, Dearest, except this to thee,
Which now upon my fingers thoughtfully,
I ring out to the full brown length and say
"Take it."   My day of youth went yesterday;
My hair no longer bounds to my foot's glee,
Nor plant I it from rose or myrtle-tree,
As girls do, any more: it only may
Now shade on two pale cheeks the mark of tears,
Taught drooping from the head that hangs aside   10
Through sorrow's trick.   I thought the funeral-shears
Would take this first, but Love is justified,—
Take it thou,—finding pure, from all those years,
The kiss my mother left here when she died.

— 19 —

The soul's Rialto [11] hath its merchandise;
I barter curl for curl upon that mart,
And from my poet's forehead to my heart
Receive this lock which outweighs argosies,—
As purply black, as erst to Pindar's eyes
The dim purpureal tresses gloomed athwart
The nine white Muse-brows. [12] For this counterpart, . . .
The bay-crown's shade, Belovèd, I surmise,
Still lingers on thy curl, it is so black!
Thus, with a fillet of smooth-kissing breath,   10
I tie the shadows safe from gliding back,
And lay the gift where nothing hindereth;
Here on my heart, as on thy brow, to lack
No natural heat till mine grows cold in death.

— 20 —

Beloved, my Belovèd, when I think
That thou wast in the world a year ago,
What time I sat alone here in the snow
And saw no footprint, heard the silence sink
No moment at thy voice, but, link by link,
Went counting all my chains as if that so

---

[11]**Rialto**: bridge in Venice lined with shops.

[12]The Greek poet **Pindar** (522?–443? BCE) describes the hair of the **Muses** as **purply black** in his first Pythian ode.

They never could fall off at any blow
Struck by thy possible hand,—why, thus I drink
Of life's great cup of wonder!   Wonderful,
Never to feel thee thrill the day or night   10
With personal act or speech,—nor ever cull
Some prescience of thee with the blossoms white
Thou sawest growing!   Atheists are as dull,
Who cannot guess God's presence out of sight.

— 21 —

Say over again, and yet once over again,
That thou dost love me. Though the word repeated
Should seem "a cuckoo-song," as thou dost treat it,
Remember, never to the hill or plain,
Valley and wood, without her cuckoo-strain
Comes the fresh Spring in all her green completed.
Belovèd, I, amid the darkness greeted
By a doubtful spirit-voice, in that doubt's pain
Cry, "Speak once more—thou lovest!"   Who can fear
Too many stars, though each in heaven shall roll,   10
Too many flowers, though each shall crown the year?
Say thou dost love me, love me, love me—toll
The silver iterance!—only minding, Dear,
To love me also in silence with thy soul.

— 22 —

When our two souls stand up erect and strong,
Face to face, silent, drawing nigh and nigher,
Until the lengthening wings break into fire
At either curvèd point,—what bitter wrong
Can the earth do to us, that we should not long
Be here contented!   Think.   In mounting higher,
The angels would press on us and aspire
To drop some golden orb of perfect song
Into our deep, dear silence.   Let us stay
Rather on earth, Belovèd,—where the unfit   10
Contrarious moods of men recoil away
And isolate pure spirits, and permit
A place to stand and love in for a day,
With darkness and the death-hour rounding it.

— 23 —

Is it indeed so?   If I lay here dead,
Wouldst thou miss any life in losing mine?
And would the sun for thee more coldly shine
Because of grave-damps falling round my head?
I marvelled, my Belovèd, when I read
Thy thought so in the letter.   I am thine—
But . . . *so* much to thee? Can I pour thy wine

While my hands tremble? Then my soul, instead
Of dreams of death, resumes life's lower range.
Then, love me, Love! look on me—breathe on me! 10
As brighter ladies do not count it strange,
For love, to give up acres and degree,
I yield the grave for thy sake, and exchange
My near sweet view of Heaven, for earth with thee!

— 24 —

Let the world's sharpness, like a clasping knife,
Shut in upon itself and do no harm
In this close hand of Love, now soft and warm,
And let us hear no sound of human strife
After the click of the shutting.   Life to life—
I lean upon thee, Dear, without alarm,
And feel as safe as guarded by a charm
Against the stab of worldlings, who if rife
Are weak to injure.   Very whitely still
The lilies of our lives may reassure   10
Their blossoms from their roots, accessible
Alone to heavenly dews that drop not fewer,
Growing straight, out of man's reach, on the hill.
God only, who made us rich, can make us poor.

— 25 —

A heavy heart, Belovèd, have I borne
From year to year until I saw thy face,
And sorrow after sorrow took the place
Of all those natural joys as lightly worn
As the stringed pearls, each lifted in its turn
By a beating heart at dance-time.   Hopes apace
Were changed to long despairs, till God's own grace
Could scarcely lift above the world forlorn
My heavy heart.   Then *thou* didst bid me bring
And let it drop adown thy calmly great   10
Deep being!   Fast it sinketh, as a thing
Which its own nature doth precipitate,
While thine doth close above it, mediating
Betwixt the stars and the unaccomplished fate.

— 26 —

I lived with visions for my company
Instead of men and women, years ago,
And found them gentle mates, nor thought to know
A sweeter music than they played to me.
But soon their trailing purple was not free
Of this world's dust, their lutes did silent grow,
And I myself grew faint and blind below
Their vanishing eyes.   Then THOU didst come—to be,

Belovèd, what they seemed.   Their shining fronts,
Their songs, their splendours (better, yet the
    same,   10
As river-water hallowed into fonts),
Met in thee, and from out thee overcame
My soul with satisfaction of all wants:
Because God's gifts put man's best dreams to shame.

— 27 —

My own Belovèd, who hast lifted me
From this drear flat of earth where I was thrown,
And, in betwixt the languid ringlets, blown
A life-breath, till the forehead hopefully
Shines out again, as all the angels see,
Before thy saving kiss!   My own, my own,
Who camest to me when the world was gone,
And I who looked for only God, found *thee!*
I find thee; I am safe, and strong, and glad.
As one who stands in dewless asphodel[13]   10
Looks backward on the tedious time he had
In the upper life,—so I, with bosom-swell,
Makes witness, here, between the good and bad,
That Love, as strong as Death, retrieves as well.

— 28 —

My letters! all dead paper, mute and white!
And yet they seem alive and quivering
Against my tremulous hands which loose the string
And let them drop down on my knee to-night.
This said,—he wished to have me in his sight
Once, as a friend: this fixed a day in spring
To come and touch my hand . . . a simple thing,
Yet I wept for it!—this, . . . the paper's light . . .
Said, *Dear, I love thee;* and I sank and quailed
As if God's future thundered on my past.   10
This said, *I am thine*—and so its ink has paled
With lying at my heart that beat too fast.
And this . . . O Love, thy words have ill availed
If, what this said, I dared repeat at last!

— 29 —

I think of thee!—my thoughts do twine and bud
About thee, as wild vines, about a tree,
Put out broad leaves, and soon there's nought to see
Except the straggling green which hides the wood.
Yet, O my palm-tree, be it understood

---

[13]**asphodel**: plant that grows in the Elysian fields of the classical
afterworld.

I will not have my thoughts instead of thee
Who art dearer, better!   Rather, instantly
Renew thy presence; as a strong tree should,
Rustle thy boughs and set thy trunk all bare,
And let these bands of greenery which insphere
    thee   10
Drop heavily down,—burst, shattered, everywhere!
Because, in this deep joy to see and hear thee
And breathe within thy shadow a new air,
I do not think of thee—I am too near thee.

— 30 —

I see thine image through my tears to-night,
And yet to-day I saw thee smiling.   How
Refer the cause?—Belovèd, is it thou
Or I, who makes me sad?   The acolyte
Amid the chanted joy and thankful rite
May so fall flat, with pale insensate brow,
On the altar-stair.   I hear thy voice and vow,
Perplexed, uncertain, since thou art out of sight,
As he, in his swooning ears, the choir's Amen.
Belovèd, dost thou love? or did I see all   10
The glory as I dreamed, and fainted when
Too vehement light dilated my ideal,
For my soul's eyes?   Will that light come again,
As now these tears come—falling hot and real?

— 31 —

Thou comest! all is said without a word.
I sit beneath thy looks, as children do
In the noon-sun, with souls that tremble through
Their happy eyelids from an unaverred
Yet prodigal inward joy.   Behold, I erred
In that last doubt! and yet I cannot rue
The sin most, but the occasion—that we two
Should for a moment stand unministered
By a mutual presence.   Ah, keep near and close,
Thou dovelike help! and, when my fears would
    rise,   10
With thy broad heart serenely interpose:
Brood down with thy divine sufficiencies
These thoughts which tremble when bereft of those,
Like callow birds left desert to the skies.

— 32 —

The first time that the sun rose on thine oath
To love me, I looked forward to the moon
To slacken all those bonds which seemed too soon
And quickly tied to make a lasting troth.

Quick-loving hearts, I thought, may quickly loathe;
And, looking on myself, I seemed not one
For such man's love!—more like an out-of-tune
Worn viol, a good singer would be wroth
To spoil his song with, and which, snatched in haste,
Is laid down at the first ill-sounding note.   10
I did not wrong myself so, but I placed
A wrong on *thee*.   For perfect strains may float
'Neath master-hands, from instruments defaced,—
And great souls, at one stroke, may do and doat.

— 33 —

Yes, call me by my pet-name! let me hear
The name I used to run at, when a child,
From innocent play, and leave the cowslips piled,
To glance up in some face that proved me dear
With the look of its eyes.   I miss the clear
Fond voices which, being drawn and reconciled
Into the music of Heaven's undefiled,
Call me no longer.   Silence on the bier,
While I call God—call God!—So let thy mouth
Be heir to those who are now exanimate.   10
Gather the north flowers to complete the south,
And catch the early love up in the late.
Yes, call me by that name,—and I, in truth,
With the same heart, will answer and not wait.

— 34 —

With the same heart, I said, I'll answer thee
As those, when thou shalt call me by my name—
Lo, the vain promise! is the same, the same,
Perplexed and ruffled by life's strategy?
When called before, I told how hastily
I dropped my flowers or brake off from a game,
To run and answer with the smile that came
At play last moment, and went on with me
Through my obedience.   When I answer now,
I drop a grave thought, break from solitude;   10
Yet still my heart goes to thee—ponder how—
Not as to a single good, but all my good!
Lay thy hand on it, best one, and allow
That no child's foot could run fast as this blood.

— 35 —

If I leave all for thee, wilt thou exchange
And be all to me?   Shall I never miss
Home-talk and blessing and the common kiss
That comes to each in turn, nor count it strange,
When I look up, to drop on a new range
Of walls and floors, another home than this?

Nay, wilt thou fill that place by me which is
Filled by dead eyes too tender to know change?
That's hardest.   If to conquer love, has tried,
To conquer grief, tries more, as all things prove;   10
For grief indeed is love and grief beside.
Alas, I have grieved so I am hard to love.
Yet love me—wilt thou?   Open thine heart wide,
And fold within the wet wings of thy dove.

— 36 —

When we met first and loved, I did not build
Upon the event with marble.   Could it mean
To last, a love set pendulous between
Sorrow and sorrow?   Nay, I rather thrilled,
Distrusting every light that seemed to gild
The onward path, and feared to overlean
A finger even.   And, though I have grown serene
And strong since then, I think that God has willed
A still renewable fear . . . O love, O troth . . .
Lest these enclaspèd hands should never hold,   10
This mutual kiss drop down between us both
As an unowned thing, once the lips being cold.
And Love, be false! if *he*, to keep one oath,
Must lose one joy, by his life's star foretold.

— 37 —

Pardon, oh, pardon, that my soul should make,
Of all that strong divineness which I know
For thine and thee, an image only so
Formed of the sand, and fit to shift and break.
It is that distant years which did not take
Thy sovranty, recoiling with a blow,
Have forced my swimming brain to undergo
Their doubt and dread, and blindly to forsake
Thy purity of likeness and distort
Thy worthiest love to a worthless counterfeit: 10
As if a shipwrecked Pagan, safe in port,
His guardian sea-god to commemorate,
Should set a sculptured porpoise, gills a-snort
And vibrant tail, within the temple-gate.

— 38 —

First time he kissed me, he but only kissed
The fingers of this hand wherewith I write;
And ever since, it grew more clean and white,
Slow to world-greetings, quick with its "Oh, list,"
When the angels speak.   A ring of amethyst
I could not wear here, plainer to my sight,
Than that first kiss.   The second passed in height
The first, and sought the forehead, and half missed,

Half falling on the hair.   O beyond meed!
That was the chrism of love, which love's own
    crown,   10
With sanctifying sweetness, did precede.
The third upon my lips was folded down
In perfect, purple state; since when, indeed,
I have been proud and said, "My love, my own."

— 39 —

Because thou hast the power and own'st the grace
To look through and behind this mask of me
(Against which years have beat thus blanchingly
With their rains), and behold my soul's true face,
The dim and weary witness of life's race,—
Because thou hast the faith and love to see,
Through that same soul's distracting lethargy,
The patient angel waiting for a place
In the new Heavens,—because nor sin nor woe,
Nor God's infliction, nor death's neighbourhood, 10
Nor all which others viewing, turn to go,
Nor all which makes me tired of all, self-viewed,—
Nothing repels thee, . . . Dearest, teach me so
To pour out gratitude, as thou dost, good!

— 40 —

Oh, yes!   they love through all this world of ours!
I will not gainsay love, called love forsooth.
I have heard love talked in my early youth,
And since, not so long back but that the flowers
Then gathered, smell still.   Mussulmans and Giaours[14]
Throw kerchiefs at a smile, and have no ruth
For any weeping.   Polypheme's white tooth
Slips on the nut if, after frequent showers,
The shell is over-smooth,—and not so much
Will turn the thing called love, aside to hate   10
Or else to oblivion.   But thou art not such
A lover, my Belovèd!   thou canst wait
Through sorrow and sickness, to bring souls to touch,
And think it soon when others cry "Too late."

— 41 —

I thank all who have loved me in their hearts,
With thanks and love from mine.   Deep thanks to all
Who paused a little near the prison-wall
To hear my music in its louder parts
Ere they went onward, each one to the mart's

Or temple's occupation, beyond call.
But thou, who, in my voice's sink and fall
When the sob took it, thy divinest Art's
Own instrument didst drop down at thy foot
To hearken what I said between my tears, . . .   10
Instruct me how to thank thee!   Oh, to shoot
My soul's full meaning into future years,
That *they* should lend it utterance, and salute
Love that endures, from Life that disappears!

— 42 —

"My future will not copy fair my past"[15]—
I wrote that once; and thinking at my side
My ministering life-angel justified
The word by his appealing look upcast
To the white throne of God, I turned at last,
And there, instead, saw thee, not unallied
To angels in thy soul!   Then I, long tried
By natural ills, received the comfort fast,
While budding, at thy sight, my pilgrim's staff
Gave out green leaves with morning dews
    impearled.   10
I seek no copy now of life's first half:
Leave here the pages with long musing curled,
And write me new my future's epigraph,
New angel mine, unhoped for in the world!

— 43 —

How do I love thee?   Let me count the ways.
I love thee to the depth and breadth and height
My soul can reach, when feeling out of sight
For the ends of Being and ideal Grace.
I love thee to the level of everyday's
Most quiet need, by sun and candle-light.
I love thee freely, as men strive for Right;
I love thee purely, as they turn from Praise.
I love thee with the passion put to use
In my old griefs, and with my childhood's faith. 10
I love thee with a love I seemed to lose
With my lost saints,—I love with the breath,
Smiles, tears, of all my life!—and, if God choose,
I shall but love thee better after death.

— 44 —

Belovèd, thou hast brought me many flowers
Plucked in the garden, all the summer through
And winter, and it seemed as if they grew

---

[14]**Giaours**: Turkish term of reproach for non-**Mussulmans**, especially Christians. **Polypheme**: Polyphemus, one-eyed giant in Greek mythology.

[15]*"My future . . . past"*: a quotation from Barrett Browning's sonnet "Past and Future" (1844).

In this close room, nor missed the sun and showers.
So, in the like name of that love of ours,
Take back these thoughts which here unfolded too,
And which on warm and cold days I withdrew
From my heart's ground.   Indeed, those beds and
　　　bowers
Be overgrown with bitter weeds and rue,
And wait thy weeding; yet here's eglantine,　　　　10
Here's ivy!—take them, as I used to do
Thy flowers, and keep them where they shall not pine.
Instruct thine eyes to keep their colours true,
And tell thy soul their roots are left in mine.

　　　　　　　　　　　　　　　　　　1850

from Aurora Leigh ✓
First Book

Of writing many books there is no end;[1]
And I who have written much in prose and verse
For others' uses, will write now for mine,—
Will write my story for my better self,
As when you paint your portrait for a friend,
Who keeps it in a drawer and looks at it
Long after he has ceased to love you, just
To hold together what he was and is.
I, writing thus, am still what men call young;
I have not so far left the coasts of life　　　　10
To travel inward,[2] that I cannot hear
That murmur of the outer Infinite
Which unweaned babies smile at in their sleep
When wondered at for smiling; not so far,
But still I catch my mother at her post
Beside the nursery door, with finger up,
"Hush, hush—here's too much noise!" while her sweet
　　　eyes
Leap forward, taking part against her word
In the child's riot.　Still I sit and feel
My father's slow hand, when she had left us both,　20
Stroke out my childish curls across his knee,
And hear Assunta's daily jest (she knew
He liked it better than a better jest)

Inquire how many golden scudi[3] went
To make such ringlets.　O my father's hand,
Stroke heavily, heavily the poor hair down,
Draw, press the child's head closer to thy knee!
I'm still too young, too young, to sit alone.

I write.　My mother was a Florentine,
Whose rare blue eyes were shut from seeing me　　30
When scarcely I was four years old, my life
A poor spark snatched up from a failing lamp
Which went out therefore.　She was weak and frail;
She could not bear the joy of giving life,
The mother's rapture slew her.　If her kiss
Had left a longer weight upon my lips
It might have steadied the uneasy breath,
And reconciled and fraternised my soul
With the new order.　As it was, indeed,
I felt a mother-want about the world,　　　　40
And still went seeking, like a bleating lamb
Left out at night in shutting up the fold,—
As restless as a nest-deserted bird
Grown chill through something being away, though what
It knows not.　I, Aurora Leigh, was born
To make my father sadder, and myself
Not overjoyous, truly.　Women know
The way to rear up children (to be just),
They know a simple, merry, tender knack
Of tying sashes, fitting baby-shoes,　　　　50
And stringing pretty words that make no sense,
And kissing full sense into empty words,
Which things are corals to cut life upon,
Although such trifles: children learn by such,
Love's holy earnest in a pretty play
And get not over-early solemnised,
But seeing, as in a rose-bush, Love's Divine
Which burns and hurts not,—not a single bloom,—
Become aware and unafraid of Love.
Such good do mothers.　Fathers love as well　60
—Mine did, I know,—but still with heavier brains,
And wills more consciously responsible,
And not as wisely, since less foolishly;
So mothers have God's license to be missed.

My father was an austere Englishman,
Who, after a dry lifetime spent at home
In college-learning, law, and parish talk,
Was flooded with a passion unaware,
His whole provisioned and complacent past
Drowned out from him that moment.　As he stood　70

---

[1] **Of writing . . . end**: see Ecclesiastes 12:12.

[2] See Wordsworth's "Ode: Intimations of Immortality" (1807) 165–171 for the image of growing up as traveling inland (**inward**) from the immortal sea. Aurora is now in her late twenties.

---

[3] **scudi**: old Italian coins.

In Florence, where he had come to spend a month
And note the secret of Da Vinci's[4] drains,
He musing somewhat absently perhaps
Some English question . . . whether men should pay
The unpopular but necessary tax
With left or right hand—in the alien sun
In that great square of the Santissima[5]
There drifted past him (scarcely marked enough
To move his comfortable island scorn)
A train of priestly banners, cross and psalm,   80
The white-veiled rose-crowned maidens holding up
Tall tapers, weighty for such wrists, aslant
To the blue luminous tremor of the air,
And letting drop the white wax as they went
To eat the bishop's wafer at the church;
From which long trail of chanting priests and girls,
A face flashed like a cymbal on his face
And shook with silent clangour brain and heart,
Transfiguring him to music.   Thus, even thus,
He too received his sacramental gift   90
With eucharistic meanings; for he loved.

And thus beloved, she died.   I've heard it said
That but to see him in the first surprise
Of widower and father, nursing me,
Unmothered little child of four years old,
His large man's hands afraid to touch my curls,
As if the gold would tarnish,—his grave lips
Contriving such a miserable smile
As if he knew needs must, or I should die,
And yet 'twas hard,—would almost make the
          stones   100
Cry out[6] for pity.   There's a verse he set
In Santa Croce to her memory,—
"Weep for an infant too young to weep much
When death removed this mother"—stops the mirth
To-day on women's faces when they walk
With rosy children hanging on their gowns,
Under the cloister to escape the sun
That scorches in the piazza.   After which
He left our Florence and made haste to hide
Himself, his prattling child, and silent grief,   110
Among the mountains above Pelago;[7]

Because unmothered babes, he thought, had need
Of mother nature more than others use,
And Pan's white goats, with udders warm and full
Of mystic contemplations, come to feed
Poor milkless lips of orphans like his own—
Such scholar-scraps he talked, I've heard from friends,
For even prosaic men who wear grief long
Will get to wear it as a hat aside
With a flower stuck in't.   Father, then, and
          child,   120
We lived among the mountains many years,
God's silence on the outside of the house,
And we who did not speak too loud within,
And old Assunta to make up the fire,
Crossing herself whene'er a sudden flame
Which lightened from the firewood, made alive
That picture of my mother on the wall.
The painter drew it after she was dead,
And when the face was finished, throat and hands,
Her cameriera[8] carried him, in hate   130
Of the English-fashioned shroud, the last brocade
She dressed in at the Pitti;[9] "he should paint
No sadder thing than that," she swore, "to wrong
Her poor signora."   Therefore very strange
The effect was.   I, a little child, would crouch
For hours upon the floor with knees drawn up,
And gaze across them, half in terror, half
In adoration, at the picture there,—
That swan-like supernatural white life
Just sailing upward from the red stiff silk   140
Which seemed to have no part in it nor power
To keep it from quite breaking out of bounds.
For hours I sat and stared.   Assunta's awe
And my poor father's melancholy eyes
Still pointed that way.   That way went my thoughts
When wandering beyond sight.   And as I grew
In years, I mixed, confused, unconsciously,
Whatever I last read or heard or dreamed,
Abhorrent, admirable, beautiful,
Pathetical, or ghastly, or grotesque,   150
With still that face . . . which did not therefore change,
But kept the mystic level of all forms,
Hates, fears, and admirations, was by turns
Ghost, fiend, and angel, fairy, witch, and sprite,
A dauntless Muse who eyes a dreadful Fate,

---

[4]Leonardo **Da Vinci** (1452–1519): painter, sculptor, architect, and engineer.

[5]**left or right hand**: see Matthew 6:3. **Santissima**: a church.

[6]**stones/Cry out**: Luke 19:40. **Santa Croce**: church in Florence.

[7]**Pelago**: village near Florence. **Pan**: goat-god of rural nature.

---

[8]**cameriera**: female servant.

[9]**Pitti** Palace: residence of the grand dukes of Tuscany.

A loving Psyche who loses sight of Love,[10]
A still Medusa with mild milky brows
All curdled and all clothed upon with snakes
Whose slime falls fast as sweat will; or anon
Our Lady of the Passion, stabbed with swords   160
Where the Babe sucked; or Lamia in her first
Moonlighted pallor, ere she shrunk and blinked
And shuddering wriggled down to the unclean;
Or my own mother, leaving her last smile
In her last kiss upon the baby-mouth
My father pushed down on the bed for that,—
Or my dead mother, without smile or kiss,
Buried at Florence.   All which images,
Concentred on the picture, glassed themselves
Before my meditative childhood, as   170
The incoherencies of change and death
Are represented fully, mixed and merged,
In the smooth fair mystery of perpetual Life.
And while I stared away my childish wits
Upon my mother's picture (ah, poor child!),
My father, who through love had suddenly
Thrown off the old conventions, broken loose
From chin-bands of the soul, like Lazarus,[11]
Yet had no time to learn to talk and walk
Or grow anew familiar with the sun,—   180
Who had reached to freedom, not to action, lived,
But lived as one entranced, with thoughts, not
          aims,—
Whom love had unmade from a common man
But not completed to an uncommon man,—
My father taught me what he had learnt the best
Before he died and left me,—grief and love.
And, seeing we had books among the hills,
Strong words of counselling souls confederate
With vocal pines and waters,—out of books
He taught me all the ignorance of men,   190
And how God laughs in heaven when any man
Says "Here I'm learned; this, I understand;
In that, I am never caught at fault or doubt."
He sent the schools to school, demonstrating
A fool will pass for such through one mistake,
While a philosopher will pass for such,
Through said mistakes being ventured in the gross

And heaped up to a system.
                    I am like,
They tell me, my dear father.   Broader brows
Howbeit, upon a slenderer undergrowth   200
Of delicate features,—paler, near as grave;
But then my mother's smile breaks up the whole,
And makes it better sometimes than itself.
So, nine full years, our days were hid with God
Among his mountains: I was just thirteen,
Still growing like the plants from unseen roots
In tongue-tied Springs,—and suddenly awoke
To full life and life's needs and agonies
With an intense, strong, struggling heart beside
A stone-dead father.   Life, struck sharp on death, 210
Makes awful lightning.   His last word was "Love—"
"Love, my child, love, love!"—(then he had done with grief)
"Love, my child."   Ere I answered he was gone,
And none was left to love in all the world.

There, ended childhood.   What succeeded next
I recollect as, after fevers, men
Thread back the passage of delirium,
Missing the turn still, baffled by the door;
Smooth endless days, notched here and there with knives,
A weary, wormy darkness, spurred i' the flank   220
With flame, that it should eat and end itself
Like some tormented scorpion.   Then at last
I do remember clearly how there came
A stranger with authority, not right
(I thought not), who commanded, caught me up
From old Assunta's neck; how, with a shriek,
She let me go,—while I, with ears too full
Of my father's silence to shriek back a word,
In all a child's astonishment at grief
Stared at the wharf-edge where she stood and
          moaned,   230
My poor Assunta, where she stood and moaned!
The white walls, the blue hills, my Italy,
Drawn backward from the shuddering steamer-deck,
Like one in anger drawing back her skirts
Which suppliants catch at.   Then the bitter sea
Inexorably pushed between us both
And, sweeping up the ship with my despair,
Threw us out as a pasture to the stars.

Ten nights and days we voyaged on the deep;
Ten nights and days without the common face   240
Of any day or night; the moon and sun
Cut off from the green reconciling earth,
To starve into a blind ferocity

---

[10]**Psyche:** mortal woman who married Cupid, or Eros (**Love**). **Medusa** had **snakes** for hair; those who looked at her turned to stone. **Lamia:** snake who takes a woman's shape.

[11]**Chin-bands:** cloth band used for corpses. **Lazarus:** raised from the dead by Jesus (John 11).

And glare unnatural; the very sky
(Dropping its bell-net down upon the sea,
As if no human heart should 'scape alive)
Bedraggled with the desolating salt,
Until it seemed no more that holy heaven
To which my father went.   All new and strange;
The universe turned stranger, for a child.   250

Then, land!—then, England!   oh, the frosty cliffs
Looked cold upon me.   Could I find a home
Among those mean red houses through the fog?
And when I heard my father's language first
From alien lips which had no kiss for mine
I wept aloud, then laughed, then wept, then wept,
And some one near me said the child was mad
Through much sea-sickness.   The train swept us on:
Was this my father's England? the great isle?
The ground seemed cut up from the fellowship   260
Of verdure, field from field, as man from man;
The skies themselves looked low and positive,
As almost you could touch them with a hand,
And dared to do it they were so far off
From God's celestial crystals; all things blurred
And dull and vague.   Did Shakespeare and his mates
Absorb the light here?—not a hill or stone
With heart to strike a radiant colour up
Or active outline on the indifferent air.

I think I see my father's sister stand   270
Upon the hall-step of her country-house
To give me welcome.   She stood straight and calm,
Her somewhat narrow forehead braided tight
As if for taming accidental thoughts
From possible pulses; brown hair pricked with gray
By frigid use of life (she was not old,
Although my father's elder by a year),
A nose drawn sharply, yet in delicate lines;
A close mild mouth, a little soured about
The ends, through speaking unrequited loves   280
Or peradventure niggardly half-truths;
Eyes of no colour,—once they might have smiled,
But never, never have forgot themselves
In smiling; cheeks, in which was yet a rose
Of perished summers, like a rose in a book,
Kept more for ruth than pleasure,—if past bloom,
Past fading also.
                    She had lived, we'll say,
A harmless life, she called a virtuous life,
A quiet life, which was not life at all
(But that, she had not lived enough to know),   290

Between the vicar and the county squires,
The lord-lieutenant looking down sometimes
From the empyrean to assure their souls
Against chance vulgarisms, and, in the abyss,
The apothecary, looked on once a year
To prove their soundness of humility.
The poor-club exercised her Christian gifts
Of knitting stockings, stitching petticoats,
Because we are of one flesh,[12] after all,
And need one flannel (with a proper sense   300
Of difference in the quality)—and still
The book-club, guarded from your modern trick
Of shaking dangerous questions from the crease,
Preserved her intellectual.   She had lived
A sort of cage-bird life, born in a cage,
Accounting that to leap from perch to perch
Was act and joy enough for any bird.
Dear heaven, how silly are the things that live
In thickets, and eat berries!
                              I, alas,
A wild bird scarcely fledged, was brought to her
     cage,   310
And she was there to meet me.   Very kind.
Bring the clean water, give out the fresh seed.

She stood upon the steps to welcome me,
Calm, in black garb. I clung about her neck,—
Young babes, who catch at every shred of wool
To draw the new light closer, catch and cling
Less blindly.   In my ears my father's word
Hummed ignorantly, as the sea in shells,
"Love, love, my child."   She, black there with my grief,
Might feel my love—she was his sister once—   320
I clung to her.   A moment she seemed moved,
Kissed me with cold lips, suffered me to cling,
And drew me feebly through the hall into
The room she sat in.
                        There, with some strange spasm
Of pain and passion, she wrung loose my hands
Imperiously, and held me at arm's length,
And with two grey-steel naked-bladed eyes
Searched through my face,—ay, stabbed it through and
     through,
Through brows and cheeks and chin, as if to find
A wicked murderer in my innocent face,   330

---

[12]The poor-club provided clothing for the poor. one flesh: see Ephesians 5:29–31. The book-club provided books and conversation for its members.

If not here, there perhaps.   Then, drawing breath,
She struggled for her ordinary calm—
And missed it rather,—told me not to shrink,
As if she had told me not to lie or swear,—
"She loved my father and would love me too
As long as I deserved it."   Very kind.

I understood her meaning afterward;
She thought to find my mother in my face,
And questioned it for that.   For she, my aunt,
Had loved my father truly, as she could,   340
And hated, with the gall of gentle souls,
My Tuscan mother who had fooled away
A wise man from wise courses, a good man
From obvious duties, and, depriving her,
His sister, of the household precedence,
Had wronged his tenants, robbed his native land,
And made him mad, alike by life and death,
In love and sorrow.   She had pored for years
What sort of woman could be suitable
To her sort of hate, to entertain it with,   350
And so, her very curiosity
Became hate too, and all the idealism
She ever used in life was used for hate,
Till hate, so nourished, did exceed at last
The love from which it grew, in strength and heat,
And wrinkled her smooth conscience with a sense
Of disputable virtue (say not, sin)
When Christian doctrine was enforced at church.

And thus my father's sister was to me
My mother's hater.   From that day she did   360
Her duty to me (I appreciate it
In her own word as spoken to herself),
Her duty, in large measure, well pressed[13] out
But measured always.   She was generous, bland,
More courteous than was tender, gave me still
The first place,—as if fearful that God's saints
Would look down suddenly and say "Herein
You missed a point, I think, through lack of love."
Alas, a mother never is afraid
Of speaking angerly to any child,   370
Since love, she knows, is justified of love.

And I, I was a good child on the whole,
A meek and manageable child.   Why not?
I did not live, to have the faults of life:
There seemed more true life in my father's grave

Than in all England.   Since *that* threw me off
Who fain would cleave (his latest will, they say,
Consigned me to his land), I only thought
Of lying quiet there where I was thrown
Like sea-weed on the rocks, and suffering her   380
To prick me to a pattern with her pin,
Fibre from fibre, delicate leaf from leaf,
And dry out from my drowned anatomy
The last sea-salt left in me.

                     So it was.
I broke the copious curls upon my head
In braids, because she liked smooth-ordered hair.
I left off saying my sweet Tuscan words
Which still at any stirring of the heart
Came up to float across the English phrase
As lilies (*Bene* or *Che che*),[14] because   390
She liked my father's child to speak his tongue.
I learnt the collects and the catechism,
The creeds, from Athanasius back to Nice,
The Articles, the Tracts *against* the times
(By no means Buonaventure's "Prick of Love"),
And various popular synopses of
Inhuman doctrines never taught by John,[15]
Because she liked instructed piety.
I learnt my complement of classic French
(Kept pure of Balzac[16] and neologism)   400
And German also, since she liked a range
Of liberal education,—tongues, not books.
I learnt a little algebra, a little
Of the mathematics,—brushed with extreme flounce
The circle of the sciences, because
She misliked women who are frivolous.
I learnt the royal genealogies
Of Oviedo, the internal laws
Of the Burmese empire,—by how many feet
Mount Chimborazo outsoars Teneriffe.   410
What navigable river joins itself

---

[14]*Bene:* Good. *Che che:* What!

[15]**collects:** short prayers for Church services. The Athanasian
and Nicene **creeds** and the 39 **Articles** contained basic doctrines of
the Anglican Church. **Tracts:** the Oxford Movement's *Tracts for the
Times* (1833–1841), written mostly by John Henry Newman and
John Keble, asserted Catholic principles within the Anglican
Church. **Buonaventure:** St. Bonaventure (1221–1274), author of
mystic works of devotion. **John:** author of the fourth gospel.

[16]Honoré de **Balzac** (1799–1850): French novelist whose books
were considered unfit for Englishwomen to read.

---

[13]**measure . . . pressed:** see Luke 6:38.

To Lara, and what census of the year five
Was taken at Klagenfurt,[17]—because she liked
A general insight into useful facts.
I learnt much music,—such as would have been
As quite impossible in Johnson's[18] day
As still it might be wished—fine sleights of hand
And unimagined fingering, shuffling off
The hearer's soul through hurricanes of notes
To a noisy Tophet; and I drew . . . costumes   420
From French engravings, nereids neatly draped
(With smirks of simmering godship): I washed in
Landscapes from nature (rather say, washed out).
I danced the polka and Cellarius,
Spun glass, stuffed birds, and modelled flowers in wax,
Because she liked accomplishments in girls.
I read a score of books on womanhood
To prove, if women do not think at all,
They may teach thinking (to a maiden aunt
Or else the author),—books that boldly assert   430
Their right of comprehending husband's talk
When not too deep, and even of answering
With pretty "may it please you," or "so it is,"—
Their rapid insight and fine aptitude,
Particular worth and general missionariness,
As long as they keep quiet by the fire
And never say "no" when the world says "ay,"
For that is fatal,—their angelic reach
Of virtue, chiefly used to sit and darn,
And fatten household sinners,—their, in brief,   440
Potential faculty in everything
Of abdicating power in it: she owned
She liked a woman to be womanly,
And English women, she thanked God and sighed
(Some people always sigh in thanking God)
Were models to the universe.   And last
I learnt cross-stitch, because she did not like
To see me wear the night with empty hands
A-doing nothing.   So, my shepherdess
Was something after all (the pastoral saints   450

Be praised for't), leaning lovelorn with pink eyes
To match her shoes, when I mistook the silks;
Her head uncrushed by that round weight of hat
So strangely similar to the tortoise-shell
Which slew the tragic poet.[19]
                                    By the way,
The works of women are symbolical.
We sew, sew, prick our fingers, dull our sight,
Producing what? A pair of slippers, sir,
To put on when you're weary—or a stool
To stumble over and vex you . . . "curse that
          stool!"   460
Or else at best, a cushion, where you lean
And sleep, and dream of something we are not
But would be for your sake.   Alas, alas!
This hurts most, this—that, after all, we are paid
The worth of our work, perhaps.
                                    In looking down
Those years of education (to return)
I wonder if Brinvilliers[20] suffered more
In the water-torture . . . flood succeeding flood
To drench the incapable throat and split the veins . . .
Than I did. Certain of your feebler souls   470
Go out in such a process; many pine
To a sick, inodorous light; my own endured:
I had relations in the Unseen, and drew
The elemental nutriment and heat
From nature, as earth feels the sun at nights,
Or as a babe sucks surely in the dark.
I kept the life thrust on me, on the outside
Of the inner life with all its ample room
For heart and lungs, for will and intellect,
Inviolable by conventions.   God,   480
I thank thee for that grace of thine!
                                    At first
I felt no life which was not patience,—did
The thing she bade me, without heed to a thing
Beyond it, sat in just the chair she placed,
With back against the window, to exclude
The sight of the great lime-tree on the lawn,
Which seemed to have come on purpose from the woods
To bring the house a message,—ay, and walked

---

[17]Gonzalez Fernandez de **Oviedo** y Valdez (1478–1557): Spanish
historian whose history of Spanish grandees was never published.
Chimborazo: in the Andes. **Teneriffe**: in the Canary Islands. **Lara**: in
Spain. **Klagenfurt**: city in Austria founded in the 12th century.

[18]**impossible . . . Johnson**: allusion to an anecdote reported by
Sir John Hawkins (1719–1789) in *The Life of Samuel Johnson* (1787),
319n. **Tophet**: see Isaiah 30.33. **nereids**: sea-nymphs. **Cellarius**: a
kind of waltz.

---

[19]The **tragic poet** Aeschylus was said to have died (456? BCE)
when an eagle dropped a **tortoise** on his bald head, thinking it a
stone on which to break the **shell**.

[20]Marie d'Aubray, marquise de **Brinvilliers** (1630–1676): notorious poisoner.

Demurely in her carpeted low rooms,
As if I should not, hearkening my own steps,   490
Misdoubt I was alive.   I read her books,
Was civil to her cousin, Romney Leigh,   *cousin*
Gave ear to her vicar, tea to her visitors,
And heard them whisper, when I changed a cup
(I blushed for joy at that),—"The Italian child,
For all her blue eyes and her quiet ways,
Thrives ill in England: she is paler yet
Than when we came the last time; she will die."

"Will die." My cousin, Romney Leigh, blushed too,
With sudden anger, and approaching me   500
Said low between his teeth, "You're wicked now?
You wish to die and leave the world a-dusk
For others, with your naughty light blown out?"
I looked into his face defyingly;
He might have known that, being what I was,
'Twas natural to like to get away
As far as dead folk can: and then indeed
Some people make no trouble when they die.
He turned and went abruptly, slammed the door,
And shut his dog out.
                        Romney, Romney Leigh.   510
I have not named my cousin hitherto,
And yet I used him as a sort of friend;
My elder by few years, but cold and shy
And absent . . . tender, when he thought of it,
Which scarcely was imperative, grave betimes,
As well as early master of Leigh Hall,
Whereof the nightmare sat upon his youth,
Repressing all its seasonable delights,
And agonising with a ghastly sense
Of universal hideous want and wrong   520
To incriminate possession.   When he came
From college to the country, very oft
He crossed the hill on visits to my aunt,
With gifts of blue grapes from the hothouses,
A book in one hand,—mere statistics (if
I chanced to lift the cover), count of all
The goats whose beards grow sprouting down toward hell
Against God's separative judgment-hour.[21]
And she, she almost loved him,—even allowed
That sometimes he should seem to sigh my way;   530
It made him easier to be pitiful,
And sighing was his gift.   So, undisturbed,
At whiles she let him shut my music up

And push my needles down, and lead me out
To see in that south angle of the house
The figs grow black as if by a Tuscan rock,
On some light pretext.   She would turn her head
At other moments, go to fetch a thing,
And leave me breath enough to speak with him,
For his sake; it was simple.
                        Sometimes too   540
He would have saved me utterly, it seemed,
He stood and looked so.
                        Once, he stood so near,   *construdi'g touch*
He dropped a sudden hand upon my head
Bent down on woman's work, as soft as rain—
But then I rose and shook it off as fire,
The stranger's touch that took my father's place
Yet dared seem soft.
                        I used him for a friend
Before I ever knew him for a friend.
'Twas better, 'twas worse also, afterward:
We came so close, we saw our differences   550
Too intimately.   Always Romney Leigh
Was looking for the worms, I for the gods.
A godlike nature his; the gods look down,
Incurious of themselves; and certainly
'Tis well I should remember, how, those days,
I was a worm too, and he looked on me.

A little by his act perhaps, yet more
By something in me, surely not my will,
I did not die.   But slowly, as one in swoon,
To whom life creeps back in the form of death,   560
With a sense of separation, a blind pain
Of blank obstruction, and a roar i' the ears
Of visionary chariots which retreat
As earth grows clearer . . . slowly, by degrees;
I woke, rose up . . . where was I? in the world;
For uses therefore I must count worth while.

I had a little chamber in the house,
As green as any privet-hedge a bird
Might choose to build in, though the nest itself
Could show but dead-brown sticks and straws; the
        walls   570
Were green, the carpet was pure green, the straight
Small bed was curtained greenly, and the folds
Hung green about the window which let in
The out-door world with all its greenery.
You could not push your head out and escape
A dash of dawn-dew from the honeysuckle,
But so you were baptized into the grace

---

[21]**goats . . . judgment-hour:** see Matthew 25:31–41.

And privilege of seeing. . . .
                              First, the lime
(I had enough there, of the lime, be sure,—
My morning-dream was often hummed away   580
By the bees in it); past the lime, the lawn,
Which, after sweeping broadly round the house,
Went trickling through the shrubberies in a stream
Of tender turf, and wore and lost itself
Among the acacias, over which you saw
The irregular line of elms by the deep lane
Which stopped the grounds and dammed the overflow
Of arbutus and laurel.   Out of sight
The lane was; sunk so deep, no foreign tramp
Nor drover of wild ponies out of Wales   590
Could guess if lady's hall or tenant's lodge
Dispensed such odours,—though his stick well-crooked
Might reach the lowest trail of blossoming briar
Which dipped upon the wall.   Behind the elms,
And through their tops, you saw the folded hills
Striped up and down with hedges (burly oaks
Projecting from the line to show themselves),
Through which my cousin Romney's chimneys smoked
As still as when a silent mouth in frost
Breathes, showing where the woodlands hid Leigh
         Hall;   600
While, far above, a jut of table-land,
A promontory without water, stretched,—
You could not catch it if the days were thick,
Or took it for a cloud; but, otherwise,
The vigorous sun would catch it up at eve
And use it for an anvil till he had filled
The shelves of heaven with burning thunder-bolts,
Protesting against night and darkness:—then,
When all his setting trouble was resolved
To a trance of passive glory, you might see   610
In apparition on the golden sky
(Alas, my Giotto's [22] background!) the sheep run
Along the fine clear outline, small as mice
That run along a witch's scarlet thread.

Not a grand nature.   Not my chestnut-woods
Of Vallombrosa,[23] cleaving by the spurs
To the precipices.   Not my headlong leaps
Of waters, that cry out for joy or fear
In leaping through the palpitating pines,
Like a white soul tossed out to eternity   620

With thrills of time upon it.   Not indeed
My multitudinous mountains, sitting in
The magic circle, with the mutual touch
Electric, panting from their full deep hearts
Beneath the influent heavens, and waiting for
Communion and commission.   Italy
Is one thing, England one.
                              On English ground
You understand the letter,—ere the fall
How Adam lived in a garden.   All the fields
Are tied up fast with hedges, nosegay-like;   630
The hills are crumpled plains, the plains parterres,
The trees, round, woolly, ready to be clipped,
And if you seek for any wilderness
You find, at best, a park.   A nature tamed
And grown domestic like a barn-door fowl,
Which does not awe you with its claws and beak,
Nor tempt you to an eyrie too high up,
But which, in cackling, sets you thinking of
Your eggs to-morrow at breakfast, in the pause
Of finer meditation.
                              Rather say,   640
A sweet familiar nature, stealing in
As a dog might, or child, to touch your hand
Or pluck your gown, and humbly mind you so
Of presence and affection, excellent
For inner uses, from the things without.

I could not be unthankful, I who was
Entreated thus and holpen.[24] In the room
I speak of, ere the house was well awake,
And also after it was well asleep,
I sat alone, and drew the blessing in   650
Of all that nature.   With a gradual step,
A stir among the leaves, a breath, a ray,
It came in softly, while the angels made
A place for it beside me.   The moon came,
And swept my chamber clean of foolish thoughts.
The sun came, saying, "Shall I lift this light
Against the lime-tree, and you will not look?
I make the birds sing—listen!   but, for you,
God never hears your voice, excepting when
You lie upon the bed at nights and weep."   660

Then, something moved me.   Then, I wakened up
More slowly than I verily write now,
But wholly, at last, I wakened, opened wide
The window and my soul, and let the airs

---

[22]**Giotto** (1266?–1337?): Florentine painter and architect.

[23]**Vallombrosa**: forest near Florence.

[24]**holpen**: helped.

And out-door sights sweep gradual gospels in,
Regenerating what I was.   O, Life,
How oft we throw it off and think,— "Enough,
Enough of life in so much!—here's a cause
For rupture;—herein we must break with Life,
Or be ourselves unworthy; here we are wronged,   670
Maimed, spoiled for aspiration: farewell, Life!"
And so, as froward babes, we hide our eyes
And think all ended.— Then, Life calls to us
In some transformed, apocalyptic voice,
Above us, or below us, or around:
Perhaps we name it Nature's voice, or Love's,
Tricking ourselves, because we are more ashamed
To own our compensations than our griefs:
Still, Life's voice!—still, we make our peace with Life.

And I, so young then, was not sullen.   Soon   680
I used to get up early, just to sit
And watch the morning quicken in the gray,
And hear the silence open like a flower
Leaf after leaf,—and stroke with listless hand
The woodbine through the window, till at last
I came to do it with a sort of love,
At foolish unaware: whereat I smiled,—
A melancholy smile, to catch myself
Smiling for joy.

  Capacity for joy
Admits temptation.   It seemed, next, worth while   690
To dodge the sharp sword set against my life;
To slip down stairs through all the sleepy house,
As mute as any dream there, and escape
As a soul from the body, out of doors,
Glide through the shrubberies, drop into the lane,
And wander on the hills an hour or two,
Then back again before the house should stir.
Or else I sat on in my chamber green,
And lived my life, and thought my thoughts, and prayed
My prayers without the vicar; read my books   700
Without considering whether they were fit
To do me good.   Mark, there.   We get no good
By being ungenerous, even to a book,
And calculating profits,—so much help
By so much reading.   It is rather when
We gloriously forget ourselves and plunge
Soul-forward, headlong, into a book's profound,
Impassioned for its beauty and salt of truth—
'Tis then we get the right good from a book.

I read much.   What my father taught before   710
From many a volume, Love re-emphasised

Upon the self-same pages: Theophrast
Grew tender with the memory of his eyes,
And Ælian[25] made mine wet.   The trick of Greek
And Latin he had taught me, as he would
Have taught me wrestling or the game of fives
If such he had known,—most like a shipwrecked man
Who heaps his single platter with goats' cheese
And scarlet berries; or like any man
Who loves but one, and so gives all at once,   720
Because he has it, rather than because
He counts it worthy.   Thus, my father gave;
And thus, as did the women formerly
By young Achilles,[26] when they pinned a veil
Across the boy's audacious front, and swept
With tuneful laughs the silver-fretted rocks,
He wrapt his little daughter in his large
Man's doublet, careless did it fit or no.
But, after I had read for memory,
I read for hope.   The path my father's foot   730
Had trod me out (which suddenly broke off
What time he dropped the wallet of the flesh
And passed), alone I carried on, and set
My child-heart 'gainst the thorny underwood,
To reach the grassy shelter of the trees.
Ah babe i' the wood, without a brother-babe!
My own self-pity, like the red-breast bird,
Flies back to cover all that past with leaves.

Sublimest danger, over which none weeps,
When any young wayfaring soul goes forth   740
Alone, unconscious of the perilous road,
The day-sun dazzling in his limpid eyes,
To thrust his own way, he an alien, through
The world of books! Ah, you!—you think it fine,
You clap hands—"A fair day!"—you cheer him on,
As if the worst, could happen, were to rest
Too long beside a fountain.   Yet, behold,
Behold!—the world of books is still the world,
And worldings in it are less merciful
And more puissant.   For the wicked there   750
Are winged like angels; every knife that strikes
Is edged from elemental fire to assail

---

[25]**Theophrastus** (371?–286 BCE): philosopher, pupil and successor of Aristotle. **Ælian**: Claudius Aelianus (170?–235?), Roman rhetorician who wrote in Greek, especially stories about animals. **fives**: ball game.

[26]Knowing he would die in the Trojan War, **Achilles'** mother hid him dressed as a woman so the Greeks would not find him.

A spiritual life; the beautiful seems right
By force of beauty, and the feeble wrong
Because of weakness; power is justified
Though armed against Saint Michael; many a crown
Covers bald foreheads.   In the book-world, true,
There's no lack, neither, of God's saints and kings,
That shake the ashes of the grave aside
From their calm locks and undiscomfited   760
Look steadfast truths against Time's changing mask.
True, many a prophet teaches in the roads;
True, many a seer pulls down the flaming heavens
Upon his own head in strong martyrdom
In order to light men a moment's space.
But stay!—who judges?—who distinguishes
'Twixt Saul and Nahash[27] justly, at first sight,
And leaves king Saul precisely at the sin,
To serve king David? who discerns at once
The sound of the trumpets, when the trumpets
       blow   770
For Alaric as well as Charlemagne?
Who judges wizards, and can tell true seers
From conjurers? the child, there?   Would you leave
That child to wander in a battle-field
And push his innocent smile against the guns;
Or even in a catacomb,—his torch
Grown ragged in the fluttering air, and all
The dark a-mutter round him? not a child.

I read books bad and good—some bad and good
At once (good aims not always make good books: 780
Well-tempered spades turn up ill-smelling soils
In digging vineyards even); books that prove
God's being so definitely, that man's doubt
Grows self-defined the other side the line,
Made atheist by suggestion; moral books,
Exasperating to license; genial books,
Discounting from the human dignity;
And merry books, which set you weeping when
The sun shines,—ay, and melancholy books,
Which make you laugh that any one should weep 790
In this disjointed life for one wrong more.

The world of books is still the world, I write,
And both worlds have God's providence, thank God,

To keep and hearten: with some struggle, indeed,
Among the breakers, some hard swimming through
The deeps—I lost breath in my soul sometimes
And cried "God save me if there's any God,"
But, even so, God saved me; and, being dashed
From error on to error, every turn
Still brought me nearer to the central truth.   800

I thought so.   All this anguish in the thick
Of men's opinions . . . press and counter-press,
Now up, now down, now underfoot, and now
Emergent . . . all the best of it, perhaps,
But throws you back upon a noble trust
And use of your own instinct,—merely proves
Pure reason stronger than bare inference
At strongest.   Try it,—fix against heaven's wall
The scaling-ladders of school logic—mount
Step by step!—sight goes faster; that still ray   810
Which strikes out from you, how, you cannot tell,
And why, you know not (did you eliminate,
That such as you indeed should analyse?)
Goes straight and fast as light, and high as God.

The cygnet finds the water, but the man
Is born in ignorance of his element
And feels out blind at first, disorganised
By sin i' the blood,—his spirit-insight dulled
And crossed by his sensations.   Presently
He feels it quicken in the dark sometimes,   820
When, mark, be reverent, be obedient,
For such dumb motions of imperfect life
Are oracles of vital Deity
Attesting the Hereafter.   Let who says
"The soul's a clean white paper," rather say,
A palimpsest, a prophet's holograph
Defiled, erased and covered by a monk's,—
The apocalypse, by a Longus![28] poring on
Which obscene text, we may discern perhaps
Some fair, fine trace of what was written once,   830
Some upstroke of an alpha and omega
Expressing the old scripture.
                       Books, books, books!
I had found the secret of a garret-room
Piled high with cases in my father's name,

---

[27]**Saul and Nahash**: 1 Samuel 11. On Saul and **David** see 1
Samuel 16ff. **Alaric** (370–410): Visigoth chieftain whose army
sacked Rome in 410, marking the fall of the Roman Empire.
Charlemagne (742–814): leader of the Christian Holy Roman
Empire.

[28]**palimpsest**: manuscript written over an effaced earlier text.
apocalypse: Revelation. **Longus**: 3rd-century Greek writer of pastoral and erotic romances. **alpha and omega**: Greek letters; see
Revelation 1:8.

Piled high, packed large,—where, creeping in and out
Among the giant fossils of my past,
Like some small nimble mouse between the ribs
Of a mastodon, I nibbled here and there
At this or that box, pulling through the gap,
In heats of terror, haste, victorious joy,   840
The first book first.   And how I felt it beat
Under my pillow, in the morning's dark,
An hour before the sun would let me read!
My books!   At last because the time was ripe,
I chanced upon the poets.
                            As the earth
Plunges in fury, when the internal fires
Have reached and pricked her heart, and, throwing flat
The marts and temples, the triumphal gates
And towers of observation, clears herself
To elemental freedom—thus, my soul,   850
At poetry's divine first finger-touch,
Let go conventions and sprang up surprised,
Convicted[29] of the great eternities
Before two worlds.
                            What's this, Aurora Leigh,
You write so of the poets, and not laugh?
Those virtuous liars, dreamers after dark,
Exaggerators of the sun and moon,
And soothsayers in a tea-cup?
                            I write so
Of the only truth-tellers now left to God,
The only speakers of essential truth,   860
Opposed to relative, comparative,
And temporal truths; the only holders by
His sun-skirts, through conventional gray glooms;
The only teachers who instruct mankind
From just a shadow on a charnel-wall
To find man's veritable stature out
Erect, sublime,—the measure of a man,
And that's the measure of an angel, says
The apostle.[30] Ay, and while your common men
Lay telegraphs, gauge railroads, reign, reap, dine,   870
And dust the flaunty carpets of the world
For kings to walk on, or our president,
The poet suddenly will catch them up
With his voice like a thunder,—"This is soul,
This is life, this word is being said in heaven,

Here's God down on us! what are you about?"
How all those workers start amid their work,
Look round, look up, and feel, a moment's space,
That carpet-dusting, though a pretty trade,
Is not the imperative labour after all.   880

My own best poets, am I one with you,
That thus I love you,—or but one through love?
Does all this smell of thyme about my feet
Conclude my visit to your holy hill
In personal presence, or but testify
The rustling of your vesture through my dreams
With influent odours?   When my joy and pain,
My thought and aspiration like the stops
Of pipe or flute, are absolutely dumb
Unless melodious, do you play on me   890
My pipers,—and if, sooth, you did not blow,
Would no sound come? or is the music mine,
As a man's voice or breath is called his own,
Inbreathed by the Life-breather?   There's a doubt
For cloudy seasons!
                            But the sun was high
When first I felt my pulses set themselves
For concord; when the rhythmic turbulence
Of blood and brain swept outward upon words,
As wind upon the alders, blanching them
By turning up their under-natures till   900
They trembled in dilation.   O delight
And triumph of the poet, who would say
A man's mere "yes," a woman's common "no,"
A little human hope of that or this,
And says the word so that it burns you through
With a special revelation, shakes the heart
Of all the men and women in the world,
As if one came back from the dead and spoke,
With eyes too happy, a familiar thing
Become divine i' the utterance! while for him   910
The poet, speaker, he expands with joy;
The palpitating angel in his flesh
Thrills inly with consenting fellowship
To those innumerous spirits who sun themselves
Outside of time.
                            O life, O poetry,
—Which means life in life! cognisant of life
Beyond this blood-beat, passionate for truth
Beyond these senses!—poetry, my life,
My eagle, with both grappling feet still hot
From Zeus's thunder, who hast ravished me   920
Away from all the shepherds, sheep, and dogs,

---

[29]**Convicted:** convinced.

[30]**measure . . . apostle:** Revelation 21:17.

And set me in the Olympian roar and round
Of luminous faces for a cup-bearer,[31]
To keep the mouths of all the godheads moist
For everlasting laughters,—I myself
Half drunk across the beaker with their eyes!
How those gods look!
                    Enough so, Ganymede,
We shall not bear above a round or two.
We drop the golden cup at Heré's foot
And swoon back to the earth,—and find ourselves 930
Face-down among the pine-cones, cold with dew,
While the dogs bark, and many a shepherd scoffs,
"What's come now to the youth?"   Such ups and downs
Have poets.
            Am I such indeed?   The name
Is royal, and to sign it like a queen
Is what I dare not,—though some royal blood
Would seem to tingle in me now and then,
With sense of power and ache,—with imposthumes
And manias usual to the race.   Howbeit
I dare not: 'tis too easy to go mad   940
And ape a Bourbon[32] in a crown of straws;
The thing's too common.
                        Many fervent souls
Strike rhyme on rhyme, who would strike steel on steel
If steel had offered, in a restless heat
Of doing something.   Many tender souls
Have strung their losses on a rhyming thread,
As children cowslips:—the more pains they take,
The work more withers.   Young men, ay, and maids,
Too often sow their wild oats in tame verse,
Before they sit down under their own vine[33]   950
And live for use.   Alas, near all the birds
Will sing at dawn,—and yet we do not take
The chaffering swallow for the holy lark.
In those days, though, I never analysed,
Not even myself.   Analysis comes late.
You catch a sight of Nature, earliest,
In full front sun-face, and your eyelids wink
And drop before the wonder of't; you miss
The form, through seeing the light.   I lived, those days,
And wrote because I lived—unlicensed else;   960
My heart beat in my brain. Life's violent flood

Abolished bounds,—and, which my neighbour's field,
Which mine, what mattered? it is thus in youth!
We play at leap-frog over the god Term;[34]
The love within us and the love without
Are mixed, confounded; if we are loved or love,
We scarce distinguish: thus, with other power;
Being acted on and acting seem the same:
In that first onrush of life's chariot-wheels,
We know not if the forest move or we.   970

And so, like most young poets, in a flush
Of individual life I poured myself
Along the veins of others, and achieved
Mere lifeless imitations of live verse,
And made the living answer for the dead,
Profaning nature.   "Touch not, do not taste,
Nor handle,"[35]—we're too legal, who write young:
We beat the phorminx[36] till we hurt our thumbs,
As if still ignorant of counterpoint;
We call the Muse,—"O Muse, benignant
    Muse,"—   980
As if we had seen her purple-braided head,
With the eyes in it, start between the boughs
As often as a stag's.   What make-believe,
With so much earnest! what effete results
From virile efforts! what cold wire-drawn odes
From such white heats!—bucolics,[37] where the cows
Would scare the writer if they splashed the mud
In lashing off the flies,—didactics, driven
Against the heels of what the master said;
And counterfeiting epics, shrill with trumps   990
A babe might blow between two straining cheeks
Of bubbled rose, to make his mother laugh;
And elegiac griefs, and songs of love,
Like cast-off nosegays picked up on the road,
The worse for being warm: all these things, writ
On happy mornings, with a morning heart,
That leaps for love, is active for resolve,
Weak for art only.   Oft, the ancient forms
Will thrill, indeed, in carrying the young blood.
The wine-skins, now and then, a little warped,   1000
Will crack even, as the new wine gurgles in.
Spare the old bottles!—spill not the new wine.[38]

---

[31]**Zeus** in the form of an **eagle** carried the beautiful boy **Ganymede** off to Olympus and made him the gods' **cup-bearer**.

[32]**Bourbon**: member of one of the great ruling families of Europe.

[33]**under . . . vine**: 1 Kings 4:25, Micah 4:4.

---

[34]**Term**: Roman **god** representing boundary marks.

[35]**"Touch not . . . handle"**: see Colossians 2:21.

[36]**phorminx**: ancient Greek stringed instrument.

[37]**bucolics**: pastoral verse.

[38]**old bottles . . . new wine**: see Matthew 9:17.

By Keats's soul, the man who never stepped
In gradual progress like another man,
But, turning grandly on his central self,
Ensphered himself in twenty perfect years
And died, not young (the life of a long life
Distilled to a mere drop, falling like a tear
Upon the world's cold cheek to make it burn
For ever); by that strong excepted soul,   1010
I count it strange and hard to understand
That nearly all young poets should write old.
That Pope was sexagenary at sixteen,
And beardless Byron academical,
And so with others. It may be perhaps
Such have not settled long and deep enough
In trance, to attain to clairvoyance,—and still
The memory mixes with the vision, spoils,
And works it turbid.
                    Or perhaps, again,
In order to discover the Muse-Sphinx,   1020
The melancholy desert must sweep round,
Behind you as before.—
                        For me, I wrote
False poems, like the rest, and thought them true
Because myself was true in writing them.
I peradventure have writ true ones since
With less complacence.
                        But I could not hide
My quickening inner life from those at watch.
They saw a light at a window, now and then,
They had not set there: who had set it there?
My father's sister started when she caught   1030
My soul agaze in my eyes.   She could not say
I had no business with a sort of soul,
But plainly she objected,—and demurred
That souls were dangerous things to carry straight
Through all the spilt saltpetre of the world.
She said sometimes "Aurora, have you done
Your task this morning? have you read that book?
And are you ready for the crochet here?"—
As if she said "I know there's something wrong;
I know I have not ground you down enough   1040
To flatten and bake you to a wholesome crust
For household uses and proprieties,
Before the rain has got into my barn
And set the grains a-spouting.   What, you're green
With out-door impudence? you almost grow?"
To which I answered, "Would she hear my task,
And verify my abstract of the book?
Or should I sit down to the crochet work?

[margin note: Poetry demands maturity]

Was such her pleasure?"   Then I sat and teased
The patient needle till it split the thread,   1050
Which oozed off from it in meandering lace
From hour to hour.   I was not, therefore, sad;
My soul was singing at a work apart
Behind the wall of sense, as safe from harm
As sings the lark when sucked up out of sight
In vortices of glory and blue air.

And so, through forced work and spontaneous work,
The inner life informed the outer life,
Reduced the irregular blood to a settled rhythm,
Made cool the forehead with fresh-sprinkling
                                    dreams,   1060
And, rounding to the spheric soul the thin,
Pined body, struck a colour up the cheeks
Though somewhat faint.   I clenched my brows across
My blue eyes greatening in the looking-glass,
And said "We'll live, Aurora! we'll be strong.
The dogs are on us—but we will not die."

Whoever lives true life will love true love.
I learnt to love that England. Very oft,
Before the day was born, or otherwise
Through secret windings of the afternoons,   1070
I threw my hunters off and plunged myself
Among the deep hills, as a hunted stag
Will take the waters, shivering with the fear
And passion of the course.   And when at last
Escaped, so many a green slope built on slope
Betwixt me and the enemy's house behind,
I dared to rest, or wander, in a rest
Made sweeter for the step upon the grass,
And view the ground's most gentle dimplement
(As if God's finger touched but did not press   1080
In making England), such an up and down
Of verdure,—nothing too much up or down,
A ripple of land; such little hills, the sky
Can stoop to tenderly and the wheatfields climb;
Such nooks of valleys lined with orchises,
Fed full of noises by invisible streams;
And open pastures where you scarcely tell
White daisies from white dew,—at intervals
The mythic oaks and elm-trees standing out
Self-poised upon their prodigy of shade,—   1090
I thought my father's land was worthy too
Of being my Shakespeare's.
                        Very oft alone,
Unlicensed; not unfrequently with leave
To walk the third with Romney and his friend

The rising painter, Vincent Carrington,
Whom men judge hardly as bee-bonneted,
Because he holds that, paint a body well,
You paint a soul by implication, like
The grand first Master.   Pleasant walks! for if   1100
He said "When I was last in Italy,"
It sounded as an instrument that's played
Too far off for the tune—and yet it's fine
To listen.
        Often we walked only two
If cousin Romney pleased to walk with me.
We read, or talked, or quarrelled, as it chanced.
We were not lovers, nor even friends well-matched:
Say rather, scholars upon different tracks,
And thinkers disagreed: he, overfull
Of what is, and I, haply, overbold
For what might be.
                  But then the thrushes sang,   1110
And shook my pulses and the elms' new leaves:
At which I turned, and held my finger up,
And bade him mark that, howsoe'er the world
Went ill, as he related, certainly
The thrushes still sang in it.   At the word
His brow would soften,—and he bore with me
In melancholy patience, not unkind,
While breaking into voluble ecstasy
I flattered all the beauteous country round,
As poets use, the skies, the clouds, the fields,   1120
The happy violets hiding from the roads
The primroses run down to, carrying gold;
The tangled hedgerows, where the cows push out
Impatient horns and tolerant churning mouths
'Twixt dripping ash-boughs,—hedgerows all alive
With birds and gnats and large white butterflies
Which look as if the May-flower had caught life
And palpitated forth upon the wind;
Hills, vales, woods, netted in a silver mist,
Farms, granges, doubled up among the hills;   1130
And cattle grazing in the watered vales,
And cottage-chimneys smoking from the woods,
And cottage-gardens smelling everywhere,
Confused with smell of orchards.   "See," I said,
"And see!   is God not with us on the earth?
And shall we put Him down by aught we do?
Who says there's nothing for the poor and vile
Save poverty and wickedness? behold!"
And ankle-deep in English grass I leaped
And clapped my hands, and called all very fair.   1140
In the beginning when God called all good,

[handwritten margin note: Sense of order in natural world]

Even then was evil near us, it is writ;
But we indeed who call things good and fair,
The evil is upon us while we speak;
Deliver us from evil, let us pray.

                              1856, 1859

A Curse For a Nation[1]

— PROLOGUE —

I heard an angel speak last night,
        And he said "Write!
Write a Nation's curse for me,
And send it over the Western Sea."

I faltered, taking up the word:
        "Not so, my lord!
If curses must be, choose another
To send thy curse against my brother.

"For I am bound by gratitude,
        By love and blood,   10
To brothers of mine across the sea,
Who stretch out kindly hands to me."

"Therefore," the voice said, "shalt thou write
        My curse to-night.
From the summits of love a curse is driven,
As lightning is from the tops of heaven."

"Not so," I answered. "Evermore
        My heart is sore
For my own land's sins: for little feet
Of children bleeding along the street: 20

"For parked-up honours that gainsay
        The right of way:
For almsgiving through a door that is
Not open enough for two friends to kiss:

"For love of freedom which abates
        Beyond the Straits:[2]
For patriot virtue starved to vice on
Self-praise, self-interest, and suspicion:

"For an oligarchic parliament,
        And bribes well-meant.   30
What curse to another land assign,
When heavy-souled for the sins of mine?"

---

[1]**Nation:** United States.

[2]The **Straits** of Gibraltar mark the SW boundary of Europe.

"Therefore," the voice said, "shalt thou write
    My curse to-night.
Because thou hast strength to see and hate
A foul thing done *within* thy gate."

"Not so," I answered once again.
    "To curse, choose men.
For I, a woman, have only known
How the heart melts and the tears run down."   40

"Therefore," the voice said, "shalt thou write
    My curse to-night.
Some women weep and curse, I say
(And no one marvels), night and day.

"And thou shalt take their part to-night,
    Weep and write.
A curse from the depths of womanhood
Is very salt, and bitter, and good."

So thus I wrote, and mourned indeed,
    What all may read.   50
And thus, as was enjoined on me,
I send it over the Western Sea.

— THE CURSE —

1

Because ye have broken your own chain
    With the strain
Of brave men climbing a Nation's height,
Yet thence bear down with brand and thong
On souls of others,—for this wrong
    This is the curse.   Write.

Because yourselves are standing straight
    In the state   60
Of Freedom's foremost acolyte,
Yet keep calm footing all the time
On writhing bond-slaves,—for this crime
    This is the curse.   Write.

Because ye prosper in God's name,
    With a claim
To honour in the old world's sight,
Yet do the fiend's work perfectly
In strangling martyrs,—for this lie
    This is the curse.   Write.   70

2

Ye shall watch while kings conspire
Round the people's smouldering fire,
    And, warm for your part,

Shall never dare—O shame!
To utter the thought into flame
    Which burns at your heart.
      This is the curse.   Write.

Ye shall watch while nations strive
With the bloodhounds, die or survive,
    Drop faint from their jaws,   80
Or throttle them backward to death;
And only under your breath
    Shall favour the cause.
      This is the curse.   Write.

Ye shall watch while strong men draw
The nets of feudal law
    To strangle the weak;
And, counting the sin for a sin,
Your soul shall be sadder within
    Than the word ye shall speak.   90
      This is the curse.   Write.

When good men are praying erect
That Christ may avenge His elect
    And deliver the earth,
The prayer in your ears, said low,
Shall sound like the tramp of a foe
    That's driving you forth.
      This is the curse.   Write.

When wise men give you their praise,
They shall praise in the heat of the phrase,   100
    As if carried too far.
When ye boast your own charters kept true,
Ye shall blush; for the thing which ye do
    Derides what ye are.
      This is the curse.   Write.

When fools cast taunts at your gate,
Your scorn ye shall somewhat abate
    As ye look o'er the wall;
For your conscience, tradition, and name
Explode with a deadlier blame   110
    Than the worst of them all.
      This is the curse.   Write.

Go, wherever ill deeds shall be done,
Go, plant your flag in the sun
    Beside the ill-doers!
And recoil from clenching the curse
Of God's witnessing Universe
    With a curse of yours.
      THIS is the curse.   Write.

1856, 1860

Lord Walter's Wife

— 1 —

"But why do you go?" said the lady, while both sat under
the yew,
And her eyes were alive in their depth, as the kraken[1]
beneath the sea-blue.

— 2 —

"Because I fear you," he answered,—"because you are far
too fair,
And able to strangle my soul in a mesh of your gold-
coloured hair."

— 3 —

"Oh, that," she said, "is no reason! Such knots are quickly
undone,
And too much beauty, I reckon, is nothing but too much sun."

— 4 —

"Yet farewell so," he answered;—"the sunstroke's fatal at
times.
I value your husband, Lord Walter, whose gallop rings still
from the limes."

— 5 —

"Oh, that," she said, "is no reason. You smell a rose through
a fence:
If two should smell it, what matter? who grumbles, and
where's the pretence?"   10

— 6 —

"But I," he replied, "have promised another, when love was
free,
To love her alone, alone, who alone and afar loves me."

— 7 —

"Why, that," she said, "is no reason. Love's always free, I am
told.
Will you vow to be safe from the headache on Tuesday,
and think it will hold?"

— 8 —

"But you," he replied, "have a daughter, a young little child,
who was laid

---

[1]**kraken:** mythical sea monster.

In your lap to be pure; so I leave you: the angels would
make me afraid."

— 9 —

"Oh, that," she said, "is no reason. The angels keep out of
the way;
And Dora, the child, observes nothing, although you
should please me and stay."

— 10 —

At which he rose up in his anger,—"Why, now, you no
longer are fair!
Why, now, you no longer are fatal, but ugly and hateful,
I swear."   20

— 11 —

At which she laughed out in her scorn: "These men! Oh,
these men overnice,
Who are shocked if a colour not virtuous is frankly put on
by a vice."

— 12 —

Her eyes blazed upon him—"And *you!* You bring us your
vices so near
That we smell them! You think in our presence a thought
'twould defame us to hear!

— 13 —

"What reason had you, and what right,—I appeal to your
soul from my life,—
To find me too fair as a woman? Why, sir, I am pure, and
a wife.

— 14 —

"Is the day-star too fair up above you? It burns you not.
Dare you imply
I brushed you more close than the star does, when Walter
had set me as high?

— 15 —

"If a man finds a woman too fair, he means simply adapted
too much
To uses unlawful and fatal. The praise!—shall I thank you
for such?   30

— 16 —

"Too fair?—not unless you misuse us! and surely if, once in
a while,
You attain to it, straightway you call us no longer too fair,
but too vile.

— 17 —

"A moment,—I pray your attention!—I have a poor word
in my head
I must utter, though womanly custom would set it down
better unsaid.

— 18 —

"You grew, sir, pale to impertinence, once when I showed
you a ring.
You kissed my fan when I dropped it. No matter!—I've
broken the thing.

— 19 —

"You did me the honour, perhaps, to be moved at my side
now and then
In the senses—a vice, I have heard, which is common to
beasts and some men.

— 20 —

"Love's a virtue for heroes!—as white as the snow on high hills,
And immortal as every great soul is that struggles, endures,
and fulfils.   40

— 21 —

"I love my Walter profoundly,—you, Maude, though you
faltered a week,
For the sake of . . . what was it—an eyebrow? or, less still, a
mole on a cheek?

— 22 —

"And since, when all's said, you're too noble to stoop to the
frivolous cant
About crimes irresistible, virtues that swindle, betray and
supplant,

— 23 —

"I determined to prove to yourself that, whate'er you might
dream or avow
By illusion, you wanted precisely no more of me than you
have now.

— 24 —

"There! Look me full in the face!—in the face. Understand,
if you can,
That the eyes of such women as I am are clean as the palm
of a man.

— 25 —

"Drop his hand, you insult him. Avoid us for fear we should
cost you a scar—

You take us for harlots, I tell you, and not for the women
we are.   50

— 26 —

"You wronged me: but then I considered . . . there's Walter!
And so at the end
I vowed that he should not be mulcted, by me, in the hand
of a friend.

— 27 —

"Have I hurt you indeed? We are quits then. Nay, friend of
my Walter, be mine!
Come, Dora, my darling, my angel, and help me to ask him
to dine."

1862

The Best Thing in the World

What's the best thing in the world?
June-rose, by May-dew impearled;
Sweet south-wind, that means no rain;
Truth, not cruel to a friend;
Pleasure, not in haste to end;
Beauty, not self-decked and curled
Till its pride is over-plain;
Light, that never makes you wink;
Memory, that gives no pain;
Love, when, *so*, you're loved again.   10
What's the best thing in the world?
—Something out of it, I think.

1862

A Musical Instrument

— 1 —

What was he doing, the great god Pan,[1]
    Down in the reeds by the river?
Spreading ruin and scattering ban,
Splashing and paddling with hoofs of a goat,
And breaking the golden lilies afloat
    With the dragon-fly on the river.

---

[1] **the great god Pan:** pursued the nymph Syrinx, who to escape
him was turned into a reed, from which Pan carved the first flute.

— 2 —

He tore out a reed, the great god Pan,
From the deep cool bed of the river:
The limpid water turbidly ran,
And the broken lilies a-dying lay,   10
And the dragon-fly had fled away,
Ere he brought it out of the river.

— 3 —

High on the shore sat the great god Pan
While turbidly flowed the river;
And hacked and hewed as a great god can,
With his hard bleak steel at the patient reed,
Till there was not a sign of the leaf indeed
To prove it fresh from the river.

— 4 —

He cut it short, did the great god Pan,
(How tall it stood in the river!)   20
Then drew the pith, like the heart of a man,
Steadily from the outside ring,
And notched the poor dry empty thing
In holes, as he sat by the river.

— 5 —

"This is the way," laughed the great god Pan
(Laughed while he sat by the river),
"The only way, since gods began
To make sweet music, they could succeed."
Then, dropping his mouth to a hole in the reed,
He blew in power by the river.   30

— 6 —

Sweet, sweet, sweet, O Pan!
Piercing sweet by the river!
Blinding sweet, O great god Pan!
The sun on the hill forgot to die,
And the lilies revived, and the dragon-fly
Came back to dream on the river.

— 7 —

Yet half a beast is the great god Pan,
To laugh as he sits by the river,
Making a poet out of a man:
The true gods sigh for the cost and pain,—   40
For the reed which grows nevermore again
As a reed with the reeds in the river.

1862

Mother and Poet[1]

(Turin, after news from Gaeta, 1861)

— 1 —

Dead! One of them shot by the sea in the east,
And one of them shot in the west by the sea.
Dead! both my boys! When you sit at the feast
And are wanting a great song for Italy free,
Let none look at *me*!

— 2 —

Yet I was a poetess only last year,
And good at my art, for a woman, men said;
But *this* woman, *this*, who is agonised here,
—The east sea and west sea rhyme on in her head
For ever instead.   10

— 3 —

What art can a woman be good at? Oh, vain!
What art *is* she good at, but hurting her breast
With the milk-teeth of babes, and a smile at the pain?
Ah boys, how you hurt! you were strong as you pressed,
And I proud, by that test.

— 4 —

What art's for a woman? To hold on her knees
Both darlings! to feel all their arms round her throat,
Cling, strangle a little! to sew by degrees
And 'broider the long-clothes and neat little coat;
To dream and to doat.   20

— 5 —

To teach them . . . It stings there! I made them indeed
Speak plain the word *country*. I taught them, no doubt,
That a country's a thing men should die for at need.
I prated of liberty, rights, and about
The tyrant cast out.

— 6 —

And when their eyes flashed . . . O my beautiful eyes! . . .
I exulted; nay, let them go forth at the wheels

---

[1]**Mother and Poet**: Laura Savio (Olimpia Savio Rossi, 1815–1889), ardent Italian patriot, active in political and literary circles, author of poems, essays, a play, and a posthumously published memoir.

Of the guns, and denied not. But then the surprise
    When one sits quite alone! Then one weeps, then one
      kneels!
        God, how the house feels!   30

— 7 —

At first, happy news came, in gay letters moiled
    With my kisses,—of camp-life and glory, and how
They both loved me; and, soon coming home to be spoiled
    In return would fan off every fly from my brow
      With their green laurel-bough.[2]

— 8 —

Then was triumph at Turin: "Ancona was free!"
    And some one came out of the cheers in the street,
With a face pale as stone, to say something to me.
    My Guido was dead! I fell down at his feet,
      While they cheered in the street.   40

— 9 —

I bore it; friends soothed me; my grief looked sublime
    As the ransom of Italy. One boy remained
To be leant on and walked with, recalling the time
    When the first grew immortal, while both of us strained
      To the height he had gained.

— 10 —

And letters still came, shorter, sadder, more strong,
    Writ now but in one hand, "I was not to faint,—
One loved me for two—would be with me ere long:
    And *Viva l'Italia!*—*he* died for, our saint,
      Who forbids our complaint."   50

— 11 —

My Nanni would add, "he was safe, and aware
    Of a presence that turned off the balls,—was imprest
It was Guido himself, who knew what I could bear,
    And how 'twas impossible, quite dispossessed
      To live on for the rest."

— 12 —

On which, without pause, up the telegraph line
    Swept smoothly the next news from Gaeta:—*Shot.*
Tell his mother. Ah, ah, "his," "their" mother,—not "mine,"
    No voice says "*My* mother" again to me. What!
      You think Guido forgot?   60

— 13 —

Are souls straight so happy that, dizzy with Heaven,
    They drop earth's affections, conceive not of woe?
I think not. Themselves were too lately forgiven
    Through THAT Love and Sorrow which reconciled so
      The Above and Below.

— 14 —

O Christ of the five wounds, who look'dst through the dark
    To the face of Thy mother! consider, I pray,
How we common mothers stand desolate, mark,
    Whose sons, not being Christs, die with eyes turned
      away,
      And no last word to say!   70

— 15 —

Both boys dead? but that's out of nature. We all
    Have been patriots, yet each house must always keep
    one.
'Twere imbecile, hewing out roads to a wall;
    And, when Italy's made, for what end is it done
      If we have not a son?

— 16 —

Ah, ah, ah! when Gaeta's taken, what then?
    When the fair wicked queen[3] sits no more at her sport
Of the fire-balls of death crashing souls out of men?
    When the guns of Cavalli with final retort
      Have cut the game short?   80

— 17 —

When Venice and Rome keep their new jubilee,
    When your flag takes all heaven for its white, green,
    and red,
When *you* have your country from mountain to sea,
    When King Victor has Italy's crown on his head,[4]
      (And *I* have my Dead)—

— 18 —

What then? Do not mock me. Ah, ring your bells low,
    And burn your lights faintly! *My* country is *there,*

---

[2]**laurel**: the traditional reward of both victors and poets.

[3]**queen**: Maria, wife of the King of Naples against whom these battles were fought. **Cavalli**: general commanding siege of Gaeta.

[4]**Venice** became part of the new **Italy** in 1866, **Rome** in 1870. The Italian flag is **white, green, and red. Victor** Emmanuel II (1820–1878), king of Sardinia, became the first **King** of a united **Italy** in 1861.

Above the star pricked by the last peak of snow:
   My Italy's THERE, with my brave civic Pair,
      To disfranchise despair!   90

— 19 —

Forgive me. Some women bear children in strength,
   And bite back the cry of their pain in self-scorn;
But the birth-pangs of nations will wring us at length
   Into wail such as this—and we sit on forlorn
      When the man-child is born.

— 20 —

Dead! One of them shot by the sea in the east,
   And one of them shot in the west by the sea.
Both! both my boys! If in keeping the feast
   You want a great song for your Italy free,
      Let none look at *me!*   100
                                1862

Letter[1] from Robert Browning to Elizabeth Barrett

New Cross, Hatcham, Surrey.
[January 10, 1845]

I love your verses with all my heart, dear Miss Barrett,—and this is no off-hand complimentary letter that I shall write,—whatever else, no prompt matter-of-course recognition of your genius and there a graceful and natural end of the thing: since the day last week when I first read your poems,[2] I quite laugh to remember how I have been turning and turning again in my mind what I should be able to tell you of their effect upon me—for in the first flush of delight I thought I would this once get out of my habit of purely passive enjoyment, when I do really enjoy, and thoroughly justify my admiration—perhaps even, as a loyal fellow-craftsman should, try and find fault and do you some little good to be proud of hereafter!—but nothing comes of it all—so into me has it gone, and part of me has it become, this great living poetry of yours, not a flower of which but

took root and grew . . oh, how different that is from lying to be dried and pressed flat and prized highly and put in a book with a proper account at top and bottom, and shut up and put away . . and the book called a "Flora," besides! After all, I need not give up the thought of doing that, too, in time; because even now, talking with whoever is worthy, I can give a reason for my faith in one and another excellence, the fresh strange music, the affluent language, the exquisite pathos and true new brave thought—but in this addressing myself to you, your own self, and for the first time, my feeling rises altogether. I do, as I say, love these Books with all my heart—and I love you too: do you know I was once not very far from seeing . . really seeing you? Mr Kenyon[3] said to me one morning "would you like to see Miss Barrett?"—then he went to announce me,—then he returned . . you were too unwell—and now it is years ago—and I feel as at some untoward passage in my travels—as if I had been close, so close, to some world's-wonder in chapel or crypt, . . only a screen to push and I might have entered—but there was some slight . . so it now seems . . slight and just-sufficient bar to admission, and the half-opened door shut, and I went home my thousands of miles, and the sight was never to be!

Well, these Poems were to be—and this true thankful joy and pride with which I feel myself

                  Yours ever faithfully,
                  ROBERT BROWNING.
                          1899

Letter to Robert Browning from Elizabeth Barrett

50 Wimpole Street.
Jan. 11. 1845—

I thank you, dear M[r]. Browning, from the bottom of my heart. You meant to give me pleasure by your letter—and even if the object had not been answered, I ought still to thank you. But it is thoroughly answered. Such a letter from such a hand! Sympathy is dear—very dear to me: but the sympathy of a poet & of such a poet, is the quintessence of sympathy to me! Will you take back my gratitude for it?—agreeing too that, of all the commerce done in the world,

---

[1]The **Letters** are given here as transcribed from the manuscripts. Dots indicate the Brownings' punctuation, not editorial omissions.

[2]**poems:** Barrett's *Poems* (1844) contained "Lady Geraldine's Courtship," in which she praised Brownings' poetry for showing "a heart within blood-tinctured, of a veined humanity" (164).

---

[3]John **Kenyon** (1784–1856): Barrett's cousin.

from Tyre to Carthage,[1] the exchange of sympathy for gratitude is the most princely thing?

For the rest you draw me on with your kindness. It is difficult to get rid of people when you once have given them too much pleasure—*that* is a fact, & we will not stop for the moral of it. What I was going to say . . after a little natural hesitation . . is, that if ever you emerge without inconvenient effort from your "passive state," & will *tell* me of such faults as rise to the surface & strike you as important in my poems, (for of course, I do not think of troubling you with criticism in detail) you will confer a lasting obligation on me, and one which I shall value so much, that I covet it at a distance. I do not pretend to any extraordinary meekness under criticism—and it is possible enough that I might not be altogether obedient to yours. But with my high respect for your power in your Art & your experience as an artist, it w^d. be quite impossible for me to hear a general observation of yours on what appear to you my master-faults, without being the better for it hereafter in some way. I ask for only a sentence or two of general observation—and I do not ask even for *that*, so as to teaze you—but in the humble, low voice, which is so excellent a thing in women[2]—particularly when they go a-begging! The most frequent general criticism I receive, is, I think, upon the style—"if I *would* but change my style!"—But *that* is an objection (is'nt it?) to the writer bodily? Buffon says, & every sincere writer must feel, that *"Le style c'est l'homme—"*[3] a fact, however, scarcely calculated to lessen the objection, with certain critics.

---

[1]**Tyre** (in Lebanon) and its colony **Carthage** (near Tunis) were ancient commercial and trading cities.

[2]**low voice . . . women**: see *King Lear* 5.3.277–78.

[3]Charles **Buffon** (1707–1788): author of *Discours sur le style*, (1753). *"Le style c'est l'homme"*: "The style is the man."

Is it indeed true that I was so near to the pleasure & honour of making your acquaintance?—and can it be true that you look back upon the lost opportunity with any regret?——BUT, . . . you know, . . if you had entered the "crypt," you might have caught cold, or been tired to death, & *wished* yourself "a thousand miles off,"—which w^d. have been worse than travelling them. It is not my interest however to put such thoughts in your head about its' being "all for the best"!—& I would rather hope (as I do) that what I lost by one chance I may recover by some future one. Winters shut me up as they do dormouse's eyes: in the spring, *we shall see*: & I am so much better that I seem turning round to the outward world again. And in the meantime, I have learnt to know your voice, not merely from the poetry but from the kindness in it—M^r. Kenyon often speaks of you—dear M^r. Kenyon!—who most unspeakably, or only speakably with tears in my eyes, . . has been my friend & helper, & my book's friend & helper! critic & sympathizer . . true friend of all hours! You know him well enough, I think, to understand that I must be grateful to him.

I am writing too much, notwithstanding,—and notwithstanding that I am writing too much, I will write of one thing more. I will say that I am your debtor, not only for this cordial letter & for all the pleasure which came with it, but in other ways, & those the highest: & I will say that while I live to follow this divine art of poetry, . . in proportion to my love for it & my devotion to it, I must be a devout admirer & student of your works. This is in my heart to say to you—& I say it.

And, for the rest, I am proud to remain

Your obliged & faithful
ELIZABETH B BARRETT.
1899

ALFRED TENNYSON

(1809–1892)

Walt Whitman called him the Boss. Queen Victoria made him Poet Laureate in 1850 and raised him to the peerage in 1884. As early as the 1840s, Carlyle and other men of letters finagled him a government pension, and by the 1860s he had entered the tiny circle of poets who have ever, anywhere, become rich by writing verse. Such a career bespeaks extraordinary gifts, among them the gift of imagining a special relationship with the reading public and the spirit of the British nation, during an era when both were momentously changing and it was far from clear what role they expected modern poetry to play.

The role that Alfred Tennyson found for poetry drew primarily—and paradoxically, in light of his huge public success—on a deep fund of melancholy. He steps onto the poetic scene around 1830 as a connoisseur of heartbreak. From early poems like "Mariana" and "Oenone" all the way through to his final lyrics of delicately muted longing, he explores the losses of love and faith, seeking compensation in bonds between the self and other sufferers and between the chastened present and a richer past. This psychic economy of loss, along with an unflagging tact for deftly resonant phrasing, made Tennyson the prince of elegists at a time when the influence of Romanticism had predisposed poets toward commemorative modes of imaginative reflection. Almost as impressive as Tennyson's superb ear and knowledge of the sorrowing heart was the versatility with which he adapted both traditional and new literary genres to elegiac ends: dramatic monologue in "Locksley Hall" and "Tithonus," *Maud* and "Rizpah"; confessional autobiography in *In Memoriam*; bourgeois realist narrative in "Enoch Arden"; and national epic in *Idylls of the King* (represented here by its earliest installment, "Morte d'Arthur").

Tennyson was born into the large family of a well-educated but professionally stymied country clergyman whose black moods, heavy drinking, and early death darkened his children's lives. In 1828 Tennyson took to Cambridge, along with the melancholia bred by this upbringing, a talent for poetry that won him an honored place among the Apostles, an undergraduate society including several members who later attained national prominence. With their encouragement—especially that of his intimate friend Arthur Henry Hallam, a Londoner of brilliant prospects—the emerging poet followed up an 1827 book of accomplished juvenilia with the important *Poems* of 1830 and 1832. Then in 1833 Hallam died of a stroke, in distant Vienna, without warning. The effect of this sudden loss on Tennyson's already brooding imagination is inestimable. Although he would publish next to nothing for a decade, he drafted in rapid succession the germs of nearly all his most significant later works. Chief among these was *In Memoriam A. H. H.* (1850), which telescopes two decades' grief and recovery into a narrative of three years. *In Memoriam* offers an idealized yet emotionally compelling account of Tennyson's inward life across the 1830s and 1840s, a time when his outward life consisted in an extended bohemian bachelorhood diversified by family responsibilities, a languidly protracted courtship (he married Emily Sellwood in 1850), a spectacularly unsuccessful business investment, and a series of visits to a sanatorium that treated depression by diet and long body wraps in a wet sheet.

In Memoriam is at bottom a work of intense subjectivity whose wells of feeling the poet himself cannot fathom. Yet much of the success the poem enjoyed among Victorian readers is due to the inventive finesse with which Tennyson connects this private experience to the collective experience of his generation. The mourner's personal grief and renewal mirror the losses and gains that Victorians faced in the shifting religious and scientific, technological and commercial aspects of their lives; it was Tennyson's genius to find in geology, for example, metaphors for the cataclysmic or imperceptibly gradual forces that were transforming the landscape of the Victorian mind. Such imaginative linkage between the personal and the communal had also distinguished Tennyson's 1842 *Poems* and his romance-in-charade about women's higher education, *The Princess* (1847). *Maud* in 1855 and the four-book *Idylls of the King* in 1859 pursued the interaction of private with public causes surprisingly far into the terrain of daily life that was concurrently occupied in Victorian literature by the novel. At a time when prose fiction did not yet have the high prestige that traditionally belonged to poetry, Tennyson offered readers many of the pleasures provided by the novel while reassuring them about the value of literature and the dignity of the literary calling.

That calling, to which was added for more than forty years the vocation of Poet Laureate, placed Tennyson under unique pressures. His wife despite her invalidism became a shrewd career manager, his son Hallam a compliant amanuensis and archivist (whose notes on individual poems are sometimes quoted here). The Tennyson home became an attraction to tourists hoping for a glimpse of the long-haired, bearded poet patrolling his acres in cape and sombrero. Every celebrity of the day felt obliged to pay a social call on Tennyson, and every poetaster felt entitled to make a professional one. Worse than these annoyances of fame was the expectation, from the 1870s onward, that he would pontificate in the manner of a sage and articulate imperial Britain's virtue and merit. Although this job was by the highest standard of integrity an impossible one, Tennyson nevertheless discharged it with honor. He kept up with current events on the global scene and in the sphere of ideas and scientific research, combining a sharp layman's curiosity with a visionary's apprehension of consequences. He largely avoided the occupational hazard of toadying to power in exhibition verse: his Wellington ode exhorts to national virtue under pretext of praise, and his famous verses on the fate of the Light Brigade derive their bitter pathos from the fact that "Someone had blundered."

In matters of ultimate belief Tennyson's compromises between intellectual agnosticism and an impulse to reverence are notoriously vague, yet they are honestly vague. He merely *hopes* to see his Pilot after crossing the bar of death, and this is as strongly as he puts the matter. When *In Memoriam* declares, "There lives more faith in honest doubt, / Believe me, than in half the creeds," he means it—all the way up to the witty deprecation of that tell-tale "Believe." From his unique vantage point at the microphone of Victorian culture, Tennyson entrusted to the public a cluster of insecurities that were broadly shared, if imprecisely understood. He made them the more bearable through the authority of a poetic voice, a feel for the nuanced weight of words, that remained sure even when nothing else did.

Mariana

Mariana in the moated grange.

Measure for Measure[1]

With blackest moss the flower-plots
    Were thickly crusted, one and all:
The rusted nails fell from the knots
    That held the pear to the gable-wall.
The broken sheds look'd sad and strange:
    Unlifted was the clinking latch;
    Weeded and worn the ancient thatch
Upon the lonely moated grange.
        She only said, "My life is dreary,
            He cometh not," she said;   10
        She said, "I am aweary, aweary,
            I would that I were dead!"

Her tears fell with the dews at even;
    Her tears fell ere the dews were dried;
She could not look on the sweet heaven,
    Either at morn or eventide.
After the flitting of the bats,
    When thickest dark did trance the sky,
    She drew her casement-curtain by,
And glanced athwart the glooming flats.   20
        She only said, "The night is dreary,
            He cometh not," she said;
        She said, "I am aweary, aweary,
            I would that I were dead!"

Upon the middle of the night,
    Waking she heard the night-fowl crow:
The cock sung out an hour ere light:
    From the dark fen the oxen's low
Came to her: without hope of change,
    In sleep she seem'd to walk forlorn,   30
    Till cold winds woke the gray-eyed morn
About the lonely moated grange.
        She only said, "The day is dreary,
            He cometh not," she said;
        She said, "I am aweary, aweary,
            I would that I were dead!"

About a stone-cast from the wall
    A sluice with blacken'd waters slept,
And o'er it many, round and small,
    The cluster'd marish-mosses crept.   40
Hard by a poplar shook alway,
    All silver-green with gnarlèd bark:
    For leagues no other tree did mark
The level waste, the rounding gray.
        She only said, "My life is dreary,
            He cometh not," she said;
        She said, "I am aweary, aweary,
            I would that I were dead!"

And ever when the moon was low,
    And the shrill winds were up and away,   50
In the white curtain, to and fro,
    She saw the gusty shadow sway.
But when the moon was very low,
    And wild winds bound within their cell,
    The shadow of the poplar fell
Upon her bed, across her brow.
        She only said, "The night is dreary,
            He cometh not," she said;
        She said, "I am aweary, aweary,
            I would that I were dead!"   60

All day within the dreamy house,
    The doors upon their hinges creak'd;
The blue fly sung in the pane; the mouse
    Behind the mouldering wainscot shriek'd,
Or from the crevice peer'd about.
    Old faces glimmer'd thro' the doors,
    Old footsteps trod the upper floors,
Old voices called her from without.
        She only said, "My life is dreary,
            He cometh not," she said;   70
        She said, "I am aweary, aweary,
            I would that I were dead!"

The sparrow's chirrup on the roof,
    The slow clock ticking, and the sound
Which to the wooing wind aloof
    The poplar made, did all confound
Her sense; but most she loathed the hour
    When the thick-moted sunbeam lay
    Athwart the chambers, and the day
Was sloping toward his western bower.   80
        Then, said she, "I am very dreary,
            He will not come," she said;
        She wept, "I am aweary, aweary,
            Oh God, that I were dead!"

[1]**moated grange:** *Measure for Measure* 3.1 (end of scene).

1830

Song

— 1 —

A spirit haunts the year's last hours
Dwelling amid these yellowing bowers.
　　To himself he talks;
For at eventide, listening earnestly,
At his work you may hear him sob and sigh
　　In the walks;
　　Earthward he boweth the heavy stalks
Of the mouldering flowers.
　　Heavily hangs the broad sunflower
　　　　Over its grave i' the earth so chilly;　10
　　Heavily hangs the hollyhock,
　　　　Heavily hangs the tiger-lily.

— 2 —

The air is damp, and hush'd, and close,
As a sick man's room when he taketh repose
　　An hour before death;
My very heart faints and my whole soul grieves
At the moist rich smell of the rotting leaves,
　　And the breath
　　Of the fading edges of box beneath,
And the year's last rose.　　　　　　　　　20
　　Heavily hangs the broad sunflower
　　　　Over its grave i' the earth so chilly;
　　Heavily hangs the hollyhock,
　　　　Heavily hangs the tiger-lily.

　　　　　　　　　　　　　　　　1830

The Kraken[1]

Below the thunders of the upper deep;
Far, far beneath in the abysmal sea,
His ancient, dreamless, uninvaded sleep
The Kraken sleepeth: faintest sunlights flee
About his shadowy sides: above him swell
Huge sponges of millennial growth and height;

And far away into the sickly light,
From many a wondrous grot and secret cell
Unnumber'd and enormous polypi
Winnow with giant arms the slumbering green. 10
There hath he lain for ages and will lie
Battening upon huge seaworms in his sleep,
Until the latter fire shall heat the deep;[2]
Then once by man and angels to be seen,
In roaring he shall rise and on the surface die.

　　　　　　　　　　　　　　　　1830

The Hesperides

"Hesperus and his daughters three,
That sing about the golden tree."

　　　　　　　　　　　　　　　Comus[1]

The North-wind fall'n, in the new-starréd night
Zidonian Hanno,[2] voyaging beyond
The hoary promontory of Soloë
Past Thymiaterion, in calméd bays,
Between the southern and the western Horn,
Heard neither warbling of the nightingale,
Nor melody of the Libyan lotus flute
Blown seaward from the shore; but from a slope
That ran bloom-bright into the Atlantic blue,
Beneath a highland leaning down a weight　　10
Of cliffs, and zoned below with cedar shade,
Came voices, like the voices in a dream,
Continuous, till he reached the outer sea.

— SONG —

1

The golden apple, the golden apple, the hallowed fruit,
Guard it well, guard it warily,
Singing airily,

---

[2]**latter fire . . . deep**: see Revelation 8:8–9.

[1]**"Hesperus . . . golden tree"**: Milton, *Comus* (1634) 982–83, referring to the fabled western garden of Hesperus, the evening star, protected by his daughters and the dragon whom their singing keeps awake. The theft of the Hesperides' golden apples was the eleventh labor of Hercules.

[2]**Hanno**: Carthaginian (**Zidonian**) mariner of the 5th century BCE who mapped the west coast of Africa, founding **Thymiaterion** and building a temple at **Soloë** in present-day Morocco.

---

[1]**Kraken**: fabulous sea creature described by Scandinavian bishop Erik Pontoppidan (1698–1764) in *The Natural History of Norway* (trans. 1755).

Standing about the charmèd root.
Round about all is mute,
As the snow-field on the mountain-peaks,
As the sand-field at the mountain-foot.   20
Crocodiles in briny creeks
Sleep and stir not: all is mute.
If ye sing not, if ye make false measure,
We shall lose eternal pleasure,
Worth eternal want of rest.
Laugh not loudly: watch the treasure
Of the wisdom of the West.
In a corner wisdom whispers. Five and three
(Let it not be preached abroad) make an awful mystery.[3]
For the blossom unto threefold music bloweth;   30
Evermore it is born anew;
And the sap to threefold music floweth,
From the root
Drawn in the dark,
Up to the fruit,
Creeping under the fragrant bark,
Liquid gold, honeysweet, thro' and thro'.
Keen-eyed Sisters, singing airily,
Looking warily
Every way,   40
Guard the apple night and day,
Lest one from the East come and take it away.

2

Father Hesper, Father Hesper, watch, watch, ever and aye,
Looking under silver hair with a silver eye.
Father, twinkle not thy steadfast sight;
Kingdoms lapse, and climates change, and races die;
Honor comes with mystery;
Hoarded wisdom brings delight.
Number, tell them over and number
How many the mystic fruit-tree holds   50
Lest the red-combed dragon slumber
Rolled together in purple folds.
Look to him, father, lest he wink, and the golden apple
    be stol'n away,
For his ancient heart is drunk with overwatchings night
    and day,
Round about the hallowed fruit-tree curled—
Sing away, sing aloud evermore in the wind, without stop,
Lest his scalèd eyelid drop,

For he is older than the world.
If he waken, we waken,
Rapidly levelling eager eyes.   60
If he sleep, we sleep,
Dropping the eyelid over the eyes.
If the golden apple be taken,
The world will be overwise.
Five links, a golden chain, are we,
Hesper, the dragon, and sisters three,
Bound about the golden tree.

3

Father Hesper, Father Hesper, watch, watch, night and day,
Lest the old wound of the world be healèd,
The glory unsealèd,   70
The golden apple stol'n away,
And the ancient secret revealèd.
Look from west to east along:
Father, old Himala weakens, Caucasus[4] is bold and strong.
Wandering waters unto wandering waters call;
Let them clash together, foam and fall.
Out of watchings, out of wiles,
Comes the bliss of secret smiles.
All things are not told to all.
Half-round the mantling night is drawn,   80
Purple fringèd with even and dawn.
Hesper hateth Phosphor,[5] evening hateth morn.

4

Every flower and every fruit the redolent breath
Of this warm sea-wind ripeneth,
Arching the billow in his sleep;
But the land-wind wandereth,
Broken by the highland-steep,
Two streams upon the violet deep;
For the western sun and the western star,
And the low west-wind, breathing afar,   90
The end of the day and beginning of night
Make the apple holy and bright;
Holy and bright, round and full, bright and blest,
Mellowed in a land of rest;
Watch it warily day and night;
All good things are in the west.
Till mid noon the cool east light

---

[3]**Five and three:** numbers portending enigmatic **mystery** by suggesting numerological meanings (which scholarship has yet to uncover).

[4]**Himala:** great mountain range of India. **Caucasus:** mountain range dividing Europe from Asia, here representing the idea that empire migrates westward.

[5]**Phosphor:** the morning star.

Is shut out by the tall hillbrow;
But when the full-faced sunset yellowly
Stays on the flowering arch of the bough,   100
The luscious fruitage clustereth mellowly,
Golden-kernelled, golden-cored,
Sunset-ripened above on the tree.
The world is wasted with fire and sword,
But the apple of gold hangs over the sea.
Five links, a golden chain are we,
Hesper, the dragon, and sisters three,
Daughters three,
Bound about
The gnarléd bole of the charméd tree.   110
The golden apple, the golden apple, the hallowed fruit,
Guard it well, guard it warily,
Watch it warily,
Singing airily,
Standing about the charméd root.

                                                   1832

The Lady of Shalott[1]

— PART 1 —

On either side the river lie
Long fields of barley and of rye,
That clothe the wold and meet the sky;
And thro' the field the road runs by
    To many-tower'd Camelot;
And up and down the people go,
Gazing where the lilies blow
Round an island there below,
    The island of Shalott.

Willows whiten, aspens quiver,   10
Little breezes dusk and shiver
Thro' the wave that runs for ever
By the island in the river
    Flowing down to Camelot.
Four gray walls, and four gray towers,
Overlook a space of flowers,
And the silent isle imbowers
    The Lady of Shalott.

By the margin, willow-veil'd,
Slide the heavy barges trail'd   20

By slow horses; and unhail'd
The shallop flitteth silken-sail'd
    Skimming down to Camelot:
But who hath seen her wave her hand?
Or at the casement seen her stand?
Or is she known in all the land,
    The Lady of Shalott?

Only reapers, reaping early
In among the bearded barley,
Hear a song that echoes cheerly   30
From the river winding clearly,
    Down to tower'd Camelot;
And by the moon the reaper weary,
Piling sheaves in uplands airy,
Listening, whispers" 'Tis the fairy
    Lady of Shalott."

— PART 2 —

There she weaves by night and day
A magic web with colours gay.
She has heard a whisper say,
A curse is on her if she stay   40
    To look down to Camelot.
She knows not what the curse may be,
And so she weaveth steadily,
And little other care hath she,
    The Lady of Shalott.

And moving thro' a mirror[2] clear
That hangs before her all the year,
Shadows of the world appear.
There she sees the highway near
    Winding down to Camelot: 50
There the river eddy whirls,
And there the surly village-churls,
And the red cloaks of market girls,
    Pass onward from Shalott.

Sometimes a troop of damsels glad,
An abbot on an ambling pad,[3]
Sometimes a curly shepherd-lad,
Or long-hair'd page in crimson clad,
    Goes by to tower'd Camelot;
And sometimes thro' the mirror blue   60
The knights come riding two and two:
She hath no loyal knight and true,
    The Lady of Shalott.

---

[1]**Shalott**: imaginary location derived from the Italian Scalotta in Tennyson's medieval Arthurian source. The 1832 version differs significantly from the 1842 revision printed here.

[2]**mirror**: a tool of the tapestry weaver, who while knotting the rough side sees in the mirror how the finished side will look.
[3]**pad**: horse.

But in her web she still delights
To weave the mirror's magic sights,
For often thro' the silent nights
A funeral, with plumes and lights
    And music, went to Camelot;
Or when the moon was overhead,
Came two young lovers lately wed;   70
"I am half sick of shadows," said
    The Lady of Shalott.

yearing

— PART 3 —

A bow-shot from her bower-eaves,
He rode between the barley-sheaves,
The sun came dazzling thro' the leaves,
And flamed upon the brazen greaves
    Of bold Sir Lancelot.
A red-cross knight for ever kneel'd
To a lady in his shield,
That sparkled on the yellow field,   80
    Beside remote Shalott.

The gemmy bridle glitter'd free,
Like to some branch of stars we see
Hung in the golden Galaxy.
The bridle bells rang merrily
    As he rode down to Camelot:
And from his blazon'd baldric slung
A mighty silver bugle hung,
And as he rode his armor rung,
    Beside remote Shalott.   90

All in the blue unclouded weather
Thick-jewell'd shone the saddle-leather,
The helmet and the helmet-feather
Burn'd like one burning flame together,
    As he rode down to Camelot;
As often thro' the purple night,
Below the starry clusters bright,
Some bearded meteor, trailing light,
    Moves over still Shalott.

His broad clear brow in sunlight glow'd;   100
On burnish'd hooves his war-horse trode;
From underneath his helmet flow'd
His coal-black curls as on he rode,
    As he rode down to Camelot.
From the bank and from the river
He flash'd into the crystal mirror,
"Tirra lirra," by the river
    Sang Sir Lancelot.

She left the web, she left the loom,
She made three paces thro' the room,   110
She saw the water-lily bloom,
She saw the helmet and the plume,
    She look'd down to Camelot.
Out flew the web and floated wide;
The mirror crack'd from side to side;
"The curse is come upon me," cried
    The Lady of Shalott.

— PART 4 —

In the stormy east-wind straining,
The pale yellow woods were waning,
The broad stream in his banks complaining,   120
Heavily the low sky raining
    Over tower'd Camelot;
Down she came and found a boat
Beneath a willow left afloat.
And round about the prow she wrote
    The Lady of Shalott.

And down the river's dim expanse
Like some bold seër in a trance,
Seeing all his own mischance—
With a glassy countenance   130
    Did she look to Camelot.
And at the closing of the day
She loosed the chain, and down she lay;
The broad stream bore her far away,
    The Lady of Shalott.

Lying, robed in snowy white
That loosely flew to left and right—
The leaves upon her falling light—
Thro' the noises of the night
    She floated down to Camelot: 140
And as the boat-head wound along
The willowy hills and fields among,
They heard her singing her last song,
    The Lady of Shalott.

Heard a carol, mournful, holy,
Chanted loudly, chanted lowly,
Till her blood was frozen slowly,
And her eyes were darken'd wholly,
    Turn'd to tower'd Camelot.
For ere she reach'd upon the tide   150
The first house by the water-side,
Singing in her song she died,
    The Lady of Shalott.

Under tower and balcony,
By garden-wall and gallery,
A gleaming shape she floated by,
Dead-pale between the houses high,
    Silent into Camelot.
Out upon the wharfs they came,
Knight and burgher, lord and dame,   160
And round the prow they read her name,
    The Lady of Shalott.

Who is this? and what is here?
And in the lighted palace near
Died the sound of royal cheer;
And they cross'd themselves for fear,
    All the knights at Camelot:
But Lancelot mused a little space;
He said, "She has a lovely face;
God in his mercy lend her grace,   170
    The Lady of Shalott."

            1832, 1842

Œnone

There lies a vale in Ida,[1] lovelier
Than all the valleys of Ionian hills.
The swimming vapour slopes athwart the glen,
Puts forth an arm, and creeps from pine to pine,
And loiters, slowly drawn. On either hand
The lawns and meadow-ledges midway down
Hang rich in flowers, and far below them roars
The long brook falling thro' the clov'n ravine
In cataract after cataract to the sea.
Behind the valley topmost Gargarus   10
Stands up and takes the morning; but in front
The gorges, opening wide apart, reveal
Troas and Ilion's column'd citadel,
The crown of Troas.
          Hither came at noon
Mournful Œnone,[2] wandering forlorn

Of Paris, once her playmate on the hills.
Her cheek had lost the rose, and round her neck
Floated her hair or seem'd to float in rest.
She, leaning on a fragment twined with vine,
Sang to the stillness, till the mountain-shade   20
Sloped downward to her seat from the upper cliff.

    "O mother Ida, many-fountain'd Ida,
Dear mother Ida, harken ere I die.
For now the noonday quiet holds the hill:
The grasshopper is silent in the grass:
The lizard, with his shadow on the stone,
Rests like a shadow, and the winds are dead.
The purple flower droops, the golden bee
Is lily-cradled; I alone awake.
My eyes are full of tears, my heart of love,   30
My heart is breaking, and my eyes are dim,
And I am all aweary of my life.

    "O mother Ida, many-fountain'd Ida,
Dear mother Ida, harken ere I die.
Hear me, O Earth, hear me, O Hills, O Caves
That house the cold crown'd snake! O mountain brooks,
I am the daughter of a River-God,
Hear me, for I will speak, and build up all
My sorrow with my song, as yonder walls
Rose slowly to a music slowly breathed,   40
A cloud that gather'd shape; for it may be
That, while I speak of it, a little while
My heart may wander from its deeper woe.

    "O mother Ida, many-fountain'd Ida,
Dear mother Ida, harken ere I die.
I waited underneath the dawning hills,
Aloft the mountain lawn was dewy-dark,
And dewy-dark aloft the mountain pine:
Beautiful Paris, evil-hearted Paris,
Leading a jet-black goat white-horn'd,
        white-hooved,   50
Came up from reedy Simois[3] all alone.

    "O mother Ida, harken ere I die.
Far-off the torrent call'd me from the cleft:
Far up the solitary morning smote
The streaks of virgin snow. With down-dropt eyes
I sat alone; white-breasted like a star
Fronting the dawn he moved; a leopard skin
Droop'd from his shoulder, but his sunny hair
Cluster'd about his temples like a God's:
And his cheek brighten'd as the foam-bow brightens 60

---

[1]**Ida**: mountain in **Ionian** (westernmost) region of Asia Minor bordering the Aegean Sea and including **Troas**, the territory around the ancient city of **Troy** or **Ilion**, which is visible from **Gargarus**, Mt. Ida's summit.

[2]**Œnone**: a nymph, daughter of a river god and of the mountain mother to whom she addresses her lament. **Paris**: Trojan prince who abandoned Œnone for Helen—the beautiful Greek queen who will be immortalized as Helen of Troy—in consequence of the events the poem narrates.

---

[3]**Simois**: river on the plain of Troy.

When the wind blows the foam, and all my heart
Went forth to embrace him coming ere he came.

"Dear mother Ida, harken ere I die.
He smiled, and opening out his milk-white palm
Disclosed a fruit of pure Hesperian[4] gold,
That smelt ambrosially, and while I look'd
And listen'd, the full-flowing river of speech
Came down upon my heart.

                          " 'My own Œnone,
Beautiful-brow'd Œnone, my own soul,
Behold this fruit, whose gleaming rind ingraven   70
"For the most fair," would seem to award it thine,
As lovelier than whatever Oread[5] haunt
The knolls of Ida, loveliest in all grace
Of movement, and the charm of married brows.'

"Dear mother Ida, harken ere I die.
He prest the blossom of his lips to mine,
And added, 'This was cast upon the board,
When all the full-faced presence of the Gods
Ranged in the halls of Peleus;[6] whereupon
Rose feud, with question unto whom 'twere due: 80
But light-foot Iris brought it yester-eve,
Delivering, that to me, by common voice
Elected umpire, Herè comes to-day,
Pallas and Aphroditè,[7] claiming each
This meed of fairest. Thou, within the cave
Behind yon whispering tuft of oldest pine,
Mayst well behold them unbeheld, unheard
Hear all, and see thy Paris judge of Gods.'

"Dear mother Ida, harken ere I die.
It was the deep midnoon: one silvery cloud   90
Had lost his way between the piney sides
Of this long glen. Then to the bower they came,
Naked they came to that smooth-swarded bower,
And at their feet the crocus brake like fire,
Violet, amaracus,[8] and asphodel,
Lotos and lilies; and a wind arose,
And overhead the wandering ivy and vine,
This way and that, in many a wild festoon

Ran riot, garlanding the gnarled boughs
With bunch and berry and flower thro' and thro'.   100

"O mother Ida, harken ere I die.
On the tree-tops a crested peacock lit,
And o'er him flow'd a golden cloud, and lean'd
Upon him, slowly dropping fragrant dew.
Then first I heard the voice of her, to whom
Coming thro' Heaven, like a light that grows
Larger and clearer, with one mind the Gods
Rise up for reverence. She to Paris made
Proffer of royal power, ample rule
Unquestion'd, overflowing revenue   110
Wherewith to embellish state, 'from many a vale
And river-sunder'd champaign clothed with corn,
Or labour'd mine undrainable of ore.
Honour,' she said, 'and homage, tax and toll,
From many an inland town and haven large,
Mast-throng'd beneath her shadowing citadel
In glassy bays among her tallest towers.'

"O mother Ida, harken ere I die.
Still she spake on and still she spake of power,
'Which in all action is the end of all;   120
Power fitted to the season; wisdom-bred
And throned of wisdom—from all neighbour crowns
Alliance and allegiance, till thy hand
Fail from the sceptre-staff. Such boon from me,
From me, Heaven's Queen, Paris, to thee king-born,
A shepherd all thy life but yet king-born,
Should come most welcome, seeing men, in power
Only, are likest Gods, who have attain'd
Rest in a happy place and quiet seats
Above the thunder, with undying bliss   130
In knowledge of their own supremacy.'

"Dear mother Ida, harken ere I die.
She ceased, and Paris held the costly fruit
Out at arm's-length, so much the thought of power
Flatter'd his spirit; but Pallas where she stood
Somewhat apart, her clear and bared limbs
O'erthwarted with the brazen-headed spear
Upon her pearly shoulder leaning cold,
The while, above, her full and earnest eye
Over her snow-cold breast and angry cheek   140
Kept watch, waiting decision, made reply.

" 'Self-reverence, self-knowledge, self-control,
These three alone lead life to sovereign power.
Yet not for power (power of herself
Would come uncall'd for) but to live by law,
Acting the law we live by without fear;

---

[4]**Hesperian**: from the garden of Hesperus; see "The Hesperides," page 383.

[5]**Oread**: mountain nymph.

[6]**Peleus**: Greek king, father of Achilles. **Iris**: divine messenger, goddess of the rainbow.

[7]**Herè**: wife of Zeus and queen of Olympus. **Pallas Athene**: goddess of wisdom. **Aphroditè**: goddess of beauty.

[8]**amaracus**: aromatic medicinal plant (dittany).

And, because right is right, to follow right
Were wisdom in the scorn of consequence.'

    "Dear mother Ida, harken ere I die.
Again she said: 'I woo thee not with gifts.   150
Sequel of guerdon[9] could not alter me
To fairer. Judge thou me by what I am,
So shalt thou find me fairest.
                                Yet, indeed,
If gazing on divinity disrobed
Thy mortal eyes are frail to judge of fair,
Unbias'd by self-profit, oh! rest thee sure
That I shall love thee well and cleave to thee,
So that my vigour, wedded to thy blood,
Shall strike within thy pulses, like a God's,
To push thee forward thro' a life of shocks,   160
Dangers, and deeds, until endurance grow
Sinew'd with action, and the full-grown will,
Circled thro' all experiences, pure law,
Commeasure perfect freedom.'
                                "Here she ceas'd,
And Paris ponder'd, and I cried, 'O Paris,
Give it to Pallas!' but he heard me not,
Or hearing would not hear me, woe is me!

    "O mother Ida, many-fountain'd Ida,
Dear mother Ida, harken ere I die.
Idalian Aphroditè beautiful,   170
Fresh as the foam, new-bathed in Paphian[10] wells,
With rosy slender fingers backward drew
From her warm brows and bosom her deep hair
Ambrosial, golden round her lucid throat
And shoulder: from the violets her light foot
Shone rosy-white, and o'er her rounded form
Between the shadows of the vine-bunches
Floated the glowing sunlights, as she moved.

    "Dear mother Ida, harken ere I die.   180
She with a subtle smile in her mild eyes,
The herald of her triumph, drawing nigh
Half-whisper'd in his ear, 'I promise thee
The fairest and most loving wife in Greece,'[11]
She spoke and laugh'd; I shut my sight for fear;
But when I look'd, Paris had raised his arm,
And I beheld great Herè's angry eyes,

As she withdrew into the golden cloud,
And I was left alone within the bower;
And from that time to this I am alone,
And I shall be alone until I die.   190

    "Yet, mother Ida, harken ere I die.
Fairest—why fairest wife? am I not fair?
My love hath told me so a thousand times.
Methinks I must be fair, for yesterday,
When I past by, a wild and wanton pard,
Eyed like the evening star, with playful tail
Crouch'd fawning in the weed. Most loving is she?
Ah me, my mountain shepherd, that my arms
Were wound about thee, and my hot lips prest
Close, close to thine in that quick-falling dew   200
Of fruitful kisses, thick as Autumn rains
Flash in the pools of whirling Simois!

    "O mother, hear me yet before I die.
They came, they cut away my tallest pines,
My tall dark pines, that plumed the craggy ledge
High over the blue gorge, and all between
The snowy peak and snow-white cataract
Foster'd the callow eaglet—from beneath
Whose thick mysterious boughs in the dark morn
The panther's roar came muffled, while I sat   210
Low in the valley. Never, never more
Shall lone Œnone see the morning mist
Sweep thro' them; never see them overlaid
With narrow moon-lit slips of silver cloud,
Between the loud stream and the trembling stars.

    "O mother, hear me yet before I die.
I wish that somewhere in the ruin'd folds,
Among the fragments tumbled from the glens,
Or the dry thickets, I could meet with her
The Abominable,[12] that uninvited came   220
Into the fair Peleïan banquet-hall,
And cast the golden fruit upon the board,
And bred this change; that I might speak my mind,
And tell her to her face how much I hate
Her presence, hated both of Gods and men.

    "O mother, hear me yet before I die.
Hath he not sworn his love a thousand times,
In this green valley, under this green hill,
Ev'n on this hand, and sitting on this stone?
Seal'd it with kisses? water'd it with tears?   230
O happy tears, and how unlike to these!
O happy Heaven, how canst thou see my face?

---

[9]**Sequel of guerdon**: addition of reward. [Tennyson's note]

[10]**Idalian**: of Mt. Ida. **Paphian**: from Paphos, site of a major temple to Aphrodite.

[11]**wife**: Helen, already married to the Greek King Menelaus, who will respond to her abduction by inciting the Trojan War.

---

[12]**the Abominable**: Eris, goddess of strife.

O happy earth, how canst thou bear my weight?
O death, death, death, thou ever-floating cloud,
There are enough unhappy on this earth,
Pass by the happy souls, that love to live:
I pray thee, pass before my light of life,
And shadow all my soul, that I may die.
Thou weighest heavy on the heart within,
Weigh heavy on my eyelids: let me die.   240

"O mother, hear me yet before I die.
I will not die alone, for fiery thoughts
Do shape themselves within me, more and more,
Whereof I catch the issue, as I hear
Dead sounds at night come from the inmost hills,
Like footsteps upon wool. I dimly see
My far-off doubtful purpose, as a mother
Conjectures of the features of her child
Ere it is born: her child!—a shudder comes
Across me: never child be born of me,   250
Unblest, to vex me with his father's eyes!

"O mother, hear me yet before I die.
Hear me, O earth. I will not die alone,
Lest their shrill happy laughter come to me
Walking the cold and starless road of Death
Uncomforted, leaving my ancient love
With the Greek woman. I will rise and go
Down into Troy, and ere the stars come forth
Talk with the wild Cassandra,[13] for she says
A fire dances before her, and a sound   260
Rings ever in her ears of armed men.
What this may be I know not, but I know
That, wheresoe'er I am by night and day,
All earth and air seem only burning fire."

                              1832, 1842

To ————[1]

With the Following Poem

I send you here a sort of allegory,
(For you will understand it) of a soul,
A sinful soul possess'd of many gifts,

---

[13]**Cassandra:** Trojan princess gifted/cursed by Apollo to make prophecies that were always true and never believed.

[1]**To** ————: addressed to Tennyson's college acquaintance R. C. Trench, who had warned, "Tennyson, we cannot live in Art."

A spacious garden full of flowering weeds,
A glorious Devil, large in heart and brain,
That did love Beauty only, (Beauty seen
In all varieties of mould and mind)
And Knowledge for its beauty; or if Good,
Good only for its beauty, seeing not
That Beauty, Good, and Knowledge are three sisters 10
That doat upon each other, friends to man,
Living together under the same roof,
And never can be sunder'd without tears.
And he that shuts Love out, in turn shall be
Shut out from Love, and on her threshold lie
Howling in outer darkness. Not for this
Was common clay[2] ta'en from the common earth
Moulded by God, and temper'd with the tears
Of angels to the perfect shape of man.

                              1832, 1842

The Palace of Art

I built my soul a lordly pleasure-house,
    Wherein at ease for aye to dwell.
I said, "O Soul, make merry and carouse,
    Dear soul, for all is well."

A huge crag-platform, smooth as burnish'd brass,
    I chose. The ranged ramparts bright
From level meadow-bases of deep grass
    Suddenly scaled the light.

Thereon I built it firm. Of ledge or shelf
    The rock rose clear, or winding stair.   10
My soul would live alone unto herself
    In her high palace there.

And "while the world runs round and round," I said,
    "Reign thou apart, a quiet king,
Still as, while Saturn whirls, his stedfast shade
    Sleeps on his luminous ring."[3]

To which my soul made answer readily:
    "Trust me, in bliss I shall abide
In this great mansion, that is built for me,
    So royal-rich and wide."   20

---

[2]**common clay:** see Genesis 2:7.

[3]**Saturn . . . ring:** The shadow of Saturn thrown on the luminous ring, though the planet revolves in ten and a half hours, appears to be motionless. [Hallam Tennyson's note]

* * * *

Four courts I made, East, West and South and North,
   In each a squared lawn, wherefrom
The golden gorge of dragons spouted forth
   A flood of fountain-foam.

And round the cool green courts there ran a row
   Of cloisters, branch'd like mighty woods,
Echoing all night to that sonorous flow
   Of spouted fountain-floods.

And round the roofs a gilded gallery
   That lent broad verge to distant lands,   30
Far as the wild swan wings, to where the sky
   Dipt down to sea and sands.

From those four jets four currents in one swell
   Across the mountain stream'd below
In misty folds, that floating as they fell
   Lit up a torrent-bow.

And high on every peak a statue seem'd
   To hang on tiptoe, tossing up
A cloud of incense of all odour steam'd
   From out a golden cup.   40

So that she thought, "And who shall gaze upon
   My palace with unblinded eyes,
While this great bow will waver in the sun,
   And that sweet incense rise?"

For that sweet incense rose and never fail'd,
   And, while day sank or mounted higher,
The light aërial gallery, golden-rail'd,
   Burnt like a fringe of fire.

Likewise, the deep-set windows, stain'd and traced,
   Would seem slow-flaming crimson fires   50
From shadow'd grots of arches interlaced,
   And tipt with frost-like spires.

* * * *

Full of long-sounding corridors it was,
   That over-vaulted grateful gloom,
Thro' which the livelong day my soul did pass,
   Well-pleased, from room to room.

Full of great rooms and small the palace stood,
   All various, each a perfect whole
From living Nature, fit for every mood
   And change of my still soul.   60

For some were hung with arras green and blue,
   Showing a gaudy summer-morn,

Where with puff'd cheek the belted hunter blew
   His wreathed bugle-horn.

One seem'd all dark and red—a tract of sand,
   And some one pacing there alone,
Who paced for ever in a glimmering land,
   Lit with a low large moon.

One show'd an iron coast and angry waves.
   You seem'd to hear them climb and call   70
And roar rock-thwarted under bellowing caves,
   Beneath the windy wall.

And one, a full-fed river winding slow
   By herds upon an endless plain,
The ragged rims of thunder brooding low,
   With shadow-streaks of rain.

And one, the reapers at their sultry toil.
   In front they bound the sheaves. Behind
Were realms of upland, prodigal in oil,
   And hoary[4] to the wind.   80

And one a foreground black with stones and slags,
   Beyond, a line of heights, and higher
All barr'd with long white cloud the scornful crags,
   And highest, snow and fire.

And one, an English home—gray twilight pour'd
   On dewy pastures, dewy trees,
Softer than sleep—all things in order stored,
   A haunt of ancient Peace.

Nor these alone, but every landscape fair,
   As fit for every mood of mind,   90
Or gay, or grave, or sweet, or stern, was there,
   Not less than truth design'd.

* * * *

Or the maid-mother by a crucifix.
   In tracts of pasture sunny-warm.
Beneath branch-work of costly sardonyx
   Sat smiling, babe in arm.

Or in a clear-wall'd city on the sea,
   Near gilded organ-pipes, her hair
Wound with white roses, slept Saint Cecily;[5]
   An angel look'd at her.   100

---

[4]**hoary:** The underside of the olive leaf is white. [Tennyson's note]

[5]**Saint Cecily:** Cecilia, patron saint of sacred music.

Or thronging all one porch of Paradise
    A group of Houris bow'd to see
The dying Islamite, with hands and eyes
    That said, We wait for thee.

Or mythic Uther's deeply-wounded son[6]
    In some fair space of sloping greens
Lay, dozing in the vale of Avalon,
    And watch'd by weeping queens.

Or hollowing one hand against his ear,
    To list a foot-fall, ere he saw   110
The wood-nymph, stay'd the Ausonian king[7] to hear
    Of wisdom and of law.

Or over hills with peaky tops engrail'd,
    And many a tract of palm and rice,
The throne of Indian Cama[8] slowly sail'd
    A summer fann'd with spice.

Or sweet Europa's[9] mantle blew unclasp'd,
    From off her shoulder backward borne:
From one hand droop'd a crocus: one hand grasp'd
    The mild bull's golden horn.   120

Or else flush'd Ganymede,[10] his rosy thigh
    Half-buried in the Eagle's down,
Sole as a flying star shot thro' the sky
    Above the pillar'd town.

Nor these alone: but every legend fair
    Which the supreme Caucasian[11] mind
Carved out of Nature for itself was there,
    Not less than life design'd.

        *   *   *   *

Then in the towers I placed great bells that swung,
    Moved of themselves, with silver sound;   130
And with choice paintings of wise men I hung
    The royal dais round.

For there was Milton like a seraph strong,
    Beside him Shakespeare bland and mild;
And there the world-worn Dante grasp'd his song,
    And somewhat grimly smiled.

And there the Ionian father[12] of the rest;
    A million wrinkles carved his skin;
A hundred winters show'd upon his breast,
    From cheek and throat and chin.   140

Above, the fair hall-ceiling stately-set
    Many an arch high up did lift,
And angels rising and descending[13] met
    With interchange of gift.

Below was all mosaic choicely plann'd
    With cycles of the human tale
Of this wide world, the times of every land
    So wrought they will not fail.

The people here, a beast of burden slow,
    Toil'd onward, prick'd with goads and stings;   150
Here play'd, a tiger, rolling to and fro
    The heads and crowns of kings;

Here rose, an athlete, strong to break or bind
    All force in bonds that might endure,
And here once more like some sick man declined,
    And trusted any cure.

But over these she trod: and those great bells
    Began to chime. She took her throne:
She sat betwixt the shining Oriels,
    To sing her songs alone.   160

And thro' the topmost Oriels' coloured flame
    Two godlike faces gazed below;
Plato the wise, and large-brow'd Verulam,[14]
    The first of those who know.

And all those names that in their motion were
    Full-welling fountain-heads of change,
Betwixt the slender shafts were blazon'd fair
    In diverse raiment strange:

Thro' which the lights, rose, amber, emerald, blue,
    Flush'd in her temples and her eyes,   170

---

[6]**Uther's . . . son:** King Arthur, who was borne from the battle-field to the island of **Avalon.**

[7]**wood-nymph:** Egeria, who gave the laws to Numa Pompilius, legendary **Ausonian king** of what would be Rome (7th century BCE).

[8]**Cama:** Brahma's son, Hindu god of love.

[9]**Europa:** beautiful maiden abducted by Zeus in the form of a bull.

[10]**Ganymede:** beautiful youth abducted by Zeus's **eagles.**

[11]**Caucasian:** European, derived by immigration from the mountainous Caucasus.

[12]**Ionian father:** Homer, thought to have lived in **Ionia,** western Asia Minor.

[13]**angels . . . descending:** see Jacob's ladder in Genesis 28:12.

[14]**Oriels:** large bay windows. **Verulam:** Francis Bacon (1561–1626), first Baron of Verulam.

And from her lips, as morn from Memnon,[15] drew
   Rivers of melodies.

No nightingale delighteth to prolong
   Her low preamble all alone,
More than my soul to hear her echo'd song
   Throb thro' the ribbed stone;

Singing and murmuring in her feastful mirth,
   Joying to feel herself alive,
Lord over Nature, Lord of the visible earth,
   Lord of the senses five;   180

Communing with herself: "All these are mine,
   And let the world have peace or wars,
'Tis one to me." She—when young night divine
   Crown'd dying day with stars,

Making sweet close of his delicious toils—
   Lit light in wreaths and anadems,
And pure quintessences of precious oils
   In hollow'd moons of gems,

To mimic heaven; and clapt her hands and cried,
   "I marvel if my still delight   190
In this great house so royal-rich, and wide,
   Be flatter'd to the height.

"O all things fair to sate my various eyes!
   O shapes and hues that please me well!
O silent faces of the Great and Wise,
   My Gods, with whom I dwell!

"O God-like isolation which art mine,
   I can but count thee perfect gain,
What time I watch the darkening droves of swine
   That range on yonder plain.   200

"In filthy sloughs they roll a prurient skin,
   They graze and wallow, breed and sleep;
And oft some brainless devil enters in,
   And drives them to the deep."

Then of the moral instinct would she prate
   And of the rising from the dead,
As hers by right of full-accomplish'd Fate;
   And at the last she said:

"I take possession of man's mind and deed.
   I care not what the sects may brawl.   210

I sit as God holding no form of creed,
   But contemplating all."

       *   *   *   *

Full oft the riddle of the painful earth
   Flash'd thro' her as she sat alone,
Yet not the less held she her solemn mirth,
   And intellectual throne.

And so she throve and prosper'd: so three years
   She prosper'd; on the fourth she fell,
Like Herod,[16] when the shout was in his ears,
   Struck thro' with pangs of hell.   220

Lest she should fail and perish utterly,
   God, before whom ever lie bare
The abysmal deeps of Personality,
   Plagued her with sore despair.

When she would think, where'er she turn'd her sight
   The airy hand confusion wrought,
Wrote, "Mene, mene,"[17] and divided quite
   The kingdom of her thought.

Deep dread and loathing of her solitude
   Fell on her, from which mood was born   230
Scorn of herself; again, from out that mood
   Laughter at her self-scorn.

"What! is not this my place of strength," she said,
   "My spacious mansion built for me,
Whereof the strong foundation-stones were laid
   Since my first memory?"

But in dark corners of her palace stood
   Uncertain shapes; and unawares
On white-eyed phantasms weeping tears of blood,
   And horrible nightmares,   240

And hollow shades enclosing hearts of flame,
   And, with dim fretted foreheads all,
On corpses three-months-old at noon she came,
   That stood against the wall.

A spot of dull stagnation, without light
   Or power of movement, seem'd my soul,
'Mid onward-sloping motions infinite
   Making for one sure goal.

---

[15]**Memnon**: Ethiopian king whose statue in Egyptian Thebes was damaged by an earthquake in 27 BCE and afterwards emitted music when first touched by the sun each day.

[16]**Herod**: see Acts 12:21–23.

[17]"**Mene, mene**": the original writing on the wall; see Daniel 5:5–6, 17–30.

A still salt pool, lock'd in with bars of sand,
    Left on the shore; that hears all night   250
The plunging seas draw backward from the land
    Their moon-led waters white.

A star that with the choral starry dance
    Join'd not, but stood, and standing saw
The hollow orb of moving Circumstance[18]
    Roll'd round by one fix'd law.

Back on herself her serpent pride had curl'd
    "No voice," she shriek'd in that lone hall,
"No voice breaks thro' the stillness of this world:
    One deep, deep silence all!"   260

She, mouldering with the dull earth's mouldering sod,
    Inwrapt tenfold in slothful shame,
Lay there exiled from eternal God,
    Lost to her place and name;

And death and life she hated equally,
    And nothing saw, for her despair,
But dreadful time, dreadful eternity,
    No comfort anywhere;

Remaining utterly confused with fears,
    And ever worse with growing time,   270
And ever unrelieved by dismal tears,
    And all alone in crime:

Shut up as in a crumbling tomb, girt round
    With blackness as a solid wall,
Far off she seem'd to hear the dully sound
    Of human footsteps fall.

As in strange lands a traveller walking slow,
    In doubt and great perplexity,
A little before moon-rise hears the low
    Moan of an unknown sea;   280

And knows not if it be thunder, or a sound
    Of rocks thrown down, or one deep cry
Of great wild beasts; then thinketh, "I have found
    A new land, but I die."

She howl'd aloud, "I am on fire within.
    There comes no murmur of reply.
What is it that will take away my sin,
    And save me lest I die?"

So when four years were wholly finished,
    She threw her royal robes away.   290

---

[18]**Circumstance**: Some old writer calls the Heavens "the Circumstance." . . . Here it is more or less a play on the word. [Tennyson's note]

"Make me a cottage in the vale," she said,
    "Where I may mourn and pray.

"Yet pull not down my palace towers, that are
    So lightly, beautifully built.
Perchance I may return with others there
    When I have purged my guilt."

                1832, 1842

The Lotos-Eaters

"Courage!" he[1] said, and pointed toward the land,
"This mounting wave will roll us shoreward soon."
In the afternoon they came unto a land
In which it seemed always afternoon.
All round the coast the languid air did swoon,
Breathing like one that hath a weary dream.
Full-faced above the valley stood the moon;
And like a downward smoke, the slender stream
Along the cliff to fall and pause and fall did seem.

A land of streams! some, like a downward smoke,   10
Slow-dropping veils of thinnest lawn, did go;
And some thro' wavering lights and shadows broke,
Rolling a slumbrous sheet of foam below.
They saw the gleaming river seaward flow
From the inner land; far off, three mountain-tops,
Three silent pinnacles of aged snow,
Stood sunset-flush'd: and, dew'd with showery drops,
Up-clomb the shadowy pine above the woven copse.

The charmed sunset linger'd low adown
In the red West: thro' mountain clefts the dale   20
Was seen far inland, and the yellow down
Border'd with palm, and many a winding vale
And meadow, set with slender galingale;
A land where all things always seem'd the same!
And round about the keel with faces pale,
Dark faces pale against that rosy flame,
The mild-eyed melancholy Lotos-eaters came.

Branches they bore of that enchanted stem,
Laden with flower and fruit, whereof they gave
To each, but whoso did receive of them,   30
And taste, to him the gushing of the wave
Far far away did seem to mourn and rave
On alien shores; and if his fellow spake,

---

[1]**he**: Odysseus, who encounters lotos-eaters in *Odyssey* 9.

His voice was thin, as voices from the grave;
And deep-asleep he seem'd, yet all awake,
And music in his ears his beating heart did make.

They sat them down upon the yellow sand,
Between the sun and moon upon the shore;
And sweet it was to dream of Fatherland,
Of child, and wife, and slave; but evermore   40
Most weary seem'd the sea, weary the oar,
Weary the wandering fields of barren foam.
Then some one said, "We will return no more;"
And all at once they sang, "Our island home
Is far beyond the wave; we will no longer roam."

— CHORIC SONG —

1

There is sweet music here that softer falls
Than petals from blown roses on the grass,
Or night-dews on still waters between walls
Of shadowy granite, in a gleaming pass;
Music that gentlier on the spirit lies,   50
Than tir'd eyelids upon tir'd eyes;
Music that brings sweet sleep down from the blissful skies.
Here are cool mosses deep,
And thro' the moss the ivies creep,
And in the stream the long-leaved flowers weep,
And from the craggy ledge the poppy hangs in sleep.

2

Why are we weigh'd upon with heaviness,
And utterly consumed with sharp distress,
While all things else have rest from weariness?
All things have rest: why should we toil alone,   60
We only toil, who are the first of things,
And make perpetual moan,
Still from one sorrow to another thrown:
Nor ever fold our wings,
And cease from wanderings,
Nor steep our brows in slumber's holy balm;
Nor harken what the inner spirit sings,
"There is no joy but calm!"
Why should we only toil, the roof and crown of things?

3

Lo! in the middle of the wood,   70
The folded leaf is woo'd from out the bud
With winds upon the branch, and there
Grows green and broad, and takes no care,
Sun-steep'd at noon, and in the moon
Nightly dew-fed; and turning yellow
Falls, and floats adown the air.

Lo! sweeten'd with the summer light,
The full-juiced apple, waxing over-mellow,
Drops in a silent autumn night.
All its allotted length of days,   80
The flower ripens in its place,
Ripens and fades, and falls, and hath no toil,
Fast-rooted in the fruitful soil.

4

Hateful is the dark-blue sky,
Vaulted o'er the dark-blue sea.
Death is the end of life; ah, why
Should life all labour be?
Let us alone. Time driveth onward fast,
And in a little while our lips are dumb.
Let us alone. What is it that will last?   90
All things are taken from us, and become
Portions and parcels of the dreadful Past.
Let us alone. What pleasure can we have
To war with evil? Is there any peace
In ever climbing up the climbing wave?
All things have rest, and ripen toward the grave
In silence; ripen, fall, and cease:
Give us long rest or death, dark death, or dreamful ease.

5

How sweet it were, hearing the downward stream,
With half-shut eyes ever to seem   100
Falling asleep in a half-dream!
To dream and dream, like yonder amber light,
Which will not leave the myrrh-bush on the height;
To hear each other's whisper'd speech;
Eating the Lotos day by day,
To watch the crisping ripples on the beach,
And tender curving lines of creamy spray;
To lend our hearts and spirits wholly
To the influence of mild-minded melancholy;
To muse and brood and live again in memory,   110
With those old faces of our infancy
Heap'd over with a mound of grass,
Two handfuls of white dust, shut in an urn of brass!

6

Dear is the memory of our wedded lives,
And dear the last embraces of our wives
And their warm tears: but all hath suffer'd change:
For surely now our household hearths are cold:
Our sons inherit us: our looks are strange:
And we should come like ghosts to trouble joy.
Or else the island princes over-bold   120

Have eat our substance, and the minstrel sings
Before them of the ten years' war in Troy,
And our great deeds, as half-forgotten things.
Is there confusion in the little isle?
Let what is broken so remain.
The Gods are hard to reconcile:
'Tis hard to settle order once again.
There *is* confusion worse than death,
Trouble on trouble, pain on pain,
Long labour unto aged breath,   130
Sore task to hearts worn out by many wars
And eyes grown dim with gazing on the pilot-stars.

7

But, propt on beds of amaranth and moly,[2]
How sweet (while warm airs lull us, blowing lowly)
With half-dropt eyelid still,
Beneath a heaven dark and holy,
To watch the long bright river drawing slowly
His waters from the purple hill—
To hear the dewy echoes calling
From cave to cave thro' the thick-twined vine—   140
To watch the emerald-colour'd water falling
Thro' many a woven acanthus-wreath divine!
Only to hear and see the far-off sparkling brine,
Only to hear were sweet, stretch'd out beneath the pine.

8

The Lotos blooms below the barren peak:
The Lotos blows by every winding creek:
All day the wind breathes low with mellower tone:
Thro' every hollow cave and alley lone
Round and round the spicy downs the yellow
      Lotos-dust is blown.
We have had enough of action, and of motion we, 150
Roll'd to starboard, roll'd to larboard, when the surge
      was seething free,
Where the wallowing monster spouted his foam-
      fountains in the sea.
Let us swear an oath, and keep it with an equal mind,
In the hollow Lotos-land to live and lie reclined
On the hills like Gods together, careless of mankind.
For they lie beside their nectar, and the bolts are hurl'd
Far below them in the valleys, and the clouds are lightly curl'd

Round their golden houses, girdled with the gleaming
      world:
Where they smile in secret, looking over wasted lands,
Blight and famine, plague and earthquake, roaring deeps
      and fiery sands,   160
Clanging fights, and flaming towns, and sinking ships,
      and praying hands.
But they smile, they find a music centred in a
      doleful song
Steaming up, a lamentation and an ancient tale
      of wrong,
Like a tale of little meaning tho' the words are strong;
Chanted from an ill-used race of men that cleave the soil,
Sow the seed, and reap the harvest with enduring toil,
Storing yearly little dues of wheat, and wine and oil;
Till they perish and they suffer—some, 'tis whisper'd—
      down in hell
Suffer endless anguish, others in Elysian valleys dwell,
Resting weary limbs at last on beds of asphodel.   170
Surely, surely, slumber is more sweet than toil, the shore
Than labour in the deep mid-ocean, wind and wave
      and oar;
Oh rest ye, brother mariners, we will not wander more.
                                                  1832, 1842

St. Simeon Stylites[1]

Altho' I be the basest of mankind,
From scalp to sole one slough and crust of sin,
Unfit for earth, unfit for heaven, scarce meet
For troops of devils, mad with blasphemy,
I will not cease to grasp the hope I hold
Of saintdom, and to clamor, mourn, and sob,
Battering the gates of heaven with storms of prayer,
Have mercy, Lord, and take away my sin!
      Let this avail, just, dreadful, mighty God,
This not be all in vain, that thrice ten years,   10
Thrice multiplied by superhuman pangs,
In hungers and in thirsts, fevers and cold,
In coughs, aches, stitches, ulcerous throes and cramps,
A sign betwixt the meadow and the cloud
Patient on this tall pillar I have borne

---

[2]**amaranth**: imaginary flower blooming eternally. **moly**: magical flowering herb that in *Odyssey* 10 immunizes Odysseus against the witchcraft of Circe.

---

[1]**St. Simeon**: Syrian Christian of the 5th century who aspired to become the outstanding ascetic of his time. **Stylites**: of the pillar, this one being 40 cubits (60 feet) high.

Rain, wind, frost, heat, hail, damp, and sleet, and snow;
And I had hoped that ere this period closed
Thou wouldst have caught me up into thy rest,
Denying not these weather-beaten limbs
The meed of saints, the white robe and the palm.   20
    O, take the meaning, Lord! I do not breathe,
Not whisper, any murmur of complaint.
Pain heap'd ten-hundred-fold to this, were still
Less burthen, by ten-hundred-fold, to bear,
Than were those lead-like tons of sin that crush'd
My spirit flat before thee.
                O Lord, Lord,
Thou knowest I bore this better at the first,
For I was strong and hale of body then;
And tho' my teeth, which now are dropt away,
Would chatter with the cold, and all my beard   30
Was tagg'd with icy fringes in the moon,
I drown'd the whoopings of the owl with sound
Of pious hymns and psalms, and sometimes saw
An angel stand and watch me, as I sang.
Now am I feeble grown; my end draws nigh.
I hope my end draws nigh; half deaf I am,
So that I scarce can hear the people hum
About the column's base, and almost blind,
And scarce can recognize the fields I know;
And both my thighs are rotted with the dew;   40
Yet cease I not to clamor and to cry,
While my stiff spine can hold my weary head,
Till all my limbs drop piecemeal from the stone,
Have mercy, mercy! take away my sin!
    O Jesus, if thou wilt not save my soul,
Who may be saved? who is it may be saved?
Who may be made a saint if I fail here?
Show me the man hath suffer'd more than I.
For did not all thy martyrs die one death?
For either they were stoned, or crucified,   50
Or burn'd in fire, or boil'd in oil, or sawn
In twain beneath the ribs; but I die here
To-day, and whole years long, a life of death.
Bear witness, if I could have found a way—
And heedfully I sifted all my thought—
More slowly-painful to subdue this home
Of sin, my flesh, which I despise and hate,
I had not stinted practice, O my God!
    For not alone this pillar-punishment,
Not this alone I bore; but while I lived   60
In the white convent down the valley there,
For many weeks about my loins I wore
The rope that haled the buckets from the well,

turn around

Twisted as tight as I could knot the noose,
And spake not of it to a single soul,
Until the ulcer, eating thro' my skin,
Betray'd my secret penance, so that all
My brethren marvell'd greatly. More than this
I bore, whereof, O God, thou knowest all.
    Three winters, that my soul might grow to thee,   70
I lived up there on yonder mountain-side.
My right leg chain'd into the crag, I lay
Pent in a roofless close of ragged stones;
Inswathed sometimes in wandering mist, and twice
Black'd with thy branding thunder, and sometimes
Sucking the damps for drink, and eating not,
Except the spare chance-gift of those that came
To touch my body and be heal'd, and live.
And they say then that I work'd miracles,
Whereof my fame is loud amongst mankind,   80
Cured lameness, palsies, cancers. Thou, O God,
Knowest alone whether this was or no.
Have mercy, mercy! cover all my sin!
    Then, that I might be more alone with thee,
Three years I lived upon a pillar, high
Six cubits, and three years on one of twelve;
And twice three years I crouch'd on one that rose
Twenty by measure; last of all, I grew
Twice ten long weary, weary years to this,
That numbers forty cubits from the soil.   90
    I think that I have borne as much as this—
Or else I dream—and for so long a time,
If I may measure time by yon slow light,
And this high dial, which my sorrow crowns—
So much—even so.
              And yet I know not well,
For that the evil ones come here, and say,
"Fall down, O Simeon; thou hast suffer'd long
For ages and for ages!" then they prate
Of penances I cannot have gone thro',
Perplexing me with lies; and oft I fall,   100
Maybe for months, in such blind lethargies
That Heaven, and Earth, and Time are choked.
                      But yet
Bethink thee, Lord, while thou and all the saints
Enjoy themselves in heaven, and men on earth
House in the shade of comfortable roofs,
Sit with their wives by fires, eat wholesome food,
And wear warm clothes, and even beasts have stalls,
I, 'tween the spring and downfall of the light,
Bow down one thousand and two hundred times,
To Christ, the Virgin Mother, and the saints;   110

Or in the night, after a little sleep,
I wake; the chill stars sparkle; I am wet
With drenching dews, or stiff with crackling frost.
I wear an undress'd goatskin on my back;
A grazing iron collar grinds my neck;
And in my weak, lean arms I lift the cross,
And strive and wrestle with thee till I die.
O, mercy, mercy! wash away my sin!

    O Lord, thou knowest what a man I am;
A sinful man, conceived and born in sin.   120
'Tis their own doing; this is none of mine;
Lay it not to me. Am I to blame for this,
That here come those that worship me? Ha! ha!
They think that I am somewhat. What am I?
The silly people take me for a saint,
And bring me offerings of fruit and flowers;
And I, in truth—thou wilt bear witness here—
Have all in all endured as much, and more
Than many just and holy men, whose names
Are register'd and calendar'd for saints.   130

    Good people, you do ill to kneel to me.
What is it I can have done to merit this?
I am a sinner viler than you all.
It may be I have wrought some miracles,
And cured some halt and maim'd; but what of that?
It may be no one, even among the saints,
May match his pains with mine; but what of that?
Yet do not rise; for you may look on me,
And in your looking you may kneel to God.
Speak! is there any of you halt or maim'd?   140
I think you know I have some power with Heaven
From my long penance; let him speak his wish.

    Yes, I can heal him. Power goes forth from me.
They say that they are heal'd. Ah, hark! they shout
"Saint Simeon Stylites." Why, if so,
God reaps a harvest in me. O my soul,
God reaps a harvest in thee! If this be,
Can I work miracles and not be saved?
This is not told of any. They were saints.
It cannot be but that I shall be saved,   150
Yea, crown'd a saint. They shout, "Behold a saint!"
And lower voices saint me from above.
Courage, Saint Simeon! This dull chrysalis
Cracks into shining wings, and hope ere death
Spreads more and more and more, that God hath now
Sponged and made blank of crimeful record all
My mortal archives.
           O my sons, my sons,
I, Simeon of the pillar, by surname

Stylites, among men; I, Simeon,
The watcher on the column till the end;   160
I, Simeon, whose brain the sunshine bakes;
I, whose bald brows in silent hours become
Unnaturally hoar with rime, do now
From my high nest of penance here proclaim
That Pontius and Iscariot[2] by my side
Show'd like fair seraphs. On the coals I lay,
A vessel full of sin; all hell beneath
Made me boil over. Devils pluck'd my sleeve,
Abaddon and Asmodeus[3] caught at me.
I smote them with the cross; they swarm'd again.   170
In bed like monstrous apes they crush'd my chest;
They flapp'd my light out as I read; I saw
Their faces grow between me and my book;
With coltlike whinny and with hoggish whine
They burst my prayer. Yet this way was left,
And by this way I 'scaped them. Mortify
Your flesh, like me, with scourges and with thorns;
Smite, shrink not, spare not. If it may be, fast
Whole Lents, and pray. I hardly, with slow steps,
With slow, faint steps, and much exceeding pain,   180
Have scrambled past those pits of fire, that still
Sing in mine ears. But yield not me the praise;
God only thro' his bounty hath thought fit,
Among the powers and princes of this world,
To make me an example to mankind,
Which few can reach to. Yet I do not say
But that a time may come—yea, even now,
Now, now, his footsteps smite the threshold stairs
Of life—I say, that time is at the doors
When you may worship me without reproach;   190
For I will leave my relics in your land,
And you may carve a shrine about my dust,
And burn a fragrant lamp before my bones,
When I am gather'd to the glorious saints.

    While I spake then, a sting of shrewdest pain
Ran shrivelling thro' me, and a cloudlike change,
In passing, with a grosser film made thick
These heavy, horny eyes. The end! the end!
Surely the end! What's here? a shape, a shade,
A flash of light. Is that the angel there   200
That holds a crown? Come, blessed brother, come!

---

[2]**Pontius** Pilate: judge who sentenced Jesus to death. Judas **Iscariot**: disciple who betrayed Jesus.

[3]**Abaddon and Asmodeus**: especially wicked biblical demons; see Revelation 9:11 and Tobit 3:8.

I know thy glittering face. I waited long;
My brows are ready. What! deny it now?
Nay, draw, draw, draw nigh. So I clutch it. Christ!
'Tis gone; 'tis here again; the crown! the crown!
So now't is fitted on and grows to me,
And from it melt the dews of Paradise,
Sweet! sweet! spikenard, and balm, and frankincense.
Ah! let me not be fool'd, sweet saints; I trust
That I am whole, and clean, and meet for Heaven. 210
     Speak, if there be a priest, a man of God,
Among you there, and let him presently
Approach, and lean a ladder on the shaft,
And climbing up into my airy home,
Deliver me the blessed sacrament;
For by the warning of the Holy Ghost,
I prophesy that I shall die to-night,

A quarter before twelve.
                         But thou, O Lord,
Aid all this foolish people; let them take
Example, pattern; lead them to thy light.   220
1833   *1842*

Ulysses[1]

It little profits that an idle king,[2]
By this still hearth, among these barren crags,
Match'd with an aged wife, I mete and dole
Unequal laws unto a savage race,
That hoard, and sleep, and feed, and know not me.

I cannot rest from travel; I will drink
Life to the lees: all times I have enjoy'd
Greatly, have suffer'd greatly, both with those
That loved me, and alone; on shore, and when
Thro' scudding drifts the rainy Hyades[3]   10
Vext the dim sea: I am become a name;

---

[1]**Ulysses:** The poem was written soon after Arthur Hallam's death, and it gives the feeling about the need of going forward and braving the struggle of life perhaps more simply than anything in *In Memoriam.* [Tennyson's note] See Dante, *Inferno* 26.

[2]**idle king:** restored to his throne after decades of war and travel, and now taking final leave of his home, his **wife** Penelope, and their son **Telemachus.**

[3]**Hyades:** star cluster whose October appearance above the horizon marks the start of the **rainy** season.

For always roaming with a hungry heart
Much have I seen and known; cities of men
And manners, climates, councils, governments,
Myself not least, but honour'd of them all;
And drunk delight of battle with my peers,
Far on the ringing plains of windy Troy.
I am a part of all that I have met;
Yet all experience is an arch wherethro'
Gleams that untravell'd world, whose margin fades 20
For ever and for ever when I move.
How dull it is to pause, to make an end,
To rust unburnish'd, not to shine in use!
As tho' to breathe were life. Life piled on life
Were all too little, and of one to me
Little remains: but every hour is saved
From that eternal silence, something more,
A bringer of new things; and vile it were
For some three suns to store and hoard myself,
And this gray spirit yearning in desire   30
To follow knowledge like a sinking star,
Beyond the utmost bound of human thought.

     This is my son, mine own Telemachus,
To whom I leave the sceptre and the isle—
Well-loved of me, discerning to fulfil
This labour, by slow prudence to make mild
A rugged people, and thro' soft degrees
Subdue them to the useful and the good.
Most blameless is he, centred in the sphere
Of common duties, decent not to fail   40
In offices of tenderness, and pay
Meet adoration to my household gods,
When I am gone. He works his work, I mine.

     There lies the port; the vessel puffs her sail:
There gloom the dark broad seas. My mariners,
Souls that have toil'd, and wrought, and thought with me—
That ever with a frolic welcome took
The thunder and the sunshine, and opposed
Free hearts, free foreheads—you and I are old;
Old age hath yet his honour and his toil;   50
Death closes all: but something ere the end,
Some work of noble note, may yet be done,
Not unbecoming men that strove with Gods.
The lights begin to twinkle from the rocks:
The long day wanes: the slow moon climbs: the deep
Moans round with many voices. Come, my friends.
'Tis not too late to seek a newer world.
Push off, and sitting well in order smite
The sounding furrows; for my purpose holds

To sail beyond the sunset, and the baths   60
Of all the western stars, until I die.
It may be that the gulfs will wash us down:
It may be we shall touch the Happy Isles,[4]
And see the great Achilles, whom we knew.
Tho' much is taken, much abides; and tho'
We are not now that strength which in old days
Moved earth and heaven, that which we are, we are;
One equal temper of heroic hearts,
Made weak by time and fate, but strong in will
To strive, to seek, to find, and not to yield.   70

1833   1842

The Epic

At Francis Allen's on the Christmas-eve,—
The game of forfeits done—the girls all kiss'd
Beneath the sacred bush[1] and past away—
The parson Holmes, the poet Everard Hall,
The host, and I sat round the wassail-bowl,
Then half-way ebb'd: and there we held a talk,
How all the old honour had from Christmas gone,
Or gone, or dwindled down to some odd games
In some odd nooks like this; till I, tired out
With cutting eights that day upon the pond,   10
Where, three times slipping from the outer edge,
I bump'd the ice into three several stars,
Fell in a doze; and half-awake I heard
The parson taking wide and wider sweeps,
Now harping on the church-commissioners,[2]
Now hawking at Geology and schism;
Until I woke, and found him settled down
Upon the general decay of faith
Right thro' the world, "at home was little left,
And none abroad: there was no anchor, none,   20

To hold by." Francis, laughing, clapt his hand
On Everard's shoulder, with "I hold by him."
"And I," quoth Everard, "by the wassail-bowl."
"Why yes," I said, "we knew your gift that way
At college: but another which you had,
I mean of verse (for so we held it then),
What came of that?" "You know," said Frank, "he burnt
His epic, his King Arthur, some twelve books"—
And then to me demanding why? "Oh, sir,
He thought that nothing new was said, or else   30
Something so said 'twas nothing—that a truth
Looks freshest in the fashion of the day:
God knows: he has a mint of reasons: ask.
It pleased me well enough." "Nay, nay," said Hall,
"Why take the style of those heroic times?
For nature brings not back the Mastodon,
Nor we those times; and why should any man
Remodel models? these twelve books of mine
Were faint Homeric echoes, nothing-worth,
Mere chaff and draff, much better burnt." "But I,"   40
Said Francis, "pick'd the eleventh from this hearth
And have it: keep a thing, its use will come.
I hoard it as a sugar-plum for Holmes."
He laugh'd, and I, tho' sleepy, like a horse
That hears the corn-bin open, prick'd my ears;
For I remember'd Everard's college fame
When we were Freshmen: then at my request
He brought it; and the poet little urged,
But with some prelude of disparagement,
Read, mouthing out his hollow oes and aes,   50
Deep-chested music, and to this result.

Morte d'Arthur[1]

So all day long the noise of battle roll'd
Among the mountains by the winter sea;
Until King Arthur's table, man by man,
Had fallen in Lyonnesse[2] about their Lord,
King Arthur: then, because his wound was deep,
The bold Sir Bedivere uplifted him,

---

[4]**Happy Isles**: paradisial afterworld reserved for heroes like **Achilles**.

[1]**sacred bush**: mistletoe, by the 1830s already a self-consciously "traditional" Christmas observance like the **game of forfeits** and the **wassail-bowl**.

[2]**church-commissioners**: charged in 1836 to investigate abuse of ecclesiastical revenues. **Geology**: subversive of religious orthodoxy; see pages 50–62. **schism**: sectarian division resulting from debates within the national Church.

[1]**Morte d'Arthur**: Arthur's death; title of Tennyson's source, Sir Thomas Malory's 15th-century prose compilation of Arthurian stories.

[2]**Lyonnesse**: legendary country in extreme SW England.

Sir Bedivere the last of all his knights,
And bore him to a chapel nigh the field,
A broken chancel with a broken cross,
That stood on a dark strait of barren land.   10
On one side lay the Ocean, and on one
Lay a great water, and the moon was full.

　Then spake King Arthur to Sir Bedivere:
"The sequel of to-day unsolders all
The goodliest fellowship of famous knights
Whereof this world holds record. Such a sleep
They sleep—the men I loved. I think that we
Shall never more, at any future time,
Delight our souls with talk of knightly deeds,
Walking about the gardens and the halls   20
Of Camelot, as in the days that were.
I perish by this people which I made,—
Tho' Merlin sware that I should come again
To rule once more—but let what will be, be,
I am so deeply smitten thro' the helm
That without help I cannot last till morn.
Thou therefore take my brand Excalibur,
Which was my pride: for thou rememberest how
In those old days, one summer noon, an arm
Rose up from out the bosom of the lake,   30
Clothed in white samite, mystic, wonderful,
Holding the sword—and how I row'd across
And took it, and have worn it, like a king:
And, wheresoever I am sung or told
In aftertime, this also shall be known:
But now delay not: take Excalibur,
And fling him far into the middle mere:
Watch what thou seëst, and lightly bring me word."

　To him replied the bold Sir Bedivere:
"It is not meet, Sir King, to leave thee thus,   40
Aidless, alone, and smitten thro' the helm.
A little thing may harm a wounded man.
Yet I thy hest will all perform at full,
Watch what I see, and lightly bring thee word."

　So saying, from the ruin'd shrine he stept
And in the moon athwart the place of tombs,
Where lay the mighty bones of ancient men,
Old knights, and over them the sea-wind sang
Shrill, chill, with flakes of foam. He, stepping down
By zig-zag paths, and juts of pointed rock,   50
Came on the shining levels of the lake.

　There drew he forth the brand Excalibur,
And o'er him, drawing it, the winter moon,

Brightening the skirts of a long cloud, ran forth
And sparkled keen with frost against the hilt:
For all the haft twinkled with diamond sparks,
Myriads of topaz-lights, and jacinth-work
Of subtlest jewellery. He gazed so long
That both his eyes were dazzled, as he stood,
This way and that dividing the swift mind,   60
In act to throw: but at the last it seem'd
Better to leave Excalibur conceal'd
There in the many-knotted waterflags,
That whistled stiff and dry about the marge.
So strode he back slow to the wounded King.

　Then spake King Arthur to Sir Bedivere:
"Hast thou perform'd my mission which I gave?
What is it thou hast seen? or what hast heard?"

　And answer made the bold Sir Bedivere:
"I heard the ripple washing in the reeds,   70
And the wild water lapping on the crag."

　To whom replied King Arthur, faint and pale:
"Thou hast betray'd thy nature and thy name,
Not rendering true answer, as beseem'd
Thy feälty, nor like a noble knight:
For surer sign had follow'd, either hand,
Or voice, or else a motion of the mere.
This is a shameful thing for men to lie.
Yet now, I charge thee, quickly go again
As thou art lief and dear, and do the thing   80
I bad thee, watch, and lightly bring me word."

　Then went Sir Bedivere the second time
Across the ridge, and paced beside the mere,
Counting the dewy pebbles, fix'd in thought;
But when he saw the wonder of the hilt,
How curiously and strangely chased, he smote
His palms together, and he cried aloud,

　"And if indeed I cast the brand away,
Surely a precious thing, one worthy note,
Should thus be lost for ever from the earth,   90
Which might have pleased the eyes of many men.
What good should follow this, if this were done?
What harm, undone? deep harm to disobey,
Seeing obedience is the bond of rule.
Were it well to obey then, if a king demand
An act unprofitable, against himself?
The King is sick, and knows not what he does.
What record, or what relic of my lord
Should be to aftertime, but empty breath
And rumors of a doubt? but were this kept,   100

Stored in some treasure-house of mighty kings,
Some one might show it at a joust of arms,
Saying, 'King Arthur's sword, Excalibur,
Wrought by the lonely maiden of the Lake.
Nine years she wrought it, sitting in the deeps
Upon the hidden bases of the hills.'
So might some old man speak in the aftertime
To all the people, winning reverence.
But now much honour and much fame were lost."

    So spake he, clouded with his own conceit,   110
And hid Excalibur the second time,
And so strode back slow to the wounded King.

    Then spoke King Arthur, breathing heavily:
"What is it thou hast seen? or what hast heard?"

    And answer made the bold Sir Bedivere:
"I heard the water lapping on the crag,
And the long ripple washing in the reeds."

    To whom replied King Arthur, much in wrath:
"Ah, miserable and unkind, untrue,
Unknightly, traitor-hearted! Woe is me!   120
Authority forgets a dying king,
Laid widow'd of the power in his eye
That bow'd the will. I see thee what thou art,
For thou, the latest-left of all my knights,
In whom should meet the offices of all,
Thou wouldst betray me for the precious hilt;
Either from lust of gold, or like a girl
Valuing the giddy pleasure of the eyes.
Yet, for a man may fail in duty twice,
And the third time may prosper, get thee hence: 130
But, if thou spare to fling Excalibur,
I will arise and slay thee with my hands."

    Then quickly rose Sir Bedivere, and ran,
And, leaping down the ridges lightly, plunged
Among the bulrush-beds, and clutch'd the sword,
And strongly wheel'd and threw it. The great brand
Made lightnings in the splendour of the moon,
And flashing round and round, and whirl'd in an arch,
Shot like a streamer of the northern morn,
Seen where the moving isles of winter[3] shock   140
By night, with noises of the northern sea.
So flash'd and fell the brand Excalibur:
But ere he dipt the surface, rose an arm
Clothed in white samite, mystic, wonderful,

And caught him by the hilt, and brandish'd him
Three times, and drew him under in the mere.
And lightly went the other to the King.

    Then spoke King Arthur, drawing thicker breath:
"Now see I by thine eyes that this is done.
Speak out: what is it thou hast heard, or seen?"   150

    And answer made the bold Sir Bedivere:
"Sir King, I closed mine eyelids, lest the gems
Should blind my purpose, for I never saw,
Nor shall see, here or elsewhere, till I die,
Not tho' I live three lives of mortal men,
So great a miracle as yonder hilt.
Then with both hands I flung him, wheeling him;
But when I look'd again, behold an arm,
Clothed in white samite, mystic, wonderful,
That caught him by the hilt, and brandish'd him   160
Three times, and drew him under in the mere."

    And answer made King Arthur, breathing hard:
"My end draws nigh; 'tis time that I were gone.
Make broad thy shoulders to receive my weight,
And bear me to the margin; yet I fear
My wound hath taken cold, and I shall die."

    So saying, from the pavement he half rose,
Slowly, with pain, reclining on his arm,
And looking wistfully with wide blue eyes
As in a picture. Him Sir Bedivere   170
Remorsefully regarded thro' his tears,
And would have spoken, but he found not words,
Then took with care, and kneeling on one knee,
O'er both his shoulders drew the languid hands,
And rising bore him thro' the place of tombs.

    But, as he walk'd, King Arthur panted hard,
Like one that feels a nightmare on his bed
When all the house is mute. So sigh'd the King,
Muttering and murmuring at his ear, "Quick, quick!
I fear it is too late, and I shall die."   180
But the other swiftly strode from ridge to ridge,
Clothed with his breath, and looking, as he walk'd,
Larger than human on the frozen hills.
He heard the deep behind him, and a cry
Before. His own thought drove him, like a goad.
Dry clash'd his harness in the icy caves
And barren chasms, and all to left and right
The bare black cliff clang'd round him, as he based
His feet on juts of slippery crag that rang
Sharp-smitten with the dint of armed heels—   190
And on a sudden, lo! the level lake,
And the long glories of the winter moon.

---

[3]**northern morn**: aurora borealis. **isles of winter**: icebergs.

Then saw they how there hove a dusky barge,
Dark as a funeral scarf from stem to stern,
Beneath them; and descending they were ware
That all the decks were dense with stately forms
Black-stoled, black-hooded, like a dream—by these
Three Queens[4] with crowns of gold—and from them rose
A cry that shiver'd to the tingling stars,
And, as it were one voice, an agony   200
Of lamentation, like a wind, that shrills
All night in a waste land, where no one comes,
Or hath come, since the making of the world.

Then murmur'd Arthur, "Place me in the barge,"
And to the barge they came. There those three Queens
Put forth their hands, and took the King, and wept.
But she, that rose the tallest of them all
And fairest, laid his head upon her lap,
And loosed the shatter'd casque, and chafed his hands,
And call'd him by his name, complaining loud,   210
And dropping bitter tears against his brow
Striped with dark blood: for all his face was white
And colourless, and like the wither'd moon
Smote by the fresh beam of the springing east;
And all his greaves and cuisses dash'd with drops
Of onset; and the light and lustrous curls—
That made his forehead like a rising sun
High from the daïs-throne—were parch'd with dust;
Or, clotted into points and hanging loose,
Mix'd with the knightly growth that fringed
     his lips.   220
So like a shatter'd column lay the King;
Not like that Arthur who, with lance in rest,
From spur to plume a star of tournament,
Shot thro' the lists at Camelot, and charged
Before the eyes of ladies and of kings.

Then loudly cried the bold Sir Bedivere,
"Ah! my Lord Arthur, whither shall I go?
Where shall I hide my forehead and my eyes?
For now I see the true old times are dead,
When every morning brought a noble chance,   230
And every chance brought out a noble knight.

---

[4]**Three Queens**: In the original *Morte d'Arthur* one was King Arthur's sister, Queen Morgan le Fay; the other was the Queen of Northgalis; the third was the Queen of the Waste Lands. Some say that the three Queens are Faith, Hope, and Charity. [Tennyson's note] Tennyson added: They are three of the noblest of women. They are also those three Graces, but they are much more. I hate to be tied down to say, *"This means that,"* because the thought within the image is much more than any one interpretation.

Such times have been not since the light that led
The holy Elders with the gift of myrrh.
But now the whole ROUND TABLE is dissolved
Which was an image of the mighty world;
And I, the last, go forth companionless,
And the days darken round me, and the years,
Among new men, strange faces, other minds."

And slowly answered Arthur from the barge:
"The old order changeth, yielding place to new,   240
And God fulfils Himself in many ways,
Lest one good custom should corrupt the world.
Comfort thyself: what comfort is in me?
I have lived my life, and that which I have done
May He within Himself make pure! but thou,
If thou shouldst never see my face again,
Pray for my soul. More things are wrought by prayer
Than this world dreams of. Wherefore, let thy voice
Rise like a fountain for me night and day.
For what are men better than sheep or goats   250
That nourish a blind life within the brain,
If, knowing God, they lift not hands of prayer
Both for themselves and those who call them friend?
For so the whole round earth is every way
Bound by gold chains about the feet of God.
But now farewell. I am going a long way
With these thou seëst—if indeed I go—
(For all my mind is clouded with a doubt)
To the island-valley of Avilion;
Where falls not hail, or rain, or any snow,   260
Nor ever wind blows loudly; but it lies
Deep-meadow'd, happy, fair with orchard-lawns
And bowery hollows crown'd with summer sea,
Where I will heal me of my grievous wound."

So said he, and the barge with oar and sail
Moved from the brink, like some full-breasted swan
That, fluting a wild carol ere her death,
Ruffles her pure cold plume, and takes the flood
With swarthy webs. Long stood Sir Bedivere
Revolving many memories, till the hull   270
Look'd one black dot against the verge of dawn,
And on the mere the wailing died away.

[THE EPIC]

Here ended Hall, and our last light, that long   52
Had wink'd and threaten'd darkness, flared and fell:
At which the Parson, sent to sleep with sound,
And waked with silence, grunted "Good!" but we
Sat rapt: it was the tone with which he read—
Perhaps some modern touches here and there

Redeem'd it from the charge of nothingness—
Or else we loved the man, and prized his work;
I know not: but we sitting, as I said,   60
The cock crew loud; as at that time of year
The lusty bird takes every hour for dawn:
Then Francis, muttering, like a man ill-used,
"There now—that's nothing!" drew a little back,
And drove his heel into the smoulder'd log,
That sent a blast of sparkles up the flue:
And so to bed; where yet in sleep I seem'd
To sail with Arthur under looming shores,
Point after point; till on to dawn, when dreams
Begin to feel the truth and stir of day,   70
To me, methought, who waited with a crowd,
There came a bark that, blowing forward, bore
King Arthur, like a modern gentleman
Of stateliest port; and all the people cried,
"Arthur is come again: he cannot die."
Then those that stood upon the hills behind
Repeated—"Come again, and thrice as fair;"
And, further inland, voices echo'd—"Come
With all good things, and war shall be no more."
At this a hundred bells began to peal,   80
That with the sound I woke, and heard indeed
The clear church-bells ring in the Christmas-morn.
1833, 1837   *1842*

Break, Break, Break

Break, break, break,
    On thy cold gray stones, O Sea!
And I would that my tongue could utter
    The thoughts that arise in me.

O, well for the fisherman's boy,
    That he shouts with his sister at play!
O, well for the sailor lad,
    That he sings in his boat on the bay!

And the stately ships go on
    To their haven under the hill;   10
But O for the touch of a vanish'd hand,
    And the sound of a voice that is still!

Break, break, break,
    At the foot of thy crags, O Sea!
But the tender grace of a day that is dead
    Will never come back to me.

1842

Locksley Hall

Comrades, leave me here a little, while as yet 'tis early
        morn;
Leave me here, and when you want me, sound upon the
        bugle-horn.

'Tis the place, and all around it, as of old, the curlews call,
Dreary gleams about the moorland flying over Locksley Hall:

Locksley Hall, that in the distance overlooks the sandy
        tracts,
And the hollow ocean-ridges roaring into cataracts.

Many a night from yonder ivied casement, ere I went to
        rest,
Did I look on great Orion[1] sloping slowly to the West.

Many a night I saw the Pleiads, rising thro' the mellow
        shade,
Glitter like a swarm of fire-flies tangled in a silver braid.
        10

Here about the beach I wander'd, nourishing a youth
        sublime
With the fairy tales of science, and the long result of Time;

When the centuries behind me like a fruitful land reposed;
When I clung to all the present for the promise that it
        closed:

When I dipt into the future far as human eye could see;
Saw the Vision of the world, and all the wonder that
        would be.—

In the Spring a fuller crimson comes upon the robin's
        breast;
In the Spring the wanton lapwing gets himself another crest;

In the Spring a livelier iris changes on the burnish'd dove;
In the Spring a young man's fancy lightly turns to thoughts
        of love.   20

Then her cheek was pale and thinner than should be for
        one so young,
And her eyes on all my motions with a mute observance
        hung.

And I said, "My cousin Amy, speak, and speak the truth
        to me,
Trust me, cousin, all the current of my being sets to thee."

---

[1]**Orion**: constellation of the hunter, who pursues the **Pleiads**,
seven sisters who are daughters of the titan Atlas.

On her pallid cheek and forehead came a colour and a
 light,
As I have seen the rosy red flushing in the northern night.

And she turn'd—her bosom shaken with a sudden storm
 of sighs—
All the spirit deeply dawning in the dark of hazel eyes—

Saying, "I have hid my feelings, fearing they should do
 me wrong,"
Saying, "Dost thou love me, cousin?" weeping, "I have loved
 thee long."   30

Love took up the glass of Time, and turn'd it in his
 glowing hands;
Every moment, lightly shaken, ran itself in golden sands.

Love took up the harp of Life, and smote on all the chords
 with might;
Smote the chord of Self, that, trembling, pass'd in music
 out of sight.

Many a morning on the moorland did we hear the copses
 ring,
And her whisper throng'd my pulses with the fulness of
 the Spring.

Many an evening by the waters did we watch the stately
 ships,
And our spirits rush'd together at the touching of the lips.

O my cousin, shallow-hearted! O my Amy, mine no more!
O the dreary, dreary moorland! O the barren, barren
 shore!   40

Falser than all fancy fathoms, falser than all songs have
 sung,
Puppet to a father's threat, and servile to a shrewish tongue!

Is it well to wish thee happy?—having known me—to
 decline
On a range of lower feelings and a narrower heart than
 mine!

Yet it shall be: thou shalt lower to his level day by day,
What is fine within thee growing coarse to sympathise
 with clay.

As the husband is, the wife is: thou art mated with
 a clown,
And the grossness of his nature will have weight to drag
 thee down.

He will hold thee, when his passion shall have spent its
 novel force,
Something better than his dog, a little dearer than his
 horse.   50

What is this? his eyes are heavy: think not they are glazed
 with wine.
Go to him: it is thy duty: kiss him: take his hand in thine.

It may be my lord is weary, that his brain is overwrought:
Soothe him with thy finer fancies, touch him with thy
 lighter thought.

He will answer to the purpose, easy things to understand—
Better thou wert dead before me, tho' I slew thee with
 my hand!

Better thou and I were lying, hidden from the heart's
 disgrace,
Roll'd in one another's arms, and silent in a last embrace.

Cursed be the social wants that sin against the strength
 of youth!
Cursed be the social lies that warp us from the
 living truth!   60

Cursed be the sickly forms that err from honest Nature's rule!
Cursed be the gold that gilds the straiten'd forehead of
 the fool!

Well—'tis well that I should bluster!—Hadst thou less
 unworthy proved—
Would to God—for I had loved thee more than ever wife
 was loved.

Am I mad, that I should cherish that which bears but bitter
 fruit?
I will pluck it from my bosom, tho' my heart be at the root.

Never, tho' my mortal summers to such length of years
 should come
As the many-winter'd crow that leads the clanging rookery
 home.

Where is comfort? in division of the records of the mind?
Can I part her from herself, and love her, as I knew her,
 kind?   70

I remember one that perish'd: sweetly did she speak
 and move:
Such a one do I remember, whom to look at was to love.

Can I think of her as dead, and love her for the love
 she bore?
No—she never loved me truly: love is love for evermore.

Comfort? comfort scorn'd of devils! this is truth the
 poet[2] sings,
That a sorrow's crown of sorrow is remembering happier
 things.

---

[2] **the poet:** see Dante, *Inferno* 5.121–23.

Drug thy memories, lest thou learn it, lest thy heart be
    put to proof,
In the dead unhappy night, and when the rain is on the
    roof.

Like a dog, he hunts in dreams, and thou art staring at
    the wall,
Where the dying night-lamp flickers, and the shadows
    rise and fall.   80

Then a hand shall pass before thee, pointing to his
    drunken sleep,
To thy widow'd marriage-pillows, to the tears that thou
    wilt weep.

Thou shalt hear the "Never, never," whisper'd by the
    phantom years,
And a song from out the distance in the ringing of thine
    ears;

And an eye shall vex thee, looking ancient kindness on
    thy pain.
Turn thee, turn thee on thy pillow: get thee to thy rest
    again.

Nay, but Nature brings thee solace; for a tender voice
    will cry.
'Tis a purer life than thine; a lip to drain thy trouble dry.

Baby lips will laugh me down: my latest rival brings
    thee rest.
Baby fingers, waxen touches, press me from the mother's
    breast.   90

O, the child too clothes the father with a dearness not
    his due.
Half is thine and half is his: it will be worthy of the two.

O, I see thee old and formal, fitted to thy petty part,
With a little hoard of maxims preaching down a daughter's
    heart.

"They were dangerous guides the feelings—she herself
    was not exempt—
Truly, she herself had suffer'd"—Perish in thy self-
    contempt!

Overlive it—lower yet—be happy! wherefore should I care?
I myself must mix with action, lest I wither by despair.

What is that which I should turn to, lighting upon days
    like these?
Every door is barr'd with gold, and opens but to golden
    keys.   100

Every gate is throng'd with suitors, all the markets overflow.
I have but an angry fancy: what is that which I should do?

I had been content to perish, falling on the foeman's
    ground,
When the ranks are roll'd in vapour, and the winds are laid
    with sound.[3]

But the jingling of the guinea helps the hurt that Honour
    feels,
And the nations do but murmur, snarling at each other's
    heels.

Can I but relive in sadness? I will turn that earlier page.
Hide me from my deep emotion, O thou wondrous
    Mother-Age!

Make me feel the wild pulsation that I felt before the strife,
When I heard my days before me, and the tumult of my
    life;   110

Yearning for the large excitement that the coming years
    would yield,
Eager-hearted as a boy when first he leaves his father's field,

And at night along the dusky highway near and nearer
    drawn,
Sees in heaven the light of London flaring like a dreary
    dawn;

And his spirit leaps within him to be gone before him then,
Underneath the light he looks at, in among the throngs
    of men:

Men, my brothers, men the workers, ever reaping
    something new:
That which they have done but earnest of the things that
    they shall do.

For I dipt into the future, far as human eye could see,
Saw the Vision of the world, and all the wonder that
    would be;   120

Saw the heavens fill with commerce, argosies of magic sails,
Pilots of the purple twilight, dropping down with costly
    bales;

Heard the heavens fill with shouting, and there rain'd a
    ghastly dew
From the nations' airy navies grappling in the central blue;

Far along the world-wide whisper of the south-wind
    rushing warm,
With the standards of the peoples plunging thro' the
    thunderstorm;

---

[3] **sound:** the roar of gunfire, thought to calm the **wind.**

Till the war-drum throbb'd no longer, and the battle-flags
 were furl'd
In the Parliament of man, the Federation of the world.

There the common sense of most shall hold a fretful realm
 in awe,
And the kindly earth shall slumber, lapt in universal
 law.   130

So I triumph'd ere my passion sweeping thro' me left
 me dry,
Left me with the palsied heart, and left me with the
 jaundiced eye;

Eye, to which all order festers, all things here are out of
 joint:
Science moves, but slowly slowly, creeping on from point
 to point:

Slowly comes a hungry people, as a lion, creeping nigher,
Glares at one that nods and winks behind a slowly-dying
 fire.

Yet I doubt not thro' the ages one increasing purpose runs,
And the thoughts of men are widen'd with the process of
 the suns.

What is that to him that reaps not harvest of his youthful
 joys,
Tho' the deep heart of existence beat for ever like a
 boy's?   140

Knowledge comes, but wisdom lingers, and I linger on
 the shore,
And the individual withers, and the world is more and more.

Knowledge comes, but wisdom lingers, and he bears a
 laden breast,
Full of sad experience, moving toward the stillness of
 his rest.

Hark, my merry comrades call me, sounding on the
 bugle-horn,
They to whom my foolish passion were a target for their
 scorn:

Shall it not be scorn to me to harp on such a moulder'd
 string?
I am shamed thro' all my nature to have loved so slight
 a thing.

Weakness to be wroth with weakness! woman's pleasure,
 woman's pain—
Nature made them blinder motions bounded in a shallower
 brain: 150

Woman is the lesser man, and all thy passions, match'd
 with mine,
Are as moonlight unto sunlight, and as water unto wine—

Here at least, where nature sickens, nothing. Ah, for
 some retreat
Deep in yonder shining Orient, where my life began
 to beat;

Where in wild Mahratta-battle[4] fell my father evil-starr'd;—
I was left a trampled orphan, and a selfish uncle's ward.

Or to burst all links of habit—there to wander far away,
On from island unto island at the gateways of the day.

Larger constellations burning, mellow moons and happy
 skies,
Breadths of tropic shade and palms in cluster, knots of
 Paradise.   160

Never comes the trader, never floats an European flag,
Slides the bird o'er lustrous woodland, swings the trailer
 from the crag;

Droops the heavy-blossom'd bower, hangs the heavy-
 fruited tree—
Summer isles of Eden lying in dark-purple spheres of sea.

There methinks would be enjoyment more than in this
 march of mind,
In the steamship, in the railway, in the thoughts that
 shake mankind.

There the passions cramp'd no longer shall have scope
 and breathing space;
I will take some savage woman, she shall rear my dusky
 race.

Iron-jointed, supple-sinew'd, they shall dive, and they
 shall run,
Catch the wild goat by the hair, and hurl their lances in
 the sun;   170

Whistle back the parrot's call, and leap the rainbows of
 the brooks,
Not with blinded eyesight poring over miserable books—

Fool, again the dream, the fancy! but I *know* my words are
 wild,
But I count the gray barbarian lower than the Christian
 child.

---

[4]**Mahratta:** Bombay troops whose defeat in 1817–1818 consolidated British supremacy in India.

I, to herd with narrow foreheads, vacant of our glorious
  gains,
Like a beast with lower pleasures, like a beast with lower
  pains!

Mated with a squalid savage—what to me were sun or
  clime?
I the heir of all the ages, in the foremost files of time—

I that rather held it better men should perish one by one,
Than that earth should stand at gaze like Joshua's moon
  in Ajalon![5]   180

Not in vain the distance beacons. Forward, forward let
  us range,
Let the great world spin for ever down the ringing grooves
  of change.[6]

Thro' the shadow of the globe we sweep into the
  younger day:
Better fifty years of Europe than a cycle of Cathay.

Mother-Age (for mine I knew not) help me as when life
  begun:
Rift the hills, and roll the waters, flash the lightnings, weigh
  the Sun.

O, I see the crescent promise of my spirit hath not set.
Ancient founts of inspiration well thro' all my fancy yet.

Howsoever these things be, a long farewell to Locksley
  Hall!
Now for me the woods may wither, now for me the
  roof-tree fall.   190
Comes a vapour from the margin, blackening over heath
  and holt,
Cramming all the blast before it, in its breast a thunderbolt.

Let it fall on Locksley Hall, with rain or hail, or fire or
  snow;
For the mighty wind arises, roaring seaward, and I go.
                                                   1842

from **The Princess**
Sweet and Low[1]

Sweet and low, sweet and low,
  Wind of the western sea,
Low, low, breathe and blow,
  Wind of the western sea!
Over the rolling waters go,
Come from the dying moon, and blow,
  Blow him again to me;
While my little one, while my pretty one sleeps.

Sleep and rest, sleep and rest,
  Father will come to thee soon;   10
Rest, rest, on mother's breast,
  Father will come to thee soon;
Father will come to his babe in the nest,
Silver sails all out of the west
  Under the silver moon;
Sleep, my little one, sleep, my pretty one, sleep.
                                           1850

Tears, Idle Tears

  Tears, idle tears, I know not what they mean,
Tears from the depth of some divine despair
Rise in the heart, and gather to the eyes,
In looking on the happy autumn-fields,
And thinking of the days that are no more.

  Fresh as the first beam glittering on a sail,
That brings our friends up from the underworld,
Sad as the last which reddens over one
That sinks with all we love below the verge;
So sad, so fresh, the days that are no more.   10

  Ah, sad and strange as in dark summer dawns
The earliest pipe of half-awaken'd birds
To dying ears, when unto dying eyes
The casement slowly grows a glimmering square;
So sad, so strange, the days that are no more.

---

[5]**Joshua**, general of the Israelites, orders the sun to pause and the
moon to stand still in **Ajalon** valley (Joshua 10:12–14).

[6]**grooves:** When I went by the first train from Liverpool to Manchester (1830) I thought that the wheels ran in a groove. . . . Then I
made this line. [Tennyson's note]

---

[1]**Sweet and Low:** This and the next three unrhymed lyrics come
from *The Princess*, an idyllic, elaborately narrated book about the
founding, infiltration, and demise of a women's university, published by Tennyson in 1847 before any such institution existed in
Britain. This lyric was added to the revised edition of 1850.

Dear as remember'd kisses after death,
And sweet as those by hopeless fancy feign'd
On lips that are for others; deep as love,
Deep as first love, and wild with all regret;
O Death in Life, the days that are no more!   20

1847

Now Sleeps the Crimson Petal[1]

Now sleeps the crimson petal, now the white,
Nor waves the cypress in the palace walk;
Nor winks the gold fin in the porphyry font.
The fire-fly wakens; waken thou with me.

Now droops the milkwhite peacock like a ghost,
And like a ghost she glimmers on to me.

Now lies the Earth all Danaë[2] to the stars,
And all thy heart lies open unto me.

Now slides the silent meteor on, and leaves
A shining furrow, as thy thoughts in me.   10

Now folds the lily all her sweetness up,
And slips into the bosom of the lake.
So fold thyself, my dearest, thou, and slip
Into my bosom and be lost in me.

1847

Come Down, O Maid

Come down, O maid, from yonder mountain height.
What pleasure lives in height (the shepherd sang),
In height and cold, the splendour of the hills?
But cease to move so near the heavens, and cease
To glide a sunbeam by the blasted pine,
To sit a star upon the sparkling spire;
And come, for Love is of the valley, come,
For Love is of the valley, come thou down
And find him; by the happy threshold, he,
Or hand in hand with Plenty in the maize,   10
Or red with spirted purple of the vats,
Or foxlike in the vine; nor cares to walk
With Death and Morning on the silver horns,
Nor wilt thou snare him in the white ravine,

Nor find him dropt upon the firths of ice,[1]
That huddling slant in furrow-cloven falls
To roll the torrent out of dusky doors.
But follow; let the torrent dance thee down
To find him in the valley; let the wild
Lean-headed eagles yelp alone, and leave   20
The monstrous ledges there to slope, and spill
Their thousand wreaths of dangling water-smoke,
That like a broken purpose waste in air.
So waste not thou, but come; for all the vales
Await thee; azure pillars[2] of the hearth
Arise to thee; the children call, and I
Thy shepherd pipe, and sweet is every sound,
Sweeter thy voice, but every sound is sweet;
Myriads of rivulets hurrying thro' the lawn,
The moan of doves in immemorial elms,   30
And murmuring of innumerable bees.

1847

In Memoriam A. H. H.

—OBIT MDCCCXXXIII[1]—

Strong Son of God, immortal Love,
    Whom we, that have not seen thy face,
    By faith, and faith alone, embrace,
Believing where we cannot prove;

---

[1]**firths of ice**: glacier from which a **torrent** issues.

[2]**azure pillars**: smoke ascending in blue columns from the **hearth** amid still air.

[1]*In Memoriam A. H. H.*: In 1833 Tennyson's closest friend, Arthur Henry Hallam, died without warning at 22. *In Memoriam* puts into a loose but effective elegiac sequence—quite different from the sequence of composition—the quatrain lyrics that Tennyson began producing shortly thereafter and kept composing for 17 years. The process of mourning gradually absorbed not only the survivor's memories but also his response to new-breaking scientific and religious developments. Tennyson continued to revise and even add to the poem in later decades, but the version we print is substantially the one that was acclaimed in 1850 as the literary statement of its generation. The four-by-four *In Memoriam* stanza variably frames, and through reiteration inculcates, the overall theme of loss and recovery. The poem also rhymes (and differs) with itself in larger units: the holiday and anniversary sections, the paired lyrics (2/39, 3/59, 7/119), the pervasive habit of self-questioning. The interplay of dainty or bookish circumlocution with lapidary aplomb, and of both with a searing neediness, has stirred and comforted readers for a century and a half.

---

[1]**Now Sleeps the Crimson Petal**: derived in structure and imagery from the ghazal, a Persian poetic form.

[2]**Danaë**: daughter of King Acrisius, who shut her up in a roofless tower where she was impregnated by Zeus in a shower of gold; her demigod son Perseus was associated by Victorian mythographers with Persia.

Thine are these orbs of light and shade;[2]
    Thou madest Life in man and brute;
    Thou madest Death; and lo, thy foot
Is on the skull which thou hast made.

Thou wilt not leave us in the dust:
    Thou madest man, he knows not why,   10
    He thinks he was not made to die;
And thou hast made him: thou art just.

Thou seemest human and divine,
    The highest, holiest manhood, thou:
    Our wills are ours, we know not how;
Our wills are ours, to make them thine.

Our little systems have their day;
    They have their day and cease to be:
    They are but broken lights of thee,
And thou, O Lord, art more than they.   20

We have but faith: we cannot know;
    For knowledge is of things we see;
    And yet we trust it comes from thee,
A beam in darkness: let it grow.

Let knowledge grow from more to more,
    But more of reverence in us dwell;
    That mind and soul, according well,
May make one music as before,

But vaster. We are fools and slight;
    We mock thee when we do not fear: 30
    But help thy foolish ones to bear;
Help thy vain worlds to bear thy light.

Forgive what seem'd my sin in me;
    What seem'd my worth since I began;
    For merit lives from man to man,
And not from man, O Lord, to thee.

Forgive my grief for one removed,
    Thy creature, whom I found so fair.
    I trust he lives in thee, and there
I find him worthier to be loved.   40

Forgive these wild and wandering cries,
    Confusions of a wasted youth;
    Forgive them where they fail in truth,
And in thy wisdom make me wise.
                                    1849

— 1 —

I held it truth, with him who sings[3]
    To one clear harp in divers tones,
    That men may rise on stepping-stones
Of their dead selves to higher things.

But who shall so forecast the years
    And find in loss a gain to match?
    Or reach a hand thro' time to catch
The far-off interest of tears?

Let Love clasp Grief lest both be drown'd,
    Let darkness keep her raven gloss: 10
    Ah, sweeter to be drunk with loss,
To dance with death, to beat the ground,

Than that the victor Hours should scorn
    The long result of love, and boast,
    "Behold the man that loved and lost,
But all he was is overworn."

— 2 —

Old Yew, which graspest at the stones
    That name the under-lying dead,
    Thy fibres net the dreamless head,
Thy roots are wrapt about the bones.

The seasons bring the flower again,
    And bring the firstling to the flock;
    And in the dusk of thee, the clock
Beats out the little lives of men.

O not for thee the glow, the bloom,
    Who changest not in any gale,   10
    Nor branding summer suns avail
To touch thy thousand years of gloom:

And gazing on thee, sullen tree,
    Sick for thy stubborn hardihood,
    I seem to fail from out my blood
And grow incorporate into thee.

— 3 —

O Sorrow, cruel fellowship,
    O Priestess in the vaults of Death,
    O sweet and bitter in a breath,
What whispers from thy lying lip?

"The stars," she whispers, "blindly run;
    A web is wov'n across the sky;
    From out waste places comes a cry,
And murmurs from the dying sun:

---

[2]**orbs of . . . shade:** Sun and moon. [Tennyson's note]

[3]**him who sings:** I alluded to Goethe's creed. [Tennyson's note]
creed: 19th-century progressivism.

"And all the phantom, Nature, stands—
    With all the music in her tone,   10
    A hollow echo of my own,—
A hollow form with empty hands."

And shall I take a thing so blind,
    Embrace her as my natural good;
    Or crush her, like a vice of blood,
Upon the threshold of the mind?

— 4 —

To Sleep I give my powers away;
    My will is bondsman to the dark;
    I sit within a helmless bark,
And with my heart I muse and say:

O heart, how fares it with thee now,
    That thou should'st fail from thy desire,
    Who scarcely darest to inquire,
"What is it makes me beat so low?"

Something it is which thou hast lost,
    Some pleasure from thine early years.   10
    Break, thou deep vase of chilling tears,
That grief hath shaken into frost![4]

Such clouds of nameless trouble cross
    All night below the darken'd eyes;
    With morning wakes the will, and cries,
"Thou shalt not be the fool of loss."

— 5 —

I sometimes hold it half a sin
    To put in words the grief I feel;
    For words, like Nature, half reveal
And half conceal the Soul within.

But, for the unquiet heart and brain,
    A use in measured language lies;
    The sad mechanic exercise,
Like dull narcotics, numbing pain.

In words, like weeds,[5] I'll wrap me o'er,
    Like coarsest clothes against the cold: 10
    But that large grief which these enfold
Is given in outline and no more.

---

[4] **shaken into frost:** Water can be brought below freezing-point and not turn into ice—if it be kept still; but if it be moved suddenly it turns into ice and may break the vase. [Tennyson's note]

[5] **weeds:** clothes, especially a mourner's.

— 6 —

One writes, that "Other friends remain,"
    That "Loss is common to the race"—
    And common is the commonplace,
And vacant chaff well meant for grain.

That loss is common would not make
    My own less bitter, rather more:
    Too common! Never morning wore
To evening, but some heart did break.

O father, wheresoe'er thou be,
    Who pledgest now thy gallant son;   10
    A shot, ere half thy draught be done,
Hath still'd the life that beat from thee.

O mother, praying God will save
    Thy sailor,—while thy head is bow'd,
    His heavy-shotted hammock-shroud
Drops in his vast and wandering grave.

Ye know no more than I who wrought
    At that last hour to please him well;
    Who mused on all I had to tell,
And something written, something thought;   20

Expecting still his advent home;
    And ever met him on his way
    With wishes, thinking, "here to-day,"
Or "here to-morrow will he come."

O somewhere, meek, unconscious dove,
    That sittest ranging golden hair;
    And glad to find thyself so fair,
Poor child, that waitest for thy love!

For now her father's chimney glows
    In expectation of a guest;   30
    And thinking "this will please him best,"
She takes a riband or a rose;

For he will see them on to-night;
    And with the thought her colour burns;
    And, having left the glass, she turns
Once more to set a ringlet right;

And, even when she turn'd, the curse
    Had fallen, and her future Lord
    Was drown'd in passing thro' the ford,
Or kill'd in falling from his horse.   40

O what to her shall be the end?
    And what to me remains of good?
    To her, perpetual maidenhood,
And unto me no second friend.

— 7 —

Dark house, by which once more I stand
  Here in the long unlovely street,
  Doors, where my heart was used to beat
So quickly, waiting for a hand,

A hand that can be clasp'd no more—
  Behold me, for I cannot sleep,
  And like a guilty thing I creep
At earliest morning to the door.

He is not here,[6] but far away
  The noise of life begins again,   10
  And ghastly thro' the drizzling rain
On the bald street breaks the blank day.

— 8 —

A happy lover who has come
  To look on her that loves him well,
  Who 'lights and rings the gateway bell,
And learns her gone and far from home;

He saddens, all the magic light
  Dies off at once from bower and hall,
  And all the place is dark, and all
The chambers emptied of delight:

So find I every pleasant spot
  In which we two were wont to meet,   10
  The field, the chamber and the street,
For all is dark where thou art not.

Yet as that other, wandering there
  In those deserted walks, may find
  A flower beat with rain and wind,
Which once she foster'd up with care;

So seems it in my deep regret,
  O my forsaken heart, with thee
  And this poor flower of poesy
Which little cared for fades not yet.   20

But since it pleased a vanish'd eye,
  I go to plant it on his tomb,
  That if it can it there may bloom,
Or dying, there at least may die.

— 9 —

Fair ship, that from the Italian shore
  Sailest the placid ocean-plains
  With my lost Arthur's loved remains,
Spread thy full wings, and waft him o'er.

So draw him home to those that mourn
  In vain; a favourable speed
  Ruffle thy mirror'd mast, and lead
Thro' prosperous floods his holy urn.

All night no ruder air perplex
  Thy sliding keel, till Phosphor,[7] bright   10
  As our pure love, thro' early light
Shall glimmer on the dewy decks.

Sphere all your lights around, above;
  Sleep, gentle heavens, before the prow;
  Sleep, gentle winds, as he sleeps now,
My friend, the brother of my love;

My Arthur, whom I shall not see
  Till all my widow'd race be run;
  Dear as the mother to the son,
More than my brothers are to me.   20

— 10 —

I hear the noise about thy keel;
  I hear the bell struck in the night:
  I see the cabin-window bright;
I see the sailor at the wheel.

Thou bring'st the sailor to his wife,
  And travell'd men from foreign lands;
  And letters unto trembling hands;
And, thy dark freight, a vanish'd life.

So bring him: we have idle dreams:
  This look of quiet flatters thus   10
  Our home-bred fancies: O to us,
The fools of habit, sweeter seems

To rest beneath the clover sod,
  That takes the sunshine and the rains,
  Or where the kneeling hamlet drains
The chalice of the grapes of God;

Than if with thee the roaring wells
  Should gulf him fathom-deep in brine;
  And hands so often clasp'd in mine,
Should toss with tangle and with shells.   20

---

[6]**He is not here:** Luke 24:6.

[7]**Phosphor:** the morning star.

— 11 —

Calm is the morn without a sound,
    Calm as to suit a calmer grief,
    And only thro' the faded leaf
The chestnut pattering to the ground:

Calm and deep peace on this high wold,
    And on these dews that drench the furze,
    And all the silvery gossamers
That twinkle into green and gold:

Calm and still light on yon great plain
    That sweeps with all its autumn bowers,   10
    And crowded farms and lessening towers,
To mingle with the bounding main:

Calm and deep peace in this wide air,
    These leaves that redden to the fall;
    And in my heart, if calm at all,
If any calm, a calm despair:

Calm on the seas, and silver sleep,
    And waves that sway themselves in rest,
    And dead calm in that noble breast
Which heaves but with the heaving deep.   20

— 12 —

Lo, as a dove when up she springs
    To bear thro' Heaven a tale of woe,
    Some dolorous message knit below
The wild pulsation of her wings;

Like her I go; I cannot stay;
    I leave this mortal ark behind,
    A weight of nerves without a mind,
And leave the cliffs, and haste away

O'er ocean-mirrors rounded large,
    And reach the glow of southern skies,   10
    And see the sails at distance rise,
And linger weeping on the marge,

And saying; "Comes he thus, my friend?
    Is this the end of all my care?"
    And circle moaning in the air:
"Is this the end? Is this the end?"

And forward dart again, and play
    About the prow, and back return
    To where the body sits, and learn
That I have been an hour away.   20

— 13 —

Tears of the widower, when he sees
    A late-lost form that sleep reveals,
    And moves his doubtful arms, and feels
Her place is empty, fall like these;

Which weep a loss for ever new,
    A void where heart on heart reposed;
    And, where warm hands have prest and closed,
Silence, till I be silent too.

Which weep the comrade of my choice,
    An awful thought, a life removed,   10
    The human-hearted man I loved,
A Spirit, not a breathing voice.

Come Time, and teach me, many years,
    I do not suffer in a dream;
    For now so strange do these things seem,
Mine eyes have leisure for their tears;

My fancies time to rise on wing,
    And glance about the approaching sails,
    As tho' they brought but merchants' bales,
And not the burthen that they bring.   20

— 14 —

If one should bring me this report,
    That thou[8] hadst touch'd the land to-day,
    And I went down unto the quay,
And found thee lying in the port;

And standing, muffled round with woe,
    Should see thy passengers in rank
    Come stepping lightly down the plank,
And beckoning unto those they know;

And if along with these should come
    The man I held as half-divine;   10
    Should strike a sudden hand in mine,
And ask a thousand things of home;

And I should tell him all my pain,
    And how my life had droop'd of late,
    And he should sorrow o'er my state
And marvel what possess'd my brain;

And I perceived no touch of change,
    No hint of death in all his frame,
    But found him all in all the same,
I should not feel it to be strange.   20

---

[8]**thou:** the ship carrying Hallam's body back to England (also
sections 9, 10, 15, 17).

— 15 —

To-night the winds begin to rise
    And roar from yonder dropping day:
    The last red leaf is whirl'd away,
The rooks are blown about the skies;

The forest crack'd, the waters curl'd,
    The cattle huddled on the lea;
    And wildly dash'd on tower and tree
The sunbeam strikes along the world:

And but for fancies, which aver
    That all thy motions gently pass   10
    Athwart a plane of molten glass,
I scarce could brook the strain and stir

That makes the barren branches loud;
    And but for fear it is not so,[9]
    The wild unrest that lives in woe
Would dote and pore on yonder cloud

That rises upward always higher,
    And onward drags a labouring breast,
    And topples round the dreary west,
A looming bastion fringed with fire.   20

— 16 —

What words are these have fall'n from me?
    Can calm despair and wild unrest
    Be tenants of a single breast,
Or sorrow such a changeling be?

Or doth she only seem to take
    The touch of change in calm or storm;
    But knows no more of transient form
In her deep self, than some dead lake

That holds the shadow of a lark
    Hung in the shadow of a heaven?   10
    Or has the shock, so harshly given,
Confused me like the unhappy bark

That strikes by night a craggy shelf,
    And staggers blindly ere she sink?
    And stunn'd me from my power to think
And all my knowledge of myself;

And made me that delirious man
    Whose fancy fuses old and new,
    And flashes into false and true,
And mingles all without a plan?   20

---

[9]**but . . . not so:** if I were not afraid that my **fancies** of a glassy-smooth passage are illusions.

— 17 —

Thou comest, much wept for: such a breeze
    Compell'd thy canvas, and my prayer
    Was as the whisper of an air
To breathe thee over lonely seas.

For I in spirit saw thee move
    Thro' circles of the bounding sky,
    Week after week: the days go by:
Come quick, thou bringest all I love.

Henceforth, wherever thou may'st roam,
    My blessing, like a line of light,   10
    Is on the waters day and night,
And like a beacon guards thee home.

So may whatever tempest mars
    Mid-ocean, spare thee, sacred bark;
    And balmy drops in summer dark
Slide from the bosom of the stars.

So kind an office hath been done,
    Such precious relics brought by thee;
    The dust of him I shall not see
Till all my widow'd race be run.   20

— 18 —

'Tis well; 'tis something; we may stand
    Where he in English earth is laid,
    And from his ashes may be made
The violet of his native land.

'Tis little; but it looks in truth
    As if the quiet bones were blest
    Among familiar names to rest
And in the places of his youth.

Come then, pure hands, and bear the head
    That sleeps or wears the mask of sleep,   10
    And come, whatever loves to weep,
And hear the ritual of the dead.

Ah yet, ev'n yet, if this might be,
    I, falling on his faithful heart,
    Would breathing thro' his lips impart
The life that almost dies in me;

That dies not, but endures with pain,
    And slowly forms the firmer mind,
    Treasuring the look it cannot find,
The words that are not heard again.   20

— 19 —

The Danube to the Severn[10] gave
 The darken'd heart that beat no more;
 They laid him by the pleasant shore,
And in the hearing of the wave.

There twice a day the Severn fills;
 The salt sea-water passes by,
 And hushes half the babbling Wye,
And makes a silence in the hills.

The Wye is hush'd nor moved along,
 And hush'd my deepest grief of all,   30
 When fill'd with tears that cannot fall,
I brim with sorrow drowning song.

The tide flows down, the wave again
 Is vocal in its wooded walls;
 My deeper anguish also falls,
And I can speak a little then.

— 20 —

The lesser griefs that may be said,
 That breathe a thousand tender vows,
 Are but as servants in a house
Where lies the master newly dead;

Who speak their feeling as it is,
 And weep the fulness from the mind:
 "It will be hard," they say, "to find
Another service such as this."

My lighter moods are like to these,
 That out of words a comfort win;   10
 But there are other griefs within,
And tears that at their fountain freeze;

For by the hearth the children sit
 Cold in that atmosphere of Death,
 And scarce endure to draw the breath,
Or like to noiseless phantoms flit:

But open converse is there none,
 So much the vital spirits sink
 To see the vacant chair, and think,
"How good! how kind! and he is gone."   20

— 21 —

I sing to him that rests below,
 And, since the grasses round me wave,
 I take the grasses of the grave,
And make them pipes whereon to blow.

The traveller hears me now and then,
 And sometimes harshly will he speak:
 "This fellow would make weakness weak,
And melt the waxen hearts of men."

Another answers, "Let him be,
 He loves to make parade of pain,   10
 That with his piping he may gain
The praise that comes to constancy."

A third is wroth: "Is this an hour
 For private sorrow's barren song,
 When more and more the people throng
The chairs and thrones of civil power?

"A time to sicken and to swoon,
 When Science reaches forth her arms
 To feel from world to world, and charms
Her secret from the latest moon?"   20

Behold, ye speak an idle thing:
 Ye never knew the sacred dust:
 I do but sing because I must,
And pipe but as the linnets sing:

And one is glad; her note is gay,
 For now her little ones have ranged;
 And one is sad; her note is changed,
Because her brood is stol'n away.

— 22 —

The path by which we twain did go,
 Which led by tracts that pleased us well,
 Thro' four sweet years[11] arose and fell,
From flower to flower, from snow to snow:

And we with singing cheer'd the way,
 And, crown'd with all the season lent,
 From April on to April went,
And glad at heart from May to May:

But where the path we walk'd began
 To slant the fifth autumnal slope,   10
 As we descended following Hope,
There sat the Shadow fear'd of man;

---

[10]**Danube, Severn:** rivers beginning and completing the waterway by which Hallam's body has returned from Vienna for burial in Clevedon (SW England). **Wye:** tributary to the Severn; see Wordsworth, "Tintern Abbey."

---

[11]**four sweet years:** from 1829, when Tennyson met Hallam, until his death in 1833.

Who broke our fair companionship,
   And spread his mantle dark and cold,
   And wrapt thee formless in the fold,
And dull'd the murmur on thy lip,

And bore thee where I could not see
   Nor follow, tho' I walk in haste,
   And think, that somewhere in the waste
The Shadow sits and waits for me.   20

— 23 —

Now, sometimes in my sorrow shut,
   Or breaking into song by fits,
   Alone, alone, to where he sits,
The Shadow cloak'd from head to foot,

Who keeps the keys of all the creeds,[12]
   I wander, often falling lame,
   And looking back to whence I came,
Or on to where the pathway leads;

And crying, How changed from where it ran
   Thro' lands where not a leaf was dumb;   10
   But all the lavish hills would hum
The murmur of a happy Pan:[13]

When each by turns was guide to each,
   And Fancy light from Fancy caught,
   And Thought leapt out to wed with Thought
Ere Thought could wed itself with Speech;

And all we met was fair and good,
   And all was good that Time could bring,
   And all the secret of the Spring
Moved in the chambers of the blood;   20

And many an old philosophy
   On Argive heights divinely sang,
   And round us all the thicket rang
To many a flute of Arcady.[14]

— 24 —

And was the day of my delight
   As pure and perfect as I say?
   The very source and fount of Day
Is dash'd with wandering isles of night.[15]

---

[12]**keys of . . . creeds:** After death we shall learn the truth of all beliefs. [Tennyson's note]

[13]**Pan:** god of woods, pastures, and pastoral poetry.

[14]**Argive:** from the Greek city of Argos. **Arcady:** Arcadia, mountain haunt of pastoral poetry, which is traditionally sung to the shepherd's **flute.**

[15]**isles of night:** sun spots.

If all was good and fair we met,
   This earth had been the Paradise
   It never look'd to human eyes
Since our first Sun arose and set.

And is it that the haze of grief
   Makes former gladness loom so great?   10
   The lowness of the present state,
That sets the past in this relief?

Or that the past will always win
   A glory from its being far;
   And orb into the perfect star
We saw not, when we moved therein?

— 25 —

I know that this was Life,—the track
   Whereon with equal feet we fared;
   And then, as now, the day prepared
The daily burden for the back.

But this it was that made me move
   As light as carrier-birds in air;
   I loved the weight I had to bear,
Because it needed help of Love:

Nor could I weary, heart or limb,
   When mighty Love would cleave in twain   10
   The lading of a single pain,
And part it, giving half to him.

— 26 —

Still onward winds the dreary way;
   I with it; for I long to prove
   No lapse of moons can canker Love,
Whatever fickle tongues may say.

And if that eye which watches guilt
   And goodness, and hath power to see
   Within the green the moulder'd tree,
And towers fall'n as soon as built—

Oh, if indeed that eye foresee
   Or see (in Him is no before)   10
   In more of life true life no more
And Love the indifference to be,

Then might I find, ere yet the morn
   Breaks hither over Indian seas,
   That Shadow waiting with the keys,
To shroud me from my proper scorn.[16]

---

[16]**my proper scorn:** scorn of myself. [Tennyson's note]

— 27 —

I envy not in any moods
    The captive void of noble rage,
    The linnet born within the cage,
That never knew the summer woods:

I envy not the beast that takes
    His license in the field of time,
    Unfetter'd by the sense of crime,
To whom a conscience never wakes;

Nor, what may count itself as blest,
    The heart that never plighted troth   10
    But stagnates in the weeds of sloth;
Nor any want-begotten rest.

I hold it true, whate'er befall;
    I feel it, when I sorrow most;
    'Tis better to have loved and lost
Than never to have loved at all.

— 28 —

The time draws near the birth of Christ:
    The moon is hid; the night is still;
    The Christmas bells from hill to hill
Answer each other in the mist.

Four voices of four hamlets round,
    From far and near, on mead and moor,
    Swell out and fail, as if a door
Were shut between me and the sound:

Each voice four changes on the wind,
    That now dilate, and now decrease,   10
    Peace and goodwill, goodwill and peace,
Peace and goodwill, to all mankind.

This year I slept and woke with pain,
    I almost wish'd no more to wake,
    And that my hold on life would break
Before I heard those bells again:

But they my troubled spirit rule,
    For they controll'd me when a boy;
    They bring me sorrow touch'd with joy,
The merry merry bells of Yule.   20

— 29 —

With such compelling cause to grieve
    As daily vexes household peace,
    And chains regret to his decease,
How dare we keep our Christmas-eve;

Which brings no more a welcome guest
    To enrich the threshold of the night
    With shower'd largess of delight
In dance and song and game and jest?

Yet go, and while the holly boughs
    Entwine the cold baptismal font,   10
    Make one wreath more for Use and Wont,
That guard the portals of the house;

Old sisters of a day gone by,
    Gray nurses, loving nothing new;
    Why should they miss their yearly due
Before their time? They too will die.

— 30 —

With trembling fingers did we weave
    The holly round the Christmas hearth;
    A rainy cloud possess'd the earth,
And sadly fell our Christmas-eve.

At our old pastimes in the hall
    We gambol'd, making vain pretence
    Of gladness, with an awful sense
Of one mute Shadow watching all.

We paused: the winds were in the beech:
    We heard them sweep the winter land;   10
    And in a circle hand-in-hand
Sat silent, looking each at each.

Then echo-like our voices rang;
    We sung, tho' every eye was dim,
    A merry song we sang with him
Last year: impetuously we sang:

We ceased: a gentler feeling crept
    Upon us: surely rest is meet:
    "They rest," we said, "their sleep is sweet,"
And silence follow'd, and we wept.   20

Our voices took a higher range;
    Once more we sang: "They do not die
    Nor lose their mortal sympathy,
Nor change to us, although they change;

"Rapt from the fickle and the frail
    With gather'd power, yet the same,
    Pierces the keen seraphic flame
From orb to orb, from veil to veil."

Rise, happy morn, rise, holy morn,
    Draw forth the cheerful day from night: 30
    O Father, touch the east, and light
The light that shone when Hope was born.

— 31 —

When Lazarus[17] left his charnel-cave,
    And home to Mary's house return'd,
    Was this demanded—if he yearn'd
To hear her weeping by his grave?

"Where wert thou, brother, those four days?"
    There lives no record of reply,
    Which telling what it is to die
Had surely added praise to praise.

From every house the neighbours met,
    The streets were fill'd with joyful sound,   10
    A solemn gladness even crown'd
The purple brows of Olivet.

Behold a man raised up by Christ!
    The rest remaineth unreveal'd;
    He told it not; or something seal'd
The lips of that Evangelist.

— 32 —

Her eyes are homes of silent prayer,
    Nor other thought her mind admits
    But, he was dead, and there he sits,
And he that brought him back is there.

Then one deep love doth supersede
    All other, when her ardent gaze
    Roves from the living brother's face,
And rests upon the Life indeed.

All subtle thought, all curious fears,
    Borne down by gladness so complete,   10
    She bows, she bathes the Saviour's feet
With costly spikenard and with tears.

Thrice blest whose lives are faithful prayers,
    Whose loves in higher love endure;
    What souls possess themselves so pure,
Or is there blessedness like theirs?

— 33 —

O thou that after toil and storm
    Mayst seem to have reach'd a purer air,
    Whose faith has centre everywhere,
Nor cares to fix itself to form,

Leave thou thy sister when she prays,
    Her early Heaven, her happy views;
    Nor thou with shadow'd hint confuse
A life that leads melodious days.

Her faith thro' form is pure as thine,
    Her hands are quicker unto good: 10
    Oh, sacred be the flesh and blood
To which she links a truth divine!

See thou, that countest reason ripe
    In holding by the law within,
    Thou fail not in a world of sin,
And ev'n for want of such a type.

— 34 —

My own dim life should teach me this,
    That life shall live for evermore,
    Else earth is darkness at the core,
And dust and ashes all that is;

This round of green, this orb of flame,
    Fantastic beauty; such as lurks
    In some wild Poet, when he works
Without a conscience or an aim.

What then were God to such as I?
    'Twere hardly worth my while to choose   10
    Of things all mortal, or to use
A little patience ere I die;

'Twere best at once to sink to peace,
    Like birds the charming serpent draws,
    To drop head-foremost in the jaws
Of vacant darkness and to cease.

— 35 —

Yet if some voice that man could trust
    Should murmur from the narrow house,
    "The cheeks drop in; the body bows;
Man dies: nor is there hope in dust:"

Might I not say? "Yet even here,
    But for one hour, O Love, I strive
    To keep so sweet a thing alive:"
But I should turn mine ears and hear

The moanings of the homeless sea,
    The sound of streams that swift or slow   10
    Draw down Æonian hills,[18] and sow
The dust of continents to be;

---

[17]**Lazarus**: resurrected by Jesus at the home of his sisters Martha and **Mary** in Bethany, on Mount **Olivet** near Jerusalem. The story occurs in the gospel of John the **Evangelist** (11:1–45).

---

[18]**Aeonian**: immeasurably ancient; with the geological implication that "old as the hills" does not mean "everlasting."

And Love would answer with a sigh,
　　"The sound of that forgetful shore[19]
　　Will change my sweetness more and more,
Half-dead to know that I shall die."

O me, what profits it to put
　　An idle case? If Death were seen
　　At first as Death, Love had not been,
Or been in narrowest working shut,　　　　20

Mere fellowship of sluggish moods,
　　Or in his coarsest Satyr-shape
　　Had bruised the herb and crush'd the grape,
And bask'd and batten'd in the woods.

— 36 —

Tho' truths in manhood darkly join,
　　Deep-seated in our mystic frame,
　　We yield all blessing to the name
Of Him that made them current coin;

For Wisdom dealt with mortal powers,
　　Where truth in closest words shall fail,
　　When truth embodied in a tale
Shall enter in at lowly doors.

And so the Word had breath, and wrought
　　With human hands the creed of creeds　　　10
　　In loveliness of perfect deeds,
More strong than all poetic thought;

Which he may read that binds the sheaf,
　　Or builds the house, or digs the grave,
　　And those wild eyes that watch the wave
In roarings round the coral reef.[20]

— 37 —

Urania[21] speaks with darken'd brow:
　　"Thou pratest here where thou art least;
　　This faith has many a purer priest,
And many an abler voice than thou.

"Go down beside thy native rill,
　　On thy Parnassus set thy feet,
　　And hear thy laurel whisper sweet
About the ledges of the hill."

And my Melpomene replies,
　　A touch of shame upon her cheek:　　　　10
　　"I am not worthy ev'n to speak
Of thy prevailing mysteries;

"For I am but an earthly Muse,
　　And owning but a little art
　　To lull with song an aching heart,
And render human love his dues;

"But brooding on the dear one dead,
　　And all he said of things divine,
　　(And dear to me as sacred wine
To dying lips is all he said),　　　　20

"I murmur'd, as I came along,
　　Of comfort clasp'd in truth reveal'd;
　　And loiter'd in the master's field,
And darken'd sanctities with song."

— 38 —

With weary steps I loiter on,
　　Tho' always under alter'd skies
　　The purple from the distance dies,
My prospect and horizon gone.

No joy the blowing season gives,
　　The herald melodies of spring,
　　But in the songs I love to sing
A doubtful gleam of solace lives.

If any care for what is here
　　Survive in spirits render'd free,　　　　10
　　Then are these songs I sing of thee
Not all ungrateful to thine ear.

— 39 —

Old warder of these buried bones,
　　And answering now my random stroke
　　With fruitful cloud and living smoke,[22]
Dark yew, that graspest at the stones

---

[19]**forgetful shore**: conflates Lethe, mythological river of mortal oblivion, with the ceaseless tide of geological change now audible to modern minds.

[20]**wild eyes . . . coral reef**: the Pacific Islanders. [Tennyson's note]

[21]**Urania** (muse of astronomy—and Milton) and her sister **Melpomene** (muse of tragedy) dwell on Mount **Parnassus**.

[22]**cloud . . . smoke**: pollen from the **yew** (also addressed in section 2), which bears male and female flowers on separate plants.

And dippest toward the dreamless head,
    To thee too comes the golden hour
    When flower is feeling after flower;
But Sorrow—fixt upon the dead,

And darkening the dark graves of men,—
    What whisper'd from her lying lips?   10
    Thy gloom is kindled at the tips,
And passes into gloom again.

— 40 —

Could we forget the widow'd hour
    And look on Spirits breathed away,
    As on a maiden in the day
When first she wears her orange-flower![23]

When crown'd with blessing she doth rise
    To take her latest leave of home,
    And hopes and light regrets that come
Make April of her tender eyes;

And doubtful joys the father move,
    And tears are on the mother's face,   10
    As parting with a long embrace
She enters other realms of love;

Her office there to rear, to teach,
    Becoming as is meet and fit
    A link among the days, to knit
The generations each with each;

And, doubtless, unto thee is given
    A life that bears immortal fruit
    In those great offices that suit
The full-grown energies of heaven.   20

Ay me, the difference I discern!
    How often shall her old fireside
    Be cheer'd with tidings of the bride,
How often she herself return,

And tell them all they would have told,
    And bring her babe, and make her boast,
    Till even those that miss'd her most
Shall count new things as dear as old:

But thou and I have shaken hands,
    Till growing winters lay me low;   30
    My paths are in the fields I know
And thine in undiscover'd lands.

— 41 —

Thy spirit ere our fatal loss
    Did ever rise from high to higher;
    As mounts the heavenward altar-fire,
As flies the lighter thro' the gross.

But thou art turn'd to something strange,
    And I have lost the links that bound
    Thy changes; here upon the ground,
No more partaker of thy change.

Deep folly! yet that this could be—
    That I could wing my will with might   10
    To leap the grades of life and light,
And flash at once, my friend, to thee.

For tho' my nature rarely yields
    To that vague fear implied in death;
    Nor shudders at the gulfs beneath,
The howlings from forgotten fields;

Yet oft when sundown skirts the moor
    An inner trouble I behold,
    A spectral doubt which makes me cold,
That I shall be thy mate no more,   20

Tho' following with an upward mind
    The wonders that have come to thee,
    Thro' all the secular to-be,[24]
But evermore a life behind.

— 42 —

I vex my heart with fancies dim:
    He still outstript me in the race;
    It was but unity of place
That made me dream I rank'd with him.

And so may Place retain us still,
    And he the much-beloved again,
    A lord of large experience, train
To riper growth the mind and will:

And what delights can equal those
    That stir the spirit's inner deeps,   10
    When one that loves but knows not, reaps
A truth from one that loves and knows?

---

[23]**orange-flower**: bridal symbol.

[24]**secular to-be**: aeons of the future. [Tennyson's note]

— 43 —

If Sleep and Death be truly one,
　　And every spirit's folded bloom
　　Thro' all its intervital[25] gloom
In some long trance should slumber on;

Unconscious of the sliding hour,
　　Bare of the body, might it last,
　　And silent traces of the past
Be all the colour of the flower:

So then were nothing lost to man;
　　So that still garden of the souls　　　　　10
　　In many a figured leaf enrolls
The total world since life began;

And love will last as pure and whole
　　As when he loved me here in Time,
　　And at the spiritual prime
Rewaken with the dawning soul.

— 44 —

How fares it with the happy dead?
　　For here the man is more and more;
　　But he forgets the days before
God shut the doorways of his head.[26]

The days have vanish'd, tone and tint,
　　And yet perhaps the hoarding sense
　　Gives out at times (he knows not whence)
A little flash, a mystic hint;

And in the long harmonious years
　　(If Death so taste Lethean[27] springs),　　　10
　　May some dim touch of earthly things
Surprise thee ranging with thy peers.

If such a dreamy touch should fall,
　　O turn thee round, resolve the doubt;
　　My guardian angel will speak out
In that high place, and tell thee all.

— 45 —

The baby new to earth and sky,
　　What time his tender palm is prest
　　Against the circle of the breast,
Has never thought that "this is I":

---

[25]**intervital**: between this life and the life to come.

[26]**doorways . . . head**: closing of the skull after babyhood. [Tennyson's note]

[27]**Lethean**: of Lethe, river of oblivion in classical mythology.

But as he grows he gathers much,
　　And learns the use of "I," and "me,"
　　And finds "I am not what I see,
And other than the things I touch."

So rounds he to a separate mind
　　From whence clear memory may begin,　　　10
　　As thro' the frame that binds him in
His isolation grows defined.

This use may lie in blood and breath,
　　Which else were fruitless of their due,
　　Had man to learn himself anew
Beyond the second birth of Death.

— 46 —

We ranging down this lower track,
　　The path we came by, thorn and flower,
　　Is shadow'd by the growing hour,
Lest life should fail in looking back.

So be it: there no shade can last
　　In that deep dawn behind the tomb,
　　But clear from marge to marge shall bloom
The eternal landscape of the past;

A lifelong tract of time reveal'd;
　　The fruitful hours of still increase;　　　10
　　Days order'd in a wealthy peace,
And those five years its richest field.

O Love, thy province were not large,
　　A bounded field, nor stretching far;
　　Look also, Love, a brooding star,
A rosy warmth from marge to marge.

— 47 —

That each, who seems a separate whole,
　　Should move his rounds, and fusing all
　　The skirts of self again, should fall
Remerging in the general Soul,

Is faith as vague as all unsweet:
　　Eternal form shall still divide
　　The eternal soul from all beside;
And I shall know him when we meet:

And we shall sit at endless feast,
　　Enjoying each the other's good:　　　10
　　What vaster dream can hit the mood
Of Love on earth? He seeks at least

Upon the last and sharpest height,
  Before the spirits fade away,
  Some landing-place, to clasp and say,
"Farewell! We lose ourselves in light."

— 48 —

If these brief lays, of Sorrow born,
  Were taken to be such as closed
  Grave doubts and answers here proposed,
Then these were such as men might scorn:

Her care is not to part and prove;
  She takes, when harsher moods remit,
  What slender shade of doubt may flit,
And makes it vassal unto love:

And hence, indeed, she sports with words,
  But better serves a wholesome law,   10
  And holds it sin and shame to draw
The deepest measure from the chords:

Nor dare she trust a larger lay,
  But rather loosens from the lip
  Short swallow-flights of song, that dip
Their wings in tears, and skim away.

— 49 —

From art, from nature, from the schools,
  Let random influences glance,
  Like light in many a shiver'd lance
That breaks about the dappled pools:

The lightest wave of thought shall lisp,
  The fancy's tenderest eddy wreathe,
  The slightest air of song shall breathe
To make the sullen surface crisp.[28]

And look thy look, and go thy way,
  But blame not thou the winds that make   10
  The seeming-wanton ripple break,
The tender-pencil'd shadow play.

Beneath all fancied hopes and fears
  Ay me, the sorrow deepens down,
  Whose muffled motions blindly drown
The bases of my life in tears.

— 50 —

Be near me when my light is low,
  When the blood creeps, and the nerves prick
  And tingle; and the heart is sick,
And all the wheels of Being slow.

Be near me when the sensuous frame
  Is rack'd with pangs that conquer trust;
  And Time, a maniac scattering dust,
And Life, a Fury slinging flame.

Be near me when my faith is dry,
  And men the flies of latter spring,   10
  That lay their eggs, and sting and sing
And weave their petty cells and die.

Be near me when I fade away,
  To point the term of human strife,
  And on the low dark verge of life
The twilight of eternal day.

— 51 —

Do we indeed desire the dead
  Should still be near us at our side?
  Is there no baseness we would hide?
No inner vileness that we dread?

Shall he for whose applause I strove,
  I had such reverence for his blame,
  See with clear eye some hidden shame
And I be lessen'd in his love?

I wrong the grave with fears untrue:
  Shall love be blamed for want of faith?   10
  There must be wisdom with great Death:
The dead shall look me thro' and thro'.

Be near us when we climb or fall:
  Ye watch, like God, the rolling hours
  With larger other eyes than ours,
To make allowance for us all.

— 52 —

I cannot love thee as I ought,
  For love reflects the thing beloved;
  My words are only words, and moved
Upon the topmost froth of thought.

"Yet blame not thou thy plaintive song,"
  The Spirit of true love replied;
  "Thou canst not move me from thy side,
Nor human frailty do me wrong.

"What keeps a spirit wholly true
  To that ideal which he bears?   10
  What record? not the sinless years[29]
That breathed beneath the Syrian blue:

---

[28]**crisp:** curl, ripple. [Hallam Tennyson's note]

[29]**sinless years:** the life of Jesus in Palestine or **Syria.**

"So fret not, like an idle girl,
    That life is dash'd with flecks of sin.
    Abide: thy wealth is gather'd in,
When Time hath sunder'd shell from pearl."

— 53 —

How many a father have I seen,
    A sober man, among his boys,
    Whose youth was full of foolish noise,
Who wears his manhood hale and green:

And dare we to this fancy give,
    That had the wild oat not been sown,
    The soil, left barren, scarce had grown
The grain by which a man may live?

Or, if we held the doctrine sound
    For life outliving heats of youth,   10
    Yet who would preach it as a truth
To those that eddy round and round?

Hold thou the good: define it well:
    For fear divine Philosophy
    Should push beyond her mark, and be
Procuress to the Lords of Hell.

— 54 —

Oh yet we trust that somehow good
    Will be the final goal of ill,
    To pangs of nature, sins of will,
Defects of doubt, and taints of blood;

That nothing walks with aimless feet;
    That not one life shall be destroy'd,
    Or cast as rubbish to the void,
When God hath made the pile complete;

That not a worm is cloven in vain;
    That not a moth with vain desire   10
    Is shrivell'd in a fruitless fire,
Or but subserves another's gain.

Behold, we know not anything;
    I can but trust that good shall fall
    At last—far off—at last, to all,
And every winter change to spring.

So runs my dream: but what am I?
    An infant crying in the night:
    An infant crying for the light:
And with no language but a cry.   20

— 55 —

The wish, that of the living whole
    No life may fail beyond the grave,
    Derives it not from what we have
The likest God within the soul?

Are God and Nature then at strife,
    That Nature lends such evil dreams?
    So careful of the type she seems,
So careless of the single life;

That I, considering everywhere
    Her secret meaning in her deeds,   10
    And finding that of fifty seeds
She often brings but one to bear,

I falter where I firmly trod,
    And falling with my weight of cares
    Upon the great world's altar-stairs
That slope thro' darkness up to God,

I stretch lame hands of faith, and grope,
    And gather dust and chaff, and call
    To what I feel is Lord of all,
And faintly trust the larger hope.   20

— 56 —

"So careful of the type?" but no.
    From scarped cliff and quarried stone
    She cries, "A thousand types are gone:
I care for nothing, all shall go.

"Thou makest thine appeal to me:
    I bring to life, I bring to death:
    The spirit does but mean the breath:
I know no more." And he, shall he,

Man, her last work, who seem'd so fair,
    Such splendid purpose in his eyes,   10
    Who roll'd the psalm to wintry skies,
Who built him fanes of fruitless prayer,

Who trusted God was love indeed
    And love Creation's final law—
    Tho' Nature, red in tooth and claw
With ravine, shriek'd against his creed—

Who loved, who suffer'd countless ills,
    Who battled for the True, the Just,
    Be blown about the desert dust,
Or seal'd within the iron hills?[30]   20

---

[30]**within . . . hills:** like fossils of extinct species in cliffs and quarries.

No more? A monster then, a dream,
   A discord. Dragons of the prime,[31]
   That tare each other in their slime,
Were mellow music match'd with him.

O life as futile, then, as frail!
   O for thy voice to soothe and bless!
   What hope of answer, or redress?
Behind the veil, behind the veil.

— 57 —

Peace; come away: the song of woe
   Is after all an earthly song:
   Peace; come away: we do him wrong
To sing so wildly: let us go.

Come; let us go: your cheeks are pale;
   But half my life I leave behind:
   Methinks my friend is richly shrined;
But I shall pass; my work will fail.

Yet in these ears, till hearing dies,
   One set slow bell will seem to toll   10
   The passing of the sweetest soul
That ever look'd with human eyes.

I hear it now, and o'er and o'er,
   Eternal greetings to the dead;
   And "Ave, Ave, Ave,"[32] said,
"Adieu, adieu" for evermore.

— 58 —

In those sad words I took farewell:
   Like echoes in sepulchral halls,
   As drop by drop the water falls
In vaults and catacombs, they fell;

And, falling, idly broke the peace
   Of hearts that beat from day to day,
   Half-conscious of their dying clay,
And those cold crypts where they shall cease.

The high Muse answer'd: "Wherefore grieve
   Thy brethren with a fruitless tear?   10
   Abide a little longer here,
And thou shalt take a nobler leave."

— 59 —

O Sorrow, wilt thou live with me
   No casual mistress, but a wife,
   My bosom-friend and half of life;
As I confess it needs must be;

O Sorrow, wilt thou rule my blood,
   Be sometimes lovely like a bride,
   And put thy harsher moods aside,
If thou wilt have me wise and good.

My centred passion cannot move,
   Nor will it lessen from to-day;   10
   But I'll have leave at times to play
As with the creature of my love;

And set thee forth, for thou art mine,
   With so much hope for years to come,
   That, howsoe'er I know thee, some
Could hardly tell what name were thine.

— 60 —

He past; a soul of nobler tone:
   My spirit loved and loves him yet,
   Like some poor girl whose heart is set
On one whose rank exceeds her own.

He mixing with his proper sphere,
   She finds the baseness of her lot,
   Half jealous of she knows not what,
And envying all that meet him there.

The little village looks forlorn;
   She sighs amid her narrow days,   10
   Moving about the household ways,
In that dark house where she was born.

The foolish neighbours come and go,
   And tease her till the day draws by:
   At night she weeps, "How vain am I!
How should he love a thing so low?"

— 61 —

If, in thy second state sublime,
   Thy ransom'd reason[33] change replies
   With all the circle of the wise,
The perfect flower of human time;

---

[31]**Dragons of the prime**: dinosaurs of early time.

[32]**Ave**: Latin greeting.

[33]**ransom'd reason**: intellect now redeemed, in heaven, from sinful error.

And if thou cast thine eyes below,
  How dimly character'd and slight,
  How dwarf'd a growth of cold and night,
How blanch'd with darkness must I grow!

Yet turn thee to the doubtful shore,
  Where thy first form was made a man;   10
  I loved thee, Spirit, and love, nor can
The soul of Shakspeare love thee more.

— 62 —

Tho' if an eye that's downward cast
  Could make thee somewhat blench or fail,
  Then be my love an idle tale,
And fading legend of the past;

And thou, as one that once declined,
  When he was little more than boy,
  On some unworthy heart with joy,
But lives to wed an equal mind;

And breathes a novel world, the while
  His other passion wholly dies,   10
  Or in the light of deeper eyes
Is matter for a flying smile.

— 63 —

Yet pity for a horse o'er-driven,
  And love in which my hound has part,
  Can hang no weight upon my heart
In its assumptions up to heaven;

And I am so much more than these,
  As thou, perchance, art more than I,
  And yet I spare them sympathy,
And I would set their pains at ease.

So mayst thou watch me where I weep,
  As, unto vaster motions bound,   10
  The circuits of thine orbit round
A higher height, a deeper deep.

— 64 —

Dost thou look back on what hath been,
  As some divinely gifted man,
  Whose life in low estate began
And on a simple village green;

Who breaks his birth's invidious bar,
  And grasps the skirts of happy chance,
  And breasts the blows of circumstance,
And grapples with his evil star;

Who makes by force his merit known
  And lives to clutch the golden keys,   10
  To mould a mighty state's decrees,
And shape the whisper of the throne;

And moving up from high to higher,
  Becomes on Fortune's crowning slope
  The pillar of a people's hope,
The centre of a world's desire;

Yet feels, as in a pensive dream,
  When all his active powers are still,
  A distant dearness in the hill,
A secret sweetness in the stream,   20

The limit of his narrower fate,
  While yet beside its vocal springs
  He play'd at counsellors and kings,
With one that was his earliest mate;

Who ploughs with pain his native lea
  And reaps the labour of his hands,
  Or in the furrow musing stands;
"Does my old friend remember me?"

— 65 —

Sweet soul, do with me as thou wilt;
  I lull a fancy trouble-tost
  With "Love's too precious to be lost,
A little grain shall not be spilt."

And in that solace can I sing,
  Till out of painful phases wrought
  There flutters up a happy thought,
Self-balanced on a lightsome wing:

Since we deserved the name of friends,
  And thine effect so lives in me,   10
  A part of mine may live in thee
And move thee on to noble ends.

— 66 —

You thought my heart too far diseased;
  You wonder when my fancies play
  To find me gay among the gay,
Like one with any trifle pleased.

The shade by which my life was crost,
  Which makes a desert in the mind,
  Has made me kindly with my kind,
And like to him whose sight is lost;

Whose feet are guided thro' the land,
    Whose jest among his friends is free,   10
    Who takes the children on his knee,
And winds their curls about his hand:

He plays with threads, he beats his chair
    For pastime, dreaming of the sky;
    His inner day can never die,
His night of loss is always there.

— 67 —

When on my bed the moonlight falls,
    I know that in thy place of rest
    By that broad water[34] of the west,
There comes a glory on the walls;

Thy marble bright in dark appears,
    As slowly steals a silver flame
    Along the letters of thy name,
And o'er the number of thy years.

The mystic glory swims away;
    From off my bed the moonlight dies;   10
    And closing eaves of wearied eyes
I sleep till dusk is dipt in gray:

And then I know the mist is drawn
    A lucid veil from coast to coast,
    And in the dark church like a ghost
Thy tablet glimmers to the dawn.

— 68 —

When in the down I sink my head,
    Sleep, Death's twin-brother, times my breath;
    Sleep, Death's twin-brother, knows not Death,
Nor can I dream of thee as dead:

I walk as ere I walk'd forlorn,
    When all our path was fresh with dew,
    And all the bugle breezes blew
Reveillée to the breaking morn.

But what is this? I turn about,
    I find a trouble in thine eye,   10
    Which makes me sad I know not why,
Nor can my dream resolve the doubt:

But ere the lark hath left the lea
    I wake, and I discern the truth;
    It is the trouble of my youth
That foolish sleep transfers to thee.

— 69 —

I dream'd there would be Spring no more,
    That Nature's ancient power was lost:
    The streets were black with smoke and frost,
They chatter'd trifles at the door:

I wander'd from the noisy town,
    I found a wood with thorny boughs:
    I took the thorns to bind my brows,
I wore them like a civic crown:

I met with scoffs, I met with scorns
    From youth and babe and hoary hairs: 10
    They call'd me in the public squares
The fool that wears a crown of thorns:

They call'd me fool, they call'd me child:
    I found an angel of the night;
    The voice was low, the look was bright;
He look'd upon my crown and smiled:

He reach'd the glory of a hand,
    That seem'd to touch it into leaf:
    The voice was not the voice of grief,
The words were hard to understand.   20

— 70 —

I cannot see the features right,
    When on the gloom I strive to paint
    The face I know; the hues are faint
And mix with hollow masks of night;

Cloud-towers by ghostly masons wrought,
    A gulf that ever shuts and gapes,
    A hand that points, and palled shapes
In shadowy thoroughfares of thought;

And crowds that stream from yawning doors,
    And shoals of pucker'd faces drive;   10
    Dark bulks that tumble half alive,
And lazy lengths on boundless shores;

Till all at once beyond the will
    I hear a wizard music roll,
    And thro' a lattice on the soul
Looks thy fair face and makes it still.

— 71 —

Sleep, kinsman thou to death and trance
    And madness, thou hast forged at last
    A night-long Present of the Past
In which we went thro' summer France.[35]

---

[34]**broad water:** the Severn estuary (see section 19).

[35]**summer France:** a tour Tennyson and Hallam made in 1830.

Hadst thou such credit with the soul?
   Then bring an opiate trebly strong,
   Drug down the blindfold sense of wrong
That so my pleasure may be whole;

While now we talk as once we talk'd
   Of men and minds, the dust of change,   10
   The days that grow to something strange,
In walking as of old we walk'd

Beside the river's wooded reach,
   The fortress, and the mountain ridge,
   The cataract flashing from the bridge,
The breaker breaking on the beach.

— 72 —

Risest thou thus, dim dawn, again,
   And howlest, issuing out of night,
   With blasts that blow the poplar white,
And lash with storm the streaming pane?

Day, when my crown'd estate begun
   To pine in that reverse of doom,
   Which sicken'd every living bloom,
And blurr'd the splendour of the sun;

Who usherest in the dolorous hour
   With thy quick tears that make the rose   10
   Pull sideways, and the daisy close
Her crimson fringes to the shower;

Who might'st have heaved a windless flame
   Up the deep East, or, whispering, play'd
   A chequer-work of beam and shade
Along the hills, yet look'd the same.

As wan, as chill, as wild as now;
   Day, mark'd as with some hideous crime,
   When the dark hand struck down thro' time,
And cancell'd nature's best: but thou,   20

Lift as thou may'st thy burthen'd brows
   Thro' clouds that drench the morning star,
   And whirl the ungarner'd sheaf afar,
And sow the sky with flying boughs,

And up thy vault with roaring sound
   Climb thy thick noon, disastrous day;
   Touch thy dull goal of joyless gray,
And hide thy shame beneath the ground.

— 73 —

So many worlds, so much to do,
   So little done, such things to be,
   How know I what had need of thee,
For thou wert strong as thou wert true?

The fame is quench'd that I foresaw,
   The head hath miss'd an earthly wreath:
   I curse not nature, no, nor death;
For nothing is that errs from law.

We pass; the path that each man trod
   Is dim, or will be dim, with weeds: 10
   What fame is left for human deeds
In endless age? It rests with God.

O hollow wraith of dying fame,
   Fade wholly, while the soul exults,
   And self-infolds the large results
Of force that would have forged a name.

— 74 —

As sometimes in a dead man's face,
   To those that watch it more and more,
   A likeness, hardly seen before,
Comes out—to some one of his race:

So, dearest, now thy brows are cold,
   I see thee what thou art, and know
   Thy likeness to the wise below,
Thy kindred with the great of old.

But there is more than I can see,
   And what I see I leave unsaid,   10
   Nor speak it, knowing Death has made
His darkness beautiful with thee.

— 75 —

I leave thy praises unexpress'd
   In verse that brings myself relief,
   And by the measure of my grief
I leave thy greatness to be guess'd;

What practice howsoe'er expert
   In fitting aptest words to things,
   Or voice the richest-toned that sings,
Hath power to give thee as thou wert?

I care not in these fading days
   To raise a cry that lasts not long,   10
   And round thee with the breeze of song
To stir a little dust of praise.

Thy leaf has perish'd in the green,
   And, while we breathe beneath the sun,
   The world which credits what is done
Is cold to all that might have been.

So here shall silence guard thy fame;
   But somewhere, out of human view,
   Whate'er thy hands are set to do
Is wrought with tumult of acclaim.   20

— 76 —

Take wings of fancy, and ascend,
    And in a moment set thy face
    Where all the starry heavens of space
Are sharpen'd to a needle's end;

Take wings of foresight; lighten thro'
    The secular abyss[36] to come,
    And lo, thy deepest lays are dumb
Before the mouldering of a yew;

And if the matin songs, that woke
    The darkness of our planet, last,   10
    Thine own shall wither in the vast,
Ere half the lifetime of an oak.

Ere these have clothed their branchy bowers
    With fifty Mays, thy songs are vain;
    And what are they when these remain
The ruin'd shells of hollow towers?

— 77 —

What hope is here for modern rhyme
    To him, who turns a musing eye
    On songs, and deeds, and lives, that lie
Foreshorten'd in the tract of time?

These mortal lullabies of pain
    May bind a book, may line a box,
    May serve to curl a maiden's locks;
Or when a thousand moons shall wane

A man upon a stall may find,
    And, passing, turn the page that tells   10
    A grief, then changed to something else,
Sung by a long-forgotten mind.

But what of that? My darken'd ways
    Shall ring with music all the same;
    To breathe my loss is more than fame,
To utter love more sweet than praise.

— 78 —

Again at Christmas did we weave
    The holly round the Christmas hearth;
    The silent snow possess'd the earth,
And calmly fell our Christmas-eve:

The yule-clog[37] sparkled keen with frost,
    No wing of wind the region swept,
    But over all things brooding slept
The quiet sense of something lost.

As in the winters left behind,
    Again our ancient games had place,   10
    The mimic picture's breathing grace,
And dance and song and hoodman-blind.

Who show'd a token of distress?
    No single tear, no mark of pain:
    O sorrow, then can sorrow wane?
O grief, can grief be changed to less?

O last regret, regret can die!
    No—mixt with all this mystic frame,
    Her deep relations are the same,
But with long use her tears are dry.   20

— 79 —

"More than my brothers are to me,"—
    Let this not vex thee, noble heart!
    I know thee of what force thou art
To hold the costliest love in fee.[38]

But thou and I are one in kind,
    As moulded like in Nature's mint;
    And hill and wood and field did print
The same sweet forms in either mind.

For us the same cold streamlet curl'd
    Thro' all his eddying coves; the same   10
    All winds that roam the twilight came
In whispers of the beauteous world.

At one dear knee we proffer'd vows,
    One lesson from one book we learn'd,
    Ere childhood's flaxen ringlet turn'd
To black and brown on kindred brows.

And so my wealth resembles thine,
    But he was rich where I was poor,
    And he supplied my want the more
As his unlikeness fitted mine.   20

— 80 —

If any vague desire should rise,
    That holy Death ere Arthur died
    Had moved me kindly from his side,
And dropt the dust on tearless eyes;

Then fancy shapes, as fancy can,
    The grief my loss in him had wrought,
    A grief as deep as life or thought,
But stay'd in peace with God and man.

---

[36]**secular abyss:** the ages upon ages to be. [Tennyson's note]

[37]**yule-clog:** dialect variant of yule-log.

---

[38]**in fee:** in possession. The poet addresses his brother Charles.

I make a picture in the brain;
   I hear the sentence that he speaks;   10
   He bears the burthen of the weeks
But turns his burthen into gain.

His credit thus shall set me free;
   And, influence-rich to soothe and save,
   Unused example from the grave
Reach out dead hands to comfort me.

— 81 —

Could I have said[39] while he was here,
   "My love shall now no further range;
   There cannot come a mellower change,
For now is love mature in ear."

Love, then, had hope of richer store:
   What end is here to my complaint?
   This haunting whisper makes me faint,
"More years had made me love thee more."

But Death returns an answer sweet:
   "My sudden frost was sudden gain,   10
   And gave all ripeness to the grain,
It might have drawn from after-heat."

— 82 —

I wage not any feud with Death
   For changes wrought on form and face;
   No lower life that earth's embrace
May breed with him, can fright my faith.

Eternal process moving on,
   From state to state the spirit walks;
   And these are but the shatter'd stalks,
Or ruin'd chrysalis of one.

Nor blame I Death, because he bare
   The use of virtue out of earth: 10
   I know transplanted human worth
Will bloom to profit, otherwhere.

For this alone on Death I wreak
   The wrath that garners in my heart;
   He put our lives so far apart
We cannot hear each other speak.

— 83 —

Dip down upon the northern shore,
   O sweet new-year delaying long;
   Thou doest expectant nature wrong;
Delaying long, delay no more.

What stays thee from the clouded noons,
   Thy sweetness from its proper place?
   Can trouble live with April days,
Or sadness in the summer moons?

Bring orchis, bring the foxglove spire,
   The little speedwell's darling blue,   10
   Deep tulips dash'd with fiery dew,
Laburnums, dropping-wells of fire.

O thou, new-year, delaying long,
   Delayest the sorrow in my blood,
   That longs to burst a frozen bud
And flood a fresher throat with song.

— 84 —

When I contemplate all alone
   The life that had been thine below,
   And fix my thoughts on all the glow
To which thy crescent would have grown;

I see thee sitting crown'd with good,
   A central warmth diffusing bliss
   In glance and smile, and clasp and kiss,
On all the branches of thy blood;

Thy blood, my friend, and partly mine;
   For now the day was drawing on,   10
   When thou should'st link thy life with one
Of mine own house, and boys of thine

Had babbled "Uncle" on my knee;
   But that remorseless iron hour
   Made cypress of her orange flower,[40]
Despair of Hope, and earth of thee.

I seem to meet their least desire,
   To clap their cheeks, to call them mine.
   I see their unborn faces shine
Beside the never-lighted fire.   20

I see myself an honour'd guest,
   Thy partner in the flowery walk
   Of letters, genial table-talk,
Or deep dispute, and graceful jest;

While now thy prosperous labour fills
   The lips of men with honest praise,
   And sun by sun the happy days
Descend below the golden hills

---

[39]**Could I have said:** Would that I could have said. [Tennyson's note]

[40]**cypress:** for mourning. **orange:** for wedding. Hallam was engaged to marry the poet's sister Emily.

With promise of a morn as fair;
   And all the train of bounteous hours   30
   Conduct by paths of growing powers,
To reverence and the silver hair;

Till slowly worn her earthly robe,
   Her lavish mission richly wrought,
   Leaving great legacies of thought,
Thy spirit should fail from off the globe;

What time mine own might also flee,
   As link'd with thine in love and fate,
   And, hovering o'er the dolorous strait
To the other shore, involved in thee,   40

Arrive at last the blessed goal,
   And He that died in Holy Land
   Would reach us out the shining hand
And take us as a single soul.

What reed was that on which I leant?
   Ah, backward fancy, wherefore wake
   The old bitterness again, and break
The low beginnings of content.

— 85 —[41]

This truth came borne with bier and pall,
   I felt it, when I sorrow'd most,
   'Tis better to have loved and lost,
Than never to have loved at all—

O true in word, and tried in deed,
   Demanding, so to bring relief
   To this which is our common grief,
What kind of life is that I lead;

And whether trust in things above
   Be dimm'd of sorrow, or sustain'd;   10
   And whether love for him have drain'd
My capabilities of love;

Your words have virtue such as draws
   A faithful answer from the breast,
   Thro' light reproaches, half exprest,
And loyal unto kindly laws.

My blood an even tenor kept,
   Till on mine ear this message falls,
   That in Vienna's fatal walls
God's finger touch'd him, and he slept.   20

---

[41]Section **85** is apparently addressed to Edmund Lushington, who married the poet's sister Cecilia in 1842.

The great Intelligences fair
   That range above our mortal state,
   In circle round the blessed gate,
Received and gave him welcome there;

And led him thro' the blissful climes,
   And show'd him in the fountain fresh
   All knowledge that the sons of flesh
Shall gather in the cycled times.

But I remain'd, whose hopes were dim,
   Whose life, whose thoughts were little worth,   30
   To wander on a darken'd earth,
Where all things round me breathed of him.

O friendship, equal-poised control,
   O heart, with kindliest motion warm,
   O sacred essence, other form,
O solemn ghost, O crowned soul!

Yet none could better know than I,
   How much of act at human hands
   The sense of human will demands
By which we dare to live or die.   40

Whatever way my days decline,
   I felt and feel, tho' left alone,
   His being working in mine own,
The footsteps of his life in mine;

A life that all the Muses deck'd
   With gifts of grace, that might express
   All-comprehensive tenderness,
All-subtilising intellect:

And so my passion hath not swerved
   To works of weakness, but I find   50
   An image comforting the mind,
And in my grief a strength reserved.

Likewise the imaginative woe,
   That loved to handle spiritual strife,
   Diffused the shock thro' all my life,
But in the present broke the blow.

My pulses therefore beat again
   For other friends that once I met;
   Nor can it suit me to forget
The mighty hopes that make us men.   60

I woo your love: I count it crime
   To mourn for any overmuch;
   I, the divided half of such
A friendship as had master'd Time;

Which masters Time indeed, and is
    Eternal, separate from fears:
    The all-assuming months and years
Can take no part away from this:

But Summer on the steaming floods,
    And Spring that swells the narrow brooks,   70
    And Autumn, with a noise of rooks,
That gather in the waning woods,

And every pulse of wind and wave
    Recalls, in change of light or gloom,
    My old affection of the tomb,
And my prime passion in the grave:

My old affection of the tomb,
    A part of stillness, yearns to speak:
    "Arise, and get thee forth and seek
A friendship for the years to come.   80

"I watch thee from the quiet shore;
    Thy spirit up to mine can reach;
    But in dear words of human speech
We two communicate no more."

And I, "Can clouds of nature stain
    The starry clearness of the free?
    How is it? Canst thou feel for me
Some painless sympathy with pain?"

And lightly does the whisper fall;
    " 'Tis hard for thee to fathom this;   90
    I triumph in conclusive bliss,
And that serene result of all."

So hold I commerce with the dead;
    Or so methinks the dead would say;
    Or so shall grief with symbols play
And pining life be fancy-fed.

Now looking to some settled end,
    That these things pass, and I shall prove
    A meeting somewhere, love with love,
I crave your pardon, O my friend;   100

If not so fresh, with love as true,
    I, clasping brother-hands, aver
    I could not, if I would, transfer
The whole I felt for him to you.

For which be they that hold apart
    The promise of the golden hours?
    First love, first friendship, equal powers,
That marry with the virgin heart.

Still mine, that cannot but deplore,
    That beats within a lonely place,   110
    That yet remembers his embrace,
But at his footstep leaps no more,

My heart, tho' widow'd, may not rest
    Quiet in the love of what is gone,
    But seeks to beat in time with one
That warms another living breast.

Ah, take the imperfect gift I bring,
    Knowing the primrose yet is dear,
    The primrose of the later year,
As not unlike to that of Spring.   120

— 86 —

Sweet after showers, ambrosial air,
    That rollest from the gorgeous gloom
    Of evening over brake and bloom
And meadow, slowly breathing bare

The round of space, and rapt below
    Thro' all the dewy-tassell'd wood,
    And shadowing down the horned flood
In ripples, fan my brows and blow

The fever from my cheek, and sigh
    The full new life that feeds thy breath   10
    Throughout my frame, till Doubt and Death,
Ill brethren, let the fancy fly

From belt to belt of crimson seas
    On leagues of odour streaming far,
    To where in yonder orient star
A hundred spirits whisper "Peace."

— 87 —

I past beside the reverend walls
    In which of old I wore the gown;[42]
    I roved at random thro' the town,
And saw the tumult of the halls;

And heard once more in college fanes
    The storm their high-built organs make,
    And thunder-music, rolling, shake
The prophet blazon'd on the panes;

---

[42]**wore the gown**: at Trinity College, Cambridge, where Tennyson and Hallam were students and members of the Apostles, a debating society (stanza 6).

And caught once more the distant shout,
 The measured pulse of racing oars   10
 Among the willows; paced the shores
And many a bridge, and all about

The same gray flats again, and felt
 The same, but not the same; and last
 Up that long walk of limes I past
To see the rooms in which he dwelt.

Another name was on the door:
 I linger'd; all within was noise
 Of songs, and clapping hands, and boys
That crash'd the glass and beat the floor; 20

Where once we held debate, a band
 Of youthful friends, on mind and art,
 And labour, and the changing mart,
And all the framework of the land;

When one would aim an arrow fair,
 But send it slackly from the string;
 And one would pierce an outer ring,
And one an inner, here and there;

And last the master-bowman, he,
 Would cleave the mark. A willing ear 30
 We lent him. Who, but hung to hear
The rapt oration flowing free

From point to point, with power and grace
 And music in the bounds of law,
 To those conclusions when we saw
The God within him light his face,

And seem to lift the form, and glow
 In azure orbits heavenly-wise;
 And over those ethereal eyes
The bar of Michael Angelo.[43] 40

— 88 —

Wild bird,[44] whose warble, liquid sweet,
 Rings Eden thro' the budded quicks,
 O tell me where the senses mix,
O tell me where the passions meet,

Whence radiate: fierce extremes employ
 Thy spirits in the darkening leaf,
 And in the midmost heart of grief
Thy passion clasps a secret joy:

And I—my harp would prelude woe—
 I cannot all command the strings; 10
 The glory of the sum of things
Will flash along the chords and go.

— 89 —

Witch-elms that counterchange the floor
 Of this flat lawn with dusk and bright;
 And thou, with all thy breadth and height
Of foliage, towering sycamore;

How often, hither wandering down,
 My Arthur found your shadows fair,
 And shook to all the liberal air
The dust and din and steam of town:

He brought an eye for all he saw;
 He mixt in all our simple sports; 10
 They pleased him, fresh from brawling courts
And dusty purlieus of the law.

O joy to him in this retreat,
 Immantled in ambrosial dark,
 To drink the cooler air, and mark
The landscape winking thro' the heat:

O sound to rout the brood of cares,
 The sweep of scythe in morning dew,
 The gust that round the garden flew,
And tumbled half the mellowing pears! 20

O bliss, when all in circle drawn
 About him, heart and ear were fed
 To hear him, as he lay and read
The Tuscan poets on the lawn:

Or in the all-golden afternoon
 A guest, or happy sister, sung,
 Or here she brought the harp and flung
A ballad to the brightening moon:

Nor less it pleased in livelier moods,
 Beyond the bounding hill to stray, 30
 And break the livelong summer day
With banquet in the distant woods;

Whereat we glanced from theme to theme,
 Discuss'd the books to love or hate,
 Or touch'd the changes of the state,
Or threaded some Socratic dream;

But if I praised the busy town,
 He loved to rail against it still,
 For "ground in yonder social mill
We rub each other's angles down, 40

---

[43]**bar**: The broad bar of frontal bone over the eyes of **Michael Angelo**. [Tennyson's note]

[44]**Wild bird**: nightingale. **budded quicks**: hedgerows of quickset thorn.

"And merge" he said "in form and gloss
    The picturesque of man and man."
    We talk'd: the stream beneath us ran,
The wine-flask lying couch'd in moss,

Or cool'd within the glooming wave;
    And last, returning from afar,
    Before the crimson-circled star[45]
Had fall'n into her father's grave,

And brushing ankle-deep in flowers,
    We heard behind the woodbine veil   50
    The milk that bubbled in the pail,
And buzzings of the honied hours.

— 90 —

He tasted love with half his mind,
    Nor ever drank the inviolate spring
    Where nighest heaven, who first could fling
This bitter seed among mankind;

That could the dead, whose dying eyes
    Were closed with wail, resume their life,
    They would but find in child and wife
An iron welcome when they rise:

'Twas well, indeed, when warm with wine,
    To pledge them with a kindly tear,   10
    To talk them o'er, to wish them here,
To count their memories half divine;

But if they came who past away,
    Behold their brides in other hands;
    The hard heir strides about their lands,
And will not yield them for a day.

Yea, tho' their sons were none of these,
    Not less the yet-loved sire would make
    Confusion worse than death, and shake
The pillars of domestic peace.   20

Ah dear, but come thou back to me:
    Whatever change the years have wrought
    I find not yet one lonely thought
That cries against my wish for thee.

— 91 —

When rosy plumelets tuft the larch,
    And rarely pipes the mounted thrush;
    Or underneath the barren bush
Flits by the sea-blue bird of March;

Come, wear the form by which I know
    Thy spirit in time among thy peers;
    The hope of unaccomplish'd years
Be large and lucid round thy brow.

When summer's hourly-mellowing change
    May breathe, with many roses sweet,   10
    Upon the thousand waves of wheat,
That ripple round the lonely grange;

Come: not in watches of the night,
    But where the sunbeam broodeth warm,
    Come, beauteous in thine after form,
And like a finer light in light.

— 92 —

If any vision should reveal
    Thy likeness, I might count it vain
    As but the canker of the brain;
Yea, tho' it spake and made appeal

To chances where our lots were cast
    Together in the days behind,
    I might but say, I hear a wind
Of memory murmuring the past.

Yea, tho' it spake and bared to view
    A fact within the coming year;   10
    And tho' the months, revolving near,
Should prove the phantom-warning true,

They might not seem thy prophecies,
    But spiritual presentiments,
    And such refraction of events
As often rises ere they rise.[46]

— 93 —

I shall not see thee. Dare I say
    No spirit ever brake the band
    That stays him from the native land
Where first he walk'd when claspt in clay?

No visual shade of some one lost,
    But he, the Spirit himself, may come
    Where all the nerve of sense is numb;
Spirit to Spirit, Ghost to Ghost.

---

[45]**crimson-circled star**: Venus, a planet generated by the sun, joins its **father's grave** when it sinks after sunset.

[46]**refraction . . . rise**: The heavenly bodies are seen above the horizon, by refraction, before they actually rise. [Tennyson's note]

O, therefore from thy sightless range
    With gods in unconjectured bliss,   10
    O, from the distance of the abyss
Of tenfold-complicated change,[47]

Descend, and touch, and enter; hear
    The wish too strong for words to name;
    That in this blindness of the frame
My Ghost may feel that thine is near.

— 94 —

How pure at heart and sound in head,
    With what divine affections bold
    Should be the man whose thought would hold
An hour's communion with the dead.

In vain shalt thou, or any, call
    The spirits from their golden day,
    Except, like them, thou too canst say,
My spirit is at peace with all.

They haunt the silence of the breast,
    Imaginations calm and fair,   10
    The memory like a cloudless air,
The conscience as a sea at rest:

But when the heart is full of din,
    And doubt beside the portal waits,
    They can but listen at the gates,
And hear the household jar within.

— 95 —

By night we linger'd on the lawn,
    For underfoot the herb was dry;
    And genial warmth; and o'er the sky
The silvery haze of summer drawn;

And calm that let the tapers burn
    Unwavering: not a cricket chirr'd:
    The brook alone far-off was heard,
And on the board the fluttering urn:[48]

And bats went round in fragrant skies,
    And wheel'd or lit the filmy shapes[49]   10
    That haunt the dusk, with ermine capes
And woolly breasts and beaded eyes;

While now we sang old songs that peal'd
    From knoll to knoll, where, couch'd at ease,
    The white kine glimmer'd, and the trees
Laid their dark arms about the field.

But when those others, one by one,
    Withdrew themselves from me and night,
    And in the house light after light
Went out, and I was all alone,   20

A hunger seized my heart; I read
    Of that glad year which once had been,
    In those fall'n leaves which kept their green,
The noble letters of the dead:

And strangely on the silence broke
    The silent-speaking words, and strange
    Was love's dumb cry defying change
To test his worth; and strangely spoke

The faith, the vigour, bold to dwell
    On doubts that drive the coward back,   30
    And keen thro' wordy snares to track
Suggestion to her inmost cell.

So word by word, and line by line,
    The dead man touch'd me from the past,
    And all at once it seem'd at last
The living soul[50] was flash'd on mine,

And mine in this was wound, and whirl'd
    About empyreal heights of thought,
    And came on that which is, and caught
The deep pulsations of the world,   40

Æonian[51] music measuring out
    The steps of Time—the shocks of Chance—
    The blows of Death. At length my trance
Was cancell'd, stricken thro' with doubt.

Vague words! but ah, how hard to frame
    In matter-moulded forms of speech,
    Or ev'n for intellect to reach
Thro' memory that which I became:

Till now the doubtful dusk reveal'd
    The knolls once more where, couch'd at ease,   50
    The white kine glimmer'd, and the trees
Laid their dark arms about the field:

---

[47]**tenfold-complicated**: Refers to the ten heavens of Dante. [Hallam Tennyson's note]

[48]**fluttering urn**: tea urn over a flame on the table (**board**).

[49]**filmy shapes**: Moths. [Tennyson's note]

[50]**The living soul**: The Deity, maybe. [Tennyson's note] Until 1872 the line read "His living soul," with "his" for "this" in the line that follows.

[51]**Aeonian**: age-old.

And suck'd from out the distant gloom
    A breeze began to tremble o'er
    The large leaves of the sycamore,
And fluctuate all the still perfume,

And gathering freshlier overhead,
    Rock'd the full-foliaged elms, and swung
    The heavy-folded rose, and flung
The lilies to and fro, and said   60

"The dawn, the dawn," and died away;
    And East and West, without a breath,
    Mixt their dim lights, like life and death,
To broaden into boundless day.

— 96 —

You say, but with no touch of scorn,
    Sweet-hearted, you, whose light-blue eyes
    Are tender over drowning flies,
You tell me, doubt is Devil-born.

I know not: one indeed I knew
    In many a subtle question versed,
    Who touch'd a jarring lyre at first,
But ever strove to make it true:

Perplext in faith, but pure in deeds,
    At last he beat his music out.   10
    There lives more faith in honest doubt,
Believe me, than in half the creeds.

He fought his doubts and gather'd strength,
    He would not make his judgment blind,
    He faced the spectres of the mind
And laid them: thus he came at length

To find a stronger faith his own;
    And Power was with him in the night,
    Which makes the darkness and the light,
And dwells not in the light alone,   20

But in the darkness and the cloud,
    As over Sinaï's peaks[52] of old,
    While Israel made their gods of gold,
Altho' the trumpet blew so loud.

— 97 —

My love has talk'd with rocks and trees;
    He finds on misty mountain-ground
    His own vast shadow glory-crown'd;
He sees himself in all he sees.

Two partners of a married life—
    I look'd on these and thought of thee
    In vastness and in mystery,
And of my spirit as of a wife.

These two—they dwelt with eye on eye,
    Their hearts of old have beat in tune,   10
    Their meetings made December June,
Their every parting was to die.

Their love has never past away;
    The days she never can forget
    Are earnest that he loves her yet,
Whate'er the faithless people say.

Her life is lone, he sits apart,
    He loves her yet, she will not weep,
    Tho' rapt in matters dark and deep
He seems to slight her simple heart.   20

He thrids the labyrinth of the mind,
    He reads the secret of the star,
    He seems so near and yet so far,
He looks so cold: she thinks him kind.

She keeps the gift of years before,
    A wither'd violet is her bliss:
    She knows not what his greatness is,
For that, for all, she loves him more.

For him she plays, to him she sings
    Of early faith and plighted vows;   30
    She knows but matters of the house,
And he, he knows a thousand things.

Her faith is fixt and cannot move,
    She darkly feels him great and wise,
    She dwells on him with faithful eyes,
"I cannot understand: I love."

— 98 —

You leave us: you will see the Rhine,
    And those fair hills I sail'd below,
    When I was there with him; and go
By summer belts of wheat and vine

To where he breathed his latest breath,
    That City.[53] All her splendour seems
    No livelier than the wisp that gleams
On Lethe in the eyes of Death.

---

[52]**Sinaï's peaks:** see Exodus 19:16–19.

[53]**That City:** Vienna, where Hallam died in 1833, having toured Germany with Tennyson the year before. The Viennese river **Danube** is compared to **Lethe**, infernal river of oblivion.

Let her great Danube rolling fair
    Enwind her isles, unmark'd of me: 10
    I have not seen, I will not see
Vienna; rather dream that there,

A treble darkness, Evil haunts
    The birth, the bridal; friend from friend
    Is oftener parted, fathers bend
Above more graves, a thousand wants

Gnarr[54] at the heels of men, and prey
    By each cold hearth, and sadness flings
    Her shadow on the blaze of kings:
And yet myself have heard him say,   20

That not in any mother town
    With statelier progress to and fro
    The double tides of chariots flow
By park and suburb under brown

Of lustier leaves; nor more content,
    He told me, lives in any crowd,
    When all is gay with lamps, and loud
With sport and song, in booth and tent,

Imperial halls, or open plain;
    And wheels the circled dance, and breaks   30
    The rocket molten into flakes
Of crimson or in emerald rain.

— 99 —

Risest thou thus, dim dawn, again,
    So loud with voices of the birds,
    So thick with lowings of the herds,
Day, when I lost the flower of men;

Who tremblest thro' thy darkling red
    On yon swoll'n brook that bubbles fast
    By meadows breathing of the past,
And woodlands holy to the dead;

Who murmurest in the foliaged eaves
    A song that slights the coming care,   10
    And Autumn laying here and there
A fiery finger on the leaves;

Who wakenest with thy balmy breath
    To myriads on the genial earth,
    Memories of bridal, or of birth,
And unto myriads more, of death.

O wheresoever those may be,
    Betwixt the slumber of the poles,
    To-day they count as kindred souls;
They know me not, but mourn with me.   20

— 100[55] —

I climb the hill: from end to end
    Of all the landscape underneath,
    I find no place that does not breathe
Some gracious memory of my friend;

No gray old grange, or lonely fold,
    Or low morass and whispering reed,
    Or simple stile from mead to mead,
Or sheepwalk up the windy wold;

Nor hoary knoll of ash and haw
    That hears the latest linnet trill,   10
    Nor quarry trench'd along the hill
And haunted by the wrangling daw;

Nor runlet tinkling from the rock;
    Nor pastoral rivulet that swerves
    To left and right thro' meadowy curves,
That feed the mothers of the flock;

But each has pleased a kindred eye,
    And each reflects a kindlier day;
    And, leaving these, to pass away,
I think once more he seems to die.   20

— 101 —

Unwatch'd, the garden bough shall sway,
    The tender blossom flutter down,
    Unloved, that beech will gather brown,
This maple burn itself away;

Unloved, the sun-flower, shining fair,
    Ray round with flames her disk of seed,
    And many a rose-carnation feed
With summer spice the humming air;

Unloved, by many a sandy bar,
    The brook shall babble down the plain,   10
    At noon or when the lesser wain[56]
Is twisting round the polar star;

---

[55]Sections **100–105** commemorate the Tennysons' moving in 1837 from their home in Somersby, Lincolnshire.

[56]**lesser wain**: the constellation Ursa minor (also known as the little dipper or wagon), which terminates in Polaris, the north **star**.

---

[54]**Gnarr**: growl or snarl.

Uncared for, gird the windy grove,
    And flood the haunts of hern and crake;
    Or into silver arrows break
The sailing moon in creek and cove;

Till from the garden and the wild
    A fresh association blow,
    And year by year the landscape grow
Familiar to the stranger's child;   20

As year by year the labourer tills
    His wonted glebe, or lops the glades;
    And year by year our memory fades
From all the circle of the hills.

— 102 —

We leave the well-beloved place
    Where first we gazed upon the sky;
    The roofs, that heard our earliest cry,
Will shelter one of stranger race.

We go, but ere we go from home,
    As down the garden-walks I move,
    Two spirits of a diverse love
Contend for loving masterdom.

One whispers, "Here thy boyhood sung
    Long since its matin song, and heard   10
    The low love-language of the bird
In native hazels tassel-hung."

The other answers, "Yea, but here
    Thy feet have stray'd in after hours
    With thy lost friend among the bowers
And this hath made them trebly dear."

These two have striven half the day,
    And each prefers his separate claim,
    Poor rivals in a losing game,
That will not yield each other way.   20

I turn to go: my feet are set
    To leave the pleasant fields and farms;
    They mix in one another's arms
To one pure image of regret.

— 103 —

On that last night before we went
    From out the doors where I was bred,
    I dream'd a vision of the dead,
Which left my after-morn content.

Methought I dwelt within a hall,
    And maidens with me: distant hills
    From hidden summits fed with rills
A river sliding by the wall.

The hall with harp and carol rang.
    They sang of what is wise and good   10
    And graceful. In the centre stood
A statue veil'd, to which they sang;

And which, tho' veil'd, was known to me,
    The shape of him I loved, and love
    For ever: then flew in a dove
And brought a summons from the sea:

And when they learnt that I must go
    They wept and wail'd, but led the way
    To where a little shallop lay
At anchor in the flood below;   20

And on by many a level mead,
    And shadowing bluff that made the banks,
    We glided winding under ranks
Of iris, and the golden reed;

And still as vaster grew the shore
    And roll'd the floods in grander space,
    The maidens gather'd strength and grace
And presence, lordlier than before;

And I myself, who sat apart
    And watch'd them, wax'd in every limb;   30
    I felt the thews of Anakim,[57]
The pulses of a Titan's heart;

As one would sing the death of war,
    And one would chant the history
    Of that great race, which is to be,
And one the shaping of a star;

Until the forward-creeping tides
    Began to foam, and we to draw
    From deep to deep, to where we saw
A great ship lift her shining sides.   40

The man we loved was there on deck,
    But thrice as large as man he bent
    To greet us. Up the side I went,
And fell in silence on his neck:

---

[57]**Anakim:** Biblical giants (Deuteronomy 2:10–11, 9:1–2). **Titan:** gigantic classical deity.

Whereat those maidens with one mind
   Bewail'd their lot; I did them wrong:
   "We served thee here," they said, "so long,
And wilt thou leave us now behind?"

So rapt I was, they could not win
   An answer from my lips, but he   50
   Replying, "Enter likewise ye
And go with us:" they enter'd in.

And while the wind began to sweep
   A music out of sheet and shroud,
   We steer'd her toward a crimson cloud
That landlike slept along the deep.

— 104 —

The time draws near the birth of Christ;
   The moon is hid, the night is still;
   A single church below the hill
Is pealing, folded in the mist.

A single peal of bells below,
   That wakens at this hour of rest
   A single murmur in the breast,
That these are not the bells I know.

Like strangers' voices here they sound,
   In lands where not a memory strays,   10
   Nor landmark breathes of other days,
But all is new unhallow'd ground.

— 105 —

To-night ungather'd let us leave
   This laurel, let this holly stand:
   We live within the stranger's land,
And strangely falls our Christmas-eve.

Our father's dust is left alone
   And silent under other snows:
   There in due time the woodbine blows,
The violet comes, but we are gone.

No more shall wayward grief abuse
   The genial hour with mask and mime;
   For change of place, like growth of time,
Has broke the bond of dying use.

Let cares that petty shadows cast,
   By which our lives are chiefly proved,
   A little spare the night I loved,
And hold it solemn to the past.

But let no footstep beat the floor,
   Nor bowl of wassail mantle warm;
   For who would keep an ancient form
Thro' which the spirit breathes no more?   20

Be neither song, nor game, nor feast;
   Nor harp be touch'd, nor flute be blown;
   No dance, no motion, save alone
What lightens in the lucid east

Of rising worlds by yonder wood.
   Long sleeps the summer in the seed;
   Run out your measured arcs, and lead
The closing cycle rich in good.

— 106 —

Ring out, wild bells, to the wild sky,
   The flying cloud, the frosty light:
   The year is dying in the night;
Ring out, wild bells, and let him die.

Ring out the old, ring in the new,
   Ring, happy bells, across the snow:
   The year is going, let him go;
Ring out the false, ring in the true.

Ring out the grief that saps the mind,
   For those that here we see no more;   10
   Ring out the feud of rich and poor,
Ring in redress to all mankind.

Ring out a slowly dying cause,
   And ancient forms of party strife;
   Ring in the nobler modes of life,
With sweeter manners, purer laws.

Ring out the want, the care, the sin,
   The faithless coldness of the times;
   Ring out, ring out my mournful rhymes,
But ring the fuller minstrel in.   20

Ring out false pride in place and blood,
   The civic slander and the spite;
   Ring in the love of truth and right,
Ring in the common love of good.

Ring out old shapes of foul disease;
   Ring out the narrowing lust of gold;
   Ring out the thousand wars of old,
Ring in the thousand years of peace.

Ring in the valiant man and free,
   The larger heart, the kindlier hand;   30
   Ring out the darkness of the land,
Ring in the Christ that is to be.

— 107 —

It is the day[58] when he was born,
  A bitter day that early sank
  Behind a purple-frosty bank
Of vapour, leaving night forlorn.

The time admits not flowers or leaves
  To deck the banquet. Fiercely flies
  The blast of North and East, and ice
Makes daggers at the sharpen'd eaves,

And bristles all the brakes and thorns
  To yon hard crescent, as she hangs   10
  Above the wood which grides[59] and clangs
Its leafless ribs and iron horns

Together, in the drifts that pass
  To darken on the rolling brine
  That breaks the coast. But fetch the wine,
Arrange the board and brim the glass;

Bring in great logs and let them lie,
  To make a solid core of heat;
  Be cheerful-minded, talk and treat
Of all things ev'n as he were by;   20

We keep the day. With festal cheer,
  With books and music, surely we
  Will drink to him, whate'er he be,
And sing the songs he loved to hear.

— 108 —

I will not shut me from my kind,
  And, lest I stiffen into stone,
  I will not eat my heart alone,
Nor feed with sighs a passing wind:

What profit lies in barren faith,
  And vacant yearning, tho' with might
  To scale the heaven's highest height,
Or dive below the wells of Death?

What find I in the highest place,
  But mine own phantom chanting hymns?   10
  And on the depths of death there swims
The reflex of a human face.

I'll rather take what fruit may be
  Of sorrow under human skies:
  'Tis held that sorrow makes us wise,
Whatever wisdom sleep with thee.

---

[58]**the day**: Hallam's birthday, February 1.

[59]**grides**: grates

— 109 —

Heart-affluence in discursive talk
  From household fountains never dry;
  The critic clearness of an eye,
That saw thro' all the Muses' walk;

Seraphic intellect and force
  To seize and throw the doubts of man;
  Impassion'd logic, which outran
The hearer in its fiery course;

High nature amorous of the good,
  But touch'd with no ascetic gloom;   10
  And passion pure in snowy bloom
Thro' all the years of April blood;

A love of freedom rarely felt,
  Of freedom in her regal seat
  Of England; not the schoolboy heat,
The blind hysterics of the Celt;

And manhood fused with female grace
  In such a sort, the child would twine
  A trustful hand, unask'd, in thine,
And find his comfort in thy face;   20

All these have been, and thee mine eyes
  Have look'd on: if they look'd in vain,
  My shame is greater who remain,
Nor let thy wisdom make me wise.

— 110 —

Thy converse drew us with delight,
  The men of rathe and riper years:
  The feeble soul, a haunt of fears,
Forgot his weakness in thy sight.

On thee the loyal-hearted hung,
  The proud was half disarm'd of pride,
  Nor cared the serpent at thy side
To flicker with his double tongue.

The stern were mild when thou wert by,
  The flippant put himself to school   10
  And heard thee, and the brazen fool
Was soften'd, and he knew not why;

While I, thy nearest, sat apart,
  And felt thy triumph was as mine;
  And loved them more, that they were thine,
The graceful tact, the Christian art;

Nor mine the sweetness or the skill,
  But mine the love that will not tire,
  And, born of love, the vague desire
That spurs an imitative will.   20

— 111 —

The churl in spirit, up or down
  Along the scale of ranks, thro' all,
  To him who grasps a golden ball,
By blood a king, at heart a clown;

The churl in spirit, howe'er he veil
  His want in forms for fashion's sake,
  Will let his coltish nature break
At seasons thro' the gilded pale:

For who can always act? but he,
  To whom a thousand memories call,   10
  Not being less but more than all
The gentleness he seem'd to be,

Best seem'd the thing he was, and join'd
  Each office of the social hour
  To noble manners, as the flower
And native growth of noble mind;

Nor ever narrowness or spite,
  Or villain fancy fleeting by,
  Drew in the expression of an eye,
Where God and Nature met in light;   20

And thus he bore without abuse
  The grand old name of gentleman,
  Defamed by every charlatan,
And soil'd with all ignoble use.

— 112 —

High wisdom holds my wisdom less,
  That I, who gaze with temperate eyes
  On glorious insufficiencies,
Set light by narrower perfectness.

But thou, that fillest all the room
  Of all my love, art reason why
  I seem to cast a careless eye
On souls, the lesser lords[60] of doom.

For what wert thou? some novel power
  Sprang up for ever at a touch,   10
  And hope could never hope too much,
In watching thee from hour to hour,

Large elements in order brought,
  And tracts of calm from tempest made,
  And world-wide fluctuation sway'd
In vassal tides that follow'd thought.

— 113 —

'Tis held that sorrow makes us wise;
  Yet how much wisdom sleeps with thee
  Which not alone had guided me,
But served the seasons that may rise;

For can I doubt, who knew thee keen
  In intellect, with force and skill
  To strive, to fashion, to fulfil—
I doubt not what thou wouldst have been:

A life in civic action warm,
  A soul on highest mission sent,   10
  A potent voice of Parliament,
A pillar steadfast in the storm,

Should licensed boldness gather force,
  Becoming, when the time has birth,
  A lever to uplift the earth
And roll it in another course,

With thousand shocks that come and go,
  With agonies, with energies,
  With overthrowings, and with cries,
And undulations to and fro.   20

— 114 —

Who loves not Knowledge? Who shall rail
  Against her beauty? May she mix
  With men and prosper! Who shall fix
Her pillars? Let her work prevail.

But on her forehead sits a fire:
  She sets her forward countenance
  And leaps into the future chance,
Submitting all things to desire.

Half-grown as yet, a child, and vain—
  She cannot fight the fear of death.   10
  What is she, cut from love and faith,
But some wild Pallas[61] from the brain

Of Demons? fiery-hot to burst
  All barriers in her onward race
  For power. Let her know her place;
She is the second, not the first.

---

[60]**lesser lords:** Those that have free-will, but less intellect. [Tennyson's note]

[61]**Pallas:** goddess of wisdom, born from the forehead of her father Zeus.

A higher hand must make her mild,
    If all be not in vain; and guide
    Her footsteps, moving side by side
With wisdom, like the younger child: 20

For she is earthly of the mind,
    But Wisdom heavenly of the soul.
    O, friend, who camest to thy goal
So early, leaving me behind,

I would the great world grew like thee,
    Who grewest not alone in power
    And knowledge, but by year and hour
In reverence and in charity.

— 115 —

Now fades the last long streak of snow,
    Now burgeons every maze of quick
    About the flowering squares,[62] and thick
By ashen roots the violets blow.

Now rings the woodland loud and long,
    The distance takes a lovelier hue,
    And drown'd in yonder living blue
The lark becomes a sightless song.

Now dance the lights on lawn and lea,
    The flocks are whiter down the vale,   10
    And milkier every milky sail
On winding stream or distant sea;

Where now the seamew pipes, or dives
    In yonder greening gleam, and fly
    The happy birds, that change their sky
To build and brood; that live their lives

From land to land; and in my breast
    Spring wakens too; and my regret
    Becomes an April violet,
And buds and blossoms like the rest.   20

— 116 —

Is it, then, regret for buried time
    That keenlier in sweet April wakes,
    And meets the year, and gives and takes
The colours of the crescent prime?

Not all: the songs, the stirring air,
    The life re-orient out of dust,
    Cry thro' the sense to hearten trust
In that which made the world so fair.

---

[62]**squares**: rural fields shaped like a **maze** by hedgerows of **quick**set thorn. **ashen**: of the ash tree.

Not all regret: the face will shine
    Upon me, while I muse alone;   10
    And that dear voice, I once have known,
Still speak to me of me and mine:

Yet less of sorrow lives in me
    For days of happy commune dead;
    Less yearning for the friendship fled,
Than some strong bond which is to be.

— 117 —

O days and hours, your work is this
    To hold me from my proper place,
    A little while from his embrace,
For fuller gain of after bliss:

That out of distance might ensue
    Desire of nearness doubly sweet;
    And unto meeting when we meet,
Delight a hundredfold accrue,

For every grain of sand that runs,
    And every span of shade that steals,   10
    And every kiss of toothed wheels,
And all the courses of the suns.

— 118 —

Contemplate all this work of Time,
    The giant labouring in his youth;
    Nor dream of human love and truth,
As dying Nature's earth and lime;

But trust that those we call the dead
    Are breathers of an ampler day
    For ever nobler ends. They say,
The solid earth whereon we tread

In tracts of fluent heat began,
    And grew to seeming-random forms,   10
    The seeming prey of cyclic storms,
Till at the last arose the man;

Who throve and branch'd from clime to clime,
    The herald of a higher race,
    And of himself in higher place,
If so he type this work of time

Within himself, from more to more;
    Or, crown'd with attributes of woe
    Like glories, move his course, and show
That life is not as idle ore,   20

But iron dug from central gloom,
    And heated hot with burning fears,
    And dipt in baths of hissing tears,
And batter'd with the shocks of doom

To shape and use. Arise and fly
   The reeling Faun, the sensual feast;
   Move upward, working out the beast,
And let the ape and tiger die.

— 119 —

Doors, where my heart was used to beat
   So quickly, not as one that weeps
   I come once more; the city sleeps;
I smell the meadow in the street;

I hear a chirp of birds; I see
   Betwixt the black fronts long-withdrawn
   A light-blue lane of early dawn,
And think of early days and thee,

And bless thee, for thy lips are bland,
   And bright the friendship of thine eye;   10
   And in my thoughts with scarce a sigh
I take the pressure of thine hand.

— 120 —

I trust I have not wasted breath:
   I think we are not wholly brain,
   Magnetic mockeries; not in vain,
Like Paul[63] with beasts, I fought with Death;

Not only cunning casts in clay:
   Let Science prove we are, and then
   What matters Science unto men,
At least to me? I would not stay.

Let him, the wiser man who springs
   Hereafter, up from childhood shape   10
   His action like the greater ape,
But I was *born* to other things.

— 121 —

Sad Hesper o'er the buried sun
   And ready, thou, to die with him,
   Thou watchest all things ever dim
And dimmer, and a glory done:

The team is loosen'd from the wain,
   The boat is drawn upon the shore;
   Thou listenest to the closing door,
And life is darken'd in the brain.

Bright Phosphor, fresher for the night,
   By thee the world's great work is heard   10
   Beginning, and the wakeful bird;
Behind thee comes the greater light:

The market boat is on the stream,
   And voices hail it from the brink;
   Thou hear'st the village hammer clink,
And see'st the moving of the team.

Sweet Hesper-Phosphor,[64] double name
   For what is one, the first, the last,
   Thou, like my present and my past,
Thy place is changed; thou art the same.   20

— 122 —

Oh, wast thou with me, dearest, then,
   While I rose up against my doom,
   And yearn'd to burst the folded gloom,
To bare the eternal Heavens again,

To feel once more, in placid awe,
   The strong imagination roll
   A sphere of stars about my soul,
In all her motion one with law;

If thou wert with me, and the grave
   Divide us not, be with me now,   10
   And enter in at breast and brow,
Till all my blood, a fuller wave,

Be quicken'd with a livelier breath,
   And like an inconsiderate boy,
   As in the former flash of joy,
I slip the thoughts of life and death;

And all the breeze of Fancy blows,
   And every dew-drop paints a bow,
   The wizard lightnings deeply glow,
And every thought breaks out a rose.   20

— 123 —

There rolls the deep where grew the tree.
   O earth, what changes hast thou seen!
   There where the long street roars, hath been
The stillness of the central sea.

The hills are shadows, and they flow
   From form to form, and nothing stands;
   They melt like mist, the solid lands,
Like clouds they shape themselves and go.

But in my spirit will I dwell,
   And dream my dream, and hold it true;   10
   For tho' my lips may breathe adieu,
I cannot think the thing farewell.

---

[63]**Paul:** see 1 Corinthians 15:32.

[64]**Hesper-Phosphor:** The evening star is also the morning star, death and sorrow brighten into death and hope. [Tennyson's note]

— 124 —

That which we dare invoke to bless;
    Our dearest faith; our ghastliest doubt;
    He, They, One, All; within, without;
The Power in darkness whom we guess;

I found Him not in world or sun,
    Or eagle's wing, or insect's eye;
    Nor thro' the questions men may try,
The petty cobwebs we have spun:

If e'er when faith had fall'n asleep,
    I heard a voice "believe no more"   10
    And heard an ever-breaking shore
That tumbled in the Godless deep;

A warmth within the breast would melt
    The freezing reason's colder part,
    And like a man in wrath the heart
Stood up and answer'd "I have felt."

No, like a child in doubt and fear:
    But that blind clamour made me wise;
    Then was I as a child that cries,
But, crying, knows his father near;   20

And what I am beheld again
    What is, and no man understands;
    And out of darkness came the hands
That reach thro' nature, moulding men.

Knowle is limike

— 125 —

Whatever I have said or sung,
    Some bitter notes my harp would give,
    Yea, tho' there often seem'd to live
A contradiction on the tongue,

Yet Hope had never lost her youth;
    She did but look through dimmer eyes;
    Or Love but play'd with gracious lies,
Because he felt so fix'd in truth:

Hope in Faith

And if the song were full of care,
    He breathed the spirit of the song;   10
    And if the words were sweet and strong
He set his royal signet there;

Abiding with me till I sail
    To seek thee on the mystic deeps,
    And this electric force, that keeps
A thousand pulses dancing, fail.

— 126 —

Love is and was my Lord and King,
    And in his presence I attend
    To hear the tidings of my friend,
Which every hour his couriers bring.

Love is and was my King and Lord,
    And will be, tho' as yet I keep
    Within his court on earth, and sleep
Encompass'd by his faithful guard,

And hear at times a sentinel
    Who moves about from place to place,   10
    And whispers to the worlds of space,
In the deep night, that all is well.

— 127 —

And all is well, tho' faith and form
    Be sunder'd in the night of fear;
    Well roars the storm to those that hear
A deeper voice across the storm,

Proclaiming social truth shall spread,
    And justice, ev'n tho' thrice again
    The red fool-fury of the Seine[65]
Should pile her barricades with dead.

But ill for him that wears a crown,
    And him, the lazar, in his rags: 10
    They tremble, the sustaining crags;
The spires of ice are toppled down,

And molten up, and roar in flood;
    The fortress crashes from on high,
    The brute earth lightens to the sky,
And the great Æon sinks in blood,

And compass'd by the fires of Hell;
    While thou, dear spirit, happy star,
    O'erlook'st the tumult from afar,
And smilest, knowing all is well.   20

— 128 —

The love that rose on stronger wings,
    Unpalsied when he met with Death,
    Is comrade of the lesser faith
That sees the course of human things.

---

[65]**Seine**: river in Paris, bloody scene of the French Revolution of 1789–1795 and insurrections in 1830 and 1848.

No doubt vast eddies in the flood
 Of onward time shall yet be made,
 And throned races may degrade;
Yet O ye mysteries of good,

Wild Hours that fly with Hope and Fear,
 If all your office had to do   10
 With old results that look like new;
If this were all your mission here,

To draw, to sheathe a useless sword,
 To fool the crowd with glorious lies,
 To cleave a creed in sects and cries,
To change the bearing of a word,

To shift an arbitrary power,
 To cramp the student at his desk,
 To make old bareness picturesque
And tuft with grass a feudal tower;   20

Why then my scorn might well descend
 On you and yours. I see in part
 That all, as in some piece of art,
Is toil coöperant to an end.

— 129 —

Dear friend, far off, my lost desire,
 So far, so near in woe and weal;
 O loved the most, when most I feel
There is a lower and a higher;

Known and unknown; human, divine;
 Sweet human hand and lips and eye;
 Dear heavenly friend that canst not die,
Mine, mine, for ever, ever mine;

Strange friend, past, present, and to be;
 Loved deeplier, darklier understood; 10
 Behold, I dream a dream of good,
And mingle all the world with thee.

— 130 —

Thy voice is on the rolling air;
 I hear thee where the waters run;
 Thou standest in the rising sun,[66]
And in the setting thou art fair.

What art thou then? I cannot guess;
 But tho' I seem in star and flower
 To feel thee some diffusive power,
I do not therefore love thee less:

My love involves the love before;
 My love is vaster passion now;   10
 Tho' mix'd with God and Nature thou,
I seem to love thee more and more.

Far off thou art, but ever nigh;
 I have thee still, and I rejoice;
 I prosper, circled with thy voice;
I shall not lose thee tho' I die.

— 131 —

O living will that shalt endure
 When all that seems shall suffer shock,
 Rise in the spiritual rock,
Flow thro' our deeds and make them pure,

That we may lift from out of dust
 A voice as unto him that hears,
 A cry above the conquer'd years
To one that with us works, and trust,

With faith that comes of self-control,
 The truths that never can be proved 10
 Until we close with all we loved,
And all we flow from, soul in soul.

[EPILOGUE]

O true and tried, so well and long,
 Demand not thou a marriage lay;
 In that it is thy marriage day[67]
Is music more than any song.

Nor have I felt so much of bliss
 Since first he told me that he loved
 A daughter of our house; nor proved
Since that dark day a day like this;

Tho' I since then have number'd o'er
 Some thrice three years: they went and came, 10
 Remade the blood and changed the frame,
And yet is love not less, but more;

No longer caring to embalm
 In dying songs a dead regret,
 But like a statue solid-set,
And moulded in colossal calm.

Regret is dead, but love is more
 Than in the summers that are flown,
 For I myself with these have grown
To something greater than before;   20

---

[66]**Thou standest . . . sun:** see Revelation 19:17.

[67]**marriage day:** written on the occasion of the 1842 marriage of Cecilia Tennyson to Edmund Lushington (see section 85).

Which makes appear the songs I made
   As echoes out of weaker times,
   As half but idle brawling rhymes,
The sport of random sun and shade.

But where is she, the bridal flower,
   That must be made a wife ere noon?
   She enters, glowing like the moon
Of Eden on its bridal bower:

On me she bends her blissful eyes
   And then on thee; they meet thy look   30
   And brighten like the star that shook
Betwixt the palms of paradise.

O when her life was yet in bud,
   He too foretold the perfect rose.
   For thee she grew, for thee she grows
For ever, and as fair as good.

And thou art worthy; full of power;
   As gentle; liberal-minded, great,
   Consistent; wearing all that weight
Of learning lightly like a flower.   40

But now set out: the noon is near,
   And I must give away the bride;
   She fears not, or with thee beside
And me behind her, will not fear.

For I that danced her on my knee,
   That watch'd her on her nurse's arm,
   That shielded all her life from harm
At last must part with her to thee;

Now waiting to be made a wife,
   Her feet, my darling, on the dead;   50
   Their pensive tablets round her head,
And the most living words of life

Breathed in her ear. The ring is on,
   The "wilt thou" answer'd, and again
   The "wilt thou" ask'd, till out of twain
Her sweet "I will" has made you one.

Now sign your names, which shall be read,
   Mute symbols of a joyful morn,
   By village eyes as yet unborn;
The names are sign'd, and overhead   60

Begins the clash and clang that tells
   The joy to every wandering breeze;
   The blind wall rocks, and on the trees
The dead leaf trembles to the bells.

O happy hour, and happier hours
   Await them. Many a merry face
   Salutes them—maidens of the place,
That pelt us in the porch with flowers.

O happy hour, behold the bride
   With him to whom her hand I gave.   70
   They leave the porch, they pass the grave
That has to-day its sunny side.

To-day the grave is bright for me,
   For them the light of life increased,
   Who stay to share the morning feast,
Who rest to-night beside the sea.

Let all my genial spirits advance
   To meet and greet a whiter sun;
   My drooping memory will not shun
The foaming grape of eastern France.   80

It circles round, and fancy plays,
   And hearts are warm'd and faces bloom,
   As drinking health to bride and groom
We wish them store of happy days.

Nor count me all to blame if I
   Conjecture of a stiller guest,
   Perchance, perchance, among the rest,
And, tho' in silence, wishing joy.

But they must go, the time draws on,
   And those white-favour'd horses wait;   90
   They rise, but linger; it is late;
Farewell, we kiss, and they are gone.

A shade falls on us like the dark
   From little cloudlets on the grass,
   But sweeps away as out we pass
To range the woods, to roam the park,

Discussing how their courtship grew,
   And talk to others that are wed,
   And how she look'd, and what he said,
And back we come at fall of dew.   100

Again the feast, the speech, the glee,
   The shade of passing thought, the wealth
   Of words and wit, the double health,
The crowning cup, the three-times-three,

And last the dance;—till I retire:
   Dumb is that tower which spake so loud,
   And high in heaven the streaming cloud,
And on the downs a rising fire:

And rise, O moon, from yonder down,
   Till over down and over dale   110
   All night the shining vapour sail
And pass the silent-lighted town,

The white-faced halls, the glancing rills,
   And catch at every mountain head,
   And o'er the friths that branch and spread
Their sleeping silver thro' the hills;

And touch with shade the bridal doors,
   With tender gloom the roof, the wall;
   And breaking let the splendour fall
To spangle all the happy shores   120

By which they rest, and ocean sounds,
   And, star and system rolling past,
   A soul shall draw from out the vast
And strike his being into bounds,

And, moved thro' life of lower phase,
   Result in man, be born and think,
   And act and love, a closer link
Betwixt us and the crowning race

Of those that, eye to eye, shall look
   On knowledge; under whose command   130
   Is Earth and Earth's, and in their hand
Is Nature like an open book;

No longer half-akin to brute,
   For all we thought and loved and did,
   And hoped, and suffer'd, is but seed
Of what in them is flower and fruit;

Whereof the man, that with me trod
   This planet, was a noble type
   Appearing ere the times were ripe,
That friend of mine who lives in God,   140

That God, which ever lives and loves,
   One God, one law, one element,
   And one far-off divine event,
To which the whole creation moves.

1850

The Eagle

Fragment

He clasps the crag with crooked hands;
Close to the sun in lonely lands,
Ring'd with the azure world, he stands.

The wrinkled sea beneath him crawls;
He watches from his mountain walls,
And like a thunderbolt he falls.

1851

Ode on the Death of the Duke of Wellington

— 1 —

Bury the Great Duke
   With an empire's lamentation,[1]
Let us bury the Great Duke
   To the noise of the mourning of a mighty nation,
Mourning when their leaders fall,
Warriors carry the warrior's pall,
And sorrow darkens hamlet and hall.

— 2 —

Where shall we lay the man whom we deplore?
Here, in streaming London's central roar.
Let the sound of those he wrought for,   10
And the feet of those he fought for,
Echo round his bones for evermore.

— 3 —

Lead out the pageant: sad and slow,
As fits an universal woe,
Let the long, long procession go,
And let the sorrowing crowd about it grow,
And let the mournful martial music blow;
The last great Englishman is low.

— 4 —

Mourn, for to us he seems the last,
Remembering all his greatness in the Past.   20
No more in soldier fashion will he greet
With lifted hand the gazer in the street.

---

[1] **an empire's lamentation**: Tennyson's first major production as Poet Laureate describes and evaluates the ostentatious state funeral of Arthur Wellesley, Duke of Wellington (1769–1852).

O friends, our chief state-oracle is mute:
Mourn for the man of long-enduring blood,
The statesman-warrior, moderate, resolute,
Whole in himself, a common good.
Mourn for the man of amplest influence,
Yet clearest of ambitious crime,
Our greatest yet with least pretence,
Great in council and great in war,   30
Foremost captain of his time,
Rich in saving common-sense,
And, as the greatest only are,
In his simplicity sublime.
O good gray head which all men knew,
O voice from which their omens all men drew,
O iron nerves to true occasion true,
O fall'n at length that tower of strength
Which stood four-square to all the winds that blew!
Such was he whom we deplore.   40
The long self-sacrifice of life is o'er.
The great World-victor's victor[2] will be seen no more.

— 5 —

All is over and done:
Render thanks to the Giver,
England, for thy son.
Let the bell be toll'd.
Render thanks to the Giver,
And render him to the mould.
Under the cross of gold
That shines over city and river,   50
There he shall rest for ever
Among the wise and the bold.
Let the bell be toll'd:
And a reverent people behold
The towering car, the sable steeds:
Bright let it be with its blazon'd deeds,
Dark in its funeral fold.
Let the bell be toll'd:
And a deeper knell in the heart be knoll'd;
And the sound of the sorrowing anthem roll'd   60
Thro' the dome of the golden cross;
And the volleying cannon thunder his loss;
He knew their voices of old.
For many a time in many a clime
His captain's-ear has heard them boom
Bellowing victory, bellowing doom:
When he with those deep voices wrought,

Guarding realms and kings from shame;
With those deep voices our dead captain taught
The tyrant, and asserts his claim   70
In that dread sound to the great name,
Which he has worn so pure of blame,
In praise and in dispraise the same,
A man of well-attemper'd frame.
O civic muse, to such a name,
To such a name for ages long,
To such a name,
Preserve a broad approach of fame,
And ever-echoing avenues of song.

— 6 —

Who is he that cometh, like an honour'd guest,   80
With banner and with music, with soldier and with priest,
With a nation weeping, and breaking on my rest?
Mighty Seaman,[3] this is he
Was great by land as thou by sea.
Thine island loves thee well, thou famous man,
The greatest sailor since our world began.
Now, to the roll of muffled drums,
To thee the greatest soldier comes;
For this is he
Was great by land as thou by sea;   90
His foes were thine; he kept us free;
O give him welcome, this is he
Worthy of our gorgeous rites,
And worthy to be laid by thee;
For this is England's greatest son,
He that gain'd a hundred fights,
Nor ever lost an English gun;
This is he that far away
Against the myriads of Assaye[4]
Clash'd with his fiery few and won;   100
And underneath another sun,
Warring on a later day,
Round affrighted Lisbon[5] drew
The treble works, the vast designs
Of his labour'd rampart-lines,
Where he greatly stood at bay,
Whence he issued forth anew,
And ever great and greater grew,

---

[2]**World-victor's victor:** Wellington commanded the army that decisively overthrew Napoleon at Waterloo in 1815.

[3]**Mighty Seaman:** Horatio Nelson (1758–1805), Wellington's naval counterpart during the Napoleonic wars. Observing a convention of the civic ode, Tennyson gives voice, and then reply, to Nelson's shade.

[4]**Assaye:** site in India of a Wellington victory (1803).

[5]**Lisbon:** at the battle of Torres Vedras in Portugal (1810).

Beating from the wasted vines
Back to France her banded swarms,   110
Back to France with countless blows,
Till o'er the hills her eagles flew
Beyond the Pyrenean pines,
Follow'd up in valley and glen
With blare of bugle, clamour of men,
Roll of cannon and clash of arms,
And England pouring on her foes.
Such a war had such a close.
Again their ravening eagle rose
In anger, wheel'd on Europe-shadowing wings,   120
And barking for the thrones of kings;
Till one that sought but Duty's iron crown
On that loud sabbath[6] shook the spoiler down;
A day of onsets of despair!
Dash'd on every rocky square
Their surging charges foam'd themselves away;
Last, the Prussian trumpet blew;
Thro' the long-tormented air
Heaven flash'd a sudden jubilant ray,
And down we swept and charged and overthrew.   130
So great a soldier taught us there,
What long-enduring hearts could do
In that world-earthquake, Waterloo!
Mighty Seaman, tender and true,
And pure as he from taint of craven guile.
O saviour of the silver-coasted isle,
O shaker of the Baltic and the Nile,
If aught of things that here befall
Touch a spirit among things divine,
If love of country move thee there at all,   140
Be glad, because his bones are laid by thine!
And thro' the centuries let a people's voice
In full acclaim,
A people's voice,
The proof and echo of all human fame,
A people's voice, when they rejoice
At civic revel and pomp and game,
Attest their great commander's claim
With honour, honour, honour, honour to him,
Eternal honour to his name.   150

— 7 —

A people's voice! we are a people yet.
Tho' all men else their nobler dreams forget,
Confused by brainless mobs and lawless Powers;

Thank Him who isled us here, and roughly set
His Briton in blown seas and storming showers,
We have a voice, with which to pay the debt
Of boundless love and reverence and regret
To those great men who fought, and kept it ours.
And keep it ours, O God, from brute control;
O Statesmen, guard us, guard the eye, the soul   160
Of Europe, keep our noble England whole,
And save the one true seed of freedom sown
Betwixt a people and their ancient throne,
That sober freedom out of which there springs
Our loyal passion for our temperate kings;
For, saving that, ye help to save mankind
Till public wrong be crumbled into dust,
And drill the raw world for the march of mind,
Till crowds at length be sane and crowns be just.
But wink no more in slothful overtrust.   170
Remember him who led your hosts;
He bad you guard the sacred coasts.
Your cannons moulder on the seaward wall;
His voice is silent in your council-hall
For ever; and whatever tempests lour
For ever silent; even if they broke
In thunder, silent; yet remember all
He spoke among you, and the Man who spoke;
Who never sold the truth to serve the hour,
Nor palter'd with Eternal God for power;   180
Who let the turbid streams of rumour flow
Thro' either babbling world of high and low;
Whose life was work, whose language rife
With rugged maxims hewn from life;
Who never spoke against a foe;
Whose eighty winters freeze with one rebuke
All great self-seekers trampling on the right:
Truth-teller was our England's Alfred[7] named;
Truth-lover was our English Duke;
Whatever record leap to light   190
He never shall be shamed.

— 8 —

Lo! the leader in these glorious wars
Now to glorious burial slowly borne,
Follow'd by the brave of other lands,
He, on whom from both her open hands
Lavish Honour shower'd all her stars,
And affluent Fortune emptied all her horn.
Yet, let all good things await
Him who cares not to be great,

---

[6]**loud sabbath**: the Sunday when the battle of Waterloo was fought.

[7]**Alfred**: 9th-century Saxon king.

But as he saves or serves the state.   200
Not once or twice in our rough island-story,
The path of duty was the way to glory:
He that walks it, only thirsting
For the right, and learns to deaden
Love of self, before his journey closes,
He shall find the stubborn thistle bursting
Into glossy purples, which outredden
All voluptuous garden-roses.
Not once or twice in our fair island-story,
The path of duty was the way to glory: 210
He, that ever following her commands,
On with toil of heart and knees and hands,
Thro' the long gorge to the far light has won
His path upward, and prevail'd,
Shall find the toppling crags of Duty scaled
Are close upon the shining table-lands
To which our God Himself is moon and sun.
Such was he: his work is done.
But while the races of mankind endure
Let his great example stand   220
Colossal, seen of every land,
And keep the soldier firm, the statesman pure:
Till in all lands and thro' all human story
The path of duty be the way to glory:
And let the land whose hearths he saved from shame
For many and many an age proclaim
At civic revel and pomp and game,
And when the long-illumined cities flame,
Their ever-loyal iron leader's fame,
With honour, honour, honour, honour to him,   230
Eternal honour to his name.

— 9 —

Peace, his triumph will be sung
By some yet unmolded tongue
Far on in summers that we shall not see:
Peace, it is a day of pain
For one about whose patriarchal knee
Late the little children clung:
O peace, it is a day of pain
For one upon whose hand and heart and brain
Once the weight and fate of Europe hung.   240
Ours the pain, be his the gain!
More than is of man's degree
Must be with us, watching here
At this, our great solemnity.
Whom we see not we revere;
We revere, and we refrain
From talk of battles loud and vain,

And brawling memories all too free
For such a wise humility
As befits a solemn fane: 250
We revere, and while we hear
The tides of Music's golden sea
Setting toward eternity,
Uplifted high in heart and hope are we,
Until we doubt not that for one so true
There must be other nobler work to do
Than when he fought at Waterloo,
And Victor he must ever be.
For tho' the Giant Ages heave the hill
And break the shore, and evermore   260
Make and break, and work their will;
Tho' world on world in myriad myriads roll
Round us, each with different powers,
And other forms of life than ours,
What know we greater than the soul?
On God and Godlike men we build our trust.
Hush, the Dead March wails in the people's ears:
The dark crowd moves, and there are sobs and tears:
The black earth yawns: the mortal disappears;
Ashes to ashes, dust to dust;   270
He is gone who seem'd so great.—
Gone; but nothing can bereave him
Of the force he made his own
Being here, and we believe him
Something far advanced in State,
And that he wears a truer crown
Than any wreath that man can weave him.
Speak no more of his renown,
Lay your earthly fancies down,
And in the vast cathedral leave him.   280
God accept him, Christ receive him.

                                        1852

~

The Charge of the Light Brigade

— 1 —

Half a league, half a league,
Half a league onward,
All in the valley of Death
    Rode the six hundred.
"Forward the Light Brigade!
Charge for the guns!" he said.
Into the valley of Death
    Rode the six hundred.

— 2 —

"Forward, the Light Brigade!"
Was there a man dismay'd?   10
Not tho' the soldier knew
     Some one had blunder'd.[1]
     Theirs not to make reply,
     Theirs not to reason why,
     Theirs but to do and die.
     Into the valley of Death
     Rode the six hundred.

— 3 —

Cannon to right of them,
Cannon to left of them,
Cannon in front of them   20
     Volley'd and thunder'd;
Storm'd at with shot and shell,
Boldly they rode and well,
Into the jaws of Death,
Into the mouth of hell
     Rode the six hundred.

— 4 —

Flash'd all their sabres bare,
Flash'd as they turn'd in air
Sabring the gunners there,
Charging an army, while   30
     All the world wonder'd.
Plunged in the battery-smoke
Right thro' the line they broke;
Cossack and Russian
Reel'd from the sabre-stroke
     Shatter'd and sunder'd.
Then they rode back, but not,
     Not the six hundred.

— 5 —

Cannon to right of them,
Cannon to left of them,   40
Cannon behind them
     Volley'd and thunder'd;

Storm'd at with shot and shell,
While horse and hero fell,
They that had fought so well
Came thro' the jaws of Death,
Back from the mouth of hell,
All that was left of them,
     Left of six hundred.

— 6 —

When can their glory fade?   50
O the wild charge they made!
     All the world wonder'd.
Honor the charge they made!
Honor the Light Brigade,
     Noble six hundred!

                                        1854

~

Maud: A Monodrama[1]

— PART I —

I

1

I hate the dreadful hollow behind the little wood,
Its lips in the field above are dabbled with blood-red heath,
The red-ribb'd ledges drip with a silent horror of blood,
And Echo there, whatever is ask'd her, answers "Death."

2

For there in the ghastly pit long since a body was found,
His who had given me life—O father! O God! was it well?—
Mangled, and flatten'd, and crush'd, and dinted into the
     ground:
There yet lies the rock that fell with him when he fell.

---

[1]**Some one had blunder'd**: Tennyson wrote this poem "in a few minutes, after reading the description in the *Times* in which occurred the phrase 'some one had blundered,' and this was the origin of the metre of his poem" (Hallam Tennyson). The light brigade, a mere cavalry detachment, had fatally complied with a mistaken order to ride straight at the entrenched Russian artillery at Balaklava, early in the Crimean War.

[1]**Monodrama**: Tennyson added this generic subtitle for his favorite poem—initially called in manuscript *Maud or the Madness*—two decades after its first publication. A dramatic piece for a single voice, it unfolds the fluctuating moods of Maud's lover, "a morbid, poetic soul, under the blighting influence of a recklessly speculative age" (Tennyson's note). These moods reflect the alienated speaker's evolving reaction to family histories, personal encounters, and current events, which the reader must infer from lyric to lyric, within the larger ambiance of class and gender norms that the speaker regards with intense ambivalence yet ultimately obeys. The experimental versification modulates with his mood, and corresponds to the often violent, sometimes protomodernist imagery.

3

Did he fling himself down? who knows? for a vast
    speculation had fail'd,
And ever he mutter'd and madden'd, and ever wann'd
    with despair,   10
And out he walk'd when the wind like a broken worldling
    wail'd,
And the flying gold of the ruin'd woodlands drove thro'
    the air.

4

I remember the time, for the roots of my hair were stirr'd
By a shuffled step, by a dead weight trail'd, by a whisper'd
    fright,
And my pulses closed their gates with a shock on my heart
    as I heard
The shrill-edged shriek of a mother divide the shuddering
    night.

5

Villainy somewhere! whose? One says, we are villains all.
Not he: his honest fame should at least by me be maintained:
But that old man, now lord of the broad estate and the Hall,
Dropt off gorged from a scheme that had left us flaccid
    and drain'd.   20

6

Why do they prate of the blessings of Peace? we have made
    them a curse,
Pickpockets, each hand lusting for all that is not its own;
And lust of gain, in the spirit of Cain, is it better or worse
Than the heart of the citizen hissing in war on his own
    hearthstone?

7

But these are the days of advance, the works of the men of
    mind,
When who but a fool would have faith in a tradesman's
    ware or his word?
Is it peace or war? Civil war, as I think, and that of a kind
The viler, as underhand, not openly bearing the sword.

8

Sooner or later I too may passively take the print
Of the golden age—why not? I have neither hope
    nor trust;   30
May make my heart as a millstone, set my face as a flint,
Cheat and be cheated, and die: who knows? we are ashes
    and dust.

9

Peace sitting under her olive, and slurring the days gone by,
When the poor are hovell'd and hustled together, each sex,
    like swine,
When only the ledger lives, and when only not all men lie;
Peace in her vineyard—yes!—but a company forges the
    wine.

10

And the vitriol madness flushes up in the ruffian's head,
Till the filthy by-lane rings to the yell of the trampled wife,
And chalk and alum and plaster are sold to the poor for
    bread,
And the spirit of murder works in the very means
    of life,   40

11

And Sleep must lie down arm'd, for the villainous centre-
    bits[2]
Grind on the wakeful ear in the hush of the moonless
    nights,
While another is cheating the sick of a few last gasps, as
    he sits
To pestle a poison'd poison behind his crimson lights.

12

When a Mammonite mother kills her babe for a burial fee,
And Timour-Mammon[3] grins on a pile of children's bones,
Is it peace or war? better, war! loud war by land and by sea,
War with a thousand battles, and shaking a hundred
    thrones!

13

For I trust if an enemy's fleet came yonder round by the hill,
And the rushing battle-bolt sang from the three-decker out
    of the foam,   50
That the smooth-faced snubnosed rogue would leap from
    his counter and till,
And strike, if he could, were it but with his cheating
    yardwand,[4] home.—

---

[2]**centre-bits**: burglars' drills.

[3]**Timour**: Tamerlane, 14th-century Mongol conqueror. **Mammon**: near-eastern god of wealth, prominent in Carlyle's denunciation (page 190) of the way commercial greed corrodes community decencies, producing the evils these stanzas itemize: wife-beating, burglary, child abuse, the adulteration of wine, bread, and medicine.

[4]**three-decker**: warship. **cheating yardwand**: tradesman's false measure.

14

What! am I raging alone as my father raged in his mood?
Must *I* too creep to the hollow and dash myself down
    and die
Rather than hold by the law that I made, nevermore to
    brood
On a horror of shatter'd limbs and a wretched swindler's lie?

15

Would there be sorrow for *me*? there was *love* in the
    passionate shriek,
Love for the silent thing that had made false haste to
    the grave—
Wrapt in a cloak, as I saw him, and thought he would
    rise and speak
And rave at the lie and the liar, ah God, as he used
    to rave.   60

16

I am sick of the Hall and the hill, I am sick of the moor and
    the main.
Why should I stay? can a sweeter chance ever come to
    me here?
O, having the nerves of motion as well as the nerves of pain,
Were it not wise if I fled from the place and the pit and
    the fear?

17

Workmen up at the Hall!—they are coming back from
    abroad;
The dark old place will be gilt by the touch of a millionaire:
I have heard, I know not whence, of the singular beauty
    of Maud;
I play'd with the girl when a child; she promised then
    to be fair.

18

Maud with her venturous climbings and tumbles and
    childish escapes,
Maud the delight of the village, the ringing joy of
    the Hall,   70
Maud with her sweet purse-mouth when my father dangled
    the grapes,
Maud the beloved of my mother, the moon-faced darling
    of all,—

19

What is she now? My dreams are bad. She may bring me
    a curse.

No, there is fatter game on the moor; she will let me alone.
Thanks, for the fiend best knows whether woman or man
    be the worse.
I will bury myself in myself, and the Devil may pipe to
    his own.

II

Long have I sigh'd for a calm: God grant I may find it at
    last!
It will never be broken by Maud, she has neither savour
    nor salt,
But a cold and clear-cut face, as I found when her carriage
    past,
Perfectly beautiful: let it be granted her: where is
    the fault?   80
All that I saw (for her eyes were downcast, not to be seen)
Faultily faultless, icily regular, splendidly null,
Dead perfection, no more; nothing more, if it had not been
For a chance of travel, a paleness, an hour's defect of
    the rose,
Or an underlip, you may call it a little too ripe, too full,
Or the least little delicate aquiline curve in a sensitive nose,
From which I escaped heart-free, with the least little touch
    of spleen.

III

Cold and clear-cut face, why come you so cruelly meek,
Breaking a slumber in which all spleenful folly was drown'd,
Pale with the golden beam of an eyelash dead on
    the cheek,   90
Passionless, pale, cold face, star-sweet on a gloom
    profound;
Womanlike, taking revenge too deep for a transient wrong
Done but in thought to your beauty, and even as pale
    as before
Growing and fading and growing upon me without a sound,
Luminous, gemlike, ghostlike, deathlike, half the night long
Growing and fading and growing, till I could bear it no
    more,
But arose, and all by myself in my own dark garden ground,
Listening now to the tide in its broad-flung shipwrecking
    roar,
Now to the scream of a madden'd beach dragg'd down by
    the wave,
Walk'd in a wintry wind by a ghastly glimmer
    and found   100
The shining daffodil dead, and Orion[5] low in his grave.

---

[5]**Orion**: winter constellation.

IV

1

A million emeralds break from the ruby-budded lime
In the little grove where I sit—ah, wherefore cannot I be
Like things of the season gay, like the bountiful season bland,
When the far-off sail is blown by the breeze of softer clime,
Half-lost in the liquid azure bloom of a crescent of sea,
The silent sapphire-spangled marriage ring of the land?

2

Below me, there, is the village, and looks how quiet and
    small!
And yet bubbles o'er like a city, with gossip, scandal, and
    spite;
And Jack on his ale-house bench has as many lies as
    a Czar;   110
And here on the landward side, by a red rock, glimmers
    the Hall;
And up in the high Hall-garden I see her pass like a light;
But sorrow seize me if ever that light be my leading star!

3

When have I bow'd to her father, the wrinkled head of
    the race?
I met her to-day with her brother, but not to her brother
    I bow'd:
I bow'd to his lady-sister as she rode by on the moor;
But the fire of a foolish pride flash'd over her beautiful face.
O child, you wrong your beauty, believe it, in being so
    proud;
Your father has wealth well-gotten, and I am nameless
    and poor.

4

I keep but a man and a maid, ever ready to slander and
    steal;   120
I know it, and smile a hard-set smile, like a stoic, or like
A wiser epicurean, and let the world have its way:
For nature is one with rapine, a harm no preacher can heal;
The Mayfly is torn by the swallow, the sparrow spear'd by
    the shrike,
And the whole little wood where I sit is a world of plunder
    and prey.

5

We are puppets, Man in his pride, and Beauty fair in her
    flower;
Do we move ourselves, or are moved by an unseen hand at
    a game

That pushes us off from the board, and others ever succeed?
Ah yet, we cannot be kind to each other here for an hour;
We whisper, and hint, and chuckle, and grin at a brother's
    shame;   130
However we brave it out, we men are a little breed.

6

A monstrous eft[6] was of old the Lord and Master of Earth,
For him did his high sun flame, and his river billowing ran,
And he felt himself in his force to be Nature's crowning
    race.
As nine months go to the shaping an infant ripe for his
    birth,
So many a million of ages have gone to the making of man:
He now is first, but is he the last? is he not too base?

7

The man of science himself is fonder of glory, and vain,
An eye well-practised in nature, a spirit bounded and poor;
The passionate heart of the poet is whirl'd into folly
    and vice.   140
I would not marvel at either, but keep a temperate brain;
For not to desire or admire, if a man could learn it,
    were more
Than to walk all day like the sultan of old in a garden
    of spice.

8

For the drift of the Maker is dark, an Isis[7] hid by the veil.
Who knows the ways of the world, how God will bring
    them about?
Our planet is one, the suns are many, the world is wide.
Shall I weep if a Poland fall? shall I shriek if a Hungary fail?[8]
Or an infant civilization be ruled with rod or with knout?
I have not made the world, and He that made it will guide.

9

Be mine a philosopher's life in the quiet woodland
    ways,   150
Where if I cannot be gay let a passionless peace be
    my lot,
Far-off from the clamour of liars belied in the hubbub
    of lies;

---

[6]**monstrous eft**: dinosaur, one of "the great old lizards of geology." [Tennyson's note]

[7]**Isis**: ancient Egyptian goddess.

[8]**Poland**: occupied by Russia in the 1840s. **Hungary**: suppressed
by Austrian empire after 1848 uprising.

From the long-neck'd geese of the world that are ever
    hissing dispraise
Because their natures are little, and, whether he heed it
    or not,
Where each man walks with his head in a cloud of
    poisonous flies.

10

And most of all would I flee from the cruel madness of love,
The honey of poison-flowers and all the measureless ill.
Ah Maud, you milkwhite fawn, you are all unmeet for a wife.
Your mother is mute in her grave as her image in marble
    above;
Your father is ever in London, you wander about at your
    will;   160
You have but fed on the roses and lain in the lilies of life.

V

1

A voice by the cedar tree
In the meadow under the Hall!
She is singing an air that is known to me,
A passionate ballad gallant and gay,
A martial song like a trumpet's call!
Singing alone in the morning of life,
In the happy morning of life and of May,
Singing of men that in battle array,
Ready in heart and ready in hand,   170
March with banner and bugle and fife
To the death, for their native land.

2

Maud with her exquisite face,
And wild voice pealing up to the sunny sky,
And feet like sunny gems on an English green,
Maud in the light of her youth and her grace,
Singing of Death, and of Honour that cannot die,
Till I well could weep for a time so sordid and mean,
And myself so languid and base.

3

Silence, beautiful voice!   180
Be still, for you only trouble the mind
With a joy in which I cannot rejoice,
A glory I shall not find.
Still! I will hear you no more,
For your sweetness hardly leaves me a choice
But to move to the meadow and fall before
Her feet on the meadow grass, and adore,

Not her, who is neither courtly nor kind,
Not her, not her, but a voice.

VI

1

Morning arises stormy and pale,   190
No sun, but a wannish glare
In fold upon fold of hueless cloud,
And the budded peaks of the wood are bow'd,
Caught and cuff'd by the gale:
I had fancied it would be fair.

2

Whom but Maud should I meet
Last night, when the sunset burn'd
On the blossom'd gable-ends
At the head of the village street,
Whom but Maud should I meet?   200
And she touch'd my hand with a smile so sweet,
She made me divine amends
For a courtesy not return'd.

3

And thus a delicate spark
Of glowing and growing light
Thro' the livelong hours of the dark
Kept itself warm in the heart of my dreams,
Till at last when the morning came
Ready to burst in a colour'd flame;
In a cloud, it faded, and seems   210
But an ashen-gray delight.

4

What if with her sunny hair,
And smile as sunny as cold,
She meant to weave me a snare
Of some coquettish deceit,
Cleopatra-like as of old
To entangle me when we met,
To have her lion roll in a silken net
And fawn at a victor's feet.

5

Ah, what shall I be at fifty   220
Should Nature keep me alive,
If I find the world so bitter
When I am but twenty-five?
Yet, if she were not a cheat,
If Maud were all that she seem'd,

And her smile were all that I dream'd,
Then the world were not so bitter
But a smile could make it sweet.

6

What if tho' her eye seem'd full
Of a kind intent to me,   230
What if that dandy-despot, he,
That jewell'd mass of millinery,
That oil'd and curl'd Assyrian bull[9]
Smelling of musk and of insolence,
Her brother, from whom I keep aloof,
Who wants the finer politic sense
To mask, tho' but in his own behoof,
With a glassy smile his brutal scorn—
What if he had told her yestermorn
How prettily for his own sweet sake   240
A face of tenderness might be feign'd,
And a moist mirage in desert eyes,
That so, when the rotten hustings shake
In another month to his brazen lies,
A wretched vote may be gain'd.

7

For a raven ever croaks, at my side,
Keep watch and ward, keep watch and ward,
Or thou wilt prove their tool.
Yea, too, myself from myself I guard,
For often a man's own angry pride   250
Is cap and bells for a fool.

8

Perhaps the smile and tender tone
Came out of her pitying womanhood,
For am I not, am I not, here alone
So many a summer since she died,
My mother, who was so gentle and good?
Living alone in an empty house,
Here half-hid in the gleaming wood,
Where I hear the dead at midday moan,
And the shrieking rush of the wainscot mouse,   260
And my own sad name in corners cried,
When the shiver of dancing leaves is thrown
About its echoing chambers wide,
Till a morbid hate and horror have grown

Of a world in which I have hardly mixt,
And a morbid eating lichen fixt
On a heart half-turn'd to stone.

9

O heart of stone, are you flesh, and caught
By that you swore to withstand?
For what was it else within me wrought   270
But, I fear, the new strong wine of love,
That made my tongue so stammer and trip
When I saw the treasured splendour, her hand,
Come sliding out of her sacred glove,
And the sunlight broke from her lip?

10

I have play'd with her when a child;
She remembers it now we meet.
Ah, well, well, well, I *may* be beguiled
By some coquettish deceit.
Yet, if she were not a cheat,   280
If Maud were all that she seem'd,
And her smile had all that I dream'd,
Then the world were not so bitter
But a smile could make it sweet.

VII

1

Did I hear it half in a doze
    Long since, I know not where?
Did I dream it an hour ago,
    When asleep in this arm-chair?

2

Men were drinking together,
    Drinking and talking of me;   290
"Well, if it prove a girl, the boy
    Will have plenty: so let it be."

3

Is it an echo of something
    Read with a boy's delight,
Viziers nodding together
    In some Arabian night?

4

Strange, that I hear two men,
    Somewhere, talking of me;
"Well, if it prove a girl, my boy
    Will have plenty: so let it be."   300

---

[9]**Assyrian bull:** massive imperial sculpture excavated at Nineveh and delivered to the British Museum in early 1850s. See Layard's account, page 108; also D.G. Rossetti's "The Burden of Nineveh" (page 804).

VIII

She came to the village church,
And sat by a pillar alone;
An angel watching an urn
Wept over her, carved in stone;
And once, but once, she lifted her eyes,
And suddenly, sweetly, strangely blush'd
To find they were met by my own;
And suddenly, sweetly, my heart beat stronger
And thicker, until I heard no longer
The snowy-banded, dilettante,   310
Delicate-handed priest intone;
And thought, is it pride? and mused and sigh'd,
"No surely, now it cannot be pride."

IX

I was walking a mile,
More than a mile from the shore,
The sun look'd out with a smile
Betwixt the cloud and the moor,
And riding at set of day
Over the dark moor land,
Rapidly riding far away,   320
She waved to me with her hand.
There were two at her side,
Something flash'd in the sun,
Down by the hill I saw them ride,
In a moment they were gone:
Like a sudden spark
Struck vainly in the night,
Then returns the dark
With no more hope of light.

X

1

Sick, am I sick of a jealous dread?   330
Was not one of the two at her side
This new-made lord, whose splendour plucks
The slavish hat from the villager's head?
Whose old grandfather has lately died,
Gone to a blacker pit, for whom
Grimy nakedness dragging his trucks
And laying his trams[10] in a poison'd gloom
Wrought, till he crept from a gutted mine
Master of half a servile shire,

And left his coal all turn'd into gold   340
To a grandson, first of his noble line,
Rich in the grace all women desire,
Strong in the power that all men adore,
And simper and set their voices lower,
And soften as if to a girl, and hold
Awe-stricken breaths at a work divine,
Seeing his gewgaw castle[11] shine,
New as his title, built last year,
There amid perky larches and pine,
And over the sullen-purple moor   350
(Look at it) pricking a cockney ear.

2

What, has he found my jewel out?
For one of the two that rode at her side
Bound for the Hall, I am sure was he:
Bound for the Hall, and I think for a bride.
Blithe would her brother's acceptance be.
Maud could be gracious too, no doubt
To a lord, a captain, a padded shape,
A bought commission, a waxen face,
A rabbit mouth that is ever agape—   360
Bought? what is it he cannot buy?
And therefore splenetic, personal, base,
A wounded thing with a rancorous cry,
At war with myself and a wretched race,
Sick, sick to the heart of life, am I.

3

Last week came one to the county town,
To preach our poor little army down,
And play the game of the despot kings,
Tho' the state has done it and thrice as well.
This broad-brimm'd hawker[12] of holy things,   370
Whose ear is cramm'd with his cotton, and rings
Even in dreams to the chink of his pence,
This huckster put down war! can he tell
Whether war be a cause or a consequence?
Put down the passions that make earth Hell!
Down with ambition, avarice, pride,
Jealousy, down! cut off from the mind
The bitter springs of anger and fear;
Down too, down at your own fireside,

---

[10]**trucks** and **trams**: miners' wagons and wheelbarrows.

[11]**gewgaw castle**: ostentatious mansion in nouveau-riche manner suited to **cockney** (citified) taste.

[12]**broad-brimm'd hawker**: Quaker-hatted pacifist lecturer, made rich in the **cotton** trade.

With the evil tongue and the evil ear,   380
For each is at war with mankind.

4

I wish I could hear again
The chivalrous battle-song
That she warbled alone in her joy!
I might persuade myself then
She would not do herself this great wrong,
To take a wanton dissolute boy
For a man and leader of men.

5

Ah God, for a man with heart, head, hand,
Like some of the simple great ones gone   390
For ever and ever by,
One still strong man in a blatant land,
Whatever they call him, what care I,
Aristocrat, democrat, autocrat—one
Who can rule and dare not lie.

6

And ah for a man to arise in me,
That the man I am may cease to be!

XI

1

O let the solid ground
    Not fail beneath my feet
Before my life has found   400
    What some have found so sweet;
Then let come what come may,
What matter if I go mad,
I shall have had my day.

2

Let the sweet heavens endure,
    Not close and darken above me
Before I am quite quite sure
    That there is one to love me;
Then let come what come may
To a life that has been so sad,   410
I shall have had my day.

XII

1

Birds in the high Hall-garden
    When twilight was falling,

Maud, Maud, Maud, Maud,
    They were crying and calling.

2

Where was Maud? in our wood;
    And I, who else?, was with her,
Gathering woodland lilies,
    Myriads blow together.

3

Birds in our wood sang   420
    Ringing thro' the valleys,
Maud is here, here, here
    In among the lilies.

4

I kiss'd her slender hand,
    She took the kiss sedately;
Maud is not seventeen,
    But she is tall and stately.

5

I to cry out on pride
    Who have won her favour!
O Maud were sure of heaven   430
    If lowliness could save her.

6

I know the way she went
    Home with her maiden posy,
For her feet have touch'd the meadows
    And left the daisies rosy.[13]

7

Birds in the high Hall-garden
    Were crying and calling to her,
Where is Maud, Maud, Maud?
    One is come to woo her.

8

Look, a horse at the door,   440
    And little King Charley[14] snarling!
Go back, my lord, across the moor,
    You are not her darling.

---

[13]**rosy**: If you tread on the daisy, it turns up a rosy underside.
[Tennyson's note]

[14]**King Charley**: Maud's pet spaniel.

XIII

1

Scorn'd, to be scorn'd by one that I scorn,
Is that a matter to make me fret?
That a calamity hard to be borne?
Well, he may live to hate me yet.
Fool that I am to be vext with his pride!
I past him, I was crossing his lands;
He stood on the path a little aside;   450
His face, as I grant, in spite of spite,
Has a broad-blown comeliness, red and white,
And six feet two, as I think, he stands;
But his essences turn'd the live air sick,
And barbarous opulence jewel-thick
Sunn'd itself on his breast and his hands.

2

Who shall call me ungentle, unfair?
I long'd so heartily then and there
To give him the grasp of fellowship;
But while I past he was humming an air,   460
Stopt, and then with a riding whip
Leisurely tapping a glossy boot,
And curving a contumelious lip,
Gorgonised[15] me from head to foot
With a stony British stare.

3

Why sits he here in his father's chair?
That old man never comes to his place:
Shall I believe him ashamed to be seen?
For only once, in the village street,
Last year, I caught a glimpse of his face,   470
A gray old wolf and a lean.
Scarcely, now, would I call him a cheat;
For then, perhaps, as a child of deceit,
She might by a true descent be untrue;
And Maud is as true as Maud is sweet:
Tho' I fancy her sweetness only due
To the sweeter blood by the other side;
Her mother has been a thing complete,
However she came to be so allied.
And fair without, faithful within,   480
Maud to him is nothing akin:

Some peculiar mystic grace
Made her only the child of her mother,
And heap'd the whole inherited sin
On that huge scapegoat of the race,
All, all upon the brother.

4

Peace, angry spirit, and let him be!
Has not his sister smiled on me?

XIV

1

Maud has a garden of roses
And lilies fair on a lawn;   490
There she walks in her state
And tends upon bed and bower,
And thither I climb'd at dawn
And stood by her garden-gate;
A lion ramps at the top,
He is claspt by a passion-flower.

2

Maud's own little oak-room
(Which Maud, like a precious stone
Set in the heart of the carven gloom,
Lights with herself, when alone   500
She sits by her music and books
And her brother lingers late
With a roystering company) looks
Upon Maud's own garden-gate:
And I thought as I stood, if a hand, as white
As ocean-foam in the moon, were laid
On the hasp of the window, and my Delight
Had a sudden desire, like a glorious ghost, to glide,
Like a beam of the seventh Heaven,[16] down to my side,
There were but a step to be made.   510

3

The fancy flatter'd my mind,
And again seem'd overbold;
Now I thought that she cared for me,
Now I thought she was kind
Only because she was cold.

---

[15]**Gorgonised**: petrified as if by the face of Medusa, the mythological Gorgon.

[16]**seventh Heaven**: in classical cosmology, the outermost celestial sphere.

4

I heard no sound where I stood
But the rivulet on from the lawn
Running down to my own dark wood;
Or the voice of the long sea-wave as it swell'd
Now and then in the dim-gray dawn;   520
But I look'd, and round, all round the house I beheld
The death-white curtain drawn;
Felt a horror over me creep,
Prickle my skin and catch my breath,
Knew that the death-white curtain meant but sleep,
Yet I shudder'd and thought like a fool of the sleep of death.

XV

So dark a mind within me dwells,
    And I make myself such evil cheer,
That if *I* be dear to some one else,
    Then some one else may have much to fear;   530
But if *I* be dear to some one else,
    Then I should be to myself more dear.
Shall I not take care of all that I think,
Yea even of wretched meat and drink,
If I be dear,
If I be dear to some one else.

XVI

1

This lump of earth has left his estate
The lighter by the loss of his weight;
And so that he find what he went to seek,
And fulsome Pleasure clog him, and drown   540
His heart in the gross mud-honey of town,
He may stay for a year who has gone for a week:
But this is the day when I must speak,
And I see my Oread[17] coming down,
O this is the day!
O beautiful creature, what am I
That I dare to look her way;
Think I may hold dominion sweet,
Lord of the pulse that is lord of her breast,
And dream of her beauty with tender dread,   550
From the delicate Arab arch of her feet
To the grace that, bright and light as the crest
Of a peacock, sits on her shining head,
And she knows it not: O, if she knew it,
To know her beauty might half undo it.

---

[17]**Oread**: mountain nymph.

I know it the one bright thing to save
My yet young life in the wilds of Time,
Perhaps from madness, perhaps from crime,
Perhaps from a selfish grave.

2

What, if she be fasten'd to this fool lord,   560
Dare I bid her abide by her word?
Should I love her so well if she
Had given her word to a thing so low?
Shall I love her as well if she
Can break her word were it even for me?
I trust that it is not so.

3

Catch not my breath, O clamorous heart,
Let not my tongue be a thrall to my eye,
For I must tell her before we part,
I must tell her, or die.   570

XVII

Go not, happy day,
    From the shining fields,
Go not, happy day,
    Till the maiden yields.
Rosy is the West,
    Rosy is the South,
Roses are her cheeks,
    And a rose her mouth
When the happy Yes
    Falters from her lips,   580
Pass and blush the news
    Over glowing ships;
Over blowing seas,
    Over seas at rest,
Pass the happy news,
    Blush it thro' the West;
Till the red man dance
    By his red cedar-tree,
And the red man's babe
    Leap, beyond the sea.   590
Blush from West to East,
    Blush from East to West,
Till the West is East,
    Blush it thro' the West.
Rosy is the West,
    Rosy is the South,
Roses are her cheeks,
    And a rose her mouth.

XVIII

1

I have led her home, my love, my only friend.
There is none like her, none.   600
And never yet so warmly ran my blood
And sweetly, on and on
Calming itself to the long-wish'd-for end,
Full to the banks, close on the promised good.

2

None like her, none.
Just now the dry-tongued laurels' pattering talk
Seem'd her light foot along the garden walk,
And shook my heart to think she comes once more;
But even then I heard her close the door,
The gates of heaven are closed, and she is gone.   610

3

There is none like her, none,
Nor will be when our summers have deceased.
O, art thou sighing for Lebanon
In the long breeze that streams to thy delicious East,
Sighing for Lebanon,
Dark cedar,[18] tho' thy limbs have here increased,
Upon a pastoral slope as fair,
And looking to the South, and fed
With honey'd rain and delicate air,
And haunted by the starry head   620
Of her whose gentle will has changed my fate,
And made my life a perfumed altar-flame;
And over whom thy darkness must have spread
With such delight as theirs of old, thy great
Forefathers of the thornless garden, there
Shadowing the snow-limb'd Eve from whom she came.

4

Here will I lie, while these long branches sway,
And you fair stars that crown a happy day
Go in and out as if at merry play,
Who am no more so all forlorn   630
As when it seem'd far better to be born
To labour and the mattock-harden'd hand,
Than nursed at ease and brought to understand

A sad astrology,[19] the boundless plan
That makes you tyrants in your iron skies,
Innumerable, pitiless, passionless eyes,
Cold fires, yet with power to burn and brand
His nothingness into man.

5

But now shine on, and what care I,
Who in this stormy gulf have found a pearl   640
The countercharm of space and hollow sky,
And do accept my madness, and would die
To save from some slight shame one simple girl.

6

Would die; for sullen-seeming Death may give
More life to Love than is or ever was
In our low world, where yet 'tis sweet to live.
Let no one ask me how it came to pass;
It seems that I am happy, that to me
A livelier emerald twinkles in the grass,
A purer sapphire melts into the sea.   650

7

Not die; but live a life of truest breath,
And teach true life to fight with mortal wrongs.
O, why should Love, like men in drinking-songs,
Spice his fair banquet with the dust of death?
Make answer, Maud my bliss,
Maud made my Maud by that long loving kiss,
Life of my life, wilt thou not answer this?
"The dusky strand of Death inwoven here
With dear Love's tie, makes Love himself more dear."

8

Is that enchanted moan only the swell   660
Of the long waves that roll in yonder bay?
And hark the clock within, the silver knell
Of twelve sweet hours that past in bridal white,
And died to live, long as my pulses play;
But now by this my love has closed her sight
And given false death her hand, and stol'n away
To dreamful wastes where footless fancies dwell
Among the fragments of the golden day.
May nothing there her maiden grace affright!
Dear heart, I feel with thee the drowsy spell.   670

---

[18]The **cedar** of **Lebanon**, celebrated in the Bible (Psalm 104:16), casts a **shadow** both literal and figural, linking Maud's garden with the Eden of **Eve**.

[19]**sad astrology**: modern astronomy, for of old astrology was thought to sympathise with and rule man's fate. [Tennyson's note]

My bride to be, my evermore delight,
My own heart's heart, my ownest own, farewell;
It is but for a little space I go:
And ye meanwhile far over moor and fell
Beat to the noiseless music of the night!
Has our whole earth gone nearer to the glow
Of your soft splendours that you look so bright?
I have climb'd nearer out of lonely Hell.
Beat, happy stars, timing with things below,
Beat with my heart more blest than heart can tell,   680
Blest, but for some dark undercurrent woe
That seems to draw—but it shall not be so:
Let all be well, be well.

XIX

1

Her brother is coming back to-night,
Breaking up my dream of delight.

2

My dream? do I dream of bliss?
I have walk'd awake with Truth.
O when did a morning shine
So rich in atonement as this
For my dark-dawning youth,   690
Darken'd watching a mother decline
And that dead man at her heart and mine:
For who was left to watch her but I?
Yet so did I let my freshness die.

3

I trust that I did not talk
To gentle Maud in our walk
(For often in lonely wanderings
I have cursed him even to lifeless things)
But I trust that I did not talk,
Not touch on her father's sin: 700
I am sure I did but speak
Of my mother's faded cheek
When it slowly grew so thin
That I felt she was slowly dying
Vext with lawyers and harass'd with debt:
For how often I caught her with eyes all wet,
Shaking her head at her son and sighing
A world of trouble within!

4

And Maud too, Maud was moved
To speak of the mother she loved   710

As one scarce less forlorn,
Dying abroad and it seems apart
From him who had ceased to share her heart,
And ever mourning over the feud,
The household Fury sprinkled with blood
By which our houses are torn:
How strange was what she said,
When only Maud and the brother
Hung over her dying bed—
That Maud's dark father and mine   720
Had bound us one to the other,
Betrothed us over their wine,
On the day when Maud was born;
Seal'd her mine from her first sweet breath.
Mine, mine by a right, from birth till death.
Mine, mine—our fathers have sworn.

5

But the true blood spilt had in it a heat
To dissolve the precious seal on a bond,
That, if left uncancell'd, had been so sweet:
And none of us thought of a something beyond,   730
A desire that awoke in the heart of the child,
As it were a duty done to the tomb,
To be friends for her sake, to be reconciled;
And I was cursing them and my doom,
And letting a dangerous thought run wild
While often abroad in the fragrant gloom
Of foreign churches—I see her there,
Bright English lily, breathing a prayer
To be friends, to be reconciled!

6

But then what a flint is he!   740
Abroad, at Florence, at Rome,
I find whenever she touch'd on me
This brother had laugh'd her down,
And at last, when each came home,
He had darken'd into a frown,
Chid her, and forbid her to speak
To me, her friend of the years before;
And this was what had redden'd her cheek
When I bow'd to her on the moor.

7

Yet Maud, altho' not blind   750
To the faults of his heart and mind,
I see she cannot but love him,
And says he is rough but kind,

And wishes me to approve him,
And tells me, when she lay
Sick once, with a fear of worse,
That he left his wine and horses and play,
Sat with her, read to her, night and day,
And tended her like a nurse.

8

Kind? but the deathbed desire   760
Spurn'd by this heir of the liar—
Rough but kind? yet I know
He has plotted against me in this,
That he plots against me still.
Kind to Maud? that were not amiss.
Well, rough but kind; why, let it be so:
For shall not Maud have her will?

9

For, Maud, so tender and true,
As long as my life endures
I feel I shall owe you a debt,   770
That I never can hope to pay;
And if ever I should forget
That I owe this debt to you
And for your sweet sake to yours;
O then, what then shall I say?—
If ever I *should* forget,
May God make me more wretched
Than ever I have been yet!

10

So now I have sworn to bury
All this dead body of hate,
I feel so free and so clear   780
By the loss of that dead weight,
That I should grow light-headed, I fear,
Fantastically merry;
But that her brother comes, like a blight
On my fresh hope, to the Hall to-night.

XX

1

Strange, that I felt so gay,
Strange, that *I* tried to-day
To beguile her melancholy;
The Sultan, as we name him,—   790
She did not wish to blame him—
But he vext her and perplext her
With his worldly talk and folly:

Was it gentle to reprove her
For stealing out of view
From a little lazy lover
Who but claims her as his due?
Or for chilling his caresses
By the coldness of her manners,
Nay, the plainness of her dresses?   800
Now I know her but in two,
Nor can pronounce upon it
If one should ask me whether
The habit, hat, and feather,
Or the frock and gipsy bonnet
Be the neater and completer;
For nothing can be sweeter
Than maiden Maud in either.

2

But to-morrow, if we live,
Our ponderous squire will give   810
A grand political dinner
To half the squirelings near;
And Maud will wear her jewels,
And the bird of prey will hover,
And the titmouse hope to win her
With his chirrup at her ear.

3

A grand political dinner
To the men of many acres,
A gathering of the Tory,
A dinner and then a dance   820
For the maids and marriage-makers,
And every eye but mine will glance
At Maud in all her glory.

4

For I am not invited,
But, with the Sultan's pardon,
I am all as well delighted,
For I know her own rose-garden,
And mean to linger in it
Till the dancing will be over;
And then, oh then, come out to me   830
For a minute, but for a minute,
Come out to your own true lover,
That your true lover may see
Your glory also, and render
All homage to his own darling,
Queen Maud in all her splendour.

XXI

Rivulet crossing my ground,
And bringing me down from the Hall
This garden-rose that I found,
Forgetful of Maud and me,　　　　　　840
And lost in trouble and moving round
Here at the head of a tinkling fall,
And trying to pass to the sea;
O Rivulet, born at the Hall,
My Maud has sent it by thee
(If I read her sweet will right)
On a blushing mission to me,
Saying in odour and colour, "Ah, be
Among the roses to-night."

XXII

1

Come into the garden, Maud,　　　　　850
　　For the black bat, night, has flown,
Come into the garden, Maud,
　　I am here at the gate alone;
And the woodbine spices are wafted abroad,
　　And the musk of the rose is blown.

2

For a breeze of morning moves,
　　And the planet of Love[20] is on high,
Beginning to faint in the light that she loves
　　On a bed of daffodil sky,
To faint in the light of the sun she loves,　　860
　　To faint in his light, and to die.

3

All night have the roses heard
　　The flute, violin, bassoon;
All night has the casement jessamine stirr'd
　　To the dancers dancing in tune;
Till a silence fell with the waking bird,
　　And a hush with the setting moon.

4

I said to the lily, "There is but one
　　With whom she has heart to be gay.
When will the dancers leave her alone?　　870
　　She is weary of dance and play."

---

[20]**planet of Love:** Venus, the morning star.

Now half to the setting moon are gone,
　　And half to the rising day;
Low on the sand and loud on the stone
　　The last wheel echoes away.

5

I said to the rose, "The brief night goes
　　In babble and revel and wine.
O young lord-lover, what sighs are those,
　　For one that will never be thine?
But mine, but mine," so I sware to the rose,　　880
　　"For ever and ever, mine."

6

And the soul of the rose went into my blood,
　　As the music clash'd in the hall;
And long by the garden lake I stood,
　　For I heard your rivulet fall
From the lake to the meadow and on to the wood,
　　Our wood, that is dearer than all;

7

From the meadow your walks have left so sweet
　　That whenever a March-wind sighs
He sets the jewel-print of your feet　　890
　　In violets blue as your eyes,
To the woody hollows in which we meet
　　And the valleys of Paradise.

8

The slender acacia would not shake
　　One long milk-bloom on the tree;
The white lake-blossom fell into the lake
　　As the pimpernel dozed on the lea;
But the rose was awake all night for your sake,
　　Knowing your promise to me;
The lilies and roses were all awake,　　900
　　They sigh'd for the dawn and thee.

9

Queen rose of the rosebud garden of girls,
　　Come hither, the dances are done,
In gloss of satin and glimmer of pearls,
　　Queen lily and rose in one;
Shine out, little head, sunning over with curls,
　　To the flowers, and be their sun.

10

There has fallen a splendid tear
　　From the passion-flower at the gate.

She is coming, my dove, my dear;   910
    She is coming, my life, my fate;
The red rose cries, "She is near, she is near;"
    And the white rose weeps, "She is late;"
The larkspur listens, "I hear, I hear;"
    And the lily whispers, "I wait."

11

She is coming, my own, my sweet;
    Were it ever so airy a tread,
My heart would hear her and beat,
    Were it earth in an earthy bed;[21]
My dust would hear her and beat,   920
    Had I lain for a century dead;
Would start and tremble under her feet,
    And blossom in purple and red.

— PART II —

I

1

"The fault was mine, the fault was mine"—
Why am I sitting here so stunn'd and still,
Plucking the harmless wild-flower on the hill?—
It is this guilty hand!—
And there rises ever a passionate cry
From underneath in the darkening land[22]—
What is it, that has been done?
O dawn of Eden bright over earth and sky,
The fires of Hell brake out of thy rising sun,
The fires of Hell and of Hate;   10
For she, sweet soul, had hardly spoken a word,
When her brother ran in his rage to the gate,
He came with the babe-faced lord;
Heap'd on her terms of disgrace,
And while she wept, and I strove to be cool,
He fiercely gave me the lie,
Till I with as fierce an anger spoke,
And he struck me, madman, over the face,
Struck me before the languid fool,
Who was gaping and grinning by: 20
Struck for himself an evil stroke;
Wrought for his house an irredeemable woe;
For front to front in an hour we stood,

And a million horrible bellowing echoes broke
From the red-ribb'd hollow behind the wood,
And thunder'd up into Heaven the Christless code,
That must have life for a blow.
Ever and ever afresh they seem'd to grow.
Was it he lay there with a fading eye?
"The fault was mine," he whisper'd, "fly!"   30
Then glided out of the joyous wood
The ghastly Wraith of one that I know;
And there rang on a sudden a passionate cry,
A cry for a brother's blood:
It will ring in my heart and my ears, till I die, till I die.

2

Is it gone? my pulses beat—
What was it? a lying trick of the brain?
Yet I thought I saw her stand,
A shadow there at my feet,
High over the shadowy land.   40
It is gone; and the heavens fall in a gentle rain,
When they should burst and drown with deluging storms
The feeble vassals of wine and anger and lust,
The little hearts that know not how to forgive:
Arise, my God, and strike, for we hold Thee just,
Strike dead the whole weak race of venomous worms,
That sting each other here in the dust;
We are not worthy to live.

II

1

See what a lovely shell,
Small and pure as a pearl,   50
Lying close to my foot,
Frail, but a work divine,
Made so fairily well
With delicate spire and whorl,
How exquisitely minute,
A miracle of design!

2

What is it? a learned man
Could give it a clumsy name.
Let him name it who can,
The beauty would be the same.   60

3

The tiny cell is forlorn,
Void of the little living will
That made it stir on the shore.

---

[21]**earth in an earthy bed:** see 1 Corinthians 15:47–52.

[22]**darkening land:** see Genesis 4:10 (Cain's guilt for a brother's blood).

Did he stand at the diamond door
Of his house in a rainbow frill?
Did he push, when he was uncurl'd,
A golden foot or a fairy horn
Thro' his dim water-world?

4

Slight, to be crush'd with a tap
Of my finger-nail on the sand,   70
Small, but a work divine,
Frail, but of force to withstand,
Year upon year, the shock
Of cataract seas that snap
The three-decker's oaken spine
Athwart the ledges of rock,
Here on the Breton strand!

5

Breton,[23] not Briton; here
Like a shipwreck'd man on a coast
Of ancient fable and fear—   80
Plagued with a flitting to and fro,
A disease, a hard mechanic ghost
That never came from on high
Nor ever arose from below,
But only moves with the moving eye,
Flying along the land and the main—
Why should it look like Maud?
Am I to be overawed
By what I cannot but know
Is a juggle born of the brain?   90

6

Back from the Breton coast,
Sick of a nameless fear,
Back to the dark sea-line
Looking, thinking of all I have lost;
An old song vexes my ear,
But that of Lamech[24] is mine.

7

For years, a measureless ill,
For years, for ever, to part—

---

[23]**Breton:** in Brittany (NW France). The speaker is now a
fugitive from British laws against dueling.

[24]**Lamech:** see Genesis 4:23–24.

But she, she would love me still;
And as long, O God, as she   100
Have a grain of love for me,
So long, no doubt, no doubt,
Shall I nurse in my dark heart,
However weary, a spark of will
Not to be trampled out.

8

Strange, that the mind, when fraught
With a passion so intense
One would think that it well
Might drown all life in the eye,—
That it should, by being so overwrought,   110
Suddenly strike on a sharper sense
For a shell, or a flower, little things
Which else would have been past by!
And now I remember, I,
When he lay dying there,
I noticed one of his many rings
(For he had many, poor worm) and thought
It is his mother's hair.

9

Who knows if he be dead?
Whether I need have fled?   120
Am I guilty of blood?
However this may be,
Comfort her, comfort her, all things good,
While I am over the sea!
Let me and my passionate love go by,
But speak to her all things holy and high,
Whatever happen to me!
Me and my harmful love go by;
But come to her waking, find her asleep,
Powers of the height, Powers of the deep,   130
And comfort her tho' I die!

III

Courage, poor heart of stone!
I will not ask thee why
Thou canst not understand
That thou art left for ever alone:
Courage, poor stupid heart of stone.—
Or if I ask thee why,
Care not thou to reply:
She is but dead, and the time is at hand
When thou shalt more than die.   140

IV

1

O that 'twere possible[25]
After long grief and pain
To find the arms of my true love
Round me once again!

2

When I was wont to meet her
In the silent woody places
By the home that gave me birth,
We stood tranced in long embraces
Mixt with kisses sweeter, sweeter
Than anything on earth.   150

3

A shadow flits before me,
Not thou, but like to thee:
Ah Christ, that it were possible
For one short hour to see
The souls we loved, that they might tell us
What and where they be.

4

It leads me forth at evening,
It lightly winds and steals
In a cold white robe before me,
When all my spirit reels   160
At the shouts, the leagues of lights,
And the roaring of the wheels.

5

Half the night I waste in sighs,
Half in dreams I sorrow after
The delight of early skies;
In a wakeful doze I sorrow
For the hand, the lips, the eyes,
For the meeting of the morrow,
The delight of happy laughter,
The delight of low replies.   170

6

'Tis a morning pure and sweet,
And a dewy splendour falls

On the little flower that clings
To the turrets and the walls;
'Tis a morning pure and sweet,
And the light and shadow fleet;
She is walking in the meadow,
And the woodland echo rings;
In a moment we shall meet;
She is singing in the meadow   180
And the rivulet at her feet
Ripples on in light and shadow
To the ballad that she sings.

7

Do I hear her sing as of old,
My bird with the shining head,
My own dove with the tender eye?
But there rings on a sudden a passionate cry,
There is some one dying or dead,
And a sullen thunder is roll'd;
For a tumult shakes the city,   190
And I wake, my dream is fled;
In the shuddering dawn, behold,
Without knowledge, without pity,
By the curtains of my bed
That abiding phantom cold.

8

Get thee hence, nor come again,
Mix not memory with doubt,
Pass, thou deathlike type of pain,
Pass and cease to move about!
'Tis the blot upon the brain   200
That *will* show itself without.

9

Then I rise, the eavedrops fall,
And the yellow vapours choke
The great city sounding wide;
The day comes, a dull red ball
Wrapt in drifts of lurid smoke
On the misty river-tide.

10

Thro' the hubbub of the market
I steal, a wasted frame,
It crosses here, it crosses there,   210
Thro' all that crowd confused and loud,
The shadow still the same;
And on my heavy eyelids
My anguish hangs like shame.

---

[25]**O that 'twere possible**: written 1833–1834, following Hallam's death, and published 1837. Tennyson later explained the genesis of *Maud* as an attempt to provide this moment with a narrative context.

11

Alas for her that met me,
That heard me softly call,
Came glimmering thro' the laurels
At the quiet evenfall,
In the garden by the turrets
Of the old manorial hall.   220

12

Would the happy spirit descend
From the realms of light and song,
In the chamber or the street,
As she looks among the blest,
Should I fear to greet my friend
Or to say "Forgive the wrong,"
Or to ask her, "Take me, sweet,
To the regions of thy rest"?

13

But the broad light glares and beats,
And the shadow flits and fleets   230
And will not let me be;
And I loathe the squares and streets,
And the faces that one meets,
Hearts with no love for me:
Always I long to creep
Into some still cavern deep,
There to weep, and weep, and weep
My whole soul out to thee.

V

1

Dead, long dead,[26]
Long dead!   240
And my heart is a handful of dust,
And the wheels go over my head,
And my bones are shaken with pain,
For into a shallow grave they are thrust,
Only a yard beneath the street,
And the hoofs of the horses beat, beat,
The hoofs of the horses beat,
Beat into my scalp and my brain,
With never an end to the stream of passing feet,
Driving , hurrying, marrying, burying,   250
Clamour and rumble, and ringing and clatter,
And here beneath it is all as bad,

---

[26]**Dead, long dead**: Tennyson reportedly composed this entire madhouse lyric in 20 minutes.

For I thought the dead had peace, but it is not so;
To have no peace in the grave, is that not sad?
But up and down and to and fro,
Ever about me the dead men go;
And then to hear a dead man chatter
Is enough to drive one mad.

2

Wretchedest age, since Time began,
They cannot even bury a man;   260
And tho' we paid our tithes in the days that are gone,
Not a bell was rung, not a prayer was read.
It is that which makes us loud in the world of the dead;
There is none that does his work, not one;
A touch of their office might have sufficed,
But the churchmen fain would kill their church,
As the churches have kill'd their Christ.

3

See, there is one of us sobbing,
No limit to his distress;
And another, a lord of all things, praying   270
To his own great self, as I guess;
And another, a statesman there, betraying
His party-secret, fool, to the press;
And yonder a vile physician, blabbing
The case of his patient—all for what?
To tickle the maggot born in an empty head,
And wheedle a world that loves him not,
For it is but a world of the dead.

4

Nothing but idiot gabble!
For the prophecy given of old   280
And then not understood,
Has come to pass as foretold;
Nor let any man think for the public good,
But babble, merely for babble.
For I never whisper'd a private affair
Within the hearing of cat or mouse,
No, not to myself in the closet alone,
But I heard it shouted at once from the top of the house;
Everything came to be known.
Who told *him* we were there?   290

5

Not that gray old wolf, for he came not back
From the wilderness, full of wolves, where he used to lie;
He has gather'd the bones for his o'ergrown whelp to crack;
Crack them now for yourself, and howl, and die.

6

Prophet, curse me the blabbing lip,
And curse me the British vermin, the rat;
I know not whether he came in the Hanover ship,[27]
But I know that he lies and listens mute
In an ancient mansion's crannies and holes:
Arsenic, arsenic, sure, would do it,   300
Except that now we poison our babes, poor souls!
It is all used up for that.

7

Tell him now: she is standing here at my head;
Not beautiful now, not even kind;
He may take her now; for she never speaks her mind,
But is ever the one thing silent here.
She is not of us, as I divine;
She comes from another stiller world of the dead,
Stiller, not fairer than mine.

8

But I know where a garden grows,   310
Fairer than aught in the world beside,
All made up of the lily and rose
That blow by night, when the season is good,
To the sound of dancing music and flutes:
It is only flowers, they had no fruits,
And I almost fear they are not roses, but blood;
For the keeper was one, so full of pride,
He linkt a dead man there to a spectral bride;
For he, if he had not been a Sultan of brutes,
Would he have that hole in his side?   320

9

But what will the old man say?
He laid a cruel snare in a pit
To catch a friend of mine one stormy day;
Yet now I could even weep to think of it;
For what will the old man say
When he comes to the second corpse in the pit?

10

Friend, to be struck by the public foe,
Then to strike him and lay him low,
That were a public merit, far,

Whatever the Quaker holds, from sin;   330
But the red life spilt for a private blow—
I swear to you, lawful and lawless war
Are scarcely even akin.

11

O me, why have they not buried me deep enough?
Is it kind to have made me a grave so rough,
Me, that was never a quiet sleeper?
Maybe still I am but half-dead;
Then I cannot be wholly dumb;
I will cry to the steps above my head
And somebody, surely, some kind heart will come 340
To bury me, bury me
Deeper, ever so little deeper.

— PART III —

1

My life has crept so long on a broken wing
Thro' cells of madness, haunts of horror and fear,
That I come to be grateful at last for a little thing:
My mood is changed, for it fell at a time of year
When the face of night is fair on the dewy downs,
And the shining daffodil dies, and the Charioteer[28]
And starry Gemini hang like glorious crowns
Over Orion's grave low down in the west,
That like a silent lightning under the stars
She seem'd to divide in a dream from a band of the blest, 10
And spoke of a hope for the world in the coming wars—
"And in that hope, dear soul, let trouble have rest,
Knowing I tarry for thee," and pointed to Mars
As he glow'd like a ruddy shield on the Lion's breast.[29]

2

And it was but a dream, yet it yielded a dear delight
To have look'd, tho' but in a dream, upon eyes so fair,
That had been in a weary world my one thing bright;
And it was but a dream, yet it lighten'd my despair
When I thought that a war would arise in defence of
     the right,
That an iron tyranny now should bend or cease,   20
The glory of manhood stand on his ancient height,
Nor Britain's one sole God be the millionaire:

---

[27]**Hanover ship**: The Jacobites asserted that the brown Norwegian rat came to England with the House of Hanover. [Hallam Tennyson's note] Hard-line **Jacobites** repeatedly sought to restore the deposed Stuarts to the throne that was occupied for most of the 18th century by kings imported from **Hanover**, Germany.

[28]**Charioteer, Gemini, Orion**: descending constellations in early spring.

[29]**Lion**: the constellation Leo. The presence of the planet Mars in Leo symbolizes Britain's engagement against Russia in the Crimean War (1854–1856).

No more shall commerce be all in all, and Peace
Pipe on her pastoral hillock a languid note,
And watch her harvest ripen, her herd increase,
Nor the cannon-bullet rust on a slothful shore,
And the cobweb woven across the cannon's throat
Shall shake its threaded tears in the wind no more.

3

And as months ran on and rumour of battle grew,
"It is time, it is time, O passionate heart," said I   30
(For I cleaved to a cause that I felt to be pure and true),
"It is time, O passionate heart and morbid eye,
That old hysterical mock-disease should die."
And I stood on a giant deck and mix'd my breath
With a loyal people shouting a battle cry,
Till I saw the dreary phantom arise and fly
Far into the North, and battle, and seas of death.

4

Let it go or stay, so I wake to the higher aims
Of a land that has lost for a little her lust of gold,
And love of a peace that was full of wrongs
          and shames,   40
Horrible, hateful, monstrous, not to be told;
And hail once more to the banner of battle unroll'd!
Tho' many a light shall darken, and many shall weep
For those that are crush'd in the clash of jarring claims,
Yet God's just wrath shall be wreak'd on a giant liar;[30]
And many a darkness into the light shall leap,
And shine in the sudden making of splendid names,
And noble thought be freër under the sun,
And the heart of a people beat with one desire;
For the peace, that I deem'd no peace, is over
          and done,   50
And now by the side of the Black and the Baltic deep,[31]
And deathful-grinning mouths of the fortress, flames
The blood-red blossom of war with a heart of fire.

5

Let it flame or fade, and the war roll down like a wind,
We have proved we have hearts in a cause, we are noble still,
And myself have awaked, as it seems, to the better mind;
It is better to fight for the good than to rail at the ill;
I have felt with my native land, I am one with my kind,
I embrace the purpose of God, and the doom assign'd.

                                        1855

---

[30]**giant liar**: the Russian tsar, whose broken promise was a cause of the war.

[31]**Black** Sea: location of the Crimean peninsula.

Tithonus[1]

The woods decay, the woods decay and fall,
The vapors weep their burthen to the ground,
Man comes and tills the field and lies beneath,
And after many a summer dies the swan.
Me only cruel immortality
Consumes; I wither slowly in thine arms,
Here at the quiet limit of the world,
A white-hair'd shadow roaming like a dream
The ever-silent spaces of the East,
Far-folded mists, and gleaming halls of morn.   10

Alas! for this gray shadow, once a man—
So glorious in his beauty and thy choice,
Who madest him thy chosen, that he seem'd
To his great heart none other than a God!
I ask'd thee, "Give me immortality."
Then didst thou grant mine asking with a smile,
Like wealthy men who care not how they give.
But thy strong Hours indignant work'd their wills,
And beat me down and marr'd and wasted me,
And tho' they could not end me, left me maim'd   20
To dwell in presence of immortal youth,
Immortal age beside immortal youth,
And all I was in ashes. Can thy love,
Thy beauty, make amends, tho' even now,
Close over us, the silver star, thy guide,
Shines in those tremulous eyes that fill with tears
To hear me? Let me go; take back thy gift.
Why should a man desire in any way
To vary from the kindly race of men,
Or pass beyond the goal of ordinance   30
Where all should pause, as is most meet for all?

A soft air fans the cloud apart; there comes
A glimpse of that dark world where I was born.
Once more the old mysterious glimmer steals
From thy pure brows, and from thy shoulders pure,
And bosom beating with a heart renew'd.
Thy cheek begins to redden thro' the gloom,
Thy sweet eyes brighten slowly close to mine,
Ere yet they blind the stars, and the wild team
Which love thee, yearning for thy yoke, arise,   40

---

[1]**Tithonus**: beloved of Eos, goddess of the dawn, who granted his request for eternal life but did not confer eternal youth. Eos appears in the poem as woman, goddess, and natural phenomenon.

And shake the darkness from their loosen'd manes,
And beat the twilight into flakes of fire.

Lo! ever thus thou growest beautiful
In silence, then before thine answer given
Departest, and thy tears are on my cheek.
Why wilt thou ever scare me with thy tears,
And make me tremble lest a saying learnt,
In days far-off, on the dark earth, be true?
"The Gods themselves cannot recall their gifts."

Ay me! ay me! with what another heart   50
In days far-off, and with what other eyes
I used to watch—if I be he that watch'd—
The lucid outline forming round thee; saw
The dim curls kindle into sunny rings;
Changed with thy mystic change, and felt my blood
Glow with the glow that slowly crimson'd all
Thy presence and thy portals, while I lay,
Mouth, forehead, eyelids, growing dewy-warm
With kisses balmier than half-opening buds
Of April, and could hear the lips that kiss'd   60
Whispering I knew not what of wild and sweet,
Like that strange song I heard Apollo sing,
While Ilion[2] like a mist rose into towers.

Yet hold me not for ever in thine East;
How can my nature longer mix with thine?
Coldly thy rosy shadows bathe me, cold
Are all thy lights, and cold my wrinkled feet
Upon thy glimmering thresholds, when the steam
Floats up from those dim fields about the homes
Of happy men that have the power to die,   70
And grassy barrows of the happier dead.
Release me, and restore me to the ground.
Thou seëst all things, thou wilt see my grave;
Thou wilt renew thy beauty morn by morn,
I earth in earth forget these empty courts,
And thee returning on thy silver wheels.
1833   1860

<hr>

Hendecasyllabics

O you chorus of indolent reviewers,
Irresponsible, indolent reviewers,

<hr>

[2]**Ilion**: Troy, whose legendary walls were built to the music of **Apollo**.

Look, I come to the test, a tiny poem
All composed in a metre of Catullus,[1]
All in quantity, careful of my motion,
Like the skater on ice that hardly bears him,
Lest I fall unawares before the people,
Waking laughter in indolent reviewers.
Should I flounder awhile without a tumble
Thro' this metrification of Catullus,   10
They should speak to me not without a welcome,
All that chorus of indolent reviewers.
Hard, hard, hard is it, only not to tumble,
So fantastical is the dainty metre.
Wherefore slight me not wholly, nor believe me
Too presumptuous, indolent reviewers.
O blatant Magazines, regard me rather—
Since I blush to belaud myself a moment—
As some rare little rose, a piece of inmost
Horticultural art, or half coquette-like   20
Maiden, not to be greeted unbenignly.
                                              1863

<hr>

Enoch Arden

    Long lines of cliff breaking have left a chasm;
And in the chasm are foam and yellow sands;
Beyond, red roofs about a narrow wharf
In cluster; then a moulder'd church; and higher
A long street climbs to one tall-tower'd mill;
And high in heaven behind it a gray down
With Danish barrows;[1] and a hazel-wood,
By autumn nutters haunted, flourishes
Green in a cuplike hollow of the down.
Here on this beach a hundred years ago,   10
Three children of three houses, Annie Lee,
The prettiest little damsel in the port,
And Philip Ray, the miller's only son,
And Enoch Arden, a rough sailor's lad

<hr>

[1]**metre of Catullus**: eleven-syllable line associated with the Latin poet of the 1st century BCE. Tennyson published this elegant stunt as one of three "Attempts at Classical Metres in Quantity," where **quantity** involves syllable length rather than the stress norm of English prosody—although these lines also manifest the five-beat measure of blank verse.

[1]**Danish barrows**: tombs left along the NE coast of England by Viking invaders during the Middle Ages.

Made orphan by a winter shipwreck, play'd
Among the waste and lumber of the shore,
Hard coils of cordage, swarthy fishing-nets,
Anchors of rusty fluke, and boats updrawn;
And built their castles of dissolving sand
To watch them overflow'd, or following up   20
And flying the white breaker, daily left
The little footprint daily wash'd away.

    A narrow cave ran in beneath the cliff;
In this the children play'd at keeping house.
Enoch was host one day, Philip the next,
While Annie still was mistress; but at times
Enoch would hold possession for a week:
"This is my house and this my little wife."
"Mine too," said Philip; "turn and turn about;"
When, if they quarrell'd, Enoch stronger-made   30
Was master. Then would Philip, his blue eyes
All flooded with the helpless wrath of tears,
Shriek out, "I hate you, Enoch," and at this
The little wife would weep for company,
And pray them not to quarrel for her sake,
And say she would be little wife to both.

    But when the dawn of rosy childhood past,
And the new warmth of life's ascending sun
Was felt by either, either fixt his heart
On that one girl; and Enoch spoke his love,   40
But Philip loved in silence; and the girl
Seem'd kinder unto Philip than to him;
But she loved Enoch, tho' she knew it not,
And would if ask'd deny it. Enoch set
A purpose evermore before his eyes,
To hoard all savings to the uttermost,
To purchase his own boat, and make a home
For Annie; and so prosper'd that at last
A luckier or a bolder fisherman,
A carefuller in peril, did not breathe   50
For leagues along that breaker-beaten coast
Than Enoch. Likewise had he served a year
On board a merchantman, and made himself
Full sailor;[2] and he thrice had pluck'd a life
From the dread sweep of the down-streaming seas,
And all men look'd upon him favorably.
And ere he touch'd his one-and-twentieth May
He purchased his own boat, and made a home
For Annie, neat and nestlike, halfway up
The narrow street that clamber'd toward the mill. 60

Then, on a golden autumn eventide
The younger people making holiday,
With bag and sack and basket, great and small,
Went nutting to the hazels. Philip stay'd—
His father lying sick and needing him—
An hour behind; but as he climb'd the hill,
Just where the prone edge of the wood began
To feather toward the hollow, saw the pair,
Enoch and Annie, sitting hand-in-hand,
His large gray eyes and weather-beaten face   70
All-kindled by a still and sacred fire,
That burn'd as on an altar. Philip look'd,
And in their eyes and faces read his doom;
Then, as their faces drew together, groan'd,
And slipt aside, and like a wounded life
Crept down into the hollows of the wood;
There, while the rest were loud in merrymaking,
Had his dark hour unseen, and rose and past
Bearing a lifelong hunger in his heart.

    So these were wed, and merrily rang the bells, 80
And merrily ran the years, seven happy years,
Seven happy years of health and competence,
And mutual love and honorable toil,
With children, first a daughter. In him woke,
With his first babe's first cry, the noble wish
To save all earnings to the uttermost,
And give his child a better bringing-up
Than his had been, or hers; a wish renew'd,
When two years after came a boy to be
The rosy idol of her solitudes,   90
While Enoch was abroad on wrathful seas,
Or often journeying landward; for in truth
Enoch's white horse, and Enoch's ocean-spoil[3]
In ocean-smelling osier, and his face,
Rough-redden'd with a thousand winter gales,
Not only to the market-cross were known,
But in the leafy lanes behind the down,
Far as the portal-warding lion-whelp
And peacock yew-tree of the lonely Hall,[4]
Whose Friday fare was Enoch's ministering.   100

    Then came a change, as all things human change.
Ten miles to northward of the narrow port
Open'd a larger haven. Thither used

---

[2]**Full sailor:** able-bodied seaman, a nautical rank.

[3]**ocean-spoil:** catch of fish, in a basket (**osier**).

[4]**portal-warding lion-whelp:** gateway statue. **peacock yew-tree:** topiary garden sculpture. Both are marks of the **Hall**, where gentlefolk live.

Enoch at times to go by land or sea;
And once when there, and clambering on a mast
In harbor, by mischance he slipt and fell.
A limb was broken when they lifted him;
And while he lay recovering there, his wife
Bore him another son, a sickly one.
Another hand crept too across his trade   110
Taking her bread and theirs; and on him fell,
Altho' a grave and staid God-fearing man,
Yet lying thus inactive, doubt and gloom.
He seem'd, as in a nightmare of the night,
To see his children leading evermore
Low miserable lives of hand-to-mouth,
And her he loved a beggar. Then he pray'd,
"Save them from this, whatever comes to me."
And while he pray'd, the master of that ship
Enoch had served in, hearing his mischance,   120
Came, for he knew the man and valued him,
Reporting of his vessel China-bound,
And wanting yet a boatswain. Would he go?
There yet were many weeks before she sail'd,
Sail'd from this port. Would Enoch have the place?
And Enoch all at once assented to it,
Rejoicing at that answer to his prayer.

    So now that shadow of mischance appear'd
No graver than as when some little cloud
Cuts off the fiery highway of the sun,   130
And isles a light in the offing. Yet the wife—
When he was gone—the children—what to do?
Then Enoch lay long-pondering on his plans:
To sell the boat—and yet he loved her well—
How many a rough sea had he weather'd in her!
He knew her, as a horseman knows his horse—
And yet to sell her—then with what she brought
Buy goods and stores—set Annie forth in trade
With all that seamen needed or their wives—
So might she keep the house while he was gone.   140
Should he not trade himself out yonder? go
This voyage more than once? yea, twice or thrice—
As oft as needed—last, returning rich,
Become the master of a larger craft,
With fuller profits lead an easier life,
Have all his pretty young ones educated,
And pass his days in peace among his own.

    Thus Enoch in his heart determined all;
Then moving homeward came on Annie pale,
Nursing the sickly babe, her latest-born.   150
Forward she started with a happy cry,

And laid the feeble infant in his arms;
Whom Enoch took, and handled all his limbs,
Appraised his weight and fondled fatherlike,
But had no heart to break his purposes
To Annie, till the morrow, when he spoke.

    Then first since Enoch's golden ring had girt
Her finger, Annie fought against his will;
Yet not with brawling opposition she,
But manifold entreaties, many a tear,   160
Many a sad kiss by day, by night, renew'd—
Sure that all evil would come out of it—
Besought him, supplicating, if he cared
For her or his dear children, not to go.
He not for his own self caring, but her,
Her and her children, let her plead in vain;
So grieving held his will, and bore it thro'.

    For Enoch parted with his old sea-friend,
Bought Annie goods and stores, and set his hand
To fit their little streetward sitting-room   170
With shelf and corner for the goods and stores.
So all day long till Enoch's last at home,
Shaking their pretty cabin, hammer and axe,
Auger and saw, while Annie seem'd to hear
Her own death-scaffold raising, shrill'd and rang,
Till this was ended, and his careful hand,—
The space was narrow,—having order'd all
Almost as neat and close as Nature packs
Her blossom or her seedling, paused; and he,
Who needs would work for Annie to the last,   180
Ascending tired, heavily slept till morn.

    And Enoch faced this morning of farewell
Brightly and boldly. All his Annie's fears,
Save as his Annie's, were a laughter to him.
Yet Enoch as a brave God-fearing man
Bow'd himself down, and in that mystery
Where God-in-man is one with man-in-God,
Pray'd for a blessing on his wife and babes,
Whatever came to him; and then he said:
"Annie, this voyage by the grace of God   190
Will bring fair weather yet to all of us.
Keep a clean hearth and a clear fire for me,
For I'll be back, my girl, before you know it;"
Then lightly rocking baby's cradle, "and he,
This pretty, puny, weakly little one,—
Nay—for I love him all the better for it—
God bless him, he shall sit upon my knees
And I will tell him tales of foreign parts,

And make him merry, when I come home again.
Come, Annie, come, cheer up before I go."   200

    Him running on thus hopefully she heard,
And almost hoped herself; but when he turn'd
The current of his talk to graver things
In sailor fashion roughly sermonizing
On providence and trust in heaven, she heard,
Heard and not heard him; as the village girl,
Who sets her pitcher underneath the spring,
Musing on him that used to fill it for her,
Hears and not hears, and lets it overflow.

    At length she spoke: "O Enoch, you are wise;   210
And yet for all your wisdom well know I
That I shall look upon your face no more."

    "Well, then," said Enoch, "I shall look on yours.
Annie, the ship I sail in passes here"—
He named the day;—"get you a seaman's glass,
Spy out my face, and laugh at all your fears."

    But when the last of those last moments came:
"Annie, my girl, cheer up, be comforted,
Look to the babes, and till I come again
Keep everything shipshape, for I must go.   220
And fear no more for me; or if you fear,
Cast all your cares on God; that anchor holds.
Is He not yonder in those uttermost
Parts of the morning? if I flee to these,
Can I go from Him? and the sea is His,
The sea is His; He made it."[5]

             Enoch rose,
Cast his strong arms about his drooping wife,
And kiss'd his wonder-stricken little ones;
But for the third, the sickly one, who slept
After a night of feverous wakefulness,   230
When Annie would have raised him Enoch said,
"Wake him not, let him sleep; how should the child
Remember this?" and kiss'd him in his cot.
But Annie from her baby's forehead clipt
A tiny curl, and gave it; this he kept
Thro' all his future, but now hastily caught
His bundle, waved his hand, and went his way.

    She, when the day that Enoch mention'd came,
Borrow'd a glass, but all in vain. Perhaps
She could not fix the glass to suit her eye;   240

Perhaps her eye was dim, hand tremulous;
She saw him not, and while he stood on deck
Waving, the moment and the vessel past.

    Even to the last dip of the vanishing sail
She watch'd it, and departed weeping for him;
Then, tho' she mourn'd his absence as his grave,
Set her sad will no less to chime with his,
But throve not in her trade, not being bred
To barter, nor compensating the want
By shrewdness, neither capable of lies,   250
Nor asking overmuch and taking less,
And still foreboding "what would Enoch say?"
For more than once, in days of difficulty
And pressure, had she sold her wares for less
Than what she gave in buying what she sold.
She fail'd and sadden'd knowing it; and thus,
Expectant of that news which never came,
Gain'd for her own a scanty sustenance,
And lived a life of silent melancholy.

    Now the third child was sickly-born and grew   260
Yet sicklier, tho' the mother cared for it
With all a mother's care; nevertheless,
Whether her business often call'd her from it,
Or thro' the want of what it needed most,
Or means to pay the voice[6] who best could tell
What most it needed—howsoe'er it was,
After a lingering,—ere she was aware,—
Like the caged bird escaping suddenly,
The little innocent soul flitted away.

    In that same week when Annie buried it,   270
Philip's true heart, which hunger'd for her peace,—
Since Enoch left he had not look'd upon her,—
Smote him, as having kept aloof so long.
"Surely," said Philip, "I may see her now,
May be some little comfort;" therefore went,
Past thro' the solitary room in front,
Paused for a moment at an inner door,
Then struck it thrice, and, no one opening,
Enter'd, but Annie, seated with her grief,
Fresh from the burial of her little one,   280
Cared not to look on any human face,
But turn'd her own toward the wall and wept.
Then Philip standing up said falteringly,
"Annie, I came to ask a favor of you."

---

[5]**The sea . . . made it:** Psalm 95:5. Enoch's farewell is a pastiche of scripture passages: see 1 Peter 5:7, Hebrews 6:19, Psalm 139:9.

---

[6]**pay the voice:** afford a doctor's fees.

He spoke; the passion in her moan'd reply,
"Favor from one so sad and so forlorn
As I am!" half abash'd him; yet unask'd,
His bashfulness and tenderness at war,
He set himself beside her, saying to her:

"I came to speak to you of what he wish'd,   290
Enoch, your husband. I have ever said
You chose the best among us—a strong man;
For where he fixt his heart he set his hand
To do the thing he will'd, and bore it thro'.
And wherefore did he go this weary way,
And leave you lonely? not to see the world—
For pleasure?—nay, but for the wherewithal
To give his babes a better bringing up
Than his had been, or yours; that was his wish.
And if he come again, vext will he be   300
To find the precious morning hours were lost.
And it would vex him even in his grave,
If he could know his babes were running wild
Like colts about the waste. So, Annie, now—
Have we not known each other all our lives?
I do beseech you by the love you bear
Him and his children not to say me nay—
For, if you will, when Enoch comes again
Why then he shall repay me—if you will,
Annie—for I am rich and well-to-do.   310
Now let me put the boy and girl to school;
This is the favor that I came to ask."

Then Annie with her brows against the wall
Answer'd, "I cannot look you in the face;
I seem so foolish and so broken down.
When you came in my sorrow broke me down;
And now I think your kindness breaks me down.
But Enoch lives; that is borne in on me;
He will repay you. Money can be repaid;
Not kindness such as yours."

                    And Philip ask'd, 320
"Then you will let me, Annie?"

                    There she turn'd,
She rose, and fixt her swimming eyes upon him,
And dwelt a moment on his kindly face,
Then calling down a blessing on his head
Caught at his hand, and wrung it passionately,
And past into the little garth beyond.

So lifted up in spirit he moved away.
Then Philip put the boy and girl to school,
And bought them needful books, and every way,

Like one who does his duty by his own,   330
Made himself theirs; and tho' for Annie's sake,
Fearing the lazy gossip of the port,
He oft denied his heart his dearest wish,
And seldom crost her threshold, yet he sent
Gifts by the children, garden-herbs and fruit,
The late and early roses from his wall,
Or conies from the down, and now and then,
With some pretext of fineness in the meal
To save the offence of charitable, flour
From his tall mill that whistled on the waste.   340

But Philip did not fathom Annie's mind;
Scarce could the woman, when he came upon her,
Out of full heart and boundless gratitude
Light on a broken word to thank him with.
But Philip was her children's all-in-all;
From distant corners of the street they ran
To greet his hearty welcome heartily;
Lords of his house and of his mill were they,
Worried his passive ear with petty wrongs
Or pleasures, hung upon him, play'd with him   350
And call'd him Father Philip. Philip gain'd
As Enoch lost, for Enoch seem'd to them
Uncertain as a vision or a dream,
Faint as a figure seen in early dawn
Down at the far end of an avenue,
Going we know not where; and so ten years,
Since Enoch left his hearth and native land,
Fled forward, and no news of Enoch came.

It chanced one evening Annie's children long'd
To go with others nutting to the wood,   360
And Annie would go with them; then they begg'd
For Father Philip, as they call'd him, too.
Him, like the working bee in blossom-dust,
Blanch'd with his mill, they found; and saying to him,
"Come with us, Father Philip," he denied;
But when the children pluck'd at him to go,
He laugh'd, and yielded readily to their wish,
For was not Annie with them? and they went.

But after scaling half the weary down,
Just where the prone edge of the wood began   370
To feather toward the hollow, all her force
Fail'd her; and sighing, "Let me rest," she said.
So Philip rested with her well-content;
While all the younger ones with jubilant cries
Broke from their elders, and tumultuously
Down thro' the whitening hazels made a plunge
To the bottom, and dispersed, and bent or broke

The lithe reluctant boughs to tear away
Their tawny clusters, crying to each other
And calling, here and there, about the wood.   380

But Philip sitting at her side forgot
Her presence, and remember'd one dark hour
Here in this wood, when like a wounded life
He crept into the shadow. At last he said,
Lifting his honest forehead, "Listen, Annie,
How merry they are down yonder in the wood.
Tired, Annie?" for she did not speak a word.
"Tired?" but her face had fallen upon her hands;
At which, as with a kind of anger in him,
"The ship was lost," he said, "the ship was lost!   390
No more of that! why should you kill yourself
And make them orphans quite?" And Annie said,
"I thought not of it; but—I know not why—
Their voices make me feel so solitary."

Then Philip coming somewhat closer spoke:
"Annie, there is a thing upon my mind,
And it has been upon my mind so long
That, tho' I know not when it first came there,
I know that it will out at last. O Annie,
It is beyond all hope, against all chance,   400
That he who left you ten long years ago
Should still be living; well, then—let me speak.
I grieve to see you poor and wanting help;
I cannot help you as I wish to do
Unless—they say that women are so quick—
Perhaps you know what I would have you know—
I wish you for my wife. I fain would prove
A father to your children; I do think
They love me as a father; I am sure
That I love them as if they were mine own;   410
And I believe, if you were fast my wife,
That after all these sad uncertain years
We might be still as happy as God grants
To any of his creatures. Think upon it;
For I am well-to-do—no kin, no care,
No burthen, save my care for you and yours,
And we have known each other all our lives,
And I have loved you longer than you know."

Then answer'd Annie—tenderly she spoke:
"You have been as God's good angel in our house.   420
God bless you for it, God reward you for it,
Philip, with something happier than myself.
Can one love twice? can you be ever loved
As Enoch was? what is it that you ask?"
"I am content," he answer'd, "to be loved

A little after Enoch." "O," she cried,
Scared as it were, "dear Philip, wait a while.
If Enoch comes—but Enoch will not come—
Yet wait a year, a year is not so long.
Surely I shall be wiser in a year.   430
O, wait a little!" Philip sadly said,
"Annie, as I have waited all my life
I well may wait a little." "Nay," she cried,
"I am bound: you have my promise—in a year.
Will you not bide your year as I bide mine?"
And Philip answer'd, "I will bide my year."

Here both were mute, till Philip glancing up
Beheld the dead flame of the fallen day
Pass from the Danish barrow overhead;
Then, fearing night and chill for Annie, rose   440
And sent his voice beneath him thro' the wood.
Up came the children laden with their spoil;
Then all descended to the port, and there
At Annie's door he paused and gave his hand,
Saying gently, "Annie, when I spoke to you,
That was your hour of weakness. I was wrong,
I am always bound to you, but you are free."
Then Annie weeping answer'd, "I am bound."

She spoke; and in one moment as it were,
While yet she went about her household ways,   450
Even as she dwelt upon his latest words,
That he had loved her longer than she knew,
That autumn into autumn flash'd again,
And there he stood once more before her face,
Claiming her promise. "Is it a year?" she ask'd.
"Yes, if the nuts," he said, "be ripe again;
Come out and see." But she—she put him off—
So much to look to—such a change—a month—
Give her a month—she knew that she was bound—
A month—no more. Then Philip with his eyes   460
Full of that lifelong hunger, and his voice
Shaking a little like a drunkard's hand,
"Take your own time, Annie, take your own time."
And Annie could have wept for pity of him;
And yet she held him on delayingly
With many a scarce-believable excuse,
Trying his truth and his long-sufferance,
Till half another year had slipt away.

By this the lazy gossips of the port,
Abhorrent of a calculation crost,   470
Began to chafe as at a personal wrong.
Some thought that Philip did but trifle with her;
Some that she but held off to draw him on;

And others laugh'd at her and Philip too,
As simple folk that knew not their own minds;
And one, in whom all evil fancies clung
Like serpent eggs together, laughingly
Would hint at worse in either. Her own son
Was silent, tho' he often look'd his wish;
But evermore the daughter prest upon her   480
To wed the man so dear to all of them
And lift the household out of poverty;
And Philip's rosy face contracting grew
Careworn and wan; and all these things fell on her
Sharp as reproach.

                 At last one night it chanced
That Annie could not sleep, but earnestly
Pray'd for a sign, "My Enoch, is he gone?"
Then compass'd round by the blind wall of night
Brook'd not the expectant terror of her heart,
Started from bed, and struck herself a light,   490
Then desperately seized the holy Book,
Suddenly set it wide to find a sign,
Suddenly put her finger on the text,
"Under the palm-tree."[7] That was nothing to her,
No meaning there; she closed the Book and slept.
When lo! her Enoch sitting on a height,
Under a palm-tree, over him the sun.
"He is gone," she thought, "he is happy, he is singing
Hosanna in the highest;[8] yonder shines
The Sun of Righteousness, and these be palms   500
Whereof the happy people strowing cried
'Hosanna in the highest!' " Here she woke,
Resolved, sent for him and said wildly to him,
"There is no reason why we should not wed."
"Then for God's sake," he answer'd, "both our sakes,
So you will wed me, let it be at once."

    So these were wed, and merrily rang the bells,
Merrily rang the bells, and they were wed.
But never merrily beat Annie's heart.
A footstep seem'd to fall beside her path,   510
She knew not whence; a whisper on her ear,
She knew not what; nor loved she to be left
Alone at home, nor ventured out alone.
What ail'd her then that, ere she enter'd, often
Her hand dwelt lingeringly on the latch,

Fearing to enter? Philip thought he knew:
Such doubts and fears were common to her state,
Being with child; but when her child was born,
Then her new child was as herself renew'd,
Then the new mother came about her heart,   520
Then her good Philip was her all-in-all,
And that mysterious instinct wholly died.

    And where was Enoch? Prosperously sail'd
The ship "Good Fortune," tho' at setting forth
The Biscay,[9] roughly ridging eastward, shook
And almost overwhelm'd her, yet unvext
She slipt across the summer of the world,
Then after a long tumble about the Cape
And frequent interchange of foul and fair,
She passing thro' the summer world again,   530
The breath of heaven came continually
And sent her sweetly by the golden isles,
Till silent in her oriental haven.

    There Enoch traded for himself, and bought
Quaint monsters for the market of those times,
A gilded dragon also for the babes.
Less lucky her home-voyage: at first indeed
Thro' many a fair sea-circle, day by day,
Scarce-rocking, her full-busted figure-head
Stared o'er the ripple feathering from her bows: 540
Then follow'd calms, and then winds variable,
Then baffling, a long course of them; and last
Storm, such as drove her under moonless heavens
Till hard upon the cry of "breakers" came
The crash of ruin, and the loss of all
But Enoch and two others. Half the night,
Buoy'd upon floating tackle and broken spars,
These drifted, stranding on an isle at morn
Rich, but the loneliest in a lonely sea.

    No want was there of human sustenance,   550
Soft fruitage, mighty nuts, and nourishing roots;
Nor save for pity was it hard to take
The helpless life so wild that it was tame.
There in a seaward-gazing mountain-gorge
They built, and thatch'd with leaves of palm, a hut,
Half hut, half native cavern. So the three,
Set in this Eden of all plenteousness,
Dwelt with eternal summer, ill-content.

---

[7]**"Under the palm-tree"**: Judges 4:5.

[8]**Hosanna ... highest**: John 12:13. **Sun of Righteousness**:
Malachi 4:2.

[9]**Biscay**: bay W of France and N of Spain. Enoch's ship passes
around the **Cape** of Good Hope and through the E Indian **golden
isles** to China, twice crossing the equator (**summer world**).

For one, the youngest, hardly more than boy,
Hurt in that night of sudden ruin and wreck,   560
Lay lingering out a five-years' death-in-life.
They could not leave him. After he was gone,
The two remaining found a fallen stem;
And Enoch's comrade, careless of himself,
Fire-hollowing[10] this in Indian fashion, fell
Sun-stricken, and that other lived alone.
In those two deaths he read God's warning "wait."

    The mountain wooded to the peak, the lawns
And winding glades high up like ways to heaven,
The slender coco's drooping crown of plumes,   570
The lightning flash of insect and of bird,
The lustre of the long convolvuluses
That coil'd around the stately stems, and ran
Even to the limit of the land, the glows
And glories of the broad belt of the world,—
All these he saw; but what he fain had seen
He could not see, the kindly human face,
Nor ever hear a kindly voice, but heard
The myriad shriek of wheeling ocean-fowl,
The league-long roller thundering on the reef,   580
The moving whisper of huge trees that branch'd
And blossom'd in the zenith, or the sweep
Of some precipitous rivulet to the wave,
As down the shore he ranged, or all day long
Sat often in the seaward-gazing gorge,
A shipwreck'd sailor, waiting for a sail.
No sail from day to day, but every day
The sunrise broken into scarlet shafts
Among the palms and ferns and precipices;
The blaze upon the waters to the east;   590
The blaze upon his island overhead;
The blaze upon the waters to the west;
Then the great stars that globed themselves in heaven,
The hollower-bellowing ocean, and again
The scarlet shafts of sunrise—but no sail.

    There often as he watch'd or seem'd to watch,
So still the golden lizard on him paused,
A phantom made of many phantoms moved
Before him haunting him, or he himself
Moved haunting people, things, and places, known   600
Far in a darker isle beyond the line;[11]
The babes, their babble, Annie, the small house,

---

[10]**Fire-hollowing:** making a canoe from the tree trunk.

[11]**line:** equator.

The climbing street, the mill, the leafy lanes,
The peacock yew-tree and the lonely Hall,
The horse he drove, the boat he sold, the chill
November dawns and dewy-glooming downs,
The gentle shower, the smell of dying leaves,
And the low moan of leaden-color'd seas.

    Once likewise, in the ringing of his ears,
Tho' faintly, merrily—far and far away—   610
He heard the pealing of his parish bells;
Then, tho' he knew not wherefore, started up
Shuddering, and when the beauteous hateful isle
Return'd upon him, had not his poor heart
Spoken with That which being everywhere
Lets none who speaks with Him seem all alone,
Surely the man had died of solitude.

    Thus over Enoch's early-silvering head
The sunny and rainy seasons came and went
Year after year. His hopes to see his own,   620
And pace the sacred old familiar fields,
Not yet had perish'd, when his lonely doom
Came suddenly to an end. Another ship—
She wanted water—blown by baffling winds,
Like the "Good Fortune," from her destined course,
Stay'd by this isle, not knowing where she lay;
For since the mate had seen at early dawn
Across a break on the mist-wreathen isle
The silent water slipping from the hills,
They sent a crew that landing burst away   630
In search of stream or fount, and fill'd the shores
With clamour. Downward from his mountain gorge
Stept the long-hair'd, long-bearded solitary,
Brown, looking hardly human, strangely clad,
Muttering and mumbling, idiot-like it seem'd,
With inarticulate rage, and making signs
They knew not what; and yet he led the way
To where the rivulets of sweet water ran,
And ever as he mingled with the crew,
And heard them talking, his long-bounden tongue 640
Was loosen'd, till he made them understand;
Whom, when their casks were fill'd, they took aboard.
And there the tale he utter'd brokenly,
Scarce-credited at first but more and more,
Amazed and melted all who listen'd to it;
And clothes they gave him and free passage home,
But oft he work'd among the rest and shook
His isolation from him. None of these
Came from his country, or could answer him,
If question'd, aught of what he cared to know.   650

And dull the voyage was with long delays,
The vessel scarce sea-worthy; but evermore
His fancy fled before the lazy wind
Returning, till beneath a clouded moon
He like a lover down thro' all his blood
Drew in the dewy meadowy morning-breath
Of England, blown across her ghostly wall.[12]
And that same morning officers and men
Levied a kindly tax upon themselves,
Pitying the lonely man, and gave him it;   660
Then moving up the coast they landed him,
Even in that harbor whence he sail'd before.

There Enoch spoke no word to any one,
But homeward—home—what home? had he a home?—
His home, he walk'd. Bright was that afternoon,
Sunny but chill; till drawn thro' either chasm,
Where either haven open'd on the deeps,
Roll'd a sea-haze and whelm'd the world in gray,
Cut off the length of highway on before,
And left but narrow breadth to left and right   670
Of wither'd holt or tilth or pasturage.
On the nigh-naked tree the robin piped
Disconsolate, and thro' the dripping haze
The dead weight of the dead leaf bore it down.
Thicker the drizzle grew, deeper the gloom;
Last, as it seem'd, a great mist-blotted light
Flared on him, and he came upon the place.

Then down the long street having slowly stolen,
His heart foreshadowing all calamity,
His eyes upon the stones, he reach'd the home   680
Where Annie lived and loved him, and his babes
In those far-off seven happy years were born;
But finding neither light nor murmur there—
A bill of sale gleam'd thro' the drizzle—crept
Still downward thinking, "dead or dead to me!"

Down to the pool and narrow wharf he went,
Seeking a tavern which of old he knew,
A front of timber-crost antiquity,
So propt, worm-eaten, ruinously old,
He thought it must have gone; but he was gone   690
Who kept it, and his widow Miriam Lane,
With daily-dwindling profits held the house;
A haunt of brawling seamen once, but now
Stiller, with yet a bed for wandering men.
There Enoch rested silent many days.

---

[12]**ghostly wall**: white cliffs of Dover.

But Miriam Lane was good and garrulous,
Nor let him be, but often breaking in,
Told him, with other annals of the port,
Not knowing—Enoch was so brown, so bow'd,
So broken—all the story of his house: 700
His baby's death, her growing poverty,
How Philip put her little ones to school,
And kept them in it, his long wooing her,
Her slow consent and marriage, and the birth
Of Philip's child; and o'er his countenance
No shadow past, nor motion. Any one,
Regarding, well had deem'd he felt the tale
Less than the teller; only when she closed,
"Enoch, poor man, was cast away and lost,"
He, shaking his gray head pathetically,   710
Repeated muttering, "cast away and lost;"
Again in deeper inward whispers, "lost!"

But Enoch yearn'd to see her face again:
"If I might look on her sweet face again,
And know that she is happy." So the thought
Haunted and harass'd him, and drove him forth,
At evening when the dull November day
Was growing duller twilight, to the hill.
There he sat down gazing on all below;
There did a thousand memories roll upon him,   720
Unspeakable for sadness. By and by
The ruddy square of comfortable light,
Far-blazing from the rear of Philip's house,
Allured him, as the beacon-blaze allures
The bird of passage, till he madly strikes
Against it and beats out his weary life.

For Philip's dwelling fronted on the street,
The latest house to landward; but behind,
With one small gate that open'd on the waste,
Flourish'd a little garden square and wall'd,   730
And in it throve an ancient evergreen,
A yew-tree, and all round it ran a walk
Of shingle, and a walk divided it.
But Enoch shunn'd the middle walk and stole
Up by the wall, behind the yew; and thence
That which he better might have shunn'd, if griefs
Like his have worse or better, Enoch saw.

For cups and silver on the burnish'd board
Sparkled and shone; so genial was the hearth;
And on the right hand of the hearth he saw   740
Philip, the slighted suitor of old times,
Stout, rosy, with his babe across his knees;

And o'er her second father stoopt a girl,
A later but a loftier Annie Lee,
Fair-hair'd and tall, and from her lifted hand
Dangled a length of ribbon and a ring
To tempt the babe, who rear'd his creasy arms,
Caught at and ever miss'd it, and they laugh'd;
And on the left hand of the hearth he saw
The mother glancing often toward her babe,   750
But turning now and then to speak with him,
Her son, who stood beside her tall and strong,
And saying that which pleased him, for he smiled.

Now when the dead man come to life beheld
His wife his wife no more, and saw the babe
Hers, yet not his, upon the father's knee,
And all the warmth, the peace, the happiness,
And his own children tall and beautiful,
And him, that other, reigning in his place,
Lord of his rights and of his children's love—   760
Then he, tho' Miriam Lane had told him all,
Because things seen are mightier than things heard,
Stagger'd and shook, holding the branch, and fear'd
To send abroad a shrill and terrible cry,
Which in one moment, like the blast of doom,
Would shatter all the happiness of the hearth.

He therefore turning softly like a thief,
Lest the harsh shingle should grate underfoot,
And feeling all along the garden-wall,
Lest he should swoon and tumble and be found,   770
Crept to the gate, and open'd it and closed,
As lightly as a sick man's chamber-door,
Behind him, and came out upon the waste.

And there he would have knelt, but that his knees
Were feeble, so that falling prone he dug
His fingers into the wet earth, and pray'd:

'Too hard to bear! why did they take me thence?
O God Almighty, blessed Saviour, Thou
That didst uphold me on my lonely isle,
Uphold me, Father, in my loneliness   780
A little longer! aid me, give me strength
Not to tell her, never to let her know.
Help me not to break in upon her peace.
My children too! must I not speak to these?
They know me not. I should betray myself.
Never! no father's kiss for me—the girl
So like her mother, and the boy, my son.'

There speech and thought and nature fail'd a little,
And he lay tranced; but when he rose and paced

Back toward his solitary home again,   790
All down the long and narrow street he went
Beating it in upon his weary brain,
As tho' it were the burthen of a song,
"Not to tell her, never to let her know."

He was not all unhappy. His resolve
Upbore him, and firm faith, and evermore
Prayer from a living source within the will,
And beating up thro' all the bitter world,
Like fountains of sweet water in the sea,
Kept him a living soul. "This miller's wife,"   800
He said to Miriam, "that you spoke about,
Has she no fear that her first husband lives?"
"Ay, ay, poor soul," said Miriam, "fear enow!
If you could tell her you had seen him dead,
Why, that would be her comfort;" and he thought,
"After the Lord has call'd me she shall know,
I wait His time;" and Enoch set himself,
Scorning an alms, to work whereby to live.
Almost to all things could he turn his hand.
Cooper he was and carpenter, and wrought   810
To make the boatmen fishing-nets, or help'd
At lading and unlading the tall barks
That brought the stinted commerce of those days,
Thus earn'd a scanty living for himself.
Yet since he did but labor for himself,
Work without hope, there was not life in it
Whereby the man could live; and as the year
Roll'd itself round again to meet the day
When Enoch had return'd, a languor came
Upon him, gentle sickness, gradually   820
Weakening the man, till he could do no more,
But kept the house, his chair, and last his bed.
And Enoch bore his weakness cheerfully.
For sure no gladlier does the stranded wreck
See thro' the gray skirts of a lifting squall
The boat that bears the hope of life approach
To save the life despair'd of, than he saw
Death dawning on him, and the close of all.

For thro' that dawning gleam'd a kindlier hope
On Enoch thinking, "after I am gone,   830
Then may she learn I loved her to the last."
He call'd aloud for Miriam Lane and said:
"Woman, I have a secret—only swear,
Before I tell you—swear upon the book
Not to reveal it, till you see me dead."
"Dead," clamour'd the good woman, "hear him talk!
I warrant, man, that we shall bring you round."

"Swear," added Enoch sternly, "on the book;"
And on the book, half-frighted, Miriam swore.
Then Enoch rolling his gray eyes upon her,   840
"Did you know Enoch Arden of this town?"
"Know him?" she said, "I knew him far away.
Ay, ay, I mind him coming down the street;
Held his head high, and cared for no man, he."
Slowly and sadly Enoch answer'd her:
"His head is low, and no man cares for him.
I think I have not three days more to live;
I am the man." At which the woman gave
A half-incredulous, half-hysterical cry:
"You Arden, you! nay,—sure he was a foot   850
Higher than you be." Enoch said again:
"My God has bow'd me down to what I am;
My grief and solitude have broken me;
Nevertheless, know you that I am he
Who married—but that name has twice been changed—
I married her who married Philip Ray.
Sit, listen." Then he told her of his voyage,
His wreck, his lonely life, his coming back,
His gazing in on Annie, his resolve,
And how he kept it. As the woman heard,   860
Fast flow'd the current of her easy tears,
While in her heart she yearn'd incessantly
To rush abroad all round the little haven,
Proclaiming Enoch Arden and his woes;
But awed and promise-bounden she forbore,
Saying only, "See your bairns before you go!
Eh, let me fetch 'em, Arden," and arose
Eager to bring them down, for Enoch hung
A moment on her words, but then replied:

"Woman, disturb me not now at the last,   870
But let me hold my purpose till I die.
Sit down again; mark me and understand,
While I have power to speak. I charge you now,
When you shall see her, tell her that I died
Blessing her, praying for her, loving her;
Save for the bar between us, loving her
As when she laid her head beside my own.
And tell my daughter Annie, whom I saw
So like her mother, that my latest breath
Was spent in blessing her and praying for her.   880
And tell my son that I died blessing him.
And say to Philip that I blest him too;
He never meant us anything but good.
But if my children care to see me dead,
Who hardly knew me living, let them come,
I am their father; but she must not come,

For my dead face would vex her after-life.
And now there is but one of all my blood
Who will embrace me in the world-to-be.
This hair is his, she cut it off and gave it,   890
And I have borne it with me all these years,
And thought to bear it with me to my grave;
But now my mind is changed, for I shall see him,
My babe in bliss. Wherefore when I am gone,
Take, give her this, for it may comfort her;
It will moreover be a token to her
That I am he."

He ceased; and Miriam Lane
Made such a voluble answer promising all,
That once again he roll'd his eyes upon her
Repeating all he wish'd, and once again   900
She promised.

Then the third night after this,
While Enoch slumber'd motionless and pale,
And Miriam watch'd and dozed at intervals,
There came so loud a calling of the sea[13]
That all the houses in the haven rang.
He woke, he rose, he spread his arms abroad,
Crying with a loud voice, "A sail! a sail!
I am saved;" and so fell back and spoke no more.

So past the strong heroic soul away.
And when they buried him the little port   910
Had seldom seen a costlier funeral.

1864

The Higher Pantheism[1]

The sun, the moon, the stars, the seas, the hills and the
  plains,—
Are not these, O Soul, the Vision of Him who reigns?

Is not the Vision He, tho' He be not that which He seems?
Dreams are true while they last, and do we not live in
  dreams?

---

[13]**calling of the sea**: a clear night with a sea-sound on the shore
in calm. [Tennyson's note]

[1]**Pantheism**: doctrine that God is coextensive with the cosmos.
Tennyson's title alludes to the **Higher** Criticism, which doubted
the literal truth of the Bible while seeking to reground faith on a
more spiritual level: see pages 67–70. Swinburne's parody (page
972) insinuates that Tennyson's elevation was mainly rhetorical.

Earth, these solid stars, this weight of body and limb,
Are they not sign and symbol of thy division from Him?

Dark is the world to thee; thyself art the reason why,
For is He not all but thou, that hast power to feel "I am I"?

Glory about thee, without thee; and thou fulfillest thy
    doom,
Making Him broken gleams and a stifled splendor and
    gloom.   10

Speak to Him, thou, for He hears, and Spirit with Spirit
    can meet—
Closer is He than breathing, and nearer than hands and
    feet.

God is law, say the wise; O Soul, and let us rejoice,
For if He thunder by law the thunder is yet His voice.

Law is God, say some; no God at all, says the fool,[2]
For all we have power to see is a straight staff bent in
    a pool;

And the ear of man cannot hear, and the eye of man
    cannot see;[3]
But if we could see and hear, this Vision—were it not He?

                        1869

Rizpah[1]

— 1 —

Wailing, wailing, wailing, the wind over land and sea—
And Willy's voice in the wind, "O mother, come out to
    me."
Why should he call me to-night, when he knows that I
    cannot go?
For the downs are as bright as day, and the full moon
    stares at the snow.

— 2 —

We should be seen, my dear; they would spy us out of
    the town.
The loud black nights for us, and the storm rushing over
    the down,

When I cannot see my own hand, but am led by the
    creak of the chain,
And grovel and grope for my son till I find myself
    drenched with the rain.

— 3 —

Anything fallen again? nay—what was there left to fall?
I have taken them home, I have number'd the bones, I
    have hidden them all.   10
What am I saying? and what are *you*? do you come as a
    spy?
Falls? what falls? who knows? As the tree falls so must it
    lie.[2]

— 4 —

Who let her in? how long has she been? you—what
    have you heard?
Why did you sit so quiet? you never have spoken a word.
O—to pray with me—yes—a lady—none of their spies—
But the night has crept into my heart, and begun to
    darken my eyes.

— 5 —

Ah—you, that have lived so soft, what should *you* know
    of the night,
The blast and the burning shame and the bitter frost and
    the fright?
I have done it, while you were asleep—you were only
    made for the day.
I have gather'd my baby together—and now you may go
    your way.   20

— 6 —

Nay—for it's kind of you, Madam, to sit by an old dying
    wife.
But say nothing hard of my boy, I have only an hour of
    life.
I kiss'd my boy in the prison, before he went out to die.
"They dared me to do it," he said, and he never has told
    me a lie.
I whipt him for robbing an orchard once when he was
    but a child—
"The farmer dared me to do it," he said; he was always
    so wild—
And idle—and couldn't be idle—my Willy—he never
    could rest.
The King should have made him a soldier, he would
    have been one of his best.

---

[2]**fool:** see Psalm 14:1.

[3]**And the ear . . . see:** see Isaiah 64:4, 1 Corinthians 2:9.

[1]Based on a 1793 incident Tennyson read about in a popular magazine. The published title—an allusion to 2 Samuel 21:8–14, where Rizpah defends her hanged son's bones—replaced his initial working title "Bones."

---

[2]**As the tree . . . lie:** see Ecclesiastes 11:3.

— 7 —

But he lived with a lot of wild mates, and they never
    would let him be good;
They swore that he dare not rob the mail, and he swore
    that he would;   30
And he took no life, but he took one purse, and when all
    was done
He flung it among his fellows—"I'll none of it," said
    my son.

— 8 —

I came into court to the Judge and the lawyers. I told
    them my tale,
God's own truth—but they kill'd him, they kill'd him for
    robbing the mail.
They hang'd him in chains for a show—we had always
    borne a good name—
To be hang'd for a thief—and then put away—isn't that
    enough shame?
Dust to dust—low down—let us hide! but they set him
    so high
That all the ships of the world could stare at him,
    passing by.
God 'ill pardon the hell-black raven and horrible fowls
    of the air,
But not the black heart of the lawyer who kill'd him and
    hang'd him there.   40

— 9 —

And the jailer forced me away. I had bid him my last
    goodbye;
They had fasten'd the door of his cell. "O mother!" I
    heard him cry.
I couldn't get back tho' I tried, he had something further
    to say,
And now I never shall know it. The jailer forced me
    away.

— 10 —

Then since I couldn't but hear that cry of my boy that
    was dead,
They seized me and shut me up: they fasten'd me down
    on my bed.
"Mother, O mother!"—he call'd in the dark to me year
    after year—
They beat me for that, they beat me—you know that I
    couldn't but hear;
And then at the last they found I had grown so stupid
    and still

They let me abroad again—but the creatures had
    worked their will.   50

— 11 —

Flesh of my flesh was gone, but bone of my bone[3] was
    left—
I stole them all from the lawyers—and you, will you call
    it a theft?—
My baby, the bones that had suck'd me, the bones that
    had laughed and had cried—
Theirs? O no! they are mine—not theirs—they had
    moved in my side.

— 12 —

Do you think I was scared by the bones? I kiss'd 'em, I
    buried 'em all—
I can't dig deep, I am old—in the night by the
    churchyard wall.
My Willy 'ill rise up whole when the trumpet of
    judgment 'ill sound,
But I charge you never to say that I laid him in holy
    ground.[4]

— 13 —

They would scratch him up—they would hang him
    again on the cursed tree.
Sin? O, yes—we are sinners, I know—let all that be,   60
And read me a Bible verse of the Lord's good will toward
    men—
"Full of compassion and mercy, the Lord"—let me hear
    it again;
"Full of compassion and mercy—long-suffering."[5] Yes,
    O, yes!
For the lawyer is born but to murder—the Saviour lives
    but to bless.
He 'll never put on the black cap except for the worst of
    the worst,
And the first may be last—I have heard it in church—
    and the last may be first.
Suffering—O long-suffering—yes, as the Lord must
    know,
Year after year in the mist and the wind and the shower
    and the snow.

---

[3]**Flesh . . . bone**: see Genesis 2:23.

[4]**holy ground**: hanged criminals were denied consecrated burial.

[5]**"Full . . . long-suffering"**: Psalms 86:15.

— 14 —

Heard, have you? what? they have told you he never
    repented his sin.
How do they know it? are *they* his mother? are *you* of his
    kin?   70
Heard! have you ever heard, when the storm on the
    downs began,
The wind that 'ill wail like a child and the sea that 'ill
    moan like a man?

— 15 —

Election, Election and Reprobation[6]—it's all very well.
But I go to-night to my boy, and I shall not find him in
    Hell.
For I cared so much for my boy that the Lord has look'd
    into my care,
And He means me I'm sure to be happy with Willy, I
    know not where.

— 16 —

And if *he* be lost—but to save *my* soul, that is all your
    desire:
Do you think that I care for *my* soul if my boy be gone
    to the fire?
I have been with God in the dark—go, go, you may
    leave me alone—
You never have borne a child—you are just as hard as a
    stone.   80

— 17 —

Madam, I beg your pardon! I think that you mean to be
    kind,
But I cannot hear what you say for my Willy's voice in
    the wind—
The snow and the sky so bright—he used but to call in
    the dark,
And he calls to me now from the church and not from
    the gibbet—for hark!
Nay—you can hear it yourself—it is coming—shaking
    the walls—
Willy—the moon's in a cloud——Good-night. I am
    going. He calls.

1880

---

[6]**Election and Reprobation**: Calvinist terms for salvation and
damnation.

"Frater Ave atque Vale"[1]

Row us out from Desenzano, to your Sirmione row!
So they row'd, and there we landed—"O venusta Sirmio!"[2]
There to me thro' all the groves of olive in the summer
    glow,
There beneath the Roman ruin where the purple flowers
    grow,
Came that "Ave atque Vale" of the Poet's hopeless woe,
Tenderest of Roman poets nineteen hundred years ago,
"Frater Ave atque Vale"—as we wander'd to and fro
Gazing at the Lydian[3] laughter of the Garda Lake below
Sweet Catullus's all-but-island, olive-silvery Sirmio!

1883

Demeter and Persephone

(In Enna[1])

Faint as a climate-changing bird that flies
All night across the darkness, and at dawn
Falls on the threshold of her native land,
And can no more, thou camest, O my child,
Led upward by the God of ghosts and dreams,
Who laid thee at Eleusis,[2] dazed and dumb
With passing thro' at once from state to state,

---

[1]**"Frater Ave atque Vale"**: Brother, hello and goodbye (from
Catullus, 1st century BCE).

[2]**O venusta Sirmio**: O lovely Sirmione (also **Catullus**). The
counterpoint between Italian and Latin names for this peninsula
(accessible by boat from **Desenzano** on Lake **Garda**) implies other
contrasts between present and past: Tennyson and Catullus,
tourists and ruins, the poet's brother Charles (died 1879) and
Arthur Hallam (died 1833: see *In Memoriam*, section 57).

[3]**Lydian**: ancestor nation (from present-day Turkey) claimed by
the Etruscan forerunners of ancient Rome. **all-but-island**: English
rendering of Latin *paeninsula*.

[1]**Enna**: valley in Sicily where **Persephone**, daughter of the earth
goddess **Demeter**, has been abducted by the god of the underworld
to become his queen. She returns from **Hades** to the light by Zeus's
ruling that she shall spend nine months a year with her mother but
the rest underground, when her mother's grief makes winter.

[2]**God of ghosts and dreams**: Hermes, escort of the dead. **Eleusis**: Greek city, home to the cult of Demeter.

Until I brought thee hither, that the day,
When here thy hands let fall the gather'd flower,
Might break thro' clouded memories once again   10
On thy lost self. A sudden nightingale
Saw thee, and flash'd into a frolic of song
And welcome; and a gleam as of the moon,
When first she peers along the tremulous deep,
Fled wavering o'er thy face, and chased away
That shadow of a likeness to the king
Of shadows, thy dark mate. Persephone!
Queen of the dead no more—my child! Thine eyes
Again were human-godlike, and the Sun
Burst from a swimming fleece of winter gray,   20
And robed thee in his day from head to feet—
"Mother!" and I was folded in thine arms.

   Child, those imperial, disimpassion'd eyes
Awed even me at first, thy mother—eyes
That oft had seen the serpent-wanded power[3]
Draw downward into Hades with his drift
Of flickering spectres, lighted from below
By the red race of fiery Phlegethon;
But when before have Gods or men beheld
The Life that had descended re-arise,   30
And lighted from above him by the Sun?
So mighty was the mother's childless cry,
A cry that rang thro' Hades, Earth, and Heaven!

   So in this pleasant vale we stand again,
The field of Enna, now once more ablaze
With flowers that brighten as thy footstep falls,
All flowers—but for one black blur of earth
Left by that closing chasm, thro' which the car
Of dark Aïdoneus[4] rising rapt thee hence.
And here, my child, tho' folded in thine arms,   40
I feel the deathless heart of motherhood
Within me shudder, lest the naked glebe
Should yawn once more into the gulf, and thence
The shrilly whinnyings of the team of Hell,
Ascending, pierce the glad and songful air,
And all at once their arch'd necks, midnight-maned,
Jet upward thro' the midday blossom. No!
For, see, thy foot has touch'd it; all the space

Of blank earth-baldness clothes itself afresh,
And breaks into the crocus-purple hour   50
That saw thee vanish.

                Child, when thou wert gone,
I envied human wives, and nested birds,
Yea, the cubb'd lioness; went in search of thee
Thro' many a palace, many a cot, and gave
Thy breast to ailing infants in the night,
And set the mother waking in amaze
To find her sick one whole; and forth again
Among the wail of midnight winds, and cried,
"Where is my loved one? Wherefore do ye wail?"
And out from all the night an answer shrill'd,   60
"We know not, and we know not why we wail."
I climb'd on all the cliffs of all the seas,
And ask'd the waves that moan about the world,
"Where? do ye make your moaning for my child?"
And round from all the world the voices came,
"We know not, and we know not why we moan."
"Where?" and I stared from every eagle-peak,
I thridded the black heart of all the woods,
I peer'd thro' tomb and cave, and in the storms
Of autumn swept across the city, and heard   70
The murmur of their temples chanting me,
Me, me, the desolate mother! "Where?"—and turn'd,
And fled by many a waste, forlorn of man,
And grieved for man thro' all my grief for thee,—
The jungle rooted in his shatter'd hearth,
The serpent coil'd about his broken shaft,
The scorpion crawling over naked skulls;—
I saw the tiger in the ruin'd fane
Spring from his fallen God, but trace of thee
I saw not; and far on, and, following out   80
A league of labyrinthine darkness, came
On three gray heads[5] beneath a gleaming rift.
"Where?" and I heard one voice from all the three,
"We know not, for we spin the lives of men,
And not of Gods, and know not why we spin!
There is a Fate beyond us." Nothing knew.

   Last as the likeness of a dying man,
Without his knowledge, from him flits to warn
A far-off friendship that he comes no more,
So he, the God of dreams, who heard my cry,   90
Drew from thyself the likeness of thyself

---

[3]**serpent-wanded power:** Hermes'. **Phlegethon:** fiery river in Hades.

[4]**Aïdoneus:** god of the underworld, also called Dis, Hades, Pluto; brother to Zeus.

---

[5]**three gray heads:** the Fates, who spin mortals' destiny.

Without thy knowledge, and thy shadow past
Before me, crying, "The Bright one in the highest
Is brother of the Dark one in the lowest,
And Bright and Dark have sworn that I, the child
Of thee, the great Earth-Mother, thee, the Power
That lifts her buried life from gloom to bloom,
Should be for ever and for evermore
The Bride of Darkness."
                  So the Shadow wail'd.
Then I, Earth-Goddess, cursed the Gods
    of heaven.   100
I would not mingle with their feasts; to me
Their nectar smack'd of hemlock on the lips,
Their rich ambrosia tasted aconite.
The man, that only lives and loves an hour,
Seem'd nobler than their hard eternities.
My quick tears kill'd the flower, my ravings hush'd
The bird, and lost in utter grief I fail'd
To send my life thro' olive-yard and vine
And golden-grain, my gift to helpless man.
Rain-rotten died the wheat, the barley-spears   110
Were hollow-husk'd, the leaf fell, and the Sun,
Pale at my grief, drew down before his time
Sickening, and Ætna[6] kept her winter snow.

    Then He, the brother of this Darkness, He
Who still is highest, glancing from his height
On earth a fruitless fallow, when he miss'd
The wonted steam of sacrifice, the praise
And prayer of men, decreed that thou shouldst dwell
For nine white moons of each whole year with me,
Three dark ones in the shadow with thy king.   120

    Once more the reaper in the gleam of dawn
Will see me by the landmark far away,
Blessing his field, or seated in the dusk
Of even, by the lonely threshing-floor,
Rejoicing in the harvest and the grange.

    Yet I, Earth-Goddess, am but ill-content
With them who still are highest. Those gray heads,
What meant they by their "Fate beyond the Fates"
But younger kindlier Gods to bear us down,
As we bore down the Gods before us?[7] Gods,   130
To quench, not hurl the thunderbolt, to stay,
Not spread the plague, the famine; Gods indeed,

To send the noon into the night and break
The sunless halls of Hades into Heaven?
Till thy dark lord accept and love the Sun,
And all the Shadow die into the Light,
When thou shalt dwell the whole bright year with me,
And souls of men, who grew beyond their race,
And made themselves as Gods against the fear
Of Death and Hell; and thou that hast from men,   140
As Queen of Death, that worship which is Fear,
Henceforth, as having risen from out the dead,
Shalt ever send thy life along with mine
From buried grain thro' springing blade, and bless
Their garner'd autumn also, reap with me,
Earth-Mother, in the harvest hymns of Earth
The worship which is Love, and see no more
The Stone, the Wheel, the dimly-glimmering lawns
Of that Elysium,[8] all the hateful fires
Of torment, and the shadowy warrior glide   150
Along the silent field of Asphodel.

                               1889

Far—Far—Away[1]

(For Music)

What sight so lured him thro' the fields he knew
As where earth's green stole into heaven's own hue,
                  Far—Far—away?

What sound was dearest in his native dells?
The mellow lin-lan-lone of evening bells
                  Far—far—away?

What vague world-whisper, mystic pain or joy,
Thro' those three words would haunt him when a boy,
                  Far—far—away?

A whisper from his dawn of life? a breath   10
From some fair dawn beyond the doors of death
                  Far—far—away?

---

[6]**Aetna**: Mount Etna, volcano in Sicily.

[7]**Gods before us**: Titans, who reigned before Olympian gods unseated them.

[8]**Stone, Wheel**: instruments of underworld torment undergone by Sisyphus and Ixion. **Elysium**: where ghosts of heroes lived in flowering fields.

[1]Before I could read I was in the habit on a stormy day of spreading my arms to the wind and crying out, "I hear a voice that's speaking in the wind," and the words "far, far away" had always a strange charm for me. [Tennyson's note]

Far, far, how far? from o'er the gates of birth,
The faint horizons, all the bounds, of earth,
          Far—far—away?

What charm in words, a charm no words could give?
O dying words, can Music make you live
          Far—far—away?

           1889

To the Marquis of Dufferin and Ava

— 1 —

At times our Britain cannot rest,
   At times her steps are swift and rash;
   She moving, at her girdle clash
The golden keys of East and West.

— 2 —

Not swift or rash, when late she lent
   The sceptres of her West, her East,
   To one,[1] that ruling has increased
Her greatness and her self-content.

— 3 —

Your rule has made the people love
   Their ruler. Your viceregal days   10
   Have added fulness to the phrase
Of "Gauntlet in the velvet glove."

— 4 —

But since your name will grow with Time,
   Not all, as honouring your fair fame
   Of Statesman, have I made the name
A golden portal to my rhyme:

— 5 —

But more, that you and yours may know
   From me and mine, how dear a debt
   We owed you, and are owing yet
To you and yours, and still would owe.   20

---

[1]**to one:** Lord **Dufferin** (1826–1902), Governor-General of India, who had befriended Tennyson's son Lionel (born 1854) when he fell ill with fever in 1886 and embarked on a homeward trip he did not survive.

— 6 —

For he—your India was his Fate,
   And drew him over sea to you—
   He fain had ranged her thro' and thro',
To serve her myriads and the State,—

— 7 —

A soul that, watch'd from earliest youth,
   And on thro' many a brightening year,
   Had never swerved for craft or fear,
By one side-path, from simple truth;

— 8 —

Who might have chased and claspt Renown
   And caught her chaplet here—and there   30
   In haunts of jungle-poison'd air
The flame of life went wavering down;

— 9 —

But ere he left your fatal shore,
   And lay on that funereal boat,
   Dying, "Unspeakable" he wrote
"Their kindness," and he wrote no more;

— 10 —

And sacred is the latest word;
   And now the Was, the Might-have-been,
   And those lone rites I have not seen,
And one drear sound I have not heard,   40

— 11 —

Are dreams that scarce will let me be,
   Not there to bid my boy farewell,
   When That within the coffin fell,
Fell—and flash'd into the Red Sea,

— 12 —

Beneath a hard Arabian moon
   And alien stars. To question, why
   The sons before the fathers die,
Not mine! and I may meet him soon;

— 13 —

But while my life's late eve endures,
   Nor settles into hueless gray,   50
   My memories of his briefer day
Will mix with love for you and yours.

           1889

~

Crossing the Bar

Sunset and evening star,
   And one clear call for me!
And may there be no moaning of the bar,
   When I put out to sea,

But such a tide as moving seems asleep,
   Too full for sound and foam,
When that which drew from out the boundless deep
   Turns again home.

Twilight and evening bell,
   And after that the dark!   10

And may there be no sadness of farewell,
   When I embark;

For tho' from out our bourne of Time and Place
   The flood may bear me far,
I hope to see my Pilot face to face[1]
   When I have crost the bar.

1889

---

[1]**Pilot:** that Divine and Unseen Who is always guiding us. [Tennyson's note] **face to face:**1 Corinthians 13:12. Tennyson requested that this poem have last place in editions of his poetry.

CHARLES DARWIN

(1809–1882)

The most influential scientist of the nineteenth century, Charles Darwin was born into a prosperous, well-connected family at a time when science was mostly a gentleman's hobby. He did not need to earn a living, but his father, a successful country doctor, sent him to Edinburgh to study medicine and then to Cambridge so that he could become a clergyman. In neither place did he show more than occasional interest in the required curriculum. At Cambridge, however, he met eminent scientists who encouraged his passion for beetles, geology, and other aspects of nature, and after graduating he went as a volunteer naturalist on the *Beagle*, a ship heading for South America to pursue scientific investigations. The voyage lasted five years, during which Darwin wrote important papers and made observations of flora and fauna, geological phenomena, and human communities that were to set the course for his life's work. He was preparing to make his greatest single contribution to evolutionary theory by filling the gap that had hindered the theory's acceptance: the apparent lack of a mechanism by which one species could evolve into another. Darwin's solution to the problem (arrived at simultaneously by another world-wandering naturalist, Alfred Wallace) was the "struggle for existence," through which only the most "fit" individuals and varieties survived and reproduced. Although no explanation for how variations arise within species was then available, plant and animal breeders had long known how to select and perpetuate particular variations, and Darwin argued that such "selection" has always occurred in nature.

The impact of *On the Origin of Species* was and remains immense, both on specialists and on the general public. It sets forth with devastating clarity and completeness a "law" encompassing all living things (humans implicitly among them), illustrated by a mass of examples taken sometimes from the English countryside or village life, sometimes from exotic places: from books, articles, and data sent to Darwin by correspondents all over the world, and from his own observations. With great imaginative cogency, it invites the reader to set aside first impressions and conventional ideas, to look beneath the bright appearances of nature and "see"— Darwin's insistent, recurrent verb—ceaseless change and interplay, complex but orderly sequences of causes, and also struggle and pain. Darwin's pervasively metaphorical language creates an image of "Nature" that accords with Tennyson's prevision in *In Memoriam* (published almost a decade before) of "Nature red in tooth and claw," who "care[s] for nothing"—the nightmarish opposite of the loving Christian God. The intricate workings of nature as imaginatively depicted by Darwin are astonishing and beautiful, and they are regularly reinforced by analogy to emergent forms of systems analysis such as Victorian political economy. But they leave no place for a creator, a designer, or the interventions of providential power, let alone for the story of creation told in Genesis.

Darwin himself tried, in his life as in his rhetoric, not to pursue disturbing implications of the theory. He became an invalid and recluse, devoting himself wholly to his family and his work. He had entered Cambridge believing without question in the "strict and literal truth of every word of the Bible," and although he became an agnostic (a word coined by his champion, Thomas Henry Huxley) he left others to fight the battle for evolutionary theory against religious fundamentalists and other opponents. As early as the voyage of the *Beagle*, however, he had observed indigenous peoples with a naturalist's eye, and in *The Descent of Man* he applies the theory of evolution directly to humans and human culture, with a particular emphasis on the mechanism of sexual selection. The entanglement of this topic with contemporary social mores and prejudices proved too deep for even Darwin to withstand, and the *Descent* lent his authority to current ideas about the inferiority of women and non-Europeans.

Darwin's brief, unpretentious *Autobiography* interweaves his apparently "innate" interest in observing and collecting natural objects, his sensitivity to suffering, and his fear of inflicting pain. It also shows how his aesthetic susceptibility ended in a nervous, anaesthetic recoil from the sublime, the tragic, the pathetic—indeed, from all literary representations except happy ones: a response, perhaps, to the pathos of the natural world as revealed by the lens of his own powerful imagination.

from Voyage of the *Beagle*
Tierra del Fuego

December 17th, 1832.—Having now finished with Patagonia and the Falkland Islands,[1] I will describe our first arrival in Tierra del Fuego.[1] A little after noon we doubled Cape St. Diego, and entered the famous strait of Le Maire. We kept close to the Fuegian shore, but the outline of the rugged, inhospitable Staten-land was visible amidst the clouds. In the afternoon we anchored in the Bay of Good Success. While entering we were saluted in a manner becoming the inhabitants of this savage land. A group of Fuegians partly concealed by the entangled forest, were perched on a wild point overhanging the sea; and as we passed by, they sprang up and waving their tattered cloaks sent forth a loud and sonorous shout. The savages followed the ship, and just before dark we saw their fire, and again heard their wild cry. The harbour consists of a fine piece of water half surrounded by low rounded mountains of clay-slate, which are covered to the water's edge by one dense gloomy forest. A single glance at the landscape was sufficient to show me how widely different it was from any thing I had ever beheld. At night it blew a gale of wind, and heavy squalls from the mountains swept past us. It would have been a bad time out at sea, and we, as well as others, may call this Good Success Bay.

In the morning the Captain[2] sent a party to communicate with the Fuegians. When we came within hail, one of the four natives who were present advanced to receive us, and began to shout most vehemently, wishing to direct us where to land. When we were on shore the party looked rather alarmed, but continued talking and making gestures with great rapidity. It was without exception the most curious and interesting spectacle I ever beheld: I could not have believed how wide was the difference between savage and civilized man: it is greater than between a wild and domesticated animal, inasmuch as in man there is a greater power of improvement. The chief spokesman was old, and appeared to be the head of the family; the three others were powerful young men, about six feet high. The women and children had been sent away. These Fuegians are a very different race from the stunted, miserable wretches farther westward; and they seem closely allied to the famous Patagonians of the Strait of Magellan. Their only garment consists of a mantle made of guanaco skin, with the wool outside; this they wear just thrown over their shoulders, leaving their persons as often exposed as covered. Their skin is of a dirty coppery red colour.

The old man had a fillet of white feathers tied round his head, which partly confined his black, coarse, and entangled hair. His face was crossed by two broad transverse bars; one, painted bright red, reached from ear to ear and included the upper lip; the other, white like chalk, extended above and parallel to the first, so that even his eyelids were thus coloured. The other two men were ornamented by streaks of black powder, made of charcoal. The party altogether closely resembled the devils which come on the stage in plays like Der Freischutz.[3]

---

[1]**Patagonia:** plateau in S Argentina. **Falkland Islands:** British colony 300 miles NE of **Tierra del Fuego,** archipelago at the tip of S America.

[2]**Captain:** Robert Fitzroy (1805–1865), hydrographer and meteorologist.

[3]*Der Freischutz* (1821): German Romantic opera by Carl Maria von Weber (1786–1826), with wilderness settings and supernatural beings.

Their very attitudes were abject, and the expression of their countenances distrustful, surprised, and startled. After we had presented them with some scarlet cloth, which they immediately tied round their necks, they became good friends. This was shown by the old man patting our breasts, and making a chuckling kind of noise, as people do when feeding chickens. I walked with the old man, and this demonstration of friendship was repeated several times; it was concluded by three hard slaps, which were given me on the breast and back at the same time. He then bared his bosom for me to return the compliment, which being done, he seemed highly pleased. The language of these people, according to our notions, scarcely deserves to be called articulate. Captain Cook[4] has compared it to a man clearing his throat, but certainly no European ever cleared his throat with so many hoarse, guttural, and clicking sounds.

They are excellent mimics: as often as we coughed or yawned, or made any odd motion, they immediately imitated us. Some of our party began to squint and look awry; but one of the young Fuegians (whose whole face was painted black, excepting a white band across his eyes) succeeded in making far more hideous grimaces. They could repeat with perfect correctness each word in any sentence we addressed them, and they remembered such words for some time. Yet we Europeans all know how difficult it is to distinguish apart the sounds in a foreign language. Which of us, for instance, could follow an American Indian through a sentence of more than three words? All savages appear to possess, to an uncommon degree, this power of mimicry. I was told, almost in the same words, of the same ludicrous habit among the Caffres: the Australians, likewise, have long been notorious for being able to imitate and describe the gait of any man, so that he may be recognized. How can this faculty be explained? is it a consequence of the more practised habits of perception and keener senses, common to all men in a savage state, as compared with those long civilized?

When a song was struck up by our party, I thought the Fuegians would have fallen down with astonishment. With equal surprise they viewed our dancing; but one of the young men, when asked, had no objection to a little waltzing. Little accustomed to Europeans as they appeared to be, yet they knew and dreaded our fire-arms; nothing would tempt them to take a gun in their hands. They begged for knives, calling them by the Spanish word "cuchilla." They explained also what they wanted, by acting as if they had a piece of blubber in their mouth, and then pretending to cut instead of tear it.

I have not as yet noticed the Fuegians whom we had on board. During the former voyage of the *Adventure* and *Beagle* in 1826 to 1830, Captain Fitz Roy seized on a party of natives, as hostages for the loss of a boat, which had been stolen, to the great jeopardy of a party employed on the survey; and some of these natives, as well as a child whom he bought for a pearl-button, he took with him to England, determining to educate them and instruct them in religion at his own expense. To settle these natives in their own country, was one chief inducement to Captain Fitz Roy to undertake our present voyage; and before the Admiralty had resolved to send out this expedition, Captain Fitz Roy had generously chartered a vessel, and would himself have taken them back. The natives were accompanied by a missionary, R. Matthews; of whom and of the natives, Captain Fitz Roy has published a full and excellent account. Two men, one of whom died in England of the small-pox, a boy and a little girl, were originally taken; and we had now on board, York Minster, Jemmy Button (whose name expresses his purchase-money), and Fuegia Basket. York Minster was a full-grown, short, thick, powerful man: his disposition was reserved, taciturn, morose, and when excited violently passionate; his affections were very strong towards a few friends on board; his intellect good. Jemmy Button was a universal favourite, but likewise passionate; the expression of his face at once showed his nice disposition. He was merry and often laughed, and was remarkably sympathetic with any one in pain: when the water was rough, I was often a little sea-sick, and he used to come to me and say in a plaintive voice, "Poor, poor fellow!" but the notion, after his aquatic life, of a man being sea-sick, was too ludicrous, and he was generally obliged to turn on one side to hide a smile or laugh, and then he would repeat his "Poor, poor fellow!" He was of a patriotic disposition; and he liked to praise his own tribe and country, in which he truly said there were "plenty of trees," and he abused all the other tribes: he stoutly declared that there was no Devil in his land. Jemmy was short, thick, and fat, but vain of his personal appearance; he used to wear gloves, his hair was neatly cut, and he was distressed if his well-polished shoes were dirtied. He was fond of admiring himself in a looking-glass; and a merry-faced little Indian boy from the Rio Negro, whom we had for some months on board, soon perceived this, and used to mock him: Jemmy, who was always rather jealous of the attention paid to this little boy, did not at all like this, and used to say, with rather a contemptuous twist of his head, "Too much skylark." It seems yet wonderful to me, when I think over all his many good qualities, that he should have been of the same race,

---

[4]James **Cook** (1728–1779): British navigator and explorer.

and doubtless partaken of the same character, with the miserable, degraded savages whom we first met here. Lastly, Fuegia Basket was a nice, modest, reserved young girl, with a rather pleasing but sometimes sullen expression, and very quick in learning anything, especially languages. This she showed in picking up some Portuguese and Spanish, when left on shore for only a short time at Rio de Janeiro and Monte Video, and in her knowledge of English. York Minster was very jealous of any attention paid to her; for it was clear he determined to marry her as soon as they were settled on shore.

Although all three could both speak and understand a good deal of English, it was singularly difficult to obtain much information from them, concerning the habits of their countrymen: this was partly owing to their apparent difficulty in understanding the simplest alternative. Every one accustomed to very young children, knows how seldom one can get an answer even to so simple a question as whether a thing is black *or* white; the idea of black or white seems alternately to fill their minds. So it was with these Fuegians, and hence it was generally impossible to find out, by cross-questioning, whether one had rightly understood anything which they had asserted. Their sight was remarkably acute: it is well known that sailors, from long practice, can make out a distant object much better than a landsman; but both York and Jemmy were much superior to any sailor on board: several times they have declared what some distant object has been, and though doubted by every one, they have proved right, when it has been examined through a telescope. They were quite conscious of this power; and Jemmy, when he had any little quarrel with the officer on watch, would say, "Me see ship, me no tell."

It was interesting to watch the conduct of the savages, when we landed, towards Jemmy Button: they immediately perceived the difference between him and ourselves, and held much conversation one with another on the subject. The old man addressed a long harangue to Jemmy, which it seems was to invite him to stay with them. But Jemmy understood very little of their language, and was, moreover, thoroughly ashamed of his countrymen. When York Minster afterwards came on shore, they noticed him in the same way, and told him he ought to shave; yet he had not twenty dwarf hairs on his face, whilst we all wore our untrimmed beards. They examined the colour of his skin, and compared it with ours. One of our arms being bared, they expressed the liveliest surprise and admiration at its whiteness, just in the same way in which I have seen the ourang-outang do at the Zoological Gardens. . . .

. . . The climate is certainly wretched: the summer solstice was now passed, yet every day snow fell on the hills, and in the valleys there was rain, accompanied by sleet. The thermometer generally stood about 45°, but in the night fell to 38° or 40°. From the damp and boisterous state of the atmosphere, not cheered by a gleam of sunshine, one fancied the climate even worse than it really was.

While going one day on shore near Wollaston Island, we pulled alongside a canoe with six Fuegians. These were the most abject and miserable creatures I anywhere beheld. On the east coast the natives, as we have seen, have guanaco cloaks, and on the west, they possess seal-skins. Amongst these central tribes the men generally have an otter-skin, or some small scrap about as large as a pocket-handkerchief, which is barely sufficient to cover their backs as low down as their loins. It is laced across the breast by strings, and according as the wind blows, it is shifted from side to side. But these Fuegians in the canoe were quite naked, and even one full-grown woman was absolutely so. It was raining heavily, and the fresh water, together with the spray, trickled down her body. In another harbour not far distant, a woman, who was suckling a recently-born child, came one day alongside the vessel, and remained there out of mere curiosity, whilst the sleet fell and thawed on her naked bosom, and on the skin of her naked baby! These poor wretches were stunted in their growth, their hideous faces bedaubed with white paint, their skins filthy and greasy, their hair entangled, their voices discordant, and their gestures violent. Viewing such men, one can hardly make oneself believe that they are fellow-creatures, and inhabitants of the same world. It is a common subject of conjecture what pleasure in life some of the lower animals can enjoy: how much more reasonably the same question may be asked with respect to these barbarians! At night, five or six human beings, naked and scarcely protected from the wind and rain of this tempestuous climate, sleep on the wet ground coiled up like animals. Whenever it is low water, winter or summer, night or day, they must rise to pick shell-fish from the rocks; and the women either dive to collect sea-eggs, or sit patiently in their canoes, and with a baited hair-line without any hook, jerk out little fish. If a seal is killed, or the floating carcass of a putrid whale discovered, it is a feast; and such miserable food is assisted by a few tasteless berries and fungi.

They often suffer from famine: I heard Mr. Low, a sealing-master intimately acquainted with the natives of this country, give a curious account of the state of a party of one hundred and fifty natives on the west coast, who were very thin and in great distress. A succession of gales prevented the women from getting shell-fish on the rocks, and they could not go out in their canoes to catch seal. A small party of these men one morning set out, and the other Indians explained to him, that they were going a four days' journey for food: on their return, Low went to meet them, and he found them excessively tired, each man carrying a great square piece of putrid whales-blubber with a hole in the middle, through which they put their heads, like the Gauchos do through their ponchos or cloaks. As soon as the blubber was brought into a wigwam, an old man cut off thin slices, and muttering over them, broiled them for a minute, and distributed them to the famished party, who during this time preserved a profound silence. Mr. Low believes that whenever a whale is cast on shore, the natives bury large pieces of it in the sand, as a resource in time of famine; and a native boy, whom he had on board, once found a stock thus buried. The different tribes when at a war are cannibals. From the concurrent, but quite independent evidence of the boy taken by Mr. Low, and of Jemmy Button, it is certainly true, that when pressed in winter by hunger, they kill and devour their old women before they kill their dogs: the boy, being asked by Mr. Low why they did this, answered, "Doggies catch otters, old women no." This boy described the manner in which they are killed by being held over smoke and thus choked; he imitated their screams as a joke, and described the parts of their bodies which are considered best to eat. Horrid as such a death by the hands of their friends and relatives must be, the fears of the old women, when hunger begins to press, are more painful to think of; we were told that they then often run away into the mountains, but that they are pursued by the men and brought back to the slaughter-house at their own fire-sides!

Captain Fitz Roy could never ascertain that the Fuegians have any distinct belief in a future life. They sometimes bury their dead in caves, and sometimes in the mountain forests; we do not know what ceremonies they perform. Jemmy Button would not eat land-birds, because "eat dead men:" they are unwilling even to mention their dead friends. We have no reason to believe that they perform any sort of religious worship; though perhaps the muttering of the old man before he distributed the putrid blubber to his famished party, may be of this nature. Each family or tribe has a wizard or conjuring doctor, whose office we could never clearly ascertain. Jemmy believed in dreams, though not, as I have said, in the devil: I do not think that our Fuegians were much more superstitious than some of the sailors; for an old quarter-master firmly believed that the successive heavy gales, which we encountered off Cape Horn, were caused by our having the Fuegians on board. The nearest approach to a religious feeling which I heard of, was shown by York Minster, who, when Mr.

Bynoe shot some very young ducklings as specimens, declared in the most solemn manner, "Oh Mr. Bynoe, much rain, snow, blow much." This was evidently a retributive punishment for wasting human food. In a wild and excited manner he also related, that his brother, one day whilst returning to pick up some dead birds which he had left on the coast, observed some feathers blown by the wind. His brother said (York imitating his manner), "What that?" and crawling onwards, he peeped over the cliff, and saw "wild man" picking his birds; he crawled a little nearer, and then hurled down a great stone and killed him. York declared for a long time afterwards storms raged, and much rain and snow fell. As far as we could make out, he seemed to consider the elements themselves as the avenging agents: it is evident in this case, how naturally, in a race a little more advanced in culture, the elements would become personified. What the "bad wild men" were, has always appeared to me most mysterious: from what York said, when we found the place like the form of a hare, where a single man had slept the night before, I should have thought that they were thieves who had been driven from their tribes; but other obscure speeches made me doubt this; I have sometimes imagined that the most probable explanation was that they were insane.

The different tribes have no government or chief; yet each is surrounded by other hostile tribes, speaking different dialects, and separated from each other only by a deserted border or neutral territory: the cause of their warfare appears to be the means of subsistence. Their country is a broken mass of wild rocks, lofty hills, and useless forests: and these are viewed through mists and endless storms. The habitable land is reduced to the stones on the beach; in search of food they are compelled unceasingly to wander from spot to spot, and so steep is the coast, that they can only move about in their wretched canoes. They cannot know the feeling of having a home, and still less that of domestic affection; for the husband is to the wife a brutal master to a laborious slave. Was a more horrid deed ever perpetrated, than that witnessed on the west coast by Byron,[5] who saw a wretched mother pick up her bleeding dying infant-boy, whom her husband had mercilessly dashed on the stones for dropping a basket of sea-eggs! How little can the higher powers of the mind be brought into play: what is there for imagination to picture, for reason to compare, for judgment to decide upon? to knock a limpet from the rock does not require even cunning, that lowest power of the mind. Their skill in some respects may

---

[5]John **Byron** (1723–1786) circumnavigated the globe.

be compared to the instinct of animals; for it is not improved by experience: the canoe, their most ingenious work, poor as it is, has remained the same, as we know from Drake,[6] for the last two hundred and fifty years.

Whilst beholding these savages, one asks, whence have they come? What could have tempted, or what change compelled a tribe of men, to leave the fine regions of the north, to travel down the Cordillera[7] or backbone of America, to invent and build canoes, which are not used by the tribes of Chile, Peru, and Brazil, and then to enter on one of the most inhospitable countries within the limits of the globe? Although such reflections must at first seize on the mind, yet we may feel sure that they are partly erroneous. There is no reason to believe that the Fuegians decrease in number; therefore we must suppose that they enjoy a sufficient share of happiness, of whatever kind it may be, to render life worth having. Nature by making habit omnipotent, and its effects hereditary, has fitted the Fuegian to the climate and the productions of his miserable country.... (Chapter 10)

1839, 1860

∼

from On the Origin of Species
Struggle for Existence

Before entering on the subject of this chapter, I must make a few preliminary remarks, to show how the struggle for existence bears on Natural Selection. It has been seen in the last chapter that amongst organic beings in a state of nature there is some individual variability: indeed I am not aware that this has ever been disputed. It is immaterial for us whether a multitude of doubtful forms be called species or sub-species or varieties; what rank, for instance, the two or three hundred doubtful forms of British plants are entitled to hold, if the existence of any well-marked varieties be admitted. But the mere existence of individual variability and of some few well-marked varieties, though necessary as the foundation for the work, helps us but little in understanding how species arise in nature. How have all those exquisite adaptations of one part of the organisation to another part, and to the conditions of life, and of one organic being to an-

other being, been perfected? We see these beautiful co-adaptations most plainly in the woodpecker and the mistle-toe; and only a little less plainly in the humblest parasite which clings to the hairs of a quadruped or feathers of a bird; in the structure of the beetle which dives through the water, in the plumed seed which is wafted by the gentlest breeze; in short, we see beautiful adaptations everywhere and in every part of the organic world.

Again, it may be asked, how is it that varieties, which I have called incipient species, become ultimately converted into good and distinct species, which in most cases obviously differ from each other far more than do the varieties of the same species? How do those groups of species, which constitute what are called distinct genera, and which differ from each other more than do the species of the same genus, arise? All these results, as we shall more fully see in the next chapter, follow from the struggle for life. Owing to this struggle, variations, however slight and from whatever cause proceeding, if they be in any degree profitable to the individuals of a species, in their infinitely complex relations to other organic beings and to their physical conditions of life, will tend to the preservation of such individuals, and will generally be inherited by the offspring. The offspring, also, will thus have a better chance of surviving, for, of the many individuals of any species which are periodically born, but a small number can survive. I have called this principle, by which each slight variation, if useful, is preserved, by the term Natural Selection, in order to mark its relation to man's power of selection. But the expression often used by Mr. Herbert Spencer of the Survival of the Fittest is more accurate, and is sometimes equally convenient. We have seen that man by selection can certainly produce great results, and can adapt organic beings to his own uses, through the accumulation of slight but useful variations, given to him by the hand of Nature. But Natural Selection, as we shall hereafter see, is a power incessantly ready for action, and is as immeasurably superior to man's feeble efforts, as the works of Nature are to those of Art.

We will now discuss in a little more detail the struggle for existence. In my future work this subject will be treated, as it well deserves, at greater length. The elder De Candolle[1] and Lyell have largely and philosophically shown that all organic beings are exposed to severe competition. In regard to plants, no one has treated this subject with more spirit and ability than W. Herbert, Dean of Manchester, evidently the

---

[6]Sir Francis **Drake** (1540–1596) visited Tierra del Fuego while circumnavigating the globe.

[7]**Cordillera**: mountain ranges that make up the Andes.

---

[1]Augustin Pyrame **de Candolle** (1778–1841): Swiss botanist. William **Herbert** (1778–1847): clergyman, poet, botanist.

result of his great horticultural knowledge. Nothing is easier than to admit in words the truth of the universal struggle for life, or more difficult—at least I have found it so—than constantly to bear this conclusion in mind. Yet unless it be thoroughly engrained in the mind, the whole economy of nature, with every fact on distribution, rarity, abundance, extinction, and variation, will be dimly seen or quite misunderstood. We behold the face of nature bright with gladness, we often see superabundance of food; we do not see or we forget, that the birds which are idly singing round us mostly live on insects or seeds, and are thus constantly destroying life; or we forget how largely these songsters, or their eggs, or their nestlings, are destroyed by birds and beasts of prey; we do not always bear in mind, that, though food may be now superabundant, it is not so at all seasons of each recurring year.

— THE TERM, STRUGGLE FOR EXISTENCE, USED IN A LARGE SENSE —

I should premise that I use this term in a large and metaphorical sense including dependence of one being on another, and including (which is more important) not only the life of the individual, but success in leaving progeny. Two canine animals, in a time of dearth, may be truly said to struggle with each other which shall get food and live. But a plant on the edge of a desert is said to struggle for life against the drought, though more properly it should be said to be dependent on the moisture. A plant which annually produces a thousand seeds, of which only one of an average comes to maturity, may be more truly said to struggle with the plants of the same and other kinds which already clothe the ground. The mistletoe is dependent on the apple and a few other trees, but can only in a far-fetched sense be said to struggle with these trees, for, if too many of these parasites grow on the same tree, it languishes and dies. But several seedling mistletoes, growing close together on the same branch, may more truly be said to struggle with each other. As the mistletoe is disseminated by birds, its existence depends on them; and it may metaphorically be said to struggle with other fruit-bearing plants, in tempting the birds to devour and thus disseminate its seeds. In these several senses, which pass into each other, I use for convenience' sake the general term of Struggle for Existence.

— GEOMETRICAL RATIO OF INCREASE —

A struggle for existence inevitably follows from the high rate at which all organic beings tend to increase. Every being, which during its natural lifetime produces several eggs or seeds, must suffer destruction during some period of its life, and during some season or occasional year, otherwise, on the principle of geometrical increase, its numbers would quickly become so inordinately great that no country could support the product. Hence, as more individuals are produced than can possibly survive, there must in every case be a struggle for existence, either one individual with another of the same species, or with the individuals of distinct species, or with the physical conditions of life. It is the doctrine of Malthus[2] applied with manifold force to the whole animal and vegetable kingdoms; for in this case there can be no artificial increase of food, and no prudential restraint from marriage. Although some species may be now increasing, more or less rapidly, in numbers, all cannot do so, for the world would not hold them.

There is no exception to the rule that every organic being naturally increases at so high a rate, that, if not destroyed, the earth would soon be covered by the progeny of a single pair. Even slow-breeding man has doubled in twenty-five years, and at this rate, in less than a thousand years, there would literally not be standing-room for his progeny. Linnæus[3] has calculated that if an annual plant produced only two seeds—and there is no plant so unproductive as this—and their seedlings next year produced two, and so on, then in twenty years there would be a million plants. The elephant is reckoned the slowest breeder of all known animals, and I have taken some pains to estimate its probable minimum rate of natural increase; it will be safest to assume that it begins breeding when thirty years old, and goes on breeding till ninety years old, bringing forth six young in the interval, and surviving till one hundred years old; if this be so, after a period of from 740 to 750 years there would be nearly nineteen million elephants alive, descended from the first pair.

But we have better evidence on this subject than mere theoretical calculations, namely, the numerous recorded cases of the astonishingly rapid increase of various animals in a state of nature, when circumstances have been favourable to them during two or three following seasons. Still more striking is the evidence from our domestic animals of many kinds which have run wild in several parts of the world; if the statements of the rate of increase of slow-breeding cattle and horses in South America, and latterly in Australia, had not been well authenticated, they would have been incredible. So it is with plants; cases could be given of

---

[2]Thomas Robert **Malthus** (1766–1834): economist who showed that unchecked population growth will always outrun food supply.

[3]Carolus **Linnæus** (1707–1778): Swedish botanist and naturalist.

introduced plants which have become common throughout whole islands in a period of less than ten years. Several of the plants, such as the cardoon and a tall thistle, which are now the commonest over the wide plains of La Plata, clothing square leagues of surface almost to the exclusion of every other plant, have been introduced from Europe; and there are plants which now range in India, as I hear from Dr. Falconer[4] from Cape Comorin to the Himalaya, which have been imported from America since its discovery. In such cases, and endless others could be given, no one supposes, that the fertility of the animals or plants has been suddenly and temporarily increased in any sensible degree. The obvious explanation is that the conditions of life have been highly favourable, and that there has consequently been less destruction of the old and young, and that nearly all the young have been enabled to breed. Their geometrical ratio of increase, the result of which never fails to be surprising, simply explains their extraordinarily rapid increase and wide diffusion in their new homes.

In a state of nature almost every full-grown plant annually produces seed, and amongst animals there are very few which do not annually pair. Hence we may confidently assert, that all plants and animals are tending to increase at a geometrical ratio,—that all would rapidly stock every station in which they could anyhow exist,—and that this geometrical tendency to increase must be checked by destruction at some period of life. Our familiarity with the larger domestic animals tends, I think, to mislead us: we see no great destruction falling on them, but we do not keep in mind that thousands are annually slaughtered for food, and that in a state of nature an equal number would have somehow to be disposed of.

The only difference between organisms which annually produce eggs or seeds by the thousand, and those which produce extremely few, is, that the slow–breeders would require a few more years to people, under favourable conditions, a whole district, let it be ever so large. The condor lays a couple of eggs and the ostrich a score, and yet in the same country the condor may be the more numerous of the two: the Fulmar petrel lays but one egg, yet it is believed to be the most numerous bird in the world. One fly deposits hundreds of eggs, and another, like the hippobosca, a single one; but this difference does not determine how many individuals of the two species can be supported in a district. A large number of eggs is of some importance

to those species which depend on a fluctuating amount of food, for it allows them rapidly to increase in number. But the real importance of a large number of eggs or seeds is to make up for much destruction at some period of life; and this period in the great majority of cases is an early one. If an animal can in any way protect its own eggs or young, a small number may be produced, and yet the average stock be fully kept up; but if many eggs or young are destroyed, many must be produced, or the species will become extinct. It would suffice to keep up the full number of a tree, which lived on an average for a thousand years, if a single seed were produced once in a thousand years, supposing that this seed were never destroyed and could be ensured to germinate in a fitting place. So that, in all cases, the average number of any animal or plant depends only indirectly on the number of its eggs or seeds.

In looking at Nature, it is most necessary to keep the foregoing considerations always in mind—never to forget that every single organic being may be said to be striving to the utmost to increase in numbers; that each lives by a struggle at some period of its life; that heavy destruction inevitably falls either on the young or old, during each generation or at recurrent intervals. Lighten any check, mitigate the destruction ever so little, and the number of the species will almost instantaneously increase to any amount. . . .

— COMPLEX RELATIONS OF ALL ANIMALS AND PLANTS TO EACH OTHER IN THE STRUGGLE FOR EXISTENCE —

Many cases are on record showing how complex and unexpected are the checks and relations between organic beings, which have to struggle together in the same country. I will give only a single instance, which, though a simple one, interested me. In Staffordshire, on the estate of a relation, where I had ample means of investigation, there was a large and extremely barren heath, which had never been touched by the hand of man; but several hundred acres of exactly the same nature had been enclosed twenty-five years previously and planted with Scotch fir. The change in the native vegetation of the planted part of the heath was most remarkable, more than is generally seen in passing from one quite different soil to another: not only the proportional numbers of the heath-plants were wholly changed, but twelve species of plants (not counting grasses and carices) flourished in the plantations, which could not be found on the heath. The effect on the insects must have been still greater, for six insectivorous birds were very common in the plantations, which were not to be seen on the heath; and the heath was frequented by two or three distinct insectivorous birds. Here

[4]Hugh **Falconer** (1808–1865): Scottish paleontologist and botanist.

we see how potent has been the effect of the introduction of a single tree, nothing whatever else having been done, with the exception of the land having been enclosed, so that cattle could not enter. But how important an element enclosure is, I plainly saw near Farnham, in Surrey. Here there are extensive heaths, with a few clumps of old Scotch firs on the distant hill–tops: within the last ten years large spaces have been enclosed, and self-sown firs are now springing up in multitudes, so close together that all cannot live. When I ascertained that these young trees had not been sown or planted, I was so much surprised at their numbers that I went to several points of view, whence I could examine hundreds of acres of the unenclosed heath, and literally I could not see a single Scotch fir, except the old planted clumps. But on looking closely between the stems of the heath, I found a multitude of seedlings and little trees which had been perpetually browsed down by the cattle. In one square yard, at a point some hundred yards distant from one of the old clumps, I counted thirty-two little trees; and one of them, with twenty-six rings of growth, had, during many years tried to raise its head above the stems of the heath, and had failed. No wonder that, as soon as the land was enclosed, it became thickly clothed with vigorously growing young firs. Yet the heath was so extremely barren and so extensive that no one would ever have imagined that cattle would have so closely and effectually searched it for food.

Here we see that cattle absolutely determine the existence of the Scotch fir; but in several parts of the world insects determine the existence of cattle. Perhaps Paraguay offers the most curious instance of this; for here neither cattle nor horses nor dogs have ever run wild, though they swarm southward and northward in a feral state; and Azara and Rengger[5] have shown that this is caused by the greater number in Paraguay of a certain fly, which lays its eggs in the navels of these animals when first born. The increase of these flies, numerous as they are, must be habitually checked by some means, probably by other parasitic insects. Hence, if certain insectivorous birds were to decrease in Paraguay, the parasitic insects would probably increase; and this would lessen the number of the navel-frequenting flies—then cattle and horses would become feral, and this would certainly greatly alter (as indeed I have observed in parts of South America) the vegetation: this again would largely affect the insects; and this, as we have just seen in Staffordshire, the insectivorous birds, and so onward in ever-increasing circles of complexity. Not that under nature the relations will ever be as simple as this. Battle within battle must be continually recurring with varying success; and yet in the long-run the forces are so nicely balanced, that the face of nature remains for long periods of time uniform, though assuredly the merest trifle would give the victory to one organic being over another. Nevertheless, so profound is our ignorance, and so high our presumption, that we marvel when we hear of the extinction of an organic being; and as we do not see the cause, we invoke cataclysms to desolate the world, or invent laws on the duration of the forms of life! . . .

In the case of every species, many different checks, acting at different periods of life, and during different seasons or years, probably come into play; some one check or some few being generally the most potent; but all will concur in determining the average number or even the existence of the species. In some cases it can be shown that widely–different checks act on the same species in different districts. When we look at the plants and bushes clothing an entangled bank, we are tempted to attribute their proportional numbers and kinds to what we call chance. But how false a view is this! Every one has heard that when an American forest is cut down, a very different vegetation springs up; but it has been observed that ancient Indian ruins in the Southern United States, which must formerly have been cleared of trees, now display the same beautiful diversity and proportion of kinds as in the surrounding virgin forest. What a struggle must have gone on during long centuries between the several kinds of trees, each annually scattering its seeds by the thousand; what war between insect and insect—between insects, snails, and other animals with birds and beasts of prey—all striving to increase, all feeding on each other, or on the trees, their seeds and seedlings, or on the other plants which first clothed the ground and thus checked the growth of the trees! Throw up a handful of feathers, and all fall to the ground according to definite laws; but how simple is the problem where each shall fall compared to that of the action and reaction of the innumerable plants and animals which have determined, in the course of centuries, the proportional numbers and kinds of trees now growing on the old Indian ruins!

The dependency of one organic being on another, as of a parasite on its prey, lies generally between beings remote in the scale of nature. This is likewise sometimes the case with those which may be strictly said to struggle with each other for existence, as in the case of locusts and grass-feeding quadrupeds. But the struggle will almost invariably be most severe between the individuals of the same species,

---

[5]Felix de **Azara**(1746–1821): Spanish explorer. John Rudolph **Rengger** (1795–1832): Swiss doctor who wrote about Paraguay.

for they frequent the same districts, require the same food, and are exposed to the same dangers. In the case of varieties of the same species, the struggle will generally be almost equally severe, and we sometimes see the contest soon decided: for instance, if several varieties of wheat be sown together, and the mixed seed be resown, some of the varieties which best suit the soil or climate, or are naturally the most fertile, will beat the others and so yield more seed, and will consequently in a few years supplant the other varieties. To keep up a mixed stock of even such extremely close varieties as the variously–coloured sweet peas, they must be each year harvested separately, and the seed then mixed in due proportion, otherwise the weaker kinds will steadily decrease in number and disappear. So again with the varieties of sheep; it has been asserted that certain mountain–varieties will starve out other mountain–varieties, so that they cannot be kept together. The same result has followed from keeping together different varieties of the medicinal leech. It may even be doubted whether the varieties of any of our domestic plants or animals have so exactly the same strength, habits, and constitution, that the original proportions of a mixed stock (crossing being prevented) could be kept up for half-a-dozen generations, if they were allowed to struggle together, in the same manner as beings in a state of nature, and if the seed or young were not annually preserved in due proportion.

— STRUGGLE FOR LIFE MOST SEVERE BETWEEN INDIVIDUALS AND VARIETIES OF THE SAME SPECIES —

As the species of the same genus usually have, though by no means invariably, much similarity in habits and constitution, and always in structure, the struggle will generally be more severe between them, if they come into competition with each other, than between the species of distinct genera. We see this in the recent extension over parts of the United States of one species of swallow having caused the decrease of another species. The recent increase of the missel-thrush in parts of Scotland has caused the decrease of the song-thrush. How frequently we hear of one species of rat taking the place of another species under the most different climates! In Russia the small Asiatic cockroach has everywhere driven before it its great congener.[6] In Australia the imported hive-bee is rapidly exterminating the small, stingless native bee. One species of charlock has been known to supplant another species; and so in other cases.

We can dimly see why the competition should be most severe between allied forms, which fill nearly the same place in the economy of nature; but probably in no one case could we precisely say why one species has been victorious over another in the great battle of life.

A corollary of the highest importance may be deduced from the foregoing remarks, namely, that the structure of every organic being is related, in the most essential yet often hidden manner, to that of all the other organic beings, with which it comes into competition for food or residence, or from which it has to escape, or on which it preys. This is obvious in the structure of the teeth and talons of the tiger; and in that of the legs and claws of the parasite which clings to the hair on the tiger's body. But in the beautifully plumed seed of the dandelion, and in the flattened and fringed legs of the water-beetle, the relation seems at first confined to the elements of air and water. Yet the advantage of plumed seeds no doubt stands in the closest relation to the land being already thickly clothed with other plants so that the seeds may be widely distributed and fall on unoccupied ground. In the water-beetle, the structure of its legs, so well adapted for diving, allows it to compete with other aquatic insects, to hunt for its own prey, and to escape serving as prey to other animals.

The store of nutriment laid up within the seeds of many plants seem at first sight to have no sort of relation to other plants. But from the strong growth of young plants produced from such seeds, as peas and beans, when sown in the midst of long grass, it may be suspected that the chief use of the nutriment in the seed is to favour the growth of the seedlings, whilst struggling with other plants growing vigorously all around.

Look at a plant in the midst of its range! why does it not double or quadruple its numbers? We know that it can perfectly well withstand a little more heat or cold, dampness or dryness, for elsewhere it ranges into slightly hotter or colder, damper or drier districts. In this case we can clearly see that if we wish in imagination to give the plant the power of increasing in number, we should have to give it some advantage over its competitors, or over the animals which prey on it. On the confines of its geographical range, a change of constitution with respect to climate would clearly be an advantage to our plant; but we have reason to believe that only a few plants or animals range so far, that they are destroyed exclusively by the rigour of the climate. Not until we reach the extreme confines of life, in the Arctic regions or on the borders of an utter desert, will competition cease. The land may be extremely cold or dry, yet there will be competition between some few species, or

---

[6]**congener:** member of the same kind or class. **charlock:** weed.

between the individuals of the same species, for the warmest or dampest spots.

Hence we can see that when a plant or animal is placed in a new country amongst new competitors, the conditions of its life will generally be changed in an essential manner, although the climate may be exactly the same as in its former home. If its average numbers are to increase in its new home, we should have to modify it in a different way to what we should have had to do in its native country; for we should have to give it some advantage over a different set of competitors or enemies.

It is good thus to try in imagination to give to any one species an advantage over another. Probably in no single instance should we know what to do. This ought to convince us of our ignorance on the mutual relations of all organic beings; a conviction as necessary, as it is difficult to acquire. All that we can do, is to keep steadily in mind that each organic being is striving to increase in a geometrical ratio; that each at some period of its life, during some season of the year, during each generation or at intervals, has to struggle for life and to suffer great destruction. When we reflect on this struggle, we may console ourselves with the full belief, that the war of nature is not incessant, that no fear is felt, that death is generally prompt, and that the vigorous, the healthy, and the happy survive and multiply. (Chapter 3)

Natural Selection; or the Survival of the Fittest

How will the struggle for existence, briefly discussed in the last chapter, act in regard to variation? Can the principle of selection, which we have seen is so potent in the hands of man, apply under nature? I think we shall see that it can act most efficiently. Let the endless number of slight variations and individual differences occurring in our domestic productions, and, in a lesser degree, in those under nature, be borne in mind; as well as the strength of the hereditary tendency. Under domestication, it may be truly said that the whole organisation becomes in some degree plastic. But the variability, which we almost universally meet with in our domestic productions, is not directly produced, as Hooker and Asa Gray[7] have well remarked, by man; he can neither originate varieties, nor prevent their occurrence; he can only preserve and accumulate such as do occur. Unintentionally he exposes organic beings to new and changing conditions of life, and variability ensues; but similar changes of condi-

tions might and do occur under nature. Let it also be borne in mind how infinitely complex and close-fitting are the mutual relations of all organic beings to each other and to their physical conditions of life; and consequently what infinitely varied diversities of structure might be of use to each being under changing conditions of life. Can it, then, be thought improbable, seeing that variations useful to man have undoubtedly occurred, that other variations useful in some way to each being in the great and complex battle of life, should occur in the course of many successive generations? If such do occur, can we doubt (remembering that many more individuals are born than can possibly survive) that individuals having any advantage, however slight, over others, would have the best chance of surviving and of procreating their kind? On the other hand, we may feel sure that any variation in the least degree injurious would be rigidly destroyed. This preservation of favourable individual differences and variations, and the destruction of those which are injurious, I have called Natural Selection, or the Survival of the Fittest. Variations neither useful nor injurious would not be affected by natural selection, and would be left either a fluctuating element, as perhaps we see in certain polymorphic species, or would ultimately become fixed, owing to the nature of the organism and the nature of the conditions.

Several writers have misapprehended or objected to the term Natural Selection. Some have even imagined that natural selection induces variability, whereas it implies only the preservation of such variations as arise and are beneficial to the being under its conditions of life. No one objects to agriculturists speaking of the potent effects of man's selection; and in this case the individual differences given by nature, which man for some object selects, must of necessity first occur. Others have objected that the term selection implies conscious choice in the animals which become modified; and it has even been urged that, as plants have no volition, natural selection is not applicable to them! In the literal sense of the word, no doubt, natural selection is a false term; but who ever objected to chemists speaking of the elective affinities of the various elements?—and yet an acid cannot strictly be said to elect the base with which it in preference combines. It has been said that I speak of natural selection as an active power or Deity; but who objects to an author speaking of the attraction of gravity as ruling the movements of the planets? Every one knows what is meant and is implied by such metaphorical expressions; and they are almost necessary for brevity. So again it is difficult to avoid personifying the word Nature; but I mean by Nature, only the aggregate action and product of many natural laws, and by laws the sequence of events as ascertained by us.

---

[7]Sir Joseph Dalton **Hooker** (1817–1911): English botanist. **Asa Gray** (1810–1888): U.S. botanist.

With a little familiarity such superficial objections will be forgotten.

We shall best understand the probable course of natural selection by taking the case of a country undergoing some slight physical change, for instance, of climate. The proportional numbers of its inhabitants will almost immediately undergo a change, and some species will probably become extinct. We may conclude, from what we have seen of the intimate and complex manner in which the inhabitants of each country are bound together, that any change in the numerical proportions of the inhabitants, independently of the change of climate itself, would seriously affect the others. If the country were open on its borders, new forms would certainly immigrate, and this would likewise seriously disturb the relations of some of the former inhabitants. Let it be remembered how powerful the influence of a single introduced tree or mammal has been shown to be. But in the case of an island, or of a country partly surrounded by barriers, into which new and better adapted forms could not freely enter, we should then have places in the economy of nature which would assuredly be better filled up, if some of the original inhabitants were in some manner modified; for, had the area been open to immigration, these same places would have been seized on by intruders. In such cases, slight modifications, which in any way favoured the individuals of any species, by better adapting them to their altered conditions, would tend to be preserved; and natural selection would have free scope for the work of improvement.

We have good reason to believe, as shown in the first chapter, that changes in the conditions of life give a tendency to increased variability; and in the foregoing cases the conditions have changed, and this would manifestly be favourable to natural selection, by affording a better chance of the occurrence of profitable variations. Unless such occur, natural selection can do nothing. Under the term of "variations," it must never be forgotten that mere individual differences are included. As man can produce a great result with his domestic animals and plants by adding up in any given direction individual differences, so could natural selection, but far more easily from having incomparably longer time for action. Nor do I believe that any great physical change, as of climate, or any unusual degree of isolation to check immigration, is necessary in order that new and unoccupied places should be left, for natural selection to fill up by improving some of the varying inhabitants. For as all the inhabitants of each country are struggling together with nicely balanced forces, extremely slight modifications in the structure or habits of one species would often give it an advantage over others; and still further modifications of the same kind would often still further increase the advantage, as long as the species continued under the same conditions of life and profited by similar means of subsistence and defence. No country can be named in which all the native inhabitants are now so perfectly adapted to each other and to the physical conditions under which they live, that none of them could be still better adapted or improved; for in all countries, the natives have been so far conquered by naturalised productions, that they have allowed some foreigners to take firm possession of the land. And as foreigners have thus in every country beaten some of the natives, we may safely conclude that the natives might have been modified with advantage, so as to have better resisted the intruders.

As man can produce, and certainly has produced, a great result by his methodical and unconscious means of selection, what may not natural selection effect? Man can act only on external and visible characters: Nature, if I may be allowed to personify the natural preservation or survival of the fittest, cares nothing for appearances, except in so far as they are useful to any being. She can act on every internal organ, on every shade of constitutional difference, on the whole machinery of life. Man selects only for his own good: Nature only for that of the being which she tends. Every selected character is fully exercised by her, as is implied by the fact of their selection. Man keeps the natives of many climates in the same country; he seldom exercises each selected character in some peculiar and fitting manner; he feeds a long and a short beaked pigeon on the same food; he does not exercise a long-backed or long-legged quadruped in any peculiar manner; he exposes sheep with long and short wool to the same climate. He does not allow the most vigorous males to struggle for the females. He does not rigidly destroy all inferior animals, but protects during each varying season, as far as lies in his power, all his productions. He often begins his selection by some half-monstrous form; or at least by some modification prominent enough to catch the eye or to be plainly useful to him. Under nature, the slightest differences of structure or constitution may well turn the nicely–balanced scale in the struggle for life, and so be preserved. How fleeting are the wishes and efforts of man! how short his time! and consequently how poor will be his results, compared with those accumulated by Nature during whole geological periods! Can we wonder, then, that Nature's productions should be far "truer" in character than man's productions; that they should be infinitely better adapted to the most complex conditions of life, and should plainly bear the stamp of far higher workmanship?

It may metaphorically be said that natural selection is daily and hourly scrutinising, throughout the world, the slightest variations; rejecting those that are bad, preserving and adding up all that are good; silently and insensibly working, *whenever and wherever opportunity offers*, at the improvement of each organic being in relation to its organic and inorganic conditions of life. We see nothing of these slow changes in progress, until the hand of time has marked the lapse of ages, and then so imperfect is our view into long-past geological ages, that we see only that the forms of life are now different from what they formerly were.

In order that any great amount of modification should be effected in a species, a variety when once formed must again, perhaps after a long interval of time, vary or present individual differences of the same favourable nature as before; and these must be again preserved, and so onwards, step by step. Seeing that individual differences of the same kind perpetually recur, this can hardly be considered as an unwarrantable assumption. But whether it is true, we can judge only by seeing how far the hypothesis accords with and explains the general phenomena of nature. On the other hand, the ordinary belief that the amount of possible variation is a strictly limited quantity is likewise a simple assumption.

Although natural selection can act only through and for the good of each being, yet characters and structures, which we are apt to consider as of very trifling importance, may thus be acted on. When we see leaf-eating insects green, and bark-feeders mottled-gray; the alpine ptarmigan white in winter, the red grouse the colour of heather, we must believe that these tints are of service to these birds and insects in preserving them from danger. Grouse, if not destroyed at some period of their lives, would increase in countless numbers; they are known to suffer largely from birds of prey; and hawks are guided by eyesight to their prey—so much so, that on parts of the Continent persons are warned not to keep white pigeons, as being the most liable to destruction. Hence natural selection might be effective in giving the proper colour to each kind of grouse, and in keeping that colour, when once acquired, true and constant. Nor ought we to think that the occasional destruction of an animal of any particular colour would produce little effect: we should remember how essential it is in a flock of white sheep to destroy a lamb with the faintest trace of black. We have seen how the colour of the hogs, which feed on the "paint-root" in Virginia, determines whether they shall live or die. In plants, the down on the fruit and the colour of the flesh are considered by botanists as characters of the most trifling importance: yet we hear from an excellent horticulturist, Downing,[8] that in the United States

smooth-skinned fruits suffer far more from a beetle, a Curculio, than those with down: that purple plums suffer far more from a certain disease than yellow plums; whereas another disease attacks yellow-fleshed peaches far more than those with other coloured flesh. If, with all the aids of art, these slight differences make a great difference in cultivating the several varieties, assuredly, in a state of nature, where the trees would have to struggle with other trees and with a host of enemies, such differences would effectually settle which variety, whether a smooth or downy, a yellow or a purple fleshed fruit, should succeed.

In looking at many small points of difference between species, which, as far as our ignorance permits us to judge, seem quite unimportant, we must not forget that climate, food, &, have no doubt produced some direct effect. It is also necessary to bear in mind that, owing to the law of correlation, when one part varies, and the variations are accumulated through natural selection, other modifications, often of the most unexpected nature, will ensue.

As we see that those variations which, under domestication, appear at any particular period of life, tend to reappear in the offspring at the same period;—for instance, in the shape, size, and flavour of the seeds of the many varieties of our culinary and agricultural plants; in the caterpillar and cocoon stages of the varieties of the silk-worm; in the eggs of poultry, and in the colour of the down of their chickens; in the horns of our sheep and cattle when nearly adult;—so in a state of nature natural selection will be enabled to act on and modify organic beings at any age, by the accumulation of variations profitable at that age, and by their inheritance at a corresponding age. If it profit a plant to have its seeds more and more widely disseminated by the wind, I can see no greater difficulty in this being effected through natural selection, than in the cotton-planter increasing and improving by selection the down in the pods on his cotton-trees. Natural selection may modify and adapt the larva of an insect to a score of contingencies, wholly different from those which concern the mature insect; and these modifications may effect, through correlation, the structure of the adult. So, conversely, modifications in the adult may affect the structure of the larva; but in all cases natural selection will ensure that they shall not be injurious: for if they were so, the species would become extinct.

Natural selection will modify the structure of the young in relation to the parent, and of the parent in relation to the young. In social animals it will adapt the structure of each individual for the benefit of the whole community; if the community profits by the selected change. What natural selection cannot do, is to modify the

---

[8]Andrew Jackson **Downing** (1815–1852): U.S. horticulturalist.

structure of one species, without giving it any advantage, for the good of another species; and though statements to this effect may be found in works of natural history, I cannot find one case which will bear investigation. A structure used only once in an animal's life, if of high importance to it, might be modified to any extent by natural selection; for instance, the great jaws possessed by certain insects, used exclusively for opening the cocoon—or the hard tip to the beak of unhatched birds, used for breaking the eggs. It has been asserted, that of the best short-beaked tumbler-pigeons a greater number perish in the egg than are able to get out of it; so that fanciers assist in the act of hatching. Now, if nature had to make the beak of a full-grown pigeon very short for the bird's own advantage, the process of modification would be very slow, and there would be simultaneously the most rigorous selection of all the young birds within the egg, which had the most powerful and hardest beaks, for all with weak beaks would inevitably perish; or, more delicate and more easily broken shells might be selected, the thickness of the shell being known to vary like every other structure.

It may be well here to remark that with all beings there must be much fortuitous destruction, which can have little or no influence on the course of natural selection. For instance a vast number of eggs or seeds are annually devoured, and these could be modified through natural selection only if they varied in some manner which protected them from their enemies. Yet many of these eggs or seeds would perhaps, if not destroyed, have yielded individuals better adapted to their conditions of life than any of those which happened to survive. So again a vast number of mature animals and plants, whether or not they be the best adapted to their conditions, must be annually destroyed by accidental causes, which would not be in the least degree mitigated by certain changes of structure or constitution which would in other ways be beneficial to the species. But let the destruction of the adults be ever so heavy, if the number which can exist in any district be not wholly kept down by such causes,—or again let the destruction of eggs or seeds be so great that only a hundredth or a thousandth part are developed,—yet of those which do survive, the best adapted individuals, supposing that there is any variability in a favourable direction, will tend to propagate their kind in larger numbers than the less well adapted. If the numbers be wholly kept down by the causes just indicated, as will often have been the case, natural selection will be powerless in certain beneficial directions; but this is no valid objection to its efficiency at other times and in other ways; for we are far from having any reason to suppose that many species ever undergo modification and improvement at the same time in the same area. . . .

— SUMMARY OF CHAPTER —

If under changing conditions of life organic beings present individual differences in almost every part of their structure, and this cannot be disputed; if there be, owing to their geometrical rate of increase, a severe struggle for life at some age, season, or year, and this certainly cannot be disputed; then, considering the infinite complexity of the relations of all organic beings to each other and to their conditions of life, causing an infinite diversity in structure, constitution and habits, to be advantageous to them, it would be a most extraordinary fact if no variations had ever occurred useful to each being's own welfare, in the same manner as so many variations have occurred useful to man. But if variations useful to any organic being ever do occur, assuredly individuals thus characterised will have the best chance of being preserved in the struggle for life; and from the strong principle of inheritance, these will tend to produce offspring similarly characterised. This principle of preservation, or the survival of the fittest, I have called natural selection. It leads to the improvement of each creature in relation to its organic and inorganic conditions of life; and consequently, in most cases, to what must be regarded as an advance in organisation. Nevertheless, low and simple forms will long endure if well fitted for their simple conditions of life.

Natural selection, on the principle of qualities being inherited at corresponding ages, can modify the egg, seed or young, as easily as the adult. Amongst many animals, sexual selection will have given its aid to ordinary selection, by assuring to the most vigorous and best adapted males the greatest number of offspring. Sexual selection will also give characters useful to the males alone, in their struggles or rivalry with other males; and these characters will be transmitted to one sex or to both sexes, according to the form of inheritance which prevails.

Whether natural selection has really thus acted in adapting the various forms of life to their several conditions and stations, must be judged by the general tenor and balance of evidence given in the following chapters. But we have already seen how it entails extinction; and how largely extinction has acted in the world's history, geology plainly declares. Natural Selection, also, leads to divergence of character; for the more organic beings diverge in structure, habits, and constitution, by so much the more can a large number be supported on the area,—of which we see proof by looking to the inhabitants of any small spot, and to the productions naturalised in foreign lands. Therefore, during the modification of the descendants of any one species, and during the incessant struggle of all species to increase in numbers, the more diversified the descendants become, the better will be their chance of success in the battle for life. Thus the small differences distinguishing varieties of the same species, steadily tend to increase, till they equal the greater differences between species of the same genus, or even of distinct genera.

We have seen that it is the common, the widely diffused and widely–ranging species, belonging to the larger genera within each class, which vary most; and these tend to transmit to their modified offspring that superiority which now makes them dominant in their own countries. Natural selection, as has just been remarked, leads to divergence of character and to much extinction of the less improved and intermediate forms of life. On these principles, the nature of the affinities, and the generally well–defined distinctions between the innumerable organic beings in each class throughout the world, may be explained. It is a truly wonderful fact—the wonder of which we are apt to overlook from familiarity—that all animals and all plants throughout all time and space should be related to each other in groups, subordinate to groups, in the manner which we everywhere behold—namely, varieties of the same species most closely related, species of the same genus less closely and unequally related, forming sections and sub-genera, species of distinct genera much less closely related, and genera related in different degrees, forming sub-families, families, orders, sub-classes and classes. The several subordinate groups in any class cannot be ranked in a single file, but seem clustered round points, and these round other points, and so on in almost endless cycles. If species had been independently created, no explanation would have been possible of this kind of classification; but it is explained through inheritance and the complex action of natural selection, entailing extinction and divergence of character, as we have seen illustrated in the diagram.

The affinities of all the beings of the same class have sometimes been represented by a great tree. I believe this simile largely speaks the truth. The green and budding twigs may represent existing species; and those produced during former years may represent the long succession of extinct species. At each period of growth all the growing twigs have tried to branch out on all sides, and to overtop and kill the surrounding twigs and branches, in the same manner as species and groups of species have at all times overmastered other species in the great battle for life. The limbs divided into great branches, and these into lesser and lesser branches, were themselves once, when the tree was young, budding twigs; and this connection of the former and present buds by ramifying branches may well represent the classification of all extinct and living species in groups subordinate to groups. Of the many twigs which flourished when the tree was a mere bush, only two or three, now grown into great branches, yet survive and bear the other branches; so with the species which lived during long-past geological periods, very few have left living and modified descendants. From the first growth of the tree, many a limb and branch has decayed and dropped off; and these fallen branches of various sizes may represent those families, and genera which have now no living representatives, and which are known to us only in a fossil state. As we here and there see a thin straggling branch springing from a fork low down in a tree, and which by some chance has been favoured and is still alive on its summit, so we occasionally see an animal like the Ornithorhynchus or Lepidosiren,[9] which in some small degree connects by its affinities two large branches of life, and which has apparently been saved from fatal competition by having inhabited a protected station. As buds give rise by growth to fresh buds, and these, if vigorous, branch out and overtop on all sides many a feebler branch, so by generation I believe it has been with the great Tree of Life, which fills with its dead and broken branches the crust of the earth, and covers the surface with its ever-branching and beautiful ramifications. (Chapter 4)

Difficulties of the Theory

— ORGANS OF EXTREME PERFECTION AND COMPLICATION —

To suppose that the eye with all its inimitable contrivances for adjusting the focus to different distances, for admitting different amounts of light, and for the correction of spherical and chromatic aberration, could have been formed by natural selection, seems, I freely confess, absurd in the highest degree. When it was first said that the sun stood still and the world turned round, the common sense of mankind declared the doctrine false; but the old saying of *Vox populi, vox Dei*,[10] as every philosopher knows, cannot be trusted in science. Reason tells me, that if numerous gradations from a simple and imperfect eye to one complex and perfect can be shown to exist, each grade being useful to its possessor, as is certainly the case; if further, the eye ever varies and the

---

[9]**Ornithorhynchus:** platypus. **Lepidosiren:** lungfish.

[10]*Vox populi, vox Dei:* The people's voice is the voice of God.

variations be inherited, as is likewise certainly the case; and if such variations should be useful to any animal under changing conditions of life, then the difficulty of believing that a perfect and complex eye could be formed by natural selection, though insuperable by our imagination, should not be considered as subversive of the theory. How a nerve comes to be sensitive to light, hardly concerns us more than how life itself originated; but I may remark that, as some of the lowest organisms, in which nerves cannot be detected, are capable of perceiving light, it does not seem impossible that certain sensitive elements in their sarcode should become aggregated and developed into nerves, endowed with this special sensibility.

In searching for the gradations through which an organ in any species has been perfected, we ought to look exclusively to its lineal progenitors; but this is scarcely ever possible, and we are forced to look to other species and genera of the same group, that is to the collateral descendants from the same parent-form, in order to see what gradations are possible, and for the chance of some gradations having been transmitted in an unaltered or little altered condition. But the state of the same organ in distinct classes may incidentally throw light on the steps by which it has been perfected.

The simplest organ which can be called an eye consists of an optic nerve, surrounded by pigment-cells and covered by translucent skin, but without any lens or other refractive body. We may, however, according to M. Jourdain, descend even a step lower and find aggregates of pigment-cells, apparently serving as organs of vision, without any nerves, and resting merely on sarcodic tissue.[11] Eyes of the above simple nature are not capable of distinct vision, and serve only to distinguish light from darkness. In certain star-fishes, small depressions in the layer of pigment which surrounds the nerve are filled, as described by the author just quoted, with transparent gelatinous matter, projecting with a convex surface, like the cornea in the higher animals. He suggests that this serves not to form an image, but only to concentrate the luminous rays and render their perception more easy. In this concentration of the rays we gain the first and by far the most important step towards the formation of a true, picture-forming eye; for we have only to place the naked extremity of the optic nerve, which in some of the lower animals lies deeply buried in the body, and in some near the surface, at the right distance from the concentrating apparatus, and an image will be formed on it.

In the great class of the Articulata,[12] we may start from an optic nerve simply coated with pigment, the latter sometimes forming a sort of pupil, but destitute of a lens or other optical contrivance. With insects it is now known that the numerous facets on the cornea of their great compound eyes form true lenses, and that the cones include curiously modified nervous filaments. But these organs in the Articulata are so much diversified that Müller formerly made three main classes with seven subdivisions, besides a fourth main class of aggregated simple eyes.

When we reflect on these facts, here given much too briefly, with respect to the wide, diversified, and graduated range of structure in the eyes of the lower animals; and when we bear in mind how small the number of all living forms must be in comparison with those which have become extinct, the difficulty ceases to be very great in believing that natural selection may have converted the simple apparatus of an optic nerve, coated with pigment and invested by transparent membrane, into an optical instrument as perfect as is possessed by any member of the Articulata class.

He who will go thus far, ought not to hesitate to go one step further, if he finds on finishing this volume that large bodies of facts, otherwise inexplicable, can be explained by the theory of modification through natural selection; he ought to admit that a structure even as perfect as an eagle's eye might thus be formed, although in this case he does not know the transitional states. It has been objected that in order to modify the eye and still preserve it as a perfect instrument, many changes would have to be effected simultaneously, which, it is assumed, could not be done through natural selection; but as I have attempted to show in my work on the variation of domestic animals, it is not necessary to suppose that the modifications were all simultaneous, if they were extremely slight and gradual. Different kinds of modification would, also, serve for the same general purpose: as Mr. Wallace[13] has remarked, "if a lens has too short or too long a focus, it may be amended either by an alteration of curvature, or an alteration of density; if the curvature be irregular, and the rays do not converge to a point, then any increased regularity of curvature will be an improvement. So the contraction of the iris and the muscular movements of the eye are neither of them essential to

---

[11]**sarcodic tissue:** protoplasm.

[12]**Articulata:** bottom-dwelling marine invertebrates.

[13]Alfred Russel **Wallace** (1823–1913): explorer and naturalist whose essay on evolution and natural selection prompted Darwin to publish his own theories.

vision, but only improvements which might have been added and perfected at any stage of the construction of the instrument." Within the highest division of the animal kingdom, namely, the Vertebrata, we can start from an eye so simple, that it consists, as in the lancelet, of a little sack of transparent skin, furnished with a nerve and lined with pigment, but destitute of any other apparatus. In fishes and reptiles, as Owen[14] has remarked, "The range of gradations of dioptric structures is very great." It is a significant fact that even in man, according to the high authority of Virchow,[15] the beautiful crystalline lens is formed in the embryo by an accumulation of epidermic cells, lying in a sack-like fold of the skin; and the vitreous body is formed from embryonic sub–cutaneous tissue. To arrive, however, at a just conclusion regarding the formation of the eye, with all its marvellous yet not absolutely perfect characters, it is indispensable that the reason should conquer the imagination; but I have felt the difficulty far too keenly to be surprised at others hesitating to extend the principle of natural selection to so startling a length.

It is scarcely possible to avoid comparing the eye with a telescope. We know that this instrument has been perfected by the long-continued efforts of the highest human intellects; and we naturally infer that the eye has been formed by a somewhat analogous process. But may not this inference be presumptuous? Have we any right to assume that the Creator works by intellectual powers like those of man? If we must compare the eye to an optical instrument, we ought in imagination to take a thick layer of transparent tissue, with spaces filled with fluid, and with a nerve sensitive to light beneath, and then suppose every part of this layer to be continually changing slowly in density, so as to separate into layers of different densities and thicknesses, placed at different distances from each other, and with the surfaces of each layer slowly changing in form. Further we must suppose that there is a power, represented by natural selection or the survival of the fittest, always intently watching each slight alteration in the transparent layers; and carefully preserving each which, under varied circumstances, in any way or in any degree, tends to produce a distincter image. We must suppose each new state of the instrument to be multiplied by the million; each to be preserved until a better one is produced, and then the old ones to be all de-

stroyed. In living bodies, variation will cause the slight alterations, generation will multiply them almost infinitely, and natural selection will pick out with unerring skill each improvement. Let this process go on for millions of years; and during each year on millions of individuals of many kinds; and may we not believe that a living optical instrument might thus be formed as superior to one of glass, as the works of the Creator are to those of man? (Chapter 6)

Recapitulation and Conclusion

. . . Authors of the highest eminence seem to be fully satisfied with the view that each species has been independently created. To my mind it accords better with what we know of the laws impressed on matter by the Creator, that the production and extinction of the past and present inhabitants of the world should have been due to secondary causes, like those determining the birth and death of the individual. When I view all beings not as special creations, but as the lineal descendants of some few beings which lived long before the first bed of the Cambrian system was deposited, they seem to me to become ennobled. Judging from the past, we may safely infer that not one living species will transmit its unaltered likeness to a distinct futurity. And of the species now living very few will transmit progeny of any kind to a far distant futurity; for the manner in which all organic beings are grouped, shows that the greater number of species in each genus, and all the species in many genera, have left no descendants, but have become utterly extinct. We can so far take a prophetic glance into futurity as to foretell that it will be the common and widely spread species, belonging to the larger and dominant groups within each class, which will ultimately prevail and procreate new and dominant species. As all the living forms of life are the lineal descendants of those which lived long before the Cambrian epoch, we may feel certain that the ordinary succession by generation has never once been broken, and that no cataclysm has desolated the whole world. Hence we may look with some confidence to a secure future of great length. And as natural selection works solely by and for the good of each being, all corporeal and mental endowments will tend to progress toward perfection.

It is interesting to contemplate a tangled bank, clothed with many plants of many kinds, with birds singing on the bushes, with various insects flitting about, and with worms crawling through the damp earth, and to reflect that these elaborately constructed forms, so different from each other, and dependent upon each other in so

---

[14]Sir Richard **Owen** (1804–1892): anatomist, paleontologist, zoologist.

[15]Rudolf **Virchow** (1821–1902): German pathologist and epidemiologist.

complex a manner, have all been produced by laws acting around us. These laws, taken in the largest sense, being Growth with reproduction; Inheritance which is almost implied by Reproduction; Variability from the indirect and direct action of the conditions of life, and from use and disuse: a Ratio of Increase so high as to lead to a Struggle for Life, and as a consequence to Natural Selection, entailing Divergence of Character and the Extinction of less improved forms. Thus, from the war of nature, from famine and death, the most exalted object which we are capable of conceiving, namely, the production of the higher animals, directly follows. There is grandeur in this view of life, with its several powers, having been originally breathed by the Creator into a few forms or into one; and that, whilst this planet has gone cycling on according to the fixed law of gravity, from so simple a beginning endless forms most beautiful and most wonderful have been, and are being evolved. (Chapter 15)

1859

~

from The Descent of Man
Secondary Sexual Characters of Man

With mankind the differences between the sexes are greater than in most of the Quadrumana, but not so great as in some, for instance, the mandrill.[1] Man on an average is considerably taller, heavier, and stronger than woman, with squarer shoulders and more plainly-pronounced muscles. Owing to the relation which exists between muscular development and the projection of the brows, the superciliary ridge is generally more marked in man than in woman. His body, and especially his face, is more hairy, and his voice has a different and more powerful tone. In certain races the women are said to differ slightly in tint from the men. For instance, Schweinfurth;[2] in speaking of a negress belonging to the Monbuttoos, who inhabit the interior of Africa a few degrees north of the Equator, says, "Like all her race, she had a skin several shades lighter than her husband's, being something of the colour of half-roasted coffee." As the women labour in the fields and are quite unclothed, it is not

likely that they differ in colour from the men owing to less exposure to the weather. European women are perhaps the brighter coloured of the two sexes, as may be seen when both have been equally exposed.

Man is more courageous, pugnacious and energetic than woman, and has a more inventive genius. His brain is absolutely larger, but whether or not proportionately to his larger body, has not, I believe, been fully ascertained. In woman the face is rounder; the jaws and the base of the skull smaller; the outlines of the body rounder, in parts more prominent; and her pelvis is broader than in man; but this latter character may perhaps be considered rather as a primary than a secondary sexual character. She comes to maturity at an earlier age than man.

As with animals of all classes, so with man, the distinctive characters of the male sex are not fully developed until he is nearly mature; and if emasculated they never appear. The beard, for instance, is a secondary sexual character, and male children are beardless, though at an early age they have abundant hair on the head. It is probably due to the rather late appearance in life of the successive variations whereby man has acquired his masculine characters, that they are transmitted to the male sex alone. Male and female children resemble each other closely, like the young of so many other animals in which the adult sexes differ widely; they likewise resemble the mature female much more closely than the mature male. The female, however, ultimately assumes certain distinctive characters, and in the formation of her skull, is said to be intermediate between the child and the man. . . .

All the secondary sexual characters of man are highly variable, even within the limits of the same race; and they differ much in the several races. These two rules hold good generally throughout the animal kingdom. In the excellent observations made on board the *Novara*,[3] the male Australians were found to exceed the females by only 65 millim. in height, whilst with the Javans the average excess was 218 millim.; so that in this latter race the difference in height between the sexes is more than thrice as great as with the Australians. Numerous measurements were carefully made of the stature, the circumference of the neck and chest, the length of the back-bone and of the arms, in various races; and nearly all these measurements shew that the males differ much more from one another than do the females. This fact indicates that, as far as these characters are concerned,

---

[1]**Quadrumana**: literally "four-handed," the great apes. **mandrill**: baboon-like African monkey.

[2]Georg August **Schweinfurth** (1836–1925): German botanist and traveller, whose *Heart of Africa* (1873) Darwin here quotes.

[3]*Novara*: Austrian frigate whose 1857–1859 travels issued in scientific publications a decade later.

it is the male which has been chiefly modified, since the several races diverged from their common stock. . . .

— LAW OF BATTLE —

With savages, for instance, the Australians, the women are the constant cause of war both between members of the same tribe and between distinct tribes. So no doubt it was in ancient times; "nam fuit ante Helenam mulier teterrima belli causa."[4] With some of the North American Indians, the contest is reduced to a system. That excellent observer, Hearne,[5] says:— "It has ever been the custom among these people for the men to wrestle for any woman to whom they are attached; and, of course, the strongest party always carries off the prize. A weak man, unless he be a good hunter, and well-beloved, is seldom permitted to keep a wife that a stronger man thinks worth his notice. This custom prevails throughout all the tribes, and causes a great spirit of emulation among their youth, who are upon all occasions, from their childhood, trying their strength and skill in wrestling." With the Guanas of South America, Azara[6] states that the men rarely marry till twenty years old or more, as before that age they cannot conquer their rivals.

Other similar facts could be given; but even if we had no evidence on this head, we might feel almost sure, from the analogy of the higher Quadrumana, that the law of battle had prevailed with man during the early stages of his development. The occasional appearance at the present day of canine teeth which project above the others, with traces of a diastema or open space for the reception of the opposite canines, is in all probability a case of reversion to a former state, when the progenitors of man were provided with these weapons, like so many existing male Quadrumana. It was remarked in a former chapter that as man gradually became erect, and continually used his hands and arms for fighting with sticks and stones, as well as for the other purposes of life, he would have used his jaws and teeth less and less. The jaws, together with their muscles, would then have been reduced through disuse, as would the teeth through the not well understood principles of correlation and economy of growth; for we everywhere see that parts, which are no longer of service, are reduced in size. By such steps the original inequality between the jaws and teeth in the two sexes of mankind would ultimately have been obliterated.

The case is almost parallel with that of many male Ruminants,[7] in which the canine teeth have been reduced to mere rudiments, or have disappeared, apparently in consequence of the development of horns. As the prodigious difference between the skulls of the two sexes in the orang and gorilla stands in close relation with the development of the immense canine teeth in the males, we may infer that the reduction of the jaws and teeth in the early male progenitors of man must have led to a most striking and favourable change in his appearance.

There can be little doubt that the greater size and strength of man, in comparison with woman, together with his broader shoulders, more developed muscles, rugged outline of body, his greater courage and pugnacity, are all due in chief part to inheritance from his half-human male ancestors. These characters would, however, have been preserved or even augmented during the long ages of man's savagery, by the success of the strongest and boldest men, both in the general struggle for life and in their contests for wives; a success which would have ensured their leaving a more numerous progeny than their less favoured brethren. It is not probable that the greater strength of man was primarily acquired through the inherited effects of his having worked harder than woman for his own subsistence and that of his family; for the women in all barbarous nations are compelled to work at least as hard as the men. With civilised people the arbitrament of battle for the possession of the women has long ceased; on the other hand, the men, as a general rule, have to work harder than the women for their joint subsistence, and thus their greater strength will have been kept up.

— DIFFERENCE IN THE MENTAL POWERS OF THE TWO SEXES —

With respect to differences of this nature between man and woman, it is probable that sexual selection has played a highly important part. I am aware that some writers doubt whether there is any such inherent difference; but this is at least probable from the analogy of the lower animals which present other secondary sexual characters. No one disputes that the bull differs in disposition from the cow, the wildboar from the sow, the stallion from the mare, and, as is well known to the keepers of menageries, the males of the larger apes from the females. Woman seems to differ from man in mental disposition, chiefly in her greater tenderness

---

[4]"**nam fuit . . . causa**": for woman was a fearsome cause of war long before Helen.

[5]Samuel **Hearne** (1745–1792): English fur-trading explorer who wrote *A Journey . . . to the Northern Ocean* (1795).

[6]Felix de **Azara** (1746–1821): Spanish explorer.

---

[7]**Ruminants**: suborder including giraffes, cattle, sheep, and goats.

and less selfishness; and this holds good even with savages, as shewn by a well-known passage in Mungo Park's Travels,[8] and by statements made by many other travellers. Woman, owing to her maternal instincts, displays these qualities towards her infants in an eminent degree; therefore it is likely that she would often extend them towards her fellow-creatures. Man is the rival of other men; he delights in competition, and this leads to ambition which passes too easily into selfishness. These latter qualities seem to be his natural and unfortunate birthright. It is generally admitted that with woman the powers of intuition, of rapid perception, and perhaps of imitation, are more strongly marked than in man; but some, at least, of these faculties are characteristic of the lower races, and therefore of a past and lower state of civilisation.

The chief distinction in the intellectual powers of the two sexes is shewn by man's attaining to a higher eminence, in whatever he takes up, than can woman—whether requiring deep thought, reason, or imagination, or merely the use of the senses and hands. If two lists were made of the most eminent men and women in poetry, painting, sculpture, music (inclusive both of composition and performance), history, science, and philosophy, with half-a-dozen names under each subject, the two lists would not bear comparison. We may also infer, from the law of the deviation from averages, so well illustrated by Mr. Galton[9] in his work on "Hereditary Genius," that if men are capable of a decided pre-eminence over women in many subjects, the average of mental power in man must be above that of woman.

Amongst the half-human progenitors of man, and amongst savages, there have been struggles between the males during many generations for the possession of the females. But mere bodily strength and size would do little for victory, unless associated with courage, perseverance, and determined energy. With social animals, the young males have to pass through many a contest before they win a female, and the older males have to retain their females by renewed battles. They have, also, in the case of mankind, to defend their females, as well as their young, from enemies of all kinds, and to hunt for their joint subsistence. But to avoid enemies or to attack them with success, to capture wild animals, and to fashion weapons, requires the aid of the higher mental faculties, namely, observation, reason, in-

vention, or imagination. These various faculties will thus have been continually put to the test and selected during manhood; they will, moreover, have been strengthened by use during this same period of life. Consequently, in accordance with the principle often alluded to, we might expect that they would at least tend to be transmitted chiefly to the male offspring at the corresponding period of manhood.

Now, when two men are put into competition, or a man with a woman, both possessed of every mental quality in equal perfection, save that one has higher energy, perseverance, and courage, the latter will generally become more eminent in every pursuit, and will gain the ascendancy.[10] He may be said to possess genius—for genius has been declared by a great authority to be patience; and patience, in this sense, means unflinching, undaunted perseverance. But this view of genius is perhaps deficient; for without the higher powers of the imagination and reason, no eminent success can be gained in many subjects. These latter faculties, as well as the former, will have been developed in man, partly through Sexual Selection,—that is, through the contest of rival males, and partly through Natural Selection,—that is, from success in the general struggle for life; and as in both cases the struggle will have been during maturity, the characters gained will have been transmitted more fully to the male than to the female offspring. It accords in a striking manner with this view of the modification and reinforcement of many of our mental faculties by sexual selection, that, firstly, they notoriously undergo a considerable change at puberty, and, secondly, that eunuchs remain throughout life inferior in these same qualities. Thus man has ultimately become superior to woman. It is, indeed, fortunate that the law of the equal transmission of characters to both sexes prevails with mammals; otherwise it is probable that man would have become as superior in mental endowment to woman, as the peacock is in ornamental plumage to the peahen.

It must be borne in mind that the tendency in characters acquired by either sex late in life, to be transmitted to the same sex at the same age, and of early acquired characters to be transmitted to both sexes, are rules which, though general, do not always hold. If they always held good, we might conclude (but I here exceed my proper bounds) that the inherited effects of the early education of boys and girls would

---

[8]**Mungo Park** (1771–1806): Scottish explorer, author of *Travels in the Interior Districts of Africa* (1797).

[9]Sir Francis **Galton** (1822–1911): eugenicist and statistician.

[10]**ascendancy**: J. Stuart Mill remarks, "The things in which man most excels woman are those which require most plodding, and long hammering at single thoughts." What is this but energy and perseverance? [Darwin's note, citing Mill's 1869 *Subjection of Women*]

be transmitted equally to both sexes; so that the present inequality in mental power between the sexes would not be effaced by a similar course of early training; nor can it have been caused by their dissimilar early training. In order that woman should reach the same standard as man, she ought, when nearly adult, to be trained to energy and perseverance, and to have her reason and imagination exercised to the highest point; and then she would probably transmit these qualities chiefly to her adult daughters. All women, however, could not be thus raised, unless during many generations those who excelled in the above robust virtues were married, and produced offspring in larger numbers than other women. As before remarked of bodily strength, although men do not now fight for their wives, and this form of selection has passed away, yet during manhood, they generally undergo a severe struggle in order to maintain themselves and their families; and this will tend to keep up or even increase their mental powers, and, as a consequence, the present inequality between the sexes.[11] . . . (Part 3, Chapter 19)

1871, 1877

from Autobiography

A German Editor having written to me to ask for an account of the development of my mind and character with some sketch of my autobiography, I have thought that the attempt would amuse me, and might possibly interest my children or their children. I know that it would have interested me greatly to have read even so short and dull a sketch of the mind of my grandfather written by himself, and what he thought and did and how he worked. I have attempted to write the following account of myself, as if I were a dead man in another world looking back at my own life. Nor have I found this difficult, for life is nearly over with me. I have taken no pains about my style of writing.

I was born at Shrewsbury on February 12th, 1809. I have heard my Father say that he believed that persons with powerful minds generally had memories extending far back to a very early period of life. This is not my case for my earliest recollection goes back only to when I was a few months over four years old, when we went to near Abergele for sea-bathing, and I recollect some events and places there with some little distinctness.

My mother died in July 1817, when I was a little over eight years old, and it is odd that I can remember hardly anything about her except her death-bed, her black velvet gown, and her curiously constructed work-table. I believe that my forgetfulness is partly due to my sisters, owing to their great grief, never being able to speak about her or mention her name; and partly to her previous invalid state. In the spring of this same year I was sent to a day-school in Shrewsbury where I staid a year. Before going to school I was educated by my sister Caroline, but I doubt whether this plan answered. I have been told that I was much slower in learning than my younger sister Catherine, and I believe that I was in many ways a naughty boy. Caroline was extremely kind, clever and zealous; but she was too zealous in trying to improve me; for I clearly remember after this long interval of years, saying to myself when about to enter a room where she was—"What will she blame me for now?" and I made myself dogged so as not to care what she might say.

By the time I went to this day-school my taste for natural history, and more especially for collecting, was well developed. I tried to make out the names of plants, and collected all sorts of things, shells, seals, franks, coins, and minerals. The passion for collecting, which leads a man to be a systematic naturalist, a virtuoso or a miser, was very strong in me, and was clearly innate, as none of my sisters or brother ever had this taste.

One little event during this year has fixed itself very firmly in my mind, and I hope that it has done so from my conscience having been afterwards sorely troubled by it; it is curious as showing that apparently I was interested at this early age in the variability of plants! I told another little boy (I believe it was Leighton,[1] who afterwards became a well-known Lichenologist and botanist) that I could produce variously coloured Polyanthuses and Primroses by watering them with certain coloured fluids, which was of course a monstrous fable, and had never been tried by me. I may here also confess that as a little boy I was much given to inventing deliberate falsehoods, and this was always done for the sake of causing excitement. For instance, I once

---

[11]**sexes**: An observation by Vogt bears on this subject: he says, "It is a remarkable circumstance, that the difference between the sexes, as regards the cranial cavity, increases with the development of the race, so that the male European excels much more the female, than the negro the negress. Welcker confirms this statement of Huschke from his measurement of negro and German skulls." But Vogt admits ("Lectures on Man," Engl. translat. 1864, p. 81) that more observations are requisite on this point. [Darwin's note]

---

[1]William Allport **Leighton** (1805–1889).

gathered much valuable fruit from my Father's trees and hid them in the shrubbery, and then ran in breathless haste to spread the news that I had discovered a hoard of stolen fruit.

About this time, or as I hope at a somewhat earlier age, I sometimes stole fruit for the sake of eating it; and one of my schemes was ingenious. The kitchen garden was kept locked in the evening, and was surrounded by a high wall, but by the aid of neighbouring trees I could easily get on the coping. I then fixed a long stick into the hole at the bottom of a rather large flower-pot, and by dragging this upwards pulled off peaches and plums, which fell into the pot and the prizes were thus secured. When a very little boy I remember stealing apples from the orchard, for the sake of giving them away to some boys and young men who lived in a cottage not far off, but before I gave them the fruit I showed off how quickly I could run and it is wonderful that I did not perceive that the surprise and admiration which they expressed at my powers of running, was given for the sake of the apples. But I well remember that I was delighted at them declaring that they had never seen a boy run so fast!

I remember clearly only one other incident during the years whilst at Mr. Case's daily school—namely, the burial of a dragoon-soldier; and it is surprising how clearly I can still see the horse with the man's empty boots and carbine suspended to the saddle, and the firing over the grave. This scene deeply stirred whatever poetic fancy there was in me.

In the summer of 1818 I went to Dr. Butler's great school in Shrewsbury,[2] and remained there for seven years till Mid-summer 1825, when I was sixteen years old. I boarded at this school, so that I had the great advantage of living the life of a true school-boy; but as the distance was hardly more than a mile to my home, I very often ran there in the longer intervals between the callings over and before locking up at night. This I think was in many ways advantageous to me by keeping up home affections and interests. I remember in the early part of my school life that I often had to run very quickly to be in time, and from being a fleet runner was generally successful; but when in doubt I prayed earnestly to God to help me, and I well remember that I attributed my success to the prayers and not to my quick running, and marvelled how generally I was aided. . . .

I can say in my own favour that I was as a boy humane, but I owed this entirely to the instruction and example of my sisters. I doubt indeed whether humanity is a natural or innate quality. I was very fond of collecting eggs, but I never took more than a single egg out of a bird's nest, except on one single occasion, when I took all, not for their value, but from a sort of bravado.

I had a strong taste for angling, and would sit for any number of hours on the bank of a river or pond watching the float; when at Maer[3] I was told that I could kill the worms with salt and water, and from that day I never spitted a living worm, though at the expense, probably, of some loss of success.

Once as a very little boy, whilst at the day-school, or before that time, I acted cruelly, for I beat a puppy I believe, simply from enjoying the sense of power; but the beating could not have been severe, for the puppy did not howl, of which I feel sure as the spot was near to the house. This act lay heavily on my conscience, as is shown by my remembering the exact spot where the crime was committed. It probably lay all the heavier from my love of dogs being then, and for a long time afterwards, a passion. Dogs seemed to know this, for I was an adept in robbing their love from their masters.

Nothing could have been worse for the development of my mind than Dr. Butler's school, as it was strictly classical, nothing else being taught except a little ancient geography and history. The school as a means of education to me was simply a blank. During my whole life I have been singularly incapable of mastering any language. Especial attention was paid to verse-making, and this I could never do well. I had many friends, and got together a grand collection of old verses, which by patching together, sometimes aided by other boys, I could work into any subject. Much attention was paid to learning by heart the lessons of the previous day; this I could effect with great facility learning forty or fifty lines of Virgil or Homer, whilst I was in morning chapel; but this exercise was utterly useless, for every verse was forgotten in forty-eight hours. I was not idle, and with the exception of versification, generally worked conscientiously at my classics, not using cribs. The sole pleasure I ever received from such studies, was from some of the odes of Horace, which I admired greatly. When I left the school I was for my age neither high nor low in it; and I believe that I was considered by all my masters and by my Father as a very ordinary boy, rather below the common standard in intellect. To my deep mortification my father once said to me, "You care for nothing but shooting, dogs,

---

[2]Samuel **Butler** (1774–1839): bishop and author, headmaster of **Shrewsbury**, a leading public school.

[3]**Maer**: the house of his uncle, the pottery heir Josiah Wedgwood, whose youngest daughter Darwin married.

and rat-catching, and you will be a disgrace to yourself and all your family." But my father, who was the kindest man I ever knew, and whose memory I love with all my heart, must have been angry and somewhat unjust when he used such words. . . .

Looking back as well as I can at my character during my school life, the only qualities which at this period promised well for the future, were, that I had strong and diversified tastes, much zeal for whatever interested me, and a keen pleasure in understanding any complex subject or thing. I was taught Euclid by a private tutor, and I distinctly remember the intense satisfaction which the clear geometrical proofs gave me. I remember with equal distinctness the delight which my uncle gave me (the father of Francis Galton) by explaining the principle of the vernier[4] of a barometer. With respect to diversified tastes, independently of science, I was fond of reading various books, and I used to sit for hours reading the historical plays of Shakespeare, generally in an old window in the thick walls of the school. I read also other poetry, such as the recently published poems of Byron, Scott, and Thomson's *Seasons*.[5] I mention this because later in life I wholly lost, to my great regret, all pleasure from poetry of any kind, including Shakespeare. In connection with pleasure from poetry I may add that in 1822 a vivid delight in scenery was first awakened in my mind, during a riding tour on the borders of Wales, and which has lasted longer than any other aesthetic pleasure. . . .

During these two years[6] I was led to think much about religion. Whilst on board the *Beagle* I was quite orthodox, and I remember being heartily laughed at by several of the officers (though themselves orthodox) for quoting the Bible as an unanswerable authority on some point of morality. I suppose it was the novelty of the argument that amused them. But I had gradually come, by this time, to see that the Old Testament from its manifestly false history of the world, with the Tower of Babel, the rainbow as a sign, etc., etc., and from its attributing to God the feelings of a revengeful tyrant, was no more to be trusted than the sacred books of the Hindoos, or the beliefs of any barbarians. The question then continually rose before my mind and would

not be banished,—is it credible that if God were now to make a revelation to the Hindoos, would he permit it to be connected with the belief in Vishnu, Siva, &c., as Christianity is connected with the Old Testament. This appeared to me utterly incredible.

By further reflecting that the clearest evidence would be requisite to make any sane man believe in the miracles by which Christianity is supported,—that the more we know of the fixed laws of nature the more incredible do miracles become,—that the men at that time were ignorant and credulous to a degree almost incomprehensible by us,—that the Gospels cannot be proved to have been written simultaneously with the events,—that they differ in many important details, far too important as it seemed to me to be admitted as the usual inaccuracies of eye-witnesses,—by such reflections as these, which I give not as having the least novelty or value, but as they influenced me, I gradually came to disbelieve in Christianity as a divine revelation. The fact that many false religions have spread over large portions of the earth like wild-fire had some weight with me. Beautiful as is the morality of the New Testament, it can hardly be denied that its perfection depends in part on the interpretation which we now put on metaphors and allegories.

But I was very unwilling to give up my belief;—I feel sure of this for I can well remember often and often inventing day-dreams of old letters between distinguished Romans and manuscripts being discovered at Pompeii or elsewhere which confirmed in the most striking manner all that was written in the Gospels. But I found it more and more difficult, with free scope given to my imagination, to invent evidence which would suffice to convince me. Thus disbelief crept over me at a very slow rate, but was at last complete. The rate was so slow that I felt no distress, and have never since doubted even for a single second that my conclusion was correct. I can indeed hardly see how anyone ought to wish Christianity to be true; for if so the plain language of the text seems to show that the men who do not believe, and this would include my Father, Brother and almost all my best friends, will be everlastingly punished.

And this is a damnable doctrine.

Although I did not think much about the existence of a personal God until a considerably later period of my life, I will here give the vague conclusions to which I have been driven. The old argument of design in nature, as given by Paley,[7] which formerly seemed to me so conclusive, fails,

---

[4]Francis **Galton** (1822–1911): anthropologist and eugenicist. **vernier**: scale for obtaining precise measurements.

[5]*The Seasons* (1726–1730): cycle of poems about nature by James **Thomson** (1700–1748).

[6]**two years**: October 1836–January 1839, between leaving the *Beagle* and his marriage. Parts of the following passages on religious belief were cut by Darwin's family before publication.

---

[7]William **Paley** (1743–1805): his **argument of design**—that because the world seems to have been designed, there must exist a deity who designed it—was a leading casualty of the *Origin of Species*.

now that the law of natural selection has been discovered. We can no longer argue that, for instance, the beautiful hinge of a bivalve shell must have been made by an intelligent being, like the hinge of a door by man. There seems to be no more design in the variability of organic beings and in the action of natural selection, than in the course which the wind blows. Everything in nature is the result of fixed laws. But I have discussed this subject at the end of my book on the *Variation of Domestic Animals and Plants*,[8] and the argument there given has never, as far as I can see, been answered.

But passing over the endless beautiful adaptations which we everywhere meet with, it may be asked how can the generally beneficent arrangement of the world be accounted for? Some writers indeed are so much impressed with the amount of suffering in the world, that they doubt if we look to all sentient beings, whether there is more of misery or of happiness,—whether the world as a whole is a good or a bad one. According to my judgment happiness decidedly prevails, though this would be very difficult to prove. If the truth of this conclusion be granted, it harmonises well with the effects which we might expect from natural selection. If all the individuals of any species were habitually to suffer to an extreme degree they would neglect to propagate their kind; but we have no reason to believe that this has ever or at least often occurred. Some other considerations, moreover, lead to the belief that all sentient beings have been formed so as to enjoy, as a general rule, happiness.

Every one who believes, as I do, that all the corporeal and mental organs (excepting those which are neither advantageous or disadvantageous to the possessor) of all beings have been developed through natural selection, or the survival of the fittest, together with use or habit, will admit that these organs have been formed so that their possessors may compete successfully with other beings, and thus increase in number. Now an animal may be led to pursue that course of action which is the most beneficial to the species by suffering, such as pain, hunger, thirst, and fear,—or by pleasure, as in eating and drinking and in the propagation of the species, &c. or by both means combined, as in the search for food. But pain or suffering of any kind, if long continued, causes depression and lessens the power of action; yet is well adapted to make a creature guard itself against any great or sudden evil. Pleasurable sensations, on the other hand, may be long continued without any depressing effect; on the contrary they stimulate the whole system to increased action. Hence it has come to pass that most or all sentient beings have been developed in such a manner through natural selection, that pleasurable sensations serve as their habitual guides. We see this in the pleasure from exertion, even occasionally from great exertion of the body or mind,—in the pleasure of our daily meals, and especially in the pleasure derived from sociability and from loving our families. The sum of such pleasures as these, which are habitual or frequently recurrent, give, as I can hardly doubt, to most sentient beings an excess of happiness over misery, although many occasionally suffer much. Such suffering, is quite compatible with the belief in Natural Selection, which is not perfect in its action, but tends only to render each species as successful as possible in the battle for life with other species, in wonderfully complex and changing circumstances.

That there is much suffering in the world no one disputes. Some have attempted to explain this in reference to man by imagining that it serves for his moral improvement. But the number of men in the world is as nothing compared with that of all other sentient beings, and these often suffer greatly without any moral improvement. A being so powerful and so full of knowledge as a God who could create the universe, is to our finite minds omnipotent and omniscient, and it revolts our understanding to suppose that his benevolence is not unbounded, for what advantage can there be in the sufferings of millions of the lower animals throughout almost endless time? This very old argument from the existence of suffering against the existence of an intelligent first cause seems to me a strong one; whereas, as just remarked, the presence of much suffering agrees well with the view that all organic beings have been developed through variation and natural selection. . . .

Nothing is more remarkable than the spread of scepticism or rationalism during the latter half of my life. Before I was engaged to be married, my father advised me to conceal carefully my doubts, for he said that he had known extreme misery thus caused with married persons. Things went on pretty well until the wife or husband became out of health, and then some women suffered miserably by doubting about the salvation of their husbands, thus making them likewise to suffer. My father added that he had known during his whole long life only three women who were sceptics; and it should be remembered that he knew well a multitude of persons and possessed extraordinary power of winning confidence. When I asked him who the three women were, he had to own with respect to one of them, his sister-in-law Kitty Wedgwood, that he had no good evidence, only the vaguest hints, aided by the conviction that so clear-sighted a woman could not be a believer. At the present time, with my small acquaintance, I know (or have

---

[8] *Variation of Animals and Plants under Domestication* (1868).

known) several married ladies, who believe very little more than their husbands. My father used to quote an unanswerable argument, by which an old lady, a Mrs Barlow, who suspected him of unorthodoxy, hoped to convert him:— "Doctor, I know that sugar is sweet in my mouth, and I know that my Redeemer liveth." . . . .

I have said that in one respect my mind has changed during the last twenty or thirty years. Up to the age of thirty, or beyond it, poetry of many kinds, such as the works of Milton, Gray, Byron, Wordsworth, Coleridge, and Shelley, gave me great pleasure, and even as a schoolboy I took intense delight in Shakespeare, especially in the historical plays. I have also said that formerly pictures gave me considerable, and music very great delight. But now for many years I cannot endure to read a line of poetry: I have tried lately to read Shakespeare, and found it so intolerably dull that it nauseated me. I have also almost lost any taste for pictures or music.—Music generally sets me thinking too energetically on what I have been at work on, instead of giving me pleasure. I retain some taste for fine scenery, but it does not cause me the exquisite delight which it formerly did. On the other hand, novels which are works of the imagination, though not of a very high order, have been for years a wonderful relief and pleasure to me, and I often bless all novelists. A surprising number have been read aloud to me, and I like all if moderately good, and if they do not end unhappily—against which a law ought to be passed. A novel, according to my taste, does not come into the first class unless it contains some person whom one can thoroughly love, and if it be a pretty woman all the better.

This curious and lamentable loss of the higher aesthetic tastes is all the odder, as books on history, biographies and travels (independently of any scientific facts which they may contain), and essays on all sorts of subjects interest me as much as ever they did. My mind seems to have become a kind of machine for grinding general laws out of large collections of facts, but why this should have caused the atrophy of that part of the brain alone, on which the higher tastes depend, I cannot conceive. A man with a mind more highly organised or better constituted than mine, would not I suppose have thus suffered; and if I had to live my life again I would have made a rule to read some poetry and listen to some music at least once every week; for perhaps the parts of my brain now atrophied could thus have been kept active through use. The loss of these tastes is a loss of happiness, and may possibly be injurious to the intellect, and more probably to the moral character, by enfeebling the emotional part of our nature.

My books have sold largely in England, have been translated into many languages, and passed through several editions in foreign countries. I have heard it said that the success of a work abroad is the best test of its enduring value. I doubt whether this is at all trustworthy; but judged by this standard my name ought to last for a few years. Therefore it may be worth while for me to try to analyse the mental qualities and the conditions on which my success has depended; though I am aware that no man can do this correctly.

I have no great quickness of apprehension or wit which is so remarkable in some clever men, for instance Huxley. I am therefore a poor critic: a paper or book, when first read, generally excites my admiration, and it is only after considerable reflection that I perceive the weak points. My power to follow a long and purely abstract train of thought is very limited; I should, moreover, never have succeeded with metaphysics or mathematics. My memory is extensive, yet hazy: it suffices to make me cautious by vaguely telling me that I have observed or read something opposed to the conclusion which I am drawing, or on the other hand in favour of it; and after a time I can generally recollect where to search for my authority. So poor in one sense is my memory, that I have never been able to remember for more than a few days a single date or a line of poetry.

Some of my critics have said, "Oh, he is a good observer, but has no power of reasoning." I do not think that this can be true, for the *Origin of Species* is one long argument from the beginning to the end, and it has convinced not a few able men. No one could have written it without having some power of reasoning. I have a fair share of invention and of common sense or judgment, such as every fairly successful lawyer or doctor must have, but not I believe, in any higher degree.

On the favourable side of the balance, I think that I am superior to the common run of men in noticing things which easily escape attention, and in observing them carefully. My industry has been nearly as great as it could have been in the observation and collection of facts. What is far more important, my love of natural science has been steady and ardent. This pure love has, however, been much aided by the ambition to be esteemed by my fellow naturalists. From my early youth, I have had the strongest desire to understand or explain whatever I observed,—that is, to group all facts under some general laws. These causes combined have given me the patience to reflect or ponder for any number of years over any unexplained problem. As far as I can judge, I am not apt to follow blindly the lead of other men. I have steadily endeavoured to keep my mind free, so as to give up any hypothesis, however much beloved (and I cannot resist forming one on every subject), as soon as facts are shown to be opposed to it. Indeed I have had no choice but to act in this manner, for with the exception of the Coral Reefs,[9] I cannot remember a single first-formed hypothesis which had not after a time to be given up or greatly modified. This has naturally led me to distrust greatly deductive reasoning in the mixed sciences. On the other hand, I am not very sceptical,—a frame of mind which I believe to be injurious to the progress of science; a good deal of scepticism in a scientific man is advisable to avoid much loss of time; for I have met with not a few men, who I feel sure have often thus been deterred from experiment or observations, which would have proved directly or indirectly serviceable. . . .

1876

1887, 1958

---

[9]**Coral Reefs:** *The Structure and Distribution of Coral Reefs* (1842), Darwin's greatest geological work.

EDWARD FITZGERALD

(1809–1883)

The self-effacing translator whose anonymous version of the *Rubáiyát of Omar Khayyám* has become perhaps the most widely read of all Victorian poems had his well-to-do family to thank for lifelong financial independence, but not for much else. He was the seventh of eight children, several of whom went insane. His mother was a social-climbing heiress who had the family name changed to hers, evidently with little objection from the breezy and mainly absent sportsman who was his father. A series of moves from the North Sea coast to London to boarding school to the university at Cambridge set patterns of drifting anomie that his later life confirmed and his masterpiece enshrined.

FitzGerald's correspondence reveals a genius for friendship with his university chum William Makepeace Thackeray; with Alfred Tennyson, whom he also met through Cambridge connections (and for several years helped support financially); and with his later London acquaintance Thomas Carlyle. But these were bantering friendships that prospered more in letters than in person. FitzGerald was attracted in a more direct way to handsome younger men, a few serious crushes punctuating a lifetime of intermittent casual relationships. These two aspects of comradely affection combined in his lightweight Platonic dialogue *Euphranor* (1851), which championed the healthy joys of youth over book learning and thus anticipated, in upbeat mode, the philosophy of the *Rubáiyát*. In succeeding years he published at his own expense *Polonius* (an 1852 anthology of quotations) and the one book to which he ever attached his name: *Six Dramas of Calderón, Freely Translated by Edward FitzGerald* (1853).

These works appeared while marriage was pending to Lucy Barton, whose unofficial guardian FitzGerald had become on her poet-father's death. He apparently proposed out of a misplaced sense of duty, and when the marriage finally came to pass in 1856 it was a disaster that did not last a year. During the next miserable months he turned his hand to the verses of Omar Khayyám (1048–1131), ancient Persian tent-stitcher, mathematician-astronomer, and poet. He was pleased by Omar's wry epicurean philosophy of reduced expectations and short-term returns, and also by his deft handling of the *rubai*, a pithy quatrain in an *aaxa* rhyme scheme that FitzGerald had acquired just enough Persian to savor. In triangulation with Omar and with his tutor in Oriental languages—a self-taught, good-looking merchant's son named Edward Cowell who would go on to be a Cambridge professor—FitzGerald embarked on the most satisfactory relationship of his life, which he prolonged after the translation appeared in 1859 by preparing enlarged and reshuffled versions in 1868, 1872, and 1879.

The FitzGerald *Rubáiyát* is not a scholarly rendering of the hundreds of stanzas Omar left behind, but something stranger and rarer. It spans long distances of culture, language, and history by respecting, rather than seeking to erase, the foreignness of its source. This tact emerges locally in the regular retention of unglossed Persian terms as so many badges of travel, artifacts of an irreducible difference that haunts the practice of translation. The poem strikingly illustrates the pattern of the life he lived as if it too were in translation, always at one or two removes from immediacy or commitment; the success of his *Rubáiyát* owes much to his personal investment in its ethos of resignation to things as they unobligingly but tolerably are. The philosophy FitzGerald found in Omar Khayyám had the freshness of disillusioned candor in a world of rampant hypocrisy and self-deception, and its freshness has endeared his translation to half a dozen generations of readers. The *Rubáiyát* repudiates not only phoniness but also the earnest kind of repudiation that is liable to turn into phoniness at another level. Like the unattached bachelor whose solitude it sweetened, and like very little else in the literature of his generation, the *Rubáiyát* keeps its cool.

Rubáiyát of Omar Khayyám

— 1 —

Wake! For the Sun who scatter'd into flight
The Stars before him from the Field of Night,
    Drives Night along with them from Heav'n, and strikes
The Sultán's Turret with a Shaft of Light.

— 2 —

Before the phantom of False morning died,
Methought a Voice within the Tavern cried,
    "When all the Temple is prepared within,
Why nods the drowsy Worshipper outside?"

— 3 —

And, as the Cock crew, those who stood before
The Tavern shouted—"Open then the Door!   10
    You know how little while we have to stay,
And, once departed, may return no more."

— 4 —

Now the New Year reviving old Desires,
The thoughtful Soul to Solitude retires,
    Where the WHITE HAND OF MOSES[1] on the Bough
Puts out, and Jesus from the Ground suspires.

— 5 —

Iram indeed is gone with all his Rose,
And Jamshyd's Sev'n-ring'd Cup[2] where no one knows;
    But still a Ruby kindles in the Vine,
And many a Garden by the Water blows.   20

— 6 —

And David's lips are lockt; but in divine
High-piping Pehlevi,[3] with "Wine! Wine! Wine!
    Red Wine!"—the Nightingale cries to the Rose
That sallow cheek of her's to' incarnadine.

— 7 —

Come, fill the Cup, and in the fire of Spring
Your Winter-garment of Repentance fling:
    The Bird of Time has but a little way
To flutter—and the Bird is on the Wing.

— 8 —

Whether at Naishápúr[4] or Babylon,
Whether the Cup with sweet or bitter run,   30
    The Wine of Life keeps oozing drop by drop,
The Leaves of Life keep falling one by one.

— 9 —

Each Morn a thousand Roses brings, you say;
Yes, but where leaves the Rose of Yesterday?
    And this first Summer month that brings the Rose
Shall take Jamshyd and Kaikobád away.

— 10 —

Well, let it take them! What have we to do
With Kaikobád the Great, or Kaikhosrú?[5]
    Let Zál and Rustum bluster as they will,
Or Hátim call to Supper—heed not you.   40

---

[1]**White Hand of Moses**: Exodus iv.6, where Moses draws forth his Hand—not, according to the Persians, *"leprous as snow,"*—but *white*, as our May-Blossom in Spring perhaps. According to them also the Healing Power of Jesus resided in his Breath. [FitzGerald's note]

[2]**Iram, Jamshyd**: Iram, planted by King Shaddád, and now sunk somewhere in the Sands of Arabia. Jamshyd's Sev'n-ring'd Cup was typical of the 7 Heavens, 7 Planets, 7 Seas, &c., and was a *Divining Cup*. [FitzGerald's note]

[3]**David**: psalmist and king. **Pehlevi**: ancient Persian literary language.

[4]**Naishápúr**: birthplace of Omar Khayyám.

[5]**Kaikobád**: Persian dynastic head. **Kaikhosrú**: Persian conqueror. **Zál, Rustum**: heroic warriors. **Hátim**: Persian poet and host.

— 11 —

With me along the strip of Herbage strewn
That just divides the desert from the sown,
    Where name of Slave and Sultán is forgot—
And Peace to Mahmúd[6] on his golden Throne!

— 12 —

A Book of Verses underneath the Bough,
A Jug of Wine, a Loaf of Bread—and Thou
    Beside me singing in the Wilderness—
Oh, Wilderness were Paradise enow!

— 13 —

Some for the Glories of this World; and some
Sigh for the Prophet's Paradise to come;   50
    Ah, take the Cash, and let the Credit go,
Nor heed the rumble of a distant Drum!

— 14 —

Look to the blowing Rose about us—"Lo,
Laughing," she says, "into the world I blow,
    At once the silken tassel of my Purse
Tear, and its Treasure on the Garden throw."

— 15 —

And those who husbanded the Golden grain,
And those who flung it to the winds like Rain,
    Alike to no such aureate Earth are turn'd
As, buried once, Men want dug up again.   60

— 16 —

The Worldly Hope men set their Hearts upon
Turns Ashes—or it prospers; and anon,
    Like Snow upon the Desert's dusty Face,
Lighting a little hour or two—was gone.

— 17 —

Think, in this batter'd Caravanserai[7]
Whose Portals are alternate Night and Day,
    How Sultán after Sultán with his Pomp
Abode his destin'd Hour, and went his way.

— 18 —

They say the Lion and the Lizard keep
The Courts where Jamshyd gloried and drank deep: 70
    And Bahrám,[8] that great Hunter—the Wild Ass
Stamps o'er his Head, but cannot break his Sleep.

— 19 —

I sometimes think that never blows so red
The Rose as where some buried Cæsar bled;
    That every Hyacinth the Garden wears
Dropt in her Lap from some once lovely Head.

— 20 —

And this reviving Herb whose tender Green
Fledges the River-Lip on which we lean—
    Ah, lean upon it lightly! for who knows
From what once lovely Lip it springs unseen!   80

— 21 —

Ah, my Belovéd, fill the Cup that clears
TO-DAY of past Regret and future Fears:
    To-morrow!—Why, To-morrow I may be
Myself with Yesterday's Sev'n thousand Years.

— 22 —

For some we loved, the loveliest and the best
That from his Vintage rolling Time hath prest,
    Have drunk their Cup a Round or two before,
And one by one crept silently to rest.

— 23 —

And we that now make merry in the Room
They left, and Summer dresses in new bloom,   90
    Ourselves must we beneath the Couch of Earth
Descend—ourselves to make a Couch—for whom?

— 24 —

Ah, make the most of what we yet may spend,
Before we too into the Dust descend;
    Dust into Dust, and under Dust, to lie,
Sans Wine, sans Song, sans Singer, and—sans End!

— 25 —

Alike for those who for TO-DAY prepare,
And those that after some TO-MORROW stare,
    A Muezzin from the Tower of Darkness cries,
"Fools! your Reward is Neither Here nor There."   100

---

[6]**Mahmúd**: Persian sultan.

[7]**Caravanserai**: inn.

[8]**Bahrám**: Persian ruler, lost in a swamp while hunting a wild ass.

— 26 —

Why, all the Saints and Sages who discuss'd,
Of the two Worlds so wisely—they are thrust
    Like foolish Prophets forth; their Words to Scorn
Are scatter'd, and their Mouths are stopt with Dust.

— 27 —

Myself when young did eagerly frequent
Doctor and Saint, and heard great argument
    About it and about: but evermore
Came out by the same door where in I went.

— 28 —

With them the seed of Wisdom did I sow,
And with mine own hand wrought to make it grow; 110
    And this was all the Harvest that I reap'd—
"I came like Water, and like Wind I go."

— 29 —

Into this Universe, and *Why* not knowing
Nor *Whence*, like Water willy-nilly flowing
    And out of it, as Wind along the Waste,
I know not *Whither*, willy-nilly blowing.

— 30 —

What, without asking, hither hurried *Whence?*
And, without asking, *Whither* hurried hence!
    Oh, many a Cup of this forbidden Wine[9]
Must drown the memory of that insolence!   120

— 31 —

Up from Earth's Centre through the Seventh Gate
I rose, and on the Throne of Saturn[10] sate,
    And many a Knot unravel'd by the Road;
But not the Master-knot of Human Fate.

— 32 —

There was the Door to which I found no Key;
There was the Veil through which I might not see;
    Some little talk awhile of ME and THEE
There was—and then no more of THEE and ME.

— 33 —

Earth could not answer; nor the Seas that mourn
In flowing Purple, of their Lord forlorn;   130
    Nor rolling Heaven, with all his Signs reveal'd
And hidden by the sleeve of Night and Morn.

— 34 —

Then of the THEE IN ME who works behind
The Veil, I lifted up my hands to find
    A Lamp amid the Darkness; and I heard,
As from Without—"THE ME WITHIN THEE blind!"

— 35 —

Then to the Lip of this poor earthen Urn
I lean'd, the Secret of my Life to learn:
    And Lip to Lip it murmur'd—"While you live,
Drink!—for, once dead, you never shall return."   140

— 36 —

I think the Vessel, that with fugitive
Articulation answer'd, once did live,
    And drink; and Ah! the passive Lip I kiss'd,
How many Kisses might it take—and give!

— 37 —

For I remember stopping by the way
To watch a Potter thumping his wet Clay:
    And with its all-obliterated Tongue
It murmur'd—"Gently Brother, gently, pray!"

— 38 —

And has not such a Story from of Old
Down Man's successive generations roll'd   150
    Of such a clod of saturated Earth
Cast by the Maker into Human mould?[11]

---

[9]**forbidden Wine:** Islam forbids the consumption of alcohol.

[10]**Saturn:** Lord of the seventh Heaven. [FitzGerald's note]

[11]**Human mould:** One of the Persian poets—Attár, I think—has a pretty story about this. A thirsty Traveller dips his hand into a Spring of Water to drink from. By-and-by comes another who draws up and drinks from an earthen Bowl, and then departs, leaving his Bowl behind him. The first Traveller takes it up for another draught; but is surprised to find that the same Water which had tasted sweet from his own hand tastes bitter from the earthen Bowl. But a Voice—from Heaven, I think—tells him the clay from which the Bowl is made was once Man; and, into whatever shape renew'd, can never lose the bitter flavour of Mortality. [FitzGerald's note]

— 39 —

And not a drop that from our Cups we throw
For Earth to drink of, but may steal below
    To quench the fire of Anguish in some Eye
There hidden—far beneath, and long ago.

— 40 —

As then the Tulip for her morning sup
Of Heav'nly Vintage from the soil looks up,
    Do you devoutly do the like, till Heav'n
To Earth invert you—like an empty Cup.   160

— 41 —

Perplext no more with Human or Divine,
To-morrow's tangle to the winds resign,
    And lose your fingers in the tresses of
The Cypress-slender Minister of Wine.

— 42 —

And if the Wine you drink, the Lip you press,
End in what All begins and ends in—Yes;
    Think then you are TO-DAY what YESTERDAY
You were—TO-MORROW you shall not be less.

— 43 —

So when the Angel of the darker Drink
At last shall find you by the river-brink,   170
    And, offering his Cup, invite your Soul
Forth to your Lips to quaff—you shall not shrink.

— 44 —

Why, if the Soul can fling the Dust aside,
And naked on the Air of Heaven ride,
    Were 't not a Shame—were 't not a Shame for him
In this clay carcase crippled to abide?

— 45 —

'Tis but a Tent where takes his one day's rest
A Sultán to the realm of Death addrest;
    The Sultán rises, and the dark Ferrásh[12]
Strikes, and prepares it for another Guest.   180

— 46 —

And fear not lest Existence closing your
Account, and mine, should know the like no more;
    The Eternal Sákí[13] from that Bowl has pour'd
Millions of Bubbles like us, and will pour.

— 47 —

When You and I behind the Veil are past,
Oh, but the long, long while the World shall last
    Which of our Coming and Departure heeds
As the Sea's self should heed a pebble-cast.

— 48 —

A Moment's Halt—a momentary taste
Of BEING from the Well amid the Waste—   190
    And Lo!—the phantom Caravan has reach'd
The NOTHING it set out from—Oh, make haste!

— 49 —

Would you that spangle of Existence spend
About THE SECRET—quick about it, Friend!
    A Hair perhaps divides the False and True;
And upon what, prithee, does life depend?

— 50 —

A Hair perhaps divides the False and True;
Yes; and a single Alif[14] were the clue—
    Could you but find it—to the Treasure-house,
And peradventure to THE MASTER too;   200

— 51 —

Whose secret Presence, through Creation's veins
Running Quicksilver-like eludes your pains;
    Taking all shapes from Máh to Máhi;[15] and
They change and perish all—but He remains;

— 52 —

A moment guess'd—then back behind the Fold
Immerst of Darkness round the Drama roll'd
    Which, for the Pastime of Eternity,
He doth Himself contrive, enact, behold.

---

[13]**Sákí**: wine-bearer.

[14]**Alif**: first letter of the Arabic alphabet, made by a single vertical stroke.

[15]**from Máh to Máhi**: from bottom to top (literally, from fish to moon).

---

[12]**Ferrásh**: servant.

— 53 —

But if in vain, down on the stubborn floor
Of Earth, and up to Heav'n's unopening Door,   210
   You gaze TO-DAY, while You are You—how then
TO-MORROW, You when shall be You no more?

— 54 —

Waste not your Hour, nor in the vain pursuit
Of This and That endeavour and dispute;
   Better be jocund with the fruitful Grape
Than sadden after none, or bitter, Fruit.

— 55 —

You know, my Friends, with what a brave Carouse
I made a Second Marriage in my house;
   Divorced old barren Reason from my Bed,
And took the Daughter of the Vine to Spouse.   220

— 56 —

For "IS" and "IS-NOT" though with Rule and Line,
And "UP-AND-DOWN" by Logic I define,
   Of all that one should care to fathom, I
Was never deep in anything but—Wine.

— 57 —

Ah, but my Computations,[16] People say
Reduced the Year to better reckoning?—Nay,
   'Twas only striking from the Calendar
Unborn To-morrow and dead Yesterday.

— 58 —

And lately, by the Tavern Door agape,
Came shining through the Dusk an Angel Shape   230
   Bearing a Vessel on his Shoulder; and
He bid me taste of it; and 't was—the Grape!

— 59 —

The Grape that can with Logic absolute
The Two-and-Seventy jarring Sects[17] confute:
   The sovereign Alchemist that in a trice
Life's leaden metal into Gold transmute:

— 60 —

The mighty Mahmúd,[18] Allah-breathing Lord,
That all the misbelieving and black Horde
   Of Fears and Sorrows that infest the Soul
Scatters before him with his whirlwind Sword.   240

— 61 —

Why, be this Juice the growth of God, who dare
Blaspheme the twisted tendril as a Snare?
   A Blessing, we should use it, should we not?
And if a Curse—why, then, Who set it there?

— 62 —

I must abjure the Balm of Life, I must,
Scared by some After-reckoning ta'en on trust,
   Or lured with Hope of some Diviner Drink,
To fill the Cup—when crumbled into Dust!

— 63 —

Oh, threats of Hell and Hopes of Paradise!
One thing at least is certain—*This* Life flies,   250
   One thing is certain and the rest is Lies;
The Flower that once has blown for ever dies.

— 64 —

Strange, is it not? that of the myriads who
Before us pass'd the door of Darkness through,
   Not one returns to tell us of the Road,
Which to discover we must travel too.

— 65 —

The Revelations of Devout and Learn'd
Who rose before us, and as Prophets burn'd,
   Are all but Stories, which, awoke from Sleep
They told their comrades, and to Sleep return'd.   260

— 66 —

I sent my Soul through the Invisible,
Some letter of that After-life to spell:
   And by and by my Soul return'd to me,
And answer'd "I Myself am Heav'n and Hell:"

---

[16]**Computations**: Omar, an astronomer, updated the calendar.

[17]**Sects**: The Seventy-two Religions supposed to divide the World, *including* Islamism, as some think: but others not. [FitzGerald's note]

---

[18]**Mahmúd**: Alluding to Sultan Mahmúd's Conquest of India and its dark people. [FitzGerald's note]

— 67 —

Heav'n but the Vision of fulfill'd Desire,
And Hell the Shadow from a Soul on fire
    Cast on the Darkness into which Ourselves,
So late emerg'd from, shall so soon expire.

— 68 —

We are no other than a moving row
Of Magic Shadow-shapes that come and go   270
    Round with the Sun-illumin'd Lantern held
In Midnight by the Master of the Show;

— 69 —

But helpless Pieces of the Game He plays
Upon this Chequer-board of Nights and Days.
    Hither and thither moves, and checks, and slays,
And one by one back in the Closet lays.

— 70 —

The Ball no question makes of Ayes and Noes,
But Here or There as strikes the Player goes,
    And He that toss'd you down into the Field,
He knows about it all—HE knows—HE knows![19]   280

— 71 —

The Moving Finger writes; and, having writ,
Moves on: nor all your Piety nor Wit
    Shall lure it back to cancel half a Line,
Nor all your Tears wash out a Word of it.

— 72 —

And that inverted Bowl they call the Sky,
Whereunder crawling coop'd we live and die,
    Lift not your hands to It for help—for it
As impotently moves as you or I.

— 73 —

With Earth's first Clay They did the Last Man knead,
And there of the Last Harvest sow'd the Seed: 290
    And the first Morning of Creation wrote
What the Last Dawn of Reckoning shall read.

— 74 —

YESTERDAY This Day's Madness did prepare;
TO-MORROW'S Silence, Triumph, or Despair:
    Drink! for you know not whence you came, nor why:
Drink! for you know not why you go, nor where.

— 75 —

I tell you this—When, started from the Goal,
Over the flaming shoulders of the Foal
    Of Heav'n Parwin and Mushtari[20] they flung,
In my predestin'd Plot of Dust and Soul   300

— 76 —

The Vine had struck a fibre: which about
If clings my Being—let the Dervish[21] flout;
    Of my Base metal may be filed a Key,
That shall unlock the Door he howls without.

— 77 —

And this I know: whether the one True Light
Kindle to Love, or Wrath-consume me quite,
    One flash of It within the Tavern caught
Better than in the Temple lost outright.

— 78 —

What! out of senseless Nothing to provoke
A conscious Something to resent the yoke   310
    Of unpermitted Pleasure, under pain
Of Everlasting Penalties, if broke!

— 79 —

What! from his helpless Creature be repaid
Pure Gold for what he lent him dross-allay'd—
    Sue for a Debt we never did contract,
And cannot answer—Oh, the sorry trade!

— 80 —

Oh Thou, who didst with pitfall and with gin
Beset the Road I was to wander in,
    Thou wilt not with Predestin'd Evil round
Enmesh, and then impute my Fall to Sin!   320

---

[19]He . . . knows: A very mysterious Line in the Original:
    O dánad O dánad O dánad O———breaking off something
like our Wood-pigeon's Note, which she is said to take up just
where she left off. [FitzGerald's note]

[20]flaming . . . Foal: constellation named the Little Horse. Parwin: Pleiades. Mushtari: Jupiter.

[21]Dervish: member of the Sufi sect, to whose allegorical mysticism FitzGerald believed Omar was firmly opposed.

— 81 —

Oh, Thou, who Man of baser Earth didst make,
And ev'n with Paradise devise the Snake:
    For all the Sin wherewith the Face of Man
Is blacken'd—Man's forgiveness give—and take!

•   •   •   •   •   •   •   •   •

— 82 —

As under cover of departing Day
Slunk hunger-stricken Ramazán[22] away,
    Once more within the Potter's house alone
I stood, surrounded by the Shapes of Clay.

— 83 —

Shapes of all Sorts and Sizes, great and small,
That stood along the floor and by the wall;   330
    And some loquacious vessels were; and some
Listen'd perhaps, but never talk'd at all.

— 84 —

Said one among them—"Surely not in vain
My substance of the common Earth was ta'en
    And to this Figure moulded, to be broke,
Or trampled back to shapeless Earth again."

— 85 —

Then said a Second—"Ne'er a peevish Boy
Would break the Bowl from which he drank in joy;
    And He that with his hand the Vessel made
Will surely not in after Wrath destroy."   340

— 86 —

After a momentary silence spake
Some Vessel of a more ungainly make:
    "They sneer at me for leaning all awry:
What! did the Hand then of the Potter shake?"

— 87 —

Whereat some one of the loquacious Lot—
I think a Súfi pipkin—waxing hot—
    "All this of Pot and Potter—Tell me then,
Who is the Potter, pray, and who the Pot?"

— 88 —

"Why," said another, "Some there are who tell
Of one who threatens he will toss to Hell   350
    The luckless Pots he marr'd in making—Pish!
He's a Good Fellow, and 't will all be well."

— 89 —

"Well," murmur'd one, "Let whoso make or buy,
My Clay with long Oblivion is gone dry:
    But fill me with the old familiar Juice,
Methinks I might recover by and by."

— 90 —

So while the Vessels one by one were speaking,
The little Moon look'd in that all were seeking:
    And then they jogg'd each other, "Brother! Brother!
Now for the Porter's shoulder-knot a-creaking!"   360

•   •   •   •   •   •   •   •   •

— 91 —

Ah, with the Grape my fading Life provide,
And wash the Body whence the Life has died,
    And lay me, shrouded in the living Leaf,
By some not unfrequented Garden-side.

— 92 —

That ev'n my buried Ashes such a snare
Of Vintage shall fling up into the Air
    As not a True-believer passing by
But shall be overtaken unaware.

— 93 —

Indeed the Idols I have loved so long
Have done my credit in this World much wrong: 370
    Have drown'd my Glory in a shallow Cup,
And sold my Reputation for a Song.

— 94 —

Indeed, indeed, Repentance oft before
I swore—but was I sober when I swore?
    And then and then came Spring, and Rose-in-hand
My thread-bare Penitence apieces tore.

---

[22]**Ramazán**: At the Close of the Fasting Month, Ramazán (which makes the Musulman unhealthy and unamiable), the first Glimpse of the New Moon (who rules their Division of the Year) is looked for with the utmost Anxiety, and hailed with Acclamation. [FitzGerald's note; see rubai 90]

— 95 —

And much as Wine has play'd the Infidel,
And robb'd me of my Robe of Honour—Well,
    I wonder often what the Vintners buy
One half so precious as the stuff they sell.   380

— 96 —

Yet Ah, that Spring should vanish with the Rose!
That Youth's sweet-scented manuscript should close!
    The Nightingale that in the branches sang,
Ah whence, and whither flown again, who knows!

— 97 —

Would but the Desert of the Fountain yield
One glimpse—if dimly, yet indeed, reveal'd,
    To which the fainting Traveller might spring,
As springs the trampled herbage of the field!

— 98 —

Would but some wingéd Angel ere too late
Arrest the yet unfolded Roll of Fate,   390
    And make the stern Recorder otherwise
Enregister, or quite obliterate!

— 99 —

Ah Love! could you and I with Him conspire
To grasp this sorry Scheme of Things entire,
    Would not we shatter it to bits—and then
Re-mould it nearer to the Heart's desire!

•   •   •   •   •   •   •   •   •   •

— 100 —

Yon rising Moon that looks for us again—
How oft hereafter will she wax and wane;
    How oft hereafter rising look for us
Through this same Garden—and for *one* in vain!   400

— 101 —

And when like her, oh Sákí, you shall pass
Among the Guests Star-scatter'd on the Grass,
    And in your joyous errand reach the spot
Where I made One—turn down an empty Glass!

TAMAM.[23]

1859, 1879

───────────────

[23]**TAMAM:** It is ended.

ELIZABETH GASKELL

(1810–1865)

Elizabeth Gaskell's biography of Charlotte Brontë (1816–1855) brings together two major Victorian writers. They first met in 1850, when both were established novelists. Brontë, although younger, had published two novels, and Gaskell one. Gaskell's warmth and charm thawed Brontë's prickly shyness; she was one of the few people whose homes Brontë visited and one of even fewer whom Brontë invited to visit her. Three months after Brontë's death, her father asked Gaskell to write her biography. Erroneous and often scurrilous notions had long been afloat about the author of *Jane Eyre* (1847), and Gaskell welcomed the chance to vindicate her friend.

Gaskell had been brought up by her aunt in a pleasant country town with a large extended family nearby. She began her education at home and then attended an excellent boarding school until she was sixteen. In 1832 she married Arthur Gaskell, a Unitarian minister in Manchester who interspersed his ministerial duties with editing a newspaper and teaching English history and literature. They had a stillborn child, then four daughters and a son who died at the age of two. To distract herself from grief after her son's death she wrote *Mary Barton* (1848), a novel drawing on her knowledge of the great industrial city she lived in and aiming to promote understanding between manufacturers and workers. *Mary Barton* was an immediate success despite fierce criticism of its sympathetic presentation of workers' grievances. It was followed by other novels and stories, including *Ruth* (1853), which was even more controversial because its heroine is depicted as virtuous despite bearing a child out of wedlock. Gaskell was a sociable, hardworking woman who kept a distinguished literary career, a busy household, and an extensive social life all comfortably afloat; she often wrote in the dining room, with the doors open to the world around her.

Her imagination was forcibly impressed by the contrasting bleakness of Charlotte Brontë's situation. She admired Brontë's strong religious faith, her fortitude in suffering, her noble character, and her powerful genius. There was perfect material for a novelist in the strange, sad history (outlined in our introduction to Emily Brontë) of the six gifted siblings of whom Charlotte was the last survivor, as well as in Charlotte's sudden fame, her devotion to her sisters and widowed father, her long-delayed marriage and her death soon thereafter. Gaskell vigorously rebutted the charges of "coarseness" aroused by the violence and sexual passion in Brontë's novels and those of her sisters Emily and Anne, which were often attributed to a single author. The crudeness and profligacy described in their books reflected, she says, their harsh surroundings and the terrible behavior of their brother, Branwell. She emphasizes the austerity and innocence of the sisters' lives and depicts her heroine as in every way "womanly": domestic, devoted to family, self-sacrificing. But she also traces the uneasy coexistence and often conflicting claims of womanly virtue on the one hand and imaginative genius on the other.

In her book we hear many voices. Writing as a sympathetic friend and occasional participant in the story, Gaskell told as much as she could in Brontë's own words. Not only did she collect Brontë's letters and draw on her published writings; she also visited or corresponded with people who had known her or her family and made their voices part of the record too. The book thus takes its place at an intersection between the proliferating biographies of the period, which typically took the form of a shapeless and adulatory "life and letters," and the polyphonic Victorian novel. The greatest of Victorian biographies, it fully rehabilitated its subject's reputation and set the terms for endless reworkings of the Brontë legend. It is largely due to Gaskell's book that the grim parsonage at Haworth is one of the most visited literary sites in England, the stony village and wild moors neatly signposted in many languages.

from Life of Charlotte Brontë

The Leeds and Skipton railway runs along a deep valley of the Aire; a slow and sluggish stream, compared to the neighbouring river of Wharfe. Keighley station is on this line of railway, about a quarter of a mile from the town of the same name. The number of inhabitants and the importance of Keighley have been very greatly increased during the last twenty years, owing to the rapidly extended market for worsted manufactures, a branch of industry that mainly employs the factory population of this part of Yorkshire, which has Bradford for its centre and metropolis.

Keighley is in process of transformation from a populous, old-fashioned village, into a still more populous and flourishing town. It is evident to the stranger, that as the gable-ended houses, which obtrude themselves corner-wise on the widening street, fall vacant, they are pulled down to allow of greater space for traffic, and a more modern style of architecture. The quaint and narrow shop-windows of fifty years ago, are giving way to large panes and plate-glass. Nearly every dwelling seems devoted to some branch of commerce. In passing hastily through the town, one hardly perceives where the necessary lawyer and doctor can live, so little appearance is there of any dwellings of the professional middle-class, such as abound in our old cathedral towns. In fact, nothing can be more opposed than the state of society, the modes of thinking, the standards of reference on all points of morality, manners, and even politics and religion, in such a new manufacturing place as Keighley in the north, and any stately, sleepy, picturesque cathedral town in the south. Yet the aspect of Keighley promises well for future stateliness, if not picturesqueness. Grey stone abounds; and the rows of houses built of it have a kind of solid grandeur connected with their uniform and enduring lines. The frame-work of the doors, and the lintels of the windows, even in the smallest dwellings, are made of blocks of stone. There is no painted wood to require continual beautifying, or else present a shabby aspect; and the stone is kept scrupulously clean by the notable Yorkshire housewives.

Such glimpses into the interior as a passer-by obtains, reveal a rough abundance of the means of living, and diligent and active habits in the women. But the voices of the people are hard, and their tones discordant, promising little of the musical taste that distinguishes the district, and which has already furnished a Carrodus[1] to the musical world. The names over the shops (of which the one just given is a sample) seem strange even to an inhabitant of the neighbouring county, and have a peculiar smack and flavour of the place.

The town of Keighley never quite melts into country on the road to Haworth, although the houses become more sparse as the traveller journeys upwards to the grey round hills that seem to bound his journey in a westerly direction. First come some villas; just sufficiently retired from the road to show that they can scarcely belong to any one liable to be summoned in a hurry, at the call of suffering or danger, from his comfortable fire-side; the lawyer, the doctor, and the clergyman, live at hand, and hardly in the suburbs, with a screen of shrubs for concealment.

In a town one does not look for vivid colouring; what there may be of this is furnished by the wares in the shops, not by foliage or atmospheric effects; but in the country some brilliancy and vividness seems to be instinctively expected, and there is consequently a slight feeling of disappointment at the grey neutral tint of every object, near or far off, on the way from Keighley to Haworth. The distance is about four miles; and, as I have said, what with villas, great worsted factories, rows of workmen's houses, with here and there an old-fashioned farm-house and outbuildings, it can hardly be called "country" any part of the way. For two miles the road passes over tolerably level ground, distant hills on the left, a "beck"[2] flowing through meadows on the right, and furnishing water power, at certain points, to the factories built on its banks. The air is dim and lightless with the smoke from all these habitations and places of business. The soil in the valley (or "bottom," to use the local

---

[1]John Tiplady **Carrodus** (1836–1895): violinist and composer.
[2]"**beck**": brook.

term) is rich; but, as the road begins to ascend, the vegetation becomes poorer; it does not flourish, it merely exists; and, instead of trees, there are only bushes and shrubs about the dwellings. Stone dykes are everywhere used in place of hedges; and what crops there are, on the patches of arable land, consist of pale, hungry-looking, grey-green oats. Right before the traveller on this road rises Haworth village; he can see it for two miles before he arrives, for it is situated on the side of a pretty steep hill, with a background of dun and purple moors, rising and sweeping away yet higher than the church, which is built at the very summit of the long narrow street. All round the horizon there is this same line of sinuous wave-like hills; the scoops into which they fall only revealing other hills beyond, of similar colour and shape, crowned with wild, bleak moors—grand, from the ideas of solitude and loneliness which they suggest, or oppressive from the feeling which they give of being pent-up by some monotonous and illimitable barrier, according to the mood of mind in which the spectator may be.

For a short distance the road appears to turn away from Haworth, as it winds round the base of the shoulder of a hill; but then it crosses a bridge over the "beck," and the ascent through the village begins. The flag-stones with which it is paved are placed end-ways, in order to give a better hold to the horses' feet; and, even with this help, they seem to be in constant danger of slipping backwards. The old stone houses are high compared to the width of the street, which makes an abrupt turn before reaching the more level ground at the head of the village, so that the steep aspect of the place, in one part, is almost like that of a wall. But this surmounted, the church lies a little off the main road on the left; a hundred yards, or so, and the driver relaxes his care, and the horse breathes more easily, as they pass into the quiet little by-street that leads to Haworth Parsonage. The churchyard is on one side of this lane, the school-house and the sexton's dwelling (where the curates formerly lodged) on the other.

The parsonage stands at right angles to the road, facing down upon the church; so that, in fact, parsonage, church, and belfried school-house, form three sides of an irregular oblong, of which the fourth is open to the fields and moors that lie beyond. The area of this oblong is filled up by a crowded churchyard, and a small garden or court in front of the clergyman's house. As the entrance to this from the road is at the side, the path goes round the corner into the little plot of ground. Underneath the windows is a narrow flower-border, carefully tended in days of yore, although only the most hardy plants could be made to grow there. Within the stone wall, which keeps out the surrounding churchyard, are bushes of elder and lilac; the rest of the ground is occupied by a square grass-plot and a gravel walk.

The house is of grey stone, two stories high, heavily roofed with flags,[3] in order to resist the winds that might strip off a lighter covering. It appears to have been built about a hundred years ago, and to consist of four rooms on each story; the two windows on the right (as the visitor stands with his back to the church, ready to enter in at the front door) belonging to Mr. Brontë's study, the two on the left to the family sitting-room. Everything about the place tells of the most dainty order, the most exquisite cleanliness. The doorsteps are spotless; the small old-fashioned window-panes glitter like looking-glass. Inside and outside of that house cleanliness goes up into its essence, purity.

The little church lies, as I mentioned, above most of the houses in the village; and the graveyard rises above the church, and is terribly full of upright tombstones. The chapel or church claims greater antiquity than any other in that part of the kingdom; but there is no appearance of this in the external aspect of the present edifice, unless it be in the two eastern windows, which remain unmodernized, and in the lower part of the steeple. . . .

The interior of the church is common-place; it is neither old enough nor modern enough to compel notice. The pews are of black oak, with high divisions; and the names of those to whom they belong are painted in white letters on the doors. There are neither brasses, nor altar-tombs, nor monuments, but there is a mural tablet on the right-hand side of the communion-table, bearing the following inscription:—

HERE
LIE THE REMAINS OF
MARIA BRONTË, WIFE
OF THE
REV. P. BRONTË, A.B., MINISTER OF HAWORTH.
HER SOUL
DEPARTED TO THE SAVIOUR, SEPT. 15TH, 1821,
IN THE 39TH YEAR OF HER AGE.
"Be ye also ready: for in such an hour as ye think not the Son of Man cometh."—Matthew xxiv. 44.
ALSO HERE LIE THE REMAINS OF
MARIA BRONTË, DAUGHTER OF THE AFORESAID;
SHE DIED ON THE
6TH OF MAY, 1825, IN THE 12TH YEAR OF HER AGE;
AND OF
ELIZABETH BRONTË, HER SISTER,
WHO DIED JUNE 15TH, 1825, IN THE 11TH YEAR OF HER AGE.
"Verily I say unto you, Except ye be converted, and become as little children, ye shall not enter into the kingdom of heaven."—Matthew xviii.3.

---

[3]**flags:** slabs of rock.

HERE ALSO LIE THE REMAINS OF
PATRICK BRANWELL BRONTË,
WHO DIED SEPT. 24TH, 1848, AGED 30 YEARS;
AND OF
EMILY JANE BRONTË,
WHO DIED DEC. 19TH, 1848, AGED 29 YEARS,
SON AND DAUGHTER OF THE
REV. P. BRONTË, INCUMBENT.
THIS STONE IS ALSO DEDICATED TO THE
MEMORY OF ANNE BRONTË,
YOUNGEST DAUGHTER OF THE REV. P. BRONTË, A.B.
SHE DIED, AGED 27 YEARS, MAY 28TH, 1849,
AND WAS BURIED AT THE OLD CHURCH, SCARBORO'.

At the upper part of this tablet ample space is allowed between the lines of the inscription; when the first memorials were written down, the survivors, in their fond affection, thought little of the margin and verge they were leaving for those who were still living. But as one dead member of the household follows another fast to the grave, the lines are pressed together, and the letters become small and cramped. After the record of Anne's death, there is room for no other.

But one more of that generation—the last of that nursery of six little motherless children—was yet to follow, before the survivor, the childless and widowed father, found his rest. On another tablet, below the first, the following record has been added to that mournful list:—

ADJOINING LIE THE REMAINS OF
CHARLOTTE, WIFE
OF THE
REV. ARTHUR BELL NICHOLLS, A.B.,
AND DAUGHTER OF THE REV. P. BRONTË., A.B., INCUMBENT.
SHE DIED MARCH 31ST, 1855, IN THE 39TH
YEAR OF HER AGE.

(Volume 1, Chapter 1)

. . . From their first going to Haworth, their walks were directed rather out towards the heathery moors, sloping upwards behind the parsonage, than towards the long descending village street. A good old woman, who came to nurse Mrs. Brontë in the illness—an internal cancer—which grew and gathered upon her, not many months after her arrival at Haworth, tells me that at that time the six little creatures[4] used to walk out, hand in hand, towards the glorious wild moors, which in after days they loved so passionately; the elder ones taking thoughtful care for the toddling wee things.

They were grave and silent beyond their years; subdued, probably, by the presence of serious illness in the house; for, at the time which my informant speaks of, Mrs. Brontë was confined to the bed-room from which she never came forth alive. "You would not have known there was a child in the house, they were such still, noiseless, good little creatures. Maria would shut herself up" (Maria, but seven!) "in the children's study with a newspaper, and be able to tell one everything when she came out; debates in parliament, and I don't know what all. She was as good as a mother to her sisters and brother. But there never were such good children. I used to think them spiritless, they were so different to any children I had ever seen. They were good little creatures. Emily was the prettiest."

Mrs. Brontë was the same patient, cheerful person as we have seen her formerly; very ill, suffering great pain, but seldom if ever complaining; at her better times begging her nurse to raise her in bed to let her see her clean the grate, "because she did it as it was done in Cornwall,"[5] devotedly fond of her husband, who warmly repaid her affection, and suffered no one else to take the night-nursing; but, according to my informant, the mother was not very anxious to see much of her children, probably because the sight of them, knowing how soon they were to be left motherless, would have agitated her too much. So the little things clung quietly together, for their father was busy in his study and in his parish, or with their mother, and they took their meals alone; sat reading, or whispering low, in the "children's study," or wandered out on the hill-side, hand in hand. . . . (Volume 1, Chapter 3)

. . . When the sisters met at home in the Christmas holidays, they talked over their lives, and the prospect which they afforded of employment and remuneration. They felt that it was a duty to relieve their father of the burden of their support, if not entirely, or that of all three, at least that of one or two; and, naturally, the lot devolved upon the elder ones to find some occupation which would enable them to do this. They knew that they were never likely to inherit much money. Mr. Brontë had but a small stipend, and was both charitable and liberal. Their aunt[6] had an

---

[4]The six Brontë children were Maria (1814–1825), Elizabeth (1815–1825), Charlotte (1816–1855), Patrick Branwell (1817–1848), Emily (1818–1848), and Anne (1820–1849).

[5]**Cornwall**: home of Maria Branwell Brontë (1783–1821) in SW England.

[6]**aunt**: Elizabeth Branwell (1776–1842) came to live with the family after Mrs. Brontë died.

annuity of 50*l.*, but it reverted to others at her death, and her nieces had no right, and were the last persons in the world to reckon upon her savings. What could they do? Charlotte and Emily were trying teaching, and, as it seemed, without much success. The former, it is true, had the happiness of having a friend for her employer, and of being surrounded by those who knew her and loved her; but her salary was too small for her to save out of it; and her education did not entitle her to a larger. The sedentary and monotonous nature of the life, too, was preying upon her health and spirits, although, with necessity "as her mistress," she might hardly like to acknowledge this even to herself. But Emily—that free, wild, untameable spirit, never happy nor well but on the sweeping moors that gathered round her home—that hater of strangers, doomed to live amongst them, and not merely to live but to slave in their service— what Charlotte could have borne patiently for herself, she could not bear for her sister. And yet what to do? She had once hoped that she herself might become an artist, and so earn her livelihood; but her eyes had failed her in the minute and useless labour which she had imposed upon herself with a view to this end.

It was the household custom among these girls to sew till nine o'clock at night. At that hour, Miss Branwell generally went to bed, and her nieces' duties for the day were accounted done. They put away their work,[7] and began to pace the room backwards and forwards, up and down,—as often with the candles extinguished, for economy's sake, as not,—their figures glancing into the fire-light, and out into the shadow, perpetually. At this time, they talked over past cares, and troubles; they planned for the future, and consulted each other as to their plans. In after years this was the time for discussing together the plots of their novels. And again, still later, this was the time for the last surviving sister to walk alone, from old accustomed habit, round and round the desolate room, thinking sadly upon the "days that were no more." But this Christmas of 1836 was not without its hopes and daring aspirations. They had tried their hands at story-writing, in their miniature magazine, long ago; they all of them "made out" perpetually. They had likewise attempted to write poetry; and had a modest confidence that they had achieved a tolerable success. But they knew that they might deceive themselves, and that sisters' judgments of each other's productions were likely to be too partial to be depended upon. So Charlotte, as the eldest, resolved to write to Southey.[8] I believe (from an expression in a letter

to be noticed hereafter), that she also consulted Coleridge; but I have not met with any part of that correspondence.

On December 29th, her letter to Southey was despatched; and from an excitement not unnatural in a girl who has worked herself up to the pitch of writing to a Poet Laureate and asking his opinion of her poems, she used some high-flown expressions, which, probably, gave him the idea that she was a romantic young lady, unacquainted with the realities of life. . . .

January and February of 1837 had passed away, and still there was no reply from Southey. Probably she had lost expectation and almost hope when at length, in the beginning of March, she received the letter inserted in Mr. C. C. Southey's life of his Father,[9] vol. iv. p. 327.

After accounting for his delay in replying to hers by the fact of a long absence from home, during which his letters had accumulated, whence "it has lain unanswered till the last of a numerous file, not from disrespect or indifference to its contents, but because in truth it is not an easy task to answer it, nor a pleasant one to cast a damp over the high spirits and the generous desires of youth," he goes on to say: "What you are I can only infer from your letter, which appears to be written in sincerity, though I may suspect that you have used a fictitious signature. Be that as it may, the letter and the verses bear the same stamp, and I can well understand the state of mind they indicate."

*   *   *   *   *   *

"It is not my advice that you have asked as to the direction of your talents, but my opinion of them, and yet the opinion may be worth little, and the advice much. You evidently possess, and in no inconsiderable degree, what Wordsworth calls the 'faculty of verse.' I am not depreciating it when I say that in these times it is not rare. Many volumes of poems are now published every year without attracting public attention, any one of which if it had appeared half a century ago, would have obtained a high reputation for its author. Whoever, therefore, is ambitious of distinction in this way ought to be prepared for disappointment.

"But it is not with a view to distinction that you should cultivate this talent, if you consult your own happiness. I, who have made literature my profession, and devoted my life to it, and have never for a moment repented of the deliberate choice, think myself, nevertheless, bound in duty to caution every young man who applies as an aspirant to me for encouragement and advice, against taking so perilous a course. You will say that a woman has no need of such a caution; there can be no peril in it for her. In a certain sense

---

[7]**work**: sewing.

[8]Robert **Southey** (1774–1843): Poet Laureate from 1813.

[9]Charles Cuthbert **Southey**: *The Life and Correspondence of Robert Southey* (1849–1850), 6:327–330.

this is true; but there is a danger of which I would, with all kindness and all earnestness, warn you. The day dreams in which you habitually indulge are likely to induce a distempered state of mind; and in proportion as all the ordinary uses of the world seem to you flat and unprofitable,[10] you will be unfitted for them without becoming fitted for anything else. Literature cannot be the business of a woman's life, and it ought not to be. The more she is engaged in her proper duties, the less leisure will she have for it, even as an accomplishment and a recreation. To those duties you have not yet been called, and when you are you will be less eager for celebrity. You will not seek in imagination for excitement, of which the vicissitudes of this life, and the anxieties from which you must not hope to be exempted, be your state what it may, will bring with them but too much.

"But do not suppose that I disparage the gift which you possess; nor that I would discourage you from exercising it. I only exhort you so to think of it, and so to use it, as to render it conducive to your own permanent good. Write poetry for its own sake; not in a spirit of emulation, and not with a view to celebrity; the less you aim at that the more likely you will be to deserve and finally to obtain it. So written, it is wholesome both for the heart and soul; it may be made the surest means, next to religion, of soothing the mind and elevating it. You may embody in it your best thoughts and your wisest feelings, and in so doing discipline and strengthen them.

"Farewell, madam. It is not because I have forgotten that I was once young myself, that I write to you in this strain; but because I remember it. You will neither doubt my sincerity nor my good will; and however ill what has here been said may accord with your present views and temper, the longer you live the more reasonable it will appear to you. Though I may be but an ungracious adviser, you will allow me, therefore, to subscribe myself, with the best wishes for your happiness here and hereafter, your true friend,

"ROBERT SOUTHEY."

I was with Miss Brontë when she received Mr. Cuthbert Southey's note, requesting her permission to insert the foregoing letter in his father's life. She said to me, "Mr. Southey's letter was kind and admirable; a little stringent, but it did me good."

It is partly because I think it so admirable, and partly because it tends to bring out her character, as shown in the

---

[10]**uses . . . unprofitable:** see *Hamlet* 1.2.133–134.

following reply, that I have taken the liberty of inserting the foregoing extracts from it.

"*March 16th.*

"SIR,

"I cannot rest till I have answered your letter, even though by addressing you a second time I should appear a little intrusive; but I must thank you for the kind and wise advice you have condescended to give me. I had not ventured to hope for such a reply; so considerate in its tone, so noble in its spirit. I must suppress what I feel, or you will think me foolishly enthusiastic.

"At the first perusal of your letter, I felt only shame and regret that I had ever ventured to trouble you with my crude rhapsody; I felt a painful heat rise to my face when I thought of the quires of paper I had covered with what once gave me so much delight, but which now was only a source of confusion; but, after I had thought a little and read it again and again, the prospect seemed to clear. You do not forbid me to write; you do not say that what I write is utterly destitute of merit. You only warn me against the folly of neglecting real duties, for the sake of imaginative pleasures; of writing for the love of fame; for the selfish excitement of emulation. You kindly allow me to write poetry for its own sake, provided I leave undone nothing which I ought to do, in order to pursue that single, absorbing, exquisite gratification. I am afraid, sir, you think me very foolish. I know the first letter I wrote to you was all senseless trash from beginning to end; but I am not altogether the idle dreaming being it would seem to denote. My father is a clergyman of limited, though competent income, and I am the eldest of his children. He expended quite as much in my education as he could afford in justice to the rest. I thought it therefore my duty, when I left school, to become a governess. In that capacity I find enough to occupy my thoughts all day long, and my head and hands too, without having a moment's time for one dream of the imagination. In the evenings, I confess, I do think, but I never trouble any one else with my thoughts. I carefully avoid any appearance of pre-occupation and eccentricity, which might lead those I live amongst to suspect the nature of my pursuits. Following my father's advice—who from my childhood has counselled me just in the wise and friendly tone of your letter—I have endeavoured not only attentively to observe all the duties a woman ought to fulfil, but to feel deeply interested in them. I don't always succeed, for sometimes when I'm teaching or sewing I would rather be reading or writing; but I try to deny myself; and my father's approbation amply rewarded me for the privation. Once more allow me to thank you with sincere gratitude. I trust I shall never more feel ambitious to see my name in print: if the wish should rise I'll look at Southey's letter, and suppress it. It is honour enough for me that I have written to him, and received an answer. That letter is consecrated; no one shall ever see it, but papa and my brother and sisters. Again I thank you. This incident, I suppose, will be renewed no more; if I live to be an old woman, I shall remember it thirty years hence as a bright dream. The signature which you suspected of being fictitious is my real name. Again, therefore, I must sign myself,

"*C. BRONTË.*

"P.S.—Pray, sir, excuse me for writing to you a second time; I could not help writing, partly to tell you how thankful I am for your kindness, and partly to let you know that your advice shall not be wasted; however sorrowfully and reluctantly it may be at first followed. . . .

"*C. B.*"

(Volume 1, Chapter 8)

. . . Henceforward Charlotte Brontë's existence becomes divided into two parallel currents—her life as Currer Bell,[11] the author; her life as Charlotte Brontë, the woman. There were separate duties belonging to each character—not opposing each other; not impossible, but difficult to be reconciled. When a man becomes an author, it is probably merely a change of employment to him. He takes a portion of that time which has hitherto been devoted to some other study or pursuit; he gives up something of the legal or medical profession, in which he has hitherto endeavoured to serve others, or relinquishes part of the trade or business by which he has been striving to gain a livelihood; and another merchant, or lawyer, or doctor, steps into his vacant place, and probably does as well as he. But no other can take up the quiet regular duties of the daughter, the wife, or the mother, as well as she whom God has appointed to fill that particular place: a woman's principal work in life is hardly left to her own choice; nor can she drop the domestic charges devolving on her as an individual, for the exercise of the most splendid talents that were ever bestowed. And yet she must not shrink from the extra responsibility implied by the very fact of her possessing such talents. She must not hide her gift in a

napkin;[12] it was meant for the use and service of others. In a humble and faithful spirit must she labour to do what is not impossible, or God would not have set her to do it.

I put into words what Charlotte Brontë put into actions.

The year 1848 opened with sad domestic distress.[13] It is necessary, however painful, to remind the reader constantly of what was always present to the hearts of father and sisters at this time. It is well that the thoughtless critics, who spoke of the sad and gloomy views of life presented by the Brontës in their tales, should know how such words were wrung out of them by the living recollection of the long agony they suffered. It is well, too, that they who have objected to the representation of coarseness and shrank from it with repugnance, as if such conceptions arose out of the writers, should learn, that, not from the imagination—not from internal conception—but from the hard cruel facts, pressed down, by external life, upon their very senses, for long months and years together, did they write out what they saw, obeying the stern dictates of their consciences. They might be mistaken. They might err in writing at all, when their afflictions were so great that they could not write otherwise than they did of life. It is possible that it would have been better to have described only good and pleasant people, doing only good and pleasant things (in which case they could hardly have written at any time): all I say is, that never, I believe, did women, possessed of such wonderful gifts, exercise them with a fuller feeling of responsibility for their use. As to mistakes, they stand now—as authors as well as women—before the judgment-seat of God.

"*Jan. 11th, 1848.*

"We have not been very comfortable here at home lately. Branwell has, by some means, contrived to get more money from the old quarter, and has led us a sad life. . . . Papa is harassed day and night; we have little peace; he is always sick; has two or three times fallen down in fits; what will be the ultimate end, God knows. But who is without their drawback, their scourge, their skeleton behind the curtain? It remains only to do one's best, and endure with patience what God sends."

I suppose that she had read Mr. Lewes' review[14] on "Recent Novels," when it appeared in the December of the

---

[11]**Currer Bell:** pseudonym under which *Jane Eyre* appeared in 1847.

[12]**talents . . . napkin:** see Matthew 25:14–29.

[13]**distress:** Branwell's now-habitual drunkenness and violence.

[14]**review:** George Henry **Lewes** (1817–1878) reviewed *Jane Eyre* in *Fraser's Magazine* (1847). He also wrote Brontë a letter about the book.

last year, but I find no allusion to it till she writes to him on January 12th, 1848.

"Dear Sir,—I thank you then sincerely for your generous review; and it is with the sense of double content I express my gratitude, because I am now sure the tribute is not superfluous or obtrusive. You were not severe on 'Jane Eyre;' you were very lenient. I am glad you told me my faults plainly in private, for in your public notice you touch on them so lightly, I should perhaps have passed them over, thus indicated, with too little reflection.

"I mean to observe your warning about being careful how I undertake new works; my stock of materials is not abundant, but very slender; and, besides, neither my experience, my acquirements, nor my powers, are sufficiently varied to justify my ever becoming a frequent writer. I tell you this, because your article in 'Frazer' left in me an uneasy impression that you were disposed to think better of the author of 'Jane Eyre' than that individual deserved; and I would rather you had a correct than a flattering opinion of me, even though I should never see you.

"If I ever *do* write another book, I think I will have nothing of what you call 'melodrama;' I *think* so, but I am not sure. I *think*, too, I will endeavour to follow the counsel which shines out of Miss Austen's 'mild eyes,' 'to finish more and be more subdued;' but neither am I sure of that. When authors write best, or, at least, when they write most fluently, an influence seems to waken in them, which becomes their master—which will have its own way— putting out of view all behests but its own, dictating certain words, and insisting on their being used, whether vehement or measured in their nature; new-moulding characters, giving unthought-of turns to incidents, rejecting carefully-elaborated old ideas, and suddenly creating and adopting new ones.

"Is it not so? And should we try to counteract this influence? Can we indeed counteract it?

"I am glad that another work of yours will soon appear; most curious shall I be to see whether you will write up to your own principles, and work out your own theories. You did not do it altogether in 'Ranthorpe'[15]—at least not in the latter part; but the first portion was, I think, nearly without fault; then it had a pith, truth, significance in it, which gave the book sterling value; but to write so, one must have seen and known a great deal, and I have seen and known very little.

"Why do you like Miss Austen so very much? I am puzzled on that point. What induced you to say that you would have rather written 'Pride and Prejudice,' or 'Tom Jones,' than any of the Waverley Novels?[16]

"I had not seen 'Pride and Prejudice' till I read that sentence of yours, and then I got the book. And what did I find? An accurate daguerreotyped portrait of a commonplace face; a carefully-fenced, highly-cultivated garden, with neat borders and delicate flowers; but no glance of a bright vivid physiognomy, no open country, no fresh air, no blue hill, no bonny beck. I should hardly like to live with her ladies and gentlemen, in their elegant but confined houses. These observations will probably irritate you, but I shall run the risk.

"Now I can understand admiration of George Sand;[17] for though I never saw any of her works which I admired throughout (even 'Consuelo,' which is the best, or the best that I have read, appears to me to couple strange extravagance with wondrous excellence), yet she has a grasp of mind, which, if I cannot fully comprehend, I can very deeply respect; she is sagacious and profound;—Miss Austen is only shrewd and observant.

"Am I wrong—or, were you hasty in what you said? If you have time, I should be glad to hear further on this subject; if not, or if you think the question frivolous, do not trouble yourself to reply.—I am, yours respectfully,

"C. BELL." . . .

Let us return from Currer Bell to Charlotte Brontë. The winter in Haworth had been a sickly season. Influenza had prevailed amongst the villagers, and where there was a real need for the presence of the clergyman's daughters, they were never found wanting, although they were shy of bestowing mere social visits on the parishioners. They had themselves suffered from the epidemic; Anne severely, as in her case it had been attended with cough and fever enough to make her elder sisters very anxious about her.

There is no doubt that the proximity of the crowded churchyard rendered the Parsonage unhealthy, and occasioned much illness to its inmates. Mr. Brontë represented the unsanitary state of Haworth pretty forcibly to the Board of Health; and, after the requisite visits from their officers, obtained a recommendation that all future interments in the churchyard should be forbidden, a new graveyard opened on the hill-side, and means set on foot for obtaining a

---

[15]*Ranthorpe* (1847): novel by Lewes.

[16]*Pride and Prejudice* (1813): by Jane Austen. *Tom Jones* (1749): by Henry Fielding. **Waverley Novels** (1814–18): by Sir Walter Scott.

[17]**George Sand** (Aurore Dupin, Baronne Dudevant, 1804–1876): French author of many novels, including *Consuelo* (1843).

water-supply to each house, instead of the weary, hard-worked housewives having to carry every bucketful, from a distance of several hundred yards, up a steep street. But he was baffled by the rate-payers;[18] as, in many a similar instance, quantity carried it against quality, numbers against intelligence. And thus we find that illness often assumed a low typhoid form in Haworth, and fevers of various kinds visited the place with sad frequency. . . .

But the dark cloud was hanging over that doomed household, and gathering blackness every hour.

On October the 9th, she thus writes:—

'The past three weeks have been a dark interval in our humble home. Branwell's constitution had been failing fast all the summer; but still neither the doctors nor himself thought him so near his end as he was. He was entirely confined to his bed but for one single day, and was in the village two days before his death. He died, after twenty minutes' struggle, on Sunday morning, September 24th. He was perfectly conscious till the last agony came on. His mind had undergone the peculiar change which frequently precedes death, two days previously; the calm of better feelings filled it; a return of natural affection marked his last moments. He is in God's hands now; and the All-Powerful is likewise the All-Merciful. A deep conviction that he rests at last—rests well after his brief, erring, suffering, feverish life—fills and quiets my mind now. The final separation, the spectacle of his pale corpse, gave me more acute, bitter pain than I could have imagined. Till the last hour comes, we never know how much we can forgive, pity, regret a near relative. All his vices were and are nothing now. We remember only his woes. Papa was acutely distressed at first, but, on the whole, has borne the event well. Emily and Anne are pretty well, though Anne is always delicate, and Emily has a cold and cough at present. It was my fate to sink at the crisis, when I should have collected my strength. Headache and sickness came on first on the Sunday; I could not regain my appetite. Then internal pain attacked me. I became at once much reduced. It was impossible to touch a morsel. At last, bilious fever declared itself. I was confined to bed a week,—a dreary week. But thank God! health seems now returning. I can sit up all day, and take moderate nourishment. The doctor said at first, I should be very slow in recovering, but I seemed to get on faster than he anticipated. I am truly *much better*.'

I have heard, from one who attended Branwell in his last illness, that he resolved on standing up to die. He had

repeatedly said, that as long as there was life there was strength of will to do what it chose; and when the last agony began, he insisted on assuming the position just mentioned.

"Oct. 29th, 1848.

"I think I have now nearly got over the effects of my late illness, and am almost restored to my normal condition of health. I sometimes wish that it was a little higher, but we ought to be content with such blessings as we have, and not pine after those that are out of our reach. I feel much more uneasy about my sister than myself just now. Emily's cold and cough are very obstinate. I fear she has pain in her chest, and I sometimes catch a shortness in her breathing, when she has moved at all quickly. She looks very thin and pale. Her reserved nature occasions me great uneasiness of mind. It is useless to question her; you get no answers. It is still more useless to recommend remedies; they are never adopted. Nor can I shut my eyes to Anne's great delicacy of constitution. The late sad event has, I feel, made me more apprehensive than common. I cannot help feeling much depressed sometimes. I try to leave all in God's hands; to trust in His goodness; but faith and resignation are difficult to practise under some circumstances. The weather has been most unfavourable for invalids of late; sudden changes of temperature, and cold penetrating winds have been frequent here. Should the atmosphere become more settled, perhaps a favourable effect might be produced on the general health, and these harassing colds and coughs be removed. Papa has not quite escaped, but he has so far stood it better than any of us. You must not mention my going to——this winter. I could not, and would not, leave home on any account. Miss——has been for some years out of health now. These things make one *feel*, as well as *know*, that this world is not our abiding-place. We should not knit human ties too close, or clasp human affections too fondly. They must leave us, or we must leave them, one day. God restore health and strength to all who need it!"

I go on now with her own affecting words in the biographical notice of her sisters.

"But a great change approached. Affliction came in that shape which to anticipate is dread; to look back on grief. In the very heat and burden of the day, the labourers failed over their work. My sister Emily first declined. . . . Never in all her life had she lingered over any task that lay before her, and she did not linger now. She sank rapidly. She made haste to leave us. . . . Day by day, when I saw with what a front she met suffering, I looked on her with an anguish of wonder and love. I have seen nothing like it; but, indeed, I have never seen her parallel in anything. Stronger than a man, simpler than a child, her nature stood alone. The awful point was, that, while full of ruth for others, on herself she had no pity; the spirit was inexorable to the flesh; from the trembling hand, the unnerved limbs, the fading eyes, the same service was exacted as they had rendered in health. To stand by and witness this, and not dare to remonstrate, was a pain no words can render."

In fact, Emily never went out of doors after the Sunday succeeding Branwell's death. She made no complaint; she would not endure questioning; she rejected sympathy and help. Many a time did Charlotte and Anne drop their sewing, or cease from their writing, to listen with wrung hearts to the failing step, the laboured breathing, the frequent pauses, with which their sister climbed the short staircase; yet they dared not notice what they observed, with pangs of suffering even deeper than hers. They dared not notice it in words, far less by the caressing assistance of a helping arm or hand. They sat, still and silent.

"*Nov. 23rd, 1848.*

"I told you Emily was ill, in my last letter. She has not rallied yet. She is *very* ill. I believe, if you were to see her, your impression would be that there is no hope. A more hollow, wasted, pallid aspect I have not beheld. The deep tight cough continues; the breathing after the least exertion is a rapid pant; and these symptoms are accompanied by pains in the chest and side. Her pulse, the only time she allowed it to be felt, was found to beat 115 per minute. In this state she resolutely refuses to see a doctor; she will give no explanation of her feelings, she will scarcely allow her feelings to be alluded to. Our position is, and has been for some weeks, exquisitely painful. God only knows how all this is to terminate. More than once, I have been forced boldly to regard the terrible event of her loss as possible, and even probable. But nature shrinks from such thoughts. I think Emily seems the nearest thing to my heart in the world."

When a doctor had been sent for, and was in the very house, Emily refused to see him. Her sisters could only describe to him what symptoms they had observed; and the medicines which he sent she would not take, denying that she was ill. . . .

But Emily was growing rapidly worse. I remember Miss Brontë's shiver at recalling the pang she felt when, after having searched in the little hollows and sheltered crevices of the moors for a lingering spray of heather—just one spray, however withered—to take in to Emily, she saw that the flower was not recognised by the dim and indifferent eyes. Yet, to the last, Emily adhered tenaciously to her habits of independence. She would suffer no one to assist her. Any effort to do so roused the old stern spirit. One Tuesday morning, in December, she arose and dressed herself as usual, making many a pause, but doing everything for herself, and even endeavouring to take up her employment of sewing: the servants looked on, and knew what the catching, rattling breath, and the glazing of the eye too surely foretold; but she kept at her work; and Charlotte and Anne, though full of unspeakable dread, had still the faintest spark of hope. On that morning Charlotte wrote thus,—probably in the very presence of her dying sister:—

"*Tuesday.*

"I should have written to you[19] before, if I had had one word of hope to say; but I have not. She grows daily weaker. The physician's opinion was expressed too obscurely to be of use. He sent some medicine, which she would not take. Moments so dark as these I have never known. I pray for God's support to us all. Hitherto He has granted it."

The morning drew on to noon. Emily was worse: she could only whisper in gasps. Now, when it was too late, she said to Charlotte, "If you will send for a doctor, I will see him now." About two o'clock she died.

"*Dec. 21st, 1848.*

"Emily suffers no more from pain or weakness now. She never will suffer more in this world. She is gone, after a hard, short conflict. She died on *Tuesday*, the very day I wrote to you. I thought it very possible she might be with us still for weeks; and a few hours afterwards, she was in eternity. Yes; there is no Emily in time or on earth now. Yesterday we put her poor, wasted, mortal frame quietly under the church pavement. We are very calm at present. Why should we be otherwise? The anguish of seeing her suffer is over; the spectacle of the pains of death is gone by; the funeral day is past. We feel she is at peace. No need now to tremble for the hard frost and the keen wind. Emily does not feel them. She died in a time of promise. We saw her taken from life in its prime. But it is God's will, and the place where she is gone is better than that she has left.

"God has sustained me, in a way that I marvel at, through such agony as I had not conceived. I now look at

---

[19]**you:** Brontë's friend from schooldays Ellen Nussey (1817–1897).

Anne, and wish she were well and strong; but she is neither; nor is Papa. Could you now come to us for a few days? I would not ask you to stay long. Write and tell me if you could come next week, and by what train. I would try to send a gig for you to Keighley. You will, I trust, find us tranquil. Try to come. I never so much needed the consolation of a friend's presence. Pleasure, of course, there would be none for you in the visit, except what your kind heart would teach you to find in doing good to others."

As the old, bereaved father and his two surviving children followed the coffin to the grave, they were joined by Keeper, Emily's fierce, faithful bull-dog. He walked alongside of the mourners, and into the church, and stayed quietly there all the time that the burial service was being read. When he came home, he lay down at Emily's chamber door, and howled pitifully for many days. Anne Brontë drooped and sickened more rapidly from that time; and so ended the year 1848. (Volume 2, Chapter 2)

1857

SAMUEL SMILES

(1812–1904)

Trained in medicine at Edinburgh University, Smiles soon turned his attention instead to the body politic. He moved from his native Scotland to the north of England, whose factory cities were the great laboratory of industrialization, and became editor of the *Leeds Times*, a radical newspaper in the Victorian sense of that adjective. Neither militant nor socialist, the paper opposed the Corn Laws (import tariffs on grain); it advocated free trade and, within limits, the workers' rights that were articulated in the People's Charter (see page 14). When in the later 1840s the Charter failed and popular revolutions on the Continent fizzled, Smiles like many others began lobbying for public education and libraries, institutions that ministered to the national good through individual rather than political improvement. He concurrently turned from journalism to railroad management and consolidation, first at Leeds and then in London, producing as his first best-seller a biography (1857) of George Stephenson, father of the British railway. His next book, *Self-Help*, made Smiles a household name, with 20,000 copies in circulation during the first year (1859) and a quarter million copies by century's end: each chapter interspersed a no-nonsense commendation of middle-class virtues with scores of anecdotes and thumbnail biographies showing how those virtues led to success in all walks of life. Smiles later tried his hand at other kinds of writing—history books, even an autobiography—but his stock in trade remained the widely popular *Self-Help* formula behind titles that speak for themselves: *Character* (1871), *Thrift* (1875), *Duty* (1880), *Life and Labour* (1887).

What to this day we call self-help literature did not begin with Smiles: nineteenth-century antecedents include numerous pamphlets and magazines aimed at readers with little or no education or money, and behind these lies a long tradition of wisdom writing that goes back to the Biblical book of Proverbs. Still, *Self-Help* displays with exceptional clarity the premium on *individualism*—a word new to the language in 1827, as was *self-help* in 1831—that was so striking a feature of Victorian middle-class culture and so paradoxical an ingredient in that culture's cohesiveness. Carlyle had declared that "History is the essence of innumerable biographies"; Smiles went on to distill from innumerable biographies the essence of a practical morality. The real-life stories of *Self-Help* urge us to embrace virtue because it *works*.

Smiles is as deliberately drab a stylist as Carlyle or Ruskin is charismatic; he wants the practical wisdom of experience to emerge as if inscribed not by literature (he expressly devalues mere book-learning) but by life. His self-effacing prose is a stylistic accomplishment noteworthy precisely for what is likely to pass without notice: its plainness of diction, its repetition of key terms, and its regular use of epigraphs and imbedded quotations to which readers are invited to help themselves. *Self-Help* strikes a rhetorical balance between authority and equality, between the writer's need to claim the privilege of a hearing and the lecturer's awareness—enforced by much practice in public speaking—that nobody will listen who suspects him of putting on airs. Smiles acknowledged the existence of separate social classes, but he had no use for either snobbery or resentment and did all he could to facilitate class cooperation rather than struggle. His roster of self-helping heroes yokes the nobly born with the bootstrap hoister, as joint laborers for a public good that is rooted in independence. His flat style was part of an overall leveling and liberating campaign that has had as wide an influence as any author's in this anthology. Witness the palace chamber that the sultan's viceroy in Egypt covered, around the turn of the century, with Smilesian maxims done in Arabic calligraphy; or spend a few minutes in the self-help section of any bookstore.

from Self-Help; With Illustrations of Character and Conduct

The origin of this book may be briefly told.

Some fifteen years since, the author was requested to deliver an address before the members of some evening classes, which had been formed in a northern town[1] for mutual improvement, under the following circumstances:

Two or three young men of the humblest rank resolved to meet in the winter evenings for the purpose of improving themselves by exchanging knowledge with each other. Their first meetings were held in the room of a cottage in which one of the members lived; and, as others shortly joined them, the place soon became inconveniently filled. When summer set in, they adjourned to the cottage garden outside, and the classes were then held in the open air, round a little boarded hut used as a garden-house, in which those who officiated as teachers set the sums, and gave forth the lessons of the evening. When the weather was fine, the youths might be seen, until a late hour, hanging round the door of the hut like a cluster of bees; but sometimes a sudden shower of rain would dash the sums from their slates, and disperse them for the evening unsatisfied.

Winter, with its cold nights, was drawing near, and what were they to do for shelter? Their numbers had by this time so increased that no room of an ordinary cottage could accommodate them. But they were youths of pluck, and determined to go forward with the work they had taken in hand. They resolved, therefore, to hire a room; and, on making inquiry, they found a large, dingy apartment to let, which had been used as a temporary cholera hospital. No tenant could be found for the place, which was avoided as if a plague still clung to it. But the mutual improvement youths, nothing daunted, hired the cholera room, lit it up, placed a few benches and a deal table in it, and began their winter classes. The place soon presented a busy and cheer-

ful appearance in the evenings. The teaching may have been, as no doubt it was, of a very rude and imperfect sort, but it was done with a will. Those who knew a little taught those who knew less, improving themselves while they improved the others, and, at all events, setting before them a good working example. Thus these youths—and there were also grown men among them—proceeded to teach themselves and each other, reading and writing, arithmetic and geography, and even mathematics, chemistry, and some of the modern languages.

About a hundred young men had thus come together, when, growing ambitious, they desired to have lectures delivered to them; and then it was that the author became acquainted with their proceedings. A party of them waited on him for the purpose of inviting him to deliver an introductory address, or, as they expressed it, "to talk to them a bit," prefacing the request by a modest statement of what they had done and what they were doing. He could not fail to be touched by the admirable self-helping spirit which they had displayed; and, though entertaining but slight faith in popular lecturing, he felt that a few words of encouragement, honestly and sincerely uttered, might not be without some good effect. And in this spirit he addressed them on more than one occasion, citing examples of what other men had done as illustrations of what each might, in a greater or less degree, do for himself, and pointing out that their happiness and well-being as individuals in after life must necessarily depend mainly upon themselves—upon their own diligent self-culture, self-discipline, and self-control—and, above all, on that honest and upright performance of individual duty which is the glory of manly character.

There was nothing in the slightest degree new or original in his counsel, which was as old as the Proverbs of Solomon, and possibly quite as familiar. But, old-fashioned though the advice may have been, it was welcomed. The youths went forward in their course; worked on with energy and resolution; and, reaching manhood, they went forth in various directions into the world, where many of them now occupy positions of trust and usefulness. Several years after the incidents referred to, the subject was unexpectedly recalled to the author's recollection by an evening visit from a

---

[1] **northern town:** Leeds, industrial center of Yorkshire.

young man, apparently fresh from the work of a foundry, who explained that he was now an employer of labor and a thriving man; and he was pleased to remember with gratitude the words spoken in all honesty to him and to his fellow-pupils years before, and even to attribute some measure of his success in life to the endeavors which he had made to work up to their spirit.

The author's personal interest having in this way been attracted to the subject of Self-Help, he was accustomed to add to the memoranda from which he had addressed these young men, and to note down occasionally in his leisure evening moments, after the hours of business, the results of such reading, observation, and experience of life as he conceived to bear upon it. One of the most prominent illustrations cited in his earlier addresses, was that of George Stephenson, the engineer; and the original interest of the subject, as well as the special facilities and opportunities which the author possessed for illustrating Mr. Stephenson's[2] life and career, induced him to prosecute it at his leisure, and eventually to publish his biography. The present volume is written in a similar spirit, as it has been similar in its origin. The illustrative sketches of character introduced are, however, necessarily less elaborately treated, being busts rather than full-length portraits, and in many of the cases only some striking feature has been noted, the lives of individuals, as indeed of nations, often concentrating their lustre and interest in a few passages. Such as the book is the author now leaves it in the hands of the reader, in the hope that the lessons of industry, perseverance, and self-culture which it contains will be found useful and instructive, as well as generally interesting. (Introduction)

Self-Help—National and Individual

"The worth of a state, in the long run, is the worth of the individuals composing it."—J. S. Mill.
"We put too much faith in systems, and look too little to men."—B. Disraeli.[3]

"Heaven helps those who help themselves" is a well-worn maxim, embodying in a small compass the results of vast human experience. The spirit of self-help is the root of all genuine growth in the individual; and, exhibited in the lives of many, it constitutes the true source of national vigor and strength. Help from without is often enfeebling in its effects, but help from within invariably invigorates. Whatever is done *for* men or classes, to a certain extent takes away the stimulus and necessity of doing for themselves; and where men are subjected to over-guidance and over-government, the inevitable tendency is to render them comparatively helpless.

Even the best institutions can give a man no active aid. Perhaps the utmost they can do is to leave him *free* to develop himself and improve his individual condition. But in all times men have been prone to believe that their happiness and well-being were to be secured by means of institutions rather than by their own conduct; hence the value of legislation as an agent in human advancement has always been greatly over-estimated. To constitute the millionth part of a Legislature by voting for one or two men once in three or five years, however conscientiously this duty may be performed, can exercise but little active influence upon any man's life and character. Moreover, it is every day becoming more clearly understood, that the function of government is negative and restrictive rather than positive and active, being resolvable principally into protection—protection of life, liberty, and property. Hence the chief "reforms" of the last fifty years have consisted mainly in abolitions and disenactments.[4] But there is no power of law that can make the idle man industrious, the thriftless provident, or the drunken sober, though every individual can be each and all of these if he will, by the exercise of his own free powers of action and self-denial. Indeed, all experience serves to prove that the worth and strength of a state depend far less upon the form of its institutions than upon the character of its men; for the nation is only the aggregate of individual conditions, and civilization itself is but a question of personal improvement.

National progress is the sum of individual industry, energy, and uprightness, as national decay is of individual idleness, selfishness, and vice. What we are accustomed to decry as great social evils will, for the most part, be found to be only the outgrowth of our own perverted life; and though we may endeavor to cut them down and extirpate them by means of law, they will only spring up again with fresh luxuriance in some other form, unless the individual

---

[2]George **Stephenson** (1781–1848): inventor of the steam locomotive and railroad pioneer.

[3]Benjamin **Disraeli** (1804–1881): author and Conservative MP, twice Prime Minister.

[4]**abolitions and disenactments:** repeal, for example, of laws that discriminated against non-Anglican religious denominations (1820s), and of the Corn Laws, protectionist legislation that enriched landowners by elevating the price of grain (1846).

conditions of human life and character are radically improved. If this view be correct, then it follows that the highest patriotism and philanthropy consist, not so much in altering laws and modifying institutions, as in helping and stimulating men to elevate and improve themselves by their own free and independent action as individuals.

The government of a nation itself is usually found to be but the reflex of the individuals composing it. The government that is ahead of the people will be inevitably dragged down to their level, as the government that is behind them will in the long run be dragged up. In the order of nature, the collective character of a nation will as surely find its befitting results in its law and its government, as water finds its own level. The noble people will be nobly ruled, and the ignorant and corrupt ignobly. Indeed, liberty is quite as much a moral as a political growth—the result of free individual action, energy, and independence. It may be of comparatively little consequence how a man is governed from without, while every thing depends upon how he governs himself from within. The greatest slave is not he who is ruled by a despot, great though that evil be, but he who is the thrall of his own moral ignorance, selfishness, and vice. There have been, and perhaps there still are, so-called patriots abroad, who hold it to be the greatest stroke for liberty to kill a tyrant, forgetting that the tyrant usually represents only too faithfully the millions of people over whom he reigns. But nations who are enslaved at heart can not be freed by any mere changes of masters or of institutions; and so long as the fatal delusion prevails that liberty solely depends upon and consists in government, so long will such changes, no matter at what cost they be effected, have as little practical and lasting result as the shifting figures in a phantasmagoria. The solid foundations of liberty must rest upon individual character, which is also the only sure guarantee for social security and national progress. In this consists the real strength of English liberty. Englishmen feel that they are free, not merely because they live under those free institutions which they have so laboriously built up, but because each member of society has to a greater or less extent got the root of the matter within himself; and they continue to hold fast and enjoy their liberty, not by freedom of speech merely, but by their steadfast life and energetic action as free individual men.

Such as England is, she has been made by the thinking and working of many generations, the action of even the least significant person having contributed toward the production of the general result. Laborious and patient men of all ranks—cultivators of the soil and explorers of the mine—inventors and discoverers—tradesmen, mechanics, and laborers—poets, thinkers, and politicians—all have worked together, one generation carrying forward the labors of another, building up the character of the country, and establishing its prosperity on solid foundations. This succession of noble workers—the artisans of civilization—has created order out of chaos in industry, science, and art; and as our forefathers labored for us, and we have succeeded to the inheritance which they have bequeathed to us, so is it our duty to hand it down, not only unimpaired, but improved, to our successors.

This spirit of self-help, as exhibited in the energetic action of individuals, has in all times been a marked feature in the English character, and furnishes the true measure of our power as a nation. Rising above the heads of the mass, there have always been a series of individuals distinguished beyond others who have commanded the public homage. But our progress has been owing also to multitudes of smaller and unknown men. Though only the generals' names may be remembered in the history of any great campaign, it has been mainly through the individual valor and heroism of the privates that victories have been won. And life, too, is a "soldiers' battle," the greatest workers in all times having been men in the ranks. Many are the lives of men unwritten, which have nevertheless as powerfully influenced civilization and progress as the more fortunate Great whose names are recorded in biography. Even the humblest person, who sets before his fellows an example of industry, sobriety, and upright honesty of purpose in life, has a present as well as a future influence upon the well-being of his country; for his life and character pass unconsciously into the lives of others, and propagate good example for all time to come.

Biographies of great, but especially of good men, are, nevertheless, most instructive and useful, as helps, guides, and incentives to others. Some of the best are almost equivalent to Gospels—teaching high living, high thinking, and energetic action for their own and the world's good. British biography is studded over, as "with patines of bright gold,"[5] with illustrious examples of the power of self-help, of patient purpose, resolute working, and steadfast integrity, issuing in the formation of truly noble and manly character; exhibiting, in language not to be misunderstood, what it is in the power of each to accomplish for himself; and illustrating the efficacy of self-respect and self-reliance in enabling men of even the humblest rank to work out for themselves an honorable competency and a solid reputation.

Foreign observers have been keen to note, as one of the most marked characteristics of the Englishman, his

---

[5]"with . . . gold": *Merchant of Venice* 5.1.59.

strong individuality and distinctive personal energy, refusing to merge himself in institutions, but retaining throughout his perfect freedom of thought, and speech, and action. "Que j'aime la hardiesse Anglaise! que j'aime les gens qui disent ce qu'ils pensent!" was the expressive exclamation of Voltaire.[6] It is this strong individualism which makes and keeps the Englishman really free, and brings out fully the action of the social body. The energies of the strong form so many living centres of action round which other individual energies group and cluster themselves; thus the life of all is quickened, and, on great occasions, a powerful energetic action of the nation is secured.

It is this energy of individual life and example acting throughout society which constitutes the best practical education of Englishmen. Schools, academies, and colleges give but the merest beginnings of culture in comparison with it. Far higher and more practical is the life-education daily given in our homes, in the streets, behind counters, in workshops, at the loom and the plow, in counting-houses and manufactories, and in all the busy haunts of men. This is the education that fits Englishmen for doing the work and acting the part of free men. This is that final instruction as members of society which Schiller[7] designated "the education of the human race," consisting in action, conduct, self-culture, self-control—all that tends to discipline a man truly, and fit him for the proper performance of the duties and business of life—a kind of education not to be learned from books, or acquired by any amount of mere literary training. With his usual weight of words, Bacon[8] observes that "Studies teach not their own use; but that is a wisdom without them, and above them, won by observation:" a remark that holds true of actual life as well as of the cultivation of the intellect itself; for all observation tends to illustrate and enforce the lesson that a man perfects himself by work much more than by reading—that it is life rather than literature, action rather than study, and character rather than biography, that tends perpetually to renovate mankind. . . .

The instances of men in this country who, by dint of persevering application and energy, have raised themselves from the humblest ranks of industry to eminent positions of usefulness and influence in society, are indeed so numerous that they have long ceased to be regarded as exceptional. Looking at some of the more remarkable instances, it might almost be said that early encounter with difficulty and adverse circumstances was the necessary and indispensable condition of success. The House of Commons has always contained a considerable number of such self-raised men—fitting representatives of the industrial character of the British people; and it is to the credit of our Legislature that such men have received due honor there. When the late Joseph Brotherton,[9] member for Salford, in the course of the discussion on the Ten Hours Bill, detailed with true pathos the hardships and fatigues to which he had been subjected when working as a factory boy in a cotton-mill, and described the resolution which he had then formed, that if ever it was in his power he would endeavor to ameliorate the condition of that class, Sir James Graham[10] rose immediately after him, and declared, amid the cheers of the House, that he did not before know that Mr. Brotherton's origin had been so humble, but that it rendered him more proud than he had ever before been of the House of Commons, to think that a person risen from that condition should be able to sit side by side, on equal terms, with the hereditary gentry of the land. . . . (Chapter 1)

Energy and Courage

"Den muthigen gehort die Welt."[11]—*German Proverb.*
"In every work that he began . . . he did it with all his heart and prospered."—*2 Chron.*, xxxi., 21.

There is a famous speech recorded of an old Norseman, thoroughly characteristic of the Teuton. "I believe neither in idols nor demons," said he; "I put my sole trust in my own strength of body and soul." The ancient crest of a pickaxe with the motto of "Either I will find a way or make one," was an expression of the same sturdy independence and practical materialism, which to this day distinguishes the descendants of the Northmen. Indeed, nothing could be more characteristic of the Scandinavian mythology than that it

---

[6]"**Que j'aime . . . pensent!**": How I love English hardihood! How I love people who say what they think! **Voltaire** (François-Marie Arouet, 1694–1778): French Enlightenment author and philosopher.

[7]Friedrich von **Schiller** (1759–1805): German poet, playwright, and literary theorist.

[8]Francis **Bacon** (1561–1626): statesman, philosopher, and author, quoted here from his pithy 1607 *Essayes.*

[9]**Joseph Brotherton** (1783–1857): Manchester cotton magnate and MP.

[10]**Sir James Graham** (1792–1861): part author of the 1832 Reform Bill who served in several Whig governments. The **Ten Hours Bill** restricted laborers' workday.

[11]"**Den muthigen . . . Welt**": The world obeys the courageous.

had a god with a hammer.[12] A man's character is seen in small matters; and from even so slight a test as the mode in which a man wields a hammer, his energy may in some measure be inferred. Thus an eminent Frenchman hit off in a single phrase the characteristic quality of the inhabitants of a particular district, in which a friend of his proposed to settle and buy land. "Beware," said he, "of making a purchase there; I know the men of that department; the pupils who come from it to our veterinary school at Paris *do not strike hard upon the anvil;* they want energy; and you will not get a satisfactory return on any capital you may invest there." A fine and just appreciation of character, indicating the accurate and thoughtful observer, and strikingly illustrative of the fact that it is the energy of the individual men that gives strength to a state, and confers a value even upon the very soil which they cultivate. As the French proverb has it, "Tant vaut l'homme, tant vaut sa terre."[13]

The cultivation of this quality is of the greatest importance, resolute determination in the pursuit of worthy objects being the foundation of all true greatness of character. Energy enables a man to force his way through irksome drudgery and dry details, and carries him onward and upward in every station in life. It accomplishes more than genius, with not one half the disappointment and peril. It is not even eminent talent that is required to insure success in any pursuit so much as purpose—not merely the power to achieve, but the will to labor energetically and perseveringly. Hence energy of will may be defined to be the very central power of character in a man—in a word, it is the Man himself. It gives impulse to his every action, and soul to every effort. True hope is based on it, and it is hope that gives the real perfume to life. There is a fine heraldic motto on a broken helmet in Battle Abbey, "L'espoir est ma force,"[14] which might be the motto of every man's life. "Woe unto him that is faint-hearted," says the son of Sirach. There is, indeed, no blessing equal to the possession of a stout heart. Even if a man fail in his efforts, it will be a great satisfaction to him to enjoy the consciousness of having done his best. In humble life nothing can be more cheering and beautiful than to see a man combating suffering by patience, triumphing in his integrity, and who, when his feet are bleeding and his limbs failing him, still walks upon his courage. . . .

It is *will*—force of purpose—that enables a man to do or be whatever he sets his mind on being or doing. A holy man was accustomed to say, "Whatever you wish, that you are; for such is the force of our will, joined to the Divine, that whatever we wish to be, seriously, and with a true intention, that we become. No one ardently wishes to be submissive, patient, modest, or liberal, who does not become what he wishes." The story is told of a working carpenter, who was observed one day planing a magistrate's bench which he was repairing with more than usual carefulness, and when asked the reason, he replied, "Because I wish to make it easy against the time when I come to sit upon it myself." And, singularly enough, the man actually lived to sit upon that very bench as a magistrate.

Whatever theoretical conclusions logicians may have formed as to the freedom of the will, each individual feels that practically he is free to choose between good and evil—that he is not like a mere straw thrown upon the water to mark the direction of the current, but that he has within him the power of a strong swimmer, and is capable of striking out for himself, of buffeting with the waves, and directing to a great extent his own independent course. There is no absolute constraint upon our volitions, and we feel and know that we are not bound, as by a spell, with reference to our actions. It would paralyze all desire of excellence were we to think otherwise. The entire business and conduct of life, with its domestic rules, its social arrangements, and its public institutions, proceed upon the practical conviction that the will is free. Without this, where would be responsibility? and what the advantage of teaching, advising, preaching, reproof, and correction? What were the use of laws were it not the universal belief, as it is the universal fact, that men obey them or not very much as they individually determine? In every moment of our life, conscience is proclaiming that our will is free. It is the only thing that is wholly ours, and it rests solely with ourselves individually whether we give it the right or the wrong direction. Our habits or our temptations are not our masters, but we of them. Even in yielding, conscience tells us we might resist; and that, were we determined to master them, there would not be required for that purpose a stronger resolution than we know ourselves to be capable of exercising. . . .

One of Napoleon's favorite maxims was, "The truest wisdom is a resolute determination." His life, beyond most others, vividly showed what a powerful and unscrupulous will could accomplish. He threw his whole force of body and mind direct upon his work. Imbecile rulers and the

---

[12]**a god:** Thor.

[13]**"Tant vaut . . . sa terre":** As is a man's worth, such is his land's.

[14]**Battle Abbey:** in SE England, founded by William the Conqueror after the Battle of Hastings (11th century). **"L'espoir est ma force":** Hope is my strength. Jesus the **son of Sirach** (2nd century BCE) wrote the apocryphal book Ecclesiasticus (2:13 quoted here).

nations they governed went down before him in succession. He was told that the Alps stood in the way of his armies: "There shall be no Alps," he said, and the road across the Simplon[15] was constructed, through a district formerly almost inaccessible. "Impossible," said he, "is a word only to be found in the dictionary of fools." He was a man who toiled terribly, sometimes employing and exhausting four secretaries at a time. He spared no one, not even himself. His influence inspired other men, and put a new life into them. "I made my generals out of mud," he said. But all was of no avail; for Napoleon's intense selfishness was his ruin, and the ruin of France, which he left a prey to anarchy. His life taught the lesson that power, however energetically wielded, without beneficence, is fatal to its possessor and its subjects; and that knowledge, or knowingness, without goodness, is but the incarnate principle of Evil.

Our own Wellington[16] was a far greater man; not less resolute, firm, and persistent, but much more self-denying, conscientious, and truly patriotic. Napoleon's aim was "Glory;" Wellington's watchword, like Nelson's, was "Duty." The former word, it is said, does not once occur in his dispatches; the latter often, but never accompanied by any high-sounding professions. The greatest difficulties could neither embarrass nor intimidate Wellington, his energy invariably rising in proportion to the obstacles to be surmounted. The patience, the firmness, the resolution, with which he bore through the maddening vexations and gigantic difficulties of the Peninsular campaigns, is, perhaps, one of the sublimest things to be found in history. In Spain, Wellington not only exhibited the genius of the general, but the comprehensive wisdom of the statesman. Though his natural temper was irritable in the extreme, his high sense of duty enabled him to restrain it, and to those about him his patience seemed absolutely inexhaustible. His great character stands untarnished by ambition, by avarice, or any low passion. Though a man of powerful individuality, he yet displayed a great variety of endowment. The equal of Napoleon in generalship, he was as prompt, vigorous, and daring as Clive,[17] as wise a statesman as Cromwell, and as pure and high-minded as Washington. The great Welling-

ton left behind him an enduring reputation, founded on toilsome campaigns won by skillful combination, by fortitude which nothing could exhaust, by sublime daring, and perhaps still sublimer patience. . . .

The life of Granville Sharp is another striking example of the same power of individual energy—a power which was afterward transfused into the noble band of workers in the cause of Slavery Abolition, prominent among whom were Clarkson, Wilberforce, Buxton, and Brougham.[18] But, giants though these men were in this cause, Granville Sharp was the first, and perhaps the greatest of them all, in point of perseverance, energy, and intrepidity. He began life as apprentice to a linen-draper on Tower Hill; but, leaving that business after his apprenticeship was out, he next entered as a clerk in the Ordnance Office, and it was while engaged in that humble position that he carried on in his spare hours the work of Negro Emancipation. He was always, even when an apprentice, ready to undertake any amount of volunteer labor where any useful purpose was to be served. Thus, while learning the linen-drapery business, a fellow-apprentice, who lodged in the same house, and was a Unitarian, led him into frequent discussions on religious subjects, in the course of which the Unitarian youth insisted that Granville's Trinitarian misconception of certain passages of Scripture arose from his want of acquaintance with the Greek tongue, on which he immediately set to work in his evening hours, and shortly acquired an intimate knowledge of Greek. A similar controversy with another fellow-apprentice, a Jew, as to the interpretation of the prophecies, led him, in like manner, to undertake and overcome the difficulties of Hebrew.

But the circumstance which gave the bias and direction to the main labors of his life originated in his generosity and benevolence. It was in this wise. His brother William, a surgeon in Mincing Lane, gave gratuitous advice to the poor, and among the numerous applicants for relief at his surgery was a poor African named Jonathan Strong. It appeared that the negro had been so brutally treated by his master, a Barbadoes lawyer then in London, that he had been thereby rendered lame and almost blind, and was altogether unable to work; and his owner, regarding him as no longer of the

---

[15]**Simplon:** Alpine pass between Switzerland and Italy.

[16]Arthur Wellesley, Duke of **Wellington** (1769–1852): commander of British armies during Napoleonic wars. Horatio **Nelson** (1758–1805): his naval counterpart.

[17]Robert **Clive** (1725–1774): military hero and diplomat in British India. Oliver **Cromwell** (1599–1658): parliamentary general who was made Lord Protector (1653).

[18]Thomas **Clarkson** (1760–1846), William **Wilberforce** (1759–1833), Thomas Fowell **Buxton** (1786–1845), Henry **Brougham** (1778–1868): parliamentary abolitionists who extended to the British Empire the principle, previously established through the efforts of **Granville Sharp** (1735–1813), that slavery might not exist on British soil.

slightest value as a chattel, but likely only to involve him in expense, at once turned him adrift into the streets of London. This poor man, a mass of disease, supported himself by begging for a time, until he found his way to William Sharp, who gave him some medicine, and shortly after got him admitted to St. Bartholomew's Hospital, where he was cured. On coming out of the hospital, the two brothers supported the negro in order to keep him off the streets, but they had not the least suspicion at the time that any one had a claim upon his person. They even succeeded in obtaining a situation for Strong with an apothecary, in whose service he remained for two years; and it was while he was attending his mistress behind a hackney-coach that his former owner, the Barbadoes lawyer, recognized him, and determined to recover possession of the slave, again rendered valuable by the restoration of his health. The lawyer employed two of the lord-mayor's officers to apprehend Strong, and he was lodged in the Compter[19] until he could be shipped off to the West Indies. The negro, bethinking him in his captivity of the kind services which Granville Sharp had rendered him in his great distress some years before, dispatched a letter to him requesting his help. Sharp had forgotten the name of Strong, but he sent a messenger to make inquiries, who returned saying that the keepers denied having any such person in their charge. His suspicions were roused, and he went forthwith to the prison, and insisted upon seeing Jonathan Strong. He was admitted, and recognized the poor negro, now in custody as a recaptured slave. Mr. Sharp charged the master of the prison at his own peril not to deliver up Strong to any person whatever until he had been carried before the lord-mayor, to whom Sharp immediately went, and obtained a summons against those persons who had seized and imprisoned Strong without a warrant. The parties appeared before the lord-mayor accordingly, and it appeared from the proceedings that Strong's former master had already sold him to a new one, who produced the bill of sale and claimed the negro as his property. As no charge of offense was made against Strong, and as the lord-mayor was incompetent to deal with the legal question as to Strong's liberty or otherwise, he discharged him, and the slave followed his benefactor out of court, no one daring to touch him. The man's owner immediately gave Sharp notice of an action to recover possession of his negro slave, of whom he

had been robbed; and now commenced that protracted and energetic movement in favor of the enslaved negro which forms one of the brightest pages in English history.

About this time (1767), the personal liberty of the Englishman, though cherished as a theory, was subject to grievous infringements, and was almost daily violated. The impressment of men for the sea service was constantly practiced, and, besides the press-gangs,[20] there were regular bands of kidnappers employed in London and all the large towns of the kingdom to seize men for the East India Company's service; and, when the men were not wanted for India, they were shipped off to the planters in the American colonies. Negro slaves were openly advertised for sale in the London and Liverpool newspapers. For instance, the Gazetteer of April 18th, 1769, classed together for sale, "at the Bull and Gate Inn, Holborn, a chestnut gelding, a Tim whisky, and a well-made, good-tempered black boy." Rewards were then offered, as now in the slave states of America, for recovering and securing fugitive slaves, and for conveying them down to certain specified ships in the river. That no shame was felt at the open recognition of slavery is apparent from an advertisement in the Daily Advertiser of the 16th May, 1768, offering a reward to whoever would apprehend a negro boy and bring him, or send tidings of him to Mr. Alderman Beckford, in Pall Mall. The Public Advertiser of the 28th November, 1769, contains this advertisement: "TO BE SOLD, a black girl, the property of J. B——, eleven years of age, who is tolerably handy, works at her needle tolerably well, and speaks English perfectly well; is of an excellent temper, and willing disposition. Inquire of Mr. Owen, at the Angel Inn, behind St. Clement's Church in the Strand." Such was the state of matters when Granville Sharp threw himself, body and soul, into his great work. Though only a clerk in a public office, without any personal influence whatever, and armed only with integrity and boldness in a good cause, he was enabled in the issue effectually to vindicate the personal liberty of the subject, and to establish as a fact what up to that time had been but a theory—that the slave who sets his foot on British ground becomes at that instant free! . . . (Chapter 7)

1859

---

[19]**Compter:** London debtors' prison.

[20]**press-gangs:** naval recruiters who forced men into service (**impressment**).

ROBERT BROWNING

(1812–1889)

Browning grew up in a comfortable suburban home where he lived until well into his thirties. His father had rejected lucrative prospects on a West Indian plantation after witnessing the slave system and returned to a modest bank clerkship in London, which enabled him to indulge passions for books and art and to pass them on to his precocious son along with the run of a very large library. When his pious Nonconformist mother brought home the poems of Shelley, her teenaged son embraced not only Shelley's vegetarianism but his atheism too. Within a year or so he reentered the Christian fold, to stay there for good; but the double-jointed experience of conversion and apostasy proved formative. Bored by a term at the new University of London, he announced his vocation as a poet and trained for it by studying Johnson's *Dictionary* cover to cover, and with results: Browning's works display the most extensive vocabulary of any writer's in English. He began to frequent circles where theological and social radicalism flourished in a mix of Unitarian and Utilitarian traditions that, fed by new thought from abroad, became his de facto university. The adolescent who had lost his faith, and then lost his loss of faith, was growing into the poetic psychologist who would care less *what* people believed than *how*. His interest in ideas would always be subordinate to curiosity about the relation ideas bear to character; his creativity would be most fully engaged by case studies of extremity or compromise, failure or inconclusiveness in the experiments of life.

Browning's own experiments were for a long while inconclusive. He traveled on the Continent, especially in Italy, and took part in a diplomatic mission to Russia that savored of espionage. He developed expertise in the musical and visual arts, read books on everything, and published volumes of verse that were extraordinarily promising although limited in appeal. The confessional monologue *Pauline* (1833) struck John Stuart Mill with its "morbid and intense self-consciousness." Wordsworth admired the closet drama *Paracelsus* (1835), which the impresario William Macready liked well enough to launch Browning on a decade of unsuccessful attempts to write for the London stage. But the chief labor of his early years, the six-book epic *Sordello* (1840), demanded so much learning and effort that almost no one managed to read it through. Browning went back to the drawing board and produced a highly original lyrical drama (*Pippa Passes*, 1841) and two collections featuring what he called "dramatic lyrics": poems in which the speech of a single character, caught at a critical juncture, reveals perhaps unwittingly a situation of considerable psychological, historical, and moral complexity.

These poems are brilliant prototypes of the dramatic monologue, the distinctively Victorian genre with which Browning's name is permanently linked; but even in affordable pamphlet form they failed to win the kind of attention readers were paying to poets like Tennyson and Elizabeth Barrett. The latter was nevertheless among Browning's admirers, and when a mutual friend arranged for an exchange of letters in 1845, it occasioned a meeting of minds that blossomed into love. Secretly married a year later, the Brownings made their home in Florence to preserve Elizabeth's fragile health, which soon improved to the point where the couple could socialize, tour Italy and France, and produce a son. During fifteen years of marriage they both wrote their greatest poetry, including Robert's superb collection

Men and Women (1855). Throughout this time he was best known as the spouse of a literary celebrity, and on her death he returned to London as England's most famous widower to raise their son and win broader recognition in his own right. *Dramatis Personae* (1864) was his first book to require more than one printing, and with it he stepped at last towards adding a substantial readership to the professional esteem he enjoyed among emerging writers like the PreRaphaelites, Pater and Hardy, George Eliot and Henry James. His renown peaked in the 1880s with the founding of the Browning Society—an unprecedented tribute to a living author—at whose study sessions the old poet would sometimes put in a genial, bemused appearance. His last words expressed gratification at hearing that his final volume had sold out on the day of issue.

During his latter decades Browning steadily published lyrics that, running a gamut from the quizzically indirect to the chest-thumpingly affirmative, cemented a reputation for elliptical shorthand syntax, colloquial dash, and versification that was dissonant but not therefore unmusical. He also produced a series of long narrative experiments, including his masterpiece *The Ring and the Book* (1868–1869). This epic reconstruction of an obscure seventeenth-century Italian murder case—based on documents he boasts of having found at a flea market—compounds the oddity of its topic by dividing the storytelling across a wide spectrum of bystanders and participants, thereby enforcing a challenging modern perspectivism in matters of knowledge and judgment. Readers have found similar challenges in his dramatic monologues, which elicit varied and often conflicting measures of psychological analysis, imaginative sympathy, and moral evaluation. Even lyrics like "One Word More" or "House," where the poet himself seems to speak out, invite us to consider the mysterious cleavings of identity or the ways in which evasiveness can be the same as self-display. An exasperated Hardy worried how Browning's intellectual audacity could coexist with his Christian optimism; an appreciative James declared, on the poet's interment at Westminster Abbey, that none of the great had ever been so strange, none of the strange so great.

~

Porphyria's Lover

The rain set early in to-night,
   The sullen wind was soon awake,
It tore the elm-tops down for spite,
   And did its worst to vex the lake:
   I listened with heart fit to break.
When glided in Porphyria; straight
   She shut the cold out and the storm,
And kneeled and made the cheerless grate
   Blaze up, and all the cottage warm;
   Which done, she rose, and from her form   10
Withdrew the dripping cloak and shawl,
   And laid her soiled gloves by, untied
Her hat and let the damp hair fall,
   And, last, she sat down by my side
   And called me. When no voice replied,

She put my arm about her waist,
   And made her smooth white shoulder bare,
And all her yellow hair displaced,
   And, stooping, made my cheek lie there,
   And spread, o'er all, her yellow hair,   20
Murmuring how she loved me—she
   Too weak, for all her heart's endeavor,
To set its struggling passion free
   From pride, and vainer ties dissever,
   And give herself to me forever.
But passion sometimes would prevail,
   Nor could to-night's gay feast restrain
A sudden thought of one so pale
   For love of her, and all in vain:
   So, she was come through wind and rain.   30
Be sure I looked up at her eyes
   Happy and proud; at last I knew

Porphyria worshipped me; surprise
    Made my heart swell, and still it grew
    While I debated what to do.
That moment she was mine, mine, fair,
    Perfectly pure and good: I found
A thing to do, and all her hair
    In one long yellow string I wound
    Three times her little throat around,   40
And strangled her. No pain felt she;
    I am quite sure she felt no pain.
As a shut bud that holds a bee,
    I warily oped her lids: again
    Laughed the blue eyes without a stain.
And I untightened next the tress
    About her neck; her cheek once more
Blushed bright beneath my burning kiss:
    I propped her head up as before,
    Only, this time my shoulder bore   50
Her head, which droops upon it still:
    The smiling rosy little head,
So glad it has its utmost will,
    That all it scorned at once is fled,
    And I, its love, am gained instead!
Porphyria's love: she guessed not how
    Her darling one wish would be heard.
And thus we sit together now,
    And all night long we have not stirred,
    And yet God has not said a word!   60

                   1836

My Last Duchess

Ferrara[1]

That's my last Duchess painted on the wall,
Looking as if she were alive. I call
That piece a wonder, now: Frà Pandolf's hands
Worked busily a day, and there she stands.
Will 't please you sit and look at her? I said
"Frà Pandolf" by design, for never read
Strangers like you that pictured countenance,
The depth and passion of its earnest glance,

---

[1]**Ferrara:** city in N Italy whose 16th-century Duke Alfonso II,
and his wife Lucrezia de' Medici, are thought to be the originals for
this poem, which when first published was titled "Italy." The other
characters are Browning's inventions.

But to myself they turned (since none puts by
The curtain I have drawn for you, but I)   10
And seemed as they would ask me, if they durst,
How such a glance came there; so, not the first
Are you to turn and ask thus. Sir, 'twas not
Her husband's presence only, called that spot
Of joy into the Duchess' cheek: perhaps
Frà Pandolf chanced to say "Her mantle laps
Over my lady's wrist too much," or "Paint
Must never hope to reproduce the faint
Half-flush that dies along her throat"; such stuff
Was courtesy, she thought, and cause enough   20
For calling up that spot of joy. She had
A heart—how shall I say?—too soon made glad,
Too easily impressed; she liked whate'er
She looked on, and her looks went everywhere.
Sir, 'twas all one! My favour at her breast,
The dropping of the daylight in the West,
The bough of cherries some officious fool
Broke in the orchard for her, the white mule
She rode with round the terrace—all and each
Would draw from her alike the approving speech,   30
Or blush, at least. She thanked men,—good! but thanked
Somehow—I know not how—as if she ranked
My gift of a nine-hundred-years-old name
With anybody's gift. Who'd stoop to blame
This sort of trifling? Even had you skill
In speech—(which I have not)—to make your will
Quite clear to such an one, and say, "Just this
Or that in you disgusts me; here you miss,
Or there exceed the mark"—and if she let
Herself be lessoned so, nor plainly set   40
Her wits to yours, forsooth, and made excuse,
—E'en then would be some stooping; and I choose
Never to stoop. Oh sir, she smiled, no doubt,
Whene'er I passed her; but who passed without
Much the same smile? This grew; I gave commands;
Then all smiles stopped together. There she stands
As if alive. Will 't please you rise? We'll meet
The company below, then. I repeat,
The Count your master's known munificence
Is ample warrant that no just pretence   50
Of mine for dowry will be disallowed;
Though his fair daughter's self, as I avowed
At starting, is my object. Nay, we'll go
Together down, sir! Notice Neptune, though,
Taming a sea-horse, thought a rarity,
Which Claus of Innsbruck cast in bronze for me!

                   1842

Count Gismond

Aix in Provence[1]

— 1 —

Christ God who savest man, save most
   Of men Count Gismond who saved me!
Count Gauthier, when he chose his post,
   Chose time and place and company
To suit it; when he struck at length
My honour, 'twas with all his strength.

— 2 —

And doubtlessly ere he could draw
   All points to one, he must have schemed!
That miserable morning saw
   Few half so happy as I seemed,   10
While being dressed in queen's array
To give our tourney prize away.

— 3 —

I thought they loved me, did me grace
   To please themselves; 'twas all their deed;
God makes, or fair or foul, our face;
   If showing mine so caused to bleed
My cousins' hearts, they should have dropped
A word, and straight the play had stopped.

— 4 —

They, too, so beauteous! Each a queen
   By virtue of her brow and breast;
Not needing to be crowned, I mean,   20
   As I do. E'en when I was dressed,
Had either of them spoke, instead
Of glancing sideways with still head!

— 5 —

But no: they let me laugh, and sing
   My birthday song quite through, adjust
The last rose in my garland, fling
   A last look on the mirror, trust
My arms to each an arm of theirs,
And so descend the castle-stairs—   30

— 6 —

And come out on the morning-troop
   Of merry friends who kissed my cheek,
And called me queen, and made me stoop
   Under the canopy—(a streak
That pierced it, of the outside sun,
Powdered with gold its gloom's soft dun)—

— 7 —

And they could let me take my state
   And foolish throne amid applause
Of all come there to celebrate
   My queen's-day—Oh I think the cause   40
Of much was, they forgot no crowd
Makes up for parents in their shroud!

— 8 —

However that be, all eyes were bent
   Upon me, when my cousins cast
Theirs down; 'twas time I should present
   The victor's crown, but . . . there, 'twill last
No long time . . . the old mist again
Blinds me as then it did. How vain!

— 9 —

See! Gismond's at the gate, in talk
   With his two boys: I can proceed.   50
Well, at that moment, who should stalk
   Forth boldly—to my face, indeed—
But Gauthier, and he thundered "Stay!"
And all stayed. "Bring no crowns, I say!

— 10 —

"Bring torches! Wind the penance-sheet
   About her! Let her shun the chaste,
Or lay herself before their feet!
   Shall she whose body I embraced
A night long, queen it in the day?
For honor's sake no crowns, I say!"   60

— 11 —

I? What I answered? As I live,
   I never fancied such a thing
As answer possible to give.
   What says the body when they spring
Some monstrous torture-engine's whole
Strength on it? No more says the soul.

---

[1] **Aix in Provence:** city in Provence (S France), medieval center for chivalric practices of courtly love. When first published the poem was titled "France."

— 12 —

Till out strode Gismond; then I knew
    That I was saved. I never met
His face before, but, at first view,
    I felt quite sure that God had set   70
Himself to Satan; who would spend
A minute's mistrust on the end?

— 13 —

He strode to Gauthier, in his throat
    Gave him the lie, then struck his mouth
With one back-handed blow that wrote
    In blood men's verdict there. North, South,
East, West, I looked. The lie was dead,
And damned, and truth stood up instead.

— 14 —

This glads me most, that I enjoyed
    The heart of the joy, with my content   80
In watching Gismond unalloyed
    By any doubt of the event:
God took that on him—I was bid
Watch Gismond for my part: I did.

— 15 —

Did I not watch him while he let
    His armorer just brace his greaves,
Rivet his hauberk, on the fret[2]
    The while! His foot . . . my memory leaves
No least stamp out, nor how anon
He pulled his ringing gauntlets on.   90

— 16 —

And e'en before the trumpet's sound
    Was finished, prone lay the false knight,
Prone as his lie, upon the ground:
    Gismond flew at him, used no sleight
O' the sword, but open-breasted drove,
Cleaving till out the truth he clove.

— 17 —

Which done, he dragged him to my feet
    And said, "Here die, but end thy breath
In full confession, lest thou fleet
    From my first, to God's second death!   100

Say, hast thou lied?" And, "I have lied
To God and her," he said, and died.

— 18 —

Then Gismond kneeling to me, asked
    —What safe my heart holds, though no word
Could I repeat now, if I tasked
    My powers forever, to a third
Dear even as you are. Pass the rest
Until I sank upon his breast.

— 19 —

Over my head his arm he flung
    Against the world; and scarce I felt   110
His sword (that dripped by me and swung)
    A little shifted in its belt:
For he began to say the while
How South our home lay many a mile.

— 20 —

So 'mid the shouting multitude
    We two walked forth to never more
Return. My cousins have pursued
    Their life, untroubled as before
I vexed them. Gauthier's dwelling-place
God lighten! May his soul find grace!   120

— 21 —

Our elder boy has got the clear
    Great brow; tho' when his brother's black
Full eye shows scorn, it . . . Gismond here?
    And have you brought my tercel[3] back?
I just was telling Adela
How many birds it struck since May.

1842

Soliloquy of the Spanish Cloister

— 1 —

Gr-r-r—there go, my heart's abhorrence!
    Water your damned flower-pots, do!
If hate killed men, Brother Lawrence,
    God's blood, would not mine kill you!

---

[2]**greaves**: armored leggings. **hauberk**: chest armor. **on the fret**: impatient.

[3]**tercel**: male hunting falcon.

What? your myrtle-bush wants trimming?
  Oh, that rose has prior claims—
Needs its leaden vase filled brimming?
  Hell dry you up with its flames!

— 2 —

At the meal we sit together:
  Salve tibi![1] I must hear   10
Wise talk of the kind of weather,
  Sort of season, time of year:
Not a plenteous cork-crop: scarcely
  Dare we hope oak-galls,[2] *I doubt:*
What's the Latin name for "parsley"?
  What's the Greek name for Swine's Snout?[3]

— 3 —

Whew! We'll have our platter burnished,
  Laid with care on our own shelf!
With a fire-new spoon we're furnished,
  And a goblet for ourself,   20
Rinsed like something sacrificial
  Ere 'tis fit to touch our chaps—
Marked with L for our initial!
  (He-he! There his lily snaps!)

— 4 —

Saint, forsooth! While brown Dolores
  Squats outside the Convent bank
With Sanchicha, telling stories,
  Steeping tresses in the tank,
Blue-black, lustrous, thick like horsehairs,
  —Can't I see his dead eye glow.   30
Bright as 'twere a Barbary corsair's?[4]
  (That is, if he'd let it show!)

— 5 —

When he finishes refection,
  Knife and fork he never lays
Cross-wise, to my recollection,
  As do I, in Jesu's praise.
I the Trinity illustrate,
  Drinking watered orange-pulp—

In three sips the Arian[5] frustrate;
  While he drains his at one gulp.   40

— 6 —

Oh, those melons! If he's able
  We're to have a feast! so nice!
One goes to the Abbot's table,
  All of us get each a slice.
How go on your flowers? None double?
  Not one fruit-sort can you spy?
Strange!—And I, too, at such trouble,
  Keep them close-nipped on the sly!

— 7 —

There's a great text in Galatians,[6]
  Once you trip on it, entails   50
Twenty-nine distinct damnations,
  One sure, if another fails:
If I trip him just a-dying,
  Sure of heaven as sure can be,
Spin him round and send him flying
  Off to hell, a Manichee?[7]

— 8 —

Or, my scrofulous[8] French novel
  On gray paper with blunt type!
Simply glance at it, you grovel
  Hand and foot in Belial's[9] gripe: 60
If I double down its pages
  At the woeful sixteenth print,
When he gathers his greengages,[10]
  Ope a sieve and slip it in't?

— 9 —

Or, there's Satan!—one might venture
  Pledge one's soul to him, yet leave
Such a flaw in the indenture
  As he'd miss till, past retrieve,

---

[1]*Salve tibi!:* Greetings to you!

[2]*oak-galls:* leaf growths prized as sources of tannin for curing and dyeing.

[3]**Swine's Snout:** dandelion.

[4]**Barbary corsair:** pirate of the Barbary Coast (N Africa).

[5]**Arian:** heretic who denies the Trinity.

[6]**Galatians** 3:10 alludes to litanies of curses in Deuteronomy 27 and 28.

[7]**Manichee:** believer in the Manichean heresy that an evil force shares power with God; thus a damnable heretic.

[8]**scrofulous:** contaminated.

[9]**Belial:** devil of lust.

[10]**greengages:** small green plums. **sieve:** basket.

Blasted lay that rose-acacia
    We're so proud of! *Hy, Zy, Hine. . . .*   70
'St, there's Vespers! *Plena gratiâ,*
    Ave, Virgo![11] Gr-r-r—you swine!

                                1842

Home-Thoughts, from Abroad

— 1 —

Oh, to be in England
Now that April's there,
And whoever wakes in England
Sees, some morning, unaware,
That the lowest boughs and the brushwood sheaf
Round the elm-tree bole are in tiny leaf,
While the chaffinch sings on the orchard bough
In England—now!

— 2 —

And after April, when May follows,
And the whitethroat builds, and all the swallows! 10
Hark, where my blossomed pear-tree in the hedge
Leans to the field and scatters on the clover
Blossoms and dewdrops—at the bent spray's edge—
That's the wise thrush; he sings each song twice over,
Lest you should think he never could recapture
The first fine careless rapture!
And though the fields look rough with hoary dew,
All will be gay when noontide wakes anew
The buttercups, the little children's dower
—Far brighter than this gaudy melon-flower! 20

                                1845

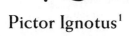

Pictor Ignotus[1]

Florence, 15—

I could have painted pictures like that youth's
    Ye praise so. How my soul springs up! No bar

Stayed me—ah, thought which saddens while it soothes!
    —Never did fate forbid me, star by star,
To outburst on your night with all my gift
    Of fires from God: nor would my flesh have shrunk
From seconding my soul, with eyes uplift
    And wide to heaven, or, straight like thunder, sunk
To the centre, of an instant; or around
    Turned calmly and inquisitive, to scan 10
The license and the limit, space and bound,
    Allowed to truth made visible in man.
And, like that youth ye praise so, all I saw,
    Over the canvas could my hand have flung,
Each face obedient to its passion's law,
    Each passion clear proclaimed without a tongue;
Whether Hope rose at once in all the blood,
    A-tiptoe for the blessing of embrace,
Or Rapture drooped the eyes, as when her brood
    Pull down the nesting dove's heart to its place; 20
Or Confidence lit swift the forehead up,
    And locked the mouth fast, like a castle braved,[2]—
O human faces, hath it spilt, my cup?
    What did ye give me that I have not saved?
Nor will I say I have not dreamed (how well!)
    Of going—I, in each new picture,—forth,
As, making new hearts beat and bosoms swell,
    To Pope or Kaiser, East, West, South, or North,
Bound for the calmly-satisfied great State,
    Or glad aspiring little burgh, it went, 30
Flowers cast upon the car which bore the freight,
    Through old streets named afresh[3] from the event,
Till it reached home, where learned age should greet
    My face, and youth, the star not yet distinct
Above his hair, lie learning at my feet—
    Oh, thus to live, I and my picture, linked
With love about, and praise, till life should end,
    And then not go to heaven, but linger here,
Here on my earth, earth's every man my friend,—
    The thought grew frightful, 'twas so wildly dear! 40
But a voice changed it. Glimpses of such sights
    Have scared me, like the revels through a door
Of some strange house of idols at its rites!
    This world seemed not the world it was before:
Mixed with my loving trusting ones, there trooped
    . . . Who summoned those cold faces that begun

---

[11]*Hy, Zy, Hine . . .* : abortive summons to Satan? **Vespers:** evening prayers. *Plena . . . Virgo* (Hail, Virgin, full of grace): slightly unorthodox version of Latin prayer to Mary.

[1]Pictor Ignotus: Painter unknown (museum or catalogue notation).

---

[2]**braved:** threatened.

[3]**streets named afresh:** as happened when Florence celebrated a Madonna painted by Cimabue (13th century).

To press on me and judge me? Though I stooped
    Shrinking, as from the soldiery a nun,
They drew me forth, and spite of me . . . enough!
    These buy and sell our pictures, take and give, 50
Count them for garniture and household-stuff,
    And where they live needs must our pictures live
And see their faces, listen to their prate,
    Partakers of their daily pettiness,
Discussed of,—"This I love, or this I hate,
    This likes[4] me more, and this affects me less!"
Wherefore I chose my portion. If at whiles
    My heart sinks, as monotonous I paint
These endless cloisters and eternal aisles
    With the same series, Virgin, Babe and Saint, 60
With the same cold calm beautiful regard,—
    At least no merchant traffics in my heart;
The sanctuary's gloom at least shall ward
    Vain tongues from where my pictures stand apart:
Only prayer breaks the silence of the shrine
    While, blackening in the daily candle-smoke,
They moulder on the damp wall's travertine,[5]
    'Mid echoes the light footstep never woke.
So, die my pictures! surely, gently die!
    O youth, men praise so,—holds their praise its
        worth? 70
Blown harshly, keeps the trump its golden cry?
    Tastes sweet the water with such specks of earth?

                                1845

The Bishop Orders His Tomb at Saint Praxed's Church[1]

Rome, 15—

Vanity, saith the preacher, vanity![2]
Draw round my bed: is Anselm keeping back?
Nephews[3]—sons mine . . . ah God, I know not! Well—
She, men would have to be your mother once,
Old Gandolf envied me, so fair she was!

What's done is done, and she is dead beside,
Dead long ago, and I am Bishop since,
And as she died so must we die ourselves,
And thence ye may perceive the world's a dream.
Life, how and what is it? As here I lie 10
In this state-chamber, dying by degrees,
Hours and long hours in the dead night, I ask
"Do I live, am I dead?" Peace, peace seems all.
Saint Praxed's ever was the church for peace;
And so, about this tomb of mine. I fought
With tooth and nail to save my niche, ye know:
—Old Gandolf cozened me, despite my care;
Shrewd was that snatch from out the corner South
He graced his carrion with, God curse the same!
Yet still my niche is not so cramped but thence 20
One sees the pulpit o' the epistle-side,[4]
And somewhat of the choir, those silent seats,
And up into the aery dome where live
The angels, and a sunbeam's sure to lurk:
And I shall fill my slab of basalt there,
And 'neath my tabernacle[5] take my rest,
With those nine columns round me, two and two,
The odd one at my feet where Anselm stands:
Peach-blossom marble all, the rare, the ripe
As fresh-poured red wine of a mighty pulse. 30
—Old Gandolf with his paltry onion-stone,[6]
Put me where I may look at him! True peach,
Rosy and flawless: how I earned the prize!
Draw close: that conflagration of my church
—What then? So much was saved if aught were missed!
My sons, ye would not be my death? Go dig
The white-grape vineyard where the oil-press stood,
Drop water gently till the surface sink,
And if ye find . . . Ah, God I know not, I! . . .
Bedded in store of rotten fig-leaves soft, 40
And corded up in a tight olive-frail,
Some lump, ah God, of *lapis lazuli*,[7]
Big as a Jew's head cut off at the nape,
Blue as a vein o'er the Madonna's breast . . .
Sons, all have I bequeathed you, villas, all,
That brave Frascati[8] villa with its bath,

---

[4]**likes**: pleases.

[5]**travertine**: white limestone.

[1]**St. Praxed's**: church in Rome named for 2nd-century female martyr.

[2]**Vanity . . . vanity**: Ecclesiastes 1:2.

[3]**Nephews**: traditional euphemism for bastard sons.

---

[4]**epistle-side**: right side as viewed from congregation.

[5]**tabernacle**: canopy.

[6]**onion-stone**: cipollino, cheap greenish marble that splits into sheets.

[7]**frail**: rush basket. *lapis lazuli*: semiprecious blue stone.

[8]**Frascati**: resort SE of Rome.

So, let the blue lump poise between my knees,
Like God the Father's globe on both his hands
Ye worship in the Jesu Church[9] so gay,
For Gandolf shall not choose but see and burst!   50
Swift as a weaver's shuttle fleet our years:
Man goeth to the grave,[10] and where is he?
Did I say basalt for my slab, sons? Black—
'Twas ever antique-black[11] I meant! How else
Shall ye contrast my frieze to come beneath?
The bas-relief in bronze ye promised me,
Those Pans and Nymphs ye wot of, and perchance
Some tripod, thyrsus, with a vase or so,
The Saviour at his sermon on the mount,
Saint Praxed in a glory,[12] and one Pan   60
Ready to twitch the Nymph's last garment off,
And Moses with the tables . . . but I know
Ye mark me not! What do they whisper thee,
Child of my bowels,[13] Anselm? Ah, ye hope
To revel down my villas while I gasp
Bricked o'er with beggar's mouldy travertine[14]
Which Gandolf from his tomb-top chuckles at!
Nay, boys, ye love me—all of jasper, then!
'Tis jasper ye stand pledged to, lest I grieve.
My bath must needs be left behind, alas!   70
One block, pure green as a pistachio-nut,
There's plenty jasper somewhere in the world—
And have I not Saint Praxed's ear to pray
Horses for ye, and brown Greek manuscripts,
And mistresses with great smooth marbly limbs?
—That's if ye carve my epitaph aright,
Choice Latin, picked phrase, Tully's[15] every word,
No gaudy ware like Gandolf's second line—
Tully, my masters? Ulpian serves his need!
And then how I shall lie through centuries,   80
And hear the blessed mutter of the mass,
And see God made and eaten all day long,
And feel the steady candle-flame, and taste
Good strong thick stupefying incense-smoke!

For as I lie here, hours of the dead night,
Dying in state and by such slow degrees,
I fold my arms as if they clasped a crook,[16]
And stretch my feet forth straight as stone can point,
And let the bedclothes, for a mortcloth,[17] drop
Into great laps and folds of sculptor's-work: 90
And as yon tapers dwindle, and strange thoughts
Grow, with a certain humming in my ears,
About the life before I lived this life,
And this life too, popes, cardinals and priests,
Saint Praxed at his sermon on the mount,
Your tall pale mother with her talking eyes,
And new-found agate urns as fresh as day,
And marble's language, Latin pure, discreet,
—Aha, ELUCESCEBAT[18] quoth our friend?
No Tully, said I, Ulpian at the best!   100
Evil and brief hath been my pilgrimage.[19]
All *lapis*, all, sons! Else I give the Pope
My villas! Will ye ever eat my heart?
Ever your eyes were as a lizard's quick,
They glitter like your mother's for my soul,
Or ye would heighten my impoverished frieze,
Piece out its starved design, and fill my vase
With grapes, and add a vizor and a Term,[20]
And to the tripod ye would tie a lynx
That in his struggle throws the thyrsus down,   110
To comfort me on my entablature[21]
Whereon I am to lie till I must ask
"Do I live, am I dead?" There, leave me, there!
For ye have stabbed me with ingratitude
To death—ye wish it—God, ye wish it! Stone—
Gritstone,[22] a-crumble! Clammy squares which sweat
As if the corpse they keep were oozing through—
And no more *lapis* to delight the world!
Well, go! I bless ye. Fewer tapers there,
But in a row: and, going, turn your backs   120
—Ay, like departing altar-ministrants,
And leave me in my church, the church for peace,

---

[9]**Jesu Church**: ornate 16th-century Church of Il Gesù in Rome.

[10]**Swift . . . shuttle**: see Job 7:6. **Man goeth . . . grave**: Job 21:13.

[11]**antique-black**: marble more costly than **basalt**.

[12]**tripod**: pagan festival trophy, also used by oracles. **thyrsus**: ornamented staff in Bacchic revels. **glory**: halo.

[13]**child of my bowels**: see 2 Samuel 16:11.

[14]**travertine**: white limestone.

[15]**Tully**: Marcus Tullius Cicero (106–43 BCE), model of Latin prose, unlike Domitius **Ulpianus** (3rd-century Roman jurist).

[16]**crook**: shepherd staff, bishop's emblem.

[17]**mortcloth**: funeral pall.

[18]ELUCESCEBAT: He was illustrious (in somewhat decadent Latin).

[19]**Evil . . . pilgrimage**: Genesis 47:9.

[20]**vizor**: reveler's mask. **Term**: bust on a pedestal.

[21]**entablature**: stone slab.

[22]**Gristone**: sandstone.

That I may watch at leisure if he leers—
Old Gandolf—at me, from his onion-stone,
As still he envied me, so fair she was!

1845

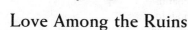

Meeting at Night

— 1 —

The gray sea and the long black land;
And the yellow half-moon large and low;
And the startled little waves that leap
In fiery ringlets from their sleep,
As I gain the cove with pushing prow,
And quench its speed i' the slushy sand.

— 2 —

Then a mile of warm sea-scented beach;
Three fields to cross till a farm appears;
A tap at the pane, the quick sharp scratch
And blue spurt of a lighted match,   10
And a voice less loud, thro' its joys and fears,
Than the two hearts beating each to each!

1845

Parting at Morning

Round the cape of a sudden came the sea,
And the sun looked over the mountain's rim:
And straight was a path of gold for him,[1]
And the need of a world of men for me.

1845

Love Among the Ruins

— 1 —

Where the quiet-coloured end of evening smiles,
    Miles and miles
On the solitary pastures where our sheep
    Half-asleep
Tinkle homeward thro' the twilight, stray or stop
    As they crop—

----

[1] **him:** the sun.

Was the site once of a city great and gay,
    (So they say)
Of our country's very capital, its prince
    Ages since   10
Held his court in, gathered councils, wielding far
    Peace or war.

— 2 —

Now,—the country does not even boast a tree,
    As you see,
To distinguish slopes of verdure, certain rills
    From the hills
Intersect and give a name to, (else they run
    Into one)
Where the domed and daring palace shot its spires
    Up like fires   20
O'er the hundred-gated circuit of a wall
    Bounding all,
Made of marble, men might march on nor be pressed,
    Twelve abreast.

— 3 —

And such plenty and perfection, see, of grass
    Never was!
Such a carpet as, this summer-time, o'erspreads
    And embeds
Every vestige of the city, guessed alone,
    Stock or stone—   30
Where a multitude of men breathed joy and woe
    Long ago;
Lust of glory pricked their hearts up, dread of shame
    Struck them tame;
And that glory and that shame alike, the gold
    Bought and sold.

— 4 —

Now,—the single little turret that remains
    On the plains,
By the caper overrooted, by the gourd
    Overscored,   40
While the patching houseleek's[1] head of blossom winks
    Through the chinks—
Marks the basement whence a tower in ancient time
    Sprang sublime,
And a burning ring, all round, the chariots traced
    As they raced,

----

[1] **caper, gourd, houseleek:** trailing plants common in S Europe.

And the monarch and his minions and his dames
    Viewed the games.

— 5 —

And I know, while thus the quiet-coloured eve
    Smiles to leave   50
To their folding, all our many-tinkling fleece
    In such peace,
And the slopes and rills in undistinguished gray
    Melt away—
That a girl with eager eyes and yellow hair
    Waits me there
In the turret whence the charioteers caught soul
    For the goal,
When the king looked, where she looks now,
        breathless, dumb
    Till I come.   60

— 6 —

But he looked upon the city, every side,
    Far and wide,
All the mountains topped with temples, all the glades'
    Colonnades,
All the causeys,[2] bridges, aqueducts,—and then,
    All the men!
When I do come, she will speak not, she will stand,
    Either hand
On my shoulder, give her eyes the first embrace
    Of my face   70
Ere we rush, ere we extinguish sight and speech
    Each on each.

— 7 —

In one year they sent a million fighters forth
    South and North,
And they built their gods a brazen pillar high
    As the sky,
Yet reserved a thousand chariots in full force—
    Gold, of course.
Oh heart! oh blood that freezes, blood that burns!
    Earth's returns   80
For whole centuries of folly, noise and sin!
    Shut them in,
With their triumphs and their glories and the rest!
    Love is best.

                                                            1855

---

[2]**causeys**: raised paths or highways.

A Woman's Last Word

— 1 —

Let's contend no more, Love,
    Strive nor weep:
All be as before, Love,
    —Only sleep!

— 2 —

What so wild as words are?
    I and thou
In debate, as birds are,
    Hawk on bough!

— 3 —

See the creature stalking
    While we speak!   10
Hush and hide the talking,
    Cheek on cheek!

— 4 —

What so false as truth is,
    False to thee?
Where the serpent's tooth is
    Shun the tree—

— 5 —

Where the apple reddens
    Never pry—
Lest we lose our Edens,
    Eve and I.   20

— 6 —

Be a god and hold me
    With a charm!
Be a man and fold me
    With thine arm!

— 7 —

Teach me, only teach, Love!
    As I ought
I will speak thy speech, Love,
    Think thy thought—

— 8 —

Meet, if thou require it,
    Both demands,   30

Laying flesh and spirit
　　In thy hands.

　　　— 9 —
That shall be to-morrow,
　　Not to-night:
I must bury sorrow
　　Out of sight:

　　　— 10 —
—Must a little weep, Love,
　　(Foolish me!)
And so fall asleep, Love,
　　Loved by thee.　　　　　　　　　　　40
　　　　　　　　　　　　　　　　1855

Fra Lippo Lippi[1]

I am poor brother Lippo, by your leave!
You need not clap your torches to my face.
Zooks,[2] what's to blame? you think you see a monk!
What, 't is past midnight, and you go the rounds,
And here you catch me at an alley's end
Where sportive ladies leave their doors ajar?
The Carmine's[3] my cloister: hunt it up,
Do,—harry out, if you must show your zeal,
Whatever rat, there, haps on his wrong hole,
And nip each softling of a wee white mouse,　　10
Weke, weke, that's crept to keep him company!
Aha, you know your betters! Then, you'll take
Your hand away that's fiddling on my throat,
And please to know me likewise. Who am I?
Why, one, sir, who is lodging with a friend
Three streets off—he's a certain . . . how d' ye call?
Master—a . . . Cosimo of the Medici,[4]
I' the house that caps the corner. Boh! you were best!
Remember and tell me, the day you're hanged,
How you affected such a gullet's-gripe!　　　20
But you, sir, it concerns you that your knaves

Pick up a manner nor discredit you:
Zooks, are we pilchards,[5] that they sweep the streets
And count fair prize what comes into their net?
He's Judas to a tittle, that man is!
Just such a face!　Why, sir, you make amends.
Lord, I'm not angry!　Bid your hangdogs go
Drink out this quarter-florin[6] to the health
Of the munificent House that harbours me
(And many more beside, lads! more beside!)　　30
And all's come square again.　I'd like his face—
His, elbowing on his comrade in the door
With the pike and lantern,—for the slave that holds
John Baptist's head a-dangle by the hair
With one hand ("Look you, now," as who should say)
And his weapon in the other, yet unwiped!
It's not your chance to have a bit of chalk,
A wood-coal or the like? or you should see!
Yes, I'm the painter, since you style me so.
What, brother Lippo's doings, up and down,　　40
You know them and they take you? like enough!
I saw the proper twinkle in your eye—
'Tell you, I liked your looks at very first.
Let's sit and set things straight now, hip to haunch.
Here's spring come, and the nights one makes up bands
To roam the town and sing out carnival,
And I've been three weeks shut within my mew,
A-painting for the great man, saints and saints
And saints again.　I could not paint all night—
Ouf! I leaned out of window for fresh air.　　50
There came a hurry of feet and little feet,
A sweep of lute-strings, laughs, and whiffs of song,[7]—
Flower o' the broom,
Take away love, and our earth is a tomb!
Flower o' the quince,
I let Lisa go, and what good in life since?
Flower o' the thyme—and so on. Round they went.
Scarce had they turned the corner when a titter
Like the skipping of rabbits by moonlight,—three slim
　　shapes,
And a face that looked up . . . zooks, sir, flesh
　　and blood,　　　　　　　　　　　　　60
That's all I'm made of! Into shreds it went,
Curtain and counterpane and coverlet,

---

[1]**Fra Lippo Lippi** (1405–1469): painter-monk, early exponent of naturalism in art.

[2]**Zooks:** mild oath (Gadzooks).

[3]Santa Maria del **Carmine**: Carmelite monastery in Florence.

[4]**Cosimo of the Medici** (1389–1464): Florentine banker and grandee, Lippo's patron.

[5]**pilchards:** sardines.

[6]**florin:** Florentine gold coin.

[7]**whiffs of song:** Browning's imitation of *stornelli,* extemporized Italian street lyrics.

All the bed-furniture—a dozen knots,
There was a ladder! Down I let myself,
Hands and feet, scrambling somehow, and so dropped,
And after them.   I came up with the fun
Hard by Saint Laurence,[8] hail fellow, well met,—
Flower o' the rose,
If I've been merry, what matter who knows?
And so as I was stealing back again   70
To get to bed and have a bit of sleep
Ere I rise up to-morrow and go work
On Jerome[9] knocking at his poor old breast
With his great round stone to subdue the flesh,
You snap me of the sudden. Ah, I see!
Though your eye twinkles still, you shake your head—
Mine's shaved[10]—a monk, you say—the sting's in that!
If Master Cosimo announced himself,
Mum's the word naturally; but a monk!
Come, what am I a beast for? tell us, now!   80
I was a baby when my mother died
And father died and left me in the street.
I starved there, God knows how, a year or two
On fig-skins, melon-parings, rinds and shucks,
Refuse and rubbish.   One fine frosty day,
My stomach being empty as your hat,
The wind doubled me up and down I went.
Old Aunt Lapaccia trussed me with one hand,
(Its fellow was a stinger as I knew)
And so along the wall, over the bridge,   90
By the straight cut to the convent.   Six words there,
While I stood munching my first bread that month:
"So, boy, you're minded," quoth the good fat father
Wiping his own mouth, 'twas refection-time,—
"To quit this very miserable world?
"Will you renounce" . . . "the mouthful of bread?" thought I;
By no means!   Brief, they made a monk of me;
I did renounce the world, its pride and greed,
Palace, farm, villa, shop and banking-house,
Trash, such as these poor devils of Medici   100
Have given their hearts to—all at eight years old.
Well, sir, I found in time, you may be sure,
'Twas not for nothing—the good bellyful,
The warm serge and the rope that goes all round,
And day-long blessed idleness beside!

"Let's see what the urchin's fit for"—that came next.
Not overmuch their way, I must confess.
Such a to-do!   They tried me with their books:
Lord, they'd have taught me Latin in pure waste!
Flower o' the clove,   110
All the Latin I construe is, "amo" I love!
But, mind you, when a boy starves in the streets
Eight years together, as my fortune was,
Watching folk's faces to know who will fling
The bit of half-stripped grape-bunch he desires,
And who will curse or kick him for his pains,—
Which gentleman processional and fine,
Holding a candle to the Sacrament,
Will wink and let him lift a plate and catch
The droppings of the wax to sell again,   120
Or holla for the Eight[11] and have him whipped,—
How say I?—nay, which dog bites, which lets drop
His bone from the heap of offal in the street,—
Why, soul and sense of him grow sharp alike,
He learns the look of things, and none the less
For admonition from the hunger-pinch.
I had a store of such remarks, be sure,
Which, after I found leisure, turned to use.
I drew men's faces on my copy-books,
Scrawled them within the antiphonary's marge,[12]   130
Joined legs and arms to the long music-notes,
Found eyes and nose and chin for A's and B's,
And made a string of pictures of the world
Betwixt the ins and outs of verb and noun,
On the wall, the bench, the door. The monks looked black.
"Nay," quoth the Prior, "turn him out, d' ye say?
"In no wise.   Lose a crow and catch a lark.
"What if at last we get our man of parts,
"We Carmelites, like those Camaldolese
"And Preaching Friars,[13] to do our church up fine   140
"And put the front on it that ought to be!"
And hereupon he bade me daub away.
Thank you! my head being crammed, the walls a blank,
Never was such prompt disemburdening.
First, every sort of monk, the black and white,[14]
I drew them, fat and lean: then, folk at church,
From good old gossips waiting to confess

---

[8]**Saint Laurence**: Church of San Lorenzo.

[9]**Saint Jerome** (347?–420): Biblical translator, theologian, monk,
ascetic.

[10]**shaved**: tonsured, in token of obedient poverty—and chastity.

---

[11]**Eight**: Florence magistrates.

[12]**antiphonary's marge**: margin of a hymn book.

[13]**Carmelites, Camaldolese, Preaching Friars**: monastic orders.

[14]**black and white**: Carmelites and Dominicans.

Their cribs[15] of barrel-droppings, candle-ends,—
To the breathless fellow at the altar-foot,
Fresh from his murder, safe and sitting there   150
With the little children round him in a row
Of admiration, half for his beard and half
For that white anger of his victim's son
Shaking a fist at him with one fierce arm,
Signing himself with the other because of Christ
(Whose sad face on the cross sees only this
After the passion of a thousand years)
Till some poor girl, her apron o'er her head,
(Which the intense eyes looked through) came at eve
On tiptoe, said a word, dropped in a loaf,   160
Her pair of earrings and a bunch of flowers
(The brute took growling), prayed, and so was gone.
I painted all, then cried " 'Tis ask and have;
"Choose, for more's ready!"—laid the ladder flat,
And showed my covered bit of cloister-wall.
The monks closed in a circle and praised loud
Till checked, taught what to see and not to see,
Being simple bodies—"That's the very man!
Look at the boy who stoops to pat the dog!
That woman's like the Prior's niece[16] who comes   170
To care about his asthma: it's the life!"
But there my triumph's straw-fire flared and funked;
Their betters took their turn to see and say:
The Prior and the learned pulled a face
And stopped all that in no time. "How? what's here?
Quite from the mark of painting, bless us all!
Faces, arms, legs and bodies like the true
As much as pea and pea! it's devil's-game!
Your business is not to catch men with show,
With homage to the perishable clay,   180
But lift them over it, ignore it all,
Make them forget there's such a thing as flesh.
Your business is to paint the souls of men—
Man's soul, and it's a fire, smoke . . . no, it's not . . .
It's vapour done up like a new-born babe—
(In that shape when you die it leaves your mouth)
It's . . . well, what matters talking, it's the soul!
Give us no more of body than shows soul!
Here's Giotto,[17] with his Saint a-praising God,
That sets us praising,—why not stop with him?   190

Why put all thoughts of praise out of our head
With wonder at lines, colours, and what not?
Paint the soul, never mind the legs and arms!
Rub all out, try at it a second time.
Oh, that white smallish female with the breasts,
She's just my niece . . . Herodias,[18] I would say,—
Who went and danced and got men's heads cut off!
Have it all out!"   Now, is this sense, I ask?
A fine way to paint soul, by painting body
So ill, the eye can't stop there, must go further   200
And can't fare worse!   Thus, yellow does for white
When what you put for yellow's simply black,
And any sort of meaning looks intense
When all beside itself means and looks nought.
Why can't a painter lift each foot in turn,
Left foot and right foot, go a double step,
Make his flesh liker and his soul more like,
Both in their order?   Take the prettiest face,
The Prior's niece . . . patron-saint—is it so pretty
You can't discover if it means hope, fear,   210
Sorrow or joy? won't beauty go with these?
Suppose I've made her eyes all right and blue,
Can't I take breath and try to add life's flash,
And then add soul and heighten them threefold?
Or say there's beauty with no soul at all—
(I never saw it—put the case the same—)
If you get simple beauty and nought else,
You get about the best thing God invents:
That's somewhat: and you'll find the soul you have missed,
Within yourself, when you return him thanks.   220
"Rub all out!" Well, well, there's my life, in short,
And so the thing has gone on ever since.
I'm grown a man no doubt, I've broken bounds:
You should not take a fellow eight years old
And make him swear to never kiss the girls.
I'm my own master, paint now as I please—
Having a friend, you see, in the Corner-house!
Lord, it's fast holding by the rings in front—
Those great rings serve more purposes than just
To plant a flag in, or tie up a horse!   230
And yet the old schooling sticks, the old grave eyes
Are peeping o'er my shoulder as I work,
The heads shake still—"It's art's decline, my son!
You're not of the true painters, great and old;
Brother Angelico's the man, you'll find;

---

[15]**cribs**: petty thefts.

[16]**niece**: euphemism for mistress.

[17]**Giotto** di Bondone (1276–1337): greatest painter in the stylized mode preceding the Renaissance.

---

[18]**Herodias**: see the story of Salome's dance in Matthew 14.

Brother Lorenzo[19] stands his single peer:
Fag on at flesh, you'll never make the third!"
Flower o' the pine,
You keep your mistr . . . manners, and I'll stick to mine!
I'm not the third, then: bless us, they must know!   240
Don't you think they're the likeliest to know,
They with their Latin? So, I swallow my rage,
Clench my teeth, suck my lips in tight, and paint
To please them—sometimes do and sometimes don't;
For, doing most, there's pretty sure to come
A turn, some warm eve finds me at my saints—
A laugh, a cry, the business of the world—
(Flower o' the peach,
Death for us all, and his own life for each!)
And my whole soul revolves, the cup runs over,   250
The world and life's too big to pass for a dream,
And I do these wild things in sheer despite,
And play the fooleries you catch me at,
In pure rage! The old mill-horse, out at grass
After hard years, throws up his stiff heels so,
Although the miller does not preach to him
The only good of grass is to make chaff.
What would men have? Do they like grass or no—
May they or mayn't they? all I want's the thing
Settled for ever one way. As it is,   260
You tell too many lies and hurt yourself:
You don't like what you only like too much,
You do like what, if given you at your word,
You find abundantly detestable.
For me, I think I speak as I was taught;
I always see the garden and God there
A-making man's wife: and, my lesson learned,
The value and significance of flesh,
I can't unlearn ten minutes afterwards.

You understand me: I'm a beast, I know.   270
But see, now—why, I see as certainly
As that the morning-star's about to shine,
What will hap some day. We've a youngster here
Comes to our convent, studies what I do,
Slouches and stares and lets no atom drop:
His name is Guidi—he'll not mind the monks—
They call him Hulking Tom,[20] he lets them talk—

He picks my practice up—he'll paint apace,
I hope so—though I never live so long,
I know what's sure to follow. You be judge!   280
You speak no Latin more than I, belike;
However, you're my man, you've seen the world
—The beauty and the wonder and the power,
The shapes of things, their colours, lights and shades,
Changes, surprises,—and God made it all!
—For what? Do you feel thankful, ay or no,
For this fair town's face, yonder river's line,
The mountain round it and the sky above,
Much more the figures of man, woman, child,
These are the frame to? What's it all about?   290
To be passed over, despised? or dwelt upon,
Wondered at? oh, this last of course!—you say.
But why not do as well as say,—paint these
Just as they are, careless what comes of it?
God's works—paint anyone, and count it crime
To let a truth slip. Don't object, "His works
Are here already; nature is complete:
Suppose you reproduce her—(which you can't)
There's no advantage! you must beat her, then."
For, don't you mark? we're made so that we love   300
First when we see them painted, things we have passed
Perhaps a hundred times nor cared to see;
And so they are better, painted—better to us,
Which is the same thing. Art was given for that;
God uses us to help each other so,
Lending our minds out. Have you noticed, now,
Your cullion's hanging[21] face? A bit of chalk,
And trust me but you should, though! How much more,
If I drew higher things with the same truth!
That were to take the Prior's pulpit-place,   310
Interpret God to all of you! Oh, oh,
It makes me mad to see what men shall do
And we in our graves! This world's no blot for us,
Nor blank; it means intensely, and means good:
To find its meaning is my meat and drink.
"Ay, but you don't so instigate to prayer!"
Strikes in the Prior: "when your meaning's plain
It does not say to folk—remember matins,[22]
Or, mind you fast next Friday!" Why, for this
What need of art at all? A skull and bones,   320
Two bits of stick nailed crosswise, or, what's best,
A bell to chime the hour with, does as well.
I painted a Saint Laurence six months since

---

[19]Fra **Angelico** (1400–1455), **Lorenzo** Monaco (1370?–1425?): painter-monks.

[20]Tommaso **Guidi** (1401–1428): in fact, Lippo's precursor in painterly realism, not as here his disciple (better known by his nickname Masaccio or **Hulking Tom**).

---

[21]**cullion**: scumbag, fit for **hanging**.

[22]**matins**: morning worship.

At Prato,[23] splashed the fresco in fine style:
"How looks my painting, now the scaffold's down?"
I ask a brother: "Hugely," he returns—
"Already not one phiz[24] of your three slaves
Who turn the Deacon off his toasted side,
But 's scratched and prodded to our heart's content,
The pious people have so eased their own   330
With coming to say prayers there in a rage:
We get on fast to see the bricks beneath.
Expect another job this time next year,
For pity and religion grow i' the crowd—
Your painting serves its purpose!" Hang the fools!

    —That is—you'll not mistake an idle word
Spoke in a huff by a poor monk, God wot,
Tasting the air this spicy night which turns
The unaccustomed head like Chianti wine!
Oh, the church knows! don't misreport me, now!   340
It's natural a poor monk out of bounds
Should have his apt word to excuse himself:
And hearken how I plot to make amends.
I have bethought me: I shall paint a piece
. . . There 's for you! Give me six months, then go, see
Something in Sant' Ambrogio's![25] Bless the nuns!
They want a cast o' my office. I shall paint
God in the midst, Madonna and her babe,
Ringed by a bowery flowery angel-brood,
Lilies and vestments and white faces, sweet   350
As puff on puff of grated orris-root[26]
When ladies crowd to Church at midsummer.
And then i' the front, of course a saint or two—
Saint John,[27] because he saves the Florentines,
Saint Ambrose, who puts down in black and white
The convent's friends and gives them a long day,
And Job, I must have him there past mistake,
The man of Uz[28] (and Us without the z,
Painters who need his patience). Well, all these
Secured at their devotion, up shall come   360
Out of a corner when you least expect,
As one by a dark stair into a great light,
Music and talking, who but Lippo! I!—

Mazed, motionless and moonstruck—I'm the man!
Back I shrink—what is this I see and hear?
I, caught up with my monk's-things by mistake,
My old serge gown and rope that goes all round,
I, in this presence, this pure company!
Where's a hole, where's a corner for escape?
Then steps a sweet angelic slip of a thing   370
Forward, puts out a soft palm—"Not so fast!"
—Addresses the celestial presence, "nay—
He made you and devised you, after all,
Though he's none of you! Could Saint John there draw—
His camel-hair make up a painting-brush?
We come to brother Lippo for all that,
Iste perfecit opus!"[29] So, all smile—
I shuffle sideways with my blushing face
Under the cover of a hundred wings
Thrown like a spread of kirtles when you're gay   380
And play hot cockles,[30] all the doors being shut,
Till, wholly unexpected, in there pops
The hothead husband! Thus I scuttle off
To some safe bench behind, not letting go
The palm of her, the little lily thing
That spoke the good word for me in the nick,
Like the Prior's niece . . . Saint Lucy,[31] I would say.
And so all's saved for me, and for the church
A pretty picture gained. Go, six months hence!
Your hand, sir, and good-bye: no lights, no lights! 390
The street's hushed, and I know my own way back,
Don't fear me! there's the grey beginning. Zooks!

                                              1855

~

A Toccata of Galuppi's[1]

— 1 —

Oh Galuppi, Baldassaro, this is very sad to find!
I can hardly misconceive you; it would prove me deaf and
    blind;
But although I take your meaning, 'tis with such a heavy
    mind!

---

[23]**Saint Laurence:** 3rd-century martyr roasted on a grid. **Prato:** town near Florence whose church contains Lippi paintings.

[24]**phiz:** face.

[25]**Sant' Ambrogio** (St. Ambrose): Florentine church where Lippo painted the **piece** here described, *The Coronation of the Virgin.*

[26]**orris-root:** root of the iris, **grated** for its scent.

[27]**Saint John:** John the Baptist, patron saint of Florence.

[28]**Uz:** patient **Job**'s homeland.

[29]*Iste perfecit opus* (This man accomplished the work): legend appearing on a scroll in a corner of the *Coronation* canvas next to a face Browning believed to be Lippo's.

[30]**kirtles:** skirts. **gay:** horny. **hot cockles:** children's blindfold game, here with sexual innuendo.

[31]**Saint Lucy:** 4th-century virgin martyr, patron saint of eyesight.

[1]**Toccata:** showy keyboard piece. Baldassaro **Galuppi** (1706–1785): Venetian composer.

— 2 —

Here you come with your old music, and here's all the
    good it brings.
What, they lived once thus at Venice where the merchants
    were the kings,
Where Saint Mark's is, where the Doges used to wed the
    sea with rings?[2]

— 3 —

Ay, because the sea's the street there; and 'tis arched
    by . . . what you call
    . . . Shylock's bridge[3] with houses on it, where they kept
    the carnival:
I was never out of England—it's as if I saw it all.

— 4 —

Did young people take their pleasure when the sea was
    warm in May?   10
Balls and masks begun at midnight, burning ever to
    mid-day,
When they made up fresh adventures for the morrow,
    do you say?

— 5 —

Was a lady such a lady, cheeks so round and lips so
    red,—
On her neck the small face buoyant, like a bell-flower on
    its bed,
O'er the breast's superb abundance where a man might
    base his head?

— 6 —

Well, and it was graceful of them—they'd break talk off
    and afford
—She, to bite her mask's black velvet—he, to finger on his
    sword,
While you sat and played Toccatas, stately at the
    clavichord?[4]

— 7 —

What? Those lesser thirds[5] so plaintive, sixths diminished,
    sigh on sigh,
Told them something? Those suspensions, those
    solutions—"Must we die?"   20
Those commiserating sevenths—"Life might last! we can
    but try!"

— 8 —

"Were you happy?"—"Yes."—"And are you still as
    happy?"—"Yes. And you?"
—"Then, more kisses!"—"Did I stop them, when a million
    seemed so few?"
Hark, the dominant's persistence till it must be answered to!

— 9 —

So, an octave struck the answer. Oh, they praised you, I
    dare say!
"Brave Galuppi! that was music! good alike at grave and gay!
I can always leave off talking when I hear a master play!"

— 10 —

Then they left you for their pleasure: till in due time, one
    by one,
Some with lives that came to nothing, some with deeds as
    well undone,
Death stepped tacitly and took them where they never see
    the sun.   30

— 11 —

But when I sit down to reason, think to take my stand nor
    swerve,
While I triumph o'er a secret wrung from nature's close
    reserve,
In you come with your cold music till I creep thro' every
    nerve.

— 12 —

Yes, you, like a ghostly cricket, creaking where a house was
    burned:
"Dust and ashes, dead and done with, Venice spent what
    Venice earned.
The soul, doubtless, is immortal—where a soul can be
    discerned.

---

[2]Saint Mark's: basilica of Venice. Doges: chief magistrates of
Venice, who annually cast ceremonial rings into the ocean to celebrate the city's maritime power.

[3]Shylock's bridge: the Rialto, spanning the Grand Canal, Shy-
lock's place of business in The Merchant of Venice.

[4]clavichord: precursor of the piano.

---

[5]lesser thirds: intervals of three semitones (minor thirds). sixths
diminished: intervals one semitone higher than fifths (harmonically
unsettled). suspensions: unresolved chords. solutions: chordal passages from dissonance to consonance. sevenths: penultimate
chords (equivalent to dominant of line 24) en route to perfect cadence of the tonic octave (line 25).

— 13 —

"Yours for instance: you know physics, something of
  geology,
Mathematics are your pastime; souls shall rise in their
  degree;
Butterflies may dread extinction,—you'll not die, it
  cannot be!

— 14 —

"As for Venice and her people, merely born to bloom
  and drop,   40
Here on earth they bore their fruitage, mirth and folly
  were the crop:
What of soul was left, I wonder, when the kissing had
  to stop?

— 15 —

"Dust and ashes!" So you creak it, and I want the heart to
  scold.
Dear dead women, with such hair, too—what's become of
  all the gold
Used to hang and brush their bosoms? I feel chilly and
  grown old.

                                                              1855

By the Fire-side

— 1 —

How well I know what I mean to do
  When the long dark autumn-evenings come:
And where, my soul, is thy pleasant hue?
  With the music of all thy voices, dumb
In life's November too!

— 2 —

I shall be found by the fire, suppose,
  O'er a great wise book as beseemeth age,
While the shutters flap as the cross-wind blows,
  And I turn the page, and I turn the page,
Not verse now, only prose!   10

— 3 —

Till the young ones whisper, finger on lip,
  "There he is at it, deep in Greek:
Now then, or never, out we slip
  To cut from the hazels by the creek
A mainmast for our ship!"

— 4 —

I shall be at it indeed, my friends:
  Greek puts already on either side
Such a branch-work forth as soon extends
  To a vista opening far and wide,
And I pass out where it ends.   20

— 5 —

The outside-frame, like your hazel-trees:
  But the inside-archway widens fast,
And a rarer sort succeeds to these,
  And we slope to Italy at last
And youth, by green degrees.

— 6 —

I follow wherever I am led,
  Knowing so well the leader's hand:
Oh woman-country, wooed not wed,
  Loved all the more by earth's male-lands,
Laid to their hearts instead!   30

— 7 —

Look at the ruined chapel again
  Half-way up in the Alpine gorge!
Is that a tower, I point you plain,
  Or is it a mill, or an iron-forge
Breaks solitude in vain?

— 8 —

A turn, and we stand in the heart of things;
  The woods are round us, heaped and dim;
From slab to slab how it slips and springs,
  The thread of water single and slim,
Through the ravage some torrent brings!   40

— 9 —

Does it feed the little lake below?
  That speck of white just on its marge
Is Pella;[1] see, in the evening-glow,
  How sharp the silver spear-heads charge
When Alp meets heaven in snow!

— 10 —

On our other side is the straight-up rock;
  And a path is kept 'twixt the gorge and it

---

[1] **Pella:** village on Lake Orta in the Italian Piedmont. While the
poem is often, and with cause, read autobiographically, the Brownings never visited this region.

By boulder-stones where lichens mock
    The marks on a moth, and small ferns fit
Their teeth to the polished block.   50

— 11 —

Oh the sense of the yellow mountain-flowers,
    And thorny balls, each three in one,
The chestnuts throw on our path in showers!
    For the drop of the woodland fruit's begun,
These early November hours,

— 12 —

That crimson the creeper's leaf across
    Like a splash of blood, intense, abrupt,
O'er a shield else gold from rim to boss,[2]
    And lay it for show on the fairy-cupped
Elf-needled mat of moss,   60

— 13 —

By the rose-flesh mushrooms, undivulged
    Last evening—nay, in to-day's first dew
Yon sudden coral nipple bulged,
    Where a freaked[3] fawn-coloured flaky crew
Of toadstools peep indulged.

— 14 —

And yonder, at foot of the fronting ridge
    That takes the turn to a range beyond,
Is the chapel reached by the one-arched bridge
    Where the water is stopped in a stagnant pond
Danced over by the midge.   70

— 15 —

The chapel and bridge are of stone alike,
    Blackish-grey and mostly wet;
Cut hemp-stalks steep in the narrow dyke.
    See here again, how the lichens fret
And the roots of the ivy strike!

— 16 —

Poor little place, where its one priest comes
    On a festa-day, if he comes at all,
To the dozen folk from their scattered homes,
    Gathered within that precinct small
By the dozen ways one roams—   80

— 17 —

To drop from the charcoal-burners' huts,
    Or climb from the hemp-dressers' low shed,
Leave the grange where the woodman stores his nuts,
    Or the wattled cote where the fowlers[4] spread
Their gear on the rock's bare juts.

— 18 —

It has some pretension too, this front,
    With its bit of fresco half-moon-wise
Set over the porch, Art's early wont:
    'Tis John in the Desert,[5] I surmise,
But has borne the weather's brunt—   90

— 19 —

Not from the fault of the builder, though,
    For a pent-house[6] properly projects
Where three carved beams make a certain show,
    Dating—good thought of our architect's—
'Five, six, nine, he lets you know.

— 20 —

And all day long a bird sings there,
    And a stray sheep drinks at the pond at times;
The place is silent and aware;
    It has had its scenes, its joys and crimes,
But that is its own affair.   100

— 21 —

My perfect wife, my Leonor,[7]
    Oh heart, my own, oh eyes, mine too,
Whom else could I dare look backward for,
    With whom beside should I dare pursue
The path grey heads abhor?

— 22 —

For it leads to a crag's sheer edge with them;
    Youth, flowery all the way, there stops—
Not they; age threatens and they contemn,
    Till they reach the gulf wherein youth drops,
One inch from life's safe hem!   110

---

[2]**boss:** raised center of a **shield.**

[3]**freaked:** streaked.

[4]**wattled cote:** thatched shed. **fowlers:** bird hunters.

[5]**John in the Desert:** John the Baptist in the wilderness (Mark 1:3–6).

[6]**pent-house:** protective roof.

[7]**Leonor:** faithful wife in Beethoven's opera *Fidelio* (1805).

— 23 —

With me, youth led . . . I will speak now,
    No longer watch you as you sit
Reading by fire-light, that great brow
    And the spirit-small hand propping it,
Mutely, my heart knows how—

— 24 —

When, if I think but deep enough,
    You are wont to answer, prompt as rhyme;
And you, too, find without rebuff
    Response your soul seeks many a time
Piercing its fine flesh-stuff.   120

— 25 —

My own, confirm me! If I tread
    This path back, is it not in pride
To think how little I dreamed it led
    To an age so blest that, by its side,
Youth seems the waste instead?

— 26 —

My own, see where the years conduct!
    At first, 'twas something our two souls
Should mix as mists do; each is sucked
    In each now: on, the new stream rolls,
Whatever rocks obstruct.   130

— 27 —

Think, when our one soul understands
    The great Word which makes all things new,[8]
When earth breaks up and heaven expands,
    How will the change strike me and you
In the house not made with hands?

— 28 —

Oh I must feel your brain prompt mine,
    Your heart anticipate my heart,
You must be just before, in fine,
    See and make me see, for your part,
New depths of the divine!   140

— 29 —

But who could have expected this
    When we two drew together first

Just for the obvious human bliss,
    To satisfy life's daily thirst
With a thing men seldom miss?

— 30 —

Come back with me to the first of all,
    Let us lean and love it over again,
Let us now forget and now recall,
    Break the rosary in a pearly rain,
And gather what we let fall!   150

— 31 —

What did I say?—that a small bird sings
    All day long, save when a brown pair
Of hawks from the wood float with wide wings
    Strained to a bell: 'gainst noon-day glare
You count the streaks and rings.

— 32 —

But at afternoon or almost eve
    'Tis better; then the silence grows
To that degree, you half believe
    It must get rid of what it knows,
Its bosom does so heave.   160

— 33 —

Hither we walked then, side by side,
    Arm in arm and cheek to cheek,
And still I questioned or replied,
    While my heart, convulsed to really speak,
Lay choking in its pride.

— 34 —

Silent the crumbling bridge we cross,
    And pity and praise the chapel sweet,
And care about the fresco's loss,
    And wish for our souls a like retreat,
And wonder at the moss.   170

— 35 —

Stoop and kneel on the settle[9] under,
    Look through the window's grated square:
Nothing to see! For fear of plunder,
    The cross is down and the altar bare,
As if thieves don't fear thunder.

---

[8]**all things new:** Revelation 21:5. **house . . . hands:** 2 Corinthians 5:1.

---

[9]**settle:** bench.

— 36 —

We stoop and look in through the grate,
   See the little porch and rustic door,
Read duly the dead builder's date;
   Then cross the bridge that we crossed before,
Take the path again—but wait!   180

— 37 —

Oh moment, one and infinite!
   The water slips o'er stock and stone;
The West is tender, hardly bright:
   How grey at once is the evening grown—
One star, its chrysolite![10]

— 38 —

We two stood there with never a third,
   But each by each, as each knew well:
The sights we saw and the sounds we heard,
   The lights and the shades made up a spell
Till the trouble grew and stirred.   190

— 39 —

Oh, the little more, and how much it is!
   And the little less, and what worlds away!
How a sound shall quicken content to bliss,
   Or a breath suspend the blood's best play,
And life be a proof of this!

— 40 —

Had she willed it, still had stood the screen
   So slight, so sure, 'twixt my love and her:
I could fix her face with a guard between,
   And find her soul as when friends confer,
Friends—lovers that might have been.   200

— 41 —

For my heart had a touch of the woodland-time,
   Wanting to sleep now over its best.
Shake the whole tree in the summer-prime,
   But bring to the last leaf no such test!
"Hold the last fast!" runs the rhyme.

— 42 —

For a chance to make your little much,
   To gain a lover and lose a friend,
Venture the tree and a myriad such,

---

[10]**chrysolite:** olive-colored precious stone.

When nothing you mar but the year can mend:
But a last leaf—fear to touch!   210

— 43 —

Yet should it unfasten itself and fall
   Eddying down till it find your face
At some slight wind—best chance of all!
   Be your heart henceforth its dwelling-place
You trembled to forestall!

— 44 —

Worth how well, those dark grey eyes,
   That hair so dark and dear, how worth
That a man should strive and agonize,
   And taste a veriest hell on earth
For the hope of such a prize!   220

— 45 —

You might have turned and tried a man,
   Set him a space to weary and wear,
And prove which suited more your plan,
   His best of hope or his worst despair,
Yet end as he began.

— 46 —

But you spared me this, like the heart you are,
   And filled my empty heart at a word.
If two lives join, there is oft a scar,
   They are one and one, with a shadowy third;
One near one is too far.   230

— 47 —

A moment after, and hands unseen
   Were hanging the night around us fast;
But we knew that a bar was broken between
   Life and life: we were mixed at last
In spite of the mortal screen.

— 48 —

The forests had done it; there they stood;
   We caught for a moment the powers at play:
They had mingled us so, for once and good,
   Their work was done—we might go or stay,
They relapsed to their ancient mood.   240

— 49 —

How the world is made for each of us!
   How all we perceive and know in it

Tends to some moment's product thus,
    When a soul declares itself—to wit,
By its fruit,[11] the thing it does!

— 50 —

Be hate that fruit or love that fruit,
    It forwards the general deed of man,
And each of the Many helps to recruit
    The life of the race by a general plan;
Each living his own, to boot.   250

— 51 —

I am named and known by that moment's feat;
    There took my station and degree;
So grew my own small life complete,
    As nature obtained her best of me—
One born to love you, sweet!

— 52 —

And to watch you sink by the fire-side now
    Back again, as you mutely sit
Musing by fire-light, that great brow
    And the spirit-small hand propping it,
Yonder, my heart knows how!   260

— 53 —

So, earth has gained by one man the more,
    And the gain of earth must be heaven's gain too;
And the whole is well worth thinking o'er
    When autumn comes: which I mean to do
One day, as I said before.

                                                    1855

~

An Epistle
Containing the Strange Medical
Experience of Karshish,
the Arab Physician

Karshish, the picker-up of learning's crumbs,
The not-incurious in God's handiwork
(This man's-flesh he hath admirably made,
Blown like a bubble, kneaded like a paste,

---

[11]**fruit**: see Matthew 7:16–20.

To coop up and keep down on earth a space
That puff of vapour from his mouth, man's soul)
—To Abib, all-sagacious in our art,
Breeder in me of what poor skill I boast,
Like me inquisitive how pricks and cracks
Befall the flesh through too much stress and strain,   10
Whereby the wily vapour fain would slip
Back and rejoin its source before the term,—
And aptest in contrivance (under God)
To baffle it by deftly stopping such:—
The vagrant Scholar to his Sage at home
Sends greeting (health and knowledge, fame with peace)
Three samples of true snakestone[1]—rarer still,
One of the other sort, the melon-shaped,
(But fitter, pounded fine, for charms than drugs)
And writeth now the twenty-second time.   20

    My journeyings were brought to Jericho:[2]
Thus I resume. Who studious in our art
Shall count a little labour unrepaid?
I have shed sweat enough, left flesh and bone
On many a flinty furlong of this land.
Also, the country-side is all on fire
With rumours of a marching hitherward:
Some say Vespasian[3] cometh, some, his son.
A black lynx snarled and pricked a tufted ear;
Lust of my blood inflamed his yellow balls: 30
I cried and threw my staff and he was gone.
Twice have the robbers stripped and beaten me,
And once a town declared me for a spy;
But at the end, I reach Jerusalem,
Since this poor covert where I pass the night,
This Bethany,[4] lies scarce the distance thence
A man with plague-sores at the third degree
Runs till he drops down dead. Thou laughest here!
'Sooth, it elates me, thus reposed and safe,
To void the stuffing of my travel-scrip   40
And share with thee whatever Jewry yields.
A viscid choler is observable
In tertians, I was nearly bold to say;

---

[1]**snakestone**: used against snakebite.

[2]**Jericho**: settlement on W bank of Jordan River.

[3]**Vespasian** (9–79): commander of Roman invasion of Palestine (66), Emperor of Rome (69–79).

[4]**Bethany**: home of Lazarus, whose revival by Jesus after death (John 11) forms the topic of Karshish's letter to his mentor Abib.

And falling-sickness[5] hath a happier cure
Than our school wots of: there's a spider here
Weaves no web, watches on the ledge of tombs,
Sprinkled with mottles on an ash-grey back;
Take five and drop them . . . but who knows his mind,
The Syrian runagate I trust this to?
His service payeth me a sublimate[6]   50
Blown up his nose to help the ailing eye.
Best wait: I reach Jerusalem at morn,
There set in order my experiences,
Gather what most deserves, and give thee all—
Or I might add, Judæa's gum-tragacanth[7]
Scales off in purer flakes, shines clearer-grained,
Cracks 'twixt the pestle and the porphyry,
In fine exceeds our produce. Scalp-disease
Confounds me, crossing so with leprosy—
Thou hadst admired one sort I gained at Zoar[8]—   60
But zeal outruns discretion. Here I end.

     Yet stay: my Syrian blinketh gratefully,
Protesteth his devotion is my price—
Suppose I write what harms not, though he steal?
I half resolve to tell thee, yet I blush,
What set me off a-writing first of all.
An itch I had, a sting to write, a tang!
For, be it this town's barrenness—or else
The Man had something in the look of him—
His case has struck me far more than 'tis worth.   70
So, pardon if—(lest presently I lose
In the great press of novelty at hand
The care and pains this somehow stole from me)
I bid thee take the thing while fresh in mind,
Almost in sight—for, wilt thou have the truth?
The very man is gone from me but now,
Whose ailment is the subject of discourse.
Thus then, and let thy better wit help all!

     'Tis but a case of mania—subinduced
By epilepsy, at the turning-point   80
Of trance prolonged unduly some three days:
When, by the exhibition[9] of some drug
Or spell, exorcization, stroke of art

Unknown to me and which 't were well to know,
The evil thing out-breaking all at once
Left the man whole and sound of body indeed,—
But, flinging (so to speak) life's gates too wide,
Making a clear house of it too suddenly,
The first conceit[10] that entered might inscribe
Whatever it was minded on the wall   90
So plainly at that vantage, as it were,
(First come, first served) that nothing subsequent
Attaineth to erase those fancy-scrawls
The just-returned and new-established soul
Hath gotten now so thoroughly by heart
That henceforth she will read or these or none.
And first—the man's own firm conviction rests
That he was dead (in fact they buried him)
—That he was dead and then restored to life
By a Nazarene physician of his tribe: 100
—'Sayeth, the same bade "Rise," and he did rise.
"Such cases are diurnal," thou wilt cry.
Not so this figment!—not, that such a fume,
Instead of giving way to time and health,
Should eat itself into the life of life,
As saffron tingeth flesh, blood, bones and all!
For see, how he takes up the after-life.
The man—it is one Lazarus a Jew,
Sanguine, proportioned, fifty years of age,
The body's habit wholly laudable,   110
As much, indeed, beyond the common health
As he were made and put aside to show.
Think, could we penetrate by any drug
And bathe the wearied soul and worried flesh,
And bring it clear and fair, by three days' sleep!
Whence has the man the balm that brightens all?
This grown man eyes the world now like a child.
Some elders of his tribe, I should premise,
Led in their friend, obedient as a sheep,
To bear my inquisition. While they spoke,   120
Now sharply, now with sorrow,—told the case,—
He listened not except I spoke to him,
But folded his two hands and let them talk,
Watching the flies that buzzed: and yet no fool.
And that's a sample how his years must go.
Look, if a beggar, in fixed middle-life,
Should find a treasure,—can he use the same
With straitened habits and with tastes starved small,
And take at once to his impoverished brain

---

[5]**viscid choler**: thick fluid. **tertians**: fevers with 3-day cycle.
falling sickness: epilepsy.

[6]**sublimate**: medicine in form of a powdered distillate.

[7]**gum-tragacanth**: binding agent gathered from shrubs and
ground against smooth rock (here **porphyry**) with a **pestle**.

[8]**Zoar**: town near Dead Sea.

[9]**exhibition**: administration.

[10]**conceit**: notion.

The sudden element that changes things,   130
That sets the undreamed-of rapture at his hand
And puts the cheap old joy in the scorned dust?
Is he not such an one as moves to mirth—
Warily parsimonious, when no need,
Wasteful as drunkenness at undue times?
All prudent counsel as to what befits
The golden mean, is lost on such an one:
The man's fantastic will is the man's law.
So here—we call the treasure knowledge, say,
Increased beyond the fleshly faculty—   140
Heaven opened to a soul while yet on earth,
Earth forced on a soul's use while seeing heaven:
The man is witless of the size, the sum,
The value in proportion of all things,
Or whether it be little or be much.
Discourse to him of prodigious armaments
Assembled to besiege his city now,
And of the passing of a mule with gourds—
'Tis one! Then take it on the other side,
Speak of some trifling fact,—he will gaze rapt   150
With stupor at its very littleness,
(Far as I see) as if in that indeed
He caught prodigious import, whole results;
And so will turn to us the bystanders
In ever the same stupor (note this point)
That we too see not with his opened eyes.
Wonder and doubt come wrongly into play,
Preposterously, at cross purposes.
Should his child sicken unto death,—why, look
For scarce abatement of his cheerfulness,   160
Or pretermission[11] of the daily craft!
While a word, gesture, glance from that same child
At play or in the school or laid asleep,
Will startle him to an agony of fear,
Exasperation, just as like. Demand
The reason why—" 'tis but a word," object—
"A gesture"—he regards thee as our lord,
Who lived there in the pyramid alone,
Looked at us (dost thou mind?) when, being young,
We both would unadvisedly recite   170
Some charm's beginning, from that book of his,
Able to bid the sun throb wide and burst
All into stars, as suns grown old are wont.
Thou and the child have each a veil alike

Thrown o'er your heads, from under which ye both
Stretch your blind hands and trifle with a match
Over a mine of Greek fire,[12] did ye know!
He holds on firmly to some thread of life—
(It is the life to lead perforcedly)
Which runs across some vast distracting orb   180
Of glory on either side that meagre thread,
Which, conscious of, he must not enter yet—
The spiritual life around the earthly life:
The law of that is known to him as this,
His heart and brain move there, his feet stay here.
So is the man perplext with impulses
Sudden to start off crosswise, not straight on,
Proclaiming what is right and wrong across,
And not along, this black thread through the blaze—
"It should be" baulked by "here it cannot be."   190
And oft the man's soul springs into his face
As if he saw again and heard again
His sage that bade him "Rise" and he did rise.
Something, a word, a tick o' the blood within
Admonishes: then back he sinks at once
To ashes, who was very fire before,
In sedulous recurrence to his trade
Whereby he earneth him the daily bread;
And studiously the humbler for that pride,
Professedly the faultier that he knows   200
God's secret, while he holds the thread of life.
Indeed the especial marking of the man
Is prone submission to the heavenly will—
Seeing it, what it is, and why it is.
'Sayeth, he will wait patient to the last
For that same death which must restore his being
To equilibrium, body loosening soul
Divorced even now by premature full growth:
He will live, nay, it pleaseth him to live
So long as God please, and just how God please.   210
He even seeketh not to please God more
(Which meaneth, otherwise) than as God please.
Hence, I perceive not he affects to preach
The doctrine of his sect whate'er it be,
Make proselytes as madmen thirst to do:
How can he give his neighbour the real ground,
His own conviction? Ardent as he is—
Call his great truth a lie, why, still the old
"Be it as God please" reassureth him.
I probed the sore as thy disciple should: 220

---

[11]**pretermission**: neglect.

[12]**Greek fire**: early form of gunpowder.

"How, beast," said I, "this stolid carelessness
Sufficeth thee, when Rome is on her march
To stamp out like a little spark thy town,
Thy tribe, thy crazy tale and thee at once?"
He merely looked with his large eyes on me.
The man is apathetic, you deduce?
Contrariwise, he loves both old and young,
Able and weak, affects the very brutes
And birds—how say I? flowers of the field—
As a wise workman recognizes tools   230
In a master's workshop, loving what they make.
Thus is the man as harmless as a lamb:
Only impatient, let him do his best,
At ignorance and carelessness and sin—
An indignation which is promptly curbed:
As when in certain travel I have feigned
To be an ignoramus in our art
According to some preconceived design,
And happed to hear the land's practitioners,
Steeped in conceit sublimed by ignorance,   240
Prattle fantastically on disease,
Its cause and cure—and I must hold my peace!

       Thou wilt object—Why have I not ere this
Sought out the sage himself, the Nazarene
Who wrought this cure, inquiring at the source,
Conferring with the frankness that befits?
Alas! it grieveth me, the learned leech
Perished in a tumult many years ago,
Accused,—our learning's fate,—of wizardry,
Rebellion, to the setting up a rule   250
And creed prodigious as described to me.
His death, which happened when the earthquake[13] fell
(Prefiguring, as soon appeared, the loss
To occult learning in our lord the sage
Who lived there in the pyramid alone)
Was wrought by the mad people—that's their wont!
On vain recourse, as I conjecture it,
To his tried virtue, for miraculous help—
How could he stop the earthquake? That's their way!
The other imputations must be lies: 260
But take one, though I loathe to give it thee,
In mere respect for any good man's fame.
(And after all, our patient Lazarus
Is stark mad; should we count on what he says?
Perhaps not: though in writing to a leech
'Tis well to keep back nothing of a case.)
This man so cured regards the curer, then,

As—God forgive me! who but God himself,
Creator and sustainer of the world,
That came and dwelt in flesh on it awhile!   270
—'Sayeth that such an one was born and lived,
Taught, healed the sick, broke bread at his own house,
Then died, with Lazarus by, for aught I know,
And yet was . . . what I said nor choose repeat,
And must have so avouched himself, in fact,
In hearing of this very Lazarus
Who saith—but why all this of what he saith?
Why write of trivial matters, things of price
Calling at every moment for remark?
I noticed on the margin of a pool   280
Blue-flowering borage, the Aleppo sort,[14]
Aboundeth, very nitrous. It is strange!

       Thy pardon for this long and tedious case,
Which, now that I review it, needs must seem
Unduly dwelt on, prolixly set forth!
Nor I myself discern in what is writ
Good cause for the peculiar interest
And awe indeed this man has touched me with.
Perhaps the journey's end, the weariness
Had wrought upon me first. I met him thus: 290
I crossed a ridge of short sharp broken hills
Like an old lion's cheek teeth. Out there came
A moon made like a face with certain spots
Multiform, manifold and menacing:
Then a wind rose behind me. So we met
In this old sleepy town at unaware,
The man and I. I send thee what is writ.
Regard it as a chance, a matter risked
To this ambiguous Syrian—he may lose,
Or steal, or give it thee with equal good.   300
Jerusalem's repose shall make amends
For time this letter wastes, thy time and mine;
Till when, once more thy pardon and farewell!

       The very God! think, Abib; dost thou think?
So, the All-Great, were the All-Loving too—
So, through the thunder comes a human voice
Saying, "O heart I made, a heart beats here!
Face, my hands fashioned, see it in myself!
Thou hast no power nor mayst conceive of mine,
But love I gave thee, with myself to love,   310
And thou must love me who have died for thee!"
The madman saith He said so: it is strange.

                                                       1855

---

[13]**earthquake**: after the death of Jesus (Matthew 27:51).

[14]**borage**: stimulant herb. **Aleppo**: Syrian town.

"Childe Roland to the Dark Tower Came"[1]

(See Edgar's song in "Lear")

— 1 —

My first thought was, he lied in every word,
    That hoary cripple, with malicious eye
    Askance to watch the working of his lie
On mine, and mouth scarce able to afford
Suppression of the glee, that pursed and scored
    Its edge, at one more victim gained thereby.

— 2 —

What else should he be set for, with his staff?
    What, save to waylay with his lies, ensnare
    All travellers who might find him posted there,
And ask the road? I guessed what skull-like laugh   10
Would break, what crutch 'gin write my epitaph
    For pastime in the dusty thoroughfare,

— 3 —

If at his counsel I should turn aside
    Into that ominous tract which, all agree,
    Hides the Dark Tower. Yet acquiescingly
I did turn as he pointed: neither pride
Nor hope rekindling at the end descried,
    So much as gladness that some end might be.

— 4 —

For, what with my whole world-wide wandering,
    What with my search drawn out thro' years,
        my hope   20
    Dwindled into a ghost not fit to cope
With that obstreperous joy success would bring,—
I hardly tried now to rebuke the spring
    My heart made, finding failure in its scope.

— 5 —

As when a sick man very near to death
    Seems dead indeed, and feels begin and end
    The tears and takes the farewell of each friend,

And hears one bid the other go, draw breath
Freelier outside, ("since all is o'er," he saith,
    "And the blow fallen no grieving can amend;")   30

— 6 —

While some discuss if near the other graves
    Be room enough for this, and when a day
    Suits best for carrying the corpse away,
With care about the banners, scarves and staves:
And still the man hears all, and only craves
    He may not shame such tender love and stay.

— 7 —

Thus, I had so long suffered in this quest,
    Heard failure prophesied so oft, been writ
    So many times among "The Band"—to wit,
The knights who to the Dark Tower's search
        addressed   40
Their steps—that just to fail as they, seemed best,
    And all the doubt was now—should I be fit?

— 8 —

So, quiet as despair, I turned from him,
    That hateful cripple, out of his highway
    Into the path he pointed. All the day
Had been a dreary one at best, and dim
Was settling to its close, yet shot one grim
    Red leer to see the plain catch its estray.[2]

— 9 —

For mark! no sooner was I fairly found
    Pledged to the plain, after a pace or two,   50
    Than, pausing to throw backward a last view
O'er the safe road, 'twas gone; grey plain all round:
Nothing but plain to the horizon's bound.
    I might go on; nought else remained to do.

— 10 —

So, on I went. I think I never saw
    Such starved ignoble nature; nothing throve:
    For flowers—as well expect a cedar grove!
But cockle, spurge,[3] according to their law
Might propagate their kind, with none to awe,
    You'd think; a burr had been a treasure-trove.   60

— 11 —

No! penury, inertness and grimace,
    In some strange sort, were the land's portion. "See

---

[1]**"Childe Roland . . . Came:"** from **Edgar's song** at end of *King Lear* 3.4. **Childe:** knight in training. **Roland:** hero of the French epic *Le Chanson de Roland* (Song of Roland, 12th century) and of Ariosto's *Orlando Furioso* (1532).

[2]**estray:** stray animal.
[3]**cockle, spurge:** prickly and bitter weeds.

Or shut your eyes," said Nature peevishly,
"It nothing skills:[4] I cannot help my case:
'Tis the Last Judgment's fire must cure this place,
    Calcine its clods and set my prisoners free."

— 12 —

If there pushed any ragged thistle-stalk
    Above its mates, the head was chopped; the bents[5]
    Were jealous else. What made those holes and rents
In the dock's harsh swarth leaves, bruised as
        to baulk   70
All hope of greenness? 'tis a brute must walk
    Pashing their life out, with a brute's intents.

— 13 —

As for the grass, it grew as scant as hair
    In leprosy; thin dry blades pricked the mud
    Which underneath looked kneaded up with blood.
One stiff blind horse, his every bone a-stare,
Stood stupefied, however he came there:
    Thrust out past service from the devil's stud!

— 14 —

Alive? he might be dead for aught I know,
    With that red gaunt and colloped[6] neck a-strain, 80
    And shut eyes underneath the rusty mane;
Seldom went such grotesqueness with such woe;
I never saw a brute I hated so;
    He must be wicked to deserve such pain.

— 15 —

I shut my eyes and turned them on my heart.
    As a man calls for wine before he fights,
    I asked one draught of earlier, happier sights,
Ere fitly I could hope to play my part.
Think first, fight afterwards—the soldier's art:
    One taste of the old time sets all to rights.   90

— 16 —

Not it! I fancied Cuthbert's reddening face
    Beneath its garniture of curly gold,
    Dear fellow, till I almost felt him fold
An arm in mine to fix me to the place,
That way he used. Alas, one night's disgrace!
    Out went my heart's new fire and left it cold.

— 17 —

Giles then, the soul of honour—there he stands
    Frank as ten years ago when knighted first.
    What honest man should dare (he said) he durst.
Good—but the scene shifts—faugh! what hang-man
        hands   100
Pin to his breast a parchment? His own bands
    Read it. Poor traitor, spit upon and curst!

— 18 —

Better this present than a past like that;
    Back therefore to my darkening path again!
    No sound, no sight as far as eye could strain.
Will the night send a howlet[7] or a bat?
I asked: when something on the dismal flat
    Came to arrest my thoughts and change their train.

— 19 —

A sudden little river crossed my path
    As unexpected as a serpent comes.   110
    No sluggish tide congenial to the glooms;
This, as it frothed by, might have been a bath
For the fiend's glowing hoof—to see the wrath
    Of its black eddy bespate[8] with flakes and spumes.

— 20 —

So petty yet so spiteful! All along,
    Low scrubby alders kneeled down over it;
    Drenched willows flung them headlong in a fit
Of mute despair, a suicidal throng:
The river which had done them all the wrong,
    Whate'er that was, rolled by, deterred no whit. 120

— 21 —

Which, while I forded,—good saints, how I feared
    To set my foot upon a dead man's cheek,
    Each step, or feel the spear I thrust to seek
For hollows, tangled in his hair or beard!
—It may have been a water-rat I speared,
    But, ugh! it sounded like a baby's shriek.

— 22 —

Glad was I when I reached the other bank.
    Now for a better country. Vain presage!
    Who were the stragglers, what war did they wage,
Whose savage trample thus could pad the dank 130

---

[4]**It nothing skills**: it makes no difference. **Calcine**: burn to powder.

[5]**bents**: coarse grasses. **dock**: burdock.

[6]**colloped**: in ridged folds.

[7]**howlet**: owl.

[8]**bespate**: spattered.

Soil to a plash? Toads in a poisoned tank,
    Or wild cats in a red-hot iron cage—

— 23 —

The fight must so have seemed in that fell cirque.[9]
    What penned them there, with all the plain to choose?
    No foot-print leading to that horrid mews,
None out of it. Mad brewage set to work
Their brains, no doubt, like galley-slaves the Turk
    Pits for his pastime, Christians against Jews.

— 24 —

And more than that—a furlong on—why, there!
    What bad use was that engine for, that wheel,   140
    Or brake,[10] not wheel—that harrow fit to reel
Men's bodies out like silk? with all the air
Of Tophet's[11] tool, on earth left unaware,
    Or brought to sharpen its rusty teeth of steel.

— 25 —

Then came a bit of stubbed ground, once a wood,
    Next a marsh, it would seem, and now mere earth
    Desperate and done with; (so a fool finds mirth,
Makes a thing and then mars it, till his mood
Changes and off he goes!) within a rood[12]—
    Bog, clay and rubble, sand and stark
      black dearth.   150

— 26 —

Now blotches rankling, coloured gay and grim,
    Now patches where some leanness of the soil's
    Broke into moss or substances like boils;
Then came some palsied oak, a cleft in him
Like a distorted mouth that splits its rim
    Gaping at death, and dies while it recoils.

— 27 —

And just as far as ever from the end!
    Nought in the distance but the evening, nought
    To point my footstep further! At the thought,
A great black bird, Apollyon's[13] bosom-friend,   160
Sailed past, nor beat his wide wing dragon-penned
    That brushed my cap—perchance the guide I sought.

[9]**fell cirque:** fearsome arena. **mews:** stable yard.

[10]**brake:** toothed machine for processing fibers.

[11]**Tophet:** Hell.

[12]**rood:** quarter-acre.

[13]**Apollyon:** winged devil from Revelation 9:11 who appears in Bunyan's *Pilgrim's Progress* (1678) with **dragon** wings.

— 28 —

For, looking up, aware I somehow grew,
    'Spite of the dusk, the plain had given place
    All round to mountains—with such name to grace
Mere ugly heights and heaps now stolen in view.
How thus they had surprised me,—solve it, you!
    How to get from them was no clearer case.

— 29 —

Yet half I seemed to recognize some trick
    Of mischief happened to me, God
      knows when—   170
    In a bad dream perhaps. Here ended, then,
Progress this way. When, in the very nick
Of giving up, one time more, came a click
    As when a trap shuts—you're inside the den!

— 30 —

Burningly it came on me all at once,
    This was the place! those two hills on the right,
    Crouched like two bulls locked horn in horn in fight;
While to the left, a tall scalped mountain . . . Dunce,
Dotard, a-dozing at the very nonce,[14]
    After a life spent training for the sight!   180

— 31 —

What in the midst lay but the Tower itself?
    The round squat turret, blind as the fool's heart,
    Built of brown stone, without a counterpart
In the whole world. The tempest's mocking elf
Points to the shipman thus the unseen shelf
    He strikes on, only when the timbers start.[15]

— 32 —

Not see? because of night perhaps?—why, day
    Came back again for that! before it left,
    The dying sunset kindled through a cleft:
The hills, like giants at a hunting, lay,   190
Chin upon hand, to see the game at bay,—
    "Now stab and end the creature—to the heft!"[16]

— 33 —

Not hear? when noise was everywhere! it tolled
    Increasing like a bell. Names in my ears
    Of all the lost adventurers my peers,—
How such a one was strong, and such was bold,

[14]**nonce:** moment.

[15]**start:** break loose.

[16]**heft:** hilt.

And such was fortunate, yet each of old
 Lost, lost! one moment knelled the woe of years.

— 34 —

There they stood, ranged along the hill-sides, met
 To view the last of me, a living frame   200
 For one more picture! in a sheet of flame
I saw them and I knew them all. And yet
Dauntless the slug-horn[17] to my lips I set,
 And blew. "Childe Roland to the Dark Tower came."

1855

How It Strikes a Contemporary

I only knew one poet in my life:
And this, or something like it, was his way.

 You saw go up and down Valladolid,[1]
A man of mark, to know next time you saw.
His very serviceable suit of black
Was courtly once and conscientious still,
And many might have worn it, though none did:
The cloak, that somewhat shone and showed the threads,
Had purpose, and the ruff, significance.
He walked and tapped the pavement with his cane, 10
Scenting the world, looking it full in face,
An old dog, bald and blindish, at his heels.
They turned up, now, the alley by the church,
That leads nowhither; now, they breathed themselves
On the main promenade just at the wrong time:
You'd come upon his scrutinizing hat,
Making a peaked shade blacker than itself
Against the single window spared some house
Intact yet with its mouldered Moorish work,—
Or else surprise the ferrel[2] of his stick   20
Trying the mortar's temper 'tween the chinks
Of some new shop a-building, French and fine.
He stood and watched the cobbler at his trade,
The man who slices lemons into drink,
The coffee-roaster's brazier, and the boys
That volunteer to help him turn its winch.
He glanced o'er books on stalls with half an eye,
And fly-leaf ballads[3] on the vendor's string,

---

[17]**slug-horn**: bugle.

[1]**Valladolid**: town in NW Spain.

[2]**ferrel**: metal tip.

[3]**fly-leaf ballads**: rhymed tales printed on separate sheets.

And broad-edge bold-print posters by the wall.
He took such cognizance of men and things, 30
If any beat a horse, you felt he saw;
If any cursed a woman, he took note;
Yet stared at nobody,—you stared at him,
And found, less to your pleasure than surprise,
He seemed to know you and expect as much.
So, next time that a neighbour's tongue was loosed,
It marked the shameful and notorious fact,
We had among us, not so much a spy,
As a recording chief-inquisitor,
The town's true master if the town but knew! 40
We merely kept a governor for form,
While this man walked about and took account
Of all thought, said and acted, then went home,
And wrote it fully to our Lord the King
Who has an itch to know things, he knows why,
And reads them in his bedroom of a night.
Oh, you might smile! there wanted not a touch,
A tang of . . . well, it was not wholly ease
As back into your mind the man's look came.
Stricken in years a little,—such a brow 50
His eyes had to live under!—clear as flint
On either side the formidable nose
Curved, cut and coloured like an eagle's claw.
Had he to do with A.'s surprising fate?
When altogether old B. disappeared
And young C. got his mistress,—was't our friend,
His letter to the King, that did it all?
What paid the bloodless man for so much pains?
Our Lord the King has favourites manifold,
And shifts his ministry some once a month; 60
Our city gets new governors at whiles,—
But never word or sign, that I could hear,
Notified to this man about the streets
The King's approval of those letters conned
The last thing duly at the dead of night.
Did the man love his office? Frowned our Lord,
Exhorting when none heard—"Beseech me not!
Too far above my people,—beneath me!
I set the watch,—how should the people know?
Forget them, keep me all the more in mind!" 70
Was some such understanding 'twixt the two?

 I found no truth in one report at least—
That if you tracked him to his home, down lanes
Beyond the Jewry,[4] and as clean to pace,

---

[4]**Jewry**: Jewish quarter.

You found he ate his supper in a room
Blazing with lights, four Titians[5] on the wall,
And twenty naked girls to change his plate!
Poor man, he lived another kind of life
In that new stuccoed third house by the bridge,
Fresh-painted, rather smart than otherwise!   80
The whole street might o'erlook him as he sat,
Leg crossing leg, one foot on the dog's back,
Playing a decent cribbage with his maid
(Jacynth, you're sure her name was) o'er the cheese
And fruit, three red halves of starved winter-pears,
Or treat of radishes in April. Nine,
Ten, struck the church clock, straight to bed went he.

    My father, like the man of sense he was,
Would point him out to me a dozen times;
" 'St—'St," he'd whisper, "the Corregidor!"[6]   90
I had been used to think that personage
Was one with lacquered breeches, lustrous belt,
And feathers like a forest in his hat,
Who blew a trumpet and proclaimed the news,
Announced the bull-fights, gave each church its turn,
And memorized[7] the miracle in vogue!
He had a great observance from us boys;
We were in error; that was not the man.

    I'd like now, yet had haply been afraid,
To have just looked, when this man came to die,   100
And seen who lined the clean gay garret-sides
And stood about the neat low truckle-bed,
With the heavenly manner of relieving guard.
Here had been, mark, the general-in-chief,
Thro' a whole campaign of the world's life and death,
Doing the King's work all the dim day long,
In his old coat and up to knees in mud,
Smoked like a herring, dining on a crust,—
And, now the day was won, relieved at once!
No further show or need for that old coat,   110
You are sure, for one thing! Bless us, all the while
How sprucely we are dressed out, you and I!
A second, and the angels alter that.
Well, I could never write a verse,—could you?
Let's to the Prado[8] and make the most of time.

                                   1855

---

[5]**Titians:** paintings by Venetian master Titian (1488–1576).

[6]**Corregidor:** chief Spanish municipal magistrate.

[7]**memorized:** commemorated.

[8]**Prado:** main promenade in Madrid.

Memorabilia

— 1 —

Ah, did you once see Shelley[1] plain,
    And did he stop and speak to you
And did you speak to him again?
    How strange it seems and new!

— 2 —

But you were living before that,
    And also you are living after;
And the memory I started at—
    My starting moves your laughter.

— 3 —

I crossed a moor, with a name of its own
    And a certain use in the world no doubt,   10
Yet a hand's-breadth of it shines alone
    'Mid the blank miles round about:

— 4 —

For there I picked up on the heather
    And there I put inside my breast
A moulted feather, an eagle-feather!
    Well, I forget the rest.

                                    1855

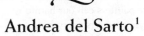

Andrea del Sarto[1]

(Called "The Faultless Painter")

But do not let us quarrel any more,
No, my Lucrezia; bear with me for once:
Sit down and all shall happen as you wish.

---

[1]Percy Bysshe **Shelley** (1792–1822): Romantic poet repeatedly emulated and apostrophized by the young Browning; see the *Essay on Shelley*, page 592. A friend of Browning's reported his telling how, in a London bookshop, "a stranger came in, who, in the course of conversation with the bookseller, spoke of something that Shelley had once said to him. Suddenly the stranger paused, and burst into laughter as he observed me staring at him with blanched face."

[1]**Andrea del Sarto** (1486–1531): Florentine painter known for **faultless** draftsmanship.

You turn your face, but does it bring your heart?
I'll work then for your friend's friend, never fear,
Treat his own subject after his own way,
Fix his own time, accept too his own price,
And shut the money into this small hand
When next it takes mine. Will it? tenderly?
Oh, I'll content him,—but to-morrow, Love!   10
I often am much wearier than you think,
This evening more than usual, and it seems
As if—forgive now—should you let me sit
Here by the window with your hand in mine
And look a half-hour forth on Fiesole,[2]
Both of one mind, as married people use,
Quietly, quietly the evening through,
I might get up to-morrow to my work
Cheerful and fresh as ever. Let us try.
To-morrow, how you shall be glad for this!   20
Your soft hand is a woman of itself,
And mine the man's bared breast she curls inside.
Don't count the time lost, neither; you must serve
For each of the five pictures we require:
It saves a model. So! keep looking so—
My serpentining beauty, rounds on rounds!
—How could you ever prick those perfect ears,
Even to put the pearl there! oh, so sweet—
My face, my moon, my everybody's moon,
Which everybody looks on and calls his,   30
And, I suppose, is looked on by in turn,
While she looks—no one's: very dear, no less.
You smile? why, there's my picture ready made,
There's what we painters call our harmony!
A common greyness silvers everything,—
All in a twilight, you and I alike
—You, at the point of your first pride in me
(That's gone you know),—but I, at every point;
My youth, my hope, my art, being all toned down
To yonder sober pleasant Fiesole.   40
There's the bell clinking from the chapel-top;
That length of convent-wall across the way
Holds the trees safer, huddled more inside;
The last monk leaves the garden; days decrease,
And autumn grows, autumn in everything.
Eh? the whole seems to fall into a shape
As if I saw alike my work and self
And all that I was born to be and do,
A twilight-piece. Love, we are in God's hand.
How strange now, looks the life he makes us lead;   50

So free we seem, so fettered fast we are!
I feel he laid the fetter: let it lie!
This chamber for example—turn your head—
All that's behind us! You don't understand
Nor care to understand about my art,
But you can hear at least when people speak:
And that cartoon,[3] the second from the door
—It is the thing, Love! so such things should be—
Behold Madonna!—I am bold to say.
I can do with my pencil what I know,   60
What I see, what at bottom of my heart
I wish for, if I ever wish so deep—
Do easily, too—when I say, perfectly,
I do not boast, perhaps: yourself are judge,
Who listened to the Legate's[4] talk last week,
And just as much they used to say in France.
At any rate 'tis easy, all of it!
No sketches first, no studies, that's long past:
I do what many dream of, all their lives,
—Dream? strive to do, and agonize to do,   70
And fail in doing. I could count twenty such
On twice your fingers, and not leave this town,
Who strive—you don't know how the others strive
To paint a little thing like that you smeared
Carelessly passing with your robes afloat,—
Yet do much less, so much less, Someone says,
(I know his name, no matter)—so much less!
Well, less is more, Lucrezia: I am judged.
There burns a truer light of God in them,
In their vexed beating stuffed and stopped-up brain,   80
Heart, or whate'er else, than goes on to prompt
This low-pulsed forthright craftsman's hand of mine.
Their works drop groundward, but themselves, I know,
Reach many a time a heaven that's shut to me,
Enter and take their place there sure enough,
Though they come back and cannot tell the world.
My works are nearer heaven, but I sit here.
The sudden blood of these men! at a word—
Praise them, it boils, or blame them, it boils too.
I, painting from myself and to myself,   90
Know what I do, am unmoved by men's blame
Or their praise either. Somebody remarks
Morello's[5] outline there is wrongly traced,
His hue mistaken; what of that? or else,
Rightly traced and well ordered; what of that?

---

[2]**Fiesole:** hillside suburb NE of Florence.

[3]**cartoon:** preparatory sketch.
[4]**Legate:** Pope's envoy.
[5]**Morello:** mountain N of Florence.

Speak as they please, what does the mountain care?
Ah, but a man's reach should exceed his grasp,
Or what's a heaven for? All is silver-grey
Placid and perfect with my art: the worse!
I know both what I want and what might gain,   100
And yet how profitless to know, to sigh
"Had I been two, another and myself,
Our head would have o'erlooked the world!" No doubt.
Yonder's a work now, of that famous youth
The Urbinate who died five years ago.
('Tis copied, George Vasari[6] sent it me.)
Well, I can fancy how he did it all,
Pouring his soul, with kings and popes to see,
Reaching, that heaven might so replenish him,
Above and through his art—for it gives way;   110
That arm is wrongly put—and there again—
A fault to pardon in the drawing's lines,
Its body, so to speak: its soul is right,
He means right—that, a child may understand.
Still, what an arm! and I could alter it:
But all the play, the insight and the stretch—
Out of me, out of me! And wherefore out?
Had you enjoined them on me, given me soul,
We might have risen to Rafael, I and you!
Nay, Love, you did give all I asked, I think—   120
More than I merit, yes, by many times.
But had you—oh, with the same perfect brow,
And perfect eyes, and more than perfect mouth,
And the low voice my soul hears, as a bird
The fowler's pipe, and follows to the snare—
Had you, with these the same, but brought a mind!
Some women do so. Had the mouth there urged
"God and the glory! never care for gain.
The present by the future, what is that?
Live for fame, side by side with Agnolo![7]   130
Rafael is waiting: up to God, all three!"
I might have done it for you. So it seems:
Perhaps not. All is as God over-rules.
Beside, incentives come from the soul's self;
The rest avail not. Why do I need you?
What wife had Rafael, or has Agnolo?
In this world, who can do a thing, will not;
And who would do it, cannot, I perceive:

Yet the will's somewhat—somewhat, too, the power—
And thus we half-men struggle. At the end,   140
God, I conclude, compensates, punishes.
'Tis safer for me, if the award be strict,
That I am something underrated here,
Poor this long while, despised, to speak the truth.
I dared not, do you know, leave home all day,
For fear of chancing on the Paris lords.[8]
The best is when they pass and look aside;
But they speak sometimes; I must bear it all.
Well may they speak! That Francis, that first time,
And that long festal year at Fontainebleau!   150
I surely then could sometimes leave the ground,
Put on the glory, Rafael's daily wear,
In that humane great monarch's golden look,—
One finger in his beard or twisted curl
Over his mouth's good mark that made the smile,
One arm about my shoulder, round my neck,
The jingle of his gold chain in my ear,
I painting proudly with his breath on me,
All his court round him, seeing with his eyes,
Such frank French eyes, and such a fire of souls   160
Profuse, my hand kept plying by those hearts,—
And, best of all, this, this, this face beyond,
This in the background, waiting on my work,
To crown the issue with a last reward!
A good time, was it not, my kingly days?
And had you not grown restless . . . but I know—
'Tis done and past; 'twas right, my instinct said;
Too live the life grew, golden and not grey,
And I'm the weak-eyed bat no sun should tempt
Out of the grange whose four walls make his world.   170
How could it end in any other way?
You called me, and I came home to your heart.
The triumph was—to reach and stay there; since
I reached it ere the triumph, what is lost?
Let my hands frame your face in your hair's gold,
You beautiful Lucrezia that are mine!
"Rafael did this, Andrea painted that;
The Roman's[9] is the better when you pray,
But still the other's Virgin was his wife—"
Men will excuse me. I am glad to judge   180
Both pictures in your presence; clearer grows
My better fortune, I resolve to think.

---

[6]**Urbinate:** the painter Rafael (1483–1520), from the town of Urbino. Giorgio **Vasari** (1511–1574): author of *Lives of the Most Eminent Italian Architects, Painters, and Sculptors* (1568), the major source for Browning's painter poems.

[7]**Agnolo:** Michelangelo (1475–1564).

---

[8]**Paris lords:** nobles visiting Florence who know about Andrea's embezzlement of French funds obtained at **Fontainebleau** from King **Francis I.**

[9]**Roman's:** Madonna by Rafael in Rome.

For, do you know, Lucrezia, as God lives,
Said one day Agnolo, his very self,
To Rafael . . . I have known it all these years . . .
(When the young man was flaming out his thoughts
Upon a palace-wall for Rome to see,
Too lifted up in heart because of it)
"Friend, there's a certain sorry little scrub
Goes up and down our Florence, none cares how, 190
Who, were he set to plan and execute
As you are, pricked on by your popes and kings,
Would bring the sweat into that brow of yours!"
To Rafael's!—And indeed the arm is wrong.
I hardly dare . . . yet, only you to see,
Give the chalk here—quick, thus the line should go!
Ay, but the soul! he's Rafael! rub it out!
Still, all I care for, if he spoke the truth,
(What he? why, who but Michel Agnolo?
Do you forget already words like those?) 200
If really there was such a chance, so lost,—
Is, whether you're—not grateful—but more pleased.
Well, let me think so. And you smile indeed!
This hour has been an hour! Another smile?
If you would sit thus by me every night
I should work better, do you comprehend?
I mean that I should earn more, give you more.
See, it is settled dusk now; there's a star;
Morello's gone, the watch-lights[10] show the wall,
The cue-owls speak the name we call them by. 210
Come from the window, love,—come in, at last,
Inside the melancholy little house
We built to be so gay with. God is just.
King Francis may forgive me: oft at nights
When I look up from painting, eyes tired out,
The walls become illumined, brick from brick
Distinct, instead of mortar, fierce bright gold,
That gold of his I did cement them with!
Let us but love each other. Must you go?
That Cousin[11] here again? he waits outside? 220
Must see you—you, and not with me? Those loans?
More gaming debts to pay? you smiled for that?
Well, let smiles buy me! have you more to spend?
While hand and eye and something of a heart
Are left me, work's my ware, and what's it worth?
I'll pay my fancy. Only let me sit

The grey remainder of the evening out,
Idle, you call it, and muse perfectly
How I could paint, were I but back in France,
One picture, just one more—the Virgin's face, 230
Not yours this time! I want you at my side
To hear them—that is, Michel Agnolo—
Judge all I do and tell you of its worth.
Will you? To-morrow, satisfy your friend.
I take the subjects for his corridor,
Finish the portrait out of hand—there, there,
And throw him in another thing or two
If he demurs; the whole should prove enough
To pay for this same Cousin's freak. Beside,
What's better and what's all I care about, 240
Get you the thirteen scudi[12] for the ruff!
Love, does that please you? Ah, but what does he,
The Cousin! what does he to please you more?

    I am grown peaceful as old age to-night.
I regret little, I would change still less.
Since there my past life lies, why alter it?
The very wrong to Francis!—it is true
I took his coin, was tempted and complied,
And built this house and sinned, and all is said.
My father and my mother died of want. 250
Well, had I riches of my own? you see
How one gets rich! Let each one bear his lot.
They were born poor, lived poor, and poor they died:
And I have laboured somewhat in my time
And not been paid profusely. Some good son
Paint my two hundred pictures—let him try!
No doubt, there's something strikes a balance. Yes,
You loved me quite enough, it seems to-night.
This must suffice me here. What would one have?
In heaven, perhaps, new chances, one
      more chance— 260
Four great walls in the New Jerusalem,
Meted on each side by the angel's reed,
For Leonard,[13] Rafael, Agnolo and me
To cover—the three first without a wife,
While I have mine! So—still they overcome
Because there's still Lucrezia,—as I choose.

    Again the Cousin's whistle! Go, my Love.

1855

---

[10]**watch-lights**: carried by night watchmen along the walled street.

    [11]**Cousin**: Lucrezia's gambling lover.

[12]**scudi**: coins.

[13]**New Jerusalem, angel's reed**: see Revelation 21:2,15.
Leonard: Leonardo da Vinci (1452–1519).

In a Year

— 1 —

Never any more,
  While I live,
Need I hope to see his face
  As before.
Once his love grown chill,
  Mine may strive:
Bitterly we re-embrace,
  Single still.

— 2 —

Was it something said,
  Something done,   10
Vexed him? was it touch of hand,
  Turn of head?
Strange! that very way
  Love begun:
I as little understand
  Love's decay.

— 3 —

When I sewed or drew,
  I recall
How he looked as if I sung,
  —Sweetly too.   20
If I spoke a word,
  First of all
Up his cheek the colour sprung,
  Then he heard.

— 4 —

Sitting by my side,
  At my feet,
So he breathed but air I breathed,
  Satisfied!
I, too, at love's brim
  Touched the sweet: 30
I would die if death bequeathed
  Sweet to him.

— 5 —

"Speak, I love thee best!"
  He exclaimed:
"Let thy love my own foretell!"
  I confessed:

— 6 —

"Clasp my heart on thine
  Now unblamed,
Since upon thy soul as well
  Hangeth mine!"   40

Was it wrong to own,
  Being truth?
Why should all the giving prove
  His alone?
I had wealth and ease,
  Beauty, youth:
Since my lover gave me love,
  I gave these.

— 7 —

That was all I meant,
  —To be just,   50
And the passion I had raised,
  To content.
Since he chose to change
  Gold for dust,
If I gave him what he praised
  Was it strange?

— 8 —

Would he loved me yet,
  On and on,
While I found some way undreamed
  —Paid my debt!   60
Gave more life and more,
  Till, all gone,
He should smile "She never seemed
  Mine before.

— 9 —

"What, she felt the while,
  Must I think?
Love's so different with us men!"
  He should smile:
"Dying for my sake—
  White and pink!   70
Can't we touch these bubbles then
  "But they break?"

— 10 —

Dear, the pang is brief,
  Do thy part,

Have thy pleasure! How perplexed
   Grows belief!
Well, this cold clay clod
   Was man's heart:
Crumble it, and what comes next?
   Is it God?   80

                   1855

Popularity

— 1 —

Stand still, true poet that you are!
   I know you; let me try and draw you.
Some night you'll fail us: when afar
   You rise, remember one man saw you,
Knew you, and named a star!

— 2 —

My star, God's glow-worm! Why extend
   That loving hand of his which leads you,
Yet locks you safe from end to end
   Of this dark world, unless he needs you,
Just saves your light to spend?   10

— 3 —

His clenched hand shall unclose at last,
   I know, and let out all the beauty:
My poet holds the future fast,
   Accepts the coming ages' duty,
Their present for this past.

— 4 —

That day, the earth's feast-master's brow
   Shall clear, to God the chalice raising;
"Others give best at first, but thou
   Forever set'st our table praising,
Keep'st the good wine till now!"[1]   20

— 5 —

Meantime, I'll draw you as you stand,
   With few or none to watch and wonder:
I'll say—a fisher, on the sand

By Tyre[2] the old, with ocean-plunder,
A netful, brought to land.

— 6 —

Who has not heard how Tyrian shells
   Enclosed the blue, that dye of dyes
Whereof one drop worked miracles,
   And coloured like Astarte's[3] eyes
Raw silk the merchant sells?   30

— 7 —

And each bystander of them all
   Could criticize, and quote tradition
How depths of blue sublimed some pall[4]
   —To get which, pricked a king's ambition;
Worth sceptre, crown and ball.

— 8 —

Yet there's the dye, in that rough mesh,
   The sea has only just o'erwhispered!
Live whelks, each lip's beard dripping fresh,
   As if they still the water's lisp heard
Through foam the rock-weeds thresh.   40

— 9 —

Enough to furnish Solomon
   Such hangings for his cedar-house,[5]
That, when gold-robed he took the throne
   In that abyss of blue, the Spouse
Might swear his presence shone

— 10 —

Most like the centre-spike of gold
   Which burns deep in the blue-bell's womb,
What time, with ardours manifold,
   The bee goes singing to her groom,
Drunken and overbold.   50

— 11 —

Mere conchs! not fit for warp or woof![6]
   Till cunning come to pound and squeeze

---

[1]**"Keep'st . . . till now!"**: see John 2:9–10 (where Jesus turns water to wine).

[2]**Tyre**: ancient Phoenician seaport.

[3]**Astarte**: Middle Eastern goddess of sex and war.

[4]**sublimed some pall**: beautified a robe.

[5]**Solomon . . . cedar-house**: see 1 Kings 7:2–3. **Spouse**: beloved in Song of Solomon.

[6]**for warp or woof**: for textile use.

And clarify,—refine to proof
  The liquor filtered by degrees,
While the world stands aloof.

— 12 —

And there's the extract, flasked and fine,
  And priced and saleable at last!
And Hobbs, Nobbs, Stokes and Nokes[7] combine
  To paint the future from the past,
Put blue into their line.   60

— 13 —

Hobbs hints blue,—straight he turtle[8] eats:
  Nobbs prints blue,—claret crowns his cup:
Nokes outdares Stokes in azure feats,—
  Both gorge. Who fished the murex[9] up?
What porridge had John Keats?

                                       1855

Two in the Campagna[1]

— 1 —

I wonder do you feel to-day
  As I have felt since, hand in hand,
We sat down on the grass, to stray
  In spirit better through the land,
This morn of Rome and May?

— 2 —

For me, I touched a thought, I know,
  Has tantalized me many times,
(Like turns of thread the spiders throw
  Mocking across our path) for rhymes
To catch at and let go.   10

— 3 —

Help me to hold it! First it left
  The yellowing fennel, run to seed

---

[7]**Hobbs . . . Nokes:** run-of-the-mill imitators.

[8]**turtle, claret:** expensive gourmet fare, as against poor **porridge**.

[9]**murex:** mollusk yielding purple dye.

[1]**Campagna** (also **champaign**, line 21): plains around Rome containing ancient ruins.

There, branching from the brickwork's cleft,
  Some old tomb's ruin: yonder weed
Took up the floating weft,[2]

— 4 —

Where one small orange cup amassed
  Five beetles,—blind and green they grope
Among the honey-meal: and last,
  Everywhere on the grassy slope
I traced it. Hold it fast!   20

— 5 —

The champaign with its endless fleece
  Of feathery grasses everywhere!
Silence and passion, joy and peace,
  An everlasting wash of air—
Rome's ghost since her decease.

— 6 —

Such life here, through such lengths of hours,
  Such miracles performed in play,
Such primal naked forms of flowers,
  Such letting nature have her way
While heaven looks from its towers!   30

— 7 —

How say you? Let us, O my dove,
  Let us be unashamed of soul,
As earth lies bare to heaven above!
  How is it under our control
To love or not to love?

— 8 —

I would that you were all to me,
  You that are just so much, no more.
Nor yours nor mine, nor slave nor free!
  Where does the fault lie? What the core
O' the wound, since wound must be?   40

— 9 —

I would I could adopt your will,
  See with your eyes, and set my heart
Beating by yours, and drink my fill
  At your soul's springs,—your part my part
In life, for good and ill.

---

[2]**weft:** threads of a web.

— 10 —

No. I yearn upward, touch you close,
    Then stand away. I kiss your cheek,
Catch your soul's warmth,—I pluck the rose
    And love it more than tongue can speak—
Then the good minute goes.   50

— 11 —

Already how am I so far
    Out of that minute? Must I go
Still like the thistle-ball, no bar,
    Onward, whenever light winds blow,
Fixed by no friendly star?

— 12 —

Just when I seemed about to learn!
    Where is the thread now? Off again!
The old trick! Only I discern—
    Infinite passion, and the pain
Of finite hearts that yearn.   60

           1855

One Word More

To. E. B. B.[1]

— 1 —

There they are, my fifty men and women
Naming me the fifty poems finished!
Take them, Love, the book and me together:
Where the heart lies, let the brain lie also.

— 2 —

Rafael made a century of sonnets,[2]
Made and wrote them in a certain volume
Dinted with the silver-pointed pencil
Else he only used to draw Madonnas:
These, the world might view—but one, the volume.

Who that one, you ask? Your heart instructs you.   10
Did she live and love it all her life-time?
Did she drop, his lady of the sonnets,
Die, and let it drop beside her pillow
Where it lay in place of Rafael's glory,
Rafael's cheek so duteous and so loving—
Cheek, the world was wont to hail a painter's,
Rafael's cheek, her love had turned a poet's?

— 3 —

You and I would rather read that volume,
(Taken to his beating bosom by it)
Lean and list the bosom-beats of Rafael,   20
Would we not? than wonder at Madonnas—
Her, San Sisto names, and Her, Foligno,
Her, that visits Florence in a vision,
Her, that's left with lilies in the Louvre[3]—
Seen by us and all the world in circle.

— 4 —

You and I will never read that volume.
Guido Reni,[4] like his own eye's apple
Guarded long the treasure-book and loved it.
Guido Reni dying, all Bologna
Cried, and the world cried too, "Ours, the treasure!"   30
Suddenly, as rare things will, it vanished.

— 5 —

Dante once prepared to paint an angel:[5]
Whom to please? You whisper "Beatrice."
While he mused and traced it and retraced it,
(Peradventure with a pen corroded
Still by drops of that hot ink he dipped for,
When, his left-hand i' the hair o' the wicked,
Back he held the brow and pricked its stigma,
Bit into the live man's flesh for parchment,
Loosed him, laughed to see the writing rankle,   40
Let the wretch go festering through Florence)—
Dante, who loved well because he hated,

---

[1]**E. B. B.:** Elizabeth Barrett Browning, to whom this closing lyric written in **London** (line 145) dedicates the 50 dramatic poems of *Men and Women.*

[2]**century of sonnets:** anecdote about **Rafael** (1483–1520) told in *Lives of the Most Eminent Italian Architects, Painters, and Sculptors* (1568) by Giorgio Vasari (1511–1574), Browning's major source on Renaissance artists.

[3]**San Sisto . . . the Louvre:** Madonnas by Rafael, respectively the Sistine Madonna, Madonna di **Foligno,** Madonna del Granduca, and La Belle Jardinière.

[4]**Guido Reni** (1575–1642): baroque painter from **Bologna.**

[5]**Dante . . . an angel:** story told in Dante's *Vita Nuova (New Life),* a book about his love for **Beatrice** (nicknamed **Bice**). The parenthetical image that follows, drawn from *Inferno* 32.97, describes the writing of the *Divine Comedy,* which includes a number of Dante's contemporaries among the damned.

Hated wickedness that hinders loving,
Dante standing, studying his angel,—
In there broke the folk of his Inferno.
Says he—"Certain people of importance"
(Such he gave his daily dreadful line to)
"Entered and would seize, forsooth, the poet."
Says the poet—"Then I stopped my painting."

— 6 —

You and I would rather see that angel,   50
Painted by the tenderness of Dante,
Would we not?—than read a fresh Inferno.

— 7 —

You and I will never see that picture.
While he mused on love and Beatrice,
While he softened o'er his outlined angel,
In they broke, those "people of importance:"
We and Bice bear the loss for ever.

— 8 —

What of Rafael's sonnets, Dante's picture?
This: no artist lives and loves, that longs not
Once, and only once, and for one only,   60
(Ah, the prize!) to find his love a language
Fit and fair and simple and sufficient—
Using nature that's an art to others,
Not, this one time, art that's turned his nature.
Ay, of all the artists living, loving,
None but would forego his proper dowry,—
Does he paint? he fain would write a poem,—
Does he write? he fain would paint a picture,
Put to proof art alien to the artist's,
Once, and only once, and for one only,   70
So to be the man and leave the artist,
Gain the man's joy, miss the artist's sorrow.

— 9 —

Wherefore? Heaven's gift takes earth's abatement!
He who smites the rock[6] and spreads the water,
Bidding drink and live a crowd beneath him,
Even he, the minute makes immortal,
Proves, perchance, but mortal in the minute,
Desecrates, belike, the deed in doing.
While he smites, how can he but remember,
So he smote before, in such a peril,   80

When they stood and mocked—"Shall smiting help us?"
When they drank and sneered—"A stroke is easy!"
When they wiped their mouths and went their journey,
Throwing him for thanks—"But drought was pleasant."
Thus old memories mar the actual triumph;
Thus the doing savours of disrelish;
Thus achievement lacks a gracious somewhat;
O'er-importuned brows becloud the mandate,
Carelessness or consciousness—the gesture.
For he bears an ancient wrong about him,   90
Sees and knows again those phalanxed faces,
Hears, yet one time more, the 'customed prelude—
"How shouldst thou, of all men, smite, and save us?"
Guesses what is like to prove the sequel—
"Egypt's flesh-pots[7]—nay, the drought was better."

— 10 —

Oh, the crowd must have emphatic warrant!
Theirs, the Sinai-forehead's cloven brilliance,[8]
Right-arm's rod-sweep, tongue's imperial fiat.
Never dares the man put off the prophet.

— 11 —

Did he love one face from out the thousands,   100
(Were she Jethro's daughter, white and wifely,
Were she but the Æthiopian bondslave,)[9]
He would envy yon dumb patient camel,
Keeping a reserve of scanty water
Meant to save his own life in the desert;
Ready in the desert to deliver
(Kneeling down to let his breast be opened)
Hoard and life together for his mistress.

— 12 —

I shall never, in the years remaining,
Paint you pictures, no, nor carve you statues,   110
Make you music that should all-express me;
So it seems: I stand on my attainment.
This of verse alone, one life allows me;
Verse and nothing else have I to give you.
Other heights in other lives, God willing:
All the gifts from all the heights, your own, Love!

---

[6]**He who smites the rock:** Moses in Exodus 17:6.

[7]**Egypt's fleshpots:** Exodus 16:3.

[8]**Sinai . . . brilliance:** see Exodus 33:20–23; 34:29–35. **rod-sweep:** Aaron's rod in Exodus 7:19–20.

[9]**Jethro's daughter . . . bondslave:** Moses' two wives (Exodus 2:21, Numbers 12:1).

— 13 —

Yet a semblance of resource avails us—
Shade so finely touched, love's sense must seize it.
Take these lines, look lovingly and nearly,
Lines I write the first time and the last time.   120
He who works in fresco, steals a hair-brush,
Curbs the liberal hand, subservient proudly,
Cramps his spirit, crowds its all in little,
Makes a strange art of an art familiar,
Fills his lady's missal-marge with flowerets.
He who blows thro' bronze, may breathe thro' silver,
Fitly serenade a slumbrous princess.
He who writes, may write for once as I do.[10]

— 14 —

Love, you saw me gather men and women,
Live or dead or fashioned by my fancy,   130
Enter each and all, and use their service,
Speak from every mouth,—the speech, a poem.
Hardly shall I tell my joys and sorrows,
Hopes and fears, belief and disbelieving:
I am mine and yours—the rest be all men's,
Karshish, Cleon, Norbert[11] and the fifty.
Let me speak this once in my true person,
Not as Lippo, Roland or Andrea,
Though the fruit of speech be just this sentence:
Pray you, look on these my men and women,   140
Take and keep my fifty poems finished;
Where my heart lies, let my brain lie also!
Poor the speech; be how I speak, for all things.

— 15 —

Not but that you know me! Lo, the moon's self!
Here in London, yonder late in Florence,
Still we find her face, the thrice-transfigured.
Curving on a sky imbrued with colour,
Drifted over Fiesole by twilight,
Came she, our new crescent of a hair's-breadth.
Full she flared it, lamping Samminiato,[12]   150
Rounder 'twixt the cypresses and rounder,
Perfect till the nightingales applauded.

---

[10]**writes . . . as I do:** in trochaic pentameter, used by Browning
only in this poem.

[11]**Cleon, Norbert:** dramatic speakers in *Men and Women.*

[12]**Fiesole:** hillside suburb NE of the Brownings' home in Florence. **Samminiato:** San Miniato al Monte, hillside church SE of
Florence.

Now, a piece of her old self, impoverished,
Hard to greet, she traverses the houseroofs,
Hurries with unhandsome thrift of silver,
Goes dispiritedly, glad to finish.

— 16 —

What, there's nothing in the moon noteworthy?
Nay: for if that moon could love a mortal,
Use, to charm him (so to fit a fancy),
All her magic ('t is the old sweet mythos)[13]   160
She would turn a new side to her mortal,
Side unseen of herdsman, huntsman, steersman—
Blank to Zoroaster on his terrace,
Blind to Galileo on his turret,
Dumb to Homer, dumb to Keats—him, even!
Think, the wonder of the moonstruck mortal—
When she turns round, comes again in heaven,
Opens out anew for worse or better!
Proves she like some portent of an iceberg
Swimming full upon the ship it founders,   170
Hungry with huge teeth of splintered crystals?
Proves she as the paved work of a sapphire
Seen by Moses when he climbed the mountain?
Moses, Aaron, Nadab and Abihu[14]
Climbed and saw the very God, the Highest,
Stand upon the paved work of a sapphire.
Like the bodied heaven in his clearness
Shone the stone, the sapphire of that paved work,
When they ate and drank and saw God also!

— 17 —

What were seen? None knows, none ever
            shall know.   180
Only this is sure—the sight were other,
Not the moon's same side, born late in Florence,
Dying now impoverished here in London.
God be thanked, the meanest of his creatures
Boasts two soul-sides, one to face the world with,
One to show a woman when he loves her!

— 18 —

This I say of me, but think of you, Love!
This to you—yourself my moon of poets!
Ah, but that's the world's side, there's the wonder,

---

[13]**mythos:** of Diana's love for Endymion, subject of a long poetic
romance by **Keats** (1818). **Zoroaster:** Persian astrological magus
and prophet (6th century BCE).

[14]**sapphire, Nadab and Abihu:** see Exodus 24:9–10.

Thus they see you, praise you, think they know you! 190
There, in turn I stand with them and praise you—
Out of my own self, I dare to phrase it.
But the best is when I glide from out them,
Cross a step or two of dubious twilight,
Come out on the other side, the novel
Silent silver lights and darks undreamed of,
Where I hush and bless myself with silence.

— 19 —

Oh, their Rafael of the dear Madonnas,
Oh, their Dante of the dread Inferno,
Wrote one song—and in my brain I sing it,   200
Drew one angel—borne, see, on my bosom!

R. B.
1855

Caliban upon Setebos

or Natural Theology in the Island[1]

"Thou thoughtest that I was altogether such a one as thyself."[2]

['Will[3] sprawl, now that the heat of day is best,
Flat on his belly in the pit's much mire,
With elbows wide, fists clenched to prop his chin,
And, while he kicks both feet in the cool slush,
And feels about his spine small eft-things[4] course,
Run in and out each arm, and make him laugh:
And while above his head a pompion-plant,
Coating the cave-top as a brow its eye,
Creeps down to touch and tickle hair and beard,
And now a flower drops with a bee inside,   10
And now a fruit to snap at, catch and crunch,—
He looks out o'er yon sea which sunbeams cross
And recross till they weave a spider-web,
(Meshes of fire, some great fish breaks at times)

And talks to his own self, howe'er he please,
Touching that other, whom his dam called God.
Because to talk about Him, vexes—ha,
Could He but know! and time to vex is now,
When talk is safer than in winter-time.
Moreover Prosper and Miranda sleep[5]   20
In confidence he drudges at their task,
And it is good to cheat the pair, and gibe,
Letting the rank tongue blossom into speech.]

Setebos, Setebos, and Setebos!
'Thinketh, He dwelleth i' the cold o' the moon.

'Thinketh He made it, with the sun to match,
But not the stars; the stars came otherwise;
Only made clouds, winds, meteors, such as that:
Also this isle, what lives and grows thereon,
And snaky sea which rounds and ends the same.   30

'Thinketh, it came of being ill at ease:
He hated that He cannot change His cold,
Nor cure its ache. 'Hath spied an icy fish
That longed to 'scape the rock-stream where she lived,
And thaw herself within the lukewarm brine
O' the lazy sea, her stream thrusts far amid,
A crystal spike 'twixt two warm walls of wave;
Only, she ever sickened, found repulse
At the other kind of water, not her life,
(Green-dense and dim-delicious, bred o' the sun)   40
Flounced back from bliss she was not born to breathe,
And in her old bounds buried her despair,
Hating and loving warmth alike: so He.

'Thinketh, He made thereat the sun, this isle,
Trees and the fowls here, beast and creeping thing.
Yon otter, sleek-wet, black, lithe as a leech;
Yon auk, one fire-eye in a ball of foam,
That floats and feeds; a certain badger brown,
He hath watched hunt with that slant white-wedge eye
By moonlight; and the pie with the long tongue   50
That pricks deep into oakwarts[6] for a worm,
And says a plain word when she finds her prize,
But will not eat the ants; the ants themselves
That build a wall of seeds and settled stalks
About their hole—He made all these and more,
Made all we see, and us, in spite: how else?
He Himself could not make a second self

---

[1]**Caliban**: aboriginal islander in *The Tempest*, enslaved by Prospero. **Setebos**: Caliban's god. **Natural Theology**: conception of God derived from observation of nature; see page 52.

[2]"**Thou . . . thyself**": Psalm 50:21, where the speaker is God.

[3]**Will**: Caliban refers to himself in the third and first person interchangeably.

[4]**eft-things**: reptiles. **pompion**: pumpkin.

[5]**his dam**: Caliban's mother Sycorax, mentioned in *The Tempest*, where **Miranda** is **Prospero's** daughter.

[6]**pie**: magpie. **oakwarts**: growths on tree trunk.

To be His mate: as well have made Himself:
He would not make what He mislikes or slights,
An eyesore to Him, or not worth His pains;   60
But did, in envy, listlessness or sport,
Make what Himself would fain, in a manner, be—
Weaker in most points, stronger in a few,
Worthy, and yet mere playthings all the while,
Things He admires and mocks too,—that is it!
Because, so brave, so better though they be,
It nothing skills[7] if He begin to plague.
Look now, I melt a gourd-fruit into mash,
Add honeycomb and pods, I have perceived,
Which bite like finches when they bill and kiss,—   70
Then, when froth rises bladdery,[8] drink up all,
Quick, quick, till maggots scamper through my brain;
Last, throw me on my back i' the seeded thyme,
And wanton, wishing I were born a bird.
Put case, unable to be what I wish,
I yet could make a live bird out of clay:
Would not I take clay, pinch my Caliban
Able to fly?—for, there, see, he hath wings,
And great comb like the hoopoe's to admire,
And there, a sting to do his foes offence,   80
There, and I will that he begin to live,
Fly to yon rock-top, nip me off the horns
Of grigs[9] high up that make the merry din,
Saucy through their veined wings, and mind me not.
In which feat, if his leg snapped, brittle clay,
And he lay stupid-like,—why, I should laugh;
And if he, spying me, should fall to weep,
Beseech me to be good, repair his wrong,
Bid his poor leg smart less or grow again,—
Well, as the chance were, this might take or else   90
Not take my fancy: I might hear his cry,
And give the manikin three legs for one,
Or pluck the other off, leave him like an egg,
And lessoned he was mine and merely clay.
Were this no pleasure, lying in the thyme,
Drinking the mash, with brain become alive,
Making and marring clay at will? So He.
'Thinketh, such shows nor right nor wrong in Him
Nor kind, nor cruel: He is strong and Lord.
'Am strong myself compared to yonder crabs   100
That march now from the mountain to the sea;

'Let twenty pass, and stone the twenty-first,
Loving not, hating not, just choosing so.
'Say, the first straggler that boasts purple spots
Shall join the file, one pincer twisted off;
'Say, this bruised fellow shall receive a worm,
And two worms he whose nippers end in red:
As it likes me each time, thus I do: so He.

Well then, 'supposeth He is good i' the main,
Placable if His mind and ways were guessed,   110
But rougher than His handiwork, be sure!
Oh, He hath made things worthier than Himself,
And envieth that, so helped, such things do more
Than He who made them! What consoles but this?
That they, unless through Him, do nought at all,
And must submit: what other use in things?
'Hath cut a pipe of pithless elder-joint
That, blown through, gives exact the scream o' the jay
When from her wing you twitch the feathers blue:
Sound this, and little birds that hate the jay   120
Flock within stone's throw, glad their foe is hurt:
Put case such pipe could prattle and boast forsooth
I catch the birds, I am the crafty thing,
I make the cry my maker cannot make
"With his great round mouth; he must blow through mine!"
Would not I smash it with my foot? So He.

But wherefore rough, why cold and ill at ease?
Aha, that is a question! Ask, for that,
What knows,—the something over Setebos
That made Him, or He, may be, found and fought, 130
Worsted, drove off and did to nothing, perchance.
There may be something quiet o'er His head,
Out of His reach, that feels nor joy nor grief,
Since both derive from weakness in some way.
I joy because the quails come; would not joy
Could I bring quails here when I have a mind:
This Quiet, all it hath a mind to, doth.
'Esteemeth stars the outposts of its couch,
But never spends much thought nor care that way.
It may look up, work up,—the worse for those   140
It works on! 'Careth but for Setebos
The many-handed as a cuttle-fish,[10]
Who, making Himself feared through what He does,
Looks up, first, and perceives he cannot soar
To what is quiet and hath happy life;
Next looks down here, and out of very spite

---

[7]**It nothing skills**: it does no good.

[8]**bladdery**: bubbling.

[9]**grigs**: crickets.

---

[10]**cuttle-fish**: squid.

Makes this a bauble-world to ape yon real,
These good things to match those, as hips[11] do grapes.
'Tis solace making baubles, ay, and sport.
Himself peeped late, eyed Prosper at his books   150
Careless and lofty, lord now of the isle:
Vexed, 'stitched a book of broad leaves, arrow-shaped,
Wrote thereon, he knows what, prodigious words;
Has peeled a wand and called it by a name;
Weareth at whiles for an enchanter's robe
The eyed skin of a supple ocelot;
And hath an ounce[12] sleeker than youngling mole,
A four-legged serpent he makes cower and couch,
Now snarl, now hold its breath and mind his eye,
And saith she is Miranda and my wife.   160
'Keeps for his Ariel[13] a tall pouch-bill crane
He bids go wade for fish and straight disgorge;
Also a sea-beast, lumpish, which he snared,
Blinded the eyes of, and brought somewhat tame,
And split its toe-webs, and now pens the drudge
In a hole o' the rock, and calls him Caliban;
A bitter heart that bides its time and bites.
'Plays thus at being Prosper in a way,
Taketh his mirth with make-believes: so He.

His dam held that the Quiet made all things   170
Which Setebos vexed only: 'holds not so.
Who made them weak, meant weakness He might vex.
Had He meant other, while His hand was in,
Why not make horny eyes no thorn could prick,
Or plate my scalp with bone against the snow,
Or overscale my flesh 'neath joint and joint,
Like an orc's[14] armour? Ay,—so spoil His sport!
He is the One now: only He doth all.

'Saith, He may like, perchance, what profits Him.
Ay, himself loves what does him good; but why?   180
'Gets good no otherwise. This blinded beast
Loves whoso places flesh-meat on his nose,
But, had he eyes, would want no help, would hate
Or love, just as it liked him: He hath eyes.
Also it pleaseth Setebos to work,
Use all His hands, and exercise much craft,
By no means for the love of what is worked.
'Tasteth, himself, no finer good i' the world

When all goes right, in this safe summer-time,
And he wants little, hungers, aches not much,   190
Than trying what to do with wit and strength.
'Falls to make something: 'piled yon pile of turfs,
And squared and stuck there squares of soft white chalk,
And, with a fish-tooth, scratched a moon on each,
And set up endwise certain spikes of tree,
And crowned the whole with a sloth's skull a-top,
Found dead i' the woods, too hard for one to kill.
No use at all i' the work, for work's sole sake;
'Shall some day knock it down again: so He.

'Saith He is terrible: watch His feats in proof!   200
One hurricane will spoil six good months' hope.
He hath a spite against me, that I know.
Just as He favours Prosper, who knows why?
So it is, all the same, as well I find.
'Wove wattles half the winter, fenced them firm
With stone and stake to stop she-tortoises
Crawling to lay their eggs here: well, one wave,
Feeling the foot of Him upon its neck,
Gaped as a snake does, lolled out its large tongue,
And licked the whole labour flat: so much for spite!   210
'Saw a ball[15] flame down late (yonder it lies)
Where, half an hour before, I slept i' the shade:
Often they scatter sparkles: there is force!
'Dug up a newt He may have envied once
And turned to stone, shut up inside a stone.
Please Him and hinder this?—What Prosper does?
Aha, if he would tell me how. Not He!
There is the sport: discover how or die!
All need not die, for of the things o' the isle
Some flee afar, some dive, some run up trees;   220
Those at His mercy,—why, they please Him most
When . . when . . well, never try the same way twice!
Repeat what act has pleased, He may grow wroth.
You must not know His ways, and play Him off,
Sure of the issue. 'Doth the like himself:
'Spareth a squirrel that it nothing fears
But steals the nut from underneath my thumb,
And when I threat, bites stoutly in defence:
'Spareth an urchin[16] that contrariwise,
Curls up into a ball, pretending death   230
For fright at my approach: the two ways please.
But what would move my choler more than this,
That either creature counted on its life

---

[11]**hips**: inedible fruit of the rose.

[12]**ounce**: leopard.

[13]**Ariel**: a spirit, Prospero's other servant.

[14]**orc**: sea monster.

---

[15]**ball**: meteorite.

[16]**urchin**: hedgehog.

To-morrow, next day and all days to come,
Saying forsooth in the inmost of its heart,
"Because he did so yesterday with me,
And otherwise with such another brute,
So must he do henceforth and always."—Ay?
'Would teach the reasoning couple what "must" means!
'Doth as he likes, or wherefore Lord? So He.   240

'Conceiveth all things will continue thus,
And we shall have to live in fear of Him
So long as He lives, keeps His strength: no change,
If He have done His best, make no new world
To please Him more, so leave off watching this,—
If He surprise[17] not even the Quiet's self
Some strange day,—or, suppose, grow into it
As grubs grow butterflies: else, here are we,
And there is He, and nowhere help at all.

'Believeth with the life, the pain shall stop.   250
His dam held different, held that after death
He both plagued enemies and feasted friends:
Idly! He doth His worst in this our life,
Giving just respite lest we die through pain,
Saving last pain for worst,—with which, an end.
Meanwhile, the best way to escape His ire
Is, not to seem too happy. 'Sees, himself,
Yonder two flies, with purple films and pink,
Bask on the pompion-bell above: kills both.
'Sees two black painful beetles roll their ball   260
On head and tail as if to save their lives:
'Moves them the stick away they strive to clear.

Even so, 'would have Him misconceive, suppose
This Caliban strives hard and ails no less,
And always, above all else, envies Him;
Wherefore he mainly dances on dark nights,
Moans in the sun, get under holes to laugh,
And never speaks his mind save housed as now:
Outside, 'groans, curses. If He caught me here,
O'erheard this speech, and asked "What
          chucklest at?"   270
'Would, to appease Him, cut a finger off,
Or of my three kid yearlings burn the best,
Or let the toothsome apple rot on tree,
Or push my tame beast for the orc to taste:
While myself lit a fire, and made a song
And sung it, *"What I hate, be consecrate*
"To celebrate Thee and Thy state, no mate
"For Thee; what see for envy in poor me?"

Hoping the while, since evils sometimes mend,
Warts rub away and sores are cured with slime,   280
That some strange day, will either the Quiet catch
And conquer Setebos, or likelier He
Decrepit may doze, doze, as good as die.

[What, what? A curtain o'er the world at once!
Crickets stop hissing; not a bird—or, yes,
There scuds His raven that hath told Him all!
It was fool's play, this prattling! Ha! The wind
Shoulders the pillared dust, death's house o' the move,
And fast invading fires begin! White blaze—
A tree's head snaps—and there, there, there, there, there,   290
His thunder follows! Fool to gibe at Him!
Lo! 'Lieth flat and loveth Setebos!
'Maketh his teeth meet through his upper lip,
Will let those quails fly, will not eat this month
One little mess of whelks, so he may 'scape!]

                                        1864

Abt Vogler[1]

(After he has been extemporizing upon the musical instrument of his invention)

— 1 —

Would that the structure brave, the manifold music I build,
     Bidding my organ obey, calling its keys to their work,
Claiming each slave of the sound, at a touch, as when
          Solomon willed
     Armies of angels that soar, legions of demons that lurk,
Man, brute, reptile, fly,—alien of end and of aim,
     Adverse, each from the other heaven-high, hell-deep
          removed,—
Should rush into sight at once as he named the ineffable
          Name,[2]
     And pile him a palace straight, to pleasure the princess
          he loved!

---

[17]**surprise:** ambush.

[1]Abbé or **Abt** Georg Joseph **Vogler** (1749–1814): German composer, celebrated improviser on a portable keyboard.

[2]**ineffable Name:** Jehovah or Yahweh, inscribed according to
legend on a signet ring that gave King Solomon command over the
spirit world.

— 2 —

Would it might tarry like his, the beautiful building of
      mine,
    This which my keys in a crowd pressed and
         importuned to raise!   10
Ah, one and all, how they helped, would dispart now and
      now combine,
    Zealous to hasten the work, heighten their master his
         praise!
And one would bury his brow with a blind plunge down
      to hell,
    Burrow awhile and build, broad on the roots of things,
Then up again swim into sight, having based me my
      palace well,
    Founded it, fearless of flame, flat on the nether springs.

— 3 —

And another would mount and march, like the excellent
      minion he was,
    Ay, another and yet another, one crowd but with many
         a crest
Raising my rampired[3] walls of gold as transparent as glass,
    Eager to do and die, yield each his place to
         the rest: 20
For higher still and higher (as a runner tips with fire,
    When a great illumination surprises a festal night—
Outlining round and round Rome's dome[4] from space to
      spire)
    Up, the pinnacled glory reached, and the pride of my
         soul was in sight.

— 4 —

In sight? Not half! for it seemed, it was certain, to match
      man's birth,
    Nature in turn conceived, obeying an impulse as I;
And the emulous heaven yearned down, made effort to
      reach the earth,
    As the earth had done her best, in my passion, to scale
         the sky:
Novel splendours burst forth, grew familiar and dwelt
      with mine,
    Not a point nor peak but found and fixed its
         wandering star;   30
Meteor-moons, balls of blaze: and they did not pale
      nor pine,

For earth had attained to heaven, there was no more
      near nor far.

— 5 —

Nay more; for there wanted not who walked in the glare
      and glow,
    Presences plain in the place; or, fresh from the
         Protoplast,[5]
Furnished for ages to come, when a kindlier wind should
      blow,
    Lured now to begin and live, in a house to their liking
         at last;
Or else the wonderful Dead who have passed through the
      body and gone,
    But were back once more to breathe in an old
         world worth their new:
What never had been, was now; what was, as it shall
      be anon;
    And what is,—shall I say, matched both? for I was
         made perfect too.   40

— 6 —

All through my keys that gave their sounds to a wish of
      my soul,
    All through my soul that praised as its wish flowed
         visibly forth,
All through music and me! For think, had I painted the
      whole,
    Why, there it had stood, to see, nor the process so
         wonder-worth:
Had I written the same, made verse—still, effect proceeds
      from cause,
    Ye know why the forms are fair, ye hear how the tale
         is told;
It is all triumphant art, but art in obedience to laws,
    Painter and poet are proud in the artist-list enrolled:—

— 7 —

But here is the finger of God, a flash of the will that can,
    Existent behind all laws, that made them and, lo,
         they are!   50
And I know not if, save in this, such gift be allowed to man,
    That out of three sounds he frame, not a fourth sound,
         but a star.

---

[3]**rampired**: with ramparts.
[4]**Rome's dome**: St. Peter's.

[5]**Protoplast**: the first created substance (protoplasm); the First
Maker (God).

Consider it well: each tone of our scale in itself is nought;
   It is everywhere in the world—loud, soft, and all is said:
Give it to me to use! I mix it with two in my thought:
   And, there! Ye have heard and seen: consider and bow
      the head!

— 8 —

Well, it is gone at last, the palace of music I reared;
   Gone! and the good tears start, the praises that come
      too slow;
For one is assured at first, one scarce can say that he feared,
   That he even gave it a thought, the gone thing was
      to go.   60
Never to be again! But many more of the kind
   As good, nay, better perchance: is this your comfort
      to me?
To me, who must be saved because I cling with my mind
   To the same, same self, same love, same God: ay,
      what was, shall be.

— 9 —

Therefore to whom turn I but to thee, the ineffable Name?
   Builder and maker, thou, of houses not made with
      hands![6]
What, have fear of change from thee who art ever the same?
   Doubt that thy power can fill the heart that thy power
      expands?
There shall never be one lost good! What was, shall live
    as before;
   The evil is null, is nought, is silence implying
      sound;   70
What was good shall be good, with, for evil, so much
    good more;
   On the earth the broken arcs; in the heaven, a perfect
      round.

— 10 —

All we have willed or hoped or dreamed of good shall exist;
   Not its semblance, but itself; no beauty, nor good, nor
      power
Whose voice has gone forth, but each survives for the
    melodist
   When eternity affirms the conception of an hour.
The high that proved too high, the heroic for earth too hard,
   The passion that left the ground to lose itself in the sky,
Are music sent up to God by the lover and the bard;
   Enough that he heard it once: we shall hear it
      by-and-by.   80

— 11 —

And what is our failure here but a triumph's evidence
   For the fulness of the days? Have we withered or
      agonized?
Why else was the pause prolonged but that singing might
    issue thence?
   Why rushed the discords in but that harmony should
      be prized?
Sorrow is hard to bear, and doubt is slow to clear,
   Each sufferer says his say, his scheme of the weal
      and woe:
But God has a few of us whom he whispers in the ear;
   The rest may reason and welcome: 'tis we musicians
      know.

— 12 —

Well, it is earth with me; silence resumes her reign:
   I will be patient and proud, and soberly
      acquiesce.   90
Give me the keys. I feel for the common chord again,
   Sliding by semitones, till I sink to the minor,—yes,
And I blunt it into a ninth,[7] and I stand on alien ground,
   Surveying awhile the heights I rolled from into the deep;
Which, hark, I have dared and done, for my resting-place
    is found,
   The C Major of this life: so, now I will try to sleep.

                     1864

~

Youth and Art

— 1 —

It once might have been, once only:
   We lodged in a street together,
You, a sparrow on the housetop lonely,
   I, a lone she-bird of his feather.

— 2 —

Your trade was with sticks and clay,
   You thumbed, thrust, patted and polished,
Then laughed "They will see some day
   "Smith made, and Gibson[1] demolished."

---

[7]**ninth**: complex dissonance, from which the music returns to
the tonic **C Major**.

[1]**Smith**: the sculptor-in-training whom the speaker (née **Kate
Brown**, former voice student) recalls her crush on. John **Gibson**
(1790–1866): well-known sculptor.

---

[6]**not made with hands**: 2 Corinthians 5:1.

— 3 —

My business was song, song, song;
   I chirped, cheeped, trilled and twittered,   10
"Kate Brown's on the boards ere long,
   "And Grisi's[2] existence embittered!"

— 4 —

I earned no more by a warble
   Than you by a sketch in plaster;
You wanted a piece of marble,
   I needed a music-master.

— 5 —

We studied hard in our styles,
   Chipped each at a crust like Hindoos,
For air looked out on the tiles,
   For fun watched each other's windows.   20

— 6 —

You lounged, like a boy of the South,
   Cap and blouse—nay, a bit of beard too;
Or you got it, rubbing your mouth
   With fingers the clay adhered to.

— 7 —

And I—soon managed to find
   Weak points in the flower-fence facing,
Was forced to put up a blind
   And be safe in my corset-lacing.

— 8 —

No harm! It was not my fault
   If you never turned your eye's tail up   30
As I shook upon E *in alt*,
   Or ran the chromatic scale[3] up:

— 9 —

For spring bade the sparrows pair,
   And the boys and girls gave guesses,
And stalls in our street looked rare
   With bulrush and watercresses.

— 10 —

Why did not you pinch a flower
   In a pellet of clay and fling it?

Why did not I put a power
   Of thanks in a look, or sing it?   40

— 11 —

I did look, sharp as a lynx,
   (And yet the memory rankles)
When models arrived, some minx
   Tripped up-stairs, she and her ankles.

— 12 —

But I think I gave you as good!
   "That foreign fellow,—who can know
"How she pays, in a playful mood,
   "For his tuning her that piano?"

— 13 —

Could you say so, and never say
   "Suppose we join hands and fortunes,   50
"And I fetch her from over the way,
   "Her, piano, and long tunes and short tunes?"

— 14 —

No, no: you would not be rash,
   Nor I rasher and something over:
You've to settle yet Gibson's hash,
   And Grisi yet lives in clover.

— 15 —

But you meet the Prince at the Board,
   I'm queen myself at *bals-paré*,[4]
I've married a rich old lord,
   And you're dubbed knight and an R. A.[5]   60

— 16 —

Each life unfulfilled, you see;
   It hangs still, patchy and scrappy:
We have not sighed deep, laughed free,
   Starved, feasted, despaired,—been happy.

— 17 —

And nobody calls you a dunce,
   And people suppose me clever:
This could but have happened once,
   And we missed it, lost it for ever.

1864

---

[2]Giulia **Grisi** (1811–1869): famous soprano.

[3]**E** *in alt*: high E. **chromatic scale:** including all semitones.

[4]**Prince:** unspecified member of the royal family. **Board:** generic commission. *bals-paré:* full-dress balls.

[5]**R. A.:** member of the Royal Academy of Art and thus an establishment artist.

Amphibian[1]

— 1 —

The fancy I had to-day,
   Fancy which turned a fear!
I swam far out in the bay,
   Since waves laughed warm and clear.

— 2 —

I lay and looked at the sun,
   The noon-sun looked at me:
Between us two, no one
   Live creature, that I could see.

— 3 —

Yes! There came floating by
   Me, who lay floating too,   10
Such a strange butterfly!
   Creature as dear as new:

— 4 —

Because the membraned wings
   So wonderful, so wide,
So sun-suffused, were things
   Like soul and nought beside.

— 5 —

A handbreadth over head!
   All of the sea my own,
It owned the sky instead;
   Both of us were alone.   20

— 6 —

I never shall join its flight,
   For, nought buoys flesh in air.
If it touch the sea—good night!
   Death sure and swift waits there.

— 7 —

Can the insect feel the better
   For watching the uncouth play
Of limbs that slip the fetter,
   Pretend as they were not clay?

— 8 —

Undoubtedly I rejoice
   That the air comports so well   30
With a creature which had the choice
   Of the land once. Who can tell?

— 9 —

What if a certain soul[2]
   Which early slipped its sheath,
And has for its home the whole
   Of heaven, thus look beneath,

— 10 —

Thus watch one who, in the world,
   Both lives and likes life's way,
Nor wishes the wings unfurled
   That sleep in the worm, they say?   40

— 11 —

But sometimes when the weather
   Is blue, and warm waves tempt
To free oneself of tether,
   And try a life exempt

— 12 —

From worldly noise and dust,
   In the sphere which overbrims
With passion and thought,—why, just
   Unable to fly, one swims!

— 13 —

By passion and thought upborne,
   One smiles to oneself—"They fare   50
Scarce better, they need not scorn
   Our sea, who live in the air!"

— 14 —

Emancipate[3] through passion
   And thought, with sea for sky,
We substitute, in a fashion,
   For heaven—poetry:

— 15 —

Which sea, to all intent,
   Gives flesh such noon-disport

---

[1]**Amphibian**: published as prologue to *Fifine at the Fair*, a long monologue delivered by Don Juan on the spiritual and worldly aspects of sexual love.

[2]**a certain soul**: Elizabeth Barrett Browning, who had died a decade before.

[3]**Emancipate**: emancipated (past participle).

As a finer element
    Affords the spirit-sort.   60

— 16 —

Whatever they are, we seem:
    Imagine the thing they know;
All deeds they do, we dream;
    Can heaven be else but so?

— 17 —

And meantime, yonder streak
    Meets the horizon's verge;
That is the land, to seek
    If we tire or dread the surge:

— 18 —

Land the solid and safe—
    To welcome again (confess!)   70
When, high and dry, we chafe
    The body, and don the dress.

— 19 —

Does she look, pity, wonder
    At one who mimics flight,
Swims—heaven above, sea under,
    Yet always earth in sight?

        1872

from Aristophanes' Apology

Thamuris marching,[1]—lyre and song of Thrace—
(Perpend[2] the first, the worst of woes that were
Allotted lyre and song, ye poet-race!)

Thamuris from Oichalia, feasted there
By kingly Eurutos of late, now bound
For Dorion at the uprise broad and bare

Of Mount Pangaios[3] (ore with earth enwound
Glittered beneath his footstep)—marching gay
And glad, Thessalia through, came, robed and crowned,

From triumph on to triumph, mid a ray   10
Of early morn,—came, saw and knew the spot
Assigned him for his worst of woes, that day.

Balura[4]—happier while its name was not—
Met him, but nowise menaced; slipt aside,
Obsequious river, to pursue its lot

Of solacing the valley—say, some wide
Thick busy human cluster, house and home,
Embanked for peace, or thrift that thanks the tide.

Thamuris, marching, laughed "Each flake of foam"
(As sparklingly the ripple raced him by)   20
"Mocks slower clouds adrift in the blue dome!"

For Autumn was the season; red the sky
Held morn's conclusive signet of the sun
To break the mists up, bid them blaze and die.

Morn had the mastery as, one by one
All pomps produced themselves along the tract
From earth's far ending to near heaven begun.

Was there a ravaged tree? it laughed compact
With gold, a leaf-ball crisp, high-brandished now,
Tempting to onset frost which late attacked.   30

Was there a wizened shrub, a starveling bough,
A fleecy thistle filched from by the wind,
A weed, Pan's[5] trampling hoof would disallow?

Each, with a glory and a rapture twined
About it, joined the rush of air and light
And force: the world was of one joyous mind.

Say not the birds flew! they forebore their right—
Swam, revelling onward in the roll of things.
Say not the beasts' mirth bounded! that was flight—

How could the creatures leap, no lift of wings?   40
Such earth's community of purpose, such
The ease of earth's fulfilled imaginings,—

So did the near and far appear to touch
I' the moment's transport,—that an interchange
Of function, far with near, seemed scarce too much;

---

[1]**Thamuris**: ancient poet already legendary for Homer; see *Iliad* 2.594–600, on his visit to King **Eurutos** of **Oichalia** and the disastrous contest with the Muses at **Dorion** that left him a maimed, imbecile mute. The poet's association with **Thrace** and **Thessaly** in N Greece affiliates him with Orphic inspiration—and tragic arrogance, which is the cautionary point stressed by the conservative comedian **Aristophanes** (5th century BCE) as he chants this terza rima outburst 5,188 lines into Browning's enormous symposium-monologue.

[2]**Perpend**: ponder.

[3]**Pangaios**: Thracian mountain with gold and silver deposits.

[4]**Balura** (Castaway): river into which Thamuris cast his lyre when blinded by the Muses.

[5]**Pan**: goat-god of flocks.

And had the rooted plant aspired to range
With the snake's license, while the insect yearned
To glow fixed as the flower, it were not strange—

No more than if the fluttery tree-top turned
To actual music, sang itself aloft;   50
Or if the wind, impassioned chantress, earned

The right to soar embodied in some soft
Fine form all fit for cloud-companionship,
And, blissful, once touch beauty chased so oft.

Thamuris, marching, let no fancy slip
Born of the fiery transport; lyre and song
Were his, to smite with hand and launch from lip—

Peerless recorded, since the list grew long
Of poets (saith Homeros) free to stand
Pedestalled mid the Muses' temple-throng,   60

A statued service, laurelled, lyre in hand,
(Ay, for we see them)—Thamuris of Thrace
Predominating foremost of the band.

Therefore the morn-ray that enriched his face,
If it gave lambent chill, took flame again
From flush of pride; he saw, he knew the place.

What wind arrived with all the rhythms from plain,
Hill, dale, and that rough wildwood interspersed?
Compounding these to one consummate strain,

It reached him, music; but his own outburst   70
Of victory concluded the account,
And that grew song which was mere music erst.

"Be my Parnassos, thou Pangaian mount!
And turn thee, river, nameless hitherto!
Famed shalt thou vie with famed Pieria's fount![6]

"Here I await the end of this ado:
Which wins—Earth's poet or the Heavenly Muse." . . .
                                                        1875

~

House

— 1 —

Shall I sonnet-sing you about myself?
    Do I live in a house you would like to see?

Is it scant of gear, has it store of pelf?[1]
    "Unlock my heart with a sonnet-key?"[2]

— 2 —

Invite the world, as my betters have done?
    "Take notice: this building remains on view,
Its suites of reception every one,
    Its private apartment and bedroom too;

— 3 —

"For a ticket, apply to the Publisher."
    No: thanking the public, I must decline.   10
A peep through my window, if folk prefer;
    But, please you, no foot over threshold of mine!

— 4 —

I have mixed with a crowd and heard free talk
    In a foreign land where an earthquake chanced:
And a house stood gaping, nought to baulk
    Man's eye wherever he gazed or glanced.

— 5 —

The whole of the frontage shaven sheer,
    The inside gaped: exposed to day,
Right and wrong and common and queer,
    Bare, as the palm of your hand, it lay.   20

— 6 —

The owner? Oh, he had been crushed, no doubt!
    "Odd tables and chairs for a man of wealth!
What a parcel of musty old books about!
    He smoked,—no wonder he lost his health!

— 7 —

"I doubt if he bathed before he dressed.
    A brasier?—the pagan, he burned perfumes!
You see it is proved, what the neighbours guessed:
    His wife and himself had separate rooms."

— 8 —

Friends, the goodman of the house at least
    Kept house to himself till an earthquake came: 30
'Tis the fall of its frontage permits you feast
    On the inside arrangement you praise or blame.

---

[6]**Parnassos, Pieria's fount**: Muses' sacred mountain and spring.

---

[1]**pelf**: wealth.

[2]**"Unlock . . . key"**: see Wordsworth, "Scorn not the sonnet" (1827) 2–3: "with this key / Shakespeare unlocked his heart."

—9—

Outside should suffice for evidence:
    And whoso desires to penetrate
Deeper, must dive by the spirit-sense—
    No optics like yours, at any rate!

—10—

"Hoity toity! A street to explore,
    Your house the exception! *'With this same key*
Shakespeare unlocked his heart,' once more!"
    Did Shakespeare? If so, the less Shakespeare he!   40

      1876

Adam, Lilith,[1] and Eve

One day it thundered and lightened.
Two women, fairly frightened,
Sank to their knees, transformed, transfixed,
At the feet of the man who sat betwixt;
And "Mercy!" cried each—"if I tell the truth
Of a passage in my youth!"

Said This: "Do you mind the morning
I met your love with scorning?
As the worst of the venom left my lips,
I thought 'If, despite this lie, he strips   10
The mask from my soul with a kiss—I crawl
His slave,—soul, body and all!' "

Said That: "We stood to be married;
The priest, or someone, tarried;
'If Paradise-door prove locked?' smiled you.
I thought, as I nodded, smiling too,
'Did one, that's away, arrive—nor late
Nor soon should unlock Hell's gate!' "

It ceased to lighten and thunder.
Up started both in wonder,   20
Looked round and saw that the sky was clear,
Then laughed "Confess you believed us, Dear!"
"I saw through the joke!" the man replied
They re-seated themselves beside.

      1883

---

[1]**Lilith:** demon seductress who was, in Jewish legend, **Adam's** first wife.

Why I Am a Liberal[1]

"Why?" Because all I haply can and do,
    All that I am now, all I hope to be,—
    Whence comes it save from fortune setting free
Body and soul the purpose to pursue,
God traced for both? If fetters, not a few,
    Of prejudice, convention, fall from me,
    These shall I bid men—each in his degree
Also God-guided—bear, and gayly too?

    But little do or can the best of us:
That little is achieved through Liberty.   10
    Who, then, dares hold, emancipated thus,
His fellow shall continue bound? Not I,
    Who live, love, labour freely, nor discuss
A brother's right to freedom. That is "Why."

      1885

from Asolando[1]
Prologue

"The Poet's age is sad: for why?
    In youth, the natural world could show
No common object but his eye
    At once involved with alien glow—
His own soul's iris-bow.[2]

"And now a flower is just a flower:
    Man, bird, beast are but beast, bird, man—
Simply themselves, uncinct by dower[3]
    Of dyes which, when life's day began,
Round each in glory ran."   10

Friend, did you need an optic glass,
    Which were your choice? A lens to drape

---

[1]**Why I Am a Liberal:** also title of the book in which this sonnet appears with other contributions from eminent Victorian Liberals.

[1]*Asolando:* title of Browning's last collection (1889), coined to mean "amusing oneself at random" from the name of **Asolo,** a hillside village near Venice.

[2]**iris-bow:** rainbow; see opening strophes of Wordsworth's "Intimations" ode (1807), here parodied.

[3]**uncinct:** not circled. **dower:** gift.

In ruby, emerald, chrysopras,[4]
   Each object—or reveal its shape
Clear outlined, past escape,

The naked very thing?—so clear
   That, when you had the chance to gaze,
You found its inmost self appear
   Through outer seeming—truth ablaze,
Not falsehood's fancy-haze?   20

How many a year, my Asolo,
   Since—one step just from sea to land—
I found you, loved yet feared you so—
   For natural objects seemed to stand
Palpably fire-clothed!   No—

No mastery of mine o'er these!
   Terror with beauty, like the Bush[5]
Burning but unconsumed.   Bend knees,
   Drop eyes to earthward!   Language?   Tush!
Silence 'tis awe decrees.   30

And now?   The lambent flame is—where?
   Lost from the naked world: earth, sky,
Hill, vale, tree, flower,—Italia's rare
   O'er-running beauty crowds the eye—
But flame? The Bush is bare.

Hill, vale, tree, flower—they stand distinct,
   Nature to know and name.   What then?
A Voice spoke thence which straight unlinked
   Fancy from fact: see, all's in ken:
Has once my eyelid winked?   40

No, for the purged ear apprehends
   Earth's import, not the eye late dazed:
The Voice said "Call my works thy friends!
   At Nature dost thou shrink amazed?
God is it who transcends."

1889

~

from An Essay on Shelley

An opportunity having presented itself for the acquisition of a series of unedited letters by Shelley, all more or less directly supplementary to and illustrative of the collection already published by Mr. Moxon,[1] that gentleman has decided on securing them. They will prove an acceptable addition to a body of correspondence, the value of which towards a right understanding of its author's purpose and work, may be said to exceed that of any similar contribution exhibiting the worldly relations of a poet whose genius has operated by a different law.

Doubtless we accept gladly the biography of an objective poet, as the phrase now goes; one whose endeavour has been to reproduce things external (whether the phenomena of the scenic universe, or the manifested action of the human heart and brain) with an immediate reference, in every case, to the common eye and apprehension of his fellow men, assumed capable of receiving and profiting by this reproduction. It has been obtained through the poet's double faculty of seeing external objects more clearly, widely, and deeply, than is possible to the average mind, at the same time that he is so acquainted and in sympathy with its narrower comprehension as to be careful to supply it with no other materials than it can combine into an intelligible whole. The auditory of such a poet will include, not only the intelligences which, save for such assistance, would have missed the deeper meaning and enjoyment of the original objects, but also the spirits of a like endowment with his own, who, by means of his abstract, can forthwith pass to the reality it was made from, and either corroborate their impressions of things known already, or supply themselves with new from whatever shows in the inexhaustible variety of existence may have hitherto escaped their knowledge. Such a poet is properly the ποιητης,[2] the fashioner; and the thing fashioned, his poetry, will of necessity be substantive, projected from himself and distinct. We are ignorant what the inventor of "Othello" conceived of that fact as he beheld it in completeness, how he accounted for it, under what known law he registered its nature, or to what unknown law he traced its coincidence. We learn only what he intended we should learn by that particular exercise of his power,—the fact itself,—which, with its infinite significances, each of us receives for the first time as a creation, and is hereafter left to deal with, as, in proportion to his own intelligence, he best may. We are ignorant, and would fain be otherwise.

Doubtless, with respect to such a poet, we covet his biography. We desire to look back upon the process of gathering together in a lifetime, the materials of the work we

---

[4]**chrysopras:** golden-green precious stone.

[5]**Bush:** see Exodus 3:2.

---

[1]Edward **Moxon** (1801–1858): Browning's friend and 1840s publisher who solicited this essay, then suppressed it on determining that the alleged Shelley letters were forgeries.

[2]ποιητης, (poietes): maker, poet.

behold entire; of elaborating, perhaps under difficulty and with hindrance, all that is familiar to our admiration in the apparent facility of success. And the inner impulse of this effort and operation, what induced it? Did a soul's delight in its own extended sphere of vision set it, for the gratification of an insuppressible power, on labour, as other men are set on rest? Or did a sense of duty or of love lead it to communicate its own sensations to mankind? Did an irresistible sympathy with men compel it to bring down and suit its own provision of knowledge and beauty to their narrow scope? Did the personality of such an one stand like an open watch-tower in the midst of the territory it is erected to gaze on, and were the storms and calms, the stars and meteors, its watchman was wont to report of, the habitual variegation of his every-day life, as they glanced across its open roof or lay reflected on its four-square parapet? Or did some sunken and darkened chamber of imagery witness, in the artificial illumination of every storied compartment we are permitted to contemplate, how rare and precious were the outlooks through here and there an embrasure upon a world beyond, and how blankly would have pressed on the artificer the boundary of his daily life, except for the amorous diligence with which he had rendered permanent by art whatever came to diversify the gloom? Still, fraught with instruction and interest as such details undoubtedly are, we can, if needs be, dispense with them. The man passes, the work remains. The work speaks for itself, as we say: and the biography of the worker is no more necessary to an understanding or enjoyment of it, than is a model or anatomy of some tropical tree, to the right tasting of the fruit we are familiar with on the market-stall,—or a geologist's map and stratification, to the prompt recognition of the hill-top, our land-mark of every day.

We turn with stronger needs to the genius of an opposite tendency—the subjective poet of modern classification. He, gifted like the objective poet with the fuller perception of nature and man, is impelled to embody the thing he perceives, not so much with reference to the many below as to the one above him, the supreme Intelligence which apprehends all things in their absolute truth,—an ultimate view ever aspired to, if but partially attained, by the poet's own soul. Not what man sees, but what God sees—the *Ideas* of Plato,[3] seeds of creation lying burningly on the Divine Hand—it is toward these that he struggles. Not with the combination of humanity in action, but with the primal elements of humanity he has to do; and he digs where he stands,—preferring to seek them in his own soul as the near-

est reflex of that absolute Mind, according to the intuitions of which he desires to perceive and speak. Such a poet does not deal habitually with the picturesque groupings and tempestuous tossings of the forest-trees, but with their roots and fibres naked to the chalk and stone. He does not paint pictures and hang them on the walls, but rather carries them on the retina of his own eyes: we must look deep into his human eyes, to see those pictures on them. He is rather a seer, accordingly, than a fashioner, and what he produces will be less a work than an effluence. That effluence cannot be easily considered in abstraction from his personality,—being indeed the very radiance and aroma of his personality, projected from it but not separated. Therefore, in our approach to the poetry, we necessarily approach the personality of the poet; in apprehending it we apprehend him, and certainly we cannot love it without loving him. Both for love's and for understanding's sake we desire to know him, and as readers of his poetry must be readers of his biography also.

I shall observe, in passing, that it seems not so much from any essential distinction in the faculty of the two poets or in the nature of the objects contemplated by either, as in the more immediate adaptability of these objects to the distinct purpose of each, that the objective poet, in his appeal to the aggregate human mind, chooses to deal with the doings of men (the result of which dealing, in its pure form, when even description, as suggesting a describer, is dispensed with, is what we call dramatic poetry), while the subjective poet, whose study has been himself, appealing through himself to the absolute Divine mind, prefers to dwell upon those external scenic appearances which strike out most abundantly and uninterruptedly his inner light and power, selects that silence of the earth and sea in which he can best hear the beating of his individual heart, and leaves the noisy, complex, yet imperfect exhibitions of nature in the manifold experience of man around him, which serve only to distract and suppress the working of his brain. These opposite tendencies of genius will be more readily described in their artistic effect than in their moral spring and cause. Pushed to an extreme and manifested as a deformity, they will be seen plainest of all in the fault of either artist, when subsidiarily to the human interest of his work his occasional illustrations from scenic nature are introduced as in the earlier works of the originative painters[4]— men and women filling the foreground with consummate mastery, while mountain, grove and rivulet show like an

---

[3]**Ideas of Plato**: supersensible realities behind perceptible phenomena.

[4]**originative painters**: early Renaissance artists, whose humanist portraits Browning finds dwindled into mere "**figures**" for a later picturesque school.

anticipatory revenge on that succeeding race of landscape-painters whose "figures" disturb the perfection of their earth and sky. It would be idle to inquire, of these two kinds of poetic faculty in operation, which is the higher or even rarer endowment. If the subjective might seem to be the ultimate requirement of every age, the objective, in the strictest state, must still retain its original value. For it is with this world, as starting point and basis alike, that we shall always have to concern ourselves: the world is not to be learned and thrown aside, but reverted to and relearned. The spiritual comprehension may be infinitely subtilised, but the raw material it operates upon, must remain. There may be no end of the poets who communicate to us what they see in an object with reference to their own individuality; what it was before they saw it, in reference to the aggregate human mind, will be as desirable to know as ever. Nor is there any reason why these two modes of poetic faculty may not issue hereafter from the same poet in successive perfect works, examples of which, according to what are now considered the exigences of art, we have hitherto possessed in distinct individuals only. A mere running in of the one faculty upon the other, is, of course, the ordinary circumstance. Far more rarely it happens that either is found so decidedly prominent and superior, as to be pronounced comparatively pure: while of the perfect shield, with the gold and the silver side set up for all comers to challenge, there has yet been no instance. Either faculty in its eminent state is doubtless conceded by Providence as a best gift to men, according to their especial want. There is a time when the general eye has, so to speak, absorbed its fill of the phenomena around it, whether spiritual or material, and desires rather to learn the exacter significance of what it possesses, than to receive any augmentation of what is possessed. Then is the opportunity for the poet of loftier vision, to lift his fellows, with their half-apprehensions, up to his own sphere, by intensifying the import of details and rounding the universal meaning. The influence of such an achievement will not soon die out. A tribe of successors (Homerides)[5] working more or less in the same spirit, dwell on his discoveries and reinforce his doctrine; till, at unawares, the world is found to be subsisting wholly on the shadow of a reality, on sentiments diluted from passions, on the tradition of a fact, the convention of a moral, the straw of last year's harvest. Then is the imperative call for the appearance of another sort of poet, who shall at once replace this intellectual rumination of food swallowed long ago, by a

supply of the fresh and living swathe; getting at new substance by breaking up the assumed wholes into parts of independent and unclassed value, careless of the unknown laws for recombining them (it will be the business of yet another poet to suggest those hereafter), prodigal of objects for men's outer and not inner sight, shaping for their uses a new and different creation from the last, which it displaces by the right of life over death,—to endure until, in the inevitable process, its very sufficiency to itself shall require, at length, an exposition of its affinity to something higher,—when the positive yet conflicting facts shall again precipitate themselves under a harmonising law, and one more degree will be apparent for a poet to climb in that mighty ladder, of which, however cloud-involved and undefined may glimmer the topmost step, the world dares no longer doubt that its gradations ascend.

Such being the two kinds of artists, it is naturally, as I have shown, with the biography of the subjective poet that we have the deeper concern. Apart from his recorded life altogether, we might fail to determine with satisfactory precision to what class his productions belong, and what amount of praise is assignable to the producer. Certainly, in the face of any conspicuous achievement of genius, philosophy, no less than sympathetic instinct, warrants our belief in a great moral purpose having mainly inspired even where it does not visibly look out of the same. Greatness in a work suggests an adequate instrumentality; and none of the lower incitements, however they may avail to initiate or even effect many considerable displays of power, simulating the nobler inspiration to which they are mistakenly referred, have been found able, under the ordinary conditions of humanity, to task themselves to the end of so exacting a performance as a poet's complete work. As soon will the galvanism, that provokes to violent action the muscles of a corpse, induce it to cross the chamber steadily: sooner. The love of displaying power for the display's sake, the love of riches, of distinction, of notoriety,—the desire of a triumph over rivals, and the vanity in the applause of friends,—each and all of such whetted appetites grow intenser by exercise and increasingly sagacious as to the best and readiest means of self-appeasement,—while for any of their ends, whether the money or the pointed finger of the crowd, or the flattery and hate to heart's content, there are cheaper prices to pay, they will all find soon enough, than the bestowment of a life upon a labour, hard, slow, and not sure. Also, assuming the proper moral aim to have produced a work, there are many and various states of an aim: it may be more intense than clear-sighted, or too easily satisfied with a lower field of activity than a steadier aspiration would reach. All the bad

---

[5]**Homerides** (children of Homer): derivative latecomers.

poetry in the world (accounted poetry, that is, by its affinities) will be found to result from some one of the infinite degrees of discrepancy between the attributes of the poet's soul, occasioning a want of correspondency between his work and the verities of nature,—issuing in poetry, false under whatever form, which shows a thing not as it is to mankind generally, nor as it is to the particular describer, but as it is supposed to be for some unreal neutral mood, midway between both and of value to neither, and living its brief minute simply through the indolence of whoever accepts it or his incapacity to denounce a cheat. Although of such depths of failure there can be no question here, we must in every case betake ourselves to the review of a poet's life ere we determine some of the nicer questions concerning his poetry,—more especially if the performance we seek to estimate aright, has been obstructed and cut short of completion by circumstances,—a disastrous youth or a premature death. We may learn from the biography whether his spirit invariably saw and spoke from the last height to which it had attained. An absolute vision is not for this world, but we are permitted a continual approximation to it, every degree of which in the individual, provided it exceed the attainment of the masses, must procure him a clear advantage. Did the poet ever attain to a higher platform than where he rested and exhibited a result? Did he know more than he spoke of?

I concede however, in respect to the subject of our study as well as some few other illustrious examples, that the unmistakable quality of the verse would be evidence enough, under usual circumstances, not only of the kind and degree of the intellectual but of the moral constitution of Shelley: the whole personality of the poet shining forward from the poems, without much need of going further to seek it. The "Remains"[6]—produced within a period of ten years, and at a season of life when other men of at all comparable genius have hardly done more than prepare the eye for future sight and the tongue for speech—present us with the complete enginery of a poet, as signal in the excellence of its several adaptitudes as transcendent in the combination of effects,—examples, in fact, of the whole poet's function of beholding with an understanding keen-

ness the universe, nature and man, in their actual state of perfection in imperfection,—of the whole poet's virtue of being untempted by the manifold partial developments of beauty and good on every side, into leaving them the ultimates he found them,—induced by the facility of the gratification of his own sense of those qualities, or by the pleasure of acquiescence in the short-comings of his predecessors in art, and the pain of disturbing their conventionalisms,—the whole poet's virtue, I repeat, of looking higher than any manifestation yet made of both beauty and good, in order to suggest from the utmost actual realisation of the one a corresponding capability in the other, and out of the calm, purity and energy of nature, to reconstitute and store up for the forthcoming stage of man's being, a gift in repayment of that former gift, in which man's own thought and passion had been lavished by the poet on the else-incompleted magnificence of the sunrise, the else-uninterpreted mystery of the lake,—so drawing out, lifting up, and assimilating this ideal of a future man, thus descried as possible, to the present reality of the poet's soul already arrived at the higher state of development and still aspirant to elevate and extend itself in conformity with its still-improving perceptions of, no longer the eventual Human, but the actual Divine. In conjunction with which noble and rare powers, came the subordinate power of delivering these attained results to the world in an embodiment of verse more closely answering to and indicative of the process of the informing spirit, (failing as it occasionally does, in art, only to succeed in highest art),—with a diction more adequate to the task in its natural and acquired richness, its material colour and spiritual transparency,—the whole being moved by and suffused with a music at once of the soul and the sense, expressive both of an external might of sincere passion and an internal fitness and consonancy,—than can be attributed to any other writer whose record is among us. Such was the spheric poetical faculty of Shelley, as its own self-sufficing central light, radiating equally through immaturity and accomplishment, through many fragments and occasional completion, reveals it to a competent judgment. . . . [7]

1851, 1881

---

[6]"**Remains**": in numerous legitimate and pirated editions of poetry and prose issued since Shelley's death in 1822.

[7]The remainder of the essay tries to argue away Shelley's apparent moral lapses.

EDWARD LEAR

(1812–1888)

If excellence in the writing of nonsense is fostered by experience of life's absurdities, then Edward Lear got off to a strong start. Next to the last of twenty-one children, a number ridiculous even by Victorian standards, he was just old enough to feel the pratfall when his stockbroker father lost most of the family's money. At the age of six he developed seizures, a few years later fits of depression, then asthma attacks—each an uncontrollably random condition that accompanied him through life. From boyhood Lear excelled at fine drawing, and in 1827 he and the much older sister who had raised him moved from the suburbs into London, where he propped up their meager household on the sale of sketches and illustrations for book publishers and for the British Museum. Then in 1832 he moved to a Lancashire nobleman's estate to paint the exotic menagerie assembled there. Wit and charm won the young draftsman entry into the extended family, and he delighted the children with funny verses improvised in the little "limerick" stanza he had discovered in a recently published book.

That nowadays everybody knows limericks is due to Lear's hugely popular *Book of Nonsense* (1846). The secret lay in his exploitation of the preposterous constraint imposed by the limerick form. Lear understood how well suited the limerick was to supercondensed narrative, and he quickly learned how much funnier it was if the plot of the form trumped the plot of the story—that is, if the return in the last line of the rhyme from line 1 bestowed solemn formal approval on a development that came out of nowhere and signified nothing. In the handful of limericks offered here, some semblance of logic admittedly motivates the chilly Old Man's call for hot toast and the dyspeptic old Person's swearing off rabbits. But we move deeper into Lear country when the absurd dancing of the Old Man of Whitehaven provokes an equally absurd attack that acts out the violence intrinsic to the limerick's non sequitur. We come fully to the heart of the matter with the Old Man who eternally pulls on the bell to no end whatsoever—except the end of the poem, whose rhyme hangs around (like the frazzled figure in Lear's drawing) in irresolute suspense.

Lear, too, seemed busily waiting for a life that never quite emerged. As failing eyesight and bronchial afflictions made specimen illustration impossible and Britain's damp climate intolerable, he chose Italy as his headquarters for travel, sketching and painting, and the preparation of a string of British books picturing vistas from all around the Mediterranean. During visits to London he gave drawing lessons to Queen Victoria, and around 1850 he formed a fervent and apparently unrequited attachment to Edward Lushington, Tennyson's brother-in-law. Through Lushington, with whom he remained friends, he met a lifelong idol in Alfred Tennyson and a confidante in Tennyson's wife Emily; the project of illustrating Tennyson's complete poems, while never consummated, became something of an obsession. Both health and inclination committed Lear well into the 1870s to a nomadic existence that he recorded in drawings, oils, travelogue diaries—and, obliquely, in the peculiar blend of footloose fantasy and wistful drift that informs the best of his *Nonsense Songs* (1871) and *Laughable Lyrics* (1876).

There was an Old Man of the coast,
Who placidly sat on a post;
But when it was cold he relinquished his hold,
And called for some hot buttered toast.

1846

There was an Old Man of Whitehaven,[1]
Who danced a quadrille with a Raven;
But they said—"It's absurd, to encourage this bird!"
So they smashed that Old Man of Whitehaven.

1846

There was an old Person whose habits,
Induced him to feed upon Rabbits;
When he'd eaten eighteen, he turned perfectly green,
Upon which he relinquished those habits.

1846

There was an Old Man who said, "Well!
Will *nobody* answer this bell?
I have pulled day and night, till my hair has grown white,
But nobody answers this bell!"

1846

There was an Old Man of Nepaul,
From his horse had a terrible fall;
But, though split quite in two, by some very strong glue,
They mended that Man of Nepaul.

1846

There was an old man who screamed out
Whenever they knocked him about;
So they took off his boots, And fed him with fruits,
And continued to knock him about.

1871

---

[1]**Whitehaven:** seaport on NW coast of England.

There was an old man, who when little
Fell casually into a kettle;
But, growing too stout, He could never get out,
So he passed all his life in that kettle.

1871

~

The Owl and the Pussy-Cat

— 1 —

The Owl and the Pussy-cat went to sea
   In a beautiful pea-green boat,
They took some honey, and plenty of money,
   Wrapped up in a five-pound note.
The Owl looked up to the stars above,
   And sang to a small guitar,
"O lovely Pussy! O Pussy, my love,
   What a beautiful Pussy you are,
     You are,
     You are!   10
What a beautiful Pussy you are!"

— 2 —

Pussy said to the Owl, "You elegant fowl!
   How charmingly sweet you sing!
O let us be married! too long we have tarried:
   But what shall we do for a ring?"
They sailed away, for a year and a day,
   To the land where the Bong-tree[1] grows
And there in a wood a Piggy-wig stood
   With a ring at the end of his nose,
     His nose,   20
     His nose,
   With a ring at the end of his nose.

[1]**Bong-tree:** Lear's invention, unknown to botany, though it does reappear in "The Dong with a Luminous Nose."

— 3 —

"Dear Pig, are you willing to sell for one shilling
   Your ring?" Said the Piggy, "I will."
So they took it away, and were married next day
   By the Turkey who lives on the hill.
They dined on mince, and slices of quince,
   Which they ate with a runcible spoon;[2]
And hand in hand, on the edge of the sand,
   They danced by the light of the moon,   30
     The moon,
     The moon,
They danced by the light of the moon.

1871

~

The Dong with a Luminous Nose

When awful darkness and silence reign
Over the great Gromboolian plain,[1]
   Through the long, long wintry nights;—
When the angry breakers roar
As they beat on the rocky shore;—
   When Storm-clouds brood on the towering heights
Of the Hills of the Chankly Bore:—

[2]**runcible spoon:** Lear's coinage, subsequently used to name a curved eating utensil with 3 broad prongs.

[1]**Gromboolian plain, Chankly Bore, Bong-tree, Zemmery Fidd, Twangum Tree:** fanciful onomatopoetic inventions all.

Then, through the vast and gloomy dark,
There moves what seems a fiery spark,
   A lonely spark with silvery rays   10
   Piercing the coal-black night,—
   A Meteor strange and bright:—
Hither and thither the vision strays,
   A single lurid light.
Slowly it wanders,—pauses,—creeps,—
Anon it sparkles,—flashes and leaps;
And ever as onward it gleaming goes
A light on the Bong-tree stems it throws.
And those who watch at that midnight hour
From Hall or Terrace, or lofty Tower,   20
Cry, as the wild light passes along,—
      "The Dong!—the Dong!
    'The wandering Dong through the forest goes!
     'The Dong! the Dong!
    'The Dong with a luminous Nose!"

      Long years ago
   The Dong was happy and gay,
Till he fell in love with a Jumbly Girl[2]
   Who came to those shores one day,
For the Jumblies came in a sieve, they did,—   30
Landing at eve near the Zemmery Fidd
   Where the Oblong Oysters grow,
   And the rocks are smooth and gray.
And all the woods and the valleys rang
With the Chorus they daily and nightly sang,—
     "Far and few, far and few,
     Are the lands where the Jumblies live;
     Their heads are green, and their hands are blue
     And they went to sea in a sieve."

Happily, happily passed those days!   40
   While the cheerful Jumblies staid;
   They danced in circlets all night long,
   To the plaintive pipe of the lively Dong,
     In moonlight, shine, or shade.
For day and night he was always there
By the side of the Jumbly Girl so fair,
With her sky-blue hands, and her sea-green hair.
Till the morning came of that hateful day
When the Jumblies sailed in their sieve away,
And the Dong was left on the cruel shore   50
Gazing—gazing for evermore,—
Ever keeping his weary eyes on
That pea-green sail on the far horizon,—
Singing the Jumbly Chorus still

As he sate all day on the grassy hill,—
     "Far and few, far and few,
     Are the lands where the Jumblies live;
     Their heads are green, and their hands are blue,
     And they went to sea in a sieve."

But when the sun was low in the West,   60
   The Dong arose and said;—
—"What little sense I once possessed
   Has quite gone out of my head!"—
And since that day he wanders still
By lake and forest, marsh and hill,
Singing—"O somewhere, in valley or plain
'Might I find my Jumbly Girl again!
'For ever I'll seek by lake and shore
'Till I find my Jumbly Girl once more!"

Playing a pipe with silvery squeaks,   70
Since then his Jumbly Girl he seeks,
And because by night he could not see,
He gathered the bark of the Twangum Tree
On the flowery plain that grows.
And he wove him a wondrous Nose,—
A Nose as strange as a Nose could be!
Of vast proportions and painted red,
And tied with cords to the back of his head.
   —In a hollow rounded space it ended
   With a luminous Lamp within suspended,   80
     All fenced about
      With a bandage stout
      To prevent the wind from blowing it out;—
   And with holes all round to send the light,
   In gleaming rays on the dismal night.

And now each night, and all night long,
Over those plains still roams the Dong;
And above the wail of the Chimp and Snipe
You may hear the squeak of his plaintive pipe
While ever he seeks, but seeks in vain   90
To meet with his Jumbly Girl again;
Lonely and wild—all night he goes,—
The Dong with a luminous Nose!
And all who watch at the midnight hour,
From Hall or Terrace, or lofty Tower,
Cry, as they trace the Meteor bright,
Moving along through the dreary night,—
   "This is the hour when forth he goes,
   The Dong with a luminous Nose!
   'Yonder—over the plain he goes;   100
     He goes!
     He goes;
   The Dong with a luminous Nose!"

---

[2]**Jumbly Girl**: allusion to Lear's nonsense poem "The Jumblies"
(1871), directly quoted in the italicized refrain.

                                        1877

EMILY BRONTË

(1818–1848)

The fifth in a family of six brilliantly talented children, Emily Brontë grew up in the grim, iso-lated village of Haworth in Yorkshire where her father was the clergyman. Her mother and two oldest sisters died when Emily was very young, and the one boy, Branwell, squandered his chances of study and employment and returned home for a squalid decline into dishon-esty, drunkenness, opium, and early death. But Charlotte achieved enduring fame as the au-thor of *Jane Eyre* and other novels; Anne, the youngest, published two interesting novels; and Emily wrote one of the best-known books in the English language, *Wuthering Heights*, as well as some remarkable poetry. (On these and related matters, see Elizabeth Gaskell's *Life of Charlotte Brontë*, pages 524–533.)

Fiercely independent and physically courageous—famous anecdotes include her mastery of large, savage dogs—Emily Brontë was also extremely reclusive. Away from Haworth she was miserable. Since the girls would have to earn their living after their father's death unless they married, they were educated to be teachers. Emily went away to school (the dreadful "Lowood" of *Jane Eyre*) briefly as a child; in 1838 she taught at a boarding school; and in 1842 she studied in Brussels to improve her qualifications in French and German. She seemed scarcely able to survive away from home, however, and after 1842 she remained in Haworth and took responsibility for the household.

As children the Brontës amused themselves by creating elaborate fantasy worlds—ongo-ing, proliferating narratives about distant lands inhabited by a shifting multitude of aristo-crats, soldiers, politicians, and bold, passionate men and women—that provided their apprenticeship as writers. Eventually Charlotte and Branwell took charge of one kingdom, called Angria, and Emily and Anne another, Gondal. In diary notes Emily depicts Gondal, the parsonage, and the British government on the same plane of reality; in 1837 she wrote: "Aunt working in the little Room papa gone out Tabby [the servant] in the kitchen—The Emperors and Empresses of Gondal and Gaaldine preparing to depart from Gaaldine to Gondal to prepare for the coronation which will be on the 12th of July Queen Victoria as-cended the throne this month." As late as 1845 Gondal still flourished, providing imaginative pleasure, practice in composing narrative, and a context for Emily Brontë's poetry. The Gondal prose narratives have disappeared, but one of the surviving notebooks into which Emily transcribed her poems was titled "Gondal Poems," and in many of these, Gondal names or initials identify the speaker or the situation. It is often impossible, however, to tell whether a poem refers specifically to Gondal; and indeed, given the interweaving of Gondal and Yorkshire in the poet's imagination, perhaps it hardly matters. She removed all Gondal names from the published versions.

The sisters' first publication occurred when Charlotte found and read some of Emily's poems and recognized their extraordinary merit. *Poems by Currer, Ellis, and Acton Bell* (that is, Charlotte, Emily, and Anne) appeared in 1846, but the book sold only two copies in its first year. In 1847 they all published novels: Charlotte's *Jane Eyre* was a sensational success, and Emily's *Wuthering Heights* and Anne's *Agnes Grey*, assumed by many to be by the same hand, were widely noticed. Critics recognized the brilliance, originality, and power of Ellis Bell's book, although some professed to be shocked by its depictions of rough manners, cruelty, and passion—qualities often summed up in the word "coarseness"—or were puzzled by its complex narrative strategies.

Within her fiercely guarded private space Emily Brontë found a realm of breathtaking freedom. Her poems are often mysterious, sometimes because they refer to unexplained Gondal stories, but more generally because of the extraordinary flexibility of characters, values, and situations. It is often hard to guess the speakers' gender, since both women and men range the world, assert their individuality, and proclaim their passions like Byronic heroes. Opposites—such as demonic and divine, imprisonment and freedom, domination and submission—shift and merge. Images of captivity and confinement, derived from Gothic and Romantic tales and embellished no doubt in innumerable Gondal dungeons, become occasions for flights of imaginative vision and revels of psychic liberty. In spiritual terms, materiality confines the soul; in gender terms, the Romantic poets' conception of Nature as female creates (for Brontë as for other women poets) a trap to which gender identity condemns the speaking self. But the poetry as a whole celebrates the triumph of visionary freedom despite—or perhaps because of—the constriction of earthly bonds. One might extend the analogy to the verse itself, which develops great richness of music and meaning within strict and apparently very simple formal limits.

When Emily Brontë died, only the twenty-one poems in the 1846 volume had been published. Charlotte edited (and titled and revised) seventeen more in 1850 when she reissued *Wuthering Heights*, and the rest gradually emerged into print during the twentieth century. Poems that Emily Brontë herself revised for publication in 1846 we print as she did; the rest we give as they appear in manuscript.

The night is darkening round me
The wild winds coldly blow
But a tyrant spell has bound me
And I cannot cannot go

The giant trees are bending
Their bare boughs weighed with snow
And the storm is fast descending
And yet I cannot go

Clouds beyond Clouds above me
Wastes beyond Wastes below   10
But nothing drear can move me
I will not cannot go
1837   1902

I am the only being whose doom
No tongue would ask no eye would mourn
I've never caused a thought of gloom
A smile of joy since I was born

In secret pleasure—secret tears
This changful life has slipped away
As freindless after 18 years
As lone as on my natal day

There have been times I cannot hide
There have been hours when this was drear   10
When my sad soul forgot its pride
And longed for one to love me here

But those were in the early glow
of feelings not subdued by care
And they have died so long ago
I hardly now beleive they were

First melted off the hope of youth
Then Fanceys rainbow fast withdrew
And then experience told me truth
in mortal bosoms never grew   20

T'was greif enough to think mankind
All [¹] searvile insincere
But worse to trust to my own mind
And find the same corruption there
1839   1910

---

¹Gap in the manuscript.

The Night Wind[1]

In summer's mellow midnight
A cloudless moon shone through
Our open parlour window
And rosetrees wet with dew—

I sat in silent musing—
The soft wind waved my hair
It told me Heaven was glorious
And sleeping Earth was fair—

I needed not its breathing
To bring such thoughts to me   10
But still it wispered lowly
"How dark the woods will be!—

"The thick leaves in my murmer
"Are rustling like a dream,
"And all their myriad voices
"Instinct with spirit seem"

I said, "go gentle singer,
"Thy wooing voice is kind
"But do not think its music
"Has power to reach my mind—   20

"play with the scented flower,
"The young tree's supple bough—
"And leave my human feelings
"In their own course to flow"

The Wanderer would not leave me
Its kiss grew warmer still—
"O come," it sighed so sweetly
"I'll win thee 'gainst thy will—

"Have we not been from childhood friends?
"Have I not loved thee long?   30
"As long as thou hast loved the night
"Whose silence wakes my song?

"And when thy heart is resting
"Beneath the churcheyard stone
"I shall have time for mourning
"And thou for being alone"—
1840   1850

The Old Stoic

Riches I hold in light esteem;
    And Love I laugh to scorn;
And lust of fame was but a dream
    That vanished with the morn:

And if I pray, the only prayer
    That moves my lips for me
Is, "Leave the heart that now I bear,
    And give me liberty!"

Yes, as my swift days near their goal,
    'Tis all that I implore;   10
In life and death, a chainless soul,
    With courage to endure.
1841   1846

Shall Earth no more inspire thee,
Thou lonely dreamer now?
Since passion may not fire thee
Shall Nature cease to bow?

Thy mind is ever moving
In regions dark to thee;
Recall its useless roving—
Come back and dwell with me—

I know my mountain breezes
Enchant and soothe thee still—   10
I know my sunshine pleases
Despite thy wayward will—

When day with evening blending
Sinks from the summer sky,
I've seen thy spirit bending
In fond[1] idolatry—

I've whached thee every hour—
I know my mighty sway—
I know my magic power
To drive thy greifs away—   20

Few hearts to mortals given
On earth so wildly pine

---

[1]**The Night Wind:** The title may have been added by Charlotte Brontë.

[1]**fond:** foolish.

Yet none would ask a Heaven
More like the Earth than thine—

Then let my winds caress thee—
Thy comrade let me be—
Since nought beside can bless thee—
Return and dwell with me—
1841   *1850*

~

Aye there it is! It wakes to night
Sweet thoughts that will not die
And feeling's fires flash all as bright
As in the years gone by!—

And I can tell by thine altered cheek
And by thy kindled gaze
And by the words thou scearce dost speak,
How wildly fancy plays—

Yes I could swear that glorious wind
Has swept the world aside   10
Has dashed its memory from thy mind
Like foam-bells from the tide—

And thou art now a spirit pouring
Thy presence into all—
The essence of the Tempest's roaring
And of the Tempest's fall—

A universal influence
From Thine own influence free—
A principle of life intense
Lost to mortality—   20

Thus truely when that breast is cold
Thy prisoned soul shall rise
The Dungeon mingle with the mould—
The captive with the skies—
1841   *1850*

~

To Imagination

When weary with the long day's care,
    And earthly change from pain to pain,
And lost and ready to despair,
    Thy kind voice calls me back again:

Oh, my true friend! I am not lone,
While thou canst speak with such a tone!

So hopeless is the world without;
    The world within I doubly prize;
Thy world, where guile, and hate, and doubt,
    And cold suspicion never rise;   10
Where thou, and I, and Liberty,
Have undisputed sovereignty.

What matters it, that, all around,
    Danger, and guilt, and darkness lie,
If but within our bosom's bound
    We hold a bright, untroubled sky,
Warm with ten thousand mingled rays
Of suns that know no winter days?

Reason, indeed, may oft complain
    For Nature's sad reality,   20
And tell the suffering heart, how vain
    Its cherished dreams must always be;
And Truth may rudely trample down
The flowers of Fancy, newly-blown:

But, thou art ever there, to bring
    The hovering vision back, and breathe
New glories o'er the blighted spring,
    And call a lovelier Life from Death,
And whisper, with a voice divine,
Of real worlds, as bright as thine.   30

I trust not to thy phantom bliss,
    Yet, still, in evening's quiet hour,
With never-failing thankfulness,
    I welcome thee, Benignant Power;
Sure solacer of human cares,
And sweeter hope, when hope despairs!
1844   *1846*

~

Plead for Me

Oh, thy bright eyes must answer now,
When Reason, with a scornful brow,
Is mocking at my overthrow!
Oh, thy sweet tongue must plead for me
And tell, why I have chosen thee!

Stern Reason is to judgment come,
Arrayed in all her forms of gloom:
Wilt thou, my advocate, be dumb?
No, radiant angel, speak and say,
Why I did cast the world away.   10

Why I have persevered to shun
The common paths that others run,
And on a strange road journeyed on,
Heedless, alike, of wealth and power—
Of glory's wreath and pleasure's flower.

These, once, indeed, seemed Beings Divine;
And they, perchance, heard vows of mine,
And saw my offerings on their shrine;
But, careless gifts are seldom prized,
And *mine* were worthily despised.   20

So, with a ready heart I swore
To seek their altar-stone no more;
And gave my spirit to adore
Thee, ever-present, phantom thing;
My slave, my comrade, and my king,

A slave, because I rule thee still;
Incline thee to my changeful will,
And make thy influence good or ill:
A comrade, for by day and night
Thou art my intimate delight,—   30

My darling pain that wounds and sears
And wrings a blessing out from tears
By deadening me to earthly cares;
And yet, a king, though Prudence well
Have taught thy subject to rebel.

And am I wrong to worship, where
Faith cannot doubt, nor hope despair,
Since my own soul can grant my prayer?
Speak, God of visions, plead for me,
And tell why I have chosen thee!   40
1844   *1846*

Have I forgot, my only Love, to love thee,
Severed at last by Time's all-severing wave?

Now, when alone, do my thoughts no longer hover
Over the mountains, on that northern shore,
Resting their wings where heath and fern-leaves cover
Thy noble heart for ever, ever more?

Cold in the earth—and fifteen wild Decembers,
From those brown hills, have melted
        into spring: 10
Faithful, indeed, is the spirit that remembers
After such years of change and suffering!

Sweet Love of youth, forgive, if I forget thee,
While the world's tide is bearing me along;
Other desires and other hopes beset me,
Hopes which obscure, but cannot do thee wrong!

No later light has lightened up my heaven,
No second morn has ever shone for me;
All my life's bliss from thy dear life was given,
All my life's bliss is in the grave with thee.   20

But, when the days of golden dreams
        had perished,
And even Despair was powerless to destroy;
Then did I learn how existence could
        be cherished,
Strengthened, and fed without the aid of joy.

Then did I check the tears of useless passion—
Weaned my young soul from yearning after thine;
Sternly denied its burning wish to hasten
Down to that tomb already more than mine.

And, even yet, I dare not let it languish,
Dare not indulge in memory's rapturous pain;   30
Once drinking deep of that divinest anguish,
How could I seek the empty world again?
1845   *1846*

❧ Remembrance[1]

Cold in the earth—and the deep snow piled above thee,
Far, far, removed, cold in the dreary grave!

---

[1]**Remembrance:** The manuscript version has a header, "R Alcona
to J Brenzaida," and other Gondal references.

❧ Death

Death! that struck when I was most confiding
In my certain faith of joy to be—
Strike again, Time's withered branch dividing
From the fresh root of Eternity!

Leaves, upon Time's branch, were
    growing brightly,
Full of sap, and full of silver dew;
Birds beneath its shelter gathered nightly;
Daily round its flowers the wild bees flew.

Sorrow passed, and plucked the
    golden blossom;
Guilt stripped off the foliage in its pride;   10
But, within its parent's kindly bosom,
Flowed for ever Life's restoring tide.

Little mourned I for the parted gladness,
For the vacant nest and silent song—
Hope was there, and laughed me out of sadness;
Whispering, "Winter will not linger long!"

And, behold! with tenfold increase blessing,
Spring adorned the beauty-burdened spray;
Wind and rain and fervent heat, caressing,
Lavished glory on that second May!   20

High it rose—no winged grief could sweep it;
Sin was scared to distance with its shine;
Love, and its own life, had power to keep it
From all wrong—from every blight but thine!

Cruel Death! The young leaves droop
    and languish;
Evening's gentle air may still restore—
No! the morning sunshine mocks my anguish—
Time, for me, must never blossom more!

Strike it down, that other boughs may flourish
Where that perished sapling used to be;   30
Thus, at least, its mouldering corpse will nourish
That from which it sprung—Eternity.

1845   *1846*

Stars

Ah! why, because the dazzling sun
    Restored our Earth to joy,
Have you departed, every one,
    And left a desert sky?

All through the night, your glorious eyes
    Were gazing down in mine,
And, with a full heart's thankful sighs,
    I blessed that watch divine.

I was at peace, and drank your beams
    As they were life to me;   10
And revelled in my changeful dreams,
    Like petrel[1] on the sea.

Thought followed thought, star followed star,
    Through boundless regions, on;
While one sweet influence, near and far,
    Thrilled through, and proved us one!

Why did the morning dawn to break
    So great, so pure, a spell;
And scorch with fire, the tranquil cheek,
    Where your cool radiance fell?   20

Blood-red, he rose, and, arrow-straight,
    His fierce beams struck my brow;
The soul of nature, sprang, elate,
    But *mine* sank sad and low!

My lids closed down, yet through their veil,
    I saw him, blazing, still,
And steep in gold the misty dale,
    And flash upon the hill.

I turned me to the pillow, then,
    To call back night, and see   30
Your worlds of solemn light, again,
    Throb with my heart, and me!

It would not do—the pillow glowed,
    And glowed both roof and floor;
And birds sang loudly in the wood,
    And fresh winds shook the door;

The curtains waved, the wakened flies
    Were murmuring round my room,
Imprisoned there, till I should rise,
    And give them leave to roam.   40

Oh, stars, and dreams, and gentle night;
    Oh, night and stars return!
And hide me from the hostile light,
    That does not warm, but burn;

That drains the blood of suffering men;
    Drinks tears, instead of dew;
Let me sleep through his blinding reign,
    And only wake with you!

1845   *1846*

---

[1]**petrel:** sea bird.

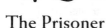

The Prisoner

A Fragment[1]

In the dungeon-crypts, idly did I stray,
Reckless of the lives wasting there away;
"Draw the ponderous bars! open, Warder stern!"
He dared not say me nay—the hinges harshly turn.

"Our guests are darkly lodged," I whisper'd, gazing through
The vault, whose grated eye showed heaven more grey
    than blue;
(This was when glad spring laughed in awaking pride;)
"Aye, darkly lodged enough!" returned my sullen guide.

Then, God forgive my youth; forgive my careless tongue;
I scoffed, as the chill chains on the damp flag-stones
    rung: 10
"Confined in triple walls, art thou so much to fear,
That we must bind thee down and clench thy fetters here?"

The captive raised her face, it was as soft and mild
As sculptured marble saint, or slumbering unwean'd child;
It was so soft and mild, it was so sweet and fair,
Pain could not trace a line, nor grief a shadow there!

The captive raised her hand and pressed it to her brow;
"I have been struck," she said, "and I am suffering now;
Yet these are little worth, your bolts and irons strong,
And, were they forged in steel, they could not hold
    me long."   20

Hoarse laughed the jailor grim: "Shall I be won to hear;
Dost think, fond, dreaming wretch, that *I* shall grant thy
    prayer?
Or, better still, wilt melt my master's heart with groans?
Ah! sooner might the sun thaw down these granite stones.

"My master's voice is low, his aspect bland and kind,
But hard as hardest flint, the soul that lurks behind;
And I am rough and rude, yet not more rough to see
Than is the hidden ghost[2] that has its home in me."

"About her lips there played a smile of almost scorn,
"My friend," she gently said, "you have not heard me
    mourn;   30
When you my kindred's lives, *my* lost life, can restore,
Then may I weep and sue,—but never, friend, before!

"Still, let my tyrants know, I am not doomed to wear
Year after year in gloom, and desolate despair;
A messenger of Hope, comes every night to me,
And offers for short life, eternal liberty.

"He comes with western winds, with evening's wandering
    airs,
With that clear dusk of heaven that brings the thickest
    stars.
Winds take a pensive tone, and stars a tender fire,
And visions rise, and change, that kill me with
    desire.   40

"Desire for nothing known in my maturer years,
When Joy grew mad with awe, at counting future tears.
When, if my spirit's sky was full of flashes warm,
I knew not whence they came, from sun, or
    thunder storm.

"But, first, a hush of peace—a soundless calm descends;
The struggle of distress, and fierce impatience ends.
Mute music soothes my breast, unuttered harmony,
That I could never dream, till Earth was lost to me.

"Then dawns the Invisible; the Unseen its truth reveals;
My outward sense is gone, my inward essence feels: 50
Its wings are almost free—its home, its harbour found,
Measuring the gulph, it stoops, and dares the
    final bound.

"Oh, dreadful is the check—intense the agony—
When the ear begins to hear, and the eye begins to see;
When the pulse begins to throb, the brain to think again,
The soul to feel the flesh, and the flesh to feel the chain.

"Yet I would lose no sting, would wish no torture less,
The more that anguish racks, the earlier it will bless;
And robed in fires of hell, or bright with heavenly shine,
If it but herald death, the vision is divine!"   60

She ceased to speak, and we, unanswering, turned
    to go—
We had no further power to work the captive woe:
Her cheek, her gleaming eye, declared that man
    had given
A sentence, unapproved, and overruled by Heaven.

                                    1846

---

[1]"**The Prisoner:**" All but the final stanza were extracted for publication by Brontë from a manuscript poem beginning "Silent is the House—all are laid asleep." The manuscript is headed "Julian M——and A. G. Rochelle—," names from Gondal; it tells how Julian found Rochelle in his dungeon, released her, nursed her back to health, and won her love.

[2]**ghost:** soul.

No coward soul is mine[1]
No trembler in the world's storm troubled sphere
I see Heaven's glories shine
And Faith shines equal arming me from Fear

O God within my breast
Almighty ever-present Deity
Life, that in me hast rest
As I,—Undying Life, have power in thee

Vain are the thousand creeds
That move men's hearts, unutterably vain,   10
Worthless as withered weeds
Or idlest froth amid the boundless main

To waken doubt in one
Holding so fast by thy infinity
So surely anchored on
The steadfast rock of Immortality

With wide-embracing love
Thy Spirit animates eternal years
Pervades and broods above,
Changes, sustains, dissolves, creates and rears   20

Though Earth and moon were gone
And suns and universes ceased to be
And Thou wert left alone
Every Exsistance would exsist in thee

There is not room for Death
Nor atom that his might could render void
Since Thou art Being and Breath
And what thou art may never be destroyed
1846   1850

~

I'm happiest when most away
I can bear my soul from its home of clay
On a windy night when the moon is bright
And the eye can wander through worlds of light

When I am not and none beside
Nor earth nor sea nor cloudless sky
But only spirit wandering wide
Through infinite imensity
1910

---

[1] **"No coward soul is mine"**: In 1850 Charlotte Brontë mistakenly identified this poem as "the last lines my sister Emily ever wrote."

JOHN RUSKIN

(1819–1900)

Ruskin's boyhood, recorded in his episodic autobiography *Praeterita* (Things Gone By), was strictly overseen yet also conspicuously indulged. He was the only child of parents whose Scottish rectitude was mellowed by the increasing prosperity of his father, a sherry importer who would leave his grown son a very rich man. No expense of time or money was spared in the young Ruskin's education, beginning at his Evangelical mother's knee with repeated traversals of the Bible that profoundly shaped his own prose. As he grew up he was tutored at his suburban home in a variety of subjects, among them the art of drawing, in which he became accomplished. Left much to himself, with few toys or playmates, he also developed precocious powers of observation and a lifelong habit of peremptory judgment. The exceptionally close family made a long tour each year (the British Isles, then the Continent), and when Ruskin went to Oxford in 1837 his mother moved from London into lodgings nearby.

At Oxford, Ruskin attracted some notice, including the poetry prize for 1840, but gained neither academic distinction nor the usual undergraduate friendships, which he seems not to have wanted. His ambition emerged, however, the year after he took his lackluster degree, when a pamphlet undertaken in defense of his favorite artist, J. M. W. Turner, expanded dramatically into *Modern Painters* (1843). This remarkable book won its anonymous author esteem in the new field of critical art appreciation, confirmed his vocation as a prodigy in virtuoso prose, and laid down the main lines of thought about nature and art, truth and imagination, reality and structure, that the rest of his thirty-odd books would pursue. An exhausting self-directed study of Italian art led to a second volume of *Modern Painters* (1846), a work of much expanded range that added an historical dimension to his assertion of art's responsibility to render faithfully the appearances of God's creation. In *The Seven Lamps of Architecture* (1849) he analyzed architectural technique and, significantly, the social conditions that went with it.

These books having made Ruskin famous, *The Stones of Venice* (1851–1853) and three further volumes of *Modern Painters* (1856–1860) consolidated his reputation, which he began using as cultural capital to purchase a hearing for the original and unpopular views that he stubbornly broadcast throughout the second half of his career. Already in "The Nature of Gothic" a meditation on architecture opens into a searing polemic on the ethics of consumption in industrial society. By the end of the decade his magazine series on political economy (including "The Veins of Wealth," presented here) aroused such indignation that the editor shut it down. Ruskin increasingly argued his case about the moral and social implications of Victorian taste in lectures at workingmen's colleges and girls' schools, or in public halls across Britain, like the one in Yorkshire where he affronted a business audience in 1864 with "Traffic." In 1869 he was elected Slade Professor of Fine Art at Oxford, a position he retained with some intermission into the 1880s. Books published during these years dealt in his strongly personal way with such matters as mineralogy, ornithology, botany, and meteorology as well as literature, myth, and art.

Ruskin's public campaigns took place against the background of a catastrophic private life. His 1848 marriage to Euphemia Gray, a decade younger than he, was annulled at her request after six years, having never been sexually consummated; within a year she had married

John Everett Millais, one of Ruskin's PreRaphaelite protégés. In 1858 he acknowledged to himself that his Christian belief had disappeared. In the same year he met nine-year-old Rose La Touche, to whom he became obsessively attached, repeatedly proposing marriage until she died insane in 1875. His own sanity wavered; the deaths of his parents left him emotionally isolated, and the world's indifference to his efforts to change it drove him to barely contained frenzy. Financially independent in the 1870s, he acquired a splendid home in the beautiful English Lake District and sank substantial sums into the Guild of St. George, a utopian agrarian commune he founded on feudal socialist principles "in defiance of the world."

In that spirit of defiance he also adopted the valiant, lonely expedient of publishing a monthly letter to the workers of England called *Fors Clavigera* (Fortune the Club-Bearer), and kept it up from 1871 to 1884. Inaccessible to most of its nominal addressees, *Fors* became in effect a long self-published soliloquy, the serial ruminations of a genius distressed by the diversity of social ills he witnessed and convinced of their systematic mutual reinforcement. The method of *Fors* is evident in the cut-and-paste tactics of Ruskin's late "Storm-Cloud" lecture, and it persisted into the writing of *Praeterita*. The method looks in retrospect like a distillation of his method ever since *Modern Painters*, for the enchanting pyrotechnic scatter of his writing as it appears in the following excerpts is not a by-product of anthologization but an essential element of style. Associative fluency and flagrant digressiveness suggest the interrelation of diverse natural, social, and aesthetic phenomena—the sage's equivalent for the multiplotted complexities of the Victorian social novel.

Ruskin's curiosity about the realities of nature remained unquenchably, incorrigibly naïve: from his early insistence that not even Turner could properly paint a wave crashing on the beach to his flatfooted apocalypticism in the late "Storm-Cloud" about how England's weather was literally changing, he flaunted the obstinacy of an amateur. The quarrels he sporadically picked with Victorian scientists concerned, not the facts of nature, but the need to integrate those facts within a coherent human perspective. Perspective was what Ruskin's studies in the visual arts, too, were about: art, he argued, offers a viewpoint on natural and social truth, and the critical study of art shows how viewpoints are constructed, maintained, and subject to historical change. The most inclusive perspective turns out to be the cultural critic's; and, as no one did more than Ruskin to establish the authority of cultural criticism, it is salutary to recall the eccentricity of his own position. In his intimate relations he could be a loving son or a sort of amorous uncle, in his social posture a visionary utopian or what he himself called a "violent" reactionary, in his manner of address a boy wonder or a patriarch. What he could not be was a mate, a contemporary, a man speaking to men. But his eccentricity was the secret of his command over Victorian readers: standing outside the circle, he could tell them what they saw, what the world they were making looked like, and what such visions meant in human terms.

from **Modern Painters**

Of Water, as Painted by Turner

. . . It will be remembered that it was said above, that Turner[1] was the only painter who had ever represented the surface of calm or the *force* of agitated water. He obtains this expression of force in falling or running water by fearless and full rendering of its forms. He never loses himself and his subject in the splash of the fall—his presence of mind never fails as he goes down; he does not blind us with the spray, or veil the countenance of his fall with its own drapery. A little crumbling white, or lightly rubbed paper, will soon give the effect of indiscriminate foam; but nature gives more than foam—she shows beneath it, and through it, a peculiar character of exquisitely studied form bestowed on every wave and line of fall; and it is this variety of definite character which Turner always aims at, rejecting, as much as possible, everything that conceals or overwhelms it. Thus, in the Upper Fall of the Tees,[2] though the whole basin of the fall is blue and dim with the rising vapour, yet the whole attention of the spectator is directed to that which it was peculiarly difficult to render, the concentric zones and delicate curves of the falling water itself; and it is impossible to express with what exquisite accuracy these are given. They are the characteristic of a powerful stream descending without impediment or break, but from a narrow channel, so as to expand as it falls. They are the constant form which such a stream assumes as it descends; and yet I think it would be difficult to point to another instance of their being rendered in art. You will find nothing in the waterfalls even of our best painters, but springing lines of parabolic descent, and splashing, shapeless foam; and, in consequence, though they may make you understand the swiftness of the water, they never let you feel the weight of it; the stream in their hands looks *active*, not *supine*, as if it leaped, not as if it fell. Now water will leap a little way, it will leap down a weir or over a stone, but it *tumbles* over a high fall like this; and it is when we have lost the parabolic line, and arrived at the catenary,[3]—when we have lost the *spring* of the fall, and arrived at the *plunge* of it, that we begin really to feel its weight and wildness. Where water takes its first leap from the top, it is cool, and collected, and uninteresting, and mathematical, but it is when it finds that it has got into a scrape, and has farther to go than it thought for, that its character comes out; it is then that it begins to writhe, and twist, and sweep out zone after zone in wilder stretching as it falls, and to send down the rocket-like, lance-pointed, whizzing shafts at its sides, sounding for the bottom. And it is this prostration, this hopeless abandonment of its ponderous power to the air, which is always peculiarly expressed by Turner, and especially in the case before us; while our other artists, keeping to the parabolic line, where they do not lose themselves in smoke and foam, make their cataract look muscular and wiry, and may consider themselves fortunate if they can keep it from stopping. I believe the majesty of motion which Turner has given by these concentric catenary lines must be felt even by those who have never seen a high waterfall, and therefore cannot appreciate their exquisite fidelity to nature.

In the Chain Bridge over the Tees, this passiveness and swinging of the water to and fro are yet more remarkable; while we have another characteristic of a great waterfall given to us, that the wind, in this instance coming up the valley against the current, takes the spray up off the edges, and carries it back in little torn, reverted rags and threads, seen in delicate form against the darkness on the left. But we must understand a little more about the nature of running water before we can appreciate the drawing either of this, or any other of Turner's torrents.

When water, not in very great body, runs in a rocky bed much interrupted by hollows, so that it can rest every now and then in a pool as it goes along, it does not acquire a continuous velocity of motion. It pauses after every leap, and curdles about, and rests a little, and then goes on again; and if in this comparatively tranquil and rational state of mind it meets with an obstacle, as a rock or stone, it parts on each side of it with a little bubbling foam, and goes round; if it comes to a step in its bed, it leaps it lightly, and then after a little plashing at the bottom, stops again to take breath. But if its bed be on a continuous slope, not much interrupted by hollows, so that it cannot rest, or if its own mass be so increased by flood that its usual resting-places are not sufficient for it, but that it is perpetually pushed out of them by the following current, before it has had time to tranquillize itself, it of course gains velocity with every yard that it runs; the impetus got at one leap is carried to the credit of the next, until the whole stream becomes one mass of unchecked, accelerating motion. Now when water in this state comes to an obstacle, it does not part at it, but clears it,

---

[1]J. M. W. **Turner** (1775–1851): landscape painter and hero of Ruskin's book.

[2]*Upper Fall of the Tees*: depiction of a Yorkshire waterfall, first of several Turner canvases and engravings this chapter discusses.

[3]**parabolic line, catenary**: respectively the shallower (bending) and steeper (straightening) slopes of a vertical parabola.

like a race-horse; and when it comes to a hollow, it does not fill it up and run out leisurely at the other side, but it rushes down into it and comes up again on the other side, as a ship into the hollow of the sea. Hence the whole appearance of the bed of the stream is changed, and all the lines of the water altered in their nature. The quiet stream is a succession of leaps and pools; the leaps are light and springy, and parabolic, and make a great deal of splashing when they tumble into the pool; then we have a space of quiet curdling water, and another similar leap below. But the stream when it has gained an impetus takes the shape of its bed, never stops, is equally deep and equally swift everywhere, goes down into every hollow, not with a leap, but with a swing, not foaming, nor splashing, but in the bending line of a strong sea-wave, and comes up again on the other side, over rock and ridge, with the ease of a bounding leopard; if it meet a rock three or four feet above the level of its bed, it will neither part nor foam, nor express any concern about the matter, but clear it in a smooth dome of water, without apparent exertion, coming down again as smoothly on the other side; the whole surface of the surge being drawn into parallel lines by its extreme velocity, but foamless, except in places where the form of the bed opposes itself at some direct angle to such a line of fall, and causes a breaker; so that the whole river has the appearance of a deep and raging sea, with this only difference, that the torrent-waves always break backwards, and sea-waves forwards. Thus, then, in the water which has gained an impetus, we have the most exquisite arrangements of curved lines, perpetually changing from convex to concave, and *vice versa*, following every swell and hollow of the bed with their modulating grace, and all in unison of motion, presenting perhaps the most beautiful series of inorganic forms which nature can possibly produce; for the sea runs too much into similar and concave curves with sharp edges, but every motion of the torrent is united, and all its curves are modifications of beautiful line. . . .

As the right rendering of the Alps depends on power of drawing snow, so the right painting of the sea must depend, at least in all coast scenery, in no small measure on the power of drawing foam. Yet there are two conditions of foam of invariable occurrence on breaking waves, of which I have never seen the slightest record attempted; first the thick creamy curdling overlapping massy form which remains for a moment only after the fall of the wave, and is seen in perfection in its running up the beach; and secondly, the thin white coating into which this subsides, which opens into oval gaps and clefts, marbling the waves over their whole surface, and connecting the breakers on a flat shore by long dragging streams of white.

It is evident that the difficulty of expressing either of these two conditions must be immense. The lapping and curdling form is difficult enough to catch even when the lines of its undulation alone are considered; but the lips, so to speak, which lie along these lines, are full, projecting, and marked by beautiful light and shade; each has its high light, a gradation into shadow of indescribable delicacy, a bright reflected light and a dark cast shadow; to draw all this requires labour, and care, and firmness of work, which, as I imagine, must always, however skilfully bestowed, destroy all impression of wildness, accidentalism, and evanescence, and so kill the sea. Again, the openings in the thin subsided foam in their irregular modifications of circular and oval shapes dragged hither and thither, would be hard enough to draw even if they could be seen on a flat surface; instead of which, every one of the openings is seen in undulation on a tossing surface, broken up over small surges and ripples, and so thrown into perspectives of the most hopeless intricacy. Now it is not easy to express the lie of a pattern with oval openings on the folds of drapery. I do not know that any one under the mark of Veronese or Titian[4] could even do this as it ought to be done, yet in drapery much stiffness and error may be overlooked; not so in sea,—the slightest inaccuracy, the slightest want of flow and freedom in the line, is attached by the eye in a moment of high treason, and I believe success to be impossible.

Yet there is not a wave or any violently agitated sea on which both these forms do not appear, the latter especially, after some time of storm, extends over their whole surfaces; the reader sees, therefore, why I said that sea could only be painted by means of more or less dexterous conventionalisms, since two of its most enduring phenomena cannot be represented at all.

Again, as respects the form of breakers on an even shore, there is difficulty of no less formidable kind. There is in them an irreconcilable mixture of fury and formalism. Their hollow surface is marked by parallel lines, like those of a smooth mill-weir,[5] and graduated by reflected and transmitted lights of the most wonderful intricacy, its curve being at the same time necessarily of mathematical purity and precision; yet at the top of this curve, when it nods over, there is a sudden laxity and giving way, the water swings and jumps along the ridge like a shaken chain, and the motion runs from part to part as it does through a

---

[4]Paolo **Veronese** (1528–1588), **Titian** (1490?–1576): Venetian painters.

[5]**mill-weir**: dam built to provide water for turning a mill.

serpent's body. Then the wind is at work on the extreme edge, and instead of letting it fling itself off naturally, it supports it, and drives it back, or scrapes it off, and carries it bodily away; so that the spray at the top is in a continual transition between forms projected by their own weight, and forms blown and carried off with their weight overcome; then at last, when it has come down, who shall say what shape that may be called, which shape has none of the great crash where it touches the beach.

I think it is that last crash which is the great taskmaster. Nobody can do anything with it. I have seen Copley Fielding[6] come very close to the jerk and nod of the lifted threatening edge, curl it very successfully, and without any look of its having been in papers, down nearly to the beach, but the final fall has no thunder in it. Turner has tried hard for it once or twice, but it will not do. The moment is given in the Sidon of the Bible Illustrations, and more elaborately in a painting of Bamborough; in both these cases there is little foam at the bottom, and the fallen breaker looks like a wall, yet grand always; and in the latter picture very beautifully assisted in expression by the tossing of a piece of cable, which some figures are dragging ashore, and which the breaker flings into the air as it falls. Perhaps the most successful rendering of the forms was in the Hero and Leander, but there the drawing was rendered easier by the powerful effect of light which disguised the foam.

It is not, however, from the shore that Turner usually studies his sea. Seen from the land, the curl of the breakers, even in nature, is somewhat uniform and monotonous; the size of the waves out at sea is uncomprehended, and those nearer the eye seem to succeed and resemble each other, to move slowly to the beach, and to break in the same lines and forms.

Afloat even twenty yards from the shore, we receive a totally different impression. Every wave around us appears vast—every one different from all the rest—and the breakers present, now that we see them with their backs towards us, the grand, extended, and varied lines of long curvature, which are peculiarly expressive both of velocity and power. Recklessness, before unfelt, is manifested in the mad, perpetual, changeful, undirected motion, not of wave after wave, as it appears from the shore, but of the very same water rising and falling. Of waves that successively approach and break, each appears to the mind a separate individual, whose part being performed, it perishes, and is

succeeded by another; and there is nothing in this to impress us with the idea of restlessness, any more than in any successive and continuous functions of life and death. But it is when we perceive that it is no succession of wave, but the same water constantly rising, and crashing, and recoiling, and rolling in again in new forms and with fresh fury, that we perceive the perturbed spirit, and feel the intensity of its unwearied rage. The sensation of power is also trebled; for not only is the vastness of apparent size much increased, but the whole action is different; it is not a passive wave rolling sleepily forward until it tumbles heavily, prostrated upon the beach, but a sweeping exertion of tremendous and living strength, which does not now appear to *fall*, but to *burst* upon the shore; which never perishes, but recoils and recovers. . . .

Few people, comparatively, have ever seen the effect on the sea of a powerful gale continued without intermission for three or four days and nights, and to those who have not, I believe it must be unimaginable, not from the mere force or size of surge, but from the complete annihilation of the limit between sea and air. The water from its prolonged agitation is beaten, not into mere creaming foam, but into masses of accumulated yeast,[7] which hang in ropes and wreaths from wave to wave, and where one curls over to break, form a festoon like a drapery, from its edge; these are taken up by the wind, not in dissipating dust, but bodily, in writhing, hanging, coiling masses, which make the air white and thick as with snow, only the flakes are a foot or two long each; the surges themselves are full of foam in their very bodies, underneath, making them white all through, as the water is under a great cataract; and their masses, being thus half water and half air, are torn to pieces by the wind whenever they rise, and carried away in roaring smoke, which chokes and strangles like actual water. Add to this, that when the air has been exhausted of its moisture by long rain, the spray of the sea is caught by it . . . and covers its surface not merely with the smoke of finely divided

---

[6]Anthony Vandyke **Copley Fielding** (1787–1855): watercolorist, Ruskin's boyhood drawing teacher.

[7]**yeast:** The "yesty waves" of Shakspeare have made the likeness familiar, and probably most readers take the expression as merely equivalent to "foamy;" but Shakspeare knew better. Sea-foam does not, under ordinary circumstances, last a moment after it is formed, but disappears, as above described, in a mere white film. But the foam of a prolonged tempest is altogether different; it is "whipped" foam,—thick, permanent, and, in a foul or discolored sea, very ugly, especially in the way it hangs about the tops of the waves, and gathers into clotted concretions before the driving wind. The sea looks truly working or fermenting. [Ruskin's note] The quotation is from *Macbeth* 4.1.53.

water, but with boiling mist; imagine also the low rain-clouds brought down to the very level of the sea, as I have often seen them, whirling and flying in rags and fragments from wave to wave; and finally, conceive the surges themselves in their utmost pitch of power, velocity, vastness, and madness, lifting themselves in precipices and peaks, furrowed with their whirl of ascent, through all this chaos; and you will understand that there is indeed no distinction left between the sea and air; that no object, nor horizon, nor any landmark or natural evidence of position is left; that the heaven is all spray, and the ocean all cloud, and that you can see no farther in any direction than you could see through a cataract. Suppose the effect of the first sunbeam sent from above to show this annihilation to itself, and you have the sea picture of the Academy,[8] 1842—the Snowstorm, one of the very grandest statements of sea-motion, mist, and light that has ever been put on canvas, even by Turner. Of course it was not understood; his finest works never are; but there was some apology for the public's not comprehending this, for few people have had the opportunity of seeing the sea at such a time, and when they have, cannot face it. To hold by a mast or a rock, and watch it, is a prolonged endurance of drowning which few people have courage to go through. To those who have, it is one of the noblest lessons of nature.

But, I think, the noblest sea that Turner has ever painted, and, if so, the noblest certainly ever painted by man, is that of the Slave Ship, the chief Academy picture of the Exhibition of 1840. It is a sunset on the Atlantic after prolonged storm; but the storm is partially lulled, and the torn and streaming rain-clouds are moving in scarlet lines to lose themselves in the hollow of the night. The whole surface of sea included in the picture is divided into two ridges of enormous swell, not high, nor local, but a low, broad heaving of the whole ocean, like the lifting of its bosom by deep-drawn breath after the torture of the storm. Between these two ridges, the fire of the sunset falls along the trough of the sea, dyeing it with an awful but glorious light, the intense and lurid splendor which burns like gold and bathes like blood. Along this fiery path and valley, the tossing waves by which the swell of the sea is restlessly divided, lift themselves in dark, indefinite, fantastic forms, each casting a faint and ghastly shadow behind it along the illumined foam. They do not rise everywhere, but three or four together in wild groups, fitfully and furiously, as the under strength of the swell compels or permits them; leaving between them treacherous spaces of level and whirling water, now lighted with green and lamp-like fire, now flashing back the gold of the declining sun, now fearfully dyed from above with the indistinguishable images of the burning clouds, which fall upon them in flakes of crimson and scarlet, and give to the reckless waves the added motion of their own fiery flying. Purple and blue, the lurid shadows of the hollow breakers are cast upon the mist of the night, which gathers cold and low, advancing like the shadow of death upon the guilty[9] ship as it labours amidst the lightning of the sea, its thin masts written upon the sky in lines of blood, girded with condemnation in that fearful hue which signs the sky with horror, and mixes its flaming flood with the sunlight,—and cast far along the desolate heave of the sepulchral waves, incarnadines the multitudinous sea.[10]

I believe, if I were reduced to rest Turner's immortality upon any single work, I should choose this. Its daring conception—ideal in the highest sense of the word—is based on the purest truth, and wrought out with the concentrated knowledge of a life; its colour is absolutely perfect, not one false or morbid hue in any part or line, and so modulated that every square inch of canvas is a perfect composition; its drawing as accurate as fearless; the ship buoyant, bending, and full of motion; its tones as true as they are wonderful; and the whole picture dedicated to the most sublime of subjects and impressions—(completing thus the perfect system of all truth, which we have shown to be formed by Turner's works)—the power, majesty, and deathfulness of the open, deep, illimitable Sea. (Volume 1, Part 2, Section 5, Chapter 3)

1843

from **The Stones of Venice**
The Nature of Gothic

. . . I believe, then, that the characteristic or moral elements of Gothic are the following, placed in the order of their importance:

1. Savageness.	4. Grotesqueness.
2. Changefulness.	5. Rigidity.
3. Naturalism.	6. Redundance.

---

[8]**Academy:** annual exhibition of the Royal Academy of Arts in London.

[9]**guilty:** She is a slaver, throwing her slaves overboard. The near sea is encumbered with corpses. [Ruskin's note]

[10]**incarnadines . . . sea:** see *Macbeth* 2.2.61.

These characters are here expressed as belonging to the building; as belonging to the builder, they would be expressed thus: 1. Savageness, or Rudeness. 2. Love of Change. 3. Love of Nature. 4. Disturbed Imagination. 5. Obstinacy. 6. Generosity. And I repeat, that the withdrawal of any one, or any two, will not at once destroy the Gothic character of a building, but the removal of a majority of them will. I shall proceed to examine them in their order.

SAVAGENESS. I am not sure when the word "Gothic" was first generically applied to the architecture of the North; but I presume that, whatever the date of its original usage, it was intended to imply reproach, and express the barbaric character of the nations among whom that architecture arose. It never implied that they were literally of Gothic lineage, far less that their architecture had been originally invented by the Goths[1] themselves; but it did imply that they and their buildings together exhibited a degree of sternness and rudeness, which, in contradistinction to the character of Southern and Eastern nations, appeared like a perpetual reflection of the contrast between the Goth and the Roman in their first encounter. And when that fallen Roman, in the utmost impotence of his luxury, and insolence of his guilt, became the model for the imitation of civilized Europe, at the close of the so-called Dark ages, the word Gothic became a term of unmitigated contempt, not unmixed with aversion. From that contempt, by the exertion of the antiquaries and architects of this century, Gothic architecture has been sufficiently vindicated; and perhaps some among us, in our admiration of the magnificent science of its structure, and sacredness of its expression, might desire that the term of ancient reproach should be withdrawn, and some other, of more apparent honourableness, adopted in its place. There is no chance, as there is no need, of such a substitution. As far as the epithet was used scornfully, it was used falsely; but there is no reproach in the word, rightly understood; on the contrary, there is a profound truth, which the instinct of mankind almost unconsciously recognizes. It is true, greatly and deeply true, that the architecture of the North is rude and wild; but it is not true, that, for this reason, we are to condemn it, or despise. Far otherwise: I believe it is in this very character that it deserves our profoundest reverence.

The charts of the world which have been drawn up by modern science have thrown into a narrow space the expression of a vast amount of knowledge, but I have never yet seen any one pictorial enough to enable the spectator to imagine the kind of contrast in physical character which exists between Northern and Southern countries. We know the differences in detail, but we have not that broad glance and grasp which would enable us to feel them in their fulness. We know that gentians grow on the Alps, and olives on the Apennines; but we do not enough conceive for ourselves that variegated mosaic of the world's surface which a bird sees in its migration, that difference between the district of the gentian and of the olive which the stork and the swallow see far off, as they lean upon the sirocco wind.[2] Let us, for a moment, try to raise ourselves even above the level of their flight, and imagine the Mediterranean lying beneath us like an irregular lake, and all its ancient promontories sleeping in the sun: here and there an angry spot of thunder, a grey stain of storm, moving upon the burning field; and here and there a fixed wreath of white volcano smoke, surrounded by its circle of ashes; but for the most part a great peacefulness of light, Syria and Greece, Italy and Spain, laid like pieces of a golden pavement into the sea-blue, chased, as we stoop nearer to them, with bossy beaten work of mountain chains, and glowing softly with terraced gardens, and flowers heavy with frankincense, mixed among masses of laurel, and orange and plumy palm, that abate with their grey-green shadows the burning of the marble rocks, and of the ledges of porphyry sloping under lucent sand. Then let us pass farther towards the north, until we see the orient colors change gradually into a vast belt of rainy green, where the pastures of Switzerland, and poplar valleys of France, and dark forests of the Danube and Carpathians stretch from the mouths of the Loire to those of the Volga, seen through clefts in grey swirls of rain-cloud and flaky veils of the mist of the brooks, spreading low along the pasture lands: and then, farther north still, to see the earth heave into mighty masses of leaden rock and heathy moor, bordering with a broad waste of gloomy purple that belt of field and wood, and splintering into irregular and grisly islands amidst the northern seas, beaten by storm and chilled by ice-drift, and tormented by furious pulses of contending tide, until the roots of the last forests fail from among the hill ravines, and the hunger of the north wind bites their peaks into barrenness; and, at last, the wall of ice, durable like iron, sets, deathlike, its white teeth against us out of the polar twilight. And, having once traversed in thought its gradation of the zoned iris[3] of the earth in all its material

---

[1]**Goths:** ancient Germanic people.

[2]**sirocco:** wind that blows northward across the Mediterranean into Europe.

[3]**iris:** prism.

vastness, let us go down nearer to it, and watch the parallel change in the belt of animal life: the multitudes of swift and brilliant creatures that glance in the air and sea, or tread the sands of the southern zone; striped zebras and spotted leopards, glistening serpents, and birds arrayed in purple and scarlet. Let us contrast their delicacy and brilliancy of color, and swiftness of motion, with the frost-cramped strength, and shaggy covering, and dusky plumage of the northern tribes; contrast the Arabian horse with the Shetland, the tiger and leopard with the wolf and bear, the antelope with the elk, the bird of paradise with the osprey: and then, submissively acknowledging the great laws by which the earth and all that it bears are ruled throughout their being, let us not condemn, but rejoice at the expression by man of his own rest in the statutes of the lands that gave him birth. Let us watch him with reverence as he sets side by side the burning gems, and smoothes with soft sculpture the jasper pillars, that are to reflect a ceaseless sunshine, and rise into a cloudless sky: but not with less reverence let us stand by him, when, with rough strength and hurried stroke, he smites an uncouth animation out of the rocks which he has torn from among the moss of the moorland, and heaves into the darkened air the pile of iron buttress and rugged wall, instinct with work of an imagination as wild and wayward as the northern sea; creations of ungainly shape and rigid limb, but full of wolfish life; fierce as the winds that beat and changeful as the clouds that shade them.

There is, I repeat, no degradation, no reproach in this, but all dignity and honourableness; and we should err grievously in refusing either to recognise as an essential character of the existing architecture of the North, or to admit as a desirable character in that which it yet may be, this wildness of thought, and roughness of work; this look of mountain brotherhood between the cathedral and the Alp; this magnificence of sturdy power, put forth only the more energetically because the fine finger-touch was chilled away by the frosty wind, and the eye dimmed by the moor-mist, or blinded by the hail; this outspeaking of the strong spirit of men who may not gather redundant fruitage from the earth, nor bask in dreamy benignity of sunshine, but must break the rock for bread, and cleave the forest for fire, and show, even in what they did for their delight, some of the hard habits of the arm and heart that grew on them as they swung the axe or pressed the plough.

If, however, the savageness of Gothic architecture, merely as an expression of its origin among Northern nations, may be considered, in some sort, a noble character, it possesses a higher nobility still, when considered as an index, not of climate, but of religious principle.

In . . . the first volume of this work, it was noticed that the systems of architectural ornament, properly so called, might be divided into three:—1. Servile ornament, in which the execution or power of the inferior workman is entirely subjected to the intellect of the higher;—2. Constitutional ornament, in which the executive inferior power is, to a certain point, emancipated and independent, having a will of its own, yet confessing its inferiority and rendering obedience to higher powers;—and 3. Revolutionary ornament, in which no executive inferiority is admitted at all. I must here explain the nature of these divisions at somewhat greater length.

Of Servile ornament, the principal schools are the Greek, Ninevite,[4] and Egyptian; but their servility is of different kinds. The Greek master-workman was far advanced in knowledge and power above the Assyrian or Egyptian. Neither he nor those for whom he worked could endure the appearance of imperfection in anything; and, therefore, what ornament he appointed to be done by those beneath him was composed of mere geometrical forms,—balls, ridges, and perfectly symmetrical foliage,—which could be executed with absolute precision by line and rule, and were as perfect in their way when completed, as his own figure sculpture. The Assyrian and Egyptian, on the contrary, less cognizant of accurate form in anything, were content to allow their figure sculpture to be executed by inferior workmen, but lowered the method of its treatment to a standard which every workman could reach, and then trained him by discipline so rigid, that there was no chance of his falling beneath the standard appointed. The Greek gave to the lower workman no subject which he could not perfectly execute. The Assyrian gave him subjects which he could only execute imperfectly, but fixed a legal standard for his imperfection. The workman was, in both systems, a slave.[5]

But in the mediæval, or especially Christian, system of ornament, this slavery is done away with altogether; Christianity having recognized, in small things as well as great, the individual value of every soul. But it not only recognizes its value; it confesses its imperfection, in only bestowing

---

[4]**Ninevite**: of Nineveh in ancient Assyria.

[5]**slave**: The third kind of ornament, the Renaissance, is that in which the inferior detail becomes principal, the executor of every minor portion being required to exhibit skill and possess knowledge as great as that which is possessed by the master of the design; and in the endeavor to endow him with this skill and knowledge, his own original power is overwhelmed, and the whole building becomes a wearisome exhibition of well-educated imbecility. [Ruskin's note]

dignity upon the acknowledgment of unworthiness. That admission of lost power and fallen nature, which the Greek or Ninevite felt to be intensely painful, and, as far as might be, altogether refused, the Christian makes daily and hourly, contemplating the fact of it without fear, as tending, in the end, to God's greater glory. Therefore, to every spirit which Christianity summons to her service, her exhortation is: Do what you can, and confess frankly what you are unable to do; neither let your effort be shortened for fear of failure, nor your confession silenced for fear of shame. And it is, perhaps, the principal admirableness of the Gothic schools of architecture, that they thus receive the results of the labor of inferior minds; and out of fragments full of imperfection, and betraying that imperfection in every touch, indulgently raise up a stately and unaccusable whole.

But the modern English mind has this much in common with that of the Greek, that it intensely desires, in all things, the utmost completion or perfection compatible with their nature. This is a noble character in the abstract, but becomes ignoble when it causes us to forget the relative dignities of the nature itself, and to prefer the perfectness of the lower nature to the imperfection of the higher; not considering that as, judged by such a rule, all the brute animals would be preferable to man, because more perfect in their functions and kind, and yet are always held inferior to him, so also in the works of man, those which are more perfect in their kind are always inferior to those which are, in their nature, liable to more faults and shortcomings. For the finer the nature, the more flaws it will show through the clearness of it; and it is a law of this universe, that the best things shall be seldomest seen in their best form. The wild grass grows well and strongly, one year with another; but the wheat is, according to the greater nobleness of its nature, liable to the bitterer blight. And therefore, while in all things that we see, or do, we are to desire perfection, and strive for it, we are nevertheless not to set the meaner thing, in its narrow accomplishment, above the nobler thing, in its mighty progress; not to esteem smooth minuteness above shattered majesty; not to prefer mean victory to honourable defeat; not to lower the level of our aim, that we may the more surely enjoy the complacency of success. But, above all, in our dealings with the souls of other men, we are to take care how we check, by severe requirement or narrow caution, efforts which might otherwise lead to a noble issue; and, still more, how we withhold our admiration from great excellences, because they are mingled with rough faults. Now, in the make and nature of every man, however rude or simple, whom we employ in manual labour, there are some powers for better things: some tardy imagination, torpid capacity of emotion, tottering steps of thought, there are, even at the worst; and in

most cases it is all our own fault that they *are* tardy or torpid. But they cannot be strengthened, unless we are content to take them in their feebleness, and unless we prize and honour them in their imperfection above the best and most perfect manual skill. And this is what we have to do with all our labourers; to look for the *thoughtful* part of them, and get that out of them, whatever we lose for it, whatever faults and errors we are obliged to take with it. For the best that is in them cannot manifest itself, but in company with much error. Understand this clearly: You can teach a man to draw a straight line, and to cut one; to strike a curved line, and to carve it; and to copy and carve any number of given lines or forms, with admirable speed and perfect precision; and you find his work perfect of its kind: but if you ask him to think about any of those forms, to consider if he cannot find any better in his own head, he stops; his execution becomes hesitating; he thinks, and ten to one he thinks wrong; ten to one he makes a mistake in the first touch he gives to his work as a thinking being. But you have made a man of him for all that. He was only a machine before, an animated tool.

And observe, you are put to stern choice in this matter. You must either make a tool of the creature, or a man of him. You cannot make both. Men were not intended to work with the accuracy of tools, to be precise and perfect in all their actions. If you will have that precision out of them, and make their fingers measure degrees like cog-wheels, and their arms strike curves like compasses, you must unhumanize them. All the energy of their spirits must be given to make cogs and compasses of themselves. All their attention and strength must go to the accomplishment of the mean act. The eye of the soul must be bent upon the finger-point, and the soul's force must fill all the invisible nerves that guide it, ten hours a day, that it may not err from its steely precision, and so soul and sight be worn away, and the whole human being be lost at last—a heap of sawdust, so far as its intellectual work in this world is concerned; saved only by its Heart, which cannot go into the form of cogs and compasses, but expands, after the ten hours are over, into fireside humanity. On the other hand, if you will make a man of the working creature, you cannot make a tool. Let him but begin to imagine, to think, to try to do anything worth doing; and the engine-turned precision is lost at once. Out come all his roughness, all his dulness, all his incapability; shame upon shame, failure upon failure, pause after pause: but out comes the whole majesty of him also; and we know the height of it only, when we see the clouds settling upon him. And, whether the clouds be bright or dark, there will be transfiguration behind and within them.

And now, reader, look round this English room of yours, about which you have been proud so often, because the work of it was so good and strong, and the ornaments of it so finished. Examine again all those accurate mouldings, and perfect polishings, and unerring adjustments of the seasoned wood and tempered steel. Many a time you have exulted over them, and thought how great England was, because her slightest work was done so thoroughly. Alas! if read rightly, these perfectnesses are signs of a slavery in our England a thousand times more bitter and more degrading than that of the scourged African, or helot Greek.[6] Men may be beaten, chained, tormented, yoked like cattle, slaughtered like summer flies, and yet remain in one sense, and the best sense, free. But to smother their souls within them, to blight and hew into rotting pollards[7] the suckling branches of their human intelligence, to make the flesh and skin which, after the worm's work on it, is to see God, into leathern thongs to yoke machinery with,—this it is to be slave-masters indeed; and there might be more freedom in England, though her feudal lords' lightest words were worth men's lives, and though the blood of the vexed husbandman dropped in the furrows of her fields, than there is while the animation of her multitudes is sent like fuel to feed the factory smoke, and the strength of them is given daily to be wasted into the fineness of a web, or racked into the exactness of a line.

And, on the other hand, go forth again to gaze upon the old cathedral front, where you have smiled so often at the fantastic ignorance of the old sculptors: examine once more those ugly goblins, and formless monsters, and stern statues, anatomiless and rigid; but do not mock at them, for they are signs of the life and liberty of every workman who struck the stone; a freedom of thought, and rank in scale of being, such as no laws, no charters, no charities can secure; but which it must be the first aim of all Europe at this day to regain for her children.

Let me not be thought to speak wildly or extravagantly. It is verily this degradation of the operative into a machine, which, more than any other evil of the times, is leading the mass of the nations everywhere into vain, incoherent, destructive struggling for a freedom of which they cannot explain the nature to themselves. Their universal outcry against wealth, and against nobility, is not forced from them either by the pressure of famine, or the sting of mortified pride. These do much, and have done much in all ages; but the foundations of society were never yet shaken as they are at this day. It is not that men are ill fed, but that they have no pleasure in the work by which they make their bread, and therefore look to wealth as the only means of pleasure. It is not that men are pained by the scorn of the upper classes, but they cannot endure their own; for they feel that the kind of labor to which they are condemned is verily a degrading one, and makes them less than men. Never had the upper classes so much sympathy with the lower, or charity for them, as they have at this day, and yet never were they so much hated by them: for, of old, the separation between the noble and the poor was merely a wall built by law; now it is a veritable difference in level of standing, a precipice between upper and lower grounds in the field of humanity, and there is pestilential air at the bottom of it. I know not if a day is ever to come when the nature of right freedom will be understood, and when men will see that to obey another man, to labour for him, yield reverence to him or to his place, is not slavery. It is often the best kind of liberty,—liberty from care. The man who says to one, Go, and he goeth, and to another, Come, and he cometh,[8] has, in most cases, more sense of restraint and difficulty than the man who obeys him. The movements of the one are hindered by the burden on his shoulder; of the other, by the bridle on his lips: there is no way by which the burden may be lightened; but we need not suffer from the bridle if we do not champ at it. To yield reverence to another, to hold ourselves and our lives at his disposal, is not slavery; often, it is the noblest state in which a man can live in this world. There is, indeed, a reverence which is servile, that is to say, irrational or selfish: but there is also noble reverence, that is to say, reasonable and loving; and a man is never so noble as when he is reverent in this kind; nay, even if the feeling pass the bounds of mere reason, so that it be loving, a man is raised by it. Which had, in reality, most of the serf nature in him,—the Irish peasant who was lying in wait yesterday for his landlord, with his musket muzzle thrust through the ragged hedge; or that old mountain servant, who, 200 years ago, at Inverkeithing,[9] gave up his own life and the lives of his seven sons for his chief?— and as each fell, calling forth his brother to the death, "Another for Hector!" And therefore, in all ages and all countries, reverence has been paid and sacrifice made by men to each other, not only without complaint, but rejoicingly; and famine, and peril, and sword, and all evil, and all shame, have been borne willingly in the causes of masters and kings; for all these gifts of the heart ennobled the men who gave, not less than the men who received them, and

---

[6]**helot**: member of servant class in ancient Sparta.

[7]**pollards**: trees lopped of their branches.

[8]**Go . . . cometh**: Matthew 8:9.

[9]**Inverkeithing**: where, according to Scott's *Fair Maid of Perth* (1828), a family gave their lives for Sir **Hector** Maclean.

nature prompted, and God rewarded the sacrifice. But to feel their souls withering within them, unthanked, to find their whole being sunk into an unrecognized abyss, to be counted off into a heap of mechanism, numbered with its wheels, and weighed with its hammer strokes;—this nature bade not,—this God blesses not,—this humanity for no long time is able to endure.

We have much studied and much perfected, of late, the great civilized invention of the division of labour; only we give it a false name. It is not, truly speaking, the labour that is divided; but the men:—Divided into mere segments of men—broken into small fragments and crumbs of life; so that all the little piece of intelligence that is left in a man is not enough to make a pin, or a nail, but exhausts itself in making the point of a pin, or the head of a nail. Now it is a good and desirable thing, truly, to make many pins in a day; but if we could only see with what crystal sand their points were polished,—sand of human soul, much to be magnified before it can be discerned for what it is,—we should think there might be some loss in it also. And the great cry that rises from all our manufacturing cities, louder than their furnace blast, is all in very deed for this,—that we manufacture everything there except men; we blanch cotton, and strengthen steel, and refine sugar, and shape pottery; but to brighten, to strengthen, to refine, or to form a single living spirit, never enters into our estimate of advantages. And all the evil to which that cry is urging our myriads can be met only in one way: not by teaching nor preaching, for to teach them is but to show them their misery, and to preach to them, if we do nothing more than preach, is to mock at it. It can be met only by a right understanding, on the part of all classes, of what kinds of labour are good for men, raising them, and making them happy; by a determined sacrifice of such convenience, or beauty, or cheapness as is to be got only by the degradation of the workman; and by equally determined demand for the products and results of healthy and ennobling labour.

And how, it will be asked, are these products to be recognized, and this demand to be regulated? Easily: by the observance of three broad and simple rules:

1. Never encourage the manufacture of any article not absolutely necessary, in the production of which *Invention* has no share.
2. Never demand an exact finish for its own sake, but only for some practical or noble end.
3. Never encourage imitation or copying of any kind, except for the sake of preserving record of great works.

The second of these principles is the only one which directly rises out of the consideration of our immediate sub-

ject; but I shall briefly explain the meaning and extent of the first also, reserving the enforcement of the third for another place.

1. Never encourage the manufacture of anything not necessary, in the production of which invention has no share.

For instance. Glass beads are utterly unnecessary, and there is no design or thought employed in their manufacture. They are formed by first drawing out the glass into rods; these rods are chopped up into fragments of the size of beads by the human hand, and the fragments are then rounded in the furnace. The men who chop up the rods sit at their work all day, their hands vibrating with a perpetual and exquisitely timed palsy, and the beads dropping beneath their vibration like hail. Neither they, nor the men who draw out the rods, or fuse the fragments, have the smallest occasion for the use of any single human faculty; and every young lady, therefore, who buys glass beads is engaged in the slave-trade,[10] and in a much more cruel one than that which we have so long been endeavouring to put down.

But glass cups and vessels may become the subjects of exquisite invention; and if in buying these we pay for the invention, that is to say for the beautiful form, or color, or engraving, and not for mere finish of execution, we are doing good to humanity.

So, again, the cutting of precious stones, in all ordinary cases, requires little exertion of any mental faculty; some tact and judgment in avoiding flaws, and so on, but nothing to bring out the whole mind. Every person who wears cut jewels merely for the sake of their value is, therefore, a slave-driver.

But the working of the goldsmith, and the various designing of grouped jewellery and enamel-work, may become the subject of the most noble human intelligence. Therefore, money spent in the purchase of well-designed plate, of precious engraved vases, cameos, or enamels, does good to humanity; and, in work of this kind, jewels may be employed to heighten its splendour; and their cutting is then a price paid for the attainment of a noble end, and thus perfectly allowable.

I shall perhaps press this law farther elsewhere, but our immediate concern is chiefly with the second, namely, never to demand an exact finish, when it does not lead to a noble end. For observe, I have only dwelt upon the rudeness of Gothic, or any other kind of imperfectness, as admirable,

---

[10]**slave-trade:** abolished in Britain 1807, in British colonies 1833.

where it was impossible to get design or thought without it. If you are to have the thought of a rough and untaught man, you must have it in a rough and untaught way; but from an educated man, who can without effort express his thoughts in an educated way, take the graceful expression, and be thankful. Only *get* the thought, and do not silence the peasant because he cannot speak good grammar, or until you have taught him his grammar. Grammar and refinement are good things, both, only be sure of the better thing first. And thus in art, delicate finish is desirable from the greatest masters, and is always given by them. In some places Michael Angelo, Leonardo, Phidias, Perugino, Turner,[11] all finished with the most exquisite care; and the finish they give always leads to the fuller accomplishment of their noble purposes. But lower men than these cannot finish, for it requires consummate knowledge to finish consummately, and then we must take their thoughts as they are able to give them. So the rule is simple: Always look for invention first, and after that, for such execution as will help the invention, and as the inventor is capable of without painful effort, and *no more.* Above all, demand no refinement of execution where there is no thought, for that is slaves' work, unredeemed. Rather choose rough work than smooth work, so only that the practical purpose be answered, and never imagine there is reason to be proud of anything that may be accomplished by patience and sandpaper.

I shall only give one example, which however will show the reader what I mean, from the manufacture already alluded to, that of glass. Our modern glass is exquisitely clear in its substance, true in its form, accurate in its cutting. We are proud of this. We ought to be ashamed of it. The old Venice glass was muddy, inaccurate in all its forms, and clumsily cut, if at all. And the old Venetian was justly proud of it. For there is this difference between the English and Venetian workman, that the former thinks only of accurately matching his patterns, and getting his curves perfectly true and his edges perfectly sharp, and becomes a mere machine for rounding curves and sharpening edges, while the old Venetian cared not a whit whether his edges were sharp or not, but he invented a new design for every glass that he made, and never moulded a handle or a lip without a new fancy in it. And therefore, though some Venetian glass is ugly and clumsy enough, when made by clumsy and uninventive workmen, other Venetian glass is so

lovely in its forms that no price is too great for it; and we never see the same form in it twice. Now you cannot have the finish and the varied form too. If the workman is thinking about his edges, he cannot be thinking of his design; if of his design, he cannot think of his edges. Choose whether you will pay for the lovely form or the perfect finish, and choose at the same moment whether you will make the worker a man or a grindstone.

Nay, but the reader interrupts me,—"If the workman can design beautifully, I would not have him kept at the furnace. Let him be taken away and made a gentleman, and have a studio, and design his glass there, and I will have it blown and cut for him by common workmen, and so I will have my design and my finish too."

All ideas of this kind are founded upon two mistaken suppositions: the first, that one man's thoughts can be, or ought to be, executed by another man's hands; the second, that manual labour is a degradation, when it is governed by intellect.

On a large scale, and in work determinable by line and rule, it is indeed both possible and necessary that the thoughts of one man should be carried out by the labor of others; in this sense I have already defined the best architecture to be the expression of the mind of manhood by the hands of childhood. But on a smaller scale, and in a design which cannot be mathematically defined, one man's thoughts can never be expressed by another: and the difference between the spirit of touch of the man who is inventing, and of the man who is obeying directions, is often all the difference between a great and a common work of art. How wide the separation is between original and second-hand execution, I shall endeavour to show elsewhere; it is not so much to our purpose here as to mark the other and more fatal error of despising manual labour when governed by intellect; for it is no less fatal an error to despise it when thus regulated by intellect, than to value it for its own sake. We are always in these days endeavouring to separate the two; we want one man to be always thinking, and another to be always working, and we call one a gentleman, and the other an operative; whereas the workman ought often to be thinking, and the thinker often to be working, and both should be gentlemen, in the best sense. As it is, we make both ungentle, the one envying, the other despising, his brother; and the mass of society is made up of morbid thinkers, and miserable workers. Now it is only by labour that thought can be made healthy, and only by thought that labour can be made happy, and the two cannot be separated with impunity. It would be well if all of us were good handicraftsmen in some kind, and the dishonour of manual

---

[11]**Phidias** (490?–430 BCE): Athenian sculptor. **Perugino** (1450?–1523): Italian painter. J. M. W. **Turner** (1775–1851): English artist, hero of Ruskin's *Modern Painters*.

labour done away with altogether; so that though there should still be a trenchant distinction of race between nobles and commoners, there should not, among the latter, be a trenchant distinction of employment, as between idle and working men, or between men of liberal and illiberal professions. All professions should be liberal, and there should be less pride felt in peculiarity of employment, and more in excellence of achievement. And yet more, in each several profession, no master should be too proud to do its hardest work. The painter should grind his own colours; the architect work in the mason's yard with his men; the master-manufacturer be himself a more skilful operative than any man in his mills; and the distinction between one man and another be only in experience and skill, and the authority and wealth which these must naturally and justly obtain.

I should be led far from the matter in hand, if I were to pursue this interesting subject. Enough, I trust, has been said to show the reader that the rudeness or imperfection which at first rendered the term "Gothic" one of reproach is indeed, when rightly understood, one of the most noble characters of Christian architecture, and not only a noble but an *essential* one. It seems a fantastic paradox, but it is nevertheless a most important truth, that no architecture can be truly noble which is *not* imperfect. And this is easily demonstrable. For since the architect, whom we will suppose capable of doing all in perfection, cannot execute the whole with his own hands, he must either make slaves of his workmen in the old Greek, and present English fashion, and level his work to a slave's capacities, which is to degrade it; or else he must take his workmen as he finds them, and let them show their weaknesses together with their strength, which will involve the Gothic imperfection, but render the whole work as noble as the intellect of the age can make it.

But the principle may be stated more broadly still. I have confined the illustration of it to architecture, but I must not leave it as if true of architecture only. Hitherto I have used the words imperfect and perfect merely to distinguish between work grossly unskilful, and work executed with average precision and science; and I have been pleading that any degree of unskilfulness should be admitted, so only that the labourer's mind had room for expression. But, accurately speaking, no good work whatever can be perfect, and *the demand for perfection is always a sign of a misunderstanding of the ends of art.*

This for two reasons, both based on everlasting laws. The first, that no great man ever stops working till he has reached his point of failure; that is to say, his mind is always far in advance of his powers of execution, and the latter will now and then give way in trying to follow it; besides that he will always give to the inferior portions of his work only such inferior attention as they require; and according to his greatness he becomes so accustomed to the feeling of dissatisfaction with the best he can do, that in moments of lassitude or anger with himself he will not care though the beholder be dissatisfied also. I believe there has only been one man who would not acknowledge this necessity, and strove always to reach perfection, Leonardo; the end of his vain effort being merely that he would take ten years to a picture, and leave it unfinished. And therefore, if we are to have great men working at all, or less men doing their best, the work will be imperfect, however beautiful. Of human work none but what is bad can be perfect, in its own bad way.[12]

The second reason is, that imperfection is in some sort essential to all that we know of life. It is the sign of life in a mortal body, that is to say, of a state of progress and change. Nothing that lives is, or can be, rigidly perfect; part of it is decaying, part nascent. The foxglove blossom,—a third part bud, a third part past, a third part in full bloom,—is a type of the life of this world. And in all things that live there are certain irregularities and deficiencies which are not only signs of life, but sources of beauty. No human face is exactly the same in its lines on each side, no leaf perfect in its lobes, no branch in its symmetry. All admit irregularity as they imply change; and to banish imperfection is to destroy expression, to check exertion, to paralyse vitality. All things are literally better, lovelier, and more beloved for the imperfections which have been divinely appointed, that the law of human life may be Effort, and the law of human judgment, Mercy.

Accept this then for a universal law, that neither architecture nor any other noble work of man can be good unless it be imperfect; and let us be prepared for the otherwise strange fact, which we shall discern clearly as we approach the period of the Renaissance, that the first cause of the fall of the arts of Europe was a relentless requirement of perfection, incapable alike either of being silenced by veneration for greatness, or softened into forgiveness of simplicity. . . .

The fifth element above named was RIGIDITY; and this character I must endeavour carefully to define, for neither

---

[12]**bad way:** The Elgin marbles are supposed by many to be "perfect." In the most important portions they indeed approach perfection, but only there. The draperies are unfinished, the hair and wool of the animals are unfinished, and the entire bas-reliefs of the frieze are roughly cut. [Ruskin's note]

the word I have used, nor any other that I can think of, will express it accurately. For I mean, not merely stable, but *active* rigidity; the peculiar energy which gives tension to movement, and stiffness to resistance, which makes the fiercest lightning forked rather than curved, and the stoutest oak-branch angular rather than bending, and is as much seen in the quivering of the lance as in the glittering of the icicle.

I have before had occasion . . . to note some manifestations of this energy or fixedness; but it must be still more attentively considered here, as it shows itself throughout the whole structure and decoration of Gothic work. Egyptian and Greek buildings stand, for the most part, by their own weight and mass, one stone passively incumbent on another: but in the Gothic vaults and traceries there is a stiffness analogous to that of the bones of a limb, or fibres of a tree; an elastic tension and communication of force from part to part, and also a studious expression of this throughout every visible line of the building. And, in like manner, the Greek and Egyptian ornament is either mere surface engraving, as if the face of the wall had been stamped with a seal, or its lines are flowing, lithe, and luxuriant; in either case, there is no expression of energy in framework of the ornament itself. But the Gothic ornament stands out in prickly independence, and frosty fortitude, jutting into crockets,[13] and freezing into pinnacles; here starting up into a monster, there germinating into a blossom; anon knitting itself into a branch, alternately thorny, bossy, and bristly, or writhed into every form of nervous entanglement; but, even when most graceful, never for an instant languid, always quickset; erring, if at all, ever on the side of brusquerie.

The feelings or habits in the workman which give rise to this character in the work, are more complicated and various than those indicated by any other sculptural expression hitherto named. There is, first, the habit of hard and rapid working; the industry of the tribes of the North, quickened by the coldness of the climate, and giving an expression of sharp energy to all they do . . . as opposed to the languor of the Southern tribes, however much of fire there may be in the heart of that languor, for lava itself may flow languidly. There is also the habit of finding enjoyment in the signs of cold, which is never found, I believe, in the inhabitants of countries south of the Alps. Cold is to them an unredeemed evil, to be suffered, and forgotten as soon as may be; but the long winter of the North forces the Goth (I mean the En-glishman, Frenchman, Dane, or German), if he would lead a happy life at all, to find sources of happiness in foul weather as well as fair, and to rejoice in the leafless as well as in the shady forest. And this we do with all our hearts; finding perhaps nearly as much contentment by the Christmas fire as in the summer sunshine, and gaining health and strength on the ice-fields of winter, as well as among the meadows of spring. So that there is nothing adverse or painful to our feelings in the cramped and stiffened structure of vegetation checked by cold; and instead of seeking, like the Southern sculptor, to express only the softness of leafage nourished in all tenderness, and tempted into all luxuriance by warm winds and glowing rays, we find pleasure in dwelling upon the crabbed, perverse, and morose animation of plants that have known little kindness from earth or heaven, but, season after season, have had their best efforts palsied by frost, their brightest buds buried under snow, and their goodliest limbs lopped by tempest.

There are many subtle sympathies and affections which join to confirm the Gothic mind in this peculiar choice of subject; and when we add to the influence of these, the necessities consequent upon the employment of a rougher material, compelling the workman to seek for vigour of effect, rather than refinement of texture or accuracy of form, we have direct and manifest causes for much of the difference between the northern and southern cast of conception: but there are indirect causes holding a far more important place in the Gothic heart, though less immediate in their influence on design. Strength of will, independence of character, resoluteness of purpose, impatience of undue control, and that general tendency to set the individual reason against authority, and the individual deed against destiny, which, in the Northern tribes, has opposed itself throughout all ages to the languid submission, in the Southern, of thought to tradition, and purpose to fatality, are all more or less traceable in the rigid lines, vigourous and various masses, and daringly projecting and independent structure of the Northern Gothic ornament: while the opposite feelings are in like manner legible in the graceful and softly guided waves and wreathed bands, in which Southern decoration is constantly disposed; in its tendency to lose its independence, and fuse itself into the surface of the masses upon which it is traced; and in the expression seen so often, in the arrangement of those masses themselves, of an abandonment of their strength to an inevitable necessity, or a listless repose.

There is virtue in the measure, and error in the excess, of both these characters of mind, and in both of the styles which they have created; the best architecture, and the best temper,

_____

[13]**crockets:** small ornaments placed along an inclined pediment or pinnacle.

are those which unite them both; and this fifth impulse of the Gothic heart is therefore that which needs most caution in its indulgence. It is more definitely Gothic than any other, but the best Gothic building is not that which is *most* Gothic: it can hardly be too frank in its confession of rudeness, hardly too rich in its changefulness, hardly too faithful in its naturalism; but it may go too far in its rigidity, and, like the great Puritan spirit in its extreme, lose itself either in frivolity of division, or perversity of purpose. It actually did so in its later times; but it is gladdening to remember that in its utmost nobleness, the very temper which has been thought most adverse to it, the Protestant spirit of self-dependence and inquiry, was expressed in its every line. Faith and aspiration there were, in every Christian ecclesiastical building, from the first century to the fifteenth; but the moral habits to which England in this age owes the kind of greatness that she has,— the habits of philosophical investigation, of accurate thought, of domestic seclusion and independence, of stern self-reliance, and sincere upright searching into religious truth,— were only traceable in the features which were the distinctive creation of the Gothic schools, in the veined foliage, and thorny fret-work, and shadowy niche, and buttressed pier, and fearless height of subtle pinnacle and crested tower, sent like an "unperplexed question up to Heaven."[14] . . . (Volume 2, Chapter 6)

1853

from **Unto This Last**
The Veins of Wealth

The answer which would be made by any ordinary political economist to the statements contained in the preceding paper,[1] is in few words as follows:—

"It is indeed true that certain advantages of a general nature may be obtained by the development of social affections. But political economists never professed, nor profess,

---

[14] "unperplexed . . . Heaven": slightly misquoting Elizabeth Barrett Browning, *Casa Guidi Windows* (1851) 1.69–70, on Giotto's campanile in Florence.

[1] **preceding paper:** "The Roots of Honour," first of four essays published in *The Cornhill Magazine* in 1860 until halted by public outcry, and revised for book publication in 1862 as *Unto this Last*. The book title, drawn from the parable of the laborers in the vineyard (Matthew 20:13), underscores Ruskin's challenge to classical economics' endorsement of self-interest and his controversial advocacy of wage regulation.

to take advantages of a general nature into consideration. Our science is simply the science of getting rich. So far from being a fallacious or visionary one, it is found by experience to be practically effective. Persons who follow its precepts do actually become rich, and persons who disobey them become poor. Every capitalist of Europe has acquired his fortune by following the known laws of our science, and increases his capital daily by an adherence to them. It is vain to bring forward tricks of logic, against the force of accomplished facts. Every man of business knows by experience how money is made, and how it is lost."

Pardon me. Men of business do indeed know how they themselves made their money, or how, on occasion, they lost it. Playing a long-practised game, they are familiar with the chances of its cards, and can rightly explain their losses and gains. But they neither know who keeps the bank of the gambling-house, nor what other games may be played with the same cards, nor what other losses and gains, far away among the dark streets, are essentially, though invisibly, dependent on theirs in the lighted rooms. They have learned a few, and only a few, of the laws of mercantile economy; but not one of those of political economy.

Primarily, which is very notable and curious, I observe that men of business rarely know the meaning of the word "rich." At least, if they know, they do not in their reasonings allow for the fact, that it is a relative word, implying its opposite "poor" as positively as the word "north" implies its opposite "south." Men nearly always speak and write as if riches were absolute, and it were possible, by following certain scientific precepts, for everybody to be rich. Whereas riches are a power like that of electricity, acting only through inequalities or negations of itself. The force of the guinea you have in your pocket depends wholly on the default of a guinea in your neighbour's pocket. If he did not want it, it would be of no use to you; the degree of power it possesses depends accurately upon the need or desire he has for it,—and the art of making yourself rich, in the ordinary mercantile economist's sense, is therefore equally and necessarily the art of keeping your neighbour poor.

I would not contend in this matter (and rarely in any matter) for the acceptance of terms. But I wish the reader clearly and deeply to understand the difference between the two economies, to which the terms "Political" and "Mercantile" might not unadvisedly be attached.

Political economy (the economy of a State, or of citizens) consists simply in the production, preservation, and distribution, at fittest time and place, of useful or pleasurable things. The farmer who cuts his hay at the right time; the shipwright who drives his bolts well home in sound wood; the builder who lays good bricks in well-tempered mortar; the housewife who takes care of her furniture in the parlour, and guards against all waste in her kitchen; and the singer who rightly disciplines, and never overstrains her voice, are all political economists in the true and final sense: adding continually to the riches and well-being of the nation to which they belong.

But mercantile economy, the economy of "merces"[2] or of "pay," signifies the accumulation, in the hands of individuals, of legal or moral claim upon, or power over, the labour of others; every such claim implying precisely as much poverty or debt on one side, as it implies riches or right on the other.

It does not, therefore, necessarily involve an addition to the actual property, or well-being of the State in which it exists. But since this commercial wealth, or power over labour, is nearly always convertible at once into real property, while real property is not always convertible at once into power over labour, the idea of riches among active men in civilized nations generally refers to commercial wealth; and in estimating their possessions, they rather calculate the value of their horses and fields by the number of guineas they could get for them, than the value of their guineas by the number of horses and fields they could buy with them.

There is, however, another reason for this habit of mind: namely, that an accumulation of real property is of little use to its owner, unless, together with it, he has commercial power over labour. Thus, suppose any person to be put in possession of a large estate of fruitful land, with rich beds of gold in its gravel; countless herds of cattle in its pastures; houses, and gardens, and storehouses full of useful stores: but suppose, after all, that he could get no servants? In order that he may be able to have servants, some one in his neighbourhood must be poor, and in want of his gold— or his corn. Assume that no one is in want of either, and that no servants are to be had. He must, therefore, bake his own bread, make his own clothes, plough his own ground, and shepherd his own flocks. His gold will be as useful to him as any other yellow pebbles on his estate. His stores must rot, for he cannot consume them. He can eat no more than another man could eat, and wear no more than another man could wear. He must lead a life of severe and common labour to procure even ordinary comforts; he will be ultimately unable to keep either houses in repair, or fields in cultivation; and forced to content himself with a poor man's

portion of cottage and garden, in the midst of a desert of waste land, trampled by wild cattle, and encumbered by ruins of palaces, which he will hardly mock at himself by calling "his own."

The most covetous of mankind would, with small exultation, I presume, accept riches of this kind on these terms. What is really desired, under the name of riches, is, essentially, power over men; in its simplest sense, the power of obtaining for our own advantage the labour of servant, tradesman, and artist; in wider sense, authority of directing large masses of the nation to various ends (good, trivial, or hurtful, according to the mind of the rich person). And this power of wealth of course is greater or less in direct proportion to the poverty of the men over whom it is exercised, and in inverse proportion to the number of persons who are as rich as ourselves, and who are ready to give the same price for an article of which the supply is limited. If the musician is poor, he will sing for small pay, as long as there is only one person who can pay him; but if there be two or three, he will sing for the one who offers him most. And thus the power of the riches of the patron (always imperfect and doubtful, as we shall see presently, even when most authoritative) depends first on the poverty of the artist, and then on the limitation of the number of equally wealthy persons, who also want seats at the concert. So that, as above stated, the art of becoming "rich," in the common sense, is not absolutely nor finally the art of accumulating much money for ourselves, but also of contriving that our neighbours shall have less. In accurate terms, it is "the art of establishing the maximum inequality in our own favour."

Now, the establishment of such inequality cannot be shown in the abstract to be either advantageous or disadvantageous to the body of the nation. The rash and absurd assumption that such inequalities are necessarily advantageous, lies at the root of most of the popular fallacies on the subject of political economy. For the eternal and inevitable law in this matter is, that the beneficialness of the inequality depends, first, on the methods by which it was accomplished; and, secondly, on the purposes to which it is applied. Inequalities of wealth, unjustly established, have assuredly injured the nation in which they exist during their establishment; and, unjustly directed, injure it yet more during their existence. But inequalities of wealth, justly established, benefit the nation in the course of their establishment; and, nobly used, aid it yet more by their existence. That is to say, among every active and well-governed people, the various strength of individuals, tested by full exertion and specially applied to various need, issues in unequal, but harmonious results, receiving

---

[2]"**merces**" (wages): Ruskin's etymological argument pits a "mercantile" science of wealth against a "political" science of the commonwealth (Greek *polis*).

reward or authority according to its class and service;[3] while, in the inactive or ill-governed nation, the gradations of decay and the victories of treason work out also their own rugged system of subjection and success; and substitute, for the melodious inequalities of concurrent power, the iniquitous dominances and depressions of guilt and misfortune.

Thus the circulation of wealth in a nation resembles that of the blood in the natural body. There is one quickness of the current which comes of cheerful emotion or wholesome exercise; and another which comes of shame or of fever. There is a flush of the body which is full of warmth and life; and another which will pass into putrefaction.

The analogy will hold down even to minute particulars. For as diseased local determination of the blood involves depression of the general health of the system, all morbid local action of riches will be found ultimately to involve a weakening of the resources of the body politic.

---

[3] I have been naturally asked several times with respect to the sentence in the first of these papers, "the bad workmen unemployed," "But what are you to do with your bad unemployed workmen?" Well, it seems to me the question might have occurred to you before. Your housemaid's place is vacant—you give twenty pounds a year—two girls come for it, one neatly dressed, the other dirtily; one with good recommendations, the other with none. You do not, under these circumstances, usually ask the dirty one if she will come for fifteen pounds, or twelve; and, on her consenting, take her instead of the well-recommended one. Still less do you try to beat both down by making them bid against each other, till you can hire both, one at twelve pounds a year, and the other at eight. You simply take the one fittest for the place, and send away the other, not perhaps concerning yourself quite as much as you should with the question which you now impatiently put to me, "What is to become of her?" For, all that I advise you to do, is to deal with workmen as with servants; and verily the question is of weight: "Your bad workman, idler, and rogue—what are you to do with him?"

We will consider of this presently: remember that the administration of a complete system of national commerce and industry cannot be explained in full detail within the space of twelve pages. Meantime, consider whether, there being confessedly some difficulty in dealing with rogues and idlers, it may not be advisable to produce as few of them as possible. If you examine into the history of rogues, you will find they are as truly manufactured articles as anything else, and it is just because our present system of political economy gives so large a stimulus to that manufacture that you may know it to be a false one. We had better seek for a system which will develop honest men, than for one which will deal cunningly with vagabonds. Let us reform our schools, and we shall find little reform needed in our prisons. [Ruskin's note]

The mode in which this is produced may be at once understood by examining one or two instances of the development of wealth in the simplest possible circumstances.

Suppose two sailors cast away on an uninhabited coast, and obliged to maintain themselves there by their own labour for a series of years.

If they both kept their health, and worked steadily and in amity with each other, they might build themselves a convenient house, and in time come to possess a certain quantity of cultivated land, together with various stores laid up for future use. All these things would be real riches or property; and, supposing the men both to have worked equally hard, they would each have right to equal share or use of it. Their political economy would consist merely in careful preservation and just division of these possessions. Perhaps, however, after some time one or other might be dissatisfied with the results of their common farming; and they might in consequence agree to divide the land they had brought under the spade into equal shares, so that each might thenceforward work in his own field, and live by it. Suppose that after this arrangement had been made, one of them were to fall ill, and be unable to work on his land at a critical time—say of sowing or harvest.

He would naturally ask the other to sow or reap for him.

Then his companion might say, with perfect justice, "I will do this additional work for you; but if I do it, you must promise to do as much for me at another time. I will count how many hours I spend on your ground, and you shall give me a written promise to work for the same number of hours on mine, whenever I need your help, and you are able to give it."

Suppose the disabled man's sickness to continue, and that under various circumstances, for several years, requiring the help of the other, he on each occasion gave a written pledge to work, as soon as he was able, at his companion's orders, for the same number of hours which the other had given up to him. What will the positions of the two men be when the invalid is able to resume work?

Considered as a "Polis," or state, they will be poorer than they would have been otherwise: poorer by the withdrawal of what the sick man's labour would have produced in the interval. His friend may perhaps have toiled with an energy quickened by the enlarged need, but in the end his own land and property must have suffered by the withdrawal of so much of his time and thought from them: and the united property of the two men will be certainly less than it would have been if both had remained in health and activity.

But the relations in which they stand to each other are also widely altered. The sick man has not only pledged his labour for some years, but will probably have exhausted his own share of the accumulated stores, and will be in consequence for some time dependent on the other for food, which he can only "pay" or reward him for by yet more deeply pledging his own labour.

Supposing the written promises to be held entirely valid (among civilized nations their validity is secured by legal measures[4]), the person who had hitherto worked for both might now, if he chose, rest altogether, and pass his time in idleness, not only forcing his companion to redeem all the engagements he had already entered into, but exacting from him pledges for further labour, to an arbitrary amount, for what food he had to advance to him.

There might not, from first to last, be the least illegality (in the ordinary sense of the word) in the arrangement; but if a stranger arrived on the coast at this advanced epoch of their political economy, he would find one man commercially Rich; the other commercially Poor. He would see, perhaps, with no small surprise, one passing his days in idleness; the other labouring for both, and living sparely, in the hope of recovering his independence at some distant period.

This is, of course, an example of one only out of many ways in which inequality of possession may be established between different persons, giving rise to the Mercantile forms of Riches and Poverty. In the instance before us, one of the men might from the first have deliberately chosen to be idle, and to put his life in pawn for present ease; or he might have mismanaged his land, and been compelled to have recourse to his neighbour for food and help, pledging his future labour for it. But what I want the reader to note especially is the fact, common to a large number of typical

cases of this kind, that the establishment of the mercantile wealth which consists in a claim upon labour, signifies a political diminution of the real wealth which consists in substantial possessions.

Take another example, more consistent with the ordinary course of affairs of trade. Suppose that three men, instead of two, formed the little isolated republic, and found themselves obliged to separate, in order to farm different pieces of land at some distance from each other along the coast: each estate furnishing a distinct kind of produce, and each more or less in need of the material raised on the other. Suppose that the third man, in order to save the time of all three, undertakes simply to superintend the transference of commodities from one farm to the other; on condition of receiving some sufficiently remunerative share of every parcel of goods conveyed, or of some other parcel received in exchange for it.

If this carrier or messenger always brings to each estate, from the other, what is chiefly wanted, at the right time, the operations of the two farmers will go on prosperously, and the largest possible result in produce, or wealth, will be attained by the little community. But suppose no intercourse between the landowners is possible, except through the travelling agent; and that, after a time, this agent, watching the course of each man's agriculture, keeps back the articles with which he has been entrusted until there comes a period of extreme necessity for them, on one side or other, and then exacts in exchange for them all that the distressed farmer can spare of other kinds of produce: it is easy to see that by ingeniously watching his opportunities, he might possess himself regularly of the greater part of the superfluous produce of the two estates, and at last, in some year of severest trial or scarcity, purchase both for himself and maintain the former proprietors thenceforward as his labourers or servants.

This would be a case of commercial wealth acquired on the exactest principles of modern political economy. But more distinctly even than in the former instance, it is manifest in this that the wealth of the State, or of the three men considered as a society, is collectively less than it would have been had the merchant been content with juster profit. The operations of the two agriculturists have been cramped to the utmost; and the continual limitations of the supply of things they wanted at critical times, together with the failure of courage consequent on the prolongation of a struggle for mere existence, without any sense of permanent gain, must have seriously diminished the effective results of their labour; and the stores finally accumulated in the merchant's hands will not in any wise be of equivalent value to those

---

[4]**legal measures**: The disputes which exist respecting the real nature of money arise more from the disputants examining its functions on different sides, than from any real dissent in their opinions. All money, properly so called, is an acknowledgment of debt; but as such, it may either be considered to represent the labour and property of the creditor, or the idleness and penury of the debtor. The intricacy of the question has been much increased by the (hitherto necessary) use of marketable commodities, such as gold, silver, salt, shells, etc., to give intrinsic value or security to currency; but the final and best definition of money is that it is a documentary promise ratified and guaranteed by the nation to give or find a certain quantity of labour on demand. A man's labour for a day is a better standard of value than a measure of any produce, because no produce ever maintains a consistent rate of productibility. [Ruskin's note]

which, had his dealings been honest, would have filled at once the granaries of the farmers and his own.

The whole question, therefore, respecting not only the advantage, but even the quantity, of national wealth, resolves itself finally into one of abstract justice. It is impossible to conclude, of any given mass of acquired wealth, merely by the fact of its existence, whether it signifies good or evil to the nation in the midst of which it exists. Its real value depends on the moral sign attached to it, just as sternly as that of a mathematical quantity depends on the algebraical sign attached to it. Any given accumulation of commercial wealth may be indicative, on the one hand, of faithful industries, progressive energies, and productive ingenuities; or, on the other, it may be indicative of mortal luxury, merciless tyranny, ruinous chicane.[5] Some treasures are heavy with human tears, as an ill-stored harvest with untimely rain; and some gold is brighter in sunshine than it is in substance.

And these are not, observe, merely moral or pathetic attributes of riches, which the seeker of riches may, if he chooses, despise; they are, literally and sternly, material attributes of riches, depreciating or exalting, incalculably, the monetary signification of the sum in question. One mass of money is the outcome of action which has created,—another, of action which has annihilated,—ten times as much in the gathering of it; such and such strong hands have been paralyzed, as if they had been numbed by night-shade: so many strong men's courage broken, so many productive operations hindered; this and the other false direction given to labour, and lying image of prosperity set up, on Dura plains dug into seven-times-heated furnaces.[6] That which seems to be wealth may in verity be only the gilded index of far-reaching ruin; a wrecker's handful of coin gleaned from the beach to which he has beguiled an argosy; a camp-follower's bundle of rags unwrapped from the breasts of goodly soldiers dead; the purchase-pieces of potter's fields,[7] wherein shall be buried together the citizen and the stranger.

And therefore, the idea that directions can be given for the gaining of wealth, irrespectively of the consideration of its moral sources, or that any general and technical law of purchase and gain can be set down for national practice, is perhaps the most insolently futile of all that ever beguiled

---

[5]**chicane:** trickery.

[6]**Dura plains:** where Shadrach, Meshach, and Abednego refuse to worship an image of gold and are cast alive into a fiery **furnace;** see Daniel 3.

[7]**potter's fields:** graveyards for paupers; see Matthew 27:3–7.

men through their vices. So far as I know, there is not in history record of anything so disgraceful to the human intellect as the modern idea that the commercial text, "Buy in the cheapest market and sell in the dearest," represents, or under any circumstances could represent, an available principle of national economy. Buy in the cheapest market?— yes; but what made your market cheap? Charcoal may be cheap among your roof timbers after a fire, and bricks may be cheap in your streets after an earthquake; but fire and earthquake may not therefore be national benefits. Sell in the dearest?—Yes, truly; but what made your market dear? You sold your bread well to-day: was it to a dying man who gave his last coin for it, and will never need bread more; or to a rich man who to-morrow will buy your farm over your head; or to a soldier on his way to pillage the bank in which you have put your fortune?

None of these things you can know. One thing only you can know: namely, whether this dealing of yours is a just and faithful one, which is all you need concern yourself about respecting it; sure thus to have done your own part in bringing about ultimately in the world a state of things which will not issue in pillage or in death. And thus every question concerning these things merges itself ultimately in the great question of justice. . . .

It has been shown that the chief value and virtue of money consists in its having power over human beings; that, without this power, large material possessions are useless, and to any person possessing such power, comparatively unnecessary. But power over human beings is attainable by other means than by money. As I said a few pages back, the money power is always imperfect and doubtful; there are many things which cannot be reached with it, others which cannot be retained by it. Many joys may be given to men which cannot be bought for gold, and many fidelities found in them which cannot be rewarded with it.

Trite enough,—the reader thinks. Yes: but it is not so trite,—I wish it were,—that in this moral power, quite inscrutable and immeasurable though it be, there is a monetary value just as real as that represented by more ponderous currencies. A man's hand may be full of invisible gold, and the wave of it, or the grasp, shall do more than another's with a shower of bullion. This invisible gold, also, does not necessarily diminish in spending. Political economists will do well some day to take heed of it, though they cannot take measure.

But farther. Since the essence of wealth consists in its authority over men, if the apparent or nominal wealth fail in this power, it fails in essence; in fact, ceases to be wealth at all. It does not appear lately in England, that our authority over men is absolute. The servants show some disposition to rush riotously upstairs, under an impression that their wages are not regularly paid.[8] We should augur ill of any gentleman's property to whom this happened every other day in his drawing-room.

So, also, the power of our wealth seems limited as respects the comfort of the servants, no less than their quietude. The persons in the kitchen appear to be ill-dressed, squalid, half-starved. One cannot help imagining that the riches of the establishment must be of a very theoretical and documentary character.

Finally. Since the essence of wealth consists in power over men, will it not follow that the nobler and the more in number the persons are over whom it has power, the greater the wealth? Perhaps it may even appear, after some consideration, that the persons themselves *are* the wealth—that these pieces of gold with which we are in the habit of guiding them, are, in fact, nothing more than a kind of Byzantine harness or trappings, very glittering and beautiful in barbaric sight, wherewith we bridle the creatures; but that if these same living creatures could be guided without the fretting and jingling of the Byzants[9] in their mouths and ears, they might themselves be more valuable than their bridles. In fact, it may be discovered that the true veins of wealth are purple—and not in Rock, but in Flesh—perhaps even that the final outcome and consummation of all wealth is in the producing as many as possible full-breathed, bright-eyed, and happy-hearted human creatures. Our modern wealth, I think, has rather a tendency the other way;—most political economists appearing to consider multitudes of human creatures not conducive to wealth, or at best conducive to it only by remaining in a dim-eyed and narrow-chested state of being.

Nevertheless, it is open, I repeat, to serious question, which I leave to the reader's pondering, whether, among national manufactures, that of Souls of a good quality may not at last turn out a quite leadingly lucrative one? Nay, in some far-away and yet undreamt-of hour, I can even imagine that England may cast all thoughts of possessive wealth back to the barbaric nations among whom they first arose; and that, while the sands of the Indus and adamant of Golconda may yet stiffen the housings of the charger,[10] and flash from the

turban of the slave, she, as a Christian mother, may at last attain to the virtues and the treasures of a Heathen one, and be able to lead forth her Sons, saying,—

"These are MY *Jewels."*[11]

(Chapter 2)

1860, 1862

from **Traffic**[1]

(Delivered in the Town Hall, Bradford)

My good Yorkshire friends, you asked me down here among your hills that I might talk to you about this Exchange you are going to build: but earnestly and seriously asking you to pardon me, I am going to do nothing of the kind. I cannot talk, or at least can say very little, about this same Exchange. I must talk of quite other things, though not willingly; I could not deserve your pardon, if when you invited me to speak on one subject, I *willfully* spoke on another. But I cannot speak, to purpose, of anything about which I do not care; and most simply and sorrowfully I have to tell you, in the outset, that I do *not* care about this Exchange of yours.

If, however, when you sent me your invitation, I had answered, "I won't come, I don't care about the Exchange of Bradford," you would have been justly offended with me, not knowing the reasons of so blunt a carelessness. So I have come down, hoping that you will patiently let me tell you why, on this, and many other such occasions, I now remain silent, when formerly I should have caught at the opportunity of speaking to a gracious audience.

In a word, then, I do not care about this Exchange—because *you* don't; and because you know perfectly well I cannot make you. Look at the essential circumstances of the case, which you, as business men, know perfectly well, though perhaps you think I forget them. You are going to spend £30,000, which to you, collectively, is nothing; the buying a new coat is, as to the cost of it, a much more important matter of consideration to me than building a new Exchange is to you. But you think you may as well have the

---

[8]**not regularly paid:** builders had gone on strike in 1859.

[9]**Byzants:** gold coins of Byzantium.

[10]**Indus, Golconda:** Indian sources of gold and diamonds (**adamant**). **housings:** trappings of a warhorse (**charger**).

[11]*"These . . . Jewels":* the plain-dressed Roman matron Cornelia, introducing a bejeweled visitor to her sons, who grew up to be the Gracchi (social reformers of 2nd century BCE).

[1]**Traffic:** trade, business. Ruskin gave this lecture in 1864 and published it in 1866.

right thing for your money. You know there are a great many odd styles of architecture about; you don't want to do anything ridiculous; you hear of me, among others, as a respectable architectural man-milliner: and you send for me, that I may tell you the leading fashion; and what is, in our shops, for the moment, the newest and sweetest thing in pinnacles.

Now, pardon me for telling you frankly, you cannot have good architecture merely by asking people's advice on occasion. All good architecture is the expression of national life and character; and it is produced by a prevalent and eager national taste, or desire for beauty. And I want you to think a little of the deep significance of this word "taste;" for no statement of mine has been more earnestly or oftener controverted than that good taste is essentially a moral quality. "No," say many of my antagonists, "taste is one thing, morality is another. Tell us what is pretty; we shall be glad to know that; but preach no sermons to us."

Permit me, therefore, to fortify this old dogma of mine somewhat. Taste is not only a part and an index of morality—it is the ONLY morality. The first, and last, and closest trial question to any living creature is, "What do you like?" Tell me what you like, and I'll tell you what you are. Go out into the street, and ask the first man or woman you meet, what their "taste" is, and if they answer candidly, you know them, body and soul. "You, my friend in the rags, with the unsteady gait, what do *you* like?" "A pipe and a quartern[2] of gin." I know you. "You, good woman, with the quick step and tidy bonnet, what do you like?" "A swept hearth and a clean tea-table, and my husband opposite me, and a baby at my breast." Good, I know you also. "You, little girl with the golden hair and the soft eyes, what do you like?" "My canary, and a run among the wood hyacinths." "You, little boy with the dirty hands and the low forehead, what do you like?" "A shy at the sparrows, and a game at pitch-farthing." Good; we know them all now. What more need we ask?

"Nay," perhaps you answer: "we need rather to ask what these people and children do, than what they like. If they *do* right, it is no matter that they like what is wrong; and if they *do* wrong, it is no matter that they like what is right. Doing is the great thing; and it does not matter that the man likes drinking, so that he does not drink; nor that the little girl likes to be kind to her canary, if she will not learn her lessons; nor that the little boy likes throwing stones at the sparrows, if he goes to the Sunday-school." In-

deed, for a short time, and in a provisional sense, this is true. For if, resolutely, people do what is right, in time they come to like doing it. But they only are in a right moral state when they *have* come to like doing it; and as long as they don't like it, they are still in a vicious state. The man is not in health of body who is always thirsting for the bottle in the cupboard, though he bravely bears his thirst; but the man who heartily enjoys water in the morning and wine in the evening, each in its proper quantity and time. And the entire object of true education is to make people not merely *do* the right things, but *enjoy* the right things—not merely industrious, but to love industry—not merely learned, but to love knowledge—not merely pure, but to love purity—not merely just, but to hunger and thirst after justice.[3] . . .

. . . Believe me, without farther instance, I could show you, in all time, that every nation's vice, or virtue, was written in its art: the soldiership of early Greece; the sensuality of late Italy; the visionary religion of Tuscany; the splendid human energy and beauty of Venice. I have no time to do this to-night (I have done it elsewhere before now); but I proceed to apply the principle to ourselves in a more searching manner.

I notice that among all the new buildings that cover your once wild hills, churches and schools are mixed in due, that is to say, in large proportion, with your mills and mansions, and I notice also that the churches and schools are almost always Gothic, and the mansions and mills are never Gothic. Will you allow me to ask precisely the meaning of this? For, remember, it is peculiarly a modern phenomenon. When Gothic was invented, houses were Gothic as well as churches; and when the Italian style superseded the Gothic, churches were Italian as well as houses. If there is a Gothic spire to the cathedral of Antwerp, there is a Gothic belfry to the Hôtel de Ville[4] at Brussels; if Inigo Jones builds an Italian Whitehall, Sir Christopher Wren builds an Italian St. Paul's. But now you live under one school of architecture, and worship under another. What do you mean by doing this? Am I to understand that you are thinking of changing your architecture back to Gothic; and that you treat your churches experimentally, because it does not matter what mistakes you make in a church? Or am I to understand that you consider Gothic a pre-eminently sacred and beautiful mode of building, which you think, like the

---

[2]**quartern:** one-fourth of a pint.

[3]**hunger and thirst:** Matthew 5:6.

[4]**Hôtel de Ville, Whitehall:** centers of government. **Inigo Jones** (1573–1652), **Sir Christopher Wren** (1632–1723): English architects.

fine frankincense, should be mixed for the tabernacle only, and reserved for your religious services? For if this be the feeling, though it may seem at first as if it were graceful and reverent, you will find that, at the root of the matter, it signifies neither more nor less than that you have separated your religion from your life.

For consider what a wide significance this fact has; and remember that it is not you only, but all the people of England, who are behaving thus just now.

You have all got into the habit of calling the church "the house of God." I have seen, over the doors of many churches, the legend actually carved, "*This* is the house of God, and this is the gate of heaven."[5] Now, note where that legend comes from, and of what place it was first spoken. A boy leaves his father's house to go on a long journey on foot, to visit his uncle; he has to cross a wild hill-desert; just as if one of your own boys had to cross the wolds[6] of Westmoreland, to visit an uncle at Carlisle. The second or third day your boy finds himself somewhere between Hawes and Brough, in the midst of the moors, at sunset. It is stony ground, and boggy; he cannot go one foot farther that night. Down he lies, to sleep, on Wharnside, where best he may, gathering a few of the stones together to put under his head—so wild the place is, he cannot get anything but stones. And there, lying under the broad night, he has a dream; and he sees a ladder set up on the earth, and the top of it reaches to heaven, and the angels of God are ascending and descending upon it. And when he wakes out of his sleep, he says, "How dreadful is this place; surely, this is none other than the house of God, and this is the gate of heaven." This PLACE, observe; not this church; not this city; not this stone, even, which he puts up for a memorial—the piece of flint on which his head has lain. But this *place*; this windy slope of Wharnside; this moorland hollow, torrent-bitten, snow-blighted; this *any* place where God lets down the ladder. And how are you to know where that will be? or how are you to determine where it may be, but by being ready for it always? Do you know where the lightning is to fall next? You *do* know that, partly; you can guide the lightning; but you cannot guide the going forth of the Spirit, which is that lightning when it shines from the east to the west.[7]

But the perpetual and insolent warping of that strong verse to serve a merely ecclesiastical purpose is only one of the thousand instances in which we sink back into gross Judaism.[8] We call our churches "temples." Now, you know, or ought to know, they are *not* temples. They have never had, never can have, anything whatever to do with temples. They are "synagogues"—"gathering places"—where you gather yourselves together as an assembly; and by not calling them so, you again miss the force of another mighty text—"Thou, when thou prayest, shall not be as the hypocrites are; for they love to pray standing in the *churches*" [we should translate it], "that they may be seen of men. But thou, when thou prayest, enter into thy closet, and when thou hast shut thy door, pray to thy Father"—which is, not in chancel nor in aisle, but "in secret."[9]

Now, you feel, as I say this to you—I know you feel—as if I were trying to take away the honour of your churches. Not so; I am trying to prove to you the honour of your houses and your hills; I am trying to show you—not that the Church is not sacred—but that the whole Earth is. I would have you feel, what careless, what constant, what infectious sin there is in all modes of thought, whereby, in calling your churches only "holy," you call your hearths and homes profane; and have separated yourselves from the heathen by casting all your household gods to the ground, instead of recognizing, in the place of their many and feeble Lares, the presence of your One and Mighty Lord and Lar.[10]

"But what has all this to do with our Exchange?" you ask me, impatiently. My dear friends, it has just everything to do with it; on these inner and great questions depend all the outer and little ones; and if you have asked me down here to speak to you, because you had before been interested in anything I have written, you must know that all I have yet said about architecture was to show this. The book[11] I called "The Seven Lamps" was to show that certain right states of temper and moral feeling were the magic powers by which all good architecture, without exception, had been produced. "The Stones of Venice" had, from beginning to end, no other aim than to show that the Gothic architecture of Venice had arisen out of, and indicated in all its features, a state of pure national faith, and of domestic virtue; and that its Renaissance architecture had arisen out of, and in all its features indicated, a state of concealed national infidelity, and of domestic corruption.

---

[5]"*This* is . . . **heaven**": Genesis 28:17 (the story of Jacob's ladder).

[6]**wolds**: wooded hills. The places named are in NW England.

[7]**from the east to the west**: see Matthew 24:27.

[8]**gross Judaism**: idolatry, priestcraft.

[9]**"in secret"**: Matthew 6:5–6.

[10]**Lar**: household god (plural **Lares**).

[11]**book**: *The Seven Lamps of Architecture* (1849).

And now, you ask me what style is best to build in; and how can I answer, knowing the meaning of the two styles, but by another question—do you mean to build as Christians or as Infidels? And still more—do you mean to build as honest Christians or as honest Infidels? as thoroughly and confessedly either one or the other? You don't like to be asked such rude questions. I cannot help it; they are of much more importance than this Exchange business; and if they can be at once answered, the Exchange business settles itself in a moment. But, before I press them further, I must ask leave to explain one point clearly. In all my past work, my endeavour has been to show that good architecture is essentially religious—the production of a faithful and virtuous, not of an infidel and corrupted people. But in the course of doing this, I have had also to show that good architecture is not *ecclesiastical*. People are so apt to look upon religion as the business of the clergy, not their own, that the moment they hear of anything depending on "religion," they think it must also have depended on the priesthood; and I have had to take what place was to be occupied between these two errors, and fight both, often with seeming contradiction. Good architecture is the work of good and believing men; therefore, you say, at least some people say, "Good architecture must essentially have been the work of the clergy, not of the laity." No—a thousand times no; good architecture has always been the work of the commonalty, *not* of the clergy. What, you say, those glorious cathedrals—the pride of Europe—did their builders not form Gothic architecture? No; they corrupted Gothic architecture. Gothic was formed in the baron's castle, and the burgher's street. It was formed by the thoughts, and hands, and powers of free citizens and soldier-kings. By the monk it was used as an instrument for the aid of his superstition; when that superstition became a beautiful madness, and the best hearts of Europe vainly dreamed and pined in the cloister, and vainly raged and perished in the crusade—through that fury of perverted faith and wasted war, the Gothic rose also to its loveliest, most fantastic, and, finally, most foolish dreams; and, in those dreams, was lost.

I hope, now, that there is no risk of your misunderstanding me when I come to the gist of what I want to say to-night—when I repeat, that every great national architecture has been the result and exponent of a great national religion. You can't have bits of it here, bits there—you must have it everywhere, or nowhere. It is not the monopoly of a clerical company—it is not the exponent of a theological dogma—it is not the hieroglyphic writing of an initiated priesthood; it is the manly language of a people inspired by resolute and common purpose, and rendering resolute and common fidelity to the legible laws of an undoubted God.

Now, there have as yet been three distinct schools of European architecture. I say, European, because Asiatic and African architectures belong so entirely to other races and climates, that there is no question of them here; only, in passing, I will simply assure you that whatever is good or great in Egypt, and Syria, and India, is just good or great for the same reasons as the buildings on our side of the Bosphorus. We Europeans, then, have had three great religions: the Greek, which was the worship of the God of Wisdom and Power; the Mediæval, which was the Worship of the God of Judgment and Consolation; the Renaissance, which was the worship of the God of Pride and Beauty; these three we have had—they are past—and now, at last, we English have got a fourth religion, and a God of our own, about which I want to ask you. But I must explain these three old ones first.

I repeat, first, the Greeks essentially worshipped the God of Wisdom; so that whatever contended against their religion—to the Jews a stumbling-block—was, to the Greeks—*Foolishness*.[12]

The first Greek idea of Deity was that expressed in the word, of which we keep the remnant in our words *"Di*-urnal" and *"Di*-vine"—the god of *Day*, Jupiter the revealer. Athena is his daughter, but especially daughter of the Intellect, springing armed from the head. We are only with the help of recent investigation beginning to penetrate the depth of meaning couched under the Athenaic symbols; but I may note rapidly, that her ægis,[13] the mantle with the serpent fringes, in which she often, in the best statues, is represented as folding up her left hand for better guard, and the Gorgon on her shield, are both representative mainly of the chilling horror and sadness (turning men to stone, as it were), of the outmost and superficial spheres of knowledge—that knowledge which separates, in bitterness, hardness, and sorrow, the heart of the full-grown man from the heart of the child. For out of imperfect knowledge spring terror, dissension, danger, and disdain; but from perfect knowledge, given by the full-revealed Athena, strength and peace, in sign of which she is crowned with the olive spray, and bears the resistless spear.

This, then, was the Greek conception of purest Deity, and every habit of life, and every form of his art developed

---

[12]"to the Jews . . . *Foolishness*": see 1 Corinthians 1:23.

[13]**aegis**: Athena's shield.

themselves from the seeking this bright, serene, resistless wisdom; and setting himself, as a man, to do things evermore rightly and strongly;[14] not with any ardent affection or ultimate hope; but with a resolute and continent energy of will, as knowing that for failure there was no consolation, and for sin there was no remission. And the Greek architecture rose unerring, bright, clearly defined, and self-contained.

Next followed in Europe the great Christian faith, which was essentially the religion of Comfort. Its great doctrine is the remission of sins; for which cause it happens, too often, in certain phases of Christianity, that sin and sickness themselves are partly glorified, as if, the more you had to be healed of, the more divine was the healing. The practical result of this doctrine, in art, is a continual contemplation of sin and disease, and of imaginary states of purification from them; thus we have an architecture conceived in a mingled sentiment of melancholy and aspiration, partly severe, partly luxuriant, which will bend itself to every one of our needs, and every one of our fancies, and be strong or weak with us, as we are strong or weak ourselves. It is, of all architecture, the basest, when base people build it—of all, the noblest, when built by the noble.

And now note that both these religions—Greek and Mediæval—perished by falsehood in their own main purpose. The Greek religion of Wisdom perished in a false philosophy—"Oppositions of science, falsely so-called."[15] The Mediæval religion of Consolation perished in false comfort; in remission of sins given lyingly. It was the selling of absolution that ended the Mediæval faith; and I can tell you more, it is the selling of absolution which, to the end of time, will mark false Christianity. Pure Christianity gives her remission of sins only by *ending* them; but false Christianity gets her remission of sins by *compounding for* them. And there are many ways of compounding for them. We English have beautiful little quiet ways of buying absolu-

tion, whether in low Church or high, far more cunning than any of Tetzel's[16] trading.

Then, thirdly, there followed the religion of Pleasure, in which all Europe gave itself to luxury, ending in death. First, *bals masqués*[17] in every saloon, and then guillotines in every square. And all these three worships issue in vast temple-building. Your Greek worshiped Wisdom, and built you the Parthenon—the Virgin's temple. The Mediæval worshiped Consolation, and built you Virgin temples also—but to our Lady of Salvation. Then the Revivalist[18] worshiped beauty, of a sort, and built you Versailles, and the Vatican. Now, lastly, will you tell me what *we* worship, and what *we* build?

You know we are speaking always of the real, active, continual, national worship; that by which men act while they live; not that which they talk of when they die. Now, we have, indeed, a nominal religion, to which we pay tithes of property and sevenths of time; but we have also a practical and earnest religion, to which we devote nine-tenths of our property and sixth-sevenths of our time. And we dispute a great deal about the nominal religion; but we are all unanimous about this practical one, of which I think you will admit that the ruling goddess may be best generally described as the "Goddess of Getting-on," or "Britannia of the Market." The Athenians had an "Athena Agoraia," or Minerva of the Market; but she was a subordinate type of their goddess, while our Britannia Agoraia is the principal type of ours. And all your great architectural works, are, of course, built to her. It is long since you built a great cathedral; and how you would laugh at me, if I proposed building a cathedral on the top of one of these hills of yours, taking it for an Acropolis! But your railroad mounds, prolonged masses of Acropolis; your railroad stations, vaster than the Parthenon, and innumerable; your chimneys, how much more mighty and costly than cathedral spires! your harbor-piers; your warehouses; your exchanges!—all these are built to your great Goddess of "Getting-on;" and she has formed, and will continue to form, your architecture, as long as you worship her; and it is quite vain to ask me to tell you how to build to *her*; you know far better than I.

There might indeed, on some theories, be a conceivably good architecture for Exchanges—that is to say if there were any heroism in the fact or deed of exchange, which

---

[14]**rightly and strongly**: It is an error to suppose that the Greek worship, or seeking, was chiefly of Beauty. It was essentially of Rightness and Strength, founded on Forethought: the principal character of Greek art is not Beauty, but Design: and the Dorian Apollo-worship and Athenian Virgin-worship are both expressions of adoration of divine Wisdom and Purity. Next to these great deities rank, in power over the national mind, Dionysus and Ceres, the givers of human strength and life: then, for heroic example, Hercules. There is no Venus-worship among the Greeks in the great times: and the Muses are essentially teachers of Truth, and of its harmonies. [Ruskin's note]

[15]**"Oppositions . . . so-called"**: 1 Timothy 6:20.

[16]Johann **Tetzel** (1465?–1519): trafficker in papal indulgences who provoked Martin Luther's initial protest against the Church.

[17]*bals masqués*: masked balls.

[18]**Revivalist**: neoclassical Renaissance man.

might be typically carved on the outside of your building. For, you know, all beautiful architecture must be adorned with sculpture or painting; and for sculpture or painting, you must have a subject. And hitherto it has been a received opinion among the nations of the world that the only right subjects for either, were *heroisms* of some sort. Even on his pots and his flagons, the Greek put a Hercules slaying lions, or an Apollo slaying serpents, or Bacchus slaying melancholy giants, and earth-born despondencies. On his temples, the Greek put contests of great warriors in founding states, or of gods with evil spirits. On his houses and temples alike, the Christian put carvings of angels conquering devils; or of hero-martyrs exchanging this world for another; subject inappropriate, I think, to our manner of exchange here. And the Master of Christians not only left his followers without any orders as to the sculpture of affairs of exchange on the outside of buildings, but gave some strong evidence of his dislike of affairs of exchange within them. And yet there might surely be a heroism in such affairs; and all commerce become a kind of selling of doves,[19] not impious. The wonder has always been great to me, that heroism has never been supposed to be in anywise consistent with the practice of supplying people with food, or clothes; but rather with that of quartering one's self upon them for food, and stripping them of their clothes. Spoiling of armour is an heroic deed in all ages; but the selling of clothes, old, or new, has never taken any colour of magnanimity. Yet one does not see why feeding the hungry and clothing the naked should ever become base businesses, even when engaged in on a large scale. If one could contrive to attach the notion of conquest to them anyhow? so that, supposing there were anywhere an obstinate race, who refused to be comforted, one might take some pride in giving them compulsory comfort; and as it were, "occupying a country" with one's gifts, instead of one's armies? If one could only consider it as much a victory to get a barren field sown, as to get an earned field stripped; and contend who should build villages, instead of who should "carry" them. Are not all forms of heroism, conceivable in doing these serviceable deeds? You doubt who is strongest? It might be ascertained by push of spade, as well as push of sword. Who is wisest? There are witty things to be thought of in planning other business than campaigns. Who is bravest? There are always the elements to fight with stronger than men; and nearly as merciless.

The only absolutely and unapproachably heroic element in the soldier's work seems to be—that he is paid little for it—and regularly: while you traffickers, and exchangers, and others occupied in presumably benevolent business, like to be paid much for it—and by chance. I never can make out how it is that a knight-errant does not expect to be paid for his trouble, but a peddler-errant always does—that people are willing to take hard knocks for nothing, but never to sell ribbons cheap—that they are ready to go on fervent crusades to recover the tomb of a buried God, never on any travels to fulfill the orders of a living God—that they will go anywhere barefoot to preach their faith, but must be well bribed to practice it, and are perfectly ready to give the Gospel gratis, but never the loaves and fishes.[20]

If you chose to take the matter up on any such soldierly principle, to do your commerce, and your feeding of nations, for fixed salaries; and to be as particular about giving people the best food, and the best cloth, as soldiers are about giving them the best gunpowder, I could carve something for you on your exchange worth looking at. But I can only at present suggest decorating its frieze with pendant purses; and making its pillars broad at the base for the sticking of bills. And in the innermost chambers of it there might be a statue of Britannia of the Market, who may have, perhaps advisably, a partridge for her crest, typical at once of her courage in fighting for noble ideas; and of her interest in game; and round its neck the inscription in golden letters, "Perdix fovit quæ non peperit."[21] Then, for her spear, she might have a weaver's beam; and on her shield, instead of her Cross, the Milanese boar,[22] semi-fleeced, with the town of Gennesaret proper, in the field and the legend "In the best market," and her corslet, of leather, folded over her heart in the shape of a purse, with thirty slits in it for a piece of money[23] to go in at, on each day of the month. And I doubt not but that people would come to see your exchange, and its goddess, with applause.

Nevertheless, I want to point out to you certain strange characters in this goddess of yours. She differs from the great Greek and Mediæval deities essentially in two

---

[19]**selling of doves**: see Matthew 21:12–13.

[20]**loaves and fishes**: see Mark 6:38–44.

[21]"**Perdix . . . peperit**": Jerem. xvii.11 (best in Septuagint and Vulgate): "As the partridge, fostering what she brought not forth, so he that getteth riches, not by right, shall leave them in the midst of his days, and at his end shall be a fool." [Ruskin's note] **Septuagint, Vulgate**: Greek and Latin versions of the Bible.

[22]**boar**: symbol of Milan, covered half with bristles, half with fleece. **Gennesaret**: see Luke 5:4–10.

[23]**thirty . . . money**: price of Judas' betrayal (Matthew 26–27).

CAP·t·ism

things—first, as to the continuance of her presumed power; secondly, as to the extent of it.

I. As to the Continuance.

The Greek Goddess of Wisdom gave continual increase of wisdom, as the Christian Spirit of Comfort (or Comforter) continual increase of comfort. There was no question, with these, of any limit or cessation of function. But with your Agora Goddess, that is just the most important question. Getting on—but where to? Gathering together—but how much? Do you mean to gather always—never to spend?

If so, I wish you joy of your goddess, for I am just as well off as you, without the trouble of worshiping her at all. But if you do not spend, somebody else will—somebody else must. And it is because of this (among many other such errors) that I have fearlessly declared your so-called science of Political Economy to be no science; because, namely, it has omitted the study of exactly the most important branch of the business—the study of *spending*. For spend you must, and as much as you make, ultimately. You gather corn: will you bury England under a heap of grain; or will you, when you have gathered, finally eat? You gather gold: will you make your house-roofs of it, or pave your streets with it? That is still one way of spending it. But if you keep it, that you may get more, I'll give you more; I'll give you all the gold you want—all you can imagine—if you can tell me what you'll do with it. You shall have thousands of gold-pieces; thousands of thousands—millions—mountains, of gold; where will you keep them? Will you put an Olympus of silver upon a golden Pelion—make Ossa like a wart?[24] Do you think the rain and dew would then come down to you, in the streams from such mountains, more blessedly than they will down the mountains which God has made for you, of moss and whinstone? But it is not gold that you want to gather! What is it? greenbacks? No; not those neither. What is it then—is it ciphers after a capital I? Cannot you practice writing ciphers, and write as many as you want? Write ciphers for an hour every morning, in a big book, and say every evening, I am worth all those noughts more than I was yesterday. Won't that do? Well, what in the name of Plutus[25] is it you want? Not gold, not greenbacks, not ciphers after a capital I? You will have to answer, after all, "No; we want, somehow or other, money's *worth*." Well, what is that? Let your Goddess of Getting-on discover it, and let her learn to stay therein.

II. But there is yet another question to be asked respecting this Goddess of Getting-on. The first was of the continuance of her power; the second is of its extent.

Pallas and the Madonna were supposed to be all the world's Pallas, and all the world's Madonna. They could teach all men, and they could comfort all men. But, look strictly into the nature of the power of your Goddess of Getting-on; and you will find she is the Goddess—not of everybody's getting on—but only of somebody's getting on. This is a vital, or rather deathful, distinction. Examine it in your own ideal of the state of national life which this Goddess is to evoke and maintain. I asked you what it was, when I was last here;[26] you have never told me. Now, shall I try to tell you?

Your ideal of human life, then is, I think, that it should be passed in a pleasant undulating world, with iron and coal everywhere underneath it. On each pleasant bank of this world is to be a beautiful mansion with two wings; and stables, and coach-houses; a moderately sized park; a large garden and hot-houses; and pleasant carriage-drives through the shrubberies. In this mansion are to live the favoured votaries of the Goddess; the English gentleman, with his gracious wife, and his beautiful family; always able to have the boudoir and the jewels for the wife, and the beautiful ball dresses for the daughters, and hunters[27] for the sons, and a shooting in the Highlands for himself. At the bottom of the bank, is to be the mill; not less than a quarter of a mile long; with a steam-engine at each end, and two in the middle, and a chimney three hundred feet high. In this mill are to be in constant employment from eight hundred to a thousand workers, who never drink, never strike, always go to church on Sunday, and always express themselves in respectful language.

Is not that, broadly, and in the main features, the kind of thing you propose to yourselves? It is very pretty indeed seen from above; not at all so pretty, seen from below. For, observe, while to one family this deity is indeed the Goddess of Getting on, to a thousand families she is the Goddess of *not* Getting on. "Nay," you say, "they have all their chance." Yes, so has every one in a lottery, but there must always be the same number of blanks. "Ah! but in a lottery it is not skill and intelligence which take the lead, but blind chance." What then! do you think the old practice, that "they should take who have the power, and they should

---

[24]**Pelion, Ossa**: mountains piled on each other during the war of the giants and gods in Greek myth. **wart**: see *Hamlet* 5.1.270.

[25]**Plutus**: god of wealth.

[26]**last here**: in 1859, for a lecture.

[27]**hunters**: horses trained for the hunt. **shooting**: exclusive hunting right.

keep who can,"[28] is less iniquitous, when the power has become power of brains instead of fist? and that, though we may not take advantage of a child's or a woman's weakness, we may of a man's foolishness? "Nay, but finally, work must be done, and some one must be at the top, some one at the bottom." Granted, my friends. Work must always be, and captains of work must always be; and if you in the least remember the tone of any of my writings, you must know that they are thought unfit for this age, because they they are always insisting on need of government, and speaking with scorn of liberty. But I beg you to observe that there is wide difference between being captains or governors of work, and taking the profits of it. It does not follow, because you are general of an army, that you are to take all the treasure or land, it wins (if it fight for treasure or land); neither, because you are king of a nation, that you are to consume all the profits of the nation's work. Real kings, on the contrary, are known invariably by their doing quite the reverse of this—by their taking the least possible quantity of the nation's work for themselves. There is no test of real kinghood so infallible as that. Does the crowned creature live simply, bravely, unostentatiously? probably he *is* a King. Does he cover his body with jewels, and his table with delicates? in all probability he is *not* a King. It is possible he may be, as Solomon was; but that is when the nation shares his splendour with him. Solomon made gold, not only to be in his own palace as stones, but to be in Jerusalem as stones.[29] But even so, for the most part, these splendid kinghoods expire in ruin, and only the true kinghoods live, which are of royal labourers governing loyal labourers; who, both leading rough lives, establish the true dynasties. Conclusively you will find that because you are king of a nation, it does not follow that you are to gather for yourself all the wealth of that nation; neither, because you are king of a small part of the nation, and lord over the means of its maintenance—over field, or mill, or mine, are you to take all the produce of that piece of the foundation of national existence for yourself.

You will tell me I need not preach against these things, for I cannot mend them. No, good friends, I cannot; but you can, and you will; or something else can and will. Do you think these phenomena are to stay always in their present power or aspect? All history shows, on the contrary, that to be the exact thing they never can do. Change *must*

come; but it is ours to determine whether change of growth, or change of death. Shall the Parthenon be in ruins on its rock, and Bolton priory[30] in its meadow, but these mills of yours be the consummation of the buildings of the earth, and their wheels be as the wheels of eternity? Think you that "men may come, and men may go," but—mills—go on forever?[31] Not so; out of these, better or worse shall come; and it is for you to choose which.

I know that none of this wrong is done with deliberate purpose. I know, on the contrary, that you wish your workmen well; that you do much for them, and that you desire to do more for them, if you saw your way to it safely. I know that many of you have done, and are every day doing whatever you feel to be in your power; and that even all this wrong and misery are brought about by a warped sense of duty, each of you striving to do his best, without noticing that this best is essentially and centrally the best for himself, not for others. And all this has come of the spreading of that thrice accursed, thrice impious doctrine of the modern economist, that "To do the best for yourself, is finally to do the best for others." Friends, our great Master said not so; and most absolutely we shall find this world is not made so. . . .

1866

from The Storm-Cloud of the Nineteenth Century

Let me first assure my audience that I have no *arrière pensée* in the title chosen for this lecture.[1] I might, indeed, have meant, and it would have been only too like me to mean, any number of things by such a title;—but, to-night, I mean simply what I have said, and propose to bring to your notice a series of cloud phenomena, which, so far as I can weigh existing evidence, are peculiar to our own times; yet which have not hitherto received any special notice or description from meteorologists.

[30]**Bolton priory:** 12th-century ruin near Bradford.

[31]**"men may come . . . forever":** satirically adapting Tennyson's "The Brook" (1855) 34.

[1]*arrière pensée:* ulterior motive. **this lecture:** first of two delivered at the London Institution in February 1884. The eruption of the Indonesian volcano Krakatoa the year before had affected atmospheric light around the world.

[28]**"they should . . . who can":** Wordsworth, "Rob Roy's Grave" (1807) 39–40.

[29]**Solomon . . . as stones:** see 1 Kings 10:27.

So far as the existing evidence, I say, of former literature can be interpreted, the storm-cloud—or more accurately plague-cloud, for it is not always stormy—which I am about to describe to you, never was seen but by now living, or *lately* living eyes. It is not yet twenty years that this—I may well call it, wonderful—cloud has been, in its essence, recognizable. There is no description of it, so far as I have read, by any ancient observer. Neither Homer nor Virgil, neither Aristophanes nor Horace, acknowledge any such clouds among those compelled by Jove. Chaucer has no word of them, nor Dante; Milton none, nor Thomson.[2] In modern times, Scott, Wordsworth, and Byron are alike unconscious of them; and the most observant and descriptive of scientific men, De Saussure, is utterly silent concerning them. Taking up the traditions of air from the year before Scott's death, I am able, by my own constant and close observation, to certify you that in the forty following years (1831 to 1871 approximately—for the phenomena in question came on gradually)—no such clouds as these are, and are now often for months without intermission, were ever seen in the skies of England, France, or Italy.

In those old days, when weather was fine, it was luxuriously fine; when it was bad—it was often abominably bad, but it had its fit of temper and was done with it—it didn't sulk for three months without letting you see the sun,—nor send you one cyclone inside out, every Saturday afternoon, and another outside in, every Monday morning.

In fine weather the sky was either blue or clear in its light; the clouds, either white or golden, adding to, not abating, the lustre of the sky. In wet weather, there were two different species of clouds,—those of beneficent rain, which for distinction's sake I will call the non-electric rain-cloud, and those of storm, usually charged highly with electricity. The beneficent rain-cloud was indeed often extremely dull and grey for days together, but gracious nevertheless, felt to be doing good, and often to be delightful after drought; capable also of the most exquisite colouring, under certain conditions; and continually traversed in clearing by the rainbow:—and, secondly, the storm-cloud, always majestic, often dazzlingly beautiful, and felt also to be beneficent in its own way, affecting the mass of the air with vital agitation, and purging it from the impurity of all morbific[3] elements. . . .

Every cloud that can be, is thus primarily definable: "Visible vapour of water floating at a certain height in the air." The second clause of this definition, you see, at once implies that there is such a thing as visible vapour of water which does *not* float at a certain height in the air. You are all familiar with one extremely cognizable variety of that sort of vapour—London Particular;[4] but that especial blessing of metropolitan society is only a strongly-developed and highly-seasoned condition of a form of watery vapour which exists just as generally and widely at the bottom of the air, as the clouds do—on what, for convenience' sake, we may call the top of it;—only as yet, thanks to the sagacity of scientific men, we have got no general name for the bottom cloud, though the whole question of cloud nature begins in this broad fact, that you have one kind of vapour that lies to a certain depth on the ground, and another that floats at a certain height in the sky. Perfectly definite, in both cases, the surface level of the earthly vapour, and the roof level of the heavenly vapour, are each of them drawn within the depth of a fathom. Under *their* line, drawn for the day and for the hour, the clouds will not stoop, and above *theirs*, the mists will not rise. Each in their own region, high or deep, may expatiate at their pleasure; within that, they climb, or decline,—within that they congeal or melt away; but below their assigned horizon the surges of the cloud sea may not sink, and the floods of the mist lagoon may not be swollen.

That is the first idea you have to get well into your minds concerning the abodes of this visible vapour; next, you have to consider the manner of its visibility. Is it, you have to ask, with cloud vapour, as with most other things, that they are seen when they are there, and not seen when they are not there? or has cloud vapour so much of the ghost in it, that it can be visible or invisible as it likes, and may perhaps be all unpleasantly and malignantly there, just as much when we don't see it, as when we do? To which I answer, comfortably and generally, that, on the whole, a cloud is where you see it, and isn't where you don't; that, when there's an evident and honest thunder-cloud in the northeast, you needn't suppose there's a surreptitious and slinking one in the north-west;—when there's a visible fog at Bermondsey,[5] it doesn't follow there's a spiritual one, more than usual, at the West End: and when you get up to the clouds, and can walk into them or out of them, as you like, you find when you're in them they wet your whiskers, or take

---

[2]James **Thomson** (1700–1748): poet of *The Seasons* (1730). Horace Bénédict **de Saussure** (1740–1799): Swiss physicist, geologist, and early mountaineer.

[3]**morbific**: causing disease.

[4]**London Particular**: dense fog.

[5]**Bermondsey**: in E London. The other places mentioned are also in London.

out your curls, and when you're out of them, they don't; and therefore you may with probability assume—not with certainty, observe, but with probability—that there's more water in the air where it damps your curls than where it doesn't. If it gets much denser than that, it will begin to rain; and then you may assert, certainly with safety, that there is a shower in one place, and not in another; and not allow the scientific people to tell you that the rain is everywhere, but palpable in Tooley Street, and impalpable in Grosvenor Square.

That, I say, is broadly and comfortably so on the whole,—and yet with this kind of qualification and farther condition in the matter. If you watch the steam coming strongly out of an engine-funnel,—at the top of the funnel it is transparent,—you can't see it, though it is more densely and intensely there than anywhere else. Six inches out of the funnel it becomes snow-white,—you see it, and you see it, observe, exactly where it is,—it is then a real and proper cloud. Twenty yards off the funnel it scatters and melts away; a little of it sprinkles you with rain if you are underneath it, but the rest disappears; yet it is still there;—the surrounding air does not absorb it all into space in a moment; there is a gradually diffusing current of invisible moisture at the end of the visible stream—an invisible, yet quite substantial, vapour; but not, according to our definition, a cloud, for a cloud is vapour *visible*.

Then the next bit of the question, of course, is, What makes the vapour visible, when it is so? Why is the compressed steam transparent, the loose steam white, the dissolved steam transparent again?

The scientific people tell you that the vapour becomes visible, and chilled, as it expands. Many thanks to them; but can they show us any reason why particles of water should be more opaque when they are separated than when they are close together, or give us any idea of the difference of the state of a particle of water, which won't *sink* in the air, from that of one that won't *rise* in it?

And here I must parenthetically give you a little word of, I will venture to say, extremely useful, advice about scientific people in general. Their first business is, of course, to tell you things that are so, and do happen,—as that, if you warm water, it will boil; if you cool it, it will freeze; and if you put a candle to a cask of gunpowder, it will blow you up. Their second, and far more important business, is to tell you what you had best do under the circumstances,—put the kettle on in time for tea; powder your ice and salt, if you have a mind for ices[6] and obviate the chance of explosion

by not making the gunpowder. But if, beyond this safe and beneficial business, they ever try to *explain* anything to you, you may be confident of one of two things,—either that they know nothing (to speak of) about it, or that they have only seen one side of it—and not only haven't seen, but usually have no mind to see, the other. . . .

. . . Now at last, entering on my immediate subject, I shall best introduce it to you by reading an entry in my diary which gives progressive description of the most gentle aspect of the modern plague-cloud.

Bolton Abbey,[7] *4th July,* 1875
"Half-past eight, morning; the first bright morning for the last fortnight.

"At half-past five it was entirely clear, and entirely calm; the moorlands glowing, and the Wharfe glittering in sacred light, and even the thin-stemmed field-flowers quiet as stars, in the peace in which—

'All trees and simples, great and small,
    That balmy leaf do bear,
Than they were painted on a wall,
    No more to move, nor steir.'[8]

"But, an hour ago, the leaves at my window first shook slightly. They are now trembling *continuously*, as those of all the trees, under a gradually rising wind, of which the tremulous action scarcely permits the direction to be defined,—but which falls and returns in fits of varying force, like those which precede a thunderstorm—never wholly ceasing: the direction of its upper current is shown by a few ragged white clouds, moving fast from the north, which rose, at the time of the first leaf-shaking, behind the edge of the moors in the east.

"This wind is the plague-wind of the eighth decade of years in the nineteenth century; a period which will assuredly be recognized in future meteorological history as one of phenomena hitherto unrecorded in the courses of nature, and characterized pre-eminently by the almost ceaseless action of this calamitous wind. While I have been writing these sentences, the white clouds above specified have increased to twice the size they had when I began to write; and in about two hours from this time—say by eleven

---

[6]**powder**: crush. **ices**: iced desserts.

[7]**Bolton Abbey**: 12th-century ruin by the River **Wharfe** in Yorkshire.

[8]**"All trees . . . steir"**: misquoting Alexander Hume, "Of the Day Estivall" (1599) 77–80. **simples**: herbs.

o'clock, if the wind continue,—the whole sky will be dark with them, as it was yesterday, and has been through prolonged periods during the last five years. I first noticed the definite character of this wind, and of the clouds it brings with it, in the year 1871, describing it then in the July number of *Fors Clavigera*; but little, at that time, apprehending either its universality, or any probability of its annual continuance. I am able now to state positively that its range of power extends from the North of England to Sicily; and that it blows more or less during the whole of the year, except the early autumn. This autumnal abdication is, I hope, beginning: it blew but feebly yesterday, though without intermission, from the north, making every shady place cold, while the sun was burning; its effect on the sky being only to dim the blue of it between masses of ragged cumulus. To-day it has entirely fallen; and there seems hope of bright weather, the first for me since the end of May, when I had two fine days at Aylesbury;[9] the third, May 28th, being black again from morning to evening. There seems to be some reference to the blackness caused by the prevalence of this wind in the old French name of Bise, '*grey* wind'; and, indeed, one of the darkest and bitterest days of it I ever saw was at Vevay in 1872."

The first time I recognized the clouds brought by the plague-wind as distinct in character was in walking back from Oxford, after a hard day's work, to Abingdon, in the early spring of 1871: it would take too long to give you any account this evening of the particulars which drew my attention to them; but during the following months I had too frequent opportunities of verifying my first thoughts of them, and on the first of July in that year wrote the description of them which begins the *Fors Clavigera* of August, thus:—

> It is the first of July, and I sit down to write by the dismallest light that ever yet I wrote by; namely, the light of this midsummer morning, in mid-England (Matlock, Derbyshire), in the year 1871.
>
> For the sky is covered with grey cloud;—not rain-cloud, but a dry black veil, which no ray of sunshine can pierce; partly diffused in mist, feeble mist, enough to make distant objects unintelligible, yet without any substance, or wreathing, or colour of its own. And everywhere the leaves of the trees are shaking fitfully, as they do before a thunderstorm; only not violently, but enough to

show the passing to and fro of a strange, bitter, blighting wind. Dismal enough, had it been the first morning of its kind that summer had sent. But during all this spring, in London, and at Oxford, through meagre March, through changelessly sullen April, through despondent May, and darkened June, morning after morning has come grey-shrouded thus.

And it is a new thing to me, and a very dreadful one. I am fifty years old, and more; and since I was five, have gleaned the best hours of my life in the sun of spring and summer mornings; and I never saw such as these, till now.

And the scientific men are busy as ants, examining the sun and the moon, and the seven stars, and can tell me all about *them*, I believe, by this time; and how they move, and what they are made of.

And I do not care, for my part, two copper spangles how they move, nor what they are made of. I can't move them any other way than they go, nor make them of anything else, better than they are made. But I would care much and give much, if I could be told where this bitter wind comes from, and what *it* is made of.

For, perhaps, with forethought, and fine laboratory science, one might make it of something else.

It looks partly as if it were made of poisonous smoke; very possibly it may be: there are at least two hundred furnace chimneys in a square of two miles on every side of me. But mere smoke would not blow to and fro in that wild way. It looks more to me as if it were made of dead men's souls—such of them as are not gone yet where they have to go, and may be flitting hither and thither, doubting, themselves, of the fittest place for them.

You know, if there *are* such things as souls, and if ever any of them haunt places where they have been hurt, there must be many above us, just now, displeased enough!

The last sentence refers of course to the battles of the Franco-German campaign,[10] which was especially horrible to me, in its digging, as the Germans should have known, a

---

moat flooded with waters of death between the two nations for a century to come.

Since that Midsummer day, my attention, however otherwise occupied, has never relaxed in its record of the phenomena characteristic of the plague-wind; and I now define for you, as briefly as possible, the essential signs of it.

(1.) It is a wind of darkness,—all the former conditions of tormenting winds, whether from the north or east, were more or less capable of co-existing with sunlight, and often with steady and bright sunlight; but whenever, and wherever the plague-wind blows, be it but for ten minutes, the sky is darkened instantly.

(2.) It is a malignant *quality* of wind, unconnected with any one quarter of the compass; it blows indifferently from all, attaching its own bitterness and malice to the worst characters of the proper winds of each quarter. It will blow either with drenching rain, or dry rage, from the south,— with ruinous blasts from the west,—with bitterest chills from the north,—and with venomous blight from the east.

Its own favourite quarter, however, is the south-west, so that it is distinguished in its malignity equally from the Bise of Provence, which is a north wind always, and from our own old friend, the east.

(3.) It always blows *tremulously*, making the leaves of the trees shudder as if they were all aspens, but with a peculiar fitfulness which gives them—and I watch them this moment as I write—an expression of anger as well as of fear and distress. You may see the kind of quivering, and hear the ominous whimpering, in the gusts that precede a great thunderstorm; but plague-wind is more panic-struck, and feverish; and its sound is a hiss instead of a wail.

When I was last at Avallon, in South France, I went to see *Faust*[11] played at the little country theatre: it was done with scarcely any means of pictorial effect, except a few old curtains, and a blue light or two. But the night on the Brocken was nevertheless extremely appalling to me,—a strange ghastliness being obtained in some of the witch scenes merely by fine management of gesture and drapery; and in the phantom scenes, by the half-palsied, half-furious, faltering or fluttering past of phantoms stumbling as into graves; as if of not only soulless, but senseless, Dead, moving with the very action, the rage, the decrepitude, and the trembling of the plague-wind.

(4.) Not only tremulous at every moment, it is also *intermittent* with a rapidity quite unexampled in former weather. There are, indeed, days—and weeks, on which it blows without cessation, and is as inevitable as the Gulf Stream; but also there are days when it is contending with healthy weather, and on such days it will remit for half an hour, and the sun will begin to show itself, and then the wind will come back and cover the whole sky with clouds in ten minutes; and so on, every half-hour, through the whole day; so that it is often impossible to go on with any kind of drawing in colour, the light being never for two seconds the same from morning till evening.

(5.) It degrades, while it intensifies, ordinary storm; but before I read you any description of its efforts in this kind, I must correct an impression which has got abroad through the papers, that I speak as if the plague-wind blew now always, and there were no more any natural weather. On the contrary, the winter of 1878–9 was one of the most healthy and lovely I ever saw ice in;—Coniston lake[12] shone under the calm clear frost in one marble field, as strong as the floor of Milan Cathedral, half a mile across and four miles down; and the first entries in my diary which I read you shall be from the 22nd to 26th June, 1876, of perfectly lovely and natural weather:—

Sunday, 25th June, 1876

Yesterday, an entirely glorious sunset, unmatched in beauty since that at Abbeville,[13]—deep scarlet, and purest rose, on purple grey, in bars; and stationary, plumy, sweeping filaments above in upper sky, like *'using up the brush,'* said Joanie;[14] remaining in glory, every moment best, changing from one good into another, (but only in colour or light— *form steady*,) for half an hour full, and the clouds afterwards fading into the grey against amber twilight, *stationary in the same form for about two hours*, at least. The darkening rose tint remained till half-past ten, the grand time being at nine.

The day had been fine,—exquisite green light on afternoon hills.

Monday, 26th June, 1876

"Yesterday an entirely perfect summer light on the Old Man;[15] Lancaster Bay all clear; Ingleborough and the great Pennine fault as on a map. Divine beauty of western colour

---

[11]*Faust*: drama (1808, 1832) by Johann Wolfgang van Goethe (1749–1832).

[12]**Coniston**: the lake beside Ruskin's Lake District home, Brantwood.

[13]**Abbeville**: in N France.

[14]**Joanie**: Joan Agnew Severn, Ruskin's cousin and attendant.

[15]**Old Man** of Coniston: Lake District peak. **Ingleborough**: summit in N Yorkshire. **Pennine**: range of Yorkshire hills.

on thyme and rose,—then twilight of clearest *warm* amber far into night, of *pale* amber all night long; hills dark-clear against it.

"And so it continued, only growing more intense in blue and sunlight, all day. After breakfast, I came in from the well under strawberry bed, to say I had never seen anything like it, so pure or intense, in Italy; and so it went glowing on, cloudless, with soft north wind, all day."

16th July

"The sunset almost too bright *through the blinds* for me to read Humboldt[16] at tea by,—finally, new moon like a lime-light, reflected on breeze-struck water; traces, across dark calm, of reflected hills."

These extracts are, I hope, enough to guard you against the absurdity of supposing that it all only means that I am myself soured, or doting, in my old age, and always in an ill humour. Depend upon it, when old men are worth anything, they are better-humoured than young ones; and have learned to see what good there is, and pleasantness, in the world they are likely so soon to have orders to quit.

Now then—take the following sequences of accurate description of thunderstorm, *with* plague-wind.

22nd June, 1876

"Thunderstorm; pitch dark, with no *blackness*,—but deep, high, *filthiness* of lurid, yet not sublimely lurid, smoke-cloud; dense manufacturing mist; fearful squalls of shivery wind, making Mr. Severn's[17] sail quiver like a man in a fever fit—all about four, afternoon—but only two or three claps of thunder, and feeble, though near, flashes. I never saw such a dirty, weak, foul storm. It cleared suddenly after raining all afternoon, at half-past eight to nine, into pure, natural weather,—low rain-clouds on quite clear, green, wet hills."

Brantwood, 13th August, 1879

"The most terrific and horrible thunderstorm, this morning, I ever remember. It waked me at six, or a little before—then rolling incessantly, like railway luggage trains, quite ghastly in its mockery of them—the air one loathsome mass of sultry and foul fog, like smoke; scarcely raining at all, but increasing to heavier rollings, with flashes quivering vaguely through all the air, and at last terrific double streams of reddish-violet fire, not forked or zigzag, but rippled rivulets—two at the same instant some twenty to thirty degrees apart, and lasting on the eye at least half a second, with grand artillery-peals following; not rattling crashes, or irregular cracklings, but delivered volleys. It lasted an hour, then passed off, clearing a little, without rain to speak of,—not a glimpse of blue,—and now, half-past seven, seems settling down again into Manchester devil's darkness.[18]

"Quarter to eight, morning.—Thunder returned, all the air collapsed into one black fog, the hills invisible, and scarcely visible the opposite shore; heavy rain in short fits, and frequent, though less formidable, flashes, and shorter thunder. While I have written this sentence the cloud has again dissolved itself, like a nasty solution in a bottle, with miraculous and unnatural rapidity, and the hills are in sight again; a double-forked flash—rippled, I mean, like the others—starts into its frightful ladder of light between me and Wetherlam, as I raise my eyes. All black above, a rugged spray cloud on the Eaglet. (The 'Eaglet' is my own name for the bold and elevated crag to the west of the little lake above Coniston mines. It had no name among the country people, and is one of the most conspicuous features of the mountain chain, as seen from Brantwood.)

"Half-past eight.—Three times light and three times dark since last I wrote, and the darkness seeming each time as it settles more loathsome, at last stopping my reading in mere blindness. One lurid gleam of white cumulus in upper lead-blue sky, seen for half a minute through the sulphurous chimney-pot vomit of blackguardly cloud beneath, where its rags were thinnest."

Thursday, 22nd Feb., 1883

"Yesterday a fearfully dark mist all afternoon, with steady, south plague-wind of the bitterest, nastiest, poisonous blight, and fretful flutter. I could scarcely stay in the wood for the horror of it. To-day, really rather bright blue, and bright semi-cumuli, with the frantic Old Man blowing sheaves of lancets and chisels across the lake—not in strength enough, or whirl enough, to raise it in spray, but tracing every squall's outline in black on the silver grey waves, and whistling meanly, and as if on a flute made of a file."

---

[16]Alexander von **Humboldt** (1769–1859): German geologist and early ecologist.

[17]**Mr. Severn:** Joan Severn's husband Arthur, sailing on Coniston Water.

---

[18]**Manchester devil's darkness:** industrial-strength gloom.

Sunday, 17th August, 1879

"Raining in foul drizzle, slow and steady; sky pitch-dark, and I just get a little light by sitting in the bow-window; diabolic clouds over everything: and looking over my kitchen garden yesterday, I found it one miserable mass of weeds gone to seed, the roses in the higher garden putrefied into brown sponges, feeling like dead snails; and the half-ripe strawberries all rotten at the stalks."

(6.) And now I come to the most important sign of the plague-wind and the plague-cloud: that in bringing on their peculiar darkness, they *blanch* the sun instead of reddening it. And here I must note briefly to you the uselessness of observation by instruments, or machines, instead of eyes. In the first year when I had begun to notice the specialty of the plague-wind, I went of course to the Oxford observatory to consult its registrars. They have their anemometer always on the twirl, and can tell you the force, or at least the pace, of a gale, by day or night. But the anemometer can only record for you how often it has been driven round, not at all whether it went round *steadily*, or went round *trembling*. And on that point depends the entire question whether it is a plague breeze or a healthy one: and what's the use of telling you whether the wind's strong or not, when it can't tell you whether it's a strong medicine, or a strong poison?

But again—you have your *sun*-measure, and can tell exactly at any moment how strong, or how weak, or how wanting, the sun is. But the sun-measurer can't tell you whether the rays are stopped by a dense *shallow* cloud, or a thin *deep* one. In healthy weather, the sun is hidden behind a cloud, as it is behind a tree; and, when the cloud is past, it comes out again, as bright as before. But in plague-wind, the sun is choked out of the whole heaven, all day long, by a cloud which may be a thousand miles square and five miles deep.

And yet observe: that thin, scraggy, filthy, mangy, miserable cloud, for all the depth of it, can't turn the sun red, as a good, business-like fog does with a hundred feet or so of itself. By the plague-wind every breath of air you draw is polluted, half round the world; in a London fog the air itself is pure, though you choose to mix up dirt with it, and choke yourself with your own nastiness.

Now I'm going to show you a diagram of a sunset in entirely pure weather, above London smoke. I saw it and sketched it from my old post of observation—the top garret of my father's house at Herne Hill. There, when the wind is south, we are outside of the smoke and above it; and this diagram, admirably enlarged from my own drawing by my, now in all things best aide-de-camp, Mr.

Collingwood,[19] shows you an old-fashioned sunset—the sort of thing Turner and I used to have to look at,—(nobody else ever would) constantly. Every sunset and every dawn, and fine weather, had something of the sort to show us. This is one of the last pure sunsets I ever saw, about the year 1876,—and the point I want you to note in it is, that the air being pure, the smoke on the horizon, though at last it hides the sun, yet hides it through gold and vermilion. Now, don't go away fancying there's any exaggeration in that study. The *prismatic* colours, I told you, were simply impossible to paint; these, which are transmitted colours, can indeed be suggested, but no more. The brightest pigment we have would look dim beside the truth.

I should have liked to have blotted down for you a bit of plague-cloud to put beside this; but Heaven knows, you can see enough of it nowadays without any trouble of mine; and if you want, in a hurry, to see what the sun looks like through it, you've only to throw a bad half-crown into a basin of soap and water.

Blanched Sun,—blighted grass,—blinded man.—If, in conclusion, you ask me for any conceivable cause or meaning of these things—I can tell you none, according to your modern beliefs; but I can tell you what meaning it would have borne to the men of old time. Remember, for the last twenty years, England, and all foreign nations, either tempting her, or following her, have blasphemed the name of God deliberately and openly; and have done iniquity by proclamation, every man doing as much injustice to his brother as it is in his power to do. Of states in such moral gloom every seer of old predicted the physical gloom, saying, "The light shall be darkened in the heavens thereof, and the stars shall withdraw their shining."[20] All Greek, all Christian, all Jewish prophecy insists on the same truth through a thousand myths; but of all the chief, to former thought, was the fable of the Jewish warrior[21] and prophet, for whom the sun hasted not to go down, with which I leave you to compare at leisure the physical result of your own wars and prophecies, as declared by your own elect journal not fourteen days ago,—that the Empire of England, on which formerly the sun never set, has become one on which he never rises.

What is best to be done, do you ask me? The answer is plain. Whether you can affect the signs of the sky or not, you *can* the signs of the times.[22] Whether you can bring the

---

[19]William **Collingwood**: collaborator and biographer of Ruskin.

[20]"The light . . . their shining": Joel 2:10.

[21]Jewish warrior: see Joshua 10:13.

[22]signs of the times: Matthew 16:3; see also Carlyle's essay, page 165.

sun back or not, you can assuredly bring back your own cheerfulness, and your own honesty. You may not be able to say to the winds, "Peace; be still,"[23] but you can cease from the insolence of your own lips, and the troubling of your own passions. And all *that* it would be extremely well to do, even though the day *were* coming when the sun should be as darkness, and the moon as blood.[24] But, the paths of rectitude and piety once regained, who shall say that the promise of old time would not be found to hold for us also?—"Bring ye all the tithes into my storehouse, and prove me now herewith, saith the Lord God, if I will not open you the windows of heaven, and pour you out a blessing, that there shall not be room enough to receive it."[25] (Lecture 1)

1884

from Praeterita

I have written these sketches[1] of effort and incident in former years for my friends; and for those of the public who have been pleased by my books.

I have written them therefore, frankly, garrulously, and at ease; speaking, of what it gives me joy to remember, at any length I like—sometimes very carefully of what I think it may be useful for others to know; and passing in total silence things which I have no pleasure in reviewing, and which the reader would find no help in the account of. My described life has thus become more amusing than I expected to myself, as I summoned its long past scenes for present scrutiny:—its main methods of study, and principles of work, I feel justified in commending to other students; and very certainly any habitual readers of my books will understand them better, for having knowledge as complete as I can give them of the personal character which, without endeavour to conceal, I yet have never taken pains to display, and even, now and then, felt some freakish pleasure in exposing to the chance of misinterpretation.

I write these few prefatory words on my father's birthday, in what was once my nursery in his old house,—to which he brought my mother and me, sixty-two years since, I being then four years old. What would otherwise in the following pages have been little more than an old man's recreation in gathering visionary flowers in fields of youth, has taken, as I wrote, the nobler aspect of a dutiful offering at the grave of parents who trained my childhood to all the good it could attain, and whose memory makes declining life cheerful in the hope of being soon again with them.

HERNE HILL, 10TH MAY, 1885.

(Preface)

The Springs of Wandel

I am, and my father was before me, a violent Tory of the old school,—Walter Scott's school, that is to say, and Homer's. I name these two out of the numberless great Tory writers, because they were my own two masters. I had Walter Scott's novels, and the *Iliad* (Pope's translation),[2] for constant reading when I was a child, on week-days: on Sunday, their effect was tempered by *Robinson Crusoe* and the *Pilgrim's Progress*; my mother having it deeply in her heart to make an evangelical clergyman of me. Fortunately, I had an aunt more evangelical than my mother; and my aunt gave me cold mutton for Sunday's dinner, which—as I much preferred it hot—greatly diminished the influence of the *Pilgrim's Progress*; and the end of the matter was, that I got all the noble imaginative teaching of Defoe and Bunyan, and yet—am not an evangelical clergyman.

I had, however, still better teaching than theirs, and that compulsorily, and every day of the week.

Walter Scott and Pope's Homer were reading of my own election, and my mother forced me, by steady daily toil, to learn long chapters of the Bible by heart; as well as to read it every syllable through, aloud, hard names and all, from Genesis to the Apocalypse, about once a year: and to that discipline—patient, accurate, and resolute—I owe, not only a knowledge of the book, which I find occasionally serviceable, but much of my general power of taking pains, and the best part of my taste in literature. From Walter Scott's novels I might easily, as I grew older, have fallen to other people's novels; and Pope might, perhaps, have led me to take Johnson's English, or Gibbon's,[3] as types of language; but, once knowing the 32nd of Deuteronomy, the

---

[23]"**Peace; be still**": Mark 4:39.

[24]**sun, moon**: see Joel 2:31.

[25]"**Bring . . . receive it**": Malachi 3:10.

[1]**these sketches**: memoirs intermittently written as Ruskin's mental health permitted, and issued serially in 1885–1889, adding to material published during early 1880s in *Fors Clavigera*.

[2]**Pope's** *Iliad:* completed 1720. *Robinson Crusoe* (1719): by Daniel Defoe (1660–1731). *Pilgrim's Progress* (1678): by John Bunyan (1628–1688).

[3]Samuel **Johnson** (1709–1784): man of letters. Edward **Gibbon** (1737–1794): historian of Roman empire.

119th Psalm, the 15th of 1st Corinthians, the Sermon on the Mount, and most of the Apocalypse, every syllable by heart, and having always a way of thinking with myself what words meant, it was not possible for me, even in the foolishest times of youth, to write entirely superficial or formal English; and the affectation of trying to write like Hooker and George Herbert[4] was the most innocent I could have fallen into.

From my own chosen masters, then, Scott and Homer, I learned the Toryism which my best after-thought has only served to confirm.

That is to say, a most sincere love of kings, and dislike of everybody who attempted to disobey them. Only, both by Homer and Scott, I was taught strange ideas about kings, which I find for the present much obsolete; for, I perceived that both the author of the *Iliad* and the author of *Waverley*[5] made their kings, or king-loving persons, do harder work than anybody else. Tydides or Idomeneus always killed twenty Trojans to other people's one, and Redgauntlet speared more salmon than any of the Solway fishermen; and—which was particularly a subject of admiration to me—I observed that they not only did more, but in proportion to their doings *got* less, than other people—nay, that the best of them were even ready to govern for nothing! and let their followers divide any quantity of spoil or profit. Of late it has seemed to me that the idea of a king has become exactly the contrary of this, and that it has been supposed the duty of superior persons generally to govern less, and get more, than anybody else. So that it was, perhaps, quite as well that in those early days my contemplation of existent kingship was a very distant one.

The aunt who gave me cold mutton on Sundays was my father's sister: she lived at Bridge-end, in the town of Perth,[6] and had a garden full of gooseberry-bushes, sloping down to the Tay, with a door opening to the water, which ran past it, clear-brown over the pebbles three or four feet deep; swift-eddying,—an infinite thing for a child to look down into.

My father began business as a wine-merchant, with no capital, and a considerable amount of debts bequeathed him by my grandfather. He accepted the bequest, and paid them all before he began to lay by anything for himself,—for which his best friends called him a fool, and I, without expressing any opinion as to his wisdom, which I knew in such matters to be at least equal to mine, have written on the granite slab over his grave that he was "an entirely honest merchant." As days went on he was able to take a house in Hunter Street, Brunswick Square,[7] No. 54, (the windows of it, fortunately for me, commanded a view of a marvellous iron post, out of which the water-carts were filled through beautiful litle trapdoors, by pipes like boa-constrictors; and I was never weary of contemplating that mystery, and the delicious dripping consequent); and as years went on, and I came to be four or five years old, he could command a postchaise and pair for two months in the summer, by help of which, with my mother and me, he went the round of his country customers (who liked to see the principal of the house his own traveller); so that, at a jog-trot pace, and through the panoramic opening of the four windows of a postchaise, made more panoramic still to me because my seat was a little bracket in front, (for we used to hire the chaise regularly for the two months out of Long Acre, and so could have it bracketed and pocketed as we liked,) I saw all the high-roads, and most of the cross ones, of England and Wales; and great part of lowland Scotland, as far as Perth, where every other year we spent the whole summer: and I used to read the *Abbot* at Kinross, and the *Monastery* in Glen Farg, which I confused with "Glendearg," and thought that the White Lady had as certainly lived by the streamlet in that glen of the Ochils, as the Queen of Scots in the island of Loch Leven.[8]

To my farther great benefit, as I grew older, I thus saw nearly all the noblemen's houses in England; in reverent and healthy delight of uncovetous admiration,—perceiving, as soon as I could perceive any political truth at all, that it was probably much happier to live in a small house, and have Warwick Castle to be astonished at, than to live in Warwick Castle and have nothing to be astonished at; but that, at all events, it would not make Brunswick Square in the least more pleasantly habitable, to pull Warwick Castle down. And at this day, though I have kind invitations enough to visit America, I could not, even for a couple

---

[4]Richard **Hooker** (1554?–1600): Anglican theologian and bishop. **George Herbert** (1593–1633): Anglican priest and poet.

[5]*Waverley* (1814): historical novel by Scott. **Tydides** (Diomedes), **Idomeneus**: Homeric warrior kings. **Redgauntlet**: royalist chief in Scott's eponymous 1824 novel. **Solway** Firth: estuary between NW England and Scotland.

[6]**Perth**: in SE Scotland on the River **Tay**.

[7]**Brunswick Square**: in N London.

[8]*The Abbot, The Monastery*: historical novels of 1820 by Scott. **Kinross, Glen Farg, Ochils, Loch Leven**: in SE Scotland. **White Lady** of Avenel: ghost in Scott's *Monastery*. **Queen of Scots**: Mary Tudor (1542–1587).

of months, live in a country so miserable as to possess no castles.

Nevertheless, having formed my notion of kinghood chiefly from the FitzJames of the *Lady of the Lake*,[9] and of noblesse from the Douglas there, and the Douglas in *Marmion*, a painful wonder soon arose in my child-mind, why the castles should now be always empty. Tantallon was there; but no Archibald of Angus:—Stirling, but no Knight of Snowdoun. The galleries and gardens of England were beautiful to see—but his Lordship and her Ladyship were always in town, said the housekeepers and gardeners. Deep yearning took hold of me for a kind of "Restoration," which I began slowly to feel that Charles the Second had not altogether effected, though I always wore a gilded oak-apple very piously in my button-hole on the 29th of May.[10] It seemed to me that Charles the Second's Restoration had been, as compared with the Restoration I wanted, much as that gilded oak-apple to a real apple. And as I grew wiser, the desire for sweet pippins instead of bitter ones, and Living Kings instead of dead ones, appeared to me rational as well as romantic; and gradually it has become the main purpose of my life to grow pippins, and its chief hope, to see Kings.

I have never been able to trace these prejudices to any royalty of descent: of my father's ancestors I know nothing, nor of my mother's more than that my maternal grandmother was the landlady of the Old King's Head in Market Street, Croydon;[11] and I wish she were alive again, and I could paint her Simone Memmi's King's Head, for a sign.

My maternal grandfather was, as I have said, a sailor, who used to embark, like Robinson Crusoe, at Yarmouth, and come back at rare intervals, making himself very delightful at home. I have an idea he had something to do with the herring business, but am not clear on that point; my mother never being much communicative concerning it. He spoiled her, and her (younger) sister, with all his heart, when he was at home; unless there appeared any tendency to equivocation, or imaginative statements, on the part of the children, which were always unforgiveable. My mother being once perceived by him to have distinctly told him a lie, he sent the servant out forthwith to buy an entire bundle of new broom twigs to whip her with. "They did not hurt me so much as one" (twig) "would have done," said my mother, "but I *thought* a good deal of it."

My grandfather was killed at two-and-thirty, by trying to ride, instead of walk, into Croydon; he got his leg crushed by his horse against a wall; and died of the hurt's mortifying. My mother was then seven or eight years old, and, with her sister, was sent to quite a fashionable (for Croydon) day-school, Mrs. Rice's: where my mother was taught evangelical principles, and became the pattern girl and best needlewoman in the school; and where my aunt absolutely refused evangelical principles, and became the plague and pet of it.

My mother, being a girl of great power, with not a little pride, grew more and more exemplary in her entirely conscientious career, much laughed at, though much beloved, by her sister; who had more wit, less pride, and no conscience. At last my mother, formed into a consummate housewife, was sent for to Scotland to take care of my paternal grandfather's house; who was gradually ruining himself; and who at last effectually ruined, and killed, himself. My father came up to London; was a clerk in a merchant's house for nine years, without a holiday; then began business on his own account; paid his father's debts; and married his exemplary Croydon cousin.

Meantime my aunt had remained in Croydon, and married a baker. By the time I was four years old, and beginning to recollect things,—my father rapidly taking higher commercial position in London,—there was traceable—though to me, as a child, wholly incomprehensible,—just the least possible shade of shyness on the part of Hunter Street, Brunswick Square, towards Market Street, Croydon. But whenever my father was ill,—and hard work and sorrow had already set their mark on him,—we all went down to Croydon to be petted by my homely aunt; and walk on Duppas Hill, and on the heather of Addington.

My aunt lived in the little house still standing—or which was so four months ago—the fashionablest in Market Street, having actually two windows over the shop, in the second story; but I never troubled myself about that superior part of the mansion, unless my father happened to be making drawings in Indian ink, when I would sit reverently by and watch; my chosen domains being, at all other times, the shop, the bakehouse, and the stones round the spring of crystal water at the back door (long since let down into the modern sewer); and my chief companion, my aunt's dog,

---

[9]**FitzJames**: James V of Scotland, known by this alias and also as the **Knight of Snowdoun** (at **Stirling** Castle) in Scott's *Lady of the Lake* (1810). **Douglas**: heroic 15th-century earl in Scott's *Marmion* (1808), where the castle of **Tantallon** and the earl **Archibald of Angus** also figure.

[10]**29th of May**: birthday of **Charles** II, whose **Restoration** to the throne in 1660 was celebrated by royalists wearing the **oak-apple** (oak-leaf gall), to commemorate his oak-tree hideout after the Battle of Worcester (1651).

[11]**Croydon**: S London suburb. **Simone Memmi**: 14th-century Italian painter.

Towzer, whom she had taken pity on when he was a snap-pish, starved vagrant; and made a brave and affectionate dog of: which was the kind of thing she did for every living creature that came in her way, all her life long.

Contented, by help of these occasional glimpses of the rivers of Paradise, I lived until I was more than four years old in Hunter Street, Brunswick Square, the greater part of the year; for a few weeks in the summer breathing country air by taking lodgings in small cottages (real cottages, not vil-las, so-called) either about Hampstead, or at Dulwich,[12] at "Mrs. Ridley's," the last of a row in a lane which led out into the Dulwich fields on one side, and was itself full of butter-cups in spring, and blackberries in autumn. But my chief re-maining impressions of those days are attached to Hunter Street. My mother's general principles of first treatment were, to guard me with steady watchfulness from all avoid-able pain or danger; and, for the rest, to let me amuse myself as I liked, provided I was neither fretful nor troublesome. But the law was, that I should find my own amusement. No toys of any kind were at first allowed;—and the pity of my Croydon aunt for my monastic poverty in this respect was boundless. On one of my birthdays, thinking to overcome my mother's resolution by splendour of temptation, she bought the most radiant Punch and Judy she could find in all the Soho[13] bazaar—as big as a real Punch and Judy, all dressed in scarlet and gold, and that would dance, tied to the leg of a chair. I must have been greatly impressed, for I remember well the look of the two figures, as my aunt her-self exhibited their virtues. My mother was obliged to ac-cept them; but afterwards quietly told me it was not right that I should have them; and I never saw them again.

Nor did I painfully wish, what I was never permitted for an instant to hope, or even imagine, the possession of such things as one saw in toy-shops. I had a bunch of keys to play with, as long as I was capable only of pleasure in what glittered and jingled; as I grew older, I had a cart, and a ball; and when I was five or six years old, two boxes of well-cut wooden bricks. With these modest, but, I still think, entirely sufficient possessions, and being always sum-marily whipped if I cried, did not do as I was bid, or tum-bled on the stairs, I soon attained serene and secure methods of life and motion; and could pass my days con-tentedly in tracing the squares and comparing the colours of my carpet;—examining the knots in the wood of the floor, or counting the bricks in the opposite houses; with raptur-ous intervals of excitement during the filling of the water-cart, through its leathern pipe, from the dripping iron post at the pavement edge; or the still more admirable proceed-ings of the turn-cock, when he turned and turned till a foun-tain sprang up in the middle of the street. But the carpet, and what patterns I could find in bed-covers, dresses, or wall-papers to be examined, were my chief resources, and my attention to the particulars in these was soon so accu-rate, that when at three and a half I was taken to have my portrait painted by Mr. Northcote, I had not been ten min-utes alone with him before I asked him why there were holes in his carpet. The portrait in question represents a very pretty child with yellow hair, dressed in a white frock like a girl, with a broad light-blue sash and blue shoes to match; the feet of the child wholesomely large in propor-tion to its body; and the shoes still more wholesomely large in proportion to the feet. . . . (Volume 1, Chapter 1)

Herne-Hill Almond Blossoms

. . . The actual height of the long ridge of Herne Hill,[14] above Thames,—at least above the nearly Thames-level of its base at Camberwell Green, is, I conceive, not more than one hundred and fifty feet: but it gives the whole of this fall on both sides of it in about a quarter of a mile; forming, east and west, a succession of quite beautiful pleasure-ground and gardens, instantly dry after rain, and in which, for chil-dren, running down is pleasant play, and rolling a roller up, vigorous work. The view from the ridge on both sides was, before railroads came, entirely lovely: westward at evening, almost sublime, over softly wreathing distances of domestic wood;—Thames herself not visible, nor any fields except immediately beneath; but the tops of twenty square miles of politely inhabited groves. On the other side, east and south, the Norwood hills, partly rough with furze, partly wooded with birch and oak, partly in pure green bramble copse, and rather steep pasture, rose with the promise of all the rustic loveliness of Surrey and Kent in them, and with so much of space and height in their sweep, as gave them some fellow-ship with hills of true hill-districts. Fellowship now incon-ceivable, for the Crystal Palace,[15] without ever itself

---

[12]**Hampstead, Dulwich**: villages N and S of London.

[13]**Soho**: London neighborhood.

[14]**Herne Hill**: site of the villa S of London to which the Ruskins moved in 1823, and from which Ruskin dated the first installments of *Praeterita* (see Preface). **Camberwell**: village S of London.

[15]**Crystal Palace**: glass hall housing the Great Exhibition of 1851 in Hyde Park, dismantled and rebuilt 1854 at Sydenham, S of London.

attaining any true aspect of size, and possessing no more sublimity than a cucumber frame between two chimneys, yet by its stupidity of hollow bulk, dwarfs the hills at once; so that now one thinks of them no more but as three long lumps of clay, on lease for building. But then, the Norwood, or North wood, so called as it was seen from Croydon, in opposition to the South wood of the Surrey downs, drew itself in sweeping crescent good five miles round Dulwich to the south, broken by lanes of ascent, Gipsy Hill, and others; and, from the top, commanding views towards Dartford, and over the plain of Croydon,—in contemplation of which I one day frightened my mother out of her wits by saying "the eyes were coming out of my head!" She thought it was an attack of coup-de-soleil.[16]

Central in such amphitheatre, the crowning glory of Herne Hill was accordingly, that, after walking along its ridge southward from London through a mile of chestnut, lilac, and apple trees, hanging over the wooden palings on each side—suddenly the trees stopped on the left, and out one came on the top of a field sloping down to the south into Dulwich valley—open field animate with cow and buttercup, and below, the beautiful meadows and high avenues of Dulwich; and beyond, all that crescent of the Norwood hills; a footpath, entered by a turnstile, going down to the left, always so warm that invalids could be sheltered there in March, when to walk elsewhere would have been death to them; and so quiet, that whenever I had anything difficult to compose or think of, I used to do it rather there than in our own garden. The great field was separated from the path and road only by light wooden open palings, four feet high, needful to keep the cows in. Since I last composed, or meditated there, various improvements have taken place; first the neighbourhood wanted a new church, and built a meagre Gothic one with a useless spire, for the fashion of the thing, at the side of the field; then they built a parsonage behind it, the two stopping out half the view in that direction. Then the Crystal Palace came, for ever spoiling the view through all its compass, and bringing every show-day, from London, a flood of pedestrians down the footpath, who left it filthy with cigar ashes for the rest of the week: then the railroads came, and expatiating roughs by every excursion train, who knocked the palings about, roared at the cows, and tore down what branches of blossom they could reach over the palings on the enclosed side. Then the residents on the enclosed side built a brick wall to defend themselves. Then the path got to be insufferably hot as well as dirty,

and was gradually abandoned to the roughs, with a policeman on watch at the bottom. Finally, this year, a six foot high close paling has been put down the other side of it, and the processional excursionist has the liberty of obtaining what notion of the country air and prospect he may, between the wall and that, with one bad cigar before him, another behind him, and another in his mouth.

I do not mean this book to be in any avoidable way disagreeable or querulous; but expressive generally of my native disposition—which, though I say it, is extremely amiable, when I'm not bothered: I will grumble elsewhere when I must, and only notice this injury alike to the resident and excursionist at Herne Hill, because questions of right-of-way are now of constant occurrence; and in most cases, the mere *path* is the smallest part of the old Right, truly understood. The Right is of the cheerful view and sweet air which the path commanded.

Also, I may note in passing, that for all their talk about Magna Charta, very few Englishmen are aware that one of the main provisions of it is that Law should not be sold;[17] and it seems to me that the law of England might preserve Banstead and other downs free to the poor of England, without charging me, as it has just done, a hundred pounds for its temporary performance of that otherwise unremunerative duty.

I shall have to return over the ground of these early years, to fill gaps, after getting on a little first; but will yet venture here the tediousness of explaining that my saying "in Herne Hill garden all fruit was forbidden," only meant, of course, forbidden unless under defined restriction; which made the various gatherings of each kind in its season a sort of harvest festival; and which had this further good in its apparent severity, that, although in the at last indulgent aeras, the peach which my mother gathered for me when she was sure it was ripe, and the cherry pie for which I had chosen the cherries red all round, were, I suppose, of more ethereal flavour to me than they could have been to children allowed to pluck and eat at their will; still, the unalloyed and long continuing pleasure given me by our fruit-tree avenue was in its blossom, not in its bearing. For the general epicurean enjoyment of existence, potatoes well browned, green pease well boiled,—broad beans of the true bitter,—and the pots of damson and currant for whose annual filling we were dependent more on the greengrocer than the garden, were a

---

[16]**coup-de-soleil**: sunstroke.

[17]**sold**: "To no one will We sell, to no one will We deny or defer, Right or Justice." [Ruskin's note] **Banstead**: a **down** (long chalk ridge) in Surrey, S of London.

hundredfold more important to me than the dozen or two of nectarines of which perhaps I might get the halves of three,—(the other sides mouldy)—or the bushel or two of pears which went directly to the storeshelf. So that, very early indeed in my thoughts of trees, I had got at the principle given fifty years afterwards in Proserpina,[18] that the seeds and fruits of them were for the sake of the flowers, not the flowers for the fruit. The first joy of the year being in its snow-drops, the second, and cardinal one, was in the almond blossom,—every other garden and woodland gladness following from that in an unbroken order of kindling flower and shadowy leaf; and for many and many a year to come,—until indeed, the whole of life became autumn to me,—my chief prayer for the kindness of heaven, in its flowerful seasons, was that the frost might not touch the almond blossom. (Volume 1, Chapter 2)

Schaffhausen and Milan

. . . The Black Forest! The fall of Schaffhausen![19] The chain of the Alps! within one's grasp for Sunday! What a Sunday, instead of customary Walworth and the Dulwich fields! My impassioned petition at last carried it, and the earliest morning saw us trotting over the bridge of boats to Kehl, and in the eastern light I well remember watching the line of the Black Forest hills enlarge and rise, as we crossed the plain of the Rhine. "Gates of the hills"; opening for me to a new life—to cease no more; except at the Gates of the Hills whence one returns not.

And so, we reached the base of the Schwarzwald,[20] and entered an ascending dingle; and scarcely, I think, a quarter of an hour after entering, saw our first "Swiss cottage." How much it meant to all of us,—how much prophesied to me, no modern traveller could the least conceive, if I spent days in trying to tell him. A sort of triumphant shriek—like all the railway whistles going off at once at Clapham Junction[21]—has gone up from the Fooldom of Europe at the destruction of the myth of William Tell. To us, every word of it was true—but mythically luminous with more than mortal truth; and here, under the black woods, glowed the visible, beautiful, tangible testimony to it in the purple larch timber, carved to exquisiteness by the joy of peasant life, continuous, motionless there in the pine

shadow on its ancestral turf,—unassailed and unassailing, in the blessedness of righteous poverty, of religious peace.

The myth of William Tell[22] is destroyed forsooth? and you have tunnelled Gothard, and filled, it may be, the Bay of Uri,—and it was all for you and your sake that the grapes dropped blood from the press of St. Jacob, and the pine club struck down horse and helm in Morgarten Glen?[23]

Difficult enough for you to imagine, that old travellers' time when Switzerland was yet the land of the Swiss, and the Alps had never been trod by foot of man. Steam, never heard of yet, but for short fair weather crossing at sea (were there paddle-packets across Atlantic? I forget). Any way, the roads by land were safe; and entered once into this mountain Paradise, we wound on through its balmy glens, past cottage after cottage on their lawns, still glistering in the dew.

The road got into more barren heights by the mid-day, the hills arduous; once or twice we had to wait for horses, and we were still twenty miles from Schaffhausen at sunset; it was past midnight when we reached her closed gates. The disturbed porter had the grace to open them—not quite wide enough; we carried away one of our lamps in collision with the slanting bar as we drove through the arch. How much happier the privilege of dreamily entering a mediæval city, though with the loss of a lamp, than the free ingress of being jammed between a dray and a tramcar at a railroad station!

It is strange that I but dimly recollect the following morning; I fancy we must have gone to some sort of church or other; and certainly, part of the day went in admiring the bow-windows projecting into the clean streets. None of us seem to have thought the Alps would be visible without profane exertion in climbing hills. We dined at four, as usual, and the evening being entirely fine, went out to walk, all of us,—my father and mother and Mary and I.

We must have still spent some time in town-seeing, for it was drawing towards sunset, when we got up to some sort of garden promenade—west of the town, I believe; and high above the Rhine, so as to command the open country across it to the south and west. At which open country of low undulation, far into blue,—gazing as at one of our own distances from Malvern of Worcestershire, or Dorking of Kent,—suddenly—behold—beyond!

There was no thought in any of us for a moment of their being clouds. They were clear as crystal, sharp on the

---

[18]*Proserpina:* title of Ruskin's book on botany (1875–1886).

[19]**Black Forest, Schaffhausen:** German and Swiss scenery on the tour Ruskin took with his parents and cousin Mary in 1833.

[20]**Schwarzwald:** Black Forest.

[21]**Clapham Junction:** major railroad interchange in S London.

[22]**William Tell:** legendary hero of Swiss struggle for independence. **Gothard:** Swiss mountain pass tunneled in early 1880s. **Uri:** canton in central Switzerland.

[23]**St. Jacob, Morgarten:** sites of Swiss victories against French (1444) and Austrians (1315).

pure horizon sky, and already tinged with rose by the sinking sun. Infinitely beyond all that we had ever thought or dreamed,—the seen walls of lost Eden could not have been more beautiful to us; not more awful, round heaven, the walls of sacred Death.

It is not possible to imagine, in any time of the world, a more blessed entrance into life, for a child of such a temperament as mine. True, the temperament belonged to the age: a very few years,—within the hundred,—before that, no child could have been born to care for mountains, or for the men that lived among them, in that way. Till Rousseau's[24] time, there had been no "sentimental" love of nature; and till Scott's, no such apprehensive love of "all sorts and conditions of men," not in the soul merely, but in the flesh. St. Bernard of La Fontaine,[25] looking out to Mont Blanc with his child's eyes, sees above Mont Blanc the Madonna; St. Bernard of Talloires, not the Lake of Annecy, but the dead between Martigny and Aosta. But for me, the Alps and their people were alike beautiful in their snow, and their humanity; and I wanted, neither for them nor myself, sight of any thrones in heaven but the rocks, or of any spirits in heaven but the clouds.

Thus, in perfect health of life and fire of heart, not wanting to be anything but the boy I was, not wanting to have anything more than I had; knowing of sorrow only just so much as to make life serious to me, not enough to slacken in the least its sinews; and with so much of science mixed with feeling as to make the sight of the Alps not only the revelation of the beauty of the earth, but the opening of the first page of its volume,—I went down that evening from the garden-terrace of Schaffhausen with my destiny fixed in all of it that was to be sacred and useful. To that terrace, and the shore of the Lake of Geneva, my heart and faith return to this day, in every impulse that is yet nobly alive in them, and every thought that has in it help or peace. . . . (Volume 1, Chapter 6)

The Simplon

. . . For all other rivers there is a surface, and an underneath, and a vaguely displeasing idea of the bottom. But the Rhone flows like one lambent jewel; its surface is nowhere, its ethereal self is everywhere, the iridescent rush and translucent strength of it blue to the shore, and radiant to the depth.

Fifteen feet thick, of not flowing, but flying water; not water, neither,—melted glacier, rather, one should call it; the force of the ice is with it, and the wreathing of the clouds, the gladness of the sky, and the continuance of Time.

Waves of clear sea are, indeed, lovely to watch, but they are always coming or gone, never in any taken shape to be seen for a second. But here was one mighty wave that was always itself, and every fluted swirl of it, constant as the wreathing of a shell. No wasting away of the fallen foam, no pause for gathering of power, no helpless ebb of discouraged recoil; but alike through bright day and lulling night, the never-pausing plunge, and never-fading flash, and never-hushing whisper, and, while the sun was up, the ever-answering glow of unearthly aquamarine, ultramarine, violet-blue, gentian-blue, peacock-blue, river-of-paradise blue, glass of a painted window melted in the sun, and the witch of the Alps[26] flinging the spun tresses of it for ever from her snow.

The innocent way, too, in which the river used to stop to look into every little corner. Great torrents always seem angry, and great rivers too often sullen; but there is no anger, no disdain, in the Rhone. It seemed as if the mountain stream was in mere bliss at recovering itself again out of the lake-sleep, and raced because it rejoiced in racing, fain yet to return and stay. There were pieces of wave that danced all day as if Perdita[27] were looking on to learn; there were little streams that skipped like lambs and leaped like chamois; there were pools that shook the sunshine all through them, and were rippled in layers of overlaid ripples, like crystal sand; there were currents that twisted the light into golden braids, and inlaid the threads with turquoise enamel; there were strips of stream that had certainly above the lake been millstreams, and were looking busily for mills to turn again; there were shoots of stream that had once shot fearfully into the air, and now sprang up again laughing that they had only fallen a foot or two;—and in the midst of all the gay glittering and eddied lingering, the noble bearing by of the midmost depth, so mighty, yet so terrorless and harmless, with its swallows skimming instead of petrels, and the dear old decrepit town[28] as safe in the

[24]Jean-Jacques **Rousseau** (1712–1778): Swiss author, early exponent of Romantic exaltation of nature. **"all sorts . . . men"**: from a prayer in the Anglican liturgy.

[25]**St. Bernard of La Fontaine** or Clairvaux (1090–1153): founder of the Cistercian order of monks. **St. Bernard of Talloires** or Montjoux (11th century): builder of Alpine hospices, namesake of famous rescue dogs.

[26]**witch of the Alps**: from Byron's *Manfred* (1817).

[27]**Perdita**: heroine of Shakespeare's *Winter's Tale*, compared to a wave when she dances (4.4.140–142).

[28]**town**: Geneva.

embracing sweep of it as if it were set in a brooch of sapphire. (Volume 2, Chapter 5)

Joanna's Care

. . . I draw back to my own home,[29] twenty years ago, permitted to thank Heaven once more for the peace, and hope, and loveliness of it, and the Elysian walks with Joanie, and Paradisiacal with Rosie, under the peach-blossom branches by the little glittering stream which I had paved with crystal for them. I had built behind the highest cluster of laurels a reservoir, from which, on sunny afternoons, I could let a quite rippling film of water run for a couple of hours down behind the hayfield, where the grass in spring still grew fresh and deep. There used to be always a corncrake[30] or two in it. Twilight after twilight I have hunted that bird, and never once got glimpse of it: the voice was always at the other side of the field, or in the inscrutable air or earth. And the little stream had its falls, and pools, and imaginary lakes. Here and there it laid for itself lines of graceful sand; there and here it lost itself under beads of chalcedony. It wasn't the Liffey, nor the Nith, nor the Wandel;[31] but the two girls were surely a little cruel to call it "The Gutter"! Happiest times, for all of us, that ever were to be; not but that Joanie and her Arthur[32] are giddy enough, both of them yet, with their five little ones, but they have been sorely anxious about me, and I have been sorrowful enough for myself, since ever I lost sight of that peach-blossom avenue. "Eden-land" Rosie calls it sometimes in her letters. Whether its tiny river were of the waters of Abana, or Euphrates, or Thamesis,[33] I know not, but they were sweeter to my thirst than the fountains of Trevi or Branda.

How things bind and blend themselves together! The last time I saw the Fountain of Trevi, it was from Arthur's father's room—Joseph Severn's, where we both took Joanie to see him in 1872, and the old man made a sweet drawing of his pretty daughter-in-law, now in her schoolroom; he himself then eager in finishing his last picture of the Marriage in Cana,[34] which he had caused to take place under a vine trellis, and delighted himself by painting the crystal and ruby glittering of the changing rivulet of water out of the Greek vase, glowing into wine. Fonte Branda I last saw with Charles Norton,[35] under the same arches where Dante saw it. We drank of it together, and walked together that evening on the hills above, where the fireflies among the scented thickets shone fitfully in the still undarkened air. *How* they shone! moving like fine-broken starlight through the purple leaves. How they shone! through the sunset that faded into thunderous night as I entered Siena three days before, the white edges of the mountainous clouds still lighted from the west, and the openly golden sky calm behind the Gate of Siena's heart, with its still golden words, "Cor magis tibi Sena pandit,"[36] and the fireflies everywhere in sky and cloud rising and falling, mixed with the lightning, and more intense than the stars.

> BRANTWOOD,
> *JUNE 19TH, 1889.*
> 1885–1889

(Volume 3, Chapter 4)

---

[29]**home:** Brantwood, on Coniston Water in the Lake District (NW England), purchased 1871. **Joanie:** Joan Agnew Severn, Ruskin's cousin, nurse, and attendant of his last years. **Rosie:** Rose La Touche (1848–1875), with whom Ruskin was in love from 1858 until her death.

[30]**corncrake:** summer bird that frequents planted fields.

[31]**Liffey, Nith, Wandel:** rivers near the first homes of Rose (Ireland), Joan (Scotland), and Ruskin (S London).

[32]**Arthur** Severn: husband of Joan, son of painter **Joseph Severn** (1790–1879), who had nursed the dying John Keats.

[33]**Abana, Euphrates:** rivers of healing in Damascus and Babylon. **Thamesis:** the Thames. **Trevi, Branda:** fountains in Rome and Siena.

[34]**Cana:** where Jesus changed water into wine (John 2).

[35]**Charles** Eliot Norton (1827–1908): American man of letters, Ruskin's literary executor, whom he visited in Siena 1870. **Dante:** see *Inferno* 30.78.

[36]**"Cor magis . . . pandit":** Siena opens her heart to you more.

VICTORIA

(1819–1901)

Throughout her secluded and rather lonely childhood Princess Victoria knew she was likely to become Queen of England, but she was carefully trained in obedience and self-control. Her father, an impoverished royal duke, died when she was an infant, and she was brought up in London by her German mother. Her education was conducted by a German governess and a British clergyman with an eye to her possible high destiny, emphasizing moral and religious instruction, history, carefully selected readings in English literature, and a little Latin as well as German and French. Despite her isolation and the uncertainty of her position, she resisted the attempts of her mother and her mother's chief adviser to secure their own power and future influence, and when she became Queen in 1837 at the age of eighteen she immediately established her independence from them. She relied for practical instruction in the business of government on the Prime Minister, Lord Melbourne, while her mother's brother Leopold, who had become King of the Belgians, advised her on such matters as maintaining a regal distance from her subjects, including prime ministers. She took her duties as monarch with the utmost seriousness. For the public, the virtuous and dignified young queen was a delightful contrast to her mad, crude, unhealthy, and profligate predecessors.

In 1840 she married a poor but handsome and high-minded German prince a few months younger than herself, with whom she was very much in love. Like Victoria, Albert (who received the title of Prince Consort) was driven by a strong conscience and a powerful sense of duty; he was more intellectual, however, and more meticulous and hard working. Her energies were drained by pregnancy and childbirth—she bore nine children in seventeen years—and Albert assumed many responsibilities both for himself and on her behalf. When he died in 1861 she went into a lifelong state of mourning that was excessive even by the standards of an age that lavished apparently endless attention on the ritual commemoration of the dead.

For almost all her life Victoria kept a diary, and six years into her widowhood she published *Leaves from the Journal of Our Life in the Highlands*, selections recording her happiest times. In a rather small and simple castle in the Scottish Highlands she had lived with her husband and children, relatively unencumbered by attendants or ceremony—only one policeman on guard, and rough, picturesque Highlanders to accompany them when Victoria rode her pony, Albert shot stags, or the royal couple went fishing in a rowboat and took a picnic lunch. Illustrated with her own sketches, simple and direct in tone, the book is innocent, sentimental, and above all domestic. It omits almost entirely the affairs of state that were always part of Victoria's daily life. An immediate best-seller, the book was reprinted several times. Its apparently artless simplicity seemed a shining example of the feminine ideal, and the virtues it embodied were solidly middle-class. Its attention to homely matters and to servants horrified many in her own circle and offered an irresistible object for parody, but it reinforced the image of the Queen as the kindly and sympathetic "mother of her people" and shored up her popularity with a public that was losing patience with her long withdrawal into private grief.

This canny public exploitation of the personal is typical of the paradoxes represented by Victoria, as by her era. She was a small, homely woman imbued with awe-inspiring royal dignity; a scoffer at the idea of women's rights who delighted in her role as Queen and Empress;

and a passionately devoted wife whose apparently perfect marriage concealed fits of depression and struggles for power. She magnificently exemplified the fecundity of the ideal Victorian marriage, but although fond of children she did not like pregnancy or infants. Her grief-sodden widowhood was punctuated by scandalous rumors about her Highland attendant John Brown, who makes his first public appearance in *Leaves*. And of course the idyllic simplicity described in the book relies for its effectiveness on the author's royal identity, as she is well aware.

Besides composing her diaries, most of which were destroyed after her death by a daughter who wished to protect family privacy, Victoria carried on an immense correspondence. Her candid and affectionate letters to her eldest daughter, "Vicky," provide the most revealing picture we have of the woman who gave her name, for better and worse, to the Victorian age.

from Leaves from the Journal of Our Life in the Highlands

Loch Muich

September 16, 1850

We reached the hut at three o'clock. At half-past four we walked down to the loch, and got into the boat with our people: Duncan, Brown,[1] P. Cotes,[2] and Leys rowing. They rowed mostly towards the opposite side, which is very fine indeed, and deeply furrowed by the torrents, which form glens and corries[3] where birch and alder trees grow close to the water's edge. We landed on a sandy spot below a fine glen, through which flows the *Black Burn*. It was very dry here; but still very picturesque, with alder-trees and mountain-ash in full fruit overhanging it. We afterwards landed at our usual place at the head of the loch, which is magnificent; and rode back. A new road has been made, and an excellent one it is, winding along above the lake.

The moon rose, and was beautifully reflected on the lake, which, with its steep green hills, looked lovely. To add to the beauty, poetry, and wildness of the scene, Cotes played in the boat; the men, who row very quickly and well now, giving an occasional shout when he played a reel. It reminded me of Sir Walter Scott's lines in *The Lady of the Lake*:[4]—

> "Ever, as on they bore, more loud
> And louder rung the pibroch proud.
> At first the sound, by distance tame,
> Mellow'd along the waters came,
> And, lingering long by cape and bay,
> Wail'd every harsher note away."

We were home at a little past seven; and it was so still and pretty as we entered the wood, and saw the light flickering from our humble little abode.

Building the Cairn on Craig Gowan, &c.

Monday, October 11, 1852

This day has been a very happy, lucky, and memorable one—our last! A fine morning.

---

[1]The same who, in 1858, became my regular attendant out of doors everywhere in the Highlands; who commenced as gillie in 1849, and was selected by Albert and me to go with my carriage. In 1851 he entered our service permanently, and began in that year leading my pony, and advanced step by step by his good conduct and intelligence. His attention, care, and faithfulness cannot be exceeded; and the state of my health, which of late years has been sorely tried and weakened, renders such qualifications most valuable, and indeed, most needful in a constant attendant upon all occasions. He has since, most deservedly, been promoted to be an upper servant, and my permanent personal attendant. (December, 1865). He has all the independence and elevated feelings peculiar to the Highland race, and is singularly straightforward, simple-minded, kind-hearted, and disinterested; always ready to oblige; and of a discretion rarely to be met with. He is now in his fortieth year. His father was a small farmer, who lived at the Bush on the opposite side to Balmoral. He is the second of nine brothers,—three of whom have died—two are in Australia and New Zealand, two are living in the neighbourhood of Balmoral; and the youngest, Archie (Archiebald) is valet to our son Leopold, and is an excellent, trustworthy young man. [Victoria's note] **gillie:** attendant to a Highland chief.

[2]Now, since some years, piper to Farquharson of Invercauld. [Victoria's note]

[3]**glens and corries:** Highland valleys and hollows.

[4]*The Lady of the Lake* (1810): 2.355–360. **pibroch:** a Highland air played on a bagpipe.

Albert had to see Mr. Walpole,[5] and therefore it was nearly eleven o'clock before we could go up to the top of *Craig Gowan,* to see the cairn built, which was to commemorate our taking possession of this dear place; the old cairn having been pulled down. We set off with all the children, ladies, gentlemen, and a few of the servants, including Macdonald and Grant, who had not already gone up; and at the *Moss House,* which is half way, Mackay met us, and preceded us, playing, Duncan and Donald Stewart[6] going before him, to the highest point of *Craig Gowan;* where were assembled all the servants and tenants, with their wives and children and old relations. All our little friends were there: Mary Symons and Lizzie Stewart, the four Grants, and several others.

I then placed the first stone, after which Albert laid one, then the children, according to their ages. All the ladies and gentlemen placed one; and then every one came forward at once, each person carrying a stone and placing it on the cairn. Mr. and Mrs. Anderson were there; Mackay played; and whisky was given to all. It took, I am sure, an hour building; and whilst it was going on, some merry reels were danced on a stone opposite. All the old people (even the gardener's wife from *Corbie Hall,* near *Abergeldie,*) danced; and many of the children, Mary Symons and Lizzie Stewart especially, danced so nicely; the latter with her hair all hanging down. Poor dear old "Monk," Sir Robert Gordon's faithful old dog, was sitting there amongst us all. At last, when the cairn, which is, I think, seven or eight feet high, was nearly completed, Albert climbed up to the top of it, and placed the last stone; after which three cheers were given. It was a gay, pretty, and touching sight; and I felt almost inclined to cry. The view was so beautiful over the dear hills; the day so fine; the whole so *gemüthlich.*[7] May God bless this place, and allow us yet to see it and enjoy it many a long year!

After luncheon, Albert decided to walk through the wood for the last time, to have a last chance, and allowed Vicky[8] and me to go with him. At half-past three o'clock we started, got out at Grant's, and walked up part of *Carrop,* in-

tending to go along the upper path, when a stag was heard to roar, and we all turned into the wood. We crept along, and got into the middle path. Albert soon left us to go lower, and we sat down to wait for him; presently we heard a shot—then complete silence—and, after another pause of some little time, three more shots. This was again succeeded by complete silence. We sent some one to look, who shortly after returned, saying the stag had been twice hit and they were after him. Macdonald next went, and in about five minutes we heard "Solomon" give tongue, and knew he had the stag at bay. We listened a little while, and then began moving down hoping to arrive in time; but the barking had ceased, and Albert had already killed the stag; and on the road he lay, a little way beyond *Invergelder*—the beauty that we had admired yesterday evening. He was a magnificent animal, and I sat down and scratched a little sketch of him on a bit of paper that Macdonald had in his pocket, which I put on a stone—while Albert and Vicky, with the others, built a little cairn to mark the spot. We heard, after I had finished my little scrawl, and the carriage had joined us, that another stag had been seen near the road; and we had not gone as far as the "Irons,"[9] before we saw one below the road, looking so handsome. Albert jumped out and fired—the animal fell, but rose again, and went on a little way, and Albert followed. Very shortly after, however, we heard a cry, and ran down and found Grant and Donald Stewart pulling up a stag with a very pretty head. Albert had gone on, Grant went after him, and I and Vicky remained with Donald Stewart, the stag, and the dogs. I sat down to sketch, and poor Vicky, unfortunately, seated herself on a wasp's nest, and was much stung. Donald Stewart rescued her, for I could not, being myself too much alarmed. Albert joined us in twenty minutes, unaware of having killed the stag. What a delightful day! But sad that it should be the last day! Home by half-past six. We found our beautiful stag had arrived, and admired him much.

Visits to the Old Women

Saturday, September 26, 1857

Albert went out with Alfred for the day, and I walked out with the two girls and Lady Churchill,[10] stopped at the

---

[5]Spencer Horatio **Walpole** (1806–1898): the Home Secretary.

[6]**Stewart:** One of the keepers, whom we found here in 1848. He is an excellent man, and was much liked by the Prince; he always led the dogs when the Prince went out stalking. He lives in the Western Lodge, close to Grant's house, which was built for him by the Prince. [Victoria's note] **Mackay:** My Piper from the year 1843, considered almost the first in Scotland, who was recommended by the Marquis of Breadalbane; he unfortunately went out of his mind in the year 1854, and died in 1855. A brother of his was Piper to the Duke of Sussex. [Victoria's note]

[7]*gemüthlich:* genial, full of good feeling.

[8]**Vicky:** Princess Victoria (1840–1901), her eldest child.

[9]These "Irons" are the levers of an old saw-mill which was pulled down, and they were left there to be sold—between thirty and forty years ago—and have remained there ever since, not being considered worth selling, on account of the immense trouble of transporting them. [Victoria's note]

[10]**Alfred** (1844–1900), their second son. **girls:** Victoria and Alice (1843–1878). Lady Jane **Churchill** (1826–1900): Lady of the Bedchamber to the Queen.

shop and made some purchases for poor people and others; drove a little way, got out and walked up the hill to *Balnacroft*, Mrs. P. Farquharson's, and she walked round with us to some of the cottages to show me where the poor people lived, and to tell them who I was. Before we went into any we met an old woman, who, Mrs. Farquharson said, was very poor, eighty-eight years old, and mother to the former distiller. I gave her a warm petticoat, and the tears rolled down her old cheeks, and she shook my hands, and prayed God to bless me: it was very touching.

I went into a small cabin of old Kitty Kear's, who is eighty-six years old—quite erect, and who welcomed us with a great air of dignity. She sat down and spun. I gave her, also, a warm petticoat; she said, "May the Lord ever attend ye and yours, here and hereafter; and may the Lord be a guide to ye, and keep ye from all harm." She was quite surprised at Vicky's height; great interest is taken in her. We went on to a cottage (formerly Jean Gordon's), to visit old widow Symons, who is "past fourscore," with a nice rosy face, but was bent quite double; she was most friendly, shaking hands with us all, asking which was I, and repeating many kind blessings: "May the Lord attend ye with mirth and with joy; may He ever be with ye in this world, and when ye leave it." To Vicky, when told she was going to be married, she said, "May the Lord be a guide to ye in your future, and may every happiness attend ye." She was very talkative; and when I said I hoped to see her again, she expressed an expectation that "she should be called any day," and so did Kitty Kear.[11]

We went into three other cottages: to Mrs. Symons's (daughter-in-law to the old widow living next door), who had an "unwell boy;" then across a little burn to another old woman's and afterwards peeped into Blair the fiddler's. We drove back, and got out again to visit old Mrs. Grant (Grant's mother), who is so tidy and clean, and to whom I gave a dress and handkerchief, and she said, "You're too kind to me, you're over kind to me, ye give me more every year, and I get older every year." After talking some time with her, she said, "I am happy to see ye looking so nice." She had tears in her eyes, and speaking of Vicky's going, said, "I'm very sorry, and I think she is sorry hersel';" and, having said she feared she would not see her (the Princess) again, said: "I am very sorry I said that, but I meant no harm; I always say just what I think, not what is fut" (fit). Dear old lady; she is such a pleasant person.

Really the affection of these good people, who are so hearty and so happy to see you, taking interest in everything, is very touching and gratifying.

1868

from Letters[1]

Buckingham Palace, June 9, 1858

I mean to try and write you a long letter, and to pour out all my feelings of joy and thankfulness. Dearest Papa's return is of course the sunshine of which you said you had a gleam. And I feel as if it were hardly possible to be true—so great and irrepressible is the happiness. But I am so glad, so thankful he made this journey;[2] I am sure it has done him so much good, refreshed and cheered him—as he is so plagued and fagged with work and I think he looks so well—so much better than when he went! And then it gave him such pleasure, it gave you such pleasure, and it was I'm sure of great use in many ways—to you and to Fritz and lastly it is almost as if I have seen you myself—so much do I feel I see through his eyes! All he told and tells me pleases me much though I am grieved at some discomforts you have for instance your bedroom being in this dreadful heat over the kitchen is awful! Can't that be altered? I must also repeat that what you say about your feelings towards your husband are only those which I have ever felt and shall ever feel! But I cannot ever think or admit that anyone can be as blessed as I am with such a husband and such a perfection as a husband; for Papa has been and is everything to me. I had led a very unhappy life as a child—had no scope for my very violent feelings of affection—had no brothers and sisters to live with—never had had a father—from my unfortunate circumstances was not on a comfortable or at all intimate or confidential footing with my mother (so different from you to me)—much as I love her now—and did not know what a happy domestic life was! All this is the complete contrast to your happy childhood and home. Consequently I owe everything to dearest Papa. He was my father, my protector, my guide and adviser in all and everything, my mother (I might almost say) as well as my husband. I suppose no-one ever was so completely

---

[11]**Kitty Kear:** She died in Jan. 1865. [Victoria's note]

[1]**Letters:** to her eldest daughter, Victoria, who had married in January 1858 and gone to live in Berlin. Her husband (**Fritz**) was Prince Frederick William of Prussia (1831–1888), who became King of Prussia and Emperor of Germany a few months before his death.

[2]**journey:** Albert had visited their daughter in Berlin.

altered and changed in every way as I was by dearest Papa's blessed influence. Papa's position towards me is therefore of a very peculiar character and when he is away I feel quite paralysed. I did my best during his absence—and he was much pleased with my "stewardship". Dear Papa praised Fritz very much—and said he was so kind and good and anxious to do everything to please us—and was devoted to you. And this is a great great comfort to us both so far away as we are. . . .

Stoneleigh Abbey, Kenilworth, June 15, 1858
. . . Broiled and exhausted and done up as I am by a worse heat than Paris I must write to you as I fear I shall not have much time tomorrow. Imagine a railway journey with heat and dust (for we had to have both windows open) flying in, and sun shining like a pine house! But today think to be out from 11 to 5 exposed to the most fearful sun (like Paris) driving about in the streets of Birmingham with seven hundred thousand people out—and then receiving addresses in a stifling town hall—and then finding the air so heated as to be unable, coming home, to open the windows and I think you would have a sick headache! Really it is Paris over again only with the thickness and heaviness of English atmosphere! But a finer reception I never saw; exceeding Manchester, and the decorations so beautiful—such quantities of wreaths and flags and guidons all through the streets, such order kept, no walking crowd, and such very kind and loyal inscriptions, you and Fritz not forgotten. Many Prussian flags and you and Fritz on a sort of transparency. But you must read the account, dear child, for it is really quite an event, and the Park and Aston Hall[3] very curious. And they are so fond of dearest Papa here. This was formerly one of the most radical towns in England! I was there and at Aston Hall 28 years ago! I was a year older than Louise. Yesterday it was deliciously cool on driving and arriving here—but today even the cool river, the Avon flowing under our windows—and the splendid woods (I never saw finer timber) does no good and I dread the night. This is a beautiful place—an old seat—and everything so well arranged and kept. The old Abbey part is very old indeed; as old as Queen Elizabeth. We have charming rooms only sadly hot this evening.

15TH. So far I got before dinner, and can hardly hold my pen for the awful steaming heat this morning after a heavy thunderstorm and violent rain during the night which was too fearfully hot! Still I think it will get better as soon as the steaming is over—so many people ask kindly after you and say I must so feel the separation which God knows I do. . . .

What you say of the pride of giving life to an immortal soul is very fine, dear, but I own I cannot enter into that; I think much more of our being like a cow or a dog at such moments; when our poor nature becomes so very animal and unecstatic—but for you, dear, if you are sensible and reasonable not in ecstasy nor spending your day with nurses and wet nurses, which is the ruin of many a refined and intellectual young lady, without adding to her real maternal duties, a child will be a great resource. Above all, dear, do remember never to lose the modesty of a young girl towards others (without being prude); though you are married don't become a matron at once to whom everything can be said, and who minds saying nothing herself—I remained particular to a degree (indeed feel so now) and often feel shocked at the confidences of other married ladies. I fear abroad they are very indelicate about these things. Think of me who at that first time, very unreasonable, and perfectly furious as I was to be caught, having to have drawing rooms and levées and made to sit down—and be stared at and take every sort of precaution. . . .

Windsor Castle, April 20, 1859
I have this very moment received your dear letter of the 18th and thank you much for it. I am glad you bear out what I said about our dear correspondence. It is an immense pleasure and comfort to me, for it is dreadful to live so far off and always separated. I really think I shall never let your sisters marry—certainly not to be so constantly away and see so little of their parents—as till now, you have done, contrary to all that I was originally promised and told. I am so glad to see that you so entirely enter into all my feelings as a mother. Yes, dearest, it is an awful moment to have to give one's innocent child up to a man, be he ever so kind and good—and to think of all that she must go through! I can't say what I suffered, what I felt—what struggles I had to go through—(indeed I have not quite got over it yet) and that last night when we took you to your room, and you cried so much, I said to Papa as we came back "after all, it is like taking a poor lamb to be sacrificed". You now know—what I meant, dear. I know that God has willed it so and that these are the trials which we poor women must go through; no father, no man can feel this! Papa never would enter into it all! As in fact he seldom can in my very violent feelings. It really makes me shudder when I look around at all your sweet, happy, unconscious sisters—and think that I must give them up too—one by one!! Our dear Alice,[4] has

---

[3]She was in Birmingham for the opening of the great Jacobean mansion and grounds of **Aston Hall**.

[4]Princess **Alice** (1843–1878) married the Grand Duke of Hesse-Darmstadt in 1862.

seen and heard more (of course not what no one ever can know before they marry and before they have had children) than you did, from your marriage—and quite enough to give her a horror rather of marrying. . . .

The Rosenau, August 27, 1863
Many, many thanks for your dear beautiful letter received this morning. How true every word is! Yes, dear child, I do deserve pity for my lot is a terrible one! I long for peace and quiet, and to be able to rest and dwell only on my adored angel; and that necessary quiet is never allowed me! Worried and worn and worked and constantly struggling against the attempts to force me to do more, when I feel worn out by what I have to do—by the awful responsibility! It must indeed be a sad sight to see me standing alone, with a few orphans, when we were ever together! God bless and protect you in your trying and painful position! I have no answer from the King! You may be quite easy as to my interview with the Emperor.[5]

Osborne, December 18, 1867
I wished to answer what you said about the bar between high and low. What you say about it is most true but alas!

that is the great danger in England now, and one which alarms all right-minded and thinking people.

The higher classes—especially the aristocracy (with of course exceptions and honourable ones)—are so frivolous, pleasure-seeking, heartless, selfish, immoral and gambling that it makes one think (just as the Dean of Windsor[6] said to me the other evening) of the days before the French Revolution. The young men are so ignorant, luxurious and self-indulgent—and the young women so fast, frivolous and imprudent that the danger really is very great, and they ought to be warned. The lower classes are becoming so well-informed, are so intelligent and earn their bread and riches so deservedly—that they cannot and ought not to be kept back—to be abused by the wretched, ignorant, high-born beings who live only to kill time. They must be warned and frightened or some dreadful crash will take place. What I can, I do and will do—but Bertie[7] ought to set a good example in these respects by not countenancing even any of these horrid people.

1964, 1968, 1971

---

[5]**Emperor:** Napoleon III (1808–1873).

[6]**Dean of Windsor:** Gerald Wellesley (1809–1882).

[7]**Bertie:** Albert Edward (1841–1910), Prince of Wales. His lively social life displeased his mother, whom he succeeded as King Edward VII.

ARTHUR HUGH CLOUGH

(1819–1861)

At school and at Oxford Arthur Hugh Clough (rhymes with "rough") was admired for his intellectual brilliance and moral seriousness and expected to do great things, but he soon came to seem an example of unfulfilled promise and wasted powers. His failure has often been ascribed to excessive conscientiousness, in particular the questioning of religious belief that was endemic among intellectual young men around midcentury. Many have thought him the victim of Thomas Arnold, the charismatic reforming headmaster of Rugby who inculcated in his best pupils an extremely high ideal of scrupulous and strenuous morality, intellectual rigor, and religious earnestness. Since his family had moved to South Carolina, where his father was a merchant in the cotton trade, Rugby School was Clough's substitute for home, and he thoroughly imbibed Dr. Arnold's values. At Oxford, however, the strongest influence during his undergraduate years was that of John Henry Newman and the movement towards Catholicism, of which Thomas Arnold was the chief opponent. Clough also responded to a third religious current, the Higher Critics' questioning of the Bible's historical status. He fell prey to self-doubt, anxiety, and depression, and—first sign of troubles to come—did not do well in his examinations. He won a fellowship nonetheless and became a popular teacher with a wide circle of friends, but in 1848 he resigned his fellowship rather than subscribe to the Thirty-Nine Articles that defined the doctrines of the Church of England, to which he could no longer fully assent.

After leaving Oxford he could not find congenial employment and eventually set off for the United States. There he was welcomed by Boston intellectuals (including Ralph Waldo Emerson) and thought of starting a school. In 1853, however, he returned to England, where his fiancée had been waiting with increasing impatience for him to decide which country to settle in. He found a job in the Education Office and got married. The work was not very interesting, however, and there was little prospect of advancement. His health weakened, while his energies were drained by assisting Florence Nightingale, his wife's cousin: he not only helped with her report on the health of the British Army but also took care of many business matters and ordinary chores. In an attempt to recover his strength he went to Italy, where he died. The tone of most later commentary was set by Matthew Arnold, who had been one of Clough's closest friends at Oxford. In his elegy "Thyrsis," Arnold wrote that Clough "of his own will went away" from the world of modern strife and doubt.

As a poet Clough made little impression during his lifetime. His rough rhythms and unsettling irony puzzled many readers, while sexual frankness, religious questioning, and what Victorians referred to as "morbid self-consciousness" repelled others. Much of his most daring and interesting work remained unfinished. In 1848 he published *The Bothie of Tober-na-Vuolich: A Long-Vacation Pastoral*, a high-spirited, rollicking narrative about a group of undergraduates that ends with the radical, idealistic hero marrying a poor but well-educated country girl and emigrating to New Zealand to become a farmer and build a better world. A volume of poems by Clough and a friend appeared in 1849 to mixed reviews. But *Amours de Voyage*, although written in 1849, was published before his death only in the United States, anonymously serialized in the *Atlantic Monthly* in 1858. Many other poems first appeared in the posthumous *Poems and Prose Remains* (1869).

Amours de Voyage is a sort of epistolary novel in verse based on Clough's visit to Rome in 1849 while the French were besieging the new Roman Republic. During the political upheavals of the 1840s Clough was an enthusiastic radical, and he arrived in Rome carrying a gift from Thomas Carlyle to Giuseppe Mazzini, one of the leaders of the movement for Italian reunification. The hero of *Amours de Voyage*, Claude, like Clough himself, is a highly educated young Englishman who is in Rome just when Clough was, and some of his letters about Rome and Roman affairs closely resemble Clough's own. Like the hero of Tennyson's *Maud*, Claude imagines himself a kind of Hamlet: a man who thinks too much to trust his own feelings or commit himself to action. He finds it hard to take himself seriously, either in politics or in love. His hyperintellectual self-consciousness is mirrored in the verse form: dactylic hexameters, the meter of classical epic, composed chiefly of dactyls (long-short-short) clumped in threes around a medial pause.

Róme disap / póints me / múch,— // I / hárdly as / yét under / stánd, but
Rúbbishy / séems the / wórd // that / móst ex / áctly would / súit it.

Hexameters do not come naturally in English verse, and while Clough's move with astonishing fluency and ease, they retain a self-conscious, faintly parodic ring that echoes Claude's own inability to take either himself or classical grandeur quite seriously. In the face of great art and heroic events he is that quintessentially awkward modern figure, the tourist. The seriocomic tone, layered quotations and allusions, and complex, inward-turning ironies make this poem more accessible, perhaps, to readers whose expectations have been shaped by T. S. Eliot, W. H. Auden, and the modernist tradition than to a Victorian audience.

ὕμνος ἄυμνος[1]
[Hymnos Ahymnos]

O thou whose image in the shrine
Of human spirits dwells divine;
Which from that precinct once conveyed,
To be to outer day displayed,
Doth vanish, part, and leave behind.
Mere blank and void of empty mind,
Which wilful fancy seeks in vain
With casual shapes to fill again—

O thou that in our bosoms' shrine
Dost dwell, because unknown, divine!   10
I thought to speak, I thought to say,
"The light is here," "behold the way,"
"The voice was thus," and "thus the word,"
And "thus I saw," and "that I heard,"—
But from the lips but half essayed
The imperfect utterance fell unmade.

O thou, in that mysterious shrine
Enthroned, as we must say, divine!

I will not frame one thought of what
Thou mayest either be or not.   20
I will not prate of "thus" and "so,"
And be profane with "yes" and "no."
Enough that in our soul and heart
Thou, whatsoe'er thou may'st be, art.

Unseen, secure in that high shrine
Acknowledged present and divine,
I will not ask some upper air,
Some future day, to place thee there;
Nor say, nor yet deny, Such men
Or women saw thee thus and then: 30
Thy name was such, and there or here
To him or her thou didst appear.

Do only thou in that dim shrine,
Unknown or known, remain, divine;
There, or if not, at least in eyes
That scan the fact that round them lies.
The hand to sway, the judgment guide,
In sight and sense thyself divide:
Be thou but there,—in soul and heart,
I will not ask to feel thou art.   40

---

[1]ὕμνος ἄυμνος: A hymn, yet not a hymn. [Clough's note]

1851

~

Say not the struggle nought availeth,
    The labour and the wounds are vain,
The enemy faints not, nor faileth,
    And as things have been, things remain.

If hopes were dupes, fears may be liars;
    It may be, in yon smoke concealed,
Your comrades chase e'en now the fliers,
    And, but for you, possess the field.

For while the tired waves, vainly breaking,
    Seem here no painful inch to gain,   10
Far back through creeks and inlets making
    Came, silent, flooding in, the main,

And not by eastern windows only,
    When daylight comes, comes in the light,
In front the sun climbs slow, how slowly,
    But westward, look, the land is bright.

                                    1855

~

Amours de Voyage

Oh, you are sick of self-love, Malvolio,
And taste with a distempered appetite![1]
                        Shakspeare

Il doutait de tout, même de l'amour.[2]
                        French Novel

Solvitur ambulando.[3]
                        Solutio Sophismatum

Flevit amores
Non elaboratum ad pedem.[4]
                        Horace

— CANTO 1 —

Over the great windy waters, and over the clear crested summits,
    Unto the sun and the sky, and unto the perfecter earth,

---

[1]*Oh, you are sick . . . appetite!: Twelfth Night* 1.5.96–97.

[2]*Il doutait . . . l'amour:* He doubted everything, even love.

[3]*Solutio Sophismaturn:* a solution of logical fallaces. *Solvitur ambulando:* It is resolved by walking, (traditional refutation of theories that flout common sense).

[4]*Flevit . . . ad pedem:* Horace, *Epodes* 14.11–12. He lamented his loves in unelaborated verse.

Come, let us go,—to a land wherein gods of the old time wandered,
    Where every breath even now changes to ether divine.
Come, let us go; though withal a voice whisper, "The world that we live in,
    Whithersoever we turn, still is the same narrow crib;
'Tis but to prove limitation, and measure a cord, that we travel;
    Let who would 'scape and be free go to his chamber and think;
'Tis but to change idle fancies for memories wilfully falser;
    'Tis but to go and have been."—Come, little bark! let us go.   10

1 CLAUDE TO EUSTACE

Dear Eustatio, I write that you may write me an answer,
Or at the least to put us again *en rapport* with each other.
Rome disappoints me much,—St Peter's,[5] perhaps, in
    especial;
Only the Arch of Titus and view from the Lateran
    please me:
This, however, perhaps, is the weather, which truly is
    horrid.
Greece must be better, surely; and yet I am feeling so
    spiteful,
That I could travel to Athens, to Delphi, and Troy, and
    Mount Sinai,
Though but to see with my eyes that these are vanity also.
    Rome disappoints me much; I hardly as yet understand,
    but
Rubbishy seems the word that most exactly would suit it.   20
All the foolish destructions, and all the sillier savings,
All the incongruous things of past incompatible ages,
Seem to be treasured up here to make fools of present and
    future.
Would to Heaven the old Goths[6] had made a cleaner sweep
    of it!
Would to Heaven some new ones would come and destroy
    these churches!
However, one can live in Rome as also in London.
Rome is better than London, because it is other than
    London.
It is a blessing, no doubt, to be rid, at least for a time, of
All one's friends and relations,—yourself (forgive me!)
    included,—
All the *assujettissement*[7] of having been what one has been,   30
What one thinks one is, or thinks that others suppose one;

---

[5]**St. Peter's:** the great cathedral of Rome. **Arch of Titus, Lateran** (Church of St. John Lateran): here as elsewhere Claude mentions the famous buildings and monuments of Rome.

[6]**Goths:** Germanic peoples who sacked Rome.

[7]*assujettissement:* subjection, constraint.

Yet, in despite of all, we turn like fools to the English.
Vernon has been my fate; who is here the same that you
    knew him,—
Making the tour, it seems, with friends of the name of
    Trevellyn.

2 CLAUDE TO EUSTACE

Rome disappoints me still; but I shrink and adapt myself
    to it.
Somehow a tyrannous sense of a superincumbent
    oppression
Still, wherever I go, accompanies ever, and makes me
Feel like a tree (shall I say?) buried under a ruin of
    brick-work.
Rome, believe me, my friend, is like its own Monte
    Testaceo,[8]
Merely a marvellous mass of broken and castaway
    wine-pots.   40
Ye gods! what do I want with this rubbish of ages departed,
Things that Nature abhors, the experiments that she has
    failed in?
What do I find in the Forum? An archway and two or three
    pillars.
Well, but St Peter's? Alas, Bernini[9] has filled it with
    sculpture!
No one can cavil, I grant, at the size of the great Coliseum.
Doubtless the notion of grand and capacious and massive
    amusement,
This the old Romans had; but tell me, is this an idea?
Yet of solidity much, but of splendour little is extant:
"Brickwork I found thee, and marble I left thee!" their
    Emperor[10] vaunted;
"Marble I thought thee, and brickwork I find thee!" the
    Tourist may answer.   50

3 GEORGINA TREVELLYN TO LOUISA

At last, dearest Louisa, I take up my pen to address you.
Here we are, you see, with the seven-and-seventy boxes,
Courier, Papa and Mamma, the children, and Mary and
    Susan:
Here we all are at Rome, and delighted of course with
    St Peter's,
And very pleasantly lodged in the famous Piazza di Spagna.

Rome is a wonderful place, but Mary shall tell you about it;
Not very gay, however; the English are mostly at Naples;
There are the A.s, we hear, and most of the W. party.
George, however, is come; did I tell you about his
    mustachios?
Dear, I must really stop, for the carriage, they tell me, is
    waiting.   60
Mary will finish; and Susan is writing, they say, to Sophia.
Adieu, dearest Louise,—evermore your faithful Georgina.
Who can a Mr Claude be whom George has taken to be
    with?
Very stupid, I think, but George says so *very* clever.

4 CLAUDE TO EUSTACE

No, the Christian faith, as at any rate I understood it,
With its humiliations and exaltations combining,
Exaltations sublime, and yet diviner abasements,
Aspirations from something most shameful here upon
    earth and
In our poor selves to something most perfect above in
    the heavens,—
No, the Christian faith, as I, at least, understood it,   70
Is not here, O Rome, in any of these thy churches;
Is not here, but in Freiburg, or Rheims, or Westminster
    Abbey.[11]
What in thy Dome I find, in all thy recenter efforts,
Is a something, I think, more *rational* far, more earthly,
Actual, less ideal, devout not in scorn and refusal,
But in a positive, calm, Stoic-Epicurean acceptance.[12]
This I begin to detect in St Peter's and some of the churches,
Mostly in all that I see of the sixteenth-century masters;
Overlaid of course with infinite gauds and gewgaws,
Innocent, playful follies, the toys and trinkets of
    childhood,   80
Forced on maturer years, as the serious one thing needful,
By the barbarian will of the rigid and ignorant Spaniard.[13]

Curious work, meantime, re-entering society; how we
Walk a livelong day, great Heaven, and watch our shadows!
What our shadows seem, forsooth, we will ourselves be.
Do I look like that? you think me that: then I am that.

---

[8]**Monte Testaceo**: artificial hill made of clay fragments.

[9]Gian Lorenzo **Bernini** (1598–1680): Baroque sculptor and architect.

[10]**Emperor**: Augustus (63 BCE–14).

[11]**Freiburg, Rheims, Westminster Abbey**: churches in the Gothic style, which was considered more spiritual by most Victorians than Roman architecture.

[12]**Stoic-Epicurean**: classical philosophies teaching resignation and calm.

[13]**one thing needful**: Luke 10:42. **Spaniard**: St. Ignatius Loyola (1491–1556), founder of the Jesuit order.

5 CLAUDE TO EUSTACE

Luther,[14] they say, was unwise; like a half-taught German,
    he could not
See that old follies were passing most tranquilly out of
    remembrance;
Leo the Tenth was employing all efforts to clear out abuses;
Jupiter, Juno, and Venus, Fine Arts, and Fine Letters, the
    Poets,   90
Scholars, and Sculptors, and Painters, were quietly clearing
    away the
Martyrs, and Virgins, and Saints, or at any rate Thomas
    Aquinas:
He must forsooth make a fuss and distend his huge
    Wittenberg lungs, and
Bring back Theology once yet again in a flood[15] upon
    Europe:
Lo you, for forty days from the windows of heaven
    it fell; the
Waters prevail on the earth yet more for a hundred
    and fifty;
Are they abating at last? the doves that are sent to
    explore are
Wearily fain to return, at the best with a leaflet of
    promise,—
Fain to return, as they went, to the wandering wave-tost
    vessel,—
Fain to re-enter the roof which covers the clean and the
    unclean,—   100
Luther, they say, was unwise; he didn't see how things
    were going;
Luther was foolish,—but, O great God! what call you
    Ignatius?[16]
O my tolerant soul, be still! but you talk of barbarians,
Alaric, Attila, Genseric;[17]—why, they came, they
    killed, they
Ravaged, and went on their way; but these vile, tyrannous
    Spaniards,

These are here still,—how long, O ye Heavens, in the
    country of Dante?
These, that fanaticized Europe, which now can forget them,
    release not
This, their choicest of prey, this Italy; here you see them,—
Here, with emasculate pupils, and gimcrack churches of
    Gesu,[18]
Pseudo-learning and lies, confessional-boxes and
    postures,—   110
Here, with metallic beliefs and regimental devotions,—
Here, overcrusting with slime, perverting, defacing,
    debasing,
Michel Angelo's[19] dome, that had hung the Pantheon in
    heaven,
Raphael's Joys and Graces, and thy clear stars, Galileo!

6 CLAUDE TO EUSTACE

Which of three Misses Trevellyn is it that Vernon shall
    marry
Is not a thing to be known; for our friend is one of those
    natures
Which have their perfect delight in the general tender-
    domestic,
So that he trifles with Mary's shawl, ties Susan's bonnet,
Dances with all, but at home is most, they say, with
    Georgina,
Who is, however, *too* silly in my apprehension for
    Vernon.   120
I, as before when I wrote, continue to see them a little;
Not that I like them much or care a *bajocco*[20] for Vernon,
But I am slow at Italian, have not many English
    acquaintance,
And I am asked, in short, and am not good at excuses.
Middle-class people these, bankers very likely, not wholly
Pure of the taint of the shop; will at table d'hôte[21] and
    restaurant
Have their shilling's worth, their penny's pennyworth even:
Neither man's aristocracy this, nor God's, God knoweth!

---

[14]Martin **Luther** (1483–1546) began the Protestant Reformation at **Wittenburg** during the papacy of **Leo the Tenth** (1510–1521), a notable patron of the arts. St. **Thomas Aquinas** (1224/5–1274): Scholastic theologian.

[15]**flood**: see Genesis 7, 8. **leaflet**: Genesis 8:11. **clean . . . unclean**: Genesis 7:8.

[16]St. **Ignatius** Loyola: see note 13.

[17]**Alaric** (370?–410): Visigothic king. **Attila**: 5th-century king of the Huns. **Genseric** (390?–477): king of the Vandals, invaders of Italy.

---

[18]**Gesu**: main church of the Jesuits, with lavish Baroque decoration.

[19]**Michel Angelo**: Michelangelo Buonarotti (1475–1564), sculptor, painter, architect, designed the great dome of St. Peter's, higher than the dome of the **Pantheon**, an ancient temple to the classical gods; he said he would raise the Pantheon in the air. **Raphael** Sanzio (1483–1520): painter.

[20]*bajocco*: small coin.

[21]**table d'hôte**: meal at a hotel. **restaurant**: accented on second syllable.

Yet they are fairly descended, they give you to know,
    well connected;
Doubtless somewhere in some neighbourhood have,
    and are careful to keep, some   130
Threadbare-genteel relations, who in their turn are
    enchanted
Grandly among county people to introduce at assemblies
To the unpennied cadets[22] our cousins with excellent
    fortunes.
Neither man's aristocracy this, nor God's, God knoweth!

7 CLAUDE TO EUSTACE

Ah, what a shame, indeed, to abuse these most worthy
    people!
Ah, what a sin to have sneered at their innocent rustic
    pretensions!
Is it not laudable really, this reverent worship of station?
Is it not fitting that wealth should tender this homage to
    culture?
Is it not touching to witness these efforts, if little availing,
Painfully made, to perform the old ritual service of
    manners?   140
Shall not devotion atone for the absence of knowledge?
    and fervour
Palliate, cover, the fault of a superstitious observance?
Dear, dear, what do I say? but, alas! just now, like Iago,
I can be nothing at all, if it is not critical wholly;
So in fantastic height, in coxcomb exaltation,
Here in the Garden[23] I can walk, can freely concede to
    the Maker
That the works of his hand are all very good: his creatures,
Beast of the field and fowl, he brings them before me; I
    name them;
That which I name them, they are,—the bird, the beast,
    and the cattle.
But for Adam,—alas, poor critical coxcomb Adam!   150
But for Adam there is not found an help-meet for him.

8 CLAUDE TO EUSTACE

No, great dome of Agrippa,[24] thou art not Christian!
    canst not,
Strip and replaster and daub and do what they will with
    thee, be so!

---

[22]**cadets:** younger sons.

[23]**Garden:** see Genesis 1, 2.

[24]**dome of Agrippa:** the Pantheon, built by Marcus Agrippa
(63?–14 BCE) and later turned into a Christian church.

Here underneath the great porch of colossal Corinthian
    columns,
Here as I walk, do I dream of the Christian belfries above
    them?
Or on a bench as I sit and abide for long hours, till thy
    whole vast
Round grows dim as in dreams to my eyes, I repeople thy
    niches,
Not with the Martyrs, and Saints, and Confessors, and
    Virgins, and children,
But with the mightier forms of an older, austerer worship;
And I recite to myself, how   160
           Eager for battle here
    Stood Vulcan, here matronal Juno,
        And with the bow to his shoulder faithful
    He who with pure dew laveth of Castaly
    His flowing locks, who holdeth of Lycia
    The oak forest and the wood that bore him,
    Delos' and Patara's own Apollo.[25]

9 CLAUDE TO EUSTACE

Yet it is pleasant, I own it, to be in their company; pleasant,
Whatever else it may be, to abide in the feminine presence.
Pleasant, but wrong, will you say? But this happy, serene
    coexistence   170
Is to some poor soft souls, I fear, a necessity simple,
Meat and drink and life, and music, filling with sweetness,
Thrilling with melody sweet, with harmonies strange
    overwhelming,
All the long-silent strings of an awkward, meaningless fabric.
Yet as for that, I could live, I believe, with children; to
    have those
Pure and delicate forms encompassing, moving about you,
This were enough, I could think; and truly with glad
    resignation
Could from the dream of romance, from the fever of
    flushed adolescence,
Look to escape and subside into peaceful avuncular
    functions.
Nephews and nieces! alas, for as yet I have none! and,
    moreover,   180
Mothers are jealous, I fear me, too often, too rightfully;
    fathers
Think they have title exclusive to spoiling their own little
    darlings;

---

[25]**Eager . . . Apollo:** translation of Horace, *Odes* 3.4.58–64,
which Clough quotes in a footnote.

And by the law of the land, in despite of Malthusian
doctrine,[26]
No sort of proper provision is made for that most patriotic,
Most meritorious subject, the childless and bachelor uncle.

10 CLAUDE TO EUSTACE

Ye, too, marvellous Twain,[27] that erect on the Monte
Cavallo
Stand by your rearing steeds in the grace of your
motionless movement,
Stand with your upstretched arms and tranquil regardant
faces,
Stand as instinct with life in the might of immutable
manhood,—
O ye mighty and strange, ye ancient divine ones of
Hellas,   190
Are ye Christian too? to convert and redeem and
renew you,
Will the brief form have sufficed, that a Pope has set up
on the apex
Of the Egyptian stone that o'ertops you, the Christian
symbol?
And ye, silent, supreme in serene and victorious marble,
Ye that encircle the walls of the stately Vatican chambers,
Juno and Ceres, Minerva, Apollo, the Muses and Bacchus,
Ye unto whom far and near come posting the Christian
pilgrims,
Ye that are ranged in the halls of the mystic Christian
pontiff,
Are ye also baptized? are ye of the Kingdom of Heaven?
Utter, O some one, the word that shall reconcile Ancient
and Modern!   200
Am I to turn me for this unto thee, great Chapel of Sixtus?[28]

11 CLAUDE TO EUSTACE

These are the facts. The uncle, the elder brother, the
squire (a
Little embarrassed, I fancy), resides in a family place in
Cornwall, of course; "Papa is in business," Mary informs me;
He's a good sensible man, whatever his trade is. The
mother

Is—shall I call it fine?—herself she would tell you
refined, and
Greatly, I fear me, looks down on my bookish and
maladroit manners;
Somewhat affecteth the blue,[29] would talk to me often
of poets;
Quotes, which I hate, Childe Harold; but also appreciates
Wordsworth;
Sometimes adventures on Schiller; and then to religion
diverges;   210
Questions me much about Oxford; and yet, in her loftiest
flights, still
Grates the fastidious ear with the slightly mercantile
accent.

Is it contemptible, Eustace,—I'm perfectly ready to
think so,—
Is it,—the horrible pleasure of pleasing inferior people?
I am ashamed my own self; and yet true it is, if disgraceful,
That for the first time in life I am living and moving with
freedom.
I, who never could talk to the people I meet with my
uncle,—
I, who have always failed,—I, trust me, can suit the
Trevellyns;
I, believe me,—great conquest,—am liked by the country
bankers.
And I am glad to be liked, and like in return very
kindly.   220
So it proceeds; *Laissez faire, laissez aller*,[30]—such is the
watchword.
Well, I know there are thousands as pretty and hundreds
as pleasant,
Girls by the dozen as good, and girls in abundance with
polish
Higher and manners more perfect than Susan or Mary
Trevellyn.
Well, I know, after all, it is only juxtaposition,—
Juxtaposition, in short; and what is juxtaposition?

12 CLAUDE TO EUSTACE

But I am in for it now,—*laissez faire*, of a truth, *laissez aller*.
Yes, I am going,—I feel it, I feel and cannot recall it,—

---

[26]**Malthusian doctrine:** Thomas Malthus (1766–1834) argued that because population growth naturally exceeds food supply, reproduction must be deliberately limited.

[27]**Twain:** statues of Castor and Pollux.

[28]**Chapel of Sixtus:** Sistine Chapel, in the Vatican, built by pope Sixtus IV, completed in 1473, contains Michelangelo's frescoes.

[29]**the blue:** bluestocking, or female intellectual. **Childe Harold:** Byron's *Childe Harold's Pilgrimage* (1812–1818) was an immensely popular travel poem. Friedrich von **Schiller** (1759–1805): German dramatist, poet, literary theorist.

[30]*Laissez . . . aller:* Let it be, let it go.

Fusing with this thing and that, entering into all sorts of
    relations,
Tying I know not what ties, which, whatever they are, I
    know one thing,   230
Will, and must, woe is me, be one day painfully broken,—
Broken with painful remorses, with shrinkings of soul,
    and relentings,
Foolish delays, more foolish evasions, most foolish
    renewals.
But I have made the step, have quitted the ship of Ulysses;
Quitted the sea and the shore, passed into the magical
    island;
Yet on my lips is the *moly*, medicinal, offered of Hermes.[31]
I have come into the precinct, the labyrinth[32] closes
    around me,
Path into path rounding slyly; I pace slowly on, and the
    fancy,
Struggling awhile to sustain the long sequences, weary,
    bewildered,
Fain must collapse in despair; I yield, I am lost and know
    nothing;   240
Yet in my bosom unbroken remaineth the clew; I shall
    use it.
Lo, with the rope on my loins I descend through the fissure;
    I sink, yet
Inly secure in the strength of invisible arms up above me;
Still, wheresoever I swing, wherever to shore, or to shelf, or
Floor of cavern untrodden, shell-sprinkled, enchanting, I
    know I
Yet shall one time feel the strong cord tighten about me,—
Feel it relentless, upbear me from spots I would rest in; and
    though the
Rope sway wildly, I faint, crags wound me, from crag unto
    crag re-
Bounding, or, wide in the void, I die ten deaths, ere the
    end I
Yet shall plant firm foot on the broad lofty spaces I quit,
    shall   250
Feel underneath me again the great massy strengths of
    abstraction,
Look yet abroad from the height o'er the sea whose salt
    wave I have tasted.

13 Georgina Trevellyn to Louisa——

Dearest Louisa,—Inquire, if you please, about Mr
    Claude——.
He has been once at R., and remembers meeting the H.s.
Harriet L., perhaps, may be able to tell you about him.
It is an awkward youth, but still with very good manners;
Not without prospects, we hear; and, George says, highly
    connected.
Georgy declares it absurd, but Mamma is alarmed, and
    insists he has
Taken up strange opinions and may be turning a Papist.
Certainly once he spoke of a daily service he
    went to.   260
"Where?" we asked, and he laughed and answered, "At the
    Pantheon."
This was a temple, you know, and now is a Catholic
    church; and
Though it is said that Mazzini[33] has sold it for Protestant
    service,
Yet I suppose the change can hardly as yet be effected.
Adieu again,—evermore, my dearest, your loving Georgina.

P.S. by Mary Trevellyn

I am to tell you, you say, what I think of our last new
    acquaintance.
Well, then, I think that George has a very fair right to be
    jealous.
I do not like him much, though I do not dislike being with
    him.
He is what people call, I suppose, a superior man, and
Certainly seems so to me; but I think he is frightfully
    selfish.   270

Alba,[34] *thou findest me still, and, Alba, thou findest me ever,*
    Now from the Capitol steps, now over Titus's Arch,
Here from the large grassy spaces that spread from the Lateran portal,
    Towering o'er aqueduct lines lost in perspective between,
Or from a Vatican window, or bridge, or the high Coliseum,
    Clear by the garlanded line cut of the Flavian ring.[35]
Beautiful can I not call thee, and yet thou hast power to o'ermaster,
    Power of mere beauty; in dreams, Alba, thou hauntest me still.
Is it religion? I ask me; or is it a vain superstition?
    Slavery abject and gross? service, too feeble, of truth?   280

---

[31]**Hermes** gave **Ulysses** the herb *moly* to protect him from being transformed into a beast by the enchantress Circe on her **island;** *Odyssey* 10.

[32]In Greek myth Theseus sought the monster Minotaur in a **labyrinth,** unwinding a thread as a clue (**clew**) to guide him back.

[33]Giuseppe **Mazzini** (1805–1872): a leader of the Italian liberation movement and the Roman Republic.

[34]**Alba:** legendary city, precursor of Rome.

[35]**Flavian ring:** Coliseum.

Is it an idol I bow to, or is it a god that I worship?
    Do I sink back on the old, or do I soar from the mean?
So through the city I wander and question, unsatisfied ever,
    Reverent so I accept, doubtful because I revere.

— CANTO 2 —

Is it illusion? or does there a spirit from perfecter ages,
    Here, even yet, amid loss, change, and corruption, abide?
Does there a spirit we know not, though seek, though we find,
        comprehend not
    Here to entice and confuse, tempt and evade us, abide?
Lives in the exquisite grace of the column disjointed and single,
    Haunts the rude masses of brick garlanded gayly with vine,
E'en in the turret fantastic surviving that springs from the ruin,
    E'en in the people itself? is it illusion or not?
Is it illusion or not that attracteth the pilgrim transalpine,
    Brings him a dullard and dunce hither to pry and to stare?   10
Is it illusion or not that allures the barbarian stranger,
    Brings him with gold to the shrine, brings him in arms to
        the gate?

1 CLAUDE TO EUSTACE

What do the people say, and what does the government
    do?[36]—you
Ask, and I know not at all. Yet fortune will favour your
    hopes; and
I, who avoided it all, am fated, it seems, to describe it.
I, who nor meddle nor make in politics,—I who sincerely
Put not my trust in leagues nor any suffrage by ballot,
Never predicted Parisian millenniums, never beheld a
New Jerusalem coming down dressed like a bride out
    of heaven
Right on the Place de la Concorde,—I, nevertheless,
    let me say it,   20
Could in my soul of souls, this day, with the Gaul at
    the gates, shed
One true tear for thee, thou poor little Roman republic!
France, it is foully done! and you, my stupid old England,—
You, who a twelvemonth ago said nations must choose for
    themselves, you

---

[36]The Pope had fled from Rome and a **republic** had been declared. After the abortive uprisings of 1848, political authority over
most of Italy had been reasserted by Austria-Hungary and France.
French troops (the **Gaul,** like the ancient barbarian invaders)
landed at **Civita Vecchia** on April 25, 1849, to attack Rome and
reinstall the pope. **New Jerusalem:** see Revelation 21:9–10. **Place
de la Concorde:** in Paris. **Apollo:** the Apollo Belvedere, famous
Roman statue.

Could not, of course, interfere,—you, now, when a nation
    has chosen—
Pardon this folly! *The Times* will, of course, have announced
    the occasion,
Told you the news of to-day; and although it was slightly
    in error
 When it proclaimed as a fact the Apollo was sold to a
    Yankee,
You may believe when it tells you the French are at Civita
    Vecchia.

2 CLAUDE TO EUSTACE

Dulce it is, and *decorum,*[37] no doubt, for the country to
    fall,—to   30
Offer one's blood an oblation to Freedom, and die for the
    Cause; yet
Still, individual culture is also something, and no man
Finds quite distinct the assurance that he of all others is
    called on,
Or would be justified, even, in taking away from the world
    that
Precious creature, himself. Nature sent him here to abide
    here;
Else why sent him at all? Nature wants him still, it is likely.
On the whole, we are meant to look after ourselves; it is
    certain
Each has to eat for himself, digest for himself, and in
    general
Care for his own dear life, and see to his own preservation;
Nature's intentions, in most things uncertain, in this most
    plain are decisive;   40
These, on the whole, I conjecture the Romans will follow,
    and I shall.
    So we cling to our rocks like limpets; Ocean may
        bluster,
Over and under and round us; we open our shells to
    imbibe our
Nourishment, close them again, and are safe, fulfilling the
    purpose
Nature intended,—a wise one, of course, and a noble, we
    doubt not.
Sweet it may be and decorous, perhaps, for the country to
    die; but,
On the whole, we conclude the Romans won't do it, and
    I sha'n't.

---

[37]*Dulce . . . decorum:* it is sweet and proper (to die for one's country); Horace, *Odes* 3.2.12.

3 CLAUDE TO EUSTACE

Will they fight? They say so. And will the French? I can
    hardly,
Hardly think so; and yet—He is come, they say, to Palo,
He is passed from Monterone, at Santa Severa[38]   50
He hath laid up his guns. But the Virgin, the Daughter
    of Roma,
She hath despised thee and laughed thee to scorn,—the
    Daughter of Tiber,
She hath shaken her head and built barricades against thee!
Will they fight? I believe it. Alas! 'tis ephemeral folly,
Vain and ephemeral folly, of course, compared with
    pictures,
Statues, and antique gems!—Indeed: and yet indeed too,
Yet methought, in broad day did I dream—tell it not in
    St James's,[39]
Whisper it not in thy courts, O Christ Church!—yet did I,
    waking,
Dream of a cadence that sings, *Si tombent nos jeunes héros, la*
Terre en produit de nouveaux contre vous tous prêts à se battre;   60
Dreamt of great indignations and angers transcendental,
Dreamt of a sword at my side and a battle-horse
    underneath me.

4 CLAUDE TO EUSTACE

Now supposing the French or the Neapolitan[40] soldier
Should by some evil chance come exploring the Maison
    Serny
(Where the family English are all to assemble for safety),
Am I prepared to lay down my life for the British female?
Really, who knows? One has bowed and talked, till, little
    by little,
All the natural heat has escaped of the chivalrous spirit.
Oh, one conformed, of course; but one doesn't die for good
    manners,
Stab or shoot, or be shot, by way of graceful attention. 70
No, if it should be at all, it should be on the barricades
    there;
Should I incarnadine ever this inky pacifical finger,

---

[38]**Palo . . . Santa Severa:** stages in the advance of French troops.
Virgin . . . Tiber: see 2 Kings 19:21.

[39]**tell it not:** see 2 Samuel 1:20. **St. James's:** area of London
men's clubs. **Christ Church:** Oxford college. *Si tombent . . . battre:* If
our young heroes fall, the earth will produce new ones ready to
fight against you; from the French anthem *La Marseillaise.*

[40]**Neapolitan:** the reactionary Kingdom of Naples opposed the
Republic.

Sooner far should it be for this vapour of Italy's freedom,
Sooner far by the side of the d——d and dirty plebeians.
Ah, for a child in the street I could strike; for the full-blown
    lady—
Somehow, Eustace, alas! I have not felt the vocation.
Yet these people of course will expect, as of course, my
    protection,
Vernon in radiant arms stand forth for the lovely Georgina,
And to appear, I suppose, were but common civility.
    Yes, and
Truly I do not desire they should either be killed or
    offended.   80
Oh, and of course you will say, "When the time comes,
    you will be ready."
Ah, but before it comes, am I to presume it will be so?
What I cannot feel now, am I to suppose that I shall feel?
Am I not free to attend for the ripe and indubious instinct?
Am I forbidden to wait for the clear and lawful perception?
Is it the calling of man to surrender his knowledge and
    insight,
For the mere venture of what may, perhaps, be the virtuous
    action?
Must we, walking our earth, discerning a little, and hoping
Some plain visible task shall yet for our hands be assigned
    us,—
Must we abandon the future for fear of omitting the
    present,   90
Quit our own fireside hopes at the alien call of a neighbour,
To the mere possible shadow of Deity offer the victim?
And is all this, my friend, but a weak and ignoble refining,
Wholly unworthy the head or the heart of Your Own
    Correspondent?

5 CLAUDE TO EUSTACE

Yes, we are fighting at last, it appears. This morning as
    usual,
Murray, as usual, in hand, I enter the Caffè Nuovo;
Seating myself with a sense as it were of a change in the
    weather,
Not understanding, however, but thinking mostly of
    Murray,[41]
And, for to-day is their day, of the Campidoglio Marbles,
Caffè-latte! I call to the waiter,— and *Non c' è latte,*   100

---

[41]John **Murray** (1778–1843) published a series of guidebooks;
Claude would be using the *Handbook for . . . Central Italy* (1843),
which directs tourists to statuary in the Piazza del **Campidoglio.**
Non c' è latte: there's no milk. *nero:* black coffee.

This is the answer he makes me, and this the sign of a
    battle.
So I sit; and truly they seem to think any one else more
Worthy than me of attention. I wait for my milkless *nero*,
Free to observe undistracted all sorts and sizes of persons,
Blending civilian and soldier in strangest costume, coming
    in, and
Gulping in hottest haste, still standing, their coffee,—
    withdrawing
Eagerly, jangling a sword on the steps, or jogging a
    musket
Slung to the shoulder behind. They are fewer, moreover,
    than usual,
Much, and silenter far; and so I begin to imagine
Something is really afloat. Ere I leave, the Caffè is
    empty,   110
Empty too the streets, in all its length the Corso[42]
Empty, and empty I see to my right and left the Condotti.
    Twelve o'clock, on the Pincian Hill, with lots of
        English,
Germans, Americans, French,—the Frenchmen, too, are
    protected,—
So we stand in the sun, but afraid of a probable shower;
So we stand and stare, and see, to the left of St Peter's,
Smoke, from the cannon, white,—but that is at intervals
    only,—
Black, from a burning house, we suppose, by the
    Cavalleggieri;[43]
And we believe we discern some lines of men descending
Down through the vineyard-slopes, and catch a bayonet
    gleaming.   120
Every ten minutes, however,—in this there is no
    misconception,—
Comes a great white puff from behind Michel Angelo's
    dome, and
After a space the report of a real big gun,—not the
    Frenchman's?—
That must be doing some work. And so we watch and
    conjecture.
    Shortly, an Englishman comes, who says he has been
        to St Peter's,
Seen the Piazza and troops, but that is all he can tell us;
So we watch and sit, and, indeed, it begins to be
    tiresome.—
All this smoke is outside; when it has come to the inside,

It will be time, perhaps, to descend and retreat to our
    houses.
    Half past one, or two. The report of small arms
        frequent,   130
Sharp and savage indeed; that cannot all be for nothing:
So we watch and wonder; but guessing is tiresome, very.
Weary of wondering, watching, and guessing, and
    gossiping idly,
Down I go, and pass through the quiet streets with the
    knots of
National Guards patrolling, and flags hanging out at the
    windows,
English, American, Danish,—and, after offering to help an
Irish family moving *en masse* to the Maison Serny,
After endeavouring idly to minister balm to the trembling
Quinquagenarian fears of two lone British spinsters,
Go to make sure of my dinner before the enemy
    enter.   140
But by this there are signs of stragglers returning; and
    voices
Talk, though you don't believe it, of guns and prisoners
    taken;
And on the walls you read the first bulletin of the
    morning.—
This is all that I saw, and all I know of the battle.

6 CLAUDE TO EUSTACE

Victory! Victory!—Yes! ah, yes, thou republican Zion,
Truly the kings of the earth are gathered and gone by
    together;
Doubtless they marvelled to witness such things, were
    astonished, and so forth.[44]
Victory! Victory! Victory!—Ah, but it is, believe me,
Easier, easier far, to intone the chant of the martyr
Than to indite any pæan of any victory. Death may   150
Sometimes be noble; but life, at the best, will appear an
    illusion.
While the great pain is upon us, it is great; when it is over,
Why, it is over. The smoke of the sacrifice rises to heaven,
Of a sweet savour, no doubt, to Somebody;[45] but on the
    altar,
Lo, there is nothing remaining but ashes and dirt and ill
    odour.
    So it stands, you perceive; the labial muscles, that
        swelled with

---

[42]**Corso, Condotti:** major streets.

[43]**Cavalleggieri:** light cavalry.

[44]**Zion . . . astonished:** see Psalms 48:1–5.

[45]**sacrifice . . . Somebody:** see Leviticus 1:9.

Vehement evolution of yesterday Marseillaises,[46]
Articulations sublime of defiance and scorning, to-day col-
Lapse and languidly mumble, while men and women and
    papers
Scream and re-scream to each other the chorus of Victory.
    Well, but   160
I am thankful they fought, and glad that the Frenchmen
    were beaten.

7 CLAUDE TO EUSTACE

So, I have seen a man killed! An experience that, among
    others!
Yes, I suppose I have; although I can hardly be certain,
And in a court of justice could never declare I had seen it.
But a man was killed, I am told, in a place where I saw
Something; a man was killed, I am told, and I saw something.
    I was returning home from St Peter's; Murray, as usual,
Under my arm, I remember; had crossed the St Angelo
    bridge; and
Moving towards the Condotti, had got to the first
    barricade, when
Gradually, thinking still of St Peter's, I became
    conscious   170
Of a sensation of movement opposing me,—tendency
    this way
(Such as one fancies may be in a stream when the wave of
    the tide is
Coming and not yet come,—a sort of poise and retention);
So I turned, and, before I turned, caught sight of stragglers
Heading a crowd, it is plain, that is coming behind that
    corner.
Looking up, I see windows filled with heads; the Piazza,
Into which you remember the Ponte St Angelo enters,
Since I passed, has thickened with curious groups; and
    now the
Crowd is coming, has turned, has crossed that last
    barricade, is
Here at my side. In the middle they drag at something.
    What is it?   180
Ha! bare swords in the air, held up! There seem to be voices
Pleading and hands putting back; official, perhaps; but the
    swords are
Many, and bare in the air. In the air? They descend; they
    are smiting
Hewing, chopping—At what? In the air once more
    upstretched! And

Is it blood that's on them? Yes, certainly blood! Of whom,
    then?
Over whom is the cry of this furor of exultation?
    While they are skipping and screaming, and dancing
        their caps on the points of
Swords and bayonets, I to the outskirts back, and ask a
Mercantile-seeming by-stander, "What is it?" and he,
    looking always
That way, makes me answer, "A Priest, who was trying
    to fly to   190
The Neapolitan army,"—and thus explains the proceeding.
    You didn't see the dead man? No;—I began to be
        doubtful;
I was in black myself, and didn't know what mightn't
    happen;—
But a National Guard close by me, outside of the hubbub,
Broke his sword with slashing a broad hat covered with
    dust,—and
Passing away from the place with Murray under my arm, and
Stooping, I saw through the legs of the people the legs of
    a body.
    You are the first, do you know, to whom I have
        mentioned the matter.
Whom should I tell it to, else?—these girls?—the Heavens
    forbid it!—
Quidnuncs at Monaldini's?—idlers upon the Pincian?[47] 200
    If I rightly remember, it happened on that afternoon when
Word of the nearer approach of a new Neapolitan army
First was spread. I began to bethink me of Paris Septembers,[48]
Thought I could fancy the look of the old 'Ninety-two. On
    that evening
Three or four, or, it may be, five, of these people were
    slaughtered.
Some declare they had, one of them, fired on a sentinel;
    others
Say they were only escaping; a Priest, it is currently stated,
Stabbed a National Guard on the very Piazza Colonna:
History, Rumour of Rumours, I leave it to thee to
    determine!
    But I am thankful to say the government seems to have
        strength to   210
Put it down; it has vanished, at least; the place is most
    peaceful.

---

[46]**Marseillaises:** French national anthems.

[47]**Quidnuncs at Monaldini's:** gossips at the British reading
room. **Pincian:** hill near the fashionable center of Rome.

[48]**Paris Septembers:** the Reign of Terror in 1792 during the
French Revolution.

Through the Trastevere walking last night, at nine of the
    clock, I
Found no sort of disorder; I crossed by the Island-bridges,
So by the narrow streets to the Ponte Rotto, and onwards
Thence, by the Temple of Vesta, away to the great
    Coliseum,
Which at the full of the moon is an object worthy a visit.

8 GEORGINA TREVELLYN TO LOUISA——

Only think, dearest Louisa, what fearful scenes we have
    witnessed!

             *   *   *

George has just seen Garibaldi,[49] dressed up in a long
    white cloak, on
Horseback, riding by, with his mounted negro
    behind him:
This is a man, you know, who came from America
    with him,   220
Out of the woods, I suppose, and uses a *lasso* in fighting,
Which is, I don't quite know, but a sort of noose, I
    imagine;
This he throws on the heads of the enemy's men in a
    battle,
Pulls them into his reach, and then most cruelly kills
    them:
Mary does not believe, but we heard it from an Italian.
Mary allows she was wrong about Mr Claude *being selfish;*
He was *most* useful and kind on the terrible thirtieth of
    April.[50]
Do not write here any more; we are starting directly for
    Florence:
We should be off to-morrow, if only Papa could
    get horses;
All have been seized everywhere for the use of this
    dreadful Mazzini.   230
P.S.
    Mary has seen thus far.—I am really so angry, Louisa,—
Quite out of patience, my dearest! What can the man be
    intending!
I am quite tired; and Mary, who might bring him to in a
    moment,
Lets him go on as he likes, and neither will help nor dismiss
    him.

---

[49]Giuseppe **Garibaldi** (1807–1882): military leader of the Italian
reunification movement. **negro**: Aguyar, Garibaldi's friend and
bodyguard from Uruguay.

[50]The French attacked on **April 30**.

9 CLAUDE TO EUSTACE

It is most curious to see what a power a few calm words (in
Merely a brief proclamation) appear to possess on the people.
Order is perfect, and peace; the city is utterly tranquil;
And one cannot conceive that this easy and *nonchalant*
    crowd, that
Flows like a quiet stream through street and market-place,
    entering
Shady recesses and bays of church, *osteria*,[51] and *caffè*,   240
Could in a moment be changed to a flood as of molten lava,
Boil into deadly wrath and wild homicidal delusion.
    Ah, 'tis an excellent race,—and even in old degradation,
Under a rule that enforces to flattery, lying, and cheating,
E'en under Pope and Priest, a nice and natural people.
Oh, could they but be allowed this chance of
    redemption!—but clearly
That is not likely to be. Meantime, notwithstanding
    all journals,
Honour for once to the tongue and the pen of the
    eloquent writer!
Honour to speech! and all honour to thee, thou noble
    Mazzini!

10 CLAUDE TO EUSTACE

I am in love, meantime, you think; no doubt you would
    think so.   250
I am in love, you say; with those letters, of course, you
    would say so.
I am in love, you declare. I think not so; yet I grant you
It is a pleasure, indeed, to converse with this girl. Oh,
    rare gift,
Rare felicity, this! she can talk in a rational way, can
Speak upon subjects that really are matters of mind and of
    thinking,
Yet in perfection retain her simplicity; never, one moment,
Never, however you urge it, however you tempt her,
    consents to
Step from ideas and fancies and loving sensations to
    those vain
Conscious understandings that vex the minds of man-kind.
No, though she talk, it is music; her fingers desert not the
    keys; 'tis   260
Song, though you hear in the song the articulate vocables
    sounded,
Syllabled singly and sweetly the words of melodious meaning.
    I am in love, you say; I do not think so exactly.

---

[51]*osteria*: inn.

11 CLAUDE TO EUSTACE

There are two different kinds, I believe, of human
    attraction:
One which simply disturbs, unsettles, and makes you
    uneasy,
And another that poises, retains, and fixes and holds you.
I have no doubt, for myself, in giving my voice for the
    latter.
I do not wish to be moved, but growing where I was
    growing,
There more truly to grow, to live where as yet I had
    languished.
I do not like being moved: for the will is excited; and
    action   270
Is a most dangerous thing; I tremble for something
    factitious,
Some malpractice of heart and illegitimate process;
We are so prone to these things with our terrible notions
    of duty.

12 CLAUDE TO EUSTACE

Ah, let me look, let me watch, let me wait, unhurried,
    unprompted!
Bid me not venture on aught that could alter or end what
    is present!
Say not, Time flies, and Occasion, that never returns, is
    departing!
Drive me not out, ye ill angels with fiery swords, from my
    Eden,[52]
Waiting, and watching, and looking! Let love be its own
    inspiration!
Shall not a voice, if a voice there must be, from the airs
    that environ,
Yea, from the conscious heavens, without our knowledge
    or effort,   280
Break into audible words? and love be its own inspiration?

13 CLAUDE TO EUSTACE

Wherefore and how I am certain, I hardly can tell; but
    it *is* so.
She doesn't like me, Eustace; I think she never will
    like me.
Is it my fault, as it is my misfortune, my ways are not
    her ways?
Is it my fault, that my habits and modes are dissimilar
    wholly?

---

[52]**angels . . . Eden:** Genesis 3:24.

'Tis not her fault, 'tis her nature, her virtue, to
    misapprehend them:
'Tis not her fault, 'tis her beautiful nature, not ever to
    know me.
Hopeless it seems,—yet I cannot, though hopeless,
    determine to leave it:
She goes,—therefore I go; she moves,—I move, not to
    lose her.

14 CLAUDE TO EUSTACE

Oh, 'tisn't manly, of course, 'tisn't manly, this method of
    wooing;   290
'Tisn't the way very likely to win. For the woman, they
    tell you,
Ever prefers the audacious, the wilful, the vehement hero;
She has no heart for the timid, the sensitive soul; and for
    knowledge,—
Knowledge, O ye Gods!—when did they appreciate
    knowledge?
Wherefore should they, either? I am sure I do not desire it.
    Ah, and I feel too, Eustace, she cares not a tittle about
    me!
(Care about me, indeed! and do I really expect it?)
But my manner offends; my ways are wholly repugnant;
Every word that I utter estranges, hurts, and repels her;
Every moment of bliss that I gain, in her exquisite
    presence,   300
Slowly, surely, withdraws her, removes her, and severs her
    from me.
Not that I care very much!—any way, I escape from the
    boy's own
Folly, to which I am prone, of loving where it is easy.
Not that I mind very much! Why should I? I am not in
    love, and
Am prepared, I think, if not by previous habit,
Yet in the spirit beforehand for this and all that is like it;
It is an easier matter for us contemplative creatures,
Us, upon whom the pressure of action is laid so lightly;
We discontented indeed with things in particular, idle,
Sickly, complaining, by faith in the vision of things in
    general,   310
Manage to hold on our way without, like others
    around us,
Seizing the nearest arm to comfort, help, and support us.
Yet, after all, my Eustace, I know but little about it.
All I can say for myself, for present alike and for past, is,
Mary Trevellyn, Eustace, is certainly worth your
    acquaintance.
You couldn't come, I suppose, as far as Florence, to see her?

15 GEORGINA TREVELLYN TO LOUISA ——

. . . . . . To-morrow we're starting for Florence,
Truly rejoiced, you may guess, to escape from republican
  terrors;
Mr C. and Papa to escort us; we by *vettura*[53]
Through Siena, and Georgy to follow and join us by
  Leghorn.   320
Then——Ah, what shall I say, my dearest? I tremble in
  thinking!
You will imagine my feelings,—the blending of hope and
  of sorrow!
How can I bear to abandon Papa and Mamma and my
  Sisters?
Dearest Louisa, indeed it is very alarming; but trust me
Ever, whatever may change, to remain your loving
  Georgina.

P.S. BY MARY TREVELLYN

. . . . . . "Do I like Mr Claude any better?"
I am to tell you,—and, "Pray, is it Susan or I that attract
  him?"
This he never has told, but Georgina could certainly
  ask him.
All I can say for myself is, alas! that he rather repels me.
There! I think him agreeable, but also a little repulsive. 330
So be content, dear Louisa; for one satisfactory marriage
Surely will do in one year for the family you would
  establish;
Neither Susan nor I shall afford you the joy of a second.

P.S. BY GEORGINA TREVELLYN

Mr Claude, you must know, is behaving a little bit better;
He and Papa are great friends; but he really is too *shilly-*
  shally,—
So unlike George! Yet I hope that the matter is going
  on fairly.
I shall, however, get George, before he goes, to say
  something.
Dearest Louisa, how delightful, to bring young people
  together!

———————

Is it to Florence we follow, or are we to tarry yet longer,
  E'en amid clamour of arms, here in the city of old,   340
Seeking from clamour of arms in the Past and the Arts to be hidden,
  Vainly 'mid Arts and the Past seeking one life to forget?

Ah, fair shadow, scarce seen, go forth! for anon he shall follow,—
  He that beheld thee, anon, whither thou leadest, must go!
Go, and the wise, loving Muse, she also will follow and find thee!
  She, should she linger in Rome, were not dissevered from thee!

— CANTO 3 —

Yet to the wondrous St Peter's, and yet to the solemn Rotonda,
  Mingling with heroes and gods, yet to the Vatican walls,
Yet may we go, and recline, while a whole mighty world seems above us
  Gathered and fixed to all time into one roofing supreme;
Yet may we, thinking on these things, exclude what is meaner around us;
  Yet, at the worst of the worst, books and a chamber remain;
Yet may we think, and forget, and possess our souls in resistance.—
  Ah, but away from the stir, shouting, and gossip of war,
Where, upon Apennine slope,[54] with the chestnut the oak-trees immingle,
  Where amid odorous copse bridle-paths wander and wind,   10
Where under mulberry-branches the diligent rivulet sparkles,
  Or amid cotton and maize peasants their waterworks ply,
Where, over fig-tree and orange in tier upon tier still repeated,
  Garden on garden upreared, balconies step to the sky,—
Ah, that I were, far away from the crowd and the streets of the city,
  Under the vine-trellis laid, O my beloved, with thee!

1 MARY TREVELLYN TO MISS ROPER,—
ON THE WAY TO FLORENCE

Why doesn't Mr Claude come with us? you ask.—We
  don't know.
You should know better than we. He talked of the Vatican
  marbles;
But I can't wholly believe that this was the actual reason,—
He was so ready before, when we asked him to come and
  escort us.   20
Certainly he is odd, my dear Miss Roper. To change so
Suddenly, just for a whim, was not quite fair to the party,—
Not quite right. I declare, I really almost am offended:
I, his great friend, as you say, have doubtless a title to be so.
Not that I greatly regret it, for dear Georgina distinctly
Wishes for nothing so much as to show her adroitness. But,
  oh, my
Pen will not write any more;—let us say nothing further
  about it.
              *   *   *
Yes, my dear Miss Roper, I certainly called him repulsive;
So I think him, but cannot be sure I have used the expression
Quite as your pupil should; yet he does most truly
  repel me.   30

———————

[53]*vettura:* carriage.

[54]**Apennine slope:** mountains near Rome.

Was it to you I made use of the word? or who was it
   told you?
Yes, repulsive; observe, it is but when he talks of ideas,
That he is quite unaffected, and free, and expansive, and easy;
I could pronounce him simply a cold intellectual being.—
When does he make advances?—He thinks that women
   should woo him;
Yet, if a girl should do so, would be but alarmed and
   disgusted.
She that should love him must look for small love in
   return,—like the ivy
On the stone wall, must expect but a rigid and niggard
   support, and
E'en to get that must go searching all round with her
   humble embraces.

2 CLAUDE TO EUSTACE,—*FROM ROME*

Tell me, my friend, do you think that the grain would
   sprout in the furrow,   40
Did it not truly accept as its *summum* and *ultimum bonum*[55]
That mere common and may-be indifferent soil it is set in?
Would it have force to develop and open its young
   cotyledons,[56]
Could it compare, and reflect, and examine one thing with
   another?
Would it endure to accomplish the round of its natural
   functions,
Were it endowed with a sense of the general scheme of
   existence?
   While from Marseilles in the steamer we voyaged to
      Civita Vecchia,
Vexed in the squally seas as we lay by Capraja and Elba,[57]
Standing, uplifted, alone on the heaving poop of the vessel,
Looking around on the waste of the rushing incurious
   billows,   50
"This is Nature," I said: "we are born as it were from her
   waters,
Over her billows that buffet and beat us, her offspring
   uncared-for,
Casting one single regard of a painful victorious knowledge,
Into her billows that buffet and beat us we sink and are
   swallowed."
This was the sense in my soul, as I swayed with the poop of
   the steamer;

And as unthinking I sat in the hall of the famed Ariadne,[58]
Lo, it looked at me there from the face of a Triton in
   marble.
It is the simpler thought, and I can believe it the truer.
Let us not talk of growth; we are still in our Aqueous Ages.

3 CLAUDE TO EUSTACE

Farewell, Politics, utterly! What can I do? I cannot   60
Fight, you know; and to talk I am wholly ashamed. And
   although I
Gnash my teeth when I look in your French or your English
   papers,
What is the good of that? Will swearing, I wonder, mend
   matters?
Cursing and scolding repel the assailants? No, it is idle;
No, whatever befalls, I will hide, will ignore or forget it.
Let the tail shift for itself; I will bury my head. And
   what's the
Roman Republic to me, or I to the Roman Republic?[59]
   Why not fight?—In the first place, I haven't so much as
      a musket.
In the next, if I had, I shouldn't know how I should use it.
In the third, just at present I'm studying ancient
   marbles.   70
In the fourth, I consider I owe my life to my country.
In the fifth,—I forget, but four good reasons are ample.
Meantime, pray, let 'em fight, and be killed. I delight in
   devotion.
So that I 'list[60] not, hurrah for the glorious army of martyrs!
Sanguis martyrum semen Ecclesiæ; though it would seem this
Church is indeed of the purely Invisible, Kingdom-come
   kind:
Militant here on earth! Triumphant, of course, then,
   elsewhere!
Ah, good Heaven, but I would I were out far away from
   the pother!

4 CLAUDE TO EUSTACE

Not, as we read in the words of the olden-time
   inspiration,
Are there two several trees in the place we are set to
   abide in;   80

55*summum . . . bonum:* highest and final good.

56**cotyledons:** leaves in the embryo of a seed.

57**Capraja and Elba:** islands.

58**Ariadne, Triton** (semihuman sea creature): mythological
sculptures in the Vatican.

59**what's . . . Republic?:** see *Hamlet* 2.2.593.

60'**list:** enlist. *Sanguis . . . Ecclesiae:* the blood of martyrs is the
seed of the church.

But on the apex most high of the Tree of Life in the Garden,[61]
Budding, unfolding, and falling, decaying and flowering
    ever,
Flowering is set and decaying the transient blossom of
    Knowledge,—
Flowering alone, and decaying, the needless, unfruitful
    blossom.
      Or as the cypress-spires by the fair-flowing stream
        Hellespontine,
Which from the mythical tomb of the godlike Protesilaüs[62]
Rose sympathetic in grief to his lovelorn Laodamia,
Evermore growing, and, when in their growth to the
    prospect attaining,
Over the low sea-banks, of the fatal Ilian city,
Withering still at the sight which still they upgrow to
    encounter.   90
      Ah, but ye that extrude from the ocean your helpless
        faces,
Ye over stormy seas leading long and dreary processions,
Ye, too, brood of the wind, whose coming is whence we
    discern not,
Making your nest on the wave, and your bed on the crested
    billow,
Skimming rough waters, and crowding wet sands that the
    tide shall return to,
Cormorants, ducks, and gulls, fill ye my imagination!
Let us not talk of growth; we are still in our Aqueous Ages.

5 Mary Trevellyn to Miss Roper,—*from Florence*

Dearest Miss Roper,—Alas! we are all at Florence quite
    safe, and
You, we hear, are shut up! indeed, it is sadly distressing!
We were most lucky, they say, to get off when we did
    from the troubles.   100
Now you are really besieged! they tell us it soon will be
    over;
Only I hope and trust without any fight in the city.
Do you see Mr Claude?—I thought he might do
    something for you.
I am quite sure on occasion he really would wish to be
    useful.
What is he doing? I wonder;—still studying Vatican marbles?
Letters, I hope, pass through. We trust your brother is
    better.

6 Claude to Eustace

Juxtaposition, in fine; and what is juxtaposition?
Look you, we travel along in the railway-carriage, or
    steamer,
And, *pour passer le temps*,[63] till the tedious journey be ended,
Lay aside paper or book, to talk with the girl that is next
    one;   110
And, *pour passer le temps*, with the terminus all but in prospect,
Talk of eternal ties and marriages made in heaven.
    Ah, did we really accept with a perfect heart the illusion!
Ah, did we really believe that the Present indeed is the Only!
Or through all transmutation, all shock and convulsion of
    passion,
Feel we could carry undimmed, unextinguished, the light of
    our knowledge!
    But for his funeral train which the bridegroom sees
      in the distance,
Would he so joyfully, think you, fall in with the marriage-
    procession?
But for that final discharge, would he dare to enlist in that
    service?
But for that certain release, ever sign to that perilous
    contract?   120
But for that exit secure, ever bend to that treacherous
    doorway?—
Ah, but the bride, meantime,—do you think she sees it as
    he does?
    But for the steady fore-sense of a freer and larger
      existence,
Think you that man could consent to be circumscribed here
    into action?
But for assurance within of a limitless ocean divine, o'er
Whose great tranquil depths unconscious the wind-tost
    surface
Breaks into ripples of trouble that come and change and
    endure not,—
But that in this, of a truth, we have our being, and
    know it,
Think you we men could submit to live and move[64] as we
    do here?
Ah, but the women,—God bless them!—they don't
    think at all about it.   130
    Yet we must eat and drink, as you say. And as
      limited beings

---

[61]**Tree . . . Garden**: Genesis 2:9.

[62]**Protesilaüs**: died by the Hellespont on his way to Troy (the
Ilian city) and was mourned by his wife **Laodamia**.

[63]*pour . . . temps*: to pass the time.

[64]**have our being, live and move**: see Acts 17:28.

Scarcely can hope to attain upon earth to an Actual
     Abstract,
Leaving to God contemplation, to His hands knowledge
     confiding,
Sure that in us if it perish, in Him it abideth and dies not,
Let us in His sight accomplish our petty particular
     doings,—
Yes, and contented sit down to the victual that He has
     provided.
Allah is great, no doubt, and Juxtaposition his prophet.[65]
Ah, but the women, alas! they don't look at it in that way.
     Juxtaposition is great;—but, my friend, I fear me, the
     maiden
Hardly would thank or acknowledge the lover that sought
     to obtain her,   140
Not as the thing he would wish, but the thing he must even
     put up with,—
Hardly would tender her hand to the wooer that candidly
     told her
That she is but for a space, an *ad-interim* solace and
     pleasure,—
That in the end she shall yield to a perfect and absolute
     something,
Which I then for myself shall behold, and not another,—
Which, amid fondest endearments, meantime I forget not,
     forsake not.
Ah, ye feminine souls, so loving and so exacting,
Since we cannot escape, must we even submit to deceive
     you?
Since, so cruel is truth, sincerity shocks and revolts you,
Will you have us your slaves to lie to you, flatter and—
     leave you?   150

7 CLAUDE TO EUSTACE

Juxtaposition is great,—but, you tell me, affinity greater.
Ah, my friend, there are many affinities, greater and lesser,
Stronger and weaker; and each, by the favour of
     juxtaposition,
Potent, efficient, in force,—for a time; but none, let me
     tell you,
Save by the law of the land and the ruinous force of the
     will, ah,
None, I fear me, at last quite sure to be final and perfect.
Lo, as I pace in the street, from the peasant-girl to the
     princess,
Homo sum, nihil humani a me alienum puto,—

Vir sum, nihil fæminei,[66]—and e'en to the uttermost circle,
All that is Nature's is I, and I all things that are Nature's. 160
Yes, as I walk, I behold, in a luminous, large intuition,
That I can be and become anything that I meet with or
     look at:
I am the ox in the dray, the ass with the garden-stuff
     panniers;
I am the dog in the doorway, the kitten that plays in the
     window,
On sunny slab of the ruin the furtive and fugitive lizard,
Swallow above me that twitters, and fly that is buzzing
     about me;
Yea, and detect, as I go, by a faint but a faithful assurance,
E'en from the stones of the street, as from rocks or trees
     of the forest,
Something of kindred, a common, though latent vitality,
     greet me;
And, to escape from our strivings, mistakings, misgrowths,
     and perversions,   170
Fain could demand to return to that perfect and primitive
     silence,
Fain be enfolded and fixed, as of old, in their rigid embraces.

8 CLAUDE TO EUSTACE

And as I walk on my way, I behold them consorting and
     coupling;
Faithful it seemeth, and fond, very fond, very probably
     faithful;
All as I go on my way, with a pleasure sincere and unmingled.
     Life is beautiful, Eustace, entrancing, enchanting to
     look at;
As are the streets of a city we pace while the carriage is
     changing,
As a chamber filled-in with harmonious, exquisite pictures,
Even so beautiful Earth; and could we eliminate only
This vile hungering impulse, this demon within us of
     craving,   180
Life were beatitude, living a perfect divine satisfaction.

9 CLAUDE TO EUSTACE

Mild monastic faces in quiet collegiate cloisters:
So let me offer a single and celibatarian phrase, a
Tribute to those whom perhaps you do not believe I can
     honour.

---

[65]**Allah ... prophet:** Allah is most great, Muhammed is his
prophet (Muslim call to prayer).

---

[66]*Homo sum ... faeminei:* I am a man (human), nothing human
do I consider alien to me; I am a man (male), nothing female. . . .
The first line is from Terence's 2nd-century BCE comedy *The Self-
Tormentor* 1.77.

But, from the tumult escaping, 'tis pleasant, of drumming
and shouting,
Hither, oblivious awhile, to withdraw, of the fact or the
falsehood,
And amid placid regards and mildly courteous greetings
Yield to the calm and composure and gentle abstraction
that reign o'er
Mild monastic faces in quiet collegiate cloisters.
　　Terrible word, Obligation! You should not, Eustace,
　　　　you should not,　　　　　　　　　　　　　　　　190
No, you should not have used it. But, O great Heavens!
　　I repel it.
Oh, I cancel, reject, disavow, and repudiate wholly
Every debt in this kind, disclaim every claim, and dishonour,
Yea, my own heart's own writing, my soul's own signature!
　　Ah, no!
I will be free in this; you shall not, none shall, bind me.
No, my friend, if you wish to be told, it was this above
　　all things,
This that charmed me, ah, yes, even this, that she held
　　me to nothing.
No, I could talk as I pleased; come close; fasten ties, as
　　I fancied;
Bind and engage myself deep;—and lo, on the following
　　morning
It was all e'en as before, like losings in games played for
　　nothing.　　　　　　　　　　　　　　　　　　　　200
Yes, when I came, with mean fears in my soul, with a
　　semi-performance
At the first step breaking down in its pitiful rôle of evasion,
When to shuffle I came, to compromise, not meet,
　　engagements,
Lo, with her calm eyes there she met me and knew nothing
　　of it,—
Stood unexpecting, unconscious. *She* spoke not of obligations,
Knew not of debt,—ah, no, I believe you, for excellent
　　reasons.

10 CLAUDE TO EUSTACE

Hang this thinking, at last! what good is it? oh, and what evil!
Oh, what mischief and pain! like a clock in a sick man's
　　chamber,
Ticking and ticking, and still through each covert of
　　slumber pursuing.
　　What shall I do to thee, O thou Preserver of Men?[67]
　　　　Have compassion;　　　　　　　　　　　　　　210
Be favourable, and hear! Take from me this regal knowledge;

---

[67]**Preserver of Men**: Job 7:20.

Let me, contented and mute, with the beasts of the field,
　　my brothers,
Tranquilly, happily lie,—and eat grass, like
　　Nebuchadnezzar![68]

11 CLAUDE TO EUSTACE

Tibur is beautiful, too, and the orchard slopes, and the Anio
Falling, falling yet, to the ancient lyrical cadence;[69]
Tibur and Anio's tide; and cool from Lucretilis ever,
With the Digentian stream, and with the Bandusian
　　fountain,
Folded in Sabine recesses, the valley and villa of Horace:—
So not seeing I sung; so seeing and listening say I,
Here as I sit by the stream, as I gaze at the cell of the
　　Sibyl,　　　　　　　　　　　　　　　　　　　　220
Here with Albunea's home and the grove of Tiburnus
　　beside me;
Tivoli beautiful is, and musical, O Teverone,
Dashing from mountain to plain, thy parted impetuous
　　waters!
Tivoli's waters and rocks; and fair under Monte Gennaro
(Haunt even yet, I must think, as I wander and gaze, of
　　the shadows,
Faded and pale, yet immortal, of Faunus, the Nymphs, and
　　the Graces),
Fair in itself, and yet fairer with human completing
　　creations,
Folded in Sabine recesses the valley and villa of Horace:—
So not seeing I sung; so now—Nor seeing, nor hearing,
Neither by waterfall lulled, nor folded in sylvan
　　embraces,　　　　　　　　　　　　　　　　　　230
Neither by cell of the Sibyl, nor stepping the Monte
　　Gennaro,
Seated on Anio's bank, nor sipping Bandusian waters,
But on Montorio's[70] height, looking down on the tile-clad
　　streets, the
Cupolas, crosses, and domes, the bushes and kitchen-
　　gardens,
Which, by the grace of the Tiber, proclaim themselves
　　Rome of the Romans,—
But on Montorio's height, looking forth to the vapoury
　　mountains,

---

[68]**eat grass . . . Nebuchadnezzar**: see Daniel 4:33.

[69]**Tibur . . . cadence**: from the classical poet Horace's *Odes*
1.7.12–14, a passage Clough quotes in a note. The next lines describe hills outside Rome associated with Horace. **Albunea**: local
goddess. **Sybil**: ecstatic prophetess.

[70]**Montorio**: hill in Rome.

Cheating the prisoner Hope with illusions of vision and
  fancy,—
But on Montorio's height, with these weary soldiers by me,
Waiting till Oudinot[71] enter, to reinstate Pope and Tourist.

12 MARY TREVELLYN TO MISS ROPER

Dear Miss Roper,—It seems, George Vernon, before we
  left Rome, said   240
Something to Mr Claude about what they call his
  attentions.
Susan, two nights ago, for the first time, heard this from
  Georgina.
It is *so* disagreeable and *so* annoying to think of!
If it could only be known, though we may never meet him
  again, that
It was all George's doing, and we were entirely
  unconscious,
It would extremely relieve—Your ever affectionate Mary.

P.S. (1)

Here is your letter arrived this moment, just as I wanted.
So you have seen him,—indeed,—and guessed,—how
  dreadfully clever!
What did he really say? and what was your answer exactly?
Charming!—but wait for a moment, I haven't read through
  the letter.   250

P.S. (2)

Ah, my dearest Miss Roper, do just as you fancy
  about it.
If you think it sincerer to tell him I know of it, do so.
Though I should most extremely dislike it, I know I could
  manage.
It is the simplest thing, but surely wholly uncalled for.
Do as you please; you know I trust implicitly to you.
Say whatever is right and needful for ending the matter.
Only don't tell Mr Claude, what I will tell you as a secret,
That I should like very well to show him myself I forget it.

P.S. (3)

I am to say that the wedding is finally settled for
  Tuesday.
Ah, my dear Miss Roper, you surely, surely can manage   260
Not to let it appear that I know of that odious matter.
It would be pleasanter far for myself to treat it exactly
As if it had not occurred; and I do not think he would like it.

I must remember to add, that as soon as the wedding is over
We shall be off, I believe, in a hurry, and travel to Milan;
There to meet friends of Papa's, I am told, at the Croce di
  Malta;
Then I cannot say whither, but not at present to England.

13 CLAUDE TO EUSTACE

Yes, on Montorio's height for a last farewell of the city,—
So it appears; though then I was quite uncertain about it.
So, however, it was. And now to explain the
  proceeding.   270
  I was to go, as I told you, I think, with the people to
    Florence.
Only the day before, the foolish family Vernon
Made some uneasy remarks, as we walked to our lodging
  together,
As to intentions, forsooth, and so forth. I was astounded,
Horrified quite; and obtaining just then, as it happened,
  an offer
(No common favour) of seeing the great Ludovisi
  collection,
Why, I made this a pretence, and wrote that they must
  excuse me.
How could I go? Great Heaven! to conduct a permitted
  flirtation
Under those vulgar eyes, the observed of such observers![72]
Well, but I now, by a series of fine diplomatic
  inquiries,   280
Find from a sort of relation, a good and sensible woman,
Who is remaining at Rome with a brother too ill for
  removal,
That it was wholly unsanctioned, unknown,—not, I think,
  by Georgina:
She, however, ere this,—and that is the best of the story,—
She and the Vernon, thank Heaven, are wedded and
  gone—honey-mooning.
So—on Montorio's height for a last farewell of the city.
Tibur I have not seen, nor the lakes that of old I had
  dreamt of;
Tibur I shall not see, nor Anio's waters, nor deep en-
Folded in Sabine recesses the valley and villa of Horace;
Tibur I shall not see;—but something better I shall see.   290
  Twice I have tried before, and failed in getting the
    horses;
Twice I have tried and failed: this time it shall not be a
  failure.

---

[71]**Oudinot**, the French commander, entered Rome July 3.

[72]**observed . . . observers:** see *Hamlet* 3.3.153.

Therefore farewell, ye hills, and ye, ye envineyarded ruins.
* Therefore farewell, ye walls, palaces, pillars, and domes!*
Therefore farewell, far seen, ye peaks of the mythic Albano,
* Seen from Montorio's height, Tibur and Æsula's hills!*
Ah, could we once, ere we go, could we stand, while, to ocean descending,
* Sinks o'er the yellow dark plain slowly the yellow broad sun,*
Stand, from the forest emerging at sunset, at once in the champaign,
* Open, but studded with trees, chestnuts umbrageous and old,*   300
E'en in those fair open fields that incurve to thy beautiful hollow,
* Nemi, imbedded in wood, Nemi, inurned in the hill!—*
Therefore farewell, ye plains, and ye hills, and the City Eternal!
* Therefore farewell! We depart, but to behold you again!*

— CANTO 4 —

Eastward, or Northward, or West? I wander and ask as I wander,
* Weary, yet eager and sure, Where shall I come to my love?*
Whitherward hasten to seek her? Ye daughters of Italy, tell me,
* Graceful and tender and dark, is she consorting with you?*
Thou that out-climbest the torrent, that tendest thy goats to the summit,
* Call to me, child of the Alp, has she been seen on the heights?*
Italy, farewell I bid thee! for whither she leads me, I follow.
* Farewell the vineyard! for I, where I but guess her, must go.*
Weariness welcome, and labour, wherever it be, if at last it
* Bring me in mountain or plain into the sight of my love.*   10

1 CLAUDE TO EUSTACE,—*FROM FLORENCE*

Gone from Florence; indeed; and that is truly provoking;—
Gone to Milan, it seems; then I go also to Milan.
Five days now departed; but they can travel but slowly;—
I quicker far; and I know, as it happens, the house they
    will go to.—
Why, what else should I do? Stay here and look at the
    pictures,
Statues, and churches? Alack, I am sick of the statues
    and pictures!—
No, to Bologna, Parma, Piacenza, Lodi, and Milan,
Off go we to-night,—and the Venus go to the Devil![73]

2 CLAUDE TO EUSTACE,—*FROM BELLAGGIO*

Gone to Como, they said; and I have posted to Como.
There was a letter left; but the *cameriere*[74] had lost it.   20
Could it have been for me? They came, however, to Como,
And from Como went by the boat,—perhaps to the
    Splügen,—

Or to the Stelvio, say, and the Tyrol; also it might be
By Porlezza across to Lugano, and so to the Simplon
Possibly, or the St Gothard,—or possibly, too, to Baveno,
Orta, Turin, and elsewhere. Indeed, I am greatly
    bewildered.

3 CLAUDE TO EUSTACE,—*FROM BELLAGGIO*

I have been up the Splügen, and on the Stelvio also:
Neither of these can I find they have followed; in no one
    inn, and
This would be odd, have they written their names. I have
    been to Porlezza;
There they have not been seen, and therefore not at
    Lugano.   30
What shall I do? Go on through the Tyrol, Switzerland,
    Deutschland,
Seeking, an inverse Saul, a kingdom, to find only asses?
    There is a tide,[75] at least in the *love* affairs of mortals,
Which, when taken at flood, leads on to the happiest
    fortune,—
Leads to the marriage-morn and the orange-flowers and
    the altar,
And the long lawful line of crowned joys to crowned
    joys succeeding.—
Ah, it has ebbed with me! Ye gods, and when it was
    flowing,
Pitiful fool that I was, to stand fiddle-faddling in that way!

4 CLAUDE TO EUSTACE,—*FROM BELLAGGIO*

I have returned and found their names in the book at
    Como.
Certain it is I was right, and yet I am also in error.   40
Added in feminine hand, I read, *By the boat to Bellaggio.*—
So to Bellaggio again, with the words of her writing to
    aid me.
Yet at Bellaggio I find no trace, no sort of remembrance.
So I am here, and wait, and know every hour will remove
    them.

5 CLAUDE TO EUSTACE,—*FROM BELLAGGIO*

I have but one chance left,—and that is going to Florence.
But it is cruel to turn. The mountains seem to demand
    me,—
Peak and valley from far to beckon and motion me onward.
Somewhere amid their folds she passes whom fain I would
    follow;

---

[73]The Medici **Venus**: famous sculpture in Florence. Claude continues N to **Bellaggio** and SE Switzerland and then returns to Italy.

[74]*cameriere*: hotel clerk.

[75]**Saul**: see 1 Samuel 9. **There is a tide**: *Julius Caesar* 4.3.218.

Somewhere among those heights she haply calls me to
　　seek her.
Ah, could I hear her call! could I catch the glimpse of
　　her raiment!　　　　　　　　　　　　　　　　　50
Turn, however, I must, though it seem I turn to desert her;
For the sense of the thing is simply to hurry to Florence,
Where the certainty yet may be learnt, I suppose, from
　　the Ropers.

6 MARY TREVELLYN, *FROM LUCERNE* TO MISS ROPER, *AT FLORENCE*

Dear Miss Roper,—By this you are safely away, we are
　　hoping,
Many a league from Rome; erelong we trust we shall
　　see you.
How have you travelled? I wonder;—was Mr Claude
　　your companion?
As for ourselves, we went from Como straight to Lugano;
So by the Mount St Gothard; we meant to go by
　　Porlezza,
Taking the steamer, and stopping, as you had advised, at
　　Bellaggio,
Two or three days or more; but this was suddenly
　　altered,　　　　　　　　　　　　　　　　　　　60
After we left the hotel, on the very way to the steamer.
So we have seen, I fear, not one of the lakes in perfection.
　　Well, he is not come; and now, I suppose, he will
　　　　not come.
What will you think, meantime?—and yet I must really
　　confess it;—
What will you say? I wrote him a note. We left in a hurry,
Went from Milan to Como, three days before we
　　expected.
But I thought, if he came all the way to Milan, he really
Ought not to be disappointed; and so I wrote three lines to
Say I had heard he was coming, desirous of joining our
　　party;—
If so, then I said, we had started for Como, and
　　meant to　　　　　　　　　　　　　　　　　　70
Cross the St Gothard, and stay, we believed, at Lucerne,
　　for the summer.
Was it wrong? and why, if it was, has it failed to
　　bring him?
Did he not think it worth while to come to Milan?
　　He knew (you
Told him) the house we should go to. Or may it, perhaps,
　　have miscarried?
Any way, now, I repent, and am heartily vexed that I
　　wrote it.

There is a home[76] *on the shore of the Alpine sea, that upswelling*
　　High up the mountain-sides spreads in the hollow between;
Wilderness, mountain, and snow from the land of the olive conceal it;
　　Under Pilatus's hill low by its river it lies:
Italy, utter the word, and the olive and vine will allure not,—　　80
　　Wilderness, forest, and snow will not the passage impede;
Italy, unto thy cities receding, the clew to recover,
　　Hither, recovered the clew, shall not the traveller haste?

— CANTO 5 —

There is a city,[77] *upbuilt on the quays of the turbulent Arno,*
　　Under Fiesole's heights,—thither are we to return?
There is a city that fringes the curve of the inflowing waters,
　　Under the perilous hill fringes the beautiful bay,—
Parthenope do they call thee?—the Siren, Neapolis, seated
　　Under Vesevus's hill,—are we receding to thee?—
Sicily, Greece, will invite, and the Orient;—or are we to turn to
　　England, which may after all be for its children the best?

1 MARY TREVELLYN, *AT LUCERNE,* TO MISS ROPER, *AT FLORENCE*

So you are really free, and living in quiet at Florence;
That is delightful news;—you travelled slowly and
　　safely;　　　　　　　　　　　　　　　　　　10
Mr Claude got you out; took rooms at Florence before you;
Wrote from Milan to say so; had left directly for Milan,
Hoping to find us soon;—*if he could, he would, you are certain.*—
Dear Miss Roper, your letter has made me exceedingly
　　happy.
　　You are quite sure, you say, he asked you about our
　　　　intentions;
You had not heard as yet of Lucerne, but told him of
　　Como.—
Well, perhaps he will come;—however, I will not expect it.
Though you say you are sure,—*if he can, he will, you are certain.*
O my dear, many thanks from your ever affectionate Mary.

2 CLAUDE TO EUSTACE

　　　　　　　　　　　　　　　　　　Florence.
Action will furnish belief,—but will that belief be the
　　true one?　　　　　　　　　　　　　　　　20
This is the point, you know. However, it doesn't much
　　matter.

---

[76]**home:** Lucerne, in Switzerland. **Pilatus:** mountain on W shore
of Lake Lucerne.

[77]**city . . . Arno:** Florence, north of Rome. **city . . . bay:** Naples,
south of Rome.

What one wants, I suppose, is to predetermine the action,
So as to make it entail, not a chance-belief, but the true
  one.
Out of the question, you say; *if a thing isn't wrong, we may do it.*
Ah! but this *wrong*, you see—but I do not know that it
  matters.
  Eustace, the Ropers are gone, and no one can tell me
    about them.

Pisa.

Pisa, they say they think; and so I follow to Pisa,
Hither and thither inquiring, I weary of making inquiries;
I am ashamed, I declare, of asking people about it.—
Who are your friends? You said you had friends who would
  certainly know them.   30

Florence.

But it is idle, moping, and thinking, and trying to fix her
Image more and more in, to write the old perfect
  inscription
Over and over again upon every page of remembrance.
  I have settled to stay at Florence to wait for your answer.
Who are your friends? Write quickly and tell me. I wait for
  your answer.

3 Mary Trevellyn to Miss Roper, *at Lucca Baths*

You are at Lucca Baths, you tell me, to stay for the summer;
Florence was quite too hot; you can't move further at
  present.
Will you not come, do you think, before the summer is
  over?
  Mr C. got you out with very considerable trouble;
And he was useful and kind, and seemed so happy to
  serve you;   40
Didn't stay with you long, but talked very openly to you;
Made you almost his confessor, without appearing to know
  it,—
What about?—and you say you didn't need his confessions.
O my dear Miss Roper, I dare not trust what you tell me!
  Will he come, do you think? I am really so sorry for
    him!
They didn't give him my letter at Milan, I feel pretty
  certain.
You had told him Bellaggio. We didn't go to Bellaggio;
So he would miss our track, and perhaps never come to
  Lugano,
Where we were written in full, *To Lucerne across the St Gothard.*
But he could write to you;—you would tell him where
  you were going.   50

4 Claude to Eustace

Let me, then, bear to forget her. I will not cling to her
  falsely;
Nothing factitious or forced shall impair the old happy
  relation.
I will let myself go, forget, not try to remember;
I will walk on my way, accept the chances that
  meet me,
Freely encounter the world, imbibe these alien airs, and
Never ask if new feelings and thoughts are of her or
  of others.
Is she not changing, herself?—the old image would only
  delude me.
I will be bold, too, and change,—if it must be. Yet if in
  all things,
Yet if I do but aspire evermore to the Absolute only,
I shall be doing, I think, somehow, what she will be
  doing;—   60
I shall be thine, O my child, some way, though I know
  not in what way.
Let me submit to forget her; I must; I already forget her.

5 Claude to Eustace

Utterly vain is, alas! this attempt at the Absolute,—
  wholly!
I, who believed not in her, because I would fain believe
  nothing,
Have to believe as I may, with a wilful, unmeaning
  acceptance.
I, who refused to enfasten the roots of my floating
  existence
In the rich earth, cling now to the hard, naked rock that is
  left me—
Ah! she was worthy, Eustace,—and that, indeed, is my
  comfort,—
Worthy a nobler heart than a fool such as I could have
  given.

———————

Yes, it relieves me to write, though I do not send, and
  the chance that   70
Takes may destroy my fragments. But as men pray,
  without asking
Whether One really exist to hear or do anything for
  them,—
Simply impelled by the need of the moment to turn to
  a Being
In a conception of whom there is freedom from all
  limitation,—

So in your image I turn to an *ens rationis*[78] of friendship.
Even so write in your name I know not to whom nor in
what wise.

———————

There was a time, methought it was but lately departed,
When, if a thing was denied me, I felt I was bound to
attempt it;
Choice alone should take, and choice alone should
surrender.
There was a time, indeed, when I had not retired thus
early,   80
Languidly thus, from pursuit of a purpose I once had
adopted.
But it is over, all that! I have slunk from the perilous
field in
Whose wild struggle of forces the prizes of life are
contested.
It is over, all that! I am a coward, and know it.
Courage in me could be only factitious, unnatural, useless.

———————

Comfort has come to me here in the dreary streets of
the city,
Comfort—how do you think?—with a barrel-organ to
bring it.
Moping along the streets, and cursing my day as I
wandered,
All of a sudden my ear met the sound of an English
psalm-tune.
Comfort me it did, till indeed I was very near crying.   90
Ah, there is some great truth, partial, very likely, but
needful,
Lodged, I am strangely sure, in the tones of the English
psalm-tune.
Comfort it was at least; and I must take without question
Comfort, however it come, in the dreary streets of the city.

———————

What with trusting myself, and seeking support from
within me,
Almost I could believe I had gained a religious assurance,
Formed in my own poor soul a great moral basis to rest on.
Ah, but indeed I see, I feel it factitious entirely;
I refuse, reject, and put it utterly from me;
I will look straight out, see things, not try to evade
them;   100
Fact shall be fact for me; and the Truth the Truth as ever,

———————

Flexible, changeable, vague, and multiform, and doubtful.—
Off, and depart to the void, thou subtle, fanatical tempter!

———————

I shall behold thee again (is it so?) at a new visitation,
O ill genius thou! I shall, at my life's dissolution,
(When the pulses are weak, and the feeble light of the
reason
Flickers, an unfed flame retiring slow from the socket),
Low on a sick-bed laid, hear one, as it were, at the
doorway,
And, looking up, see thee, standing by, looking emptily
at me;
I shall entreat thee then, though now I dare to refuse
thee,—   110
Pale and pitiful now, but terrible then to the dying.—
Well, I will see thee again, and while I can, will repel thee.

6 CLAUDE TO EUSTACE

Rome is fallen,[79] I hear, the gallant Medici taken,
Noble Manara slain, and Garibaldi has lost *il Moro*,—
Rome is fallen; and fallen, or falling, heroical Venice.
I, meanwhile, for the loss of a single small chit of a girl, sit
Moping and mourning here,—for her, and myself much
smaller.
   Whither depart the souls of the brave that die in the
   battle,
Die in the lost, lost fight, for the cause that perishes with
them?
Are they upborne from the field on the slumberous pinions
of angels   120
Unto a far-off home, where the weary rest from their labour,
And the deep wounds are healed, and the bitter and
burning moisture
Wiped from the generous eyes? or do they linger, unhappy,
Pining, and haunting the grave of their by-gone hope and
endeavour?
   All declamation, alas! though I talk, I care not for
   Rome, nor
Italy; feebly and faintly, and but with the lips, can lament the
Wreck of the Lombard youth,[80] and the victory of the
oppressor.
Whither depart the brave?—God knows; I certainly do not.

———————

[78]*ens rationis:* a being merely mental.

[79]**Rome is fallen:** Rome surrendered at the end of June. Giacomo
Medici and Luciano **Manara:** republican commanders. *il Moro:* Aguyar; see note 49. **Venice** too revolted in 1848 but fell to Austria in
1849.

[80]**Lombard youth:** Lombardy briefly threw off Austrian rule in
1848.

7 Mary Trevellyn to Miss Roper

He has not come as yet; and now I must not expect it.
You have written you say, to friends at Florence, to
    see him,   130
If he perhaps should return;—but that is surely unlikely.
Has he not written to you?—he did not know your
    direction.
Oh, how strange never once to have told him where you
    were going!
Yet if he only wrote to Florence, that would have
    reached you.
If what you say he said was true, why has he not done so?
Is he gone back to Rome, do you think, to his Vatican
    marbles?—
O my dear Miss Roper, forgive me! do not be angry!—
You have written to Florence;—your friends would
    certainly find him.
Might you not write to him?—but yet it is so little likely!
I shall expect nothing more.—Ever yours, your
    affectionate Mary.   140

8 Claude to Eustace

I cannot stay at Florence, not even to wait for a letter.
Galleries only oppress me. Remembrance of hope I had
    cherished
(Almost more than as hope, when I passed through
    Florence the first time)
Lies like a sword in my soul. I am more a coward than ever,
Chicken-hearted, past thought. The *caffes* and waiters
    distress me.
All is unkind, and, alas! I am ready for any one's kindness.
Oh, I knew it of old, and knew it, I thought, to perfection,
If there is any one thing in the world to preclude all
    kindness,
It is the need of it,—it is this sad, self-defeating
    dependence.
Why is this, Eustace? Myself, were I stronger, I think I
    could tell you.   150
But it is odd when it comes. So plumb I the deeps of
    depression,
Daily in deeper, and find no support, no will, no purpose.
All my old strengths are gone. And yet I shall have to do
    something.
Ah, the key of our life, that passes all wards, opens all
    locks,
Is not *I will*, but *I must*. I must,—I must,—and I do it.

After all, do I know that I really cared so about her?
Do whatever I will, I cannot call up her image;

For when I close my eyes, I see, very likely, St Peter's,
Or the Pantheon façade, or Michel Angelo's figures,
Or, at a wish, when I please, the Alban hills and the
    Forum,—   160
But that face, those eyes,—ah no, never anything like them;
Only, try as I will, a sort of featureless outline,
And a pale blank orb, which no recollection will add to.
After all perhaps there was something factitious about it:
I have had pain, it is true; I have wept; and so have the actors.

At the last moment I have your letter, for which I was waiting.
I have taken my place, and see no good in inquiries.
Do nothing more, good Eustace, I pray you. It only will
    vex me.
Take no measures. Indeed, should we meet, I could not
    be certain;
All might be changed, you know. Or perhaps there was
    nothing to be changed.   170
It is a curious history, this; and yet I foresaw it;
I could have told it before. The Fates, it is clear, are against us;
For it is certain enough that I met with the people you
    mention;
They were at Florence the day I returned there, and spoke
    to me even;
Stayed a week, saw me often; departed, and whither I
    know not.
Great is Fate, and is best. I believe in Providence partly.
What is ordained is right, and all that happens is ordered.
Ah, no, that isn't it. But yet I retain my conclusion.
I will go where I am led, and will not dictate to the chances.
Do nothing more, I beg. If you love me, forbear
    interfering.   180

9 Claude to Eustace

Shall we come out of it all, some day, as one does from a
    tunnel?
Will it be all at once, without our doing or asking,
We shall behold clear day, the trees and meadows about us,
And the faces of friends, and the eyes we loved looking
    at us?
Who knows? Who can say? It will not do to suppose it.

10 Claude to Eustace,—*from Rome*

Rome will not suit me, Eustace; the priests and soldiers
    possess it;
Priests and soldiers;—and, ah! which is worst, the priest or
    the soldier?
    Politics, farewell, however! For what could I do? with
      inquiring,

Talking, collating the journals, go fever my brain about
 things o'er
Which I can have no control. No, happen whatever may
 happen,   190
Time, I suppose, will subsist; the earth will revolve on
 its axis;
People will travel; the stranger will wander as now in
 the city;
Rome will be here, and the Pope the *custode*[81] of Vatican
 marbles.
  I have no heart, however, for any marble or fresco;
I have essayed it in vain; 'tis vain as yet to essay it;
But I may haply resume some day my studies in this kind;
Not as the Scripture says, is, I think, the fact. Ere our
 death-day,
Faith, I think, does pass, and Love; but Knowledge
 abideth.[82]
Let us seek Knowledge;—the rest must come and go as
 it happens.
Knowledge is hard to seek, and harder yet to adhere to. 200
Knowledge is painful often; and yet when we know, we
 are happy.
Seek it, and leave mere Faith and Love to come with the
 chances.
As for Hope,—to-morrow I hope to be starting for Naples.
Rome will not do, I see, for many very good reasons.
  Eastward, then, I suppose, with the coming of winter,
  to Egypt.

11 MARY TREVELLYN TO MISS ROPER

You have heard nothing; of course, I know you can have
 heard nothing.
Ah, well, more than once I have broken my purpose, and
 sometimes,
Only too often, have looked for the little lake-steamer to
 bring him.
But it is only fancy,—I do not really expect it.
Oh, and you see I know so exactly how he would
 take it: 210
Finding the chances prevail against meeting again, he
 would banish
Forthwith every thought of the poor little possible
 hope, which
I myself could not help, perhaps, thinking only too much of;

He would resign himself, and go. I see it exactly.
So I also submit, although in a different manner.
  Can you not really come? We go very shortly to England.

      ——————

So go forth to the world, to the good report and the evil?
 Go, little book! thy tale, is it not evil and good?
Go, and if strangers revile, pass quietly by without answer.
 Go, and if curious friends ask of thy rearing and age,   220
Say, "I am flitting about many years from brain unto brain of
 Feeble and restless youths born to inglorious days;
But,' so finish the word, 'I was writ in a Roman chamber,
 When from Janiculan[83] *heights thundered the cannon of France."*
1849   1858

The Latest Decalogue[1]

Thou shalt have one God only; who
Would be at the expense of two?
No graven images may be
Worshipped, except the currency:
Swear not at all; for for thy curse
Thine enemy is none the worse:
At church on Sunday to attend
Will serve to keep the world thy friend:
Honour thy parents; that is, all
From whom advancement may befall: 10
Thou shalt not kill; but needst not strive
Officiously to keep alive:
Do not adultery commit;
Advantage rarely comes of it:
Thou shalt not steal; an empty feat,
When it's so lucrative to cheat:
Bear not false witness; let the lie
Have time on its own wings to fly:
Thou shalt not covet; but tradition
Approves all forms of competition.   20

The sum of all is, thou shalt love,
If any body, God above:
At any rate shall never labour
More than thyself to love thy neighbour.
                 1862

---

[81]*custode*: custodian.

[82]**Faith . . . abideth**: see 1 Corinthians 13:8–13, which Claude
contradicts.

[83]**Janiculan**: one of the hills of Rome.

[1]**Decalogue**: the Ten Commandments (Exodus 20:3–17).

JEAN INGELOW

(1820–1897)

Jean Ingelow was one of the most popular poets of the Victorian period. Her 1863 *Poems* went through thirty editions and her books sold especially well in America; her fantasy for children, *Mopsa the Fairy*, was often reprinted in the twentieth century. Much of her poetry is narrative, but she had a nice sense of rhythm and meter and was known mostly for her lyrics. Although the diction is often archaic or "poetic," the flow of the verse is usually smooth and clear, with a bias towards tripping measures that are kept fresh by deft syncopation, as in the choral trill "It's we two, it's we two" from "Like a Laverock in the Lift". Many of her poems were set to music and frequently sung. She upholds conventional values—joy in the beauty of nature, trust in a benevolent God, acceptance of woman's duty to love and submit—but there are occasional signs of a darker vision as well as dissatisfaction with women's role and some murmurs of unrest, particularly in her longer narratives.

The daughter of a banker and shipper who fell from prosperity into bankruptcy and genteel poverty, Ingelow was the eldest in a large family. Her early years were spent in a house overlooking the water in Lincolnshire, and the sea is a familiar presence in her poetry. In 1850 the family moved to London, where she produced several volumes of poetry, novels, and books for children. Her literary acquaintances included Tennyson, another poet from Lincolnshire and the one who most influenced her, Robert Browning; and Christina Rossetti, who expressed joking envy of her success.

Divided

— 1 —

An empty sky, a world of heather,
   Purple of foxglove, yellow of broom;[1]
We two among them wading together,
   Shaking out honey, treading perfume.

Crowds of bees are giddy with clover,
   Crowds of grasshoppers skip at our feet,
Crowds of larks at their matins[2] hang over,
   Thanking the Lord for a life so sweet.

Flusheth the rise with her purple favour,
   Gloweth the cleft with her golden ring,   10
'Twixt the two brown butterflies waver,
   Lightly settle, and sleepily swing.

We two walk till the purple dieth
   And short dry grass under foot is brown,
But one little streak at a distance lieth
   Green like a ribbon to prank[3] the down.

— 2 —

Over the grass we stepped unto it,
   And God He knoweth how blithe we were!
Never a voice to bid us eschew it:
   Hey the green ribbon that showed so fair!   20

Hey the green ribbon! we kneeled beside it,
   We parted the grasses dewy and sheen;
Drop over drop there filtered and slided,
   A tiny bright beck that trickled between.

Tinkle, tinkle, sweetly it sung to us,
   Light was our talk as of faëry bells;
Faëry wedding-bells faintly rung to us
   Down in their fortunate parallels.

---

[1]**broom:** shrub with yellow flowers.

[2]**matins:** morning song or prayer.

[3]**prank:** dress brightly.

Hand in hand, while the sun peered over,
　　We lapped the grass on that youngling spring; 30
Swept back its rushes, smoothed its clover,
　　And said, "Let us follow it westering."

— 3 —

A dappled sky, a world of meadows,
　　Circling above us the black rooks fly
Forward, backward; lo, their dark shadows
　　Flit on the blossoming tapestry.

Flit on the beck,[4] for her long grass parteth
　　As hair from a maid's bright eyes blown back;
And, lo, the sun like a lover darteth
　　His flattering smile on her wayward track.   40

Sing on! we sing in the glorious weather
　　Till one steps over the tiny strand,
So narrow, in sooth, that still together
　　On either brink we go hand in hand.

The beck grows wider, the hands must sever.
　　On either margin, our songs all done,
We move apart, while she singeth ever,
　　Taking the course of the stooping sun.

He prays, "Come over"—I may not follow;
　　I cry, "Return"—but he cannot come: 50
We speak, we laugh, but with voices hollow;
　　Our hands are hanging, our hearts are numb.

— 4 —

A breathing sigh, a sigh for answer,
　　A little talking of outward things;
The careless beck is a merry dancer,
　　Keeping sweet time to the air she sings.

A little pain when the beck grows wider;
　　"Cross to me now—for her wavelets swell":
"I may not cross"—and the voice beside her
　　Faintly reacheth, though heeded well.   60

No backward path; ah! no returning;
　　No second crossing that ripple's flow:
"Come to me now, for the west is burning;
　　Come ere it darkens;"—"Ah, no! ah, no!"

Then cries of pain, and arms outreaching—
　　The beck grows wider and swift and deep:
Passionate words as of one beseeching—
　　The loud beck drowns them; we walk, and weep.

— 5 —

A yellow moon in splendour drooping,
　　A tired queen with her state oppressed,   70
Low by rushes and swordgrass stooping,
　　Lies she soft on the waves at rest.

The desert heavens have felt her sadness;
　　Her earth will weep her some dewy tears;
The wild beck ends her tune of gladness,
　　And goeth stilly as soul that fears.

We two walk on in our grassy places
　　On either marge of the moonlit flood,
With the moon's own sadness in our faces,
　　Where joy is withered, blossom and bud.   80

— 6 —

A shady freshness, chafers whirring,
　　A little piping of leaf-hid birds;
A flutter of wings, a fitful stirring,
　　A cloud to the eastward snowy as curds.

Bare grassy slopes, where kids are tethered,
　　Round valleys like nests all ferny-lined;
Round hills, with fluttering tree-tops feathered,
　　Swell high in their freckled robes behind.

A rose-flush tender, a thrill, a quiver,
　　When golden gleams to the tree-tops glide;   90
A flashing edge for the milk-white river,
　　The beck, a river—with still sleek tide.

Broad and white, and polished as silver,
　　On she goes under fruit-laden trees;
Sunk in leafage cooeth the culver,[5]
　　And 'plaineth of love's disloyalties.

Glitters the dew and shines the river,
　　Up comes the lily and dries her bell;
But two are walking apart for ever,
　　And wave their hands for a mute farewell.   100

— 7 —

A braver swell, a swifter sliding;
　　The river hasteth, her banks recede:
Wing-like sails on her bosom gliding
　　Bear down the lily and drown the reed.

---

[4]**beck:** brook.

[5]**culver:** wood-pigeon.

Stately prows are rising and bowing
  (Shouts of mariners winnow the air),
And level sands for banks endowing
  The tiny green ribbon that showed so fair.

While, O my heart! as white sails shiver,
  And crowds are passing, and banks stretch wide,   110
How hard to follow, with lips that quiver,
  That moving speck on the far-off side.

Farther, farther—I see it—know it—
  My eyes brim over, it melts away:
Only my heart to my heart shall show it
  As I walk desolate day by day.

— 8 —

And yet I know past all doubting, truly—
  A knowledge greater than grief can dim—
I know, as he loved, he will love me duly—
  Yea better—e'en better than I love him.   120

And as I walk by the vast calm river,
  The awful river so dread to see,
I say, "Thy breadth and thy depth for ever
  Are bridged by his thoughts that cross to me."

1863

from **Supper at the Mill**

When sparrows build, and the leaves break forth,
  My old sorrow wakes and cries,
For I know there is dawn in the far, far north,
  And a scarlet sun doth rise;
Like a scarlet fleece the snow-field spreads,
  And the icy founts run free,
And the bergs begin to bow their heads,
  And plunge, and sail in the sea.

O my lost love, and my own, own love,
  And my love that loved me so!   10
Is there never a chink in the world above
  Where they listen for words from below?
Nay, I spoke once, and I grieved thee sore,
  I remember all that I said,
And now thou wilt hear me no more—no more
  Till the sea gives up her dead.

Thou didst set thy foot on the ship, and sail
  To the ice-fields and the snow;
Thou wert sad, for thy love did naught avail,
  And the end I could not know;   20
How could I tell I should love thee to-day,
  Whom that day I held not dear?
How could I know I should love thee away
  When I did not love thee anear?

We shall walk no more through the sodden plain.
  With the faded bents[1] o'erspread,
We shall stand no more by the seething main
  While the dark wrack drives o'erhead;
We shall part no more in the wind and the rain,
  Where thy last farewell was said: 30
But perhaps I shall meet thee and know thee again
  When the sea gives up her dead.

1863

A Raven in a White Chine[1]

I saw when I looked up, on either hand,
  A pale high chalk-cliff, reared aloft in white;
A narrowing rent soon closed toward the land—
  Toward the sea an open yawning bight.

The polished tide, with scarce a hint of blue,
  Washed in the bight;[2] above with angry moan
A raven, that was robbed, sat up in view,
  Croaking and crying on a ledge alone.

"Stand on thy nest, spread out thy fateful wings,
  With sullen hungry love bemoan thy brood,   10
For boys have wrung their necks, those imp-like things,
  Whose beaks dripped crimson daily at their food.

"Cry, thou black prophetess! cry, and despair,
  None love thee, none! Their father was thy foe,
Whose father in his youth did know thy lair,
  And steal thy little demons long ago.

"Thou madest many childless for their sake,
  And picked out many eyes that loved the light.
Cry, thou black prophetess! sit up, awake,
  Forebode; and ban them through the desolate night."20

---

[1]**bents**: stiff, reedy grasses.

[1]**Chine**: ravine.

[2]**bight**: bay.

Lo! while I spake it, with a crimson hue
    The dipping sun endowed that silver flood,
And all the cliffs flushed red, and up she flew,
    The bird, as mad to bathe in airy blood.

"Nay, thou may'st cry, the omen is not thine,
    Thou aged priestess of fell doom, and fate.
It is not blood: thy gods are making wine,
    They spilt the must[3] outside their city gate,

"And stained their azure pavement with the lees;
    They will not listen though thou cry aloud.   30
Old Chance, thy dame, sits mumbling at her ease,
    Nor hears; the fair hag, Luck, is in her shroud.

"They heed not, they withdraw the sky-hung sign:
    Thou hast no charm against the favourite race;
Thy gods pour out for it, not blood, but wine:
    There is no justice in their dwelling-place!

"Safe in their father's house the boys shall rest,
    Though thy fell brood doth stark and silent lie;
Their unborn sons may yet despoil thy nest:
    Cry, thou black prophetess! lift up! cry, cry."   40

1867

Like a Laverock in the Lift[1]

— 1 —

It's we two, it's we two, it's we two for ay,
All the world and we two, and Heaven be our stay.
Like a laverock in the lift, sing, O bonny bride!
All the world was Adam once, with Eve by his side.

— 2 —

What's the world, my lass, my love!—what can it do?
I am thine, and thou art mine; life is sweet and new.

---

[3]**must**: crushed grapes.

[1]**laverock**: lark. **lift**: air, sky.

If the world have missed the mark, let it stand by,
For we two have gotten leave, and once more we'll try.

— 3 —

Like a laverock in the lift, sing, O bonny bride!
It's we two, it's we two, happy side by side.   10
Take a kiss from me thy man; now the song begins:
"All is made afresh for us, and the brave heart wins."

— 4 —

When the darker days come, and no sun will shine,
Thou shalt dry my tears, lass, and I'll dry thine.
It's we two, it's we two, while the world's away,
Sitting by the golden sheaves on our wedding-day.

1869

Compensation

One launched a ship, but she was wrecked at sea;
    He built a bridge, but floods have borne it down,
He meant much good, none came: strange destiny,
    His corn lies sunk, his bridge bears none to town,
    Yet good he had not meant became his crown;
For once at work, when even as nature free,
    From thought of good he was, or of renown,
God took the work for good and let good be.
So wakened with a trembling after sleep,
    Dread Mona Roa[1] yields her fateful store;   10
All gleaming hot the scarlet rivers creep,
    And fanned of great-leaved palms slip to the shore,
Then stolen to unplumbed wastes of that far deep,
    Lay the foundations for one island more.

1871

---

[1]**Mona Roa**: Mauna Loa, volcano in Hawaii.

RUDENT, wise, and happy men who have selected their libraries as a squirrel lays by his winter hoard—without one decayed or hollow nut in the lot—have, of course, on their shelves the ELEVEN VOLUMES OF PUNCH. There they stand—(hear you not HANDEL's organ ?)—

"In burning row !"

On the shelves of Windsor Castle Library, *Punch* has eleven magnificent coats of gorgeous crimson, "smeared with gold." For, representing English Letters and English Art, *Punch* is the pet of the Palace, and is cherished by his QUEEN and his Prince with a condescending tenderness unknown even to royal pups and royal parrots. How often has a Cabinet Council broken up, leaving some state riddle still unsolved, when, not to mention names, the Highest Lady in the Land has consulted the crimson-coated *Punch*, and straightway the enigma has been clear as sunbeam !

Amid the shades of venerable Lambeth, clothed in morocco of episcopal purple, and shouldered on either side by tall saints and corpulent fathers, stands *Punch*—the delight and monitor of Archbishops ; Bishops ; Deans ; Prebends ; and Church Pluralists—(holy men, with twenty hands, and a loaf or a fish in either of them)—in particular !

In the Court of Chancery, bound—(the word has a terrible significance)—in law-calf, *Punch*, dilated into Eleven Volumes, gives a fragrance to mustiness, and casts a rosy colour upon parchment, that then does *not* appear the dead, discoloured skin of flayed Justice.

Richard Doyle, from *Punch, or the London Charivari*, volume 12 (1847)

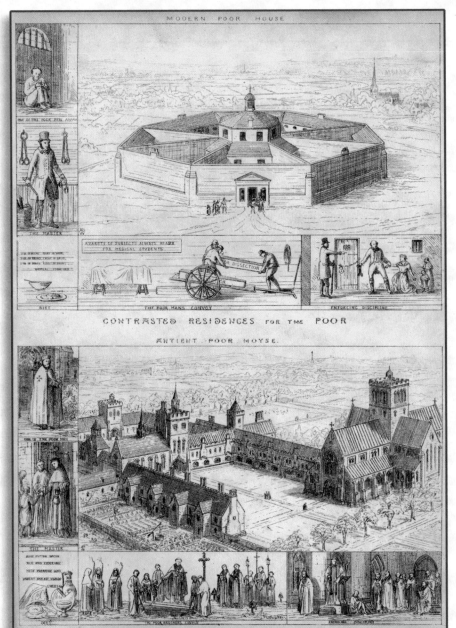

A. Welby Pugin, *Contrasted Residences for the Poor*, from *Contrasts: or,
A Parallel between the Noble Edifices of the Middle Ages, and Corresponding Buildings
of the Present Day, Shewing the Present Decay of Taste* (1841)

THE LADY OF SHALOTT.

PART I.

I.

On either side the river lie
Long fields of barley and of rye,
That clothe the wold and meet the sky;
And thro' the field the road runs by
　　　To many-tower'd Camelot;

William Holman Hunt, from Tennyson, *Poems* (1857)

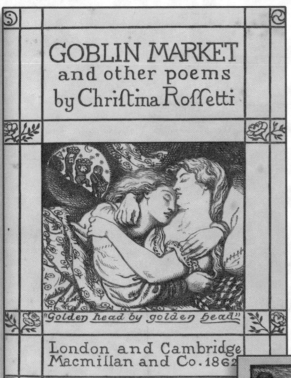

GOBLIN MARKET
and other poems
by Christina Rossetti

"Golden head by golden head"

London and Cambridge
Macmillan and Co. 1862

Dante Gabriel Rossetti, from
Christina Rossetti, *Goblin
Market and Other Poems* (1862)

"Buy from us with @ golden curl"

F. S. Cary, The Valentine, from
The Keepsake, edited by Miss Power (1856)

from *Peter Parley's Annual:
A Christmas & New Year's Present
for Young People* (1860)

Aubrey Beardsley, from
The Yellow Book, volume 1 (1894)

Charles Ricketts, from Oscar
Wilde, *The Sphinx* (1894)

from William Booth, *In Darkest England, and the Way Out* (1890)

"STRONGEST AND BEST."—*Health.*

Fry's

Pure Concentrated

Cocoa

By SPECIAL APPOINTMENT to HER MOST GRACIOUS MAJESTY

200 GOLD MEDALS & DIPLOMAS

from *The Illustrated London News*, Diamond Jubilee Edition (1897)

FLORENCE NIGHTINGALE

(1820–1910)

A brilliant and passionate child, Florence Nightingale received an exceptionally fine education at home under her father's superintendence. Her father was an intellectual, her mother beautiful and fashionable, her family sociable and rich. Nightingale herself was handsome, charming, witty, and a great success in the most sparkling society. But she despised her easy, pointless life; restless and unhappy, she lived in daydreams she could not dispel. She loved dancing and opera and the great world, but she had a deep streak of mysticism and an overwhelming need to serve God and suffering humanity. She heard her first clear divine call when she was still in her teens, and at twenty-four she realized that hospital work was her vocation. The little nursing she was able to do in her family and the local village showed her that sympathy and kindness were not enough, that to nurse effectively she needed training; but there seemed no way to get it. At that time hospitals were squalid institutions for the poor; nurses, drawn from the lowest classes of society, were untrained and notorious for drunkenness and sexual immorality. Nightingale's parents and sister were appalled at the suggestion that she degrade herself to such a level. Their unremitting opposition held her back but left her unappeased; she even refused to marry the highly suitable man she was in love with. In 1853 she wrote "Cassandra," an impassioned outcry against upper-class women's stifling, useless lives, part of a work called *Selections for Thought* that was privately printed but not published in her lifetime.

It was not until 1850 that she was allowed to train at a religious nursing community in Germany, and she did not move out of the family home and go to work organizing a new hospital until 1853. In the meantime, however, she traveled and observed and collected information about hospitals, studying reports in secret and preparing for her life's work. Her opportunity came during the Crimean War (1854–1856). The British army was in administrative chaos, its medical division disorganized and badly led, with few doctors, no nurses, and almost no supplies. The large number of casualties combined with a cholera epidemic brought appalling suffering, which was reported in the London *Times* by Britain's first war correspondent. The public was outraged, and Nightingale was grudgingly allowed to set off with a group of nurses.

Arriving at Scutari on the Bosporus, she met with indifference or hostility. Her efforts to clean up the filthy hospitals and provide adequate food and care were frustrated at every turn. But with patience, tact, iron self-control, and powerful connections in London, she made significant progress nonetheless. The fame spread back to England of the "lady with the lamp" who moved through the dark wards bringing comfort. She was present, she said, at two thousand deathbeds. The men worshipped her, and for the rest of her life she thought of them as her "children." When the inglorious war ended she was its only hero. And by her care for the ordinary soldiers, almost all of whom came from the ranks of the poor and were regarded—not least by their officers—as hardly human, she initiated a transformation in the way they were treated by the army and viewed by the public.

Extraordinary though she was as a hospital nurse, Nightingale was even more extraordinary as a planner and administrator. She loved statistics and was indefatigable in collecting, interpreting, and explaining them. Back in England, she made detailed plans for the reorganization of medical and sanitary services in the army, in civilian hospitals and public health, and eventually for British India as well, and she used her great personal magnetism to get powerful men to work for their implementation. She carried on many different projects simultaneously, all of them difficult and some, such as her plans for irrigation to alleviate hunger in India, vast in scope. Because women were assumed to be incapable of administration, she could work only indirectly, shunning publicity so effectively that for the last decades of her life most people assumed she was dead. Withdrawing from society and directing operations of all sorts by way of an immense correspondence and private meetings with the men who carried out her projects, she drove herself and her helpers mercilessly and was an invalid for many years. Most of what she wrote consisted of correspondence in pursuit of her aims or reports for official purposes only. Her most popular work, *Notes on Nursing*, shows the characteristic combination of high moral purpose, profound human sympathy, far-reaching principle, and acute organization of detail that made her the most famous woman in Victorian England, apart from the queen herself, and the most admired person, bar none.

from Cassandra

"Yet I would spare no pang,
    Would wish no torture less,
The more that anguish racks,
    The earlier it will bless."[1]

Give us back our suffering, we cry to Heaven in our hearts—suffering rather than indifferentism; for out of nothing comes nothing. But out of suffering may come the cure. Better have pain than paralysis! A hundred struggle and drown in the breakers. One discovers the new world. But rather, ten times rather, die in the surf, heralding the way to that new world, than stand idly on the shore!

Passion, intellect, moral activity—these three have never been satisfied in woman. In this cold and oppressive conventional atmosphere, they cannot be satisfied. To say more on this subject would be to enter into the whole history of society, of the present state of civilization.

Look at that lizard—"It is not hot," he says, "I like it. The atmosphere which enervates you is life to me." The state of society which some complain of makes others happy. Why should these complain to those? *They* do not suffer. *They* would not understand it, any more than that lizard would comprehend the sufferings of a Shetland sheep.

The progressive world is necessarily divided into two classes—those who take the best of what there is and enjoy it—those who wish for something better and try to create it. Without these two classes, the world would be badly off. They are the very conditions of progress, both the one and the other. Were there none who were discontented with what they have, the world would never reach anything better. And, through the other class, which is constantly taking the best of what the first is creating for them, a balance is secured, and that which is conquered is held fast. But with neither class must we quarrel for not possessing the privileges of the other. The laws of the nature of each make it impossible.

Is discontent a privilege?

Yes, it is a privilege to suffer for your race—a privilege not reserved to the Redeemer and the martyrs alone, but one enjoyed by numbers in every age.

The common-place life of thousands; and in that is its only interest—its only merit as a history: viz. that it *is* the type of common sufferings—the story of one who has not the courage to resist nor to submit to the civilization of her time—is this.

Poetry and imagination begin life. A child will fall on its knees on the gravel walk at the sight of a pink hawthorn in full flower, when it is by itself, to praise God for it.

Then comes intellect. It wishes to satisfy the wants which intellect creates for it. But there is a physical, not moral, impossibility of supplying the wants of the intellect in the state of civilization at which we have arrived. The stimulus, the training, the time, are all three wanting to us;

---

[1]**"Yet I . . . will bless"**: Emily Brontë, "The Prisoner. A Fragment," 57–58 (see page 605).

or, in other words, the means and inducements are not there.

Look at the poor lives which we lead. It is a wonder that we are so good as we are, not that we are so bad. In looking round we are struck with the power of the organizations we see, not with their want of power. Now and then, it is true, we are conscious that *there* is an inferior organization, but, in general, just the contrary. Mrs A has the imagination, the poetry of a Murillo,[2] and has sufficient power of execution to show that she might have had a great deal more. Why is she not a Murillo? From a material difficulty, not a mental one. If she has a knife and fork in her hands during three hours of the day, she cannot have a pencil or brush. Dinner is the great sacred ceremony of this day, the great sacrament. To be absent from dinner is equivalent to being ill. Nothing else will excuse us from it. Bodily incapacity is the only apology valid. If she has a pen and ink in her hands during other three hours, writing answers for the penny post; again, she cannot have her pencil, and so *ad infinitum* through life. People have no type before them in their lives, neither fathers and mothers, nor the children themselves. They look at things in detail. They say, "It is very desirable that A, my daughter, should go to such a party, should know such a lady, should sit by such a person." It is true. But what standard have they before them? of the nature and destination of man? The very words are rejected as pedantic. But might they not, at least, have a type in their minds that such an one might be a discoverer through her intellect, such another through her art, a third through her moral power?

Women often try one branch of intellect after another in their youth, *e.g.*, mathematics. But that, least of all, is compatible with the life of "society." It is impossible to follow up anything systematically. Women often long to enter some man's profession where they would find direction, competition (or rather opportunity of measuring the intellect with others), and, above all, time.

In those wise institutions, mixed as they are with many follies, which will last as long as the human race lasts, because they are adapted to the wants of the human race; those institutions which we call monasteries, and which, embracing much that is contrary to the laws of nature, are yet better adapted to the union of the life of action and that of thought than any other mode of life with which we are acquainted; in many such, four and a half

hours, at least, are daily set aside for thought, rules are given for thought, training and opportunity afforded. Among us, there is *no* time appointed for this purpose, and the difficulty is that, in our social life, we must be always doubtful whether we ought not to be with somebody else or be doing something else.

Are men better off than women in this?

If one calls upon a friend in London and sees her son in the drawing-room, it strikes one as odd to find a young man sitting idling in his mother's drawing-room in the morning. For men, who are seen much in those haunts, there is no end of the epithets we have; "knights of the carpet," "drawing-room heroes," "ladies' men." But suppose we were to see a number of men in the morning sitting round a table in the drawing-room, looking at prints, doing worsted work,[3] and reading little books, how we should laugh! A member of the House of Commons was once known to do worsted work. Of another man was said, "His only fault is that he is too good; he drives out with his mother every day in the carriage, and if he is asked anywhere he answers that he must dine with his mother, but, if she can spare him, he will come in to tea, and he does not come."

Now, why is it more ridiculous for a man than for a woman to do worsted work and drive out every day in the carriage? Why should we laugh if we were to see a parcel of men sitting round a drawing-room table in the morning, and think it all right if they were women?

Is man's time more valuable than woman's? or is the difference between man and woman this, that woman has confessedly nothing to do?

Women are never supposed to have any occupation of sufficient importance *not* to be interrupted, except "suckling their fools";[4] and women themselves have accepted this, have written books to support it, and have trained themselves so as to consider whatever they do as *not* of such value to the world or to others, but that they can throw it up at the first "claim of social life". They have accustomed themselves to consider intellectual occupation as a merely selfish amusement, which it is their "duty" to give up for every trifler more selfish than themselves.

A young man (who was afterwards useful and known in his day and generation) when busy reading and sent for by his proud mother to shine in some morning visit, came; but, after it was over, he said, "Now, remember, this is not to

---

[2]Bartolomé Estéban **Murillo** (1617?–1682): Spanish religious painter.

[3]**worsted work**: embroidery done with fine soft wool on canvas.

[4]"**suckling their fools**": see *Othello* 2.1.162.

happen again. I came that you might not think me sulky, but I shall not come again". But for a young woman to send such a message to her mother and sisters, how impertinent it would be! A woman of great administrative powers said that she never undertook anything which she "could not throw by at once, if necessary".

How do we explain then the many cases of women who have distinguished themselves in classics, mathematics, even in politics?

Widowhood, ill-health, or want of bread, these three explanations or excuses are supposed to justify a woman in taking up an occupation. In some cases, no doubt, an indomitable force of character will suffice without any of these three, but such are rare.

But see how society fritters away the intellects of those committed to her charge! It is said that society is necessary to sharpen the intellect. But what do we seek society for? It does sharpen the intellect, because it is a kind of *tour-de-force* to say something at a pinch,—unprepared and uninterested with any subject, to improvise something under difficulties. But what "go we out for to seek"? To take the chance of some one having something to say which we want to hear? or of our finding something to say which *they* want to hear? You have a little to say, but not much. You often make a stipulation with some one else, "Come in ten minutes, for I shall not be able to find enough to spin out longer than that." You are not to talk of anything very interesting, for the essence of society is to prevent any long conversations and all *tête-à-têtes*. "Glissez, n'appuyez pas"[5] is its very motto. The praise of a good *"maîtresse de maison"* consists in this, that she allows no one person to be too much absorbed in, or too long about, a conversation. She always recalls them to their "duty". People do not go into the company of their fellow-creatures for what would seem a very sufficient reason, namely, that they have something to say to them, or something that they want to hear from them; but in the vague hope that they may find something to say.

Then as to solitary opportunities. Women never have half an hour in all their lives (excepting before or after anybody is up in the house) that they can call their own, without fear of offending or of hurting some one. Why do people sit up so late, or, more rarely, get up so early? Not because the day is not long enough, but because they have "no time in the day to themselves."

If we do attempt to do anything in company, what is the system of literary exercise which we pursue? Everybody reads aloud out of their own book or newspaper—or, every five minutes, something is said. And what is it to be "read aloud to"? The most miserable exercise of the human intellect. Or rather, is it any exercise at all? It is like lying on one's back, with one's hands tied and having liquid poured down one's throat. Worse than that, because suffocation would immediately ensue and put a stop to this operation. But no suffocation would stop the other.

So much for the satisfaction of the intellect. Yet for a married woman in society, it is even worse. A married woman was heard to wish that she could break a limb that she might have a little time to herself. Many take advantage of the fear of "infection" to do the same.

It is a thing *so* accepted among women that they have nothing to do, that one woman has not the least scruple in saying to another, "I will come and spend the morning with you." And you would be thought quite surly and absurd, if you were to refuse it on the plea of occupation. Nay, it is thought a mark of amiability and affection, if you are "on such terms" that you can "come in" "any morning you please".

In a country house, if there is a large party of young people, "You will spend the morning with us," they say to the neighbours, "we will drive together in the afternoon," "to-morrow we will make an expedition, and we will spend the evening together". And this is thought friendly, and spending time in a pleasant manner. So women play through life. Yet time is the most valuable of all things. If they had come every morning and afternoon and robbed us of half-a-crown we should have had redress from the police. But it is laid down, that our time is of no value. If you offer a morning visit to a professional man, and say, "I will just stay an hour with you, if you will allow me, till so and so comes back to fetch me"; it costs him the earnings of an hour, and therefore he has a right to complain. But women have no right, because it is *"only* their time".

Women have no means given them, whereby they *can* resist the "claims of social life". They are taught from their infancy upwards that it is wrong, ill-tempered, and a misunderstanding of "woman's mission"[6] (with a great M.) if they do not allow themselves *willingly* to be interrupted at all hours. If a woman has once put in a claim to be treated as a man by some work of science or art or literature, which she can *show* as the "fruit of her leisure", then she will be considered justified in *having* leisure (hardly, perhaps, even

---

[5]*tête-à-têtes*: intimate talks. **"Glissez . . . pas"**: Glide, don't bear down (from L.-S. Mercier, *Tableau de Paris* [1782], chapter 37). *"maîtresse de maison"*: lady of the house.

---

[6]**"woman's mission"**: see Sarah Lewis, pages 86–87.

then). But if not, not. If she has nothing to show, she must resign herself to her fate. (Section 2)

"L'enthousiasme et la faiblesse d'un temps où l'intelligence monte très haut, entraînée par l'imagination, et tombe très bas, écrasée par une réalité, sans poésie et sans grandeur."[7]

Women dream till they have no longer the strength to dream; those dreams against which they so struggle, so honestly, vigorously, and conscientiously, and so in vain, yet which are their life, without which they could not have lived; those dreams go at last. All their plans and visions seem vanished, and they know not where; gone, and they cannot recall them. They do not even remember them. And they are left without the food either of reality or of hope.

Later in life, they neither desire nor dream, neither of activity, nor of love, nor of intellect. The last often survives the longest. They wish, if their experiences would benefit anybody, to give them to some one. But they never find an hour free in which to collect their thoughts, and so discouragement becomes ever deeper and deeper, and they less and less capable of undertaking anything.

It seems as if the female spirit of the world were mourning everlastingly over blessings, *not* lost, but which she has never had, and which, in her discouragement, she feels that she never will have, they are so far off.

The more complete a woman's organization, the more she will feel it, till at last there shall arise a woman, who will resume, in her own soul, all the sufferings of her race, and that woman will be the Saviour of her race.

Jesus Christ raised women above the condition of mere slaves, mere ministers to the passions of the man, raised them by his sympathy, to be ministers of God. He gave them moral activity. But the Age, the World, Humanity, must give them the means to exercise this moral activity, must give them intellectual cultivation, spheres of action.

There is perhaps no century where the woman shows so meanly as in this.[8] Because her education seems entirely

to have parted company with her vocation; there is no longer unity between the woman as inwardly developed, and as outwardly manifested.

In the last century it was not so. In the succeeding one let us hope that it will no longer be so.

But now she is like the Archangel Michael as he stands upon Saint Angelo[9] at Rome. She has an immense provision of wings, which seem as if they would bear her over earth and heaven; but when she tries to use them, she is petrified into stone, her feet are grown into the earth, chained to the bronze pedestal.

Nothing can well be imagined more painful than the present position of woman, unless, on the one hand, she renounces all outward activity and keeps herself within the magic sphere, the bubble of her dreams; or, on the other, surrendering all aspiration, she gives herself to her real life, soul and body. For those to whom it is possible, the latter is best, for out of activity may come thought, out of mere aspiration can come nothing.

But now—when the young imagination is so high and so developed, and reality is so narrow and conventional—there is no more parallelism between life in the thought and life in the actual than between the corpse, which lies motionless in its narrow bed, and the spirit, which, in our imagination, is at large among the stars.

The ideal life is passed in noble schemes of good consecutively followed up, of devotion to a great object, of sympathy given and received for high ideas and generous feelings. The actual life is passed in sympathy given and received for a dinner, a party, a piece of furniture, a house built or a garden laid out well, in devotion to your guests—(a too real devotion, for it implies that of all your time)—in schemes of schooling for the poor, which you follow up perhaps in an odd quarter of an hour, between luncheon and driving out in the carriage—broth and dripping are included in the plan—and the rest of your time goes in ordering the dinner, hunting for a governess for your children, and sending pheasants and apples to your poorer relations. Is there anything in *this* life which can be called an Incarnation of the ideal life within? Is it a wonder that the unhappy woman should prefer to keep them entirely separate? not to take the bloom off her Ideal by mixing it up with her Actual; not to make her Actual still more unpalatable by trying to *inform* it with her Ideal? And then she is blamed, and her own sex unites against her, for not being content with the "day of small things". She is told that "trifles make the sum of human things"; they do indeed. She is contemptuously

---

[7]"**L'enthousiasme . . . grandeur**": "The rapture and weakness of a time when the mind rises very high, carried away by imagination, and falls very low, crushed by a reality without poetry and without grandeur" (George Sand, *Lélia* [1833]).

[8]At almost every period of social life, we find, as it were, two undercurrents running different ways. There is the noble woman who dreams the following out her useful vocation; but there is also the selfish dreamer now, who is ever turning to something new, regardless of the expectations she has voluntarily excited, who is ever talking about "making a life for herself", heedless that she is spoiling another life, undertaken, perhaps, at her own bidding. This is the ugly reverse of the medal. [Nightingale's note]

---

[9]**Saint Angelo**: castle in Rome.

asked, "Would she abolish domestic life?" Men are afraid that their houses will not be so comfortable, that their wives will make themselves "remarkable"—women, that they will make themselves distasteful to men; they write books (and very wisely) to teach themselves to dramatize "little things," to persuade themselves that "domestic life is their sphere" and to idealize the "sacred hearth". Sacred it is indeed. Sacred from the touch of their sons almost as soon as they are out of childhood—from its dulness and its tyrannous trifling *these* recoil. Sacred from the grasp of their daughters' affections, upon which it has so light a hold that they seize the first opportunity of marriage, *their* only chance of emancipation. The "sacred hearth"; sacred to their husband's sleep, their sons' absence in the body and their daughters' in mind.

Oh! mothers, who talk about this hearth, how much do you know of your sons' real life, how much of your daughters' imaginary one? Awake, ye women, all ye that sleep, awake! If this domestic life were so very good, would your young men wander away from it, your maidens think of something else?

The time is come when women must do something more than the "domestic hearth," which means nursing the infants, keeping a pretty house, having a good dinner and an entertaining party.

You say, "It is true, our young men see visions, and our maidens dream dreams,[10] but what of? Does not the woman intend to marry, and have over again what she has at home? and the man ultimately too?" Yes, but not the same; she *will* have the same, that is, if circumstances are not altered to prevent it; but her *idéal* is very different, though that *idéal* and the reality will never come together to mould each other. And it is not only the unmarried woman who dreams. The married woman also holds long imaginary conversations but too often. (Section 5)

We live in the world, it is said, and must walk in its ways.

Was Christ called a complainer against the world? Yet all these great teachers and preachers must have had a most deep and ingrained sense, a continual gnawing feeling of the miseries and wrongs of the world. Otherwise they would not have been impelled to devote life and death to redress them. Christ, Socrates, Howard,[11] they must have had no ear for the joys, compared to that which they had for the sorrows of the world.

They acted, however, and we complain. The great reformers of the world turn into the great misanthropists, if circumstances or organisation do not permit them to act. Christ, if He had been a woman, might have been nothing but a great complainer. Peace be with the misanthropists! They have made a step in progress; the next will make them great philanthropists; they are divided but by a line.

The next Christ will perhaps be a female Christ. But do we see one woman who looks like a female Christ? or even like 'the messenger before' her "face," to go before her and prepare the hearts and minds for her?

To this will be answered that half the inmates of Bedlam begin in this way, by fancying that they are "the Christ."[12]

People talk about imitating Christ, and imitate Him in the little trifling formal things, such as washing the feet, saying his prayer, and so on; but if any one attempts the real imitation of Him, there are no bounds to the outcry with which the presumption of that person is condemned.

For instance, Christ was saying something to the people one day, which interested Him very much, and interested them very much; and Mary and his brothers came in the middle of it, and wanted to interrupt Him, and take Him home to dinner, very likely—(how natural that story is! does it not speak more home than any historic evidences of the Gospel's reality?), and He, instead of being angry with their interruption of Him in such an important work for some trifling thing, answers, "Who is my mother? and who are my brethren? Whosoever shall do the will of my Father which is in heaven, the same is my brother and sister and mother."[13] But if *we* were to say that, we should be accused of "destroying the family tie, of diminishing the obligation of the home duties."

---

[10]**young men . . . dreams**: see Joel 2:28, Acts 2:17.

[11]John **Howard** (1726?–1790) inspected and wrote about prisons in Britain and abroad.

[12]It is quite true that insanity, sensuality, and monstrous fraud have constantly assumed to be "the Christ," *vide* the *Agapemone*, and the Mormons. "Believing" a man by the name of Prince "to be the tabernacle of God on earth," poor deluded women transfer to him all their stock in the Three per Cents. We hear of the Mormons, etc., being the "recipients and mouth-pieces of God's spirit." They profess to be "incarnations of the Deity," "witnesses of the Almighty, solely knowing God's will, and being the medium of communicating it to man," and so forth. It does not appear to us that this blasphemy is very dangerous to the cause of true religion in general, any more than forgery is very dangerous to commerce in general. It is the universal dishonesty in religion, as in trade, which is really dangerous. [Nightingale's note] *Agapemone*: a contemporary religious community in England holding everything in common and expecting the imminent second coming of Christ.

[13]**Christ . . . one day**: see Matthew 12:46–50.

He might well say, "Heaven and earth shall pass away, but my words shall not pass away."[14] His words will never pass away. If He had said, "Tell them that I am engaged at this moment in something very important; that the instruction of the multitude ought to go before any personal ties; that I will remember to come when I have done", no one would have been impressed by His words; but how striking is that, "Behold my mother and my brethren!" (Section 6)

The dying woman to her mourners:—"Oh! if you knew how gladly I leave this life, how much more courage I feel to take the chance of another, than of anything I see before me in this, you would put on your wedding-clothes instead of mourning for me!"

"But", they say, "so much talent! so many gifts! such good which you might have done!"

"The world will be put back some little time by my death", she says; "you see I estimate my powers at least as highly as you can; but it is by the death which has taken place some years ago in me, not by the death which is about to take place now." And so is the world put back by the death of every one who has to sacrifice the development of his or her peculiar gifts (which were meant, not for selfish gratification, but for the improvement of that world) to conventionality.

"My people were like children playing on the shore of the eighteenth century. I was their hobby-horse, their plaything; and they drove me to and fro, dear souls! never weary of the play themselves, till I, who had grown to woman's estate and to the ideas of the nineteenth century, lay down exhausted, my mind closed to hope, my heart to strength.

"Free—free—oh! divine freedom, art thou come at last? Welcome, beautiful death!"

Let neither name nor date be placed on her grave, still less the expression of regret or of admiration; but simply the words, "I believe in God." (Section 7)

1860

from Notes on Nursing

Observations of the Sick

... Vast has been the increase of knowledge in pathology—that science which teaches us the final change produced by disease on the human frame—scarce any in the art

of observing the signs of the change while in progress. Or, rather, is it not to be feared that observation, as an essential part of medicine, has been declining?

Which of us has not heard fifty times, from one or another, a nurse, or a friend of the sick, aye, and a medical friend too, the following remark:—"So A is worse, or B is dead. I saw him the day before; I thought him so much better; there certainly was no appearance from which one could have expected so sudden (?) a change." I have never heard any one say, though one would think it the more natural thing, "There *must* have been *some* appearance, which I should have seen if I had but looked; let me try and remember what there was, that I may observe another time." No, this is not what people say. They boldly assert that there was nothing to observe, not that their observation was at fault.

Let people who have to observe sickness and death look back and try to register in their observation the appearances which have preceded relapse, attack, or death, and not assert that there were none, or that there were not the *right* ones.[1]

A want of the habit of observing conditions and an inveterate habit of taking averages are each of them often equally misleading.

Men whose profession like that of medical men leads them to observe only, or chiefly, palpable and permanent organic changes are often just as wrong in their opinion of the result as those who do not observe at all. For instance, there is a broken leg; the surgeon has only to look at it once to know; it will not be different if he sees it in the morning to what it would have been had he seen it in the evening. And in whatever conditions the patient is, or is likely to be, there will still be the broken leg, until it is set. The same with many organic diseases. An experienced physician has but to feel the pulse once, and he knows that there is aneurism which will kill some time or other.

But with the great majority of cases, there is nothing of the kind; and the power of forming any correct opinion as to

---

[14]"**Heaven . . . away**": Mark 13:31.

[1]**the *right* ones**: It falls to few ever to have had the opportunity of observing the different aspects which the human face puts on at the sudden approach of certain forms of death by violence; and as it is knowledge of little use, I only mention it here as being the most startling example of what I mean. In the nervous temperament the face becomes pale (this is the only *recognised* effect); in the sanguine temperament purple; in the bilious yellow, or every manner of colour in patches. Now, it is generally supposed that paleness is the one indication of almost any violent change in the human being, whether from terror, disease, or anything else. There can be no more false observation. Granted, it is the one recognised livery, as I have said— *de rigueur* in novels, but nowhere else. [Nightingale's note]

the result must entirely depend upon an enquiry into all the conditions in which the patient lives. In a complicated state of society in large towns, death, as every one of great experience knows, is far less often produced by any one organic disease than by some illness, after many other diseases, producing just the sum of exhaustion necessary for death. There is nothing so absurd, nothing so misleading as the verdict one so often hears: So-and-so has no organic disease,—there is no reason why he should not live to extreme old age; sometimes the clause is added, sometimes not: Provided he has quiet, good food, good air, &c., &c., &c.: the verdict is repeated by ignorant people *without* the latter clause; or there is no possibility of the conditions of the latter clause being obtained; and this, the *only* essential part of the whole, is made of no effect. I have heard a physician, deservedly eminent, assure the friends of a patient of his recovery. Why? Because he had now prescribed a course, every detail of which the patient had followed for years. And because he had forbidden a course which the patient could not by any possibility alter.[2]

Undoubtedly a person of no scientific knowledge whatever but of observation and experience in these kinds of conditions, will be able to arrive at a much truer guess as to the probable duration of life of members of a family or inmates of a house, than the most scientific physician to whom the same persons are brought to have their pulse felt; no enquiry being made into their conditions.

In Life Insurance and such like societies, were they instead of having the person examined by the medical man, to have the houses, conditions, ways of life, of these persons examined, at how much truer results would they arrive! W. Smith appears a fine hale man, but it might be known that the next cholera epidemic he runs a bad chance. Mr. and Mrs. J. are a strong healthy couple, but it might be known that they live in such a house, in such a part of London, so near the river that they will kill four-fifths of their children; which of the children will be the ones to survive might also be known.

Averages again seduce us away from minute observation. "Average mortalities" merely tell that so many per cent. die in this town and so many in that, per annum. But whether A or B will be among these, the "average rate" of course does not tell. We know, say, that from 22 to 24 per 1,000 will die in London next year. But minute enquiries into conditions enable us to know that in such a district, nay, in such a street,—or even on one side of that street, in such a particular house, or even on one floor of that particular house, will be the excess of mortality, that is, the person will die who ought not to have died before old age.

Now, would it not very materially alter the opinion of whoever were endeavouring to form one, if he knew that from that floor, of that house, of that street the man came.

Much more precise might be our observations even than this, and much more correct our conclusions.

It is well known that the same names may be seen constantly recurring on workhouse[3] books for generations. That is, the persons were born and brought up, and will be born and brought up, generation after generation, in the conditions which make paupers. Death and disease are like the workhouse, they take from the same family, the same house, or in other words, the same conditions. Why will we not observe what they are?

The close observer may safely predict that such a family, whether its members marry or not, will become extinct; that such another will degenerate morally and physically. But who learns the lesson? On the contrary, it may be well known that the children die in such a house at the rate of 8 out of 10; one would think that nothing more need be said; for how could Providence speak more distinctly? yet nobody listens, the family goes on living there till it dies out, and then some other family takes it. Neither would they listen "if one rose from the dead."[4] . . . (Chapter 13)

. . . To sum up:—the answer to two of the commonest objections urged, one by women themselves, the other by men, against the desirableness of sanitary knowledge for women, *plus* a caution, comprises the whole argument for the art of nursing.

(1.) It is often said by men, that it is unwise to teach women anything about these laws of health, because they will take to physicking,—that there is a great deal too much of amateur physicking as it is, which is indeed true. One eminent physician told me that he had known more calomel given, both at a pinch and for a continuance, by mothers, governesses, and nurses, to children than he had ever heard

---

[2]**a course . . . alter:** I have known two cases, the one of a man who intentionally and repeatedly displaced a dislocation, and was kept and petted by all the surgeons; the other of one who was pronounced to have nothing the matter with him, there being no organic change perceptible, but who died within the week. In both these cases, it was the nurse who, by accurately pointing out what she had accurately observed, to the doctors, saved the one case from persevering in a fraud, the other from being discharged when actually in a dying state. . . . [Nightingale's note]

[3]**workhouse:** institution for paupers.

[4]**"if one . . . dead":** see Luke 16:31.

of a physician prescribing in all his experience. Another says, that women's only idea in medicine is calomel and aperients. This is undeniably too often the case. There is nothing ever seen in any professional practice like the reckless physicking by amateur females.[5] But this is just what the really experienced and observing nurse does not do; she neither physics herself nor others. And to cultivate in things pertaining to health observation and experience in women who are mothers, governesses or nurses, is just the way to do away with amateur physicking, and if the doctors did but know it, to make the nurses obedient to them,—helps to them instead of hindrances. Such education in women would indeed diminish the doctor's work—but no one really believes that doctors wish that there should be more illness, in order to have more work.

(2.) It is often said by women, that they cannot know anything of the laws of health, or what to do to preserve their children's health, because they can know nothing of "Pathology," or cannot "dissect,"—a confusion of ideas which it is hard to attempt to disentangle. Pathology teaches the harm that disease has done. But it teaches nothing more. We know nothing of the principle of health, the positive of which pathology is the negative, except from observation and experience. And nothing but observation and experience will teach us the ways to maintain or to bring back the state of health. It is often thought that medicine is the curative process. It is no such thing; medicine is the surgery of functions, as surgery proper is that of limbs and organs. Neither can do anything but remove obstructions; neither can cure; nature alone cures. Surgery removes the bullet out of the limb, which is an obstruction to cure, but nature heals the wound. So it is with medicine; the function of an organ becomes obstructed; medicine, so far as we know, assists nature to remove the obstruction, but does nothing more. And what nursing has to do in either case, is to put the patient in the best condition for nature to act upon him. Generally, just the contrary is done, You think fresh air, and quiet and cleanliness extravagant, perhaps dangerous, luxuries, which should be given to the patient only when quite convenient, and medicine the *sine qua non*,[6] the panacea. If I have succeeded in any measure in dispelling this illusion, and in showing what true nursing is, and what it is not, my object will have been answered.

Now for the caution:—

(3.) It seems a commonly received idea among men and even among women themselves that it requires nothing but a disappointment in love, the want of an object, a general disgust, or incapacity for other things, to turn a woman into a good nurse.

This reminds one of the parish where a stupid old man was set to be schoolmaster because he was "past keeping the pigs."

Apply the above receipt for making a good nurse to making a good servant. And the receipt will be found to fail.

Yet popular novelists of recent days have invented ladies disappointed in love or fresh out of the drawing-room turning into the war-hospitals to find their wounded lovers, and when found, forthwith abandoning their sick-ward for their lover, as might be expected. Yet in the estimation of the authors, these ladies were none the worse for that, but on the contrary were heroines of nursing.

What cruel mistakes are sometimes made by benevolent men and women in matters of business about which they can know nothing and think they know a great deal.

The everyday management of a large ward, let alone of a hospital—the knowing what are the laws of life and death for men, and what the laws of health for wards—(and wards are healthy or unhealthy, mainly according to the knowledge or ignorance of the nurse)—are not these matters of sufficient importance and difficulty to require learning by experience and careful inquiry, just as much as any other art? They do not come by inspiration to the lady disappointed in love, nor to the poor workhouse drudge hard up for a livelihood.

And terrible is the injury which has followed to the sick from such wild notions! . . . (Conclusion)

1859

---

[5]**amateur females**: I have known many ladies who, having once obtained a "blue pill" prescription from a physician, gave and took it as a common aperient two or three times a week—with what effect may be supposed. . . . It is very seldom indeed, that by choosing your diet, you cannot regulate your own bowels; and every woman may watch herself to know what kind of diet will do this. [Nightingale's note] **aperient**: laxative.

[6]*sine qua non*: indispensable (literally: without which, nothing).

HERBERT SPENCER

(1820–1903)

The longwinded, surprisingly affable *Autobiography* that was published shortly after Herbert Spencer's death tells this representative tale from his boyhood: having been farmed out at age thirteen for a holiday among relatives he did not like, he trekked more than a hundred miles home on foot in just three days, sleepless and sustained by bread, water, and beer. Here was an individual with a mind of his own, undaunted by hard work or long distance. The child was father to the man: strength of purpose and capaciousness of scope are the salient features of Spencer's diversified intellectual output. An early scientific bent led him into engineering during the railroad boom of the 1830s and 1840s (years later he found time to patent a mechanical sickbed), but in early adulthood his curiosity turned towards inventing a science of society. He took editorial positions with a Birmingham political journal advocating universal male suffrage and with the prestigious London *Economist*, and began publishing formidable books on government, society, the science of mind, and education. All were written from a pronounced liberal-individualist standpoint compatible both with his most-quoted phrase, "the survival of the fittest," and with his agitation in later years against aggression and war.

Eventually the relentless generalizing power of Spencer's mind brought him to envision a science of science: an overview of human knowledge based on materialist premises and integrated by an evolutionary paradigm. In 1860 he announced the plan of constructing what he called the "Synthetic Philosophy," in a sequence of volumes that were to cover not only biology, sociology, and psychology but metaphysics and ethics as well. Although the plan was never fully completed, Spencer accomplished enough of it to engage not only scientists but also imaginative writers like George Eliot (an admirer though with reservations) and Alfred Tennyson (a grumbling but respectful adversary). His comprehensive ambition was laid out in 1862 in *First Principles*, which included a revised version of an essay he had published five years before on "Progress: Its Law and Cause." That revised essay, excerpted here, provides in short compass a sense of the breathtaking panorama of change within which Spencer helped his contemporaries locate themselves, not without some complacency at finding that the crowning result of the evolutionary process turned out to be British Victorian man.

from Progress: Its Law and Cause

... The investigations of Wolff, Goethe, and Von Baer,[1] have established the truth that the series of changes gone through during the development of a seed into a tree, or an ovum into an animal, constitute an advance from homogeneity of structure to heterogeneity of structure. In its primary stage, every germ consists of a substance that is uniform throughout, both in texture and chemical composition. The first step is the appearance of a difference between two parts of this substance; or, as the phenomenon is called in physiological language, a differentiation. Each of these differentiated divisions presently begins itself to exhibit some contrast of parts; and by and by these secondary differentiations become as definite as the original one. This process is continuously repeated—is simultaneously going

---

[1]Christian Freiherr **Wolff** (1679–1754): German philosopher and scientist. Johann Wolfgang von **Goethe** (1749–1832): German man of letters and science. Karl Ernst, Ritter **von Baer** (1792–1876): German embryologist.

on in all parts of the growing embryo; and by endless such differentiations there is finally produced that complex combination of tissues and organs constituting the adult animal or plant. This is the history of all organisms whatever. It is settled beyond dispute that organic progress consists in a change from the homogeneous to the heterogeneous.

Now, we propose in the first place to show, that this law of organic progress is the law of all progress. Whether it be in the development of the Earth, in the development of Life upon its surface, in the development of Society, of Government, of Manufactures, of Commerce, of Language, Literature, Science, Art, this same evolution of the simple into the complex, through successive differentiations, holds throughout. From the earliest traceable cosmical changes down to the latest results of civilization, we shall find that the transformation of the homogeneous into the heterogeneous, is that in which Progress essentially consists.

With the view of showing that *if* the Nebular Hypothesis[2] be true, the genesis of the solar system supplies one illustration of this law, let us assume that the matter of which the sun and planets consist was once in a diffused form; and that from the gravitation of its atoms there resulted a gradual concentration. By the hypothesis, the solar system in its nascent state existed as an indefinitely extended and nearly homogeneous medium—a medium almost homogeneous in density, in temperature, and in other physical attributes. The first advance towards consolidation resulted in a differentiation between the occupied space which the nebulous mass still filled, and the unoccupied space which it previously filled. There simultaneously resulted a contrast in density and a contrast in temperature, between the interior and the exterior of this mass. And at the same time there arose throughout it rotatory movements, whose velocities varied according to their distances from its centre. These differentiations increased in number and degree until there was evolved the organized group of sun, planets, and satellites, which we now know—a group which presents numerous contrasts of structure and action among its members. There are the immense contrasts between the sun and planets, in bulk and in weight; as well as the subordinate contrasts between one planet and another, and between the planets and their satellites. There is the similarly marked contrast between the sun as almost stationary, and the planets as moving round him with great velocity; while there are the secondary contrasts between the velocities and periods of the several planets, and between their simple revolutions and the double ones of their satellites, which have to move round their primaries while moving round the sun. There is the yet further strong contrast between the sun and the planets in respect of temperature; and there is reason to suppose that the planets and satellites differ from each other in their proper heat, as well as in the heat they receive from the sun.

When we bear in mind that, in addition to these various contrasts, the planets and satellites also differ in respect to their distances from each other and their primary; in respect to the inclinations of their orbits, the inclinations of their axes, their times of rotation on their axes, their specific gravities, and their physical constitutions; we see what a high degree of heterogeneity the solar system exhibits, when compared with the almost complete homogeneity of the nebulous mass out of which it is supposed to have originated.

Passing from this hypothetical illustration, which must be taken for what it is worth, without prejudice to the general argument, let us descend to a more certain order of evidence. It is now generally agreed among geologists that the Earth was at first a mass of molten matter; and that it is still fluid and incandescent at the distance of a few miles beneath its surface. Originally, then, it was homogeneous in consistence, and, in virtue of the circulation that takes place in heated fluids, must have been comparatively homogeneous in temperature; and it must have been surrounded by an atmosphere consisting partly of the elements of air and water, and partly of those various other elements which assume a gaseous form at high temperatures. That slow cooling by radiation which is still going on at an inappreciable rate, and which, though originally far more rapid than now, necessarily required an immense time to produce any decided change, must ultimately have resulted in the solidification of the portion most able to part with its heat—namely, the surface. In the thin crust thus formed we have the first marked differentiation. A still further cooling, a consequent thickening of this crust, and an accompanying deposition of all solidifiable elements contained in the atmosphere, must finally have been followed by the condensation of the water previously existing as vapour. A second marked differentiation must thus have arisen: and as the condensation must have taken place on the coolest parts of the surface—namely, about the poles—there must thus have resulted the first geographical distinction of parts. To these illustrations of growing heterogeneity, which, though deduced from the known laws of matter, may be regarded as more or less hypothetical, Geology adds an extensive series that have been inductively

---

[2]**Nebular Hypothesis**: advanced by Pierre Simon Laplace (1749–1827), whose 1796 *System of the World* proposed that the sun and planets had condensed from a cloud (nebula) of gas and dust.

established. Its investigations show that the Earth has been continually becoming more heterogeneous in virtue of the multiplication of the strata which form its crust; further, that it has been becoming more heterogeneous in respect of the composition of these strata, the latter of which, being made from the detritus of the older ones, are many of them rendered highly complex by the mixture of materials they contain; and that this heterogeneity has been vastly increased by the action of the Earth's still molten nucleus upon its envelope, whence have resulted not only a great variety of igneous rocks, but the tilting up of sedimentary strata at all angles, the formation of faults and metallic veins, the production of endless dislocations and irregularities. Yet again, geologists teach us that the Earth's surface has been growing more varied in elevation—that the most ancient mountain systems are the smallest, and the Andes and Himalayas the most modern; while in all probability there have been corresponding changes in the bed of the ocean. As a consequence of these ceaseless differentiations, we now find that no considerable portion of the Earth's exposed surface is like any other portion, either in contour, in geologic structure, or in chemical composition; and that in most parts it changes from mile to mile in all these characteristics.

Moreover, it must not be forgotten that there has been simultaneously going on a gradual differentiation of climates. As fast as the Earth cooled and its crust solidified, there arose appreciable differences in temperature between those parts of its surface most exposed to the sun and those less exposed. Gradually, as the cooling progressed, these differences became more pronounced; until there finally resulted those marked contrasts between regions of perpetual ice and snow, regions where winter and summer alternately reign for periods varying according to the latitude, and regions where summer follows summer with scarcely an appreciable variation. At the same time the successive elevations and subsidences of different portions of the Earth's crust, tending as they have done to the present irregular distribution of land and sea, have entailed various modifications of climate beyond those dependent on latitude; while a yet further series of such modifications have been produced by increasing differences of elevation in the land, which have in sundry places brought arctic, temperate, and tropical climates to within a few miles of each other. And the general result of these changes is, that not only has every extensive region its own meteorologic conditions, but that every locality in each region differs more or less from others in those conditions, as in its structure, its contour, its soil. Thus, between our existing Earth, the phenomena of whose varied crust neither geographers, geologists, mineral-

ogists, nor meteorologists have yet enumerated, and the molten globe out of which it was evolved, the contrast in heterogeneity is sufficiently striking. . . .

Whether an advance from the homogeneous to the heterogeneous is or is not displayed in the biological history of the globe, it is clearly enough displayed in the progress of the latest and most heterogeneous creature—Man. It is alike true that, during the period in which the Earth has been peopled, the human organism has grown more heterogeneous among the civilized divisions of the species; and that the species, as a whole, has been growing more heterogeneous in virtue of the multiplication of races and the differentiation of these races from each other.

In proof of the first of these positions, we may cite the fact that, in the relative development of the limbs, the civilized man departs more widely from the general type of the placental mammalia than do the lower human races. While often possessing well-developed body and arms, the Papuan has extremely small legs: thus reminding us of the quadrumana,[3] in which there is no great contrast in size between the hind and fore limbs. But in the European, the greater length and massiveness of the legs has become very marked—the fore and hind limbs are relatively more heterogeneous. Again, the greater ratio which the cranial bones bear to the facial bones illustrates the same truth. Among the vertebrata in general, progress is marked by an increasing heterogeneity in the vertebral column, and more especially in the vertebræ constituting the skull: the higher forms being distinguished by the relatively larger size of the bones which cover the brain, and the relatively smaller size of those which form the jaw, &c. Now, this characteristic, which is stronger in Man than in any other creature, is stronger in the European than in the savage. Moreover, judging from the greater extent and variety of faculty he exhibits, we may infer that the civilized man has also a more complex or heterogeneous nervous system than the uncivilized man: and indeed the fact is in part visible in the increased ratio which his cerebrum bears to the subjacent ganglia.

If further elucidation be needed, we may find it in every nursery. The infant European has sundry marked points of resemblance to the lower human races; as in the flatness of the alæ[4] of the nose, the depression of its bridge, the divergence and forward opening of the nostrils, the

_____

[3]quadrumana (four-handed): order of mammals including monkeys, apes, baboons, and lemurs.

[4]alæ: nostrils.

form of the lips, the absence of a frontal sinus, the width between the eyes, the smallness of the legs. Now, as the developmental process by which these traits are turned into
those of the adult European, is a continuation of that
change from the homogeneous to the heterogeneous displayed during the previous evolution of the embryo, which
every physiologist will admit; it follows that the parallel developmental process by which the like traits of the barbarous races have been turned into those of the civilized
races, has also been a continuation of the change from the
homogeneous to the heterogeneous. The truth of the second position—that Mankind, as a whole, have become
more heterogeneous—is so obvious as scarcely to need illustration. Every work on Ethnology, by its divisions and
subdivisions of races, bears testimony to it. Even were we to
admit the hypothesis that Mankind originated from several
separate stocks, it would still remain true, that as, from each
of these stocks, there have sprung many now widely different tribes, which are proved by philological evidence to
have had a common origin, the race as a whole is far less
homogeneous than it once was. Add to which, that we
have, in the Anglo-Americans, an example of a new variety
arising within these few generations; and that, if we may
trust to the description of observers, we are likely soon to
have another such example in Australia.

On passing from Humanity under its individual form,
to Humanity as socially embodied, we find the general law
still more variously exemplified. The change from the homogeneous to the heterogeneous is displayed equally in the
progress of civilization as a whole, and in the progress of
every tribe or nation; and is still going on with increasing
rapidity. As we see in existing barbarous tribes, society in its
first and lowest form is a homogeneous aggregation of individuals having like powers and like functions: the only
marked difference of function being that which accompanies difference of sex. Every man is warrior, hunter, fisherman, tool-maker, builder; every woman performs the same
drudgeries; every family is self-sufficing, and save for purposes of aggression and defence, might as well live apart
from the rest. Very early, however, in the process of social
evolution, we find an incipient differentiation between the
governing and the governed. Some kind of chieftainship
seems coeval with the first advance from the state of separate wandering families to that of a nomadic tribe. The authority of the strongest makes itself felt among a body of
savages as in a herd of animals, or a posse of schoolboys. At
first, however, it is indefinite, uncertain; is shared by others
of scarcely inferior power; and is unaccompanied by any
difference in occupation or style of living: the first ruler kills

his own game, makes his own weapons, builds his own hut,
and economically considered, does not differ from others of
his tribe. Gradually, as the tribe progresses, the contrast between the governing and the governed grows more decided.
Supreme power becomes hereditary in one family; the head
of that family, ceasing to provide for his own wants, is
served by others; and he begins to assume the sole office of
ruling.

At the same time there has been arising a co-ordinate
species of government—that of Religion. As all ancient
records and traditions prove, the earliest rulers are regarded
as divine personages. The maxims and commands they uttered during their lives are held sacred after their deaths,
and are enforced by their divinely-descended successors;
who in their turns are promoted to the pantheon of the
race, there to be worshipped and propitiated along with
their predecessors: the most ancient of whom is the
supreme god, and the rest subordinate gods. For a long time
these connate forms of government—civil and religious—
continue closely associated. For many generations the king
continues to be the chief priest, and the priesthood to be
members of the royal race. For many ages religious law continues to contain more or less of civil regulation, and civil
law to possess more or less of religious sanction; and even
among the most advanced nations these two controlling
agencies are by no means completely differentiated from
each other.

Having a common root with these, and gradually diverging from them, we find yet another controlling
agency—that of Manners or ceremonial usages. All titles of
honour are originally the names of the god-king; afterwards
of God and the king; still later of persons of high rank; and
finally come, some of them, to be used between man and
man. All forms of complimentary address were at first the
expressions of submission from prisoners to their conqueror, or from subjects to their ruler, either human or divine—expressions that were afterwards used to propitiate
subordinate authorities, and slowly descended into ordinary
intercourse. All modes of salutation were once obeisances
made before the monarch and used in worship of him after
his death. Presently others of the god-descended race were
similarly saluted; and by degrees some of the salutations
have become the due of all. Thus, no sooner does the originally homogeneous social mass differentiate into the governed and the governing parts, than this last exhibits an
incipient differentiation into religious and secular—Church
and State; while at the same time there begins to be differentiated from both, that less definite species of government
which rules our daily intercourse—a species of government

which, as we may see in heralds' colleges,[5] in books of the peerage, in masters of ceremonies, is not without a certain embodiment of its own. Each of these is itself subject to successive differentiations. In the course of ages, there arises, as among ourselves, a highly complex political organization of monarch, ministers, lords and commons, with their subordinate administrative departments, courts of justice, revenue offices, &c., supplemented in the provinces by municipal governments, county governments, parish or union governments—all of them more or less elaborated. By its side there grows up a highly complex religious organization, with its various grades of officials, from archbishops down to sextons, its colleges, convocations, ecclesiastical courts, &c.; to all which must be added the ever multiplying independent sects, each with its general and local authorities. And at the same time there is developed a highly complex aggregation of customs, manners, and temporary fashions, enforced by society at large, and serving to control those minor transactions between man and man which are not regulated by civil and religious law. Moreover it is to be observed that this ever increasing heterogeneity in the governmental appliances of each nation, has been accompanied by an increasing heterogeneity in the governmental appliances of different nations; all of which are more or less unlike in their political systems and legislation, in their creeds and religious institutions, in their customs and ceremonial usages.

Simultaneously there has been going on a second differentiation of a more familiar kind; that, namely, by which the mass of the community has been segregated into distinct classes and orders of workers. While the governing part has undergone the complex development above detailed, the governed part has undergone an equally complex development, which has resulted in that minute division of labour characterizing advanced nations. It is needless to trace out this progress from its first stages, up through the caste divisions of the East and the incorporated guilds of Europe, to the elaborate producing and distributing organization existing among ourselves. Political economists have long since described the evolution which, beginning with a tribe whose members severally perform the same actions each for himself, ends with a civilized community whose members severally perform different actions for each other; and they have further pointed out the changes through which the solitary producer of any one commodity is transformed into a combination of producers who, united under

a master, take separate parts in the manufacture of such commodity. But there are yet other and higher phases of this advance from the homogeneous to the heterogeneous in the industrial organization of society.

Long after considerable progress has been made in the division of labour among different classes of workers, there is still little or no division of labour among the widely separated parts of the community; the nation continues comparatively homogeneous in the respect that in each district the same occupations are pursued. But when roads and other means of transit become numerous and good, the different districts begin to assume different functions, and to become mutually dependent. The calico manufacture locates itself in this county, the woollen-cloth manufacture in that; silks are produced here, lace there; stockings in one place, shoes in another; pottery, hardware, cutlery, come to have their special towns; and ultimately every locality becomes more or less distinguished from the rest by the leading occupation carried on in it. Nay, more, this subdivision of functions shows itself not only among the different parts of the same nation, but among different nations. That exchange of commodities which free-trade promises so greatly to increase, will ultimately have the effect of specializing, in a greater or less degree, the industry of each people. So that beginning with a barbarous tribe, almost if not quite homogeneous in the functions of its members, the progress has been, and still is, towards an economic aggregation of the whole human race; growing ever more heterogeneous in respect of the separate functions assumed by separate nations, the separate functions assumed by the local sections of each nation, the separate functions assumed by the many kinds of makers and traders in each town, and the separate functions assumed by the workers united in producing each commodity.

Not only is the law thus clearly exemplified in the evolution of the social organism, but it is exemplified with equal clearness in the evolution of all products of human thought and action, whether concrete or abstract, real or ideal. Let us take Language as our first illustration.

The lowest form of language is the exclamation, by which an entire idea is vaguely conveyed through a single sound; as among the lower animals. That human language ever consisted solely of exclamations, and so was strictly homogeneous in respect of its parts of speech, we have no evidence. But that language can be traced down to a form in which nouns and verbs are its only elements, is an established fact. In the gradual multiplication of parts of speech out of these primary ones—in the differentiation of verbs into active and passive, of nouns into abstract and concrete—in the rise of distinctions of mood, tense, person, of number and

---

[5]**heralds' colleges:** for certifying aristocratic rank.

case—in the formation of auxiliary verbs, of adjectives, adverbs, pronouns, prepositions, articles—in the divergence of those orders, genera, species, and varieties of parts of speech by which civilized races express minute modifications of meaning—we see a change from the homogeneous to the heterogeneous. And it may be remarked, in passing, that it is more especially in virtue of having carried this subdivision of function to a greater extent and completeness, that the English language is superior to all others.[6]

Another aspect under which we may trace the development of language is the differentiation of words of allied meanings. Philology early disclosed the truth that in all languages words may be grouped into families having a common ancestry. An aboriginal name applied indiscriminately to each of an extensive and ill-defined class of things or actions, presently undergoes modifications by which the chief divisions of the class are expressed. These several names springing from the primitive root, themselves become the parents of other names still further modified. And by the aid of those systematic modes which presently arise, of making derivations and forming compound terms expressing still smaller distinctions, there is finally developed a tribe of words so heterogeneous in sound and meaning, that to the uninitiated it seems incredible that they should have had a common origin. Meanwhile from other roots there are being evolved other such tribes, until there results a language of some sixty thousand or more unlike words, signifying as many unlike objects, qualities, acts.

Yet another way in which language in general advances from the homogeneous to the heterogeneous, is in the multiplication of languages. Whether as Max Müller and Bunsen[7] think, all languages have grown from one stock, or whether, as some philologists say, they have grown from two or more stocks, it is clear that since large families of languages, as the Indo-European, are of one parentage, they have become distinct through a process of continuous divergence. The same diffusion over the Earth's surface which has led to the differentiation of the race, has simultaneously led to a differentiation of their speech: a truth which we see further illustrated in each nation by the peculiarities of dialect found in several districts. Thus the progress of Language conforms to the general law, alike in the evolution of languages, in the evolution of families of words, and in the evolution of parts of speech. . . .

Strange as it seems then, we find it no less true, that all forms of written language, of painting, and of sculpture, have a common root in the politico-religious decorations of ancient temples and palaces. Little resemblance as they now have, the bust that stands on the console, the landscape that hangs against the wall, and the copy of the *Times* lying upon the table, are remotely akin; not only in nature, but by extraction. The brazen face of the knocker which the postman has just lifted, is related not only to the woodcuts of the *Illustrated London News* which he is delivering, but to the characters of the *billet-doux*[8] which accompanies it. Between the painted window, the prayer-book on which its light falls, and the adjacent monument, there is consanguinity. The effigies on our coins, the signs over shops, the figures that fill every ledger, the coats of arms outside the carriage panel, and the placards inside the omnibus, are, in common with dolls, bluebooks, paper-hangings, lineally descended from the rude sculpture-paintings in which the Egyptians represented the triumphs and worship of their god-kings. Perhaps no example can be given which more vividly illustrates the multiplicity and heterogeneity of the products that in course of time may arise by successive differentiations from a common stock. . . .

. . . Going back to the early time when the deeds of the god-king, chanted and mimetically represented in dances round his altar, were further narrated in picture-writings on the walls of temples and palaces, and so constituted a rude literature, we might trace the development of Literature through phases in which, as in the Hebrew Scriptures, it presents in one work theology, cosmogony, history, biography, civil law, ethics, poetry; through other phases in which, as in the Iliad, the religious, martial, historical, the epic, dramatic, and lyric elements are similarly commingled; down to its present heterogeneous development, in which its divisions and subdivisions are so numerous and varied as to defy complete classification. Or we might trace out the evolution of Science; beginning with the era in which it was not yet differentiated from Art, and was, in union with Art, the handmaid of Religion; passing through the era in which the sciences were so few and rudimentary, as to be simultaneously cultivated by the same philosophers; and ending with the era in which the genera and species are so numerous that few can enumerate them, and no one can adequately grasp

---

[6]**English . . . others:** added 1862, apparently with reference to the atrophy of declensions and conjugations in English and their replacement by prepositions and auxiliary verbs.

[7]F. Max **Müller** (1823–1900): German philologist and mythographer, professor at Oxford. Christian Karl Josias **Bunsen** (1791–1860): Prussian scholar, envoy to Britain.

[8]*Illustrated London News:* picture magazine of news and arts founded 1842. *billet-doux:* love letter.

even one genus. Or we might do the like with Architecture, with the Drama, with Dress.

But doubtless the reader is already weary of illustrations; and our promise has been amply fulfilled. We believe we have shown beyond question, that that which the German physiologists have found to be the law of organic development, is the law of all development. The advance from the simple to the complex, through a process of successive differentiations, is seen alike in the earliest changes of the Universe to which we can reason our way back; and in the earliest changes which we can inductively establish; it is seen in the geologic and climatic evolution of the Earth, and of every single organism on its surface; it is seen in the evolution of Humanity, whether contemplated in the civilized individual, or in the aggregation of races; it is seen in the evolution of Society in respect alike of its political, its religious, and its economical organization; and it is seen in the evolution of all those endless concrete and abstract products of human activity which constitute the environment of our daily life. From the remotest past which Science can fathom, up to the novelties of yesterday, that in which Progress essentially consists, is the transformation of the homogeneous into the heterogeneous.

And now, from this uniformity of procedure, may we not infer some fundamental necessity whence it results? May we not rationally seek for some all-pervading principle which determines this all-pervading process of things? Does not the universality of the *law* imply a universal *cause?*

That we can fathom such cause, noumenally[9] considered, is not to be supposed. To do this would be to solve that ultimate mystery which must ever transcend human intelligence. But it still may be possible for us to reduce the law of all Progress, above established, from the condition of an empirical generalization, to the condition of a rational generalization. . . .

. . . The only obvious respect in which all kinds of Progress are alike, is, that they are modes of *change;* and hence, in some characteristic of changes in general, the desired solution will probably be found. We may suspect *à priori*[10] that in some law of change lies the explanation of this universal transformation of the homogeneous into the heterogeneous.

Thus much premised, we pass at once to the statement of the law, which is this:—*Every active force produces more than one change—every cause produces more than one effect.*

Before this law can be duly comprehended, a few examples must be looked at. When one body is struck against another, that which we usually regard as the effect, is a change of position or motion in one or both bodies. But a moment's thought shows us that this is a careless and very incomplete view of the matter. Besides the visible mechanical result, sound is produced; or, to speak accurately, a vibration in one or both bodies, and in the surrounding air: and under some circumstances we call this the effect. Moreover, the air has not only been made to vibrate, but has had sundry currents caused in it by the transit of the bodies. Further, there is a disarrangement of the particles of the two bodies in the neighbourhood of their point of collision; amounting in some cases to a visible condensation. Yet more, this condensation is accompanied by the disengagement of heat. In some cases a spark—that is, light—results, from the incandescence of a portion struck off; and sometimes this incandescence is associated with chemical combination.

Thus, by the original mechanical force expended in the collision, at least five, and often more, different kinds of changes have been produced. Take, again, the lighting of a candle. Primarily this is a chemical change consequent on a rise of temperature. The process of combination having once been set going by extraneous heat, there is a continued formation of carbonic acid, water, &c.—in itself a result more complex than the extraneous heat that first caused it. But accompanying this process of combination there is a production of heat; there is a production of light; there is an ascending column of hot gases generated; there are currents established in the surrounding air. Moreover, the decomposition of one force into many forces does not end here: each of the several changes produced becomes the parent of further changes. The carbonic acid given off will by and by combine with some base; or under the influence of sunshine give up its carbon to the leaf of a plant. The water will modify the hygrometric state[11] of the air around; or, if the current of hot gases containing it come against a cold body, will be condensed: altering the temperature, and perhaps the chemical state, of the surface it covers. The heat given out melts the subjacent tallow, and expands whatever it warms. The light, falling on various substances, calls forth from them reactions by which it is modified; and so divers colours are produced. Similarly even with these secondary actions, which may be traced out into ever-multiplying ramifications, until they become too minute to be appreciated. And thus it is with all changes whatever. No case can be named in which an active force does not evolve forces of

---

[9]**noumenally**: as apprehended by intuition rather than phenomenal perception.

[10]*à priori*: as a matter of principle.

---

[11]**hygrometric state**: degree of humidity.

several kinds, and each of these, other groups of forces. Universally the effect is more complex than the cause.

Doubtless the reader already foresees the course of our argument. This multiplication of results, which is displayed in every event of to-day, has been going on from the beginning; and is true of the grandest phenomena of the universe as of the most insignificant. From the law that every active force produces more than one change, it is an inevitable corollary that through all time there has been an ever-growing complication of things. Starting with the ultimate fact that every cause produces more than one effect, we may readily see that throughout creation there must have gone on, and must still go on, a never-ceasing transformation of the homogeneous into the heterogeneous. But let us trace out this truth in detail. . . .

. . . Should the Nebular Hypothesis ever be established, then it will become manifest that the Universe at large, like every organism, was once homogeneous; that as a whole, and in every detail, it has unceasingly advanced towards greater heterogeneity; and that its heterogeneity is still increasing. It will be seen that as in each event of to-day, so from the beginning, the decomposition of every expended force into several forces has been perpetually producing a higher complication; that the increase of heterogeneity so brought about is still going on, and must continue to go on; and that thus Progress is not an accident, not a thing within human control, but a beneficent necessity.

A few words must be added on the ontological bearings of our argument. Probably not a few will conclude that here is an attempted solution of the great questions with which Philosophy in all ages has perplexed itself. Let none thus deceive themselves. Only such as know not the scope and the limits of Science can fall into so grave an error. The foregoing generalizations apply, not to the genesis of things in themselves, but to their genesis as manifested to the human consciousness. After all that has been said, the ultimate mystery remains just as it was. The explanation of that which is explicable, does but bring out into greater clearness the inexplicableness of that which remains behind. However we may succeed in reducing the equation to its lowest terms, we are not thereby enabled to determine the unknown quantity: on the contrary, it only becomes more manifest that the unknown quantity can never be found.

Little as it seems to do so, fearless inquiry tends continually to give a firmer basis to all true Religion. The timid sectarian, alarmed at the progress of knowledge, obliged to abandon one by one the superstitions of his ancestors, and daily finding his cherished beliefs more and more shaken, secretly fears that all things may some day be explained; and has a corresponding dread of Science: thus evincing the profoundest of all infidelity—the fear lest the truth be bad. On the other hand, the sincere man of science, content to follow wherever the evidence leads him, becomes by each new inquiry more profoundly convinced that the Universe is an insoluble problem. Alike in the external and the internal worlds, he sees himself in the midst of perpetual changes, of which he can discover neither the beginning nor the end. If, tracing back the evolution of things, he allows himself to entertain the hypothesis that all matter once existed in a diffused form, he finds it utterly impossible to conceive how this came to be so; and equally, if he speculates on the future, he can assign no limit to the grand succession of phenomena ever unfolding themselves before him. On the other hand, if he looks inward, he perceives that both terminations of the thread of consciousness are beyond his grasp: he cannot remember when or how consciousness commenced, and he cannot examine the consciousness that at any moment exists; for only a state of consciousness that is already past can become the object of thought, and never one which is passing.

When, again, he turns from the succession of phenomena, external or internal, to their essential nature, he is equally at fault. Though he may succeed in resolving all properties of objects into manifestations of force, he is not thereby enabled to realize what force is; but finds, on the contrary, that the more he thinks about it, the more he is baffled. Similarly, though analysis of mental actions may finally bring him down to sensations as the original materials out of which all thought is woven, he is none the forwarder; for he cannot in the least comprehend sensation—cannot even conceive how sensation is possible. Inward and outward things he thus discovers to be alike inscrutable in their ultimate genesis and nature. He sees that the Materialist and Spiritualist controversy is a mere war of words; the disputants being equally absurd—each believing he understands that which it is impossible for any man to understand. In all directions his investigations eventually bring him face to face with the unknowable; and he ever more clearly perceives it to be the unknowable. He learns at once the greatness and the littleness of human intellect—its power in dealing with all that comes within the range of experience; its impotence in dealing with all that transcends experience. He feels, with a vividness which no others can, the utter incomprehensibleness of the simplest fact, considered in itself. He alone truly *sees* that absolute knowledge is impossible. He alone *knows* that under all things there lies an impenetrable mystery.

1857, 1862

MATTHEW ARNOLD

(1822–1888)

In what is perhaps the quintessential expression of mid-Victorian malaise, the speaker of "Dover Beach" tells his beloved that although the world spread out before them looks "like a land of dreams," it has really "neither joy, nor love, nor light, / Nor certitude, nor peace, nor help for pain." Traditional faith has died and nothing has replaced it. Arnold's poetry self-consciously inhabits a moment of historical transition, "between two worlds, / One dead, the other powerless to be born." As a poet he laments this impasse; as a critic he tries to lead the way out.

What Arnold called "criticism" addresses many forms of cultural production, primarily but not exclusively written texts. Its aim is to discover "the best that has been thought and said in the world" and, by disseminating its findings, to "make reason and the will of God prevail." Great poetry, Arnold asserted, would replace religion, which would itself survive only as poetry, not dogma. He put his faith in what came to be called the literary canon: a set of "classic" texts that represents the highest insights of the human spirit and should therefore form the basis of all education. This idea was attacked in Arnold's lifetime by those (like Thomas Henry Huxley) who thought he slighted the claims of science or represented the interests only of a small elite. Later it was remarked that a canon consisting almost entirely of works from western Europe could hardly be "universal," as Arnoldians have claimed. Nonetheless, the belief that great literature forms and elevates our character, and that the habit of critically reading both literary and nonliterary texts enables us to evaluate the world we live in, still inspires students and teachers of literature, whatever they may think of the canon as Arnold formulated it.

Everything in Arnold's education and experience prepared him for a position of cultural authority. As the eldest son of Thomas Arnold, the headmaster of Rugby School who gave new intellectual and moral seriousness to classical pedagogy, he had the finest possible training in the Greek and Latin literature that formed the basis of elite education in England. In the Lake District, where the Arnolds and their numerous children spent vacations, William Wordsworth was their neighbor and much-revered friend, and Matthew read the other Romantic poets on his own. At Rugby he was casual about schoolwork, adopting a dandyish manner—aloof, charming, debonair—that enabled him to elude his parents' anxious scrutiny; but he astonished them by winning a scholarship to Oxford. At Oxford he cut chapel, lost money at cards, and paid little attention to the required curriculum, but he read assiduously in books that interested him and won a fellowship despite taking an undistinguished degree. After leaving Oxford he became private secretary to Lord Lansdowne, a cabinet minister from whose grand London house he observed the doings of the magnates who governed England, and still had ample time for going to parties, thinking about politics, and writing poetry.

Arnold's carefree, self-assured manner was belied, however, by the four volumes of poetry he published between 1849 and 1855. These describe a world in which classical certainties, Christian faith, and Wordsworth's joyous and sublime vision of nature are revealed as myths that can no longer inspire creativity or sustain belief. Romantic love, too, eludes his poetic speakers, whose worst misery is that they are losing the power to feel. Plangent and elegiac, Arnold's poems are suffused with nostalgia for a free, spontaneous, authentic emotional life that has been stunted, he thinks, by the "unpoetical" modern world.

After a brief love affair (about which little is known although much has been conjectured, and which may have been mostly imaginary) with a woman he calls in his poems "Marguerite," Arnold fell in love with the daughter of a conservative judge. The judge, like many fathers in Victorian literature and life, disapproved of his daughter's unsettled and impecunious suitor; but in 1851, instead of waiting a decade like Tennyson or eloping like Elizabeth Barrett and Robert Browning, Arnold found a job that satisfied the judge and enabled him to marry. The government had recently begun giving grants to primary schools for the poor—the first step in the long road to providing state education for everyone—and Arnold was hired as one of the inspectors who traveled around the country checking the condition and performance of these schools. Unlike almost all other major nineteenth-century writers, he worked for most of his adult life at a job that was often tedious and unsatisfying. The writer who was to argue for state action to deal with social ills was himself part of the burgeoning bureaucracy of the modern state.

The result was that he came to know English society pretty much from top to bottom. Belonging by birth, training, and marriage to the small circle of upper-middle-class professionals who increasingly were administering both English culture and the British state, on his tours of inspection he visited the homes of middle-class Dissenters whom he would otherwise never have met, and he sometimes mingled socially with the aristocracy. He examined the children of the poor in arithmetic and reading, evaluated the progress of student teachers who were making their way upward into the middle class, and in 1857 was elected Professor of Poetry at Oxford.

After the early 1850s he wrote very few poems. As a critic, however, he became increasingly fluent, influential, and wide-ranging. At first he mostly discussed literary works. Then he argued in a series of witty and extremely provocative essays that England needed to reform itself through "culture," by which he meant, in the widest sense, the knowledge and habits of mind formed by the right kind of reading. In "The Function of Criticism at the Present Time," he reads a newspaper paragraph about a woman referred to only by her surname, Wragg, who has been arrested for child murder. This lesson in cultural criticism is notorious for its fastidious shudder at poor Wragg's name, but it is notable most of all for the force with which it drives home the connection between the newspaper's dehumanizing language and the human misery it reports. In *Culture and Anarchy*, Arnold analyzes with similar vividness the class structure that retarded social progress, describing the nation as divided into Barbarians (aristocracy), Philistines (middle class), and Populace (working class). His ideal was a classless society in which every person could attain a fully developed human life; but this, he argued, would require Englishmen to abandon their worship of individual freedom so that a centralized state could provide, for example, universal primary and secondary education. His last great project was to save Christianity from the Philistines' dogmatic and socially divisive sectarianism by applying literary criticism to the Bible. Like the other "Higher Critics" he regarded the Bible as a book produced like any other by human beings at specific moments in human history, and by reading it as "poetry" (that is, as literature) he hoped to save it for the growing number of people, especially those from the more educated working class, who believed that its narratives were not literally true. If poetry was what mattered in the Bible, then secular poems too could contain saving power. The very best English poetry—including Wordsworth's, which Arnold found false as philosophy but true as an emotional interpretation of the world—provides, he asserted, spiritual sustenance, consolation, and joy.

Like many of his contemporaries, Arnold was morally committed to a democratic ideal but uncomfortable with the cultural climate it seemed to imply. He especially disliked the bumptious hypermasculinity that he saw in middle-class Englishmen—harsh, self-congratulatory, addicted to politics and money making, eager to act, unwilling to think, insensitive to beauty, and contemptuously indifferent to delicacy of feeling. His poetic protagonists shrink from the Philistine world but have nowhere else to go. As a critic, however, Arnold tries to show how society can be remade, articulating a role for literature and criticism that has profoundly influenced pedagogic and humanistic ideals throughout the English-speaking world.

Shakespeare

Others abide our question. Thou art free.
We ask and ask—Thou smilest and art still,
Out-topping knowledge. For the loftiest hill,
Who to the stars uncrowns his majesty,

Planting his steadfast footsteps in the sea,
Making the heaven of heavens his dwelling-place,
Spares but the cloudy border of his base
To the foil'd searching of mortality;

And thou, who didst the stars and sunbeams know,
Self-school'd, self-scann'd, self-honour'd, self-secure,   10
Didst tread on earth unguess'd at.—Better so!

All pains the immortal spirit must endure,
All weakness which impairs, all griefs which bow,
Find their sole speech in that victorious brow.

                                                1849

Resignation
To Fausta[1]

To die be given us, or attain!
Fierce work it were, to do again.
So pilgrims, bound for Mecca, pray'd
At burning noon; so warriors said,

Scarf'd with the cross, who watch'd the miles
Of dust which wreathed their struggling files
Down Lydian mountains;[2] so, when snows
Round Alpine summits, eddying rose,
The Goth, bound Rome-wards; so the Hun,
Crouch'd on his saddle, while the sun   10
Went lurid down o'er flooded plains
Through which the groaning Danube strains
To the drear Euxine;[3]—so pray all,
Whom labours, self-ordain'd, enthrall;
Because they to themselves propose
On this side the all-common close
A goal which, gain'd, may give repose.
So pray they; and to stand again
Where they stood once, to them were pain;
Pain to thread back and to renew   20
Past straits, and currents long steer'd through.

But milder natures, and more free—
Whom an unblamed serenity
Hath freed from passions, and the state
Of struggle these necessitate;
Whom schooling of the stubborn mind
Hath made, or birth hath found, resign'd—
These mourn not, that their goings pay
Obedience to the passing day.
These claim not every laughing Hour   30
For handmaid to their striding power;
Each in her turn, with torch uprear'd,
To await their march; and when appear'd,
Through the cold gloom, with measured race,
To usher for a destined space

---

[1]**Fausta:** Arnold's older sister Jane, who was living with her mother in their Lake District home and was frustrated by her inability to find serious, satisfying activity. The poem commemorates a walk taken by the older Arnold children with their father (who died in 1842) ten years earlier; the landscape is that celebrated by Wordsworth.

---

[2]**Lydian:** in Asia Minor. **Mecca** is the holy place of Islam; the **warriors** wearing the **cross** are Christian crusaders.

[3]**Euxine:** Black Sea.

(Her own sweet errands all forgone)
The too imperious traveller on.
These, Fausta, ask not this; nor thou,
Time's chafing prisoner, ask it now!

We left, just ten years since, you say,   40
That wayside inn we left to-day.
Our jovial host, as forth we fare,
Shouts greeting from his easy chair.
High on a bank our leader stands,
Reviews and ranks his motley bands,
Makes clear our goal to every eye—
The valley's western boundary.
A gate swings to! our tide hath flow'd
Already from the silent road.
The valley-pastures, one by one,   50
Are threaded, quiet in the sun;
And now beyond the rude stone bridge
Slopes gracious up the western ridge.
Its woody border, and the last
Of its dark upland farms is past—
Cool farms, with open-lying stores,
Under their burnish'd sycamores;
All past! and through the trees we glide,
Emerging on the green hill-side.
There climbing hangs, a far-seen sign,   60
Our wavering, many-colour'd line;
There winds, upstreaming slowly still
Over the summit of the hill.
And now, in front, behold outspread
Those upper regions we must tread!
Mild hollows, and clear heathy swells,
The cheerful silence of the fells.
Some two hours' march with serious air,
Through the deep noontide heats we fare;
The red-grouse, springing at our sound,   70
Skims, now and then, the shining ground;
No life, save his and ours, intrudes
Upon these breathless solitudes.
O joy! again the farms appear.
Cool shade is there, and rustic cheer;
There springs the brook will guide us down,
Bright comrade, to the noisy town.
Lingering, we follow down; we gain
The town, the highway, and the plain.
And many a mile of dusty way,   80
Parch'd and road-worn, we made that day;
But, Fausta, I remember well,
That as the balmy darkness fell

We bathed our hands with speechless glee,
That night, in the wide-glimmering sea.

Once more we tread this self-same road,
Fausta, which ten years since we trod;
Alone we tread it, you and I,
Ghosts of that boisterous company.
Here, where the brook shines, near its head,   90
In its clear, shallow, turf-fringed bed;
Here, whence the eye first sees, far down,
Capp'd with faint smoke, the noisy town;
Here sit we, and again unroll,
Though slowly, the familiar whole.
The solemn wastes of heathy hill
Sleep in the July sunshine still;
The self-same shadows now, as then,
Play through this grassy upland glen;
The loose dark stones on the green way   100
Lie strewn, it seems, where then they lay;
On this mild bank above the stream,
(You crush them!) the blue gentians gleam.
Still this wild brook, the rushes cool,
The sailing foam, the shining pool!
These are not changed; and we, you say,
Are scarce more changed, in truth, than they.

The gipsies, whom we met below,
They, too, have long roam'd to and fro;
They ramble, leaving, where they pass,   110
Their fragments on the cumber'd grass.
And often to some kindly place
Chance guides the migratory race,
Where, though long wanderings intervene,
They recognise a former scene.
The dingy tents are pitch'd; the fires
Give to the wind their wavering spires;
In dark knots crouch round the wild flame
Their children, as when first they came;
They see their shackled beasts again   120
Move, browsing, up the gray-wall'd lane.
Signs are not wanting, which might raise
The ghost in them of former days—
Signs are not wanting, if they would;
Suggestions to disquietude.
For them, for all, time's busy touch,
While it mends little, troubles much.
Their joints grow stiffer—but the year
Runs his old round of dubious cheer;
Chilly they grow—yet winds in March,   130
Still, sharp as ever, freeze and parch;

They must live still—and yet, God knows,
Crowded and keen the country grows;
It seems as if, in their decay,
The law grew stronger every day.
So might they reason, so compare,
Fausta, times past with times that are.
But no!—they rubb'd through yesterday
In their hereditary way,
And they will rub through, if they can,   140
To-morrow on the self-same plan,
Till death arrive to supersede,
For them, vicissitude and need.

The poet, to whose mighty heart
Heaven doth a quicker pulse impart,
Subdues that energy to scan
Not his own course, but that of man.
Though he move mountains, though his day
Be pass'd on the proud heights of sway,
Though he hath loosed a thousand chains,   150
Though he hath borne immortal pains,
Action and suffering though he know—
He hath not lived, if he lives so.
He sees, in some great-historied land,
A ruler of the people stand,
Sees his strong thought in fiery flood
Roll through the heaving multitude;
Exults—yet for no moment's space
Envies the all-regarded place.
Beautiful eyes meet his—and he   160
Bears to admire uncravingly;
They pass—he, mingled with the crowd,
Is in their far-off triumphs proud.
From some high station he looks down,
At sunset, on a populous town;
Surveys each happy group, which fleets,
Toil ended, through the shining streets,
Each with some errand of its own—
And does not say: *I am alone.*
He sees the gentle stir of birth   170
When morning purifies the earth;
He leans upon a gate and sees
The pastures, and the quiet trees.
Low, woody hill, with gracious bound,
Folds the still valley almost round;
The cuckoo, loud on some high lawn,
Is answer'd from the depth of dawn;
In the hedge straggling to the stream,
Pale, dew-drench'd, half-shut roses gleam;

But, where the farther side slopes down,   180
He sees the drowsy new-waked clown[4]
In his white quaint-embroider'd frock
Make, whistling, tow'rd his mist-wreathed flock—
Slowly, behind his heavy tread,
The wet, flower'd grass heaves up its head.
Lean'd on his gate, he gazes—tears
Are in his eyes, and in his ears
The murmur of a thousand years.
Before him he sees life unroll,
A placid and continuous whole—   190
That general life, which does not cease,
Whose secret is not joy, but peace;
That life, whose dumb wish is not miss'd
If birth proceeds, if things subsist;
The life of plants, and stones, and rain,
The life he craves—if not in vain
Fate gave, what chance shall not control,
His sad lucidity of soul.

You listen—but that wandering smile,
Fausta, betrays you cold the while!   200
Your eyes pursue the bells of foam
Wash'd, eddying, from this bank, their home.
Those gipsies, so your thoughts I scan,
Are less, the poet more, than man.
They feel not, though they move and see;
Deeper the poet feels; but he
Breathes, when he will, immortal air,
Where Orpheus[5] and where Homer are.
In the day's life, whose iron round
Hems us all in, he is not bound;   210
He leaves his kind, o'erleaps their pen,
And flees the common life of men.
He escapes thence, but we abide—
Not deep the poet sees, but wide.

The world in which we live and move
Outlasts aversion, outlasts love,
Outlasts each effort, interest, hope,
Remorse, grief, joy;—and were the scope
Of these affections wider made,
Man still would see, and see dismay'd,   220
Beyond his passion's widest range,
Far regions of eternal change.

---

[4] **clown:** countryman.

[5] **Orpheus:** mythic poet and musician.

Nay, and since death, which wipes out man,
Finds him with many an unsolved plan,
With much unknown, and much untried,
Wonder not dead, and thirst not dried,
Still gazing on the ever full
Eternal mundane spectacle—
This world in which we draw our breath,
In some sense, Fausta, outlasts death.   230

Blame thou not, therefore, him who dares
Judge vain beforehand human cares;
Whose natural insight can discern
What through experience others learn;
Who needs not love and power, to know
Love transient, power an unreal show;
Who treads at ease life's uncheer'd ways—
Him blame not, Fausta, rather praise!
Rather thyself for some aim pray
Nobler than this, to fill the day;   240
Rather that heart, which burns in thee,
Ask, not to amuse, but to set free;
Be passionate hopes not ill resign'd
For quiet, and a fearless mind.
And though fate grudge to thee and me
The poet's rapt security,
Yet they, believe me, who await
No gifts from chance, have conquer'd fate.
They, winning room to see and hear,
And to men's business not too near,   250
Through clouds of individual strife
Draw homeward to the general life.
Like leaves by suns not yet uncurl'd;
To the wise, foolish; to the world,
Weak;—yet not weak, I might reply.
Not foolish, Fausta, in His eye,
To whom each moment in its race,
Crowd as we will its neutral space,
Is but a quiet watershed
Whence, equally, the seas of life and death are fed.   260

Enough, we live!—and if a life,
With large results so little rife,
Though bearable, seem hardly worth
This pomp of worlds, this pain of birth;
Yet, Fausta, the mute turf we tread,
The solemn hills around us spread,
This stream which falls incessantly,
The strange-scrawl'd rocks, the lonely sky,
If I might lend their life a voice,
Seem to bear rather than rejoice.   270

And even could the intemperate prayer
Man iterates, while these forbear,
For movement, for an ampler sphere,
Pierce Fate's impenetrable ear;
Not milder is the general lot
Because our spirits have forgot,
In action's dizzying eddy whirl'd,
The something that infects the world.

                                    1849

The Forsaken Merman

Come, dear children, let us away;
Down and away below!
Now my brothers call from the bay,
Now the great winds shoreward blow,
Now the salt tides seaward flow;
Now the wild white horses play,
Champ and chafe and toss in the spray.
Children dear, let us away!
This way, this way!

Call her once before you go—   10
Call once yet!
In a voice that she will know:
"Margaret! Margaret!"
Children's voices should be dear
(Call once more) to a mother's ear;
Children's voices, wild with pain—
Surely she will come again!
Call her once and come away;
This way, this way!
"Mother dear, we cannot stay!   20
The wild white horses foam and fret."
Margaret! Margaret!

Come, dear children, come away down;
Call no more!
One last look at the white-wall'd town,
And the little grey church on the windy shore,
Then come down!
She will not come though you call all day;
Come away, come away!

Children dear, was it yesterday   30
We heard the sweet bells over the bay?
In the caverns where we lay,

Through the surf and through the swell,
The far-off sound of a silver bell?
Sand-strewn caverns, cool and deep,
Where the winds are all asleep;
Where the spent lights quiver and gleam,
Where the salt weed sways in the stream,
Where the sea-beasts, ranged all round,
Feed in the ooze of their pasture-ground;   40
Where the sea-snakes coil and twine,
Dry their mail and bask in the brine;
Where great whales come sailing by,
Sail and sail, with unshut eye,
Round the world for ever and aye?
When did music come this way?
Children dear, was it yesterday?

Children dear, was it yesterday
(Call yet once) that she went away?
Once she sate with you and me,   50
On a red gold throne in the heart of the sea,
And the youngest sate on her knee.
She comb'd its bright hair, and she tended it well,
When down swung the sound of a far-off bell.
She sigh'd, she look'd up through the clear green sea;
She said: "I must go, for my kinsfolk pray
In the little grey church on the shore to-day.
'Twill be Easter-time in the world—ah me!
And I lose my poor soul, Merman! here with thee."
I said: "Go up, dear heart, through the waves;   60
Say thy prayer, and come back to the kind sea-caves!"
She smiled, she went up through the surf in the bay.
Children dear, was it yesterday?

    Children dear, were we long alone?
"The sea grows stormy, the little ones moan;
Long prayers," I said, "in the world they say;
Come!" I said; and we rose through the surf in the bay.
We went up the beach, by the sandy down
Where the sea-stocks bloom, to the white-wall'd town;
Through the narrow paved streets, where all was still,   70
To the little grey church on the windy hill.
From the church came a murmur of folk at their prayers,
But we stood without in the cold blowing airs.
We climb'd on the graves, on the stones worn with rains,
And we gazed up the aisle through the small leaded
        panes.
She sate by the pillar; we saw her clear:
"Margaret, hist! come quick, we are here!
Dear heart," I said, "we are long alone;
The sea grows stormy, the little ones moan."

But, ah, she gave me never a look,   80
For her eyes were seal'd to the holy book!
Loud prays the priest; shut stands the door.
Come away, children, call no more!
Come away, come down, call no more!

    Down, down, down!
Down to the depths of the sea!
She sits at her wheel in the humming town,
Singing most joyfully.
Hark what she sings: "O joy, O joy,
For the humming street, and the child with its toy!   90
For the priest, and the bell, and the holy well;
For the wheel where I spun,
And the blessed light of the sun!"
And so she sings her fill,
Singing most joyfully,
Till the spindle drops from her hand,
And the whizzing wheel stands still.
She steals to the window, and looks at the sand,
And over the sand at the sea;
And her eyes are set in a stare;   100
And anon there breaks a sigh,
And anon there drops a tear,
From a sorrow-clouded eye,
And a heart sorrow-laden,
A long, long sigh;
For the cold strange eyes of a little Mermaiden
And the gleam of her golden hair.

    Come away, away children;
Come children, come down!
The hoarse wind blows coldly;   110
Lights shine in the town.
She will start from her slumber
When gusts shake the door;
She will hear the winds howling,
Will hear the waves roar.
We shall see, while above us
The waves roar and whirl,
A ceiling of amber,
A pavement of pearl.
Singing: "Here came a mortal,   120
But faithless was she!
And alone dwell for ever
The kings of the sea."
But, children, at midnight,
When soft the winds blow,
When clear falls the moonlight,
When spring-tides are low;

When sweet airs come seaward
From heaths starr'd with broom,
And high rocks throw mildly   130
On the blanch'd sands a gloom;
Up the still, glistening beaches,
Up the creeks we will hie,
Over banks of bright seaweed
The ebb-tide leaves dry.
We will gaze, from the sand-hills,
At the white, sleeping town;
At the church on the hill-side—
And then come back down.
Singing: "There dwells a loved one,   140
But cruel is she!
She left lonely for ever
The kings of the sea."

1849

Isolation. To Marguerite[1]

We were apart; yet, day by day,
I bade my heart more constant be.
I bade it keep the world away,
And grow a home for only thee;
Nor fear'd but thy love likewise grew,
Like mine, each day, more tried, more true.

The fault was grave! I might have known,
What far too soon, alas! I learn'd—
The heart can bind itself alone,
And faith may oft be unreturn'd.   10
Self-sway'd our feelings ebb and swell—
Thou lov'st no more;—Farewell! Farewell!

Farewell!—and thou, thou lonely heart,
Which never yet without remorse
Even for a moment didst depart
From thy remote and spheréd course
To haunt the place where passions reign—
Back to thy solitude again!

Back! with the conscious thrill of shame
Which Luna felt, that summer-night,   20
Flash through her pure immortal frame,
When she forsook the starry height

To hang over Endymion's[2] sleep
Upon the pine-grown Latmian steep.

Yet she, chaste queen, had never proved
How vain a thing is mortal love,
Wandering in Heaven, far removed.
But thou hast long had place to prove
This truth—to prove, and make thine own:
"Thou hast been, shalt be, art, alone."   30

Or, if not quite alone, yet they
Which touch thee are unmating things—
Ocean and clouds and night and day;
Lorn autumns and triumphant springs;
And life, and others' joy and pain,
And love, if love, of happier men.

Of happier men—for they, at least,
Have *dream'd* two human hearts might blend
In one, and were through faith released
From isolation without end   40
Prolong'd; nor knew, although not less
Alone than thou, their loneliness.

1857

To Marguerite—Continued

Yes! in the sea of life enisled,
With echoing straits between us thrown,
Dotting the shoreless watery wild,
We mortal millions live *alone*.
The islands feel the enclasping flow,
And then their endless bounds they know.

But when the moon their hollows lights,
And they are swept by balms of spring,
And in their glens, on starry nights,
The nightingales divinely sing;   10
And lovely notes, from shore to shore,
Across the sounds and channels pour—

Oh! then a longing like despair
Is to their farthest caverns sent;
For surely once, they feel, we were
Parts of a single continent!

----

[1]The poems to **Marguerite** are part of "Switzerland," a sequence recounting the failure of a mysterious love affair.

[2]**Luna:** moon goddess in love with **Endymion,** a shepherd on Mt. Latmos.

Now round us spreads the watery plain—
Oh might our marges meet again!

Who order'd, that their longing's fire
Should be, as soon as kindled, cool'd?   20
Who renders vain their deep desire?—
A God, a God their severance ruled!
And bade betwixt their shores to be
The unplumb'd, salt, estranging sea.

                                              1852

The Buried Life

Light flows our war of mocking words, and yet,
Behold, with tears mine eyes are wet!
I feel a nameless sadness o'er me roll.
Yes, yes, we know that we can jest,
We know, we know that we can smile!
But there's a something in this breast,
To which thy light words bring no rest,
And thy gay smiles no anodyne.
Give me thy hand, and hush awhile,
And turn those limpid eyes on mine,   10
And let me read there, love! thy inmost soul.

Alas! is even love too weak
To unlock the heart, and let it speak?
Are even lovers powerless to reveal
To one another what indeed they feel?
I knew the mass of men conceal'd
Their thoughts, for fear that if reveal'd
They would by other men be met
With blank indifference, or with blame reproved;
I knew they lived and moved   20
Trick'd in disguises, alien to the rest
Of men, and alien to themselves—and yet
The same heart beats in every human breast!

But we, my love!—doth a like spell benumb
Our hearts, our voices?—must we too be dumb?

Ah! well for us, if even we,
Even for a moment, can get free
Our heart, and have our lips unchain'd;
For that which seals them hath been deep-ordain'd!
Fate, which foresaw   30
How frivolous a baby man would be—
By what distractions he would be possess'd,

How he would pour himself in every strife,
And well-nigh change his own identity—
That it might keep from his capricious play
His genuine self, and force him to obey
Even in his own despite his being's law,
Bade through the deep recesses of our breast
The unregarded river of our life
Pursue with indiscernible flow its way;   40
And that we should not see
The buried stream, and seem to be
Eddying at large in blind uncertainty,
Though driving on with it eternally.

But often, in the world's most crowded streets,
But often, in the din of strife,
There rises an unspeakable desire
After the knowledge of our buried life;
A thirst to spend our fire and restless force
In tracking out our true, original course;   50
A longing to inquire
Into the mystery of this heart which beats
So wild, so deep in us—to know
Whence our lives come and where they go.
And many a man in his own breast then delves,
But deep enough, alas! none ever mines.
And we have been on many thousand lines,
And we have shown, on each, spirit and power;
But hardly have we, for one little hour,
Been on our own line, have we been ourselves—   60
Hardly had skill to utter one of all
The nameless feelings that course through our breast,
But they course on for ever unexpress'd.
And long we try in vain to speak and act
Our hidden self, and what we say and do
Is eloquent, is well—but 'tis not true!
And then we will no more be rack'd
With inward striving, and demand
Of all the thousand nothings of the hour
Their stupefying power;   70
Ah yes, and they benumb us at our call!
Yet still, from time to time, vague and forlorn,
From the soul's subterranean depth upborne
As from an infinitely distant land,
Come airs, and floating echoes, and convey
A melancholy into all our day.

Only—but this is rare—
When a belovéd hand is laid in ours,
When, jaded with the rush and glare
Of the interminable hours,   80

Our eyes can in another's eyes read clear,
When our world-deafen'd ear
Is by the tones of a loved voice caress'd—
A bolt is shot back somewhere in our breast,
And a lost pulse of feeling stirs again.
The eye sinks inward, and the heart lies plain,
And what we mean, we say, and what we would, we know.
A man becomes aware of his life's flow,
And hears its winding murmur; and he sees
The meadows where it glides, the sun, the breeze.   90

And there arrives a lull in the hot race
Wherein he doth for ever chase
That flying and elusive shadow, rest.
An air of coolness plays upon his face,
And an unwonted calm pervades his breast.
And then he thinks he knows
The hills where his life rose,
And the sea where it goes.

                                          1852

The Scholar-Gipsy

Go, for they call you, shepherd, from the hill;
    Go, shepherd, and untie the wattled cotes![1]
        No longer leave thy wistful flock unfed,
    Nor let thy bawling fellows rack their throats,
        Nor the cropp'd herbage shoot another head.
            But when the fields are still,
    And the tired men and dogs all gone to rest,
        And only the white sheep are sometimes seen
        Cross and recross the strips of moon-blanch'd green,
Come, shepherd, and again begin the quest!   10

Here, where the reaper was at work of late—
    In this high field's dark corner, where he leaves
        His coat, his basket, and his earthen cruse,
    And in the sun all morning binds the sheaves,
        Then here, at noon, comes back his stores to use—
            Here will I sit and wait,
    While to my ear from uplands far away
        The bleating of the folded flocks is borne,
        With distant cries of reapers in the corn—
All the live murmur of a summer's day.   20

Screen'd is this nook o'er the high, half-reap'd field,
    And here till sun-down, shepherd! will I be.
        Through the thick corn the scarlet poppies peep,
    And round green roots and yellowing stalks I see
        Pale pink convolvulus in tendrils creep;
            And air-swept lindens yield
    Their scent, and rustle down their perfumed showers
        Of bloom on the bent grass where I am laid,
        And bower me from the August sun with shade;
And the eye travels down to Oxford's towers.   30

And near me on the grass lies Glanvil's book[2]—
    Come, let me read the oft-read tale again!
        The story of the Oxford scholar poor,
    Of pregnant parts and quick inventive brain,
        Who, tired of knocking at preferment's[3] door,
            One summer-morn forsook
    His friends, and went to learn the gipsy-lore,
        And roam'd the world with that wild brotherhood,
        And came, as most men deem'd, to little good,
But came to Oxford and his friends no more.   40

But once, years after, in the country-lanes,
    Two scholars, whom at college erst he knew,
        Met him, and of his way of life enquired;
    Whereat he answer'd, that the gipsy-crew,
        His mates, had arts to rule as they desired
            The workings of men's brains,
    And they can bind them to what thoughts they will.
        "And I," he said, "the secret of their art,
        When fully learn'd, will to the world impart;
But it needs heaven-sent moments for this skill."   50

This said, he left them, and return'd no more.—
    But rumours hung about the country-side,
        That the lost Scholar long was seen to stray,
    Seen by rare glimpses, pensive and tongue-tied,
        In hat of antique shape, and cloak of grey,
            The same the gipsies wore.
    Shepherds had met him on the Hurst in spring;
        At some lone alehouse in the Berkshire moors,
        On the warm ingle-bench, the smock-frock'd boors[4]
Had found him seated at their entering,   60

---

[2]**book**: Joseph **Glanvill** (1636–1680), *The Vanity of Dogmatizing* (1661).

[3]**preferment**: appointment to a position in the Church.

[4]**boors**: country laborers; **the Hurst** (a hill) and the places mentioned in the next stanzas are in the countryside around Oxford.

---

[1]**wattled cotes**: sheds made of woven branches.

But, 'mid their drink and clatter, he would fly.
   And I myself seem half to know thy looks,
      And put the shepherds, wanderer! on thy trace;
   And boys who in lone wheatfields scare the rooks
      I ask if thou hast pass'd their quiet place;
         Or in my boat I lie
   Moor'd to the cool bank in the summer-heats,
      'Mid wide grass meadows which the sunshine fills,
      And watch the warm, green-muffled Cumner hills,
   And wonder if thou haunt'st their shy retreats.   70

For most, I know, thou lov'st retired ground!
   Thee at the ferry Oxford riders blithe,
      Returning home on summer-nights, have met
   Crossing the stripling Thames at Bab-lock-hithe,
      Trailing in the cool stream thy fingers wet,
         As the punt's rope chops round;
   And leaning backward in a pensive dream,
      And fostering in thy lap a heap of flowers
      Pluck'd in shy fields and distant Wychwood bowers,
   And thine eyes resting on the moonlit stream.   80

And then they land, and thou art seen no more!—
   Maidens, who from the distant hamlets come
      To dance around the Fyfield elm in May,
   Oft through the darkening fields have seen thee roam,
      Or cross a stile into the public way.
         Oft thou hast given them store
   Of flowers—the frail-leaf'd, white anemony,
      Dark bluebells drench'd with dews of summer eves,
      And purple orchises with spotted leaves—
   But none hath words she can report of thee.   90

And above Godstow Bridge, when hay-time's here
   In June, and many a scythe in sunshine flames,
      Men who through those wide fields of breezy grass
   Where black-wing'd swallows haunt the glittering
         Thames,
      To bathe in the abandon'd lasher[5] pass,
         Have often pass'd thee near
   Sitting upon the river bank o'ergrown;
      Mark'd thine outlandish garb, thy figure spare,
      Thy dark vague eyes, and soft abstracted air—
   But, when they came from bathing, thou wast gone! 100

At some lone homestead in the Cumner hills,
   Where at her open door the housewife darns,
      Thou hast been seen, or hanging on a gate
   To watch the threshers in the mossy barns.

Children, who early range these slopes and late
      For cresses from the rills,
   Have known thee eying, all an April-day,
      The springing pastures and the feeding kine;
      And mark'd thee, when the stars come out and shine,
   Through the long dewy grass move slow away.   110

In autumn, on the skirts of Bagley Wood—
   Where most the gipsies by the turf-edged way
      Pitch their smoked tents, and every bush you see
   With scarlet patches tagg'd and shreds of grey,
      Above the forest-ground called Thessaly—
         The blackbird, picking food,
   Sees thee, nor stops his meal, nor fears at all;
      So often has he known thee past him stray,
      Rapt, twirling in thy hand a wither'd spray,
   And waiting for the spark from heaven to fall.   120

And once, in winter, on the causeway chill
   Where home through flooded fields foot-travellers go,
      Have I not pass'd thee on the wooden bridge,
   Wrapt in thy cloak and battling with the snow,
      Thy face tow'rd Hinksey and its wintry ridge?
         And thou hast climb'd the hill,
   And gain'd the white brow of the Cumner range;
      Turn'd once to watch, while thick the snowflakes
         fall,
      The line of festal light in Christ-Church hall[6]—
   Then sought thy straw in some sequester'd grange.   130

But what—I dream! Two hundred years are flown
   Since first thy story ran through Oxford halls,
      And the grave Glanvil did the tale inscribe
   That thou wert wander'd from the studious walls
      To learn strange arts, and join a gipsy-tribe;
         And thou from earth art gone
   Long since, and in some quiet churchyard laid—
      Some country-nook, where o'er thy unknown grave
      Tall grasses and white flowering nettles wave,
   Under a dark, red-fruited yew-tree's shade.   140

—No, no, thou hast not felt the lapse of hours!
   For what wears out the life of mortal men?
      'Tis that from change to change their being rolls;
      'Tis that repeated shocks, again, again,
      Exhaust the energy of strongest souls
         And numb the elastic powers.

---

[5]**lasher**: weir.

[6]**Christ Church**: an Oxford college.

Till having used our nerves with bliss and teen,
    And tired upon a thousand schemes our wit,
      To the just-pausing Genius[7] we remit
    Our worn-out life, and are—what we have been.   150

Thou hast not lived, why should'st thou perish, so?
    Thou hadst *one* aim, *one* business, *one* desire;
      Else wert thou long since number'd with the dead!
    Else hadst thou spent, like other men, thy fire!
      The generations of thy peers are fled,
        And we ourselves shall go;
    But thou possessest an immortal lot,
      And we imagine thee exempt from age
      And living as thou liv'st on Glanvil's page,
    Because thou hadst—what we, alas! have not.   160

For early didst thou leave the world, with powers
    Fresh, undiverted to the world without,
      Firm to their mark, not spent on other things;
    Free from the sick fatigue, the languid doubt,
      Which much to have tried, in much been baffled,
        brings.
        O life unlike to ours!
Who fluctuate idly without term or scope,
    Of whom each strives, nor knows for what he strives,
    And each half lives a hundred different lives;
Who wait like thee, but not, like thee, in hope.   170

Thou waitest for the spark from heaven! and we,
    Light half-believers of our casual creeds,
      Who never deeply felt, nor clearly will'd,
    Whose insight never has borne fruit in deeds,
      Whose vague resolves never have been fulfill'd;
        For whom each year we see
Breeds new beginnings, disappointments new;
    Who hesitate and falter life away,
    And lose to-morrow the ground won to-day—
Ah! do not we, wanderer! await it too?   180

Yes, we await it!—but it still delays,
    And then we suffer! and amongst us one,[8]
      Who most has suffer'd, takes dejectedly
    His seat upon the intellectual throne;
      And all his store of sad experience he
        Lays bare of wretched days;

Tells us his misery's birth and growth and signs,
    And how the dying spark of hope was fed,
    And how the breast was soothed, and how the head,
    And all his hourly varied anodynes.   190

This for our wisest! and we others pine,
    And wish the long unhappy dream would end,
      And waive all claim to bliss, and try to bear;
    With close-lipp'd patience for our only friend,
      Sad patience, too near neighbour to despair—
        But none has hope like thine!
Thou through the fields and through the woods dost stray,
    Roaming the country-side, a truant boy,
    Nursing thy project in unclouded joy,
And every doubt long blown by time away.   200

O born in days when wits were fresh and clear,
    And life ran gaily as the sparkling Thames;
      Before this strange disease of modern life,
    With its sick hurry, its divided aims,
      Its heads o'ertax'd, its palsied hearts, was rife—
        Fly hence, our contact fear!
Still fly, plunge deeper in the bowering wood!
    Averse, as Dido[9] did with gesture stern
    From her false friend's approach in Hades turn,
Wave us away, and keep thy solitude!   210

Still nursing the unconquerable hope,
    Still clutching the inviolable shade,
      With a free, onward impulse brushing through,
    By night, the silver'd branches of the glade—
      Far on the forest-skirts, where none pursue.
        On some mild pastoral slope
Emerge, and resting on the moonlit pales
    Freshen thy flowers as in former years
    With dew, or listen with enchanted ears,
From the dark dingles,[10] to the nightingales!   220

But fly our paths, our feverish contact fly!
    For strong the infection of our mental strife,
      Which, though it gives no bliss, yet spoils for rest;
    And we should win thee from thy own fair life,
      Like us distracted, and like us unblest.
        Soon, soon thy cheer would die,

---

[7]**Genius:** spirit of the age.

[8]**one:** identified by Arnold as Johann Wolfgang von Goethe (1749–1832), German poet, novelist, and sage.

[9]**Dido:** queen of Carthage who, having killed herself when her lover Aeneas deserted her, refuses to greet him in **Hades** (*Aeneid* 6.469–473).

[10]**dingles:** wooded hollows.

Thy hopes grow timorous, and unfix'd thy powers,
 And thy clear aims be cross and shifting made;
 And then thy glad perennial youth would fade,
Fade, and grow old at last, and die like ours. 230

Then fly our greetings, fly our speech and smiles!
 —As some grave Tyrian[11] trader, from the sea,
 Descried at sunrise an emerging prow
Lifting the cool-hair'd creepers stealthily,
 The fringes of a southward-facing brow
  Among the Ægæan isles;
And saw the merry Grecian coaster come,
 Freighted with amber grapes, and Chian wine,
 Green, bursting figs, and tunnies steep'd in brine—
And knew the intruders on his ancient home, 240

The young light-hearted masters of the waves—
 And snatch'd his rudder, and shook out more sail;
 And day and night held on indignantly
O'er the blue Midland waters with the gale,
 Betwixt the Syrtes and soft Sicily,
  To where the Atlantic raves
Outside the western straits;[12] and unbent sails
 There, where down cloudy cliffs, through sheets
  of foam,
 Shy traffickers, the dark Iberians come;
And on the beach undid his corded bales. 250

         1853

Stanzas from the Grande Chartreuse[1]

Through Alpine meadows soft-suffused
With rain, where thick the crocus blows,
Past the dark forges long disused,
The mule-track from Saint Laurent goes.

---

[11]**Tyrian**: from Tyre, ancient Phoenician seaport, whose colonists founded Carthage.

[12]**Midland**: Mediterranean. **Syrtes**: shallow waters near Africa. **western straits**: Straits of Gibraltar; here, the limits of the known world. **Iberians**: Spanish or Portuguese.

[1]Arnold and his wife visited the **Grande Chartreuse**, a Carthusian monastery in the French Alps, on their honeymoon in 1851. The first stanzas describe their ascent to it: the **Dead Guier** (Guiers Mort) is a river.

The bridge is cross'd, and slow we ride,
Through forest, up the mountain-side.

The autumnal evening darkens round,
The wind is up, and drives the rain;
While, hark! far down, with strangled sound
Doth the Dead Guier's stream complain, 10
Where that wet smoke, among the woods,
Over his boiling cauldron broods.

Swift rush the spectral vapours white
Past limestone scars with ragged pines,
Showing—then blotting from our sight!—
Halt—through the cloud-drift something shines!
High in the valley, wet and drear,
The huts of Courrerie appear.

Strike leftward! cries our guide; and higher
Mounts up the stony forest-way. 20
At last the encircling trees retire;
Look! through the showery twilight grey
What pointed roofs are these advance?—
A palace of the Kings of France?

Approach, for what we seek is here!
Alight, and sparely sup, and wait
For rest in this outbuilding near;
Then cross the sward and reach that gate.
Knock; pass the wicket! Thou art come
To the Carthusians' world-famed home. 30

The silent courts, where night and day
Into their stone-carved basins cold
The splashing icy fountains play—
The humid corridors behold!
Where, ghostlike in the deepening night,
Cowl'd forms brush by in gleaming white.

The chapel, where no organ's peal
Invests the stern and naked prayer—
With penitential cries they kneel
And wrestle; rising then, with bare 40
And white uplifted faces stand,
Passing the Host from hand to hand;

Each takes, and then his visage wan
Is buried in his cowl once more.
The cells!—the suffering Son of Man
Upon the wall—the knee-worn floor—
And where they sleep, that wooden bed,
Which shall their coffin be, when dead!

The library, where tract and tome
Not to feed priestly pride are there,   50
To hymn the conquering march of Rome,
Nor yet to amuse, as ours are!
They paint of souls the inner strife,
Their drops of blood, their death in life.

The garden, overgrown—yet mild,
See, fragrant herbs are flowering there!
Strong children of the Alpine wild`
Whose culture is the brethren's care;
Of human tasks their only one,
And cheerful works beneath the sun.   60

Those halls, too, destined to contain
Each its own pilgrim-host of old,
From England, Germany, or Spain—
All are before me! I behold
The House, the Brotherhood austere!
—And what am I, that I am here?

For rigorous teachers seized my youth,
And purged its faith, and trimm'd its fire,
Show'd me the high, white star of Truth,
There bade me gaze, and there aspire.   70
Even now their whispers pierce the gloom:
What dost thou in this living tomb?

Forgive me, masters of the mind!
At whose behest I long ago
So much unlearnt, so much resign'd—
I come not here to be your foe!
I seek these anchorites, not in ruth,
To curse and to deny your truth;

Not as their friend, or child, I speak!
But as, on some far northern strand,   80
Thinking of his own Gods, a Greek
In pity and mournful awe might stand
Before some fallen Runic stone[2]
For both were faiths, and both are gone.

Wandering between two worlds, one dead,
The other powerless to be born,
With nowhere yet to rest my head,
Like these, on earth I wait forlorn.
Their faith, my tears, the world deride—
I come to shed them at their side.   90

Oh, hide me in your gloom profound,
Ye solemn seats of holy pain!
Take me, cowl'd forms, and fence me round,
Till I possess my soul again;
Till free my thoughts before me roll,
Not chafed by hourly false control!

For the world cries your faith is now
But a dead time's exploded dream;
My melancholy, sciolists[3] say,
Is a pass'd mode, an outworn theme—   100
As if the world had ever had
A faith, or sciolists been sad!

Ah, if it *be* pass'd, take away,
At least, the restlessness, the pain;
Be man henceforth no more a prey
To these out-dated stings again!
The nobleness of grief is gone—
Ah, leave us not the fret alone!

But—if you cannot give us ease—
Last of the race of them who grieve   110
Here leave us to die out with these
Last of the people who believe!
Silent, while years engrave the brow;
Silent—the best are silent now.

Achilles ponders in his tent,[4]
The kings of modern thought are dumb;
Silent they are, though not content,
And wait to see the future come.
They have the grief men had of yore,
But they contend and cry no more.   120

Our fathers water'd with their tears
This sea of time whereon we sail,
Their voices were in all men's ears
Who pass'd within their puissant hail.
Still the same ocean round us raves,
But we stand mute, and watch the waves.

For what avail'd it, all the noise
And outcry of the former men?—
Say, have their sons achieved more joys,
Say, is life lighter now than then?   130
The sufferers died, they left their pain—
The pangs which tortured them remain.

---

[2]**Runic stone**: stone inscribed in ancient Teutonic alphabet, associated with magic and mystery.

[3]**sciolists**: superficial pretenders to knowledge.

[4]In the *Iliad* **Achilles** sulks in his **tent**, refusing to fight because he has been slighted.

What helps it now, that Byron bore,
With haughty scorn which mock'd the smart,
Through Europe to the Ætolian shore[5]
The pageant of his bleeding heart?
That thousands counted every groan,
And Europe made his woe her own?

What boots it, Shelley! that the breeze
Carried thy lovely wail away,   140
Musical through Italian trees
Which fringe thy soft blue Spezzian bay?[6]
Inheritors of thy distress
Have restless hearts one throb the less?

Or are we easier, to have read,
O Obermann![7] the sad, stern page,
Which tells us how thou hidd'st thy head
From the fierce tempest of thine age
In the lone brakes of Fontainebleau,[8]
Or chalets near the Alpine snow?   150

Ye slumber in your silent grave!—
The world, which for an idle day
Grace to your mood of sadness gave,
Long since hath flung her weeds away.
The eternal trifler breaks your spell;
But we—we learnt your lore too well!

Years hence, perhaps, may dawn an age,
More fortunate, alas! than we,
Which without hardness will be sage,
And gay without frivolity.   160
Sons of the world, oh, speed those years;
But, while we wait, allow our tears!

Allow them! We admire with awe
The exulting thunder of your race;
You give the universe your law,
You triumph over time and space!
Your pride of life, your tireless powers,
We laud them, but they are not ours.

We are like children rear'd in shade
Beneath some old-world abbey wall,   170
Forgotten in a forest-glade,
And secret from the eyes of all.
Deep, deep the greenwood round them waves,
Their abbey, and its close of graves!

But, where the road runs near the stream,
Oft through the trees they catch a glance
Of passing troops in the sun's beam—
Pennon, and plume, and flashing lance!
Forth to the world those soldiers fare,
To life, to cities, and to war!   180

And through the wood, another way,
Faint bugle-notes from far are borne,
Where hunters gather, staghounds bay,
Round some fair forest-lodge at morn.
Gay dames are there, in sylvan green;
Laughter and cries—those notes between!

The banners flashing through the trees
Make their blood dance and chain their eyes;
That bugle-music on the breeze
Arrests them with a charm'd surprise.   190
Banner by turns and bugle woo:
Ye shy recluses, follow too!

O children, what do ye reply?—
"Action and pleasure, will ye roam
Through these secluded dells to cry
And call us?—but too late ye come!
Too late for us your call ye blow,
Whose bent was taken long ago.

"Long since we pace this shadow'd nave;
We watch those yellow tapers shine,   200
Emblems of hope over the grave,
In the high altar's depth divine;
The organ carries to our ear
Its accents of another sphere.

"Fenced early in this cloistral round
Of reverie, of shade, of prayer,
How should we grow in other ground?
How should we flower in foreign air?
—Pass, banners, pass, and bugles, cease;
And leave our desert[9] to its peace!"   210

                                                1855

---

[5]**Ætolian shore:** Byron died in Greece in 1824.

[6]**Spezzian bay:** Shelley drowned in the Gulf of Spezzia in 1822.

[7]**Obermann:** character created by Étienne Pivert de Senancour (1770–1846) whose melancholy musings on life and nature inspired Arnold to two poems and an essay.

[8]**brakes:** thickets. **Fontainebleau:** town in N France with a great chateau and extensive forest.

---

[9]**desert:** wilderness.

Thyrsis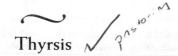

A monody, to commemorate the author's friend,
Arthur Hugh Clough, *who died at Florence,* 1861[1]

How changed is here each spot man makes or fills!
  In the two Hinkseys nothing keeps the same;
    The village street its haunted mansion lacks,
  And from the sign is gone Sibylla's name,[2]
    And from the roofs the twisted chimney-stacks—
      Are ye too changed, ye hills?
  See, 'tis no foot of unfamiliar men
    To-night from Oxford up your pathway strays!
  Here came I often, often, in old days—
Thyrsis and I; we still had Thyrsis then.   10

Runs it not here, the track by Childsworth Farm,
  Past the high wood, to where the elm-tree crowns
    The hill behind whose ridge the sunset flames?
  The signal-elm, that looks on Ilsley Downs,
    The Vale, the three lone weirs, the youthful
        Thames?—
      This winter-eve is warm,
  Humid the air! leafless, yet soft as spring,
    The tender purple spray on copse and briers!
  And that sweet city with her dreaming spires,
She needs not June for beauty's heightening,   20

Lovely all times she lies, lovely to-night!—
  Only, methinks, some loss of habit's power
    Befalls me wandering through this upland dim.
  Once pass'd I blindfold here, at any hour;
    Now seldom come I, since I came with him.
      That single elm-tree bright
  Against the west—I miss it! is it gone?
    We prized it dearly; while it stood, we said,
    Our friend, the Gipsy-Scholar, was not dead;
While the tree lived, he in these fields lived on.   30

Too rare, too rare, grow now my visits here,
  But once I knew each field, each flower, each stick;
    And with the country-folk acquaintance made
  By barn in threshing-time, by new-built rick.
    Here, too, our shepherd-pipes we first assay'd.
      Ah me! this many a year
  My pipe is lost, my shepherd's holiday!
    Needs must I lose them, needs with heavy heart
    Into the world and wave of men depart;
But Thyrsis of his own will went away.   40

It irk'd him to be here, he could not rest.
  He loved each simple joy the country yields,
    He loved his mates; but yet he could not keep,
  For that a shadow lour'd on the fields,
    Here with the shepherds and the silly sheep.
      Some life of men unblest
  He knew, which made him droop, and fill'd his head.
    He went; his piping took a troubled sound
    Of storms that rage outside our happy ground;
He could not wait their passing, he is dead.   50

So, some tempestuous morn in early June,
  When the year's primal burst of bloom is o'er,
    Before the roses and the longest day—
  When garden-walks and all the grassy floor
    With blossoms red and white of fallen May
      And chestnut-flowers are strewn—
  So have I heard the cuckoo's parting cry,
    From the wet field, through the vext garden-trees,
    Come with the volleying rain and tossing breeze:
  The bloom is gone, and with the bloom go I!   60

Too quick despairer, wherefore wilt thou go?
  Soon will the high Midsummer pomps come on,
    Soon will the musk carnations break and swell,
  Soon shall we have gold-dusted snapdragon,
    Sweet-William with his homely cottage-smell,
      And stocks in fragrant blow;
  Roses that down the alleys shine afar,
    And open, jasmine-muffled lattices,
    And groups under the dreaming garden-trees,
And the full moon, and the white evening-star.   70

He hearkens not! light comer, he is flown!
  What matters it? next year he will return,
    And we shall have him in the sweet spring-days,
  With whitening hedges, and uncrumpling fern,
    And blue-bells trembling by the forest-ways,
      And scent of hay new-mown.

---

[1]**Thyrsis**, a shepherd in Virgil's *Eclogues* 7, represents **Clough**, Arnold's closest friend at Oxford, who Arnold rather unfairly says had withdrawn from the problem-ridden modern world. The poem, like "The Scholar-Gipsy," is set in the Oxford countryside, to which the English place names refer.

[2]**Sibylla**: an innkeeper.

But Thyrsis never more we swains shall see;
  See him come back, and cut a smoother reed,
  And blow a strain the world at last shall heed—
For Time, not Corydon,[3] hath conquer'd thee!   80

Alack, for Corydon no rival now!—
  But when Sicilian shepherds lost a mate,
    Some good survivor with his flute would go,
  Piping a ditty sad for Bion's[4] fate;
    And cross the unpermitted ferry's flow,
      And relax Pluto's brow,
  And make leap up with joy the beauteous head
    Of Proserpine, among whose crowned hair
    Are flowers first open'd on Sicilian air,
And flute his friend, like Orpheus, from the dead.[5]   90

O easy access to the hearer's grace
  When Dorian shepherds sang to Proserpine!
    For she herself had trod Sicilian fields,
  She knew the Dorian water's gush divine,
    She knew each lily white which Enna yields,
      Each rose with blushing face;
  She loved the Dorian pipe, the Dorian strain.
    But ah, of our poor Thames she never heard![6]
    Her foot the Cumner cowslips never stirr'd;
And we should tease her with our plaint in vain!   100

Well! wind-dispersed and vain the words will be,
  Yet, Thyrsis, let me give my grief its hour
    In the old haunt, and find our tree-topp'd hill!
  Who, if not I, for questing here hath power?
    I know the wood which hides the daffodil,
      I know the Fyfield tree,
  I know what white, what purple fritillaries
    The grassy harvest of the river-fields,
    Above by Ensham, down by Sandford, yields,
And what sedged brooks are Thames's tributaries;   110

I know these slopes; who knows them if not I?—
  But many a dingle on the loved hill-side,
    With thorns once studded, old, white-blossom'd
      trees,
  Where thick the cowslips grew, and far descried
    High tower'd the spikes of purple orchises,
      Hath since our day put by
  The coronals of that forgotten time;
    Down each green bank hath gone the ploughboy's
      team,
    And only in the hidden brookside gleam
Primroses, orphans of the flowery prime.   120

Where is the girl, who by the boatman's door,
  Above the locks, above the boating throng,
    Unmoor'd our skiff when through the Wytham
      flats,
  Red loosestrife and blond meadow-sweet among
    And darting swallows and light water-gnats,
      We track'd the shy Thames shore?
  Where are the mowers, who, as the tiny swell
    Of our boat passing heaved the river-grass,
    Stood with suspended scythe to see us
      pass?—
They all are gone, and thou art gone as well!   130

Yes, thou art gone! and round me too the night
  In ever-nearing circle weaves her shade.
    I see her veil draw soft across the day,
  I feel her slowly chilling breath invade
    The cheek grown thin, the brown hair sprent with
      grey;
      I feel her finger light
  Laid pausefully upon life's headlong train;—
    The foot less prompt to meet the morning dew,
    The heart less bounding at emotion new,
And hope, once crush'd, less quick to spring
      again.   140

And long the way appears, which seem'd so short
  To the less practised eye of sanguine youth;
    And high the mountain-tops, in cloudy air,
  The mountain-tops where is the throne of Truth,
    Tops in life's morning-sun so bright and bare!
      Unbreachable the fort
  Of the long-batter'd world uplifts its wall;
    And strange and vain the earthly turmoil grows,
    And near and real the charm of thy repose,
And night as welcome as a friend would fall.   150

---

[3]**Corydon**: a shepherd who competes with Thyrsis in playing music on rustic pipes.

[4]**Bion**: Greek poet, 2nd century BCE, who according to the classical *Lament for Bion* lived mostly in Sicily.

[5]**unpermitted ferry's flow**: river Styx, which only the dead cross. **Pluto, Proserpine**: king and queen of the underworld. **Orpheus'** music won his dead wife back from the underworld.

[6]**Dorian**: ancient Greek. **Enna**: valley in Sicily associated with ancient cult of Proserpine. **Thames**: river of Oxford.

But hush! the upland hath a sudden loss
    Of quiet!—Look, adown the dusk hill-side,
       A troop of Oxford hunters going home,
    As in old days, jovial and talking, ride!
       From hunting with the Berkshire hounds they
          come.
        Quick! let me fly, and cross
   Into yon farther field!—'Tis done; and see,
       Back'd by the sunset, which doth glorify
       The orange and pale violet evening-sky,
   Bare on its lonely ridge, the Tree! the Tree!   160

I take the omen! Eve lets down her veil,
    The white fog creeps from bush to bush about,
       The west unflushes, the high stars grow bright,
    And in the scatter'd farms the lights come out.
       I cannot reach the signal-tree to-night,
         Yet, happy omen, hail!
   Hear it from thy broad lucent Arno-vale[7]
       (For there thine earth-forgetting eyelids keep
       The morningless and unawakening sleep
   Under the flowery oleanders pale),   170

Hear it, O Thyrsis, still our tree is there!—
    Ah, vain! These English fields, this upland dim,
       These brambles pale with mist engarlanded,
    That lone, sky-pointing tree, are not for him;
       To a boon southern country he is fled,
         And now in happier air,
   Wandering with the great Mother's[8] train divine
       (And purer or more subtle soul than thee,
       I trow, the mighty Mother doth not see)
   Within a folding of the Apennine,   180

Thou hearest the immortal chants of old!—
    Putting his sickle to the perilous grain
       In the hot cornfield of the Phrygian king,
    For thee the Lityerses-song again
       Young Daphnis with his silver voice doth sing;
        Sings his Sicilian fold,

His sheep, his hapless love, his blinded eyes—
    And how a call celestial round him rang,
       And heavenward from the fountain-brink he sprang,
   And all the marvel of the golden skies.[9]   190

There thou art gone, and me thou leavest here
    Sole in these fields! yet will I not despair.
       Despair I will not, while I yet descry
    'Neath the mild canopy of English air
       That lonely tree against the western sky.
         Still, still these slopes, 'tis clear,
   Our Gipsy-Scholar haunts, outliving thee!
       Fields where soft sheep from cages pull the hay,
       Woods with anemonies in flower till May,
   Know him a wanderer still; then why not me?   200

A fugitive and gracious light he seeks,
    Shy to illumine; and I seek it too.
       This does not come with houses or with gold,
   With place, with honour, and a flattering crew;
       'Tis not in the world's market bought and sold—
         But the smooth-slipping weeks
   Drop by, and leave its seeker still untired;
       Out of the heed of mortals he is gone,
       He wends unfollow'd, he must house alone;
   Yet on he fares, by his own heart inspired.   210

Thou too, O Thyrsis, on like quest wast bound;
    Thou wanderedst with me for a little hour!
       Men gave thee nothing; but this happy quest,
   If men esteem'd thee feeble, gave thee power,
       If men procured thee trouble, gave thee rest.
         And this rude Cumner ground,
   Its fir-topped Hurst, its farms, its quiet fields,
       Here cam'st thou in thy jocund youthful time,
       Here was thine height of strength, thy golden prime!
   And still the haunt beloved a virtue yields.   220

What though the music of thy rustic flute
    Kept not for long its happy, country tone;
       Lost it too soon, and learnt a stormy note
   Of men contention-tost, of men who groan,
       Which task'd thy pipe too sore, and tired thy throat—
         It fail'd, and thou wast mute!

---

[7]**Arno**: river of Florence, where Clough was buried.

[8]**great Mother**: Demeter, earth goddess and mother of Proserpine. **Apennine**: Italian mountain chain.

---

[9]**Daphnis**, a Sicilian shepherd, went to **Phrygia** in Asia Minor where the king **Lityerses** challenged newcomers to a grain-reaping contest in which the loser was put to death; Lityerses' death was the subject of a harvest-**song**. Daphnis was **blinded** by a jealous nymph and raised to heaven by his father, Hermes.

Yet hadst thou alway visions of our light,
    And long with men of care thou couldst not stay,
    And soon thy foot resumed its wandering way,
Left human haunt, and on alone till night.   230

Too rare, too rare, grow now my visits here!
  'Mid city-noise, not, as with thee of yore,
    Thyrsis! in reach of sheep-bells is my home.
—Then through the great town's harsh, heart-wearying
      roar,
    Let in thy voice a whisper often come,
      To chase fatigue and fear:
  Why faintest thou? I wander'd till I died.
    Roam on! The light we sought is shining still.
    Dost thou ask proof? Our tree yet crowns the hill,
Our Scholar travels yet the loved hill-side.   240

                                 1866

Dover Beach[1]

The sea is calm to-night.
The tide is full, the moon lies fair
Upon the straits;—on the French coast the light
Gleams and is gone; the cliffs of England stand,
Glimmering and vast, out in the tranquil bay.
Come to the window, sweet is the night-air!
Only, from the long line of spray
Where the sea meets the moon-blanch'd land,
Listen! you hear the grating roar
Of pebbles which the waves draw back, and fling,   10
At their return, up the high strand,
Begin, and cease, and then again begin,
With tremulous cadence slow, and bring
The eternal note of sadness in.

Sophocles[2] long ago
Heard it on the Ægæan, and it brought
Into his mind the turbid ebb and flow
Of human misery; we
Find also in the sound a thought,
Hearing it by this distant northern sea.   20

The Sea of Faith
Was once, too, at the full, and round earth's shore
Lay like the folds of a bright girdle[3] furl'd.
But now I only hear
Its melancholy, long, withdrawing roar,
Retreating, to the breath
Of the night-wind, down the vast edges drear
And naked shingles[4] of the world.

Ah, love, let us be true
To one another! for the world, which seems   30
To lie before us like a land of dreams,
So various, so beautiful, so new,
Hath really neither joy, nor love, nor light,
Nor certitude, nor peace, nor help for pain;
And we are here as on a darkling plain
Swept with confused alarms of struggle and flight,
Where ignorant armies clash by night.[5]
   1851?   *1867*

Preface to *Poems*, 1853

In two small volumes of Poems, published anonymously, one in 1849, the other in 1852, many of the poems which compose the present volume have already appeared. The rest are now published for the first time.

    I have, in the present collection, omitted the poem[1] from which the volume published in 1852 took its title. I have done so, not because the subject of it was a Sicilian Greek born between two and three thousand years ago, although many persons would think this a sufficient reason. Neither have I done so because I had, in my own opinion, failed in the delineation which I intended to effect. I intended to delineate the feelings of one of the last of the Greek religious philosophers, one of the family of Orpheus

---

[1]**Dover:** main port for crossing the English Channel to France. In 1851 Arnold and his wife visited Dover soon after their marriage and again during their honeymoon.

[2]**Sophocles:** Greek dramatist, 5th century BCE.

---

[3]**girdle:** belt, sash.

[4]**shingles:** pebbly beaches.

[5]**ignorant . . . night:** allusion to Thucydides' history of the Peloponnesian War (5th century BCE).

[1]**poem:** *Empedocles on Etna,* a closet drama about an ancient Greek philosopher in whom thought has overworn feeling and who leaps into the volcano to be reunited with the universe. This is Arnold's first and most severely classicizing critical essay, prescribing a kind of poetry he himself could not write and proscribing the kind he did.

and Musaeus,[2] having survived his fellows, living on into a time when the habits of Greek thought and feeling had begun fast to change, character to dwindle, the influence of the Sophists to prevail. Into the feelings of a man so situated there entered much that we are accustomed to consider as exclusively modern; how much, the fragments of Empedocles himself which remain to us are sufficient at least to indicate. What those who are familiar only with the great monuments of early Greek genius suppose to be its exclusive characteristics, have disappeared; the calm, the cheerfulness, the disinterested objectivity have disappeared; the dialogue of the mind with itself has commenced; modern problems have presented themselves; we hear already the doubts, we witness the discouragement, of Hamlet and of Faust.[3]

The representation of such a man's feelings must be interesting, if consistently drawn. We all naturally take pleasure, says Aristotle,[4] in any imitation or representation whatever: this is the basis of our love of poetry: and we take pleasure in them, he adds, because all knowledge is naturally agreeable to us; not to the philosopher only, but to mankind at large. Every representation therefore which is consistently drawn may be supposed to be interesting, inasmuch as it gratifies this natural interest in knowledge of all kinds. What is *not* interesting, is that which does not add to our knowledge of any kind; that which is vaguely conceived and loosely drawn; a representation which is general, indeterminate, and faint, instead of being particular, precise, and firm.

Any accurate representation may therefore be expected to be interesting; but, if the representation be a poetical one, more than this is demanded. It is demanded, not only that it shall interest, but also that it shall inspirit and rejoice the reader: that it shall convey a charm, and infuse delight. For the Muses, as Hesiod[5] says, were born that they might be "a forgetfulness of evils, and a truce from cares": and it is not enough that the poet should add to the knowledge of men, it is required of him also that he should add to their happiness. "All Art," says Schiller,[6] "is dedicated to Joy, and there is no higher and no more serious problem, than how to make men happy. The right Art is that alone, which creates the highest enjoyment."

A poetical work, therefore, is not yet justified when it has been shown to be an accurate, and therefore interesting representation; it has to be shown also that it is a representation from which men can derive enjoyment. In presence of the most tragic circumstances, represented in a work of Art, the feeling of enjoyment, as is well known, may still subsist: the representation of the most utter calamity, of the liveliest anguish, is not sufficient to destroy it: the more tragic the situation, the deeper becomes the enjoyment; and the situation is more tragic in proportion as it becomes more terrible.

What then are the situations, from the representation of which, though accurate, no poetical enjoyment can be derived? They are those in which the suffering finds no vent in action; in which a continuous state of mental distress is prolonged, unrelieved by incident, hope, or resistance; in which there is everything to be endured, nothing to be done. In such situations there is inevitably something morbid, in the description of them something monotonous. When they occur in actual life, they are painful, not tragic; the representation of them in poetry is painful also.

To this class of situations, poetically faulty as it appears to me, that of Empedocles, as I have endeavoured to represent him, belongs; and I have therefore excluded the poem from the present collection.

And why, it may be asked, have I entered into this explanation respecting a matter so unimportant as the admission or exclusion of the poem in question? I have done so, because I was anxious to avow that the sole reason for its exclusion was that which has been stated above; and that it has not been excluded in deference to the opinion which many critics of the present day appear to entertain against subjects chosen from distant times and countries: against the choice, in short, of any subjects but modern ones.

"The poet," it is said, and by an intelligent critic,[7] "the poet who would really fix the public attention must leave the exhausted past, and draw his subjects from matters of present import, and *therefore* both of interest and novelty."

Now this view I believe to be completely false. It is worth examining, inasmuch as it is a fair sample of a class of critical dicta everywhere current at the present day, having a philosophical form and air, but no real basis in fact; and which are calculated to vitiate the judgement of readers of poetry, while they exert, so far as they are adopted, a misleading influence on the practice of those who make it.

---

[2]**Orpheus, Musaeus:** legendary Greek poets.

[3]**Faust:** in *Faust* (1808, 1832) by Johann Wolfgang von Goethe (1749–1832).

[4]**Aristotle:** in *Poetics*.

[5]**Hesiod:** Greek poet, 7th century BCE.

[6]Friedrich von **Schiller** (1759–1805): German dramatist, poet, critic.

---

[7]**critic:** Robert S. Rintoul (1787–1858) in *The Spectator* (1853).

What are the eternal objects of poetry, among all nations and at all times? They are actions; human actions; possessing an inherent interest in themselves, and which are to be communicated in an interesting manner by the art of the poet. Vainly will the latter imagine that he has everything in his own power; that he can make an intrinsically inferior action equally delightful with a more excellent one by his treatment of it. He may indeed compel us to admire his skill, but his work will possess, within itself, an incurable defect.

The poet, then, has in the first place to select an excellent action; and what actions are the most excellent? Those, certainly, which most powerfully appeal to the great primary human affections: to those elementary feelings which subsist permanently in the race, and which are independent of time. These feelings are permanent and the same; that which interests them is permanent and the same also. The modernness or antiquity of an action, therefore, has nothing to do with its fitness for poetical representation; this depends upon its inherent qualities. To the elementary part of our nature, to our passions, that which is great and passionate is eternally interesting; and interesting solely in proportion to its greatness and to its passion. A great human action of a thousand years ago is more interesting to it than a smaller human action of to-day, even though upon the representation of this last the most consummate skill may have been expended, and though it has the advantage of appealing by its modern language, familiar manners, and contemporary allusions, to all our transient feelings and interests. These, however, have no right to demand of a poetical work that it shall satisfy them; their claims are to be directed elsewhere. Poetical works belong to the domain of our permanent passions: let them interest these, and the voice of all subordinate claims upon them is at once silenced.

Achilles, Prometheus, Clytemnestra, Dido[8]—what modern poem presents personages as interesting, even to us moderns, as these personages of an "exhausted past"? We have the domestic epic dealing with the details of modern life which pass daily under our eyes; we have poems representing modern personages in contact with the problems of modern life, moral, intellectual, and social; these works have been produced by poets the most distinguished of their nation and time; yet I fearlessly assert that *Hermann and Dorothea, Childe Harold, Jocelyn, The Excursion,* leave the reader cold in comparison with the effect produced upon him by the latter books of the *Iliad,* by the *Oresteia,* or by the episode of Dido.[9] And why is this? Simply because in the three last-named cases the action is greater, the personages nobler, the situations more intense: and this is the true basis of the interest in a poetical work, and this alone.

It may be urged, however, that past actions may be interesting in themselves, but that they are not to be adopted by the modern poet, because it is impossible for him to have them clearly present to his own mind, and he cannot therefore feel them deeply, nor represent them forcibly. But this is not necessarily the case. The externals of a past action, indeed, he cannot know with the precision of a contemporary; but his business is with its essentials. The outward man of Oedipus[10] or of Macbeth, the houses in which they lived, the ceremonies of their courts, he cannot accurately figure to himself; but neither do they essentially concern him. His business is with their inward man; with their feelings and behaviour in certain tragic situations, which engage their passions as men; these have in them nothing local and casual; they are as accessible to the modern poet as to a contemporary.

The date of an action, then, signifies nothing: the action itself, its selection and construction, this is what is all-important. This the Greeks understood far more clearly than we do. The radical difference between their poetical theory and ours consists, as it appears to me, in this: that, with them, the poetical character of the action in itself, and the conduct of it, was the first consideration; with us, attention is fixed mainly on the value of the separate thoughts and images which occur in the treatment of an action. They regarded the whole; we regard the parts. With them, the action predominated over the expression of it; with us, the expression predominates over the action. Not that they failed in expression, or were inattentive to it; on the contrary, they are the highest models of expression, the unapproached masters of the *grand style.* But their expression is so excellent because it is so admirably kept in its right degree of prominence; because it is so simple and so well subordinated; because it draws its force directly from the pregnancy of the matter which it conveys. For what reason was the Greek tragic poet confined to so limited a range of subjects? Because there are so few actions which unite in themselves, in the highest degree, the conditions of excellence:

[8]**Achilles, Prometheus, Clytemnestra, Dido**: in Homer's *Iliad,* Aeschylus' *Prometheus Bound* and *Agamemnon,* Virgil's *Aeneid.*

[9]*Hermann and Dorothea, Childe Harold, Jocelyn, The Excursion*: long poems by Goethe (1797), Byron (1812–1818), Lamartine (1836), Wordsworth (1814). *Oresteia*: trilogy by Aeschylus, which includes the *Agamemnon.*

[10]**Oedipus**: in Sophocles' *Oedipus the King* and *Oedipus at Colonus.*

and it was not thought that on any but an excellent subject could an excellent poem be constructed. A few actions, therefore, eminently adapted for tragedy, maintained almost exclusive possession of the Greek tragic stage. Their significance appeared inexhaustible; they were as permanent problems, perpetually offered to the genius of every fresh poet. This too is the reason of what appears to us moderns a certain baldness of expression in Greek tragedy; of the triviality with which we often reproach the remarks of the chorus, where it takes part in the dialogue: that the action itself, the situation of Orestes, or Merope, or Alcmaeon,[11] was to stand the central point of interest, unforgotten, absorbing, principal; that no accessories were for a moment to distract the spectator's attention from this; that the tone of the parts was to be perpetually kept down, in order not to impair the grandiose effect of the whole. The terrible old mythic story on which the drama was founded stood, before he entered the theatre, traced in its bare outlines upon the spectator's mind; it stood in his memory, as a group of statuary, faintly seen, at the end of a long and dark vista: then came the poet, embodying outlines, developing situations, not a word wasted, not a sentiment capriciously thrown in: stroke upon stroke, the drama proceeded: the light deepened upon the group; more and more it revealed itself to the rivetted gaze of the spectator: until at last, when the final words were spoken, it stood before him in broad sunlight, a model of immortal beauty.

This was what a Greek critic demanded; this was what a Greek poet endeavoured to effect. It signified nothing to what time an action belonged. We do not find that the *Persae* occupied a particularly high rank among the dramas of Aeschylus, because it represented a matter of contemporary interest: this was not what a cultivated Athenian required. He required that the permanent elements of his nature should be moved; and dramas of which the action, though taken from a long-distant mythic time, yet was calculated to accomplish this in a higher degree than that of the *Persae*, stood higher in his estimation accordingly. The Greeks felt, no doubt, with their exquisite sagacity of taste, that an action of present times was too near them, too much mixed up with what was accidental and passing, to form a sufficiently grand, detached, and self-subsistent object for a tragic poem. Such objects belonged to the domain of the comic poet, and of the lighter kinds of poetry. For the more serious kinds, for *pragmatic* poetry, to use an excellent expres-

sion of Polybius,[12] they were more difficult and severe in the range of subjects which they permitted. Their theory and practice alike, the admirable treatise of Aristotle, and the unrivalled works of their poets, exclaim with a thousand tongues—"All depends upon the subject; choose a fitting action, penetrate yourself with the feeling of its situations; this done, everything else will follow."

But for all kinds of poetry alike there was one point on which they were rigidly exacting; the adaptability of the subject to the kind of poetry selected, and the careful construction of the poem.

How different a way of thinking from this is ours! We can hardly at the present day understand what Menander[13] meant, when he told a man who inquired as to the progress of his comedy that he had finished it, not having yet written a single line, because he had constructed the action of it in his mind. A modern critic would have assured him that the merit of his piece depended on the brilliant things which arose under his pen as he went along. We have poems which seem to exist merely for the sake of single lines and passages; not for the sake of producing any total-impression. We have critics who seem to direct their attention merely to detached expressions, to the language about the action, not to the action itself. I verily think that the majority of them do not in their hearts believe that there is such a thing as a total-impression to be derived from a poem at all, or to be demanded from a poet; they think the term a common-place of metaphysical criticism. They will permit the poet to select any action he pleases, and to suffer that action to go as it will, provided he gratifies them with occasional bursts of fine writing, and with a shower of isolated thoughts and images. That is, they permit him to leave their poetical sense ungratified, provided that he gratifies their rhetorical sense and their curiosity. Of his neglecting to gratify these, there is little danger. He needs rather to be warned against the danger of attempting to gratify these alone; he needs rather to be perpetually reminded to prefer his action to everything else; so to treat this, as to permit its inherent excellences to develop themselves, without interruption from the intrusion of his personal peculiarities: most fortunate, when he most entirely succeeds in effacing himself, and in enabling a noble action to subsist as it did in nature.

---

[11]**Orestes, Merope, Alcmaeon:** named by Aristotle's *Poetics* as subjects of Greek tragedies.

[12]**Polybius (?200–?118 BCE):** **Greek** historian of Rome who called his histories **pragmatic.**

[13]**Menander:** Athenian writer of comedies, 4th-3rd centuries BCE.

But the modern critic not only permits a false practice; he absolutely prescribes false aims.—"A true allegory of the state of one's own mind in a representative history," the poet is told, "is perhaps the highest thing that one can attempt in the way of poetry."—And accordingly he attempts it. An allegory of the state of one's own mind, the highest problem of an art which imitates actions! No assuredly, it is not, it never can be so: no great poetical work has ever been produced with such an aim. *Faust* itself, in which something of the kind is attempted, wonderful passages as it contains, and in spite of the unsurpassed beauty of the scenes which relate to Margaret, *Faust* itself, judged as a whole, and judged strictly as a poetical work, is defective: its illustrious author, the greatest poet of modern times, the greatest critic of all times, would have been the first to acknowledge it; he only defended his work, indeed, by asserting it to be "something incommensurable."

The confusion of the present times is great, the multitude of voices counselling different things bewildering, the number of existing works capable of attracting a young writer's attention and of becoming his models, immense. What he wants is a hand to guide him through the confusion, a voice to prescribe to him the aim which he should keep in view, and to explain to him that the value of the literary works which offer themselves to his attention is relative to their power of helping him forward on his road towards this aim. Such a guide the English writer at the present day will nowhere find. Failing this, all that can be looked for, all indeed that can be desired, is, that his attention should be fixed on excellent models; that he may reproduce, at any rate, something of their excellence, by penetrating himself with their works and by catching their spirit, if he cannot be taught to produce what is excellent independently.

Foremost among these models for the English writer stands Shakespeare: a name the greatest perhaps of all poetical names; a name never to be mentioned without reverence. I will venture, however, to express a doubt, whether the influence of his works, excellent and fruitful for the readers of poetry, for the great majority, has been of unmixed advantage to the writers of it. Shakespeare indeed chose excellent subjects; the world could afford no better than Macbeth, or Romeo and Juliet, or Othello: he had no theory respecting the necessity of choosing subjects of present import, or the paramount interest attaching to allegories of the state of one's own mind; like all great poets, he knew well what constituted a poetical action; like them, wherever he found such an action, he took it; like them, too, he found his best in past times. But to these general characteristics of all great poets he added a special one of

his own; a gift, namely, of happy, abundant, and ingenious expression, eminent and unrivalled: so eminent as irresistibly to strike the attention first in him, and even to throw into comparative shade his other excellences as a poet. Here has been the mischief. These other excellences were his fundamental excellences *as a poet;* what distinguishes the artist from the mere amateur, says Goethe, is *Architectonicè* in the highest sense; that power of execution, which creates, forms, and constitutes: not the profoundness of single thoughts, not the richness of imagery, not the abundance of illustration. But these attractive accessories of a poetical work being more easily seized than the spirit of the whole, and these accessories being possessed by Shakespeare in an unequalled degree, a young writer having recourse to Shakespeare as his model runs great risk of being vanquished and absorbed by them, and, in consequence, of reproducing, according to the measure of his power, these, and these alone. Of this preponderating quality of Shakespeare's genius, accordingly, almost the whole of modern English poetry has, it appears to me, felt the influence. To the exclusive attention on the part of his imitators to this it is in a great degree owing, that of the majority of modern poetical works the details alone are valuable, the composition worthless. In reading them one is perpetually reminded of that terrible sentence on a modern French poet—*il dit tout ce qu'il veut, mais malheureusement il n'a rien à dire.*[14]

Let me give an instance of what I mean. I will take it from the works of the very chief among those who seem to have been formed in the school of Shakespeare: of one whose exquisite genius and pathetic death render him for ever interesting. I will take the poem of *Isabella, or the Pot of Basil,* by Keats. I choose this rather than the *Endymion,* because the latter work (which a modern critic has classed with the *Fairy Queen!*),[15] although undoubtedly there blows through it the breath of genius, is yet as a whole so utterly incoherent, as not strictly to merit the name of a poem at all. The poem of *Isabella,* then, is a perfect treasure-house of graceful and felicitous words and images: almost in every stanza there occurs one of those vivid and picturesque turns of expression, by which the object is made to flash upon the eye of the mind, and which thrill the reader with a sudden delight. This one short poem contains, perhaps, a greater number of happy single expressions which one could quote than all the extant tragedies of Sophocles. But the action, the story? The action in itself is an excellent one; but so feebly is

---

[14]*Il dit . . . à dire:* He says whatever he wants, but unfortunately he has nothing to say.

[15]*Fairy Queen:* Edmund Spenser's *The Faerie Queene* (1590–1596).

it conceived by the poet, so loosely constructed, that the effect produced by it, in and for itself, is absolutely null. Let the reader, after he has finished the poem of Keats, turn to the same story in the *Decameron*:[16] he will then feel how pregnant and interesting the same action has become in the hands of a great artist, who above all things delineates his object; who subordinates expression to that which it is designed to express.

I have said that the imitators of Shakespeare, fixing their attention on his wonderful gift of expression, have directed their imitation to this, neglecting his other excellences. These excellences, the fundamental excellences of poetical art, Shakespeare no doubt possessed them—possessed many of them in a splendid degree; but it may perhaps be doubted whether even he himself did not sometimes give scope to his faculty of expression to the prejudice of a higher poetical duty. For we must never forget that Shakespeare is the great poet he is from his skill in discerning and firmly conceiving an excellent action, from his power of intensely feeling a situation, of intimately associating himself with a character; not from his gift of expression, which rather even leads him astray, degenerating sometimes into a fondness for curiosity of expression, into an irritability of fancy, which seems to make it impossible for him to say a thing plainly, even when the press of the action demands the very directest language, or its level character the very simplest. Mr. Hallam,[17] than whom it is impossible to find a saner and more judicious critic, has had the courage (for at the present day it needs courage) to remark, how extremely and faultily difficult Shakespeare's language often is. It is so: you may find main scenes in some of his greatest tragedies, *King Lear* for instance, where the language is so artificial, so curiously tortured, and so difficult, that every speech has to be read two or three times before its meaning can be comprehended. This over-curiousness of expression is indeed but the excessive employment of a wonderful gift—of the power of saying a thing in a happier way than any other man; nevertheless, it is carried so far that one understands what M. Guizot[18] meant, when he said that Shakespeare appears in his language to have tried all styles except that of simplicity. He has not the severe and scrupulous self-restraint of the ancients, partly no doubt, because he had a far less cultivated and exacting audience. He

has indeed a far wider range than they had, a far richer fertility of thought; in this respect he rises above them. In his strong conception of his subject, in the genuine way in which he is penetrated with it, he resembles them, and is unlike the moderns. But in the accurate limitation of it, the conscientious rejection of superfluities, the simple and rigorous development of it from the first line of his work to the last, he falls below them, and comes nearer to the moderns. In his chief works, besides what he has of his own, he has the elementary soundness of the ancients; he has their important action and their large and broad manner: but he has not their purity of method. He is therefore a less safe model; for what he has of his own is personal, and inseparable from his own rich nature; it may be imitated and exaggerated, it cannot be learned or applied as an art. He is above all suggestive; more valuable, therefore, to young writers as men than as artists. But clearness of arrangement, rigour of development, simplicity of style—these may to a certain extent be learned: and these may, I am convinced, be learned best from the ancients, who although infinitely less suggestive than Shakespeare, are thus, to the artist, more instructive.

What, then, it will be asked, are the ancients to be our sole models? the ancients with their comparatively narrow range of experience, and their widely different circumstances? Not, certainly, that which is narrow in the ancients, nor that in which we can no longer sympathize. An action like the action of the *Antigone* of Sophocles, which turns upon the conflict between the heroine's duty to her brother's corpse and that to the laws of her country, is no longer one in which it is possible that we should feel a deep interest. I am speaking too, it will be remembered, not of the best sources of intellectual stimulus for the general reader, but of the best models of instruction for the individual writer. This last may certainly learn of the ancients, better than anywhere else, three things which it is vitally important for him to know:—the all-importance of the choice of a subject; the necessity of accurate construction; and the subordinate character of expression. He will learn from them how unspeakably superior is the effect of the one moral impression left by a great action treated as a whole, to the effect produced by the most striking single thought or by the happiest image. As he penetrates into the spirit of the great classical works, as he becomes gradually aware of their intense significance, their noble simplicity, and their calm pathos, he will be convinced that it is this effect, unity and profoundness of moral impression, at which the ancient poets aimed; that it is this which constitutes the grandeur of their works, and which makes them immortal. He will desire to direct his own efforts towards producing the same effect. Above all, he will deliver himself from the jargon of

---

[16]*Decameron*: collection of stories by Giovanni Boccaccio (1313–1375).

[17]Henry **Hallam** (1777–1859): historian.

[18]François **Guizot** (1787–1874): French political leader and historian.

modern criticism, and escape the danger of producing poetical works conceived in the spirit of the passing time, and which partake of its transitoriness.

The present age makes great claims upon us: we owe it service, it will not be satisfied without our admiration. I know not how it is, but their commerce with the ancients appears to me to produce, in those who constantly practice it, a steadying and composing effect upon their judgement, not of literary works only, but of men and events in general. They are like persons who have had a very weighty and impressive experience: they are more truly than others under the empire of facts, and more independent of the language current among those with whom they live. They wish neither to applaud nor to revile their age: they wish to know what it is, what it can give them, and whether this is what they want. What they want, they know very well; they want to educe and cultivate what is best and noblest in themselves: they know, too, that this is no easy task— χαλεπὸν, as Pittacus said, χαλεπὸν ἐσθλὸν ἔμμεναι[19]— and they ask themselves sincerely whether their age and its literature can assist them in the attempt. If they are endeavouring to practice any art, they remember the plain and simple proceedings of the old artists, who attained their grand results by penetrating themselves with some noble and significant action, not by inflating themselves with a belief in the pre-eminent importance and greatness of their own times. They do not talk of their mission, nor of interpreting their age, nor of the coming poet; all this, they know, is the mere delirium of vanity; their business is not to praise their age, but to afford to the men who live in it the highest pleasure which they are capable of feeling. If asked to afford this by means of subjects drawn from the age itself, they ask what special fitness the present age has for supplying them. They are told that it is an era of progress, an age commissioned to carry out the great ideas of industrial development and social amelioration. They reply that with all this they can do nothing; that the elements they need for the exercise of their art are great actions, calculated powerfully and delightfully to affect what is permanent in the human soul; that so far as the present age can supply such actions, they will gladly make use of them; but that an age wanting in moral grandeur can with difficulty supply such, and an age of spiritual discomfort with difficulty be powerfully and delightfully affected by them.

A host of voices will indignantly rejoin that the present age is inferior to the past neither in moral grandeur nor in spiritual health. He who possesses the discipline I speak of will content himself with remembering the judgements passed upon the present age, in this respect, by the two men, the one of strongest head, the other of widest culture, whom it has produced; by Goethe and by Niebuhr.[20] It will be sufficient for him that he knows the opinions held by these two great men respecting the present age and its literature; and that he feels assured in his own mind that their aims and demands upon life were such as he would wish, at any rate, his own to be; and their judgement as to what is impeding and disabling such as he may safely follow. He will not, however, maintain a hostile attitude towards the false pretensions of his age; he will content himself with not being overwhelmed by them. He will esteem himself fortunate if he can succeed in banishing from his mind all feelings of contradiction, and irritation, and impatience; in order to delight himself with the contemplation of some noble action of a heroic time, and to enable others, through his representation of it, to delight in it also.

I am far indeed from making any claim, for myself, that I possess this discipline; or for the following poems, that they breathe its spirit. But I say, that in the sincere endeavour to learn and practice, amid the bewildering confusion of our times, what is sound and true in poetical art, I seemed to myself to find the only sure guidance, the only solid footing, among the ancients. They, at any rate, knew what they wanted in Art, and we do not. It is this uncertainty which is disheartening, and not hostile criticism. How often have I felt this when reading words of disparagement or of cavil: that it is the uncertainty as to what is really to be aimed at which makes our difficulty, not the dissatisfaction of the critic, who himself suffers from the same uncertainty. *Non me tua fervida terrent Dicta; Dii me terrent, et Jupiter hostis.*[21]

Two kinds of *dilettanti*, says Goethe, there are in poetry: he who neglects the indispensable mechanical part, and thinks he has done enough if he shows spirituality and feeling; and he who seeks to arrive at poetry merely by mechanism, in which he can acquire an artisan's readiness, and is without soul and matter. And he adds, that the first does most harm to Art, and the last to himself. If we must be *dilettanti*: if it is impossible for us, under the circumstances amidst which we live, to think clearly, to feel nobly, and to delineate firmly: if we cannot attain to the mastery of the great artists—let us, at least, have so much respect for our Art as to prefer it to

---

[19] χαλεπὸν ἐσθλὸν ἔμμεναι: It is hard to be excellent. **Pittacus**: Greek statesman and sage, 7th century BCE.

[20] Barthold **Niebuhr** (1776–1831): German historian of ancient Rome.

[21] *Non me . . . Jupiter hostis:* Your fiery words don't scare me; the gods scare me, and Jupiter my enemy (*Aeneid* 12.894–95).

ourselves: let us not bewilder our successors: let us transmit to them the practice of Poetry, with its boundaries and wholesome regulative laws, under which excellent works may again, perhaps, at some future time, be produced, not yet fallen into oblivion through our neglect, not yet condemned and cancelled by the influence of their eternal enemy, Caprice.

1853

~

The Function of Criticism at the Present Time

Many objections have been made to a proposition which, in some remarks of mine on translating Homer, I ventured to put forth; a proposition about criticism, and its importance at the present day. I said: "Of the literature of France and Germany, as of the intellect of Europe in general, the main effort, for now many years, has been a critical effort; the endeavour, in all branches of knowledge, theology, philosophy, history, art, science, to see the object as in itself it really is."[1] I added, that owing to the operation in English literature of certain causes, "almost the last thing for which one would come to English literature is just that very thing which now Europe most desires,—criticism"; and that the power and value of English literature was thereby impaired. More than one rejoinder declared that the importance I here assigned to criticism was excessive, and asserted the inherent superiority of the creative effort of the human spirit over its critical effort. And the other day, having been led by Mr. Shairp's excellent notice of Wordsworth[2] to turn again to his biography, I found, in the words of this great man, whom I, for one, must always listen to with the pro-

foundest respect, a sentence passed on the critic's business, which seems to justify every possible disparagement of it. Wordsworth says in one of his letters:

"The writers in these publications" (the Reviews), "while they prosecute their inglorious employment, cannot be supposed to be in a state of mind very favourable for being affected by the finer influences of a thing so pure as genuine poetry."

And a trustworthy reporter of his conversation quotes a more elaborate judgment to the same effect:

"Wordsworth holds the critical power very low, infinitely lower than the inventive; and he said to-day that if the quantity of time consumed in writing critiques on the works of others were given to original composition, of whatever kind it might be, it would be much better employed; it would make a man find out sooner his own level, and it would do infinitely less mischief. A false or malicious criticism may do much injury to the minds of others; a stupid invention, either in prose or verse, is quite harmless."

It is almost too much to expect of poor human nature, that a man capable of producing some effect in one line of literature, should, for the greater good of society, voluntarily doom himself to impotence and obscurity in another. Still less is this to be expected from men addicted to the composition of the "false or malicious criticism" of which Wordsworth speaks. However, everybody would admit that a false or malicious criticism had better never have been written. Everybody, too, would be willing to admit, as a general proposition, that the critical faculty is lower than the inventive. But is it true that criticism is really, in itself, a baneful and injurious employment; is it true that all time given to writing critiques on the works of others would be much better employed if it were given to original composition, of whatever kind this may be? Is it true that Johnson had better have gone on producing more *Irenes* instead of writing his *Lives of the Poets*;[3] is it certain that Wordsworth himself was better employed in making his Ecclesiastical Sonnets than when he made his celebrated Preface so full of criticism, and criticism of the works of others? Wordsworth was himself a great critic, and it is to be sincerely regretted that he has not left us more criticism; Goethe[4] was one of the greatest of critics, and we may sincerely congratulate ourselves that he has left us so much criticism. Without

---

[1]**"Of the literature . . . really is"**: *On Translating Homer* (1861), Lecture 2.

[2]I cannot help thinking that a practice, common in England during the last century, and still followed in France, of printing a notice of this kind,—a notice by a competent critic,—to serve as an introduction to an eminent author's works, might be revived among us with advantage. To introduce all succeeding editions of Wordsworth, Mr. Shairp's notice might, it seems to me, excellently serve; it is written from the point of view of an admirer, nay, of a disciple, and that is right; but then the disciple must be also, as in this case he is, a critic, a man of letters, not, as too often happens, some relation or friend with no qualification for his task except affection for his author. John Campbell **Shairp** (1819–1885): college friend of Arnold's. **notice:** *North British Review*, 1864.

[3]Samuel **Johnson** (1709–1784). *Irene: A Tragedy* (1749). *Lives of the English Poets* (1779, 1781).

[4]Johann Wolfgang von **Goethe** (1749–1832): German Romantic poet and novelist.

wasting time over the exaggeration which Wordsworth's judgment on criticism clearly contains, or over an attempt to trace the causes,—not difficult, I think, to be traced,—which may have led Wordsworth to this exaggeration, a critic may with advantage seize an occasion for trying his own conscience, and for asking himself of what real service, at any given moment, the practice of criticism either is or may be made to his own mind and spirit, and to the minds and spirits of others.

The critical power is of lower rank than the creative. True; but in assenting to this proposition, one or two things are to be kept in mind. It is undeniable that the exercise of a creative power, that a free creative activity, is the highest function of man; it is proved to be so by man's finding in it his true happiness. But it is undeniable, also, that men may have the sense of exercising this free creative activity in other ways than in producing great works of literature or art; if it were not so, all but a very few men would be shut out from the true happiness of all men. They may have it in well-doing, they may have it in learning, they may have it even in criticising. This is one thing to be kept in mind. Another is, that the exercise of the creative power in the production of great works of literature or art, however high this exercise of it may rank, is not at all epochs and under all conditions possible; and that therefore labour may be vainly spent in attempting it, which might with more fruit be used in preparing for it, in rendering it possible. This creative power works with elements, with materials; what if it has not those materials, those elements, ready for its use? In that case it must surely wait till they are ready. Now, in literature,—I will limit myself to literature, for it is about literature that the question arises,—the elements with which the creative power works are ideas; the best ideas on every matter which literature touches, current at the time. At any rate we may lay it down as certain that in modern literature no manifestation of the creative power not working with these can be very important or fruitful. And I say *current* at the time, not merely accessible at the time; for creative literary genius does not principally show itself in discovering new ideas, that is rather the business of the philosopher. The grand work of literary genius is a work of synthesis and exposition, not of analysis and discovery; its gift lies in the faculty of being happily inspired by a certain intellectual and spiritual atmosphere, by a certain order of ideas, when it finds itself in them; of dealing divinely with these ideas, presenting them in the most effective and attractive combinations,—making beautiful works with them, in short. But it must have the atmosphere, it must find itself amidst the order of ideas, in order to work freely; and these it is not so easy to command. This is why great creative epochs in literature are so rare, this is why there is so much that is unsatisfactory in the productions of many men of real genius; because, for the creation of a master-work of literature two powers must concur, the power of the man and the power of the moment, and the man is not enough without the moment; the creative power has, for its happy exercise, appointed elements, and those elements are not in its own control.

Nay, they are more within the control of the critical power. It is the business of the critical power, as I said in the words already quoted, "in all branches of knowledge, theology, philosophy, history, art, science, to see the object as in itself it really is." Thus it tends, at last, to make an intellectual situation of which the creative power can profitably avail itself. It tends to establish an order of ideas, if not absolutely true, yet true by comparison with that which it displaces; to make the best ideas prevail. Presently these new ideas reach society, the touch of truth is the touch of life, and there is a stir and growth everywhere; out of this stir and growth come the creative epochs of literature.

Or, to narrow our range, and quit these considerations of the general march of genius and of society,—considerations which are apt to become too abstract and impalpable,—every one can see that a poet, for instance, ought to know life and the world before dealing with them in poetry; and life and the world being in modern times very complex things, the creation of a modern poet, to be worth much, implies a great critical effort behind it; else it must be a comparatively poor, barren, and short-lived affair. This is why Byron's poetry had so little endurance in it, and Goethe's so much; both Byron and Goethe had a great productive power, but Goethe's was nourished by a great critical effort providing the true materials for it, and Byron's was not; Goethe knew life and the world, the poet's necessary subjects, much more comprehensively and thoroughly than Byron. He knew a great deal more of them, and he knew them much more as they really are.

It has long seemed to me that the burst of creative activity in our literature, through the first quarter of this century, had about it in fact something premature; and that from this cause its productions are doomed, most of them, in spite of the sanguine hopes which accompanied and do still accompany them, to prove hardly more lasting than the productions of far less splendid epochs. And this prematureness comes from its having proceeded without having its proper data, without sufficient materials to work with. In other words, the English poetry of the first quarter of this century, with plenty of energy, plenty of creative force, did not know enough. This makes Byron so empty of matter, Shelley so incoherent, Wordsworth even, profound as he is, yet so wanting in completeness and variety. Wordsworth cared little for books, and disparaged Goethe. I admire Wordsworth, as he is, so much that I cannot wish him different; and it is vain, no doubt, to imagine such a man different from what he is, to suppose that he *could* have been different. But surely the one thing wanting to make Wordsworth an even greater poet than he is,—his thought richer, and his influence of wider application,— was that he should have read more books, among them, no doubt, those of that Goethe whom he disparaged without reading him.

But to speak of books and reading may easily lead to a misunderstanding here. It was not really books and reading that lacked to our poetry at this epoch: Shelley had plenty of reading, Coleridge had immense reading. Pindar and Sophocles,[5]—as we all say so glibly, and often with so little discernment of the real import of what we are saying,—had not many books; Shakespeare was no deep reader. True; but in the Greece of Pindar and Sophocles, in the England of Shakespeare, the poet lived in a current of ideas in the highest degree animating and nourishing to the creative power; society was, in the fullest measure, permeated by fresh thought, intelligent and alive. And this state of things is the true basis for the creative power's exercise, in this it finds its data, its materials, truly ready for its hand; all the books and reading in the world are only valuable as they are helps to this. Even when this does not actually exist, books and reading may enable a man to construct a kind of semblance of it in his own mind, a world of knowledge and intelligence in which he may live and work. This is by no means an equivalent to the artist for the nationally diffused life and thought of the epochs of Sophocles or Shakespeare; but, besides that it may be a means of preparation for such epochs, it does really constitute, if many share in it, a quickening and sustaining atmosphere of great value. Such an atmosphere the many-sided learning and the long and widely combined critical effort of Germany formed for Goethe, when he lived and worked. There was no national glow of life and thought there as in the Athens of Pericles or the England of Elizabeth. That was the poet's weakness. But there was a sort of equivalent for it in the complete culture and unfettered thinking of a large body of Germans. That was his strength. In the England of the first quarter of this century

there was neither a national glow of life and thought, such as we had in the age of Elizabeth, nor yet a culture and a force of learning and criticism such as were to be found in Germany. Therefore the creative power of poetry wanted, for success in the highest sense, materials and a basis; a thorough interpretation of the world was necessarily denied to it.

At first sight it seems strange that out of the immense stir of the French Revolution and its age should not have come a crop of works of genius equal to that which came out of the stir of the great productive time of Greece, or out of that of the Renascence, with its powerful episode the Reformation. But the truth is that the stir of the French Revolution took a character which essentially distinguished it from such movements as these. These were, in the main, disinterestedly intellectual and spiritual movements; movements in which the human spirit looked for its satisfaction in itself and in the increased play of its own activity. The French Revolution took a political, practical character. The movement, which went on in France under the old *régime*, from 1700 to 1789, was far more really akin than that of the Revolution itself to the movement of the Renascence; the France of Voltaire and Rousseau[6] told far more powerfully upon the mind of Europe than the France of the Revolution. Goethe reproached this last expressly with having "thrown quiet culture back." Nay, and the true key to how much in our Byron, even in our Wordsworth, is this!—that they had their source in a great movement of feeling, not in a great movement of mind. The French Revolution, however,—that object of so much blind love and so much blind hatred,— found undoubtedly its motive-power in the intelligence of men, and not in their practical sense; this is what distinguishes it from the English Revolution of Charles the First's time. This is what makes it a more spiritual event than our Revolution, an event of much more powerful and worldwide interest, though practically less successful; it appeals to an order of ideas which are universal, certain, permanent. 1789 asked of a thing, Is it rational? 1642 asked of a thing, Is it legal? or, when it went furthest, Is it according to conscience? This is the English fashion, a fashion to be treated, within its own sphere, with the highest respect; for its success, within its own sphere, has been prodigious. But what is law in one place is not law in another; what is law here today is not law even here to-morrow; and as for conscience,

---

[5]In 5th-century Athens, **Pindar** was the foremost poet, **Sophocles** a great dramatist, and **Pericles** the leading statesman.

[6]**Voltaire** (François-Marie Arouet, 1694–1778), Jean-Jacques **Rousseau** (1712–1778): French authors and philosophers. **1789**: the French Revolution. The English Revolution began in **1642**.

what is binding on one man's conscience is not binding on another's. The old woman who threw her stool at the head of the surpliced minister in St. Giles's Church at Edinburgh obeyed an impulse to which millions of the human race may be permitted to remain strangers. But the prescriptions of reason are absolute, unchanging, of universal validity; *to count by tens is the easiest way of counting*— that is a proposition of which every one, from here to the Antipodes, feels the force; at least I should say so if we did not live in a country where it is not impossible that any morning we may find a letter in the *Times* declaring that a decimal coinage is an absurdity. That a whole nation should have been penetrated with an enthusiasm for pure reason, and with an ardent zeal for making its prescriptions triumph, is a very remarkable thing, when we consider how little of mind, or anything so worthy and quickening as mind, comes into the motives which alone, in general, impel great masses of men. In spite of the extravagant direction given to this enthusiasm, in spite of the crimes and follies in which it lost itself, the French Revolution derives from the force, truth, and universality of the ideas which it took for its law, and from the passion with which it could inspire a multitude for these ideas, a unique and still living power; it is,—it will probably long remain,—the greatest, the most animating event in history. And as no sincere passion for the things of the mind, even though it turn out in many respects an unfortunate passion, is ever quite thrown away and quite barren of good, France has reaped from hers one fruit—the natural and legitimate fruit though not precisely the grand fruit she expected: she is the country in Europe where *the people* is most alive.

But the mania for giving an immediate political and practical application to all these fine ideas of the reason was fatal. Here an Englishman is in his element: on this theme we can all go on for hours. And all we are in the habit of saying on it has undoubtedly a great deal of truth. Ideas cannot be too much prized in and for themselves, cannot be too much lived with; but to transport them abruptly into the world of politics and practice, violently to revolutionise this world to their bidding,—that is quite another thing. There is the world of ideas and there is the world of practice; the French are often for suppressing the one and the English the other; but neither is to be suppressed. A member of the House of Commons said to me the other day: "That a thing is an anomaly, I consider to be no objection to it whatever." I venture to think he was wrong; that a thing is an anomaly *is* an objection to it, but absolutely and in the sphere of ideas: it is not necessarily, under such and such circumstances, or at such and such a moment, an objection to it in the sphere of politics and practice. Joubert[7] has said beautifully: "*C'est la force et le droit qui règlent toutes choses dans le monde; la force en attendant le droit.*" (Force and right are the governors of this world; force till right is ready.) Force till right is ready; and till right is ready, force, the existing order of things, is justified, is the legitimate ruler. But right is something moral, and implies inward recognition, free assent of the will; we are not ready for right,—*right*, so far as we are concerned, *is not ready*,—until we have attained this sense of seeing it and willing it. The way in which for us it may change and transform force, the existing order of things, and become, in its turn, the legitimate ruler of the world, should depend on the way in which, when our time comes, we see it and will it. Therefore for other people enamoured of their own newly discerned right, to attempt to impose it upon us as ours, and violently to substitute their right for our force, is an act of tyranny, and to be resisted. It sets at nought the second great half of our maxim, *force till right is ready.* This was the grand error of the French Revolution; and its movement of ideas, by quitting the intellectual sphere and rushing furiously into the political sphere, ran, indeed, a prodigious and memorable course, but produced no such intellectual fruit as the movement of ideas of the Renascence, and created, in opposition to itself, what I may call an *epoch of concentration.* The great force of that epoch of concentration was England; and the great voice of that epoch of concentration was Burke.[8] It is the fashion to treat Burke's writings on the French Revolution as superannuated and conquered by the event; as the eloquent but unphilosophical tirades of bigotry and prejudice. I will not deny that they are often disfigured by the violence and passion of the moment, and that in some directions Burke's view was bounded, and his observation therefore at fault. But on the whole, and for those who can make the needful corrections, what distinguishes these writings is their profound, permanent, fruitful, philosophical truth. They contain the true philosophy of an epoch of concentration, dissipate the heavy atmosphere which its own nature is apt to engender round it, and make its resistance rational instead of mechanical.

But Burke is so great because, almost alone in England, he brings thought to bear upon politics, he saturates politics with thought. It is his accident that his ideas were at the service of an epoch of concentration, not of an epoch of

---

[7]Joseph **Joubert** (1754–1824): right-wing French moralist.

[8]Edmund **Burke** (1729–1797): statesman and writer, whose *Reflections on the Revolution in France* (1790) focused conservative opposition in Britain.

expansion; it is his characteristic that he so lived by ideas, and had such a source of them welling up within him, that he could float even an epoch of concentration and English Tory politics with them. It does not hurt him that Dr. Price[9] and the Liberals were enraged with him; it does not even hurt him that George the Third and the Tories were enchanted with him. His greatness is that he lived in a world which neither English Liberalism nor English Toryism is apt to enter;—the world of ideas, not the world of catchwords and party habits. So far is it from being really true of him that he "to party gave up what was meant for mankind,"[10] that at the very end of his fierce struggle with the French Revolution, after all his invectives against its false pretensions, hollowness, and madness, with his sincere convictions of its mischievousness, he can close a memorandum on the best means of combating it, some of the last pages he ever wrote,—the *Thoughts on French Affairs*, in December 1791,—with these striking words:—

"The evil is stated, in my opinion, as it exists. The remedy must be where power, wisdom, and information, I hope, are more united with good intentions than they can be with me. I have done with this subject, I believe, for ever. It has given me many anxious moments for the last two years. *If a great change is to be made in human affairs, the minds of men will be fitted to it; the general opinions and feelings will draw that way. Every fear, every hope will forward it; and then they who persist in opposing this mighty current in human affairs, will appear rather to resist the decrees of Providence itself, than the mere designs of men. They will not be resolute and firm, but perverse and obstinate.*"

That return of Burke upon himself has always seemed to me one of the finest things in English literature, or indeed in any literature. That is what I call living by ideas: when one side of a question has long had your earnest support, when all your feelings are engaged, when you hear all round you no language but one, when your party talks this language like a steam-engine and can imagine no other,— still to be able to think, still to be irresistibly carried, if so it be, by the current of thought to the opposite side of the question, and, like Balaam,[11] to be unable to speak anything *but what the Lord has put in your mouth.* I know nothing more striking, and I must add that I know nothing more un-English.

For the Englishman in general is like my friend the Member of Parliament, and believes, point-blank, that for a thing to be an anomaly is absolutely no objection to it whatever. He is like the Lord Auckland of Burke's day, who, in a memorandum on the French Revolution, talks of certain "miscreants, assuming the name of philosophers, who have presumed themselves capable of establishing a new system of society." The Englishman has been called a political animal, and he values what is political and practical so much that ideas easily become objects of dislike in his eyes, and thinkers, "miscreants," because ideas and thinkers have rashly meddled with politics and practice. This would be all very well if the dislike and neglect confined themselves to ideas transported out of their own sphere, and meddling rashly with practice; but they are inevitably extended to ideas as such, and to the whole life of intelligence; practice is everything, a free play of the mind is nothing. The notion of the free play of the mind upon all subjects being a pleasure in itself, being an object of desire, being an essential provider of elements without which a nation's spirit, whatever compensations it may have for them, must, in the long run, die of inanition, hardly enters into an Englishman's thoughts. It is noticeable that the word *curiosity*, which in other languages is used in a good sense, to mean, as a high and fine quality of man's nature, just this disinterested love of a free play of the mind on all subjects, for its own sake,— it is noticeable, I say, that this word has in our language no sense of the kind, no sense but a rather bad and disparaging one. But criticism, real criticism, is essentially the exercise of this very quality. It obeys an instinct prompting it to try to know the best that is known and thought in the world, irrespectively of practice, politics, and everything of the kind; and to value knowledge and thought as they approach this best, without the intrusion of any other considerations whatever. This is an instinct for which there is, I think, little original sympathy in the practical English nature, and what there was of it has undergone a long benumbing period of blight and suppression in the epoch of concentration which followed the French Revolution.

But epochs of concentration cannot well endure for ever; epochs of expansion, in the due course of things, follow them. Such an epoch of expansion seems to be opening in this country. In the first place all danger of a hostile forcible pressure of foreign ideas upon our practice has long disappeared; like the traveller in the fable,[12] therefore, we begin to wear our cloak a little more loosely. Then, with a

---

[9]Richard **Price** (1723–1791): Nonconformist minister whose enthusiasm for the Revolution evoked Burke's rebuke.

[10]"**to party . . . mankind**": Oliver Goldsmith (1730–1774), "Retaliation" (1774) 32.

[11]**Balaam**: Numbers 22:38.

---

[12]**fable**: Aesop's fable of the wind and sun.

long peace, the ideas of Europe steal gradually and amicably in, and mingle, though in infinitesimally small quantities at a time, with our own notions. Then, too, in spite of all that is said about the absorbing and brutalising influence of our passionate material progress, it seems to me indisputable that this progress is likely, though not certain, to lead in the end to an apparition of intellectual life; and that man, after he has made himself perfectly comfortable and has now to determine what to do with himself next, may begin to remember that he has a mind, and that the mind may be made the source of great pleasure. I grant it is mainly the privilege of faith, at present, to discern this end to our railways, our business, and our fortune-making; but we shall see if, here as elsewhere, faith is not in the end the true prophet. Our ease, our travelling, and our unbounded liberty to hold just as hard and securely as we please to the practice to which our notions have given birth, all tend to beget an inclination to deal a little more freely with these notions themselves, to canvass them a little, to penetrate a little into their real nature. Flutterings of curiosity, in the foreign sense of the word, appear amongst us, and it is in these that criticism must look to find its account. Criticism first; a time of true creative activity, perhaps,—which, as I have said, must inevitably be preceded amongst us by a time of criticism,—hereafter, when criticism has done its work.

It is of the last importance that English criticism should clearly discern what rule for its course, in order to avail itself of the field now opening to it, and to produce fruit for the future, it ought to take. The rule may be summed up in one word,—*disinterestedness*. And how is criticism to show disinterestedness? By keeping aloof from what is called "the practical view of things"; by resolutely following the law of its own nature, which is to be a free play of the mind on all subjects which it touches. By steadily refusing to lend itself to any of those ulterior, political, practical considerations about ideas, which plenty of people will be sure to attach to them, which perhaps ought often to be attached to them, which in this country at any rate are certain to be attached to them quite sufficiently, but which criticism has really nothing to do with. Its business is, as I have said, simply to know the best that is known and thought in the world, and by in its turn making this known, to create a current of true and fresh ideas. Its business is to do this with inflexible honesty, with due ability; but its business is to do no more, and to leave alone all questions of practical consequences and applications, questions which will never fail to have due prominence given to them. Else criticism, besides being really false to its own nature, merely continues in the old rut which it has hitherto followed in this country, and will certainly miss the chance now given to it. For what is at present the bane of criticism in this country? It is that practical considerations cling to it and stifle it. It subserves interests not its own. Our organs of criticism are organs of men and parties having practical ends to serve, and with them those practical ends are the first thing and the play of mind the second; so much play of mind as is compatible with the prosecution of those practical ends is all that is wanted. An organ like the *Revue des Deux Mondes*,[13] having for its main function to understand and utter the best that is known and thought in the world, existing, it may be said, as just an organ for a free play of the mind, we have not. But we have the *Edinburgh Review*, existing as an organ of the old Whigs, and for as much play of mind as may suit its being that; we have the *Quarterly Review*, existing as an organ of the Tories, and for as much play of mind as may suit its being that; we have the *British Quarterly Review*, existing as an organ of the political Dissenters, and for as much play of mind as may suit its being that; we have the *Times*, existing as an organ of the common, satisfied, well-to-do Englishman, and for as much play of mind as may suit its being that. And so on through all the various fractions, political and religious, of our society; every fraction has, as such, its organ of criticism, but the notion of combining all fractions in the common pleasure of a free disinterested play of mind meets with no favour. Directly this play of mind wants to have more scope, and to forget the pressure of practical considerations a little, it is checked, it is made to feel the chain. We saw this the other day in the extinction, so much to be regretted, of the *Home and Foreign Review*. Perhaps in no organ of criticism in this country was there so much knowledge, so much play of mind; but these could not save it. The *Dublin Review* subordinates play of mind to the practical business of English and Irish Catholicism, and lives. It must needs be that men should act in sects and parties, that each of these sects and parties should have its organ, and should make this organ subserve the interests of its action; but it would be well, too, that there should be a criticism, not the minister of these interests, not their enemy, but absolutely and entirely independent of them. No other criticism will ever attain any real authority or make any real way towards its end,—the creating a current of true and fresh ideas.

It is because criticism has so little kept in the pure intellectual sphere, has so little detached itself from practice, has been so directly polemical and controversial, that it has so ill accomplished, in this country, its best spiritual work;

---

[13]*Revue des Deux Mondes:* French intellectual periodical.

which is to keep man from a self-satisfaction which is retarding and vulgarising, to lead him towards perfection, by making his mind dwell upon what is excellent in itself, and the absolute beauty and fitness of things. A polemical practical criticism makes men blind even to the ideal imperfection of their practice, makes them willingly assert its ideal perfection, in order the better to secure it against attack; and clearly this is narrowing and baneful for them. If they were reassured on the practical side, speculative considerations of ideal perfection they might be brought to entertain, and their spiritual horizon would thus gradually widen. Sir Charles Adderley[14] says to the Warwickshire farmers:

"Talk of the improvement of breed! Why, the race we ourselves represent, the men and women, the old Anglo-Saxon race, are the best breed in the whole world. . . . The absence of a too enervating climate, too unclouded skies, and a too luxurious nature, has produced so vigorous a race of people, and has rendered us so superior to all the world."

Mr. Roebuck[15] says to the Sheffield cutlers:

"I look around me and ask what is the state of England? Is not property safe? Is not every man able to say what he likes? Can you not walk from one end of England to the other in perfect security? I ask you whether, the world over or in past history, there is anything like it? Nothing. I pray that our unrivalled happiness may last."

Now obviously there is a peril for poor human nature in words and thoughts of such exuberant self-satisfaction, until we find ourselves safe in the streets of the Celestial City.

> *Das wenige verschwindet leicht dem Blicke*
> *Der vorwärts sieht, wie viel noch übrig bleibt—*

says Goethe;[16] "the little that is done seems nothing when we look forward and see how much we have yet to do." Clearly this is a better line of reflection for weak humanity, so long as it remains on this earthly field of labour and trial.

But neither Sir Charles Adderley nor Mr. Roebuck is by nature inaccessible to considerations of this sort. They only lose sight of them owing to the controversial life we all lead, and the practical form which all speculation takes with us. They have in view opponents whose aim is not ideal, but practical; and in their zeal to uphold their own practice against these innovators, they go so far as even to attribute to this practice an ideal perfection. Somebody has been

wanting to introduce a six-pound franchise, or to abolish church-rates,[17] or to collect agricultural statistics by force, or to diminish local self-government. How natural, in reply to such proposals, very likely improper or ill-timed, to go a little beyond the mark and to say stoutly, "Such a race of people as we stand, so superior to all the world! The old Anglo-Saxon race, the best breed in the whole world! I pray that our unrivalled happiness may last! I ask you whether, the world over or in past history, there is anything like it?" And so long as criticism answers this dithyramb by insisting that the old Anglo-Saxon race would be still more superior to all others if it had no church-rates, or that our unrivalled happiness would last yet longer with a six-pound franchise, so long will the strain, "The best breed in the whole world!" swell louder and louder, everything ideal and refining will be lost out of sight, and both the assailed and their critics will remain in a sphere, to say the truth, perfectly unvital, a sphere in which spiritual progression is impossible. But let criticism leave church-rates and the franchise alone, and in the most candid spirit, without a single lurking thought of practical innovation, confront with our dithyramb this paragraph on which I stumbled in a newspaper immediately after reading Mr. Roebuck:

"A shocking child murder has just been committed at Nottingham. A girl named Wragg left the workhouse there on Saturday morning with her young illegitimate child. The child was soon afterwards found dead on Mapperly Hills, having been strangled. Wragg is in custody."[18]

Nothing but that; but, in juxtaposition with the absolute eulogies of Sir Charles Adderley and Mr. Roebuck, how eloquent, how suggestive are those few lines! "Our old Anglo-Saxon breed, the best in the whole world!"—how much that is harsh and ill-favoured there is in this best! *Wragg!* If we are to talk of ideal perfection, of "the best in the whole world," has any one reflected what a touch of grossness in our race, what an original short-coming in the more delicate spiritual perceptions, is shown by the natural growth amongst us of such hideous names,—Higginbottom, Stiggins, Bugg! In Ionia and Attica[19] they were luckier in this respect than "the best race in the world"; by the Ilissus there

---

[14]**Sir Charles Adderley** (1814–1905): Conservative MP.

[15]John Arthur **Roebuck** (1801–1879): Benthamite MP.

[16]**Goethe**: *Iphigenie auf Tauris* (1787) 1.2. 91–92.

[17]A **six-pound franchise** would have given the vote to owners or leasers of property worth six pounds a year. **church-rates**: taxes to maintain the church, abolished 1868.

[18]Elizabeth **Wragg** was sentenced to 20 years' penal servitude for manslaughter on March 13, 1865.

[19]**Ionia, Attica**: regions of ancient Greece. **Ilissus**: river in Greece.

was no Wragg, poor thing! And "our unrivalled happiness",— what an element of grimness, bareness, and hideousness mixes with it and blurs it; the workhouse, the dismal Mapperly Hills—how dismal those who have seen them will remember;—the gloom, the smoke, the cold, the strangled illegitimate child! "I ask you whether, the world over or in past history, there is anything like it?" Perhaps not, one is inclined to answer; but at any rate, in that case, the world is very much to be pitied. And the final touch,— short, bleak and inhuman: *Wragg is in custody*. The sex lost in the confusion of our unrivalled happiness; or (shall I say?) the superfluous Christian name lopped off by the straightforward vigour of our old Anglo-Saxon breed! There is profit for the spirit in such contrasts as this; criticism serves the cause of perfection by establishing them. By eluding sterile conflict, by refusing to remain in the sphere where alone narrow and relative conceptions have any worth and validity, criticism may diminish its momentary importance, but only in this way has it a chance of gaining admittance for those wider and more perfect conceptions to which all its duty is really owed. Mr. Roebuck will have a poor opinion of an adversary who replies to his defiant songs of triumph only by murmuring under his breath, *Wragg is in custody*; but in no other way will these songs of triumph be induced gradually to moderate themselves, to get rid of what in them is excessive and offensive, and to fall into a softer and truer key.

It will be said that it is a very subtle and indirect action which I am thus prescribing for criticism, and that, by embracing in this manner the Indian virtue of detachment[20] and abandoning the sphere of practical life, it condemns itself to a slow and obscure work. Slow and obscure it may be, but it is the only proper work of criticism. The mass of mankind will never have any ardent zeal for seeing things as they are; very inadequate ideas will always satisfy them. On these inadequate ideas reposes, and must repose, the general practice of the world. That is as much as saying that whoever sets himself to see small things as they are will find himself one of a very small circle; but it is only by this small circle resolutely doing its own work that adequate ideas will ever get current at all. The rush and roar of practical life will always have a dizzying and attracting effect upon the most collected spectator, and tend to draw him into its vortex; most of all will this be the case where that life is so powerful as it is in England. But it is only by remaining collected, and

refusing to lend himself to the point of view of the practical man, that the critic can do the practical man any service; and it is only by the greatest sincerity in pursuing his own course, and by at last convincing even the practical man of his sincerity, that he can escape misunderstandings which perpetually threaten him.

For the practical man is not apt for fine distinctions, and yet in these distinctions truth and the highest culture greatly find their account. But it is not easy to lead a practical man,—unless you reassure him as to your practical intentions, you have no chance of leading him,—to see that a thing which he has always been used to look at from one side only, which he greatly values, and which, looked at from that side, quite deserves, perhaps, all the prizing and admiring which he bestows upon it,—that this thing, looked at from another side, may appear much less beneficent and beautiful, and yet retain all its claims to our practical allegiance. Where shall we find language innocent enough, how shall we make the spotless purity of our intentions evident enough, to enable us to say to the political Englishman that the British Constitution itself, which, seen from the practical side, looks such a magnificent organ of progress and virtue, seen from the speculative side,—with its compromises, its love of facts, its horror of theory, its studied avoidance of clear thoughts,—that, seen from this side, our august Constitution sometimes looks,—forgive me, shade of Lord Somers![21]—a colossal machine for the manufacture of Philistines? How is Cobbett to say this and not be misunderstood, blackened as he is with the smoke of a lifelong conflict in the field of political practice? how is Mr. Carlyle to say it and not be misunderstood, after his furious raid into this field with his *Latter-day Pamphlets?* how is Mr. Ruskin, after his pugnacious political economy? I say, the critic must keep out of the region of immediate practice in the political, social, humanitarian sphere if he wants to make a beginning for that more free speculative treatment of things, which may perhaps one day make its benefits felt even in this sphere, but in a natural and thence irresistible manner.

Do what he will, however, the critic will still remain exposed to frequent misunderstandings, and nowhere so much as in this country. For here people are particularly indisposed even to comprehend that without this free disinterested treatment of things, truth and the highest culture are out of the question. So immersed are they in practical

---

[20]**Indian virtue:** Arnold had earlier been enthusiastic about the *Bhagavad-Gita*, one of the Hindu scriptures, which teaches **detachment** from desire for earthly goods.

[21]**Lord Somers** (1651–1716): statesman and lawyer. **Philistines:** Arnold's name for the self-satisfied middle class; see 1 Samuel 17.

life, so accustomed to take all their notions from this life and its processes, that they are apt to think that truth and culture themselves can be reached by the processes of this life, and that it is an impertinent singularity to think of reaching them in any other. "We are all *terræ filii*,"[22] cries their eloquent advocate; "all Philistines together. Away with the notion of proceeding by any other course than the course dear to the Philistines; let us have a social movement, let us organise and combine a party to pursue truth and new thought, let us call it *the liberal party*, and let us all stick to each other, and back each other up. Let us have no nonsense about independent criticism, and intellectual delicacy, and the few and the many. Don't let us trouble ourselves about foreign thought; we shall invent the whole thing for ourselves as we go along. If one of us speaks well, applaud him; if one of us speaks ill, applaud him too; we are all in the same movement, we are all liberals, we are all in pursuit of truth." In this way the pursuit of truth becomes really a social, practical, pleasurable affair, almost requiring a chairman, a secretary, and advertisements; with the excitement of an occasional scandal, with a little resistance to give the happy sense of difficulty overcome; but, in general, plenty of bustle and very little thought. To act is so easy, as Goethe says; to think is so hard! It is true that the critic has many temptations to go with the stream, to make one of the party movement, one of these *terræ filii*; it seems ungracious to refuse to be a *terræ filius* when so many excellent people are; but the critic's duty is to refuse, or, if resistance is vain, at least to cry with Obermann: *Périssons en résistant.*[23]

How serious a matter it is to try and resist, I had ample opportunity of experiencing when I ventured some time ago to criticise the celebrated first volume of Bishop Colenso.[24]

The echoes of the storm which was then raised I still, from time to time, hear grumbling round me. That storm arose out of a misunderstanding almost inevitable. It is a result of no little culture to attain to a clear perception that science and religion are two wholly different things. The multitude will for ever confuse them; but happily that is of no great real importance, for while the multitude imagines itself to live by its false science, it does really live by its true religion. Dr. Colenso, however, in his first volume did all he could to strengthen the confusion, and to make it dangerous. He did this with the best intentions, I freely admit, and with the most candid ignorance that this was the natural effect of what he was doing; but, says Joubert, "Ignorance, which in matters of morals extenuates the crime, is itself, in intellectual matters, a crime of the first order." I criticised Bishop Colenso's speculative confusion. Immediately there was a cry raised: "What is this? here is a liberal attacking a liberal. Do not you belong to the movement? are you not a friend of truth? Is not Bishop Colenso in pursuit of truth? then speak with proper respect of his book. Dr. Stanley[25] is another friend of truth, and you speak with proper respect of his book; why make these invidious differences? both books are excellent, admirable, liberal; Bishop Colenso's perhaps the most so, because it is the boldest, and will have the best practical consequences for the liberal cause. Do you want to encourage to the attack of a brother liberal his, and your, and our implacable enemies, the *Church and State Review* or the *Record*,—the High Church rhinoceros and the Evangelical hyaena? Be silent, therefore; or rather speak, speak as loud as ever you can! and go into ecstasies over the eighty and odd pigeons."[26]

But criticism cannot follow this coarse and indiscriminate method. It is unfortunately possible for a man in pursuit of truth to write a book which reposes upon a false conception. Even the practical consequences of a book are to genuine criticism no recommendation of it, if the book is, in the highest sense, blundering. I see that a lady[27] who herself, too, is in pursuit of truth, and who writes with great ability, but a little too much, perhaps, under the influence of the practical spirit of the English liberal movement, classes

---

[22]*terrae filii*: sons of earth.

[23]*Périssons en résistant*: let us die resisting. **Obermann**: see Arnold's "Stanzas from the Grande Chartreuse," note 7.

[24]So sincere is my dislike to all personal attack and controversy, that I abstain from reprinting, at this distance of time from the occasion which called them forth, the essays in which I criticised Dr. Colenso's book; I feel bound, however, after all that has passed, to make here a final declaration, of my sincere impenitence for having published them. Nay, I cannot forbear repeating yet once more, for his benefit and that of his readers, this sentence from my original remarks upon him. *There is truth of science and truth of religion; truth of science does not become truth of religion till it is made religious.* And I will add: Let us have all the science there is from the men of science; from the men of religion let us have religion. [Arnold's note] John **Colenso**, Bishop of Natal (1814–1883), author of *The Pentateuch . . . Critically Examined* (1862); see page 68.

[25]Arthur Penrhyn **Stanley** (1815–1881), Dean of Westminster and biographer of Thomas Arnold, was one of Colenso's few clerical defenders.

[26]Colenso had argued that a Biblical account concerning **pigeons** was mathematically impossible.

[27]**lady**: Frances Power **Cobbe**, who discusses Colenso in *Broken Lights* (1864).

Bishop Colenso's book and M. Renan's[28] together, in her survey of the religious state of Europe, as facts of the same order, works, both of them, of "great importance"; "great ability, power, and skill"; Bishop Colenso's, perhaps, the most powerful; at least, Miss Cobbe gives special expression to her gratitude that to Bishop Colenso "has been given the strength to grasp, and the courage to teach, truths of such deep import." In the same way, more than one popular writer has compared him to Luther. Now it is just this kind of false estimate which the critical spirit is, it seems to me, bound to resist. It is really the strongest possible proof of the low ebb at which, in England, the critical spirit is, that while the critical hit in the religious literature of Germany is Dr. Strauss's book,[29] in that of France M. Renan's book, the book of Bishop Colenso is the critical hit in the religious literature of England. Bishop Colenso's book reposes on a total misconception of the essential elements of the religious problem, as that problem is now presented for solution. To criticism, therefore, which seeks to have the best that is known and thought on this problem, it is, however well meant, of no importance whatever. M. Renan's book attempts a new synthesis of the elements furnished to us by the Four Gospels. It attempts, in my opinion, a synthesis, perhaps premature, perhaps impossible, certainly not successful. Up to the present time, at any rate, we must acquiesce in Fleury's sentence on such recastings of the Gospel story: *Quiconque s'imagine la pouvoir mieux écrire, ne l'entend pas.*[30] M. Renan had himself passed by anticipation a like sentence on his own work, when he said: "If a new presentation of the character of Jesus were offered to me, I would not have it; its very clearness would be, in my opinion, the best proof of its insufficiency." His friends may with perfect justice rejoin that at the sight of the Holy Land, and of the actual scene of the Gospel-story, all the current of M. Renan's thoughts may have naturally changed, and a new casting of that story irresistibly suggested itself to him; and that this is just a case for applying Cicero's maxim: Change of mind is not inconsistency— *nemo doctus unquam mutationem consilii inconstantiam dixit esse.*[31]

Nevertheless, for criticism, M. Renan's first thought must still be the truer one, as long as his new casting so fails more fully to commend itself, more fully (to use Coleridge's happy phrase about the Bible) to *find* us. Still M. Renan's attempt is, for criticism, of the most real interest and importance, since, with all its difficulty, a fresh synthesis of the New Testament *data*—not a making war on them, in Voltaire's fashion, not a leaving them out of mind, in the world's fashion, but the putting a new construction upon them, the taking them from under the old, traditional, conventional point of view and placing them under a new one,—is the very essence of the religious problem, as now presented; and only by efforts in this direction can it receive a solution.

Again, in the same spirit in which she judges Bishop Colenso, Miss Cobbe, like so many earnest liberals of our practical race, both here and in America, herself sets vigorously about a positive reconstruction of religion, about making a religion of the future out of hand, or at least setting about making it. We must not rest, she and they are always thinking and saying, in negative criticism, we must be creative and constructive; hence we have such works as her recent *Religious Duty*, and works still more considerable, perhaps, by others, which will be in every one's mind. These works often have much ability; they often spring out of sincere convictions, and a sincere wish to do good; and they sometimes, perhaps, do good. Their fault is (if I may be permitted to say so) one which they have in common with the British College of Health, in the New Road. Every one knows the British College of Health; it is that building with the lion and the statue of the Goddess Hygeia before it; at least I am sure about the lion, though I am not absolutely certain about the Goddess Hygeia. This building does credit, perhaps, to the resources of Dr. Morrison[32] and his disciples; but it falls a good deal short of one's idea of what a British College of Health ought to be. In England, where we hate public interference and love individual enterprise, we have a whole crop of places like the British College of Health; the grand name without the grand thing. Unluckily, creditable to individual enterprise as they are, they tend to impair our taste by making us forget what more grandiose, noble, or beautiful character properly belongs to a public institution. The same may be said of the religions of the future of Miss Cobbe and others. Creditable, like the British College of Health, to the resources of their authors, they

---

[28]Ernest **Renan** (1823–1892): author of *La Vie de Jésus* (1863), a secular biography.

[29]David Friedrich **Strauss** (1808–1874): demythologizing author of *The Life of Christ Critically Examined* (1835–1836).

[30]*Quiconque . . . ne l'entend pas:* Whoever thinks he could write it better, doesn't understand it. Claude **Fleury** (1640–1723): ecclesiastical writer.

[31]**Cicero** (106–43 BCE): Roman orator and writer. *nemo . . . dixit esse:* no educated person ever calls a change of opinion inconstancy.

[32]James **Morrison** (1770–1840) called himself "the Hygeist" and dispensed vegetable pills. Chapter 4 of Carlyle's *Past and Present* is named for him.

yet tend to make us forget what more grandiose, noble, or beautiful character properly belongs to religious constructions. The historic religions, with all their faults, have had this; it certainly belongs to the religious sentiment, when it truly flowers, to have this; and we impoverish our spirit if we allow a religion of the future without it. What then is the duty of criticism here? To take the practical point of view, to applaud the liberal movement and all its works,— its New Road religions of the future into the bargain,—for their general utility's sake? By no means; but to be perpetually dissatisfied with these works, while they perpetually fall short of a high and perfect ideal.

For criticism, these are elementary laws; but they never can be popular, and in this country they have been very little followed, and one meets with immense obstacles in following them. That is a reason for asserting them again and again. Criticism must maintain its independence of the practical spirit and its aims. Even with well-meant efforts of the practical spirit it must express dissatisfaction, if in the sphere of the ideal they seem impoverishing and limiting. It must not hurry on to the goal because of its practical importance. It must be patient, and know how to wait; and flexible, and know how to attach itself to things and how to withdraw from them. It must be apt to study and praise elements that for the fulness of spiritual perfection are wanted, even though they belong to a power which in the practical sphere may be maleficent. It must be apt to discern the spiritual shortcomings or illusions of powers that in the practical sphere may be beneficent. And this without any notion of favouring or injuring, in the practical sphere, one power or the other; without any notion of playing off, in this sphere, one power against the other. When one looks, for instance, at the English Divorce Court,—an institution which perhaps has its practical conveniences, but which in the ideal sphere is so hideous; an institution which neither makes divorce impossible nor makes it decent, which allows a man to get rid of his wife, or a wife of her husband, but makes them drag one another first, for the public edification, through a mire of unutterable infamy,—when one looks at this charming institution, I say, with its crowded trials, its newspaper reports, and its money compensations, this institution in which the gross unregenerate British Philistine has indeed stamped an image of himself,—one may be permitted to find the marriage theory of Catholicism refreshing and elevating. Or when Protestantism, in virtue of its supposed rational and intellectual origin, gives the law to criticism too magisterially, criticism may and must remind it that its pretensions, in this respect, are illusive and do it harm; that the Reformation was a moral rather than an intellectual event; that Luther's theory of grace no more exactly reflects the mind of the spirit than Bossuet's philosophy of history reflects it; and that there is no more antecedent probability of the Bishop of Durham's stock of ideas being agreeable to perfect reason than of Pope Pius the Ninth's.[33] But criticism will not on that account forget the achievements of Protestantism in the practical and moral sphere; nor that, even in the intellectual sphere, Protestantism, though in a blind and stumbling manner, carried forward the Renascence, while Catholicism threw itself violently across its path.

I lately heard of a man of thought and energy contrasting the want of ardour and movement which he now found amongst young men in this country with what he remembered in his own youth, twenty years ago. "What reformers we were then!" he exclaimed; "What a zeal we had! how we canvassed every institution in Church and State, and were prepared to remodel them all on first principles!" He was inclined to regret, as a spiritual flagging, the lull which he saw. I am disposed rather to regard it as a pause in which the turn to a new mode of spiritual progress is being accomplished. Everything was long seen, by the young and ardent amongst us, in inseparable connection with politics and practical life. We have pretty well exhausted the benefits of seeing things in this connection, we have got all that can be got by so seeing them. Let us try a more disinterested mode of seeing them; let us betake ourselves more to the serener life of the mind and spirit. This life, too, may have its excesses and dangers; but they are not for us at present. Let us think of quietly enlarging our stock of true and fresh ideas, and not, as soon as we get an idea or half an idea, be running out with it into the street, and trying to make it rule there. Our ideas will, in the end, shape the world all the better for maturing a little. Perhaps in fifty years' time it will in the English House of Commons be an objection to an institution that it is an anomaly, and my friend the Member of Parliament will shudder in his grave. But let us in the meanwhile rather endeavour that in twenty years' time it may, in English literature, be an objection to a proposition that it is absurd. That will be a change so vast, that the imagination almost fails to grasp it. *Ab integro sæclorum nascitur ordo*.[34]

---

[33]Jacques-Bénigne **Bossuet** (1627–1704): Catholic bishop who defended the French Church against Papal authority. **Bishop of Durham**: Charles Thomas Baring (1807–1879), an Evangelical (Anglican). **Pius the Ninth**: Pope (1846–1878).

[34]*Ab integro . . . ordo*: the great order of the centuries begins anew (Virgil, *Eclogues* 4.5).

If I have insisted so much on the course which criticism must take where politics and religion are concerned, it is because, where these burning matters are in question, it is most likely to go astray. I have wished, above all, to insist on the attitude which criticism should adopt towards things in general; on its right tone and temper of mind. But then comes another question as to the subject-matter which literary criticisms should most seek. Here, in general, its course is determined for it by the idea which is the law of its being; the idea of a disinterested endeavour to learn and propagate the best that is known and thought in the world, and thus to establish a current of fresh and true ideas. By the very nature of things, as England is not all the world, much of the best that is known and thought in the world cannot be of English growth, must be foreign; by the nature of things, again, it is just this that we are least likely to know, while English thought is streaming in upon us from all sides, and takes excellent care that we shall not be ignorant of its existence. The English critic of literature, therefore, must dwell much on foreign thought, and with particular heed on any part of it, which, while significant and fruitful in itself, is for any reason specially likely to escape him. Again, judging is often spoken of as the critic's one business, and so in some sense it is; but the judgment which almost insensibly forms itself in a fair and clear mind, along with fresh knowledge, is the valuable one; and thus knowledge, and ever fresh knowledge, must be the critic's great concern for himself. And it is by communicating fresh knowledge, and letting his own judgment pass along with it,—but insensibly, and in the second place, not the first, as a sort of companion and clue, not as an abstract lawgiver,—that the critic will generally do most good to his readers. Sometimes, no doubt, for the sake of establishing an author's place in literature, and his relation to a central standard (and if this is not done, how are we to get at our *best in the world?*) criticism may have to deal with a subject-matter so familiar that fresh knowledge is out of the question, and then it must be all judgment; an enunciation and detailed application of principles. Here the great safeguard is never to let oneself become abstract, always to retain an intimate and lively consciousness of the truth of what one is saying, and, the moment this fails us, to be sure that something is wrong. Still under all circumstances, this mere judgment and application of principles is, in itself, not the most satisfactory work to the critic; like mathematics, it is tautological, and cannot well give us, like fresh learning, the sense of creative activity.

But stop, some one will say; all this talk is of no practical use to us whatever; this criticism of yours is not what we have in our minds when we speak of criticism; when we speak of critics and criticism, we mean critics and criticism of the current English literature of the day; when you offer to tell criticism its function, it is to this criticism that we expect you to address yourself. I am sorry for it, for I am afraid I must disappoint these expectations. I am bound by my own definition of criticism: *a disinterested endeavour to learn and propagate the best that is known and thought in the world.* How much of current English literature comes into this "best that is known and thought in the world"? Not very much I fear; certainly less, at this moment, than of the current literature of France or Germany. Well, then, am I to alter my definition of criticism, in order to meet the requirements of a number of practising English critics, who, after all, are free in their choice of a business? That would be making criticism lend itself just to one of those alien practical considerations, which, I have said, are so fatal to it. One may say, indeed, to those who have to deal with the mass—so much better disregarded—of current English literature, that they may at all events endeavour, in dealing with this, to try it, so far as they can, by the standard of the best that is known and thought in the world; one may say, that to get anywhere near this standard, every critic should try and possess one great literature, at least, besides his own; and the more unlike his own, the better. But, after all, the criticism I am really concerned with,—the criticism which alone can much help us for the future, the criticism which, throughout Europe, is at the present day meant, when so much stress is laid on the importance of criticism and the critical spirit,—is a criticism which regards Europe as being, for intellectual and spiritual purposes, one great confederation, bound to a joint action and working to a common result; and whose members have, for their proper outfit, a knowledge of Greek, Roman, and Eastern antiquity, and of one another. Special, local, and temporary advantages being put out of account, that modern nation will in the intellectual and spiritual sphere make most progress, which most thoroughly carries out this program. And what is that but saying that we too, all of us, as individuals, the more thoroughly we carry it out, shall make the more progress?

There is so much inviting us!—what are we to take? what will nourish us in growth towards perfection? That is the question which, with the immense field of life and of literature lying before him, the critic has to answer; for himself first, and afterwards for others. In this idea of the critic's business the essays brought together in the following pages have had their origin; in this idea, widely different as are their subjects, they have, perhaps, their unity.

I conclude with what I said at the beginning: to have the sense of creative activity is the great happiness and the great proof of being alive, and it is not denied to criticism to have it; but then criticism must be sincere, simple, flexible, ardent, ever widening its knowledge. Then it may have, in no contemptible measure, a joyful sense of creative activity; a sense which a man of insight and conscience will prefer to what he might derive from a poor, starved, fragmentary, inadequate creation. And at some epochs no other creation is possible.

Still, in full measure, the sense of creative activity belongs only to genuine creation; in literature we must never forget that. But what true man of letters ever can forget it? It is no such common matter for a gifted nature to come into possession of a current of true and living ideas, and to produce amidst the inspiration of them, that we are likely to underrate it. The epochs of Æschylus and Shakespeare make us feel their pre-eminence. In an epoch like those is, no doubt, the true life of literature; there is the promised land, toward which criticism can only beckon. That promised land it will not be ours to enter, and we shall die in the wilderness:[35] but to have desired to enter it, to have saluted it from afar, is already, perhaps, the best distinction among contemporaries; it will certainly be the best title to esteem with posterity.

1864, 1865

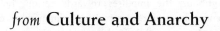

from Culture and Anarchy

In one of his speeches a short time ago, that fine speaker and famous Liberal, Mr. Bright,[1] took occasion to have a fling at the friends and preachers of culture. "People who talk about what they call *culture!*" said he, contemptuously; "by which they mean a smattering of the two dead languages of Greek and Latin." And he went on to remark, in a strain with which modern speakers and writers have made us very familiar, how poor a thing this culture is, how little good it can do to the world, and how absurd it is for its possessors to set much store by it. And the other day a younger Liberal than Mr. Bright, one of a school whose mission it is to bring into order and system that body of truth with which the earlier Liberals merely fumbled, a member of the University of Oxford, and a very clever writer, Mr. Frederic

Harrison,[2] developed, in the systematic and stringent manner of his school, the thesis which Mr. Bright had propounded in only general terms. "Perhaps the very silliest cant of the day," said Mr. Frederic Harrison, "is the cant about culture. Culture is a desirable quality in a critic of new books, and sits well on a possessor of *belles lettres*; but as applied to politics, it means simply a turn for small fault-finding, love of selfish ease, and indecision in action. The man of culture is in politics one of the poorest mortals alive. For simple pedantry and want of good sense no man is his equal. No assumption is too unreal, no end is too unpractical for him. But the active exercise of politics requires common sense, sympathy, trust, resolution, and enthusiasm, qualities which your man of culture has carefully rooted up, lest they damage the delicacy of his critical olfactories. Perhaps they are the only class of responsible beings in the community who cannot with safety be entrusted with power."

Now for my part I do not wish to see men of culture asking to be entrusted with power; and, indeed, I have freely said, that in my opinion the speech most proper, at present, for a man of culture to make to a body of his fellow-countrymen who get him into a committee-room, is Socrates's: *Know thyself!* and this is not a speech to be made by men wanting to be entrusted with power. For this very indifference to direct political action I have been taken to task by the *Daily Telegraph*, coupled, by a strange perversity of fate, with just that very one of the Hebrew prophets whose style I admire the least, and called "an elegant Jeremiah." It is because I say (to use the words which the *Daily Telegraph* puts in my mouth):—"You mustn't make a fuss because you have no vote,—that is vulgarity; you mustn't hold big meetings to agitate for reform bills and to repeal corn laws,—that is the very height of vulgarity,"—it is for this reason that I am called sometimes an elegant Jeremiah, sometimes a spurious Jeremiah, a Jeremiah about the reality of whose mission the writer in the *Daily Telegraph* has his doubts. It is evident, therefore, that I have so taken my line as not to be exposed to the whole brunt of Mr. Frederic Harrison's censure. Still, I have often spoken in praise of culture, I have striven to make all my works and ways serve the interests of culture. I take culture to be something a great deal more than what Mr. Frederic Harrison and others call it: "a desirable quality in a critic of new books." Nay, even though to a certain extent I am disposed to agree with Mr. Frederic Harrison, that men of culture are just the class

---

[35]Moses died **in the wilderness** before the Israelites entered the **promised land;** Deuteronomy 32:48–52, 34:1–6.

[1]John **Bright** (1811–1889): MP representing manufacturing class.

[2]**Frederic Harrison** (1831–1923): Positivist lawyer and writer.

liberal, open minded

of responsible beings in this community of ours who cannot properly, at present, be entrusted with power, I am not sure that I do not think this the fault of our community rather than of the men of culture. In short, although, like Mr. Bright and Mr. Frederic Harrison, and the editor of the *Daily Telegraph*, and a large body of valued friends of mine, I am a Liberal, yet I am a Liberal tempered by experience, reflection, and renouncement, and I am, above all, a believer in culture. Therefore I propose now to try and inquire, in the simple unsystematic way which best suits both my taste and my powers, what culture really is, what good it can do, what is our own special need of it; and I shall seek to find some plain grounds on which a faith in culture,—both my own faith in it and the faith of others,—may rest securely. (Introduction)

Sweetness and Light

The disparagers of culture make its motive curiosity; sometimes, indeed, they make its motive mere exclusiveness and vanity. The culture which is supposed to plume itself on a smattering of Greek and Latin is a culture which is begotten by nothing so intellectual as curiosity; it is valued either out of sheer vanity and ignorance or else as an engine of social and class distinction, separating its holder, like a badge or title, from other people who have not got it. No serious man would call this *culture*, or attach any value to it, as culture, at all. To find the real ground for the very different estimate which serious people will set upon culture, we must find some motive for culture in the terms of which may lie a real ambiguity; and such a motive the word *curiosity* gives us.

I have before now pointed out that we English do not, like the foreigners, use this word in a good sense as well as in a bad sense. With us the word is always used in a somewhat disapproving sense. A liberal and intelligent eagerness about the things of the mind may be meant by a foreigner when he speaks of curiosity, but with us the word always conveys a certain notion of frivolous and unedifying activity. In the *Quarterly Review*, some little time ago, was an estimate of the celebrated French critic, M. Sainte-Beuve,[3] and a very inadequate estimate it in my judgment was. And its inadequacy consisted chiefly in this: that in our English way it left out of sight the double sense really involved in the word *curiosity*, thinking enough was said to stamp M. Sainte-Beuve with blame if it was said that he was impelled in his

operations as a critic by curiosity, and omitting either to perceive that M. Sainte-Beuve himself, and many other people with him, would consider that this was praiseworthy and not blameworthy, or to point out why it ought really to be accounted worthy of blame and not of praise. For as there is a curiosity about intellectual matters which is futile, and merely a disease, so there is certainly a curiosity,—a desire after the things of the mind simply for their own sakes and for the pleasure of seeing them as they are,—which is, in an intelligent being, natural and laudable. Nay, and the very desire to see things as they are implies a balance and regulation of mind which is not often attained without fruitful effort, and which is the very opposite of the blind and diseased impulse of mind which is what we mean to blame when we blame curiosity. Montesquieu[4] says: "The first motive which ought to impel us to study is the desire to augment the excellence of our nature, and to render an intelligent being yet more intelligent." This is the true ground to assign for the genuine scientific passion, however manifested, and for culture, viewed simply as a fruit of this passion; and it is a worthy ground, even though we let the term *curiosity* stand to describe it.

But there is of culture another view, in which not solely the scientific passion, the sheer desire to see things as they are, natural and proper in an intelligent being, appears as the ground of it. There is a view in which all the love of our neighbour, the impulses towards action, help, and beneficence, the desire for removing human error, clearing human confusion, and diminishing human misery, the noble aspiration to leave the world better and happier than we found it,—motives eminently such as are called social,—come in as part of the grounds of culture, and the main and pre-eminent part. Culture is then properly described not as having its origin in curiosity, but as having its origin in the love of perfection; it is *a study of perfection*. It moves by the force, not merely or primarily of the scientific passion for pure knowledge, but also of the moral and social passion for doing good. As, in the first view of it, we took for its worthy motto Montesquieu's words: "To render an intelligent being yet more intelligent!" so, in the second view of it, there is no better motto which it can have than these words of Bishop Wilson:[5] "To make reason and the will of God prevail!"

Only, whereas the passion for doing good is apt to be overhasty in determining what reason and the will of God

---

[3]Charles-Augustin **Sainte-Beuve** (1804–1869): French literary critic whom Arnold regarded as a model.

[4]Charles-Louis de Secondat, Baron de **Montesquieu** (1689–1755): French political philosopher.

[5]Thomas **Wilson** (1663–1755): **Bishop** of Sodor and Man.

say, because its turn is for acting rather than thinking and it wants to be beginning to act; and whereas it is apt to take its own conceptions, which proceed from its own state of development and share in all the imperfections and immaturities of this, for a basis of action; what distinguishes culture is, that it is possessed by the scientific passion as well as by the passion of doing good; that it demands worthy notions of reason and the will of God, and does not readily suffer its own crude conceptions to substitute themselves for them. And knowing that no action or institution can be salutary and stable which is not based on reason and the will of God, it is not so bent on acting and instituting, even with the great aim of diminishing human error and misery ever before its thoughts, but that it can remember that acting and instituting are of little use, unless we know how and what we ought to act and to institute.

This culture is more interesting and more far-reaching than that other, which is founded solely on the scientific passion for knowing. But it needs times of faith and ardour, times when the intellectual horizon is opening and widening all round us, to flourish in. And is not the close and bounded intellectual horizon within which we have long lived and moved now lifting up, and are not new lights finding free passage to shine in upon us? For a long time there was no passage for them to make their way in upon us, and then it was of no use to think of adapting the world's action to them. Where was the hope of making reason and the will of God prevail among people who had a routine which they had christened reason and the will of God, in which they were inextricably bound, and beyond which they had no power of looking? But now the iron force of adhesion to the old routine,—social, political, religious,—has wonderfully yielded; the iron force of exclusion of all which is new has wonderfully yielded. The danger now is, not that people should obstinately refuse to allow anything but their old routine to pass for reason and the will of God, but either that they should allow some novelty or other to pass for these too easily, or else that they should underrate the importance of them altogether, and think it enough to follow action for its own sake, without troubling themselves to make reason and the will of God prevail therein. Now, then, is the moment for culture to be of service, culture which believes in making reason and the will of God prevail, believes in perfection, is the study and pursuit of perfection, and is no longer debarred, by a rigid invincible exclusion of whatever is new, from getting acceptance for its ideas, simply because they are new.

The moment this view of culture is seized, the moment it is regarded not solely as the endeavour to see things as they are, to draw towards a knowledge of the universal order which seems to be intended and aimed at in the world, and which it is a man's happiness to go along with or his misery to go counter to,—to learn, in short, the will of God,—the moment, I say, culture is considered not merely as the endeavour to *see* and *learn* this, but as the endeavour, also, to make it *prevail*, the moral, social, and beneficent character of culture becomes manifest. The mere endeavour to see and learn the truth for our own personal satisfaction is indeed a commencement for making it prevail, a preparing the way for this, which always serves this, and is wrongly, therefore, stamped with blame absolutely in itself and not only in its caricature and degeneration. But perhaps it has got stamped with blame, and disparaged with the dubious title of curiosity, because in comparison with this wider endeavour of such great and plain utility it looks selfish, petty, and unprofitable.

And religion, the greatest and most important of the efforts by which the human race has manifested its impulse to perfect itself,—religion, that voice of the deepest human experience,—does not only enjoin and sanction the aim which is the great aim of culture, the aim of setting ourselves to ascertain what perfection is and to make it prevail; but also, in determining generally in what human perfection consists, religion comes to a conclusion identical with that which culture,—culture seeking the determination of this question through *all* the voices of human experience which have been heard upon it, of art, science, poetry, philosophy, history, as well as of religion, in order to give a greater fulness and certainty to its solution,—likewise reaches. Religion says: *The kingdom of God is within you;*[6] and culture, in like manner, places human perfection in an *internal* condition, in the growth and predominance of our humanity proper, as distinguished from our animality. It places it in the ever-increasing efficacy and in the general harmonious expansion of those gifts of thought and feeling, which make the peculiar dignity, wealth, and happiness of human nature. As I have said on a former occasion: "It is in making endless additions to itself, in the endless expansion of its powers, in endless growth in wisdom and beauty, that the spirit of the human race finds its ideal. To reach this ideal, culture is an indispensable aid, and that is the true value of culture."[7] Not a having and a resting, but a growing and a becoming, is the character of perfection as culture conceives it; and here, too, it coincides with religion.

---

[6]*The kingdom . . . within you:* Luke 17:21.

[7]**It is . . . culture**": Arnold is quoting his *A French Eton* (1864).

And because men are all members of one great whole, and the sympathy which is in human nature will not allow one member to be indifferent to the rest or to have a perfect welfare independent of the rest, the expansion of our humanity, to suit the idea of perfection which culture forms, must be a *general* expansion. Perfection, as culture conceives it, is not possible while the individual remains isolated. The individual is required, under pain of being stunted and enfeebled in his own development if he disobeys, to carry others along with him in his march towards perfection, to be continually doing all he can to enlarge and increase the volume of the human stream sweeping thitherward. And here, once more, culture lays on us the same obligation as religion, which says, as Bishop Wilson has admirably put it, that "to promote the kingdom of God is to increase and hasten one's own happiness."

But, finally, perfection,—as culture from a thorough disinterested study of human nature and human experience learns to conceive it,—is a harmonious expansion of *all* the powers, which make the beauty and worth of human nature, and is not consistent with the overdevelopment of any one power at the expense of the rest. Here culture goes beyond religion, as religion is generally conceived by us.

If culture, then, is a study of perfection, and of harmonious perfection, general perfection, and perfection which consists in becoming something rather than in having something, in an inward condition of the mind and spirit, not in an outward set of circumstances,—it is clear that culture, instead of being the frivolous and useless thing which Mr. Bright, and Mr. Frederic Harrison, and many other Liberals are apt to call it, has a very important function to fulfil for mankind. And this function is particularly important in our modern world, of which the whole civilisation is, to a much greater degree than the civilisation of Greece and Rome, mechanical and external, and tends constantly to become more so. But above all in our own country has culture a weighty part to perform, because here that mechanical character, which civilisation tends to take everywhere, is shown in the most eminent degree. Indeed nearly all the characters of perfection, as culture teaches us to fix them, meet in this country with some powerful tendency which thwarts them and sets them at defiance. The idea of perfection as an *inward* condition of the mind and spirit is at variance with the mechanical and material civilisation in esteem with us, and nowhere, as I have said, so much in esteem as with us. The idea of perfection as a *general* expansion of the human family is at variance with our strong individualism, our hatred of all limits to the unrestrained swing of the individual's personality, our maxim of "every man for himself." Above all, the idea of perfection as a *harmonious* expansion of human nature is at variance with our want of flexibility, with our inaptitude for seeing more than one side of a thing, with our intense energetic absorption in the particular pursuit we happen to be following. So culture has a rough task to achieve in this country. Its preachers have, and are likely long to have, a hard time of it, and they will much oftener be regarded, for a great while to come, as elegant or spurious Jeremiahs than as friends and benefactors. That, however, will not prevent their doing in the end good service if they persevere. And, meanwhile, the mode of action they have to pursue, and the sort of habits they must fight against, ought to be made quite clear for every one to see, who may be willing to look at the matter attentively and dispassionately.

Faith in machinery is, I said, our besetting danger; often in machinery most absurdly disproportioned to the end which this machinery, if it is to do any good at all, is to serve; but always in machinery, as if it had a value in and for itself. What is freedom but machinery? what is population but machinery? what is coal but machinery? what are railroads but machinery? what is wealth but machinery? what are, even, religious organisations but machinery? Now almost every voice in England is accustomed to speak of these things as if they were precious ends in themselves, and therefore had some of the characters of perfection indisputably joined to them. I have before now noticed Mr. Roebuck's[8] stock argument for proving the greatness and happiness of England as she is, and for quite stopping the mouths of all gainsayers. Mr. Roebuck is never weary of reiterating this argument of his, so I do not know why I should be weary of noticing it. "May not every man in England say what he likes?"—Mr. Roebuck perpetually asks; and that, he thinks, is quite sufficient, and when every man may say what he likes, our aspirations ought to be satisfied. But the aspirations of culture, which is the study of perfection, are not satisfied, unless what men say, when they may say what they like, is worth saying,—has good in it, and more good than bad. In the same way the *Times*, replying to some foreign strictures on the dress, looks, and behaviour of the English abroad, urges that the English ideal is that every one should be free to do and to look just as he likes. But culture indefatigably tries, not to make what each raw person may like the rule by which he fashions himself; but to draw ever nearer to a sense of what is indeed beautiful, graceful, and becoming, and to get the raw person to like that.

---

[8]John Arthur **Roebuck** (1801–1879): see "The Function of Criticism at the Present Time," note 15.

And in the same way with respect to railroads and coal. Every one must have observed the strange language current during the late discussions as to the possible failures of our supplies of coal. Our coal, thousands of people were saying, is the real basis of our national greatness; if our coal runs short, there is an end of the greatness of England. But what *is* greatness?—culture makes us ask. Greatness is a spiritual condition worthy to excite love, interest, and admiration; and the outward proof of possessing greatness is that we excite love, interest, and admiration. If England were swallowed up by the sea to-morrow, which of the two, a hundred years hence, would most excite the love, interest, and admiration of mankind,—would most, therefore, show the evidences of having possessed greatness,—the England of the last twenty years, or the England of Elizabeth, of a time of splendid spiritual effort, but when our coal, and our industrial operations depending on coal, were very little developed? Well, then, what an unsound habit of mind it must be which makes us talk of things like coal or iron as constituting the greatness of England, and how salutary a friend is culture, bent on seeing things as they are, and thus dissipating delusions of this kind and fixing standards of perfection that are real!

Wealth, again, that end to which our prodigious works for material advantage are directed,—the commonest of commonplaces tells us how men are always apt to regard wealth as a precious end in itself; and certainly they have never been so apt thus to regard it as they are in England at the present time. Never did people believe anything more firmly than nine Englishmen out of ten at the present day believe that our greatness and welfare are proved by our being so very rich. Now, the use of culture is that it helps us, by means of its spiritual standard of perfection, to regard wealth as but machinery, and not only to say as a matter of words that we regard wealth as but machinery, but really to perceive and feel that it is so. If it were not for this purging effect wrought upon our minds by culture, the whole world, the future as well as the present, would inevitably belong to the Philistines.[9] The people who believe most that our greatness and welfare are proved by our being very rich, and who most give their lives and thoughts to becoming rich, are just the very people whom we call Philistines. Culture says: "Consider these people, then, their way of life, their habits, their manners, the very tones of their voice; look at them attentively; observe the literature they read, the things which give them pleasure, the words which come forth out of their mouths, the thoughts which make the furniture of their minds; would any amount of wealth be worth having with the condition that one was to become just like these people by having it?" And thus culture begets a dissatisfaction which is of the highest possible value in stemming the common tide of men's thoughts in a wealthy and industrial community, and which saves the future, as one may hope, from being vulgarised, even if it cannot save the present.

Population, again, and bodily health and vigour, are things which are nowhere treated in such an unintelligent, misleading, exaggerated way as in England. Both are really machinery; yet how many people all around us do we see rest in them and fail to look beyond them! Why, one has heard people, fresh from reading certain articles of the *Times* on the Registrar-General's returns of marriages and births in this country, who would talk of our large English families in quite a solemn strain, as if they had something in itself beautiful, elevating, and meritorious in them; as if the British Philistine would have only to present himself before the Great Judge with his twelve children, in order to be received among the sheep as a matter of right!

But bodily health and vigour, it may be said, are not to be classed with wealth and population as mere machinery; they have a more real and essential value. True; but only as they are more intimately connected with a perfect spiritual condition than wealth or population are. The moment we disjoin them from the idea of a perfect spiritual condition, and pursue them, as we do pursue them, for their own sake and as ends in themselves, our worship of them becomes as mere worship of machinery, as our worship of wealth or population, and as unintelligent and vulgarising a worship as that is. Every one with anything like an adequate idea of human perfection has distinctly marked this subordination to higher and spiritual ends of the cultivation of bodily vigour and activity. "Bodily exercise profiteth little; but godliness is profitable unto all things," says the author of the Epistle to Timothy. And the utilitarian Franklin[10] says just as explicitly:—"Eat and drink such an exact quantity as suits the constitution of thy body, *in reference to the services of the mind.*" But the point of view of culture, keeping the mark of human perfection simply and broadly in view, and not assigning to this perfection, as religion or utilitarianism assigns to it, a special and limited character, this point of view, I say, of culture is best given by these words of Epictetus:[11]—"It is a sign of ἀφυΐα," says he,—that is, of a nature

[9]**Philistines**: self-satisfied middle class; see 1 Samuel 17.

[10]**1 Timothy** 4:8. Benjamin **Franklin** (1706–1790): quoted from *Poor Richard's Almanack* (1742).

[11]**Epictetus**: Greek Stoic philosopher (55–135?).

not finely tempered,—"to give yourselves up to things which relate to the body; to make, for instance, a great fuss about exercise, a great fuss about eating, a great fuss about drinking, a great fuss about walking, a great fuss about riding. All these things ought to be done merely by the way: the formation of the spirit and character must be our real concern." This is admirable; and, indeed, the Greek word εὐφυΐα, a finely tempered nature, gives exactly the notion of perfection as culture brings us to conceive it: a harmonious perfection, a perfection in which the characters of beauty and intelligence are both present, which unites "the two noblest of things,"—as Swift, who of one of the two, at any rate, had himself all too little, most happily calls them in his *Battle of the Books*,[12]—"the two noblest of things, *sweetness and light.*" The εὐφυής is the man who tends towards sweetness and light; the ἀφυής, on the other hand, is our Philistine. The immense spiritual significance of the Greeks is due to their having been inspired with this central and happy idea of the essential character of human perfection; and Mr. Bright's misconception of culture, as a smattering of Greek and Latin, comes itself after all, from this wonderful significance of the Greeks having affected the very machinery of our education, and is in itself a kind of homage to it.

In thus making sweetness and light to be characters of perfection, culture is of like spirit with poetry, follows one law with poetry. Far more than on our freedom, our population, and our industrialism, many amongst us rely upon our religious organisations to save us. I have called religion a yet more important manifestation of human nature than poetry, because it has worked on a broader scale for perfection, and with greater masses of men. But the idea of beauty and of a human nature perfect on all its sides, which is the dominant idea of poetry, is a true and invaluable idea, though it has not yet had the success that the idea of conquering the obvious faults of our animality, and of a human nature perfect on the moral side,—which is the dominant idea of religion,—has been enabled to have; and it is destined, adding to itself the religious idea of a devout energy, to transform and govern the other.

The best art and poetry of the Greeks, in which religion and poetry are one, in which the idea of beauty and of a human nature perfect on all sides adds to itself a religious and devout energy, and works in the strength of that, is on this account of such surpassing interest and instructiveness for us, though it was,—as, having regard to the human race in general, and, indeed, having regard to the Greeks themselves, we must own,—a premature attempt, an attempt which for success needed the moral and religious fibre in humanity to be more braced and developed than it had yet been. But Greece did not err in having the idea of beauty, harmony, and complete human perfection, so present and paramount. It is impossible to have this idea too present and paramount; only, the moral fibre must be braced too. And we, because we have braced the moral fibre, are not on that account in the right way, if at the same time the idea of beauty, harmony, and complete human perfection, is wanting or misapprehended amongst us; and evidently it *is* wanting or misapprehended at present. And when we rely as we do on our religious organisations, which in themselves do not and cannot give us this idea, and think we have done enough if we make them spread and prevail, then, I say, we fall into our common fault of overvaluing machinery.

Nothing is more common than for people to confound the inward peace and satisfaction which follows the subduing of the obvious faults of our animality with what I may call absolute inward peace and satisfaction,—the peace and satisfaction which are reached as we draw near to complete spiritual perfection, and not merely to moral perfection, or rather to relative moral perfection. No people in the world have done more and struggled more to attain this relative moral perfection than our English race has. For no people in the world has the command to *resist the devil, to overcome the wicked one*,[13] in the nearest and most obvious sense of those words, had such a pressing force and reality. And we have had our reward, not only in the great worldly prosperity which our obedience to this command has brought us, but also, and far more, in great inward peace and satisfaction. But to me few things are more pathetic than to see people, on the strength of the inward peace and satisfaction which their rudimentary efforts towards perfection have brought them, employ, concerning their incomplete perfection and the religious organisations within which they have found it, language which properly applies only to complete perfection, and is a far-off echo of the human soul's prophecy of it. Religion itself, I need hardly say, supplies them in abundance with this grand language. And very freely do they use it; yet it is really the severest possible criticism of such an incomplete perfection as alone we have yet reached through our religious organisations.

The impulse of the English race towards moral development and self-conquest has nowhere so powerfully manifested itself as in Puritanism. Nowhere has Puritanism found

---

[12]Jonathan **Swift** (1667–1745). *Battle of the Books* (1704).

[13]*resist the devil*: James 4:7. *overcome the wicked one*: 1 John 2:13–14.

so adequate an expression as in the religious organisation of the Independents. The modern Independents have a newspaper, the *Nonconformist*, written with great sincerity and ability. The motto, the standard, the profession of faith which this organ of theirs carries aloft, is: "The Dissidence of Dissent and the Protestantism of the Protestant religion." There is sweetness, light, and an ideal of complete harmonious human perfection! One need not go to culture and poetry to find language to judge it. Religion, with its instinct for perfection, supplies language to judge it, language, too, which is in our mouths every day. "Finally, be of one mind, united in feeling," says St. Peter. There is an ideal which judges the Puritan ideal: "The Dissidence of Dissent and the Protestantism of the Protestant religion!" And religious organisations like this are what people believe in, rest in, would give their lives for! Such, I say, is the wonderful virtue of even the beginnings of perfection, of having conquered even the plain faults of our animality, that the religious organisation which has helped us to do it can seem to us something precious, salutary, and to be propagated, even when it wears such a brand of imperfection on its forehead as this. And men have got such a habit of giving to the language of religion a special application, of making it a mere jargon, that for the condemnation which religion itself passes on the shortcomings of their religious organisations they have no ear; they are sure to cheat themselves and to explain this condemnation away. They can only be reached by the criticism which culture, like poetry, speaking a language not to be sophisticated, and resolutely testing these organisations by the ideal of a human perfection complete on all sides, applies to them.

But men of culture and poetry, it will be said, are again and again failing, and failing conspicuously, in the necessary first stage to a harmonious perfection, in the subduing of the great obvious faults of our animality, which it is the glory of these religious organisations to have helped us to subdue. True, they do often so fail. They have often been without the virtues as well as the faults of the Puritan; it has been one of their dangers that they so felt the Puritan's faults that they too much neglected the practice of his virtues. I will not, however, exculpate them at the Puritan's expense. They have often failed in morality, and morality is indispensable. And they have been punished for their failure, as the Puritan has been rewarded for his performance. They have been punished wherein they erred; but their ideal of beauty, of sweetness and light, and a human nature complete on all its sides, remains the true ideal of perfection still; just as the Puritan's ideal of perfection remains narrow and inadequate, although for what he did well he has been

richly rewarded. Notwithstanding the mighty results of the Pilgrim Fathers' voyage, they and their standard of perfection are rightly judged when we figure to ourselves Shakespeare or Virgil,—souls in whom sweetness and light, and all that in human nature is most humane, were eminent,—accompanying them on their voyage, and think what intolerable company Shakespeare and Virgil would have found them! In the same way let us judge the religious organisations which we see all around us. Do not let us deny the good and the happiness which they have accomplished; but do not let us fail to see clearly that their idea of human perfection is narrow and inadequate, and that the Dissidence of Dissent and the Protestantism of the Protestant religion will never bring humanity to its true goal. As I said with regard to wealth: Let us look at the life of those who live in and for it,—so I say with regard to the religious organisations. Look at the life imaged in such a newspaper as the *Nonconformist*,—a life of jealousy of the Establishment, disputes, tea-meetings, openings of chapels, sermons; and then think of it as an ideal of a human life completing itself on all sides, and aspiring with all its organs after sweetness, light, and perfection! . . .

The pursuit of perfection, then, is the pursuit of sweetness and light. He who works for sweetness and light, works to make reason and the will of God prevail. He who works for machinery, he who works for hatred, works only for confusion. Culture looks beyond machinery, culture hates hatred; culture has one great passion, the passion for sweetness and light. It has one even yet greater!—the passion for making them *prevail*. It is not satisfied till we *all* come to a perfect man; it knows that the sweetness and light of the few must be imperfect until the raw and unkindled masses of humanity are touched with sweetness and light. If I have not shrunk from saying that we must work for sweetness and light, so neither have I shrunk from saying that we must have a broad basis, must have sweetness and light for as many as possible. Again and again I have insisted how those are the happy moments of humanity, how those are the marking epochs of a people's life, how those are the flowering times for literature and art and all the creative power of genius, when there is a *national* glow of life and thought, when the whole of society is in the fullest measure permeated by thought, sensible to beauty, intelligent and alive. Only it must be *real* thought and *real* beauty; *real* sweetness and *real* light. Plenty of people will try to give the masses, as they call them, an intellectual food prepared and adapted in the way they think proper for the actual condition of the masses. The ordinary popular literature is an example of this way of working on the masses. Plenty of people will try to indoctrinate the masses with the set of ideas and judgments constituting the creed of their own profession or party. Our religious and political organisations give an example of this way of working on the masses. I condemn neither way; but culture works differently. It does not try to teach down to the level of inferior classes; it does not try to win them for this or that sect of its own, with ready-made judgments and watchwords. It seeks to do away with classes; to make the best that has been thought and known in the world current everywhere; to make all men live in an atmosphere of sweetness and light, where they may use ideas, as it uses them itself, freely,—nourished, and not bound by them.

This is the *social idea;* and the men of culture are the true apostles of equality. The great men of culture are those who have had a passion for diffusing, for making prevail, for carrying from one end of society to the other, the best knowledge, the best ideas of their time; who have laboured to divest knowledge of all that was harsh, uncouth, difficult, abstract, professional, exclusive; to humanise it, to make it efficient outside the clique of the cultivated and learned, yet still remaining the *best* knowledge and thought of the time, and a true source, therefore, of sweetness and light. Such a man was Abelard in the Middle Ages, in spite of all his imperfections; and thence the boundless emotion and enthusiasm which Abelard excited. Such were Lessing and Herder[14] in Germany, at the end of the last century; and their services to Germany were in this way inestimably precious. Generations will pass, and literary monuments will accumulate, and works far more perfect than the works of Lessing and Herder will be produced in Germany; and yet the names of these two men will fill a German with a reverence and enthusiasm such as the names of the most gifted masters will hardly awaken. And why? Because they *humanised* knowledge; because they broadened the basis of life and intelligence; because they worked powerfully to diffuse sweetness and light, to make reason and the will of God prevail. With Saint Augustine they said: "Let us not leave thee alone to make in the secret of thy knowledge, as thou didst before the creation of the firmament, the division of light from darkness; let the children of thy spirit, placed in their firmament, make their light shine upon the earth, mark the division of night and day, and announce the revolution of the times; for the old order is passed, and the new arises; the night is spent, the day is come forth; and thou shalt crown the year with thy blessing, when thou shalt send forth labourers into thy harvest sown by other hands than theirs; when thou shalt send forth new labourers to new seed-times, whereof the harvest shall be not yet."[15] (Chapter 1)

Doing as One Likes

I have been trying to show that culture is, or ought to be, the study and pursuit of perfection; and that of perfection as pursued by culture, beauty and intelligence, or, in other words, sweetness and light, are the main characters. But hitherto I have been insisting chiefly on beauty, or sweetness, as a character of perfection. To complete rightly my design, it evidently remains to speak also of intelligence, or light, as a character of perfection.

First, however, I ought perhaps to notice that, both here and on the other side of the Atlantic, all sorts of objections are raised against the "religion of culture," as the objectors mockingly call it, which I am supposed to be promulgating. It is said to be a religion proposing parmaceti, or some scented salve or other, as a cure for human miseries; a religion breathing a spirit of cultivated inaction, making its believer refuse to lend a hand at uprooting the definite evils on all sides of us, and filling him with antipathy against the reforms and reformers which try to extirpate them. In general, it is summed up as being not practical, or,—as some critics familiarly put it,—all moonshine. That Alcibiades,[16] the editor of the *Morning Star*, taunts me, as its promulgator, with living out of the world and knowing nothing of life and men. That great austere toiler, the editor of the *Daily Telegraph*, upbraids me,—but kindly, and more in sorrow than in anger,—for trifling with æsthetics and poetical fancies, while he himself, in that arsenal of his in Fleet Street, is bearing the burden and heat of the day. An intelligent American newspaper, the *Nation*, says that it is very easy to sit in one's study and find fault with the course of modern society, but the thing is to propose practical improvements for it. While, finally, Mr. Frederic Harrison, in a very good-tempered and witty satire, which makes me quite understand his having apparently achieved such a conquest of my young Prussian friend, Arminius,[17] at last gets moved to an almost stern moral impatience, to behold, as he says,

---

[14]Peter **Abelard** (1079–1142): French theologian and philosopher. Gotthold Ephraim **Lessing** (1729–1781), Johann Gottfried **Herder** (1744–1803): German writers.

[15]**Saint Augustine** (354–430): *Confessions* 13.18.

[16]**Alcibiades** (450?–404 BCE): brilliant and ambitious pupil of Socrates.

[17]In "Culture: A Dialogue" (1867) **Harrison** used **Arminius**, a character in Arnold's *Friendship's Garland*, to satirize Arnold.

"Death, sin, cruelty stalk among us, filling their maws with innocence and youth," and me, in the midst of the general tribulation, handing out my pouncet-box.

It is impossible that all these remonstrances and re-proofs should not affect me, and I shall try my very best, in completing my design and in speaking of light as one of the characters of perfection, and of culture as giving us light, to profit by the objections I have heard and read, and to drive at practice as much as I can, by showing the communica-tions and passages into practical life from the doctrine which I am inculcating.

It is said that a man with my theories of sweetness and light is full of antipathy against the rougher or coarser movements going on around him, that he will not lend a hand to the humble operation of uprooting evil by their means, and that therefore the believers in action grow im-patient with him. But what if rough and coarse action, ill-calculated action, action with insufficient light, is, and has for a long time been, our bane? What if our urgent want now is, not to act at any price, but rather to lay in a stock of light for our difficulties? In that case, to refuse to lend a hand to the rougher and coarser movements going on round us, to make the primary need, both for oneself and others, to consist in enlightening ourselves and qualifying ourselves to act less at random, is surely the best and in real truth the most practical line our endeavours can take. So that if I can show what my opponents call rough or coarse action, but what I would rather call random and ill-regulated action,—action with insufficient light, action pur-sued because we like to be doing something and doing it as we please, and do not like the trouble of thinking and the severe constraint of any kind of rule,—if I can show this to be, at the present moment, a practical mischief and danger-ous to us, then I have found a practical use for light in cor-recting this state of things, and have only to exemplify how, in cases which fall under everybody's observation, it may deal with it.

When I began to speak of culture, I insisted on our bondage to machinery, on our proneness to value machin-ery as an end in itself, without looking beyond it to the end for which alone, in truth, it is valuable. Freedom, I said, was one of those things which we thus worshipped in itself, without enough regarding the ends for which freedom is to be desired. In our common notions and talk about freedom, we eminently show our idolatry of machinery. Our preva-lent notion is,—and I quoted a number of instances to prove it,—that it is a most happy and important thing for a man merely to be able to do as he likes. On what he is to do when he is thus free to do as he likes, we do not lay so much stress. Our familiar praise of the British Constitution under which we live, is that it is a system of checks,—a sys-tem which stops and paralyses any power in interfering with the free action of individuals. To this effect Mr. Bright, who loves to walk in the old ways of the Constitution, said forcibly in one of his great speeches, what many other peo-ple are every day saying less forcibly, that the central idea of English life and politics is *the assertion of personal liberty*. Evi-dently this is so; but evidently, also, as feudalism, which with its ideas and habits of subordination was for many cen-turies silently behind the British Constitution, dies out, and we are left with nothing but our system of checks, and our notion of its being the great right and happiness of an En-glishman to do as far as possible what he likes, we are in danger of drifting towards anarchy. We have not the no-tion, so familiar on the Continent and to antiquity, of *the State*,—the nation in its collective and corporate character, entrusted with stringent powers for the general advantage, and controlling individual wills in the name of an interest wider than that of individuals. We say, what is very true, that this notion is often made instrumental to tyranny; we say that a State is in reality made up of the individuals who compose it, and that every individual is the best judge of his own interests. Our leading class is an aristocracy, and no aristocracy likes the notion of a State-authority greater than itself, with a stringent administrative machinery supersed-ing the decorative inutilities of lord-lieutenancy, deputy-lieutenancy, and the *posse comitatus*,[18] which are all in its own hands. Our middle class, the great representative of trade and Dissent, with its maxims of every man for himself in business, every man for himself in religion, dreads a power-ful administration which might somehow interfere with it; and besides, it has its own decorative inutilities of vestry-manship and guardianship, which are to this class what lord-lieutenancy and the county magistracy are to the aris-tocratic class, and a stringent administration might either take these functions out of its hands, or prevent its exercis-ing them in its own comfortable, independent manner, as at present.

Then as to our working class. This class, pressed con-stantly by the hard daily compulsion of material wants, is naturally the very centre and stronghold of our national idea, that it is man's ideal right and felicity to do as he likes. I think I have somewhere related how M. Michelet[19] said to

---

[18]*posse comitatus:* legally authorized armed force.

[19]Jules **Michelet** (1798–1874): French historian whom Arnold met in Paris.

me of the people of France, that it was "a nation of barbarians civilised by the conscription." He meant that through their military service the idea of public duty and of discipline was brought to the mind of these masses, in other respects so raw and uncultivated. Our masses are quite as raw and uncultivated as the French; and so far from their having the idea of public duty and of discipline, superior to the individual's self-will, brought to their mind by a universal obligation of military service, such as that of the conscription,—so far from their having this, the very idea of a conscription is so at variance with our English notion of the prime right and blessedness of doing as one likes, that I remember the manager of the Clay Cross[20] works in Derbyshire told me during the Crimean war, when our want of soldiers was much felt and some people were talking of a conscription, that sooner than submit to a conscription the population of that district would flee to the mines, and lead a sort of Robin Hood life under ground.

For a long time, as I have said, the strong feudal habits of subordination and deference continued to tell upon the working class. The modern spirit has now almost entirely dissolved those habits, and the anarchical tendency of our worship of freedom in and for itself, of our superstitious faith, as I say, in machinery, is becoming very manifest. More and more, because of this our blind faith in machinery, because of our want of light to enable us to look beyond machinery to the end for which machinery is valuable, this and that man, and this and that body of men, all over the country, are beginning to assert and put in practice an Englishman's right to do what he likes; his right to march where he likes, meet where he likes, enter where he likes, hoot as he likes, threaten as he likes, smash as he likes. All this, I say, tends to anarchy; and though a number of excellent people, and particularly my friends of the Liberal or progressive party, as they call themselves, are kind enough to reassure us by saying that these are trifles, that a few transient outbreaks of rowdyism signify nothing, that our system of liberty is one which itself cures all the evils which it works, that the educated and intelligent classes stand in overwhelming strength and majestic repose, ready, like our military force in riots, to act at a moment's notice,—yet one finds that one's Liberal friends generally say this because they have such faith in themselves and their nostrums, when they shall return, as the public welfare requires, to place and power. But this faith of theirs one cannot exactly share, when one has so long had them and their nostrums at

work, and sees that they have not prevented our coming to our present embarrassed condition. And one finds, also, that the outbreaks of rowdyism tend to become less and less of trifles, to become more frequent rather than less frequent; and that meanwhile our educated and intelligent classes remain in their majestic repose, and somehow or other, whatever happens, their overwhelming strength, like our military force in riots, never does act.

How, indeed, *should* their overwhelming strength act, when the man who gives an inflammatory lecture, or breaks down the park railings[21] or invades a Secretary of State's office, is only following an Englishman's impulse to do as he likes; and our own conscience tells us that we ourselves have always regarded this impulse as something primary and sacred? Mr. Murphy[22] lectures at Birmingham, and showers on the Catholic population of that town "words," says the Home Secretary, "only fit to be addressed to thieves or murderers." What then? Mr. Murphy has his own reasons of several kinds. He suspects the Roman Catholic Church of designs upon Mrs. Murphy; and he says if mayors and magistrates do not care for their wives and daughters, he does. But, above all, he is doing as he likes; or, in worthier language, asserting his personal liberty. "I will carry out my lectures if they walk over my body as a dead corpse; and I say to the Mayor of Birmingham that he is my servant while I am in Birmingham, and as my servant he must do his duty and protect me." Touching and beautiful words, which find a sympathetic chord in every British bosom! The moment it is plainly put before us that a man is asserting his personal liberty, we are half disarmed; because we are believers in freedom, and not in some dream of a right reason to which the assertion of our freedom is to be subordinated. Accordingly, the Secretary of State had to say that although the lecturer's language was "only fit to be addressed to thieves or murderers," yet, "I do not think he is to be deprived, I do not think that anything I have said could justify the inference that he is to be deprived, of the right of protection in a place built by him for the purpose of these lectures; because the language was not language which afforded grounds for a criminal prosecution." No, nor to be silenced by Mayor, or Home Secretary, or any administrative authority on earth, simply on their notion of what is discreet and reasonable! This is in perfect consonance

---

[20]**Clay Cross**: coal-mining town.

[21]In July 1866 demonstrators supporting the Second Reform Bill (1867) tore down the **railings** in Hyde Park, London; the Hyde Park riots became Arnold's main symbol of anarchy.

[22]William **Murphy**: anti-Catholic lecturer.

with our public opinion, and with our national love for the assertion of personal liberty.

In quite another department of affairs, an experienced and distinguished Chancery Judge[23] relates an incident which is just to the same effect as this of Mr. Murphy. A testator bequeathed £300 a year, to be for ever applied as a pension to some person who had been unsuccessful in literature, and whose duty should be to support and diffuse, by his writings, the testator's own views, as enforced in the testator's publications. The views were not worth a straw, and the bequest was appealed against in the Court of Chancery on the ground of its absurdity; but, being only absurd, it was upheld, and the so-called charity was established. Having, I say, at the bottom of our English hearts a very strong belief in freedom, and a very weak belief in right reason, we are soon silenced when a man pleads the prime right to do as he likes, because this is the prime right for ourselves too; and even if we attempt now and then to mumble something about reason, yet we have ourselves thought so little about this and so much about liberty, that we are in conscience forced, when our brother Philistine with whom we are meddling turns boldly round upon us and asks: *Have you any light?*—to shake our heads ruefully, and to let him go his own way after all.

There are many things to be said on behalf of this exclusive attention of ours to liberty, and of the relaxed habits of government which it has engendered. It is very easy to mistake or to exaggerate the sort of anarchy from which we are in danger through them. We are not in danger from Fenianism,[24] fierce and turbulent as it may show itself; for against this our conscience is free enough to let us act resolutely and put forth our overwhelming strength the moment there is any real need for it. In the first place, it never was any part of our creed that the great right and blessedness of an Irishman, or, indeed, of anybody on earth except an Englishman, is to do as he likes; and we can have no scruple at all about abridging, if necessary, a non-Englishman's assertion of personal liberty. The British Constitution, its checks, and its prime virtues, are for Englishmen. We may extend them to others out of love and kindness; but we find no real divine law written on our hearts constraining us

so to extend them. And then the difference between an Irish Fenian and an English rough is so immense, and the case, in dealing with the Fenian, so much more clear! He is so evidently desperate and dangerous, a man of a conquered race, a Papist, with centuries of ill-usage to inflame him against us, with an alien religion established in his country by us at his expense, with no admiration of our institutions, no love of our virtues, no talents for our business, no turn for our comfort! Show him our symbolical Truss Manufactory[25] on the finest site in Europe, and tell him that British industrialism and individualism can bring a man to that, and he remains cold! Evidently, if we deal tenderly with a sentimentalist like this, it is out of pure philanthropy.

But with the Hyde Park rioter how different! He is our own flesh and blood; he is a Protestant; he is framed by nature to do as we do, hate what we hate, love what we love; he is capable of feeling the symbolical force of the Truss Manufactory; the question of questions, for him, is a wages question. That beautiful sentence Sir Daniel Gooch quoted to the Swindon workmen, and which I treasure as Mrs. Gooch's Golden Rule, or the Divine Injunction "Be ye Perfect"[26] done into British,—the sentence Sir Daniel Gooch's mother repeated to him every morning when he was a boy going to work:—*"Ever remember, my dear Dan, that you should look forward to being some day manager of that concern!"*—this truthful maxim is perfectly fitted to shine forth in the heart of the Hyde Park rough also, and to be his guiding-star through life. He has no visionary schemes of revolution and transformation, though of course he would like his class to rule, as the aristocratic class like their class to rule, and the middle class theirs. But meanwhile our social machine is a little out of order; there are a good many people in our paradisiacal centres of industrialism and individualism taking the bread out of one another's mouths. The rough has not yet quite found his groove and settled down to his work, and so he is just asserting his personal liberty a little, going where he likes, assembling where he likes, bawling as he likes, hustling as he likes. Just as the rest of us,—as the country squires in the aristocratic class, as the political dissenters in the middle class,—he has no idea of a *State*, of the nation in its collective and corporate character controlling, as government, the free swing of this or that one of its members in the name of the higher reason of all of them, his own as well as that of others. He sees the rich, the aristocratic class, in

---

[23]The Court of **Chancery**, which dealt with contracts, trusts, and issues not covered by specific laws, was infamous for procedural delays; Dickens' *Bleak House* (1853) was the most famous of many attacks on it.

[24]**Fenianism**: movement supporting Irish independence with acts of terrorism.

[25]Coles's **Truss Manufactury**: in London's Trafalgar Square.

[26]**Sir Daniel Gooch** (1816–1889): railway pioneer, inventor, MP. "**Be ye Perfect**": Matthew 5:48.

occupation of the executive government, and so if he is stopped from making Hyde Park a bear-garden or the streets impassable, he says he is being butchered by the aristocracy.

His apparition is somewhat embarrassing, because too many cooks spoil the broth; because, while the aristocratic and middle classes have long been doing as they like with great vigour, he has been too undeveloped and submissive hitherto to join in the game; and now, when he does come, he comes in immense numbers, and is rather raw and rough. But he does not break many laws, or not many at one time; and, as our laws were made for very different circumstances from our present (but always with an eye to Englishmen doing as they like), and as the clear letter of the law must be against our Englishman who does as he likes and not only the spirit of the law and public policy, and as Government must neither have any discretionary power nor act resolutely on its own interpretation of the law if any one disputes it, it is evident our laws give our playful giant, in doing as he likes, considerable advantage. Besides, even if he can be clearly proved to commit an illegality in doing as he likes, there is always the resource of not putting the law in force, or of abolishing it. So he has his way, and if he has his way he is soon satisfied for the time. However, he falls into the habit of taking it oftener and oftener, and at last begins to create by his operations a confusion of which mischievous people can take advantage, and which, at any rate, by troubling the common course of business throughout the country, tends to cause distress, and so to increase the sort of anarchy and social disintegration which had previously commenced. And thus that profound sense of settled order and security, without which a society like ours cannot live and grow at all, sometimes seems to be beginning to threaten us with taking its departure.

Now, if culture, which simply means trying to perfect oneself, and one's mind as part of oneself, brings us light, and if light shows us that there is nothing so very blessed in merely doing as one likes, that the worship of the mere freedom to do as one likes is worship of machinery, that the really blessed thing is to like what right reason ordains, and to follow her authority, then we have got a practical benefit out of culture. We have got a much wanted principle, a principle of authority, to counteract the tendency to anarchy which seems to be threatening us.

But how to organise this authority, or to what hands to entrust the wielding of it? How to get your *State,* summing up the right reason of the community, and giving effect to it, as circumstances may require, with vigour? And here I think I see my enemies waiting for me with a hungry joy in their eyes. But I shall elude them.

The *State,* the power most representing the right reason of the nation, and most worthy, therefore, of ruling,—of exercising, when circumstances require it, authority over us all,—is for Mr. Carlyle the aristocracy. For Mr. Lowe,[27] it is the middle class with its incomparable Parliament. For the Reform League, it is the working class, the class with "the brightest powers of sympathy and readiest powers of action." Now culture, with its disinterested pursuit of perfection, culture, simply trying to see things as they are in order to seize on the best and to make it prevail, is surely well fitted to help us to judge rightly, by all the aids of observing, reading, and thinking, the qualifications and titles to our confidence of these three candidates for authority, and can thus render us a practical service of no mean value. . . .

Well, then, what if we tried to rise above the idea of class to the idea of the whole community, *the State,* and to find our centre of light and authority there? Every one of us has the idea of country, as a sentiment; hardly any one of us has the idea of *the State,* as a working power. And why? Because we habitually live in our ordinary selves, which do not carry us beyond the ideas and wishes of the class to which we happen to belong. And we are all afraid of giving to the State too much power, because we only conceive of the State as something equivalent to the class in occupation of the executive government, and are afraid of that class abusing power to its own purposes. If we strengthen the State with the aristocratic class in occupation of the executive government, we imagine we are delivering ourselves up captive to the ideas and wishes of our fierce aristocratical baronet; if with the middle class in occupation of the executive government, to those of our truculent middle-class Dissenting minister; if with the working class, to those of its notorious tribune, Mr. Bradlaugh.[28] And with much justice; owing to the exaggerated notion which we English, as I have said, entertain of the right and blessedness of the mere doing as one likes, of the affirming oneself, and oneself just as it is. People of the aristocratic class want to affirm their ordinary selves, their likings and dislikings; people of the middle class the same, people of the working class the same. By our every day selves, however, we are separate, personal, at war; we are only safe from one

---

[27]Robert **Lowe** (1811–1892): leading Liberal politician whose educational policies Arnold vigorously opposed.

[28]In the section omitted above, Sir Thomas Bateson, MP (the **baronet**), Rev. Cattle, a Wesleyan **minister,** and Charles **Bradlaugh** (1833–1891), radical politician and free-thought advocate, represent the three classes.

another's tyranny when no one has any power; and this safety, in its turn, cannot save us from anarchy. And when, therefore, anarchy presents itself as a danger to us, we know not where to turn.

But by our *best self* we are united, impersonal, at harmony. We are in no peril from giving authority to this, because it is the truest friend we all of us can have; and when anarchy is a danger to us, to this authority we may turn with sure trust. Well, and this is the very self which culture, or the study of perfection, seeks to develop in us; at the expense of our old untransformed self, taking pleasure only in doing what it likes or is used to do, and exposing us to the risk of clashing with every one else who is doing the same! So that our poor culture, which is flouted as so unpractical, leads us to the very ideas capable of meeting the great want of our present embarrassed times! We want an authority, and we find nothing but jealous classes, checks, and a deadlock; culture suggests the idea of *the State*. We find no basis for a firm State-power in our ordinary selves; culture suggests one to us in our *best self*.

It cannot but acutely try a tender conscience to be accused, in a practical country like ours, of keeping aloof from the work and hope of a multitude of earnest-hearted men, and of merely toying with poetry and æsthetics. So it is with no little sense of relief that I find myself thus in the position of one who makes a contribution in aid of the practical necessities of our times. The great thing, it will be observed, is to find our *best* self, and to seek to affirm nothing but that; not,—as we English with our over-value for merely being free and busy have been so accustomed to do,—resting satisfied with a self which comes uppermost long before our best self, and affirming that with blind energy. In short,—to go back yet once more to Bishop Wilson,—of these two excellent rules of Bishop Wilson's for a man's guidance: "Firstly, never go against the best light you have; secondly, take care that your light be not darkness," we English have followed with praiseworthy zeal the first rule, but we have not given so much heed to the second. We have gone manfully according to the best light we have; but we have not taken enough care that this should be really the best light possible for us, that it should not be darkness. And, our honesty being very great, conscience has whispered to us that the light we were following, our ordinary self, was, indeed, perhaps, only an inferior self, only darkness; and that it would not do to impose this seriously on all the world.

But our best self inspires faith, and is capable of affording a serious principle of authority. For example. We are on our way to what the late Duke of Wellington, with his strong sagacity, foresaw and admirably described as "a revolution by due course of law." This is undoubtedly,—if we are still to live and grow, and this famous nation is not to stagnate and dwindle away on the one hand, or, on the other, to perish miserably in mere anarchy and confusion,—what we are on the way to. Great changes there must be, for a revolution cannot accomplish itself without great changes; yet order there must be, for without order a revolution cannot accomplish itself by due course of law. So whatever brings risk of tumult and disorder, multitudinous processions in the streets of our crowded towns, multitudinous meetings in their public places and parks,—demonstrations perfectly unnecessary in the present course of our affairs,—our best self, or right reason, plainly enjoins us to set our faces against. It enjoins us to encourage and uphold the occupants of the executive power, whoever they may be, in firmly prohibiting them. But it does this clearly and resolutely, and is thus a real principle of authority, because it does it with a free conscience; because in thus provisionally strengthening the executive power, it knows that it is not doing this merely to enable our aristocratical baronet to affirm himself as against our working-men's tribune, or our middle-class Dissenter to affirm himself as against both. It knows that it is establishing *the State*, or organ of our collective best self, of our national right reason. And it has the testimony of conscience that it is stablishing the State on behalf of whatever great changes are needed, just as much as on behalf of order; stablishing it to deal just as stringently, when the time comes, with our baronet's aristocratical prejudices, or with the fanaticism of our middle-class Dissenter, as it deals with Mr. Bradlaugh's street-processions. (Chapter 2)

Hebraism and Hellenism

This fundamental ground[29] is our preference of doing to thinking. Now this preference is a main element in our nature, and as we study it we find ourselves opening up a number of large questions on every side.

Let me go back for a moment to Bishop Wilson, who says: "First, never go against the best light you have; secondly, take care that your light be not darkness." We show, as a nation, laudable energy and persistence in walking according to the best light we have, but are not quite careful enough, perhaps, to see that our light be not darkness. This is only another version of the old story that energy is our strong

---

[29]At the end of the preceding section Arnold sets out to find the **fundamental ground** of British habits and practice.

point and favourable characteristic, rather than intelligence. But we may give to this idea a more general form still, in which it will have a yet larger range of application. We may regard this energy driving at practice, this paramount sense of the obligation of duty, self-control, and work, this earnestness in going manfully with the best light we have, as one force. And we may regard the intelligence driving at those ideas which are, after all, the basis of right practice, the ardent sense for all the new and changing combinations of them which man's development brings with it, the indomitable impulse to know and adjust them perfectly, as another force. And these two forces we may regard as in some sense rivals,—rivals not by the necessity of their own nature, but as exhibited in man and his history,—and rivals dividing the empire of the world between them. And to give these forces names from the two races of men who have supplied the most signal and splendid manifestations of them, we may call them respectively the forces of Hebraism and Hellenism. Hebraism and Hellenism,—between these two points of influence moves our world. At one time it feels more powerfully the attraction of one of them, at another time of the other; and it ought to be, though it never is, evenly and happily balanced between them.

The final aim of both Hellenism and Hebraism, as of all great spiritual disciplines, is no doubt the same: man's perfection or salvation. The very language which they both of them use in schooling us to reach this aim is often identical. Even when their language indicates by variation,— sometimes a broad variation, often a but slight and subtle variation,—the different courses of thought which are uppermost in each discipline, even then the unity of the final end and aim is still apparent. To employ the actual words of that discipline with which we ourselves are all of us most familiar, and the words of which, therefore, come most home to us, that final end and aim is "that we might be partakers of the divine nature."[30] These are the words of a Hebrew apostle, but of Hellenism and Hebraism alike this is, I say, the aim. When the two are confronted, as they very often are confronted, it is nearly always with what I may call a rhetorical purpose; the speaker's whole design is to exalt and enthrone one of the two, and he uses the other only as a foil and to enable him the better to give effect to his purpose. Obviously, with us, it is usually Hellenism which is thus reduced to minister to the triumph of Hebraism. There is a sermon on Greece and the Greek spirit by a man never to be mentioned without interest and re-

spect, Frederick Robertson,[31] in which this rhetorical use of Greece and the Greek spirit, and the inadequate exhibition of them necessarily consequent upon this, is almost ludicrous, and would be censurable if it were not to be explained by the exigencies of a sermon. On the other hand, Heinrich Heine,[32] and other writers of his sort, give us the spectacle of the tables completely turned, and of Hebraism brought in just as a foil and contrast to Hellenism, and to make the superiority of Hellenism more manifest. In both these cases there is injustice and misrepresentation. The aim and end of both Hebraism and Hellenism is, as I have said, one and the same, and this aim and end is august and admirable.

Still, they pursue this aim by very different courses. The uppermost idea with Hellenism is to see things as they really are; the uppermost idea with Hebraism is conduct and obedience. Nothing can do away with this ineffaceable difference. The Greek quarrel with the body and its desires is, that they hinder right thinking; the Hebrew quarrel with them is, that they hinder right acting. "He that keepeth the law, happy is he"; "Blessed is the man that feareth the Eternal, that delighteth greatly in his commandments"[33]—that is the Hebrew notion of felicity; and, pursued with passion and tenacity, this notion would not let the Hebrew rest till, as is well known, he had at last got out of the law a network of prescriptions to enwrap his whole life, to govern every moment of it, every impulse, every action. The Greek notion of felicity, on the other hand, is perfectly conveyed in these words of a great French moralist: "C'est le bonheur des hommes,"[34]—when? when they abhor that which is evil?—no; when they exercise themselves in the law of the Lord day and night?—no; when they die daily?—no; when they walk about the New Jerusalem with palms in their hands?—no; but when they think aright, when their thought hits: "quand ils pensent juste." At the bottom of both the Greek and the Hebrew notion is the desire, native in man, for reason and the will of God, the feeling after the universal order,—in a word, the love of God. But, while Hebraism seizes upon certain plain, capital intimations of the universal order, and

[30]"that we . . . nature": 2 Peter 1:4.

[31]Frederick Robertson (1816–1853): influential Anglican clergyman.

[32]Heinrich Heine (1797–1856): German poet, born and brought up as a Jew, who converted to Protestantism for practical reasons.

[33]"He . . . happy is he": Proverbs 29:18. "Blessed . . . commandments": Psalms 112:1.

[34]French moralist: Sainte-Beuve. "C'est le bonheur des hommes": it is men's happiness.

rivets itself, one may say, with unequalled grandeur of earnestness and intensity on the study and observance of them, the bent of Hellenism is to follow, with flexible activity, the whole play of the universal order, to be apprehensive of missing any part of it, of sacrificing one part to another, to slip away from resting in this or that intimation of it, however capital. An unclouded clearness of mind, an unimpeded play of thought, is what this bent drives at. The governing idea of Hellenism is *spontaneity of consciousness;* that of Hebraism, *strictness of conscience.*

Christianity changed nothing in this essential bent of Hebraism to set doing above knowing. Self-conquest, self-devotion, the following not our own individual will, but the will of God, *obedience,* is the fundamental idea of this form, also, of the discipline to which we have attached the general name of Hebraism. Only, as the old law and the network of prescriptions with which it enveloped human life were evidently a motive-power not driving and searching enough to produce the result aimed at,—patient continuance in well-doing, self-conquest,—Christianity substituted for them boundless devotion to that inspiring and affecting pattern of self-conquest offered by Jesus Christ; and by the new motive-power, of which the essence was this, though the love and admiration of Christian churches have for centuries been employed in varying, amplifying, and adorning the plain description of it, Christianity, as St. Paul truly says, "establishes the law," and in the strength of the ampler power which she has thus supplied to fulfil it, has accomplished the miracles, which we all see, of her history. . . .

Yet there is a very important difference between the defeat inflicted on Hellenism by Christianity eighteen hundred years ago, and the check given to the Renascence by Puritanism. The greatness of the difference is well measured by the difference in force, beauty, significance, and usefulness, between primitive Christianity and Protestantism. Eighteen hundred years ago it was altogether the hour of Hebraism. Primitive Christianity was legitimately and truly the ascendant force in the world at that time, and the way of mankind's progress lay through its full development. Another hour in man's development began in the fifteenth century, and the main road of his progress then lay for a time through Hellenism. Puritanism was no longer the central current of the world's progress, it was a side stream crossing the central current and checking it. The cross and the check may have been necessary and salutary, but that does not do away with the essential difference between the main stream of man's advance and a cross or side stream. For more than two hundred years the main stream of man's advance has moved towards knowing himself and the world, seeing things as they are, spontaneity of consciousness; the main impulse of a great part, and that the strongest part, of our nation has been towards strictness of conscience. They have made the secondary the principal at the wrong moment, and the principal they have at the wrong moment treated as secondary. This contravention of the natural order has produced, as such contravention always must produce, a certain confusion and false movement, of which we are now beginning to feel, in almost every direction, the inconvenience. In all directions our habitual courses of action seem to be losing efficaciousness, credit, and control, both with others and even with ourselves. Everywhere we see the beginnings of confusion, and we want a clue to some sound order and authority. This we can only get by going back upon the actual instincts and forces which rule our life, seeing them as they really are, connecting them with other instincts and forces, and enlarging our whole view and rule of life. (Chapter 4)

Our Liberal Practitioners

But an unpretending writer, without a philosophy based on inter-dependent, subordinate, and coherent principles, must not presume to indulge himself too much in generalities. He must keep close to the level ground of common fact, the only safe ground for understandings without a scientific equipment. Therefore, since I have spoken so slightingly of the practical operations in which my friends and countrymen are at this moment engaged for the removal of certain definite evils, I am bound to take, before concluding, some of those operations and to make them, if I can, show the truth of what I have advanced. . . .

If here again, therefore, we minister better to the diseased spirit of our time by leading it to think about the operation our Liberal friends have in hand,[35] than by lending a hand to this operation ourselves, let us see, before we dismiss from our view the practical operations of our Liberal friends, whether the same thing does not hold good as to their celebrated industrial and economical labours also. Their great work of this kind is, of course, their free-trade policy. This policy, as having enabled the poor man to eat untaxed bread, and as having wonderfully augmented trade, we are accustomed to speak of with a kind of thankful solemnity. It is chiefly on their having been our leaders in this policy that Mr. Bright founds for himself and his friends

---

[35]In this final chapter Arnold has been analyzing various **Liberal** causes.

the claim, so often asserted by him, to be considered guides of the blind, teachers of the ignorant, benefactors slowly and laboriously developing in the Conservative party and in the country that which Mr. Bright is fond of calling *the growth of intelligence*,—the object, as is well known, of all the friends of culture also, and the great end and aim of the culture that we preach.

Now, having first saluted free-trade and its doctors with all respect, let us see whether even here, too, our Liberal friends do not pursue their operations in a mechanical way, without reference to any firm intelligible law of things, to human life as a whole, and human happiness; and whether it is not more for our good, at this particular moment at any rate, if, instead of worshipping free-trade with them Hebraistically, as a kind of fetish, and helping them to pursue it as an end in and for itself, we turn the free stream of our thought upon their treatment of it, and see how this is related to the intelligible law of human life, and to national well-being and happiness. In short, suppose we Hellenise a little with free-trade, as we Hellenised with the Real Estate Intestacy Bill, and with the disestablishment of the Irish Church by the power of the Nonconformists' antipathy to religious establishments,[36] and see whether what our reprovers beautifully call ministering to the diseased spirit of our time is best done by the Hellenising method of proceeding, or by the other.

But first let us understand how the policy of free-trade really shapes itself for our Liberal friends, and how they practically employ it as an instrument of national happiness and salvation. For as we said that it seemed clearly right to prevent the Church-property of Ireland from being all taken for the benefit of the Church of a small minority, so it seems clearly right that the poor man should eat untaxed bread, and, generally, that restrictions and regulations which, for the supposed benefit of some particular person or class of persons, make the price of things artificially high here, or artificially low there, and interfere with the natural flow of trade and commerce, should be done away with. But in the policy of our Liberal friends free-trade means more than this, and is specially valued as a stimulant to the production of wealth, as they call it, and to the increase of the trade, business, and population of the country. We have already

seen how these things,—trade, business, and population,—are mechanically pursued by us as ends precious in themselves, and are worshipped as what we call fetishes; and Mr. Bright, I have already said, when he wishes to give the working class a true sense of what makes glory and greatness, tells it to look at the cities it has built, the railroads it has made, the manufactures it has produced. So to this idea of glory and greatness the free-trade which our Liberal friends extol so solemnly and devoutly, has served,—to the increase of trade, business, and population; and for this it is prized. Therefore, the taxing of the poor man's bread has, with this view of national happiness, been used not so much to make the existing poor man's bread cheaper or more abundant, but rather to create more poor men to eat it; so that we cannot precisely say that we have fewer poor men than we had before free-trade, but we can say with truth that we have many more centres of industry, as they are called, and much more business, population, and manufactures. And if we are sometimes a little troubled by our multitude of poor men, yet we know the increase of manufactures and population to be such a salutary thing in itself, and our free-trade policy begets such an admirable movement, creating fresh centres of industry and fresh poor men here, while we were thinking about our poor men there, that we are quite dazzled and borne away, and more and more industrial movement is called for, and our social progress seems to become one triumphant and enjoyable course of what is sometimes called, vulgarly, outrunning the constable.

If, however, taking some other criterion of man's well-being than the cities he has built and the manufactures he has produced, we persist in thinking that our social progress would be happier if there were not so many of us so very poor, and in busying ourselves with notions of in some way or other adjusting the poor man and business one to the other, and not multiplying the one and the other mechanically and blindly, then our Liberal friends, the appointed doctors of free-trade, take us up very sharply. "Art is long," says the *Times*, "and life is short; for the most part we settle things first and understand them afterwards. Let us have as few theories as possible; what is wanted is not the light of speculation. If nothing worked well of which the theory was not perfectly understood, we should be in sad confusion. The relations of labour and capital, we are told, are not understood, yet trade and commerce, on the whole, work satisfactorily." I quote from the *Times* of only the other day. But thoughts like these, as I have often pointed out, are thoroughly British thoughts, and we have been familiar with them for years.

---

[36]Liberals advocated modestly changing the laws governing inheritance and disestablishing the **Irish Church** (i.e., the Anglican Church in Ireland). Arnold believed in **religious establishments**, although not in preferential treatment of the Protestant Church of England in Catholic Ireland.

Or, if we want more of a philosophy of the matter than this, our free-trade friends have two axioms for us, axioms laid down by their justly esteemed doctors, which they think ought to satisfy us entirely. One is, that, other things being equal, the more population increases, the more does production increase to keep pace with it; because men by their numbers and contact call forth all manner of activities and resources in one another and in nature, which, when men are few and sparse, are never developed. The other is, that, although population always tends to equal the means of subsistence, yet people's notions of what subsistence is enlarge as civilisation advances, and take in a number of things beyond the bare necessaries of life; and thus, therefore, is supplied whatever check on population is needed. But the error of our friends is precisely, perhaps, that they apply axioms of this sort as if they were self-acting laws which will put themselves into operation without trouble or planning on our part, if we will only pursue free-trade, business, and population zealously and staunchly. Whereas the real truth is, that, however the case might be under other circumstances, yet in fact, as we now manage the matter, the enlarged conception of what is included in *subsistence* does not operate to prevent the bringing into the world of numbers of people who but just attain to the barest necessaries of life or who even fail to attain to them; while, again, though production may increase as population increases, yet it seems that the production may be of such a kind, and so related, or rather non-related, to population, that the population may be little the better for it.

For instance, with the increase of population since Queen Elizabeth's time the production of silk-stockings has wonderfully increased, and silk-stockings have become much cheaper, and procurable in greater abundance by many more people, and tend perhaps, as population and manufactures increase, to get cheaper and cheaper, and at last to become, according to Bastiat's[37] favourite image, a common free property of the human race, like light and air. But bread and bacon have not become much cheaper with the increase of population since Queen Elizabeth's time, nor procurable in much greater abundance by many more people; neither do they seem at all to promise to become, like light and air, a common free property of the human race. And if bread and bacon have not kept pace with our population, and we have many more people in want of them now than in Queen Elizabeth's time, it seems vain to tell us that silk-stockings have kept pace with our population, or even

more than kept pace with it, and that we are to get our comfort out of that.

In short, it turns out that our pursuit of free-trade, as of so many other things, has been too mechanical. We fix upon some object, which in this case is the production of wealth, and the increase of manufactures, population, and commerce through free-trade, as a kind of one thing needful, or end in itself; and then we pursue it staunchly and mechanically, and say that it is our duty to pursue it staunchly and mechanically, not to see how it is related to the whole intelligible law of things and to full human perfection, or to treat it as the piece of machinery, of varying value as its relations to the intelligible law of things vary, which it really is.

So it is of no use to say to the *Times*, and to our Liberal friends rejoicing in the possession of their talisman of free-trade, that about one in nineteen of our population is a pauper, and that, this being so, trade and commerce can hardly be said to prove by their satisfactory working that it matters nothing whether the relations between labour and capital are understood or not; nay, that we can hardly be said not to be in sad confusion. For here our faith in the staunch mechanical pursuit of a fixed object comes in, and covers itself with that imposing and colossal necessitarianism of the *Times* which we have before noticed. And this necessitarianism, taking for granted that an increase in trade and population is a good in itself, one of the chiefest of goods, tells us that disturbances of human happiness caused by ebbs and flows in the tide of trade and business, which, on the whole, steadily mounts, are inevitable and not to be quarreled with. This firm philosophy I seek to call to mind when I am in the East of London, whither my avocations often lead me; and, indeed, to fortify myself against the depressing sights which on these occasions assail us, I have transcribed from the *Times* one strain of this kind, full of the finest economical doctrine, and always carry it about with me. The passage is this:—

"The East End is the most commercial, the most industrial, the most fluctuating region of the metropolis. It is always the first to suffer; for it is the creature of prosperity, and falls to the ground the instant there is no wind to bear it up. The whole of that region is covered with huge docks, shipyards, manufactories, and a wilderness of small houses, all full of life and happiness in brisk times, but in dull times withered and lifeless, like the deserts we read of in the East. Now their brief spring is over. There is no one to blame for this; it is the result of Nature's simplest laws!" We must all agree that it is impossible that anything can be firmer than this, or show a surer faith in the working of free-trade, as our Liberal friends understand and employ it.

---

[37]Frédéric **Bastiat** (1801–1850): French economist.

But, if we still at all doubt whether the indefinite multi-plication of manufactories and small houses can be such an absolute good in itself as to counterbalance the indefinite multiplication of poor people, we shall learn that this multi-plication of poor people, too, is an absolute good in itself, and the result of divine and beautiful laws. This is indeed a favourite thesis with our Philistine friends, and I have al-ready noticed the pride and gratitude with which they re-ceive certain articles in the *Times*, dilating in thankful and solemn language on the majestic growth of our population. But I prefer to quote now, on this topic, the words of an in-genious young Scotch writer, Mr. Robert Buchanan, [38] be-cause he invests with so much imagination and poetry this current idea of the blessed and even divine character which the multiplying of population is supposed in itself to have. "We move to multiplicity," says Mr. Robert Buchanan. "If there is one quality which seems God's, and his exclusively, it seems that divine philoprogenitiveness, that passionate love of distribution and expansion into living forms. Every animal added seems a new ecstasy to the Maker; every life added, a new embodiment of his love. He would *swarm* the earth with beings. There are never enough. Life, life, life,— faces gleaming, hearts beating, must fill every cranny. Not a corner is suffered to remain empty. The whole earth breeds, and God glories."

It is a little unjust, perhaps, to attribute to the Divinity exclusively this philoprogenitiveness, which the British Philistine, and the poorer class of Irish, may certainly claim to share with him; yet how inspiriting is here the whole strain of thought! and these beautiful words, too, I carry about with me in the East of London, and often read them there. They are quite in agreement with the popular lan-guage one is accustomed to hear about children and large families, which describes children as *sent*. And a line of po-etry, which Mr. Robert Buchanan throws in presently after the poetical prose I have quoted,—

"'Tis the old story of the fig-leaf time"—

this fine line, too, naturally connects itself, when one is in the East of London, with the idea of God's desire to *swarm* the earth with beings; because the swarming of the earth with beings does indeed, in the East of London, so seem to revive *the old story of the fig-leaf time*, such a number of the peo-ple one meets there having hardly a rag to cover them; and the more the swarming goes on, the more it promises to re-

vive this old story. And when the story is perfectly revived, the swarming quite completed, and every cranny choke-full, then, too, no doubt, the faces in the East of London will be gleaming faces, which Mr. Robert Buchanan says it is God's desire they should be, and which every one must perceive they are not at present, but, on the contrary, very miserable. . . . (Chapter 6)

And so we bring to an end what we had to say in praise of culture, and in evidence of its special utility for the circum-stances in which we find ourselves, and the confusion which environs us. Through culture seems to lie our way, not only to perfection, but even to safety. Resolutely refusing to lend a hand to the imperfect operations of our Liberal friends, disregarding their impatience, taunts, and reproaches, firmly bent on trying to find in the intelligible laws of things a firmer and sounder basis for future practice than any which we have at present, and believing this search and discovery to be, for our generation and circumstances, of yet more vital and pressing importance than practice itself, we never-theless may do more, perhaps, we poor disparaged followers of culture, to make the actual present, and the frame of soci-ety in which we live, solid and seaworthy, than all which our bustling politicians can do. . . .

Pericles was perhaps the most perfect public speaker who ever lived, for he was the man who most perfectly combined thought and wisdom with feeling and eloquence. Yet Plato brings in Alcibiades declaring, that men went away from the oratory of Pericles, saying it was very fine, it was very good, and afterwards thinking no more about it; but they went away from hearing Socrates talk, he says, with the point of what he had said sticking fast in their minds, and they could not get rid of it. Socrates has drunk his hemlock and is dead; but in his own breast does not every man carry about with him a possible Socrates, in that power of a disinterested play of consciousness upon his stock notions and habits, of which this wise and admirable man gave all through his lifetime the great example, and which was the secret of his incomparable influence? And he who leads men to call forth and exercise in themselves this power, and who busily calls it forth and exercises it in him-self, is at the present moment, perhaps, as Socrates was in his time, more in concert with the vital working of men's minds, and more effectually significant, than any House of Commons' orator, or practical operator in politics.

Every one is now boasting of what he has done to edu-cate men's minds and to give things the course they are tak-ing. Mr. Disraeli educates, Mr. Bright educates, Mr. Beales educates.[39] We, indeed, pretend to educate no one, for we are still engaged in trying to clear and educate ourselves. But we are sure that the endeavour to reach, through culture, the firm intelligible law of things, we are sure that the detaching ourselves from our stock notions and habits, that a more free play of consciousness, an increased desire for sweetness and light, and all the bent which we call Hellenising, is the master impulse even now of the life of our nation and of humanity,—somewhat obscurely perhaps for this actual moment, but decisively and certainly for the immediate future; and that those who work for this are the sovereign educators.

Docile echoes of the eternal voice, pliant organs of the infinite will, such workers are going along with the essential movement of the world; and this is their strength, and their happy and divine fortune. For if the believers in action, who are so impatient with us and call us effeminate, had had the same good fortune, they would, no doubt, have surpassed us in this sphere of vital influence by all the superiority of their genius and energy over ours. But now we go the way the human race is going, while they abolish the Irish Church by the power of the Nonconformists' antipathy to establishments, or they enable a man to marry his deceased wife's sister.[40] (Conclusion)

1869

from The Study of Poetry[1]

"The future of poetry is immense, because in poetry, where it is worthy of its high destinies, our race, as time goes on, will find an ever surer and surer stay. There is not a creed which is not shaken, not an accredited dogma which is not shown to be questionable, not a received tradition which does not threaten to dissolve. Our religion has materialised itself in the fact, in the supposed fact; it has attached its emotion to the fact, and now the fact is failing it. But for poetry the idea is everything; the rest is a world of illusion, of divine illusion. Poetry attaches its emotion to the idea; the idea *is* the fact. The strongest part of our religion to-day is its unconscious poetry."[2]

Let me be permitted to quote these words of my own, as uttering the thought which should, in my opinion, go with us and govern us in all our study of poetry. In the present work it is the course of one great contributory stream to the world-river of poetry that we are invited to follow. We are here invited to trace the stream of English poetry. But whether we set ourselves, as here, to follow only one of the several streams that make the mighty river of poetry, or whether we seek to know them all, our governing thought should be the same. We should conceive of poetry worthily, and more highly than it has been the custom to conceive of it. We should conceive of it as capable of higher uses, and called to higher destinies, than those which in general men have assigned to it hitherto. More and more mankind will discover that we have to turn to poetry to interpret life for us, to console us, to sustain us. Without poetry, our science will appear incomplete; and most of what now passes with us for religion and philosophy will be replaced by poetry. Science, I say, will appear incomplete without it. For finely and truly does Wordsworth call poetry "the impassioned expression which is in the countenance of all science"; and what is a countenance without its expression? Again, Wordsworth finely and truly calls poetry "the breath and finer spirit of all knowledge":[3] our religion, parading evidences such as those on which the popular mind relies now; our philosophy, pluming itself on its reasonings about causation and finite and infinite being; what are they but the shadows and dreams and false shows of knowledge? The day will come when we shall wonder at ourselves for having trusted to them, for having taken them seriously; and the more we perceive their hollowness, the more we shall prize "the breath and finer spirit of knowledge" offered to us by poetry.

But if we conceive thus highly of the destinies of poetry, we must also set our standard for poetry high, since poetry, to be capable of fulfilling such high destinies, must be poetry of a high order of excellence. We must accustom ourselves to a high standard and to a strict judgment. Sainte-Beuve[4] relates that Napoleon one day said, when

---

[39]Benjamin **Disraeli** (1804–1881): novelist, MP, leader of the Conservative party, Prime Minister in 1868 and later. Edmond **Beales** (1803–1881): radical lawyer and political activist.

[40]Liberals made repeated attempts to legalize marriage between a man and his **deceased wife's sister**, which Arnold felt violated delicate family feeling in the name of freedom.

[1]"**The Study of Poetry**": introduction to an anthology, *The English Poets*, ed. T. H. Ward. Arnold's provision of translations suggests that he hopes for a wide general audience.

[2]"**The future . . . unconscious poetry**": from Arnold's introduction to *The Hundred Greatest Men* (1879).

[3]The quotations are from **Wordsworth**, Preface to 2nd ed. of *Lyrical Ballads* (1800).

[4]Charles-Augustin **Sainte-Beuve** (1804–1869): French literary critic whom Arnold regarded as a model.

somebody was spoken of in his presence as a charlatan: "Charlatan as much as you please; but where is there *not* charlatanism?"—"Yes," answers Sainte-Beuve, "in politics, in the art of governing mankind, that is perhaps true. But in the order of thought, in art, the glory, the eternal honour is that charlatanism shall find no entrance; herein lies the inviolableness of that noble portion of man's being." It is admirably said, and let us hold fast to it. In poetry, which is thought and art in one, it is the glory, the eternal honour, that charlatanism shall find no entrance; that this noble sphere be kept inviolate and inviolable. Charlatanism is for confusing or obliterating the distinctions between excellent and inferior, sound and unsound or only half-sound, true and untrue or only half-true. It is charlatanism, conscious or unconscious, whenever we confuse or obliterate these. And in poetry, more than anywhere else, it is unpermissible to confuse or obliterate them. For in poetry the distinction between excellent and inferior, sound and unsound or only half-sound, true and untrue or only half-true, is of paramount importance. It is of paramount importance because of the high destinies of poetry. In poetry, as a criticism of life under the conditions fixed for such a criticism by the laws of poetic truth and poetic beauty, the spirit of our race will find, we have said, as time goes on and as other helps fail, its consolation and stay. But the consolation and stay will be of power in proportion to the power of the criticism of life. And the criticism of life will be of power in proportion as the poetry conveying it is excellent rather than inferior, sound rather than unsound or half-sound, true rather than untrue or half-true.

The best poetry is what we want; the best poetry will be found to have a power of forming, sustaining, and delighting us, as nothing else can. A clearer, deeper sense of the best in poetry, and of the strength and joy to be drawn from it, is the most precious benefit which we can gather from a poetical collection such as the present. And yet in the very nature and conduct of such a collection there is inevitably something which tends to obscure in us the consciousness of what our benefit should be, and to distract us from the pursuit of it. We should therefore steadily set it before our minds at the outset, and should compel ourselves to revert constantly to the thought of it as we proceed.

Yes; constantly in reading poetry, a sense for the best, the really excellent, and of the strength and joy to be drawn from it, should be present in our minds and should govern our estimate of what we read. But this real estimate, the only true one, is liable to be superseded, if we are not watchful, by two other kinds of estimate, the historic estimate and the personal estimate, both of which are fallacious. A poet or a poem may count to us historically, they

may count to us on grounds personal to ourselves, and they may count to us really. They may count to us historically. The course of development of a nation's language, thought, and poetry, is profoundly interesting; and by regarding a poet's work as a stage in this course of development we may easily bring ourselves to make it of more importance as poetry than in itself it really is, we may come to use a language of quite exaggerated praise in criticising it; in short, to over-rate it. So arises in our poetic judgments the fallacy caused by the estimate which we may call historic. Then, again, a poet or a poem may count to us on grounds personal to ourselves. Our personal affinities, likings, and circumstances, have great power to sway our estimate of this or that poet's work, and to make us attach more importance to it as poetry than in itself it really possesses, because to us it is, or has been, of high importance. Here also we over-rate the object of our interest, and apply to it a language of praise which is quite exaggerated. And thus we get the source of a second fallacy in our poetic judgments—the fallacy caused by an estimate which we may call personal.

Both fallacies are natural. It is evident how naturally the study of the history and development of a poetry may incline a man to pause over reputations and works once conspicuous but now obscure, and to quarrel with a careless public for skipping, in obedience to mere tradition and habit, from one famous name or work in its national poetry to another, ignorant of what it misses, and of the reason for keeping what it keeps, and of the whole process of growth in its poetry. The French have become diligent students of their own early poetry, which they long neglected; the study makes many of them dissatisfied with their so-called classical poetry, the court-tragedy of the seventeenth century, a poetry which Pellisson[5] long ago reproached with its want of the true poetic stamp, with its *politesse stérile et rampante*, but which nevertheless has reigned in France as absolutely as if it had been the perfection of classical poetry indeed. The dissatisfaction is natural; yet a lively and accomplished critic, M. Charles d'Héricault, the editor of Clément Marot,[6] goes too far when he says that "the cloud of glory playing round a classic is a mist as dangerous to the future of a literature as it is intolerable for the purposes of history." "It hinders," he goes on, "it hinders us from seeing more than one single point, the culminating and exceptional point; the summary, fictitious and arbitrary, of a

---

[5]Paul Pellisson (1624–1693): French critic. *politesse . . . rampante:* sterile and servile politeness.

[6]**Charles d'Héricault** (1823–1899): historian. **Clément Marot:** 16th-century French poet.

thought and of a work. It substitutes a halo for a physiognomy, it puts a statue where there was once a man, and hiding from us all trace of the labour, the attempts, the weaknesses, the failures, it claims not study but veneration; it does not show us how the thing is done, it imposes upon us a model. Above all, for the historian this creation of classic personages is inadmissible; for it withdraws the poet from his time, from his proper life, it breaks historical relationships, it blinds criticism by conventional admiration, and renders the investigation of literary origins unacceptable. It gives us a human personage no longer, but a God seated immovable amidst His perfect work, like Jupiter on Olympus; and hardly will it be possible for the young student, to whom such work is exhibited at such a distance from him, to believe that it did not issue ready made from that divine head."

All this is brilliantly and tellingly said, but we must plead for a distinction. Everything depends on the reality of a poet's classic character. If he is a dubious classic, let us sift him; if he is a false classic, let us explode him. But if he is a real classic, if his work belongs to the class of the very best (for this is the true and right meaning of the word *classic, classical*), then the great thing for us is to feel and enjoy his work as deeply as ever we can, and to appreciate the wide difference between it and all work which has not the same high character. This is what is salutary, this is what is formative; this is the great benefit to be got from the study of poetry. Everything which interferes with it, which hinders it, is injurious. True, we must read our classic with open eyes, and not with eyes blinded with superstition; we must perceive when his work comes short, when it drops out of the class of the very best, and we must rate it, in such cases, at its proper value. But the use of this negative criticism is not in itself, it is entirely in its enabling us to have a clearer sense and a deeper enjoyment of what is truly excellent. To trace the labour, the attempts, the weaknesses, the failures of a genuine classic, to acquaint oneself with his time and his life and his historical relationships, is mere literary dilettantism unless it has that clear sense and deeper enjoyment for its end. It may be said that the more we know about a classic the better we shall enjoy him; and, if we lived as long as Methuselah[7] and had all of us heads of perfect clearness and wills of perfect steadfastness, this might be true in fact as it is plausible in theory. But the case here is much the same as the case with the Greek and Latin studies of our schoolboys. The elaborate philological groundwork which we require them to lay is in theory an admirable preparation

for appreciating the Greek and Latin authors worthily. The more thoroughly we lay the groundwork, the better we shall be able, it may be said, to enjoy the authors. True, if time were not so short, and schoolboys' wits not so soon tired and their power of attention exhausted; only, as it is, the elaborate philological preparation goes on, but the authors are little known and less enjoyed. So with the investigator of "historic origins" in poetry. He ought to enjoy the true classic all the better for his investigations; he often is distracted from the enjoyment of the best, and with the less good he overbusies himself, and is prone to over-rate it in proportion to the trouble which it has cost him.

The idea of tracing historic origins and historical relationships cannot be absent from a compilation like the present. And naturally the poets to be exhibited in it will be assigned to those persons for exhibition who are known to prize them highly, rather than to those who have no special inclination towards them. Moreover the very occupation with an author, and the business of exhibiting him, disposes us to affirm and amplify his importance. In the present work, therefore, we are sure of frequent temptation to adopt the historic estimate, or the personal estimate, and to forget the real estimate; which latter, nevertheless, we must employ if we are to make poetry yield us its full benefit. So high is that benefit, the benefit of clearly feeling and of deeply enjoying the really excellent, the truly classic in poetry, that we do well, I say, to set it fixedly before our minds as our object in studying poets and poetry, and to make the desire of attaining it the one principle to which, as the *Imitation* says, whatever we may read or come to know, we always return. *Cum multa legeris et cognoveris, ad unum semper oportet redire principium.*[8]

The historic estimate is likely in especial to affect our judgment and our language when we are dealing with ancient poets; the personal estimate when we are dealing with poets our contemporaries, or at any rate modern. The exaggerations due to the historic estimate are not in themselves, perhaps, of very much gravity. Their report hardly enters the general ear; probably they do not always impose even on the literary men who adopt them. But they lead to a dangerous abuse of language. So we hear Caedmon,[9] amongst our own poets, compared to Milton. I have already noticed the enthusiasm of one accomplished French critic for "historic

---

[7]**Methuselah**: see Genesis 5:21–27.

[8]*Cum multa . . . principium*: a phrase Arnold frequently copied in his personal notebooks and translates in the preceding sentence; from *The Imitation of Christ*, by Thomas À Kempis (1379/80–1471), theologian.

[9]**Caedmon**: Old English poet, 2nd century BCE.

origins." Another eminent French critic, M. Vitet,[10] comments upon that famous document of the early poetry of his nation, the *Chanson de Roland*. It is indeed a most interesting document. The *joculator* or *jongleur* Taillefer, who was with William the Conqueror's army at Hastings, marched before the Norman troops, so said the tradition, singing "of Charlemagne and of Roland and of Oliver, and of the vassals who died at Roncevaux"; and it is suggested that in the *Chanson de Roland* by one Turoldus or Théroulde, a poem preserved in a manuscript of the twelfth century in the Bodleian Library at Oxford, we have certainly the matter, perhaps even some of the words, of the chant which Taillefer sang. The poem has vigour and freshness; it is not without pathos. But M. Vitet is not satisfied with seeing in it a document of some poetic value, and of very high historic and linguistic value; he sees in it a grand and beautiful work, a monument of epic genius. In its general design he finds the grandiose conception, in its details he finds the constant union of simplicity with greatness, which are the marks, he truly says, of the genuine epic, and distinguish it from the artificial epic of literary ages. One thinks of Homer; this is the sort of praise which is given to Homer, and justly given. Higher praise there cannot well be, and it is the praise due to epic poetry of the highest order only, and to no other. Let us try, then, the *Chanson de Roland* at its best. Roland, mortally wounded, lays himself down under a pine-tree, with his face turned towards Spain and the enemy—

De plusurs choses à remembrer li prist,
De tantes teres cume li bers cunquist,
De dulce France, des humes de sun lign,
De Carlemagne sun seignor ki l'nurrit.[11]

That is primitive work, I repeat, with an undeniable poetic quality of its own. It deserves such praise, and such praise is sufficient for it. But now turn to Homer—

῝Ως φάτο· τοὺς δ᾿ ἤδη κάτεχεν φυσίζοος αἶα
ἐν Λακεδαίμονι αὖθι, φίλῃ ἐν πατρίδι γαίῃ."[12]

We are here in another world, another order of poetry altogether; here is rightly due such supreme praise as that which M. Vitet gives to the *Chanson de Roland*. If our words are to have any meaning, if our judgments are to have any solidity, we must not heap that supreme praise upon poetry of an order immeasurably inferior.

Indeed there can be no more useful help for discovering what poetry belongs to the class of the truly excellent, and can therefore do us most good, than to have always in one's mind lines and expressions of the great masters, and to apply them as a touchstone[13] to other poetry. Of course we are not to require this other poetry to resemble them; it may be very dissimilar. But if we have any tact we shall find them, when we have lodged them well in our minds, an infallible touchstone for detecting the presence or absence of high poetic quality, and also the degree of this quality, in all other poetry which we may place beside them. Short passages, even single lines, will serve our turn quite sufficiently. Take the two lines which I have just quoted from Homer, the poet's comment on Helen's mention of her brothers;— or take his

Ἇ δειλώ, τί σφῶϊ δόμεν Πηλῆϊ ἄνακτι
θνητῷ; ὑμεῖς δ᾿ ἐστὸν ἀγήρω τ᾿ ἀθανάτω τε.
ἦ ἵνα δυστήνοισι μετ᾿ ἀνδράσιν ἄλγε᾿ ἔχητον;[14]

the address of Zeus to the horses of Peleus;—or take finally his

Καὶ σέ, γέρον, τὸ πρὶν μὲν ἀκούομεν ὄλβιον εἶναι.[15]

the words of Achilles to Priam, a suppliant before him. Take that incomparable line and a half of Dante, Ugolino's tremendous words—

Io no piangeva; sì dentro impietrai.
Piangevan elli . . .[16]

---

[10]Louis **Vitet** (1802–1873).

[11]"Then began he to call many things to remembrance,—all the lands which his valour conquered, and pleasant France, and the men of his lineage, and Charlemagne his liege lord who nourished him."—*Chanson de Roland*, iii, 939–942. [Arnold's note]

[12]"So said she; they long since in Earth's soft arms were reposing,/ There, in their own dear land, their fatherland, Lacedaemon."—*Iliad*, iii, 243, 244 (translated by Dr. Hawtrey). [Arnold's note] **Helen** of Troy, for whom the Trojan war was fought, looks out on the battlefield hoping to see her brothers.

[13]**touchstone**: in alchemy, something that when touched to an unknown metal can identify true gold.

[14]"Ah, unhappy pair, why gave we you to King Peleus, to a mortal? but ye are without old age, and immortal. Was it that with men born to misery ye might have sorrow?"—*Iliad*, xvii, 443–445. [Arnold's note] **Peleus**: father of Achilles.

[15]"Nay, and thou too, old man, in former days wast, as we hear, happy."—*Iliad*, xxiv, 543. [Arnold's note] **Priam**: king of Troy, who begs the body of his son Hector from **Achilles**, who killed him.

[16]"I wailed not, so of stone grew I within;—*they* wailed."—*Inferno*, xxxiii, 49, 50. [Arnold's note] Ugolino and his sons were locked in a tower where they starved to death.

take the lovely words of Beatrice to Virgil—

> Io son fatta da Dio, sua mercè, tale,
> Che la vostra miseria non mi tange,
> Nè fiamma d'esto incendio non m'assale . . . [17]

take the simple, but perfect, single line—

> In la sua volontade è nostra pace.[18]

Take of Shakespeare a line or two of Henry the Fourth's ex-postulation with sleep—

> Wilt thou upon the high and giddy mast
> Seal up the ship-boy's eyes, and rock his brains
> In cradle of the rude imperious surge . . . [19]

and take, as well, Hamlet's dying request to Horatio—

> If thou didst ever hold me in thy heart,
> Absent thee from felicity awhile,
> And in this harsh world draw thy breath in pain
> To tell my story . . . [20]

Take of Milton that Miltonic passage—

> Darken'd so, yet shone
> Above them all the archangel; but his face
> Deep scars of thunder had intrench'd, and care
> Sat on his faded cheek . . . [21]

add two such lines as—

> And courage never to submit or yield
> And what is else not to be overcome . . . [22]

and finish with the exquisite close to the loss of Proserpine, the loss

> . . . which cost Ceres all that pain
> To seek her through the world.[23]

---

[17]"Of such sort hath God, thanked be His mercy, made me, that your misery toucheth me not, neither doth the flame of this fire strike me."—*Inferno*, ii, 91–93. [Arnold's note] The speaker is **Beatrice**, Dante's beloved.

[18]"In his will is our peace."—*Paradiso*, iii, 85. [Arnold's note]

[19]*2 Henry IV* 3.1.18–20.

[20]*Hamlet* 5.2.288–291.

[21]*Paradise Lost* 1.599–602.

[22]*Paradise Lost* 1.108–109.

[23]*Paradise Lost* 4.271–72. The earth-goddess **Ceres** sought her daughter **Proserpine**, who had been carried off to the underworld.

These few lines, if we have tact and can use them, are enough even of themselves to keep clear and sound our judgments about poetry, to save us from fallacious estimates of it, to conduct us to a real estimate.

The specimens I have quoted differ widely from one another, but they have in common this: the possession of the very highest poetical quality. If we are thoroughly penetrated by their power, we shall find that we have acquired a sense enabling us, whatever poetry may be laid before us, to feel the degree in which a high poetical quality is present or wanting there. Critics give themselves great labour to draw out what in the abstract constitutes the characters of a high quality of poetry. It is much better simply to have recourse to concrete examples;—to take specimens of poetry of the high, the very highest quality, and to say: The characters of a high quality of poetry are what is expressed *there*. They are far better recognised by being felt in the verse of the master, than by being perused in the prose of the critic. Nevertheless if we are urgently pressed to give some critical account of them, we may safely, perhaps, venture on laying down, not indeed how and why the characters arise, but where and in what they arise. They are in the matter and substance of the poetry, and they are in its manner and style. Both of these, the substance and matter on the one hand, the style and manner on the other, have a mark, an accent, of high beauty, worth, and power. But if we are asked to define this mark and accent in the abstract, our answer must be: No, for we should thereby be darkening the question, not clearing it. The mark and accent are as given by the substance and matter of that poetry, by the style and manner of that poetry, and of all other poetry which is akin to it in quality.

Only one thing we may add as to the substance and matter of poetry, guiding ourselves by Aristotle's profound observation that the superiority of poetry over history consists in its possessing a higher truth and a higher seriousness (φιλοσοφώτερον καὶ σπουδαιότερον). Let us add, therefore, to what we have said, this: that the substance and matter of the best poetry acquire their special character from possessing, in an eminent degree, truth and seriousness. We may add yet further, what is in itself evident, that to the style and manner of the best poetry their special character, their accent, is given by their diction, and, even yet more, by their movement. And though we distinguish between the two characters, the two accents, of superiority, yet they are nevertheless vitally connected one with the other. The superior character of truth and seriousness, in the matter and substance of the best poetry, is inseparable from the superiority of diction and movement marking its style and manner. The two superiorities are closely related, and are in steadfast proportion one to the other. So far as high poetic truth and seriousness are wanting to a poet's matter and substance, so far also, we may be sure, will a high poetic stamp of diction and movement be wanting to his style and manner. In proportion as this high stamp of diction and movement, again, is absent from a poet's style and manner, we shall find, also, that high poetic truth and seriousness are absent from his substance and matter.

So stated, these are but dry generalities; their whole force lies in their application. And I could wish every student of poetry to make the application of them for himself. Made by himself, the application would impress itself upon his mind far more deeply than made by me. Neither will my limits allow me to make any full application of the generalities above propounded; but in the hope of bringing out, at any rate, some significance in them, and of establishing an important principle more firmly by their means, I will, in the space which remains to me, follow rapidly from the commencement the course of our English poetry with them in my view. . . .

At any rate the end to which the method and the estimate are designed to lead, and from leading to which, if they do lead to it, they get their whole value,—the benefit of being able clearly to feel and deeply to enjoy the best, the truly classic, in poetry,—is an end, let me say it once more at parting, of supreme importance. We are often told that an era is opening in which we are to see multitudes of a common sort of readers, and masses of a common sort of literature; that such readers do not want and could not relish anything better than such literature, and that to provide it is becoming a vast and profitable industry. Even if good literature entirely lost currency with the world, it would still be abundantly worth while to continue to enjoy it by oneself. But it never will lose currency with the world, in spite of momentary appearances; it never will lose supremacy. Currency and supremacy are insured to it, not indeed by the world's deliberate and conscious choice, but by something far deeper,—by the instinct of self-preservation in humanity.

1880

FRANCES POWER COBBE

(1822–1904)

Frances Power Cobbe was a journalist who delighted in her profession. She particularly enjoyed the seven years she spent writing short essays for a newspaper, the *Echo*, which allowed her the participation in public affairs and access to a clergyman's role that her gender otherwise denied her.

> To be in touch with the most striking events of the whole world, and enjoy the privilege of giving your opinion on them to 50,000 or 100,000 readers within a few hours, this struck me . . . as something for which many prophets and preachers of old would have given a house full of silver and gold. And I was to be *paid!*

"It was *my pulpit*," she said, "with permission to make in it (what other pulpits lack so sadly!) such jokes as pleased me."

Unlike the clergymen whose solemnity she laughs at, she had to provide her own training for that pulpit, since her schooling although fashionable and expensive was intellectually very poor. She left school at sixteen and returned to Ireland, where her parents lived comfortably in the country. The local parson taught her Greek and geometry, and she pursued a strenuous course of self-education. The most important event of her early years was a prolonged crisis of faith (described in our excerpt from her autobiography) from which she emerged as a theist believing in the two crucial tenets of Broad Church Victorian faith, personal immortality and the existence of a loving God. When she told her father about her fall from Anglican orthodoxy he refused to speak to her and sent her away from home for almost a year, after which they lived uneasily together until his death in 1856. During that time her first book appeared: an *Essay on the Theory of Intuitive Morals* (1855), based on her reading of Kant's philosophy, published anonymously to avoid offending her relatives, and attacked in the religious press as unfeminine and un-Christian. After her father died, however, she was free to travel and to devote herself openly to writing, philanthropy, and feminism. Her intellectual accomplishments and high social connections provided access to influential people and made possible a leading role in many social causes, especially the care and education of poor girls, university education for women, women's rights and suffrage, and anti-vivisectionism. She was particularly effective as a writer on feminist issues, buttressing her arguments with vigorous wit and a stunning array of factual details.

Cobbe exalted the traditionally feminine virtues of sympathy and love. She defined women as "Human Beings of the Mother Sex" and said that her voluminous writings did not include reviews of other people's books because she hated the idea of giving pain. Through her leadership in the anti-vivisection movement she opposed "the vice of scientific cruelty," setting humane values against the exaltation of intellect and power by such leading defenders of vivisection as Darwin and Huxley. She braved the bastions of "culture," too, with writings on ethics and religion that won her the mockery of Matthew Arnold in "The Function of Criticism at the Present Time" (see page 736). Writing enabled her to support herself as a single woman and at the same time to further feminist causes and the social renovation that she hoped was near at hand.

from Criminals, Idiots, Women, and Minors

. . . At the head of this paper I have placed the four categories under which persons are now excluded from many civil, and all political rights in England. They were complacently quoted this year by the *Times* as every way fit and proper exceptions; but yet it has appeared to not a few, that the place assigned to Women among them is hardly any longer suitable. To a woman herself who is aware that she has never committed a Crime; who fondly believes that she is not an Idiot; and who is alas! only too sure she is no longer a Minor, there naturally appears some incongruity in placing her, for such important purposes, in an association wherein otherwise she would scarcely be likely to find herself. But in all seriousness, the question presses, Ought Englishwomen of full age, at the present state of affairs, to be considered as having legally attained majority? or ought they permanently to be considered, for all civil and political purposes, as minors? This, we venture to think, is the real point at issue between the friends and opponents of "women's rights," and it would save, perhaps, not a little angry feeling and aimless discussion, were we to keep it well in view and not allow ourselves to be drawn off into collateral debates about equality and abstract rights. Let us admit (if it be desired) that the pupilage in which women have been hitherto kept has been often inevitable, and sometimes salutary. The question is, should it be prolonged indefinitely? . . .

What, in the first place, of the Justice of giving all a woman's property to her husband? The argument is that the wife gets an ample *quid pro quo*.[1] *Does* she get it under the existing law? That is the simple question.

In the first place, many husbands are unable, from fault or from misfortune, to maintain their wives. Of this law takes no note, proceeding on reasoning which may be reduced to the syllogism:

A man who supports his wife ought to have all her property;
Most men support their wives;
Therefore, all men ought to have all the property of their wives.

Let us suppose the managers of a public institution to engage with a contractor, to pay him 1,000*l.* on the nail for the supply of the institution with provisions for a year. At the end of a month the contractor has spent the 1,000*l.* on his own devices and is bankrupt. The institution starves accordingly. What, in such case, do we think of the managers who gave the 1,000*l.* without security for the fulfilment of the contract, and what do we think of the contractor? But are not hundreds of husbands in the position of the contractor, yet rather pitied than blamed by public opinion? And is not the law in such cases precisely in the position of the reckless managers? When all that a woman possesses in the present and future is handed over unreservedly by the law to her husband, is there the smallest attempt at obtaining security that he on his part can fulfil that obligation which is always paraded as the equivalent, namely, the obligation to support her for the rest of her life? Nay, he is not so much as asked to promise he will reserve any portion of her money for such purpose, or reminded of his supposed obligation. If he spend 10,000*l.* of her fortune in a week in paying his own debts, and incapacitate himself for ever from supporting her and her children, the law has not one word to say against him.

But waiving the point of the *inability* of many husbands to fulfil their side of the understood engagement, one thing, at all events, it must behove the law to do. Having enforced her part on the woman, it is bound to enforce his part on the man, *to the utmost of his ability.* The legal act by which a man puts his hand in his wife's pocket, or draws her money out of the savings' bank, is perfectly clear, easy, inexpensive. The corresponding process by which the wife can obtain food and clothing from her husband when he neglects to provide it—what may it be? Where is it described? How is it rendered safe and easy to every poor woman who may chance to need its protection? When we are assured that men are always so careful of the interests of the women for whom they legislate, that it is quite needless for women to seek political freedom to protect themselves, we might be inclined to take it for granted that here, if anywhere, here where the very life and subsistence of women are concerned, the legislation of their good friends and protectors in their behalf would have been as stringent and as clear as words could make it. We should expect to find the very easiest and simplest mode of redress laid open to every hapless creature thus reduced to want by him to whom the law itself has given all she has ever earned, or inherited. Nay, seeing the hesitation wherewith any wife would prosecute the husband with whom she still tries to live, and the exceeding cowardice and baseness of the act of maltreating so helpless a dependant, it might not have been too much had the law exercised as much severity in such a case as if the offender had voluntarily starved his ass or his sheep, and the Society for the Prevention of Cruelty to Animals were his prosecutors.

---

[1]*quid pro quo:* something exchanged for something else.

But this is the imaginary, what is the actual fact? Simply that the woman's remedy for her husband's neglect to provide her with food, has been practically found unattainable. The law which has robbed her so straightforwardly, has somehow forgotten altogether to secure for her the supposed compensation. Since 1857, if the husband altogether forsake his home for years together, the wife may obtain from the magistrate a protection order, and prevent him from seizing her property. But, if he come back just often enough to keep within the technical period fixed as desertion, and take from her everything she may have earned, or which charitable people may have given her, then there is absolutely no resource for her at all. The Guardians of her Union, if she ask to be admitted into the workhouse,[2] may, if they please, receive her and prosecute her husband at the petty sessions for putting the parish to the expense of supporting his wife. But the guardians are not obliged to admit her, and the trouble and cost of prosecution is an argument which frequently weighs with them against doing so. Then, as if to add insult to injury, when the poor wretch, driven from the shelter of the workhouse, and perhaps on the point of bearing a child to the wretch who is starving her, goes to the magistrate to implore protection,—what answer does she receive? She is told that he cannot hear her complaint; that she cannot sue her husband, as he and she are one in the eye of the law.

Again, the Common Law fails to secure justice to the wife, not only during her husband's life, but after his death. The following story was published many years ago in the *Westminster Review* as having then recently occurred. We cannot vouch otherwise for its veracity, and must quote from memory, but if it be only taken as a hypothetical case, what a lesson does it convey! A gentleman of landed estate in the north of England became involved in debt and finally ruined and reduced to actual want. His wife, a lady of ability and spirit, finding him incapable of any effort for their joint support, opened a little shop for millinery in the county town. Her old friends gave her their custom, and her taste and industry made it a thriving business. For many years she maintained her husband and herself, till at last having realised a little competency, and grown old and feeble, she sold her shop and retired to spend, as she hoped, in peace with her husband the remaining years of her life. After a short time, however, the husband died, duly nursed and tended to the last by his wife. When he was dead he was found to have left a will by which he bequeathed every shilling of his wife's earnings to a mistress he had secretly maintained. Either the wife had originally married without a settlement, or her settlements had not contemplated so singular a fact as her earning a fortune. The husband's will therefore was perfectly valid, *and was executed.*

So much for the Justice of the Common Law. What now shall we say to its Expediency? The matter seems to lie thus. Men are generally more wise in worldly matters; more generally able and intelligent, and their wives habitually look up to them with even ridiculously exaggerated confidence and admiration. Such being the case, it would naturally happen, were there no law in the case, that the husband should manage all the larger business of the family. The law then *when the husband is really wise and good* is a dead letter. But for the opposite cases, exceptions though they be, yet alas! too numerous, where the husband is a fool, a gambler, a drunkard, and where the wife is sensible, frugal, devoted to the interests of the children,—is it indeed expedient that the whole and sole power should be lodged in the husband's hands; the power not only over all they already have in common, but the power over all she can ever earn in future? Such a law must paralyse the energy of any woman less than a heroine of maternal love. How many poor wives has it driven to despair, as one time after another they have been legally robbed of their hard won earnings, who can calculate? One such hapless one, we are told, when her lawful tyrant came home as usual, drunk with the spoils of her starving children, took up some wretched relic of their ruined household and smote him to death. She was a murderess. In former times she would have been burnt alive for "petty treason" for killing her lord and master. But what was the law which gave to that reckless savage a power the same as that of a slave-holder of the South over his slave?

It is continually repeated *in this connection only* that laws cannot take note of exceptional cases; they must be laid down to suit the majority, and the minority must do as best they can. But is there any other department of public justice in which the same principle is applied? What else is law *for*, but to be "a terror to evil doers"?[3]—always, as we trust, in a minority in the community. The greater number of people are honest, and neither steal their neighbours' goods nor break into their houses. Yet the law takes pretty sharp account of thieves and burglars.

Setting up an ideal of perfect marriage union sounds very well. But what would it be to set up an ideal, say,

---

[2]**workhouse**: where the poor were maintained in deliberately harsh conditions, managed by parishes combined into **Unions**.

[3]**"terror to evil doers"**: see Romans 13:3.

between rich and poor, and to assume that what ought to be their relation in a Christian country actually is so? A new Poor Law based on the hypothesis that the Sermon on the Mount[4] forms the rule of English life, to which the exceptions were too trifling to be regarded, would be at all events a novelty in legislation. Or rather, would it not correspond in spirit with the law we have been considering? The poor woman whose husband has robbed her earnings, who leaves her and her children to starve and then goes unpunished because the law can only recognise the relation of husband and wife as it ought to be, and he and she are one before the law,—that poor soul's case would resemble closely enough that of a pauper who should be told that the law can only recognise the relation of rich and poor as it ought to be, and that as every one who had two coats must be assumed to give to him who has none, and from him that would borrow nobody can be supposed to turn away, the striking of a Poor's Rate[5] in a Christian land must be wholly superfluous.

It is one of the numerous anomalies connected with women's affairs, that when they are under debate the same argument which would be held to determine other questions in one way is felt to settle theirs in another. If for instance it be proved of any other class of the community, that it is peculiarly liable to be injured, imposed on, and tyrannised over (e.g. the children who work in factories), it is considered to follow as a matter of course, that the law must step in for its protection. But it is the alleged *helplessness* of married women which, it is said, makes it indispensable to give all the support of the law, *not* to them, but to the stronger persons with whom they are unequally yoked. "Woman is physically, mentally, and morally inferior to man." Therefore it follows—what?—that the law should give to her bodily weakness, her intellectual dulness, her tottering morality, all the support and protection which it is possible to interpose between so poor a creature and the strong being always standing over her? By no means. Quite the contrary of course. The husband being already physically, mentally, and morally his wife's superior must in justice receive from the law additional strength by being constituted absolute master of her property. Do we not seem to hear one of the intelligent keepers in the Zoological Gardens explaining to a party of visitors:

"This, ladies and gentlemen, is an inoffensive bird, the *Mulier Anglicana*.[6] The beak is feeble, and the claws unsuited for grubbing for worms. It seems to be only intelligent in building its nest, or taking care of its young, to whom it is peculiarly devoted, as well as to its mate. Otherwise it is a very simple sort of bird, picking up any crumbs which are thrown to it, and never touching carrion like the vulture or intoxicating fluids like the maccaw. Therefore you see, ladies and gentlemen, as it is so helpless, we put that strong chain round its leg, and fasten it to its nest, and make the bars of its cage exceptionally strong. As to its rudimentary wings we always break them early, for greater security; though I have heard Professor Huxley say that he is convinced it could never fly far with them, under any circumstances."

Such is the argument from the feebleness of women to the expediency of weakening any little independent spirit they might possibly found on the possession of a trifle of money. "To him that hath shall be given, and he shall have more abundantly; but from her that hath not, shall be taken away even that which it seemeth she has a right to have."[7] The text is a hard one, in an ethical point of view.

But the great and overwhelming argument against the Expediency of the Common Law in this matter is the simple fact that no parent or guardian possessed of means sufficient to evade it by a marriage settlement[8] ever dreams of permitting his daughter or ward to undergo its (supposed) beneficial action. The parent who neglected to demand such a settlement from a man before he gave him his daughter, would be thought to have failed in the performance of one of his most obvious and imperative duties. Even the law itself in its highest form in the realm (that of the Court of Chancery) invariably requires settlements for its wards. How then can it be argued that the same rule is generally considered expedient, yet invariably evaded by all who have means to evade it? . . .

With such examples before us it truly seems wanton to talk of Expediency.[9] The only persons for whom the existing law is expedient are fortune-hunters, who, if they can befool young women of property so far as to induce them to elope, are enabled thereby to grasp all their inheritance. Were there no such law as the cession of the wife's property on marriage, there would be considerably fewer of those

---

[4]**Sermon on the Mount**: Matthew 5–7.

[5]**Poor's Rate**: tax to support the poor.

[6]*Mulier Anglicana*: English woman, wife.

[7]**"To him . . . to have"**: see Matthew 25:29.

[8]**marriage settlement**: money or property ensured to the wife in a marriage contract.

[9]**Expediency**: It is satisfactory to know that separate property and the right of contract has been accorded to married women by the new law of India, compiled by some of the ablest lawyers in this country. [Cobbe's note]

disgusting and miserable alliances where the man marries solely to become possessed of his wife's money.

But, as we have said already, there is an argument which has more force in determining legislation about marriage than either considerations of Justice or of Expediency. It is the sentiment entertained by the majority of men on the subject; the ideal they have formed of wedlock, the poetical vision in their minds of a wife's true relation to her husband. Legislators talk in Parliament with a certain conviction that the principles of fairness and policy are the only ones to be referred to *there*. But whenever the subject is freely discussed, in private or in a newspaper, there is sure to burst out sooner or later the real feeling at bottom. Nothing can be more amusing than to watch such spontaneous outbreaks of the natural man in the dignified columns of the *Times*, or the hard-hitting periods of a well-known writer in the *Pall Mall Gazette*. Let us try to fathom this sentiment, for till we understand it we are but fighting our battles in the dark. Is it not this—that a woman's whole life and being, her soul, body, time, property, thought, and care, ought to be given to her husband; that nothing short of such absorption in him and his interests makes her a true wife; and that when she is thus absorbed even a very mediocre character and inferior intellect can make a man happy in a sense no splendour of endowments can otherwise do? Truly I believe this is the feeling at the bottom of nearly all men's hearts, and of the hearts of thousands of women also. There is no use urging that it is a gigantic piece of egotism in a man to desire such a marriage. Perhaps it is natural for him to do so, and perhaps it is natural for a great number of women to give just such absorbed adoring affection. Perhaps it is a tribute to the infinite nature of all love, that for those who know each other best, as a wife knows her husband, there is no limit to human affection. At all events it seems a fact that the typical Man (if we may call him so), desires such love, and the typical Woman is ready to give it to him. He is impatient at the notion of a marriage in which this conception of absolute absorption of his wife's interests in his own shall not be fulfilled; and, so far as legislation can create such an ideal, he is resolved that it shall do so.

So far all is plain and natural, but the question is this: Supposing such marriages to be the most desirable, do men set the right way about securing them, by making such laws as the Common Law of England? Is perfect love to be called out by perfect dependence? Does an empty purse necessarily imply a full heart? Is a generous-natured woman likely to be won or rather to be alienated and galled by being made to feel she has no choice but submission? Surely there is great fallacy in this direction. The idea which we are all agreed ought to be realised in marriage is that of the highest possible Union. But what *is* that most perfect Union? Have we not taken it in a most gross commercial sense, as if even here we were a nation of shopkeepers? Let us go into this matter a little carefully. It is rather instructive.

Husband and wife, in the eye of the poet, the divine, and—shall we say, the Judge of the Divorce Court? are "not twain, but one flesh."[10] I know not whether Mr. Darwin will sanction that theory concerning the Origin of Species, which tells us that

> Man came from Nothing, and by the same plan,
> Woman was made from the rib of a man;

or whether Dr. Carpenter and Professor Huxley have verified the anatomical doctrine instilled by our nurses, that in consequence of Adam's sacrifice of his rib, men have ever since had one rib fewer than women. Still, however learned physiologists may decide this obscure problem, we shall all agree that it is a noble Oriental metaphor, to describe a wife's relation to her husband as "bone of his bone, and flesh of his flesh."[11] But the union of two human beings may, as preachers say, be considered three ways. Firstly, there is the sort of union between any friends who are greatly attached to one another; a union oftenest seen, perhaps, between two sisters, who each have full liberty to come and go, and dispose of their separate resources, but who yet manage commonly to live in harmony and affection, and not unfrequently to bring up a whole batch of little nephews and nieces in their common abode. Two such we know, who for many years have kept the same account at their banker's, and say that they find only one serious objection to the plan—they can never make each other a present!

Secondly, there is the Union of the celebrated Siamese twins, who are tied together—not by Mother Church but by Mother Nature—so effectually that Sir William Fergusson and Sir William Wilde[12] are equally powerless to release them. Each of them has, however, the satisfaction of dragging about his brother as much as he is dragged himself;

---

[10]"not twain . . . one flesh": Mark 10:8.

[11]**Dr. William Benjamin Carpenter** (1813–1885): ally of Huxley and Darwin, specialist in anatomy and physiology. "**bone . . . flesh**": Genesis 2:23.

[12]**Siamese twins**: Chang and Eng (1811–1874), joined at the waist, toured Europe in the 1830s and again in 1869. **Sir William Fergusson** (1808–1877), **Sir William Wilde** (1815–1876): eminent surgeons.

and if either have a pocket, the other must needs have every facility of access thereto.

Lastly, for the most absolute type of Union of all, we must seek an example in the Tarantula Spider. As most persons are aware, when one of these delightful creatures is placed under a glass with a companion of his own species a little smaller than himself, he forthwith gobbles him up; making him thus, in a very literal manner, "bone of his bone" (supposing tarantulas to have any bones) "and flesh of his flesh." The operation being completed, the victorious spider visibly acquires double bulk, and thenceforth may be understood to "represent the family" in the most perfect manner conceivable.

Now, of these three types of union, it is singular that the only one which seems to have approved itself, in a pecuniary point of view, to the legislative wisdom of England should be that of the Tarantula. Unless a man be allowed to eat up the whole of a woman's fortune, there is apparently no union possible between their interests. Partnerships, limited liabilities, and all other devices for amalgamation of property are here considered inadmissible. The way in which brothers and sisters settle their affairs when they reside under the same roof would never suffice, it seems, to keep things straight between those who hold a yet more tender and trustful relationship.

Englishmen have, perhaps beyond all men, generous hearts and chivalrous natures. They delight in such glorious lines as that of their own poet[13]:

> Yet were life a charnel, where
> Love lay coffined with Despair;
> Yet were Truth a sacred lie,
> Love were lust—if Liberty
> Lent not life its soul of light,
> Hope its iris of delight,
> Truth its prophet's robe to wear,
> Love its power to give and bear.

Is it possible that one of them, whose eye kindles over such words, seriously believes that his own mother, sister, daughter, is made of such different clay from himself, as that for *her*, abject dependence is calculated to create and foster love, while for *him* it would be gall and wormwood, turning his affection into bitterness and revolt?

Truly I am persuaded it is not *thanks* to the Common Law, but in *spite* thereof, that there are so many united and happy homes in England. . . .

1868

---

[13]**poet:** P. B. Shelley, *Hellas* (1822) 38–45.

from **Life of Frances Power Cobbe**
Religion

. . . The notion of "getting to Heaven" by means of a faithful pilgrimage through this "Vale of Tears" was the prominent feature I think, always, in my father's religion, and naturally took great hold on me. When the day came whereon I began to doubt whether there were any Heaven to be reached, that moral earthquake, as was inevitable, shook not only my religion but my morality to their foundations; and my experience of the perils of those years has made me ever since anxious to base religion in every young mind on ground liable to no such catastrophes. The danger came to me on this wise.

Up to my eleventh year, my little life inward and outward had flown in a bright and even current. Looking back at it and comparing my childhood with that of others I seem to have been—probably from the effects of solitude—*devout* beyond what was normal at my age. I used to spend a great deal of time secretly reading the Bible and that dullest of dull books, "The Whole Duty of Man"[1] (the latter a curious foretaste of my subsequent life-long interest in the study of ethics),—not exactly enjoying them but happy in the feeling that I was somehow approaching God. I used to keep awake at night to repeat various prayers and (wonderful to remember!) the Creed and Commandments! I made all sorts of severe rules for myself, and if I broke them, manfully mulcted myself of any little pleasures or endured some small self-imposed penance. Of none of these things had any one, even my dear mother, the remotest idea, except once when I felt driven like a veritable Cain, by my agonized conscience to go and confess to her that I had said in a recent rage (to myself), *"Curse them all!"* referring to my family in general and to my governess in particular! The tempest of my tears and sobs on this occasion evidently astonished her, and I remember lying exhausted on the floor in a recess in her bedroom, for a long time before I was able to move.

But the hour of doubt and difficulty was approaching. The first question which ever arose in my mind was concerning the miracle of the Loaves and Fishes.[2] I can recall

---

[1]*The Whole Duty of Man* (1658): by Richard Allestree (1619–1681).

[2]**Loaves and Fishes:** see Matthew 14.

the scene vividly. It was a winter's night; my father was reading the Sunday evening sermon in the dining-room. The servants, whose attendance was *de rigueur*, were seated in a row down the room. My father faced them, and my mother and I and my governess sat round the fire near him. I was opposite the beautiful classic black marble mantel-piece, surmounted with an antique head of Jupiter Serapis[3] (all photographed on my brain even now), and listening with all my might, as in duty bound, to the sermon which described the miracle of the Loaves and Fishes. "How did it happen exactly?" I began cheerfully to think, quite imagining I was doing the right thing to try to understand it all. "Well! first there were the fishes and the loaves. But what was done to them? Did the fish grow and grow as they were eaten and broken? And the bread the same? No! that is non-sense. And then the twelve basketsful taken up at the end, when there was not nearly so much at the beginning. It is not possible!" "O Heavens! (was the next thought) *I am doubting the Bible!* God forgive me! I must never think of it again."

But the little rift had begun, and as time went on other difficulties arose. Nothing very seriously, however, dis-tracted my faith or altered the intensity of my religious feel-ings for the next two years, till in October, 1836, I was sent to school as I have narrated in the last chapter, at Brighton, and a new description of life opened. At school I came under influence of two kinds. One was the preaching of the Evangelical Mr. Vaughan, in whose church (Christ Church) were our seats; and I recall vividly the emotion with which one winter's night I listened to his sermon on the great theme, "Though your sins be as scarlet, they shall be white as wool."[4] The sense of "the exceeding sinfulness of sin," the rapturous joy of purification therefrom, came home to me, and as I walked back to school with the waves thundering up the Brighton beach beside us and the wind tossing the clouds in the evening sky overhead, the whole tremendous realities of the moral life seemed borne in on my heart. On the other hand, the perpetual overstrain of school-work, and unjust blame and penalty for failure to do what it was impossible to accomplish in the given time, drove me to all sorts of faults for which I hated and despised myself. When I knelt by my bed at night, after the schoolfellow who shared my room was, as I fancied, asleep, she would get up and pound my head with a bolster, laughing and crying out, "Get up, you horrid hypocrite; get up! I'll go on beating you

till you do!" It was not strange if, under such circumstances, my beautiful childish religion fell into abeyance and my conscience into disquietude. But, as I have narrated, I came home at sixteen, and then, once more able to enjoy the soli-tude of the woods and of my own bedroom and its inner study where no one intruded, the old feelings, tinged with deep remorse for the failures of my school life and for many present faults (amongst others a very bitter and unforgiving temper) come back with fresh vigour. I have always consid-ered that in that summer in my seventeenth year I went through what Evangelical Christians call "conversion." Reli-gion became the supreme interest of life; and the sense that I was pardoned its greatest joy. I was, of course, a Christian of the usual Protestant type, finding infinite pleasure in the simple old "Communion" of those pre-ritualistic[5] days, and in endless Bible readings to myself. Sometimes I rose in the early summer dawn and read a whole Gospel before I dressed. I think I never ran up into my room in the daytime for any change of attire without glancing into the book and carrying away some echo of what I believed to be "God's Word." Nobody knew anything about all this, of course; but as time went on there were great and terrible perturbations in my inner life, and these perhaps I did not always succeed in concealing from the watchful eyes of my dear mother.

So far as I can recall, the ideas of Christ and of God the Father were for all practical religious purposes identified in my young mind. it was as God upon earth,—the Re-deemer God, that I worshipped Jesus. To be pardoned through his "atonement" and at death to enter Heaven were the religious objects of life. But a new and most disturbing element here entered my thoughts. How did anybody know all that story of Galilee to be true? How could we believe the miracles? I had read very carefully Gibbon's[6] XV. and XVI. chapters and other books enough to teach me that everything in historical Christianity had been questioned; and my own awakening critical, and reasoning, and above all, ethical, faculties supplied fresh crops of doubts of the truth of the story and of the morality of much of the Old Testament history, and of the scheme of Atonement itself.

Then ensued four years on which I look back as pitiful in the extreme. In complete mental solitude and great igno-rance, I found myself facing all the dread problems of human existence. For a long time my intense desire to remain a

---

[3]**Jupiter Serapis**: Alexandrian (Greco-Egyptian) sun god.

[4]**"Though . . . wool"**: see Isaiah 1:18.

[5]**pre-ritualistic**: Keble, Newman, and others emphasized Church ritual in the 1830s and 1840s.

[6]Edward **Gibbon** (1737–1794): rationalist, skeptical author of *The Decline and Fall of the Roman Empire* (1776–1788).

Christian predominated, and brought me back from each return to skepticism in a passion of repentance and prayer to Christ to take my life or my reason sooner than allow me to stray from his fold. In those days no such thing was heard of as "Broad" interpretations of Scripture doctrines. We were fifty years before "Lux Mundi" and thirty before even "Essays and Reviews."[7] To be a "Christian," then, was to believe implicitly in the verbal inspiration of every word of the Bible, and to adore Christ as "very God of very God." With such implicit belief it was permitted to hope we might, by a good life and through Christ's Atonement, attain after death to Heaven. Without the faith or the good life it was certain we should go to Hell. It was taught us all that to be good only from fear of Hell was not the highest motive; the *highest* motive was the hope of Heaven! Had anything like modern rationalizing theories of the Atonement, or modern expositions of the Bible stories, or finally modern loftier doctrines of disinterested morality and religion, been known to me at this crisis of my life, it is possible that the whole course of my spiritual history would have been different. But of all such "raising up the astral spirits of dead creeds," as Carlyle called it, or as Broad Churchmen say, "liberating the kernel of Christianity from the husk," I knew, and could know nothing. Evangelical Christianity in 1840 presented itself as a thing to be taken whole, or rejected wholly; and for years the alternations went on in my poor young heart and brain, one week or month of rational and moral disbelief, and the next of vehement, remorseful return to the faith which I supposed could alone give me the joy of religion. As time went on, and my reading supplied me with a little more knowledge and my doubts deepened and accumulated, the returns to Christian faith grew fewer and shorter, and, as I had no idea of the possibility of reaching any other vital religion, I saw all that had made to me the supreme joy and glory of life fade out of it, while that motive which had been presented to me as the mainspring of duty and curb of passion, namely, the Hope of Heaven, vanished as a dream. I always had, as I have described, somewhat of that *mal-du-ciel* which Lamartine[8] talks of, that longing, as from the very depths of our being, for an Eden of Divine eternal love. I could scarcely in those days read even such poor stuff as the song

of the Peri in Moore's "Lalla Rookh" (not to speak of Bunyan's vision of the Celestial City)[9] without tears rushing to my eyes. But this, I saw, must all go with the rest. If, as Clough was saying, all unknown to me, about that same time,—

"Christ is not risen, no!
He lies and moulders low;"

if all the Christian revelation were a mass of mistakes and errors, no firmer ground on which to build than the promises of Mahomet, or of Buddha, or of the Old Man of the Mountain,[10]—of course there was (so far as I saw) no reason left for believing in any Heaven at all, or any life after death. Neither had the Moral Law, which had come to me through that supposed revelation on Sinai and the Mount of Galilee, any claim to my obedience other than might be made out by identifying it with principles common to heathen and Christian alike; an identity of which, at that epoch, I had as yet only the vaguest ideas. In short my poor young soul was in a fearful dilemma. On the one hand I had the choice to accept a whole mass of dogmas against which my reason and conscience rebelled; on the other, to abandon those dogmas and strive no more to believe the incredible, or to revere what I instinctively condemned; and then, as a necessary sequel, to cast aside the laws of Duty which I had hitherto cherished; to cease to pray or take the sacrament; and to relinquish the hope of a life beyond the grave.

It was not very wonderful, if, as I think I can recall, my disposition underwent a considerable change for the worse while all these tremendous questions were being debated in my solitary walks in the woods and by the seashore, and in my room at night over my Gibbon or my Bible. I know I was often bitter and morose and selfish; and then came the alternate spell of paroxysms of self-reproach and fanciful self-tormentings.

The life of a young woman in such a home as mine is so guarded round on every side and the instincts of a girl are so healthy, that the dangers incurred even in such a spiritual landslip as I have described are very limited compared to

---

[7]*Lux Mundi* (light of the world): *A Series of Studies in the Religion of the Incarnation* (1889), edited by Bishop Charles Gore (1853–1932), directed Anglican theology toward science and social action. *Essays and Reviews:* see Benjamin Jowett, page 66.

[8]*mal-du-ciel:* heaven-sickness. Alphonse de **Lamartine** (1790–1869): French poet.

[9]*Lalla Rookh* (1817): popular verse romance by Thomas Moore (1779–1852). John **Bunyan** (1628–1688): author of *The Pilgrim's Progress* (1678), in which Christian takes an allegorical pilgrimage to the **Celestial City**. The following quotation is from **Clough's** "Easter Day" (1849).

[10]**Old Man of the Mountain:** Crusaders' name for Rashid ad-Din (d. 1192), Syrian leader.

what they must inevitably be in the case of young men or of women less happily circumstanced. It has been my profound sense of the awful perils of such a downfall of faith as I experienced, the peril of moral shipwreck without compass or anchorage amid the tempests of youth, which has spurred me ever since to strive to forestall for others the hour of danger.

At last my efforts to believe in orthodox Christianity ceased altogether. In the summer after my twentieth birthday I had reached the end of the long struggle. The complete downfall of Evangelicalism—which seems to have been effected in George Eliot's strong brain in a single fortnight of intercourse with Mr. and Mrs. Bray[11]—had taken in my case four long years of miserable mental conflict and unspeakable pain. It left me with something as nearly like a *Tabula rasa*[12] of faith as can well be imagined. I definitely disbelieved in human immortality and in a supernatural revelation. The existence of God I neither denied nor affirmed. I felt I had no means of coming to any knowledge of Him. I was, in fact (long before the word was invented), precisely—an Agnostic.

One day, while thus literally creedless, I wandered out alone as was my wont into a part of our park a little more wild than the rest, where deer were formerly kept, and sat down among the rocks and the gorse which was then in its summer glory of odorous blossoms, ever since rich to me with memories of that hour. It was a sunny day in May, and after reading a little of my favourite Shelley, I fell, as often happened, into mournful thought. I was profoundly miserable; profoundly conscious of the deterioration and sliding down of all my feelings and conduct from the high ambitions of righteousness and holiness which had been mine in the days of my Christian faith and prayer; and at the same time I knew that the whole scaffolding of that higher life had fallen to pieces and could never be built up again. While I was thus musing despairingly, something stirred within me, and I asked myself, "Can I not rise once more, conquer my faults, and live up to my own idea of what is right and good? Even though there be no life after death, I may yet deserve my own respect here and now, and if there be a God He must approve me."

The resolution was made very seriously. I came home to begin a new course and to cultivate a different spirit. Was

it strange that in a few days I began instinctively, and almost without reflection, to pray again? No longer did I make any kind of effort to believe this thing or the other about God. I simply addressed Him as the Lord of conscience, whom I implored to strengthen my good resolutions, to forgive my faults, "to lift me out of the mire and clay and set my feet upon a rock and order my goings."[13] Of course, there was Christian sentiment and the results of Christian training in all I felt and did. I could no more have cast them off than I could have leaped off my shadow. But of dogmatical Christianity there was never any more. I have never from that time, now more than fifty years ago, attached, or wished I could attach, credence to any part of what Dr. Martineau[14] has called the "Apocalyptic side of Christianity," nor (I may add with thankfulness) have I ever lost faith in God. . . .

I may here conclude the story of my religious life extending through the years after the above described momentous change. After a time, occupied in part with study and with efforts to be useful to our poor neighbors and to my parents, my Deism was lifted to a higher plane by one of those inflowings of truth which seem the simplest things in the world, but are as rain on the dry ground in summer to the mind which receives them. One day while praying quietly, the thought came to me with extraordinary lucidity: "God's Goodness is what *I mean* by Goodness! It is not a mere title, like the 'Majesty' of a King. He has really that character which we call 'Good.' He is Just, as I understand Justice, only more perfectly just. He is Good as I understand Goodness, only more perfectly good. He is not good in time and tremendous in eternity; not good to some of His creatures and cruel to others, but wholly, eternally, universally good. If I could know and understand all His acts from eternity, there would not be one which would not deepen my reverence and call forth my adoring praise."

To some readers this discovery may seem a mere platitude and truism: the assertion of a thing which they have never failed to understand. To me it was a real revelation which transformed my religion from one of reverence only into one of vivid love for that Infinite Goodness which I then beheld unclouded. The deep shadow left for years on my soul by the doctrine of eternal Hell had rolled away at last. Another truth came home to me many years later, and not till after I had written my first book. It was one night,

---

[11]Charles **Bray** (1811–1884) and his wife Caroline Hennell (1814–1905) influenced George Eliot (see Charles Hennell, page 63.)

[12]*Tabula rasa:* clean slate.

[13]"to lift . . . my goings": Psalm 40:2.

[14]James **Martineau** (1805–1900): Unitarian theologian and philosopher, brother of Harriet Martineau.

after sitting up late in my room reading (for once) no grave work, but a pretty little story by Mrs. Gaskell. Up to that time I had found the pleasures of knowledge the keenest of all, and gloried in the old philosopher's *dictum*, "Man was created to know and to contemplate." I looked on the pleasures of the affections as secondary and inferior to those of the intellect, and I strove to perform my duties to those around me, rather in a spirit of moral rectitude and obedience to law than in one of loving-kindness. Suddenly again it came to me to see that Love is greater than Knowledge; that it is more beautiful to serve our brothers freely and tenderly, than to "hive up learning with each studious year,"[15] to compassionate the failures of others and ignore them

---

[15]"**hive . . . studious year**": see Byron, *Childe Harold's Pilgrimage* 3 (1816) 995.

when possible, rather than undertake the hard process (I always found it so!) of forgiveness of injuries; to say, "What may I be allowed to do to help and bless this one—or that?" rather than "What am I bound by duty to do for him, or her; and how little will suffice?" As these thoughts swelled in my heart, I threw myself down in a passion of happy tears, and passed most of the night thinking how I should work out what I had learned. I had scarcely fallen asleep towards morning when I was waked by the intelligence that one of the servants, a young laundress, was dying. I hurried to the poor woman's room, which was at a great distance from mine, and found all the men and women servants collected around her. She wished for some one to pray for her, and there was no one to do it but myself, and so, while the innocent girl's soul passed away, I led, for the first and only time, the prayers of my father's household. . . . (Chapter 4)

1894

COVENTRY PATMORE

(1823–1896)

Coventry Patmore's *The Angel in the House* took ordinary, uneventful middle-class marriage as the subject uniquely suited to modern poetry. At first reviewers laughed at the "bard of the tea-tables" when they noticed him at all, finding the poem tepid and tedious, and "The Angel in the House" quickly became a catchphrase for idealized Victorian womanhood as well as a convenient shorthand for jokes about women and marriage. (Patmore himself meant by the "Angel" not a woman but the spirit of Love.) But as this notoriety suggests, sales were good. Ruskin recommended the poem to girls and women in "Of Queens' Gardens" (1865), and in 1887 it was reprinted in a very cheap edition that drew many new readers. By the end of the century more than a million copies are said to have been sold. The Angel was then pretty much forgotten until Virginia Woolf invoked her in "The Death of the Moth" (1942) to symbolize the ideal that had to be destroyed before women could be free. Unassertive, self-sacrificing, sympathetic, pure, "immensely charming," and with never a "mind or wish of her own," the Angel, Woolf says, "bothered me and wasted my time and so tormented me that at last I killed her." Thus memorialized in her annihilation, the Angel resumed her symbolic existence.

The poet who was to become the laureate of connubial love married a clergyman's daughter at the age of twenty-four. Son of a writer and editor, he had attended school only for six months, when a teenager in France; he had published essays and poems and become an assistant librarian at the British Museum. The first installment of *The Angel in the House*, "The Betrothal," appeared in 1854, followed by "The Espousals" (1856), "Faithful for Ever" (1860), and "Victories of Love" (1863). In 1862 Patmore's wife died of consumption, having borne six children, and in 1864 he converted to Catholicism and married an heiress whose fortune enabled him to quit his job and buy a country estate. His second wife died in 1880, and in the following year he married the children's governess, who bore his seventh child. He continued the nuptial theme, among others, in a series of odes collected as *The Unknown Eros*, and elaborated in prose the mystical and sacramental theories of love that increasingly inform his verse. Wedded love, he asserted, is the symbol and revelation of divine love: in relation to Christ, the soul of man is like a betrothed wife. The social implications of this idea were extremely conservative, as was Patmore's thought in almost every sphere. For him, the difference between the sexes was the central fact of human existence, and although he deplored male aggression when untempered by female influence, he mocked women's doomed attempts to rebel against their "privilege of subordination to men."

For years Patmore tinkered with the text of *The Angel in the House*, revising and rearranging, adding or removing large chunks. The poem consequently exists in a bewildering variety of versions. Basically, however, it consists of four books, two about the courtship and marriage of a couple loosely based on Patmore and his first wife, and two (sometimes separately titled "The Victories of Love") focusing on other characters in the story. The books are divided into cantos, each with a set of lyrical meditations ("Preludes") followed by a narrative section in the lover's voice. Most of the poem is in octosyllabic quatrains, often echoing Tennyson's *In Memoriam*. For the odes, however, Patmore developed a freer, more flexible form in which lines vary greatly in length and pauses are counted as parts of the metrical feet.

His poetry remains of interest for the technical skill it displays; the sometimes humorous, sometimes profoundly sad moments of psychological insight; and the insistence that humdrum domesticity is not out of place in the precincts of poetry.

from The Angel in the House

The Prologue

— 1 —

"Mine is no horse with wings,[1] to gain
    The region of the spheral chime;
He does but drag a rumbling wain,
    Cheer'd by the coupled bells of rhyme;
And if at Fame's bewitching note
    My homely Pegasus pricks an ear,
The world's cart-collar hugs his throat,
    And he's too sage to kick or rear."

— 2 —

Thus ever answer'd Vaughan his Wife,
    Who, more than he, desired his fame;   10
But, in his heart, his thoughts were rife
    How for her sake to earn a name.
With bays[2] poetic three times crown'd,
    And other college honours won,
He, if he chose, might be renown'd,
    He had but little doubt, she none;
And in a loftier phrase he talk'd
    With her, upon their Wedding Day,
(The eighth,) while through the fields they walk'd,
    Their children shouting by the way.   20

— 3 —

"Not careless of the gift of song,
    Nor out of love with noble fame,
I, meditating much and long
    What I should sing, how win a name,
Considering well what theme unsung,
    What reason worth the cost of rhyme,
Remains to loose the poet's tongue
    In these last days, the dregs of time,

Learn that to me, though born so late,
    There does, beyond desert, befall   30
(May my great fortune make me great!)
    The first of themes, sung last of all.
In green and undiscover'd ground,
    Yet near where many others sing,
I have the very well-head found
    Whence gushes the Pierian Spring."[3]

— 4 —

Then she: "What is it, Dear? The Life
    Of Arthur, or Jerusalem's Fall?"
Neither: your gentle self, my Wife,
    And love, that grows from one to all.   40
And if I faithfully proclaim
    Of these the exceeding worthiness,
Surely the sweetest wreath of Fame
    Shall, to your hope, my brows caress;
And if, by virtue of my choice
    Of this, the most heart-touching theme
That ever tuned a poet's voice,
    I live, as I am bold to dream,
To be delight to many days,
    And into silence only cease   50
When those are still, who shared their bays
    With Laura and with Beatrice,[4]
Imagine, Love, how learned men
    Will deep-conceiv'd devices find,
Beyond my purpose and my ken,
    An ancient bard of simple mind
You, Sweet, his Mistress, Wife, and Muse,
    Were you for mortal woman meant?
Your praises give a hundred clues
    To mythological intent!   60

---

[1]**horse with wings: Pegasus**, in Greek myth, often associated with poetry. **wain:** wagon.

[2]**bays:** poet's crown of laurel.

[3]**Pierian Spring:** well of inspiration associated with the Muses, in NE Greece.

[4]**Laura, Beatrice:** beloved women celebrated in the poetry of Petrarch and Dante, respectively.

And, severing thus the truth from trope,
  In you the Commentators see,
Outlines occult of abstract scope,
  A future for philosophy!
Your arm's on mine! these are the meads
  In which we pass our living days;
There Avon[5] runs, now hid with reeds,
  Now brightly brimming pebbly bays;
Those are our children's songs that come
  With bells and bleatings of the sheep;   70
And there, in yonder English home,
  We thrive on mortal food and sleep!"
She laugh'd. How proud she always was
  To feel how proud he was of her!
But he had grown distraught, because
  The Muse's mood began to stir.

— 5 —

His purpose with performance crown'd,
  He to his well-pleased Wife rehears'd,
When next their Wedding Day came round,
  His leisure's labour, "Book the First."   80

The Cathedral Close

— PRELUDES —

1 THE IMPOSSIBILITY

Lo, love's obey'd by all. 'Tis right
  That all should know what they obey,
Lest erring conscience damp delight,
  And folly laugh our joys away.
Thou Primal Love, who grantest wings
  And voices to the woodland birds,
Grant me the power of saying things
  Too simple and too sweet for words!

2 LOVE'S REALITY

I walk, I trust, with open eyes;
  I've travell'd half my worldly course;
And in the way behind me lies
  Much vanity and some remorse;
I've lived to feel how pride may part
  Spirits, tho' match'd like hand and glove;
I've blush'd for love's abode, the heart;
  But have not disbelieved in love;

Nor unto love, sole mortal thing
  Of worth immortal, done the wrong   10
To count it, with the rest that sing,
  Unworthy of a serious song;
And love is my reward; for now,
  When most of dead'ning time complain,
The myrtle[6] blooms upon my brow,
  Its odour quickens all my brain.

3 THE POET'S CONFIDENCE

The richest realm of all the earth
  Is counted still a heathen land:
Lo, I, like Joshua,[7] now go forth
  To give it into Israel's hand.
I will not hearken blame or praise;
  For so should I dishonour do
To that sweet Power by which these Lays
  Alone are lovely, good, and true;
Nor credence to the world's cries give;
  Which ever preach and still prevent   10
Pure passion's high prerogative
  To make, not follow, precedent.
From love's abysmal ether rare
  If I to men have here made known
New truths, they, like new stars, were there
  Before, though not yet written down.
Moving but as the feelings move,
  I run, or loiter with delight,
Or pause to mark where gentle Love
  Persuades the soul from height to height.   20
Yet, know ye, though my words are gay
  As David's dance, which Michol[8] scorn'd,
If kindly you receive the Lay,
  You shall be sweetly help'd and warn'd.

—THE CATHEDRAL CLOSE—

— 1 —

Once more I came to Sarum Close,[9]
  With joy half memory, half desire,
And breathed the sunny wind that rose
  And blew the shadows o'er the Spire,

---

[6]**myrtle:** evergreen shrub, classical emblem of love.

[7]**Joshua:** see Joshua 1:1–6.

[8]**David's dance, Michol** (Michal): see 2 Samuel 6:16.

[9]**Sarum:** old name for Salisbury, cathedral city in S England.
Close: precinct of the cathedral, where the presiding **Dean** lives.

---

[5]**Avon:** river in S England.

And toss'd the lilac's scented plumes,
    And sway'd the chestnut's thousand cones,
And fill'd my nostrils with perfumes,
    And shaped the clouds in waifs and zones,
And wafted down the serious strain
    Of Sarum bells, when, true to time,   10
I reach'd the Dean's, with heart and brain
    That trembled to the trembling chime.

— 2 —

'Twas half my home, six years ago.
    The six years had not alter'd it:
Red-brick and ashlar, long and low,
    With dormers and with oriels lit.
Geranium, lychnis, rose array'd
    The windows, all wide open thrown;
And some one in the Study play'd
    The Wedding March of Mendelssohn.[10]   20
And there it was I last took leave:
    'Twas Christmas: I remember'd now
The cruel girls, who feign'd to grieve,
    Took down the evergreens; and how
The holly into blazes woke
    The fire, lighting the large, low room,
A dim, rich lustre of old oak
    And crimson velvet's glowing gloom.

— 3 —

No change had touch'd Dean Churchill: kind,
    By widowhood more than winters bent,   30
And settled in a cheerful mind,
    As still forecasting heaven's content.
Well might his thoughts be fix'd on high,
    Now she was there! Within her face
Humility and dignity
    Were met in a most sweet embrace.
She seem'd expressly sent below
    To teach our erring minds to see
The rhythmic change of time's swift flow
    As part of still eternity.   40
Her life, all honour, observed, with awe
    Which cross experience could not mar,
The fiction of the Christian law
    That all men honourable are;

And so her smile at once conferr'd
    High flattery and benign reproof;
And I, a rude boy, strangely stirr'd,
    Grew courtly in my own behoof.
The years, so far from doing her wrong,
    Anointed her with gracious balm,   50
And made her brows more and more young
    With wreaths of amaranth and palm.[11]

— 4 —

Was this her eldest, Honor, prude,
    Who would not let me pull the swing;
Who, kiss'd at Christmas, call'd me rude,
    And, sobbing low, refused to sing?
How changed! In shape no slender Grace,
    But Venus; milder than the dove;
Her mother's air: her Norman face;
    Her large sweet eyes, clear lakes of love.   60
Mary I knew. In former time
    Ailing and pale, she thought that bliss
Was only for a better clime,
    And, heavenly overmuch, scorn'd this.
I, rash with theories of the right,
    Which stretch'd the tether of my Creed,
But did not break it, held delight
    Half discipline. We disagreed.
She told the Dean I wanted grace.
    Now she was kindest of the three,   70
And soft wild roses deck'd her face.
    And, what, was this my Mildred, she
To herself and all a sweet surprise?
    My Pet, who romp'd and roll'd a hoop?
I wonder'd where those daisy eyes
    Had found their touching curve and droop.

— 5 —

Unmannerly times! But now we sat
    Stranger than strangers; till I caught
And answer'd Mildred's smile; and that
    Spread to the rest, and freedom brought.   80
The Dean talk'd little, looking on,
    Of three such daughters justly vain.
What letters they had had from Bonn,
    Said Mildred, and what plums from Spain!

---

[10]Felix **Mendelssohn** (1809–1847): German composer.

[11]**amaranth:** everlasting flower. **palm:** symbol of excellence, victory, martyrdom.

By Honor I was kindly task'd
    To excuse my never coming down
From Cambridge; Mary smiled and ask'd
    Were Kant and Goethe[12] yet outgrown?
And, pleased, we talk'd the old days o'er;
    And, parting, I for pleasure sigh'd.   90
To be there as a friend, (since more,)
    Seem'd then, seems still, excuse for pride;
For something that abode endued
    With temple-like repose, an air
Of life's kind purposes pursued
    With order'd freedom sweet and fair.
A tent pitch'd in a world not right
    It seem'd, whose inmates, every one,
On tranquil faces bore the light
    Of duties beautifully done,   100
And humbly, though they had few peers,
    Kept their own laws, which seem'd to be
The fair sum of six thousand years'[13]
    Traditions of civility.

                                 1854, 1878

The Toys

My little Son, who look'd from thoughtful eyes
And moved and spoke in quiet grown-up wise,
Having my law the seventh time disobey'd,
I struck him, and dismiss'd
With hard words and unkiss'd,
His Mother, who was patient, being dead.
Then, fearing lest his grief should hinder sleep,
I visited his bed,
But found him slumbering deep,
    With darken'd eyelids, and their lashes yet   10
From his late sobbing wet.
And I, with moan,
Kissing away his tears, left others of my own;
For, on a table drawn beside his head,
He had put, within his reach,
A box of counters and a red-vein'd stone,
A piece of glass abraded by the beach

And six or seven shells,
A bottle with bluebells
And two French copper coins, ranged there with
        careful art,   20
To comfort his sad heart.
So when that night I pray'd
To God, I wept, and said:
Ah, when at last we lie with tranced breath,
Not vexing Thee in death,
And Thou rememberest of what toys
We made our joys,
How weakly understood,
Thy great commanded good,
Then, fatherly not less   30
Than I whom Thou hast moulded from the clay
Thou'lt leave Thy wrath, and say,
"I will be sorry for their childishness."

The Azalea

There, where the sun shines first
    Against our room,
She train'd the gold Azalea, whose perfume
She, Spring-like, from her breathing grace dispersed.
Last night the delicate crests of saffron bloom,
For that their dainty likeness watch'd and nurst,
Were just at point to burst.
At dawn I dream'd, O God, that she was dead,
And groan'd aloud upon my wretched bed,
And waked, ah, God, and did not waken her,   10
But lay, with eyes still closed,
Perfectly bless'd in the delicious sphere
By which I knew so well that she was near,
My heart to speechless thankfulness composed
Till 'gan to stir
A dizzy somewhat in my troubled head—
It *was* the azalea's breath, and she *was* dead!
The warm night had the lingering buds disclosed,
And I had fall'n asleep with to my breast
A chance-found letter press'd   20
In which she said,
"So, till to-morrow eve, my Own adieu!
Parting's well-paid with soon again to meet,
Soon in your arms to feel so small and sweet,
Sweet to myself that am so sweet to you!"

---

[12]Immanuel **Kant** (1724–1804): German philosopher. Johann Wolfgang von **Goethe** (1749–1832): German Romantic writer.

[13]**six thousand years**: age of the world as traditionally computed from the Bible.

Departure

It was not like your great and gracious ways!
Do you, that have nought other to lament,
Never, my Love, repent
Of how, that July afternoon,
You went,
With sudden, unintelligible phrase,
And frighten'd eye,
Upon your journey of so many days,
Without a single kiss, or a good-bye?
I knew, indeed, that you were parting soon;   10
And so we sate, within the low sun's rays,
You whispering to me, for your voice was weak;
Your harrowing praise.
Well, it was well,
To hear you such things speak,
And I could tell
What made your eyes a growing gloom of love,
As a warm South-wind sombres a March grove.
And it was like your great and gracious ways
To turn your talk on daily things, my Dear,   20
Lifting the luminous, pathetic lash
To let the laughter flash,
Whilst I drew near,
Because you spoke so low that I could scarcely hear.
But all at once to leave me at the last,
More at the wonder than the loss aghast,
With huddled, unintelligible phrase,
And frighten'd eye,
And go your journey of all days
With not one kiss, or a good-bye,   30
And the only loveless look the look with which
        you pass'd:
'Twas all unlike your great and gracious ways.

                                                        1877

ADELAIDE ANNE PROCTER

(1825–1864)

When Adelaide Procter became a pseudonymous contributor to Charles Dickens' journal *Household Words*, the staff fabricated an identity for her that shows what mid-Victorian women poets were expected to be. "We settled somehow, to our complete satisfaction," Dickens explained in his introduction to a posthumous collection of her poems, "that she was a governess in a family; that she went to Italy in that capacity, and returned; and that she had long been in the same family." They assumed, that is, that she was poor, dependent, and emotionally deprived. They were, however, quite wrong. Her father, Bryan Waller Procter, was a successful London lawyer and popular poet who wrote under the name of Barry Cornwall, and from childhood she had moved familiarly in the literary world. She also displayed considerable independence of spirit. An energetic feminist, she worked to increase employment opportunities for women, was active in various philanthropic works, and converted to Catholicism. Dickens found her death a more pleasing object of contemplation than the unseemly exertions to which he attributed her illness:

> All the restlessness gone then, and all the sweet patience of her natural disposition purified by the resignation of her soul, she lay upon her bed through the whole round of changes of the seasons. She lay upon her bed through fifteen months. In all that time, her old cheerfulness never quitted her. In all that time, not an impatient or a querulous minute can be remembered. . . . Her sister entering as they raised her, she said: "It has come at last!" And with a bright and happy smile, looked upward, and departed.

This highly stylized, quintessentially Victorian deathbed scene by the great master of deathbed scenes reduces Procter's vigorous and independent character to a sentimental cliché. In her lifetime Procter's poetry sold better than that of any living poet except Tennyson; her immensely popular "A Lost Chord," which was set to music by the distinguished composer Arthur Sullivan (of Gilbert and Sullivan), may be taken to typify public taste around midcentury, in instructive contrast to Elizabeth Barrett Browning's "A Musical Instrument" or Robert Browning's "Abt Vogler." Often, however, Procter's poetry expresses unexpected subtleties, questions established values, and speaks out more strongly on behalf of the outcast and oppressed than her mainstream popularity might lead us to expect.

Envy

He was the first always: Fortune
    Shone bright in his face.
I fought for years; with no effort
    He conquered the place:
We ran; my feet were all bleeding,
    But he won the race.

Spite of his many successes,
    Men loved him the same;
My one pale ray of good fortune
    Met scoffing and blame.   10
When we erred, they gave him pity,
    But me—only shame.

My home was still in the shadow,
    His lay in the sun:
I longed in vain: what he asked for
    It straightway was done.
Once I staked all my heart's treasure.
    We played—and he won.

Yes; and just now I have seen him,
    Cold, smiling, and blest,   20
Laid in his coffin. God help me!
    While he is at rest,
I am cursed still to live:—even
    Death loved him the best.

1859

A Lost Chord

Seated one day at the Organ,
    I was weary and ill at ease,
And my fingers wandered idly
    Over the noisy keys.

I do not know what I was playing,
    Or what I was dreaming then;
But I struck one chord of music,
    Like the sound of a great Amen.

It flooded the crimson twilight,
    Like the close of an Angel's Psalm,   10
And it lay on my fevered spirit
    With a touch of infinite calm.

It quieted pain and sorrow,
    Like love overcoming strife;
It seemed the harmonious echo
    From our discordant life.

It linked all perplexed meanings
    Into one perfect peace,
And trembled away into silence
    As if it were loth to cease.   20

I have sought, but I seek it vainly,
    That one lost chord divine,
That came from the soul of the Organ,
    And entered into mine.

It may be that Death's bright angel
    Will speak in that chord again,
It may be that only in Heaven
    I shall hear that grand Amen.

1860

The Requital

Loud roared the Tempest,
    Fast fell the sleet;
A little Child Angel
    Passed down the street,
With trailing pinions,
    And weary feet.

The moon was hidden;
    No stars were bright;
So she could not shelter
In heaven that night,   10
For the Angels' ladders
    Are rays of light.

She beat her wings
    At each window-pane,
And pleaded for shelter,
    But all in vain:—
"Listen," they said,
    "To the pelting rain!"

She sobbed, as the laughter
And mirth grew higher,   20
"Give me rest and shelter
    Beside your fire,
And I will give you
    Your heart's desire."

The dreamer sat watching
　　His embers gleam,
While his heart was floating
　　Down hope's bright stream;
. . . So he wove her wailing
　　Into his dream.　　　　　30

The worker toiled on,
　　For his time was brief;
The mourner was nursing
　　Her own pale grief:
They heard not the promise
　　That brought relief.

But fiercer the Tempest
　　Rose than before,
When the Angel paused
　　At a humble door,　　　40
And asked for shelter
　　And help once more.

A weary woman,
　　Pale, worn, and thin,
With the brand upon her
　　Of want and sin,
Heard the Child Angel
　　And took her in.

Took her in gently,
　　And did her best　　　50
To dry her pinions;
　　And made her rest
With tender pity
　　Upon her breast.

When the eastern morning
　　Grew bright and red,
Up the first sunbeam
　　The Angel fled;
Having kissed the woman
　　And left her—dead.　　60

1860

~

A Woman's Last Word[1]

Well—the links are broken,
　　All is past;
This farewell, when spoken,
　　Is the last.

---

[1]"**A Woman's Last Word**": see Robert Browning's poem of the same ambiguous name and halting meter (page 552).

I have tried and striven
　　All in vain;
Such bonds must be riven,
　　Spite of pain,
And never, never, never
　　Knit again.　　　　　10

So I tell you plainly,
　　It must be:
I shall try, not vainly,
　　To be free;
Truer, happier chances
　　Wait me yet,
While you, through fresh fancies,
　　Can forget;—
And life has nobler uses
　　Than Regret.　　　　　20

All past words retracing,
　　One by one,
Does not help effacing
　　What is done.
Let it be. O, stronger
　　Links can break!
Had we dreamed still longer
　　We could wake,—
Yet let us part in kindness
　　For Love's sake.　　　30

Bitterness and sorrow
　　Will at last,
In some bright to-morrow,
　　Heal their past;
But future hearts will never
　　Be as true
As mine was—is ever,
　　Dear, for you. . . . .
. .Then must we part, when loving
　　As we do?　　　　　40

1861

~

Homeless

It is cold, dark midnight, yet listen
　　To that patter of tiny feet!
Is it one of your dogs, fair lady,
　　Who whines in the bleak cold street?
Is it one of your silken spaniels
　　Shut out in the snow and the sleet?

My dogs sleep warm in their baskets,
  Safe from the darkness and snow;
All the beasts in our Christian England,
  Find pity wherever they go—   10
(Those are only the homeless children
  Who are wandering to and fro).

Look out in the gusty darkness,—
  I have seen it again and again,
That shadow, that flits so slowly
  Up and down past the window pane:—
It is surely some criminal lurking
  Out there in the frozen rain?

Nay, our criminals all are sheltered,
  They are pitied and taught and fed: 20
That is only a sister-woman
  Who has got neither food nor bed,—
And the Night cries, "Sin to be living,"
  And the River cries, "Sin to be dead."

Look out at that farthest corner
  Where the wall stands blank and bare:—
Can that be a pack which a Pedler
  Has left and forgotten there?
His goods lying out unsheltered
  Will be spoilt by the damp night-air.   30

Nay;—goods in our thrifty England
  Are not left to lie and grow rotten,
For each man knows the market value
  Of silk or woollen or cotton . . .
But in counting the riches of England
  I think our Poor are forgotten.

Our Beasts and our Thieves and our Chattels
  Have weight for good or for ill;
But the Poor are only His image,
  His presence, His word, His will;—   40
And so Lazarus lies at our doorstep
  And Dives[1] neglects him still.

                                          1862

---

[1]**Lazarus, Dives**: rich man and beggar; see Luke 16:19–26.

THOMAS HENRY HUXLEY

(1825–1895)

Thomas Huxley was the spokesman for Victorian science in its militant and triumphal aspect. Not only did he fight the battle for evolutionary theory that Darwin himself shrank from; he led the onslaught against the social, religious, and educational establishment whose claims to authority evolutionary theory implicitly defied. His first great public coup took place at a meeting of the British Association for the Advancement of Science in 1860, when an eminent bishop sneeringly inquired whether he was descended from apes on his grandmother's or grandfather's side. Huxley replied:

> If . . . the question is put to me would I rather have a miserable ape for a grandfather or a man highly endowed by nature and possessed of great means of influence and yet who employs these faculties and that influence for the mere purpose of introducing ridicule into a grave scientific discussion, I unhesitatingly affirm my preference for the ape.

Huxley invented the term "agnosticism" in 1869 for the belief that whatever may lie behind material phenomena is unknowable and therefore irrelevant to scientific argument. Scientific habits of mind—respect for the laws of nature, commitment to seeking truth—could, he believed, transform society. He presented his views in clear, strong, lively, witty prose, and with tremendous moral assertiveness; as the title of his collection of essays *Lay Sermons* suggests, he was the preacher and prophet of a new, anti–theological religion. He is remembered as "Darwin's bulldog," but "Pope Huxley" was an equally apt nickname.

His own life exemplified the struggle of Victorian science for status and recognition. He became a leader of the intellectual elite, loaded with academic and public honors, but the story of how he reached that position might have come from the pages of Samuel Smiles' *Self-Help*. Huxley was mostly self-educated: he taught himself algebra, geometry, physics, chemistry, physiology, history, Latin, and Greek, and learned French from an older sister. Formal schooling began when he was eight at a private school near London where his father taught, but ended two years later when the school closed. The family moved north to the poverty-ridden city of Coventry, where at thirteen he was apprenticed to his brother-in-law, a doctor. At fifteen he became apprentice to another doctor, this time in one of the most desperately miserable London slums. With grim determination he acquired formal training at a hospital, which led to a position as surgeon's mate in the navy. From 1846 to 1850 he traveled as surgeon and naturalist on the *Rattlesnake*, and like Darwin voyaging on the *Beagle* (these names are not, despite appearances, allegorical) enlarged his view of the world and laid the foundations of his later work. In the mid-Victorian period, however, science was not yet a profession that offered regular training, school and university positions, and research massively financed by government; and Huxley had a hard time finding employment that would allow him to continue his research. In later years he fought for scientific education, the professionalization of research, and the principle of advancement by merit.

"A Liberal Education; and Where to Find It" is a speech given at the opening of a Working Men's College of which Huxley, who was a hero among the working classes, was the principal. It is a stinging denunciation of the elitist system of classical education: part of an ongoing public debate, in which Huxley and Matthew Arnold were the main contestants, about whether science should replace the classics at the center of the curriculum. In Huxley's most potent rhetoric, the essay elevates Darwinian Nature to the position of ruling deity, a relentless, unpitying, supernatural schoolmistress whose laws man (Huxley's language is decidedly masculine) must learn and obey. These laws seem to uphold the ideology of the new industrial order even as they offer some relief from its worst effects. Huxley came increasingly to feel, however, the need for values more humane than those enforced by Nature, and to deplore the idea (known as "Social Darwinism") that the "struggle for existence" should serve as an ethical norm; "Evolution and Ethics" is the most powerful statement of this later view. His "Autobiography," designed less for self-revelation than for warding off public scrutiny, is comparatively restrained; it glosses over the hardships and social degradations of his youth even as it jabs at the social system that had tried to exclude him. The allusions to religion that frame and intersperse the narrative indicate, lightly but surely, the arch-agnostic's sense of being engaged in a profoundly religious—and successful—struggle for reform.

from A Liberal Education; and Where to Find It

The business which the South London Working Men's College has undertaken is a great work; indeed, I might say, that Education, with which that college proposes to grapple, is the greatest work of all those which lie ready to a man's hand just at present.

And, at length, this fact is becoming generally recognised. You cannot go anywhere without hearing a buzz of more or less confused and contradictory talk on this subject—nor can you fail to notice that, in one point at any rate, there is a very decided advance upon like discussions in former days. Nobody outside the agricultural interest now dares to say that education is a bad thing. If any representative of the once large and powerful party, which, in former days, proclaimed this opinion, still exists in a semifossil state, he keeps his thoughts to himself. In fact, there is a chorus of voices, almost distressing in their harmony, raised in favour of the doctrine that education is the great panacea for human troubles, and that, if the country is not shortly to go to the dogs, everybody must be educated.

The politicians tell us, "you must educate the masses because they are going to be masters." The clergy join in the cry for education, for they affirm that the people are drifting away from church and chapel into the broadest infidelity. The manufacturers and the capitalists swell the chorus lustily. They declare that ignorance makes bad workmen;

that England will soon be unable to turn out cotton goods, or steam engines, cheaper than other people; and then, Ichabod! Ichabod! the glory will be departed from us.[1] And a few voices are lifted up in favour of the doctrine that the masses should be educated because they are men and women with unlimited capacities of being, doing, and suffering, and that it is as true now, as ever it was, that the people perish for lack of knowledge.

These members of the minority, with whom I confess I have a good deal of sympathy, are doubtful whether any of the other reasons urged in favour of the education of the people are of much value—whether, indeed, some of them are based upon either wise or noble grounds of action. They question if it be wise to tell people that you will do for them, out of fear of their power, what you have left undone, so long as your only motive was compassion for their weakness and their sorrows. And, if ignorance of everything which it is needful a ruler should know is likely to do so much harm in the governing classes of the future, why is it, they ask reasonably enough, that such ignorance in the governing classes of the past has not been viewed with equal horror?

Compare the average artisan and the average country squire, and it may be doubted if you will find a pin to choose between the two in point of ignorance, class feeling,

---

[1]Ichabod . . . from us: 1 Samuel 4:21. the people perish . . . knowledge: see Hosea 4:6.

or prejudice. It is true that the ignorance is of a different sort—that the class feeling is in favour of a different class, and that the prejudice has a distinct favour of wrong-headedness in each case—but it is questionable if the one is either a bit better, or a bit worse, than the other. The old protectionist theory is the doctrine of trades unions as applied by the squires, and the modern trades unionism is the doctrine of the squires applied by the artisans. Why should we be worse off under one *régime* than under the other?

Again, this sceptical minority asks the clergy to think whether it is really want of education which keeps the masses away from their ministrations—whether the most completely educated men are not as open to reproach on this score as the workmen; and whether, perchance, this may not indicate that it is not education which lies at the bottom of the matter?

Once more, these people, whom there is no pleasing, venture to doubt whether the glory which rests upon being able to undersell all the rest of the world, is a very safe kind of glory—whether we may not purchase it too dear; especially if we allow education, which ought to be directed to the making of men, to be diverted into a process of manufacturing human tools, wonderfully adroit in the exercise of some technical industry, but good for nothing else.

And, finally, these people inquire whether it is the masses alone who need a reformed and improved education. They ask whether the richest of our public schools might not well be made to supply knowledge, as well as gentlemanly habits, a strong class feeling, and eminent proficiency in cricket. They seem to think that the noble foundations of our old universities are hardly fulfilling their functions in their present posture of half-clerical seminaries, half racecourses, where men are trained to win a senior wranglership, or a double-first, as horses are trained to win a cup, with as little reference to the needs of after-life in the case of the man as in that of the racer. And, while as zealous for education as the rest, they affirm that, if the education of the richer classes were such as to fit them to be the leaders and the governors of the poorer; and, if the education of the poorer classes were such as to enable them to appreciate really wise guidance and good governance; the politicians need not fear mob-law, nor the clergy lament their want of flocks, nor the capitalists prognosticate the annihilation of the prosperity of the country.

Such is the diversity of opinion upon the why and the wherefore of education. And my hearers will be prepared to expect that the practical recommendations which are put forward are not less discordant. There is a loud cry for compulsory education. We English, in spite of constant experi-

ence to the contrary, preserve a touching faith in the efficacy of acts of parliament; and I believe we should have compulsory education in the course of next session, if there were the least probability that half a dozen leading statesmen of different parties would agree what that education should be.

Some hold that education without theology is worse than none. Others maintain, quite as strongly, that education with theology is in the same predicament. But this is certain, that those who hold the first opinion can by no means agree what theology should be taught; and that those who maintain the second are in a small minority.

At any rate "make people learn to read, write, and cipher," say a great many; and the advice is undoubtedly sensible as far as it goes. But, as has happened to me in former days, those who, in despair of getting anything better, advocate this measure, are met with the objection that it is very like making a child practise the use of a knife, fork, and spoon, without giving it a particle of meat. I really don't know what reply is to be made to such an objection.

But it would be unprofitable to spend more time in disentangling, or rather in showing up the knots in, the ravelled skeins of our neighbours. Much more to the purpose is to ask if we possess any clue of our own which may guide us among these entanglements. And by way of a beginning, let us ask ourselves—What is education? Above all things, what is our ideal of a thoroughly liberal education?—of that education which, if we could begin life again, we would give ourselves—of that education which, if we could mould the fates to our own will, we would give our children. Well, I know not what may be your conceptions upon this matter, but I will tell you mine, and I hope I shall find that our views are not very discrepant.

Suppose it were perfectly certain that the life and fortune of every one of us would, one day or other, depend upon his winning or losing a game at chess. Don't you think that we should all consider it to be a primary duty to learn at least the names and the moves of the pieces; to have a notion of a gambit, and a keen eye for all the means of giving and getting out of check? Do you not think that we should look with a disapprobation amounting to scorn, upon the father who allowed his son, or the state which allowed its members, to grow up without knowing a pawn from a knight?

Yet it is a very plain and elementary truth, that the life, the fortune, and the happiness of every one of us, and, more or less, of those who are connected with us, do depend upon our knowing something of the rules of a game infinitely more difficult and complicated than chess. It is a game which has been played for untold ages, every man and woman of us being one of the two players in a game of his or her own. The chess-board is the world, the pieces are the phenomena of the universe, the rules of the game are what we call the laws of Nature. The player on the other side is hidden from us. We know that his play is always fair, just, and patient. But also we know, to our cost, that he never overlooks a mistake, or makes the smallest allowance for ignorance. To the man who plays well, the highest stakes are paid, with that sort of overflowing generosity with which the strong shows delight in strength. And one who plays ill is checkmated—without haste, but without remorse.

My metaphor will remind some of you of the famous picture in which Retzsch[2] has depicted Satan playing at chess with man for his soul. Substitute for the mocking fiend in that picture, a calm, strong angel who is playing for love, as we say, and would rather lose than win—and I should accept it as an image of human life.

Well, what I mean by Education is learning the rules of this mighty game. In other words, education is the instruction of the intellect in the laws of Nature, under which name I include not merely things and their forces, but men and their ways; and the fashioning of the affections and of the will into an earnest and loving desire to move in harmony with those laws. For me, education means neither more nor less than this. Anything which professes to call itself education must be tried by this standard, and if it fails to stand the test, I will not call it education, whatever may be the force of authority, or of numbers, upon the other side.

It is important to remember that, in strictness, there is no such thing as an uneducated man. Take an extreme case. Suppose that an adult man, in the full vigour of his faculties, could be suddenly placed in the world, as Adam is said to have been, and then left to do as he best might. How long would he be left uneducated? Not five minutes. Nature would begin to teach him, through the eye, the ear, the touch, the properties of objects. Pain and pleasure would be at his elbow telling him to do this and avoid that; and by slow degrees the man would receive an education, which, if narrow, would be thorough, real, and adequate to his circumstances, though there would be no extras and very few accomplishments.

And if to this solitary man entered a second Adam, or, better still, an Eve, a new and greater world, that of social

and moral phenomena, would be revealed. Joys and woes, compared with which all others might seem but faint shadows, would spring from the new relations. Happiness and sorrow would take the place of the coarser monitors, pleasure and pain; but conduct would still be shaped by the observation of the natural consequences of actions; or, in other words, by the laws of the nature of man.

To every one of us the world was once as fresh and new as to Adam. And then, long before we were susceptible of any other mode of instruction, Nature took us in hand, and every minute of waking life brought its educational influence, shaping our actions into rough accordance with Nature's laws, so that we might not be ended untimely by too gross disobedience. Nor should I speak of this process of education as past, for any one, be he as old as he may. For every man, the world is as fresh as it was at the first day, and as full of untold novelties for him who has the eyes to see them. And Nature is still continuing her patient education of us in that great university, the universe, of which we are all members—Nature having no Test-Acts.[3]

Those who take honours in Nature's university, who learn the laws which govern men and things and obey them, are the really great and successful men in this world. The great mass of mankind are the "Poll,"[4] who pick up just enough to get through without much discredit. Those who won't learn at all are plucked; and then you can't come up again. Nature's pluck means extermination.

Thus the question of compulsory education is settled so far as Nature is concerned. Her bill on that question was framed and passed long ago. But, like all compulsory legislation, that of Nature is harsh and wasteful in its operation. Ignorance is visited as sharply as wilful disobedience—incapacity meets with the same punishment as crime. Nature's discipline is not even a word and a blow, and the blow first; but the blow without the word. It is left to you to find out why your ears are boxed.

The object of what we commonly call education—that education in which man intervenes and which I shall distinguish as artificial education—is to make good these defects in Nature's methods; to prepare the child to receive Nature's education, neither incapably nor ignorantly, nor with wilful

---

[2]Friedrich **Retzsch** (1779–1857): German painter.

[3]**Test-Acts**: laws requiring adherence to Church of England for membership in Parliament and municipal office, repealed 1828–1829. Religious tests for university entrance and degrees were abolished in 1871.

[4]"**Poll**": students who pass without honors. **plucked**: failed in an examination.

disobedience; and to understand the preliminary symptoms of her displeasure, without waiting for the box on the ear. In short, all artificial education ought to be an anticipation of natural education. And a liberal education is an artificial education, which has not only prepared a man to escape the great evils of disobedience to natural laws, but has trained him to appreciate and to seize upon the rewards, which Nature scatters with as free a hand as her penalties.

That man, I think, has had a liberal education, who has been so trained in youth that his body is the ready servant of his will, and does with ease and pleasure all the work that, as a mechanism, it is capable of; whose intellect is a clear, cold, logic engine, with all its parts of equal strength, and in smooth working order; ready, like a steam engine, to be turned to any kind of work, and spin the gossamers as well as forge the anchors of the mind; whose mind is stored with a knowledge of the great and fundamental truths of Nature and of the laws of her operations; one who, no stunted ascetic, is full of life and fire, but whose passions are trained to come to heel by a vigorous will, the servant of a tender conscience; who has learned to love all beauty, whether of Nature or of art, to hate all vileness, and to respect others as himself.

Such an one and no other, I conceive, has had a liberal education; for he is, as completely as a man can be, in harmony with Nature. He will make the best of her, and she of him. They will get on together rarely; she as his ever beneficent mother; he as her mouth-piece, her conscious self, her minister and interpreter.

Where is such an education as this to be had? Where is there any approximation to it? Has any one tried to found such an education? Looking over the length and breadth of these islands, I am afraid that all these questions must receive a negative answer. Consider our primary schools, and what is taught in them. A child learns:—

1. To read, write, and cipher, more or less well; but in a very large proportion of cases not so well as to take pleasure in reading, or to be able to write the commonest letter properly.
2. A quantity of dogmatic theology, of which the child, nine times out of ten, understands next to nothing.
3. Mixed up with this, so as to seem to stand or fall with it, a few of the broadest and simplest principles of morality. This, to my mind, is much as if a man of science should make the story of the fall of the apple in Newton's garden, an integral part of the doctrine of gravitation, and teach it as of equal authority with the law of the inverse squares.

4. A good deal of Jewish history and Syrian geography, and, perhaps, a little something about English history and the geography of the child's own country. But I doubt if there is a primary school in England in which hangs a map of the hundred in which the village lies, so that the children may be practically taught by it what a map means.
5. A certain amount of regularity, attentive obedience, respect for others: obtained by fear, if the master be incompetent or foolish; by love and reverence, if he be wise.

So far as this school course embraces a training in the theory and practice of obedience to the moral laws of Nature, I gladly admit, not only that it contains a valuable educational element, but that, so far, it deals with the most valuable and important part of all education. Yet, contrast what is done in this direction with what might be done; with the time given to matters of comparatively no importance; with the absence of any attention to things of the highest moment; and one is tempted to think of Falstaff's bill and "the halfpenny worth of bread to all that quantity of sack."[5]

Let us consider what a child thus "educated" knows, and what it does not know. Begin with the most important topic of all—morality, as the guide of conduct. The child knows well enough that some acts meet with approbation and some with disapprobation. But it has never heard that there lies in the nature of things a reason for every moral law, as cogent and as well defined as that which underlies every physical law; that stealing and lying are just as certain to be followed by evil consequences, as putting your hand in the fire, or jumping out of a garret window. Again, though the scholar may have been made acquainted, in dogmatic fashion, with the broad laws of morality, he has had no training in the application of those laws to the difficult problems which result from the complex conditions of modern civilization. Would it not be very hard to expect any one to solve a problem in conic sections who had merely been taught the axioms and definitions of mathematical science?

A workman has to bear hard labour, and perhaps privation, while he sees others rolling in wealth, and feeding their dogs with what would keep his children from starvation. Would it not be well to have helped that man to calm the natural promptings of discontent by showing him, in his youth, the necessary connexion of the moral law which

---

[5] sack: wine; see 1 Henry IV 2.5.492.

prohibits stealing with the stability of society—by proving to him, once for all, that it is better for his own people, better for himself, better for future generations, that he should starve than steal? If you have no foundation of knowledge, or habit of thought, to work upon, what chance have you of persuading a hungry man that a capitalist is not a thief "with a circumbendibus?"[6] And if he honestly believes that, of what avail is it to quote the commandment against stealing, when he proposes to make the capitalist disgorge?

Again, the child learns absolutely nothing of the history or the political organization of his own country. His general impression is, that everything of much importance happened a very long while ago; and that the Queen and the gentlefolks govern the country much after the fashion of King David and the elders and nobles of Israel—his sole models. Will you give a man with this much information a vote? In easy times he sells it for a pot of beer. Why should he not? It is of about as much use to him as a chignon, and he knows as much what to do with it, for any other purpose. In bad times, on the contrary, he applies his simple theory of government, and believes that his rulers are the cause of his sufferings—a belief which sometimes bears remarkable practical fruits.

Least of all, does the child gather from this primary "education" of ours a conception of the laws of the physical world, or of the relations of cause and effect therein. And this is the more to be lamented, as the poor are especially exposed to physical evils, and are more interested in removing them than any other class of the community. If any one is concerned in knowing the ordinary laws of mechanics one would think it is the hand-labourer, whose daily toil lies among levers and pulleys; or among the other implements of artisan work. And if any one is interested in the laws of health, it is the poor workman, whose strength is wasted by ill-prepared food, whose health is sapped by bad ventilation and bad drainage, and half whose children are massacred by disorders which might be prevented. Not only does our present primary education carefully abstain from hinting to the workman that some of his greatest evils are traceable to mere physical agencies, which could be removed by energy, patience, and frugality; but it does worse—it renders him, so far as it can, deaf to those who could help him, and tries to substitute an Oriental submission to what is falsely declared to be the will of God, for his natural tendency to strive after a better condition.

What wonder then, if very recently, an appeal has been made to statistics for the profoundly foolish purpose of showing that education is of no good—that it diminishes neither misery, nor crime, among the masses of mankind? I reply, why should the thing which has been called education do either the one or the other? If I am a knave or a fool, teaching me to read and write won't make me less of either one or the other—unless somebody shows me how to put my reading and writing to wise and good purposes.

Suppose any one were to argue that medicine is of no use, because it could be proved statistically, that the percentage of deaths was just the same, among people who had been taught how to open a medicine chest, and among those who did not so much as know the key by sight. The argument is absurd; but it is not more preposterous than that against which I am contending. The only medicine for suffering, crime, and all the other woes of mankind, is wisdom. Teach a man to read and write, and you have put into his hands the great keys of the wisdom box. But it is quite another matter whether he ever opens the box or not. And he is as likely to poison as to cure himself, if, without guidance, he swallows the first drug that comes to hand. In these times a man may as well be purblind, as unable to read— lame, as unable to write. But I protest that, if I thought the alternative were a necessary one, I would rather that the children of the poor should grow up ignorant of both these mighty arts, than that they should remain ignorant of that knowledge to which these arts are means.

It may be said that all these animadversions may apply to primary schools, but that the higher schools, at any rate, must be allowed to give a liberal education. In fact, they professedly sacrifice everything else to this object.

Let us inquire into this matter. What do the higher schools, those to which the great middle class of the country sends its children, teach, over and above the instruction given in the primary schools? There is a little more reading and writing of English. But, for all that, every one knows that it is a rare thing to find a boy of the middle or upper classes who can read aloud decently, or who can put his thoughts on paper in clear and grammatical (to say nothing of good or elegant) language. The "ciphering" of the lower schools expands into elementary mathematics in the higher; into arithmetic, with a little algebra, a little Euclid. But I doubt if one boy in five hundred has ever heard the explanation of a rule of arithmetic, or knows his Euclid otherwise than by rote.

Of theology, the middle class schoolboy gets rather less than poorer children, less absolutely and less relatively, because there are so many other claims upon his attention. I venture to say that, in the great majority of cases, his ideas

---

[6]**circumbendibus:** long–winded evasion.

on this subject when he leaves school are of the most shadowy and vague description, and associated with painful impressions of the weary hours spent in learning collects and catechism by heart.

Modern geography, modern history, modern literature; the English language as a language; the whole circle of the sciences, physical, moral, and social, are even more completely ignored in the higher than in the lower schools. Up till within a few years back, a boy might have passed through any one of the great public schools with the greatest distinction and credit, and might never so much as have heard of one of the subjects I have just mentioned. He might never have heard that the earth goes round the sun; that England underwent a great revolution in 1688, and France another in 1789; that there once lived certain notable men called Chaucer, Shakspeare, Milton, Voltaire, Goethe, Schiller. The first might be a German and the last an Englishman for anything he could tell you to the contrary. And as for science, the only idea the word would suggest to his mind would be dexterity in boxing.

I have said that this was the state of things a few years back, for the sake of the few righteous who are to be found among the educational cities of the plain.[7] But I would not have you too sanguine about the result, if you sound the minds of the existing generation of public schoolboys, on such topics as those I have mentioned.

Now let us pause to consider this wonderful state of affairs; for the time will come when Englishmen will quote it as the stock example of the stolid stupidity of their ancestors in the nineteenth century. The most thoroughly commercial people, the greatest voluntary wanderers and colonists the world has ever seen, are precisely the middle classes of this country. If there be a people which has been busy making history on the great scale for the last three hundred years— and the most profoundly interesting history—history which, if it happened to be that of Greece or Rome, we should study with avidity—it is the English. If there be a people which, during the same period, has developed a remarkable literature, it is our own. If there be a nation whose prosperity depends absolutely and wholly upon their mastery over the forces of Nature, upon their intelligent apprehension of, and obedience to, the laws of the creation and distribution of wealth, and of the stable equilibrium of the forces of society, it is precisely this nation. And yet this is what these wonderful people tell their sons:—"At the cost of from one to two thousand pounds of our hard earned money, we devote twelve of the most precious years of your lives to school.

There you shall toil, or be supposed to toil; but there you shall not learn one single thing of all those you will most want to know, directly you leave school and enter upon the practical business of life. You will in all probability go into business, but you shall not know where, or how, any article of commerce is produced, or the difference between an export or an import, or the meaning of the word 'capital.' You will very likely settle in a colony, but you shall not know whether Tasmania is part of New South Wales, or *vice versâ*.

"Very probably you may become a manufacturer, but you shall not be provided with the means of understanding the working of one of your own steam-engines, or the nature of the raw products you employ; and, when you are asked to buy a patent, you shall not have the slightest means of judging whether the inventor is an imposter who is contravening the elementary principles of science, or a man who will make you as rich as Crœsus.

"You will very likely get into the House of Commons. You will have to take your share in making laws which may prove a blessing or a curse to millions of men. But you shall not hear one word respecting the political organization of your country; the meaning of the controversy between free-traders and protectionists shall never have been mentioned to you; you shall not so much as know that there are such things as economical laws.

"The mental power which will be of most importance in your daily life will be the power of seeing things as they are without regard to authority; and of drawing accurate general conclusions from particular facts. But at school and at college you shall know of no source of truth but authority; nor exercise your reasoning faculty upon anything but deduction from that which is laid down by authority.

"You will have to weary your soul with work, and many a time eat your bread in sorrow and in bitterness, and you shall not have learned to take refuge in the great source of pleasure without alloy, the serene resting-place for worn human nature,—the world of art."

Said I not rightly that we are a wonderful people? I am quite prepared to allow, that education entirely devoted to these omitted subjects might not be a completely liberal education. But is an education which ignores them all, a liberal education? Nay, is it too much to say that the education which should embrace these subjects and no others, would be a real education, though an incomplete one; while an education which omits them is really not an education at all, but a more or less useful course of intellectual gymnastics?

For what does the middle-class school put in the place of all these things which are left out? It substitutes what is

---

[7]**cities of the plain:** Sodom and Gomorrah; see Genesis 19.

usually comprised under the compendious title of the "classics"—that is to say, the languages, the literature, and the history of the ancient Greeks and Romans, and the geography of so much of the world as was known to these two great nations of antiquity. Now, do not expect me to depreciate the earnest and enlightened pursuit of classical learning. I have not the least desire to speak ill of such occupations, nor any sympathy with those who run them down. On the contrary, if my opportunities had lain in that direction, there is no investigation into which I could have thrown myself with greater delight than that of antiquity.

What science can present greater attractions than philology? How can a lover of literary excellence fail to rejoice in the ancient masterpieces? And with what consistency could I, whose business lies so much in the attempt to decipher the past, and to build up intelligible forms out of the scattered fragments of long-extinct beings, fail to take a sympathetic, though an unlearned, interest in the labour of a Niebuhr, a Gibbon, or a Grote?[8] Classical history is a great section of the palæontology of man; and I have the same double respect for it as for other kinds of palæontology—that is to say, a respect for the facts which it establishes as for all facts, and a still greater respect for it as a preparation for the discovery of a law of progress.

But if the classics were taught as they might be taught—if boys and girls were instructed in Greek and Latin, not merely as languages, but as illustrations of philological science; if a vivid picture of life on the shores of the Mediterranean, two thousand years ago, were imprinted on the minds of scholars; if ancient history were taught, not as a weary series of feuds and fights, but traced to its causes in such men placed under such conditions; if, lastly, the study of the classical books were followed in such a manner as to impress boys with their beauties, and with the grand simplicity of their statement of the everlasting problems of human life, instead of with their verbal and grammatical peculiarities; I still think it as little proper that they should form the basis of a liberal education for our contemporaries, as I should think it fitting to make that sort of palæontology with which I am familiar, the back-bone of modern education.

It is wonderful how close a parallel to classical training could be made out of that palæontology to which I refer. In the first place I could get up an osteological primer so arid, so pedantic in its terminology, so altogether distasteful to the youthful mind, as to beat the recent famous production of the head-masters out of the field in all these excellences. Next, I could exercise my boys upon easy fossils, and bring out all their powers of memory and all their ingenuity in the application of my osteo-grammatical rules to the interpretation, or construing, of those fragments. To those who had reached the higher classes, I might supply odd bones to be built up into animals, giving great honour and reward to him who succeeded in fabricating monsters most entirely in accordance with the rules. That would answer to verse-making and essay-writing in the dead languages.

To be sure, if a great comparative anatomist were to look at these fabrications he might shake his head, or laugh. But what then? Would such a catastrophe destroy the parallel?[9] What think you would Cicero, or Horace, say to the production of the best sixth form going? And would not Terence stop his ears and run out if he could be present at an English performance of his own plays? Would Hamlet, in the mouths of a set of French actors, who should insist on pronouncing English after the fashion of their own tongue, be more hideously ridiculous?

But it will be said that I am forgetting the beauty, and the human interest, which appertain to classical studies. To this I reply that it is only a very strong man who can appreciate the charms of a landscape, as he is toiling up a steep hill, along a bad road. What with short-windedness, stones, ruts, and a pervading sense of the wisdom of rest and be thankful, most of us have little enough sense of the beautiful under these circumstances. The ordinary schoolboy is precisely in this case. He finds Parnassus[10] uncommonly steep, and there is no chance of his having much time or inclination to look about him till he gets to the top. And nine times out of ten he does not get to the top.

But if this be a fair picture of the results of classical teaching at its best—and I gather from those who have authority to speak on such matters that it is so—what is to be said of classical teaching at its worst, or in other words, of the classics of our ordinary middle-class schools? I will tell you. It means getting up endless forms and rules by heart. It means turning Latin and Greek into English, for the mere sake of being able to do it, and without the smallest regard to the worth, or worthlessness, of the author read. It means the learning of innumerable, not always decent, fables in

---

[8]Barthold Georg **Niebuhr** (1776–1831), Edward **Gibbon** (1737–1794), George **Grote** (1794–1871): classical historians.

[9]**Cicero, Horace, Terence:** Roman prose writer, poet, dramatist of the 1st and 2nd centuries BCE.

[10]**Parnassus:** mountain in Greece associated with poetic inspiration. The *Gradus ad* [way to] *Parnassum* was a school handbook of Greek and Latin prosody.

such a shape that the meaning they once had is dried up into utter trash; and the only impression left upon a boy's mind is, that the people who believed such things must have been the greatest idiots the world ever saw. And it means, finally, that after a dozen years spent at this kind of work, the sufferer shall be incompetent to interpret a passage in an author he has not already got up; that he shall loathe the sight of a Greek or Latin book; and that he shall never open, or think of, a classical writer again, until, wonderful to relate, he insists upon submitting his sons to the same process.

These be your gods, O Israel! For the sake of this net result (and respectability) the British father denies his children all the knowledge they might turn to account in life, not merely for the achievement of vulgar success, but for guidance in the great crises of human existence. This is the stone he offers to those whom he is bound by the strongest and tenderest ties to feed with bread.

If primary and secondary education are in this unsatisfactory state, what is to be said to the universities? This is an awful subject, and one I almost fear to touch with my unhallowed hands; but I can tell you what those say who have authority to speak.

The Rector of Lincoln College,[11] in his lately published, valuable "Suggestions for Academical Organization with especial reference to Oxford," tells us:—

"The colleges were, in their origin, endowments, not for the elements of a general liberal education, but for the prolonged study of special and professional faculties by men of riper age. The universities embraced both these objects. The colleges, while they incidentally aided in elementary education, were specially devoted to the highest learning. . . . .

"This was the theory of the middle-age university and the design of collegiate foundations in their origin. Time and circumstances have brought about a total change. The colleges no longer promote the researches of science, or direct professional study. Here and there college walls may shelter an occasional student, but not in larger proportions than may be found in private life. Elementary teaching of youths under twenty is now the only function performed by the university, and almost the only object of college endowments. Colleges were homes for the life-study of the highest and most abstruse parts of knowledge. They have become boarding schools in which the elements of the learned languages are taught to youths."

---

[11]**Rector:** Mark Pattison (1813–1884), Oxford scholar and contributor to *Essays and Reviews* (see page 66).

If Mr. Pattison's high position, and his obvious love and respect for his university, be insufficient to convince the outside world that language so severe is yet no more than just, the authority of the Commissioners who reported on the University of Oxford in 1850 is open to no challenge. Yet they write:—

"It is generally acknowledged that both Oxford and the country at large suffer greatly from the absence of a body of learned men devoting their lives to the cultivation of science, and to the direction of academical education.

"The fact that so few books of profound research emanate from the University of Oxford materially impairs its character as a seat of learning, and consequently its hold on the respect of the nation."

Cambridge can claim no exemption from the reproaches addressed to Oxford. And thus there seems no escape from the admission that what we fondly call our great seats of learning are simply "boarding schools" for bigger boys; that learned men are not more numerous in them than out of them; that the advancement of knowledge is not the object of fellows of colleges; that, in the philosophic calm and meditative stillness of their greenswarded courts, philosophy does not thrive and meditation bears few fruits.

It is my great good fortune to reckon amongst my friends resident members of both universities, who are men of learning and research, zealous cultivators of science, keeping before their minds a noble ideal of a university, and doing their best to make that ideal a reality; and, to me, they would necessarily typify the universities, did not the authoritative statements I have quoted compel me to believe that they are exceptional, and not representative men. Indeed, upon calm consideration, several circumstances lead me to think that the Rector of Lincoln College and the Commissioners cannot be far wrong.

I believe there can be no doubt that the foreigner who should wish to become acquainted with the scientific, or the literary, activity of modern England, would simply lose his time and his pains if he visited our universities with that object.

And, as for works of profound research on any subject, and, above all, in that classical lore for which the universities profess to sacrifice almost everything else, why, a third-rate, poverty-stricken German university turns out more produce of that kind in one year, than our vast and wealthy foundations elaborate in ten.

Ask the man who is investigating any question, profoundly and thoroughly—be it historical, philosophical, philological, physical, literary, or theological; who is trying to make himself master of any abstract subject (except, perhaps, political economy and geology, both of which are intensely Anglican sciences) whether he is not compelled to read half a dozen times as many German, as English, books? And whether, of these English books, more than one in ten is the work of a fellow of a college, or a professor of an English university?

Is this from any lack of power in the English as compared with the German mind? The countrymen of Grote and of Mill, of Faraday, of Robert Brown,[12] of Lyell, and of Darwin, to go no further back than the contemporaries of men of middle age, can afford to smile at such a suggestion. England can show now, as she has been able to show in every generation since civilization spread over the West, individual men who hold their own against the world, and keep alive the old tradition of her intellectual eminence.

But, in the majority of cases, these men are what they are in virtue of their native intellectual force, and of a strength of character which will not recognize impediments. They are not trained in the courts of the Temple of Science, but storm the walls of that edifice in all sorts of irregular ways, and with much loss of time and power, in order to obtain their legitimate positions.

Our universities not only do not encourage such men; do not offer them positions, in which it should be their highest duty to do, thoroughly, that which they are most capable of doing; but, as far as possible, university training shuts out of the minds of those among them, who are subjected to it, the prospect that there is anything in the world for which they are specially fitted. Imagine the success of the attempt to still the intellectual hunger of any of the men I have mentioned, by putting before him, as the object of existence, the successful mimicry of the measure of a Greek song, or the roll of Ciceronian prose! Imagine how much success would be likely to attend the attempt to persuade such men, that the education which leads to perfection in such elegancies is alone to be called culture; while the facts of history, the process of thought, the conditions of moral and social existence, and the laws of physical nature, are left to be dealt with as they may, by outside barbarians!

It is not thus that the German universities, from being beneath notice a century ago, have become what they are now—the most intensely cultivated and the most productive intellectual corporations the world has ever seen.

The student who repairs to them sees in the list of classes and of professors a fair picture of the world of knowledge. Whatever he needs to know there is some one ready to teach him, some one competent to discipline him in the way of learning; whatever his special bent, let him but be able and diligent, and in due time he shall find distinction and a career. Among his professors, he sees men whose names are known and revered throughout the civilized world; and their living example infects him with a noble ambition, and a love for the spirit of work.

The Germans dominate the intellectual world by virtue of the same simple secret as that which made Napoleon the master of old Europe. They have declared *la carrière ouverte aux talents*,[13] and every Bursch marches with a professor's gown in his knapsack. Let him become a great scholar, or man of science, and ministers will compete for his services. In Germany, they do not leave the chance of his holding the office he would render illustrious to the tender mercies of a hot canvass, and the final wisdom of a mob of country parsons.[14]

In short, in Germany, the universities are exactly what the Rector of Lincoln and the Commissioners tell us the English universities are not; that is to say, corporations "of learned men devoting their lives to the cultivation of science, and the direction of academical education." They are not "boarding schools for youths," nor clerical seminaries; but institutions for the higher culture of men, in which the theological faculty is of no more importance, or prominence, than the rest; and which are truly "universities," since they strive to represent and embody the totality of human knowledge, and to find room for all forms of intellectual activity.

May zealous and clear-headed reformers like Mr. Pattison succeed in their noble endeavours to shape our universities towards some such ideal as this, without losing what is valuable and distinctive, in their social tone! But until they have succeeded, a liberal education will be no more obtainable in our Oxford and Cambridge Universities than in our public schools.

If I am justified in my conception of the ideal of a liberal education; and if what I have said about the existing educational institutions of the country is also true, it is clear that the two have no sort of relation to one another; that

---

[12]Michael **Faraday** (1791–1867): physicist and chemist. **Robert Brown** (1773–1858): botanist.

[13]*la carrière . . . talents:* career open to ability. **Bursch:** university student.

[14]**canvass . . . parsons:** Many appointments at Oxford and Cambridge were voted on by graduates and by college fellows who were **country parsons** rather than scholars.

the best of our schools and the most complete of our university trainings give but a narrow, one-sided, and essentially illiberal education—while the worst give what is really next to no education at all. The South London Working-Men's College could not copy any of these institutions if it would. I am bold enough to express the conviction that it ought not if it could.

For what is wanted is the reality and not the mere name of a liberal education; and this College must steadily set before itself the ambition to be able to give that education sooner or later. At present we are but beginning, sharpening our educational tools, as it were, and, except a modicum of physical science, we are not able to offer much more than is to be found in an ordinary school.

Moral and social science—one of the greatest and most fruitful of our future classes, I hope—at present lacks only one thing in our programme, and that is a teacher. A considerable want, no doubt; but it must be recollected that it is much better to want a teacher than to want the desire to learn.

Further, we need what, for want of a better name, I must call Physical Geography. What I mean is that which the Germans call "*Erdkunde.*" It is a description of the earth, of its place and relation to other bodies; of its general structure, and of its great features—winds, tides, mountains, plains; of the chief forms of the vegetable and animal worlds, of the varieties of man. It is the peg upon which the greatest quantity of useful and entertaining scientific information can be suspended.

Literature is not upon the College programme; but I hope some day to see it there. For literature is the greatest of all sources of refined pleasure, and one of the great uses of a liberal education is to enable us to enjoy that pleasure. There is scope enough for the purposes of liberal education in the study of the rich treasures of our own language alone. All that is needed is direction, and the cultivation of a refined taste by attention to sound criticism. But there is no reason why French and German should not be mastered sufficiently to read what is worth reading in those languages, with pleasure and with profit.

And finally, by-and-by, we must have History; treated not as a succession of battles and dynasties; not as a series of biographies; not as evidence that Providence has always been on the side of either Whigs or Tories; but as the development of man in times past, and in other conditions than our own.

But, as it is one of the principles of our College to be self-supporting, the public must lead, and we must follow, in these matters. If my hearers take to heart what I have said about liberal education, they will desire these things, and I doubt not we shall be able to supply them. But we must wait till the demand is made.

1868

~

from Evolution and Ethics

. . . But there is another aspect of the cosmic process, so perfect as a mechanism, so beautiful as a work of art. Where the cosmopoietic[1] energy works through sentient beings, there arises, among its other manifestations, that which we call pain or suffering. This baleful product of evolution increases in quantity and in intensity, with advancing grades of animal organization, until it attains its highest level in man. Further, the consummation is not reached in man, the mere animal; nor in man, the whole or half savage; but only in man, the member of an organized polity. And it is a necessary consequence of his attempt to live in this way; that is, under those conditions which are essential to the full development of his noblest powers.

Man, the animal, in fact, has worked his way to the headship of the sentient world, and has become the superb animal which he is, in virtue of his success in the struggle for existence.[2] The conditions having been of a certain order, man's organization has adjusted itself to them better than that of his competitors in the cosmic strife. In the case of mankind, the self-assertion, the unscrupulous seizing upon all that can be grasped, the tenacious holding of all that can be kept, which constitute the essence of the struggle for existence, have answered. For his successful progress, throughout the savage state, man has been largely indebted to those qualities which he shares with the ape and the tiger; his exceptional physical organization; his cunning, his sociability, his curiosity, and his imitativeness; his ruthless and ferocious destructiveness when his anger is roused by opposition.

But, in proportion as men have passed from anarchy to social organization, and in proportion as civilization has grown in worth, these deeply ingrained serviceable qualities have become defects. After the manner of successful persons, civilized man would gladly kick down the ladder by which he has climbed. He would be only too pleased to see

---

[1]**cosmopoietic:** cosmos–making.

[2]**struggle for existence,** like **survival of the fittest** (below), is a key term in Darwin's *The Origin of Species* (see page 493).

"the ape and tiger die."[3] But they decline to suit his convenience; and the unwelcome intrusion of these boon companions of his hot youth into the ranged existence of civil life adds pains and griefs, innumerable and immeasurably great, to those which the cosmic process necessarily brings on the mere animal. In fact, civilized man brands all these ape and tiger promptings with the name of sins; he punishes many of the acts which flow from them as crimes; and, in extreme cases, he does his best to put an end to the survival of the fittest of former days by axe and rope.

I have said that civilized man has reached this point; the assertion is perhaps too broad and general; I had better put it that ethical man has attained thereto. The science of ethics professes to furnish us with a reasoned rule of life; to tell us what is right action and why it is so. Whatever differences of opinion may exist among experts, there is a general consensus that the ape and tiger methods of the struggle for existence are not reconcilable with sound ethical principles. . . .

The propounders of what are called the "ethics of evolution," when the "evolution of ethics" would usually better express the object of their speculations, adduce a number of more or less interesting facts and more or less sound arguments, in favour of the origin of the moral sentiments, in the same way as other natural phenomena, by a process of evolution. I have little doubt, for my own part, that they are on the right track; but as the immoral sentiments have no less been evolved, there is, so far, as much natural sanction for the one as the other. The thief and the murderer follow nature just as much as the philanthropist. Cosmic evolution may teach us how the good and the evil tendencies of man may have come about; but, in itself, it is incompetent to furnish any better reason why what we call good is preferable to what we call evil than we had before. Some day, I doubt not, we shall arrive at an understanding of the evolution of the æsthetic faculty; but all the understanding in the world will neither increase nor diminish the force of the intuition that this is beautiful and that is ugly.

There is another fallacy which appears to me to pervade the so-called "ethics of evolution." It is the notion that because, on the whole, animals and plants have advanced in perfection of organization by means of the struggle for existence and the consequent "survival of the fittest"; therefore men in society, men as ethical beings, must look to the same process to help them towards perfection. I suspect that this fallacy has arisen out of the unfortunate ambiguity of the phrase "survival of the fittest." "Fittest" has a connotation of "best"; and about

"best" there hangs a moral flavour. In cosmic nature, however, what is "fittest" depends upon the conditions. Long since, I ventured to point out that if our hemisphere were to cool again, the survival of the fittest might bring about, in the vegetable kingdom, a population of more and more stunted and humbler and humbler organisms, until the "fittest" that survived might be nothing but lichens, diatoms, and such microscopic organisms as those which give red snow its colour; while, if it became hotter, the pleasant valleys of the Thames and Isis[4] might be uninhabitable by any animated beings save those that flourish in a tropical jungle. They, as the fittest, the best adapted to the changed conditions, would survive.

Men in society are undoubtedly subject to the cosmic process. As among other animals, multiplication goes on without cessation, and involves severe competition for the means of support. The struggle for existence tends to eliminate those less fitted to adapt themselves to the circumstances of their existence. The strongest, the most self-assertive, tend to tread down the weaker. But the influence of the cosmic process on the evolution of society is the greater the more rudimentary its civilization. Social progress means a checking of the cosmic process at every step and the substitution for it of another, which may be called the ethical process; the end of which is not the survival of those who may happen to be the fittest, in respect of the whole of the conditions which obtain, but of those who are ethically the best.[5]

As I have already urged, the practice of that which is ethically best—what we call goodness or virtue—involves a

---

[3]"the ape and tiger die": Tennyson, *In Memoriam* 118.28.

[4]The **Thames** river near Oxford is often called **Isis**. This lecture was delivered in Oxford in 1893.

[5]**best:** Of course, strictly speaking, social life, and the ethical process in virtue of which it advances towards perfection, are part and parcel of the general process of evolution, just as the gregarious habit of innumerable plants and animals, which has been of immense advantage to them, is so. A hive of bees is an organic polity, a society in which the part played by each member is determined by organic necessities. Queens, workers, and drones are, so to speak, castes, divided from one another by marked physical barriers. Among birds and mammals, societies are formed, of which the bond in many cases seems to be purely psychological; that is to say, it appears to depend upon the liking of the individuals for one another's company. The tendency of individuals to over self-assertion is kept down by fighting. Even in these rudimentary forms of society, love and fear come into play, and enforce a greater or less renunciation of self-will. To this extent the general cosmic process begins to be checked by a rudimentary ethical process, which is, strictly speaking, part of the former, just as the "governor" in a steam engine is part of the mechanism of the engine. [Huxley's note]

course of conduct which, in all respects, is opposed to that which leads to success in the cosmic struggle for existence. In place of ruthless self-assertion it demands self-restraint; in place of thrusting aside, or treading down, all competitors, it requires that the individual shall not merely respect, but shall help his fellows; its influence is directed, not so much to the survival of the fittest, as to the fitting of as many as possible to survive. It repudiates the gladiatorial theory of existence. It demands that each man who enters into the enjoyment of the advantages of a polity shall be mindful of his debt to those who have laboriously constructed it; and shall take heed that no act of his weakens the fabric in which he has been permitted to live. Laws and moral precepts are directed to the end of curbing the cosmic process and reminding the individual of his duty to the community, to the protection and influence of which he owes, if not existence itself, at least the life of something better than a brutal savage.

It is from neglect of these plain considerations that the fanatical individualism of our time attempts to apply the analogy of cosmic nature to society. Once more we have a misapplication of the stoical injunction[6] to follow nature; the duties of the individual to the state are forgotten, and his tendencies to self-assertion are dignified by the name of rights. It is seriously debated whether the members of a community are justified in using their combined strength to constrain one of their number to contribute his share to the maintenance of it; or even to prevent him from doing his best to destroy it. The struggle for existence, which has done such admirable work in cosmic nature, must, it appears, be equally beneficent in the ethical sphere. Yet if that which I have insisted upon is true; if the cosmic process has no sort of relation to moral ends; if the imitation of it by man is inconsistent with the first principles of ethics; what becomes of this surprising theory?

Let us understand, once for all, that the ethical progress of society depends, not on imitating the cosmic process, still less in running away from it, but in combating it. It may seem an audacious proposal thus to pit the microcosm against the macrocosm and to set man to subdue nature to his higher ends; but I venture to think that the great intellectual difference between the ancient times with which we have been occupied and our day, lies in the solid foundation we have acquired for the hope that such an enterprise may meet with a certain measure of success.

The history of civilization details the steps by which men have succeeded in building up an artificial world within the cosmos. Fragile reed as he may be, man, as Pascal says, is a thinking reed:[7] there lies within him a fund of energy, operating intelligently and so far akin to that which pervades the universe, that it is competent to influence and modify the cosmic process. In virtue of his intelligence, the dwarf bends the Titan to his will. In every family, in every polity that has been established, the cosmic process in man has been restrained and otherwise modified by law and custom; in surrounding nature, it has been similarly influenced by the art of the shepherd, the agriculturist, the artisan. As civilization has advanced, so has the extent of this interference increased; until the organized and highly developed sciences and arts of the present day have endowed man with a command over the course of non-human nature greater than that once attributed to the magicians. The most impressive, I might say startling, of these changes have been brought about in the course of the last two centuries; while a right comprehension of the process of life and of the means of influencing its manifestations is only just dawning upon us. We do not yet see our way beyond generalities; and we are befogged by the obtrusion of false analogies and crude anticipations. But Astronomy, Physics, Chemistry, have all had to pass through similar phases, before they reached the stage at which their influence became an important factor in human affairs. Physiology, Psychology, Ethics, Political Science, must submit to the same ordeal. Yet it seems to me irrational to doubt that, at no distant period, they will work as great a revolution in the sphere of practice.

The theory of evolution encourages no millennial anticipations. If, for millions of years, our globe has taken the upward road, yet, some time, the summit will be reached and the downward route[8] will be commenced. The most

---

[6]**stoical injunction:** Stoics were Greek and Roman philosophers.

[7]**thinking reed:** "L'homme n'est qu'un roseau, le plus faible de la nature, mais c'est un roseau pensant. Il ne faut pas que l'univers entier s'arme pour l'écraser. Une vapeur, une goutte d'eau, suffit pour le tuer. Mais quand l'univers l'écraiserait, l'homme serait encore plus noble que ce qui le tue, parce qu'il sait qu'il meurt; et l'avantage que l'univers a sur lui, l'univers n'en sait rien."—*Pensées de Pascal.* [Huxley's note] Man is only a reed, the weakest thing in nature, but he is a thinking reed. The whole universe need not take up arms to annihilate him. A vapor, a drop of water, suffices to kill him. But even though the universe annihilated him, man would still be more noble than what kills him, because he knows that he dies; and the victory that the universe has over him, the universe knows nothing about. The *Pensées* (Thoughts) of Blaise **Pascal** (1623–1662), French mathematician, physicist, and philosopher, were published in 1670.

[8]**downward route:** According to Huxley the cosmos evolves from simplicity to the highest differentiation and back to simplicity.

daring imagination will hardly venture upon the suggestion that the power and the intelligence of man can ever arrest the procession of the great year.

Moreover, the cosmic nature born with us and, to a large extent, necessary for our maintenance, is the outcome of millions of years of severe training, and it would be folly to imagine that a few centuries will suffice to subdue its masterfulness to purely ethical ends. Ethical nature may count upon having to reckon with a tenacious and powerful enemy as long as the world lasts. But, on the other hand, I see no limit to the extent to which intelligence and will, guided by sound principles of investigation, and organized in common effort, may modify the conditions of existence, for a period longer than that now covered by history. And much may be done to change the nature of man himself. The intelligence which has converted the brother of the wolf into the faithful guardian of the flock ought to be able to do something towards curbing the instincts of savagery in civilized men.

But if we may permit ourselves a larger hope of abatement of the essential evil of the world than was possible to those who, in the infancy of exact knowledge, faced the problem of existence more than a score of centuries ago, I deem it an essential condition of the realization of that hope that we should cast aside the notion that the escape from pain and sorrow is the proper object of life.

We have long since emerged from the heroic childhood of our race, when good and evil could be met with the same "frolic welcome"[9]; the attempts to escape from evil, whether Indian or Greek, have ended in flight from the battle-field; it remains to us to throw aside the youthful overconfidence and the no less youthful discouragement of nonage. We are grown men, and must play the man

> strong in will
> To strive, to seek, to find, and not to yield,

cherishing the good that falls in our way, and bearing the evil, in and around us, with stout hearts set on diminishing it. So far, we all may strive in one faith towards one hope:

> It may be that the gulfs will wash us down,
> It may be we shall touch the Happy Isles,

> . . . . but something ere the end,
> Some work of noble note may yet be done.

1894

---

[9]"**frolic welcome**": This and the following quotations are from Tennyson's "Ulysses."

from Autobiography

And when I consider, in one view, the many things. . . . . . which I have upon my hands, I feel the burlesque of being employed in this manner at my time of life. But, in another view, and taking in all circumstances, these things, as trifling as they may appear, no less than things of greater importance, seem to be put upon me to do. . . . . .
Bishop Butler to the Duchess of Somerset[1]

The "many things" to which the Duchess's correspondent here refers are the repairs and improvements of the episcopal seat at Auckland. I doubt if the great apologist, greater in nothing than in the simple dignity of his character, would have considered the writing an account of himself as a thing which could be put upon him to do whatever circumstances might be taken in. But the good bishop lived in an age when a man might write books and yet be permitted to keep his private existence to himself; in the pre-Boswellian[2] epoch, when the germ of the photographer lay in the womb of the distant future, and the interviewer who pervades our age was an unforeseen, indeed unimaginable, birth of time.

At present, the most convinced believer in the aphorism "Bene qui latuit, bene vixit,"[3] is not always able to act up to it. An importunate person informs him that his portrait is about to be published and will be accompanied by a biography which the importunate person proposes to write. The sufferer knows what that means; either he undertakes to revise the "biography" or he does not. In the former case, he makes himself responsible; in the latter, he allows the publication of a mass of more or less fulsome inaccuracies for which he will be held responsible by those who are familiar with the prevalent art of self-advertisement. On the whole, it may be better to get over the "burlesque of being employed in this manner" and do the thing himself.

It was by reflections of this kind that, some years ago, I was led to write and permit the publication of the subjoined sketch.

---

[1]Joseph **Butler** (1692–1752): Anglican bishop, apologist for revealed religion. **Duchess of Somerset:** Frances Seymour (1699–1754).

[2]**Boswellian:** James Boswell (1740–1795) wrote the intimate and detailed *Life of Samuel Johnson* (1791).

[3]**Bene . . . vixit**": He has lived well who has lived unobtrusively (Ovid, *Tristia* 3.4a.25).

I was born about eight o'clock in the morning on the 4th of May, 1825, at Ealing, which was, at that time, as quiet a little country village as could be found within half-a-dozen miles of Hyde Park Corner. Now it is a suburb of London with, I believe, 30,000 inhabitants. My father was one of the masters in a large semi-public school which at one time had a high reputation. I am not aware that any portents preceded my arrival in this world, but, in my childhood, I remember hearing a traditional account of the manner in which I lost the chance of an endowment of great practical value. The windows of my mother's room were open, in consequence of the unusual warmth of the weather. For the same reason, probably, a neighbouring beehive had swarmed, and the new colony, pitching on the window-sill, was making its way into the room when the horrified nurse shut down the sash. If that well-meaning woman had only abstained from her ill-timed interference, the swarm might have settled on my lips, and I should have been endowed with that mellifluous[4] eloquence which, in this country, leads far more surely than worth, capacity, or honest work, to the highest places in Church and State. But the opportunity was lost, and I have been obliged to content myself through life with saying what I mean in the plainest of plain language, than which, I suppose, there is no habit more ruinous to a man's prospects of advancement. . . .

I have next to nothing to say about my childhood. In later years my mother, looking at me almost reproachfully, would sometimes say, "Ah! you were such a pretty boy!" whence I had no difficulty in concluding that I had not fulfilled my early promise in the matter of looks. In fact, I have a distinct recollection of certain curls of which I was vain, and of a conviction that I closely resembled that handsome, courtly gentleman, Sir Herbert Oakley, who was vicar of our parish, and who was as a god to us country folk, because he was occasionally visited by the then Prince George of Cambridge.[5] I remember turning my pinafore wrong side forwards in order to represent a surplice, and preaching to my mother's maids in the kitchen as nearly as possible in Sir Herbert's manner one Sunday morning when the rest of the family were at church. That is the earliest indication I can call to mind of the strong clerical affinities which my friend Mr. Herbert Spencer has always ascribed to me, though I fancy they have for the most part remained in a latent state.

My regular school training was of the briefest, perhaps fortunately, for though my way of life has made me acquainted with all sorts and conditions of men, from the highest to the lowest, I deliberately affirm that the society I fell into at school was the worst I have ever known. We boys were average lads, with much the same inherent capacity for good and evil as any others; but the people who were set over us cared about as much for our intellectual and moral welfare as if they were baby-farmers.[6] We were left to the operation of the struggle for existence among ourselves, and bullying was the least of the ill practices current among us. Almost the only cheerful reminiscence in connection with the place which arises in my mind is that of a battle I had with one of my classmates, who had bullied me until I could stand it no longer. I was a very slight lad, but there was a wild-cat element in me which, when roused, made up for lack of weight, and I licked my adversary effectually. However, one of my first experiences of the extremely rough-and-ready nature of justice, as exhibited by the course of things in general, arose out of the fact that I—the victor—had a black eye, while he—the vanquished—had none, so that I got into disgrace and he did not. We made it up, and thereafter I was unmolested. One of the greatest shocks I ever received in my life was to be told a dozen years afterwards by the groom who brought me my horse in a stable-yard in Sydney that he was my quondam antagonist. He had a long story of family misfortune to account for his position, but at that time it was necessary to deal very cautiously with mysterious strangers in New South Wales, and on inquiry I found that the unfortunate young man had not only been "sent out,"[7] but had undergone more than one colonial conviction.

As I grew older, my great desire was to be a mechanical engineer, but the fates were against this and, while very young, I commenced the study of medicine under a medical brother-in-law. But, though the Institute of Mechanical Engineers would certainly not own me, I am not sure that I have not all along been a sort of mechanical engineer *in partibus infidelium.*[8] I am now occasionally horrified to think how very little I ever knew or cared about medicine as the art of healing. The only part of my professional course which really and deeply interested me was physiology, which is the mechanical engineering of living machines; and, notwithstanding that natural science has been my proper business, I

---

[4]**mellifluous:** honeyed.

[5]**Prince George:** Victoria's first cousin, later Duke of **Cambridge** (1819–1904).

[6]**baby-farmers:** people who lodged and took care of babies for profit. **struggle for existence:** key term in Darwin's *Origin of Species.*

[7]**"sent out":** transported as a convicted criminal.

[8]**in partibus infidelium:** in the lands of the unbelievers.

am afraid there is very little of the genuine naturalist in me. I never collected anything, and species work was always a burden to me; what I cared for was the architectural and engineering part of the business, the working out the wonderful unity of plan in the thousands and thousands of diverse living constructions, and the modifications of similar apparatuses to serve diverse ends. The extraordinary attraction I felt towards the study of the intricacies of living structure nearly proved fatal to me at the outset. I was a mere boy—I think between thirteen and fourteen years of age—when I was taken by some older student friends of mine to the first *post-mortem* examination I ever attended. All my life I have been most unfortunately sensitive to the disagreeables which attend anatomical pursuits, but on this occasion my curiosity overpowered all other feelings, and I spent two or three hours in gratifying it. I did not cut myself, and none of the ordinary symptoms of dissection-poison supervened, but poisoned I was somehow, and I remember sinking into a strange state of apathy. By way of a last chance, I was sent to the care of some good, kind people, friends of my father's, who lived in a farmhouse in the heart of Warwickshire. I remember staggering from my bed to the window on the bright spring morning after my arrival, and throwing open the casement. Life seemed to come back on the wings of the breeze, and to this day the faint odour of wood-smoke, like that which floated across the farm-yard in the early morning, is as good to me as the "sweet south upon a bed of violets."[9] I soon recovered, but for years I suffered from occasional paroxysms of internal pain, and from that time my constant friend, hypochondriacal dyspepsia, commenced his half century of co-tenancy of my fleshy tabernacle.

Looking back on my "Lehrjahre,"[10] I am sorry to say that I do not think that any account of my doings as a student would tend to edification. In fact, I should distinctly warn ingenuous youth to avoid imitating my example. I worked extremely hard when it pleased me, and when it did not—which was a very frequent case—I was extremely idle (unless making caricatures of one's pastors and masters is to be called a branch of industry), or else wasted my energies in wrong directions. I read everything I could lay hands upon, including novels, and took up all sorts of pursuits to drop them again quite as speedily. No doubt it was very largely my own fault, but the only instruction from which I ever obtained the proper effect of education was that which

I received from Mr. Wharton Jones, who was the lecturer on physiology at the Charing Cross School of Medicine. The extent and precision of his knowledge impressed me greatly, and the severe exactness of his method of lecturing was quite to my taste. I do not know that I have ever felt so much respect for anybody as a teacher before or since. I worked hard to obtain his approbation, and he was extremely kind and helpful to the youngster who, I am afraid, took up more of his time than he had any right to do. It was he who suggested the publication of my first scientific paper—a very little one—in the *Medical Gazette* of 1845, and most kindly corrected the literary faults which abounded in it, short as it was; for at that time, and for many years afterwards, I detested the trouble of writing, and would take no pains over it.

It was in the early spring of 1846, that, having finished my obligatory medical studies and passed the first M.B. examination at the London University—though I was still too young to qualify at the College of Surgeons—I was talking to a fellow-student (the present eminent physician, Sir Joseph Fayrer), and wondering what I should do to meet the imperative necessity for earning my own bread, when my friend suggested that I should write to Sir William Burnett, at that time Director-General for the Medical Service of the Navy, for an appointment. I thought this rather a strong thing to do, as Sir William was personally unknown to me, but my cheery friend would not listen to my scruples, so I went to my lodgings and wrote the best letter I could devise. . . .

Life on board Her Majesty's ships in those days was a very different affair from what it is now, and ours was exceptionally rough, as we were often many months without receiving letters or seeing any civilised people but ourselves. In exchange, we had the interest of being about the last voyagers, I suppose, to whom it could be possible to meet with people who knew nothing of fire-arms—as we did on the south Coast of New Guinea—and of making acquaintance with a variety of interesting savage and semi-civilised people. But, apart from experience of this kind and the opportunities offered for scientific work, to me, personally, the cruise was extremely valuable. It was good for me to live under sharp discipline; to be down on the realities of existence by living on bare necessaries; to find out how extremely well worth living life seemed to be when one woke up from a night's rest on a soft plank, with the sky for canopy and cocoa and weevilly biscuit the sole prospect for breakfast; and, more especially, to learn to work for the sake of what I got for myself out of it, even if it all went to the bottom and I along with it. My brother officers were as good

---

[9]"sweet south . . . violets": misquoted from *Twelfth Night* 1.1.5–6. **hypochondriacal**: melancholy, depressive.

[10]"Lehrjahre": years of apprenticeship.

fellows as sailors ought to be and generally are, but, naturally, they neither knew nor cared anything about my pursuits, nor understood why I should be so zealous in pursuit of the objects which my friends, the middies, christened "Buffons," after the title conspicuous on a volume of the "Suites à Buffon,"[11] which stood on my shelf in the chart room.

During the four years of our absence, I sent home communication after communication to the "Linnean Society," with the same result as that obtained by Noah when he sent the raven out of his ark. Tired at last of hearing nothing about them, I determined to do or die, and in 1849 I drew up a more elaborate paper and forwarded it to the Royal Society.[12] This was my dove, if I had only known it. But owing to the movements of the ship, I heard nothing of that either until my return to England in the latter end of the year 1850, when I found that it was printed and published, and that a huge packet of separate copies awaited me. When I hear some of my young friends complain of want of sympathy and encouragement, I am inclined to think that my naval life was not the least valuable part of my education. . . .

The last thing that it would be proper for me to do would be to speak of the work of my life, or to say at the end of the day whether I think I have earned my wages or not. Men are said to be partial judges of themselves. Young men may be, I doubt if old men are. Life seems terribly foreshortened as they look back, and the mountain they set themselves to climb in youth turns out to be a mere spur of immeasurably higher ranges when, with failing breath, they reach the top. But if I may speak of the objects I have had

more or less definitely in view since I began the ascent of my hillock, they are briefly these: To promote the increase of natural knowledge and to forward the application of scientific methods of investigation to all the problems of life to the best of my ability, in the conviction which has grown with my growth and strengthened with my strength, that there is no alleviation for the sufferings of mankind except veracity of thought and of action, and the resolute facing of the world as it is when the garment of make-believe by which pious hands have hidden its uglier features is stripped off.

It is with this intent that I have subordinated any reasonable, or unreasonable, ambition for scientific fame which I may have permitted myself to entertain to other ends; to the popularisation of science; to the development and organisation of scientific education; to the endless series of battles and skirmishes over evolution; and to untiring opposition to that ecclesiastical spirit, that clericalism, which in England, as everywhere else, and to whatever denomination it may belong, is the deadly enemy of science.

In striving for the attainment of these objects, I have been but one among many, and I shall be well content to be remembered, or even not remembered, as such. Circumstances, among which I am proud to reckon the devoted kindness of many friends, have led to my occupation of various prominent positions, among which the Presidency of the Royal Society is the highest. It would be mock modesty on my part, with these and other scientific honours which have been bestowed upon me, to pretend that I have not succeeded in the career which I have followed, rather because I was driven into it than of my own free will; but I am afraid I should not count even these things as marks of success if I could not hope that I had somewhat helped that movement of opinion which has been called the New Reformation.

1889   *1893*

---

[11]**middies:** midshipmen, ranking just below commissioned officers. **Suites à Buffon** (*Sequels to Buffon*): work on two-winged flies (diptera) by Georges-Louis Leclerc, Count de Buffon (1707–1788), French naturalist.

[12]**Royal Society:** Britain's oldest scientific society, founded 1661.

DANTE GABRIEL ROSSETTI

(1828–1882)

The provocative sensuousness of much of Dante Rossetti's work, along with his disorderly way of life—drink, drugs, mistresses, a menagerie of odd animals in his London house—made him the exemplary English figure of the bohemian artist. As both poet and painter he was at the center of the PreRaphaelite movement, which dominated the artistic landscape in the third quarter of the century and culminated in the Decadent and Symbolist movements of the fin de siècle. Rossetti had grown up steeped in the Italian poetic tradition and in the habit of writing verse. His father, an Italian political exile with a lifelong devotion to Dante, taught Italian at King's College, London; his half-English, half-Italian mother had been a governess. Dante Gabriel left regular schooling after his thirteenth year to study art and in 1848 became one of the originators of the PreRaphaelite Brotherhood, a group of young men who declared allegiance to nature in rebellion against conventions of modern art that they traced back to the Italian Renaissance painter Raphael. They wanted to paint the world in its true bright colors and clear detail, while at the same time drawing their subjects from Biblical and legendary sources that lent themselves to vivid treatment, rather than from the gray contemporary world. They also wanted to take the art world by storm: their short-lived journal *The Germ* and their habit of affixing a mysterious "PRB" to their canvasses declared the emergence of an aggressively modern movement. When their first works were scoffed at, Ruskin came to the rescue with a defense of their moral seriousness and fidelity to nature. The PRB lasted only a few years and was partly a game to its exuberant young participants; but the name stuck, as did the basic principles, even when most of the founders had become respectable and successful. The fact that some of the PreRaphaelites took each other, their wives, and their mistresses for models, and fell in and out of love with the same women, gave an additional popular fascination to their work and made it easy to forget the difference between life and art.

Poets to whom the "PreRaphaelite" designation can at least sometimes be applied include, besides Rossetti himself, Swinburne, Morris, Meredith, and above all Rossetti's younger sister Christina. The distinguishing aspects of PreRaphaelitism include medieval, religious, literary, or vaguely supernatural subjects executed with dreamlike realism and precision of detail; highly wrought surfaces and elaborate patterns of ornamentation; and a fascination with powerful, enigmatic, beautiful women: some sinful, some pure, but all with an abundance of long thick hair. In Rossetti's poetic world self-conscious, inward-turning, self-regarding beauty characterizes women and works of art alike.

Rossetti had mixed feelings about success in the art market, where his paintings went to embellish the nouveau-riche life of industrial cities that he deplored. His poetry was more private and more transgressive. Only three volumes appeared in his lifetime: translations of Dante and other early Italian poets in 1861 and collections of original poems in 1870 and 1881. The history of *Poems* (1870) is emblematic both of gender relations in the mid-Victorian art world and of the kind of anecdote that proliferated around the PRB. Rossetti had been in love with Elizabeth Siddal, a poet and painter and also the model (as Christina Rossetti points out in "In an Artist's Studio," page 845) for many of his paintings and drawings. They became engaged in 1852 but did not marry until 1860, by which time he was involved with other women and she was very ill. She died in 1862 from an overdose of an opiate, which may have been accidental but was probably suicide. Rossetti, remorseful, buried his poems in her coffin. In 1869, however, he had the manuscripts disinterred, disinfected, and cleaned, and he published them along with more recent work, including poems about another woman.

Rossetti's poetry includes such diverse works as Browningesque dramatic monologues, tormented lyrics of futility and desire, reflections on the rise and death of empires, faux-medieval ballads, and *The House of Life*: a sonnet-sequence that inhabits what is simultaneously an astrological "house," an architectural structure, and a desperately antidomestic home ruled by the god of love. In the conjoining of poetry and painting his only predecessor is Blake, whom the PreRaphaelites jubilantly rediscovered after decades of neglect (see Swinburne, page 926). Rossetti's most famous single work, "The Blessed Damozel," exists in both media. Moments of visual framing and particularity in his poems remind us that he was a painter, and his paintings' subjects often come from poems. Women, ideal or earthly, divine or dangerous, salvific or corrupt, loom in poems and paintings alike. But what most profoundly unifies his artistic world is the merging of the erotic and the spiritual and, more generally, the search for transcendental meaning in the visible world. His sacramental vision, like his ideal of love, comes from Dante; but because the beliefs that sustained Dante's symbolic structure are gone, Rossetti's visions are often troubled and perplexing. When the speaker in "The Woodspurge" tells us that the flower "has a cup of three," is he suggesting that nature has, or does not have, sacramental meaning? Both the implicit posing of the question and the refusal to answer it typify Victorian aestheticism's delicate, precarious balancing of faith and doubt, religion and art.

Rossetti's last years were marred by psychological and physical collapse, addiction to drugs and alcohol, and paranoid delusions: an object-lesson, many contemporaries thought, of the dangers of living for art.

~

The Blessed Damozel[1]

The blessed damozel leaned out
  From the gold bar of Heaven;
Her eyes were deeper than the depth
  Of waters stilled at even;
She had three lilies in her hand,
  And the stars in her hair were seven.

Her robe, ungirt from clasp to hem,
  No wrought flowers did adorn,

But a white rose of Mary's gift,
  For service meetly worn;   10
Her hair that lay along her back
  Was yellow like ripe corn.

Herseemed she scarce had been a day
  One of God's choristers;
The wonder was not yet quite gone
  From that still look of hers;
Albeit, to them she left, her day
  Had counted as ten years.

(To one, it is ten years of years.
    . . . Yet now, and in this place,   20
Surely she leaned o'er me—her hair
  Fell all about my face. . . .
Nothing: the autumn-fall of leaves.
  The whole year sets apace.)

---

[1]**Damozel**: damsel. The poem is matched with a painting (1876–1877): the Damozel leans down and the much smaller reclining figure of the lover looks up at her from a small compartment at the bottom of the canvas.

It was the rampart of God's house
   That she was standing on;
By God built over the sheer depth
   The which is Space begun;
So high, that looking downward thence
   She scarce could see the sun.   30

It lies in Heaven, across the flood
   Of ether, as a bridge.
Beneath, the tides of day and night
   With flame and darkness ridge
The void, as low as where this earth
   Spins like a fretful midge.

Around her, lovers, newly met
   'Mid deathless love's acclaims,
Spoke evermore among themselves
   Their heart-remembered names;   40
And the souls mounting up to God
   Went by her like thin flames.

And still she bowed herself and stooped
   Out of the circling charm;
Until her bosom must have made
   The bar she leaned on warm,
And the lilies lay as if asleep
   Along her bended arm.

From the fixed place of Heaven she saw
   Time like a pulse shake fierce   50
Through all the worlds. Her gaze still strove
   Within the gulf to pierce
Its path; and now she spoke as when
   The stars sang in their spheres.

The sun was gone now; the curled moon
   Was like a little feather
Fluttering far down the gulf; and now
   She spoke through the still weather.
Her voice was like the voice the stars
   Had when they sang together.   60

(Ah sweet! Even now, in that bird's song,
   Strove not her accents there,
Fain to be hearkened? When those bells
   Possessed the mid-day air,
Strove not her steps to reach my side
   Down all the echoing stair?)

"I wish that he were come to me,
   For he will come," she said.
"Have I not prayed in Heaven?—on earth,
   Lord, Lord, has he not pray'd?   70

Are not two prayers a perfect strength?
   And shall I feel afraid?

"When round his head the aureole clings,
   And he is clothed in white,
I'll take his hand and go with him
   To the deep wells of light;
As unto a stream we will step down,
   And bathe there in God's sight.

"We two will stand beside that shrine,
   Occult, withheld, untrod,   80
Whose lamps are stirred continually
   With prayer sent up to God;
And see our old prayers, granted, melt
   Each like a little cloud.

"We two will lie i' the shadow of
   That living mystic tree
Within whose secret growth the Dove[2]
   Is sometimes felt to be,
While every leaf that His plumes touch
   Saith His Name audibly.   90

"And I myself will teach to him,
   I myself, lying so,
The songs I sing here; which his voice
   Shall pause in, hushed and slow,
And find some knowledge at each pause,
   Or some new thing to know."

(Alas! We two, we two, thou say'st!
   Yea, one wast thou with me
That once of old. But shall God lift
   To endless unity   100
The soul whose likeness with thy soul
   Was but its love for thee?)

"We two," she said, "will seek the groves
   Where the lady Mary is,
With her five handmaidens, whose names
   Are five sweet symphonies,
Cecily, Gertrude, Magdalen,
   Margaret and Rosalys.

"Circlewise sit they, with bound locks
   And foreheads garlanded;   110
Into the fine cloth white like flame
   Weaving the golden thread,
To fashion the birth-robes for them
   Who are just born, being dead.

---

[2]**Dove:** the Holy Ghost.

"He shall fear, haply, and be dumb:
    Then will I lay my cheek
To his, and tell about our love,
    Not once abashed or weak:
And the dear Mother will approve
    My pride, and let me speak.   120

"Herself shall bring us, hand in hand,
    To Him round whom all souls
Kneel, the clear-ranged unnumbered heads
    Bowed with their aureoles:
And angels meeting us shall sing
    To their citherns and citoles.[3]

"There will I ask of Christ the Lord
    Thus much for him and me:—
Only to live as once on earth
    With Love,—only to be,   130
As then awhile, for ever now
    Together, I and he."

She gazed and listened and then said,
    Less sad of speech than mild,—
"All this is when he comes." She ceased.
    The light thrilled towards her, fill'd
With angels in strong level flight.
    Her eyes prayed, and she smil'd.

(I saw her smile.) But soon their path
    Was vague in distant spheres: 140
And then she cast her arms along
    The golden barriers,
And laid her face between her hands,
    And wept. (I heard her tears.)

                1850

My Sister's Sleep[1]

She fell asleep on Christmas Eve:
    At length the long-ungranted shade
    Of weary eyelids overweigh'd
The pain nought else might yet relieve.

Our mother, who had leaned all day
    Over the bed from chime to chime,
    Then raised herself for the first time,
And as she sat her down, did pray.

Her little work-table was spread
    With work to finish. For the glare   10
    Made by her candle, she had care
To work some distance from the bed.

Without, there was a cold moon up,
    Of winter radiance sheer and thin;
    The hollow halo it was in
Was like an icy crystal cup.

Through the small room, with subtle sound
    Of flame, by vents the fireshine drove
    And reddened. In its dim alcove
The mirror shed a clearness round.   20

I had been sitting up some nights,
    And my tired mind felt weak and blank;
    Like a sharp strengthening wine it drank
The stillness and the broken lights.

Twelve struck. That sound, by dwindling years
    Heard in each hour, crept off; and then
    The ruffled silence spread again,
Like water that a pebble stirs.

Our mother rose from where she sat:
    Her needles, as she laid them down,   30
    Met lightly, and her silken gown
Settled: no other noise than that.

"Glory unto the Newly Born!"
    So, as said angels,[2] she did say;
    Because we were in Christmas Day,
Though it would still be long till morn.

Just then in the room over us
    There was a pushing back of chairs,
    As some who had sat unawares
So late, now heard the hour, and rose.   40

With anxious softly-stepping haste
    Our mother went where Margaret lay,
    Fearing the sounds o'erheard—should they
Have broken her long watched-for rest!

---

[3]**citherns, citoles**: stringed musical instruments.

[1]**"My Sister's Sleep"**: This little poem, written in 1847, was printed in a periodical at the outset of 1850. The metre, which is used by several old English writers, became celebrated a month or two later on the publication of "In Memoriam." [Rossetti's note]

[2]**angels**: see Luke 2:9–14.

She stooped an instant, calm, and turned;
   But suddenly turned back again;
   And all her features seemed in pain
With woe, and her eyes gazed and yearned.

For my part, I but hid my face,
   And held my breath, and spoke no word: 50
   There was none spoken; but I heard
The silence for a little space.

Our mother bowed herself and wept:
   And both my arms fell, and I said,
   "God knows I knew that she was dead."
And there, all white, my sister slept.

Then kneeling, upon Christmas morn
   A little after twelve o'clock,
   We said, ere the first quarter struck,
"Christ's blessing on the newly born!"   60

1850

The Burden of Nineveh[1]

In our Museum galleries
To-day I lingered o'er the prize
Dead Greece vouchsafes to living eyes,—
Her Art for ever in fresh wise
   From hour to hour rejoicing me.
Sighing I turned at last to win
Once more the London dirt and din;
And as I made the swing-door spin
And issued, they were hoisting in
   A wingèd beast from Nineveh.   10

A human face the creature wore,
And hoofs behind and hoofs before,
And flanks with dark runes fretted o'er.
'Twas bull, 'twas mitred Minotaur,[2]
   A dead disbowelled mystery:
The mummy of a buried faith
Stark from the charnel without scathe,

Its wings stood for the light to bathe,—
Such fossil cerements as might swathe
   The very corpse of Nineveh.   20

The print of its first rush-wrapping,
Wound ere it dried, still ribbed the thing.
What song did the brown maidens sing,
From purple mouths alternating,
   When that was woven languidly?
What vows, what rites, what prayers preferr'd,
What songs has the strange image heard?
In what blind vigil stood interr'd
For ages, till an English word
   Broke silence first at Nineveh?   30

Oh when upon each sculptured court,
Where even the wind might not resort,—
O'er which Time passed, of like import
With the wild Arab boys at sport,—
   A living face looked in to see:—
Oh seemed it not—the spell once broke—
As though the carven warriors woke,
As though the shaft the string forsook,
The cymbals clashed, the chariots shook,
   And there was life in Nineveh?   40

On London stones our sun anew
The beast's recovered shadow threw.
(No shade that plague of darkness knew,
No light, no shade, while older grew
   By ages the old earth and sea.)
Lo thou! could all thy priests have shown
Such proof to make thy godhead known?
From their dead Past thou liv'st alone;
And still thy shadow is thine own,
   Even as of yore in Nineveh.   50

That day whereof we keep record,
When near thy city-gates the Lord
Sheltered His Jonah[3] with a gourd,
This sun, (I said) here present, pour'd
   Even thus this shadow that I see.
This shadow has been shed the same
From sun and moon,—from lamps which came
For prayer,—from fifteen days of flame,
The last, while smouldered to a name
   Sardanapalus'[4] Nineveh.   60

---

[1]"The Burden of Nineveh": Nahum 1:1. **Burden**: a load to be carried, also the refrain or theme of a song. **Nineveh**: ancient Assyrian city whose supposed ruins A. H. Layard excavated (see pages 107–109), sending many of its monuments to the British **Museum galleries**.

[2]**Minotaur**: fabulous monster of ancient Crete, with the body of a man and the head of a bull.

---

[3]**Jonah**: see Jonah 4:6.

[4]**Sardanapalus**: legendary king of Assyria who burned himself, his treasures, and his concubines and servants.

Within thy shadow, haply, once
Sennacherib[5] has knelt, whose sons
Smote him between the altar-stones:
Or pale Semiramis her zones
    Of gold, her incense brought to thee,
In love for grace, in war for aid: . . . .
Ay, and who else?. . . . till 'neath thy shade
Within his trenches newly made
Last year the Christian knelt and pray'd—
    Not to thy strength—in Nineveh.[6]   70

Now, thou poor god, within this hall
Where the blank windows blind the wall
From pedestal to pedestal,
The kind of light shall on thee fall
    Which London takes the day to be:
While school-foundations in the act
Of holiday, three files compact,
Shall learn to view thee as a fact
Connected with that zealous tract:[7]
    "ROME,—Babylon and Nineveh."   80

Deemed they of this, those worshippers,
When, in some mythic chain of verse
Which man shall not again rehearse,
The faces of thy ministers
    Yearned pale with bitter ecstasy?
Greece, Egypt, Rome,—did any god
Before whose feet men knelt unshod
Deem that in this unblest abode
Another scarce more unknown god
    Should house with him, from Nineveh?   90

Ah! in what quarries lay the stone
From which this pillared pile has grown
Unto man's need how long unknown,
Since thy vast temples, court and cone,
    Rose far in desert history?
Ah! what is here that does not lie
All strange to thine awakened eye?

Ah! what is here can testify
(Save that dumb presence of the sky)
    Unto thy day and Nineveh?   100

Why, of those mummies in the room
Above, there might indeed have come
One out of Egypt to thy home,
An alien. Nay, but were not some
    Of these thine own "antiquity"?
And now,—they and their gods and thou
All relics here together,—now
Whose profit? whether bull or cow,
Isis or Ibis,[8] who or how,
    Whether of Thebes or Nineveh?   110

The consecrated metals found,
And ivory tablets, underground,
Winged teraphim[9] and creatures crown'd
When air and daylight filled the mound,
    Fell into dust immediately.
And even as these, the images
Of awe and worship,—even as these,—
So, smitten with the sun's increase,
Her glory mouldered and did cease
    From immemorial Nineveh.   120

The day her builders made their halt,
Those cities of the lake of salt[10]
Stood firmly 'stablished without fault,
Made proud with pillars of basalt,
    With sardonyx and porphyry.
The day that Jonah bore abroad
To Nineveh the voice of God,
A brackish lake lay in his road,
Where erst Pride fixed her sure abode,
    As then in royal Nineveh.   130

The day when he, Pride's lord[11] and Man's,
Showed all the kingdoms at a glance
To Him before whose countenance
The years recede, the years advance,
    And said, Fall down and worship me:—

---

[5]**Sennacherib**: king of Assyria (704–681 BCE), who rebuilt and beautified Nineveh. **sons**: see 2 Kings 19:37. **Semiramis**: wife of Ninus, mythical founder of Nineveh.

[6]**in Nineveh**: During the excavations, the Tiyari workmen held their services in the shadow of the great bulls. (*Layard's "Nineveh,"* ch. ix.) [Rossetti's note]

[7]**tract**: denouncing the Roman Catholic Church as the sinful modern equivalent of **Babylon and Nineveh**.

---

[8]**Isis**: ancient Egyptian goddess. The Egyptian god of wisdom, Thoth, had the bird's head of an **Ibis**. **Thebes**: ancient capital of upper Egypt.

[9]**teraphim**: ancient Semitic idols or images.

[10]**cities of the lake of salt**: cities along the river Jordan and the Dead Sea; see Joshua 1:1–16. **brackish lake**: Dead Sea.

[11]**Pride's lord**: the devil tempting Jesus; see Luke 4:5–7.

'Mid all the pomp beneath that look,
Then stirred there, haply, some rebuke,
Where to the wind the Salt Pools shook,
And in those tracts, of life forsook,
    That knew thee not, O Nineveh!   140

Delicate harlot![12] On thy throne
Thou with a world beneath thee prone
In state for ages sat'st alone;
And needs were years and lustres flown
    Ere strength of man could vanquish thee:
Whom even thy victor foes must bring,
Still royal, among maids that sing
As with doves' voices, taboring
Upon their breasts, unto the King,—
    A kingly conquest, Nineveh!   150

. . . Here woke my thought. The wind's slow sway
Had waxed; and like the human play
Of scorn that smiling spreads away,
The sunshine shivered off the day:
    The callous wind, it seemed to me,
Swept up the shadow from the ground:
And pale as whom the Fates astound,
The god forlorn stood winged and crown'd:
Within I knew the cry lay bound
    Of the dumb soul of Nineveh.   160

And as I turned, my sense half shut
Still saw the crowds of kerb and rut
Go past as marshalled to the strut
Of ranks in gypsum quaintly cut.
    It seemed in one same pageantry
They followed forms which had been erst;
To pass, till on my sight should burst
That future of the best or worst
When some may question which was first,
    Of London or of Nineveh.   170

For as that Bull-god once did stand
And watched the burial-clouds of sand,
Till these at last without a hand
Rose o'er his eyes, another land,
    And blinded him with destiny:—
So may he stand again; till now,
In ships of unknown sail and prow,
Some tribe of the Australian plough
Bear him afar,—a relic now
    Of London, not of Nineveh!   180

Or it may chance indeed that when
Man's age is hoary among men,—
His centuries threescore and ten,—
His furthest childhood shall seem then
    More clear than later times may be:
Who, finding in this desert place
This form, shall hold us for some race
That walked not in Christ's lowly ways,
But bowed its pride and vowed its praise
    Unto the god of Nineveh.   190

The smile rose first,—anon drew nigh
The thought: . . . Those heavy wings spread high,
So sure of flight, which do not fly;
That set gaze never on the sky;
    Those scriptured flanks it cannot see;
Its crown, a brow-contracting load;
Its planted feet which trust the sod: . . .
(So grew the image as I trod:)
O Nineveh, was this thy God,—
    Thine also, mighty Nineveh?   200
                            1856

Jenny

"Vengeance of Jenny's case! Fie on her! Never name her, child!"—(Mrs. Quickly.)[1]

Lazy laughing languid Jenny,
Fond of a kiss and fond of a guinea,[2]
Whose head upon my knee to-night
Rests for a while, as if grown light
With all our dances and the sound
To which the wild tunes spun you round:
Fair Jenny mine, the thoughtless queen
Of kisses which the blush between
Could hardly make much daintier;
Whose eyes are as blue skies, whose hair   10
Is countless gold incomparable:
Fresh flower, scarce touched with signs that tell
Of Love's exuberant hotbed:—Nay,
Poor flower left torn since yesterday

---

[12]**harlot:** Nahum 3:4. **lustres:** 5-year periods; also splendors. **maids:** Nahum 2:7.

[1]**"Vengeance . . . child!"**: *Merry Wives of Windsor* 4.1.53–54. The quotation continues: "if she be a whore."

[2]**guinea:** gold coin worth one pound plus one shilling, last produced 1813.

Until to-morrow leave you bare;
Poor handful of bright spring-water
Flung in the whirlpool's shrieking face;
Poor shameful Jenny, full of grace
Thus with your head upon my knee;—
Whose person or whose purse may be   20
The lodestar of your reverie?

This room of yours, my Jenny, looks
A change from mine so full of books,
Whose serried ranks hold fast, forsooth,
So many captive hours of youth,—
The hours they thieve from day and night
To make one's cherished work come right,
And leave it wrong for all their theft,
Even as to-night my work was left:
Until I vowed that since my brain   30
And eyes of dancing seemed so fain,
My feet should have some dancing too:—
And thus it was I met with you.
Well, I suppose 'twas hard to part,
For here I am. And now, sweetheart,
You seem too tired to get to bed.

It was a careless life I led
When rooms like this were scarce so strange
Not long ago. What breeds the change,—
The many aims or the few years?   40
Because to-night it all appears
Something I do not know again.

The cloud's not danced out of my brain—
The cloud that made it turn and swim
While hour by hour the books grew dim.
Why, Jenny, as I watch you there,—
For all your wealth of loosened hair,
Your silk ungirdled and unlac'd
And warm sweets open to the waist,
All golden in the lamplight's gleam,—   50
You know not what a book you seem,
Half-read by lightning in a dream!
How should you know, my Jenny? Nay,
And I should be ashamed to say:—
Poor beauty, so well worth a kiss!
But while my thought runs on like this
With wasteful whims more than enough,
I wonder what you're thinking of.

If of myself you think at all,
What is the thought?—conjectural   60
On sorry matters best unsolved?—
Or inly is each grace resolved

To fit me with a lure?—or (sad
To think!) perhaps you're merely glad
That I'm not drunk or ruffianly
And let you rest upon my knee.

For sometimes, were the truth confess'd,
You're thankful for a little rest,—
Glad from the crush to rest within,
From the heart-sickness and the din   70
Where envy's voice at virtue's pitch
Mocks you because your gown is rich;
And from the pale girl's dumb rebuke,
Whose ill-clad grace and toil-worn look
Proclaim the strength that keeps her weak
And other nights than yours bespeak;
And from the wise unchildish elf,
To schoolmate lesser than himself,
Pointing you out, what thing you are:—
Yes, from the daily jeer and jar,   80
From shame and shame's outbraving too,
Is rest not sometimes sweet to you?—
But most from the hatefulness of man
Who spares not to end what he began,
Whose acts are ill and his speech ill,
Who, having used you at his will,
Thrusts you aside, as when I dine
I serve the dishes and the wine.

Well, handsome Jenny mine, sit up:
I've filled our glasses, let us sup,   90
And do not let me think of you,
Lest shame of yours suffice for two.
What, still so tired? Well, well then, keep
Your head there, so you do not sleep;
But that the weariness may pass
And leave you merry, take this glass.
Ah! lazy lily hand, more bless'd
If ne'er in rings it had been dress'd
Nor ever by a glove conceal'd!

Behold the lilies of the field,   100
They toil not neither do they spin;
(So doth the ancient text[3] begin,—
Not of such rest as one of these
Can share.) Another rest and ease
Along each summer-sated path
From its new lord the garden hath,
Than that whose spring in blessings ran
Which praised the bounteous husbandman,

---

[3]**ancient text:** Matthew 6:28.

Ere yet, in days of hankering breath,
The lilies sickened unto death.   110

   What, Jenny, are your lilies dead?
Aye, and the snow-white leaves are spread
Like winter on the garden-bed.
But you had roses left in May,—
They were not gone too. Jenny, nay,
But must your roses die, and those
Their purfled buds that should unclose?
Even so; the leaves are curled apart,
Still red as from the broken heart,
And here's the naked stem of thorns.   120

   Nay, nay, mere words. Here nothing warns
As yet of winter. Sickness here
Or want alone could waken fear,—
Nothing but passion wrings a tear.
Except when there may rise unsought
Haply at times a passing thought
Of the old days which seem to be
Much older than any history
That is written in any book;
When she would lie in fields and look   130
Along the ground through the blown grass,
And wonder where the city was.
Far out of sight, whose broil and bale
They told her then for a child's tale.

   Jenny, you know the city now.
A child can tell the tale there, how
Some things which are not yet enroll'd
In market-lists are bought and sold
Even till the early Sunday light,
When Saturday night is market-night   140
Everywhere, be it dry or wet,
And market-night in the Haymarket.[4]
Our learned London children know,
Poor Jenny, all your pride and woe;
Have seen your lifted silken skirt
Advertise dainties through the dirt;
Have seen your coach-wheels splash rebuke
On virtue; and have learned your look
When, wealth and health slipped past, you stare
Along the streets alone, and there,   150
Round the long park, across the bridge,
The cold lamps at the pavement's edge

Wind on together and apart,
A fiery serpent for your heart.

   Let the thoughts pass, an empty cloud!
Suppose I were to think aloud,—
What if to her all this were said?
Why, as a volume seldom read
Being opened halfway shuts again,
So might the pages of her brain   160
Be parted at such words, and thence
Close back upon the dusty sense.
For is there hue or shape defin'd
In Jenny's desecrated mind,
Where all contagious currents meet,
A Lethe[5] of the middle street?
Nay, it reflects not any face,
Nor sound is in its sluggish pace,
But as they coil those eddies clot,
And night and day remember not.   170

   Why, Jenny, you're asleep at last!—
Asleep, poor Jenny, hard and fast,—
So young and soft and tired; so fair,
With chin thus nestled in your hair,
Mouth quiet, eyelids almost blue
As if some sky of dreams shone through!

   Just as another woman sleeps!
Enough to throw one's thoughts in heaps
Of doubt and horror,—what to say
Or think,—this awful secret sway,   180
The potter's power over the clay![6]
Of the same lump (it has been said)
For honour and dishonour made,
Two sister vessels. Here is one.

   My cousin Nell is fond of fun,
And fond of dress, and change, and praise.
So mere a woman in her ways:
And if her sweet eyes rich in youth
Are like her lips that tell the truth,
My cousin Nell is fond of love.   190
And she's the girl I'm proudest of.
Who does not prize her, guard her well?
The love of change, in cousin Nell,
Shall find the best and hold it dear;
The unconquered mirth turn quieter

---

[4]**Haymarket**: street in London's theater district, notorious for prostitution.

[5]**Lethe**: river of forgetfulness in the classical underworld; here, open sewer.

[6]**potter's power . . . sister vessels**: see Romans 9:21.

Not through her own, through others' woe:
The conscious pride of beauty glow
Beside another's pride in her,
One little part of all they share.
For Love himself shall ripen these   200
In a kind soil to just increase
Through years of fertilizing peace.

    Of the same lump (as it is said)
For honour and dishonour made,
Two sister vessels. Here is one.

    It makes a goblin of the sun.

    So pure,—so fall'n! How dare to think
Of the first common kindred link?
Yet, Jenny, till the world shall burn
It seems that all things take their turn;   210
And who shall say but this fair tree
May need, in changes that may be,
Your children's children's charity?
Scorned then, no doubt, as you are scorn'd!
Shall no man hold his pride forewarn'd
Till in the end, the Day of Days,
At Judgment, one of his own race,
As frail and lost as you, shall rise,—
His daughter, with his mother's eyes?

    How Jenny's clock ticks on the shelf!   220
Might not the dial scorn itself
That has such hours to register?
Yet as to me, even so to her
Are golden sun and silver moon,
In daily largesse of earth's boon,
Counted for life-coins to one tune.
And if, as blindfold fates are toss'd,
Through some one man this life be lost,
Shall soul not somehow pay for soul?

    Fair shines the gilded aureole   230
In which our highest painters place
Some living woman's simple face.
And the stilled features thus descried
As Jenny's long throat droops aside,—
The shadows where the cheeks are thin,
And pure wide curve from ear to chin,—
With Raffael's,[7] Leonardo's hand
To show them to men's souls, might stand,

Whole ages long, the whole world through,
For preachings of what God can do.   240
What has man done here? How atone,
Great God, for this which man has done?
And for the body and soul which by
Man's pitiless doom must now comply
With lifelong hell, what lullaby
Of sweet forgetful second birth
Remains? All dark. No sign on earth
What measure of God's rest endows
The many mansions of his house.

    If but a woman's heart might see   250
Such erring heart unerringly
For once! But that can never be.

    Like a rose shut in a book
In which pure women may not look,
For its base pages claim control
To crush the flower within the soul;
Where through each dead rose-leaf that clings,
Pale as transparent Psyche-wings,[8]
To the vile text, are traced such things
As might make lady's cheek indeed   260
More than a living rose to read;
So nought save foolish foulness may
Watch with hard eyes the sure decay;
And so the life-blood of this rose,
Puddled with shameful knowledge, flows
Through leaves no chaste hand may unclose;
Yet still it keeps such faded show
Of when 'twas gathered long ago,
That the crushed petals' lovely grain,
The sweetness of the sanguine stain,   270
Seen of a woman's eyes, must make
Her pitiful heart, so prone to ache,
Love roses better for its sake:—
Only that this can never be:—
Even so unto her sex is she.

    Yet, Jenny, looking long at you,
The woman almost fades from view.
A cipher[9] of man's changeless sum
Of lust, past, present, and to come,
Is left. A riddle that one shrinks   280
To challenge from the scornful sphinx.

---

[7]**Raffael**: Raphael Sanzio (1483–1520), who like **Leonardo** da Vinci (1452–1519) painted Madonnas and saints.

[8]**Psyche**: Cupid's beloved, pictured with **wings** and emblematized in the butterfly.

[9]**cipher**: zero, which alters the value of other numbers.

Like a toad within a stone
Seated while Time crumbles on;
Which sits there since the earth was curs'd
For Man's transgression at the first;
Which, living through all centuries,
Not once has seen the sun arise;
Whose life, to its cold circle charmed,
The earth's whole summers have not warmed;
Which always—whitherso the stone   290
Be flung—sits there, deaf, blind, alone;
Aye, and shall not be driven out
Till that which shuts him round about
Break at the very Master's stroke,
And the dust thereof vanish as smoke,
And the seed of Man vanish as dust:—
Even so within this world is Lust.

Come, come, what use in thoughts like this?
Poor little Jenny, good to kiss,—
You'd not believe by what strange roads   300
Thought travels, when your beauty goads
A man to-night to think of toads!
Jenny, wake up. . . . Why, there's the dawn!

And there's an early waggon drawn
To market, and some sheep that jog
Bleating before a barking dog;
And the old streets come peering through
Another night that London knew;
And all as ghostlike as the lamps.

So on the wings of day decamps   310
My last night's frolic. Glooms begin
To shiver off as lights creep in
Past the gauze curtains half drawn-to,
And the lamp's doubled shade grows blue,—
Your lamp, my Jenny, kept alight,
Like a wise virgin's,[10] all one night!
And in the alcove coolly spread
Glimmers with dawn your empty bed;
And yonder your fair face I see
Reflected lying on my knee,   320
Where teems with first foreshadowings
Your pier-glass scrawled with diamond rings:[11]
And on your bosom all night worn
Yesterday's rose now droops forlorn
But dies not yet this summer morn.

And now without, as if some word
Had called upon them that they heard,
The London sparrows far and nigh
Clamour together suddenly;
And Jenny's cage-bird grown awake   330
Here in their song his part must take,
Because here too the day doth break.

And somehow in myself the dawn
Among stirred clouds and veils withdrawn
Strikes greyly on her. Let her sleep.
But will it wake her if I heap
These cushions thus beneath her head
Where my knee was? No,—there's your bed,
My Jenny, while you dream. And there
I lay among your golden hair   340
Perhaps the subject of your dreams,
These golden coins.
                    For still one deems
That Jenny's flattering sleep confers
New magic on the magic purse,—
Grim web, how clogged with shrivelled flies!
Between the threads fine fumes arise
And shape their pictures in the brain.
There roll no streets in glare and rain,
Nor flagrant man-swine whets his tusk;
But delicately sighs in musk   350
The homage of the dim boudoir;
Or like a palpitating star
Thrilled into song, the opera-night
Breathes faint in the quick pulse of light;
Or at the carriage-window shine
Rich wares for choice; or, free to dine,
Whirls through its hour of health (divine
For her) the concourse of the Park.
And though in the discounted dark
Her functions there and here are one,   360
Beneath the lamps and in the sun
There reigns at least the acknowledged belle
Apparelled beyond parallel.
Ah, Jenny, yes, we know your dreams.

For even the Paphian Venus[12] seems
A goddess o'er the realms of love,
When silver-shrined in shadowy grove:
Aye, or let offerings nicely plac'd
But hide Priapus[13] to the waist,

---

[10]**wise virgin**: Matthew 25.

[11]**pier-glass . . . rings**: mirror on which Jenny's clients scratched
their names.

[12]**Paphian Venus**: goddess of love associated with the city of Paphos, whose devotees were prostitutes.

[13]**Priapus**: classical phallic god of procreation.

And whoso looks on him shall see   370
An eligible deity.

    Why, Jenny, waking here alone
May help you to remember one,
Though all the memory's long outworn
Of many a double-pillowed morn.
I think I see you when you wake,
And rub your eyes for me, and shake
My gold, in rising, from your hair,
A Danaë[14] for a moment there.

    Jenny, my love rang true! for still   380
Love at first sight is vague, until
That tinkling makes him audible.

    And must I mock you to the last,
Ashamed of my own shame,—aghast
Because some thoughts not born amiss
Rose at a poor fair face like this?
Well, of such thoughts so much I know:
In my life, as in hers, they show,
By a far gleam which I may near,
A dark path I can strive to clear.   390

    Only one kiss. Good-bye, my dear.
1848   *1870*

The Woodspurge[1]

The wind flapped loose, the wind was still,
Shaken out dead from tree and hill:
I had walked on at the wind's will,—
I sat now, for the wind was still.

Between my knees my forehead was,—
My lips, drawn in, said not Alas!
My hair was over in the grass,
My naked ears heard the day pass.

My eyes, wide open, had the run
Of some ten weeds to fix upon;   10
Among those few, out of the sun,
The woodspurge flowered, three cups in one.

From perfect grief there need not be
Wisdom or even memory:
One thing then learnt remains to me,—
The woodspurge has a cup of three.
1856   *1870*

Sudden Light

I have been here before,
    But when or how I cannot tell:
I know the grass beyond the door,
    The sweet keen smell,
The sighing sound, the lights around the shore.

You have been mine before,—
    How long ago I may not know:
But just when at that swallow's soar
    Your neck turned so,
Some veil did fall,—I knew it all of yore.   10

Then, now,—perchance again! . . .
    O round mine eyes your tresses shake!
Shall we not lie as we have lain
    Thus for Love's sake,
And sleep, and wake, yet never break the chain?
                                    1870

The Ballad of Dead Ladies[1]

Tell me now in what hidden way is
    Lady Flora[2] the lovely Roman?
Where's Hipparchia, and where is Thaïs,
    Neither of them the fairer woman?
    Where is Echo, beheld of no man,
Only heard on river and mere,—
    She whose beauty was more than human? . . .
But where are the snows of yester-year?

---

[14]**Danaë**: woman in Greek mythology with whom Zeus, disguised as a shower of gold, had sexual relations.

[1]**Woodspurge**: small green wildflower with two long cuplike petals hanging from the middle of each flower, making the appearance of two cups suspended from a third.

[1]"**The Ballad of Dead Ladies**": translated from "Balade des dames du temps jadis" by François Villon (1431–1463?), French lyric poet. Formally this is a French *ballade*, not an English ballad.

[2]**Flora, Hipparchia, Thaïs**: courtesans of antiquity. **Echo**: nymph in Greek myth who became only a reverberating voice.

Where's Héloise, the learned nun,
     For whose sake Abeillard,[3] I ween,   10
Lost manhood and put priesthood on?
     (From Love he won such dule and teen!)
     And where, I pray you, is the Queen[4]
Who willed that Buridan should steer
     Sewed in a sack's mouth down the Seine? . . .
But where are the snows of yester-year?

White Queen Blanche,[5] like a queen of lilies,
     With a voice like any mermaiden,—
Bertha Broadfoot, Beatrice, Alice,
     And Ermengarde the lady of Maine,—   20
     And that good Joan whom Englishmen
At Rouen doomed and burned her there,—
     Mother of God, where are they then?..
But where are the snows of yester-year?

Nay, never ask this week, fair lord,
     Where they are gone, nor yet this year,
Save with thus much for an overword,—
     But where are the snows of yester-year?

                                              1870

For "The Wine of Circe"

By Edward Burne-Jones[1]

Dusk-haired and gold-robed o'er the golden wine
     She stoops, wherein, distilled of death and shame,
     Sink the black drops; while, lit with fragrant flame,
Round her spread board the golden sunflowers shine.

---

[3]**Abeillard**: Peter Abelard (1079–1142), French theologian, and his pupil **Héloise** (1098?–1164) secretly married; when this was discovered, Abelard was castrated, he became a monk and she a nun. **dule and teen**: grief and pain.

[4]**Queen**: Margaret of Burgundy was said to have her discarded lovers tied in sacks and thrown in the Seine, among them the philosopher Jean **Buridan** (1300–1358).

[5]**Queen Blanche** of Castille (1185–1252). **Bertha Broadfoot**: Bertrada (d. 783), Frankish queen, mother of Charlemagne; appears with **Beatrice** and **Alice** in a medieval romance. **Ermengarde** (d. 1126): countess of Anjou. **Joan**: Joan of Arc (1412–1431).

[1]*The Wine of Circe*: painting by **Edward Burne-Jones** (1833–1898), PreRaphaelite. Circe's wine turns men into beasts (*Odyssey* 10.210ff). This sonnet is one of a series Rossetti devoted to paintings.

Doth Helios here with Hecatè[2] combine
     (O Circe, thou their votaress!) to proclaim
     For these thy guests all rapture in Love's name,
Till pitiless Night gave Day the countersign?

Lords of their hour, they come. And by her knee
     Those cowering beasts, their equals heretofore,   10
Wait; who with them in new equality
     To-night shall echo back the sea's dull roar
     With a vain wail from passion's tide-strown shore
Where the dishevelled seaweed hates the sea.

                                              1870

from The House of Life: A Sonnet-Sequence

A Sonnet is a moment's monument,—
     Memorial from the Soul's eternity
     To one dead deathless hour. Look that it be,
Whether for lustral rite or dire portent,
Of its own arduous fulness reverent:
     Carve it in ivory or in ebony,
     As Day or Night may rule; and let Time see
Its flowering crest impearled and orient.

A Sonnet is a coin: its face reveals
     The soul,—its converse, to what Power 'tis due:—   10
Whether for tribute to the august appeals
     Of Life, or dower in Love's high retinue,
It serve; or, 'mid the dark wharf's cavernous breath,
In Charon's[1] palm it pay the toll to Death.

2 BRIDAL BIRTH

As when desire, long darkling, dawns, and first
     The mother looks upon the newborn child,
     Even so my Lady stood at gaze and smiled
When her soul knew at length the Love it nurs'd.
Born with her life, creature of poignant thirst
     And exquisite hunger, at her heart Love lay
     Quickening in darkness, till a voice that day
Cried on him, and the bonds of birth were burst.

---

[2]**Helios**: Circe's father, the sun god. **Hecatè**: goddess associated with sorcery, the underworld, and the moon.

[1]**Charon**: ferryman to the classical underworld, whose fee was paid with coins placed in the mouths of the dead.

Now, shadowed by his wings, our faces yearn
    Together, as his full-grown feet now range   10
      The grove, and his warm hands our
          couch prepare:
Till to his song our bodiless souls in turn
    Be born his children, when Death's nuptial change
      Leaves us for light the halo of his hair.

5 HEART'S HOPE

By what word's power, the key of paths untrod,
    Shall I the difficult deeps of Love explore,
    Till parted waves of Song yield up the shore
Even as that sea which Israel crossed dryshod?[2]
For lo! in some poor rhythmic period,
    Lady, I fain would tell how evermore
    Thy soul I know not from thy body, nor
Thee from myself, neither our love from God.

Yea, in God's name, and Love's, and thine, would I
    Draw from one loving heart such evidence   10
As to all hearts all things shall signify;
    Tender as dawn's first hill-fire, and intense
    As instantaneous penetrating sense,
In Spring's birth-hour, of other Springs gone by.

6 THE KISS

What smouldering senses in death's sick delay
    Or seizure of malign vicissitude
    Can rob this body of honour, or denude
This soul of wedding-raiment worn to-day?
For lo! even now my lady's lips did play
    With these my lips such consonant interlude
    As laurelled Orpheus[3] longed for when he wooed
The half-drawn hungering face with that last lay.

I was a child beneath her touch,—a man
    When breast to breast we clung, even I
      and she,—   10
    A spirit when her spirit looked through me,—
A god when all our life-breath met to fan
Our life-blood, till love's emulous ardors ran,
    Fire within fire, desire in deity.

6A NUPTIAL SLEEP[4]

At length their long kiss severed, with sweet smart:
    And as the last slow sudden drops are shed
    From sparkling eaves when all the storm has fled,
So singly flagged the pulses of each heart.
Their bosoms sundered, with the opening start
    Of married flowers to either side outspread
    From the knit stem; yet still their mouths, burnt red,
Fawned on each other where they lay apart.

Sleep sank them lower than the tide of dreams,
    And their dreams watched them sink, and
      slid away.   10
Slowly their souls swam up again, through gleams
    Of watered light and dull drowned waifs of day;
Till from some wonder of new woods and streams
    He woke, and wondered more: for there she lay.

10 THE PORTRAIT

O Lord of all compassionate control,
    O Love! let this my lady's picture glow
    Under my hand to praise her name, and show
Even of her inner self the perfect whole:
That he who seeks her beauty's furthest goal,
    Beyond the light that the sweet glances throw
    And refluent wave of the sweet smile, may know
The very sky and sea-line of her soul.

Lo! it is done. Above the enthroning throat
    The mouth's mould testifies of voice and kiss,   10
      The shadowed eyes remember and foresee.
Her face is made her shrine. Let all men note
    That in all years (O Love, thy gift is this!)
      They that would look on her must come to me.

18 GENIUS IN BEAUTY

Beauty like hers is genius. Not the call
    Of Homer's or of Dante's heart sublime,—
    Not Michael's[5] hand furrowing the zones
      of time,—
Is more with compassed mysteries musical;

---

[2]**parted waves . . . dryshod:** see Exodus 14:21–22.

[3]**Orpheus:** poet in Greek mythology whose lay (song) almost won his dead wife back from the underworld. The **laurel** wreath signifies poetic prowess.

---

[4]**Nuptial Sleep:** Rossetti omitted this sonnet, which had been harshly attacked by Robert Buchanan (see page 146), from the completed 1881 edition; his brother William Michael replaced it in the posthumous edition of 1904.

[5]**Michael:** Michelangelo Buonarrotti (1475–1564): sculptor, painter, architect, and sonneteer.

Nay, not in Spring's or Summer's sweet footfall
 More gathered gifts exuberant Life bequeaths
 Than doth this sovereign face, whose love-spell breathes
Even from its shadowed contour on the wall.

As many men are poets in their youth,
 But for one sweet-strung soul the wires prolong 10
 Even through all change the indomitable song;
So in likewise the envenomed years, whose tooth
Rends shallower grace with ruin void of ruth,
 Upon this beauty's power shall wreak no wrong.

19 SILENT NOON

Your hands lie open in the long fresh grass,—
 The finger-points look through like rosy blooms:
 Your eyes smile peace. The pasture gleams
  and glooms
'Neath billowing skies that scatter and amass.
All round our nest, far as the eye can pass,
 Are golden kingcup-fields with silver edge
 Where the cow-parsley skirts the hawthorn-hedge.
'T is visible silence, still as the hour-glass.

Deep in the sun-searched growths the dragon-fly
Hangs like a blue thread loosened from the sky:— 10
 So this wing'd hour is dropt to us from above.
Oh! clasp we to our hearts, for deathless dower,
This close-companioned inarticulate hour
 When twofold silence was the song of love.

49, 50, 51, 52 WILLOWWOOD
— 1 —

I sat with Love upon a woodside well,
 Leaning across the water, I and he;
 Nor ever did he speak nor looked at me,
But touched his lute wherein was audible
The certain secret thing he had to tell:
 Only our mirrored eyes met silently
 In the low wave; and that sound came to be
The passionate voice I knew; and my tears fell.

And at their fall, his eyes beneath grew hers;
And with his foot and with his wing-feathers 10
 He swept the spring that watered my
  heart's drouth.
Then the dark ripples spread to waving hair,
And as I stooped, her own lips rising there
 Bubbled with brimming kisses at my mouth.

— 2 —

And now Love sang: but his was such a song,
 So meshed with half-remembrance hard to free,
 As souls disused in death's sterility
May sing when the new birthday tarries long.
And I was made aware of a dumb throng
 That stood aloof, one form by every tree,
 All mournful forms, for each was I or she,
The shades of those our days that had no tongue.

They looked on us, and knew us and were known;
 While fast together, alive from the abyss, 10
 Clung the soul-wrung implacable close kiss;
And pity of self through all made broken moan
Which said, "For once, for once, for once alone!"
 And still Love sang, and what he sang was this:—

— 3 —

"O ye, all ye that walk in Willowwood,
 That walk with hollow faces burning white;
What fathom-depth of soul-struck widowhood,
 What long, what longer hours, one lifelong night,
Ere ye again, who so in vain have wooed
 Your last hope lost, who so in vain invite
Your lips to that their unforgotten food,
 Ere ye, ere ye again shall see the light!

Alas! the bitter banks in Willowwood,
 With tear-spurge[6] wan, with blood-wort[6] burning
  red: 10
Alas! if ever such a pillow could
 Steep deep the soul in sleep till she were dead,—
Better all life forget her than this thing,
That Willowwood should hold her wandering!"

— 4 —

So sang he: and as meeting rose and rose
 Together cling through the wind's wellaway
 Nor change at once, yet near the end of day
The leaves drop loosened where the heart-stain glows,—
So when the song died did the kiss unclose;
 And her face fell back drowned, and was as grey
 As its grey eyes; and if it ever may
Meet mine again I know not if Love knows.

---

[6]**tear-spurge:** plant that exudes milky fluid. **blood-wort:** red-leaved or red-rooted plant.

Only I know that I leaned low and drank
A long draught from the water where she sank,   10
   Her breath and all her tears and all her soul:
And as I leaned, I know I felt Love's face
Pressed on my neck with moan of pity and grace,
   Till both our heads were in his aureole.[7]

70 THE HILL SUMMIT

This feast-day of the sun, his altar there
   In the broad west has blazed for vesper-song;
   And I have loitered in the vale too long
And gaze now a belated worshipper.
Yet may I not forget that I was 'ware,
   So journeying, of his face at intervals
   Transfigured where the fringed horizon falls,—
A fiery bush with coruscating hair.

And now that I have climbed and won this height,
   I must tread downward through the sloping shade   10
And travel the bewildered tracks till night.
   Yet for this hour I still may here be stayed
   And see the gold air and the silver fade
And the last bird fly into the last light.
1853

74 ST. LUKE THE PAINTER[8]

Give honour unto Luke Evangelist;
   For he it was (the aged legends say)
   Who first taught Art to fold her hands and pray.
Scarcely at once she dared to rend the mist
Of devious symbols: but soon having wist
   How sky-breadth and field-silence and this day
   Are symbols also in some deeper way,
She looked through these to God and was God's priest.

And if, past noon, her toil began to irk,
   And she sought talismans, and turned in vain   10
     To soulless self-reflections of man's skill,—
     Yet now, in this the twilight, she might still
   Kneel in the latter grass to pray again,
Ere the night cometh and she may not work.[9]
1849

77 SOUL'S BEAUTY

Under the arch of Life, where love and death,
   Terror and mystery, guard her shrine, I saw
   Beauty enthroned; and though her gaze
     struck awe,
I drew it in as simply as my breath.
Hers are the eyes which, over and beneath,
   The sky and sea bend on thee,—which can draw,
   By sea or sky or woman, to one law,
The allotted bondman of her palm and wreath.

This is that Lady Beauty, in whose praise
   Thy voice and hand shake still,—long known
     to thee   10
     By flying hair and fluttering hem,—the beat
     Following her daily of thy heart and feet,
   How passionately and irretrievably,
In what fond flight, how many ways and days!

78 BODY'S BEAUTY

Of Adam's first wife, Lilith,[10] it is told
   (The witch he loved before the gift of Eve,)
   That, ere the snake's, her sweet tongue
     could deceive,
And her enchanted hair was the first gold.
And still she sits, young while the earth is old,
   And, subtly of herself contemplative,
   Draws men to watch the bright web she
     can weave,
Till heart and body and life are in its hold.

The rose and poppy are her flowers; for where
   Is he not found, O Lilith, whom shed scent   10
And soft-shed kisses and soft sleep shall snare?
   Lo! as that youth's eyes burned at thine, so went
   Thy spell through him, and left his straight neck
     bent
And round his heart one strangling golden hair.

83 BARREN SPRING

Once more the changed year's turning wheel returns:
   And as a girl sails balanced in the wind,
   And now before and now again behind
Stoops as it swoops, with cheek that laughs and
     burns,—

---

[7]**aureole**: glorifying halo.

[8]**St.Luke**: author of the third gospel.

[9]**night cometh . . . work**: see John 9:4.

[10]**Lilith** appears in Jewish folklore and rabbinical literature.

So Spring comes merry towards me here, but earns
   No answering smile from me, whose life is twin'd
   With the dead boughs that winter still must bind,
And whom to-day the Spring no more concerns.

Behold, this crocus is a withering flame;
   This snowdrop, snow; this apple-blossom's part   10
   To breed the fruit that breeds the serpent's art.
Nay, for these Spring-flowers, turn thy face
     from them,
Now stay till on the year's last lily-stem
   The white cup shrivels round the golden heart.

97 A SUPERSCRIPTION

Look in my face; my name is Might-have-been;
   I am also called No-more, Too-late, Farewell;
   Unto thine ear I hold the dead-sea shell
Cast up thy Life's foam-fretted feet between;
Unto thine eyes the glass where that is seen
   Which had Life's form and Love's, but by my spell
   Is now a shaken shadow intolerable,
Of ultimate things unuttered the frail screen.

Mark me, how still I am! But should there dart
   One moment through thy soul the soft surprise   10
   Of that winged Peace which lulls the breath
     of sighs,—

Then shalt thou see me smile, and turn apart
Thy visage to mine ambush at thy heart
   Sleepless with cold commemorative eyes.

101 THE ONE HOPE

When vain desire at last and vain regret
   Go hand in hand to death, and all is vain,
   What shall assuage the unforgotten pain
And teach the unforgetful to forget?
Shall Peace be still a sunk stream long unmet,—
   Or may the soul at once in a green plain
   Stoop through the spray of some sweet
     life-fountain
And cull the dew-drenched flowering amulet?

Ah! when the wan soul in that golden air
   Between the scriptured petals softly blown   10
   Peers breathless for the gift of grace unknown,—
Ah! let none other alien spell soe'er
But only the one Hope's one name be there,—
   Not less nor more, but even that word alone.

1849—1880   1868—1881

from The Stealthy School of Criticism

. . . The primary accusation, on which this writer[1] grounds all the rest, seems to be that others and myself "extol fleshliness as the distinct and supreme end of poetic and pictorial art; aver that poetic expression is greater than poetic thought; and, by inference, that the body is greater than the soul, and sound superior to sense."

As my own writings are alone formally dealt with in the article, I shall confine my answer to myself; and this must first take unavoidably the form of a challenge to prove so broad a statement. It is true, some fragmentary pretence at proof is put in here and there throughout the attack, and thus far an opportunity is given of contesting the assertion.

A Sonnet entitled *Nuptial Sleep* is quoted and abused at page 338 of the *Review*, and is there dwelt upon as a "whole poem," describing "merely animal sensations." It is no more a whole poem, in reality, than is any single stanza of any poem throughout the book. The poem, written chiefly in sonnets, and of which this is one sonnet-stanza, is entitled *The House of Life*; and even in my first published instalment of the whole work (as contained in the volume under notice) ample evidence is included that no such passing phase of description as the one headed *Nuptial Sleep* could possibly be put forward by the author of *The House of Life* as his own representative view of the subject of love. In proof of this, I will direct attention (among the love-sonnets of this poem) to Nos. 2, 8, 11, 17, 28, and more especially 13, which, indeed, I had better print here.

LOVE-SWEETNESS

"Sweet dimness of her loosened hair's downfall
   About thy face; her sweet hands round thy head
   In gracious fostering union garlanded;
Her tremulous smiles; her glances' sweet recall
Of love; her murmuring sighs memorial;
   Her mouth's culled sweetness by thy kisses shed
   On cheeks and neck and eyelids, and so led
Back to her mouth which answers there for all:—

<hr>

[1] **this writer:** Rossetti is replying to Robert Buchanan's "The Fleshly School of Poetry" (see pages 144–148). Buchanan had used the pseudonym Thomas Maitland.

"What sweeter than these things, except the thing
    In lacking which all these would lose their sweet:—
    The confident heart's still fervour; the swift beat
And soft subsidence of the spirit's wing
Then when it feels, in cloud-girt wayfaring,
    The breath of kindred plumes against its feet?"

Any reader may bring any artistic charge he pleases against the above sonnet; but one charge it would be impossible to maintain against the writer of the series in which it occurs, and that is, the wish on his part to assert that the body is greater than the soul. For here all the passionate and just delights of the body are declared—somewhat figuratively, it is true, but unmistakably—to be as naught if not ennobled by the concurrence of the soul at all times. Moreover, nearly one half of this series of sonnets has nothing to do with love, but treats of quite other life-influences. I would defy any one to couple with fair quotation of Sonnets 29, 30, 31, 39, 40, 41, 43, or others, the slander that their author was not impressed, like all other thinking men, with the responsibilities and higher mysteries of life; while Sonnets 35, 36, and 37, entitled *The Choice*, sum up the general view taken in a manner only to be evaded by conscious insincerity. Thus much for *The House of Life*, of which the sonnet *Nuptial Sleep* is one stanza, embodying, for its small constituent share, a beauty of natural universal function, only to be reprobated in art if dwelt on (as I have shown that it is not here) to the exclusion of those other highest things of which it is the harmonious concomitant.

At page 342, an attempt is made to stigmatize four short quotations as being specially "my own property," that is, (for the context shows the meaning,) as being grossly sensual; though all guiding reference to any precise page or poem in my book is avoided here. The first of these unspecified quotations is from the *Last Confession*; and is the description referring to the harlot's laugh, the hideous character of which, together with its real or imagined resemblance to the laugh heard soon afterwards from the lips of one long cherished as an ideal, is the immediate cause which makes the maddened hero of the poem a murderer. Assailants may say what they please; but no poet or poetic reader will blame me for making the incident recorded in these seven lines as repulsive to the reader as it was to the hearer and beholder. Without this, the chain of motive and result would remain obviously incomplete. Observe also that these are but seven lines in a poem of some five hundred, not one other of which could be classed with them.

A second quotation gives the last two lines *only* of the following sonnet, which is the first of four sonnets in *The House of Life* jointly entitled *Willowwood*:—

"I sat with Love upon a woodside well,
    Leaning across the water, I and he;
    Nor ever did he speak nor looked at me,
But touched his lute wherein was audible
The certain secret thing he had to tell:
    Only our mirrored eyes met silently
    In the low wave; and that sound seemed to be
The passionate voice I knew; and my tears fell.

"And at their fall, his eyes beneath grew hers;
And with his foot and with his wing-feathers
    He swept the spring that watered my heart's drouth.
Then the dark ripples spread to waving hair,
And as I stooped, her own lips rising there
    Bubbled with brimming kisses at my mouth."

The critic has quoted (as I said) only the last two lines, and he has italicized the second as something unbearable and ridiculous. Of course the inference would be that this was really my own absurd bubble-and-squeak[2] notion of an actual kiss. The reader will perceive at once, from the whole sonnet transcribed above, how untrue such an inference would be. The sonnet describes a dream or trance of divided love momentarily re-united by the longing fancy; and in the imagery of the dream, the face of the beloved rises through deep dark waters to kiss the lover. Thus the phrase, "Bubbled with brimming kisses," etc., bears purely on the special symbolism employed, and from that point of view will be found, I believe, perfectly simple and just.

A third quotation is from *Eden Bower*, and says,

"What more prize than love to impel thee?
Grip and lip my limbs as I tell thee!"

Here again no reference is given; and naturally the reader would suppose that a human embrace is described. The embrace, on the contrary, is that of a fabled snake-woman and a snake. It would be possible still, no doubt, to object on other grounds to this conception; but the ground inferred and relied on for full effect by the critic is none the less an absolute misrepresentation. These three extracts, it will be admitted, are virtually, though not verbally, garbled with malicious intention; and the same is the case, as I have shown, with the sonnet called *Nuptial Sleep* when purposely treated as a "whole poem."

---

[2]**bubble-and-squeak:** meat or potatoes fried with cabbage.

The last of the four quotations grouped by the critic as conclusive examples consists of two lines from *Jenny*. Neither some thirteen years ago, when I wrote this poem, nor last year when I published it, did I fail to foresee impending charges of recklessness and aggressiveness, or to perceive that even some among those who could really *read* the poem, and acquit me on these grounds, might still hold that the thought in it had better have dispensed with the situation which serves it for framework. Nor did I omit to consider how far a treatment from without might here be possible. But the motive powers of art reverse the requirement of science, and demand first of all an *inner* standing-point. The heart of such a mystery as this must be plucked[3] from the very world in which it beats or bleeds; and the beauty and pity, the self-questionings and all-questionings which it brings with it, can come with full force only from the mouth of one alive to its whole appeal, such as the speaker put forward in the poem,—that is, of a young and thoughtful man of the world. To such a speaker, many half-cynical revulsions of feeling and reverie, and a recurrent presence of the impressions of beauty (however artificial) which first brought him within such a circle of influence, would be inevitable features of the dramatic relations portrayed. Here again I can give the lie, in hearing of honest readers, to the base or trivial ideas which my critic labours to connect with the poem. There is another little charge, however, which this minstrel in mufti brings against *Jenny*, namely, one of plagiarism from that very poetic self of his which the tutelary prose does but enshroud for the moment. This question can, fortunately, be settled with ease by others who have read my critic's poems; and thus I need the less regret that, not happening myself to be in that position, I must be content to rank with those who cannot pretend to an opinion on the subject.

It would be humiliating, need one come to serious detail, to have to refute such an accusation as that of "binding oneself by solemn league and covenant to extol fleshliness as the distinct and supreme end of poetic and pictorial art"; and one cannot but feel that here every one will think it allowable merely to pass by with a smile the foolish fellow who has brought a charge thus framed against any reasonable man. Indeed, what I have said already is substantially enough to refute it, even did I not feel sure that a fair balance of my poetry must, of itself, do so in the eyes of every candid reader. I say nothing of my pictures; but those who know them will laugh at the idea. That I may, nevertheless,

take a wider view than some poets or critics, of how much, in the material conditions absolutely given to man to deal with as distinct from his spiritual aspirations, is admissible within the limits of Art,—this, I say, is possible enough; nor do I wish to shrink from such responsibility. But to state that I do so to the ignoring or overshadowing of spiritual beauty, is an absolute falsehood, impossible to be put forward except in the indulgence of prejudice or rancour.

I have selected, amid much railing on my critic's part, what seemed the most representative indictment against me, and have, so far, answered it. Its remaining clauses set forth how others and myself "aver that poetic expression is greater than poetic thought... and sound superior to sense"—an accusation elsewhere, I observe, expressed by saying that we "wish to create form for its own sake." If writers of verse are to be listened to in such arraignment of each other, it might be quite competent of me to prove, from the works of my friends in question, that no such thing is the case with them; but my present function is to confine myself to my own defence. This, again, it is difficult to do quite seriously. It is no part of my undertaking to dispute the verdict of any "contemporary," however contemptuous or contemptible, on my own measure of executive success; but the accusation cited above is not against the poetic value of certain work, but against its primary and (by assumption) its admitted aim. And to this I must reply that so far, assuredly, not even Shakespeare himself could desire more arduous human tragedy for development in Art than belongs to the themes I venture to embody, however incalculably higher might be his power of dealing with them. What more inspiring for poetic effort than the terrible Love turned to Hate,—perhaps the deadliest of all passion-woven complexities,—which is the theme of *Sister Helen*, and, in a more fantastic form, of *Eden Bower*—the surroundings of both poems being the mere machinery of a central universal meaning? What, again, more so than the savage penalty exacted for a lost ideal, as expressed in the *Last Confession*;—than the outraged love for man and burning compensations in art and memory of *Dante at Verona*;—than the baffling problems which the face of *Jenny* conjures up;—or than the analysis of passion and feeling attempted in *The House of Life*, and others among the more purely lyrical poems? I speak here, as does my critic in the clause adduced, of *aim*, not of *achievement*; and so far, the mere summary is instantly subversive of the preposterous imputation. To assert that the poet whose matter is such as this aims chiefly at "creating form for its own sake," is, in fact, almost an ingenuous kind of dishonesty; for surely it delivers up the asserter at once, bound hand and foot, to the tender mercies of contradictory proof.

---

[3]**heart . . . mystery:** see *Hamlet* 3.2.350.

Yet this may fairly be taken as an example of the spirit in which a constant effort is here made against me to appeal to those who either are ignorant of what I write, or else belong to the large class too easily influenced by an assumption of authority in addressing them. The false name appended to the article must, as is evident, aid this position vastly; for who, after all, would not be apt to laugh at seeing one poet confessedly come forward as aggressor against another in the field of criticism?

It would not be worth while to lose time and patience in noticing minutely how the system of misrepresentation is carried into points of artistic detail,—giving us, for example, such statements as that the burthen employed in the ballad of *Sister Helen* "is repeated with little or no alteration through thirty-four verses," whereas the fact is, that the alteration of it in every verse is the very scheme of the poem.

But these are minor matters quite thrown into the shade by the critic's more daring sallies. In addition to the class of attack I have answered above, the article contains, of course, an immense amount of personal paltriness; as, for instance, attributions of my work to this, that, or the other absurd derivative source; or again, pure nonsense (which can have no real meaning even to the writer) about "one art getting hold of another, and imposing on it its conditions and limitations"; or, indeed, what not besides? However, to such antics as this, no more attention is possible than that which Virgil enjoined Dante[4] to bestow on the meaner phenomena of his pilgrimage. . . .

1871

---

[4]**Virgil enjoined Dante:** see *Inferno* 30.145–148.

GEORGE MEREDITH

(1828–1909)

The son of a prosperous tailor (a socially awkward fact he preferred to conceal), George Meredith studied in Germany, worked briefly as a law clerk, and then became a successful journalist, novelist, and poet. In addition, from 1862 to 1894 he augmented his income and exerted considerable literary influence as reader for a major publisher, Chapman and Hall. He was associated with the PreRaphaelite movement, sharing a London house for a few years with Dante Rossetti and Swinburne until he tired of their bohemian way of life. His novels were much admired by intellectuals but less popular with the general public; their style was poetical, witty, elaborate, and usually rather difficult. Their topics were very much of the moment, reflecting scientific ideas about development and progress, supporting ideals of liberty, and celebrating the advent of the intelligent and independent "new woman."

In 1849 Meredith married Mary Ellen Nicolls, a brilliant and beautiful widow nine years older than he. She was the daughter of a well-known Romantic satirist and novelist, Thomas Love Peacock, and the young couple moved in literary circles and collaborated in literary projects. But in 1858 she left her husband and their child and went off with a PreRaphaelite painter. Out of this bitter experience Meredith wrote his best-known poem, the sequence of modified sonnets called *Modern Love*. The poem alters the actual events considerably: the wife falls in love with another man but does not consummate this passion or actually leave her husband. Instead, she rounds off the story by committing suicide after her husband has so-laced his hurt pride with a lover ("My Lady") of his own. The protagonists are highly intelligent, sophisticated, and self-conscious—a very "modern" couple. The husband can be bitterly ironical about his own jealousy, self-righteousness, and rage, and is adept at psychological analysis. "We are betrayed," he says, "by what is false within." Like many other Victorian poets, Meredith used the events of his life to explore the relationship between poetic conventions and modern habits of mind, exploiting the discrepancy between them to turn his own experience into poetry.

Modern Love

The Promise in Disturbance

How low when angels fall their black descent,
Our primal thunder tells: known is the pain
Of music, that nigh throning wisdom went,
And one false note cast wailful to the insane.
Now seems the language heard of Love as rain
To make a mire where fruitfulness was meant.
The golden harp gives out a jangled strain,
Too like revolt from heaven's Omnipotent.
But listen in the thought; so may there come
Conception of a newly-added chord,   10
Commanding space beyond where ear has home.
In labour of the trouble at its fount,
Leads Life to an intelligible Lord
The rebel discords up the sacred mount.

                                                      1892

— 1 —

By this he knew she wept with waking eyes:
That, at his hand's light quiver by her head,
The strange low sobs that shook their common bed,
Were called into her with a sharp surprise,
And strangled mute, like little gaping snakes,
Dreadfully venomous to him. She lay
Stone-still, and the long darkness flowed away
With muffled pulses. Then, as midnight makes
Her giant heart of Memory and Tears
Drink the pale drug of silence, and so beat
Sleep's heavy measure, they from head to feet   10
Were moveless, looking through their dead black years,
By vain regret scrawled over the blank wall.
Like sculptured effigies they might be seen
Upon their marriage-tomb, the sword between;
Each wishing for the sword that severs all.

— 2 —

It ended, and the morrow brought the task.
Her eyes were guilty gates, that let him in
By shutting all too zealous for their sin:
Each sucked a secret, and each wore a mask.
But, oh, the bitter taste her beauty had!
He sickened as at breath of poison-flowers:
A languid humour stole among the hours,
And if their smiles encountered, he went mad,
And raged deep inward, till the light was brown

Before his vision, and the world, forgot,   10
Looked wicked as some old dull murder-spot.
A star with lurid beams, she seemed to crown
The pit of infamy: and then again
He fainted on his vengefulness, and strove
To ape the magnanimity of love,
And smote himself, a shuddering heap of pain.

— 3 —

This was the woman; what now of the man?
But pass him. If he comes beneath a heel,
He shall be crushed until he cannot feel,
Or, being callous, haply till he can.
But he is nothing:—nothing? Only mark
The rich light striking out from her on him!
Ha! what a sense it is when her eyes swim
Across the man she singles, leaving dark
All else! Lord God, who mad'st the thing so fair,
See that I am drawn to her even now!   10
It cannot be such harm on her cool brow
To put a kiss? Yet if I meet him there!
But she is mine! Ah, no! I know too well
I claim a star whose light is overcast:
I claim a phantom-woman in the Past.
The hour has struck, though I heard not the bell!

— 4 —

All other joys of life he strove to warm,
And magnify, and catch them to his lip:
But they had suffered shipwreck with the ship,
And gazed upon him sallow from the storm.
Or if Delusion came, 't was but to show
The coming minute mock the one that went.
Cold as a mountain in its star-pitched tent,
Stood high Philosophy, less friend than foe:
Whom self-caged Passion, from its prison-bars,
Is always watching with a wondering hate.   10
Not till the fire is dying in the grate,
Look we for any kinship with the stars.
Oh, wisdom never comes when it is gold,
And the great price we pay for it full worth:
We have it only when we are half earth.
Little avails that coinage to the old!

— 5 —

A message from her set his brain aflame.
A world of household matters filled her mind,
Wherein he saw hypocrisy designed:
She treated him as something that is tame,
And but at other provocation bites.
Familiar was her shoulder in the glass,
Through that dark rain: yet it may come to pass
That a changed eye finds such familiar sights
More keenly tempting than new loveliness.
The "What has been" a moment seemed his own: 10
The splendours, mysteries, dearer because known,
Nor less divine: Love's inmost sacredness
Called to him, "Come!"—In his restraining start,
Eyes nurtured to be looked at scarce could see
A wave of the great waves of Destiny
Convulsed at a checked impulse of the heart.

— 6 —

It chanced his lips did meet her forehead cool.
She had no blush, but slanted down her eye.
Shamed nature, then, confesses love can die:
And most she punishes the tender fool
Who will believe what honours her the most!
Dead! is it dead? She has a pulse, and flow
Of tears, the price of blood-drops, as I know,
For whom the midnight sobs around Love's ghost,
Since then I heard her, and so will sob on.
The love is here; it has but changed its aim.   10
O bitter barren woman! what's the name?
The name, the name, the new name thou hast won?
Behold me striking the world's coward stroke!
That will I not do, though the sting is dire.
—Beneath the surface this, while by the fire
They sat, she laughing at a quiet joke.

— 7 —

She issues radiant from her dressing-room,
Like one prepared to scale an upper sphere:
—By stirring up a lower, much I fear!
How deftly that oiled barber lays his bloom!
That long-shanked dapper Cupid with frisked curls
Can make known women torturingly fair;
The gold-eyed serpent dwelling in rich hair,
Awakes beneath his magic whisks and twirls.
His art can take the eyes from out my head,
Until I see with eyes of other men;   10

While deeper knowledge crouches in its den,
And sends a spark up:—is it true we are wed?
Yea! filthiness of body is most vile,
But faithlessness of heart I do hold worse.
The former, it were not so great a curse
To read on the steel-mirror of her smile.

— 8 —

Yet it was plain she struggled, and that salt
Of righteous feeling made her pitiful.
Poor twisting worm, so queenly beautiful!
Where came the cleft between us? whose the fault?
My tears are on thee, that have rarely dropped
As balm for any bitter wound of mine:
My breast will open for thee at a sign!
But, no: we are two reed-pipes, coarsely stopped:
The God once filled them with his mellow breath;
And they were music till he flung them down,   10
Used! used! Hear now the discord-loving clown
Puff his gross spirit in them, worse than death!
I do not know myself without thee more:
In this unholy battle I grow base:
If the same soul be under the same face,
Speak, and a taste of that old time restore!

— 9 —

He felt the wild beast in him betweenwhiles
So masterfully rude, that he would grieve
To see the helpless delicate thing receive
His guardianship through certain dark defiles.
Had he not teeth to rend, and hunger too?
But still he spared her. Once: "Have you no fear?"
He said: 'twas dusk; she in his grasp; none near.
She laughed: "No, surely; am I not with you?"
And uttering that soft starry "you," she leaned
Her gentle body near him, looking up;   10
And from her eyes, as from a poison-cup,
He drank until the flittering eyelids screened.
Devilish malignant witch! and oh, young beam
Of heaven's circle-glory! Here thy shape
To squeeze like an intoxicating grape—
I might, and yet thou goest safe, supreme.

— 10 —

But where began the change; and what's my crime?
The wretch condemned, who has not been arraigned,
Chafes at his sentence. Shall I, unsustained,
Drag on Love's nerveless body thro' all time?

I must have slept, since now I wake. Prepare,
You lovers, to know Love a thing of moods:
Not like hard life, of laws. In Love's deep woods,
I dreamt of loyal Life:—the offence is there!
Love's jealous woods about the sun are curled;
At least, the sun far brighter there did beam.—   10
My crime is, that the puppet of a dream,
I plotted to be worthy of the world.
Oh, had I with my darling helped to mince
The facts of life, you still had seen me go
With hindward feather and with forward toe,
Her much-adored delightful Fairy Prince!

— 11 —

Out in the yellow meadows, where the bee
Hums by us with the honey of the Spring,
And showers of sweet notes from the larks on wing,
Are dropping like a noon-dew, wander we.
Or is it now? or was it then? for now,
As then, the larks from running rings pour showers:
The golden foot of May is on the flowers,
And friendly shadows dance upon her brow.
What's this, when Nature swears there is no change
To challenge eyesight? Now, as then, the grace   10
Of heaven seems holding earth in its embrace.
Nor eyes, nor heart, has she to feel it strange?
Look, woman, in the West. There wilt thou see
An amber cradle near the sun's decline:
Within it, featured even in death divine,
Is lying a dead infant, slain by thee.

— 12 —

Not solely that the Future she destroys,
And the fair life which in the distance lies
For all men, beckoning out from dim rich skies:
Nor that the passing hour's supporting joys
Have lost the keen-edged flavour, which begat
Distinction in old times, and still should breed
Sweet Memory, and Hope,—earth's modest seed,
And heaven's high-prompting: not that the world is flat
Since that soft-luring creature I embraced
Among the children of Illusion went: 10
Methinks with all this loss I were content,
If the mad Past, on which my foot is based,
Were firm, or might be blotted: but the whole
Of life is mixed: the mocking Past will stay:
And if I drink oblivion of a day,
So shorten I the stature of my soul.

— 13 —

"I play for Seasons; not Eternities!"
Says Nature, laughing on her way. "So must
All those whose stake is nothing more than dust!"
And lo, she wins, and of her harmonies
She is full sure! Upon her dying rose
She drops a look of fondness, and goes by,
Scarce any retrospection in her eye;
For she the laws of growth most deeply knows,
Whose hands bear, here, a seed-bag—there, an urn.
Pledged she herself to aught, 'twould mark her end!   10
This lesson of our only visible friend
Can we not teach our foolish hearts to learn?
Yes! yes!—but oh, our human rose is fair
Surpassingly! Lose calmly Love's great bliss,
When the renewed for ever of a kiss
Whirls life within the shower of loosened hair!

— 14 —

What soul would bargain for a cure that brings
Contempt the nobler agony to kill?
Rather let me bear on the bitter ill,
And strike this rusty bosom with new stings!
It seems there is another veering fit,
Since on a gold-haired lady's eyeballs pure
I looked with little prospect of a cure,
The while her mouth's red bow loosed shafts of wit.
Just heaven! can it be true that jealousy
Has decked the woman thus? and does her head   10
Swim somewhat for possessions forfeited?
Madam, you teach me many things that be.
I open an old book, and there I find,
That "Women still may love whom they deceive."
Such love I prize not, madam: by your leave,
The game you play at is not to my mind.

— 15 —

I think she sleeps; it must be sleep, when low
Hangs that abandoned arm toward the floor;
The face turned with it. Now make fast the door.
Sleep on: it is your husband, not your foe.
The Poet's black stage-lion[1] of wronged love
Frights not our modern dames:—well if he did!
Now will I pour new light upon that lid,
Full-sloping like the breasts beneath. "Sweet dove,

---

[1]**stage-lion**: Shakespeare's Othello.

Your sleep is pure. Nay, pardon: I disturb.
I do not? good!" Her waking infant-stare   10
Grows woman to the burden my hands bear:
Her own handwriting to me when no curb
Was left on Passion's tongue. She trembles through;
A woman's tremble—the whole instrument:—
I show another letter lately sent.
The words are very like: the name is new.

— 16 —

In our old shipwrecked days there was an hour,
When in the firelight steadily aglow,
Joined slackly, we beheld the red chasm grow
Among the clicking coals. Our library-bower
That eve was left to us: and hushed we sat
As lovers to whom Time is whispering.
From sudden-opened doors we heard them sing:
The nodding elders mixed good wine with chat.
Well knew we that Life's greatest treasure lay
With us, and of it was our talk. "Ah, yes!   10
Love dies!" I said: I never thought it less.
She yearned to me that sentence to unsay.
Then when the fire domed blackening, I found
Her cheek was salt against my kiss, and swift
Up the sharp scale of sobs her breast did lift:—
Now am I haunted by that taste! that sound!

— 17 —

At dinner, she is hostess, I am host.
Went the feast ever cheerfuller? She keeps
The Topic over intellectual deeps
In buoyancy afloat. They see no ghost.
With sparkling surface-eyes we ply the ball:
It is in truth a most contagious game:
HIDING THE SKELETON, shall be its name.
Such play as this the devils might appal!
But here's the greater wonder; in that we,
Enamoured of an acting nought can tire,   10
Each other, like true hypocrites, admire;
Warm-lighted looks, Love's ephemerioe,[2]
Shoot gaily o'er the dishes and the wine.
We waken envy of our happy lot.
Fast, sweet, and golden, shows the marriage-knot.
Dear guests, you now have seen Love's corpse-light[3] shine.

— 18 —

Here Jack and Tom are paired with Moll and Meg.
Curved open to the river-reach is seen
A country merry-making on the green.
Fair space for signal shakings of the leg.
That little screwy[4] fiddler from his booth,
Whence flows one nut-brown stream, commands the joints
Of all who caper here at various points.
I have known rustic revels in my youth:
The May-fly pleasures of a mind at ease.
An early goddess was a country lass: 10
A charmed Amphion-oak[5] she tripped the grass.
What life was that I lived? The life of these?
Heaven keep them happy! Nature they seem near.
They must, I think, be wiser than I am;
They have the secret of the bull and lamb.
'Tis true that when we trace its source, 'tis beer.

— 19 —

No state is enviable. To the luck alone
Of some few favoured men I would put claim.
I bleed, but her who wounds I will not blame.
Have I not felt her heart as 'twere my own
Beat thro' me? could I hurt her? heaven and hell!
But I could hurt her cruelly! Can I let
My Love's old time-piece to another set,
Swear it can't stop, and must for ever swell?
Sure, that's one way Love drifts into the mart
Where goat-legged buyers throng. I see not plain:—   10
My meaning is, it must not be again.
Great God! the maddest gambler throws his heart.
If any state be enviable on earth,
'Tis yon born idiot's, who, as days go by,
Still rubs his hands before him, like a fly,
In a queer sort of meditative mirth.

— 20 —

I am not of those miserable males
Who sniff at vice, and daring not to snap,
Do therefore hope for heaven. I take the hap
Of all my deeds. The wind that fills my sails
Propels; but I am helmsman. Am I wrecked,

---

[2]ephemerioe: creatures of a day.

[3]corpse-light: a lambent flame by a grave, an omen of death.

[4]screwy: tipsy. nut-brown stream: ale.

[5]Amphion: mythological singer whose music charmed rocks and trees into motion.

I know the devil has sufficient weight
To bear: I lay it not on him, or fate.
Besides, he's damned. That man I do suspect
A coward, who would burden the poor deuce[6]
With what ensues from his own slipperiness.   10
I have just found a wanton-scented tress
In an old desk, dusty for lack of use.
Of days and nights it is demonstrative,
That, like some aged star, gleam luridly
If for those times I must ask charity.
Have I not any charity to give?

— 21 —

We three are on the cedar-shadowed lawn;
My friend being third. He who at love once laughed
Is in the weak rib by a fatal shaft
Struck through, and tells his passion's bashful dawn
And radiant culmination, glorious crown,
When "this" she said: went "thus": most wondrous she.
Our eyes grow white, encountering: that we are three,
Forgetful; then together we look down.
But he demands our blessing; is convinced
That words of wedded lovers must bring good.   10
We question; if we dare! or if we should!
And pat him, with light laugh. We have not winced.
Next, she has fallen. Fainting points the sign
To happy things in wedlock. When she wakes,
She looks the star that thro' the cedar shakes:
Her lost moist hand clings mortally to mine.

— 22 —

What may the woman labour to confess?
There is about her mouth a nervous twitch.
'Tis something to be told, or hidden:—which?
I get a glimpse of hell in this mild guess.
She has desires of touch, as if to feel
That all the household things are things she knew.
She stops before the glass. What sight in view?
A face that seems the latest to reveal!
For she turns from it hastily, and tossed
Irresolute, steals shadow-like to where   10
I stand; and wavering pale before me there,
Her tears fall still as oak-leaves after frost.
She will not speak. I will not ask. We are
League-sundered by the silent gulf between.
You burly lovers on the village green,
Yours is a lower, and a happier star!

---

[6]**deuce:** devil.

— 23 —

'Tis Christmas weather, and a country house
Receives us: rooms are full: we can but get
An attic-crib. Such lovers will not fret
At that, it is half-said. The great carouse
Knocks hard upon the midnight's hollow door,
But when I knock at hers, I see the pit.
Why did I come here in that dullard fit?
I enter, and lie couched upon the floor.
Passing, I caught the coverlet's quick beat:—
Come, Shame, burn to my soul! and Pride, and Pain—   10
Foul demons that have tortured me, enchain!
Out in the freezing darkness the lambs bleat.
The small bird stiffens in the low starlight.
I know not how , but shuddering as I slept,
I dreamed a banished angel to me crept:
My feet were nourished on her breasts all night.

— 24 —

The misery is greater, as I live!
To know her flesh so pure, so keen her sense,
That she does penance now for no offence,
Save against Love. The less can I forgive!
The less can I forgive, though I adore
That cruel lovely pallor which surrounds
Her footsteps; and the low vibrating sounds
That come on me, as from a magic shore.
Low are they, but most subtle to find out
The shrinking soul. Madam, 'tis understood   10
When women play upon their womanhood,
It means, a Season gone. And yet I doubt
But I am duped. That nun-like look waylays
My fancy. Oh! I do but wait a sign!
Pluck out the eyes of pride! thy mouth to mine!
Never! though I die thirsting. Go thy ways!

— 25 —

You like not that French novel? Tell me why.
You think it quite unnatural. Let us see.
The actors are, it seems, the usual three:
Husband, and wife and lover. She—but fie!
In England we'll not hear of it. Edmond
The lover, her devout chagrin doth share;
Blanc-mange and absinthe[7] are his penitent fare,
Till his pale aspect makes her over-fond:

---

[7]**Blanc-mange, absinthe, rosbif:** sweet white jelly, liqueur, roast
beef.

So, to preclude fresh sin, he tries rosbif.
Meantime the husband is no more abused: 10
Auguste forgives her ere the tear is used.
Then hangeth all on one tremendous IF:—
If she will choose between them. She does choose;
And takes her husband, like a proper wife.
Unnatural? My dear, these things are life:
And life, some think, is worthy of the Muse.

— 26 —

Love ere he bleeds, an eagle in high skies,
Has earth beneath his wings: from reddened eve
He views the rosy down. In vain they weave
The fatal web below while far he flies.
But when the arrow strikes him, there's a change.
He moves but in the track of his spent pain,
Whose red drops are the links of a harsh chain,
Binding him to the ground, with narrow range.
A subtle serpent then has Love become.
I had the eagle in my bosom erst: 10
Henceforward with the serpent I am cursed.
I can interpret where the mouth is dumb.
Speak, and I see the side-lie of a truth.
Perchance my heart may pardon you this deed:
But be no coward:—you that made Love bleed,
You must bear all the venom of his tooth!

— 27 —

Distraction is the panacea, Sir!
I hear my oracle of Medicine say.
Doctor! that same specific yesterday
I tried, and the result will not deter
A second trial. Is the devil's line
Of golden hair, or raven black, composed?
And does a cheek, like any sea-shell rosed,
Or clear as widowed sky, seem most divine?
No matter, so I taste forgetfulness.
And if the devil snare me, body and mind,   10
Here gratefully I score:—he seeméd kind,
When not a soul would comfort my distress!
O sweet new world, in which I rise new made!
O Lady, once I gave love: now I take!
Lady, I must be flattered. Shouldst thou wake
The passion of a demon, be not afraid.

— 28 —

I must be flattered. The imperious
Desire speaks out. Lady, I am content

To play with you the game of Sentiment,
And with you enter on paths perilous;
But if across your beauty I throw light,
To make it threefold, it must be all mine.
First secret; then avowed. For I must shine
Envied,—I, lessened in my proper sight!
Be watchful of your beauty, Lady dear!
How much hangs on that lamp you cannot tell.   10
Most earnestly I pray you, tend it well:
And men shall see me as a burning sphere;
And men shall mark you eyeing me, and groan
To be the God of such a grand sunflower!
I feel the promptings of Satanic power,
While you do homage unto me alone.

— 29 —

Am I failing? For no longer can I cast
A glory round about this head of gold.
Glory she wears, but springing from the mould;
Not like the consecration of the Past!
Is my soul beggared? Something more than earth
I cry for still: I cannot be at peace
In having Love upon a mortal lease.
I cannot take the woman at her worth!
Where is the ancient wealth wherewith I clothed
Our human nakedness, and could endow   10
With spiritual splendour a white brow
That else had grinned at me the fact I loathed?
A kiss is but a kiss now! and no wave
Of a great flood that whirls me to the sea.
But, as you will! we'll sit contentedly,
And eat our pot of honey on the grave.

— 30 —

What are we first? First, animals; and next
Intelligences at a leap, on whom
Pale lies the distant shadow of the tomb,
And all that draweth on the tomb for text.
Into which state comes Love, the crowning sun:
Beneath whose light the shadow loses form.
We are the lords of life, and life is warm.
Intelligence and instinct now are one.
But nature says: "My children most they seem
When they least know me: therefore I decree   10
That they shall suffer." Swift doth young Love flee,
And we stand wakened, shivering from our dream.
Then if we study Nature we are wise.
Thus do the few who live but with the day:

The scientific animals are they.—
Lady, this is my sonnet to your eyes.

— 31 —

This golden head has wit in it. I live
Again, and a far higher life, near her.
Some women like a young philosopher;
Perchance because he is diminutive.
For woman's manly god must not exceed
Proportions of the natural nursing size.
Great poets and great sages draw no prize
With women: but the little lap-dog breed,
Who can be hugged, or on a mantel-piece
Perched up for adoration, these obtain   10
Her homage. And of this we men are vain?
Of this! 'Tis ordered for the world's increase!
Small flattery! Yet she has that rare gift
To beauty, Common Sense. I am approved.
It is not half so nice as being loved,
And yet I do prefer it. What's my drift?

— 32 —

Full faith I have she holds that rarest gift
To beauty, Common Sense. To see her lie
With her fair visage an inverted sky
Bloom-covered, while the underlids uplift,
Would almost wreck the faith; but when her mouth
(Can it kiss sweetly? sweetly!) would address
The inner me that thirsts for her no less,
And has so long been languishing in drouth,
I feel that I am matched; that I am man!
One restless corner of my heart or head,   10
That holds a dying something never dead,
Still frets, though Nature giveth all she can.
It means, that woman is not, I opine,
Her sex's antidote. Who seeks the asp
For serpents' bites? 'Twould calm me could I clasp
Shrieking Bacchantes[8] with their souls of wine!

— 33 —

"In Paris, at the Louvre, there have I seen
The sumptuously-feathered angel[9] pierce
Prone Lucifer, descending. Looked he fierce,
Showing the fight a fair one? Too serene!

---

[8]**Bacchantes:** female followers of Bacchus, god of wine.

[9]**angel:** painting of St. Michael by **Raphael** (1483–1520).

The young Pharsalians[10] did not disarray
Less willingly their locks of floating silk:
That suckling mouth of his, upon the milk
Of heaven might still be feasting through the fray.
Oh, Raphael! when men the Fiend do fight,
They conquer not upon such easy terms.   10
Half serpent in the struggle grow these worms.
And does he grow half human, all is right."
This to my Lady in a distant spot,
Upon the theme: *While mind is mastering clay,*
Gross clay invades it. If the spy you play,
My wife, read this! Strange love-talk, is it not?

— 34 —

Madam would speak with me. So, now it comes:
The Deluge or else Fire! She's well; she thanks
My husbandship. Our chain on silence clanks.
Time leers between, above his twiddling thumbs.
Am I quite well? Most excellent in health!
The journals, too, I diligently peruse.
Vesuvius[11] is expected to give news:
Niagara is no noisier. By stealth
Our eyes dart scrutinizing snakes. She's glad
I'm happy, says her quivering under-lip.   10
"And are not you?" "How can I be?" "Take ship!
For happiness is somewhere to be had."
"Nowhere for me!" Her voice is barely heard.
I am not melted, and make no pretence.
With commonplace I freeze her, tongue and sense.
Niagara or Vesuvius is deferred.

— 35 —

It is no vulgar nature I have wived.
Secretive, sensitive, she takes a wound
Deep to her soul, as if the sense had swooned,
And not a thought of vengeance had survived.
No confidences has she: but relief
Must come to one whose suffering is acute.
O have a care of natures that are mute!
They punish you in acts: their steps are brief.
What is she doing? What does she demand
From Providence or me? She is not one   10
Long to endure this torpidly, and shun
The drugs that crowd about a woman's hand.

---

[10]**Pharsalians:** Plutarch (46?–120?) reports in *The Parallel Lives* that handsome young soldiers fled when Julius Caesar's troops threatened to injure their faces in the battle of Pharsalus.

[11]**Vesuvius:** volcano in Italy.

At Forfeits[12] during snow we played, and I
Must kiss her. "Well performed!" I said: then she:
"'Tis hardly worth the money, you agree?"
Save her? What for? To act this wedded lie!

— 36 —

My Lady unto Madam makes her bow.
The charm of women is, that even while
You're probed by them for tears, you yet may smile,
Nay, laugh outright, as I have done just now.
The interview was gracious: they anoint
(To me aside) each other with fine praise:
Discriminating compliments they raise,
That hit with wondrous aim on the weak point:
My Lady's nose of Nature might complain.
It is not fashioned aptly to express   10
Her character of large-browed steadfastness.
But Madam says: Thereof she may be vain!
Now, Madam's faulty feature is a glazed
And inaccessible eye, that has soft fires,
Wide gates, at love-time, only. This admires
My Lady. At the two I stand amazed.

— 37 —

Along the garden terrace, under which
A purple valley (lighted at its edge
By smoky torch-flame on the long cloud-ledge
Whereunder dropped the chariot) glimmers rich,
A quiet company we pace, and wait
The dinner-bell in præ-digestive calm.
So sweet up violet banks the Southern balm
Breathes round, we care not if the bell be late:
Though here and there grey seniors question Time
In irritable coughings. With slow foot   10
The low rosed moon, the face of Music mute,
Begins among her silent bars to climb.
As in and out, in silvery dusk, we thread,
I hear the laugh of Madam, and discern
My Lady's heel before me at each turn.
Our tragedy, is it alive or dead?

— 38 —

Give to imagination some pure light
In human form to fix it, or you shame
The devils with that hideous human game:—

Imagination urging appetite!
Thus fallen have earth's greatest Gogmagogs,[13]
Who dazzle us, whom we can not revere:
Imagination is the charioteer
That, in default of better, drives the hogs.
So, therefore, my dear Lady, let me love!
My soul is arrowy to the light in you.   10
You know me that I never can renew
The bond that woman broke: what would you have?
'Tis Love, or Vileness! not a choice between,
Save petrifaction! What does Pity here?
She killed a thing, and now it's dead, 'tis dear.
Oh, when you counsel me, think what you mean!

— 39 —

She yields: my Lady in her noblest mood
Has yielded: she, my golden-crownëd rose!
The bride of every sense! more sweet than those
Who breathe the violet breath of maidenhood.
O visage of still music in the sky!
Soft moon! I feel thy song, my fairest friend!
True harmony within can apprehend
Dumb harmony without. And hark! 'tis nigh!
Belief has struck the note of sound: a gleam
Of living silver shows me where she shook   10
Her long white fingers down the shadowy brook,
That sings her song, half waking, half in dream.
What two come here to mar this heavenly tune?
A man is one: the woman bears my name,
And honour. Their hands touch! Am I still tame?
God, what a dancing spectre seems the moon!

— 40 —

I bade my Lady think what she might mean.
Know I my meaning, I? Can I love one,
And yet be jealous of another? None
Commits such folly. Terrible Love, I ween,
Has might, even dead, half sighing to upheave
The lightless seas of selfishness amain:
Seas that in a man's heart have no rain
To fall and still them. Peace can I achieve,
By turning to this fountain-source of woe,
This woman, who's to Love as fire to wood?   10
She breathed the violet breath of maidenhood
Against my kisses once! but I say, No!
The thing is mocked at! Helplessly afloat,

---

[12]**Forfeits**: game in which players must perform tasks, such as kissing.

[13]**Gogmagogs**: giants; see Revelation 20:8.

I know not what I do, whereto I strive,
The dread that my old love may be alive
Has seized my nursling new love by the throat.

— 41 —

How many a thing which we cast to the ground,
When others pick it up becomes a gem!
We grasp at all the wealth it is to them;
And by reflected light its worth is found.
Yet for us still 'tis nothing! and that zeal
Of false appreciation quickly fades.
This truth is little known to human shades,
How rare from their own instinct 'tis to feel!
They waste the soul with spurious desire,
That is not the ripe flame upon the bough.   10
We two have taken up a lifeless vow
To rob a living passion: dust for fire!
Madam is grave, and eyes the clock that tells
Approaching midnight. We have struck despair
Into two hearts. O, look we like a pair
Who for fresh nuptials joyfully yield all else?

— 42 —

I am to follow her. There is much grace
In woman when thus bent on martyrdom.
They think that dignity of soul may come,
Perchance, with dignity of body. Base!
But I was taken by that air of cold
And statuesque sedateness, when she said
"I'm going"; lit a taper, bowed her head,
And went, as with the stride of Pallas[14] bold.
Fleshly indifference horrible! The hands
Of Time now signal: O, she's safe from me!   10
Within those secret walls what do I see?
Where first she set the taper down she stands:
Not Pallas: Hebe[15] shamed! Thoughts black as death,
Like a stirred pool in sunshine break. Her wrists
I catch: she faltering, as she half resists,
"You love . . . ? love . . . ? love . . . ?" all on an indrawn breath.

— 43 —

Mark where the pressing wind shoots javelin-like
Its skeleton shadow on the broad-backed wave!
Here is a fitting spot to dig Love's grave;

---

[14]**Pallas**: Athena, Greek goddess of wisdom.

[15]**Hebe**: young goddess, cupbearer of the Greek gods.

Here where the ponderous breakers plunge and strike,
And dart their hissing tongues high up the sand:
In hearing of the ocean, and in sight
Of those ribbed wind-streaks running into white.
If I the death of Love had deeply planned,
I never could have made it half so sure,
As by the unblest kisses which upbraid   10
The full-waked sense; or failing that, degrade!
'Tis morning: but no morning can restore
What we have forfeited. I see no sin:
The wrong is mixed. In tragic life, God wot,
No villain need be! Passions spin the plot:
We are betrayed by what is false within.

— 44 —

They say, that Pity in Love's service dwells,
A porter at the rosy temple's gate.
I missed him going: but it is my fate
To come upon him now beside his wells;
Whereby I know that I Love's temple leave,
And that the purple doors have closed behind.
Poor soul! if, in those early days unkind,
The power to sting had been but power to grieve,
We now might with an equal spirit meet,
And not be matched like innocence and vice.   10
She for the Temple's worship has paid price,
And takes the coin of Pity as a cheat.
She sees through simulation to the bone:
What's best in her impels her to the worst:
Never, she cries, shall Pity soothe Love's thirst,
Or foul hypocrisy for truth atone!

— 45 —

It is the season of the sweet wild rose,
My Lady's emblem in the heart of me!
So golden-crownëd shines she gloriously,
And with that softest dream of blood she glows:
Mild as an evening heaven round Hesper bright!
I pluck the flower, and smell it, and revive
The time when in her eyes I stood alive.
I seem to look upon it out of Night.
Here's Madam, stepping hastily. Her whims
Bid her demand the flower, which I let drop.   10
As I proceed, I feel her sharply stop,
And crush it under heel with trembling limbs.
She joins me in a cat-like way, and talks
Of company, and even condescends
To utter laughing scandal of old friends.
These are the summer days, and these our walks.

— 46 —

At last we parley: we so strangely dumb
In such a close communion! It befell
About the sounding of the Matin-bell,[16]
And lo! her place was vacant, and the hum
Of loneliness was round me. Then I rose,
And my disordered brain did guide my foot
To that old wood where our first love-salute
Was interchanged: the source of many throes!
There did I see her, not alone. I moved
Toward her, and made proffer of my arm.   10
She took it simply, with no rude alarm;
And that disturbing shadow passed reproved.
I felt the pained speech coming, and declared
My firm belief in her, ere she could speak.
A ghastly morning came into her cheek,
While with a widening soul on me she stared.

— 47 —

We saw the swallows gathering in the sky,
And in the osier-isle we heard them noise.
We had not to look back on summer joys,
Or forward to a summer of bright dye:
But in the largeness of the evening earth
Our spirits grew as we went side by side.
The hour became her husband and my bride.
Love that had robbed us so, thus blessed our dearth!
The pilgrims of the year waxed very loud
In multitudinous chatterings, as the flood   10
Full brown came from the West, and like pale blood
Expanded to the upper crimson cloud.
Love, that had robbed us of immortal things,
This little moment mercifully gave,
Where I have seen across the twilight wave
The swan sail with her young beneath her wings.

— 48 —

Their sense is with their senses all mixed in,
Destroyed by subtleties these women are!
More brain, O Lord, more brain! or we shall mar
Utterly this fair garden we might win.
Behold! I looked for peace, and thought it near.
Our inmost hearts had opened, each to each.
We drank the pure daylight of honest speech.
Alas! that was the fatal draught, I fear.

For when of my lost Lady came the word,
This woman, O this agony of flesh!   10
Jealous devotion bade her break the mesh,
That I might seek that other like a bird.
I do adore the nobleness! despise
The act! She has gone forth, I know not where.
Will the hard world my sentience of her share?
I feel the truth; so let the world surmise.

— 49 —

He found her by the ocean's moaning verge,
Nor any wicked change in her discerned;
And she believed his old love had returned,
Which was her exultation, and her scourge.
She took his hand, and walked with him, and seemed
The wife he sought, though shadow-like and dry.
She had one terror, lest her heart should sigh,
And tell her loudly she no longer dreamed.
She dared not say, "This is my breast: look in."
But there's a strength to help the desperate weak.   10
That night he learned how silence best can speak
The awful things when Pity pleads for Sin.
About the middle of the night her call
Was heard, and he came wondering to the bed.
"Now kiss me, dear! it may be, now!" she said.
Lethe[17] had passed those lips, and he knew all.

— 50 —

Thus piteously Love closed what he begat:
The union of this ever-diverse pair!
These two were rapid falcons in a snare,
Condemned to do the flitting of the bat.
Lovers beneath the singing sky of May,
They wandered once; clear as the dew on flowers:
But they fed not on the advancing hours:
Their hearts held cravings for the buried day.
Then each applied to each that fatal knife,
Deep questioning, which probes to endless dole.   10
Ah, what a dusty answer gets the soul
When hot for certainties in this our life!—
In tragic hints here see what evermore
Moves dark as yonder midnight ocean's force,
Thundering like ramping hosts of warrior horse,
To throw that faint thin line upon the shore!

1862, 1892

---

[16]**Matin-bell:** bell for morning prayer.

[17]**Lethe:** river of oblivion in Hades; here, the poison she has drunk.

Lucifer in Starlight

On a starred night Prince Lucifer uprose.
Tired of his dark dominion swung the fiend
Above the rolling ball in cloud part screened,
Where sinners hugged their spectre of repose.
Poor prey to his hot fit of pride were those.
And now upon his western wing he leaned,
Now his huge bulk o'er Afric's sands careened,
Now the black planet shadowed Arctic snows.
Soaring through wider zones that pricked his scars
With memory of the old revolt from Awe,   10
He reached a middle height, and at the stars,
Which are the brain of heaven, he looked, and sank.
Around the ancient track marched, rank on rank,
The army of unalterable law.

                                                    1883

Dirge in Woods

A wind sways the pines,
          And below
Not a breath of wild air;
Still as the mosses that glow
On the flooring and over the lines
Of the roots here and there.
The pine-tree drops its dead;
They are quiet, as under the sea.
Overhead, overhead
Rushes life in a race,   10
As the clouds the clouds chase;
          And we go,
And we drop like the fruits of the tree,
          Even we,
          Even so.

                                              1870, 1888

MARGARET OLIPHANT

(1828–1897)

One of the most prolific writers in this anthology, Margaret Oliphant published ninety-two novels, eight collections of stories, twenty-five other books, and hundreds of articles. For most of her life she also had sole emotional and financial responsibility for her children, and sometimes for other family members too. (Most eminent Victorian women writers were unmarried, and few of the others had more than one child; men who had children generally had wives to take care of them.) She often wrote late at night and early in the morning, when everyone else was sleeping. Not surprisingly her greatest work, the *Autobiography*, is largely a meditation on the conflict between career and motherhood.

Margaret Oliphant Wilson was born in Scotland and always kept up her Scottish connections, although when she was ten the family moved to Liverpool, where her father worked as a low-paid clerk in the Customs House. They lived quietly and frugally and there is no record of Margaret ever attending school, but her well-read mother kept her provided with books. She published her first novel at twenty-one. When she was twenty-four she married her cousin Francis (Frank) Oliphant, a painter ten years older than herself who earned a living designing stained-glass windows, and they settled in London. There she tended to the household and bore six children, three of whom died in infancy, while writing novels, stories, and essays for the famous and influential *Blackwood's Edinburgh Magazine*. She was "alarmed and saddened" when another woman writer, Mary Howitt, told her that too much mental work on the part of the mother could cause the death of babies.

Frank's small workshop business failed, he fell ill with tuberculosis, and in 1859 they went south for warmer weather. He died in Rome, leaving his pregnant wife with two small children and substantial debts. She returned first to Edinburgh and then to England, and had written her way to a precarious security when her eldest child, Maggie, suddenly died while they were visiting Rome again in 1864. Even then, with only a month's break in the serialized novel that was currently appearing in *Blackwood's*, Oliphant kept on writing, and she gradually recovered her equilibrium. Generous and hospitable, with many friends although shy in company, she was usually in debt and sometimes on the brink of financial disaster, but she kept her household comfortably afloat. Eventually she settled near Eton, the leading boys' school in England, so that her two sons could attend as day students. When her elder brother lost his money and then his health, she took his son into her home and sent him to Eton too. Two nieces also became part of her family. But her sons did not live up to their early promise, and both they and her nephew died young.

Oliphant wrote biographies, literary history and criticism, reviews, and essays on almost every kind of subject; but she was best known as a novelist. The plots of her novels are generally perfunctory, but they contain sharply drawn characters and shrewd delineations of how people actually, rather than conventionally, think and feel. Stories of young love culminating (or not) in marriage—most novelists' essential stock in trade—did not much interest her, although she used them because they were popular and convenient. Much of her best fiction portrays women who never marry, husbands and wives who care little for each other, and other subjects that were common in life though rare in fiction. Her finest work includes stories of the supernatural that explore elusive shades of psychological experience.

The *Autobiography* was written over a period of many years, usually under the pressure of strong emotion. It contemplates a life that fit no conventional pattern: her literary career was what justified an autobiography, but the experiences that mattered most to her were familial and domestic. Like the life it examines, the book has no determinate shape. Oliphant's supple prose follows the flow of memory and traces the turns of the mind as it tries to account for itself. She does not begin at the beginning, and as she meditates on past and present she circles forward and back. She assumed that after her death someone would excise anything that seemed too personal for publication. As edited by her niece and cousin in 1899, the sections were arranged to form a chronological narrative, with the most painful passages omitted. The text we give here is from the 1990 edition by Elisabeth Jay, which gives the full manuscript in the order in which the parts were written.

from Autobiography

Albano, March 13 [1864][1]

I keep on always upbraiding and reproaching God. I can't help thinking of the question somebody once asked a grieving woman, Have you not yet forgiven God? I feel like that myself. So many burdens as I have, so much to do, so little help in this hard way of life, he might have left me my little band of children unbroken. By then the perfect number, and oh my firstborn, my only daughter, my Maggie. How He sows children broadcast about this world, how they swarm untaught, uncared for by the score in these Italian villages, living in beggary and wretchedness. Oh my Lord why didst thou grudge to me the one blossom of womankind that I thought my own. In the days of Job when affliction was considered a direct punishment for sin and in later days when people had taken up the idea, I know not on what foundation that it was the faithful, the righteous who were tried with unceasing troubles, it must have been easier to accept the judgements of God—but what can one say? I am neither better nor worse than my brother Frank who has never known a trouble in his family—I am neither better nor worse than my dear friend who is so much happier, so much more blessed than I, but I am smitten and they are spared—why is it?—God has put upon me a great many things to do—Frank left me *not* only with my children to work for, but with many encumbrances to clear off—and

W.[2] is entirely dependent both for his living and for such guidance as is possible upon me—I have been wilful and extravagant in many things but I have not shrunk from any of my duties—I have faced the burden and borne it and never tried to put off any part of it upon the shoulders of others—God help me—does this make me think that I had a right to demand from him that divine cordial of happiness which I have been enjoying for these years past, but which now he has deprived me of? If I feel so is that not enough to show how needful was the blow—but God is not like man—He sees our foolishness—he pities us as a father his children—so must I come round again to the one misused unfailing answer—God must ever have a reason—The reason must have been sufficient since it pleased Him.

I was reading of Charlotte Brontë[3] the other day, and could not help comparing myself with the picture more or less as I read. I don't suppose my powers are equal to hers—my work to myself looks perfectly pale and colourless beside hers—but yet I have had far more experience and, I think, a fuller conception of life. I have learned to take perhaps more a man's view of mortal affairs,—to feel that the love between men and women, the marrying and giving in marriage, occupy in fact so small a portion of either existence or thought.

---

[1] **Albano:** town near Rome. Oliphant's daughter Maggie had died in Rome on January 27, 1864, aged 10.

[2] **W.:** her brother Willie, an alcoholic whom she supported until his death in 1885. The **Frank** who left her (by dying) was her husband.

[3] See Elizabeth Gaskell's 1857 biography of **Charlotte Brontë** (1816-1855) page 524.

When I die I know what people will say of me: they will give me credit for courage (which I almost think is not courage but insensibility), and for honesty and honourable dealing; they will say I did my duty with a kind of steadiness, not knowing how I have rebelled and groaned under the rod. Scarcely anybody who cares to speculate further will know what to say of my working power and my own conception of it; for, except one or two, even my friends will scarcely believe how little possessed I am with any thought of it all,—how little credit I feel due to me, how accidental most things have been, and how entirely a matter of daily labour, congenial work, sometimes now and then the expression of my own heart, almost always the work most pleasant to me, this has been. I wonder if God were to try me with the loss of this gift, such as it is, whether I should feel it much? If I could live otherwise I do not think I should. If I could move about the house, and serve my children with my own hands, I know I should be happier. But this is vain talking; only I know very well that for years past neither praise nor blame has quickened my pulse ten beats that I am aware of. This insensibility saves me some pain, but it must also lose me a great deal of pleasure.

Capri.[4]

I have not written anything for several weeks that I could help writing—Letters have come to be a pain and trouble to me—I wrote almost eagerly at first because the utterance was something like crying; it relieved me and exhausted me and exhaustion is a great blessing when trouble is great. I even went so far as to write to Mr. Maurice[5] who had sent me some words of kindness, asking him if he knew any explanation of this terrible enigma God had given me to read—a vain question to ask of anyone. He writes to me as they all write to me—and failing of anything else, tells me that he thinks it is my work in the world to tell truths which are not likely to be welcome to my contemporaries and that this is a baptism of fire—this is the last desperate shift of human consolation. It is kindly as well as solemnly meant—meant to comfort me and stimulate me and warm me. What can anyone say to me—I know it is vain to accept any explanation, any light upon this darkness. Nobody on earth can tell me any more than I can tell myself, though I ask night and day why God has bereaved my life. He has done so that is all—and what I have to do is to take up my cross

and endure—as for teaching anybody God knows I have nothing to teach—I may put the long musings of my agony into words, but Tennyson has done it already far better than I can[6]—and how can I who sit in darkness show any light to my neighbours. And then they say God will give me compensation. Thus people speak in their perplexity and sympathy, not knowing what to say. . . . But now comes in the question which is between God and me—What He demands of me is that I should trust to Him entirely for her welfare, and though my heart is breaking I will, I will. For it is all so strange. She was my compensation for the solitude of my life. My boys, God bless them, if they are spared must go away from me, must leave me. My daughter would have been at least for all the sweet years of her youth my constant companion by night and day. Now in this innermost chamber of the heart which no man except a husband can enter and he but a little, I am alone always, alone in the world for ever. Help me, Oh help me Lord. I am a poor helpless woman without any strength and thou hast snatched away the props on which I leant. Stand by me and grant me a little patience till I die. . . .

Windsor,[7] *1st February* 1885.
Twenty-one years have passed since I wrote what is on the opposite page. I have just been reading it all with tears; sorry, very sorry for that poor soul who has lived through so much since. Twenty-one years is a little lifetime. It is curious to think that I was not very young, nearly thirty-six, at that time, and that I am not very old, nearly fifty-seven, now. Life though it is short, is very long, and contains so much. And one does not, to one's consciousness, change as one's outward appearance and capabilities do. Doesn't Mrs Somerville[8] say that, so far from feeling old, she was not always quite certain (up in the seventies) whether she was quite grown up! I entirely understand the feeling, though I have had enough, one would think, to make one feel old. Since the time when that most unexpected, most terrible blow overtook me in Rome—where her father had died four years before—I have had trials which, I say it with full knowledge of all the ways of mental suffering, have been harder than sorrow. I have lived a laborious life, incessant work, incessant anxiety, and in the last nine years or so pangs of disappointment and misery beyond description,

---

[4]**Capri**: island near Naples.

[5]Frederick Denison **Maurice** (1805–1872): clergyman, writer, Christian Socialist.

[6]See **Tennyson**, *In Memoriam.*

[7]**Windsor**: town on the Thames across from Eton College, site of Windsor Castle, the chief royal residence.

[8]Mary **Somerville**: see page 42.

anguish that has no comfort in it, nor even the feeling that God's hand is in it, for though he permits it alas, yet He is not the creator of wrong doing.[9] Nor can I say, "It is thy will", as I did in other calamities. And yet so strange, so capricious is this human being, that I would not say I have had an unhappy life. I have said this to one or two friends who know faintly without details what I have had to go through, and astonished them.... Sometimes I am miserable—always there is in me the sense that I may have active cause to be so at any moment—always the gnawing pangs of anxiety, and deep, deep dissatisfaction beyond words, and the sense of helplessness, which of itself is despair. And yet there are times when my heart jumps up in the old unreasonable way, and I am,—yes, happy—though the word seems so inappropriate—without any cause for it, with so many causes the other way. I wonder whether this is want of feeling, or mere temperament and elasticity, or if it is a special compensation—"Werena my heart licht I wa' deed"[10]—Grizel Hume must have had the same.

I have been tempted to begin writing by George Eliot's life[11]—with that curious kind of self-compassion which one cannot get clear of. I wonder if I am a little envious of her? I always avoid considering formally what my own mind is worth. I have never had any theory on the subject. I have written because it gave me pleasure, because it came natural to me, because it was like talking or breathing, besides the big fact that it was necessary for me to work for my children. That, however, was not the first motive, so that when I laugh inquiries off and say that it is my trade, I do it only by way of eluding the question which I have neither time nor wish to enter into. Anthony Trollope's talk about the characters[12] in his books astonished me beyond measure, and I am totally incapable of talking about anything I have ever done in that way. As he was a thoroughly sensible genuine man, I suppose he was quite sincere in what he says of them,—or was it that he was driven into a fashion of self-explanation which belongs to the time, and which I am following now though in another way? I feel that my care-lessness of asserting my claim is very much against me with everybody. It is so natural to think that if the workman himself is indifferent about his work, there can't be much in it that is worth thinking about. I am not indifferent, yet I should rather like to forget it all, to wipe out all the books, to silence those compliments about my industry, &c., which I always turn off with a laugh. I suppose this is really pride, with a mixture of Scotch shyness, and a good deal of that uncomprehended, unexplainable feeling which made Mrs Carlyle[13] reply with a jibe, which meant only a whimsical impulse to take the side of opposition, and the strong Scotch sense of the absurdity of a chorus of praise, but which looks so often like detraction and bitterness, and has now definitely been accepted as such by the public in general. I don't find words to express it adequately, but I feel it strenuously in my own case. When people comment upon the number of books I have written, and I say that I am so far from being proud of that fact that I should like at least half of them forgotten, they stare—and yet it is quite true; and even here I could no more go solemnly into them, and tell why I had done this or that, than I could fly. They are my work, which I like in the doing, which is my natural way of occupying myself, which are never so good as I meant them to be. And when I have said that, I have said all that it is in me to say.

I don't quite know why I should put this all down. I suppose because George Eliot's life has, as I said above, stirred me up to an involuntary confession. How I have been handicapped in life! Should I have done better if I had been kept, like her, in a mental greenhouse and taken care of? This is one of the things it is perfectly impossible to tell. In all likelihood our minds and our circumstances are so arranged that, after all, the possible way is the way that is best; yet it is a little hard sometimes not to feel with Browning's Andrea,[14] that the men who have no wives, who have given themselves up to their art, have had an almost unfair advantage over us who have been given perhaps more than one Lucrezia to take care of. And to feel with him that perhaps in the after-life four square walls in the New Jerusalem may be given for another trial! I used to be intensely impressed in the Laurence Oliphants[15] with that curious

[9]The **wrong doing** that caused her **disappointment and misery** was that of her elder son, Cyril (1856–1890), who had entered Oxford 9 years before.

[10]"**Werena . . . deed**": Were my heart not light I would die; from the Scottish poet Lady **Grizel Hume** Baillie (1665–1746).

[11]Oliphant reviewed John Cross's 1885 **life** of **George Eliot** for *Blackwood's*.

[12]**Anthony Trollope** (1815–1882) asserts in *Autobiography* (1883) that his **characters** seem to him fully alive.

[13]Jane Welsh **Carlyle** (1801–1866): wife of Thomas Carlyle and, like Oliphant's mother, a sharp-witted Scotswoman; Oliphant's friend for many years.

[14]**Browning's Andrea**: see "Andrea del Sarto," page 571.

[15]**Laurence Oliphant** (1829–1888): novelist, journalist, and mystic, not related to Margaret.

freedom from human ties which I have never known; and that they felt it possible to make up their minds to do what was best, without any sort of *arrière pensée*,[16] without having to consider whether they could or not. Curious freedom! I have never known what it was. I have always had to think of other people, and to plan everything—for my own pleasure, it is true, very often, but always in subjection to the necessity which bound me to them. On the whole, I have had a great deal of my own way, and have insisted upon getting what I wished, but only at the cost of infinite labour, and of carrying a whole little world with me wherever I moved. I have not been able to rest, to please myself, to take the pleasures that have come in my way, but have always been forced to go on without a pause. When my poor brother's family fell upon my hands,[17] and especially when there was question of Frank's education, I remember that I said to myself, having then perhaps a little stirring of ambition, that I must make up my mind to think no more of that, and that to bring up the boys for the service of God was better than to write a fine novel, supposing even that it was in me to do so. Alas! the work has been done; the education is over; my good Frank, my steady, good boy, is dead—and the rest—. It seemed rather a fine thing to make that resolution (though in reality I had no choice); but now I think that if I had taken the other way, which seemed the less noble, it might have been better for all of us. I might have done better work. I should in all probability have earned nearly as much for half the production had I done less; and I might have had the satisfaction of knowing that there was something laid up for them and for my old age; while they[18] might have learned habits of work which now seem beyond recall. Who can tell? I did with much labour what I thought the best, and there is only a might have been on the other side.

In this my resolution which I did make, I was after all, only following my instincts, it being in reality easier to me to keep on with a flowing sail, to keep my household and make a number of people comfortable at the cost of incessant work, and an occasional great crisis of anxiety, than to live the self-restrained life which the greater artist imposes upon himself.

What casuists we are on our own behalf!—this is altogether self-defence. And I know I am giving myself the air

of being *au fond*[19] a finer sort of character than the others. I may as well take the little satisfaction to myself, for nobody will give it to me. No one even will mention me in the same breath with George Eliot. And that is just. It is a little justification to myself to think how much better off she was,—no trouble in all her life as far as appears, but the natural one of her father's death—and perhaps coolnesses with her brothers and sisters, though that is not said. And though her marriage,[20] so called, is not one that most of us would have ventured on, still it seems to have secured her a caretaker and worshipper unrivalled—little nasty body though he looked, and hideous in nastiness as his previous story was.

I think she must have been a dull woman with a great genius distinct from herself, something like the gift of the old prophets, which they sometimes exercised with only a dim sort of perception what it meant. But this is a thing to be said only with bated breath, and perhaps further thought on the subject may change my mind soon. She took herself with tremendous seriousness, that is evident, and was always on duty, never relaxing, her letters ponderous beyond description—and those to the Hennell[21] party giving one the idea of a mutual improvement society for the exchange of essays.

Let me be done with this—I wonder if I will ever have time to put a few autobiographical bits down before I die. I am in very little danger of having my life written. No one belonging to me has energy enough to do it, or even to gather the fragments for some one else and that is all the better in this point of view—for what could be said of me? George Eliot and George Sand[22] make me half inclined to cry over my poor little unappreciated self—"Many love me (*i.e.*, in a sort of a way), but by none am I enough beloved." These two bigger women did things which I have never felt the least temptation to do—but how very much enjoyment they seem to have got out of their life, how much more praise and homage and honour! I would not buy their fame with their disadvantages, but I do feel very small, very obscure, beside them, rather a failure all round, never securing

---

[16]*arrière pensée*: mental reservation.

[17]Her **brother** Frank lost his money in 1868; she sent his son **Frank,** who was to die in India in 1879, to Eton.

[18]**they**: her sons.

[19]*au fond*: at bottom.

[20]**marriage**: George Eliot and George Henry Lewes (1817–1878) lived together as husband and wife until his death; his wife was still living and had borne two children by another man.

[21]Eliot had several friends in the **Hennell** family, including Sara Hennell (1812–1899), Caroline Hennell Bray (1814–1905), and Charles Hennell (1809–1850). See page 62.

[22]**George Sand** (1804–1876): famous and prolific French woman novelist.

any strong affection, and throughout my life, though I have had all the usual experiences of woman, never impressing anybody,—what a droll little complaint!—why should I? I acknowledge frankly that there is nothing in me—a fat, little, commonplace woman, rather tongue-tied—to impress any one; and yet there is a sort of whimsical injury in it which makes me sorry for myself.

Feb. 8th.

Here, then, for a little try at the autobiography. I ought to be doing some work, getting on a little in advance for to-morrow, which gives a special zest to doing nothing:[23] to doing what has no need to be done—and Sunday evenings have always been a time to *fantasticare*, to do what one pleased; and I have dropped out of the letter I used to do on these occasions, having—which, by the way, is a little sad when one comes to think of it—no one to write to, of anything that is beneath the surface. Curious! I had scarcely realised it before. Now for a beginning.

I remember nothing of Wallyford, where I was born, but opened my eyes to life, so far as I remember, in the village of Lasswade, where we lived in a little house, I think, on the road to Dalkeith. I recollect the wintry road ending to my consciousness in a slight ascent with big ash-trees forming a sort of arch; underneath which I fancy was a toll-bar, the way into the world appropriately barred by that turnpike. But no, that was not the way into the world; for the world was Edinburgh, the coach for which, I am almost sure, went the other way through the village and over the bridge to the left hand, starting from somewhere close to Mr Todd the baker's shop, of which I have a faint and kind recollection. It was by that way that Frank came home on Saturday nights to spend Sunday at home, walking out from Edinburgh (about six miles) to walk in again on Monday in the dark winter mornings. I recollect nothing about the summer mornings when he set out on that walk, but remember vividly like a picture the Monday mornings in winter; the fire burning cheerfully and candles on the breakfast-table, all dark but with a subtle sense of morning, though it seemed a kind of dissipation to be up so long before the day. I can see myself, a small creature seated on a stool by the fire, toasting a cake of dough which was brought for me by the baker with the prematurely early rolls, which were for Frank. (This dough was the special feature of the morning to me, and I suppose I had it only on these occasions.)

And my mother, who never seemed to sit down in the strange, little, warm, bright picture, but to hover about the table pouring out tea, supplying everything he wanted to her boy (how proud, how fond of him!—her eyes liquid and bright with love as she hovered about); and Frank, the dearest of companions so long—then long separated, almost alienated, brought back again at the end to my care to linger out his life here, and die old and suffering and deteriorated, he and I so far apart. How bright he was then, how good always to me, how fond of his little sister!—impatient by moments, good always. And he was a kind of god to me—my Frank, as I always called him. I remember once weeping bitterly over a man singing in the street, a buttoned-up, shabby-genteel man, whom, on being questioned why I cried, I acknowledged I thought like my Frank. That was when he was absent, and my mother's anxiety reflected in a child's mind went, I suppose, the length of fancying that Frank too might have to sing in the street. (He would have come off very badly in that case, for he did not know one tune from another, much less could he sing a note!) How well I recollect the appearance of the man in his close-buttoned black coat, with his dismal song, and the acute anguish of the thought that Frank might have come to that for anything I knew. Frank, however, never gave very much anxiety; it was Willie, poor Willie, who was our sore and constant trouble—Willie, who lives still in Rome, as he has done for the last two-or three-and-twenty years—nearly a quarter of a century—among strangers who are kind to him, wanting nothing, I hope, yet also having outlived everything. I shrank from going to see him when I was in Italy, which was wrong; but how can I return to Rome, and how could he have come to me?—poor Willie! the handsomest, brightest of us all, with eyes that ran over with fun and laughter—and the hair which we used to say he had to poll, like Absalom[24] so many times a-year. Alas!

What I recollect in Lasswade besides the Monday morning aforesaid is not much. I remember standing at the smithy with brother Willie, on some occasion when the big boy was very unwillingly charged with his little sister to take somewhere or other,—standing in the dark, wondering at the sparks as they flew up and the dark figures of the smith and his men; and I remember playing on the road opposite the house, where there was a low wall over which the Esk and the country beyond could be seen (I think), playing with two little kittens, who were called Lord Brougham and Lord Grey. It must have been immediately after the passing

---

[23]**doing nothing:** This is exactly what Sir Walter says in his *Diary*, only published in 1890, so I was like him in this without knowing it. [Oliphant's note] *fantasticare:* to fancy, to muse.

[24]**poll:** cut short. **Absalom:** see 2 Samuel 14:25–26.

of the Reform Bill,[25] and I suppose this was why the kittens bore such names. We were all tremendously political and Radical, my mother especially and Frank. Likewise I recollect with the most vivid clearness on what must have been a warm still summer day, lying on my back in the grass, the little blue speedwells in which are very distinct before me, and looking up into the sky. The depths of it, the blueness of it, the way in which it seemed to move and fly and avoid the gaze which could not penetrate beyond that profound unfathomable blue,—the bliss of lying there doing nothing, trying to look into it, growing giddy with the effort, with a sort of vague realisation of the soft swaying of the world in space! I feel the giddiness in my brain still, and the happiness, as if I had been the first discoverer of that wonderful sky. All my little recollections are like pictures to which the meaning, naturally, is put long afterwards. I did not know the world moved or anything about it, being under six at most; but I can feel the sensation of the small head trying to fix that great universe, and in the effort growing dizzy and going round. . . .

[1891]

When I look back on my life, among the happy moments which I can recollect is one which is so curiously common and homely, with nothing in it, that it is strange even to record such a recollection, and yet it embodied more happiness to me than almost any real occasion as might be supposed for happiness. It was the moment after dinner when I used to run up-stairs to see that all was well in the nursery, and then to turn into my room on my way down again to wash my hands, as I had a way of doing before I took up my evening work, which was generally needlework, something to make for the children. My bedroom had three windows in it, one looking out upon the gardens I have mentioned, the other two into the road. It was light enough with the lamp-light outside for all I wanted. I can see it now, the glimmer of the outside lights, the room dark, the faint reflection in the glasses, and my heart full of joy and peace—for what?—for nothing—that there was no harm anywhere, the children well above stairs and their father below. I had few of the pleasures of society, no gaiety at all. I was eight-and-twenty, going down-stairs as light as a feather, to the little frock I was making. My husband also gone back for an hour or two after dinner to his work, and well—and the bairns well. I can feel now the sensation of that sweet calm and ease and peace.

I have always said it is in these unconsidered moments that happiness is—not in things or events that may be

supposed to cause it. How clear it is over these more than thirty years! . . .

[1894]

Into the midst of this half-childish gaiety there came a very sudden and alarming interruption. My brother Frank had married at the same time as I myself did, and had lived a very humdrum but happyish life with a wife who suited him, and had now four children—a boy and three girls. He had been in rather delicate health for a year or two, and had fallen into rather a nervous condition, his hand shaking very much so that it was difficult for him to write, though he still could do his work. For this reason I heard from them rarely, as Jeanie, his wife, was a bad correspondent too. One morning very suddenly, and in the most painful and disagreeable way, I heard that he had got into great trouble about money, and was, in fact, a ruined man. It was the thunderbolt out of the clear sky, which is always so tremendous. I spent a day of misery, expecting him to come to me, not knowing what to expect, and fearing all sorts of things. A day or two after I went to look for him, and found him absent and his wife in great trouble. His health, from what I now heard, was altogether shattered; and it was that as much as anything else which had brought his affairs into the most hopeless muddle, from which there seemed no escape. They had not very much money at any time, but what they had had somehow slipped through his fingers. His wife and I did everything we could, but that was very little. He was a man without an expensive taste, the most innocent, the most domestic of men, but what he had had always slipped through his fingers, as I well knew. Poor dear Frank! how well I remembered the use he made of one of my mother's Scotch proverbs to justify some new small expense following a bigger one which he would allow to be imprudent. "Well," he would say, half-coaxing, half-apologetic, "what's the use of eating the coo and worrying[26] on her tail?" Alas! he had choked on the tail this time without remedy, and the only thing to be done was to wind up the affairs as well as was possible, and to further the little family, whom he could not live without, after him, which was what we did accordingly, with a prompt action which was some relief to our heavy hearts. We neither of us had a word of blame on our lips or a thought of anger in our hearts. Frank and Nelly, the two elder children, came to me, and Jeanie with her two little girls (my two girls this many a year, and now the only comfort of my life) joined her husband in France. It was a terrible break in life, and affected me in many ways permanently; but after the shock of seeing that chasm opening at our feet, and all their life shattered to pieces, everything quieted down

---

[25]**Lord Brougham** (1778–1868), **Lord Grey** (1764–1845): leading advocates of the **Reform Bill** of 1832.

[26]**coo:** cow. **worrying:** choking.

again. The children were well. Oh, magic of life that made everything go smooth! they had taken no harm. They had their lives before them, and unbounded possibilities of making everything right. I am not sure that I had not a sort of secret satisfaction in getting Frank, my nephew, into my hands, thinking, with that complacency with which we always look at our own doings, that I could now train him for something better than they had thought of. This was in 1868. My Cyril was twelve and at Eton, having his room at his tutor's, and living precisely like other Eton boys, though coming home to sleep, which was one of the greatest happinesses in my life. Frank was fourteen, a big strong boy. I planned to send him to Eton too, but coming home for his meals, which was much less expensive, as I could not afford the other for him, and it answered very well. He was always the best of boys, manful, and a steady worker. Cyril had begun to be by this time noted as one of the cleverest boys, far on for his age, and promising everything, besides the brightest, wittiest, most sparkling little fellow, as he always was. I used to make it my boast that both my boys received Frank as a true brother, and never would have allowed me, had I wished it, to give them any pleasure or advantage which he did not share. Nelly after a while went to her mother's sister, Mrs Sime, and so we all settled down. If Denny[27] publishes this, or any part of it, she will, of course, or any one else who may have the charge of it, cut out any of these details she pleases. It is not likely that such family details would be of interest to the public.

And yet, as a matter of fact, it is exactly those family details that are interesting,—the human story in all its chapters. I have often said, however, that none of us with any of the strong sense of family credit which used to be so general, but is not so, I think, now, could ever really tell what were perhaps the best and most creditable things in our own life, since by the strange fate which attends us human creatures, what is most creditable to one is often least creditable to another. These things steal out; they are divined in most cases, and then forgotten. Therefore all can never be told of any family story, except at the cost of family honour, and that pride which is the most pardonable of all pride, the determination to keep unsullied a family name. This catastrophe was tremendous in appearance, and yet was more or less a good thing for the children, whose prospects seemed to be utterly ruined,—not for the parents. Poor Jeanie—not strong enough, I suppose, to bear what fell upon her, as she had not been strong enough to do anything to prevent it—died most unexpectedly in her sleep, in a mild attack of fever which excited no

alarm. My brother had been glad to get an appointment among the employees of a railway that was being made by the Walkers,[28] of all places in the world, in Hungary, and went there with his wife and the little girls. I forget how long they were there,—only a very short time. The shock of their downfall was over, they were more or less happy to be together, and Frank and Nelly were happy enough here. We had returned to all our little gaieties again, our theatricals,—our boating, and the rest,—without much thought on my part, I fear, of the additional responsibility I had upon me of another boy to educate and set out in the world. We were all assembled, a merry party enough, one summer evening, after an afternoon on the river, at a late meal,—a sort of supper,—when a telegram was put into my hand. I remember the look of the long table and all the bright faces round it, the pretty summer dishes, salad, and pink salmon, and ornamented sweet things, and many flowers, the men and boys in their flannels, the girls in their light summer dresses,—everything light and bright. I have often said that it was the only telegram I ever received without a certain tremor of anxiety. Captain Gun,[29] who was there, had been uncertain of his coming on this particular day, and a good many telegrams on that subject had been passing between us. I held the thing in my hand and looked across at him, and said, "This time it cannot be from you." Then I opened it with the laugh in my mouth, and this is what I read: "Jeanie is dead, and I am in despair." It was like a scene in a tragedy. They all saw the change in my face, but I dreaded to say anything, for there was her son sitting by, my good Frank, as gay as possible. He was only about fifteen, or perhaps sixteen. We managed to keep it from him till next morning, not to give him that shock in the midst of his pleasure; and somehow the supper got completed without any one knowing what had happened.

A very short time after my poor brother came home with the two little white-faced, forlorn children, with their big eyes. I never thought but that it must kill him, but it did not; though, when I met them at Victoria,[30] I thought I never should have got him safely back, even to Windsor. He was completely shattered, like a man in a palsy, for a time scarcely able to stand or to speak, but not so overwhelmed with grief as I expected. Grief is the strangest thing, or rather it is very wonderful in how many different ways people take those blows, which from outside seem as if they must be final. Especially is it so in the closest of human connections, that

---

[27]**Denny:** Oliphant's niece Janet Mary Oliphant Wilson, whom she raised after her brother Frank's death.

[28]**Walkers:** Thomas and Charles Walker, railway contractors, the former an eminent engineer.

[29]**Captain Gun:** an officer stationed nearby.

[30]**Victoria:** London railway station.

between man and wife. People who have seemed to be all the world to each other are parted so, and the survivor, who is for the moment as my poor brother said "in despair," shows the most robust power of bearing it, and is so soon himself or herself again, that one, confounded and half-ashamed, feels that one is half-ridiculous to have expected anything different. Frank, poor fellow, had got over his sorrow on the long journey. He came to me like a child glad to get home, not much disturbed about anything that could happen. He lived for about six years after, for a great part of the time in tolerable comfort, but, so far as work was concerned, was capable of no more. The shaking of his hand was never cured, nor even sufficiently improved to make writing of any kind possible. He settled down to a kind of quiet life, read his newspaper, took his walk, sat in his easy-chair in the dining-room or in his own room for the rest of the day, was pleased with Frank's progress and with Nelly's love for reading, and with his little girls, and so got through his life, I think, not unhappily. But he and I, who had been so much to each other once, were nothing to each other now. I sometimes thought he looked at me as a kind of stepmother to his children, and we no longer thought alike on almost any subject: he had drifted one way and I another. He did not even take very much interest in me, and I fear he often irritated me. Poor Frank! it was sometimes a great trial, and I often wonder how the life went on, on the whole, so well as it did. He entertained delusive hopes for a time of going back and of being able to do something; but they were evidently from the first delusions and nothing more, and it did not hurt him so much as might have been thought when they vanished,—he had too little strength to feel it, I suppose.

Of course I had to face a prospect considerably changed by this great addition to my family. I had been obliged to work pretty hard before to meet all the too great expenses of the house. Now four people were added to it, very small two of them, but the others not inexpensive members of the house. I remember making a kind of pretence to myself that I had to think it over, to make a great decision, to give up what hopes I might have had of doing now my very best, and to set myself steadily to make as much money as I could, and do the best I could for the three boys. I think that in some pages of my old book I have put this down with a little half-sincere attempt at a heroical attitude. I don't think, however, that there was any reality in it. I never did nor could, of course, hesitate for a moment as to what had to be done. It had to be done, and that was enough, and there is no doubt that it was much more congenial to me to drive on and keep everything going, with a certain scorn of the increased work, and metaphorical toss of my head, as if it mattered! than it ever would have been to

labour with an artist's fervour and concentration to produce a masterpiece. One can't be two things or serve two masters. Which was God and which was mammon[31] in that individual case it would be hard to say, perhaps; for once in a way mammon, meaning the money which fed my flock, was in a kind of a poor way God, so far as the necessities of that crisis went. And the wonder was that we did it, I can't tell how, economising, I fear, very little, never knowing quite at the beginning of the year how the ends would come together at Christmas, always with troublesome debts and forestalling of money earned, so that I had generally eaten up the price of a book before it was printed, but always—thank God for it!—so far successfully that, though always owing somebody, I never owed anybody to any unreasonable amount or for any unreasonable extent of time, but managed to pay everything and do everything, to stint nothing, to give them all that was happy and pleasant and of good report[32] through all those dear and blessed boyish years. I confess that it was not done in the noblest way, with those strong efforts of self-control and economy which some people can exercise. I could not do that, or at least did not, but I could work. And I did work, joyfully, with pleasure in it and in my life, sometimes with awful moments when I did not know how I should ever pass some dreadful corner, where the way seemed to end and the rocks to close in: but the corner was always rounded, the road opened up again.

I recollect one of these moments especially, I forget the date: I always do forget dates, but the circumstances were these. We were a family of eight, children included, two boys at Eton, almost always guests in the house,—every kind of thing (in our modest way) going on, small dinner-parties, and a number of mild amusements, when it so happened that I came to a pause and found that every channel was closed and no place for any important work. I had always a lightly flowing stream of magazine articles, &c., and refused no work that was offered to me; but the course of life could not have been carried on on these, and a large sum was wanted at brief intervals to clear the way. I had, I think, a novel written, but did not know where I should find a place for it. Literary business arrangements were not organised then as now—there was no such thing as a literary agent. Serials in magazines were published in much less number, magazines themselves being not half so many (and a good thing too!). The consequence was that I seemed to be at a dead standstill. It was like nothing but what I have

---

[31]**mammon:** demon of avarice; see Matthew 6:24.

[32]See Philippians 4:8.

already said,—a mountainous road making a sharp turn round a corner, when it seems to disappear altogether, as if it ended there in the closing in of the cliffs. I was miserably anxious, not knowing where to turn or what to do, hoping every morning would bring me some proposal, waiting upon God, if I may use the word (I did the thing with the most complete faith,—what could I else?), for the opening up of that closed way. One evening I got a letter from a man whose name I did not know, asking if he could come to see me about a business matter. I forget whether he mentioned the name of the "Graphic," then just established,—I think not; at all events there was nothing in the letter to make me think it of any importance. I replied, however (I didn't always reply so quickly), appointing the second day after to receive him. I had decided to go to London next day to see if I could persuade some one to take my novel and give a good price for it. I think it was to Mr George Smith[33] I went, who was very kind and gracious, as was his wont, but would have nothing to say to me. I fancy I went somewhere else, but I had no success. I recollect coming home in a kind of despair, and being met at the door when it was opened to me by the murmur of the merry house, the cheerful voices, the overflowing home,—every corner full and warm as if it had a steady income and secure revenue at its back. My brother, I remember, who I suppose had seen some cloud on my face before I left, came forward to meet me with some trivial question, hoping I had not felt cold or taken cold or something, which in the state of despair in which I was had a sort of exasperating effect upon me; but they were all dispersing over the house to get ready for dinner, and I escaped further notice. No one thought anything more than that I was dull or cross for the rest of the evening. I used to work very late then, always till two in the morning (it is past three at this moment, 18th, nay, 19th April 1895, but this is no longer usual with me). I can't remember whether I worked that night, but I think it was one of the darkest nights (oh, no, no, that I should say so! they were all safe and well), at least a very dreadful moment, and I could not think what I should do.

Next morning came my visitor. He came from the "Graphic": he wanted a story, I think the first they had had. He wanted it very soon, the first instalments within a week or two; and after a little talk and negotiation, he came to the conclusion that they would give me £1300. The road did run round that corner after all. Our Father in heaven had

settled it all the time for the children; there had never been any doubt. I was absolutely without hope or help. I did not know where to turn, and here, in a moment, all was clear again—the road free in the sunshine, the cloud in a moment rolled away. . . .

With that year[34] began a new life, one of which I cannot speak much. That was the burden and heat of the day: my anxieties were sometimes almost more than I could bear. I had gone through many trials, as I thought, and God knows many of them had been hard enough, but then I knew to the depths of my heart what the yoke was and how heavy. Many times I have woke in the morning feeling in myself that image of Shelley's "Prometheus," which in my youth I had vexed my husband by not appreciating, except in what seemed to me the picture rather than the poem, the man chained on the rock, with the vultures swooping down upon him. Their cruel beaks I seemed to feel in my heart the moment I awoke. Ah me, alas! pain ever, for ever,[35] God alone knows what was the anguish of these years. And yet now I think of *ces beaux jours quand j'étais si malheureuse*, the moments of relief were so great and so sweet that they seemed compensation for the pain,—I remembered no more the anguish. Lately in my many sad musings it has been brought very clearly before my mind how often all the horrible tension, the dread, the anxiety which there are no words strong enough to describe,—which devoured me, but which I had to conceal often behind a smiling face,—would yield in a moment, in the twinkling of an eye, at the sound of a voice, at the first look, into an ineffable ease and the overwhelming happiness of relief from pain, which is, I think, our highest human sensation, higher and more exquisite than any positive enjoyment in this world. It used to sweep over me like a wave, sometimes when I opened a door, sometimes in a letter,—in all simple ways. I cannot explain, but if this should ever come to the eye of any woman in the passion and agony of motherhood, she will more or less understand. I was thinking lately, or rather, as sometimes happens, there was suddenly presented to my mind, like a suggestion from some one else, the recollection of these ineffable happinesses, and it seemed to me that it meant that which would be when one pushed through that last door and was met—oh, by what, by whom?—by instant relief. The wave of sudden ease and warmth and peace and joy. I

---

[33]**George Smith** (1824–1901): Smith & Elder published many major Victorian writers.

[34]**that year:** 1875.

[35]**Ah me . . . for ever:** P.B. Shelley, *Prometheus Unbound* (1820) 24. Prometheus is **chained** on a **rock;** **vultures** gnaw at his liver. *ces beaux jours . . . malheureuse:* those fine days when I was so unhappy.

felt, to tell the truth, that it was one of them who brought that to my mind, and I said to myself, "I will not want any explanation, I will not ask any question,—the first touch, the first look, will be enough, as of old, yet better than of old."

I do injustice to those whom I love above all things by speaking thus, and yet what can I say? My dearest, bright, delightful boy[36] missed somehow his footing, how can I tell how? I often think that I had to do with it, as well as what people call inherited tendencies, and, alas! the perversity of youth, which he never outgrew. He had done everything too easily in the beginning of his boyish career, by natural impulse and that kind of genius which is so often deceptive in youth, and when he came to that stage in which hard work was necessary against the competition of the hard working, he could not believe how much more effort was necessary. Notwithstanding all distractions he took a second-class at Oxford,—a great disappointment, yet not disgraceful after all. And I will not say that, except at the first keen moment of pain, I was in any way bitterly disappointed. *Tout peut se réparer.*[37] I always felt so to the end, and perhaps he thought I took it lightly, and that it did not so much matter. Then it was one of my foolish ways to take my own work very lightly, and not to let them know how hard pressed I was sometimes, so that he never, I am sure, was convinced how serious it was in that way, and certainly never was convinced that he could not, when the moment came, right himself and recover lost way. But only the moment, God bless him! did not come till God took it in His own hands. Another theory I have thought of with many tears lately. I had another foolish way of laughing at the superior people, the people who took themselves too seriously,—the boys of pretension, and all the strong intellectualisms. This gave him, perhaps, or helped him to form, a prejudice against the good and reading men, who have so many affectations, poor boys, and led him towards those so often inferior, all inferior to himself, who had the naturalness along with the folly of youth. Why should I try to explain? He went out of the world, leaving a love-song or two behind him and the little volume of "De Musset,"[38] of which much was so well done, and yet some so badly done, and nothing more to show for his life. And I to watch it all going on day by day and year by year!

My Cecco[39] took the first steps in the same way; but, thanks be to God, righted himself and overcame—not in time enough to save his career at Oxford, but so as to be all that I had hoped,—always my very own, my dearest companion, choosing me before all others. What a companion he was, everybody who knew us knows: full of knowledge, full of humour—a most accomplished man, though to me always a boy. He did not make friends easily, and he had few; but those whom he had were very fond of him, and all our immediate surroundings looked up to him with an affectionate admiration which I cannot describe. "I don't know, but I will ask Cecco," was what we all said. He had not much more than emerged from the desert of temptation and trial, bringing balm and healing to me, when he fell ill. When his illness first was declared, it seemed to me that my misery was more than I could bear. I remember that we all went to the Holy Communion together the Sunday before we left for Pau,[40] and that as I went up to kneel at the altar I was so nearly overcome, that Cyril put his hand on my arm and gripped it almost roughly to recall me to myself. And then the whole world seemed to come back again into the sun after a time; he got so much better, and the warm summer of the Queen's Jubilee year[41] seemed to complete what Pau had begun. And he passed his examination for the British Museum, coming out first, and his life seemed now to be ordered in a safe place—in the work he loved. Alas! Then Sir Andrew Clark[42] would not pass him, but other doctors gave the best of hopes. And he did a great deal of good work, and finally went to the Library here; and we had many blinks of happiness, both in the winter on the Riviera and at home. I cannot tell what he was to me—consulting me about everything, desiring to have me with him, to walk with me and talk to me, only put out of humour when I was drawn away or occupied by other things. When he was absent he wrote to me every day. I never went out but he was there to give me his arm. I seem to feel it now—the dear, thin, but firm arm. In the last four years after Cyril was taken from us, we were nearer and nearer. I can hear myself saying "Cecco and I." It was the constant phrase. But all through he was getting weaker; and I knew it, and tried not to know.

And now here I am all alone.

I cannot write any more.

1899, 1990

---

[36]**boy:** Cyril.

[37]*Tout . . . réparer:* Everything can be redeemed.

[38]Cyril wrote a book on the French poet Alfred **de** Musset (1810–1857), published just before he died.

[39]**Cecco:** her younger son, Francis (1859–1894).

[40]**Pau:** spa in SW France.

[41]**Queen's Jubilee year:** 1887, her 50th on the throne.

[42]**Sir Andrew Clark** (1826–1893): physician. Cecco found employment at the Royal **Library,** Windsor.

CHRISTINA GEORGINA ROSSETTI

(1830–1894)

It was understood in the Rossetti household once Christina reached her teens that she was to be the poet of the family. The youngest of four talented children, she had the clearest poetic gift and calling. And the publication of her poetry was largely a family affair. An uncle had her first book privately printed (1847); her entrepreneurial brother Dante Gabriel acted as editor, illustrator, and agent for *Goblin Market* (1862) and the books of poetry that followed; her scholarly brother William in a posthumous edition of her works drew the picture of obedient piety and erotic sublimation that established her reputation as a Victorian "poetess" for much of the twentieth century. This picture was misleadingly incomplete, but it was not all wrong. It was Christina Rossetti (not her older sister, who was first a governess, later an Anglican nun) who stayed home to care for her father in the 1840s, then her brother in the 1870s, then her mother in the 1880s. After 1871 a dangerous and disfiguring thyroid condition further restricted her range of activity.

At twenty and again at thirty-five, Rossetti gave serious consideration to offers of marriage, but eventually declined on grounds of religious incompatibility. Her High Church orthodoxy formed part of a complex network of allegiances—to family, to social service (rehabilitating fallen women, extirpating child prostitution), and to her own creative inspiration. These allegiances may have constrained her choices, but such constraint also provided coherence and purpose. Self-suppression did not come easily to Rossetti, as childhood tantrums and adult episodes of nervous prostration suggest. Still, for her as for Elizabeth Barrett Browning (whom she revered) and Emily Dickinson (whom she read with keen approval in her last years), limitation seems to have made possible an intensity of writerly concentration that nineteenth-century marriage ordinarily foreclosed to women.

Nor was Rossetti's life as housebound as it might appear. The Italian intellectuals who regularly visited her expatriate father made vivid both the family legend of descent from Petrarch's Laura and her uncle John Polidori's connection with Byron and the Shelleys. The household was bilingual, and Rossetti read and composed in Italian as well as English. Around 1850 she tested her poetic voice as a sort of honorary sister to the PreRaphaelite Brotherhood, holding her own in versification contests and publishing several poems in their short-lived avant-garde journal *The Germ*. When *Goblin Market* appeared a decade later it was the PreRaphaelites' first literary success. Rossetti placed poems in leading periodicals, wrote autobiographical short fiction, and formed friendships with feminists who ran journals and a press of their own. As her books came out in the 1860s, and a collected *Poems* in 1875, reviewers ranked her high among the women poets of the day; requests arrived to anthologize her lyrics or set them to music, and she was asked to write encyclopedia articles on Italian literature. She enjoyed the acquaintance and regard of poets as diverse as Robert Browning, Jean Ingelow, Augusta Webster, and A. C. Swinburne. In later decades she published under the auspices of the Society for the Promotion of Christian Knowledge half a dozen books whose strictly devotional character, as our final excerpts show, embraced a fresh responsiveness to nature and Scripture.

Freshness of response and powerful creativity within chosen limits steadfastly observed: the temper of Rossetti's art matched that of her life. Her best-known poem, "Goblin Market," is a teasingly enigmatic story of forbidden fruit that takes the transgression and reinstatement of rules as its narrative theme and also as its formal artistic agenda. Victorian readers were enchanted by the apparent childishness of its fairy-tale narrative, deftly irregular verse, and reassuring moral; later readers have been fascinated by the way its suffused eroticism undermines the conventional values it seems to uphold. Rossetti never wrote anything like it again—nor has anyone else—yet the interplay that "Goblin Market" stages between impatience and restraint energizes much of her best work. The nursery rhymes of *Sing-Song* mingle a child's wonder with mischievous riddlings that reflect a bilingual poet's feeling for the mystery of words. "Winter: My Secret" gives nothing away except the open secret of playfulness itself: the more the lines flirt with a disclosure they never make, the firmer the reader's awareness of contents—possibly dangerous contents—stored under pressure.

Rossetti's lyricism renders this sense of hard-won composure supremely well, usually with the aim of clarifying the emotional obscurities that oppression and sentimentality have created and maintained. Many of her poems, including the famous song "When I am dead, my dearest" and the sonnet sequence *Monna Innominata*, are responses to poems about women written by men. "Goblin Market" can be read as an answer to her brother's "Jenny" (page 806). Some poems expose the woman artist's double role as subject and object of art and desire; others challenge rigid definitions of female virtue. Most often her lyrics perform strenuous acts of recontainment—especially the difficult acceptance of deprivation in a spirit of loving obedience to God—acts that are the more remarkable for their ruthless serenity of manner. Her artistic vision is steady, like her exceptionally regular rhythm; her poetic bearing is as cool as her diction is pure. Wasting no motion, she practices a breathtaking economy of means. Faith in an unseen world and a life to come purges her imagination to confront this world without the distortions of desire, regret, or even hope. The lucidity with which she probes the fallen, broken heart might seem inhuman were her poems not at the same time so charitable towards the throes they record.

In deference to prevailing gender ideology, her brother William framed Rossetti as a songstress of artless spontaneity. Still, he recognized the artistic perfection of her work: "There is no poet with a more marked instinct for fusing the thought into the image, and the image into the thought: the fact is always to her emotional, not merely positive, and the emotion clothed in sensible shape, not merely abstract." This praise from 1866 might pass as Arthur Hallam's of Tennyson in 1830 (see page 133) or Arthur Symons' of Symbolism in 1900 (see page 152)—or for that matter as S. T. Coleridge's definition of poetry in 1815, or Ezra Pound's a hundred years later. Yet by mid-Victorian times devotional poetry, although very popular, was no longer in the serious literary mainstream, and the next century found Rossetti's orthodox strictness strange and uncongenial—so much so that readers mistook it for mere conventionality and ignored the questioning of ordinary gender politics that impels much of what she wrote. By the turn of the twenty-first century, however, her richness of reference, complexity of thought and feeling, and minimalist poetics of creative withholding have been more rightly valued, and she has taken her place as one of the foremost poets of her age.

Despair

— 1 —

Up rose the moon in glory,
    And glittered on the sea;
Up rose the stars around her,
    Making the darkness flee.

— 2 —

The nightingale's wild warbling
    Rang in the far-off wood;
When in his Father's castle
    A mournful figure stood.

— 3 —

His heart was almost bursting,
    He madly beat his breast;   10
As, in low plaintive accents,
    His grief he thus exprest.

— 4 —

"Stars, shroud yourselves in darkness!
    Pale moon, withdraw thy light!
Let darkness hide the ocean
    For ever from my sight;

— 5 —

"Hide cottage, town and city;—
    Appear no more, thou Sun!
But let in foreign countries
    Thy cheering race be run.   20

— 6 —

"For I have lost my loved one!
    Low lies she in her grave!
Speak not to me of pleasure,
    For her I could not save.

— 7 —

"Hark to the distant murmur
    As waves break on the shore"—
When lo! a light came flashing
    Along the corridor.

— 8 —

The mystic form that bore it
    He scarcely could discern;   30
Its flowing robe was blackness—
    Higher the flame doth burn—

— 9 —

He cried, "What art thou, Spirit
    So luminous and bright?"
A voice said, "I'm the maid, Sir,
    A bringing in the light."

1844   *1990*

The P.R.B.[1]

The P.R.B. is in its decadence:—
For Woolner in Australia cooks his chops;
And Hunt is yearning for the land of Cheops;
D. G. Rossetti shuns the vulgar optic;
While William M. Rossetti merely lops
His B.s[2] in English disesteemed as Coptic;
Calm Stephens in the twilight smokes his pipe
But long the dawning of his public day;
And he at last, the champion, great Millais
Attaining academic opulence   10
Winds up his signature with A.R.A.:—
So rivers merge in the perpetual sea,
So luscious fruit must fall when over ripe,
And so the consummated P.R.B.

1853   *1895*

In an Artist's Studio

One face looks out from all his canvases,
    One selfsame figure sits or walks or leans:
    We found her hidden just behind those screens,
That mirror gave back all her loveliness.

---

[1]**P.R.B.**: PreRaphaelite Brotherhood; see page 800. Rossetti was excluded on gender grounds but had two actual Brotherhood brothers in **D. G.** and **William M.** (1829–1919). Thomas **Woolner** (1825–1892): sculptor who emigrated briefly to **Australia** around 1850. William Holman **Hunt** (1827–1910): painter who traveled in 1854 to Egypt (site of the ancient pyramid of **Cheops**). F. G. **Stephens** (1836-1909): painter and art critic. John Everett **Millais** (1829-1896): painter and illustrator. **A.R.A.**: Associate of the Royal Academy of Arts.

[2]**lops / His B.s**: publishes critiques of his brothers, who in turn call his **English** as incomprehensible as **Coptic** (Egyptian).

A queen in opal or in ruby dress,
    A nameless girl in freshest summer-greens,
    A saint, an angel—every canvas means
The same one meaning, neither more nor less.
He feeds upon her face by day and night,
    And she with true kind eyes looks back on him,   10
Fair as the moon and joyful as the light:
    Not wan with waiting, not with sorrow dim;
Not as she is, but was when hope shone bright;
    Not as she is, but as she fills his dream.

1856   1896

A Birthday

My heart is like a singing bird
    Whose nest is in a watered shoot;
My heart is like an apple tree
    Whose boughs are bent with thickset fruit;
My heart is like a rainbow shell
    That paddles in a halcyon[1] sea;
My heart is gladder than all these
    Because my love is come to me.

Raise me a dais of silk and down;
    Hang it with vair[2] and purple dyes;   10
Carve it with doves and pomegranates,
    And peacocks with a hundred eyes;
Work it in gold and silver grapes,
    In leaves and silver fleurs-de-lys
Because the birthday of my life
    Is come, my love is come to me.

                                     1861

Up-Hill

Does the road wind up-hill all the way?
    Yes, to the very end.
Will the day's journey take the whole long day?
    From morn to night, my friend.

---

[1]**halcyon**: calm.

[2]**vair**: squirrel fur used in medieval apparel.

But is there for the night a resting-place?
    A roof for when the slow dark hours begin.
May not the darkness hide it from my face?
    You cannot miss that inn.

Shall I meet other wayfarers at night?
    Those who have gone before.   10
Then must I knock, or call when just in sight?
    They will not keep you standing at that door.

Shall I find comfort, travel-sore and weak?
    Of labour you shall find the sum.
Will there be beds for me and all who seek?
    Yea, beds for all who come.

                                     1861

Goblin Market

Morning and evening
Maids heard the goblins cry:
"Come buy our orchard fruits,
Come buy, come buy:
Apples and quinces,
Lemons and oranges,
Plump unpecked cherries,
Melons and raspberries,
Bloom-down-cheeked peaches,
Swart-headed mulberries,   10
Wild free-born cranberries,
Crab-apples, dewberries,
Pine-apples, blackberries,
Apricots, strawberries;—
All ripe together
In summer weather,—
Morns that pass by,
Fair eves that fly;
Come buy, come buy:
Our grapes fresh from the vine,   20
Pomegranates full and fine,
Dates and sharp bullaces,
Rare pears and greengages,
Damsons and bilberries,
Taste them and try:
Currants and gooseberries,
Bright-fire-like barberries,
Figs to fill your mouth,
Citrons from the South,

Sweet to tongue and sound to eye;   30
Come buy, come buy."

    Evening by evening
Among the brookside rushes,
Laura bowed her head to hear,
Lizzie veiled her blushes:
Crouching close together
In the cooling weather,
With clasping arms and cautioning lips,
With tingling cheeks and finger tips.
"Lie close," Laura said,   40
Pricking up her golden head:
"We must not look at goblin men,
We must not buy their fruits:
Who knows upon what soil they fed
Their hungry thirsty roots?"
"Come buy," call the goblins
Hobbling down the glen.
"Oh," cried Lizzie, "Laura, Laura,
You should not peep at goblin men."
Lizzie covered up her eyes,   50
Covered close lest they should look;
Laura reared her glossy head,
And whispered like the restless brook:
"Look, Lizzie, look, Lizzie,
Down the glen tramp little men.
One hauls a basket,
One bears a plate,
One lugs a golden dish
Of many pounds' weight.
How fair the vine must grow   60
Whose grapes are so luscious;
How warm the wind must blow
Through those fruit bushes."
"No," said Lizzie: "No, no, no;
Their offers should not charm us,
Their evil gifts would harm us."
She thrust a dimpled finger
In each ear, shut eyes and ran:
Curious Laura chose to linger
Wondering at each merchant man.   70
One had a cat's face,
One whisked a tail,
One tramped at a rat's pace,
One crawled like a snail,
One like a wombat[1] prowled obtuse and furry,
One like a ratel tumbled hurry skurry.

She heard a voice like voice of doves
Cooing all together:
They sounded kind and full of loves
In the pleasant weather.   80

    Laura stretched her gleaming neck
Like a rush-imbedded swan,
Like a lily from the beck,[2]
Like a moonlit poplar branch,
Like a vessel at the launch
When its last restraint is gone.

    Backwards up the mossy glen
Turned and trooped the goblin men,
With their shrill repeated cry,
"Come buy, come buy."   90
When they reached where Laura was
They stood stock still upon the moss,
Leering at each other,
Brother with queer brother;
Signalling each other,
Brother with sly brother.
One set his basket down,
One reared his plate;
One began to weave a crown
Of tendrils, leaves, and rough nuts brown   100
(Men sell not such in any town);
One heaved the golden weight
Of dish and fruit to offer her:
"Come buy, come buy," was still their cry.
Laura stared but did not stir,
Longed but had no money:
The whisk-tailed merchant bade her taste
In tones as smooth as honey,
The cat-faced purr'd,
The rat-paced spoke a word   110
Of welcome, and the snail-paced even was heard;
One parrot-voiced and jolly
Cried "Pretty Goblin" still for "Pretty Polly";—
One whistled like a bird.

    But sweet-tooth Laura spoke in haste:
"Good folk, I have no coin;
To take were to purloin:
I have no copper in my purse,
I have no silver either,
And all my gold is on the furze[3]   120
That shakes in windy weather

[1]**wombat:** burrowing marsupial. **ratel:** badger.

[2]**beck:** brook.

[3]**furze:** yellow-flowering shrub.

Above the rusty heather."
"You have much gold upon your head,"
They answered all together:
"Buy from us with a golden curl."
She clipped a precious golden lock,
She dropped a tear more rare than pearl,
Then sucked their fruit globes fair or red:
Sweeter than honey from the rock,[4]
Stronger than man-rejoicing wine,   130
Clearer than water flowed that juice;
She never tasted such before,
How should it cloy with length of use?
She sucked and sucked and sucked the more
Fruits which that unknown orchard bore;
She sucked until her lips were sore;
Then flung the emptied rinds away
But gathered up one kernel-stone,
And knew not was it night or day
As she turned home alone.   140

    Lizzie met her at the gate
Full of wise upbraidings:
"Dear, you should not stay so late,
Twilight is not good for maidens;
Should not loiter in the glen
In the haunts of goblin men.
Do you not remember Jeanie,
How she met them in the moonlight,
Took their gifts both choice and many,
Ate their fruits and wore their flowers   150
Plucked from bowers
Where summer ripens at all hours?
But ever in the noonlight
She pined and pined away;
Sought them by night and day,
Found them no more, but dwindled and grew grey;
Then fell with the first snow,
While to this day no grass will grow
Where she lies low:
I planted daisies there a year ago   160
That never blow.
You should not loiter so."
"Nay, hush," said Laura:
"Nay, hush, my sister:
I ate and ate my fill,
Yet my mouth waters still;
To-morrow night I will

Buy more": and kissed her:
"Have done with sorrow;
I'll bring you plums to-morrow   170
Fresh on their mother twigs,
Cherries worth getting;
You cannot think what figs
My teeth have met in,
What melons icy-cold
Piled on a dish of gold
Too huge for me to hold,
What peaches with a velvet nap,
Pellucid grapes without one seed:
Odorous indeed must be the mead   180
Whereon they grow, and pure the wave they drink
With lilies at the brink,
And sugar-sweet their sap."

    Golden head by golden head,
Like two pigeons in one nest,
Folded in each other's wings,
They lay down in their curtained bed:
Like two blossoms on one stem,
Like two flakes of new-fall'n snow,
Like two wands of ivory   190
Tipped with gold for awful kings.
Moon and stars gazed in at them,
Wind sang to them lullaby,
Lumbering owls forbore to fly,
Not a bat flapped to and fro
Round their nest:
Cheek to cheek and breast to breast
Locked together in one nest.

    Early in the morning
When the first cock crowed his warning,   200
Neat like bees, as sweet and busy,
Laura rose with Lizzie:
Fetched in honey, milked the cows,
Aired and set to rights the house,
Kneaded cakes of whitest wheat,
Cakes for dainty mouths to eat,
Next churned butter, whipped up cream,
Fed their poultry, sat and sewed;
Talked as modest maidens should:
Lizzie with an open heart,   210
Laura in an absent dream,
One content, one sick in part;
One warbling for the mere bright day's delight,
One longing for the night.

---

[4]**honey from the rock:** see Psalm 81:16.

At length slow evening came:
They went with pitchers to the reedy brook;
Lizzie most placid in her look,
Laura most like a leaping flame.
They drew the gurgling water from its deep;
Lizzie plucked purple and rich golden flags,[5]   220
Then turning homewards said: "The sunset flushes
Those furthest loftiest crags;
Come, Laura, not another maiden lags,
No wilful squirrel wags,
The beasts and birds are fast asleep."
But Laura loitered still among the rushes
And said the bank was steep.

And said the hour was early still,
The dew not fall'n, the wind not chill:
Listening ever, but not catching   230
The customary cry,
"Come buy, come buy,"
With its iterated jingle
Of sugar-baited words:
Not for all her watching
Once discerning even one goblin
Racing, whisking, tumbling, hobbling;
Let alone the herds
That used to tramp along the glen,
In groups or single,   240
Of brisk fruit-merchant men.

Till Lizzie urged, "O Laura, come;
I hear the fruit-call, but I dare not look:
You should not loiter longer at this brook:
Come with me home.
The stars rise, the moon bends her arc,
Each glowworm winks her spark,
Let us get home before the night grows dark:
For clouds may gather
Though this is summer weather,   250
Put out the lights and drench us through;
Then if we lost our way what should we do?"

Laura turned cold as stone
To find her sister heard that cry alone,
That goblin cry,
"Come buy our fruits, come buy."
Must she then buy no more such dainty fruit?

Must she no more such succous pasture[6] find,
Gone deaf and blind?
Her tree of life drooped from the root: 260
She said not one word in her heart's sore ache;
But peering thro' the dimness, naught discerning,
Trudged home, her pitcher dripping all the way;
So crept to bed, and lay
Silent till Lizzie slept;
Then sat up in a passionate yearning,
And gnashed her teeth for baulked desire, and wept
As if her heart would break.

Day after day, night after night,
Laura kept watch in vain   270
In sullen silence of exceeding pain.
She never caught again the goblin cry:
"Come buy, come buy";—
She never spied the goblin men
Hawking their fruits along the glen:
But when the moon waxed bright
Her hair grew thin and grey;
She dwindled, as the fair full moon doth turn
To swift decay and burn
Her fire away.   280

One day remembering her kernel-stone
She set it by a wall that faced the south;
Dewed it with tears, hoped for a root,
Watched for a waxing shoot,
But there came none;
It never saw the sun,
It never felt the trickling moisture run:
While with sunk eyes and faded mouth
She dreamed of melons, as a traveller sees
False waves in desert drouth   290
With shade of leaf-crowned trees,
And burns the thirstier in the sandful breeze.

She no more swept the house,
Tended the fowls or cows,
Fetched honey, kneaded cakes of wheat,
Brought water from the brook:
But sat down listless in the chimney-nook
And would not eat.

Tender Lizzie could not bear
To watch her sister's cankerous care   300

---

[5]**flags:** irises.

[6]**succous pasture:** succulent food.

Yet not to share.
She night and morning
Caught the goblins' cry:
"Come buy our orchard fruits,
Come buy, come buy":—
Beside the brook, along the glen,
She heard the tramp of goblin men,
The voice and stir
Poor Laura could not hear;
Longed to buy fruit to comfort her,   310
But feared to pay too dear.
She thought of Jeanie in her grave,
Who should have been a bride;
But who for joys brides hope to have
Fell sick and died
In her gay prime,
In earliest Winter time,
With the first glazing rime,[7]
With the first snow-fall of crisp Winter time.

　　Till Laura dwindling   320
Seemed knocking at Death's door:
Then Lizzie weighed no more
Better and worse;
But put a silver penny in her purse,
Kissed Laura, crossed the heath with clumps of furze
At twilight, halted by the brook:
And for the first time in her life
Began to listen and look.

　　Laughed every goblin
When they spied her peeping: 330
Came towards her hobbling,
Flying, running, leaping,
Puffing and blowing,
Chuckling, clapping, crowing,
Clucking and gobbling,
Mopping and mowing,
Full of airs and graces,
Pulling wry faces,
Demure grimaces,
Cat-like and rat-like,   340
Ratel- and wombat-like,
Snail-paced in a hurry,
Parrot-voiced and whistler,
Helter skelter, hurry skurry,
Chattering like magpies,
Fluttering like pigeons,

Gliding like fishes,—
Hugged her and kissed her,
Squeezed and caressed her:
Stretched up their dishes,   350
Panniers, and plates:
"Look at our apples
Russet and dun,
Bob[8] at our cherries,
Bite at our peaches,
Citrons and dates,
Grapes for the asking,
Pears red with basking
Out in the sun,
Plums on their twigs;   360
Pluck them and suck them,
Pomegranates, figs."—

　　"Good folk," said Lizzie,
Mindful of Jeanie:
"Give me much and many":—
Held out her apron,
Tossed them her penny.
"Nay, take a seat with us,
Honour and eat with us,"
They answered grinning: 370
"Our feast is but beginning.
Night yet is early,
Warm and dew-pearly,
Wakeful and starry:
Such fruits as these
No man can carry;
Half their bloom would fly,
Half their dew would dry,
Half their flavour would pass by.
Sit down and feast with us,   380
Be welcome guest with us,
Cheer you and rest with us."—
"Thank you," said Lizzie: "But one waits
At home alone for me:
So without further parleying,
If you will not sell me any
Of your fruits though much and many,
Give me back my silver penny
I tossed you for a fee."—
They began to scratch their pates,   390
No longer wagging, purring,
But visibly demurring,
Grunting and snarling.

---

[7]**rime**: frost.

[8]**Bob**: catch at with the mouth.

One called her proud,
Cross-grained, uncivil;
Their tones waxed loud,
Their looks were evil.
Lashing their tails
They trod and hustled her,
Elbowed and jostled her,   400
Clawed with their nails,
Barking, mewing, hissing, mocking,
Tore her gown and soiled her stocking,
Twitched her hair out by the roots,
Stamped upon her tender feet,
Held her hands and squeezed their fruits
Against her mouth to make her eat.

    White and golden Lizzie stood,
Like a lily in a flood,—
Like a rock of blue-veined stone   410
Lashed by tides obstreperously,—
Like a beacon left alone
In a hoary roaring sea,
Sending up a golden fire,—
Like a fruit-crowned orange-tree,
White with blossoms honey-sweet,
Sore beset by wasp and bee,—
Like a royal virgin town
Topped with gilded dome and spire
Close beleaguered by a fleet   420
Mad to tug her standard down.

    One may lead a horse to water,
Twenty cannot make him drink.
Though the goblins cuffed and caught her,
Coaxed and fought her,
Bullied and besought her,
Scratched her, pinched her black as ink,
Kicked and knocked her,
Mauled and mocked her,
Lizzie uttered not a word;   430
Would not open lip from lip
Lest they should cram a mouthful in:
But laughed in heart to feel the drip
Of juice that syruped all her face,
And lodged in dimples of her chin,
And streaked her neck which quaked like curd.
At last the evil people
Worn out by her resistance
Flung back her penny, kicked their fruit
Along whichever road they took,   440
Not leaving root or stone or shoot;

Some writhed into the ground,
Some dived into the brook
With ring and ripple,
Some scudded on the gale without a sound,
Some vanished in the distance.

    In a smart, ache, tingle,
Lizzie went her way;
Knew not was it night or day;
Sprang up the bank, tore thro' the furze,   450
Threaded copse and dingle;[9]
And heard her penny jingle
Bouncing in her purse,—
Its bounce was music to her ear.
She ran and ran
As if she feared some goblin man
Dogged her with gibe or curse
Or something worse:
But not one goblin skurried after,
Nor was she pricked by fear;   460
The kind heart made her windy-paced
That urged her home quite out of breath with haste
And inward laughter.

    She cried, "Laura," up the garden,
"Did you miss me?
Come and kiss me.
Never mind my bruises,
Hug me, kiss me, suck my juices
Squeezed from goblin fruits for you,
Goblin pulp and goblin dew.   470
Eat me, drink me, love me;
Laura, make much of me:
For your sake I have braved the glen
And had to do with goblin merchant men."

    Laura started from her chair,
Flung her arms up in the air,
Clutched her hair:
"Lizzie, Lizzie, have you tasted
For my sake the fruit forbidden?
Must your light like mine be hidden,   480
Your young life like mine be wasted,
Undone in mine undoing
And ruined in my ruin,
Thirsty, cankered, goblin-ridden?"—
She clung about her sister,
Kissed and kissed and kissed her:

---

[9]**copse:** small wood. **dingle:** valley.

Tears once again
Refreshed her shrunken eyes,
Dropping like rain
After long sultry drouth;   490
Shaking with anguish, fear, and pain,
She kissed and kissed her with a hungry mouth.

    Her lips began to scorch,
That juice was wormwood[10] to her tongue,
She loathed the feast:
Writhing as one possessed she leaped and sung,
Rent all her robe, and wrung
Her hands in lamentable haste,
And beat her breast.
Her locks streamed like the torch   500
Borne by a racer at full speed,
Or like the mane of horses in their flight,
Or like an eagle when she stems[11] the light
Straight toward the sun,
Or like a caged thing freed,
Or like a flying flag when armies run.

    Swift fire spread through her veins, knocked at her heart,
Met the fire smouldering there
And overbore its lesser flame;
She gorged on bitterness without a name: 510
Ah! fool, to choose such part
Of soul-consuming care!
Sense failed in the mortal strife:
Like the watch-tower of a town
Which an earthquake shatters down,
Like a lightning-stricken mast,
Like a wind-uprooted tree
Spun about,
Like a foam-topped waterspout
Cast down headlong in the sea,   520
She fell at last;
Pleasure past and anguish past,
Is it death or is it life?

    Life out of death.
That night long Lizzie watched by her,
Counted her pulse's flagging stir,
Felt for her breath,
Held water to her lips, and cooled her face
With tears and fanning leaves:

---

[10]**wormwood**: bitter medicinal plant.

[11]**stems**: makes headway against.

But when the first birds chirped about their eaves,   530
And early reapers plodded to the place
Of golden sheaves,
And dew-wet grass
Bowed in the morning winds so brisk to pass,
And new buds with new day
Opened of cup-like lilies on the stream,
Laura awoke as from a dream,
Laughed in the innocent old way,
Hugged Lizzie but not twice or thrice;
Her gleaming locks showed not one thread
    of grey,   540
Her breath was sweet as May
And light danced in her eyes.

    Days, weeks, months, years,
Afterwards, when both were wives
With children of their own;
Their mother-hearts beset with fears,
Their lives bound up in tender lives;
Laura would call the little ones
And tell them of her early prime,
Those pleasant days long gone   550
Of not-returning time:
Would talk about the haunted glen,
The wicked quaint fruit-merchant men,
Their fruits like honey to the throat
But poison in the blood;
(Men sell not such in any town:)
Would tell them how her sister stood
In deadly peril to do her good,
And win the fiery antidote:
Then joining hands to little hands   560
Would bid them cling together,
"For there is no friend like a sister
In calm or stormy weather;
To cheer one on the tedious way,
To fetch one if one goes astray,
To lift one if one totters down,
To strengthen whilst one stands."

                  1862

A Triad

Three sang of love together: one with lips
    Crimson, with cheeks and bosom in a glow,

Flushed to the yellow hair and finger-tips;
   And one there sang who soft and smooth as snow
   Bloomed like a tinted hyacinth at a show;
And one was blue with famine after love,
   Who like a harpstring snapped rang harsh and low
The burden of what those were singing of.
One shamed herself in love; one temperately
   Grew gross in soulless love, a sluggish wife;   10
One famished died for love. Thus two of three
   Took death for love and won him after strife;
One droned in sweetness like a fattened bee:
   All on the threshold, yet all short of life.

                                        1862

Love from the North

I had a love in soft south land,
   Beloved through April far in May;
He waited on my lightest breath,
   And never dared to say me nay.

He saddened if my cheer was sad,
   But gay he grew if I was gay;
We never differed on a hair,
   My yes his yes, my nay his nay.

The wedding hour was come, the aisles
   Were flushed with sun and flowers that day;   10
I pacing balanced in my thoughts:
   "It's quite too late to think of nay."—

My bridegroom answered in his turn,
   Myself had almost answered "yea:"
When through the flashing nave I heard
   A struggle and resounding "nay."

Bridemaids and bridegroom shrank in fear,
   But I stood high who stood at bay:
"And if I answer yea, fair Sir,
   What man art thou to bar with nay?"   20

He was a strong man from the north,
   Light-locked, with eyes of dangerous grey:
"Put yea by for another time
   In which I will not say thee nay."

He took me in his strong white arms,
   He bore me on his horse away
O'er crag, morass, and hairbreadth pass,
   But never asked me yea or nay.

He made me fast with book and bell,[1]
   With links of love he makes me stay;   30
Till now I've neither heart nor power
   Nor will nor wish to say him nay.

                                        1862

Cousin Kate

I was a cottage-maiden
   Hardened by sun and air,
Contented with my cottage-mates,
   Not mindful I was fair.
Why did a great lord find me out
   And praise my flaxen hair?
Why did a great lord find me out
   To fill my heart with care?

He lured me to his palace-home—
   Woe's me for joy thereof—   10
To lead a shameless shameful life,
   His plaything and his love.
He wore me like a golden knot,
   He changed me like a glove:
So now I moan an unclean thing
   Who might have been a dove.

O Lady Kate, my Cousin Kate,
   You grew more fair than I:
He saw you at your father's gate,
   Chose you and cast me by.   20
He watched your steps along the lane,
   Your sport among the rye:
He lifted you from mean estate
   To sit with him on high.

Because you were so good and pure
   He bound you with his ring:
The neighbours call you good and pure,
   Call me an outcast thing.
Even so I sit and howl in dust,
   You sit in gold and sing: 30
Now which of us has tenderer heart?
   You had the stronger wing.

---

[1]**book and bell**: emblems of witchcraft, derived from Church rites of excommunication.

O Cousin Kate, my love was true,
   Your love was writ in sand:
If he had fooled not me but you,
   If you stood where I stand,
He had not won me with his love
   Nor bought me with his land:
I would have spit into his face
   And not have taken his hand.   40

Yet I've a gift you have not got
   And seem not like to get:
For all your clothes and wedding-ring
   I've little doubt you fret.
My fair-haired son, my shame, my pride,
   Cling closer, closer yet:
Your sire would give broad lands for one
   To wear his coronet.

                          1862

Remember

Remember me when I am gone away,
   Gone far away into the silent land;
   When you can no more hold me by the hand,
Nor I half turn to go yet turning stay.
Remember me when no more day by day
   You tell me of our future that you plann'd:
   Only remember me; you understand
It will be late to counsel then or pray.
Yet if you should forget me for a while
   And afterwards remember, do not grieve: 10
   For if the darkness and corruption leave
   A vestige of the thoughts that once I had,
Better by far you should forget and smile
   Than that you should remember and be sad.

                          1862

After Death

The curtains were half drawn, the floor was swept
   And strewn with rushes, rosemary and may[1]
   Lay thick upon the bed on which I lay,
Where through the lattice ivy-shadows crept.

---

[1]**may:** hawthorn blossom.

He leaned above me, thinking that I slept
   And could not hear him; but I heard him say:
   "Poor child, poor child": and as he turned away
Came a deep silence, and I knew he wept.
He did not touch the shroud, or raise the fold
   That hid my face, or take my hand in his,   10
   Or ruffle the smooth pillows for my head:
   He did not love me living; but once dead
He pitied me; and very sweet it is
To know he still is warm though I am cold.

                          1862

The Hour and the Ghost

— BRIDE —

O Love, love, hold me fast,
He draws me away from thee;
I cannot stem the blast,
Nor the cold strong sea:
Far away a light shines
Beyond the hills and pines;
It is lit for me.

— BRIDEGROOM —

I have thee close, my dear,
No terror can come near;
Only far off the northern light shines clear.   10

— GHOST —

Come with me, fair and false,
To our home, come home.
It is my voice that calls:
Once thou wast not afraid
When I woo'd, and said,
"Come, our nest is newly made"—
Now cross the tossing foam.

— BRIDE —

Hold me one moment longer!
He taunts me with the past,
His clutch is waxing stronger;   20
Hold me fast, hold me fast.

He draws me from thy heart,
And I cannot withhold:
He bids my spirit depart
With him into the cold:—
Oh bitter vows of old!

— BRIDEGROOM —

Lean on me, hide thine eyes:
Only ourselves, earth and skies,
Are present here: be wise.

— GHOST —

Lean on me, come away,   30
I will guide and steady:
Come, for I will not stay:
Come, for house and bed are ready.
Ah sure bed and house,
For better and worse, for life and death,
Goal won with shortened breath!
Come, crown our vows.

— BRIDE —

One moment, one more word,
While my heart beats still,
While my breath is stirred   40
By my fainting will.
O friend, forsake me not,
Forget not as I forgot:
But keep thy heart for me,
Keep thy faith true and bright;
Through the lone cold winter night
Perhaps I may come to thee.

— BRIDEGROOM —

Nay peace, my darling, peace:
Let these dreams and terrors cease:
Who spoke of death or change or aught but ease?   50

— GHOST —

O fair frail sin,
O poor harvest gathered in!
Thou shalt visit him again
To watch his heart grow cold:
To know the gnawing pain
I knew of old;
To see one much more fair
Fill up the vacant chair,
Fill his heart, his children bear;

While thou and I together,   60
In the outcast weather,
Toss and howl and spin.

                                                    1862

Echo

Come to me in the silence of the night;
  Come in the speaking silence of a dream;
Come with soft rounded cheeks and eyes as bright
    As sunlight on a stream;
      Come back in tears,
O memory, hope, love of finished years.

O dream how sweet, too sweet, too bitter sweet,
  Whose wakening should have been in Paradise,
Where souls brimfull of love abide and meet;
    Where thirsting longing eyes   10
      Watch the slow door
That opening, letting in, lets out no more.

Yet come to me in dreams, that I may live
  My very life again though cold in death:
Come back to me in dreams, that I may give
    Pulse for pulse, breath for breath:
      Speak low, lean low,
As long ago, my love, how long ago.

                                                    1862

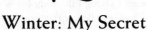

Winter: My Secret

I tell my secret? No indeed, not I:
Perhaps some day, who knows?
But not to-day; it froze, and blows, and snows,
And you're too curious: fie!
You want to hear it? well:
Only, my secret's mine, and I won't tell.

Or, after all, perhaps there's none:
Suppose there is no secret after all,
But only just my fun.
To-day's a nipping day, a biting day;   10
In which one wants a shawl,
A veil, a cloak, and other wraps:
I cannot ope to every one who taps,
And let the draughts come whistling through my hall;

Come bounding and surrounding me,
Come buffeting, astounding me,
Nipping and clipping through my wraps and all.
I wear my mask for warmth: who ever shows
His nose to Russian snows
To be pecked at by every wind that blows?   20
You would not peck? I thank you for good will,
Believe, but leave that truth untested still.

Spring's an expansive time: yet I don't trust
March with its peck of dust,
Nor April with its rainbow-crowned brief showers,
Nor even May, whose flowers
One frost may wither through the sunless hours.

Perhaps some languid summer day,
When drowsy birds sing less and less,
And golden fruit is ripening to excess,   30
If there's not too much sun nor too much cloud,
And the warm wind is neither still not loud,
Perhaps my secret I may say,
Or you may guess.

1857   1862

Shut Out

The door was shut. I looked between
    Its iron bars; and saw it lie,
    My garden, mine, beneath the sky,
Pied with all flowers bedewed and green.

From bough to bough the song-birds crossed,
    From flower to flower the moths and bees:
    With all its nests and stately trees
It had been mine, and it was lost.

A shadowless spirit kept the gate,
    Blank and unchanging like the grave.   10
    I, peering through, said: "Let me have
Some buds to cheer my outcast state."

He answered not. "Or give me, then,
    But one small twig from shrub or tree;
    And bid my home remember me
Until I come to it again."

The spirit was silent; but he took
    Mortar and stone to build a wall;
    He left no loophole great or small
Through which my straining eyes
    might look.   20

So now I sit here quite alone,
    Blinded with tears; nor grieve for that,
    For nought is left worth looking at
Since my delightful land is gone.

A violet bed is budding near,
    Wherein a lark has made her nest;
    And good they are, but not the best;
And dear they are, but not so dear.

                                           1862

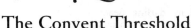

Song

When I am dead, my dearest,
    Sing no sad songs for me;
Plant thou no roses at my head,
    Nor shady cypress tree:
Be the green grass above me
    With showers and dewdrops wet:
And if thou wilt, remember,
    And if thou wilt, forget.

I shall not see the shadows,
    I shall not feel the rain;   10
I shall not hear the nightingale
    Sing on as if in pain:
And dreaming through the twilight
    That doth not rise nor set,
Haply I may remember,
    And haply may forget.

                                           1862

The Convent Threshold

There's blood between us, love, my love,
There's father's blood, there's brother's blood;
And blood's a bar I cannot pass.
I choose the stairs that mount above,
Stair after golden sky-ward stair,
To city and to sea of glass.[1]
My lily feet are soiled with mud,
With scarlet mud which tells a tale

---

[1] **sea of glass:** Revelation 15:2.

Of hope that was, of guilt that was,
Of love that shall not yet avail;   10
Alas, my heart, if I could bare
My heart, this selfsame stain is there:
I seek the sea of glass and fire
To wash the spot, to burn the snare;
Lo, stairs are meant to lift us higher:
Mount with me, mount the kindled stair.

    Your eyes look earthward, mine look up.
I see the far-off city grand,
Beyond the hills a watered land,
Beyond the gulf a gleaming strand   20
Of mansions where the righteous sup;
Who sleep at ease among their trees,
Or wake to sing a cadenced hymn
With Cherubim and Seraphim.[2]
They bore the Cross, they drained the cup,
Racked, roasted, crushed, wrenched limb from limb,
They the offscouring of the world:
The heaven of starry heavens unfurled,
The sun before their face is dim.

    You looking earthward, what see you?   30
Milk-white, wine-flushed among the vines,
Up and down leaping, to and fro,
Most glad, most full, made strong with wines,
Blooming as peaches pearled with dew,
Their golden windy hair afloat,
Love-music warbling in their throat,
Young men and women come and go.

    You linger, yet the time is short:
Flee for your life, gird up your strength
To flee; the shadows stretched at length   40
Show that day wanes, that night draws nigh;
Flee to the mountain, tarry not.
Is this a time for smile and sigh,
For songs among the secret trees
Where sudden blue birds nest and sport?
The time is short and yet you stay:
To-day, while it is called to-day,
Kneel, wrestle, knock, do violence, pray;
To-day is short, to-morrow nigh:
Why will you die? why will you die?   50

    You sinned with me a pleasant sin:
Repent with me, for I repent.
Woe's me the lore I must unlearn!

Woe's me that easy way we went,
So rugged when I would return!
How long until my sleep begin,
How long shall stretch these nights and days?
Surely, clean Angels cry, she[3] prays;
She laves her soul with tedious tears:
How long must stretch these years and years?   60

    I turn from you my cheeks and eyes,
My hair which you shall see no more—
Alas for joy that went before,
For joy that dies, for love that dies!
Only my lips still turn to you,
My livid lips that cry, Repent!
O weary life, O weary Lent,
O weary time whose stars are few!

    How should I rest in Paradise,
Or sit on steps of heaven alone?   70
If Saints and Angels spoke of love,
Should I not answer from my throne,
Have pity upon me, ye my friends,
For I have heard the sound thereof.
Should I not turn with yearning eyes,
Turn earthwards with a pitiful pang?
Oh save me from a pang in heaven!
By all the gifts we took and gave,
Repent, repent, and be forgiven.
This life is long, but yet it ends;   80
Repent and purge your soul and save:
No gladder song the morning stars[4]
Upon their birthday morning sang
Than Angels sing when one repents.

    I tell you what I dreamed last night.
A spirit with transfigured face
Fire-footed clomb an infinite space.
I heard his hundred pinions clang,
Heaven-bells rejoicing rang and rang,
Heaven-air was thrilled with subtle scents,   90
Worlds spun upon their rushing cars:
He mounted shrieking "Give me light!"
Still light was poured on him, more light;
Angels, Archangels he outstripped,
Exultant in exceeding might,
And trod the skirts of Cherubim.
Still "Give me light," he shrieked; and dipped

---

[2]**Cherubim, Seraphim:** heavenly orders above the archangels.

[3]**she:** the "I" who speaks the poem.

[4]**morning stars:** see Job 38:7.

His thirsty face, and drank a sea,
Athirst with thirst it could not slake.
I saw him, drunk with knowledge, take   100
From aching brows the aureole[5] crown—
His locks writhed like a cloven snake—
He left his throne to grovel down
And lick the dust of Seraphs' feet:
For what is knowledge duly weighed?
Knowledge is strong, but love is sweet;
Yea all the progress he had made
Was but to learn that all is small
Save love, for love is all in all.

    I tell you what I dreamed last night.   110
It was not dark, it was not light,
Cold dews had drenched my plenteous hair
Through clay; you came to seek me there,
And "Do you dream of me?" you said.
My heart was dust that used to leap
To you; I answered half asleep:
"My pillow is damp, my sheets are red,
There's a leaden tester[6] to my bed:
Find you a warmer playfellow,
A warmer pillow for your head,   120
A kinder love to love than mine."
You wrung your hands: while I, like lead,
Crushed downwards through the sodden earth:
You smote your hands but not in mirth,
And reeled but were not drunk with wine.

    For all night long I dreamed of you:
I woke and prayed against my will,
Then slept to dream of you again.
At length I rose and knelt and prayed.
I cannot write the words I said,   130
My words were slow, my tears were few;
But through the dark my silence spoke
Like thunder. When this morning broke
My face was pinched, my hair was grey,
And frozen blood was on the sill
Where stifling in my struggle I lay.

    If now you saw me you would say:
Where is the face I used to love?
And I would answer: Gone before;
It tarries veiled in Paradise.   140
When once the morning star shall rise,
When earth with shadow flees away

---

[5]aureole: halo.

[6]tester: canopy.

And we stand safe within the door,
Then you shall lift the veil thereof.
Look up, rise up: for far above
Our palms are grown, our place is set;
There we shall meet as once we met,
And love with old familiar love.

1862

A Better Resurrection

I have no wit, no words, no tears;
    My heart within me like a stone
Is numbed too much for hopes or fears;
    Look right, look left, I dwell alone;
I lift mine eyes, but dimmed with grief
    No everlasting hills I see;
My life is in the falling leaf:
    O Jesus, quicken me.

My life is like a faded leaf,
    My harvest dwindled to a husk;   10
Truly my life is void and brief
    And tedious in the barren dusk;
My life is like a frozen thing,
    No bud nor greenness can I see:
Yet rise it shall—the sap of Spring;
    O Jesus, rise in me.

My life is like a broken bowl,
    A broken bowl that cannot hold
One drop of water for my soul
    Or cordial in the searching cold;   20
Cast in the fire the perished thing,
    Melt and remould it, till it be
A royal cup for Him my King:
    O Jesus, drink of me.

1862

Good Friday

Am I a stone, and not a sheep,
    That I can stand, O Christ, beneath Thy cross,
    To number drop by drop Thy Blood's slow loss,
And yet not weep?

Not so those women[1] loved
  Who with exceeding grief lamented Thee;
    Not so fallen Peter[2] weeping bitterly;
Not so the thief was moved;

Not so the Sun and Moon
  Which hid their faces in a starless sky,   10
A horror of great darkness at broad noon[3]—
  I, only I.

Yet give not o'er,
  But seek Thy sheep, true Shepherd of the flock;
Greater than Moses, turn and look once more
  And smite a rock.[4]

                      1864

Amor Mundi[1]

"Oh where are you going with your love-locks flowing,
  On the west wind blowing along this valley track?"
"The downhill path is easy, come with me an it
    please ye,
  We shall escape the uphill by never turning back."

So they two went together in glowing August weather,
  The honey-breathing heather lay to their left
    and right;
And dear she was to doat on, her swift feet seemed to
  float on
  The air like soft twin pigeons too sportive to alight.

"Oh what is that in heaven where grey cloud-flakes
  are seven,
  Where blackest clouds hang riven just at the rainy
    skirt?"   10
"Oh, that's a meteor sent us, a message dumb,
  portentous,
  An undeciphered solemn signal of help or hurt."

"Oh what is that glides quickly where velvet flowers grow
  thickly,
  Their scent comes rich and sickly?" "A scaled and
    hooded worm."

---

[1]those women: see Luke 23:27.
[2]Peter: see Matthew 26:75. thief: Luke 23:39–43.
[3]darkness . . . noon: see Deuteronomy 28:29, Luke 23:44–45.
[4]smite a rock: Exodus 17:6.
[1]"Amor Mundi": Love of the World.

"Oh what's that in the hollow, so pale I quake to follow?"
  "Oh that's a thin dead body which waits the eternal
    term."
"Turn again, O my sweetest,—turn again, false and
  fleetest:
  This beaten way thou beatest, I fear, is hell's own track."
"Nay, too steep for hill mounting; nay, too late for cost
  counting:
  This downhill path is easy, but there's no turning back." 20

                      1865

Twice

I took my heart in my hand,
  (O my love, O my love),
I said: Let me fall or stand,
  Let me live or die,
But this once hear me speak—
  (O my love, O my love)—
Yet a woman's words are weak;
  You should speak, not I.

You took my heart in your hand
  With a friendly smile,   10
With a critical eye you scanned,
  Then set it down,
And said: It is still unripe,
  Better wait awhile;
Wait while the skylarks pipe,
  Till the corn grows brown.

As you set it down it broke—
  Broke, but I did not wince;
I smiled at the speech you spoke,
  At your judgment that I heard: 20
But I have not often smiled
  Since then, nor questioned since,
Nor cared for corn-flowers wild,
  Nor sung with the singing bird.

I take my heart in my hand,
  O my God, O my God,
My broken heart in my hand:
  Thou hast seen, judge Thou.
My hope was written on sand,
  O my God, O my God: 30
Now let Thy judgment stand—
  Yea, judge me now.

This contemned of[1] a man,
    This marred one heedless day,
This heart take Thou to scan
    Both within and without:
Refine with fire its gold,
    Purge Thou its dross away—
Yea hold it in Thy hold,
    Whence none can pluck it out.   40

I take my heart in my hand—
    I shall not die, but live—
Before Thy face I stand;
    I, for Thou callest such:
All that I have I bring,
    All that I am I give;
Smile Thou and I shall sing,
    But shall not question much.

                      1866

Memory

— 1 —

I nursed it in my bosom while it lived,
    I hid it in my heart when it was dead.
In joy I sat alone; even so I grieved
    Alone, and nothing said.

I shut the door to face the naked truth,
    I stood alone—I faced the truth alone,
Stripped bare of self-regard or forms or ruth
    Till first and last were shown.

I took the perfect balances and weighed;
    No shaking of my hand disturbed the poise;   10
Weighed, found it wanting: not a word I said,
    But silent made my choice.

None know the choice I made; I make it still.
    None know the choice I made and broke my heart,
Breaking mine idol: I have braced my will
    Once, chosen for once my part.

I broke it at a blow, I laid it cold,
    Crushed in my deep heart where it used to live.
My heart dies inch by inch; the time grows old,
    Grows old in which I grieve.   20

1857   *1866*

---

[1]**contemned of:** scorned by.

— 2 —

I have a room whereinto no one enters
    Save I myself alone:
    There sits a blessed memory on a throne,
There my life centres;

While winter comes and goes—oh tedious comer!—
    And while its nip-wind blows;
    While bloom the bloodless lily and warm rose
Of lavish summer.

If any should force entrance he might see there
    One buried yet not dead,   30
    Before whose face I no more bow my head
Or bend my knee there;

But often in my worn life's autumn weather
    I watch there with clear eyes,
    And think how it will be in Paradise
When we're together.

1865   *1866*

The Lowest Place

    Give me the lowest place: not that I dare
        Ask for that lowest place, but Thou hast died
    That I might live and share
        Thy glory by Thy side.

    Give me the lowest place: or if for me
        That lowest place too high, make one more low
    Where I may sit and see
        My God and love Thee so.

                      1866

By the Sea

    Why does the sea moan evermore?
        Shut out from heaven it makes its moan,
    It frets against the boundary shore;
        All earth's full rivers cannot fill
        The sea, that drinking thirsteth still.

    Sheer miracles of loveliness
        Lie hid in its unlooked-on bed:
    Anemones, salt, passionless,
        Blow flower-like; just enough alive
        To blow and multiply and thrive.   10

Shells quaint with curve, or spot, or spike,
    Encrusted live things argus-eyed,[1]
All fair alike, yet all unlike,
    Are born without a pang, and die
Without a pang, and so pass by.

                      1866

A Christmas Carol

In the bleak mid-winter
    Frosty wind made moan,
Earth stood hard as iron,
    Water like a stone;
Snow had fallen, snow on snow,
    Snow on snow,
In the bleak mid-winter
    Long ago.

Our God, Heaven cannot hold Him
    Nor earth sustain;   10
Heaven and earth shall flee away
    When He comes to reign:
In the bleak mid-winter
    A stable-place sufficed
The Lord God Almighty
    Jesus Christ.

Enough for Him whom cherubim
    Worship night and day,
A breastful of milk
    And a mangerful of hay;   20
Enough for Him whom angels
    Fall down before,
The ox and ass and camel
    Which adore.

Angels and archangels
    May have gathered there,
Cherubim and seraphim
    Throng'd the air,
But only His mother
    In her maiden bliss   30
Worshipped the Beloved
    With a kiss.

What can I give Him,
    Poor as I am?

If I were a shepherd
    I would bring a lamb,
If I were a wise man
    I would do my part,—
Yet what I can I give Him,
    Give my heart.   40

                      1872

Paradise

Once in a dream I saw the flowers
    That bud and bloom in Paradise;
    More fair they are than waking eyes
Have seen in all this world of ours.
And faint the perfume-bearing rose,
    And faint the lily on its stem,
And faint the perfect violet
        Compared with them.

I heard the songs of Paradise:
    Each bird sat singing in his place;   10
    A tender song so full of grace
It soared like incense to the skies.
Each bird sat singing to his mate
    Soft cooing notes among the trees:
The nightingale herself were cold
        To such as these.

I saw the fourfold River[1] flow,
    And deep it was, with golden sand;
    It flowed between a mossy land
With murmured music grave and low.   20
It hath refreshment for all thirst,
    For fainting spirits strength and rest;
Earth holds not such a draught as this
        From east to west.

The Tree of Life stood budding there,
    Abundant with its twelvefold fruits;[2]
    Eternal sap sustains its roots,
Its shadowing branches fill the air.
    Its leaves are healing for the world,
    Its fruit the hungry world can feed,   30
Sweeter than honey to the taste
        And balm indeed.

---

[1]**argus-eyed**: like the mythic watchman Argus with 100 eyes.

[1]**fourfold River**: in Eden; see Genesis 2:10–14.

[2]**twelvefold fruits**: from the tree of life in Revelation 22:2.

I saw the gate called Beautiful[3]
   And looked, but scarce could look within;
   I saw the golden streets begin,
And outskirts of the glassy pool.
Oh harps, oh crowns of plenteous stars,
   Oh green palm branches many-leaved—
Eye hath not seen, nor ear hath heard,
   Nor heart conceived.[4]   40

I hope to see these things again,
   But not as once in dreams by night;
   To see them with my very sight,
And touch and handle and attain:
To have all Heaven beneath my feet
   For narrow way that once they trod;
To have my part with all the saints,
   And with my God.

                  1875

from Sing-Song

What are heavy? sea-sand and sorrow:
What are brief? to-day and to-morrow:
What are frail? Spring blossoms and youth:
What are deep? the ocean and truth.

A toadstool comes up in a night,—
   Learn the lesson, little folk:—
An oak grows on a hundred years,
   But then it is an oak.

A pin has a head, but has no hair;
A clock has a face, but no mouth there;
Needles have eyes, but they cannot see;
A fly has a trunk without lock or key;
A timepiece may lose, but cannot win;
A corn-field dimples without a chin;
A hill has no leg, but has a foot;
A wine-glass a stem, but not a root;

A watch has hands, but no thumb or finger;
A boot has a tongue, but is no singer;   10
Rivers run, though they have no feet;
A saw has teeth, but it does not eat;
Ash-trees have keys,[1] yet never a lock;
And baby crows, without being a cock.

When the cows come home the milk is coming,
Honey's made while the bees are humming;
Duck and drake on the rushy lake,
And the deer live safe in the breezy brake[2];
And timid, funny, brisk little bunny
Winks his nose and sits all sunny.

When a mounting skylark sings
   In the sunlit summer morn,
I know that heaven is up on high,
   And on earth are fields of corn.

But when a nightingale sings
   In the moonlit summer even,
I know not if earth is merely earth,
   Only that heaven is heaven.

Who has seen the wind?
   Neither I nor you:
But when the leaves hang trembling
   The wind is passing thro'.

Who has seen the wind?
   Neither you nor I:
But when the trees bow down their heads
   The wind is passing by.

An emerald is as green as grass;
   A ruby red as blood;
A sapphire shines as blue as heaven;
   A flint lies in the mud.

---

[3]**gate called Beautiful**: in Jerusalem; see Acts 3:2.
[4]**Eye hath . . . conceived**: 1 Corinthians 2:9.

[1]**keys**: fruits of the ash tree.
[2]**brake**: rough or marshy land.

A diamond is a brilliant stone,
　　To catch the world's desire;
An opal holds a fiery spark;
　　But a flint holds fire.

If stars dropped out of heaven,
　　And if flowers took their place,
The sky would still look very fair,
　　And fair earth's face.

Winged angels might fly down to us
　　To pluck the stars,
But we could only long for flowers
　　Beyond the cloudy bars.

1872

Monna Innominata[1]

A Sonnet of Sonnets

Beatrice,[2] immortalized by "altissimo poeta ... cotanto amante," Laura,[3] celebrated by a great though an inferior bard,—have alike paid the exceptional penalty of exceptional honour, and have come down to us resplendent with charms, but (at least, to my apprehension) scant of attractiveness.

These heroines of world-wide fame were preceded by a bevy of unnamed ladies "donne innominate" sung by a school of less conspicuous poets; and in that land and that period[4] which gave simultaneous birth to Catholics, to Albigenses, and to Troubadours, one can imagine many a lady as sharing her lover's poetic aptitude, while the barrier between them might be one held sacred by both, yet not such as to render mutual love incompatible with mutual honour.

Had such a lady spoken for herself, the portrait left us might have appeared more tender, if less dignified, than any

drawn even by a devoted friend. Or had the Great Poetess[5] of our own day and nation only been unhappy instead of happy, her circumstances would have invited her to bequeath to us, in lieu of the "Portuguese Sonnets," an inimitable "donna innominata" drawn not from fancy but from feeling, and worthy to occupy a niche beside Beatrice and Laura.

— 1 —

"Lo dì che han detto a' dolci amici addio."[6]—DANTE.
"Amor, con quanto sforzo oggi mi vinci!"[7]—PETRARCA.

Come back to me, who wait and watch for you:—
　　Or come not yet, for it is over then,
　　And long it is before you come again,
So far between my pleasures are and few.
While, when you come not, what I do I do
　　Thinking "Now when he comes," my sweetest "when:"
　　For one man is my world of all the men
This wide world holds; O love, my world is you.
Howbeit, to meet you grows almost a pang
　　Because the pang of parting comes so soon;   10
　　My hope hangs waning, waxing, like a moon
　　Between the heavenly days on which we meet:
Ah me, but where are now the songs I sang
　　When life was sweet because you called them sweet?

— 2 —

"Era già l'ora che volge il desio."[8]—DANTE.
"Ricorro al tempo ch' io vi vidi prima."[9]—PETRARCA.

I wish I could remember that first day,
　　First hour, first moment of your meeting me,
　　If bright or dim the season, it might be
Summer or Winter for aught I can say;
So unrecorded did it slip away,
　　So blind was I to see and to foresee,
　　So dull to mark the budding of my tree
That would not blossom yet for many a May.

---

[1]**Monna Innominata:** Unnamed Lady.

[2]**Beatrice** Portinari (1266?–1290): beloved of Dante (1265–1321), the "altissimo poeta ..." (highest poet who loved so well).

[3]**Laura** de Noves of Avignon (1314–1348): beloved of the **bard** Francesco Petrarca (1304–1374).

[4]**that land, that period:** medieval Provence in S France, home of the heretical **Albigenses** (12th and 13th centuries) and minstrel **Troubadours.**

[5]**Great Poetess:** Elizabeth Barrett Browning, author of *Sonnets from the Portuguese* (1850, page 351).

[6]**"Lo dì ... addio":** On the day they have said farewell to their sweet friends (*Purgatorio* 8.3).

[7]**"Amor ... vinci!":** Love, with what force you vanquish me today! (*Rime* 85.12).

[8]**"Era ... desio":** It was now the hour that bends desire back (*Purgatorio* 8.1).

[9]**"Ricorro ... prima":** I recur to the time I saw you first (*Rime* 20.3).

If only I could recollect it, such
   A day of days! I let it come and go   10
   As traceless as a thaw of bygone snow;
It seemed to mean so little, meant so much;
If only now I could recall that touch,
   First touch of hand in hand—Did one but know!

— 3 —

"O ombre vane, fuor che ne l'aspetto!"[10]—DANTE.
"Immaginata guida la conduce."[11]—PETRARCA.

I dream of you to wake: would that I might
   Dream of you and not wake but slumber on;
   Nor find with dreams the dear companion gone,
As Summer ended Summer birds take flight.
In happy dreams I hold you full in sight,
   I blush again who waking look so wan;
   Brighter than sunniest day that ever shone,
In happy dreams your smile makes day of night.
Thus only in a dream we are at one,
   Thus only in a dream we give and take   10
      The faith that maketh rich who take or give;
   If thus to sleep is sweeter than to wake,
      To die were surely sweeter than to live,
Though there be nothing new beneath the sun.

— 4 —

"Poca favilla gran fiamma seconda."[12]—DANTE.
"Ogni altra cosa, ogni pensier va fore,
   E sol ivi con voi rimansi amore."[13]—PETRARCA.

I loved you first: but afterwards your love
   Outsoaring mine, sang such a loftier song
As drowned the friendly cooings of my dove.
   Which owes the other most? my love was long,
   And yours one moment seemed to wax more strong;
I loved and guessed at you, you construed me
And loved me for what might or might not be—
   Nay, weights and measures do us both a wrong.

For verily love knows not "mine" or "thine;"
   With separate "I" and "thou" free love has done,   10
   For one is both and both are one in love:
Rich love knows nought of "thine that is not mine;"
   Both have the strength and both the length thereof,
   Both of us of the love which makes us one.

— 5 —

"Amor che a nulla amato amar perdona."[14]—DANTE.
"Amor m'addusse in sì gioiosa spene."[15]—PETRARCA.

O my heart's heart, and you who are to me
   More than myself myself, God be with you,
   Keep you in strong obedience leal[16] and true
To Him whose noble service setteth free,
Give you all good we see or can foresee,
   Make your joys many and your sorrows few,
   Bless you in what you bear and what you do,
Yea, perfect you as He would have you be.
So much for you; but what for me, dear friend?
   To love you without stint and all I can   10
To-day, to-morrow, world without an end;
   To love you much and yet to love you more,
   As Jordan at his flood sweeps either shore;
Since woman is the helpmeet made for man.

— 6 —

"Or puoi la quantitate
Comprender de l'amor che a te mi scalda."[17]—DANTE
"Non vo' che da tal nodo amor mi scioglia."[18]—PETRARCA.

Trust me, I have not earned your dear rebuke,
   I love, as you would have me, God the most;
   Would lose not Him, but you, must one be lost,
Nor with Lot's wife[19] cast back a faithless look
Unready to forego what I forsook;
   This say I, having counted up the cost,
   This, though I be the feeblest of God's host,
The sorriest sheep Christ shepherds with His crook.

---

[10]"**O ombre . . . l'aspetto!**": O shadows empty of everything but semblance! (*Purgatorio* 2.79).

[11]"**Immaginata . . . conduce**": An imaginary guide conducts her (*Rime* 277.9).

[12]"**Poca . . . seconda**": A small spark fosters a great flame (*Paradiso* 1.34).

[13]"**Ogni . . . amore**": Every other thing, every thought, departs, and love alone remains there with you (*Rime* 72.44–45).

[14]"**Amor . . . perdona**": Love, who exempts from loving no one who is loved (*Inferno* 5.103).

[15]"**Amor . . . spene**": Love led me into such joyous hope (*Rime* 56.11).

[16]**leal**: loyal.

[17]"**Or puoi . . . scalda**": Now you can comprehend the quantity of love that burns for you within me (*Purgatorio* 21.133–134).

[18]"**Non . . . scioglia**": I don't want love to release me from such a knot (*Rime* 59.17).

[19]**Lot's wife**: see Genesis 19.

Yet while I love my God the most, I deem
    That I can never love you overmuch;   10
        I love Him more, so let me love you too;
    Yea, as I apprehend it, love is such
I cannot love you if I love not Him,
        I cannot love Him if I love not you.

— 7 —

"Qui primavera sempre ed ogni frutto."[20]—DANTE.
"Ragionando con meco ed io con lui."[21]—PETRARCA.

"Love me, for I love you"—and answer me,
    "Love me, for I love you"—so shall we stand
    As happy equals in the flowering land
Of love, that knows not a dividing sea.
Love builds the house on rock and not on sand,
    Love laughs what while[22] the winds rave desperately;
And who hath found love's citadel unmanned?
    And who hath held in bonds love's liberty?
My heart's a coward though my words are brave—
    We meet so seldom, yet we surely part   10
So often; there's a problem for your art!
        Still I find comfort in his Book,[23] who saith,
Though jealousy be cruel as the grave,
        And death be strong, yet love is strong as death.

— 8 —

"Come dicesse a Dio: D'altro non calme."[24]—DANTE.
"Spero trovar pietà non che perdono."[25]—PETRARCA.

"I, if I perish, perish"—Esther[26] spake:
    And bride of life or death she made her fair
    In all the lustre of her perfumed hair
And smiles that kindle longing but to slake.

She put on pomp of loveliness, to take
    Her husband through his eyes at unaware;
    She spread abroad her beauty for a snare,
Harmless as doves and subtle as a snake.
She trapped him with one mesh of silken hair,
    She vanquished him by wisdom of her wit,   10
        And built her people's house that it should stand:—
        If I might take my life so in my hand,
And for my love to Love put up my prayer,
    And for love's sake by Love be granted it!

— 9 —

"O dignitosa coscienza e netta!"[27]—DANTE.
"Spirto più acceso di virtuti ardenti."[28]—PETRARCA.

Thinking of you, and all that was, and all
    That might have been and now can never be,
    I feel your honored excellence, and see
Myself unworthy of the happier call:
For woe is me who walk so apt to fall,
    So apt to shrink afraid, so apt to flee,
    Apt to lie down and die (ah, woe is me !)
Faithless and hopeless turning to the wall.
And yet not hopeless quite nor faithless quite,
Because not loveless; love may toil all night,   10
    But take at morning; wrestle[29] till the break
        Of day, but then wield power with God and man:—
        So take I heart of grace as best I can,
Ready to spend and be spent for your sake.

— 10 —

"Con miglior corso e con migliore stella."[30]—DANTE.
"La vita fugge e non s'arresta un' ora."[31]—PETRARCA.

Time flies, hope flags, life plies a wearied wing;
    Death following hard on life gains ground apace;
    Faith runs with each and rears an eager face,
Outruns the rest, makes light of everything,

---

[20]"**Qui . . . frutto**": Here is spring forever and every fruit (*Purgatorio* 28.143).

[21]"**Ragionando . . . lui**": Conversing with me, and I with him (*Rime* 35.14).

[22]**what while**: when.

[23]**his Book**: see Song of Solomon 8:6.

[24]"**Come . . . calme**": As if he were to say to God, "I care for nothing else" (*Purgatorio* 8.12).

[25]"**Spero . . . perdono**": I hope to find pity, not merely pardon (*Rime* 1.8).

[26]**Esther**: Jewish wife of the Persian king Ahasuerus; see Esther 4:16.

---

[27]"**O dignitosa . . . netta!**": O dignified and pure conscience! (*Purgatorio* 3.8).

[28]"**Spirto . . . ardenti**": Spirit most lit with ardent virtues (*Rime* 283.3).

[29]**wrestle**: see Genesis 32:24 (Jacob and the angel).

[30]"**Con . . . stella**": With a better course and a better star (*Paradiso* 1.40).

[31]"**La vita . . . un' ora**": Life flees, and stays not an hour (*Rime* 272.1).

Spurns earth, and still finds breath to pray and sing;
   While love ahead of all uplifts his praise,
   Still asks for grace and still gives thanks for grace,
Content with all day brings and night will bring.
Life wanes; and when love folds his wings above
   Tired hope, and less we feel his conscious pulse,   10
     Let us go fall asleep, dear friend, in peace:
     A little while, and age and sorrow cease;
   A little while, and life reborn annuls
Loss and decay and death, and all is love.

— 11 —

"Vien dietro a me e lascia dir le genti."[32]—DANTE.
"Contando i casi della vita nostra."[33]—PETRARCA.

Many in aftertimes will say of you
   "He loved her"—while of me what will they say?
   Not that I loved you more than just in play,
For fashion's sake as idle women do.
Even let them prate; who know not what we knew
   Of love and parting in exceeding pain,
   Of parting hopeless here to meet again,
Hopeless on earth, and heaven is out of view.
But by my heart of love laid bare to you,
   My love that you can make not void nor vain,   10
Love that foregoes you but to claim anew
     Beyond this passage of the gate of death,
I charge you at the Judgment make it plain
     My love of you was life and not a breath.

— 12 —

"Amor, che ne la mente mi ragiona."[34]—DANTE.
"Amor vien nel bel viso di costei."[35]—PETRARCA.

If there be any one can take my place
   And make you happy whom I grieve to grieve,
   Think not that I can grudge it, but believe
I do commend you to that nobler grace,

That readier wit than mine, that sweeter face;
   Yea, since your riches make me rich, conceive
   I too am crowned, while bridal crowns I weave,
And thread the bridal dance with jocund pace.
For if I did not love you, it might be
   That I should grudge you some one dear delight;   10
     But since the heart is yours that was mine own,
   Your pleasure is my pleasure, right my right,
Your honorable freedom makes me free,
     And you companioned I am not alone.

— 13 —

"E drizzeremo glí occhi al Primo Amore."[36]—DANTE.
"Ma trovo peso non da le mie braccia."[37]—PETRARCA.

If I could trust mine own self with your fate,
   Shall I not rather trust it in God's hand?
   Without Whose Will one lily doth not stand,
Nor sparrow fall at his appointed date;
   Who numbereth the innumerable sand,
Who weighs the wind and water with a weight,[38]
To Whom the world is neither small nor great,
   Whose knowledge foreknew every plan we planned.
Searching my heart for all that touches you,
   I find there only love and love's goodwill   10
Helpless to help and impotent to do,
   Of understanding dull, of sight most dim;
   And therefore I commend you back to Him
Whose love your love's capacity can fill.

— 14 —

"E la Sua Volontade è nostra pace."[39]—DANTE.
"Sol con questi pensier, con altre chiome."[40]—PETRARCA.

Youth gone, and beauty gone if ever there
   Dwelt beauty in so poor a face as this;
   Youth gone and beauty, what remains of bliss?
I will not bind fresh roses in my hair,

---

[32]"Vien dietro . . . le genti": Come after me, and let people talk (Purgatorio 5.13).

[33]"Contando . . . nostra": Recounting the casualties of our life (Rime 285.12).

[34]"Amor . . . ragiona": Love, who speaks within my mind (Purgatorio 2.112).

[35]"Amor . . . costei": Love comes into the beautiful face of this lady (Rime 13.2).

[36]"E drizzeremo . . . Amore": And we will direct our eyes to the First Love (Paradiso 32.142).

[37]"Ma . . . braccia": But I find a burden that is not for my arms (Rime 20.5).

[38]sparrow, sand, weight: see Matthew 10:29, Ecclesiasticus 1:2, Job 28:25.

[39]"E la Sua . . . pace": And His Will is our peace (Paradiso 3.85).

[40]"Sol . . . chiome": Alone with these thoughts, and with altered locks of hair (Rime 30.32).

To shame a cheek at best but little fair,—
    Leave youth his roses, who can bear a thorn,—
I will not seek for blossoms anywhere,
    Except such common flowers as blow with corn.
Youth gone and beauty gone, what doth remain?
    The longing of a heart pent up forlorn,   10
        A silent heart whose silence loves and longs;
        The silence of a heart which sang its songs
    While youth and beauty made a summer morn,
Silence of love that cannot sing again.

1881

A Fisher-Wife

The soonest mended, nothing said;
    And help may rise from east or west;
But my two hands are lumps of lead,
    My heart sits leaden in my breast.

O north wind swoop not from the north,
    O south wind linger in the south,
Oh come not raving raging forth,
    To bring my heart into my mouth;

For I've a husband out at sea,
    Afloat on feeble planks of wood;   10
He does not know what fear may be;
    I would have told him if I could.

I would have locked him in my arms,
    I would have hid him in my heart;
For oh! the waves are fraught with harms,
    And he and I so far apart.

1881

Birchington Churchyard[1]

A lowly hill which overlooks a flat,
    Half sea, half country side;
A flat-shored sea of low-voiced creeping tide
Over a chalky, weedy mat.

A hill of hillocks, flowery and kept green
    Round Crosses raised for hope,
    With many-tinted sunsets where the slope
Faces the lingering western sheen.

A lowly hope, a height that is but low,
    While Time sets solemnly,   10
    While the tide rises of Eternity,
Silent and neither swift nor slow.

1882

Everything that is born must die;
    Everything that can sigh may sing;
Rocks in equal balance, low or high,
    Everything.

    Honeycomb is weighed against a sting;
Hope and fear take turns to touch the sky;
    Height and depth respond alternating.

O my soul, spread wings of love to fly,
    Wings of dove that soars on home-bound wing;
Love trusts Love, till Love shall justify   10
    Everything.

1885

An Echo from Willow-wood

"O ye, all ye that walk in willow-wood."[1]—D. G. Rossetti

Two gazed into a pool, he gazed and she,
    Not hand in hand, yet heart in heart, I think,
    Pale and reluctant on the water's brink,
As on the brink of parting which must be.
Each eyed the other's aspect, she and he,
    Each felt one hungering heart leap up and sink,
    Each tasted bitterness which both must drink,
There on the brink of life's dividing sea.
Lilies upon the surface, deep below
    Two wistful faces craving each for each,   10
        Resolute and reluctant without speech:—
A sudden ripple made the faces flow,
    One moment joined, to vanish out of reach:
        So those hearts joined, and ah were parted so.

1890

---

[1]**Birchington**: where Rossetti's brother Dante Gabriel was buried, SE coast of England.

[1]"**O ye . . . willow-wood**": first line of third "Willow-wood" sonnet from Dante Gabriel Rossetti's *The House of Life*; see page 812.

O Lord, when Thou didst call me, didst Thou know
   My heart disheartened thro' and thro',
   Still hankering after Egypt[1] full in view
Where cucumbers and melons grow?
         —"Yea, I knew."—

But, Lord, when Thou didst choose me, didst Thou know
   How marred I was and withered too,
   Nor rose for sweetness nor for virtue rue,[2]
Timid and rash, hasty and slow?
         —"Yea, I knew."—   10

My Lord, when Thou didst love me, didst Thou know
   How weak my efforts were, how few,
   Tepid to love and impotent to do,
Envious to reap while slack to sow?
         —"Yea, I knew."—

Good Lord, Who knowest what I cannot know
   And dare not know, my false, my true,
   My new, my old; Good Lord, arise and do
If loving Thou hast known me so.
         —"Yea, I knew."—   20
                        1892

"Where their worm dieth not, and the fire is not quenched."[1]

In tempest and storm blackness of darkness for ever,
   A fire unextinguished, a worm's indestructible swarm;
Where no hope shall ever be more, and love shall be never,
     In tempest and storm;
   Where the form of all things is fashionless, void of all
       form;
Where from death that severeth all, the soul cannot sever
     In tempest and storm.
                       1892

Lord, grant us calm, if calm can set forth Thee;
   Or tempest, if a tempest set Thee forth;
   Wind from the east or west or south or north,

Or congelation[1] of a silent sea,
With stillness of each tremulous aspen tree.

Still let fruit fall, or hang upon the tree;
   Still let the east and west, the south and north,
Curb in their winds, or plough a thundering sea;
   Still let the earth abide to set Thee forth,
Or vanish like a smoke to set forth Thee.   10
                       1892

A Pause

They made the chamber sweet with flowers and leaves,
   And the bed sweet with flowers on which I lay;
   While my soul, love-bound, loitered on its way.
I did not hear the birds about the eaves,
Nor hear the reapers talk among the sheaves:
   Only my soul kept watch from day to day,
   My thirsty soul kept watch for one away:—
Perhaps he loves, I thought, remembers, grieves.
At length there came the step upon the stair,
   Upon the lock the old familiar hand: 10
Then first my spirit seemed to scent the air
   Of Paradise; then first the tardy sand
Of time ran golden; and I felt my hair
   Put on a glory, and my soul expand.
                       1896

Sleeping at last, the trouble and tumult over,
   Sleeping at last, the struggle and horror past,
Cold and white, out of sight of friend and of lover,
     Sleeping at last.

   No more a tired heart downcast or overcast,
No more pangs that wring or shifting fears that hover,
   Sleeping at last in a dreamless sleep locked fast.

Fast asleep. Singing birds in their leafy cover
   Cannot wake her, nor shake her the gusty blast.
Under the purple thyme and the purple clover   10
     Sleeping at last.
                       1896

---

[1]**Egypt:** see Numbers 11:5.

[2]**rue:** herbal flower.

[1]**"Where . . . quenched":** Mark 9:44. The poem is a roundelay.

---

[1]**congelation:** freezing.

~

from **Seek and Find**[1]

Stars

"Behold the height of the stars, how high they are!" Job 22.12.

There is something awe-striking, overwhelming, in contemplation of the stars. Their number, magnitudes, distances, orbits, we know not: any multitude our unaided eyes discern is but an instalment of that vaster multitude which the telescope reveals; and of this the heightened and yet again heightened power bringing to light more and more stars, opens before us a vista unmeasured, incalculable. Knowledge runs apace: and our globe which once seemed large is now but a small planet among planets, while not one of our group of planets is large as compared with its central sun; and the sun itself may be no more than a sub-centre, it and all its system coursing but as satellites and sub-satellites around a general centre; and this again,—what of this? Is even this remote centre truly central, or is it no more than yet another sub-centre revolving around some point of overruling attraction, and swaying with it the harmonious encircling dance of its attendant worlds? Thus while knowledge runs apace, ignorance keeps ahead of knowledge: and all which the deepest students know proves to themselves, yet more convincingly than to others, that much more exists which still they know not. As saints in relation to spiritual wisdom, so sages in relation to intellectual wisdom, eating they yet hunger and drinking they yet thirst (Ecclus. 24.21).[2]

Deep only can call to deep: still, we who occupy comparative shallows of intelligence are not wholly debarred from the admiration and delights of noble contemplations. We can marvel over the many tints of the heavenly bodies, ruddy, empurpled, golden, or by contrast pale; we can understand the conclusion, though we cannot follow the process by which analysis of a ray certifies various component elements as existing in the orb which emits it; we can realise mentally how galaxies, which by reason of remoteness present to our eyes a mere modification of sky-colour, are truly a host of distinct luminaries; we can long to know more of belts and atmospheres; we can ponder reverently

over interstellar spaces so vast as to exhaust the attractive force of suns and more than suns.

And we can make of what we know and of what we know not stepping-stones towards heaven, adoring our Creator for all that He is and that His creatures are not; adoring Him also for what many of our fellows already are, and for what we ourselves are and may become. We shall not run to waste in idle curiosity if we bear in mind that "knowledge puffeth up, but charity edifieth" (1 Cor. 8.1), and that whoso understood all mysteries and all knowledge, not having charity would be nothing (13.2). The innumerable number of the stars will profit us while we bear in mind that, though we know not, God telleth their number and "calleth them all by their names" (Ps. 147.4). Their material light will become to us light spiritual, if, because "they that turn many to righteousness" shall shine "as the stars for ever and ever" (Dan. 12.3), zeal burn within us not for our own righteousness only, but for our neighbour's also. The awful familiar heavens now by fixed laws exhibiting motions, influences, aspects, phenomena (now, but not for ever after this present temporal fashion), are even now night by night instructing pious souls who watch and pray and wait for their beloved Lord.

"Seek Him that maketh the seven stars and Orion" (Amos 5.8).

Ice and Snow

"Hast thou entered into the treasures of the snow?
or hast thou seen the treasures of the hail?" Job 38.22.

The beauty of Snow needs no proof. Perfect in whiteness, feathery in lightness, it often floats down with hesitation as if it belonged to air rather than to earth: yet once resting on that ground it seemed loath to touch, it silently and surely accomplishes its allotted task; it fills up chasms, levels inequalities, cloaks imperfections, arrests the evaporation of heat, nurses vegetation; it prepares floods for arid watercourses, and abundant moisture for roots and seeds. Snow, as we are familiar with it, is uncertain in its arrival and brief in its stay; having done its work it vanishes utterly, becoming as though it had never been. Not so in northern regions and on mountain-ranges where it occupies a permanent habitation: there it wraps itself in mist or overlooks the clouds, and thence not in silence but in thunder it rushes down upon the valleys. The beauties of snow are not exhausted when we have watched it afloat in air, or heaped in dazzling whiteness on the earth, or even when we have beheld it on mountain-heights flushed with pure rosiness at the fall of day: the microscope is required to reveal to us the

---

[1]*Seek and Find:* subtitled *A Double Series of Short Studies of the Benedicte,* a sequence of meditations on a Lenten prayer in praise of the elements of the creation.

[2]**Ecclus.:** the apocryphal book Ecclesiasticus.

exquisite symmetry of its crystals, starry, foliated, mimicking with minute perfection features of the firmament and of the flower-bed.

In symbolic analogies we find snow suggestive both of guilt and of cleansing. The whiteness of leprosy, that loathsome type of more loathsome sin, is "as snow" (Exod. 4.6; Num. 12.10; 2 Kings 5.27): while in the other sense Psalmist and Prophet bring forward material snow as a standard of spiritual purification; David saying, "Wash me, and I shall be whiter than snow" (Ps. 51.7), and Isaiah, "Though your sins be as scarlet, they shall be as white as snow" (Isa. 1.18). Job also in one of his passionate appeals cries out from instinctive feeling if not from close reasoning, "If I wash myself with snow water, and make my hands never so clean. . . ." (Job 9.30); thus attributing to *"snow"* water an exceptional purifying virtue.

Ice, viewed as hail, seems exclusively, or almost exclusively, in the Inspired Text, to be or to represent a weapon of God's wrath and righteous vengeance; and this is its aspect whether we study prophets or historians, the Old Testament or the New. Following a scheme of chronology which makes Job a contemporary of Moses, we hear about thirty years before the Exodus this purpose of the hail indicated to Job by Almighty God Himself: "Hast thou seen the treasures of the hail, which I have reserved against the time of trouble, against the day of battle and war?" (Job 38.22,23); and the earliest hailstorm recorded in Holy Scripture is that which scourged Egypt with its seventh plague, "The Lord rained hail upon the land of Egypt" (Exod. 9.23), and to which passages in the Psalms refer (78.47,48; 105.32,33). So also in the wars of Joshua the hail fought on God's side, and slew more of the army of the Amorites than did the sword of the children of Israel (Josh. 10.11). David, again, celebrating his deliverance from his enemies, and especially from Saul, describes his troubles under figure of a flood ready to engulph him, and his rescue as achieved by a manifestation of the Divine Presence, amid mighty convulsions of nature, "hail stones and coals of fire" (Ps. 18.4–17). Isaiah (28.2,17; 30.30; and presumably 32.19), and Ezekiel (13.10–14; 38.22), name hail in their prophecies of vengeance: Haggai mentions it among the agents of an unavailing Divine discipline (Hag. 2.17): St. John thrice beholds it in awful vision (Rev. 8.7; 11.19; 16.21).

If the weapon be mighty, mightier is He Who wields it: nevertheless, if it be good to tremble before God's judgments, it is yet better to confide in His mercy and love. Let us, not neglecting the performance of either duty, add to both humility; and carry our heads as it were low, in memory of that wheat and rye which not being grown up escaped unscathed, while the forwarder flax and barley[3] were smitten.

"Enter into the rock, and hide thee in the dust, for fear of the Lord, and for the glory of His Majesty. The lofty looks of man shall be humbled, and the haughtiness of men shall be bowed down, and the Lord alone shall be exalted in that day" (Isa. 2.10,11).

1879

from Called to Be Saints[1]

St. Andrew, Apostle
30 November

The Daisy

We are well placed where God places us.

The daisy, scattered over many soils, blows the whole year round in genial weather, and though less plentiful in November than in milder months, its rarity may then be viewed as choiceness, for throughout November flowers are few. The daisy must almost always be precursor and companion of some blossom more gorgeous, or more beautiful, or more fragrant than itself: yet not for this does it shrink from opening wide its star towards the sky, and tipping its white disk with a pink nimbus when it expands in sunshine; even in shade it wears no sadder colour than a spotless white. Its centre, or heart, or eye, is of pure gold. Its very name, day's-eye, shows how it courts the sun, and closes against darkness. Its leaves grow habitually close to the ground, though sometimes a leaf or two unfolds along the flower-stalk: yet low-growing as they are, and springing in profusion amid the meadow grasses, a certain acridity protects them from being made havock of altogether and devoured by the grazing cattle which trample them under foot. Grass is tall enough to tower above and hide a daisy; yet the daisy will more readily spread and supersede the grass, than the grass it. Not the petals only, but the leaves also of the daisy are often tinged with pink; as though its allotted beauty and joy overflowed its capacity to hold them.

---

[3]**wheat . . . barley:** see Exodus 9:31–32.

[1]*Called to Be Saints:* based on the 24 chief holy days of the Anglican calendar, a book of seven-fold meditations each ending with consideration of a seasonal wildflower.

Small as this plant is, it both spreads rapidly and is at the same time multiplied by seed; it is "mother of thousands of millions."[2]

God giveth it a body as it hath pleased Him, and to every seed his own body.—1 Cor. 15.38.

All Saints
1 November

The Arbutus and Grass

Great and small.

Even in small matters the end implies a certain solemnity; the last opportunity to be utilized or missed, the last occasion of gain or loss. Often as I have let slip what cannot be regained, two points of my own experience stand out vividly: once, when little realizing how nearly I had despised my last chance, I yet did in bare time do what must shortly have been for ever left undone; and again, when I fulfilled a promise which beyond calculation there remained but scant leisure to fulfil.

Our last Apostle[3] might, I thought, suitably commend to us fruit rather than flowers. Our last and widest Saints' Day, embracing height and depth, honour and humility, shall put on for its garland that which is lofty entwined with that which is very lowly.

Puny in a forest, yet in a shrubbery of grand and stately presence, the Arbutus or Strawberry Tree wears all at one time the panoply of its beauties; combining the blossom of a late flowering season, with ripened fruit from the preceding autumn, and with dark rich foliage in profusion. Its so-called strawberry sprouts rather after the manner of a cherry; but a red and roughened surface invites for it the former name: like its namesake it is edible, though of a far less delicious flavour. The blossom hangs in bunches, and is of a waxen semblance, white, greenish, or pink: each individual floweret approaches certain heath blossoms in size and shape, being rounded and lipped like a minute bottle. Nor do even leaves, flowers, and fruit exhaust the simultaneous graces of the Arbutus: the tree itself branches boldly and nobly, and by a general darkness throws out the fairness of its efflorescence.

At the foot of the Arbutus and of the plant-world in general, trodden at all seasons by all feet, live and thrive the Grasses; stripped of which, earth would lack half her refreshing charm. At the tropics they often match trees in stature; in arctic regions they maintain their ground with no less persistent vitality. They compose a numerous tribe, numbered by hundreds and frequenting every latitude. Most precious of all their charms to us seems their inexhaustible verdure, parched indeed by summer drought but renewed by a shower of rain: sun they need, and air, and moisture; these given, they clothe the ground with a living carpet which snow cannot nip or tempest destroy, yet which a breeze can break up into a sea of ripples, and of which each component blade is straight-veined pointing skywards. In its modest flowering season, however, when the pointed stalk shoots up to a slim tallness and prepares to shed its harvest of seed, then Grass rallies not under trampling foot or stress of weather but is laid low by the assault of even a slight pressure.

The beauty of Grasses whether in blossom or in seed is widely varied, and in some instances truly exquisite. One like miniature barley grows a beard, another showers a weeping oat-like head, another droops a thick rose-tinted plume; one is invested with purple knops,[4] a second feathers greenly, a third displays prevalent whiteness; the leaf of a fourth hangs like a striped ribbon; and yet another, sweetened by an enduring scent, turns a hayrick into a nosegay.

All these and many more we include under the common name of Grass: but other specimens there are of more honourable standing and of yet higher service in our economy, which belong to the same tribe, and being analyzed reveal some of the same constituents. Grasses contain sugar, and the sugar-cane claims kindred with them: they are stiffened by flint, and flint imparts stiffness to the cereal[5] straws. Rice and rye belong to the Grass connection; barley and oats recognise not mere likenesses among the Grasses, but humble kinsfolk: the very "corn of wheat" is itself the most noble member of the common family.

From the Grasses no less than from the heavenly host, from mankind at large, even from Apostles, we gather one same reiterated lesson: Angels share one nature with devils, sanctified souls with souls nigh unto cursing, St. Matthias with Judas Iscariot, the very staff of our life with the noxious darnel.[6] And thus the perfections of our Very God's very Humanity urge us to fear and hope: though we are of

---

[2]"**mother . . . millions**": Genesis 24:60.

[3]**Apostles**: St. Stephen and St. John Evangelist, **last** in the calendar (December 26 and 27) but treated earlier in Rossetti's sequence.

[4]**knops**: knobs.

[5]**cereal**: edible grain.

[6]**St. Matthias** took the place of **Judas Iscariot** among Jesus' apostles after Judas' betrayal (Acts 1:21–26). **darnel**: poisonous ryegrass.

one blood with Him we may not be of one mind, may never become like Him, may never see Him as He is; on the other hand (blessed be God), though we languish ready to perish, yet is He our Brother Who loveth us, Who can be touched with the feeling of our infirmities, and is able to save them to the uttermost that come unto God by Him.

I will cause the shower to come down in his season; there shall be showers of blessing. And the tree of the field shall yield her fruit, and the earth shall yield her increase.— Ezek. 34.26,27.

Light is our sorrow for it ends to-morrow,
    Light is our death which cannot hold us fast;
So brief a sorrow can be scarcely sorrow,
    Or death be death so quickly past.

One night, no more, of pain that turns to pleasure,
    One night, no more, of weeping weeping sore;
And then the heaped-up measure beyond measure,
    In quietness for evermore.

Our face is set like flint against our trouble,
    Yet many things there are which comfort us,
This bubble is a rainbow-coloured bubble,
    This bubble-life tumultuous.

Our sails are set to cross the tossing river,
    Our face is set to reach Jerusalem;
We toil awhile, but then we rest for ever,
    Sing with all Saints and rest with them.

1881

LEWIS CARROLL
(CHARLES LUTWIDGE DODGSON)

(1832–1898)

The eldest boy in a family of eight children, Dodgson arrived at Oxford in 1851 badly shaken by his years at Rugby School, where he had been bullied for his stammering shyness and lost to illness the hearing in one ear. Oxford suited him far better; he dug in to stay. He earned high honors in mathematics and classics, and after his first year accepted a scholarship that was his for life on the double condition of taking holy orders, as he did in 1861, and remaining unmarried, as he did until death. A mathematics tutorship awarded on graduation assured him permanent residence in Christ Church College, where he remained for the rest of his years. He met his teaching obligations faithfully, published some capable but undistinguished work on algebra and geometry, and in his capacity as a church deacon preached a few sermons and officiated occasionally at baptisms and funerals. The retired life of a university don left Dodgson the leisure in which to achieve distinction as an amateur photographer who had two specialties: rather stiff portraits of famous Victorians, and remarkably—not to say scandalously—informal portraits of children, especially little girls in fancy dress or no dress at all. He destroyed many of his thousands of recorded negatives, including all nudes, but the strength of personality in many of the child portraits that survive suggests his uncanny ability to hold his young sitters' amused interest and put them at their ease.

The qualities that must have charmed these children are apparent in the imaginative writing Dodgson published under the name Lewis Carroll, derived via Latin from a reversal of his first and middle names. The *Alice* books that ensued from summer outings in 1862 with a set of Oxford child-friends made Lewis Carroll an author as celebrated as any in this anthology. It is less well known that he attached the same pseudonym to his publications in the field of logic: these notes, games, and inquiries into the rules for making sense and assessing consequence (especially *Symbolic Logic*, 1896) have a great deal in common with the amusements of *Alice's Adventures in Wonderland* (1865) and *Through the Looking-Glass and What Alice Found There* (1871). While Dodgson's strictly Euclidean geometry affirmed the consistency of a system built on self-evident propositions, Carroll's speculatively constructivist logic exposed the arbitrariness of a system built on ungrounded postulates. So did his narrative non sequiturs in the *Alice* books; so did his puns, making ordinary language suddenly opaque, and his parodies, infiltrating Victorian conventions of sentimental instruction with a preposterous content. The nonsense of Edward Lear a generation earlier *makes fun*, with a hilarious humor that is giddy from the start and stays that way; Carrollian nonsense, in a witty process of logical transformation, *makes fun of* something—and its favorite target is established ways of making sense. Children and childlike readers love Lewis Carroll for articulating their suspicion that there is something funny about the sober truth: that it is imposed by adult force and founded on assumptions that are no more inherently plausible than the options they exclude—options that a sufficiently elastic imagination can always revive.

Father William[1]

"You are old, Father William," the young man said,
　"And your hair has become very white;
And yet you incessantly stand on your head—
　Do you think, at your age, it is right?"

"In my youth," Father William replied to his son,
　"I feared it might injure the brain;
But, now that I'm perfectly sure I have none,
　Why, I do it again and again."

"You are old," said the youth, "as I mentioned before,
　And have grown most uncommonly fat;   10
Yet you turned a back-somersault in at the door—
　Pray, what is the reason of that?"

"In my youth," said the sage, as he shook his grey locks,
　"I kept all my limbs very supple
By the use of this ointment—one shilling the box—
　Allow me to sell you a couple?"

"You are old," said the youth, "and your jaws are too weak
　For anything tougher than suet;
Yet you finished the goose, with the bones and the beak—
　Pray, how did you manage to do it?"   20

"In my youth," said his father, "I took to the law,
　And argued each case with my wife;
And the muscular strength, which it gave to my jaw,
　Has lasted the rest of my life."

"You are old," said the youth, "one would hardly suppose
　That your eye was as steady as ever;
Yet you balanced an eel on the end of your nose—
　What made you so awfully clever?"

"I have answered three questions, and that is enough,"
　Said his father; "don't give yourself airs!   30
Do you think I can listen all day to such stuff?
　Be off, or I'll kick you down stairs!"

　　　　　　　　　　　　　　　　　　　　　　　　　　1865

Yet what are all such gaieties to me
　Whose thoughts are full of indices and surds?[1]
$x^2 + 7x + 53$
　$= \dfrac{11}{3}$.

　　　　　　　　　　　　　　　　　　　　　　　　　　1869

Jabberwocky[1]

'Twas brillig, and the slithy toves
　Did gyre and gimble in the wabe;
All mimsy were the borogoves,
　And the mome raths outgrabe.

"Beware the Jabberwock, my son!
　The jaws that bite, the claws that catch!
Beware the Jubjub bird, and shun
　The frumious Bandersnatch!"

---

[1]**indices:** exponents. **surds:** irrational numbers.

[1]"Well, *'toves'* are something like badgers—they're something like lizards—and they're something like corkscrews."

"They must be very curious-looking creatures."

"They are that," said Humpty Dumpty, "also they make their nests under sun-dials—also they live on cheese."

"And what's to *'gyre'* and to *'gimble'*?"

"To *'gyre'* is to go round and round like a gyroscope. To *'gimble'* is to make holes like a gimblet."

"And *'the wabe'* is the grass-plot round a sundial, I suppose?" said Alice, surprised at her own ingenuity.

"Of course it is. It's called *'wabe,'* you know, because it goes a long way before it, and a long way behind it——"

"And a long way beyond it on each side," Alice added.

"Exactly so. Well then, *'mimsy'* is flimsy 'and miserable' (there's another portmanteau for you). And a *'borogove'* is a thin shabby-looking bird with its feathers sticking out all round—something like a live mop."

"And then *'mome raths'*?" said Alice. "I'm afraid I'm giving you a great deal of trouble."

"Well, a *'rath'* is a sort of green pig: but *'mome'* I'm not certain about. I think it's short for 'from home'—meaning that they'd lost their way, you know."

"And what does *'outgrabe'* mean?"

"Well, *'outgribing'* is something between bellowing and whistling, with a kind of sneeze in the middle: however, you'll hear it done, maybe—down in the wood yonder—and when you've once heard it you'll be *quite* content." (*Through the Looking-Glass*, ch. 6)

---

[1]**"Father William"**: from *Alice's Adventures in Wonderland*, chapter 5. The poem parodies "The Old Man's Comforts and How He Gained Them" (1799) by Robert Southey (1774–1843).

He took his vorpal sword in hand:
    Long time the manxome foe he sought—   10
So rested he by the Tumtum tree,
    And stood awhile in thought.

And as in uffish thought he stood,
    The Jabberwock, with eyes of flame,
Came whiffling through the tulgey wood,
    And burbled as it came!

One, two! One, two! And through and through
    The vorpal blade went snicker-snack!
He left it dead, and with its head
    He went galumphing back.   20

"And hast thou slain the Jabberwock?
    Come to my arms, my beamish boy!
O frabjous day! Callooh! Callay!"
    He chortled in his joy.

'Twas brillig, and the slithy toves
    Did gyre and gimble in the wabe;
All mimsy were the borogoves,
    And the mome raths outgrabe.

    1871

The Walrus and the Carpenter[1]

The sun was shining on the sea,
    Shining with all his might:
He did his very best to make
    The billows smooth and bright—
And this was odd, because it was
    The middle of the night.

The moon was shining sulkily,
    Because she thought the sun
Had got no business to be there
    After the day was done—   10
"It's very rude of him," she said,
    "To come and spoil the fun!"

---

[1]"**The Walrus and the Carpenter**": from *Through the Looking-Glass*, chapter 4.

The sea was wet as wet could be,
    The sands were dry as dry.
You could not see a cloud, because
    No cloud was in the sky:
No birds were flying overhead—
    There were no birds to fly.

The Walrus and the Carpenter
    Were walking close at hand;   20
They wept like anything to see
    Such quantities of sand:
"If this were only cleared away,"
    They said, "it *would* be grand!"

"If seven maids with seven mops
    Swept it for half a year,
Do you suppose," the Walrus said,
    "That they could get it clear?"
"I doubt it," said the Carpenter,
    And shed a bitter tear.   30

"O Oysters, come and walk with us!"
    The Walrus did beseech.
"A pleasant walk, a pleasant talk,
    Along the briny beach:
We cannot do with more than four,
    To give a hand to each."

The eldest Oyster looked at him,
    But never a word he said:
The eldest Oyster winked his eye,
    And shook his heavy head—   40
Meaning to say he did not choose
    To leave the oyster-bed.

But four young Oysters hurried up,
    All eager for the treat:
Their coats were brushed, their faces washed,
    Their shoes were clean and neat—
And this was odd, because, you know,
    They hadn't any feet.

Four other Oysters followed them,
    And yet another four;   50
And thick and fast they came at last,
    And more, and more, and more—
All hopping through the frothy waves,
    And scrambling to the shore.

The Walrus and the Carpenter
　　Walked on a mile or so,
And then they rested on a rock
　　Conveniently low:
And all the little Oysters stood
　　And waited in a row.   60

"The time has come," the Walrus said,
　　"To talk of many things:
Of shoes—and ships—and sealing-wax—
　　Of cabbages—and kings—
And why the sea is boiling hot—
　　And whether pigs have wings."

"But wait a bit," the Oysters cried,
　　"Before we have our chat;
For some of us are out of breath,
　　And all of us are fat!"   70
"No hurry!" said the Carpenter.
　　They thanked him much for that.

"A loaf of bread," the Walrus said,
　　"Is what we chiefly need:
Pepper and vinegar besides
　　Are very good indeed—
Now if you're ready, Oysters dear,
　　We can begin to feed."

"But not on us!" the Oysters cried,
　　Turning a little blue.   80
"After such kindness, that would be
　　A dismal thing to do!"
"The night is fine," the Walrus said.
　　"Do you admire the view?

"It was so kind of you to come!
　　And you are very nice!"
The Carpenter said nothing but
　　"Cut us another slice:
I wish you were not quite so deaf—
　　I've had to ask you twice!"   90

"It seems a shame," the Walrus said,
　　"To play them such a trick,
After we've brought them out so far,
　　And made them trot so quick!"
The Carpenter said nothing but
　　"The butter's spread too thick!"

"I weep for you," the Walrus said:
　　"I deeply sympathize."
With sobs and tears he sorted out
　　Those of the largest size,   100
Holding his pocket-handkerchief
　　Before his streaming eyes.

"O Oysters," said the Carpenter,
　　"You've had a pleasant run!
Shall we be trotting home again?"
　　But answer came there none—
And this was scarcely odd, because
　　They'd eaten every one.
                                          1871

The White Knight's Ballad[1]

I'll tell thee everything I can;
　　There's little to relate.
I saw an aged aged man,
　　A-sitting on a gate.
"Who are you, aged man?" I said.
　　"And how is it you live?"
And his answer trickled through my head
　　Like water through a sieve.

He said "I look for butterflies
　　That sleep among the wheat: 10
I make them into mutton-pies,
　　And sell them in the street.
I sell them unto men," he said,
　　"Who sail on stormy seas;
And that's the way I get my bread—
　　A trifle, if you please."

But I was thinking of a plan
　　To dye one's whiskers green,
And always use so large a fan
　　That they could not be seen.   20
So, having no reply to give
　　To what the old man said,
I cried "Come, tell me how you live!"
　　And thumped him on the head.

---

[1]"**The White Knight's Ballad**": from *Through the Looking-Glass*, chapter 8. The poem, a parody of Wordsworth's "Resolution and Independence" (1807), first appeared in the short-lived humor monthly *The Train* in 1856 under the title "Upon the Lonely Moor."

His accents mild took up the tale:
    He said "I go my ways,
And when I find a mountain-rill,
    I set it in a blaze;
And thence they make a stuff they call
    Rowland's Macassar Oil—[2]   30
Yet twopence-halfpenny is all
    They give me for my toil."

But I was thinking of a way
    To feed oneself on batter,
And so go on from day to day
    Getting a little fatter.
I shook him well from side to side,
    Until his face was blue:
"Come, tell me how you live," I cried
    "And what it is you do!"   40

He said "I hunt for haddocks' eyes
    Among the heather bright,
And work them into waistcoat-buttons
    In the silent night.
And these I do not sell for gold
    Or coin of silvery shine,
But for a copper halfpenny,
    And that will purchase nine.

"I sometimes dig for buttered rolls,
    Or set limed[3] twigs for crabs;   50
I sometimes search the grassy knolls
    For wheels of hansom-cabs.

And that's the way" (he gave a wink)
    "By which I get my wealth—
And very gladly will I drink
    Your Honour's noble health."

I heard him then, for I had just
    Completed my design
To keep the Menai bridge[4] from rust
    By boiling it in wine.   60
I thanked him much for telling me
    The way he got his wealth,
But chiefly for his wish that he
    Might drink my noble health.

And now, if e'er by chance I put
    My fingers into glue,
Or madly squeeze a right-hand foot
    Into a left-hand shoe,
Or if I drop upon my toe
    A very heavy weight,   70
I weep, for it reminds me so
Of that old man I used to know—
Whose look was mild, whose speech was slow,
Whose hair was whiter than the snow,
Whose face was very like a crow,
With eyes, like cinders, all aglow,
Who seemed distracted with his woe,
Who rocked his body to and fro,
And muttered mumblingly and low,
As if his mouth were full of dough,   80
Who snorted like a buffalo—
That summer evening long ago
    A-sitting on a gate.

1871

---

[2]**Rowland's Macassar Oil**: popular hair preparation, named after a region of Indonesia. See advertisement after page 684.

[3]**limed**: smeared with sticky lime to catch birds.

[4]**Menai bridge**: early suspension bridge, built 1819–1826, across the Menai strait, N Wales.

WILLIAM MORRIS

(1834–1896)

Advances in the division of labor leave us abashed at the range of cultural tasks an eminent Victorian could creditably perform. Yet even among Victorians the versatility of William Morris had no equal. Lyric poet and teller of long tales, translator of epics, library lecturer, soapbox demagogue—Morris was all these and more, yet his more than twenty volumes represent, on the whole, a kind of inspired moonlighting. Writing was his after-hours recreation, an outlet for the superabundant vitality he devoted mainly to designing and making beautiful objects and imagining and struggling for a just society.

Born to parents made rich by inheritance and investment, Morris spent his life and much of his fortune in inventive and increasingly overt rebellion against the conditions of his wealth. He arrived at Oxford in 1853 a confirmed neo-medievalist with High-Church allegiances; and the old romances, chronicles, and myths he devoured there furnished topics for much of the poetry he would soon write. Meanwhile John Ruskin's analysis of Gothic art in the recent *Stones of Venice* served, as Morris later said, "to give form to my discontent," implanting a radicalism that was to flourish decades later. Art usurped religion as the focus of his undergraduate energies: he entered an architect's office in 1856 but, coming under the PreRaphaelite influence of Edward Burne-Jones, D. G. Rossetti, and others, rapidly became a painter and poet instead. The painterly poems in his 1858 *Defence of Guenevere* collection sum up Morris' interests to date: medieval materials furnish these poems with images and emotions whose brilliant rendition in primary colors combines detailed Tennysonian sensuousness with historical and contextual implication learned from Browning. At once vivid and enigmatic, the energy of these PreRaphaelite poems crowds moral purpose virtually out of the picture.

In 1859 Morris married Jane Burden, a stableman's daughter and artist's model whose beauty epitomized the PreRaphaelite ideal. Two years later he established what would become Morris and Company, an upscale design firm that occupied him for decades weaving and dyeing cloth, staining glass, creating wallpaper, and inventing among other furniture the simple, comfortable Morris chair. His most enduring legacy was as the founder and chief exponent of what came to be known as "arts and crafts": a practical faith in the aesthetic and moral value of simple flowing attire, homemade pots and fabrics, hand-produced furniture and books, and other forms of resistance to mass production and consumption. If everyone did as he did—practiced a variety of arts with curiosity and enthusiasm—then the degraded modern body and alienated modern mind might recover their broken harmony, he believed, and society regain its lost communal joy.

In his spare time Morris composed narrative verse, sometimes hundreds of lines at a stretch, rehearsing old Greek and Norse legends in a leisurely style whose evenness of flow prompts comparison to the clean-lined patterns for wallpaper and fabric that filled his days. Reversing the practice of his *Guenevere* volume, Morris now subordinated special effects to the pleasures, including pleasantly suffusive melancholy, of the tale itself. The accumulated result was the serial *Earthly Paradise* (1868–1870), one of the longest poems in the English language, a resounding bestseller, and—with its enormous scale and unhurried pace—an anthologist's despair. Morris' characteristic response to this success was to turn a new corner. He became absorbed in Northern mythology, studied the old sagas, visited Iceland, and with a tutor's help issued translations of Icelandic texts. In *Sigurd the Volsung* (1876) he produced a book-length version of these and other Germanic materials that was at once a remarkably faithful treatment and a highly original Victorian poem, which in its stark nobility could hardly have been more different from the wistful ease of the writing he had done a decade before.

Something in the tragically committed heroism of the Volsung saga seems to have awakened a new civic impulse pushing Morris into public life. He wrote open letters critical of British foreign policy, founded an organization in defense of ancient church architecture, and gave public lectures on art's relation to society (the first of which is excerpted here). Grappling with this last theme and its unfinished Ruskinian business took him ever deeper into analysis of the social fabric, and into the proposals for political and economic redesign that swirled through the turbulent end of the century. In the mid-1880s Morris joined one socialist organization, founded another, read Karl Marx and other communists, edited the radical journal *Commonweal*, and in rallies and strategy sessions placed his wealth and prestige at the disposal of the British movement for workers' rights and economic equality. He opened a new vein of propagandistic writing—call it social science fiction—that included time-traveling utopian prose romances (notably *News from Nowhere*, 1890) and a revolutionary verse idyll based on the 1870 communist uprising in Paris. He also translated the *Odyssey*, the *Aeneid*, and *Beowulf* into forms of the vernacular British ballad that Morris hoped might restore these epics to the people.

Troubled physically by gout and bruised politically by leftist infighting, Morris stepped back after 1890 from the front lines—though not from ideological commitment, as the late "How I Became a Socialist" demonstrates—to concentrate on a last intersection point of literature, art, and economics: the printed book. His Kelmscott Press combined paper craft, ink manufacture, original font designs, and handpress techniques to set a new standard for fine book production with editions of Tennyson, Chaucer, and earlier writings of his own. He remained an active writer, producing translations, socialist tracts, and a series of romances—composed in a strange full prose developed from a lifetime of verse- and speech-making—that imagine forms of sexual and social happiness he did not find in Victorian life. Morris' reiterated refusal of the poet laureateship after 1892 confirms his literary standing—and reminds us that he had attained it nearly as an afterthought.

The Defence of Guenevere[1]

But, knowing now that they would have her speak,
She threw her wet hair backward from her brow,
Her hand close to her mouth touching her cheek,

As though she had had there a shameful blow,
And feeling it shameful to feel ought but shame
All through her heart, yet felt her cheek burned so,

She must a little touch it; like one lame
She walked away from Gauwaine,[2] with her head
Still lifted up; and on her cheek of flame

The tears dried quick; she stopped at last and said: 10
O knights and lords, it seems but little skill[3]
To talk of well-known things past now and dead.

---

[1] **Guenevere**: Arthur's queen, on trial for adultery with Launcelot.

[2] **Gauwaine**: Arthur's nephew, her accuser.

[3] **skill**: use.

God wot[4] I ought to say, I have done ill,
And pray you all forgiveness heartily!
Because you must be right, such great lords; still

Listen, suppose your time were come to die,
And you were quite alone and very weak;
Yea, laid a dying while very mightily

The wind was ruffling up the narrow streak
Of river through your broad lands running well;   20
Suppose a hush should come, then some one speak:

"One of these cloths is heaven, and one is hell,
Now choose one cloth for ever; which they be,
I will not tell you, you must somehow tell

Of your own strength and mightiness; here, see!"
Yea, yea, my lord, and you to ope your eyes,
At foot of your familiar bed to see

A great God's angel standing, with such dyes,
Not known on earth, on his great wings, and hands,
Held out two ways, light from the inner skies   30

Showing him well, and making his commands
Seem to be God's commands, moreover, too,
Holding within his hands the cloths on wands;

And one of these strange choosing cloths was blue,
Wavy and long, and one cut short and red;
No man could tell the better of the two.

After a shivering half-hour you said:
"God help! heaven's colour, the blue;" and he said, "hell."
Perhaps you then would roll upon your bed,

And cry to all good men that loved you well,   40
"Ah Christ! if only I had known, known, known;"
Launcelot went away, then I could tell,

Like wisest man how all things would be, moan,
And roll and hurt myself, and long to die,
And yet fear much to die for what was sown.

Nevertheless you, O Sir Gauwaine, lie,
Whatever may have happened through these years,
God knows I speak truth, saying that you lie.

Her voice was low at first, being full of tears,
But as it cleared, it grew full loud and shrill,   50
Growing a windy shriek in all men's ears,

A ringing in their startled brains, until
She said that Gauwaine lied, then her voice sunk,
And her great eyes began again to fill,

Though still she stood right up, and never shrunk,
But spoke on bravely, glorious lady fair!
Whatever tears her full lips may have drunk,

She stood, and seemed to think, and wrung her hair,
Spoke out at last with no more trace of shame,
With passionate twisting of her body there: 60

It chanced upon a day that Launcelot came
To dwell at Arthur's court: at Christmas-time
This happened; when the heralds sung his name,

Son of King Ban of Benwick,[5] seemed to chime
Along with all the bells that rang that day,
O'er the white roofs, with little change of rhyme.

Christmas and whitened winter passed away,
And over me the April sunshine came,
Made very awful with black hail-clouds, yea

And in the Summer I grew white with flame,   70
And bowed my head down: Autumn, and the sick
Sure knowledge things would never be the same,

However often Spring might be most thick
Of blossoms and buds, smote on me, and I grew
Careless of most things, let the clock tick, tick,

To my unhappy pulse, that beat right through
My eager body; while I laughed out loud,
And let my lips curl up at false or true,

Seemed cold and shallow without any cloud.
Behold my judges, then the cloths were brought;   80
While I was dizzied thus, old thoughts would crowd,

Belonging to the time ere I was bought
By Arthur's great name and his little love;
Must I give up for ever then, I thought,

That which I deemed would ever round me move
Glorifying all things; for a little word,
Scarce ever meant at all, must I now prove

Stone-cold for ever? Pray you, does the Lord
Will that all folks should be quite happy and good?
I love God now a little, if this cord   90

Were broken, once for all what striving could
Make me love anything in earth or heaven?
So day by day it grew, as if one should

Slip slowly down some path worn smooth and even,
Down to a cool sea on a summer day;
Yet still in slipping there was some small leaven

---

[4]**God wot:** God knows.

[5]**King Ban of Benwick:** Launcelot's father, a Breton king.

Of stretched hands catching small stones by the way,
Until one surely reached the sea at last,
And felt strange new joy as the worn head lay

Back, with the hair like sea-weed; yea all past   100
Sweat of the forehead, dryness of the lips,
Washed utterly out by the dear waves o'ercast,

In the lone sea, far off from any ships!
Do I not know now of a day in Spring?
No minute of that wild day ever slips

From out my memory; I hear thrushes sing,
And wheresoever I may be, straightway
Thoughts of it all come up with most fresh sting:

I was half mad with beauty on that day,
And went without my ladies all alone,   110
In a quiet garden walled round every way;

I was right joyful of that wall of stone,
That shut the flowers and trees up with the sky,
And trebled all the beauty: to the bone,

Yea right through to my heart, grown very shy
With weary thoughts, it pierced, and made me glad;
Exceedingly glad, and I knew verily,

A little thing just then had made me mad;
I dared not think, as I was wont to do,
Sometimes, upon my beauty; if I had   120

Held out my long hand up against the blue,
And, looking on the tenderly darken'd fingers,
Thought that by rights one ought to see quite through,

There, see you, where the soft still light yet lingers,
Round by the edges; what should I have done,
If this had joined with yellow spotted singers,

And startling green drawn upward by the sun?
But shouting, loosed out, see now! all my hair,
And trancedly stood watching the west wind run

With faintest half-heard breathing sound: why there 130
I lose my head e'en now in doing this;
But shortly listen: In that garden fair

Came Launcelot walking; this is true, the kiss
Wherewith we kissed in meeting that spring day,
I scarce dare talk of the remember'd bliss,

When both our mouths went wandering in one way,
And aching sorely, met among the leaves;
Our hands being left behind strained far away.

Never within a yard of my bright sleeves
Had Launcelot come before: and now, so nigh!   140
After that day why is it Guenevere grieves?

Nevertheless you, O Sir Gauwaine, lie,
Whatever happened on through all those years,
God knows I speak truth, saying that you lie.

Being such a lady could I weep these tears
If this were true? A great queen such as I
Having sinn'd this way, straight her conscience sears;

And afterwards she liveth hatefully,
Slaying and poisoning, certes[6] never weeps:
Gauwaine be friends now, speak me lovingly.   150

Do I not see how God's dear pity creeps
All through your frame, and trembles in your mouth?
Remember in what grave your mother[7] sleeps,

Buried in some place far down in the south,
Men are forgetting as I speak to you;
By her head sever'd in that awful drouth

Of pity that drew Agravaine's fell blow,
I pray your pity! let me not scream out
For ever after, when the shrill winds blow

Through half your castle-locks! let me not shout   160
For ever after in the winter night
When you ride out alone! in battle-rout

Let not my rusting tears make your sword light!
Ah! God of mercy, how he turns away!
So, ever must I dress me[8] to the fight,

So: let God's justice work! Gauwaine, I say,
See me hew down your proofs: yea all men know
Even as you said how Mellyagraunce[9] one day,

One bitter day in *la Fausse Garde*, for so
All good knights held it after, saw: 170
Yea, sirs, by cursed unknightly outrage; though

You, Gauwaine, held his word without a flaw,
This Mellyagraunce saw blood upon my bed:
Whose blood then pray you? is there any law

To make a queen say why some spots of red
Lie on her coverlet? or will you say:
Your hands are white, lady, as when you wed,

---

[6]**certes**: surely.

[7]**your mother**: accused of infidelity and killed by **Agravaine**, Gauwaine's brother.

[8]**dress me**: brace myself.

[9]**Mellyagraunce**: knight and accuser who formerly abducted Guenevere from her bed in the castle afterward called *Fausse Garde* (False Guard) and whom Launcelot killed in ordeal by combat.

Where did you bleed? and must I stammer out, Nay,
I blush indeed, fair lord, only to rend
My sleeve up to my shoulder, where there lay   180

A knife-point last night: so must I defend
The honour of the Lady Guenevere?
Not so, fair lords, even if the world should end

This very day, and you were judges here
Instead of God. Did you see Mellyagraunce
When Launcelot stood by him? what white fear

Curdled his blood, and how his teeth did dance,
His side sink in? as my knight cried and said:
Slayer of unarm'd men, here is a chance!

Setter of traps, I pray you guard your head,   190
By God I am so glad to fight with you,
Stripper of ladies, that my hand feels lead

For driving weight; hurrah now! draw and do,
For all my wounds are moving in my breast,
And I am getting mad with waiting so.

He struck his hands together o'er the beast,
Who fell down flat, and grovell'd at his feet,
And groan'd at being slain so young: At least,

My knight said, rise you, sir, who are so fleet
At catching ladies, half-arm'd will I fight,   200
My left side all uncovered! then I weet,[10]

Up sprang Sir Mellyagraunce with great delight
Upon his knave's face; not until just then
Did I quite hate him, as I saw my knight

Along the lists look to my stake and pen[11]
With such a joyous smile, it made me sigh
From agony beneath my waist-chain, when

The fight began, and to me they drew nigh;
Ever Sir Launcelot kept him on the right,
And traversed warily, and ever high   210

And fast leapt caitiff's[12] sword, until my knight
Sudden threw up his sword to his left hand,
Caught it, and swung it; that was all the fight,

Except a spout of blood on the hot land;
For it was hottest summer; and I know
I wonder'd how the fire, while I should stand,

And burn, against the heat, would quiver so,
Yards above my head; thus these matters went;
Which things were only warnings of the woe

That fell on me. Yet Mellyagraunce was shent,[13]   220
For Mellyagraunce had fought against the Lord;
Therefore, my lords, take heed lest you be blent[14]

With all this wickedness; say no rash word
Against me, being so beautiful; my eyes,
Wept all away to grey, may bring some sword

To drown you in your blood; see my breast rise,
Like waves of purple sea, as here I stand;
And how my arms are moved in wonderful wise,

Yea also at my full heart's strong command,
See through my long throat how the words go up   230
In ripples to my mouth; how in my hand

The shadow lies like wine within a cup
Of marvellously colour'd gold; yea now
This little wind is rising, look you up,

And wonder how the light is falling so
Within my moving tresses: will you dare,
When you have looked a little on my brow,

To say this thing is vile? or will you care
For any plausible lies of cunning woof,[15]
When you can see my face with no lie there   240

For ever? am I not a gracious proof?
But in your chamber Launcelot was found:
Is there a good knight then would stand aloof,

When a queen says with gentle queenly sound:
O true as steel come now and talk with me,
I love to see your step upon the ground

Unwavering, also well I love to see
That gracious smile light up your face, and hear
Your wonderful words, that all mean verily

The thing they seem to mean: good friend, so dear   250
To me in everything, come here to-night,
Or else the hours will pass most dull and drear;

If you come not, I fear this time I might
Get thinking over much of times gone by,
When I was young, and green hope was in sight:

---

[10]weet: know.

[11]stake and pen: where she was chained for burning had Launcelot not defeated Mellyagraunce.

[12]caitiff: coward.

[13]shent: ruined.

[14]blent: blended, also blinded.

[15]woof: weave, fabrication.

For no man cares now to know why I sigh;
And no man comes to sing me pleasant songs,
Nor any brings me the sweet flowers that lie

So thick in the gardens; therefore one so longs
To see you, Launcelot; that we may be   260
Like children once again, free from all wrongs

Just for one night. Did he not come to me?
What thing could keep true Launcelot away
If I said, Come? there was one less than three

In my quiet room that night, and we were gay;
Till sudden I rose up, weak, pale, and sick,
Because a bawling broke our dream up, yea

I looked at Launcelot's face and could not speak,
For he looked helpless too, for a little while;
Then I remember how I tried to shriek,   270

And could not, but fell down; from tile to tile
The stones they threw up rattled o'er my head
And made me dizzier; till within a while

My maids were all about me, and my head
On Launcelot's breast was being soothed away
From its white chattering, until Launcelot said:

By God! I will not tell you more to-day,
Judge any way you will: what matters it?
You know quite well the story of that fray,

How Launcelot still'd their bawling, the mad fit   280
That caught up Gauwaine: all, all, verily,
But just that which would save me; these things flit.

Nevertheless you, O Sir Gauwaine, lie,
Whatever may have happen'd these long years,
God knows I speak truth, saying that you lie!

All I have said is truth, by Christ's dear tears.
She would not speak another word, but stood
Turn'd sideways; listening, like a man who hears

His brother's trumpet sounding through the wood
Of his foes' lances. She lean'd eagerly,   290
And gave a slight spring sometimes, as she could

At last hear something really; joyfully
Her cheek grew crimson, as the headlong speed
Of the roan charger drew all men to see,
The knight who came was Launcelot at good need.

1858

~

Concerning Geffray Teste Noire

And if you meet the Canon of Chimay,[1]
    As going to Ortaise you well may do,
Greet him from John of Castel Neuf, and say,
    All that I tell you, for all this is true.

This Geffray Teste Noire was a Gascon thief,
    Who, under shadow of the English name,
Pilled[2] all such towns and countries as were lief
    To King Charles and St. Denis; thought it blame

If anything escaped him; so my lord,
    The Duke of Berry,[3] sent Sir John Bonne Lance,   10
And other knights, good players with the sword,
    To check this thief, and give the land a chance.

Therefore we set our bastides[4] round the tower
    That Geffray held, the strong thief! like a king,
High perch'd upon the rock of Ventadour,[5]
    Hopelessly strong by Christ! It was mid spring,

When first I joined the little army there
    With ten good spears; Auvergne is hot, each day
We sweated armed before the barrier;
    Good feats of arms were done there often. Eh?   20

Your brother was slain there? I mind me now,
    A right good man-at-arms, God pardon him!
I think 'twas Geffray smote him on the brow
    With some spiked axe, and while he totter'd, dim

About the eyes, the spear of Alleyne Roux[6]
    Slipped through his camaille and his throat; well, well!
Alleyne is paid now; your name Alleyne too?
    Mary! how strange! but this tale I would tell:

---

[1]**Canon of Chimay**: Jean Froissart (1333?–1400), recorder of chivalric manners and chronicler of the Hundred Years' War, who identified **Teste Noire** (Blackhead) as Breton, not **Gascon**. **Ortaise**: town in S France. **John of Castel Neuf** (New Castle): Morris' invention.

[2]**Pilled**: pillaged. **lief**: precious. **King Charles** VI of France (1368–1422). **St. Denis**: patron saint of France.

[3]**Duke of Berry**: Jean de France (1340–1416), third son of King John II (1319–1364) and a major contender during the Hundred Years' War. **Bonne Lance**: Morris' invention.

[4]**bastides**: temporary siege towers.

[5]**Ventadour**: castle in **Auvergne** (central France) purchased by Teste Noire and used as a raiding base.

[6]**Alleyne Roux**: Geffray's nephew. **camaille**: hooded cape.

For spite of all our bastides, damned Blackhead
    Would ride abroad whene'er he chose to ride,   30
We could not stop him; many a burgher bled
    Dear gold all round his girdle; far and wide

The villaynes[7] dwelt in utter misery
    'Twixt us and thief Sir Geffray; hauled this way
By Sir Bonne Lance at one time; he gone by,
    Down comes this Teste Noire on another day.

And therefore they dig up the stone, grind corn,
    Hew wood, draw water, yea, they lived, in short,
As I said just now, utterly forlorn,
    Till this our knave and blackhead was out-fought.40

So Bonne Lance fretted, thinking of some trap
    Day after day, till on a time he said:
John of Newcastle, if we have good hap,
    We catch our thief in two days. How? I said.

Why, Sir, to-day he rideth out again,
    Hoping to take well certain sumpter[8] mules
From Carcassonne, going with little train,
    Because, forsooth, he thinketh us mere fools;

But if we set an ambush in some wood,
    He is but dead: so, Sir, take thirty spears   50
To Verville forest, if it seem you good.
    Then felt I like the horse in Job,[9] who hears

The dancing trumpet sound, and we went forth;
    And my red lion on the spear-head flapped,
As faster than the cool wind we rode north,
    Towards the wood of Verville; thus it happed.

We rode a soft pace on that day, while spies
    Got news about Sir Geffray: the red wine
Under the road-side bush was clear; the flies,
    The dragon-flies I mind me most, did shine   60

In brighter arms than ever I put on;
    So: Geffray, said our spies, would pass that way
Next day at sundown: then he must be won;
    And so we enter'd Verville wood next day,

In the afternoon; through it the highway runs,
    'Twixt copses of green hazel, very thick,
And underneath, with glimmering of suns,
    The primroses are happy; the dews lick

The soft green moss: "Put cloths about your arms,
    Lest they should glitter; surely they will go   70
In a long thin line, watchful for alarms,
    With all their carriages of booty; so,

Lay down my pennon in the grass: Lord God!
    What have we lying here? will they be cold,
I wonder, being so bare, above the sod,
    Instead of under? This was a knight too, fold

Lying on fold of ancient rusted mail;
    No plate[10] at all, gold rowels to the spurs,
And see the quiet gleam of turquoise pale
    Along the ceinture; but the long time blurs   80

Even the tinder of his coat to nought,
    Except these scraps of leather; see how white
The skull is, loose within the coif![11] He fought
    A good fight, maybe, ere he was slain quite.

No armour on the legs too; strange in faith!
    A little skeleton for a knight, though: ah!
This one is bigger, truly without scathe
    His enemies escaped not! ribs driven out far;

That must have reach'd the heart, I doubt: how now,
    What say you, Aldovrand, a woman? why?"   90
"Under the coif a gold wreath on the brow,
    Yea, see the hair not gone to powder, lie,

Golden, no doubt, once: yea, and very small,
    This for a knight; but for a dame, my lord,
These loose-hung bones seem shapely still, and tall.
    Didst ever see a woman's bones, my Lord?"

Often, God help me! I remember when
    I was a simple boy, fifteen years old,
The Jacquerie[12] froze up the blood of men
    With their fell deeds, not fit now to be told.   100

God help again! we enter'd Beauvais town,
    Slaying them fast, whereto I help'd, mere boy
As I was then; we gentles cut them down,
    These burners and defilers, with great joy.

Reason for that, too, in the great church there
    These fiends had lit a fire, that soon went out,
The church at Beauvais being so great and fair:
    My father, who was by me, gave a shout

---

[7]**villaynes:** feudal serfs.

[8]**sumpter:** baggage. **Carcassonne:** fortified town in SW France.

[9]**horse in Job:** see Job 39:25.

[10]**plate:** solid metal armor. **rowels:** rotating disks. **ceinture:** belt.

[11]**coif:** metal skullcap.

[12]**Jacquerie:** peasant uprising, begun 1358 at **Beauvais** in N France.

Between a beast's howl and a woman's scream,
    Then, panting, chuckled to me: "John, look! look! 110
Count the dames' skeletons!" From some bad dream
    Like a man just awaked, my father shook;

And I, being faint with smelling the burnt bones,
    And very hot with fighting down the street,
And sick of such a life, fell down, with groans
    My head went weakly nodding to my feet.

—An arrow had gone through her tender throat,
    And her right wrist was broken; then I saw
The reason why she had on that war-coat,
    Their story came out clear without a flaw;   120

For when he knew that they were being waylaid,
    He threw it over her, yea, hood and all;
Whereby he was much hack'd, while they were stay'd
    By those their murderers; many an one did fall

Beneath his arm, no doubt, so that he clear'd
    Their circle, bore his death-wound out of it;
But as they rode, some archer least afear'd
    Drew a strong bow, and thereby she was hit.

Still as he rode he knew not she was dead,
    Thought her but fainted from her broken wrist,   130
He bound with his great leathern belt: she bled?
    Who knows! he bled too, neither was there miss'd

The beating of her heart, his heart beat well
    For both of them, till here, within this wood,
He died scarce sorry; easy this to tell;
    After these years the flowers forget their blood.

How could it be? never before that day,
    However much a soldier I might be,
Could I look on a skeleton and say
    I care not for it, shudder not: now see,   140

Over those bones I sat and pored for hours,
    And thought, and dream'd, and still I scarce could see
The small white bones that lay upon the flowers,
    But evermore I saw the lady; she

With her dear gentle walking leading in,
    By a chain of silver twined about her wrists,
Her loving knight, mounted and arm'd to win
    Great honour for her, fighting in the lists.

O most pale face, that brings such joy and sorrow
    Into men's hearts (yea, too, so piercing sharp   150
That joy is, that it marcheth nigh to sorrow
    For ever, like an overwinded harp).

Your face must hurt me always: pray you now,
    Doth it not hurt you too? seemeth some pain
To hold you always, pain to hold your brow
    So smooth, unwrinkled ever; yea again,

Your long eyes where the lids seem like to drop,
    Would you not, lady, were they shut fast, feel
Far merrier? there so high they will not stop,
    They are most sly to glide forth and to steal   160

Into my heart; I kiss their soft lids there,
    And in green gardens scarce can stop my lips
From wandering on your face, but that your hair
    Falls down and tangles me, back my face slips.

Or say your mouth, I saw you drink red wine
    Once at a feast; how slowly it sank in,
As though you fear'd that some wild fate might twine
    Within that cup, and slay you for a sin.

And when you talk your lips do arch and move
    In such wise that a language new I know   170
Besides their sound; they quiver, too, with love
    When you are standing silent; know this, too,

I saw you kissing once, like a curved sword
    That bites with all its edge, did your lips lie,
Curled gently, slowly, long time could afford
    For caught-up breathings: like a dying sigh

They gather'd up their lines and went away,
    And still kept twitching with a sort of smile,
As likely to be weeping presently;
    Your hands too, how I watch'd them all
        the while!   180

Cry out St. Peter now, quoth Aldovrand;
    I cried, St. Peter! broke out from the wood
With all my spears; we met them hand to hand,
    And shortly slew them; natheless, by the rood,

We caught not Blackhead then, or any day;
    Months after that he died at last in bed,
From a wound pick'd up at a barrier-fray;
    That same year's end a steel bolt in the head,

And much bad living kill'd Teste Noire at last;
    John Froissart knoweth he is dead by now,   190
No doubt, but knoweth not this tale just past;
    Perchance then you can tell him what I show.

In my new castle, down beside the Eure,[13]
    There is a little chapel of squared stone,
Painted inside and out; in green nook pure
    There did I lay them, every wearied bone;

---

[13]**Eure:** river in N France.

And over it they lay, with stone-white hands
    Clasped fast together, hair made bright with gold;
This Jaques Picard,[14] known through many lands,
    Wrought cunningly; he's dead now: I am old.   200

1858

The Blue Closet[1]

— THE DAMOZELS —[2]

Lady Alice, lady Louise,
Between the wash of the tumbling seas
We are ready to sing, if so ye please;
So lay your long hands on the keys;
    Sing, *Laudate pueri.*[3]

And ever the great bell overhead
Boom'd in the wind a knell for the dead,
Though no one toll'd it, a knell for the dead.

— LADY LOUISE —

Sister, let the measure swell
Not too loud; for you sing not well   10
If you drown the faint boom of the bell;
    He is weary, so am I.

And ever the chevron[4] overhead
Flapp'd on the banner of the dead;
(Was he asleep, or was he dead?)

— LADY ALICE —

Alice the Queen, and Louise the Queen,
Two damozels wearing purple and green,
Four lone ladies dwelling here
From day to day and year to year;
And there is none to let us go;   20
To break the locks of the doors below,
Or shovel away the heaped-up snow;
And when we die no man will know

---

[14]**Jaques Picard**: Morris' invention.

[1]**"The Blue Closet"**: title of a D. G. Rossetti watercolor (1856–1857) commissioned by Morris, depicting two queens playing instruments and two ladies singing.

[2]**Damozels**: noble maidens.

[3]*Laudate pueri* (Praise, O ye servants): Latin version of Psalm 113:1.

[4]**chevron**: zigzag line in heraldry.

That we are dead; but they give us leave,
Once every year on Christmas-eve,
To sing in the Closet Blue one song;
And we should be so long, so long,
If we dared, in singing; for dream on dream,
They float on in a happy stream;
Float from the gold strings, float from the keys,   30
Float from the open'd lips of Louise;
But, alas! the sea-salt oozes through
The chinks of the tiles of the Closet Blue;

And ever the great bell overhead
Booms in the wind a knell for the dead,
The wind plays on it a knell for the dead.

— THEY SING ALL TOGETHER —

How long ago was it, how long ago,
He came to this tower with hands full of snow?

Kneel down, O love Louise, kneel down! he said,
And sprinkled the dusty snow over my head.   40

He watch'd the snow melting, it ran through my hair,
Ran over my shoulders, white shoulders and bare.

I cannot weep for thee, poor love Louise,
For my tears are all hidden deep under the seas;

In a gold and blue casket she keeps all my tears,
But my eyes are no longer blue, as in old years;

Yea, they grow grey with time, grow small and dry,
I am so feeble now, would I might die.

And in truth the great bell overhead
Left off his pealing for the dead,   50
Perchance, because the wind was dead.

Will he come back again, or is he dead?
O! is he sleeping, my scarf round his head?

Or did they strangle him as he lay there,
With the long scarlet scarf I used to wear?

Only I pray thee, Lord, let him come here!
Both his soul and his body to me are most dear.

Dear Lord, that loves me, I wait to receive
Either body or spirit this wild Christmas-eve.

Through the floor shot up a lily red,   60
With a patch of earth from the land of the dead,
For he was strong in the land of the dead.

What matter that his cheeks were pale,
   His kind kiss'd lips all grey?
O, love Louise, have you waited long?
   O, my lord Arthur, yea.

What if his hair that brush'd her cheek
   Was stiff with frozen rime?[5]
His eyes were grown quite blue again,
   As in the happy time.   70

O, love Louise, this is the key
   Of the happy golden land!
O, sisters, cross the bridge with me,
   My eyes are full of sand.
What matter that I cannot see,
   If ye take me by the hand?

And ever the great bell overhead,
And the tumbling seas mourn'd for the dead;
For their song ceased, and they were dead.

                  1858

~

The Tune of Seven Towers[1]

No one goes there now:
   For what is left to fetch away
From the desolate battlements all arow,[2]
   And the lead roof heavy and grey?
Therefore, said fair Yoland of the flowers,
This is the tune of Seven Towers.

No one walks there now;
   Except in the white moonlight
The white ghosts walk in a row;
   If one could see it, an awful sight,   10
Listen! said fair Yoland of the flowers,
This is the tune of Seven Towers.

But none can see them now,
   Though they sit by the side of the moat,
Feet half in the water, there in a row,
   Long hair in the wind afloat.
Therefore, said fair Yoland of the flowers,
This is the tune of Seven Towers.

---

[5]**rime**: frost.

[1]**"The Tune of Seven Towers"**: title of a D. G. Rossetti water-color, commissioned by Morris in 1857, depicting a seated lady playing the zither to a gentleman and a lady-in-waiting.

[2]**arow**: in a row.

If any will go to it now,
   He must go to it all alone,   20
Its gates will not open to any row
   Of glittering spears: will *you* go alone?
Listen! said fair Yoland of the flowers,
This is the tune of Seven Towers.

By my love go there now,
   To fetch me my coif away,
My coif and my kirtle,[3] with pearls arow,
   Oliver, go to-day!
Therefore, said fair Yoland of the flowers,
This is the tune of Seven Towers.   30

I am unhappy now,
   I cannot tell you why;
If you go, the priests and I in a row
   Will pray that you may not die.
Listen! said fair Yoland of the flowers,
This is the tune of Seven Towers.

If you will go for me now,
   I will kiss your mouth at last;
      [She sayeth inwardly.]
   (*The graves stand gray in a row.*)   40
   Oliver, hold me fast!
Therefore, said fair Yoland of the flowers,
This is the tune of Seven Towers.

                  1858

~

The Haystack in the Floods

Had she come all the way for this,
To part at last without a kiss?
Yea, had she borne the dirt and rain
That her own eyes might see him slain
Beside the haystack in the floods?

Along the dripping leafless woods,
The stirrup touching either shoe,
She rode astride as troopers do;
With kirtle kilted[1] to her knee,
To which the mud splash'd wretchedly;   10
And the wet dripp'd from every tree
Upon her head and heavy hair,
And on her eyelids broad and fair;
The tears and rain ran down her face.

---

[3]**coif**: cap. **kirtle**: gown.

[1]**kirtle kilted**: long skirt tucked up.

By fits and starts they rode apace,
And very often was his place
Far off from her; he had to ride
Ahead, to see what might betide
When the roads cross'd; and sometimes, when
There rose a murmuring from his men,   20
Had to turn back with promises.
Ah me! she had but little ease;
And often for pure doubt and dread
She sobb'd, made giddy in the head
By the swift riding; while, for cold,
Her slender fingers scarce could hold
The wet reins; yea, and scarcely, too,
She felt the foot within her shoe
Against the stirrup: all for this,
To part at last without a kiss   30
Beside the haystack in the floods.

For when they near'd that old soak'd hay,
They saw across the only way
That Judas, Godmar, and the three
Red running lions dismally
Grinn'd from his pennon,[2] under which
In one straight line along the ditch,
They counted thirty heads.

                    So then,
While Robert turn'd round to his men,
She saw at once the wretched end,   40
And, stooping down, tried hard to rend
Her coif[3] the wrong way from her head,
And hid her eyes; while Robert said:
Nay, love, 'tis scarcely two to one,
At Poictiers[4] where we made them run
So fast: why, sweet my love, good cheer,
The Gascon frontier is so near,
Nought after this.

                    But: O! she said,
My God! my God! I have to tread
The long way back without you; then   50
The court at Paris; those six men;[5]

The gratings of the Chatelet;
The swift Seine on some rainy day
Like this, and people standing by,
And laughing, while my weak hands try
To recollect how strong men swim.[6]
All this, or else a life with him,
For which I should be damned at last,
Would God that this next hour were past!

He answer'd not, but cried his cry,   60
St. George for Marny![7] cheerily;
And laid his hand upon her rein.
Alas! no man of all his train
Gave back that cheery cry again;
And, while for rage his thumb beat fast
Upon his sword-hilt, some one cast
About his neck a kerchief long,
And bound him.

                Then they went along
To Godmar; who said: Now, Jehane,
Your lover's life is on the wane   70
So fast, that, if this very hour
You yield not as my paramour,
He will not see the rain leave off:
Nay, keep your tongue from gibe and scoff,
Sir Robert, or I slay you now.

She laid her hand upon her brow,
Then gazed upon the palm, as though
She thought her forehead bled, and: No!
She said, and turn'd her head away,
As there were nothing else to say,   80
And everything were settled: red
Grew Godmar's face from chin to head:
Jehane, on yonder hill there stands
My castle, guarding well my lands;
What hinders me from taking you,
And doing that I list to do
To your fair wilful body, while
Your knight lies dead?

                    A wicked smile
Wrinkled her face, her lips grew thin,
A long way out she thrust her chin: 90
You know that I should strangle you
While you were sleeping; or bite through

---

[2]**pennon**: banner.

[3]**coif**: cap.

[4]**Poictiers**: town in W France where English defeated French forces in 1356. The English knight Sir Robert de Marny and his French lady Jehane are riding across enemy territory to the English-held **Gascon frontier**.

[5]**six men**: panel of judges at the **Chatelet**, a Paris courthouse and prison.

---

[6]**swim**: Jehane if captured will undergo trial (ordeal) by water, in which sinking proves innocence, staying afloat guilt.

[7]**St. George**: patron saint of England. **Marny**: the speaker's family name.

Your throat, by God's help: ah! she said,
Lord Jesus, pity your poor maid!
For in such wise they hem me in,
I cannot choose but sin and sin,
Whatever happens: yet I think
They could not make me eat or drink,
And so should I just reach my rest.

Nay, if you do not my behest,   100
O Jehane! though I love you well,
Said Godmar, would I fail to tell
All that I know? Foul lies, she said.
Eh? lies, my Jehane? by God's head,
At Paris folks would deem them true!
Do you know, Jehane, they cry for you:
Jehane the brown! Jehane the brown!
Give us Jehane to burn or drown!
Eh! gag me Robert! Sweet my friend,
This were indeed a piteous end   110
For those long fingers, and long feet,
And long neck, and smooth shoulders sweet;
An end that few men would forget
That saw it. So, an hour yet:
Consider, Jehane, which to take
Of life or death!

          So, scarce awake,
Dismounting, did she leave that place,
And totter some yards: with her face
Turn'd upward to the sky she lay,
Her head on a wet heap of hay,   120
And fell asleep: and while she slept,
And did not dream, the minutes crept
Round to the twelve again; but she,
Being waked at last, sigh'd quietly,
And strangely childlike came, and said:
I will not. Straightway Godmar's head,
As though it hung on strong wires, turn'd
Most sharply round, and his face burn'd.

For Robert, both his eyes were dry,
He could not weep, but gloomily   130
He seem'd to watch the rain; yea, too,
His lips were firm; he tried once more
To touch her lips; she reach'd out, sore
And vain desire so tortured them,
The poor grey lips, and now the hem
Of his sleeve brush'd them.

          With a start
Up Godmar rose, thrust them apart;

From Robert's throat he loosed the bands
Of silk and mail; with empty hands
Held out, she stood and gazed, and saw,   140
The long bright blade without a flaw
Glide out from Godmar's sheath, his hand
In Robert's hair; she saw him bend
Back Robert's head; she saw him send
The thin steel down; the blow told well,
Right backward the knight Robert fell,
And moaned as dogs do, being half dead,
Unwitting, as I deem: so then
Godmar turn'd grinning to his men,
Who ran, some five or six, and beat   150
His head to pieces at their feet.

Then Godmar turn'd again and said:
So, Jehane, the first fitte[8] is read!
Take note, my lady, that your way
Lies backward to the Chatelet!
She shook her head and gazed awhile
At her cold hands with a rueful smile,
As though this thing had made her mad.

This was the parting that they had
Beside the haystack in the floods.   160

              1858

Two Red Roses across the Moon

There was a lady lived in a hall,
Large of her eyes, and slim and tall;
And ever she sung from noon to noon,
Two red roses across the moon.

There was a knight came riding by
In early spring, when the roads were dry;
And he heard that lady sing at the noon,
Two red roses across the moon.

Yet none the more he stopp'd at all,
But he rode a-gallop past the hall;   10
And left that lady singing at noon,
Two red roses across the moon.

Because, forsooth, the battle was set,
And the scarlet and blue had got to be met,
He rode on the spur till the next warm noon:
Two red roses across the moon.

---

[8]**fitte:** part of a ballad tale.

But the battle was scatter'd from hill to hill,
From the windmill to the watermill;
And he said to himself, as it near'd the noon,
Two red roses across the moon.   20

You scarce could see for the scarlet and blue,
A golden helm or a golden shoe:
So he cried, as the fight grew thick at the noon,
Two red roses across the moon!

Verily then the gold bore through
The huddled spears of the scarlet and blue;
And they cried, as they cut them down at the noon,
Two red roses across the moon!

I trow[1] he stopp'd when he rode again
By the hall, though draggled sore with the rain;   30
And his lips were pinch'd to kiss at the noon
Two red roses across the moon.

Under the may[2] she stoop'd to the crown,
All was gold, there was nothing of brown;
And the horns blew up in the hall at noon,
Two red roses across the moon.

                                                    1858

~

from The Earthly Paradise

An Apology

Of Heaven or Hell I have no power to sing,
I cannot ease the burden of your fears,
Or make quick-coming death a little thing,
Or bring again the pleasure of past years,
Nor for my words shall ye forget your tears,
Or hope again for aught that I can say,
The idle singer of an empty day.

But rather, when aweary of your mirth,
From full hearts still unsatisfied ye sigh,
And, feeling kindly unto all the earth,   10
Grudge every minute as it passes by,
Made the more mindful that the sweet days die—
—Remember me a little then I pray,
The idle singer of an empty day.

---

[1] **trow:** believe.

[2] **may:** blossoming hawthorn.

The heavy trouble, the bewildering care
That weighs us down who live and earn our bread,
These idle verses have no power to bear;
So let me sing of names remembered,
Because they, living not, can ne'er be dead,
Or long time take their memory quite away   20
From us poor singers of an empty day.

Dreamer of dreams, born out of my due time,
Why should I strive to set the crooked straight?
Let it suffice me that my murmuring rhyme
Beats with light wing against the ivory gate,[1]
Telling a tale not too importunate
To those who in the sleepy region stay,
Lulled by the singer of an empty day.

Folk say, a wizard to a northern king
At Christmas-tide such wondrous things did show,   30
That through one window men beheld the spring,
And through another saw the summer glow,
And through a third the fruited vines a-row,
While still, unheard, but in its wonted way,
Piped the drear wind of that December day.

So with this Earthly Paradise it is,
If ye will read aright, and pardon me,
Who strive to build a shadowy isle of bliss
Midmost the beating of the steely sea,
Where tossed about all hearts of men must be: 40
Whose ravening monsters mighty men shall slay,
Not the poor singer of an empty day.

                                                    1868

~

from The Lesser Arts

. . . I have not undertaken to talk to you[1] of Architecture, Sculpture, and Painting, in the narrower sense of those words, since, most unhappily as I think, these master-arts, these arts more specially of the intellect, are at the present day divorced from decoration in its narrower sense. Our

---

[1] **ivory gate:** portal of false dreams.

[1] **you:** London artisans of the Trades' Guild of Learning, to whom Morris delivered this, his first public lecture, in 1877. His lecture title "The Decorative Arts: Their Relation to Modern Life and Progress" was retained for pamphlet publication in 1878 and changed with some irony to "The Lesser Arts" for inclusion in *Hopes and Fears for Art* (1882).

subject is that great body of art, by means of which men have at all times more or less striven to beautify the familiar matters of everyday life: a wide subject, a great industry; both a great part of the history of the world, and a most helpful instrument to the study of that history.

A very great industry indeed, comprising the crafts of house-building, painting, joinery and carpentry, smiths' work, pottery and glass-making, weaving, and many others: a body of art most important to the public in general, but still more so to us handicraftsmen; since there is scarce anything that they use, and that we fashion, but it has always been thought to be unfinished till it has had some touch or other of decoration about it. True it is that in many or most cases we have got so used to this ornament, that we look upon it as if it had grown of itself, and note it no more than the mosses on the dry sticks with which we light our fires. So much the worse! for there *is* the decoration, or some pretence of it, and it has, or ought to have, a use and a meaning. For, and this is at the root of the whole matter, everything made by man's hands has a form, which must be either beautiful or ugly; beautiful if it is in accord with Nature, and helps her; ugly if it is discordant with Nature, and thwarts her; it cannot be indifferent: we, for our parts, are busy or sluggish, eager or unhappy, and our eyes are apt to get dulled to this eventfulness of form in those things which we are always looking at. Now it is one of the chief uses of decoration, the chief part of its alliance with nature, that it has to sharpen our dulled senses in this matter: for this end are those wonders of intricate patterns interwoven, those strange forms invented, which men have so long delighted in: forms and intricacies that do not necessarily imitate nature, but in which the hand of the craftsman is guided to work in the way that she does, till the web, the cup, or the knife, look as natural, nay as lovely, as the green field, the river bank, or the mountain flint.

To give people pleasure in the things they must perforce *use*, that is one great office of decoration; to give people pleasure in the things they must perforce *make*, that is the other use of it.

Does not our subject look important enough now? I say that without these arts, our rest would be vacant and uninteresting, our labour mere endurance, mere wearing away of body and mind.

As for that last use of these arts, the giving us pleasure in our work, I scarcely know how to speak strongly enough of it; and yet if I did not know the value of repeating a truth again and again, I should have to excuse myself to you for saying any more about this, when I remember how a great man now living has spoken of it: I mean my friend Professor John Ruskin:[2] if you read the chapter in the 2nd vol. of his *Stones of Venice* entitled, "On the Nature of Gothic, and the Office of the Workman therein," you will read at once the truest and the most eloquent words that can possibly be said on the subject. What I have to say upon it can scarcely be more than an echo of his words, yet I repeat there is some use in reiterating a truth, lest it be forgotten; so I will say this much further: we all know what people have said about the curse of labour, and what heavy and grievous nonsense are the more part of their words thereupon; whereas indeed the real curses of craftsmen have been the curse of stupidity, and the curse of injustice from within and from without: no, I cannot suppose there is anybody here who would think it either a good life, or an amusing one, to sit with one's hands before one doing nothing—to live like a gentleman, as fools call it.

Nevertheless there *is* dull work to be done, and a weary business it is setting men about such work, and seeing them through it, and I would rather do the work twice over with my own hands than have such a job: but now only let the arts which we are talking of beautify our labour, and be widely spread, intelligent, well understood both by the maker and the user, let them grow in one word *popular*, and there will be pretty much an end of dull work and its wearing slavery; and no man will any longer have an excuse for talking about the curse of labour, no man will any longer have an excuse for evading the blessing of labour. I believe there is nothing that will aid the world's progress so much as the attainment of this; I protest there is nothing in the world that I desire so much as this, wrapped up, as I am sure it is, with changes political and social, that in one way or another we all desire.

Now if the objection be made, that these arts have been the handmaids of luxury, of tyranny and of superstition, I must needs say that it is true in a sense; they have been so used, as many other excellent things have been. But it is also true that, among some nations, their most vigorous and freest times have been the very blossoming times of art: while at the same time, I must allow that these decorative arts have flourished among oppressed peoples, who have seemed to have no hope of freedom: yet I do not think that we shall be wrong in thinking that at such times, among such peoples, art, at least, was free; when it has not been, when it has really been gripped by superstition, or by luxury, it has straightway begun to sicken under that grip. Nor must you forget that when men say popes, kings, and emperors

---

[2]Ruskin: see page 613.

built such and such buildings, it is a mere way of speaking. You look in your history-books to see who built Westminster Abbey, who built St. Sophia at Constantinople, and they tell you Henry III., Justinian the Emperor.[3] Did they? or, rather, men like you and me, handicraftsmen, who have left no names behind them, nothing but their work?

Now as these arts call people's attention and interest to the matters of every-day life in the present, so also, and that I think is no little matter, they call our attention at every step to that history, of which, I said before, they are so great a part; for no nation, no state of society, however rude, has been wholly without them: nay, there are peoples not a few, of whom we know scarce anything, save that they thought such and such forms beautiful. So strong is the bond between history and decoration, that in the practice of the latter we cannot, if we would, wholly shake off the influence of past times over what we do at present. I do not think it is too much to say that no man, however original he may be, can sit down to-day and draw the ornament of a cloth, or the form of an ordinary vessel or piece of furniture, that will be other than a development or a degradation of forms used hundreds of years ago; and these, too, very often, forms that once had a serious meaning, though they are now become little more than a habit of the hand; forms that were once perhaps the mysterious symbols of worships and beliefs now little remembered or wholly forgotten. Those who have diligently followed the delightful study of these arts are able as if through windows to look upon the life of the past:—the very first beginnings of thought among nations whom we cannot even name; the terrible empires of the ancient East; the free vigour and glory of Greece; the heavy weight, the firm grasp of Rome; the fall of her temporal Empire which spread so wide about the world all that good and evil which men can never forget, and never cease to feel; the clashing of East and West, South and North, about her rich and fruitful daughter Byzantium; the rise, the dissensions, and the waning of Islam; the wanderings of Scandinavia; the Crusades; the foundation of the States of modern Europe; the struggles of free thought with ancient dying system—with all these events and their meaning is the history of popular art interwoven; with all this, I say, the careful student of decoration as an historical industry must be familiar. When I think of this, and the usefulness of all this knowledge, at a time when history has become so earnest a study amongst us as

to have given us, as it were, a new sense: at a time when we so long to know the reality of all that has happened, and are to be put off no longer with the dull records of the battles and intrigues of kings and scoundrels,—I say when I think of all this, I hardly know how to say that this interweaving of the Decorative Arts with the history of the past is of less importance than their dealings with the life of the present: for should not these memories also be a part of our daily life?

And now let me recapitulate a little before I go further, before we begin to look into the condition of the arts at the present day. These arts, I have said, are part of a great system invented for the expression of a man's delight in beauty: all peoples and times have used them; they have been the joy of free nations, and the solace of oppressed nations; religion has used and elevated them, has abused and degraded them; they are connected with all history, and are clear teachers of it; and, best of all, they are the sweeteners of human labour, both to the handicraftsman, whose life is spent in working in them, and to people in general who are influenced by the sight of them at every turn of the day's work: they make our toil happy, our rest fruitful.

And now if all I have said seems to you but mere open-mouthed praise of these arts, I must say that it is not for nothing that what I have hitherto put before you has taken that form.

It is because I must now ask you this question: All these good things—will you have them? will you cast them from you?

Are you surprised at my question—you, most of whom, like myself, are engaged in the actual practice of the arts that are, or ought to be, popular?

In explanation, I must somewhat repeat what I have already said. Time was when the mystery and wonder of handicrafts were well acknowledged by the world, when imagination and fancy mingled with all things made by man; and in those days all handicraftsmen were *artists*, as we should now call them. But the thought of man became more intricate, more difficult to express; art grew a heavier thing to deal with, and its labour was more divided among great men, lesser men, and little men; till that art, which was once scarce more than a rest of body and soul, as the hand cast the shuttle or swung the hammer, became to some men so serious a labour, that their working lives have been one long tragedy of hope and fear, joy and trouble. This was the growth of art: like all growth, it was good and fruitful for awhile; like all fruitful growth, it grew into decay; like all decay of what was once fruitful, it will grow into something new.

---

[3]**St. Sophia**: cathedral of **Constantinople** built during the reign of **Justinian** (483–565). **Henry III** (1207–1272), King of England.

Into decay; for as the arts sundered into the greater and the lesser, contempt on one side, carelessness on the other arose, both begotten of ignorance of that *philosophy* of the Decorative Arts, a hint of which I have tried just now to put before you. The artist came out from the handicraftsmen, and left them without hope of elevation, while he himself was left without the help of intelligent, industrious sympathy. Both have suffered; the artist no less than the workman. It is with art as it fares with a company of soldiers before a redoubt,[4] when the captain runs forward full of hope and energy, but looks not behind him to see if his men are following, and they hang back, not knowing why they are brought there to die. The captain's life is spent for nothing, and his men are sullen prisoners in the redoubt of Unhappiness and Brutality.

I must in plain words say of the Decorative Arts, of all the arts, that it is not so much that we are inferior in them to all who have gone before us, but rather that they are in a state of anarchy and disorganisation, which makes a sweeping change necessary and certain.

So that again I ask my question, All that good fruit which the arts should bear, will you have it? will you cast it from you? Shall that sweeping change that must come, be the change of loss or of gain?

We who believe in the continuous life of the world, surely we are bound to hope that the change will bring us gain and not loss, and to strive to bring that gain about.

Yet how the world may answer my question, who can say? A man in his short life can see but a little way ahead, and even in mine, wonderful and unexpected things have come to pass. I must needs say that therein lies my hope rather than in all I see going on round about us. Without disputing that if the imaginative arts perish, some new thing, at present unguessed of, *may* be put forward to supply their loss in men's lives, I cannot feel happy in that prospect, nor can I believe that mankind will endure such a loss for ever: but in the meantime the present state of the arts and their dealings with modern life and progress seem to me to point, in appearance at least, to this immediate future; that the world, which has for a long time busied itself about other matters than the arts, and has carelessly let them sink lower and lower, till many not uncultivated men, ignorant of what they once were, and hopeless of what they might yet be, look upon them with mere contempt; that the world, I say, thus busied and hurried, will one day wipe the slate, and be clean rid in her impatience of the whole matter with all this tangle and trouble.

---

[4]**redoubt**: stronghold.

And then—what then?

Even now amid the squalor of London it is hard to imagine what it will be. Architecture, Sculpture, Painting, with the crowd of lesser arts that belong to them, these, together with Music and Poetry, will be dead and forgotten, will no longer excite or amuse people in the least: for, once more, we must not deceive ourselves; the death of one art means the death of all; the only difference in their fate will be that the luckiest will be eaten the last—the luckiest, or the unluckiest: in all that has to do with beauty the invention and ingenuity of man will have come to a dead stop; and all the while Nature will go on with her eternal recurrence of lovely changes—spring, summer, autumn, and winter; sunshine, rain, and snow; storm and fair weather; dawn, noon, and sunset; day and night—ever bearing witness against man that he has deliberately chosen ugliness instead of beauty, and to live where he is strongest amidst squalor or blank emptiness.

You see, sirs, we cannot quite imagine it; any more, perhaps, than our forefathers of ancient London, living in the pretty, carefully whitened houses, with the famous church and its huge spire rising above them,—than they, passing about the fair gardens running down to the broad river, could have imagined a whole county or more covered over with hideous hovels, big, middle-sized, and little, which should one day be called London.

Sirs, I say that this dead blank of the arts that I more than dread is difficult even now to imagine; yet I fear that I must say that if it does not come about, it will be owing to some turn of events which we cannot at present foresee: but I hold that if it does happen, it will only last for a time, that it will be but a burning up of the gathered weeds, so that the field may bear more abundantly. I hold that men would wake up after a while, and look round and find the dullness unbearable, and begin once more inventing, imitating, and imagining, as in earlier days.

That faith comforts me, and I can say calmly, if the blank space must happen, it must, and amidst its darkness the new seed must sprout. So it has been before: first comes birth, and hope scarcely conscious of itself; then the flower and fruit of mastery, with hope more than conscious enough, passing into insolence, as decay follows ripeness; and then—the new birth again.

Meantime it is the plain duty of all who look seriously on the arts to do their best to save the world from what at the best will be a loss, the result of ignorance and unwisdom; to prevent, in fact, that most discouraging of all changes, the supplying the place of an extinct brutality by a new one; nay, even if those who really care for the arts are so weak and few that they can do nothing else, it may be their business to keep alive some tradition, some memory of the past, so that the new life when it comes may not waste itself more than enough in fashioning wholly new forms for its new spirit.

To what side then shall those turn for help, who really understand the gain of a great art in the world, and the loss of peace and good life that must follow from the lack of it? I think that they must begin by acknowledging that the ancient art, the art of unconscious intelligence, as one should call it, which began without a date, at least so long ago as those strange and masterly scratchings on mammoth-bones and the like found but the other day in the drift—that this art of unconscious intelligence is all but dead; that what little of it is left lingers among half-civilised nations, and is growing coarser, feebler, less intelligent year by year; nay, it is mostly at the mercy of some commercial accident, such as the arrival of a few shiploads of European dye-stuffs or a few dozen orders from European merchants: this they must recognise, and must hope to see in time its place filled by a new art of conscious intelligence, the birth of wiser, simpler, freer ways of life than the world leads now, than the world has ever led.

I said, *to see* this in time; I do not mean to say that our own eyes will look upon it: it may be so far off, as indeed it seems to some, that many would scarcely think it worth while thinking of: but there are some of us who cannot turn our faces to the wall, or sit deedless because our hope seems somewhat dim; and, indeed, I think that while the signs of the last decay of the old art with all the evils that must follow in its train are only too obvious about us, so on the other hand there are not wanting signs of the new dawn beyond that possible night of the arts, of which I have before spoken; this sign chiefly, that there are some few at least, who are heartily discontented with things as they are, and crave for something better, or at least some promise of it—this best of signs: for I suppose that if some half-dozen men at any time earnestly set their hearts on something coming about which is not discordant with nature, it will come to pass one day or other; because it is not by accident that an idea comes into the heads of a few; rather they are pushed on, and forced to speak or act by something stirring in the heart of the world which would otherwise be left without expression.

By what means then shall those work who long for reform in the arts, and who shall they seek to kindle into eager desire for possession of beauty, and better still, for the development of the faculty that creates beauty?

People say to me often enough: If you want to make your art succeed and flourish, you must make it the fashion:

a phrase which I confess annoys me; for they mean by it that I should spend one day over my work to two days in trying to convince rich, and supposed influential people, that they care very much for what they really do not care in the least, so that it may happen according to the proverb: *Bell-wether*[5] *took the leap, and we all went over.* Well, such advisers are right if they are content with the thing lasting but a little while; say till you can make a little money—if you don't get pinched by the door shutting too quickly: otherwise they are wrong: the people they are thinking of have too many strings to their bow, and can turn their backs too easily on a thing that fails, for it to be safe work trusting to their whims: it is not their fault, they cannot help it, but they have no chance of spending time enough over the arts to know anything practical of them, and they must of necessity be in the hands of those who spend their time in pushing fashion this way and that for their own advantage.

Sirs, there is no help to be got out of these latter, or those who let themselves be led by them: the only real help for the decorative arts must come from those who work in them; nor must they be led, they must lead.

You whose hands make those things that should be works of art, you must be all artists, and good artists too, before the public at large can take real interest in such things; and when you have become so, I promise you that you shall lead the fashion; fashion shall follow your hands obediently enough.

That is the only way in which we can get a supply of intelligent popular art: a few artists of the kind so-called now, what can they do working in the teeth of difficulties thrown in their way by what is called Commerce, but which should be called greed of money? working helplessly among the crowd of those who are ridiculously called manufacturers, *i.e.* handicraftsmen, though the more part of them never did a stroke of hand-work in their lives, and are nothing better than capitalists and salesmen. What can these grains of sand do, I say, amidst the enormous mass of work turned out every year which professes in some way to be decorative art, but the decoration of which no one heeds except the salesmen who have to do with it, and are hard put to it to supply the cravings of the public for something new, not for something pretty?

The remedy, I repeat, is plain if it can be applied; the handicraftsman, left behind by the artist when the arts sundered, must come up with him, must work side by side with him: apart from the difference between a great master and a

---

[5]*Bell-wether:* lead ram in a flock.

scholar, apart from the differences of the natural bent of men's minds, which would make one man an imitative, and another an architectural or decorative artist, there should be no difference between those employed on strictly ornamental work; and the body of artists dealing with this should quicken with their art all makers of things into artists also, in proportion to the necessities and uses of the things they would make.

I know what stupendous difficulties, social and economical, there are in the way of this; yet I think that they seem to be greater than they are: and of one thing I am sure, that no real living decorative art is possible if this is impossible.

It is not impossible, on the contrary it is certain to come about, if you are at heart desirous to quicken the arts; if the world will, for the sake of beauty and decency, sacrifice some of the things it is so busy over (many of which I think are not very worthy of its trouble), art will begin to grow again; as for those difficulties above mentioned, some of them I know will in any case melt away before the steady change of the relative conditions of men; the rest, reason and resolute attention to the laws of nature, which are also the laws of art, will dispose of little by little: once more, the way will not be far to seek, if the will be with us.

Yet, granted the will, and though the way lies ready to us, we must not be discouraged if the journey seem barren enough at first, nay, not even if things seem to grow worse for a while: for it is natural enough that the very evil which has forced on the beginning of reform should look uglier, while on the one hand life and wisdom are building up the new, and on the other folly and deadness are hugging the old to them.

In this, as in all other matters, lapse of time will be needed before things seem to straighten, and the courage and patience that does not despise small things lying ready to be done; and care and watchfulness, lest we begin to build the wall ere the footings are well in; and always through all things much humility that is not easily cast down by failure, that seeks to be taught, and is ready to learn.

For your teachers, they must be Nature and History: as for the first, that you must learn of it is so obvious that I need not dwell upon that now: hereafter, when I have to speak more of matters of detail, I may have to speak of the manner in which you must learn of Nature. As to the second I do not think that any man but one of the highest genius could do anything in these days without much study of ancient art, and even he would be much hindered if he lacked it. If you think that this contradicts what I said about the death of that ancient art, and the necessity I implied for

an art that should be characteristic of the present day, I can only say that, in these times of plenteous knowledge and meagre performance, if we do not study the ancient work directly and learn to understand it, we shall find ourselves influenced by the feeble work all round us, and shall be copying the better work through the copyists and *without* understanding it, which will by no means bring about intelligent art. Let us therefore study it wisely, be taught by it, kindled by it; all the while determining not to imitate or repeat it; to have either no art at all, or an art which we have made our own. . . .

There is a great deal of sham work in the world, hurtful to the buyer, more hurtful to the seller, if he only knew it, most hurtful to the maker: how good a foundation it would be towards getting good Decorative Art, that is ornamental workmanship, if we craftsmen were to resolve to turn out nothing but excellent workmanship in all things, instead of having, as we too often have now, a very low average standard of work, which we often fall below.

I do not blame either one class or another in this matter, I blame all: to set aside our own class of handicraftsmen, of whose shortcomings you and I know so much that we need talk no more about it, I know that the public in general are set on having things cheap, being so ignorant that they do not know when they get them nasty also; so ignorant that they neither know nor care whether they give a man his due: I know that the manufacturers (so called) are so set on carrying out competition to its utmost, competition of cheapness, not of excellence, that they meet the bargain-hunters half way, and cheerfully furnish them with nasty wares at the cheap rate they are asked for, by means of what can be called by no prettier name than fraud. England has of late been too much busied with the counting-house and not enough with the workshop: with the result that the counting-house at the present moment is rather barren of orders.

I say all classes are to blame in this matter, but also I say that the remedy lies with the handicraftsmen, who are not ignorant of these things like the public, and who have no call to be greedy and isolated like the manufacturers or middlemen; the duty and honour of educating the public lies with them, and they have in them the seeds of order and organisation which make that duty the easier.

When will they see to this and help to make men of us all by insisting on this most weighty piece of manners; so that we may adorn life with the pleasure of cheerfully *buying* goods at their due price; with the pleasure of *selling* goods that we could be proud of both for fair price and fair workmanship: with the pleasure of working soundly and without haste at *making* goods that we could be proud of?—much the greatest pleasure of the three is that last, such a pleasure as, I think, the world has none like it.

You must not say that this piece of manners lies out of my subject: it is essentially a part of it and most important: for I am bidding you learn to be artists, if art is not to come to an end amongst us: and what is an artist but a workman who is determined that, whatever else happens, his work shall be excellent? or, to put it in another way: the decoration of workmanship, what is it but the expression of man's pleasure in successful labour? But what pleasure can there be in *bad* work, in *un*successful labour; why should we decorate *that*? and how can we bear to be always unsuccessful in our labour?

As greed of unfair gain, wanting to be paid for what we have not earned, cumbers our path with this tangle of bad work, of sham work, so that heaped-up money which this greed has brought us (for greed will have its way, like all other strong passions), this money, I say, gathered into heaps little and big, with all the false distinction which so unhappily it yet commands amongst us, has raised up against the arts a barrier of the love of luxury and show, which is of all obvious hindrances the worst to overpass: the highest and most cultivated classes are not free from the vulgarity of it, the lower are not free from its pretence. I beg you to remember both as a remedy against this, and as explaining exactly what I mean, that nothing can be a work of art which is not useful; that is to say, which does not minister to the body when well under command of the mind, or which does not amuse, soothe, or elevate the mind in a healthy state. What tons upon tons of unutterable rubbish pretending to be works of art in some degree would this maxim clear out of our London houses, if it were understood and acted upon! To my mind it is only here and there (out of the kitchen) that you can find in a well-to-do house things that are of any use at all: as a rule all the decoration (so called) that has got there is there for the sake of show, not because anybody likes it. I repeat, this stupidity goes through all classes of society: the silk curtains in my Lord's drawing-room are no more a matter of art to him than the powder in his footman's hair; the kitchen in a country farmhouse is most commonly a pleasant and homelike place, the parlour dreary and useless.

Simplicity of life, begetting simplicity of taste, that is, a love for sweet and lofty things, is of all matters most necessary for the birth of the new and better art we crave for; simplicity everywhere, in the palace as well as in the cottage.

Still more is this necessary, cleanliness and decency everywhere, in the cottage as well as in the palace: the lack of that is a serious piece of *manners* for us to correct: that

lack and all the inequalities of life, and the heaped-up thoughtlessness and disorder of so many centuries that cause it: and as yet it is only a very few men who have begun to think about a remedy for it in its widest range: even in its narrower aspect, in the defacements of our big towns by all that commerce brings with it, who heeds it? who tries to control their squalor and hideousness? there is nothing but thoughtlessness and recklessness in the matter: the helplessness of people who don't live long enough to do a thing themselves, and have not manliness and foresight enough to begin the work, and pass it on to those that shall come after them.

Is money to be gathered? cut down the pleasant trees among the houses, pull down ancient and venerable buildings for the money that a few square yards of London dirt will fetch; blacken rivers, hide the sun and poison the air with smoke and worse, and it's nobody's business to see to it or mend it: that is all that modern commerce, the counting house forgetful of the workshop, will do for us herein.

And Science—we have loved her well, and followed her diligently, what will she do? I fear she is so much in the pay of the counting-house, the counting-house and the drill-sergeant, that she is too busy, and will for the present do nothing. Yet there are matters which I should have thought easy for her; say for example teaching Manchester how to consume its own smoke, or Leeds how to get rid of its superfluous black dye without turning it into the river, which would be as much worth her attention as the production of the heaviest of heavy black silks, or the biggest of useless guns. Anyhow, however it be done, unless people care about carrying on their business without making the world hideous, how can they care about Art? I know it will cost much both of time and money to better these things even a little; but I do not see how these can be better spent than in making life cheerful and honourable for others and for ourselves; and the gain of good life to the country at large that would result from men seriously setting about the bettering of the decency of our big towns would be priceless, even if nothing specially good befell the arts in consequence: I do not know that it would; but I should begin to think matters hopeful if men turned their attention to such things, and I repeat that, unless they do so, we can scarcely even begin with any hope our endeavours for the bettering of the arts.

Unless something or other is done to give all men some pleasure for the eyes and rest for the mind in the aspect of their own and their neighbours' houses, until the contrast is less disgraceful between the fields where beasts live and the streets where men live, I suppose that the practice of the arts must be mainly kept in the hands of a few highly cultivated men, who can go often to beautiful places, whose education enables them, in the contemplation of the past glories of the world, to shut out from their view the everyday squalors that the most of men move in. Sirs, I believe that art has such sympathy with cheerful freedom, open-heartedness and reality, so much she sickens under selfishness and luxury, that she will not live thus isolated and exclusive. I will go further than this and say that on such terms I do not wish her to live. I protest that it would be a shame to an honest artist to enjoy what he had huddled up to himself of such art, as it would be for a rich man to sit and eat dainty food amongst starving soldiers in a beleaguered fort.

I do not want art for a few, any more than education for a few, or freedom for a few.

No, rather than art should live this poor thin life among a few exceptional men, despising those beneath them for an ignorance for which they themselves are responsible, for a brutality that they will not struggle with,—rather than this, I would that the world should indeed sweep away all art for awhile, as I said before I thought it possible she might do; rather than the wheat should rot in the miser's granary, I would that the earth had it, that it might yet have a chance to quicken in the dark.

I have a sort of faith, though, that this clearing away of all art will not happen, that men will get wiser, as well as more learned; that many of the intricacies of life, on which we now pride ourselves more than enough, partly because they are new, partly because they have come with the gain of better things, will be cast aside as having played their part, and being useful no longer. I hope that we shall have leisure from war,—war commercial, as well as war of the bullet and the bayonet; leisure from the knowledge that darkens counsel; leisure above all from the greed of money, and the craving for that overwhelming distinction that money now brings: I believe that as we have even now partly achieved LIBERTY, so we shall one day achieve EQUALITY, which, and which only, means FRATERNITY, and so have leisure from poverty and all its griping, sordid cares.

Then having leisure from all these things, amidst renewed simplicity of life we shall have leisure to think about our work, that faithful daily companion, which no man any longer will venture to call the Curse of labour: for surely then we shall be happy in it, each in his place, no man grudging at another; no one bidden to be any man's *servant*, every one scorning to be any man's *master*: men will then assuredly be happy in their work, and that happiness will assuredly bring forth decorative, noble, *popular* art. . . .

1878

How I Became a Socialist

I am asked by the Editor[1] to give some sort of a history of the above conversion, and I feel that it may be of some use to do so, if my readers will look upon me as a type of a certain group of people, but not so easy to do clearly, briefly, and truly. Let me, however, try. But first, I will say what I mean by being a Socialist, since I am told that the word no longer expresses definitely and with certainty what it did ten years ago. Well, what I mean by Socialism is a condition of society in which there should be neither rich nor poor, neither master nor master's man, neither idle nor overworked, neither brain-sick brain workers, nor heart-sick hand workers, in a word, in which all men would be living in equality of condition, and would manage their affairs unwastefully, and with the full consciousness that harm to one would mean harm to all—the realization at last of the meaning of the word COMMONWEALTH.

Now this view of Socialism which I hold to-day, and hope to die holding, is what I began with; I had no transitional period, unless you may call such a brief period of political radicalism during which I saw my ideal clear enough, but had no hope of any realization of it. That came to an end some months before I joined the (then) Democratic Federation, and the meaning of my joining that body was that I had conceived a hope of the realization of my ideal. If you ask me how much of a hope, or what I thought we Socialists then living and working would accomplish towards it, or when there would be effected any change in the face of society, I must say, I do not know. I can only say that I did not measure my hope, nor the joy that it brought me at the time. For the rest, when I took that step I was blankly ignorant of economics; I had never so much as opened Adam Smith, or heard of Ricardo, or of Karl Marx.[2] Oddly enough, I *had* read some of Mill, to wit, those posthumous papers of his (published, was it, in the *Westminster Review* or

---

[1] **Editor:** of *Justice*, organ of the Social Democratic Federation (founded in 1881 as the **Democratic Federation**), which Morris had joined in 1883, then quit with others to form the Socialist League in 1884. Estranged from the increasingly Anarchist-dominated League after 1890, Morris wrote this essay as a gesture of reconciliation with the more moderate and centrist SDF.

[2] **Adam Smith** (1723–1790): classic exponent of free-market economics. David **Ricardo** (1772–1823): political economist in the British tradition. **Karl Marx** (1818–1883): economic and political philosopher in the continental tradition, founder of communism.

the *Fortnightly*?) in which he attacks Socialism in its Fourierist[3] guise. In those papers he put the arguments, as far as they go, clearly and honestly, and the result, so far as I was concerned, was to convince me that Socialism was a necessary change, and that it was possible to bring it about in our own days. Those papers put the finishing touch to my conversion to Socialism. Well, having joined a Socialist body (for the Federation soon became definitely Socialist), I put some conscience into trying to learn the economical side of Socialism, and even tackled Marx, though I must confess that, whereas I thoroughly enjoyed the historical part of *Capital*,[4] I suffered agonies of confusion of the brain over reading the pure economics of that great work. Anyhow, I read what I could, and will hope that some information stuck to me from my reading; but more, I must think, from continuous conversation with such friends as Bax and Hyndman and Scheu,[5] and the brisk course of propaganda meetings which were going on at the time, and in which I took my share. Such finish to what of education in practical Socialism as I am capable of I received afterwards from some of my Anarchist friends, from whom I learned, quite against their intention, that Anarchism was impossible, much as I learned from Mill against *his* intention that Socialism was necessary.

But in this telling how I fell into *practical* Socialism I have begun, as I perceive, in the middle, for in my position of a well-to-do man, not suffering from the disabilities which oppress a working man at every step, I feel that I might never have been drawn into the practical side of the question if an ideal had not forced me to seek towards it. For politics as politics, i.e., not regarded as a necessary if cumbersome and disgustful means to an end, would never have attracted me, nor when I had become conscious of the wrongs of society as it now is, and the oppression of poor people, could I have ever believed in the possibility of a *partial* setting right of those wrongs. In other words, I could never have been such a fool as to believe in the happy and "respectable" poor.

If, therefore, my ideal forced me to look for practical Socialism, what was it that forced me to conceive of an ideal? Now, here comes in what I said (in this paper) of my being a type of a certain group of mind.

Before the uprising of *modern* Socialism almost all intelligent people either were, or professed themselves to be, quite contented with the civilization of this century. Again, almost all of these really were thus contented, and saw nothing to do but to perfect the said civilization by getting rid of a few ridiculous survivals of the barbarous ages. To be short, this was the *Whig*[6] frame of mind, natural to the modern prosperous middle-class men, who, in fact, as far as mechanical progress is concerned, have nothing to ask for, if only Socialism would leave them alone to enjoy their plentiful style.

But besides these contented ones there were others who were not really contented, but had a vague sentiment of repulsion to the triumph of civilization, but were coerced into silence by the measureless power of Whiggery. Lastly, there were a few who were in open rebellion against the said Whiggery—a few, say two, Carlyle and Ruskin. The latter, before my days of practical Socialism, was my master towards the ideal aforesaid, and, looking backward, I cannot help saying, by the way, how deadly dull the world would have been twenty years ago but for Ruskin! It was through him that I learned to give form to my discontent, which I must say was not by any means vague. Apart from the desire to produce beautiful things, the leading passion of my life has been and is hatred of modern civilization. What shall I say of it now, when the words are put into my mouth, my hope of its destruction—what shall I say of its supplanting by Socialism?

What shall I say concerning its mastery of and its waste of mechanical power, its commonwealth so poor, its enemies of the commonwealth so rich, its stupendous organization—for the misery of life! Its contempt of simple pleasures which everyone could enjoy but for its folly? Its eyeless vulgarity which has destroyed art, the one certain solace of labour? All this I felt then as now, but I did not know why it was so. The hope of the past times was gone, the struggles of mankind for many ages had produced nothing but this sordid, aimless, ugly confusion; the immediate future seemed to me likely to intensify all the present evils by sweeping away the last survivals of the days before the dull squalor of civilization had settled down on the world.

---

[3] J. S. **Mill**'s largely sympathetic critique of the socialism of Charles **Fourier** (1772–1837) and others was posthumously published in 1879 in the *Fortnightly Review*.

[4] *Capital*: Marx's *Das Kapital* (1867), which Morris read in French translation in 1883.

[5] Henry Mayers **Hyndman** (1842–1921): foremost British Marxist, authoritarian leader of the Social Democratic Federation. Ernest Belfort **Bax** (1854–1926), Andreas **Scheu** (1844–1927): early Marxists who joined Morris in the Socialist League.

---

[6] *Whig*: party of limited bourgeois liberalism that had triumphed with the 1832 Reform Bill.

This was a bad look-out indeed, and, if I may mention myself as a personality and not as a mere type, especially so to a man of my disposition, careless of metaphysics and religion, as well as of scientific analysis, but with a deep love of the earth and the life on it, and a passion for the history of the past of mankind. Think of it! Was it all to end in a counting-house on the top of a cinder-heap, with Podsnap's drawing-room in the offing,[7] and a Whig committee dealing out champagne to the rich and margarine to the poor in such convenient proportions as would make all men contented together, though the pleasure of the eyes was gone from the world, and the place of Homer was to be taken by Huxley? Yet, believe me, in my heart, when I really forced myself to look towards the future, that is what I saw in it, and, as far as I could tell, scarce anyone seemed to think it worth while to struggle against such a consummation of civilization. So there I was in for a fine pessimistic end of life, if it had not somehow dawned on me that amidst all this filth of civilization the seeds of a great change, what we others call Social-Revolution, were beginning to germinate. The whole face of things was changed to me by that discovery, and all I had to do then in order to become a Socialist was to hook myself on to the practical movement, which, as before said, I have tried to do as well as I could.

To sum up, then, the study of history and the love and practice of art forced me into a hatred of the civilization which, if things were to stop as they are, would turn history into inconsequent nonsense, and make art a collection of the curiosities of the past, which would have no serious relation to the life of the present.

But the consciousness of revolution stirring amidst our hateful modern society prevented me, luckier than many others of artistic perceptions, from crystallizing into a mere railer against "progress" on the one hand, and on the other from wasting time and energy in any of the numerous schemes by which the quasi-artistic of the middle classes hope to make art grow when it has no longer any root, and thus I became a practical Socialist.

A last word or two. Perhaps some of our friends will say, what have we to do with these matters of history and art? We want by means of Social-Democracy to win a decent livelihood, we want in some sort to live, and that at once. Surely anyone who professes to think that the question of art and cultivation must go before that of the knife and fork (and there are some who do propose that) does not understand what art means, or how that its roots must have a soil of a thriving and unanxious life. Yet it must be remembered that civilization has reduced the workman to such a skinny and pitiful existence, that he scarcely knows how to frame a desire for any life much better than that which he now endures perforce. It is the province of art to set the true ideal of a full and reasonable life before him, a life to which the perception and creation of beauty, the enjoyment of real pleasure that is, shall be felt to be as necessary to man as his daily bread, and that no man, and no set of men, can be deprived of this except by mere opposition, which should be resisted to the utmost.

1894

---

[7]**Podsnap:** self-important philistine in Dickens' novel *Our Mutual Friend* (1864). **in the offing:** in prospect.

ALGERNON CHARLES SWINBURNE

(1837–1909)

Son of an earl's daughter and a sea captain who became an admiral, Swinburne grew up on the Isle of Wight, an only son surrounded by doting sisters. Island-bred, he became a fearless swimmer, and his delight in the sea resounds in the imagery and rolling cadences of his verse. He attended Eton, where he became addicted to the pains and pleasures of flagellation, and Oxford, where he met a convivial group of young PreRaphaelites including Dante Rossetti and William Morris. Swinburne neglected his studies, failed his examinations, and left without a degree. Unabashed by failure at the university that had expelled his poetic idol Shelley, he settled in London, sharing a house for a while with Rossetti and George Meredith and giving himself full time to literature. He had been writing plays in the Elizabethan manner since childhood and now published two such plays, several essays and stories, and *Atalanta in Calydon* (1865), a verse drama modeled on the severity and violence of Greek tragedy. *Atalanta* introduces some of Swinburne's central themes: fatal women, the destructiveness of love, the cruelty or indifference of the gods, the allure of death.

Atalanta was received, on the whole, with admiration. A storm of outrage, however, greeted *Poems and Ballads* in the following year. Poems apparently celebrating sadomasochism, necrophilia, and other forms of sexual deviancy shocked moralists, while attacks on Christian values provoked accusations of blasphemy. Critics gleefully denounced Swinburne with phrases that seem infected by his own swinging rhetoric: "the spurious passion of a putrescent imagination," "nameless shameless abominations," "feverish carnality." The publisher withdrew the volume from sale, fearing prosecution. Swinburne defended himself vigorously in *Notes on Poems and Reviews* and found a new publisher, but *Poems and Ballads* did not lose its scandalous sting. *Songs before Sunrise* (1871), celebrating republican and revolutionary movements in Italy and France, added political offenses to the other counts against him. *Poems and Ballads: Second Series* (1878) was less provocative and more cordially received. His other works include faux-Elizabethan verse dramas, a second Greek tragedy, several long poems on medieval themes, some prose fiction, translations, hoaxes, parodies, unpublished writings on flagellation, and more. He wrote excellent and impassioned literary criticism too, his fiery temperament leading to extremes of adulation and excoriation. A precise, even pedantic Hellenist, a scholar of Jacobean drama and much else besides, he was one of the first to champion Blake, Baudelaire, and other revolutionary modern writers.

The sheer pleasure of reading Swinburne's verse has led many critics to dismiss it as "mere" music, sound devoid of sense. Carried along by mesmeric, unstoppable cadences, lulled by intricate verbal repetitions, the reader cannot grasp the sense of the words or pause to ponder them. But the swell of sound is cunningly varied, and sound and sense meet in a complex interplay that is designed at once to induce altered states and to provoke reflection on them. Long syntactic structures are held in suspension, while the vocabulary is kept surprisingly simple. Short monosyllables of the most general and generic kind (love, fate, life, death, night, day, all, none) abound, and a profusion of negatives fills poems like "A Forsaken Garden" with ghostly presences that are annihilated even as they arise. Swinburne is the poet of ecstatic, almost intolerably heightened feeling and language, and also the poet of the dissolution of feeling, language, and the self. T. S. Eliot complained in a brilliantly appreciative and unfair essay that although Swinburne's poetry is "genuine," its apparently self-generating language gives only "the hallucination of meaning." Still, Eliot had to admit that despite its length "The Triumph of Time," for instance, contains nothing that is not essential, and later critics have shown that Swinburne's language will in fact sustain the minute attention to meaning that it superficially seems to discourage.

Other obstacles to interpretation include strange imagery, often drawn from the literature of classical Greece or contemporary France. Swinburne exploits with deliberate provocativeness the deep-seated British association of France with sexual corruption; and his picture of ancient Greece, like Walter Pater's, gives the lie to the sublime sanity, calm objectivity, and purity of form that for Matthew Arnold and other Victorians was the classical ideal. Swinburne celebrated instead the semimythic figure of Sappho, traditionally the greatest of lyric poets, whom he presents in "Anactoria" and elsewhere as a shamelessly sensual lesbian as well as a suicide. Distracted by the exciting subject matter, critics were slow to recognize the ethic of stoic endurance that undergirds his attacks on Christianity, the tender sensitivity to psychic pleasure and bodily pain that is the ground note of his sensuality, his principled opposition to tyranny, or the varying kinds of courage with which his speakers face up to the loss of love and the allure of death, his central themes.

Even readers who disapprove on moral grounds can delight in the intoxicating beauty of Swinburne's verse. His technical virtuosity—he mastered many poetic forms, and his metrics are varied yet distinctive—is remarkable. At the same time, his verse lends itself irresistibly to parody, which no one has done better than Swinburne himself in "Poeta Loquitur." It is often hard to tell when and if seriousness modulates into self-parody in a work like the impudently blasphemous, gleefully masochistic "Dolores," about which Swinburne disarmingly wrote to a friend, "I have added yet four more jets of boiling and gushing infamy to the perennial and poisonous fountain of Dolores." The capacity for deliberate self-parody is rare in poets; it shows both Swinburne's good nature and a rather disconcerting detachment from some of his most provocative work.

With a small nervous body, a big head, wild red hair, an excitable temperament, and an inability to hold his liquor, Swinburne aroused wonder and dismay in person as well as in print. Rumors of outrageous remarks and tales of drunken misbehavior swirled around him. He wore out his health, alienated most of his old friends, and ended his days in controlled sobriety under the watchful care of a respectable lawyer-poet in suburban London, writing all the while and publishing his last collection of poems in 1904.

from **Atalanta in Calydon**

— CHORUS —

When the hounds of spring are on winter's traces,
  The mother of months[1] in meadow or plain
Fills the shadows and windy places
  With lisp of leaves and ripple of rain;
And the brown bright nightingale amorous
Is half assuaged for Itylus,[2]
For the Thracian ships and the foreign faces,
  The tongueless vigil, and all the pain.

Come with bows bent and with emptying of quivers,
  Maiden most perfect, lady of light,   10
With a noise of winds and many rivers,
  With a clamour of waters, and with might;
Bind on thy sandals, O thou most fleet,
Over the splendour and speed of thy feet;
For the faint east quickens, the wan west shivers,
  Round the feet of the day and the feet of the night.

Where shall we find her, how shall we sing to her,
  Fold our hands round her knees, and cling?
O that man's heart were as fire and could spring to her,
  Fire, or the strength of the streams that spring!   20
For the stars and the winds are unto her
As raiment, as songs of the harp-player;
For the risen stars and the fallen cling to her,
  And the south-west wind and the west wind sing.

For winter's rains and ruins are over,
  And all the season of snows and sins;
The days dividing lover and lover,
  The light that loses, the night that wins;
And time remembered is grief forgotten,
And frosts are slain and flowers begotten,   30
And in green underwood and cover
  Blossom by blossom the spring begins.

The full streams feed on flower of rushes,
  Ripe grasses trammel a travelling foot,
The faint fresh flame of the young year flushes
  From leaf to flower and flower to fruit;

And fruit and leaf are as gold and fire,
And the oat is heard above the lyre,[3]
And the hoofèd heel of a satyr crushes
  The chestnut-husk at the chestnut-root.   40

And Pan by noon and Bacchus by night,
  Fleeter of foot than the fleet-foot kid,
Follows with dancing and fills with delight
  The Maenad and the Bassarid;[4]
And soft as lips that laugh and hide
The laughing leaves of the trees divide,
And screen from seeing and leave in sight
  The god pursuing, the maiden hid.

The ivy falls with the Bacchanal's hair
  Over her eyebrows hiding her eyes;   50
The wild vine slipping down leaves bare
  Her bright breast shortening into sighs;
The wild vine slips with the weight of its leaves
But the berried ivy catches and cleaves
To the limbs that glitter, the feet that scare
  The wolf that follows, the fawn that flies.

                                                1865

— CHORUS —

Before the beginning of years
  There came to the making of man
Time, with a gift of tears;
  Grief, with a glass that ran;
Pleasure, with pain for leaven;
  Summer, with flowers that fell;
Remembrance fallen from heaven,
  And madness risen from hell;
Strength without hands to smite;
  Love that endures for a breath: 10
Night, the shadow of light,
  And life, the shadow of death.
And the high gods took in hand
  Fire, and the falling of tears,
And a measure of sliding sand
  From under the feet of the years;
And froth and drift of the sea;
  And dust of the labouring earth;
And bodies of things to be
  In the houses of death and of birth;   20

---

[1]**mother of months:** Artemis, goddess of the moon and the hunt.

[2]**Itylus** was killed by his mother, Procne, after her husband Tereus, the **Thracian** king, had brought home in his **ships** and then raped, mutilated, and made **tongueless** Procne's sister Philomela, who was later transformed into a **nightingale**.

---

[3]**oat:** Pan's pastoral flute. **lyre:** Apollo's harp.

[4]**Maenad, Bassarid, Bacchanal:** female votaries of Dionysus.

And wrought with weeping and laughter,
    And fashioned with loathing and love
With life before and after
    And death beneath and above,
For a day and a night and a morrow,
    That his strength might endure for a span
With travail and heavy sorrow,
    The holy spirit of man.
From the winds of the north and the south
    They gathered as unto strife;   30
They breathed upon his mouth,
    They filled his body with life;
Eyesight and speech they wrought
    For the veils of the soul therein,
A time for labour and thought,
    A time to serve and to sin;
They gave him light in his ways,
    And love, and a space for delight,
And beauty and length of days,
    And night, and sleep in the night.   40
His speech is a burning fire;
    With his lips he travaileth;
In his heart is a blind desire,
    In his eyes foreknowledge of death;
He weaves, and is clothed with derision;
    Sows and he shall not reap;
His life is a watch or a vision
    Between a sleep and a sleep.

                                  1865

~

The Leper

Nothing is better, I well think,
    Than love; the hidden well-water
Is not so delicate to drink:
    This was well seen of me and her.

I served her in a royal house;
    I served her wine and curious meat.
For will to kiss between her brows,
    I had no heart to sleep or eat.

Mere scorn God knows she had of me,
    A poor scribe, nowise great or fair,   10
Who plucked his clerk's hood back to see
    Her curled-up lips and amorous hair.

I vex my head with thinking this.
    Yea, though God always hated me,
And hates me now that I can kiss
    Her eyes, plait up her hair to see

How she then wore it on the brows,
    Yet am I glad to have her dead
Here in this wretched wattled house
    Where I can kiss her eyes and head.   20

Nothing is better, I well know,
    Than love; no amber in cold sea
Or gathered berries under snow:
    That is well seen of her and me.

Three thoughts I make my pleasure of:
    First I take heart and think of this:
That knight's gold hair she chose to love,
    His mouth she had such will to kiss.

Then I remember that sundawn
    I brought him by a privy way   30
Out at her lattice, and thereon
    What gracious words she found to say.

(Cold rushes for such little feet—
    Both feet could lie into my hand.
A marvel was it of my sweet
    Her upright body could so stand.)

"Sweet friend, God give you thank and grace;
    Now am I clean and whole of shame,
Nor shall men burn me in the face
    For my sweet fault that scandals them."   40

I tell you over word by word.
    She, sitting edgewise on her bed,
Holding her feet, said thus. The third,
    A sweeter thing than these, I said.

God, that makes time and ruins it
    And alters not, abiding God,
Changed with disease her body sweet,
    The body of love wherein she abode.

Love is more sweet and comelier
    Than a dove's throat strained out to sing.   50
All they spat out and cursed at her
    And cast her forth for a base thing.

They cursed her, seeing how God had wrought
    This curse to plague her, a curse of his.
Fools were they surely, seeing not
    How sweeter than all sweet she is.

He that had held her by the hair,
    With kissing lips blinding her eyes,
Felt her bright bosom, strained and bare,
    Sigh under him, with short mad cries   60

Out of her throat and sobbing mouth
    And body broken up with love,
With sweet hot tears his lips were loth
    Her own should taste the savour of.

Yea, he inside whose grasp all night
    Her fervent body leapt or lay,
Stained with sharp kisses red and white,
    Found her a plague to spurn away.

I hid her in this wattled house,
    I served her water and poor bread.   70
For joy to kiss between her brows
    Time upon time I was nigh dead.

Bread failed; we got but well-water
    And gathered grass with dropping seed;
I had such joy of kissing her,
    I had small care to sleep or feed.

Sometimes when service made me glad
    The sharp tears leapt between my lids,
Falling on her, such joy I had
    To do the service God forbids.   80

"I pray you let me be at peace,
    Get hence, make room for me to die."
She said that: her poor lip would cease,
    Put up to mine, and turn to cry.

I said, "Bethink yourself how love
    Fared in us twain, what either did;
Shall I unclothe my soul thereof?
    That I should do this, God forbid."

Yea, though God hateth us, he knows
    That hardly in a little thing   90
Love faileth of the work it does
    Till it grow ripe for gathering.

Six months, and now my sweet is dead
    A trouble takes me; I know not
If all were done well, all well said,
    No word or tender deed forgot.

Too sweet, for the least part in her,
    To have shed life out by fragments; yet,
Could the close mouth catch breath and stir,
    I might see something I forget.   100

Six months, and I sit still and hold
    In two cold palms her cold two feet.
Her hair, half grey half ruined gold,
    Thrills me and burns me in kissing it.

Love bites and stings me through, to see
    Her keen face made of sunken bones.
Her worn-off eyelids madden me,
    That were shot through with purple once.

She said, "Be good with me; I grow
    So tired for shame's sake, I shall die   110
If you say nothing": even so.
    And she is dead now, and shame put by.

Yea, and the scorn she had of me
    In the old time, doubtless vexed her then.
I never should have kissed her. See
    What fools God's anger makes of men!

She might have loved me a little too,
    Had I been humbler for her sake.
But that new shame could make love new
    She saw not—yet her shame did make.   120

I took too much upon my love,
    Having for such mean service done
Her beauty and all the ways thereof,
    Her face and all the sweet thereon.

Yea, all this while I tended her,
    I know the old love held fast his part,
I know the old scorn waxed heavier,
    Mixed with sad wonder, in her heart.

It may be all my love went wrong—
    A scribe's work writ awry and blurred,   130
Scrawled after the blind evensong[1]—
    Spoilt music with no perfect word.

But surely I would fain have done
    All things the best I could. Perchance
Because I failed, came short of one,
    She kept at heart that other man's.

I am grown blind with all these things:
    It may be now she hath in sight

---

[1]**evensong**: evening church service.

Some better knowledge; still there clings
    The old question. Will not God do right?[2]   140

1866

---

[2]En ce temps-là estoyt dans ce pays grand nombre de ladres et de meseaulx, ce dont le roy eut grand desplaisir, veu que Dieu dust en estre moult griefvement courroucé. Ores il advint qu'une noble damoyselle appelée Yolande de Sallières estant atteincte et touste guastée de ce vilain mal, tous ses amys et ses parens ayant devant leurs yeux la paour de Dieu la firent issir fors de leurs maisons et oncques ne voulurent recepvoir ni reconforter chose mauldicte de Dieu et à tous les hommes puante et abhominable. Ceste dame avoyt esté moult belle et gracieuse de formes, et de son corps elle estoyt large et de vie lascive. Pourtant nul des amans qui l'avoyent souventesfois accollée et basiée moult tendrement ne voulust plus héberger si laide femme et si détestable pescheresse. Ung seul clerc qui feut premièrement son lacquays et son entremetteur en matière d'amour la reçut chez luy et la récéla dans une petite cabane. Là mourut la meschinette de grande misère et de male mort: et après elle décéda ledist clerc qui pour grand amour l'avoyt six mois durant soignée, lavée, habillée et deshabillée tous les jours de ses mains propres. Mesme dist-on que ce meschant homme et mauldict clerc se remémourant de la grande beauté passée et guastée de ceste femme se délectoyt maintesfois à la baiser sur sa bouche orde et lépreuse et l'accoller doulcement de ses mains amoureuses. Aussy est-il mort de ceste mesme maladie abhominable. Cecy advint près Fontainebellant en Gastinois. Et quand ouyt le roy Philippe ceste adventure moult en estoyt esmerveillé. [Swinburne's note, citing the *Grandes Chroniques de France*, 1505, a veritable source of medieval history but one in which this passage does not occur] Swinburne's evidently forged antique French may be translated as follows: In that time there was in this land a great number of unclean lepers, which much displeased the king, seeing hence that God must be most grievously angered. Now it came to pass that, a noble damsel called Yolande de Sallières being stricken and wasted away by this base disease, all her friends and relations having the fear of God before their eyes sent her from their houses, and none would receive or comfort a thing accursed of God and to all men foul and abominable. This lady had been most fair and graceful of form, free of her body and of a lascivious life. Yet none of the lovers who had oftentimes very tenderly embraced and kissed her was yet willing to shelter so ugly a woman and so hateful a sinner. One clerk alone, who was formerly her lackey and go-between in affairs of love, took her in and harbored her in a little hut. There the wretched woman died in great misery an evil death; and there died after her the said clerk, who out of great love had for six months nursed, bathed, dressed, and undressed her every day with his own hands. It is even said that this naughty man and accursed clerk, remembering the woman's bygone, wasted beauty, often took delight in kissing her upon her foul and leprous mouth and embracing her sweetly with his amorous hands. Thus he perished of this same abominable sickness. This came to pass near Fontainebellant-en-Gastinois. And when King Philippe heard of this occurrence he marveled at it greatly.

~

The Triumph of Time

Before our lives divide for ever,
    While time is with us and hands are free,
(Time, swift to fasten and swift to sever
    Hand from hand, as we stand by the sea)
I will say no word that a man might say
Whose whole life's love goes down in a day;
For this could never have been; and never,
    Though the gods and the years relent, shall be.

Is it worth a tear, is it worth an hour,
    To think of things that are well outworn?   10
Of fruitless husk and fugitive flower,
    The dream foregone and the deed forborne?
Though joy be done with and grief be vain,
Time shall not sever us wholly in twain;
Earth is not spoilt for a single shower;
    But the rain has ruined the ungrown corn.

It will grow not again, this fruit of my heart,
    Smitten with sunbeams, ruined with rain.
The singing seasons divide and depart,
    Winter and summer depart in twain.   20
It will grow not again, it is ruined at root,
The bloodlike blossom, the dull red fruit;
Though the heart yet sickens, the lips yet smart,
    With sullen savour of poisonous pain.

I have given no man of my fruit to eat;
    I trod the grapes, I have drunken the wine.
Had you eaten and drunken and found it sweet,
    This wild new growth of the corn and vine,
This wine and bread without lees or leaven,
We had grown as gods, as the gods in heaven,   30
Souls fair to look upon, goodly to greet,
    One splendid spirit, your soul and mine.

In the change of years, in the coil of things,
    In the clamour and rumour of life to be,
We, drinking love at the furthest springs,
    Covered with love as a covering tree,
We had grown as gods, as the gods above,
Filled from the heart to the lips with love,
Held fast in his hands, clothed warm with his wings,
    O love, my love, had you loved but me!   40

We had stood as the sure stars stand, and moved
    As the moon moves, loving the world; and seen
Grief collapse as a thing disproved,
    Death consume as a thing unclean.
Twain halves of a perfect heart, made fast
Soul to soul while the years fell past;
Had you loved me once, as you have not loved;
    Had the chance been with us that has not been.

I have put my days and dreams out of mind,
    Days that are over, dreams that are done.   50
Though we seek life through, we shall surely find
    There is none of them clear to us now, not one.
But clear are these things; the grass and the sand,
Where, sure as the eyes reach, ever at hand,
With lips wide open and face burnt blind,
    The strong sea-daisies feast on the sun.

The low downs lean to the sea; the stream,
    One loose thin pulseless tremulous vein,
Rapid and vivid and dumb as a dream,
    Works downward, sick of the sun and the rain;   60
No wind is rough with the rank rare flowers;
The sweet sea, mother of loves and hours,
Shudders and shines as the grey winds gleam,
    Turning her smile to a fugitive pain.

Mother of loves that are swift to fade,
    Mother of mutable winds and hours.
A barren mother, a mother-maid,
    Cold and clean as her faint salt flowers.
I would we twain were even as she,
Lost in the night and the light of the sea,   70
Where faint sounds falter and wan beams wade,
    Break, and are broken, and shed into showers.

The loves and hours of the life of a man,
    They are swift and sad, being born of the sea.
Hours that rejoice and regret for a span,
    Born with a man's breath, mortal as he;
Loves that are lost ere they come to birth,
Weeds of the wave, without fruit upon earth.
I lose what I long for, save what I can,
    My love, my love, and no love for me!   80

It is not much that a man can save
    On the sands of life, in the straits of time,
Who swims in sight of the great third wave[1]
    That never a swimmer shall cross or climb.

Some waif washed up with the strays and spars
That ebb-tide shows to the shore and the stars;
Weed from the water, grass from a grave,
    A broken blossom, a ruined rhyme.

There will no man do for your sake, I think,
    What I would have done for the least word said.   90
I had wrung life dry for your lips to drink,
    Broken it up for your daily bread:
Body for body and blood for blood,
As the flow of the full sea risen to flood
That yearns and trembles before it sink,
    I had given, and lain down for you, glad and dead.

Yea, hope at highest and all her fruit,
    And time at fullest and all his dower,
I had given you surely, and life to boot,
    Were we once made one for a single hour.   100
But now, you are twain, you are cloven apart,
Flesh of his flesh,[2] but heart of my heart;
And deep in one is the bitter root,
    And sweet for one is the lifelong flower.

To have died if you cared I should die for you, clung
    To my life if you bade me, played my part
As it pleased you—these were the thoughts that stung,
    The dreams that smote with a keener dart
Than shafts of love or arrows of death;
These were but as fire is, dust, or breath,   110
Or poisonous foam on the tender tongue
    Of the little snakes that eat my heart.

I wish we were dead together to-day,
    Lost sight of, hidden away out of sight,
Clasped and clothed in the cloven clay,
    Out of the world's way, out of the light,
Out of the ages of worldly weather,
Forgotten of all men altogether,
As the world's first dead, taken wholly away,
    Made one with death, filled full of the night.   120

How we should slumber, how we should sleep,
    Far in the dark with the dreams and the dews!
And dreaming, grow to each other, and weep,
    Laugh low, live softly, murmur and muse;
Yea, and it may be, struck through by the dream,
Feel the dust quicken and quiver, and seem
Alive as of old to the lips, and leap
    Spirit to spirit as lovers use.

---

[1] **third wave**: tradition holds every third wave to be greater than the two before and after.

[2] **flesh of his flesh**: see Genesis 2:23.

Sick dreams and sad of a dull delight;
  For what shall it profit when men are dead   130
To have dreamed, to have loved with the whole soul's
    might,
  To have looked for day when the day was fled?
Let come what will, there is one thing worth,
To have had fair love in the life upon earth:
To have held love safe till the day grew night,
  While skies had colour and lips were red.

Would I lose you now? would I take you then,
  If I lose you now that my heart has need?
And come what may after death to men,
  What thing worth this will the dead years breed?   140
Lose life, lose all; but at least I know,
O sweet life's love, having loved you so,
Had I reached you on earth, I should lose not again,
  In death nor life, nor in dream or deed.

Yea, I know this well: were you once sealed mine,
  Mine in the blood's beat, mine in the breath,
Mixed into me as honey in wine,
  Not time, that sayeth and gainsayeth,
Nor all strong things had severed us then;
Not wrath of gods, nor wisdom of men,   150
Nor all things earthly, nor all divine,
  Nor joy nor sorrow, nor life nor death.

I had grown pure as the dawn and the dew,
  You had grown strong as the sun or the sea.
But none shall triumph a whole life through:
  For death is one, and the fates are three.
At the door of life, by the gate of breath,
There are worse things waiting for men than death;
Death could not sever my soul and you,
  As these have severed your soul from me.   160

You have chosen and clung to the chance they sent you,
  Life sweet as perfume and pure as prayer.
But will it not one day in heaven repent you?
  Will they solace you wholly, the days that were?
Will you lift up your eyes between sadness and bliss,
Meet mine, and see where the great love is,
And tremble and turn and be changed? Content you;
  The gate is strait; I shall not be there.

But you, had you chosen, had you stretched hand,
  Had you seen good such a thing were done,   170
I too might have stood with the souls that stand
  In the sun's sight, clothed with the light of the sun;

But who now on earth need care how I live?
Have the high gods anything left to give,
Save dust and laurels and gold and sand?
  Which gifts are goodly; but I will none.

O all fair lovers about the world,
  There is none of you, none, that shall comfort me.
My thoughts are as dead things, wrecked and whirled
  Round and round in a gulf of the sea;   180
And still, through the sound and the straining stream,
Through the coil and chafe, they gleam in a dream,
The bright fine lips so cruelly curled,
  And strange swift eyes where the soul sits free.

Free, without pity, withheld from woe,
  Ignorant; fair as the eyes are fair.
Would I have you change now, change at a blow,
  Startled and stricken, awake and aware?
Yea, if I could, would I have you see
My very love of you filling me,   190
And know my soul to the quick, as I know
  The likeness and look of your throat and hair?

I shall not change you. Nay, though I might,
  Would I change my sweet one love with a word?
I had rather your hair should change in a night,
  Clear now as the plume of a black bright bird;
Your face fail suddenly, cease, turn grey,
Die as a leaf that dies in a day.
I will keep my soul in a place out of sight,
  Far off, where the pulse of it is not heard.   200

Far off it walks, in a bleak blown space,
  Full of the sound of the sorrow of years.
I have woven a veil for the weeping face,
  Whose lips have drunken the wine of tears;
I have found a way for the failing feet,
A place for slumber and sorrow to meet;
There is no rumour about the place,
  Nor light, nor any that sees or hears.

I have hidden my soul out of sight, and said
  "Let none take pity upon thee, none   210
Comfort thy crying: for lo, thou art dead,
  Lie still now, safe out of sight of the sun.
Have I not built thee a grave, and wrought
Thy grave-clothes on thee of grievous thought,
With soft spun verses and tears unshed,
  And sweet light visions of things undone?

"I have given thee garments and balm and myrrh,
　　And gold, and beautiful burial things.
But thou, be at peace now, make no stir;
　　Is not thy grave as a royal king's?　　　　　　　　　220
Fret not thyself though the end were sore;
Sleep, be patient, vex me no more.
Sleep; what hast thou to do with her?
　　The eyes that weep, with the mouth that sings?"

Where the dead red leaves of the years lie rotten,
　　The cold old crimes and the deeds thrown by,
The misconceived and the misbegotten,
　　I would find a sin to do ere I die,
Sure to dissolve and destroy me all through,
That would set you higher in heaven, serve you　　　230
And leave you happy, when clean forgotten,
　　As a dead man out of mind, am I.

Your lithe hands draw me, your face burns through me,
　　I am swift to follow you, keen to see;
But love lacks might to redeem or undo me;
　　As I have been, I know I shall surely be;
"What should such fellows as I do?"[3] Nay,
My part were worse if I chose to play;
For the worst is this after all; if they knew me,
　　Not a soul upon earth would pity me.　　　　　　　240

And I play not for pity of these; but you,
　　If you saw with your soul what man am I,
You would praise me at least that my soul all through
　　Clove to you, loathing the lives that lie;
The souls and lips that are bought and sold,
The smiles of silver and kisses of gold,
The lapdog loves that whine as they chew,
　　The little lovers that curse and cry.

There are fairer women, I hear; that may be;
　　But I, that I love you and find you fair,　　　　　　250
Who are more than fair in my eyes if they be,
　　Do the high gods know or the great gods care?
Though the swords in my heart for one were seven,
Would the iron hollow of doubtful heaven,
That knows not itself whether night-time or day be,
　　Reverberate words and a foolish prayer?

I will go back to the great sweet mother,
　　Mother and lover of men, the sea.
I will go down to her, I and none other,
　　Close with her, kiss her and mix her with me.　　260

Cling to her, strive with her, hold her fast:
O fair white mother, in days long past
Born without sister, born without brother,
　　Set free my soul as thy soul is free.

O fair green-girdled mother of mine,
　　Sea, that art clothed with the sun and the rain,
Thy sweet hard kisses are strong like wine,
　　Thy large embraces are keen like pain.
Save me and hide me with all thy waves,
Find me one grave of thy thousand graves,　　　　　270
Those pure cold populous graves of thine
　　Wrought without hand in a world without stain.

I shall sleep, and move with the moving ships,
　　Change as the winds change, veer in the tide;
My lips will feast on the foam of thy lips,
　　I shall rise with thy rising, with thee subside;
Sleep, and not know if she be, if she were,
Filled full with life to the eyes and hair,
As a rose is fulfilled to the roseleaf tips
　　With splendid summer and perfume and pride.　　280

This woven raiment of nights and days,
　　Were it once cast off and unwound from me,
Naked and glad would I walk in thy ways,
　　Alive and aware of thy ways and thee;
Clear of the whole world, hidden at home,
Clothed with the green and crowned with the foam,
A pulse of the life of thy straits and bays,
　　A vein in the heart of the streams of the sea.

Fair mother, fed with the lives of men,
　　Thou art subtle and cruel of heart, men say.　　　290
Thou hast taken, and shalt not render again;
　　Thou art full of thy dead, and cold as they.
But death is the worst that comes of thee;
Thou art fed with our dead, O mother, O sea,
But when hast thou fed on our hearts? or when,
　　Having given us love, hast thou taken away?

O tender-hearted, O perfect lover,
　　Thy lips are bitter, and sweet thine heart.
The hopes that hurt and the dreams that hover,
　　Shall they not vanish away and apart?　　　　　　300
But thou, thou art sure, thou art older than earth;
Thou art strong for death and fruitful of birth;
Thy depths conceal and thy gulfs discover;
　　From the first thou wert; in the end thou art.

---

[3]"**What should . . . I do?**" *Hamlet* 3.1.125.

And grief shall endure not for ever, I know.
  As things that are not shall these things be;
We shall live through seasons of sun and of snow,
  And none be grievous as this to me.
We shall hear, as one in a trance that hears,
The sound of time, the rhyme of the years;   310
Wrecked hope and passionate pain will grow
  As tender things of a spring-tide sea.

Sea-fruit that swings in the waves that hiss,
  Drowned gold and purple and royal rings.
And all time past, was it all for this?
  Times unforgotten, and treasures of things?
Swift years of liking and sweet long laughter,
That wist not well of the years thereafter
Till love woke, smitten at heart by a kiss,   320
  With lips that trembled and trailing wings?

There lived a singer in France of old
  By the tideless dolorous midland sea.[4]
In a land of sand and ruin and gold
  There shone one woman, and none but she.
And finding life for her love's sake fail,
Being fain to see her, he bade set sail,
Touched land, and saw her as life grew cold,
  And praised God, seeing; and so died he.

Died, praising God for his gift and grace:
  For she bowed down to him weeping, and said   330
"Live"; and her tears were shed on his face
  Or ever the life in his face was shed.
The sharp tears fell through her hair, and stung
Once, and her close lips touched him and clung
Once, and grew one with his lips for a space;
  And so drew back, and the man was dead.

O brother, the gods were good to you.
  Sleep, and be glad while the world endures.
Be well content as the years wear through;
  Give thanks for life, and the loves and lures; 340
Give thanks for life, O brother, and death,
For the sweet last sound of her feet, her breath,
For gifts she gave you, gracious and few,
  Tears and kisses, that lady of yours.

Rest, and be glad of the gods; but I,
  How shall I praise them, or how take rest?
There is not room under all the sky
  For me that know not of worst or best,

Dream or desire of the days before,
  Sweet things or bitterness, any more.   350
Love will not come to me now though I die,
  As love came close to you, breast to breast.

I shall never be friends again with roses;
  I shall loathe sweet tunes, where a note grown strong
Relents and recoils, and climbs and closes,
  As a wave of the sea turned back by song.
There are sounds where the soul's delight takes fire,
Face to face with its own desire;
A delight that rebels, a desire that reposes;
  I shall hate sweet music my whole life long.   360

The pulse of war and passion of wonder,
  The heavens that murmur, the sounds that shine,
The stars that sing and the loves that thunder,
  The music burning at heart like wine,
An armed archangel whose hands raise up
All senses mixed in the spirit's cup
Till flesh and spirit are molten in sunder—
  These things are over, and no more mine.

These were a part of the playing I heard
  Once, ere my love and my heart were at strife;   370
Love that sings and hath wings as a bird,
  Balm of the wound and heft of the knife.
Fairer than earth is the sea, and sleep
Than overwatching of eyes that weep,
Now time has done with his one sweet word,
  The wine and leaven of lovely life.

I shall go my ways, tread out my measure,
  Fill the days of my daily breath
With fugitive things not good to treasure,
  Do as the world doth, say as it saith;   380
But if we had loved each other—O sweet,
Had you felt, lying under the palms of your feet,
The heart of my heart, beating harder with pleasure
  To feel you tread it to dust and death—

Ah, had I not taken my life up and given
  All that life gives and the years let go,
The wine and honey, the balm and leaven,
  The dreams reared high and the hopes brought low?
Come life, come death, not a word be said;
Should I lose you living, and vex you dead?   390
I never shall tell you on earth; and in heaven,
  If I cry to you then, will you hear or know?

---

[4]**singer in France:** Jaufré Rudel, 13th-century troubadour who
sailed the Mediterranean (**midland sea**) to die by his beloved.

1866

Anactoria[1]

τίνος αὖ τὺ πειθοῖ
μάψ σαγηνεύσας φιλότατα;
Sappho.

My life is bitter with thy love; thine eyes
Blind me, thy tresses burn me, thy sharp sighs
Divide my flesh and spirit with soft sound,
And my blood strengthens, and my veins abound.
I pray thee sigh not, speak not, draw not breath;
Let life burn down, and dream it is not death.
I would the sea had hidden us, the fire
(Wilt thou fear that, and fear not my desire?)
Severed the bones that bleach, the flesh that cleaves,
And let our sifted ashes drop like leaves.   10
I feel thy blood against my blood: my pain
Pains thee, and lips bruise lips, and vein stings vein.
Let fruit be crushed on fruit, let flower on flower,
Breast kindle breast, and either burn one hour.
Why wilt thou follow lesser loves? are thine
Too weak to bear these hands and lips of mine?
I charge thee for my life's sake, O too sweet
To crush love with thy cruel faultless feet,
I charge thee keep thy lips from hers or his,
Sweetest, till theirs be sweeter than my kiss: 20
Lest I too lure, a swallow for a dove,
Erotion or Erinna[2] to my love.
I would my love could kill thee; I am satiated
With seeing thee live, and fain would have thee dead.
I would earth had thy body as fruit to eat,
And no mouth but some serpent's found thee sweet.
I would find grievous ways to have thee slain,
Intense device, and superflux of pain;
Vex thee with amorous agonies, and shake
Life at thy lips, and leave it there to ache;   30
Strain out thy soul with pangs too soft to kill,
Intolerable interludes, and infinite ill;
Relapse and reluctation[3] of the breath,
Dumb tunes and shuddering semitones of death.
I am weary of all thy words and soft strange ways,
Of all love's fiery nights and all his days,

And all the broken kisses salt as brine
That shuddering lips make moist with waterish wine,
And eyes the bluer for all those hidden hours
That pleasure fills with tears and feeds from flowers,   40
Fierce at the heart with fire that half comes through,
But all the flower-like white stained round with blue;
The fervent underlid, and that above
Lifted with laughter or abashed with love;
Thine amorous girdle, full of thee and fair,
And leavings of the lilies in thine hair.
Yea, all sweet words of thine and all thy ways,
And all the fruit of nights and flower of days,
And stinging lips wherein the hot sweet brine
That Love[4] was born of burns and foams like wine,   50
And eyes insatiable of amorous hours,
Fervent as fire and delicate as flowers,
Coloured like night at heart, but cloven through
Like night with flame, dyed round like night with blue,
Clothed with deep eyelids under and above—
Yea, all thy beauty sickens me with love;
Thy girdle empty of thee and now not fair,
And ruinous lilies in thy languid hair.
Ah, take no thought for Love's sake; shall this be,
And she who loves thy lover not love thee?   60
Sweet soul, sweet mouth of all that laughs and lives,
Mine is she, very mine; and she forgives.
For I beheld in sleep the light that is
In her high place in Paphos,[5] heard the kiss
Of body and soul that mix with eager tears
And laughter stinging through the eyes and ears;
Saw Love, as burning flame from crown to feet,
Imperishable, upon her storied seat;
Clear eyelids lifted toward the north and south,
A mind of many colours, and a mouth   70
Of many tunes and kisses; and she bowed,
With all her subtle face laughing aloud,
Bowed down upon me, saying, "Who doth thee wrong,
Sappho?"[6] but thou—thy body is the song,
Thy mouth the music; thou art more than I,
Though my voice die not till the whole world die;
Though men that hear it madden; though love weep,
Though nature change, though shame be charmed to sleep.

---

[1]**Anactoria** is a woman in the poems of **Sappho** (7th century BCE), Greek woman poet of whose works only fragments survive. Epigraph: "By what persuasion did you again snare love in vain?"; a corrupt reading from Sappho's fragment 1, an address to Aphrodite.

[2]**Erotion**: name meaning *loved one*. **Erinna**: woman poet once thought contemporary with Sappho.

[3]**reluctation**: resistance.

---

[4]**Love** (and **queen**, below): Aphrodite.

[5]**Paphos**: Aphrodite's island birthplace.

[6]**"Who . . . Sappho?"**: Aphrodite's words here and below are translated from Sappho's fragment 1.

Ah, wilt thou slay me lest I kiss thee dead?
Yet the queen laughed from her sweet heart and said: 80
"Even she that flies shall follow for thy sake,
And she shall give thee gifts that would not take,
Shall kiss that would not kiss thee" (yea, kiss me)
"When thou wouldst not"—when I would not kiss thee!
Ah, more to me than all men as thou art,
Shall not my songs assuage her at the heart?
Ah, sweet to me as life seems sweet to death,
Why should her wrath fill thee with fearful breath?
Nay, sweet, for is she God alone? hath she
Made earth and all the centuries of the sea,   90
Taught the sun ways to travel, woven most fine
The moonbeams, shed the starbeams forth as wine,
Bound with her myrtles,[7] beaten with her rods,
The young men and the maidens and the gods?
Have we not lips to love with, eyes for tears,
And summer and flower of women and of years?
Stars for the foot of morning, and for noon
Sunlight, and exaltation of the moon;
Waters that answer waters, fields that wear
Lilies, and languor of the Lesbian[8] air?   100
Beyond those flying feet of fluttered doves,
Are there not other gods for other loves?
Yea, though she scourge thee, sweetest, for my sake,
Blossom not thorns, and flowers not blood should break.
Ah that my lips were tuneless lips, but pressed
To the bruised blossom of thy scourged white breast!
Ah that my mouth for Muses' milk were fed
On the sweet blood thy sweet small wounds had bled!
That with my tongue I felt them, and could taste
The faint flakes from thy bosom to the waist!   110
That I could drink thy veins as wine, and eat
Thy breasts like honey! that from face to feet
Thy body were abolished and consumed,
And in my flesh thy very flesh entombed!
Ah, ah, thy beauty! like a beast it bites,
Stings like an adder, like an arrow smites.
Ah sweet, and sweet again, and seven times sweet,
The paces and the pauses of thy feet!
Ah sweeter than all sleep or summer air
The fallen fillets fragrant from thine hair!   120
Yea, though their alien kisses do me wrong,
Sweeter thy lips than mine with all their song;
Thy shoulders whiter than a fleece of white,
And flower-sweet fingers, good to bruise or bite

As honeycomb of the inmost honey-cells,
With almond-shaped and roseleaf-coloured shells,
And blood like purple blossom at the tips
Quivering; and pain made perfect in thy lips
For my sake when I hurt thee; O that I
Durst crush thee out of life with love, and die,   130
Die of thy pain and my delight, and be
Mixed with thy blood and molten into thee!
Would I not plague thee dying overmuch?
Would I not hurt thee perfectly? not touch
Thy pores of sense with torture, and make bright
Thine eyes with bloodlike tears and grievous light!
Strike pang from pang as note is struck from note,
Catch the sob's middle music in thy throat,
Take thy limbs living, and new-mould with these
A lyre of many faultless agonies?   140
Feed thee with fever and famine and fine drouth,
With perfect pangs convulse thy perfect mouth,
Make thy life shudder in thee and burn afresh,
And wring thy very spirit through the flesh?
Cruel? but love makes all that love him well
As wise as heaven and crueller than hell.
Me hath love made more bitter toward thee
Than death toward man; but were I made as he
Who hath made all things to break them one by one
If my feet trod upon the stars and sun   150
And souls of men as his have alway trod,
God knows I might be crueller than God.
For who shall change with prayers or thanksgivings
The mystery of the cruelty of things?
Or say what God above all gods and years,
With offering and blood-sacrifice of tears,
With lamentation from strange lands, from graves
Where the snake pastures, from scarred mouth of slaves,
From prison, and from plunging prows of ships
Through flamelike foam of the sea's closing lips—   160
With thwartings of strange signs, and wind–blown hair
Of comets, desolating the dim air,
When darkness is made fast with seals and bars,
And fierce reluctance of disastrous stars,
Eclipse, and sound of shaken hills, and wings
Darkening, and blind inexpiable things—
With sorrow of labouring moons, and altering light
And travail of the planets of the night,
And weeping of the weary Pleiads[9] seven,
Feeds the mute melancholy lust of heaven?   170

---

[7]**myrtles:** sacred to Aphrodite, as are **doves.**

[8]**Lesbian:** from Lesbos, Sappho's island.

[9]**Pleiads:** mythic sisters, transformed into a constellation.

Is not this incense bitterness, his meat
Murder? his hidden face and iron feet
Hath not man known, and felt them on their way
Threaten and trample all things and every day?
Hath he not sent us hunger? who hath cursed
Spirit and flesh with longing? filled with thirst
Their lips who cried unto him? who bade exceed
The fervid will, fall short the feeble deed,
Bade sink the spirit and the flesh aspire,
Pain animate the dust of dead desire,   180
And life yield up her flower to violent fate?
Him would I reach, him smite, him desecrate,
Pierce the cold lips of God with human breath,
And mix his immortality with death.
Why hath he made us? what had all we done
That we should live and loathe the sterile sun,
And with the moon wax paler as she wanes,
And pulse by pulse feel time grow through our veins?
Thee too the years shall cover; thou shalt be
As the rose born of one same blood with thee,   190
As a song sung, as a word said, and fall
Flower-wise, and be not any more at all,
Nor any memory of thee anywhere;
For never Muse has bound above thine hair
The high Pierian[10] flowers whose graft outgrows
All summer kinship of the mortal rose
And colour of deciduous days, nor shed
Reflex and flush of heaven about thine head,
Nor reddened brows made pale by floral grief
With splendid shadow from that lordlier leaf.   200
Yea, thou shalt be forgotten like spilt wine,
Except these kisses of my lips on thine
Brand them with immortality; but me—
Men shall not see bright fire nor hear the sea,
Nor mix their hearts with music, nor behold
Cast forth of heaven with feet of awful gold
And plumeless wings that make the bright air blind,
Lightning, with thunder for a hound behind
Hunting through fields unfurrowed and unsown—
But in the light and laughter, in the moan   210
And music, and in grasp of lip and hand
And shudder of water that makes felt on land
The immeasurable tremor of all the sea,
Memories shall mix and metaphors of me.
Like me shall be the shuddering calm of night,
When all the winds of the world for pure delight

Close lips that quiver and fold up wings that ache:
When nightingales are louder for love's sake,
And leaves tremble like lute-strings or like fire;
Like me the one star swooning with desire   220
Even at the cold lips of the sleepless moon,
As I at thine; like me the waste white noon,
Burnt through with barren sunlight; and like me
The land-stream and the tide-stream in the sea.
I am sick with time as these with ebb and flow,
And by the yearning in my veins I know
The yearning sound of waters; and mine eyes
Burn as that beamless fire which fills the skies
With troubled stars and travailing things of flame;
And in my heart the grief consuming them   230
Labours, and in my veins the thirst of these,
And all the summer travail of the trees
And all the winter sickness; and the earth,
Filled full with deadly works of death and birth,
Sore spent with hungry lusts of birth and death,
Has pain like mine in her divided breath;
Her spring of leaves is barren, and her fruit
Ashes; her boughs are burdened, and her root
Fibrous and gnarled with poison; underneath
Serpents have gnawn it through with tortuous teeth   240
Made sharp upon the bones of all the dead,
And wild birds rend her branches overhead.
These, woven as raiment for his word and thought,
These hath God made, and me as these, and wrought
Song, and hath lit it at my lips; and me
Earth shall not gather though she feed on thee.
As a shed tear shalt thou be shed; but I—
Lo, earth may labour, men live long and die,
Years change and stars, and the high God devise
New things, and old things wane before his eyes   250
Who wields and wrecks them, being more strong
        than they—
But, having made me, me he shall not slay.
Nor slay nor satiate, like those herds of his
Who laugh and live a little, and their kiss
Contents them, and their loves are swift and sweet,
And sure death grasps and gains them with slow feet,
Love they or hate they, strive or bow their knees—
And all these end; he hath his will of these.
Yea, but albeit he slay me, hating me—
Albeit he hide me in the deep dear sea   260
And cover me with cool wan foam, and ease
This soul of mine as any soul of these,
And give me water and great sweet waves, and make
The very sea's name lordlier for my sake,

---

[10]**Pierian**: from Pieria, mountain home of the Muses.

The whole sea sweeter—albeit I die indeed
And hide myself and sleep and no man heed,
Of me the high God hath not all his will.
Blossom of branches, and on each high hill
Clear air and wind, and under in clamorous vales
Fierce noises of the fiery nightingales,   270
Buds burning in the sudden spring like fire,
The wan washed sand and the waves' vain desire,
Sails seen like blown white flowers at sea, and words
That bring tears swiftest, and long notes of birds
Violently singing till the whole world sings—
I Sappho shall be one with all these things,
With all high things forever; and my face
Seen once, my songs once heard in a strange place,
Cleave to men's lives, and waste the days thereof
With gladness and much sadness and long love.   280
Yea, they shall say, earth's womb has borne in vain
New things, and never this best thing again;
Borne days and men, borne fruits and wars and wine,
Seasons and songs, but no song more like mine.
And they shall know me as ye who have known me here,
Last year when I loved Atthis,[11] and this year
When I love thee; and they shall praise me, and say
"She hath all time as all we have our day,
Shall she not live and have her will"—even I?
Yea, though thou diest, I say I shall not die.   290
For these shall give me of their souls, shall give
Life, and the days and loves wherewith I live,
Shall quicken me with loving, fill with breath,
Save me and serve me, strive for me with death.
Alas, that neither moon nor snow nor dew
Nor all cold things can purge me wholly through,
Assuage me nor allay me nor appease,
Till supreme sleep shall bring me bloodless ease;
Till time wax faint in all his periods;
Till fate undo the bondage of the gods,   300
And lay, to slake and satiate me all through,
Lotus and Lethe[12] on my lips like dew,
And shed around and over and under me
Thick darkness and the insuperable sea.

1866

Hymn to Proserpine[1]

(After the Proclamation in Rome of the Christian Faith)

Vicisti, Galilæe[2]

I have lived long enough, having seen one thing, that love
    hath an end;
Goddess and maiden and queen, be near me now and
    befriend.
Thou art more than the day or the morrow, the seasons that
    laugh or that weep;
For these give joy and sorrow; but thou, Proserpina, sleep.
Sweet is the treading of wine, and sweet the feet of the dove;
But a goodlier gift is thine than foam of the grapes or love.
Yea, is not even Apollo, with hair and harpstring of gold,
A bitter God to follow, a beautiful God to behold?
I am sick of singing: the bays[3] burn deep and chafe: I am
    fain
To rest a little from praise and grievous pleasure and
    pain.   10
For the Gods we know not of, who give us our daily breath,
We know they are cruel as love or life, and lovely as death.
O Gods dethroned and deceased, cast forth, wiped out
    in a day!
From your wrath is the world released, redeemed from your
    chains, men say.
New Gods are crowned in the city; their flowers have
    broken your rods;
They are merciful, clothed with pity, the young
    compassionate Gods.
But for me their new device is barren, the days are bare;
Things long past over suffice, and men forgotten that were.
Time and the Gods are at strife; ye dwell in the midst
    thereof,
Draining a little life from the barren breasts of love.   20
I say to you, cease, take rest; yea, I say to you all, be at peace,
Till the bitter milk of her breast and the barren bosom
    shall cease.

---

[11]**Atthis:** woman in Sappho's verse.

[12]**Lotus, Lethe:** flower and river of oblivion.

---

[1]**Proserpine:** Roman goddess, queen of the underworld.

[2]**Proclamation:** after Constantine I proclaimed Christianity the official religion of the Roman Empire in the early 4th century, his nephew Julian tried to reestablish paganism, reportedly dying with the words *Vicisti, Galilaee* (You win, Galilean).

[3]**bays:** poet's laurel wreath.

Wilt thou yet take all, Galilean? but these thou shalt not take,
The laurel, the palms and the pæan, the breast of the
  nymphs in the brake;
Breasts more soft than a dove's that tremble with tenderer
  breath;
And all the wings of the Loves, and all the joy before death;
All the feet of the hours that sound as a single lyre,
Dropped and deep in the flowers, with strings that flicker
  like fire.
More than these wilt thou give, things fairer than all
  these things?
Nay, for a little we live, and life hath mutable wings.   30
A little while and we die; shall life not thrive as it may?
For no man under the sky lives twice, outliving his day.
And grief is a grievous thing, and a man hath enough of
  his tears:
Why should he labour, and bring fresh grief to blacken
  his years?
Thou hast conquered, O pale Galilean; the world has
  grown grey from thy breath;
We have drunken of things Lethean,[4] and fed on the
  fulness of death.
Laurel is green for a season, and love is sweet for a day;
But love grows bitter with treason, and laurel outlives
  not May.
Sleep, shall we sleep after all? for the world is not sweet
  in the end;
For the old faiths loosen and fall, the new years ruin
  and rend.   40
Fate is a sea without shore, and the soul is a rock that
  abides;
But her ears are vexed with the roar and her face with the
  foam of the tides.
O lips that the live blood faints in, the leavings of racks
  and rods!
O ghastly glories of saints, dead limbs of gibbeted Gods!
Though all men abase them before you in spirit, and all
  knees bend,
I kneel not neither adore you, but standing, look to the end.
All delicate days and pleasant, all spirits and sorrows are cast
Far out with the foam of the present that sweeps to the surf
  of the past:
Where beyond the extreme sea-wall, and between the
  remote sea-gates,
Waste water washes, and tall ships founder, and deep
  death waits: 50

Where, mighty with deepening sides, clad about with the
  seas as with wings,
And impelled of invisible tides, and fulfilled of unspeakable
  things,
White-eyed and poisonous-finned, shark-toothed and
  serpentine-curled,
Rolls, under the whitening wind of the future, the wave of
  the world.
The depths stand naked in sunder behind it, the storms
  flee away;
In the hollow before it the thunder is taken and snared as
  a prey;
In its sides is the north-wind bound; and its salt is of all
  men's tears;
With light of ruin, and sound of changes, and pulse of years:
With travail of day after day, and with trouble of hour
  upon hour;
And bitter as blood is the spray; and the crests are as fangs
  that devour: 60
And its vapour and storm of its steam as the sighing of
  spirits to be;
And its noise as the noise in a dream; and its depth as the
  roots of the sea:
And the height of its heads as the height of the utmost
  stars of the air:
And the ends of the earth at the might thereof tremble,
  and time is made bare.
Will ye bridle the deep sea with reins, will ye chasten the
  high sea with rods?
Will ye take her to chain her with chains, who is older
  than all ye Gods?
All ye as a wind shall go by, as a fire shall ye pass and be past;
Ye are Gods, and behold, ye shall die, and the waves be
  upon you at last.
In the darkness of time, in the deeps of the years, in the
  changes of things,
Ye shall sleep as a slain man sleeps, and the world shall
  forget you for kings.   70
Though the feet of thine high priests tread where thy
  lords and our forefathers trod,
Though these that were Gods are dead, and thou being
  dead art a God,
Though before thee the throned Cytherean[5] be fallen,
  and hidden her head,
Yet thy kingdom shall pass, Galilean, thy dead shall go
  down to thee dead.

---

[4]**Lethean**: from the underworld river of forgetfulness.

[5]**Cytherean**: Venus.

Of the maiden thy mother men sing as a goddess with
    grace clad around;
Thou art throned where another was king; where another
    was queen she is crowned.
Yea, once we had sight of another: but now she is queen,
    say these.
Not as thine, not as thine was our mother, a blossom of
    flowering seas,
Clothed round with the world's desire as with raiment, and
    fair as the foam,
And fleeter than kindled fire, and a goddess, and mother
    of Rome.[6]   80
For thine came pale and a maiden, and sister to sorrow;
    but ours,
Her deep hair heavily laden with odour and colour of
    flowers,
White rose of the rose-white water, a silver splendour, a
    flame,
Bent down unto us that besought her, and earth grew
    sweet with her name.
For thine came weeping, a slave among slaves, and
    rejected; but she
Came flushed from the full-flushed wave, and imperial,
    her foot on the sea.
And the wonderful waters knew her, the winds and the
    viewless ways,
And the roses grew rosier, and bluer the sea-blue stream
    of the bays.
Ye are fallen, our lords, by what token? we wist that ye
    should not fall.
Ye were all so fair that are broken; and one more fair than
    ye all.   90
But I turn to her still, having seen she shall surely abide
    in the end;
Goddess and maiden and queen, be near me now and
    befriend.
O daughter of earth, of my mother, her crown and
    blossom of birth,
I am also, I also, thy brother; I go as I came unto earth.
In the night where thine eyes are as moons are in heaven,
    the night where thou art,
Where the silence is more than all tunes, where sleep
    overflows from the heart,

Where the poppies are sweet as the rose in our world,
    and the red rose is white,
And the wind falls faint as it blows with the fume of the
    flowers of the night.
And the murmur of spirits that sleep in the shadow of Gods
    from afar
Grows dim in thine ears and deep as the deep dim soul
    of a star,   100
In the sweet low light of thy face, under heavens untrod
    by the sun,
Let my soul with their souls find place, and forget what is
    done and undone.
Thou art more than the Gods who number the days of
    our temporal breath;
For these give labour and slumber; but thou, Proserpina,
    death.
Therefore now at thy feet I abide for a season in silence.
    I know
I shall die as my fathers died, and sleep as they sleep;
    even so.
For the glass of the years is brittle wherein we gaze for
    a span;
A little soul for a little bears up this corpse which is
    man.[7]
So long I endure, no longer; and laugh not again, neither
    weep.
For there is no God found stronger than death; and death
    is a sleep.   110
                        1866

Hermaphroditus[1]

— 1 —

Lift up thy lips, turn round, look back for love,
    Blind love that comes by night and casts out rest;
    Of all things tired thy lips look weariest,
Save the long smile that they are wearied of.

---

[7]**A little . . . man:** ψυχάριον εἶ βαστάζον νεκρόν.—Epictetus.
[Swinburne's note, citing the 1st-century Stoic Epictetus, as reported by Marcus Aurelius (121–180): You are a little soul bearing
a corpse.]

[1]**Hermaphroditus:** youth who, when the nymph **Salmacis** (line
53) wished that they might never be parted, fused with her into one
double-sexed body.

---

[6]**mother of Rome:** Venus was the mother of Rome's founder,
Aeneas.

Ah sweet, albeit no love be sweet enough,
    Choose of two loves and cleave unto the best;
Two loves at either blossom of thy breast
Strive until one be under and one above.
Their breath is fire upon the amorous air,
    Fire in thine eyes and where thy lips suspire: 10
And whosoever hath seen thee, being so fair;
    Two things turn all his life and blood to fire;
A strong desire begot on great despair,
    A great despair cast out by strong desire.

— 2 —

Where between sleep and life some brief space is,
    With love like gold bound round about the head,
    Sex to sweet sex with lips and limbs is wed,
Turning the fruitful feud of hers and his
To the waste wedlock of a sterile kiss;
    Yet from them something like as fire is shed
    That shall not be assuaged till death be dead,
Though neither life nor sleep can find out this.
Love made himself of flesh that perisheth
    A pleasure-house for all the loves his kin;   10
But on the one side sat a man like death,
    And on the other a woman sat like sin.[2]
So with veiled eyes and sobs between his breath
    Love turned himself and would not enter in.

— 3 —

Love, is it love or sleep or shadow or light
    That lies between thine eyelids and thine eyes?
    Like a flower laid upon a flower it lies,
Or like the night's dew laid upon the night.
Love stands upon thy left hand and thy right,
    Yet by no sunset and by no moonrise
    Shall make thee man and ease a woman's sighs,
Or make thee woman for a man's delight.
To what strange end hath some strange god made fair
    The double blossom of two fruitless flowers?   10
Hid love in all the folds of all thy hair,
    Fed thee on summers, watered thee with showers,
Given all the gold that all the seasons wear
    To thee that art a thing of barren hours?

— 4 —

Yea, love, I see; it is not love but fear.
    Nay, sweet, it is not fear but love, I know;
    Or wherefore should thy body's blossom blow
So sweetly, or thine eyelids leave so clear
Thy gracious eyes that never made a tear—
    Though for their love our tears like blood should flow,
    Though love and life and death should come and go,
So dreadful, so desirable, so dear?
 Yea, sweet, I know; I saw in what swift wise
    Beneath the woman's and the water's kiss   10
    Thy moist limbs melted into Salmacis,
And the large light turned tender in thine eyes,
And all thy boy's breath softened into sighs;
    But Love being blind, how should he know of this?
Au Musée du Louvre, Mars 1863.[3]

                            1866

Stage Love

When the game began between them for a jest,
He played king and she played queen to match the best;
Laughter soft as tears, and tears that turned to laughter,
These were things she sought for years and sorrowed after.

Pleasure with dry lips, and pain that walks by night;
All the sting and all the stain of long delight;
These were things she knew not of, that knew not of her,
When she played at half a love with half a lover.

Time was chorus, gave them cues to laugh or cry;
They would kill, befool, amuse him, let him die;   10
Set him webs to weave to-day and break to-morrow,
Till he died for good in play, and rose in sorrow.

What the years mean; how time dies and is not slain;
How love grows and laughs and cries and wanes again;
These were things she came to know, and take their
    measure,
When the play was played out so for one man's pleasure.

                            1866

---

[2] **a man . . . like sin:** see *Paradise Lost* 2.648ff, where Sin and her incestuous son Death flank the gates of hell.

[3] *Au . . . Louvre:* At the Louvre Museum in Paris, which contains several hermaphroditic statues.

The Garden of Proserpine[1]

Here, where the world is quiet;
    Here, where all trouble seems
Dead winds' and spent waves' riot
    In doubtful dreams of dreams;
I watch the green field growing
For reaping folk and sowing,
For harvest-time and mowing,
    A sleepy world of streams.

I am tired of tears and laughter,
    And men that laugh and weep;   10
Of what may come hereafter
    For men that sow to reap:
I am weary of days and hours,
Blown buds of barren flowers,
Desires and dreams and powers
    And everything but sleep.

Here life has death for neighbour,
    And far from eye or ear
Wan waves and wet winds labour,
    Weak ships and spirits steer;   20
They drive adrift, and whither
They wot not who make thither;[2]
But no such winds blow hither,
    And no such things grow here.

No growth of moor or coppice,
    No heather-flower or vine,
But bloomless buds of poppies,
    Green grapes of Proserpine,
Pale beds of blowing rushes
Where no leaf blooms or blushes   30
Save this whereout she crushes
    For dead men deadly wine.

Pale, without name or number,
    In fruitless fields of corn,
They bow themselves and slumber
    All night till light is born;
And like a soul belated,
In hell and heaven unmated,
By cloud and mist abated
    Comes out of darkness morn.   40

Though one were strong as seven,
    He too with death shall dwell,
Nor wake with wings in heaven,
    Nor weep for pains in hell;
Though one were fair as roses,
His beauty clouds and closes;
And well though love reposes,
    In the end it is not well.

Pale, beyond porch and portal,
    Crowned with calm leaves, she stands   50
Who gathers all things mortal
    With cold immortal hands;
Her languid lips are sweeter
Than love's who fears to greet her
To men that mix and meet her
    From many times and lands.

She waits for each and other,
    She waits for all men born;
Forgets the earth her mother,[3]
    The life of fruits and corn;   60
And spring and seed and swallow
Take wing for her and follow
Where summer song rings hollow
    And flowers are put to scorn.

There go the loves that wither,
    The old loves with wearier wings;
And all dead years draw thither,
    And all disastrous things;
Dead dreams of days forsaken,
Blind buds that snows have shaken,   70
Wild leaves that winds have taken,
    Red strays of ruined springs.

We are not sure of sorrow,
    And joy was never sure;
To-day will die to-morrow;
    Time stoops to no man's lure;
And love, grown faint and fretful,
With lips but half regretful
Sighs, and with eyes forgetful
    Weeps that no loves endure.   80

From too much love of living,
    From hope and fear set free,
We thank with brief thanksgiving
    Whatever gods may be

---

[1]**Proserpine**: Roman goddess, queen of the underworld.

[2]**wot**: know. **make thither**: travel there.

[3]**her mother**: Ceres, **earth** and harvest goddess.

That no life lives for ever;
That dead men rise up never;
That even the weariest river
    Winds somewhere safe to sea.

Then star nor sun shall waken,
    Nor any change of light: 90
Nor sound of waters shaken,
    Nor any sound or sight:
Nor wintry leaves nor vernal,
Nor days nor things diurnal;
Only the sleep eternal
    In an eternal night.

                                          1866

Ave atque Vale[1]

In Memory of Charles Baudelaire

Nous devrions pourtant lui porter quelques fleurs;
Les morts, les pauvres morts, ont de grandes douleurs,
Et quand Octobre souffle, émondeur des vieux arbres,
Son vent mélancolique à l'entour de leurs marbres,
Certe, ils doivent trouver les vivants bien ingrats.
                  —"Les Fleurs du Mal."

— 1 —

Shall I strew on thee rose or rue or laurel,[2]
    Brother, on this that was the veil of thee?
    Or quiet sea-flower moulded by the sea,
Or simplest growth of meadow-sweet or sorrel,
    Such as the summer-sleepy Dryads[3] weave,
    Waked up by snow-soft sudden rains at eve?

Or wilt thou rather, as on earth before,
    Half-faded fiery blossoms, pale with heat
    And full of bitter summer, but more sweet
To thee than gleanings of a northern shore   10
    Trod by no tropic feet?

— 2 —

For always thee the fervid languid glories
    Allured of heavier suns in mightier skies;
    Thine ears knew all the wandering watery sighs
Where the sea sobs round Lesbian[4] promontories,
    The barren kiss of piteous wave to wave
    That knows not where is that Leucadian grave
Which hides too deep the supreme head of song.
    Ah, salt and sterile as her kisses were,
    The wild sea winds her and the green gulfs bear   20
Hither and thither, and vex and work her wrong,
    Blind gods that cannot spare.

— 3 —

Thou sawest, in thine old singing season, brother,
    Secrets and sorrows unbeheld of us:
    Fierce loves, and lovely leaf-buds poisonous,
Bare to thy subtler eye, but for none other
    Blowing by night in some unbreathed-in clime;
    The hidden harvest of luxurious time,
Sin without shape, and pleasure without speech;
    And where strange dreams in a tumultuous sleep   30
    Make the shut eyes of stricken spirits weep;
And with each face thou sawest the shadow on each,
    Seeing as men sow men reap.[5]

— 4 —

O sleepless heart and sombre soul unsleeping,
    That were athirst for sleep and no more life
    And no more love, for peace and no more strife!
Now the dim gods of death have in their keeping
    Spirit and body and all the springs of song,
    Is it well now where love can do no wrong,

---

[1]**Ave atque Vale**: Hail and Farewell; from Catullus' 1st–century elegy for his brother. Swinburne was among the first English reviewers to praise **Baudelaire** (1821–1867), from whose **Les Fleurs du Mal** (*The Flowers of Evil*, 1857) the epigraph is drawn: We should, however, take him some flowers; / The dead, the poor dead, suffer greatly, / And when October, pruner of trees, sends / His melancholy wind around their tombs, / Surely they must find the living very ungrateful ("La Servante au Grand Coeur").

[2]**rose, rue, laurel**: symbols of love, grief, poetry.

[3]**Dryads**: wood nymphs.

[4]**Lesbian**: from Lesbos, island of the poet Sappho, who according to legend died leaping from a cliff on the island Leucas (**Leucadian**) into the sea.

[5]**as . . . reap**: see Galatians 6:7.

Where stingless pleasure has no foam or fang   40
  Behind the unopening closure of her lips?
  Is it not well where soul from body slips
And flesh from bone divides without a pang
  As dew from flower-bell drips?

— 5 —

It is enough; the end and the beginning
  Are one thing to thee, who art past the end.
  O hand unclasped of unbeholden friend,
For thee no fruits to pluck, no palms for winning,
  No triumph and no labour and no lust,
  Only dead yew-leaves and a little dust.   50
O quiet eyes wherein the light saith nought,
  Whereto the day is dumb, nor any night
  With obscure finger silences your sight,
Nor in your speech the sudden soul speaks thought,
  Sleep, and have sleep for light.

— 6 —

Now all strange hours and all strange loves are over,
  Dreams and desires and sombre songs and sweet,
  Hast thou found place at the great knees and feet
Of some pale Titan-woman[6] like a lover,
  Such as thy vision here solicited,   60
  Under the shadow of her fair vast head,
The deep division of prodigious breasts,
  The solemn slope of mighty limbs asleep,
  The weight of awful tresses that still keep
The savour and shade of old-world pine-forests
  Where the wet hill-winds weep?

— 7 —

Hast thou found any likeness for thy vision?
  O gardener of strange flowers, what bud, what bloom,
  Hast thou found sown, what gathered in the gloom?
What of despair, of rapture, of derision,   70
  What of life is there, what of ill or good?
  Are the fruits grey like dust or bright like blood?
Does the dim ground grow any seed of ours,
  The faint fields quicken any terrene root,
  In low lands where the sun and moon are mute
And all the stars keep silence? Are there flowers
  At all, or any fruit?

---

[6]**Titan-woman**: see Baudelaire's poem "La Géante" (The Giantess).

— 8 —

Alas, but though my flying song flies after,
  O sweet strange elder singer, thy more fleet
  Singing, and footprints of thy fleeter feet,   80
Some dim derision of mysterious laughter
  From the blind tongueless warders of the dead,
  Some gainless glimpse of Proserpine's veiled head,
Some little sound of unregarded tears
  Wept by effaced unprofitable eyes,
  And from pale mouths some cadence of dead sighs—
These only, these the hearkening spirit hears,
  Sees only such things rise.

— 9 —

Thou art far too far for wings of words to follow,
  Far too far off for thought or any prayer.   90
  What ails us with thee, who art wind and air?
What ails us gazing where all seen is hollow?
  Yet with some fancy, yet with some desire,
  Dreams pursue death as winds a flying fire,
Our dreams pursue our dead and do not find.
  Still, and more swift than they, the thin flame flies,
  The low light fails us in elusive skies,
Still the foiled earnest ear is deaf, and blind
  Are still the eluded eyes.

— 10 —

Not thee, O never thee, in all time's changes,   100
  Not thee, but this the sound of thy sad soul,
  The shadow of thy swift spirit, this shut scroll
I lay my hand on, and not death estranges
  My spirit from communion of thy song—
  These memories and these melodies that throng
Veiled porches of a Muse funereal—
  These I salute, these touch, these clasp and fold
  As though a hand were in my hand to hold,
Or through mine ears a mourning musical
  Of many mourners rolled.   110

— 11 —

I among these, I also, in such station
  As when the pyre was charred, and piled the sods,
  And offering to the dead made, and their gods,
The old mourners had, standing to make libation,
  I stand, and to the gods and to the dead
  Do reverence without prayer or praise, and shed

Offering to these unknown, the gods of gloom,
And what of honey and spice my seedlands bear,
And what I may of fruits in this chilled air,
And lay, Orestes-like,[7] across the tomb   120
A curl of severed hair.

— 12 —

But by no hand nor any treason stricken,
Not like the low-lying head of Him, the King,
The flame that made of Troy a ruinous thing,
Thou liest, and on this dust no tears could quicken
There fall no tears like theirs that all men hear
Fall tear by sweet imperishable tear
Down the opening leaves of holy poets' pages.
Thee not Orestes, not Electra[8] mourns;
But bending us-ward with memorial urns   130
The most high Muses that fulfil all ages
Weep, and our God's[9] heart yearns.

— 13 —

For, sparing of his sacred strength, not often
Among us darkling here the lord of light
Makes manifest his music and his might
In hearts that open and in lips that soften
With the soft flame and heat of songs that shine.
Thy lips indeed he touched with bitter wine,
And nourished them indeed with bitter bread;
Yet surely from his hand thy soul's food came,   140
The fire that scarred thy spirit at his flame
Was lighted, and thine hungering heart he fed
Who feeds our hearts with fame.

— 14 —

Therefore he too now at thy soul's sunsetting,
God of all suns and songs, he too bends down
To mix his laurel with thy cypress crown,[10]
And save thy dust from blame and from forgetting.
Therefore he too, seeing all thou wert and art,
Compassionate, with sad and sacred heart,

Mourns thee of many his children the last dead,   150
And hallows with strange tears and alien sighs
Thine unmelodious mouth and sunless eyes,
And over thine irrevocable head
Sheds light from the under skies.

— 15 —

And one weeps with him in the ways Lethean,[11]
And stains with tears her changing bosom chill:
That obscure Venus of the hollow hill,
That thing transformed which was the Cytherean,
With lips that lost their Grecian laugh divine
Long since, and face no more called Erycine;   160
A ghost, a bitter and luxurious god.
Thee also with fair flesh and singing spell
Did she, a sad and second prey, compel
Into the footless places once more trod,
And shadows hot from hell.

— 16 —

And now no sacred staff shall break in blossom,
No choral salutation lure to light
A spirit sick with perfume and sweet night
And love's tired eyes and hands and barren bosom.
There is no help for these things; none to mend   170
And none to mar; not all our songs, O friend,
Will make death clear or make life durable.
Howbeit with rose and ivy and wild vine
And with wild notes about this dust of thine
At least I fill the place where white dreams dwell
And wreathe an unseen shrine.

— 17 —

Sleep; and if life was bitter to thee, pardon,
If sweet, give thanks; thou hast no more to live;
And to give thanks is good, and to forgive.
Out of the mystic and the mournful garden   180
Where all day through thine hands in barren braid
Wove the sick flowers[12] of secrecy and shade,

---

[7]**Orestes**: put a lock of **hair** on the tomb of his murdered father, **King** Agamemnon, who led the Greek armies against **Troy**.

[8]**Electra**: Orestes' sister.

[9]**our God**: Apollo, god of poetry, music, and the sun (**lord of light**).

[10]**laurel**: Apollo's emblem of poetic renown. **cypress**: emblem of death.

---

[11]**Lethean**: of the classical river of oblivion. This stanza and the next concern **Venus**, worshipped on the island of Cythera (**Cytherean**) and on Mt. Eryx in Sicily (**Erycine**). In a medieval legend retold by Swinburne in "Laus Veneris" (1866), Tannhäuser's adoration of Venus is rewarded when his **sacred staff** blossoms.

[12]**sick flowers**: Baudelaire's *Fleurs du Mal*.

Green buds of sorrow and sin, and remnants grey,
    Sweet-smelling, pale with poison, sanguine-hearted,
    Passions that sprang from sleep and thoughts that
        started,
Shall death not bring us all as thee one day
    Among the days departed?

— 18 —

For thee, O now a silent soul, my brother,
    Take at my hands this garland, and farewell.
    Thin is the leaf, and chill the wintry smell,   190
And chill the solemn earth, a fatal mother,
    With sadder than the Niobean[13] womb,
    And in the hollow of her breasts a tomb.
Content thee, howsoe'er, whose days are done;
    There lies not any troublous thing before,
    Nor sight nor sound to war against thee more,
For whom all winds are quiet as the sun,
    All waters as the shore.

                        1868, 1878

A Forsaken Garden

In a coign[1] of the cliff between lowland and highland,
    At the sea-down's[2] edge between windward and lee,
Walled round with rocks as an inland island,
    The ghost of a garden fronts the sea.
A girdle of brushwood and thorn encloses
    The steep square slope of the blossomless bed
Where the weeds that grew green from the graves of
        its roses
        Now lie dead.

The fields fall southward, abrupt and broken,
    To the low last edge of the long lone land.   10
If a step should sound or a word be spoken,
    Would a ghost not rise at the strange guest's hand?
So long have the grey bare walks lain guestless,
    Through branches and briars if a man make way,
He shall find no life but the sea-wind's, restless
        Night and day.

---

[13]**Niobean:** Niobe's children were struck dead in punishment for
maternal pride.

[1]**coign:** jutting angle.

[2]**sea-down:** grassy coastal upland.

The dense hard passage is blind and stifled
    That crawls by a track none turn to climb
To the strait waste place that the years have rifled
    Of all but the thorns that are touched not of time.   20
The thorns he spares when the rose is taken;
    The rocks are left when he wastes the plain.
The wind that wanders, the weeds wind-shaken,
    These remain.

Not a flower to be pressed of the foot that falls not;
    As the heart of a dead man the seed-plots are dry;
From the thicket of thorns whence the nightingale
    calls not,
    Could she call, there were never a rose to reply.
Over the meadows that blossom and wither
    Rings but the note of a sea-bird's song;   30
Only the sun and the rain come hither
        All year long.

The sun burns sere and the rain dishevels
    One gaunt bleak blossom of scentless breath.
Only the wind here hovers and revels
    In a round where life seems barren as death.
Here there was laughing of old, there was weeping,
    Haply, of lovers none ever will know,
Whose eyes went seaward a hundred sleeping
        Years ago.   40

Heart handfast in heart as they stood, "Look thither,"
    Did he whisper? "look forth from the flowers to the sea;
For the foam-flowers endure when the rose-blossoms
    wither,
    And men that love lightly may die—but we?"
And the same wind sang and the same waves whitened,
    And or ever the garden's last petals were shed,
In the lips that had whispered, the eyes that had lightened,
    Love was dead.

Or they loved their life through, and then went whither?
    And were one to the end—but what end who
        knows?   50
Love deep as the sea as a rose must wither,
    As the rose-red seaweed that mocks the rose.
Shall the dead take thought for the dead to love them?
    What love was ever as deep as a grave?
They are loveless now as the grass above them
        Or the wave.

All are at one now, roses and lovers,
    Not known of the cliffs and the fields and the sea.
Not a breath of the time that has been hovers
    In the air now soft with a summer to be.   60

Not a breath shall there sweeten the seasons hereafter
 Of the flowers or the lovers that laugh now or weep,
When as they that are free now of weeping and laughter
  We shall sleep.

Here death may deal not again for ever;
 Here change may come not till all change end.
From the graves they have made they shall rise up never,
 Who have left nought living to ravage and rend.
Earth, stones, and thorns of the wild ground growing,
 While the sun and the rain live, these shall be; 70
Till a last wind's breath upon all these blowing
  Roll the sea.

Till the slow sea rise and the sheer cliff crumble,
 Till terrace and meadow the deep gulfs drink,
Till the strength of the waves of the high tides humble
 The fields that lessen, the rocks that shrink,
Here now in his triumph where all things falter,
 Stretched out on the spoils that his own hand spread,
As a god self-slain on his own strange altar,
  Death lies dead. 80

          1876, 1878

A Ballad of Dreamland

I hid my heart in a nest of roses,
 Out of the sun's way, hidden apart;
In a softer bed than the soft white snow's is,
 Under the roses I hid my heart.
 Why would it sleep not? why should it start,
When never a leaf of the rose-tree stirred?
 What made sleep flutter his wings and part?
Only the song of a secret bird.

Lie still, I said, for the wind's wing closes,
 And mild leaves muffle the keen sun's dart; 10
Lie still, for the wind on the warm sea dozes,
 And the wind is unquieter yet than thou art.
 Does a thought in thee still as a thorn's wound smart?
Does the fang still fret thee of hope deferred?
 What bids the lids of thy sleep dispart?
Only the song of a secret bird.

The green land's name that a charm encloses,
 It never was writ in the traveller's chart,
And sweet on its trees as the fruit that grows is,
 It never was sold in the merchant's mart. 20

The swallows of dreams through its dim fields dart,
And sleep's are the tunes in its tree-tops heard;
 No hound's note wakens the wildwood hart,
Only the song of a secret bird.

— ENVOI —

In the world of dreams I have chosen my part,
 To sleep for a season and hear no word
Of true love's truth or of light love's art,
 Only the song of a secret bird.

          1878

The Roundel[1]

A roundel is wrought as a ring or a starbright sphere,
With craft of delight and with cunning of sound unsought,
That the heart of the hearer may smile if to pleasure his ear
 A roundel is wrought.

Its jewel of music is carven of all or of aught—
Love, laughter, or mourning—remembrance of rapture or
  fear—
That fancy may fashion to hang in the ear of thought.

As a bird's quick song runs round, and the hearts in us hear
Pause answer to pause, and again the same strain caught,
So moves the device whence, round as a pearl or tear, 10
 A roundel is wrought.

          1883

The Higher Pantheism[1] in a Nutshell

One, who is not, we see: but one, whom we see not, is:
Surely this is not that: but that is assuredly this.

What, and wherefore, and whence? for under is over and
  under:
If thunder could be without lightning, lightning could be
  without thunder.

---

 [1]**Roundel**: also called *rondeau*, a poetic form with two alternating rhymes and a cycling refrain. Swinburne published an entire volume of these poems in 1883.

 [1]**Pantheism**: belief that God is coextensive with the universe. The poem parodies Tennyson's "The Higher Pantheism," page 480).

Doubt is faith in the main: but faith, on the whole, is
   doubt:
We cannot believe by proof: but could we believe
   without?

Why, and whither, and how? for barley and rye are not
   clover:
Neither are straight lines curves: yet over is under and over.

Two and two may be four: but four and four are not eight:
Fate and God may be twain: but God is the same thing
   as fate.   10

Ask a man what he thinks, and get from a man what he
   feels:
God, once caught in the fact, shows you a fair pair of heels.

Body and spirit are twins: God only knows which is which:
The soul squats down in the flesh, like a tinker drunk in
   a ditch.

More is the whole than a part: but half is more than the
   whole:
Clearly, the soul is the body: but is not the body the soul?

One and two are not one: but one and nothing is two:
Truth can hardly be false, if falsehood cannot be true.

Once the mastodon was: pterodactyls were common
   as cocks:
Then the mammoth was God: now is He a prize ox.   20

Parallels all things are: yet many of these are askew:
You are certainly I: but certainly I am not you.

Springs the rock from the plain, shoots the stream from
   the rock:
Cocks exist for the hen: but hens exist for the cock.

God, whom we see not, is: and God, who is not, we see:
Fiddle, we know, is diddle: and diddle, we take it, is dee.
                                    1880

Sonnet for a Picture[1]

That nose is out of drawing. With a gasp,
   She pants upon the passionate lips that ache
   With the red drain of her own mouth, and make
A monochord of colour. Like an asp,

One lithe lock wriggles in his rutilant[2] grasp.
   Her bosom is an oven of myrrh, to bake
   Love's white warm shewbread[3] to a browner cake.
The lock his fingers clench has burst its hasp.
The legs are absolutely abominable.
   Ah! what keen overgust of wild-eyed woes   10
   Flags in that bosom, flushes in that nose?
Nay! Death sets riddles for desire to spell,
   Responsive. What red hem earth's passion sews,
But may be ravenously unripped in hell?
                                 1880

Poeta Loquitur[1]

If a person conceives an opinion
   That my verses are stuff that will wash,
Or my Muse has one plume on her pinion,
   That person's opinion is bosh.
My philosophy, politics, free-thought!
   Are worth not three skips of a flea,
And the emptiest of thoughts that can be thought
   Are mine on the sea.

In a maze of monotonous murmur
   Where reason roves ruined by rhyme,   10
In a voice neither graver nor firmer
   Than the bells on a fool's cap chime,
A party pretentiously pensive,
   With a Muse that deserves to be skinned,
Makes language and metre offensive
   With rhymes on the wind.

A perennial procession of phrases
   Pranked primly, though pruriently prime,
Precipitates preachings on praises
   In a ruffianly riot of rhyme   20
Through the pressure of print on my pages:
   But reckless the reader must be
Who imagines me one of the sages
   That steer through Time's sea.

---

[2]**rutilant**: shining.

[3]**shewbread**: in Jewish tradition, loaves laid by the altar every Sabbath and eaten at the end of the week by priests.

[1]**Poeta Loquitur**: The Poet Speaks.

[1]**Sonnet**: parody of such poems as D. G. Rossetti's "For The Wine of Circe,'" page 812.

Mad mixtures of Frenchified offal
    With insults to Christendom's creed,
Blind blasphemy, schoolboylike scoff, all
    These blazon me blockhead indeed.
I conceive myself obviously some one
    Whose audience will never be thinned,   30
But the pupil must needs be a rum one
    Whose teacher is wind.

In my poems, with ravishing rapture
    Storm strikes me and strokes me and stings:
But I'm scarcely the bird you might capture
    Out of doors in the thick of such things.
I prefer to be well out of harm's way
    When tempest makes tremble the tree,
And the wind with omnipotent arm-sway
    Makes soap of the sea.   40

Hanging hard on the rent rags of others,
    Who before me did better, I try
To believe them my sisters and brothers,
    Though I know what a low lot am I.
The mere sight of a church sets me yelping
    Like a boy that at football is shinned!
But the cause must indeed be past helping
    Whose gospel is wind!

All the pale past's red record of history
    Is dusty with damnable deeds;   50
But the future's mild motherly mystery
    Peers pure of all crowns and all creeds.
Truth dawns on time's resonant ruin,
    Frank, fulminant, fragrant, and free:
And apparently this is the doing
    Of wind on the sea.

Fame flutters in front of pretension
    Whose flagstaff is flagrantly fine:
And it cannot be needful to mention
    That such beyond question is mine.   60
Some singers indulging in curses,
    Though sinful, have splendidly sinned:
But my would-be maleficent verses
    Are nothing but wind.

1917

~

from Notes on Poems and Reviews

. . . The question at issue is wider than any between a single writer and his critics, or it might well be allowed to

drop. It is this: whether or not the first and last requisite of art is to give no offence; whether or not all that cannot be lisped in the nursery or fingered in the schoolroom is therefore to be cast out of the library; whether or not the domestic circle is to be for all men and writers the outer limit and extreme horizon of their world of work. For to this we have come; and all students of art must face the matter as it stands. Who has not heard it asked, in a final and triumphant tone, whether this book or that can be read aloud by her mother to a young girl? whether such and such a picture can properly be exposed to the eyes of young persons? If you reply that this is nothing to the point, you fall at once into the ranks of the immoral. Never till now, and nowhere but in England, could so monstrous an absurdity rear for one moment its deformed and eyeless head. In no past century were artists ever bidden to work on these terms; nor are they now, except among us. The disease, of course, afflicts the meanest members of the body with most virulence. Nowhere is cant at once so foul-mouthed and so tight-laced as in the penny, twopenny, threepenny, or sixpenny press. Nothing is so favourable to the undergrowth of real indecency as this overshadowing foliage of fictions, this artificial network of proprieties. *L'Arioste rit au soleil, l'Arétin ricane à l'ombre.*[1] The whiter the sepulchre without, the ranker the rottenness within. Every touch of plaster is a sign of advancing decay. The virtue of our critical journals is a dowager of somewhat dubious antecedents: every day that thins and shrivels her cheek thickens and hardens the paint on it; she consumes more chalk and ceruse than would serve a whole courtful of crones. "It is to be presumed," certainly, that in her case "all is not sweet, all is not sound."[2] The taint on her fly-blown reputation is hard to overcome by patches and perfumery. Literature, to be worthy of men, must be large, liberal, sincere; and cannot be chaste if it be prudish. Purity and prudery cannot keep house together. Where free speech and fair play are interdicted, foul hints and vile suggestions are hatched into fetid life. And if literature indeed is not to deal with the full life of man and the whole nature of things, let it be cast aside with the rods and rattles of childhood. Whether

---

[1] *L'Arioste . . . l'ombre:* An Ariosto laughs in broad daylight, an Aretino snickers in the dark. Ludovico **Ariosto** (1474–1533) wrote the freethinking romance *Orlando Furioso,* Pietro **Aretino** (1492–1556) the *Sonetti Lussuriosi* ("Lewd Sonnets"). The idea of hypocrisy recalls the whited **sepulchre** of Matthew 23:27.

[2] **"all is not . . . sound"**: Ben Jonson, *Epicoene* (1609) 1.1.90. Swinburne published *A Study of Ben Jonson* in 1889.

it affect to teach or to amuse, it is equally trivial and contemptible to us; only less so than the charge of immorality. Against how few really great names has not this small and dirt-encrusted pebble been thrown! A reputation seems imperfect without this tribute also: one jewel is wanting to the crown. It is good to be praised by those whom all men should praise; it is better to be reviled by those whom all men should scorn.

Various chances and causes must have combined to produce a state of faith or feeling which would turn all art and literature "into the line of children." One among others may be this: where the heaven of invention holds many stars at once, there is no fear that the highest and largest will either efface or draw aside into its orbit all lesser lights. Each of these takes its own way and sheds its proper lustre. But where one alone is dominant in heaven, it is encircled by a pale procession of satellite moons, filled with shallow and stolen radiance. Thus, with English versifiers now, the idyllic form is alone in favour. The one great and prosperous poet of the time[3] has given out the tune, and the hoarser choir takes it up. His highest lyrical work remains unimitated, being in the main inimitable. But the trick of tone which suits an idyl is easier to assume; and the note has been struck so often that the shrillest songsters can affect to catch it up. We have idyls good and bad, ugly and pretty; idyls of the farm and the mill; idyls of the dining-room and the deanery; idyls of the gutter and the gibbet. If the Muse of the minute will not feast with "gigmen"[4] and their wives, she must mourn with costermongers and their trulls. I fear the more ancient Muses are guests at neither house of mourning nor house of feasting.

For myself, I begrudge no man his taste or his success; I can enjoy and applaud all good work, and would always, when possible, have the workman paid in full. There is much excellent and some admirable verse among the poems of the day: to none has it given more pleasure than to me, and from none, had I been a man of letters to whom the ways were open, would it have won heartier applause. I have never been able to see what should attract men to the profession of criticism but the noble pleasure of praising. But I have no right to claim a place in the silver flock of idyllic swans. I have never worked for praise or pay, but simply by impulse, and to please myself; I must therefore, it is to be feared, remain where I am, shut out from the communion of these. At all events, I shall not be hounded into emulation of other men's work by the baying of unleashed beagles. There are those with whom I do not wish to share the praise of their praisers. I am content to abide a far different judgment:—

> I write as others wrote
> On Sunium's height.[5]

I need not be over-careful to justify my ways in other men's eyes; it is enough for me that they also work after their kind, and earn the suffrage, as they labour after the law, of their own people. The idyllic form is best for domestic and pastoral poetry. It is naturally on a lower level than that of tragic or lyric verse. Its gentle and maidenly lips are somewhat narrow for the stream and somewhat cold for the fire of song. It is very fit for the sole diet of girls; not very fit for the sole sustenance of men.

When England has again such a school of poetry, so headed and so followed, as she has had at least twice before, or as France has now;[6] when all higher forms of the various art are included within the larger limits of a stronger race; then, if such a day should ever rise or return upon us, it will be once more remembered that the office of adult art is neither puerile nor feminine, but virile; that its purity is not that of the cloister or the harem; that all things are good in its sight, out of which good work may be produced. Then the press will be as impotent as the pulpit to dictate the laws and remove the landmarks of art; and those will be laughed at who demand from one thing the qualities of another—who seek for sermons in sonnets and morality in music. Then all accepted work will be noble and chaste in the wider masculine sense, not truncated and curtailed, but outspoken and full-grown; art will be pure by instinct and fruitful by nature, no clipped and forced growth of unhealthy heat and unnatural air; all baseness and all triviality will fall off from it, and be forgotten; and no one will then need to assert, in defence of work done for the work's sake, the simple laws of his art which no one will then be permitted to impugn.

1866

---

[3]**poet:** Tennyson, who had been publishing **idyllic** verse since the 1840s.

[4]**"gigmen":** Carlyle's phrase for well-to-do owners of fine carriages. **house . . . of feasting:** see Ecclesiastes 7:2.

[5]**Sunium:** mountainous cape near Athens. Swinburne quotes from an 1853 epigram by W. S. Landor (1775–1864), "Wearers of rings and chains."

[6]**such . . . now:** the epochs of Shakespeare, Shelley, and Baudelaire.

~

from William Blake: A Critical Essay

. . . In a time of critical reason and definite division, he[1] was possessed by a fervour and fury of belief; among sane men who had disproved most things and proved the rest, here was an evident madman who believed a thing, one may say, only insomuch as it was incapable of proof. He lived and worked out of all rule, and yet by law. He had a devil, and its name was Faith. No materialist has such belief in bread and meat as Blake had in the substance underlying appearance which he christened god or spectre, devil or angel, as the fit took him; or rather as he saw it from one or the other side. His faith was absolute and hard, like a pure fanatic's; there was no speculation in him. What could be made of such a man in a country fed and clothed with the teapot pieties of Cowper and the tape-yard infidelities of Paine?[2] Neither set would have to do with him; was he not a believer? and was he not a blasphemer? His licence of thought and talk was always of the maddest, or seemed so in the ears of his generation. People remember at this day with horror and pity the impression of his daring ways of speech, but excuse him still on the old plea of madness. Now on his own ground no man was ever more sane or more reverent. His outcries on various matters of art or morals were in effect the mere expression, not of reasonable dissent, but of violent belief. No artist of equal power had ever a keener and deeper regard for the meaning and teaching— what one may call the moral—of art. He sang and painted as men write or preach. Indifference was impossible to him. Thus every shred of his work has some life, some blood, infused or woven into it. In such a vast tumbling chaos of relics as he left behind to get in time disentangled and cast into shape, there are naturally inequalities enough; rough sides and loose sides, weak points and helpless knots, before which all mere human patience or comprehension recoils and reels back. But in all, at all times, there is the one invaluable quality of actual life. . . .

. . . It is not easy, but it is requisite, to realise the perpetual freshness and fulness of belief, the inalterable vigour and fervour of spirit with which Blake, heretic and mystic as he may have been, worshipped and worked; by which he was throughout life possessed and pursued. Above all gods or

dæmons of creation and division, he beheld by faith in a perfect man a supreme God. "Though I have been very unhappy, I am so no longer. I am again emerged into the light of day; I still (and shall to eternity) embrace Christianity, and adore Him who is the express image of God."[3] In the light of his especial faith all visible things were fused into the intense heat and sharpened into the keen outline of vision. He walked and laboured under other heavens, on another earth, than the earth and the heaven of material life:

> "With a blue sky spread over with wings,
> And a mild sun that mounts and sings;
> With trees and fields full of fairy elves
> And little devils who fight for themselves;
> With angels planted in hawthorn bowers,
> And God Himself in the passing hours."

All this was not a mere matter of creed or opinion, much less of decoration or ornament to his work. It was, as we said, his element of life, inhaled at every breath with the common air, mixed into his veins with their natural blood. It was an element almost painfully tangible and actual; an absolute medium or state of existence, inevitable, inexplicable, insuperable. To him the veil of outer things seemed always to tremble with some breath behind it: seemed at times to be rent in sunder with clamour and sudden lightning. All the void of earth and air seemed to quiver with the passage of sentient wings and palpitate under the pressure of conscious feet. Flowers and weeds, stars and stones, spoke with articulate lips and gazed with living eyes. Hands were stretched towards him from beyond the darkness of material nature, to tempt or to support, to guide or to restrain. His hardest facts were the vaguest allegories of other men. To him all symbolic things were literal, all literal things symbolic. About his path and about his bed, around his ears and under his eyes, an infinite play of spiritual life seethed and swarmed or shone and sang. Spirits imprisoned in the husk and shell of earth consoled or menaced him. Every leaf bore a growth of angels; the pulse of every minute sounded as the falling foot of God; under the rank raiment of weeds, in the drifting down of thistles, strange faces frowned and white hair fluttered; tempters and allies, wraiths of the living and phantoms of the dead, crowded and made populous the winds that blew about him, the fields and hills over which he gazed. . . . (Chapter 1)

---

[1] **he**: William Blake (1757–1827), eldest of the major Romantics and still the obscurest at his death. The 1868 book here excerpted was the first full-length critical study of Blake.

[2] William **Cowper** (1731–1800), celebrated sentimentalist poet, and Tom **Paine** (1737–1809), radical publicist, stake out between them the 18th-century literary landscape in which Blake grew up.

---

[3] **"Though . . . image of God"**: quoted, like the verse passage that follows, from Blake's letters (November 22, 1802).

. . . Art is not like fire or water, a good servant and bad master; rather the reverse. She will help in nothing, of her own knowledge or freewill: upon terms of service you will get worse than nothing out of her. Handmaid of religion, exponent of duty, servant of fact, pioneer of morality, she cannot in any way become; she would be none of these things though you were to bray her in a mortar. All the battering in the world will never hammer her into fitness for such an office as that. It is at her peril, if she tries to do good: one might say, borrowing terms from the other party,[4] "she shall not try that under penalty of death and damnation." Her business is not to do good on other grounds, but to be good on her own: all is well with her while she sticks fast to that. To ask help or furtherance from her in any extraneous good work is exactly as rational as to expect lyrical beauty of form and flow in a logical treatise. The contingent result of having good art about you and living in a time of noble writing or painting may no doubt be this; that the spirit and mind of men then living will receive on some points a certain exaltation and insight caught from the influence of such forms and colours of verse or painting; will become for one thing incapable of tolerating bad work, and capable therefore of reasonably relishing the best; which of course implies and draws with it many other advantages of a sort you may call moral or spiritual. But if the artist does his work with an eye to such results or for the sake of bringing about such improvements, he will too probably fail even of them. Art for art's sake first of all, and afterwards we may suppose all the rest shall be added to her (or if not she need hardly be overmuch concerned); but from the man who falls to artistic work with a moral purpose, shall be taken away even that which he has—whatever of capacity for doing well in either way he may have at starting. A living critic[5] of incomparably delicate insight and subtly good sense, himself "impeccable" as an artist, calls this "the heresy of instruction" (*l'hérésie de l'enseignement*): one might call it, for the sake of a shorter and more summary name, the great moral heresy. Nothing can be imagined more futile; nothing so ruinous. Once let art humble herself, plead excuses, try at any compromise with the Puritan principle of doing good, and she is worse than dead. Once let her turn apologetic, and promise or imply that she really will now be "loyal to fact" and useful to men in general (say, by furthering their moral work or improving their moral nature), she is no longer of any human use or value. The one fact for her which is worth taking account of is simply mere excellence of verse or colour, which

involves all manner of truth and loyalty necessary to her wellbeing. That is the important thing; to have her work supremely well done, and to disregard all contingent consequences. You may extract out of Titian's[6] work or Shakespeare's any moral or immoral inference you please; it is none of their business to see after that. Good painting or writing, on any terms, is a thing quite sufficiently in accordance with fact and reality for them. Supplant art by all means if you can; root it out and try to plant in its place something useful or at least safe, which at all events will not impede the noble moral labour and trammel the noble moral life of Puritanism. But in the name of sense and fact itself let us have done with all abject and ludicrous pretence of coupling the two in harness or grafting the one on the other's stock: let us hear no more of the moral mission of earnest art; let us no longer be pestered with the frantic and flatulent assumptions of quasi-secular clericalism willing to think the best of all sides, and ready even, with consecrating hand, to lend meritorious art and poetry a timely pat or shove. Philistia[7] had far better (always providing it be possible) crush art at once, hang or burn it out of the way, than think of plucking out its eyes and setting it to grind moral corn in the Philistine mills; which it is certain not to do at all well. Once and again the time has been that there was no art worth speaking of afloat anywhere in the world; but there never has been or can have been a time when art, or any kind of art worth having, took active service under Puritanism, or indulged for its part in the deleterious appetite of saving souls or helping humanity in general along the way of labour and progress.[8] Let no artist or poet listen to the bland bark of those porter dogs of the Puritan kingdom even when they fawn and flirt with tongue or tail. *Cave canem.*[9] That Cerberus of the portals of Philistia will swallow your honey-cake

---

[4]**other party**: orthodox religion.

[5]**critic**: Charles Baudelaire (1821–1867), whose death while this book was in press prompted Swinburne's elegy "Ave atque Vale."

[6]**Titian** (1488–1576): Venetian painter.

[7]**Philistia**: Biblical kingdom where Samson was blinded and enslaved to labor in the **mills** (see Judges 16).

[8]**progress**: There are exceptions, we are told from the first, to all rules; and the sole exception to this one is great enough to do all but establish a rival rule. But, as I have tried already to say, the work—all the work—of Victor Hugo is in its essence artistic, in its accident alone philanthropic or moral. I call this the sole exception, not being aware that the written work of Dante or Shelley did ever tend to alter the material face of things; though they may have desired that it should, and though their unwritten work may have done so. Accidentally of course a poet's work may tend towards some moral or actual result; that is beside the question. [Swinburne's note] In 1872 Swinburne published a review essay on the French Romantic author **Victor Hugo** (1802–1885).

[9]*Cave canem*: Beware of the dog. **Cerberus**: guard dog at the gate of Hades, bribed with a **honey-cake**.

to no purpose; if he does not turn and rend you, his slaver as he licks your hand will leave it impotent and palsied for all good work. . . .

This old war—not (as some would foolishly have it defined) a war between facts and fancies, reason and romance, poetry and good sense, but simply between the imagination which apprehends the spirit of a thing and the understanding which dissects the body of a fact—this strife which can never be decided or ended—was for Blake the most important question possible. He for one, madman or no madman, had the sense to see that the one thing utterly futile to attempt was a reconciliation between two sides of life and thought which have no community of work or aim imaginable. This is no question of reconciling contraries. Admit all the implied pretensions of art, they remain simply nothing to science; accept all the actual deductions of science, they simply signify nothing to art. The eternal "Après?"[10] is answer enough for both in turn. "True, then, if you will have it; but what have we to do with your good or bad poetries and paintings?" "Undeniably; but what are we to gain by your deductions and discoveries, right or wrong?" The betrothal of art and science were a thing harder to bring about and more profitless to proclaim than "the marriage of heaven and hell."[11] It were better not to

fight, but to part in peace; but better certainly to fight than to temporize, where no reasonable truce can be patched up. Poetry or art based on loyalty to science is exactly as absurd (and no more) as science guided by art or poetry. Neither in effect can coalesce with the other and retain a right to exist. Neither can or (while in its sober senses) need wish to destroy the other; but they must go on their separate ways, and in this life their ways can by no possibility cross. Neither can or (unless in some fit of fugitive insanity) need wish to become valuable or respectable to the other: each must remain, on its own ground and to its own followers, a thing of value and deserving respect. To art, that is best which is most beautiful; to science, that is best which is most accurate; to morality, that is best which is most virtuous. Change or quibble upon the simple and generally accepted significance of these three words, "beautiful," "accurate," "virtuous," and you may easily (if you please, or think it worth while) demonstrate that the aim of all three is radically one and the same; but if any man be correct in thinking this exercise of the mind worth the expenditure of his time, that time must indeed be worth very little. You can say (but had perhaps better not say) that beauty is the truthfullest, accuracy the most poetic, and virtue the most beautiful of things; but a man of ordinary or decent insight will perceive that you have merely reduced an affair of things to an affair of words—shifted the body of one thing into the clothes of another—and proved actually nothing. . . . (Chapter 2)

1868

---

[10]"Après?": And then what?

[11]"the marriage of heaven and hell": title of Blake's prophetic manifesto of 1792.

AUGUSTA WEBSTER

(1837–1894)

The daughter of a vice admiral, Augusta Davies spent her early years on ships and by the sea. Most of her education was informal and self-acquired. She learned Greek in order, she said, to help a younger brother, taught herself Italian and Spanish, and improved her French in Paris and Geneva. When her parents moved to Cambridge in 1851 she attended classes at the Cambridge School of Art; later she was expelled from the South Kensington Art School for whistling. In 1863 she married a Cambridge University lecturer and lawyer, Thomas Webster, with whom she had one child, and around 1870 they moved to London.

She began her literary career with a volume of poems in 1860 and went on to publish a novel, translations of Aeschylus' *Prometheus Bound* and Euripides' *Medea*, more poems, and several verse dramas. She also wrote regularly for periodicals. In the *Examiner* she published graceful and humorous essays on literary, social, and political topics, which she collected under the misleadingly modest title *A Housewife's Opinions* (1879), and from 1884 until her death she reviewed more than 150 books, mostly poetry, for a prominent journal, the *Athenaeum*. With little patience for moralizing cant and a sharp eye for the economic causes of social conditions, she became a prominent feminist activist and a skilled public speaker, supporting women's rights to employment, university education, and the franchise. In 1879 and 1885 she was elected to the London School Board by large majorities.

Although not widely popular, Webster's poetry commanded respect. Her "masculine" qualities—her learning, her unsentimental confrontation of economic and social evils, and her forceful intellect—were much remarked by reviewers. Christina Rossetti considered her "by far the most formidable" of women poets, and Rossetti's brother William Michael declared *The Sentence* (1887), Webster's blank-verse play about the most depraved of Roman emperors, Caligula, "the supreme thing amid the work of *all* British poetesses." She was interested in aberrant points of view and extreme, even macabre, psychological conditions, but also in ordinary people and uneventful lives, and her dramatic monologues explore the mysteries and contingencies of identity and the subtle ways in which circumstances shape character. The speaker of "A Castaway" explains the social and economic causes of prostitution. "By the Looking-Glass," with its pervasive echoes of the lonely, self-conscious speaker of Tennyson's *Maud*, is one of several depictions of women who can define themselves only in terms of their attractiveness to men. Webster is particularly interested in marriages between unformed, ill-educated young women and older, more self-confident men: "Betrothed" gives a man's account of such a relationship, "The Happiest Girl in the World" a woman's. ("The Happiest Girl in the World," which Victorian reviewers found delightfully pretty and simple, may strike modern readers as a masterpiece of irony.) Some short lyrics delicately explore phases and failures of love, and the uncompleted sonnet sequence *Mother and Daughter* carries the exploration of female identity into the realm of maternal experience.

Of the essays in *A Housewife's Opinions*, Webster wrote that

though written for immediate appearance in those lighter columns of weekly journals which everyone reads and no one recalls, they had, even the most jesting of them, all the care and thought I could have given work meant to last . . . the matters to which I have tried, in one guise or another, to give help or hindrance are no mere momentary questions begun and ended with the talk of the week.

These shrewdly practical essays address such topics as "Matrimony as a Means of Livelihood," "Husband-Hunting and Match-Making," and "The Novel-Making Trade"; those included here represent two of her major concerns, the fight for women's suffrage and the complexities of selfhood.

In her major collection of dramatic monologues, *Portraits* (1870), Webster took the strikingly modern tack of not beginning each line with a capital letter, but in response to reviewers' objections she retreated to conventional usage in the third edition (1893). We give the 1870 versions here.

By the Looking-Glass

Alone at last in my room—
How sick I grow of the glitter and din,
Of the lips that smile and the voices that prate
To a ballroom tune for the fashion's sake:
Light and laughters without, but what within?
Are these like me? Do the pleasure and state
Weary them under the seeming they make?—
But I see all through my gloom.

For why should a light young heart
Not leap to a merry moving air,   10
Not laugh with the joy of the flying hour
And feed upon pleasure just for a while?
But the right of a woman is being fair,
And her heart must starve if she miss that dower,
For how should she purchase the look and the smile?
And I have not had my part.

A girl, and so plain a face!
Once more, as I learn by heart every line
In the pitiless mirror, night by night,
Let me try to think it is not my own.   20
Come, stranger with features something like mine,
Let me place close by you the tell-tale light;
Can I find in you now some charm unknown,
Only one softening grace?

Alas! it is I, I, I,
Ungainly, common. The other night
I heard one say "Why, she is not so plain.
See, the mouth is shapely, the nose not ill."

If I could but believe his judgement right!
But I try to dupe my eyesight in vain,   30
For I, who have partly a painter's skill,
I cannot put knowledge by.

He had not fed, as I feed
On beauty, till beauty itself must seem
Me, my own, a part and essence of me,
My right and my being—Why! how am I plain?
I feel as if this were almost a dream
From which I should waken, as it might be,
And open my eyes on beauty again
And know it myself indeed.   40

Oh idle! oh folly! look,
There, looking back from the glass, is my fate,
A clumsy creature smelling of earth,
What fancy could lend her the angel's wings?
She looks like a boorish peasant's fit mate.
Why! what a mock at the pride of birth,
Fashioned by nature for menial things,
With her name in the red-bound book.[1]

Oh! to forget me a while,
Feeling myself but as one in the throng,   50
Losing myself in the joy of my youth!
Then surely some pleasure might lie in my reach.
But the sense of myself is ever strong,
And I read in all eyes the bitter truth,
And I fancy scorning in every speech
And mocking in every smile.

---

[1] **the red-bound book**: listing of families in the aristocracy or gentry.

Ah! yes, it was so to-night,
And I moved so heavily through the dance,
And answered uncouthly like one ill taught,
And knew that ungentleness seemed on my brow, 60
While it was but pain at each meeting glance,
For I knew that all who looked at me thought
"How ugly she is! one sees it more now
With the other young faces so bright."

I might be more like the rest,
Like those that laugh with a girlish grace
And make bright nothings an eloquence;
I might seem gentler and softer souled;
But I needs must shape myself to my place,
Softness in me would seem clumsy pretence, 70
Would they not deem my laughters bold?
I hide in myself as is best.

Do I grow bitter sometimes?
They say it, ah me! and I fear it is true,
And I shrink from that curse of bitterness,
And I pray on my knees that it may not come;
But how should I envy—they say that I do—
All the love which others' young lives may bless?
Because *my* age will be lone in its home
Do I weep at the wedding chimes? 80

Ah no, for they judge me ill,
Judging me doubtless by that which I look,
Do I not joy for another's delight?
Do I not grieve for another's regret?
And I have been true where others forsook
And kind where others bore hatred and spite,
For there I could think myself welcome—and yet
My care is unpitied still.

Yes, who can think it such pain
Not to be fair "Such a trifling thing." 90
And "Goodness may be where beauty is not"
And "How weak to sorrow for outward show!"
Ah! if they knew what a poisonful sting
Has this sense of shame, how a woman's lot
Is darkened throughout!—Oh yes I know
How weak—but I know in vain.

　I hoped in vain, for I thought,
When first I grew to a woman's days,
Woman enough to feel what it means
To be a woman and not be fair, 100
That I need not sigh for the voice of praise
And the beauty's triumph in courtly scenes

Where she queens with her maiden-royal air,
Ah! and so worshipped and sought.

But I, oh my dreaming! deemed
With a woman's yearning and faith in love,
With a woman's faith in her lovingness,
That that joy might brighten on me, even me,
For which all the force of my nature strove,
Joy of daily smiles and voices that bless, 110
And one deeper other love it might be—
Hush, *that* was wrong to have dreamed.

I thank God, I have not loved,
Loved as one says it whose life has gone out
Into another's for evermore,
Loved as I know what love might be
Writhing but living through poison of doubt,
Drinking the gall of the sweetness before,
Drinking strange deep strength from the bitter lee—
Love, love in a falsehood proved! 120

Loving him on to the end,
Through the weary weeping hours of the night,
Through the wearier laughing hours of the day;
Knowing him less than the love I gave,
But this one fond dream left my life for its light
To do him some service and pass away;
Not daring, for sin, to think of the grave
Lest it seemed the only friend.

Thank God that it was not so,
And I have my scatheless maidenly pride, 130
But it might have been—for did he not speak
With that slow sweet cadence that seemed made deep
By a meaning—Hush! he has chosen his bride.
Oh! happy smile on her lips and her cheek,
My darling! And I have no cause to weep,
I have not bowed me so low.

But would he have wooed in vain?
Would not my heart have leaped to his will,
If he had not changed?—How, *changed* do I say?
Was I not mocked with an idle thought, 140
Dreaming and dreaming so foolishly still?
By the sweet glad smile and the winning way
And the grace of beauty alone is love bought.
He woo me! Am I not plain?

But yet I was not alone
To fancy I might be something to him.
They thought it, I know, though it seems so wild
Now, in this bitterer Now's hard light.

Vain that I was! could his sight grow dim?
How could he love me? But she, when she smiled   150
Once, the first once, by her beauty's right
Had made all his soul her own.

It is well that no busy tongue
Has vexed her heart with those bygone tales.
But I think he fears he did me some wrong,
I see him watch me at times, and his cheek
Crimsons a little, a little pales,
If his eye meets mine for a moment long.
But he need not fear, I am not so weak
Though I *am* a woman and young.   160

I had not grown to my love,
Though it might have been. And I give no blame:
Nothing was spoken to bind him to me,
Nothing had been that could make him think
My heart beat stronger and fast when he came,
And if he *had* loved me, was he not free,
When the fancy passed, to loose that vague link
That only such fancy wove?

No he has done no such ill
But that I can bear it, nor shame in my heart   170
To call him my brother and see her his,
The one little pearl that gleams through our gloom:
He has no dishonour to bar them apart.
I loving her so, am rested in this;
Else I would speak though I spoke her doom,
Though grief had the power to kill.

When she came a while ago,
My young fair sister bright with her bloom,
Back to a home which is little glad,
I thought "Here is one who should know no care,   180
A little wild bird flown into a room
From its far free woods; will she droop and grow sad?
But, here even, love smiles upon one so fair.
And I too might feel that glow."

But now she will fly away!
Ah me! and I love her so deep in my heart
And worship her beauty as he might do.
If I could but have kept her a little time!
Ah she will go! So the sunbeams depart
That brightened the winter's sky into blue,   190
And the dews of the chill dusk freeze into rime,
And cold cold mists hang grey.

I think she loved me till now—
Nay doubtless she loves me quietly yet,
But his lightest fancy is more, far more,
To her than all the love that I live.
But I cannot blame (as if love were a debt)
That, though I love, he is held far before;
And is it not well that a bride should give
All, all her heart with her vow?   200

But ah, if I smiled more sweet
And spoke more soft as one fairer could,
Had not love indeed been more surely mine?
Folly to say that a woman's grace
Is only strong o'er a man's light mood!
Even the hearts of the nearest incline
With a gentler thought to the lovely face,
And the winning eyes that entreat.

But I—yes flicker pale light,
Fade into darkness and hide it away,   210
The poor dull face that looks out from the glass,
Oh wearily wearily back to me!
Yes, I will sleep, for my wild thoughts stray
Weakly, selfishly—yes let them pass,
Let self and this sadness of self leave me free,
Lost in the peace of the night.

                                    1866

Circe[1]

The sun drops luridly into the west;
darkness has raised her arms to draw him down
before the time, not waiting as of wont
till he has come to her behind the sea;
and the smooth waves grow sullen in the gloom
and wear their threatening purple; more and more
the plain of waters sways and seems to rise
convexly from its level of the shores;
and low dull thunder rolls along the beach:
there will be storm at last, storm, glorious storm.   10

    Oh welcome, welcome, though it rend my bowers,
scattering my blossomed roses like the dust,
splitting the shrieking branches, tossing down

---

[1] **Circe**: goddess in *Odyssey* 10 who entertains travelers on her island with a magic potion that turns men into beasts. Odysseus' men become swine, but he is protected by a magical herb and stays with Circe a year before resuming his journey home.

my riotous vines with their young half-tinged grapes
like small round amethysts or beryls strung
tumultuously in clusters, though it sate
its ravenous spite among my goodliest pines
standing there round and still against the sky
that makes blue lakes between their sombre tufts,
or harry from my silvery olive slopes   20
some hoary king whose gnarled fantastic limbs
wear crooked armour of a thousand years;
though it will hurl high on my flowery shores
the hostile wave that rives at the poor sward
and drags it down the slants, that swirls its foam
over my terraces, shakes their firm blocks
of great bright marbles into tumbled heaps,
and makes my pleached and mossy labyrinths,
where the small odorous blossoms grow like stars
strewn in the milky way, a briny marsh.   30
What matter? let it come and bring me change,
breaking the sickly sweet monotony.

I am too weary of this long bright calm;
always the same blue sky, always the sea
the same blue perfect likeness of the sky,
one rose to match the other that has waned,
to-morrow's dawn the twin of yesterday's;
and every night the ceaseless crickets chirp
the same long joy and the late strain of birds
repeats their strain of all the even month;   40
and changelessly the petty plashing surfs
bubble their chiming burden round the stones;
dusk after dusk brings the same languid trance
upon the shadowy hills, and in the fields
the waves of fireflies come and go the same,
making the very flash of light and stir
vex one like dronings of the spinning wheel.

Give me some change. Must life be only sweet,
all honey-pap as babes would have their food?
And, if my heart must always be adrowse   50
in a hush of stagnant sunshine, give me then
something outside me stirring; let the storm
break up the sluggish beauty, let it fall
beaten below the feet of passionate winds,
and then to-morrow waken jubilant
in a new birth: let me see subtle joy
of anguish and of hopes, of change and growth.

What fate is mine who, far apart from pains
and fears and turmoils of the cross-grained world,
dwell, like a lonely god, in a charmed isle   60
where I am first and only, and, like one

who should love poisonous savours more than mead,
long for a tempest on me and grow sick
of resting, and divine free carelessness!
Oh me, I am a woman, not a god;[2]
yea, those who tend me even are more than I,
my nymphs who have the souls of flowers and birds
singing and blossoming immortally.

Ah me! these love a day and laugh again,
and loving, laughing, find a full content;   70
but I know nought of peace, and have not loved.

Where is my love? Does some one cry for me,
not knowing whom he calls? does his soul cry
for mine to grow beside it, grow in it?
does he beseech the gods to give him me,
the one unknown rare woman by whose side
no other woman, thrice as beautiful,
should once seem fair to him; to whose voice heard
in any common tones no sweetest sound
of love made melody on silver lutes,   80
or singing like Apollo's when the gods
grow pale with happy listening, might be peered
for making music to him; whom once found
there will be no more seeking anything?

Oh love, oh love, oh love, art not yet come
out of the waiting shadows into life?
art not yet come after so many years
that I have longed for thee? Come! I am here.

Not yet. For surely I should feel a sound
of his far answering, if now in the world   90
he sought me who will seek me—Oh ye gods
will he not seek me? Is it all a dream?
will there be never never such a man?
will there be only these, these bestial things
who wallow in my styes, or mop and mow
among the trees, or munch in pens and byres,
or snarl and filch behind their wattled coops;
these things who had believed that they were men?

Nay but he *will* come. Why am I so fair,
and marvellously minded, and with sight   100
which flashes suddenly on hidden things,
as the gods see who do not need to look?
why wear I in my eyes that stronger power
than basilisks,[3] whose gaze can only kill,

---

[2]**not a God**: Homer's Circe, daughter of Helios the sun-god and
granddaughter of Oceanus, is indeed a goddess.

[3]**basilisks**: fabulous serpents whose breath and look are fatal.

to draw men's souls to me to live or die
as I would have them? why am I given pride
which yet longs to be broken, and this scorn
cruel and vengeful for the lesser men
who meet the smiles I waste for lack of him
and grow too glad? why am I who I am,   110
but for the sake of him whom fate will send
one day to be my master utterly,
that he should take me, the desire of all,
whom only he in the world could bow to him?

Oh sunlike glory of pale glittering hairs,
bright as the filmy wires my weavers take
to make me golden gauzes; oh deep eyes,
darker and softer than the bluest dusk
of August violets, darker and deep
like crystal fathomless lakes in summer noons;   120
oh sad sweet longing smile; oh lips that tempt
my very self to kisses; oh round cheeks,
tenderly radiant with the even flush
of pale smoothed coral; perfect lovely face
answering my gaze from out this fleckless pool;
wonder of glossy shoulders, chiselled limbs;
should I be so your lover as I am,
drinking an exquisite joy to watch you thus
in all a hundred changes through the day,
but that I love you for him till he comes,   130
but that my beauty means his loving it?

Oh, look! a speck on this side of the sun,
coming—yes, coming with the rising wind
that frays the darkening cloud-wrack on the verge
and in a little while will leap abroad,
spattering the sky with rushing blacknesses,
dashing the hissing mountainous waves at the stars.
'Twill drive me that black speck a shuddering hulk
caught in the buffeting waves, dashed impotent
from ridge to ridge, will drive it in the night   140
with that dull jarring crash upon the beach,
and the cries for help and the cries of fear and hope.

And then to-morrow they will thoughtfully,
with grave low voices, count their perils up,
and thank the gods for having let them live,
and tell of wives or mothers in their homes,
and children, who would have such loss in them
that they must weep, and may be I weep too,
with fancy of the weepings had they died.
And the next morrow they will feel their ease   150
and sigh with sleek content, or laugh elate,
tasting delights of rest and revelling,

music and perfumes, joyaunce for the eyes
of rosy faces and luxurious pomps,
the savour of the banquet and the glow
and fragrance of the wine-cup; and they'll talk
how good it is to house in palaces
out of the storms and struggles, and what luck
strewed their good ship on our accessless coast.
Then the next day the beast in them will wake,   160
and one will strike and bicker, and one swell
with puffed up greatness, and one gibe and strut
in apish pranks, and one will line his sleeve
with pilfered booties, and one snatch the gems
out of the carven goblets as they pass,
one will grow mad with fever of the wine,
and one will sluggishly besot himself,
and one be lewd, and one be gluttonous;
and I shall sickly look, and loathe them all.

Oh my rare cup! my pure and crystal cup,   170
with not one speck of colour to make false
the passing lights, or flaw to make them swerve!
My cup of Truth! How the lost fools will laugh
and thank me for my boon, as if I gave
some momentary flash of the gods' joy,
to drink where I have drunk and touch the touch
of my lips with their own! Aye, let them touch.

Too cruel am I? And the silly beasts,
crowding around me when I pass their way,
glower on me and, although they love me still,   180
(with their poor sorts of love such as they could,)
call wrath and vengeance to their humid eyes
to scare me into mercy, or creep near
with piteous fawnings, supplicating bleats.
Too cruel? Did I choose them what they are?
or change them from themselves by poisonous charms?
But any draught, pure water, natural wine,
out of my cup, revealed them to themselves
and to each other. Change? there was no change;
only disguise gone from them unawares: 190
and had there been one right true man of them
he would have drunk the draught as I had drunk,
and stood unchanged, and looked me in the eyes,
abashing me before him. But these things—
why, which of them has even shown the kind
of some one nobler beast? Pah, yapping wolves
and pitiless stealthy wild-cats, curs and apes
and gorging swine and slinking venomous snakes
all false and ravenous and sensual brutes
that shame the Earth that bore them, these they are.   200

Lo, lo! the shivering blueness darting forth
on half the heavens, and the forked thin fire
strikes to the sea: and hark, the sudden voice
that rushes through the trees before the storm,
and shuddering of the branches. Yet the sky
is blue against them still, and early stars
glimmer above the pine-tops; and the air
clings faint and motionless around me here.

Another burst of flame—and the black speck
shows in the glare, lashed onwards. It were well   210
I bade make ready for our guests to-night.

1870

The Happiest Girl in the World

A week ago; only a little week:
it seems so much much longer, though that day
is every morning still my yesterday;
as all my life 'twill be my yesterday,
for all my life is morrow to my love.
Oh fortunate morrow! Oh sweet happy love!

A week ago; and I am almost glad
to have him now gone for this little while,
that I may think of him and tell myself
what to be his means, now that I am his,   10
and know if mine is love enough for him,
and make myself believe it all is true.

A week ago; and it seems like a life,
and I have not yet learned to know myself:
I am so other than I was, so strange,
grown younger and grown older all in one;
and I am not so sad and not so gay;
and I think nothing, only hear him think.

That morning, waking, I remembered him
"Will he be here to-day? he often comes;—   20
and is it for my sake or to kill time?"
and, wondering "Will he come?" I chose the dress
he seemed to like the best, and hoped for him;
and did not think I could quite love him yet.
And did I love him then with all my heart?
or did I wait until he held my hands
and spoke "Say, shall it be?" and kissed my brow,
and I looked at him and he knew it all?

And did I love him from the day we met?
but I more gladly danced with some one else   30
who waltzed more smoothly and was merrier:
and did I love him when he first came here?
but I more gladly talked with some one else
whose words were readier and who sought me more.
When did I love him? How did it begin?

The small green spikes of snowdrops in the spring
are there one morning ere you think of them;
still we may tell what morning they pierced up:
June rosebuds stir and open stealthily,
and every new-blown rose is a surprise;   40
still we can date the day when one unclosed:
but how can I tell when my love began?

Oh, was it like the young pale twilight star
that quietly breaks on the vacant sky,
is sudden there and perfect while you watch,
and, though you watch, you have not seen it dawn,
the star that only waited and awoke?

But he knows when he loved me; for he says
the first time we had met he told a friend
"The sweetest dewy daisy of a girl,   50
but not the solid stuff to make a wife;"
and afterwards the first time he was here,
when I had slipped away into our field
to watch alone for sunset brightening on
and heard them calling me, he says he stood
and saw me come along the coppice walk
beneath the green and sparkling arch of boughs,
and, while he watched the yellow lights that played
with the dim flickering shadows of the leaves
over my yellow hair and soft pale dress,   60
flitting across me as I flitted through,
he whispered inly, in so many words,
"I see my wife; this is my wife who comes,
and seems to bear the sunlight on with her."
and that was when he loved me, so he says.

Yet is he quite sure? was it only then?
and had he had no thought which I could feel?
for why was it I knew that he would watch,
and all the while thought in my silly heart,
as I advanced demurely, it was well   70
I had on the pale dress with sweeping folds
which took the light and shadow tenderly,
and that the sunlights touched my hair and cheek,
because he'd note it all and care for it?

Oh vain and idle poor girl's heart of mine,
content with that coquettish mean content!
He, with his man's straight purpose, thinking "wife,"
and I but that 'twas pleasant to be fair
and that 'twas pleasant he should count me fair.
But oh, to think he should be loving me   80
and I be no more moved out of myself!
The sunbeams told him, but they told me nought,
except that maybe I was looking well.
And oh had I but known! Why did no bird,
trilling its own sweet lovesong, as I passed,
so musically marvellously glad,
sing one for me too, sing me "It is he,"
sing "Love him," and "You love him: it is he,"
that I might then have loved him when he loved,
that one dear moment might be date to both?   90

And must I not be glad he hid his thought
and did not tell me then, when it was soon
and I should have been startled, and not known
how he is just the one man I can love,
and, only with some pain lest he were pained,
and nothing doubting, should have answered "No."
How strange life is! I should have answered "No."
Oh, can I ever be half glad enough
he is so wise and patient and could wait!

He waited as you wait the reddening fruit   100
which helplessly is ripening on the tree,
and not because it tries or longs or wills,
only because the sun will shine on it:
but he who waited was himself that sun.

Oh was it worth the waiting? was it worth?
For I am half afraid love is not love,
this love which only makes me rest in him
and be so happy and so confident,
this love which makes me pray for longest days
that I may have them all to use for him,   110
this love which almost makes me yearn for pain
that I might have borne something for his sake,
this love which I call love, is less than love.
Where are the fires and fevers and the pangs?
where is the anguish of too much delight,
and the delirious madness at a kiss,
the flushing and the paling at a look,
and passionate ecstasy of meeting hands?
where is the eager weariness at time
that will not bate a single measured hour   120
to speed to us the far-off wedding day?
I am so calm and wondering, like a child

who, led by a firm hand it knows and trusts
along a stranger country beautiful
with a bewildering beauty to new eyes
if they be wise to know what they behold,
finds newness everywhere but no surprise,
and takes the beauty as an outward part
of being led so kindly by the hand.
I am so cold: is mine but a child's heart,   130
and not a woman's fit for such a man?
Alas am I too cold, am I too dull,
can I not love him as another could?
And oh, if love be fire, what love is mine
that is but like the pale subservient moon
who only asks to be earth's minister?
And, oh, if love be whirlwind, what is mine
that is but like a little even brook
which has no aim but flowing to the sea,
and sings for happiness because it flows?   140

Ah well, I would that I could love him more
and not be only happy as I am;
I would that I could love him to his worth,
with that forgetting all myself in him,
that subtle pain of exquisite excess,
that momentary infinite sharp joy,
I know by books but cannot teach my heart:
and yet I think my love must needs be love,
since he can read me through—oh happy strange,
my thoughts that were my secrets all for me   150
grown instantly his open easy book!—
since he can read me through, and is content.

And yesterday, when they all went away,
save little Amy with her daisy chains,
and left us in that shadow of tall ferns,
and the child, leaning on me, fell asleep,
and I, tired by the afternoon long walk,
said "I could almost gladly sleep like her,"
did he not answer, drawing down my head,
"Sleep, darling, let me see you rest on me,"   160
and when the child, awaking, wakened me,
did he not say "Dear, you have made me glad,
for, seeing you so sleeping peacefully,
I feel that you do love me utterly,
no questionings, no regrettings, but at rest."

Oh yes, my good true darling, you said well
"No questionings, no regrettings, but at rest:"
what should I question, what should I regret,
now I have you who are my hope and rest?

I am the feathery wind-wafted seed   170
that flickered idly half a merry morn,
now thralled into the rich life-giving earth
to root and bud and waken into leaf
and make it such poor sweetness as I may;
the prisoned seed that never more shall float
the frolic playfellow of summer winds
and mimic the free changeful butterfly;
the prisoned seed that prisoned finds its life
and feels its pulses stir, and grows, and grows.
Oh love, who gathered me into yourself,   180
oh love, I am at rest in you, and live.

And shall I for so many coming days
be flower and sweetness to him? Oh pale flower,
grow, grow, and blossom out, and fill the air,
feed on his richness, grow, grow, blossom out,
and fill the air, and be enough for him.

Oh crystal music of the air-borne lark,
so falling, nearer, nearer, from the sky,
are you a message to me of dear hopes?
oh trilling gladness, flying down to earth,   190
have you brought answer of sweet prophecy?
have you brought answer to the thoughts in me?
Oh happy answer, and oh happy thoughts!
and which is the bird's carol, which my heart's?

My love, my love, my love! And I shall be
so much to him, so almost everything:
and I shall be the friend whom he will trust,
and I shall be the child whom he will teach,
and I shall be the servant he will praise,
and I shall be the mistress he will love,   200
and I shall be his wife. Oh days to come,
will ye not pass like gentle rhythmic steps
that fall to sweetest music noiselessly?

But I have known the lark's song half sound sad,
and I have seen the lake, which rippled sun,
toss dimmed and purple in a sudden wind;
and let me laugh a moment at my heart
that thinks the summer-time must all be fair,
that thinks the good days always must be good:
yes let me laugh a moment—may be weep.   210

But no, but no, not laugh; for through my joy
I have been wise enough to know the while
some tears and some long hours are in all lives,
in every promised land some thorn-plants grow,
some tangling weeds as well as laden vines:
and no, not weep; for is not my land fair,

my land of promise flushed with fruit and bloom?
and who would weep for fear of scattered thorns?
and very thorns bear oftentimes sweet fruits.

Oh the black storm that breaks across the lake   220
ruffles the surface, leaves the deeps at rest—
deep in our hearts there always will be rest:
oh summer storms fall sudden as they rose,
the peaceful lake forgets them while they die—
our hearts will always have it summer time.

All rest, all summer time. My love, my love,
I know it will be so; you are so good,
and I, near you, shall grow at last like you;
and you are tender, patient—oh I know
you will bear with me, help me, smile to me,   230
and let me make you happy easily;
and I, what happiness could I have more
than that dear labour of a happy wife?
I would not have another. Is it wrong,
and is it selfish that I cannot wish,
that I, who yet so love the clasping hand
and innocent fond eyes of little ones,
I cannot wish that which I sometimes read
is women's dearest wish hid in their love,
to press a baby creature to my breast?   240
Oh is it wrong? I would be all for him,
not even children coming 'twixt us two
to call me from his service to serve them;
and maybe they would steal too much of love,
for, since I cannot love him now enough,
what would my heart be halved? or would it grow?
But he perhaps would love me something less,
finding me not so always at his side.

Together always, that was what he said;
together always. Oh dear coming days!   250
O dear dear present days that pass too fast,
although they bring such rainbow morrows on!
that pass so fast, and yet, I know not why,
seem always to encompass so much time.
And I should fear I were too happy now,
and making this poor world too much my Heaven,
but that I feel God nearer and it seems
as if I had learned His love better too.

So late already! The sun dropping down,
and under him the first long line of red—   260
my truant should be here again by now,
is come maybe. I will not seek him, I;
he would be vain and think I cared too much;

I will wait here, and he shall seek for me,
and I will carelessly——Oh his dear step—
he sees me, he is coming; my own love!

                                        1870

A Castaway[1]

Poor little diary, with its simple thoughts,
its good resolves, its "Studied French an hour,"
"Read Modern History," "Trimmed up my grey hat,"
"Darned stockings," "Tatted," "Practised my new song,"
"Went to the daily service," "Took Bess soup,"
"Went out to tea." Poor simple diary!
and did *I* write it? Was I this good girl,
this budding colourless young rose of home?
did I so live content in such a life,
seeing no larger scope, nor asking it,   10
than this small constant round—old clothes to mend,
new clothes to make, then go and say my prayers,
or carry soup, or take a little walk
and pick the ragged-robins[2] in the hedge?
Then for ambition, (was there ever life
that could forego that?) to improve my mind
and know French better and sing harder songs;
for gaiety, to go, in my best white
well washed and starched and freshened with new bows,
and take tea out to meet the clergyman.   20
No wishes and no cares, almost no hopes,
only the young girl's hazed and golden dreams
that veil the Future from her.

                    So long since:
and now it seems a jest to talk of me
as if I could be one with her, of me
who am. . . . . . me.

                    And what is that? My looking-glass
answers it passably; a woman sure,
no fiend, no slimy thing out of the pools,
a woman with a ripe and smiling lip
that has no venom in its touch I think,   30
with a white brow on which there is no brand;
a woman none dare call not beautiful,
not womanly in every woman's grace.

Aye let me feed upon my beauty thus,
be glad in it like painters when they see
at last the face they dreamed but could not find
look from their canvass on them, triumph in it,
the dearest thing I have. Why, 'tis my all,
let me make much of it: is it not this,
this beauty, my own curse at once and tool
to snare men's souls—(I know what the good say   40
of beauty in such creatures)—is it not this
that makes me feel myself a woman still,
some little pride, some little—

                    Here's a jest!
what word will fit the sense but modesty?
A wanton I but modest!

                    Modest, true;
I'm not drunk in the streets, ply not for hire
at infamous corners with my likenesses
of the humbler kind; yes, modesty's my word—
'twould shape my mouth well too, I think I'll try: 50
"Sir, Mr What-you-will, Lord Who-knows-what,
my present lover or my next to come,
value me at my worth, fill your purse full,
for I am modest; yes, and honour me
as though your schoolgirl sister or your wife
could let her skirts brush mine or talk of me;
for I am modest."

                    Well, I flout myself:
but yet, but yet——

                    Fie, poor fantastic fool,
why do I play the hypocrite alone,
who am no hypocrite with others by?   60
where should be my "But yet"? I am that thing
called half a dozen dainty names, and none
dainty enough to serve the turn and hide
the one coarse English worst that lurks beneath:
just that, no worse, no better.

                    And, for me,
I say let no one be above her trade;
I own my kindredship with any drab
who sells herself as I, although she crouch
in fetid garrets and I have a home
all velvet and marqueterie and pastilles,   70
although she hide her skeleton in rags
and I set fashions and wear cobweb lace:
the difference lies but in my choicer ware,
that I sell beauty and she ugliness;
our traffic's one—I'm no sweet slaver-tongue

---

[1]**Castaway**: a sexually fallen woman; see 1 Corinthians 9:27.

[2]**ragged-robins**: purple flowers.

to gloze upon it and explain myself
a sort of fractious angel misconceived—
our traffic's one: I own it. And what then?
I know of worse that are called honourable.
Our lawyers, who, with noble eloquence   80
and virtuous outbursts, lie to hang a man,
or lie to save him, which way goes the fee:
our preachers, gloating on your future hell
for not believing what they doubt themselves:
our doctors, who sort poisons out by chance,
and wonder how they'll answer, and grow rich:
our journalists, whose business is to fib
and juggle truths and falsehoods to and fro:
our tradesmen, who must keep unspotted names
and cheat the least like stealing that they can: 90
our——all of them, the virtuous worthy men
who feed on the world's follies, vices, wants,
and do their businesses of lies and shams
honestly, reputably, while the world
claps hands and cries "good luck," which of their trades,
their honourable trades, barefaced like mine,
all secrets brazened out, would shew more white?

And whom do I hurt more than they? as much?
The wives? Poor fools, what do I take from them
worth crying for or keeping? If they knew   100
what their fine husbands look like seen by eyes
that may perceive there are more men than one!
But, if they can, let them just take the pains
to keep them: 'tis not such a mighty task
to pin an idiot to your apron-string;
and wives have an advantage over us,
(the good and blind ones have), the smile or pout
leaves them no secret nausea at odd times.
Oh they could keep their husbands if they cared,
but 'tis an easier life to let them go,   110
and whimper at it for morality.

Oh! those shrill carping virtues, safely housed
from reach of even a smile that should put red
on a decorous cheek, who rail at us
with such a spiteful scorn and rancourousness,
(which maybe is half envy at the heart),
and boast themselves so measurelessly good
and us so measurelessly unlike them,
what is their wondrous merit that they stay
in comfortable homes whence not a soul   120
has ever thought of tempting them, and wear
no kisses but a husband's upon lips
there is no other man desires to kiss—
refrain in fact from sin impossible?

How dare they hate us so? what have they done,
what borne, to prove them other than we are?
What right have they to scorn us—glass-case saints,
Dianas under lock and key—what right
more than the well-fed helpless barn-door fowl
to scorn the larcenous wild-birds?

              Pshaw, let be!   130
Scorn: or no scorn, what matter for their scorn?
I have outfaced my own—that's harder work.
Aye let their virtuous malice dribble on—
mock snowstorms on the stage—I'm proof long since:
I have looked coolly on my what and why,
and I accept myself.

            Oh I'll endorse
the shamefullest revilings mouthed at me,
cry "True! Oh perfect picture! Yes, that's I!"
and add a telling blackness here and there,
and then dare swear you, every nine of ten,   140
my judges and accusers, I'd not change
my conscience against yours, you who tread out
your devil's pilgrimage along the roads
that take in church and chapel, and arrange
a roundabout and decent way to hell.

Well, mine's a short way and a merry one:
so says my pious hash of ohs and ahs,
choice texts and choicer threats, appropriate names,
(Rahabs and Jezebels), some fierce Tartuffe[3]
hurled at me through the post. We had rare fun   150
over that tract digested with champagne.
Where is it? where's my rich repertory
of insults biblical? *'I prey on souls'*—
only my men have oftenest none I think:
'I snare the simple ones'—but in these days
there seem to be none simple and none snared,
and most men have their favourite sinnings planned
to do them civilly and sensibly:
'I braid my hair'—but braids are out of date:
'I paint my cheeks'—I always wear them pale: 160
'I—'

Pshaw! the trash is savourless to-day:
one cannot laugh alone. There, let it burn.
What, does the windy dullard think one needs
his wisdom dove-tailed on to Solomon's,
his threats out-threatening God's, to teach the news

---

[3]**Rahab, Jezebel:** wicked women in the Old Testament; see
Joshua 2:1–24, 2 Kings 9:29–37. **Tartuffe:** religious hypocrite in
Molière's play of that name (1664).

that those who need not sin have safer souls?
We know it, but we've bodies to save too;
and so we earn our living.

     Well lit, tract!
at least you've made me a good leaping blaze.
Up, up, how the flame shoots! and now 'tis dead. 170
Oh proper finish, preaching to the last—
no such bad omen either; sudden end,
and no sad withering horrible old age.
How one would clutch at youth to hold it tight!
and then to know it gone, to see it gone,
be taught its absence by harsh careless looks,
to live forgotten, solitary, old—
the cruellest word that ever woman learns.
Old—that's to be nothing, or to be at best
a blurred memorial that in better days   180
there was a woman once with such a name.
No, no, I could not bear it: death itself
shews kinder promise. . . . . . even death itself,
since it must come one day—

     Oh this grey gloom!
This rain, rain, rain, what wretched thoughts it brings!
Death: I'll not think of it.

     Will no one come?
'Tis dreary work alone.

     Why did I read
that silly diary? Now, sing song, ding dong,
come the old vexing echoes back again,
church bells and nursery good-books, back again 190
upon my shrinking ears that had forgotten—
I hate the useless memories: 'tis fools' work
singing the hacknied dirge of 'better days:'
best take Now kindly, give the past good-bye,
whether it were a better or a worse.

  Yes, yes, I listened to the echoes once,
the echoes and the thoughts from the old days.
The worse for me: I lost my richest friend,
and that was all the difference. For the world
I would not have that flight known. How they'd roar: 200
"What! Eulalie, when she refused us all,
'ill' and 'away,' was doing Magdalene,
tears, ashes, and her Bible, and then off
to hide her in a Refuge[4] . . . for a week!"

A wild whim that, to fancy I could change
my new self for my old, because I wished!
Since then, when in my languid days there comes
that craving, like homesickness, to go back
to the good days, the dear old stupid days,
to the quiet and the innocence, I know 210
'tis a sick fancy and try palliatives.

  What is it? You go back to the old home,
and 'tis not *your* home, has no place for you,
and, if it had, you could not fit you in it.
And could I fit me to my former self?
If I had had the wit, like some of us,
to sow my wild-oats into three per cents,[5]
could I not find me shelter in the peace
of some far nook where none of them would come,
nor whisper travel from this scurrilous world, 220
that gloats and moralizes through its leers,
to blast me with my fashionable shame?
There I might—oh my castle in the clouds!
and where's its rent?—but there, were there a there,
I might again live the grave blameless life
among such simple pleasures, simple cares:
but could they be my pleasures, be my cares?
The blameless life, but never the content—
never. How could I henceforth be content
in any life but one that sets the brain 230
in a hot merry fever with its stir?
what would there be in quiet rustic days,
each like the other, full of time to think,
to keep one bold enough to live at all?
Quiet is hell, I say—as if a woman
could bear to sit alone, quiet all day,
and loathe herself, and sicken on her thoughts.

  They tried it at the Refuge, and I failed:
I could not bear it. Dreary hideous room,
coarse pittance, prison rules, one might bear these 240
and keep one's purpose; but so much alone,
and then made faint and weak and fanciful
by change from pampering to half-famishing—
good God, what thoughts come! Only one week more
and 'twould have ended: but in one day more
I must have killed myself. And I loathe death,
the dreadful foul corruption, with who knows
what future after it.

     Well, I came back,
back to my slough. Who says I had my choice?

---

[4]**Magdalene**: archetypal repentant fallen woman; see Luke 7:36–50. **Refuge**: institution for reforming prostitutes.

[5]**wild-oats**: youthful misbehavior. **three per cents**: investments.

Could I stay there to die of some mad death?   250
and if I rambled out into the world,
sinless but penniless, what else were that
but slower death, slow pining shivering death
by misery and hunger? Choice! what choice
of living well or ill? could I have that?
And who would give it me? I think indeed
if some kind hand, a woman's—I hate men—
had stretched itself to help me to firm ground,
taken a chance and risked my falling back,
I could have gone my way not falling back: 260
but, let her be all brave, all charitable,
how could she do it? Such a trifling boon,
a little work to live by, 'tis not much,
and I might have found will enough to last:
but where's the work? More sempstresses than shirts;
and defter hands at white work[6] than are mine
drop starved at last: dressmakers, milliners,
too many too they say; and then their trades
need skill, apprenticeship. And who so bold
as hire me for their humblest drudgery?   270
not even for scullery slut;[7] not even, I think,
for governess, although they'd get me cheap.
And after all it would be something hard,
with the marts for decent women overfull,
if I could elbow in and snatch a chance
and oust some good girl so, who then perforce
must come and snatch her chance among our crowd.

Why, if the worthy men who think all's done
if we'll but come where we can hear them preach,
could bring us all, or any half of us,   280
into their fold, teach all us wandering sheep,
or only half of us, to stand in rows
and baa them hymns and moral songs, good lack,
what would they do with us? what could they do?
Just think! with were't but half of us on hand
to find work for . . . or husbands. Would they try
to ship us to the colonies for wives?[8]

Well, well, I know the wise ones talk and talk:
"Here's cause, here's cure:" "No, here it is and here:"
and find society to blame, or law,   290

---

[6]**white work**: embroidery with white thread on white cloth, very
damaging to the eyesight.

[7]**scullery slut**: maid who does coarse kitchen work.

[8]**ship . . . wives**: reformed prostitutes were often sent to the
colonies, where there were more men than women, while in England there were thought to be too many marriageable women.

the Church, the men, the women, too few schools,
too many schools, too much, too little taught:
somewhere or somehow someone is to blame:
but I say all the fault's with God himself
who puts too many women in the world.
We ought to die off reasonably and leave
as many as the men want, none to waste.
Here's cause; the woman's superfluity:
and for the cure, why, if it were the law,
say, every year, in due percentages,   300
balancing them with men as the times need,
to kill off female infants, 'twould make room;
and some of us would not have lost too much,
losing life ere we know what it *can* mean.

The other day I saw a woman weep
beside her dead child's bed: the little thing
lay smiling, and the mother wailed half mad,
shrieking to God to give it back again.
I could have laughed aloud: the little girl
living had but her mother's life to live;   310
there she lay smiling, and her mother wept
to know her gone!

              My mother would have wept.

Oh mother, mother, did you ever dream,
you good grave simple mother, you pure soul
no evil could come nigh, did you once dream
in all your dying cares for your lone girl
left to fight out her fortune all alone
that there would be *this* danger?—for *your* girl,
taught by you, lapped in a sweet ignorance,
scarcely more wise of what things sin could be   320
than some young child a summer six months old,
where in the north the summer makes a day,
of what is darkness . . . darkness that will come
to-morrow suddenly. Thank God at least
for this much of my life, that when you died,
that when you kissed me dying, not a thought
of this made sorrow for you, that I too
was pure of even fear.

              Oh yes, I thought,
still new in my insipid treadmill life,
(my father so late dead), and hopeful still   330
there might be something pleasant somewhere in it,
some sudden fairy come, no doubt, to turn
my pumpkin to a chariot, I thought then
that I might plod, and plod, and drum the sounds
of useless facts into unwilling ears,

tease children with dull questions half the day,
then con dull answers in my room at night
ready for next day's questions, mend quill pens
and cut my fingers, add up sums done wrong
and never get them right; teach, teach, and teach—   340
what I half knew, or not at all—teach, teach
for years, a lifetime—*I!*

                    And yet, who knows?
it might have been, for I was patient once,
and willing, and meant well; it might have been
had I but still clung on in my first place—
a safe dull place, where mostly there were smiles
but never merry-makings; where all days
jogged on sedately busy, with no haste;
where all seemed measured out, but margins broad:
a dull home but a peaceful, where I felt   350
my pupils would be dear young sisters soon,
and felt their mother take me to her heart,
motherly to all lonely harmless things.
But I must have a conscience, must blurt out
my great discovery of my ignorance!
And who required it of me? And who gained?
What did it matter for a more or less
the girls learnt in their schoolbooks, to forget
in their first season? We did well together:
they loved me and I them: but I went off   360
to housemaid's pay, six crossgrained brats to teach,
wrangles and jangles, doubts, disgrace . . . then this;
and they had a perfection found for them,
who has all ladies' learning in her head
abridged and scheduled, speaks five languages,
knows botany and conchology and globes,
draws, paints, plays, sings, embroiders, teaches all
on a patent method never known to fail:
and now they're finished and, I hear, poor things,
are the worst dancers and worst dressers out.   370
And where's their profit of those prison years
all gone to make them wise in lesson books?
who wants his wife to know weeds' Latin names?
who ever chose a girl for saying dates?
or asked if she had learned to trace a map?

    Well, well, the silly rules this silly world
makes about women! This is one of them.
Why must there be pretence of teaching them
what no one ever cares that they should know,
what, grown out of the schoolroom, they cast off   380
like the schoolroom pinafore, no better fit
for any use of real grown-up life,

for any use to her who seeks or waits
the husband and the home, for any use,
for any shallowest pretence of use,
to her who has them? Do I not know this,
I like my betters, that a woman's life,
her natural life, her good life, her one life,
is in her husband, God on earth to her,
and what she knows and what she can and is   390
is only good as it brings good to him?

    Oh God, do I not know it? I the thing
of shame and rottenness, the animal
that feed men's lusts and prey on them, I, I,
who should not dare to take the name of wife
on my polluted lips, who in the word
hear but my own reviling, I know that.
I could have lived by the rule, how content:
my pleasure to make him some pleasure, pride
to be as he would have me, duty, care,   400
to fit all to his taste, rule my small sphere
to his intention; then to lean on him,
be guided, tutored, loved—no not that word,
that *loved* which between men and women means
all selfishness, all putrid talk, all lust,
all vanity, all idiocy—not loved
but cared for. I've been loved myself, I think,
some once or twice since my poor mother died,
but *cared for*, never:—that's a word for homes,
kind homes, good homes, where simple children come   410
and ask their mother is this right or wrong,
because they know she's perfect, cannot err;
their father told them so, and he knows all,
being so wise and good and wonderful,
even enough to scold even her at times
and tell her everything she does not know.
Ah the sweet nursery logic!

                    Fool! thrice fool!
do I hanker after that too? Fancy me
infallible nursery saint, live code of law!
me preaching! teaching innocence to be good!—   420
a mother!

                    Yet the baby thing that woke
and wailed an hour or two, and then was dead,
was mine, and had he lived. . . . . . why then my name
would have been mother. But 'twas well he died:
I could have been no mother, I, lost then
beyond his saving. Had he come before
and lived, come to me in the doubtful days

when shame and boldness had not grown one sense,
for his sake, with the courage come of him,
I might have struggled back.

                But how? But how?   430
His father would not then have let me go:
his time had not yet come to make an end
of my 'for ever' with a hireling's fee
and civil light dismissal. None but him
to claim a bit of bread of if I went,
child or no child: would he have given it me?
He! no; he had not done with me. No help,
no help, no help. Some ways can be trodden back,
but never our way, we who one wild day
have given goodbye to what in our deep hearts   440
the lowest woman still holds best in life,
good name—good name though given by the world
that mouths and garbles with its decent prate,
and wraps it in respectable grave shams,
and patches conscience partly by the rule
of what one's neighbour thinks but something more
by what his eyes are sharp enough to see.
How I could scorn it with its Pharisees,[9]
if it could not scorn me: but yet, but yet—
oh God, if I could look it in the face!   450

    Oh I am wild, am ill, I think, to night:
will no one come and laugh with me? No feast,
no merriment to-night. So long alone!
Will no one come?

              At least there's a new dress
to try, and grumble at—they never fit
to one's ideal. Yes, a new rich dress,
with lace like this too, that's a soothing balm
for any fretting woman, cannot fail,
I've heard men say it . . . and they know so well
what's in all women's hearts, especially   460
women like me.

           No help! no help! no help!
How could it be? It was too late long since—
even at the first too late. Whose blame is that?
there are some kindly people in the world,
but what can they do? If one hurls oneself
into a quicksand, what can be the end,
but that one sinks and sinks? Cry out for help?

---

[9]**Pharisees**: Jewish partisans criticized by Jesus as rigid upholders
of religious law.

Ah yes, and, if it came, who is so strong
to strain from the firm ground and lift one out?
And how, so firmly clutching the stretched hand,   470
as death's pursuing terror bids, even so,
how can one reach firm land, having to foot
the treacherous crumbling soil that slides and gives
and sucks one in again? Impossible path!
No, why waste struggles, I or any one?
what is must be. What then? I, where I am,
sinking and sinking; let the wise pass by
and keep their wisdom for an apter use,
let me sink merrily as I best may.

    Only, I think, my brother—I forgot   480
he stopped his brotherhood some years ago—
but if he had been just so much less good
as to remember mercy. Did he think
how once I was his sister, prizing him
as sisters do, content to learn for him
the lesson girls with brothers all must learn,
to do without?

             I have heard girls lament
that doing so without all things one would,
but I saw never aught to murmur at,
for men must be made ready for their work,   490
and women all have more or less their chance
of husbands to work for them, keep them safe
like summer roses in soft greenhouse air
that never guess 'tis winter out of doors:
no, I saw never aught to murmur at,
content with stinted fare and shabby clothes
and cloistered silent life to save expense,
teaching myself out of my borrowed books,
while he for some one pastime, (needful true
to keep him of his rank, 'twas not his fault),   500
spent in a month what could have given me
my teachers for a year.

                 'Twas no one's fault:
for could he be launched forth on the rude sea
of this contentious world and left to find
oars and the boatman's skill by some good chance?
'Twas no one's fault: yet still he might have thought
of our so different youths, and owned at least
'tis pitiful when a mere nerveless girl,
untutored, must put forth upon that sea,
not in the woman's true place, the wife's place,   510
to trust a husband and be borne along,
but impotent blind pilot to herself.

Merciless, merciless—like the prudent world
that will not have the flawed soul prank itself
with a hoped second virtue, will not have
the woman fallen once lift up herself. . . . . .
lest she should fall again. Oh how his taunts,
his loathing fierce reproaches, scarred and seared,
like branding iron hissing in a wound!
And it was true—*that* killed me: and I felt   520
a hideous hopeless shame kill out my heart,
and knew myself for ever that he said,
that which I was—Oh it was true, true, true.

No, not true then. I was not all that then.
Oh, I have drifted on before mad winds
and made ignoble shipwreck, not to-day
could any breeze of heaven prosper me
into the track again, nor any hand
snatch me out of the whirlpool I have reached;
but then?

                    Nay he judged very well: he knew   530
repentance was too dear a luxury
for a beggar's buying, knew it earns no bread—
and knew me a too base and nerveless thing
to bear my first fault's sequel and just die.
And how could he have helped me? Held my hand,
owned me for his, fronted the angry world
clothed with my ignominy? Or maybe
taken me to his home to damn him worse?
What did I look for? for what less would serve
that he could do, a man without a purse?   540
He meant me well, he sent me that five pounds,
much to him then; and, if he bade me work
and never vex him more with news of me,
we both knew him too poor for pensioners.[10]
I see he did his best; I could wish now
sending it back I had professed some thanks.

But there! I was too wretched to be meek:
it seemed to me as if he, every one,
the whole great world, were guilty of my guilt,
abettors and avengers: in my heart   550
I gibed them back their gibings; I was wild.

I see clear now and know one has one's life
in hand at first to spend or spare or give
like any other coin; spend it or give
or drop it in the mire, can the world see
you get your value for it, or bar back

the hurrying of its marts to grope it up
and give it back to you for better use?
And if you spend or give that is your choice;
and if you let it slip that's your choice too,   560
you should have held it firmer. Yours the blame,
and not another's, not the indifferent world's
which goes on steadily, statistically,
and count by censuses not separate souls—
and if it somehow needs to its worst use
so many lives of women, useless else,
it buys us of ourselves, we could hold back,
free all of us to starve, and some of us,
(those who have done no ill and are in luck),
to slave their lives out and have food and clothes   570
until they grow unserviceably old.

Oh I blame no one—scarcely even myself.
It was to be: the very good in me
has always turned to hurt; all I thought right
at the hot moment, judged of afterwards,
shows reckless.

                    Why, look at it, had I taken
the pay my dead child's father offered me
for having been its mother, I could then
have kept life in me, (many have to do it,
that swarm in the back alleys, on no more,   580
cold sometimes, mostly hungry, but they live);
I could have gained a respite trying it,
and maybe found at last some humble work
to eke the pittance out. Not I, forsooth,
I must have spirit, must have womanly pride,
must dash back his contemptuous wages, I,
who had not scorned to earn them, dash them back
the fiercer that he dared to count our boy
in my appraising: and yet now I think
I might have taken it for my dead boy's sake;   590
it would have been *his* gift.

                    But I went forth
with my fine scorn, and whither did it lead?
Money's the root of evil[11] do they say?
money is virtue, strength: money to me
would then have been repentance: could I live
upon my idiot's pride?

                    Well, it fell soon.
I had prayed Edward might believe me dead,
and yet I begged of him—That's like me too,

---

[10]**pensioners**: recipients of a regular allowance.

[11]**Money . . . evil**: see 1 Timothy 6:10.

beg of him and then send him back his alms!
What if he gave as to a whining wretch   600
that holds her hand and lies? I am less to him
than such a one; her rags do him no wrong,
but I, I, wrong him merely that I live,
being his sister. Could I not at least
have still let him forget me? But 'tis past:
and naturally he may hope I am long dead.

    Good God! to think that we were what we were
one to the other . . . and now!

                     He has done well;
married a sort of heiress, I have heard,
a dapper little madam, dimple cheeked   610
and dimple brained, who makes him a good wife—
No doubt she'd never own but just to him,
and in a whisper, she can even suspect
that we exist, we other women things:
what would she say if she could learn one day
she has a sister-in-law! So he and I
must stand apart till doomsday.

                    But the jest,
to think how she would look!—Her fright, poor thing!
The notion!—I could laugh outright. . . . . . or else,
for I feel near it, roll on the ground and sob.   620

    Well, after all, there's not much difference
between the two sometimes.

                Was that the bell?
Some one at last, thank goodness. There's a voice,
and that's a pleasure. Whose though? Ah I know.
Why did she come alone, the cackling goose?
why not have brought her sister?—she tells more
and titters less. No matter; half a loaf
is better than no bread.

             Oh, is it you?
Most welcome, dear: one gets so moped alone.

                          1870

                  ~

While the woods were green,
"Oh!" she sang, "my heart is new,
    Leaping, longing, in my breast:
Let him come that loves me true,

Let him come that I love best,
I will tell him what I mean,
Now the wood-birds tell it too,
    Now the woods are green."

    While the woods were bare,
"Oh!" she sighed, "my heart is grey,   10
    Shrinking, shivering, in my breast:
Love me, hate me, as they may,
    None of them do I love best:
Let me be alone with care,
Now the wood-birds hide away,
    Now the woods are bare."

                      1879, 1881

Betrothed

I did not think to love her. As we go
    We pluck a hedge-rose blushing in its sheath,
Fresh, and at hand; and not the less we know
    That where rich garden blossoms take the breath
With eddying sweets and wear a thousand hues
We shall be fain to linger and to choose.
        And who indeed
    Would pass the garden by to choose the weed,
The little wayside rose we hold and lose?

Fair; and so loving. With the young surprise   10
    Of children who still newly understand
Their right and wrong out of their mother's eyes,
    She watches for my thought. Her trustful hand
Creeps into mine and rests. Ah, little one,
Hadst thou loved less I had not been undone;
        My wayside rose.
    I love thee, sweet: some hopes have found their close
Ere yet their aim; some joys ceased unbegun.

I had not thought to love her. She is fair;
    But I had pictured eyes which, meeting mine,   20
Should kindle something in me that was there
    But waited Her arousing; I divine
A love, that was to be, past hence unborn,
The sun o'erclouded ere it rose at morn.
        I love thee, yes:
    Let hopes be dead which thou couldst never guess.
Sweet, could I let thy blossom drop unworn?

                      1881

Beyond the Shadow

Some quick kind tears, some easy sorrow,
    And then 'tis past.
'Twas sad; yet sadness has its morrow;
Blue skies succeed skies overcast:
    Why should grief last?

Something that's passing, something dying.
    Well, weep one's fill,
Spend grief's sweet courtesy, go sighing;
But violets break from snow-time's chill:
    Who can mourn still?   10

Aye, let me pass. No life will miss me
    Save few first days.
A shudder, stooping down to kiss me,
A little love and tardy praise;
    Then the old ways.

                                       1881

Siste Viator[1]

    What is it that is dead?
Somewhere there is a grave, and something lies
Cold in the ground and stirs not for my sighs,
    Nor songs that I can make, nor smiles from me,
Nor tenderest foolish words that I have said;
    Something that was has hushed and will not be.

    Did it go yesterday?
Or did it wane away with the old years?
There hath not been farewell, nor watchers' tears,
    Nor hopes, nor vain reprieves, nor strife with death,   10
Nor lingering in a meted out delay;
    None closed the eyes nor felt the latest breath.

    But, be there joyous skies,
It is not in their sunshine; in the night
It is not in the silence, and the light
    Of all the silver stars; the flowers asleep
Dream no more of it, nor their morning eyes
    Betray the secrets it has bidden them keep.

---

[1]**Siste Viator:** Pause, wayfarer.

Birds that go singing now
Forget it and leave sweetness meaningless;   20
The fitful nightingale, that feigns distress
    To sing it all away, flows on by rote;
The seeking lark, in very heaven, I trow,
    Shall find no memory to inform his note.

    The voices of the shore
Chime not with it for burden; in the wood,
Where it was soul of the vast solitude,
    It hath forsook the stillness; dawn and day
And the deep-thoughted dusk know it no more;
    It is no more the freshness of the May.   30

    Joy hath it not for heart;
Nor music for its second, subtler, tongue,
Sounding what music's self hath never sung;
    Nor very Sorrow needs it help her weep.
Vanished from everywhere! what was a part
    Of all and everywhere; lost into sleep!

    What was it ere it went?
Whence had it birth? What is its name to call,
That gone unmissed has left a want in all?
    Or shall I cry on Youth, in June-time still?   40
Or cry on Hope, who long since am content?
    Or Love, who hold him ready at my will?

    What is it that is dead?
Breath of a flower? sea-freshness on a wind?
Oh, dearest, what is that that we should find,
    If you and I at length could win it back?
What have we lost and know not it hath fled?
    Heart of my heart, could it be love we lack?

                                     1881

from Mother and Daughter[1]

    — 7 —

Her father lessons me I at times am hard,
    Chiding a moment's fault as too grave ill,
    And let some little blot my vision fill,
Scanning her with a narrow near regard.

---

[1]*Mother and Daughter:* During the 1890s Webster left unfinished
a set of 27 sonnets that adapt traditional themes of the amatory
sonnet sequence to a mother's love for her daughter.

True. Love's unresting gaze is self-debarred
    From all sweet ignorance, and learns a skill,
    Not painless, of such signs as hurt love's will,
That would not have its prize one tittle marred.

Alas! Who rears and loves a dawning rose
    Starts at a speck upon one petal's rim: 10
Who sees a dusk creep in the shrined pearl's glows,
    Is ruined at once: "My jewel growing dim!"
I watch one bud that on my bosom blows,
    I watch one treasured pearl for me and him.

— 8 —

A little child she, half defiant came
    Reasoning her case—'twas not so long ago—
    "I cannot mind your scolding, for I know
However bad I were you'd love the same."
And I, what countering answer could I frame?
    'Twas true, and true, and God's self told her so.
    One does but ask one's child to smile and grow,
And each rebuke has love for its right name.

And yet, methinks, sad mothers who for years,
    Watching the child pass forth that was their boast,   10
Have counted all the footsteps by new fears
Till even lost fears seem hopes whereof they're reft
And of all mother's good love sole is left—
    Is their Love, Love, or some remembered ghost?

— 16 —

She will not have it that my day wanes low,
    Poor of the fire its drooping sun denies,
    That on my brow the thin lines write good-byes
Which soon may be read plain for all to know,
Telling that I have done with youth's brave show;
    Alas! and done with youth in heart and eyes,
    With wonder and with far expectancies,
Save but to say "I knew such long ago."

She will not have it. Loverlike to me,
    She with her happy gaze finds all that's best,   10
She sees this fair and that unfretted still,
    And her own sunshine over all the rest:
So she half keeps me as she'd have me be,
And I forget to age, through her sweet will.

— 27 —

Since first my little one lay on my breast
    I never needed such a second good,
    Nor felt a void left in my motherhood
She filled not always to the utterest.

The summer linnet, by glad yearnings pressed,
    Builds room enough to house a callow brood:
    I prayed not for another child—nor could;
My solitary bird had my heart's nest.

But she is cause that any baby thing
    If it but smile, is one of mine in truth,   10
    And every child becomes my natural joy:
And, if my heart gives all youth fostering,
    Her sister, brother, seems the girl or boy:
    My darling makes me mother to their youth.

                                    1895

An Irrepressible Army

The defect which Napoleon is said to have pointed out in English soldiers certainly seems to exist equally in English women; they do not know that they have lost the battle, and they go on all the same.[1] They will not understand their case and retreat—and that is very hard on their antagonists, for it cannot be but disheartening and confusing to any combatants to find the out-manœuvred troops who ought, if they had but the sense to see it, to be flying from the field in disorder, obtusely standing to their guns and attacking and advancing and behaving themselves altogether as if it was they who were winning. Defeating such troops naturally gets fatiguing before the fight is over, and the result of their obtuseness is apt to be that their defeats culminate in a signal victory at last. And a signal victory is what the Women's Suffrage women resolutely affirm that they will have; they look upon a check as a mere matter of detail, part of the process. Such an incident, they consider, may not be exactly agreeable but it was to be looked for, and now it has happened the next thing is to go on going forward. Each time their Bill has been thrown out in Parliament they have instantly set to work holding more public meetings, printing more pamphlets, signing more petitions, and all the while they have steadily, and even rapidly, gained ground. And they accept with more than equanimity the augmenting violence of their opponents in the House of Commons, looking upon it as quite a cheering circumstance, "for," say

---

[1]**Lost . . . the same:** Bills to allow women to vote in parliamentary elections were considered in 1867 (in an amendment proposed by J. S. Mill) and almost annually in the 1870s. In 1870 women became eligible to vote for and serve on local school boards, as Webster did; suffrage in national elections was not achieved until 1918.

they, "the tremendousness of the efforts made to whip up a majority against us is in itself an assurance of the progress we are making; if the measure could be defeated with little trouble, only little trouble would be taken."

Their Bill to remove the Electoral Disabilities of Women has been six times rejected. No matter—or rather all the better; six is just a nice number for failures. That spider Robert Bruce[2] saw six times fail to throw her thread and succeed the seventh is reported to have been similarly observed by other victors in a defeat stage of victory. As the Women's Suffrage women, whether from housewifely conscientiousness pure and uncorrupt or from Machiavellian policy, make it a point of honour to be notable, one must not venture to assume that any of them, sitting brooding in her own chamber at home, caught sight of the prognosticating insect at work on her walls; but she may have remarked one when she took her walks abroad, or in the house of a non-suffrage friend, and may have been inspirited for the coming effort. At all events, spider or no spider, the effort is to be. And there is no secret about it; the enemy is forewarned. Paragraphs in a dozen newspapers, evidently on authority, have informed all whom it may concern that there is to be another battle next session; the Bill will be voted on the seventh time.

The phalanx stands united, nothing changed in it; but there is a new leader. Mr. Jacob Bright, it is announced, has been compelled by the state of his health to relinquish that post, and Mr. Leonard Courtney[3] accepts it. The Women's Suffragites may safely be congratulated on the successor they have found to the leader who has so long and so well earned their gratitude. To begin with, Mr. Courtney is a dauntless champion. His courage and his ears can stand any amount of assault. His recent prowess will be remembered— how when the oxen encompassed him, gaping upon him with their mouths as it were a ramping and a roaring lion, he stood Van Amburgh[4]-like amid them, drank a glass of water, and went on with his speech. His advocacy of the cause of which he is now elected chief advocate is no new matter; he

was earnest for it when it was not merely unfashionable but unpopular. He is known to be possessed, not only of highly educated and proved ability, but of that practical perception of means and possibilities which is of all qualities—excepting perhaps the quality of selfishness—the surest safeguard against the fascinations of crotchets. It may perhaps without too much rashness be inferred from the Bulls of Basan[5] episode just referred to that he is obstinate; and obstinacy is a very fine gift in the leader of a reform movement.

The demand of the Women's Suffrage societies continues to be what it was, in spite of the tempting provocation of their opponents to widen it to cover the case of married women.[6] They accept with placidity—especially the married ones—any statements that may be made about the superiority, moral and mental, of wives to spinsters and widows; they are quite willing to admit that it will be a pity the advantages of the wisdom and experience of the women enhanced by husbands should be lost to the nation simply because they are so enhanced, but they are not going to run the risk of asking too much. They content themselves with taking the electoral qualification as they find it and claiming that all and any women who have this qualification, with no disqualification apart from the fact of womanhood, should be allowed to vote; if, because of laws which affect the status and property of married women, only spinsters and widows can fulfil the conditions, they do not hold themselves responsible for the exclusion of the British matrons so highly venerated—once a year—in the House of Commons. They do not feel themselves called on to defend it; and they do not feel themselves called on to insist on a revision of the conditions of married life as a preliminary to asking for the suffrage for such women as are at present living under precisely the conditions prescribed by the electoral laws for electors. Probably they find it all the easier to keep within the limits prescribed them by those confounders of logic, things as they are, that they take it that there can be no real division of the interests of spinster, wife, and widow, so long as every one woman has the possibility of being in turn all the three. This is a view of the case which seems to escape certain orators who, in the edifying thrills of a comprehensive uxoriousness, raise the war-cry of all the married women against all the single ones, and, so to speak, shy their wives' wedding-rings in their aunts' and sisters' faces.

[2]**Robert Bruce:** Robert I (1274–1329), king of Scotland, said to have been inspired by watching a **spider** persist despite repeated failures.

[3]**Jacob Bright** (1821–1899), **Leonard Courtney** (1832–1918): advocates for women's suffrage in Parliament in the 1870s. On June 6, 1877, Courtney was shouted and jeered, but undeterred, when he spoke in the House of Commons.

[4]Isaac **Van Amburgh** (1801–1865): animal trainer for P. T. Barnum.

[5]**Bulls of Basan:** see Psalms 22:12–13.

[6]**married women:** barred by law from holding property in their own name, and thus from voting even when property, instead of gender, became the basis of franchise.

But, supposing Mr. Courtney, like a modern and more fortunate Conon, to have led on the 11,000 virgins, more or less, not to shipwreck and martyrdom[7] but, by good steering and good fighting, to the reward of the franchise in this world, what will they do with it? "Plunge England into interminable war," says one; "Sacrifice the honour of the country for the sake of peace," says another; "Bring us under the yoke of the priesthood, and set up an abject conservatism," says one; "Abolish morality and masculine authority, and hurry us into political anarchy," says another. There are fears that they will make matrimony illegal, suppress cooking, and have the Prime Minister chosen for his good looks and his skill at lawn-tennis. It is also apprehended that they will at once throw off all their present customs, tastes, virtues, and attractions—which, as is well known, are the compensations bestowed on them by nature for the absence of a vote—and will become coarse-featured unmannerly hybrids, men-hating, and hateful to men. They will wear coats and trousers, they will refuse to sew on shirt-buttons, they will leave off *poudre de riz* and auricomiferous waters,[8] they will be Bishops and Judges, and will break all the commandments. And they will wind up by enacting a law against men which will compel the men to rise in arms to resist it, and there will be a sanguinary pitched battle between all the males and all the females in the country, in which the physical force of thews and sinews will prevail and so most of the women will be shot down, and then everybody left alive can start fair again and there will be no more votes for women.

Qui vivra verra.[9] The women will get their votes some day, for the men will get tired of refusing them. And then it will probably be found out that it was never worth while to refuse. Women will be women, and men will be men, as before, and no less able than before to dazzle themselves with each other's merits when in love and to discern each other's defects when out of love. In matters of legislation their interests will be found to be the same, with the same modifications by the same circumstances, in ninety-nine cases out of a hundred; and the hundredth will be some matter specially affecting women, in which it will come to be admitted that it is, in the long run, to the advantage of men also that women should have a voice. The women, as a class, will be the better by all the educating and nerving influence of the suffrage and its stamp of equal rights and responsibilities, and the men, as a class, will be none the worse; while, as a nation, men and women together will gain by the removal of an unnecessary inequality, which, like all unnecessary inequalities, disturbs the balance of relations and lessens the just importance of superiorities that really have their reason.

1877, 1879

Poets and Personal Pronouns

There is no objection against the use of human lay figures[1] by the novelist which does not equally apply to their use by the poet; and, from the solely artistic point of view, the objections in the case of the poet are yet stronger than in the case of the novelist. We ask from the novelist a definiteness and possibility for each personage, a suitability of conduct, language, and sentiment, to the epoch and theatre of events chosen, which shall make the story read as true: but we ask of the poet that his personages shall not be sharply definite, shall not even in drama be definite with the minute definiteness of the novel, while it shall seem impossible for them not to be, or to be other than they are; and we ask a suitability not so much to a given epoch and theatre as to always and everywhere, no matter under what disguise of date and story. The poet has therefore yet greater need than the novelist of that full conception of the character he is treating which can only come from creation. He need not, of course, create in the sense that the personage or the events he is interpreting shall not have pre-existed in fact or fiction; on the contrary, the highest powers of creative imagination have usually found their fittest exercise in intensified pourtrayal of the men and women and events of history or of legends and tales. It seems as if the resistance, so to speak, offered to the plastic despotism of the artist by characteristics accepted, not made, called forth a subtler and a stronger skill than if he had worked with the limitlessness of free invention. The poet creates as the sculptor does; he need not make the stone as well as the statue. His function is not, like the novelist's, to devise new stories, but to make old stories new. But the men and women he pourtrays must have been born again in his brain; they must be his by creation, not by copying. It will not answer, if he wants to

---

[7]**11,000 virgins**: led by St. Ursula, legend has it, to find Cynan (or **Conon**) Meiriadog, but met by shipwreck and martyrdom.

[8]*poudre de riz*: face powder made from pulverized rice. **auricomiferous waters**: used to make hair blond.

[9]*Qui vivra verra*: who lives (longest) will see (most).

---

[1]**lay figures**: jointed models of the **human** body used by artists; puppets.

poetise the mood of a good man conscious of temptation, to take the clergyman of his parish and try to imagine what he would feel if he could be in such a position; nor will it be inspiring, artistically speaking, if he needs a villain triumphant, to select his most hostile reviewer to sit for a likeness. For even supposing that he really could look into an individual heart as the oculist, by the proper arrangement of lens and light, can look into an individual eye, and that, being thus enabled to map out an *absolutely* true copy of the man, he could, by virtue of the poetic instinct of fitness, provide it with exactly and only such accessory incidents and surroundings as should keep it *relatively* true to nature, the successful result would be no poet's success. Nobody wants the poet so to draw characters that each shall seem the presentment of some special person known in the flesh; that is an aim to be left to the novelist—the nature of whose art and materials renders him fifty-fold more competent to fulfil it. We look to the poet for feelings, thoughts, actions if need be, represented in a way which shall affect us as the manifest expression of what our very selves must have felt and thought and done if we had been those he puts before us and in their cases. He must make us feel this not only of what we ourselves, being ourselves, could come to think and feel and do in like circumstances, but of what no circumstances could possibly call out in us. One may be hopelessly incapacitated by a limp and considerate mental temperament from ever becoming a murderer even in a moment's thought, and for the matter of that so may the poet, but if the poet describes the sensations of an intending murderer he has to make one feel that he has found out just what one's sensations would be if one could have been capable of thinking about committing murder. Or one may be impermeable to any more ecstatic love than goes to make a matrimonial choice in a comfortable way, but the poet describing the passion of love must make one feel that one knows it all for a fact, that those are just one's own sentiments—or at least what one's own sentiments would be if one were of the sort to fall in love. Not many have it in us to be Iagos, but we feel sure that, if we were to be an Iago, we should be *that* Iago.

And yet, with the very nature of the poet's delineation to show that he cannot effect it in reference to individual models, it is the poet especially whom the general public are wont to assume to have filled his canvases with direct studies from living lay figures. People will not understand that he embodies his conception, say, of modesty and girlhood, in some fair girl-shape of his imagination, without measuring to the pattern of somebody he knows who is a girl and is modest; or his conception of martial valour in a soldier whose personality grew in his own brain, instead of setting down the results of his contemplations of some distinguished officer of his acquaintance. He writes a poem about an unnatural grandmother; people guess which of his two grandmothers it was who endeavoured to poison him in his youth and left him with such an unpleasant feeling about it; and, if it is quite certain that he never had a grandmother, then the question is which of the grandmothers of his confidential friends he has had for heroine. Points of personal description are seized on in the most ludicrous way for identifying purposes: must not Lady Blanche Dove be the "fair fierce fiend" and the "passionate Upas blight"[2] of Mr. Bayleaf's poem "The Golden-haired Witch;" for has she not golden hair and is she not fair, and, though she does not strike ordinary observers as ferocious or passionate or anything but a very meek well-behaved young lady, yet was she not believed to have, in her quiet way, let Mr. Bayleaf pay her a good deal of attention before he engaged himself to the lady with dark hair he is going to marry? And whom can Mr. Bayleaf mean in his poem of "The False Lover's Return" by the hero with "low pale brow" and "strong and eager gait," but his friend Captain Steadyman who has got a low forehead and does usually walk fast, and who, having been to India, did return, and who, being good-looking and in the army, might very likely have flirted with Mr. Bayleaf's sister or some other lady Mr. Bayleaf knew? It would be interesting to know how many young ladies were, on the strength of the least little aquiline curve in their delicate noses[3] and the having been more or less frequently in the same room with the laureate, or somewhere where he could if he pleased perceive their noses, declared with absoluteness "the Original of Tennyson's Maud." The present writer was favoured with the sight of one, and heard of five or six; others were understood to be plentiful. Nothing seems more likely.

But more especially still is the poet believed to be his own lay figure. He is taken as offering his readers the presentment of himself, his hopes, his loves, his sorrows, his guilts and remorses, his history and psychology generally. Some people so thoroughly believe this to be the proper view of the poet's position towards the public that they will despise a man as a hypocrite because, after having written and printed, "I am the bridegroom of Despair," or "No wine

---

[2]**Upas**: Javanese tree with intensely poisonous juice, thought to destroy any living thing that approached it. **Bayleaf**: laurel, traditional crown for poets.

[3]**least . . . noses**: see Tennyson's *Maud* I.86, page 452.

but the wine of death for me," or some such unsociable sentiment, he goes out to dinners and behaves like anybody else. One even hears it adduced as a fault in the moral character of poets generally that they do not feel all they write—meaning that they do not feel it in their own persons, part of their own experience. It is heartily to be hoped of most of them that they do not. Turn over the pages of any dozen poets now living, men and women, and take all their utterances for their own in their own persons, suppose the first personal pronoun not artistically vicarious but standing for the writer's substantive self; what an appalling dozen of persons! Not to speak of those legions of love-affairs simultaneously carried on in which they indulge—although some of them, being married and moving in respectable society, ought long ago to have "renounced all others"—not to speak of these, what sort of existences can they be that allow of all the miscellaneous tragedies and idylls which appear to diversify the days of these multifarious beings? and how do they preserve their reason through such a conflicting variety of emotions, sonnet by sonnet and stanza by stanza? We have only to try to imagine what, if I meant I, must be the mental state of these writers of many emotions, to see, in the fact of their being able to correct their proofs and get their books through press, consoling evidence that, as a rule, I does not mean I.

There are exceptions to the rule. Every now and then even a reticent poet does distinctly express emotions which belong to him in his actual life, and not in that life of interpretership which in some ways he feels as even more real to him than the actual. Naturally he will do so chiefly, or only, as to moods which belong to all human nature, and which would find like expression whether he expressed them in his own ego or in an imagined one; they will be poems, not biography. And there have been poets who, accepting the popular theory of poetry being, as it were, confessional, have systematically put their personality forward. Yet where this is obvious it is not always real. The burst of sorrow has many a time had its ostensible subject hit upon only when it was wanted for the printers; the anger and withering scorn have found their theme in something that happened after the taunts and the rhymes were irrevocably fixed; the dirge has had to wait for a death to make it relevant; the love poem has had to be antedated to give it an appropriate motive. Byron's most Byronic heroes were certainly less a portrait of him than he of them; he made them and then imitated them. Where a poet falls into the popular fallacy and takes it that the public have a right to form a theory of his life from his writings and to expect him to be consistent to it, he is quite likely to become, with unconscious

hypocrisy, a claimant to virtues which are too hard for him or "le fanfaron des vices qu'il n'a pas."[4] In his interpreter life he knows the bitter and the sweet of love, as what poet does not; but he conceives it incumbent upon him to have an "object" and, like Don Quixote, looks for his Dulcinea.[5] So with the other passions; he knows them, he possesses them; as a part of the interpreter life he feels them with a completeness and intensity which experience of them in himself as a study of actual life can in no way increase and could lessen; but he feels that he ought to get at them somehow in his private capacity and practise them up, like a young lady with her show pieces. The hate of hate, the scorn of scorn,[6] will not answer the purpose; he must hate Jones and scorn Robinson. He tries to do it, and he says in verse that he has done it.

Nothing is truer than that the poet sings because he must.[7] He sings because singing is his sixth sense, and because it is so bound up with all the others that if you deprived him of it he would feel as if they too were leaving him. Yet you can reduce even the linnet's song to rule—whether the linnet is aware of a rule or no—and the rule of the poet's expression seems to be that it is not the revealing of him but of themselves to others; and to him the revealing of them and himself among them. At all events, few poets are even ostensibly autobiographical; and it is hard on them to investigate them as if they were putting themselves through a process of vivisection for the public to see how they were getting on inside.

Their difficulty comes from the personal pronoun they have to use; and it is only by some reform here that they can escape misconception from the majority of nonliterary readers. If instead of I they took to the editorial We, for instance, a man might thus write:—

We loved, she was unworth our heart;
  We scorned her, but loved not again

without the public thinking him disrespectful to his wife from any point of view: or he might begin, "We wept alone o'er him we slew," without fear of his readers thinking him a case for the police. But then poets are so fond of saying "we" in an emphatic manner as short for the particular *she* and I, and confusion might arise. The use of a little i instead of a big I might have some effect as a sort of modest disclaimer of the writer's personality in the matter; but the printers

---

[4]"**le fanfaron . . . n'a pas**": boaster of vices he does not have.

[5]**Dulcinea**: idealized beloved of Cervantes' **Don Quixote**.

[6]**hate . . . scorn**: see Tennyson, "The Poet" (1830) 3–4.

[7]**sings . . . must**: see Tennyson, *In Memoriam* 21.23–24.

would never stand that. Our vernacular "says he" and "says she" interspersed among the I's with a prudent frequentness would give considerable protection; but then if they were inserted in the matter of the poems they would put the metres out, and if they were relegated to footnotes or marginal arguments the very readers they were meant for would be just those who would never look at them. The indefinite "one" might be of some avail; but scarcely sufficient, because it is so frequently used as a more bashful but equally individual I that it does not convey the required distinction. On the whole the editorial pronoun, the "We" and the "Our" and the "Us," is what can most safely be recommended to poets for their future protection.

1878, 1879

WALTER PATER

(1839–1894)

Pater's life was as tame as his writing was incendiary. His surgeon father having died young, he grew up under his mother's protection and then, when she too died shortly after he went off to boarding school, under an aunt's; throughout the second half of his life he shared a quiet home with his two sisters. Yet this impeccable university don and bourgeois house-holder was at the same time Britain's primary exponent of the countercultural creed that be-came fin-de-siècle aestheticism. His profound decorum and reserve may have owed something to the caution that a scholarship boy learned at class-conscious Victorian Ox-ford—especially when making his way, as Pater did, towards a permanent teaching appoint-ment (classics and history of philosophy). The need for discretion remained as his influence grew: he knew contemporary German ideas and French literature suspiciously well, regarded all metaphysics, including Christianity, with skepticism, and harbored, even if he never in-dulged, a strong erotic inclination towards his own sex.

To judge from his autobiographical "The Child in the House," Pater's temperament was turned inward from the start. His acute juvenile receptivity to impressions of texture and shade, like his tenacious memory for the etched detail of those impressions, showed a mental disposition that flourished in conditions of seclusion. Pater secured these conditions through employment in a university that many contemporaries considered the secular equivalent of a monastery, and through life residence as a child in the house of memory. In this double re-treat he pursued an aestheticism that its detractors view as super-sophisticated selfishness, its adherents as a challenging modern self-discipline.

The method of this discipline is hard to define: Ruskinian connoisseurship, but more an amateur's than an expert's; Arnoldian criticism, but without pretension to any standard be-yond the critic's taste; Wildean brilliance, but without the sparkle of paradox or spotlight of celebrity, and certainly without the compulsion to practice the hedonism one preaches. But *preaching* is the wrong word for the way Pater influenced Wilde and others who fell under his spell. He deliberated, insinuated, and supposed, captivating readers through what the first paragraph of his epoch-making book *The Renaissance* quietly calls "suggestive and penetrating things said by the way." His ornately supple sentences do not so much arrive at a destination as execute an itinerary, delighting in the by-play of modifiers that, revolving their topic in the changing light of the mind, qualify or develop or half retract what their subject and pred-icate propose.

To entertain an idea by slipping away from it for a better look: something like this habit of mind also emerged in the bibliographical fortunes of the closest thing to a manifesto Pater ever wrote. The unforgettable paragraphs that advised readers to burn with a hard, gemlike flame and multiply heightened sensation for its own sake appeared first in an 1869 review of William Morris' poems, then provided the Conclusion to *The Renaissance* in 1873, were sup-pressed in the edition of 1877, and were finally restored with an apologetic warning in 1888. By that time, of course, the damage was done: aestheticism was well established, and its pro-ponents (including Pater) had become the objects of parody in novels, operettas, and essays (see Max Beerbohm's "Diminuendo," which closes this anthology). Pater stood by his ideas for twenty years, then, but rather as if he were an interested bystander. In marked contrast to

Carlyle, Newman, Ruskin, and Arnold, he never became a polemical lecturer or pamphleteer. Instead he stuck to his study, writing and rewriting prose that obliges readers to adopt, as they read, his deliberate way of seeing: the attentive poise, the vigilant hesitancy, in which the Paterian consciousness discriminates its impression of a text or an artwork or an historical contingency.

Fascinated by time and mortality, Pater had little patience with history as it was normally written. Both *Studies in the History of the Renaissance* (1873) and the historical novel *Marius the Epicurean: His Sensations and Ideas* (1885) replace the grand, all-explanatory nineteenth-century narrative of progress with detached, casually sequential episodes of intense imaginative experience. Pater wrote as if the history of art and ideas were itself an art, ideas a kind of taste in the brain. This aesthetic counter-historicism makes him a pivotal figure in the history of Victorian and modern literature. His insistence on the truth of individual subjectivity nourishes a tendency, lurking in Victorian sage writing since Carlyle's, to subordinate argument to rhetoric. His rhetoric of elements and forces, quantity and precision, indicates a surprising convergence between late-century aestheticism and the discourse of science, especially the geological and evolutionary vision of ceaseless transformation and flux. Even more striking is the way his sinuous style eroticizes rhetoric itself, "proposing frankly to give nothing but the highest quality to your moments as they pass." Pater's body English—his slow pitch to the senses, his feel for the physique of language—fleshes out practices of literary seduction that were foreshadowed in Newman and Ruskin, while his suasive style registers the irrational drift of desire. The symbolic evocativeness of his prose was recognized by W. B. Yeats as a living influence when he printed a paragraph on the *Mona Lisa* from Pater's essay on Leonardo da Vinci as the first poem in the 1936 *Oxford Book of Modern Verse*.

from Preface to *The Renaissance*

Many attempts have been made by writers on art and poetry to define beauty in the abstract, to express it in the most general terms, to find some universal formula for it. The value of these attempts has most often been in the suggestive and penetrating things said by the way. Such discussions help us very little to enjoy what has been well done in art or poetry, to discriminate between what is more and what is less excellent in them, or to use words like beauty, excellence, art, poetry, with a more precise meaning than they would otherwise have. Beauty, like all other qualities presented to human experience, is relative; and the definition of it becomes unmeaning and useless in proportion to its abstractness. To define beauty, not in the most abstract but in the most concrete terms possible, to find not its universal formula, but the formula which expresses most adequately this or that special manifestation of it, is the aim of the true student of aesthetics.

"To see the object as in itself it really is,"[1] has been justly said to be the aim of all true criticism whatever; and in æsthetic criticism the first step towards seeing one's object as it really is, is to know one's own impression as it really is, to discriminate it, to realise it distinctly. The objects with which æsthetic criticism deals—music, poetry, artistic and accomplished forms of human life—are indeed receptacles of so many powers or forces: they possess, like the products of nature, so many virtues or qualities. What is this song or picture, this engaging personality presented in life or in a book, to *me*? What effect does it really produce on me? Does it give me pleasure? and if so, what sort or degree of pleasure? How is my nature modified by its presence, and under its influence? The answers to these questions are the original facts with which the æsthetic critic has to do; and, as in the study of light, of morals, of number, one must realise

---

[1]"**To see . . . really is**": quoting Arnold's "The Function of Criticism"; see page 728.

such primary data for one's self, or not at all. And he who experiences these impressions strongly, and drives directly at the discrimination and analysis of them, has no need to trouble himself with the abstract question what beauty is in itself, or what its exact relation to truth or experience— metaphysical questions, as unprofitable as metaphysical questions elsewhere. He may pass them all by as being, answerable or not, of no interest to him.

The æsthetic critic, then, regards all the objects with which he has to do, all works of art, and the fairer forms of nature and human life, as powers or forces producing pleasurable sensations, each of a more or less peculiar or unique kind. This influence he feels, and wishes to explain, by analysing and reducing it to its elements. To him, the picture, the landscape, the engaging personality in life or in a book, *La Gioconda*, the hills of Carrara, Pico of Mirandola,[2] are valuable for their virtues, as we say, in speaking of a herb, a wine, a gem; for the property each has of affecting one with a special, a unique, impression of pleasure. Our education becomes complete in proportion as our susceptibility to these impressions increases in depth and variety. And the function of the æsthetic critic is to distinguish, to analyse, and separate from its adjuncts, the virtue by which a picture, a landscape, a fair personality in life or in a book, produces this special impression of beauty or pleasure, to indicate what the source of that impression is, and under what conditions it is experienced. His end is reached when he has disengaged that virtue, and noted it, as a chemist notes some natural element, for himself and others; and the rule for those who would reach this end is stated with great exactness in the words of a recent critic of Sainte-Beuve:— *De se borner à connaître de près les belles choses, et à s'en nourrir en exquis amateurs, en humanistes accomplis.*[3]

What is important, then, is not that the critic should possess a correct abstract definition of beauty for the intellect, but a certain kind of temperament, the power of being deeply moved by the presence of beautiful objects. He will remember always that beauty exists in many forms. To him all periods, types, schools of taste, are in themselves equal.

---

[2] *La Gioconda:* the famous Mona Lisa (1505?), so called because the sitter, Lisa Gherardini, was wife to Francesco del Giocondo; subject of Pater's best-known prose poem, page 957. Statues of **Carrara** marble are discussed in *The Renaissance*, which devotes a chapter to the humanist **Pico** (1463–1494).

[3] *De se borner . . . accomplis:* To restrict themselves to knowing beautiful things firsthand, and to develop themselves as sensitive amateurs, as accomplished humanists. The words are those of Charles-Augustin **Sainte-Beuve** (1804–1869) himself.

In all ages there have been some excellent workmen, and some excellent work done. The question he asks is always:—In whom did the stir, the genius, the sentiment of the period find itself? where was the receptacle of its refinement, its elevation, its taste? "The ages are all equal," says William Blake, "but genius is always above its age."[4]

Often it will require great nicety to disengage this virtue from the commoner elements with which it may be found in combination. Few artists, not Goethe[5] or Byron even, work quite cleanly, casting off all *débris*, and leaving us only what the heat of their imagination has wholly fused and transformed. Take, for instance, the writings of Wordsworth. The heat of his genius, entering into the substance of his work, has crystallised a part, but only a part, of it; and in that great mass of verse there is much which might well be forgotten. But scattered up and down it, sometimes fusing and transforming entire compositions, like the Stanzas on *Resolution and Independence*, or the *Ode on the Recollections of Childhood*, sometimes, as if at random, depositing a fine crystal here or there, in a matter it does not wholly search through and transmute, we trace the action of his unique, incommunicable faculty, that strange, mystical sense of a life in natural things, and of man's life as a part of nature, drawing strength and colour and character from local influences, from the hills and streams, and from natural sights and sounds. Well! that is the *virtue*, the active principle in Wordsworth's poetry; and then the function of the critic of Wordsworth is to follow up that active principle, to disengage it, to mark the degree in which it penetrates his verse. . . .

1873

from Leonardo da Vinci

In Vasari's life of Leonardo da Vinci[1] as we now read it there are some variations from the first edition. There, the painter who has fixed the outward type of Christ for succeeding centuries was a bold speculator, holding lightly by other men's beliefs, setting philosophy above Christianity. Words of his, trenchant enough to justify this impression, are not

---

[4] "The ages . . . age": from **Blake's** annotations to *The Works of Sir Joshua Reynolds* (1798).

[5] Johann Wolfgang von **Goethe** (1749–1832): German Romantic writer.

[1] Giorgio **Vasari** (1511–1574): *Lives of the Most Excellent Italian Painters* (1550).

recorded, and would have been out of keeping with a genius of which one characteristic is the tendency to lose itself in a refined and graceful mystery. The suspicion was but the time-honoured mode in which the world stamps its appreciation of one who has thoughts for himself alone, his high indifference, his intolerance of the common forms of things; and in the second edition the image was changed into something fainter and more conventional. But it is still by a certain mystery in his work, and something enigmatical beyond the usual measure of great men, that he fascinates, or perhaps half repels. His life is one of sudden revolts, with intervals in which he works not at all, or apart from the main scope of his work. By a strange fortune the pictures on which his more popular fame rested disappeared early from the world, like the *Battle of the Standard;* or are mixed obscurely with the product of meaner hands, like the *Last Supper.*[2] His type of beauty is so exotic that it fascinates a larger number than it delights, and seems more than that of any other artist to reflect ideas and views and some scheme of the world within; so that he seemed to his contemporaries to be the possessor of some unsanctified and secret wisdom; as to Michelet[3] and others to have anticipated modern ideas. He trifles with his genius, and crowds all his chief work into a few tormented years of later life; yet he is so possessed by his genius that he passes unmoved through the most tragic events, overwhelming his country and friends, like one who comes across them by chance on some secret errand. . . .

Curiosity and the desire of beauty—these are the two elementary forces in Leonardo's genius; curiosity often in conflict with the desire of beauty, but generating, in union with it, a type of subtle and curious grace.

The movement of the fifteenth century was twofold; partly the Renaissance, partly also the coming of what is called the "modern spirit," with its realism, its appeal to experience. It comprehended a return to antiquity, and a return to nature. Raphael[4] represents the return to antiquity, and Leonardo the return to nature. In this return to nature, he was seeking to satisfy a boundless curiosity by her perpetual surprises, a microscopic sense of finish by her *finesse,* or delicacy of operation, that *subtilitas naturae* which Bacon[5]

notices. So we find him often in intimate relations with men of science,—with Fra Luca Paccioli[6] the mathematician, and the anatomist Marc Antonio della Torre. His observations and experiments fill thirteen volumes of manuscript; and those who can judge describe him as anticipating long before, by rapid intuition, the later ideas of science. He explained the obscure light of the unilluminated part of the moon, knew that the sea had once covered the mountains which contain shells, and of the gathering of the equatorial waters above the polar.

He who thus penetrated into the most secret parts of nature preferred always the more to the less remote, what, seeming exceptional, was an instance of law more refined, the construction about things of a peculiar atmosphere and mixed lights. He paints flowers with such curious felicity that different writers have attributed to him a fondness for particular flowers, as Clement the cyclamen, and Rio[7] the jasmin; while, at Venice, there is a stray leaf from his portfolio dotted all over with studies of violets and the wild rose. In him first appears the taste for what is *bizarre* or *recherché* in landscape; hollow places full of the green shadow of bituminous rocks, ridged reefs of trap-rock which cut the water into quaint sheets of light,—their exact antitype is in our own western seas[8]; all the solemn effects of moving water. You may follow it springing from its distant source among the rocks on the heath of the *Madonna of the Balances,* passing, as a little fall, into the treacherous calm of the *Madonna of the Lake,* as a goodly river next, below the cliffs of the *Madonna of the Rocks,* washing the white walls of its distant villages, stealing out in a network of divided streams in *La Gioconda* to the seashore of the *Saint Anne*[9]—that delicate place, where the wind passes like the hand of some fine etcher over the surface, and the untorn shells are lying thick upon the sand, and the tops of the rocks, to which the waves never rise, are green with grass, grown fine as hair. It is the landscape, not of dreams or of fancy, but of places far withdrawn, and hours selected from a thousand with a miracle of *finesse.*

---

[2]*Battle of the Standard* (or *of Anghiari*): painted around 1513. *Last Supper:* painted 1495–1497.

[3]Jules **Michelet** (1798–1874): French historian.

[4]**Raphael** of Urbino (1483–1520): Renaissance painter and architect.

[5]*subtilitas naturae:* subtlety of nature, quoting Sir Francis **Bacon** (1561–1626), *Novum Organum* (1620) 1.10.

[6]**Fra Luca Paccioli** (d. 1514): geometer, architect, and early statistician.

[7]Charles **Clément** (1821–1887): French art historian and critic. Alexis-François **Rio** (1797–1894): French theologian and art historian.

[8]**trap-rock:** dark columnar rock, as found in the Cornish headlands along Britain's **western seas.**

[9]*Madonna of . . . Saint Anne:* paintings by Leonardo conjecturally dated 1480–1508 and known by various names in Pater's day and ours.

Through Leonardo's strange veil of sight things reach him so; in no ordinary night or day, but as in faint light of eclipse, or in some brief interval of falling rain at daybreak, or through deep water.

And not into nature only; but he plunged also into human personality, and became above all a painter of portraits; faces of a modelling more skilful than has been seen before or since, embodied with a reality which almost amounts to illusion, on the dark air. To take a character as it was, and delicately sound its stops, suited one so curious in observation, curious in invention. He painted thus the portraits of Ludovico's mistresses, Lucretia Crivelli and Cecilia Galerani the poetess, of Ludovico himself, and the Duchess Beatrice.[10] The portrait of Cecilia Galerani is lost, but that of Lucretia Crivelli has been identified with *La Belle Feronière* of the Louvre, and Ludovico's pale, anxious face still remains in the Ambrosian library. Opposite is the portrait of Beatrice d'Este, in whom Leonardo seems to have caught some presentiment of early death, painting her precise and grave, full of the refinement of the dead, in sad earth-coloured raiment, set with pale stones.

Sometimes this curiosity came in conflict with the desire of beauty; it tended to make him go too far below that outside of things in which art really begins and ends. This struggle between the reason and its ideas, and the senses, the desire of beauty, is the key to Leonardo's life at Milan—his restlessness, his endless re-touchings, his odd experiments with colour. How much must he leave unfinished, how much recommence! His problem was the transmutation of ideas into images. What he had attained so far had been the mastery of that earlier Florentine style, with its naïve and limited sensuousness. Now he was to entertain in this narrow medium those divinations of a humanity too wide for it, that larger vision of the opening world, which is only not too much for the great, irregular art of Shakespeare; and everywhere the effort is visible in the work of his hands. This agitation, this perpetual delay, give him an air of weariness and *ennui*. To others he seems to be aiming at an impossible effect, to do something that art, that painting, can never do. . . .

La Gioconda is, in the truest sense, Leonardo's masterpiece, the revealing instance of his mode of thought and work. In suggestiveness, only the *Melancholia* of Dürer[11] is comparable to it; and no crude symbolism disturbs the effect of its subdued and graceful mystery. We all know the face and hands of the figure, set in its marble chair, in that circle of fantastic rocks, as in some faint light under sea. Perhaps of all ancient pictures time has chilled it least.[12] As often happens with works in which invention seems to reach its limit, there is an element in it given to, not invented by, the master. In that inestimable folio of drawings, once in the possession of Vasari, were certain designs by Verrocchio,[13] faces of such impressive beauty that Leonardo in his boyhood copied them many times. It is hard not to connect with these designs of the elder, by-past master, as with its germinal principle, the unfathomable smile, always with a touch of something sinister in it, which plays over all Leonardo's work. Besides, the picture is a portrait. From childhood we see this image defining itself on the fabric of his dreams; and but for express historical testimony, we might fancy that this was but his ideal lady, embodied and beheld at last. What was the relationship of a living Florentine to this creature of his thought? By what strange affinities had the dream and the person grown up thus apart, and yet so closely together? Present from the first incorporeally in Leonardo's brain, dimly traced in the designs of Verrocchio, she is found present at last in *Il Giocondo's* house. That there is much of mere portraiture in the picture is attested by the legend that by artificial means, the presence of mimes and flute-players, that subtle expression was protracted on the face. Again, was it in four years and by renewed labour never really completed, or in four months and as by stroke of magic, that the image was projected?

The presence that rose thus so strangely beside the waters, is expressive of what in the ways of a thousand years men had come to desire. Hers is the head upon which all "the ends of the world are come,"[14] and the eyelids are a little weary. It is a beauty wrought out from within upon the flesh, the deposit, little cell by cell, of strange thoughts and fantastic reveries and exquisite passions. Set it for a moment beside one of those white Greek goddesses or beautiful women of antiquity, and how would they be troubled by this beauty, into which the soul with all its maladies has passed! All the thoughts and experience of the world have etched and moulded there, in that which they have of power to refine and make expressive the outward form, the animalism of Greece, the lust of Rome, the mysticism of the

---

[10]**Ludovico Sforza** (1452–1508): Duke of Milan, Leonardo's patron from 1482 to 1499. **Duchess Beatrice** (1475–1497): Ludovico's wife. The "lost" portrait of **Cecilia Galerani** is now thought to be Leonardo's 1491 *Portrait of a Lady with an Ermine*.

[11]Albrecht **Dürer** (1471–1528): German painter and engraver.

[12]**least:** Yet for Vasari there was some further magic of crimson in the lips and cheeks, lost for us. [Pater's note]

[13]Andrea del **Verrocchio** (1435–1488): Leonardo's teacher.

[14]"the ends . . . are come": 1 Corinthians 10:11.

middle age with its spiritual ambition and imaginative loves, the return of the Pagan world, the sins of the Borgias.[15] She is older than the rocks among which she sits; like the vampire, she has been dead many times, and learned the secrets of the grave; and has been a diver in deep seas, and keeps their fallen day about her; and trafficked for strange webs with Eastern merchants and, as Leda, was the mother of Helen of Troy, and, as Saint Anne, the mother of Mary; and all this has been to her but as the sound of lyres and flutes, and lives only in the delicacy with which it has moulded the changing lineaments, and tinged the eyelids and the hands. The fancy of a perpetual life, sweeping together ten thousand experiences, is an old one; and modern philosophy has conceived the idea of humanity as wrought upon by, and summing up in itself, all modes of thought and life. Certainly Lady Lisa might stand as the embodiment of the old fancy, the symbol of the modern idea.

During these years at Florence Leonardo's history is the history of his art; for himself, he is lost in the bright cloud of it. The outward history begins again in 1502, with a wild journey through central Italy, which he makes as the chief engineer of Cæsar Borgia.[16] The biographer, putting together the stray jottings of his manuscripts, may follow him through every day of it, up the strange tower of Siena, elastic like a bent bow, down to the seashore at Piombino, each place appearing as fitfully as in a fever dream.

One other great work was left for him to do, a work all trace of which soon vanished, *The Battle of the Standard*, in which he had Michelangelo for his rival. The citizens of Florence, desiring to decorate the walls of the great council-chamber, had offered the work for competition, and any subject might be chosen from the Florentine wars of the fifteenth century. Michelangelo chose for his cartoon an incident of the war with Pisa, in which the Florentine soldiers, bathing in the Arno, are surprised by the sound of trumpets, and run to arms. His design has reached us only in an old engraving, which helps us less perhaps than our remembrance of the background of his *Holy Family* in the *Uffizii*[17] to imagine in what superhuman form, such as might have beguiled the heart of an earlier world, those figures ascended out of the water. Leonardo chose an incident from the battle of Anghiari, in which two parties of soldiers fight for a standard. Like Michelangelo's, his cartoon is lost, and

has come to us only in sketches, and in a fragment of Rubens.[18] Through the accounts given we may discern some lust of terrible things in it, so that even the horses tore each other with their teeth. And yet one fragment of it, in a drawing of his at Florence, is far different—a waving field of lovely armour, the chased[19] edgings running like lines of sunlight from side to side. Michelangelo was twenty-seven years old; Leonardo more than fifty; and Raphael, then nineteen years of age, visiting Florence for the first time, came and watched them as they worked.

We catch a glimpse of Leonardo again, at Rome in 1514, surrounded by his mirrors and vials and furnaces, making strange toys that seemed alive of wax and quicksilver. The hesitation which had haunted him all through life, and made him like one under a spell, was upon him now with double force. No one had ever carried political indifferentism farther; it had always been his philosophy to "fly before the storm"[20]; he is for the Sforzas, or against them, as the tide of their fortune turns. Yet now, in the political society of Rome, he came to be suspected of secret French sympathies. It paralysed him to find himself among enemies; and he turned wholly to France, which had long courted him.

France was about to become an Italy more Italian than Italy itself. Francis the First, like Lewis the Twelfth before him, was attracted by the *finesse* of Leonardo's work; *La Gioconda* was already in his cabinet, and he offered Leonardo the little *Château de Clou*, with its vineyards and meadows, in the pleasant valley of the Masse, just outside the walls of the town of Amboise, where, especially in the hunting season, the court then frequently resided. *A Monsieur Lyonard, peinteur du Roy pour Amboyse*—so the letter of Francis the First[21] is headed. It opens a prospect, one of the most interesting in the history of art, where, in a peculiarly blent atmosphere, Italian art dies away as a French exotic.[22]

Two questions remain, after much busy antiquarianism, concerning Leonardo's death—the question of the exact form of his religion, and the question whether Francis the First was present at the time. They are of about equally little

---

[15]**Borgias:** family notorious for worldly prelacy and ruthless politics.

[16]Cesare **Borgia** (1476–1507): the original Machiavellian prince.

[17]*Uffizii:* gallery in Florence.

[18]**cartoon:** artist's full-size working design. Peter Paul **Rubens** (1577–1640): Flemish baroque painter.

[19]**chased:** embossed or engraved.

[20]"**fly before the storm**": adapting Shelley's *Alastor* (1816) 345.

[21]*A Monsieur Lyonard . . . Amboyse:* To Master Leonardo, painter to the king at Amboise. **Clou** or Cloux was near the palace of **Francis I** at Amboise in the Loire valley.

[22]**exotic:** plant of foreign extraction.

importance in the estimate of Leonardo's genius. The directions in his will concerning the thirty masses and the great candles for the church of Saint Florentin[23] are things of course, their real purpose being immediate and practical; and on no theory of religion could these hurried offices be of much consequence. We forget them in speculating how one who had been always so desirous of beauty, but desired it always in such precise and definite forms, as hands or flowers or hair, looked forward now into the vague land, and experienced the last curiosity.

1869

Conclusion to *The Renaissance*

Λέγει που Ἡράκλειτος ὅτι πάντα χωρεῖ καὶ οὐδὲν μένει[1]

To regard all things and principles of things as inconstant modes or fashions has more and more become the tendency of modern thought. Let us begin with that which is without—our physical life. Fix upon it in one of its more exquisite intervals, the moment, for instance, of delicious recoil from the flood of water in summer heat. What is the whole physical life in that moment but a combination of natural elements to which science gives their names? But those elements, phosphorus and lime and delicate fibres, are present not in the human body alone: we detect them in places most remote from it. Our physical life is a perpetual motion of them—the passage of the blood, the waste and repairing of the lenses of the eye, the modification of the tissues of the brain under every ray of light and sound—processes which science reduces to simpler and more elementary forces. Like the elements of which we are composed, the action of these forces extends beyond us: it rusts iron and ripens corn. Far out on every side of us those elements are broadcast, driven in many currents; and birth and gesture and death and the springing of violets from the grave are but a few out of ten thousand resultant combinations. That clear, perpetual outline of face and limb is but an image of ours, under which we group them—a design in a web, the actual threads of which pass out beyond it. This at least of flamelike our life has, that it is but the concurrence, renewed from moment to moment, of forces parting sooner or later on their ways.

Or if we begin with the inward world of thought and feeling, the whirlpool is still more rapid, the flame more eager and devouring. There it is no longer the gradual darkening of the eye, the gradual fading of colour from the wall—movements of the shore-side, where the water flows down indeed, though in apparent rest—but the race of the mid-stream, a drift of momentary acts of sight and passion and thought. At first sight experience seems to bury us under a flood of external objects, pressing upon us with a sharp and importunate reality, calling us out of ourselves in a thousand forms of action. But when reflexion begins to play upon those objects they are dissipated under its influence; the cohesive force seems suspended like some trick of magic; each object is loosed into a group of impressions—colour, odour, texture—in the mind of the observer. And if we continue to dwell in thought on this world, not of objects in the solidity with which language invests them, but of impressions, unstable, flickering, inconsistent, which burn and are extinguished with our consciousness of them, it contracts still further: the whole scope of observation is dwarfed into the narrow chamber of the individual mind. Experience, already reduced to a group of impressions, is ringed round for each one of us by that thick wall of personality through which no real voice has ever pierced on its way to us, or from us to that which we can only conjecture to be without. Every one of those impressions is the impression of the individual in his isolation, each mind keeping as a solitary prisoner its own dream of a world. Analysis goes a step farther still, and assures us that those impressions of the individual mind to which, for each one of us, experience dwindles down, are in perpetual flight; that each of them is limited by time, and that as time is infinitely divisible, each of them is infinitely divisible also; all that is actual in it being a single moment, gone while we try to apprehend it, of which it may ever be more truly said that it has ceased to be than that it is. To such a tremulous wisp constantly re-forming itself on the stream, to a single sharp impression, with a sense in it, a relic more or less fleeting, of such moments gone by, what is real in our life fines itself down. It is with this movement, with the passage and dissolution of impressions, images, sensations, that analysis leaves off—that continual vanishing away, that strange, perpetual weaving and unweaving of ourselves.

---

[23]**Saint Florentin:** church at the Amboise palace, Leonardo's gravesite.

[1]**Conclusion:** This brief "Conclusion" was omitted in the second edition of this book, as I conceived it might possibly mislead some of those young men into whose hands it might fall. On the whole, I have thought it best to reprint it here, with some slight changes which bring it closer to my original meaning. I have dealt more fully in *Marius the Epicurean* with the thoughts suggested by it. [Pater's 1888 note; he published his novel *Marius* in 1885] Epigraph: Heracleitus says, "all things give way; nothing remains." [Pater's translation of Plato's *Cratylus* 402A, where a 4th-century BCE philosopher cites a 6th-century BCE one]

Philosophiren, says Novalis, *ist dephlegmatisiren, vivificiren.*[2] The service of philosophy, of speculative culture, towards the human spirit, is to rouse, to startle it to a life of constant and eager observation. Every moment some form grows perfect in hand or face; some tone on the hills or the sea is choicer than the rest; some mood of passion or insight or intellectual excitement is irresistibly real and attractive to us,—for that moment only. Not the fruit of experience, but experience itself, is the end. A counted number of pulses only is given to us of a variegated, dramatic life. How may we see in them all that is to be seen in them by the finest senses? How shall we pass most swiftly from point to point, and be present always at the focus where the greatest number of vital forces unite in their purest energy?

To burn always with this hard, gemlike flame, to maintain this ecstasy, is success in life. In a sense it might even be said that our failure is to form habits: for, after all, habit is relative to a stereotyped world, and meantime it is only the roughness of the eye that makes any two persons, things, situations, seem alike. While all melts under our feet, we may well grasp at any exquisite passion, or any contribution to knowledge that seems by a lifted horizon to set the spirit free for a moment, or any stirring of the senses, strange dyes, strange colours, and curious odours, or work of the artist's hands, or the face of one's friend. Not to discriminate every moment some passionate attitude in those about us, and in the very brilliancy of their gifts some tragic dividing of forces on their ways, is, on this short day of frost and sun, to sleep before evening. With this sense of the splendour of our experience and of its awful brevity, gathering all we are into one desperate effort to see and touch, we shall hardly have time to make theories about the things we see and touch. What we have to do is to be for ever curiously testing new opinions and courting new impressions, never acquiescing in a facile orthodoxy of Comte, or of Hegel,[3] or of our own. Philosophical theories or ideas, as points of view, instruments of criticism, may help us to gather up what might otherwise pass unregarded by us. "Philosophy is the microscope of thought."[4] The theory or idea or system which requires of us the sacrifice of any part of this experience, in consideration of some interest into which we cannot enter, or some abstract theory we have not identified with ourselves, or of what is only conventional, has no real claim upon us.

One of the most beautiful passages of Rousseau is that in the sixth book of the *Confessions*, where he describes the awakening in him of the literary sense. An undefinable taint of death had clung always about him, and now in early manhood he believed himself smitten by mortal disease. He asked himself how he might make as much as possible of the interval that remained; and he was not biassed by anything in his previous life when he decided that it must be by intellectual excitement, which he found just then in the clear, fresh writings of Voltaire. Well! we are all *condamnés*, as Victor Hugo says: we are all under sentence of death but with a sort of indefinite reprieve—*les hommes sont tous condamnés à mort avec des sursis indéfinis:*[5] we have an interval, and then our place knows us no more. Some spend this interval in listlessness, some in high passions, the wisest, at least among "the children of this world,"[6] in art and song. For our one chance lies in expanding that interval, in getting as many pulsations as possible into the given time. Great passions may give us this quickened sense of life, ecstasy and sorrow of love, the various forms of enthusiastic activity, disinterested or otherwise, which come naturally to many of us. Only be sure it is passion—that it does yield you this fruit of a quickened, multiplied consciousness. Of such wisdom, the poetic passion, the desire of beauty, the love of art for its own sake, has most. For art comes to you proposing frankly to give nothing but the highest quality to your moments as they pass, and simply for those moments' sake.

1868, 1888

~

The Child in the House[1]

As Florian Deleal walked, one hot afternoon, he overtook by the wayside a poor aged man, and, as he seemed weary with the road, helped him on with the burden which he

---

[2]*Philosophiren . . . vivificiren:* To philosophize is to cast off sluggishness, to bring oneself to life. **Novalis:** pen name of Friedrich Leopold von Hardenberg (1772–1801), German Romantic poet.

[3]Auguste **Comte** (1798–1857): French empiricist philosopher. Georg Wilhelm Friedrich **Hegel** (1770–1831): German idealist philosopher.

[4]**"Philosophy . . . thought"**: Victor Hugo (1802–1885), *Les Misérables* (1862), book 2, chapter 2.

[5]**"les hommes . . . indéfinis"**: We are all under sentence of death but with a sort of indefinite reprieve. [Pater's 1893 translation of Hugo's phrase in *Le dernier jour d'un condamné* (A Condemned Man's Last Day, 1832)]

[6]**"the children of this world"**: Luke 16:8.

[1]**The Child in the House**: autobiographical, although under a veil of fiction thick enough to discourage identifications other than Florian's with Pater. Pater wanted to publish the piece anonymously, but the *Macmillan's Magazine* editor persuaded him to sign it.

carried, a certain distance

carried, a certain distance. And as the man told his story, it chanced that he named the place, a little place in the neighbourhood of a great city, where Florian had passed his earliest years, but which he had never since seen, and, the story told, went forward on his journey comforted. And that night, like a reward for his pity, a dream of that place came to Florian, a dream which did for him the office of the finer sort of memory, bringing its object to mind with a great clearness, yet, as sometimes happens in dreams, raised a little above itself, and above ordinary retrospect. The true aspect of the place, especially of the house there in which he had lived as a child, the fashion of its doors, its hearths, its windows, the very scent upon the air of it, was with him in sleep for a season; only, with tints more musically blent on wall and floor, and some finer light and shadow running in and out along its curves and angles, and with all its little carvings daintier. He awoke with a sigh at the thought of almost thirty years which lay between him and that place, yet with a flutter of pleasure still within him at the fair light, as if it were a smile, upon it. And it happened that this accident of his dream was just the thing needed for the beginning of a certain design he then had in view, the noting, namely, of some things in the story of his spirit—in that process of brain-building by which we are, each one of us, what we are. With the image of the place so clear and favourable upon him, he fell to thinking of himself therein, and how his thoughts had grown up to him. In that half-spiritualised house he could watch the better, over again, the gradual expansion of the soul which had come to be there—of which indeed, through the law which makes the material objects about them so large an element in children's lives, it had actually become a part; inward and outward being woven through and through each other into one inextricable texture—half, tint and trace and accident of homely colour and form, from the wood and the bricks; half, mere soul-stuff, floated thither from who knows how far. In the house and garden of his dream he saw a child moving, and could divide the main streams at least of the winds that had played on him, and study so the first stage in that mental journey.

The *old house*, as when Florian talked of it afterwards he always called it, (as all children do, who can recollect a change of home, soon enough but not too soon to mark a period in their lives) really was an old house; and an element of French descent in its inmates—descent from Watteau,[2] the old court-painter, one of whose gallant pieces still

hung in one of the rooms—might explain, together with some other things, a noticeable trimness and comely whiteness about everything there—the curtains, the couches, the paint on the walls with which the light and shadow played so delicately; might explain also the tolerance of the great poplar in the garden, a tree most often despised by English people, but which French people love, having observed a certain fresh way its leaves have of dealing with the wind, making it sound, in never so slight a stirring of the air, like running water.

The old-fashioned, low wainscoting went round the rooms, and up the staircase with carved balusters and shadowy angles, landing half-way up at a broad window, with a swallow's nest below the sill, and the blossom of an old pear-tree showing across it in late April, against the blue, below which the perfumed juice of the find of fallen fruit in autumn was so fresh. At the next turning came the closet which held on its deep shelves the best china. Little angel faces and reedy flutings stood out round the fire-place of the children's room. And on the top of the house, above the large attic, where the white mice ran in the twilight—an infinite, unexplored wonderland of childish treasures, glass beads, empty scent-bottles still sweet, thrum[3] of coloured silks, among its lumber—a flat space of roof, railed round, gave a view of the neighbouring steeples; for the house, as I said, stood near a great city, which sent up heavenwards, over the twisting weather-vanes, not seldom, its beds of rolling cloud and smoke, touched with storm or sunshine. But the child of whom I am writing did not hate the fog because of the crimson lights which fell from it sometimes upon the chimneys, and the whites which gleamed through its openings, on summer mornings, on turret or pavement. For it is false to suppose that a child's sense of beauty is dependent on any choiceness or special fineness, in the objects which present themselves to it, though this indeed comes to be the rule with most of us in later life; earlier, in some degree, we see inwardly; and the child finds for itself, and with unstinted delight, a difference for the sense, in those whites and reds through the smoke on very homely buildings, and in the gold of the dandelions at the roadside, just beyond the houses, where not a handful of earth is virgin and untouched, in the lack of better ministries to its desire of beauty.

This house then stood not far beyond the gloom and rumours of the town, among high garden-wall, bright all summer-time with Golden-rod, and brown-and-golden

---

[2]Jean-Antoine **Watteau** (1684–1721): French painter.

[3]**thrum**: remnants of woven fabric.

Wall-flower—*Flos Parietis*, as the children's Latin-reading father taught them to call it, while he was with them. Tracing back the threads of his complex spiritual habit, as he was used in after years to do, Florian found that he owed to the place many tones of sentiment afterwards customary with him, certain inward lights under which things most naturally presented themselves to him. The coming and going of travellers to the town along the way, the shadow of the streets, the sudden breath of the neighbouring gardens, the singular brightness of bright weather there, its singular darknesses which linked themselves in his mind to certain engraved illustrations in the old big Bible at home, the coolness of the dark, cavernous shops round the great church, with its giddy winding stair up to the pigeons and the bells—a citadel of peace in the heart of the trouble—all this acted on his childish fancy, so that ever afterwards the like aspects and incidents never failed to throw him into a well-recognised imaginative mood, seeming actually to have become a part of the texture of his mind. Also, Florian could trace home to this point a pervading preference in himself for a kind of comeliness and dignity, an *urbanity* literally, in modes of life, which he connected with the pale people of towns, and which made him susceptible to a kind of exquisite satisfaction in the trimness and well-considered grace of certain things and persons he afterwards met with, here and there, in his way through the world.

So the child of whom I am writing lived on there quietly; things without thus ministering to him, as he sat daily at the window with the birdcage hanging below it, and his mother taught him to read, wondering at the ease with which he learned, and at the quickness of his memory. The perfume of the little flowers of the lime-tree fell through the air upon them like rain; while time seemed to move ever more slowly to the murmur of the bees in it, till it almost stood still on June afternoons. How insignificant, at the moment, seem the influences of the sensible things which are tossed and fall and lie about us, so, or so, in the environment of early childhood. How indelibly, as we afterwards discover, they affect us; with what capricious attractions and associations they figure themselves on the white paper, the smooth wax, of our ingenuous souls, as "with lead in the rock for ever,"[4] giving form and feature, and as it were assigned house-room in our memory, to early experiences of feeling and thought, which abide with us ever afterwards, thus, and not otherwise. The realities and passions, the rumours of the greater world without, steal in upon us, each by its own special little passage-way, through the wall of custom about us; and never afterwards quite detach themselves from this or that accident, or trick, in the mode of their first entrance to us. Our susceptibilities, the discovery of our powers, manifold experiences—our various experiences of the coming and going of bodily pain, for instance—belong to this or the other well-remembered place in the material habitation—that little white room with the window across which the heavy blossoms could beat so peevishly in the wind, with just that particular catch or throb, such a sense of teasing in it, on gusty mornings; and the early habitation thus gradually becomes a sort of material shrine or sanctuary of sentiment; a system of visible symbolism interweaves itself through all our thoughts and passions; and irresistibly, little shapes, voices, accidents—the angle at which the sun in the morning fell on the pillow—become parts of the great chain wherewith we are bound.

Thus far, for Florian, what all this had determined was a peculiarly strong sense of home—so forcible a motive with all of us—prompting to us our customary love of the earth, and the larger part of our fear of death, that revulsion we have from it, as from something strange, untried, unfriendly; though life-long imprisonment, they tell you, and final banishment from home is a thing bitterer still; the looking forward to but a short space, a mere childish *goûter*[5] and dessert of it, before the end, being so great a resource of effort to pilgrims and wayfarers, and the soldier in distant quarters, and lending, in lack of that, some power of solace to the thought of sleep in the home churchyard, at least—dead cheek by dead cheek, and with the rain soaking in upon one from above.

So powerful is this instinct, and yet accidents like those I have been speaking of so mechanically determine it; its essence being indeed the early familiar, as constituting our ideal, or typical conception, of rest and security. Out of so many possible conditions, just this for you and that for me, brings ever the unmistakeable realisation of the delightful *chez soi*;[6] this for the Englishman, for me and you, with the closely-drawn white curtain and the shaded lamp; that, quite other, for the wandering Arab, who folds his tent every morning, and makes his sleeping-place among haunted ruins, or in old tombs.

With Florian then the sense of home became singularly intense, his good fortune being that the special character of

---

[4]"with lead . . . forever": Job 19:24.

[5]*goûter*: snack.

[6]*chez soi*: at home.

his home was in itself so essentially home-like. As after many wanderings I have come to fancy that some parts of Surrey and Kent are, for Englishmen, the true landscape, true home-counties,[7] by right, partly, of a certain earthy warmth in the yellow of the sand below their gorse-bushes, and of a certain grey-blue mist after rain, in the hollows of the hills there, welcome to fatigued eyes, and never seen farther south; so I think that the sort of house I have described, with precisely those proportions of red-brick and green, and with a just perceptible monotony in the subdued order of it, for its distinguishing note, is for Englishmen at least typically home-life. And so for Florian that general human instinct was reinforced by this special home-likeness in the place his wandering soul had happened to light on, as, in the second degree, its body and earthly tabernacle; the sense of harmony between his soul and its physical environment became, for a time at least, like perfectly played music, and the life led there singularly tranquil and filled with a curious sense of self-possession. The love of security, of an habitually undisputed standing-ground or sleeping-place, came to count for much in the generation and correcting of his thoughts, and afterwards as a salutary principle of restraint in all his wanderings of spirit. The wistful yearning towards home, in absence from it, as the shadows of evening deepened, and he followed in thought what was doing there from hour to hour, interpreted to him much of a yearning and regret he experienced afterwards, towards he knew not what, out of strange ways of feeling and thought in which, from time to time, his spirit found itself alone; and in the tears shed in such absences there seemed always to be some soul-subduing foretaste of what his last tears might be.

And the sense of security could hardly have been deeper, the quiet of the child's soul being one with the quiet of its home, a place "inclosed" and "sealed."[8] But upon this assured place, upon the child's assured soul which resembled it, there came floating in from the larger world without, as at windows left ajar unknowingly, or over the high garden walls, two streams of impressions, the sentiments of beauty and pain—recognitions of the visible, tangible, audible loveliness of things, as a very real and somewhat tyrannous element in them—and of the sorrow of the world, of grown people and children and animals, as

a thing not to be put by[9] in them. From this point he could trace two predominant processes of mental change in him—the growth of an almost diseased sensibility to the spectacle of suffering, and, parallel with this, the rapid growth of a certain capacity of fascination by bright colour and choice form—the sweet curvings, for instance, of the lips of those who seemed to him comely persons, modulated in such delicate unison to the things they said or sang,—marking early the activity in him of a more than customary sensuousness, "the lust of the eye,"[10] as the Preacher says, which might lead him, one day, how far! Could he have foreseen the weariness of the way! In music sometimes the two sorts of impressions came together, and he would weep, to the surprise of older people. Tears of joy too the child knew, also to older people's surprise; real tears, once, of relief from long-strung, childish expectation, when he found returned at evening, with new roses in her cheeks, the little sister who had been to a place where there was a wood, and brought back for him a treasure of fallen acorns, and black crow's feathers, and his peace at finding her again near him mingled all night with some intimate sense of the distant forest, the rumour of its breezes, with the glossy blackbirds aslant and the branches lifted in them, and of the perfect nicety of the little cups that fell. So those two elementary apprehensions of the tenderness and of the colour in things grew apace in him, and were seen by him afterwards to send their roots back into the beginnings of life.

Let me note first some of the occasions of his recognition of the element of pain in things—incidents, now and again, which seemed suddenly to awake in him the whole force of that sentiment which Goethe has called the *Weltschmerz*,[11] and in which the concentrated sorrow of the world seemed suddenly to lie heavy upon him. A book lay in an old book-case, of which he cared to remember one picture—a woman sitting, with hands bound behind her, the dress, the cap, the hair, folded with a simplicity which touched him strangely, as if not by her own hands, but with some ambiguous care at the hands of others—Queen Marie Antoinette, on her way to execution—we all remember

---

[7]**Surrey, Kent:** parts of S England known as **home-counties** because they were nearest to London.

[8]**"inclosed" and "sealed":** Song of Solomon 4:12: "A garden inclosed is my sister, my spouse; a spring shut up, a fountain sealed."

[9]**not to be put by:** see Wordsworth's "Intimations" ode (1807) 121.

[10]**"the lust of the eye":** 1 John 2:16, apparently conflated with Ecclesiastes 6:9.

[11]*Weltschmerz:* world-pain. Pater credits Johann Wolfgang von **Goethe** (1749–1832) with a coinage attributable to a contemporary German Romantic, Jean Paul (1763–1825).

David's[12] drawing, meant merely to make her ridiculous. The face that had been so high had learned to be mute and resistless; but out of its very resistlessness, seemed now to call on men to have pity, and forbear; and he took note of that, as he closed the book, as a thing to look at again, if he should at any time find himself tempted to be cruel. Again, he would never quite forget the appeal in the small sister's face, in the garden under the lilacs, terrified at a spider lighted on her sleeve. He could trace back to the look then noted a certain mercy he conceived always for people in fear, even of little things, which seemed to make him, though but for a moment, capable of almost any sacrifice of himself. Impressible, susceptible persons, indeed, who had had their sorrows, lived about him; and this sensibility was due in part to the tacit influence of their presence, enforcing upon him habitually the fact that there are those who pass their days, as a matter of course, in a sort of "going quietly." Most poignantly of all he could recall, in unfading minutest circumstance, the cry on the stair, sounding bitterly through the house, and struck into his soul for ever, of an aged woman, his father's sister, come now to announce his death in distant India; how it seemed to make the aged woman like a child again; and, he knew not why, but this fancy was full of pity to him. There were the little sorrows of the dumb animals too—of the white angora, with a dark tail like an ermine's, and a face like a flower, who fell into a lingering sickness, and became quite delicately human in its valetudinarianism,[13] and came to have a hundred different expressions of voice—how it grew worse and worse, till it began to feel the light too much for it, and at last, after one wild morning of pain, the little soul flickered away from the body, quite worn to death already, and now but feebly retaining it.

So he wanted another pet; and as there were starlings about the place, which could be taught to speak, one of them was caught, and he meant to treat it kindly; but in the night its young ones could be heard crying after it, and the responsive cry of the mother-bird towards them; and at last, with the first light, though not till after some debate with himself, he went down and opened the cage, and saw a sharp bound of the prisoner up to her nestlings; and therewith came the sense of remorse,—that he too was become an accomplice in moving, to the limit of his small power, the springs and handles of that great machine in things, constructed so ingeniously to play pain-fugues on the delicate nerve-work of living creatures.

I have remarked how, in the process of our brain-building, as the house of thought in which we live gets itself together, like some airy bird's-nest of floating thistle-down and chance straws, compact at last, little accidents have their consequence; and thus it happened that, as he walked one evening, a garden gate, usually closed, stood open; and lo! within, a great red hawthorn in full flower, embossing heavily the bleached and twisted trunk and branches, so aged that there were but few green leaves thereon—a plumage of tender, crimson fire out of the heart of the dry wood. The perfume of the tree had now and again reached him, in the currents of the wind, over the wall, and he had wondered what might be behind it, and was now allowed to fill his arms with the flowers—flowers enough for all the old blue-china pots along the chimney-piece, making fête[14] in the children's room. Was it some periodic moment in the expansion of soul within him, or mere trick of heat in the heavily-laden summer air? But the beauty of the thing struck home to him feverishly; and in dreams all night he loitered along a magic roadway of crimson flowers, which seemed to open ruddily in thick, fresh masses about his feet, and fill softly all the little hollows in the banks on either side. Always afterwards, summer by summer, as the flowers came on, the blossom of the red hawthorn still seemed to him absolutely the reddest of all things; and the goodly crimson, still alive in the works of old Venetian masters or old Flemish tapestries, called out always from afar the recollection of the flame in those perishing little petals, as it pulsed gradually out of them, kept long in the drawers of an old cabinet. Also then, for the first time, he seemed to experience a passionateness in his relation to fair outward objects, an inexplicable excitement in their presence, which disturbed him, and from which he half longed to be free. A touch of regret or desire mingled all night with the remembered presence of the red flowers, and their perfume in the darkness about him; and the longing for some undivided, entire possession of them was the beginning of a revelation to him, growing ever clearer, with the coming of the gracious summer guise of fields and trees and persons in each succeeding year, of a certain, at times seemingly exclusive, predominance in his interests, of beautiful physical things, a kind of tyranny of the senses over him.

In later years he came upon philosophies which occupied him much in the estimate of the proportion of the sensuous

---

[12]Jacques-Louis **David** (1748–1825): French neoclassical painter and visual propagandist.

[13]**valetudinarianism**: hypochondria.

---

[14]*fête*: celebration.

and the ideal elements in human knowledge, the relative parts they bear in it; and, in his intellectual scheme, was led to assign very little to the abstract thought, and much to its sensible vehicle or occasion. Such metaphysical speculation did but reinforce what was instinctive in his way of receiving the world, and for him, everywhere, that sensible vehicle or occasion became, perhaps only too surely, the necessary concomitant of any perception of things, real enough to be of any weight or reckoning, in his house of thought. There were times when he could think of the necessity he was under of associating all thoughts to touch and sight, as a sympathetic link between himself and actual, feeling, living objects; a protest in favour of real men and women against mere grey, unreal abstractions; and he remembered gratefully how the Christian religion, hardly less than the religion of the ancient Greeks, translating so much of its spiritual verity into things that may be seen, condescends in part to sanction this infirmity, if so it be, of our human existence, wherein the world of sense is so much with us,[15] and welcomed this thought as a kind of keeper and sentinel over his soul therein. But certainly, he came more and more to be unable to care for, or think of soul but as in an actual body, or of any world but that wherein are water and trees, and where men and women look, so or so, and press actual hands. It was the trick even his pity learned, fastening those who suffered in anywise to his affections by a kind of sensible attachments. He would think of Julian, fallen into incurable sickness, as spoiled in the sweet blossom of his skin like pale amber, and his honey-like hair; of Cecil, early dead, as cut off from the lilies, from golden summer days, from women's voices; and then what comforted him a little was the thought of the turning of the child's flesh to violets in the turf above him. And thinking of the very poor, it was not the things which most men care most for that he yearned to give them; but fairer roses, perhaps, and power to taste quite as they will, at their ease and not task-burdened, a certain desirable, clear light in the new morning, through which sometimes he had noticed them, quite unconscious of it, on their way to their early toil.

So he yielded himself to these things, to be played upon by them like a musical instrument, and began to note with deepening watchfulness, but always with some puzzled, unutterable longing in his enjoyment, the phases of the seasons and of the growing or waning day, down even to the shadowy changes wrought on bare wall or ceiling—

---

[15]**the world . . . with us**: conflates two Wordsworth phrases, from "The World Is Too Much With Us" (1807) and *The Excursion* (1814) 9.214.

the light cast up from the snow, bringing out their darkest angles; the brown light in the cloud, which meant rain; that almost too austere clearness, in the protracted light of the lengthening day, before warm weather began, as if it lingered but to make a severer workday, with the school-books opened earlier and later; that beam of June sunshine, at last, as he lay awake before the time, a way of gold-dust across the darkness; all the humming, the freshness, the perfume of the garden seemed to lie upon it—and coming in one afternoon in September, along the red gravel walk, to look for a basket of yellow crab-apples left in the cool, old parlour, he remembered it the more, and how the colours struck upon him, because a wasp on one bitten apple stung him, and he felt the passion of sudden, severe pain. For this too brought its curious reflexions; and, in relief from it, he would wonder over it—how it had then been with him—puzzled at the depth of the charm or spell over him, which lay, for a little while at least, in the mere absence of pain; once, especially, when an older boy taught him to make flowers of sealing-wax, and he had burnt his hand badly at the lighted taper, and been unable to sleep. He remembered that also afterwards, as a sort of typical thing—a white vision of heat about him, clinging closely, through the languid scent of the ointments put upon the place to make it well.

Also, as he felt this pressure upon him of the sensible world, then, as often afterwards, there would come another sort of curious questioning how the last impressions of eye and ear might happen to him, how they would find him—the scent of the last flower, the soft yellowness of the last morning, the last recognition of some object of affection, hand or voice; it could not be but that the latest look of the eyes, before their final closing, would be strangely vivid; one would go with the hot tears, the cry, the touch of the wistful bystander, impressed how deeply on one! or would it be, perhaps, a mere frail retiring of all things, great or little, away from one, into a level distance?

For with this desire of physical beauty mingled itself early the fear of death—the fear of death intensified by the desire of beauty. Hitherto he had never gazed upon dead faces, as sometimes, afterwards, at the *Morgue* in Paris, or in that fair cemetery at Munich, where all the dead must go and lie in state before burial, behind glass windows, among the flowers and incense and holy candles—the aged clergy with their sacred ornaments, the young men in their dancing-shoes and spotless white linen—after which visits, those waxen, resistless faces would always live with him for many days, making the broadest sunshine sickly. The child had heard indeed of the death of his father, and how, in the Indian station, a fever had taken him, so that though not in action he had yet died as a soldier; and hearing of the "res-urrection of the just,"[16] he could think of him as still abroad in the world, somehow, for his protection—a grand, though perhaps rather terrible figure, in beautiful soldier's things, like the figure in the picture of Joshua's Vision[17] in the Bible—and of that, round which the mourners moved so softly, and afterwards with such solemn singing, as but a wornout garment left at a deserted lodging. So it was, until on a summer day he walked with his mother through a fair churchyard. In a bright dress he rambled among the graves, in the gay weather, and so came, in one corner, upon an open grave for a child—a dark space on the brilliant grass— the black mould lying heaped up round it, weighing down the little jewelled branches of the dwarf rose-bushes in flower. And therewith came, full-grown, never wholly to leave him, with the certainty that even children do some-times die, the physical horror of death, with its wholly self-ish recoil from the association of lower forms of life, and the suffocating weight above. No benign, grave figure in beauti-ful soldier's things any longer abroad in the world for his protection! only a few poor, piteous bones; and above them, possibly, a certain sort of figure he hoped not to see. For sit-ting one day in the garden below an open window, he heard people talking, and could not but listen, how, in a sleepless hour, a sick woman had seen one of the dead sitting beside her, come to call her hence; and from the broken talk evolved with much clearness the notion that not all those dead people had really departed to the churchyard, nor were quite so motionless as they looked, but led a secret, half-fugitive life in their old homes, quite free by night, though sometimes visible in the day, dodging from room to room, with no great goodwill towards those who shared the place with them. All night the figure sat beside him in the reveries of his broken sleep, and was not quite gone in the morning—an odd, irreconcileable new member of the household, making the sweet familiar chambers unfriendly and suspect by its uncertain presence. He could have hated the dead he had pitied so, for being thus. Afterwards he came to think of those poor, home-returning ghosts, which all men have fancied to themselves—the *revenants*[18]—pathet-ically, as crying, or beating with vain hands at the doors, as the wind came, their cries distinguishable in it as a wilder inner note. But, always making death more unfamiliar still, that old experience would ever, from time to time, return to

him; even in the living he sometimes caught its likeness; at any time or place, in a moment, the faint atmosphere of the chamber of death would be breathed around him, and the image with the bound chin, the quaint smile, the straight, stiff feet, shed itself across the air upon the bright carpet, amid the gayest company, or happiest communing with himself.

To most children the sombre questionings to which impressions like these attach themselves, if they come at all, are actually suggested by religious books, which therefore they often regard with much secret distaste, and dismiss, as far as possible, from their habitual thoughts as a too de-pressing element in life. To Florian such impressions, these misgivings as to the ultimate tendency of the years, of the relationship between life and death, had been suggested spontaneously in the natural course of his mental growth by a strong innate sense for the soberer tones in things, further strengthened by actual circumstances; and religious senti-ment, that system of biblical ideas in which he had been brought up, presented itself to him as a thing that might soften and dignify, and light up as with a "lively hope,"[19] a melancholy already deeply settled in him. So he yielded himself easily to religious impressions, and with a kind of mystical appetite for sacred things; the more as they came to him through a saintly person who loved him tenderly, and believed that this early pre-occupation with them al-ready marked the child out for a saint. He began to love, for their own sakes, church lights, holy days, all that belonged to the comely order of the sanctuary, the secrets of its white linen, and holy vessels, and fonts of pure water; and its hier-atic purity and simplicity became the type of something he desired always to have about him in actual life. He pored over the pictures in religious books, and knew by heart the exact mode in which the wrestling angel grasped Jacob, how Jacob looked in his mysterious sleep, how the bells and pomegranates were attached to the hem of Aaron's vest-ment,[20] sounding sweetly as he glided over the turf of the holy place. His way of conceiving religion came then to be in effect what it ever afterwards remained—a sacred history indeed, but still more a sacred ideal, a transcendent version or representation, under intenser and more expressive light and shade, of human life and its familiar or exceptional inci-dents, birth, death, marriage, youth, age, tears, joy, rest, sleep, waking—a mirror, towards which men might turn

---

16"resurrection of the just": Luke 14:14.

17Joshua's Vision: Joshua 5:13–15.

18*revenants*: ghosts.

19"lively hope": 1 Peter 1:3.

20Jacob: Genesis 32:24, 28:11–15. **Aaron's vestment**: Exodus 39:24–26.

away their eyes from vanity and dullness, and see themselves therein as angels, with their daily meat and drink, even, become a kind of sacred transaction—a complementary strain or burden, applied to our every-day existence, whereby the stray snatches of music in it re-set themselves, and fall into the scheme of some higher and more consistent harmony. A place adumbrated itself in his thoughts, wherein those sacred personalities, which are at once the reflex and the pattern of our nobler phases of life, housed themselves; and this region in his intellectual scheme all subsequent experience did but tend still further to realise and define. Some ideal, hieratic persons he would always need to occupy it and keep a warmth there. And he could hardly understand those who felt no such need at all, finding themselves quite happy without such heavenly companionship, and sacred double of their life, beside them.

Thus a constant substitution of the typical for the actual took place in his thoughts. Angels might be met by the way, under English elm or beech-tree; mere messengers seemed like angels, bound on celestial errands; a deep mysticity brooded over real meetings and partings; marriages were made in heaven; and deaths also, with hands of angels thereupon, to bear soul and body quietly asunder, each to its appointed rest. All the acts and accidents of daily life borrowed a sacred colour and significance; the very colours of things became themselves weighty with meanings like the sacred stuffs of Moses' tabernacle,[21] full of penitence or peace. Sentiment, congruous in the first instance only with those divine transactions, the deep, effusive unction of the House of Bethany, was assumed as the due attitude for the reception of our every-day existence; and for a time he walked through the world in a sustained, not unpleasurable awe, generated by the habitual recognition, beside every circumstance and event of life, of its celestial correspondent.

Sensibility—the desire of physical beauty—a strange biblical awe, which made any reference to the unseen act on him like solemn music—these qualities the child took away with him, when, at about the age of twelve years, he left the old house, and was taken to live in another place. He had never left home before, and, anticipating much from this change, had long dreamed over it, jealously counting the days till the time fixed for departure should come; had been a little careless about others even, in his strong desire for it—when Lewis fell sick, for instance, and they must wait still two days longer. At last the morning came, very fine; and all

things—the very pavement with its dust, at the roadside—seemed to have a white, pearl-like lustre in them. They were to travel by a favourite road on which he had often walked a certain distance, and on one of those two prisoner days, when Lewis was sick, had walked farther than ever before, in his great desire to reach the new place. They had started and gone a little way when a pet bird was found to have been left behind, and must even now—so it presented itself to him—have already all the appealing fierceness and wild self-pity at heart of one left by others to perish of hunger in a closed house; and he returned to fetch it, himself in hardly less stormy distress. But as he passed in search of it from room to room, lying so pale, with a look of meekness in their denudation, and at last through that little, stripped white room, the aspect of the place touched him like the face of one dead; and a clinging back towards it came over him, so intense that he knew it would last long, and spoiling all his pleasure in the realisation of a thing so eagerly anticipated. And so, with the bird found, but himself in an agony of home-sickness, thus capriciously sprung up within him, he was driven quickly away, far into the rural distance, so fondly speculated on, of that favourite country-road.

1878

from **Postscript to** *Appreciations*

αἰνεῖ δὲ παλαιὸν μὲν οἶνον, ἄνθεα δ' ὕμνων νεωτέρων[1]

The words, *classical* and *romantic*, although, like many other critical expressions, sometimes abused by those who have understood them too vaguely or too absolutely, yet define two real tendencies in the history of art and literature. Used in an exaggerated sense, to express a greater opposition between those tendencies than really exists, they have at times tended to divide people of taste into opposite camps. But in that *House Beautiful*, which the creative minds of all generations—the artists and those who have treated life in the spirit of art—are always building together, for the refreshment of the human spirit, these oppositions cease; and the *Interpreter* of the *House Beautiful*,[2] the true æsthetic critic, uses

---

[21]**Moses' tabernacle:** see Exodus 25–27. **House of Bethany:** see Matthew 26:6–13.

[1]αἰνεῖ . . . νεωτέρων: When you praise the old wine, praise too the flowers of newer songs (Pindar's *Olympian Odes* 9.48–49). Pater first published this essay in 1876 as "Romanticism."

[2]*Interpreter, House Beautiful:* from John Bunyan's *Pilgrim's Progress* (1678).

these divisions, only so far as they enable him to enter into the peculiarities of the objects with which he has to do. The term *classical*, fixed, as it is, to a well-defined literature, and a well-defined group in art, is clear, indeed; but then it has often been used in a hard, and merely scholastic sense, by the praisers of what is old and accustomed, at the expense of what is new, by critics who would never have discovered for themselves the charm of any work, whether new or old, who value what is old, in art or literature, for its accessories, and chiefly for the conventional authority that has gathered about it—people who would never really have been made glad by any Venus fresh-risen from the sea, and who praise the Venus of old Greece and Rome, only because they fancy her grown now into something staid and tame.

And as the term, *classical*, has been used in a too absolute, and therefore in a misleading sense, so the term, *romantic*, has been used much too vaguely, in various accidental senses. The sense in which Scott is called a romantic writer is chiefly this; that, in opposition to the literary tradition of the last century, he loved strange adventure, and sought it in the Middle Age. Much later, in a Yorkshire village, the spirit of romanticism bore a more really characteristic fruit in the work of a young girl, Emily Brontë, the romance of *Wuthering Heights*[3]; the figures of Hareton Earnshaw, of Catherine Linton, and of Heathcliff—tearing open Catherine's grave, removing one side of her coffin, that he may really lie beside her in death—figures so passionate, yet woven on a background of delicately beautiful, moorland scenery, being typical examples of that spirit. In Germany, again, that spirit is shown less in Tieck, its professional representative, than in Meinhold,[4] the author of *Sidonia the Sorceress* and the *Amber-Witch*. In Germany and France, within the last hundred years, the term has been used to describe a particular school of writers; and, consequently, when Heine criticises the *Romantic School* in Germany—that movement which culminated in Goethe's *Goetz von Berlichingen*; or when Théophile Gautier criticises the romantic movement in France,[5] where, indeed, it bore its most characteristic fruits, and its play is hardly yet over, where, by a certain audacity,

or *bizarrerie* of motive, united with faultless literary execution, it still shows itself in imaginative literature, they use the word, with an exact sense of special artistic qualities, indeed; but use it, nevertheless, with a limited application to the manifestation of those qualities at a particular period. But the romantic spirit is, in reality, an ever-present, an enduring principle, in the artistic temperament; and the qualities of thought and style which that, and other similar uses of the word *romantic* really indicate, are indeed but symptoms of a very continuous and widely working influence.

Though the words *classical* and *romantic*, then, have acquired an almost technical meaning, in application to certain developments of German and French taste, yet this is but one variation of an old opposition, which may be traced from the very beginning of the formation of European art and literature. From the first formation of anything like a standard of taste in these things, the restless curiosity of their more eager lovers necessarily made itself felt, in the craving for new motives, new subjects of interest, new modifications of style. Hence, the opposition between the classicists and the romanticists—between the adherents, in the culture of beauty, of the principles of liberty, and authority, respectively—of strength, and order or what the Greeks called κοσμιότης.[6]

Sainte-Beuve, in the third volume of the *Causeries du Lundi*,[7] has discussed the question, *What is meant by a classic?* It was a question he was well fitted to answer, having himself lived through many phases of taste, and having been in earlier life an enthusiastic member of the romantic school: he was also a great master of that sort of "philosophy of literature," which delights in tracing traditions in it, and the way in which various phases of thought and sentiment maintain themselves, through successive modifications, from epoch to epoch. His aim, then, is to give the word *classic* a wider and, as he says, a more generous sense than it commonly bears, to make it expressly *grandiose et flottant*;[8] and, in doing this, he develops, in a masterly manner, those qualities of measure, purity, temperance, of which it is the especial function of classical art and literature, whatever meaning, narrower or wider, we attach to the term, to take care.

The charm, therefore, of what is classical, in art or literature, is that of the well-known tale, to which we can,

---

[3] *Wuthering Heights*: published 1847. Sir Walter **Scott**: died 1832. On **Brontë's Yorkshire** see Elizabeth Gaskell, page 524.

[4] Johann Ludwig **Tieck** (1773–1853). Wilhelm **Meinhold** (1797–1851).

[5] Heinrich **Heine** (1797–1856): *The Romantic School*, 1836. Johann Wolfgang von **Goethe** (1749–1832): *Goetz von Berlichingen*, 1773. **Théophile Gautier** (1811–1872): *The History of Romanticism*, 1874.

[6] κοσμιότης: orderliness; here Pater associates authority with classicism and liberty with romanticism.

[7] Charles-Augustin **Sainte-Beuve** (1804–1869): French critic whose *Causeries du Lundi* (1851–1862) or "Monday Chats" collected his weekly essays from Paris newspapers.

[8] *grandiose et flottant*: grand and flowing.

nevertheless, listen over and over again, because it is told so well. To the absolute beauty of its artistic form, is added the accidental, tranquil, charm of familiarity. There are times, indeed, at which these charms fail to work on our spirits at all, because they fail to excite us. *"Romanticism,"* says Stendhal, "is the art of presenting to people the literary works which, in the actual state of their habits and beliefs, are capable of giving them the greatest possible pleasure; *classicism,* on the contrary, of presenting them with that which gave the greatest possible pleasure to their grandfathers."[9] But then, beneath all changes of habits and beliefs, our love of that mere abstract proportion—of music—which what is classical in literature possesses, still maintains itself in the best of us, and what pleased our grandparents may at least tranquillise us. The "classic" comes to us out of the cool and quiet of other times, as the measure of what a long experience has shown will at least never displease us. And in the classical literature of Greece and Rome, as in the classics of the last century, the essentially classical element is that quality of order in beauty, which they possess, indeed, in a pre-eminent degree, and which impresses some minds to the exclusion of everything else in them.

It is the addition of strangeness to beauty, that constitutes the romantic character in art; and the desire of beauty being a fixed element in every artistic organisation, it is the addition of curiosity to this desire of beauty, that constitutes the romantic temper. Curiosity and the desire of beauty,[10] have each their place in art, as in all true criticism. When one's curiosity is deficient, when one is not eager enough for new impressions, and new pleasures, one is liable to value mere academical proprieties too highly, to be satisfied with worn-out or conventional types, with the insipid ornament of Racine,[11] or the prettiness of that later Greek sculpture, which passed so long for true Hellenic work; to miss those places where the handiwork of nature, or of the artist, has been most cunning; to find the most stimulating products of art a mere irritation. And when one's curiosity is in excess, when it overbalances the desire of beauty, then one is liable to value in works of art what is inartistic in them; to be satisfied with what is exaggerated in art, with productions like some of those of the romantic school in Germany; not to

distinguish, jealously enough, between what is admirably done, and what is done not quite so well, in the writings, for instance, of Jean Paul.[12] And if I had to give instances of these defects, then I should say, that Pope, in common with the age of literature to which he belonged, had too little curiosity, so that there is always a certain insipidity in the effect of his work, exquisite as it is; and, coming down to our own time, that Balzac[13] had an excess of curiosity—curiosity not duly tempered with the desire of beauty.

But, however falsely those two tendencies may be opposed by critics, or exaggerated by artists themselves, they are tendencies really at work at all times in art, moulding it, with the balance sometimes a little on one side, sometimes a little on the other, generating, respectively, as the balance inclines on this side or that, two principles, two traditions, in art, and in literature so far as it partakes of the spirit of art. If there is a great overbalance of curiosity, then, we have the grotesque in art: if the union of strangeness and beauty, under very difficult and complex conditions, be a successful one, if the union be entire, then the resultant beauty is very exquisite, very attractive. With a passionate care for beauty, the romantic spirit refuses to have it, unless the condition of strangeness be first fulfilled. Its desire is for a beauty born of unlikely elements, by a profound alchemy, by a difficult initiation, by the charm which wrings it even out of terrible things; and a trace of distortion, of the grotesque, may perhaps linger, as an additional element of expression, about its ultimate grace. . . .

For, although temperament has much to do with the generation of the romantic spirit, and although this spirit, with its curiosity, its thirst for a curious beauty, may be always traceable in excellent art (traceable even in Sophocles) yet still, in a limited sense, it may be said to be a product of special epochs. Outbreaks of this spirit, that is, come naturally with particular periods—times, when, in men's approaches towards art and poetry, curiosity may be noticed to take the lead, when men come to art and poetry, with a deep thirst for intellectual excitement, after a long *ennui,* or in reaction against the strain of outward, practical things: in the later Middle Age, for instance; so that medieval poetry, centering in Dante, is often opposed to Greek and Roman poetry, as romantic poetry to the classical. What the romanticism of Dante is, may be estimated, if we compare the lines in which Virgil describes the hazel-wood, from whose

---

[9]**"Romanticism . . . grandfathers"**: from *Racine et Shakespeare* (1823–1825) by **Stendhal** (pen name of Henri Beyle, 1783–1842).

[10]**curiosity and the desire of beauty**: "the two elementary forces in Leonardo's genius" in Pater's own 1869 "Leonardo da Vinci" (see page 955).

[11]Jean **Racine** (1639–1699): French tragic dramatist.

---

[12]**Jean Paul**: pen name of Johann Paul Friedrich Richter (1763–1825), German Romantic novelist.

[13]Honoré de **Balzac** (1799–1850): French novelist.

broken twigs flows the blood of Polydorus, not without the expression of a real shudder at the ghastly incident, with the whole canto of the *Inferno*, into which Dante[14] has expanded them, beautifying and softening it, meanwhile, by a sentiment of profound pity. And it is especially in that period of intellectual disturbance, immediately preceding Dante, amid which the romance languages define themselves at last, that this temper is manifested. Here, in the literature of Provence,[15] the very name of *romanticism* is stamped with its true signification: here we have indeed a romantic world, grotesque even, in the strength of its passions, almost insane in its curious expression of them, drawing all things into its sphere, making the birds, nay! lifeless things, its voices and messengers, yet so penetrated with the desire for beauty and sweetness, that it begets a wholly new species of poetry, in which the *Renaissance* may be said to begin. The last century was pre-eminently a classical age, an age in which, for art and literature, the element of a comely order was in the ascendant; which, passing away, left a hard battle to be fought between the classical and the romantic schools. Yet, it is in the heart of this century, of Goldsmith and Stothard, of Watteau and the *Siècle de Louis XIV.*—in one of its central, if not most characteristic figures, in Rousseau[16]—that the modern or French romanticism really originates. But, what in the eighteenth century is but an exceptional phenomenon, breaking through its fair reserve and discretion only at rare intervals, is the habitual guise of the nineteenth, breaking through it perpetually, with a feverishness, an incomprehensible straining and excitement, which all experience to some degree, but yearning also, in the genuine children of the romantic school, to be *énergique, frais, et dispos*—for those qualities of energy, freshness, comely order; and often, in Murger, in Gautier, in Victor Hugo,[17] for instance, with singular felicity attaining them. . . .

Romanticism, then, although it has its epochs, is in its essential characteristics rather a spirit which shows itself at all times, in various degrees, in individual workmen and their work, and the amount of which criticism has to estimate in them taken one by one, than the peculiarity of a time or a school. Depending on the varying proportion of curiosity and the desire of beauty, natural tendencies of the artistic spirit at all times, it must always be partly a matter of individual temperament. The eighteenth century in England has been regarded as almost exclusively a classical period; yet William Blake,[18] a type of so much which breaks through what are conventionally thought the influences of that century, is still a noticeable phenomenon in it, and the reaction in favour of naturalism in poetry begins in that century, early. There are, thus, the born romanticists and the born classicists. There are the born classicists who start with *form*, to whose minds the comeliness of the old, immemorial, well-recognised types in art and literature, have revealed themselves impressively; who will entertain no matter which will not go easily and flexibly into them; whose work aspires only to be a variation upon, or study from, the older masters. " 'Tis art's decline, my son!"[19] they are always saying, to the progressive element in their own generation; to those who care for that which in fifty years' time every one will be caring for. On the other hand, there are the born romanticists, who start with an original, untried *matter*, still in fusion; who conceive this vividly, and hold by it as the essence of their work; who, by the very vividness and heat of their conception, purge away, sooner or later, all that is not organically appropriate to it, till the whole effect adjusts itself in clear, orderly, proportionate form; which form, after a very little time, becomes classical in its turn.

The romantic or classical character of a picture, a poem, a literary work, depends, then, on the balance of certain qualities in it; and in this sense, a very real distinction may be drawn between good classical and good romantic work. But all critical terms are relative; and there is at least a valuable suggestion in that theory of Stendhal's, that all good art was romantic in its day. In the beauties of Homer and Pheidias,[20] quiet as they now seem, there must have been, for those who confronted them for the first time, excitement and surprise, the sudden, unforeseen satisfaction of the desire of beauty. Yet the *Odyssey*, with its marvellous adventure, is more romantic

---

[14]**Virgil:** see *Aeneid* 3.19–72. **Dante:** see *Inferno* 13.

[15]**literature of Provence:** troubadour poetry from the feudal courts of southern France, northern Italy, and Spain.

[16]Oliver **Goldsmith** (1730–1774): Anglo-Irish poet, playwright and novelist. Thomas **Stothard** (1755–1834): English painter. Jean-Antoine **Watteau** (1684–1721): French painter. *Siècle de Louis XIV:* Voltaire's 1751 study of the Louis Quatorze epoch. Jean-Jacques **Rousseau** (1712–1778): Swiss author and philosopher.

[17]*énergique, frais, et dispos:* vigorous, fresh, and poised (quoting Sainte-Beuve). Henri **Murger** (1822–1861): French novelist. **Victor Hugo** (1802–1885): French Romantic poet, playwright, and novelist.

[18]**William Blake** (1757–1827): visionary artist and poet who first attained wide recognition in Pater's lifetime. See Swinburne, page 926.

[19]" 'Tis art's decline, my son": see Robert Browning's "Fra Lippo Lippi" 233.

[20]**Pheidias** (490?–430 BCE): Athenian sculptor.

than the *Iliad*, which nevertheless contains, among many other romantic episodes, that of the immortal horses of Achilles, who weep at the death of Patroclus. Æschylus is more romantic than Sophocles, whose *Philoctetes*,[21] were it written now, might figure, for the strangeness of its motive and the perfectness of its execution, as typically romantic; while, of Euripides, it may be said, that his method in writing his plays is to sacrifice readily almost everything else, so that he may attain the fulness of a single romantic effect. These two tendencies, indeed, might be applied as a measure or standard, all through Greek and Roman art and poetry, with very illuminating results; and for an analyst of the romantic principle in art, no exercise would be more profitable, than to walk through the collection of classical antiquities at the Louvre, or the British Museum, or to examine some representative collection of Greek coins, and note how the element of curiosity, of the love of strangeness, insinuates itself into classical design, and record the effects of the romantic spirit there, the traces of struggle, of the grotesque even, though overbalanced here by sweetness; as in the sculpture of Chartres and Rheims, the real sweetness of mind in the sculptor is often overbalanced by the grotesque, by the rudeness of his strength.

Classicism, then, means for Stendhal, for that younger enthusiastic band of French writers whose unconscious method he formulated into principles, the reign of what is pedantic, conventional, and narrowly academical in art; for him, all good art is romantic. To Sainte-Beuve, who understands the term in a more liberal sense, it is the characteristic of certain epochs, of certain spirits in every epoch, not given to the exercise of original imagination, but rather to the working out of refinements of manner on some authorised matter; and who bring to their perfection, in this way, the elements of sanity, of order and beauty in manner. In general criticism, again, it means the spirit of Greece and Rome, of some phases in literature and art that may seem of equal authority with Greece and Rome, the age of Louis the Fourteenth, the age of Johnson[22]; though this is at best an uncritical use of the term, because in Greek and Roman work there are typical examples of the romantic spirit. But explain the terms as we may, in application to particular epochs, there are these two elements always recognisable; united in perfect art—in Sophocles, in Dante, in the highest work of Goethe, though not always absolutely balanced there; and these two elements may be not inappropriately termed the classical and romantic tendencies.

Material for the artist, motives of inspiration, are not yet exhausted: our curious, complex, aspiring age still abounds in subjects for æsthetic manipulation by the literary as well as by other forms of art. For the literary art, at all events, the problem just now is, to induce order upon the contorted, proportionless accumulation of our knowledge and experience, our science and history, our hopes and disillusion, and, in effecting this, to do consciously what has been done hitherto for the most part too unconsciously, to write our English language as the Latins wrote theirs, as the French write, as scholars should write. Appealing, as he may, to precedent in this matter, the scholar will still remember that if "the style is the man"[23] it is also the age: that the nineteenth century too will be found to have had its style, justified by necessity—a style very different, alike from the baldness of an impossible "Queen Anne" revival, and an incorrect, incondite exuberance, after the mode of Elizabeth[24]: that we can only return to either at the price of an impoverishment of form or matter, or both, although, an intellectually rich age such as ours being necessarily an eclectic one, we may well cultivate some of the excellences of literary types so different as those: that in literature as in other matters it is well to unite as many diverse elements as may be: that the individual writer or artist, certainly, is to be estimated by the number of graces he combines, and his power of interpenetrating them in a given work. To discriminate schools, of art, of literature, is, of course, part of the obvious business of literary criticism: but, in the work of literary production, it is easy to be overmuch occupied concerning them. For, in truth, the legitimate contention is, not of one age or school of literary art against another, but of all successive schools alike, against the stupidity which is dead to the substance, and the vulgarity which is dead to form.

1876, 1888

from Style

Since all progress of mind consists for the most part in differentiation, in the resolution of an obscure and complex

---

[21]*Philoctetes*: Greek tragedy (409 BCE) based on a grotesque affliction, a festering wound.

[22]**age of Louis the Fourteenth, age of Johnson**: eras of French and English neoclassicism.

[23]**"the style is the man"**: from Comte de Buffon's address to the Académie Française in 1753.

[24]**"Queen Anne" revival, mode of Elizabeth**: two fashions in Victorian architecture as well as literature.

object into its component aspects, it is surely the stupidest of losses to confuse things which right reason has put asunder, to lose the sense of achieved distinctions, the distinction between poetry and prose, for instance, or, to speak more exactly, between the laws and characteristic excellences of verse and prose composition. On the other hand, those who have dwelt most emphatically on the distinction between prose and verse, prose and poetry, may sometimes have been tempted to limit the proper functions of prose too narrowly; and this again is at least false economy, as being, in effect, the renunciation of a certain means or faculty, in a world where after all we must needs make the most of things. Critical efforts to limit art *a priori*,[1] by anticipations regarding the natural incapacity of the material with which this or that artist works, as the sculptor with solid form, or the prose-writer with the ordinary language of men, are always liable to be discredited by the facts of artistic production; and while prose is actually found to be a coloured thing with Bacon, picturesque with Livy and Carlyle, musical with Cicero and Newman, mystical and intimate with Plato and Michelet and Sir Thomas Browne, exalted or florid, it may be, with Milton and Taylor,[2] it will be useless to protest that it can be nothing at all, except something very tamely and narrowly confined to mainly practical ends—a kind of "good round-hand;"[3] as useless as the protest that poetry might not touch prosaic subjects as with Wordsworth, or an abstruse matter as with Browning, or treat contemporary life nobly as with Tennyson. In subordination to one essential beauty in all good literary style, in all literature as a fine art, as there are many beauties of poetry so the beauties of prose are many, and it is the business of criticism to estimate them as such; as it is good in the criticism of verse to look for those hard, logical, and quasi-prosaic excellences which that too has, or needs. To find in the poem, amid the flowers, the allusions, the mixed perspectives, of *Lycidas*[4] for instance, the thought, the logical structure:—how wholesome! how delightful! as to identify in prose what we call the poetry, the imaginative power, not treating it as out of place and a kind of vagrant

intruder, but by way of an estimate of its rights, that is, of its achieved powers, there.

Dryden,[5] with the characteristic instinct of his age, loved to emphasise the distinction between poetry and prose, the protest against their confusion with each other, coming with somewhat diminished effect from one whose poetry was so prosaic. In truth, his sense of prosaic excellence affected his verse rather than his prose, which is not only fervid, richly figured, poetic, as we say, but vitiated, all unconsciously, by many a scanning line.[6] Setting up correctness, that humble merit of prose, as the central literary excellence, he is really a less correct writer than he may seem, still with an imperfect mastery of the relative pronoun. It might have been foreseen that, in the rotations of mind, the province of poetry in prose would find its assertor; and, a century after Dryden, amid very different intellectual needs, and with the need therefore of great modifications in literary form, the range of the poetic force in literature was effectively enlarged by Wordsworth.[7] The true distinction between prose and poetry he regarded as the almost technical or accidental one of the absence or presence of metrical beauty, or, say! metrical restraint; and for him the opposition came to be between verse and prose of course; but, as the essential dichotomy in this matter, between imaginative and unimaginative writing, parallel to De Quincey's[8] distinction between "the literature of power and the literature of knowledge," in the former of which the composer gives us not fact, but his peculiar sense of fact, whether past or present.

Dismissing then, under sanction of Wordsworth, that harsher opposition of poetry to prose, as savouring in fact of the arbitrary psychology of the last century, and with it the prejudice that there can be but one only beauty of prose style, I propose here to point out certain qualities of all literature as a fine art, which, if they apply to the literature of fact, apply still more to the literature of the imaginative sense of fact, while they apply indifferently to verse and prose, so far as either is really imaginative—certain conditions of true art in both alike, which conditions may also contain in them the secret of the proper discrimination and guardianship of the peculiar excellences of either.

---

[1]*a priori*: by theoretical reasoning, not from experience.

[2]**Livy** (Titus Livius, 59 BCE–17?): Roman historian. Marcus Tullius **Cicero** (106–43 BCE): Roman statesman and orator. Jules **Michelet** (1798–1874): French historian. **Sir Thomas Browne** (1605–1682): English physician and author. Jeremy **Taylor** (1613–1667): Anglican churchman.

[3]"**good round-hand**": fine penmanship.

[4]*Lycidas*: Milton's famous elegy (1638).

[5]John **Dryden** (1631–1700): English dramatist, poet, and critic. See his critical essay *Of Dramatic Poesie* (1668).

[6]**scanning line**: passage exhibiting metrical regularity.

[7]**Wordsworth**: in the Preface to *Lyrical Ballads* (1800).

[8]Thomas **De Quincey** (1785–1859): English writer, quoted from a review essay of 1848 on Pope.

The line between fact and something quite different from external fact is, indeed, hard to draw. In Pascal,[9] for instance, in the persuasive writers generally, how difficult to define the point where, from time to time, argument which, if it is to be worth anything at all, must consist of facts or groups of facts, becomes a pleading—a theorem no longer, but essentially an appeal to the reader to catch the writer's spirit, to think with him, if one can or will—an expression no longer of fact but of his sense of it, his peculiar intuition of a world, prospective, or discerned below the faulty conditions of the present, in either case changed somewhat from the actual world. In science, on the other hand, in history so far as it conforms to scientific rule, we have a literary domain where the imagination may be thought to be always an intruder. And as, in all science, the functions of literature reduce themselves eventually to the transcribing of fact, so all the excellences of literary form in regard to science are reducible to various kinds of painstaking; this good quality being involved in all "skilled work" whatever, in the drafting of an act of parliament, as in sewing. Yet here again, the writer's sense of fact, in history especially, and in all those complex subjects which do but lie on the borders of science, will still take the place of fact, in various degrees. Your historian, for instance, with absolutely truthful intention, amid the multitude of facts presented to him must needs select, and in selecting assert something of his own humour, something that comes not of the world without but of a vision within. So Gibbon[10] moulds his unwieldy material to a preconceived view. Livy, Tacitus, Michelet, moving full of poignant sensibility amid the records of the past, each, after his own sense, modifies—who can tell where and to what degree?—and becomes something else than a transcriber; each, as he thus modifies, passing into the domain of art proper. For just in proportion as the writer's aim, consciously or unconsciously, comes to be the transcribing, not of the world, not of mere fact, but of his sense of it, he becomes an artist, his work *fine* art; and good art (as I hope ultimately to show) in proportion to the truth of his presentment of that sense; as in those humbler or plainer functions of literature also, truth—truth to bare fact, there—is the essence of such artistic quality as they may have. Truth! there can be no merit, no craft at all, without that. And further, all beauty is in the long run only *fineness* of

truth, or what we call expression, the finer accommodation of speech to that vision within.

—The transcript of his sense of fact rather than the fact, as being preferable, pleasanter, more beautiful to the writer himself. In literature, as in every other product of human skill, in the moulding of a bell or a platter for instance, wherever this sense asserts itself, wherever the producer so modifies his work as, over and above its primary use or intention, to make it pleasing (to himself, of course, in the first instance) there, "fine" as opposed to merely serviceable art, exists. Literary art, that is, like all art which is in any way imitative or reproductive of fact—form, or colour, or incident—is the representation of such fact as connected with soul, of a specific personality, in its preferences, its volition and power.

Such is the matter of imaginative or artistic literature—this transcript, not of mere fact, but of fact in its infinite variety, as modified by human preference in all its infinitely varied forms. It will be good literary art not because it is brilliant or sober, or rich, or impulsive, or severe, but just in proportion as its representation of that sense, that soul-fact, is true, verse being only one department of such literature, and imaginative prose, it may be thought, being the special art of the modern world. That imaginative prose should be the special and opportune art of the modern world results from two important facts about the latter: first, the chaotic variety and complexity of its interests, making the intellectual issue, the really master currents of the present time incalculable—a condition of mind little susceptible of the restraint proper to verse form, so that the most characteristic verse of the nineteenth century has been lawless verse; and secondly, an all-pervading naturalism, a curiosity about everything whatever as it really is, involving a certain humility of attitude, cognate to what must, after all, be the less ambitious form of literature. And prose thus asserting itself as the special and privileged artistic faculty of the present day, will be, however critics may try to narrow its scope, as varied in its excellence as humanity itself reflecting on the facts of its latest experience—an instrument of many stops, meditative, observant, descriptive, eloquent, analytic, plaintive, fervid. Its beauties will be not exclusively "pedestrian": it will exert, in due measure, all the varied charms of poetry, down to the rhythm which, as in Cicero, or Michelet, or Newman, at their best, gives its musical value to every syllable.

The literary artist is of necessity a scholar, and in what he proposes to do will have in mind, first of all, the scholar and the scholarly conscience—the male conscience in this matter, as we must think it, under a system of education which still to so large an extent limits real scholarship to men. In his self-criticism, he supposes always that sort of

---

[9]Blaise **Pascal** (1623–1662): French mathematician, physicist, and theologian.

[10]Edward **Gibbon** (1737–1794): author of *History of the Decline and Fall of the Roman Empire* (1776–1788). **Tacitus** (56–120?): Roman historian.

reader who will go (full of eyes) warily, considerately, though without consideration for him, over the ground which the female conscience traverses so lightly, so amiably. For the material in which he works is no more a creation of his own than the sculptor's marble. Product of a myriad various minds and contending tongues, compact of obscure and minute association, a language has its own abundant and often recondite laws, in the habitual and summary recognition of which scholarship consists. A writer, full of a matter he is before all things anxious to express, may think of those laws, the limitations of vocabulary, structure, and the like, as a restriction, but if a real artist will find in them an opportunity. His punctilious observance of the proprieties of his medium will diffuse through all he writes a general air of sensibility, of refined usage. *Exclusiones debitæ naturæ*—the exclusions, or rejections, which nature demands—we know how large a part these play, according to Bacon,[11] in the science of nature. In a somewhat changed sense, we might say that the art of the scholar is summed up in the observance of those rejections demanded by the nature of his medium, the material he must use. Alive to the value of an atmosphere in which every term finds its utmost degree of expression, and with all the jealousy of a lover of words, he will resist a constant tendency on the part of the majority of those who use them to efface the distinctions of language, the facility of writers often reinforcing in this respect the work of the vulgar. He will feel the obligation not of the laws only, but of those affinities, avoidances, those mere preferences, of his language, which through the associations of literary history have become a part of its nature, prescribing the rejection of many a neology,[12] many a license, many a gipsy phrase which might present itself as actually expressive. His appeal, again, is to the scholar, who has great experience in literature, and will show no favour to short-cuts, or hackneyed illustration, or an affectation of learning designed for the unlearned. Hence a contention, a sense of self-restraint and renunciation, having for the susceptible reader the effect of a challenge for minute consideration; the attention of the writer, in every minutest detail, being a pledge that it is worth the reader's while to be attentive too, that the writer is dealing scrupulously with his instrument, and therefore, indirectly, with the reader himself also, that he has the science of the instrument he plays on, perhaps, after all, with a freedom which in such case will be the freedom of a master.

For meanwhile, braced only by those restraints, he is really vindicating his liberty in the making of a vocabulary, an entire system of composition, for himself, his own true manner; and when we speak of the manner of a true master we mean what is essential in his art. Pedantry being only the scholarship of *le cuistre*[13] (we have no English equivalent) he is no pedant, and does but show his intelligence of the rules of language in his freedoms with it, addition or expansion, which like the spontaneities of manner in a well-bred person will still further illustrate good taste.—The right vocabulary! Translators have not invariably seen how all-important that is in the work of translation, driving for the most part at idiom or construction; whereas, if the original be first-rate, one's first care should be with its elementary particles, Plato, for instance, being often reproducible by an exact following, with no variation in structure, of word after word, as the pencil follows a drawing under tracing-paper, so only each word or syllable be not of false colour, to change my illustration a little.

Well! that is because any writer worth translating at all has winnowed and searched through his vocabulary, is conscious of the words he would select in systematic reading of a dictionary, and still more of the words he would reject were the dictionary other than Johnson's;[14] and doing this with his peculiar sense of the world ever in view, in search of an instrument for the adequate expression of that, he begets a vocabulary faithful to the colouring of his own spirit, and in the strictest sense original. That living authority which language needs lies, in truth, in its scholars, who recognising always that every language possesses a genius, a very fastidious genius, of its own, expand at once and purify its very elements, which must needs change along with the changing thoughts of living people. Ninety years ago, for instance, great mental force, certainly, was needed by Wordsworth, to break through the consecrated poetic associations of a century, and speak the language that was his, that was to become in a measure the language of the next generation. But he did it with the tact of a scholar also. English, for a quarter of a century past, has been assimilating the phraseology of pictorial art; for half a century, the phraseology of the great German metaphysical movement of eighty years ago; in part also the language of mystical theology: and none but pedants will regret a great consequent increase of its resources. For many years to come its enterprise may well lie in the naturalisation of the vocabulary of science, so only

---

[11]Francis **Bacon** (1561–1626): philosopher, statesman, and essayist. *Exclusiones debitae naturae:* from his *Novum Organum* (1620) 2.18.

[12]**neology:** new word.

[13]*cuistre:* petty chef.

[14]Samuel **Johnson** (1709–1784): compiled *A Dictionary of the English Language* (1755).

it be under the eye of a sensitive scholarship—in a liberal naturalisation of the ideas of science too, for after all the chief stimulus of good style is to possess a full, rich, complex matter to grapple with. The literary artist, therefore, will be well aware of physical science; science also attaining, in its turn, its true literary ideal. And then, as the scholar is nothing without the historic sense, he will be apt to restore not really obsolete or really worn-out words, but the finer edge of words still in use: *ascertain, communicate, discover*—words like these it has been part of our "business" to misuse. And still, as language was made for man, he will be no authority for correctnesses which, limiting freedom of utterance, were yet but accidents in their origin; as if one vowed not to say *"its,"* which ought to have been in Shakespeare; *"his"* and *"hers,"* for inanimate objects, being but a barbarous and really inexpressive survival. Yet we have known many things like this. Racy Saxon monosyllables, close to us as touch and sight, he will intermix readily with those long, savoursome, Latin words, rich in "second intention."[15] In this late day certainly, no critical process can be conducted reasonably without eclecticism. Of such eclecticism we have a justifying example in one of the first poets of our time. How illustrative of monosyllabic effect, of sonorous Latin, of the phraseology of science, of metaphysic, of colloquialism even, are the writings of Tennyson; yet with what a fine, fastidious scholarship throughout!

A scholar writing for the scholarly, he will of course leave something to the willing intelligence of his reader. "To go preach to the first passer-by," says Montaigne,[16] "to become tutor to the ignorance of the first I meet, is a thing I abhor;" a thing, in fact, naturally distressing to the scholar, who will therefore ever be shy of offering uncomplimentary assistance to the reader's wit. To really strenuous minds there is a pleasurable stimulus in the challenge for a continuous effort on their part, to be rewarded by securer and more intimate grasp of the author's sense. Self-restraint, a skilful economy of means, *ascêsis,*[17] that too has a beauty of its own; and for the reader supposed there will be an æsthetic satisfaction in that frugal closeness of style which makes the most of a word, in the exaction from every sentence of a precise relief, in the just spacing out of word to thought, in the logically filled space connected always with the delightful sense of difficulty overcome.

Different classes of persons, at different times, make, of course, very various demands upon literature. Still, scholars, I suppose, and not only scholars, but all disinterested lovers of books, will always look to it, as to all other fine art, for a refuge, a sort of cloistral refuge, from a certain vulgarity in the actual world. A perfect poem like *Lycidas,* a perfect fiction like *Esmond,*[18] the perfect handling of a theory like Newman's *Idea of a University,* has for them something of the uses of a religious "retreat." Here, then, with a view to the central need of a select few, those "men of a finer thread" who have formed and maintain the literary ideal, everything, every component element, will have undergone exact trial, and, above all, there will be no uncharacteristic or tarnished or vulgar decoration, permissible ornament being for the most part structural, or necessary. As the painter in his picture, so the artist in his book, aims at the production by honourable artifice of a peculiar atmosphere. "The artist," says Schiller,[19] "may be known rather by what he *omits*"; and in literature, too, the true artist may be best recognised by his tact of omission. For to the grave reader words too are grave; and the ornamental word, the figure, the accessory form or colour or reference, is rarely content to die to thought precisely at the right moment, but will inevitably linger awhile, stirring a long "brainwave" behind it of perhaps quite alien associations.

Just there, it may be, is the detrimental tendency of the sort of scholarly attentiveness of mind I am recommending. But the true artist allows for it. He will remember that, as the very word ornament indicates what is in itself nonessential, so the "one beauty" of all literary style is of its very essence, and independent, in prose and verse alike, of all removable decoration; that it may exist in its fullest lustre, as in Flaubert's *Madame Bovary,* for instance, or in Stendhal's *Le Rouge et Le Noir,* in a composition utterly unadorned, with hardly a single suggestion of visibly beautiful things. Parallel, allusion, the allusive way generally, the flowers in the garden:—he knows the narcotic force of these upon the negligent intelligence to which any *diversion,* literally, is welcome, any vagrant intruder, because one can go wandering away with it from the immediate subject. Jealous, if he have a really quickening motive within, of all that does not hold directly to that, of the facile, the otiose, he will never depart from the strictly pedestrian process, unless he gains a ponderable something thereby. Even assured of its congruity, he will still question its serviceableness. Is it worth while,

---

[15]**"second intention"**: denotation not of objects but of relations derived from objects.

[16]Michel de **Montaigne** (1533–1592): French essayist, quoted here from "Of the Art of Conversing."

[17]*ascêsis:* self-discipline.

[18]*Esmond: The History of Henry Esmond, Esq.* (1852), novel by W. M. Thackeray (1811–1863).

[19]Friedrich von **Schiller** (1759–1805): German poet and aesthetic theorist.

can we afford, to attend to just that, to just that figure or literary reference, just then?—Surplusage! he will dread that, as the runner on his muscles. For in truth all art does but consist in the removal of surplusage, from the last finish of the gem-engraver blowing away the last particle of invisible dust, back to the earliest divination of the finished work to be, lying somewhere, according to Michelangelo's fancy, in the rough-hewn block of stone.

And what applies to figure or flower must be understood of all other accidental or removable ornaments of writing whatever; and not of specific ornament only, but of all that latent colour and imagery which language as such carries in it. A lover of words for their own sake, to whom nothing about them is unimportant, a minute and constant observer of their physiognomy, he will be on the alert not only for obviously mixed metaphors of course, but for the metaphor that is mixed in all our speech, though a rapid use may involve no cognition of it. Currently recognising the incident, the colour, the physical elements or particles in words like *absorb, consider, extract*, to take the first that occur, he will avail himself of them, as further adding to the resources of expression. The elementary particles of language will be realised as colour and light and shade through his scholarly living in the full sense of them. Still opposing the constant degradation of language by those who use it carelessly, he will not treat coloured glass as if it were clear; and while half the world is using figure unconsciously, will be fully aware not only of all that latent figurative texture in speech, but of the vague, lazy, half-formed personification—a rhetoric, depressing, and worse than nothing, because it has no really rhetorical motive—which plays so large a part there, and, as in the case of more ostentatious ornament, scrupulously exact of it, from syllable to syllable, its precise value.

So far I have been speaking of certain conditions of the literary art arising out of the medium or material in or upon which it works, the essential qualities of language and its aptitudes for contingent ornamentation, matters which define scholarship as science and good taste respectively. They are both subservient to a more intimate quality of good style: more intimate, as coming nearer to the artist himself. The otiose, the facile, surplusage: why are these abhorrent to the true literary artist, except because, in literary as in all other art, structure is all-important, felt, or painfully missed, everywhere?—that architectural conception of work, which foresees the end in the beginning and never loses sight of it, and in every part is conscious of all the rest, till the last sentence does but, with undiminished vigour, unfold and justify the first—a condition of literary art, which, in contradistinction to another quality of the artist

himself, to be spoken of later, I shall call the necessity of *mind* in style.

An acute philosophical writer, the late Dean Mansel[20] (a writer whose works illustrate the literary beauty there may be in closeness, and with obvious repression or economy of a fine rhetorical gift) wrote a book, of fascinating precision in a very obscure subject, to show that all the technical laws of logic are but means of securing, in each and all of its apprehensions, the unity, the strict identity with itself, of the apprehending mind. All the laws of good writing aim at a similar unity or identity of the mind in all the processes by which the word is associated to its import. The term is right, and has its essential beauty, when it becomes, in a manner, what it signifies, as with the names of simple sensations. To give the phrase, the sentence, the structural member, the entire composition, song, or essay, a similar unity with its subject and with itself:—style is in the right way when it tends towards that. All depends upon the original unity, the vital wholeness and identity, of the initiatory apprehension or view. So much is true of all art, which therefore requires always its logic, its comprehensive reason—insight, foresight, retrospect, in simultaneous action—true, most of all, of the literary art, as being of all the arts most closely cognate to the abstract intelligence. Such logical coherency may be evidenced not merely in the lines of composition as a whole, but in the choice of a single word, while it by no means interferes with, but may even prescribe, much variety, in the building of the sentence for instance, or in the manner, argumentative, descriptive, discursive, of this or that part or member of the entire design. The blithe, crisp sentence, decisive as a child's expression of its needs, may alternate with the long-contending, victoriously intricate sentence; the sentence, born with the integrity of a single word, relieving the sort of sentence in which, if you look closely, you can see much contrivance, much adjustment, to bring a highly qualified matter into compass at one view. For the literary architecture, if it is to be rich and expressive, involves not only foresight of the end in the beginning, but also development or growth of design, in the process of execution, with many irregularities, surprises, and afterthoughts; the contingent as well as the necessary being subsumed under the unity of the whole. As truly, to the lack of such architectural design, of a single, almost visual, image, vigorously informing an entire, perhaps very intricate, composition, which shall be austere, ornate, argumentative, fanciful, yet true from first to last to that vision within, may be attributed those weaknesses of

---

[20]Henry Longueville **Mansel** (1820–1871): English philosopher and Anglican theologian, published *Prolegomena Logica* (1851).

conscious or unconscious repetition of word, phrase, motive, or member of the whole matter, indicating, as Flaubert was aware, an original structure in thought not organically complete. With such foresight, the actual conclusion will most often get itself written out of hand, before, in the more obvious sense, the work is finished. With some strong and leading sense of the world, the tight hold of which secures true *composition* and not mere loose accretion, the literary artist, I suppose, goes on considerately, setting joint to joint, sustained by yet restraining the productive ardour, retracing the negligences of his first sketch, repeating his steps only that he may give the reader a sense of secure and restful progress, readjusting mere assonances even, that they may soothe the reader, or at least not interrupt him on his way; and then, somewhere before the end comes, is burdened, inspired, with his conclusion, and betimes delivered of it, leaving off, not in weariness and because he finds *himself* at an end, but in all the freshness of volition. His work now structurally complete, with all the accumulating effect of secondary shades of meaning, he finishes the whole up to the just proportion of that ante-penultimate conclusion, and all becomes expressive. The house he has built is rather a body he has informed. And so it happens, to its greater credit, that the better interest even of a narrative to be recounted, a story to be told, will often be in its second reading. And though there are instances of great writers who have been no artists, an unconscious tact sometimes directing work in which we may detect, very pleasurably, many of the effects of conscious art, yet one of the greatest pleasures of really good prose literature is in the critical tracing out of that conscious artistic structure, and the pervading sense of it as we read. Yet of poetic literature too; for, in truth, the kind of constructive intelligence here supposed is one of the forms of the imagination.

That is the special function of mind, in style. Mind and soul:—hard to ascertain philosophically, the distinction is real enough practically, for they often interfere, are sometimes in conflict, with each other. Blake, in the last century, is an instance of preponderating soul, embarrassed, at a loss, in an era of preponderating mind. As a quality of style, at all events, soul is a fact, in certain writers—the way they have of absorbing language, of attracting it into the peculiar spirit they are of, with a subtlety which makes the actual result seem like some inexplicable inspiration. By mind, the literary artist reaches us, through static and objective indications of design in his work, legible to all. By soul, he reaches us, somewhat capriciously perhaps, one and not another, through vagrant sympathy and a kind of immediate contact. Mind we cannot choose but approve where we recognise it; soul may repel us, not because we misunderstand it. The way in which theological interests sometimes avail themselves of

language is perhaps the best illustration of the force I mean to indicate generally in literature, by the word *soul*. Ardent religious persuasion may exist, may make its way, without finding any equivalent heat in language: or, again, it may enkindle words to various degrees, and when it really takes hold of them doubles its force. Religious history presents many remarkable instances in which, through no mere phrase-worship, an unconscious literary tact has, for the sensitive, laid open a privileged pathway from one to another. "The altar-fire," people say, "has touched those lips!" The Vulgate, the English Bible, the English Prayer-Book, the writings of Swedenborg, the Tracts for the Times:[21]—there, we have instances of widely different and largely diffused phases of religious feeling in operation as soul in style. But something of the same kind acts with similar power in certain writers of quite other than theological literature, on behalf of some wholly personal and peculiar sense of theirs. Most easily illustrated by theological literature, this quality lends to profane writers a kind of religious influence. At their best, these writers become, as we say sometimes, "prophets"; such character depending on the effect not merely of their matter, but of their matter as allied to, in "electric affinity"[22] with, peculiar form, and working in all cases by an immediate sympathetic contact, on which account it is that it may be called soul, as opposed to mind, in style. And this too is a faculty of choosing and rejecting what is congruous or otherwise, with a drift towards unity—unity of atmosphere here, as there of design—soul securing colour (or perfume, might we say?) as mind secures form, the latter being essentially finite, the former vague or infinite, as the influence of a living person is practically infinite. There are some to whom nothing has any real interest, or real meaning except as operative in a given person; and it is they who best appreciate the quality of soul in literary art. They seem to know a *person*, in a book, and make way by intuition: yet, although they thus enjoy the completeness of a personal information, it is still a characteristic of soul, in this sense of the word, that it does but suggest what can never be uttered, not as being different from, or more obscure than, what actually gets said,

---

[21]**"altar-fire"**: see Isaiah 6:6–7. **Vulgate**: St. Jerome's 4th–century Latin Bible. **English Bible**: King James translation of 1611, replaced in 1880s by the Revised Version. **English Prayer-Book**: standard Anglican liturgy, dating from 1662. Emanuel **Swedenborg** (1688–1772): Swedish theologian. **Tracts for the Times** (1833–1841): polemical writings by Newman and others from the Catholic revivalist Oxford Movement.

[22]**"electric affinity"**: electrochemical attraction; see the novel *Elective Affinities* (1809), by Johann Wolfgang von Goethe (1749–1832).

but as containing that plenary substance of which there is only one phase or facet in what is there expressed. . . .

In this way, according to the well-known saying, "The style is the man,"[23] complex or simple, in his individuality, his plenary sense of what he really has to say, his sense of the world; all cautions regarding style arising out of so many natural scruples as to the medium through which alone he can expose that inward sense of things, the purity of this medium, its laws or tricks of refraction: nothing is to be left there which might give conveyance to any matter save that. Style in all its varieties, reserved or opulent, terse, abundant, musical, stimulant, academic, so long as each is really characteristic or expressive, finds thus its justification, the sumptuous good taste of Cicero being as truly the man himself, and not another, justified, yet insured inalienably to him, thereby, as would have been his portrait by Raffaelle, in full consular splendour, on his ivory chair.

A relegation, you may say perhaps—a relegation of style to the subjectivity, the mere caprice, of the individual, which must soon transform it into mannerism. Not so! since there is, under the conditions supposed, for those elements of the man, for every lineament of the vision within, the one word, the one acceptable word, recognisable by the sensitive, by others "who have intelligence" in the matter, as absolutely as ever anything can be in the evanescent and delicate region of human language. The style, the manner, would be the man, not in his unreasoned and really uncharacteristic caprices, involuntary or affected, but in absolutely sincere apprehension of what is most real to him. But let us hear our French guide[24] again.—

"Styles," says Flaubert's commentator, "*Styles*, as so many peculiar moulds, each of which bears the mark of a particular writer, who is to pour into it the whole content of his ideas, were no part of his theory. What he believed in was *Style*: that is to say, a certain absolute and unique manner of expressing a thing, in all its intensity and colour. For him the *form* was the work itself. As in living creatures, the blood, nourishing the body, determines its very contour and external aspect, just so, to his mind, the *matter*, the basis, in a work of art, imposed, necessarily, the unique, the just expression, the measure, the rhythm—the *form* in all its characteristics."

If the style be the man, in all the colour and intensity of a veritable apprehension, it will be in a real sense "impersonal."

I said, thinking of books like Victor Hugo's *Les Misérables*,[25] that prose literature was the characteristic art of the nineteenth century, as others, thinking of its triumphs since the youth of Bach, have assigned that place to music. Music and prose literature are, in one sense, the opposite terms of art; the art of literature presenting to the imagination, through the intelligence, a range of interests, as free and various as those which music presents to it through sense. And certainly the tendency of what has been here said is to bring literature too under those conditions, by conformity to which music takes rank as the typically perfect art. If music be the ideal of all art whatever, precisely because in music it is impossible to distinguish the form from the substance or matter, the subject from the expression, then, literature, by finding its specific excellence in the absolute correspondence of the term to its import, will be but fulfilling the condition of all artistic quality in things everywhere, of all good art.

Good art, but not necessarily great art; the distinction between great art and good art depending immediately, as regards literature at all events, not on its form, but on the matter. Thackeray's *Esmond*, surely, is greater art than *Vanity Fair*,[26] by the greater dignity of its interests. It is on the quality of the matter it informs or controls, its compass, its variety, its alliance to great ends, or the depth of the note of revolt, or the largeness of hope in it, that the greatness of literary art depends, as *The Divine Comedy, Paradise Lost, Les Misérables, The English Bible*, are great art. Given the conditions I have tried to explain as constituting good art;—then, if it be devoted further to the increase of men's happiness, to the redemption of the oppressed, or the enlargement of our sympathies with each other, or to such presentment of new or old truth about ourselves and our relation to the world as may ennoble and fortify us in our sojourn here, or immediately, as with Dante, to the glory of God, it will be also great art; if, over and above those qualities I summed up as mind and soul—that colour and mystic perfume, and that reasonable structure, it has something of the soul of humanity in it, and finds its logical, its architectural place, in the great structure of human life.

1888

---

[23]"**The style is the man**": from Comte de Buffon's 1753 address to the Académie Française.

[24]**French guide**: Guy de Maupassant (1850–1893), fiction writer and disciple of **Flaubert**.

[25]**Victor Hugo** (1802–1855): author of *Les Misérables* (1862).

[26]*Vanity Fair*: novel published 1847–1848 by Thackeray, author of *Esmond*.

THOMAS HARDY

(1840–1928)

Thomas Hardy was born in Dorset, a predominantly rural area in the west of England that, fictionalized under the name of Wessex, became the setting for most of his novels and poems. His father was a master mason and builder. He attended a good local school where he became proficient in practical subjects, and at the age of sixteen was apprenticed to an architect who specialized in restoring (that is, altering to suit modern notions of antique style) old churches. He kept up his studies on his own, however, continuing the Latin he had learned in school and teaching himself Greek. At twenty-one he went to London, where he worked as an architect's assistant and finally recognized that he could not fulfill his longtime dream of becoming a clergyman. His knowledge of the classics was insufficient for entrance to Cambridge; and besides, he was losing his faith in a benevolent deity and coming to see the world as ruled by, at best, blind chance.

He returned home in 1867, still working as an architect but resolved to attempt a literary career. His first novel was published in 1871. His novels were too dark and strange to attract publishers or readers right away—indeed, Hardy never lost his power to shock and repel—but they were successful enough for him to give up his job as an architect. In 1874 he married a woman whose social status was higher than his own (a fact of importance to both of them) and moved back to London.

Although as a novelist Hardy is unquestionably a Victorian, as a poet he is often thought of as belonging to the twentieth century. His first volume of poetry, *Wessex Poems*, did not appear until 1898, when the fame of his novels was well established and he had stopped writing them. His grim vision of nature and human life suited modernist sensibilities, as did his quirky music, unusual stanza forms, and strange vocabulary. He scornfully defied what he called in 1898 the prevailing notion of poetry as "the art of saying nothing with mellifluous preciosity." But he had been writing poems since he was a young man, and his vision reflected nineteenth-century realities: commercial and social upheaval of rooted traditions, scientific abolition of received certitudes, reconsideration of knowledge and morals by such pessimistic philosophers as Hardy's favorite, Schopenhauer. In versecraft, too, Hardy apprenticed himself to nineteenth-century masters of formal innovation, particularly Shelley, Browning, and his near-contemporary Swinburne. Like his Dorset exemplar, William Barnes, he often used dialect and obsolete or even invented words, and imitated the halting, hesitant rhythms of ordinary speech. He emphasized, he said, stress rather than syllable, poetic texture rather than poetic veneer, and in accord with the neo-Gothic tradition he had learned as an architect, he valued irregularity and the appearance of spontaneity in verse as well as buildings. (Critics, he complained, understood neither his innovative metrics nor his sense of humor, regarding "verses of a satirical, dry, caustic, or farcical cast . . . with the deepest seriousness.") Hardy often said that he rated his poetry higher than his fiction, a judgment that would have seemed entirely perverse to his contemporaries but in which many readers now concur.

Hap[1]

If but some vengeful god would call to me
From up the sky, and laugh: "Thou suffering thing,
Know that thy sorrow is my ecstasy,
That thy love's loss is my hate's profiting!"

Then would I bear it, clench myself, and die,
Steeled by the sense of ire unmerited;
Half-eased in that a Powerfuller than I
Had willed and meted me the tears I shed.

But not so. How arrives it joy lies slain,
And why unblooms the best hope ever sown?   10
—Crass Casualty obstructs the sun and rain,
And dicing Time for gladness casts a moan. . . .
These purblind[2] Doomsters had as readily strown
Blisses about my pilgrimage as pain.
1866   *1898*

Neutral Tones

We stood by a pond that winter day,
And the sun was white, as though chidden[1] of God,
And a few leaves lay on the starving sod;
    —They had fallen from an ash, and were gray.

Your eyes on me were as eyes that rove
Over tedious riddles of years ago;
And some words played between us to and fro
    On which lost the more by our love.

The smile on your mouth was the deadest thing
Alive enough to have strength to die;   10
And a grin of bitterness swept thereby
    Like an ominous bird a-wing. . . .

Since then, keen lessons that love deceives,
And wrings with wrong, have shaped to me
Your face, and the God-curst sun, and a tree,
    And a pond edged with grayish leaves.
1867   *1898*

Her Initials

Upon a poet's page I wrote
Of old two letters of her name;
Part seemed she of the effulgent thought
Whence that high singer's rapture came.
—When now I turn the leaf the same
Immortal light illumes the lay,[1]
But from the letters of her name
The radiance has waned away!
1869   *1898*

A Sign-Seeker

I mark the months in liveries dank and dry,
    The noontides many-shaped and hued;
    I see the nightfall shades subtrude,
And hear the monotonous hours clang negligently by.

I view the evening bonfires of the sun
    On hills where morning rains have hissed;
    The eyeless countenance of the mist
Pallidly rising when the summer droughts are done.

I have seen the lightning-blade, the leaping star,
    The cauldrons of the sea in storm,   10
    Have felt the earthquake's lifting arm,
And trodden where abysmal fires and snow-cones are.

I learn to prophesy the hid eclipse,
    The coming of eccentric orbs;
    To mete[1] the dust the sky absorbs,
To weigh the sun, and fix the hour each planet dips.

I witness fellow earth-men surge and strive;
    Assemblies meet, and throb, and part;
    Death's sudden finger, sorrow's smart;
—All the vast various moils[2] that mean a world alive.   20

But that I fain would wot[3] of shuns my sense—
    Those sights of which old prophets tell,
    Those signs the general word so well
As vouchsafed their unheed, denied my long suspense.

---

[1]**Hap:** chance.
[2]**purblind:** half blind.
[1]**chidden:** scolded.

---

[1]**lay:** song, poem meant to be sung.

[1]**mete:** measure.
[2]**moils:** toils.
[3]**wot:** know.

In graveyard green, where his pale dust lies pent
  To glimpse a phantom parent, friend,
  Wearing his smile, and "Not the end!"
Outbreathing softly: that were blest enlightenment;

Or, if a dead Love's lips, whom dreams reveal
  When midnight imps of King Decay   30
  Delve sly to solve me back to clay,
Should leave some print to prove her spirit-kisses real;

Or, when Earth's Frail lie bleeding of her Strong,
  If some Recorder, as in Writ,
  Near to the weary scene should flit
And drop one plume as pledge that Heaven inscrolls
  the wrong.

—There are who, rapt to heights of trancelike trust,
  These tokens claim to feel and see,
  Read radiant hints of times to be—
Of heart to heart returning after dust to dust.   40

Such scope is granted not to lives like mine . . .
  I have lain in dead men's beds, have walked
  The tombs of those with whom I had talked,
Called many a gone and goodly one to shape a sign,

And panted for response. But none replies;
  No warnings loom, nor whisperings
  To open out my limitings,
And Nescience[4] mutely muses: When a man falls he lies.

                                1898

Friends Beyond

William Dewy , Tranter Reuben, Farmer Ledlow late at
  plough,
  Robert's kin, and John's, and Neds,
And the Squire, and Lady Susan,[1] lie in Mellstock
  churchyard now!

"Gone," I call them, gone for good, that group of local
  hearts and heads;
  Yet at mothy curfew-tide,[2]
And at midnight when the noon-heat breathes it back from
  walls and leads,[3]

---

[4]**Nescience**: ignorance.

[1]**William . . . Susan**: real people and characters from Hardy's
fiction.

[2]**curfew-tide**: time of the evening curfew-bell.

[3]**leads**: roofs.

They've a way of whispering to me—fellow-wight who
  yet abide[4]—
  In the muted, measured note
Of a ripple under archways, or a lone cave's stillicide:[5]

"We have triumphed: this achievement turns the bane[6]
  to antidote,   10
  Unsuccesses to success,
Many thought-worn eves and morrows to a morrow
  free of thought.

"No more need we corn and clothing, feel of old terrestial
  stress;
  Chill detraction stirs no sigh;
Fear of death has even bygone us: death gave all that we
  possess."

W. D.—"Ye mid[7] burn the old bass-viol that I set such
  value by."
Squire.—"You may hold the manse in fee,[8]
  You may wed my spouse, may let my children's memory
  of me die."

Lady S.—"You may have my rich brocades, my laces; take
  each household key;
  Ransack coffer, desk, bureau;   20
  Quiz the few poor treasures hid there, con[9] the letters
  kept by me."

Far.—"Ye mid zell my favourite heifer, ye mid let the
  charlock[10] grow,
  Foul the grinterns,[11] give up thrift."
Far. Wife.—"If ye break my best blue china, children, I shan't
  care or ho."[12]

All.—"We've no wish to hear the tidings, how the people's
  fortunes shift;
  What your daily doings are;
Who are wedded, born, divided; if your lives beat slow
  or swift.

---

[4]**wight**: creature. **abide**: remain.

[5]**stillicide**: falling of water drops.

[6]**bane**: poison.

[7]**mid**: may.

[8]**manse**: manor. **in fee**: by inherited right.

[9]**Quiz**: mock. **con**: peruse.

[10]**zell**: sell. **charlock**: weed.

[11]**grinterns**: granary compartments.

[12]**ho**: be anxious.

"Curious not the least are we if our intents you make
    or mar,
    If you quire to our old tune.
If the City stage still passes, if the weirs still roar afar."   30

—Thus, with very gods' composure, freed those crosses
    late and soon
    Which, in life, the Trine allow
(Why, none witteth),[13] and ignoring all that haps beneath
    the moon,

William Dewy, Tranter Reuben, Farmer Ledlow late at
    plough,
    Robert's kin, and John's, and Ned's,
And the Squire, and Lady Susan, murmur mildly to
    me now.

                                                          1898

Thoughts of Phena[1]

At News of Her Death

Not a line of her writing have I,
    Not a thread of her hair,
No mark of her late time as dame in her dwelling,
    whereby
    I may picture her there;
And in vain do I urge my unsight
    To conceive my lost prize
At her close, whom I knew when her dreams were
    upbrimming with light,
    And with laughter her eyes.

What scenes spread around her last days,
    Sad, shining, or dim?   10
Did her gifts and compassions enray and enarch her
    sweet ways
    With an aureate nimb?[2]
Or did life-light decline from her years,
    And mischances control
Her full day-star; unease, or regret, or forebodings, or fears
    Disennoble her soul?

---

[13]**Trine**: Trinity. **witteth**: knows.

[1]**Phena**: Tryphena Spark (1851–1890), Hardy's cousin, thought
to have been his lover and once his fiancée.

[2]**enray**: surround with rays, illuminate. **enarch**: arch over.
aureate nimb: golden halo.

Thus I do but the phantom retain
    Of the maiden of yore
As my relic; yet haply the best of her—fined[3] in
    my brain
    It may be the more   20
That no line of her writing have I,
    Nor a thread of her hair,
No mark of her late time as dame in her dwelling, whereby
    I may picture her there.

1890   *1898*

Nature's Questioning

When I look forth at dawning, pool,
    Field, flock, and lonely tree,
    All seem to gaze at me
Like chastened children sitting silent in a school;

    Their faces dulled, constrained, and worn,
        As though the master's ways
        Through the long teaching days
Had cowed them till their early zest was overborne.

    Upon them stirs in lippings[1] mere
        (As if once clear in call,   10
        But now scarce breathed at all)—
"We wonder, ever wonder, why we find us here!

    "Has some Vast Imbecility,
        Mighty to build and blend,
        But impotent to tend,
Framed us in jest, and left us now to hazardry?

    "Or come we of an Automaton
        Unconscious of our pains? . . .
        Or are we live remains
Of Godhead dying downwards, brain and eye
    now gone?   20

    "Or is it that some high Plan betides,
        As yet not understood,
        Of Evil stormed by Good,
We the Forlorn Hope over which Achievement
    strides?"

---

[3]**fined**: refined.

[1]**lippings**: weakly spoken words.

Thus things around. No answerer I. . . .
   Meanwhile the winds, and rains,
   And Earth's old glooms and pains
Are still the same, and Life and Death are neighbours nigh.

1898

The Impercipient

(At a Cathedral Service)

That with this bright believing band
   I have no claim to be,
That faiths by which my comrades stand
   Seem fantasies to me,
And mirage-mists their Shining Land,
   Is a strange destiny.

Why thus my soul should be consigned
   To infelicity,
Why always I must feel as blind
   To sights my brethren see,   10
Why joys they've found I cannot find,
   Abides a mystery.

Since heart of mine knows not that ease
   Which they know; since it be
That He who breathes All's Well to these
   Breathes no All's-Well to me,
My lack might move their sympathies
   And Christian charity!

I am like a gazer who should mark
   An inland company   20
Standing upfingered, with, "Hark! hark!
   The glorious distant sea!"
And feel, "Alas, 'tis but yon dark
   And wind-swept pine to me!"

Yet I would bear my shortcomings
   With meet tranquillity,
But for the charge that blessed things
   I'd liefer[1] not have be.
O, doth a bird deprived of wings
   Go earth-bound wilfully!   30

    .   .   .

Enough. As yet disquiet clings
   About us. Rest shall we.

1898

---

[1]**liefer**: rather.

Heiress and Architect

For A. W. Blomfield[1]

She sought the Studios, beckoning to her side
An arch-designer, for she planned to build.
He was of wise contrivance, deeply skilled
In every intervolve of high and wide—
   Well fit to be her guide.

   "Whatever it be,"
   Responded he,
With cold, clear voice, and cold, clear view,
"In true accord with prudent fashionings
For such vicissitudes as living brings,   10
And thwarting not the law of stable things,
   That will I do."

"Shape me," she said, "high halls with tracery
And open ogive-work,[2] that scent and hue
Of buds, and travelling bees, may come in through,
The note of birds, and singings of the sea,
   For these are much to me."

   "An idle whim!"
   Broke forth from him
Whom nought could warm to gallantries: 20
"Cede all these buds and birds, the zephyr's call,
And scents, and hues, and things that falter all,
And choose as best the close and surly wall,
   For winters freeze."

"Then frame," she cried, "wide fronts of crystal glass,
That I may show my laughter and my light—
Light like the sun's by day, the stars' by night—
Till rival heart-queens, envying, wail, 'Alas,
   Her glory!' as they pass."

   "O maid misled!"   30
   He sternly said
Whose facile foresight pierced her dire;
"Where shall abide the soul when, sick of glee,
It shrinks, and hides, and prays no eye may see?
Those house them best who house for secrecy,
   For you will tire."

---

[1]Sir Arthur **Blomfield** (1829–1899): president of the Architectural Association, noted renovator of churches.

[2]**ogive-work**: diagonal ribs in Gothic vaulting.

"A little chamber, then, with swan and dove
Ranged thickly, and engrailed with rare device
Of reds and purples, for a Paradise
Wherein my Love may greet me, I my Love,   40
    When he shall know thereof?"

        "This, too, is ill,"
        He answered still,
The man who swayed her like a shade.
"An hour will come when sight of such sweet nook
Would bring a bitterness too sharp to brook,
When brighter eyes have won away his look;
        For you will fade."

Then said she faintly: "O, contrive some way—
Some narrow winding turret, quite mine own,   50
To reach a loft where I may grieve alone!
It is a slight thing; hence do not, I pray,
    This last dear fancy slay!"

        "Such winding ways
        Fit not your days,"
Said he, the man of measuring eye;
"I must even fashion as the rule declares,
To wit: Give space (since life ends unawares)
To hale a coffined corpse adown the stairs;
        For you will die."   60
1867

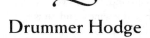

Drummer Hodge

— 1 —

They throw in Drummer Hodge, to rest
    Uncoffined—just as found:
His landmark is a kopje-crest
    That breaks the veldt[1] around;
And foreign constellations west
    Each night above his mound.

— 2 —

Young Hodge the Drummer never knew—
    Fresh from his Wessex home—
The meaning of the broad Karoo,
    The Bush,[2] the dusty loam,   10
And why uprose to nightly view
    Strange stars amid the gloom.

— 3 —

Yet portion of that unknown plain
    Will Hodge for ever be;
His homely Northern breast and brain
    Grow to some Southern tree,
And strange-eyed constellations reign
    His stars eternally.

                                    1899, 1902

I Look into My Glass

I look into my glass,
And view my wasting skin,
And say, "Would God it came to pass
My heart had shrunk as thin!"

For then, I, undistrest
By hearts grown cold to me,
Could lonely wait my endless rest
With equanimity.

But Time, to make me grieve,
Part steals, lets part abide;
And shakes this fragile frame at eve   10
With throbbings of noontide.

                                    1898

The Ruined Maid

"O 'Melia, my dear, this does everything crown!
Who could have supposed I should meet you in Town?
And whence such fair garments, such prosperi-ty?"—
"O didn't you know I'd been ruined?" said she.

—"You left us in tatters, without shoes or socks,
Tired of digging potatoes, and spudding up docks;[1]
And now you've gay bracelets and bright feathers three!"—
"Yes: that's how we dress when we're ruined," said she.

---

[1]**kopje, veldt**: small hill, grassy plateau in S Africa, where Hodge died in the Boer War (1899–1902).

[2]**Karoo**: barren plateau in S Africa. **Bush**: colonialist term for uncleared land with thick vegetation.

[1]**spudding**: digging. **docks**: coarse weeds.

1898

—"At home in the barton[2] you said 'thee' and 'thou,'
And 'thik oon,' and 'theäs oon,' and 't'other'; but now   10
Your talking quite fits 'ee for high compa-ny!"—
"Some polish is gained with one's ruin," said she.

—"Your hands were like paws then, your face blue and
    bleak
But now I'm bewitched by your delicate cheek,
And your little gloves fit as on any la-dy!"—
"We never do work when we're ruined," said she.

—"You used to call home-life a hag-ridden dream,
And you'd sigh, and you'd sock; but at present you seem
To know not of megrims[3] or melancho-ly!"—
"True. One's pretty lively when ruined," said she.   20

—"I wish I had feathers, a fine sweeping gown,
And a delicate face, and could strut about Town!"—
"My dear—a raw country girl, such as you be,
Cannot quite expect that. You ain't ruined," said she.
1866   *1901*

In Tenebris[1]

— I —

"Percussus sum sicut foenum, et aruit cor meum."—*Ps.* ci.[2]

    Wintertime nighs;
But my bereavement-pain
It cannot bring again:
    Twice no one dies.

    Flower-petals flee;
But, since it once hath been,
No more that severing scene
    Can harrow me.

    Birds faint in dread:
I shall not lose old strength   10
In the lone frost's black length:
    Strength long since fled!

    Leaves freeze to dun;
But friends can not turn cold
This season as of old
    For him with none.

    Tempests may scath;
But love can not make smart
Again this year his heart
    Who no heart hath.   20

    Black is night's cope;
But death will not appal
One who, past doubtings all,
    Waits in unhope.
1896   *1901*

In Tenebris

— II —

"Considerabam ad dexteram, et videbam; et non erat qui
cognosceret me. . . . Non est qui requirat animam meam."—
Ps. cxli.[1]

When the clouds' swoln bosoms echo back the shouts of
    the many and strong
That things are all as they best may be, save a few to be
    right ere long,
And my eyes have not the vision in them to discern what to
    these is so clear,
The blot seems straightway in me alone; one better he were
    not here.

The stout upstanders say, All's well with us: ruers have
    nought to rue!
And what the potent say so oft, can it fail to be somewhat
    true?
Breezily go they, breezily come; their dust smokes around
    their career,
Till I think I am one born out of due time,[2] who has no
    calling here.

---

[2]**barton:** farmyard.

[3]**megrims:** low spirits.

[1]**In Tenebris:** in darkness.

[2]"**Percussus . . . meum**": "My heart is smitten, and withered like
grass" (Psalm 102:4).

---

[1]"**Considerabam . . . meam**": "I looked on my right hand, and
beheld, but there was no man that would know me, refuge failed
me: no man cared for my soul" (Psalm 142:4–5).

[2]**one . . . time:** 1 Corinthians 15:8.

Their dawns bring lusty joys, it seems; their evenings all
    that is sweet;
Our times are blessed times, they cry: Life shapes it as is
    most meet,   10
And nothing is much the matter; there are many smiles
    to a tear;
Then what is the matter is I, I say. Why should such an one
    be here? . . .

Let him in whose ears the low-voiced Best is killed by the
    clash of the First,
Who holds that if way to the Better there be, it exacts a full
    look at the Worst,
Who feels that delight is a delicate growth cramped by
    crookedness, custom, and fear,
Get him up and be gone as one shaped awry; he disturbs
    the order here.

1896   1901

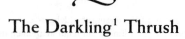

The Darkling[1] Thrush

I leant upon a coppice gate
    When Frost was spectre-gray,
And Winter's dregs made desolate
    The weakening eye of day.

The tangled bine[2]-stems scored the sky
    Like strings of broken lyres,
And all mankind that haunted nigh
    Had sought their household fires.

The land's sharp features seemed to be
    The Century's corpse outleant,   10
His crypt the cloudy canopy,
    The wind his death-lament.
The ancient pulse of germ and birth
    Was shrunken hard and dry,
And every spirit upon earth
    Seemed fervourless as I.

At once a voice arose among
    The bleak twigs overhead
In a full-hearted evensong[3]
    Of joy illimited;   20
An aged thrush, frail, gaunt, and small,
    In blast-beruffled plume,
Had chosen thus to fling his soul
    Upon the growing gloom.

So little cause for carolings
    Of such ecstatic sound
Was written on terrestrial things
    Afar or nigh around,
That I could think there trembled through
    His happy good-night air   30
Some blessed Hope, whereof he knew
    And I was unaware.

31 December 1900   1901

---

[1]**Darkling**: in the dark.

[2]**bine**: woodbine or other twining shrub.

[3]**evensong**: evening prayer service with music.

GERARD MANLEY HOPKINS

(1844–1889)

Among the many younger Victorians who followed John Henry Newman out of comfortable Anglican households through Oxford into the Church of Rome, Hopkins had the greatest literary gift. Newman corresponded with him before his undergraduate conversion in 1866, saw him appointed to teach at the Birmingham Oratory, and then gave his blessing when the young man decided to enter the Society of Jesus, whose strenuous discipline, Newman predicted, would supply what Hopkins was looking for. After eight years of retreat and training, scholarship and self-examination, he was ordained a priest in 1877, dividing the rest of his short life between parish duties and the work of a classics instructor at English Jesuit schools and eventually at University College in Dublin.

Newman may have seen in Hopkins an intensity of focused individuality comparable to his own, and a corresponding need for outward rigor to shape it. Such a need informed the poetry Hopkins wrote at Oxford, which was verbally lush yet bound to themes of ascetic renunciation; it also emerged in the severity with which, at the start of his Jesuit training, he burned every scrap he could find and resolved to write no more verse. He did, however, continue during the early 1870s to keep notebooks that shimmer with descriptive power, directed mostly towards aspects of the natural world. In these journals Hopkins was laying the ground for a poetic vocation that might be consistent with his priestly one, practicing the sacramental apprehension of a divine reality at work within the beauty of creation. In particular—and Hopkins' studies in medieval philosophy confirmed his orientation towards the particular, the *haecceitas* or "thisness" of energetic perception—he invented a special vocabulary for rendering such experiences of radiant insight as his Oxford tutor Walter Pater would call "privileged moments" or the Jesuit-trained modernist James Joyce "epiphanies." Hopkins wrote of a vista or detail in terms of *inscape* (unique and essential form) and *instress* (energy sustaining inscape and communicating it to a perceiver). His notebook prose, briefly represented here, anticipated his later verse by bringing out the *stress* in instress, through a freshly imagined, sinewy language that strives to render bodily the phenomena it describes. Language itself, Hopkins taught himself to believe, might when reverently used disclose the etymology and syntax of the world, the plot and interrelatedness of God's works. The poet who rejoiced at "the dearest freshness deep down things" sought a counterpart for that wealth deep down in the roots of words, which his notes explore as if to find a philologer's stone, an alchemical clue to the holiness of the Logos or Christian Word.

When a group of refugee nuns from Germany perished in a terrible shipwreck off the English coast late in 1875, the news seized Hopkins' imagination and—having first scrupulously gotten permission to do so—he exploded into verse after seven years of silence with "The Wreck of the *Deutschland*." This ecstatic ode correlates the storm and stress of a maritime disaster (Hopkins' father, incidentally, worked in shipping insurance) with confessions of spiritual agony and celebrations of martyrdom, all performed within an intricate stanza and according to a metrical principle that broke with centuries of standard prosody. This principle of "sprung rhythm," which Hopkins employed and refined in the extraordinarily inventive poems he went on to write, observes a strict account of stresses but takes great license with unstressed syllables. The result is a verbal music both extravagant and sophisticated, scored for the voice or inner ear (sometimes with actual notation, which we minimize in this edition), and easily bewildering to a mind already tasked by the pace and agility of Hopkins' tropes and his batteries of multiple-epithet-compounds. Such strong stuff, despite the orthodoxy of its content, was too much for the Catholic literary magazines in which Hopkins sought publication; with just a handful of exceptions his work circulated only in manuscript during his lifetime. Correspondence with family members and poet friends provided all the audience he required and challenged him to produce—pretty clearly with a larger posterity in mind—elucidations of theory and practice that readers still find helpful. In 1918, three decades after his death, one of these friends brought out an edition of the poems that was faithful to Hopkins' intentions. The timing could not have been better: a postwar audience that was almost ready for *The Waste Land* welcomed the posthumous debut of a genius whom the Victorians had rejected and who in so many ways had rejected the Victorians.

Hopkins' aberrant prosody, and the enormous pressure under which he places language by dint of metaphorical condensation and structural constraint—much of his work obeys the demands of the Petrarchan sonnet—present his editors with an annotation problem that is perhaps insoluble. Where a new word is coined in almost every poem or a new use found for an old one, where triple meanings for a phrase are not rare and double meanings almost business as usual, the explication of each ambiguity would drive readers to distraction; worse, it would spoil their pleasure at discovering verbal inscapes on their own. We therefore leave it to be seen, for instance, that in "Heaven-Haven" *springs* and *fail* each can play subject to the other's verb; that in "The Wreck of the *Deutschland*" *blear share* (88) names both a plough's blade and life's grim portion; that *charged* in "God's Grandeur" conveys electricity, freight, and assault all at once; that in "The Windhover" the verb *Buckle*, merging statement with command, also merges the contradictory meanings of a clasp and a collapse. The footnotes that do appear chiefly explain antiquated or dialect words, exceptionally twisted syntax, and Hopkins' most important textual or ritual allusions.

Heaven-Haven

A Nun Takes the Veil

I have desired to go
   Where springs not fail,
To fields where flies no sharp and sided hail
   And a few lilies blow.

And I have asked to be
   Where no storms come,
Where the green swell is in the havens dumb,
   And out of the swing of the sea.

1864

The Habit of Perfection[1]

Elected Silence, sing to me
And beat upon my whorlèd ear,
Pipe me to pastures still and be
The music that I care to hear.

---

[1]**Habit**: custom or disposition; also religious attire, given Hopkins' manuscript subtitle "The Novice."

1918

Shape nothing, lips; be lovely-dumb:
It is the shut, the curfew sent
From there where all surrenders come
Which only makes you eloquent.

Be shellèd, eyes, with double dark
And find the uncreated light: 10
This ruck and reel which you remark
Coils, keeps, and teases simple sight.

Palate, the hutch of tasty lust,
Desire not to be rinsed with wine:
The can must be so sweet, the crust
So fresh that come in fasts divine!

Nostrils, your careless breath that spend
Upon the stir and keep of pride,
What relish shall the censers send
Along the sanctuary side!   20

O feel-of-primrose hands, O feet
That want the yield of plushy sward,
But you shall walk the golden street
And you unhouse and house the Lord.[2]

And, Poverty, be thou the bride
And now the marriage feast begun,
And lily-coloured clothes provide
Your spouse not laboured-at nor spun.[3]
1866   *1918*

The Wreck of the *Deutschland*[1]

To the
happy memory of five Franciscan nuns
exiles by the Falck Laws
drowned between midnight and morning of
Dec. 7th, 1875[2]

— PART THE FIRST —

1

Thou mastering me
God! giver of breath and bread;
World's strand, sway of the sea;
Lord of living and dead;

Thou hast bound bones and veins in me, fastened
    me flesh,
And after it almost unmade, what with dread,
    Thy doing: and dost thou touch me afresh?
Over again I feel thy finger and find thee.

2

I did say yes
O at lightning and lashed rod;   10
Thou heardst me truer than tongue confess
Thy terror, O Christ, O God;

---

[1]Note—Be pleased, reader, since the rhythm in which the following poem is written is new, strongly to mark the beats of the measure, according to the number belonging to each of the eight lines of the stanza, as the indentation guides the eye, namely two and three and four and three and five and five and four and six; not disguising the rhythm and rhyme, as some readers do, who treat poetry as if it were prose fantastically written to rule (which they mistakenly think the perfection of reading), but laying on the beats too much stress rather than too little; nor caring whether one, two, three, or more syllables go to a beat, that is to say, whether two or more beats follow running—as there are three running in the third line of the first stanza—or with syllables between, as commonly; nor whether the line begin with a beat or not; but letting the scansion run on from one line into the next, without break to the end of the stanza: since the dividing of the lines is more to fix the places of the necessary rhymes than for any pause in the measure. Only let this be observed in the reading, that, where more than one syllable goes to a beat, then if the beating syllable is of its nature strong, the stress laid on it must be stronger the greater the number of syllables belonging to it, the voice treading and dwelling: but if on the contrary it is by nature light, then the greater the number of syllables belonging to it the less is the stress to be laid on it, the voice passing flyingly over all the syllables of the foot and in some manner distributing among them all the stress of the one beat. Which syllables however are strong and which light is better told by the ear than by any instruction that could be in short space given: but for an example, in the stanza which is fifth from the end of the poem and in the 6th line the first two beats are very strong and the more the voice dwells on them the more it fetches out the strength of the syllables they rest upon, the next two beats are very light and escaping, and the last, as well as those which follow in the next line, are of a mean strength, such as suits narrative. And so throughout let the stress be made to fetch out both the strength of the syllables and the meaning and feeling of the words. [Hopkins' note]

[2]**Falck Laws:** German legislation passed in the 1870s (spearheaded by Dr. **Falck**, minister of Public Worship), penalizing Catholics, confiscating Church property, and expelling members of religious orders from the country. On the composition of this ode see the letter to R. W. Dixon, page 1004.

---

[2]**golden street:** see Revelation 21:21. **the Lord:** Christ's body, the eucharistic bread in its tabernacle on the altar.

[3]**lily-coloured . . . nor spun:** see Matthew 6:28–29.

Thou knowest the walls, altar and hour and night:
  The swoon of a heart that the sweep and the hurl of
    thee trod
    Hard down with a horror of height:
And the midriff astrain with leaning of, laced with fire
  of stress.

3

    The frown of his face
  Before me, the hurtle[3] of hell
  Behind, where, where was a, where was a place?—
    I whirled out wings that spell[4]   20
And fled with a fling of the heart to the heart of
  the Host.[5]—
My heart, but you were dovewinged, I can tell,
  Carrier-witted, I am bold to boast,
To flash from the flame to the flame then, tower from the
  grace to the grace.

4

    I am soft sift
  In an hourglass—at the wall
  Fast, but mined with a motion, a drift,
    And it crowds and it combs[6] to the fall;
I steady as a water in a well, to a poise, to a pane,
But roped with, always, all the way down from the tall 30
  Fells or flanks of the voel,[7] a vein
Of the gospel proffer, a pressure, a principle, Christ's gift.

5

    I kiss my hand
  To the stars, lovely-asunder
  Starlight, wafting him out of it; and
    Glow, glory in thunder;
Kiss my hand to the dappled-with-damson[8] west:
Since, tho' he is under the world's splendour and wonder,
  His mystery must be instressed, stressed;
For I greet him the days I meet him, and bless when I
  understand.   40

---

[3]**hurtle**: clash.

[4]**that spell**: at that time.

[5]**Host**: eucharistic body of Christ, here also keeper of the house
to which the speaker speeds, **dovewinged**, with the homing instinct
of a **Carrier** pigeon: see Psalm 55:6.

[6]**combs**: topples (like a breaking wave).

[7]**Fells, voel**: bare mountains (terms respectively from N British
and Welsh, the latter rhyming with *coil*).

[8]**damson**: deep purple.

6

    Not out of his bliss
  Springs the stress felt
  Nor first from heaven (and few know this)
    Swings the stroke dealt—
Stroke and a stress that stars and storms deliver,
That guilt is hushed by, hearts are flushed by and
  melt—
  But it rides time like riding a river
(And here the faithful waver, the faithless fable and miss).

7

    It dates from day
  Of his going in Galilee;[9]   50
  Warm-laid grave of a womb-life grey;
    Manger, maiden's knee;
The dense and the driven Passion,[10] and frightful sweat:
Thence the discharge of it, there its swelling to be,
  Though felt before, though in high flood yet—
What none would have known of it, only the heart, being
  hard at bay,

8

    Is out with it! Oh,
  We lash with the best or worst
  Word last! How a lush-kept plush-capped sloe[11]
    Will, mouthed to flesh-burst,   60
Gush!—flush the man, the being with it, sour or sweet,
Brim, in a flash, full!—Hither then, last or first,
  To hero of Calvary, Christ,'s feet—
Never ask if meaning it, wanting it, warned of it—men go.

9

    Be adored among men,
  God, three-numberèd form;
  Wring thy rebel, dogged in den,
    Man's malice, with wrecking and storm.
Beyond saying sweet, past telling of tongue,
Thou art lightning and love, I found it, a winter and
  warm;   70
  Father and fondler of heart thou hast wrung:
Hast thy dark descending and most art merciful then.

---

[9]**Galilee**: N Palestine, main scene of Jesus' life and ministry.

[10]**Passion**: Jesus' crucifixion, on the hill of **Calvary** (stanza 8).

[11]**sloe**: plumlike fruit of the blackthorn bush.

10

With an anvil-ding[12]
And with fire in him forge thy will
Or rather, rather then, stealing as Spring
   Through him, melt him but master him still:
Whether at once, as once at a crash Paul,[13]
Or as Austin, a lingering-out sweet skill,
   Make mercy in all of us, out of us all
Mastery, but be adored, but be adored King.   80

— PART THE SECOND —

11

"Some find me a sword; some
The flange[14] and the rail; flame,
Fang, or flood" goes Death on drum,
   And storms bugle his fame.
But we dream we are rooted in earth—Dust!
Flesh falls within sight of us, we, though our flower
   the same,
   Wave with the meadow, forget that there must
The sour scythe cringe, and the blear share come.

12

On Saturday sailed from Bremen,[15]
American-outward-bound,   90
Take settler and seamen, tell men with women,
   Two hundred souls in the round—
O Father, not under thy feathers[16] nor ever
   as guessing
The goal was a shoal, of a fourth the doom to be
   drowned;
   Yet did the dark side of the bay of
   thy blessing
Not vault them, the million of rounds of thy mercy not
   reeve[17] even them in?

13

Into the snows she sweeps,
Hurling the haven behind,
The Deutschland, on Sunday; and so the sky keeps,
   For the infinite air is unkind,   100
And the sea flint-flake, black-backed in the regular blow,
Sitting Eastnortheast, in cursed quarter, the wind;
   Wiry and white-fiery and whirlwind-swivellèd snow
Spins to the widow-making unchilding unfathering deeps.

14

She drove in the dark to leeward,
She struck—not a reef or a rock
But the combs of a smother of sand: night drew her
   Dead to the Kentish Knock;[18]
And she beat the bank down with her bows and the ride
   of her keel:
The breakers rolled on her beam with ruinous shock;   110
   And canvas and compass, the whorl[19] and the wheel
Idle for ever to waft her or wind her with, these she endured.

15

Hope had grown grey hairs,
Hope had mourning on,
Trenched with tears, carved with cares,
   Hope was twelve hours gone;
And frightful a nightfall folded rueful a day
Nor rescue, only rocket and lightship, shone,
   And lives at last were washing away:
To the shrouds they took,—they shook in the hurling and
   horrible airs.   120

16

One stirred from the rigging to save
The wild woman-kind below,
With a rope's end round the man, handy and brave—
   He was pitched to his death at a blow,
For all his dreadnought breast and braids of thew[20]:
They could tell him for hours, dandled the to and fro
   Through the cobbled foam-fleece. What could he do
With the burl of the fountains of air, buck and the flood of
   the wave?

---

[12]**ding**: heavy blow.

[13]**Paul**: see Acts 9:3–9 for the instantaneous conversion of St. Paul, contrasted to the prolonged conversion of **Austin** (St. Augustine, 354–430).

[14]**flange**: rim of a railroad wheel.

[15]**Bremen**: German port on the North Sea. The ship sailed for New York.

[16]**feathers**: see Psalm 91:4.

[17]**reeve**: gather.

---

[18]**combs**: ridges. **Kentish Knock**: sandbar off the mouth of the Thames River.

[19]**whorl**: propeller screw.

[20]**braids of thew**: knotted muscles.

17

They fought with God's cold—
　　And they could not and fell to the deck　　130
　　(Crushed them) or water (and drowned them) or rolled
　　　With the sea-romp over the wreck.
Night roared, with the heart-break hearing a
　　　heart-broke rabble,
The woman's wailing, the crying of child without check—
Till a lioness arose breasting the babble,
A prophetess towered in the tumult, a virginal tongue told.

18

Ah, touched in your bower of bone,
　　Are you! turned for an exquisite smart,
　　Have you! make words break from me here all alone,
　　　Do you!—mother of being in me, heart.　　140
O unteachably after evil, but uttering truth,
Why, tears! is it? tears; such a melting, a madrigal start!
　　Never-eldering revel and river of youth,
What can it be, this glee? the good you have there of
　　　your own?

19

Sister, a sister calling
　　A master, her master and mine!—
　　And the inboard seas run swirling and hawling;
　　　The rash smart sloggering brine
Blinds her; but she that weather[21] sees one thing, one;
Has one fetch in her: she rears herself to divine　　150
　　Ears, and the call of the tall nun
To the men in the tops and the tackle[22] rode over the
　　　storm's brawling.

20

She was first of a five and came
　　Of a coifèd sisterhood.
　　(O Deutschland, double a desperate name!
　　　O world wide of its good!
But Gertrude, lily, and Luther,[23] are two of a town,
Christ's lily and beast of the waste wood:
　　From life's dawn it is drawn down,
Abel is Cain's brother and breasts they have sucked
　　the same.)　　160

---

[21]**that weather**: in that circumstance.

[22]**tops, tackle**: masts, rigging.

[23]**Gertrude** (13th century): German saint. Martin **Luther** (1483–1546): instigator of Protestant Reformation, born in Gertrude's **town** Eisleben.

21

Loathed for a love men knew in them,
　　Banned by the land of their birth,
　　Rhine refused them, Thames would ruin them;
　　　Surf, snow, river and earth
Gnashed: but thou art above, thou Orion[24] of light;
Thy unchancelling poising palms were weighing the
　　　worth,
　　Thou martyr-master: in thy sight
Storm flakes were scroll-leaved flowers, lily showers—sweet
　　heaven was astrew in them.

22

Five! the finding and sake[25]
　　And cipher of suffering Christ.　　170
　　Mark, the mark is of man's make[26]
　　　And the word of it Sacrificed.
But he scores it in scarlet himself on his own
　　bespoken,
Before-time-taken, dearest prizèd and priced—
　　Stigma, signal, cinquefoil[27] token
For lettering of the lamb's fleece, ruddying of the
　　rose-flake.

23

Joy fall to thee, father Francis,[28]
　　Drawn to the Life that died;
　　With the gnarls of the nails in thee, niche of the
　　　lance, his
　　Lovescape crucified　　180
And seal of his seraph-arrival! and these thy
　　daughters
And five-livèd and leavèd favour and pride,
　　Are sisterly sealed in wild waters,
To bathe in his fall-gold mercies, to breathe in his all-fire
　　glances.

---

[24]**Orion**: winter constellation of the giant hunter, figuring the God who by **unchancelling** or evicting the nuns from their church has hunted them to martyrdom.

[25]**finding and sake**: clue and trace.

[26]**make**: manufacture, also match or likeness.

[27]**cinquefoil**: five-leaved.

[28]**Francis** of Assisi (1182–1226): founder of the nuns' order, marked by stigmata of **nails** and **spear** from Christ's crucifixion (the **lovescape** or pattern of compassion).

24

Away in the loveable west,
　　On a pastoral forehead of Wales,[29]
I was under a roof here, I was at rest,
　　And they the prey of the gales;
She to the black-about air, to the breaker, the thickly
Falling flakes, to the throng that catches and quails   190
　　Was calling "O Christ, Christ, come quickly":
The cross to her she calls Christ to her, christens her
　　wild-worst Best.

25

The majesty! what did she mean?
　　Breathe, arch and original Breath.
Is it love in her of the being as her lover had been?
　　Breathe, body of lovely Death.
They were else-minded then, altogether, the men
Woke thee with a *We are perishing* in the weather of
　　Gennesareth.[30]
Or is it that she cried for the crown then,
The keener to come at the comfort for feeling the
　　combating keen?   200

26

For how to the heart's cheering
　　The down-dugged ground-hugged grey[31]
Hovers off, the jay-blue heavens appearing
　　Of pied and peeled May!
Blue-beating and hoary-glow height; or night, still
　　higher,
With belled fire and the moth-soft Milky Way,
　　What by your measure is the heaven of desire,
The treasure never eyesight got, nor was ever guessed what
　　for the hearing?[32]

27

No, but it was not these.
　　The jading and jar of the cart,   210
Time's tasking, it is fathers that asking for ease
　　Of the sodden-with-its-sorrowing heart,

Not danger, electrical horror; then further it finds
The appealing of the Passion is tenderer in
　　prayer apart:
Other, I gather, in measure her mind's
Burden, in wind's burly[33] and beat of endragonèd seas.

28

But how shall I . . . make me room there:
　　Reach me a . . . Fancy, come faster—
Strike you the sight of it? look at it loom there,
　　Thing that she . . . There then! the Master,   220
Ipse,[34] the only one, Christ, King, Head:
He was to cure the extremity where he had cast her;
　　Do, deal, lord it with living and dead;
Let him ride, her pride, in his triumph, despatch and have
　　done with his doom there.

29

Ah! there was a heart right!
　　There was single eye![35]
Read the unshapeable shock night
　　And knew the who and the why;
Wording it how but by him that present and past,
Heaven and earth are word of, worded by?—   230
　　The Simon Peter[36] of a soul! to the blast
Tarpeïan-fast, but a blown beacon of light.

30

Jesu, heart's light,
　　Jesu, maid's son,
What was the feast followed the night
　　Thou hadst glory of this nun?—
Feast of the one woman without stain.[37]
For so conceivèd, so to conceive thee is done;
　　But here was heart-throe, birth of a brain,
Word, that heard and kept thee and uttered thee
　　outright.   240

---

[29]**forehead of Wales:** the hilltop St. Beuno's College, at which Hopkins was studying.

[30]*We are perishing* . . . **Gennesareth:** see Matthew 8:25.

[31]**down-dugged ground-hugged grey:** udder-shaped low rain cloud, embraced by hills.

[32]**The treasure . . . the hearing:** see Isaiah 64:4, 1 Corinthians 2:9.

[33]**burly:** uproar.

[34]*Ipse:* Himself (spoken at the elevation of the Host during Latin mass).

[35]**single eye:** see Luke 11:34.

[36]**Simon Peter:** called the rock of the church in Matthew 16:18. **Tarpeïan:** rock in Rome from which traitors were thrown to death.

[37]**Feast:** of the Immaculate Conception (December 8, the day after the wreck), honoring the Virgin Mary as born **without stain.**

31

Well, she has thee for the pain, for the
    Patience; but pity of the rest of them!
Heart, go and bleed at a bitterer vein for the
    Comfortless unconfessed of them—
No not uncomforted: lovely-felicitous Providence
Finger of a tender of, O of a feathery delicacy, the
    breast of the
    Maiden could obey so, be a bell to, ring of it, and
Startle the poor sheep back! is the shipwrack then a harvest,
    does tempest carry the grain for thee?

32

I admire thee, master of the tides,
    Of the Yore-flood,[38] of the year's fall;   250
The recurb and the recovery of the gulf's sides,
    The girth of it and the wharf of it and the wall;
Stanching, quenching ocean of a motionable mind;
Ground of being, and granite of it: past all
    Grasp God, throned behind
Death with a sovereignty that heeds but hides, bodes
    but abides;

33

With a mercy that outrides
    The all of water, an ark
For the listener; for the lingerer with a love glides
    Lower than death and the dark;   260
A vein for the visiting of the past-prayer, pent in prison,
The-last-breath penitent spirits—the uttermost mark
    Our passion-plungèd giant risen,
The Christ of the Father compassionate, fetched in the
    storm of his strides.

34

Now burn, new born to the world,
    Double-naturèd[39] name,
The heaven-flung, heart-fleshed, maiden-furled
    Miracle-in-Mary-of-flame,
Mid-numberèd[40] he in three of the thunder-throne!
Not a dooms-day dazzle in his coming nor dark as
    he came;   270
    Kind, but royally reclaiming his own;
A released shower, let flash to the shire, not a lightning
    of fire hard-hurled.

---

[38]**Yore-flood:** the Deluge (Genesis 7).

[39]**Double-naturèd:** Christ as human and divine.

[40]**Mid-numberèd:** second person in the Trinity.

35

Dame, at our door
    Drowned, and among our shoals,
Remember us in the roads,[41] the heaven-haven of
    the reward:
    Our King back, Oh, upon English souls!
Let him easter in us, be a dayspring to the dimness of us,
    be a crimson-cresseted east,
More brightening her, rare-dear Britain, as his reign
    rolls,
Pride, rose, prince, hero of us, high-priest,
Our hearts' charity's hearth's fire, our thoughts' chivalry's
    throng's Lord.   280
1876   *1918*

The Starlight Night

Look at the stars! look, look up at the skies!
    O look at all the fire-folk sitting in the air!
    The bright boroughs, the circle-citadels there!
Down in dim woods the diamond delves! the elves'-eyes!
The grey lawns cold where gold, where quickgold[1] lies!
    Wind-beat whitebeam! airy abeles[2] set on a flare!
    Flake-doves sent floating forth at a farmyard scare!—
Ah well! it is all a purchase, all is a prize.

Buy then! bid then!—What?—Prayer, patience, alms,
    vows.
Look, look: a May-mess, like on orchard boughs!   10
    Look! March-bloom, like on mealed-with-yellow
        sallows![3]
These are indeed the barn; withindoors house
The shocks. This piece-bright paling shuts the spouse
    Christ home, Christ and his mother and all his
        hallows.[4]
1877   *1893*

---

[41]**roads:** sheltered coastal anchorage.

[1]**quickgold:** liquid gold.

[2]**whitebeam, abeles:** trees whose leaves have silver undersides.

[3]**mess:** helping of food. **sallows:** willows, here in early spring
leaf.

[4]**barn:** see Matthew 13:30. **shocks:** gathered sheaves. **paling:**
fence. **hallows:** saints.

Spring

Nothing is so beautiful as Spring—
    When weeds, in wheels, shoot long and lovely and
        lush;
    Thrush's eggs look little low heavens, and thrush
Through the echoing timber does so rinse and wring
The ear, it strikes like lightnings to hear him sing;
    The glassy peartree leaves and blooms, they brush
    The descending blue; that blue is all in a rush
With richness; the racing lambs too have fair their fling.

What is all this juice and all this joy?
    A strain of the earth's sweet being in the beginning   10
In Eden garden.—Have, get, before it cloy,

    Before it cloud, Christ, lord, and sour with sinning,
Innocent mind and Mayday in girl and boy,
    Most, O maid's child, thy choice and worthy the
        winning.

1877   1918

God's Grandeur

The world is charged with the grandeur of God.
    It will flame out, like shining from shook foil;
    It gathers to a greatness, like the ooze of oil
Crushed. Why do men then now not reck his rod?
Generations have trod, have trod, have trod;
    And all is seared with trade; bleared, smeared with
        toil;
    And wears man's smudge and shares man's smell:
        the soil
Is bare now, nor can foot feel, being shod.

And for all this, nature is never spent;
    There lives the dearest freshness deep down things; 10
And though the last lights off the black West went
    Oh, morning, at the brown brink eastward,
        springs—
Because the Holy Ghost over the bent
    World broods with warm breast and with ah! bright
        wings.

1877   1918

The Windhover[1]

To Christ our Lord

I caught this morning morning's minion,[2] king-
    dom of daylight's dauphin,[3] dapple-dawn-drawn
      Falcon, in his riding
    Of the rolling level underneath him steady air, and
      striding
High there, how he rung upon the rein of a wimpling[4] wing
In his ecstasy! then off, off forth on swing,
    As a skate's heel sweeps smooth on a bow-bend: the
      hurl and gliding
    Rebuffed the big wind. My heart in hiding
Stirred for a bird,—the achieve of, the mastery of the thing!

Brute beauty and valour and act, oh, air, pride, plume, here
    Buckle! AND the fire that breaks from thee then,
      a billion   10
Times told lovelier, more dangerous, O my chevalier[5]!

    No wonder of it: shéer plód makes plough down
      sillion[6]
Shine, and blue-bleak embers, ah my dear,
    Fall, gall themselves, and gash gold-vermilion.

1877   1918

Pied Beauty

Glory be to God for dappled things—
    For skies of couple-colour as a brinded[1] cow;
      For rose-moles all in stipple upon trout that swim;
Fresh-firecoal chestnut-falls; finches' wings;
    Landscape plotted and pieced—fold,[2] fallow, and
      plough;
      And áll trádes, their gear and tackle and trim.

---

[1]**Windhover**: small falcon.
[2]**minion**: favorite.
[3]**dauphin**: prince.
[4]**rung**: circled. **wimpling**: rippling.
[5]**chevalier**: knight.
[6]**sillion**: ploughed furrow.
[1]**brinded**: streaked.
[2]**fold**: pastureland.

All things counter, original, spare, strange;
    Whatever is fickle, freckled (who knows how?)
      With swift, slow; sweet, sour; adazzle, dim;
He fathers-forth whose beauty is past change: 10
               Praise him.[3]

1877   1918

Hurrahing in Harvest

Summer ends now; now, barbarous in beauty, the
    stooks[1] rise
Around; up above, what wind-walks! what lovely
    behaviour
Of silk-sack clouds! has wilder, wilful-wavier
Meal-drift moulded ever and melted across skies?

I walk, I lift up, I lift up heart, eyes,
Down all that glory in the heavens to glean our
    Saviour;
And, éyes, heárt, what looks, what lips yet gave you a
Rapturous love's greeting of realer, of rounder replies?

And the azurous hung hills are his world-wielding
    shoulder
Majestic—as a stallion stalwart, very-violet-sweet!—   10
These things, these things were here and but the
    beholder
Wanting; which two when they once meet,
The heart rears wings bold and bolder
And hurls for him, O half hurls earth for him off under
    his feet.

1877   1918

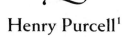

Henry Purcell[1]

The poet wishes well to the divine genius of Purcell and praises him that, whereas other musicians have given utterance to the moods of man's mind, he has, beyond that, uttered in notes the very make and species of man as created both in him and in all men generally.

Have fair fallen,[2] O fair, fair have fallen, so dear
To me, so arch-especial a spirit as heaves in Henry Purcell,
An age is now since passed, since parted; with the reversal
Of the outward sentence low lays him, listed to a heresy,[3]
    here.

Not mood in him nor meaning, proud fire or sacred fear,
Or love or pity or all that sweet notes not his might nursle:
It is the forgèd feature finds me; it is the rehearsal
Of own, of abrúpt sélf there so thrusts on, so throngs
    the ear.

Let him oh! with his air of angels then lift me, lay me!
    only I'll
Have an eye to the sakes of him, quaint moonmarks,[4]
    to his pelted plumage under   10
Wings: so some great stormfowl, whenever he has walked
    his while

The thunder-purple seabeach plumèd purple-of-thunder,
If a wuthering[5] of his palmy snow-pinions scatter a colossal
    smile
Off him, but meaning motion[6] fans fresh our wits with
    wonder.

1879   1918

---

[1]**Henry Purcell** (1659?–1695): English composer whose name was pronounced as Hopkins' rhymes suggest.

[2]**Have fair fallen:** May the **spirit** of Purcell have come to good (a subjunctive construction).

[3]**the outward . . . heresy:** the apparent damnation (which) lays him low as an attested Protestant heretic.

[4]**sakes:** distinctive markings, here the crescent-shaped **moonmarks** on a bird's feathers.

[5]**wuthering:** blustering.

[6]**but meaning motion:** although intent merely on his own action.

---

[3]**Praise him:** If this heavy double-stress is reckoned a half-line, then the 6:4.5 proportions of this curtailed or "curtal sonnet" (Hopkins) are equivalent to the classic 8:6.

[1]**stooks:** sheaves.

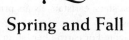

Felix Randal

Felix Randal the farrier,[1] O is he dead then? my duty all
    ended,
Who have watched his mould of man, big-boned and
    hardy-handsome
Pining, pining, till time when reason rambled in it and some
Fatal four disorders, fleshed there, all contended?

Sickness broke him. Impatient, he cursed at first, but mended
Being anointed[2] and all; though a heavenlier heart began
    some
Months earlier, since I had our sweet reprieve and ransom
Tendered to him. Ah well, God rest him all road[3] ever he
    offended!

This seeing the sick endears them to us, us too it endears.
My tongue had taught thee comfort, touch had quenched
    thy tears,   10
Thy tears that touched my heart, child, Felix, poor Felix
    Randal;

How far from then forethought of, all thy more boisterous
    years,
When thou at the random grim[4] forge, powerful amidst peers,
Didst fettle for the great grey drayhorse his bright and
    battering sandal!

1880   *1918*

Spring and Fall

To a Young Child

Márgarét, áre you gríeving
Over Goldengrove unleaving?
Leáves, like the things of man, you
With your fresh thoughts care for, can you?
Áh! ás the heart grows older
It will come to such sights colder

By and by, nor spare a sigh
Though worlds of wanwood leafmeal[1] lie;
And yet you *will* weep and know why.
Now no matter, child, the name: 10
Sórrow's spríngs áre the same.
Nor mouth had, no nor mind, expressed
What heart heard of, ghost guessed:
It ís the blight man was born for,
It is Margaret you mourn for.

1880   *1918*

As kingfishers catch fire, dragonflies draw flame;
    As tumbled over rim in roundy wells
    Stones ring; like each tucked[1] string tells, each hung bell's
Bow[2] swung finds tongue to fling out broad its name;
Each mortal thing does one thing and the same:
    Deals out that being indoors each one dwells;[3]
    Selves—goes itself; *myself* it speaks and spells,
Crying *What I do is me: for that I came.*

Í say more: the just man justices;[4]
    Keeps gráce: thát keeps all his goings graces;   10
Acts in God's eye what in God's eye he is—
    Chríst. For Christ plays in ten thousand places,
Lovely in limbs, and lovely in eyes not his
    To the Father through the features of men's faces.

1881?   *1918*

Carrion Comfort

Not, I'll not, carrion comfort, Despair, not feast on thee;
Not untwist—slack they may be—these last strands of man
In me ór, most weary, cry *I can no more.* I can;
Can something, hope, wish day come, not choose not
    to be.

---

[1]**farrier:** blacksmith.

[2]**anointed, reprieve and ransom:** rites of extreme unction and of communion.

[3]**all road:** in every way.

[4]**random:** irregular. **grim:** dirty.

---

[1]**wanwood:** decaying forest. **leafmeal:** one leaf at a time (as in *piecemeal*); also ground-up fallen leaves.

[1]**tucked:** plucked.

[2]**Bow:** yoke from which a bell hangs.

[3]**Deals out . . . dwells:** emits its inner essence ("which" is elided after **being**).

[4]**justices:** a verb.

But ah, but O thou terrible, why wouldst thou rude
    on me
Thy wring-world right foot rock? lay a lionlimb against
    me? scan
With darksome devouring eyes my bruisèd bones?
    and fan,
O in turns of tempest, me heaped there; me frantic to
    avoid thee and flee?
Why? That my chaff might fly; my grain lie, sheer and
    clear.
Nay in all that toil, that coil, since (seems) I kissed
    the rod,   10
Hand rather, my heart lo! lapped strength, stole joy,
    would laugh, chéer.
Cheer whom though? The hero whose heaven-handling
    flung me, fóot tród
Me? or me that fought him? O which one? is it each one?
    That night, that year
Of now done darkness I wretch lay wrestling with (my
    God!) my God.

1885?   *1918*

No worst, there is none. Pitched past pitch of grief,
More pangs will, schooled at forepangs, wilder wring.
Comforter,[1] where, where is your comforting?
Mary, mother of us, where is your relief?
My cries heave, herds-long; huddle in a main, a chief-
woe, world-sorrow; on an age-old anvil wince and sing—
Then lull, then leave off. Fury had shrieked "No ling-
ering! Let me be fell: force[2] I must be brief".
O the mind, mind has mountains; cliffs of fall
Frightful, sheer, no-man-fathomed. Hold them cheap   10
May who ne'er hung there. Nor does long our small
Durance deal with that steep or deep. Here! creep,
Wretch, under a comfort serves in a whirlwind: all
Life death does end and each day dies with sleep.

1885?   *1918*

I wake and feel the fell of dark, not day.
What hours, O what black hoúrs we have spent
This night! what sights you, heart, saw; ways you went!
And more must, in yet longer light's delay.

With witness I speak this. But where I say
Hours I mean years, mean life. And my lament
Is cries countless, cries like dead letters[1] sent
To dearest him that lives alas! away.

I am gall, I am heartburn. God's most deep decree
Bitter would have me taste: my taste was me;   10
Bones built in me, flesh filled, blood brimmed the curse.

Selfyeast of spirit a dull dough sours. I see
The lost are like this, and their scourge to be
As I am mine, their sweating selves; but worse.

1885?   *1918*

Spelt from Sibyl's Leaves[1]

Earnest, earthless, equal, attuneable, | vaulty, voluminous,
    . . . stupendous
Evening strains to be tíme's vást, | womb-of-all, home-of-all,
    hearse-of-all night.
Her fond yellow hornlight[2] wound to the west, | her wild
    hollow hoarlight hung to the height
Waste; her earliest stars, earlstars, | stárs principal,
    overbend us,
Fíre-féaturing heaven. For earth | her being has unbound;
    her dapple is at an end, as-
tray or aswarm, all throughther,[3] in throngs; | self in self
    steepèd and páshed—quíte
Disremembering, dísmémbering | áll now. Heart, you round
    me right

---

[1] **dead letters**: undelivered correspondence.

[1] **Sibyl**: soothsayer of classical legend whose oracular ecstasies were written down on paper **leaves**. Hopkins called this "the longest sonnet ever made."

[2] **hornlight**: as in a lantern made of thin horn.

[3] **throughther**: through one another.

---

[1] **Comforter**: the Holy Spirit.

[2] **Fury had shrieked**: My tormentor, had she been a Fury (classical goddess of vengeance), would have shrieked. **fell**: fierce. **force**: perforce, necessarily.

With: Óur évening is over us; óur night | whélms, whélms,
    ánd will end us.
Only the beakleaved boughs dragonish | damask[4] the
    tool-smooth bleak light; black,
Ever so black on it. Óur tale, O óur oracle! | Lét life,
    wáned, ah lét life wind   10
Off hér once skéined stained véined variety | upon, áll
    on twó spools; párt, pen, páck[5]
Now her áll in twó flocks, twó folds—black, white; |
    right, wrong; reckon but, reck but, mind
But thése two; wáre of a wórld where bút these | twó
    tell,[6] each off the óther; of a rack
Where, selfwrung, selfstrung, sheathe- and shelterless, |
    thóughts agaínst thoughts ín groans grínd.

1886   *1918*

That Nature Is a Heraclitean Fire[1] and of the Comfort of the Resurrection

Cloud-puffball, torn tufts, tossed pillows | flaunt forth,
    then chevy[2] on an air-
built thoroughfare: heaven-roysterers,[3] in gay-gangs | they
    throng; they glitter in marches.
Down roughcast,[4] down dazzling whitewash, | wherever
    an elm arches,
Shivelights and shadowtackle[5] in long | lashes lace, lance,
    and pair.

Delightfully the bright wind boisterous | ropes,
    wrestles, beats earth bare
Of yestertempest's creases; | in pool and rutpeel parches
Squandering ooze to squeezed | dough, crust, dust;[6]
    stanches, starches
Squadroned masks[7] and manmarks | treadmire toil there
Footfretted in it. Million-fuelèd, | nature's bonfire
    burns on.
But quench her bonniest, dearest | to her, her clearest-
    selvèd spark   10
Man, how fast his firedint, | his mark on mind, is gone!
Both are in an unfathomable, all is in an enormous dark
Drowned. O pity and indig | nation! Manshape, that shone
Sheer off, disseveral,[8] a star, | death blots black out;
    nor mark
        Is any of him at all so stark
But vastness blurs and time | beats level. Enough! the
    Resurrection,
A heart's-clarion! Away grief's gasping, | joyless days,
    dejection.
        Across my foundering deck shone
A beacon, an eternal beam. | Flesh fade, and mortal trash
Fall to the residuary worm; | world's wildfire, leave
    but ash: 20
        In a flash, at a trumpet crash,
I am all at once what Christ is, | since he was what
    I am, and
This Jack, joke, poor potsherd, | patch, matchwood,[9]
    immortal diamond,
        Is immortal diamond.

1888   *1918*

---

[4]**damask**: adorn with patterns.

[5]**part, pen, pack**: imperatives with **Let** in line 10.

[6]**tell**: count, matter.

[1]**Heraclitean Fire**: element of ceaseless flux that the Greek philosopher Heraclitus (540?–480 BCE) regarded as the basis of the cosmos.

[2]**chevy**: race.

[3]**roysterers**: hooligans.

[4]**roughcast**: plaster made of gravel and lime.

[5]**Shivelights**: splinters of light. **shadowtackle**: shadows like ships' rigging.

---

[6]**rutpeel**: marks in the earth damp from the **yestertempest** and skinned over as the wind **parches** and **squanders** (scatters) all forms into **dust**.

[7]**Squadroned masks**: squared-off, imprinted treads.

[8]**disseveral**: distinct.

[9]**Jack**: fellow. **potsherd**: see Isaiah 45:9. **patch**: fool. **matchwood**: tinder, also carbonized burnt match.

Justus quidem tu es, Domine, si disputem tecum; verumtamen justa loquar ad te: Quare via impiorum prosperatur? &c.[1]

Thou art indeed just, Lord, if I contend
With thee; but, sir, so what I plead is just.
Why do sinners' ways prosper? and why must
Disappointment all I endeavour end?

Wert thou my enemy, O thou my friend,
How wouldst thou worse, I wonder, than thou dost
Defeat, thwart me? Oh, the sots and thralls of lust
Do in spare hours more thrive than I that spend,

Sir, life upon thy cause. See, banks and brakes[2]   10
Now, leavèd how thick! lacèd they are again
With fretty chervil,[3] look, and fresh wind shakes

Them; birds build—but not I build; no, but strain,
Time's eunuch, and not breed one work that wakes.
Mine, O thou lord of life, send my roots rain.

1889   *1918*

To R. B.[1]

The fine delight that fathers thought; the strong
Spur, live and lancing like the blowpipe flame,
Breathes once and, quenchèd faster than it came,
Leaves yet the mind a mother of immortal song.

Nine months she then, nay years, nine years she long
Within her wears, bears, cares and combs the same:
The widow of an insight lost she lives, with aim
Now known and hand at work now never wrong.

Sweet fire the sire of muse, my soul needs this;
I want the one rapture of an inspiration.   10
O then if in my lagging lines you miss

---

[1] *Justus . . . prosperatur?*: Righteous art thou, O Lord, when I plead with thee: yet let me talk with thee of thy judgments: Wherefore doth the way of the wicked prosper? (Jeremiah 12:1).

[2] **brakes**: untilled fields.

[3] **fretty**: interlaced. **chervil**: parsley-like wild herb.

[1] **R. B.**: Robert Bridges (1844–1930), Hopkins' classmate at Oxford and literary executor; edited and published Hopkins' *Poems*, 1918; poet laureate 1913–1930.

The roll, the rise, the carol, the creation,
My winter world, that scarcely breathes that bliss
Now, yields you, with some sighs, our explanation.

1889   *1893*

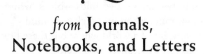

from Journals, Notebooks, and Letters

Flick, fillip, flip, fleck, flake.

Flick means to touch or strike lightly as with the end of a whip, a finger etc. To *fleck* is the next tone above flick, still meaning to touch or strike lightly (and leave a mark of the touch or stroke) but in a broader less slight manner. Hence substantively[1] a *fleck* is a piece of light, colour, substance etc. looking as though shaped or produced by such touches. *Flake* is a broad and decided *fleck*, a thin plate of something, the tone above it. Their connection is more clearly seen in the applications of the words to natural objects than in explanations. It would seem that *fillip* generally pronounced *flip* is a variation of *flick*, which however seems connected with *fly, flee, flit*, meaning to make fly off. Key to meaning of *flick, fleck* and *flake* is that of striking or cutting off the surface of a thing; in *flick* (as to flick off a fly) something little or light from the surface, while *flake* is a thin scale of surface. *Flay* is therefore connected, perhaps *flitch*. (1863 diary)

The sky minted into golden sequins.
Stars like gold tufts.
— —golden bees.
— —golden rowels.
Sky peak'd with tiny flames.
Stars like tiny-spoked wheels of fire.
Lantern of night pierced in eyelets, (or eye lets, which
        avoids ambiguity.)
Altogether peak is a good word. For sunlight through shutter, locks of hair, rays in brass knobs etc. Meadows peaked with flowers. (1864 diary)

---

[1] **substantively**: as a noun.

. . . I am meditating an essay, perhaps for the *Hexameron*,[2] on some points of poetical criticism, and it is with reference to this a little that I have composed my thoughts on Tennyson. I think then the language of verse may be divided into three kinds.[3] The first and highest is poetry proper, the language of inspiration. The word inspiration need cause no difficulty. I mean by it a mood of great, abnormal in fact, mental acuteness, either energetic or receptive, according as the thoughts which arise in it seem generated by a stress and action of the brain, or to strike into it unasked. This mood arises from various causes, physical generally, as good health or state of the air or, prosaic as it is, length of time after a meal. But I need not go into this; all that it is needful to mark is, that the poetry of inspiration can only be written in this mood of mind, even if it only last a minute, by poets themselves. Everybody of course has like moods, but not being poets what they then produce is not poetry. This second kind I call *Parnassian*.[4] It can only be spoken by poets, but it is not in the highest sense poetry. It does not require the mood of mind in which the poetry of inspiration is written. It is spoken *on and from the level* of a poet's mind, not, as in the other case, when the inspiration which is the gift of genius, raises him above himself. For I think it is the case with genius that it is not when quiescent so very much above mediocrity as the difference between the two might lead us to think, but that it has the power and privilege of rising from that level to a height utterly far from mediocrity: in other words that its greatness is *that it can be* so great. You will understand. *Parnassian* then is that language which genius speaks as fitted to its exaltation, and place among other genius, but does not sing (I have been betrayed into the whole hog of a metaphor) in its flights. Great men, poets I mean, have each their own dialect as it were of Parnassian, formed generally as they go on writing, and at last,—this is the point to be marked,—they can see things in this Parnassian way and describe them in this Parnassian tongue, without further effort of inspiration. In a poet's particular kind of Parnassian lies most of his style, of his manner, of his mannerism if you like. But I must not go farther without giving you instances of Parnassian. I shall take one from Tennyson, and from *Enoch Arden*, from a passage much quoted already and which will be no doubt often quoted, the description of Enoch's tropical island.

> The mountain wooded to the peak, the lawns
> And winding glades high up like ways to Heaven,
> The slender coco's drooping crown of plumes,
> The lightning flash of insect and of bird,
> The lustre of the long convolvuluses
> That coil'd around the stately stems, and ran
> Ev'n to the limit of the land, the glows
> And glories of the broad belt of the world,
> All these he saw.

Now it is a mark of Parnassian that one could conceive oneself writing it if one were the poet. Do not say that *if* you were Shakespear you can imagine yourself writing Hamlet, because that is just what I think you cannot conceive. In a fine piece of inspiration every beauty takes you as it were by surprise, not of course that you did not think the writer could be so great, for that is not it,—indeed I think it is a mistake to speak of people admiring Shakespear more and more as they live, for when the judgment is ripe and you have read a good deal of any writer including his best things, and carefully, then, I think, however high the place you give him, that you must have rated him equally with his merits however great they be; so that all after admiration cannot increase but keep alive this estimate, make his greatness stare into your eyes and din it into your ears, as it were, but not make it greater,—but to go on with the broken sentence, every fresh beauty could not in any way be predicted or accounted for by what one has already read. But in Parnassian pieces you feel that if you were the poet you could have gone on as he has done, you see yourself doing it, only with the difference that if you actually try, to find you cannot write his Parnassian. Well now to turn to the piece above. The glades being "like ways to Heaven," is, I think, a new thought, it is an inspiration. Not so the next line, that is pure Parnassian. If you examine it the words are choice and the description is beautiful and unexceptionable, but it does not *touch* you. The next is more Parnassian still. In the next lines I think the picture of the convolvuluses does touch; but only the picture: the words are Parnassian. It is a very good instance, for the lines are undoubtedly beautiful, but yet I could scarcely point anywhere to anything more idiomatically Parnassian, to anything which I more clearly see myself writing *qua*[5] Tennyson, than the words

> The glows
> And glories of the broad belt of the world.

---

[2]*Hexameron:* club of Oxford undergraduates with High-Church sympathies.

[3]**three kinds:** Hopkins' letter never gets to the third, which a contemporary diary entry specifies as the ordinary language of everyday use.

[4]*Parnassian:* of Parnassus, mountain sacred to the Muses.

[5]*qua:* as.

What Parnassian is you will now understand, but I must make some more remarks on it. I believe that when a poet palls on us it is because of his Parnassian. We seem to have found out his secret. Now in fact we have not found out more than this, that when he is not inspired and in his flights, his poetry does run in an intelligibly laid down path. Well, it is notorious that Shakespear does not pall, and this is because he uses, I believe, so little Parnassian. He does use some, but little. Now judging from my own experience I should say no author palls so much as Wordsworth; this is because he writes such an "intolerable deal of" Parnassian. . . (Letter to Alexander Baillie,[6] September 10/11, 1864)

For Lent. No pudding on Sundays. No tea except if to keep me awake and then without sugar. Meat only once a day. No verses in Passion Week or on Fridays. No lunch or meat on Fridays. Not to sit in armchair except can work in no other way. Ash Wednesday and Good Friday bread and water.

Drops of rain hanging on rails etc seen with only the lower rim lighted like nails (of fingers). Screws of brooks and twines. Soft chalky look with more shadowy middles of the globes of cloud on a night with a moon faint or concealed. Mealy clouds with a not brilliant moon. Blunt buds of the ash. Pencil buds of the beech. Lobes of the trees. Cups of the eyes. Gathering back the lightly hinged eyelids. Bows of the eyelids. Pencil of eyelashes. Juices of the eyeball. Eyelids like leaves, petals, caps, tufted hats, handkerchiefs, sleeves, gloves. Also of the bones sleeved in flesh. Juices of the sunrise. Joins and veins of the same. Vermilion look of the hand held against a candle with the darker parts as the middles of the fingers and especially the knuckles covered with ash. (1866 diary)

March 12—A fine sunset: the higher sky dead clear blue bridged by a broad slant causeway rising from right to left of wisped or grass cloud, the wisps lying across; the sundown yellow, moist with light but ending at the top in a foam of delicate white pearling and spotted with big tufts of cloud in colour russet between brown and purple but edged with brassy light. But what I note it all for is this: before I had always taken the sunset and the sun as quite out of gauge with each other, as indeed physically they are, for the eye after looking at the sun is blunted to everything else and if you look at the rest of the sunset you must cover the sun, but today I inscaped them[7] together and made the sun the true eye and ace of the whole, as it is. It was all active and tossing out light and started as strongly forward from the field as a long stone or a boss in the knop[8] of the chalice-stem: it is indeed by stalling it so that it falls into scape with the sky.

The next morning a heavy fall of snow. It tufted and toed the firs and yews and went on to load them till they were taxed beyond their spring. The limes, elms, and Turkey-oaks[9] it crisped beautifully as with young leaf. Looking at the elms from underneath you saw every wave in every twig (become by this the wire-like stem to a finger of snow) and to the hangers and flying sprays it restored, to the eye, the inscapes they had lost. They were beautifully brought out against the sky, which was on one side dead blue, on the other washed with gold.

At sunset the sun a crimson fireball, above one or two knots of rosy cloud middled with purple. After that, frost for two days. . . .

Sept. 24—First saw the Northern Lights. My eye was caught by beams of light and dark very like the crown of horny rays the sun makes behind a cloud. At first I thought of silvery cloud until I saw that these were more luminous and did not dim the clearness of the stars in the Bear.[10] They rose slightly radiating thrown out from the earthline. Then I saw soft pulses of light one after another rise and pass upwards arched in shape but waveringly and with the arch broken. They seemed to float, not following the warp of the sphere as falling stars look to do but free though concentrical with it. This busy working of nature wholly independent of the earth and seeming to go on in a strain of time not reckoned by our reckoning of days and years but simpler and as if correcting the preoccupation of the world

---

[7]**inscaped them:** perceived their unique and essential form or "inscape" (Hopkins' coinage); compare **scape** (visible relationship) in the next sentence.

[8]**boss in the knop:** protuberance within the knob.

[9]**Turkey-oaks:** species native to Europe (*Quercus cerris*).

[10]**Bear:** Ursa Major, the Big Dipper.

by being preoccupied with and appealing to and dated to the day of judgment was like a new witness to God and filled me with delightful fear

Oct. 20—Laus Deo[11]—the river today and yesterday. Yesterday it was a sallow glassy gold at Hodder Roughs[12] and by watching hard the banks began to sail upstream, the scaping unfolded, the river was all in tumult but not running, only the lateral motions were perceived, and the curls of froth where the waves overlap shaped and turned easily and idly.—I meant to have written more.— Today the river was wild, very full, glossy brown with mud, furrowed in permanent billows through which from head to head the water swung with a great down and up again. These heads were scalped with rags of jumping foam. But at the Roughs the sight was the burly water-backs which heave after heave kept tumbling up from the broken foam and their plump heap turning open in ropes of velvet

. . . The winter was long and hard. I made many observations on freezing. For instance the crystals in mud.—Hailstones are shaped like the cut of diamonds called brilliants.[13]—I found one morning the ground in one corner of the garden full of small pieces of potsherd from which there rose up (and not dropped off) long icicles carried on in some way each like a forepitch of the shape of the piece of potsherd it grew on, like a tooth to its root for instance, and most of them bended over and curled like so many tusks or horns or / best of all and what they looked likest when they first caught my eye / the first soft root-spurs thrown out from a sprouting chestnut. This bending of the icicle seemed so far as I could see not merely a resultant, where the smaller spars of which it was made were still straight, but to have flushed them too.—The same day and others the garden mould very crisp and meshed over with a lace-work of needles leaving (they seemed) three-cornered openings: it looked greyish and like a coat of gum on wood. Also the smaller crumbs and clods were lifted fairly up from the ground on upright ice-pillars, whether they had dropped these from themselves or drawn them from the soil: it was like a little Stonehenge—Looking down into the thick ice of our pond I found the imprisoned air-bubbles nothing at random but starting from centres and in particular one most beautifully regular white brush of them, each spur of it a curving string of beaded and diminishing bubbles—The pond, I suppose from over pressure when it was less firm, was mapped with a puzzle of very slight clefts branched with little sprigs: the pieces were odd-shaped and sized—though a square angular scaping could be just made out in the outline but the cracks ran deep through the ice markedly in planes and always the planes of the cleft on the surface. They remained and in the end the ice broke up in just these pieces (1870 journal)

. . . What you look hard at seems to look hard at you, hence the true and the false instress[14] of nature. One day early in March when long streamers were rising from over Kemble End[15] one large flake loop-shaped, not a streamer but belonging to the string, moving too slowly to be seen, seemed to cap and fill the zenith with a white shire of cloud. I looked long up at it till the tall height and the beauty of the scaping—regularly curled knots springing if I remember from fine stems, like foliation in wood or stone— had strongly grown on me. It changed beautiful changes, growing more into ribs and one stretch of running into branching like coral. Unless you refresh the mind from time to time you cannot always remember or believe how deep the inscape in things is. (1871 journal)

Is all verse poetry or all poetry verse?—Depends on definitions of both. Poetry is speech framed for contemplation of the mind by the way of hearing or speech framed to be heard for its own sake and interest even over and above its interest of meaning. Some matter and meaning is essential to it but only as an element necessary to support and employ the shape which is contemplated for its own sake. (Poetry is in fact speech only employed to carry the inscape of speech for the inscape's sake—and therefore the inscape must be dwelt on. Now if this can be done without repeating it *once* of the inscape will be enough for art and beauty and poetry but then at least the inscape must be understood as so standing by itself that it could be copied

---

[11]**Laus Deo**: Praise to God.

[12]**Hodder Roughs**: rapids in the River Hodder, near St. Mary's Hall, a Jesuit seminary in Lancashire (NW England), where Hopkins took two of his eight years' training for the priesthood.

[13]**brilliants**: diamonds cut horizontally on top and bottom.

---

[14]**instress**: Hopkins' coinage for the indwelling force, ultimately divine, that produces and sustains "inscape" (see note above).

[15]**Kemble End**: hill near St. Mary's; Hopkins is observing clouds.

and repeated. If not/ repetition, *oftening, over-and-overing, aftering* of the inscape must take place in order to detach it to the mind and in this light poetry is speech which afters and oftens its inscape, speech couched in a repeating figure and verse is spoken sound having a repeating figure.) Verse is (inscape of spoken sound, not spoken words, or speech employed to carry the inscape of spoken sound— or in the usual words) speech wholly or partially repeating the same figure of sound. Now there is speech which wholly or partially repeats the same figure of grammar and this may be framed to be heard for its own sake and interest over and above its interest of meaning. Poetry then may be couched in this, and therefore all poetry is not verse but all poetry is either verse or falls under this or some still further development of what verse is, speech wholly or partially repeating some kind of figure which is over and above meaning, at least the grammatical, historical, and logical meaning ("Poetry and Verse," lecture notes, 1873–1874)[16]

. . . Why do I employ sprung rhythm at all? Because it is the nearest to the rhythm of prose, that is the native and natural rhythm of speech, the least forced, the most rhetorical and emphatic of all possible rhythms, combining, as it seems to me, opposite and, one wd. have thought, incompatible excellences, markedness of rhythm—that is rhythm's self—and naturalness of expression—for why, if it is forcible in prose to say "lashed : rod", am I obliged to weaken this in verse, which ought to be stronger, not weaker, into "láshed birch-ród" or something?

My verse is less to be read than heard, as I have told you before; it is oratorical, that is the rhythm is so. I think if you will study what I have here said you will be much more pleased with it and may I say? converted to it.

You ask may you call it "presumptious jugglery". No, but only for this reason, that *presumptious* is not English.

I cannot think of altering anything. Why shd. I? I do not write for the public. You are my public and I hope to convert you.

You say you wd. not for any money read my poem again. Nevertheless I beg you will. Besides money, you know, there is love. If it is obscure do not bother yourself with the meaning but pay attention to the best and most intelligible stanzas, as the two last of each part and the narra-

tive of the wreck. If you had done this you wd. have liked it better and sent me some serviceable criticisms, but now your criticism is of no use, being only a protest memorialising me against my whole policy and proceedings.

I may add for your greater interest and edification that what refers to myself in the poem is all strictly and literally true and did all occur; nothing is added for poetical padding. (Letter to Robert Bridges,[17] August 21, 1877)

. . . You ask, do I write verse myself. What I had written I burnt before I became a Jesuit and resolved to write no more, as not belonging to my profession, unless it were by the wish of my superiors; so for seven years I wrote nothing but two or three little presentation pieces which occasion called for. But when in the winter of '75 the Deutschland was wrecked in the mouth of the Thames and five Franciscan nuns, exiles from Germany by the Falck Laws, aboard of her were drowned I was affected by the account and happening to say so to my rector he said that he wished someone would write a poem on the subject. On this hint I set to work and, though my hand was out at first, produced one. I had long had haunting my ear the echo of a new rhythm[18] which now I realised on paper. To speak shortly, it consists in scanning by accents or stresses alone, without any account of the number of syllables, so that a foot may be one strong syllable or it may be many light and one strong. I do not say the idea is altogether new; there are hints of it in music, in nursery rhymes and popular jingles, in the poets themselves, and, since then, I have seen it talked about as a thing possible in critics. Here are instances—"Díng, dóng, béll; Pússy's ín the wéll; Whó pút her ín? Líttle Jóhnny Thín. Whó púlled her óut? Líttle Jóhnny Stóut." For if each line has three stresses or three feet it follows that some of the feet are of one syllable only. So too "Óne, twó, Búckle my shóe" *passim*. In Campbell you have "Ánd their fléet alóng the *déep próudly* shóne"—"Ít was tén of Ápril mórn bý the chíme" etc; in Shakspere[19] "Whý shd.

[16]**lecture notes**: from Hopkins' time teaching Classics and English to Jesuit novices at Roehampton (S of London).

[17]**Robert Bridges** (1844–1930): Hopkins' Oxford classmate and chief correspondent on poetry. See the sonnet "To R. B."

[18]**new rhythm**: the "sprung rhythm" characteristic of Hopkins' verse from "The Wreck of the *Deutschland*" forward.

[19]Thomas **Campbell** (1777–1844): author of "The Battle of the Baltic" (1805). Hopkins quotes lines 5 and 14, the former inaccurately ("fleet" for "arms"). **Shakspere**: quoting *As You Like It* 3.2.120, a song often editorially emended to begin, "Why should this a desert be?" Shakespeare's name was variably spelled during the 19th century. Thomas **Moore** (1779–1852): author of *Irish Melodies* (1807).

thís désert bé?" corrected wrongly by the editors; in Moore a little melody I cannot quote; etc. But no one has professedly used it and made it the principle throughout, that I know of. Nevertheless to me it appears, I own, to be a better and more natural principle than the ordinary system, much more flexible, and capable of much greater effects. However I had to mark the stresses in blue chalk, and this and my rhymes carried on from one line into another and certain chimes suggested by the Welsh poetry I had been reading (what they call *cynghanedd*)[20] and a great many more oddnesses could not but dismay an editor's eye, so that when I offered it to our magazine the *Month*, though at first they accepted it, after a time they withdrew and dared not print it. After writing this I held myself free to compose, but cannot find it in my conscience to spend time upon it; so I have done little and shall do less. But I wrote a shorter piece[21] on the Eurydice, also in "sprung rhythm," as I call it, but simpler, shorter, and without marks, and offered the *Month* that too, but they did not like it either. Also I have written some sonnets and a few other little things; some in sprung rhythm, with various other experiments—as "outriding feet," that is parts of which do not count in the scanning (such as you find in Shakspere's later plays, but as a licence, whereas mine are rather calculated effects); others in the ordinary scanning *counterpointed* (this is counterpoint: "*Hóme to* his *móther's hóuse prívate* retúrned" and "*Bút to vánquish* by *wísdom héllish wíles'*" etc);[22] others, one or two, in common uncounterpointed rhythm. But even the impulse to write is wanting, for I have no thought of publishing.

I should add that Milton is the great standard in the use of counterpoint. In *Paradise Lost* and *Regained*, in the last more freely, it being an advance in his art, he employs counterpoint more or less everywhere, markedly now and then; but the choruses of *Samson Agonistes* are in my judgment counterpointed throughout; that is, each line (or nearly so) has two different coexisting scansions. But when you reach that point the secondary or "mounted rhythm," which is necessarily a sprung rhythm, overpowers the original or conventional one and then this becomes superfluous and may be got rid of; by taking that last step you reach simple sprung rhythm. Milton must have known this but had reasons for not taking it. . . . (Letter to R. W. Dixon,[23] October 5, 1878)

"Homo creatus est"[24]—Aug. 20 1880: during this retreat, which I am making at Liverpool, I have been thinking about creation and this thought has led the way naturally through the exercises hitherto. I put down some thoughts.—We may learn that all things are created by consideration of the world without or of ourselves the world within. The former is the consideration commonly dwelt on, but the latter takes on the mind more hold. I find myself both as man and as myself something most determined and distinctive, at pitch, more distinctive and higher pitched than anything else I see; I find myself with my pleasures and pains, my powers and my experiences, my deserts and guilt, my shame and sense of beauty, my dangers, hopes, fears, and all my fate, more important to myself than anything I see. And when I ask where does all this throng and stack of being, so rich, so distinctive, so important, come from / nothing I see can answer me. And this whether I speak of human nature or of my individuality, my selfbeing. For human nature, being more highly pitched, selved, and distinctive than anything in the world, can have been developed, evolved, condensed, from the vastness of the world not anyhow or by the working of common powers but only by one of finer or higher pitch and determination than itself and certainly than any that elsewhere we see, for this power had to force forward the starting or stubborn elements to the one pitch required. And this is much more true when we consider the mind; when I consider my selfbeing, my consciousness and feeling of myself, that taste of myself, of *I* and *me* above and in all things, which is more distinctive than the taste of ale or alum, more distinctive than the smell of walnutleaf or camphor, and is incommunicable by any means to another man (as when I was a child I used to ask myself: What must it be to be someone else?). Nothing else in nature comes near this unspeakable stress of pitch, distinctiveness, and selving, this selfbeing of my own. Nothing explains it or resembles it, except so far as this, that other men to themselves have the same feeling. But this only multiplies the phenomena to be explained so far as the cases are like and do resemble. But to me there is no resemblance: searching nature I taste *self* but at one tankard, that of my own being. (Comments on *Spiritual Exercises* of Loyola, 1880)

---

[20]*cynghanedd:* Welsh verse rich in alliteration and internal rhyme.

[21]**shorter piece:** "The Loss of the *Eurydice*" (1878).

[22]"*Hóme to . . . wíles*": quoting Milton's *Paradise Regained* 4.639 and 1.175.

[23]**R. W. Dixon** (1833–1900): poet, Anglican priest and historian.

[24]"**Homo creatus est**": Man was created. Hopkins here meditates, during a retreat, on the preface to the *Spiritual Exercises* of St. Ignatius of Loyola (1491–1556), founder of the Jesuits.

MICHAEL FIELD

(KATHARINE BRADLEY, 1846–1914)
(EDITH COOPER, 1862–1913)

"Michael Field" was the pen name of an aunt and niece who collaboratively published several verse dramas and volumes of poetry. The younger of two daughters of the prosperous owner of a tobacco factory, Katharine Bradley was educated by tutors at home. After the death of her mother in 1868 she studied in Paris, where she enjoyed a brief passion for a glamorous Frenchman, and then returned to England to live with her sister's family. In 1875 she spent a summer at the recently opened Newnham College, Cambridge, and published a collection of poems for which she used the pseudonym "Arran Leigh," presumably in tribute to Barrett Browning's poet-heroine Aurora Leigh. She subscribed to John Ruskin's fantastic-chivalric Guild of St. George and kept up a correspondence with Ruskin that erupted in storm when Bradley declared herself an atheist. Later she had other intense friendships with artists and men of letters, but her emotional life centered on her reciprocated affection for her sister's daughter Edith.

By the time Edith Cooper was sixteen they had established their partnership, living with Edith's parents and sister, attending university lectures in classics and philosophy, and studying, reading, and writing together. They lived together for the rest of their lives. In the diary they kept together Bradley wrote, after talking with Robert Browning about his long-dead wife:

> Oh! love. I give thanks for my Persian [one of Bradley's pet names for Cooper]: those two poets, man and wife, wrote alone; each wrote, but did not bless or quicken one another at their work; *we are closer married.*

Each apparently did her actual writing alone in her own room, but they edited each other's work and published only as Michael Field. The poems "It was deep April" and "A Girl" celebrate their collaboration.

Michael Field made his first appearance in 1884 with two well-received verse plays, one based on classical legend, one on English history. In 1889 they published *Long Ago*, a series of lyrics extrapolated from fragments of Sappho's poetry and spoken in Sappho's voice, as if Sappho were a third in their collaboration. Sappho has lived in legend since ancient times as the greatest of all lyric poets, although her work survives almost entirely in tiny fragments. Many poets had used her as a model, but the poems in *Long Ago* are presented more as imitations of imagined Sapphic originals than as modern reinterpretations. Perhaps the most thoroughgoing of all late-century revisions of high Victorian classicism, *Long Ago* considers the delights and perplexities of love in a lush setting of meadows, groves, and streams peopled mostly by Greek gods and lovers and presided over by Aphrodite, goddess of beauty and love. Several poems are based on Sappho's legendary unrequited passion for Phaon the fisherman, or the poet Alcaeus' equally unrequited love for her, but most concern a group of women. By the 1880s poets such as Baudelaire and Swinburne had used the figure of Sappho with direct reference to lesbianism (Sappho being from the island of Lesbos), but in England the idea of female homosexuality was just beginning to be formulated as a clinical category. While it is extremely difficult to assess sexual attitudes (to say nothing of sexual behavior) from more than a century ago, close friendships and verbal expressions of love between women were fairly common, and apparently most people saw nothing transgressive either in the poems or in Bradley and Cooper's friendship.

Their second collection of poems, *Sight and Song* (1892), describes pictures in museums. An experiment in ekphrasis—translation from visual into verbal art—the book abounds in sensuous, erotically charged description. Succeeding collections are increasingly varied. *Underneath the Bough* (1893) is mostly about love, usually in classical landscapes or English meadows and gardens. Poems published after the turn of the century extend the range of moods and subjects. In 1907 Bradley and Cooper, like many writers associated with aestheticism, converted to the Roman Catholic Church.

The intricately wrought verse of Michael Field, with its delicate metrical irregularities and verbal surprises, its subtle artificialities and studied naturalness, displays considerable formal inventiveness. As befits the collaborative project, the poems characteristically express reciprocity, equality, and even identity between lover and beloved, human and divine, or opposing states of mind, and, most fundamentally, between the poetic speaker and the object of desire. Untroubled by conventional oppositions of gender, these poems effortlessly achieve the equality between poets and lovers that Barrett Browning's *Sonnets from the Portuguese* struggles for. The difficulty of choosing pronouns to talk about Michael Field (female or male? singular or plural?) is a continual reminder of the poems' escape from conventional terms of identity.

The early work of Michael Field was well reviewed, and George Meredith and Robert Browning were among those who privately expressed approbation. In 1936 William Butler Yeats, another early admirer, included nine of their poems in the *Oxford Book of Modern Verse*. Although artistic collaboration was fairly frequent around the turn of the century, however, it goes against the Romantic idea of genius, and the fact that the collaborators were soon discovered to be women worked against them. Their poems appeared only in small, elegantly artistic editions, and even in their lifetime ceased to attract attention. They were rediscovered at the end of the twentieth century.

Χρύσεοι δ' ἐρέβινθοι ἐπ' ἀϊνων ἐφύοντο[1]

Where with their boats the fishers land
Grew golden pulse along the sand;
It tangled Phaon's[2] feet—away
He spurned the trails, and would not stay;
Its stems and yellow flowers in vain
Withheld him: can my arms detain
The fugitive? If that might be,
If I could win him from the sea,
Then subtly I would draw him down
'Mid the bright vetches; in a crown   10
My art should teach him to entwine
Their thievish rings, and keep him mine.

                                        1889

Ταῖς κάλαις ὔμμιν [τὸ] νόημα τὢμον οὐ διάμειπτον[1]

Maids, not to you my mind doth change;
Men I defy, allure, estrange,
Prostrate, make bond or free:
Soft as the stream beneath the plane[2]
To you I sing my love's refrain;
Between us is no thought of pain,
          Peril, satiety.

Soon doth a lover's patience tire,
But ye to manifold desire
Can yield response, ye know   10
When for long, museful days I pine,
The presage at my heart divine;[3]
To you I never breathe a sign
          Of inward want or woe.

When injuries my spirit bruise,
Allaying virtue ye infuse
With unobtrusive skill:
And if care frets ye come to me
As fresh as nymph from stream or tree,
And with your soft vitality   20
          My weary bosom fill.

                                        1889

Ἄλλα, μὴ μεγαλύνεο δακτυλίῳ πέρι[1]

Come, Gorgo, put the rug in place,
          And passionate recline;
I love to see thee in thy grace,
          Dark, virulent, divine.
But wherefore thus thy proud eyes fix
          Upon a jewelled band?
Art thou so glad the sardonyx
          Becomes thy shapely hand?
Bethink thee! 'Tis for such as thou
          Zeus leaves his lofty seat;[2]   10
'Tis at thy beauty's bidding how
          Man's mortal life shall fleet;
Those fairest hands—dost thou forget
          Their power to thrill and cling?
O foolish woman, dost thou set
          Thy pride upon a ring?

                                        1889

Διὸς παῖς ὁ χρυσός, κεῖνον οὐ σῆς οὐδὲ κὶς δάπτει,[1]

Yea, gold is son of Zeus: no rust
          Its timeless light can stain;
The worm that brings man's flesh to dust
          Assaults its strength in vain:
More gold than gold the love I sing,
A hard, inviolable thing.

---

[1]**Χρύσεοι . . . ἐφύοντο:** And golden pulse grew on the shore. This and the following three poems from *Long Ago* expand on the fragments of Sappho's poetry that appear as epigraphs. **pulse:** leguminous plants, like **vetches.**

[2]**Phaon:** fisherman for love of whom Sappho, according to ancient tradition, killed herself.

[1]**Ταῖς . . . διάμειπτον:** To you lovely maids my thoughts do not change.

[2]**plane:** tall spreading tree.

[3]**presage . . . divine:** perceive through sympathy the foreboding in my heart.

---

[1]**Ἄλλα . . . πέρι:** But do not be proud because of a ring.

[2]**Zeus:** king of the gods, who often came to earth to make love to beautiful women.

[1]**Διὸς . . . δάπτει:** Gold is the child of Zeus, no moth nor worm devours it.

Men say the passions should grow old
    With waning years; my heart
Is incorruptible as gold,
    'Tis my immortal part: 10
Nor is there any god can lay
On love the finger of decay.

                1889

Ah me, if I grew sweet to man[1]
It was but as a rose that can
No longer keep the breath that heaves
And swells among its folded leaves.

The pressing fragrance would unclose
The flower, and I became a rose,
That unimpeachable and fair
Planted an odour in the air.

No art I used men's love to draw;
I lived but by my being's law,   10
As roses are by heaven designed
To bring the honey to the wind.

I found there is scant sun in spring,
I found the blast a riving thing;
Yet even ruined roses can
No other than be sweet to man.

            1890, 1893

A Portrait

Bartolommeo Veneto[1]

The Städel'sche Institut at Frankfurt

A crystal, flawless beauty on the brows
Where neither love nor time has conquered space
On which to live; her leftward smile endows
The gazer with no tidings from the face;
About the clear mounds of the lip it winds with silvery pace

---

[1]**Ah me, if I grew sweet to man**: This lyric is sung by Mary
Queen of Scots in Field's play *The Tragic Mary*.

[1]**Bartolommeo Veneto**: 16th-century Italian painter.

And in the umber eyes it is a light
Chill as a glowworm's when the moon embrowns an
    August night.

She saw her beauty often in the glass,
Sharp on the dazzling surface, and she knew
The haughty custom of her grace must pass: 10
Though more persistent in all charm it grew
As with a desperate joy her hair across her throat
    she drew
In crinkled locks stiff as dead, yellow snakes . . .
Until at last within her soul the resolution wakes.

She will be painted, she who is so strong
In loveliness, so fugitive in years:
Forth to the field she goes and questions long
Which flowers to choose of those the summer bears;
She plucks a violet larkspur,—then a columbine appears
    Of perfect yellow,—daisies choicely wide;   20
These simple things with finest touch she gathers in
    her pride.

Next on her head, veiled with well-bleachen white
And bound across the brow with azure-blue,
She sets the box-tree leaf and coils it tight
In spiky wreath of green, immortal hue;
Then, to the prompting of her strange, emphatic
    insight true,
She bares one breast, half-freeing it of robe,
And hangs green-water gem and cord beside the naked
    globe.

So was she painted and for centuries
Has held the fading field-flowers in her hand   30
Austerely as a sign. O fearful eyes
And soft lips of the courtesan who planned
To give her fragile shapeliness to art, whose reason
    spanned
Her doom, who bade her beauty in its cold
And vacant eminence persist for all men to behold!

She had no memories save of herself
And her slow-fostered graces, naught to say
Of love in gift or boon; her cruel pelf
Had left her with no hopes that grow and stay;
She found default in everything that happened night
    or day,   40
Yet stooped in calm to passion's dizziest strife
And gave to art a fair, blank form, unverified by life.

Thus has she conquered death: her eyes are fresh,
Clear as her frontlet jewel, firm in shade
And definite as on the linen mesh
Of her white hood the box-tree's sombre braid,
That glitters leaf by leaf and with the year's waste will
    not fade.
The small, close mouth, leaving no room for breath,
In perfect, still pollution smiles—Lo, she has conquered
    death!

1892

A Pen-Drawing of Leda

Sodoma[1]

The Grand Duke's Palace at Weimar

'Tis Leda lovely, wild and free,
    Drawing her gracious Swan down through the grass
        to see
    Certain round eggs without a speck:
One hand plunged in the reeds and one dinting the
        downy neck,
    Although his hectoring bill
    Gapes toward her tresses,
She draws the fondled creature to her will.

    She joys to bend in the live light
Her glistening body toward her love, how much more
        bright!
    Though on her breast the sunshine lies   10
And spreads its affluence on the wide curves of her waist
        and thighs,
    To her meek, smitten gaze
    Where her hand presses
The Swan's white neck sink Heaven's concentred rays.

1892

Ah, Eros[1] doth not always smite
    With cruel, shining dart,
Whose bitter point with sudden might
    Rends the unhappy heart—
Not thus forever purple-stained,
    And sore with steely touch,
Else were its living fountain drained
    Too oft and overmuch.
O'er it sometimes the boy will deign
    Sweep the shaft's feathered end;
And friendship rises without pain
    Where the white plumes descend.

1893

When high Zeus first peopled earth,
    As sages say,
All were children of one birth,
Helpless nurslings. Doves and bees
Tended their soft infancies:
Hand to hand they tossed the ball,
And none smiled to see the play,
    Nor stood aside
    In pride
And pleasure of their youthful day.   10
    All waxed gray,
Mourning in companies the winter dearth:
    Whate'er they saw befall
    Their neighbours, they
    Felt in themselves; so lay
    On life a pall.

Zeus at the confusion smiled,
    And said, "From hence
Man by change must be beguiled;
Age with royalties of death,   20
Childhood, sweeter than its breath,
Will be won, if we provide
Generation's difference."
    Wisely he planned;
    The tiny hand,

---

[1]Zeus, king of the gods, made love in the form of a swan to
Leda, who gave birth to four children, including Helen of Troy.
ll **Sodoma:** Giovanni Bazzi (1477–1549), Italian painter.

---

[1]**Eros:** youthful god of love in Greek mythology whose arrows
cause erotic passion.

In eld's weak palm found providence,
   And each through influence
Of things beholden and not borne grew mild:
   Youths by the old man's side
      Their turbulence   30
      To crystal sense
      Saw clarified.

Dear, is not the story's truth
      Most manifest?
Had our lives been twinned, forsooth,
We had never had one heart:
By time set a space apart,
We are bound by such close ties
None can tell of either breast
      The native sigh   40
        Who try
To learn with whom the Muse is guest.
   How sovereignly I'm blest

To see and smell the rose of my own youth
   In thee: how pleasant lies
      My life, at rest
   From dream, its hope expressed
      Before mine eyes.

                     1893

A Girl,
   Her soul a deep-wave pearl
Dim, lucent of all lovely mysteries;
   A face flowered for heart's ease,[1]
   A brow's grace soft as seas
   Seen through faint forest-trees:
   A mouth, the lips apart,
Like aspen-leaflets trembling in the breeze
From her tempestuous heart.
Such: and our souls so knit,   10
I leave a page half-writ—
      The work begun
Will be to heaven's conception done,
      If she come to it.

                   1893

---

[1]**heart's ease:** heartsease is an old name for pansies.

Noon

Full summer and at noon; from a waste bed
Convolvulus, musk-mallow,[1] poppies spread
The triumph of the sunshine overhead.

Blue on refulgent ash-trees lies the heat;
It tingles on the hedge-rows; the young wheat
Sleeps, warm in golden verdure, at my feet.

The pale, sweet grasses of the hayfield blink;
The heath-moors, as the bees of honey drink,
Suck the deep bosom of the day. To think

Of all that beauty by the light defined   10
None shares my vision! Sharply on my mind
Presses the sorrow: fern and flower are blind.

                     1893

An Apple-Flower

I felt my leaves fall free,
   I felt the wind and sun,
At my heart a honey-bee:
   And life was done.

                     1893

Unbosoming

The love that breeds
   In my heart for thee!
As the iris is full, brimful of seeds,
And all that it flowered for among the reeds
Is packed in a thousand vermilion-beads
That push, and riot, and squeeze, and clip,
Till they burst the sides of the silver scrip,
And at last we see
What the bloom, with its tremulous, bowery fold
Of zephyr-petal[1] at heart did hold: 10

---

[1]**convolvulus, musk-mallow:** wildflowers.

[1]**zephyr:** flowering plant (zephyranth) with waving stalks; soft breeze; kind of butterfly.

So my breast is rent
With the burthen and strain of its great content;
For the summer of fragrance and sighs is dead,
The harvest-secret is burning red,
And I would give thee, after my kind,
The final issues of heart and mind.

1893

Love rises up some days
From a blue couch of light
　　Upon the summer sky;
He wakes, and waking plays
With beams and dewdrops white;
His laugh is like the sunniest rain,
　　And patters through his voice;
He is so lovely, tolerant, and sane,
　　That the heart questions why
It doth not, every hour it beats, rejoice.　　10

Yet sometimes Love awakes
On a black, hellish bed,
　　And rises up as hate:
He drinks the hurtful lakes,
He joys to toss and spread
Sparkles of pitchy, rankling flame,
　　He joys to play with death;
But when we look on him he is the same
　　Quaint child we blest of late,
And every word that once he said he saith.　　20

1893

It was deep April, and the morn
　　Shakspere was born;[1]
The world was on us, pressing sore;
My Love and I took hands and swore,
　　Against the world, to be

Poets and lovers evermore,
To laugh and dream on Lethe's shore,
To sing to Charon[2] in his boat,
Heartening the timid souls afloat;
Of judgment never to take heed,　　10
But to those fast-locked souls to speed,
Who never from Apollo[3] fled,
Who spent no hour among the dead;
　　Continually
　　　With them to dwell,
Indifferent to heaven and hell.

1893

Cyclamens[1]

They are terribly white:
　　There is snow on the ground,
And a moon on the snow at night;
The sky is cut by the winter light;
Yet I, who have all these things in ken,
Am struck to the heart by the chiselled white
　　Of this handful of cyclamen.

1893

To Christina Rossetti

Lady, we would behold thee moving bright
As Beatrice or Matilda[1] 'mid the trees,
Alas! thy moan was as a moan for ease
And passage through cool shadows to the night:
Fleeing from love, hadst thou not poet's right
To slip into the universe? The seas
Are fathomless to rivers drowned in these,
And sorrow is secure in leafy light.

---

[2]**Charon:** ferryman of the dead across the rivers of Hades. **Lethe:** river of forgetfulness in Hades.

[3]**Apollo:** Greek god associated with the sun and music.

[1]**cyclamens:** flowers.

[1]**Beatrice, Matilda:** blessed spirits in Dante's *Divine Comedy;* **Beatrice** was the object of Dante's ideal love.

---

[1]**April 23:** the date of **Shakespeare**'s death, traditionally taken as his birthday too; also St. George's Day, honoring the patron saint of England.

Ah, had this secret touched thee, in a tomb
Thou hadst not buried thy enchanting self,   10
As happy Syrinx murmuring with the wind,
Or Daphne[2] thrilled through all her mystic bloom,
From safe recess as genius or as elf,
Thou hadst breathed joy in earth and in thy kind.

1896

Your rose is dead,
    They said,
The Grand Mogul[1]—for so her splendour
Exceeded, masterful, it seemed her due
By dominant male titles to commend her:
    But I, her lover, knew
That myriad-coloured blackness, wrought with fire,
Was woman to the rage of my desire.
    My rose was dead? She lay
Against the sulphur, lemon and blush-gray   10
Of younger blooms, transformed, morose,
Her shrivelling petals gathered round her close,
    And where before,
Coils twisted thickest at her core
A round, black hollow: it had come to pass
Hints of tobacco, leather, brass,
Confounded, gave her texture and her colour.
I watched her, as I watched her, growing duller,
    Majestic in recession
    From flesh to mould.   20
My rose is dead—I echo the confession,
    And they pass to pluck another;
While I, drawn on to vague, prodigious pleasure,
    Fondle my treasure.
O sweet, let death prevail
Upon you, as your nervous outlines thicken
And totter, as your crimsons stale,
I feel fresh rhythms quicken;
Fresh music follows you. Corrupt, grow old,
Drop inwardly to ashes, smother   30
Your burning spices, and entoil
My senses till you sink a clod of fragrant soil!

1898

[2]**Syrinx** escaped Pan's amorous embrace by being turned into a reed, from which the first flute was made. **Daphne** fleeing Apollo was turned into a laurel tree.

[1]*Grand Mogul:* European name for the Emperor of Delhi.

Grass in Spring

Spring!
    The light is stronger, the air is shuddering,
The sky is smiling through sun-clouds that shall be
        showers,
And the grass is caught imagining
    Flowers.

1898

Stream and Pool[1]

Mine is the eddying foam and the broken current,
Thine the serene-flowing tide, the unshattered rhythm;
Light touches me on the surface with glints of sunshine,
Dives in thy bosom disclosing a mystic river:
Ruffling, the wind takes the crest of my waves resurgent,
Stretches his pinions at poise on thy even ripples:
What is my song but the tumult of chafing forces,
What is thy silence, Beloved, but enchanted music!

1898

I love you with my life—'tis so I love you;
    I give you as a ring
The cycle of my days till death:
    I worship with the breath
That keeps me in the world with you and spring:
And God may dwell behind, but not above you.

Mine, in the dark, before the world's beginning:
    The claim of every sense,
    Secret and source of every need;
    The goal to which I speed,   10
And at my heart a vigour more immense
Than will itself to urge me to its winning.

1895?   *1908*

[1]**Stream and Pool:** The first of three poems in imitation of classical meters, grouped as "Metrum Praxillae"; Praxilla was a woman poet of ancient Greece.

The Mummy Invokes His Soul

Down to me quickly, down! I am such dust,
Baked, pressed together; let my flesh be fanned
With thy fresh breath; come from thy reedy land
Voiceful with birds; divert me, for I lust
To break, to crumble—prick with pores this crust!—
And fall apart, delicious, loosening sand.
Oh, joy, I feel thy breath, I feel thy hand
That searches for my heart, and trembles just
Where once it beat. How light thy touch, thy frame!
Surely thou perchest on the summer trees . . .   10
And the garden that we loved? Soul, take thine ease,
I am content, so thou enjoy the same
Sweet terraces and founts, content, for thee,
To burn in this immense torpidity.

1897?   1908

Good Friday

There is wild shower and winter on the main.
Foreign and hostile, as the flood of Styx,[1]
The rumbling water: and the clouds that mix
And drop across the land, and drive again
Whelm as they pass. And yet the bitter rain,
The fierce exclusion hurt me not; I fix
My thought on the deep-blooded crucifix
My lips adore, and there is no more pain.
A Power is with me that can love, can die,
That loves, and is deserted, and abides;   10
A loneliness that craves me and enthrals:
And I am one with that extremity,
One with that strength. I hear the alien tides
No more, no more the universe appals.

1897   1908

---

[1]**Styx:** river in classical underworld.

Nests in Elms

The rooks are cawing up and down the trees!
Among their nests they caw. O sound I treasure,
Ripe as old music is, the summer's measure,
Sleep at her gossip, sylvan mysteries,
With prate and clamour to give zest of these—
In rune[1] I trace the ancient law of pleasure,
Of love, of all the busy-ness of leisure,
With dream on dream of never-thwarted ease.
O homely birds, whose cry is harbinger
Of nothing sad, who know not anything   10
Of sea-birds' loneliness, of Procne's[2] strife,
Rock round me when I die! So sweet it were
To die by open doors, with you on wing
Humming the deep security of life.

1899?   1908

Ebbtide at Sundown

How larger is remembrance than desire!
How deeper than all longing is regret!
The tide is gone, the sands are rippled yet;
The sun is gone; the hills are lifted higher,
Crested with rose. Ah, why should we require
Sight of the sea, the sun? The sands are wet,
And in their glassy flaws huge record set
Of the ebbed stream, the little ball of fire.
Gone, they are gone! But, oh, so freshly gone,
So rich in vanishing we ask not where—   10
So close upon us is the bliss that shone,
And, oh, so thickly it impregns the air!
Closer in beating heart we could not be
To the sunk sun, the far, surrendered sea.

1899?   1908

---

[1]**rune:** written character or sung verse, often magical.

[2]**Procne:** in early Greek myth, which this poem seems to follow, Procne was transformed into the nightingale, her sister Philomela into a swallow, after Procne's husband raped Philomela and cut out her tongue. In the more familiar Latin version the sisters' transformations are reversed.

OSCAR WILDE
(1854–1900)

Outrageous, indecent, immoral, morbid, degenerate, depraved—such terms of abuse were often envoked by the Aesthetic and Decadent movements of the 1890s and their presumed leader, Oscar Wilde. Like Matthew Arnold baiting the Philistines in the name of culture, Wilde enjoyed teasing the respectable middle classes. He asserted with brilliantly paradoxical wit the primacy of art over life, artifice over nature, individual self-development over conventional morality. What he loved best in the world, he said in a light-hearted moment, was "Poetry and Paradox dancing together." But he himself danced to and over the edge of danger; he spent two terrible years in prison and died in poverty and disgrace. The catastrophic conclusion to his brilliant career seemed to confirm in the most public and appalling way the fin-de-siècle notion that artists were corrupt and art corrupting.

Oscar Fingal O'Flahertie Wills Wilde's father was an eminent Dublin physician, his mother a poet who published under the name "Speranza." A brilliant classical scholar though a lazy and disdainful pupil, he studied first in Dublin, then at Oxford, where he came under the influence of John Ruskin and Walter Pater. He cultivated the deliberately outrageous persona of a dandy, elevating self-adornment and interior decoration to the status of art and mocking the virtues and values of the money-making classes with imperturbable nonchalance. Satirists were quick to retaliate, delighting in the target offered by his flamboyant self-fashioning—long hair, distinctive attire, a passion for lilies and blue china—and his memorable paradoxes. He became a man-about-town in London, published a volume of poems that was called licentious and immoral, and exploited his notoriety with a lecture tour in North America and numerous lectures in Britain. He produced reviews, essays, fairy tales and other stories, and from 1887 to 1889 edited *The Woman's World*, a journal to which he gave a strong feminist edge. He argued that art could transform the world, and in "The Soul of Man under Socialism" (1891) he imagined a noncoercive socialism under which poverty would disappear and individual personalities flourish. But there was another side to Wilde's vision, too: a "decadent" fascination with corruption and sin, that appeared in his novel *The Picture of Dorian Gray* (1890) and his drama *Salomé* (1893).

His most lucrative works were his comedies, staged with great success in London. The last and best of these, *The Importance of Being Earnest*, revalues with an impeccably light touch some of the most serious themes of Victorian literature: identity, individualism, and self-creation; nature and family values; the truth of art and its influence on life; scientific and religious controversy; the worship of money; women's education and conventional gender roles; class stereotypes (useless aristocrats, the virtuous poor); and the grand hallmark of high Victorian culture, earnestness itself.

Earnest also plays with the idea of a double life: the heroes (if that is the word for either Jack or Algy) are one person in the country, another in London. Even as the comedy was enjoying its great theatrical success, Wilde allowed the dangerous side of his own double life to be exposed to public view. Having bolstered his respectability by marrying in 1884 and becoming the father of two children, he had soon turned his attention to young men. A love affair with Lord Alfred Douglas led Lord Alfred's enraged and aggressive father, the Marquess of Queensberry, to accuse Wilde of "posing" as a Sodomite, and Wilde with astonishing recklessness sued him for libel. The ensuing trial brought into the open Wilde's dealings with male prostitutes and led to his being charged under the Criminal Law Amendment Act of 1885 (see page 97), which outlawed acts of "gross indecency" between men. After one trial ended with a hung jury the charge was brought again, resulting in the maximum penalty, two years imprisonment with hard labor.

These sensational trials fixed in the public mind the association of aestheticism, decadence, and homosexuality. There had been a growing tendency in the course of the century to relegate art to the feminine sphere, in opposition to the world of money and power, manliness and public virtue. Charges of unmanliness had been leveled against poets, and also against critics like Arnold, Ruskin, and Pater who spoke for culture and art. Dante Rossetti and Swinburne had been accused of depicting excessive and indecent sexuality. Much of Wilde's work hints at sexual transgression, particularly *Dorian Gray*. But at the trials the issue was specifically and explicitly homosexual behavior. There was talk of "the Love that dare not speak its name," a phrase from a poem by Lord Alfred Douglas. Asked by a prosecution lawyer to define it, Wilde replied:

> The "Love that dare not speak its name" in this century is such a great affection of an elder for a younger man as there was between David and Jonathan, such as Plato made the very basis of his philosophy, and such as you find in the sonnets of Michelangelo and Shakespeare. It is that deep, spiritual affection that is as pure as it is perfect. It dictates and pervades great works of art. . . . It is in this century misunderstood . . . and on account of it I am placed where I am now. It is beautiful, it is fine, it is the noblest form of affection. There is nothing unnatural about it. . . . The world mocks at it and sometimes puts one in the pillory for it.

Mocked and vilified by the press, ostracized by society, Wilde endured the modern equivalent of the pillory as well as the horrors of solitary confinement. He courageously declared that his art would be deepened and purified by his sufferings, and while he was in prison he composed a long letter to Lord Alfred Douglas that was published in expurgated form after his death under the title *De Profundis*. But after his release he wrote only a long poem, "The Ballad of Reading Gaol" (1898), the most famous prison poem in English. He died in France three and a half years after his release, a bankrupt and broken exile. Yet he remains as striking a figure to the imagination in humiliation and disgrace as when he laughingly defied the forces of respectability that destroyed him.

"I have put my genius into my life; I have put only my talent into my works." Like most of Wilde's pithy sayings, this paradoxical balancing of opposites is both true and not true. His life was a deliberately created work of art—or so he liked to think—that spun out of control and inspired, in the end, the pity and terror of tragedy. In the best of his literary works, however, and especially in his comic mode, there is a quality one is glad to call genius.

Impression du Matin[1]

The Thames nocturne of blue and gold
   Changed to a Harmony[2] in grey:
   A barge with ochre-coloured hay
Dropt from the wharf: and chill and cold

The yellow fog came creeping down
   The bridges, till the houses' walls
   Seemed changed to shadows, and S. Paul's[3]
Loomed like a bubble o'er the town.

Then suddenly arose the clang
   Of waking life; the streets were stirred   10
   With country waggons: and a bird
Flew to the glistening roofs and sang.

But one pale woman all alone,
   The daylight kissing her wan hair,
   Loitered beneath the gas lamps' flare,
With lips of flame and heart of stone.

                     1881

The Harlot's House[1]

We caught the tread of dancing feet,
We loitered down the moonlit street,
And stopped beneath the Harlot's house.

Inside, above the din and fray,
We heard the loud musicians play
The "Treues Liebes Herz" of Strauss.[2]

Like strange mechanical grotesques,
Making fantastic arabesques,
The shadows raced across the blind.

We watched the ghostly dancers spin   10
To sound of horn and violin,
Like black leaves wheeling in the wind.

Like wire-pulled automatons,
Slim silhouetted skeletons
Went sidling through the slow quadrille,

Then took each other by the hand,
And danced a stately saraband;
Their laughter echoed thin and shrill.

Sometimes a clock-work puppet pressed
A phantom lover to her breast,   20
Sometimes they seemed to try and sing,

Sometimes a horrible Marionette
Came out, and smoked its cigarette
Upon the steps like a live thing.

Then turning to my love I said,
"The dead are dancing with the dead,
The dust is whirling with the dust."

But she, she heard the violin,
And left my side, and entered in;
Love passed into the house of Lust.   30

Then suddenly the tune went false,
The dancers wearied of the waltz,
The shadows ceased to wheel and whirl,

And down the long and silent street,
The dawn with silver-sandalled feet,
Crept like a frightened girl.

                     1885

Symphony in Yellow

An omnibus across the bridge
   Crawls like a yellow butterfly,
   And, here and there, a passer-by
Shows like a little restless midge.

Big barges full of yellow hay
   Are moored against the shadowy wharf,
   And, like a yellow silken scarf,
The thick fog hangs along the quay.

The yellow leaves begin to fade
   And flutter from the Temple[1] elms,   10
   And at my feet the pale green Thames
Lies like a rod of rippled jade.

                     1889

---

[1]**Impression du Matin**: impression of the morning.

[2]**nocturne, Harmony**: terms for musical compositions, like symphony, that J. A. M. Whistler (1834–1903) used with the names of colors for many paintings, including London scenes like this one.

[3]**S. Paul's**: London cathedral with a great dome.

[1]**Harlot's House**: see Joshua 2:1.

[2]**"Treues Liebes Herz"**: "Heart of True Love," waltz by Viennese composer Johann **Strauss** (1825–1899).

---

[1]**Temple**: buildings in London on the river **Thames**.

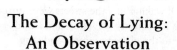

from The Picture of Dorian Gray

The Preface

The artist is the creator of beautiful things.

To reveal art and conceal the artist is art's aim.

The critic is he who can translate into another manner or a new material his impression of beautiful things.

The highest as the lowest form of criticism is a mode of autobiography.

Those who find ugly meanings in beautiful things are corrupt without being charming. This is a fault.

Those who find beautiful meanings in beautiful things are the cultivated. For these there is hope.

They are the elect to whom beautiful things mean only Beauty.

There is no such thing as a moral or an immoral book.

Books are well written, or badly written. That is all.

The nineteenth century dislike of Realism is the rage of Caliban[1] seeing his own face in a glass.

The nineteenth century dislike of Romanticism is the rage of Caliban not seeing his own face in a glass.

The moral life of man forms part of the subject-matter of the artist, but the morality of art consists in the perfect use of an imperfect medium.

No artist desires to prove anything. Even things that are true can be proved.

No artist has ethical sympathies. An ethical sympathy in an artist is an unpardonable mannerism of style.

No artist is ever morbid. The artist can express everything.

Thought and language are to the artist instruments of an art.

Vice and virtue are to the artist materials for an art.

From the point of view of form, the type of all the arts is the art of the musician. From the point of view of feeling, the actor's craft is the type.

All art is at once surface and symbol.

Those who go beneath the surface do so at their peril.

Those who read the symbol do so at their peril.

It is the spectator, and not life, that art really mirrors.

Diversity of opinion about a work of art shows that the work is new, complex, and vital.

When critics disagree the artist is in accord with himself.

We can forgive a man for making a useful thing as long as he does not admire it. The only excuse for making a useless thing is that one admires it intensely.

All art is quite useless.

1891

The Decay of Lying: An Observation

— A DIALOGUE —

PERSONS: CYRIL AND VIVIAN.

SCENE: THE LIBRARY OF A COUNTRY HOUSE IN OTTINGHAMSHIRE.

CYRIL: (*coming in through the open window from the terrace*). My dear Vivian, don't coop yourself up all day in the library. It is a perfectly lovely afternoon. The air is exquisite. There is a mist upon the woods, like the purple bloom upon a plum. Let us go and lie on the grass, and smoke cigarettes, and enjoy Nature.

VIVIAN: Enjoy Nature! I am glad to say that I have entirely lost that faculty. People tell us that Art makes us love Nature more than we loved her before; that it reveals her secrets to us; and that after a careful study of Corot and Constable[1] we see things in her that had escaped our observation. My own experience is that the more we study Art, the less we care for Nature. What Art really reveals to us is Nature's lack of design, her curious crudities, her extraordinary monotony, her absolutely unfinished condition. Nature has good intentions, of course, but, as Aristotle once said,[2] she cannot carry them out. When I look at a

---

[1]**Caliban:** see Shakespeare, *The Tempest.*

[1]Camille **Corot** (1796–1875): French landscape painter. John **Constable** (1776–1837): English landscape painter.

[2]**Aristotle** (384–322 BCE): philosopher whose most important discussion of art is the *Poetics.*

landscape I cannot help seeing all its defects. It is fortunate for us, however, that Nature is so imperfect, as otherwise we should have had no art at all. Art is our spirited protest, our gallant attempt to teach Nature her proper place. As for the infinite variety of Nature, that is a pure myth. It is not to be found in Nature herself. It resides in the imagination, or fancy, or cultivated blindness of the man who looks at her.

CYRIL: Well, you need not look at the landscape. You can lie on the grass and smoke and talk.

VIVIAN: But Nature is so uncomfortable. Grass is hard and lumpy and damp, and full of dreadful black insects. Why, even Morris' poorest workman could make you a more comfortable seat than the whole of Nature can. Nature pales before the furniture of "the street which from Oxford has borrowed its name," as the poet[3] you love so much once vilely phrased it. I don't complain. If Nature had been comfortable, mankind would never have invented architecture, and I prefer houses to the open air. In a house we all feel of the proper proportions. Everything is subordinated to us, fashioned for our use and our pleasure. Egotism itself, which is so necessary to a proper sense of human dignity, is entirely the result of indoor life. Out of doors one becomes abstract and impersonal. One's individuality absolutely leaves one. And then Nature is so indifferent, so unappreciative. Whenever I am walking in the park here, I always feel that I am no more to her than the cattle that browse on the slope, or the burdock that blooms in the ditch. Nothing is more evident than that Nature hates Mind. Thinking is the most unhealthy thing in the world, and people die of it just as they die of any other disease. Fortunately, in England at any rate, thought is not catching. Our splendid physique as a people is entirely due to our national stupidity. I only hope we shall be able to keep this great historic bulwark of our happiness for many years to come; but I am afraid that we are beginning to be over-educated; at least everybody who is incapable of learning has taken to teaching—that is really what our enthusiasm for education has come to. In the meantime, you had better go back to your wearisome uncomfortable Nature, and leave me to correct my proofs.

CYRIL: Writing an article! That is not very consistent after what you have just said.

VIVIAN: Who wants to be consistent? The dullard and the doctrinaire, the tedious people who carry out their principles to the bitter end of action, to the *reductio ad absurdum*[4] of practice. Not I. Like Emerson, I write over the door of my library the word "Whim." Besides my article is really a most salutary and valuable warning. If it is attended to, there may be a new Renaissance of Art.

CYRIL: What is the subject?

VIVIAN: I intend to call it "The Decay of Lying: A Protest."

CYRIL: Lying! I should have thought that our politicians kept up that habit.

VIVIAN: I assure you that they do not. They never rise beyond the level of misrepresentation, and actually condescend to prove, to discuss, to argue. How different from the temper of the true liar, with his frank, fearless statements, his superb irresponsibility, his healthy, natural disdain of proof of any kind! After all, what is a fine lie? Simply that which is its own evidence. If a man is sufficiently unimaginative to produce evidence in support of a lie, he might just as well speak the truth at once. No, the politicians won't do. Something may, perhaps, be urged on behalf of the Bar.[5] The mantle of the Sophist has fallen on its members. Their feigned ardours and unreal rhetoric are delightful. They can make the worse appear the better cause, as though they were fresh from Leontine schools, and have been known to wrest from reluctant juries triumphant verdicts of acquittal for their clients, even when those clients, as often happens, were clearly and unmistakeably innocent. But they are briefed[6] by the prosaic, and are not ashamed to appeal to precedent. In spite of their endeavours, the truth will out. Newspapers, even, have degenerated. They may now be absolutely relied upon. One feels it as one wades through their columns. It is always the unreadable that occurs. I am afraid that there is not

---

[4]*reductio ad absurdum*: refutation of a proposition by following it to a nonsensical conclusion. "**Whim**": see Ralph Waldo **Emerson**, "Self-Reliance" (1841).

[5]**the Bar**: lawyers. **Sophist**: 5th-century BCE Greek teacher of rhetoric, the falsifying art of persuasion. **Leontine**: from Leontini, in ancient Sicily.

[6]**briefed**: hired and instructed as legal counsel.

---

[3]"**the street . . . name**": Oxford Street, a major shopping area of London. **poet**: see Wordsworth, "Power of Music" (1807)4.

much to be said in favour of either the lawyer or the journalist. Besides, what I am pleading for is Lying in art. Shall I read you what I have written? It might do you a great deal of good.

CYRIL: Certainly, if you give me a cigarette. Thanks. By the way, what magazine do you intend it for?

VIVIAN: For the *Retrospective Review*.[7] I think I told you that the elect had revived it.

CYRIL: Whom do you mean by "the elect"?

VIVIAN: Oh, The Tired Hedonists[8] of course. It is a club to which I belong. We are supposed to wear faded roses in our button-holes when we meet, and to have a sort of cult for Domitian. I am afraid you are not eligible. You are too fond of simple pleasures.

CYRIL: I should be black-balled on the ground of animal spirits, I suppose?

VIVIAN: Probably. Besides, you are a little too old. We don't admit anybody who is of the usual age.

CYRIL: Well, I should fancy you are all a good deal bored with each other.

VIVIAN: We are. That is one of the objects of the club. Now, if you promise not to interrupt too often, I will read you my article.

CYRIL: You will find me all attention.

VIVIAN: (*reading in a very clear, musical voice*) "THE DECAY OF LYING: A PROTEST.—One of the chief causes that can be assigned for the curiously commonplace character of most of the literature of our age is undoubtedly the decay of Lying as an art, a science, and a social pleasure. The ancient historians gave us delightful fiction in the form of fact; the modern novelist presents us with dull facts under the guise of fiction. The Blue-Book[9] is rapidly becoming his ideal both for method and manner. He has his tedious '*document humain*,' his miserable little '*coin de la création*,' into which he peers with his microscope. He is to be found at the Librairie Nationale, or at the British Museum, shamelessly reading up his subject. He has not even the courage of other people's ideas, but insists on going directly to life for everything, and ultimately, between encyclopædias and personal experience, he comes to the ground, having drawn his types from the family circle or from the weekly washerwoman, and having acquired an amount of useful information from which never, even in his most meditative moments, can he thoroughly free himself.

"The loss that results to literature in general from this false ideal of our time can hardly be over-estimated. People have a careless way of talking about a 'born liar,' just as they talk about a 'born poet.' But in both cases they are wrong. Lying and poetry are arts—arts, as Plato[10] saw, not unconnected with each other—and they require the most careful study, the most disinterested devotion. Indeed, they have their technique, just as the more material arts of painting and sculpture have, their subtle secrets of form and colour, their craft-mysteries, their deliberate artistic methods. As one knows the poet by his fine music, so one can recognise the liar by his rich rhythmic utterances, and in neither case will the casual inspiration of the moment suffice. Here, as elsewhere, practice must precede perfection. But in modern days while the fashion of writing poetry has become far too common, and should, if possible, be discouraged, the fashion of lying has almost fallen into disrepute. Many a young man starts in life with a natural gift of exaggeration which, if nurtured in congenial and sympathetic surroundings, or by the imitation of the best models, might grow into something really great and wonderful. But, as a rule, he comes to nothing. He either falls into careless habits of accuracy—"

CYRIL: My dear fellow!

VIVIAN: Please don't interrupt in the middle of a sentence. "He either falls into careless habits of accuracy, or takes to frequenting the society of the aged and the well-informed. Both things are equally fatal to his imagination, as indeed they would be fatal to the imagination of anybody, and in a short time he develops a morbid and unhealthy faculty of truth-telling, begins to verify all statements made in his presence, has no hesitation in contradicting people who are much younger than himself, and often ends by writing novels which are so like life that no one can possibly believe in their probability. This is no isolated instance that we are giving. It is simply one example out of many; and if something cannot be done to check, or at least to modify, our monstrous worship of facts,

---

[7]*Retrospective Review*: a short-lived, long-defunct antiquarian periodical; Wilde is kidding.

[8]**Hedonists** regard pleasure as the highest good. **Domitian** (51–96): an exceptionally perverse Roman emperor.

[9]**Blue-Book**: government commission report. '*coin de la création*': corner of the universe.

[10]**Plato** in the *Republic* accuses poets of not representing truth.

Art will become sterile, and Beauty will pass away from the land.

"Even Mr Robert Louis Stevenson,[11] that delightful master of delicate and fanciful prose, is tainted with this modern vice, for we know positively no other name for it. There is such a thing as robbing a story of its reality by trying to make it too true, and *The Black Arrow* is so inartistic as not to contain a single anachronism to boast of, while the transformation of Dr Jekyll reads dangerously like an experiment out of the *Lancet*. As for Mr Rider Haggard, who really has, or had once, the makings of a perfectly magnificent liar, he is now so afraid of being suspected of genius that when he does tell us anything marvellous, he feels bound to invent a personal reminiscence, and to put it into a footnote as a kind of cowardly corroboration. Nor are our other novelists much better. Mr Henry James writes fiction as if it were a painful duty, and wastes upon mean motives and imperceptible 'points of view' his neat literary style, his felicitous phrases, his swift and caustic satire. Mr Hall Caine, it is true, aims at the grandiose, but then he writes at the top of his voice. He is so loud that one cannot hear what he says. Mr James Payn is an adept in the art of concealing what is not worth finding. He hunts down the obvious with the enthusiasm of a short-sighted detective. As one turns over the pages, the suspense of the author becomes almost unbearable. The horses of Mr William Black's phaeton do not soar towards the sun. They merely frighten the sky at evening into violent chromolithographic effects. On seeing them approach, the peasants take refuge in dialect. Mrs Oliphant prattles pleasantly about curates, lawn-tennis parties, domesticity, and other wearisome things. Mr Marion Crawford has immolated himself upon the altar of local colour. He is like the lady in the French comedy who keeps talking about 'le beau ciel d'Italie.' Besides, he has fallen into a bad habit of uttering moral platitudes. He is always telling us that to be good is to be good, and that to be bad is to be wicked. At times he is almost edifying. *Robert Elsmere*[12] is, of course, a masterpiece—a masterpiece of the 'genre ennuyeux,' the one form of literature that English people seem to thoroughly enjoy. A thoughtful young friend of ours once told us that it reminded him of the sort of conversation that goes on at a meat tea in the house of a serious Nonconformist family, and we can quite believe it. Indeed it is only in England that such a book could be produced. England is the home of lost ideas. As for that great and daily increasing school of novelists for whom the sun always rises in the East-End, the only thing that can be said about them is that they find life crude, and leave it raw.

"In France,[13] though nothing so deliberately tedious as *Robert Elsmere* has been produced, things are not much better. M. Guy de Maupassant, with his keen mordant irony and his hard vivid style, strips life of the few poor rags that still cover her, and shows us foul sore and festering wound. He writes lurid little tragedies in which everybody is ridiculous; bitter comedies at which one cannot laugh for very tears. M. Zola, true to the lofty principle that he lays down in one of his pronunciamientos on literature, 'L'homme de génie n'a jamais d'esprit,'[14] is determined to show that, if he has not got genius, he can at least be dull. And how well he succeeds! He is not without power. Indeed at times, as in *Germinal*, there is something almost epic in his work. But his work is entirely wrong from beginning to end, and wrong not on the ground of morals, but on the ground of art. From any ethical standpoint it is just what it should be. The author is perfectly truthful, and describes things exactly as they happen. What more can any moralist desire? We have no sympathy at all with the moral indignation of our time against M. Zola. It is simply the indignation of Tartuffe[15] on being exposed. But from the standpoint

---

[11]**Stevenson** (1850–1894): his works include *The Black Arrow* (1888), an historical novel, and *Dr Jekyll and Mr Hyde* (1886). *Lancet*: medical journal. This paragraph surveys contemporary novelists: **Haggard** (1856–1925), **James** (1843–1916), **Caine** (1853–1931), **Payn** (1830–1898). **phaeton**: horse-drawn carriage, named for the mythical youth who tried to drive the chariot of his father, the sun god. **William Black** (1841–1898) wrote *The Strange Adventures of a Phaeton* (1872). **Crawford** (1854–1909) was American. **'le beau ciel d'Italie'**: the beautiful sky of Italy.

[12]***Robert Elsmere*** (1888): best-selling novel by Mrs. Humphry Ward (1851–1920) about a young clergyman's crisis of religious faith. **ennuyeux**: boring. **East-End**: very poor section of London.

[13]This paragraph surveys contemporary French novelists: **Guy de Maupassant** (1850–1893), **Emile Zola** (1840–1902), **Alphonse Daudet** (1840–1897), **Paul Bourget** (1852–1935).

[14]**'L'homme . . . d'esprit'**: the man of genius is never witty.

[15]**Tartuffe**: hypocrite in Molière's comedy (1664).

of art, what can be said in favour of the author of *L'Assommoir*, *Nana*, and *Pot-Bouille*? Nothing. Mr Ruskin once described the characters in George Eliot's novels as being like the sweepings of a Pentonville[16] omnibus, but M. Zola's characters are much worse. They have their dreary vices, and their drearier virtues. The record of their lives is absolutely without interest. Who cares what happens to them? In literature we require distinction, charm, beauty, and imaginative power. We don't want to be harrowed and disgusted with an account of the doings of the lower orders. M. Daudet is better. He has wit, a light touch, and an amusing style. But he has lately committed literary suicide. Nobody can possibly care for Delobelle with his 'Il faut lutter pour l'art,'[17] or for Valmajour with his eternal refrain about the nightingale, or for the poet in *Jack* with his 'mots cruels,' now that we have learned from *Vingt Ans de ma Vie littéraire* that these characters were taken directly from life. To us they seem to have suddenly lost all their vitality, all the few qualities they ever possessed. The only real people are the people who never existed; and if a novelist is base enough to go to life for his personages, he should at least pretend that they are creations, and not boast of them as copies. The justification of a character in a novel is not that other persons are what they are, but that the author is what he is. Otherwise the novel is not a work of art. As for M. Paul Bourget, the master of the *roman psychologique*,[18] he commits the error of imagining that the men and women of modern life are capable of being infinitely analysed for an innumerable series of chapters. In point of fact what is interesting about people in good society—and M. Bourget rarely moves out of the Faubourg St Germain,[19] except to come to London—is the mask that each one of them wears, not the reality that lies behind the mask. It is a humiliating confession, but we are all of us made out of the same stuff. In Falstaff there is something of Hamlet, in Hamlet there is not a little of Falstaff. The fat knight has his moods of melancholy,

and the young prince his moments of coarse humour. Where we differ from each other is purely in accidentals: in dress, manner, tone of voice, religious opinions, personal appearance, tricks of habit, and the like. The more one analyses people, the more all reasons for analysis disappear. Sooner or later one comes to that dreadful universal thing called human nature. Indeed, as any one who has ever worked among the poor knows only too well, the brotherhood of man is no mere poet's dream, it is a most depressing and humiliating reality; and if a writer insists upon analysing the upper classes, he might just as well write of match-girls and coster-mongers at once." However, my dear Cyril, I will not detain you any further just here. I quite admit that modern novels have many good points. All I insist on is that, as a class, they are quite unreadable.

CYRIL: That is certainly a very grave qualification, but I must say that I think you are rather unfair in some of your strictures. I like *The Deemster*, and *The Daughter of Heth*, and *Le Disciple*, and *Mr Isaacs*,[20] and as for *Robert Elsmere* I am quite devoted to it. Not that I can look upon it as a serious work. As a statement of the problems that confront the earnest Christian it is ridiculous and antiquated. It is simply Arnold's *Literature and Dogma* with the literature left out. It is as much behind the age as Paley's *Evidences*, or Colenso's[21] method of Biblical exegesis. Nor could anything be less impressive than the unfortunate hero gravely heralding a dawn that rose long ago, and so completely missing its true significance that he proposes to carry on the business of the old firm under the new name. On the other hand, it contains several clever caricatures, and a heap of delightful quotations, and Green's[22] philosophy very pleasantly sugars the somewhat bitter pill of the author's fiction. I also cannot help expressing my surprise that you have said nothing about the two novelists whom you are al-

---

[16]**Pentonville**: in London.

[17]'**Il faut . . . l'art**': art must be struggled for. '**mots cruels**': cruel words. *Vingt Ans . . . littéraire*: Twenty Years of My Literary Life (a nonexistent book).

[18]*roman psychologique*: psychological novel.

[19]**Faubourg St Germain**: fashionable section of Paris.

[20]*The Deemster* (1887) by Hall Caine. *The Daughter of Heth* (1871) by William Black. *Le Disciple* (1889) by Paul Bourget. *Mr Isaacs* (1882) by F. Marion Crawford.

[21]Matthew **Arnold**: *Literature and Dogma* (1873). *Evidences: A View of the Evidences of Christianity* (1794) by William **Paley** (1743–1805). **Colenso**: see page 68.

[22]Thomas Hill **Green** (1836–1882): idealist philosopher, professor at Oxford.

ways reading, Balzac[23] and George Meredith. Surely they are realists, both of them?

VIVIAN: Ah! Meredith! Who can define him? His style is chaos illumined by flashes of lightning. As a writer he has mastered everything, except language: as a novelist he can do everything, except tell a story: as an artist he is everything, except articulate. Somebody in Shakespeare—Touchstone, I think—talks about a man who is always breaking his shins over his own wit,[24] and it seems to me that this might serve as the basis for a criticism of Meredith's method. But whatever he is, he is not a realist. Or rather I would say that he is a child of realism who is not on speaking terms with his father. By deliberate choice he has made himself a romanticist. He has refused to bow the knee to Baal,[25] and after all, even if the man's fine spirit did not revolt against the noisy assertions of realism, his style would be quite sufficient of itself to keep life at a respectful distance. By its means he has planted round his garden a hedge full of thorns, and red with wonderful roses. As for Balzac, he was a most remarkable combination of the artistic temperament with the scientific spirit. The latter he bequeathed to his disciples: the former was entirely his own. The difference between such a book as M. Zola's *L'Assommoir* and Balzac's *Illusions Perdues*[26] is the difference between unimaginative realism and imaginative reality. "All Balzac's characters," said Baudelaire,[27] "are gifted with the same ardour of life that animated himself. All his fictions are as deeply coloured as dreams. Each mind is a weapon loaded to the muzzle with will. The very scullions have genius." A steady course of Balzac reduces our living friends to shadows, and our acquaintances to the shadows of shades. His characters have a kind of fervent fiery-coloured existence. They dominate us, and defy scepticism. One of the greatest tragedies of my life is the death of Lucien de Rubempré.[28] It is a grief from which I have never been able to

completely rid myself. It haunts me in my moments of pleasure. I remember it when I laugh. But Balzac is no more a realist than Holbein[29] was. He created life, he did not copy it. I admit, however, that he set far too high a value on modernity of form, and that, consequently, there is no book of his that, as an artistic masterpiece, can rank with *Salammbô* or *Esmond*, or *The Cloister and the Hearth*, or the *Vicomte de Bragelonne*.

CYRIL: Do you object to modernity of form, then?

VIVIAN: Yes. It is a huge price to pay for a very poor result. Pure modernity of form is always somewhat vulgarising. It cannot help being so. The public imagine that, because they are interested in their immediate surroundings, Art should be interested in them also, and should take them as her subject-matter. But the mere fact that they are interested in these things makes them unsuitable subjects for Art. The only beautiful things, as somebody once said,[30] are the things that do not concern us. As long as a thing is useful or necessary to us, or affects us in any way, either for pain or for pleasure, or appeals strongly to our sympathies, or is a vital part of the environment in which we live, it is outside the proper sphere of Art. To Art's subject-matter we should be more or less indifferent. We should, at any rate, have no preferences, no prejudices, no partizan feeling of any kind. It is exactly because Hecuba[31] is nothing to us that her sorrows are such an admirable motive for a tragedy. I do not know anything in the whole history of literature sadder than the artistic career of Charles Reade. He wrote one beautiful book, *The Cloister and the Hearth*, a book as much above *Romola* as *Romola* is above *Daniel Deronda*,[32] and wasted the rest of his life in a foolish attempt to be modern, to draw public attention to the state of our convict prisons, and the management of our private lunatic asylums. Charles Dickens was

---

[23]Honoré de **Balzac** (1799–1850) chronicled contemporary French society in many novels and stories.

[24]**Touchstone . . . wit:** *As You Like It* 2.4.55.

[25]**Baal:** Middle Eastern god; see 1 Kings 16:30ff.

[26]*L'Assommoir* (translated as *The Drunkard*) (1877). *Illusions Perdues* (*Lost Illusions*) (1837–1843).

[27]Charles **Baudelaire** (1821–1867), in an 1859 essay on Théophile Gautier (1811–1872).

[28]**Lucien de Rubempré:** character in Balzac's *Illusions Perdues*.

[29]Hans **Holbein** (1497–1543): German portrait painter. *Salammbô* (1862) by Gustave Flaubert, *The History of Henry Esmond* (1852) by William Makepeace Thackeray (1811–1863), *The Cloister and the Hearth* (1861) by Charles Reade (1814–1884), and *Le Vicomte de Bragelonne* (1850) by Alexandre Dumas père (1802–1870): historical novels.

[30]**somebody once said:** Théophile Gautier, *Mademoiselle de Maupin* (1835), Preface.

[31]**Hecuba:** see *Hamlet* 2.2.536–537.

[32]*Romola* (1863), *Daniel Deronda* (1876): novels, respectively historical and contemporary, by George Eliot.

depressing enough in all conscience when he tried to arouse our sympathy for the victims of the poor-law administration; but Charles Reade, an artist, a scholar, a man with a true sense of beauty, raging and roaring over the abuses of contemporary life like a common pamphleteer or a sensational journalist, is really a sight for the angels to weep over. Believe me, my dear Cyril, modernity of form and modernity of subject-matter are entirely and absolutely wrong. We have mistaken the common livery of the age for the vesture of the Muses, and spend our days in the sordid streets and hideous suburbs of our vile cities when we should be out on the hillside with Apollo. Certainly we are a degraded race, and have sold our birthright[33] for a mess of facts.

CYRIL: There is something in what you say, and there is no doubt that whatever amusement we may find in reading a purely modern novel, we have rarely any artistic pleasure in re-reading it. And this is perhaps the best rough test of what is literature and what is not. If one cannot enjoy reading a book over and over again, there is no use reading it at all. But what do you say about the return to Life and Nature? This is the panacea that is always being recommended to us.

VIVIAN: I will read you what I say on that subject. The passage comes later on in the article, but I may as well give it to you now:—

"The popular cry of our time is 'Let us return to Life and Nature; they will recreate Art for us, and send the red blood coursing through her veins; they will shoe her feet with swiftness and make her hand strong.' But, alas! we are mistaken in our amiable and well-meaning efforts. Nature is always behind the age. And as for Life, she is the solvent that breaks up Art, the enemy that lays waste her house."

CYRIL: What do you mean by saying that Nature is always behind the age?

VIVIAN: Well, perhaps that is rather cryptic. What I mean is this. If we take Nature to mean natural simple instinct as opposed to self-conscious culture, the work produced under this influence is always old-fashioned, antiquated, and out of date. One touch of Nature may make the whole world kin,[34] but two touches of Nature will destroy any work of Art. If, on the other hand, we regard Nature as the collection of phenomena external to man, people only discover in her what they bring to her. She has no suggestions of her own. Wordsworth went to the lakes, but he was never a lake poet. He found in stones the sermons[35] he had already hidden there. He went moralizing about the district, but his good work was produced when he returned, not to Nature but to poetry. Poetry gave him "Laodamia," and the fine sonnets, and the Great Ode, such as it is. Nature gave him "Martha Ray" and "Peter Bell," and the address to Mr Wilkinson's spade.

CYRIL: I think that view might be questioned. I am rather inclined to believe in the "impulse from a vernal wood,"[36] though of course the artistic value of such an impulse depends entirely on the kind of temperament that receives it, so that the return to Nature would come to mean simply the advance to a great personality. You would agree with that, I fancy. However, proceed with your article.

VIVIAN: (reading) "Art begins with abstract decoration with purely imaginative and pleasurable work dealing with what is unreal and non-existent. This is the first stage. Then Life becomes fascinated with this new wonder, and asks to be admitted into the charmed circle. Art takes life as part of her rough material, recreates it, and refashions it in fresh forms, is absolutely indifferent to fact, invents, imagines, dreams, and keeps between herself and reality the impenetrable barrier of beautiful style, of decorative or ideal treatment. The third stage is when Life gets the upper hand, and drives Art out into the wilderness. This is the true decadence, and it is from this that we are now suffering.

"Take the case of the English drama. At first in the hands of the monks Dramatic Art was abstract, decorative, mythological. Then she enlisted Life in her service, and using some of life's external forms, she created an entirely new race of beings, whose sorrows were more terrible than any sorrow man has ever felt, whose joys were keener than lover's joys, who had the rage of the Titans and the calm of the gods, who had monstrous and marvellous sins, monstrous and marvellous

---

[33]**sold our birthright**: see Genesis 25:29–34.

[34]**One touch . . . kin**: see *Troilus and Cressida* 3.3.169.

[35]**stones . . . sermons**: see *As You Like It* 2.1.17. **Ode**: "Intimations of Immortality" (1807). **address**: "To the **Spade** of a Friend" (1807).

[36]**"impulse . . . wood"**: Wordsworth, "The Tables Turned" (1798) 21.

virtues. To them she gave a language different from that of actual use, a language full of resonant music and sweet rhythm, made stately by solemn cadence, or made delicate by fanciful rhyme, jewelled with wonderful words, and enriched with lofty diction. She clothed her children in strange raiment and gave them masks, and at her bidding the antique world rose from its marble tomb. A new Cæsar stalked through the streets of risen Rome, and with purple sail and flute-led oars another Cleopatra passed up the river to Antioch.[37] Old myth and legend and dream took shape and substance. History was entirely re-written, and there was hardly one of the dramatists who did not recognize that the object of Art is not simple truth but complex beauty. In this they were perfectly right. Art itself is really a form of exaggeration; and selection, which is the very spirit of art, is nothing more than an intensified mode of over-emphasis.

"But Life soon shattered the perfection of the form. Even in Shakespeare we can see the beginning of the end. It shows itself by the gradual breaking up of the blank-verse in the later plays, by the predominance given to prose, and by the over-importance assigned to characterisation. The passages in Shakespeare—and they are many—where the language is uncouth, vulgar, exaggerated, fantastic, obscene even, are entirely due to Life calling for an echo of her own voice, and rejecting the intervention of beautiful style, through which alone should Life be suffered to find expression. Shakespeare is not by any means a flawless artist. He is too fond of going directly to life, and borrowing life's natural utterance. He forgets that when Art surrenders her imaginative medium she surrenders everything. Goethe[38] says somewhere—

In der Beschränkung zeigt sich erst der Meister,

'It is in working within limits that the master reveals himself,' and the limitation, the very condition of any art is style. However, we need not linger any longer over Shakespeare's realism. *The Tempest* is the most perfect of palinodes.[39] All that we desired to point out

was, that the magnificent work of the Elizabethan and Jacobean artists contained within itself the seed of its own dissolution, and that, if it drew some of its strength from using life as rough material, it drew all its weakness from using life as an artistic method. As the inevitable result of this substitution of an imitative for a creative medium, this surrender of an imaginative form, we have the modern English melodrama. The characters in these plays talk on the stage exactly as they would talk off it; they have neither aspirations nor aspirates;[40] they are taken directly from life and reproduce its vulgarity down to the smallest detail; they present the gait, manner, costume, and accent of real people; they pass unnoticed in a third-class railway carriage. And yet how wearisome the plays are! They do not succeed in producing even that impression of reality at which they aim, and which is their only reason for existing. As a method, realism is a complete failure.

"What is true about the drama and the novel is no less true about those arts that we call the decorative arts. The whole history of these arts in Europe is the record of the struggle between Orientalism,[41] with its frank rejection of imitation, its love of artistic convention, its dislike to the actual representation of any object in Nature, and our own imitative spirit. Wherever the former has been paramount, as in Byzantium, Sicily, and Spain, by actual contact, or in the rest of Europe by the influence of the Crusades, we have had beautiful and imaginative work in which the visible things of life are transmuted into artistic conventions, and the things that Life has not are invented and fashioned for her delight. But wherever we have returned to Life and Nature, our work has always become vulgar, common, and uninteresting. Modern tapestry, with its aërial effects, its elaborate perspective, its broad expanses of waste sky, its faithful and laborious realism, has no beauty whatsoever. The pictorial glass of Germany is absolutely detestable. We are beginning to weave possible carpets in England, but only because we have returned to the method and spirit of the East. Our rugs and carpets of twenty years ago,

---

[37]**Antioch:** see *Antony and Cleopatra* 2.2.190. Wilde mistakes Tarsus for Antioch, unless he too is rewriting history.

[38]Johann Wolfgang von **Goethe** (1749–1832): quoted from his sonnet "Nature and Art."

[39]**palinodes:** poetic retractions.

[40]**aspirates:** initial "h" sounds, dropped in lower-class urban (cockney) speech.

[41]**Orientalism:** as received in the west, nonmimetic and abstract **artistic convention**, related to the Aesthetic movement and promoted in Wilde's day by the craze for Asian art and objects.

with their solemn depressing truths, their inane worship of Nature, their sordid reproductions of visible objects, have become, even to the Philistine,[42] a source of laughter. A cultured Mahomedan once remarked to us, 'You Christians are so occupied in misinterpreting the fourth commandment that you have never thought of making an artistic application of the second.' He was perfectly right, and the whole truth of the matter is this: The proper school to learn art in is not Life but Art."

And now let me read you a passage which seems to me to settle the question very completely:—

"It was not always thus. We need not say anything about the poets, for they, with the unfortunate exception of Mr Wordsworth, have been really faithful to their high mission, and are universally recognised as being absolutely unreliable. But in the works of Herodotus,[43] who, in spite of the shallow and ungenerous attempts of modern sciolists to verify his history, may justly be called the 'Father of Lies'; in the published speeches of Cicero and the biographies of Suetonius; in Tacitus at his best; in Pliny's *Natural History*; in Hanno's *Periplus*; in all the early chronicles; in the Lives of the Saints; in Froissart and Sir Thomas Mallory; in the travels of Marco Polo; in Olaus Magnus, and Aldrovandus, and Conrad Lycosthenes, with his magnificent *Prodigiorum et Ostentorum Chronicon*; in the autobiography of Benvenuto Cellini; in the memoirs of Casanuova; in Defoe's *History of the Plague*; in Boswell's *Life of Johnson*; in Napoleon's despatches, and in the works of our own Carlyle, whose *French Revolution* is one of the most fascinating historical novels ever written, facts are either kept in their proper subordinate position, or else entirely excluded on the general ground of dulness. Now, everything is changed. Facts are not merely finding a footing-place in History, but they are usurping the domain of Fancy, and have invaded the kingdom of Romance. Their chilling touch is over everything. They are vulgarising mankind. The crude commercialism of America, its materialising spirit, its indifference to the poetical side of things, and its lack of imagination and of high unattainable ideals, are entirely due to that country having adopted for its national hero a man, who, according to his own confession, was incapable of telling a lie, and it is not too much to say that the story of George Washington and the cherry-tree has done more harm, and in a shorter space of time, than any other moral tale in the whole of literature."

CYRIL: My dear boy!

VIVIAN: I assure you it is the case, and the amusing part of the whole thing is that the story of the cherry-tree is an absolute myth. However, you must not think that I am too despondent about the artistic future either of America or of our own country. Listen to this:—

"That some change will take place before this century has drawn to its close we have no doubt whatsoever. Bored by the tedious and improving conversation of those who have neither the wit to exaggerate nor the genius to romance, tired of the intelligent person whose reminiscences are always based upon memory, whose statements are invariably limited by probability, and who is at any time liable to be corroborated by the merest Philistine who happens to be present, Society sooner or later must return to its lost leader, the cultured and fascinating liar. Who he was who first, without ever having gone out to the rude chase, told the wondering cave-men at sunset how he had dragged the Megatherium from the purple darkness of its jasper cave, or slain the Mammoth in single combat and brought back its gilded tusks, we cannot tell, and not one of our modern anthropologists, for all their much boasted science, has had the ordinary courage to tell us. Whatever was his name or race, he certainly was the true founder of social intercourse. For the aim of the liar is simply to charm, to delight, to give pleasure. He is the very basis of civilized society, and without him a dinner party, even at the mansions of the great, is as dull as a lecture at the Royal Society,[44] or a debate at the Incorporated Authors, or one of Mr Burnand's farcical comedies.

"Nor will he be welcomed by society alone. Art, breaking from the prison-house of realism, will run to greet him, and will kiss his false, beautiful lips,

---

[42]**Philistine**: Matthew Arnold's term for the middle class.

[43]**Herodotus** (5th century BCE): first great classical historian. **sciolist**: superficial pretender to knowledge. This paragraph surveys works of ancient, medieval, and modern historiography.

[44]**Royal Society**: Britain's oldest and most prestigious scientific association. **Incorporated Authors**: Wilde's derisory name for the Society of Authors (founded 1884). Francis Cowley **Burnand** (1836–1917): editor and popular playwright.

knowing that he alone is in possession of the great secret of all her manifestations, the secret that Truth is entirely and absolutely a matter of style; while Life—poor, probable, uninteresting human life—tired of repeating herself for the benefit of Mr Herbert Spencer, scientific historians, and the compilers of statistics in general, will follow meekly after him, and try to reproduce, in her own simple and untutored way, some of the marvels of which he talks.

"No doubt there will always be critics who, like a certain writer in the *Saturday Review*, will gravely censure the teller of fairy tales for his defective knowledge of natural history,[45] who will measure imaginative work by their own lack of any imaginative faculty, and will hold up their inkstained hands in horror if some honest gentleman, who has never been farther than the yew-trees of his own garden, pens a fascinating book of travels like Sir John Mandeville, or, like great Raleigh, writes a whole history of the world,[46] without knowing anything whatsoever about the past. To excuse themselves they will try and shelter under the shield of him who made Prospero the magician, and gave him Caliban and Ariel as his servants, who heard the Tritons blowing their horns round the coral reefs of the Enchanted Isle, and the fairies singing to each other in a wood near Athens, who led the phantom kings in dim procession across the misty Scottish heath, and hid Hecate in a cave with the weird sisters.[47] They will call upon Shakespeare—they always do—and will quote that hackneyed passage about Art holding the mirror up to Nature,[48] forgetting that this unfortunate aphorism is deliberately said by Hamlet in order to convince the bystanders of his absolute insanity in all art matters."

CYRIL: Ahem! Another cigarette, please.

VIVIAN: My dear fellow, whatever you may say, it is merely a dramatic utterance, and no more represents Shakespeare's real views upon Art than the speeches of Iago represent his real views upon morals. But let me get to the end of the passage:

"Art finds her own perfection within, and not outside of, herself. She is not to be judged by any external standard of resemblance. She is a veil, rather than a mirror. She has flowers that no forests know of, birds that no woodland possesses. She makes and unmakes many worlds, and can draw the moon from the heaven with a scarlet thread. Hers are the 'forms more real than living man,'[49] and hers the great archetypes of which things that have existence are but unfinished copies. Nature has, in her eyes, no laws, no uniformity. She can work miracles at her will, and when she calls monsters from the deep they come. She can bid the almond tree blossom in winter, and send the snow upon the ripe cornfield. At her word the frost lays its silver finger on the burning mouth of June, and the winged lions creep out from the hollows of the Lydian hills. The dryads peer from the thicket as she passes by, and the brown fauns smile strangely at her when she comes near them. She has hawk-faced gods that worship her, and the centaurs gallop at her side."

CYRIL: I like that. I can see it. Is that the end?

VIVIAN: No. There is one more passage, but it is purely practical. It simply suggests some methods by which we could revive this lost art of Lying.

CYRIL: Well, before you read it to me, I should like to ask you a question. What do you mean by saying that life, "poor, probable, uninteresting human life," will try to reproduce the marvels of art? I can quite understand your objection to Art being treated as a mirror. You think it would reduce genius to the position of a cracked looking-glass. But you don't mean to say that you seriously believe that Life imitates art, that Life in fact is the mirror, and Art the reality?

VIVIAN: Certainly I do. Paradox though it may seem—and paradoxes are always dangerous things—it is none the less true that Life imitates art far more than Art imitates life. We have all seen in our own day in England how a certain curious and fascinating type of beauty, invented and emphasised by two imaginative painters,[50] has so influenced Life that whenever

---

[45]The *Saturday Review* in a review of Wilde's *The Happy Prince and Other Tales* (October 20, 1888) had remarked that Wilde's **natural history** "stumbled."

[46]Sir John **Mandeville**: purported author of a 14th-century travel book. Sir Walter **Raleigh** (1552?–1618) published his *History of the World* in 1614.

[47]**Prospero . . . sisters**: see Shakespeare's *Tempest*, *Midsummer Night's Dream*, and *Macbeth*.

[48]**mirror . . . Nature**: *Hamlet* 3.2.21.

[49]'**forms . . . man**': Shelley, *Prometheus Unbound* (1820) 1.748.

[50]**painters**: Dante Gabriel **Rossetti**, Edward Burne-Jones (1833–1898).

one goes to a private view or to an artistic salon one sees, here the mystic eyes of Rossetti's dream, the long ivory throat, the strange square-cut jaw, the loosened shadowy hair that he so ardently loved, there the sweet maidenhood of "The Golden Stair," the blossom-like mouth and weary loveliness of the "Laus Amoris," the passion-pale face of Andromeda, the thin hands and lithe beauty of the Vivien in "Merlin's Dream." And it has always been so. A great artist invents a type, and Life tries to copy it, to reproduce it in a popular form, like an enterprising publisher. Neither Holbein nor Vandyck[51] found in England what they have given us. They brought their types with them, and Life with her keen imitative faculty set herself to supply the master with models. The Greeks, with their quick artistic instinct, understood this, and set in the bride's chamber the statue of Hermes or of Apollo, that she might bear children as lovely as the works of art that she looked at in her rapture or her pain. They knew that Life gains from Art not merely spirituality, depth of thought and feeling, soul-turmoil or soul-peace, but that she can form herself on the very lines and colours of Art, and can reproduce the dignity of Pheidias as well as the grace of Praxiteles.[52] Hence came their objection to realism. They disliked it on purely social grounds. They felt that it inevitably makes people ugly, and they were perfectly right. We try to improve the conditions of the race by means of good air, free sunlight, wholesome water, and hideous bare buildings for the better housing of the lower orders. But these things merely produce health, they do not produce beauty. For this, Art is required, and the true disciples of the great artist are not his studio-imitators, but those who become like his works of art, be they plastic as in Greek days, or pictorial as in modern times: in a word, Life is Art's best, Art's only pupil.

As it is with the visible arts, so it is with literature. The most obvious and the vulgarest form in which this is shown is in the case of the silly boys who, after reading the adventures of Jack Sheppard or Dick Turpin,[53] pillage the stalls of unfortunate apple-women, break into sweet-shops at night, and alarm old gentlemen who are returning home from the city by leaping out on them in suburban lanes, with black masks and unloaded revolvers. This interesting phenomenon, which always occurs after the appearance of a new edition of either of the books I have alluded to, is usually attributed to the influence of literature on the imagination. But this is a mistake. The imagination is essentially creative, and always seeks for a new form. The boy-burglar is simply the inevitable result of life's imitative instinct. He is Fact, occupied as Fact usually is, with trying to reproduce Fiction, and what we see in him is repeated on an extended scale throughout the whole of life. Schopenhauer[54] has analysed the pessimism that characterises modern thought, but Hamlet invented it. The world has become sad because a puppet was once melancholy. The Nihilist, that strange martyr who has no faith, who goes to the stake without enthusiasm, and dies for what he does not believe in, is a purely literary product. He was invented by Tourgénieff, and completed by Dostoieffski. Robespierre came out of the pages of Rousseau as surely as the People's Palace rose out of the *débris* of a novel. Literature always anticipates life. It does not copy it, but moulds it to its purpose. The nineteenth century, as we know it, is largely an invention of Balzac. Our Luciens de Rubempré, our Rastignacs, and De Marsays made their first appearance on the stage of the *Comédie Humaine*. We are merely carrying out, with footnotes and unnecessary additions, the whim or fancy or creative vision of a great novelist. I once asked a lady who knew Thackeray intimately, whether he had had any model for Becky Sharp.[55] She

[53]**Jack Sheppard** (1702–1724), **Dick Turpin** (1706–1739): criminals who became heroes of W. H. Ainsworth's popular romances *Jack Sheppard* (1839) and *Rookwood* (1834).

[54]Arthur **Schopenhauer** (1788–1860): German philosopher. **Nihilists:** terrorist saboteurs who appear in the novels of Ivan **Tourgénieff** (Turgenev) (1818–1883) and Fyodor **Dostoieffski** (Dostoevsky) (1821–1881). **Robespierre** (1758–1794): a leader of the French Revolution, inspired by the writings of Jean-Jacques **Rousseau** (1712–1778). A **People's Palace,** a vast cultural institution for the poor, appeared in Walter Besant's novel *All Sorts and Conditions of Men* (1882); a similar institution opened in 1887. *Comédie Humaine:* series of novels and stories by Balzac.

[55]**Becky Sharp,** later **Mrs. Rawdon Crawley,** appears in Thackeray's novel *Vanity Fair* (1847).

[51]**Vandyck:** Anthony Van Dyck (1599–1641), Flemish painter who, like Holbein, painted the English court.

[52]**Pheidias** (5th century BCE), **Praxiteles:** (4th century BCE): Greek sculptors.

told me that Becky was an invention, but that the idea of the character had been partly suggested by a governess who lived in the neighbourhood of Kensington Square, and was the companion of a very selfish and rich old woman. I inquired what became of the governess, and she replied that, oddly enough, some years after the appearance of *Vanity Fair*, she ran away with the nephew of the lady with whom she was living, and for a short time made a great splash in society, quite in Mrs Rawdon Crawley's style, and entirely by Mrs Rawdon Crawley's methods. Ultimately she came to grief, disappeared to the Continent, and used to be occasionally seen at Monte Carlo and other gambling places. The noble gentleman from whom the same great sentimentalist drew Colonel Newcome died, a few months after *The Newcomes* had reached a fourth edition, with the word "Adsum"[56] on his lips. Shortly after Mr Stevenson published his curious psychological story of transformation, a friend of mine, called Mr Hyde, was in the north of London, and being anxious to get to a railway station, took what he thought would be a short cut, lost his way, and found himself in a network of mean, evil-looking streets. Feeling rather nervous, he began to walk extremely fast, when suddenly out of an archway ran a child right between his legs. It fell on the pavement, he tripped over it, and trampled upon it. Being of course very much frightened and a little hurt, it began to scream, and in a few seconds the whole street was full of rough people who came pouring out of the houses like ants. They surrounded him, and asked him his name. He was just about to give it when he suddenly remembered the opening incident in Mr Stevenson's story. He was so filled with horror at having realised in his own person that terrible and well written scene, and at having done accidentally, though in fact, what the Mr Hyde of fiction had done with deliberate intent, that he ran away as hard as he could go. He was, however, very closely followed, and finally he took refuge in a surgery, the door of which happened to be open, where he explained to a young assistant, who happened to be there, exactly what had occurred. The humanitarian crowd were induced to go away on his giving them a small sum of money, and as soon as

the coast was clear he left. As he passed out, the name on the brass door-plate of the surgery caught his eye. It was "Jekyll." At least it should have been.

Here the imitation, as far as it went, was of course accidental. In the following case the imitation was self-conscious. In the year 1879, just after I had left Oxford, I met at a reception at the house of one of the Foreign Ministers a woman of very curious exotic beauty. We became great friends, and were constantly together. And yet what interested me most in her was not her beauty, but her character, her entire vagueness of character. She seemed to have no personality at all, but simply the possibility of many types. Sometimes she would give herself up entirely to Art, turn her drawing-room into a studio, and spend two or three days a week at picture-galleries or museums. Then she would take to attending race-meetings, wear the most horsey clothes, and talk about nothing but betting. She abandoned religion for mesmerism, mesmerism for politics, and politics for the melodramatic excitements of philanthropy. In fact, she was a kind of Proteus,[57] and as much a failure in all her transformations as was that wondrous sea-god when Odysseus laid hold of him. One day a serial began in one of the French magazines. At that time I used to read serial stories, and I well remember the shock of surprise I felt when I came to the description of the heroine. She was so like my friend that I brought her the magazine, and she recognised herself in it immediately, and seemed fascinated by the resemblance. I should tell you, by the way, that the story was translated from some dead Russian writer, so that the author had not taken his type from my friend. Well, to put the matter briefly, some months afterwards I was in Venice, and finding the magazine in the reading-room of the hotel, I took it up casually to see what had become of the heroine. It was a most piteous tale, as the girl had ended by running away with a man absolutely inferior to her, not merely in social station, but in character and intellect also. I wrote to my friend that evening about my views on John Bellini,[58] and the admirable ices at Florio's, and the artistic value of gondolas, but added

---

[56]"**Adsum**" ("I am here"): dying words of **Colonel Newcome** in Thackeray's *The Newcomes* (1855).

[57]**Proteus**: sea-god who could change his form; see *Odyssey* 4.385ff.

[58]Giovanni **Bellini** (1430?–1516): Venetian painter. **Florio's** (Florian's): café in Venice.

a postscript to the effect that her double in the story had behaved in a very silly manner. I don't know why I added that, but I remember I had a sort of dread over me that she might do the same thing. Before my letter had reached her, she had run away with a man who deserted her in six months. I saw her in 1884 in Paris, where she was living with her mother, and I asked her whether the story had had anything to do with her action. She told me that she had felt an absolutely irresistible impulse to follow the heroine step by step in her strange and fatal progress, and that it was with a feeling of real terror that she had looked forward to the last few chapters of the story. When they appeared, it seemed to her that she was compelled to reproduce them in life, and she did so. It was a most clear example of this imitative instinct of which I was speaking, and an extremely tragic one.

However, I do not wish to dwell any further upon individual instances. Personal experience is a most vicious and limited circle. All that I desire to point out is the general principle that Life imitates Art far more than Art imitates Life, and I feel sure that if you think seriously about it you will find that it is true. Life holds the mirror up to Art, and either reproduces some strange type imagined by painter or sculptor, or realises in fact what has been dreamed in fiction. Scientifically speaking, the basis of life—the energy of life, as Aristotle would call it—is simply the desire for expression, and Art is always presenting various forms through which this expression can be attained. Life seizes on them and uses them, even if they be to her own hurt. Young men have committed suicide because Rolla[59] did so, have died by their own hand because by his own hand Werther died. Think of what we owe to the imitation of Christ, of what we owe to the imitation of Cæsar.

CYRIL: The theory is certainly a very curious one, but to make it complete you must show that Nature, no less than Life, is an imitation of Art. Are you prepared to prove that?

VIVIAN: My dear fellow, I am prepared to prove anything.

CYRIL: Nature follows the landscape painter then, and takes her effects from him?

VIVIAN: Certainly. Where, if not from the Impressionists,[60] do we get those wonderful brown fogs that come creeping down our streets, blurring the gas-lamps and changing the houses into monstrous shadows? To whom, if not to them and their master, do we owe the lovely silver mists that brood over our river, and turn to faint forms of fading grace curved bridge and swaying barge? The extraordinary change that has taken place in the climate of London during the last ten years is entirely due to this particular school of Art. You smile. Consider the matter from a scientific or a metaphysical point of view, and you will find that I am right. For what is Nature? Nature is no great mother who has borne us. She is our creation. It is in our brain that she quickens to life. Things are because we see them, and what we see, and how we see it, depends on the Arts that have influenced us. To look at a thing is very different from seeing a thing. One does not see anything until one sees its beauty. Then, and then only, does it come into existence. At present, people see fogs, not because there are fogs, but because poets and painters have taught them the mysterious loveliness of such effects. There may have been fogs for centuries in London. I dare say there were. But no one saw them, and so we do not know anything about them. They did not exist until Art had invented them. Now, it must be admitted, fogs are carried to excess. They have become the mere mannerism of a clique, and the exaggerated realism of their method gives dull people bronchitis. Where the cultured catch an effect, the uncultured catch cold. And so, let us be humane, and invite Art to turn her wonderful eyes elsewhere. She has done so already, indeed. That white quivering sunlight that one sees now in France, with its strange blotches of mauve, and its restless violet shadows, is her latest fancy, and, on the whole, Nature produces it quite admirably. Where she used to give us Corots and Daubignys, she gives us now exquisite Monets and entrancing Pisaros.[61] Indeed there are moments, rare, it is true, but still to be observed from time to time, when

---

[59]**Rolla:** hero of Alfred de Musset's *Rolla* (1833). **Werther:** hero of Goethe's *Sorrows of Young Werther* (1774). **the imitation of Christ:** title of a devotional work (1427?), by Thomas à Kempis.

[60]**Impressionists:** painters of the later 19th century, whose London **master** here is probably James McNeill Whistler (1834–1903).

[61]Camille **Corot** (1796–1875), Charles **Daubigny** (1817–1878): landscape painters, precursors of Impressionists Claude **Monet** (1840–1926) and Camille **Pisaro** (Pissarro) (1830–1903).

Nature becomes absolutely modern. Of course she is not always to be relied upon. The fact is that she is in this unfortunate position. Art creates an incomparable and unique effect, and, having done so, passes on to other things. Nature, upon the other hand, forgetting that imitation can be made the sincerest form of insult, keeps on repeating this effect until we all become absolutely wearied of it. Nobody of any real culture, for instance, ever talks nowadays about the beauty of the sunset. Sunsets are quite old-fashioned. They belong to the time when Turner[62] was the last note in Art. To admire them is a distinct sign of provincialism of temperament. Upon the other hand, they go on. Yesterday evening Mrs Arundel insisted on my going to the window, and looking at the glorious sky, as she called it. Of course, I had to look at it. She is one of those absurdly pretty Philistines, to whom one can deny nothing. And what was it? It was simply a very second-rate Turner, a Turner of a bad period, with all the painter's worst faults exaggerated and over-emphasized. Of course, I am quite ready to admit that Life very often commits the same error. She produces her false Renés[63] and her sham Vautrins, just as Nature gives us, on one day a doubtful Cuyp, and on another a more than questionable Rousseau. Still, Nature irritates one more when she does things of that kind. It seems so stupid, so obvious, so unnecessary. A false Vautrin might be delightful. A doubtful Cuyp is unbearable. However, I don't want to be too hard on Nature. I wish the Channel, especially at Hastings, did not look quite so often like a Henry Moore, grey pearl with yellow lights, but then, when Art is more varied, Nature will, no doubt, be more varied also. That she imitates Art, I don't think even her worst enemy would deny now. It is the one thing that keeps her in touch with civilized man. But have I proved my theory to your satisfaction?

CYRIL: You have proved it to my dissatisfaction, which is better. But even admitting this strange imitative instinct in Life and Nature, surely you would acknowledge that Art expresses the temper of its age, the spirit of its time, the moral and social conditions that surround it, and under whose influence it is produced.

VIVIAN: Certainly not! Art never expresses anything but itself. This is the principle of my new æsthetics; and it is this, more than that vital connection between form and substance, on which Mr Pater dwells, that makes music the type of all the arts. Of course, nations and individuals, with that healthy natural vanity which is the secret of existence, are always under the impression that it is of them that the Muses are talking, always trying to find in the calm dignity of imaginative art some mirror of their own turbid passions, always forgetting that the singer of life is not Apollo, but Marsyas.[64] Remote from reality, and with her eyes turned away from the shadows of the cave,[65] Art reveals her own perfection, and the wondering crowd that watches the opening of the marvellous, many-petalled rose fancies that it is its own history that is being told to it, its own spirit that is finding expression in a new form. But it is not so. The highest art rejects the burden of the human spirit, and gains more from a new medium or a fresh material than she does from any enthusiasm for art, or from any lofty passion, or from any great awakening of the human consciousness. She develops purely on her own lines. She is not symbolic of any age. It is the ages that are her symbols.

Even those who hold that Art is representative of time and place and people, cannot help admitting that the more imitative an art is, the less it represents to us the spirit of its age. The evil faces of the Roman emperors look out at us from the foul porphyry and spotted jasper in which the realistic artists of the day delighted to work, and we fancy that in those cruel lips and heavy sensual jaws we can find the secret of the ruin of the Empire. But it was not so. The vices of Tiberius[66] could not destroy that supreme civilization, any more than the virtues of the Antonines could save it. It fell for other, for less interesting reasons. The

---

[62]J. M. W. **Turner** (1775–1851): British landscape painter.

[63]**René**: hero of *René* (1802), a novel by Chateaubriand. **Vautrin**: criminal figure in novels by Balzac. Albert **Cuyp** (1620–1691): Dutch painter. Henri **Rousseau** (1844–1910): French painter. **Henry Moore** (1831–1895): English painter.

[64]**Marsyas**: satyr who challenged the god Apollo to a contest in music and having been defeated, was flayed alive.

[65]**shadows of the cave**: see Plato's *Republic*, book 7.

[66]**Tiberius** (42 BCE–37): Roman emperor known as vicious and cruel. **Antonines**: Antonius Pius (86–161) and Marcus Aurelius (121–180), Roman emperors renowned for virtue. **sibyls and prophets**: painted in the **Sistine** Chapel in Rome.

sibyls and prophets of the Sistine may indeed serve to interpret for some that new birth of the emancipated spirit that we call the Renaissance; but what do the drunken boors and brawling peasants of Dutch art tell us about the great soul of Holland? The more abstract, the more ideal an art is, the more it reveals to us the temper of its age. If we wish to understand a nation by means of its art, let us look at its architecture or its music.

CYRIL: I quite agree with you there. The spirit of an age may be best expressed in the abstract ideal arts, for the spirit itself is abstract and ideal. Upon the other hand, for the visible aspect of an age, for its look, as the phrase goes, we must of course go to the arts of imitation.

VIVIAN: I don't think so. After all, what the imitative arts really give us are merely the various styles of particular artists, or of certain schools of artists. Surely you don't imagine that the people of the Middle Ages bore any resemblance at all to the figures on mediæval stained glass, or in mediæval stone and wood carving, or on mediæval metal-work, or tapestries, or illuminated MSS.[67] They were probably very ordinary-looking people, with nothing grotesque, or remarkable, or fantastic in their appearance. The Middle Ages, as we know them in art, are simply a definite form of style, and there is no reason at all why an artist with this style should not be produced in the nineteenth century. No great artist ever sees things as they really are. If he did, he would cease to be an artist. Take an example from our own day. I know that you are fond of Japanese things. Now, do you really imagine that the Japanese people, as they are presented to us in art, have any existence? If you do, you have never understood Japanese art at all. The Japanese people are the deliberate self-conscious creation of certain individual artists. If you set a picture by Hokusai, or Hokkei,[68] or any of the great native painters, beside a real Japanese gentleman or lady, you will see that there is not the slightest resemblance between them. The actual people who live in Japan are not unlike the general run of English people; that is to say, they are extremely commonplace, and have nothing curious or extraordinary about them. In fact, the whole of Japan is a pure invention. There is no such country, there are no such people. One of our most charming painters[69] went recently to the Land of the Chrysanthemum in the foolish hope of seeing the Japanese. All he saw, all he had the chance of painting, were a few lanterns and some fans. He was quite unable to discover the inhabitants, as his delightful exhibition at Messrs Dowdeswell's Gallery showed only too well. He did not know that the Japanese people are, as I have said, simply a mode of style, an exquisite fancy of art. And so, if you desire to see a Japanese effect, you will not behave like a tourist and go to Tokio. On the contrary, you will stay at home, and steep yourself in the work of certain Japanese artists, and then, when you have absorbed the spirit of their style, and caught their imaginative manner of vision, you will go some afternoon and sit in the Park, or stroll down Piccadilly, and if you cannot see an absolutely Japanese effect there, you will not see it anywhere. Or, to return again to the past, take as another instance the ancient Greeks. Do you think that Greek art ever tells us what the Greek people are like? Do you believe that the Athenian women were like the stately dignified figures of the Parthenon frieze,[70] or like those marvellous goddesses who sat in the triangular pediments of the same building? If you judge from the art, they certainly were so. But read an authority, like Aristophanes for instance. You will find that the Athenian ladies laced tightly, wore high-heeled shoes, dyed their hair yellow, painted and rouged their faces, and were exactly like any silly fashionable or fallen creature of our own day. The fact is that we look back on the ages entirely through the medium of Art, and Art, very fortunately, has never once told us the truth.

CYRIL: But modern portraits by English painters, what of them? Surely they are like the people they pretend to represent?

VIVIAN: Quite so. They are so like them that a hundred years from now no one will believe in them. The only portraits in which one believes are portraits where

---

[67]**illuminated MSS:** elaborately decorated handwritten books.

[68]**Hokusai** (1760–1849), **Hokkei** (1780–1850): Japanese **painters** and printmakers.

[69]**One of our . . . painters:** Mortimer Menpes (1860–1938) exhibited paintings and prints made on a trip to Japan in 1888 at the **Dowdeswell Gallery** in London.

[70]**Parthenon frieze:** classical carvings from Athens in the British Museum. **Aristophanes** (448–388? BCE): Greek comic dramatist.

there is very little of the sitter, and a very great deal of the artist. Holbein's drawings of the men and women of his time impress us with a sense of their absolute reality. But this is simply because Holbein compelled life to accept his conditions, to restrain itself within his limitations, to reproduce his type, and to appear as he wished it to appear. It is style that makes us believe in a thing—nothing but style. Most of our modern portrait painters are doomed to absolute oblivion. They never paint what they see. They paint what the public sees, and the public never sees anything.

CYRIL: Well, after that I think I should like to hear the end of your article.

VIVIAN: With pleasure. Whether it will do any good I really cannot say. Ours is certainly the dullest and most prosaic century possible. Why, even Sleep has played us false, and has closed up the gates of ivory, and opened the gates of horn.[71] The dreams of the great middle classes of this country, as recorded in Mr Myers's two bulky volumes on the subject and in the Transactions of the Physical Society, are the most depressing things that I have ever read. There is not even a fine nightmare among them. They are commonplace, sordid, and tedious. As for the Church, I cannot conceive anything better for the culture of a country than the presence in it of a body of men whose duty it is to believe in the supernatural, to perform daily miracles, and to keep alive that mythopœic faculty which is so essential for the imagination. But in the English Church a man succeeds, not through his capacity for belief, but through his capacity for disbelief. Ours is the only Church where the sceptic stands at the altar, and where St. Thomas[72] is regarded as the ideal apostle. Many a worthy clergyman, who passes his life in admirable works of kindly charity, lives and dies unnoticed and unknown; but it is sufficient for some shallow uneducated passman out of either University to get up in his pulpit and express his doubts about Noah's ark, or Balaam's ass, or Jonah and the whale,

for half of London to flock to hear him, and to sit open-mouthed in rapt admiration at his superb intellect. The growth of common sense in the English Church is a thing very much to be regretted. It is really a degrading concession to a low form of realism. It is silly, too. It springs from an entire ignorance of psychology. Man can believe the impossible, but man can never believe the improbable. However, I must read the end of my article:—

"What we have to do, what at any rate it is our duty to do, is to revive this old art of Lying. Much of course may be done, in the way of educating the public, by amateurs in the domestic circle, at literary lunches, and at afternoon teas. But this is merely the light and graceful side of lying, such as was probably heard at Cretan[73] dinner parties. There are many other forms. Lying for the sake of gaining some immediate personal advantage, for instance—lying with a moral purpose, as it is usually called—though of late it has been rather looked down upon, was extremely popular with the antique world. Athena laughs when Odysseus tells her 'his words of sly devising,' as Mr William Morris phrases it,[74] and the glory of mendacity illumines the pale brow of the stainless hero of Euripidean tragedy, and sets among the noble women of the past the young bride of one of Horace's most exquisite odes. Later on, what at first had been merely a natural instinct was elevated into a self-conscious science. Elaborate rules were laid down for the guidance of mankind, and an important school of literature grew up round the subject. Indeed when one remembers the excellent philosophical treatise of Sanchez on the whole question, one cannot help regretting that no one has ever thought of publishing a cheap and condensed edition of the works of that great casuist. A short primer, 'When to Lie and How,' if brought out in an attractive and not too expensive a form, would no doubt command a large sale, and would prove of real practical service to many earnest and deep-thinking people. Lying for the sake of the improvement of the young, which is the basis of home education,

---

[71]In Greek myth, false **dreams** come through the **gates of ivory,** true dreams through the **gates of horn.** F. W. H. **Myers** (1843–1901): a founder of the Society for Psychical Research.

[72]**St Thomas: apostle** who doubted the resurrected Jesus; John 20:24–25. **Noah . . . whale:** miraculous Old Testament stories; Genesis 6–9, Numbers 22:22–33, Jonah 1–2.

[73]**Cretans** were reputed to be liars.

[74]**Morris** translated the *Odyssey* in 1887. **tragedy:** Euripides' *Ion* (413? BCE). **Horace,** *Odes* 3.11.35. Francisco **Sanchez** (1550?–1623): skeptical philosopher.

still lingers amongst us, and its advantages are so admirably set forth in the early books of Plato's *Republic* that it is unnecessary to dwell upon them here. It is a mode of lying for which all good mothers have peculiar capabilities, but it is capable of still further development, and has been sadly overlooked by the School Board. Lying for the sake of a monthly salary is of course well known in Fleet Street,[75] and the profession of a political leader-writer is not without its advantages. But it is said to be a somewhat dull occupation, and it certainly does not lead to much beyond a kind of ostentatious obscurity. The only form of lying that is absolutely beyond reproach is Lying for its own sake, and the highest development of this is, as we have already pointed out, Lying in Art. Just as those who do not love Plato more than Truth[76] cannot pass beyond the threshold of the Academe, so those who do not love Beauty more than Truth never know the inmost shrine of Art. The solid stolid British intellect lies in the desert sands like the Sphinx in Flaubert's marvellous tale,[77] and fantasy, *La Chimère*, dances round it, and calls to it with her false, flute-toned voice. It may not hear her now, but surely some day, when we are all bored to death with the commonplace character of modern fiction, it will hearken to her and try to borrow her wings.

"And when that day dawns, or sunset reddens, how joyous we shall all be! Facts will be regarded as discreditable, Truth will be found mourning over her fetters, and Romance, with her temper of wonder, will return to the land. The very aspect of the world will change to our startled eyes. Out of the sea will rise Behemoth and Leviathan,[78] and sail round the high-pooped galleys, as they do on the delightful maps of those ages when books on geography were actually readable. Dragons will wander about the waste places, and the phœnix will soar from her nest of fire into the air. We shall lay our hands upon the basilisk, and see the jewel in the toad's head.

Champing his gilded oats, the Hippogriff will stand in our stalls, and over our heads will float the Blue Bird singing of beautiful and impossible things, of things that are lovely and that never happen, of things that are not and that should be. But before this comes to pass we must cultivate the lost art of Lying."

CYRIL: Then we must certainly cultivate it at once. But in order to avoid making any error, I want you to tell me briefly the doctrines of the new æsthetics.

VIVIAN: Briefly, then, they are these. Art never expresses anything but itself. It has an independent life, just as Thought has, and develops purely on its own lines. It is not necessarily realistic in an age of realism, nor spiritual in an age of faith. So far from being the creation of its time, it is usually in direct opposition to it, and the only history that it preserves for us is the history of its own progress. Sometimes it returns upon its footsteps, and revives some antique form, as happened in the archaistic movement of late Greek art, and in the pre-Raphaelite movement of our own day. At other times it entirely anticipates its age, and produces in one century work that it takes another century to understand, to appreciate, and to enjoy. In no case does it reproduce its age. To pass from the art of a time to the time itself is the great mistake that all historians commit.

The second doctrine is this. All bad art comes from returning to Life and Nature, and elevating them into ideals. Life and Nature may sometimes be used as part of Art's rough material, but before they are of any real service to Art they must be translated into artistic conventions. The moment Art surrenders its imaginative medium it surrenders everything. As a method Realism is a complete failure, and the two things that every artist should avoid are modernity of form and modernity of subject-matter. To us, who live in the nineteenth century, any century is a suitable subject for art except our own. The only beautiful things are the things that do not concern us. It is, to have the pleasure of quoting myself, exactly because Hecuba is nothing to us that her sorrows are so suitable a motive for a tragedy. Besides, it is only the modern that ever becomes old-fashioned. M. Zola sits down to give us a picture of the Second Empire.[79]

---

[75]**Fleet Street:** London newspaper district.

[76]**love . . . Truth:** Aristotle reputedly said he was a friend more to truth than to Plato.

[77]**tale:** Gustave **Flaubert**, probably *The Temptation of St. Anthony* (1874).

[78]**Behemoth and Leviathan:** see Job 40–41.

---

[79]**Second Empire:** 1852–1870, reign of Napoléon III.

Who cares for the Second Empire now? It is out of date. Life goes faster than Realism, but Romanticism is always in front of Life.

The third doctrine is that Life imitates Art far more than Art imitates Life. This results not merely from Life's imitative instinct, but from the fact that the self-conscious aim of Life is to find expression, and that Art offers it certain beautiful forms through which it may realize that energy. It is a theory that has never been put forward before, but it is extremely fruitful, and throws an entirely new light upon the history of Art.

It follows, as a corollary from this, that external Nature also imitates Art. The only effects that she can show us are effects that we have already seen through poetry, or in paintings. This is the secret of Nature's charm, as well as the explanation of Nature's weakness.

The final revelation is that Lying, the telling of beautiful untrue things, is the proper aim of Art. But of this I think I have spoken at sufficient length. And now let us go out on the terrace, where "droops the milk-white peacock like a ghost,"[80] while the evening star "washes the dusk with silver." At twilight nature becomes a wonderfully suggestive effect, and is not without loveliness, though perhaps its chief use is to illustrate quotations from the poets. Come! We have talked long enough.

1889, 1891

~

The Importance of Being Earnest

A Trivial Comedy for Serious People

— THE PERSONS OF THE PLAY —

JOHN WORTHING, JP	LADY BRACKNELL
ALGERNON MONCRIEFF	HON. GWENDOLEN FAIRFAX
REVD CANON CHASUBLE, DD	CECILY CARDEW
MERRIMAN (BUTLER)	MISS PRISM (GOVERNESS)
LANE (MANSERVANT)	

---

[80]"**droops . . . ghost**": from Tennyson, "Now Sleeps the Crimson Petal." "**washes . . . silver**": William Blake, "To the Evening Star" (1783).

— THE SCENES OF THE PLAY —

Act 1
Algernon Moncrieff's flat in Half-Moon Street, W.

Act 2
The garden at the Manor House, Woolton

Act 3
Drawing-room at the Manor House, Woolton

Time
The Present

— FIRST ACT —

(Scene: Morning-room in Algernon's flat in Half-Moon Street. The room is luxuriously and artistically furnished. The sound of a piano is heard in the adjoining room. Lane is arranging afternoon tea on the table and, after the music has ceased, Algernon enters [from music-room])

ALGERNON: Did you hear what I was playing, Lane?

LANE: I didn't think it polite to listen, sir.

ALGERNON: I'm sorry for that, for your sake. I don't play accurately—anyone can play accurately—but I play with wonderful expression. As far as the piano is concerned, sentiment is my forte. I keep science for Life.

LANE: Yes, sir.

ALGERNON: And, speaking of the science of Life, have you got the cucumber sandwiches cut for Lady Bracknell?

LANE: Yes, sir. (*Hands them on a salver*)

ALGERNON: (*inspects them, takes two, and sits down on the sofa*) Oh! . . . by the way, Lane, I see from your book that on Thursday night, when Lord Shoreham and Mr Worthing were dining with me, eight bottles of champagne are entered as having been consumed.

LANE: Yes, sir; eight bottles and a pint.

ALGERNON: Why is it that at a bachelor's establishment the servants invariably drink the champagne? I ask merely for information.

LANE: I attribute it to the superior quality of the wine, sir. I have often observed that in married households the champagne is rarely of a first-rate brand.

ALGERNON: Good heavens! Is marriage so demoralizing as that?

LANE: I believe it *is* a very pleasant state, sir. I have had very little experience of it myself up to the present. I have only been married once. That was in consequence of a misunderstanding between myself and a young person.

ALGERNON: (*languidly*) I don't know that I am much interested in your family life, Lane.

LANE: No, sir; it is not a very interesting subject. I never think of it myself.

ALGERNON: Very natural, I am sure. That will do, Lane, thank you.

LANE: Thank you, sir.

(*Lane goes out*)

ALGERNON: Lane's views on marriage seem somewhat lax. Really, if the lower orders don't set us a good example, what on earth is the use of them? They seem, as a class, to have absolutely no sense of moral responsibility.

(*Enter Lane*)

LANE: Mr Ernest Worthing.

(*Enter Jack. Lane goes out*)

ALGERNON: How are you, my dear Ernest? What brings you up to town?

JACK: Oh, pleasure, pleasure! What else should bring one anywhere? Eating as usual, I see, Algy!

ALGERNON: (*stiffly*) I believe it is customary in good society to take some slight refreshment at five o'clock. Where have you been since last Thursday?

JACK: (*sitting down on the sofa*) In the country.

ALGERNON: What on earth do you do there?

JACK: (*pulling off his gloves*) When one is in town one amuses oneself. When one is in the country one amuses other people. It is excessively boring.

ALGERNON: And who are the people you amuse?

JACK: (*airily*) Oh, neighbours, neighbours.

ALGERNON: Got nice neighbours in your part of Shropshire?[1]

JACK: Perfectly horrid! Never speak to one of them.

ALGERNON: How immensely you must amuse them! (*Goes over and takes sandwich*) By the way, Shropshire is your county, is it not?

JACK: Eh? Shropshire? Yes, of course. Hallo! Why all these cups? Why cucumber sandwiches? Why such reckless extravagance in one so young? Who is coming to tea?

ALGERNON: Oh! merely Aunt Augusta and Gwendolen.

---

[1]**Shropshire**: county in W Midlands.

JACK: How perfectly delightful!

ALGERNON: Yes, that is all very well; but I am afraid Aunt Augusta won't quite approve of your being here.

JACK: May I ask why?

ALGERNON: My dear fellow, the way you flirt with Gwendolen is perfectly disgraceful. It is almost as bad as the way Gwendolen flirts with you.

JACK: I am in love with Gwendolen. I have come up to town expressly to propose to her.

ALGERNON: I thought you had come up for pleasure? . . . I call that business.

JACK: How utterly unromantic you are!

ALGERNON: I really don't see anything romantic in proposing. It is very romantic to be in love. But there is nothing romantic about a definite proposal. Why, one may be accepted. One usually is, I believe. Then the excitement is all over. The very essence of romance is uncertainty. If ever I get married, I'll certainly try to forget the fact.

JACK: I have no doubt about that, dear Algy. The Divorce Court was specially invented for people whose memories are so curiously constituted.

ALGERNON: Oh! there is no use speculating on that subject. Divorces are made in Heaven—(*Jack puts out his hand to take a sandwich. Algernon at once interferes*) Please don't touch the cucumber sandwiches. They are ordered specially for Aunt Augusta. (*Takes one and eats it*)

JACK: Well, you have been eating them all the time.

ALGERNON: That is quite a different matter. She is my aunt. (*Takes plate from below*) Have some bread and butter. The bread and butter is for Gwendolen. Gwendolen is devoted to bread and butter.

JACK: (*advancing to table and helping himself*) And very good bread and butter it is too.

ALGERNON: Well, my dear fellow, you need not eat as if you were going to eat it all. You behave as if you were married to her already. You are not married to her already, and I don't think you ever will be.

JACK: Why on earth do you say that?

ALGERNON: Well, in the first place, girls never marry the men they flirt with. Girls don't think it right.

JACK: Oh, that is nonsense!

ALGERNON: It isn't. It is a great truth. It accounts for the extraordinary number of bachelors that one sees all over the place. In the second place, I don't give my consent.

JACK: Your consent!

ALGERNON: My dear fellow, Gwendolen is my first

cousin. And before I allow you to marry her, you will have to clear up the whole question of Cecily. (*Rings bell*)

JACK: Cecily! What on earth do you mean? What do you mean, Algy, by Cecily? I don't know anyone of the name of Cecily.

(*Enter Lane*)

ALGERNON: Bring me that cigarette case Mr Worthing left in the smoking-room the last time he dined here.

LANE: Yes, sir.

(*Lane goes out*)

JACK: Do you mean to say you have had my cigarette case all this time? I wish to goodness you had let me know. I have been writing frantic letters to Scotland Yard about it. I was very nearly offering a large reward.

ALGERNON: Well, I wish you would offer one. I happen to be more than usually hard up.

JACK: There is no good offering a large reward now that the thing is found.

(*Enter Lane with the cigarette case on a salver. Algernon takes it at once. Lane goes out*)

ALGERNON: I think that is rather mean of you, Ernest, I must say. (*Opens case and examines it*) However, it makes no matter, for, now that I look at the inscription inside, I find that the thing isn't yours after all.

JACK: Of course it's mine. (*Moving to him*) You have seen me with it a hundred times, and you have no right whatsoever to read what is written inside. It is a very ungentlemanly thing to read a private cigarette case.

ALGERNON: Oh! it is absurd to have a hard and fast rule about what one should read and what one shouldn't. More than half of modern culture depends on what one shouldn't read.

JACK: I am quite aware of the fact, and I don't propose to discuss modern culture. It isn't the sort of thing one should talk of in private. I simply want my cigarette case back.

ALGERNON: Yes; but this isn't your cigarette case. This cigarette case is a present from someone of the name of Cecily, and you said you didn't know anyone of that name.

JACK: Well, if you want to know, Cecily happens to be my aunt.

ALGERNON: Your aunt!

JACK: Yes. Charming old lady she is, too. Lives at Tunbridge Wells.[2] Just give it back to me, Algy.

ALGERNON: (*retreating to back of sofa*) But why does she call herself little Cecily if she is your aunt and lives at Tunbridge Wells? (*Reading*) "From little Cecily with her fondest love."

JACK: (*moving to sofa and kneeling upon it*) My dear fellow, what on earth is there in that? Some aunts are tall, some aunts are not tall. That is a matter that surely an aunt may be allowed to decide for herself. You seem to think that every aunt should be exactly like your aunt! That is absurd! For Heaven's sake give me back my cigarette case. (*Follows Algernon round the room*)

ALGERNON: Yes. But why does your aunt call you her uncle? "From little Cecily, with her fondest love to her dear Uncle Jack." There is no objection, I admit, to an aunt being a small aunt, but why an aunt, no matter what her size may be, should call her own nephew her uncle, I can't quite make out. Besides, your name isn't Jack at all; it is Ernest.

JACK: It isn't Ernest; it's Jack.

ALGERNON: You have always told me it was Ernest. I have introduced you to every one as Ernest. You answer to the name of Ernest. You look as if your name was Ernest. You are the most earnest looking person I ever saw in my life. It is perfectly absurd your saying that your name isn't Ernest. It's on your cards. Here is one of them. (*Taking it from case*) "Mr Ernest Worthing, B.4, The Albany." I'll keep this as a proof that your name is Ernest if ever you attempt to deny it to me, or to Gwendolen, or to anyone else. (*Puts the card in his pocket*)

JACK: Well, my name is Ernest in town and Jack in the country, and the cigarette case was given to me in the country.

ALGERNON: Yes, but that does not account for the fact that your small Aunt Cecily, who lives at Tunbridge Wells, calls you her dear uncle. Come, old boy, you had much better have the thing out at once.

JACK: My dear Algy, you talk exactly as if you were a dentist. It is very vulgar to talk like a dentist when one isn't a dentist. It produces a false impression.

ALGERNON: Well, that is exactly what dentists always do. Now, go on! Tell me the whole thing. I may

---

[2]**Tunbridge Wells:** town in SE England where respectable spinsters or widows were traditionally thought to reside.

mention that I have always suspected you of being a confirmed and secret Bunburyist; and I am quite sure of it now.

JACK: Bunburyist? What on earth do you mean by a Bunburyist?

ALGERNON: I'll reveal to you the meaning of that incomparable expression as soon as you are kind enough to inform me why you are Ernest in town and Jack in the country.

JACK: Well, produce my cigarette case first.

ALGERNON: Here it is. (*Hands cigarette case*) Now produce your explanation, and pray make it improbable. (*Sits on sofa*)

JACK: My dear fellow, there is nothing improbable about my explanation at all. In fact it's perfectly ordinary. Old Mr Thomas Cardew, who adopted me when I was a little boy, made me in his will guardian to his granddaughter, Miss Cecily Cardew. Cecily, who addresses me as her uncle from motives of respect that you could not possibly appreciate, lives at my place in the country under the charge of her admirable governess, Miss Prism.

ALGERNON: Where is that place in the country, by the way?

JACK: That is nothing to you, dear boy. You are not going to be invited. . . . I may tell you candidly that the place is not in Shropshire.

ALGERNON: I suspected that, my dear fellow! I have Bunburyed all over Shropshire on two separate occasions. Now, go on. Why are you Ernest in town and Jack in the country?

JACK: My dear Algy, I don't know whether you will be able to understand my real motives. You are hardly serious enough. When one is placed in the position of guardian, one has to adopt a very high moral tone on all subjects. It's one's duty to do so. And as a high moral tone can hardly be said to conduce very much to either one's health or one's happiness, in order to get up to town I have always pretended to have a younger brother of the name of Ernest, who lives in the Albany, and gets into the most dreadful scrapes. That, my dear Algy, is the whole truth pure and simple.

ALGERNON: The truth is rarely pure and never simple. Modern life would be very tedious if it were either, and modern literature a complete impossibility!

JACK: That wouldn't be at all a bad thing.

ALGERNON: Literary criticism is not your forte, my dear fellow. Don't try it. You should leave that to people who haven't been at a University. They do it so well in the daily papers. What you really are is a Bunburyist. I was quite right in saying you were a Bunburyist. You are one of the most advanced Bunburyists I know.

JACK: What on earth do you mean?

ALGERNON: You have invented a very useful younger brother called Ernest, in order that you may be able to come up to town as often as you like. I have invented an invaluable permanent invalid called Bunbury, in order that I may be able to go down into the country whenever I choose. Bunbury is perfectly invaluable. If it wasn't for Bunbury's extraordinary bad health, for instance, I wouldn't be able to dine with you at Willis's[3] tonight, for I have been really engaged to Aunt Augusta for more than a week.

JACK: I haven't asked you to dine with me anywhere tonight.

ALGERNON: I know. You are absurdly careless about sending out invitations. It is very foolish of you. Nothing annoys people so much as not receiving invitations.

JACK: You had much better dine with your Aunt Augusta.

ALGERNON: I haven't the smallest intention of doing anything of the kind. To begin with, I dined there on Monday, and once a week is quite enough to dine with one's own relations. In the second place, whenever I do dine there I am always treated as a member of the family, and sent down with either no woman at all, or two. In the third place, I know perfectly well whom she will place me next to, tonight. She will place me next Mary Farquhar, who always flirts with her own husband across the dinner-table. That is not very pleasant. Indeed, it is not even decent . . . and that sort of thing is enormously on the increase. The amount of women in London who flirt with their own husbands is perfectly scandalous. It looks so bad. It is simply washing one's clean linen in public. Besides, now that I know you to be a confirmed Bunburyist I naturally want to talk to you about Bunburying. I want to tell you the rules.

JACK: I'm not a Bunburyist at all. If Gwendolen accepts me, I am going to kill my brother, indeed I think I'll kill him in any case. Cecily is a little too much interested in him. It is rather a bore. So I am going to get rid of Ernest. And I strongly advise you to do the

---

[3]**Willis's**: fashionable London restaurant.

same with Mr . . . with your invalid friend who has the absurd name.

ALGERNON: Nothing will induce me to part with Bunbury, and if you ever get married, which seems to me extremely problematic, you will be very glad to know Bunbury. A man who marries without knowing Bunbury has a very tedious time of it.

JACK: That is nonsense. If I marry a charming girl like Gwendolen, and she is the only girl I ever saw in my life that I would marry, I certainly won't want to know Bunbury.

ALGERNON: Then your wife will. You don't seem to realize, that in married life three is company and two is none.

JACK: (*sententiously*) That, my dear young friend, is the theory that the corrupt French Drama has been propounding for the last fifty years.

ALGERNON: Yes; and that the happy English home has proved in half the time.

JACK: For heaven's sake, don't try to be cynical. It's perfectly easy to be cynical.

ALGERNON: My dear fellow, it isn't easy to be anything nowadays. There's such a lot of beastly competition about. (*The sound of an electric bell is heard*) Ah! that must be Aunt Augusta. Only relatives, or creditors, ever ring in that Wagnerian[4] manner. Now, if I get her out of the way for ten minutes, so that you can have an opportunity for proposing to Gwendolen, may I dine with you tonight at Willis's?

JACK: I suppose so, if you want to.

ALGERNON: Yes, but you must be serious about it. I hate people who are not serious about meals. It is so shallow of them.

(*Enter Lane*)

LANE: Lady Bracknell and Miss Fairfax.

(*Algernon goes forward to meet them. Enter Lady Bracknell and Gwendolen*)

LADY BRACKNELL: Good afternoon, dear Algernon, I hope you are behaving very well.

ALGERNON: I'm feeling very well, Aunt Augusta.

LADY BRACKNELL: That's not quite the same thing. In fact the two things rarely go together. (*Sees Jack and bows to him with icy coldness*)

---

[4]**Wagnerian**: in the style of the operas of German composer Richard Wagner (1813–1883).

ALGERNON: (*to Gwendolen*) Dear me, you are smart!

GWENDOLEN: I am always smart! Aren't I, Mr Worthing?

JACK: You're quite perfect, Miss Fairfax.

GWENDOLEN: Oh! I hope I am not that. It would leave no room for developments, and I intend to develop in many directions. (*Gwendolen and Jack sit down together in the corner*)

LADY BRACKNELL: I'm sorry if we are a little late, Algernon, but I was obliged to call on dear Lady Harbury. I hadn't been there since her poor husband's death. I never saw a woman so altered; she looks quite twenty years younger. And now I'll have a cup of tea, and one of those nice cucumber sandwiches you promised me.

ALGERNON: Certainly, Aunt Augusta. (*Goes over to tea-table*)

LADY BRACKNELL: Won't you come and sit here, Gwendolen?

GWENDOLEN: Thanks, mamma, I'm quite comfortable where I am.

ALGERNON: (*picking up empty plate in horror*) Good heavens! Lane! Why are there no cucumber sandwiches? I ordered them specially.

LANE: (*gravely*) There were no cucumbers in the market this morning, sir. I went down twice.

ALGERNON: No cucumbers!

LANE: No, sir. Not even for ready money.

ALGERNON: That will do, Lane, thank you.

LANE: Thank you, sir.

(*Goes out*)

ALGERNON: I am greatly distressed, Aunt Augusta, about there being no cucumbers, not even for ready money.

LADY BRACKNELL: It really makes no matter, Algernon. I had some crumpets with Lady Harbury, who seems to me to be living entirely for pleasure now.

ALGERNON: I hear her hair has turned quite gold from grief.

LADY BRACKNELL: It certainly has changed its colour. From what cause I, of course, cannot say. (*Algernon crosses and hands tea*) Thank you. I've quite a treat for you tonight, Algernon. I am going to send you down with Mary Farquhar. She is such a nice woman, and so attentive to her husband. It's delightful to watch them.

ALGERNON: I am afraid, Aunt Augusta, I shall have to give up the pleasure of dining with you tonight after all.

LADY BRACKNELL: (*frowning*) I hope not, Algernon. It would put my table completely out. Your uncle would have to dine upstairs. Fortunately he is accustomed to that.

ALGERNON: It is a great bore, and, I need hardly say, a terrible disappointment to me, but the fact is I have just had a telegram to say that my poor friend Bunbury is very ill again. (*Exchanges glances with Jack*) They seem to think I should be with him.

LADY BRACKNELL: It is very strange. This Mr Bunbury seems to suffer from curiously bad health.

ALGERNON: Yes; poor Bunbury is a dreadful invalid.

LADY BRACKNELL: Well, I must say, Algernon, that I think it is high time that Mr Bunbury made up his mind whether he was going to live or to die. This shilly-shallying with the question is absurd. Nor do I in any way approve of the modern sympathy with invalids. I consider it morbid. Illness of any kind is hardly a thing to be encouraged in others. Health is the primary duty of life. I am always telling that to your poor uncle, but he never seems to take much notice . . . as far as any improvement in his ailments goes. I should be much obliged if you would ask Mr Bunbury, from me, to be kind enough not to have a relapse on Saturday, for I rely on you to arrange my music for me. It is my last reception, and one wants something that will encourage conversation, particularly at the end of the season when everyone has practically said whatever they had to say, which, in most cases, was probably not much.

ALGERNON: I'll speak to Bunbury, Aunt Augusta, if he is still conscious, and I think I can promise you he'll be all right by Saturday. Of course the music is a great difficulty. You see, if one plays good music, people don't listen, and if one plays bad music people don't talk. But I'll run over the programme I've drawn out, if you will kindly come into the next room for a moment.

LADY BRACKNELL: Thank you, Algernon. It is very thoughtful of you. (*Rising, and following Algernon*) I'm sure the programme will be delightful, after a few expurgations. French songs I cannot possibly allow. People always seem to think that they are improper, and either look shocked, which is vulgar, or laugh, which is worse. But German sounds a thoroughly respectable language, and indeed I believe is so. Gwendolen, you will accompany me.

GWENDOLEN: Certainly, mamma.

(*Lady Bracknell and Algernon go into the music-room, Gwendolen remains behind*)

JACK: Charming day it has been, Miss Fairfax.

GWENDOLEN: Pray don't talk to me about the weather, Mr Worthing. Whenever people talk to me about the weather, I always feel quite certain that they mean something else. And that makes me so nervous.

JACK: I do mean something else.

GWENDOLEN: I thought so. In fact, I am never wrong.

JACK: And I would like to be allowed to take advantage of Lady Bracknell's temporary absence. . . .

GWENDOLEN: I would certainly advise you to do so. Mamma has a way of coming back suddenly into a room that I have often had to speak to her about.

JACK: (*nervously*) Miss Fairfax, ever since I met you I have admired you more than any girl . . . I have ever met since . . . I met you.

GWENDOLEN: Yes, I am quite aware of the fact. And I often wish that in public, at any rate, you had been more demonstrative. For me you have always had an irresistible fascination. Even before I met you I was far from indifferent to you. (*Jack looks at her in amazement*) We live, as I hope you know, Mr Worthing, in an age of ideals. The fact is constantly mentioned in the more expensive monthly magazines, and has reached the provincial pulpits I am told; and my ideal has always been to love someone of the name of Ernest. There is something in that name that inspires absolute confidence. The moment Algernon first mentioned to me that he had a friend called Ernest, I knew I was destined to love you.

JACK: You really love me, Gwendolen?

GWENDOLEN: Passionately!

JACK: Darling! You don't know how happy you've made me.

GWENDOLEN: My own Ernest!

JACK: But you don't really mean to say that you couldn't love me if my name wasn't Ernest?

GWENDOLEN: But your name is Ernest.

JACK: Yes, I know it is. But supposing it was something else? Do you mean to say you couldn't love me then?

GWENDOLEN: (*glibly*) Ah! that is clearly a metaphysical speculation, and like most metaphysical speculations has very little reference at all to the actual facts of real life, as we know them.

JACK: Personally, darling, to speak quite candidly, I don't much care about the name of Ernest. . . . I don't think the name suits me at all.

GWENDOLEN: It suits you perfectly. It is a divine name. It has music of its own. It produces vibrations.

JACK: Well, really, Gwendolen, I must say that I think there are lots of other much nicer names. I think Jack, for instance, a charming name.

GWENDOLEN: Jack? . . . No, there is very little music in the name Jack, if any at all, indeed. It does not thrill. It produces absolutely no vibrations. . . . I have known several Jacks, and they all, without exception, were more than usually plain. Besides, Jack is a notorious domesticity for John! And I pity any woman who is married to a man called John. She would probably never be allowed to know the entrancing pleasure of a single moment's solitude. The only really safe name is Ernest.

JACK: Gwendolen, I must get christened at once—I mean we must get married at once. There is no time to be lost.

GWENDOLEN: Married, Mr Worthing?

JACK: (*astounded*) Well . . . surely. You know that I love you, and you led me to believe, Miss Fairfax, that you were not absolutely indifferent to me.

GWENDOLEN: I adore you. But you haven't proposed to me yet. Nothing has been said at all about marriage. The subject has not even been touched on.

JACK: Well . . . may I propose to you now?

GWENDOLEN: I think it would be an admirable opportunity. And to spare you any possible disappointment, Mr Worthing, I think it only fair to tell you quite frankly beforehand that I am fully determined to accept you.

JACK: Gwendolen!

GWENDOLEN: Yes, Mr Worthing, what have you got to say to me?

JACK: You know what I have got to say to you.

GWENDOLEN: Yes, but you don't say it.

JACK: Gwendolen, will you marry me? (*Goes on his knees*)

GWENDOLEN: Of course I will, darling. How long you have been about it! I am afraid you have had very little experience in how to propose.

JACK: My own one, I have never loved anyone in the world but you.

GWENDOLEN: Yes, but men often propose for practice. I know my brother Gerald does. All my girl-friends tell me so. What wonderfully blue eyes you have, Ernest! They are quite, quite, blue. I hope you will always look at me just like that, especially when there are other people present.

(*Enter Lady Bracknell*)

LADY BRACKNELL: Mr Worthing! Rise, sir, from this semi-recumbent posture. It is most indecorous.

GWENDOLEN: Mamma! (*He tries to rise; she restrains him*) I must beg you to retire. This is no place for you. Besides, Mr Worthing has not quite finished yet.

LADY BRACKNELL: Finished what, may I ask?

GWENDOLEN: I am engaged to Mr Worthing, mamma.

(*They rise together*)

LADY BRACKNELL: Pardon me, you are not engaged to anyone. When you do become engaged to someone, I, or your father, should his health permit him, will inform you of the fact. An engagement should come on a young girl as a surprise, pleasant or unpleasant, as the case may be. It is hardly a matter that she could be allowed to arrange for herself. . . . And now I have a few questions to put to you, Mr Worthing. While I am making these inquiries, you, Gwendolen, will wait for me below in the carriage.

GWENDOLEN: (*reproachfully*) Mamma!

LADY BRACKNELL: In the carriage, Gwendolen!

(*Gwendolen goes to the door. She and Jack blow kisses to each other behind Lady Bracknell's back. Lady Bracknell looks vaguely about as if she could not understand what the noise was. Finally turns round*)

Gwendolen, the carriage!

GWENDOLEN: Yes, mamma.

(*Goes out, looking back at Jack*)

LADY BRACKNELL: (*sitting down*) You can take a seat, Mr Worthing. (*Looks in her pocket for note-book and pencil*)

JACK: Thank you, Lady Bracknell, I prefer standing.

LADY BRACKNELL: (*pencil and note-book in hand*). I feel bound to tell you that you are not down on my list of eligible young men, although I have the same list as the dear Duchess of Bolton has. We work together, in fact. However, I am quite ready to enter your name, should your answers be what a really affectionate mother requires. Do you smoke?

JACK: Well, yes, I must admit I smoke.

LADY BRACKNELL: I am glad to hear it. A man should always have an occupation of some kind. There are far too many idle men in London as it is. How old are you?

JACK: Twenty-nine.

LADY BRACKNELL: A very good age to be married at. I have always been of opinion that a man who desires to get married should know either everything or nothing. Which do you know?

JACK: (*after some hesitation*) I know nothing, Lady Bracknell.

LADY BRACKNELL: I am pleased to hear it. I do not approve of anything that tampers with natural ignorance. Ignorance is like a delicate exotic fruit; touch it and the bloom is gone. The whole theory of modern education is radically unsound. Fortunately in

England, at any rate, education produces no effect whatsoever. If it did, it would prove a serious danger to the upper classes, and probably lead to acts of violence in Grosvenor Square. What is your income?

JACK: Between seven and eight thousand a year.

LADY BRACKNELL: (*makes a note in her book*) In land, or in investments?

JACK: In investments, chiefly.

LADY BRACKNELL: That is satisfactory. What between the duties expected of one during one's lifetime, and the duties exacted from one after one's death, land has ceased to be either a profit or a pleasure. It gives one position, and prevents one from keeping it up. That's all that can be said about land.

JACK: I have a country house with some land, of course, attached to it, about fifteen hundred acres, I believe; but I don't depend on that for my real income. In fact, as far as I can make out, the poachers are the only people who make anything out of it.

LADY BRACKNELL: A country house! How many bedrooms? Well, that point can be cleared up afterwards. You have a town house, I hope? A girl with a simple, unspoiled nature, like Gwendolen, could hardly be expected to reside in the country.

JACK: Well, I own a house in Belgrave Square,[5] but it is let by the year to Lady Bloxham. Of course, I can get it back whenever I like, at six months' notice.

LADY BRACKNELL: Lady Bloxham? I don't know her.

JACK: Oh, she goes about very little. She is a lady considerably advanced in years.

LADY BRACKNELL: Ah, nowadays that is no guarantee of respectability of character. What number in Belgrave Square?

JACK: 149.

LADY BRACKNELL: (*shaking her head*) The unfashionable side. I thought there was something. However, that could easily be altered.

JACK: Do you mean the fashion, or the side?

LADY BRACKNELL: (*sternly*) Both, if necessary, I presume. What are your politics?

JACK: Well, I am afraid I really have none. I am a Liberal Unionist.[6]

LADY BRACKNELL: Oh, they count as Tories. They dine with us. Or come in the evening, at any rate. Now to minor matters. Are your parents living?

---

[5]**Belgrave Square**: upper-class neighborhood in London.

[6]**Liberal Unionist**: member of the Liberal Party who opposed its leader Gladstone's support of Home Rule for Ireland.

JACK: I have lost both my parents.

LADY BRACKNELL: Both? . . . That seems like carelessness. Who was your father? He was evidently a man of some wealth. Was he born in what the Radical papers call the purple of commerce, or did he rise from the ranks of the aristocracy?

JACK: I am afraid I really don't know. The fact is, Lady Bracknell, I said I had lost my parents. It would be nearer the truth to say that my parents seem to have lost me. . . . I don't actually know who I am by birth. I was . . . well, I was found.

LADY BRACKNELL: Found!

JACK: The late Mr Thomas Cardew, an old gentleman of a very charitable and kindly disposition, found me, and gave me the name of Worthing, because he happened to have a first-class ticket for Worthing in his pocket at the time. Worthing is a place in Sussex. It is a seaside resort.

LADY BRACKNELL: Where did the charitable gentleman who had a first-class ticket for this seaside resort find you?

JACK: (*gravely*) In a hand-bag.

LADY BRACKNELL: A hand-bag?

JACK: (*very seriously*) Yes, Lady Bracknell. I was in a hand-bag—a somewhat large, black leather hand-bag, with handles to it—an ordinary hand-bag in fact.

LADY BRACKNELL: In what locality did this Mr James, or Thomas, Cardew come across this ordinary hand-bag?

JACK: In the cloak-room at Victoria Station. It was given to him in mistake for his own.

LADY BRACKNELL: The cloak-room at Victoria Station?

JACK: Yes. The Brighton line.

LADY BRACKNELL: The line is immaterial. Mr Worthing, I confess I feel somewhat bewildered by what you have just told me. To be born, or at any rate bred, in a hand-bag, whether it had handles or not, seems to me to display a contempt for the ordinary decencies of family life that reminds one of the worst excesses of the French Revolution. And I presume you know what that unfortunate movement led to? As for the particular locality in which the hand-bag was found, a cloak-room at a railway station might serve to conceal a social indiscretion—has probably, indeed, been used for that purpose before now—but it could hardly be regarded as an assured basis for a recognized position in good society.

JACK: May I ask you then what you would advise me to do? I need hardly say I would do anything in the world to ensure Gwendolen's happiness.

LADY BRACKNELL: I would strongly advise you, Mr Worthing, to try and acquire some relations as soon as possible, and to make a definite effort to produce at any rate one parent, of either sex, before the season is quite over.

JACK: Well, I don't see how I could possibly manage to do that. I can produce the hand-bag at any moment. It is in my dressing-room at home. I really think that should satisfy you, Lady Bracknell.

LADY BRACKNELL: Me, sir! What has it to do with me? You can hardly imagine that I and Lord Bracknell would dream of allowing our only daughter—a girl brought up with the utmost care—to marry into a cloak-room, and form an alliance with a parcel? Good morning, Mr Worthing!

(Lady Bracknell sweeps out in majestic indignation)

JACK: Good morning! *(Algernon, from the other room, strikes up the Wedding March. Jack looks perfectly furious, and goes to the door)* For goodness' sake don't play that ghastly tune, Algy! How idiotic you are!

(The music stops and Algernon enters cheerily)

ALGERNON: Didn't it go off all right, old boy? You don't mean to say Gwendolen refused you? I know it is a way she has. She is always refusing people. I think it is most ill-natured of her.

JACK: Oh, Gwendolen is as right as a trivet. As far as she is concerned, we are engaged. Her mother is perfectly unbearable. Never met such a Gorgon. . . . I don't really know what a Gorgon is like, but I am quite sure that Lady Bracknell is one. In any case, she is a monster, without being a myth, which is rather unfair. . . . I beg your pardon, Algy, I suppose I shouldn't talk about your own aunt in that way before you.

ALGERNON: My dear boy, I love hearing my relations abused. It is the only thing that makes me put up with them at all. Relations are simply a tedious pack of people, who haven't got the remotest knowledge of how to live, nor the smallest instinct about when to die.

JACK: Oh, that is nonsense!

ALGERNON: It isn't!

JACK: Well, I won't argue about the matter. You always want to argue about things.

ALGERNON: That is exactly what things were originally made for.

JACK: Upon my word, if I thought that, I'd shoot myself. . . . *(A pause)* You don't think there is any chance of Gwendolen becoming like her mother in about a hundred and fifty years, do you Algy?

ALGERNON: All women become like their mothers. That is their tragedy. No man does. That's his.

JACK: Is that clever?

ALGERNON: It is perfectly phrased! and quite as true as any observation in civilized life should be.

JACK: I am sick to death of cleverness. Everybody is clever nowadays. You can't go anywhere without meeting clever people. The thing has become an absolute public nuisance. I wish to goodness we had a few fools left.

ALGERNON: We have.

JACK: I should extremely like to meet them. What do they talk about?

ALGERNON: The fools? Oh! about the clever people, of course.

JACK: What fools!

ALGERNON: By the way, did you tell Gwendolen the truth about your being Ernest in town, and Jack in the country?

JACK: *(in a very patronizing manner)* My dear fellow, the truth isn't quite the sort of thing one tells to a nice sweet refined girl. What extraordinary ideas you have about the way to behave to a woman!

ALGERNON: The only way to behave to a woman is to make love to her, if she is pretty, and to someone else if she is plain.

JACK: Oh, that is nonsense.

ALGERNON: What about your brother? What about the profligate Ernest?

JACK: Oh, before the end of the week I shall have got rid of him. I'll say he died in Paris of apoplexy. Lots of people die of apoplexy, quite suddenly, don't they?

ALGERNON: Yes, but it's hereditary, my dear fellow. It's a sort of thing that runs in families. You had much better say a severe chill.

JACK: You are sure a severe chill isn't hereditary, or anything of that kind?

ALGERNON: Of course it isn't!

JACK: Very well, then. My poor brother Ernest is carried off suddenly in Paris, by a severe chill. That gets rid of him.

ALGERNON: But I thought you said that . . . Miss Cardew was a little too much interested in your poor brother Ernest? Won't she feel his loss a good deal?

JACK: Oh, that is all right. Cecily is not a silly romantic girl, I am glad to say. She has got a capital appetite, goes long walks, and pays no attention at all to her lessons.

ALGERNON: I would rather like to see Cecily.

JACK: I will take very good care you never do. She is excessively pretty, and she is only just eighteen.

ALGERNON: Have you told Gwendolen yet that you have an excessively pretty ward who is only just eighteen?

JACK: Oh! one doesn't blurt these things out to people. Cecily and Gwendolen are perfectly certain to be extremely great friends. I'll bet you anything you like that half an hour after they have met, they will be calling each other sister.

ALGERNON: Women only do that when they have called each other a lot of other things first. Now, my dear boy, if we want to get a good table at Willis's, we really must go and dress. Do you know it is nearly seven?

JACK: (irritably) Oh! it always is nearly seven.

ALGERNON: Well, I'm hungry.

JACK: I never knew you when you weren't. . . .

ALGERNON: What shall we do after dinner? Go to a theatre?

JACK: Oh no! I loathe listening.

ALGERNON: Well, let us go to the Club?

JACK: Oh, no! I hate talking.

ALGERNON: Well, we might trot round to the Empire[7] at ten?

JACK: Oh, no! I can't bear looking at things. It is so silly.

ALGERNON: Well, what shall we do?

JACK: Nothing!

ALGERNON: It is awfully hard work doing nothing. However, I don't mind hard work where there is no definite object of any kind.

(Enter Lane)

LANE: Miss Fairfax.

(Enter Gwendolen. Lane goes out)

ALGERNON: Gwendolen, upon my word!

GWENDOLEN: Algy, kindly turn your back. I have something very particular to say to Mr Worthing.

ALGERNON: Really, Gwendolen, I don't think I can allow this at all.

GWENDOLEN: Algy, you always adopt a strictly immoral attitude towards life. You are not quite old enough to do that. (Algernon retires to the fireplace)

JACK: My own darling!

GWENDOLEN: Ernest, we may never be married. From the expression on mamma's face I fear we never shall. Few parents nowadays pay any regard to what their children say to them. The old-fashioned respect for the young is fast dying out. Whatever influence I ever had over mamma, I lost at the age of three. But although she may prevent us from becoming man and wife, and I may marry someone else, and marry often, nothing that she can possibly do can alter my eternal devotion to you.

JACK: Dear Gwendolen!

GWENDOLEN: The story of your romantic origin, as related to me by mamma, with unpleasing comments, has naturally stirred the deeper fibres of my nature. Your Christian name has an irresistible fascination. The simplicity of your character makes you exquisitely incomprehensible to me. Your town address at the Albany I have. What is your address in the country?

JACK: The Manor House, Woolton, Hertfordshire.[8]

(Algernon, who has been carefully listening, smiles to himself, and writes the address on his shirt-cuff. Then picks up the Railway Guide)

GWENDOLEN: There is a good postal service, I suppose? It may be necessary to do something desperate. That of course will require serious consideration. I will communicate with you daily.

JACK: My own one!

GWENDOLEN: How long do you remain in town?

JACK: Till Monday.

GWENDOLEN: Good! Algy, you may turn round now.

ALGERNON: Thanks, I've turned round already.

GWENDOLEN: You may also ring the bell.

(Algernon rings bell)

JACK: You will let me see you to your carriage, my own darling?

GWENDOLEN: Certainly.

(Enter Lane)

JACK: I will see Miss Fairfax out.

LANE: Yes, sir.

(Jack and Gwendolen go off. Lane presents several letters on a salver, to Algernon. It is to be surmised that they are bills, as Algernon, after looking at the envelopes, tears them up)

ALGERNON: A glass of sherry, Lane.

LANE: Yes, sir.

ALGERNON: Tomorrow, Lane, I'm going Bunburying.

---

[7]**Empire:** a music hall theater, recently accused of indecency.

[8]**Hertfordshire:** one of the home counties, a short train trip from London.

LANE: Yes, sir.

ALGERNON: I shall probably not be back till Monday. You can put up my dress clothes, my smoking jacket, and all the Bunbury suits . . .

LANE: Yes, sir. (*Handing sherry*)

ALGERNON: I hope tomorrow will be a fine day, Lane.

LANE: It never is, sir.

ALGERNON: Lane, you're a perfect pessimist.

LANE: I do my best to give satisfaction, sir.

(*Enter Jack. Lane goes off*)

JACK: There's a sensible, intellectual girl! the only girl I ever cared for in my life. (*Algernon is laughing immoderately*) What on earth are you so amused at?

ALGERNON: Oh, I'm a little anxious about poor Bunbury, that is all.

JACK: If you don't take care, your friend Bunbury will get you into a serious scrape some day.

ALGERNON: I love scrapes. They are the only things that are never serious.

JACK: Oh, that's nonsense, Algy. You never talk anything but nonsense.

ALGERNON: Nobody ever does.

(*Jack looks indignantly at him, and leaves the room. Algernon lights a cigarette, reads his shirt-cuff, and smiles.*)

— SECOND ACT —

(*Scene: Garden at the Manor House. A flight of grey stone steps leads up to the house. The garden, an old-fashioned one, full of roses. Time of year, July. Basket chairs, and a table covered with books, are set under a large yew-tree. Miss Prism discovered seated at the table. Cecily is at the back, watering flowers*)

MISS PRISM: (*calling*) Cecily, Cecily! Surely such a utilitarian occupation as the watering of flowers is rather Moulton's duty than yours? Especially at a moment when intellectual pleasures await you. Your German grammar is on the table. Pray open it at page fifteen. We will repeat yesterday's lesson.

CECILY: (*coming over very slowly*) But I don't like German. It isn't at all a becoming language. I know perfectly well that I look quite plain after my German lesson.

MISS PRISM: Child, you know how anxious your guardian is that you should improve yourself in every way. He laid particular stress on your German, as he was leaving for town yesterday. Indeed, he always lays stress on your German when he is leaving for town.

CECILY: Dear Uncle Jack is so very serious! Sometimes he is so serious that I think he cannot be quite well.

MISS PRISM: (*drawing herself up*) Your guardian enjoys the best of health, and his gravity of demeanour is especially to be commended in one so comparatively young as he is. I know no one who has a higher sense of duty and responsibility.

CECILY: I suppose that is why he often looks a little bored when we three are together.

MISS PRISM: Cecily! I am surprised at you. Mr Worthing has many troubles in his life. Idle merriment and triviality would be out of place in his conversation. You must remember his constant anxiety about that unfortunate young man his brother.

CECILY: I wish Uncle Jack would allow that unfortunate young man, his brother, to come down here sometimes. We might have a good influence over him, Miss Prism. I am sure you certainly would. You know German, and geology, and things of that kind influence a man very much. (*Cecily begins to write in her diary*)

MISS PRISM: (*shaking her head*) I do not think that even I could produce any effect on a character that according to his own brother's admission is irretrievably weak and vacillating. Indeed I am not sure that I would desire to reclaim him. I am not in favour of this modern mania for turning bad people into good people at a moment's notice. As a man sows so let him reap. You must put away your diary, Cecily. I really don't see why you should keep a diary at all.

CECILY: I keep a diary in order to enter the wonderful secrets of my life. If I didn't write them down I should probably forget all about them.

MISS PRISM: Memory, my dear Cecily, is the diary that we all carry about with us.

CECILY: Yes, but it usually chronicles the things that have never happened, and couldn't possibly have happened. I believe that Memory is responsible for nearly all the three-volume novels that Mudie[9] sends us.

MISS PRISM: Do not speak slightingly of the three-volume novel, Cecily. I wrote one myself in earlier days.

CECILY: Did you really, Miss Prism? How wonderfully clever you are! I hope it did not end happily? I don't like novels that end happily. They depress me so much.

---

[9]**Mudie's:** subscription library, from which subscribers borrowed current books.

MISS PRISM: The good ended happily, and the bad unhappily. That is what Fiction means.

CECILY: I suppose so. But it seems very unfair. And was your novel ever published?

MISS PRISM: Alas! no. The manuscript unfortunately was abandoned. (*Cecily starts*) I used the word in the sense of lost or mislaid. To your work, child, these speculations are profitless.

CECILY: (*smiling*) But I see dear Dr Chasuble coming up through the garden.

MISS PRISM: (*rising and advancing*) Dr Chasuble! This is indeed a pleasure.

(*Enter Canon Chasuble*)

CHASUBLE: And how are we this morning? Miss Prism, you are, I trust, well?

CECILY: Miss Prism has just been complaining of a slight headache. I think it would do her so much good to have a short stroll with you in the Park, Dr Chasuble.

MISS PRISM: Cecily, I have not mentioned anything about a headache.

CECILY: No, dear Miss Prism, I know that, but I felt instinctively that you had a headache. Indeed I was thinking about that, and not about my German lesson, when the Rector came in.

CHASUBLE: I hope, Cecily, you are not inattentive.

CECILY: Oh, I am afraid I am.

CHASUBLE: That is strange. Were I fortunate enough to be Miss Prism's pupil, I would hang upon her lips. (*Miss Prism glares*) I spoke metaphorically.—My metaphor was drawn from bees. Ahem! Mr Worthing, I suppose, has not returned from town yet?

MISS PRISM: We do not expect him till Monday afternoon.

CHASUBLE: Ah yes, he usually likes to spend his Sunday in London. He is not one of those whose sole aim is enjoyment, as, by all accounts, that unfortunate young man his brother seems to be. But I must not disturb Egeria[10] and her pupil any longer.

MISS PRISM: Egeria? My name is Laetitia, Doctor.

CHASUBLE: (*bowing*) A classical allusion merely, drawn from the Pagan authors. I shall see you both no doubt at Evensong?

MISS PRISM: I think, dear Doctor, I will have a stroll with you. I find I have a headache after all, and a walk might do it good.

CHASUBLE: With pleasure, Miss Prism, with pleasure. We might go as far as the schools and back.

MISS PRISM: That would be delightful. Cecily, you will read your Political Economy in my absence. The chapter on the Fall of the Rupee[11] you may omit. It is somewhat too sensational. Even these metallic problems have their melodramatic side.

(*Goes down the garden with Dr Chasuble*)

CECILY: (*picks up books and throws them back on table*) Horrid Political Economy! Horrid Geography! Horrid, horrid German!

(*Enter Merriman with a card on a salver*)

MERRIMAN: Mr Ernest Worthing has just driven over from the station. He has brought his luggage with him.

CECILY: (*takes the card and reads it*) "Mr Ernest Worthing, B.4 The Albany, W." Uncle Jack's brother! Did you tell him Mr Worthing was in town?

MERRIMAN: Yes, Miss. He seemed very much disappointed. I mentioned that you and Miss Prism were in the garden. He said he was anxious to speak to you privately for a moment.

CECILY: Ask Mr Ernest Worthing to come here. I suppose you had better talk to the housekeeper about a room for him.

MERRIMAN: Yes, Miss.

(*Merriman goes off*)

CECILY: I have never met any really wicked person before. I feel rather frightened. I am so afraid he will look just like everyone else.

(*Enter Algernon, very gay and debonair*)

He does!

ALGERNON: (*raising his hat*) You are my little cousin Cecily, I'm sure.

CECILY: You are under some strange mistake. I am not little. In fact, I believe I am more than usually tall for my age. (*Algernon is rather taken aback*) But I am your cousin Cecily. You, I see from your card, are Uncle Jack's brother, my cousin Ernest, my wicked cousin Ernest.

ALGERNON: Oh! I am not really wicked at all, cousin Cecily. You mustn't think that I am wicked.

---

[10]**Egeria:** water nymph and goddess, legendary adviser to the Roman king Numa Pompilius (715–673 BCE).

[11]**Rupee:** Indian currency.

CECILY: If you are not, then you have certainly been deceiving us all in a very inexcusable manner. I hope you have not been leading a double life, pretending to be wicked and being really good all the time. That would be hypocrisy.

ALGERNON: (*looks at her in amazement*) Oh! Of course I have been rather reckless.

CECILY: I am glad to hear it.

ALGERNON: In fact, now you mention the subject, I have been very bad in my own small way.

CECILY: I don't think you should be so proud of that, though I am sure it must have been very pleasant.

ALGERNON: It is much pleasanter being here with you.

CECILY: I can't understand how you are here at all. Uncle Jack won't be back till Monday afternoon.

ALGERNON: That is a great disappointment. I am obliged to go up by the first train on Monday morning. I have a business appointment that I am anxious. . . . to miss!

CECILY: Couldn't you miss it anywhere but in London?

ALGERNON: No: the appointment is in London.

CECILY: Well, I know, of course, how important it is not to keep a business engagement, if one wants to retain any sense of the beauty of life, but still I think you had better wait till Uncle Jack arrives. I know he wants to speak to you about your emigrating.

ALGERNON: About my what?

CECILY: Your emigrating. He has gone up to buy your outfit.

ALGERNON: I certainly wouldn't let Jack buy my outfit. He has no taste in neckties at all.

CECILY: I don't think you will require neckties. Uncle Jack is sending you to Australia.

ALGERNON: Australia! I'd sooner die.

CECILY: Well, he said at dinner on Wednesday night, that you would have to choose between this world, the next world, and Australia.

ALGERNON: Oh, well! The accounts I have received of Australia and the next world are not particularly encouraging. This world is good enough for me, cousin Cecily.

CECILY: Yes, but are you good enough for it?

ALGERNON: I'm afraid I'm not that. That is why I want you to reform me. You might make that your mission, if you don't mind, cousin Cecily.

CECILY: I'm afraid I've no time, this afternoon.

ALGERNON: Well, would you mind my reforming myself this afternoon?

CECILY: It is rather Quixotic of you. But I think you should try.

ALGERNON: I will. I feel better already.

CECILY: You are looking a little worse.

ALGERNON: That is because I am hungry.

CECILY: How thoughtless of me. I should have remembered that when one is going to lead an entirely new life, one requires regular and wholesome meals. Won't you come in?

ALGERNON: Thank you. Might I have a buttonhole first? I have never any appetite unless I have a buttonhole first.

CECILY: A Maréchal Niel?[12] (*Picks up scissors*)

ALGERNON: No, I'd sooner have a pink rose.

CECILY: Why? (*Cuts a flower*)

ALGERNON: Because you are like a pink rose, cousin Cecily.

CECILY: I don't think it can be right for you to talk to me like that. Miss Prism never says such things to me.

ALGERNON: Then Miss Prism is a short-sighted old lady. (*Cecily puts the rose in his buttonhole*) You are the prettiest girl I ever saw.

CECILY: Miss Prism says that all good looks are a snare.

ALGERNON: They are a snare that every sensible man would like to be caught in.

CECILY: Oh! I don't think I would care to catch a sensible man. I shouldn't know what to talk to him about.

(*They pass into the house. Miss Prism and Dr Chasuble return*)

MISS PRISM: You are too much alone, dear Dr Chasuble. You should get married. A misanthrope I can understand—a womanthrope, never!

CHASUBLE: (*with a scholar's shudder*) Believe me, I do not deserve so neologistic a phrase. The precept as well as the practice of the Primitive Church was distinctly against matrimony.

MISS PRISM: (*sententiously*) That is obviously the reason why the Primitive Church has not lasted up to the present day. And you do not seem to realize, dear Doctor, that by persistently remaining single, a man converts himself into a permanent public temptation. Men should be more careful; this very celibacy leads weaker vessels astray.

CHASUBLE: But is a man not equally attractive when married?

MISS PRISM: No married man is ever attractive except to his wife.

CHASUBLE: And often, I've been told, not even to her.

MISS PRISM: That depends on the intellectual sympathies of the woman. Maturity can always be depended on.

---

[12]**Maréchal Niel:** a yellow rose.

Ripeness can be trusted. Young women are green. (*Dr Chasuble starts*) I spoke horticulturally. My metaphor was drawn from fruits. But where is Cecily?

CHASUBLE: Perhaps she followed us to the schools.

(*Enter Jack slowly from the back of the garden. He is dressed in the deepest mourning, with crape hatband and black gloves*)

MISS PRISM: Mr Worthing!

CHASUBLE: Mr Worthing?

MISS PRISM: This is indeed a surprise. We did not look for you till Monday afternoon.

JACK: (*shakes Miss Prism's hand in a tragic manner*) I have returned sooner than I expected. Dr Chasuble, I hope you are well?

CHASUBLE: Dear Mr Worthing, I trust this garb of woe does not betoken some terrible calamity?

JACK: My brother.

MISS PRISM: More shameful debts and extravagance?

CHASUBLE: Still leading his life of pleasure?

JACK: (*shaking his head*) Dead!

CHASUBLE: Your brother Ernest dead?

JACK: Quite dead.

MISS PRISM: What a lesson for him! I trust he will profit by it.

CHASUBLE: Mr Worthing, I offer you my sincere condolence. You have at least the consolation of knowing that you are always the most generous and forgiving of brothers.

JACK: Poor Ernest! He had many faults, but it is a sad, sad blow.

CHASUBLE: Very sad indeed. Were you with him at the end?

JACK: No. He died abroad; in Paris, in fact. I had a telegram last night from the manager of the Grand Hotel.

CHASUBLE: Was the cause of death mentioned?

JACK: A severe chill, it seems.

MISS PRISM: As a man sows, so shall he reap.

CHASUBLE: (*raising his hand*) Charity, dear Miss Prism, charity! None of us are perfect. I myself am peculiarly susceptible to draughts. Will the interment take place here?

JACK: No. He seems to have expressed a desire to be buried in Paris.

CHASUBLE: In Paris! (*Shakes his head*) I fear that hardly points to any very serious state of mind at the last. You would no doubt wish me to make some slight allusion to this tragic domestic affliction next Sunday. (*Jack presses his hand convulsively*) My sermon on the meaning of the manna[13] in the wilderness can be adapted to almost any occasion, joyful, or, as in the present case, distressing. (*All sigh*) I have preached it at harvest celebrations, christenings, confirmations, on days of humiliation and festal days. The last time I delivered it was in the Cathedral, as a charity sermon on behalf of the Society for the Prevention of Discontent among the Upper Orders. The Bishop, who was present, was much struck by some of the analogies I drew.

JACK: Ah! that reminds me, you mentioned christenings I think, Dr Chasuble? I suppose you know how to christen all right? (*Dr Chasuble looks astounded*) I mean, of course, you are continually christening, aren't you?

MISS PRISM: It is, I regret to say, one of the Rector's most constant duties in this parish. I have often spoken to the poorer classes on the subject. But they don't seem to know what thrift is.

CHASUBLE: But is there any particular infant in whom you are interested, Mr Worthing? Your brother was, I believe, unmarried, was he not?

JACK: Oh yes.

MISS PRISM: (*bitterly*) People who live entirely for pleasure usually are.

JACK: But it is not for any child, dear Doctor. I am very fond of children. No! the fact is, I would like to be christened myself, this afternoon, if you have nothing better to do.

CHASUBLE: But surely, Mr Worthing, you have been christened already?

JACK: I don't remember anything about it.

CHASUBLE: But have you any grave doubts on the subject?

JACK: I certainly intend to have. Of course I don't know if the thing would bother you in any way, or if you think I am a little too old now.

CHASUBLE: Not at all. The sprinkling, and, indeed, the immersion of adults is a perfectly canonical practice.

JACK: Immersion!

CHASUBLE: You need have no apprehensions. Sprinkling is all that is necessary, or indeed I think advisable. Our weather is so changeable. At what hour would you wish the ceremony performed?

JACK: Oh, I might trot round about five if that would suit you.

CHASUBLE: Perfectly, perfectly! In fact I have two similar ceremonies to perform at that time. A case of twins

---

[13]**manna**: food from heaven; see Exodus 16:14–15.

that occurred recently in one of the outlying cottages on your own estate. Poor Jenkins the carter, a most hard-working man.

JACK: Oh! I don't see much fun in being christened along with other babies. It would be childish. Would half-past five do?

CHASUBLE: Admirably! Admirably! (*Takes out watch*) And now, dear Mr Worthing, I will not intrude any longer into a house of sorrow. I would merely beg you not to be too much bowed down by grief. What seem to us bitter trials are often blessings in disguise.

MISS PRISM: This seems to me a blessing of an extremely obvious kind.

(*Enter Cecily from the house*)

CECILY: Uncle Jack! Oh, I am pleased to see you back. But what horrid clothes you have got on. Do go and change them.

MISS PRISM: Cecily!

CHASUBLE: My child! my child.

(*Cecily goes towards Jack; he kisses her brow in a melancholy manner*)

CECILY: What is the matter, Uncle Jack? Do look happy! You look as if you had toothache, and I have got such a surprise for you. Who do you think is in the dining-room? Your brother!

JACK: Who?

CECILY: Your brother Ernest. He arrived about half an hour ago.

JACK: What nonsense! I haven't got a brother.

CECILY: Oh, don't say that. However badly he may have behaved to you in the past he is still your brother. You couldn't be so heartless as to disown him. I'll tell him to come out. And you will shake hands with him, won't you, Uncle Jack?

(*Runs back into the house*)

CHASUBLE: These are very joyful tidings.

MISS PRISM: After we had all been resigned to his loss, his sudden return seems to me peculiarly distressing.

JACK: My brother is in the dining-room? I don't know what it all means. I think it is perfectly absurd.

(*Enter Algernon and Cecily hand in hand. They come slowly up to Jack*)

JACK: Good heavens! (*Motions Algernon away*)

ALGERNON: Brother John, I have come down from town to tell you that I am very sorry for all the trouble I

have given you, and that I intend to lead a better life in the future. (*Jack glares at him and does not take his hand*)

CECILY: Uncle Jack, you are not going to refuse your own brother's hand?

JACK: Nothing will induce me to take his hand. I think his coming down here disgraceful. He knows perfectly well why.

CECILY: Uncle Jack, do be nice. There is some good in everyone. Ernest has just been telling me about his poor invalid friend Mr Bunbury whom he goes to visit so often. And surely there must be much good in one who is kind to an invalid, and leaves the pleasures of London to sit by a bed of pain.

JACK: Oh! he has been talking about Bunbury, has he?

CECILY: Yes, he has told me all about poor Mr Bunbury, and his terrible state of health.

JACK: Bunbury! Well, I won't have him talk to you about Bunbury or about anything else. It is enough to drive one perfectly frantic.

ALGERNON: Of course I admit that the faults were all on my side. But I must say that I think that Brother John's coldness to me is peculiarly painful. I expected a more enthusiastic welcome, especially considering it is the first time I have come here.

CECILY: Uncle Jack, if you don't shake hands with Ernest I will never forgive you.

JACK: Never forgive me?

CECILY: Never, never, never!

JACK: Well, this is the last time I shall ever do it. (*Shakes hands with Algernon and glares*)

CHASUBLE: It's pleasant, is it not, to see so perfect a reconciliation? I think we might leave the two brothers together.

MISS PRISM: Cecily, you will come with us.

CECILY: Certainly, Miss Prism. My little task of reconciliation is over.

CHASUBLE: You have done a beautiful action today, dear child.

MISS PRISM: We must not be premature in our judgements.

CECILY: I feel very happy.

(*They all go off except Jack and Algernon*)

JACK: You young scoundrel, Algy, you must get out of this place as soon as possible. I don't allow any Bunburying here.

(*Enter Merriman*)

MERRIMAN: I have put Mr Ernest's things in the room next to yours, sir. I suppose that is all right?

JACK: What?

MERRIMAN: Mr Ernest's luggage, sir. I have unpacked it and put it in the room next to your own.

JACK: His luggage?

MERRIMAN: Yes, sir. Three portmanteaus, a dressing-case, two hat-boxes, and a large luncheon-basket.

ALGERNON: I am afraid I can't stay more than a week this time.

JACK: Merriman, order the dog-cart[14] at once. Mr Ernest has been suddenly called back to town.

MERRIMAN: Yes, sir.

(Goes back into the house)

ALGERNON: What a fearful liar you are, Jack. I have not been called back to town at all.

JACK: Yes, you have.

ALGERNON: I haven't heard anyone call me.

JACK: Your duty as a gentleman calls you back.

ALGERNON: My duty as a gentleman has never interfered with my pleasures in the smallest degree.

JACK: I can quite understand that.

ALGERNON: Well, Cecily is a darling.

JACK: You are not to talk of Miss Cardew like that. I don't like it.

ALGERNON: Well, I don't like your clothes. You look perfectly ridiculous in them. Why on earth don't you go up and change? It is perfectly childish to be in deep mourning for a man who is actually staying for a whole week with you in your house as a guest. I call it grotesque.

JACK: You are certainly not staying with me for a whole week as a guest or anything else. You have got to leave . . . by the four-five train.

ALGERNON: I certainly won't leave you so long as you are in mourning. It would be most unfriendly. If I were in mourning you would stay with me, I suppose. I should think it very unkind if you didn't.

JACK: Well, will you go if I change my clothes?

ALGERNON: Yes, if you are not too long. I never saw anybody take so long to dress, and with such little result.

JACK: Well, at any rate, that is better than being always over-dressed as you are.

ALGERNON: If I am occasionally a little over-dressed, I make up for it by being always immensely over-educated.

---

[14]**dog-cart**: two-wheeled vehicle drawn by horses.

JACK: Your vanity is ridiculous, your conduct an outrage, and your presence in my garden utterly absurd. However, you have got to catch the four-five, and I hope you will have a pleasant journey back to town. This Bunburying, as you call it, has not been a great success for you.

(Goes into the house)

ALGERNON: I think it has been a great success. I'm in love with Cecily, and that is everything.

(Enter Cecily at the back of the garden. She picks up the can and begins to water the flowers)

But I must see her before I go, and make arrangements for another Bunbury. Ah, there she is.

CECILY: Oh, I merely came back to water the roses. I thought you were with Uncle Jack.

ALGERNON: He's gone to order the dog-cart for me.

CECILY: Oh, is he going to take you for a nice drive?

ALGERNON: He's going to send me away.

CECILY: Then have we got to part?

ALGERNON: I am afraid so. It's a very painful parting.

CECILY: It is always painful to part from people whom one has known for a very brief space of time. The absence of old friends one can endure with equanimity. But even a momentary separation from anyone to whom one has just been introduced is almost unbearable.

ALGERNON: Thank you.

(Enter Merriman)

MERRIMAN: The dog-cart is at the door, sir.

(Algernon looks appealingly at Cecily)

CECILY: It can wait, Merriman . . . for . . . five minutes.

MERRIMAN: Yes, miss.

(Exit Merriman)

ALGERNON: I hope, Cecily, I shall not offend you if I state quite frankly and openly that you seem to me to be in every way the visible personification of absolute perfection.

CECILY: I think your frankness does you great credit, Ernest. If you will allow me, I will copy your remarks into my diary. *(Goes over to table and begins writing in diary)*

ALGERNON: Do you really keep a diary? I'd give anything to look at it. May I?

CECILY: Oh no. *(Puts her hand over it)* You see, it is simply a very young girl's record of her own thoughts and impressions, and consequently meant for publication. When it appears in volume form I hope you will order a copy. But pray, Ernest, don't stop. I delight in taking down from dictation. I have reached "absolute perfection." You can go on. I am quite ready for more.

ALGERNON: (*somewhat taken aback*) Ahem! Ahem!

CECILY: Oh, don't cough, Ernest. When one is dictating one should speak fluently and not cough. Besides, I don't know how to spell a cough. (*Writes as Algernon speaks*)

ALGERNON: (*speaking very rapidly*) Cecily, ever since I first looked upon your wonderful and incomparable beauty, I have dared to love you wildly, passionately, devotedly, hopelessly.

CECILY: I don't think that you should tell me that you love me wildly, passionately, devotedly, hopelessly. Hopelessly doesn't seem to make much sense, does it?

ALGERNON: Cecily!

(*Enter Merriman*)

MERRIMAN: The dog-cart is waiting, sir.

ALGERNON: Tell it to come round next week, at the same hour.

MERRIMAN: (*looks at Cecily, who makes no sign*) Yes, sir.

(*Merriman retires*)

CECILY: Uncle Jack would be very much annoyed if he knew you were staying on till next week, at the same hour.

ALGERNON: Oh, I don't care about Jack. I don't care for anybody in the whole world but you. I love you, Cecily. You will marry me, won't you?

CECILY: You silly boy! Of course. Why, we have been engaged for the last three months.

ALGERNON: For the last three months?

CECILY: Yes, it will be exactly three months on Thursday.

ALGERNON: But how did we become engaged?

CECILY: Well, ever since dear Uncle Jack first confessed to us that he had a younger brother who was very wicked and bad, you of course have formed the chief topic of conversation between myself and Miss Prism. And of course a man who is much talked about is always very attractive. One feels there must be something in him after all. I daresay it was foolish of me, but I fell in love with you, Ernest.

ALGERNON: Darling! And when was the engagement actually settled?

CECILY: On the 14th of February last. Worn out by your entire ignorance of my existence, I determined to end the matter one way or the other, and after a long struggle with myself I accepted you under this dear old tree here. The next day I bought this little ring in your name, and this is the little bangle with the true lovers' knot I promised you always to wear.

ALGERNON: Did I give you this? It's very pretty, isn't it?

CECILY: Yes, you've wonderfully good taste, Ernest. It's the excuse I've always given for your leading such a bad life. And this is the box in which I keep all your dear letters. (*Kneels at table, opens box, and produces letters tied up with blue ribbon*)

ALGERNON: My letters! But my own sweet Cecily, I have never written you any letters.

CECILY: You need hardly remind me of that, Ernest. I remember only too well that I was forced to write your letters for you. I wrote always three times a week, and sometimes oftener.

ALGERNON: Oh, do let me read them, Cecily!

CECILY: Oh, I couldn't possibly. They would make you far too conceited. (*Replaces box*) The three you wrote me after I had broken off the engagement are so beautiful, and so badly spelled, that even now I can hardly read them without crying a little.

ALGERNON: But was our engagement ever broken off?

CECILY: Of course it was. On the 22nd of last March. You can see the entry if you like. (*Shows diary*) "Today I broke off my engagement with Ernest. I feel it is better to do so. The weather still continues charming."

ALGERNON: But why on earth did you break it off? What had I done? I had done nothing at all. Cecily, I am very much hurt indeed to hear you broke it off. Particularly when the weather was so charming.

CECILY: It would hardly have been a really serious engagement if it hadn't been broken off at least once. But I forgave you before the week was out.

ALGERNON: (*crossing to her, and kneeling*) What a perfect angel you are, Cecily.

CECILY: You dear romantic boy. (*He kisses her, she puts her fingers through his hair*) I hope your hair curls naturally, does it?

ALGERNON: Yes, darling, with a little help from others.

CECILY: I am so glad.

ALGERNON: You'll never break off our engagement again, Cecily?

CECILY: I don't think I could break it off now that I have actually met you. Besides, of course, there is the question of your name.

ALGERNON: (*nervously*)—Yes, of course.

CECILY: You must not laugh at me, darling, but it had always been a girlish dream of mine to love someone whose name was Ernest. (*Algernon rises, Cecily also*) There is something in that name that seems to inspire absolute confidence. I pity any poor married woman whose husband is not called Ernest.

ALGERNON: But, my dear child, do you mean to say you could not love me if I had some other name?

CECILY: But what name?

ALGERNON: Oh, any name you like—Algernon—for instance . . .

CECILY: But I don't like the name of Algernon.

ALGERNON: Well, my own dear, sweet, loving little darling, I really can't see why you should object to the name of Algernon. It is not at all a bad name. In fact, it is rather an aristocratic name. Half of the chaps who get into the Bankruptcy Court are called Algernon. But seriously, Cecily . . . (*moving to her*) if my name was Algy, couldn't you love me?

CECILY: (*rising*) I might respect you, Ernest, I might admire your character, but I fear that I should not be able to give you my undivided attention.

ALGERNON: Ahem! Cecily! (*Picking up hat*) Your Rector here is, I suppose, thoroughly experienced in the practice of all the rites and ceremonials of the Church?

CECILY: Oh, yes. Dr Chasuble is a most learned man. He has never written a single book, so you can imagine how much he knows.

ALGERNON: I must see him at once on a most important christening—I mean on most important business.

CECILY: Oh!

ALGERNON: I shan't be away more than half an hour.

CECILY: Considering that we have been engaged since February the 14th, and that I only met you today for the first time, I think it is rather hard that you should leave me for so long a period as half an hour. Couldn't you make it twenty minutes?

ALGERNON: I'll be back in no time.

(*Kisses her and rushes down the garden*)

CECILY: What an impetuous boy he is! I like his hair so much. I must enter his proposal in my diary.

(*Enter Merriman*)

MERRIMAN: A Miss Fairfax has just called to see Mr Worthing. On very important business, Miss Fairfax states.

CECILY: Isn't Mr Worthing in his library?

MERRIMAN: Mr Worthing went over in the direction of the Rectory some time ago.

CECILY: Pray ask the lady to come out here; Mr Worthing is sure to be back soon. And you can bring tea.

MERRIMAN: Yes, Miss.

(*Goes out*)

CECILY: Miss Fairfax! I suppose one of the many good elderly women who are associated with Uncle Jack in some of his philanthropic work in London. I don't quite like women who are interested in philanthropic work. I think it is so forward of them.

(*Enter Merriman*)

MERRIMAN: Miss Fairfax.

(*Enter Gwendolen. Exit Merriman*)

CECILY: (*advancing to meet her*) Pray let me introduce myself to you. My name is Cecily Cardew.

GWENDOLEN: Cecily Cardew? (*Moving to her and shaking hands*) What a very sweet name! Something tells me that we are going to be great friends. I like you already more than I can say. My first impressions of people are never wrong.

CECILY: How nice of you to like me so much after we have known each other such a comparatively short time. Pray sit down.

GWENDOLEN: (*still standing up*) I may call you Cecily, may I not?

CECILY: With pleasure!

GWENDOLEN: And you will always call me Gwendolen, won't you?

CECILY: If you wish.

GWENDOLEN: Then that is all quite settled, is it not?

CECILY: I hope so.

(*A pause. They both sit down together*)

GWENDOLEN: Perhaps this might be a favourable opportunity for my mentioning who I am. My father is Lord Bracknell. You have never heard of papa, I suppose?

CECILY: I don't think so.

GWENDOLEN: Outside the family circle, papa, I am glad to say, is entirely unknown. I think that is quite as it should be. The home seems to me to be the proper sphere for the man. And certainly once a man begins to neglect his domestic duties he becomes painfully effeminate, does he not? And I don't like that. It makes men so very attractive. Cecily, mamma, whose views on education are remarkably strict, has brought me up to be extremely short-sighted; it is part of her system; so do you mind my looking at you through my glasses?

CECILY: Oh! not at all, Gwendolen. I am very fond of being looked at.

GWENDOLEN: (*after examining Cecily carefully through a lorgnette*) You are here on a short visit I suppose.

CECILY: Oh no! I live here.

GWENDOLEN: (*severely*) Really? Your mother, no doubt, or some female relative of advanced years, resides here also?

CECILY: Oh no! I have no mother, nor, in fact, any relations.

GWENDOLEN: Indeed?

CECILY: My dear guardian, with the assistance of Miss Prism, has the arduous task of looking after me.

GWENDOLEN: Your guardian?

CECILY: Yes, I am Mr Worthing's ward.

GWENDOLEN: Oh! It is strange he never mentioned to me that he had a ward. How secretive of him! He grows more interesting hourly. I am not sure, however, that the news inspires me with feelings of unmixed delight. (*Rising and going to her*) I am very fond of you, Cecily; I have liked you ever since I met you! But I am bound to state that now that I know that you are Mr Worthing's ward, I cannot help expressing a wish you were—well just a little older than you seem to be—and not quite so very alluring in appearance. In fact, if I may speak candidly—

CECILY: Pray do! I think that whenever one has anything unpleasant to say, one should always be quite candid.

GWENDOLEN: Well, to speak with perfect candour, Cecily, I wish that you were fully forty-two, and more than usually plain for your age. Ernest has a strong upright nature. He is the very soul of truth and honour. Disloyalty would be as impossible to him as deception. But even men of the noblest possible moral character are extremely susceptible to the influence of the physical charms of others. Modern, no less than Ancient History, supplies us with many most painful examples of what I refer to. If it were not so, indeed, History would be quite unreadable.

CECILY: I beg your pardon, Gwendolen, did you say Ernest?

GWENDOLEN: Yes.

CECILY: Oh, but it is not Mr Ernest Worthing who is my guardian. It is his brother—his elder brother.

GWENDOLEN: (*sitting down again*) Ernest never mentioned to me that he had a brother.

CECILY: I am sorry to say they have not been on good terms for a long time.

GWENDOLEN: Ah! that accounts for it. And now that I think of it I have never heard any man mention his brother. The subject seems distasteful to most men. Cecily, you have lifted a load from my mind. I was growing almost anxious. It would have been terrible if any cloud had come across a friendship like ours, would it not? Of course you are quite, quite sure that it is not Mr Ernest Worthing who is your guardian?

CECILY: Quite sure. (*A pause*) In fact, I am going to be his.

GWENDOLEN: (*enquiringly*) I beg your pardon?

CECILY: (*rather shy and confidingly*) Dearest Gwendolen, there is no reason why I should make a secret of it to you. Our little county newspaper is sure to chronicle the fact next week. Mr Ernest Worthing and I are engaged to be married.

GWENDOLEN: (*quite politely, rising*) My darling Cecily, I think there must be some slight error. Mr Ernest Worthing is engaged to me. The announcement will appear in the *Morning Post* on Saturday at the latest.

CECILY: (*very politely, rising*) I am afraid you must be under some misconception. Ernest proposed to me exactly ten minutes ago.

(*Shows diary*)

GWENDOLEN: (*examines diary through her lorgnette carefully*) It is very curious, for he asked me to be his wife yesterday afternoon at 5.30. If you would care to verify the incident, pray do so. (*Produces diary of her own*) I never travel without my diary. One should always have something sensational to read in the train. I am so sorry, dear Cecily, if it is any disappointment to you, but I am afraid I have the prior claim.

CECILY: It would distress me more than I can tell you, dear Gwendolen, if it caused you any mental or physical anguish, but I feel bound to point out that since Ernest proposed to you he clearly has changed his mind.

GWENDOLEN: (*meditatively*) If the poor fellow has been entrapped into any foolish promise I shall consider it my duty to rescue him at once, and with a firm hand.

CECILY: (*thoughtfully and sadly*) Whatever unfortunate entanglement my dear boy may have got into, I will never reproach him with it after we are married.

GWENDOLEN: Do you allude to me, Miss Cardew, as an entanglement? You are presumptuous. On an occasion of this kind it becomes more than a moral duty to speak one's mind. It becomes a pleasure.

CECILY: Do you suggest, Miss Fairfax, that I entrapped Ernest into an engagement? How dare you? This is no time for wearing the shallow mask of manners. When I see a spade I call it a spade.

GWENDOLEN: (satirically) I am glad to say that I have never seen a spade. It is obvious that our social spheres have been widely different.

(Enter Merriman, followed by the footman. He carries a salver, table cloth, and plate stand. Cecily is about to retort. The presence of the servants exercises a restraining influence, under which both girls chafe)

MERRIMAN: Shall I lay tea here as usual, Miss?

CECILY: (sternly, in a calm voice) Yes, as usual.

(Merriman begins to clear table and lay cloth. A long pause. Cecily and Gwendolen glare at each other.)

GWENDOLEN: Are there many interesting walks in the vicinity, Miss Cardew?

CECILY: Oh! yes! a great many. From the top of one of the hills quite close one can see five counties.

GWENDOLEN: Five counties! I don't think I should like that; I hate crowds.

CECILY: (sweetly) I suppose that is why you live in town?

(Gwendolen bites her lip, and beats her foot nervously with her parasol)

GWENDOLEN: (looking around) Quite a well-kept garden this is, Miss Cardew.

CECILY: So glad you like it, Miss Fairfax.

GWENDOLEN: I had no idea there were any flowers in the country.

CECILY: Oh, flowers are as common here, Miss Fairfax, as people are in London.

GWENDOLEN: Personally I cannot understand how anybody manages to exist in the country, if anybody who is anybody does. The country always bores me to death.

CECILY: Ah! This is what the newspapers call agricultural depression, is it not? I believe the aristocracy are suffering very much from it just at present. It is almost an epidemic amongst them, I have been told. May I offer you some tea, Miss Fairfax?

GWENDOLEN: (with elaborate politeness) Thank you. (Aside) Detestable girl! But I require tea!

CECILY: (sweetly) Sugar?

GWENDOLEN: (superciliously) No, thank you. Sugar is not fashionable any more. (Cecily looks angrily at her, takes up the tongs and puts four lumps of sugar into the cup)

CECILY: (severely) Cake or bread and butter?

GWENDOLEN: (in a bored manner) Bread and butter, please. Cake is rarely seen at the best houses nowadays.

CECILY: (cuts a very large slice of cake and puts it on the tray) Hand that to Miss Fairfax.

(Merriman does so, and goes out with footman. Gwendolen drinks the tea and makes a grimace. Puts down cup at once, reaches out her hand to the bread and butter, looks at it, and finds it is cake. Rises in indignation)

GWENDOLEN: You have filled my tea with lumps of sugar, and though I asked most distinctly for bread and butter, you have given me cake. I am known for the gentleness of my disposition, and the extraordinary sweetness of my nature, but I warn you, Miss Cardew, you may go too far.

CECILY: (rising) To save my poor, innocent, trusting boy from the machinations of any other girl there are no lengths to which I would not go.

GWENDOLEN: From the moment I saw you I distrusted you. I felt that you were false and deceitful. I am never deceived in such matters. My first impressions of people are invariably right.

CECILY: It seems to me, Miss Fairfax, that I am trespassing on your valuable time. No doubt you have many other calls of a similar character to make in the neighbourhood.

(Enter Jack)

GWENDOLEN: (catching sight of him) Ernest! My own Ernest!

JACK: Gwendolen! Darling! (Offers to kiss her)

GWENDOLEN: (drawing back) A moment! May I ask if you are engaged to be married to this young lady? (Points to Cecily)

JACK: (laughing) To dear little Cecily! Of course not! What could have put such an idea into your pretty little head?

GWENDOLEN: Thank you. You may! (Offers her cheek)

CECILY: (very sweetly) I knew there must be some misunderstanding, Miss Fairfax. The gentleman whose arm is at present round your waist is my dear guardian, Mr John Worthing.

GWENDOLEN: I beg your pardon?

CECILY: This is Uncle Jack.

GWENDOLEN: (receding) Jack! Oh!

(Enter Algernon)

CECILY: Here is Ernest.

ALGERNON: (goes straight over to Cecily without noticing anyone else) My own love! (Offers to kiss her)

CECILY: (*drawing back*) A moment, Ernest! May I ask you—are you engaged to be married to this young lady?

ALGERNON: (*looking round*) To what young lady? Good heavens! Gwendolen!

CECILY: Yes! to good heavens, Gwendolen, I mean to Gwendolen.

ALGERNON: (*laughing*) Of course not! What could have put such an idea into your pretty little head?

CECILY: Thank you. (*Presenting her cheek to be kissed*) You may. (*Algernon kisses her*)

GWENDOLEN: I felt there was some slight error, Miss Cardew. The gentleman who is now embracing you is my cousin, Mr Algernon Moncrieff.

CECILY: (*breaking away from Algernon*) Algernon Moncrieff! Oh!

(*The two girls move towards each other and put their arms round each other's waists as if for protection*)

CECILY: Are you called Algernon?

ALGERNON: I cannot deny it.

CECILY: Oh!

GWENDOLEN: Is your name really John?

JACK: (*standing rather proudly*) I could deny it if I liked. I could deny anything if I liked. But my name certainly is John. It has been John for years.

CECILY: (*to Gwendolen*) A gross deception has been practised on both of us.

GWENDOLEN: My poor wounded Cecily!

CECILY: My sweet wronged Gwendolen!

GWENDOLEN: (*slowly and seriously*) You will call me sister, will you not?

(*They embrace. Jack and Algernon groan and walk up and down*)

CECILY: (*rather brightly*) There is just one question I would like to be allowed to ask my guardian.

GWENDOLEN: An admirable idea! Mr Worthing, there is just one question I would like to be permitted to put to you. Where is your brother Ernest? We are both engaged to be married to your brother Ernest, so it is a matter of some importance to us to know where your brother Ernest is at present.

JACK: (*slowly and hesitatingly*) Gwendolen—Cecily—it is very painful for me to be forced to speak the truth. It is the first time in my life that I have ever been reduced to such a painful position, and I am really quite inexperienced in doing anything of the kind. However, I will tell you quite frankly that I have no brother Ernest. I have no brother at all. I never had a brother in my life, and I certainly have not the smallest intention of ever having one in the future.

CECILY: (*surprised*) No brother at all?

JACK: (*cheerily*) None!

GWENDOLEN: (*severely*) Had you never a brother of any kind?

JACK: (*pleasantly*) Never. Not even of any kind.

GWENDOLEN: I am afraid it is quite clear, Cecily, that neither of us is engaged to be married to anyone.

CECILY: It is not a very pleasant position for a young girl suddenly to find herself in. Is it?

GWENDOLEN: Let us go into the house. They will hardly venture to come after us there.

CECILY: No, men are so cowardly, aren't they?

(*They retire into the house with scornful looks*)

JACK: This ghastly state of things is what you call Bunburying, I suppose?

ALGERNON: Yes, and a perfectly wonderful Bunbury it is. The most wonderful Bunbury I have ever had in my life.

JACK: Well, you've no right whatsoever to Bunbury here.

ALGERNON: That is absurd. One has a right to Bunbury anywhere one chooses. Every serious Bunburyist knows that.

JACK: Serious Bunburyist! Good heavens!

ALGERNON: Well, one must be serious about something, if one wants to have any amusement in life. I happen to be serious about Bunburying. What on earth you are serious about I haven't got the remotest idea. About everything, I should fancy. You have such an absolutely trivial nature.

JACK: Well, the only small satisfaction I have in the whole of this wretched business is that your friend Bunbury is quite exploded. You won't be able to run down to the country quite so often as you used to do, dear Algy. And a very good thing too.

ALGERNON: Your brother is a little off colour, isn't he, dear Jack? You won't be able to disappear to London quite so frequently as your wicked custom was. And not a bad thing either.

JACK: As for your conduct towards Miss Cardew, I must say that your taking in a sweet, simple, innocent girl like that is quite inexcusable. To say nothing of the fact that she is my ward.

ALGERNON: I can see no possible defence at all for your deceiving a brilliant, clever, thoroughly experienced young lady like Miss Fairfax. To say nothing of the fact that she is my cousin.

JACK: I wanted to be engaged to Gwendolen, that is all. I love her.

ALGERNON: Well, I simply wanted to be engaged to Cecily. I adore her.

JACK: There is certainly no chance of your marrying Miss Cardew.

ALGERNON: I don't think there is much likelihood, Jack, of you and Miss Fairfax being united.

JACK: Well, that is no business of yours.

ALGERNON: If it was my business, I wouldn't talk about it. (*Begins to eat muffins*) It is very vulgar to talk about one's business. Only people like stockbrokers do that, and then merely at dinner parties.

JACK: How you can sit there, calmly eating muffins when we are in this horrible trouble, I can't make out. You seem to me to be perfectly heartless.

ALGERNON: Well, I can't eat muffins in an agitated manner. The butter would probably get on my cuffs. One should always eat muffins quite calmly. It is the only way to eat them.

JACK: I say it's perfectly heartless your eating muffins at all, under the circumstances.

ALGERNON: When I am in trouble, eating is the only thing that consoles me. Indeed, when I am in really great trouble, as anyone who knows me intimately will tell you, I refuse everything except food and drink. At the present moment I am eating muffins because I am unhappy. Besides, I am particularly fond of muffins. (*Rising*)

JACK: (*rising*) Well, there is no reason why you should eat them all in that greedy way. (*Takes muffins from Algernon*)

ALGERNON: (*offering tea-cake*) I wish you would have tea-cake instead. I don't like tea-cake.

JACK: Good heavens! I suppose a man may eat his own muffins in his own garden.

ALGERNON: But you have just said it was perfectly heartless to eat muffins.

JACK: I said it was perfectly heartless of you, under the circumstances. That is a very different thing.

ALGERNON: That may be. But the muffins are the same. (*He seizes the muffin-dish from Jack*)

JACK: Algy, I wish to goodness you would go.

ALGERNON: You can't possibly ask me to go without having some dinner. It's absurd. I never go without my dinner. No one ever does, except vegetarians and people like that. Besides I have just made arrangements with Dr Chasuble to be christened at a quarter to six under the name of Ernest.

JACK: My dear fellow, the sooner you give up that nonsense the better. I made arrangements this morning with Dr Chasuble to be christened myself at 5.30, and I naturally will take the name of Ernest. Gwendolen would wish it. We cannot both be christened Ernest. It's absurd. Besides, I have a perfect right to be christened if I like. There is no evidence at all that I have ever been christened by anybody. I should think it extremely probable I never was, and so does Dr Chasuble. It is entirely different in your case. You have been christened already.

ALGERNON: Yes, but I have not been christened for years.

JACK: Yes, but you have been christened. That is the important thing.

ALGERNON: Quite so. So I know my constitution can stand it. If you are not quite sure about your ever having been christened, I must say I think it rather dangerous your venturing on it now. It might make you very unwell. You can hardly have forgotten that someone very closely connected with you was very nearly carried off this week in Paris by a severe chill.

JACK: Yes, but you said yourself that a severe chill was not hereditary.

ALGERNON: It usen't to be, I know—but I daresay it is now. Science is always making wonderful improvements in things.

JACK: (*picking up the muffin-dish*) Oh, that is nonsense; you are always talking nonsense.

ALGERNON: Jack, you are at the muffins again! I wish you wouldn't. There are only two left. (*Takes them*) I told you I was particularly fond of muffins.

JACK: But I hate tea-cake.

ALGERNON: Why on earth then do you allow tea-cake to be served up for your guests? What ideas you have of hospitality!

JACK: Algernon! I have already told you to go. I don't want you here. Why don't you go!

ALGERNON: I haven't quite finished my tea yet! and there is still one muffin left.

(*Jack groans, and sinks into a chair. Algernon still continues eating*)

ACT DROP

— THIRD ACT —

(*Scene: Morning-room at the Manor House. Gwendolen and Cecily are at the window, looking out into the garden*)

GWENDOLEN: The fact that they did not follow us at once into the house, as anyone else would have done, seems to me to show that they have some sense of shame left.

CECILY: They have been eating muffins. That looks like repentance.

(*A pause*)

GWENDOLEN: They don't seem to notice us at all. Couldn't you cough?

CECILY: But I haven't got a cough.

GWENDOLEN: They're looking at us. What effrontery!

CECILY: They're approaching. That's very forward of them.

GWENDOLEN: Let us preserve a dignified silence.

CECILY: Certainly. It's the only thing to do now.

(*Enter Jack followed by Algernon. They whistle some dreadful popular air from a British Opera*)

GWENDOLEN: This dignified silence seems to produce an unpleasant effect.

CECILY: A most distasteful one.

GWENDOLEN: But we will not be the first to speak.

CECILY: Certainly not.

GWENDOLEN: Mr Worthing, I have something very particular to ask you. Much depends on your reply.

CECILY: Gwendolen, your common sense is invaluable. Mr Moncrieff, kindly answer me the following question. Why did you pretend to be my guardian's brother?

ALGERNON: In order that I might have an opportunity of meeting you.

CECILY: (*to Gwendolen*) That certainly seems a satisfactory explanation, does it not?

GWENDOLEN: Yes, dear, if you can believe him.

CECILY: I don't. But that does not affect the wonderful beauty of his answer.

GWENDOLEN: True. In matters of grave importance, style, not sincerity, is the vital thing. Mr Worthing, what explanation can you offer to me for pretending to have a brother? Was it in order that you might have an opportunity of coming up to town to see me as often as possible?

JACK: Can you doubt it, Miss Fairfax?

GWENDOLEN: I have the gravest doubts upon the subject. But I intend to crush them. This is not the moment for German scepticism. (*Moving to Cecily*) Their explanations appear to be quite satisfactory, especially Mr Worthing's. That seems to me to have the stamp of truth upon it.

CECILY: I am more than content with what Mr Moncrieff said. His voice alone inspires one with absolute credulity.

GWENDOLEN: Then you think we should forgive them?

CECILY: Yes. I mean no.

GWENDOLEN: True! I had forgotten. There are principles at stake that one cannot surrender. Which of us should tell them? The task is not a pleasant one.

CECILY: Could we not both speak at the same time?

GWENDOLEN: An excellent idea! I nearly always speak at the same time as other people. Will you take the time from me?

CECILY: Certainly. (*Gwendolen beats time with uplifted finger*)

GWENDOLEN AND CECILY: (*speaking together*) Your Christian names are still an insuperable barrier. That is all!

JACK AND ALGERNON: (*speaking together*) Our Christian names! Is that all? But we are going to be christened this afternoon.

GWENDOLEN: (*to Jack*) For my sake you are prepared to do this terrible thing?

JACK: I am.

CECILY: (*to Algernon*) To please me you are ready to face this fearful ordeal?

ALGERNON: I am!

GWENDOLEN: How absurd to talk of the equality of the sexes! Where questions of self-sacrifice are concerned, men are infinitely beyond us.

JACK: We are! (*Clasps hands with Algernon*)

CECILY: They have moments of physical courage of which we women know absolutely nothing.

GWENDOLEN: (*to Jack*) Darling!

ALGERNON: (*to Cecily*) Darling! (*They fall into each other's arms*)

(*Enter Merriman. When he enters he coughs loudly, seeing the situation*)

MERRIMAN: Ahem! Ahem! Lady Bracknell.

JACK: Good heavens!

(*Enter Lady Bracknell. The couples separate, in alarm. Exit Merriman*)

LADY BRACKNELL: Gwendolen! What does this mean?

GWENDOLEN: Merely that I am engaged to be married to Mr Worthing, mamma.

LADY BRACKNELL: Come here. Sit down. Sit down immediately. Hesitation of any kind is a sign of mental decay in the young, of physical weakness in the old. (*Turns to Jack*) Apprised, sir, of my daughter's sudden flight by her trusty maid, whose confidence I purchased by means of a small coin, I followed her at once by a luggage train. Her unhappy father is, I am glad to say, under the impression that she is attending a more than usually lengthy lecture by the University Extension Scheme on the Influence of a permanent income on Thought. I do not propose to undeceive him. Indeed I have never undeceived him on any question. I would consider it wrong. But of course, you will clearly understand that all communication between yourself and my daughter must cease immediately from this moment. On this point, as indeed on all points, I am firm.

JACK: I am engaged to be married to Gwendolen, Lady Bracknell!

LADY BRACKNELL: You are nothing of the kind, sir. And now as regards Algernon! . . . Algernon!

ALGERNON: Yes, Aunt Augusta.

LADY BRACKNELL: May I ask if it is in this house that your invalid friend Mr Bunbury resides?

ALGERNON: (*stammering*) Oh! No! Bunbury doesn't live here. Bunbury is somewhere else at present. In fact, Bunbury is dead.

LADY BRACKNELL: Dead! When did Mr Bunbury die? His death must have been extremely sudden.

ALGERNON: (*airily*) Oh! I killed Bunbury this afternoon. I mean poor Bunbury died this afternoon.

LADY BRACKNELL: What did he die of?

ALGERNON: Bunbury? Oh, he was quite exploded.

LADY BRACKNELL: Exploded! Was he the victim of a revolutionary outrage? I was not aware that Mr Bunbury was interested in social legislation. If so, he is well punished for his morbidity.

ALGERNON: My dear Aunt Augusta, I mean he was found out! The doctors found out that Bunbury could not live, that is what I mean—so Bunbury died.

LADY BRACKNELL: He seems to have had great confidence in the opinion of his physicians. I am glad, however, that he made up his mind at the last to some definite course of action, and acted under proper medical advice. And now that we have finally got rid of this Mr Bunbury, may I ask, Mr Worthing, who is that young person whose hand my nephew Algernon is now holding in what seems to me a peculiarly unnecessary manner?

JACK: That lady is Miss Cecily Cardew, my ward. (*Lady Bracknell bows coldly to Cecily*)

ALGERNON: I am engaged to be married to Cecily, Aunt Augusta.

LADY BRACKNELL: I beg your pardon?

CECILY: Mr Moncrieff and I are engaged to be married, Lady Bracknell.

LADY BRACKNELL: (*with a shiver, crossing to the sofa and sitting down*) I do not know whether there is anything peculiarly exciting in the air of this particular part of Hertfordshire, but the number of engagements that go on seems to me considerably above the proper average that statistics have laid down for our guidance. I think some preliminary enquiry on my part would not be out of place. Mr Worthing, is Miss Cardew at all connected with any of the larger railway stations in London? I merely desire information. Until yesterday I had no idea that there were any families or persons whose origin was a Terminus. (*Jack looks perfectly furious, but restrains himself*)

JACK: (*in a clear, cold voice*) Miss Cardew is the granddaughter of the late Mr Thomas Cardew of 149 Belgrave Square, S.W.; Gervase Park, Dorking, Surrey; and the Sporran, Fifeshire, N.B.[15]

LADY BRACKNELL: That sounds not unsatisfactory. Three addresses always inspire confidence, even in tradesmen. But what proof have I of their authenticity?

JACK: I have carefully preserved the Court Guides of the period. They are open to your inspection, Lady Bracknell.

LADY BRACKNELL: (*grimly*) I have known strange errors in that publication.

JACK: Miss Cardew's family solicitors are Messrs Markby, Markby, and Markby.

LADY BRACKNELL: Markby, Markby, and Markby? A firm of the very highest position in their profession. Indeed I am told that one of the Mr Markbys is occasionally to be seen at dinner parties. So far I am satisfied.

JACK: (*very irritably*) How extremely kind of you, Lady Bracknell! I have also in my possession, you will be pleased to hear, certificates of Miss Cardew's birth, baptism, whooping cough, registration, vaccination, confirmation, and the measles; both the German and the English variety.

LADY BRACKNELL: Ah! A life crowded with incident, I see; though perhaps somewhat too exciting for a young girl. I am not myself in favour of premature experiences. (*Rises, looks at her watch*) Gwendolen! the time approaches for our departure. We have not a moment to lose. As a matter of form, Mr Worthing, I had better ask you if Miss Cardew has any little fortune?

JACK: Oh! about a hundred and thirty thousand pounds in the Funds.[16] That is all. Good-bye, Lady Bracknell. So pleased to have seen you.

---

[15]**Surrey**: county just SW of London. **N.B.**: N Britain (Scotland).

[16]**in the Funds**: invested in national stocks.

LADY BRACKNELL: (*sitting down again*) A moment, Mr Worthing. A hundred and thirty thousand pounds! And in the Funds! Miss Cardew seems to me a most attractive young lady, now that I look at her. Few girls of the present day have any really solid qualities, any of the qualities that last, and improve with time. We live, I regret to say, in an age of surfaces. (*To Cecily*) Come over here, dear. (*Cecily goes across*) Pretty child! your dress is sadly simple, and your hair seems almost as Nature might have left it. But we can soon alter all that. A thoroughly experienced French maid produces a really marvellous result in a very brief space of time. I remember recommending one to young Lady Lancing, and after three months her own husband did not know her.

JACK: And after six months nobody knew her.

LADY BRACKNELL: (*glares at Jack for a few moments. Then bends, with a practised smile, to Cecily*) Kindly turn round, sweet child. (*Cecily turns completely round*) No, the side view is what I want. (*Cecily presents her profile*) Yes, quite as I expected. There are distinct social possibilities in your profile. The two weak points in our age are its want of principle and its want of profile. The chin a little higher, dear. Style largely depends on the way the chin is worn. They are worn very high, just at present. Algernon!

ALGERNON: Yes, Aunt Augusta!

LADY BRACKNELL: There are distinct social possibilities in Miss Cardew's profile.

ALGERNON: Cecily is the sweetest, dearest, prettiest girl in the whole world. And I don't care twopence about social possibilities.

LADY BRACKNELL: Never speak disrespectfully of Society, Algernon. Only people who can't get into it do that. (*To Cecily*) Dear child, of course you know that Algernon has nothing but his debts to depend upon. But I do not approve of mercenary marriages. When I married Lord Bracknell I had no fortune of any kind. But I never dreamed for a moment of allowing that to stand in my way. Well, I suppose I must give my consent.

ALGERNON: Thank you, Aunt Augusta.

LADY BRACKNELL: Cecily, you may kiss me!

CECILY: (*kisses her*) Thank you, Lady Bracknell.

LADY BRACKNELL: You may also address me as Aunt Augusta for the future.

CECILY: Thank you, Aunt Augusta.

LADY BRACKNELL: The marriage, I think, had better take place quite soon.

ALGERNON: Thank you, Aunt Augusta.

CECILY: Thank you, Aunt Augusta.

LADY BRACKNELL: To speak frankly, I am not in favour of long engagements. They give people the opportunity of finding out each other's character before marriage, which I think is never advisable.

JACK: I beg your pardon for interrupting you, Lady Bracknell, but this engagement is quite out of the question. I am Miss Cardew's guardian, and she cannot marry without my consent until she comes of age. That consent I absolutely decline to give.

LADY BRACKNELL: Upon what grounds may I ask? Algernon is an extremely, I may almost say an ostentatiously, eligible young man. He has nothing, but he looks everything. What more can one desire?

JACK: It pains me very much to have to speak frankly to you, Lady Bracknell, about your nephew, but the fact is that I do not approve at all of his moral character. I suspect him of being untruthful.

(*Algernon and Cecily look at him in indignant amazement*)

LADY BRACKNELL: Untruthful! My nephew Algernon? Impossible! He is an Oxonian.[17]

JACK: I fear there can be no possible doubt about the matter. This afternoon during my temporary absence in London on an important question of romance, he obtained admission to my house by means of the false pretence of being my brother. Under an assumed name he drank, I've just been informed by my butler, an entire pint bottle of my Perrier-Jouet, Brut, '89; a wine I was specially reserving for myself. Continuing his disgraceful deception, he succeeded in the course of the afternoon in alienating the affections of my only ward. He subsequently stayed to tea, and devoured every single muffin. And what makes his conduct all the more heartless is, that he was perfectly well aware from the first that I have no brother, that I never had a brother, and that I don't intend to have a brother, not even of any kind. I distinctly told him so myself yesterday afternoon.

LADY BRACKNELL: Ahem! Mr Worthing, after careful consideration I have decided entirely to overlook my nephew's conduct to you.

JACK: That is very generous of you, Lady Bracknell. My own decision, however, is unalterable. I decline to give my consent.

---

[17]**Oxonian**: Oxford student or graduate.

LADY BRACKNELL: (to Cecily) Come here, sweet child. (Cecily goes over) How old are you, dear?

CECILY: Well, I am really only eighteen, but I always admit to twenty when I go to evening parties.

LADY BRACKNELL: You are perfectly right in making some slight alteration. Indeed, no woman should ever be quite accurate about her age. It looks so calculating. . . . (In a meditative manner) Eighteen, but admitting to twenty at evening parties. Well, it will not be very long before you are of age and free from the restraints of tutelage. So I don't think your guardian's consent is, after all, a matter of any importance.

JACK: Pray excuse me, Lady Bracknell, for interrupting you again, but it is only fair to tell you that according to the terms of her grandfather's will Miss Cardew does not come legally of age till she is thirty-five.

LADY BRACKNELL: That does not seem to me to be a grave objection. Thirty-five is a very attractive age. London society is full of women of the very highest birth who have, of their own free choice, remained thirty-five for years. Lady Dumbleton is an instance in point. To my own knowledge she has been thirty-five ever since she arrived at the age of forty, which was many years ago now. I see no reason why our dear Cecily should not be even still more attractive at the age you mention than she is at present. There will be a large accumulation of property.

CECILY: Algy, could you wait for me till I was thirty-five?

ALGERNON: Of course I could, Cecily. You know I could.

CECILY: Yes, I felt it instinctively, but I couldn't wait all that time. I hate waiting even five minutes for anybody. It always makes me rather cross. I am not punctual myself, I know, but I do like punctuality in others, and waiting, even to be married, is quite out of the question.

ALGERNON: Then what is to be done, Cecily?

CECILY: I don't know, Mr Moncrieff.

LADY BRACKNELL: My dear Mr Worthing, as Miss Cardew states positively that she cannot wait till she is thirty-five—a remark which I am bound to say seems to me to show a somewhat impatient nature—I would beg of you to reconsider your decision.

JACK: But my dear Lady Bracknell, the matter is entirely in your own hands. The moment you consent to my marriage with Gwendolen, I will most gladly allow your nephew to form an alliance with my ward.

LADY BRACKNELL: (rising and drawing herself up) You must be quite aware that what you propose is out of the question.

JACK: Then a passionate celibacy is all that any of us can look forward to.

LADY BRACKNELL: That is not the destiny I propose for Gwendolen. Algernon, of course, can choose for himself. (Pulls out her watch) Come, dear (Gwendolen rises), we have already missed five, if not six, trains. To miss any more might expose us to comment on the platform.

(Enter Dr Chasuble)

CHASUBLE: Everything is quite ready for the christenings.

LADY BRACKNELL: The christenings, sir! Is not that somewhat premature?

CHASUBLE: (looking rather puzzled, and pointing to Jack and Algernon) Both these gentlemen have expressed a desire for immediate baptism.

LADY BRACKNELL: At their age? The idea is grotesque and irreligious! Algernon, I forbid you to be baptized. I will not hear of such excesses. Lord Bracknell would be highly displeased if he learned that that was the way in which you wasted your time and money.

CHASUBLE: Am I to understand then that there are to be no christenings at all this afternoon?

JACK: I don't think that, as things are now, it would be of much practical value to either of us, Dr Chasuble.

CHASUBLE: I am grieved to hear such sentiments from you, Mr Worthing. They savour of the heretical views of the Anabaptists,[18] views that I have completely refuted in four of my unpublished sermons. However, as your present mood seems to be one peculiarly secular, I will return to the church at once. Indeed, I have just been informed by the pew-opener that for the last hour and a half Miss Prism has been waiting for me in the vestry.

LADY BRACKNELL: (starting) Miss Prism! Did I hear you mention a Miss Prism?

CHASUBLE: Yes, Lady Bracknell. I am on my way to join her.

LADY BRACKNELL: Pray allow me to detain you for a moment. This matter may prove to be one of vital importance to Lord Bracknell and myself. Is this Miss Prism a female of repellent aspect, remotely connected with education?

CHASUBLE: (somewhat indignantly) She is the most cultivated of ladies, and the very picture of respectability.

LADY BRACKNELL: It is obviously the same person. May I ask what position she holds in your household?

---

[18]**Anabaptists**: 16th-century continental Protestants who practiced adult baptism.

CHASUBLE: (*severely*) I am a celibate, madam.

JACK: (*interposing*) Miss Prism, Lady Bracknell, has been for the last three years Miss Cardew's esteemed governess and valued companion.

LADY BRACKNELL: In spite of what I hear of her, I must see her at once. Let her be sent for.

CHASUBLE: (*looking off*) She approaches; she is nigh.

(*Enter Miss Prism hurriedly*)

MISS PRISM: I was told you expected me in the vestry, dear Canon. I have been waiting for you there for an hour and three quarters. (*Catches sight of Lady Bracknell who has fixed her with a stony glare. Miss Prism grows pale and quails. She looks anxiously round as if desirous to escape*)

LADY BRACKNELL: (*in a severe, judicial voice*) Prism! (*Miss Prism bows her head in shame*) Come here, Prism! (*Miss Prism approaches in a humble manner*) Prism! Where is that baby? (*General consternation. The Canon starts back in horror. Algernon and Jack pretend to be anxious to shield Cecily and Gwendolen from hearing the details of a terrible public scandal*) Twenty-eight years ago, Prism, you left Lord Bracknell's house, Number 104, Upper Grosvenor Square, in charge of a perambulator that contained a baby, of the male sex. You never returned. A few weeks later, through the elaborate investigations of the Metropolitan police, the perambulator was discovered at midnight standing by itself in a remote corner of Bayswater. It contained the manuscript of a three-volume novel of more than usually revolting sentimentality. (*Miss Prism starts in involuntary indignation*) But the baby was not there. (*Everyone looks at Miss Prism*) Prism! Where is that baby?

(*A pause*)

MISS PRISM: Lady Bracknell, I admit with shame that I do not know. I only wish I did. The plain facts of the case are these. On the morning of the day you mention, a day that is for ever branded on my memory, I prepared as usual to take the baby out in its perambulator. I had also with me a somewhat old, but capacious hand-bag in which I had intended to place the manuscript of a work of fiction that I had written during my few unoccupied hours. In a moment of mental abstraction, for which I can never forgive myself, I deposited the manuscript in the bassinette and placed the baby in the hand-bag.

JACK: (*who has been listening attentively*) But where did you deposit the hand-bag?

MISS PRISM: Do not ask me, Mr Worthing.

JACK: Miss Prism, this is a matter of no small importance to me. I insist on knowing where you deposited the hand-bag that contained that infant.

MISS PRISM: I left it in the cloak-room of one of the larger railway stations in London.

JACK: What railway station?

MISS PRISM: (*quite crushed*) Victoria. The Brighton line. (*Sinks into a chair*)

JACK: I must retire to my room for a moment. Gwendolen, wait here for me.

GWENDOLEN: If you are not too long, I will wait here for you all my life.

(*Exit Jack in great excitement*)

CHASUBLE: What do you think this means, Lady Bracknell?

LADY BRACKNELL: I dare not even suspect, Dr Chasuble. I need hardly tell you that in families of high position strange coincidences are not supposed to occur. They are hardly considered the thing.

(*Noises heard overhead as if some one was throwing trunks about. Everyone looks up*)

CECILY: Uncle Jack seems strangely agitated.

CHASUBLE: Your guardian has a very emotional nature.

LADY BRACKNELL: This noise is extremely unpleasant. It sounds as if he was having an argument. I dislike arguments of any kind. They are always vulgar, and often convincing.

CHASUBLE: (*looking up*) It has stopped now. (*The noise is redoubled*)

LADY BRACKNELL: I wish he would arrive at some conclusion.

GWENDOLEN: This suspense is terrible. I hope it will last.

(*Enter Jack with a hand-bag of black leather in his hand*)

JACK: (*rushing over to Miss Prism*) Is this the hand-bag, Miss Prism? Examine it carefully before you speak. The happiness of more than one life depends on your answer.

MISS PRISM: (*calmly*) It seems to be mine. Yes, here is the injury it received through the upsetting of a Gower Street[19] omnibus in younger and happier days. Here is the stain on the lining caused by the explosion of a temperance beverage, an incident that occurred at

---

[19]**Gower Street**: near University of London.

Leamington.[20] And here, on the lock, are my initials. I had forgotten that in an extravagant mood I had had them placed there. The bag is undoubtedly mine. I am delighted to have it so unexpectedly restored to me. It has been a great inconvenience being without it all these years.

JACK: (*in a pathetic voice*) Miss Prism, more is restored to you than this hand-bag. I was the baby you placed in it.

MISS PRISM: (*amazed*) You?

JACK: (*embracing her*). Yes—mother!

MISS PRISM: (*recoiling in indignant astonishment*) Mr Worthing! I am unmarried!

JACK: Unmarried! I do not deny that is a serious blow. But after all, who has the right to cast a stone[21] against one who has suffered? Cannot repentance wipe out an act of folly? Why should there be one law for men, and another for women? Mother, I forgive you. (*Tries to embrace her again*)

MISS PRISM: (*still more indignant*) Mr Worthing, there is some error. (*Pointing to Lady Bracknell*) There is the lady who can tell you who you really are.

(*A pause*)

JACK: Lady Bracknell, I hate to seem inquisitive, but would you kindly inform me who I am?

LADY BRACKNELL: I am afraid that the news I have to give you will not altogether please you. You are the son of my poor sister, Mrs Moncrieff, and consequently Algernon's elder brother.

JACK: Algy's elder brother! Then I have a brother after all. I knew I had a brother! I always said I had a brother! Cecily—how could you have ever doubted that I had a brother. (*Seizes hold of Algernon*) Dr Chasuble, my unfortunate brother. Miss Prism, my unfortunate brother. Gwendolen, my unfortunate brother. Algy, you young scoundrel, you will have to treat me with more respect in the future. You have never behaved to me like a brother in all your life.

ALGERNON: Well, not till today, old boy, I admit. I did my best, however, though I was out of practice.

(*Shakes hands*)

GWENDOLEN: (*to Jack*) My own! But what own are you? What is your Christian name, now that you have become someone else?

JACK: Good heavens!—I had quite forgotten that point. Your decision on the subject of my name is irrevocable, I suppose?

GWENDOLEN: I never change, except in my affections.

CECILY: What a noble nature you have, Gwendolen!

JACK: Then the question had better be cleared up at once. Aunt Augusta, a moment. At the time when Miss Prism left me in the hand-bag, had I been christened already?

LADY BRACKNELL: Every luxury that money could buy, including christening, had been lavished on you by your fond and doting parents.

JACK: Then I was christened! That is settled. Now, what name was I given? Let me know the worst.

LADY BRACKNELL: Being the eldest son you were naturally christened after your father.

JACK: (*irritably*) Yes, but what was my father's Christian name?

LADY BRACKNELL: (*meditatively*) I cannot at the present moment recall what the General's Christian name was. But I have no doubt he had one. He was eccentric, I admit. But only in later years. And that was the result of the Indian climate, and marriage, and indigestion, and other things of that kind.

JACK: Algy! Can't you recollect what our father's Christian name was?

ALGERNON: My dear boy, we were never even on speaking terms. He died before I was a year old.

JACK: His name would appear in the Army Lists of the period, I suppose, Aunt Augusta?

LADY BRACKNELL: The General was essentially a man of peace, except in his domestic life. But I have no doubt his name would appear in any military directory.

JACK: The Army Lists of the last forty years are here. These delightful records should have been my constant study. (*Rushes to bookcase and tears the books out*) M. Generals ... Mallam, Maxbohm, Magley—what ghastly names they have—Markby, Migsby, Mobbs, Moncrieff! Lieutenant 1840, Captain, Lieutenant-Colonel, Colonel, General 1869, Christian names, Ernest John. (*Puts book very quietly down and speaks quite calmly*) I always told you, Gwendolen, my name was Ernest, didn't I? Well, it is Ernest after all. I mean it naturally is Ernest.

LADY BRACKNELL: Yes, I remember now that the General was called Ernest. I knew I had some particular reason for disliking the name.

GWENDOLEN: Ernest! My own Ernest! I felt from the first that you could have no other name!

[20]**Leamington**: genteel health spa in the Midlands.

[21]**cast a stone**: see John 8:7.

JACK: Gwendolen, it is a terrible thing for a man to find out suddenly that all his life he has been speaking nothing but the truth. Can you forgive me?

GWENDOLEN: I can. For I feel that you are sure to change.

JACK: My own one!

CHASUBLE: (*to Miss Prism*) Laetitia! (*Embraces her*)

MISS PRISM: (*enthusiastically*) Frederick! At last!

ALGERNON: Cecily! (*Embraces her*) At last!

JACK: Gwendolen! (*Embraces her*) At last!

LADY BRACKNELL: My nephew, you seem to be displaying signs of triviality.

JACK: On the contrary, Aunt Augusta, I've now realized for the first time in my life the vital Importance of Being Earnest.

1894 (*performed 1895*)   1899

~

from De Profundis[1]

. . . I must say to myself that neither you[2] nor your father, multiplied a thousand times over, could possibly have ruined a man like me: that I ruined myself: and that nobody, great or small, can be ruined except by his own hand. I am quite ready to do so. I am trying to do so, though you may not think it at the present moment. If I have brought this pitiless indictment against you, think what an indictment I bring without pity against myself. Terrible as what you did to me was, what I did to myself was far more terrible still.

I was a man who stood in symbolic relations to the art and culture of my age. I had realised this for myself at the very dawn of my manhood, and had forced my age to realise it afterwards. Few men hold such a position in their own lifetime and have it so acknowledged. It is usually discerned, if discerned at all, by the historian, or the critic, long after both the man and his age have passed away. With me it was different. I felt it myself, and made others feel it. Byron was a symbolic figure, but his relations were to the passion of his age and its weariness of passion. Mine were to

something more noble, more permanent, of more vital issue, of larger scope.

The gods had given me almost everything. I had genius, a distinguished name, high social position, brilliancy, intellectual daring: I made art a philosophy, and philosophy an art: I altered the minds of men and the colours of things: there was nothing I said or did that did not make people wonder: I took the drama, the most objective form known to art, and made it as personal a mode of expression as the lyric or the sonnet, at the same time that I widened its range and enriched its characterisation: drama, novel, poem in rhyme, poem in prose, subtle or fantastic dialogue, whatever I touched I made beautiful in a new mode of beauty: to truth itself I gave what is false no less than what is true as its rightful province, and showed that the false and the true are merely forms of intellectual existence. I treated Art as the supreme reality, and life as a mere mode of fiction: I awoke the imagination of my century so that it created myth and legend around me: I summed up all systems in a phrase, and all existence in an epigram.

Along with these things, I had things that were different. I let myself be lured into long spells of senseless and sensual ease. I amused myself with being a *flâneur*,[3] a dandy, a man of fashion. I surrounded myself with the smaller natures and the meaner minds. I became the spendthrift of my own genius, and to waste an eternal youth gave me a curious joy. Tired of being on the heights I deliberately went to the depths in the search for new sensations. What the paradox was to me in the sphere of thought, perversity became to me in the sphere of passion. Desire, at the end, was a malady, or a madness, or both. I grew careless of the lives of others. I took pleasure where it pleased me and passed on. I forgot that every little action of the common day makes or unmakes character, and that therefore what one has done in the secret chamber one has some day to cry aloud on the housetops.[4] I ceased to be Lord over myself. I was no longer the Captain of my Soul,[5] and did not know it. I allowed you to dominate me, and your father to frighten me. I ended in horrible disgrace. There is only one thing for me now, absolute Humility: just as there is only one thing for you, absolute Humility also. You had better come down into the dust and learn it beside me.

---

[1] *De Profundis:* From the Depths. See Psalm 71:20. This excerpt is from the original letter on which the posthumously published text was based.

[2] **you:** Lord Alfred Douglas (1870–1945), a minor poet. **your father:** Sir John Sholto Douglas, Marquess of Queensberry (1844–1900).

[3] *flâneur:* idler, man about town.

[4] **cry . . . housetops:** see Luke 12:3.

[5] **Captain of my Soul:** see William Ernest Henley (1849–1903), "Invictus" (1888) 16.

I have lain in prison for nearly two years. Out of my nature has come wild despair; an abandonment to grief that was piteous even to look at: terrible and impotent rage: bitterness and scorn: anguish that wept aloud: misery that could find no voice: sorrow that was dumb. I have passed through every possible mood of suffering. Better than Wordsworth himself I know what Wordsworth meant when he said:

> Suffering is permanent, obscure, and dark
> And has the nature of Infinity.[6]

But while there were times when I rejoiced in the idea that my sufferings were to be endless, I could not bear them to be without meaning. Now I find hidden away in my nature something that tells me that nothing in the whole world is meaningless, and suffering least of all. That something hidden away in my nature, like a treasure in a field, is Humility. . . .

Perhaps there may come into my art also, no less than into my life, a still deeper note, one of greater unity of passion, and directness of impulse. Not width but intensity is the true aim of modern Art. We are no longer in Art concerned with the type. It is with the exception we have to do. I cannot put my sufferings into any form they took, I need hardly say. Art only begins where Imitation ends. But something must come into my work, of fuller harmony of words perhaps, of richer cadences, of more curious colour-effects, of simpler architectural-order, of some æsthetic quality at any rate.

When Marsyas[7] was "torn from the scabbard of his limbs"—*dalla vagina delle membre sue*, to use one of Dante's most terrible, most Tacitean phrases—he had no more song, the Greeks said. Apollo had been victor. The lyre had vanquished the reed. But perhaps the Greeks were mistaken. I hear in much modern Art the cry of Marsyas. . . . But whether or not the Phrygian Faun was silent, I cannot be. Expression is as necessary to me as leaf and blossom are to the black branches of the trees that show themselves above the prison wall and are so restless in the wind. Between my art and the world there is now a wide gulf, but between Art and myself there is none. I hope at least that there is none.

To each of us different fates have been meted out. Freedom, pleasure, amusements, a life of ease have been your lot, and you are not worthy of it. My lot has been one of public infamy, of long imprisonment, of misery, of ruin, of disgrace, and I am not worthy of it either—not yet, at any rate. I remember I used to say that I thought I could bear a real tragedy if it came to me with purple pall and a mask of noble sorrow, but that the dreadful thing about modernity was that it put Tragedy into the raiment of Comedy, so that the great realities seemed commonplace or grotesque or lacking in style. It is quite true about modernity. It has probably always been true about actual life. It is said that all martyrdoms seemed mean to the looker-on.[8] The nineteenth century is no exception to the general rule.

Everything about my tragedy has been hideous, mean, repellent, lacking in style. Our very dress makes us grotesques. We are the zanies of sorrow. We are clowns whose hearts are broken. We are specially designed to appeal to the sense of humour. On November 13th[9] 1895 I was brought down here from London. From two o'clock till half-past two on that day I had to stand on the centre platform of Clapham Junction in convict dress and handcuffed, for the world to look at. I had been taken out of the Hospital Ward without a moment's notice being given to me. Of all possible objects I was the most grotesque. When people saw me they laughed. Each train as it came up swelled the audience. Nothing could exceed their amusement. That was of course before they knew who I was. As soon as they had been informed, they laughed still more. For half an hour I stood there in the grey November rain surrounded by a jeering mob. For a year after that was done to me I wept every day at the same hour and for the same space of time. That is not such a tragic thing as possibly it sounds to you. To those who are in prison, tears are a part of every day's experience. A day in prison on which one does not weep is a day on which one's heart is hard, not a day on which one's heart is happy.

Well, now I am really beginning to feel more regret for the people who laughed than for myself. Of course when they saw me I was not on my pedestal. I was in the pillory. But it is a very unimaginative nature that only cares for people on their pedestals. A pedestal may be a very unreal thing. A pillory is a terrific reality. They should have known

---

[6]Wordsworth: see *The Borderers* (1842) 3.1543–1544.

[7]Marsyas, Phrygian Faun: satyr from Phrygia in Asia Minor who played a flute (reed) in a musical contest to which he had challenged Apollo and his lyre; defeated, he was flayed alive. *dalla vagina . . . sue*: Dante, *Paradiso* 1.21. Tacitean: in the manner of Tacitus (56–120), Roman orator and historian.

[8]martyrdoms . . . looker-on: see Ralph Waldo Emerson, "Experience" (1844).

[9]November 13th: in fact, November 20.

also how to interpret sorrow better. I have said that behind Sorrow there is always Sorrow. It were still wiser to say that behind sorrow there is always a soul. And to mock at a soul in pain is a dreadful thing. Unbeautiful are their lives who do it. In the strangely simple economy of the world people only get what they give, and to those who have not enough imagination to penetrate the mere outward of things and feel pity, what pity can be given save that of scorn?

I have told you this account of the mode of my being conveyed here simply that you should realise how hard it has been for me to get anything out of my punishment but bitterness and despair. I have however to do it, and now and then I have moments of submission and acceptance. All the spring may be hidden in a single bud, and the low ground-nest of the lark may hold the joy that is to herald the feet of many rose-red dawns, and so perhaps whatever beauty of life still remains to me is contained in some moment of surrender, abasement and humiliation. I can, at any rate, merely proceed on the lines of my own development, and by accepting all that has happened to me make myself worthy of it. . . .

1897   1905, 1962

A. E. HOUSMAN

(1859–1936)

Alfred Edward Housman entered Oxford with every assurance of success, but he neglected his studies and to his profound humiliation failed the examination for an honors degree. For ten years thereafter he worked to recover lost ground. Having established himself at the forefront of classical scholarship while employed full time in the London Patent Office, he won professorships first at the University of London and then at Cambridge. His emotional attachments were to men; he never married, and was noted for his reclusive and extremely reserved personality. Defining the "textual criticism" of which he was the acknowledged master in the driest possible terms as "the science of discovering error in texts and the art of removing it," he embraced as his main project a multi-volume edition of Manilius, a thoroughly minor Latin poet; not surprisingly, he said, the combination of a tedious author and an odious editor did not bring popular success.

His poetry, however, has been very popular indeed. There is not much of it: two volumes published in his lifetime, *A Shropshire Lad* (1896) and *Last Poems* (1922), containing just over a hundred poems, mostly very short. The main subjects are the brevity of youth, the impermanence of love, and the certainty of death. The setting is usually rural Shropshire, a world drawn from imagination and desire rather than from experience (the hills of Shropshire, Housman explained, formed the western horizon of the town in Worcestershire where he grew up). Religion has vanished, leaving courage, endurance, and pity as the essential virtues. Despite its deliberate self-limitation and easy, colloquial tone, Housman's poetry is far from simple. Delicately echoing classical, Biblical, and modern antecedents and imitating the linguistic compression of Latin poetry, it is at the same time tightly disciplined, carefully casual, and elegantly austere. Its emotion is often tinged with a delicate irony, and its reticence heightens its expressiveness and intensifies its eerie poignancy.

Housman gave a famous definition of poetry in terms of its physical effects: the bristling of the skin that stopped his razor when he shaved, a shiver down the spine, a constriction of the throat and water in the eyes, and a sensation in the pit of the stomach that went through him like a spear. By such standards, generations of readers have found his poetry to be the real thing.

from A Shropshire Lad

1
1887[1]

From Clee[2] to heaven the beacon burns,
    The shires have seen it plain,
From north and south the sign returns
    And beacons burn again.

Look left, look right, the hills are bright,
    The dales are light between,
Because 'tis fifty years to-night
    That God has saved the Queen.

Now, when the flame they watch not towers
    About the soil they trod,   10
Lads, we'll remember friends of ours
    Who shared the work with God.

To skies that knit their heartstrings right,
    To fields that bred them brave,
The saviours come not home to-night:
    Themselves they could not save.[3]

It dawns in Asia, tombstones show
    And Shropshire names are read;
And the Nile spills his overflow
    Beside the Severn's[4] dead.   20

We pledge in peace by farm and town
    The Queen they served in war,
And fire the beacons up and down
    The land they perished for.

"God save the Queen" we living sing,
    From height to height 'tis heard;
And with the rest your voices ring,
    Lads of the Fifty-third.[5]

Oh, God will save her, fear you not:
    Be you the men you've been,
Get you the sons your fathers got,   30
    And God will save the Queen.

---

[1]**1887**: Queen Victoria's Golden Jubilee.

[2]**Clee**: hills in Shropshire.

[3]**Themselves . . . save**: see Mark 15:31.

[4]**Severn**: river traversing Shropshire.

[5]**Fifty-third**: regiment from Shropshire.

2

Loveliest of trees, the cherry now
Is hung with bloom along the bough,
And stands about the woodland ride
Wearing white for Eastertide.

Now, of my threescore years and ten,[1]
Twenty will not come again,
And take from seventy springs a score,
It only leaves me fifty more.

And since to look at things in bloom
Fifty springs are little room,   10
About the woodlands I will go
To see the cherry hung with snow.

4
Réveillé

Wake: the silver dusk returning
    Up the beach of darkness brims,
And the ship of sunrise burning
    Strands upon the eastern rims.

Wake: the vaulted shadow shatters,
    Trampled to the floor it spanned,
And the tent of night in tatters
    Straws the sky-pavilioned land.

Up, lad, up, 'tis late for lying:
    Hear the drums of morning play;
Hark, the empty highways crying   10
    "Who'll beyond the hills away?"

Towns and countries woo together,
    Forelands beacon, belfries call;
Never lad that trod on leather
    Lived to feast his heart with all.

---

[1]**threescore years and ten**: see Psalm 90:10.

Up, lad: thews[1] that lie and cumber
  Sunlit pallets never thrive;
Morns abed and daylight slumber
  Were not meant for man alive.   20

Clay lies still, but blood's a rover;
  Breath's a ware that will not keep.
Up, lad: when the journey's over
  There'll be time enough to sleep.

13

When I was one-and-twenty
  I heard a wise man say,
"Give crowns and pounds and guineas
  But not your heart away;
Give pearls away and rubies
  But keep your fancy free."
But I was one-and-twenty,
  No use to talk to me.

When I was one-and-twenty
I heard him say again,   10
  "The heart out of the bosom
  Was never given in vain;
'Tis paid with sighs a plenty
  And sold for endless rue."
And I am two-and-twenty,
  And oh, 'tis true, 'tis true.

15

Look not in my eyes, for fear
  They mirror true the sight I see,
And there you find your face too clear
  And love it and be lost like me.
One the long nights through must lie
  Spent in star-defeated sighs,
But why should you as well as I
  Perish? gaze not in my eyes.

---

[1]thews: muscles or tendons.

A Grecian lad, as I hear tell,
  One that many loved in vain,   10
Looked into a forest well
  And never looked away again.
There, when the turf in springtime flowers,
  With downward eye and gazes sad,
Stands amid the glancing showers
  A jonquil, not a Grecian lad.[1]

19
To an Athlete Dying Young

The time you won your town the race
We chaired you through the market-place;
Man and boy stood cheering by,
And home we brought you shoulder-high.

To-day, the road all runners come,
Shoulder-high we bring you home,
And set you at your threshold down,
Townsman of a stiller town.

Smart lad, to slip betimes away
From fields where glory does not stay   10
And early though the laurel grows
It withers quicker than the rose.

Eyes the shady night has shut
Cannot see the record cut,
And silence sounds no worse than cheers
After earth has stopped the ears:

Now you will not swell the rout
Of lads that wore their honours out,
Runners whom renown outran
And the name died before the man.   20

So set, before its echoes fade,
The fleet foot on the sill of shade,
And hold to the low lintel up
The still-defended challenge-cup.

---

[1]**Grecian lad**: Narcissus, who was transformed into a **jonquil** (daffodil).

And round that early-laurelled head
Will flock to gaze the strengthless dead,
And find unwithered on its curls
The garland briefer than a girl's.

27

"Is my team ploughing,
    That I was used to drive
And hear the harness jingle
    When I was man alive?"

Ay, the horses trample,
    The harness jingles now;
No change though you lie under
    The land you used to plough.

"Is football[1] playing
    Along the river shore,   10
With lads to chase the leather,
    Now I stand up no more?"

Ay, the ball is flying,
    The lads play heart and soul;
The goal stands up, the keeper
    Stands up to keep the goal.

"Is my girl happy,
    That I thought hard to leave,
And has she tired of weeping
    As she lies down at eve?"   20

Ay, she lies down lightly,
    She lies not down to weep:
Your girl is well contented.
    Be still, my lad, and sleep.

"Is my friend hearty,
    Now I am thin and pine,
And has he found to sleep in
    A better bed than mine?"

Yes, lad, I lie easy,
    I lie as lads would choose;   30
I cheer a dead man's sweetheart,
    Never ask me whose.

31

On Wenlock Edge[1] the wood's in trouble;
    His forest fleece the Wrekin heaves;
The gale, it plies the saplings double,
    And thick on Severn snow the leaves.

'Twould blow like this through holt and hanger
    When Uricon[2] the city stood:
'Tis the old wind in the old anger,
    But then it threshed another wood.

Then, 'twas before my time, the Roman
    At yonder heaving hill would stare: 10
The blood that warms an English yeoman,
    The thoughts that hurt him, they were there.

There, like the wind through woods in riot,
    Through him the gale of life blew high;
The tree of man was never quiet:
    Then 'twas the Roman, now 'tis I.

The gale, it plies the saplings double,
    It blows so hard, 'twill soon be gone:
To-day the Roman and his trouble
    Are ashes under Uricon.   20

35

On the idle hill of summer,
    Sleepy with the flow of streams,
Far I hear the steady drummer
    Drumming like a noise in dreams.

Far and near and low and louder
    On the roads of earth go by,
Dear to friends and food for powder,
    Soldiers marching, all to die.

---

[1]**football:** soccer or rugby.

---

[1]**Wenlock Edge:** limestone ridge in Shropshire. **Wrekin:** prominent hill in Shropshire.

[2]**holt, hanger:** folk terms for woods. **Uricon:** Uriconium, Roman settlement in Shropshire.

East and west on fields forgotten
    Bleach the bones of comrades slain,   10
Lovely lads and dead and rotten;
    None that go return again.

Far the calling bugles hollo,
    High the screaming fife replies,
Gay the files of scarlet follow:
    Woman bore me, I will rise.

40

Into my heart an air that kills
    From yon far country blows:
What are those blue remembered hills,
    What spires, what farms are those?

That is the land of lost content,
    I see it shining plain,
The happy highways where I went
    And cannot come again.

54

With rue my heart is laden
    For golden friends I had,
For many a rose-lipt maiden
    And many a lightfoot lad.

By brooks too broad for leaping
    The lightfoot boys are laid;
The rose-lipt girls are sleeping
    In fields where roses fade.

60

Now hollow fires burn out to black,
    And lights are guttering low:
Square your shoulders, lift your pack,
    And leave your friends and go.

Oh never fear, man, nought's to dread,
    Look not left nor right:
In all the endless road you tread
    There's nothing but the night.

62

"Terence,[1] this is stupid stuff:
You eat your victuals fast enough;
There can't be much amiss, 'tis clear,
To see the rate you drink your beer.
But oh, good Lord, the verse you make,
It gives a chap the belly-ache.
The cow, the old cow, she is dead;
It sleeps well, the horned head:
We poor lads, 'tis our turn now
To hear such tunes as killed the cow.   10
Pretty friendship 'tis to rhyme
Your friends to death before their time
Moping melancholy mad:
Come, pipe a tune to dance to, lad."

Why, if 'tis dancing you would be,
There's brisker pipes than poetry.
Say, for what were hop-yards meant,
Or why was Burton built on Trent?[2]
Oh many a peer of England brews
Livelier liquor than the Muse,   20
And malt does more than Milton can

---

[1]**Terence:** *A Shropshire Lad* was originally titled "The Poems of Terence Hearsay."

[2]**Burton-on-Trent:** city known for breweries. A brewer who became rich was occasionally ennobled (made a **peer**).

To justify God's ways to man.[3]
Ale, man, ale's the stuff to drink
For fellows whom it hurts to think:
Look into the pewter pot
To see the world as the world's not.
And faith, 'tis pleasant till 'tis past:
The mischief is that 'twill not last.
Oh I have been to Ludlow[4] fair
And left my necktie God knows where,   30
And carried half way home, or near,
Pints and quarts of Ludlow beer:
Then the world seemed none so bad,
And I myself a sterling lad;
And down in lovely muck I've lain,
Happy till I woke again.
Then I saw the morning sky:
Heigho, the tale was all a lie;
The world, it was the old world yet,
I was I, my things were wet,   40
And nothing now remained to do
But begin the game anew.

Therefore, since the world has still
Much good, but much less good than ill,
And while the sun and moon endure
Luck's a chance, but trouble's sure,
I'd face it as a wise man would,
And train for ill and not for good.
'Tis true, the stuff I bring for sale
Is not so brisk a brew as ale: 50

Out of a stem that scored the hand
I wrung it in a weary land.
But take it: if the smack is sour,
The better for the embittered hour;
It should do good to heart and head
When your soul is in my soul's stead;
And I will friend you, if I may,
In the dark and cloudy day.

There was a king reigned in the east:
There, when kings will sit to feast,   60
They get their fill before they think
With poisoned meat and poisoned drink.
He gathered all that springs to birth
From the many-venomed earth;
First a little, thence to more,
He sampled all her killing store;
And easy, smiling, seasoned sound,
Sate the king when healths went round.
They put arsenic in his meat
And stared aghast to watch him eat;   70
They poured strychnine in his cup
And shook to see him drink it up:
They shook, they stared as white's their shirt:
Them it was their poison hurt.
—I tell the tale that I heard told.
Mithridates,[5] he died old.

      1896

---

[3]justify . . . man: see *Paradise Lost* 1.26.
[4]**Ludlow**: in south Shropshire.

---

[5]**Mithridates** VI (131?-63 BCE): king of Pontus (in N Asia Minor) who developed an immunity to poison by taking small doses.

MARY COLERIDGE

(1861–1907)

Mary Coleridge was the great-great-grandniece of Samuel Taylor Coleridge. Her father was a lawyer who entertained artists, poets, and scholars; Mary especially revered Robert Browning, but was too shy to speak to him when he visited. She lived all her life in her parents' London home, devoting her time to friendship, travel, art, study, and writing. Her father taught her Hebrew, and she read widely in French, German, and Italian literature and later in classical Greek, as well as in English literature and history; at twenty-six she said ruefully that she had lived half her life in books. She had a close circle of women friends but does not appear to have been sympathetic to feminism. From 1895 on she gave lessons at a Working Women's College.

She published novels, stories, essays, and reviews, achieving popular success with a dreamy, rather fantastical historical romance about love, loyalty, and betrayal, *The King with Two Faces* (1897). Her poems, although admired by other poets, were published under a pseudonym and only in very small editions. Their odd metrics and simple diction give them a casual, off-hand air, but their artlessness is deliberate. "Poetry," Coleridge said, "is making, not feeling. But . . . what is most carefully made often sounds as if it had been felt straight off, whereas what has been felt carelessly sounds as if it were made." She avoids conventional plots. "Men's stories are never anything else but men and women," the heroine of one of her stories says dismissively. "A man falls in love with a woman, a woman falls in love with a man, and then they marry or don't marry." Coleridge's poems spring instead from mysterious situations, enigmatic feelings, and fantastic settings, and work by a logic more dreamlike than discursive. Her poetic world is inhabited mostly by women. Like many other Victorian poets, Coleridge explores questions of identity, doubtings of the self, and irruptions of repressed or prohibited emotions. The intriguing spareness of her lyricism, with its sculpted, unexplained images, may be seen as anticipating the poetics of twentieth-century modernism.

The Other Side of a Mirror

I sat before my glass one day,
    And conjured up a vision bare,
Unlike the aspects glad and gay,
    That erst were found reflected there—
The vision of a woman, wild
    With more than womanly despair.

Her hair stood back on either side
    A face bereft of loveliness.
It had no envy now to hide
    What once no man on earth could guess.   10
It formed the thorny aureole
    Of hard unsanctified distress.

Her lips were open—not a sound
    Came through the parted lines of red.
Whate'er it was, the hideous wound
    In silence and in secret bled.
No sigh relieved her speechless woe,
    She had no voice to speak her dread.

And in her lurid eyes there shone
    The dying flame of life's desire,   20
Made mad because its hope was gone,
    And kindled at the leaping fire
Of jealousy, and fierce revenge,
    And strength that could not change nor tire.

Shade of a shadow in the glass,
　　O set the crystal surface free!
Pass—as the fairer visions pass—
　　Nor ever more return, to be
The ghost of a distracted hour,
　　That heard me whisper, "I am she!"   30

1882   1896

Impromptu

Gorgeous grew the common walls about me,
Floor and ceiling very Heaven became,
Music all within me and about me,
Brain on fire and heart aflame;
Yet I could not speak for shame,
And I stammered when I tried to speak the name.

Gone the light and vanished all the glory,
Clasping, grasping Fancy strives in vain;
None can sing the song or tell the story,
Walls are only walls again,   10
Now the stammering tongue speaks plain.
O, the ache of dreary dullness worse than pain.

1885   1908

Gone

About the little chambers of my heart
Friends have been coming—going—many a year.
　　The doors stand open there.
Some, lightly stepping, enter; some depart.

Freely they come and freely go, at will.
The walls give back their laughter; all day long
　　They fill the house with song.
One door alone is shut, one chamber still.

1889   1896

Mortal Combat

It is because you were my friend,
　　I fought you as the devil fights.
Whatever fortune God may send,
　　For once I set the world to rights.

And that was when I thrust you down,
　　And stabbed you twice and twice again,
Because you dared take off your crown,
　　And be a man like other men.

1890   1896

Master and Guest

There came a man across the moor,
　　Fell and foul of face was he.
　　He left the path by the cross-roads three,
And stood in the shadow of the door.

I asked him in to bed and board.
　　I never hated any man so.
　　He said he could not say me No.
He sat in the seat of my own dear lord.

"Now sit you by my side!" he said,
　　"Else may I neither eat nor drink.   10
　　You would not have me starve, I think."
He ate the offerings of the dead.

"I'll light you to your bed," quoth I.
　　"My bed is yours—but light the way!"
　　I might not turn aside nor stay;
I showed him where we twain did lie.

The cock was trumpeting the morn.
　　He said: "Sweet love, a long farewell!
　　You have kissed a citizen of Hell,
And a soul was doomed when you were born.   20

"Mourn, mourn no longer for your dear!
　　Him may you never meet above.
　　The gifts that Love hath given to Love,
Love gives away again to Fear."

                                        1896

The Witch

I have walked a great while over the snow,
And I am not tall nor strong.
My clothes are wet, and my teeth are set,
And the way was hard and long.
I have wandered over the fruitful earth,
But I never came here before.
Oh, lift me over the threshold, and let me in at the door!

The cutting wind is a cruel foe.
I dare not stand in the blast.
My hands are stone, and my voice a groan,   10
And the worst of death is past.
I am but a little maiden still,
My little white feet are sore.
Oh, lift me over the threshold, and let me in at the door!

Her voice was the voice that women have,
Who plead for their heart's desire.
She came—she came—and the quivering flame
Sank and died in the fire.
It never was lit again on my hearth
Since I hurried across the floor,   20
To lift her over the threshold, and let her in at the door.
1892   *1896*

L'Oiseau Bleu[1]

The lake lay blue below the hill.
    O'er it, as I looked, there flew
Across the waters, cold and still,
    A bird whose wings were palest blue.

The sky above was blue at last,
    The sky beneath me blue in blue.
A moment, ere the bird had passed,
    It caught his image as he flew.

1894   *1897*

---

[1]**L'Oiseau Bleu:** the blue bird.

The Nurse's Lament

The flower is withered on the stem,
The fruit hath fallen from the bough.
None knows nor thinks of them.
There's no child in the house now.

The bird that sang sings not here.
Where is the bonny lark?
When shall I behold my dear?
The fire is out, the house dark.
1895?   *1954*

Wilderspin

In the little red house by the river,
    When the short night fell,
Beside his web sat the weaver,
    Weaving a twisted spell.
Mary and the Saints deliver
    My soul from the nethermost Hell!

In the little red house by the rushes
    It grew not dark at all,
For day dawned over the bushes
    Before the night could fall.   10
Where now a torrent rushes,
    The brook ran thin and small.

In the little red house a chamber
    Was set with jewels fair;
There did a vine clamber
    Along the clambering stair,
And grapes that shone like amber
    Hung at the windows there.

Will the loom not cease whirring?
    Will the house never be still?   20
Is never a horseman stirring
    Out and about on the hill?
Was it the cat purring?
    Did some one knock at the sill?

To the little red house a rider
    Was bound to come that night.
A cup of sheeny cider
    Stood ready for his delight.
And like a great black spider,
    The weaver watched on the right.   30

To the little red house by the river
    I came when the short night fell.
I broke the web for ever,
    I broke my heart as well.
Michael[1] and the Saints deliver
    My soul from the nethermost Hell!
1897   1898

Some in a child would live, some in a book;
    When I am dead let there remain of me
Less than a word—a little passing look,
Some sign the soul had once, ere she forsook
    The form of life to live eternally.
1897   1908

The White Women[1]

Where dwell the lovely, wild white women folk,
    Mortal to man?
They never bowed their necks beneath the yoke,
They dwelt alone when the first morning broke
    And Time began.

---

[1]**Michael**: the archangel, Satan's antagonist (see Revelation 12: 7–8).

[1]**The White Women**: From a legend of Malay, told by Hugh Clifford. [Coleridge's note] Sir Hugh Charles **Clifford** (1886–1941): author of essays and stories about Malay people and customs.

Taller are they than man, and very fair,
    Their cheeks are pale,
At sight of them the tiger in his lair,
The falcon hanging in the azure air,
    The eagles quail.   10

The deadly shafts their nervous hands let fly
    Are stronger than our strongest—in their form
Larger, more beauteous, carved amazingly,
And when they fight, the wild white women cry
    The war-cry of the storm.

Their words are not as ours. If man might go
    Among the waves of Ocean when they break
And hear them—hear the language of the snow
Falling on torrents—he might also know
    The tongue they speak.   20

Pure are they as the light; they never sinned,
    But when the rays of the eternal fire
Kindle the West, their tresses they unbind
And fling their girdles to the Western wind,
    Swept by desire.

Lo, maidens to the maidens then are born,
    Strong children of the maidens and the breeze,
Dreams are not—in the glory of the morn,
Seen through the gates of ivory and horn[2]—
    More fair than these.   30

And none may find their dwelling. In the shade
    Primeval of the forest oaks they hide.
One of our race, lost in an awful glade,
Saw with his human eyes a wild white maid,
    And gazing, died.
1900   1907

---

[2]**gates of ivory and horn**: classical sources of false and of true dreams.

AMY LEVY

(1861–1889)

As a Jew in Victorian England, a Jew and a woman at Cambridge University, and an ambitious, Cambridge-educated woman in London's Anglo-Jewish community, which expected women to stay home and get married, Amy Levy was always an outsider. She became a competent professional writer at an early age, publishing stories, essays, and poems while still an undergraduate. Besides three short novels and three small volumes of verse, she wrote essays and stories for periodicals as oddly assorted as the *Gentleman's Magazine*, Oscar Wilde's *Women's World*, and the *Jewish Chronicle*. After studying modern languages at Cambridge and leaving without a degree, she lived with her parents in London. She worked for a charity, took part in the social life of literary London, and formed close friendships with a group of feminist writers and social activists.

Her fiction shows a steady concern for the plight of women who have to negotiate the pitfalls and humiliations of the marriage market and are restive within the narrow range of activity and expression society allows them. In her first and most entertaining novel, the oxymoronically titled *Romance of a Shop*, three sisters set up a photography studio in London and enjoy the satisfactions of conducting a business and earning a precarious living. Levy also wrote about Jews; while objecting to stereotyped depictions by writers like Charles Dickens and George Eliot, she gave unflattering portrayals of the Jewish upper-middle class in essays for the *Jewish Chronicle*, a weekly publication widely read by English Jews, and also in a story called "Cohen of Trinity" and her best and most successful novel, *Reuben Sachs*.

Her longer poems center on the bitterness of exclusion. "Xantippe," published when she was still an undergraduate, is an indictment of the contemptuous treatment of women in classical culture and may reflect, through the dramatic monologue form, her experience at Cambridge. But most of Levy's poetry, including all of the posthumously published *A London Plane-Tree and Other Verse*, is lyrical. Its greatest debt is to the German-Jewish poet Heinrich Heine, from whom she took the epigraph of her first book: "*Aus meinen grossen Schmerzen / Mach' ich die kleinen Lieder*" (From my great sorrows I make little songs). The lyrics are mostly brief evocations of desire and regret, alluding to stories rather than spelling them out and often following the lyric convention by which the loved object is female. Levy's lyric world is contemporary and urban, with city streets and buses and the plane-tree that "loves the town": sometimes jaunty, usually sad, deftly delineating a universe in which human love fails and the consolations of religion disappear.

Amy Levy suffered from bouts of severe depression and killed herself at the age of twenty-seven.

Xantippe[1]
(A Fragment)

What, have I waked again? I never thought
To see the rosy dawn, or ev'n this grey,
Dull, solemn stillness, ere the dawn has come.
The lamp burns low; low burns the lamp of life:
The still morn stays expectant, and my soul,
All weighted with a passive wonderment,
Waiteth and watcheth, waiteth for the dawn.
Come hither, maids; too soundly have ye slept
That should have watched me; nay, I would not chide—
Oft have I chidden, yet I would not chide   10
In this last hour;—now all should be at peace.
I have been dreaming in a troubled sleep
Of weary days I thought not to recall;
Of stormy days, whose storms are hushed long since;
Of gladsome days, of sunny days; alas
In dreaming, all their sunshine seem'd so sad,
As though the current of the dark To-Be
Had flow'd, prophetic, through the happy hours.
And yet, full well, I know it was not thus;
I mind me sweetly of the summer days,   20
When, leaning from the lattice, I have caught
The fair, far glimpses of a shining sea;
And, nearer, of tall ships which thronged the bay,
And stood out blackly from a tender sky
All flecked with sulphur, azure, and bright gold;
And in the still, clear air have heard the hum
Of distant voices; and methinks there rose
No darker fount to mar or stain the joy
Which sprang ecstatic in my maiden breast
Than just those vague desires, those hopes and fears,   30
Those eager longings, strong, though undefined,
Whose very sadness makes them seem so sweet.
What cared I for the merry mockeries
Of other maidens sitting at the loom?
Or for sharp voices, bidding me return
To maiden labour? Were we not apart—
I and my high thoughts, and my golden dreams,
My soul which yearned for knowledge, for a tongue
That should proclaim the stately mysteries
Of this fair world, and of the holy gods?   40
Then followed days of sadness, as I grew
To learn my woman-mind had gone astray,

And I was sinning in those very thoughts—
For maidens, mark, such are not woman's thoughts—
(And yet, 'tis strange, the gods who fashion us
Have given us such promptings). . . .
                       Fled the years,
Till seventeen had found me tall and strong,
And fairer, runs it, than Athenian maids
Are wont to seem; I had not learnt it well—
My lesson of dumb patience—and I stood   50
At Life's great threshold with a beating heart,
And soul resolved to conquer and attain. . . .
Once, walking 'thwart the crowded market-place,
With other maidens, bearing in the twigs
White doves for Aphrodite's sacrifice,
I saw him, all ungainly and uncouth,
Yet many gathered round to hear his words,
Tall youths and stranger-maidens—Sokrates—
I saw his face and marked it, half with awe,
Half with a quick repulsion at the shape. . . .   60
The richest gem lies hidden furthest down,
And is the dearer for the weary search;
We grasp the shining shells which strew the shore,
Yet swift we fling them from us; but the gem
We keep for aye and cherish. So a soul,
Found after weary searching in the flesh
Which half repelled our senses, is more dear,
For that same seeking, than the sunny mind
Which lavish Nature marks with thousand hints
Upon a brow of beauty. We are prone   70
To overweigh such subtle hints, then deem,
In after disappointment, we are fooled. . . .
And when, at length, my father told me all,
That I should wed me with great Sokrates,
I, foolish, wept to see at once cast down
The maiden image of a future love,
Where perfect body matched the perfect soul.
But slowly, softly did I cease to weep;
Slowly I 'gan to mark the magic flash
Leap to the eyes, to watch the sudden smile   80
Break round the mouth, and linger in the eyes;
To listen for the voice's lightest tone—
Great voice, whose cunning modulations seemed
Like to the notes of some sweet instrument.
So did I reach and strain, until at last
I caught the soul athwart the grosser flesh.
Again of thee, sweet Hope, my spirit dreamed!
I, guided by his wisdom and his love,
Led by his words, and counselled by his care,
Should lift the shrouding veil from things which be,   90

[1]**Xantippe**: notorious for her bad temper; her husband Socrates (469–399 BCE) was venerated for his wisdom and virtue.

And at the flowing fountain of his soul
Refresh my thirsting spirit. . . .
                          And indeed,
In those long days which followed that strange day
When rites and song, and sacrifice and flow'rs,
Proclaimed that we were wedded, did I learn,
In sooth, a-many lessons; bitter ones
Which sorrow taught me, and not love inspired,
Which deeper knowledge of my kind impressed
With dark insistence on reluctant brain;—
But that great wisdom, deeper, which dispels   100
Narrowed conclusions of a half-grown mind,
And sees athwart the littleness of life
Nature's divineness and her harmony,
Was never poor Xantippe's. . . .
                          I would pause
And would recall no more, no more of life,
Than just the incomplete, imperfect dream
Of early summers, with their light and shade,
Their blossom-hopes, whose fruit was never ripe;
But something strong within me, some sad chord
Which loudly echoes to the later life,   110
Me to unfold the after-misery
Urges, with plaintive wailing in my heart.
Yet, maidens, mark; I would not that ye thought
I blame my lord departed, for he meant
No evil, so I take it, to his wife.
'Twas only that the high philosopher,
Pregnant with noble theories and great thoughts,
Deigned not to stoop to touch so slight a thing
As the fine fabric of a woman's brain—
So subtle as a passionate woman's soul.   120
I think, if he had stooped a little, and cared,
I might have risen nearer to his height,
And not lain shattered, neither fit for use
As goodly household vessel, nor for that
Far finer thing which I had hoped to be. . . .
Death, holding high his retrospective lamp,
Shows me those first, far years of wedded life,
Ere I had learnt to grasp the barren shape
Of what the Fates had destined for my life.
Then, as all youthful spirits are, was I   130
Wholly incredulous that Nature meant
So little, who had promised me so much.
At first I fought my fate with gentle words,
With high endeavours after greater things;
Striving to win the soul of Sokrates,
Like some slight bird, who sings her burning love
To human master, till at length she finds

Her tender language wholly misconceived,
And that same hand whose kind caress she sought,
With fingers flippant flings the careless corn. . . .   140
I do remember how, one summer's eve,
He, seated in an arbour's leafy shade,
Had bade me bring fresh wine-skins. . . .
                          As I stood
Ling'ring upon the threshold, half concealed
By tender foliage, and my spirit light
With draughts of sunny weather, did I mark
An instant the gay group before mine eyes.
Deepest in shade, and facing where I stood,
Sat Plato,[2] with his calm face and low brows
Which met above the narrow Grecian eyes,   150
The pale, thin lips just parted to the smile,
Which dimpled that smooth olive of his cheek.
His head a little bent, sat Sokrates,
With one swart finger raised admonishing,
And on the air were borne his changing tones.
Low lounging at his feet, one fair arm thrown
Around his knee (the other, high in air
Brandish'd a brazen amphor, which yet rained
Bright drops of ruby on the golden locks
And temples with their fillets of the vine),   160
Lay Alkibiades[3] the beautiful.
And thus, with solemn tone, spake Sokrates:
"This fair Aspasia, which our Perikles[4]
Hath brought from realms afar, and set on high
In our Athenian city, hath a mind,
I doubt not, of a strength beyond her race;
And makes employ of it, beyond the way
Of women nobly gifted: woman's frail—
Her body rarely stands the test of soul;
She grows intoxicate with knowledge; throws   170
The laws of custom, order, 'neath her feet,
Feasting at life's great banquet with wide throat."
Then sudden, stepping from my leafy screen,
Holding the swelling wine-skin o'er my head,
With breast that heaved, and eyes and cheeks aflame,
Lit by a fury and a thought, I spake:
"By all great powers around us! can it be

---

[2]**Plato** (429?-347 BCE): great classical philosopher who wrote about Socrates' life and thought.

[3]**Alkibiades**: Athenian general and statesman famous for brilliance and beauty.

[4]**Aspasia**: an intellectually accomplished courtesan, mistress of the preeminent Athenian statesman, **Perikles**.

That we poor women are empirical?
That gods who fashioned us did strive to make
Beings too fine, too subtly delicate,   180
With sense that thrilled response to ev'ry touch
Of nature's, and their task is not complete?
That they have sent their half-completed work
To bleed and quiver here upon the earth?
To bleed and quiver, and to weep and weep,
To beat its soul against the marble walls
Of men's cold hearts, and then at last to sin!"
I ceased, the first hot passion stayed and stemmed
And frighted by the silence: I could see,
Framed by the arbour foliage, which the sun   190
In setting softly gilded with rich gold,
Those upturned faces, and those placid limbs;
Saw Plato's narrow eyes and niggard mouth,
Which half did smile and half did criticise,
One hand held up, the shapely fingers framed
To gesture of entreaty—"Hush, I pray,
Do not disturb her; let us hear the rest;
Follow her mood, for here's another phase
Of your black-browed Xantippe. . . ."
                           Then I saw
Young Alkibiades, with laughing lips   200
And half-shut eyes, contemptuous shrugging up
Soft, snowy shoulders, till he brought the gold
Of flowing ringlets round about his breasts.
But Sokrates, all slow and solemnly,
Raised, calm, his face to mine, and sudden spake:
"I thank thee for the wisdom which thy lips
Have thus let fall among us: prythee tell
From what high source, from what philosophies
Didst cull the sapient notion of thy words?"
Then stood I straight and silent for a breath,   210
Dumb, crushed with all that weight of cold contempt;
But swiftly in my bosom there uprose
A sudden flame, a merciful fury sent
To save me; with both angry hands I flung
The skin upon the marble, where it lay
Spouting red rills and fountains on the white;
Then, all unheeding faces, voices, eyes,
I fled across the threshold, hair unbound—
White garment stained to redness—beating heart
Flooded with all the flowing tide of hopes   220
Which once had gushed out golden, now sent back
Swift to their sources, never more to rise. . . .
I think I could have borne the weary life,
The narrow life within the narrow walls,
If he had loved me; but he kept his love

For this Athenian city and her sons;
And, haply, for some stranger-woman, bold
With freedom, thought, and glib philosophy. . . .
Ah me! the long, long weeping through the nights,
The weary watching for the pale-eyed dawn   230
Which only brought fresh grieving: then I grew
Fiercer, and cursed from out my inmost heart
The Fates which marked me an Athenian maid.
Then faded that vain fury; hope died out;
A huge despair was stealing on my soul,
A sort of fierce acceptance of my fate,—
He wished a household vessel—well 'twas good,
For he should have it! He should have no more
The yearning treasure of a woman's love,
But just the baser treasure which he sought.   240
I called my maidens, ordered out the loom,
And spun unceasing from the morn till eve;
Watching all keenly over warp and woof,
Weighing the white wool with a jealous hand.
I spun until, methinks, I spun away
The soul from out my body, the high thoughts
From out my spirit; till at last I grew
As ye have known me,—eye exact to mark
The texture of the spinning; ear all keen
For aimless talking when the moon is up,   250
And ye should be a-sleeping; tongue to cut
With quick incision, 'thwart the merry words
Of idle maidens. . . .
                  Only yesterday
My hands did cease from spinning; I have wrought
My dreary duties, patient till the last.
The gods reward me! Nay, I will not tell
The after years of sorrow; wretched strife
With grimmest foes—sad Want and Poverty;—
Nor yet the time of horror, when they bore   260
My husband from the threshold; nay, nor when
The subtle weed had wrought its deadly work.[5]
Alas! alas! I was not there to soothe
The last great moment; never any thought
Of her that loved him—save at least the charge,
All earthly, that her body should not starve. . . .
You weep, you weep; I would not that ye wept;
Such tears are idle; with the young, such grief
Soon grows to gratulation, as, "her love

---

[5]**weed**: hemlock, the deadly poison administered to Socrates in prison on his conviction for introducing strange gods and corrupting young men. See Plato, *Phaedo.*

Was withered by misfortune; mine shall grow
All nurtured by the loving," or, "her life   270
Was wrecked and shattered—mine shall smoothly sail."
Enough, enough. In vain, in vain, in vain!
The gods forgive me! Sorely have I sinned
In all my life. A fairer fate befall
You all that stand there. . . .
                              Ha! the dawn has come;
I see a rosy glimmer—nay! it grows dark;
Why stand ye so in silence? throw it wide,
The casement, quick; why tarry?—give me air—
O fling it wide, I say, and give me light!

                                                        1880

Felo De Se[1]

With Apologies to Mr. Swinburne

For repose I have sighed and have struggled; have sigh'd
    and have struggled in vain;
I am held in the Circle of Being and caught in the Circle
    of Pain.
I was wan and weary with life; my sick soul yearned for
    death;
I was weary of women and war and the sea and the wind's
    wild breath;
I cull'd sweet poppies and crush'd them, the blood ran rich
    and red:—
And I cast it in crystal chalice and drank of it till I was dead.
And the mould of the man was mute, pulseless in ev'ry
    part,
The long limbs lay on the sand with an eagle eating the
    heart.
Repose for the rotting head and peace for the putrid breast,
But for that which is "I" indeed the gods have decreed
    no rest;   10
No rest but an endless aching, a sorrow which grows
    amain:—
I am caught in the Circle of Being and held in the Circle
    of Pain.
Bitter indeed is Life, and bitter of Life the breath,
But give me life and its ways and its men, if this be Death.

Wearied I once of the Sun and the voices which clamour'd
    around:
Give them me back—in the sightless depths there is neither
    light nor sound.
Sick is my soul, and sad and feeble and faint as it felt
When (far, dim day) in the fair flesh-fane of the body it
    dwelt.
But then I could run to the shore, weeping and weary
    and weak;
See the waves' blue sheen and feel the breath of the
    breeze on my cheek: 20
Could wail with the wailing wind; strike sharply the
    hands in despair;
Could shriek with the shrieking blast, grow frenzied and
    tear the hair;
Could fight fierce fights with the foe or clutch at a human
    hand;
And weary could lie at length on the soft, sweet, saffron
    sand. . . .
I have neither a voice nor hands, nor any friend nor a foe;
I am I—just a Pulse of Pain—I am I, that is all I know.
For life, and the sickness of Life, and Death and desire to
    die,—
They have passed away like the smoke, here is nothing
    but Pain and I.

                                                        1881

Magdalen[1]

All things I can endure, save one.
The bare, blank room where is no sun;
The parcelled hours; the pallet hard;
The dreary faces here within;
The outer women's cold regard;
The Pastor's iterated "sin";—
These things could I endure, and count
No overstrain'd, unjust amount;
No undue payment for such bliss—
Yea, all things bear, save only this: 10
That you, who knew what thing would be,
Have wrought this evil unto me.

---

[1]*Felo De Se*: Suicide. Compare the versification of **Swinburne's** "Hymn to Proserpine."

[1]**Magdalen**: a 19th-century euphemism for a prostitute, referring to Mary Magdalen in the New Testament; the term also referred to institutions for the reformation of prostitutes.

It is so strange to think on still—
That you, that *you* should do me ill!
Not as one ignorant or blind,
But seeing clearly in your mind
How this must be which now has been,
Nothing aghast at what was seen.
Now that the tale is told and done,
It is so strange to think upon.   20

You were so tender with me, too!
One summer's night a cold blast blew,
Closer about my throat you drew
The half-slipt shawl of dusky blue.
And once my hand, on a summer's morn,
I stretched to pluck a rose; a thorn
Struck through the flesh and made it bleed
(A little drop of blood indeed!)
Pale grew your cheek; you stoopt and bound
Your handkerchief about the wound;   30
Your voice came with a broken sound;
With the deep breath your breast was riven;
I wonder, did God laugh in Heaven?

How strange, that *you* should work my woe!
How strange! I wonder, do you know
How gladly, gladly I had died
(And life was very sweet that tide)
To save you from the least, light ill?
How gladly I had borne your pain.
With one great pulse we seem'd to thrill,—   40
Nay, but we thrill'd with pulses twain.

Even if one had told me this,
"A poison lurks within your kiss,
Gall that shall turn to night his day:"
Thereon I straight had turned away—
Ay, tho' my heart had crack'd with pain—
And never kiss'd your lips again.

At night, or when the daylight nears,
I hear the other women weep;
My own heart's anguish lies too deep   50
For the soft rain and pain of tears.
I think my heart has turn'd to stone,
A dull, dead weight that hurts my breast;
Here, on my pallet-bed alone,
I keep apart from all the rest.
Wide-eyed I lie upon my bed,
I often cannot sleep all night;
The future and the past are dead,
There is no thought can bring delight.

All night I lie and think and think;   60
If my heart were not made of stone,
But flesh and blood, it needs must shrink
Before such thoughts. Was ever known
A woman with a heart of stone?

The doctor says that I shall die.
It may be so, yet what care I?
Endless reposing from the strife?
Death do I trust no more than life.
For one thing is like one arrayed,
And there is neither false nor true;   70
But in a hideous masquerade
All things dance on, the ages through.
And good is evil, evil good;
Nothing is known or understood
Save only Pain. I have no faith
In God or Devil, Life or Death.

The doctor says that I shall die.
You, that I knew in days gone by,
I fain would see your face once more,
Con well its features o'er and o'er;   80
And touch your hand and feel your kiss,
Look in your eyes and tell you this:
That all is done, that I am free;
That you, through all eternity,
Have neither part nor lot in me.

                                                                1884

A Farewell

(*After Heine*[1])

The sad rain falls from Heaven,
A sad bird pipes and sings;
I am sitting here at my window
And watching the spires of "King's."[2]

O fairest of all fair places,
Sweetest of all sweet towns!
With the birds, and the greyness and greenness,
And the men in caps and gowns.[3]

---

[1]Heinrich **Heine** (1797–1856): German-Jewish poet.

[2]"King's": King's College, Cambridge.

[3]caps and gowns: worn by members of the university, including undergraduates.

All they that dwell within thee,
   To leave are ever loth,   10
For one man gets friends, and another
   Gets honour, and one gets both.

The sad rain falls from Heaven;
   My heart is great with woe—
I have neither a friend nor honour,
   Yet I am sorry to go.

                     1884

On the Threshold

O God, my dream! I dreamed that you were dead;
Your mother hung above the couch and wept
Whereon you lay all white, and garlanded
With blooms of waxen whiteness. I had crept
Up to your chamber-door, which stood ajar,
And in the doorway watched you from afar,
Nor dared advance to kiss your lips and brow.
I had no part nor lot in you, as now;
Death had not broken between us the old bar;
Nor torn from out my heart the old, cold sense   10
Of your misprision and my impotence.

                     1889

A Reminiscence

It is so long gone by, and yet
   How clearly now I see it all!
The glimmer of your cigarette,
   The little chamber, narrow and tall.

Perseus,[1] your picture in its frame;
   (How near they seem and yet how far!)
The blaze of kindled logs; the flame
   Of tulips in a mighty jar.

Florence and spring-time: surely each
   Glad things unto the spirit saith.   10
Why did you lead me in your speech
   To these dark mysteries of death?

                     1889

---

[1]Perseus: statue by Benvenuto Cellini in Florence, where Levy visited with friends in 1885.

The Old House

In through the porch and up the silent stair;
   Little is changed, I know so well the
      ways;—
Here, the dead came to meet me; it was there
   The dream was dreamed in unforgotten
      days.

But who is this that hurries on before,
   A flitting shade the brooding shades among?—
She turned,—I saw her face,—O God, it wore
   The face I used to wear when I was young!

I thought my spirit and my heart were tamed
   To deadness; dead the pangs that agonise.   10
The old grief springs to choke me.—I am shamed
   Before that little ghost with eager eyes.

O turn away, let her not see, not know!
   How should she bear it, how should
      understand?
O hasten down the stairway, haste and go,
   And leave her dreaming in the silent land.

                     1889

London in July

What ails my senses thus to cheat?
   What is it ails the place,
That all the people in the street
   Should wear one woman's face?

The London trees are dusty-brown
   Beneath the summer sky;
My love, she dwells in London town,
   Nor leaves it in July.

O various and intricate maze,
   Wide waste of square and street;   10
Where, missing through unnumbered days,
   We twain at last may meet!

And who cries out on crowd and mart?
   Who prates of stream and sea?
The summer in the city's heart—
   That is enough for me.

                     1889

A Ballad of Religion and Marriage[1]

Swept into limbo is the host
    Of heavenly angels, row on row;
The Father, Son, and Holy Ghost,
    Pale and defeated, rise and go.
The great Jehovah is laid low,
    Vanished his burning bush and rod—
Say, are we doomed to deeper woe?
    Shall marriage go the way of God?

Monogamous, still at our post,
    Reluctantly we undergo   10
Domestic round of boiled and roast,
    Yet deem the whole proceeding slow.

Daily the secret murmurs grow;
    We are no more content to plod
Along the beaten paths—and so
    Marriage must go the way of God.

Soon, before all men, each shall toast
    The seven strings unto his bow,[2]
Like beacon fires along the coast,
    The flames of love shall glance and glow.   20
Nor let nor hindrance man shall know,
    From natal bath to funeral sod;
Perennial shall his pleasures flow
    When marriage goes the way of God.

Grant, in a million years at most,
    Folk shall be neither pairs nor odd—
Alas! we sha'n't be there to boast
    "Marriage has gone the way of God!"

1915

---

[1]**Ballad of . . . Marriage**: printed in an edition of 12 copies "for private circulation" after Levy's death.

[2]To have two **strings** to one's **bow** is, proverbially, to have two lovers.

WILLIAM BUTLER YEATS

(1865–1939)

Many readers consider Yeats the greatest English-language poet of the twentieth century, yet he also deserves notice as a twilight luminary of Victorianism. Anglo-Irish by descent and upbringing—as a boy he moved often with his family to and from Dublin, London, and Sligo on the Irish west coast—Yeats grew up in the bohemian milieu that his father, a painter, had embraced when throwing over the law for art. The young Yeats stayed young a long time, seeking a vocation in art school and in the writing of verses, ransacking imaginative and spiritual literature for something to believe in, dabbling in the theosophical, mystical practices that late-Victorian seekers pieced together from the world's traditions. He was also given to courting beautiful and unattainable women, notably Maud Gonne, whom he met in 1889 and to whom he directly or indirectly wrote love poetry for much of his life. Her fiery nationalism kindled his earlier study of Celtic folkways into a smoldering political flame, which brought him into the public arena at a critical juncture in Irish history: he organized literary societies among the nationalist Fenians and involved himself in the founding and management of the national Abbey Theatre; he became a senator of the Irish Free State in 1922, and in the next year won Ireland its first Nobel Prize for literature. Little of this spotlighted public life enters the poems Yeats wrote during the 1880s and 1890s, which remain fine flowers of the Decadent and Symbolist poetics that his associate Arthur Symons was then articulating (see page 148). Lyrics of passionate unfulfillment, oblivious or disdainful of politics and commerce, they reject the discursive introspection of earlier Victorian verse and fix their emotion in elementary, evocative images, set against a deliberately simplified mythic or pastoral background. Exquisite in itself, the Victorian poetry of Yeats is also important for literary history, looking back through PreRaphaelitism to the Romantic sensuousness of early Tennyson, and ahead to the twentieth-century modernism that thought it could sweep Victorian poetics under the carpet.

The Falling of the Leaves

Autumn is over the long leaves that love us,
And over the mice in the barley sheaves;
Yellow the leaves of the rowan above us,
And yellow the wet wild-strawberry leaves.
The hour of the waning of love has beset us,
And weary and worn are our sad souls now;
Let us part, ere the season of passion forget us,
With a kiss and a tear on thy drooping brow.

1889

The Lake Isle of Innisfree

I will arise and go now, and go to Innisfree,[1]
And a small cabin build there, of clay and wattles[2] made:

---

[1]**Innisfree:** island in Lough Gill, Sligo, associated with fairy folklore.

[2]**wattles:** interwoven twigs. Yeats modeled this fancied retreat on his reading of Thoreau's *Walden* (1854).

Nine bean-rows will I have there, a hive for the honey-bee,
And live alone in the bee-loud glade.

And I shall have some peace there, for peace comes
    dropping slow,
Dropping from the veils of the morning to where the
    cricket sings;
There midnight's all a glimmer, and noon a purple glow,
And evening full of the linnet's wings.

I will arise and go now, for always night and day
I hear lake water lapping with low sounds by the shore; 10
While I stand on the roadway, or on the pavements grey,
I hear it in the deep heart's core.

                              1890

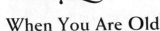

When You Are Old

When you[1] are old and grey and full of sleep,
And nodding by the fire, take down this book,
And slowly read, and dream of the soft look
Your eyes had once, and of their shadows deep;

How many loved your moments of glad grace,
And loved your beauty with love false or true,
But one man loved the pilgrim soul in you,
And loved the sorrows of your changing face;

And bending down beside the glowing bars,
Murmur, a little sadly, how Love fled   10
And paced upon the mountains overhead
And hid his face amid a crowd of stars.

                              1892

Who Goes with Fergus?

Who will go drive with Fergus[1] now,
And pierce the deep wood's woven shade,
And dance upon the level shore?

---

[1]**you:** in the first instance, Maud Gonne (1865–1953), although the poem is based on a courtly love sonnet by French poet Pierre Ronsard (1524–1585).

[1]**Fergus:** legendary king of Ulster in N Ireland, who has just added to his practical statecraft the contrary powers of a poetic visionary.

Young man, lift up your russet brow,
And lift your tender eyelids, maid,
And brood on hopes and fear no more.

And no more turn aside and brood
Upon love's bitter mystery;
For Fergus rules the brazen cars,
And rules the shadows of the wood,   10
And the white breast of the dim sea
And all dishevelled wandering stars.

                              1892

The Song of Wandering Aengus[1]

I went out to the hazel wood,
Because a fire was in my head,
And cut and peeled a hazel wand,
And hooked a berry to a thread;
And when white moths were on the wing,
And moth-like stars were flickering out,
I dropped the berry in a stream
And caught a little silver trout.

When I had laid it on the floor
I went to blow the fire aflame,   10
But something rustled on the floor,
And some one called me by my name:
It had become a glimmering girl
With apple blossom in her hair
Who called me by my name and ran
And faded through the brightening air.

Though I am old with wandering
Through hollow lands and hilly lands,
I will find out where she has gone,
And kiss her lips and take her hands;   20
And walk among long dappled grass,
And pluck till time and times are done
The silver apples of the moon,
The golden apples of the sun.

                              1897

---

[1]**Aengus:** god of love, youth, and poetry.

He Hears the Cry of the Sedge

I wander by the edge
Of this desolate lake
Where wind cries in the sedge:
Until the axle break
That keeps the stars in their round,
And hands hurl in the deep
The banners of East and West,
And the girdle¹ of light is unbound,
Your breast will not lie by the breast
Of your beloved in sleep.   10

1898

He Wishes for the Cloths
of Heaven

Had I the heavens' embroidered cloths,
Enwrought with golden and silver light,
The blue and the dim and the dark cloths
Of night and light and the half-light,
I would spread the cloths under your feet:
But I, being poor, have only my dreams;
I have spread my dreams under your feet;
Tread softly because you tread on my dreams.

1899

---

¹**axle, banners, girdle**: cosmological images drawn from no specific myth; their undoing signifies the end of the world.

The Cap and Bells

The jester walked in the garden:
The garden had fallen still;
He bade his soul rise upward
And stand on her window-sill.

It rose in a straight blue garment,
When owls began to call:
It had grown wise-tongued by thinking
Of a quiet and light footfall;

But the young queen would not listen;
She rose in her pale night-gown;   10
She drew in the heavy casement
And pushed the latches down.

He bade his heart go to her,
When the owls called out no more;
In a red and quivering garment
It sang to her through the door.

It had grown sweet-tongued by dreaming
Of a flutter of flower-like hair;
But she took up her fan from the table
And waved it off on the air.   20

"I have cap and bells," he pondered,
"I will send them to her and die";
And when the morning whitened
He left them where she went by.

She laid them upon her bosom,
Under a cloud of her hair,
And her red lips sang them a love-song
Till stars grew out of the air.

She opened her door and her window,
And the heart and the soul came through,   30
To her right hand came the red one,
To her left hand came the blue.

They set up a noise like crickets,
A chattering wise and sweet,
And her hair was a folded flower
And the quiet of love in her feet.

1899

RUDYARD KIPLING

(1865–1936)

Poet of Empire, spokesman for imperialist ideology, and author of stories that brought India magically alive for English readers, Rudyard Kipling took as his imaginative territory the borderlands of nation, race, class, and (in children's stories) species. He was born of English parents in Bombay, where his father had just taken a position as artist-craftsman at a school. His first six years were spent in what seemed retrospectively like paradise: living mostly among Indian servants, he spoke Hindi, saw the city with them, and listened to their songs and tales. Then, as was customary, his parents sent him and his younger sister "home" to England, where for the next six years they lived with a couple who treated Rudyard with exceptional cruelty. After that he spent happier times with his relatives (who included Edward Burne-Jones, a leading PreRaphaelite painter, and Stanley Baldwin, a cousin his own age who became Prime Minister) and attended a military prep school. In 1882 he rejoined his parents and sister in India, where he worked for a newspaper and began publishing poems and tales about Anglo-Indian life. He left India in 1888, bearing with him the inspiration for most of his best work, above all his enduringly popular stories for or about children: the *Jungle Books* (1894–1895), tales of a boy who is raised in India by wolves; the funny, incantatory creation myths of the *Just-So Stories* (1902); and *Kim* (1901), a novel about an Irish orphan who roams through India with eager observation and delight.

Barrack-Room Ballads (1892), speaking for the good-natured, patriotic, and sometimes sardonic common soldier ("Tommy"), was an immense popular success, and for the rest of his life Kipling enjoyed the kind of instant international celebrity that developing networks of communication had just begun to make possible. Many of his lines became enduringly famous: "The female of the species is more deadly than the male"; "East is East and West is West, and never the twain shall meet"; and the bluff and bracing "If you can keep your head when all about you / Are losing theirs and blaming it on you . . . You'll be a Man, my son." His poems often started as a melody in his head, and some, set to music, were sung for generations; their literary antecedents are Browning and Swinburne, their context the popular music hall. T. S. Eliot praised his "consummate gift of word, phrase, and rhythm." Kipling also produced some fine lesser-known prose works, unmarked by the strident imperialist ideology for which he was both adulated and despised. He became increasingly bellicose and reactionary, however, and after the controversial Boer War (1899–1902), which he fervently supported, his popularity declined. He had already become an object of derision among liberals and intellectuals, who could see no literary merit in work that was so outrageously popular and supported all the worst ideas. Fame and honors continued to accrue to him, however, culminating in 1907 with an Oxford doctorate and the Nobel Prize for literature.

The Ballad of East and West

Oh, East is East, and West is West, and never the twain shall meet,
Till Earth and Sky stand presently at God's great Judgment Seat;
But there is neither East nor West, Border, nor Breed, nor Birth,
When two strong men stand face to face, tho' they come from the ends of
the earth!

Kamal is out with twenty men to raise the Border side,
And he has lifted the Colonel's mare that is the Colonel's
pride:
He has lifted her out of the stable-door between the dawn
and the day,
And turned the calkins[1] upon her feet, and ridden her far
away.
Then up and spoke the Colonel's son that led a troop of
the Guides:[2]
"Is there never a man of all my men can say where Kamal
hides?"   10
Then up and spoke Mahommed Khan, the son of the
Ressaldar,[3]
"If ye know the track of the morning-mist, ye know where
his pickets are.
At dusk he harries the Abazai—[4]at dawn he is into Bonair,
But he must go by Fort Bukloh to his own place to fare,
So if ye gallop to Fort Bukloh as fast as a bird can fly,
By the favour of God ye may cut him off ere he win to the
Tongue of Jagai,
But if he be passed the Tongue of Jagai, right swiftly turn
ye then,
For the length and the breadth of that grisly plain is sown
with Kamal's men.
There is rock to the left, and rock to the right, and low lean
thorn between,
And ye may hear a breech-bolt snick where never a man
is seen."   20
The Colonel's son has taken a horse, and a raw rough dun
was he,

With the mouth of a bell and the heart of Hell, and the
head of the gallows-tree.
The Colonel's son to the Fort has won, they bid him stay
to eat—
Who rides at the tail of a Border thief, he sits not long at
his meat.
He's up and away from Fort Bukloh as fast as he can fly,
Till he was aware of his father's mare in the gut of the
Tongue of Jagai,
Till he was aware of his father's mare with Kamal upon
her back,
And when he could spy the white of her eye, he made the
pistol crack.
He has fired once, he has fired twice, but the whistling ball
went wide.
"Ye shoot like a soldier," Kamal said. "Show now if ye can
ride."   30
It's up and over the Tongue of Jagai, as blown dust-devils
go,
The dun he fled like a stag of ten, but the mare like a
barren doe.
The dun he leaned against the bit and slugged his head
above,
But the red mare played with the snaffle-bars, as a maiden
plays with a glove.
There was rock to the left and rock to the right, and low
lean thorn between,
And thrice he heard a breech-bolt snick tho' never a man
was seen.
They have ridden the low moon out of the sky, their hoofs
drum up the dawn,
The dun he went like a wounded bull, but the mare like a
new-roused fawn.
The dun he fell at a water-course—in a woful heap
fell he,
And Kamal has turned the red mare back, and pulled the
rider free.   40
He has knocked the pistol out of his hand—small room
was there to strive,
"'Twas only by favour of mine," quoth he, "ye rode so long
alive:
There was not a rock for twenty mile, there was not a
clump of tree,
But covered a man of my own men with his rifle cocked on
his knee.
If I had raised my bridle-hand, as I have held it low,
The little jackals that flee so fast, were feasting all in a row:
If I had bowed my head on my breast, as I have held it
high,

---

[1]**calkins:** edges of horseshoes, reversed to confuse pursuers.

[2]**Guides:** highly decorated corps of mostly native soldiers in British India.

[3]**Ressaldar:** native captain in an Indian cavalry regiment.

[4]**Abazai, Bonair, Fort Bukloh, Tongue of Jagai, Peshawur, Khyber:** points of military importance leading from the British headquarters to a native stronghold.

The kite that whistles above us now were gorged till she
    could not fly."
Lightly answered the Colonel's son:—"Do good to bird
    and beast,
But count who come for the broken meats before thou
    makest a feast.   50
If there should follow a thousand swords to carry my
    bones away,
Belike the price of a jackal's meal were more than a thief
    could pay.
They will feed their horse on the standing crop, their men
    on the garnered grain,
The thatch of the byres will serve their fires when all the
    cattle are slain.
But if thou thinkest the price be fair,—thy brethren wait
    to sup,
The hound is kin to the jackal-spawn,—howl, dog, and
    call them up!
And if thou thinkest the price be high, in steer and gear
    and stack,
Give me my father's mare again, and I'll fight my own
    way back!"
Kamal has gripped him by the hand and set him upon
    his feet.
"No talk shall be of dogs," said he, "when wolf and grey
    wolf meet.   60
May I eat dirt if thou hast hurt of me in deed or breath;
What dam of lances brought thee forth to jest at the dawn
    with Death?"
Lightly answered the Colonel's son: "I hold by the blood
    of my clan:
Take up the mare for my father's gift—by God, she has
    carried a man!"
The red mare ran to the Colonel's son, and nuzzled against
    his breast,
"We be two strong men," said Kamal then, "but she loveth
    the younger best.
So she shall go with a lifter's dower, my turquoise-studded
    rein,
My broidered saddle and saddle-cloth, and silver stirrups
    twain."
The Colonel's son a pistol drew and held it muzzle-end,
"Ye have taken the one from a foe," said he; "will ye take
    the mate from a friend?"   70
"A gift for a gift," said Kamal straight; "a limb for the risk of
    a limb.
Thy father has sent his son to me, I'll send my son to him!"
With that he whistled his only son, that dropped from a
    mountain-crest—

He trod the ling[5] like a buck in spring, and he looked like
    a lance in rest.
"Now here is thy master," Kamal said, "who leads a troop of
    the Guides,
And thou must ride at his left side as shield on shoulder
    rides.
Till Death or I cut loose the tie, at camp and board and
    bed,
Thy life is his—thy fate it is to guard him with
    thy head.
So thou must eat the White Queen's meat, and all her foes
    are thine,
And thou must harry thy father's hold for the peace of
    the Border-line,   80
And thou must make a trooper tough and hack thy way
    to power—
Belike they will raise thee to Ressaldar when I am hanged in
    Peshawur."

They have looked each other between the eyes, and there
    they found no fault,
They have taken the Oath of the Brother-in-Blood on
    leavened bread and salt:
They have taken the Oath of the Brother-in-Blood on fire
    and fresh-cut sod,
On the hilt and the haft of the Khyber knife, and the
    Wondrous Names of God.
The Colonel's son he rides the mare and Kamal's boy
    the dun,
And two have come back to Fort Bukloh where there went
    forth but one.
And when they drew to the Quarter-Guard, full twenty
    swords flew clear—
There was not a man but carried his feud with the blood
    of the mountaineer.   60
"Ha' done! ha' done!" said the Colonel's son. "Put up the
    steel at your sides!
Last night ye had struck at a Border thief—tonight 'tis a
    man of the Guides!"

Oh, East is East, and West is West, and never the two shall meet,
Till Earth and Sky stand presently at God's great Judgment Seat;
But there is neither East nor West, Border, nor Breed, nor Birth,
When two strong men stand face to face, tho' they come from the ends
    of the earth.

                   1889, 1893

---

[5]**ling:** heather.

Mandalay

By the old Moulmein[1] Pagoda, lookin' eastward to
   the sea,
There's a Burma girl a-settin', and I know she thinks o' me;
For the wind is in the palm-trees, and the temple-bells
   they say:
"Come you back, you British soldier; come you back to
   Mandalay!"
     Come you back to Mandalay,
     Where the old Flotilla lay:
     Can't you 'ear their paddles chunkin' from Rangoon
       to Mandalay?
     On the road to Mandalay,
     Where the flyin'-fishes play,
     An' the dawn comes up like thunder outer China
       'crost the Bay!   10

'Er petticoat was yaller an' 'er little cap was green,
An' 'er name was Supi-yaw-lat—jes' the same as Theebaw's[2]
   Queen,
An' I seed her first a-smokin' of a whackin' white cheroot,
An' a-wastin' Christian kisses on an 'eathen idol's foot:
     Bloomin' idol made o' mud—
     Wot they called the Great Gawd Budd[3]—
     Plucky lot she cared for idols when I kissed 'er
       where she stud!
     On the road to Mandalay . . .

When the mist was on the rice-fields an' the sun was
   droppin' slow,
She'd git 'er little banjo an' she'd sing *"Kulla-lo-lo!"*   20
With 'er arm upon my shoulder an' 'er cheek agin'
   my cheek
We useter watch the steamers an' the *hathis*[4] pilin' teak.
     Elephints a-pilin' teak
     In the sludgy, squdgy creek,
     Where the silence 'ung that 'eavy you was 'arf afraid
       to speak!
     On the road to Mandalay . . .

---

[1]**Moulmein, Mandalay, Rangoon:** towns in **Burma** (modern
Myanmar). **Flotilla:** fleet of small boats.

[2]**Theebaw** (Thibaw): king of Burma (1878–1885), whose rule
ended when Britain annexed Burma.

[3]**Budd:** Buddha.

[4]*hathis:* elephants.

But that's all shove be'ind me—long ago an' fur away,
An' there ain't no 'busses runnin' from the Bank to
   Mandalay;
An' I'm learnin' 'ere in London what the ten-year
   soldier tells:
"If you've 'eard the East a-callin', you won't never 'eed
   naught else."   30
     No! you won't 'eed nothin' else
     But them spicy garlic smells,
     An' the sunshine an' the palm-trees an' the tinkly
       temple-bells;
     On the road to Mandalay . . .

I am sick o' wastin' leather on these gritty pavin'-stones,
An' the blasted Henglish drizzle wakes the fever in
   my bones;
Tho' I walks with fifty 'ousemaids outer Chelsea to
   the Strand,
An' they talks a lot o' lovin', but wot do they understand?
     Beefy face an' grubby 'and—
     Law! wot do they understand?   40
     I've a neater, sweeter maiden in a cleaner, greener
       land!
     On the road to Mandalay . . .

Ship me somewheres east of Suez, where the best is like
   the worst,
Where there aren't no Ten Commandments an' a man
   can raise a thirst;
For the temple-bells are callin', an' it's there that I would be—
By the old Moulmein Pagoda, looking lazy at the sea;
     On the road to Mandalay,
     Where the old Flotilla lay,
     With our sick beneath the awnings when we went
       to Mandalay!
     On the road to Mandalay,   50
     Where the flyin'-fishes play,
     An' the dawn comes up like thunder outer China
       'crost the Bay!

                  1890, 1892

Tommy

I went into a public-'ouse to get a pint o' beer,
The publican' e up an' sez, "We serve no red-coats here."
The girls be'ind the bar they laughed an' giggled fit to die,
I outs into the street again an' to myself sez I:

O it's Tommy this, an' Tommy that, an' "Tommy,
    go away";
But it's "Thank you, Mister Atkins," when the band
    begins to play,
The band begins to play, my boys, the band begins
    to play,
O it's "Thank you, Mister Atkins," when the band
    begins to play.

I went into a theatre as sober as could be,
They gave a drunk civilian room, but 'adn't none for me;   10
They sent me to the gallery or round the music-'alls,
But when it comes to fightin', Lord! they'll shove me in
    the stalls!
    For it's Tommy this, an' Tommy that, an' "Tommy,
        wait outside";
    But it's "Special train for Atkins" when the trooper's
        on the tide,
    The troopship's on the tide, my boys, the troopship's
        on the tide,
    O it's "Special train for Atkins" when the trooper's on
        the tide.

Yes, makin' mock o' uniforms that guard you while you
    sleep
Is cheaper than them uniforms, an' they're starvation
    cheap;
An' hustlin' drunken soldiers when they're goin' large a bit
Is five times better business than paradin' in full kit.   20
    Then it's Tommy this, an' Tommy that, an' "Tommy,
        'ow's yer soul?"
    But it's "Thin red line of 'eroes" when the drums
        begin to roll,
    The drums begin to roll, my boys, the drums begin
        to roll,
    O it's "Thin red line of 'eroes" when the drums begin
        to roll.

We aren't no thin red 'eroes, nor we aren't no blackguards
    too,
But single men in barricks, most remarkable like you;
An' if sometimes our conduck isn't all your fancy paints,
Why, single men in barricks don't grow into plaster saints;
    While it's Tommy this, an' Tommy that, an' "Tommy,
        fall be'ind,"
    But it's "Please to walk in front, sir," when there's
        trouble in the wind,   30
    There's trouble in the wind, my boys, there's trouble
        in the wind,
    O it's "Please to walk in front, sir," when there's
        trouble in the wind.

You talk o' better food for us, an' schools, an' fires, an' all:
We'll wait for extry rations if you treat us rational.
Don't mess about the cook-room slops, but prove it to
    our face
The Widow's Uniform is not the soldier-man's disgrace.
    For it's Tommy this, an' Tommy that, an' "Chuck him
        out, the brute!"
    But it's "Saviour of 'is country" when the guns begin
        to shoot;
    An' it's Tommy this, an' Tommy that, an' anything
        you please;
    An' Tommy ain't a bloomin' fool—you bet that Tommy
        sees!   40
                  1890, 1892

The Widow at Windsor

'Ave you 'eard o' the Widow at Windsor[1]
    With a hairy gold crown on 'er 'ead?
She 'as ships on the foam—she 'as millions at 'ome,
    An' she pays us poor beggars in red.
        (Ow, poor beggars in red!)
There's 'er nick on the cavalry 'orses,
    There's 'er mark on the medical stores—
An' 'er troopers you'll find with a fair wind be'ind
    That takes us to various wars.
        (Poor beggars!—barbarious wars!)   10
        Then 'ere's to the Widow at Windsor,
           An' 'ere's to the stores an' the guns,
        The men an' the 'orses what makes up the forces
           O' Missis Victorier's sons.
        (Poor beggars! Victorier's sons!)

Walk wide o' the Widow at Windsor,
    For 'alf o' Creation she owns:
We 'ave bought 'er the same with the sword an' the flame,
    An' we've salted it down with our bones.
        (Poor beggars!—it's blue with our bones!)   20
Hands off o' the sons o' the Widow,
    Hands off o' the goods in 'er shop,
For the Kings must come down an' the Emperors frown
    When the Widow at Windsor says "Stop!"
        (Poor beggars!—we're sent to say "Stop!")

---

[1]**Windsor**: Royal Castle W of London.

Then 'ere's to the Lodge o' the Widow,
    From the Pole to the Tropics it runs—
To the Lodge that we tile with the rank an'
        the file,
    An' open in form with the guns.
        (Poor beggars!—it's always they guns!)   30

We 'ave 'eard o' the Widow at Windsor,
    It's safest to let 'er alone:
For 'er sentries we stand by the sea an' the land
    Wherever the bugles are blown.
        (Poor beggars!—an' don't we get blown!)
Take 'old o' the Wings o' the Mornin',
    An' flop round the earth till you're dead;
But you won't get away from the tune that they play
    To the bloomin' old rag over'ead.
        (Poor beggars!—it's 'ot over'ead!)   40
    Then 'ere's to the sons o' the Widow,
        Wherever, 'owever they roam.
    'Ere's all they desire, an' if they require
        A speedy return to their 'ome.
        (Poor beggars!—they'll never see 'ome!)
                                    1890, 1892

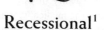

Recessional[1]

God of our fathers, known of old,
    Lord of our far-flung battle-line,
Beneath whose awful Hand we hold
    Dominion over palm and pine—
Lord God of Hosts, be with us yet,
Lest we forget—lest we forget![2]

The tumult and the shouting dies;
    The captains and the kings depart:
Still stands Thine ancient sacrifice,
    An humble and a contrite heart.[3]   10
Lord God of Hosts, be with us yet,
Lest we forget—lest we forget!

Far-called, our navies melt away;
    On dune and headland sinks the fire:
Lo, all our pomp of yesterday
    Is one with Nineveh and Tyre![4]
Judge of the Nations, spare us yet,
Lest we forget—lest we forget!

If, drunk with sight of power, we loose
    Wild tongues that have not Thee in awe,   20
Such boastings as the Gentiles use,
    Or lesser breeds without the Law[5]—
Lord God of Hosts, be with us yet,
Lest we forget—lest we forget!

For heathen heart that puts her trust
    In reeking tube and iron shard,
All valiant dust that builds on dust,
    And guarding, calls not Thee to guard,
For frantic boast and foolish word—
Thy Mercy on Thy People, Lord!
                            Amen.   30
                        1897, 1903

The White Man's Burden[1]

Take up the White Man's burden—
    Send forth the best ye breed—
Go bind your sons to exile
    To serve your captives' need;
To wait in heavy harness,
    On fluttered folk and wild—
Your new-caught, sullen peoples,
    Half-devil and half-child.

Take up the White Man's burden—
    In patience to abide,   10
To veil the threat of terror
    And check the show of pride;

---

[1]Recessional: hymn sung at the end of a church service. Published in the year of Victoria's Diamond Jubilee (60th year on the throne).

[2]lest we forget: see Deuteronomy 6:12.

[3]humble . . . heart: Psalms 51:17.

[4]Nineveh and Tyre: cities in ancient Assyria and Phoenicia.

[5]Gentiles, in Romans 2:14, "have not the law." lesser breeds: colonialist rivals.

[1]White Man's Burden: phrase that became current in the controversy about the U.S. acquisition of the Philippines after the Spanish–American war of 1898.

By open speech and simple,
    An hundred times made plain,
To seek another's profit,
    And work another's gain.

Take up the White Man's burden—
    The savage wars of peace—
Fill full the mouth of Famine
    And bid the sickness cease.   20
And when your goal is nearest
    The end for others sought,
Watch Sloth and heathen Folly
    Bring all your hope to naught.

Take up the White Man's burden—
    No tawdry rule of kings,
But toil of serf and sweeper—
    The tale of common things.
The ports ye shall not enter,
    The roads ye shall not tread,   30
Go make them with your living,
    And mark them with your dead.

Take up the White Man's burden—
    And reap his old reward:
The blame of those ye better,
    The hate of those ye guard—

The cry of hosts ye humour
    (Ah, slowly!) toward the light:—
"Why brought ye us from bondage,
    Our loved Egyptian night?"[2]   40

Take up the White Man's burden—
    Ye dare not stoop to less—
Nor call too loud on Freedom
    To cloak your weariness;
By all ye cry or whisper,
    By all ye leave or do,
The silent, sullen peoples
    Shall weigh your Gods and you.

Take up the White Man's burden—
    Have done with childish days—   50
The lightly proffered laurel,
    The easy, ungrudged praise.
Comes now, to search your manhood
    Through all the thankless years,
Cold, edged with dear-bought wisdom,
    The judgment of your peers!

1899, 1903

---

[2]**Egyptian night:** see Exodus 16:2–3.

ERNEST DOWSON

(1867–1900)

Both the world-weary, enervated music of Ernest Dowson's verse and his melancholy, drifting, often sordid way of life seemed to epitomize the English Decadent movement as it faded out at the century's end. Dowson knew French literature—from which English Decadent authors drew examples and sustenance—better than English, having spent much of his youth in France because of his father's failing health. He also developed an enthusiasm for Latin poetry that proved useful at Oxford, for which his total lack of formal schooling had left him otherwise ill prepared. Having left Oxford without a degree, he spent his days working as bookkeeper for the family's failing business (a drydock on the Thames) and his nights in bohemian London. He succumbed to alcohol, frequented prostitutes, published some poems that gained some recognition, and like many other Decadent artists converted to Catholicism. He also fell in love with a girl barely in her teens, the daughter of an immigrant restaurant keeper, and to his friends' dismay declared his intention to marry her when she grew up even though she showed little interest in marrying him. By the time he was twenty-seven the long-declining family business had foundered, both his parents had died (his father probably, his mother certainly a suicide), and he had contracted tuberculosis.

Dowson spent much of his time thereafter on the continent, especially in Paris, occasionally producing poems, stories, or translations to keep himself from absolute penury. He still drank too much, ate and washed too little, and haunted shabby and disreputable places. As his friend Arthur Symons, whose essays did much to define the Aesthetic and Decadent movements, rather unkindly put it: "That curious love of the sordid, so common an affectation of the modern decadent, and with him so expressively genuine, grew upon him, and dragged him into yet more sorry corners." He met French writers and for a while spent time with Oscar Wilde in his post-prison exile, but as he grew ever poorer and sicker he cut himself off from old friends. The girl he loved grew up and married a waiter. Dowson returned to London, where a friend almost as poor as himself came upon him by chance and took him home to die.

Dowson published very little and is best known for a handful of elaborately wrought, inward-turning poems that draw on the pessimistic elegance of Latin poetry and the more immediately decadent literature of France. He refined his art within a narrow, almost monastically disciplined emotional range: a distillation of Swinburne without the will to shock, Levy without bitterness, Hardy without irony. He is remembered in popular culture by phrases epitomizing a single chord of feeling: the days of wine and roses, gone with the wind. "Yes," said Symons, summing up both Dowson and the fin-de-siècle that Dowson had come to represent, "in these few, evasive, immaterial snatches of song, I find, implied for the most part, hidden away like a secret, all the fever and turmoil and the unattained dreams of a life which has itself had much of the swift, disastrous, and suicidal energy of genius."

Non Sum Qualis Eram Bonae sub Regno Cynarae[1]

Last night, ah, yesternight, betwixt her lips and mine
There fell thy shadow, Cynara! thy breath was shed
Upon my soul between the kisses and the wine;
And I was desolate and sick of an old passion,
    Yea, I was desolate and bowed my head:
I have been faithful to thee, Cynara! in my fashion.

All night upon mine heart I felt her warm heart beat,
Night-long within mine arms in love and sleep she lay;
Surely the kisses of her bought red mouth were sweet;
But I was desolate and sick of an old passion,   10
    When I awoke and found the dawn was gray:
I have been faithful to thee, Cynara! in my fashion.

I have forgot much, Cynara! gone with the wind,
Flung roses, roses riotously with the throng,
Dancing, to put thy pale, lost lilies out of mind;
But I was desolate and sick of an old passion,
    Yea, all the time, because the dance was long:
I have been faithful to thee, Cynara! in my fashion.

I cried for madder music and for stronger wine,
But when the feast is finished and the lamps expire,   20
Then falls thy shadow, Cynara! the night is thine;
And I am desolate and sick of an old passion,
    Yea hungry for the lips of my desire:
I have been faithful to thee, Cynara! in my fashion.

                1891, 1896

Vitae Summa Brevis Spem Nos Vetat Incohare Longam[1]

They are not long, the weeping and the laughter,
    Love and desire and hate:
I think they have no portion in us after
    We pass the gate.

They are not long, the days of wine and roses:
    Out of a misty dream
Our path emerges for a while, then closes
    Within a dream.

                1896

Benedictio Domini[1]

Without, the sullen noises of the street!
    The voice of London, inarticulate,
Hoarse and blaspheming, surges in to meet
    The silent blessing of the Immaculate.[2]

Dark is the church, and dim the worshippers,
    Hushed with bowed heads as though by some
        old spell,
While through the incense-laden air there stirs
    The admonition of a silver bell.

Dark is the church, save where the altar stands,
    Dressed like a bride, illustrious with light,   10
Where one old priest exalts with tremulous hands
    The one true solace of man's fallen plight.

Strange silence here: without, the sounding street
    Heralds the world's swift passage to the fire:
O Benediction, perfect and complete!
    When shall men cease to suffer and desire?

                1896

Spleen[1]

I was not sorrowful, I could not weep,
And all my memories were put to sleep.

I watched the river grow more white and strange,
All day till evening I watched it change.

---

[1] **Benedictio Domini** (the blessing of the Lord): Benediction is a rite of Roman Catholicism.

[2] **the Immaculate:** the immaculately conceived Virgin Mary.

[1] **Spleen:** organ thought to cause melancholy. Charles Baudelaire (1821–1861) and Paul Verlaine (1844–1896), French poets who greatly influenced the English Decadent movement, both used this title for poems.

---

[1] **Non Sum . . . Cynarae:** I am not as I was under good Cynara's rule. Horace, *Odes* 4.1.3. **Cynara:** conventional name for a woman in Latin poetry.

[1] **Vitae Summa . . . Longam:** Life's short span forbids us to entertain long hopes. Horace, *Odes* 1.4.15.

All day till evening I watched the rain
Beat wearily upon the window pane.

I was not sorrowful, but only tired
Of everything that ever I desired.

Her lips, her eyes, all day became to me
The shadow of a shadow utterly.   10

All day mine hunger for her heart became
Oblivion, until the evening came,

And left me sorrowful, inclined to weep,
With all my memories that could not sleep.

1896

Villanelle[1] of the Poet's Road

Wine and woman and song,
    Three things garnish our way:
Yet is day over long.

Lest we do our youth wrong,
    Gather them while we may:
Wine and woman and song.

Three things render us strong,
    Vine leaves, kisses and bay;[2]
Yet is day over long.

---

[1]**Villanelle**: poem with five stanzas of three lines and a final quatrain, with only two rhymes.

[2]**bay**: leaves that crown poets.

Unto us they belong,   10
    Us the bitter and gay,
Wine and woman and song.

We, as we pass along,
    Are sad that they will not stay;
Yet is day over long.

Fruits and flowers among,
    What is better than they:
Wine and woman and song?
    Yet is day over long.

1899

A Last Word

Let us go hence: the night is now at hand;
The day is overworn, the birds all flown;
And we have reaped the crops the gods have sown;
Despair and death; deep darkness o'er the land,
Broods like an owl; we cannot understand
Laughter or tears, for we have only known
Surpassing vanity: vain things alone
Have driven our perverse and aimless band.
Let us go hence, somewhither strange and cold,
To Hollow Lands where just men and unjust   10
Find end of labour, where's rest for the old,
Freedom to all from love and fear and lust.
Twine our torn hands! O pray the earth enfold
Our life-sick hearts and turn them into dust.

1895, 1899

MAX BEERBOHM

(1872–1956)

The Incomparable Max—so George Bernard Shaw hailed his successor as London's major drama critic in 1898—belongs to the literary history of the twentieth century. His dainty coda "Diminuendo" appears here as light dessert for those who have feasted with Oscar Wilde and others on the special pleasures of Victorian belatedness—that is, on the elegant mischief that pinpoint irony can make with the ponderous legacy of nineteenth-century literature. A slightly younger generation of writers would create Modernism by dynamiting the Victorian mansion, rifling the remains, and building with them a literary architecture designed to look new from the ground up. Max Beerbohm, by contrast, stayed indoors, in what had dwindled to a modest suburban villa, and played with what he found there. Already in his twenties he had become "incomparable" in the arts of comparison itself, mocking the Victorians' pieties with their own voices, for which he had an unparalleled ear and a fastidious but genuine affection.

Like D. G. Rossetti (to whom he would return in a 1922 book), or Pater (chief figure of fun in "Diminuendo"), or Wilde (whose *Intentions* was the only book he admitted reading at Oxford), Beerbohm wrote under a keen, potentially disabling suspicion that the nineteenth-century mechanization and commodification of literary production had spoiled all the words, tropes, and plots. Like those earlier aesthetes he sought refuge, and expressive freedom, along a fine line of ambivalent elaboration, now parroting and now parodying mainstream models. Moreover, because these precursors had already succeeded, and attracted plodding imitators—because Beerbohm came along so very late in the belatedness game—he adopted the extreme, unrepeatable strategy of sheer ventriloquism: deadpan imitation of styles of writing and feeling that had gone comatose but that mockery with the right touch might yet tickle into fresh life. The sparkling decade of *Zuleika Dobson* (1911), *A Christmas Garland* (1912), and *Seven Men* (1919) lay ahead of him, but the appearance of "Diminuendo" in the twenty-four-year-old author's solemnly titled volume *The Works of Max Beerbohm* pointed the way. Speaking only in the voices of others, masked Max the pure *persona* told fin-de-siècle truth more faithfully than any shopworn sincerity could do.

Diminuendo[1]

In the year of grace 1890, and in the beautiful autumn of that year, I was a freshman at Oxford. I remember how

---

my tutor asked me what lectures I wished to attend, and how he laughed when I said that I wished to attend the lectures of Mr. Walter Pater. Also I remember how, one morning soon after, I went into Ryman's to order some foolish engraving for my room, and there saw, peering into a portfolio, a small, thick, rock-faced man, whose top-hat and gloves of *bright* dog-skin struck one of the many discords in that little city of learning or laughter. The serried bristles of his moustachio made for him a false-military air. I think I nearly went down when they told me that this was Pater.

Not that even in those more decadent days of my childhood did I admire the man as a stylist. Even then I was angry that he should treat English as a dead language, bored by that sedulous ritual wherewith he laid out every sentence as in a shroud—hanging, like a widower, long over its marmoreal beauty or ever he could lay it at length in his book, its sepulchre. From that laden air, the so cadaverous murmur of that sanctuary, I would hook it at the beck of any jade.[2] The writing of Pater had never, indeed, appealed to me, ἀλλ' αἰεί, having regard to the couth solemnity of his mind, to his philosophy, his rare erudition, τινα φῶτα μέγαν καὶ καλὸν ἐδέγμην.[3] And I suppose it was when at length I saw him that I first knew him to be fallible.

At school I had read *Marius the Epicurean*[4] in bed and with a dark lantern. Indeed, I regarded it mainly as a tale of adventure, quite as fascinating as *Midshipman Easy*,[5] and far less hard to understand, because there were no nautical terms in it. Marryat, moreover, never made me wish to run away to sea, whilst certainly Pater did make me wish for more "colour" in the curriculum, for a renaissance of the Farrar[6] period, when there was always "a sullen spirit of revolt against the authorities"; when lockers were always being broken into and marks falsified, and small boys prevented from saying their prayers, insomuch that they vowed they would no longer buy brandy for their seniors. In some schools, I am told, the pretty old custom of roasting a fourth-form boy, whole, upon Founder's Day[7] still survives. But in my school there was less sentiment. I ended by acquiescing in the slow revolution of its wheel of work and play. I felt that at Oxford, when I should be of age to matriculate, a "variegated dramatic life"[8] was waiting for me. I was not a little too sanguine, alas!

How sad was my coming to the university! Where were those sweet conditions I had pictured in my boyhood?

Those antique contrasts? Did I ride, one sunset, through fens on a palfrey, watching the gold reflections on Magdalen[9] Tower? Did I ride over Magdalen Bridge and hear the consonance of evening-bells and cries from the river below? Did I rein in to wonder at the raised gates of Queen's, the twisted pillars of St. Mary's, the little shops, lighted with tapers? Did bull-pups snarl at me, or dons, with bent backs, acknowledge my salute? Any one who knows the place as it is, must see that such questions are purely rhetorical. To him I need not explain the disappointment that beset me when, after being whirled in a cab from the station to a big hotel, I wandered out into the streets. *On aurait dit*[10] a bit of Manchester through which Apollo had once passed; for here, among the hideous trams and the brand-new bricks—here, glared at by the electric-lights that hung from poles, screamed at by boys with the *Echo* and the *Star*[11]—here, in a riot of vulgarity, were remnants of beauty, as I discerned. There were only remnants.

Soon also I found that the life of the place, like the place, had lost its charm and its tradition. Gone were the contrasts that made it wonderful. That feud between undergraduates and dons—latent, in the old days, only at times when it behoved the two academic grades to unite against the townspeople—was one of the absurdities of the past. The townspeople now looked just like undergraduates, and the dons just like townspeople. So splendid was the train-service between Oxford and London that, with hundreds of passengers daily, the one had become little better than a suburb of the other. What more could extensionists demand? As for me, I was disheartened. Bitter were the comparisons I drew between my coming to Oxford and the coming of Marius to Rome. Could it be that there was at length no beautiful environment wherein a man might sound the harmonies of his soul? Had civilization made beauty, besides adventure, so rare? I wondered what counsel Pater, insistent always upon contact with comely things, would offer to one who could nowhere find them. I had been wondering that very day when I went into Ryman's and saw him there.

When the tumult of my disillusioning was past, my mind grew clearer. I discerned that the scope of my quest for emotion must be narrowed. That abandonment of one's self to life, that merging of one's soul in bright waters, so often suggested in Pater's writing, were a counsel impossible

---

[2]**hook it**: run off. **beck**: provocation. **jade**: woman.

[3]τινα . . . ἐδέγμην: but always I expected some great and noble man (*Odyssey* 9.513).

[4]*Marius the Epicurean*: philosophical historical novel (1885) by Pater.

[5]*Mr. Midshipman Easy*: swashbuckling historical novel (1836) by Frederick **Marryat** (1792–1848).

[6]F. W. **Farrar** (1831–1903): schoolmaster at Harrow, author of moralistic school tale *Eric; or Little by Little* (1858).

[7]*Founder's Day*: boarding-school holiday.

[8]"**variegated dramatic life**": this and all subsequent quotations are from the "Conclusion" to Pater's *Renaissance* (see page 930).

[9]**Magdalen, Queen's, St. Mary's**: colleges at Oxford.

[10]*On aurait dit*: one would have said.

[11]*Echo, Star*: cheap newspapers.

for today. The quest of emotions must be no less keen, certainly, but the manner of it must be changed forthwith. To unswitch myself from my surroundings, to guard my soul from contact with the unlovely things that compassed it about, therein lay my hope. I must approach the Benign Mother[12] with great caution. And so, while most of the freshmen were doing her honor with wine and song and wreaths of smoke, I stood aside, pondered. In such seclusion I passed my first term—ah, how often did I wonder whether I was not wasting my days, and, wondering, abandon my meditations upon the right ordering of the future! Thanks be to Athene,[13] who threw her shadow over me in those moments of weak folly!

At the end of term I came to London. Around me seethed swirls, eddies, torrents, violent cross-currents of human activity. What uproar! Surely I could have no part in modern life. Yet, yet for a while, it was fascinating to watch the ways of its children. The prodigious life of the Prince of Wales[14] fascinated me above all; indeed, it still fascinates me. What experience has been withheld from His Royal Highness? Was ever so supernal a type, as he, of mere Pleasure? How often he has watched, at Newmarket,[15] the scud-a-run of quivering homuncules over the vert on horses, or, from some night-boat, the holocaust of great wharves by the side of the Thames; raced through the blue Solent; threaded *les coulisses!* He has danced in every palace of every capital, played in every club. He has hunted elephants through the jungles of India, boar through the forests of Austria, pigs over the plains of Massachusetts. From the Castle of Abergeldie[16] he has led his Princess into the frosty night, Highlanders lighting with torches the path to the deer-larder, where lay the wild things that had fallen to him on the crags. He has marched the Grenadiers to chapel through the white streets of Windsor. He has ridden through Moscow, in strange apparel, to kiss the catafalque of more than one Tzar. For him the Rajahs of India have spoiled their temples, and Blondin has crossed Niagara along the tightrope, and the Giant Guard done drill

beneath the chandeliers of the Neue Schloss.[17] Incline he to scandal, lawyers are proud to whisper their secrets in his ear. Be he gallant, the ladies are at his feet. *Ennuyé*, all the wits from Bernal Osborne to Arthur Roberts[18] have jested for him. He has been "present always at the focus where the greatest number of forces unite in their purest energy," for it is his presence that makes those forces unite.

"*Ennuyé?*" I asked. Indeed he never is. How could he be when Pleasure hangs constantly upon his arm! It is those others, overtaking her only after arduous chase, breathless and footsore, who quickly sicken of her company, and fall fainting at her feet. And for me, shod neither with rank nor riches, what folly to join the chase! I began to see how small a thing it were to sacrifice those external "experiences," so dear to the heart of Pater, by a rigid, complex civilization made so hard to gain. They gave nothing but lassitude to those who had gained them through suffering. Even to the kings and princes, who so easily gained them, what did they yield besides themselves? I do not suppose that, if we were invited to give authenticated instances of intelligence on the part of our royal pets, we could fill half a column of the *Spectator*.[19] In fact, their lives are so full they have no time for thought, the highest energy of man. Now, it was to thought that *my* life should be dedicated. Action, apart from its absorption of time, would war otherwise against the pleasures of intellect, which, for me, meant mainly the pleasures of imagination. It is only (this is a platitude) the things one has not done, the faces or places one has not seen, or seen but darkly, that have charm. It is only mystery—such mystery as besets the eyes of children—that makes things superb. I thought of the voluptuaries I had known—they seemed so sad, so ascetic almost, like poor pilgrims, raising their eyes never or ever gazing at the moon of tarnished endeavour. I thought of the round, insouciant faces of the monks at whose monastery I once broke bread, and how their eyes sparkled when they asked me of the France that lay around their walls. I thought, *pardie*,[20] of the lurid verses written by young men who, in real life, know no haunt more lurid than a literary public-house. It was, for me,

---

[12]**Benign Mother**: *alma mater*.

[13]**Athene**: goddess of wisdom, patroness of Odysseus.

[14]**Prince of Wales** (1841–1910): eldest son of Queen Victoria, the future Edward VII and a notorious playboy.

[15]**Newmarket**: race track. **homuncules**: miniature men (i.e., jockeys). **vert**: the green steeplechase course. **Solent**: strait of the English Channel between the mainland and the Isle of Wight. *les coulisses*: Channel currents known to yachters.

[16]**Abergeldie**: royal residence in Grampian mountains of Scotland.

[17]**Blondin**: stage name of Jean-François Gavelet (1824–1897), acrobat. **Giant Guard**: Prussian unit comprised of very tall soldiers. **Neue Schloss**: 14th-century castle in SW Germany.

[18]*Ennuyé*: bored. **Bernal Osborne** (1808–1882), **Arthur Roberts** (1810–1886): satirists.

[19]*Spectator*: Victorian highbrow journal, not its 18th-century namesake.

[20]*pardie*: mild, obsolete oath (from *par Dieu*, by God).

merely a problem how I could best avoid "sensations," "pulsations," and "exquisite moments" that were not purely intellectual. I would not attempt to combine both kinds, as Pater seemed to fancy a man might. I would make myself master of some small area of physical life, a life of quiet, monotonous simplicity, exempt from all outer disturbance. I would shield my body from the world that my mind might range over it, not hurt nor fettered. As yet, however, I was in my first year at Oxford. There were many reasons that I should stay there and take my degree, reasons that I did not combat. Indeed, I was content to wait for my life.

And now that I have made my adieux to the Benign Mother, I need wait no longer. I have been casting my eye over the suburbs of London. I have taken a most pleasant little villa in——ham, and here I shall make my home. Here there is no traffic, no harvest. Those of the inhabitants who do anything go away each morning and do it elsewhere. Here no vital forces unite. Nothing happens here. The days and the months will pass by me, bringing their sure recurrence of quiet events. In the spring-time I shall look out from my window and see the laburnum flowering in the little front garden. In summer cool syrups will come for me from the grocer's shop. Autumn will make the boughs of my mountain-ash scarlet, and, later, the asbestos in my grate will put forth its blossoms of flame. The infrequent cart of Buzzard or Mudie[21] will pass my window at all seasons. Nor will this be all. I shall have friends. Next door, there is a retired military man who has offered, in a most neighbourly way, to lend me his copy of the *Times*. On the other side of my house lives a charming family, who perhaps will call on me, now and again. I have seen them sally forth, at sundown, to catch the theatre-train; among them walked a young lady, the charm of whose figure was ill concealed by the neat water-proof that overspread her evening dress. Some day it may be . . . but I anticipate. These things will be but the cosy accompaniment of my days. For I shall contemplate the world.

I shall look forth from my window, the laburnum and the mountain-ash becoming mere silhouettes in the foreground of my vision. I shall look forth and, in my remoteness, appreciate the distant pageant of the world. Humanity will range itself in the columns of my morning paper. No pulse of life will escape me. The strife of politics, the intriguing of courts, the wreck of great vessels, wars, dramas, earthquakes, national griefs or joys; the strange sequels to divorces, even, and the mysterious suicides of land-agents at

Ipswich[22]—in all such phenomena I shall steep my exhaurient mind. *Delicias quoque bibliothecæ experiar.* Tragedy, comedy, chivalry, philosophy will be mine. I shall listen to their music perpetually and their colors will dance before my eyes. I shall soar from terraces of stone upon dragons with shining wings and make war upon Olympus. From the peaks of hills I shall swoop into recondite valleys and drive the pigmies, shrieking little curses, to their caverns. It may be my whim to wander through infinite parks where the deer lie under the clustering shadow of their antlers and flee lightly over the grass; to whisper with white prophets under the elms or bind a child with a daisy-chain or, with a lady, thread my way through the acacias. I shall swim down rivers into the sea and outstrip all ships. Unhindered I shall penetrate all sanctuaries and snatch the secrets of every dim confessional.

Yes! among books that charm, and give wings to the mind, will my days be spent. I shall be ever absorbing the things great men have written; with such experience I will charge my mind to the full. Nor will I try to give anything in return. Once, in the delusion that Art, loving the recluse, would make his life happy, I wrote a little for a yellow quarterly . . . and had that *succès de fiasco*[23] which is always given to a young writer of talent. But the stress of creation soon overwhelmed me. Only Art with a capital H[24] gives any consolations to her henchmen. And I, who crave no knighthood,[25] shall write no more. I shall write no more. Already I feel myself to be a trifle outmoded. I belong to the Beardsley period.[26] Younger men, with months of activity before them, with fresher schemes and notions, with newer enthusiasm, have pressed forward since then. *Cedo junioribus.*[27] Indeed, I stand aside with no regret. For to be outmoded is to be a classic, if one has written well. I have acceded to the hierarchy of good scribes and rather like my niche.

Chicago, 1895

1896

---

[22]**land-agents at Ipswich:** small-town realtors. **exhaurient:** absorbent (Beerbohm's coinage). *Delicias . . . experiar:* I shall also enjoy the pleasures of the library.

[23]**yellow quarterly:** *The Yellow Book,* Decadent periodical in which Beerbohm published "A Defence of Cosmetics" (1894); see illustration before page 820. The ellipsis here is Beerbohm's. *succès de fiasco:* acclaim due to failure (Beerbohm's coinage).

[24]**Art with a capital H:** cockney, vulgar art.

[25]**knighthood:** Beerbohm, in fact, became Sir Max in 1939.

[26]Aubrey **Beardsley** (1872–1898): *Yellow Book* art editor who printed many of Beerbohm's caricatures.

[27]*Cedo junioribus:* I yield to those who are younger.

---

[21]**Buzzard:** London confectioner. **Mudie:** lending library for novels.

CHRONOLOGY
AND
BIBLIOGRAPHIES

CHRONOLOGY

DATE	SOCIETY AND POLITICS	SCIENCE, LEARNING, AND IDEAS
1830	George IV dies, accession of William IV; Captain Swing riots against agricultural mechanization and low pay; death penalty abolished for many offenses	Comte, *Cours de philosophie positive* (–1842); Lyell, *Principles of Geology* (–1833); Manchester–Liverpool Railway opened
1831		Faraday discovers electromagnetic induction; Antarctica and magnetic North Pole discovered; dynamo and transformer invented
1832	First Reform Bill changes property requirements for voting and reorganizes constituencies	Martineau, *Illustrations of Political Economy* (–1835)
1833	Keble's National Apostasy sermon begins Oxford movement; *Tracts for the Times* (–1841); Factory Act regulates child labor in textile industry; first public education grant	
1834	Poor Law Amendment Act places the destitute in workhouses; Tolpuddle Martyrs transported to Australia for swearing oath to join a labor union; Palace of Westminster and Houses of Parliament burn	Babbage designs analytical engine (computer); McCormick patents mechanical reaper
1835	Municipal Corporations Act reforms local government	Strauss, *Das Leben Jesu*
1836	London Working-Men's Association proposes People's Charter; Marriage Act allows civil weddings; University of London chartered	Schopenhauer, *On the Will in Nature*
1837	William IV dies; Victoria crowned; birth, marriage, and death registration begins; industrial depression (–1842)	Morse invents electric telegraph
1838	National Gallery opened	regular transatlantic steamship service begun; first railroads in London
1839	Anti-Corn Law League formed; People's Charter rejected by House of Commons; Chartist riots	Daguerre invents the daguerrotype; bicycle invented

DATE	LITERATURE AND THE ARTS	EMPIRE AND WORLD
1830	Stendhal, *The Red and the Black*; Tennyson, *Poems, Chiefly Lyrical*; Delacroix, *Liberty Leading the People* (painting); *Fraser's Magazine*	fall of Charles X of France; July monarchy established under Louis-Philippe; East India Company annexes Mysore; Royal Geographical Society and Colonization Society founded
1831	Elliott, *Corn-Law Rhymes*; Hugo, *Notre–Dame de Paris*; Constable, *Waterloo Bridge* (painting)	Anglo-Ashanti treaty; Jamaica slave rebellion
1832	Goethe dies; *Faust, Part 2*; Scott dies; Constable, *The Grove, Hampstead* (painting); Berlioz, *Symphonie Fantastique*	Newfoundland granted representative government; Mazzini founds "Young Italy"
1833	Balzac, *Eugénie Grandet*; Pushkin, *Eugene Onegin*; Mendelssohn, *Italian Symphony*	slavery abolished in British colonies; Britain annexes Falkland Islands; Mehemet Ali dynasty established in Egypt
1834	Balzac, *Le Père Goriot*; Bulwer-Lytton, *The Last Days of Pompeii*; Coleridge and Lamb die	sixth Kaffir War in Cape Colony
1835	Hemans dies	Macaulay, Minute on Indian Education; East India Company monopoly over trade with India and China ends
1836	Pugin, *Contrasts*	Boer Great Trek northward into Zulu lands begins
1837	Carlyle, *The French Revolution*; Dickens, *The Pickwick Papers*	rebellions in Lower and Upper Canada; regular steamship service between London and Alexandria, Suez, and Bombay; Aborigines Protection Society
1838	Landon dies	Afghan War (–1842); commercial treaty between Britain and Turkey
1839	Turner, *The Téméraire* (painting)	first Anglo-Chinese Opium War (–1842); first British-Afghan War; Britain acquires Aden

DATE	SOCIETY AND POLITICS	SCIENCE, LEARNING, AND IDEAS
1840	Queen Victoria marries Albert, Prince of Saxe-Coburg-Gotha; penny post established; first adhesive postage stamps; Kew Gardens opened	Morse code patented
1841	Newman, *Tract 90*	Feuerbach, *The Essence of Christianity*; arc-lamp street lighting in Paris
1842	Mine Act outlaws female and child labor in underground mines; Second National Convention of Chartists, second petition rejected by Parliament; Chadwick report on working-class sanitary conditions	anæsthesia first used in surgery; Manchester–London rail line
1843		Mill, *A System of Logic*
1844	Factory Act limits working hours of women and children	Chambers, *Vestiges of the Natural History of Creation*
1845	Newman converts to Roman Catholicism; Irish potato famine (–1847), mass emigration to United States	Engels, *Condition of the Working Class in England*; pneumatic tire invented; Britannia Bridge across Menai Strait; cuneiform deciphered
1846	Corn Laws repealed	Strauss, *The Life of Jesus* (trans. Mary Ann Evans); planet Neptune discovered
1847	Ten Hours Factory Act; industrial depression (–1848)	Boole, *Mathematical Logic*; Helmholz, *On the Conservation of Energy*; chloroform first used as anaesthetic in a surgical operation
1848	Marx and Engels, *The Communist Manifesto*; cholera outbreak; Public Health Act; Hyde Park rally and presentation of Chartist petition to Parliament	breech-loading rifle invented; Mill, *Principles of Political Economy*
1849		Layard excavates Nineveh
1850	first science degrees at Oxford; Roman Catholic hierarchy restored in England	

DATE	LITERATURE AND THE ARTS	EMPIRE AND WORLD
1840	Bulwer-Lytton, *Money* (play); Turner, *The Slave Ship* (painting)	Upper and Lower Canada united and granted partial self-government; Treaty of London multilaterally limits Egyptian expansion; Britain annexes New Zealand
1841	Emerson, *Essays*; Boucicault, *London Assurance* (play); Schumann, *Symphony #1*; *Punch*	Convention of the Straits closes Bosporus to foreign fleets; Britain annexes Hong Kong; Livingstone begins missionary work in South Africa; Brooke becomes Rajah of Sarawak
1842	Gogol, *Dead Souls*; copyright act; Mudie's Circulating Library opened	Treaty of Nanking cedes Hong Kong to Britain and opens Chinese ports to British trade
1843	Carlyle, *Past and Present*; Ruskin, *Modern Painters 1*; Wordsworth becomes Poet Laureate	Britain annexes Natal and Basutoland; Britain annexes Sind (India); Maori revolts in New Zealand
1844	Dumas, *The Three Musketeers*; Turner, *Rain, Steam, and Speed* (painting)	Britain resumes control of West African settlements
1845	Disraeli, *Sybil, or The Two Nations*; Poe, *The Raven and Other Poems*; Wagner, *Tannhäuser* (opera)	first Sikh War, India (–1846); Franklin expedition seeks Northwest Passage; Anglo-French blockade of Buenos Aires
1846	Dostoevsky, *Poor Folk*	Mexican-American War; Canada-U. S. border established at 49th parallel
1847	C. Brontë, *Jane Eyre*; E. Brontë, *Wuthering Heights*; Longfellow, *Evangeline*; Thackeray, *Vanity Fair*	Italian *Risorgimento* begins; Liberia established
1848	Gaskell, *Mary Barton*; George Cruikshank, *The Drunkard's Children* (painting); PreRaphaelite Brotherhood founded; Millais, *Ophelia* (painting)	revolutions throughout Europe; Louis-Philippe abdicates; Louis-Napoléon elected president; Ferdinand I abdicates, Franz Josef becomes emperor of Austria-Hungary; second Sikh War
1849	Dickens, *David Copperfield*	Britain annexes Punjab; gold rush begins in California
1850	Wordsworth dies; *The Prelude*; Tennyson becomes Poet Laureate; *In Memoriam*; Hawthorne, *The Scarlet Letter*; *Household Words*	Australian Constitutions Act grants constitutional liberties and governmental powers; Taiping Rebellion in China

DATE	SOCIETY AND POLITICS	SCIENCE, LEARNING, AND IDEAS
1851	Great Exhibition at Crystal Palace; first science degrees at Cambridge; Jewish schools officially recognized	Comte, *Système de politique positive* (–1854); Mayhew, *London Labour and the London Poor;* Thomson publishes first and second laws of thermodynamics; telegraph cable Dover–Calais
1852	funeral of Duke of Wellington	Newman, *The Idea of a University;* Kelvin and Rankine develop refrigeration; first dirigible airship
1853	last convicts transported to Australia; mandatory smallpox vaccination begun	telegraph system established in India
1854	Civil Service reformed; Working Men's College founded in London; Oxford degrees granted to Dissenters	first transalpine railway
1855	newspaper stamp tax abolished	invention of processes enabling mass production of steel
1856	Cambridge degrees granted to Dissenters	Müller, *Comparative Mythology*
1857	Divorce and Matrimonial Causes Act allows some civil divorces; National Portrait Gallery	Buckle, *History of Civilization in England;* Gosse, *Omphalos*
1858	Jewish Disabilities Act ends legal discrimination; Lionel de Rothschild becomes first Jewish MP; property requirements for MPs abolished; Sinn Fein founded in Ireland	Darwin and Wallace propose theory of evolution
1859		Darwin, *The Origin of Species;* Mill, *On Liberty;* Nightingale, *Notes on Nursing*
1860		Burckhardt, *Civilization of the Renaissance in Italy; Essays and Reviews;* Huxley-Wilberforce debate; first ironclad warship launched
1861	death of Prince Albert; Revised Code bases elementary school funding on examinations; Royal Academy of Music; death penalty for sodomy abolished	Beeton, *Book of Household Management;* Faraday, *On the Chemical History of a Candle;* Maine, *Ancient Law*

DATE	LITERATURE AND THE ARTS	EMPIRE AND WORLD
1851	Melville, *Moby Dick*; Verdi, *Rigoletto* (opera)	Louis-Napoléon carries out coup d'état; gold rush begins in Australia
1852	Dickens, *Bleak House*; Stowe, *Uncle Tom's Cabin*; Gautier, *Emaux et Camées*; Hunt, *The Awakening Conscience*, *The Light of the World* (paintings)	Britain recognizes independence of Transvaal; Louis-Napoléon becomes Emperor Napoléon III; second Anglo-Burmese War; British invasion of Basutoland defeated
1853	C. Brontë, *Villette*; Verdi, *Il Trovatore*, *La Traviata* (operas)	Russia and Turkey at war; Legislative Council Act establishes Indian legislature
1854	Thoreau, *Walden*	Crimean War (–1856); Boers found Orange Free State, British relinquish sovereignty
1855	R. Browning, *Men and Women*; Trollope, *The Warden*; Whitman, *Leaves of Grass*; Brown, *The Last of England* (painting)	death of Nicholas I, Alexander II becomes Tsar; self-government extended in Australian colonies; Livingstone reaches and names Victoria Falls, Africa
1856	Barrett Browning, *Aurora Leigh*; Flaubert, *Madame Bovary*; Hunt, *The Scapegoat* (painting); Millais, *The Blind Girl* (painting)	second Anglo-Chinese War; Britain annexes Oudh, India; Anglo-Persian War
1857	Hughes, *Tom Brown's Schooldays*; Baudelaire, *Les Fleurs du Mal*; Museum of Ornamental Art (Victoria and Albert Museum)	Sepoy Rebellion (Indian "Mutiny"); Burton and Speke reach Lake Tanganyika
1858	Procter, *Legends and Lyrics*; Ballantyne, *The Coral Island*; *English Woman's Journal*	control of India transferred from East India Company to the Crown; Victoria proclaimed Sovereign of India
1859	Eliot, *Adam Bede*; FitzGerald, *Rubáiyát of Omar Khayyám*; Smiles, *Self-Help*; Millet, *The Angelus* (painting)	Suez Canal construction begins (–1869)
1860	Collins, *The Woman in White*; Eliot, *The Mill on the Floss*; *Cornhill Magazine*	Anglo-French forces defeat Chinese; Maori Wars, New Zealand (–1870)
1861	Palgrave, *Golden Treasury*; Braddon, *Lady Audley's Secret*; Wood, *East Lynne*	Victor Emmanuel crowned king of unified Italy; Russian serfs emancipated; British colony established in Nigeria; American Civil War begins

DATE	SOCIETY AND POLITICS	SCIENCE, LEARNING, AND IDEAS
1862	cotton famine in industrial Lancashire; Companies Act introduces corporate limited liability	Colenso, *The Pentateuch and Book of Joshua Critically Examined;* Foucault measures speed of light
1863	women take Cambridge Local Examinations	first London subway; Maxwell proposes electromagnetic theory of light; Pasteur develops process of pasteurization; Renan, *La Vie de Jésus*
1864	Contagious Diseases Acts; International Working Men's Association	Early English Text Society
1865	Women's Suffrage Committee	Lister introduces antiseptic surgery; Mendel's experiments on heredity
1866	Governor Eyre controversy; Habeas Corpus Act suspended in Ireland; Royal Aeronautical Society; cholera epidemic	Nobel invents dynamite; torpedo invented; first successful transatlantic cable
1867	Second Reform Bill; Nelson's Column unveiled in Trafalgar Square, London	Bagehot, *The English Constitution;* Marx, *Das Kapital*
1868	last public execution; first Trades Union Congress	Ballad Society; Chaucer Society; Royal Historical Society
1869	Irish Church Disestablishment Act; imprisonment for debt abolished; first women's college at Cambridge; Municipal Franchise Act gives limited votes to women	Galton, *Hereditary Genius;* Lecky, *History of European Morals;* Mill, *On the Subjection of Women;* margarine and the washing machine invented
1870	Irish Land Act; Education Act extends government responsibility for elementary education; Married Women's Property Act; examinations for entrance to Civil Service	doctrine of Papal Infallibility proclaimed; Huxley, *Lay Sermons;* Schliemann begins excavation of Troy Darwin, *The Descent of Man;* Tylor, *Primitive Culture*
1871	Oxford and Cambridge open degrees and university positions to non-Anglicans; labor unions legalized; purchase of army commissions abolished	International Bureau of Weights and Measures; Nietzsche, *The Birth of Tragedy*
1872	Secret Ballot Act; Slade School of Art opened to women	
1873	agricultural depression	typewriter and color photography invented

DATE	LITERATURE AND THE ARTS	EMPIRE AND WORLD
1862	Hugo, *Les Misérables*; C. Rossetti, *Goblin Market and Other Poems*; Turgenev, *Fathers and Sons*; Whistler, *The White Girl* (painting)	Speke reaches source of Nile; British Honduras proclaimed a colony
1863	Taylor, *The Ticket-of-Leave Man* (play); Taine, *Histoire de la littérature anglaise*; D. G. Rossetti, *Beata Beatrix* (painting); Manet, *Le dejeuner sur l'herbe* (painting)	
1864	Dickens, *Our Mutual Friend*; Gaskell, *Wives and Daughters*; Newman, *Apologia Pro Vita Sua*	first Geneva Convention for protecting sick and wounded soldiers
1865	Carroll, *Alice's Adventures in Wonderland*; Tolstoy, *War and Peace*; Brown, *Work* (painting); Wagner, *Tristan und Isolde* (opera)	Morant Bay Rebellion, Jamaica
1866	Dostoyevsky, *Crime and Punishment*; Swinburne, *Poems and Ballads*, first series; Verlaine, *Poèmes saturniens*	Austro-Prussian War ("Seven Weeks' War")
1867	Robertson, *Caste* (play); Ibsen, *Peer Gynt* (play); Strauss, "Blue Danube" (waltz)	Canada established as British dominion; diamonds discovered in South Africa; second Anglo-Burmese Commercial Treaty
1868	Browning, *The Ring and the Book*; Collins, *The Moonstone*; Alcott, *Little Women*; Wagner, *Die Meistersinger* (opera)	third Maori War, New Zealand; end of penal transportation to Australia; Britain invades Abyssinia
1869	Arnold, *Culture and Anarchy*; Flaubert, *Sentimental Education*	Suez Canal opened; Red River rebellion in Canada
1870	D. G. Rossetti, *Poems*; Delibes, *Coppélia* (ballet)	Franco-Prussian War; France forms Third Republic
1871	Eliot, *Middlemarch*; Verdi, *Aida* (opera)	Britain annexes Kimberley diamond fields, South Africa; Western Australia granted responsible government
1872	Whistler, *The Artist's Mother* (painting); Scott, Albert Memorial	Cape Colony granted responsible government
1873	Pater, *Studies in the History of the Renaissance*; Rimbaud, *Une Saison en Enfer*; Tolstoy, *Anna Karenina*	East India Company dissolved; Second Ashanti War; abolition of slave markets in Zanzibar

DATE	SOCIETY AND POLITICS	SCIENCE, LEARNING, AND IDEAS
1874	Factory Act institutes 56-hour work week; employment of children as chimney sweeps banned; London School of Medicine for Women	Stubbs, *Constitutional History of England*
1875	Public Health Act codifies sanitary laws; peaceful picketing in industrial disputes legalized	Eddy, *Science and Health*; *Encyclopaedia Britannica*, 9th edition
1876	Medical Qualification Act allows women to qualify as doctors	Bell invents telephone
1877	Phoenix Park murders in Dublin; female medical students allowed clinical training in London	Edison invents phonograph
1878	first women's college at Cambridge; Salvation Army established; Scotland Yard established	incandescent electric light invented; first electric streetlights in London; first modern microscope
1879	Irish National Land League	first telephone exchange in London; Skeat, *Etymological Dictionary of the English Language*
1880	elementary education becomes compulsory to age ten	
1881	Habeas Corpus Act suspended in Ireland; army flogging abolished; Civil Service grade of Woman Clerk established	Revised Version of New Testament
1882	Married Women's Property Act	
1883	Royal College of Music	Nietzsche, *Thus Spoke Zarathustra*; Seeley, *Expansion of England*
1884	Third Reform Bill; Fabian Society	first part of *Oxford English Dictionary* published; steam turbine invented; Revised Version of Old Testament; Greenwich Mean Time made international Standard
1885		Pasteur develops rabies inoculation; Daimler invents internal combustion engine; Benz builds first single-cylinder motor car; Stanley develops safety bicycle
1886	Contagious Diseases Acts repealed; Mansfield College founded at Oxford for religious Dissenters; Labouchere amendment; First Irish Home Rule Bill defeated	Hertz discovers electromagnetic waves
1887	Queen Victoria's golden jubilee; Bloody Sunday riots	Lang, *Myth, Ritual and Religion*; Linotype and artificial silk invented; Esperanto developed

DATE	LITERATURE AND THE ARTS	EMPIRE AND WORLD
1874	Hardy, *Far From the Madding Crowd*; first exhibition of Impressionist art; J. Strauss, *Die Fledermaus* (opera); Moussorgsky, *Boris Godunov* (opera)	Britain annexes Fiji Islands; Stanley explores Congo
1875	Twain, *Adventures of Tom Sawyer*; Monet, *Boating at Argenteuil* (painting); Bizet, *Carmen* (opera)	Britain purchases controlling interest in Suez Canal
1876	Eliot, *Daniel Deronda*; Brahms, *Symphony #1*; Wagner, *Siegfried* (opera)	Indian famine
1877	D. G. Rossetti, *Astarte Syriaca* (painting); Tchaikovsky, *Swan Lake* (ballet)	Victoria declared Empress of India; Britain annexes Transvaal, attempts to annex Boer republics
1878	Hardy, *The Return of the Native*; Gilbert and Sullivan, *H. M. S. Pinafore* (operetta)	second Afghan War; Britain occupies Cyprus
1879	Dostoevsky, *The Brothers Karamazov*; James, *Daisy Miller*; Ibsen, *A Doll's House* (play)	Britain and France reassume joint control of Egypt; Zulu War
1880	Rodin, *The Thinker* (sculpture)	First Boer War; construction of Panama Canal begins (–1914)
1881	James, *The Portrait of a Lady*; Offenbach, *Tales of Hoffman* (opera); Browning Society founded	Treaty of Pretoria establishes Transvaal Republic
1882	Gilbert and Sullivan, *Iolanthe* (operetta)	Britain occupies Cairo and Suez Canal Zone
1883	Stevenson, *Treasure Island*; Schreiner, *Story of an African Farm*	
1884	Twain, *The Adventures of Huckleberry Finn*	British protectorate established in Somaliland; Berlin Conference sets rules for partition of Africa
1885	Haggard, *King Solomon's Mines*; Zola, *Germinal*; Gilbert and Sullivan, *The Mikado* (operetta); Van Gogh, *The Potato Eaters* (painting)	Indian National Congress founded; Mahdists defeat Gordon at Khartoum (Sudan); Third Anglo-Burmese War; Southern New Guinea annexed
1886	Stevenson, *The Strange Case of Dr. Jekyll and Mr. Hyde*	Burma incorporated into Indian Empire; gold fields opened in Transvaal; Kenya becomes British colony
1887	Doyle, "A Study in Scarlet"; Haggard, *She*; Verdi, *Otello* (opera)	first Colonial Conference, London

DATE	SOCIETY AND POLITICS	SCIENCE, LEARNING, AND IDEAS
1888	Jack the Ripper murders	pneumatic bicycle tire invented; Eastman markets box camera
1889	Prevention of Cruelty to Children Act; London dock strike	first celluloid film
1890	Free Elementary Education Act	Frazer, *The Golden Bough*; Marshall, *Principles of Economics*; first moving picture shows
1891		William James, *The Principles of Psychology*
1892		Pearson, *The Grammar of Science*; electric oven invented
1893	Independent Labour Party; Second Irish Home Rule Bill defeated	Durkheim, *The Division of Labor in Society*; Bradley, *Appearance and Reality*; cinematograph invented
1894		
1895	London School of Economics	Durkheim, *The Rules of Sociological Method*; Freud and Breuer, *Studies on Hysteria*; Röntgen discovers X-rays; Lumière brothers invent cinema camera
1896		Bergson, *Matter and Memory*; Becquerel discovers radioactivity
1897	Queen Victoria's diamond jubilee; Tate Gallery	Ellis, *Studies in the Psychology of Sex* (–1910); Thomson discovers electrons; monotype typesetting machine invented
1898		Curies discover radium and polonium
1899	International Women's Congress, London	Freud, *The Interpretation of Dreams*; Veblen, *The Theory of the Leisure Class*; first motor bus; aspirin invented
1900	Independent Labour Party, Fabian Society, and Trades Unions combine to form Labour Party	Planck develops quantum theory; first flight of Zeppelin airship

DATE	LITERATURE AND THE ARTS	EMPIRE AND WORLD
1888	Ward, *Robert Elsmere*; Strindberg, *Miss Julie* (play); Rimsky-Korsakoff, *Scheherazade* (symphony); Waterhouse, *The Lady of Shalott* (painting)	Britain annexes Zululand
1889	Van Gogh, *The Starry Night* (painting)	Anglo-French territorial agreements on West Africa; British South Africa Company chartered; International Exhibition, Paris
1890	Morris, *News from Nowhere*; Dickinson, *Poems*; Ibsen, *Hedda Gabler* (play); Cèzanne, *The Card Players* (painting)	Anglo-German territorial agreements on East Africa; Brussels Act outlaws slave trade and liquor sales to "primitive" peoples
1891	Hardy, *Tess of the d'Urbervilles*; Wilde, *The Picture of Dorian Gray*	Nyasaland becomes British protectorate
1892	Doyle, *The Adventures of Sherlock Holmes*; Tchaikovsky, *The Nutcracker* (ballet); Monet, paintings of Rouen Cathedral; Toulouse-Lautrec, *Le Moulin Rouge* (painting)	Britain and Germany partition Cameroons
1893	Pinero, *The Second Mrs. Tanqueray* (play); Shaw, *Mrs. Warren's Profession* (play)	Uganda becomes British protectorate; Natal granted responsible government; World Exhibition, Chicago
1894	Hope, *The Prisoner of Zenda*; Kipling, *The Jungle Book*	Gandhi organizes Natal Indian Congress
1895	Hardy, *Jude the Obscure*; Wilde tried and imprisoned	Britain establishes East African Protectorate; Lenin joins Russian Social-Democratic Party and is exiled to Siberia
1896	Housman, *A Shropshire Lad*; Chekhov, *The Sea Gull* (play); *The Daily Mail*	Anglo-Egyptian forces begin to reconquer Sudan; Klondike gold rush begins; first modern Olympic Games, Athens
1897	Stoker, *Dracula*; Rousseau, *The Sleeping Gypsy* (painting)	
1898	Hardy, *Wessex Poems*; Shaw, *Plays Pleasant and Unpleasant*	Mahdists defeated, Sudan; Spanish-American War ended by Treaty of Paris; International Jewish Congress, Basle; formal establishment of Zionism
1899	James, *The Turn of the Screw*; Tolstoy, *Resurrection*; Bruckner, *Symphony #5*	first Peace Conference at The Hague; Geneva Convention expanded, Court of Arbitration established; second Boer War (–1902)
1900	Conrad, *Lord Jim*; Dreiser, *Sister Carrie*; Puccini, *Tosca* (opera); Sibelius, *Finlandia* (symphonic poem)	Chinese uprising ("Boxer Rebellion") suppressed by European states; Universal Exhibition, Paris

BIBLIOGRAPHIES

GENERAL

Altick, Richard D. *The English Common Reader: A Social History of the Mass Reading Public, 1800–1900.* 1998 [1967].

Bradley, Ian C. *The Call to Seriousness: The Evangelical Impact on the Victorians.* 1976.

Briggs, Asa. *Victorian Things.* 1988.

Buckley, Jerome H. *The Triumph of Time: A Study of the Victorian Concepts of Time, History, Progress and Decadence.* 1966.

Culler, A. Dwight. *The Victorian Mirror of History.* 1985.

DeLaura, David. *Hebrew and Hellene in Victorian England: Newman, Arnold, and Pater.* 1969.

Dooley, Allan C. *Author and Printer in Victorian England.* 1992.

Dowling, Linda. *Language and Decadence in the Victorian Fin de Siècle.* 1986.

Gilbert, Sandra, and Susan Gubar. *The Madwoman in the Attic: The Woman Writer and the Nineteenth-Century Literary Imagination.* 1979.

Gilmour, Robin. *The Victorian Period: The Intellectual and Cultural Context of English Literature, 1830–1890.* 1993.

Herbert, Christopher. *Culture and Anomie: Ethnographic Imagination in the Nineteenth Century.* 1991.

Hobsbawm, Eric. *The Age of Revolution 1789–1848.* 1962.
_____. *The Age of Capital 1848–1875.* 1975.

Holloway, John. *The Victorian Sage: Studies in Argument.* 1953.

Houghton, Walter E. *The Victorian Frame of Mind, 1830–1870.* 1957.

Knoepflmacher, U. C. and G. B. Tennyson, eds. *Nature and the Victorian Imagination.* 1977.

Madden, William, and George Levine, eds. *The Art of Victorian Prose.* 1968.

Mermin, Dorothy. *Godiva's Ride: Women of Letters in England, 1830–1880.* 1993.

Mitchell, Sally, ed. *Daily Life in Victorian England.* 1996.

Reed, John R. *Victorian Conventions.* 1975.

Richards, Thomas. *The Commodity Culture of Victorian Britain.* 1990.

Robbins, Ruth, and Julian Wolfreys, eds. *Victorian Identities.* 1996.

Rubinstein, W.D. *Britain's Century: A Political and Social History, 1815–1905.* 1998.

Shuttleworth, Sally, and Jenny Browne Taylor, eds. *Embodied Selves: An Anthology of Psychological Texts, 1830–1890.* 1998.

Tucker, Herbert, ed. *A Companion to Victorian Literature and Culture.* 1999.

Turner, Frank. *The Greek Heritage in Victorian Britain.* 1981.

Williams, Raymond. *Culture and Society, 1780–1950.* 1958.

Young, G. M. *Victorian England: Portrait of an Age.* 1936.

THE CONDITION OF ENGLAND

Brantlinger, Patrick. *The Spirit of Reform: British Literature and Politics, 1830–1867.* 1977.

Gallagher, Catherine. *The Industrial Reformation of English Fiction: Social Discourse and Narrative Form 1832–1867.* 1985.

Harris, Jose. *Private Lives, Public Spirit: A Social History of Great Britain, 1870–1914.* 1993.

Jones, Gareth Stedman. *Outcast London: A Study in the Relationship Between Classes in Victorian Society.* 1971.

Lucas, John. *England and Englishness: Ideas of Nationhood in English Poetry, 1688–1900.* 1990.

Perkin, Harold. *The Origins of Modern English Society 1780–1880.* 1969.

Sussman, Herbert. *Victorians and the Machine: The Literary Response to Technology.* 1968.

Thompson, E. P. *The Making of the English Working Class.* 1963.

Vicinus, Martha. *The Industrial Muse: A Study of Nineteenth Century British Working-Class Literature.* 1974.

Williams, Raymond. *The Country and the City.* 1973.

FAITH, DOUBT, AND KNOWLEDGE

Addinall, Peter. *Philosophy and Biblical Interpretation: A Study in Nineteenth-Century Conflict.* 1991.

Beer, Gillian. *Open Fields: Science in Cultural Encounter.* 1995.

Chadwick, Owen. *The Secularization of the European Mind in the Nineteenth Century.* 1975.

Frei, Hans W. *The Eclipse of Biblical Narrative.* 1974.

Gould, Stephen Jay. *Time's Arrow, Time's Cycle: Myth and Metaphor in the Discovery of Geological Time.* 1987.

Hanson, Ellis. *Decadence and Catholicism.* 1997.

Helmstadter, Richard, ed. *Freedom and Religion in the Nineteenth Century*. 1997.

————, and Bernard Lightman, eds. *Victorian Faith in Crisis: Essays on Continuity and Change in Nineteenth-Century Religious Belief*. 1990.

Jay, Elisabeth, ed. *The Evangelical and Oxford Movements*. 1983.

Levine, George, ed. *One Culture: Essays in Science and Literature*. 1987.

Morton, Peter. *The Vital Science: Biology and the Literary Imagination 1860–1900*. 1984.

Paradis, James, and Thomas Postlewait, eds. *Victorian Science and Victorian Values: Literary Perspectives*. 1981.

Shaffer, Elinor. *"Kubla Khan" and* The Fall of Jerusalem: *The Mythological School in Biblical Criticism and Secular Literature, 1770–1880*. 1975.

Turner, Frank M. *Between Science and Religion: The Reaction to Scientific Naturalism in Victorian England*. 1974.

Wheeler, Michael. *Death and the Future Life in Victorian Literature and Theology*. 1990.

Whitla, William, and Victor Shea, eds. *Essays and Reviews: The 1860 Text and Its Reading*. 2000.

GENDER AND SEXUALITY

Adams, James Eli. *Dandies and Desert Saints: Styles of Victorian Masculinity*. 1995.

Auerbach, Nina. *Romantic Imprisonment: Women and Other Glorified Outcasts*. 1985.

Craft, Christopher. *Another Kind of Love: Male Homosexual Desire in English Discourse, 1850–1920*. 1994.

Dellamora, Richard. *Masculine Desire: The Sexual Politics of Victorian Aestheticism*. 1990.

Dowling, Linda. *Hellenism and Homosexuality in Victorian Oxford*. 1994.

Helsinger, Elizabeth K., Robin Lauterbach Sheets, and William Veeder. *The Woman Question: Society and Literature in Britain and America 1837–1883*. 1983.

Langland, Elizabeth. *Nobody's Angels: Middle-Class Women and Domestic Ideology in Victorian Culture*. 1995.

Marcus, Steven. *The Other Victorians: A Study of Sexuality and Pornography in Mid-Nineteenth-Century England*. 1966.

Mason, Michael. *The Making of Victorian Sexuality*. 1994.

Moers, Ellen. *Literary Women*. 1976.

Poovey, Mary. *Uneven Developments: The Ideological Work of Gender in Mid-Victorian England*. 1988.

Sedgwick, Eve Kosofsky. *Between Men: English Literature and Male Homosocial Desire*. 1985.

————. *Epistemology of the Closet*. 1990.

Shires, Linda, ed. *Rewriting the Victorians: Theory, History and the Politics of Gender*. 1992.

Sinfield, Alan. *The Wilde Century: Effeminacy, Oscar Wilde and the Queer Movement*. 1994.

Sussman, Herbert L. *Victorian Masculinities: Manhood and Masculine Poetics in Early Victorian Literature and Art*. 1995.

Vicinus, Martha. *Independent Women: Work and Community for Single Women, 1850–1920*. 1985.

EMPIRE AND TRAVEL

Brantlinger, Patrick. *Rule of Darkness: British Literature and Imperialism, 1830–1914*. 1988.

Buzard, James. *The Beaten Track: European Tourism, Literature, and the Ways to Culture, 1800–1918*. 1993.

David, Deirdre. *Rule Britannia: Women, Empire, and Victorian Writing*. 1995.

Eldridge, C.C. *Victorian Imperialism*. 1978.

Foster, Shirley. *Across New Worlds: Nineteenth-Century Women and their Writings*. 1990.

Mills, Sara. *Discourses of Difference: An Analysis of Women's Travel Writing and Colonialism*. 1991.

Morgan, Susan. *Place Matters: Gendered Geography in Victorian Women's Travel Books about Southeast Asia*. 1996.

Pratt, Mary Louise. *Imperial Eyes: Travel Writing and Transculturation*. 1992.

Richards, Thomas. *The Imperial Archive: Knowledge and the Fantasy of Empire*. 1993.

Said, Edward. *Culture and Imperialism*. 1993.

Spurr, David. *The Rhetoric of Empire: Colonial Discourse in Journalism, Travel Writing, and Imperial Administration*. 1993.

Stocking, George W. *Victorian Anthropology*. 1987.

Suleri, Sara. *The Rhetoric of English India*. 1992.

THE FUNCTION OF POETRY

Armstrong, Isobel. *Victorian Poetry: Poetry, Poetics and Politics*. 1993.

———— and Virginia Blain, eds. *Women's Poetry, Late Romantic to Late Victorian: Gender and Genre, 1830–1900*. 1999.

Bristow, Joseph, ed. *Victorian Women Poets: Emily Brontë, Elizabeth Barrett Browning, Christina Rossetti*. 1995.

Christ, Carol. *Victorian and Modern Poetics*. 1984.

Coslett, Tess, ed. *Victorian Women Poets*. 1996.

Fraser, Hilary. *Beauty and Belief: Aesthetics and Religion in Victorian Literature*. 1986.

Griffiths, Eric. *The Printed Voice of Victorian Poetry*. 1989.

Johnson, E. D. H. *The Alien Vision of Victorian Poetry*. 1952.

Leighton, Angela, ed. *Victorian Women Poets: A Critical Reader*. 1996.

————. *Victorian Women Poets: Writing Against the Heart*. 1992.

Meisel, Perry. *The Myth of the Modern: A Study of British Literature and Criticism after 1850*. 1987.

Shaw, W. David. *The Lucid Veil: Poetic Truth in the Victorian Age*. 1987.

Slinn, E. Warwick. *The Discourse of Self in Victorian Poetry*. 1991.

Warren, Alba. *English Poetic Theory, 1825–1865*. 1950.

MATTHEW ARNOLD

Arnold: The Complete Poems, ed. K Allott. 1965: 2nd edn, ed. Miriam Allott. 1979.

Complete Prose Works, ed. Robert H. Super. 11 vols. 1960–1977.

apRoberts, Ruth. *Arnold and God*. 1983.

Bloom, Harold, ed. *Matthew Arnold*. 1987.

Culler, Dwight. *Imaginative Reason: The Poetry of Matthew Arnold*. 1966.

Dawson, Carl, and John Pfordresher, eds. *Matthew Arnold: The Critical Heritage*. 2 vols. 1973, 1979.

Gottfried, Leon. *Matthew Arnold and the Romantics*. 1963.

Honan, Park. *Matthew Arnold, A Life*. 1981.

Riede, David G. *Matthew Arnold and the Betrayal of Language*. 1988.

Trilling, Lionel. *Matthew Arnold*. 1949.

WILLIAM BARNES

The Poems of William Barnes. 2 vols, ed. Bernard Jones. 1962.

Baxter, Lucy (Barnes). *The Life of William Barnes*. 1887.

Chedzoy, Alan. *William Barnes: A Life of the Dorset Poet*. 1985.

Dugdale, Giles. *William Barnes of Dorset*. 1953.

Heath-Stubbs, John. *The Darkling Plain*. 1950.

Larkin, Philip. *Required Writing*. 1983.

Levy, William Turner. *William Barnes: The Man and the Poems*. 1960.

Parins, James W. *William Barnes*. 1984.

MAX BEERBOHM

The Works of Max Beerbohm. 1922.

Cecil, David. *Max, a Biography*. 1964.

Danson, Lawrence. *Max Beerbohm and the Act of Writing*. 1991.

Felstiner, John. *The Lies of Art: Max Beerbohm's Parody and Caricature*. 1972.

McElderry, Bruce Robert. *Max Beerbohm*. 1972.

Riewald, J. G., ed. *Remembering Max Beerbohm: Correspondence, Conversations, Criticisms*. 1991.

Viscusi, Robert. *Max Beerbohm, or, The Dandy Dante: Rereading with Mirrors*. 1986.

EMILY BRONTË

The Poems of Emily Brontë, ed. Derek Roper and Edward Chitham. 1995.

Brontë, Charlotte. "Biographical Notice of Ellis and Acton Bell." In *Wuthering Heights*, 2d edn. 1850.

Chitham, Edward. *A Life of Emily Brontë*. 1987.

Davies, Stevie. *Emily Brontë*. 1988.

Homans, Margaret. *Women Writers and Female Identity: Dorothy Wordsworth, Emily Brontë, and Emily Dickinson*. 1980.

Miller, J. Hillis. *The Disappearance of God: Five Nineteenth-Century Writers*. 1963.

Tayler, Irene. *Holy Ghosts: The Male Muses of Emily and Charlotte Brontë*. 1990.

Ratchford, Fannie. *The Brontës' Web of Childhood*. 1941.

Winnifrith, Tom, ed. *Critical Essays on Emily Brontë*. 1997.

ELIZABETH BARRETT BROWNING

Aurora Leigh, ed. Margaret Reynolds. 1996.

The Brownings' Correspondence, ed. Philip Kelley and Ronald Hudson. 14 vols. to date. 1984– .

Donaldson, Sandra, ed. *Critical Essays on Elizabeth Barrett Browning*. 1999.

————. *Elizabeth Barrett Browning: An Annotated Bibliography of the Commentary and Criticism, 1826–1990*.

Forster, Margaret. *Elizabeth Barrett Browning: A Biography*. 1988.

Leighton, Angela. *Elizabeth Barrett Browning*. 1986.

Mermin, Dorothy. *Elizabeth Barrett Browning: The Origins of a New Poetry*. 1989.

Stone, Marjorie. *Elizabeth Barrett Browning*. 1995.
Woolf, Virginia. *Flush: A Biography*. 1933.

ROBERT BROWNING

The Poems of Robert Browning, ed. John Pettigrew and Thomas J. Collins. 2 vols. 1981.
Bloom, Harold. *The Ringers in the Tower*. 1966.
Bristow, Joseph. *Robert Browning*. 1991.
Chesterton, G.K. *Robert Browning*. 1903.
Gibson, Mary Ellis, ed. *Critical Essays on Robert Browning*. 1992.
Hair, Donald. *Robert Browning's Language*. 1999.
Irvine, William and Park Honan. *The Book, the Ring, and the Poet: A Biography of Robert Browning*. 1974.
Karlin, Daniel. *The Courtship of Robert Browning and Elizabeth Barrett Browning*. 1985.
Langbaum, Robert. *The Poetry of Experience: The Dramatic Monologue in Modern Literary Tradition*. 1957.
Litzinger, Boyd and Donald Smalley, eds. *Browning: The Critical Heritage*, 1970.
Martin, Loy. *Browning's Dramatic Monologues and the Post-Romantic Subject*. 1985.
Maynard, John. *Browning's Youth*. 1977.
Slinn, E. Warwick. *Browning and the Fictions of Identity*. 1982.
Tucker, Herbert F. *Browning's Beginnings: The Art of Disclosure*. 1980.
Woolford, John. *Browning the Revisionary*. 1988.

JAMES DAWSON BURN

Autobiography of a Beggar Boy, ed. David Vincent. 1978.
Burnett, John, ed. *Useful Toil: Autobiographies of Working People from the 1820s to the 1920s*. 1994.
Gagnier, Regenia. *Subjectivities: A History of Self-Representation in Britain, 1832–1920*. 1991.

THOMAS CARLYLE

The Works of Thomas Carlyle: Centenary Edition, ed. H. D. Traill. 30 vols. 1898–1901.
apRoberts, Ruth. *The Ancient Dialect: Thomas Carlyle and Comparative Religion*. 1988.

Farrell, John P. *Revolution as Tragedy: The Dilemma of the Moderate from Scott to Arnold*. 1980.
Froude, J. A. *Thomas Carlyle: A History of the First Forty Years of his Life, 1795–1835*. 1882.
————. *Thomas Carlyle: A History of His Life in London, 1834–1881*. 1884.
Gross, John. *The Rise and Fall of the Man of Letters*. 1969.
Kaplan, Fred. *Thomas Carlyle: A Biography*. 1983.
Rosenberg, John D. *Carlyle and the Burden of History*. 1985.
Rosenberg, Phillip. *The Seventh Hero: Thomas Carlyle and the Theory of Radical Activism*. 1974.
Siegel, Jules P., ed. *Thomas Carlyle: The Critical Heritage*. 1971.
Vanden Bossche, Chris R. *Carlyle and the Search for Authority*. 1991.

LEWIS CARROLL

Alice in Wonderland, ed. Donald Gray. 1992.
Bloom, Harold, ed. *Lewis Carroll*. 1987.
Cohen, Morton. *Lewis Carroll: A Biography*. 1995.
Empson, William. *Some Versions of Pastoral*. 1935.
Guiliano, Edward and Kincaid, James R., eds. *Soaring with the Dodo: Essays on Lewis Carroll's Life and Art*. 1982.
Hutcheon, Linda. *A Theory of Parody*. 1985.
Hirsch, E. D. *The Aims of Interpretation*. 1976.
Huxley, Francis. *The Raven and the Writing Desk*. 1976.
Lecercle, Jean-Jacques. *Philosophy of Nonsense: The Intuitions of Victorian Nonsense Literature*. 1994.

ARTHUR HUGH CLOUGH

The Poems of Arthur Hugh Clough, ed. F. L. Mulhauser. 1974.
Armstrong, Isobel. *Arthur Hugh Clough*. 1962.
Biswas, Robindra. *Arthur Hugh Clough: Towards a Reconsideration*. 1972.
Chorley, Katherine. *Arthur Hugh Clough, The Uncommitted Mind*. 1962.
Goode, John. "Clough's Aqueous Poem." In *The Major Victorian Poets: Reconsiderations*, ed. Isobel Armstrong. 1969.
Houghton, Walter. *The Poetry of Clough*. 1963.
Maynard, John. *Victorian Discourses on Sexuality and Religion*. 1993.
Mermin, Dorothy. *The Audience in the Poem*. 1983.

Scott, Patrick. "The Victorianism of Clough." *Victorian Poetry* 16 (1978): 32–42.

Thorpe, Michael, ed. *Clough: The Critical Heritage.* 1972.

FRANCES POWER COBBE

Caine, Barbara. *Victorian Feminists.* 1992.

Bauer, Carol, and Lawrence Ritt. "A Husband Is a Wife-Beating Animal: Frances Power Cobbe Confronts the Wife-Abuse Problem in Victorian England." *International Journal of Women's Studies* 6 (1983): 99–118.

MARY COLERIDGE

The Collected Poems of Mary Coleridge, ed. Theresa Whistler. 1954.

Gathered Leaves From the Prose of Mary E. Coleridge, with a Memoir by Edith Sichel. 1910.

Bridges, Robert. *Collected Essays, Papers, &c.* 6, 1931.

Gilbert, Sandra, and Susan Gubar, *The Madwoman in the Attic: The Woman Writer and the Nineteenth-Century Literary Imagination.* 1979.

Jackson, Vanessa Furse, "Breaking the Quiet Surface: The Shorter Poems of Mary Coleridge." *English Literature in Transition* 39 (1996): 41–62.

MacGowran, Katherine. "The Restless Wanderer at the Gates: Hosts, Guests and Ghosts in the Poetry of Mary E. Coleridge." In *Victorian Women Poets: A Critical Reader,* ed. Angela Leighton. 1996.

CHARLES DARWIN

Darwin. 1979, ed. Philip Appleman.

Beer, Gillian. *Darwin's Plots: Evolutionary Narrative in Darwin, George Eliot, and Nineteenth-Century Fiction.* 1983.

Bowlby, John. *Charles Darwin: A New Life.* 1991.

Levine, George. *Darwin and the Novelists: Patterns of Science in Victorian Fiction.* 1988.

Rosenberg, John D. "Mr. Darwin Collects Himself." In *Nineteenth-Century Lives,* ed. Laurence S. Lockridge et al. 1989.

Young, Robert M. *Darwin's Metaphor: Nature's Place in Victorian Culture.* 1985.

ERNEST DOWSON

The Poetry of Ernest Dowson, ed. Desmond Flower. 1907.

Adams, Jad. *Madder Music, Stronger Wine: The Life of Ernest Dowson, Poet and Decadent.* 2000.

Alford, Norman. *The Rhymers' Club: Poets of the Tragic Generation.* 1994.

Longaker, J. M. *Ernest Dowson.* 1967.

Reed, John R. *Decadent Style.* 1985.

Swann, Thomas Burnett. *Ernest Dowson.* 1965.

Thornton, R. K. R. *The Decadent Dilemma.* 1983.

Tillotson, Geoffrey. *Essays in Criticism and Research.* 1967.

Yeats, W. B. *Autobiographies.* 1927.

MICHAEL FIELD

Works and Days: From the Journal of Michael Field, ed. T. and D. C. Sturge Moore. 1933.

Donoghue, Emma. *We Are Michael Field.* 1998.

Fletcher, Robert P. " 'I leave a page half-writ': Narrative Discoherence in Michael Field's *Underneath the Bough.*" In Armstrong and Blain, *Women's Poetry,* 1999.

Laird, Holly. *Women CoAuthors.* 2000.

Leighton, Angela. *Victorian Women Poets: Writing against the Heart.* 1992.

Prins, Yopie. *Victorian Sappho.* 1999.

Treby, Ivor C. *The Michael Field Catalogue: A Book of Lists.* 1998.

White, Chris. " 'Poets and lovers evermore': Interpreting Female Love in the Poetry and Journals of Michael Field." *Textual Practice* 4 (1990): 197–212.

_____. "The Tiresian Poet: Michael Field." In *Victorian Women Poets: A Critical Reader,* ed. Angela Leighton. 1996.

EDWARD FITZGERALD

Rubáiyát of Omar Khayyám: A Critical Edition, ed. Christopher Decker. 1997.

Arberry, A. J. *Omar Khayyám: A New Version Based upon Recent Discoveries.* 1952.

Black, Barbara J. *On Exhibit: Victorians and their Museums.* 2000.

D'Ambrosio, Vinnie-Marie. *Eliot Possessed: T. S. Eliot and FitzGerald's Rubáiyát.* 1989.

Gray, Erik. "Forgetting FitzGerald's *Rubáiyát*." *Studies in English Literature* 41. 2001.

Martin, Robert Bernard. *With Friends Possessed: A Life of Edward FitzGerald*. 1985.

ELIZABETH GASKELL

The Life of Charlotte Brontë, ed. J. Uglow and G. Handley. 1997.

Brodetsky, Tessa. *Elizabeth Gaskell*. 1986.

Gérin, Winifred. *Elizabeth Gaskell*. 1976.

Hughes, Linda K. and Michael Lund, *Victorian Publishing and Mrs. Gaskell's Work*. 1999.

Schor, Hilary. *Scheherazade in the Market Place*. 1986.

Stoneman, Patsy. *Elizabeth Gaskell*. 1987.

Uglow, Jenny. *Elizabeth Gaskell: A Habit of Stories*. 1993.

Unsworth, Anna. *Elizabeth Gaskell: An Independent Woman*. 1996.

THOMAS HARDY

The Complete Poems of Thomas Hardy, ed. James Gibson. 1976.

Davie, Donald. *Thomas Hardy and British Poetry*. 1972.

Miller, J. Hillis. *Thomas Hardy, Distance and Desire*. 1970.

Millgate, Michael. *Thomas Hardy: A Biography*. 1982.

Orel, Harold, ed. *Critical Essays on Hardy's Poetry*. 1995.

Page, Norman, ed. *Oxford Reader's Companion to Hardy*. 2000.

Paulin, Tom. *Thomas Hardy: The Poetry of Perception*. 1975.

Taylor, Dennis. *Hardy's Meters and Victorian Prosody*. 1988.

_____. *Hardy's Poetry, 1860–1928*. 1981.

Zeitlow, Paul. *Moments of Vision: The Poetry of Thomas Hardy*. 1974.

GERARD MANLEY HOPKINS

The Poems of Gerard Manley Hopkins, eds. W. H. Gardner and N. H. Mackenzie. 4th edn. 1990.

The Journals and Papers of Gerard Manley Hopkins, ed. Humphry House. 1959.

Brown, Daniel. *Hopkins' Idealism: Philosophy, Physics, Poetry*. 1997.

Gardner, William H. *Gerard Manley Hopkins (1844–1889): A Study of Poetic Idiosyncrasy in Relation to Poetic Tradition*. 2 vols. 1948–49.

Harris, Daniel. *Inspirations Unbidden: The "Terrible Sonnets" of Gerard Manley Hopkins*. 1982.

Mariani, Paul L. *A Commentary on the Complete Poems of Gerard Manley Hopkins*. 1970.

Martin, Robert Bernard. *Gerard Manley Hopkins: A Very Private Life*. 1991.

Saville, Julia. *A Queer Chivalry: The Homoerotic Asceticism of Gerard Manley Hopkins*. 2000.

Sulloway, Alison. *Gerard Manley Hopkins and the Victorian Temper*. 1972.

White, Norman. *Hopkins: A Literary Biography*. 1992.

A. E. HOUSMAN

Collected Poems and Selected Prose, ed. Christopher Ricks. 1988.

Bayley, John. *Housman's Poems*. 1992.

Gardner, Philip, ed. *A. E. Housman: The Critical Heritage*. 1992.

Graves, Richard Perceval. *A. E. Housman: The Scholar-Poet*. 1979.

Holden, Alan W. and J. Roy Birch, eds. *A. E. Housman: A Reassessment*. 2000.

Ricks, Christopher, ed. *A. E. Housman: A Collection of Critical Views*. 1968.

THOMAS HENRY HUXLEY

The Life and Letters of Thomas Henry Huxley, ed. Leonard Huxley. 2 vols. 1900.

Barr, Alan P., ed. *Thomas Henry Huxley's Place in Science and Letters: Centenary Essays*. 1997.

Desmond, Adrian J. *Huxley: From Devil's Disciple to Evolution's High Priest*. 1997.

Di Gregorio, Mario A. *T. H. Huxley's Place in Natural Science*. 1984.

Irvine, William. *Apes, Angels, and Victorians: Darwin, Huxley, and Evolution*. 1959.

Paradis, James G. *T. H. Huxley: Man's Place in Nature*. 1978.

JEAN INGELOW

Poems, ed. Humphrey Milford. 1913.

Auerbach, Nina, and U. C. Knoepflmacher, eds. *Forbidden Journeys: Fairy Tales and Fantasies by Victorian Women Writers*. 1992.

Knoepflmacher, U. C. "Male Patronage and Female Author-ship: The Case of John Ruskin and Jean Ingelow." *Princeton University Library Chronicle* 57 (1995):13–45.

Peters, Maureen. *Jean Ingelow: Victorian Poetess.* 1972.

Wagner, Jennifer A. "In Her 'Proper Place': Ingelow's Fable of the Female Poet and Her Community in *Gladys and Her Island." Victorian Poetry* 31 (1993): 227–240.

JOHN KEBLE

Keble's Lectures on Poetry, 1832–1841. 2 vols. Trans. Edward Kernshaw Francis. 1912.

Battiscombe, Georgina. *John Keble, A Study in Limitations.* 1963.

Edgecombe, Rodney Stenning. *Two Poets of the Oxford Movement: John Keble and John Henry Newman.* 1996.

Griffin, John R. *John Keble, Saint of Anglicanism.* 1987.

Lock, Walter. *John Keble, A Biography.* 1893.

Martin, Brian. *John Keble: Priest, Professor, and Poet.* 1976.

Prickett, Stephen. *Romanticism and Religion: The Tradition of Coleridge and Wordsworth in the Victorian Church.* 1976.

Tennyson, G. B. *Victorian Devotional Poetry: The Tractarian Mode.* 1980.

RUDYARD KIPLING

Rudyard Kipling's Verse: Definitive Edition. 1940.

Early Verse by Rudyard Kipling, 1879–1889: Unpublished, Uncollected, and Rarely Collected Poems, ed. Andrew Rutherford. 1986.

Eliot, T. S. *On Poetry and Poets.* 1941.

Gilbert, Elliott L., ed. *Kipling and the Critics.* 1965.

Green, Roger Lancelyn. *Kipling: The Critical Heritage.* 1971.

Orel, Harold, ed. *Critical Essays on Rudyard Kipling.* 1989.

Parry, Ann. *The Poetry of Rudyard Kipling.* 1992.

Ricketts, Harry. *The Unforgiving Minute: A Life of Rudyard Kipling.* 1999.

Tompkins, J. M. S. *The Art of Rudyard Kipling.* 1959.

Wilson, Angus. *The Strange Ride of Rudyard Kipling: His Life and Works.* 1978.

EDWARD LEAR

Chitty, Susan. *That Singular Person Called Lear.* 1988.

Colley, Ann C. *Edward Lear and the Critics.* 1993.

Hark, Ina Rae. *Edward Lear.* 1982.

Levi, Peter. *Edward Lear: A Biography.* 1996.

Noakes, Vivien. *Edward Lear:The Life of a Wanderer.* 1986.

Sewell, Elizabeth. *The Field of Nonsense.* 1970.

Stewart, Susan. *Nonsense: Aspects of Intertextuality in Folklore and Literature.* 1989.

AMY LEVY

The Complete Novels and Selected Writings of Amy Levy, 1861–1889, ed. Melvyn New. 1993.

Beckman, Linda Hunt. *Amy Levy: Her Life and Letters.* 2000.

Francis, Emma. "Amy Levy: Contradictions?—Feminism and Semitic Discourse." In *Victorian Women's Poetry,* eds. Isobel Armstrong and Virginia Blain. 1999.

Scheinberg, Cynthia. "'Recasting sympathy and judgement': Amy Levy, Poets, and the Victorian Dramatic Monologue." *Victorian Poetry* 35 (1997): 173–191.

Wagenknecht, Edward. In *Daughters of the Covenant: Portraits of Six Jewish Women.* 1983.

THOMAS BABINGTON MACAULAY

Complete Works of Lord Macaulay, ed. Hannah More Macaulay Trevelyan. 1898.

Clive, John. *Macaulay: The Shaping of the Historian.* 1973.

Gay, Peter. *Style in History.* 1974.

Hamburger, Joseph. *Macaulay and the Whig Tradition.* 1976.

Levine, George. *The Boundaries of Fiction: Carlyle, Macaulay, Newman.* 1968.

Millgate, Jane. *Macaulay.* 1973.

Trevelyan, George O. *The Life and Letters of Lord Macaulay.* 1876.

HARRIET MARTINEAU

Harriet Martineau on Women, ed. Gayle Graham Yates. 1985.

David, Deirdre. *Intellectual Women and Victorian Patriarchy: Harriet Martineau, Elizabeth Barrett Browning, George Eliot.* 1987.

Hoecker-Drysdale, Susan. *Harriet Martineau, First Woman Sociologist.* 1992.

Hunter, Shelagh. *Harriet Martineau: The Poetics of Moralism.* 1995.

Pichanick, Valerie Kossew. *Harriet Martineau, the Woman and Her Work, 1802–1876.* 1980.

Webb, R. K. *Harriet Martineau: A Radical Victorian.* 1960.

GEORGE MEREDITH

The Poems of George Meredith, ed. Phyllis B. Bartlett. 2 vols. 1978.

Bernstein, Carol L. *Precarious Enchantment: A Reading of Meredith's Poetry.* 1979.

Edmond, Rod. *Affairs of the Hearth: Victorian Poetry and Domestic Narrative.* 1988.

Johnson, Diane. *The True History of the First Mrs. Meredith and Other Lesser Lives.* 1972.

Kelvin, Norman. *A Troubled Eden; Nature and Society in the Works of George Meredith.* 1961.

Mermin, Dorothy. *The Audience in the Poem.* 1983.

Stevenson, Lionel. *The Ordeal of George Meredith.* 1953.

Williams, Ioan, ed. *Meredith, The Critical Heritage.* 1971.

JOHN STUART MILL

Collected Works, ed. John Robson et al. 27 vols. 1963–90.

Carlisle, Janice. *John Stuart Mill and the Writing of Character.* 1991.

Glassman, Peter. *J. S. Mill: The Evolution of a Genius.* 1985.

Gray, John and G. W. Smith, eds. *J. S. Mills' "On Liberty" in Focus.* 1991.

Laine, Michael, ed. *A Cultivated Mind: Essays on J. S. Mill Presented to John M. Robson.* 1991.

Mazlish, Bruce. *James and John Stuart Mill: Father and Son in the Nineteenth Century.* 1975.

Robson, John M. *The Improvement of Mankind: The Social and Political Thought of J. S. Mill.* 1968.

Ryan, Alan. *J. S. Mill.* 1974.

Sharpless, F. Parvin. *The Literary Criticism of John Stuart Mill.* 1967.

WILLIAM MORRIS

Collected Works, ed. May Morris. 24 vols. 1910–15.

Cumming, Elizabeth and Wendy Kaplan. *The Arts and Crafts Movement.* 1991.

Faulkner, Peter, ed. *William Morris: The Critical Heritage.* 1973.

MacCarthy, Fiona. *William Morris: A Life for Our Time.* 1994.

Mackail, J. W. *The Life of William Morris.* 2 vols. 1901.

Peterson, William. *The Kelmscott Press: A History of William Morris's Typographical Adventure.* 1991.

Skoblow, Jeffrey. *Paradise Dislocated: Morris, Poetics, Art.* 1993.

Stansky, Peter. *Redesigning the World: William Morris, the 1880's, and the Arts and Crafts.* 1985.

Thompson, E. P. *William Morris: Romantic to Revolutionary.* 1977 [1955].

Tompkins, J. M. S. *William Morris: An Approach to the Poetry.* 1988.

JOHN HENRY NEWMAN

The Letters and Diaries of John Henry Newman, ed. C. S. Dessain, T. Gornall, I.T. Ker. 31 vols. 1961–78.

Apologia Pro Vita Sua, ed. Martin J. Svaglic. 1967.

Culler, Dwight. *The Imperial Intellect: A Study of Newman's Educational Ideal.* 1955.

Gilley, Sheridan. *Newman and His Age.* 1990.

Houghton, Walter E. *The Art of Newman's "Apologia."* 1945.

Jost, Walter. *Rhetorical Thought in John Henry Newman.* 1989.

Ker, Ian T. *John Henry Newman: A Biography.* 1988.

Ker, Ian T. and Alan G. Hill, eds. *Newman After a Hundred Years.* 1990.

Pattison, Robert. *The Great Dissent: John Henry Newman and the Liberal Heresy.* 1991.

Rothblatt, Sheldon. *The Modern University and Its Discontents: The Fate of Newman's Legacies in Britain and America.* 1997.

Thomas, Stephen. *Newman and Heresy: The Anglican Years.* 1991.

FLORENCE NIGHTINGALE

"Cassandra'" and Other Selections from "Suggestion for Thought", ed. Mary Poovey. 1991.

Bullough, Vern, Bonnie Bullough, and Marietta P. Stanton, eds. *Florence Nightingale and Her Era: A Collection of New Scholarship.* 1990.

Hobbs, Colleen A. *Florence Nightingale.* 1997.

Jenkins, Ruth Y. *Reclaiming Myths of Power: Women Writers and the Victorian Spiritual Crisis.* 1995.

Seymer, Lucy Ridgely. *Florence Nightingale*. 1950.

Snyder, Katherine V. "From Novel to Essay: Gender and Revision in Florence Nightingale's 'Cassandra'." In *The Politics of the Essay: Feminist Perspectives*, eds. Ruth-Ellen Boetcher Joeres and Elizabeth Mittman. 1993.

Zemka, Sue. *Victorian Testaments: The Bible, Christology, and Literary Authority in Early-Nineteenth-Century British Culture*. 1997.

MARGARET OLIPHANT

The Autobiography of Margaret Oliphant: The Complete Text, ed. Elisabeth Jay. 1990.

Colby, Vineta and Robert A. *The Equivocal Virtue: Mrs. Oliphant and the Victorian Literary Market Place*. 1966.

Jay, Elisabeth. *Mrs. Oliphant: A Fiction to Herself*. 1995.

Trela, D. J., ed. *Margaret Oliphant: Critical Essays on a Gentle Subversive*. 1995.

Williams, Merryn. *Margaret Oliphant: A Critical Biography*. 1986.

WALTER PATER

The Renaissance: Studies in Art and Poetry: The 1893 Text, ed. Donald Hill. 1980.

Donoghue, Denis. *Walter Pater: A Lover of Strange Souls*. 1995.

Eliot, T. S. *Selected Essays*. 1930.

Hough, Graham. *The Last Romantics*. 1961.

Iser, Wolfgang. *Walter Pater: The Aesthetic Moment*. 1960.

Levey, Michael. *The Case of Walter Pater*. 1978.

Monsman, Gerald. *Walter Pater's Art of Autobiography*. 1980.

Shaffer, Elinor. *Walter Pater and the Culture of the Fin-de-Siècle*. 1995.

Williams, Carolyn. *Transfigured World: Walter Pater's Aesthetic Historicism*. 1989.

COVENTRY PATMORE

Anstruther, Ian. *Coventry Patmore's Angel: A Study of Coventry Patmore, His Wife Emily and* The Angel in the House. 1992.

Maynard, John. *Victorian Discourses on Sexuality and Religion*. 1993.

Page, Frederick. *Patmore, a Study in Poetry*. 1933.

Patmore, Derek. *The Life and Times of Coventry Patmore*. 1949.

Praz, Mario. *The Hero in Eclipse in Victorian Fiction*. 1956.

Reid, John Cowie. *The Mind and Art of Coventry Patmore*. 1957.

Weining, Mary Anthony. *Coventry Patmore*. 1981.

ADELAIDE ANNE PROCTER

Legends and Lyrics, with an introduction by Charles Dickens. 1866.

Gregory, Gill. "Adelaide Procter: A Poetics of Reserve and Passion." In *Women's Poetry*, eds. Isobel Armstrong and Virginia Blain. 1999.

_____. *The Life and Work of Adelaide Procter: Poetry, Feminism and Fathers*. 1998.

CHRISTINA GEORGINA ROSSETTI

Complete Poems: A Variorum Edition, ed. R. W. Crump. 3 vols. 1979–90.

Arseneau, Mary, Antony Harrison, and Lorrain Janzen Kooistra, eds. *The Culture of Christina Rossetti*. 1999.

Harrison, Antony H. *Christina Rossetti in Context*. 1988.

Helsinger, Elizabeth K. "Consumer Power and the Utopia of Desire: Christina Rossetti's 'Goblin Market'." *ELH* 58 (1991): 903–933.

Kent, David A., ed. *The Achievement of Christina Rossetti*. 1987.

Lootens, Tricia. *Lost Saints: Silence, Gender, and Victorian Literary Canonization*. 1996.

McGann, Jerome J. "The Religious Poetry of Christina Rossetti." *Critical Inquiry* 10 (1983): 127–144.

Marsh, Jan. *Christina Rossetti: A Writer's Life*. 1995.

Rosenblum, Dolores. *Christina Rossetti: The Poetry of Endurance*. 1986.

Woolf, Virginia. *The Second Common Reader*. 1932.

DANTE GABRIEL ROSSETTI

The Complete Poetical Works of Dante Gabriel Rossetti, ed. William Michael Rossetti. 1887.

The Complete Writings and Pictures of Dante Gabriel Rossetti: A Hypermedia Research Archive, ed. Jerome J. McGann. http://jefferson.village.virginia-edu/rossetti/

Doughty, Oswald. *A Victorian Romantic, Dante Gabriel Rossetti.* 1949.

Fennell, Francis L., ed. *Dante Gabriel Rossetti: An Annotated Bibliography.* 1982.

McGann, Jerome J. *Dante Gabriel Rossetti and the Game That Must Be Lost.* 2000.

Psomiades, Kathy Alexis. *Beauty's Body: Femininity and Representation in British Aestheticism.* 1997.

Rees, Joan. *The Poetry of Dante Gabriel Rossetti.* 1981.

Riede, David G. *Dante Gabriel Rossetti and the Limits of Victorian Vision.* 1983.

Sheets, Robin. "Pornography and Art: The Case of 'Jenny'." *Critical Inquiry* 14 (1988): 315–334.

Stein, Richard L. *The Ritual of Interpretation: The Fine Arts as Literature in Ruskin, Rossetti, and Pater.* 1975.

Stevenson, Lionel. *The Pre-Raphaelite Poets.* 1973.

JOHN RUSKIN

The Works of John Ruskin, ed. E.T. Cook and Alexander Wedderburn. 39 vols. 1903–12.

Austin, Linda M. *The Practical Ruskin: Economics and Audience in the Late Work.* 1991.

Casteras, Susan et al. *John Ruskin and the Victorian Eye.* 1993.

Helsinger, Elizabeth. *Ruskin and the Art of the Beholder.* 1982.

Hilton, Timothy. *John Ruskin: The Early Years, 1819–1859.* 1985.

_____. *John Ruskin: The Later Years.* 2000.

Hunt, John Dixon. *The Wider Sea: A Life of John Ruskin.* 1982.

Rosenberg, John D. *The Darkening Glass: A Portrait of Ruskin's Genius.* 1961.

Sawyer, Paul. *Ruskin's Poetic Argument.* 1985.

Spear, Jeffrey. *Dreams of an English Eden: Ruskin and His Tradition in Social Criticism.* 1984.

SAMUEL SMILES

Briggs, Asa. *Victorian People.* 1972.

Harrison, J.F.C. "The Victorian Gospel of Success." *Victorian Studies* 1 (1957): 158–164.

Jarvis, Adrian. *Samuel Smiles.* 1997.

Morris, R. J. "Samuel Smiles and the Genesis of Self-Help." *Historical Journal* 24 (1981): 89–109.

Smiles, Aileen. *Samuel Smiles and his Surroundings.* 1956.

Travers, Timothy. *Samuel Smiles and the Victorian Work Ethic.* 1987.

HERBERT SPENCER

Duncan, David, ed. *Life and Letters of Herbert Spencer,* 2 vols. 1908.

Kennedy, James Gettier. *Herbert Spencer.* 1978.

Paxton, Nancy L. *George Eliot and Herbert Spencer: Feminism, Evolutionism, and the Reconstruction of Gender.* 1991.

Peel, J. D.Y. *Herbert Spencer: The Evolution of a Sociologist.* 1971.

Taylor, Michael, ed. *Herbert Spencer and the Limits of the State: The Late Nineteenth-Century Debate Between Individualism and Collectivism.* 1996.

Weinstein, David. *Equal Freedom and Utility: Herbert Spencer's Liberal Utilitarianism.* 1998.

Wiltshire, David. *The Social and Political Thought of Herbert Spencer.* 1978.

ALGERNON CHARLES SWINBURNE

Complete Works of Algernon Charles Swinburne, ed. E. W. Gosse and T. J. Wise. 20 vols. 1925–27.

Hyder, Clyde Kenneth, ed. *Swinburne: The Critical Heritage.* 1970.

Louis, Margot K. *Swinburne and His Gods: The Roots and Growth of an Agnostic Poetry.* 1990.

McGann, Jerome J. *Swinburne: An Experiment in Criticism.* 1972.

Paglia, Camille. *Sexual Personae.* 1990.

Prins, Yopie. *Victorian Sappho.* 1999.

Riede, David G. *Swinburne: A Study of Romantic Mythmaking.* 1978.

Rooksby, Rikky and Nicholas Shrimpton, eds. *The Whole Music of Passion: New Essays on Swinburne.* 1993.

Rooksby, Rikky. *A.C. Swinburne: A Poet's Life.* 1997.

Rosenberg, John D. "Swinburne." *Victorian Studies* 11 (1967): 131–152.

ALFRED TENNYSON

The Poems of Tennyson, ed. Christopher Ricks. 3 vols. 1987.

Culler, A. Dwight. *The Poetry of Tennyson.* 1977.

Joseph, Gerhard. *Tennyson and the Text: The Weaver's Shuttle.* 1992.

Jump, John D., ed. *Tennyson: The Critical Heritage.* 1967.

Killham, John, ed. *Critical Essays on the Poetry of Tennyson.* 1960.

Martin, Robert. *Tennyson: The Unquiet Heart.* 1980.

Peltason, Timothy. *Reading* In Memoriam. 1985.

Ricks, Christopher. *Tennyson.* 1972.

Shaw, W. David. *Tennyson's Style.* 1976.

Sinfield, Alan. *Alfred Tennyson.* 1986.

Tucker, Herbert F. *Tennyson and the Doom of Romanticism.* 1988.

VICTORIA

Queen Victoria in Her Letters and Journals: A Selection, ed. Christopher Hibbert. 1985.

Homans, Margaret. *Royal Representations: Queen Victoria and British Culture 1837–1876.* 1998.

————, and Adrienne Munich, eds. *Remaking Queen Victoria.* 1997.

Houston, Gail Turley. *Royalties: The Queen and Victorian Writers.* 1999.

Longford, Elizabeth. *Queen Victoria: Born to Succeed.* 1965.

Munich, Adrienne. *Queen Victoria's Secrets.* 1996.

Weintraub, Stanley. *Victoria: An Intimate Biography.* 1987.

AUGUSTA WEBSTER

Portraits and Other Poems, ed. Christine Sutphin. 2000.

Brown, Susan. "Economical Representations: Dante Gabriel Rossetti's 'Jenny', Augusta Webster's 'A Castaway', and the Campaign Against the Contagious Diseases Acts." *Victorian Review* 17 (1991): 78–95.

————. "Determined Heroines: George Eliot, Augusta Webster, and Closet Drama by Victorian Women." *Victorian Poetry*, 33 (1995): 89–109.

Leighton, Angela. *Victorian Women Poets: Writing Against the Heart.* 1992.

OSCAR WILDE

Beckson, Carl, ed. *Oscar Wilde: The Critical Heritage.* 1970.

Cohen, Ed. *Talk on the Wilde Side: Toward a Genealogy of Discourse on Male Sexualities.* 1993.

Ellmann, Richard. *Oscar Wilde.* 1987.

Eltis, Sos. *Revising Wilde: Society and Subversion in the Plays of Oscar Wilde.* 1996.

Gagnier, Regenia, ed. *Critical Essays on Oscar Wilde.* 1991.

————. *Idylls of the Marketplace: Oscar Wilde and the Victorian Public.* 1986.

Hyde, H. Montgomery, ed. *The Trials of Oscar Wilde.* 1952.

Paglia, Camille. *Sexual Personae.* 1990.

Powell, Kerry. *Oscar Wilde and the Theatre of the 1890s.* 1990.

Raby, Peter. *Oscar Wilde.* 1988.

Worth, Katharine. *Oscar Wilde.* 1983.

WILLLIAM BUTLER YEATS

The Collected Poems of W.B. Yeats, ed. Richard J. Finneran. 1996.

Bloom, Harold. *Yeats.* 1970.

Finneran, Richard J., ed. *Critical Essays on W. B. Yeats.* 1987.

Foster, R. F. *W. B. Yeats: A Life.* 1997.

Eddins, Dwight. *Yeats: The Nineteenth-Century Matrix.* 1971.

Ellmann, Richard. *The Identity of Yeats.* 1954.

Grossman, Alan. *Poetic Knowledge in the Early Yeats.* 1971.

Henn, T. R. *The Lonely Tower: Studies in the Poetry of W. B. Yeats.* 1965.

Parkinson, Thomas. *W. B. Yeats, Self-Critic: A Study of His Early Verse.* 1951.

CREDITS

LITERARY

Emily Brontë. Selections from *The Poems of Emily Brontë*, ed. Derek Roper, with Edward Chitham. Oxford University Press, 1995. Reprinted by permission of Oxford University Press.

Robert Browning and Elizabeth Barrett Browning. Selections from *The Brownings' Correspondence*, edited by Philip Kelley and Ronald Hudson, volume 10. Wedgestone Press, 1992. Reprinted by permission of John Murray.

Gerard Manley Hopkins. *Selections from The Journals and Papers of Gerard Manley Hopkins*, edited by Humphry House, and completed by Graham Story (1959); *The Notebooks and Papers of Gerard Manley Hopkins*, edited with notes and a preface by Humphry House (1937); *Gerard Manley Hopkins: Selected Prose*, edited by Gerald Roberts (1980); *The Poetical Works of Gerard Manley Hopkins*, edited by Norman H. MacKenzie (1990). Reprinted by permission of Oxford University Press.

Margaret Oliphant. Selections from *Autobiography*, edited by Elisabeth Jay. Oxford University Press, 1990. Reprinted by permission of Elisabeth Jay.

Christina Rossetti. Selections from *The Complete Poems of Christina Rossetti*, edited by R. W. Crump. Copyright © 1990 by Louisiana State University Press. Reprinted by permission of Louisiana State University Press.

John Addington Symonds. Selections from *The Memoirs of John Addington Symonds*, edited by Phyllis Grosskurth. University of Chicago Press, 1984. Reprinted by permission of The London Library.

Queen Victoria. Selections from *Dearest Child: Letters between Queen Victoria and the Princess Royal 1858–1861* (1964); *Dearest Mama: Letters between Queen Victoria and the Crown Princess of Prussia 1861–1864* (1968); *Your Dear Letter: Private Correspondence of Queen Victoria and the Crown Princess of Prussia, 1865–1871* (1971). Edited by Roger Fulford. Evans Brothers. Reprinted by permission of Her Majesty Queen Elizabeth II.

Oscar Wilde. Selections from *The Complete Letters of Oscar Wilde*, edited by Merlin Holland and Rupert Hart-Davis. Letters © 1962 by Vyvyan Holland, © 1990, 1997 by Merlin Holland. Reprinted by permission of Henry Holt and Company, LLC.

ART

Richard Doyle, from *Punch, or the London Charivari*, volume 12 (1847). Special Collections Department, University of Virginia Library.

A. Welby Pugin, Contrasted Residences for the Poor, from *Contrasts: or, A Parallel between the Noble Edifices of the Middle Ages, and Corresponding Buildings of the Present Day, Shewing the Present Decay of Taste* (1841). Division of Rare and Manuscript Collections, Cornell University Library.

William Holman Hunt, from Tennyson, *Poems* (1857). Special Collections Department, University of Virginia Library.

Dante Gabriel Rossetti, from Christina Rossetti, *Goblin Market and Other Poems* (1862). Special Collections Department, University of Virginia Library.

F. S. Cary, The Valentine, from *The Keepsake*, edited by Miss Power (1856). Division of Rare and Manuscript Collections, Cornell University Library.

from *Peter Parley's Annual: A Christmas & New Year's Present for Young People* (1860). Division of Rare and Manuscript Collections, Cornell University Library.

Aubrey Beardsley, from *The Yellow Book*, volume 1 (1894). Special Collections Department, University of Virginia Library.

Charles Ricketts, from *The Sphinx*, by Oscar Wilde (1894). Special Collections Department, University of Virginia Library.

from *In Darkest England, and the Way Out*, by William Booth (1890). Division of Rare and Manuscript Collections, Cornell University Library.

from *The Illustrated London News*, Diamond Jubilee Edition (1897). Special Collections Department, University of Virginia Library.

INDEX OF AUTHORS, TITLES, AND FIRST LINES